KU-748-205

BARCLAYS WORLD OF CRICKET

The Game from A to Z

✲

General Editor
E. W. SWANTON OBE

Associate Editor
JOHN WOODCOCK

Assistant Editors
GEORGE PLUMPTRE AND A. S. R. WINLAW

Statistician
G. A. COPINGER

COLLINS PUBLISHERS
in association with
Barclays Bank International

First edition published 1966
This new edition published 1980 by Collins Publishers
14 St James's Place London SW 1
in association with Barclays Bank International Ltd
54 Lombard Street London EC 3

ISBN 0 00 216349 7

Designed by Humphrey Stone
Publishing Editor Hugh Montgomery-Massingberd

Filmset and printed in Great Britain by
BAS Printers Limited, Over Wallop
Hampshire

Contents

Foreword

SIR ANTHONY TUKE
Chairman Barclays Bank

The 1st Test Match played in this country between England and Australia took place in 1880: so Jim Swanton's book comes out during the centenary year.

1980 sees Barclays Bank represented in almost all the countries where cricket is played, and it is therefore appropriate that we should make a contribution towards the publication of this excellent book which reflects the game in all its aspects in such an interesting and informative way. I am sure that it will enhance the understanding and enjoyment of cricket wherever it is played.

Anthony Tuke

General Editor's Introduction

I BEGAN the corresponding introduction to the 1st edition of this book, printed 15 years ago, with what might be thought a blinding flash of the obvious, saying that the intention behind it was to satisfy 'anyone anxious to extend his or her general knowledge of cricket and to provide them with some entertaining, worthwhile reading in the process'. Naturally our ambition remains the same in 1980 as it was in 1965. However, I concluded by hoping that the book would help the current generation to see the game in balance and perspective, adding that 'that cannot be an easy thing for them to do nowadays with so bright a gleam focused on the present.'

How oddly such a comment reads today! For the bright gleam, looking back, seems the gentlest aura compared with the dazzling arc lights and the crescendo of sound surrounding cricket at the top in 1980. To say that there are manifestations of the modern game that affront the eye and jar the ear may seem to some an understatement. One needs a degree of optimism to suggest that the commercial over-exploitation of Test cricket, and of Test cricketers too frequently involved in one-day matches, may be merely a temporary phenomenon which the art and genius inherent in the game may reduce, in time, to acceptable levels. At this stage who can do more than earnestly hope so?

Whatever the future holds, however, this surely is a good moment to attempt another survey, wide in space and deep in time, exposing the ancient roots of cricket and tracing its growth and spread all over the Commonwealth and beyond, to some degree at least wherever English is spoken.

Hence this new edition, in the production of which I must first acknowledge gratefully not only the patronage of Barclays Bank International, but in particular the personal interest of the Barclays group chairman, Sir Anthony Tuke, who has kindly in his Foreword given the book his *imprimatur*.

This new edition shows a fundamental change from the first, and I am confident that it will be considered a change very much for the better. The radical difference in the format of *Barclays World of Cricket* is that, although the alphabetical pattern of entries is still broadly followed, the many-sided aspects of the game, instead of being lined up from A to Z willy-nilly, are now divided into eleven separate parts.

The economics of publishing being what they are, such a complete overhaul could not have been accomplished without financial help if the book were to remain within the reach of the pocket of the enthusiast – or, if not his pocket, then that of an indulgent elder. As it is, the type size, of necessity, has had to be reduced, but in compensation for this we have been able to double – to some 750 – the number of photographs. More there are and better, reflecting the great improvement in the art of cricket illustration since the 1st edition.

Despite so greatly increasing the pictorial side, by reducing the type size we have fitted about the same number of words (around three-quarters of a million) into little more than half the number of pages. Though a large book still, it is no longer true that, as a reviewer said of the 1966 edition, one almost needs a lectern to stand it on. Another improvement is the provision of a selective index, expertly compiled by J. D. Coldham, editor of the *Cricket Society Journal*.

It is a privilege to be bringing back into print the writing done for our 1st edition by several famous names now passed on: H. S. Altham, Sir Neville Cardus, E. D. R. Eagar, G. D. Martineau, Ian Peebles, R. A. Roberts, R. C. Robertson-Glasgow and A. A. Thomson. There are assembled here also some mature and well-known writers who did not contribute to the 1st edition such as Keith Dunstan, Alan Gibson, S. C. Griffith, H. F. Ellis, Robin Marlar, Gerald Pawle, Alan and Gordon Ross, and M. H. Stevenson as well as a rather later school (in the cricket sense) including Trevor Bailey, Michael Brearley, Tony Cozier, Ted Dexter, Benny Green, Kenneth Gregory, Trevor Macdonald, Geoffrey Moorhouse, Christopher Martin-Jenkins, André Odendaal, Norman de Mesquita, David Rayvern Allen, A. C. Smith and John Thicknesse, to name some. With all the other chief contributors to the 1st edition either bringing their work up to date, or writing fresh pieces, or both, there are very few names missing from the ranks of the best modern cricket-writers. These will be found at the back of the book listed under Notes on Chief Contributors. (The names of many others invited to submit shorter items are given at the end of each.) As was inevitable, much good 1st edition writing has had to be jettisoned in order to cover the eventful story of the last few years. All the main articles of the 1965 edition have had to be compressed to some extent. I feel sure however that the new writing will be rated as at least fully up to the standard of the old. I specially regret that at the last moment Diana Rait Kerr's scholarly history of the Laws up to and including the 1947 code had to give place, the compensation in this case being an Introduction to the 1980 code by the 1979–80 President of MCC, Billy Griffith, the man who did most to compile it, and the code itself with the preface to it written by the MCC Secretary, J. A. Bailey.

When commissioning and reading this fresh material I have been regularly conscious of one particular tribute to the 1st edition written in a letter to the Editor of the *Daily Telegraph* by J. W. Goldman who at that time possessed probably the biggest and best private cricket library in existence. He was disposing of it, he said, but would retain *The World of Cricket* because in all its pages there was not an unkind word. How does the new edition, which has had to chronicle so many happenings of the last 15 years so alien to the old conception of cricket, answer such a test of benevolence unalloyed? To be 'kind' on certain subjects and in respect of certain people could well be construed as just, in common parlance, 'wet'. What I hope may be said is that no *unfair* judgments have marred the general tenor of the book.

As to the Parts themselves we have aimed, naturally, to arrange them in a logical order. The History of the Game in England (PART I), is followed by articles of widely varying lengths on all the main countries, states and provinces where the game is played – 89 in all. They form PART II. In PART III come the Biographies, 320 this time, slightly more than in 1965, the addition of 75 new ones involving the painful necessity of 73 omissions. No two 'experts' would come near agreement on exactly who commands a place at the expense of whom. I will not seek to justify the new list other than to say that various aspects of service to the game, as well as degree of personal achievement on the field, were taken into account. Almost all those who have carried the weight of Test captaincy, for instance, are included.

PART IV is chiefly occupied by the long and nowadays ever more concentrated story of Test Cricket; but not exclusively since it contains, among other less explosive items, the dramatic saga of the intrusion on to the international scene of the Australian, Kerry Packer – this at a moment moreover when the cricket world was basking in the unique euphoria of the Centenary Test at Melbourne, and the game had reached a higher level of popularity and financial stability than at any time since the mid-1950s. (Retrospectively that event of March 1977 will surely be seen as a historical watershed.) For the article entitled World Series Cricket I was lucky to find in Trevor Macdonald (known to a very large public as the ITN newscaster) a man who saw more of this revolutionary version than most and who, as a West Indian, has dealt with the story in an objective, factual and thorough manner such as a duly qualified Englishman or Australian might have found more difficult to achieve.

The many Test Series which nowadays follow one another almost uninterruptedly through the calendar have been covered as fully as possible, and if it is remarked that England v Australia is disproportionately long, I can only answer that those great contests were the foundation of all international cricket, and that their status remains unchallenged – though it undoubtedly will be weakened, as will all Test cricket, if the present tendency of 'too many too often' is not promptly arrested. The greater the frequency of Test series and the larger the number of Tests in each the more the rest of first-class cricket, which is the training ground of the highest talent, becomes undervalued and less-readily supported.

This brings me to the histories of the Counties, both major and minor, and of the Universities which form PART V. Here one sees how the county game has been revived by the other worthwhile prizes subsidiary to the Championship. Competition is nowadays much more open – though the 'Big Six' of olden days, Yorkshire, Lancashire and Notts, Surrey, Middlesex and Kent are still the only ones of the 17 to have won, comfortably, more matches than they have lost. The Minor Counties also get their showing here – the department of the English game, by the way, which has changed least in recent years, and certainly none the worse for that. The ancient universities are in eclipse so far as public interest is concerned, though they remain fruitful nurseries for county players and over the last 20 years or so have also produced, as in the past, a respectable muster of Test cricketers. The history of the University Clubs of Oxford and Cambridge is too closely interwoven with the fabric of English Cricket to be subjected to more than the minimum of cutting - though the long pieces telling the stories of the University Match and Gentlemen v Players in the 1st edition – the classics of the past – have had to suffer severely from the pruning knife. For the Limited-Over Game, forming PART VI, demanded attention in all its manifestations from the 'World Cup' under Prudential patronage through the three County trophies down to the national Knock-out Championships for the Clubs and Villages. Next, in PART VII, come the first-class grounds of the world, from Lord's and Melbourne down to the English county grounds, some of which cater for a county match only once or twice a year. Long may they do so!

There follow two PARTS, VIII and IX, of a more varied character than anything hitherto. The first seeks to hold up a mirror to all cricket in the United Kingdom short of what is officially first or second-class. The scope of PART VIII takes in other countries of the UK; Services; Leagues; Clubs; Junior Cricket Organizations; Schools and Sundry Societies and Institutions which fulfil a useful function in the service of the game – all of them coming under the broad authority of the National Cricket Association. As to the selection of the schools I hope it will be accepted that all those whose names appeared in 1965 were approached again. Nearly all of them revised their entries. We did not however seek to include fresh entries, much as we would have liked to, for reasons of space. There are nearly 25,000 clubs of one kind or another throughout the United Kingdom. The fact that we have not found the space this time to record the doings of any of them individually (though many are mentioned in the special articles) has at least therefore saved us from a highly invidious choice. We have, however, given an idea of the country-wide efforts which since the last war have been made to encourage the young to play, and to avail themselves of the good coaching which they can surely find nowadays in most places if they are keen enough to look for it.

Its title, 'A Cricket Treasury', indicates the diverse character of PART IX. A bibliography is its main ingredient, but there is much else besides. The articles are mostly not obligatory inclusions but they hold their place by a combination of the quality of the writing and the fascination of the subject.

The Glossary which forms PART X seeks not only to define the language of cricket but to describe the action of the game in its various departments and also to offer at least brief instruction in the arts of batting and bowling. The new Laws forming PART XI complete the text, followed only by a select Appendix of statistics not otherwise covered.

Such in brief is the scope and arrangement of this new edition. Its complete revision has been accomplished well within 12 months, an achievement for which I am extremely grateful to the editorial staff I was fortunate enough to enrol. To John Woodcock's indefatigable efforts I must pay special tribute. His particular areas were the illustrations and the biographies, but his hand was everywhere: for me at least, with Michael Melford, Associate Editor of the 1st edition, no longer available, the long hiatus at *The Times* had this substantial compensation. To George Plumptre, fresh from Cambridge, fell the full-time job of manning our office, assembling manuscript and pictures, communicating with authors and photographers, and generally turning his hand to whatever job or contact was required. All this he accomplished with a maturity and confidence beyond his years. Of my assistant editors last time, Irving Rosenwater was otherwise engaged with the BBC and could only bring his many contributions up to date; Antony Winlaw, however, as before, looked after the information from clubs and schools. For the statistical side I am indebted to Geoffrey Copinger, a well-known student for many years responsible for the cricket records in *Wisden*. Though our authors kept their deadlines extremely well – and, incidentally, there was only one hard-worked journalist who was unable to undertake the article he was asked to write – there were certain moments when it was touch and go whether we might fall behind our schedule. On these occasions Bill Frindall, Richard Streeton, Steve Whiting and Alex Bannister gave invaluable help at short notice.

On the production side we were likewise fortunate in the high professional skills of the publishing editor, Hugh Montgomery-Massingberd, and of Humphrey Stone, who was responsible for the layout of the book.

There was help of another kind, too, from G. O. Allen and Mrs G. N. Foster, widow of the fifth of the famous brotherhood of seven. For access to their ample collection of cuttings and photographs I am grateful to them both: also to Gubby Allen for comments on some of the biographies.

Much individual help must go, I fear, unacknowledged, and sources of reference likewise; but no work on cricket can even be begun without the aid of *Wisden*, to whose successive editors I respectfully doff my cap. As to copyright I am grateful to the Committee of MCC for permission to publish the new code of Laws, and also for allowing me to quote, as in the 1st edition, from MCC's *Cricket – How to Play*, a book of brief, succinct instruction (now out of print) on the basic arts of batting and bowling. We have also made extensive demands on the MCC photographic library, thanks to the ready help of the Curator, Stephen Green.

Coming to the illustrations, one found oneself, not for the first time, confronted by a wealth of excellent photography of earlier days and also a rich choice of modern work, dating more or less from Patrick Eagar's gifted emergence in the mid-1960s and the lifting some years later of the monopolies held by one or other of the agencies on each of the English Test grounds. For the long period between the times of G. W. Beldam, early in the century, and Eagar and his school good pictures are much harder to come by – partly because much was lost in the bombing. Central Press, however, who supplied the bulk of the 1st edition photographs, have again gone to much trouble on our behalf with excellent result. I must express special thanks to Richard Wilson of Kodak for giving us the advantage of his skill and experience, and to that company for allowing us the use of the marvellously-clear Beldam prints made for their 1977 Cricket Exhibition: also to George Beldam, son of G.W. whose copyright they are.

In our search for likenesses of players I was amused to come across the phrase 'mug-shots' – which is what the professionals call a straightforward head-and-shoulders. There was some slight surprise when I preferred 'mug' to 'action', and a good many mugs of wide variety will be found deliberately scattered through the book, some smiling, some stern, some ugly, some handsome, but all in some degree expressive of character. After all, one stroke can be very much like another – especially if it be that vastly overdone leg-sweep – but not many cricketers look very like other cricketers.

As has been said and written many times by critics from Nyren to the present, cricket holds up a mirror to character in a way that a faster-moving game of briefer duration cannot do. It is this property possessed by cricket which does much to explain its fascination for so many sorts and conditions of men – and women. Equally cricket reflects the social attitudes of the day. The elegance of the Golden Age (roughly perhaps 1890–1914), which my generation were lucky enough to see after the First War in the batting of Jack Hobbs and Frank Woolley, was no accident. Nor, sad to say, is the over-obsession with money in the game today, and the deterioration of manners, of which verbal abuse is a particularly distasteful expression.

Sad to say, the triangular one-day international tournament in Australia in 1979–80 between the home country, England and the West Indies seems to have taken place at times in an utterly alien element with rowdy and violent crowds calling the tune and a very few famous players playing to the gallery in an unheard-of and contemptible way. The Test countries at the moment of writing have a burning issue on their hands in 'player-power', with which, of course, is immediately connected the upholding of the absolute authority of the umpire.

In my more pessimistic moments I think of the game in Australia and the West Indies also as a version apart in the future, wherein fast bowling with the open object of intimidation rules the day against batsmen armoured ever more heavily against it. The crowd comes to see a gladiatorial contest, craving only excitement and violence.

At least I believe the limitation of fast bowling aimed to hurt and frighten, and the encouragement of the more subtle arts of spin, will be a major challenge to authority in the 1980s, wherever the game is played. As to the current trends in Australia, it can only be hoped that there may be a reaction against them among the many Australians with a deep appreciation of cricket who, I know, have been greatly saddened by much that they have seen.

I am far from indicting the generality of modern first-class cricketers, most of whom when under strong and sensible leadership comport themselves perfectly well. Unfortunately it is the lapses from accepted standards of sportsmanship which often find their way on to the television screen, and are therefore seen and apt to be imitated by lesser players and especially by the young. It is this aspect which traditionalists like myself find so repellent.

The key surely lies in leadership – in firm captaincy resolutely backed by a responsible committee. Much of the trouble in Test cricket of late years has derived from the theory, hitherto unheard of, that all authority on the field is concentrated in the umpire – poor, wretched fellow. 'Anything goes', so long as it gets by him.

Having said so much about the responsibility of professional players in respect of standards on the field I would add that in England we are lucky in having in the Cricketers' Association a body to which all playing in English first-class cricket belong. It is responsibly led and has an amiable working relationship with the Test and County Cricket Board. It is sure to have an increasing influence in the game, and I believe that the commonsense and integrity of the big majority of county players today will ensure that that influence is to the good.

But enough of the darker side. This book aims to hold up a mirror to the whole world of cricket, and here a picture emerges of a game healthy and prospering in most of its aspects, preserved by the tireless, unselfish service to it of a multitude of people. In the end the prosperity of the game depends on the schoolmaster and the old player willing to give up their time to organize and to coach, to the various officers of the club whose labours are needed to keep it ticking over. You will be encouraged no doubt to read in Mike Stevenson's well-researched review of the last 15 years of League cricket the comment from a Lancashire League secretary, 'The crucial sphere of junior cricket has never been healthier'. This assessment, I believe, can be widely echoed. Clubs are coming more and more to ensure future supply by catching boys during school age and catering for them. The National Cricket Association will say that the total number playing in England has never been so great, and the same is true of Australia.

The women, let me add, have not been forgotten in this book, their doings recorded by that evergreen worker for the game, Miss Netta Rheinberg. An item of hers caught my eye to the effect that the Australian women cricketers who toured England in 1976 were required to pay, or somehow find, the equivalent of no less than £1,000 for the privilege. In an age of ever-increasing sponsorship – welcome as it is – it is good to know that, among the women anyway, the spirit of true amateurism is not dead.

Cricket has never lacked its eccentrics, and Benny Green, a master of such esoteric material, tells us in his article on the subject how one, Harry Bagshaw, by his decree, was buried in his umpire's coat *and with a cricket ball in his hand*. If this novel idea appeals to any of the noble fraternity in these expensive days perhaps he should specify an old ball.

My last reflection in the 1st edition was a reminder of how, despite the voluminous literature of cricket, each generation naturally finds its own heroes. Telling how shocked Plum Warner had been many years ago on discovering that an England captain had never heard of Stoddart, and saying it would horrify those of my age to find anyone ignorant of the name of Chapman, I added, 'It will no doubt astonish the middle-aged enthusiast of the year 2000 to be asked: "Cowdrey – for whom did he play?"' In 2000 indeed! I heard recently of some talk on the great postwar players to which a few small boys were listening. May was mentioned, and Graveney, and Cowdrey. 'Oh, yes, Cowdrey!' piped up one, 'and didn't his father play pretty well, too?'

Sandwich,
January 1980 E. W. SWANTON

Part I
History of the Game in England

1 Origins

E. D. R. EAGAR

CRICKET HISTORIANS since the early 19th century have sought in vain to date the birth of cricket but it will remain for ever shrouded in mystery. Many clues have been dug up as to the game's antiquity. We know, for example, that cricket was old when the Tudors were young. We know, too, that Englishmen played cricket as well as bowls at the time the Spanish Armada was sighted.

Andrew Lang wrote: 'No one invented cricket. Like almost everything else cricket was evolved.' The 18th-century historian, Joseph Strutt, suggested that 'the pleasant and manly exercise of cricket originated from club-ball'. The late H. S. Altham, greatest of all cricket historians, endorses the findings of an earlier researcher 'H. P.-T.' who had supported the derivation from club-ball.

John Nyren writing in 1833 says that this game 'appears to have been no other than the present well-known bat-and-ball'. The Rev James Pycroft in *The Cricket-Field* (1851) also identifies club-ball as 'the name which usually stood for cricket in the 13th century'. In the best-known edition of this book, edited by Mr F. S. Ashley-Cooper in 1922, the latter endorses the author's view in a summary of the evidence.

Thus we find such dedicated historians as Strutt, Pycroft and Ashley-Cooper in close accord. What was this club-ball? 'H. P.-T.' points out that it is a generic term, as football and handball used to be. It stood for any game in which a club and a ball were used. It is in fact the ancestor of most of our English ball games. We may never discover when cricket ceased to be club-ball and became itself. Cricket, in fact, just grew up.

What part of England can be termed the birthplace of the game? Hambledon in Hampshire has been known for years as the cradle of cricket. There is a popular misconception that it all started on Broadhalfpenny Down. But a cradle is no birthplace; we must look farther east for that – to Kent and to Sussex. All the evidence points to that part of England known as 'The Weald' as providing our earliest cricket grounds. Originally there was much forest in addition to downland in this area. What could be more natural than for people to seek and find relaxation in the forests whilst resting from their labours? Trees had to be cut down for building and for ships, and here also could be found the implements of play – the tree stump and the bat. In the downlands the shepherds took time off to play their own variety of club-ball. There were few 'stumps' on the downs, so a new target had to be found – the 'wicket gate', through which passed their flocks of sheep. This gate took the form of a small hurdle consisting of two uprights. The upright sticks of the wickets – the 'little gates' – were still known as stumps and across them was laid a crosspiece known to this day in Australian pastures as a bail. This was a superior target to the tree stump, for there could be no argument when the bail fell to the ground!

Originally there were but three necessities to this, as yet, unnamed game. The target, *i.e.* the stump or the wicket, and the bat and ball. The first manufactured missile for the club-ball games may well have been a shaped piece of wood. Before long the cobbler was making a ball filled with cork or some other form of stuffing around which would be stitched a leather covering. The bat is simply a hitting device – a club.

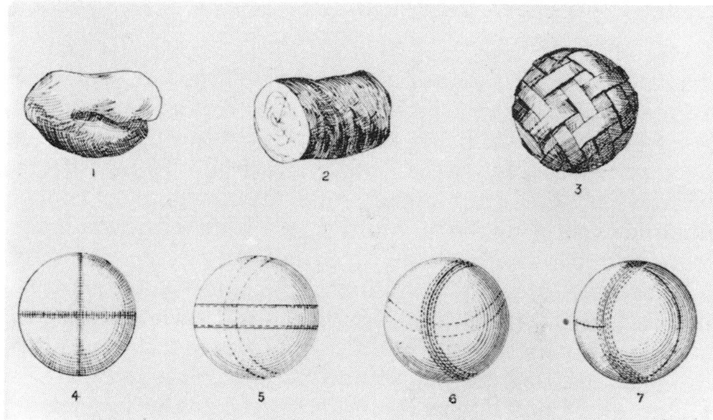

Evolution of the ball 1 stone; 2 piece of wood; 3 hidebound ball; 4 Small's ball; 5 and 6 other improved balls; 7 present-day ball.

Many of the expressions used today have their roots in history. The earliest bats were naturally weapons hacked off trees. They looked like cumbersome hockey sticks and were rounded at the end to deal with the ball bowled literally, as the word suggests, all along the ground. The word umpire is derived from the French '*non pair*' or the odd man. The score was kept by 'notching' runs with a knife on a stick. A deeper groove was 'notched' for every tenth run and to this day we refer at times to runs as 'notches'. A crease is the same word as scratch. Even when W. G. Grace first began to play in the 1860s, white-wash had not altogether superseded the creases cut in the turf.

The popping crease was set 46 inches in front of the target. In Tudor times there was a measure of 45 inches known as the cloth yard or ell, the length, in fact, of the arrows with which the British bowmen had won the Battle of Agincourt. If the 2 half inches are taken away for the creases it became a simple task for the early players to measure the distance where a batsman should take his stand.

But what of the word cricket itself? It is simply the diminutive of 'cric' – the little cric or curved staff and more especially a shepherd's staff or crook. Like so much of basic cricket vocabulary it is derived from an Anglo-Saxon word. 'Thy staff' in the Saxon version of the 23rd Psalm is simply 'cricc thin'.

In 1787, the London Society of Antiquaries published some wardrobe accounts of King Edward I. Later historians from

Pycroft onwards have sought to prove that these accounts constitute in fact the earliest mention of our game. The original quotation was, according to 'H.P.-T's' translation:

To Master John of Leek, Chaplain of Prince Edward, the King's son, for ready money disbursed for the said Prince's playing at Creag' and other sports, out of his own and deputies' hands (was paid) at Westminster, on the 10th day of March (1300) the sum of 100 shillings. And to his Chamberlain Hugo, at Newenton, in the month of March 20 shillings. In all £6.

This entry in the accounts occurred in the 28th year of the King's reign. King Edward I was proclaimed King, although absent on a crusade, in the year 1272. Pycroft observed that 'the glossaries have been searched in vain for any other name of a pastime but cricket to which the term Creag' can apply'. Creag' and cricket he, therefore, presumed to be identical.

In 1907 Ashley-Cooper wrote in similar vein

The meaning of the word Creag' has never been clearly explained, but that it referred to a game which was well-known at the end of the century is evident. . . . Creag' and cricket being presumed identical, the game must have been popular 600 years ago!

The Black Prince's grandfather and first Prince of Wales was 16 years of age in 1300. To keep him company a Gascon youth, Piers Gaveston, was being brought up at Court in repayment for services rendered to the King by his father. The apostrophe with which the word creag' ends was a common enough method of showing the diminutive 'et'. If the game was in fact 'creaget' it requires little imagination to see a foreign accountant's difficulty in attempting to embody in his Latin a native Saxon word. If, says 'H. P.-T.', the town of Newenton mentioned in those wardrobe accounts was in fact Newenden, 'it seems to clinch the matter and there seems a good case for regarding Prince Edward and his friend as the first pair of cricketers known to fame', and, we may add, for fixing the Weald as its earliest home.

All that has gone before may, to some extent, be supposition. But by the end of the 16th century the historian is on certain ground. A manuscript in the possession of the Mayor and Corporation of Guildford, dated 16 January 1598, records the evidence of a certain John Derrick, one of the coroners of the county of Surrey and 'of the age of fyfty and nyne yeares or thereabouts', concerning a disputed piece of land, to wit that

when he was a scholler in the free school of Guldeford, he and several of his fellowes did runne and play there at crickett and other plaies. And also that the same was used for the baytinge of beares in the saide towne, . . .

This is the earliest definite reference to cricket and it would seem certain that cricket was a well-known game, at least for boys, before the end of the reign of Henry VIII. In 1598 the game had become sufficiently well known to earn a place in the English version of an Italian dictionary. Giovanni Florio translated the word '*sgrittare*' as 'to make a noise as a cricket, to play cricket-a-wicket, and be merry'. Whilst a few years later, in 1611, Randle Cotgrave's French/English dictionary translated 'crosse' as 'a crosier, or Bishop's staffe; also a cricket-staffe, or the crooked staffe wherewith boys play at cricket'.

Until the Restoration cricket was, at best, a boyish pastime and, at worst, a disreputable pursuit. There was no mention of the game in a publication printed in 1618 under the title *The Kings Majesties Declaration to His Subjects concerning lawfull Sports to be used*. This Declaration listed all the 'honest exercises' that might be performed on Sunday. Mention of cricket, along with bear-baiting, was conspicuous by its absence.

In the second year of Oliver Cromwell's Protectorate (1654) the churchwardens and overseers of Eltham in Kent fined seven of their parishioners 2 shillings each for playing cricket on the Lord's Day. This was a considerable sum in those days.

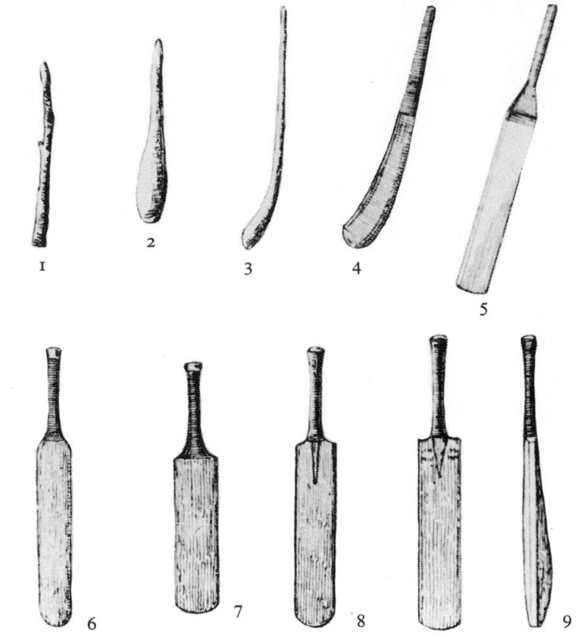

Evolution of the bat: 1 piece of stick; 2 club; 3 battes; 4 curved bat; 5 batten bat; 6 skyscraper; 7 shouldered bat; 8 spliced bat; 9 present-day bat.

Small wonder that certain Royalists sought to blacken Cromwell's character by coupling his name with 'dissolute and disorderly' pastimes. Sir William Dugdale started a legend that when the Protector was a boy – he was born in 1599 – he became 'famous for football, cricket, cudgelling and wrestling and thereby earned himself 'the name of royster'. Whatever his youthful instincts. Cromwell's major-generals disapproved of 'krickett' strongly enough to prohibit the game in Ireland; all 'sticks' and balls were to be burnt by the common hangman!

But Cromwell's revolution was in fact to have a decisive impact upon the game. Many of the aristocracy perforce had to retire to their country seats. Those who had estates in the Weald would there discover their tenants playing a rough-and-ready but lively and intriguing game. Their gambling instincts were soon aroused. Although betting was by now illegal the need for relaxation and sheer boredom were encouragement enough for small private wagers to be made as they watched the previously discredited game in practice. Interest and excitement grew and it was not long before the nobles were themselves practising and thoroughly enjoying a new and needed recreation. The Wealden 'gentlemen' gave the game their patronage. Families such as the Sackvilles of Knole House, Sevenoaks, the Sidneys of Penshurst, the Richmond family at Goodwood and the Gages of Firle were soon to fall under its spell and become leaders in its ever widening influence.

With the Restoration in 1660 the nobles came back to London with their discovery and with them their servants, many of them the original local 'players'. In the first few years of the reign of Charles II cricket became quite the 'thing' in society. There is mention of a club established at St Albans in 1666, and John Churchill, later 1st Duke of Marlborough, was known to be playing cricket at the Old St Paul's School at about this date. Before the end of the 17th century we learn from the diary of a naval chaplain, Henry Teonge, that on 6 May 1676, he and some companions in the Levant travelled to Aleppo, where the English residents in 'a fine vally by a river syde . . . had severall pastimes and sports, as duck hunting, fishing, shooting, handball, krickett, scrofilo. . .' The game had begun to spread across the world.

2 Early Days in Kent

E. D. R. EAGAR

Towns and villages in the Weald naturally predominate in all the early references to cricket in the first half of the 18th century, yet the game was spreading slowly but surely across the country. By 1729 we find it played in Gloucestershire and in that same year we have the first definite reference to Hampshire when Kent, under Mr Edwin Stead, played a combined team from Sussex, Surrey and Hampshire led by Sir William Gage. In the next few years Berkshire, Oxfordshire, Buckinghamshire, Essex and Hertfordshire had followed suit. The noble game was gradually becoming a national one.

The earliest score sheet was found by Dr Squire only a few years ago at Goodwood House, among the papers of the 2nd Duke of Richmond. It was at Goodwood House that Squire found the earliest known Laws: the Articles of Agreement for a match in 1727. The game was probably between Slindon and London and played in London on 2 June 1744.

The 2nd Duke of Richmond, a distinguished 18th-century patron in the days of bold challenges and high stakes.

The earliest description of a cricket match was written in 1706. An Old Etonian, William Goldwin, published a collection of poems in Latin under the general title *Musae Juveniles*. The poem called 'In Certamen Pilae' described a cricket match which, to all intents and purposes, seems to have been played under the code of laws published 38 years later in 1744. But the first full description was of the game in 1744 between Kent and All England. 'Cricket: An Heroic Poem' was written by a young poet named James Dance using the pseudonym of Love and goes with a rare swing from the opening lines:

Hail Cricket! Manly British game!
First of all sports! Be first alike in fame!

Kent won the match by 1 wicket due to a dropped catch by one 'W—k.' Poor Waymark! Has the missing of a sitter ever been better described:

The erring ball amazing to be told!
Slipped thro' his outstretched hand and mocked his hold.

The development of the game as the 18th century advanced can be traced to the interest of the great landowners. Age-old barriers began to be broken down as one patron after another vied with each other to get together on their estates the strongest possible team. Gardeners, gamekeepers and huntsmen would often owe their employment to their good eye or strong arm, for many of the matches arranged would be played for high stakes.

London society had taken cricket to its heart and it was now but a short step to the formation of clubs. It was in 1719 that Kent played London in the first match recorded by a representative Kentish side. To those who are content to look upon London as representative of Surrey or Middlesex this game constitutes the first county match. The more meticulous prefer to look upon the matches in 1728 as the first real contests between counties. In the 17th Earl of Leicester's Park at Penshurst, Sussex, under Sir William Gage, played Kent, led by Edwin Stead, for 50 guineas and for 'the third time this summer the Kent men have been too expert for those of Sussex'.

Whoever represented the opposition there is little doubt that Kent can justify the title given to them by Altham in his *History* when he refers to 'Kent, the First Champions'. Surrey and Sussex can make a good case for themselves at certain periods of the century but, as 'H. P.-T.' writes, 'there was no greater draw to a cricket ground than the announcement that the opponents were coming out of Kent'. More often than not they were opposed by more than one county and their occasional defeats were often accomplished with the help of 'given men' in the opposition. George Colman, the younger, wrote in 1762: 'Here's Kent, fertile in pheasants, cherries, hops, yeomen, codlings and cricketers!'

The father of Kent cricket was Edwin Stead. He died in 1735 and the *Gentleman's Magazine* noted that he was 'remarkable for several great Cricket Matches he made with the Prince of Wales, and many of the Nobility'. He retained on his staff many of the best cricketers in the county. When he died the fame of Kent continued under the leadership of the Earl of Middlesex, who became the 2nd Duke of Dorset (1711–1769) and his brother Lord John Sackville (1713–1765), well into the Hambledon era, when the Kent player, Joseph Miller, was the batsman most feared by the Hambledon men. One of the greatest patrons of the game, Sir Horatio Mann, was mainly responsible for Kent's later triumphs. Born in 1744 – the year of 'Love's' Match – he died at the age of 70 in the year before the Battle of Waterloo.

Kent's main challenger in these early years of 'county' cricket was Surrey. In 1707 Mitcham could challenge the might of London. The London Club held a place in the cricket world for almost half a century similar to that of MCC today, though its empire was on a much smaller scale. Most of the chief members of the club were in fact Surrey men but their famous Artillery Ground was situated in Middlesex. It was at this ground, described as 'the old ground' as early as 1731, that the members of the club met in 1744 to draw up the Code of Laws which received such universal approval that a match in New York in 1751 'was played according to the London Method'. The Artillery Ground was the first Mecca of cricket. It had been presented to the Honourable Artillery Company in 1638. In 1689 games were forbidden and it was not until the lifetime of 'Poor Fred' that the ground became famous.

Cricket first earned the patronage of royalty in 1723. Frederick, Prince of Wales, the son of King George II, was not a good player but he became the life and soul of Surrey cricket. He selected teams and promoted many matches at which he would entertain the players. He first played in a match in Kensington Gardens in September 1735, when he was 28 years old. His passion for the game and his frequent attendance at matches encouraged society to make the game their own.

'Poor Fred' died in 1751 at the early age of 44. His death was caused indirectly by the game he loved so well. He was hit with a cricket ball in a match at Cliveden House, in Buckinghamshire. Some months later an internal abscess, which had formed on the spot, burst and suffocated him. His death was perhaps the main reason that little was heard of Surrey cricket between 1750 and 1773. There was no patron left with enough enthusiasm to select a team of the best players from the various clubs to represent the county. It was this period, too, which coincided with the decline in the fortunes of the London Club, the emergence of White Conduit House as a serious rival to the Artillery Ground and, above all, with the rise of Hambledon.

William Beldham in old age; one of the first and most illustrious of the early players.

In 1773 Surrey emerged once more as a great cricketing force. The Earl of Tankerville deserves most credit for this revival. With immense enthusiasm and liberality he collected a strong side together which was to prove a worthy opponent for the great Kent XI.

The backbone of the Surrey XIs for the next few years were Lumpy, Yalden and Thomas White. Lumpy, whose real name was Edward Stevens, was the most famous of all bowlers until David Harris appeared on the scene. He was renowned for his accuracy and to him we owe the introduction of the third stump. Three times did Lumpy bowl right through John Small's wicket in a celebrated single-wicket match between Five of Hambledon and Five of Kent in 1775. Hambledon needed 14 runs for victory and Small, the last man, obtained them. The Hambledon men were the first to concede that this was hard luck on the bowler and soon afterwards the third stump was added. Yalden was the great wicket-keeper of the day. He was a licensed victualler at Chertsey and managed the Laleham-Burway ground.

Thomas White, better known as 'Shock' White, was for years the most successful of the Surrey batsmen. Like so many of the great players of those days he was a stout man. His highest score was 197 for Surrey and Kent v Middlesex and Hampshire in 1771. He will best be remembered for appearing against Hambledon with a bat as wide as the stumps. His bat was shaved with a knife and a law was made that the width of the bat should in future be 4 inches and a quarter.

On 5 February 1766, one of the great cricket characters of his or any other age was born at Wrecclesham, near Farnham. William Beldham died 96 years later in 1862. In his life he played with the contemporaries of 'Poor Fred', assisted Surrey to win back her former glory, came over the border to assist Hambledon at the height of her fame and lived to hear of England's first tour to Australia.

One has only to read the many announcements of the early matches to realize that betting was an integral part of the game. Indeed early editions of the Laws acknowledged the fact. Stakes of 100 or 200 guineas were commonplace. The Earl of Sandwich raised an Old Etonian side to play England in 1751 and the match was played for £1,500. It was said at the time that 'near £20,000 is depending' on the result.

There is little doubt that large sums of money did change hands and few of the early games were played purely for the game's sake. The practice continued into the early 19th century and many of the great matches were played for large stakes. Bookmakers were a common sight calling the odds in front of the old pavilion at Lord's. It was, of course, an age of gambling, but it did the game no good: with so much money at stake the temptation to 'sell' matches was very real.

The two great patrons of early Sussex cricket have already been mentioned. *The Duke who was Cricket*, as John Marshall so happily entitled his biography of the 2nd Duke of Richmond, and Sir William Gage were friendly adversaries. The last recorded match played by the Duke of Richmond's team was in 1731. It is probable that from then until 1745 when the Rebellion caused him to go to Scotland on military duty, the Duke's team played as Slindon. This village, whose cricket fame is surpassed only by the men from Hambledon, could challenge and defeat London and even county sides in the 1730s and 1740s.

The captain of Slindon and of England in 1744 was Richard Newland. He was the most famous batsman of his day, making top score in both innings against Kent in the famous match and 88 against them the following year, and Love, in his poem, refers to him as 'The Champion'. Richard Newland, who was a surgeon, left Slindon to take up a practice in Chichester. But before he retired from the game he had passed on his knowledge and technique to his nephew who, like him, was a left-handed batsman. The nephew was well taught and an apt pupil — by name, Richard Nyren.

3 The Hambledon Era, 1750–1787

E. D. R. EAGAR

Until the day that some new source of information is unearthed about this all-important period of cricket history, there is nothing that can be added to the writings and researches of the famous cricket historians. Certainly nothing could hope to replace the charm of the account of those great days handed down to us by John Nyren, son of Richard Nyren and great-nephew of Richard Newland.

John Nyren's *The Young Cricketer's Tutor* was first published by Effingham Wilson in 1833. It was 'collected and edited by Charles Cowden Clarke', an early example of a

John Nyren, to whom and to his collaborator, Charles Cowden Clarke, the game owes the immortal story of the Hambledon Men.

cricketer's 'ghost' writer! The second, and subsequent editions of the book were titled *Nyren's Cricketer's Guide*.

The two most attractive and informative editions were published early in the 20th century. The first by Gay and Bird in 1902 contained an introduction, notes and no less than 8 appendices by F. S. Ashley-Cooper. But it was left to Henry Frowde and E. V. Lucas to give us in 1907 *The Hambledon Men*, a book in which are to be found Nyren's reminiscences, Pycroft's long interview with William Beldham, the Rev. John Mitford's classic review of the book written for *The Gentleman's Magazine* and his talks with Fennex, memoirs of the old players by Haygarth and much else besides.

When was the Hambledon Club formed? The usual answer to this question is either 'in the middle of the 18th century' or more shortly '1750'. The evidence is scarcely conclusive but it would seem that the nearest we may ever get to the date of the club's formation would be nearer to 1760 than 1750. Richard Nyren was captain and secretary of Hambledon for many years. In a newspaper advertisement of 1782 he thanked the public for the many favours he had received 'during the last 20 years'. I believe, as did P. F. Thomas, that he was only one year out in his memory and that he took over the 'Bat and Ball' Inn in 1763 and the club was formed. It is an extraordinary coincidence that exactly 100 years later the Hampshire County Cricket Club came into being. The most remarkable feature in the saga of the Hambledon Club is the fact that this small village was miles from anywhere, even in these days. Two hundred years ago, when there were no cars, it must have been an adventure in itself even to find one's way to the ground. Yet this village for almost three decades attracted the chief patrons and the best cricketers in the land, to say nothing of the vast crowds who turned out for all the big matches. Nyren talks of 'many thousands'—

> 'Oh! it was a heart-stirring sight to witness the multitude forming a complete and dense circle round that noble green. Half the county would be present, and all their hearts are with us – Little Hambledon, pitted against All England was a proud thought for the Hampshire men. Defeat was glory in such a struggle – victory, indeed, made us only 'a little lower than angels'.

Why should such men as the 3rd Duke of Chandos, the Earl of Northington, the 8th Earl of Winchilsea, the 4th Duke of Richmond, and the 4th Earl of Darnley, amongst other great patrons, agree to become President of this village club? What made the 3rd Duke of Dorset, the 4th Earl of Tankerville and Sir Horatio Mann, amongst others, attend the great matches as players or spectators?

The answer lies in the fact that for about 30 years this little village became the centre of the cricket world. Here cricket grew to man's estate. Until the Hambledon era, the skills of the game had been largely a question of a good eye and great strength, depending whether one was batsman or bowler. The niceties of the game began to develop once the original Hambledon men came together.

An early minute book and a statement of accounts, kept by Richard Nyren and the Messrs Bonham, are still in existence. They were all at one time secretary of the club, and Mrs Alan Lubbock (*née* Bonham), allowed Ashley-Cooper to reproduce them in his fascinating book *The Hambledon Cricket Chronicle 1772–1796*. As was to be expected, much information can be discovered from a study of these manuscript volumes. It is an eye-opener to find that members of the club paid a subscription of 3 guineas a year in 1791 – the exact amount which members of the Hampshire County Cricket Club were required to pay up to a few years ago. Some of the members represented the club occasionally, but the players were required to pay no subscription and were, in fact, professionals. In 1782 it was decided that those who played for the County XI should receive 'on the practice days, four shillings if winners and three shillings if losers, provided they attended by twelve of the clock'. If they were not present by eleven they 'are to forfeit threepence each, to be spent amongst those that come at the appointed time'. Club meetings were not always well supported, which must have been aggravating to such an enthusiast as the Rev Charles Powlett, the chief patron. They were apt to be convivial affairs, for a terse minute reads: 'a wet day, only three members present, nine bottles of wine'. As the years rolled by attendances grew less and less and the last sad minute simply states: 'no gentlemen'. This was on 2 September 1796. The following April, Richard Nyren died, but the squarson Powlett lived on until 1809. His love of the game continued and he found solace for the demise of his beloved Hambledon in the early days of Lord's Cricket Ground.

John Nyren was born in 1764 and he certainly would have played with most, if not all, the original members of the club. Unfortunately, the scores that have been handed down to us seldom contain the initials of the players. From 1783 to 1786 it is impossible to know whether it was father or son playing in a match. But it was the son who remembered batting with Noah Mann 'when, by one stroke from a toss that he hit behind him, we got 10 runs'. This must have been in 1782, for the game took place on Windmill Down. The Duke of Dorset and other gentlemen had complained of the 'bleakness of the old place'. Broadhalfpenny is certainly bleak, but the new home could

Broadhalfpenny Down: on this bare strip of Hampshire heathland was born, by a strange quirk of cricket history, the legend of Hambledon, the village whose team drawn from the surrounding countryside was in its day a match for All-England. A game in progress between the wars.

have been little better, though it was certainly more convenient being nearer the centre of the village.

It was on Broadhalfpenny that the greatest deeds of the original Hambledon men, old John Small, William Barber, Richard Nyren, Thomas Sueter, George Leer, Thomas Brett, Edward Aburrow (nicknamed 'Curry' – no one knows why), James Aylward, William Hogsflesh, Peter Stewart ('Buck' – because of his spruceness), Richard Purchase and Richard Veck, were performed. These were the cricketers who made the village famous for all time. Most of them were Hampshire-born, and the remainder could genuinely claim a residential qualification. It was after the move to Windmill Down that the Surrey contingent joined forces with the Hampshire men to provide a team which feared no combination that could be brought against them – William Beldham and John Wells (1787), 'those anointed clod stumpers', Harry Walker (1784) and Thomas Walker 'of the scrag o' mutton frame' (1786) played only on Windmill Down, as did David Harris, who was Hampshire born – the greatest bowler of his generation.

The players wore sky-blue coats which had black velvet collars – the buttons had 'CC' for Cricketing Club engraved upon them. Beldham recalls their velvet caps, knee breeches and stockings. Shoes had buckles, a decorative but dangerous adornment, and Wells once tore his finger nail off whilst picking up the ball. Nyren records that about the years 1769 and 1770 the club had a run of ill success and was on the eve of being dissolved. Fortunately the defeat of Surrey by one run at Laleham Burway on 23 September 1771, proved sufficient encouragement for members and players to face the future with growing confidence.

We have seen how Hambledon came to be connected with the introduction of the third stump. Now, too, the shape, as well as the width, of the bat was gradually modified and began to look more like its modern counterpart. The great John Small was an early bat maker. He was also an expert ball maker whose wares kept their size and shape remarkably well even in wet weather. He could proudly hang a sign in front of his house proclaiming:

Here lives John Small,
Makes Bat and Ball,
Pitch a Wicket, Play at Cricket
with any man in England.

Small's greatest, and indeed historic, contribution to the game was his development of the basic technique of straight-bat play as the only answer to the length-ball revolution of the bowler's attack. It was surely this classic technique which enabled him once to bat for three whole days and is it not recorded that when 'Lumpy' Stevens bowled him out in Bishopsbourne Paddock in 1772, it was the first time 'for several years'?

It was in the improvement and variety of the bowling that Hambledon led the way. Length, swerve and break, all these had now to be countered and their batsmen on practice days seized every opportunity of learning how to deal with them more successfully than most of their opponents. Thus from the earliest days the Hambledon men were able to practise against Thomas Brett, the fastest and straightest bowler of his day. At the other end there was Richard Nyren himself, and as change bowlers Barber and Hogsflesh were accurate enough not to give away many runs. In those days all the bowling was medium to fast and thus the arrival on the scene of Lamborn, the 'Little Farmer', was to pose quite a new problem to batsmen for he was the first off-spinner in the game.

The early under-arm bowlers seldom practised spin and if there was a twist on the ball it was from the leg to off when delivered by a right hander. This new deceitful and teasing style of delivering the ball worried the best of their opponents and the Kent and Surrey men were 'tumbled out one after another, as if they had been picked off by a rifle Corps'.

E. D. R. Eagar, for 31 years secretary of Hampshire, when he died suddenly in 1977 was both cricketer (12 years county captain) and cricket historian, a devoted disciple of H. S. Altham and the author of the first 3 sections of the history in this book.

Unfortunately the 'Little Farmer' had little else to offer as he was no batsman and a poor field and his 'comprehension did not equal the speed of lightning'; but he was the originator of the famous saying 'Ah! it was tedious near you, Sir!' when one of his deliveries shaved the Duke of Dorset's leg stump.

It was in 1777 that the 'swarthy gypsy', Noah Mann, joined the club. He was a good bat, fielder and a very fast sprinter whom Nyren had never seen beaten. Above all he was one of the earliest exponents of the swerve. He was left-handed and the chief merit of his bowling 'consisted in giving a curve to the ball the whole way'. Poor Noah, he died at the age of 33 after falling on a fire following a party which Nyren spoke of as 'a free carouse'.

These were the early bowlers of the club but the greatest of them all was yet to come. David Harris was born at Elvetham in 1754 and first played for the club in 1782. He practised assiduously and was wonderfully accurate, compelling the batsmen to go forward in defence. Thus many of his wickets fell to catches which, in those days, were not credited to the bowler. He did not invent length bowling, but his accurate combination of length, direction, speed and leg-spin posed new problems to those initiated by Lumpy Stevens. David Harris, more than any other cricketer, was instrumental in forcing the batsman to evolve the fundamental techniques of batsmanship that we know to-day. The Rev John Mitford calls him 'the finest bowler whom the world ever rejoiced in when living, or lamented over when dead'. This tribute can be allowed to stand if it is acknowledged that he was the greatest before the introduction of round-arm or over-arm deliveries. Here is Mitford's description of his action:

His attitude, when preparing to deliver the ball, was masculine, erect and appalling. First, he stood like a soldier at drill, upright. Then with a graceful and elegant curve, he raised the fatal ball to his forehead and, drawing back his right foot, started off. Woe be to the unlucky wight who did not know how to stop those cannonades!

So much then for the bowling strength which proved so often too much for the rest of All England. For their successes they had often to thank their fieldsmen, and *The Cricketer's Tutor* makes it plain that great store was set on this vital department of the game. Thus we read of the wicket-keeper, Tom Sueter: 'What a handful of steel-hearted soldiers are in an important pass, such was Tom in keeping the wicket. I never saw his equal and have numberless times seen him stump a man out with Brett's tremendous bowling', and there were no gloves or pads in those days. Then there was George Leer, his longstop, who 'was sure as a sandbank'. If John Small, Snr, was the Hutton of his day the mantle of Bradman must,

200 years ago, have been worn by Beldham. 'Silver Billy' was primarily a Surrey player but his name has, historically, always been linked with Hambledon. In fact he did not begin to play for the club until 1787 when its power was declining and the focus of the game was destined to move elsewhere; in fact to Lord's and its club, MCC – in the formation of which, by a strange irony of history, the Earl of Winchilsea, in that very year President of Hambledon, played so decisive a part.

These were the men who brought immortal fame to the Hampshire village, who could hold their own with any team in England, and whose captain could proudly proclaim that it was never safe to 'bet your money against such men as we are'.

4 Lord's and the Early Champions, 1787–1865

A. A. THOMSON

The period between 1787, the year of the formation of Marylebone Cricket Club, and 1845, when the All-England XI, organized by William Clarke, started its 'missionary journeys' over the length and breadth of England, was for cricket an era of sweeping change and saw its development from an uncomplicated pastime of country skills and country pleasures into an institution of national importance.

The formation and rise of MCC was in itself one of the two or three most important events in the whole history of the game. The era saw in 1805 the first matches between Eton and Harrow; in 1806 between Gentlemen and Players, and in 1827 between Oxford and Cambridge. In 1815 when the Duchess of Richmond gave her historic ball on the eve of Waterloo many of the officers present came straight from a cricket match arranged for them on the outskirts of Brussels by the Duke, their commanding officer. More personally interesting than all the other events was the emergence of the great names, more famous than any so far except those of the Hambledon heroes; names that were to become embedded in the authentic history of cricket.

There is no doubt that cricket owes an immeasurable debt to Thomas Lord, the Yorkshireman, who as a young man migrated south first to Norfolk with his family and then came on to seek his fortune in London. *The story of his employment by the founders of what in 1787 became MCC and his successive renting of three grounds, the last of which became the Club's permanent home and the headquarters of cricket, is told by J. H. Fingleton in* 'Lords and the MCC' (*qv*).

By the turn of the century Lord's Ground had established itself as a cricket centre without rival. The Marylebone Cricket Club, which the White Conduit Club had become on leaving its Islington fields, took upon itself to revise the laws of cricket (through a committee of noblemen and gentlemen). Within a few years it had become recognized as the leading authority on the organization of the game.

Even when eminent players were members of powerful counties like Kent and Hampshire they still liked to have their names on its members' list. It had become uncommon, almost ridiculous, for the great matches to be played elsewhere and, then as now, it was the dream of every ambitious youngster to come to Lord's and make a century. Gradually most of the southern counties began to raise strong XIs, though there was not to be a regular County Championship for another three-quarters of a century. There were matches, however, between North and South (the South being in earlier days capable of raising sides that were much the stronger) or between an All-England XI and the 'Bs'; that is, players whose names began with that letter, which, since it could contain cricketers of the calibre of Lord Frederick Beauclerk or William Beldham or Thomas Beagley, was bound to be a formidable combination. Of the ancient fixtures at Lord's the oldest by a distance, now that Gentlemen v Players is no more, is that between Eton and Harrow. There was possibly a match between Eton and Harrow in 1800, though no score remains, but it is certain that the schools met at Lord's in 1805. Lord Byron, despite his lameness, was a member of the Harrow side, but they could not prevent their opponents from 'confoundedly' beating them by an innings. His lordship even spoke, without his customary tongue in cheek, of 'cricket's manly toil'.

There was a gap for a dozen years after this, but in the summer of 1822 there came to the Harrow XI a notable player, the young Charles Wordsworth, a nephew of the poet, who was later to captain Oxford in the first University Match. As a left-hand bowler he had so embarrassed the Eton batsmen that they took on a professional coach to help them to cope with such problems, and this engagement formed the start of a long line of Eton coaches which reached its greatest height with George Hirst in the 1920s. Other schools, too, were laying down traditions and arranging fixtures that would become historic.

Of all the great names that arose between the days of the Hambledon men and the era of the wandering XIs the greatest undoubtedly was that of the Rev Lord Frederick Beauclerk, the most gifted all-round amateur cricketer of his day. A great-grandson of Charles II by Nell Gwyn, he was an aristocrat to the tips of his bowling fingers. He had such insolent confidence in his ability that at practice he would hang his gold watch on a bail. His bowling was slow, curly and cunning. His talents as a skilled and punishing batsman were used to make centuries on the first Lord's ground at Dorset Square. In his zest, his prowess, his insistence on the 'rigour of the game' he was in his day the forerunner of the greatest of all cricketers, W. G. Grace.

Lord Frederick was not above the gambling which was rife in all sports, from horse-racing to cock-fighting. Sometimes as much as 1,000 guineas was wagered upon one game. Single-wicket matches were personal contests carrying heavy wagers, sometimes laid by players themselves and often by the general public. Lord Frederick himself boasted that he was likely to make £600 a year by betting. With such large sums at stake there was always danger and it cannot be doubted that there was some corruption or that on particular occasions players could not be bribed to play badly. It was even whispered that Lord Frederick was himself a party to some of the chicanery that went on, though this seems unlikely. On the contrary, while he supported betting, he did not approve of roguery. It was, in fact, his influence as an administrator at Lord's which called a halt to the selling of matches and secured the permanent dismissal from cricket of two well-known cricketers.

While Lord Frederick must be acquitted of corruption, he cannot be absolved from gamesmanship and bad temper. After vainly bowling at Tom Walker, 'Old Everlasting' of Hambledon, Lord Frederick flung his white hat on the ground, dancing with rage and shouting: 'You confounded old beast.' His most notorious attempt at gamesmanship recoiled on his own head. Along with a very fast underhand bowler named Howard, he arranged a 2-a-side single-wicket match for a stake of 50 guineas against the famous 'Squire' Osbaldeston and William Lambert, the most talented all-round professional of the day. At the last moment the Squire fell sick, but when he asked that the game should be delayed, Lord Frederick gave

The first Lord's: on the site of Dorset Square, used by the MCC from the club's formation in 1787 until 1809.

his characteristic, almost classic, reply: 'No, Sir. Play or pay!'

But the Squire was also a man of character. 'Lambert shall play you both,' he retorted, 'and take the stake money if he wins.' Lord Frederick, after a good deal of bluster, agreed that the game should proceed, but that the Squire must go to the wicket and score at least 1 run in order to qualify for a substitute fieldsman. This he did; then Lambert went in and scored 56. When Lord Frederick and Howard batted they finished 32 runs behind and, as the redoubtable Lambert scored another 24, they were left with 57 to make to win. Howard, put in first, was soon out, but Lord Frederick laid about him fiercely and, as the excitement of the spectators rose, it almost looked as though he might hit his way to triumph. But Lambert was full of cunning tricks and, well knowing his Lordship's choleric disposition, he began bowling a little more and more off the wicket, till the batsman, driven to exasperation, lashed out wildly at everything and was eventually bowled by a straight ball, still 14 runs short of the target.

After his retirement, Lord Frederick would sit each playing day just inside the pavilion gate at Lord's, a cigar in his mouth and at his feet his little dog, which by the intensity of its barking seemed to applaud or criticise the returning batsman. Last scene of all, that ends this strange clerical history, is the picture of Lord Frederick, sitting in his brougham, his nurse by his side, sadly surveying the scenes of his former triumphs and muttering no doubt that the glory had departed. A great personage, if not the most amiable of persons.

Among the purely amateur cricketers of the day E. H. Budd, 'Squire' Osbaldeston and the famous Wykehamist, William Ward, were the players most worthy to be compared with Lord Frederick. In the earliest days of the Gentlemen v Players series these four formed the backbone of the amateur side. Edward H. Budd was an eager cricketer and a fierce hitter. Lord Frederick said of him: 'Budd always wanted to win the game off a single ball.' He first appeared as a boy at Lord's, the original Dorset Square ground, in 1802 and was actually playing cricket half-a-century later. A dashing batsman, he wielded a massive 3 lb bat and was, like Sir Jack Hobbs, a master of the quick-footed drive.

Budd was ideally strong in build, 5 feet 10 inches in height and weighing 12 stone. 'Very clean made and powerful,' the Rev James Pycroft calls him, 'with an eye singularly keen.' The best judges, that is, the batsmen who had to cope with it, found Budd's bowling particularly difficult. In the field he was the quickest of his time, standing at midwicket with wonderfully safe hands and, by his reputation for speed in a sharp return, daring the batsmen to take short runs. In this period, the heyday of the single-wicket player, Budd was outstanding, because of his all-round capabilities. He had once, not boastfully but for the record, stated that he would play any man at single-wicket without fieldsmen, and in the post-prandial glow of an MCC dinner William Ward asked him if he stood by this.

'Undoubtedly,' said Budd. 'And for 50 guineas.'

'Then,' said Ward, 'I will produce your man.'

On the day that had been arranged Budd arrived at Lord's, where the flag was flying and the crowds were jostling. There he met Mr Brand, a well-known single-wicket player for Sussex.

'Why, Brand,' he asked, ignorant of his opponent, 'are you here to see the match?'

'No Sir,' was the the reply. 'To play in it.'

Budd went in first and Brand bowled away at ferocious pace, hitting and bruising the batsman all over his legs more severely than any modern 'bumper'. 'I was wearing nankeen knee-breeches and silk stockings,' recalled Budd ruefully, 'and there were no pads in those days.' But fiercely as he was hit, he hit out with his 3lb bat even more fiercely. When he had scored 70 furious runs, he contemplated his swelling bruises and reflected that he might be too stiff and sore on the morrow to bowl at all. He therefore smartly knocked down his own wicket, which was his only way of declaring, and then clean bowled Brand for a duck. After that he hit up 30 even quicker runs, 'declared' in his own fashion and bowled Brand for a second duck. It was an extremely satisfying victory by exactly 100 runs and, of course, 50 guineas. A vigorous and delightful character was Edward Budd and to the end of his life – he was over 90 when he died – he remained a fine all-round sportsman, always trying to win the game off the first ball.

Last and not least of the 'medieval' figures was William Lillywhite (*b* 1792), the 'Nonpareil,' a leading protagonist in the fight to legalize round-arm bowling. MCC accorded him a benefit in 1854 when despite his 61 years he bowled admirably.

The most famous of early 19th-century bowlers, William Lillywhite, came of a Sussex family. He was not only a cricketer of intelligence and skill, but a person of high integrity and these qualities gained him the nickname of the '*Nonpareil.*' With James Broadbridge, his county colleague, he practised the peccant form of bowling known as round-arm so successfully that when in 1827 Sussex and an England XI played three 'experimental' matches the county won the first two, much to the digust of the England men. In the third, an amateur, G. T. Knight, bowled round-arm for England even more effectively than Lillywhite and Broadbridge had done. The Law was amended in 1835 to allow the ball to be delivered below the level of the shoulder. It was 1864 before the bowler was allowed complete freedom as to the height of the arm.

The advent of mowing-machines, of practice nets, of scoreboards and score-cards dates from the middle of the century. The most far-reaching movement within the game around this time however began when in 1846 William Clarke, a Nottingham man, founded the All-England XI for the purpose of touring the countryside, playing against local XVIIIs and XXIIs in towns and villages on what may be called without irreverence their missionary journeys. Clarke himself, besides being a key figure in cricket history, was a remarkable, if rugged, character. Originally a bricklayer, he had in 1837 married the widow who kept the Trent Bridge Inn and with her had carried out the development of the gracious river-side ground, now for ever linked with Test cricket. Starting late, he achieved performances that sound fantastic: in the seasons spanning 1846 and 1853 he took 2,385 wickets, averaging 340 a season and never taking less than 200. In 1853, when he was 54 years old, he captured 476. True, many of his victims were rustic amateurs and, as captain, he was seldom in haste to take himself off. Nevertheless, the feat remains a prodigious one.

As well as excellent players in his own town he brought in additional high talent from the south: from Kent, Alfred Mynn and Felix, and from Sussex, Lillywhite and Dean, notable bowlers both. Acting as captain and business manager, Clarke led his team round England, to match his skilled XI against the unskilled but hopeful hordes. To budding cricketers the Grand Match of the season, played against the All-England XI, was a landmark in their lives, and the local youths would try their best to bowl a batsman of the calibre of George Parr or stand up for an over or two to Jackson, whose 'pace was very fearful'.

We have a record of a typical match at Bristol in 1855, when W. G. Grace, aged 7, watched his elder brother, E. M., a stocky lad of 13, playing for the West Gloucestershire side. E. M. achieved little with the bat, but he was as quick as a jumping cracker at long-stop and impressed Clarke so much that he gave him a bat. He also gave the boys' mother a cricketing instruction book which drew from Mrs. Grace the classic reply that, while E. M. was good, she had another son who was also promising. There is a well-known lithograph by Felix showing the All-England XI in 1847. Among them are the most eminent cricketers of the day: 'Kind and manly Alfred Mynn'; the classic batsman, Fuller Pilch; the artistic performer, Joseph Guy, not to mention such bowlers as Martingell, 'Ploughboy' Dean, and Hillyer, the Kent bowler, who, like Sobers a century later, could employ speed or spin as the occasion demanded. Later there were bowlers of daunting pace, such as the notorious John Jackson. Six feet tall and weighing 15 stone, he would think nothing of taking 15 wickets in an innings and he gained the nickname of 'Foghorn' because he blew his nose loudly every time the bails flew.

Another bowler of the terrifying kind was 'Tear 'em Tarrant', who could also be relied on virtually to scare a side out. Other talented cricketers were Diver, called 'Ducky' because of his dapper appearance; H. H. Stephenson, the Surrey all-rounder and master of both kinds of break, and another lively all-rounder, Julius Caesar, who always demanded that his full name should appear in the score-book.

It was sad, but historically inevitable, that this fine body of cricketers should in time split up among themselves, and the reason, as with many other quarrels, was economic. Some of the players, and particularly the southern professionals, felt strongly that their captain was taking too large a share of the profits of the venture and that they themselves were underpaid and exploited. After much bickering, matters finally came to a head. An indignation meeting was held after a match in Sheffield and a protest was drawn up, stating that the rebels would never play (except in county matches) under Clarke's leadership again. Clarke was adamant and the break-up could no longer be avoided. A new team, the United England XI, came into being, with Dean and Wisden, founder of the celebrated *Cricketers' Almanack*, as its moving spirits. This split might have been a tragedy for cricket, but it was not. The truth is there were far more than a mere 11 'master' cricketers in the land, and the fact that there were now two touring XIs of almost equal strength meant that the missionary work of the pioneers could spread even more widely.

Clarke died in 1856 and his work was carried on by his more genial successor, the handsome George Parr, whose biggest hits at Trent Bridge were commemorated by 'Parr's Tree'. In the side that he captained were the Yorkshire batsman, George Anderson, and Edgar Willsher, the accurate, fast left-hand bowler, whose no-balling in 1862 had created the revolutionary climate which was to end two seasons later in

All England 1847: from *left*, Guy, Parr, Martingell, A. Mynn, W. Denison, Dean, Clarke, N. Felix, O. C. Pell, Hillyer, Lillywhite, Dorrington, Pilch and Sewell.

round-arm bowling being universally allowed. Some equally famous names crop up in the United XI: William Caffyn, the 'Surrey Pet', who toured Australia in 1863 and stayed to become the first great Australian coach; Jem Grundy, a medium-paced bowler who was so accurate that he could 'drop 'em on a cheese-plate'; Tom Lockyer, first of Surrey's great wicket-keepers; and Billy Buttress, one of the best of bowlers and worst of batsmen, who said: 'If they bowls straight, they bowls me, and if I hits 'em, they catches me!'

The part played by the touring sides in cricket's progress cannot be overvalued; when they began, regular county cricket, as we now understand it, hardly existed; by the end of the period which they dominated, county clubs such as Yorkshire and Lancashire were already on their feet. Their effect in entertainment and emulation over the remoter parts of England was enormous. Indeed, they spread, and delighted in spreading, the whole art and true spirit of the game. The relationship between the two touring sides became less hostile as the years went by until it finally faded with the death of Clarke in 1856. Regularly they played a match for the Cricketers' Fund (instituted in 1857) before big crowds who knew they were watching the cream of English cricket.

Gradually, with the rise of the county clubs, the players were more frequently called on for duty nearer home and the historic necessity for their touring grew less. But of the vital importance of their role there is not the slightest doubt.

In July 1864, W. G. Grace, two days before his 16th birthday, scored 170 and 56 not out against the Gentlemen of Sussex at Brighton for a side raised by his elder brother in South Wales. And the same year was issued the first number of Wisden's *Cricketers' Almanack*, to chronicle, sometimes gloriously and always accurately, the cricketers, great and small, from that day to this.

5 W. G. Grace and his Times, 1865–1899

RONALD MASON

The last 35 years of the 19th century saw the emergence of cricket from its middle age of random potentiality into a brilliant productive period of expansion and consolidation. Before the 1860s the game at its higher levels sparked and flourished unclassified, prey to the incalculable whims and overbearing personalities of its grandees, aristocrat or autocrat, Beauclerk or Clarke, and dependent for co-ordination on the popularity and success of what were all too often glorified exhibition-matches. Nevertheless its enormous fascination and vitality captivated ever-widening areas of its native country. Through all the eccentricity and uncertainty the great names drew their great crowds: Pilch, Mynn, Felix, Clarke, Lillywhite, Wisden and others made resounding contemporary reputations whose echoes draw our wonder and admiration more than a century later.

The cricket-loving public found itself a symbol in the 1860s in the person of W. G. Grace. The Victorians, worshipping masculine authority and success, accorded the man who rapidly became a father-figure an Olympian adoration. The magnificent physique, proud dominating beard and rich, presumptuous character of this astonishing cricketer were as effective in capturing his enormous public as his specialized skill. I would suggest that, wonderful as that skill was, it could never have invested him with the potent mystique that still attaches to his name had it not been for his unusual capacity to represent in his own presence and personality the ideals to which the age itself aspired. Nothing remotely like this had happened to a cricketer before, and it is improbable that it will ever happen to one again. It elevated W. G. Grace into a national figure as well-known as Queen Victoria herself.

It is arguable there may possibly have been better players than W. G. – bowlers, fielders, all-rounders for certain, and a picked two or three batsmen of even higher resource, intelligence and technique; but nobody in the history of the whole multifarious game can compete with the comprehensiveness of this man's contribution to the history of cricket and the social history of England. By force of skill he made a well-established game into something infinitely varied and resourceful; by fortune of physique and energy of personality he presented to his country a transformed pastime, half spectacle and half science, with the power to entrap at times the imaginative sympathies of a whole nation.

Thanks to Old Clarke and the wandering XIs, a wide popularity had already spread over the length and breadth of the country, and in certain honoured centres the great pioneering counties were establishing their reputations and their characteristic flavours. It would be largely correct to say that the quality of amateur cricket was determined in the public schools and universities, and that of the professional game in the wandering circuses and the counties; so that with the gradual evolution of the nomadic mercenaries into the resolute regional settlers, first-class cricket acquired a tough professional backbone that it has never lost. In the early 1860s it was Notts who first asserted the pride of the north in its lifelong rivalry with the south; they had possessed during the 1850s in Jackson, Grundy and Bickley, the most formidable collection of bowlers in the country, to be succeeded in the next few years with apparently inexhaustible resource by the outstanding lob-bowler, Tinley, the dangerous and persistent fast-medium left-handers, J. C. Shaw and Wootton, and – as if these were not enough to establish one county for ever among the classics – the imperturbable Alfred Shaw.

Unhurried, resourceful and relentless, this greatest of English 19th-century bowlers took just over 2,000 wickets for just under 12 runs apiece in the course of twenty-seven seasons. This is a fearsome enough feat of pertinacity and endurance; enhanced by the significant tally of fact that accompanies it – he bowled in all that time 24,700 overs and nearly 17,000 of those were maidens, 4-ball mostly but the principle holds; and the runs that were hit off him in all that time, 24,107, fell short, if you can believe it, of the number of his overs. He clean bowled W. G. Grace 20 times, more often than any other bowler.

There will be more to say of this during the later decades of our period; but for more than twenty years from the end of the 1850s Notts could claim in Richard Daft the most complete professional batsman living. Here was a great cricketer with whom fame has dealt a trifle unworthily; had Grace never played, Daft's forthright if ambiguous name would have attracted more than a casual share of the honour that we all naturally accord to the greater champion.

By the side of Notts in the 1860s most other counties look tenuous. Sussex and Surrey were no match for them in names, reputations or results, though Surrey's sterling professionals, William Caffyn and Julius Caesar, gave immense quality and character to the game and in H. H. Stephenson they produced one of cricket's classic coaches whose influence extended long after his own day Middlesex had brilliance rather than body, laying down a long and attractive tradition of amateur versatility around the personalities of the celebrated Walker brotherhood of Southgate.

Even the illustrious Yorkshiremen had at this period to share the honours with their neighbours, and to allow them cumulatively over the first decade or two their rightful pride of place; for they were not solidly founded until 1863 and found their early development frustrated by a series of schisms.

Knowing Yorkshire, we can guess that their resilience was immediate and effective; and in the year of their come-back, 1867, they returned characteristically all the way to the top. They possessed in George Freeman a great fast bowler, whom W. G. at the end of his career pronounced the best he ever played against; and in Tom Emmett the first of the unbroken line of individualist characters whose toughness of fibre and resourcefulness of vitality and wit have illuminated their county's native dourness with their equally native inventiveness and gaiety.

From Notts, accuracy and persistence; from Middlesex, *panache*; from Surrey, solidity and worth; from Yorkshire, above all, character. This is the pattern of the great counties of the 1860s and it was set for 30 years and more to come, along those very lines. Lancashire was to catch up later; Kent and Sussex, predestined to greatness, were undergoing straggling and indefinite phases.

Over yet another prominent county club of the 1860s a curious fate was hanging. Cambridgeshire at the time was a powerful combination, ready and eager to be matched with any side in England, and they allied in their collective talents a most comprehensive variety of all-round skills. They had an admirable leg-spinner in Buttress and a most terrifying fast bowler in the temperamental Tarrant, nicknamed rather ominously 'Tear 'em', who bowled with deadly effect from round the wicket on the line of the batsmen's legs. Balancing these were the neat and capable all-rounder, A. J. ('Ducky') Diver, and the memorable pair of batsmen, Tom Hayward and Robert Carpenter, the one frail and neurotic but a brilliantly adaptable stylist, the other a fierce, rapacious aggressor with a fine defence and great quickness of foot.

It is much to be regretted that this wonderfully promising county's cricket history ends where it begins. The county lost its leeway among its first-class rivals and never recovered it, relying for its fame upon its lost glories. It would perhaps not be fair to forget that it may be said to have continued its honourable service to the game vicariously and a little obscurely; for it was the great Tom Hayward's even more distinguished nephew and namesake who not only gave his own considerable talents to Surrey but fostered the promise of an even greater Cambridge player, Jack Hobbs.

It was Cambridgeshire's honour to found a tradition without sharing it; to Gloucestershire belonged a far more satisfying destiny. They barely existed as a county until their colleague counties had been well and competitively established for several years; but before they were formed into the potent menace they immediately became, they had earned their final immortality. Gloucester from the beginning was the county of the Graces; and from that strange lively family of doctor's sons on the outskirts of Bristol the history of modern cricket inevitably dates and derives.

W. G. Grace is in his own person such a towering and authoritative phenomenon that it is sometimes an effort to remember that he began his career as one of an already mildly illustrious family and not as the most prominent member of the family at that. When he was born in 1848 he had already three brothers, of whom one was to achieve a ripe repute in cricket before ever W. G. began to play; and two years later arrived the youngest of his brothers, who during a too short life was more than fit to be talked of in the same breath.

In a family apparently addicted to cricket, the keenest and shrewdest was the mother who, when writing to George Parr, the manager of the All-England team, recommending to his attention her son E. M., made bold to add that she had a younger one whose back-play would make him the best of the bunch. How satisfying that history so compellingly endorsed this brilliant woman's perceptiveness; how touching and appropriate the fact that when she died, 20 and more years later, the county match in which her sons were playing at the time was there and then abandoned; and how admirable that in the enormous list of births and deaths of cricketers in *Wisden* the mother of the Graces remains there, honoured and conspicuous, the only woman's name.

'W.G.' in early manhood, when he won athletic prizes as well as setting new standards as a cricketer.

Out of this vigorous and unusual family three sons emerged to help transform the face of the game. It was E. M., the third son, 6 years old when W. G. arrived, who first caught the eye of cricketers. A character of mercurial and relentless energy, he preserved for the threescore and ten years of his vigorous life a boisterous, adolescent enthusiasm for cricket and his own part in it. At anything below the highest level he was a devastating bowler, and his close fielding was the most rapacious in the game. His batting, greatly successful, was the despair of his teachers, who were unnerved at his incorrigible cross-bat pull and the vices that derived from it; E. M. trusted to his eagle eye and whipcord wrists and scored prolifically wherever he went.

G. F., the youngest, is visible only as through a glass darkly, as after a youth of great promise and pride he was smitten with sudden illness and died when he was 30; the gayest of the Graces, the lightest and the fleetest, he hints of accomplishments of beauty and adroitness which are not excelled even by the greatest of his brothers; a free and stylish batsman and a more than useful bowler, he was in addition a glorious field, who three weeks before his death, in the first Test played in England, brought off the most famous deep field catch in history.

William Gilbert Grace graduated from the orchard into the county of his birth in the very year of its actual foundation as a county club. He was still a few days short of 16 when in 1864 he made 170 and 56 not out in a non-first-class match at Brighton, and by the next year he was accepted without incongruity as one of England's leading amateurs, playing for the Gentlemen at Lord's and the Oval and in representative matches for All-England. Perhaps the first occasion when he stamped his image with finality upon the game was the match between England and Surrey at the Oval in 1866, when at 18 years old he went in at number 5 and made 224 not out, his first century in first-class cricket. His batting came to its full maturity in the 1870s. In this decade his name and fame were established once and for all. Superb physical health, great strength and endurance, gave his resourceful skills the firm reinforcement they needed. Added to these must have been courage beyond the normal, for the wickets commonly laid out for first-class play in those years varied disconcertingly in quality and some of the greatest grounds – most notably Lord's – had a very bad reputation indeed. It was rudely said that the only resemblance between the Lord's square and a billiards table was in the pockets!

The finest of the professional batsmen, Daft, Hayward, Carpenter, faced the unpredictable horrors with brave and adroit resource; but scores were low on these wickets, the free styles of amateur batsmanship were materially inhibited. One batsman was killed at Lord's in 1870, ducking into a short ball. The extraordinary triumph of W. G. lay in the imperturbability with which he met both the probable and the actual dangers. He had all the orthodox strokes and he used them with a quite unexpected power. He gave immense strength and solidity to the art of batsmanship, where beforehand it was perhaps courage and dexterity alone that had faced the erratic combination of bowler and pitch. As a fielder of fearless vigilance he was excelled only by his brother E. M.; as a round-arm medium-pace bowler, later modifying his craft to wily, bamboozling slows, he picked up as many wickets as he wanted.

In the 1870s W.G. nobly assisted by his brothers, pulled Gloucestershire's fortunes from honourable aspiration to triumphant success. It was not until 1870 that this purely amateur side had responded to the energetic enthusiasm of Dr Grace, Snr, and challenged the great professional counties on their own terms. W. G. had a tremendous season in 1871, when he collected 2,739 runs in 35 completed innings, a fabulous feat on the shirtfront wickets of the 20th century and almost unbelievable on the puddings and dustheaps of his own time. He enjoyed another like it two years later, when for the first time in his life he did the double, (which nobody else had ever done before) and took 106 wickets to go with his 2,139 runs. In 1875 he sharply steepened up his total of wickets to as many as 191, a figure he never beat, and in the next great year of 1876 redeemed a moderate start by crowding on unprecedented canvas in August and piling up 1,278 runs in one fantastic month, a record which stood for exactly sixty years until Walter Hammond, without being in the least aware of it, beat it by 3 runs in 1936. The climax of this historic month was compressed into 8 hot days in the middle when in three consecutive innings he made 344, 177 and 318 not out, against the sweating bowlers of, respectively, Kent, Notts and Yorkshire. For the rest of the decade his personal figures, though entirely adequate, were never so impressive as this – the combination of wet seasons, growing family responsibilities and the preparation and ultimate success of his final medical examinations, affected in their sum total even his enormous energy and capacity.

Nevertheless with E. M. and G. F. vigorously backing him up, and with admirable auxiliaries both in batting and bowling, he had seen his county safely to the top. As early as 1873, the year in which the Championship Competition was first instituted in recognizable form, Gloucestershire were bracketed first with the illustrious Notts. There is some little doubt about 1874, when according to certain statisticians they won on their own, although official honours seem to have been awarded to Derbyshire, whose first-class status at this time was somewhat ambiguous; but there is no doubt whatever about 1876 and 1877 when the primacy was theirs fair and square. This was the era of their great fame and supremacy. There is a certain melancholy fitness in the fact that since 1877 Gloucester have never won the honour again; there seems a kind of fateful insistence that the story of the three Graces was never to be bettered, whatever fortune or genius (and there were plenty of each of these) might have in store.

Arthur Shrewsbury of Notts, who in the 1880s twice led England to success in Australia; according to 'W.G.' the finest professional batsman of his day.

'My Hornby and my Barlow long ago', immortalized in Francis Thompson's poem, are on the right, with two other Lancastrians of the 1880s, Pilling and Watson. A. N. ('Monkey') Hornby won 4 Championships.

Gloucestershire yielded her supremacy back to Notts from whom she had taken it; this wonderful county had no Graces, but it had solidity and variety, consistency and the hue of greatness, and until Surrey bloomed and blossomed in the 1890s Notts were the most illustrious county in cricket's history. Alfred Shaw was still there, menacing and relentless as ever, reinforced by his worthy pupil Dick Attewell, with fine auxiliary all-rounders in Barnes and Flowers. These deadly bowlers were the penetrative force that carried Notts to fame; but the huge essential weight came from the memorable batting, dour Scotton and aggressive Barnes, with the crown of their talent the great opening pair, William Gunn and Arthur Shrewsbury. These were the most illustrious openers in English cricket before Jack Hobbs in the next century linked with four supreme partners in turn to put competition and argument to shame.

It was Hornby and Barlow who led Lancashire through their triumphant seasons of the early 1880s. Hornby was a great captain and Barlow an outstanding all-rounder, but it was as run-stealing openers that they earned their fame. They were helped by an outstanding amateur in A. G. Steel, who had a prodigious schoolboy record and fulfilled all his promise (some say there has never yet been so accurate and deadly a leg-spinner), and later by an intimidating array of bowlers who by a not very creditable coincidence were all suspected of throwing. Lancashire's unquestionable talents were consequently the centre for some crucial years of certain unhappy controversies; but during these years they laid the purposeful foundations of a glorious history.

Alongside Lancashire naturally voyaged Yorkshire, who were on the threshold of a lean period but who for the present throve in the possession of Peate and Peel, two of the deadliest slow left-handers in the great history of that strange and individual class of cricketers. In the half-century and more from the 1870s Yorkshire presented to the world no less than four supreme examples of this specialist talent, Wilfred Rhodes and Hedley Verity being the other two. The Yorkshire batting in the 1880s was perhaps adequate rather than distinguished, but the great George Ulyett, a punishing and resilient all-rounder, is a 'character' name that conceals behind happy camaraderie an enormous and effective talent, while Peel more than complemented his bowling prowess with the bat.

Down south, Middlesex drew liberally on their apparently inexhaustible store of glittering amateurs, some of them strung on dazzling family chains, like the Walkers, the Lytteltons and the Studds. In the 1880s A. J. Webbe founded the Middlesex tradition of a well-established and paternal captaincy, continued so staunchly after him in later years by Plum Warner, F. T. Mann and Nigel Haig; and was followed and surpassed in renown by that very brilliant batsman and all-round athlete, A. E. Stoddart, whose reputation at one time looked like rivalling W. G.'s for popularity but whose name has in the perspective of history been dimmed by the proximity of the great batsmen of the Golden Age.

Middlesex at this stage were too spasmodic and mercurial to rival the great northern counties in any serious tussle for honours; the backbone of southern cricket during the 1880s was provided by a rehabilitated and aspirant Surrey, led by the prolific and aggressive Walter Read. But the glory that was in store for the Surrey of the 1890s was referable less to Read and to his admirable captains, John Shuter and K. J. Key, than to the two most eminent of Surrey's pre-1890 professionals, George Lohmann and Bobby Abel. Lohmann was one of the most distinguished all-rounders in all cricket; a medium-paced bowler of tireless capacity and variety, he had a subtle intelligence and surpassing athletic graces, and both W.G. and Fry declared him to be the best of his kind in their experience. He was a dashing and effective bat, and a slip fielder who seems to have been in the Hammond class. Debonair and blond, he had a reputation with the ladies as well as with Lord's. Tragically, he played himself so hard during his short career that when tuberculosis took him while he was still young he had little resistance to offer and it burned him out.

There was more than a dash of the romantic about the handsome Lohmann, but the comic sterling earthiness of the undersized Abel commended him equally to the watchers. One of the spindliest and shortest men who have ever excelled in this exacting game, he developed into one of the most resolute of all opening batsmen and an immense popular favourite at the Oval. He instituted that wonderful chain of Surrey opening batsmen that kept its links unbroken through Abel and Hayward and Hobbs and Sandham and Fishlock and, like the strongly welded side he helped to found and perpetuate, has never been seriously disrupted since.

There was widespread belief in the 1880s that W.G.'s powers were on the decline, and that this massive bearded patriarch was ripe for little but an honoured retirement. This illusion was fostered by nothing less than a nationwide public subscription; by a disturbance of the regularity of his appearances through his proper preoccupation with his medical practice; and by a consequent rather pronounced decline in his scoring consistency, reflected in a general lowering of his average.

But a new dimension appeared to prove public instinct to be mistaken, and it presented a challenge that could not be properly answered without him. Australia had entered the first-class field, and was showing early signs of annexing it.

The story of international cricket harks back, of course, to the Canadian tour of 1859 and Spiers & Pond's lucky business venture of 1861, when for the first time a team of professionals dared the Australian continent and triumphed. Two years later the experiment was repeated, and so was the success; but there was no follow-up until 1873, unless one can take into serious account the strange visit to English cricket grounds in 1868 of the attractive and unpredictable aborigines. 1873 saw W.G.'s first tour, a somewhat turbulent pilgrimage on which friendly rivalry was on occasion so stimulated that the rivalry took precedence over the friendliness; but W.G. himself had no doubt of the quality and promise of the local players, and made this cordially clear to them before he left.

The 1880 Australian team in England, whose centenary this year was marked by a special Test Match against Australia at Lord's. Back row: J. Bannerman, T. Horan, G. H. Bailey, D. W. Gregory, J. Conway, A. Bannerman, C. Bannerman, W. L. Murdoch; Front row: F. R. Spofforth, F. Allan, W. Midwinter, T. W. Garrett, H. F. Boyle.

The first Test against Australia in England was played at Kennington Oval in September 1880. Lord Harris, who led his side to victory by 5 wickets, is depicted in the act of saving 4. In those days there were apparently 6 gasometers (now 4 gasholders).

All the tourists' matches so far had been against odds, and it was 1877 before any touring team from England met an Australian side on level terms. The English travellers came to their match against a Combined Australian XI at Melbourne after a gruelling Odyssey all over Australia and New Zealand. This may serve in part as a palliation of the ominous truth that Australia won this game, the first Test Match of recorded history, by 45 runs, their great opening batsman, Charles Bannerman, first of an illustrious line, making 165 when none of his colleagues reached more than 20 in either innings. One more Test was played that tour and England saved their faces by winning it; but the victory had founded for ever the inexhaustible native self-confidence that is the outstanding characteristic of Australian cricket. The stimulus it provided gave them at last the needed crusading incentive.

The year 1878 is accordingly ear-marked for all time in the history books as the occasion of the first Australian visit to this country by cricketers accepted as first-class. D. W. Gregory, leader of a long line of cricketing Gregorys, led a talented side into an exacting tour which contained everything but Test fixtures.

The first match at Trent Bridge saw Alfred Shaw and Morley destroy the tourists on a wet wicket; and there was no great public enthusiasm for their first appearance at Lord's in late May when they arrived on a chilly, showery morning to play a powerful MCC side which was as near to a Test XI as any that they were to meet. As W.G. and Hornby came out to bat, the tourists can have been forgiven a qualm or two, but 6 hours later one of the most astonishing cricket matches ever to be played had taken its due place in the annals, and the Australians had established themselves without any fear of inadequacy. It was naturally a bowler's wicket, and it happened to be entertaining that day a handful of the game's greatest artists with the ball. A dark and menacing fast-medium bowler named F. R. Spofforth was given his turn when MCC were 26 for two in 23 balls he had taken 6 for 4 and demolished this outstanding batting side for 33. Alfred Shaw and Morley, fresh from Trent Bridge, were nearly as destructive, bundling out the Australians for 41, Shaw's 5 wickets costing 10 runs in 33 overs, and Morley's 5 yielding 31 – admirable contributions to a classic carnage. Honours were even enough, and crowds were by now pouring into Lord's as the strange rumours spread. They were rewarded by factual horrors that outdid even their fancies, for MCC, unnerved at the crisis, were at their second attempt summarily annihilated by Spofforth and H. F. Boyle, who by taking 4 for 16 and 6 for 3 respectively had their hosts out in an hour for 19.

When the Australians won by 9 wickets shortly after half-past five they had completed the most extraordinary day's work in the history of cricket, and opened therein a new chapter. They established a new standard in hostile and penetrating medium-pace bowling, superseding the Alfred Shaw techniques of attrition that had followed on the murder by W.G. of the old fast-bowling tradition. Spofforth in particular ranks now and always in the very forefront of aggressive bowlers. They nicknamed him 'the Demon', and it matched his appearance and his guile.

After the initial shock and success of the 1878 tourists, international tours followed thick and fast. Between 1878 and the turn of the century nine Australian teams landed in England and ten English parties left home in the opposite direction; by the 1890s Anglo-Australian cricket was clearly a firmly established institution. Results of the Tests were from the beginning very even, neither side ever seeming to enjoy the prolonged predominance that 20th-century conditions have sometimes ensured. In the first Test on English soil in 1880 Murdoch and W.G. got over 150 each and England won by five wickets after a thrilling game. Two years later the tables were turned, again at the Oval, when England failed by 7 runs in a crescendo of tension that is still fascinating to contemplate.

The history of the times of W. G. Grace would not be complete without a full acknowledgment of the effect of the impact of Australia on the English cricket scene. From the 1880s must be picked out the deadly twin menace of C. T. B. Turner and J. J. Ferris, medium-paced attackers of pertinacity and penetrative power. Between them they were conspicuously destructive; in the whole summer of 1888, 663 wickets fell to the touring Australians, and Turner and Ferris had 534 between them. No other Australian bowler who came to us in these closing years of the century shares their class and their honours, with the distinguished exception of tall Hugh Trumble, most accurate and dangerous of spinners, whose long and illustrious Test career runs into the next age.

The Australian batsmen who appeared in the 1890s added a new and fearsome weight to the problems of the England bowlers, showing the first evidences of a matured skill. Aggression had always been favoured in their ranks, since the days of Charles Bannerman, H. H. Massie, Lyons and Harry Trott; and if resourceful stability were needed to reinforce it, the tradition of the solid Alec Bannerman was continued by S. E. Gregory and George Giffen. These were all very good batsmen, yet only W. L. Murdoch ranked with the greatest of their English rivals. But in the mid-1890s arrived Joe Darling, a highly promising left-hander due for an impressive career as captain and administrator. Following him a year or two later came an even greater left-hander, the infinitely resolute Clem

Hill. Here, if not genius, was at least talent supremely adapted by concentration and intelligence to share most of genius' rewards. Then in the 1899 Test series, the one which saw W.G.'s last appearance, Australia's batting tradition received its crowning seal of genius when the 21-year-old Victor Trumper played the first Test match of his brief but incomparable career. Trumper's play had a beauty and an adaptability that no known batsman has ever matched; he put a grace and glory into every movement and phase of his cricket that must subtly have reflected an unusual and strangely attractive personality.

In 1890 the recently founded and short-lived County Cricket Council recommended an elaborate scheme for an inter-county league system made up of three divisions. The second-class counties fought this to the death, and killed it; and the County Championship, which was still a completely unofficial organization, was left for a dozen years longer to grow by nature rather than by rule. The 8 old-stagers continued their flourishing existence – Gloucester, Notts, Surrey, Kent, Middlesex, Sussex and the two historic northern rivals. Welcome additions now gave variety and colour to familiarity. Somerset, arriving in 1891, were followed 4 years later by Derby, Essex, Warwick, Leicester and Hampshire. Thus such names as Hewett and Palairet, and Sammy Woods, Kortright and Perrin, Pougher, Walter Mead and Wynyard were ushered in – and began at once to build new qualities and new traditions into an already rich heritage.

The decade rightly belonged to Surrey, who between 1887 and 1899 were undisputed Champions 8 times and shared it with two others once. In the 1880s it had been W. W. Read, Abel and Lohmann who had led Surrey to top place; in the 1890s the two professionals still formed the powerful nucleus, but what confounded all opposition was the resplendent striking force embodied in the two magnificent fast bowlers, Richardson and Lockwood.

This most formidable pair, as great in their generation as Gregory and McDonald or Miller and Lindwall in theirs, held Surrey's opponents at their mercy for a solid decade, striking sparks out of the hard batsman's wicket at the Oval each in their characteristic way. Together they made Surrey's victories and they made England's; and along with their penetrative powers there was allied the forthright, handsome run-making of the younger and greater Tom Hayward, who for nearly a quarter of a century was the staple of Surrey's aggressive batsmanship. It was over fifty years before Surrey reached and held such heights again.

This was not true of Yorkshire, supreme in manpower as well as in cunning and skill, who found in the 'nineties that sure touch of co-ordinated character that belongs to them above all counties. In these years Lord Hawke exercised his illustrious rule over the last of the Old Guard, Peel and Ulyett, and Brown and Tunnicliffe, the first of the new. But the greatest names operative in the Yorkshire of the 1890s were names of the future rather than the past – George Hirst and Wilfred Rhodes, Schofield Haigh and David Denton. These were still all playing in vigorous form up to the First World War, and some went on long after it. One conspicuous all-round cricketer who put his own great mark on his county and his country, whose aristocratic refinements were blended with indomitable arts and skills, was F. S. Jackson, one of the finest amateur products of a county whose toughest fibres have been professional. His triumphs, and those of his fellows, come to real fruition in the next decade.

To confront Jackson across the Pennines, Lancashire produced in this golden time two classic masters of amateur batsmanship, A. C. MacLaren and R. H. Spooner. The latter's free-flowing artistry was seen at its sweetest in later years, but MacLaren gave of his best in the 1890s in both batsmanship and leadership, making a fantastic 424 against Somerset in 1895 and playing throughout his long career with a spacious grandeur with which there are few modern parallels. He was ably backed by the all-round genius of Johnny Briggs, a left-arm spinner and cover-point of the very first order; and, of course, by Johnny Tyldesley, a little, serious man of immeasurable dependability and artistry, the first of a whole line of Tyldesleys to give their dour county colour and aggression.

Kent with J. R. Mason, Middlesex with P. F. Warner and Gregor MacGregor, Essex with C. J. Kortright and Percy Perrin, Notts with A. O. Jones, added each their quota of great amateurs to swell the ranks of the most honoured collection of amateur cricketers in the game's history. Sussex added two wonderful prizes to the collection; the first, the captivating Prince Ranjitsinhji, a very great player by all standards, of an extraordinary lightness and quickness, a figure who had his worthy successors but no true equal, a natural artist who moulded the game to the dictation of his own art; and second, that remarkable athlete-intellectual, C. B. Fry, who built his supreme batsmanship up by the pure light of rational intelligence and wit and thought his way to a commanding and memorable success. In C. L. Townsend and G. L. Jessop too, Gloucestershire had two of the most arresting amateur characters of the 1890s; the one a graceful left-hand bat and occasionally devastating leg-break bowler, the other an indestructible legend who elevated cold-blooded unorthodox hitting to a high art with his cross-batted savagery.

W.G. and his brothers, way back in the 1860s, had raised amateur cricket to a level where it had outfaced for more than a generation the supremacy of the well-founded professional masters. It was fitting that the last decade of W.G.'s own fabulous career should be honoured by this rare flowering of outstanding amateur talent. The consolidation of the first-class game as a business organization dependent on reliable

'W.G.' and F. S. Jackson around 1900: an expression of mutual respect and affection.

and regular professional resources, the emergence of a series of rare, attractive and popular professional performers, and the beginnings of economic uncertainty for the hitherto carefree and cushioned gentlemen of leisure, all made it unlikely that this conspicuous parade of brilliant individualism would ever be repeated; and in spite of wonderful temporary flashes in later years, it never was.

In the midst of all this glory, W.G., the fully acknowledged Champion, did not come to his close without one last triumphant expression of his powers. Nobody was prepared for the season of his astonishing Indian summer of 1895, when, in the course of the same celebrated May that saw Oscar Wilde tried and convicted, Grace, at the age of 46, made 1,016 runs. This unprecedented revel included 4 centuries, one of which was his hundredth. It also included the game against Kent in which he made 257 and 73 not out and was on the field throughout. He made five more centuries that season and finished with 2,346 runs and an average of over 50.

W.G. came to his close tenaciously, having passed 50 before age and temperamental differences parted him, a little regrettably, from his county. 1899 was the season of his last Test, at Trent Bridge, and his last game for Gloucestershire. He had been honoured the year before with a grand Gents v Players jubilee at Lord's, on and around his 50th birthday, and he had provided his friends and spectators with a grand individual contribution to a finely-fought match. In the next year he transferred his activities to the London County Club, which played for a few years at the Crystal Palace and which presented the spectacle of a number of promising and utilitarian cricketers circling around the central figure of the genial evergreen potentate. He was not therefore technically lost to the game; in fact he was 59 when he played his last match, at the Oval, making 15 and 25 and watching the rising young Jack Hobbs get himself a duck.

Over a span of more than 40 years W. G. Grace had seemed by his personality to carry cricket on his own from the days of its rough obscurity to the golden years of its widely accepted popularity as the most subtle and decorative of the great English games, and through the incalculable accidents of history and personality he had been accepted as a living symbol even by many who cared little for what he stood.

6 Dawn of the Modern Age, 1900–1914

I. A. R. PEEBLES

The cricket world of Edwardian England reflected the general spirit and pattern of the era. It was gay, elegant and secure; yet it was progressive. Together with racing, cricket provided the only major summer sporting entertainment. Counter attractions were few and infrequent in days before the family motor car had revolutionized the towndweller's weekend. First-class cricket was securely established. When Northants were admitted in 1905 the County Championship had recruited all its present competitors with the exception of Glamorgan. Talent was readily available. There was sufficient leisure to provide an abundance of amateurs, while the life of the modestly successful professional was prosperous and agreeable compared to the lot of the working man. County Committees ruled their own provinces with a benevolent but unquestioned authority, while MCC exercised a similar influence upon the entire English scene. Major tours were confined to Australia and South Africa, and their visits to this country were a considerable event. Club cricket flourished, as now, in a great variety of forms and qualities, from Inverness to Land's End. In the north it tended to take the sterner form of leagues and competitions. The Lancashire League and its counterparts had not yet become the off-season home of a stream of distinguished overseas performers but played to exacting standards, each team with its professional, who was usually a rising or lately retired county man. In Scotland the Western Union and counties provided high quality and keenly contested play which would draw 2,000 spectators on a Saturday afternoon. The Midland leagues of England were of much the same outlook and calibre.

In the south, as until modern times, the league system had no hold at all. Cricket was less closely organized in a wider field than the more localized communities of the provinces, and there prevailed a deeply embedded, if slightly self-conscious, attitude that the game was the thing and the pursuit of points alien to the spirit of it. The great but groundless touring clubs such as I Zingari, Free Foresters and Incogniti played Services, schools and clubs and had close connexions with country-house cricket (*qv*), a luxurious and picturesque institution much curtailed by the impoverishment of the householders after the First World War, and almost completely obliterated by the results of the Second.

Some impetus was given to the thriving urban and suburban clubs by W.G.'s arrival at Crystal Palace to inject his titanic spirit into the London County Cricket Club, which at the turn of the century survived for a few summers as a first-class entity. Amongst the many distinguished players who appeared in the large and varied fixture list was a young man named Hobbs who made some runs for Surrey against a Gentlemen of England side and earned an approving word from the Doctor. Regimental and Services cricket was enthusiastically pursued wherever the Army or Navy had reason to be, at home and abroad. The public schools had first-class facilities of their own and, although the National Playing Fields Association was yet to come, the less well-endowed schoolboys were occasionally fortunate in having open spaces such as Parker's Piece at Cambridge, or Turnham Green in London, one of which bred Tom Hayward and Jack Hobbs and the other Pat Hendren. There were still parts of England sufficiently rustic to encourage village cricket in its simplest and most attractive form.

The county captains at Lord's in 1901. Standing: D. L. A. Jephson, Surrey, G. L. Jessop, Gloucestershire, R. E. Foster, Worcestershire, S. M. J. Woods, Somerset, and J. R. Mason, Kent; seated: G. Macgregor, Middlesex, H. W. Bainbridge, Warwickshire, H. G. Owen, Essex, Lord Hawke, Yorkshire, and C. E. de Trafford, Leicestershire.

These years saw two major innovations in the technique of bowling. The first and much the more important of these innovations was the googly (*qv*), invented by B. J. T. Bosanquet, as a result of experimenting on the billiards table. There had been some – W.G. and A. G. Steel for example – who had perfected the ball bowled with the leg-break action which came straight on, but no one had hitherto succeeded in consistently making the ball *break* from the off when bowled from the back of the hand. The impact upon batsmen was tremendous. When the interpretation of the bowler's intentions had been confined to several well-defined positions of the fingers and hand the batsman could position himself confidently as soon as he had judged the length and direction of the ball. This was now no longer true in the case of the googly bowler, for a stroke correctly played on a wrong premise was disastrous where there was the slightest margin or error.

The great players, Trumper and later Hobbs, quickly counteracted this new menace by speed of foot and perfection of judgment. Trumper was, in fact, bowled by the first ball he received from Bosanquet in Australia, and it is recounted that he was later completely beaten by the first 'Bosie' he received from Hordern in a club match in Sydney. His response was characteristic. Walking down the wicket he smiled at the bowler and said, 'Where did you learn it?' Hobbs gained his experience against the superb South African quartet: Vogler, Faulkner, Schwarz and White. This was relatively, and possibly in fact, the greatest combination of pure spin ever to appear in any single team. (It is necessary to qualify this statement for the Australian trio, O'Reilly, Grimmett and Fleetwood-Smith, at their best in a more advanced age of batsmen, might have excelled the South Africans who operated largely in favourable conditions against the uninitiated.) Vogler was the greatest, and, in the opinion of his colleague, Faulkner, a bowler second only to Barnes. When the power of this school waned the cult passed from South Africa to Australia where the long line of 'Bosie' bowlers was founded by Hordern.

The second advance made in the bowler's craft was a much greater understanding of what could be done by manipulating the seam of the ball. The Philadelphian, King, had early adapted the baseball pitcher's curve whilst Hirst had perfected the in-swerve delivered left handed round the wicket. Noble discovered that by giving the ball a fuller flight, by dint of bending his knees and pitching it well up, he could influence its path through the air. These pioneers awakened others of the fast and fast-medium category to the possibilities of swerve and movement from the pitch. In earlier days Richardson had been noted for his break-back from the pitch which was ascribed to 'body-spin' caused by his fingers sweeping across the surface of the ball at the moment of delivery. It takes but a moment's reflection upon the amount of spin necessary to cause a fast ball to deviate on a hard wicket, and the meagre amount applicable with Richardson's typical thumb and two-fingered grip, to see that this explanation was quite inadequate, and that the break was caused by the ball pitching on the seam.

Once the comparatively simple device of using the seam as a rudder or fin had been grasped the cult spread rapidly and by the outbreak of the First War most new bowlers had acquired these new tricks. J. W. H. T. Douglas led the field amongst the swervers, in England, with the power to make the ball dip in either direction very late in its flight. But of all bowlers S. F. Barnes bestrode the scene, a towering figure. At a fast-medium pace he combined spin and swerve in a way which has never since been equalled or, indeed, imitated to any effective degree, except, perhaps, by Bedser's 'cut' from the leg. He mastered the 'googly' out of curiosity, but considered it superfluous to his armoury. His unique powers also had a strong influence on the batting of the day.

These innovations led to batting becoming less of an exercise in free forward-play and more of a taut watchfulness with greater emphasis on back-play. But this is not to say that stroke play was to any noticeable extent inhibited for, despite these added complications, it was an era of stroke players. Trumper was a product of the previous decade, but the early years of the century saw him at his greatest. Possibly the excessively wet English season of 1902 wherein he made 11 hundreds set the seal on his illustrious career. Jessop had also come to the fore in the 1890s but continued to devastate all forms of bowling with a mixture of shrewd, if momentary, defence and unorthodox onslaught. But the three leading batsmen in their respective countries by 1914, Hobbs, Macartney and the young H. W. Taylor, were wholly of this era. They had in common a great brilliance of stroke, Hobbs and Taylor with an impeccable orthodoxy and Macartney with an insouciance and taste for improvization in the tradition of Trumper.

Modes and manners in the Edwardian era followed a regular pattern. The delineation between amateur and professional cricketers was clear-cut and formal. The amateur, regardless of age and status, was addressed by his title or as 'Sir' by the professional, who was reciprocally called by his Christian or nickname, or, by the older school of cricketer, by his surname. Accommodation for each category was separated to the extent that, in some cases, they took the field by different gates. To modern eyes such segregation may seem feudal but, being in accord with the manners and customs of the day, it was apparently a happy and harmonious relationship, a view encouraged by the bearing and impeccable manners of the still surviving professionals, conspicuous in a less formal age.

Dress differed only in detail. It was a popular habit to wear a sash of club colours round the waist and the peak of the cap was steep and small compared to present dimensions. Boots were stouter and a really heavy sole was considered essential. The turtle-necked sweater, a most sensible garment revived for everyday wear in recent years, was slowly giving way to the V-neck. Straw hats and boaters, again colourfully bedecked, were popular for off the field wear, and the official photograph.

Apart from the dimensions of the wicket, which were then 27 inches high, by 8 inches wide, the apparatus was similar to that of the present day, differing only in detail. The bat was exactly alike in appearance and construction, but the demand for white willow was not then universal. The ball would seem large to the modern hand for it was made to the maximum legal measurements. Pads were of lighter construction than their modern counterparts, the skeleton pattern still being popular, while a modern wicket-keeper would have felt somewhat exposed in the gauntlets of the early 1900s. These latter grew stouter in the next few years, but many wicket-keepers of the era continued to seek added insulation in the shape of a good fat steak between glove and palm.

International cricket developed and prospered in the Edwardian span. Australia had been a formidable opponent ever since the defeat of James Lillywhite's team at Melbourne in 1877, a remarkable state of affairs in view of the disproportionate size of the populations. But the Australian weekend system of grade cricket did then, as it does now, bring young club cricketers into constant and immediate contact with the established masters, a privilege largely confined in England to those who played county cricket. The young Australian has usually learnt to play on true turf or concrete wickets, a very important matter in the formative stages. The love of the game coupled with the enthusiasm of a young and virile nature saw that the most was made of these advantages. By the close of the century Australia had won 20 Test Matches to England's 26, the remaining 10 matches being left drawn.

Cricket had taken root in South Africa as early as in Australia but for various reasons had flowered less rapidly. It was not until the end of the South African war that there were signs that a third first-class cricketing power was about to emerge. A team which came to England in 1901 caused no great stir, but in 1904 Frank Mitchell brought a team which did exceedingly well against the counties and the scene was set for South Africa's entry into Test Match cricket on equal terms.

The Board of Control for Test Match cricket had been formed in 1898 and as a result there was an important change in the organization of touring sides which took effect in 1903. Hitherto it had been the practice for individual cricketers to select and conduct teams to the colonies. At the request of the counties, and also its own Australian counterpart, the Melbourne Cricket Club, MCC sponsored the team to tour Australia under the captaincy of P. F. Warner in 1903–04, and thereafter all teams playing official Test Matches sailed under the blue, red and gold colours of the club. The actual 'hostilities' of the 20th century began with the visit of A. C. MacLaren's team to Australia in 1901–02. There was a dramatic prelude when MacLaren picked Barnes from the League to which he had returned after a brief and modest experience of first class cricket. But since this apparent eclipse Barnes had perfected his fast-medium leg-break and become the finest bowler in the world. MacLaren's inspiration combined with his own superb batting might have won the day had not Barnes broken down in the Third Test and dropped out of the series which was lost 4–1. It is an ironical footnote that MacLaren and his discovery, both being men of fiery spirit, generated such a degree of friction that, when it was suggested that an ill-found Tasmanian-bound ship might sink, the English captain derived a gloomy satisfaction from the thought that in the event of such a calamity his protégé would drown with the rest of them.

For the first tour of the new century, 1902, the Australians brought a very powerful side to England led by Joe Darling. Under his command he had two outstanding batsmen in Trumper and Hill and two of Australia's greatest all-rounders in Noble and Armstrong. Trumble, Saunders and Howell were all top-class bowlers, but Jones was probably past his fiery best. In the First Test at Edgbaston, what should have been the battle of well-matched giants was, owing largely to the weather, a most astonishing but one-sided affair so far as it went. After Tyldesley had made 138 of England's 376 for nine wickets declared, Hirst and Rhodes shot Australia out for 36 on a sticky wicket. In the follow-on Australia lost Trumper and Duff for 46 before the end of the match.

One need hardly say that this was not a true indication of the relative strength of the sides. The Lord's match was ruined by rain, the only remarkable feature being Hopkins's opening spell which disposed of Ranjitsinhji and Fry for 0 apiece. Sheffield produced the first result, a win for Australia due largely to the batting of Trumper and Hill and the all-round cricket of Noble. The Old Trafford match brought another win for Australia by 3 runs and provided the single and melancholy appearance of F. W. Tate. The Oval match resulted in England's only win, and that by a single wicket sustained by Hirst and Rhodes, after Jessop's century had turned a very adverse tide. This historic match brought to a fitting end a classic series wherein only the weather was less than perfect. On the homeward journey the Australians visited South Africa where they quickly mastered the intricacies of the mat and won two of the Test Matches played.

The victory of Warner's team in Australia in 1903–04 was in the nature of a pleasant surprise for its supporters and the first of many triumphs for its captain. This was another admirable series the success of which must have fortified MCC in their new responsibility for overseas tours.

The Australian team of 1905 was roundly defeated by a very strong home side. The greatest contributor to their downfall was England's captain, the Hon F. S. Jackson, whose record of winning all five tosses, heading the batting with an average of 70 and the bowling with 13 wickets at 15 apiece, was unique and astonishing. Jackson was, indeed, one of the most remarkable cricketers of his age or any other, endowed with great technical skill, a heart of real British oak and a consistently lucky star which would have excited the envy and admiration of Napoleon.

The first MCC team to Australia (1903–04), which brought back the Ashes. Standing: H. Strudwick, L. C. Braund, A. E. Knight, E. G. Arnold, A. Fielder, W. Rhodes, R. E. Foster, A. E. Relf and J. T. Tyldesley; seated: T. W. Hayward, B. J. T. Bosanquet, P. F. Warner, G. H. Hirst and A. A. Lilley.

In the following winter Warner set out again for South Africa and, although his team was not the full strength of England, it came as a severe shock that it lost the series. The South African batting was so even that the order could be reversed without ill-effect; but it was the superb googly bowling which carried the day. Bosanquet's invention had been developed to a point where it was bowled accurately, with almost complete deception and, in the case of Vogler, at around medium pace. The impact upon the uninitiated batsmen may be judged from the fact that a player as accomplished as Warner himself scored less than 90 runs in 10 completed Test innings. In 1907 the South Africans came to England, and although their spin bowling was the sensation of the year it was not quite sufficient to carry the day on English wickets. As their profound influence on the game has already been noted it may be proper to examine this unprecedented quartet in rather more detail. Vogler was generally regarded as the greatest. He ran about a dozen yards and delivered the ball at a good medium pace from a final jump more characteristic of a fast bowler. His spin was considerable and his googly not only well concealed but described by one victim as being 'like a knife'.

Schwarz was the most remarkable. Having learnt the trick of the 'wrong 'un' from watching Bosanquet he found himself the possessor of an abundance of off-spin, which merely increased when he sought to turn the ball from leg. Faulkner spun viciously and was also difficult to detect; and White, if unable to achieve quite the same venom, was a model of accuracy for his type. Those who wish to pursue this fascinating study further can turn up *Wisden* of 1908 in which R. E. Foster gives his impressions of the South African bowlers based upon practical and recent experience of their methods. The present writer had the privilege of bowling in nets with both Vogler and Faulkner and is deeply indebted to the latter for much of the information on this particular subject and of the era in general.

When the South Africans had departed, having lost the only Test Match of the three to be decided, it was time for England to revisit Australia. The series of 1907–08 showed that English cricket had receded since the glories of 1905 and the series was lost 4–1. But it was not without event and promise from the tourists' point of view. Barnes again bowled magnificently but J. N. Crawford, a youth of 21, was the most spectacular success, taking 30 wickets in Test Matches at 24 a time. Hobbs foreshadowed a unique career by scoring 83 in his first innings against Australia. Perhaps the most fascinating figure was George Gunn. Ostensibly touring Australia independently for reasons of health, he was enlisted for the Test Matches and, having scored 119 and 74 in the first, topped the averages for the series. This interlude was somehow typical of the picturesque career of a very remarkable man who, originally destined to be a professional pianist, brought to his play something of the temperament and virtuosity of the musician.

The recession continued through the following home series for, although the Australian team of 1909 was not considered to be of the first flight, it was victorious by two matches to one, two being drawn. Noble led his side with his usual acumen and Macartney emerged as an all-rounder. Bardsley completed a highly successful series by making a hundred in each innings of the last Test at the Oval. Hobbs was not in his best form, and the English batting was not particularly distinguished; but Blythe took 18 wickets in his only two matches and Woolley made his first Test appearance.

The Australian season of 1910–11 saw the South Africans outplayed despite the magnificent batting of Faulkner. The spin, so potent on the mat, failed to bite on bulli soil, and the Australian batting order was formidable and extensive. Yet when the next MCC side followed in 1911–12 the Australians were sorely bombarded by Barnes and Foster. The English batsmen were in their turn severely tried by Hordern, who bowled his leg-breaks and 'Bosies' so well that he took 32 wickets in the 5 matches for 24 apiece, an astonishing record in a side losing the rubber 4–1. English cricket at this stage had developed to its maximum strength, and the victorious side must rank as one of the most powerful ever to tour Australia.

The last season of Test Match cricket in England before the First World War was 1912. The Triangular Tournament was a bold, even grandiose, conception, largely instigated by Sir Abe Bailey. The idea of the three reigning cricket powers in action during the same season no doubt had a powerful appeal but, in the event, sanguine anticipations were soon translated into doubts and eventually into major disappointment. In practice almost every factor which could have made for success seemed to war against it. The preparations started on an ominous note when Australian cricket found itself riven with rows and feuds. The result of these disputes was that half-a-dozen of Australia's best players refused to come, and no adequate substitutes were available to make the final team fully representative. In South Africa cricket politics were commendably peaceable, but the practical material had grown thin since the days of 1907. England on her home soil had abundant resources and dominated the scene, while Australia were too strong for South Africa. To add a final chilly note it was a poor summer, and rain interfered with almost every match.

In 1913–14 an MCC side toured South Africa. On the matting Barnes's quick leg-breaks proved as deadly as on the wet English turf of 1912. In four Test Matches he took 49 wickets at an average cost of just over 10. But amidst the slaughter he met a truly great opponent in 'Herbie' Taylor, whose 508 runs in 10 innings was a major achievement, especially in light of Barnes's figures. On matting Taylor was a supreme batsman. On all wickets he was a model with a straight back-lift and a precision of footwork that brought him right back on the stumps or full stretch to the pitch of the ball. On this healthy note the international cricket scene closed for 6 long years. The records of the countries concerned within the 14 years revealed that England had won 14 times against Australia and 11 times against South Africa. Australia had beaten England in 15 matches and South Africa in 8. South Africa had succeeded in defeating England 7 times but only at Adelaide in 1911 had they ever got the better of Australia.

English county cricket was at its zenith in the years preceding the First World War. There was still some foundation for the saying that love of county was greater than love of country. The levelling, centralizing effects of broadcasting and the mass-produced motor car were still far away and to the ordinary citizen the borders of his county were very real. Where cricket was concerned the setting had all the attractions of the 1890s but the game had developed in itself and expanded. The Championship was dominated during this time by Yorkshire, who won it no less than 6 times, and by Kent who, with 4 wins, ran them close. Middlesex, Lancashire, Nottinghamshire, Warwickshire and Surrey shared what honours were left, which was a fair reflection of the balance of power.

Yorkshire, under the captaincy of Lord Hawke, who had done so much to mould them into the finest side in the table, won three times in a row from 1900 to 1902. They were essentially a complete team, with the batting of Tunnicliffe, Brown and Denton, the powerful all-round cricket of Hirst, Rhodes and Haigh, and plentiful reserves of high quality. This last asset was emphasized in 1905 when Yorkshire again took the Championship while contributing as many as five of their best players to the Test Matches against Australia.

Kent came to their best form in 1906. K. L. Hutchings batted and fielded magnificently, while Fielder, if not the fastest bowler in the country, had now mastered the ball that left the bat late in the air or off the pitch. Blythe competed with Rhodes as the leading slow left-hander and Woolley had an auspicious first season for his county. The following two seasons were less successful but in 1909 D. W. Carr arrived at the advanced age of 37 to spread destruction with a well-concealed googly. Middlesex won the Championship in 1903 and (from 1908) under the keen and skilful captaincy of P. F. Warner were always a side to be reckoned with. Albert Trott swung his 3lb bat and bowled his leg-breaks with fine effect in the early years and was succeeded as an all-rounder by his fellow Australian, Tarrant. J. T. Hearne was a model medium-paced off-spinner, and later his nephew, 'Young Jack', supported him in the role of an outstanding all-rounder.

In the north, Lancashire, champions in 1904, had a succession of illustrious names. MacLaren, J. T. Tyldesley, Brearley and Spooner were all in full force when the cessation came. For a brief period Barnes played regularly before returning to League cricket. Nottinghamshire were a Midland bastion between the great powers of north and south, whom they outstripped in 1907 and threatened at all times. Jones, the brothers Gunn, and Hardstaff, were Test players, but Wass, whose fast leg-breaks were unplayable on sticky wickets, lacked the additional equipment to rival Barnes. The other Midland county to reach the top of the table was Warwickshire who owed much, in the four seasons leading to the war, to the leadership and all-round cricket of F. R. Foster. His side was otherwise useful rather than spectacular, though it boasted, in W. G. Quaife, England's smallest batsman.

Surrey had Hobbs and Hayward and an array of supporting ''aitches'. The chief obstacle to their complete success was the difficulty of bowling sides out at the Oval after the departure of Richardson and Lockwood. Sussex were in something of the same case but, as long as Ranjitsinhji and Fry were available, they were a very difficult side to beat on the beautiful Hove wicket. But Ranjitsinhji played little after the opening years of the century and Fry moved to the neighbouring county of Hampshire. Worcestershire played upon equally fine turf, and were dependent to a large extent upon the Foster family. In 1913 Frank Chester made 3 hundreds, and his future as a player might have been amongst the very great. It was some consolation for the loss of an arm that he became the most famous of all umpires. In G. H. Simpson-Hayward Worcester had the last of the great lob bowlers. No other counties seriously challenged the strength of the big 6 but each had its moments and outstanding personalities. Essex were always resolute under the captaincy of 'Johnnie' Douglas, that splendid and determined man. Gloucestershire were always an attraction when the name of Jessop appeared in the batting order. Their neighbours had a beautiful home ground at Taunton and the batting of L. C. H. Palairet and skills of Braund to grace it. Hampshire produced Philip Mead. Derby, Leicester and the newcomers Northants had few frills but plenty of good Midland common sense and spirit. The last-named made a modest enough start but, aided by the fine cricket of S. G. Smith, were good enough to take second place in the Championship table of 1912.

University cricket over this period was at its most attractive. Life for the undergraduate was agreeable and elegant. There was an abundant supply of cricketers from the public schools and those fortunate enough to be awarded a blue played the game in its most idyllic form. When the season in the Parks or at Fenner's had been completed the teams toured, as do their present-day counterparts, but, one imagines, in rather greater comfort and, under a less exacting academic regime, in greater peace of mind. In passing one recalls the tale of one very famous university cricketer unable to recognize, let alone answer, the questions before him, writing a pithy expletive across his paper and returning to the nets. On his tutor sadly remarking to one of the examiners that he had hardly expected the hero would pass, the examiner replied that he had only written one word – but they would have passed him had that one been correctly spelt. The University Match in Edwardian times was not only an important event in the cricket world but one of considerable social consequence, rivalling the Eton and

G. H. Simpson-Hayward of Worcestershire, 'the last of the lobsters,' took over 400 wickets in the Golden Age.

Harrow. Dress was equally formal and fashionable, and many people believe that laxity in these standards is one reason why the fixture lost much of its attraction. Sir Pelham Warner was convinced that this was the case and for years fought a heroic but losing battle for grey topper and morning coat. Oxford won 5 matches between 1900 and 1914 as against 6 Cambridge victories. In 1910 Eton beat Harrow in the most famous of all school contests which, like other memorable occasions, is remembered by the name of its hero as 'Fowler's Match'.

It is not, perhaps, for the chronicler to turn advocate, but it must be fair to say that the period between 1900 and 1914 has a fascination for the student of cricket beyond any other. By accident of time it was the end of a long and gracious era. By its fertility it was the first episode in the purely modern age, for there has since been no major innovation in the actual technique of batting or bowling. It was a time of champions and personalities whose deeds and images are fresh and familiar to lovers of cricket 50 years later.

Trumper, Ranjitsinhji, Jackson, MacLaren, Hill, Noble, Fry, Jessop, Hirst and Rhodes were products of the 1890s, but they all belonged very much to the new century. Hobbs, Macartney, Faulkner, Blythe and Spooner were its products. It produced the most beautiful of all left-handers in Frank Woolley and two of the most efficient in Bardsley and Mead. The world's greatest bowler, Sydney Francis Barnes, appeared in major cricket in the first year to dominate the scene for its duration. Foster's left-handed pace from the pitch caused alarm and astonishment in England and Australia. There were exponents of every type in the highest class with but one possible and interesting exception. Despite the tremendous pace of Cotter and Kotze, the new-found craft of Fielder, and a multitude of good workaday performers, the age did not bring forth a fast bowler of the calibre of Lockwood, McDonald, Larwood or Lindwall.

It did, though, produce several very notable wicket-keepers. Lilley ended his days as England's 'keeper in 1909, having established a complete supremacy in his craft. His absence in 1907–08 had a considerable bearing on the loss of the series. His successor was Herbert Strudwick, whom any Surrey man will claim had few peers, if indeed any. He was, however, sometimes displaced by E. J. Smith, who was an adept at

1

2

3

4

5

6

7

8

9

10

11

An XI of great England cricketers all in their prime around the turn of the century as captured by the camera of George W. Beldam. The names of this hypothetical team in a likely batting order and reading from left to right are: 1 A. C. MacLaren; 2 T. W. Hayward; 3 K. S. Ranjitsinhji; 4 C. B. Fry; 5 Hon F. S. Jackson; 6 G. L. Jessop; 7 A. A. Lilley; 8 W. Rhodes; 9 B. J. T. Bosanquet; 10 S. F. Barnes; 11 T. Richardson.

The subjects were perforce photographed at close quarters in practice since these were times prior to the invention of the telephoto lens. The prints were made by Kodak from the original plates in the possession of the copyright holder, Mr G. A. Beldam, with his kind permission. These 'action shots' stand up to the most critical analysis, apart from the position of the wicket-keeper.

G. L. Jessop making a First World War recruiting speech. Shortly afterwards an accident so damaged his heart that he could never play again.

taking the fierce and awkward deliveries of his captain, F. R. Foster, and the swift turning leg-breaks of Barnes. Although David Hunter of Yorkshire never got an England cap, he was nevertheless a legend and a rare character, as indeed many wicket-keepers have been through the ages.

Much was done to spread and encourage cricket in far places. P. F. Warner – 'Plum' to the man in the street – was indefatigable in taking sides abroad, and his Harlequin cap became a beacon to all who followed cricket. The coaching scheme for boys was started at Lord's in 1902. More than 200 books and publications concerned with cricket appeared. The player-writer and attendant ghost were already to hand so that *Punch* commented acidly on a bowler with a 40 yard run that at least the batsmen would have time to form their Press opinions of him.

On 4 August 1914, 'W.G.' was 66. In his day he was said to be a better-known figure in England than Mr Gladstone himself and was, in retirement, a national institution. Victor Trumper was to enter his 38th and last year a few months later. Jack Hobbs, aged 31, was playing for Surrey against Notts at the Oval, having made 226 on the previous day. Sydney Barnes, back in the League, had by then attained the mature cricketing age of 41. Eighty miles from Sydney in a town called Bowral a little boy named Bradman was asleep in bed, looking forward to his sixth birthday at the end of the month. His incomprehension of what lay ahead was possibly no greater than that of the thousands of cricketers who heard the news and joined the cheering crowds.

7 Between the Wars, 1919–1939

MICHAEL MELFORD

The First World War caused the first interruption which organized cricket had known. During the later years of the war alarming pictures were built up of how the game would be out-of-date in the post-war world and of how first-class cricket must be radically changed if it were to survive. Some stalwarts, however, such as Lord Harris, who had been a young President of MCC nearly a quarter of a century before and who was still only in his sixties, were full of optimism. Most of the structural changes proposed were resisted, including such revolutionary masterpieces as abolishing the left-hander and penalizing the batting side when a maiden over was bowled, but it was decided to play two-day county cricket in 1919. The long hours which this involved, and the abundance of drawn matches which it brought, made it a notable failure and three-day cricket was resumed in 1920.

The leisurely prewar days were gone beyond recall and the 'country-house' type of cricket had inevitably become rarer. But club cricket was soon re-established in all its other different grades and settings. As early as August 1920, Incogniti set off to the United States for a month's tour. The Minor Counties Championship began again in 1920 while, on a loftier level, the first postwar Test Match was played in Sydney between Australia and England in the winter of that year.

The most cheerful optimists were surprised by the public enthusiasm for cricket in the early postwar years. The first English season of 1919 had been given an added distinction by the Australian Imperial Forces team which toured the country playing both two- and three-day matches under the captaincy first of C. E. Kelleway and then of H. L. Collins, who was to bring the 1926 Australians to England. It was a good side including C. E. Pellew, J. M. Gregory and W. A. Oldfield and it won twelve matches and lost 4 out of its 28 first-class games.

After leaving Britain the AIF helped to revive South African cricket by playing nine matches there and stayed together for three matches against Victoria, Queensland and New South Wales on arriving home amid great enthusiasm in January, 1920. Australian cricket standards had not perceptibly deteriorated during the war, and they found a pair of great fast bowlers as a basis for attack in Gregory and McDonald.

The level of English cricket was inevitably low and not only through lack of practice and lack of recent experience. Something of what cricket had lost, particularly in England, could be estimated from the Roll of Honour of well-known players, by no means complete, in the 1920 edition of *Wisden*. It numbered 77. Batsmen were not scarce, and when in the autumn of 1920 MCC set off for Australia under the captaincy of J. W. H. T. Douglas they left behind such players as George Gunn, Philip Mead, Holmes, Sutcliffe and Sandham. Moreover, unlike their successors after the Second World War, batsmen went on playing first-class cricket long after they had mastered their difficult craft. Hobbs was 51 when he retired in 1934. Among his contemporaries Rhodes played until he was 52, Woolley 51, Hendren 49 and Holmes 48. This must sound like longevity indeed to the modern generation which considers a first-class cricketer to have one leg in the bath-chair at 35.

Good bowlers in the immediate postwar years were few. Barnes, the giant of prewar, was 46 in 1919 and lost to first-class cricket. For a few years, until Maurice Tate's talents came to full bloom, there were no high-class fast or fast-medium bowlers in England, though among the spinners Rhodes was still a force and was to help in the recovery of the Ashes in 1926. Paradoxically in this period amateur bowling, for once, was superior in the higher levels to amateur batting. A glance at the school sides which played at Lord's in 1919 – the names of Jardine and Chapman prominent among them – will hint that the balance was soon to be redressed, but among their elders M. Falcon, E. R. Wilson, C. S. Marriott, J. C. White, P. G. H. Fender and young G. T. S. Stevens made an unusually strong hand for the Gentlemen to hold.

The prosperity of cricket is usually closely related to the weather, and the brilliant summer of 1921 gave an added momentum to the game's recovery. In the Test series, perhaps, it did a disservice by emphasizing the current difference in strength between England and Australia. England inside 12 months in 1920–21 lost 8 Tests in a row, an indignity neither country has suffered since though Australia recently has come quite close to it. But elsewhere cricketers in county, club and school teams revelled in the chance to be able to play or learn in the sun.

It was in the middle 1920s that a new and permanent problem began to emerge, as a result of cricket's expansion throughout the Empire. More and more tours were called for as standards rose and, in the jargon of a later day and in a cricketing sense, 'underdeveloped countries asked for recognition and independence'. At first they were content with tours by teams of good players happy to cut their teeth against the counties. In time they wanted Test Matches with the added implications, responsibilities and financial involvements which these bring. England, as the mother country and the only major cricket-playing country in the Northern Hemisphere whose season is perforce confined to summer, were most heavily committed. A visit to Australia every four years and an occasional briefer visit elsewhere in between had put no great strain on England's resources, but now the demands on the best players grew.

However, fewer professionals had profitable winter jobs then and so were delighted to tour abroad. Nor did they marry and acquire families as young as their successors were to do after the Second War. For the moment, therefore, while only Australia and sometimes South Africa had the strength to test the best English side, there was no shortage of players for overseas tours, so that in the winter of 1929–30, while several famous names remained at home, MCC were able to send two strong sides simultaneously to New Zealand (under A. H. H. Gilligan) and to West Indies (under the Hon F. S. G. Calthorpe).

The rise in standards in England, which began after 1921 and was the more marked because Hobbs was now fit again after his ill-health of that sunny but in many ways ill-starred summer, meant that when the Australians made their next visit to England in 1926, three days were not enough in which obtain a result. The first 4 Tests were drawn. It was agreed that the Fifth should be played to a finish, and England won back the Ashes in four days. The Australians thereafter pressed for an extension in England from 3-day Test Matches to 4 days and this was granted in 1930, though with misgivings in many quarters. It was felt that taking the best players away from their counties for as many as ten matches a season might undermine the County Championship.

By 1926 when F. E. Lacey ended his 28 years as secretary of MCC, the knighthood conferred on him testified to the standing of the game in the life of the country and Empire, and to its development since he had taken up office 28 years earlier.

The number of first-class counties rose to 17 with the admission of Glamorgan to the Championship in 1921, an event somewhat disputed at the time, for they had finished only 6th in the Minor Counties' Championship of the year before. How they advanced from the bottom place in their first season of 1921 to the royal heights of champions in 1948 is a story near to the heart of every Welshman, however wedded to Rugby football. Nor will many forget the part of J. C. Clay whose career spanned that whole period from 1921 to 1948. The game, of course, had its difficulties, though they were less formidable then than in a more competitive era later.

This perhaps is the moment to examine a broader balance of power, that in world cricket which was usually reflected by the results of series between England and Australia. England's line in the graph of success between the wars begins in 1920–21 at rock bottom, for they were beaten 5–0 in a series for the only time. It rises steadily to a peak from 1926 to 1933, though in the middle of this period Australia, just starting on the Bradman era, recovered the Ashes by winning 2–1 in England in 1930.

After a brief recession in the middle 1930s English cricket was recovering fast when the Second World War intervened. With Hammond, Barnett and Hardstaff still in their prime, Leyland and Paynter still available, and young players of the calibre of Compton, Hutton and Edrich striding forward, the batting seemed assured for many years. Verity, still pre-eminent among spinners, Bowes, Farnes and the young leg-spinner, Wright, were a strong nucleus of bowlers, and it was not too much to look forward to the early 1940s as another golden era of English cricket. When cricket was resumed,

Outside the Oval, 1926: street buskers entertain the crowd queueing to watch the Test wherein England regained the Ashes.

however, in 1946, the bowlers were no longer there in the same strength.

What, briefly, of England's other opponents? South Africa, who had made so great an advance in Test cricket after the Boer War, were slower to recover after the First World War. Restricted by their racial policy to playing against England, Australia and New Zealand, they had a rough time against Australia between the world wars, losing ten Test Matches and drawing 3 out of 13. This was not, however, quite as bleak a period as it may sound. In the previous winter South Africa at home had won the only match finished against England. Better still, in 1935 H. F. Wade's side, which included players of the class of Cameron, Mitchell, Balaskas, Crisp, A. D. Nourse, Jnr. and Viljoen, beat England at Lord's by 157 runs and, this being again the only match finished, won their first rubber in England.

In 1928 West Indies visited England for the first time as a side which had been granted Test status and played 3 Tests. They came at a time when the best England team was a very strong one, drawn perhaps from: Hobbs, Sutcliffe, Tyldesley, Hammond, Woolley, Leyland, Hendren, Chapman, Tate, Larwood, Geary, White, Duckworth, Freeman – and they lost all 3 by an innings. But 18 months later, when MCC sent teams concurrently to West Indies and New Zealand, the West Indian one under Calthorpe could only draw a series of 4. Five years later West Indies, on their own hard wickets, won 2–1 against R. E. S. Wyatt's side which was probably slightly stronger than Calthorpe's.

Not all the younger cricketing countries made the same progress. New Zealand played their first Tests against A. H. H. Gilligan's team in 1929–30, drawing 3 and losing only once. In those early days of T. C. Lowry, C. S. Dempster, M. L. Page, R. C. Blunt and W. E. Merritt, New Zealand were probably at their strongest and nearly 30 years were to pass before they won a Test Match – against West Indies in 1955–56.

India's progress was not dissimilar. After playing their first Test Match (and the only one of the tour) at Lord's in 1932, they came again 4 years later with a team captained by the Maharajah of Vizianagram which was quite as strong as any they were to send after the Second World War. Merchant, Amar Singh, Mushtaq Ali, Amarnath, Mahomed Nissar and C. K. Nayudu would have made a strong framework of any side. But this one suffered from injuries and also from the political and religious differences which were then a part of Indian life and which had caused a break in first-class cricket in India not long before.

Jack Hobbs and Herbert Sutcliffe, the best of all opening partnerships.

While towards the end of the 1920s England's commitments overseas were growing fast, the balance of power in domestic affairs at home had settled firmly north of the Trent. The history of county cricket between the wars is a tale of uninterrupted northern success after Middlesex had been Champions in 1920 and 1921. And if the war had not come, their batting headed by Robertson, Brown, Edrich and Compton, and the improved balance of the side, might have made them one of the outstanding county sides of this century, but in the years before their renaissance under R. W. V. Robins neither they nor any other southern county were able to disturb the northern monopoly.

First came a run of Yorkshire victories, four in a row beginning in 1922, the first three under G. Wilson, the last under Major A. W. Lupton. The Yorkshire team of that era, dour, skilled and experienced, contains names which have a firm place in cricket history even though some of their owners played rarely, or never, for England: Holmes, Sutcliffe, Oldroyd, Leyland, Rhodes, Kilner, Robinson, Macaulay, Waddington, Dolphin. Soundness was probably the principal virtue of the batting. The bowling had variety and accuracy and, like the fielding, gave nothing away. Runs made against Yorkshire were hard earned.

In 1925 they had one of their most decisive successes so far, winning 11 of their 21 victories by an innings and suffering no defeat. Yet next year was to mark the beginning of a lull in Yorkshire success while the honours moved across the Pennines to Lancashire, captained first by Major L. Green and, from 1929, by P. T. Eckersley.

Lancashire did not make sure of the Championship until very late in the 1926 season but with batsmen such as Hallows, Watson, Ernest Tyldesley and Makepeace – and greater depth than in recent years after them – they became a very hard side to beat. In 5 years, in fact with McDonald, the ageing but still redoubtable Australian to lead their attack, they were beaten only 5 times while they were 64 times victorious. Between 1926 and 1930 Lancashire were Champions 4 times and finished 2nd to Notts in 1929. Notts under A. W. Carr had missed the honour two years earlier in one of the most remarkable finishes in the history of the Championship. When they took the field at Swansea for their last match on 3 August, they had only to draw to become Champions; and in Glamorgan they were meeting opponents who had not won a match all the season.

A week before, Notts had easily beaten Glamorgan at Trent Bridge but now, after batting first, they were led on first innings by 142 runs. Then, caught on an ugly wicket on the 3rd morning, they were bowled out for 61 by Mercer and Ryan. So Lancashire, who had finished their programme, unexpectedly found themselves Champions. But by 1931 Yorkshire had taken over again. Except in the Australian year of 1934, when Lancashire made a temporary return to the top, and in 1936 when A. W. Richardson led Derbyshire to the only Championship in their history, Yorkshire were to be Champions every year until the war.

The recipe for success was much as before and the players at first, certainly the batsmen, had changed little. When some of them dropped out later, their replacements were of outstanding ability and the general efficiency and tightness of the side suffered not at all. Verity, Bowes, Mitchell and Wood were now in it. Hutton and Smailes were to play important parts later in the decade. From 1933 Yorkshire were directed by A. B. Sellers, a vigorous captain who was a fine cricketer and a brilliant fielder. They had won often enough with a captain chosen for his captaincy rather than for his cricketing ability. Now they grew in strength under a leader who combined both.

The lunch interval on the first day of the Third Test between England and Australia at Headingley, 1930, with Bradman leading the way already past 100. By the close of play he was 309 not out. Following behind are Woodfull, Hobbs, Hammond, Sutcliffe (half-hidden), Chapman (in a Cambridge Quidnunc cap), Geary (hand to his head) and Duleepsinhji bringing up the rear.

From a distance of half a century or so there are two chapters in the cricket history of the inter-war period which seem to dwarf all others: the career of Don Bradman and the bitter feeling between England and Australia as a result of what is now known as the Body-line tour.

They were not unconnected. Bradman first made his mark on the stage of first-class cricket in the 1927–28 season when he made two hundreds for New South Wales including one in his first Sheffield Shield match. He was only 19 but this was Australia, a young man's and a young cricketer's country, and he did not in this first season make the impact which he would certainly have done in England. However, the MCC tour of 1928–29 made his exceptional talents abundantly plain. He was eagerly awaited in England in 1930 and, for all the anticipation, he disappointed nobody. His first two innings were 236 against Worcestershire and 185 not out against Leicestershire. Those who saw his 254 at Lord's will never expect to see more complete mastery of bat over ball in a Test Match. Bradman averaged 139 in the Tests of 1930 and 98·66 through the season; and he was still only 22. Few who saw it at first-hand approved or condoned Body-line, but it must at least be seen in the context of Bradman's voracious batsmanship. The prospect of bowling for years to a devastating automaton like this was a gloomy one, particularly as there was at the time some concern about where the bowlers for the 1932–33 tour of Australia were coming from. Larwood was in his prime, but J. C. White, the hero of 1928–29, was over 40 and Tate and Geary not far short of it. It was in this atmosphere that MCC set sail in the autumn of 1932, not under the relatively gay captaincy of Chapman, who had won 4–1 four years before and had been captain for the first four tests of 1930, but under the sterner command of D. R. Jardine. Bradman, perhaps more than any one batsman in history, controlled the destiny of the Ashes. How to stop him? The melancholy answer was Body-line, the story of which earns a separate place in this book.

The tour ended in the most expensive victory – for England – that either side had ever gained; the Ashes were brought back to a cool reception and MCC held an inquiry, the ultimate outcome of which was the addition of the Intimidation clause to the Law governing Fair and Unfair Play. Gradually the clouds of dissension began to thin out. A lengthy correspondence took place between MCC and the Australian Board of Control which established a basis on which the 1934 Australian tour of England could proceed. Jardine, after taking an MCC team to India in the winter of 1933–34, declined to play against the Australians. Larwood, in the course of some unplacatory newspaper articles, did the same, and the only subsequent ruptures of the peace were caused by the bowling of Voce against the Australians and Middlesex in 1934. In 1933 the MCC Committee had agreed that any form of bowling which was obviously a direct attack upon the batsman would be an offence against the spirit of the game. The Australians, having had 'bumpers' bowled to them with a full leg-side field, now complained of a 'direct attack'. The Advisory Committee found the complaints proven and ordered Notts to apologize. This was the only open breach on the 1934 tour which ended with Australia taking the Ashes home.

A legacy of bitterness remained in Australia – or, more accurately, in the minds of some Australians – for many years to come. But by the end of 1934 it could be fairly said that a sorry chapter in cricket history was closed. The only gain was a clarification of the Law which MCC produced in November, 1934, after Board of Control and Advisory Committee meetings.

In that same month it was at last decided to experiment with an amended lbw Law. The long campaign of the Hon. R. H. Lyttelton, now carried on by F. G. J. Ford, was rewarded. A batsman could now be out to a ball pitching on the off-side of the wicket, if in the opinion of the umpire it would have hit the wicket and if his body was in a line between wicket and wicket. (Hitherto the ball had been required to pitch in a straight line between the wickets.) Partly this was intended to give the bowler a better chance than he had been having on good wickets in recent years. Mostly, perhaps, it was designed to curb excessive pad-play which, according to some, had provoked the so-called 'Body-line' bowling. Whether it had or not, the practice was tedious and unlovely.

In the first season of the experiment 483 of the 1,560 lbw decisions given against the batsman were under the new Law of lbw (N), as it was recorded in the score-book. Opinion was generally in its favour. It certainly restricted pad-play and forced the batman to play at more balls outside the off-stump. It encouraged the fast and medium-paced bowler. One of those opposed to the change was R. E. S. Wyatt, the current captain of England, who three decades later was partly responsible for a reconsideration of the Law by his call for a return to the old Law *plus* an increase in the width of the wicket as compensation to the bowler.

Don Bradman thought that the change should have been still greater and that it should not have been necessary for the batsman's leg to be between wicket and wicket. He also advocated an extension later on, when the present changes had been assimilated, to include the ball pitching outside the leg-stump. To this suggestion there is a time-honoured answer that the batsman has to put his legs somewhere. In general the change was considered a success and after two seasons of trial in England and its adoption in Australia, after some hesitation, in time for the MCC tour of 1936–37, it became law.

The early 1930s were not the most prosperous period in the game's history. A series of wet summers in England, the distaste and bad publicity spread by the Body-line controversy and, perhaps, the system of scoring in the County Championship which to some extent permitted a side to prosper by escaping defeat, had all helped towards a slackening in public interest in the game. Towards the end of the decade there was an all-round improvement. Anglo-Australian relations had been strengthened considerably during the tour of G. O. Allen's team in 1936–37. The proportion of dry summers to wet increased. Adjustments were made to the scoring in the County Championship whereby greater emphasis was placed on an outright win. Bradman still commanded the world scene, a legend in his time, while in England the young Compton was capturing the public imagination by the brilliant improvization of his strokes and the speed of his scoring.

Boys at Lord's: a social study outside the Grace Gates during the Eton and Harrow match 1937.

Not only in the higher circles was the future encouraging. Club cricket remained strong and the Universities, who had continued through the years since the First World War to provide a steady stream of fine players, further commended themselves by several excellent matches at Lord's. During the inter-war period, however, there had been a considerable change in the amateur's situation. Many fewer were now able to play regularly after leaving the university and such illustrious cricketers as G. O. Allen and R. W. V. Robins had intermittent first-class careers. The University Match had never quite become again the social event which it was up to 1914, but in the late 1930s there were strong signs of a revival and in 1939 the welcome innovation of a Saturday (instead of a Monday) start.

Eton and Harrow was still an important social occasion attracting up to 30,000 elegantly clad spectators. It was given an extra boost in 1939 by a Harrow victory, the first since 1908 when G. E. V. Crutchley, later of Oxford University and Middlesex, had been a member of the Harrow XI. When Harrow won next, 31 years later, his son, E. Crutchley, made 115 in their first innings.

After war had broken out in September 1939, there was no more first-class cricket for a long time to raise new issues and develop new players. Inevitably the immediate pre-war events stayed fresh in the cricketer's mind for seven years, and two events above all others. One undoubtedly was Len Hutton's innings of 364 at the Oval in the Fifth Test of 1938. He batted almost without fault for 13½ hours, exceeding Bradman's England-Australia Test record of 334 and steering England most of the way to their score of 903 for seven at which Hammond declared at tea on the third day. For a young man of 22 it was a prodigious feat of concentration, temperament and technique.

In England the timeless Test, on the few occasions when one had been played, had been anything but a marathon. However, in the following winter of 1938–39, the last Test played by Hammond's England team in South Africa was to sound the death knell of the cricket match played without time limit. Of the previous 4 four-day Tests, 3 had been drawn and England had actually won the other at Durban by an innings in only 3 days. The last, also at Durban, was to be played to a finish but, having been started on a Friday, it was given up as a draw after 10 days on the following Tuesday week to enable MCC to catch the ship home. The match had produced 1,981 runs and broken more than a dozen records.

The factors which made the pitch so impervious to wear were unlikely to be repeated, for they were related to the Natal climate and a local rule. This rule allowed the groundsman to roll the pitch between one day's play and the next if he thought that he would thereby improve it. After the thunderstorms to which Durban is prone at that time of year, hot sun and a rolling, the pitch was as good as new again. The impact of this match, however, was considerable and after six years of reflection no one wanted to continue with the timeless Test when in 1946 cricket started again.

Ranji and Duleep: in 1930 at the time of Duleep's 173 for England v Australia at Lord's. The Jam Sahib watched this innings in full Oriental dress. He died 3 years later aged 60. Meanwhile, in August 1932, tuberculosis had brought his nephew's cricket to an end.

8 The Postwar Scene

J. M. KILBURN

First-class cricket returned to England in 1945 with eager improvization of Victory Tests, 'friendly' county matches and festivals, and in 1946 a Championship programme was undertaken by the counties together with the Test series against India as preparation for a tour of Australia and New Zealand. Public response was unmistakably enthusiastic. The Whitsuntide match of 1945 at Lord's brought a record 3-day attendance and the Hedley Verity Memorial Fund, based on a Yorkshire and Lancashire match at Bradford, raised more than £8,000.

The 1946 summer was uncommonly wet and England was manifestly stronger than India, but spectators were ready to pay their tribute in cash and in person and through all the inconveniences of war-damaged grounds, transport and catering restrictions and limitations in publicity, cricket called with a strong and cheerful voice. County club memberships increased and new sources of patronage were discovered, first in the form of industrial backing and later by the lotteries that rocketed revenue in some cases almost to a point of embarrassment.

The quality of first-class cricket in England in the years immediately following resumption inevitably gave cause for concern. There were players of unquestionable stature, the majority of them continuing careers originating before the war, but there were many from whom necessity had withdrawn the opportunity for apprenticeship in method and tradition. In the natural reaction against hardship and compulsory discipline cricketers followed the common practice of the time in search for an easy way to fame and fortune. The survivors were few and until the hard road of experience had been travelled by a new generation England's international record remained unworthy.

Between 1946 and the beginning of Surrey's supremacy there was no dominant county. Six different teams finished at the head of the Championship and in two successive seasons, 1949 and 1950, the leadership was shared. All counties were rebuilding teams, re-establishing traditions, reconstituting principles. No other period in Championship history had spread the honours so widely or so unpredictably. No other period brought so many players of modest significance into first-class company. There was ample room at the top, even at the very top; England called on 21 players for Test duty in both 1947, when they defeated South Africa, and in 1948, when they lost to Australia.

The pattern of development emerging in this 'Restoration' period was based on two changes of law and one change in playing conditions. Before the Second World War bowling easement had been offered through the introduction of lbw (N), which had scarcely revealed its full scope by 1939. During the war an MCC Select Committee recommended increased availability of a new ball, suggesting the 55-over period that was adopted in 1946.

The consequence was emphasis on in-swing or 'in-slant' bowling. The fast-medium or medium-paced bowler directing his attention towards the leg-stump found himself the favoured of cricketers. He was rarely expensive, he was sometimes dramatically successful and he quickly discovered how to conserve both physical and mental energies. Aided and abetted by the preparation of grassy and loose-surfaced pitches in-swing bowling began to dominate cricket. It nurtured a race of courageous and acrobatic fieldsmen stationed at close range on the leg-side and it reduced wicket-keeping miracles to the comparatively commonplace.

It constrained batsmanship towards patience and deflection.

In the Fifth 'Victory Test' between England and Australia at Old Trafford in August 1945 this team won by 6 wickets and so squared the rubber: Back row: H. Elliot (Umpire), L. B. Fishlock, Sgt R. Pollard, Major F. A. Sloan, Pte G. H. Pope, Flt-Sgt W. E. Phillipson, Lieut J. D. Robertson, Lt-Col G. O. Allen and Frank Chester; front row: Flt-Sgt C. Washbrook, Sgt L. Hutton, Major-Gen T. F. N. Wilson, Flt-Lieut W. R. Hammond (captain), W/Cmdr W. H. N. Shakespeare, Lt-Col S. C. Griffith, Lieut D. V. P. Wright; in front: S/Ldr W. J. Edrich, Sgt W. B. Roberts.

Tom Webster of the *Daily Mail* recalls old faces before the MCC team for Australia is chosen in 1946.

In 1950 Hutton remarked that on his arrival at the crease he had observed a half-volley outside the off-stump and driven it for 4; in the course of a century innings he never received another. The same problems beset batsmen when the ball turned. In-swing became off-spin and over a decade in-swinger or off-spinner headed the English bowling averages, despite minor changes of law designed to loosen shackles on the batsmen.

All the tendencies of the times combined to reduce batting from the brilliant to the businesslike. Test Matches were lengthened as they increased in number and as their importance was inflated by the attention of Press and broadcast and considerations of finance. Lesser cricket took tone and model from the greater and lost both briskness and inclination to adventure. Figures in themselves brought recognition; recognition brought perquisites. They seemed to serve at the crease who only stood and waited and the steady fall in attendances was masked in balance sheets by extraneous income.

The late 1940s and almost the whole of the 1950s represented a bowler's era in cricket. The laws favoured bowling and the pitches favoured bowling. Moderate achievement came readily; great achievement, of course, demanded the qualities of greatness indispensable in any circumstances. They were evident in A. V. Bedser who played with uncommon success in the Test series of 1946 and, adding experience to ability, rose to the highest standards of his craft. Bedser's type of bowling, fast-medium in pace with late swing and finger 'cut' for variation, was always economical and, when conditions helped, triumph invariably resulted, as when he took seven wickets in each innings against the 1953 Australians at Trent Bridge.

In both method and career Alec Bedser had much in common with Maurice Tate. Great physical strength permitted long spells of bowling and long spells were necessary because circumstances left the main burden to be carried without adequate support. In their most effective personal seasons Tate and Bedser could not win the Ashes for England. They could and did, however, maintain bowling inspiration and example by classical standards. Bedser was a bowler of his time, encouraged to the easy option of in-swing, but he made himself into a bowler of all time, resolute in the preservation of accuracy, thoughtful and hard-working in the development of variations, loyal to the ideals of his vocation.

As the thread of distinction broadened and diversified, English cricket returned to supremacy. The Ashes were recovered in 1953 and held in 1954–55 and 1956; the South Africans were beaten in 1951 and 1955; a rubber in the West Indies was shared in 1953–54 and West Indies in England were defeated in 1957; New Zealand, India and Pakistan were outclassed whenever England's full resources could be brought to bear. Bowling strength invariably determined the issue. J. B. Statham, F. S. Trueman and, more briefly, F. H. Tyson ruled the realms of speed and J. C. Laker and G. A. R. Lock became dominant in spin.

Internationally they demanded little support except from the playing conditions and the remarkable catching near the wicket, of which Lock himself provided outstanding illustration, but in the wider cricket of the period there were bowlers exceeding the level of mere competence. R. Appleyard of Yorkshire, T. E. Bailey of Essex, R. Tattersall of Lancashire, P. J. Loader of Surrey and C. Gladwin and L. Jackson of Derbyshire exemplified uncommon merit in the prevailing manner of their day, and the tremendous batting figures of Edrich and Compton in 1947 were neither approached nor expected to be approached in the generation following.

In this summer of sunshine, batting unquestionably led Middlesex to the County Championship, if only because the pace of scoring offered scope for the subsequent purchase of wickets with little need for considerations of time and cost.

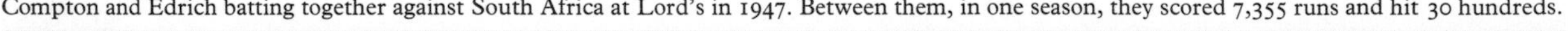
Compton and Edrich batting together against South Africa at Lord's in 1947. Between them, in one season, they scored 7,355 runs and hit 30 hundreds.

At the Oval in 1953 England, under L. Hutton's captaincy, crowned Coronation Year by winning back The Ashes.

Robertson and Brown opened the innings with 9 century partnerships in the season yet left the more glittering achievements to their successors at the crease. Compton scored 3,816 runs and Edrich 3,539, the two highest aggregates ever recorded in a season.

Figures alone guarantee Compton and Edrich high standing among the batsmen of all cricket history but their reputation rests also on character. Both were courageous cricketers, Edrich sometimes grimly so when situations were uncomfortable, Compton invariably marked by the touch of creative attainment that lifts the greatest even above the admittedly great. Edrich made 39 appearances for England, his selection depending on current form and fancy; Compton rarely set a selectorial problem because his right to be an England player whenever he was available brooked no argument.

On an equal plane of ability stood Leonard Hutton whose career was a story of success that carried its own seeds of inescapable and almost overwhelming anxieties. From his prewar performances Hutton was marked out for postwar burden. As an England and Yorkshire batsman from 1946 to the end of his career he was always the first objective of enemy assault, and experience taught him that he represented not only the protective moat and curtain wall but often enough the keep as well. He rarely found freedom to enjoy himself at the crease. Much of the England and the Yorkshire batting of his maturity carried obvious technical deficiencies and Hutton's responsibilities were heavy and continuous. He accepted them to score over 40,000 runs in a career extending from 1934 to 1955, nearly 7,000 runs in Test cricket and to complete 129 centuries.

By 1952 Hutton had become England's appointed captain and he led the side at home, in Australia, New Zealand and the West Indies before his retirement from the first-class field under the pressure of ill-health. He was a successful captain because he appreciated the basic principles of success and was stern in their application, unrelaxing in search for perfection. He felt, as a professional, the compulsion to success that came to characterize his own tenacity and flawless technique in batting. For his international achievements he was honoured by knighthood; among contemporary players his manifest ability was acknowledged the world over.

Hutton's captaincy of England as a professional player reflected the changing outlook of the times. His first appointment was not accepted with universal approval and even after he had held office there was challenge to his suitability – by comparison with the Rev D. S. Sheppard – for leadership in Australia, but in both principle and practice the reign of the amateur was approaching its end. Not only the reign but existence of the amateur in first-class cricket was declining. Economic circumstances and the social structure offered little scope for a 5-month concentration on sport without monetary recompense and sometimes at considerable cost. Full-time cricketers were compelled to make cricket provide a livelihood in one form or another. Some simply became paid players. Others accepted the sponsorship of commercial firms who derived benefit from the employment of prominent figures in sport. Administrative appointments within cricket permitted regular appearances for a few players and one or two, reaching the highest levels, found that their names commanded a substantial cash value.

The ability of professional players to undertake captaincy could not be seriously questioned after a few instances had been noted. H. E. Dollery led Warwickshire from 1949 and led them not only to the Championship in 1951 but to the highest of reputations as a well-managed and well-mannered side. Under pressure of circumstances and by the satisfaction given, captaincy by professional players came rapidly into general practice, and in 1962–63 the formal distinction between amateur and professional was officially abolished with the consequent abandonment of 'Gentlemen v Players', one of the oldest engagements in the cricketing calendar.

This development was only one sign of increasing commercialization. Another was the swing towards dependence on extraneous finance. From its beginning first-class cricket has rarely been self-supporting. Private patronage, membership subscription, public appeals and concessions in taxation all took a turn as essential supplement to gate receipts until the lottery was developed to a pitch of elaborate organization. By 1964, when Yorkshire finally succumbed, every county club was accepting donations from 'supporters' organizations controlling the funds derived from 'pools'. Apart from any moral issue involved, this departure roused minority misgivings because it meant that cricket was no longer under the financial control of cricketing interests. The private generosity and all the fund-raising devices of earlier days contained a basis of appeal in cricket itself; pools contributors imply no such concern.

Participation in Test Match and tour profits became another essential item in county balance sheets and exercised a clear and substantial influence on the course of the cricket of the period. The Test Match became paramount; the rubber dominated and almost suffocated the season's programme. Tests were increased in number and extended in time. All the countries of the ICC were accorded a nominal parity of esteem and any player chosen for a whole series would be occupied for thirty days. Tests took not only time but also public attention, stimulated by the concentrated publicity inflicted through television, radio and Press.

Inevitably, all Test cricket could not justify the claims of its presentation. Teams of unbalanced strength provided disappointing contests which were, nevertheless, accorded elaborate treatment simply because elaborate treatment had been prepared in advance and paid for in the purchase of rights. By simple arithmetic Test Matches brought money; therefore, with money an over-riding consideration, the more Test Matches the better. Test Matches, or Test Match publicity, also induced a change of outlook among players.

Publicity can be applied to people even more readily than to occasions, and leading cricketers found themselves more akin to actors on a stage than participants in a game. Their exploitation, willingly conceded in most cases, became a lucrative business for agents and promoters. Television and radio paid for interviews, newspapers and publishers paid for expressions of opinion, advertisers paid for the use of a face or a name.

Eventually the bounds of propriety were overstepped and ill-will among players and administrators was created. Ghost-writers competed in the raising of controversy and taste in interview, and advertising plunged to hitherto untouched depths. Principles of behaviour in the dressing-room and on the field became so unacceptable that the public image of cricket itself was besmirched. Umpires reported players, the Yorkshire members expressed their dissatisfaction at a special general meeting. J. H. Wardle ended his county engagement with self-revelation in newspaper articles and had an MCC invitation to tour Australia withdrawn. J. C. Laker subscribed his name to a book that cost him his membership privileges at the Oval and at Lord's. As an outcome of the several disturbances the Advisory Committee resolved upon supervision of players' public communications as part of the contracts of employment.

The cricket of the period also raised controversial issues within the laws of the game. Striving towards increased effectiveness rather than any deliberate attempt to evade law and custom led to question of the legitimacy of certain bowling practices. Some bowlers were accused of throwing, some of illegal or unfair delivery by means of drag. Murmurings of several years' duration exploded into downright protest against Australian bowling in Australia during the MCC tour of 1958–59 and against G. Griffin of South Africa in England during the 1960 season. No action was taken by umpires during the Tests in Australia, but the Australian Board of Control conducted investigations and practical experiments and adopted a definition for the throw.

Griffin, a fast-medium right-hander, came on tour after having been no-balled for throwing in his own country and was no-balled for throwing 17 times by 6 different umpires in England before he appeared in the Lord's Test. There he was no-balled 11 times in the match proper by one umpire, F. S. Lee, and again, decisively, by the other, J. S. Buller, in the subsequent exhibition game. Warm personal sympathy was extended to the bowler in his embarrassment, but cricketers everywhere recognized the need for firm handling of a growing menace to the game.

Any law dependent on opinion must leave some loophole, but with intention made manifest and co-operation achieved suspect bowling was sharply reduced in quantity, by players as willingly as by legislative authority. The long drag of the back foot in the delivery stride raised protest of such proportion that experimental law was introduced involving first arbitary limitations by umpires and eventually abandonment of the bowling crease as a measure of permitted distance.

These changes and many others covering field-placing, availability of the new-ball, pitch protection, follow-on, limitation of the playing area and innumerable adjustments in the County Championship reckoning tended towards a bewildering artificiality that left first-class cricket a somewhat distant relation to the 'meadow game with the beautiful name' that was played and watched for unsophisticated recreation. The casual spectator, as distinct from the devotee and the Test-ticket hunter, stayed away. Reformers sought to recapture crowds with a variety of enticement, minor and major. Gloucestershire offered late-evening cricket. The County Advisory Committee recommended revision of the Sunday Observance law, though without committing themselves to promotion of county cricket on Sundays.

The first knock-out competition of single-innings matches was instituted under the patronage of Gillette in 1963. Qualification rules for players were relaxed to permit easier transfer of allegiance from one county to another or easier introduction from overseas. The simplest remedy of all – concentration on vigorous, enthusiastic play – was frequently urged but not always heeded.

The influx from overseas undoubtedly added vitality to the domestic cricket. West Indians brought adventurous batting to Hampshire and Somerset. Australians brought the fascination of 'wrist-spin' bowling to Nottinghamshire, Leicestershire and Northamptonshire. New Zealand were splendidly represented in Warwickshire and Goonesena of Ceylon helped Nottinghamshire after experience at Cambridge University. For all the sturdy assistance of Walsh and Jackson, Dooland, Wight and Alley, Tribe and Livingston, their counties never took the Championship. Purchase could not outrange population and through the 1950s no new name appeared on the Roll of Champions, though Warwickshire, winners in 1951, had enjoyed only one previous success, 40 years back.

The period was, in fact, close to a monopoly for Surrey. They were joint Champions with Lancashire in 1950, 6th in 1951, and then 1st for 7 successive seasons. Their supremacy developed from a happy combination of circumstances and persisted, to some extent, through its own momentum. The longer Surrey remained Champions the stronger became expectation that they would continue as Champions. Traditionally, Championships are won by bowling and fielding. Surrey's years of triumph reinforced the tradition. They were unquestionably one of the most powerful bowling sides in county cricket history and they made the most of their resources by brilliant fielding support.

Only invidious comparison would rate the bowlers in order of merit or significance; it is sufficient to say that A. V. Bedser, Laker and Lock were supreme in their categories, that Loader played for England at home and abroad and that such

The outstanding county side of the 1950s, Surrey won 7 Championships in a row, 1952 to 1958. 1955 side – back row: R. C. E. Pratt, D. F. Cox, P. J. Loader, T. H. Clark, G. A. R. Lock, D. G. W. Fletcher, K. F. Barrington, M. D. Willett and B. Constable; front row: M. J. Stewart, E. A. Bedser, A. J. McIntyre, P. B. H. May, W. S. Surridge (Captain), A. V. Bedser, J. C. Laker and R. Swetman.

supplementary bowling as was required lacked neither talent nor endeavour. The team assembled and developed more or less together and for 5 years played under the same eager captaincy of W. S. Surridge. Surridge gave useful help to the team as a fast bowler, but he earned his highest respect as a daring and skilful close-in fieldsman and as a captain of persistently effervescent optimism. He gave heart and soul to duties that were obviously a pleasure and made far greater contribution to the Surrey side than could be measured by his batting and bowling figures.

In this period Surrey were further favoured by playing conditions at the Oval. The ruination of the ground in wartime was repaired with remarkable speed and efficiency but not without a complete change of character. The outfield that was a sore trial to feet became grassy, soft and green; the pitches that had permitted monumental scoring enabled matches to be finished in 2 days through their accommodation to early swing and later spin. Surrey possessed precisely the resources required for success, for though their batting was limited by the highest standards, the quality of P. B. H. May was as unquestionable as his achievements were distinguished, and support down the list kept the small totals usually required within the range of attainment.

In their 7 years of county conquest Surrey won more than 4 times as many matches as they lost and approaching 3 times as many as they drew. In 1955 they won 23 games out of the 28 in the Championship programme. In 1956 they beat not only county rivals but also the Australians. In 1957 they finished 94 points ahead of their nearest Championship challengers.

Surrey's deposition in 1959 represented a general relief. It was accomplished, rather against expectation, by Yorkshire who, apart from dramatic descents in 1953 and 1958, had remained nearest to the leaders with second place five times. Being nearest still left Yorkshire disappointed in themselves. In 70 years they had never gone so long without a Championship success, and even more disturbing than their fall in playing standards was the decline in playing attitude that raised comment on lack of enthusiasm in the field and dressing-room discontent that culminated in the public revelations of 1957 and 1958.

Through the years of unease the Yorkshire side always contained individuals of uncommon talent. Nobody queried the level of Hutton's batsmanship. Trueman and Close eventually fulfilled the promise of their early appearance. Appleyard took 200 wickets in his first full season only to suffer subsequent limitations by illness and injury. Watson displayed high technical competence which he transferred to Leicestershire in 1958. Wardle was an exceptionally skilful spin bowler. Yardley, who captained the side until 1955, also captained England, having justified selection on playing ability alone. When Yardley retired, W. H. H. Sutcliffe, son of Herbert, led Yorkshire for two seasons, giving way to J. R. Burnet under whom the team was reconstructed and the Championship dramatically regained. In 1960 Yorkshire turned to professional captaincy, appointing J. V. Wilson, followed by Close.

Warwickshire's Championship of 1951 was based on the inspiring leadership and admirable batting of Dollery and the bowling of Pritchard, Grove and Hollies, but it was the shared success of a self-confident team enjoying a season of good form and favourable circumstances. Neither Warwickshire nor Glamorgan, who won in 1948, remained consistent challengers for the Championship pennant, though Warwickshire under M. J. K. Smith came back to prominence in the wider scope that followed Surrey's long stranglehold on the county honours.

Changes in regulations designed to encourage faster scoring and increase the public appeal of third-day play offered a premium to sides with limited but appropriate resources. With restrictive bowling and fielding approximate balance could be maintained through the greater part of a match and the whole issue then decided by contrivance of declarations calling for brief batting assault. The 'beer' match as it came to be called ('beer and skittles') grew prevalent in the Championship to disguise true strength and weakness and to be received with mixed feelings. By the traditional outlook there was little merit in a victory through an hour's conceded hitting after general disadvantage throughout the match. Under revised principle there was call amounting to moral obligation for 'sporting' declarations to provide the artificial stimulus of a close finish by contrivance.

Hampshire, with the notably economical bowling of Shackleton, the ready scoring of Marshall and the adventurous inclination of Ingleby-Mackenzie, were splendidly equipped to seize opportunities and in 1961 they joined the list of Champions. They were outstanding but not alone in rising reputation. Northamptonshire, relieved of financial anxieties by commercial patronage and pools income, built a side that promised even more than was actually achieved, with the importation at one time or another of F. R. Brown, Subba Row, Jakeman, Barrick, Nutter, Allen and the Australians, Tribe, Livingston and Manning. The most dramatic acquisition was F. H. Tyson, who justified expectations for England but was hamstrung on the placid pitch at Northampton.

Worcestershire would have been Champions in 1962 had Yorkshire failed to win the last engagement, returning to significance when a new generation of bowling, represented by Flavell, Coldwell and Gifford, developed to fill gaps left by the departure of Perks and Jenkins. The consistency of Kenyon made a striking feature of the batting and strength was replaced by strength when internal disagreements tranferred P. E. Richardson to Kent and T. W. Graveney from Gloucestershire. In several seasons Essex gave indication of greater authority than they could finally command. With T. E. Bailey as an outstanding all-rounder of his time and D. J. Insole a notably persevering batsman and devoted captain they were always capable of extending any opponents, but consistency as a team could not be established to bring a Championship within grasp.

In sharp contrast were some falls from ancient grace. It was scarcely conceivable, in recollection of the days of Shaw and Shrewsbury, George Gunn and A. O. Jones, Larwood and Voce, that Saturday afternoon crowds at Trent Bridge should be numbered in mere hundreds, that Nottinghamshire should blush at the bottom of the Championship table. R. T. Simpson as batsman and the Australian, B. Dooland, as leg-break bowler, would have been at home in any cricketing company. At Trent Bridge they were lonely.

Lancashire began several seasons as likely Champions. Only in 1950 could they finish at the top of the table and by 1962 they were second from the bottom. Their descent made an unhappy story of neglected opportunities and weakening resolution, with splendours of individual achievement and specific match successes left to brighten the page. They rejoiced in Washbrook's batting; they had every reason for pride in Statham's bowling; they brought forward Tattersall and Pullar; they defeated Yorkshire twice in a season after an interval of 67 years. Yet they lost support so seriously that Old Trafford was in danger of becoming a shell and they were involved in public and private disagreements among their own players and with other counties. Some of their experiments in pitch-preparation, team-constructions and management did not bear the expected fruit, but even their misconceptions suggested that Lancashire did try to maintain a position among leaders of cricket thought and they were invariably the most severe critics of themselves.

Sussex and Kent based any prominence in the period more on individual contributions to cricketing distinction than on any prolonged challenge for county honours. Sussex finished 2nd to Surrey in 1953, but without causing any great uneasiness to the leaders; the consistency and the reserve strength that underpins winning sides was never a Sussex characteristic. They were also short of authoritative bowling, for though they enjoyed estimable service from Thomson and others of his fast-medium type they never provided a bowler for England after Tate. Their attraction lay in batting under a variety of styles from the shrewd conservatism of John Langridge to the unpredictable splendour of E. R. Dexter. Between the extremes of professional reliability and the impulse of the moment lay the talents of J. M. Parks, A. S. M. Oakman, G. H. G. Doggart and D. S. Sheppard.

Kent, too, were a leavening in the county cricket bakery. Bowling shortage limited Championship ambitions, for even when D. V. P. Wright was troubling the best of batsmen with leg-breaks at medium pace he could not be offered the necessary support. The traditional batting quality maintained its line with Cowdrey following Ames, and Evans enlivening almost every match in which he played through a long career as brilliant wicket-keeper and exuberant batsman. Kent passed through deep depression when the team was weak and the outlook dark, but a strong nucleus of county pride was never lost and from the early 1960s cricketing enthusiasm in the county has been steadily rekindled.

The experiences of all the counties, the complications at international level and the consequences of social change set problems of basic significance before the rulers, players and followers of first-class cricket during the 20 years following the Second World War. It was not likely that their solution should be immediate or unanimously approved. It was rather a measure of cricket's continuing appeal that problems should be considered worthy of attention and the future a matter of such wide concern. By the mid-1960s the ultimate pattern of the game was as far beyond conjecture as its departure from the sporting scene. Cricket changes because it lives; the restless and sometimes stormy water of a period is accompaniment to the surging vitality of an ocean's swell.

9 Years of Ferment, 1965–1980

ALAN GIBSON

The period in English cricket from 1965 to the dawn of the 1980s saw an intensification of the problems which Mr Kilburn adumbrated in the previous pages. One-day cricket; sponsorship; demands from the players for higher pay; the proliferation of international matches; a further decline in crowds for the County Championship; an even more drastic decline in those for such ancient institutions as the Eton v Harrow and Oxford v Cambridge matches, which, it became increasingly clear, were out of place before tiny audiences at Lord's. Overseas cricketers playing for counties multiplied, and something like a transfer-list system, if not quite so blatant as in association football, arrived. Cricketing manners and morals, at first-class level, grew worse. Finally there came Mr Packer. If Mr Kilburn's narrative does not exactly foresee Mr Packer, World Series Cricket cannot have altogether surprised him.

Let us begin comment on these changes – not all have been for the worse – with a consideration of the one-day game. This, for the counties, has produced the readiest sponsorship, and the biggest crowds. The Gillette Cup (which *Wisden* cautiously referred to in its first season as the 'knock-out championship') had begun in 1963. It was played for 65 overs a side, soon reduced to 60. As I write, it has been won 4 times by Lancashire (3 in succession, 1970–72), 3 by Sussex, twice by Yorkshire, Warwickshire and Kent, once by Gloucestershire, Northamptonshire, Middlesex and Somerset. So the honours have gone round a bit. The final, which has had a remarkable run of luck with the weather (apart from a washed-out first day in 1974) has brought large crowds to Lord's. Indeed, nowadays it is extremely difficult to get a ticket. In 1969 the John Player League was begun, 40 overs a side on Sunday afternoons. Since there was only the one afternoon, as opposed to the 3 days allowed, if necessary, for a Gillette match, the rules to ensure a finish had to be tighter. This has resulted in some absurd contests – but even the Gillette Cup has had its farcical moments, none more so than the semi-final at Lord's

Old Trafford in the gloaming: this 1971 Gillette Cup semi-final between Lancashire and Gloucestershire, delayed an hour in the afternoon because of rain, ended at 8.50 p.m. following an onslaught by David Hughes, of Lancashire. With lights on in the pavilion he said to J. D. Bond, his captain and batting partner, 'Don't worry skipper, if I can see 'em I'll hit 'em' – and did to the tune of 24 in an over. It was 10 o'clock before many of the crowd of 23,000 left for home.

in 1977, when, on the 6th day (a Championship match had been postponed to permit the extra allocation), Middlesex and Somerset played a 15-over match. The John Player League has been won 3 times by Kent, twice by Lancashire, Leicestershire and Hampshire, once by Worcestershire and Somerset.

In 1972 the Benson and Hedges Cup began. This is a competition over 55 overs, beginning as 4 little leagues and proceeding to a knock-out when the last 8 is reached. I am not at all sure it was a good idea. Partly because it is played in the earlier part of the season, it has suffered greatly from bad weather. Because of the likelihood of bad weather, 3 days were allotted to each match, and because of such a generous allotment, we have been well advanced in the season before the County Championship begins to stir much public interest. Happily some improvement in respect of the programme is in the offing. Kent have won the Benson and Hedges 3 times, Leicestershire twice, Surrey, Gloucestershire and Essex once. So Kent and Lancashire have the reputation, so far, for being the one-day (it would be more strictly correct to say limited-over) experts. When it began, the Benson and Hedges had two interesting qualities: its plan for the preliminary leagues to be played on a regional basis, and the extra point it offered for bowling sides out. For one reason and another, both of these have been abandoned.

Of the 3 one-day county competitions, the Benson and Hedges would seem to be the obvious one to go – for there is certainly one too many. On the other hand, I have seen some excellent cricket in the Benson and Hedges, and very little in the John Player League. 55 overs apiece is just about enough for two first-class sides to play a game which resembles cricket, and 40 overs is not. In any case my views are of no importance, because the competitions, or something like them, will carry on. The next edition of this work is more likely to record the death of the Three-day County Championship.

I suppose that the thing that would strike an Edwardian, and even a man of the 1920s, about this account, is the ready acceptance that has been given to Sunday cricket. Some counties began it, even in the Championship, in 1966. Rothman's International Cavaliers, in collaboration with BBC Television, popularized the 40-over match, and Rothman's must have felt themselves hard done by when the Sunday League was started, and the contract went to Player's. The decline of the traditional British Sunday is by no means altogether a bad thing (I write with feeling memories of my childhood) but I am surprised that, where such a sport as cricket was concerned, it collapsed so easily.

The Championship itself, sponsored for the first time in 1978, by Schweppes, has been won over the period 3 times by Worcestershire and Yorkshire, twice by Kent with one shared, once by Middlesex with one shared, and once each by Glamorgan, Surrey, Warwickshire, Hampshire, Leicestershire, and Essex. There has been no dominant county in the period. Yorkshire's last win, their 7th in 10 years, was in 1968. They have maintained their traditional policy of playing only Yorkshiremen born. Generally speaking, teams had less close associations with the counties they represented than was the case even in the previous decade (though Somerset, once known as 'The League of Nations', has combined improving fortunes with a good deal of local talent). Partly this was because of importation of overseas players – which steps have now been taken to reduce. They decorated our cricket, but in such numbers were discouraging for young English players. Partly it was due to the increase in special registrations. It is common for a cricketer to have played for two counties, and quite likely that he has no personal link with either. Sometimes players do not bother even to live in their counties – including captains. Illingworth, captain of Leicestershire, and Close, captain of Somerset (both, it must be made clear, good captains) continued to live in Yorkshire.

In the first 47 years of the Championship – if we accept the early starting date of 1864, which I doubt if we should – 7 counties won or shared the Championship. The magic circle was broken by Warwickshire in 1911, but not again until Derbyshire won in 1936, and then not again until Glamorgan won in 1948. 9 counties in 84 years (less the war periods) had won. From 1965 to 1979 inclusive 10 counties have won. This is an obvious indication of a levelling of standards. After the success of Essex in 1979, only Northamptonshire, Somerset and Sussex have never won a Championship, and they have all been near it.

The Championship has now become, in a sense, another limited-over competition, with 100 overs to a side in the first innings. It is widely and reasonably felt that all this limited-over cricket has had an unfortunate effect upon middle-order batting. The popularity of going in first has increased. Middle order batsmen find, so frequently, that they do not have the time to build an innings – unless there has been a bad start, which has its own problems. The effect on bowling, I am inclined to think, has been even more deleterious. Bowlers, at least in the shorter forms of the limited game, do not have to work for their wickets. Economy is all. The seamer is king, bowling to a field swiftly getting nearer the boundary. Spinners raise their pace and use a flat trajectory. 'Great performance by' (as it might be) 'Underwood', is the cry, when he has bowled his 8 overs for 15 or so for no wickets in a Sunday match, on a pitch where, bowling normally, he would have had the lot of them out. The last English Test Match leg-spinner, Hobbs of Essex – latterly of Glamorgan – is near to the end of his career. When do you see leg-spin nowadays in county cricket? From an Englishman, I mean. You see it from a batsman turning his arm over, either in an emergency or for fun. You do not often see it at other levels either, since more and more club and even village cricket is over-limited. The loss of leg-spin, one of the highest skills and beauties of the game, one of the aspects of cricket which truly approached fine art, is a tragedy.

Will it ever revive? In the present social climate (which is not to be altogether deplored: after all, cricketers were paid rather badly until the sponsors came) it is hard to see it happening, unless a genius should come along, another Barnes or O'Reilly. But the chances even of a genius are to some extent limited by his environment – including his overs. Full many a flower . . . Yet it was only in 1961 Benaud won a rubber for Australia at Old Trafford – with leg-spin.

The department in which limited-over cricket has unquestionably raised standards is fielding. Perhaps one should exclude wicket-keeping, not because today's wicket-keepers are less talented than their predecessors, but because they have much less practice at stumping, with the dominance of seam and the absence of leg-spin. In 1978 the wicket-keeper who made most dismissals was Bairstow, with 71, 10 of them stumped. Taylor, the England wicket-keeper, had 65, 9 stumped. Downton, Kent's young successor to Knott, had 60, only 4 stumped. Smith of Essex (formerly of Yorkshire) had 9 stumpings out of his 58. Stephenson of Hampshire had 10 out of his 55. The last wicket-keeper to make 100 dismissals in a season was Booth (91 caught, 9 stumped) in 1964. Ames, who did it 3 times, in 1928 and 1929 and 1932 – which still gives him 1st, 2nd, and 11th place in the order of record – stumped 48 out of 127 in 1929, 52 out of 121 in 1928, 64 out of 100 in 1932. Of course he had Freeman bowling. So we come back to the loss of leg-spin, and the changing nature of the game.

Fielding in all other positions has improved remarkably, under the stress of saving every possible run. There have been outstanding fieldsmen in the past, and even whole sides who were exceptionally good in the field: Yorkshire in the 1930s, Surrey in the 1950s, are two within my own experience (though even Yorkshire in the 1930s had Bill Bowes, not exactly a flyer except when he was bowling). I have not, I think, seen any better fieldsmen than Turner and Mitchell, Surridge and Lock. But I believe that about one third of the cricketers in the present first-class game would have been called 'outstanding' even a quarter of a century ago. It is interesting, going back further, to call in evidence E. H. D. Sewell, that stern old reporter who maintained that cricket had gone to the dogs ever since 1918, in every respect. With many other experts, he used to declare that the ideal throw from the deep should bounce a few yards before the wicket-keeper. Throwing to the wicket (not always *at* the wicket, which is often overdone) – at least English throwing to the wicket – is the most vivid illustration of fielding improvement. 'The Australians always have us beat at this', wrote Jack Hobbs, but this is no more true. Sewell was reckoned, not just by himself, a fine fieldsman, one of the best of his day when he played for Essex and London County. For several seasons he kept a record of his catching. In 1903 he caught, he says, 19 of the 23 chances offered to him. In 1904, he held 30 out of 39. He held these sometimes near the wicket, and sometimes in the deep. Yes, it is a good record, but no better than almost every member of the 1979 Essex side would expect to achieve.

As far as the success of the England team is concerned in the period under review, there were good times and bad, as there will be in any span of 15 years. Perhaps the worst time was when Lillee and Thomson demolished us in Australia in 1974–75. Perhaps the best was when Brearley's side won there, almost as conclusively, 4 years later. That victory was slightly marred, or the pleasure in it was lessened because Australia was without its 'Packer players', but Brearley had already beaten the full Australian side in England, and Illingworth's tour of 1970–71 – the only other occasion in the period when we have won a rubber in Australia – was also marred, by some ill-mannered squabbles in which England were not blameless (Perhaps this is the place sadly to observe that there has been a steady deterioration in manners, not only on the field but off. Limited-over crowds have been the worst offenders, especially on Sundays, when many spectators seem to go largely for the all-day licence. Curiously, two of the grounds worst affected have been two of the most beautiful, Taunton and Worcester.)

Despite the criticisms made of Illingworth on that 1970–71 tour – and remembering that Brearley's career is still incomplete – Illingworth was the outstanding England captain of the 15 years. Dexter was never regularly available after the Australian visit of 1964. He retired too soon, as May had done, but he had his livelihood to think of. Great cricketers were then not paid commensurately with their fame. Today, of course, things are much better in that respect, and the top ones can do very well indeed for themselves. This is partly due to sponsorship (under this heading I suppose we must include the indirect contribution made by Kerry Packer, though it is a little like praising a highly skilled burglar for the invention of an improved burglar alarm). Even the Tests are now sponsored, by Cornhill Insurance, and one-day internationals by the Prudential, including the 'World Cup'. This competition has taken place twice, in England, in 1975 and 1979.

After Dexter, M. J. K. Smith had a couple of happy and not unsuccessful years in the job. It was felt, after the First Test against the very strong West Indies tourists of 1966, that his batting was not quite good enough, and so the job reverted to Cowdrey, who had first led England in 1959. But Cowdrey had no better success, and for the last Test Close was appointed. This was a return to the 'professional' approach. Although the distinction between amateur and professional no longer existed, the types were still recognizable. All the captains since Hutton had been Oxford or Cambridge men. Close beat the West Indies, won two fairly easy series at home next summer against India and Pakistan, and would have taken the side to the West Indies in 1967–8, had it not been for an unfortunate incident at Edgbaston. He was captaining Yorkshire there in a tight match against Warwickshire, and was guilty of time-wasting. He refused to apologize, and Cowdrey replaced him for the West Indies tour. Had it not been for this needless fracas, Close would probably have remained the England captain for a long time to come. I make the reservation 'probably' because there was always a possibility, with such a stormy character, that trouble might blow up about something or other.

Time-wasting, usually by bowling overs slowly in a fourth innings, was not uncommon – nor was it new. Edgbaston provided a flagrant example, but every season would produce half a dozen minor rows. It is true to say, though, that over-rates at almost all stages of the game were getting slower. Hence the regulation to ensure that at least 20 overs are bowled in the last 'hour' of a game, and also penalties for the sides who, over the season, bowl their overs too slowly. Both of these provisions, on the whole, have worked well, though nothing is perfect. There have been instances of sides slowing up the rate in the last hour but one. And the sides with the slowest rates are often the most successful ones, who have to work their bowlers, especially their fast bowlers, hard.

After Cowdrey had won the rubber in the West Indies, once more it seemed that the captaincy was settled for a few years. He was captain in the drawn rubber against Australia in 1968, and took the side to Pakistan in the winter. An extraordinary series of chances, however, ensured that those were his last matches as captain. First was his own Achilles tendon injury early in 1969 which cost him practically the whole season.

The selectors now had to find a deputy, whom it was generally assumed would only be a stop-gap, since there was no obvious successor, if Close was still held to be *persona non grata*. Now Illingworth had fallen out with Yorkshire over the terms of renewal of his contract. Leicestershire invited him to join them, as captain. He had had no previous experience of captaincy except as a deputy, though his knowledge of the game was widely respected, and many close to the action believed he had had more to do with the run of Yorkshire successes than anybody. His merit as a player was also much admired, with the reservation that he had never done much for England, nor been assured of his place in the side. So his choice to follow Cowdrey as captain caused a good deal of surprise, not least to Illingworth himself. It must also have been something of a relief to Cowdrey, whose great ambition it was to lead an England side in Australia. Here was no thrusting

Georgetown, Guyana, April 1968: England, led by Colin Cowdrey, won back the Wisden Trophy from West Indies under Gary Sobers after a chivalrous series contested by two great sportsmen.

Two days after being deposed as England's captain, in August 1973, Ray Illingworth (*left*) and his successor, Michael Denness, were opposing captains in the County Championship. Illingworth was England's outstanding captain of the 1970s.

youngster who might make the job his own. Illingworth in fact held the job for 5 years, winning the Ashes in Australia and retaining them at home. Cowdrey was to go, in all, to Australia 6 times, 4 times as vice-captain, each time under a different captain.

The turning-point came towards the end of 1970, when England were playing a series of matches against the Rest of the World, sponsored by Guinness, put on at short notice to replace the cancelled South African tour. (These matches contained some of the best, and indeed most sporting, cricket I have ever seen, and it has always seemed to be absurd that many quibble about their 'Test' status.) Illingworth was reappointed at the beginning of the season, naturally enough since Cowdrey took some time to regain his touch, but there was a general expectation that Cowdrey would return to command for the Australian trip. However, Illingworth had a good series, and the choice went the other way. No one can say it was unjustified, though it was impossible not to feel sympathy for Cowdrey, a man who graced the game, in style and in manner, as much as any of his time.

The intention was to follow Illingworth with Lewis, who took the side to India and Pakistan in 1972–3, and became the first Welshman to captain England – if one discounts C. F. Walters, captain once as a deputy in 1934. Lewis was a good captain, not an outstanding player by Test standards, but a leader. he might have done much the same sort of job as Brearley was to do, had not his fitness wavered: but it did in the shape of persistent knee trouble, and so his vice-captain in India, Denness, took over when Illingworth (who had not been available for the Indian tour) finally stepped down. Denness, heavily beaten in Australia in 1974–75, was also unlucky, though an excellent batsman against all but the fastest bowling, because he met exceptionally strong opposition – as he had done on his first tour to the West Indies (where nevertheless he drew the rubber). A thoughtful but sometimes diffident Scot, he was not the ideal captain.

After Denness came Greig. Greig is, of course, a South African. There is nothing unusual about an England captain being born abroad, but Greig had not learnt his cricket here. I remember John Woodcock saying something to the effect that 'this could not be quite the same thing'. This mild comment caused some sharp criticism, but events told their tale. However, Greig was a good captain in most ways. We tend to forget this after all the storms associated with the Packer enterprise, and the sense of betrayal. But for so long as he threw in his lot with us, he served us well, which should not be forgotten. His England career ended with the Centenary Test at Melbourne in 1977, a remarkable match, played in the best spirit, which ended in a win for Australia by 45 runs – precisely the same margin by which they had won what is now recognized as the first Test, also at Melbourne, in 1877. Not only a remarkable match but a remarkable occasion: of 244 living Test cricketers who had played for England or Australia, 218 were able to attend. The oldest Australian was Jack Ryder, aged 87, the oldest Englishman Percy Fender, aged 84. It was the idea of Hans Ebeling, who bowled for Australia over here in 1934 and was a Vice-President of the Melbourne Cricket Club. No wonder Reg Hayter was moved to call him Hans 'Andersen' Ebeling. It was a moment of hope and rejoicing, swiftly gone, engulfed by the shock of Packer's attempted take-over with Greig his 'English' recruiting agent.

After Greig had departed with a clap of thunder, the calm philosophy of Brearley was much needed, and certainly, though there have been recurrent queries about his batting, up to the time I write he has done very well.

Before I leave the England sides of the period, I should note that India won a rubber here, for the first time, in 1971. That was a particularly pleasing success because it was achieved by spin bowling, a rarity in modern Tests. Not many countries at any time can have had a stronger hand of spinners than Bedi, Chandrasekhar, Venkataraghavan and Prasanna. The mind went back to the South Africans of 1907. New Zealand came close to winning a match against England over here in 1973, and did so, at last, in their own country in 1978. No matches have been played against South Africa since 1965 (when South Africa won in England). All of these were 3-match rubbers. Fitting two touring sides into an English season became inevitable after the proliferation of Tests and Test-playing countries.

In the Centenary Test at Melbourne in March 1977, Derek Randall, with 174 audacious runs in the 2nd innings, brought England to the verge of an unimaginable victory; here he hooks Lillee for 4.

The outstanding English batsman of the time, if one allows an earlier generation to claim Cowdrey and Dexter, has been Boycott. His first appearance for Yorkshire was in 1962, and he reached his 100th century in 1977. He is the only player to have done it in a Test match, and it was against Australia, before his own people at Headingley. He lost some sympathy among cricketers, especially in the south, by declining to play for England at a critical time. It was openly said (by Greig, that paragon of loyalty, among others) that he was scared of the fast bowlers. But Boycott is a complex man, and I do not think his motives were altogether unworthy. He seemed when young to have all the makings of a successful captain, but it has not proved so. He is a solitary man with a solitary aim. Cowdrey and John Edrich, Bill's cousin, also reached their hundred centuries during the period.

Jubilee Crowns (500 each) were awarded to both English and Australian batsmen and bowlers in the Test Series of 1977. Messrs Willis, Boycott and Greg Chappell seem suitably elated. One of the many modern faces of sponsorship.

The outstanding English bowler of the period is less easy to identify. Myself I would go for Underwood, but as fast bowling has been the dominant theme, there is a case for Snow or Willis. If you think of *county* bowlers, not even Illingworth can approach Shackleton of Hampshire, the epitome of the seamer, but much, much better than nearly all the others, despite constantly having to bowl more overs than anyone else in a season. The outstanding wicket-keeper has, not much doubt, been Knott. He must have been a regular choice even had he batted at No. 11. Incidentally, the old principle that you should always play the best wicket-keeper irrespective of his batting ability does not often apply nowadays (partly a side-effect of one-day cricket, and partly the preponderance of seam bowling: they spend so much time standing back). Parks, for instance, played in 46 Tests, and Andrew in 2, but Parks could not compare with Andrew as a wicket-keeper. Indeed, in the last Test in the West Indies as long ago as 1959–60, when Swetman was injured, and England needed a draw for the rubber, Andrew, the stand-by wicket-keeper, was left out, and Parks, who was not a member of the party but happened to be in that part of the world, was brought in. As he scored a century when the match was in the balance, the strategy was justified. Further back, in the early 1930s, Lancastrians at least maintained that Duckworth was a better wicket-keeper than Ames, and that Ames only ousted him from the Test team because of his batting: but the point is arguable, and again the results of the change were satisfactory. So this is not a new process, but it has accelerated. At county level, some excellent wicket-keepers have had to end their careers early because they could not bat well enough.

I have written already of the rise in fielding standards, and will not attempt to name an outstanding English fieldsman of the period. There are too many of them. Even if I mentioned half a dozen, it would be unfair to another half-dozen, and if I mentioned *them*, further candidates would immediately present themselves. I will, however, mention Randall, not because I am claiming he is the best, but because he is the one I have most enjoyed watching, all arms and legs and enthusiasm and capers. Some find him irritating – 'clowning', they call it – but not I. And I will suggest a best English runner-between-the-wickets for the period: Arthur Milton of Gloucestershire. Again I am not making a very serious claim: it is just that I am determined to get him in. The point about Arthur's running was that he never missed a single but never looked in a hurry: 'Roll and stroll', his colleagues used to call him.

It has been a crowded and controversial 15 years. The biggest rumpuses have been about playing South Africa, early in the period, and latterly about Packer cricket – 'World Series Cricket', as it came to be called. Both of these are treated extensively elsewhere, and I will only make one or two points. The two events are, in a sense, linked. If there had not been practically an entire high-class Test side wandering about the world unable to play Test matches for their own country, K. Packer would have found it much more difficult to acquire players. This is not the place to expound on the rights and wrongs of our cricketing association with South Africa, or to argue whether and to what extent the position has changed since the cancellation of the 1970 tour, but I have no doubt the right decision was taken at the time, and that as time goes on it will increasingly be seen that no one comes out of the business better than the present Bishop of Liverpool and Basil d'Oliveira. The affair was badly handled, and I do not mean just by MCC, but a point of crisis had been reached from which there could be no satisfactory outcome. It was very sad that players such as Procter and Barry Richards should have been deprived of illustrious Test careers, but it would have been very sad if cricket had lost its long multi-racial tradition, or if the game had divided into black and white sections. The Packer problem, in its later stages, revived this last spectre, for rather different reasons.

So I found it good news, or relatively good news, when in the middle of 1979 we heard of the agreement between K. Packer and the Australian Cricket Board. It was, so far as could be seen at the time, a victory for K. Packer. He won his original point about television rights (which he could have had without all the palaver by waiting until the contract was open to negotiation) and, with his new status as official promoter will, in practice (if he bothers) have a large say in the way cricket develops, not only in Australia. He quickly began to rearrange the Test programme, and the ICC, though with several explicit reservations, went along with him. Whether this treaty will work out it is too early to say. The long battle left many victims by the wayside, not least the Australian Broadcasting Commission. But almost any sort of agreement, or so I felt at the time, was better than none. The cricketing authorities had been a little over-confident (as MCC were over the South African business in 1970) and took a long time to realize what a pickle they were in: that a lot of people in the world 'don't play cricket'. Perhaps I may add, since nearly all the prophecies I make have the permanence of bubbles, that when the Packer plans were first announced, I wrote an article for *The Times* saying that I thought they were deplorable, but would be successful. The article was not published.

The problem of 'throwing', which had seemed so serious in the late 1950s, has only occasionally recurred, once the Australians decided not to choose any bowlers with doubtful actions for the tour of 1961. This decision was, I suspect, one of the great services of Bradman to cricket – the generosity of which can only be understood when you remember that he had been the principal target of Bodyline. The bowlers who have suffered from the stricter interpretation of the (still vague) law have been mostly those who have some unusual physical formation of the arm (such as Rhodes of Derbyshire), or those who have not, despite much trying, been able to cure themselves of habits left uncorrected when they were young (such as Cope of Yorkshire). A much bigger worry has been the bouncer. There have been many unpleasant incidents, though so far, in first-class cricket, no deaths. Lever, of Lancashire, nearly killed

Chatfield, of New Zealand, in a Test at Auckland in 1975. He was a tail-ender. So was Iqbal Qasim, of Pakistan, severely hurt by a bouncer from Willis at Edgbaston in 1978 (though he had gone in as night-watchman, and was proving difficult to dislodge). In lesser grades of cricket, where the pitches are often poor, people *have* been killed. Cricketers are imitators of what they see in the first-class game. Many attempts have been made to curb the bouncer by law, umpires have been urged to take stronger action, but the problem is unsolved. Batsmen in self-defence have taken to crash-helmets (so, less justifiably, have close fieldsmen – after all, a batsman *has* to face the ball, but a fieldsman does not have to stand at suicide short-leg). The bouncer has always been considered, in moderation, a legitimate part of a fast bowler's armoury; but perhaps the time has come for its complete abolition.

There have been some changes in the administration of the game, made in the first place so that there could be an official body with which the Minister for Sport and the Sports Council could deal. The powers of MCC (always more real than theoretical) have been merged with those of the Test and County Cricket Board, and the National Cricket Association, in the Cricket Council. The changes have not in practice been at all revolutionary, and Lord's is still the hub of the English game. One bad habit of cricket administrators, which is very far from new and shews no sign of abating, is what might be called law-mongering. In 1967 the editor of *Wisden* complained 'For the past twenty years we have had one change after another . . . Small wonder that the ordinary follower of the game has become so utterly confused . . . And what about the players? Surely this constant tampering with the rules has been of little benefit to them'. Wise words, but still it goes on. Indeed the new competitions, with their varying regulations have made things worse. The ways of settling the winners of the Championship have been altered times without number – a habit that goes back to its beginning. I long for a moratorium on changes – except to deal with a major crisis such as bouncing – for 5 years or so. Cricket is a complicated game, but we make it unnecessarily difficult for ourselves. There have been many instances of captains and even umpires being caught at a loss.

The 1979 season deserves a word of its own. Here was a further illustration of the levelling of first-class standards. The 4 competitions were shared between Essex and Somerset, the two counties who had never won anything before. Essex, as well as the Benson and Hedges, won their first Championship, by a wide margin. Somerset won the Gillette Cup and then, next day, the John Player League. Somerset's success was dramatic, because the previous year, also on consecutive days, they had lost them both. So now everyone has won something sometime. 'All have won, and all shall have prizes': a pleasing thought on which to end.

Lord's and the MCC

Lord's

J. H. FINGLETON

The histories of Lord's Ground and of the Marylebone Cricket Club are, of course, intricately and indeed inextricably intertwined. The following essay, which tells the story of the early days of the ground and the Club and their impact on an Australian visitor, and one of its distinguished honorary cricket members, may be read in conjunction with the contribution immediately following, entitled MCC

I think it was the No. 13 bus that I used to catch from the bottom of the Strand to go to Lord's. We would do some jogging past Nelson in Trafalgar Square, as he kept his good eye on things up Whitehall, and then, making speed, move out of Cockspur Street into Regent Street. It sometimes happened that long before we got to Piccadilly Circus the 'clippie', with a discernment common to those of his and her ilk on the London buses, would gather from my accent the nature of my journey. Up Regent Street, then, there would be some sharp and direful asides upon how the Australians would fare this day at Lord's, and by the time the bus had reached Oxford Street we would be on the best of swapping terms. From Oxford Street we turned into Baker Street, thence across Marylebone Road, and so on to the disembarkation point, the 'clippie' having the parting thrust. The bus largely emptied itself at the Lord's stop. Most of the ties of my travelling neighbours I could recognize – MCC, the Forty Club, an occasional Middlesex one, the Purchasers and, sometimes, the distinctive one of the Hong Kong Cricket Club or a club in South Africa. One felt an affinity with them all.

We were all off with hope to Lord's for the Test, and it was fitting, one always thought, that this particular route should have led along some of the best-known streets in the world because Lord's, of a surety, is as much part of the London scene as Buckingham Palace, the House of Commons, the National Gallery, the red double-deck buses and so on.

Some (and particularly from Australia because it is not a national characteristic of ours to take care to conceal our first impressions) have expressed disappointment on seeing Lord's for the first time. It has not the ample open-space proportions of the Sydney Cricket Ground. It has not the immense tier upon tier of concrete construction that has hidden the gaunt Melbourne ground from the adjacent parklands and given it the character of a Colosseum. Lord's lacks, for instance, the idyllic charm and splendour of the hills that frame the fields of Adelaide and Cape Town. But no other ground, as I have seen them, can compare with Lord's in its calm and peaceful majesty. The Holy of Holies it has been exaggeratedly called by some of its disciples. I prefer to think of it as the Mecca of Cricket because I think it true to say that there has never been an outstanding player from any country who hasn't played at Lord's. I saw it first in 1938, enveloped by the slight mist of a departing spring. It was awakening to a new season, full of pride in its long and historic past yet looking forward with youthful zest to more great deeds in the sun. Old Father Time, I told myself as I caught a glimpse of him over the sight-board as he was removing the bails at the day's end, knew what it was all about.

There is that thought, suggested above, of every great and good international cricketer of every age having been seen at Lord's. That is one aspect of it – the travellers to cricket's Mecca – yet there is another important one that flits through the mind as it takes in Lord's for the first time. From here the game has spread to those countries, incredibly many, in which cricket is played. From here has come the spirit of the game, the changes in Laws, the mellowed and qualified lead that spreads through the game wherever it is played. A1 at Lloyd's is a well-known distinction. To be A1 at Lord's at the end of an international career and to be accepted into life membership by this immortal club is an accolade that warms the cricketing hearts that receive it.

Lord Winchilsea, regarded as the chief founder of MCC in 1787 and Thomas Lord whom the first members encouraged to procure them a ground. In fact he found 3, the present headquarters being the last.

On hearing of Lord's for the first time one is understandably apt to associate it with the aristocracy; to imagine it as the possible cavorting (if such a term can be used in this context) place of those members of the House of Lords set free, for the nonce, from their duties of the nation. But the naming of the places is as far apart in actuality as they are in being, although membership of both has been common to many. The House of Lords is on the River Thames at Westminster; the club is in Marylebone, from which parish its name originates, some miles away.

There was a prisoner of war once who found the erroneous association to his well-being. The story is told of one Gordon Johnston who was elected a member of MCC when he was a prisoner of the Italians in 1942. His relations decided to send him the glad tidings through the diplomatic channels of the Vatican yet, knowing that cricket would mean little to the Italians, they hesitated to use the initials 'MCC' in case some sinister meaning should be attached to them. The message, then, merely stated that he had been elected a member of Lord's. The Italian interpreter concluded that one under his charge had been elevated to the peerage. From that moment on, Johnston (and his fellows profited with him) was given prisoner-of-war treatment which the Italians thought commensurate with his noble standing!

The name comes from Thomas Lord, 'the pivot around whom the formation of the Marylebone club turned'. Lord was a Yorkshireman, and his father, a substantial yeoman of Roman Catholic stock, had his lands sequestrated when he espoused the Stuart cause in the rising of 1745, so that he had to work as a labourer on the very farm which he once owned. We can imagine the feelings of the Lord family when it moved south to Norfolk, where Thomas Lord spent his young days. Thence he migrated to London and found employment at the White Conduit Club as a bowler and factotum around the club.

This club was the acorn which blossomed into the gigantic oak to be known as the Marylebone club. Formed in 1782, it was an offshoot of a convivial West End club called the '*Je-ne-sais-quoi*', some of whose members frequented the White Conduit House and played cricket matches on the adjoining fields near Islington. In spite of their club name, the cricketers did know what they wanted in the shape of a permanent cricketing home. Prompted by the Earl of Winchilsea, who could be considered the founder of MCC, and Charles Lennox, later to be the Duke of Richmond, a guarantee against loss was made to Lord if he would start a new private cricket ground. Lord was most willing and in May 1787 he opened his first ground on what is now Dorset Square. Middlesex beat Essex by 93 runs in the first game played there.

The first recorded MCC match was in June 1788, when the club beat the White Conduit club by 83 runs. Lord put a fence around the ground but the site was now an invaluable building one and became too costly for Lord's purse. The last match was played there in 1810. Foreseeing the future with some acumen, Lord in 1808 rented two fields on the St John's Wood Estate for a term of 80 years, free of land-tax and tithe, at £54 a year. The new ground was ready in 1809, so that for two years Lord had two grounds on his hands, the St John's Wood CC using the new enclosure. This club was afterwards incorporated in the MCC. The new Lord's was officially taken over on 8 May 1811, the turf having been removed from the original ground in Dorset Square so that 'the noblemen and Gentlemen of the MCC should be able to play on the same footing as before'. The move was not popular with many members of the MCC and the club did not play a single match there in 1811 or 1812 – and only 3 the following year.

But London was spreading, and yet another move was enforced upon Lord as Parliament decreed that the Regent's Canal should be cut through the centre of the ground. The Eyre family, on whose ground the second estate was situated, were willing to grant Lord another plot. So Lord lifted his roots and his turf again and made yet another headquarters, this time on the site where Lord's is today. The rent was to be £100 yearly and the ground was to open in 1814. Lord was now a man of some substance in the parish of Marylebone. He was made a member of the Marylebone Vestry in 1807 and he also conducted a wine-and-spirit business. The ground had an inauspicious beginning. Four days before it opened the landlady of the public house at the fields was handling some gunpowder (an odd substance, surely, for such a one to be handling). A spark from the fire caught it and it went off with a great bang, seriously injuring the landlady, her sister and four little girls. It cast a shadow over the first game played there which MCC won against Hertfordshire by an innings and 27 runs.

The ground was immediately popular with the players and the public, but Lord, who could have had well-developed business instincts by this time, was anxious to turn more shillings. He obtained permission from the Eyre Estate to develop the ground as a building site to enhance the value of the 68 years remaining of the lease, and plans for building houses were actually drawn up which limited the playing area to 150 sq yds. Had he been able to sell out, there would be no Lord's today.

William Ward, a director of the Bank of England and later to be MP for the City of London, saved the situation by buying Lord's interest in the ground for £5,000. Thus Lord's contact with the famous ground ceased in 1825. He continued to live in the adjoining St John's Wood Road until 1830 and died in Hampshire in 1832, aged 76. In 1835 Ward and his 4 daughters, who joined in the lease to bind any interest they had in the property, transferred it to one J. H. Dark, who gave £2,000 for it and undertook to pay the Ward family an annuity of £425 during the unexpired term of the lease, which was to be 59 years from 1834, at a yearly rental of £150. When Dark first leased Lord's there were two ponds, one in front of the present Mound stand and the other at the west end of the ground. One of the groundsmen learned to swim there. Dark, himself, lived in a house where the new Tavern Stand has been built.

E. H. Budd, in 1816, hit the first hundred at Lord's. He played with a bat weighing 3 lb which is in the pavilion today. William Ward, the saviour of the ground when Lord wished to sell it, hit 278 for the club against Norfolk in 1820 and that record as the highest score on the ground stood until Percy Holmes, of Yorkshire, hit 315 not out in 1925. Jack Hobbs beat that the next year with 316 not out, which still remains the highest score made at Lord's. Middlesex were on

The Long Room in repose. For 90 years from these windows have been witnessed many of the epics of cricket history.

the receiving end in both instances. Ward was a pretty powerful fellow. In that record innings he used a bat weighing 4 lb – and, moreover, used the same bat for 50 years.

A wooden pavilion was built in 1814, and was later enlarged and improved by Ward. In 1825, a few hours after the Winchester–Harrow match, it was destroyed by fire and all the club's original possessions, records, score-books and trophies were lost. A new pavilion was built in 1826, and was enlarged in 1865. This did service until the present pavilion was opened in 1890. A tennis court was put down in 1838 and pulled down in 1898 to make way for the Mound stand. The present tennis court behind the pavilion, to which a rackets court and squash courts were later added, was then built. In 1838 the pavilion was lighted by gas and the tavern, which had been erected by Lord when he opened the ground in 1814, had an assembly-room built over it. As far back as 1825, Eton, Harrow and Winchester used to meet at Lord's and did so until 1854 when the headmaster of Winchester, thinking London held too many temptations for his boys, forbade the fixture.

Pony races were held at Lord's in the 1840s and 1850s after the cricket season had finished. A balloon, too, once made its ascent from Lord's which, however, had nothing to rival the Oval where executions were sometimes held. Over these years the pitch and outfield at Lord's were notoriously rough. Sheep used to be brought in before a game began to nibble the outfield and only a small roller was used to condition the pitch. It is interesting that when a machine-mower made its first appearance strong objection was made to it by some members. In 1864, the first groundsman was engaged, at 25*s.* a week. A crisis arose in 1860, when the Eyre Estate sold the freehold of Lord's at a public auction. Dark and others wanted the club to bid but, strangely, they did not and the ground was bought by Isaac Moses for £7,000. When, eventually, the ground became the property of the club on 22 August 1866, £18,333 6*s.* 8*d.* had to be paid to Moses for the freehold. An Old Harrovian, William Nicholson, advanced the sum and, justly, became President of MCC in 1879.

In 1887, £18,500 was paid for 3¾ acres of what was known as Henderson's Nursery. It reputedly grew the best pineapples in England and was famed also for its tulips. Hence the origin of the Nursery end, where the practice pitches and car parks are. Four years later, MCC acquired the Clergy Female Orphan School from the then Manchester and Sheffield Railway in exchange for leave to tunnel under the practice ground. Today the British Railways own a strip of ground 40 yards wide where the arbours are situated and for which the club pay an annual rent of £200. The 99-year lease dates from May 1897.

In 1888 the Great Central Railway promoted a bill in Parliament to acquire Lord's in order to run their line through it. This would have meant the end of Lord's, but the Club made such a fuss that this part of the bill was withdrawn. Thus entrenched, the foundation stone of the present pavilion was laid in September 1889. (It was ready for the club's AGM, held then as now on the first Wednesday of May in 1890). The cost, including extras and furniture, was £21,000. There have been some internal alterations since but mostly the pavilion today is as it was first built. The Press stand was added in 1906, and was in use until the building of the splendid stand named after Sir Pelham Warner in 1958. The Press now sits at the top of this stand.

After the First World War, MCC built a new grandstand and the cantilever stands on the east side of the ground. In 1934 an additional stand for members and their friends was built between the south clock tower and the pavilion. It cost £46,000. Sir Pelham Warner was one who thought it should have been better. In Churchillian terms he once said that never in the history of cricket had so large a stand been built at such a cost to hold so few people. Sir Herbert Baker was the architect of this, as he had also been of the grandstand about which a similar criticism might have been made. However, to his eternal credit, Baker threw in a superb surprise in the Father Time weather-vane. Nobody on the committee knew that Father Time was to be placed on top of the grandstand. It is now one of the characteristics of Lord's, bails being taken off at the end of play by the Old Man with his scythe over his shoulder. In an air-raid in 1940, during the Second World War, Father Time was caught up in the cable of a barrage balloon and slid gently down on to the balcony seats. He spent the rest of the war in the committee-room. Even today, however, Lord's does not hold very big crowds. Its capacity would be about 30,000 and that with a lot of people sitting on the grass. Many a time in Tests against Australia have the gates been closed before play began. It was no uncommon occurrence to see people leave the ground after a day's play and then join the overnight queue for play next day. That, to my mind, has always been one of the saddest sights in English cricket – to see thousands queued up outside grounds with no possible hope of gaining admittance.

It was not until 1877, when Middlesex began to use Lord's as their home ground, that the area realized its full potential. It is interesting to know that the ground was of heavy clay and badly drained and the outfield always rough and treacherous. There were no boundaries – except the pavilion – no stands or fixed seats of any kind, nothing but the small old pavilion and a line of loose benches running part of the way around the ground. The MCC committee at this time was said to be stuffy and unimaginative. One who thought the club in dire danger of losing its character was the enthusiastic secretary, R. A. FitzGerald. He was intent on making Lord's the great centre of cricket but his committee was lethargic and indifferent. FitzGerald hoped to induce Middlesex to use Lord's as its home ground but there was delay and Middlesex found another London ground in Prince's. Later FitzGerald

F. R. Spofforth, the Australian 'Demon', unsurpassed as a bowler in his day and of proverbially stark hostility, looks benign enough in this Spy cartoon. When Edward Lyttelton scored the first hundred against the first Australians Spofforth presented him with his walking-stick.

persuaded MCC to invite Middlesex again, and this time they accepted.

Down the years, Lord's has had the reputation of being conservative. Evidently it was true in the last century. FitzGerald induced E. Rutter and C. E. Green to accept nomination for the committee, in order to liven it up, and Rutter relates how they sat in conclave with their elderly and reactionary fellow-members:

At first we were distinctly ignored and Charlie Green was so utterly disgusted with the supercilious manner in which he was received that he declared he would never sit on the committee again. Nor did he, but stuck to his resolve. Oddly enough, the next official appearance he made in the club was many years later (1905), when he was elected President.

Sir Pelham Warner notes that Green himself was not altogether free of reactionary tendencies. 'When I suggested early in the present century,' writes Warner, 'that there should be a wider screen at Lord's, Green remarked, "I never knew you were such a radical, Warner".' Warner, of course, was referring to the Nursery end. One wonders what the reactions of both him and Green would have been in 1964 when MCC agreed to a sight-screen being put up in front of the sacred pavilion for the first time.

The rough nature of the ground must have been a trial. It cost the life of a Nottinghamshire player, George Summers, in 1870 when a ball reared from the pitch and hit his head. He died a few days later. During 1873, the ground was relevelled and Lord's lost its proverbial reputation of being the most dangerous ground in the country.

Dr W. G. Grace was now casting his huge shadow on the game and its fields. With both bat and ball he did big things at Lord's for the Gentlemen against the Players and obviously he must have had a tremendous capacity for the game to make hundreds on such dubious pitches. In 1875, Grace made 7 and 152, run out, and took 12 for 125 against the Players. Next year in the same game he made 169 and took 9 for 122. FitzGerald resigned from the secretaryship that year, after 13 years, and it is worth noting that during his time the membership grew from 650 to 2,080. Now the famous names stream across Lord's: A. J. Webbe, A. P. Lucas, Edward and Alfred Lyttelton, A. G. Steel, I. D. Walker – and the Australians of 1878. They shocked English cricket almost immediately by beating a powerful MCC side at Lord's by nine wickets in a single day. *Wisden* describes the scene on the ground:

A stream of at least a thousand men rushed frantically up to the Pavilion, in front of which they clustered and lustily shouted, 'Well done, Australia!' 'Bravo Spofforth!' 'Boyle, Boyle!', the members of the MCC keenly joining in the applause of that maddened crowd, who shouted themselves hoarse before they left to scatter far and wide that evening the news how in one day the Australians had so easily defeated one of the strongest MCC elevens that had ever played for the famous old club.

The Australians played two other games at Lord's that year. One was against Middlesex, whom they beat by 98 runs, a game memorable for a magnificent innings of 113 by the Hon E. Lyttelton, the bearer of a renowned name in English public life and cricket, who thus became the first Englishman ever to score a century against an Australian team at Lord's. In honour of it Spofforth presented him with his walking-stick. At Lord's too the Australians played Cambridge who, under Lyttelton's captaincy, won a famous victory by an innings and 72 runs.

As an Australian perhaps one could be forgiven for noting that this first team from our country took England unawares. Nobody thought there was strength in any cricket outside of England, and so a very haphazard fixture-list was drawn up for this tour. It might be true to say that England has never since taken an Australian team in England too easily. The Australians, under W. L. Murdoch, came again in 1880 but didn't play a single game at Lord's. Trouble had arisen two years earlier over the status of Australians as amateurs, but the most trouble arose over a decision in Sydney during the tour of Lord Harris's English team when Murdoch was given run out. Oddly, Dave Gregory, the NSW captain, went on the field and asked that the English umpire, Coulthard, should be retired. There were violent crowd scenes and Lord Harris, who was assaulted in the mêlée, said he had no wish to play against an Australian team again.

The atmosphere towards my countrymen in England in 1880 was icy, but Lord Harris nobly relented and helped to arrange the first Test against England in England, at the Oval, and England won a good game by 5 wickets. Dr Grace made 152, and Murdoch 153 not out for Australia. Australia played its first Test at Lord's in 1884, England winning by an innings and 5 runs. A. G. Steel was England's hero with 148.

Lord's now became in all ways the central point of cricket. Changes in the laws emanated from there, and in 1899 a Board of Control was set up, being chaired by the President of MCC, to decide upon finance, payment of professionals, hours of play, umpires and so on. As 5 Tests were played against Australia for the first time in this year, the Board also nominated English Test selectors. The South Africans sent

J. D. Robertson was the batsman as all fell prone at the approach of a 'Doodle-bug' in 1944.

their first side to England; the West Indians followed soon afterwards and a team from Philadelphia (USA) also played at Lord's.

And so, down the years, every major visiting team has played there and, like the Australians, I'll wager every team considers that its Test at Lord's is the big match of the tour. No player has walked on to Lord's for the first time without his heart beating infinitely faster. There is something about Lord's, something in its somnolent yet majestic atmosphere, that no other ground in the world possesses. The Saturday of the Lord's Test is without parallel – a crowded ground bathed in sunshine (if the sun *is* shining), the arch-critics looking down from the boxes, Father Time keeping a gentle eye upon things, the learned 'Professors' in the Long Room (and the Press-box, might I add) passing sonorous judgment. What honour indeed – to play at Lord's on such an occasion – and happy is the cricketer who, on tour, has notched his century there.

It is an odd thing, but I sensed the traditions of Lord's most in the biggest and deepest bath I have ever seen – with the smallest plug-hole, incidentally. Lucky was the man who got first bath there, because it took an eternity to drain and refill and the gentlemen in the Long Room, not aware of our social engagements, must often have wondered as we moved with speed through their midst and scampered up the stairs for first bath after play. It was an intriguing thought to laze in that bath, ignoring the knocking at the door, and reflect that no doubt in its water had floated the whiskers of the great Doctor.

Lord's is chock-full of tranquil history and close association with the past. It is interesting to reflect upon all the great players who have gone down the steps from the pavilion, all fated to do so some day for the last time. I can see the ground again in 1948 when the clamouring thousands swarmed over it the day Don Bradman had played there for the last time. They stood in front of the pavilion and called for their hero to appear on the balcony. He did not come. Possibly he was deep in his own thoughts. I can remember seeing Miller and Lindwall walk from the field for the last time. There is something tragic in this, and yet few, I think, recognize their final curtain call when it comes. If so, they would surely pause on the threshold of the Long Room and look back with a last, longing and lingering look.

Yet, when the playing days are gone, Lord's always beckons back. Many a lovely hour have I spent in the Long Room (and, indeed, in the committee-room) just walking around, yarning and looking at the relics of other days, in which Lord's abounds. In that Long Room you will meet all manner of Englishmen. Not everybody, in the English tradition, is prepared to pass the time of day with his neighbour. Be that as it may I think all who enter Lord's are entitled to be alone with their own thoughts, if they feel that way.

Of all the manifold stories of Lord's I like best the one of two strangers in the Long Room watching a match there one day and each ignoring the other – until a workman sauntered in, covered the bust of Dr Grace and carried it off. 'My God,' said one member to the other, 'that can mean only one thing. That means war.' And it did – the Second World War. One of the most dramatic photographs ever taken at Lord's shows cricketers lying prone to the ground during a match as a Doodle-Bomb speeds overhead.

There is much at Lord's upon which I have not touched, but then Lord's has filled many a volume and my effort is but to give an Australian impression of cricket's holy of holies. It is well to reflect that from Lord's comes the sage guidance and wisdom in the game. And unlike our own Australian Cricket Board, which not even yet seems to have forgotten the great cleavage between the players and officials in 1912, Lord's

In 1973 an IRA bomb-scare at Lord's led to the stands being cleared during the England v West Indies Test. As the crowd moved on to the middle one of the umpires, 'Dicky' Bird, keeps an eye on the pitch.

gathers to its bosom those who have served the game best on the field. We in Australia suffer, as I see it, from the desire of many unknowns to impress themselves in a sphere which they never graced in a playing manner. That is the beauty of Lord's, or, at least, one beauty that impresses itself upon me. One walks with cricket's past, present and the future at Lord's. Long may Father Time reign there!

MCC

E. W. SWANTON

Foundation 1787 *Colours* Red and Yellow
Badge (for touring use) St George and the Dragon

Although MCC is coming up to its bicentenary it is doubtful whether any comparable period in its history has seen such a degree of change as the 15 years since the first edition of this book was published. In 1965 the club was guiding English cricket, it might be said, on a loose rein. In practice the counties ran Test Matches through the Board of Control and the County Championship through the Advisory County Cricket Committee, albeit the adjective signified that MCC was the final court of appeal. The club was still responsible for the tours abroad that bore its name, as it had been since 'Plum' Warner led the first MCC team to Australia in 1903–04. It had been the Melbourne Cricket Club, that other MCC, which finally persuaded Marylebone to undertake this responsibility, just as it was in answer to the counties' request that the club set up 'the Advisory'. The Laws of the game had been accepted by the club as its responsibility since 1788, the year after its inception, but aside from them the picture was always of MCC taking the lead by invitation. To Warner are ascribed the aphorisms that MCC was a private club with a public function, that it reigned but did not rule. It did so by consent rather than by dint of a constitution.

Since 1969 however there is a defined hierarchy wherein MCC takes a place within the Cricket Council (now the governing body) alongside the Test and County Cricket Board (which controls what its name implies) and the National Cricket Association (which fosters and to an extent administers all aspects of the game beneath county club level). This basic change in the control of cricket is dealt with in more detail later in this section. It is almost incidental, though not without significance, that major touring teams abroad now under the aegis of the TCCB are labelled simply 'England'. The sentimental anachronism 'MCC' has been dropped from the title though with the club's willing permission the touring colours have been retained.

While these weighty matters were taking their course in the late 1960s the club and Lord's itself were being expanded and modernized. When the Warner Stand was built immediately to the west of the pavilion in 1958 the wait for membership, then standing at around 30 years, had been greatly reduced, thanks to this increased accommodation. So 12,000 members became, first, 15,000 and today, thanks to an over-spill on the big match days into the P and Q block flanking the pavilion on the other side, 18,000 all told. Though nearly 1,000 of this 18,000 at the time of writing are on the Abroad List, more than 2,000 are Country members, and a further sizeable proportion have reached the psalmist's span and may accordingly pass through the Grace Gates less often, if no less eagerly, than of old, the strain on resources can no doubt be imagined. Moreover the present numbers put additional pressures on the administration. Yet with overheads constantly rising and a waiting-list growing year by year, what option had the Committee other than allowing the club to grow still larger?

Apart from other claims to membership in due course, the club still offers the traditional preference to young candidates who are good cricketers, giving them the chance to qualify by playing for MCC on probation. Only thus can the club fulfil a fixture-list of 250 out-matches against clubs and schools spread all over England and spilling over the borders into Scotland and Wales.

Lastly on the matter of membership the club does not forget the distinguished old Test cricketers who have given long service to the game. The list of these Honorary Cricket Members of MCC who have played for England numbers 40: all the Test-playing countries likewise have their quota.

The membership of the club is, of course, a matter of general cricket interest since MCC is, as it has always been, the maker and guardian of the Laws. Though close consultation is always maintained with the member-countries of the International Cricket Conference – and the new Code to be found in the section devoted to the Laws in this book is the latest outcome of this liaison – the instrument of change is a General Meeting of the members of MCC, such as that which confirmed the new Code on 21 November 1979.

Turning to the ground itself one notes first the major development on the site of the old Tavern and also the building of the new Tavern immediately outside the Grace Gates. It was sad but inevitable that the Tavern built in 1867/8 in place of the original put up by Thomas Lord had to be pulled down along with the adjoining dining rooms, Clock Tower, boxes and stand. This corner of the ground had seen just 100 years of history when it was replaced by the handsome new Tavern block which even ardent conservationists will admit blends harmoniously into the general picture.

The other and more recent building project is the MCC Indoor School which stands on the south corner of the Practice Ground, and through the doors of which many thousands of cricketers of every age and degree of skill have passed for practice and coaching since they were first opened in November 1977. The need had been felt for many years. That it was fulfilled at last owed most to a member, J. A. (Jack) Hayward, who made a handsome opening contribution, which was followed by subscriptions from many quarters both within the club and beyond.

So much for the various physical changes of the past 15

The most notable addition to the premises in the 1970s was the MCC Indoor School, with its 7 nets, 17 yards of run-up and the latest in club facilities and coaching aids.

F. E. Lacey, secretary 1898–1926, who led MCC firmly and shrewdly into the 20th century: the first man knighted for services to cricket.

years, made since Jack Fingleton wrote his nostalgic essay on Lord's and the MCC as seen by a famous figure in the game from Down Under. The appearance of Lord's has been given something of a face-lift, and the process must continue, without any jeopardizing of its character. The author has sketched with a fresh eye the romantic story of the early days, leaving perhaps only a closer look at the later development of the club and its handling of some major issues before one comes to what might be called the control structure of the game in England today.

There is no doubt that the expansion of MCC, and the equipping of it to keep pace with the rapid spread of the game in the 20th century was chiefly the work of Francis Lacey, who assumed the secretaryship in 1898 and on his retirement in 1926 became the first man to be knighted for his services to cricket. Hitherto the club had been run very much on a personal basis by its secretaries, of whom Henry Perkins, Lacey's predecessor, is said to have given him the advice: 'don't take any notice of the damned committee'. Perkins was a character, peppery and convivial, who is said to have ended a club dinner on the floor going through the motions of swimming, under the impression, it was said, that he was crossing the Styx. According to Warner he also gave short shrift to a member who queried some dictum of his, saying, 'do you think I'm going to be told the law by a silly beggar like you? Get out of the room.'

'Ben' Lacey, a barrister by training and only 39 when he came to Lord's, got his own way by more conventional means. It was he who instituted the system of sub-committees, each responsible to the main committee for its own department, which, much expanded, persists today. Under him the Mound Stand was built and the ground improved, the boys' Easter Classes started, the Board of Control for Test Matches, the Advisory County Cricket Committee and the Imperial Cricket Conference set up.

Early in the new century it was probably the decision to shoulder the job of raising representative sides abroad that established in the public mind the image of Lord's as the fount of authority and power. In the high noon of Empire, with the Pax Britannica apparently secure for ever. Lord's Cricket Ground was an apt symbol of the age. The membership stood now at 5,000. Amateur cricket was at its zenith, and MCC was enriched by large and fashionable crowds for the three great annual matches, Gentlemen v Players, Oxford v Cambridge and Eton v Harrow. Added to this staple fare there came, every few years, a popular bonus in the shape of a Test Match against Australia or South Africa.

In the Treasurer's chair in these prosperous times sat, as he had done since 1879 and was to do until his death in his 92nd year in 1915, a patriarchal link with the past, Sir Spencer Ponsonby-Fane. Elected in 1840 at the age of 16, he was a nephew of the Rev Lord Frederick Beauclerk; he had played with William Ward, who had saved Lord's from the builders; had taken part in the first Canterbury Week; had been one of the three founders of I Zingari; and was for *eighty* years a habitué of Lord's. Benignly he looks down from his portrait in the Committee-room on the complex and manifold affairs nowadays being conducted there. Cricket's tangible debt to Ponsonby-Fane is as the originator of the MCC Collection – that wonderful assemblage of paintings, prints, engravings, photographs, bats and cricketana of various kinds which is being perpetually added to, and, with the library, likewise expanding, is under the charge of the Curator. (The first full-time Curator, to whom the game owes a deep debt, was Diana Rait-Kerr (1945–68)). On her retirement the duty passed to the present incumbent, Stephen Green.

The Treasurer of MCC holds a position second only to that of the President of the day, whose deputy he is. As a member, *ipso facto*, of all committees, the treasurership is unpaid, semi-permanent, and to that extent more important than the presidency itself. On the death of Ponsonby-Fane (who, strangely, several times declined the office of President) the post went to Lord Harris. He exercised an influence from the treasurership on MCC and the wide world of cricket which scarcely has a parallel; though in a more democratic age since the Second World War, G. O. Allen has been at the heart of affairs to a degree which his predecessors could never have imagined. From 1916 to 1932 what Lord Harris opined generally came to pass, and it must be added that his decisions were the fruit of the widest experience of cricket in all climes and of all categories, and of a singularly shrewd knowledge of human nature. In what may be justly called Lord Harris's time the West Indies (where he, like 'Plum' Warner, was born), India (where he had been Governor of Bombay) and New Zealand were added to the company of Test-playing countries and admitted, *ipso facto*, to the ICC.

The greatest trial of MCC's diplomacy and vision, however, immediately followed Harris's death in the early days of his successor, Lord Hawke. The story of Body-line and MCC's part in avoiding a severance of cricket relations – almost, perhaps, a Commonwealth rupture – is told elsewhere in this book. There can be no doubt that the club came advantageously from the widely publicized exchange of cables which took place while their side was in Australia, beginning at the time of the Adelaide Test Match in January 1933. They supported their captain, D. R. Jardine, as they were bound to do on the facts as known to them, and before they had had any full and official report from their managers, P. F. Warner and R. C. N. Palairet. The less explosive but more difficult phase of the negotiations with Australia followed the return of the team when full evidence was available (though not in all cases called for by the committee), and the decisions had to be taken whether to implement Australia's suggestion for a change in the Law to protect the batsman against intimidation, and what came to be called 'direct attack', and also whether in the circumstances of high tension and wounded feelings the invitation to Australia to tour England in 1934 should even be allowed to stand.

It was the club's good fortune that at the AGM in May 1933, the retiring President, Lord Lewisham, nominated as his successor a distinguished lawyer in Lord Hailsham. A study of the cables that passed between the respective authorities between June and December 1933, indicates the extremely

delicate – indeed scarcely tenable – situation in which their captain's tactics had placed MCC. In the end the Australians agreed to come to England in 1934 without any real retreat by MCC from the position that everything done by their team in 1932–33 had been fair and above board. But what strong conflict of view must have existed within the MCC Committee is evident from the fact that the decision that the Australian tour to England in 1934 should still be proceeded with, which was implicit in the cable from Lord's of 12 December 1933, was only passed by 8 votes to 5. Ultimately, of course, MCC were obliged to alter the Unfair Play Law and make special provision against the type of bowling to which the Australians, and subsequently also the county captains, objected. But what if MCC had said, as they were not very far from saying: 'On the whole we think it better for you to stay at home'?

No problem of such gravity as Body-line disturbed the cricket scene for more than 30 years, but with economic pressures increasing and life becoming more complex the Lord's Committee-room came into ever more regular use as a debating chamber. Until the age of sponsorship dawned first-class cricket was generally thought to be on its last legs and the standard solution was an enquiry commission which at the request of the counties MCC used obligingly to set up. Between 1937 and 1966 the game was under scrutiny no fewer than 5 times: the Findlay Commission of 1937 was followed by those of Sir Stanley Jackson in 1944, of H. S. Altham in 1957, and of R. S. Rait-Kerr in 1961. In 1966 two major enquiries were at work simultaneously, one under MCC auspices with F. G. Mann in the chair on the delicate and crucial matter of Throwing (*qv*), and the other, which was technically the brainchild of 'the Advisory', dealing with all aspects of the first-class game. This was a specially thorough-going affair which produced two reports identified by the name of the chairman, D. G. Clark.

The years have been given in each case so that those anxious to explore the subject can do so by reference to the appropriate *Wisden*. The 1967 issue devotes 13 pages to the Clark reports – evidence of conscientious industry indeed but in after years no longer compulsive reading. Rait-Kerr, Secretary of MCC between 1936 and 1952, died soon after he started work: a more valuable monument to him was the major revision of the Laws for which he was responsible in 1947. The Throwing issue concerned MCC especially in that it was their tour to Australia in 1958–59 which brought the trouble to a head, and because it produced various suggestions for changes in the law. Temporarily at least this dangerous source of friction was resolved by the ICC (*qv*) of 1960.

Hard upon Throwing came another highly emotive subject, that of the continuation or otherwise of the distinction between amateur and professional. In 1962 by a margin of 10 to 7, the counties decided at the autumn 'Advisory' to abolish the dividing line. Henceforward all would be 'cricketers'. Technically MCC were not bound to ratify the decision, which, as the editor of *Wisden* pointed out, contradicted the view arrived at by a very strong and representative committee appointed by the club to examine the subject, whose views 'the Advisory' had accepted only four years earlier. Many hoped that the independence that went with true amateurism would be preserved as long as possible as a valuable element in the first-class game. Looking back, however, the economics of life in the 1960s must have diminished that independence almost to extinction before very long. It need only be added that though the word 'amateur' is now extinct the honourable status of 'professional' lives on in schools and in the northern leagues.

It was in May 1968 that S. C. Griffith, as Secretary of MCC, announced the future pattern for the government of the game in England which has been already referred to. Though the club welcomed the new scheme of things wherein the TCCB and the NCA (begun as the MCC Cricket Association 4 years earlier) were to enjoy autonomy under the overall umbrella of the Cricket Council, the new constitution derived from the pragmatic necessity of setting up a democratic official body which the Government could recognize in order to be able to offer financial aid in the development of the game through the newly-formed Sports Council.

For all the many years of effort on behalf of cricket willingly contributed by the club it was an untimely coincidence that at this historic moment, and before the Council had met for the first time, there came in the autumn of 1968 the malign chain of circumstances that became known as 'The d'Oliveira Affair' (*qv*). (The subject is fully dealt with elsewhere.) Within the club it divided friend from friend, and in the public mind MCC's image for a while inevitably suffered.

To know MCC well, its historical background and its modern workings, is to believe that as the owner of Lord's, the game's headquarters, as the custodian of the Laws, and as a relatively disinterested partner in the government of cricket,

OPPOSITE The match that never was: this composite picture painted by G. H. Barrable and K. Ponsonby Staples in 1887 aims to show rank and fashion watching a Test Match at Lord's. To the *extreme right* stand the Prince and Princess of Wales; *extreme left* is Lord Harris in an IZ coat with horizontal stripes talking to Lady de Grey. Another Court favourite, Lillie Langtry, looking away from the cricket (and from the Prince), is *lower-middle right*. 'W.G.' has hit Spofforth towards the extra-cover boundary where the Australian T. W. Garrett, is about to save the 4. Note the old pavilion as depicted in its last days: from an almost identical angle, RIGHT Today's view from the same angle.

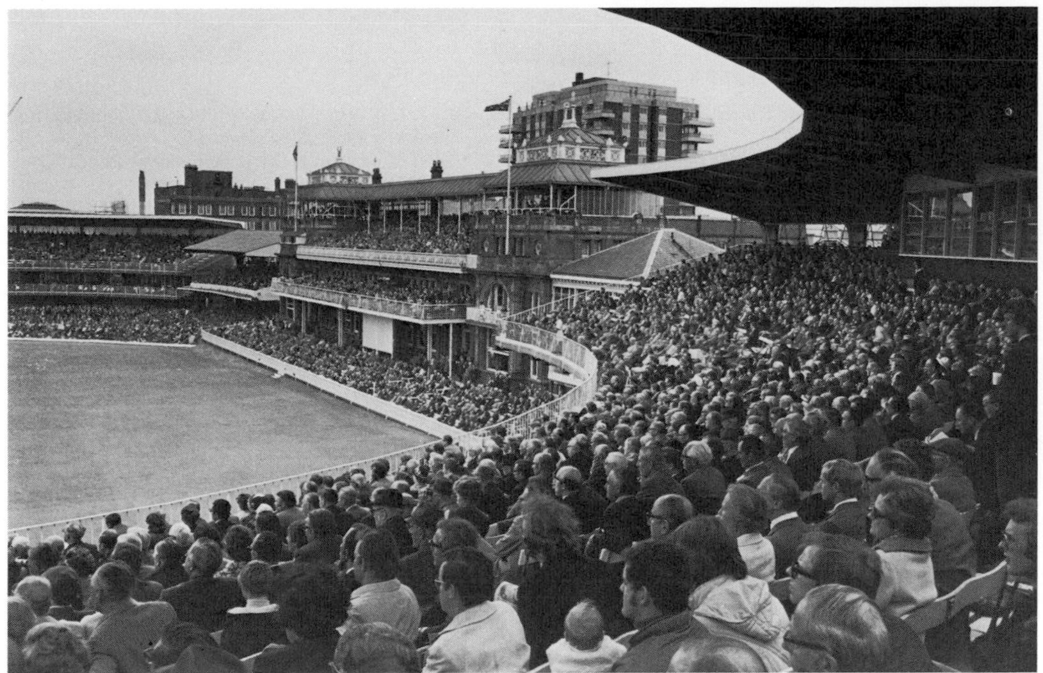

the club has a significant and important role yet to play in these times of stress, when the old values and standards are so clearly and dangerously at risk.

CHRONOLOGY

1787 Thomas Lord opened his first ground in Dorset Fields and MCC was formed

1805 First Eton v Harrow match (Lord Byron was the Harrow captain)

1806 First Gentlemen v Players match

1811 The club moved to North Bank Regent's Park

1814 The ground was moved to its third and present site

1820 William Ward scored 278 for MCC v Norfolk, the highest individual score at Lord's for 105 years

1822 Benjamin Aislabie appointed Honorary Secretary

1825 William Ward purchased the ground lease from Thomas Lord; the pavilion destroyed by fire, with the loss of all records

1827 First Oxford v Cambridge match

1835 Lease transferred by Ward to J. H. Dark who remained proprietor until 1864

1837 Jubilee of MCC celebrated by a grand North v South match

1838 Tennis Court built on the site of the present Mound Stand; the Pavilion lit by gas

1839 Lowest score – 15 by MCC v Surrey

1842 Roger Kynaston appointed Honorary Secretary

1846 First telegraph scoreboard installed

1848 First printing tent on ground erected and match cards sold; E. Hinkly took all 10 wickets for Kent v England

1850 J. Wisden took all 10 wickets for North v South (all bowled)

1858 Alfred Baillie appointed Honorary Secretary

1860 Freehold of the ground bought by Isaac Moses from the Eyre Estate for £7,000; MCC did not bid

1863 R. A. Fitzgerald appointed Honorary Secretary

1864 First groundsman engaged; lease relinquished by J. H. Dark to MCC

1865 Pavilion enlarged

1866 Freehold of the ground purchased for £18,333-6*s*-8*d* with money advanced by William Nicholson

1866/7 First grandstand erected

1867/8 Second Tavern built

1868 The position of Secretary ceased to be honorary

1871 Best bowling – 10–38 by S. E. Butler for Oxford v Cambridge; turnstiles first used

1874 Alfred Shaw took all 10 wickets for MCC v North

1876 Henry Perkins appointed Secretary

1877 Middlesex CCC first played at Lord's

1878 Australians first match at Lord's, over in one day: MCC all out for 39 and 19

1881 Members' Luncheon Room built

1884 First Test match at Lord's

1887 Centenary of MCC; 3½ acres of Henderson's Nursery purchased

1888 Bill proposing to take over the ground for railway development rejected; entrance fee raised from £1 to £5; MCC totalled 735 for 9 v Wiltshire in a Minor match

1889–90 Present Pavilion built

1891 Clergy Orphan School acquired from the Manchester & Sheffield Railway in exchange for the right to tunnel under part of the practice ground

1898 F. E. Lacey appointed Secretary; Board of Control first meeting at Lord's

1899 A. E. Trott hit a ball from M. A. Noble which struck a chimneypot and fell behind the Pavilion (MCC v Australians)

1902 Easter Cricket Classes established

1904 Advisory County Cricket Committee first Meeting at Lord's

1906 A. Fielder took all 10 wickets for Players v Gentlemen; Press Box built

1907 First Test Match v South Africa

1909 Imperial Cricket Conference inaugurated by England, Australia and South Africa

1910 'Fowler's Match': Eton 169–9 in second innings made 219 and beat Harrow by 9 runs

1914 Centenary of the Ground on its present site

1923 W. G. Grace Memorial Gates erected in St John's Wood Road

1925/6 Present Grandstand built; Father Time weathervane presented by the architect

1926 W. Findlay appointed Secretary; highest individual score – 316 not out by J. B. Hobbs for Surrey v Middlesex

1928 First Test Match v West Indies

1929 G. O. Allen took all 10 wickets for Middlesex v Lancashire

1930 Highest score: 729–6 Australia v England, 4-day match aggregate 1601 runs for 33 wickets

1931 First Test Match v New Zealand

1932 First Test Match v India

1934 Harris Memorial Garden made and 'Q' Stand built

1935 South Africa win their first Test Match in England

1936 Col R. S. Rait Kerr appointed Secretary

1937 MCC 150th anniversary; car park made on practice ground

1949 HRH The Duke of Edinburgh President of MCC; 26 retired England Cricketers made honorary cricket members of MCC

1950 West Indies win their first Test Match in England

1952 Ronald Aird appointed Secretary

1953 HRH The Duke of Edinburgh opened Memorial Gallery to the memory of cricketers of all lands who lost their lives in the two World Wars; Coronation Garden made; highest attendance – 137,915 – England v Australia (England 20 for 3 on last day saved by 4 hour partnership between W. Watson and T. E. Bailey)

1954 First Test Match v Pakistan

1958 Warner Stand opened on site of old 'A' Enclosure

1962 S. C. Griffith appointed Secretary; last Gentlemen v Players Match

1963 First Gillette Cup Final

1964 150th anniversary of the ground on its present site

1965 Imperial Cricket Conference title changed to International Cricket Conference; associate membership introduced

1967 New Tavern opened

1968 New Stand opened on the site of the old Tavern; Cricket Council formed and Board of Control and Advisory County Cricket Committee replaced by Test and County Cricket Board

1972 First Benson and Hedges Cup Final

1973 Bookmakers permitted at Lord's

1974 J. A. Bailey appointed Secretary

1975 First Prudential World Cup Series

1977 MCC Indoor School opened by G. O. Allen

OFFICERS SINCE THE SECOND WORLD WAR

PRESIDENTS

1946 General Sir Ronald Adam
1947 Lord Cornwallis
1948 The Earl of Gowrie
1949 HRH The Duke of Edinburgh
1950 Sir Pelham Warner
1951 W. Findlay
1952 The Duke of Beaufort
1953 The Earl of Rosebery
1954 Viscount Cobham
1955 Field Marshal Earl Alexander of Tunis
1956 Viscount Monckton
1957 The Duke of Norfolk
1958 Marshal of the RAF Viscount Portal
1959 H. S. Altham
1960 Sir Hubert Ashton
1961 Sir William Worsley, Bt
1962 Lt-Col Lord Nugent
1963 G. O. Allen
1964 R. H. Twining
1965 Lt-Gen Sir Oliver Leese
1966 Sir Alec Douglas-Home
1967 A. E. R. Gilligan
1968 R. Aird
1969 M. J. C. Allom
1970 Sir Cyril Hawker
1971 F. R. Brown
1972 A. M. Crawley
1973 Lord Caccia
1974 HRH The Duke of Edinburgh
1975 C. G. A. Paris
1976 W. H. Webster
1977 D. G. Clark
1978 C. H. Palmer
1979 S. C. Griffith

[*Note* By ancient tradition the President of MCC nominates his successor.]

TREASURERS

1938–49 9th Viscount Cobham
1949–63 H. S. Altham
1963–64 10th Viscount Cobham
1964–76 G. O. Allen
1977– J. G. W. Davies

SECRETARIES

1936–52 Col. R. S. Rait Kerr
1952–62 R. Aird
1962–74 S. C. Griffith
1974– J. A. Bailey

Pattern of Government

Formation of The Cricket Council, TCCB and NCA

E. W. SWANTON

Neither the heading to this article nor, I expect, its content will rivet the average reader's attention as compared with the prospect of the many more obviously fascinating items which follow. Yet, apart from the consideration that no book of this scope should skip too lightly over the subject, it is important surely that followers of the English game know something of the evolving pattern of its government and so understand something of the stresses and tensions involved, particularly since, at the moment of writing, a wholly smooth relationship as between the various parties concerned has still to emerge.

As from 1969 the game in England, as was noted in the previous article, has been reconciling itself for the first time in its history to a defined constitution with, at its head, a Cricket Council comprising the two bodies responsible for its two broad areas of activity and also the erstwhile *de facto* authority – the Test and County Cricket Board, the National Cricket Association and the Marylebone Club respectively.

The TCCB as a result of this reorganization became responsible for the administration of Test and County cricket, answerable to the Cricket Council only in so far as the activities under its control might have a significance extending to the whole English game.

The NCA, which had been set up in 1965 as the MCC Cricket Association, had a clear if quelling overall function as visualized at its foundation by MCC to coordinate and foster all aspects of the game short of the first-class; notably coaching

in all its aspects and at all levels on a national basis; the attraction of cash for the spread of the game by way of Government grants and the patronage of business and sporting trusts; the administration of national competitions as well as local ones through its 50 affiliated county associations; ground maintenance and the promotion of non-turf pitches; the encouragement of boys' cricket through such benevolent institutions as the Lord's Taverners, the Wrigley Foundation, the A. J. McAlpine Trust, Agatha Christie Ltd, etc; and the provision of advice and, if necessary, legal aid, as needed, to all clubs affiliated through their County Associations.

MCC's place within the Cricket Council derived from its immemorial function as guide, philosopher and friend to the game in all its aspects; from its ownership of Lord's, the headquarters of the TCCB and NCA; from its situation as cricket's chief source of revenue at the gate; and from its traditional position as maker and guardian of the Laws.

ABOVE The inaugural meeting of the Test and County Cricket Board in December 1968. At the top table are G. O. Allen (*standing*), J. A. Bailey, D. B. Carr, S. C. Griffith, C. G. A. Paris (Chairman, *half-hidden*), M. J. C. Allom and D. J. Insole.

RIGHT F. G. Mann, Chairman of the TCCB since 1978, was, like his father F.T., captain of both Middlesex and England. He is also Chairman of Middlesex.

It was the parlous financial situation of the game, and the prospect of a helping hand from Government, which, precipitated the setting-up by MCC and the counties of the Cricket Council. It was to be the game's ruling body in the United Kingdom, the final court of appeal, its three constituent members so represented that no one of them, be it MCC or TCCB or NCA, could outvote the other two. At first the Council wore a distinctly red-and-yellow hue since the Council was chaired by the MCC President of the day, with the Treasurer as his deputy, and the Secretary acting both for the Council and the Club. Co-opted non-voting members came soon to be added from Scotland and Ireland. The chairman of the MCCA from the outset represented the interests of the Minor Counties.

Perhaps the first time the cricket world at large became aware of the new Council's place as the ruling body was when the 1970 Labour Government called its representatives to Downing Street to request them to cancel the 1970 South African tour to England. [*See* 'The d'Oliveira Affair', PART IV]. A year later the Council came into prominence again in an unwelcome context, when, after considering the official reports on the 1970–71 MCC tour of Australia, they issued a stern but timely warning regarding conduct on the field. The following statement showed that the Council not only had teeth but was prepared to use them. The words had a stronger impact than if they had been issued by the TCCB or by MCC, whose label in respect of the title of the team was now outdated. The Council spoke for *all* cricketers when they announced in April 1971:

The Cricket Council have considered the report of the committee set up to review all aspects of the 1970–71 Australasian tour.

The Council are unanimous in expressing their pleasure at the success of the team in winning both series of Test matches.

However, the Cricket Council, as the governing body of cricket in the United Kingdom, must record their grave concern about incidents involving dissent from umpires' decisions, whether by word or deed.

While appreciating the strains and stresses under which cricket at the highest level is played, the Council must warn all players that such conduct, which is contrary to the spirit and tradition of the game and brings it into disrepute, will not be tolerated.

In dealing with such breaches of discipline the Council and the Test and County Cricket Board, through their Disciplinary Committee, will not hesitate to use their wide powers which include the termination of the registration of a player. The Selection Committee have been instructed accordingly.

Copies of this statement have been sent to all County Clubs.

LEFT C. H. Palmer, President of MCC 1978–1979 and as such Chairman of the International Cricket Conference.

RIGHT D. G. Clark, Palmer's predecessor in both offices, who helped him bear the brunt of various visits to ICC countries in earnest search for an honourable settlement of the Packer affair.

On 1 October 1974, the make-up of the Council was revised to the extent that it appointed its own Chairman, choosing F. R. Brown. Also it was to be the Secretary of the TCCB who handled the dual job. Freddie Brown was now in the seat of power, the more so when, two years later, he succeeded A. M. Crawley as Chairman of the NCA. The 3 constituent bodies henceforth supplied 5 members apiece. The President of MCC occupied the titular post of President of the Council which now sprouted three sub-committees, including an Emergency Executive to handle urgent major business.

When the Packer affair blew up, however, in May 1977, it was the International Cricket Conference and the TCCB who after Kerry Packer had met the ICC at Lord's tended to hold the stage on behalf of official cricket. It was they, not the Council, whose legal advisers advocated the termination of contracts – which Packer successfully contested.

It was probably in part the Packer case, and the disruption and internecine struggle following, which led the TCCB in the spring of 1978 to examine (yet again!) the structure of cricket administration. A working party comprising the respective chairmen of Surrey, Lancashire and Glamorgan, R. Subba Row, C. S. Rhoades and O. S. Wheatley, having decided that UK cricket badly lacked 'a focal point of identity', came up with a revolutionary plan proposing a winding-up of the Cricket Council, which would be replaced by a United Kingdom Board of Control 'based mainly on the first-class counties and the NCA'.

The new Board would meet 'infrequently' but would be 'administered' by an Executive Committee headed by a Chief Executive. MCC's role in the affairs of the game whose evolution over the best part of two centuries had owed so much to the club was a representative 'for liaison purposes'.

Happily, and not surprisingly, this recipe was not to the taste of the majority of the counties, though the feeling of many TCCB representatives could well be that the present system of cricket administration with its duplication of sub-committees and ever-increasing weight of 'paper', is top-heavy and ripe for some discreet revision which would facilitate sound decision-making. Under C. H. Palmer, F. R. Brown's successor as Chairman as from October 1979, the Council must respond positively to the mood within the TCCB.

The Board are the game's money-earners, both directly from Test and television receipts and also by means of sponsorship on an ever-increasing scale. Negotiations with overseas bodies in respect of tours and the conditions attaching to them – a ceaseless headache following the accommodation reached between the Australian Cricket Board and Kerry Packer – are undertaken in practice by the TCCB acting for the Cricket Council. It is the TCCB likewise which consults and receives proposals from the Cricketers' Association, the players' 'trade union'. Add to these things their other basic function as the administrators of the county game in all its modern diversity, and it will be realized that they have indeed plenty on their plate.

NCA, founded and financed initially by MCC, is now funded jointly by TCCB and MCC, and it is common ground between both the other parties that the nourishment of the game at its roots must be expanded to the furthest limits that funds permit.

The essence of MCC's position will have been grasped, I hope, from the preceding pages without the need to embellish further. While never seeking power, the club with its large representative membership and an authority deriving from many years of experience is anxious to continue in its traditional role of wise and friendly counsellor – not wholly disinterested, of course, in these days of economic stringency but to a degree, at least, above the heat and dust of battle. This can only be so if the Cricket Council in its triumvirate nature is maintained.

If the TCCB were to seize unfettered power, as elements within it seek, it would be the judge of its own cause in issues affecting the interests of the game as a whole. Would the voice of the ordinary cricketer be heard, one wonders? Declaring an interest in so far as I am a serving member of the MCC Committee, I believe that English cricket today needs an Upper House if its old characteristics are to be preserved.

Part II
Overseas Cricket

Cricket among the high-rise buildings of Buenos Aires, at the ground of the Belgrano AC.

Argentina

THERE IS evidence of cricket having been played in Argentina as early as 1806. After Britain had, through her brilliant envoy, Sir Woodbine Parish, recognized the young republic, Englishmen poured in and by 1823 there were some two to three thousand British subjects in Buenos Aires. With them came cricket and the first local reference to the game is to be found in the issue of 22 October of the *British Packet* – an English language newspaper founded in 1826 – which reported that the Buenos Aires Cricket Club had been formed by about 25 members who 'have lately played some excellent games at that manly exercise . . . and who might not be ashamed to take up a bat, even by the side of the men of Kent'.

The Buenos Aires Cricket Club ground at Palermo Park was the chief focus of cricket, as of other sports. It was inaugurated in 1864 with a cricket match against a team from HMS *Bombay*, the home team winning by 9 wickets. Six days later the ill-fated *Bombay* caught fire off the coast of Uruguay and sank with great loss of life. Ironically, the cricket club suffered a somewhat similar fate; in 1948, Evita Peron had the clubhouse burnt down in a fit of rage at the Englishmen's obstinate refusal to give up the ground in favour of some wild welfare scheme of hers.

The gradual influx of British capital with its staff spread out all over the country following the railway lines, and packing houses soon followed suit, concentrating mostly to the south of the city of Buenos Aires. One important concentration was to be found around the city of Tucuman, 750 miles northwest where cricket friendlies were played against Cordoba and Jujuy. In 1891 those cricket centres got together and challenged Buenos Aires and its suburbs to an annual encounter; the match was played on the BACC ground and North won the first match. Thus began the most important cricket fixture in the local cricket calendar, which still survives.

As Argentines gradually took over the specialized jobs of Englishmen, the latter moved south and the headquarters of the North committee moved to Rosario, some 200 miles northwest of Buenos Aires. The South committee had always resided in Buenos Aires. As the migration of cricketers flowed south, the dividing line between these two teams was moved right into Buenos Aires until today it has become a trial of strength between the local clubs, with Belgrano and Lomas forming South and Hurlingham, St Andrew's and BACRC (who since losing their club in 1948 moved out to Don Torcuato in the northwest and included rugby in their name) forming North. The game is played over three days at the end of the season on one of the three grounds, Hurlingham, Lomas or Belgrano.

The Argentine Cricket Association was formed just prior to the First World War but it was only 20 years later that it took complete control of all organized cricket in the country. The cricket championships today comprise Sunday and Saturday competitions, the former consisting of all-day games with 6 teams participating: two from Belgrano AC, and one each from Buenos Aires Cricket and Rugby Club, Lomas AC, Hurlingham Club, and St Andrew's FPC. Apart from the regular championship games played for The Standard cup, they also play a limited over championship for the Robin Stuart Memorial Shield with a colts team (young players under 21) replacing one of the Belgrano teams. The Saturday championship plays half-day and is more popular; up to 12 teams sometimes participate, this making it necessary to divide up the teams into two groups. The trophy for this championship – The Buenos Aires Herald Cup – and The Standard cup were given over 70 years ago. The standard of play of the Sunday division has been compared to top club cricket in London; while a composite Argentine team, it is believed, could hold its own against an average Minor County.

Except for England, probably no other country in the world has undertaken such an intensive programme of tours to and from its home base. Spanning 111 years, they include 88 tours and of these no less than 66 were against other Latin American countries – proof of the way Argentina has helped to keep the game alive in South America. The most important tours were those from England and in the last 70 years Argentina has received 7 important teams:

Lord Hawke's MCC team of 1912 included A. C. MacLaren (Lancashire), E. R. Wilson (Yorkshire) and W. Findlay (Lancashire). The rubber of three Tests was won by MCC by the odd match. S. A. Cowper scored 182 for the Southern Suburbs against this team.

P. F. Warner's MCC team of 1926–27 included G. O. Allen (Middlesex), J. C. White (Somerset), Capt T. O. Jameson (Hampshire), M. F. S. Jewell (Worcestershire) and Lord Dunglass (now Lord Home of the Hirsel). MCC won the rubber by the odd match in three. H. W. Marshall scored 105 for Argentina in the First Test.

Sir Julien Cahn's team in 1930 included P. T. Eckersley (Lancashire), J. Gunn (Notts), G. F. H. Heane (Notts), T. L. Richmond (Notts) and R. W. V. Robins (Middlesex). The visitors won the First Test, the remaining two being drawn. Col L. Green scored 102 for the visitors in the First Test.

Sir Theodore Brinckman's team in 1937–38 was one of the strongest to come. In it were R. E. S. Wyatt (Warwickshire), F. J. Durston (Middlesex), L. C. Eastman (Essex), W. F. Price (Middlesex), A. Sandham (Surrey), F. R. Santall (Warwickshire), J. M. Sims (Middlesex), M. W. Tate (Sussex), E. A. Watts (Surrey) and A. Wood (Yorkshire). Each side won a Test and the third was drawn. R. E. S. Wyatt scored 162, H. W. Dods 104 and D. Ayling took 6 wickets for 10 runs for Argentina.

G. H. G. Doggart's MCC team of 1958–59 was composed of G. H. G. Doggart (Sussex), D. B. Carr (Derby), J. A. Bailey (Essex), P. I. Bedford (Middlesex), M. H. Bushby (Cambridge University), C. B. Howland (Cambridge University), A. C. D. Ingleby-Mackenzie (Hampshire), R. V. C. Robins (Middlesex), D. M. Sayers (Kent), D. R. W. Silk (Somerset), M. J. K. Smith (Warwickshire) and O. S. Wheatley (Glamorgan). M. J. Bear (Essex) who was coaching in the Argentine also played. MCC won both Tests. Silk scored 150, while in the Tests, Carr made 144 and Smith 216 not out.

A. C. Smith's MCC team of 1964–65 was composed of A. C. Smith (Warwickshire), P. I. Bedford (Middlesex), A. R. Duff (Worcestershire), R. A. Gale (Middlesex), C. Gibson (MCC), M. G. Griffith (Sussex), R. A. Hutton (Yorkshire), R. I. Jefferson (Surrey), R. C. Kerslake (Somerset), A. R. Lewis (Glamorgan), J. D. Martin (Oxford University), D. J. Mordaunt (Berkshire) and R. C. White (Gloucestershire). MCC won both Tests. R. C. White scored 108 and in the Tests, Gale scored 132, Lewis 110 and Mordaunt 122.

Derrick Robins's XI of 1979 was composed of C. S. Cowdrey (Kent), C. W. J. Athey (Yorkshire), N. E. Briers (Leicestershire), R. G. L. Cheatle (Sussex), I. J. Gould (Middlesex), T. A. Lloyd (Warwickshire), D. N. Patel (Worcestershire), S. P. Perryman (Warwickshire), K. D. Smith (Warwickshire), G. B. Stevenson (Yorkshire), L. B. Taylor (Leicestershire), K. P. Tomlins (Middlesex), P. Whiteley (Yorkshire). Stevenson scored 103 not out, Smith 143 not out and the Derrick Robins XI won the only Test.

Argentina have received 3 other important visits in December 1969 from New Zealand (The NZ Ambassadors), in December 1971 from South Africa (Country Districts) and in March 1974 from Australia (Australian Old Collegians), all of whom brought first-class players and won each Test.

Argentine cricketers have played in England on 9 occasions: the first 6 involved teams of players then on holiday playing against local clubs. But twice (August 1926 and 1928) they were invited to play at Lords against MCC and drew the first match but lost the second. In 1932 a team of players from Argentina, Brazil and Chile led by C. H. Gibson, the great Cambridge bowler of a decade earlier, went on an extended tour of England. Seven centuries were scored, all of them by Argentines, two by H. W. Marshall, and one each by D. Ayling, A. L. S. Jackson, J. Knox, J. H. Paul and R. L. Stuart. This tour was perhaps the high peak of South American cricket and included 6 first-class matches, of which those against Oxford and Cahn's XI were handsomely won.

Forty years later, this time as the Argentine Cricket Association, they were again on tour and acquitted themselves fairly well: out of 13 matches played, they won 4, lost 2, tied 1 and drew 6. The game at Lords against MCC was lost but the Argentine put up a good fight. Finally in May 1979 the ACA sent a team to participate in the ICC Trophy for Associate Members. Although they did not win a match in their group, they did not lose any of the friendlies surrounding the official fixtures.

Argentina first started her tours abroad by going to Uruguay in 1868 and for the next 70 years 29 teams crossed the River Plate, the visits being divided equally between the two countries. But the balance of power lay heavily with Argentina; in 29 matches played they won 21 and lost 6. After the Second World War, the influx of expatriate Englishmen into Uruguay dwindled and a few sporadic matches only took place against inferior teams. In 1888 another South American country appeared on the scene to threaten Argentine supremacy, Brazil. From then until 1921 there were 6 tours, all of friendly matches, and as rivalry increased it was decided to play two-innings Tests. In the 4 subsequent tours, Argentina won 7 Tests, Brazil 2, and 3 were drawn. From 1953 on, the two countries played for the Norris Trophy. It has changed hands 4 times with Brazil the present possessors though out of 19 Tests Argentina has won 9 and lost only 3.

Argentines were the first to visit Chile and their trip in 1893 was an extraordinary Odyssey taking three-and-a-half days to reach Santiago, the Andes being crossed by mule. After the Transandine railway was built tours became more frequent and between 1920 and 1964 Argentines toured Chile 12 times and Chileans Argentina twice. Here too the balance was heavily in Argentina's favour. In 1922 J. H. Paul scored 226 for Argentina in Viña del Mar and in 1929 at Belgrano, Argentina, the home team scored their record score of 612 for 6 declared. D. Ayling scored 234 and although the Chileans lost the Test their captain J. A. S. Jackson scored a hundred in each innings.

In recent years, Peru have produced good teams and tours between the two countries have started.

K. E. BRIDGER

Australia

J. M. KILBURN

No existing records establish the advent of cricket in Australia. It came, by reasonable assumption, as an import with the first fleet. The improvization became established with the growth of the early settlements, flourished in the circumstances of favourable environment, adapted itself to the special needs of the new setting and developed an individuality with a crystallization of a national character.

Australian cricket is a variation of the English game. The essentials are common, but the details are different. Australian cricketers could not take over 'the meadow game with the beautiful name' in precisely its English form because their meadows are not precisely as English meadows. Evening light and agricultural background based on the village community are not Australian characteristics encouraging sport. Facilities for Australian cricket have had to be created in the small township as in the big city and every step in the game's progress has had to be taken deliberately, with inevitable dispute over the appropriate way ahead.

Survival demanded organization in Australian cricket. To play cricket at all the Australians have had to plan for playing cricket. They have planned and prepared the artificial pitch that in one form or another serves both picnic game in the bush and the Test Match. They have channelled their talents of play in elaborate and far-reaching administration. They have cultivated a seaborne seed to a crop of cricketing eminence.

Foundations of Australian cricket swiftly followed foundation of Australian colonies. Governor Macquarie ordered the manufacture of bats and balls in government workshops for the first recorded match in Sydney, played in 1830, between the military and civilians. In Tasmania the Hobart Club challenged the Governor's team and the crew of a visiting warship. In Victoria the first opponents of Melbourne CC were the military.

The great distances between settlements and the difficulties of travel restricted the range of early cricketers, but in each centre the competitive element came quickly into evidence. Formation of one club was spur to the formation of another, invariably with a light of challenge in the eye. Challenge stimulates the Australian in every phase of life, inconsequential activity tends to leave him uninterested. The Australian in battle is perhaps the most fearsome soldier in the world, but he is an indifferent polisher of boots and buttons. In his cricket the Australian is essentially purposeful. His aim is achievement; the Grade pennant, the State trophy, the Ashes.

From this competitive urge developed a logical organization of district cricket, State associations and the Board of Control. The benefits are manifest and manifold, few cricketers are lost through lack of opportunity. Enterprise and resolution were characteristics of Australian cricket from its inception. Sponsorship has invariably been forthcoming for a match, for an innovation, an adventure.

In 1845 the Maitland Club, encouraged by a local millowner named Honeysett, tried their wings in home and away matches with the Australian Club of Sydney. In 1851 Melbourne CC crossed stormy waters to play a Tasmanian club in Launceston, where, by contemporary account, it was difficult for the umpires to select a suitable piece of ground for the occasion. By 1871 the Norwood Club of Adelaide were asking Melbourne CC for fixtures. Seven years earlier Queensland had found backing for a representative side to challenge New South Wales.

Cricket in Australia would presumably have spread without external stimulus, but the visits of teams from England in 1859, 1861–62 and in 1863–64 were of incalculable significance. H. H. Stephenson's team, the first, was not the strongest England could have sent, but the performances of this hardy band of professionals opened Australian eyes and stirred Australian ambitions. In 15 engagements the tourists were twice defeated by opponents 22 strong. Within 15 years the Australians were ready to challenge on level terms and the Test Match era had begun.

Australian cricketers were quick to learn and keen to compete. The first tourists from England were helpful not only in satisfying the competitive urge but also because on their departure they left instructors behind. In 1862 Charles Lawrence was persuaded to stay as a coach in New South Wales and after the second tour William Caffyn accepted an engagement with Melbourne CC. Lawrence eventually led a team of aborigines to England on a tour that proved a curiosity more than a financial success. Caffyn stayed a year in Melbourne and then moved to Sydney, where he became coach to the Warwick Club, player for New South Wales and proprietor of a remunerative hairdressing business.

Caffyn noted phenomenal improvement in Australian cricket during the decade following the tour of Stephenson's team and by the 1880s was rating the colonists in every way the equals of their English contemporaries. Clubs multiplied in the expanding areas of the great cities and as the States achieved autonomy the natural tendency towards State cricket was followed.

The New South Wales Association originated from the first inter-colonial match of 1856. It was formed specifically to prepare for the return match against Victoria. The moving spirits were William Tunks as financial organizer and A. L. Park as benefactor. Close liaison with the State government was maintained to ensure use of the Sydney Domain as a playing area until the need for enclosure led to the choice of private grounds for representative occasions.

The Melbourne Cricket Ground, *c.* 1890.

Victoria had found their major ground and cricket leadership long before the Victorian Association was formed in 1875. The Melbourne Cricket Club was founded within 3 years of the foundation of Melbourne itself and, after the coming of the railway had deprived the club of its second ground, settlement was made in 'the Paddock That Grew', the present Melbourne Cricket Ground which ranks high among the modern wonders of the sporting world.

To Australians, in their propensity for abbreviation by initials, this awesome centre is simply 'MCG'. It is accepted as the most impressive sporting arena of the whole Dominion, completely circled by stands where once trees grew, a vast bowl of breathlessness that gathers crowds in excess of 100,000 a setting that by its very dominance influences play and players.

For close upon 100 years the Melbourne CC held dominance over Australian cricket. The catering firm of Spiers & Pond sponsored the first English team to tour, but their interest was commercial compensation for a failure to secure Charles Dickens with his programme of public reading. Cricketers would have sponsored the visiting cricketers had they been able to raise the capital and from the second tour to the 15th Melbourne CC underwrote the ventures. In 1887–88 their temerity cost them £3,000 because Sydney promoters invited another English team at the same time. Even with the staggering expenses demanded by W. G. Grace for his second visit in 1891–92 Melbourne CC were always willing guarantors until responsibility passed to the Board of Control.

The Melbourne success and authority was recognized but it was not left undisputed. Challenge from New South Wales was inevitable. The responsibility for English touring teams of 1894–95 and 1897–98 was shared by the trustees of Sydney Cricket Ground. In 1904 New South Wales rejected proposals for a Board of Control because they claimed the Victorian and South Australian Associations were inadequate. In Victoria the State Association lived uneasily with the Melbourne Club, and club and Association were in open dispute over any necessity for a Board of Control. The Associations of New South Wales and Victoria eventually conceded the presentation of all Test and State matches in Victoria to MCG and the Board of Control was established in 1905. New South Wales and Victoria were founder members, Queensland joined within weeks, South Australia a year later, Tasmania in 1908 and Western Australia during the First World War.

Stormy beginnings presaged a career of storms and the first thunderclouds soon gathered. By custom Australian teams touring overseas determined their own manager and a clause in the Board's constitution acknowledged this practice, subject to

A trial of strength between the Board of Control and leading players as to who should appoint the manager preceded the tour to England in 1912. Hitherto the players had done so, and when the Board shown here, were adamant, 6 of the foremost cricketers, including Clem Hill (*centre right* in light suit), responded by staying at home.

the Board's confirmation of the choice. For the 1909 tour of England the players chose Frank Laver, a Victorian with wide experience as both manager and player. The Board appointed P. A. McAlister as vice-captain and treasurer. After the tour the Board and Laver fell into dispute, the manager maintaining that some required financial information should be supplied by the treasurer rather than from managerial records. The argument became public and as issues widened on a personal basis the temperature of debate increased.

As the 1912 tour approached, the Board, without overstepping constitutional bounds, indicated that managerial appointment would be kept in their own hands. Six leading players, Hill, Armstrong, Trumper, Ransford, Cotter and Carter thereupon informed the Board that they would be unavailable for the tour unless the players could preserve the right to appoint their manager. Cricketing Australia was passionately divided over the principles and practices involved. The Board claimed compliance with constitution and rejected any dictation by players. The players remained adamant in their stand. Public meetings were called in all the major centres.

The 1912 team sailed with a Board-appointed manager but it contained 6 substitute players. The controversy left a dissatisfaction that rankled for years and has not been completely eliminated to this day.

The Board's constitution is frequently questioned. Its authority has become accepted but some of its decisions and methods have been criticized uncompromisingly down the years. Players of distinction tend to be lost to administration because they cannot reach the Board except through Association politics. Lack of frequent contact and first-hand knowledge of playing problems at international level germinates divided and parochial outlook. In its various proceedings the Board has offered examples of beneficial autocracy and misinformed intransigence.

Moments of crisis, major or minor, are almost a commonplace of the Board's existence. Major alarm was raised during the tour of Jardine's team in 1932–33 when the Board made vigorous and unsubstantiated protest against 'unsportsmanlike' visiting behaviour to inflame one of the great controversies in cricket history.

A continuous concern of Australian cricket authority has been barracking. The Australian spectator has always been inclined towards uninhibited expression of opinion. He makes no secret of likes and dislikes and sees no objection in principle to their pointed emphasis. Democracy postulates freedom of speech.

As far back as 1879 an Australian crowd followed speech with action. After an unpopular umpiring decision spectators invaded the playing area at Sydney, causing the eventual abandonment of a day's play. During the midfield uproar Lord Harris, protecting the umpire, was assaulted by a spectator, who was promptly seized by A. N. Hornby and taken to the pavilion. Hornby in his turn was attacked and the two assailants subsequently appeared in the police court, to be fined for disorderly conduct.

Tempests of disapproval were experienced by Warner's team of 1903–04 and, of course, by Jardine's team of 1932–33, but infliction of spectatorial intemperance has not been confined entirely to visiting players. Fairfax of New South Wales walked off the field for ever because of barracking during the State match.

Crowd demonstrations disrupting play are rarities but the individual barracker is virtually a background to Australian cricket, as is the over-officious gatekeeper. The barracker assumes and is granted a right to rudeness, collective and personal. His humour is crude and his memorable witticisms are few. He is essentially an exhibitionist, claiming a tolerance of custom. In their collective and appreciative character Australian crowds are generous in applause and open-handed in practical response. They subscribe lavishly to testimonials and are readily moved to sentiment. Their heroes are highly rated, their scapegoats roughly treated.

Heroes have been many and deserving from Bannerman to Bradman and beyond; Australia has offered a succession of the greatest players in the world. Bannerman made the first Test match hundred; Bradman returned career figures unparalleled in the whole history of the game. Australians have produced masters in every style and mood of play and Australians have produced leaders for every category of player, except perhaps the slow left-handed bowler of orthodox spin, whose development is geographically discouraged.

Australian cricketers established their quality and founded their traditions in the very first Test match. At Melbourne in 1877 Charles Bannerman scored a hundred, two Gregorys played, the wicket-keeping represented by Blackman was at the highest standard in the world and devotion to success was made evident. Hundreds, Gregorys and wicket-keeping and success were made features of Australian play down the years. In the first era of Anglo-Australian cricket, covering the 1870s and 1880s, the outstanding Australian personalities included Charles and Alec Bannerman, W. L. Murdoch, J. M. Blackham, C. T. B. Turner and F. R. Spofforth. These players were not the only gifted Australian cricketers of the time, but they were creators of Australian reputation and their standing in cricket history remains beyond dispute.

Sir Donald Bradman during his tour of England in 1948. For 50 years he was the greatest power in Australian cricket.

Murdoch in Australia bore comparison with W. G. Grace in England as a dominant batsman in an age of general bowling advantage. His Test match average was no higher than 32, but in his period the Test Match total below 100 was not exceptional. He scored the first Test hundred for Australia in England and he scored the first individual double century in any Test Match anywhere. He was the first Australian to record an innings of over 300 and with several other innings of over 200 he cut the pathway subsequently followed with such relish by Ponsford and Bradman.

Blackham instituted the line of superlative wicket-keepers that has graced and strengthened Australian cricket. Ill-protected by alarmingly thin gloves and pads, adorned by a black beard he established the art of wicket-keeping as a positive factor in out-cricket. He increased bowling threat by standing up to the stumps and he widened fielding scope by scorning the alliance of a long-stop. His first Test was the first of all; in his last, 17 years later, he scored 74 runs in a ninth wicket partnership of 154.

Blackham and Spofforth were associated in the later manner of Strudwick and Tate, Evans and Bedser. The wicket-keeper close to the stumps magnified the menace of fast-medium bowling. Spofforth refused to play in the first Test match in protest against the choice of Blackham as wicket-keeper; his misjudgment was made manifest by later experiences and together Blackham and Spofforth came to symbolize Australian power and outlook in cricket. Spofforth is usually placed in the category of fast bowling, but speed alone was not his basic weapon. His pace was as widely varied as his accuracy was consistent and his off-break, or break-back, was sharp and superbly controlled. His arm was high and his pre-delivery stride was a leap, but it was less for his action than for his concentrated aggression that he earned his sobriquet of the 'Demon Bowler'. The Demon thrust the lance of Australia deep into the complacency of English cricket when he took 6 wickets for 4 runs on his first appearance at Lord's.

Turner, the 'Terror', linked the youth of Australian cricketing renown with the attainment of maturity. He was briefly contemporary with Spofforth as a player but he followed him in magnificence and was more closely associated in bowling partnership with Ferris. Right-handed like Spofforth, Turner had the same devastation of sharp off-break and on his first tour of England in 1888 he took 314 wickets, though all the matches of the programme could not be rated as first-class.

The 1890s and the first decade of the 20th century brought cricket to full stature as an undertaking of sport. Tours and Test match rubbers ceased to be improvizations of private patronage. Formal government was created and accepted and the game enjoyed its share of the world's increasing material prosperity. The glow of a Golden Age radiated across the playing fields. New South Wales rejoiced in the sight of S. E. Gregory, Noble, Duff, Cotter and the immortal Victor Trumper. Victoria had Trotts and McLeods, Trumble and Ransford and a comparatively slim Armstrong. In South Australia Giffen's monumental efforts were reinforced by the splendour of Clem Hill, the determination of Darling and the brilliance of J. N. Crawford, immigrant from England.

Inter-state cricket was stimulated by the creation of the Sheffield Shield competition in the season of 1892–93. Lord Sheffield, who brought out the 12th English team, left a farewell present of £150 to be used as thought best by the Australian authority then existing under the title of Cricket Council – a short-lived forerunner of the Board of Control. The money was spent on a shield bearing the arms of Australia and the Earls of Sheffield and this trophy was put up for inter-State competition. Victoria, New South Wales and South Australia were the original contestants and were joined in 1926 by Queensland and by Western Australia after the Second World War. Victoria were the first winners of the Shield but Trumper's batting made New South Wales the most glamorous side of the period. Trumper came modestly into the first-class arena with four small innings in 1894–95, but when he had established himself his performances sparkled like crown jewels.

In England Trumper was seen at his best in 1902. In Australia he wore glory for a decade. His mastery was evident on all types of pitch, against all types of bowling. In successive matches of 1902–3 Trumper and Duff opened the innings for New South Wales with partnerships of 267 in 2 hours 15 minutes against Victoria and of 298 in 2½ hours against South Australia. In 1905–06 New South Wales were caught on a rain-affected pitch with the formidable Saunders bowling for Victoria. Trumper made a century in 57 minutes. The 1910–11 South Africans in Australia marvelled at Trumper's chanceless 214 not out which was scored at a rate of 50 runs an hour. The flame of Trumper's genius flared and dimmed under the pressures of uncertain health. He died at the age of 37 and, even in the preoccupations of world war, Australia paused to pay tribute.

Contemporary with Trumper and even more influential on his State's cricket was the South Australian left-hander Clem Hill. The South Australian Cricket Association was formed in 1871 under the spur of providing a suitable ground for fixtures with Victoria. The land leased was called The Oval and the early caretakers were beset by problems of preparation and finance. Their persistence made possible a beautiful ground in a beautiful setting.

The first representative matches were with neighbouring Victoria and it was not until 1890 that South Australia met New South Wales. By this time a South Australian reputation had been constructed round the remarkable feats of George Giffen, who as batsman and bowler virtually carried the State side on his sturdy shoulders. Giffen's responsibility and response were illustrated by the peaks of his all-round achievements. In 1890–91, in Melbourne, he played an innings of 237 and then took five wickets for 89 and seven for 103. He was given a civic welcome and a purse of sovereigns and, duly inspired, he improved on himself in the following season. Again against Victoria he scored 271, took nine for 96 and seven for 70.

After Giffen's autocracy more balance developed in the South Australian side. Darling became an Australian captain and many South Australian players won international status, yet Hill, throughout his career, remained the outstanding South Australian cricketer. His ability was inborn. His father made the first century on the Adelaide Oval and two of his brothers were State players. Clem Hill's batting approach was pugnacious and his endurance was exceptional. His figures contain 96, 97, 98 and 99 in Test match innings and 92 and 94 in the same State match; but he also scored four Test centuries. Against New South Wales in the 1900–01 season he hit 365 not out, batting for more than 8 hours.

Tasmania began inter-State matches as far back as 1851, but that primitive engagement could scarcely be termed first-class. For many years the cricket of the island made its high holiday in meetings between North and South and, later, visits from teams on tour from England served to stimulate interest and stir ambitions. Scope for gifted players is necessarily limited and some Tasmanian-bred cricketers have had to take their talents to the mainland for recognition and development.

Queensland first tested representative wings by putting a team of 22 into the field against New South Wales at Brisbane in 1864, but the Queensland Cricket Association was not formed until 1876. They had to wait 50 years for admission to the Sheffield Shield and until 1928 for the first Test match in the State.

Western Australia began inter-State ventures in the 1890s, but progress was limited by the problems of travel and it was 1912 before a Western Australia side appeared in Sydney. Between the wars playing standards and ground amenities improved steadily and the expansion of air travel became a factor of admission to the Shield in 1947.

The curtain of war fell slowly and reluctantly across Australian cricket in 1914, but by the New Year of 1916 a first-class programme had been abandoned. It returned in pageantry. A Services side known as the Australian Imperial Forces gave colour to the English season of 1919 and returned home by way of South Africa, to meet the senior States, giving assurance that neither cricketing strength nor prestige had been dissipated during the interruption. From the achievements of the AIF H. L. Collins, J. M. Gregory and W. A. Oldfield took bounding steps to world-renown.

New ideas flowed into the resumed cricket. The 8-ball over was introduced and pitch preparation and protection were advanced and standardized. Australian cricket, in common with that of the rest of the world, tended to develop as professional public entertainment. Figures loomed large in the scorebook and in the cash ledgers.

In the early 1920s the Australians were clearly kings of the cricketing world. Between 1920 and 1925 they won 11 Test matches against England and took the Ashes from 3 successive rubbers. They held, through E. A. McDonald and J. M. Gregory, the outstanding fast bowling, and their batting, collectively, was powerful beyond compare. In State and representative matches, where pitches were perfection for batting, the individual hundred was a commonplace and totals surged to the astronomical. In 1920–21 South Australia fielded in successive matches to innings of 639, 724, 802 and 770. In 1926–27 New South Wales scored 221 and 230 against Victoria and lost by an innings and 656 runs. Victoria outranged the capacity of the scoreboard with a total of 1,107.

Brilliance of batting methods was exemplified in the performances of C. G. Macartney, A. F. Kippax, C. E. Pellew, V. Y. Richardson, J. M. Taylor, T. J. E. Andrews and the hard-hitting of J. M. Gregory and J. Ryder, but endurance and accumulation became fashionable attributes. C. Kelleway, H. L. Collins and W. M. Woodfull earned their fame as defenders to the death and W. H. Ponsford opened up new territory of Australian aggregates and averages.

W. H. Ponsford and W. M. Woodfull: clothed in authority and stuffed with runs.

Ponsford of Victoria was the first Australian batsman to reach 1,000 runs in a purely domestic season. On his third appearance in first-class cricket he played, against Tasmania, an innings of 429. Four successive matches in December 1927, in which he batted 5 times, brought him 1,146 runs. His contribution to the Victorian 1,107 was 352 and counting run-getting as his well-doing he never wearied of good works. In his turn Ponsford abdicated his throne of accumulation in favour of an even greater collector – Donald George Bradman.

Bradman wasted no time over establishing his quality and indicating his ambitions. In his first appearance for New South Wales he made a hundred; in his first full season his aggregate was 1,690 and his average 93. From advent to retirement he was the biggest single factor in Australian cricket. He suffered some personal unpopularity among contemporary players. He became the principal object of a devastating bowling strategy. He endured minor public and major private grief that would have been intolerable affliction on a weaker character. Against all the pressures imposed by praise and denigration, against all the bowling that could be brought to challenge in health and in sickness, from youth to cricketing old age, he remained the Australian batsman above all others whose presence could ensure capacity crowds.

Bradman's achievements are unparalleled. His reputation as a successful batsman is unassailable. He dominated his time in the game with performances scarcely credible. His career average for 28,000 runs was 95; his Test match average was 99. He played 338 first-class innings, of which 117, more than a third, brought centuries. Many of the hundreds were not merely so; one exceeded 400, five others exceeded 300 and 31 ended somewhere between 200 and 300. Reflection on the figures takes the breath away.

In the batting era epitomized in Bradman and Ponsford, Australia also contrived a succession of distinguished bowlers. Exceptional ability was, of course, necessary for survival. The type of cricket played, based on the conditions prevailing, dictated the successful forms of bowling. There was scope for speed, there was scope for the more forthright spin of leg-break and googly. When Australia could command masters of both types at the same time, Gregory, McDonald and Mailey, they were irresistible; with Grimmett and O'Reilly in spin association they remained formidable. Australian conditions always promoted fast bowling and a line of greatness ran from Ernest Jones through Cotter, McDonald and Gregory, Lindwall and Miller to Lillee and Thomson.

Leg-break bowling and variations generally classified as 'wrist-spin' came to authority after introduction of the googly, learned by observation from Bosanquet and the South Africans. Before the First World War H. V. Hordern expressed his mastery of the young art with 32 wickets in a Test series, but world conflict and his profession of dentistry limited his cricket career. His immediate successor, A. A. Mailey, came into State cricket before the war and significantly into Test cricket in 1920–21 when he took 36 wickets in the series against England. On his first tour of England he supported Gregory and McDonald with 146 wickets. Mailey and C. V. Grimmett, the one prepared to buy wickets with elaborate spin, the other miserly in concession of runs, were in the highest ranks of their category, but even more respected by batsmen was W. J. O'Reilly who took 102 wickets in 4 rubbers against England and 774 wickets in a first-class career of brief duration in the 1930s.

Australia lost only one Test rubber to England in the 1930s. That was in 1932–33 when Anglo-Australian cricket came close to suspension in the most provocative and disturbed of all tours. England took out a powerful batting side, but their decisive superiority lay in bowling of rare speed and accuracy by Larwood under the direction of D. R. Jardine. In the essential strategy of attack Larwood directed himself towards the leg stump, setting an encirclement of fielders close to the bat. At Larwood's great pace batsmen were left little margin for stroke-making or personal comfort. The bubble of colossal totals burst with the force of atomic explosion. S. J. McCabe made a magnificent 187 not out in the First Test and Bradman made 103 not out at Melbourne, but these were the only individual hundreds for Australia in the whole rubber. The emphasis in the England bowling plan was too marked to escape attention and bitter feeling was aroused. Crisis was reached in the Third Test at Adelaide when a hastily constructed cable was sent by the Australian Board of Control to MCC accusing the England team of unsportsmanlike play. MCC rejected the undocumented allegation and offered Australian authorities the opportunity to cancel the remainder of the tour. The Australian Board withdrew their reflection on the sportsmanship of the England players and set up a committee of inquiry on whose report an amendment to the laws of cricket was eventually formulated.

The hard feelings engendered by controversy were regrettable from every point of view, but their repercussions on Australian cricket were not entirely without benefit. Public interest swelled and was maintained through Bradman's amazing scoring to such extent that even the great grounds seemed likely to be inadequate, Melbourne's accommodation and amenities were extended to host a Monday attendance of 87,798 during the 1936–37 tour. Melbourne went on building, not for cricket alone but also to house other great outdoor gatherings from football matches to Olympic Games and evangelist meetings. During the Second World War cricket grounds became temporary military camps. At one time MCG was residence for 14,000 of the American troops, who made such startling and lasting impact on the Australian way of life in the cities. For the Olympic Games of 1956 stands were rebuilt and the playing area was remodelled. Cricket drew benefit in the 1961 Test with West Indies when 90,800 spectators attended on one day.

Cricket in the presence of such crowds and in the huge arenas is cricket only distantly related to the game of the village green. It becomes cricket of wide separation between players and spectators, cricket of spectacle presented on a remote stage. The temperature of opinion tends to rise with increasing difficulties of observation. Players seen through field glasses if they are to be seen at all become objects rather than people of human endeavour and frailty, detachments for veneration or vilification. The too-distant spectator ceases to participate in the game's breathing and breeding. Inevitably bigger crowds mean diminution of spectatorial understanding and a lowering of standards in public behaviour. This trend, common to all sport the world over, has been an experience of Australian cricket since the Second World War. The Test match has become an occasion apart, almost irrelevant to the game it represents. For promoters success is measured in terms of publicity accorded. For players achievement and consequent personal advantage is dependent on the exaggerated importance attached to specific and increasingly artificial presentation.

Teams touring Australia and Australian touring teams have shown increasing reluctance to appreciate fixtures outside the Tests. Australia's huge grounds and the comparatively short first-class programme have made contrast particularly marked since 1946. There is an enormous following for Tests, very little for the Sheffield Shield.

The cricketing consequences have proved inescapable. State and Test match have not been comparable and complementary in the essence of enjoyable cricket. Test matches have become more of a purpose and a prize for the better players and to secure an end some curious means have been evolved.

Australian cricket immediately following the resumption enjoyed the same supremacy manifest after the First World War. A Services team in England and returning home through India gave notice of uncommon talent developing in K. R. Miller and A. L. Hassett and the pool in the Commonwealth was not empty with Bradman, S. G. Barnes, R. R. Lindwall, A. R. Morris and D. Tallon waiting for new or further opportunity.

The years of resettlement were triumphal, England were overwhelmed in 1946–47, in 1948 and in 1950–51, with the fast bowling of Lindwall and Miller decisive. Miller was personification of the ideals of his time. Gifted, independent in outlook, spendthrift of assets in the satisfaction of living for the moment, he pitched himself full-length into cricket with a toss of the head and a flourish of greeting. He bowled fast, he hit sixes, he held diving catches. He would have been an attraction in any team in any age. He had the good fortune to be contemporary with comparable greatness in the same teams. Bradman remained until 1948, cornerstone of Australian authority; Lindwall shared one of the most commanding fast-bowling partnerships in the whole history of cricket.

Miller bowled by the light of nature and with the vitality of splendid physique. Lindwall was professional to the ultimate degree of responsibility and conviction. He studied bowling, he studied batsmen and he studied himself. He was the Roman efficiency to Miller's Greek artistry. Efficiency brought to Lindwall 228 Test wickets and a place on the highest level of cricketers.

Self-confidence so characteristic of Bradman remained in Australian batting through Barnes, Morris, Hassett and Neil Harvey until it was whittled away by Tyson and Statham in Australia and Bedser and Laker in England. After 1956 Australian cricket needed a stimulant. The Sheffield Shield suffered declining appeal, the MCC tours of 1958–59 and 1962–63 were more notable for verbiage than for exciting cricket and the highlights of an unadventurous period had to be provided by a West Indian visit in 1960–61. The West Indians were talented but it was their zestful approach to all phases of play that drew delight from the Australian public. The First Test of the series ended in a tie, the last two batsmen run out when the scores were level.

Australia won the Second Test, West Indies the Third and the Fourth was drawn because the last Australian batting partnership held out for an hour and 50 minutes. Predictably in the atmosphere of this dramatic tour the Fifth Test at Melbourne induced a record crowd and a 2-wicket victory crowned a season of Australian delight. Cricket had flared again into Australian consciousness. The defeated yet triumphant West Indies captained by Worrell were given a departing salute by 100,000 people lining the Melbourne streets.

Richie Benaud: as player, captain, writer and a senior executive of World Series Cricket, Benaud has had a continuing influence on the game.

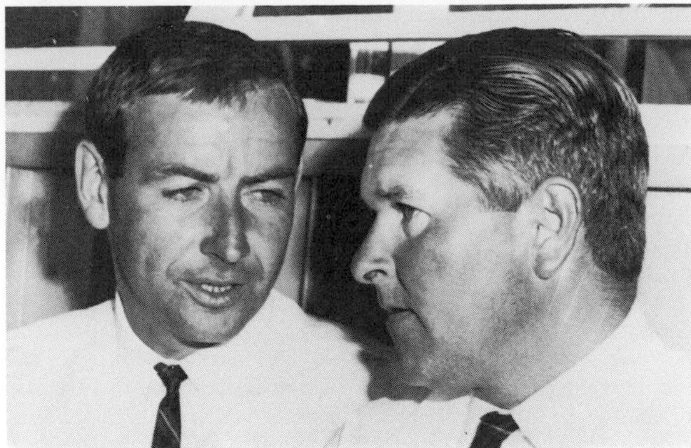

Brisbane, December 1963: Ian Meckiff *(left)* talks to Umpire Egar, who, by no-balling him for throwing, had just effectively ended Meckiff's controversial career.

Worrell's legacy of cricketing practice and principle was dissipated in the materialistic decades of the 1960s and 1970s. As cricket became more tightly bound by financial consideration, as the prizes for victory became more lavish, the means to winning became less pertinent.

The story of a nation's cricket cannot carry much significance without contrast of light and shade, without an occasional smear of dubiety disfiguring pages of glory. Australian cricket has grown in terms of humanity, with periodic human lapses, but with the ambition, the enterprise and the devotion that are among humanity's higher attributes. There has been no finer cricket than Australian cricket; there have been no greater cricketers than the greatest of Australians. The game has both reflected the development of a nation and contributed towards that development.

Australians in cricket have won the world's admiration and created figures of international renown and respect. Cricket has a home in Australia and Australians are at home in cricket everywhere.

General cricketing experiences, good and ill, have infected Australia. The bowling illegalities exemplified in throwing and dragging that scarred cricket in the late 1950s and early 1960s were sharply outlined in Australia. Recovery of the Ashes in 1958–59 was a satisfaction clouded in controversy and Australian thinking was eventually reversed to clear a way towards international collaboration over an alarming problem. More difficult to resolve because less capable of recognition and definition was the onset of changing attitudes towards sport at high level.

With the amateur sacrificed to the cult of egalitarianism and the pressure of financial demand a harsher approach began to flavour first-class cricket. The metaphors of warfare assumed a more literal meaning. By their own admission fast bowlers deliberately sought to inflict injury. Exchange of verbal insult on the field became tactical exercise. Intimidation of umpire by players, and of player by spectators became commonplace and unrebuked behaviour. Provocation by Press comment and television picture exacerbated minor irritation and created a pervading atmosphere of ill-will, some of it affected, no doubt, but some genuinely felt.

In Australia the separation of cricket as a professional pursuit and as a form of sport to be enjoyed for intrinsic merits widened to a chasm under commercial exploitation. The exploitation became an urgent and fundamental concern in the 1970s when the Packer organization, a publishing and broadcasting business, was refused a wanted television contract by the Board of Control. Packer devised a television rivalry with traditional cricket, luring prominent players in Australia and from all parts of the world with magnetic payments.

World Series Cricket, as the new venture was named, bore little more than nominal relation to traditional cricket, but the financial appeal to those invited was in many cases too strong to be resisted. The effect was felt throughout the cricket world. Established authorities applied such sanctions as they could on the principle that players could not serve two loyalties, but in Australia any continuity in Test teams was virtually eliminated. R. B. Simpson was persuaded from retirement to captain teams without Test qualifications and experience and inevitably the immediate results were uncharacteristic of Australian stature. Hogg could follow the departed Lillee and Thomson but batsmen were harder to find and took longer to meet international requirements.

The resentment towards World Series Cricket was not so much over its conception as over the dubious means of recruitment and promotion. Putting distinguished cricketers through a circus hoop to provide a television spectacle was regarded by traditionalists not only as a financial rivalry but also as a denigration of the game. Australian cricket was faced with a choice between sporting and commercial morality polarized in personalities.

The Packer organization achieved its initial purpose when, after two years of debate and disharmony, its bid for television rights was successful, but consultations and compromise could not eliminate all the unease and ill-feeling that had been created in Australian and international cricket. Money spoke loudly to players and promoters, and cricket the game suffered moral bruising to complement the physical discomforts infiltrating the practices of play.

Sheffield Shield

The Sheffield Shield is a handsome trophy, the winning of which signifies domestic supremacy in Australian cricket. It derives its name from the 3rd Earl of Sheffield who took a team to Australia in 1891–92 and gave a sum of money to the Australian Cricket Council for the advancement of the game. The Council invested the money in a shield bearing the Sheffield and Australian coats of arms. It measures 46 inches by 30 inches. Apart from the war years, the Sheffield Shield has been competed for by the leading Australian colonies (later States) beginning in 1892–93.

The original contestants were New South Wales, Victoria and South Australia, Queensland being admitted to the competition in 1926–27 and Western Australia (on a limited basis) in 1947–48. Western Australia has competed on an equal basis with the other States as from 1956–57. Despite doubts by many regarding the wisdom of further extension, Tasmania was admitted on a limited, provisional basis in 1977–78, thus bringing the competing sides to 6.

IRVING ROSENWATER

The Chappell brothers, Ian and Greg, both Australian captains, choosing a Test side with wicket-keeper Marsh.

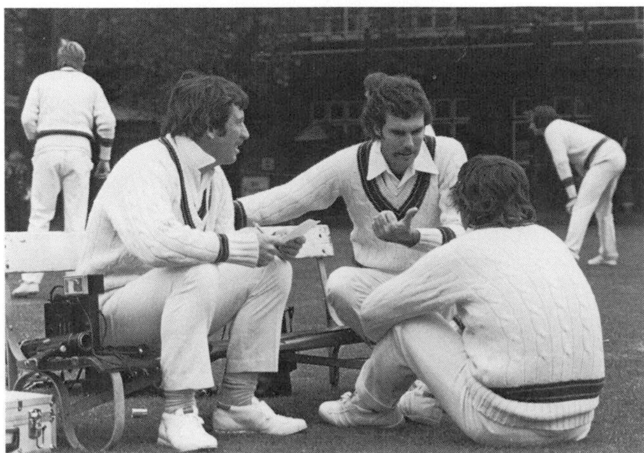

A. F. Kippax (260 not out) and J. E. H. Hooker (62) during their world-record last-wicket stand of 307 in the Sheffield Shield match between New South Wales and Victoria, Melbourne 1928–29.

WINNERS

1892–93	Victoria	1938–39	South Australia
1893–94	South Australia	1939–40	New South Wales
1894–95	Victoria	1940–46	No Competition
1895–96	New South Wales	1946–47	Victoria
1896–97	New South Wales	1947–48	Western Australia
1897–98	Victoria	1948–49	New South Wales
1898–99	Victoria	1949–50	New South Wales
1899–1900	New South Wales	1950–51	Victoria
1900–01	Victoria	1951–52	New South Wales
1901–02	New South Wales	1952–53	South Australia
1902–03	New South Wales	1953–54	New South Wales
1903–04	New South Wales	1954–55	New South Wales
1904–05	New South Wales	1955–56	New South Wales
1905–06	New South Wales	1956–57	New South Wales
1906–07	New South Wales	1957–58	New South Wales
1907–08	Victoria	1958–59	New South Wales
1908–09	New South Wales	1959–60	New South Wales
1909–10	South Australia	1960–61	New South Wales
1910–11	New South Wales	1961–62	New South Wales
1911–12	New South Wales	1962–63	Victoria
1912–13	South Australia	1963–64	South Australia
1913–14	New South Wales	1964–65	New South Wales
1914–15	Victoria	1965–66	New South Wales
1915–19	No Competition	1966–67	Victoria
1919–20	New South Wales	1967–68	Western Australia
1920–21	New South Wales	1968–69	South Australia
1921–22	Victoria	1969–70	Victoria
1922–23	New South Wales	1970–71	South Australia
1923–24	Victoria	1971–72	Western Australia
1924–25	Victoria	1972–73	Western Australia
1925–26	New South Wales	1973–74	Victoria
1926–27	South Australia	1974–75	Western Australia
1927–28	Victoria	1975–76	South Australia
1928–29	New South Wales	1976–77	Western Australia
1929–30	Victoria	1977–78	Western Australia
1930–31	Victoria	1978–79	Victoria
1931–32	New South Wales		
1932–33	New South Wales		
1933–34	Victoria		
1934–35	Victoria		
1935–36	South Australia		
1936–37	Victoria		
1937–38	New South Wales		

Summary of wins

New South Wales	36
Victoria	23
South Australia	11
Western Australia	7

New South Wales

There is an old saying that when New South Wales is strong, so too is Australia. The saying has great merit for there has been many an era, sometimes as long as a decade, when the men from New South Wales, many of them with green baggy caps, have seemed as impregnable as the Harbour Bridge.

The first cricket matches began in Sydney in 1803, back in the days of 24-inch stumps and the 4-ball over. One of the founders, back in 1826, was E. S. Gregory, who, apart from 7 daughters, was wise enough to have 6 sons, 5 of whom played for New South Wales; he launched a dynasty of cricketing Gregorys who served the State and Australia for more than a century.

The first inter-colonial match, New South Wales v Victoria, was in 1856 at the Melbourne Cricket Ground. The Victorians were amazed at the homely nature of the New South Welshmen who wore drill pants, guernseys, caps, and, most incredible of all, they played either in socks or bare feet.

There were giggles from the spectators at the antique under-arm style of the New South Wales bowler, McKone. However McKone was deadly. He took four wickets for 25 runs in the first innings and five for 11 in the second, sending Victoria down for 28 runs. There was a return match the following year, but still the elegant Victorians could not beat the homely New South Welshmen.

The first English tours to Australia were by H. H. Stephenson and George Parr. After their departure two players remained behind, those capable professionals, William Caffyn, better known as 'Terrible Billy' or the 'Surrey Pet', and Charles Lawrence. Caffyn, a dapper little man with side whiskers, taught in both Sydney and Melbourne, and these two men helped lay the foundation of Australian cricket.

Under their guidance New South Wales very quickly produced a coterie of extraordinary cricketers. There was F. R. Spofforth, called the 'Demon', who was brilliant at disguising his pace and swing. There was W. L. Murdoch, the Bradman of the 19th century. In 1882 Murdoch scored 321 not out against Victoria at a time when even a hundred was a score of prodigious majesty. That remained as the best individual score on the Sydney Cricket Ground until 20-year-old Don Bradman made 340 not out against Victoria in 1929 and followed it a year later with 452 not out against Queensland.

In 1891–92 Lord Sheffield brought to Australia a team captained by Dr W. G. Grace. His lordship was so delighted by the reception his team had in Australia that he gave the Australian Cricket Council £150 to use as it saw fit. The Council bought a Shield which bore the Sheffield and Australian coat of arms; it took 4 seasons for New South Wales to win that Shield but from 1901–2 they triumphed 6 times in a row. The talent included such men as Noble, Duff, Macartney, called the 'Governor-General' because of his majesty at the wicket, Bardsley, Syd Gregory and, of course, Trumper.

At most Australian cricket grounds there is a large photograph of Victor Trumper halfway down the wicket, bat raised high in the full power of aggression. Veterans talk of it as an adventure of a lifetime just to have seen Trumper and Duff together at the wicket. In 1902–03 Trumper and Duff scored opening partnerships of 298 and 267. Then in 1905–06 against Victoria on a bad wicket Trumper hit 101 out of 139 in 57 minutes.

Between the wars there were bowlers like the awesome 6 feet 4 inch Ted McDonald and the impish Arthur Mailey, who had great gifts as a cartoonist. Mailey depicted himself as a comical little chap with a patch on his trousers, which tended to delude batsmen regarding the devilish guile of his spin.

There was that great spin bowler, W. J. O'Reilly, called 'Tiger' because of his predatory demands for justice from the umpires. Regularly he still appears on the lists of those who like to compile the world all-time XI. Yet this was an era when

LEFT New South Wales, 1954: when they made a habit of winning the Sheffield Shield and were perhaps the best state, provincial, county or island side in the world. Front row: J. H. de Courcy, A. R. Morris, G. B. Barter (manager), K. R. Miller (captain) and O. Lambert; second row: R. B. Simpson, J. Treanor, J. W. Burke, R. Benaud, E. Cotton and J. O'Reilly; back row: R. Briggs and W. Watson.

BELOW Ken Mackay: a Queensland cap and a Queensland character. Neil Harvey and J. Ryder in the background.

batsmen produced run totals which looked more like lottery figures. There was Kippax who made 6,096 runs for New South Wales. There was Stan McCabe, a man of flawless technique, who on many a wondrous day produced batsmanship of such brilliance that Sydney-siders deserted their radios to rush to their Cricket Ground. Then young Don Bradman in the 8 years before he left for Adelaide rewrote almost every record in the book.

New South Wales, a real cricket power machine, continued its progress after the Second World War. It had the best opening bowlers in the world in Lindwall and Miller and such superb openers as Arthur Morris and S. G. Barnes; these were followed by such talent as Richie Benaud, Alan Davidson, Ian Craig, Norman O'Neill, Brian Booth and R. B. Simpson. For 9 successive seasons from 1953–54 through 1961–62 New South Wales dominated the Sheffield Shield. As if all this talent were not sufficient, the great Neil Harvey transferred to New South Wales from Victoria in 1957. Harvey's last State game was on the Sydney Cricket Ground against South Australia when he enthralled the crowd with 231 not out in 4¾ hours.

From the mid-1960s, while Western Australia rose to power, the old mother State of New South Wales went into a strange decline. Worse than that the once mighty New South Welshmen lingered near the bottom of the ladder.

During 1977–78 Bob Simpson returned to cricket to help his country after so many had left to join World Series Cricket. He was appointed co-ordinator and captain of the New South Wales team. It was a remarkable comeback after nearly 10 years and his advice and help gave steadiness and stability to New South Wales.

In 1978–79 he passed the captaincy to Andrew Hilditch, who at 21 became one of the youngest Sheffield Shield captains in history. In his first full season as captain Hilditch lifted New South Wales to third position on the ladder, thus predicting a new golden era for the State. One hoped he was correct for Australia still needed badly that age-old New South Wales muscle.

KEITH DUNSTAN

Queensland

Cricket should really be played in Queensland during those balmy, sunny winter days of June and July. Instead Queenslanders fight it out in the often steamy, tempestuous weather of January and February. There have been famous occasions when the ground at Woolloongabba has been flooded by tropical downpours and the stumps have been left floating across the wicket. So the northern State of Queensland has always been at a disadvantage compared with South Australia or Western Australia which receive almost summer-long uninterrupted sunshine.

Oddly enough some of the first Brisbane matches were played in winter. The first New South Wales v Queensland encounter was on 3 June 1864 and a curious affair it was with fieldsmen constantly falling into potholes. New South Wales fielded 11 against 22 of Queensland. The Queenslanders were terribly unimpressive and they scored 11 ducks in their second innings.

The Queensland Cricket Association was formed in 1876 but progress was slow. There was no match against South Australia until 1899 and no visit from Victoria until 1902.

Before the First World War there were some fine Queensland-bred players. There was C. Barstow, who, if not a true express bowler, had canny powers of deception and could turn the ball from the leg. There was S. J. Redgrave, a Sydney player, who came north as State coach in 1907, A. C. Y. Coningham, and that beautiful batsman Roger Hartigan, a Brisbane auctioneer who played for Australia. This was some achievement. Queenslanders then, as they do now, often cried out against the injustice of selectors. Their players always have had to achieve more, or so it is said, to gain international selection.

Queensland after much pleading was admitted to the Sheffield Shield competition in 1926. There were some good batsmen such as L. D. P. O'Connor, the first Shield captain, R. K. Oxenham, C. W. Rowe and F. C. Thompson. Young Don Tallon was an example of the problems of gaining recognition from Queensland. He first played for Queensland in 1933 when he was only 17. They called him the Paganini of wicket-keepers and, added to this, he was a brilliant forcing batsman.

During the 1938–39 season he set a world record. In the match against New South Wales he caught 9 batsmen and stumped 3 and then against Victoria he bagged 7 wickets in one innings. There was a row of hundreds, including 193 against Victoria in 1935–36, but still he did not force his way into the Australian side until 1946–47.

Distinguished Queensland players came in a stream after the Second World War. One thinks of all-rounders like Ron Archer and Tom Veivers, and of the redoubtable Ken Mackay, called 'Slasher', a fine example of that curious Australian sense of humour, slashing being precisely what Ken Mackay did not do.

There was Peter Burge who scored 22 centuries for Queensland, including 283 against New South Wales in the 1963–64 season. Sam Trimble was another, too often ignored for Australian honours. He, too, scored 22 centuries and a record 8,647 runs for his State. There was the speed bowler Tony Dell, and the remarkable P. A. Allan, who must have been close to being recommended for a knighthood when he took 10 wickets for 61 runs in one innings against Victoria in 1966.

Queensland's great and continuing frustration has been its failure to win the Sheffield Shield. So often they have just failed to get there. They were 2nd 4 times out of 5 between 1973–4 and 1977–78. Then in 1978–79, when they had only to perform comfortably well over the last two or three matches, they had an incomprehensible loss of form, which allowed Graham Yallop and his Victorians to steal the honours.

So to win the Shield has developed into a mission like the hunt for the Holy Grail. The Queensland administration has sought great imports. There was the fast bowler Ray Lindwall from New South Wales. There was Wesley Hall from the West Indies, and then, in 1973–74, Greg Chappell from South Australia. Chappell came in as captain and remained until the split caused by World Series Cricket. In his first season Chappell very nearly won the Shield off his own bat. Other imports have included Alvin Kallicharran, Majid Khan and the all-rounder Gary Cosier.

The northern weather does not help. Lost play means lost points. Yet triumph for Queensland cannot be far off. They have such talent in depth. There is A. D. Ogilvie, who hit 6 centuries during the 1977–78 season, Geoff Dymock, who has taken a record 200 wickets for his State, and J. A. Maclean, who, by 1978, had even shattered the old records of A. T. W. Grout with more than 290 dismissals behind the wickets.

KEITH DUNSTAN

South Australia

Cricket always seems to have just that much more grace and charm in Adelaide. Some other cricket grounds are more like arenas where lions might be called upon to eat Christians, but the Adelaide Oval breathes cricket and there is the lovely view across to the Cathedral and the Adelaide hills.

The game began early enough, less than two years after the founding of the colony. There was an advertisement in the *South Australian Gazette and Register* on 19 October 1839 which announced that a

> grand match will be played on Monday October 28 on the Thebarton Cricket Ground between Eleven Gentlemen of the Royal Victoria Independent Club, and Eleven Gentlemen of Adelaide, for Twenty-two guineas a-side. Wickets to be pitched at 10 o'clock.

Adelaide was always very English and the game was played with much enthusiasm, but the colony was slow in acquiring cricketing skill. The first touring English sides did not visit South Australia.

The South Australian Cricket Association began in 1871 and the Adelaide Oval, host for touring international sides ever since, saw the first ball bowled on 13 December 1873.

The visiting international side was led by the young Dr W. G. Grace, during the season of 1873–74. He was 25 and it was still possible to discern a face behind his beard. Right at the end of his tour he played the Yorke XXII at Kadina, 100 miles from Adelaide. The Yorke team was thoroughly beaten. In the second innings the 22 batsmen amassed only 13 runs with 15 ducks. Lillywhite took 13 wickets for 7 runs and McIntyre 7 wickets for 1 run.

The Adelaide XXII did rather better with 64 and 82 against England's 108 and 73. The local newspapers commented that

Adelaide's lovely Oval, with St Peter's Cathedral in the background and the Chappell brothers batting.

Dr Grace's men did not try over hard. After all, their horse-drawn coach did have to travel all night to get to Adelaide in time for the match.

From here on the determined South Australians picked up skills with almost embarrassing speed. The first match against the slightly arrogant Victorians was in 1874. Victoria just won by a margin of 15 runs. The return match in 1876 was almost a rout. South Australia won by an innings and 70 runs.

Already on the scene at this stage was the mighty George Giffen, still remembered as possibly the greatest all-rounder Australia has ever produced. He took 1000 wickets and scored 10,000 runs in first-class matches for Australian and State teams. He was a one-man match winner. For example, he caused great embarrassment for Victoria in 1891 when he scored 271 in 7 hours, and as if that was not enough he also took 16 wickets to give the home side victory by an innings and 62 runs.

Then, in the 1890s, came Clem Hill, unquestionably the best left-handed batsman in the world. At school, Prince Alfred College, he made 360 (retired) against St Peter's College, and he was chosen to play against Western Australia when he was just a few days over 16 years old. He went on to make 8,027 runs for South Australia and in one Sheffield Shield match he even beat his schoolboy record with 365.

The Sheffield Shield competition began in the season of 1892–93 with the three foundation members, New South Wales, Victoria and South Australia. South Australia had its first victory in the second year. The long hot summers of Adelaide were good for ripening grapes and superb for breeding cricketers. A contemporary of Clem Hill was Joe Darling, who captained Australia on three visits to England, a formidable gentleman, big of jaw and big of moustache. The first time he faced English bowling he scored 117 and 37 not out for South Australia against A. E. Stoddart's team in 1894.

One of the great builders of South Australian cricket was Victor Richardson, an extraordinary athlete. After the First World War he captained South Australia at both cricket and football, and he was highly skilled at tennis and golf. He was the first South Australian to score a century in each innings of a Sheffield Shield match and the gates at the Adelaide Oval are named in his honour. He was, too, the grandfather of the Chappell brothers, Ian, Greg and Trevor.

Later there were some very interesting imports, Clarrie Grimmett, born in New Zealand, the best leg-spin and googly bowler the world had seen. Then Don Bradman, after his terrible illness in 1934, switched from New South Wales to South Australia. It would be an understatement to say that he was a help in winning the Sheffield Shield that season. His first 3 innings were 117, 233 and 357. His influence was profound, as player, captain, selector and later as administrator.

After the Second World War the leisurely atmosphere of the Adelaide Oval was brightened by such players as Gil Langley, Neil Hawke, Graeme Hole and, for 3 seasons from 1961–62, the South Australian cap was worn by the great Garfield Sobers. Anyone who was present for the New South Wales match in February 1962 will have particular reason to recall this extraordinary man. He took 6 wickets for 72 runs in NSWs second innings and made 251 runs, his last century coming in 83 minutes. Even George Giffen could not have done better.

One of the most helpful and consistently inspiring characters in the history of South Australian cricket has been Les Favell. One never knew what to expect when he came to the wicket. He always batted as if he were worried about being late for dinner. By the end of the 1968–69 season he had made 7,426 runs for the State.

Barry Richards of South Africa was another to leave his mark. He was there just for the 1970–71 season, but he was like an electric power house, nothing could stop him. He played 14 innings of Sheffield Shield cricket, scored 1,538 runs at an average of 109.8, the highest total for a season by a South Australian batsman.

There were the spinners, Terry Jenner and Ashley Mallett, and the Chappell brothers, who, when they were batting well, made South Australia almost unbeatable. It was practically a State-wide tragedy when Greg Chappell moved to Queensland in 1973.

And then there was David Hookes, who rained sixes as if he were operating a trench mortar and during the season of 1976–77 seemed to make a hundred every time he went to the wicket. He did actually score a hundred in each innings in 2 successive first-class matches, 185 and 105 against Queensland and 135 and 156 against New South Wales. As long as South Australia can continue to produce cricketers like Hookes its position is secure.

KEITH DUNSTAN

Tasmania

The battle of competitive cricket has not been easy for Tasmania. First Tasmania is an island and second its entire population would fit into, say, 4 affluent Melbourne suburbs.

However, gentlemen were playing cricket in Tasmania before Melbourne was thought of, as early as 1826. Furthermore the first inter-colonial match ever to take place was between the gentlemen of Port Phillip and the gentlemen of Van Diemen's Land which took place on 11 and 12 February 1851.

The match was played at Launceston and the Van Diemen's Land team won by 2 runs with 3 wickets intact. The Victorians attributed their defeat to the bowling which was 'slow and peculiar in character.'

The defeat was certainly a shock and according to one newspaper:

> As a mark of kindness and good feeling of the Tasmanians towards the Port Phillipians, not the slightest breath of applause escaped from the multitude, numbering over 1,500, but a marked silence ensued as though they had committed a breach of hospitality to their guests.

Over the years Tasmania was never ignored. Touring international sides always called there, but if a local player wanted to earn an Australian cap there was no future for him on the island, he had to move to Victoria or perhaps South Australia. Some famous names like Ted McDonald, Badcock and Nash did this.

The change came in 1977 when Tasmania won its way into the Sheffield Shield competition. It was a lovely debut. The Vandemonians became known as 'Jack's giant Killers'. 'Jack' was the captain and coach, Jack Simmons, a wily old spin bowler and class batsman from Lancashire. His deputy was

Jack Simmons: no one has done more for Tasmanian cricket than the Lancashire player.

Jack Hampshire from Yorkshire, a true professional run-getter. Behind them they had a team of enthusiastic young Tasmanians.

Their record was this. In their first year they played themselves into the final of the Gillette Cup one-day competition where they were narrowly defeated by Western Australia. They defeated the touring Indian side twice, first in a one-day game and, then over 4 days.

During the 1978–79 season they beat the Sheffield Shield champions, Western Australia, by 4 wickets in a Shield match and then Western Australia in the final of the Gillette Cup. The match took place at Hobart and Jack Simmons described it as 'the happiest day of my life.'

There was the atmosphere of a football final and this time the Van Demonians did not remain silent as a mark of kindness and good feeling.

KEITH DUNSTAN

Victoria

Victorians man for man could be the most devoted cricket followers in the world. Certainly the greatest cricket crowds are here. Touring captains when they come to the vast cricket stadium that is the Melbourne Cricket Ground approach the occasion with a feeling of awe.

They see the world's biggest cricket arena and know the atmosphere will be akin to that of a football match. A bowler who has just been cheered or hooted by a crowd of 80,000 is unlikely to forget the experience. The greatest cricket crowd in history, 90,800, was at the Melbourne Cricket Ground on 11 February 1961 for the Fifth Test between Australia and West Indies.

If cricket seeps through the pores of Victorians very likely it is because of the Melbourne Cricket Club. Apart from the Marylebone Cricket Club no other club has contributed more to the game. This other MCC began in 1838 when Melbourne was only 3 years old and just a muddy village. On 15 November 1838, 5 gentlemen met and drew up a document agreeing to form a cricket club to be called the 'Melbourne Cricket Club' with a subscription of 1 guinea. The signatories were F. A. Powlett, R. Russell, Arthur Mundy, C. F. Mundy and George B. Smyth. They all paid their guinea and on the same day the first secretary, Mr D. G. McArthur, bought two bats and stumps for £2.0*s*.3*d*.

This club went on to rule cricket in Australia. It contracted and brought out all the early international sides. It brought from England H. H. Stephenson's XI which played here in 1862. Mr Stephenson did not mind playing Victorian sides of 18, but when he had to compete against country sides of 22, as he did on 15 occasions, he found it tiresome. There is a certain challenge to a batsman when he has to get the ball past 22 opposing fieldsmen.

Castlemaine, to its eternal glory, on 14, 15 and 17 March 1862, was the first team to beat an English XI on Victorian soil. Admittedly Castlemaine did field XXII and just possibly the abundance of champagne and lobster was a contributing factor.

It was the Melbourne Cricket Club which staged the first Test Match between England and a combined Australian side in 1877. There is a feeling of pride in the club that cricket could draw the rival colonies together 24 years before the politicians were able to do so and create a federated Commonwealth of Australia.

Legend has it that during the tour of the Hon Ivo Bligh's side of 1882–83 the famous Ashes came into being. The millionaire grazier, Sir William Clarke, who even possessed his own personal regiment, was president of the MCC. The ladies of his household incinerated some bails at his mansion, Rupertswood, Sunbury. They placed them in an urn and they have been a matter of some competition ever since.

The Melbourne Cricket Club's power as an omnipotent ruler came to an end in 1912, causing a split reminiscent of the Packer struggle of 1978. There was a dispute over which body was to provide the manager for the England tour. As a result some of Australia's greatest cricketing names resigned from

CHILDRENS FOOTWEAR PADDLE BRAND AUSTRALIA'S BEST

Audited Net Sales 132,391 Daily

Forecast: Fine; cool S.E. winds.

The Sun NEWS-PICTORIAL

2/6 HOLIDAY SUITS and COSTUMES — Cassells — 343 ELIZABETH ST. 382 CHAPEL ST., SOUTH YARRA. 45 PAISLEY STREET, FOOTSCRAY

No. 1341 MELBOURNE: WEDNESDAY, DECEMBER 29, 1926 1½d.

CRICKET HISTORY WAS MADE ON THE M.C.C. YESTERDAY, when Victoria, in piling up a magnificent 1107, broke the world's record, and Ponsford and Hendry eclipsed the best second wicket partnership for Victoria against New South Wales. But, while big things were achieved, further record-breaking feats were missed by narrow margins. Ponsford's 352 failed by 14 runs to pass the highest individual score for Shield cricket; Ryder needed only 5 more to reach 300. This picture was taken at the fall of the last wicket; the board shows the score which will be discussed by cricket enthusiasts all over the world. Andrews is removing the bails from the wicket at the Richmond end, while both the batsmen (Ellis and Blackie) are at the other. Ellis, the last man, was run out, and the Victorian innings ended at 5.55. Inset: Ryder (right) and Ellis returning to the pavilion at the 4 o'clock adjournment. Ryder hit six sixers; one almost hit the clock in the pavilion. If he had done so, Ryder would have won six cases of champagne.

Melbourne, 29 December 1926: Victoria's 1,107 all out is still the largest first-class total ever made. The front page of the *Melbourne Sun* tells the story. A. A. Mailey's bowling analysis of 62–0–362–4 is unlikely ever to be matched.

the tour – Hill, Armstrong, Trumper, Ransford, Cotter and Carter.

The Victorian Cricket Association was formed on 29 September 1875 but it was no more than a struggling organization, penniless and dependent on the MCC. After 1912 it became the proper controller of cricket in Victoria.

One thinks back to the great Victorian names John McCarthy Blackham, once called the 'Prince of Wicket-Keepers' and the first to stand up to the stumps to the medium-pace bowlers; Frank Allan 'the bowler of the century', the long, lean and deadly Hugh Trumble, the immense and imperious Warwick Armstrong, Vernon Ransford, Jack Ryder, Bill Ponsford, Bill Woodfull, Ian Johnson, Keith Miller, Lindsay Hassett, Bill Lawry and so it goes on.

The nose to nose rivals in Australian cricket have always been Victoria and New South Wales. The Sheffield Shield match played over Christmas at the Melbourne Cricket Ground is always nicely tuned as the grudge match. The most famous of all was the Christmas encounter of 1926 when Victoria set a world record 1,107 runs – Woodfull 133, Ponsford 352 and Ryder 295.

Arthur Mailey put up the remarkable figures 4 for 362. He commented: 'It was a pity Ellis was run out at the finish, just when I was striking my length.'

By 1979 New South Wales had won the Shield 36 times and Victoria 22.

After the Second World War Victoria gave to world cricket a series of dazzling players. One remembers the loping stride of Bill Johnston, the greatest medium-pacer since Hugh Trumble, the curious flick spin of Jack Iverson, the uncanny skill of

Neil Harvey when scouting around the covers, the tall athletic grace of Paul Sheahan, the batting power of Bob Cowper and, of course, Bill Lawry. As an opening bat Lawry seemed as indestructible as Ayer's Rock. His nickname was 'The Phantom.'

The Sheffield Shield was always a hard-fought competition, made the more so by the rise in power of the more junior cricketing States. Victoria under Jack Potter won in 1966–67; it won again under Bob Cowper in 1969–70 and under Keith Stackpole in 1973–74. Stackpole was an enthusiastic leader. he said this was a bigger thrill to him than his dashing career as an opening bat in Test cricket. Graham Yallop, an uncommonly young Shield captain, gave Victoria a further win in 1978–79 at a time when both he and most of his side seemed certain to be around for a long time.

KEITH DUNSTAN

John Inverarity (*right*), recently captain of Western Australia, and Australian Test-cap, and Ian Brayshaw, Western Australian cricketer and cricket-writer, after being invested with the MBE for services to cricket.

Western Australia

The most exciting event in modern Australian cricket has been the surge to power of Western Australia. West Australians dominated Australian cricket in the 1970s. Yet this used to be the forgotten State, the impoverished relation that could not afford to send teams to the East, the State which had no hope of getting a representative into an international side.

Cricket in Perth had similar origins to cricket in Melbourne and Sydney; the game was being played as early as 1835. The problem was what the historians have called 'the tyranny of distance' and that tyranny was perhaps greater than anywhere else in the world. Western Australia was and is a third of the continent and Perth might just as well have been an island out in the Pacific. To the East was the vast Nullarbor desert and the nearest cricketing capitals were almost as far off as Omsk is from London. So costs cut both ways, the neighbouring colonies were not keen on making the long sea voyage.

The Western Australian Cricketing Association was formed in 1885 and the grand event, a WACA team going on tour to the distant East, did not take place until 1892–93. It was hardly triumphant. The match at Melbourne was a hard one. W.A. made 38 and 130, Victoria scored 411, a loss by an innings and 243 runs. Not until 1912 did a team from the West adventure as far across as Sydney. If any great cricketer were born he was like the true desert rose, he learned to blush unseen. E. H. Bromley, a left-hander, did play for Australia in 1934, but he had had to move to Melbourne first.

The breakthrough came in 1947. The Eastern States admitted Western Australia, a little grudgingly, to the Sheffield Shield competition, on probation, 4 matches instead of the full 7. Keith Carmody, the inventor of the famous Carmody umbrella field, came over from Sydney as State coach. In the first match against South Australia he made 198 and Western Australia won by an innings. He had an average of 61.14 for the season as well as the beautiful satisfaction of seeing Western Australia, on its maiden debut, win the Shield.

In the early days Western Australia could get the Eastern States to Perth only by paying most of their expenses. At last full membership of the Sheffield Shield came in 1956–57. Western Australia started well enough but could not sustain it. The resolute Ken Meuleman made 234 not out against South Australia, the highest innings ever in Perth, and the happiest part of the season was an outright victory over the Victorians. Never before had the Westerners done this.

The drought between Shield wins for the West was 20 years and one could say the man who changed the climate was Tony Lock. Lock was bitterly disappointed when England did not choose him to tour Australia during 1962–63 and it was precisely the right psychological moment to invite him to Perth to coach and ply his spin for Western Australia.

His best moment came during the 1967–68 season with the deciding match on the Melbourne Cricket Ground. He took 9 wickets for 119 runs in that match and he has recalled that he knew victory was his when there was plaintive call from the outer: 'Why don't you go home to Coronation Street you bald-headed old b......'

This was just the start. In the seasons between 1970–71 and 1977–78, the great renaissance took over, Western Australia won the Sheffield Shield five times. There were a number of reasons for this. There was the captaincy of that fine batsman John Inverarity, who was as reliable as that wind, the 'Fremantle Doctor', which blows in every afternoon. Then there were the hot summers and the hard, bouncy wickets of the WACA ground, which produced a generation of Australia's finest fast bowlers.

The fast bowling tradition really began in the 1960s with Graham McKenzie, upon whose broad shoulders Australia depended for so many Test matches. Then came bowlers like Dennis Lillee, Bob Massie, Wayne Clark, Terry Alderman and Sam Gannon. As for the batting, the team seemed sometimes to take over the Australian XI, Wal Edwards, Bruce Laird, Graeme Wood, Kim Hughes, Craig Serjeant, plus wicket-keepers like Rodney Marsh and Kevin Wright.

Western Australia became the side to beat for the one-day Gillette Cup and again for the Sheffield Shield. 'WA' have always been burdened with the tag 'the Cinderella State', but Cinderella, it seemed, had found her handsome prince.

KEITH DUNSTAN

Coaching in Australia

There are many disciples of Jean Jacques Rousseau's naturalistic philosophy in Australian sport; they support the viewpoint that innate talent will always prevail over athletes with an acquired technique. Not surprisingly, therefore, there has long been an ingrained suspicion of coaching within cricket circles in this country.

Sir Donald Bradman expressed commonly-held reservations about the desirable extent of the influence of coaching, when he wrote in the foreword of the manual containing the Rothman's National Cricket Coaching Plan:

> How important is coaching? Let us get this into proper perspective at once. The greatest Test match players in history were not made great by coaching. You may check the careers of the noblest from Dr. W. G. Grace to Sir Jack Hobbs, Denis Compton, Bill O'Reilly and so on. The

story is the same. They rose to eminence through sheer natural skill, allied to the basic fundamentals and personal qualities.

Bradman goes on to set his seal of approval on coaching, provided the teaching process allows the full development of the individual's natural talents and seeks only to maximize them. It is, in my estimation, a fundamental difference between the English and Australian coaching doctrines that in Australia the coach is less categorical in his instruction and more sensitive to the individual and unorthodox differences which exist.

The lukewarm support given to coaching in Australia in the past has meant that, until recently, the teaching of cricket techniques was largely associated with the names of prominent schoolmasters such as P. L. Williams and Chester Bennett, the mentors of players of the ilk of Lindsay Hassett, Ian Johnson, Ross Gregory and the Chappell brothers. Although, in New South Wales, annual coaching clinics have been organized in country and city areas under former state players like George Lowe and Peter Philpott, State Cricket Associations for a long time pursued rather casual coaching plans, accepting help and sponsorship where and when it was offered. The *Adelaide Advertiser*, for example, and its coach, former Test opener Les Favell, have supported coaching clinics in South Australia; for two decades the Shell Company of Australia has lent its financial muscle to the organization of training sessions for young players in Junior Country Week competitions throughout Victoria. More recently, the Perth Building Society has employed former England bowler, Tony Lock, as a promotions officer and coach in Western Australia country areas.

For the most part, however, these were isolated operations and the overall neglect of coaching in Australia lay revealed when, in 1972–73, a survey conducted by the Victorian Cricket Association amongst its 1250 affiliated clubs, showed that over 80% of them had no coach and did not, in consequence, receive any guidance. Even more alarming was the fact that only 2.8% of all clubs were assisted in the coaching field by the central association.

Three years before the Victorian census was carried out, a more subjective evaluation of the deficiencies of the Australian coaching system was conducted by the Rothman's National Sports Foundation. Two years of exhaustive effort on the part of the Board of the Sports Foundation, with the co-operation of the Australian Board of Control for International Cricket, came to fruition in 1971 with the publication of the National Cricket Coaching Plan and the appointment of the former Australian wicket-keeper, Brian Taber, as the National Director of Cricket Coaching. Taber was the first National Director of Coaching of any sport in Australia. His portfolio was to:

Co-ordinate coaching throughout Australia by setting up, in co-operation with the six states, a workable system, whereby thousands of coaches with standardized coaching techniques will assist players in the skills of the game.

It was also his task to gain 'widespread acceptance of the plan in the Departments of Education.'

Like its English counterpart, this Australian format embraced a system of coaching qualifications at different levels: the Preliminary, Intermediate and Advanced certificates – an arrangement which was subsequently modified to a 4-tiered award structure. The Rothman's Coaching Plan produced a manual which, like the *MCC Cricket Coaching Book*, redefined the techniques of the sport, suggested group activities and modified games as valuable coaching methods and was backed by visual aids. Unfortunately the independence of State Cricket Associations made it impractical for the Australian Board of Control to impose on its members a uniform coaching policy, suitable for all. The Queensland Cricket Association would argue that a coaching seminar which is well suited to Sydney inner suburban clubs is totally inappropriate in Mount Isa where the lecturer has to fly more than a thousand miles from the state capital, Brisbane, and potential coaches have to travel long distances to participate. Directors of Coaching were appointed in Western Australia (Len Pavy), Victoria (Frank Tyson), South Australia (Ernie Clifton), Queensland (Tom Veivers) and New South Wales (Peter Spence). But this did not lessen the magnitude of Brian Taber's problem of maintaining a national coaching standard in states and centres which were sometimes separated by a continent of 3,000 miles. Even the conduct of an Advanced Coaching Certificate course each year in a different state capital did not bridge the standards gap or overcome the geographical problem of the national scheme.

The Rothman's National Sports Foundation recognized its lack of centralized authority when it stated in its coaching manual:

This is the key to the National Coaching Plan: that full co-operation between Cricket Associations, clubs and schools will produce not only a great upsurge in interest in the game but also better and many more cricketers.

This sentence is virtually a plea for co-operation in the coaching plan.

In Victoria, substantial financial aid for coaching came in 1975 from government sources. Shocked by the revelations of the State Association's Development Committee survey and a further census taken two years later, the Victorian Cricket Association appointed a full-time Director of Coaching. They were assisted in making the appointment by a subsidy from the State Department of Youth, Sport and Recreation, who provided 50% of the Director's salary and coaching expenses. The grant duly arrived – but with a barb in its tail: the government would not co-sponsor any coaching scheme with a tobacco company such as Rothman's. The government subsidy was substantial and could not be rejected. So Victoria passed out of the Rothman's Coaching Plan and the national scheme became as much fragmented in physical fact as it was in philosophy and operation.

In some ways Victoria's secession acted as a catalyst for the improvement of teaching in the sport. The instigation of a breakaway coaching plan caused fresh initiatives to be taken and painstaking investigations to be conducted at a high level.

Because both philosophical and physical differences are to be found within the Australian coaching camp, it is not to be assumed that they are permanent breaches. A meeting of State Directors of Coaching in 1979 recommended to the Australian Cricket Board that coaching courses within the country be standardized and that a National Coaching Committee be established to advise the Board on the maintenance and improvement of coaching. These decisions anticipated an initiative on the part of the Australian government, aimed at raising the performances of athletes in international competition by the injection of expertise into the coaching community. Moves are afoot to establish a Coaches' National Accreditation Scheme to train and accredit coaches in all sports. Government support for sporting associations seems likely to hinge upon the recognition and approval of training programmes by the Australian Coaching Council and its expert arm, the Technical Committee. With such a powerful ally as the government in the offing, the Australian Cricket Board is anxious to set its house in order. It remains to be seen whether any government can court unpopularity by condoning the support given to sport by tobacco and alcohol companies.

Government moves to train and recognize the increasingly professional status of coaches within the sporting community indicate that the scepticism with which Australian sportsmen and women formerly regarded coaching is giving way to approval. An indication of this are the indoor coaching centres that are mushrooming throughout the country. The Melbourne metropolitan area alone boasts ten such centres. The former Queensland opening batsman Sam Trimble operates an indoor school on Brisbane's Woolongabba Test Ground. The England all-rounder Barry Knight, is in a similar line of business in Sydney, whilst Norman O'Neill conducts the indoor nets on the Western Australian Cricket Association ground in conjunction with his son, Mark. South Australia have the only indoor complex owned by the State Cricket Association.

In spite of all this, though, the future of coaching in Australia may bear out the truth of a recent saying of one of this country's political leaders that: 'life was not meant to be easy.' Obstacles, however, were intended to be overcome and there is no doubt that a cohesive coaching system in Australia is not too far away.

FRANK TYSON

Ashraful Haq: 7 for 23 for Bangladesh against Fiji, May 1979, in the ICC Trophy.

Bangladesh

Fertile, but poor, Bangladesh straddles the estuary of the River Ganges. It is a country of almost 100 million people crowded into an area not much larger than that of the British Isles. As part of the old Indian province of Bengal it has long been associated with cricket. After partition, East Pakistan developed its own identity, and the first team from England to tour there was the MCC 'A' team which played at both Chittagong and Dacca in the early part of 1956 under the captaincy of Donald Carr, now the Secretary of the Test and County Cricket Board. On a matting pitch at Dacca the full Pakistan XI, not too dissimilar from the team which had defeated England at the Oval in 1954, beat this MCC side by an innings. Thereafter the matting wicket was replaced by grass and on a surface composed of rolled mud results have ever since been much harder to achieve.

In 1973 after a bloody war of independence, Muslim Bengal declared independence and faced with the problems of survival the new government of Bangladesh found itself with more urgent priorities than the furtherance of cricket. Early in 1975 the stadium in Dacca, the focal point of the entire sprawling capital city, was in such disrepair that the cricket square had sunk several inches after years of disuse. The first cricketing visitor to Dacca after Independence found a shell-torn Press Club and a Russian delegation discussing football in the single office which served as the cultural department of the Ministry of Education. Bengalis were very conscious that the only inhabitants of East Pakistan to have made the Pakistan Test side were either those posted from the west or else Muslim immigrants from the Indian state of Bihar.

Following the murder of Abdul Rahman, called the father of Bangladesh, a military regime was established which determined to revive cricket. The students and former students of Dacca University were amongst those who welcomed this encouragement and if the government saw cricket as a safety valve for youthful enthusiasm their judgment was not misplaced. During the weeks of Christmas and the New Year of 1976–77 an MCC team under the captaincy of Brian Taylor, a former captain of Essex and Test selector, toured the country playing four matches. The only result came on a matting wicket at Chittagong where the touring side won by an innings. The significant feature of the tour was the attendance of well over 40,000 during the three days of the representative match at Dacca. The next foray into international competition saw Sri Lanka victorious in Bangladesh. In 1978–79 an MCC team paid a second visit after a gap of only 2 years thus indicating its care for cricket worldwide. All three of the unofficial Test matches were drawn.

By this time the new nation had been welcomed into the international cricket community as an associate member and as such took part in the ICC Trophy, featuring 24 nations, which was the prelude to the Prudential World Cup competition of 1979. Playing in the second of the three groups of 5, out of which two semi-finalists Denmark and Canada emerged, Bangladesh had to be content with 3rd place after losing a match they felt they should have won to Denmark by 9 runs with 7 balls remaining. During a competition afflicted by wet weather, their offspin bowler, Ashraful Haq, achieved the bowling performance of the competition by taking 7–23 against Fiji. As a young all-rounder Ashraful Haq had been a member of the Pakistan Colts squad prior to independence.

The Bangladeshis are ambitious to win a place in the final rounds of the World Cup. Their problem in fielding a balanced team is akin to that faced by India: Bengalis, traditionally short of stature, do not make great fast bowlers. Nor does the tradition of drawn matches help in the long run. Easy-paced wickets which show little sign of wear are a help in bringing young batsman up to a certain level of excellence, but they afford poor experience for occasions on which the ball moves both in the air and off the wicket. Unlike the Pakistanis, who devoted considerable resources to the development of an outstanding national cricket XI by the use of a crash programme of tours such as those by the Eaglets, in a tougher economic world the Bangladeshis do not have ready access to foreign exchange.

Nonetheless from Jessore in the West, where MCC banqueted in the same circuit house used by Lord Lytton, the first Viceroy a century before, to Chittagong in the East and Sialkhot in the North, Bangladeshis can be relied upon to attend good cricket in their thousands at the well-appointed stadia mostly built during their East Pakistan period. The potential exists for thousands to play cricket. Given help, encouragement and experience, Bangladesh has a better chance than most associate members of the ICC of playing host to a full Test series before the end of the 20th century.

ROBIN MARLAR

Belgium

Cricket has been played in and around Brussels for many years. The earliest quoted example, as recorded in *Wisden*, was of a match played in 1815 before the Battle of Waterloo by the officers of the Brigade of Guards (an event which was commemorated 150 years later by a match played between the Brussels Club and the Household Brigade – which ended in a tie).

Evidence that the Brussels Cricket Club existed as early as 1866 may be seen in the pavilion at Lord's where there hangs a water colour, painted in 1870, of the 'Vallon des Anglais, Brussels, seen looking N.E., the ground of the Brussels Cricket Club opened by the Bourgmestre of Brussels in 1866'. The earliest original document in the hands of the present club is a printed leaflet bearing the names of the club's officers for 1885 – together with other details of the times of play, membership subscriptions, etc.

The following dates mark some of the milestones in the club's more recent history:

1954 The presently accepted individual performance records and team records date from this year.

1967 Brussels CC v Hampshire CCC, 10 September, at the Brussels Home Ground, then at the Royal Rasante Tennis and Hockey Club. Hampshire made 285–6 declared and Brussels, batting 12, were all out for exactly 100 in reply. The best Brussels performance was by the present Club Chairman, Ted Vorzanger, who took 2 wickets for 32 runs and was Brussels top scorer with 30.

1972 The Home Ground moved from that of the Rasante Club to the British School of Brussels, at Tervuren. The Rt Hon Edward Heath, then UK Prime Minister, became its first honorary Patron.

1973 A gala match was held at Tervuren between Brussels CC and Whitbread Wanderers, the latter featuring a number of well-known test and first-class players.

1975 The Club's Home Ground moved once more – this time from the British School to its present site at Blanden which is also the ground of the Royal Hockey Club Louvain.

1977 HM King Baudouin bestowed upon the Club the honour of becoming '*une société royale*' – hence the present name: Royal Brussels Cricket Club.

J. L. STORR-BEST

Belize

Until it changed its name on 1 June 1973, the territory now called Belize was British Honduras and was the only British possession in Central America. It has survived through its cricket history very much by its own efforts and with the minimum of encouragement from overseas sides. With a population predominantly 'Belize creole', there are only small cricketing communities in the larger towns, though the game has been played for well over a hundred years. The Belize Wanderers Cricket Club, which first flourished in the 1880s, has remained the leading side in the country and was the forerunner of a large number of clubs which grew up principally in the decade before the First World War.

Sides from Jamaica visited British Honduras in 1936, 1951, 1961 and 1962, after which a return visit was paid by the British Hondurans. The greatest event in the colony's cricket history, however, was the visit of MCC in April 1960, at the conclusion of the tour of West Indies. The 2 matches at Belize hardly extended the English cricketers – who were captained in their second game by their manager, Walter Robins – but over 4,000 turned up on each day to watch. The principal venue for the game has always been at Newtown Barracks in Belize.

IRVING ROSENWATER

Bermuda

The earliest recorded matches in Bermuda date back to the 1840s – the Garrison there lost to another army side by 3 wickets on 30 August 1844. By 1845 the Bermuda Cricket Club had been established and the game was being played regularly not only by the Garrison and Royal Navy but by local Bermudians as well; indeed, the game was described as 'a favorite amusement in Bermuda' as early as February 1846. During the remainder of the 19th century many clubs sprang up all over Bermuda, though because of the lack of opportunity in meeting strong visiting teams the colony's cricket made no great advance. The first international encounter came in March, 1891, when the Philadelphia Zingari visited Bermuda and played 3 matches against the Garrison. Although the tourists included several well-known cricketers, the Bermuda players remained undefeated and sowed the seeds of a cricketing friendship between Philadelphia and Bermuda that was to see its full flowering in the decade before the First World War.

In 1905 the first touring team – the Hamilton CC – left Bermuda to play one game in New York and six in Philadelphia. Only one game was won, but the Philadelphians were sufficiently impressed to undertake tours to Bermuda in 1907, 1908, 1910, 1911 and 1912, the Americans – J. B. King, H. V. Hordern, C. C. Morris and others notwithstanding – by no means having things all their own way. In fact they lost more matches in Bermuda than they won. In 1911 a second touring side left Bermuda – this time representative of the whole colony – and won 3 of its 5 matches on the unfamiliar wickets of Philadelphia. These were the prosperous days of Bermuda's cricket, when the brothers J. R. and G. C. Conyers and the giant T. St G. Gilbert often dealt disaster to opposing sides. In both 1912 and 1913 powerful Australian teams visited Bermuda, creating enormous enthusiasm.

Although domestic cricket in the islands continued to be played with undiminished fervour, the national strength of Bermuda declined sharply after the First World War. Tours were undertaken to America and Canada, and occasional West Indian sides visited Bermuda, but such tours had only local significance. The greatest highlight between the wars was the visit to Bermuda of Sir Julien Cahn's side in September, 1933, after matches in Canada and the United States. The five matches played on the Prospect ground were spoken of for years, and the two final matches saw the visitors very close to defeat. Like many visitors before and since they found it hard to adjust their game to matting stretched over concrete, on which nearly all cricket in Bermuda is played.

Less spectacular tours both to and from Bermuda – but not by English sides – continued until the Second World War.

Bermuda's team for the ICC Trophy, 1979: standing: C. Blades, W. Weldon, P. Caines, E. James, C. Parfitt, N. Gibbons, E. Decouto and J. Bailey; sitting: R. L. Smith (secretary), Winston Trott, Winston Reid, Rupert Irvine Scotland (manager), Gladstone Brown (captain), John Tucker, Lionel Thomas, and L. Tucker (treasurer).

Thereafter, enthusiasm to meet overseas sides gained such rapid pace that there has been a positive spate of cricket activity by Bermudians over the last quarter of a century. Many teams from the West Indies have visited the islands, and in December, 1953, an MCC side (on their way to the West Indies) played in Bermuda for the first time. E. W. Swanton's team which visited the West Indies in 1956 stopped for a game in Bermuda on their return journey. Since then, several Test sides – from England, Australia, New Zealand and Pakistan – have played there, the match at Hamilton against New Zealand in April 1972 being accorded first-class status.

The first Bermudian team to visit England was in 1960, a tour originated by W. F. ('Chummy') Hayward, MBE, for several decades now a powerful and respected force in Bermudian cricket as administrator and benefactor. He organized further tours to England in 1962 and 1978, to Canada in 1966 and 1970, and to the Bahamas in 1977. Throughout this period competitive cricket within Bermuda itself was manifested principally in the Somers Isles Cricket League and the various counties' competitions.

Central to the cricket life of Bermuda is the annual Cup Match. First played in 1902, this meeting of the two leading clubs of the islands – Somerset and St George's – is the turbulent highlight of each season, when feverish crowds of up to 15,000 watch in an atmosphere of carnival and colour on days that have been declared a public holiday by the Governor in Council. It is the sporting and social event of the year, and not even two world wars could bring a halt in the sequence of games.

The best cricketer produced by Bermuda is Alma Hunt, an all-rounder who played with some success in a trial match in 1933 in Trinidad prior to the selection of the West Indian side for England. Bermuda has never been geographically part of the West Indies, and on this score confusion arose as to the eligibility of Hunt, and he was not chosen – but he later made his mark as an outstanding professional with Aberdeenshire and indeed played for Scotland.

In 1966 Bermuda were admitted as associate members of the ICC, and it was their representative, Alma Hunt, who first proposed a tournament among the minor ICC countries that saw fruition in 1979 in the ICC Trophy in England, in which Bermuda participated with much distinction.

IRVING ROSENWATER

Brazil

The history of Brazilian cricket is the history of several clubs. In widely separated parts of this vast and rugged country, where transport and communications between the large centres of industry and commerce were extremely difficult before the age of the aeroplane, cricket clubs sprang up wherever Britons congregated in the growing towns along the eastern seaboard during the second half of the 19th century, when coffee was introduced into Brazil. Some of the clubs have long since disappeared; others, having lost most of their British members, have converted to other sports; a few, however, have survived the passage of time because they are situated in or near the two great cities, Rio de Janeiro and Sao Paulo.

The first reports of cricket games taking place in Rio are to be found in the Brazilian press in the early 1870s. There is no record of results, but the founding of the Rio Cricket Club on 15 August 1872 definitely establishes the existence of organized games. The ground was in the Rua Paysandú, at the foot of the stone quarry. The Emperor of Brazil, Dom Pedro II, and family were constant visitors at cricket matches and sports meetings. In 1898 the club set up where the Rio Cricket and Athletic Association play today.

The present Sao Paulo Athletic Club was formed in 1882, thanks to the initiative of William Fox Rule, and played at Ponte Pequeno, beyond the River Tieté, to which transportation was by one-mule tram. In 1892 an Argentine team visited Sao Paulo, only to see 12 days of continual rain, and not a ball was bowled – surely a record for international tours. In 1899 the club moved to its present grounds in the Rua Visconde de Ouro Preto but, because the club grew so quickly, the cricket ground had to be moved and after various changes settled in Santo Amaro, where the matches are still played, albeit on coconut matting.

The Santos Athletic club was founded in 1890. From a humble beginning the club developed into the rallying centre of the British colony in the coffee port of Santos. The ground is a delightful one and the pavilion, built in the later 1920s, is one of the best of its kind in Brazil. Other centres where cricket flourishes in Brazil are Morro Velho, Barretos and Recife.

In 1908 the Portuguese Minister, Conde de Selir, presented a trophy for an Inter-State competition which pitted the best players from the state of Rio de Janeiro against the best from Sao Paulo and Santos. By 1930 the influx of cricketers from England to other cities in Brazil had increased the interest in this important fixture, so the Brazilian Cricket Association donated a cup to be played for by Rio and North v Sao Paulo and South over a 3-day period once a year. But it was against Argentina that Brazil found its strongest and most consistent challenge. After 40 years of exchanging tours, a British businessman, 'Bing' Norris, gave the first cup. For 21 years Argentina reigned supreme until, in the last match played (February 1978), in an astounding reversal of fortunes and against incredible odds, Brazil regained the Norris Cup.

K. E. BRIDGER

Brunei

This independent Sultanate has had to depend on external stimulus for matches. These are against neighbouring British North Borneo (now Sabah) and Sarawak. In 1968 it lost to Sabah in the Borneo Championship. Unlike Sabah and Sarawak, which have been integrated into Malaysia, the Brunei State Cricket Association has not moved over into that country's regular Inter-State competition.

PHILIP SNOW

Burma

Cricket in Burma has had a precarious existence. F. S. Ashley-Cooper in his *Cricket Highways and Byways* says that

> cricket of a kind was played there in 1824, when British troops took Rangoon. Subsequently, there was much military cricket in the country, and even King Thebaw came partly under the fascination of the game. In 1869 and 1870 he and eight of his brothers were at a school at Mandalay kept by Dr Marles, a well-known missionary, and whilst there he batted fairly well, but refused to do his share of fielding, and was in the habit of using very injurious language to anyone who bowled him.

Although there have been some XIs composed entirely of Burmese players, cricket has been mostly the preserve of British expatriates and local Indians. Two prominent sides have been BAA and Rangoon Gymkhana; amongst their players before the Second War were W. B. Giles and Hubert Ashton. Knock-out tournaments were arranged for the Rowe Oriental Shield, no less than 34 teams participating in the first competition after the Second War.

There have been tours to Burma by sides from Ceylon (as it was then), Pakistan and India, as well as a visit by the MCC team that went to India in 1926–27. Sir Julien Cahn's team also visited in 1937. Burmese sides have toured Thailand, Malaysia and Singapore.

The Burmese Cricket Federation was established in 1947,

although since Burma divested herself of colonial status in 1948, and then became a Socialist Republic in 1962, cricket there has suffered from a lack of facilities and outside inspiration.

DAVID RAYVERN ALLEN

Canada

The first known reference to cricket in Canada was made concerning a game played at Ile Ste-Helene in Montreal in the year 1785. The site of this historic match is where the Montreal Exposition buildings now stand. The roots of Canadian cricket spring mainly from the regions of Upper Canada and in particular around the little town of York, later to become known as Toronto. The game was played by the British military and was introduced to garrison towns from the early days of the 19th century. During the 1820s cricket was encouraged and nurtured in York by George A. Barber, generally considered to be the father of Canadian cricket. Barber, who was publisher of the *Toronto Herald* and a master at Upper Canada College, was a founder of the Toronto Cricket Club in 1827 and also played a large part in introducing cricket into the college. In 1834 the first match of which there is any record took place in Hamilton between Toronto and Guelph and we have the full scores of a match between the same teams in Guelph which took place on 15 August 1835. It was Barber who instigated the historic series between the Toronto Cricket Club and Upper Canada College in 1836. These matches are still played annually and through the years both clubs have turned out a host of talented cricketers who have gone on to represent their country.

In 1844 Canada and the United States met in their first international. This was over 30 years before the famed England v Australia series began and historians believe the contest is the oldest international sporting fixture in the world. George Parr of Notts brought the first touring team to Canada from England in 1859, and although the tourists were far too strong for the locals the visit was a great success, becoming the first cricket tour in history. During these years of healthy cricket activity in the east, the game was spreading rapidly in the west. In 1864 the North West Cricket Club was formed at Winnipeg and in 1876 the famous Victoria Cricket Club was formed on the west coast. Cricket had already been played in both areas prior to the formation of these two clubs, but the game was now beginning to take hold in the west and as a result the sport was played from coast to coast.

By the time Canada became a nation in 1867, the game was so popular it was declared the national sport of the fledgling country by the first Prime Minister, Sir John A. MacDonald and his Cabinet. In 1872 the third English touring side arrived including none other than the immortal Dr. W. G. Grace, who lived up to his reputation by scoring a magnificent 142 against Toronto. 1874 was the year of the first Halifax tournament which was won by Philadelphia. This tournament was repeated in 1875 and 1892.

The first Australian team to tour Canada was the 1878 side led by W. L. Murdoch. It included such greats as Charlie Bannerman, Fred Spofforth, Dave Gregory, and John Blackham. In a match played at Montreal, Bannerman scored 125. It will be remembered he made 165 retired hurt in the first Test match at Melbourne in 1877. A weak Canadian side toured England in 1880, then in 1887 the first major tour was undertaken by an all Canadian-born team. The side toured England under the captaincy of Dr E. R. Ogden and took on several of the counties on level terms. The team far from disgraced itself, recording wins over Ireland, Derbyshire, Warwickshire, and Leicester. In 1905 and 1907 MCC teams made brief tours to the USA and Canada.

During the 1890s the Canada v USA matches surged to a new popularity with the emergence of the great American all-rounder Bart King. For 20 years King dominated cricket on the North American continent and large crowds flocked to see him perform. His achievements with bat and ball are legendary. He humbled the best batsmen of England and Australia and in 1909 took all 10 wickets clean bowled for America in an international against Ireland. Three years earlier, in 1906, he scored a mammoth 344 not out for Belmont against Merion to set a North American batting record which still stands.

Assiniboine Park, Winnipeg; the cricket pavilion in the background.

With the growth of baseball and coming of the First World War the fortunes of cricket waned. The international series with America ceased in 1912 and 20 years were to elapse before another major cricket tour of the country took place. In 1932 the Australians arrived under the captaincy of Victor Y. Richardson, grandfather of the famous Chappell brothers. The tour was most successful despite the ravages of the great depression. In a match against Western Ontario at Guelph, Don Bradman, the wonder of the age, scored 260 not out. This innings still stands as the highest individual score in Canadian cricket.

In 1935 the first tour to England by a Colts side was successfully carried out and repeated in 1937 and 1939. Also in 1939 an English Public Schools side was touring Canada when war broke out. In 1936 R. C. Mathews led a Canadian side to England for a very successful tour by a senior side which included Lew Gunn, later to become Chairman of the Canadian Cricket Association, and the brothers Bell, Clark and Billy. In 1937 G. C. Newman led an MCC side on an extensive tour of Canada playing 19 matches and losing only 1.

After the Second World War tours again became popular, as they had been many years before, and teams from overseas reappeared with a visit from MCC, led by R. W. V. Robins, in 1951. In 1954 H. B. O. Robinson led Canada on a successful visit to England in which matches were played against first-class counties, the MCC and Pakistan. 1957 marked the resumption of colts' tours to England on a biennial basis which continues to this day. In fact 1979 was the first time this sequence was broken because Canada hosted the 3rd International Youth Festival in Toronto which included under-19 teams from Holland, Denmark, Ireland, Bermuda and two from the UK. In 1958 Pakistan played a single match against Canada in Toronto at Varsity Stadium.

In 1963 the Canada v USA international series was resumed at Toronto and has been played each year on Labour Day weekend (the first weekend in September) since that date. 1968 saw the Yorkshire County Cricket Club tour Canada. In 1973 Kent County Cricket Club and Ireland visited Canada and in

The ICC Trophy, 1979: Jitendra Patel bowling for Canada.

1974 Denmark. Canada went to the UK in 1974 and to the Windward and Leeward Islands in 1976. Australia played 4 matches in Canada on their way to the first Prudential World Cup in 1975 and Canada gained world attention when the Eastern Canada side beat Australia by 5 wickets in Toronto.

Canada duly entered in 1979 the first ICC Trophy Competition for associate members and became runners-up in the competition to Sri Lanka. To get to the final of the ICC Trophy, Canada defeated Malaysia, Bangladesh and Fiji, losing only to Denmark. In the semi-final they defeated Bermuda. Sri Lanka defeated Denmark in the other semi-final. Canada were then placed in a group with Pakistan, Australia, and England. While they lost all three matches, the team played with confidence and put up good performances against Pakistan and Australia. So in the space of four weeks Canada played international matches against 9 countries, more than we had played throughout our history. The success of Canada's performance in this competition certainly raised the status of Canada's cricket ability in the eyes of the International Cricket Conference. In the 60-over one-day competition of the World Cup, Canada can claim to be 8th in the World.

In conclusion I must say a word about administration. In the latter years of the 19th century, provincial and national bodies were formed to control the game. 1880 saw Ontario form the first provincial association and on 29 March 1892 the Canadian Cricket Association was first formed. We know of a North-Western Cricket Association headed by Arthur A. Morrison in 1912 and by Dr W. E. Dean, President of the Canadian Cricket Association, in the same year. However, this body was basically an eastern Canadian organization. Its constitution was revised in 1912. In 1934 work began on revising the national organization under the chairmanship of the Hon R. C. Matthews and this resulted in a revised constitution being completed 15 April 1940. Due to the war the new organization was finally adopted on 29 July 1949.

On 1 April 1968 the Canadian Cricket Association was incorporated and in 1972 major amendments were made to the By-Laws creating a Board of Directors of 10, 1 to be President, 7 representing individual provinces and 2 at large. In 1979 the provinces represented were British Columbia, Alberta, Saskatchewan, Manitoba, Ontario, Quebec, and Nova Scotia. In the 1970s a gradual expansion of work was adopted, much of it in conjunction with the evolution of the National Sport and Recreation Centre in Ottawa. Federal Government financing enabled the CCA to carry out plans that were not even contemplated in the 1960s. More tours were arranged and coaching was given a high priority.

Canadian cricket grounds are found in public parks in the cities of Victoria, Vancouver, Edmonton, Calgary, Regina, Saskatoon, Winnipeg, London, Woodstock, Hamilton, Toronto, Ottawa, Montreal and Halifax. High-school grounds are now being used more often. There is little doubt that the playing grounds are one of the most serious problems facing all cricketing areas. Fortunately some standardization occurred during the 1960s due to the efforts of that great worker for Canadian cricket, the late Donald King, who introduced the Haydite shale pitch upon which Corotex matting is laid. While some centres use clay, concrete or grass as a base, the shale wicket has proved to be very practical for the Canadian climate. The advantages of shale are minimal maintenance and quick drainage after heavy rainstorms. Turf pitches have become almost non-existent mainly due to the lack of experience in preparation plus the high cost of maintenance.

Since the Second World War, cricket has gone through some radical expansions. The decision to hold an Inter-Provincial Tournament in 1947 in Calgary brought life back into the game after the hardships of the war years when cricket was severely weakened. Through the 1950s heavy immigration from the United Kingdom created a healthy expansion of the game lasting into the mid-1960s. In the late 1960s, a new immigration trend from the West Indies, India and Pakistan and in the 1970s from Uganda created a new era in Canadian cricket leading to a steady expansion. From 100 clubs in 1965 there were 230 teams operating in 1979 in 12 leagues in 7 provinces from Victoria to Halifax, as follows:

Province	*League*
British Columbia	Victoria and District
	BC Mainland
Alberta	Edmonton
	Calgary
Saskatchewan	Saskatchewan Cricket Association
Manitoba	Manitoba Cricket Association
Ontario	Southern Ontario Cricket Association
	Hamilton and District Cricket League
	Toronto and District Cricket Association
	Ottawa Valley Cricket Council
Quebec	Quebec Cricket Council
Nova Scotia	Nova Scotia Cricket Association

Junior cricket is operating in organized leagues in Victoria, Vancouver, Edmonton, Calgary and Toronto thus providing the feeder system to develop the cricketers of tomorrow.

KENNETH R. BULLOCK

Cayman Islands

Wherever the British flag has proudly waved there is cricket, and the Cayman Islands, one of the few territories of the British West Indies which has not become independent, are in this respect no exception. They are the most remote of all the Caribbean islands, lying 150 miles south of Cuba and 178 miles north west of Jamaica. These distances refer to the largest island, Grand Cayman, the only one where cricket is played.

Unlike most other West Indian communities, the population of Grand Cayman is of very heterogeneous descent (over 50% were accredited with 'mixed racial origin' at the last census). Since tourism and its tax-haven status opened up the island cricket has started to develop.

Until a few years ago it was played only on a stretch of wasteland, which also served as a football pitch, with a concrete strip down the middle. That field has recently been abandoned in favour of a site right alongside the air strip – the only reason it has not been used for building is its proximity to the runway. The Smith Road Oval has, therefore, taken over as the one home of cricket on Grand Cayman (it doubles as an athletics stadium as well). The pitch is excellent, consisting of a firm base of imported Jamaican clay, overlaid by a thin sack matting, but the facilities generally are inadequate. Seven teams compete every year, between April and September, for the Cricket Association Shield, *i.e.* the national league, and a six-a-side knock-out competition. The 7 teams are United, Police, School, Printers, West Bay, By-Rite and the Carlsberg Cavaliers (formerly the Heineken 'Greenies'). Most successful recently have been Printers, champions in 1977, and By-Rite, who won the shield in 1978. The Caymanian has never been as disposed to cricket as the natives of many of the other British West Indian islands. Without exception, the best cricketers on the island are immigrants, mainly from Barbados, Jamaica, Guyana and Britain. From time to time a Cayman Islands representative team is selected, for a tour or to provide strong opposition for a visiting side, but hardly ever is a Caymanian cricketer considered. Recently an overall controlling body, The Cayman Islands Cricket Association, came into being. Tours abroad are very sporadic, although exotic. Recent visits have been paid to Houston, Texas, Nassau, in The Bahamas, and the Turks and Caicos Islands. Visits by foreign clubs to Grand Cayman are also rare: the De Kieviten club from The Netherlands were the last team to take on the Caymanians on their own soil.

D. J. HARDY

Chile

Cricket has been played in Chile at various times, from Iquique in the North to Punta Arenas in the extreme South, but it is at Valparaiso that it has been played most consistently. The earliest record of cricket being played in Chile appears in *Memoirs of General Miller*, published in 1829: 'A match of cricket between the officers of the *Andromache* and those of HMS *Blossom* led to the establishment of a club, the members of which met twice a week and dined under canvas'.

The first known match to be played by a Valparaiso XI took place in 1863. Their first visit to Santiago was in 1870 and to Concepción about 1890, while Iquique paid their first visit to Valparaiso about that time. As in the case of those other three centres, the heyday of Valparaiso cricket was in the 1920s. The game was played in Iquique from the late 1860s, when the nitrate industry was opened up by British capital and enterprise. It thrived during the nitrate boom until the crisis of 1931. Games were also played against Antofagasta, Valparaiso and teams from Royal Navy visiting ships. After the Second World War interest waned, mainly – as it had done in other centres where it once flourished – because the British colony had dwindled, and the Chilean has never taken to the game. Cricket is now kept going at the Prince of Wales Country Club in Santiago by a small band of enthusiasts who enjoy the privilege of playing in what must be unique surroundings, as the ground is at the very foot of the Andes, with snow-capped peaks towering 20,000 feet above it.

K. E. BRIDGER

Commonwealth Tours

The conception of Commonwealth tours, to bring together players of more than one country on an overseas venture, first materialized in 1949–50. In that season it had been hoped in India that an MCC side would visit that country for the first time since 1933–34, but when it was known that such a visit would not be possible, the experiment of a 'mixed' side – at that time unique – was launched. A Commonwealth Team consisting of Englishmen, Australians and West Indians, in the main prominent in the Lancashire leagues, banded together under the managership of George Duckworth to give India some consolation for the absence of MCC. The late A. S. de Mello, then President of the Indian Board of Control, made the major arrangements for the tour, which was to take in India, Pakistan and Ceylon. The side on this pioneering tour was all professional. The whole venture was only possible because of the presence in England of many capable cricketers from many parts of the Commonwealth whose professional duties ended in September.

Before the Second World War, quite apart from the greater travelling difficulties which existed, such a situation did not obtain in the leagues. In 1949, however, there were such men as F. M. Worrell, C. G. Pepper, W. E. Alley and G. E. Tribe, who grouped together with some of their fellow and English cricketers under the captaincy of L. Livingston. Pessimists forecast failure, especially as many of the players had not previously known each other and the strong sense of nationalism, fostered by frequent Test Matches, was expected to keep the players 'apart'. In the event, all fears proved groundless, and the success of the tour served as a prototype for future Commonwealth ventures. Another trip to India was arranged for the following season and a third for 1953–54. Duckworth managed all three and Frank Worrell went with him each time. Among some of the famous cricketers who took part in these early Commonwealth tours were L. E. G. Ames, R. E. Marshall, J. C. Laker, W. A. Johnston, B. A. Barnett, S. Ramadhin, P. J. Loader, R. T. Simpson, D. Shackleton and R. Subba Row.

Although official tours were taking up a large part of the time and energy of leading players, by October 1959, the pattern for Commonwealth tours had been set. In that month the Transvaal Cricket Union received an attractive side under the captaincy of Denis Compton which included players who had learnt their cricket in England, Australia, New Zealand and the West Indies. That tour was managed by R. A. Roberts, one of cricket's most widely travelled writers, who later negotiated and managed 5 further Commonwealth tours. None was more ambitious than that of early 1962 when some 40,000 miles were covered in eight weeks by players from England, Australia, South Africa, West Indies, Pakistan, India, Rhodesia and East Africa – the team playing in Nairobi, Rhodesia, Pakistan, New Zealand, India and Hong Kong. Many of the world's most illustrious players took part in these tours, the captains including R. Benaud, T. W. Graveney, Ray Lindwall and Everton Weekes. Many centres which would not normally have the opportunity of seeing such players were given a thrilling glimpse of masters in action, and consistently spirited play always ensured such ventures a genuine success. Even the Greek island of Corfu was included in one itinerary.

The former Surrey and England fast bowler, A. R. Gover, raised and managed two Commonwealth teams to the Indian sub-continent, both captained by P. E. Richardson. The first, to Pakistan at the end of 1963, drew some 400,000 spectators for the three representative matches alone, some brilliant play being shown by Kanhai, Graveney, d'Oliveira and Butcher. A year later Gover took a Commonwealth side to Calcutta to celebrate the 75th anniversary of the Mohun Bagan Club, and among the tourists were M. C. Cowdrey, L. R. Gibbs, Mushtaq Mohammad and Garfield Sobers. Such tours as these – some comprising a mere 2 matches and some well over a dozen – soon became a regular feature of the international programme. Alex Bannister, the journalist, managed a Commonwealth side to Pakistan, captained by R. Benaud, early in 1968; and sides under a variety of names – such as Cavaliers and International Wanderers – have toured the West Indies and South Africa. Prominent among these have been the enterprises of Derrick Robins (*qv*). With the proliferation in recent years of Test cricket, though, the opportunities for extended Commonwealth tours are not what they once were.

IRVING ROSENWATER

Corfu

Playing cricket on Corfu is a rare experience. The pitch is matting on concrete, the outfield sporting, the surroundings outstandingly beautiful and the crowd partisan and knowledgeable – if the volume of words that pour out is anything to go by.

Cricket and ginger beer are the two remaining legacies of the British, who introduced the sport after the Napoleonic wars, and the appeal of the game to the Corfiots has survived two World Wars. In the early days they mainly played teams from the British Mediterranean Fleet. After the Second World War the British Military Mission in Corfu re-established the game and in 1962 an International XI, organized by the late Ron Roberts and including Colin Ingleby-Mackenzie, Wes Hall, Rohan Kanhai, Basil d'Oliveira and Bill Alley, placed Corfu firmly on the cricketing map.

From the late 1960s, British Airways and *The Cricketer* have been bringing teams every year for an annual Cricket Festival in September, and the season has been lengthened with many matches from clubs not only from Britain but from The Netherlands, Italy and Malta. Seven years ago the Anglo-Corfiot Cricket Association was formed with Lord Orr-Ewing as president. Thanks to many of these visitors the local sides are much better equipped and the standard has greatly improved. Members of ACCA have sponsored Corfiot players on a coaching course at Lilleshall and had the Laws of Cricket translated into Greek, as well as entertaining and arranging matches for Corfiot sides visiting this country.

The Corfiot approach gives the game a unique charm. 'Where else', Henry Blofeld has written, 'would one find a game of 33 overs a side? Where else would the umpire call 'no ball' some seconds after the batsman's stumps have been knocked over? Where else do spectators sit in comfortably armed chairs under acacia trees drinking ouzo the while, and where else are games of cricket finished in moonlight?'

The ground is the square in the centre of Corfu town in front of the old Greek royal palace, stretching out from the shops and cafés to the splendid medieval castle at the sea's edge and on 3 sides the playing area is increased by 20 yards of tarmac car park: a 4 is scored whenever a ball goes under a car.

There are 3 local clubs – Byron, Gymnastikos and Phaeax, the latter formed in 1977 to help bring on younger players. The game is controlled by the Corfu Cricket Technical Committee of SEGAS and receives some financial aid from the Greek Ministry of Sport. Visiting teams over the last 10 years have included several British naval vessels, as well as the Brandy-cask XI, Old Citizens' XI, the Eton Ramblers, the Jaipur Wanderers, Knotty Green CC, the Lord's Taverners, the Dutch club De Flamingos and the Little Aston Stragglers, as well as regular visits by Lord Orr-Ewing's XI, The Cricket Society, British Airways and *The Cricketer*, all of whom are represented on the ACCA committee.

B. G. BROCKLEHURST

The Esplanade, Corfu: a lingering look at the cricket.

Denmark

Nothing definite is on record as to when the game was introduced into Denmark, but it was mentioned in a *Collection of Gymnastic Games* in 1801 under the name of 'Gateball'. It is believed to have been played in a Copenhagen 'ball game club' in 1861, the members of which were Danes who had been to England and British railway engineers working in Denmark. The first officially recorded matches date from 1865 at Randers, in Jutland, and the two encounters in 1866 between Copenhagen and the Sorø Academy sides. In 1887 the first match of an international nature took place when the KB club of Copenhagen played a team drawn from the officers and men of the Prince of Wales's yacht, the *Osborne*, surprisingly won by the Danish team.

Only friendly matches had been played until this time, but by 1889 sufficient clubs existed over the country for the game to become incorporated into the 'Danish Ball Games Union' – an association dominated by football but including also lawn tennis. This led to regional tournaments the following year, when the Laws of Cricket were translated for the first time into Danish. The man behind the latter was the great advocate of cricket of the time, Lt-Col Hilarius Kalkau, who became President of the Union the next year. In 1890 organized tournaments began in Copenhagen and also, on a regional basis, in Jutland. Not until 1953, though, did the game succeed in breaking free from football; this was the year in which the Danish Cricket Association was founded and nationwide championships began.

Football's tendency to hold cricket back may be partly explained by the two sports overlapping. In many cases cricket is but a section of a football club and has to play second fiddle with regard to grounds. With so little cricket being played in the schools, it has to be fostered in the clubs. These number about 40.

After the First World War British teams began visiting Denmark more frequently. They included MCC, Leicester CC, Incogniti, Gentlemen of Worcestershire and Sir Julien Cahn's XI. The man behind many of these visits was R. P. Keigwin, who had shown a great interest in Danish cricket while living in Denmark. Following the Second War contacts spread chiefly through British services organizations in Germany, and these are maintained to this day. In 1954 the Oxford University side came to Denmark, including such players as Colin Cowdrey and M. J. K. Smith. This made a considerable impression, and in 1957 Cambridge followed.

Another important contact dated from 1947, which resulted in Holland's oldest club, UD, visiting Denmark the next year. In 1955 the first of the Continental 'Tests' between the two countries took place, at The Hague. The cup played for between the countries was in Dutch hands until 1972, in which year Denmark's most decisive breakthrough occurred. Denmark's next international victory was against Canada at Toronto in 1974, and this was followed the next year with an excellent win over East Africa, fresh from the Prudential Cup competition in England. In 1976 another good win was recorded in Denmark against an MCC side, and it was with

The Denmark team to England for the ICC Trophy, 1979: standing: H. Espensen, B. Rossen, O. B. Andersen, J. B. Andersen, C. Morild, jr., S. Thomsen, C. Morild, sr., M. Christensen (assistant manager); seated: O. Mortensen, H. Mortensen, K. Kristensen, K. Bus (captain), T. S. Nielsen, M. Petersson, and P. Hansen.

this background that the Danish national side prepared for its greatest adventure – the ICC Trophy competition of 1979 in England. Victories over Fiji, Malaysia, Canada and Bangladesh were well worth having.

Early individual players of note included Harald Hansen, a hitter, and the stylish Charles Buchwald, who scored 28 hundreds; later B. Pockendahl made 33 hundreds. The leg-break googly bowler, Louis Bronée, acquired a great reputation in the 1930s. It is also hardly possible to discuss Danish cricket without mentioning the Morild family, whose doyen, Thomas, played his last match in 1969 when 81. His eldest nephew, Axel, has scored most runs in Danish cricket, and history was made in 1955 when his son, Svend, fielded against Holland with his own son, Carsten, also in the side. Since then, Carsten's son, Claus, has repeated the feat with his father, for what is surely a world record.

The Danish team which played against MCC at Lord's in 1961 included the 3 young players, Henrik Mortensen, Hardy Sørensen and Klaus Buus, and it has been these who have formed the nucleus of the Danish side with Carsten Morild over the past generation.

With an absence of good outfields, a spectator public, and television publicity, the governing of the game poses a constant challenge in this amateur cricket country. With an active, home-grown coaching force now operating, however, it is hoped that the ICC Trophy successes of 1979 will give it a timely boost.

D. G. STEPTOE AND P. S. HARGREAVES

East Africa Cricket Conference

Inter-territorial matches, apart from Kenya v Uganda, developed relatively late – in the 1950s. In the same period, overseas teams invariably played all the countries in East Africa: the Pakistan Writers' Cricket Club in 1956, the Sundar CC of Bombay in 1957, including many Indian Test players, F. R. Brown's 1957–58 MCC team, a Non-European team from South Africa in 1958, which swept all before it largely through B. L. d'Oliveira, and a similarly all-powerful Gujrat Cricket Association team, full of Indian Test players including P. R. Umrigar whose 200 is the highest score in East Africa. So there was soon sufficient in common between the recently established central bodies of Kenya, Uganda and Tanzania, when contests followed between these countries, for a joint organization to be formed in 1960, mainly through the efforts of C. O. Oates, Chairman except for one year until 1976; Major H. A. Collins has succeeded to the post.

Some manifest consequences of the Conference's establishment were a combined tackling of problems, selection of teams properly named East Africa (one captained by Ramanbhai Patel played a Commonwealth XI in Nairobi in 1962), admission of East Africa as an associate member of the International Cricket Conference in 1966, and after 1966 a Quadrangular Tournament for the Sir Robert Menzies Trophy in a rota of the countries. Zambia joined in 1968 and won it in 1969 on Zambian turf. In the first comprehensive Tournament of 1968, Tanzania won, but Kenya's Akhil Lakhani excelled with hundreds against Zambia and Uganda and 2 against Tanzania, a remarkable performance.

Touring sides since the Association's inauguration have been frequent. An East African side (3 Indian players from Kenya, 2 from Tanganyika and 6 from Uganda) was heavily defeated by the 1963 MCC side at Kampala, Uganda, a match surprisingly given first-class status. Pakistan International Airways, a Muslim side captained by Hanif Mohammad and including leading Pakistan Test players, won 4 and drew 1 of its 5 matches in three territories in 1964. East Africa lost at Kampala to the Nawab of Pataudi's India team of 1967, although Upendra Patel's 105 not out and Vasant Tapu's 5 for 72 represented a real measure of opposition. A year later a draw was obtained by East Africa at Nairobi against an International XI under M. J. Stewart; Upendra Patel scored 79 and D. J. Pringle took 5 wickets in each innings for the Conference side. After an East African side (excluding Zambia) played against club sides in England, MCC with J. M. Brearley as captain and J. A. Bailey as player-manager, won 5 and drew 3 of its 8 matches throughout East Africa. The match MCC v East Africa (captained by Jawahir Shah) on Nairobi grass, was ruled first-class.

No associate member country except Sri Lanka was able at short notice to even up the number of contestants in the Prudential World Cup Competition in 1975: East Africa, captained by H. R. Shah, did, however participate but was totally outclassed. It took the advantage of that experience to the 1979 World Cup Competition, when its leading players (virtually all Indian) included Jawahir Shah and Zulfiqar Ali, and finished 2nd to Bermuda in Group I.

PHILIP SNOW

Egypt

In Egypt, cricket has been mainly the prerogative of British expatriates albeit ranking second to polo. It is impossible to establish when cricket was first played in Egypt but the Alexandria Club was formed in 1851. The Royal Navy and merchant ships which passed through Suez nearly always arranged a game at Port Said. In 1882 a British Expeditionary Force was sent and started the combination of games arranged by government officials and soldiers. The chief centres were Cairo, home of the Gezira Sporting Club with its matting pitch and grass outfield, and Alexandria which had a grass pitch. Other grass pitches were at the YMCA (Willcocks sports ground) at Maadi, and the Ministry of Education ground (home of the Egyptian club). Sand grounds were used at Heliopolis and the British Army depots at Abassia and Helmieh. Victoria College was a beautiful ground whilst the RAF headquarters was at Abukir.

Viscount Brackley took out a fairly strong MCC side in 1909, followed by I Zingari in 1914 and Free Foresters in 1927. Between the Wars the presence of battalions of the Brigade of Guards and the RAF ensured much good cricket at Alexandria and Cairo.

From 1929 until 1939, H. M. Martineau's team went to Egypt at the beginning of every April for a month's tour. Invariably the side included many of England's most prominent amateurs. The 11 tours had a consistent fixture list usually starting at Alexandria; they provided high class, entertaining cricket and enjoyed unlimited hospitality. Each tour included 2 'Tests' against All Egypt with honours, over the years, about even. One of these games, in 1934 at Gezira, produced a score of 588 for 5 declared (J. L. Guise 217 not out); this is a record total for Egypt, beating the 531 at Alexandria in 1931 and All Egypt's 507 in 1935. The All Egypt sides were made up mainly of officers with a few other ranks. Very few native players took to the game; easily the best of those who did was Abdou, a fine spin bowler and the Gezira professional.

The Second War saw a large concentration of British personnel in the Middle East, including South Africans, Australians, New Zealanders, Indians and countless English Test and county players. The leading players managed to gravitate to Cairo and Alexandria to play in matches of a high standard. W. R. Hammond made many huge scores; A. D. Nourse, Jnr, once hit 9 sixes off successive balls whilst another South African, E. A. B. Rowan, scored 5 hundreds in consecutive innings. During the latter stages of the War the RAF took part in Zonal games mostly at the Alamein ground. In 1951 the Alexandria Club celebrated its centenary and an Egyptian team came to England and played MCC at Lord's. By 1966 the Willcocks ground had become the home of the National Sporting Club, the Victoria College ground at Maadi was known as the Victory and the Heliopolis ground had disappeared under a building site.

E. E. SNOW

Falkland Islands

Here, the weather has proved insuperable. Enthusiasm was demonstrated after the First World War on the bleak, sloping Government House paddock at Stanley, both for internal matches and when ships called, but with the Wireless Telegraph Station closing down in the 1920s the game virtually froze. The enthusiasm of the Colonial Treasurer, S. G. Trees, and a dozen other British officials, warmed the cricket climate sufficiently in the mid-1950s for 4 teams including Islanders to play each other regularly and to take on Naval ships.

PHILIP SNOW

Finland

The first cricket played here as far as is known was a demonstration of the game on a field alongside the Olympic stadium in 1952. In 1975 the Helsinki Cricket Club came into being through the initiative of British and Australian representations, and today boasts a membership of some 70 people, including a few of local origin. Its chief contact is the Stockholm CC, and it has also played host to Danish clubs.

P. S. HARGREAVES

Fiji

Cricket in the Islands is long-established and follows a colourful, unusual pattern. The account written by the celebrated S. M. J. Woods of a visit there in 1910 probably owes something to literary invention. With Australian modesty he wrote of having taken, as a passing cruise passenger, 27 wickets in a single innings which he left with the score at 175 for 72 wickets, only to be chased with arrows and spears at sea. These feats and Woods himself belong properly to *The Boy's Own Paper*. Yet the first part of his tale fits in with the pattern of scores in South Sea Islands where exuberance for the game has taken the shape of communal participation. Every able-bodied male from puberty estimates himself capable of a contribution and with 90 or so fielders spread over a village green or lurking behind thatched houses or perched on branches, the batsman who manages to scramble one run may have accumulated his side's whole total. But Sammy Woods let his imagination run away in the second part of his story. Fiji had, 35 years before, forsaken its cannibalistic pursuits; a measure of its sophistication is that fifteen years before his visit a mixed team of Fijians and Europeans had toured New Zealand with distinction.

Cricket had probably been first seen in the Fijian Group in 1874 on an outlying island's white sands where ship passengers on the Sydney–San Francisco run induced natives to join in. In the 1880s under the patronage of the second Governor, Sir William des Voeux and his ADCs, Hon J. G.H. Amherst (I Zingari and MCC) and Sir Edward Wallington (Oxford, Dorset and Wiltshire), later Queen Mary's Treasurer, there were many matches between Europeans, particularly with visiting ships (Prince George, later George V, was in one in 1881 but his score did not greatly affect the total).

It was J. S. Udal, the Attorney-General (Dorset, MCC and Somerset and selected by W. G. Grace to go to Australia in 1873), who took the Fijian team the 1,000 miles to New Zealand in 1895, an ambitious undertaking well justified by 4 wins, 2 losses and 2 draws. The 6 Fijian chiefs in this side radiated their enthusiasm on their return: the game became *de rigueur* on the island of Bau where the last King of Fiji, Cakobau, had lived before his cession of the group to Queen Victoria in 1874. Cricket's fascination for this tiny island (about 20 houses of thatch and 60 male adult inhabitants) was such that, guided by an Australian, E. J. Marsden, it had the temerity in 1908 to tour Australia. The Bauans' fielding was acrobatic, their batting and bowling brisk. Just before this tour, J. Darling's team, *en route* to England in 1905, had played under M. A. Noble at Suva, the capital, against Fiji team – the first time a representative match had been played in Fiji, but only Ratu Pope among Fijians was selected. The game now consolidated itself with the help of H. S. de Maus (New Zealand's most successful all-rounder about 1900) and Austin Diamond (2nd in Australia's averages in 1907); the local players only needed first-class competition to show themselves quite able to hold their own. These included Sir Henry Scott, KC, H. B. Riley, Reginald Berkeley, M.P. and playwright, C. A. Adams, C. E. de Pennefather, C. R. Carne, H. Edmunds and F. G. Forster. In 1912 and 1913 Australian teams under S. E. Gregory and A. Diamond (including C. G. Macartney, W. Bardsley, J. N. Crawford and A. A. Mailey) played in Suva. Regrettably, there was no overseas tour in the 'twenties and 'thirties, but a touring New Zealand side in 1924 gave strong opposition.

On appointment to the Islands in 1938 as an Administrator I found the absurdity of Europeans and part-Europeans on the one hand, and Fijians and Indians on the other, continuing to play apart intolerable and managed to amalgamate them: the standards rose remarkably. The war, too, provided a real test

The Fiji team of 1948, the strongest in its history, taking the field against the first-class Province of Otago in New Zealand. Its custom was to walk in single file halfway to the wicket: from left, Philip Snow (captain); Ratu (Prince) Sir George Cakobau, Governor-General of Fiji and great-grandson of King Cakobau of Fiji (vice-captain); M. J. Fenn; Ratu Sir Edward Cakobau, Deputy Prime Minister of Fiji and son of King George II of Tonga; Kaminieli Arai; Isoa Logavatu; Petero Kubunavanua; Ilikena Bula; Mosese Bogisa; H. J. Apted and P. T. Raddock.

of local attainment with New Zealand players such as P. E. Whitelaw and N. Gallichan playing regularly in the Forces' teams. In 1942 the New Zealand Forces XI played Fiji at Lautoka. Fiji could not be totally representative but they dismissed the New Zealand side, including 7 Plunket Shield players, for 25 in one innings, Turaga's skill surmounting everything in this his last match before accidental electrocution at the Gold Mines. In 1946 the need for a Fiji Cricket Association to promote the game on an inter-racial basis was accepted at an inaugural meeting in the picturesque colonial-style bungalow of E. E. Turner, a wise Australian administrator of the game and gifted googly bowler. The most distinguished Fijians, Ratu Sir J. Lala V. Sukuna, KCMG, KBE, Médaille Militaire, BA, presided. Soon after, it was possible to organize the first tour of a totally representative Fiji team overseas for 53 years, and in 1948 I was honoured with the leadership of the side to New Zealand. Two of the 5 three-day matches with the first-class Provinces, which included their Test players, were won, and none of the two-day matches lost; but also New Zealand liked the team.

Bare feet, *sulus* (calf-length skirts) aflying, large heads of bristly hair conferring a ferocity wholly belied by amiability of countenance: these were part of the attraction. An effervescence in cutting, driving, hooking, throwing, catching, in bowling with all one's might, singing in fine harmony to the crowds, copperplate autographing, an eagerness to please: the recipe could not fail. On top of this, Ilikena Lasarusa Talebulamaineiilikenamainavaleniveivakabulaimainakulalakeba (score-cards humanely limited this to I. L. Bula) showed a mastery of technique. Magnificent high-carrying drives, rapid feet movement against slow bowling (to most Fijians pure white magic) and resounding hooks earned him 1,000 runs in 17 matches.

Ratu Sir Edward Cakobau, son of King George II of Tonga and the leading chieftainess of Bau, was a high-class all-rounder, the double of d'Oliveira in style on the field. As he was later Deputy Prime Minister, and the Prime Minister and Governor-General were also first-class cricketers, it must be the only instance of the top three positions in a country being so occupied after Independence in 1970 when Fiji became a Dominion.

Fiji's grounds are picturesque but poor, except Levuka's Nasau Park and Suva's Albert Park, which is bounded on four sides by the Grand Pacific Hotel, the imposing Government Buildings, the Botanical Gardens and a palm-hung soapstone cliff created on the lagoon edge in 1890. Albert Park is lined with royal palms and weeping-fig trees. In 1955 the West Indies team *en route* to New Zealand lost by 28 to a mere Suva side, captained by a first-class all-rounder, Ratu Sir Kamisese Mara, vice-captain of the 1954 tour and Prime Minister since independence, largely through batting by H. J. Apted and Bula (whose 246 in a later match is the highest Fiji innings) and Asaeli Driu's fine left-hand bowling. In 1959 another side in New Zealand under Nacanieli Uluiviti, who had played for Auckland and scored 40 off the first 7 balls of an 8-ball over in a top-class match in Fiji, was less successful. Shortly afterwards a team under Uluiviti, including for the first time an Indian (there are many more Indians than Fijians in the Colony), toured New South Wales country districts – a modest venture, with no three-day matches. In a Saturday game against a New South Wales XI, including K. R. Miller, J. Burke, N. C. O'Neill, R. Benaud, R. N. Harvey and A. K. Davidson, on Sydney Cricket Ground, Fiji won on the first innings.

On a tour of New Zealand under S. E. B. Snowsill in 1962, Fiji played less strong sides than previously, and while winning 8 matches and drawing 4, lost 9. Fiji was, with Ceylon and USA, the first non-Test country to be elected an associate member of the ICC in 1965. In 1968 the standard of fixtures was again lowered for a tour of New Zealand under Uluiviti: the most successful all-rounder, H. J. Apted, had been, like Bula, on all tours and was still successful but Bula in ill-health declined. A very strong Air India team visited Fiji in 1972, V. J. Manjrekar scoring a hundred. Following Hyderabad Blues' visit with Indian Test players in 1973, a club side under A. K. Sharma toured India in 1974 and did outstandingly well against strong opposition, A. L. Wadekar obtaining a hundred, as did Apenisa Waqatabu for the visitors.

1974 was Fiji's cricket centenary and I was asked to design special stamps. In 1977, for the first time, Papua New Guinea, Honiara in the Solomons and Vila in the New Hebrides were visited by Fiji, losing in the first country, drawing in the second and winning in the third. Again under F. L. C. Valentine, Fiji toured New Zealand in 1978, winning 4, drawing 7, losing 4: R. G. Jepsen was the leading batsman and Ilikena Vuli the most successful all-rounder.

For the World Cup Tournament Fiji was managed by Sir Josua Rabukawaqa, player-manager on the 1967 New Zealand Tour and former High Commissioner in the United Kingdom, and captained by Inoke Tabualevu. Fiji found the continuously wet conditions difficult to adapt to: 4 days after arrival and with virtually no practice, they were unable to cope with Denmark. Two days later Bangladesh, at one stage 54 for 8, won by 22 runs. The match with Malaysia was abandoned without a ball bowled. Canada, the finalist, won by a small margin, but in non-competitive matches Fiji beat USA and Argentina. C. A. C. Browne was the most consistent batsman, Isoa Suka a fast, accurate bowler; Valentine was still a successful swing bowler, A. L. Apted was prominent in an outstanding fielding side, whilst Uraia Sorovakatini, 46-years old with 6 tours behind him, was an agile wicket-keeper. Jaswant Singh, the only Indian, was a steady opening batsman, and M. I. Konrote, the first Rotuman to play for Fiji, flighted his left-hand spin ably.

PHILIP SNOW

Ghana

From the beginning of the century, when the Gold Coast's cricket came from sources identical with Nigeria's, the Gold Coast have been Nigeria's traditional opponents.

Sir Gordon Guggisberg, Governor, captained Gold Coast in their first representative matches, his counterpart in Nigeria being Sir Shenton Thomas. After a lapse in the fixtures from the First World War to 1926, Gold Coast were the stronger to the Second War, since when Nigeria have predominated. Players were almost exclusively European up to 1956. Prominent among them were C. D. A. Pullan, Brig M. A. Green (Army and Gloucestershire), Col L. H. Bean (Army, Sierra Leone and Dorset) and H. Vane Percy, who had played for South Africa under the name of Baumgartner.

In touring Kenya, Tanzania and Uganda in 1973, Ghana became the first national side to play outside West Africa. Clubs are building up from a low level, mostly in Accra, following a visit by MCC in 1976.

PHILIP SNOW

Gibraltar: HMS *Vanguard* v Royal Artillery, 1950.

Gibraltar

The first record of cricket on the Rock was in 1822, when it was reported in the *Gibraltar Chronicle* that the 'Gibraltar Cricket Club will play their first match on the Neutral Ground on Saturday next, 6th July.' The end of the Neutral Ground, which included a racecourse and garden, came with the building of an airstrip in the Second World War.

The Australians, under the captaincy of W. L. Murdoch, visited the Rock in 1890, both C. T. B. Turner and J. J. Ferris proving too much for the local batsmen, then, as now, mostly servicemen. In 1927 the Cryptics played there; in 1932 H. D. G. Leveson Gower took a side. In 1934 the Gibraltar Club played no fewer than 69 matches. Since the Second War many sides from elsewhere have sampled the pleasures of playing cricket in this unique setting, Essex and Yorkshire among them.

Due to a clash of interests, with hockey claiming some of the players, it was decided to withdraw from the ICC Trophy in 1979. This came of there being so few indigenous cricketers to choose from. The game has not been played in the schools in Gibraltar for some years, a fact which causes those who work to keep it going, and grow older each year, growing concern.

Gilbert Islands

Sir Arthur Grimble in his *Pattern of Islands* made known the eccentricities of the game of *kirikiti* on Ocean Island 40 years ago. They are to be found on other Micronesian islands to this day. Most of the batting is still highly unorthodox (the sandy pitches and rough outfields a temptation to lift every ball into the lapis lazuli lagoon), the fielding daringly one-handed, the bowling nothing less than a form of catapulting.

PHILIP SNOW

Hawaii

As might be expected, cricket has been hard-pressed to compete with Hawaii's other and often American-inspired attractions. Even so, D. G. Bradman was seen there in V. Y. Richardson's Australian team going to California in 1932. Worcestershire, on their world tour in 1965, dismissed Honolulu for 46 and T. W. Graveney made 85 not out, not one of his more difficult innings, no doubt, but in such a locale, one to be remembered.

PHILIP SNOW

Hong Kong

An episode in Hong Kong's history is one of the most dramatic in the history of cricket. Almost 100 years ago an entire representative team was lost. There has been nothing comparable in sporting records.

The Hong Kong Cricket Club, inaugurated in 1851 by the Armed and Civil Services, had formed the enterprising habit of having a fixture with Shanghai Cricket Club, 800 miles to the north. Indeed, the length of time Hong Kong has been touring overseas is a distinctive feature in its history, for as long ago as 1867, Hong Kong first travelled to Shanghai in return for Shanghai's first visit the year before, starting a remarkable series of inter-port fixtures. In 1882, Capt J. Dunn (Army), who had scored nearly 3,000 runs in a previous season, was the captain of the Hong Kong team of 13 touring Shanghai. On the return the P & O steamer Bokhara ran into a typhoon. Mountainous seas rolling the ship over so far so many times extinguished the engine room fires: without power the ship drifted towards the Pescadores Archipelago near Formosa. It struck an island at midnight, sinking immediately with the loss of 125 lives.

Bokhara's end in the China Sea nearly eliminated cricket in Hong Kong. But progress was resumed in 1891 with a

Hong Kong CC: the famous ground of $3\frac{1}{2}$ acres in the heart of the city valued at £50 million which until the expiry of the Government's lease was the game's headquarters in the colony. The domed building behind the sight-screen is the Law Courts, the central skyscraper the Mandarin Hotel; extreme right is the Hong Kong Club. The Hong Kong CC now occupy an excellent ground on the mainland.

fortnight's festival in Hong Kong for the 3 representative teams of Ceylon, the Straits Settlements and Hong Kong. Ceylon's visit was not returned until 1971 when Hong Kong, captained by John S. Shroff and managed by E. H. Wilson, lost there and went to Singapore (who won) and Sabah (who were defeated) in their most ambitious tour up to that date. Minor tours have been to the Philippines and Bangkok.

Associated with Hong Kong cricket have been J. M. (later Admiral of the Fleet Sir John) de Robeck, who opened the Hong Kong innings and also played in Malaya; Capt. P. Havelock Davies (Oxford); the Pearces, father and son – the latter, T.A., in 1946, after having been imprisoned by the Japanese, scored a century for Kent; Capt G. F. Grace; Col H. Owen Hughes, an outstanding President as well as captain and all-rounder; and Admiral Sir Robert Burnett. 1959 saw another impressive confluence in Hong Kong, with Bangkok and Malaya as visitors. Hong Kong defeated Bangkok, but Malaya beat Hong Kong from the extraordinary position of needing 91 to do so when the last Malayan batsman went in.

Since then, more cricket visitors have gone to Hong Kong than any other distant part. Only a summary can be given of considerable activity in the last 15 years. In 1964 MCC played 2 matches, G. Boycott making a hundred. So did Worcestershire, T. W. Graveney making 2 hundreds. E. W. Swanton's side, during a highly successful tour of the Far East in 1964, played two matches: G. St A. Sobers and S. Nurse each scored centuries. A couple of matches was often the visiting pattern, one at Hong Kong, the other at Kowloon. An International XI under M. J. Stewart in 1968 followed, and then MCC under A. R. Lewis in 1970 (B. Kwong Wo, son of the groundsman in the centre of the city and one of the few Chinese to play representative cricket, as a spin bowler, took 4 wickets and made the highest score in addition to fielding brilliantly).

Inter-port fixtures with Shanghai from 1866 ended in 1948: they are now with Malaysia and Singapore. In 1963, through a hundred by Shroff, Hong Kong beat Malaysia for the first time in 30 years. Playing Singapore in 1973, Hong Kong, under C. Myatt and including J. R. T. Barclay, won comfortably through Kwong Wo's 8 for 36. The same year they were beaten by Hyderabad Blues, captained by M. L. Jaisimha and including other Test players. Hong Kong, with English, Australian, Chinese, Indian, West Indian and Cingalese elements, was now very transitory, a factor which prevented its qualifying by residence for the ICC Associate Members' Competition in 1979 in England. Hong Kong had become an associate member in 1969. In 1973 the Midland Club Cricket Conference on tour narrowly defeated Hong Kong under Myatt, who also led a first visit to Western Australia. MCC under M. H. Denness had easy wins in 1975 in 2 single-day matches (hundreds by K. W. R. Fletcher and D. L. Amiss), playing one of the final games on the main ground, Chater Road, where the premier club, Hong Kong CC, were eventually overwhelmed on 3 sides by 2 skyscraper Banks, the Supreme Court and the Hong Kong Hilton, leaving but one side open for views of trams. The Government would not renew the lease of the world's most valuable cricket ground which had been reclaimed from the sea. Flat space being coveted above all else, after 155 years' use, the Chater Road ground was abandoned for Wongneichong, a river valley filled in among the hills with an imposing view between them from the new pavilion towards the harbour.

In 1972 Denys Roberts handed the presidency of Hong Kong Cricket Association to E. H. Wilson, captain of the Hong Kong Club and formerly of Uganda; in 1975 Sir Denys, Attorney-General, Colonial Secretary and novelist, was President of the Hong Kong Cricket Club at Wongneichong's opening. The third major club, Kowloon, founded in 1904, has been on its present ground at Cox's Road since then.

Hong Kong, with a side all European but for one Indian, toured England for the first time in 1976, playing clubs and an MCC side in 11 matches, drawing 8 and losing 3. The captain, Myatt, was outstanding as a bowler. They toured again in 1978 (under P. Davies) without winning, and they also made (under G. Foster) the first tour to Japan for 60 years, playing 2 matches on Japan's only ground Yokohama Athletic and Cricket Club, winning narrowly in one of them against a team captained by the British Ambassador, Sir Michael Wilford. Meanwhile, Hong Kong has difficulty in accommodating the many teams keen to visit them.

PHILIP SNOW

India

R. A. ROBERTS AND D. J. RUTNAGUR

If the American abroad is puzzled by the English attachment to cricket, he is dumbfounded by the Indian passion for it. Even Englishmen on first acquaintance are surprised by this manifestation of the influence of the British Raj. A great Indian patriot once said: 'The finest legacies left us by British Rule are the English language and, even more precious, the game of cricket'. Wandering through any of the great, teeming cities of the sub-continent, the visitor is astonished by the enormous enthusiasm for the game. Along Bombay's Marine Drive and on the 3 large commons in the vicinity of Churchgate, cricket is played everywhere, from first light until dusk. Open spaces in Madras and Calcutta also bustle with cricket activity. While thousands play the game, millions watch it or listen to running commentaries on the wireless. All India Radio broadcasts Test commentaries in three languages – English, Hindi and the regional tongue. Cricketers are idolized in India as footballers are in Brazil.

Stumps were first pitched on Indian soil as early as 1721, in Cambay, situated in the same western Indian region as Ranjitsinhji's Nawanagar. But that must have been an impromptu game, among sailors off a trading ship. A cricket match was a more regular sight in Calcutta, even as early as in Clive's day. The early encounters were between the Army and the settlers of the East India Company. Then, in 1792, the Calcutta Cricket Club was established on the site where Eden Gardens, the world's second largest Test ground, now stands. Its membership was restricted to Europeans and for many years the game excited no more than idle curiosity among the indigenous population. Five years after the founding of the Calcutta Cricket Club, the first recorded match in Bombay was staged.

Although it was in Calcutta that the game was first played on any significant scale, Bombay must be regarded as the birthplace of Indian cricket, for it was here that the Indians themselves began to play. One section of the community, the Parsees (whose ancestors had fled from Persia in medieval times), saw merit in playing this curious English game. They took on the Old Etonians towards the end of the 18th century, and in 1848 they formed their own club on the Esplanade Maidan, within a 6 hit of the exclusive European Club, the Bombay Gymkhana. They called it the Orient Club. Equipment could not be bought in shops those days. The British brought their own from home and the Parsees, initially, played with their cast-off implements. They learnt the game with bats

The early days in an Indian Hill station: Annandale, Simla, June 1854.

that were no more than bundles of splinters and fragments held together with string.

The Parsees beat a team of Europeans in 1877 and were so enthused by this success that they made plans to visit England and Australia as soon as possible. The trip to Australia did not come off, but the pioneering Parsees set sail for England in 1886. Their captain, Dr Patel, had had experience of English conditions while reading medicine. They won only 1 match out of 28 played, but their enthusiasm was undiminished. They undertook another trip two years later, this time winning 8 out of 31 matches and losing 11. The improved performance was due to M. E. Pavri, who took 170 wickets on the tour at less than 12 runs apiece. Like England's champion cricketer of the time, Mehlasa Pavri was a doctor and stood well over 6 feet in his socks.

Dr Pavri must have been a bowler of brisk pace for, at Eastbourne, he trimmed a bail and made it travel 50 yards, while at Norwich a stump he uprooted pitched 9 yards behind its original position. The Bombay GP was a major wicket-taker when English teams subsequently visited India. The first of them went out in 1889. It was an all-amateur side, led by G. F. Vernon, of Middlesex, and included Lord Hawke. The only defeat they suffered during a comprehensive tour of India and Ceylon (in most instances, the opposing teams were made up of expatriate Englishmen) was inflicted by the Parsees of Bombay. The tourists were bundled out for 97 and 61, Dr Pavri taking 9 wickets in the match. Lord Hawke captained another amateur side to India, only 3 years later. Vernon, this time, played under him. Another famous member of that side was the Hon F. S. Jackson, who returned to India some years later as Governor of Bengal.

The Englishmen played 20 matches on that trip and lost only 2, one of them again to the Parsees. A representative match against an All-India team, largely made up of India-based Englishmen, was won by an innings. The Parsees completed a 'hat trick' of wins against visiting sides when the Oxford Authentics toured in 1902–03. Led by K. J. Key, of Surrey, the side included the famous Worcestershire lob bowler, G. H. Simpson-Hayward, who took 103 wickets at 10 runs each. He also scored 203 against Peshawar. This tour was the starting point of larger individual scores and more substantial totals – a pattern for the future. The end of the 19th century had seen the start, even though on a very small scale, of competitive cricket in India. Beginning in 1895, the Europeans and the Parsees played each other annually in what came to be called Presidency matches.

It was Ranjitsinhji who helped to stir up the wind that spread the seeds of cricket over a wider territory. Having learnt the game at the Rajkumar College under the tutelage of Charles Magnagthen, a Cambridge man but not a Blue, the Crown Prince of Nawangar himself went to Cambridge. He was up for 2 years before his genius was allowed to express itself at Fenner's. Once this first barrier was broken, Ranji went from strength to strength. His keen eye, suppleness of body and beautiful touch inspired some of the most lyrical prose written about cricket. The fact that he was an eastern prince added to the romance.

With the agreement of the Australian captain, Harry Trott, Ranji was chosen for England in the Manchester Test of 1896, in which he contributed his immortal 154 not out. In 1897–98, he toured Australia under A. E. Stoddart and achieved further triumphs. In 1905, upon succeeding to the throne of Nawanagar, he went home to perform his princely duties. Affairs of state and the loss of an eye in a shooting accident

MCC v All India, Calcutta 1926–27: the most keenly contested match of the tour, in which 7 Europeans played for All India. MCC won by 4 wickets, Maurice Tate taking 6 for 42 and 4 for 64. The Maharajah of Patiala, wearing a turban, played for MCC.

permitted him only spasmodic appearances in English cricket thereafter. Before Indian cricket achieved its own identity, two other Indian princes played for England with great distinction – first, Ranji's own nephew, Duleepsinhji, and then, the Nawab of Pataudi.

Ranji's feats in England and the glowing tributes to his art fired the imagination of thousands back home. His fellow princes became involved, fostering cricket in their states with great zeal. Many of them sent for coaches from England and spared no expense on facilities. Thus there was rapid development in the hinterland. In Bombay, the many Presidency matches between the Europeans and the Parsees won for the game converts from other sections of the community. In 1907, the Hindus entered the lists to form the Triangular Tournament and the Mohammedans threw in their challenge in 1912. The Christians and the Jews combined to field a side called The Rest in 1937 and the competition between teams representing the religious denominations was now called the Pentangular.

This competition, always staged in Bombay, was the highlight of India's cricket calendar. The formation of a central body to organize cricket on a nationwide scale did not, however, come about until the late 1920s and a national competition on the lines of the County Championship was not started until after India had played her first Test match, in 1932, at Lord's. The first efforts to achieve international status dated back to 1911 when an All-India side toured England under Bhupinder Singh, the Maharaja of Patiala, who financed the trip as well. His Highness, whose lifestyle seemed to have been influenced by the *Tales of the Arabian Nights*, is remembered as a burly Sikh who wore a large diamond earring and hit straight sixes with great power. His touring team, unfortunately, did not do too well in England. But the performance of representative sides against the MCC team of 1926–27 indicated that India was ready to play Test cricket. The recommendation to Lord's came from the captain of MCC, Arthur Gilligan.

However, India had to form a central organizing body before she could be afforded Test status and the Board of Control for Cricket in India came into being in 1928, with an Englishman, M. E. Grant Govan, as President, and Anthony D'Mello, a flamboyant and imaginative Goan, as the Honorary Secretary. India's Test baptism was to take place at home during a tour by the MCC, in the winter of 1930–31. But the tour had to be deferred because the nationalist movement was at a high peak at the time and an English team might not have been well received. MCC went to India 3 years later, but in the meanwhile India came to England in 1932 and played one three-day Test, at Lord's. The Maharaja of Porbander, captain of the side but no great cricketer, stepped aside to allow C. K. Nayudu to lead India in her maiden Test, an honour that Nayudu, a cricketer of tremendous personality, was fully worthy of. Although beaten in this Test at Lord's, by a formidable England side, India were by no means disgraced. In fact, they had England in trouble on the opening morning, claiming three wickets for 19 runs. Those early victims included Percy Holmes and Herbert Sutcliffe, fresh from their record opening stand of 555 for Yorkshire against Essex. England's innings would have been crippled further had Douglas Jardine, top scorer with 79, not been allowed an early escape – ironically by Colah, who made a great reputation for himself as a fielder on that trip. India's heroes were their opening bowlers, Mohammad Nissar, one of the few outstanding fast bowlers India have produced, and Amar Singh, who was not as quick but could bowl with more unerring accuracy over long periods.

At least one leading England batsman of the 1920s and 1930s described Amar Singh as the finest bowler he ever played. Nissar took 5 wickets in the first innings; Amar Singh 2 in each. The great Nayudu, who had hit a record 11 sixes during an innings in Bombay against the 1926–27 MCC side, made a resolute 40 in the first innings. He was to come back to England in 1936, and he continued to play first-class cricket in India until he was in his 60s. But for him, India's entry into Test cricket had come too late. He was 37 when he played in the inaugural Test.

MCC led by Douglas Jardine – who was himself born in Bombay and whose father, a high court judge, played in the early Presidency matches – returned the Indian visit in 1933–34. England won the first and last of the 3 Test matches and the other was drawn, very much in England's favour. Besides Jardine, Hedley Verity was the only member of the party who had gone to Australia the year before. All the same, MCC were by any standards a formidable combination, reflecting the great strength of English cricket in the early

The Bombay Gymkhana ground, 1933: C. F. Walters batting for England in the first Test Match ever played on Indian soil.

Old Trafford, 1936: India take the field. Mohammed Nissar has a sweater round his neck, the Maharaj Kumar of Vizianagram (bespectacled) on his left.

1930s. The team included Arthur Mitchell, Cyril Walters, Charlie Barnett, James Langridge, Morris Nichols and Nobby Clark. The Indian bowling was seen to greater advantage than the batting. Nissar took 5 wickets in the First Test, Amar Singh, 4 for 106 in the Second and 8 wickets, including 7 in the first innings, in the Third. As for the batting, the youthful Merchant did not come off to the anticipated extent. However, another 22-year-old, Lala Amarnath, made history by scoring 118 out of a total of 258 on debut, at Bombay.

Although the Bombay Quadrangular produced a lot of good cricket and drew large crowds each day, the scope of the competition was not wide enough for it to play a major role in the building of a national side. The recruiting ground had to be widened and the newly-formed Board established in 1934 a national championship between teams representing the provinces and princely states. In honour of the country's greatest-ever cricketer, the championship cup was named the Ranji Trophy. Another constructive move by the Board was to initiate an inter-university competition which, for many years, proved of value in spotlighting young players.

But to look back again on the international scene, India returned to England for a second tour in 1936, their itinerary this time including 3 Test matches. The tour was a disappointment, injuries and adverse weather being contributory factors. The Maharajkumar of Vizianagram (or Vizzy, as he liked to be called), although captain of the side was barely a good club cricketer. Unlike the Maharaja of Porbander in 1932, he was determined to play in the Test matches, and not long before the first of these he sent the side's best all-rounder, Lala Amarnath, back to India, following an unhappy disagreement. In the Test series, which England won 2–0, India did, however, experience some moments of glory. Nissar and Amar Singh again distinguished themselves. In the second innings of the second Test, Vijay Merchant and Mushtaq Ali, batsmen of contrasting styles, had an opening partnership of 203, which equalled the tourists' total in the first innings. This stand was staged in the face of a formidable deficit, England, with Hammond scoring 167, having declared at 571 for 8. The partnership between Merchant and Mushtaq, spanning 150 minutes, contributed to a day of record scoring. No less than 588 runs were scored on that Monday, while only six wickets fell.

For obvious reasons, that 1936 series in England was India's last for ten years. But in 1937–38 they were hosts to a strong and colourful side captained by Lord Tennyson. The tour, during which Amarnath enhanced his reputation and during which Vinoo Mankad made his mark, was arranged to coincide with the opening in Bombay of the Cricket Club of India and the Brabourne Stadium. A large, modern cricket ground, which was ahead of its time, and a luxurious clubhouse to go with it were conceived by D'Mello, who always did everything in style. D'Mello had meant the CCI to be India's Lord's. The building of this new ground was a major landmark in the history of Indian cricket not only because it was the forerunner of giant stadia elsewhere in the country. The pitches at the Brabourne Stadium wrought a big change in the pattern of Indian cricket. The new ground was laid on land reclaimed from the sea, a factor which determined the pace of the pitches.

It is also true that the voracious appetite for runs of Vijay Merchant was one of the considerations in the preparation of the sort of pitches that obtained at the Brabourne Stadium during the 1940s. Merchant, who was more than a mere accumulator of runs, was not the only batsman who broke records at the Brabourne Stadium. Hazare made a double-hundred and a triple-hundred there in one season. Rusi Modi, a lean and graceful striker of the ball, also thrived. Big individual scores and massive totals became commonplace. Hitherto, only the Poona Club had the reputation of being an invariably happy hunting ground for batsmen. It is a myth that Indian pitches have always been slow and characterless. At the old Bombay Gymkhana, the contest between bat and ball was very even. Although runs were made in plenty at the Eden Gardens in Calcutta, bowlers were always happy to bowl there because a good length of grass was left on the pitches and the riverside atmosphere was amenable to swing.

At Chepauk, in Madras, decisive results were obtained as regularly as on any ground in the world. They still are. In the arid hinterland, cricket was mainly played on coir matting, which yielded prolific bounce. They bred a unique breed of medium-paced spinners. Batsmen who played on them were strong hookers and cutters. In the late 1940s, however, the Board issued a directive to replace coir by jute matting so as to bring about greater uniformity with turf wickets. The move seemed logical enough at the time, but the outcome was a higher proportion of drawn matches. Domestically, Indian cricket did not suffer from the war. In fact, it boomed because of several prominent English cricketers being either posted in India, or being available to play while in transit. Denis Compton, Joe Hardstaff and Reg Simpson were already well-known, but Paddy Corrall, Peter Cranmer, Peter Judge and Harold Butler became well-known names in the early 1940s. They all played for the Europeans in the Pentangular. Simpson (Sind) and Compton (Holkar) also played in the Ranji Trophy competition. The latter's double-hundred in the final of 1944–45 was an unforgettable experience for one of the authors of this short history of Indian cricket.

India were the tourists in England's first full postwar season. They started the tour optimistically, having done quite well against the Australian Services team during the past winter. But India lost the 3-Test series to England 1–0. India might have been a stronger side for the inclusion of Dattu Phadkar, Imtiaz Ahmed, and Ghulam Ahmed, who was developing into one of the best off-spinners in the world. Vijay Merchant, a thoughtful and dedicated cricketer, had another triumphant tour. Vinoo Mankad did the double and established himself as one of the leading all-rounders of all time. At the Oval, against Surrey, Sarwate and Bannerjee, batting at numbers 10 and 11, staged the highest-ever last-wicket partnership and turned certain defeat into a remarkable win. Rusi Modi, still at university, went back from the tour a more accomplished batsman. The following year, India went on their first-ever tour to Australia, not, unfortunately, with their strongest side. Vijay Merchant, who was elected captain, and Modi withdrew on grounds of health, Fazal Mahmood, who already looked a world-beater, had opted to live in Pakistan, which came into being after the team was picked, and Mushtaq Ali stayed back because he did not want to be away during a time of political uncertainty.

Australia, moulding themselves into the great side they were in England in 1948, were already immensely formidable and it was no surprise that the depleted Indians lost 4 out of 5 Tests. To make matters worse, India were caught on drying pitches in the first 2 Tests and when it was their turn to trap Australia on a glue pot in the third, in Sydney, the rain came back and foiled them. The Indians failed to win a state match either, though they distinguished themselves by beating an Australian XI which included Brown, Bradman, Miller, Hamence, Harvey, Dooland and Johnston. Individually, several players had a good tour. Amarnath, who led the side well, and Hazare, his vice-captain, both scored 1,000 runs, the latter becoming the first Indian to score separate hundreds in a Test match. Mankad made 2 Test hundreds and was also the highest wicket-taker on the tour, although on firmer Australian pitches his striking rate was not as high as in England a year earlier. A year later India met the West Indies for the first time, and while their batsmen held their own – with Modi the most consistent run-maker – their bowlers were hard put to it to contain the West Indies' batting strength, which was vast despite the absence of Frank Worrell. Everton Weekes filled the gap, scoring 779 runs in the series. India lost one Test and could have drawn the rubber with a win in the Fifth which ended with their having one wicket standing and needing 6 runs to win. Being in a high state of excitement the umpires drew stumps with 2½ minutes remaining.

The enthralling finish to this final Test won an increasing following for cricket and the two seasons free of international cricket before MCC paid their first postwar visit, in 1951–52, had to be filled in with tours by Commonwealth teams, assembled and managed by George Duckworth. Representative matches against these sides were excellent preparation for the home series with England. After looking as good as the below strength England side, if not a shade superior, in the first 3 Tests, which were drawn, India lost the Fourth. The Fifth at Madras made history, with India registering their first-ever Test win – by an innings and 8 runs. The heroes of this momentous win were Roy and Umrigar, with a century apiece, and Vinoo Mankad, who took 12 wickets in the match, including 8 for 55 in the first innings.

Umrigar, Roy and Manjrekar were three batsmen whose talent was honed during these matches against Commonwealth sides. All three of them were to serve India well for many years to come. Still, in the early 1950s, India continued to call on batsmen who had made their mark before or during the early years of the war. The first series India ever won was in the following season, against Pakistan, a useful side not yet adjusted to the demands of Test cricket. India played New Zealand for the first time in 1955–56 and beat them comfortably. Sandwiched between the two winning rubbers were a disastrous series in England, in 1952, a maiden tour of the West Indies and a series in Pakistan that produced five protracted draws. In England in 1952 India were beaten 3–0 in a series of four Tests, suffering from the raw fury of a young Fred Trueman. India's plight heightened the glory of Vinoo Mankad's great achievement in the Second Test at Lord's, in which he was top-scorer in both innings, with 72 and 184, and also the main wicket-taker (5 for 196) during a marathon feat of delivering 73 overs. Posterity will always recognize the Lord's Test of 1952 as Mankad's Test.

India's performance on their first West Indies tour was more distinguished. Although the West Indies possessed no outstanding fast bowlers at the time, Ramadhin and Valentine were at their peak and the three 'W's', Worrell, Walcott and Weekes, were also at the height of their powers. India did not win a Test, but they lost only one. Umrigar was a heavy scorer in that series and Subash Gupte, who was to make his home in Trinidad a decade later, was India's most incisive bowler. His performances against one of the most lethal batting combinations in Test cricket placed him among the best leg-spinners of all time. India's fielding achieved standards never reached before or after.

The second half of the 1950s was a period of heartbreak for India. They let the enemy slip through the net in the last Test of a 3-match home series with Australia. In 1958–59 they were annihilated by a West Indian side that was heading for great things – the famous rubber in Australia under Sir Frank Worrell, two years later, and triumphs over England in 1963 and 1966. But India suffered another rout in England, in 1959, losing all 5 Tests. Soon afterwards, they redeemed themselves during a splendid home series in which they scored their first-ever win over Australia.

The first series India won against any of the major cricketing powers was in 1961–62 when they beat England 2-nil. England, led by Ted Dexter, were not fully representative in that all her main fast bowlers stayed home. But of the main batsmen, only Colin Cowdrey was absent. The first three Tests were drawn. Then halfway through the series, India recruited the services of the young Nawab of Pataudi whose career had seemed to be ended the previous summer when he lost the sight of his right eye after a car accident in England. Although the most junior member of the side, Pataudi was given a say in tactical planning; his theory was that they had to hit the spinners, Allen and Lock, over the top if India were to make runs at match-winning speed. Pataudi himself, and his captain, Nari Contractor, took the lead in implementing the plan. India won the last 2 Tests and the glory for bowling out England in these Tests went to the all-rounders, Chandu Borde (leg-breaks) and Salim Durrani (orthodox left-arm spin). Durrani, a tall, good-looking man, had a touch of genius about him and although he finished with a distinguished record, having shaped more than one Indian Test victory, he never realized his full potential.

Close fielding to their spin bowlers played a major part in India's successes in the 1970s. Here Solkar catches d'Oliveira off Chandrasekhar, watched by Engineer.

Euphoria over the beating of England did not last long. Every Test was lost during the tour of the West Indies which followed. The tour, furthermore, was marred by a head injury to the captain, Nari Contractor, whose life was in danger for some days. It finished his international career and left the Nawab of Pataudi, just turned 21, as the new captain. Taking over a losing side is not easy and Pataudi's problems were compounded by the fact that two or three key members of it were approaching retirement. Umrigar, the most senior of them, called it a day soon after the tour and Manjrekar did not have long to go. Pataudi remained captain until 1969 and although New Zealand was the only country against whom he won a whole series, Pataudi could count 2 wins against Australia in separate series among his triumphs. The second of these wins (at New Delhi, in 1969) gave notice of the rising strength of India's spin attack.

With one eye practically blinded, Pataudi never quite fulfilled the promise he had held as a schoolboy and then as freshman at Oxford. But he played several unforgettable Test innings, such as his 128 not out against Australia, in 1964, his 148 against England at Headingley, and his 75 and 85 in 1967–68 at Melbourne when he had the additional handicap of a severe hamstring injury. Pataudi still had an undisputed claim to a place in the side when he lost the captaincy. His successor, Ajit Wadekar, proved a lucky and competent, if not dynamic, captain. His first assignment was to lead India in the West Indies in 1971. India won the series 1–0. The win that decided the series, in the Second Test at Port-of-Spain, was by no means a freak result, for India were on top in at least three of the four drawn Tests. That series was notable for the meteoric rise to fame of Sunil Gavaskar, picked for the tour before he had even played a full first-class season at home. Although he missed the first Test because of an infection in a fingernail, Gavaskar aggregated 774 runs in the series and performed the rare feat of scoring a hundred and a double-hundred in the last Test. He was not the only heavy scorer for India in that rubber. Dilip Sardesai, virtually the last man to be picked for the tour, contributed 642 runs. Solkar and the veteran Salim Durrani also made outstanding contributions. India might have dominated the series even more strongly had they picked Chandrasekhar and Engineer. The former was almost a forgotten man after breaking down with an ankle injury during the 1967–68 tour of Australia and Engineer was not considered because he had not played in domestic cricket during the previous season.

Both, however, were recalled for the tour of England that followed within weeks and played a major role in India's first-ever win at the Oval, which gave them the series. The run of Indian wins under Wadekar continued. Due mainly to the wizardry of the spinners they beat England 2–1 in a home series in 1972–73. Wadekar's fall, however, was as dramatic as his rise. Back in England during the summer of 1974 India were beaten in every Test, the margin of defeat widening with each Test. A reason for this shift in balance was the England selectors' judicious choice of batsmen to play spin bowling. Wadekar, therefore, went out in defeat, but with a record benefit. Since he did so India have recorded some glorious wins, though their record has been inconsistent. The outstanding achievement has probably been a win over the West Indies, at Port-of-Spain in 1976, when India scored 406 for 4 wickets in the final innings. But when they lost 3–1 to England at home the following winter it was apparent that an infusion of fresh blood was badly needed. Their declining strength was evident, too, when India resumed their cricketing rivalry with Pakistan in the autumn of 1978. The 1979 tourists in England under Venkat were unkindly treated by the weather, but Gavaskar's reputation soared still higher, and the moral victory in the Oval Test came near to redeeming all.

Talent of adequate class, however, in spite of the game's popularity in India and the increasing financial rewards for

A great day for Indian cricket: Chandrasekhar, Wadekar and Sardesai on the winners' balcony after India's victory at the Oval in 1971.

playing it at the highest level, is not always abundantly available. The fault, perhaps, lies with the structure of first-class cricket in India and the nature of the pitches at most centres. Too many state sides not worthy of first-class status may have been admitted to the Ranji Trophy tournament in the last two decades. Hence competition is not always keen enough to raise standards. Strong emphasis on first-innings lead has also had a detrimental effect in that when two strong sides meet, their main aim is a draw, with a premium on first-innings advantage. The presence of so many high-class spinners during the 1960s and the early 1970s influenced the quality of pitches. Inevitably, batsmanship suffered and bowlers of a new generation had success beyond their true ability. The great Indian spinners, Bishen Bedi, Chandrasekhar, Prasanna and Venkat all learnt and mastered this craft on good pitches.

Indian cricket's major handicap, however, is the lack of space for open air recreation. Cricket is still very much an urban game, and in towns and cities struggling to keep pace with expanding industrialization and growing populations cricket grounds are all too scarce.

The Ranji Trophy

That India's major domestic competition should be named after a man who played so little of his cricket in the country is not the only ironic thing about the Ranji Trophy. It was started 2 years after India had made her Test debut – against England at Lord's in 1932 – and at various phases during its history it has been overshadowed by other more glamorous competitions. During and after the Second War it was the Pentangular tournament, which pitted teams of Hindus, Muslims and Parsees – the major religious communities – against Europeans; more recently it has been the zonal Duleep Trophy. This competition, wherein 5 zonal teams play each other on a knock-out basis, often provides a more accurate assessment of the state of Indian cricket and selectors with a more accurate guide.

The Ranji Trophy started in the 1934–35 season and its early years were dominated by the Princely states, like Nawanagar – Ranji's old state – Holkar and Hyderabad – states which had done much to promote the game. Unlike the other major cricketing countries, the Second War did not disrupt the domestic Indian season and the decade between 1940 and 1950 was possibly the golden age of the trophy: mammoth scores, record-breaking batting feats, and a flowering of Indian classical batsmanship exemplified by Vijay Merchant. In the 1945–46 season Holkar scored 912 for 8 declared against Mysore, in the previous season Bombay and Holkar had had a match aggregate of 2,078, while in 1948–49 Maharastra and Bombay between them had a match aggregate of 2,376 which is still a world record. It was during this decade that B. B. Nimbalkar made 443 not out for Maharastra against Bombay, which ranks, after Hanif Mohammed's 499 and Bradman's 452 not out, as the highest individual innings in first class cricket.

India's emergence as an independent nation brought many social and economic changes: Princely India virtually disappeared and the city of Bombay became the dominant influence in domestic cricket. Between 1948–49 and 1978–79 Bombay won 23 out of 31 finals, holding the Trophy continuously from 1958–59 to 1972–73. Bombay's post-independence ascendancy was a reflection of the changing nature of Indian society. The game that had been introduced to the country by the East India Company in 1721, had been nurtured by the wealthy Princes of India became a necessary status symbol of the increasingly powerful commercial and industrial communities centred round the main cities, particularly Bombay. As this Western metropolis replaced Calcutta as the country's commercial capital – 75% of all Indian taxes are collected from Bombay – Indian cricket became Bombay cricket.

This process was halted only in the late 1960s and evidence of challengers to Bombay's supremacy first came in the zonal Duleep Trophy. This tournament which had started in the 1960s began to be dominated by South Zone whose team could boast almost all of India's spin – Venkat, Prasanna, Chandra, V. V. Kumar – and a fair bit of its batting: Jaisimha, Pataudi, later Viswanath and Brijesh Patel. Since the early 1970s Karnataka ably led first by Prasanna and now by Viswanath have effectively checked Bombay's claim to be undisputed rulers of domestic Indian cricket. In the 1978–79 season Delhi won the trophy for the first time.

India's size and diversity has always made this a difficult tournament to organize. After much experimentation it is now based on a zonal league system with 2 teams from each zone taking part in a knock-out competition. In the years since independence political demands have led to the creation of new states, who, like newly independent countries seeking international recognition, have aspired to recognition as cricketing powers. This has made the tournament unwieldy and resulted in lop-sided zonal matches with some teams almost permanently condemned to defeat. Though 4 days are allotted for the matches – 5 for the final – results are difficult to obtain and matches are decided on first innings result. This has fashioned a generation of Indian tactical thinking which has often left its cricketers unprepared for the different demands of international cricket. Though over the years several measures have been suggested for reform it is unlikely that radical changes will be made.

MIHIR BOSE

WINNERS

1945–46	Holkar	1955–56	Bombay
1946–47	Baroda	1956–57	Bombay
1947–48	Holkar	1957–58	Baroda
1948–49	Bombay	1958–59–1972–73	Bombay (15 years)
1949–50	Baroda	1973–74	Karnataka
1950–51	Holkar	1974–75	Bombay
1951–52	Bombay	1975–76	Bombay
1952–53	Holkar	1976–77	Bombay
1953–54	Bombay	1977–78	Karnataka
1954–55	Madras	1978–79	Delhi

Israel

Despite the British influence, it was not until 1966 that Israel Cricket became organized when the first Israel Cricket League was established with 10 clubs from as far apart as Central Galilee, Haifa, Beersheba and Ashdod.

Inspired by their dynamic first President, Max Kahan, the new league prospered, supported almost entirely by new immigrants from India and South Africa, and led by such families as the Abrahams who themselves were able to field an all-family team.

Conditions were, and still are, almost impossible. Cricket grounds as such are non-existent, matches were staged mainly on football pitches, themselves only bare earth, with the few available mats trundled from one fixture to another on any available transport.

Despite these great difficulties, the sport has grown steadily. More teams have been formed so that today there are 22 competing in a variety of competitions, and the Israel Cricket Association now has a new and enthusiastic President in South African solicitor Ivan Kantor, and a most popular and dedicated Chairman in Indian accountant Gabriel Kandli.

Cricket in Israel really began to come of age with a highly successful tour of England in 1970, and this has led to many reciprocal tours from England, Ireland and South Africa including such famous names as Ken Barrington, Basil d'Oliveira and Dennis Gamsy. A second tour was undertaken

Cricket in Israel: the Harrow club captain planting a tree at the Kibbutz Yizreel.

in 1974, but the real culmination of everyone's efforts was when Israel participated in the recent World Cup. Aided by a group of enthusiastic supporters in England, the visit was an unqualified success from every point of view. While competition results were not special, performances on and off the field against strong opposition were most creditable, and the results of many of the friendly matches reflected how much Israel cricket was improving.

The immediate targets are to establish a real and permanent cricket centre, and to work towards the day when youngsters are taught and encouraged to play the game, so that Israel itself can begin to produce its own native born cricketers, rather than rely on those who have learnt the game elsewhere.

G. DAVIS

Kenya

Kenya's port, Mombasa (which has an excellent ground) assimilated cricket from visiting ships and perhaps from Zanzibar Island. To the 3-day fixture from 1910 to 1964 at Nairobi, Officials v Settlers, was added another internal one in 1933, Europeans v Asians – with the Asians (whose Sports Association began in 1930, 3 years after Kenya Kongonis were formed for Europeans) increasingly providing stronger opposition. Pre-eminent among organizers for 34 years to 1964 was a surgeon, C. V. Braimbridge (who gained the highest honour anyone not a member of the MCC can gain – the very select honorary membership). Sir Godfrey Rhodes, K. E. Crawley and G. J. Antrobus (a first-class googly and leg-break bowler) were prominent before the Second War which provided outside stimulus. South African members of the Forces, including B. Mitchell and Athol and Eric Rowan, were seen in action, as were R. E. (later Sir Richard) Luyt (Oxford), R. I. F. McIntosh (Oxford) and H. D. Burrough (Somerset); the outstanding memory is, however, naturally enough, of a hundred by W. R. Hammond.

In 1951 Kenya first played Tanganyika (captained by C. de L. Innis, the West Indian representative) and in 1952 a Natal team visited Kenya, W. R. Endean scoring a century. The following year marked a significant change – the creation of the Kenya Cricket Association as the colony's first inter-racial organization. Africans have not however so far been conspicuous in Kenyan cricket.

In 1957–8 MCC, captained by F. R. Brown and managed by S. C. Griffith, played 9 games in East Africa, winning 3, drawing 5, losing one (to Kenya Kongonis at Nairobi, due principally to two excellent innings by P. Prodger). Another MCC side, under W. Watson and M. J. K. Smith, visited Kenya in 1963. Pitches were mats of jute rather than coconut-fibre to reduce the bounce above concrete or impacted gravel. The Kenya team drew one match, M. J. Stewart's 152 being balanced by Gursuran Singh's 107, and lost the other when R. N. S. Hobbs took 7 for 73.

The South African non-European Team touring East Africa in 1958 played a number of matches in Kenya. South Africa, whose captain, B. L. d'Oliveira, was pre-eminent, won them all. Following tours included Worcestershire's in 1965 (Narendra Patel and Akhil Lakhani scored centuries for Kenya), MCC's under J. M. Brearley in 1974, when Kenya, mostly due to Narendra's 95 and Jagoo Shah's 72, managed a draw and confined R. W. Barber to 99, and the Minor Counties' first overseas tour in 1978. Minor Counties beat Kenya Cricket Association and also East Africa in limited-over matches.

PHILIP SNOW

Kuwait

Kuwait cricket has been highlighted by the Select Kuwait Wanderers' tour of England, Denmark and Switzerland in 1979. Select Kuwait Wanderers also recently toured India, Pakistan and Bahrain under the leadership of Chatrapal Sinh, a nephew of Duleep and grand-nephew of the immortal Ranji. Cricket began in Kuwait in 1947 when the British and some western expatriates employed by the Kuwait Oil Company cleared a desert area to prepare a pitch. Messrs George Wimpey were influential in forming a formal club in 1948 known as the Magwa CC, later known as the Kuwait CC. The Hubara Club later took over conducting tournaments in Kuwait which they continue to do. The 3 teams which began to compete on a league basis were Hubare, Unity and Nakhalistan, all recreation clubs of the Kuwait Oil Company. But as interest grew more teams were formed. The Wimpey League was thus born and is still being played as the leading tournament.

Foreign teams which have so far played in Kuwait include the New Zealand Colts in 1964, Tom Graveney's international side in 1959, Joe Lister's international side in 1971 and an Air India side in 1978. Some of the unforgettable incidents have been Clive Lloyd's towering sixes, the wicket-keeping of Godfrey Evans and the bowling of Fred Trueman. Glenn Turner of New Zealand, Neil Hawke of Australia and Mohinder Amar Nath of India also toured and delighted the enthusiastic crowd.

DEREK SEMMENCE

Lord Howe Island

With a total population of only 150, two teams have been raised. But the ground is so small that only one end of the concrete pitch is covered with matting; at the over's end fieldsmen stay and batsmen change over.

PHILIP SNOW

Malawi

Nyasaland's convoluted history inhibited much development of the game. Nevertheless, the Nyasaland Cricket Club published handbooks in the 1950s. Becoming Malawi in 1964, the country has now joined the contiguous East African Cricket Conference but has not been visited by overseas teams.

PHILIP SNOW

Malaysia

First it was Straits Settlement, then Malaya, now Malaysia (absorbing both British North Borneo, which has become Sabah, and Sarawak, but losing Singapore where cricket in the Peninsula is claimed to have started in 1837). Straits Settlement toured Burma, Bangkok and Batavia as early as 1870, and in 1893 was taken by Sir Henry McMullen, Surveyor-General, to Ceylon for the first time, reciprocating Ceylon's first of many visits three years earlier. At this time triangular meetings between Ceylon, Hong Kong and Straits Settlement started in Singapore. European planters, colonial officials and members of the Forces supplied the driving force and technical skill which, by 1900, had been followed capably by Cingalese, Eurasians, Indians (in themselves Sikhs and Tamils) and Chinese.

Malaya has been fortunate in that its size permits spacious grounds not restricted by the need to locate them in valleys and jungle clearings. It has also benefited in a cricket sense from its division into natural competitive areas; and it is specially favoured by proximity to other keen cricketing countries. The grounds at Singapore, Kuala Lumpur, Ipoh and Penang, looked after by Malayans or Indians, are first-class, with imposing pavilions. With so much rainfall the wickets are of matting, except on the main grounds where grass has been tamed, sometimes to the texture of red dust.

Triumphing over lushness and humidity, inter-State cricket has attained a high standard, helped by a tradition of 3-day matches, and the major match, the Malay States v the Crown Colony, was marginally first-class for years. This class criterion is difficult to assess: it can perhaps be judged best by performances of visiting teams, such as W. A. Oldfield's XI in 1927 which was defeated at Kuala Lumpur, but won its other game. In 1909 5 Australians, M. A. Noble, F. Laver, W. W. Armstrong, A. J. Hopkins and A. Cotter, had had an easier time, but there has been much development beyond the European opposition since then. With the addition of Cingalese and Indians, the All-Malayan side of 1937, principally due to Dr H. O. Hopkins (Oxford and Worcestershire) and T. M. Hart (Oxford and Scotland), held Sir Julien Cahn's XI to a good draw. Perak and Penang also managed to make draws. A year later, however, all parts of Malaya found Ceylon under Dr. C. H. Gunasekera (Cambridge and Middlesex) too strong. Malaya's richest period may have been about 1930 when Capt G. J. Bryan (Kent and Army), D. V. Hill (Oxford and Worcestershire), G. E. Livock (RAF) and P. H. Stewart-Brown (Oxford) were playing for the Colony of Singapore which, even so, was beaten by the Federated Malay States under N. J. A. Foster (Worcestershire).

The Asiatic standard, particularly of Cingalese immigrants, had reached a higher level quicker than had been expected. Best known of the locally produced players was Lall Singh. The Sikh with the pastel-hued turbans and trim beard was picked out from Selangor, where he was born, brought up and played most of his cricket, to play for All-India under the Maharaja of Porbandar in England in 1932, his panther-like fielding leaving an indelible impression. He continued to grace Malayan cricket until after the war when there were other high-class Indian players; next in ability after them and the Europeans, Eurasians and Cingalese came the Chinese. They outnumber the Malays who, however, show promise. Outstanding individuals in Malaya have included Eu Cheow Teik, captain of Penang State, Capt E. I. M. Barrett (Hampshire and Shanghai), a prolific scorer, Capt. E. L. Armitage (Army), Capt. E. D. Dynes (Army), B. K. Castor (Essex), Capt. F. E. Hugonin (Army), Khoo Bin Kheng and Khooay Khoon Leong, both quick-footed left-hand bats.

Despite the Japanese occupation's ruinous effect on players and grounds, cricket revived quickly after the war. Its administration became more comprehensive; prewar objections to a broader basis evaporated. In 1948 the Malayan Cricket Association was established, its first president being Lim Khye Seng. The Singapore Cricket Association started in 1949. Cricket continued during the Emergency with provincial life menaced by guerrilla warfare. When State sides were augmented by members of visiting Forces, a player for Negri Sembilan was Petero Kubunavanua who had toured New Zealand in 1948 in the Fiji team. Stationed in the shadows deepening at square leg, he found himself encircled by swallows. As a distraction to his hawk-like attentions to the batsman, this was more than he could endure: with a ferocious sweep he picked one out of the air and put it in his sulu pocket. (Petero and his swallow; George Brown and his hawk; Dr Jahangir Khan and his sparrow; when else have ornithology and cricket coincided?)

In 1957 Brig M. A. Green (Gloucestershire and MCC manager in Australia) took Malaya, including H. E. Webb (Oxford), to Hong Kong in the Inter-Port fixture of 82 years' standing and won emphatically. But perspective was, as it had been 20 years earlier, again restored, at least in the estimation of their nearest competitors, Ceylon (including P. I. Pieris (Cambridge) and C. C. Inman (Leicestershire), by their touring Malaya in 1958 and again leaving unbeaten. The following year Australia en route to India under R. Benaud played against Malaya. In 1963 the Malaysian Cricket Association was established, Sabah and Sarawak affiliating, Singapore going its own way in 1965 but still playing (by invitation) in Malaysia's inter-State competition. British North Borneo's first cricket was after 1918. English residents,

The primary object of this Commonwealth tour of the Far East, arranged and managed by E. W. Swanton, in 1964 was to encourage the game in Malaysia. The team visited in turn Penang, Singapore, Kuala Lumpur, Hong Kong, Bangkok, and Calcutta where in the last match an Indian XI of Test strength was defeated by 7 wickets. Back row: K. T. Ramadhin, N. C. Pretzlik, K. Taylor, M. G. Griffith, J. D. Piachaud, T. B. L. Coghlan, R. A. Hutton and S. Nurse; front row: E. W. Swanton, Nawab of Pataudi, R. Benaud, A. C. D. Ingleby-Mackenzie (captain), G. St. A. Sobers, I. M. McLachlan and J. S. O. Haslewood (honorary treasurer).

supplemented by Australians and Chinese, were hard to beat on the grounds at Jesselton and Sandakan. As Sabah, on its first appearance in the Malaysian inter-state competition in 1969, it lost narrowly to Perak in the semi-final. In 1971 Hong Kong defeated Sabah. To encourage the new Federation of Malaysia, E. W. Swanton's side in 1964, captained by A. C. D. Ingleby-Mackenzie, played at Penang, Singapore and Kuala Lumpur, the last-named ground seeing the first appearance of an All-Malaysian National XI (against which G. St A. Sobers had 5 wickets in 5 balls but made only 0 and 1). In matches with the Malaysia Cricket Association President's XI (at Singapore, still in the Federation), the Nawab of Pataudi scored a century but Dr A. E. Delikan, a Cingalese from Penang, took 7 wickets; Sobers made a hundred at Kuala Lumpur where the Victorian-Oriental style Government Buildings and their tall Clock Tower dominate the capital's individualistic ground.

Succeeding tours were by Worcestershire, the Cricket Club of India, an International XI under M. J. Stewart, Hyderabad Blues (including Indian Test players) and the 1970 MCC side under A. R. Lewis (G. Boycott making 2 hundreds and R. M. C. Gilliat one against the Malaysian side which lost by a heavy margin). The Malaysian side toured Ceylon in 1972. Including 3 Cingalese and 3 Chinese, it lost 4 and drew 1 of the 5 matches. Elected as an associate member of the International Cricket Conference in 1967, Malaysia, which is energetically run by its Sikh secretary, Daljit Singh Gill, played in the ICC Trophy Competition in 1979 under the captaincy of Dr R. Ratnalingam but finished bottom of Group III without winning any matches.

PHILIP SNOW

Mauritius

In a Commonwealth survey it could hardly be guessed where outside the major cricket-playing parts the game had its earliest start. Mauritius claims this distinction, with records of its existence there in 1838 (although Singapore believes 1837 to be its own first date). The Mauritius CC was founded in 1845. A commendable continuity of archives shows that the game, starting in the military garrison, spread among the English community. The many Mauritians of French descent have taken to other English sports but not cricket, accounting readily enough for the present name of the club governing cricket, which has become the Mauritius Football and Hockey Club. Almost all external matches are with visiting ships, played on turf wickets on impressive grounds 1,000 feet above sea-level at Roseheill and Vacoas. The sugar industry of Mauritius has been built up by Indian immigrants whose descendants show skill at cricket, but the isolation of the island, 1,300 miles from Africa, bars development.

Mauritius had its first team from overseas in 1972 when Lusaka Nondescripts, the first Zambian team to venture abroad, made a visit. The island lost both matches, despite the notable all-round play of G. B. Naik.

PHILIP SNOW

The Netherlands

In only two countries on the continent of Europe has cricket become a regular feature of the sporting calendar – Denmark and The Netherlands. It is not generally realized that amongst the canals, the tulips and the polders cricket has been played in The Netherlands for more than a hundred years: *Wisden* notes that a club was formed in Utrecht in 1855; the oldest existing club, Koninklijke Utile Dulci in Deventer, was formed in 1875; and the Netherlands Cricket Association has been in existence since 1883, when there were already 18 clubs.

Cricket in The Netherlands has a long history, though it has remained to this day a 'minority' sport – some say an 'elite' sport – enjoyed by 3,000 or so men, women, boys and girls. There are now 60 clubs, the majority of them in the densely populated west of the country where the largest cities, Amsterdam, Rotterdam and The Hague are located. The Hague area is really the hub of Dutch cricket with over a dozen clubs and 4 of the 8 which make up the Hoofdklasse (Premier League), but the last two decades have witnessed a steady growth of the game in other parts of the country. 17 new clubs have been formed since 1960, mostly outside the big cities, although the sport is still virtually unknown in the two southernmost provinces, Zeeland and Limburg.

Competitive cricket has been played since 1891 when there were two leagues. In 1979 there were 19 senior leagues organized on a national basis (which is possible in a country only about the size of Wales) into 9 grades in which in that season 144 teams took part. There are also leagues for juniors, veterans and ladies, the latter having possessed their own governing body since 1934, and regional competitions and tournaments for juniors of all ages. All this competitive cricket, played mainly at the weekends, is concentrated into a short $3\frac{1}{2}$ month season, mid-May to the end of August. Dutch cricket clubs have extreme difficulty in playing outside this period because they invariably have to make use of the playing fields of a hockey or football club – very often a sister club in the same organization – whose requirements normally take precedence. There are no purpose-built cricket grounds as such; the matches are played on a matting wicket, laid out over a gravel base.

Cricket, like all sports in The Netherlands, is under the control of a central body, in this case the Royal Netherlands Cricket Association whose 13 committees preside over all aspects of the sport. Again just like other sports in The Netherlands, cricket is subsidized by the Ministry of Culture, Recreation and Social Welfare, and also by the Netherlands Sport Federation. Sponsors, a very important source of income for most Dutch sports, have not been attracted to cricket on any large scale; neither have the radio, television or press, who devote little time and space to the sport.

A vital element in the popularization of the game is the development of international contacts. Cricketers in The Netherlands have always been ready to entertain teams from abroad, to undertake tours and to take part in tournaments at all levels. An important factor in these international relationships has been the employment of foreign coaches, many coming over from England for the summer (the first was Arthur Bentley in 1889). Coaching courses have been held in The Netherlands, in close liaison with the NCA, since 1951 with the result that many Dutchmen themselves are now qualified coaches. In 1978 they were permitted for the first time to play in the competition, in the top two grades only. This immediately attracted younger, more active professionals than hitherto, so that in 1979 15 player/coaches were spending their summers in Holland, among them Hylton Ackerman (South Africa), David Murray (West Indies) and Mike Shrimpton (New Zealand).

The Netherlands has basically three types of representative team: various junior teams selected according to age group; a ladies' team; and, of course, the full national side. All three have been more active in the 1970s than ever before. A great deal of energy is put into promoting junior cricket by means of tournaments and coaching camps, and the colts team travelled to Canada in 1979 for an international tournament there. The ladies' team has recently been in England again on tour. The senior team has over the years been privileged to play host to most of the Test cricketing countries, all of them, in fact, except India and England.

In 1964, against the Australians, The Netherlands achieved a momentous victory in a one-day game by 3 wickets. The Australians, batting first, made 197, in reply to which the Dutch opener P. Marseille scored 77, and in a frantic flurry at the end Holland just beat the clock to signal a great day in her

The Netherlands team for the ICC Trophy, England 1979 – standing: Ted Hartman (physiotherapist), Dick Kramer, Peter Entrop, Peter van Wel, Dick Bekedam, Mar Flohil and W. van der Sloot (manager); sitting: Tony Bakker, Jan Spits, Rob van Weelde, Steven Lubbers, Chris van Schouwenburg (captain), Eduard Abendanon, Rene Schoonheim and Menso van Meurs.

cricket history. The hero of the hour was R. Onstein who hit the third ball of the final over for six and hooked the next for the winning four. Periodically, English county teams also visit the continent.

More regular fixtures for the Dutch national team are, however, against Ireland, Denmark, Free Foresters, MCC and the British Forces in Germany. These matches, varying between one-day and three-day affairs, usually provide interesting and close encounters. In recent years two further associate members of the ICC have been opponents of the Dutch team: Bermuda (in 1969) and Sri Lanka (in 1975). Every other year or so the Dutch team undertakes a short tour, usually to England, to gain experience against opposition ranging from ordinary clubs to near county standard (minor counties and county 2nd XIs are popular opponents). All in all, the national side has a wide ranging fixture list but no hardy annuals. The 1979 World Cup was The Netherlands' first opportunity to take part in an international competition at the senior level.

For the first time intensive indoor winter training was organized, under the leadership of coloured South African Dik Abed, who was for many years a professional in the Lancashire League and now lives and works in Holland. Great success was not achieved, however, partly because Holland found itself in the strongest of the three qualifying groups.

Representative cricket is by no means the only way Dutch cricketers maintain contact with the rest of the world. There are a number of invitation and touring sides active, notably The Flamingos, founded in 1921, who tour England every other year, and have a close relationship with MCC and the Free Foresters. They have also visited Corfu. For veterans, the Still Going Strong club is the Dutch equivalent of the English Forty Club and, in commemoration of 50 years' existence, organized a tournament in 1979, inviting her English, Scottish and Danish counterparts to share the celebrations. The more recently established Klaas Vervelde Touring Team has kept cricketing links open with South Africa, whilst one Dutch club, 'De Kieviten', even more exotically, visited the Cayman Islands in April 1979.

D. J. HARDY

New Caledonia

Here is a veritable cricket surprise. In this French colony the game is played with uninhibited, often rumbustious enjoyment. By women. And on Sundays. Umpires, to be neutral, must be men. So as not to be mistaken for other figures on the slag field, which is often submerged in rainwater with the players paddling barefooted, umpires always hold bats. These are the same shape as the women's, like those used for baseball. The stumps are appreciably taller than in the conventional game and are always bail-less. There are no creases and an over consists of one ball. Matches, often 15 a side, have no time limits: the two male umpires are arbiters as to which side wins. The scorer has to be a man.

The players' dress is highly-coloured, knee-length Mother Hubbards introduced by English missionaries before they showed them cricket at the end of the last century. Straw hats and frangipani flowers over the ear complete the costume. Pads and other protection are eschewed. The batswoman can always, and invariably does, employ a runner – younger than herself.

Hideously ugly factories producing a huge proportion of the world's nickel are the backdrop to the ground in the capital, Nouméa, where 14 women's teams and three from the neighbouring Loyalty Islands of Ouvea, Mare and Lifou, which are half-way between New Caledonia and New Hebrides, play at weekends in the Caledonian Cricket League.

Men in the Loyalty Islands, where there are more English than French characteristics, are now eager to take up the game: male teams have started there, but without female arbiters. In these part-Anglicized Islands a punch on the nose is a '*sikisse*' derived from 'six', the most aggressive of hits.

PHILIP SNOW

New Hebrides

In this Anglo-French Condominium cricket started on a baseball diamond left by American Forces. The Vila CC, established in 1945, became the New Hebrides Cricket Association in 1978. Polyglot pioneers were P. Colley, Commandant of British Police, J. Lançon, a French engineer-cum-planter, and J. C. Stegler of the commercial firm of Burns Philp, which gave the trophy competed for annually on the flamboyant tree-lined British Paddock of the capital, Port Vila. All cricketers are on Efate Island, one of the 80 islands in the Archipelago handicapped by poor communications: there are 150 players, 100 of them being native New Hebrideans. Prominent among the latter – all bowlers – are villagers Tafaki and Naapu and a South Pacific University student, Niroa John – and a batsman, Apete Marayawa. Bowling and fielding, not requiring the same sophistication as batting, are the strongest features of the indigenous game which is developing fast. The leading European batsman and organizer is L. D. Barrett: he captained New Hebrides against eight other countries in the 1979 South Pacific Games in Fiji (the first time that cricket has been included in this versatile tournament).

In 1976 New Hebrides made a first journey overseas to compete for the local Crompton Cup in Fiji, drawing all matches, and in 1977 Fiji returned the visit, winning a one-day game. Unlike other Pacific groups, the season is from March to November. The New Hebrides Cricket Association has to have three Patrons – the British and French Resident Commissioners and the Chief Minister, a New Hebridean.

PHILIP SNOW

New Zealand

T. P. MCLEAN

The Rossetti who asked, 'Does the road wind uphill all the way?' and who herself answered, 'Yes, to the very end', could be said to have uttered an exact and prophetic statement as to the game in cricket's southernmost seas. In the nigh on 140 years during which it has faithfully been followed and played in New Zealand, 90 were spent in achieving Test-match status. Of the 136 Tests which have been played in these last 50 years, no more than 10 have been won. Most humiliating of all was the dreadful experience against Sir Leonard Hutton's great Ashes-winning team when Tyson, Statham and the ferociously accurate Appleyard destroyed the second innings for only 26 runs.

Being of stout British stock, New Zealanders decided that this was no more than a battle, not a war. Within 3 years, they had won their first Test victory by beating Denis Atkinson's West Indians. Just over a dozen years later, New Zealand had the moral victory in a drawn series with India in India and carried on to defeat Pakistan in a series in Pakistan. G. M. Turner flourished so abundantly that all 5 of the Tests in the West Indies in 1971–72 were drawn, while in England in 1973 B. E. Congdon, in successive innings, played two memorable knocks, one of which, at Lord's, brought England perilously close to defeat. The road was still winding uphill, as it always will in a country at the whim of freakish weather and so lightly populated – 3,140,000 in 1979 spread over an area about five-sixths the size of the British Isles – as to make the game's financial burden as tormenting as Sinbad's Old Man of the Sea. But the guns of the 1812 Overture were primed; and fired they were, over and over again, when at Christchurch in 1974 and Wellington in 1978 first Australia and then England were fairly and squarely beaten.

In these later years, when New Zealand won a one-day tournament against the Australian states, and they rather than Australia figures among the semi-finalists of the 1979 Prudential World Cup, many fine New Zealand players emerged – the likes of R. J. Hadlee, one of the most competitive of 'quickies', Turner, Congdon, G. P. Howarth (a century in each innings of a Test against England), J. G. Wright, S. Boock and so on. No doubt because they were offered so many more opportunities than were available in the days of slow boats to England and elsewhere, they were sometimes deemed to be superior to their predecessors. But who, looking down the long hill up which New Zealand have climbed in cricket, could forget such a captain as T. C. Lowry, trained at Cambridge; G. R. Dickinson, a genuine fast bowler who played for his country at both cricket and rugby; C. S. Dempster, a great opening batsman; J. Cowie, a medium-fast bowler who at Sydney bowled S. J. McCabe first ball in the first innings and second ball in the second – 'How could I forget the man,' said McCabe 30 years later, 'he was a great bowler'; M. P. Donnelly, to whom the Lord's members stood after his hundred for the Gentlemen and his 206 for New Zealand; B. Sutcliffe, who in 1949 achieved an aggregate on an English tour second only to Bradman's; J. R. Reid, whose 15 sixes in an innings still ranks as a world record; W. E. Merritt, who, given the ball at the start of MCC's innings in 1931, spun out 7 batsmen for 28; G. A. Bartlett, genuinely fast, who made I. D. Craig his 'bunny' in New Zealand and who in South Africa menaced as a counter-puncher whenever the Springboks were tempted to fire in their hostile battery; and many more going all the way back to the Auckland fast bowler, W. Stemson, who in 1905 uprooted Trumper's leg-stump for 0 more or less simultaneously with the cry of 'No ball' (Stemson flung his hat upon the ground and only just restrained himself from jumping on it – whereupon Trumper, of course, scored 92 in 100 minutes).

A host of fine cricketers have made their way up that long winding hill – in one of those mythical contests in cricket's Valhalla, a New Zealand side starting off with Dempster, Turner, Sutcliffe (B.), Donnelly, Reid and having, at the tail, Cowie, R. J. Hadlee, Bartlett and Merritt would not easily suffer defeat – and, providentally, the parade of 'good 'uns' seems thicker now than before. The real problem has been to marry the talents. When first-class bowlers have been short, whatever their category, the inconsistent wickets available at both club and representative level have sometimes been to blame. When a bowler doesn't have to work for his wickets, he doesn't learn to work. Nevertheless, in terms of public interest, the game prospers. To the regret of many, the old-time first-class competition for the Plunket Shield was superseded by a tournament sponsored by Shell, in which newfangled inventions like limited overs for the first innings, and bonus points for everything short of dropped catches, tended to dissipate the incentive to get on and win the game. But a national coaching scheme initiated by the former Worcestershire and England player, Martin Horton, during the 1960s has been helpful in establishing higher standards at schoolboy level – fine teams of New Zealand youngsters have done very well in Australia – and a national cricket foundation is steadily amassing a substantial capital fund, the income from which will materially encourage future ventures.

For purposes of convenience, it can be stated that New Zealand came into being in 1840, for on 6 February of that year the Treaty of Waitangi bound the country to the British Crown and the Governor of the colony, Captain Hobson, RN, took pride in exclaiming to the aboriginal Maori race, 'Now we are one people.' Only 6 years before that, there had been reported cases of cannibalism among the Maoris. Twenty years before, they had fought a tribal battle of the utmost ferocity. And yet, within a year of the Treaty, there was cricket. As early as 28 December, 1842, amid the wassail of Christmas-time, the blues of the Wellington club, with 126 notches in 2 innings, defeated the reds, who had scored 124 – 'after which', so the *Spectator* remarked, 'they adjourned to the ship's hotel, where they partook of a true Christmas dinner of roast beef and plum pudding'. Three years later, in March 1844, the *Examiner* in Nelson reported a match by the Surveyors of the Land Company against Nelson (Nelson won) and said: 'We hail with pleasure the *revival* of the truly English game of cricket.'

So, securely, the game was planted in the growing colony; and over the decades leading up to the turn of the century, it kept pace with the growth of the population and the development of the country. As early as 1851, when the province of Canterbury was founded after the arrival of four ships from England, 500 acres of the town of Christchurch were set aside as a reserve named Hagley Park, in honour of the Lyttelton family seat in Worcestershire, and from early days cricket was played here. By 1882, Lancaster Park Oval had been brought into use by a company of which the capital was 6*s*, divided into shares of 1*s* apiece. Wellington, which had set about the game on a club basis in 1846, in 1867 established headquarters at the Basin Reserve, which had been left a swamp when a vast, convulsive earthquake a few years before raised all the land about. The Domain in Auckland came into being in 1862 and on every summer Saturday to this day, this ground is peopled by dozens of club cricketers whose wickets are spaced little more than half a good throw from each other.

By 1864, Parr's All-England XI, which was visiting Victoria, was persuaded to make a brief visit to Otago and Canterbury and teams of XXII were fielded against the tourists. By 1877, Lillywhite brought on his team from Australia and in 1878 the Australians made a visit, the consequences of which are not perhaps fully recorded in the history of Australian cricket. When set to play the Canterbury province, the Australians insisted that the locals, in accordance with custom, bat 22 men. The locals, who had pride in their prowess, resisted. They were prepared to compromise at 15, but if the Australians persisted in their demands, there would be no game. So XV it was – and perhaps, if you listen carefully, you may hear the cheers and the roars of laughter to this day; for Canterbury won.

As the game strengthened and expanded, so did the demand for technical improvements increase. The headmaster of Wellington College, J. P. Firth – known to generations as, simply, 'The Boss' – became an inspiring leader and his call-sign, 'Play the game, sir!' took on the character of a battle-cry. Professionals were engaged from England and Australia and some stayed for long periods. Albert Trott, of the Australian XI, was one incumbent, and one of the classic batsmen, C. G. Macartney – 'The Governor-General' – did duty for a season. Greatest of all was A. E. Relf, the Englishman who served three years in Auckland. It is almost certainly true that no man ever did more for the game in New Zealand. He was not only a great cricketer, he was also a great technician and coach. Under his influence, Auckland bounded to the forefront and for years was all but unbeatable. On 27 December 1894, the New Zealand Cricket Council was formed in Christchurch, and from this significant date, which roughly coincided with the establishment of the New Zealand Rugby Union, cricket took on a national character.

It was in the summer of 1906–07 that Lord Plunket, the Governor-General of New Zealand, gave a shield for competition among the first-class provinces. The first to hold the trophy was Canterbury, but under the challenge system which was then in vogue they were soon dispossessed and in a period of four seasons Auckland resisted 7 challenges. In the period of 14 years ending on 10 January 1921, there were 32 challenges of which Canterbury won 16, Auckland 14 and Wellington 2. Subsequently, the system was altered, the winner being annually discovered by the best performance in the series of matches among the first-class provinces. Lord Hawke organized a team to New Zealand in 1902–03 and subsequently gave a cup which was put into competition in the 1910–11 season. This was arranged for the minor, or second-class, provinces on a challenge basis, which is still retained, and it has been valuable in whetting the interest of hundreds of cricketers in districts that, at least in the good old days, tended to be isolated.

It should be explained that in the days before the First World War the provinces of Auckland, Wellington, Canterbury and Otago, which were centred about the metropolitan areas of Auckland, Wellington, Christchurch and Dunedin respectively, were recognized as first-class districts. In 1950–51 Central Districts was formed from the minor provinces of Taranaki, Wanganui, Hawke's Bay, Manawatu, Wairarapa, Nelson and Marlborough and to the huge delight of these places, it not only played in, but also won, the Plunket Shield at the fourth attempt. In the 1956–57 season, after further heavy pressure had been exerted upon the New Zealand Council, a 6th first-class grouping, called Northern Districts, was created from the minor and more or less contiguous provinces of Northland, Waikato, Bay of Plenty and Poverty Bay in the northern half of the North Island.

In the 120 years since the visit of Parr's All-England team, which included E. M. Grace and Julius Caesar – who, like his illustrious forbear, also came, saw and conquered – a great number of teams of all sorts and conditions have visited New Zealand. The early Australian teams included F. R. Spofforth, Trumble, W. W. Armstrong, Clem Hill and the immortal Victor Trumper; and it is scarcely a matter of argument that the greatest batting ever seen in New Zealand was from Trumper against Canterbury at the end of February 1914. In an innings of 293, he made his first century in 73 minutes, his 200 in 131 minutes and his whole innings in 180 minutes.

Meanwhile, the kindly English brought their great players. By far the longest tour of the Colony before the First World War was made by a team arranged by Lord Hawke and captained in his absence by P. F. Warner. This team included B. J. T. Bosanquet and E. M. Dowson and it played together 18 matches, ending with 2 'Tests' which were won by 7 wickets in one case and by an innings and 22 runs in the other. MCC sent a team of amateurs in 1906–07 which was captained by E. G. Wynyard and which included J. W. H. T. Douglas and this, too, played a long tour of sixteen matches. Once more there were 2 'Test' matches. It was significant of the strength of New Zealand that 2 matches were lost, 1 to Canterbury by 7 wickets and the other to New Zealand by 56 runs. Douglas performed prodigies, scoring 433 runs at 27 and taking 84 wickets at 10·5.

Following the First World War, MCC visits increased and Australian tours correspondingly declined. A. C. MacLaren plucked bouncers off his eyebrows in exhibiting his famous hook while leading a team of 1922–23 which included the New Zealander, Lowry, just down from Cambridge, and A. P. F. Chapman, who was later to marry Lowry's sister. At the end of the 1920s, A. H. H. Gilligan captained a side which included Woolley and K. S. Duleepsinhji. This was a famous occasion, for in a Test Match at Wellington the New Zealand openers, C. S. Dempster and J. E. Mills, put on 276; but the match, in spite of the bright promise of the partnership, was drawn. In 1932–33, D. R. Jardine led his team onward from the explosions of the 'Body-line' tour to New Zealand for 2 Test Matches, both of which were drawn and both of which were

England v New Zealand, the Oval, 1931: the first series between the two countries to take place in England. D. R. Jardine and T. C. Lowry were the captains.

notable for incredible displays of batting by Hammond. In the Second Test, he was unbeaten with 336, 2 runs more than the then world record Test score of D. G. Bradman's at Headingley in 1930. It was flawless batting, mounting in strength and brilliance to the climax of 4 sixes over the head of a fine left-arm quickish bowler, J. Newman, in the one over.

From the end of the Second World War, MCC excursions to New Zealand were continued and matches with England were played during the visits by the sides led by Hammond, F. R. Brown, Hutton, P. B. H. May and E. R. Dexter. In many of these, the want of confidence which Trumble had pinpointed so many years before led to some unfortunate experiences for New Zealand teams, and these culminated in the total disaster of an afternoon at Eden Park in 1955 when Statham, Tyson and Appleyard reduced the New Zealanders to one of the saddest jokes of all cricket, a second innings of 26. It was an afternoon when, putting it mildly, terror stalked abroad – terror in the hearts of administrators and cricket-lovers, too, for this sort of performance, turning a noble pastime into a caricature, could in repetition do the game irreparable harm. Australia in the 1920s dispatched a team led by W. M. Woodfull, containing W. H. Ponsford, W. A. Oldfield and the late Archie Jackson, who flashed a brilliant blade for all too short a time before he was bowled by death. The team, too, included C. V. Grimmett and at this New Zealanders took pride; for Grimmett, like Spofforth before him, was born in New Zealand. Like Spofforth, too, the immortal 'Clarrie' was a fast bowler until Australians tamed him.

H. B. Cameron led a South African team to New Zealand from Australia in the summer of 1931–32, and partly by the batting of himself, B. Mitchell and a tall, powerful man. J. A. J. Christy, and even more by the bowling of Q. McMillan and a magnificent left-arm 'quickie' in N. Quinn, won both of the Test Matches. Some 20 years later, the Springboks, captained by J. E. Cheetham, toured again, once more successfully, for this was a team of such talents as D. J. McGlew and R. A. McLean and into the bargain its previous squaring of the Test series with Australia had been achieved by fielding of the very highest quality. Meanwhile, from the postwar years, the Australians paid increasingly frequent visits. The first, in 1945–46, was almost as disastrous as the Statham-Tyson-Appleyard affair, for Lindwall and O'Reilly bowled superbly to dismiss New Zealand for 42 and 54.

Gratifyingly, this period did produce a Test Match victory, the first full-scale Test victory in New Zealand history. The first West Indian visit of 1951–52 offered Weekes, Worrell and Walcott, not to mention Ramadhin and Valentine, at their mightiest. By the time of the second West Indian visit, in 1955–56, Walcott was not playing, Worrell had other engagements and the captain was D. Atkinson. There were 4 Tests and the West Indians duly won the first 3. At the fourth, at Eden Park, the scene of shame against Hutton's team, the West Indians batted last. Even Everton Weekes, who had scored 6 hundreds in 9 innings, like the others found the bowling of H. B. Cave, a nagging right-hander dropping them on a length, or just short of it, too accurate to command. It was one of those afternoons of contagion of which cricket offers so many examples. As wickets began to fall, the New Zealand team became inspired. The crowd roared. It was victory, by 190 runs; and all that a former New Zealand captain, G. O. Rabone, could say, over and over again, was 'I'm so bloody pleased. I'm so *bloody* pleased'.

New Zealand's cricketing experiences outward bound began with a visit to Australia in 1898–99, when defeats were suffered from both Victoria and New South Wales, and were followed with a second tour, in 1913–14, when Queensland was beaten by 12 runs, South Australia was held to a draw and there were losses to both Victoria and New South Wales. Again in 1925–26, yet another tour was made. The matches with New South Wales, Victoria and South Australia were drawn and there was a loss to Queensland by an innings and 92 runs. These tours were not without stout performance. The first tour drew attention to one of New Zealand's greatest players, D. Reese, who had played first-class cricket at the age of 16 and who later played club cricket in London with that famous team which contained 'W. G.', Murdoch and other players of splendid reputation. It also is remembered for the partnership of two Otago bowlers, A. Downes, right-arm off-spinner, and A. H. Fisher, left-arm medium, who were such perfect foils that in a long career the one took 343 wickets at 15 and the other 274 at 14·7.

A climactic experience was the visit to England of the 1927 team captained by Lowry and in which Blunt, Dempster, Dacre and an extraordinary boy, W. E. Merritt, were specially prominent. Twelve of the 38 matches were second-class, but of the 26 first-class encounters the New Zealanders won 7, lost 5 and drew 14, a satisfactory achievement. Moreover, there were splendid individual performances. In the first-class matches, Dempster scored 1,430 runs at 44·68, Blunt 1,540 at 44, Lowry 1,277 at 38·69 and Mills, the talented left-hander, who had four centuries, 1,251 at 37·90. Dacre was so impressive that he later accepted an invitation to qualify for Gloucestershire. Additionally, Merritt, who was only 19, took 107 wickets with his spinners at 23·64 and Blunt, another spinner, was also most successful with 78 at 24·97. The popularity of the side was such that 4 years later another invitation was offered by MCC. This, too, was a successful tour, the more so because 3 Test Matches were arranged. Dempster, one of the outstanding batsmen in the world at the time, scored 1,778 runs at 59·26, Blunt 1,592 at 43·02 and a young 19-year-old, H. G. Vivian, scored 1,002 at 30·36 and took 64 wickets at 23·75. Merritt was still the workhorse and from 820 overs he took 99 wickets at 26·48.

Chiefest of all yields, however, was the Test Match at Lord's which England saved, for this, assuredly, epitomized the finest qualities of cricket. Though their first innings yielded only 224, New Zealand had England in thrall until Ames and Allen came together at the tail of the England innings. But the truly wonderful aspect was that in 3 days, no fewer than 1,293 runs were scored while 34 wickets fell. In 1937, New Zealand journeyed to England again. Alas, some of the great ones, Dempster, Blunt, Merritt and a superb wicket-keeper in K. C. James, had gone all of them to England. Apart from two young men, W. M. Wallace, just turned 21, and M. P. Donnelly, not yet 20, the batting was somewhat less efficient than before and the bowling lacked such a genius as Merritt. Wallace was often brilliant in scoring 1,641 runs at 41·02, while Donnelly, who had been picked out by Errol Holmes the season before as a player of special gifts, was seen to be a left-hander of exceptional promise in his run of 1,414 at 37·21. Above all, the tour was memorable for the bowling of J. A. Cowie, right-arm medium-fast, who from 860 overs took 114 wickets at 19·95. *Wisden* praised him unstintedly and indeed he had that combination of endurance, determination and spiritual fire which makes the great bowlers. But in the 3 Tests, one of which England won, the other two being drawn, the New Zealand batting, as so often in history, was seen to be better in the nets than out in the middle and the tour record of 9 won and 9 lost in 32 matches was indicative of some falling-away from the standards of 1927 and 1931.

By the record, the 1949 team's visit to England under the captaincy of W. A. Hadlee was by far the most successful experience in the whole history of New Zealand cricket. Each of the 4 Test Matches, played over 3 days, was drawn. In the programme of 32 first-class matches, 13 were won and only 1, to Oxford University, was lost. The tour averages were staggering. Donnelly, now in the fullness of his powers, scored 2,287 runs at 61·81 and his 206 in the Test at Lord's was masterful batting to the highest degree. Though regularly opening the innings, Sutcliffe amassed 2,627 runs at 59·70 and statisticians were quick to discover that only Bradman among

One of New Zealand's strongest teams, at the Oval 1949: standing: V. J. Scott, T. B. Burtt, F. L. H. Mooney, J. B. Hayes, G. O. Rabone, H. B. Cave, J. R. Reid, C. C. Burke, F. B. Smith and G. F. Cresswell; sitting: M. P. Donnelly, W. M. Wallace (vice-captain), W. A. Hadlee (captain), J. Cowie and B. Sutcliffe.

the batsmen to tour England had scored a higher aggregate of runs. V. J. Scott, Sutcliffe's partner, scored 1,572 at 40·30, and Wallace, who totalled 960 runs before the end of May and who so nearly scored his 1,000, had an aggregate of 1,722 at 49·20. There were centuries galore, 29 in all, and Wallace, Donnelly and Sutcliffe accounted for 17 of these. Altogether, the team scored 15,659 runs at an average of 39·14 a wicket.

Providentially, Sutcliffe, who was 26, and Reid, who was 21, were to remain deeply attached to New Zealand cricket. Not that they could prevent defeat in South Africa in 1953–54, even though Reid scored 1,000 runs and took fifty wickets, nor save the visit to England in 1958 from becoming a desperately unsuccessful encounter. This last, perhaps the most unfortunate experience New Zealand have had in England, began promisingly, for there were 6 wins in the first 9 matches. Then came the rain, day after day of it, and with want of match practice the team's foreseeable weaknesses, especially at the head of the innings, turned 4 of the Tests into little better than routs. The full record was 7 matches won and 6 lost out of 31 played.

Save for the triumphs scored by Dexter's team at the end of their 1962–63 tour of Australia, the history of New Zealand cricket might well have ended its first 100 years since the visit of Parr's team with a bright, golden haze on the meadow. In 18 first-class matches in South Africa in 1961–62, the New Zealand team captained by Reid won 5 and lost 2. This was satisfactory enough. What was superb, wonderful, out of this world, was the achievement of sharing the Test series with the Springboks, two wins apiece and a draw in the second match. These were the first Test Match victories New Zealand had ever scored abroad; and they were merited, that was the encouraging thing. By scoring 1,915 runs in his 30 innings Reid surpassed even the efforts in South Africa of such immortals as Hobbs and Compton.

It may be that New Zealand cricket's long uphill road would have been more easily climbed had Australia been a kindlier Big Brother. But the old Australian Board of Control between the wars was stolidly indifferent to the plight of the New Zealanders who desperately needed international competition for the benefit of their finest players and the good of the game as a whole. Even when a team was sent to New Zealand soon after the end of the Second War it was designated as a 'board' rather than an Australian team. Fortunately, MCC were warm and helpful. Many an Englishman cried aloud at the thought of cricket and yet more cricket after 5 months of battling in Australia, but they came and kept on coming. Gradually, the scope of New Zealand administration widened until the establishment of a Board of Control which more fairly represented provincial opinion than had been possible in the old days of, in effect, a self-perpetuating council based upon Christchurch. From these difficulties and discussions emerged a man, J. G. Leggat, whose legal brilliance was married to wit, charm and diplomatic skill and who had been sufficient of a batsman to play for his country. His appointment as Chairman of the Council coincided with the appointment of generous-minded men to the Australian Cricket Board. Cordiality replaced the old Australian indifference. The relationship now is secure; and the benefits of this compensate for the loss of short tours by full England teams after their long and fatiguing visits to Australia and the introduction of full strength teams from England to New Zealand, incorporated with visits to India or Pakistan.

It is a measure of the progress of New Zealand at international level that of the 136 Test matches they had played by 1979, since being granted full status in 1929–30, no fewer than 122 had been since the end of the Second War. In the old days of 4-team competition in the Plunket Shield, players obtained, even if the weather was right, 72 hours of play at first-class level in each season. Now the amount has been extended to 168 hours, or 28 days of playing-time on a 6-hour day basis. Even so, the emergence of men like Turner, who can score their 1,000 runs before the end of May, as Glenn

The New Zealand team to England, 1958: standing: J. T. Ward, J. C. Alabaster, N. S. Harford, W. R. Playle, A. R. MacGibbon, T. Meale, R. W. Blair, J. T. Sparling and A. M. Moir; sitting: E. C. Petrie, L. S. M. Miller, J. A. Hayes, H. B. Cave, J. R. Reid (captain), J. H. Phillipps (manager), B. Sutcliffe and J. W. D'Arcy.

did in 1973, or score 10 hundreds in a county season, is neither easy nor natural in a country where man is born to work, not to play. Whether Turner is the most remarkable bat New Zealand has produced is arguable. Older hands still think of C. S. Dempster, who in 15 Test innings averaged 65·72 and under modern conditions of frequent play might have plundered the bowling of all countries. Yet Turner is singular because of his professionalism, his complete absorption in his job. In this, he matches New Zealand's great left-handed golfer, R. J. Charles, who won the British Open in 1963.

The most inspirational event in New Zealand cricket was the first win at Test-match level. The defeat, on 13 March 1956, of West Indies was the equivalent, in New Zealand cricketing terms, of Bannister's immortal breakthrough to the 4-minute mile. By an extraordinary coincidence, it was again on 13 March, 18 years later, that the defeat of Australia was scored, Turner contributing 101 in New Zealand's first innings and 110 not out in the second. This victory was the sweeter because Australia's leader, I. M. Chappell, violently abused Turner at the wicket. Even so stalwart an Australian as J. H. Fingleton wrote saddeningly of Chappell's attitudes and their impact on the game. Then came 15 February 1978, the great day when G. Boycott's English team were bowled out for 64 in their second innings and New Zealand, after 48 Tests in 48 years, at last were victorious over England. The teams were roughly level pegging, 228 to New Zealand, 215 to England, after the first innings of each side. New Zealand, 75 for one at lunch, seemed set for a good score in their second knock. But bounding in like an antelope Willis then bowled at his fiercest and finest. In 7 overs he had 5 wickets. New Zealand were dismissed for 123 and England, needing 137, seemed set for victory. But Boycott played all over Collinge's second ball, a yorker, and then came Richard Hadlee, bounding in scarcely less vigorously than Willis. Hadlee's bag of 6 for 26 was irresistible; he was a national hero.

It has often been dismal, sometimes it has been dreadful, this road winding uphill all the way which New Zealand cricket has had to traverse. Yet the glories of the game with the beautiful name have been abundant. Who could forget Congdon, jaw jutting out as far as the end of his bat, as he gestured defiance at England's finest? Lillee ran in, ferociously fast, and Richard Hadlee swished him for 6, widish of mid-on. While Trueman was collecting his 250th test wicket, John Reid held on and on, mourning lost partners, until he had his 100. Then, exhausted, he left. Struck down at Johannesburg by Adcock, Sutcliffe went to hospital for his ear to be stitched and returned, head bandaged like a man from Passchendaele. To the wicket came the fast bowler, R. W. Blair, whose 19-year-old fiancée 24 hours before had been one of the 151 victims of a tragic rail-disaster in New Zealand. Not in all of Test history has there been a more emotional moment, cricketers and spectators crying in sadness for Blair and in gladness for the courage of the two men. In 10 minutes, they scored 33 runs, 25 in an over off Tayfield. In 90 minutes, Sutcliffe hit 80, striking 7 sixes with staggering brilliance.

These were New Zealanders. Not least, they were cricketers. All of these have finished their long, winding walk uphill. Happily, and forever, there will be more and more to come, of the same mould, fortitude, determination and dedication to the game that has been pursued so diligently in the far southern waters of the spinning world.

Richard Collinge had 6 wickets, including Boycott's twice, in New Zealand's first victory over England, Wellington 1978.

Plunket Shield and Shell Trophy

The Plunket Shield was presented in 1906 by the then Governor-General of New Zealand, Lord Plunket. It was first awarded in 1906–07 to Canterbury as the side with the best record that season in first-class cricket in New Zealand. Until 1921 it was played for by the major provinces on a challenge basis, and was generally held by either Canterbury or Auckland. From 1921–22 a points system and an annual table obtained. The participants for many years were Auckland, Canterbury, Otago and Wellington, joined in 1950–51 by Central Districts and in 1956–57 by Northern Districts, these being amalgamations of the smaller provinces.

The winners from 1921–22 were:

1921–22	Auckland	1950–51	Otago
1922–23	Canterbury	1951–52	Canterbury
1923–24	Wellington	1952–53	Otago
1924–25	Otago	1953–54	Central Districts
1925–26	Wellington	1954–55	Wellington
1926–27	Auckland	1955–56	Canterbury
1927–28	Wellington	1956–57	Wellington
1928–29	Auckland	1957–58	Otago
1929–30	Wellington	1958–59	Auckland
1930–31	Canterbury	1959–60	Canterbury
1931–32	Wellington	1960–61	Wellington
1932–33	Otago	1961–62	Wellington
1933–34	Auckland	1962–63	Northern Districts
1934–35	Canterbury	1963–64	Auckland
1935–36	Wellington	1964–65	Canterbury
1936–37	Auckland	1965–66	Wellington
1937–38	Auckland	1966–67	Central Districts
1938–39	Auckland	1967–68	Central Districts
1939–40	Auckland	1968–69	Auckland
1940–45	No Competition	1969–70	Otago
1945–46	Canterbury	1970–71	Central Districts
1946–47	Auckland	1971–72	Otago
1947–48	Otago	1972–73	Wellington
1948–49	Canterbury	1973–74	Wellington
1949–50	Wellington	1974–75	Otago

In 1975–76 the Plunket Shield was replaced by a fresh first-class programme in New Zealand called the Shell Series, comprising an initial round of matches on a points system for the Shell Cup, after which the teams are divided into 2 divisions for the second round, with each team playing the other teams in their section, again for points. The 2 teams with the highest aggregate number of points in each section compete in a final for the Shell Trophy.

The winners of the Shell Trophy since 1975–76 have been:

1975–76	Canterbury	1977–78	Auckland
1976–77	Otago	1978–79	Otago

IRVING ROSENWATER

Auckland

Auckland, which covers a large part of North Island, has an almost tropical climate and uniform wickets, in marked contrast to Otago in New Zealand's south. But like Otago Auckland's cricket is more than a century old, for in 1859–60 Auckland journeyed to Wellington and had the distinction of winning the first inter-provincial match ever played in New Zealand. The game was then at least 15 years old in Auckland.

Cricket languished for some time due to the great distances from Auckland to the other centres, but in 1873–74 a southern tour proved a great success. In the 1880s Auckland were the best side in New Zealand, with W. E. Barton a stylish, aggressive batsman. Greater days followed in the next decade when A. E. Relf of Sussex was engaged as coach and his work for Auckland – as well as for New Zealand cricket generally – was of the highest calibre. In the period up to the First World War L. G. Hemus was probably the best batsman New Zealand had then produced. He was outshone after the war by the dashing C. C. Dacre, soon to be joined by the graceful left-hander, J. W. E. Mills. The bowling was helped by the Sussex professionals Bowley and Wensley. T. C. Lowry played for Auckland before going to Cambridge, but Auckland's greatest successes came in the 1930s when the Plunket Shield was won 4 times in succession. W. M. Wallace and V. J. Scott were fine batsmen and J. A. Cowie the best New Zealand fast bowler of his era. Bert Sutcliffe played some of his cricket for Auckland, but since the Second War the standard of cricket in Auckland has not been as high as it was.

With increased fixtures in recent years, the aggregates of the old cricketers have been surpassed, and the heaviest scorers in recent times have been M. G. Burgess (who has captained New Zealand), R. W. Morgan and R. M. Harris. Hedley Howarth, an outstanding left-arm spin bowler, is the first Auckland bowler to exceed 300 first-class wickets. (His younger brother, Geoffrey Howarth, also born in Auckland, had two seasons with the side before going elsewhere.) In the 1960s and 1970s many wickets were also taken by J. T. Sparling, R. S. Cunis and R. E. Sutton.

IRVING ROSENWATER

Canterbury

Canterbury has always been a relatively strong centre of cricket in New Zealand, though the strength has often lain around Christchurch itself. Twenty-two of Christchurch played George Parr's English side in February, 1864, and by the 1880s both Hagley Park and Lancaster Park were in regular use. Some early enterprise had been shown when Canterbury visited Australia in 1878–79 after a famous victory had been won by a Canterbury XV which defeated the 1878 Australians before they left for England. Christchurch became the headquarters of the New Zealand Cricket Council when it was formed in 1894, Canterbury's best players at this time being the batsmen L. A. Cuff and H. Demaus. Before the First World War Canterbury's captain, D. Reese, was the best all-rounder produced to that date in New Zealand, and J. H. Bennett, a medium-pace bowler, was also a tower of strength.

Canterbury were the first holders of the Plunket Shield in 1906–07. R. C. Blunt played his early cricket for Canterbury – first appearing as a schoolboy in 1917 – and R. O. Talbot and M. L. Page were also youngsters whose promise flowered to maturity. J. L. Kerr, from Wanganui College, first played for Canterbury in 1929–30 and has rendered years of invaluable service as player, coach and administrator. Canterbury's outstanding bowler of the 1930s was W. E. Merritt, the leg-spinner who was such a prominent member of the early Test sides. W. A. Hadlee, T. B. Burtt and, more recently, R. C. Motz, G. T. Dowling, B. F. Hastings and the Hadlee brothers, have all given fine service to Canterbury.

IRVING ROSENWATER

Otago

Otago, the most southerly of the New Zealand first-class sides, is the closest to England climatically. It also can claim the oldest of New Zealand's cricketing links with England, for at Dunedin in February 1864, the first English side to play in New Zealand took the field, though the game had been known there some 15 years earlier. But George Parr's team was a spur which saw many teams grow up. Otago cricket gained much when J. C. Lawton, of Warwickshire, was engaged as coach in 1890 and he built the side into a powerful unit. J. Baker was the best batsman, and for many years, A. D. Downes, an off-break bowler, and A. H. Fisher, a fast left-hander, gathered a harvest of wickets. The season 1913–14 marked the jubilee of Otago's matches with Canterbury, which had been played without a break to that time; but Otago's bowling strength had declined and her finest days were behind her. After the First World War Otago relied mainly on J. S. Shepherd, a fine batsman, A. W. Alloo, an all-rounder, and A. Galland, who could bat, bowl and keep wicket. But her finest player was R. C. Blunt, once of Canterbury, whose greatest batting feats were reserved for Otago; he was also a very capable slow right-arm bowler. Most of Blunt's batting records were exceeded after the Second World War by Bert Sutcliffe, the most prolific batsman in New Zealand's history: his innings for Otago include scores of 385 and 355. For brief periods W. A. Hadlee and J. R. Reid appeared for Otago, and in recent years J. C. Alabaster, A. M. Moir and S. N. McGregor have all played well. G. M. Turner made his debut for the side in 1964–65 (while still a schoolboy) and for more than a decade rendered them outstanding service.

IRVING ROSENWATER

Wellington

In a broad survey of New Zealand cricket, Wellington would probably emerge as the most successful of the first-class provincial sides. Cricket was known there in the early 1840s – soon after the first settlement – and in March 1860 Wellington received a side from Auckland to see the start of first-class cricket in New Zealand. The first English side was Lillywhite's in 1876–77, by which time the Basin Reserve ground had already been in use for some years. Wellington cricket came to the fore in the 1880s, when R. V. Blacklock proved himself a fine batsman, as did his younger brother Arthur. W. S. Brice, a fast-medium bowler, performed heroically from 1902 until the late 1920s and after the First World War Wellington were the strongest side in New Zealand. J. S. Hiddleston, a powerful driver, was the best batsman in the country for a few years, and Wellington could boast also H. M. McGirr, T. C. Lowry and C. S. Dempster. The wicket-keeper, K. C. James, was well above average, as later was F. L. H. Mooney. The versatile J. R. Reid, who first came to England as a 20-year-old in 1949, performed great feats for Wellington and captained them, as well as New Zealand, with much vigour and fine spirit. The postwar bowlers of distinction have included the brothers G.F. and A. E. Cresswell, R. W. Blair, R. O. Collinge and E. J. Chatfield; and the batsmen B. A. G. Murray, B. W. Sinclair and G. P. Bilby.

IRVING ROSENWATER

Nigeria

Cricket was introduced by administrators and the Armed Services to Lagos about the end of the 19th century. Its highest level in Nigeria was for many years inter-Colonial rivalry with the Gold Coast; it was not until 1932 that the Nigeria Cricket Association was founded with jurisdiction over European cricket. The African Cricket Association started later. Multiracial organization was achieved in 1956, with a fast-medium bowler, A. O. Omolulu, as the first president. In the (primarily European) matches with Gold Coast to that date, Nigeria won twice as many matches as their opponents.

In Nigeria there is perhaps one name more isolated in the single-mindedness of his effort for the game than in the cricket history of most Commonwealth countries. F. K. Butler, who played for Hertfordshire, was a leading all-rounder for Nigeria from 1925 to 1939, an inspired administrator (secretary for many years after 1936) with a paternal interest in the native game, and also historian. There is a long list of other notable participants – Cmdr A. G. G. Webb, an outstanding secretary for Leicestershire, and generally regarded as Nigeria's best wicket-keeper; W. R. de la C. Shirley (Cambridge and Hampshire), a police officer whose performances in the series with the Gold Coast were highly successful; 3 administrative officers – A. K. Judd (Cambridge and Hampshire), T. B. G. Welch (Northamptonshire) and M. V. Spurway (Somerset); D. A. D. Sewell (Buckinghamshire); E. M. Cadogan (Army and Hampshire); R. G. W. Melsome (Army and Gloucestershire); Sir Charles Arden-Clarke, later Governor of Sarawak and first Governor-General of Ghana; General Sir Hugh Stockwell, and Sir John Maybin, Chairman of the Association before becoming Governor of Northern Rhodesia. Among distinctive Nigerian players have been N. D. Nuha, an in-and-out swing bowler. African bowling is generally better than its batting, and conventionally of a smart pace.

In 1959 Nigeria was captained for the first time by an African. Sierra Leone, the Gambia, Ghana and Nigeria, which has more clubs than the other countries put together, compete annually in a quadrangular tournament; Nigeria normally wins it. Tanzania's visit in 1974 was Nigeria's first contact with East Africa. The principal grounds are at Lagos, the capital, Enugu, Kano, Ibadan, Warri and Zaria, with matting over grass or lateritic subsoil.

PHILIP SNOW

Pakistan

R. A. ROBERTS AND D. J. RUTNAGUR

Among Pakistan's first widely-lauded exports were cricketers. Within a few years of Jinnah's Muslim state being founded in 1947, with its 2 wings, West (including a big slice of the old Northern India, Baluchistan and Sind) and East (part of Bengal), the world was sitting up to take notice of Pakistan's cricket deeds. Unless possessing an erudite background of eastern affairs, one might at times have been forgiven for assuming that cricket was more important to Pakistan than jute. The new nation, however, certainly gained enormous prestige from its early gains at cricket. The first years were studded with some brilliant successes. Like all pioneers, the cricketers who wore Pakistan's colours were fired with ambition, zeal and confidence. Test match status was accorded in 1952, and within 5 years Pakistan could point to victories over England, Australia, India and New Zealand. The first series out of the sub-continent, in England in 1954, was drawn after a famous win at the Oval. Their first-ever Test against Australia, on matting in Karachi, was won. Their maiden tour of the West Indies brought defeat in the rubber, but victory in one Test was followed by a clear-cut success in the return series at home, a year later.

This remarkable budding, however, was slow to blossom. After beating West Indies in 1959, Pakistan did not win a Test anywhere until they defeated New Zealand in a home series in 1964–65. In between they played 22 Tests, of which 8 were lost and the rest drawn. During this barren period, 2 full series against neighbouring India failed to produce a single conclusive result. Following their home win against New Zealand, another 8 years went by before Pakistan won again, and that despite the emergence of several fine cricketers. Perhaps too much had been expected after Pakistan's dramatic entry into Test cricket. It might have been more to their advantage if success had not come quite so suddenly, for the players found it hard to live up to what was so soon expected of them.

There were various reasons for this early, albeit passing, decline in fortunes. Prominent among them were the retirement of an outstanding captain in Abdul Hafeez Kardar and the fading of the powers of the great Fazal Mahmood. Another significant cause, at least in the short term, was the switch from matting to turf pitches. Lahore was always noted for turf wickets of outstanding quality but elsewhere, until the early 1960s, the game was played on matting, stretched over baked, rolled mud. The arid climate raised problems in preparing turf pitches. While they played on matting, Pakistan were well nigh invincible, mainly because Fazal used the conditions so well. The only time Pakistan were beaten on matting was at Dacca, by the Australians under Richie Benaud, in the 1959–60 series. As far as the Pakistanis' splendid maiden tour of England was concerned, their bowlers' experience on matting served them well, for in a wretched summer they found a similarity in conditions. Although matting had been the key to so much success, Pakistan cricket authorities were not reluctant to opt for turf, especially at the first-class grounds.

They appreciated that the change would be of benefit to their cricketers when playing abroad. Also, at the time, Pakistan were trying to figure more prominently in the programme of international tours, and they felt that other countries scarcely relished the prospect of playing on matting. The present generation has played no first-class cricket on the mat, so that the change to turf is no more a valid reason for a lack of Test victories, particularly with so many of the leading Pakistani players plying their trade in England. The only residual drawback of the change is that the Pakistani version of a turf pitch, being miserably slow, has made for a surfeit of slow-moving, unfinished Test matches.

The one regrettable aspect of the tremendous enthusiasm whisked up by Pakistan's early success was that big cricket had to move away from historic and traditional venues such as Lawrence Gardens (renamed Bagh-E-Jinnah) in Lahore and the Gymkhana ground in Karachi. To accommodate the increasing crowds at Test matches, new stadia were erected in both these cities. Need was felt for a stadium in Dacca too, despite the fact that cricket was not a big favourite in East Bengal. In the 24 years that it remained a part of Pakistan, the east wing contributed only one Test player, Niaz Ahmed, a seam bowler, in the mid-1960s. Even so, the loss of Dacca as a Test centre, after the birth of Bangla Desh, was still a major handicap to Pakistan.

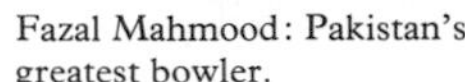

Fazal Mahmood: Pakistan's greatest bowler.

A. H. Kardar: the founder of Pakistan cricket.

In Lahore and Karachi, the vast stadia stand as monuments to the achievements of Pakistan under Kardar during the pioneering days. Seldom now, though, are they filled to the extent visualized by their builders. Crowd indiscipline, often rooted in political unrest, has become a regular feature of Test cricket in Pakistan, deterring many a genuine cricket-lover from attending. Also, to keep out the disruptive element the authorities have raised admission charges beyond the pocket of even the average man.

In two of the larger provinces of West Pakistan, Punjab and Sind, cricket took root under the British Raj and shared a common upbringing with India. The military and the schools gave Pakistan a flying start. Many of the finest sportsmen in colonial India came from the north. Polo, squash, cricket and hockey flourished. Lahore, the premier city of the region, where Rudyard Kipling worked on the old *Civil & Military Gazette*, was a major military cantonment as well as a famous seat of learning. The local garrison and officers on leave from service on the North-West Frontier played a lot of cricket in Lahore (the prints, dating from before the First World War, that adorn the walls of the Lahore Gymkhana might have come straight from Sandhurst), as did the colleges, on their picturesque grounds flanking the famous Mall. Lahore University developed many outstanding players. With few exceptions, the first international Pakistan side was the Lahore University team of the mid-1940s.

Kardar had already played for India before going up to Oxford, and several more of the first Pakistan team would have done so had the sub-continent remained as one country. In fact, with the team picked before the physical act of partition, Fazal Mahmood, as a 20-year-old fast-medium bowler of exceptional promise, was included for the projected Indian tour of Australia in 1947.

Fazal was one of the four pillars upon which the new country were able to build a future. The others were Kardar, shortly due to come down from Oxford, Imtiaz Ahmed, a wicket-keeper-batsman of unusual flair and serene disposition, and a teenage member of a remarkable family which moved across the border from the Western Indian state of Junagadh to Karachi, Hanif Mohammad. All the patience and inscrutability of the east were concentrated in Hanif's tiny frame. Imtiaz made the initial impact. The first time Pakistan put a national XI into the field was against the West Indian team of 1948–49. This was before Pakistan had been accorded Test status. In a representative match at Lahore, Pakistan gave a splendid account of themselves against a side that included Walcott, Weekes, Goddard, Christiani, Rae, Stollmeyer and Prior Jones. Pakistan earned an honourable draw through a 2nd-wicket stand of 205 between Imtiaz (who also kept wicket with distinction) and Mahommad Saeed. Both scored centuries. Mohammad Saeed, whose daughter was to marry Fazal, and whose son, Yawar Saeed, played for Somerset, will be remembered also for his organization of the frequent visits to England of the Pakistan Eaglets, teams consisting of young Test prospects. Fazal also played in that first representative match, though without any stirring success.

The visit of N. D. Howard's MCC side at the end of 1951 took Pakistan a step nearer to Test status. In the representative match at Karachi, Fazal's pronounced leg-cutter accounted for 6 victims and Pakistan went on to win. *Wisden* referred to some curious umpiring decisions, recording that not one of over thirty appeals by MCC for lbw was granted, but adding that 'Pakistan authorities were highly delighted and regarded the victory as a great claim towards their inclusion in the Imperial Cricket Conference'. Khan Mohammad took 5 wickets in Pakistan's second innings; Hanif, only 16, batted 4 hours for 64 and Kardar displayed his fighting temperament by making an unbeaten 50 when the pressure was greatest.

A year later, Pakistan were playing full Tests against their neighbours, India, who had sponsored their ICC membership. If the early encounters between them did not betray the unyielding approach of subsequent meetings, the series was not entirely free from tension. There was an unsavoury incident in Bombay with an exchange of insults between Kardar and Mankad. Pakistan still wince at recollections of their maiden Test at Delhi, which India won by an innings and 70 runs. Pakistan took revenge on the matting of Lucknow with an equally decisive triumph, Fazal capturing 12 wickets. The fluctuating theme continued: India won the Third Test and Pakistan could well have got even at Madras, in the Fourth, had rain not washed out the last two days. India, replying to a score of 344, were struggling at 175 for 6. The final Test was drawn – the starting point of a stalemate that spanned 25 years and 12 Tests.

In terms of physical comfort, the weather during the miserable 1954 summer could hardly have delighted the Pakistanis, who were making their first tour of England. For all that, it helped them to draw the series. They were routed in the Second Test at Nottingham after Denis Compton had made 278, but the First and Third were rained off when Pakistan were struggling. When Fazal laid the ground for their epic win on a rain-affected Oval pitch he came to be tagged the 'Alec Bedser of Pakistan'. This Test was Tyson's first. Pakistan were bowled out for 133, but Fazal (6 for 53) prevented England getting ahead. Wardle (7 for 56) spread havoc in Pakistan's ranks in the second innings. From 82 for 8, though, they recovered to score 164. England, needing 168 to win, seemed keen to get them in the 155 minutes that remained of the fourth day. May batted impeccably for 53 and when he left only 59 runs were wanted, with 7 wickets remaining. Then England, who had played about with their batting order, collapsed. With the last 4 wickets falling for only 19 runs on the 5th morning Pakistan won by 24 runs. Fazal took 6 wickets for the second time in the match, Imtiaz held 7 catches behind the stumps and a public holiday was declared at home. Pakistan had done remarkably well on the tour as a whole. They played some delightful cricket, winning 9 matches and losing only 3. A tour profit of £15,000 was realized despite the weather.

The prestige achieved in England turned into a millstone when Pakistan embarked upon a home series against India. All 5 Tests were drawn. In the Peshawar Test, only 638 runs were scored in 4 days; at Dacca only 710. The rivals may have thwarted each other, but on cricket as a game they inflicted a landslide defeat. Although new captains were in charge, the pattern was repeated when Pakistan next went to India. Both sides were again on the defensive, and once more all 5 Tests were drawn. Political issues kept India and Pakistan apart for 18 years after that, though in view of the aimless cricket played in these last two series it was a long time before the hiatus was regretted. Where it was never anything but a blow was to the finances of both Boards.

However, during the rest of the 1950s, Pakistan continued to do well against other visitors. New Zealand were comfortably beaten, 2–0 in a 3-Test series. In 1955–56, an MCC 'A' team went out, exclusively to tour Pakistan, but with unfortunate repercussions. Towards the end of the tour, the 'ragging' of umpire Idris Begh took place one evening at Peshawar. Though meant as a prank, it badly misfired. Idris Begh, his dignity hurt, gave a somewhat dramatized version of the incident which inflamed the whole body of cricket opinion in Pakistan. Apologies were tendered at once and Earl Alexander of Tunis, then President of MCC, offered to recall the team. Fortunately, the tour went on and MCC won the final representative match in Karachi, with Lock bowling as brilliantly as he invariably did on matting wickets. That victory did not alter the result of the series, Pakistan, led by the iron hand of Kardar, having come to Karachi with a 2–0 lead.

In 1956, on the way home from their trials in England, Australia played one Test on the Karachi mat, and found the experience against Fazal as perplexing as the off-breaks of Laker had been on suspect English turf. Miller recounts how he played forward without getting a touch at 5 successive balls from Fazal that cut away off the mat like fast leg-breaks and was dismissed by the 6th that came back at him. On the first day, Australia were bowled out for 80 and Pakistan made 15 for two. This aggregate stands as the slowest scoring rate for a full day in a Test Match, yet some of the Australians claimed it was one of the most fascinating they had encountered. On the last day, when Pakistan wanted a mere 9 runs to win with all wickets intact, the ground was packed. Pakistan celebrated, Australia went off to lick further wounds, determined to do better next time (which, of course, they did).

In the West Indies for the first time, Pakistan's batsmen often found the pace of Gilchrist too quick for them. They lost 3 of the first 4 Tests heavily, and yet had enough stuffing left to win the Fifth by an innings. Wazir Mohammad, Hanif's elder brother, made 189. Hanif himself played a remarkable part in the drawn opening Test at Bridgetown. Pakistan followed on 463 behind with most of the 6-day Test left. Hanif endured for 16 hours and 39 minutes, the longest measured innings, to score 337. He fell 27 short of Hutton's record which Sobers was to break in the Third Test. Sobers's 365 not out was a superb effort, even if Pakistan's attack was reduced to only three fit bowlers, Kardar, Fazal and Khan Mohammed.

Back at home, Hanif, having got the taste, played an innings of 499 for Karachi against Bahawalpur, the highest score yet achieved in a first-class match, and thereby hangs a tale. Hanif was run out in the last over of the day. The scoreboard had credited him with 496 and 2 or 3 minutes remained. In trying to steal the strike, he was run out. Only after he was back in the pavilion did he discover that he had made 499 and, ironically, could have afforded a little more patience. Hanif was blessed with remarkably quick reactions, boundless patience, infinite stamina and complete confidence in his sure technique. Two of his dozen Test hundreds were in one Test against England and he finished with a Test aggregate of 3,915 runs.

In 1958–59, West Indies, having successfully toured India, found their fast bowlers could not make much impression on the mat at Karachi and Dacca. They were beaten at both centres, scoring only 76 and 100 at Dacca, where Fazal took 12 wickets in the match. On turf at Lahore, West Indies won by an innings and 156. When Australia visited Pakistan a year later, their first match was a Test at Dacca. Recalling Karachi and 1956, Benaud decided to field first to study the behaviour of the mat. Mackay gave a model display of medium-paced bowling, not 'cutting' the ball with the same zip as Fazal in his palmiest days, but gaining the right amount of deviation, and maintaining a model line and length. Harvey played a superb innings, and Grout produced a fine display of calculated aggression. Australia outplayed their opponents, who were clearly beginning to miss the guiding hand of their first general, Kardar. On turf at the new National Stadium in Lahore, Pakistan were no match for Australia; Benaud, ever the opportunist, kept stressing the point that until Pakistan were able to play on turf everywhere they would struggle in the top class. At Karachi, back on the mat, the Third Test was drawn. During it, President Eisenhower became the first USA Head of State to visit a Test Match.

With Kardar and Khan gone, Fazal fading, and the mats being rolled up, Pakistan had to make a fresh start. Their 1960–61 series in India, as has already been mentioned, was a chastening experience. So was the visit of Dexter's team in 1961–62, when England lost in India but won easily enough in Pakistan. Almost immediately afterwards, Pakistan toured England for the second time. There was no repeat performance of 1954. Javed Burki, a fine player at Oxford, found the difficult job of knitting together a collection of individuals beyond his limited experience. They won only 4 of 29 matches and were outplayed in all 5 Tests, losing 4 of them. The batsmen, changing from matting to extremely slow lifeless pitches at home which allowed for little, if any, movement of the ball, could not cope in England with the necessary adjustments in technique. Yet one of their members, Mushtaq Mohammad, who played in a first-class match when only 13, in a Test at 15 and was still just under 19 at the end of this tour, was the most accomplished and exciting young batsman of the season. He had his elder brother Hanif's technique, and more of a mind to parade his abundant strokes.

Mushtaq's talents extended beyond his batting. He was also a worthy leg-spinner and, after his excellent tour in 1962, he was engaged by Northamptonshire, with whom he remained for 15 years and finished as captain. Pakistan's selectors, never reluctant to throw young players in at the deep end, quickly built up a nucleus of players to serve them for many years. In the context of young cricketers, it was a splendid idea on both sides to organize an Under-25 MCC tour of Pakistan in 1967, at a time when England were also trying to bring along young players. Mike Brearley, who was to captain England 10 years later, took out the MCC side, which included David Brown, already an established Test player, and several others who were to win their colours in the near future. Two of these, Knott and Underwood, went on to great things. In the Pakistan team were Mushtaq, Majid Khan and Wasim Bari. They were led by a wiry, athletic all-rounder, Asif Iqbal, a recent immigrant from India.

While Pakistan were endowed well enough with promising batsmen, two acute problems remained: the pace bowlers of the early years seemed irreplaceable and there was the question of the captaincy. After their brief experiment with Burki, the selectors turned to Hanif, who took command for a busy schedule of 8 Test matches during the 1964–65 season. The first of these was against Australia, who stopped off for a

Mushtaq, Hanif and Sadiq, members of Pakistan's most famous cricketing dynasty and makers, between them, of nearly 30 Test hundreds.

Karachi and an example of crowd disturbance that has often been inseparable from cricket in Pakistan.

solitary Test in Karachi on their way home from England. Hanif had the daunting task in his first match as captain of leading a side with 6 new caps. Two of them, Billy Ibadulla, already on Warwickshire's books, and Abdul Kadir, did him proud. They put on 249 for the first wicket, a partnership that was the basis of a total of 414. Thanks to a century by Bobby Simpson, Australia drew comfortably. But Pakistan had made the running. In transit to New Zealand, two months later, they faced Australia again, this time in Melbourne. Despite a big first-innings deficit, Pakistan were in no danger of defeat, due mainly to Hanif, who narrowly missed the distinction of scoring 2 separate hundreds in a Test for the second time.

All 3 Tests in New Zealand were unfinished. They were of only 4 days' duration and the weather was unkind. When New Zealand returned the visit immediately afterwards, while on their way to England, Pakistan asserted their superiority in no uncertain manner. Ironically, Hanif played his only big innings of the 3-match series in the one Test that was left unfinished. But without his 203 in the Second Test in Lahore Pakistan might well have struggled. Pakistan's record under Hanif's captaincy was without blemish till the England tour of 1967. A typically grim innings of 187 in 542 minutes gained Pakistan immunity from defeat in the First Test at Lord's, but did nothing to help the team's image. Surprisingly, it was Hanif's first Test century in England. Rain spelled their doom in the Second Test at Trent Bridge, while a misty first morning, which induced Brian Close to put them in, set the odds against them in the final Test at the Oval. Before they lost it, though, Asif and Intikhab salvaged much honour with a heroic 9th-wicket partnership of 190.

One of the high spots of a moderate tour was a whirlwind innings of 147 in only 89 minutes by Majid Khan against Glamorgan. It was hardly surprising after this that Glamorgan offered Majid terms when, next year, county cricket opened its doors more widely to overseas players. Asif (Kent) and Intikhab (Surrey) were also recruited immediately, and within the next few years no less than 8 Pakistanis were playing county cricket. The experience gained playing in so tough a school and under such varying conditions strengthened the fibre of the Pakistan team. Hanif himself remained in the side for one more series, but not as captain. Saeed Ahmed led Pakistan against England in a home series that was hurriedly arranged to replace the cancelled England tour of South Africa in 1968–69. Not only the series but each Test in it was inconclusive, and it was marred by the matches being used for expressions of political and social discontent by students and militants.

There followed a decade of change, frustration, poor luck and much squabbling. The captaincy changed hands several times. Intikhab held it for 2 terms. Under him, Pakistan won only one Test, against New Zealand, but they played some splendid cricket and victory narrowly escaped their grasp several times. One such occasion was the third Test at Headingley in 1971, when, batting last on a wearing pitch, Pakistan lost by only 25 runs. A new batting star in Zaheer Abbas rose during that series. He scored 274 in the opening Test at Edgbaston, which Pakistan dominated. Asif Masood, a pace bowler, also made a big impact, and the series might well have taken a different course had injury not deprived Pakistan of the services of Sarfraz Nawaz. In the winter of 1972–73 Pakistan lost 3–0 to Australia, though not without giving them a good run for their money in the last 2 Tests. They moved on to New Zealand where they won a 3-match series. But even before they got home, it was announced that the popular, mild-mannered Intikhab had been replaced by Majid Khan for the home series against England. In this Pakistan led on the first innings in every Test, without ever getting near to winning.

With Majid's captaincy lacking the flair of his batting, for the England tour of 1974 Pakistan turned again to the loyal Intikhab. Rain halted the first Test at Headingley when it was poised for a palpitating finish. A flooded square at Lord's placed Pakistan in desperate trouble in the second, but they escaped, and on a slow Oval pitch the final Test was also drawn. Pakistan came back to England the following summer for the first Prudential Cup competition and nearly put out the ultimate holders, West Indies. They had 8 West Indian wickets down when 101 runs were still wanted. West Indies might not have recovered to win but for some rather thoughtless field-placing by Majid, who was standing in for the indisposed Asif. In the intervening winter, Pakistan played the West Indies for the first time in 16 years. The two Test matches involved were both drawn. A long run of inconclusive Test matches at home was ended 2 years later when a depleted New Zealand side was soundly thrashed. The captain, this time, was Mushtaq.

Pakistan's next venture was a twin tour of Australia and the West Indies. A violent storm raged before the team departed, its eye being a disagreement over financial terms between Kardar, now the Board President, and 6 senior members of the side, including Mushtaq, the captain-elect. Kardar, never one to brook any challenge to his authority, directed the selectors to select a new team, excluding the rebels. This was done. But the Sports Minister intervened, overruled Kardar, and the tour went on as first planned. Kardar had little option but to bow out from the administration. There are various opinions about his leadership. But even his critics give him praise for opening membership of the Board to business and industrial undertakings, such as PIA, the Banks and the Railway. It meant a changed structure for the national competitions, but a fair proportion of cricketers were provided with secure employment.

Considering the arduous nature of the tour and the strength of the opposition, Pakistan did well against Australia (1 win, 1 loss, 1 draw) and the West Indies. In the Carribbean, they went to Kingston for the last Test with 1 win each and were beaten on a pitch of lightning pace. The final score in the rubber could quite easily have been 2-all, for Pakistan were desperately close to winning the First Test. While in the West Indies, 5 key players signed with World Series Cricket. But even without them, Pakistan held their own against England the following winter. A move before the Third Test to reinstate 3 Packer players was resisted on principle – not only by the opposition but by several members of the Pakistan side and indeed at the instigation of the then Chief Martial Law Administrator General Zia ul Haq. However, in England in 1978, Pakistan's depleted side was hopelessly outplayed.

Atrocious weather, Sarfraz's unavailability for the first 2 Tests and politicking on the sidelines ruined their prospects.

Being very sensitive to defeat, Pakistan took back their Packer players for their first series against India for 18 years. They won it decisively. The series was a triumph for both sides, because of the way they brought to it a refreshing change of approach from the old era. Zaheer, never before a success in a home series, amassed 583 runs in 5 innings. Victory was due in a large measure also to the tireless and hostile pace bowling of Sarfraz and Imran. An arrangement with Mr Packer enabled Pakistan to go to New Zealand and Australia later in the same season and again with a full side. New Zealand were beaten, though with nothing to spare, and the 2-match series in Australia was shared, a young and largely untried Australian side beating Pakistan in Perth after losing an exciting match in Melbourne. The time was clearly not far off when Asif, Majid and Mushtaq would be bowing out.

Papua New Guinea

Sir Hubert Murray, Lieutenant-Governor of Papua from 1909 to 1940, backed missionaries' introduction of cricket in the 1890s as a diversion from head-hunting: he preferred football but considered cricket more desirable administratively. Papuans have taken kindly to the game, not discouraged by a tendency of early Europeans, once having batted, to decline to field in the steaming heat and to put the Papuans in to do that kind of work. New Guinea, which was Kaiser Wilhelms Land up to the First World War, did not see cricket until 1921. In the Trobriand Islands, the game has become mixed with ritual dancing and inter-tribal displays of bombast: sides of up to 100, beflowered and befeathered, with names such as The Aeroplanes and The Scarlet Reds, are still to be seen performing in this style.

Port Moresby, Papua's capital, inaugurated a competition in 1937, mostly for Europeans. Australians in the Forces, including Arthur Morris, played during the Second War, and later Norman O'Neill coached there. Sir John Guise, part-Papuan and first Governor-General, was an accomplished player. In 1963 the races combined, and in 1972 the Papua New Guinea Board of Control was established, with the country admitted as an Associate to the International Cricket Conference in 1973. An Australian team under S. Trimble, including some Test players, then met 9 Europeans and 2 Islanders. Indigenous players were in a majority by 1975, when West Indies under Clive Lloyd called. Fiji, in a first encounter, was defeated at Port Moresby in 1977 by 4 Europeans and 7 Islanders, one of whom, Brian Amini, was captain. In 1979 Papua New Guinea was seen in England in the Associate Members' Competition for the ICC Trophy.

PHILIP SNOW

Pitcairn Island

Fletcher Christian's deliberate choice of his forbiddingly rugged refuge has not lent itself comfortably to outfields. Jungle has never been far from the pitch, in itself highly sporting, with the topographical landmarks at opposite ends of Up Ha Beans and Break Im Hip. 18th-century English and Tahitian is the vocabulary: a great benefit is the Islanders' capacity in wood-carving which embraces bats and stumps. Boundaries do not exist: everything is run. Balls are 'lorse' for an unconscionable time but always eventually recovered from palms, frangipani and flamboyant trees, liana creeper, banana and pineapple plots. While the batsmen credited with 6 runs and the search by the total male adult population of 25 continues, the women temporarily take over the pitch for under-arm contest. For these timeless and festive occasions the entire female and juvenile population of about 30 are spectators in close-slip positions. The urge to play depends on the rare visit by a European and the existence of imported balls, the making of which from Island resources is one of the few crafts beyond the ability of the mutineers' descendants. Once extremely popular, the game is, like the Island, in a serious state through desertion by nearly all between 45 and 15.

PHILIP SNOW

Portugal

It is on record that in 1736 crews of HM ships played cricket at Lisbon, and that in 1810, during the Peninsular War, Crawfurd's 'Light Horse' also played cricket there. Old scorebooks show that as far back as 1869 matches were being played by the British residents against the Channel Fleet and naval squadrons visiting Portuguese waters, and such games have continued until recent times.

Local British clubs were founded in Oporto (1855) and in Lisbon (1861), and have engaged in an annual 2-day match for

The Papua New Guinea team, ICC Trophy, 1979: standing: Lou Ao, Vele Amini, Pala Ura, Kila Alewa, Vavine Pala, Tau Ao, Charles Harrison, Brian Iga and Teio Ila (manager); sitting: La'a Aukopi, Taunao Vai, Nigel Agonia (captain), Ilinome Tarua (vice-captain), Sam Malum and Api Leka.

The visit of H. D. G. Leveson Gower's team to Portugal, April 1934. Back row: C. F. S. Buckley, Major J. T. Montgomery (umpire), J. K. Guy, W. H. Milne, H. M. Garland-Wells, J. Lynn-Robinson, M. T. Maw, D. A. M. Rome, N. Drury, A. G. Hazlerigg, R. A. Peck, M. A. Cope, G. Kevill-Davies, F. A. Johns and Rev C. G. Holland (umpire); middle row: R. W. Frazer, P. T. Eckersley, R. I. Canby, H. D. G. Leveson Gower, W. L. Warren and N. MacCaskie; bottom row: L. Barley, R. E. Fox, E. D. Rawes and J. Cronshaw.

over 100 years, the highest individual score recorded being 251 not out by M. C. Clodd in 1928. An amusing account by a sporting Lisbon journalist of the first of these encounters in 1861 was published in *Punch* on 7 June 1862.

During the last 50 years Portugal has been a favourite destination for touring sides from England, no doubt encouraged by the hospitality provided by the British residents. The Cryptics have toured Portugal on 10 occasions since their first visit in 1924, the Wine Trade CC have been out 8 times, the Dorset Rangers have made 6 visits, whilst other visitors include British Airways, Eton Ramblers, Frogs, Gentlemen of Worcester, Gibraltar, Law Society, Madrid, Old Wellingtonians, RAF Gibraltar, Sou'Westers, and Wiltshire Queries. Sides have also been taken out by the Westrys, H. D. Swan, H. D. G. Leveson Gower, R. P. Rankine and Bertie Joel.

The British residents' touring side, the 'Iberians', have visited England on 3 occasions, in 1971, 1975 and 1979, playing matches mainly in Dorset, but also several games in the home counties against old rivals in British Airways, the Law Society and the Wine Trade CC.

GORDON WHITE

St Helena

Jamestown's ground is most spectacular, the pavilion looking at 2 lofty mountains and the South Atlantic beyond. It is a long drive to the pavilion, but the ball is frequently lost in a waterfall behind square-leg or point. Trying to save the ball from this fate, an Army fielder once suffered a worse one himself. He slipped over the edge of the ground, fell down on to a protruding rock and broke his neck.

PHILIP SNOW

Samoa

William B. Churchward, British Consul 1881 to 1885 helped by HMS *Diamond* in 1884, is believed to have introduced the game to Samoa with results the like of which have scarcely been known outside the South Seas. Cricket's set-up seemed to Samoans such an opportunity for carrying on feuds under a thin veneer of courtesy and laws that the men of entire districts grappled on the village greens, 200–300 a side, with 3 batsmen at each end and a new bowler to deliver each ball with all his unsapped frenzy. Work, Wesleyanism and women all suffered in these amplitudinous struggles renewed weekly to stretch over months; so much so that in 1890 High Chief Malietoa I, the Mission and wives issued respectively proclamations, edicts and threats banishing it. The game scarcely raised its head again, even when the New Zealand mandate in the First World War succeeded the 1900 to 1914 German occupation which had outlawed it as a British-induced mania. At least so far as men are concerned. A neat touch of irony is that Samoa is now noted far beyond its coral reefs for the prowess of its women, who play it with gusto, skill, brawn and a fine disregard for meal times.

PHILIP SNOW

The Seychelles

These islands, 1,000 miles off East Africa and the beaten track, enjoy a limited amount of cricket. They are dependent on ships' calls for enthusiasm to be maintained. There is a pleasant, if small, ground on Mahé Island at Victoria, the capital. For many years M. D. Lyon (Cambridge and Somerset) was Chief Justice of this Group.

PHILIP SNOW

Shanghai

The Shanghai CC ground is now a People's Park but in its time saw a remarkably sustained inter-port rivalry with Hong Kong. From 1866 to 1948 the contest went on, with some intervals, so that the final reckoning, when there were not enough European merchants in Shanghai, was 20 victories for Hong Kong, 15 for Shanghai, 2 draws. Up to 1914 Shanghai's best player was Capt E. I. M. Barrett of the Army, Hampshire and Straits Settlements. When the latter country visited Hong Kong under that name (and later as Malaya) there was occasionally a triangular tournament with Shanghai. From 1897 to 1933, Shanghai had 5 wins, Straits Settlements 3, with 1 draw.

PHILIP SNOW

Sierra Leone and the Gambia

Opponents since Europeans introduced cricket in the late 1920s, visits took place in alternate years after 1927; now there are annual encounters. The Gambia has been too small to produce noteworthy players so far but Sierra Leone has contributed a number, including currently their leader and probably the most aggressive West Indian bowler, Stalin Adolf Fraser. The first outside teams to visit the 2 countries, which now regularly play against Nigeria and Ghana, have been an International XI under M. J. Stewart in 1968 and MCC in 1976. Principal pitches of matting on concrete are in the capitals, Freetown (Sierra Leone) and Banjul, formerly Bathurst (The Gambia).

PHILIP SNOW

Freetown, Sierra Leone: Colin Cowdrey conducts a coaching session.

Singapore

Cricket has been played in Singapore for well over a century. The game was mentioned in records as far back as 1837 when Sunday cricket in Singapore was disallowed in response to a protest. The next surviving report is a newspaper record on 20 April 1843, that 'the manly game of cricket resumed in the settlement, a match being played between Singaporeans and the "Dido"'. The first fully recorded match was played on 14 October 1852 under the title of 'A Picked Eleven vs The Club' (Singapore Cricket Club) between 6 on one side and 9 on the other. The picked lot made 11 in the first innings and 1 in the second. The Club scored 14 and 12. The next match a week later was 'a scratch match between 16 gentlemen', 8 a side. One side scored 52 and 18; the other 49 and 53. The pitch had evidently improved. The game gained popularity in the 1860s. Scoring was low and it was not until 1865 that 100 runs were scored in an innings for the first time.

The 1890s saw the beginning of inter-state cricket and also tours to Hong Kong, Shanghai, Ceylon and Batavia in which Singapore contributed many players to the Straits Settlements team (Singapore, Penang, Malacca), which usually gave a good account of itself. For instance, in 1897 the Straits touring side defeated a combined Hong Kong and Shanghai team by an innings and 231 runs.

Visits from touring teams were infrequent in the early days. There was mention of Lord Harris's visit in 1882, followed by teams from Hong Kong and Ceylon in 1891. In November 1909, 5 of the Australian Test XI, M. A. Noble, A. J. Hopkins, W. W. Armstrong, A. Cotter and F. Laver, visited Singapore on their return journey from England to Australia. Their side including local players beat Singapore and the Malay States in 2 matches in Singapore.

In 1927 C. G. Macartney's Australian team including such stars as W. A. Oldfield, W. M. Woodfull, E. R. Mayne, R. Bardsley, T. J. Andrews and S. C. Everett, played 9 matches in Malaya, winning 5, drawing 3 and losing 1. After 2 games on the Singapore Padang in which first the Singapore Cricket Club and then the Singapore State side were defeated, a Malayan side (captained by N. J. A. Foster and including several Singapore players) made history by defeating the Australians in Kuala Lumpur by 39 runs.

Another 2 international sides visited Singapore before the outbreak of the Second World War in 1941. In 1937 Sir Julien Cahn, former President of the Nottinghamshire County Cricket Club, brought out a team to tour Ceylon and Malaya, comprising Australian, English, New Zealand and South African Test and County cricketers. In 1938, Dr C. H. Gunasekara led a Ceylon team, comprising some All Ceylon players.

Although the Europeans dominated the local cricket scene in the early days, other communities such as the Ceylonese, Chinese, Eurasians and Indians, soon took up the game and showed rapid improvement and over the years have produced several distinguished cricketers in club, inter-state and other representative fixtures.

The principal annual match in Malaya before the war was the Colony (comprising the Straits Settlements of Singapore, Penang and Malacca) versus Federated Malay States series which was started in 1905 and carried on until the last war. 37 matches were played in this series of which the Federated Malay States won 20 and the Colony 10.

Since the Second World War cricket has been widely played in Singapore. Of significance was the formation in 1949 of the Singapore Cricket Association to which all the cricket playing clubs are affiliated and which has successfully organized inter-club tournaments, tours, inter-state and representative fixtures and made every effort to encourage the young.

In November 1959 the Australian team, led by Richie Benaud, en route to India, made a stop-over in Singapore and treated 5,000 spectators to entertaining and instructive cricket in the 2 matches played there against the Malayan Cricket Association President's XI and Malaya. Since then several distinguished teams of cricketers, with Ceylon, English, Indian, Pakistani and West Indian stars, including XIs led by R. A. Roberts, E. W. Swanton, Joe Lister and Derrick Robins, MCC and Indian Test Teams, and other first-class teams from Australia, Ceylon, Great Britain, India, and Pakistan have graced these shores. Their visits have proved a great success in many respects, especially in advancing the cause of cricket and enabling local enthusiasts and past, present and future cricketers to watch and learn from the fine quality and technique of the cricket produced as well as engendering goodwill and forming many friendships.

Since the Second War Singapore has participated in several inter-state matches with other States across the Causeway and in the Malaysian Cricket Association Championship for inter-state cricket, in which Singapore has figured prominently in the finals to decide the championship. Singapore has also taken a regular part and fared well in the inter-state Colts competition for under-23 group since 1966. Cricket links between Singapore and Hong Kong have been maintained since 1889 when Singapore, Hong Kong and Shanghai first began playing friendly matches with one another. Since 1965 Singapore and Malaysia have played separate fixtures with Hong Kong.

Singapore's first trip to Australia was to Perth, Western Australia, in 1967 when 7 matches were played (3 lost, 1 won, 2 drawn, 1 abandoned). This was followed by 4 subsequent trips of Singapore's youngsters to New South Wales, in 1969, 1973, 1975 and 1977, where a series of matches were played against District teams. These visits were made possible through the sponsorship and assistance of Mr Jim White, founder and

The Singapore team for the ICC Trophy, England 1979: standing: Goh Swee Heng, Lawrence Young, Harmam Singh, Chris de Silva, Rex Martens, Mohanvelu Neethianathan, Mukhtar Ahmed and Fred Martens; sitting: Sitharam Sathivail, Mahesh Mehta, Pritam Singh (captain), J. C. Cooke (manager), Sreerangam Muruthi (vice-captain), Stephen Noel Houghton and P. Ishwarlal.

patron of the Emu Club of New South Wales. In continuation of the efforts to encourage young cricketers, particularly from the schools, a Singapore Cricket Association Juniors Team (average age 18) was sent to Madras and Bangalore in December 1973.

Under the sponsorship of the Board of Control for Cricket in India, the services of a professional coach, R. B. Kenny, were made available to Singapore for the first time in 1976, to coach schoolboys and other youngsters in the Republic. 60 trainees were taught the basics in stance, back-lift, forward play, back play, bowling and fielding. On further request Kenny returned for a second coaching stint in 1977. His first week was set aside for the training of 9 prospective coaches who were taught the importance of dress, discipline and display, correct approach and right technique in batting and bowling.

In the 1970s the number of cricket grounds available in Singapore was reduced by half following the British pull-out. The British Services had at one time a dozen teams participating in the Senior and Junior Cricket Tournaments organized by the Singapore Cricket Association and between them maintained many well-kept grounds in various parts of the island, at Tanglin, Nee Soon, Gillman Barracks, Ayer Rajah, Changi, Seletar, Tengah, Sembawang and Woodlands. Currently there are two good turf wickets on the Singapore Padang, adjacent to the Esplanade in the heart of the Central Business District and opposite to the City Hall building where the historic surrender of the Japanese Armed Forces to the Allied Forces under Lord Louis Mountbatten took place in 1945. But the 2 grounds, maintained and cared for by the Singapore Cricket Club and the Singapore Recreation Club, have been the main venue of international and representative cricket matches. The playing area with a boundary radius of approximately 60 yards has a fast outfield particularly in dry weather. The grounds in a picturesque environment are adequate in size to cater for other sports, such as, hockey, rugger, soccer, softball and tennis. The remaining cricket grounds used by other sporting Clubs are located at Balestier Plain (Ceylon Sports Club, Indian Association and Singapore Chinese Recreation Club), Tanglin (Singapore Armed Forces Sports Association), Thomson Road (Police Sports Association), Seletar (Heli-Orient) and Sembawang (New Zealand Forces). These grounds have fast matting wickets on laterite which are ideal for batting.

CECIL COOKE

Solomon Islands

The second Bishop of Melanesia, J. C. Patteson, sometime captain of the Eton XI, was clubbed to death off the Solomons in 1871. A successor as Bishop, C. Wilson, who had played for Kent, encouraged cricket's appeal to Solomon Islanders, particularly by being bowled first ball on his debut. He has described with equal candour other difficulties he encountered on the New Britain grounds sloping down the steamy sides of extinct volcanoes to the sea. The spectators, including thin bush dogs and long-eared razor-backed pigs, all liked to make their presence felt. In a key match between two villages Wilson put himself on to bowl on the brink of a result. His first ball was hit into the sea. Onlookers shouted to the last pair batting to run. Wilson shouted to the fielders wading in the sea (which was too close to represent a boundary) to fling the ball in. The issue could not have been more decisive – quite unlike Newbolt's totally untenable conception of a crisis in The Close's breathless hush. The village dogs felt it imperative to take part. One in particular was unable to contain himself and, as Wilson stood poised at the wicket to intercept the ball for the certain run-out that would bring his side victory, he seized the Rt Rev's rear to effect a quite different result. Recently memorable but almost wholly conventional has been a first visit – in 1977 – to Honiara, the Island's capital, by Fiji.

PHILIP SNOW

South Africa

LOUIS DUFFUS, MICHAEL OWEN-SMITH AND ANDRÉ ODENDAAL

The first part of this article gives the broad picture of South Africa's contribution to cricket from the early part of the 19th century; the second part traces the progress of the game among the various sections of the coloured population, culminating in the establishment in 1977 of the non-racial and (theoretically) all-embracing South African Cricket Union.

Cricket in South Africa was sired by British soldiers. England had barely relaxed the law that all bowling was to be underhand, when the game started in the southern tip of the African continent. There is a strong possibility that the game was introduced when garrison troops first occupied the Cape from 1795 to 1802 during the early part of the Napoleonic Wars. A belief exists, though there is no evidence to support it, that cricket was played by one of their officers, a certain Charles Anguish, between 1795 and the date when he died, aged 28, at Cape Town in May 1797. Since British soldiers and sailors were pioneers of the game in several foreign lands it is plausible to assume that they were the first to play cricket in South Africa in the closing years of the 18th century. The first-known written reference to a match being played in South Africa was contained in this announcement which appeared, after the British had re-occupied the Cape in 1806, in *The Cape Town Gazette and African Advertiser*, the only newspaper then published:

> A grand match at cricket will be played for 1,000 dollars a side on Tuesday, January 5, 1808 between the officers of the artillery mess, having Colonel Austen of the 60th Regiment, and the officers of the Colony, with General Clavering. The wickets are to be pitched at 10 o'clock.

By 1840 Cape Town was a town of some size and civilians are also found among the players. One of them named Taylor is reported to have carried his bat for 110 through an innings of 186 for Civilians v Military on the Wynberg ground in January 1842. This was the first hundred recorded in South Africa.

In the 1840s the game became well established at Cape Town, Port Elizabeth and Pietermaritzburg. No cricket club appears to have existed at Cape Town, so that pride of place among South African cricket clubs belongs to that founded on 15 January, 1843, at a meeting in Port Elizabeth, a town of 3,000 people which had grown as a result of the introduction of the 1820 Settlers. The Port Elizabeth Cricket Club, which was reputedly the first club of any sort in the country and which still flourishes, is thus one of the oldest in the world. The City Fathers allocated to the club a piece of land on what was then an outlying suburb and is now the field at St George's Park. It was on this ground, 46 years later, that South Africa's first Test Match was played.

Meanwhile cricket was progressing at Cape Town, the Cape Town and Wynberg Cricket Club being in existence by October 1844, when a match, Cape Town v The Colony, took place on its ground. Cricket was introduced into Natal by the

45th Foot Regiment stationed at Fort Napier, Pietermaritzburg. The *Natal Witness* of 24 March 1848 refers to the playing of a match at Fort Napier. In 1850 the 45th Regiment was in the little village of Bloemfontein and issued a challenge to the residents to play any XI they put up but it is not known if a match took place. Cricket is also reported to have been played by the forces at Fort Beaufort, on the Cape Border, during the year 1851. Two civilian clubs, West End and Olympic, were started in Pietermaritzburg in January 1852, and the latter immediately challenged 'our D'Urban friends' to a match.

The existence of cricket in schools was known in the early 1850s. The game was played by the Diocesan College (founded 1849), the South African College at Cape Town and by the boys of the Port Elizabeth Academy. An Old Boy of the Diocesan College has left it on record that cricket at this time was a major sport, being played nearly all the year round in those pre-football days. Of the small populations in the hinterland more than half knew little about cricket and cared less about the game, yet it spread with the settlers as they moved north. The first recorded match in the Transvaal was played in 1861 at Potchefstroom where a club was founded 2 years later. In January 1862 the first of the long series of regular Mother Country v Colonial-Born matches was played at Cape Town. This was for many years the most important match of the Cape season, and in October 1864 the Western Province Cricket Club was formed. An important event, the first attempt to bring centres together in competition, was organized by the enterprise of Port Elizabeth in January 1876. Its municipality presented a trophy known as 'The Champion Bat'. 5 matches were played at Port Elizabeth between teams representing Cape Town, Port Elizabeth, Grahamstown and Kingwilliamstown from which the last-named emerged as victors. Five more tournaments of a similar nature took place between 1880 and 1891.

Two noteworthy events of 1888 were the opening of what were to become two of South Africa's most famous cricket grounds: Newlands, beautifully situated beneath Table Mountain, on 1 January, and the Wanderers, on a hastily levelled piece of red earth near the centre of the 3-year-old mining camp of Johannesburg, on 10 October, President Kruger's birthday. The main reason for the construction of the Wanderers was the necessity to provide a ground fit for the English touring team to play upon. For, with the game firmly established in all the towns and the fairly high standard of play reached in the semi-representative matches of the previous 12 years, the time had come for South African cricket to test its strength against sterner opposition from the game's mother country.

Major R. G. Warton, who had been attached from 1883 to 1888 to the Army General Staff in Cape Town, took a prominent part in local cricket and was a member of the Western Province Cricket Club. He was invited to negotiate for a tour of South Africa by a team of first-class cricketers. As a result of his going to England to make arrangements for the visit the side was known as Major Warton's team. C. A. Smith of Sussex was captain of the team and Major Warton manager. The team was about the strength of an average county side. Except financially, the tour was an eminent success. Matches were played on matting, set in grass outfields at the coast and on hard soil ground in the interior. The strength of the touring side proved to be quite adequate for the opposition who, in all matches except the 2 'Tests' played at Port Elizabeth and Cape Town, consisted of more than 11 players. O. R. Dunell of Port Elizabeth, who was 33, became the first captain of South Africa.

One important result of the first England visit was the inauguration of the Currie Cup tournament. To commemorate the pioneer tour Sir Donald Currie, the head of the Castle Mail Packets Company, whose ship brought the team to South Africa, presented a cup to be awarded by the English team to the side which excelled most against the visitors. Thereafter it was to be competed for by the provinces. Kimberley gained the distinction of receiving the trophy. In 1890 Transvaal lodged a challenge for the cup and the first tournament was conducted between the 2 teams, Transvaal winning by 6 wickets. Starting with these 2 teams the tournament increased to 3, then 5, until today it embraces 9 centres – 3 in the 'B' section Castle Bowl – including Zimbabwe-Rhodesia. With so many Englishmen among the inhabitants it was inevitable that cricket should be introduced to the latter country. The first record of a game appeared on 27 February 1893 in a Fort Victoria newspaper.

In the 1891–92 season a second touring team under the captaincy of W. W. Read of Surrey went through the land undefeated. Then with an enthusiasm typical of the age South Africa decided to send a team to England in 1894, the year in which the South African Cricket Association was formed. A side of 15 was chosen with H. H. Castens of Western Province as captain. It was an ill-fated journey, the team running into one of the wettest seasons known in England and the gate takings, towards expenses which exceeded £3,600, being less than £500. The collapse of the tour was only avoided by the advance of money from South African friends in England. No Test Match was played and only a few games against first-class counties.

Five more tours followed in quick succession. Lord Hawke brought teams out from England in 1895–96 and 1898–99. South Africa made trips to England in 1901 and 1904, and Australia visited South Africa for the first time in 1902–03. The visits were a tribute to the generosity and public spirit of cricket lovers for both English tours were conducted at a loss. Lord Hawke's team of 1898–99 were the first overseas players to visit Zimbabwe-Rhodesia. They played 2 matches at Bulawayo against teams of 18 and 15 and won comfortably. J. D. Logan was a spectator at both these games and in commemoration presented a cup which under his name has become the trophy for inter-centre games in this country. The season was conspicuous for the rise of J. H. Sinclair who played innings of 86 and 106, the first hundred ever scored for South Africa. M. Bisset became the country's youngest captain at the age of 22. It was Bisset who captained the 1901 team, financed by Logan, which went away during the South African War. Although South Africa suggested calling it off England insisted that the tour continue.

The admirable initiative and enthusiasm which characterized the country's cricket led in 1902 to the Australians, captained by Joe Darling, breaking their journey from England to play 6 matches. They were the first fully representative side to visit South Africa. By demonstrating new standards of the game they gave it an immense fillip. South Africa, with 3 different captains in H. M. Taberer, J. H. Anderson and E. A. Halliwell, lost 2 Tests and drew 1 but were by no means humbled. This was the prelude to the country's so-called 'Golden Age'. None gave it greater impetus than Sinclair. He scored 2 hundreds in the Tests and 1 for the Transvaal XV. The series saw the debut of Dave Nourse and the maturing of that fine bowler C. B. Llewellyn.

The 3rd South African team to tour England, in 1904, was captained by Frank Mitchell who was born in Yorkshire. This was the last time that a tour was undertaken in which no Test Matches were played. The event of the season was the development of the googly, invented by B. J. T. Bosanquet, by R. O. Schwarz. He finished the season with 96 wickets. The new style of bowling was taken up by G. A. Faulkner, A. E. Vogler and G. C. White and had a profound reaction on the country's cricket. Its first effects were evident in the fifth English tour to South Africa in 1905–06 – the first official MCC visit – the season which launched 6 years of P. W. Sherwell's captaincy and which produced some of the most accomplished cricketers in South Africa's history. Represented throughout by the same XI, they won 4 Test Matches and lost 1. The touring side, captained by P. F. Warner, was not fully representative of English cricket but it was considered strong enough to beat any XI South Africa could field.

The heyday of South Africa's googly bowlers, however, occurred during the 1907 tour of England. The team won 21 (17 first-class) of their 31 matches. England won 1 of the 3 Tests, played over 3 days, the others being drawn. Faulkner established himself as South Africa's finest all-rounder by taking 73 wickets and scoring over 1,000 runs. When the next England side, captained by H. D. G. Leveson Gower, arrived in 1909–10 Faulkner had a remarkable season. He headed the Test Match batting with an average of 60·55 and was third in the bowling with 29 wickets (average 21·89). Although the English team included several great players it was still not England at full strength. An event of significance for South Africa was the appearance of 20-year-old Herby Taylor who scored 55 and 30 for Natal in his first match against an overseas team. In 2 Test series at home South Africa had now won 7 matches and lost 3.

Their marked improvement led to the ill-fated triangular tournament in England in 1912, but before its inauguration, as a provision of their acceptance, Australia asked that South Africa should visit their country. So in 1910–11, with Sherwell as captain, a team including Faulkner,* Schwarz, Vogler, Nourse and Sinclair broke new ground on the first South African tour of Australia. It proved a disappointment in performance in spite of several individual triumphs and in fact marked the end of an age of splendid cricketers. One Test – at Adelaide – was won by 38 runs, and 4 lost. Faulkner had another wonderful tour. The idea of the triangular tournament of 1912 was initiated in South Africa, but it was because South Africa fell short of the international standard, and because of a wet summer, that the tournament failed. South Africa lost 5 of the 6 Tests and drew the other one.

The duel between the renowned England bowler S. F. Barnes, who had taken 39 wickets in the triangular Tests, and Taylor became the feature of the 1913–14 tour on which the team led by J. W. H. T. Douglas struck South Africa in the midst of lean years. Barnes had a phenomenal season, taking 49 wickets in only 4 Test Matches. Taylor was the only batsman who could play him. Like many others Taylor went to the First World War at the peak of his prowess. Before he had returned from active service, South Africa in 1919 entertained the Australian Imperial Forces team led by H. L. Collins on an unofficial visit on their way home from England. When they returned in 1921, reinforced by C. G. Macartney, E. A. McDonald, J. Ryder and A. A. Mailey, to play 6 matches under the captaincy of Collins, South Africa unexpectedly held them to 1 victory in 3 Tests.

The South African team of 1924 arriving at Southampton on the *Arundel Castle*: standing: M. J. Susskind, J. M. Blanckenberg, C. D. Dixon, S. J. Pegler, P. Allsop (manager), G. F. Bissett, H. G. Deane and A. D. Nourse; sitting: E. P. Nupen, T. A. Ward, M. J. Commaille, H. W. Taylor (captain), G. Hearne, C. P. Carter; front: R. H. Catterall and D. J. Meintjes.

At this time South Africa undertook a spate of tours – perhaps too many. There were 4 in 4 years. They suffered a sharp blow to their prestige on their 6th visit to England in 1924. The one beneficial outcome of the tour in which the team won only 8 out of 38 matches, and which concluded Taylor's record captaincy in 18 Tests, was a renewed agitation for turf wickets in South Africa. These were the last official Tests played by Nourse, the Grand Old Man of South African cricket, who was then 46. he represented his country in 52 consecutive games.

England were still not sending out their strongest teams, but the necessity to do so seemed to be approaching with an improvement in the country's standard of play during the 12 Tests played under the captaincy of H. G. Deane. He made a name for himself, when Capt R. T. Stanyforth brought out the English team in 1927–28, by his daring tactics of putting England in to bat in the last 2 matches. Both were won and South Africa shared the rubber. In 1929 Deane took an exceptionally young team to England and launched the distinguished careers of B. Mitchell, H. G. Owen-Smith and E. L. Dalton and laid the foundation for a refreshing revival in the game.

The 1930s became one of the country's most important periods of the game. Besides the maturing of a new generation of accomplished cricketers the period witnessed the inauguration of turf pitches. Natal had pioneered the introduction of grass and in 1926–27 staged the first Currie Cup match under full turf conditions. In 1930–31 during the visit of A. P. F. Chapman's team 3 Tests – 1 at Cape Town and 2 at Durban – were for the first time played on grass pitches. This series gave South Africa a rubber for the third time at home.

The following summer, after a lapse of 20 years, South Africa returned to Australia with a young side captained by H. B. Cameron. They were outclassed and were beaten in all 5 Tests by an Australian team of famous players of whom Don Bradman was in his prime. History was made when South Africa played in New Zealand for the first time. It was here that the distinguished Taylor, at the age of 41, played his 42nd and last Test.

Although the tour to Australia halted the hopeful revival made in 1929 South Africa quickly recovered. With one of their best teams ever sent abroad – under H. F. Wade in 1935 – they won their first Test and rubber in England. D. S. Tomlinson became the first Rhodesian to represent South Africa, though R. J. Crisp, then domiciled in the Western Province, had learned his cricket in Rhodesia. The only tragedy was that Cameron died, aged 30, from fever contracted on the return journey from England. It was left to Australia to disillusion the jubilant South Africans. On their 4th visit in 1935–36, without Bradman who was not available and who thus never played in South Africa, and led by V. Y. Richardson they swept through the country in a blaze of victories. The 8-ball over was then adopted in the Currie Cup tournament of 1936–37 and remained in vogue for a number of years.

The visit of W. R. Hammond's side in 1938–39 was conspicuous for 3 reasons. He led the first team to South Africa that was fully representative of English cricket, it was virtually the first all-turf-wicket tour, and his side participated in the fantastic Durban timeless Test which extended over 10 days, and remained unfinished when rain ended play on the last possible day before the return home. With 1 Test victory England won the rubber. The series provoked a general outcry against timeless Test Matches but the tour drew record crowds, and when Lord Nuffield gave £10,000 for the furtherance of school cricket he put the seal on a progressive decade.

The 6 years of war disrupted cricket's nursery and when A. Melville took the side to England in 1947 it had the high average age of 30. In the Test Matches, which for the first time against South Africa were extended to 4 days, England won 3

Alan Melville leading out his South African side in England in 1947, a particularly golden summer.

and drew 2 games. Two tours, from England under F. G. Mann in 1948–49 and Australia led by A. L. Hassett in 1949–50, followed in quick succession, but not a match was won by a local side. Mitchell, after playing in 42 Tests and compiling the highest aggregate of 3,471 runs, was dropped from the series against Australia. Nourse made his last appearances for South Africa when he captained the side in his third successive series – in England in 1951. The team's 5 victories in 30 matches equalled the poorest yet achieved, the very first first-class tour to England in 1901.

Nothing suggested that South Africa was now to embark upon a second Golden Age. 8 of the best players of 1951 were not taken to Australia in 1952–53. The bowling was acknowledged to be the weakest ever to leave the country, and J. E. Cheetham captained a young, inexperienced team for the first time in a strange country. Their chances seemed forlorn but when the summer was over they had won 2 Test Matches in Australia for the first time, shared the rubber, made a name for themselves as the most brilliant fielding side ever to represent South Africa, and changed the whole outlook of the country's cricket. New Zealand paid their first visit to South Africa in 1953–54. The winning of 4 Tests by South Africa, with 1 drawn, was the country's best result in any series up to that time.

The 3rd series of the new era played in England in 1955 was memorable for the thrilling change of fortunes when the South Africans were 2 down in the Tests. Amid high drama they won the Third Test at Old Trafford with 5 minutes to spare, won again at Leeds and lost the rubber 2–3 at the Oval. Because of an injury to Cheetham his deputy McGlew captained the team in the 2 victories. The tour reflected a welcome trend towards more forceful batting. No previous side had ever won 2 Tests in England, even though it might be argued that P. W. Sherwell's side were superior in individual talent.

The visit by P. B. H. May's team in 1956–57 coincided with the opening of a new Wanderers stadium in Johannesburg some 5 miles from the old site which had been expropriated for the extension of the railway station. Once again South Africa lagged behind. They were 2 down with 2 Tests to play and finished up sharing the series. The man of the season for South Africa was Tayfield who in taking 37 wickets in the series eclipsed the record of Vogler (36) which had stood for 47 years. When the season ended South Africa, in 4 years since Cheetham had taken an unfledged team to Australia, had played 22 Tests, won 11 and lost 7. They had won 2 series and lost 1 (by 2 matches to 3) and shared a rubber with both England and Australia. In South African cricket such successes were not long sustained and sure enough the pendulum swung back immediately – once more with Australia the cause of change. The team led by I. D. Craig in 1957–58 won the rubber by 3–0 and maintained Australia's record of never having lost a match in South Africa.

The most eventful tour South Africa has ever undertaken and one that caused controversy wherever cricket is played was the visit to England in 1960 of the side captained by McGlew. From the moment they arrived, they were the subject of demonstrations against the apartheid policy of the South African Government. They encountered a wet and depressing summer, a drastic falling off in attendances at cricket and except in one instance, that of the fast bowler N. A. T. Adcock, a decline in the general standard of play. Defensive batting was the main weakness and they lost the rubber 3–0. All other events were overshadowed by the unprecedented incidents involving the controversial action of the 21-year-old fast bowler, G. Griffin. At Lord's in the Second Test he became the first bowler no-balled for throwing in a Test in England when he was called 11 times. In spite of the penalty he performed the hat-trick. But in an exhibition match which followed the early conclusion of the Test he was so consistently no-balled by one umpire, J. S. Buller, that he had to complete his over by bowling under-arm. It was decided thereupon that he should bowl no more on the tour. No replacement was made.

The failure of any new players to develop in England made the time ripe for South Africa to build up a new team and this was now begun with the second visit of a New Zealand team to the country in 1961–62. With admirable enterprise the selectors chose no fewer than 7 new caps for the First Test and by the end of the series 10 new players had been given international experience. The tour was a triumph for New Zealand who for the first time won 2 Tests abroad and shared a rubber.

The South Africans arriving in England, 1951. The party consists of A. D. Nourse (captain), S. J. Pegler (manager), J. E. Cheetham, G. W. A. Chubb, W. R. Endean, G. M. Fullerton, N. B. F. Mann, P. N. F. Mansell, C. N. McCarthy, D. J. McGlew, R. A. McLean, M. G. Melle, A. M. B. Rowan, E. A. B. Rowan, C. B. Van Ryneveld and J. H. B. Waite.

When McGlew announced his retirement from Test cricket, history repeated itself. For the second time in 11 years South Africa were faced with sending a team to Australia, in 1963–64, under a captain who had never led a side in Test cricket. T. L. Goddard surprised Australia by drawing the series – each side won 1 Test – and in the final game at Sydney, time alone saved Australia from defeat. The fast bowling attack of P. M. Pollock and J. T. Partridge and the excellent batsmanship of R. G. Pollock and E. J. Barlow did much towards South Africa's good showing.

The 1964–65 England tour to South Africa was something of a disappointment. Following the successful visit to Australia and the fact that the England bowling attack was not as strong as usual, the South Africans were expected to do well. However, they failed to produce sufficiently attacking cricket at vital stages and England, taking advantage of winning the toss on a pitch that assisted the spin bowler as early as the second day, clinched the series by winning the First Test in Durban.

The South African visit to England for a 3-match series in 1965 introduced probably the greatest era in South Africa's history. The selection of a new captain, P. L. van der Merwe, was one of the most important factors for he had the attacking vision that was right in step with the rich array of aggressive batsmen headed by Barlow, Pollock and K. C. Bland. The latter also set a new standard in fielding and P. M. Pollock continued to advance as a fast bowler. For the second time in history South Africa won a series 1–0 in England, thanks to a brilliant hundred by R. G. Pollock in the second Test at Trent Bridge where his older brother, P. M. Pollock, backed him up with 10 wickets in the match. The 1965 South Africans restored the popularity of this country in England following the disaster of 1960 and they took home a handsome profit of £15,000.

From this point on, South Africa went from strength to strength. Australia were outclassed in two series in South Africa in 1966–67 and 1970 by 3–1 and 4–0 margins respectively. It was the first time that Australia had lost on South African soil and the South Africans compiled their highest ever Test total of 620 at Johannesburg in 1966 and improved on this with 622 for 9 at Durban in 1970. Out of this latter total R. G. Pollock made South Africa's highest ever Test score of 274.

These two series launched the tragically short international careers of two of South Africa's greatest cricketers of all time. M. J. Procter took 41 wickets in just 7 matches while B. A. Richards in one series of 4 matches scored 2 hundreds for an average of 72. In later years Richards went to play cricket in England and Australia and was responsible for the highest first-class score of all time by a South African, making 356 for South Australia against West Australia at Perth. He made 325 of them in one day.

However, within these days of glorious revival the dark clouds of international isolation were already gathering. In the 1968–69 season England were due to visit South Africa. There was immediate speculation whether B. L. d'Oliveira, a Cape coloured who had been barred from playing international cricket for his homeland by his country's racial laws, would be allowed into South Africa if he was chosen for England. Initially he was left out of the touring party but later was included when T. W. Cartwright was injured and withdrew. The South African Prime Minister, Mr B. J. Vorster, then proceeded to accuse England of mixing sport with politics, though in effect he did this himself by telling MCC that d'Oliveira was not an acceptable member of the touring team. It was a decision that brought about South Africa's isolation earlier than it might otherwise have occurred, leading to the immediate cancellation of the MCC tour.

The year 1968 also saw England lift certain restrictions on overseas professionals playing in the County Championship.

Great days in South African cricket. Brian Taber lbw to Mike Procter during one of South Africa's overwhelming victories over Australia, 1969–70. Ali Bacher and Eddie Barlow are at slip, Ian Redpath is the non-striker.

Richards and Procter were the first South Africans to avail themselves of this opportunity and more and more of their compatriots followed as they were denied the opportunity of playing Test cricket. The South African tour to England in 1970 was duly cancelled under pressure from the British Government and South Africa were informed that there could be no resumption of tours until such time as one national body was formed to administer all cricketers and merit selection was introduced as official policy. On the domestic front 1970 also saw the introduction of South Africa's first one-day Gillette Cup competition. Although it was unofficial in its first year, it was such a success that it immediately became a permanent feature on the South African calendar. Denied all cricket at Test level, South Africa's leading players had to settle for a menu of private tours organized by the cricket philanthropist, Derrick Robins. They served a purpose in maintaining communication with overseas players and administrators but because such a team was not strong enough to challenge the full might of South Africa, these tours lacked public appeal and posed financial problems. The South African Government did permit Robins to bring a multi-racial side to South Africa with the inclusion of West Indian John Shepherd and Younis Ahmed of Pakistan in 1973–74, and the following season South Africa were allowed to field a multi-racial invitation team to oppose the tourists. This was followed by a Government decision to allow an African XI to play in the Gillette Cup in 1975–76.

These concessions were too small to allow South Africa to make any meaningful progress on the road to national cricket unity and merit selection. It was a formality for the 1975 tour to England to be cancelled and Mr Boon Wallace, President of the SACA, was refused a visa to enter Australia to discuss that country's tour of South Africa in 1975–76. This tour also fell away. South African cricket had reached the lowest level of despair.

However, the 1975–76 season saw the formation of what became known as the 9-man motivating committee, consisting of 3 members of every national body, which started working towards national unity and merit selection at all levels, or 'normal cricket' as it was called. Such was their progress that a powerful International Wanderers team, managed by former Australian captain Richie Benaud and including 2 Australian captains in the Chappell brothers and a former England captain in Mike Denness, toured South Africa in March and April of 1976, playing all their matches against multi-racial opposition.

The formation of the new non-racial South African Cricket Union (SACU) in 1977 with Mr Rashid Varachia, who had played a leading part in the negotiations, as first president and Mr Wallace as his deputy, was a great step forward which placed cricket ahead of any other sport in South Africa in terms of eliminating discrimination. 1977 was also the year when Kerry Packer launched his World Series Cricket organization, buying up a majority of the world's Test cricketers. South Africa was as badly affected as any country. Without any Test cricket there was no sense of national duty to keep the best players in the country and South Africa lost the cream of their talent with some signing for Packer and others joining club teams in Australia where the financial inducements were greater than in South Africa. An important development in domestic cricket was the award of the first benefit match in South Africa to Western Province captain E. J. Barlow. The award was later withdrawn when Barlow signed for Packer, but in subsequent years benefits were awarded to R. G. Pollock and V. A. P. van der Bijl.

South Africa took a step forward in 1978 when the Emergency Committee of the Cricket Council in England accepted that South Africa had fulfilled the requirements for a return to Test cricket. At the annual meeting of the International Cricket Conference in June of that year, the ICC decided to send a fact-finding mission to South Africa. The delegation headed by ICC chairman Charles Palmer, spent March of 1979 in South Africa. West Indies, Pakistan and India refused to support the delegation which contained representatives from England, Australia, New Zealand, the United States and Bermuda. A further important step, hereabouts, was the decision of Western Province to appoint E. J. Barlow as full-time organizer, promoter and marketing manager of their cricket, thus providing both machinery to make the game financially viable in the absence of Test cricket, and also an enticement to keep South Africa's top players in South Africa.

The question of race, cricket and politics in South Africa has been one of the most sensitive subjects cricket has known in its long history. For the past decade and a half it has seldom been out of the news, but the roots of the problem extend back much further, more than a hundred years to the very beginnings of the game in that country.

In the 19th century, cricket in South Africa was predominantly a British garrison and settler game, but through contact with Englishmen, the other population groups gradually became familiar with it. The first groups to be influenced in this way were the Afrikaners, Malays and people of mixed blood in and around Cape Town where the British administration had its earliest seat. The game moved apace with the extension of British influence into the interior and soon tribal Africans – through their contacts with missionaries, teachers, traders, administrators and settlers – were being introduced to cricket.

The opening up of the diamond and gold fields in the last quarter of the century resulted in dramatic urbanization and economic integration, here again bringing a huge African proletariat into contact with European influences. In order to ensure a healthy labour force, mining houses in time provided recreational and other facilities which gave people, who would not otherwise have had the resources, the opportunities to play. Many of the outstanding names in the history of African cricket learnt to play and administer the game in this way.

It is known that cricket was played by blacks in Natal, the Transvaal, Orange Free State and present-day Lesotho by the 1890s, but far and away the greatest development took place in the Cape Colony where a more relaxed system of race relations was found and the English influence was most deeply rooted.

Contrary to the generally held belief that cricket only now is beginning to make headway amongst Africans, African cricket flourished in the Cape at the turn of the century. As early as 1884, before white cricket was organized on a provincial basis, blacks also organized inter-town tournaments, planned overseas tours and, under the 'liberal' policies which prevailed at the Cape until 1910, frequently played mixed matches in which they often acquitted themselves with distinction.

Meanwhile, in Cape Town, clubs had been formed and black cricketers, particularly the Malays, had developed a good standard of play. In 1889–90 the first centralized Malay tournament was held at Newlands with teams from Cape Town, Johannesburg and Kimberley participating, and in 1894 a Malay side was given a fixture against W. W. Read's English tourists. The tourists won easily, but L. Sammodien scored one of only two 50s recorded against the English side that year and J. 'Krom' Hendricks had figures of 4 for 50 in 25 overs. For almost 80 years, despite subsequent efforts, this remained the only match by a black side against an international touring team. The match gives an indication of the policy which prevailed in the Cape at the time. Blacks were allowed to take part in the practice sessions of white clubs. This paternalistic system prevailed until the accession to power of the National Party in 1948, after which, under apartheid, interracial contact soon dried up.

Evidence of discrimination in cricket also goes back to the earliest years. In 1894 Krom Hendricks, said by Read's English side to be one of the fastest bowlers they had encountered, was included in the final party of 15 players from which the side for the first South African tour to England was to be selected, but he was later omitted as the result of 'the greatest pressure by those in high authority in the Cape Colony'. English newspapers noted that the South Africans would regret before the season was out that they were so particular about the colour of their men. Further examples of discrimination in the early years are found in the Transvaal where no mixing was allowed and blacks were barred as spectators from matches, a fact which Lord Selborne, the British High Commissioner, publicly denounced in 1909. And so the story goes on almost unnoticed, until the d'Oliveira affair brought the facts into sharp focus much later.

We have seen that clubs were first formed, then district unions and provincial associations followed. In 1904 the first national body for black cricket, the South African Coloured Cricket Board, was established. Under the auspices of this organization black cricketers of all groups participated for more than 2 decades in centralized provincial tournaments for the Barnato Trophy (presented by Sir David Harris, chairman of the De Beers Consolidated Mines and also a Cape parliamentarian) before the various racial groups started breaking away to form independent bodies of their own.

Four black bodies functioned independently from one another and each organized regular interprovincial mass tournaments. The Independent body competed for the Sir David Harris trophy, the Bantu Board for the NRC trophy, the Indians for the Christophers Cup, and the old mother body, the SACCB, also known as the Barnato Board, which was resuscitated in 1944, still competed for the Barnato Trophy.

However, moves were soon afoot for the reconciliation of the black bodies, as a result of which the inaugural meeting of the South African Cricket Board of Control (SACBOC) took place in July 1947 under the jurisdiction of the South African Indian Cricket Union. The Barnato Board refused to be drawn into the new organization but a union of the African, Independent Coloured and Indian groups was brought about. The affiliate bodies did not lose their identity. They united at the top, but each controlled its cricketers as before at the lower levels. Mr B. D. Pavadhai was elected as the first President of SACBOC, with Mr. Rashid Varachia, present President of the South

LEFT The first President of the multi-racial South African Cricket Union, Rashid Varachia.

RIGHT Boon Wallace, (*left*) 3 times President of the South African Cricket Association and a dedicated worker towards multi-racial cricket, with Hassan Howa, spokesman for many years for Cape Coloureds.

African Cricket Union, as the first secretary. In 1951 SACBOC staged the first of 4 tournaments in which the national sides of the various black affiliates took part. In 1953 the Barnato Board was accepted as a member of SACBOC after it had agreed to change its name to the South African Malay Cricket Board.

The Africans, Coloureds, Indians and Malays competed for the last time in an inter-race tournament in Cape Town in 1958, the year in which the first-ever black touring side led by Basil d'Oliveira left for a tour of East Africa. This tour followed a similar historic visit to South Africa by a Kenya Asian side in 1956.

Events that took place on the administrative side of the 1958 inter-race tournament, however, overshadowed those on the playing side. On Sunday 27 January 1958 a meeting of all affiliate boards of SACBOC was held in the library of the Cape Town City Hall to discuss the question of racial integration in South African cricket. The Rev B. L. E. Sigamoney proposed that racialism be abolished in 'non-European' cricket. This motion was followed by 5 hours of heated debate before being carried by 12 votes to 0. (The Malay Board abstained from voting.) 'The struggle for integration on the cricket field is now over,' wrote one newspaperman. 'The result is a precedent for other sporting bodies which are debating the same problem. National cricket teams will be selected on merit not race'.

But this was not to be, because despite the affirmative nod given by the 4 African representatives, African cricketers, with a few exceptions, never took part in SACBOC's new non-racial provincial (Dadabhay tournament) and club competitions in integrated teams. Moreover these developments were seen as a threat and opposed by the Government and white sports bodies, including the South African Cricket Association (SACA), who ignored the first calls for non-racialism. When SACA, prompted by complaints to the ICC, approached the Government about mixed play in 1960, the Minister of the Interior replied that the Government was opposed to inter-racial competition and would discourage it.

The growth of the non-racial movement in South Africa, however, allied to increasing world hostility – charged by events like Sharpeville – towards South African government policies, led to intensive global pressures and protests against segregation in sport, resulting eventually in the expulsion of an increasing number of South African sports from international associations. Cricket was significantly affected for the first time when the d'Oliveira affair led to the cancellation of the MCC tour to South Africa in 1968. Faced with the threat of growing isolation, white cricketers now began to challenge segregation, and white administrators, as in other sports, began to offer concessions to black cricket in order to preserve their own international status. Some black cricketers, the Africans, responded to these overtures; others, SACBOC, rejected the gestures as acts of tokenism.

In December 1969 Mr Jack Cheetham, President of SACA, declared that in future Springbok sides would be chosen on merit alone and at the same time announced, without prior consultation with the relevant bodies, a R50,000 grant by SACA for 'assisting the development and advancement of non-white cricket.' Mr Cheetham's offers made no impression on SACBOC with whom earlier exploratory talks had also ended in deadlock. The money was rejected out of hand because it 'sought to perpetuate colour differentiation.'

The policy of SACBOC, led at this time by the flamboyant, outspoken Mr Hassan Howa, rested on considerations of principle rather than convenience. The organization decided to go it alone until genuine change was forthcoming rather than benefit temporarily from the acceptance of token and concessionary gestures. Despite hardships which resulted from SACBOC's independent stand, its players and administrators raised the standard of their cricket and organization appreciably in the 1970s. In 1970, the biennial inter-provincial mass tournaments were replaced by a series of 2-day matches. In the following season 3-day interprovincial matches were instituted and later these were run on a home-and-away basis. In 1975 the traditional Dadabhay Trophy was replaced by the Stellenbosch Farmers' Winery competition as SACBOC entered the age of air travel and sponsorship. National B-section, Under-23 and schoolboy tournaments also became regular features.

On the other hand, the Africans whose affairs, both playing-wise and organizationally, had lapsed into a parlous state in the 1960s, made use of the Cheetham offer, although agreeing fundamentally with SACBOC's non-racial principles. The co-operation with SACA was of considerable benefit to the playing standards of African cricketers. Coaching facilities were provided; a national John Passmore Schools week was started; fixtures were arranged against touring teams such as Derrick Robins's and International Wanderers' sides; the national side was included in SACA's domestic Gillette Cup competition; a tour to Zimbabwe-Rhodesia – the first by an African side outside the borders of the country – was organized; and select African cricketers played in the annual International Datsun Double-Wicket Competition.

While the playing standards of SACBOC and SAACB could not compare with those of the white SACA whose cricketers by 1970 were, arguably, the finest in the world, on the administrative side the coloured bodies held the trump cards with regard to South Africa's future in Test cricket. Once South Africa's isolation had become complete following the 1970 tour by Australia, SACA approached the problem of domestic conciliation with more urgency. Still it did not meet the standards set by SACBOC and the international community.

By now SACA was also lagging behind the demands of its top cricketers who collectively demonstrated their support for mixed cricket in a dramatic way by walking off the field during the important final trial for the selection of the Springbok team for the abortive Australian tour in 1971. But not until 1976 was unity forthcoming.

When Mr Boon Wallace succeeded Mr Cheetham as president of SACA in 1972, he stated that he believed in selection on merit and that he had a mandate from the 9 provinces to pursue that goal to its logical end. Feeling that SACA had shown a change of heart, SACBOC initiated a second meeting of the 3 governing bodies in March 1973. The meeting ended with the appointment of a sub-committee consisting of the 3 presidents who were charged with setting up a blue print for merit selection within 2 months. The meeting at which the blue print was presented, however, ended in disagreement, and the impasse remained.

While the administrators haggled, and although it had only recently become a matter of doubt whether mixed cricket was in fact illegal in South Africa, mixed cricket began to take its course in the early 1970s. By 1975 a mixed club in the real sense of the word – Aurora – had established itself despite the close attentions of the Government and its agencies; plans were going ahead for mixed leagues in the Transvaal; the first 4 blacks had joined white clubs and the first whites had crossed the colour line in the opposite direction to join SACBOC; mixed friendlies were in vogue; and calls for integration were growing steadily stronger. A further relaxation of the government's sports policy in 1973 also led to the arrival of the first mixed international touring sides and the first mixed South African invitation sides at international level.

All these events were, however, overshadowed by SACBOC's decision in February 1975 to renew the initiative to convene a cricket summit of the 3 national bodies. Eventually, almost a year later, on 18 January 1976, representatives of SACBOC, SACA and SAACB met in Johannesburg under the chairmanship of Mr Rashid Varachia, who had succeeded Mr Howa as president of SACBOC, in a meeting which was widely hailed as one of the most dramatic developments in South African sports history. That afternoon they blazoned out their message to their followers, to the rest of the cricket world, to the Vorster government and to anyone else who cared to listen: South African cricketers of all races had united and committed themselves to the path of non-racialism in a country where tradition and decree encourage exactly the opposite path. The principle was adopted that cricket in South Africa would be played on a 'normal' integrated basis, regardless of race, creed or colour and recognizing only merit, from club level upwards, under the controlling aegis of one united governing body. A 9-Man Motivating Committee consisting of 3 representatives from each of the bodies was delegated the task of effecting the change.

A good stroke during a non-white game in Port Elizabeth.

And what a task the 20-month transition to the formation of a single body controlling cricket in South Africa proved to be. But the momentum, though constantly in jeopardy, was maintained to its conclusion. At the head of it all stood Mohammad Rashid Varachia. This Bombay-born third generation South African, a wealthy businessman with 2 Dublin University-trained doctor children, kept the shaky alliance intact against all odds and with rare perspicacity and diplomacy guided South African cricket into a new era.

In March/April 1976 the first South African sides representative of all the cricket bodies in the country clashed with the strong International Wanderers side managed by Richie Benaud and captained by Greg Chappell. And in the new season starting in October of that year, integrated club leagues came to South Africa for the first time and the first black players were selected to play at provincial level in the 88 year old Currie Cup competition. Although in several areas efforts to bring cricketers of all races together failed significantly, the 1976–77 season was a roaring success in the sense that black and white cricketers played together and against each other and socialized freely on hundreds of occasions. The scene was in marked contrast to the limited and out-of-the-usual contact which had existed in years preceding this season.

The initiative was carried further during the off-season and, accompanied by the usual contretemps, it culminated on 18 September 1977 in the historic fusion of the 3 existing national bodies, the South African Cricket Board, the South African Cricket Association and the South African Cricket Board of Control, into the South African Cricket Union. Thereby, in the face of hostile societal pressures, South African cricketers of all races were officially united, for the first time in a hundred years and more, on completely equal terms in a single governing body whose constitution outlaws any discrimination based on race, creed or colour and recognizes merit as the sole criterion. Officially the racial era in cricket had come to an end.

The occasion was marred, however, by the formation 2 months later of a rival non-racial body, the South African Cricket Board. The Board was established by the sizeable faction of SACBOC followers, under the leadership of Mr Hassan Howa, who refused to be part of the new dispensation even though it accorded exactly with their demands over many years and although Mr Howa had been one of the chief architects of the constitution which governed the new South African Cricket Union.

Even this, though, was far from the end of the story. Initially Mr Howa had entered into the 'normal cricket' agreement, but from the start was a reluctant participant. The reason, it is commonly believed, even by confidants of Mr Howa, was the bitter personal feud which dated back several years between him and Mr Varachia. The feud had its origins in SACBOC leadership struggles. It was exacerbated by Mr Varachia's accession to high office in place of Mr Howa and the latter's resentment at the former's intrusion into the limelight. Mr Howa participated in the detente initiative because he could not ignore the groundswell of support for the unification moves in SACBOC ranks, but it was clear his support was grudgingly given.

The unrest which swept through South Africa after June 1976 and the uncertainty on the cricket front in the first weeks of the 1976–77 season (caused by an interfering government and ineffectual white administrators), provided Mr Howa with a new platform from which to fight. Now, having extended his demands beyond those for which he and the rest of SACBOC had fought for 20 years, capitalizing on the uncertainty on the cricket front and the sense of outrage which followed the civil unrest, and using his personal dynamism and high standing in the black community, Mr Howa began winning over supporters from the 9-Man Motivating Committee. By November 1977, when his South African Cricket Board was formed, he had formalized his support and his aims. The slogan 'no normal cricket in an abnormal society' was taken up and a policy of non co-operation was resolved upon until the prevailing political system is completely dismantled. Whereas before the call was for a separation of politics and sport and for assimilation, sport is now recognized as being an integral part of the general political system. Consequently in the two years that followed the formation of the SACU and SACB the split remained as implacable as ever. No official contact was forthcoming and relations continued to be marked by acrimony as the two bodies vied with each other for the majority support of black cricketers and the Board did its best to frustrate the Union's efforts to get South Africa readmitted to Test cricket.

NOTE
In South Africa 'Black' is the term widely used today for people who are not genetically classified as 'White' under the race laws. This definition encompasses Africans and people of mixed blood and of Malay and Indian descent. Where other terms which now give offence appear in the text – non-European, non-white, kaffir, Bantu and Coloured – they have only been retained when in widespread use during the period being analysed; for example when Africans themselves spoke of non-whites and there was a South African Bantu Cricket Union.

Currie Cup

The Currie Cup, South Africa's main domestic competition since 1899, produces some of the best first-class cricket in the world outside of Test Matches. This is because it is confined to only the leading teams, usually the 4 provinces, Transvaal, Natal, Eastern Province and Western Province, and Zimbabwe-Rhodesia.

Playing on a home and away basis, South Africa's leading cricketers thus appear in only 8 first-class matches a season. With the exclusion of South Africa from international competition, in the 1970s the Currie Cup took on new dimensions.

The lack of Test Matches was keenly felt by the players and cricket followers generally, and the unions suffered financially. But fears that interest would decline and standards fall proved groundless. South African cricket is probably as good today as it has ever been.

Because there are so few matches, there is none of the drudgery of a 7-day playing week. Players go into each 3-day, 21-hour game fresh and keen, knowing that a bad showing even in one match could cost them the competition. There is generous sponsorship, notably by South African breweries who back the Currie Cup, and Datsun, who have taken over the one-day knock-out series from Gillette, and the Provincial Unions have various incentive schemes to reward their players.

Crowds do not reach Test Match proportions, but Newlands in Capetown is packed for the traditional New Year fixture against Transvaal, and the Wanderers in Johannesburg has a festive air over Christmas when Transvaal are usually at home to Natal. In 1979, the Wanderers gates were closed on a 30,000 crowd for the Datsun Shield Final between these old rivals.

While it is difficult to assess the standard, the impression of general excellence over the years seems to be borne out by the achievements of South Africa's leading players in England and Australia. Barry Richards, Mike Procter, Eddie Barlow, Allan Lamb, Clive Rice, Garth le Roux, Ken McEwan and Kepler Wessels are among those who have played with great distinction at the highest level outside South Africa.

Wessels has been lost to the Currie Cup because of South Africa's exclusion from Test Cricket, and Australian Clubs and sponsors have also drawn away Richards. But there are others, like Transvaal batsman Henry Fotheringham and Natal's giant fast bowler Vincent Van Der Bijl, who rank close to them solely on their achievements in the Currie Cup.

Foreigners, usually English county players, occasionally appear in the Currie Cup, but the rules allow provinces to select only one visiting professional. Barry Dudleston (Leicestershire), Philippe Edmonds (Middlesex), Robin Jackman (Surrey) and Bob Woolmer (Kent) and the Australian, Johnny Gleeson, are among those who have gained regular places in Currie Cup sides in recent years.

Since 1976, when cricketers of all races came together under the South African Cricket Union, the Currie Cup has been free of racial restrictions for players and spectators. Black players have represented Western Province, Natal and Eastern Province in the 'A' section, and appear regularly in the Castle Bowl subsidiary competition, in which the leading province's 'B' teams compete against the smaller unions.

Transvaal, with ageless Graeme Pollock hitting nearly 1,000 runs after transferring from Port Elizabeth, won both the Currie Cup and Datsun Shield in 1978–79, becoming only the second team to achieve the double. They have won the Currie Cup outright 18 times and shared it 4 times. Natal have won outright 17 times and shared the cup 3 times. Western Province, led by Barlow, have twice taken the trophy in recent years, but Rhodesia and Eastern Province have never won the competition.

TREVOR BISSEKER

WINNERS

1889–90	Transvaal
1890–91	Griqualand West
1892–93	Western Province
1893–94	Western Province
1894–95	Transvaal
1896–97	Western Province
1897–98	Western Province
1902–03	Transvaal
1903–04	Transvaal
1904–05	Transvaal
1906–07	Transvaal
1908–09	Western Province
1910–11	Natal
1912–13	Natal
1920–21	Western Province
1921–22	Transvaal, Natal and Western Province tied
1923–24	Transvaal
1925–26	Transvaal
1926–27	Transvaal
1929–30	Transvaal
1931–32	Western Province
1933–34	Natal
1934–35	Transvaal
1936–37	Natal
1937–38	Transvaal and Natal tied
1946–47	Natal
1947–48	Natal
1950–51	Transvaal
1951–52	Natal
1952–53	Western Province
1954–55	Natal
1955–56	Western Province
1958–59	Transvaal
1959–60	Natal
1960–61	Natal
1962–63	Natal
1963–64	Natal
1965–66	Natal and Transvaal tied
1966–67	Natal
1967–68	Natal
1968–69	Transvaal
1969–70	Transvaal and Western Province tied
1970–71	Transvaal
1971–72	Transvaal
1972–73	Transvaal
1973–74	Natal
1974–75	Western Province
1975–76	Natal
1976–77	Natal
1977–78	Western Province
1978–79	Transvaal

Border

The district of Cape Province that surrounds East London – known as the Border – first saw cricket in about 1860. By 1876 King Williams Town were strong enough to win the tournament at Port Elizabeth and again won the tournament of 1880. Border first played first-class cricket when they entered a side in the Currie Cup of 1897–98, though a XXII of Border had already played W. W. Read's side 6 years before. In 1909–10 the side put up a good performance against MCC, one of Border's players, N. O. Norton, playing in a Test that season.

Border's best player of that era was G. P. D. Hartigan, a stylish bat and capable bowler who toured England in 1912. Probably the best bowler in Border's history was H. L. E. Promnitz who took 125 wickets in Currie Cup games between 1925 and 1937. Since the Second World War O. C. Dawson, K. N. Kirton, W. S. Farrer, P. J. Muzzell, I. Foulkes and the wicket-keeper N. Kirsten have been the most successful players. A. W. Greig began his first-class career with Border in 1965–66 and was with them for 5 years. The side has never managed to win the Currie Cup.

IRVING ROSENWATER

Eastern Province

Eastern Province may not be able to boast the strongest cricket team in South Africa but it can certainly boast the oldest. The Port Elizabeth CC were formed in January 1843, and cricket enthusiasm there has never seen a break. The first cricket tournament held in South Africa was staged at Port Elizabeth – on the St George's Park ground – in 1876. A local player, O. R. Dunell, had the honour of captaining the first South African team to play England, at Port Elizabeth in 1888–89: A. R. Innes, a fine all-rounder, also played in the match. There still exists the ball used in this historic game. But the pendulum swung away from the Eastern Province before long and she never developed into a force in South African cricket. A. E. E. Vogler played for the side before the First World War, but there was never any real challenge for Currie Cup honours. The situation did not alter between the wars, though occasional shocks were administered: MCC in 1927–28, on a perfect wicket, were shot out in under 18 overs for 49 – but Eastern Province still lost by 10 wickets. It was after 1945 that some former glory returned to Eastern Province. E. A. B. Rowan, who had found himself there during the war years, captained the side (and played an innings of 284 for them) and led them to 3rd place in the Currie Cup tournament of 1946–47. N. B. F. Mann had also joined Eastern Province by then. J. H. B. Waite played in his early years for the province, but another decline set in during the 1950s. The all-rounder, A. R. A. Murray, played well but there was not a great deal of support.

The side's batting from 1960 to 1978 was quite overshadowed by the brilliance of R. G. Pollock, a first-class cricketer since the age of 16, who, before he left to play for Transvaal, scored 8,736 runs for Eastern Province, very easily a record. His brother, P. M. Pollock, likewise, dominated the bowling between 1957 and 1972, with the record number of 268 first-class wickets for the side. In recent years C. P. Wilkins and K. S. McEwan, both captains of the side, have batted well; and M. J. Macaulay, the old Test player, after a decade's absence from the game, made a remarkable debut for Eastern Province at the age of 38 in 1977–78, taking 42 first-class wickets, the second best figures in the country. The Currie Cup, however, has still proved elusive.

IRVING ROSENWATER

Graeme and Peter Pollock, two of South Africa's most famous cricketers, both of Eastern Province.

Natal

Natal not only has one of the finest grounds in South Africa – at Kingsmead, Durban – but has one of the finest sides. In recent years, especially, her record has been second to none. Few teams can afford to visit Durban or Pietermaritzburg today with unbounded confidence. The roots of the game are deep in Natal, for cricket is recorded there in 1843. Military influence was strong in the early days and the game thrived through the Victorian age. The first of Natal's great players was A. D. Nourse, Snr, who first appeared in the late 1890s and eventually became known as the Grand Old Man of South African cricket. He was a left-hander who hit 304 not out for Natal in 1919–20 and was still playing first-class cricket beyond the age of 50. His aggregate in Currie Cup games was a record until exceeded by his son. Born at Durban a year after Nourse was the most prominent South African batsman of his day – H. W. Taylor, one of the few men to score with any ease off S. F. Barnes and a stalwart in the Natal side for many years. R. M. Poore played some of his cricket for Natal, as also did another who appeared for Hampshire, C. B. Llewellyn. But for all Natal's talent, the province only twice won the Currie Cup before the First World War.

Thereafter, though strong, Natal could not quite hold off the challenge of Transvaal. E. L. Dalton was a stylish left-hander and useful change bowler, and H. G. Deane another stylish bat and shrewd captain. I. J. Siedle scored heavily from the middle 1920s, but by far the greatest player emerged in 1931 in A. D. Nourse, Jnr, a famous son of a famous father. A strong, aggressive batsman and a magnificent player of spin bowling, he was Natal's and South Africa's batting mainstay for a generation. H. F. and W. W. Wade were other good Natal batsmen and the side were the equal of Transvaal in strength in the years before the Second World War. Since then a host of fine players have been thrown up and the Currie Cup has almost become Natal's by prescriptive right. V. I. Smith was a fine spinner who perhaps was not given sufficient opportunity, and by the middle 1950s a fine side was being moulded: D. J. McGlew, a solid opener and captain; T. L. Goddard, an all-rounder of fine calibre and McGlew's successor as captain; R. A. McLean, a talented and dashing stroke-player; H. J. Tayfield, one of the best off-spinners of his era; H. J. Keith, C. Wesley, J. C. Watkins and P. M. Dodds were all a force in the side.

In 1964–65 the 19-year-old B. A. Richards made his debut for Natal, going on to score a record number of runs and hundreds for the side, and twice passing 1,000 runs in a Currie Cup season (the only player ever to reach this target). M. J. Procter followed Richards into the side a year later, and by 1967–68 Natal had finished top of 7 successive Currie Cup competitions (including one tie with Transvaal). V. A. P. van der Bijl joined Procter to become the 2 greatest wicket-takers in Currie Cup history, Procter himself creating a new record of 59 wickets in the 1976–77 season. Natal had then had a fresh run of success, with 3 Currie Cup titles in 4 years. P. H. J. Trimborn, a fine fast bowler with 274 first-class wickets for the side, was also a great force until the mid-70s. In 1976–77 Natal became the first side ever to win both the Currie Cup and Gillette Cup in the same season. Natal's total of Currie Cup titles is only slightly behind the record of Transvaal.

IRVING ROSENWATER

North-Eastern Transvaal

As a cricket-playing entity North-Eastern Transvaal made their début in first-class cricket in 1937–38, when they finished behind Transvaal and Natal in the Currie Cup. In that first season W. A. Henderson took 4 wickets in 4 balls v Orange Free State and L. S. Brown proved himself a fine all-rounder. Xenophon Balaskas made a fleeting appearance for the side v MCC in 1938–39, and when MCC came again 10 years later Denis Compton made the occasion memorable with his fantastic 300 at Benoni in a fraction over 3 hours. In the 1950s P. C. Davies was a steady opening bat – he scored 200 v Orange Free State in 1955–56 – and J. H. Richardson a capable captain and wicket-keeper. The former 'keeper, J. D. Lindsay, had accompanied the South African side to England in 1947. More recently K. J. Funston, S. F. Burke, D. T. Lindsay, J. T. Botten and the brothers J. A. and P. L. Corbett have been among the best players. After the 1970–71 season, North-Eastern Transvaal ceased to be a first-class side, and were replaced in domestic cricket by the newly-constituted Northern Transvaal, with virtually the same players, who headed the 'B' section of the Currie Cup at the first attempt. In 1977–78 the side became the first holders of the Castle Bowl, and won it again the following year.

IRVING ROSENWATER

The Ramblers Ground, Bloemfontein, for many years the charming headquarters of the Orange Free State.

Orange Free State

Cricket was being regularly played in Bloemfontein, the capital of Orange Free State, as early as the 1850s. It was not until the Edwardian era, however – when the territory was known as the Orange River Colony – that first-class cricket was first seen, though English sides continued to play against odds. In 1913–14, when OFS decided to play MCC on level terms, their rashness was answered by defeat by an innings and 374 runs. Their teams have never been particularly strong and they have never challenged for Currie Cup honours, though in 1926–27 they showed fine form to finish 2nd to Transvaal: S. K. Coen scored 737 runs in the 6 Currie Cup games that season and shared a stand of 305 for the 2nd wicket with J. M. M. Commaille v Natal. K. G. Viljoen played some of his cricket with OFS in the 1930s and Lindsay Tuckett, like his father a Test cricketer, first played for the side at the age of 16. P. S. Heine played his early first-class cricket with Orange Free State in the 1950s, capturing many wickets for them. In 1962–63 the left-handed N. Rosendorff began his career as the most prolific run-scorer in the side's history and in due course captained them. W. T. Strydom, one of 4 Bloemfontein-born brothers who have played for OFS, has taken most wickets for the side in the Currie Cup with his medium-pace bowling.

IRVING ROSENWATER

Transvaal

There has rarely been a time in South African first-class cricket that Transvaal has not fielded a strong – and at times powerful – XI. The history of the province is scattered with the names of some of South Africa's most illustrious cricketers, and most sides expect a testing opposition on a visit to Johannesburg. Transvaal was making its influence felt in the 1880s and in 1887–88 a tournament – not a common thing in South Africa in those days – was held at Pretoria. The first side from England was met the following year, and when the Currie Cup competition was formally instituted Transvaal were the first winners. This was in 1889–90, and in the period up to the First World War Transvaal were the strongest side in the Union. They held the Currie Cup from 1903 until 1909, when it was taken from them by Western Province.

The first of South Africa's great wicket-keepers, though an Englishman by birth, was a Transvaal player – E. A. Halliwell. He came to England with the first 3 South African sides and his reputation was of the highest. The great googly bowler Vogler entered upon his professional cricket career when he went to live in the Transvaal in 1905 and he helped form one of the most formidable attacks in South Africa's history. Of the same era was the outstanding all-rounder G. A. Faulkner, one of the dominating figures in the story of South African cricket. With R. O. Schwarz, J. H. Sinclair, S. J. Pegler and G. C. White, it was not surprising that Transvaal were strong. The first time Transvaal met an Australian team was in 1919–20 when H. L. Collins's AIF side drew at Johannesburg.

The 1920s were years of almost unrelieved success for Transvaal, for having shared the Currie Cup in 1921–22 they were not to be deprived of it until 10 year later. E. P. Nupen, a great matting-wicket bowler, was consistently successful, though blind in one eye, and he eventually beat J. H. Sinclair's total aggregate of wickets in the Currie Cup. No side in South Africa has been better served by batsmen than was Transvaal in the 1930s. Bruce Mitchell, an opener to rank with the best in the world, became one of the most experienced batsmen in the country; E. A. B. Rowan, A. W. Briscoe and D. W. Begbie could all score heavily; and towards the end of the 1930s came K. G. Viljoen and Alan Melville, heavy scorers both. Up to 1937 Nupen was still taking his regular wickets. Transvaal also boasted the services of South Africa's finest wicket-keeper, H. B. Cameron, until his untimely death in his 31st year in 1935.

There were 7 Transvaal men in the 1947 South African side in England, and when the first English team played at Johannesburg after the war (in 1948–49) Transvaal replied to MCC's 513 for seven declared with 560. A. M. B. Rowan, a fine off-spinner, was now making his mark and in the following season had the incredible analysis of 9 for 19 for Transvaal against the Australians. Thereafter W. R. Endean, J. H. B. Waite, P. S. Heine and N. A. T. Adcock all added to Transvaal's strength. In a long career between 1960 and 1974, A. Bacher not only captained the side on a record 72 occasions (a record for any South African side) but became the first player to reach 5,000 runs for Transvaal in the Currie Cup, an aggregate later exceeded by the wicket-keeper B. L. Irvine. Under Bacher, Transvaal won the Currie Cup 5 successive seasons (one tied) up to 1972–73; and when R. G. Pollock made his debut for the side and scored a Transvaal record of 961 runs in the season in 1978–79, the Currie Cup was again won. Other recent players of calibre have included D. Mackay-Coghill, H. R. Lance, R. K. Muzzell and C. E. B. Rice.

IRVING ROSENWATER

Western Province

Western Province can boast a fine playing record over her years in first-class cricket and ranks as one of the 'big three' in domestic cricket in South Africa. A Western Province player, H. H. Castens, had the privilege of captaining the first South African side to visit England (in 1894), and the second side, too, was led by a Western Province man, Murray Bisset, who also did much fine administrative work for South African cricket. S. J. Snooke in the early years of the twentieth century proved himself one of the most reliable batsmen in the Cape, while J. J. Kotze was a fast bowler of remarkable stamina and ability. J. M. M. Commaille also scored heavily and J. M. Blanckenberg took many wickets. The great A. W. Nourse, Snr, played some of his cricket after the First World War for Western Province, and when almost 55 scored a double-hundred for them. In the 1920s A. J. Bell was the best turf-wicket bowler in South Africa, and H. G. Owen-Smith was one of the finest all-round sportsmen in history. D. P. B. Morkel and S. S. L. Steyn were fine batsmen, and R. J. Crisp in the 1930s was often a devastating bowler. The standard of Western Province cricket was maintained after the war and reached a particularly high level under the leadership of J. E. Cheetham in the 1950s. Cheetham's gifts as a captain have tended to overshadow his prowess as a batsman, and at one time he held the individual Currie Cup record with an innings of 271 not out for Western Province. E. R. H. Fuller was a fast-medium bowler and useful batsman and, like most of the Western Province side of his time, a brilliant fielder. J. E. Pothecary, a powerfully built medium-pace bowler, also rendered fine service.

The only side to break the Natal-Transvaal monopoly since the Second War, Western Province, owed much to E. J. Barlow, who joined them in 1968–69. He eventually broke all Western Province records for runs, hundreds, wickets and catches, as well as captaining the side over 60 times with great flair. Other fine players have included D. L. Hobson, perhaps the best leg-spin bowler in South Africa, the wicket-keeper G. P. Pfuhl, M. H. Bowditch, P. N. Kirsten and G. S. le Roux.

IRVING ROSENWATER

Sri Lanka

Sri Lanka's first cricket club was formed in 1832. The only English newspaper of the time, the *Colombo Journal*, records the first match in its edition of 3 November of that year. The scores of the first game credits the 97th Regiment with 136 'notches'. Nearly 150 years later Sri Lanka are pressing hard for Test Match status.

In 1879 the Colombo Academy (now the Royal College) played for the first time against its arch rivals, St Thomas's College, with each team including 2 masters. The first exclusively schoolboy encounter took place in 1880. The originator of this match was Ashley Walker, a master at Royal College. A Cambridge blue, he has been called the 'father of Ceylon cricket'.

In 1872 the Malay Cricket Club (Malays were recruited to the Ceylon Rifle Regiment from Java) was formed; the first Ceylonese club, started in 1873. Within 5 years the Colts CC were known as the 'Invincible Colts.' The first match between Europeans and Ceylonese took place in 1887, the Colts CC representing the Ceylonese. In 1868 the first planters' clubs (coffee in those days, rather than tea) had been formed. These hardy planters, trekking perhaps 30 miles through jungle country, played on grounds levelled out on hillsides sometimes over 6,000 feet above sea level. Although they had to contend with many county, university and public-school players the Ceylonese more than held their own in this long series of matches, which continued almost until the Second War.

In the early 1880s another Englishman, George Vanderpar, took Ceylon cricket to his heart. It was he who first arranged for English and Australian touring teams to play a 'whistle stop' game in Colombo. The Hon. Ivo Bligh's was the first to go there in 1882. The ship in which they were travelling, the *Glenroy*, collided with another soon after sailing from Colombo, enabling the Englishmen to play a second match against the Royal Dublin Fusiliers when the *Glenroy* returned for repairs. The first Australian team to make an extended tour to Ceylon was the Rev E. F. Waddy's New South Welshmen in 1914. They included 2 Test players and played in Colombo, Galle, Kandy, Darrawella and Anuradhpura.

The Ceylon Cricket Association was formed in 1922. Two prominent Ceylonese dominating the scene at this time were Dr John Rockwood, first President of the CCA, and S. P. Foenander, author of *Sixty Years of Ceylon Cricket* published in 1924. The leading Ceylonese cricketers between the wars were D. L. de Saram, Edward Kelaart, M. K. Albert, Dr C. H. Gunasekera and S. S. Jayawickrema; among Europeans, A. L. Gibson, A. E. Blair, E. H. L. Sinclair, D. A. Wright, F. A. Waldock, C. Clover-Brown and W. T. Brindley were well-known names.

MCC made their first tour of any length in 1927. They were followed by the Maharaj Kumar of Vizianagram's Indian team, which included, by special invitation, Jack Hobbs and Herbert Sutcliffe, in 1930. In 1932–33 Ceylon made their first official overseas tour, to India. The team, led by C. H.

In the days when touring teams travelled by sea, Ceylon was the scene of many landfall matches. Here the 1938 Australians are seen, all in topees, playing All-Ceylon on their way to England.

Gunasekera, was all Ceylonese and had a good record, losing only the last of their 10 matches.

In 1934 F. C. de Saram became the first Ceylonese to win a University blue; he scored 128 for Oxford against the touring Australians of that year. Three of Ceylon's leading batsmen, Jayawickrema, P. C. D. McCarthy and M. Sathasivam, played hereabouts for the Rest in the Bombay Pentangular; the leading bowlers of the time were D. S. Jayasundera, George Pereira and F. W. E. Porritt. McCarthy migrated to Australia in 1948, where he played Sheffield Shield cricket for Western Australia, the first Ceylonese to do so.

There were official visits from India (1945), the West Indians (1949) and Pakistan (1949), all for the first time, as well as from West Indian, Australian and Commonwealth (1950 and 1957) teams. In the unofficial 'Tests' Ceylon were mostly outplayed. It was not until 1964 that a new and more successful era began, under Michael Tissera, Ceylon's youngest captain who led them to victory over the Pakistan 'A' team in 1964. Of 3 unofficial 'Tests' played in India in 1964–65, also under Tissera, 2 were lost and the last, in Ahmedabad, won. With Tissera and Stanley Jayasinghe leading the way Ceylon were now a good batting side but still weak in bowling.

Tissera's successor as captain, Annura Tennekoon, scored 101 against Colin Cowdrey's MCC team in 1969, and 131 and 169 not out in successive 'Tests' against India in Ceylon in 1974. Led by Tennekoon, Ceylon, now Sri Lanka, toured Pakistan in 1974, by when their big defeats were a thing of the past. In 1975 a strong West Indian team was held to a draw in 2 unofficial 'Tests', the year in which Sri Lanka went on its first tour of England for the inaugural Prudential World Cup. In the cup matches they fared well against Australia, scoring 276 for 4 at the Oval against an attack that included Thomson, Lillee, Mallett, Walker and the two Chappells, but lost to Pakistan and West Indies.

By now tours between Sri Lanka and Pakistan, at Under-19 as well as senior level, were frequent, thanks not least to the encouragement of A. H. Kardar. In 1978 Sri Lanka went to Bangla Desh, where they did well, and an Under-19 Australian side visited Sri Lanka. With victory in the ICC Trophy in England in 1979, and a 47 run win over India in the main competition, as well as several good performances against first-class English counties, Sri Lanka looked to be making steady progress towards their ambition of official Test recognition. Tennekoon, Duleep Mendis, Bandula Warnapura and Sunil Wettimuny as batsmen, E. R. Fernando as wicket-keeper, and more than one de Silva as bowlers, formed the nucleus of a good and experienced side; and with Mr Robert Senanayake as its President Sri Lanka's Board of Control for Cricket entered the 1980s in good hands.

S. S. PERERA

Anura Tennekoon, Captain of the Sri Lankan team that won the inaugural ICC Trophy in 1979, beating Canada in the final at Worcester.

Sweden

Although interest in the game had occasionally been shown in some circles, it was not until 1951 that Sweden's first club, the Stockholm CC, was founded. It numbers almost entirely expatriate players, British Embassy staff among them, and has toured Denmark regularly for many years and made trips to both Holland and Germany.

In the mid-1970s clubs became founded in quick succession at Lund, Gothenburg, Mariestad and Jönköping, also based on expatriate players. A notable breakthrough followed in 1978, when the most recent Bjärred club was formed, consisting mainly of Swedish boys and now boasting also a team of Swedish girls. Like his Danish missionary counterpart, Henry K. Buhl, in South Schleswig, its founder, Kogs Reddy, deserves great credit for his work.

P. S. HARGREAVES

Tanzania

In the First World War, when German colonization ended in Tanganyika, cricket developed slowly, aided by tours of Kenya and Uganda sides from 1951 onwards at Dar-es-Salaam, Moshi and Tanga. Progress was certainly recorded by 1957 when F. R. Brown's MCC team in a 2-day match at Dar-es-Salaam was held to a draw, as was the 1958 South African Non-European team. Tanganyika's players were mostly Indian. In 1958 the Tanganyika Cricket Association was formed. In 1960, for the first time in contests begun in 1951, Tanganyika beat Kenya. Three Patel brothers, K.R., C.D. and R.D., with J. Solanky, have been leading players for Tanzania (from 1962). R. D. Patel's 104 in 4 hours and Solanky's 98 guaranteed a reputable draw in a match at Mombasa v MCC in 1963, while Solanky (83) and a left-armer, Vasant Tapur (5 for 39), partly resisted the MCC win over Tanzania (R. N. S. Hobbs 6 for 21). Vasant Tapu's batting also helped Tanzania draw with MCC in 1974.

PHILIP SNOW

Thailand

Matches with Hong Kong, and periodically with Kowloon CC, took place in the last century and still do in this. At the Royal Bangkok Sports Club (given regal patronage although the kings and princes of Siam, despite being educated mostly in England, have not been known to take successfully to this game), some distinguished cricketers have been seen. E. W. Swanton's XI won comfortably in 1964, as did Worcestershire in 1965, B. L. d'Oliveira making one of his ubiquitous centuries. The Cricket Club of India toured Thailand the following year and in 1968 the International XI under M. J. Stewart played a drawn match. Centuries by G. Boycott and A. Jones in an opening partnership for the 1970 MCC team under A. R. Lewis were too much by far for the Royal Bangkok Sports Club which concentrates on swimming, golf and racing. The Sports Editor of the *Bangkok Post*, Anton Perera from Ceylon, has kept this outpost's cricket going.

PHILIP SNOW

Tonga

As Tongans aim to fall not too far behind their Royal Family in height and weight, their cricketers are probably the world's largest. What they lack in agility compared with their Fijian neighbours these W. W. Armstrong-like Polynesians make up in power of swinging at, and hurling, the ball. Ten teams play constantly: the ball has to be retrieved monotonously from the adjacent Palace lawn or the Pacific. Back-stop is the most overworked man in the field. It is a pity that there has been no European knowledgeable in the game active in the Tongan Archipelago since Sir Basil Thomson (later head of Scotland Yard) – he wrote entertainingly in the 1890s of Tongan capriciousness in the field; there has, perhaps in consequence, been no Fiji v Tonga encounter.

PHILIP SNOW

Tristan da Cunha

Precipitous and, for that reason, scarcely a propitious location, for cricket. But its mild climate induced as late as 1976 the Administrator, S. G. Trees, with a handful of British officials and the remainder of Islanders, to establish 2 teams which are locked in constant rivalry on matting-covered concrete for the South Atlantic Ocean championship.

PHILIP SNOW

Uganda

Ugandan cricket, which sprang from Zanzibar at the turn of the century and centred at first around the European-run Entebbe Sports Club, was almost eliminated under the Amin tyranny. Of the dozen clubs in existence before his Asian expulsions and the economic reprisals only the Africa CC could remain active, and both the then secretary and treasurer of the Uganda CA, Y. B. S. Masembe and John Kasujja, were murdered. The present enthusiastic secretary, Dan Muzito, though hampered by foreign currency restrictions, is busily starting a national league and reviving the game in the schools.

In 1914 the first representative fixture on the East Coast, British East African Protectorate (Kenya) v Uganda, was played at Entebbe with Sir William Morris Carter, the Chief Justice, opening successfully for Uganda, and T. S. W. Thomas (later Sir Shenton Thomas, Governor of Straits Settlements at the time of Singapore's fall and, as captain also of Nigeria and Gold Coast, perhaps the most widely experienced person ever to play in colonial cricket) the best all-rounder in the Kenya side. This fixture was followed in 1920 by Uganda's return visit, after which the Uganda Kobs, the premier club for all sports, became an entity, with Carter as the first President. Hereabouts, African cricketers made tentative starts beyond the fame that Long Boy and Short Boy had attained. But they have proved slower to accept the game than the Goans and Indians who took it up about 1920. There was little to choose in standard between the 2 Asian clubs, Portuguese and British, and Europeans in Uganda's Quadrangular Tournament played the year round. Only the Africans found it difficult to hold their own but they have been more enthusiastic and prominent than in the rest of East Africa.

At Entebbe is one of the most impressive grounds in the Commonwealth. The oval is of fine turf bordered by flowering trees, and just beyond lie the beauties of Lake Victoria. Other splendid grounds, all of which have jute mats for wickets, are at Kampala and Jinja. Prominent in this part of the world where the climate is so favourable have been an administrator J. V. Wild (Cambridge) both as organizer (the Uganda Cricket Association was formed in 1952) and all-rounder, R. A. Snoxall, S. R. Hooper, Major W. V. D. Dickinson (Army and also Kenya) and H. King who transferred to Fiji. To find among those successful on the score-sheets the Portuguese names of Silva, Souza, Gama, Pinto might seem odd if it were not for having come across similar names connected with Ceylon cricket. Uganda cricket was initially associated most closely with Kenya's but 3-day representative matches started later against Tanganyika. Uganda has common ground with Malaya and Fiji in that it has only known a comprehensive Cricket Association set up since the last war. Then racial aloofness, which had not prevented different races playing against each other but had made it rare for them to be represented in one side, gave way. Against MCC touring East Africa in 1958 Uganda lost with a mostly Indian side (predominantly Sikh) at Kampala. J. A. Boucher alone batted confidently, and he alone had been able to resist Zulfiqar Ahmed when A. H. Kardar's Pakistan Cricket Writers' side had visited Uganda in 1956.

Uganda was heavily defeated by the 1963 MCC side (T. W. Cartwright 6 for 17), as was a Jinja side (J. D. F. Larter 5 for 14). In 1967 V. Noordin was 4 short of a century against India under the Nawab of Pataudi. Against the 1974 MCC side Uganda combined with Kenya but was defeated.

PHILIP SNOW

West African Cricket Association

Despite its geographical position West Africa has been a backstream for touring teams. Sir Julien Cahn's team was to have visited in 1938 but the tour fell through 'for accommodation reasons'. A combined side from the Gold Coast (C. D. A. Pullan and an African bowler, J. B. Fleischer), Sierra Leone (L. H. Bean, W. F. H. Kempster and R. Whyte, an African wicket-keeper) and Nigeria (W. R. Shirley, A. K. Judd, E. H. Cadogan, another African bowler, N. D. Nuha, and F. K. Butler, captain) had been selected.

After nearly 70 years of separate existence, these 3 countries and the Gambia inevitably followed the East African pattern, seeing advantages in a central link. Their Association was formed in 1975. The first team to be able to play in the name of West Africa played twice in 1976 against MCC under E. A. Clark. It lost at Freetown, despite 67 not out by Dworzak and 5 for 57 by S. A. Fraser, and also at Lagos because of D. C. Wing's 8 for 10. R. W. Barber and M. C. Cowdrey were in this first MCC team to West Africa but no hundreds were scored. All countries (except Ghana which drew) lost their individual matches by heavy margins.

West Africa was elected an associate member of the International Cricket Conference but through administrative changes applied too late for participation in the 1979 World Cup Competition. Unlike East Africa, West Africa's cricket is almost exclusively indigenous in its current players and leaders. Liberia (there is a cricket league in Monrovia) belongs to the federation.

PHILIP SNOW

United States of America

To some cricket enthusiasts it may appear presumptuous of the United States to claim a modest place in cricket history. A generation reared in the belief that baseball and American-rules football are the main sporting endeavours of the United States may be surprised to learn that cricket has been played more or less seriously for over 200 years. There was a time indeed when Philadelphia cricket was judged good enough to play the full strength of Australia and the first-class English counties, and when an American player on tour in England headed the first-class English bowling averages. The glory has long since departed but the tiny cricketing fraternity in the United States would like to consider that their efforts have upheld the best traditions of the game. One of the earliest mentions of cricket played in the American colonies appears to have been made by William Stephens, a planter living in Georgia. In 1737 he reported, 'Many of our townsmen, freeholders, inmates and servants were assembled in the principal square at cricket and divers other athletick sports.' Stephens knew of cricket as he was educated at Winchester and

Cambridge University before engaging as a planter in the colonies.

The New York *Weekly Post Boy* reported a match between XI of London and XI of New York, played in New York in 1751 and won by the New Yorkers, the scores being 80 and 86 against 43 and 47. It appears most likely that both XIs were drawn from residents of New York, as it is difficult to believe that a touring group would cross the Atlantic for one match, or that the state of the game would encourage such a tour. There was a notice of a cricket match at Baltimore, Maryland, in 1754 and an advertisement for cricket equipment in the New York *Independent Journal* for 19 April, 1786. The American Revolution alienated a great deal of interest in all matters English, one of the victims being the game of cricket. Before the Revolution there was an active interest in the game, and as far as possible in those days, there was some encouragement for the younger players. Even after the Revolution, the question of a name for the chief executive officer of the newly formed United States was brought up and John Adams remarked that 'there are Presidents of fire companies and cricket clubs'. It is interesting to reflect that the word 'President', as used for the chief executive of the United States, may have come about through its use by a humble cricket club.

About 1856 the idea of a visit from an England XI was discussed. (Bear in mind no England XI had ever visited any foreign country at this date.) An industrial depression gripped the United States in 1857, and talks were postponed. A Mr Waller of New York was instrumental in guaranteeing £500 for 2 matches in the United States, and on 6 September 1859, 12 professional cricketers of England met at the George Hotel, Liverpool, to embark for America on the steamer *Nova Scotian* the following morning. The team comprised Caffyn, Lockyer, H. H. Stephenson and Julius Caesar (all of Surrey), Parr, Grundy and Jackson (Notts), Wisden and John Lillywhite (Sussex), Carpenter, Hayward and Diver (Cambridgeshire) and Fred Lillywhite who acted as scorekeeper, historian and manager of the trip. History was made since it was the first overseas tour of an English Cricket XI. The little book describing the tour, first of a plethora of touring literature, is a classic of the game. The experiences of a rough passage are humorously described.

The first international game took place between England and XXII of the United States at Hoboken, New Jersey, on 3, 4 and 5 October 1859, England scoring 156 and dismissing the USA XXII for 38 and 54. There was no disgrace in the England team taking on a XXII. The early Australian games were on the same basis, and cricket in the United States was probably more advanced at that time than in Australia. At Philadelphia the XXII scored 94 and 60. England scoring 126 and 29 for 3 wickets. The little party of cricket pioneers travelled over 7,000 miles in 2 months to play 5 matches, a prodigious adventure in those mid-Victorian times. If this first tour had been followed up Test Matches between the United States and England might have followed in due course. The bitter Civil War which broke out in 1861 between the Northern and Southern States had many unforseen results, one of which was to establish baseball beyond all doubt as the national game of the United States. Before the war cricket was an established game and baseball was played more by students and children. The difficulties of getting proper cricket equipment and of marking and maintaining pitches were too great during the 4 years of war; it was easy to throw down 4 bags to mark bases and to play baseball on any ground available. Thousands of soldiers learned the game of baseball during the Civil War. When they returned to civil life the future of baseball was assured. With the ruinous war proceeding in America, the attention of English cricket tour organizers turned to Australia.

One result of the international tour, however, was to popularize cricket in Philadelphia. English XIs began to play there and good coaching and frequent games against first-class English cricketers began to lift Philadelphia cricket to an exalted spot. Jupp's English XI of 1868 played 2 games at Philadelphia, winning both easily. A study of the scoring in these early games leads one to the conclusion that the Americans were deficient in batting and bowling. Lack of coaching was evident in the batting which apparently was suffering from poor defensive methods. A batsman simply did not know how to cope with the English bowling. Over-arm bowling had been authorized by MCC in 1864 but there is no doubt that the Americans were playing an old-fashioned game and had not learned how to cope with the new type of bowling. As late as 1880 an Under-arm XI defeated a Round-arm XI at Merion, Pennsylvania, 121 to 94. This was almost 100 years after round-arm bowling was introduced in England.

Philadelphia cricket was helped by the visit of R. A. FitzGerald's amateur XI in 1872, humorously described by Mr FitzGerald in his book *Wickets in the West*. W. G. Grace made his only appearance in the United States with this team and it is of interest to record his scores:

At New York v XXII of St George's Club – 68 and 11 wkts for 8 runs.
At Philadelphia v XXII of Philadelphia – 14 and 7 and 20 wkts for 68 runs.
At Boston v XXII of Boston – 26 and 13 wkts for 35 runs.

Most early professional baseball players were former cricketers, including Harry Wright and A. G. Spalding, both of whom founded sporting goods firms which are still active today. The Philadelphians continued to outstrip other centres until the city became the focal point of American cricket. Tours were regularly made to England and the Australian XIs began to return through the United States, playing games at Philadelphia, Chicago and San Francisco. These visits were too irregular to be educational, but in 1878 the Australian XI captained by D. W. Gregory, after finishing its first tour of England, met Philadelphia on 3, 4 and 5 October. This Australian team was the historic XI which had beaten MCC at Lord's in one day, but at Philadelphia they earned only a drawn game in a match which has become historic. it was the first time an American team had played on even terms in an international match. The full Australian team – Spofforth, Blackham, the Bannermans, Murdoch, Boyle and all included – were led by 46 on first innings and honours were even at the finish. This game made the fame of Philadelphia cricket. Enthusiasm ran high in the district, young men took up the game, rich men supported it and the clubs built luxurious club houses. The cricket clubs of Philadelphia became the country clubs of their time. To this day United States international tennis matches are played at Longwood Cricket Club or at Merion. In both places, alas, regular cricket is played no more.

The Philadelphians organized a visit to England in 1884 and another in 1889, playing good clubs with some success. Lord Hawke brought a team of first-class English amateurs to Philadelphia in 1891 and the Australian team of 1893 played 2 games in the city. In the first match Philadelphia made the highest score made by an American team in first-class cricket, amassing 525 and putting the Australian Test team out twice. The Australians lost the match by an innings and 68 runs. The real hero of this game, however, was a humble railway car. The liner *Germanic* was bringing the Australian team from England and, in an effort to save valuable time, it was arranged to pick up the team at Jersey City and put them aboard railway car No. 30! Any cricketer who can imagine himself taking a long ocean voyage, being picked up by a private train, rushed 100 miles, changing at breakneck speed into flannels, then stepping out to play an international match, will appreciate the position of the Australian team. Never by a look did they excuse themselves. They took their defeat in good spirit. Local enthusiasm ran high but a local poet put the credit for the victory where it belonged:

The outstanding American cricketer was J. Barton King, who in 3 tours of England with the Philadelphians (1893–1908) established himself with the foremost critics of the day as a truly great in-swing bowler.

Who was it that whipt the Australians?
Others' glory we don't want to mar
But the victory was won and won nobly
By John Green with his fast private car!

The Australian XI of 1896 under G. H. S. Trott visited Philadelphia and played 3 games on level terms. The first 2 games were lost by handy margins but Philadelphia won the 3rd by an innings and 99 runs. It was after these experiences that the city cricketers determined to try a first-class tour of England in 1897. The Philadelphian tour of 1897 was a great success and showed the heights to which their cricket had soared in a few short years. The tour was entirely first-class; after this tour all Philadelphia matches with English county opponents were reckoned first-class until 1914. The team beat Sussex and Warwickshire and drew with Somerset, Yorkshire Notts and Oxford University. This tour also saw J. Barton King spring into the limelight for the first time. Bart King, one of the world's greatest bowlers, accomplished the best performance of the tour when he took 7 wickets for 13 against Sussex on a good wicket at Brighton. King bowled a ball which he called the 'Angler' and which he has described as an in-swinger which, if properly bowled, would change direction sharply in the last 10 or 15 feet of flight. King used this ball sparingly and against good batsmen, but he did it so successfully that from 1893 to 1912 he was one of the most feared bowlers in the world and in 1908 actually headed the first-class English bowling averages. King was undoubtedly the finest cricketer produced in America, not only for his bowling in the Golden Age of American cricket, but also for his batting, and his personal characteristics endeared him to generations of friends. This giant of the game died in 1965.

In 1897 and 1899 P. F. Warner and K. S. Ranjitsinhji took teams to Philadelphia, both with great success. It was during Warner's tour that Ralph D. Paine described the mighty hitter G. L. Jessop in lines which are still quoted:

At one end stocky Jessop frowned,
The human catapult
Who wrecks the roofs of distant towns
When set in his assault.
His mate was that perplexing man
We know as 'Looshon-Gore'.
It isn't spelt at all that way
We don't know what it's for

The Philadelphia tours of 1903 and 1908 more than held their own against the first-class counties, but the end of the glory of Philadelphia was in sight. After 1908 they played no more first-class cricket in England. The Australian team of 1912 lost to Philadelphia by 2 runs in an exciting match, and an Australian XI, visiting the United States and Canada in 1913, lost to XII of Germantown CC by 2 wickets in a game which was virtually the last American first-class match. Although the Philadelphian Pilgrims had an enjoyable tour in 1921, the games were not first-class. Since that time, apart from Haverford College, no American team toured in England until 1961 when Winnetka Cricket Club of Chicago made a valiant effort to play some club games in England – and with 10 volunteers at that!

Many reasons have been advanced for the decline of cricket as a popular game in the United States. The fact remains that the national temperament is not altogether suited for cricket's leisurely pace. Perhaps there are other reasons such as the many counter-attractions for the young generation of Americans, the lack of interest by cricket's governing bodies, the tremendous increase of spectator sports, the greater interest in sports such as golf, tennis and swimming as against team sports. The United States was one of the first countries outside England to have a magazine devoted exclusively to cricket. *The American Cricketer* was founded on 28 June 1877, and had a life of over 50 years. The last issue appeared in April 1929, but by that time much of its space was devoted to tennis and other sports, and cricket had been relegated to the back page, Complete sets of *The American Cricketer* are preserved in the library of Haverford College and the Philadelphia Library of the Historical Society of Philadelphia. The C. C. Morris Cricket Library Association was dedicated at Haverford in 1968. The organization has on view a very large collection of other American cricket memorabilia consisting of books, records, periodicals, photographs and trophies. No real central authority existed in the United States until 1961 when the United States Cricket Association was formed.

Whilst Philadelphia cricket ascended to the heights of the first-class game, there were other centres in which good class cricket was and still is played. In New York the game flourished principally because of English players who had settled in that city. The first match between the United States and Canada took place on the grounds of the St. George's Club of New York on 24 and 26 September, 1844. This game was played for $1,000 a side. The value of a dollar was much higher in those carefree days; so a great deal of importance must have been attached to this match. After a break of 51 years, the series was revived in 1963. In the first 16 games the United States and Canada each had 6 victories and 4 were drawn. The New York clubs never attained the heights of the Philadelphians but they had some good players, amongst them J. L. Poyer and B. J. Kortlang.

In New York today there are 4 leagues, and over 40 clubs play. Most of the cricket played there is carried on by West Indians who bring much enthusiasm to the game. They were responsible for the visit of the West Indian XI with several Test players in 1959 and for the visit of the Pakistan Test team in 1958. Several of the New York West Indian cricket teams have toured in the West Indies and Bermuda. It is this enthusiasm which must be allied with the enthusiasm of cricketers in other cities to make the United States Cricket Association a successful national organization. F. Fitzmaurice Kelly was secretary of Staten Island CC for many years and was associated with the game in New York for a long period. Kelly came to the United States in 1888 and after 1 year at Denver and 5 in Chicago, he was connected with New York cricket for over 40 years.

Cricket in Chicago started about 1876. Most of the players were from England. They had come to work in the thriving big city of the prairies. The Chicago Cricket Club was formed in that year and other clubs were The Wanderers CC, St George's and Pullman. Tom Armitage, a former Yorkshire county player, greatly encouraged the local players and provided some first-class coaching. In the 1890s, Chicago cricket was very strong and it is a pity that there were very few matches against Philadelphia. Lord Hawke's XI played All-Chicago, winning by an innings in a match in which the local cricketers did not shine. The Australian XI of 1896 played a match in Chicago on their way home after a successful English tour. Australia scored 235 and XV of Chicago 105 and 53. A large crowd watched the match, attracted to some extent by the fact that 2 of Chicago White Sox baseball club, 'Cap' Anson and Fred Pfeiffer, were in the cricket team.

The Australian team of 1913 played 3 games in Chicago, overwhelming the locals in all 3 games. 10 years later, after an interval due to the First World War, Chicago cricket resumed under the leadership of K. A. Auty, who encouraged young cricketers in every way. Karl André Auty, who died in Chicago in November 1959 at the age of 78, was a great American cricket enthusiast who encouraged the game at every level. During the 1930s, the Illinois Cricket Association went on regular tours to Canada, Detroit, St. Louis and Winnipeg and received 3 overseas touring teams: Sir Julien Cahn's XI, Cambridge University Vandals and the Australian XI of 1932. For the most part, the visitors were not too badly extended. A Chicago XVIII, however, on 23 July 1932, scored 186 against Australia and saw the visitors lose 6 wickets for 148 and walked away with the honour of a drawn game. The following statistics of Don Bradman's visit to Chicago are illuminating:

23 July 1932 v XVIII of Illinois b Watt	4
24 July 1932 v XVIII of Illinois c Knights b Smith	6
25 July 1932 v XVIII of Illinois b Watt	13
26 July 1932 v XVIII of Illinois c T. Williams b Foster	41

Cricket continues in Chicago due to the determination of a small but loyal group of cricketers and 12 clubs are playing in the district at present. The great days of Chicago cricket in the 1930s have long since gone but the game continues to be enjoyed at the local level.

St Louis started cricket about 1868. The game was introduced by a group of English cotton brokers who worked in the city at that time. The ground selected was in the very centre of the present city and, when a match was to be played, it was a gala day for everyone. Lunch and tea were served; ladies and gentlemen in all their finery paraded on the ground and a band was in attendance in the best tradition of 19th-century England. Some of the games attracted over 4,000 people, although there were, of course, no visiting XIs. About 12 years later the club lost their ground and removed to a piece of ground entitled 'Sportsman's Park'. This is now the home ground of the St Louis Cardinals professional baseball club. After a short sojourn there, several grounds were used prior to a move to Forest Park which is still the seat of St Louis cricket. The cricketers fight a lonely battle for the survival of their favourite game.

California cricket was played in the San Francisco area for many years after the famous gold strikes of 1849. Perhaps that was the start of cricket on the Pacific Coast. There are reports of cricket played in Placer County, California, in the 1860s and 1870s by miners who had played in Australia or England. The Australian XI of 1878 played in San Francisco, but the game is reported in *Lillywhite* of the period as being little more than a farce. Cricket continued to be played more or less intermittently in San Francisco until fairly recent times, and after the Second World War, due to an influx of immigrants from Australia, India and England, more cricket has been played than previously. There are now 10 clubs in the Northern California Association, playing a regular Schedule. The standard of the game has been constantly improving.

In Los Angeles the game became popular just before the First World War when the movie industry began to attract people from all over the world. Cricketers, too, were part of this general immigration, and cricket became part of the local scene. A cricket league with 12 clubs flourished in the early 1920s, but when they lost the grounds in 1924 it was a severe blow. The Santa Monica club managed to keep the game going and after a few years C. Aubrey Smith, the famous actor and cricketer, arrived in Los Angeles and immediately proceeded to revitalize the game. With tact and enthusiasm he breathed life into the dormant local cricket scene and founded the Hollywood Cricket Club. Several rival clubs sprang up and cricket received its share of publicity and interest which has

An illustrious group at Hollywood, California in 1937. From the left: John McCormack, Rupert Howard, Jim Sims, Walter Hammond, George Duckworth, Bob Wyatt, Nigel Bruce, Sir Aubrey Smith, Gubby Allen, Maurice Leyland, Charles Fry, Par Somerset and Boris Karloff. MCC were returning from Australia.

kept Southern California cricket going to this day. There are 13 clubs in the local Association. Cricket is also played at California Institute of Technology and the University of California in Los Angeles. Southern California met and defeated the Australian Old Collegian touring XI in 1959. It was the first victory of an American XI over foreign opposition since 1913 and created a great deal of enthusiasm.

Cricket was televised in Los Angeles in 1958. Two hours were allotted by a local station and part of a match between Corinthians and Hollywood was shown. The match proved to be exciting, and the television station received many calls and letters congratulating it on its enterprise. Due to the enthusiasm engendered, the Harlequins CC was formed entirely of ex-cricketers who had watched the transmission. Sir Aubrey Smith deserves many plaudits for his share in the encouragment of cricket. He was born in 1863, the son of a doctor. He was educated at Charterhouse where he was in the XI, and later won a blue at Cambridge. He was principally famous for his bowling which earned him the name of 'Round-the-Corner Smith', due to a slanting run-up. His bowling was fast-medium and good enough to win him a place for Sussex from 1882 to 1896 as well as frequent games with the Gentlemen. In 1888–89 he captained the first English XI to play in South Africa. He arrived in Hollywood as an accomplished actor, world famous in his field, but his first love was cricket and he aided it by every means in his power. He was knighted in 1944 as a tribute to his efforts to further Anglo-American friendship. The cricket grounds at Griffith Park, Los Angeles, were officially named the Sir C. Aubrey Smith grounds.

Cricket has been played in American universities for many years, but mostly by foreign students who are from cricket-playing countries. Harvard, Yale, Pennsylvania, Princeton and Cornell have all fielded teams. The Universities of California, Ursinus, Southern Illinois and many other universities field teams irregularly. Haverford College, a small school at Haverford, Pennsylvania, has kept the flag of inter-collegiate cricket flying in the United States for over 125 years. In 1836 the school engaged an English gardener named William Carvill who must have been a very enthusiastic cricketer. He introduced the game to some students who took it up immediately. A diary kept by an unknown student has this entry in it:

> About this time a new game was introduced amongst the students called cricket. The school was shortly divided into several clubs or associations each of which was provided with the necessary instruments for playing the game.

The school sent teams over to England in 1896, 1900, 1904, 1910 and 1914 and the last Haverford College tour was in 1925. Haverford still tours Ontario as well as playing a programme of matches against eastern clubs.

American cricket, from its earliest days, has been characterized by its *bonhomie* and good fun. Professionalism, except for paid coaches from England who held sway in Philadelphia, has never intruded on the American scene. In a land which is probably more than most given up to materialism in sport, cricket is one of the rare sports a man indulges in for its own sake. Cricket in the United States is played on turf wickets, on matting rolled over concrete, on matting stretched over abominable grass uncut and unrolled; in short, wherever an enthusiast stakes a claim, a cricket ground arises and for a short spell the magic of bat and ball can hold sway. Most of all, American cricket owes its being to enthusiasts for whom the charm of the game can never die and who lose no time in their new surroundings in spreading their gospel. Cricket was sometimes played in October or November, with icy conditions prevailing. The first tourists of all time, Lillywhite's team of 1859, played at Rochester, New York, in greatcoats and mufflers. The first cricket teams from England and Australia crossed the Great Plains in tiny rickety trains, in which depredations by bands of armed, painted Indians, in the best traditions of the Old West, were not unlikely.

Anyone from England is eagerly sought, either as player or umpire. Some of these visitors could not care less about the world of cricket, but to show their British sympathies in this Land of the Dollar, they enter into umpiring or playing duties, feeling that they are doing their all for Queen and Commonwealth.

Cricket in the United States continues to benefit from visiting teams from England, Australia, New Zealand, India, Pakistan, Ireland, Canada, Bermuda and Mexico. Recent visitors have included county teams from England such as Yorkshire and Worcester; national teams such as New Zealand; and touring teams such as the New Zealand Ambassadors, Australian Emus and Australian Old Collegians. In addition, tours have been made by club teams including Auckland University from New Zealand, an MCC Indoor Schools XI and the Australia House Cricket Club from England, British Columbia Cricket Association, Vancouver Rowing Club and Vancouver Cricket Club from Western Canada, and the Mexico City Cricket Club from Mexico. There has also been a large increase in the number of club teams touring from the United States. England has been toured by Prior Cricket Club from Philadelphia, University Cricket Club and Pasadena Cricket Club from Los Angeles and the Northern California Cricket Association. A successful tour to Jamaica was made by the Southern California Cricket Association in 1971 and the Northern California Cricket Association also made successful visits to South America and the West Indies in 1976 and the South Pacific and Hawaii in 1978.

Having been admitted to associate membership of the International Cricket Conference in 1965, the United States have been ably represented there by John Gardiner. In 1979, successful participation was achieved in the inaugural ICC Associates Competition. Other United States teams have toured England and Bermuda, and in 1973 an all-Jewish team participated in the 9th Maccabiah Games in Tel Aviv. John Marder, the first President of the United States Cricket Association was the inspiration of many of these tours. When he died in 1976 no one had done more for cricket in North America.

JOHN MARDER AND ADRIAN COLE

The USA team which competed for the ICC Trophy, 1979, comprising mostly West Indian exiles: standing: Neil Lashkari, Steve Jones, Hasib Khan, Wayne Stuger, Michael Gordon, Rex Legal and John Reid; sitting: Sri Nagesh, Kamran Khan, James Reid (manager), Anil Lashkari (captain), Ivan Atherley, Ophneal Larrier and Walter Bovell.

West Indies

C. L. R. JAMES AND P. D. B. SHORT

The British West Indian islands are part of a scattered chain in the Gulf of Mexico. Jamaica is the only one which now has over a million people. Barbados, the home of Weekes, Worrell, Walcott, Sobers and Hall, 21 miles long and 14 miles broad, has a population of a third of a million. British Guiana on the mainland of South America has a large extent of territory but its population, about twice that of Barbados, is concentrated on a thin strip of coastline. There are smaller islands with a few thousand population some of which, particularly Antigua, St Lucia and St Vincent, have produced fine cricketers. Except for British Guiana and Trinidad where there is a substantial number of East Indians, their population is about 75% Negro, 5% white and the rest mixed blood with a sprinkling of other races.

It is Barbados which has always been the traditional centre of West Indian cricket. In 1806 the St Ann's Club of Barbados was formed. There are other tantalizing Press references and it was noted that in 1861 Prince Albert, the second son of Queen Victoria, visiting the island as a midshipman, spent a great part of one day playing cricket. In 1865 Barbados played the first inter-colonial match against Demerara (now part of Guyana). In 1886 a West Indies team visited Canada and in 1887 an American team toured the West Indies. In a Barbados paper of 1867 we hear of a Mr G. R. Challenor playing against the officers. He should be remembered. He is the father of George Challenor, the first of the famous West Indian batsmen. H. B. G. Austin who was active in West Indies cricket in the last decade of the nineteenth century says that while there was much natural ability there was no method and it was the advent of a series of English teams in the 1890s, led by pioneers like Lord Hawke and Sir (then Mr) Pelham Warner, which began to give some shape and style to local play. A. E. Stoddart was one of the visitors.

Slavery had been abolished only in 1833 and even in the last quarter of the century the historian notes that the coloured people had little opportunity to develop their fascination with the game. H. B. G. Austin was a son of the Bishop of the West Indies, and his brother, M.B.G., was not only a commercial magnate of Demerara but led the Demerara team. After the experiences with English visitors a team came to England in 1900; black bowlers, making a place for themselves as professionals, were in the side. Selected as a batsman was L. S. Constantine, the father of Learie Constantine. The haphazard organization (and genuine enthusiasm) of West Indies cricket is shown by the experience of 'Old Cons', as he came to be called, even before his son became a famous cricketer. Selected to go, on the day the boat left he was seen standing disconsolately downtown. Asked if he was not going he replied no, he couldn't afford it. A public subscription was opened on the spot. A fast launch was chartered, the boat was caught before it left the Gulf of Paria and L. S. Constantine scrambled on board to hit the first West Indian century in England for West Indies v MCC at Lord's. Woods, a black professional, proved himself a good fast bowler and Ollivierre proved himself a good batsman. That is as much as can be profitably said. Lord Brackley's team, including Hayes of Surrey and Thompson of Northamptonshire, visited the West Indies in 1905, and in 1906 another visit was paid to England. The side played disappointingly. E. H. D. Sewell noted: 'It is a most extraordinary thing that the side cannot get going . . . I cannot help thinking that they may one day do something surprising.' That was West Indies cricket for many years. This time their surprise was beating Yorkshire with Rhodes, Denton, Tunnicliffe and T. L. Taylor. Watching Challenor, a boy of 19, practise at the nets at Lord's, W.G. said to take note of him: he would be heard of again. The star of the tour was S. G. Smith, all-rounder and, curiously enough for the West Indies, a slow left-hander. He qualified for Northamptonshire and played county cricket so well as to represent the Gentlemen.

Owing to the war West Indies did not visit England again till 1923 but up to 1912 MCC continued to send teams. By the outbreak of war in 1914 West Indies might have been better than they were in 1923. Challenor at home was never in better form. Tarilton had his impregnable defence and unfailing self-control. George John may have gained in experience but in 1923 – at the age of 38, some even say more – had lost his early fire. Richard Ollivierre had proved himself. In 1914 Pascall (brother-in-law of L. S. Constantine), Joe Small and Cephas Rogers were fine cricketers. Furthermore in 1914 H. B. G. Austin would still have been under 40. The disappointment with the teams of 1901 and 1906 was in 1923 happily reversed. The team improved as it played. George Challenor took his place as one of the great batsmen of the day. The combination of Gregory and McDonald being broken, George John and Francis were the finest pair of fast bowlers cricket could show. C. R. Browne confirmed his 'googly' reputation earned in England. Young Constantine promised much in every department. But Lord Harris visiting the West Indies in 1926 warned that West Indies cricket was overrated, chiefly, he thought, due to the sensational collapse before the West Indies fast bowlers of a powerful English batting side (including Hobbs) in the last match of the 1923 tour. The 1925–26 MCC team contained the youthful Hammond. West Indies did well.

George Challenor, one of the first great West Indians, batting against Surrey at the Oval in 1923.

LEFT Paddington Station, April 1933: the West Indians arrive.

OPPOSITE The first all-conquering West Indian side, at Old Trafford in 1950: from left, Johnson, Goddard (Captain), Weekes, Stollmeyer, Walcott, Gomez, Worrell and Christiani.

Despite Challenor's continued form, Lord Harris said of W. St Hill that he was the finest batsman in the West Indies. On this showing the West Indies team was granted Test status in 1928. It proved to be a miscalculation. Challenor never recaptured his earlier form. St Hill failed completely. C. R. Browne was not as effective as he had been. Francis needed reinforcement and received some from Griffith, a fast and very steady bowler. Roach, a newcomer, showed promise. But the tour was made memorable by the histrionic performance of Constantine. He hit fiercely for 1,000 runs. He took 100 wickets with bowling faster than most; no finer all-round fieldsman had yet been seen. Some matches, as a famous one against Middlesex, he seemed to win by himself alone. Unfortunately he failed in the 3 Tests and the West Indians were soundly beaten.

Yet when an MCC team visited the West Indies in 1930 West Indies had perked up enough to win the series. Roach fulfilled all his early promise and George Headley of Jamaica took the field. Only 20 years of age, he made a century 3 times and practically won the Test at Georgetown against time on a wearing wicket. West Indies seemed to have made some ground but a tour to Australia showed that they had not. Woodfull's 1930 team was too much for them. The side never caught itself until the last State match against New South Wales. The tour was saved from inconsequence by the full blossoming of Headley who was hailed by the best judges in critical Australia as a batsman *sans peur et sans reproche*. West Indies in England in 1933 were no stronger than in Australia. Headley was better than ever. Constantine, now a League cricketer, could only play intermittently and the side achieved little of note except that in Martindale Barbados produced yet another great fast bowler.

By 1935 maturity had come. In 1934 the English batsmen had concluded an exceptionally successful season against Grimmett and O'Reilly. In the West Indies in 1935, facing the pace of Martindale, Constantine and a new-comer, Hylton of Jamaica, the English batting failed in match after match. In Tests Hendren (who had had a spectacular previous tour in the West Indies) failed to pass 50. Wyatt and Holmes did that much only once and Ames alone reached a century. Headley compounded for his scores of 93 and 53 with a mammoth 270 not out. J. E. D. Sealy, who as a boy had gone to Australia, at last came into his own. Constantine in Tests did belated justice to his batting and the West Indies convincingly won the series. In 1939 much the same team visited England. They lost the First Test at Lord's, Headley adding yet another to his apparently unending list of laurels by making a hundred in each innings of a Test on the famous ground. Martindale was not the bowler he had been but Constantine played the full season and with less pace but more guile was successful throughout. By the last Test the side had found itself. England made 352 and West Indies replied with a vigorous 498. West Indies now aimed to bowl out the English side and had Keeton and Oldfield for 77. But Constantine, in addition to 78 from 92 balls, had taken 5 wickets in the first innings. Martindale failed to get a wicket and Hammond and Hutton put on 264.

The international cricket played between 1928 and 1939 had been of inestimable value. The foundations had now been properly laid, and during the war a new generation playing by themselves made some colossal individual scores whose significance was not fully appreciated until the West Indies tour of 1950. MCC sent only a moderate team to the West Indies after the war. Outstanding form was shown only by Frank Worrell, already playing League cricket in England. He apart, no one on either side stood out, and of the 4 matches, West Indies won 2, showing a clear supremacy. Worrell did not participate in the West Indian visit to India in 1948–49. Everton Weekes had not done exceptionally well in 1947–48. However he scored a hundred in the last Test and did the same in his first 4 Test innings in India. He seemed certain to make it 6 in succession when he was run out at 90; his 5 successive Test centuries remains a record. The West Indian batsmen all scored heavily. The bowling, though adequate and able to defeat India, was for the most part medium to fast and seemed inadequate for the England tour due in 1950.

The 1950 team to England created a sensation. Jeffrey Stollmeyer, one who played a great part in that tour and later captained the West Indies, had toured in 1939 and he believes that in 1950 English cricket was still far below its accustomed standards. The 1950 team accomplished some mighty deeds. Contrary to all expectation the most striking successes were the 2 slow bowlers, one 20 in April, the other 20 in May. Ramadhin from Trinidad (he had played only 2 first-class matches) spun the ball both ways and batsmen seemed unable to detect his changes. Valentine from Jamaica could get more spin from a sound wicket than any left-hander playing. The two of them bowled West Indies to victory in 3 Tests out of 4. 1950 also saw the triple efflorescence of Weekes, Worrell and Walcott, born within a few miles and a few months of each other in the island of Barbados. Worrell was all grace and style,

Weekes a terrific punisher of all bowling, Walcott a giant who could hook anything and off either foot was equally powerful in front of the wicket. The 1950 tour established 'the three Ws'. Weekes's first 3 hundreds were double hundreds. Good judges believed that better batting could not be seen than his partnership in the Nottingham Test with Worrell who ended with 261. Stollmeyer and Rae, a left-hander, regularly gave a good start. Whatever might be further needed was supplied by Gomez, a canny all-rounder. Goddard, the captain, could produce dangerous off-breaks and was able to stand anywhere and catch anything.

With this tour West Indies cricket had at last arrived. Yet the team failed in Australia in 1951–52. Gomez alone seemed to have consistent staying power with the bat. Gomez also bowled well above his usual form. Yet Valentine, with 24 wickets, again proved himself to be the best left-hand spinner in the game. One Test was won and the other 4 lost. India visited West Indies in 1952. Weekes regained all his consistent brilliance, Walcott surpassed himself and Worrell atoned for some uncertain scoring by a brilliant double century in the last Test. Despite other successful batting only the 3 Ws were really able to master the 23-year-old Gupte who here began his career as a master of the googly. To him Worrell and Weekes left the crease, Walcott on the other hand trusted to his great height.

There was one notable omission from the 1953 MCC team to the West Indies, the finest bowler in England, A. V. Bedser. The team otherwise seemed the best available. After 2 games, however, West Indies seemed set for another victorious series against England. They won the First Test and declared the second innings of the Second Test closed at 292 for 2, to win by 181 runs. Walcott, better than ever, made a dominating 220. Holt also scored heavily. MCC's batting was so drab as to evoke derision from Barbados schoolboys. Hutton, however, pulled his side together, won the next Test, drew the fourth and won the last to even the series. Compton and May helped Hutton to restore the prestige of English batting but the outstanding batting feat of the tour was in Trinidad when all 3 'Ws' set the seal on their collective reputation by each scoring a brilliant century, Weekes reaching 206. Bailey, always a dependable cricketer with both bat and ball, excelled himself in the last Test by taking 7 for 34 in the first innings. Hutton crowned his now impregnable batsmanship by making 205. The youthful Statham's bowling impressed all and if Valentine did little, Ramadhin took 23 wickets.

In 1955 the Australians, warmly welcomed by West Indian crowds, won 3 of the 5 Tests and drew the other two. Ramadhin and Valentine failed and in Tests 9 Australians averaged from 107 to 37. Walcott scored a century in each innings of a Test twice, scored yet another century and ended with a total of 827. Weekes repeatedly showed the Australians the dazzling form he had failed to show against the same bowling in Australia. Worrell, however, seemed to have lost the habit of heavy scoring.

Striving to blood young players, early in 1956 Goddard was sent to New Zealand with an experimental side. Of the 3 Ws only Weekes went. The young players (including Sobers) did little, but Weekes's first 5 innings were hundreds. Against his all-conquering stroke-play and with Ramadhin and Valentine effective as a pair, New Zealand did well to win 1 Test of the 4.

Once again West Indies, in 1957 in England, did not fulfil early expectations. Leading England by 288 runs in the first innings, West Indies seemed to have the First Test well in hand. A tremendous stand of 411 runs by May and Cowdrey for the 4th wicket nearly won the match for England. From this the West Indians never recovered. Neither Weekes nor Walcott showed consistent form, Worrell both with bat and with ball brought off some noteworthy performances, but Ramadhin, devastating as usual against the counties, in Tests never seemed to be able to recapture that first fine carefree rapture with which he had bowled out England in the first innings of the First Test. Valentine was in and out of form, mostly out. The wicket-keeping was not good, and in the end 3 Tests were lost and two drawn. Goddard was unable to cope with an English batting side 7 members of which averaged over 50 runs per innings. 'Collie' Smith twice scored hundreds in Tests. Full of courage he hit a long ball. His flighted off-spinners could not infrequently penetrate the defence of well-set Test batsmen. He fielded brilliantly anywhere. He was a brave cricketer and charming personality. His death in a motor-car accident while a League player in Lancashire was a loss not only to West Indies cricket but to cricket as a whole. In 1958 Pakistan visited the West Indies. Sobers had begun years before as a slow left-hander, had rapidly worked his way up, doing well with the bat in England in 1957. He now came to maturity, made 824 runs in Tests and by scoring 365 not out at Kingston passed the record individual score in Tests which Hutton had held since 1938. The two maestros, Walcott and Weekes, seemed to recover their old form and very welcome

Melbourne's farewell to Frank Worrell's side to Australia, 1960–61.

was off-spinner Lance Gibbs, who took 17 wickets and headed the averages. There was some fine play by Pakistani players but everything took second place to Hanif Mohammad in the First Test. Pakistan following on 473 behind, Hanif saved the game by making 337 out of 657 for 8 declared. In 1958–59 West Indies went to India and Pakistan. Worrell could not leave his studies at Manchester University and thus Hall, who had failed to impress in England in 1957, squeezed into the side. Against India Hall took 30 wickets and in 3 matches against Pakistan 16. In India another newcomer, from Jamaica, Gilchrist, bowled perhaps faster than Hall and took 26 wickets. Sobers and Kanhai, Butcher and Solomon showed that already West Indians had replacements for the 3 'Ws'. 3 Tests against India were won and 2 drawn. Pakistan lost the last Test but won the other two.

An MCC team visited the West Indies in 1959–60. 4 Tests were drawn and MCC convincingly won the Second by 256 runs. Sobers made 709 runs in Tests, scored a hundred 3 times and averaged over 100. No other West Indies batsman scored half as many. Ramadhin bowled well at times but Valentine lost his place and the fast bowling of Hall and Watson, though it raised plenty of dust, could not prevent the first 5 batsmen on the England side averaging over 40 runs per innings. Dexter made over 500 runs and though careful in defence not infrequently showed what powers were yet to come with maturity. Cowdrey after a dismal start missed scoring two hundreds in one game by only 3 runs.

In 1960–61 West Indies visited Australia. Frank Worrell took over as captain from Alexander who continued as wicket-keeper. Although the side lost 2 Tests and won only 1, history was made. The First Test at Brisbane produced a tie, the only one in the whole history of Tests. Gibbs soon took and more than adequately filled Ramadhin's place as the spin bowler of the side. Sobers, Kanhai and Hunte batted splendidly and were surpassed in figures by a new Alexander. Valentine bowled well if not as well as in 1951. Worrell showed exceptional form both as batsman and captain. In its style of play the team restored to Test cricket the *élan* of the Golden Age. Half a million citizens of Melbourne turned out spontaneously to say goodbye and to speed an early return, a demonstration unprecedented in cricket history. India visited the West Indies in 1962 and West Indies won all 5 Tests, maintaining their Australian form in every department.

The West Indies Cricket Board of Control has always been sustained by clubs in each territory which are lineal descendants of the old aristocratic clubs of the plantocracy and commercial magnates. Their services in West Indies cricket, all proportions strictly guarded, can legitimately be compared to that of MCC in Britain. In the early days they bore the financial risks, they have been tireless in arranging tournaments and visiting groups of first-class cricketers. They have organized coaching from Australia and from England. They have managed to adjust themselves to the rising self-consciousness of the West Indian community without irreparable conflicts. Best of all, no part of the Commonwealth in proportion to their numbers has produced a finer body of players. To repeat E. W. Swanton: in the West Indies the cricket ethic has shaped not only the cricketers but life as a whole.

In 1963 West Indies made the tour in England which again lifted Test cricket to a pitch of public interest and excitement which for some years it had been losing. West Indies won the First Test at Manchester and a magnificent game at Lord's ended in a draw which could easily have been a tie. The match at Edgbaston was lost but West Indies won convincingly at Leeds and, having to make over 250 in the last innings at the Oval, made them for the loss of 2 wickets. Sobers and Kanhai were great batsmen. Butcher was not far behind and Hunte did all that was required from an opening batsman. Hall maintained his reputation as a fast bowler in the great tradition and Griffith, a newcomer with real pace, showed a subtlety and adaptability which constantly broke up stands by English batsmen. Gibbs was a master of off-spin and flight. Sobers bowling either fast or a bewildering mixture of slows could have been played for bowling alone. A youthful wicket-keeper, Murray, a last-minute selection, had the honour of taking the largest number of wickets by a wicket-keeper in Tests. West Indians in the crowds contributed much to the renaissance. Yet in a great season the finest cricket on display was the captaincy of Frank Worrell. By his easy mastery of strategy and tactics, his command of his team, his respect for the traditions of the game, and his personal distinction on and off the field he won the admiration and affection of the British public. The stimulating impact of the West Indian visit reached a fitting climax in the chorus of approbation which greeted his knighthood.

Worrell had achieved his lifelong ambition of leading West Indies to victory in England. The winning of the series was the crowning glory for the first coloured West Indian to lead West Indies on tour; George Headley had captained them at home. Worrell had done more than any previous captain to mould individual West Indian talents into an efficient sportsmanlike and respected team. On his retirement he strongly recommended that the talented young Barbadian, Garfield Sobers, and not his vice-captain, Conrad Hunte, take over the captaincy. The West Indies Board accepted this recommendation and Hunte, deeply committed to Moral Rearmament, concealed the hurt and disappointment and soldiered on as vice-captain, giving Sobers his full support.

The visit of Australia to West Indies in 1964–5 brought together arguably the 2 strongest Test sides of the time. The West Indian attack was spearheaded by Hall and Griffith, backed by Sobers and the offspin of Gibbs, while the batting was in the capable hands of Hunte, Kanhai, Butcher, Nurse and the new captain himself. In the event the series, which West Indies won, was somewhat marred by a controversy over Griffith's bowling action. Richie Benaud, the former Australian captain who was covering the tour as a correspondent, was in no doubt that Griffith threw; but the West Indian board, having scrutinized films of his action, decided that any doubt should be determined by the umpires and were fortified by the fact that he had had a full tour of England in 1963 and not been called.

Although there was no international tour during the winter of 1965–66, an important milestone had been reached in the development of West Indian cricket with the introduction of the Shell Shield tournament. Sponsorship by Shell Antilles and Guyanas Ltd enabled the WICBC, always lacking financial resources, to stage an inter-territorial tournament between Barbados, Guyana, Trinidad, Jamaica and the Combined Windward and Leeward Islands. Barbados won the inaugural tournament and have dominated it since.

In 1966 the WICBC moved headquarters from Guyana to Barbados where T. N. Peirce took over the Presidency from John Dare. The emergence of West Indies as a cricket power had been achieved by the dedicated work of such administrators as Sir Errol dos Santos and Sir Lindsay Grant of Trinidad, Carl Nunes and Donald Lacey of Jamaica, John Dare and Kenny Wishart of British Guyana and Noel Peirce and Eric Inniss of Barbados. West Indian star cricketers were now being rapidly recruited as overseas professionals by English counties; a few, like Sobers and Kanhai, were also playing state cricket in Australia. This new professionalism, with its attendant contractual problems, and the intensified international Test and domestic programme, placed a heavy and increased burden on the WICBC, both financially and administratively. They were fortunate to find a secretariat in Barbados which was able to cope with the many and varied problems of the day.

In England in 1966 Sobers scored hundreds in 3 of the first 4 Tests and with his cousin, David Holford, saved his team at Lord's when England seemed certain to win. Sobers scored 722 runs during the series, more than any other West Indian on a tour of England, and finished with an average of 103. He also took 20 wickets, fielded and caught magnificently and led the team with dash and distinction. On the West Indies tour of 1966–67 West Indies defeated India, in India, 2 Tests to 0 with a 3rd Test drawn. Sobers's personal success continued; he averaged 114 with the bat and took 14 wickets in the 3-match series. This West Indian tour saw the emergence of Clive Lloyd, a young bespectacled Guyanese left-hander. Sobers returned from India a successful but very tired man; the strain was beginning to take its toll, both physically and mentally. The West Indian team, so successful in the early and mid-1960s, was beginning to disintegrate, and Sobers was about to embark upon a sequence of 31 Test matches, between 1967 and 1973, of which West Indies won only 2.

At the conclusion of the 1966 tour to England Jeffrey Stollmeyer, manager of that team, drew to the attention of the WICBC the inequity of all players being paid the same fee for the tour. Stollmeyer, with the assistance of the Board's Secretariat, established a new system of payment to players whereby each player received a basic tour fee plus an increment for each Test match previously played. Regrettably, good though the system was it was not translated into improved performance on the field by the senior players.

The little fancied MCC team under Cowdrey visited West Indies in the winter of 1967–68 and soon showed that they were not to be underrated. Hall and Griffith were not as good as they had been; Hunte had retired and an even greater strain was placed on Sobers. The first 3 Tests were drawn, then Sobers made his highly publicized declaration at the Queen's Park Oval which gave England the chance to win the match and, as it transpired, the series. Sobers manfully bore the criticism and blame which was heaped on him by the press and a disappointed West Indian public, without ever disclosing that he had consulted both the manager and vice-captain prior to his declaration. England, largely through Cowdrey and Knott, held on to save the final Test, and the series with it, with 9 wickets down in their 2nd innings.

West Indies continued, mistakenly, to rely on the old brigade for their tour of Australia in 1968–69. West Indies won the First Test to everyone's surprise but proved no match for Lawry's young bloods. Sobers, who had been the mainspring of success for so long, seemed tired and disenchanted with cricket and incapable of holding his team together. A short tour of England followed this visit to Australia and New Zealand. The selectors put the knife into the 'old brigade', cutting out Hall and Griffith in a new look team. England won the series 2–0, but the Second Test at Lord's and the Third at Headingley were both close affairs.

In the English summer of 1970 Sobers captained a strong Rest of the World team in a 5 'Test' series against England. His team included 5 South Africans. During the tour, he accepted an invitation from Eddie Barlow to play in a double-wicket tournament in Salisbury, Rhodesia. Having regard to the fact that he was the West Indian captain, to think that his visit would pass unnoticed was naïve in the extreme. He compounded matters on arrival in Barbados by stating to the press that Ian Smith, Rhodesia's Prime Minister, was a 'tremendous person'. Forbes Burnham, Prime Minister of Guyana, who had been visiting various African countries pledging Guyana's support for the guerrillas, was seriously embarrassed by Sobers's visit and reacted by stating that in future he would be 'unwelcome' in Guyana. The Indian visit was only months away and an impasse ensued. The Barbadian Government and public were outraged that one of their national heroes should be so treated. For weeks tension ran high. Mr Burnham was adamant that unless Sobers apologized he would not be permitted to play cricket in Guyana. Mr Barrow, Prime Minister of Barbados, was equally determined that Sobers should not be made to apologize.

A hastily summoned emergency meeting of the WICBC took place in Barbados on 25 October 1970. After long deliberation and consultation with the Prime Minister of Barbados and Sobers, the Board issued a statement from Sobers explaining his reasons for the visit and stating that had he known of the serious repercussions he would not have gone to Rhodesia. Mr Burnham accepted the statement and West Indian cricket breathed again.

West Indies continued their sequence of drawn and lost matches. In 1971 India won their first Test series against them, while the 1972 tour of West Indies by New Zealand produced a frustrating 5 draws. In 1973 Ian Chappell brought a strong and confident Australian team to West Indies and won the Frank Worrell Trophy by 2 matches to 0 with 3 drawn. This was the first series for 20 years that Sobers, convalescing from a cartilage operation, had not taken the field, and West Indies appointed Rohan Kanhai captain. With the help of a now rested Sobers, West Indies under Kanhai defeated England by 2 matches to 0 in a short tour of England in 1973. England, however, returned to the Caribbean under Denness in the winter of 1973–74 and much against the odds drew the 5-match series with 3 Tests drawn.

The WICBC headquarters had now moved to Jamaica where Cecil Marley took over as President, admirably supported by the experienced Donald Lacey with Allan Rae, the former West Indian opening batsman and now a barrister, playing an increasingly prominent role. West Indies now took the difficult decision to leave out both Sobers and Kanhai and appoint Lloyd as captain and Deryck Murray as vice-captain, a combination which was to play a major part in West Indian cricket history. Lloyd's first assignment was a tour of India and Pakistan in 1974–75 with a comparatively young but potentially strong team; only Gibbs of the 'Old Brigade' retained his place. In India, West Indies won a fine series 3–2, after India had squared the series at 2 all by winning the Third and Fourth Tests. The 2 Tests in Pakistan were drawn.

Blessed by warm and sunny weather, and supported by large and enthusiastic crowds, West Indies, after nearly failing against a talented Pakistan team, won the first Prudential (or World) Cup in 1975, beating Australia in the final at Lord's

West Indians in the slips, accomplices to their fast bowlers: from left, Lloyd, Julien, Gibbs, Greenidge and Rowe.

before a capacity crowd, to become the one-day Champions of the World. Lloyd played a superb match-winning innings of 102 and proudly received the Prudential Cup from the then President of MCC, the Duke of Edinburgh.

In the winter of 1975–76 Lloyd and his triumphant team, full of confidence, toured Australia, only to be convincingly defeated by Ian Chappell's men by 5 matches to 1. On their return home, West Indies entertained India and restored some lost prestige by winning the series 2–1 with 1 Test drawn. In the summer of 1976 West Indies had a successful tour of England, retaining the Wisden Trophy conclusively and touring the counties without defeat. Lloyd, Richards, Kallicharan and Fredericks all batted splendidly, while Holding, the Jamaican fast bowler, was an admirable partner for Roberts. West Indies continued their winning streak early in 1977 by defeating a strong Pakistan team in West Indies by 2–1, with two drawn Tests.

By now the secretariat of the WICBC had moved to Trinidad, where Stollmeyer had taken over as the Board's President. It was to prove the most testing time for administrators in the history of cricket generally, and of West Indian cricket in particular. In May 1977 the story of the signing of contracts by many of Australia's leading cricketers to the Australian television tycoon, Mr Kerry Packer, broke in England. As the story unfolded during the summer of 1977, it became clear that what appeared to be a players' revolution in Australia had quickly become an international cricket problem, by the active involvement of Tony Greig the England captain, Clive Lloyd, aided and abetted by Deryck Murray and Ian Chappell, in signing many of the best English, West Indian and Australian cricketers.

Stollmeyer and Rae, representing West Indies at the International Cricket Conference at Lord's, were reluctantly persuaded that 'for the sake of unanimity', the 51 players contracted to Packer be 'banned' from Test Cricket. It was clear from public reaction in West Indies that the players had the sympathy and support of the masses, and when Mr Justice Slade ruled in the High Court in London that the 'ban' constituted 'a restraint of Trade', the public, encouraged by the press and broadcasting stations, were openly hostile to West Indian cricket administrators. Early in 1978 the West Indian players contracted to World Series Cricket, reinforced by their Shell Shield colleagues, launched the full weight of a combined team against a young Australian side devoid of Packer players and led by the veteran, Bobby Simpson. West Indies' pace attack in the first 2 Tests proved to be too hostile for Simpson's immature Australians; Croft and Garner established themselves by supporting Roberts, in the absence through injury of Holding and Daniel. Not even an inspired piece of fast bowling by Jeff Thompson in the Second Test in Barbados, could save Australia from defeat. It came to light that WSC had signed 3 more West Indians during this Barbados Test – Croft, Haynes and Austin – despite the players' verbal assurance to the Board's President that they would not sign before the Guyana Test. This was, of course, a sickening blow to the WICBC, as they, more than any cricket authority, had been sympathetic to WSC.

The WICBC had asked Deryck Murray (Secretary of the WI Players' Association) for information regarding the availability of WSC players for the tour of India and Sri Lanka in 1978–79. The deadline for an answer had come and gone without any definite reply being received. It appeared that the players were trying to manoeuvre the Board into a position where they would have to treat direct with WSC in contravention of the ICC Agreement that no unilateral negotiations be carried out by member countries. The West Indian selectors, Carew, Clyde Walcott, Holt and Lloyd, met in Guyana on Sunday 26 March to select the side for the Third Test. The selectors agreed that, already being 2 up in the present series, some thought should be given to blooding players for the forthcoming tour of India. In the event, Murray, Lloyd's lieutenant, Haynes and Austin were dropped. Lloyd did not agree with Murray's omission and resigned as captain. Murray, in Trinidad, stated that the remainder of the WSC players were likely to withdraw and it was rumoured that Packer was on his way to Guyana. Stollmeyer acted quickly and positively, instructing the selectors to have replacements for the Packer players flown into Guyana, while he himself and Peter Short, the Barbados President and Board representative, arrived in Guyana late in the evening of Wednesday 29 March.

Next morning, the day before the start of the match, the WICBC members present in Guyana met with Lloyd and a delegation of WSC players. Lloyd confirmed his resignation and the withdrawal of the WSC players, but he tried, as Murray had done, to vacillate further, asking for no decision to be taken until Mr Packer arrived that evening. Time had now run out for Lloyd and the WSC players; the Board stood firm and announced that no WSC players would be considered for selection for the remainder of the tour. By the time Packer arrived that evening the matter had been resolved.

Alvin Kallicharan, the new West Indian captain, and his makeshift team narrowly lost the Third Test, played before good and well-behaved crowds at Bourda. West Indies won the Fourth Test in Trinidad, which was virtually devoid of spectator support, due to a boycott designed by certain disruptive elements to embarrass the Board. Spectator unrest in Jamaica precluded an exciting finish to the final Test which seemed to be going Australia's way. This made an unhappy finish to an unhappy tour, fought as much off the field as on it, and a financial disaster.

Mr Packer, in a photofinish, had just failed to gain control of West Indian cricket, but he soon won the biased media and sympathetic public over to his side, making out that the WICBC were the villains of the piece. In Jamaica and Barbados, special general meetings were held and resolutions passed, calling on the WICBC to negotiate directly with WSC. In Barbados Keith Walcott and Peter Short, the Barbadian representatives on the WICBC, survived a vote of no confidence by a narrow margin. The real issues had never been put to the public.

Kallicharan and his new-look West Indian team, devoid of Packer players, fought bravely but unavailingly in India. Packer's agents had meanwhile been busy in the Caribbean, trying to gain access to traditional grounds for his WSC Australians to play against WSC West Indians. There was overwhelming public support for this venture, an important factor which, coupled with the financial rewards, persuaded the bankrupt WICBC that limited co-operation with the WSC Special Committee was not only the best, but the only policy, in the prevailing circumstances. The WSC tour was played before packed stands, paying an average of 50% more than for Test matches, and was marred by crowd disturbances in Trinidad, Guyana, and, of all places, for the first time, Barbados.

The WICBC, after considerable deliberation and not a few misgivings, having regard to recent history, appointed Lloyd to lead West Indies in England in defence of the Prudential World Cup. Whether or not they were influenced by events in Australia, where the Australian Board of Control for Cricket had awarded Mr Packer's Channel 9 station the exclusive rights to televise cricket in Australia for the next 3 years, the way was now clear for an agreement between WSC and the cricket authorities.

One thing was certain: both the West Indian and Australian Boards had suffered some crippling financial blows. In future the players seemed assured that they would receive a bigger share of the financial cake and more money was coming into the game through sponsorship.

In the World Cup, West Indies did not disappoint their supporters. Pakistan were beaten in a good semi-final match at the Oval and West Indies won the final at Lord's against England, through Richards, who made a fine century, an innings from Collis King of pure magic, and a splendid spell of accurate fast bowling by Joel Garner.

Lord's 1979: West Indies win the Prudential World Cup again.

Inter-Colonials and Shell Shield

The former name given to matches and tournaments contested between the chief West Indian islands: Barbados, Trinidad and Jamaica, and British Guiana was 'Inter-colonials'. Representative cricket in the West Indies is more than a century old, the first meeting between Barbados and Demerara, as Guyana was then known, having been played on the Garrison Savannah, Barbados, and won by the home team, in 1865. Cricket clubs were by then already established in Trinidad and at Kingston, Jamaica, and in 1869 British Guiana first visited Trinidad. Distance prevented Jamaica competing against the other centres until in 1925 they sailed for the first time to Barbados.

Inter-colonial tournaments between Barbados, Trinidad and British Guiana were held in most years between 1893 and 1939, the venue being changed in regular rotation. Trinidad won 11 of these tournaments, Barbados 10 and British Guiana 5.

Owing to expense, and also to the frequent visits of representative West Indian teams to other countries, the tournament was not resumed after the war. It was revived, however, in 1964, in a different form, all 4 territories meeting each other, 2 four-day matches each being played in Barbados, Trinidad and British Guiana. This tournament attracted good support, and was won by British Guiana. Results were as follows:

	PLAYED	WON	WON ON 1ST INNS	LOST ON 1ST INNS	LOST	POINTS
British Guiana	3	1	1	1	0	20
Barbados	3	0	3	0	0	18
Trinidad	3	1	0	2	0	16
Jamaica	3	0	0	1	2	2

Win=12 pts, Win on 1st Innings=6 pts, Loss on 1st Innings=2 pts

The old inter-colonial tournaments were superseded in 1965–66 by the introduction – under the aegis of the West Indies Board of Control – of the Shell Shield, which took its name from its sponsor, the Shell Oil Company.

WINNERS

1965–66	Barbados	1973–74	Barbados
1966–67	Barbados	1974–75	Guyana
1968–69	Jamaica	1975–76	Trinidad and Barbados tied
1969–70	Trinidad	1976–77	Barbados
1970–71	Trinidad	1977–78	Barbados
1971–72	Barbados	1978–79	Barbados
1972–73	Guyana		

IRVING ROSENWATER

Antigua

Cricket has as long a history in Antigua as in most other West Indian islands. The cricket club of the 59th Foot Regiment was formed there on New Year's Day 1842, and Antiguans took to the game as rapidly as those of English descent. King George V, when a midshipman in 1882, played in Antigua, but it was not until the coming of the English touring sides in the 1890s that the island came before the public eye. R. S. Lucas's team, in the 4th match of their tour, beat Antigua by an innings in February 1895, when the home team was composed almost entirely of coloured players. Both Arthur Priestley's team and Lord Hawke's won comfortably there in 1896–97, P. F. Warner scoring 110 for Lord Hawke's side at St John's.

The Inter-Presidential Cricket Tournament was instituted, and, though it lapsed, was revived in the early 1920s. Antigua was frequently the venue of this tournament and of the Leeward Islands Tournament, with teams from Montserrat, Dominica and St Kitts taking part. The principal ground – that of the Antigua CC – is beautifully situated to the east of the capital. Representative matches against the Leeward Islands have frequently been held in Antigua, and MCC played there for the first time in 1953–54 before a crowd of over 10,000: the Leeward Islands lost by an innings and 56 runs. In 1959–60 MCC again played there – the match was first-class – and drew. The Australians (in 1955) and the Pakistanis (in 1957–58) also played there. In July–August 1956, both Jamaica Colts and British Guiana visited Antigua to play each other and also combined sides of the Leeward and Windward Islands.

St John's staged the opening fixture – Windward and Leeward Islands v Jamaica – in the new Shell tournament in January 1966, and has been a regular venue for home fixtures for Combined Islands. Likewise regular overseas sides have in recent years visited St John's to oppose the Leeward Islands: MCC in 1967–68, the New Zealanders in 1971–72, the Australians in 1972–73, MCC in 1973–74 and the Pakistanis in 1976–77. All these matches were drawn. Antigua advanced in stature when St John's was chosen for the one-day International between West Indies and Australia, watched by over 13,000, in February 1978. In April 1979 a 5-day fixture was played at St John's between the West Indian and Australian sides of World Series Cricket.

The pitches in Antigua are prepared by prisoners from a nearby jail, supervised, in this instance, by a Superintendent of Police and Umpire Douglas Sang Hue.

Antigua's most celebrated representatives on the field have been A. M. E. Roberts and I. V. A. Richards, the first Antiguans to play Test cricket. They have also represented Hampshire and Somerset respectively, and between 1959 and 1972 the Hampshire side also included the Antiguan batsman, D. A. Livingstone.

IRVING ROSENWATER

Barbados

The most easterly of the Caribbean chain of islands, Barbados – known as 'Little England' – is something of a phenomenon in the world of cricket. No more than 166 square miles in area, with great expanses of waving sugar cane, the sheer power that the game exerts among the populace has made the island cricket's richest corner of the world. In no comparable geographical space have so many great players been produced: in the last 30 or so years at least, a team of Barbadians would not have disgraced themselves against the rest of the world on the cricket field. Nowhere is there a more *concentrated* area of cricket enthusiasm and skill. In a community of such unbounded keenness, it is not surprising that the game should have a long and honoured tradition.

It is probable that cricket was played there in the 18th century, though the first Press notice appeared in 1806. Certainly by the 1830s the military had established the game as a regular feature of Barbadian life. Civilian clubs, such as St Michael's, and the schools – notably the Lodge and Codrington College – furthered the progress of the game; and they were to be joined later by Harrison College which was to produce, as its most famous old boy, Sir Pelham Warner. Maturity came to Barbadian cricket with the establishment, in 1877, of the Wanderers Club, and, 5 years later, of the Pickwick Club. Meanwhile Barbados had made history – in February 1865 – by staging the first inter-colonial cricket match ever played in the West Indies. The venue was the Garrison Savannah at Bridgetown, and the visitors, Guyana (then known as Demerara and later as British Guiana), were, perhaps significantly, soundly beaten. The first Barbados captain, F. B. Smith, was easily the highest scorer in the match with 50 not out, and he took 10 wickets as well; he was the uncle of S. G. Smith, who later was to gain fame with Trinidad and Northamptonshire. Thus representative cricket in the Caribbean was born.

Further history was made at Bridgetown – this time on the Wanderers' ground at the 'Bay' – when both British Guiana and Trinidad sent teams to compete in the first triangular tournament in 1891. Enthusiasm ran high and no fewer than 80 Bridgetown firms closed down for the afternoon when Barbados played the visiting sides. The venture was a great success, and Barbados emerged as undisputed champions of the West Indies. There emerged, too, for all to see, the genius of the Goodman brothers, who did a tremendous amount for Barbados cricket. The tall Clifford Goodman was an outstanding fast-medium bowler with a devastating lift from the pitch; while his younger brother, Percy, became the first of the great West Indian batsmen. He toured England twice – in 1900 and 1906 – and scored centuries against Derbyshire, Yorkshire and Northamptonshire. Evan and Aubrey Goodman were also Barbadian cricketers of repute, the latter becoming Attorney-General of the island.

Following this initial success, a biennial (and later an annual) tournament for a handsome trophy was instituted, to be competed for by the first-class colonies. Barbados showed her strength in these encounters by winning 7 of the 12 tournaments up to the First World War. High excitement was also engendered when the first side from England – an amateur team led by R. Slade Lucas – toured the West Indies early in 1895. The start of the tour was in Barbados, and half of Bridgetown turned out to see the Englishmen land. For the first time the famous Kensington Oval, the home of the Pickwick Club, was used for a representative match, and with Clifford Goodman taking 14 wickets for 85, Barbados won this important game by 5 wickets. Two years later Arthur Priestley's team also began their programme at Bridgetown, and Barbados won by the handsome margin of an innings and 41. Barbados, in fact, always performed particularly well against English teams of that time. R. A. Bennett's young side were beaten by an innings in 1901–02, when professionals played for Barbados for the first time, while Lord Brackley's side lost one of the colony games 3 years later. A. W. F. Somerset, who captained 2 MCC sides in the West Indies before the First War, considered Barbados a more difficult side to beat than a composite West Indian XI, so well did the Barbadians play together.

In those halcyon days – and indeed for many years afterwards – the name of H. B. G. (later Sir Harold) Austin, one of a large cricket fraternity, stood out. As an outstanding batsman and captain of the colony, his influence and popularity were such that he was freely called 'the King of Barbados'. At the age of 17 he had played against Slade Lucas's team and when 48 was still good enough to command his place in the Barbadian and West Indian sides during MCC's tour of 1925–26. But for absence in the South African War, he would have led the 1900 West Indian side in England, and did captain the sides of 1906 and 1923. His contemporary, the great George Challenor, was another idol of Barbados. A product of Harrison College, his brilliant batsmanship sent West Indian crowds wild with delight – 'Lord Runs-Come' they called him, and indeed he scored prolifically, becoming the first West Indian to make 5,000 runs in first-class cricket. The long Barbadian supremacy came to an end after the colony won the inter-colonial tournament of 1926–27. She was not to reassert herself again until the Second World War. But there were many notable names in the 1920s and 1930s apart from Challenor and Austin: P. H. Tarilton, E. L. G. Hoad, H. W. Ince, C. A. Browne and the two fast bowlers, G. N. Francis and H. C. Griffith.

The great days of Barbadian strength came back with the war, in the course of the 'goodwill' tournaments with Trinidad. C. L. Walcott was at Harrison College and F. M. Worrell was at Combermere School, while the young Everton Weekes had already caught the eye of 'Teddy' Hoad. These 3 batsmen – who were to achieve resounding fame as the famous '3 Ws' – were all born within a mile or so of each other within the space of 18 months. Barbados has been rightly called a sparkling jewel! Their deeds became part of West Indian history and their fame today, with their careers behind them, is secure for all time. First under T. N. Peirce and then under J. D. C. Goddard, Barbados was a force again.

The perfect turf pitches and keen cricketing environment which provide such regular and spirited play in all grades of their competitive cricket have kept Barbados to the fore and ensured a healthy stream of cultured batsmen and brilliant bowlers. In the 1950s and 1960s, the island's greatest adornment was Garfield Sobers (knighted in 1975), a left-handed all-rounder of incredible talent, who alone would afford Barbados a permanent place in the cricket firmament. He led Barbados to victory in the first 2 seasons of the Shell Shield when it was instituted in 1965–66. Among his contemporaries as batsmen were C. C. Hunte and S. M. Nurse, and as bowlers the great opening pair of Hall and Griffith. Later gifted players have included C. G. Greenidge, V. A. Holder, C. L. King and W. W. Daniel, all of whom – like Sobers, and, of an earlier generation, R. E. Marshall – have appeared for English counties. It seems unlikely that Barbados will ever forfeit her place as a major stronghold of West Indian cricket.

'Arise Sir Garfield': Gary Sobers is knighted by Her Majesty The Queen in Bridgetown in February 1975, not far from where he was born.

IRVING ROSENWATER

Dominica

No touring team had ever set foot in Dominica until the Duke of Norfolk's team flew in there from St Lucia in 1970. After a distinctly hazardous motor ride over the steep spine of this most luxuriant of islands they found themselves in a ground of matchless beauty within the botanical gardens of Roseau, the capital. Crowded within was a company of more than 5,000, which is about 1 in 12 in an island of more than 300 square miles. The Duke's side won a thrilling limited-over match by 8 runs despite admirable performances by the Shilligford cousins, Irving and Grayson, both of whom have represented West Indies in the 1970s. Grayson, a fastish bowler of supple physique, came to England with West Indies in 1969 while his cousin Irving, a high-class bat, was perhaps belatedly picked for the Tests against Pakistan in 1976–77, the last West Indies' home season before the Packer inroads dislocated their cricket so grievously. Dominican cricket has never been so strong as in the later 1970s when as many as 5 from this hitherto unvisited island earned selection in the same Shell Shield Islands' side.

Grenada

Although for many years not a regular stopping-place in the itinerary of touring teams, Grenada, in the Windward Islands, has a long cricket history of enthusiasm and skill in keeping with her sister West Indian islands. Grenada beat the touring Americans in 1887, but Lord Hawke's side won their 2 games there in 1896–97. Five years later Grenada and St Vincent combined to play R. A. Bennett's team in 2 matches at St George's, but again the Englishmen won both games: W. H. Mignon bowled well and he remains the only player who has hailed from Grenada and has toured with a West Indian side in England (in 1900). In 1909–10 there was played in Grenada the first competition – between Grenada, St Lucia and St Vincent – for the Cork Cup, presented by the Hon Philip Clark Cork.

MCC first visited the island in 1953–54 and did so again in 1959–60, playing the Windward Islands on each occasion. The Australian side of 1955 had a similar fixture there, as did further Australian touring sides in May 1965, April 1973 and April 1976. All these matches were played at St George's, which has also been the home venue for both the Windward Islands and Combined Islands in the Shell Shield.

Since the former matting was replaced by turf, the only private side of first-class standing to have played there in recent years is E. W. Swanton's team, who played a 3-day match at Queen's Park against the Windward Islands in March 1961, and won a keen encounter by 10 wickets.

IRVING ROSENWATER

Guyana

Guyana – or, for the greater part of her cricket history, and until May 1966, British Guiana – is situated on the South American mainland, but is none the less for that wholly cricket-conscious. Indeed, this vast country is West Indian in everything except geography. As far back as the 1840s British sailors were playing cricket at Georgetown, and the Georgetown Cricket Club itself – around which much of the colony's cricket history has revolved – has an unbroken existence of more than a hundred years. To Guyana (or Demerara, as she then was) goes the distinction of being the first West Indian territory to undertake a sea journey to another – not an unhazardous expedition a century ago. Early in 1865 a team journeyed to Barbados to play the first representative cricket in the Caribbean, and in September of the same year Barbados returned the visit.

Further distinction came to British Guiana when there was recorded for her the first hundred made in first-class cricket in the West Indies – 123 (in a total of 168) by E. F. Wright, a former Gloucestershire cricketer, against Trinidad at Georgetown in September, 1882. It was the Georgetown CC that sponsored the first tour abroad of West Indian cricketers, 14 players from British Guiana, Barbados and Jamaica visiting Canada and the United States in 1886. In 1887–88 a return visit was paid by the Americans, who had a busy trip around the Caribbean, losing by an innings when they played British Guiana at Georgetown. The Bourda ground, with its excellent wicket, was now in regular use for big cricket in British Guiana and has remained – as the home of the Georgetown Cricket Club – the chief centre of the game to this day. While never as consistent or powerful as the strong Barbados side, British Guiana had a very capable team in the years up to the end of the 19th century: Stanley Sproston and C. H. King were handsome batsmen, and Oscar Weber and W. J. Burton outstanding bowlers. But once the new century turned, British Guianese cricket slipped into decline, never really to revive itself until the mid-1920s.

Tree-ticket holders watching a Test Match from outside the Bourda Oval, Georgetown.

The Georgetown CC for many years financed the British Guiana teams in the inter-colonial tournaments, but, after winning in 1895–96, more than 30 years went by before a second success, in 1929–30. Once her strength had been reasserted, British Guiana, however, remained on top, and it was a ding-dong battle with Trinidad right through the 1930s that held the West Indian cricket stage. C. R. ('Snuffy') Browne, the first non-white West Indian to become a member of MCC; Maurice Fernandes, the wicket-keeper-batsman; C. V. Wight, the de Caires brotherhood, Berkeley Gaskin, the Christianis and Peter Bayley all played their part for British Guiana.

In 1954, with the coming to Georgetown of C. L. Walcott as an assiduous coach (as well as the inter-colonial captain), there was witnessed an emergence of talent that made the territory one of the finest sides in the world. Rohan Kanhai, Basil Butcher, Lance Gibbs and J. S. Solomon were as powerful a quartet as any side possessed, and indeed the Guianese proved themselves masters of the Caribbean when they won the Regional Tournament held early in 1964. Gibbs, of course, went on to achieve a world record total of Test wickets, and Kanhai's aggregate of runs for West Indies was exceeded only by Sobers.

The 1963–64 season saw the debuts of 2 distinguished left-handers, each to play in more than 50 Tests for the West Indies and score more than 4,000 Test runs – Roy Fredericks (also of Glamorgan) and Clive Lloyd (of Lancashire), Lloyd going on to captain West Indies regularly in Test cricket and lead them to victories in the first 2 World Cup events staged in England in 1975 and 1979. A. I. Kallicharran (also, briefly, a Test captain), yet another left-hander, has also scored prolifically for Guyana and the West Indies, as well as rendering notable service for Warwickshire. Guyana both in 1972–73 and 1974–75 won the Shell Shield competition, each time displacing the powerful Barbados side.

IRVING ROSENWATER

Jamaica

Though the largest of the West Indian cricketing islands, Jamaica developed in a cricket sense more slowly than any other of the major Caribbean territories. The Kingston Cricket Club had certainly been founded as early as 1863, but the geographical position of Jamaica – some thousand miles or more from the other cricket centres – frequently proved too insuperable a bar to her active participation in first-class cricket. It was out of the question, in the early days at least, to expect British Guiana, Barbados and Trinidad to journey to Kingston at the same time. Thus it was many years before Jamaica became an integral part of the inter-colonial Tournament, and it is probably true even today that, relatively speaking, there is not so much cricket played in Jamaica as in the other main West Indian areas.

This is not to suggest that the game in Jamaica is other than robust and well organized. The Senior Cup, Nethersole Cup, Wright Cup and sugar estates competitions are very real parts of the island's cricketing life, and Kingston on Test Match day is as vital as any. Because of the lack of top-class experience in the early days, however, the standard of cricket then was comparatively low. More than any other West Indian colony, Jamaica depended on English goodwill tours to provide infusion of spirit, and as a result she was able to develop some very fine cricketers. Rather surprisingly, as many as 7 Jamaicans (including the captain, L. R. Fyffe) were in the West Indian side that toured Canada and the United States in 1886; one of them, J. Lees (an Old Uppinghamian), headed the batting, and the giant enthusiast W. H. Farquharson the bowling. The tour suggested that Jamaica could probably hold her own if given the chance, and indeed it was in Jamaica the following year that the touring American side had the highest total made against them.

Jamaica had still not met another colony when R. Slade Lucas brought his amateur side to the West Indies in 1895. Of the 5 matches played in Jamaica, the final game was won by All-Jamaica by 8 wickets, and the colony was ready to make its first tour to meet other West Indian sides. Thus in September 1896, Jamaica sailed to Georgetown to play 2 games and Barbados was also met on the return journey: Jamaica lost all 3 matches, but a start had been made. When Arthur Priestley's side played in Jamaica in 1896–97, the Jamaicans went under in all 5 games, which served to emphasize that the colony was really not yet in the top bracket as a cricket power. In fact, in the entire period up to the First World War, Jamaica was to win only one more important match – against the visiting Philadelphians in February 1909; although the colony did win all 3 games played against a somewhat weak scratch side brought to the island by S. C. Snow in the following year. In this period J. K. Holt first showed his batting skill for Jamaica and C. S. Morrison did well as a bowler.

It was in the 1920s that Jamaica began to develop a remarkable strain of batsmen. J. K. Holt had now reached his maturity, and the stolid left-handed opener, F. R. Martin, became (in 1924–25) the first native-born Jamaican to score a century in first-class cricket. Another left-hander, R. K. Nunes, did a tremendous amount for Jamaican cricket as player, captain and administrator; and there were also E. A. Rae (like Holt, the father of a famous son), Ivan Barrow, a wicket-keeper-batsman, and C. M. Morales, another fine opener. But outshining them all, of course, was the great George Headley – compiler of mammoth scores, artist and complete batsman and most modest of men. He is unarguably the greatest adornment in the story of Jamaican cricket.

Between the wars goodwill tours to Jamaica were undertaken by 3 teams led by the Hon L. H. (later Lord) Tennyson, by Sir Julien Cahn, by Yorkshire and by a combined Oxford and Cambridge side. All these ventures were resounding successes, and the Duke of Norfolk continued the sequence by taking out a side early in 1957. By this time Allan Rae and the brilliant Alfred Valentine had left their mark on world cricket, and the spontaneous prowess of 'Collie' Smith – tragically killed in a road accident at 26 – was giving joy to his admirers. F. M. Worrell also made his home in the island (when he was not playing in England) soon after the war, and in 1962 was appointed a member of the Jamaican Senate. The Freedom of Kingston was his after his triumphant captaincy in England in 1963.

The only Jamaican batsman to approach the skill of Headley has been Lawrence Rowe, a right-hander who reached great heights in the early 1970s (including a triple-hundred in a Test against England) but whose career was sadly affected by eye trouble. In 1972–73 Michael Holding first appeared for Jamaica – a lithe and extremely fast bowler who, with Roberts of Antigua, formed an opening attack for West Indies of formidable strength. He has claims to be the most effective fast bowler in Jamaica's history.

Turf wickets have always been the rule in Jamaica, and the major ground has always been at Sabina Park in Kingston. There is also a fine ground in the north, at Montego Bay, and for many years Melbourne Park (Kingston) also staged important games. Jamaican crowds are loquacious and colourful, and tropical trees and superb mountain ridges make a backcloth of exotic attraction.

George Headley, who put Jamaica on the map, and remains their greatest cricketer.

IRVING ROSENWATER

St Kitts

In 1879 a team of Barbadian schoolboys – under the captaincy of T. G. Clarke – from Harrison College toured both St Kitts and Antigua and beat the local clubs. The side was a powerful one, but in truth the island has never been particularly strong. The earliest representative sides were predominantly European, and the touring teams of the 1890s led by R. Slade Lucas, Arthur Priestley and Lord Hawke all won by an innings margin; only once in 6 attempts did the St Kitts total exceed 100. Although St Kitts was a regular participant in the Leeward Islands Tournaments, touring sides – other than those from the Caribbean and Bermuda – seem to have ignored her for more than 60 years until in April 1961 E. W. Swanton's side played a 2-day match there on a ground levelled and relaid for the occasion, and were held to a draw. In the following year the Indians played a 3-day game at Basseterre to bring to an end their tour of the West Indies; they beat a combined Leeward and Windward Islands side by 137 runs.

In the first season of the Shell tournament (1965–66), Basseterre became a home venue for the Windward and Leeward Islands; and further major touring sides that have played at Basseterre – all against the Leeward Islands – have been the Australians in March 1965, the Indians in February 1971, and the Australians again in February 1978. No St Kitts cricketer has yet emerged into the Test arena.

IRVING ROSENWATER

St Lucia

St Lucia was luckier than some other of the smaller islands in attracting the touring teams which gave the first fillip to their cricket around the turn of the century. After a long interval the Duke of Norfolk's XI in 1970 played 3 matches on the charming Victoria Park ground. In the first 2 (a day apiece) St Lucia paraded several young cricketers of distinct promise. In the last the Windward Islands had shown something of their emerging talent before rain reminded the visitors that they have no monopoly of it during the hours of play. Four years later The Combined Islands playing at St Lucia actually defeated M. H. Denness's MCC side in a 50-over warming-up match at the start of their tour. St Lucia are lucky in having an administrator of the calibre of Julian Hunte to press their interests in the competitive world of West Indian cricket.

St Lucia spreads the gospel.

Trinidad

Trinidad is about the size of Lancashire and about as keen in her zest for cricket. Impromptu games are as prevalent here as anywhere in the West Indies, but nowhere is there a more cosmopolitan mixture of regular participants – English, French, Portuguese, Germans, Chinese, Negroes and East Indians have all played their part in the island's cricket. It has been truly said that a Trinidadian village may lack a church and it may lack a school: but a cricket-pitch is always there. The roots of cricket dig deep in Trinidad. In July 1842, the Trinidad Cricket Club was described as already being 'of very long standing', and in 1869 the colony was ready to field a representative side when she entertained a visiting team from British Guiana. In September 1882, a Trinidad side made their first venture outside the island, sailing to Georgetown, and in 1887–88 a large crowd saw Trinidad defeat the touring United States side – the first non-Caribbean team to tour the West Indies. In those days, and indeed for many years to come, the cricket of Trinidad was played on a matting wicket, because of the ravages of the mole-cricket: but the balance between bat and ball was very even, and Trinidadian cricketers could generally adapt themselves to turf when they played elsewhere.

Trinidad went to Barbados for the first time in 1891 to play in the initial triangular tournament, and early in 1893 the first of the tournaments in the recognized series was held at St Clair, Port of Spain. Trinidad, alas, were severely handicapped in these encounters by the absence from their sides of coloured men – barred following objections from British Guiana and Barbados; this situation obtained, fortunately, for no more than 10 years. However, the coloured professionals, who formed the real Trinidadian bowling strength, showed their worth when R. Slade Lucas's team came to Port of Spain in 1895 and was defeated by 8 wickets – a result which meant a great deal for Trinidad and put her firmly on the cricket map. The professional fast bowlers, Woods and Cumberbatch, were a power in the land, and Trinidad prospered under the captaincy of Aucher Warner, a brother of Sir Pelham. Aucher Warner captained the first West Indian side to visit England (in 1900), when his fellow-Trinidadians were Woods, L. S. D'Ade and L. S. Constantine, father of the famous Learie; but perhaps the finest bowler in the West Indies – Cumberbatch – was omitted. Constantine the elder, still a revered name in Trinidad's history, scored the first hundred for a West Indian side in England with 113 v MCC at Lord's in 1900.

In 1896 the Queen's Park Oval became the permanent home of major cricket in Trinidad, and the Queen's Park CC, whose ground it is, is still the most influential club. P. F. Warner – appropriately born in Trinidad – became the first man to score a hundred on the new ground when he made 119 against the Queen's Park Club itself for Lord Hawke's side in 1896–97. In this season Trinidad carried all before her when she beat both Lord Hawke's side and Arthur Priestley's side twice in the 4 big games played. A. E. Harragin, one of Trinidad's greatest sportsmen, began his career at this time, and as a batsman and captain he was destined to occupy much the same place in Trinidad as did Sir Harold Austin in Barbados.

Trinidad won 4 of the inter-colonial tournaments in the first decade of the 20th century, when a new generation of local players emerged: George John, a fast bowler; J. A. Small, a fine all-rounder; J. C. S. Rogers, a clever slow bowler; and André Cipriani, a cultured batsman who had learnt much cricket in England while studying law. There was also S. G. Smith, an almost legendary all-rounder, whose rather short career with Trinidad was supplemented later with some mighty deeds for Northamptonshire and Auckland. And L. S. Constantine was then at his very best. Trinidad twice beat the first MCC team to visit the West Indies in 1910–11, when perhaps the matting affected the Englishmen. Cipriani scored a magnificent hundred and was considered by MCC's captain to be good enough for any English first-class county.

It was after the First World War that a 19-year-old youth named Learie Constantine burst on to the Trinidad scene: a dynamic fast bowler, whirlwind batsman and incredible fielder, he became the pride of the island, though many of his

The Savannah, Port of Spain, where as many as 30 matches can be seen on a Saturday morning.

finest feats were performed elsewhere. He became the first man who ever accompanied 4 West Indian sides to England. C. A. Wiles, Clifford Roach and the graceful magic of Wilton St Hill all added to Trinidad's strength. By the time the 1930s came, with M. Grell and the two Grants displaying their skill, Trinidad was a real power. The youthful Gerry Gomez and the even younger Jeffrey Stollmeyer – as well as his brother Victor – were winning high opinions for Trinidad when war came again. But Gomez and Stollmeyer performed yeoman service for the colony (as well as for the Queen's Park Club and West Indian cricket in general) and they remain powerful influences on the destinies of Trinidad cricket. The rivalry of Maple and Shannon and of Queen's Royal College and St Mary's continues undiminished, though with little interest perhaps for the outside world. It is the great player who commands attention. Thus Sonny Ramadhin, spin bowler extraordinary, who first played his cricket at a mission school in Trinidad, became a world figure in 1950. His mysteries perplexed batsmen for years, and he is today a legend in Trinidad. Deryck Murray, of Queen's Royal College, and captain of Cambridge in 1966, has likewise gained similar honour in Trinidad as wicket-keeper and captain, and in 1977–78 became the first West Indian 'keeper to appear in 50 Tests.

There remains to be said that in July 1954 a turf wicket was finally laid at Queen's Park, thus bringing Trinidad – the birthplace of Lord Harris as well as Sir Pelham Warner – in line with the other major cricket centres of the world.

IRVING ROSENWATER

Zambia

This was the last part of East Africa to acquire cricket as it percolated from the coast. Northern Rhodesia became Zambia in 1964. In that year Zambia founded its Cricket Union. It joined the East Africa Cricket Conference (which had toured Zambia in 1967 under R. D. Patel but had been held to draws by Zambia under R. Henderson's captaincy) and its Quadrangular Tournament in 1968. The name of Philippe Edmonds (educated at Gilbert Rennie High School, Lusaka) was noted in a tour by Zambia Eagles of English clubs and schools in 1968.

PHILIP SNOW

Zanzibar

There is less history of cricket in Zanzibar than might be imagined, considering its position just off the east coast of Africa. Although cricket started earlier here from naval ships towards the close of the 19th century, than elsewhere in East Africa, interest on the island only quickened when the Navy called. But after 1950 the standard rose significantly with Indians' application to the game, Zanzibar taking part successfully in interterritorial matches with Uganda, both on Zanzibar Island and the mainland. G. C. Grant (Cambridge and West Indies) was a powerful influence for many years. Zanzibar lost to the 1958 South African Non-European touring team, and amalgamated with Tanganyika in 1962 to become Tanzania.

PHILIP SNOW

Zimbabwe

Cricket started in Rhodesia, as the country was then called, on 16 August 1890, when a match was played near Fort Victoria between units of the Pioneer Column. In the early days, most cricket was between such teams as the Police and the 'Rest of the World', Public Schools and 'all-comers', etc. But clubs gradually formed when towns were established, and a cricket league had started before 1914. Inter-town fixtures were rare because of difficulties of transport, mostly by mulecart, and of expense. There were only a few first-class fixtures.

After the First World War Rhodesian-born players emerged, and leagues started again. The Logan Cup was competed for by provinces, and turf wickets began to replace matting on the major grounds. The standard of play rapidly improved. There were visits by MCC in 1930–31 and 1938–39. The Australians came in 1936. In 1935 R. J. Crisp and D. S. Tomlinson, both Rhodesians, toured England with the South African team.

During the Second World War most young Rhodesians were away in the forces, but the game was kept alive by the Air Training Scheme, most of the club grounds being in use at the weekends. Many good players arrived in the country, and a high standard was maintained.

After the war, cricket was resumed with great enthusiasm. Up to 1939 Rhodesia had played only 12 Currie Cup matches; after 1946 they took part in every Currie Cup competition. Leagues were formed in the main centres, and the general standard rapidly improved. A Country Districts league was also formed, which played its matches in the winter and from which came several good players.

Rhodesians to have played for South Africa are P. Mansell, C. Duckworth, G. B. Lawrence, K. C. Bland, J. Partridge, A. Pithey, D. B. Pithey, J. du Preez and A. J. Traicos, besides Crisp and Tomlinson.

After the war visits were paid by MCC, Australia, New Zealand, Surrey, Worcestershire, The Cavaliers, Commonwealth teams and the International Wanderers. Rhodesia won against Surrey and Worcestershire, and twice against International Wanderers. In these matches Rhodesians were able to see many of the world's leading cricketers.

Club cricket made great strides. Professional coaches were engaged by the Rhodesian Cricket Union, to coach both clubs and schools. The standard rose steadily; two Asian clubs, in particular, became serious contenders in the major competitions.

There was keen rivalry among the schools. Each year a schoolboy team was sent to the Nuffield week, to compete with teams from all the South African provinces. And from this team came, in due course, most of the members of the Currie Cup team.

In 1966 the withdrawal of visits by official international teams meant that the public were starved of cricket at the highest level; nor could the best players gain international honours. Enthusiasm for cricket however survived the setback to a considerable extent, and with independence it must be hoped that Zimbabwe can resume, and indeed improve upon, its place among the cricketing nations.

A. P. SINGLETON

Part III
Biographies

The following 'ground-rules' may be noted: 1 The Test and Career figures to date of men still playing are not included; 2 Figures for the unofficial Test Matches between England and the Rest of the World in 1970 are not included here, but they are to be found in the STATISTICAL APPENDIX; *3 A man is designated as captain against the date of a Test series irrespective of his having served as such in one Test or all. 4 Touring dates are confined to those wherein a man has played in one or more Tests in the series in question; 5 Schools have been included wherever ascertainable.*

Bobby Abel, known as 'The Guv'nor', was the favourite of the Surrey crowd with Tom Hayward, immediately before the coming of Hobbs.

ABEL, Robert (1857–1936)

Surrey 1881–1904. England: in England 1888, 1896, 1902; in Australia 1891–92; in South Africa 1888–89.

One of the smallest of cricketers, 'Bobby' Abel ('The Guv'nor') overcame distinct physical disabilities to become a great opening batsman. H. S. Altham has described his faded and shrunken chocolate cap, slow half-waddling walk to the wicket, upright and seemingly limb-tied stance, and yet also his mastery over all types of bowling. He was 31 when, in 1888–89, he toured South Africa under Aubrey Smith, and, in the last Test at Cape Town, scored 120. Three years later he was with Lord Sheffield's team in Australia, and made 132 not out in the Second Test at Sydney. During the 1890s his triumphs increased. He was 41 when, against Somerset, he carried his bat for 357. Craig, the 'Surrey poet', had already been writing rhymes about him – one of them fitting the tune of 'Annie Rooney'. Though he made 94 against Australia at Lord's in 1896, it is always at the Oval that Abel is remembered. In 1900 'The Guv'nor' achieved 12 hundreds, passing 2,000 runs for the 6th successive year, and going on beyond 3,000 a year later, when (at the Oval) he scored 247 for the Players. One more season, and he was again past the 2,000, but also past his best, for at 45 his eyesight began to fail, and soon he was playing in glasses. This foreshadowed the end. He also took wickets, and held many catches, but it is as an opening batsman that he lives, pointing the way to Hayward and to Hobbs.

G. D. MARTINEAU

CAREER FIGURES

	INNS	NO	RUNS	HS	AVGE	100S
Batting	1007	73	33124	357*	35.46	74

Bowling 263 wkts at 24.01 Ct 587

Test Record (13)

	INNS	NO	RUNS	HS	AVGE	100S
Batting	22	2	744	132*	37·20	2

Ct 13

ADCOCK, Neil Amwin Treharne (1931–)

Grey HS and Jeppe HS. Transvaal 1952–53 to 1960–61. Natal 1960–61 to 1962–63. South Africa: in South Africa 1953–54, 1956–57, 1957–58, 1961–62; in England 1955, 1960.

The first South African fast bowler to exceed 100 wickets in Tests, Adcock's speed derived from an exceptionally tall, wiry frame and a delivery wherein the arm from a full arc remained firmly grooved in the vertical plane. E. A. B. Rowan discovered his talent while with Jeppe Old Boys and he played for South Africa after only one season in first-class cricket. He took 8 for 39 against Orange Free State at Johannesburg in 1953–54 and in the match 13 for 65. In England in 1955 he was the fastest bowler in the South African side, but a broken bone in his left foot in July hindered him. Against Australia at Durban in 1957–58 he took 6 for 43. Always hostile and superbly fit, he was at his best in England in 1960, when he easily headed both the South African first-class and Test averages, taking 108 wickets on the tour.

IRVING ROSENWATER

CAREER FIGURES

	INNS	NO	RUNS	HS	AVGE	100S
Batting	117	35	451	41	5·50	–

Bowling 405 wkts at 17.25 Ct 23

Test Record (26)

	INNS	NO	RUNS	HS	AVGE	100S
Batting	39	12	146	24	5·40	–

Bowling 104 wkts at 21·10 Ct 4

ALLEN, David Arthur (1935–)

Cotham GS. Gloucestershire 1953–1972. England: in England 1960–1964 consecutively, 1966; in Australia 1962–63, 1965–66; in South Africa 1964–65; in West Indies 1959–60; in New Zealand 1965–66; in India 1961–62; in Pakistan 1961–62.

To David Allen fell the unenviable lot of following in the wake of J. C. Laker, with a fearsome baptism bowling to the West Indian batsmen on the finest wickets in the world on the MCC tour of 1959–60. Yet he survived and became one of the best slow bowlers in England. Off 4 paces, with a lazy amble to the crease, he could bowl an accurate line for long spells, spinning the ball more than most. His leisurely air conveyed a false impression, for he was a great fighter, at his best when the odds were against the bowler. He was also a fine outfielder, with a strong and accurate arm. One thousand and one runs and 124 wickets in 1961 took him to his first double; his best batting came against the fastest bowling or when runs were most needed.

COLIN COWDREY

CAREER FIGURES

	INNS	NO	RUNS	HS	AVGE	100S
Batting	641	147	9291	121*	18·80	1

Bowling 1209 wkts at 23·64 Ct 252

Test Record (39)

	INNS	NO	RUNS	HS	AVGE	100S
Batting	51	15	918	88	25·50	–

Bowling 122 wkts at 30·97 Ct 10

G. O. B. Allen, most tireless of workers for the game, symbolizes the wisdom and experience of MCC.

ALLEN, George Oswald Browning, CBE (1902–)

Eton 1919–21. Cambridge Univ 1922–1923. Middlesex 1921–1950. England: in England 1930, 1931, 1933, 1934, 1936 (Captain); in Australia 1932–33, 1936–37 (Captain); in West Indies 1947–48 (Captain); in New Zealand 1932–33. President of MCC 1963–1964; Treasurer 1964–1976. Vice-Chairman Cricket Council 1974–1976. Selector (Chairman) 1955–1961.

G. O. B. Allen (euphoniously called 'Gubby') was born in Sydney, NSW, on 31 July 1902; but was an Etonian and of Cambridge University, Lord's, the MCC, and of the England XI after the manner born. He bowled really fast, with an action answering to classical requirements, sideways on, left shoulder seen momentarily by the batsman, then a strong urgent swing over, after a run to attack that was sturdy and galloping, and not too long. Also he could use a bat straight as a die in defence, and handsome to the eye in forward play. In Tests he took 81 wickets, averaging round about 30 each, and he scored 750 runs in these representative games, averaging 24. In the University Match of 1922 he had an impressive haul of 5 Oxford wickets for 60, and 4 for 18. He was seldom able to take part in first-class cricket day-by-day which is the reason, no doubt, why he never in a season achieved a thousand runs and a hundred wickets. His selection for the MCC Australian team of 1932–33 brought forth strong Press criticism, but his all-round performances in the Tests silenced all doubts.

In 1936 he was England's captain for the first time against India, in England, obviously a rehearsal for heavier responsibilities soon to come. In 1936–37 he was in charge of the MCC team visiting Australia, where he touched heroic heights in times of severe frustration. England won the First and Second Tests of this rubber, then lost the remaining 3, every game played to a finish. The tide turned during the 3rd engagement at Melbourne where, on a glorious New Year's Day, England dismissed, on a flawless turf, 6 Australian batsmen for 130, including Bradman, Brown and Fingleton. Rain now came to Australia's aid. On the 2nd day England, facing Australia's 200, were trapped on a frightful pitch (wickets were not entirely covered in Australia in those days). England actually got as far as 68 for 4, thanks to wonderful resistance by Hammond and Leyland. Allen – so it was, and is, argued to this day – should have declared the England innings closed and put Australia on to the 'gluepot'. But Allen could not know that the weather over the weekend would settle down again to hot summer. As events turned out, summer returned, and on a fully restored pitch Australia amassed 564. In the subsequent Test at Adelaide, England at one stage needed 245 for victory, with 7 wickets in hand; but Fleetwood-Smith clean bowled Hammond in the 1st over of the closing, decisive day. Little of fortune fell into Allen's lap. None the less, he fought the good fight gallantly. In this rubber he bowled 128 overs for 526 runs and 17 wickets; and every ball wheeling from his arm was a great-hearted effort of defiance. After the war when England's commitments were heavy and her forces inadequate he stepped into the breach and, at the age of 45, took MCC to face the formidable power of the West Indies on their own pitches.

He has since been one of the most influential of MCC figures as President for the statutory one year and in the thick of everything as Treasurer for many. For 7 years he was a remarkably successful chief of the Test Selection Committee and, altogether, a shrewd, not always visible, Grey Eminence at Lord's.

NEVILLE CARDUS

CAREER FIGURES

	INNS	NO	RUNS	HS	AVGE	100S
Batting	376	54	9232	180	28·67	11

Bowling 778 wkts at 21·22 Ct 131

Test Record (25)

	INNS	NO	RUNS	HS	AVGE	100S
Batting	33	2	750	122	24·19	1

Bowling 81 wkts at 29·37 Ct 20

ALTHAM, Harry Surtees, CBE, DSO, MC (1888–1965)

Repton 1905–1908 (Captain 1907–1908). Oxford Univ 1911–1912. Surrey 1908–1912. Hampshire 1919–1923; President 1947–1965. Treasurer MCC 1950–1963; President 1959. Chairman MCC Youth Cricket Association 1951–1965. Selector 1954 (Chairman).

Good player though he was, and great though his services to cricket were, it is as a cricket historian that Altham will be chiefly remembered by posterity. His *History of Cricket*, which originally appeared as a serial in *The Cricketer*, was first published in book form in 1926. In its later editions he collaborated with E. W. Swanton. It is a book that answers to every test, a book that one values more highly every time one returns to it, worthy alike of the greatest game and of the game with the greatest literature. After captaining one of the most famous of all school XIs, Altham played before the war with moderate success for Surrey and Oxford, but his greatest achievement was an innings of 141 which saved Hampshire from an innings defeat at Canterbury in 1921. Old habitués of the Week went back to MacLaren's 226 not out in 1896 for a comparison and years later G. J. V. Weigall called it 'the finest innings ever played at Canterbury except Bradman's 205'. He was a beautiful bat of the classic school, whose strokes might have come out of *The Jubilee Book of Cricket*, but who, being eminently practical, did not eschew the short-approach shot played over the in-fielders. He was also a splendid off-side field. For some years he captained the Harlequins on their August tour. In over 50 seasons of bowling in the nets at Winchester he taught many fine players and he also in his time gave great help with the coaching at Oxford.

At Lord's he was long a power behind the scenes, but perhaps even more notable than his 14 years as Treasurer was his work for the MCC Youth Cricket Association, of which he was the first chairman: he devoted much time to its coaching classes at Lilleshall and was co-author of *The MCC Cricket Coaching Book*. He did, besides, a great deal for Winchester rackets and indeed for Public School rackets in general. But his interests were not confined to games. He was a much loved and respected Winchester housemaster. No one can read his *History of Cricket* without realizing that he was a scholar, and he was a great authority on Winchester Cathedral and worked indefatigably for its Friends. Indeed, as Johnson said of Goldsmith, he touched nothing that he did not adorn.

R. L. ARROWSMITH

AMES, Leslie Ethelbert George, CBE (1905–)

Harvey GS, Folkestone. Kent 1926–1951. England: in England 1929, 1931–1935 consecutively, 1937, 1938; in Australia 1932–33, 1936–37; in South Africa 1938–39; in West Indies 1929–30, 1934–35; in New Zealand 1932–33. Selector 1950–1956, 1958. Secretary/Manager Kent CCC 1960–1974; President 1975. Manager MCC Under-25 in Pakistan 1966–67; MCC in West Indies 1967–68; in Ceylon and Pakistan 1968–69.

Les Ames was a batsman/wicket-keeper of the highest class, on a plane with his distinguished contemporaries, Oldfield of Australia and Cameron of South Africa. He originally applied to Kent as a batsman but, at a time when Kent was rich in talent, was advised by G. J. V. Weigall to reapply as a wicket-keeper. This advice was of as great benefit to his country as it was to the recipient. Ames started with Kent in the season of 1926. In 1931 he was preferred to Duckworth in the First Test against New Zealand, and thereafter was England's constant choice until the outbreak of war. In all he played in 47 Tests.

Ames was a fine all-round 'keeper. Taking Freeman's leg-spin not only sharpened his skill when standing up, but gave him unlimited opportunity for wicket-taking. In Australia he was equally at home standing back to Larwood and Voce. He was an orthodox, but free-scoring batsman who showed a fine full face of the bat during the operative part of the stroke.

Ames, a strongly-built man, with the dark eye and colouring of Romany blood, has been fortunate in being associated with cricket ever since joining Kent. On retirement he, as Manager as well as Secretary of Kent, combined with Colin Cowdrey, the captain, and latterly with Mike Denness to build a new era of success for the county, before finally being honoured with the Presidency of Kent and a place on the Committee of MCC.

IAN PEEBLES

CAREER FIGURES

	INNS	NO	RUNS	HS	AVGE	100S
Batting	951	95	37248	295	43·51	102

Bowling 24 wkts at 33.37 W/k: ct 698; st 415 Total 1113

Test Record (47)

	INNS	NO	RUNS	HS	AVGE	100S
Batting	72	12	2434	149	40·56	5

W/k: ct 74; st 23 Total 97

Dennis Amiss: concentration under the Indian sun.

AMISS, Dennis Leslie (1943–)

Oldknow Road Sch, Birmingham. Warwickshire 1960– . England: in England 1966, 1967, 1968, 1970, 1971, 1973–1977 consecutively; in Australia 1974–75, 1976–77; in West Indies 1973–74; in New Zealand 1974–75; in India 1972–73, 1976–77; in Pakistan 1972–73. WSC.

From 1972 until 1974 Dennis Amiss was England's most prolific batsman. In that time he scored over 2,000 runs in 20 Test matches at an average of 71. He had had a struggle to reach the top, and in his later playing years, when he became the first Test cricketer regularly to wear a crash helmet while batting, he appeared somewhat anonymously in World Series Cricket. For his 3 best years, though, he was, in more senses than one, a substantial cricketing figure.

Amiss's rise coincided with his being given the chance to open the Warwickshire innings in June 1972. Having, in May, been unsure even of a county place, by August he was going in 1st for England against Australia in one of the Prudential one-day 'internationals' and making 103. In West Indies, in 1973–74, his Test average was 82·87, his 262 not out in England's 2nd innings at Port of Spain being one of the greatest of all match-saving efforts. In Australia the following winter he foundered against the formidable speed of Thomson and Lillee, and despite one memorable come-back innings of 203 against West Indies at the Oval in 1976 he was, from 1975 onwards, marked down as being disproportionately vulnerable to the fastest bowling.

Powerfully built, with massive forearms and infinite patience, Amiss scored most of his runs off the front foot. Between pipes he made many a county hundred, usually at his own pace, though sometimes, when his eye was in, with some truly thunderous strokes.

JOHN WOODCOCK

ARLOTT, Leslie Thomas John, OBE (1914–)

At EXPO '67, the major international exposition at Montreal in 1967, the entrance to the British pavilion simply and successfully depicted the boast of a timeless civilization under the sun – it consisted solely of a plot of fresh-mown grass on which was placed nothing more than an old deckchair bathed in light. A continuous tape-recording was playing – the faint rustle of breeze on trees, the distant pock of bat on ball and an occasional drowsy smatter of applause, all as background effects to an unmistakable voice commentating endlessly on a cricket match at Worcester.

It could only have been John Arlott. For over 30 years his articulate, leisurely, confiding countryman's burr has been synonymous with the radio and cricket. After the first half-century of public broadcasting Arlott stands four-square on the plinth alongside such outstanding radio journalists as Ed Murrow, Richard Dimbleby and Alistair Cooke. He was 32 when he made his first live cricket commentary at Worcester in 1946. Since that year he has not missed one Test Match in England for the BBC.

His first job, when he left Queen Mary's School, Basingstoke, was as a clerk in a local mental hospital. In 1934 he joined the Hampshire Constabulary. Increasingly he was writing and broadcasting in his spare time. He resigned as a detective-sergeant in 1945 when the BBC appointed him first a staff producer and later a general instructor in their training school. Soon he was a prolific journalist and author as well as broadcaster; and not only about cricket, his range reflecting his tastes with such titles as *English Cheese of the South and West* and *Burgundy Vines and Wines*. But notably his biographies of F. S. Trueman and Maurice Tate remain definitive works. In 1979 he published his *Book of Cricketers*, a loving collection of essays 'about the players most enjoyed by one spectator' of which nearly half had played for Hampshire and which he admitted 'but for the intrusion of editorial conscience there would have been many more'. Before the last war he occasionally fielded as 12th man for his beloved county XI in an emergency. Since 1968 he has been a proud, caring and working President of the professional Cricketers' Association. He was responsible for bringing the South African Basil d'Oliveira to England.

For a dozen years he has been cricket correspondent of *The Guardian*, a direct custodian of the traditions of the post established by Sir Neville Cardus, his friend with whom in 1969 he combined to write *The Noblest Game*. John Arlott continues in all his works to evoke the charms and flavours of a noble game founded by obscure Judes in the English shires. He has introduced this game to millions has this talented, generous man of warm, uncomplicated tastes who lists his recreations as watching cricket, drinking wine, talking and sleeping.

FRANK KEATING

ARMSTRONG, Warwick Windridge (1879–1947)

Cumloden Sch, Melbourne, and Univ Coll, Armadale. Victoria 1898–1922, (Captain 1906–07, 1920–21). Australia: in Australia 1901–02, 1903–04, 1907–08, 1910–11, 1911–12, 1920–21 (Captain); in England 1902, 1905, 1909, 1921 (Captain); in South Africa 1902–03.

Warwick Armstrong was a cricketer on the grand scale. Upon the eve of his retirement from the game he weighed 22 stone, had achieved an all-round record excelled by very few, and had captained his country 10 times without once meeting defeat. He had, apparently, a flair for success, and it is pleasant to recall that a chance meeting with a whisky merchant, whilst playing in Glasgow on his last tour, inaugurated a new and prosperous business career when his cricketing days were done. Armstrong died in 1947, a rich man.

He started in major cricket for his native Victoria in 1898–99 and in 1901–02 played for Australia against MacLaren's side of that year. His first tour of England was under Joe Darling in 1902, after which he made 3 more in '05, '09 and '21. He would have made another in 1912 had not his stubborn, forceful character led him to join the revolt of a number of players against the Australian Board of Control. He was a great all-round success on each visit, but his full glory was reserved for his final 2 seasons. In 1920–21 he crushed England in all 5 Tests, contributing 3 hundreds from his own bat towards this destruction. Three successive victories followed in England, before the losers gained a moment's respite in a couple of welcome draws.

He was a man who spoke his mind and liked to get his way, regardless of sensitive feelings or niceties. As such he was a strong disciplinarian and somewhat dictatorial opponent. Beneath this hard exterior was a kind, generous heart which could, and did, send him travelling miles to play an outlying school single-handed, to emerge, incidentally, once more victorious. As a batsman Armstrong made sensible use of his vast physical gifts. He attacked mainly from the front foot, an unhurried lunge sending the ball scudding into the deep and beyond. On the back foot he was, like many bred on shiny hard Australian pitches, a sure and powerful square-cutter. He bowled from the back of his hand but his spin was mostly over the top. His height gave him flight and bounce, to which was coupled a remarkable and consistent accuracy. For a man of such enormous bulk his action was neat, well-balanced and easy.

A comparatively slim-line edition (*c* 1905) of Warwick Armstrong, the Falstaffian all-conquering Australian captain of 1920–21.

As a captain he was never tested by adversity, for he was a general with sufficient resources to crush all opposition in a series of orthodox set-pieces. There can be little doubt that the rough fibre of his being would have made him as thorny a defender as he was formidable a victor. His shirt is preserved in the Melbourne Pavilion, a banner appropriately spacious to the wearer and, possibly, an object of admiration and envy to rival shirtmakers.

IAN PEEBLES

CAREER FIGURES

	INNS	NO	RUNS	HS	AVGE	100S
Batting	406	61	16158	303*	46·83	45

Bowling 832 wkts at 19·71 Ct 274

Test Record (50)

	INNS	NO	RUNS	HS	AVGE	100S
Batting	84	10	2863	159*	38·68	6

Bowling 87 wkts at 33·59 Ct 44

ASHTON, Sir Hubert, KBE, MC (1898–1979)

Winchester 1915–1916 (Captain 1916). Cambridge Univ 1920–1922 (Captain 1922). Essex 1921–1939; Chairman 1941–1955; President 1955–1969. President MCC 1960–1961.

Sir Hubert Ashton was an outstanding University cricketer. In each of his 3 years he averaged over 60 for Cambridge and played for the Gentlemen at Lord's. In 1921 he made 118 against Oxford and in 1922 declared when his own score was 90. Even better remembered is his batting against the Australians in 1921. At Cambridge he made the 1st hundred scored against them that summer. For Essex he made 90. His innings of 75 had much to do with the sensational victory of MacLaren's XI at Eastbourne and for the South of England he got 65. A sound batsman, who played well forward to fast bowling, he had plenty of strokes and was a magnificent all-round field. Why, in a season when our batting and fielding were so weak, he was not picked for England it is impossible to imagine. Unfortunately his regular first-class cricket ended when he came down. One of 3 brothers who captained Cambridge in consecutive years, he had blues for soccer and hockey as well. He was MP for Chelmsford from 1950–1964.

R. L. ARROWSMITH

CAREER FIGURES

	INNS	NO	RUNS	HS	AVGE	100S
Batting	115	11	4025	236*	38·70	8

Bowling 0–14 Ct 71

ASIF IQBAL, Razvi (1943–)

Osmania Univ. Hyderabad 1959–60. Karachi 1961–62. Kent 1968– (Captain 1977). Pakistan: in Pakistan 1964–65, 1968–69, 1969–70, 1972–73, 1974–75, 1976–77, 1978–79; in England 1967, 1971, 1974; in Australia 1964–65, 1972,73, 1976–77; in West Indies 1976–77; in New Zealand 1964–65, 1972–73, 1978–79; in India 1979–80 (Captain).

Few Pakistan players have given more pleasure to spectators than Asif Iqbal. His attacking instinct, happy demeanour and feline grace have perhaps tended to mask his

Asif Iqbal: feline grace.

effectiveness. His Test hundreds have usually been scored when most needed, the best remembered being his 146 against England at the Oval in 1967. Asif's score at No. 9 and the 9th wicket stand of 190 he shared with Intikhab Alam both established new Test records. Slim, supple and always with sleeves buttoned down, Asif's fleet-footed batting is marked by wristy drives and cuts and remarkable speed between the wickets.

He first made his name with medium-fast bowling and still retains a knack for taking useful wickets. He began in Hyderabad (India) in the 1959–60 Ranji Trophy and after migrating to Pakistan embarked on his lengthy Test career 5 years later. Asif's gifts were ideally suited to Kent, whom he joined in 1968, and not least in one-day matches. As an almost inevitable process he succeeded to Pakistan's Test captaincy, a job which is never particularly secure and which he forfeited temporarily when he became first an agent and then a player for World Series Cricket. Having led Kent to a share of the Championship in 1977, his Packer connexion lost him the captaincy there too, though he continued to win matches for them with the occasional dazzling innings.

RICHARD STREETON

BAILEY, Trevor Edward (1923–)

Dulwich 1938–1942 (Captain 1941–1942). Cambridge Univ 1947–1948. Essex 1946–1967 (Captain 1961–1966). England: in England 1949, 1950, 1951, 1953–1958 consecutively; in Australia 1950–51, 1954–55, 1958–59; in South Africa 1956–57; in West Indies 1953–54; in New Zealand 1950–51, 1954–55.

Bailey's great value to the England sides with which he played was as a genuine Test-class all-rounder. Such he became when in 1949 he began a bowling partnership with A. V. Bedser which continued for 5 years, and caused more than enough worry to opposing batsmen everywhere. Such he remained until, in 1959, the arrival of E. R. Dexter hastened his exit from the England side. He was the first man to complete the double in 1949, whereafter in a span of 10 years covering tours to Australia, West Indies, New Zealand and South Africa, he completed a rare feat of making 2,000 runs and taking 100 wickets in Test Matches.

His skill reached its highest fulfilment in the mid-1950s. Lord's, 1953, was his greatest triumph, when with Watson he fought the famous rearguard action on the last day which, as it eventually turned out, regained the Ashes for England after 20 years. These two withstood the wiles of Hassett and the power of Miller and the rest of the Australian attack almost all day, and it was Bailey with his tenacious nature who set the pattern. In 1954–55 when Tyson and Statham were leading the attack in Australia, and Bedser could have been used as the 3rd seam bowler, it was Bailey who got the place because of his steady, courageous batting and fine close-to-the-wicket fielding. Bailey justified the choice by making just on 300 runs and taking 10 wickets in the series.

Nicknames have come along as inevitably as the morning sun because of his penchant for slow scoring. Those watching the game sometimes confessed to being bored by this, or even annoyed; this was nothing to the annoyance of the cricketers opposing him who found they were unable to shift this one man who stood between them and victory. Sometimes he carried defence too far, as when at Brisbane in 1958–59 we saw that dark wavy hair glinting immaculately from the other end for the 7 hours and 38 minutes he took to make 68. For this effort it was his own side that paid the price; but there were plenty of other times when almost single-handed he defied the might of Miller, Lindwall and others, steadied the ship and then got it back to calmer waters.

Trevor Bailey: Over my dead body, says Bailey to Benaud during one of the slowest Test innings ever played. At Brisbane in 1958–59 Bailey's 68 in 7 hours 38 minutes failed to save the game for England by upwards of a day.

Five times his forward and back defensive stroke have given cricket historians the chance to list him among the slowest scoring offenders of all time. Apart from the resistance at Brisbane he made 26 in 251 minutes and 8 in 125 minutes – efforts which, I suppose, must have brought some clearing of the spectators' throats. Unfortunately he is likely to be recalled in years to come only as a slow scorer instead of what he in fact was, a fine 'team man' and one of the best all-rounders to play for England – a dedicated cricketer fond of the game and believing that to be played properly it must always be played to win. About this there could be no half measures. His knowledge of the game continues to be exploited by the BBC as a regular member of their radio commentary team.

RICHIE BENAUD

CAREER FIGURES

	INNS	NO	RUNS	HS	AVGE	100S
Batting	1072	215	28642	205	33·42	28

Bowling 2082 wkts at 23·13 Ct 427

Test Record (61)

	INNS	NO	RUNS	HS	AVGE	100S
Batting	91	14	2290	134*	29·74	1

Bowling 132 wkts at 29·21 Ct 32

Warren Bardsley: left-handed opener, and Australian stalwart 1909–26.

BARDSLEY, Warren (1882–1954)

New South Wales 1903–04 to 1927–28 (Captain 1913–14 to 1914–15). Australia: in Australia 1910–11, 1911–12, 1920–21, 1924–25; in England 1909, 1912, 1921, 1926 (Captain); in South Africa 1921–22.

Warren Bardsley was one of the greatest of left-handed batsmen, as accomplished on all wickets as Clem Hill or Neil Harvey. He played with an exemplary straight bat, and his footwork on a turning pitch had the quickness and the shrewdness of the canniest Yorkshire professional of his period. He drove with easy propulsion off the front foot, and was as ready to go back on his stumps to force the ball from his pads by means of powerful wrists and forearms. He would toss his head backwards at a bumping ball with a sniff of the nose, a sign of contempt, letting it fly past a yard or so from the nose aforesaid, entirely unmoved. Only once in his career did he suffer complete frustration. During the 1911–12 rubber in Australia he was put off his balance by the formidable combination of S. F. Barnes and Frank Foster. In his years of retirement he told me that Foster 4 times in the first 4 Tests clean bowled him with deliveries terribly fast off the pitch after swinging in to his leg stump then hitting, sometimes uprooting, the off. He was actually left out of the Australian XI for the Fifth Test of this same rubber of 1911–12, in which his scores were 30, 12, 0, 16 (run out), 5, 63, 0 and 3.

Altogether Bardsley played in 41 Test Matches, usually going in 1st. At the Oval on his 1st visit to England in 1909, he achieved 2 hundreds in the same Test Match, 136 and 130; he was the 1st to perform this double accomplishment in Test cricket. At Lord's, in 1926, he carried his bat through Australia's 1st innings – 193 not out in 6½ hours against the attack of Tate, Root, Kilner, Larwood and Woolley. He and other eminent Australian batsmen – such as Trumper and Macartney – were equally great on turning pitches in England as on hard true ones in Australia, for the simple reason that wickets in Australia were then not perpetually protected from the effects of rain and sun. Bardsley was nearing his 42nd birthday when he played his monumental innings at Lord's. The soundness of his method reinsured him against any failing of eye or muscular reaction. He was also a splendid outfield.

NEVILLE CARDUS

CAREER FIGURES

	INNS	NO	RUNS	HS	AVGE	100S
Batting	376	35	17031	264	49·94	53

Bowling 0–41 Ct 113

Test Record (41)

	INNS	NO	RUNS	HS	AVGE	100S
Batting	66	5	2469	193*	40·47	6

Ct 12

BARLOW, Edgar John (1940–)

Pretoria Boys' HS. Transvaal 1959–60. Eastern Province 1964–65. Western Province 1968–69. Derbyshire 1976–1978 (Captain 1977–1978). South Africa: in South Africa 1961–62, 1964–65, 1966–67, 1969–70; in England 1965; in Australia 1963–64; in New Zealand 1963–64; Rest of the World in England 1970. WSC.

The tragedy of Eddie Barlow's career was that this gifted, highly competitive all-rounder was seen only 30 times in the Test arena because of South Africa's isolation. It was hardly surprising, therefore, that after a brief but successful excursion into county cricket, he found the blandishments of World Series Cricket impossible to resist and was among the first to join Kerry Packer.

Born in Pretoria, Barlow played at various times for Transvaal, Eastern Province and Western Province; his dynamic leadership with the latter inspired a revival of fortunes similar to that which followed in his 3 seasons with Derbyshire.

Eddie Barlow: a South African powerhouse.

A right-arm fast-medium bowler with a clever change of pace, an aggressive stroke-playing batsman and a high-class slip fielder, Barlow averaged 63 on South Africa's tour of Australia and New Zealand in 1963–64. As a rugby player, he was good enough to represent Transvaal against the All Blacks.

Among many notable achievements in the highest company, Barlow took 4 wickets in 5 balls, including the hat-trick, for the Rest of the World against England in 1970, but curiously he was not among the first flood of overseas players to appear in England when restrictions were lifted. He joined Derbyshire in 1976, taking over the captaincy from R. W. Taylor later that season. Under his guidance, a county that had struggled for too long was all but transformed. If his powers were starting to fade, he was still able to contribute match-winning performances, notably a career-best innings of 217, plus many inspired flourishes in one-day cricket. The height of intensive effort was second nature to him – a characteristic never better shown than in the Rest of the World series.

MICHAEL CAREY

CAREER FIGURES

	INNS	NO	RUNS	HS	AVGE	100S
Batting	440	25	16330	217	39·34	39

Bowling 512 wkts at 24·90 Ct 304

Test Record (30)

	INNS	NO	RUNS	HS	AVGE	100S
Batting	57	2	2516	201	45·74	6

Bowling 40 wkts at 34·05 Ct 35

BARNES, Sydney Francis (1873–1967)

Warwickshire 1894–1896. Lancashire 1899–1903. Staffordshire 1904–1934. England: in England 1902, 1909, 1912; in Australia 1901–02, 1907–08, 1911–12; in South Africa 1913–14. League Cricket 1895–1934.

Sydney Barnes, perhaps the greatest bowler in all cricket history, was born at Smethwick in Staffordshire on 19 April 1873. His appearances in county cricket were limited to a few matches for Warwickshire in the mid-1890s, and 2 full seasons for Lancashire in 1902 and

1903 in which he took 215 wickets. The rest of his regular cricket engagements were with his own county, Staffordshire, and in the North Staffordshire, Lancashire, Bradford and Central Lancashire Leagues. In both these fields his bowling figures are almost unbelievable: in 22 seasons for Staffordshire he took 1,432 wickets for 8 apiece, and in 38 summers with the Leagues his total bag was 3,741 at an average cost of 6·68; in his last year, 1934, when he was 61 years old, his wickets cost under 11 each.

But his name will, of course, always be associated with his phenomenal achievements in Test Match cricket. In 27 games between 1901 and 1914, of which by some strange selectorial mystery only 10 were in this country, he took 189 wickets for 3,106 runs, a record unrivalled alike for consistency and economy. For the 1911–12 MCC side in Australia his 34 wickets in the Tests were clearly decisive in winning the rubber, but still more sensational was his record of 34 South African wickets taken in the 3 Test Matches of the 1912 Triangular Tournament, and the 49 in four Tests – 17 for 159 in one of them – when, at the age of 40, he visited that country 18 months later. That was the last time he played for England, but men who batted against him 8 years later when in 1921 England were so outplayed by Australia, would claim that he was still the greatest bowler in the world.

The fine picture of Barnes which hangs at Lord's well reflects the formidable menace with which batsmen found themselves faced: long arms, and at the end of them a comprehensive hand with long, strong fingers, a tall, gaunt, erect and co-ordinated body, and above it a face of austere but composed hostility. A run, not long but full of life and spring, a high delivery, and the head leading a full and perfectly balanced follow-through – this was the basic machinery that commanded such control of length and direction; but the secret of his mastery lay in the supple steel of his fingers and hand. At appreciably more than medium pace he could, even in the finest weather and on the truest wickets in Australia, both swing and break the ball from off or leg. Most deadly of all was the ball which he would deliver from rather wide on the crease, move in with a late swerve the width of the wicket, and then straighten back off the ground to hit the off stump.

Art, resolution, stamina, he commanded them all. Well might a man who saw him in his prime have found himself saying, 'Here was a Caesar, when comes such another?'

H. S. ALTHAM

CAREER FIGURES

	INNS	NO	RUNS	HS	AVGE	100S
Batting	173	50	1573	93	12·78	–

Bowling 719 wkts at 17·09 Ct 65

Test Record (27)

	INNS	NO	RUNS	HS	AVGE	100S
Batting	39	9	242	38*	8·06	

Bowling 189 wkts at 16·43 Ct 12

BARNETT, Charles John (1910–)

Wycliffe Coll. Gloucestershire 1927–1948, England: in England 1933, 1936, 1937, 1938, 1947, 1948; in Australia 1936–37; in India 1933–34.

C. J. Barnett: straight in to the attack.

Barnett was arguably the last great English attacking opening batsman. If he went in at the start of play and was there at lunch, he was sure to have got his hundred or be near it, and it needed a shrewd spectator to realize that the bowling had not consisted chiefly of half-volleys varied by an occasional long-hop. In fact, he would have been driving on the rise balls of a good length or even shorter, a stroke possible only to a man possessed of strong wrists and forearms, a wonderful sense of timing and a rigidly straight bat. He was, too, a fine cutter of the shorter ball. He did not alter his tactics for a Test Match. Against Australia at Nottingham in 1938 he completed his hundred the first ball after lunch. He was a useful medium-pace opening bowler and a fine outfield.

R. L. ARROWSMITH

CAREER FIGURES

	INNS	NO	RUNS	HS	AVGE	100S
Batting	821	45	25389	259	32·71	48

Bowling 394 wkts at 30·97 Ct 318

Test Record (20)

	INNS	NO	RUNS	HS	AVGE	100S
Batting	35	4	1098	129	35·41	2

Bowling 0 wkts for 93 Ct 14

BARRINGTON, Kenneth Frank (1930–)

Katesgrove Sch, Reading. Surrey 1953–1968. England: in England 1955, 1959 to 1968 consecutively; in Australia 1962–63, 1965–66; in South Africa 1965–65; in West Indies 1959–60, 1967–68; in New Zealand 1962–63; in India 1961–62, 1963–64; in Pakistan 1961–62. Selector 1975– . Manager MCC in India, Sri Lanka and Australia 1976–77; in Pakistan and New Zealand 1977–78. Assistant Manager: in Australia 1978–79; in Australia and India 1979–80.

Ken Barrington joined Surrey from Reading in 1948, showing promise as a bowler but with ambitions of being a front-line batsman. Improving with every match, he enjoyed a successful season in the 2nd XI of 1952, played his first match for Surrey in 1953 and, such was his progress, he played for England against South Africa in 1955. Early disappointments only served to strengthen his resolution to become an England batsman, but it took him 4 years to establish himself again. In an attempt to tighten his defence he sought to eliminate every risk. Once an off-side driver, he turned himself into a back-foot player, strong on the on-side, allowing himself the cut to the off. This more frugal approach, though less attractive to watch, was infinitely more productive for him.

In 1959 he scored 2,499 runs, which earned him a place to the West Indies. After that he never looked back. In India and Pakistan in 1961–62 he scored 1,329 runs, a record for an Englishman, and 1,765 runs at an average of 80·13 in Australia and New Zealand the following winter. This included 219 not out for MCC against an Australian XI at Melbourne, 132 not out in the Fourth Test and 101 and 94 in the Fifth. In 1964 he was England's leading batsman, sharing in a stand of 246 with Dexter for the 3rd wicket in the Fourth Test at Old Trafford. Barrington went on to his highest score of 256 – a remarkable demonstration of application and self-discipline.

A useful and enthusiastic leg-spinner, he was a fine slip catcher and, into the bargain, a good safe outfielder with a powerful arm. He could also be very funny patrolling the boundary fence, particularly overseas, where he showed a deft touch with the crowds. He was a genial companion whose warm sense of humour endeared him to cricket folk everywhere. At the age of 38, his career was cut short when he suffered a mild heart attack playing in a match on the Melbourne Cricket Ground. Happily recovered, he has since devoted himself to the game as an England selector from 1976 and as manager or assistant manager on 4 successive England tours.

COLIN COWDREY

Ken Barrington: Australia at the receiving end, as they often were.

CAREER FIGURES

	INNS	NO	RUNS	HS	AVGE	100S
Batting	831	136	31714	256	45·63	76

Bowling 273 wkts at 32·61 Ct 515

Test Record (82)

	INNS	NO	RUNS	HS	AVGE	100S
Batting	131	15	6806	256	58·67	20

Bowling 29 wkts at 44·82 Ct 58

Bishen Bedi: a living legend.

BEDI, Bishen Singh (1946–)

St Francis HS (Amritsar) and Punjab Univ. Northern Punjab 1961–62– . Northamptonshire 1972–1977. India: in India 1966–67, 1969–70, 1972–73, 1974–75, 1976–77 (Captain), 1978–79; in England 1967, 1971, 1974, 1979; in Australia 1967–68, 1977–78 (Captain); in West Indies 1970–71, 1975–76 (Captain); in New Zealand 1967–68, 1975–76 (Captain); in Pakistan 1978–79 (Captain).

A spin bowler's apprenticeship is traditionally long. But Bishen Bedi was only 15 when he made his first-class debut, for Punjab, and not for a day did he look out of his depth. If he had to wait another 5 years for his 1st Test cap, it was only because Durani and Nadkarni, both outstanding left-arm spinners – although of a different type – were absolute fixtures until the mid-1960s.

Bedi's consistency of performance can be gauged from the fact that of the 68 Tests India played following his debut, Bedi figured in 64. He has in fact made the most Test appearances for India, and taken more wickets than any of his countrymen. He missed one through crossing swords with officialdom and another through injury. It is true that due to India's heavy dependence on spin bowling, Bedi had enormous scope to get wickets. At the same time, he never had the advantage of coming on after the opposition had been softened up by genuinely fast bowlers.

A beautiful, rhythmic action is the key to his control, his subtlety in variation of flight and pace, and his durability. There is a close link between Bedi's cricket philosophy and his attitude to life. The cost of living enjoyably matters as little to him as the price he pays for his wickets. His cricket is delightfully old-fashioned. Even though India were a moderate side in the 3 years he led them, Bedi was never defensively inclined.

His beard and colourful headgear (the *patka*) are symbols of his Sikh religion, which he practises devotedly. But his religious orthodoxy is very private. The world knows him as a gregarious man, an internationalist, who is as much at home in Northampton, Melbourne, Auckland, Karachi or Kingston as in his native Amritsar. Married to an Australian and father of two children, Bedi is an outspoken and controversial character, but extremely likeable.

D. J. RUTNAGUR

BEDSER, Alec Victor, OBE (1918–)

Monument Hill Cent Sch. Surrey 1939–1960. England: in England 1946–1955 consecutively; in Australia 1946–47, 1950–51, 1954–55; in South Africa 1948–49; in New Zealand 1946–47, 1950–51. Selector 1962– (Chairman 1969–). Assistant Manager in Australia and New Zealand 1962–63. Manager MCC in Australia and New Zealand 1974–75; in Australia and India 1979–80.

Alec Bedser was born in Reading within minutes of his brother Eric. He made his bow for Surrey in 1939, but his real cricketing life started postwar, in 1946. In that season he began an illustrious Test career having 11 wickets in each of his first 2 Test Matches against India. From such promising beginnings he went on to take 236 wickets in 51 Tests for 24·89 each. There were times when, like Atlas, he seemed to be carrying the whole burden of events on his broad and willing shoulders. Fifteen times he took 5 wickets or more in an innings. Running parallel to this massive role in international cricket, Alec Bedser played a leading part in Surrey's phenomenal series of 7 consecutive County Championship victories from 1952 onwards. It is probably by this achievement that he would choose to be remembered.

He was a professional and proud of it, from the steel tip of his enormous boots to the beads of perspiration on his brow. Whilst not a Nijinsky in the field, he still took 290 catches; nothing much dropped out of those capacious buckets when he got within striking range. His batting was not negligible, being firm-footed and straight. His bowling action was a model of economy and maximum effort where it mattered most. The better he bowled the louder his feet seemed to pound on the turf and the more his head jerked on his shoulders. His arm was high, only dropping in the later stages of his career, and his pace was genuine medium-fast.

The basis of his technique was the in-swing action, with his enormous hand cutting inside the ball at the moment of release. Sometimes, on pitching, the ball would continue on its course but occasionally it would straighten or 'hold its own'. The leg-cutter bowled at a slightly slower pace was delivered in a similar way and on broken or wet wickets it became the equivalent of a fast leg-break. He never used the out-swinger, only permitting himself the odd one in Sunday matches. His movement in the air was always in to the right-handed batsman and away from the left-handed. Bowling at Neil Harvey at Melbourne in 1951, the movement was so late that a sort of stalemate developed because the great Australian was unable to make contact of any sort.

A. V. Bedser: the perfect follow-through.

Bradman has gone on record as saying that Bedser in certain conditions was the most difficult bowler he ever batted against. Despite his tremendous skill his cricket was permeated by an endearing aura of pessimism. One felt that if he hit the middle stump with 10 consecutive balls he would suspect it was just a dark plot to get his own side to the batting crease. Intensely loyal to club, country and his friends his contribution to cricket continued as selector, manager and committee man. No one has ever chosen more Test teams. From 1962 until 1980 he had a permanent place on the England Selection Committee, for 12 years as Chairman. His devotion to his twin brother has become legendary. They dress alike, think alike and even talk alike. Perhaps, however, having lived through an era when the distinction between amateur and professional was discarded, he will go down as the last of the really great professionals.

JOHN WARR

CAREER FIGURES

	INNS	NO	RUNS	HS	AVGE	100S
Batting	576	181	5735	126	14·51	1

Bowling 1924 wkts at 20·41 Ct 290

Test Record (51)

	INNS	NO	RUNS	HS	AVGE	100S
Batting	71	15	714	79	12·75	–

Bowling 236 wkts at 24·89 Ct 26

BELDAM, George William (1868–1937)

Middlesex 1900–1907

George Beldam came rather late into county cricket in 1900, aged 32, but from then until 1907 made a valuable all-round contribution to Middlesex, especially in 1903 when they carried off the Championship for the first time. His crowning moment came with the Surrey match at Lord's when he made 89 and 118 against Lockwood and Richardson. He and Plum Warner were the most reliable bats in the side – in addition to which he frequently opened the bowling.

Beldam, however, earns his place in this gallery for his pioneer work as the first action photographer of sport in this country. With C. B. Fry, he published *Great Batsmen* in 1905, followed a year later by *Great Bowlers*. These books contained more than 1,000 action shots. According to the equipment of the time they were perforce taken at close quarters. It is thanks to the father of cricket photography that we get a graphic idea of how the heroes of the Golden Age looked and played. Beldam also supplied much of the text of the books written in collaboration with Fry, and also the writing which complemented Albert Chevallier Tayler's crayon drawings in *The Empire's Cricketers*. He also specialized in golfers, and is said to have introduced 'W.G.' to the game.

With the advantage of a long focus lens developed during the First World War, Herbert Fishwick, starting in 1920, made

George Beldam: helped Middlesex to the Championship of 1903 and was the father of cricket photography.

great strides in photography in Australia. In England the photographic agencies held the field until individuals, headed by Patrick Eagar, gained access to Test Match grounds in the late 1960s and early 1970s.

E. W. SWANTON

CAREER FIGURES

	INNS	NO	RUNS	HS	AVGE	100S
Batting	231	16	6513	155*	30·29	9

Bowling 107 wkts at 30·64 Ct 81

BENAUD, Richie, OBE (1930–)

Parramatta HS. New South Wales 1948–49 to 1963–64 (Captain 1955–56 to 1963–64). Australia: in Australia 1951–52, 1952–53, 1954–55, 1958–59 (Captain), 1960–61 (Captain), 1962–63 (Captain), 1963–64 (Captain); in England 1953, 1956, 1961 (Captain); in South Africa 1957–58; in West Indies 1954–55; in India 1956–57, 1959–60 (Captain); in Pakistan 1956–57, 1959–60 (Captain).

Richie Benaud owed his start in cricket to his father, an experienced Australian first-grade player, one of very few to take 20 wickets in a match. Playing for New South Wales at the age of 18, Benaud made his start in Test cricket against the West Indies in 1951–52 at the age of 21. He came to England in 1953 and 1956, playing in the home series against England in 1954–55 and in the West Indies in 1955. Yet it was not until 1957–58 in South Africa that he established himself as an all-round cricketer of the highest class; on that tour he took 106 wickets and scored 817 runs, including 4 hundreds. In India and Pakistan he excelled with 47 wickets in the 2 series and against the West Indies in 1960–61 his record was 2nd only to Davidson's. Ian Craig's illness led to the somewhat unexpected appointment of Benaud as Australian captain in 1958, following which he went on to lead Australia in 4 successive and triumphant series until the end of 1961.

He was the complete captain, an inspiring leader, thoughtful and adroit in the field and a tough competitor. Yet no one has tried harder to make Test cricket an interesting and attractive spectacle. At a time when the pull of cricket was flagging, his joint co-operation with Frank Worrell in the exciting series against West Indies in 1960–61 captured the imagination of the cricket world and did a great deal to rekindle interest. During this series Benaud suffered a strained shoulder, which limited his skill but never blunted his determination to see that his side played the right sort of cricket. Deservedly, he had the storybook finish to his playing career. One-all in the series in 1961, England looked set to win the Fourth Test Match at Old Trafford, when they needed little more than 100 to make with 9 wickets in hand. Benaud took the ball, and bowling round the wicket, dismissed Dexter, Close, May and Subba Row in 5 overs. From 150 for 1, England were all out for 201. Benaud's 6 for 70, his best performance against England, had pulled the match out of the fire and saved the Ashes for Australia. He was a magnificent close fielder. Tall and lithe, able to leap with cat-like agility, he brought off some spectacular catches. The strength of his batting lay in his driving. At the crease he always personified a sense of challenge and the will to attack.

Richie Benaud: the last great Australian spinner.

But it was as a leg-break bowler that Benaud touched the heights. An advocate of practice, practice and yet more practice, he *drove* himself to the top. From a nice rhythmical, high action he was more of a length bowler than a big spinner of the ball. He was at his most dangerous bowling into a breeze blowing from the area of third man. With clever changes of pace and a teasing flight, he was always a more fearsome proposition on the hard wickets overseas than he was in England.

In his retirement, his involvement in the game has been maintained as a journalist, a highly respected television commentator, and, while it lasted, as a senior executive in World Series Cricket.

COLIN COWDREY

CAREER FIGURES

	INNS	NO	RUNS	HS	AVGE	100S
Batting	365	44	11719	187	36·50	23

Bowling 945 wkts at 24·73 Ct 249

Test Record (63)

	INNS	NO	RUNS	HS	AVGE	100S
Batting	97	7	2201	122	24·45	3

Bowling 248 wkts at 27·03 Ct 65

Lord Birkett (*on right*): cricket's silver-tongued orator in conversation with Jack Fingleton.

BIRKETT, 1st Lord, PC (1883–1962)

William Norman, 1st Baron Birkett, one of the world's most distinguished lawyers, was a fervent lover of cricket. Throughout a brilliant career at the Bar and on the Bench, he freely confessed a ruling passion for cricket and the fascination it offered. He played for Emmanuel College when a young man at Cambridge, and later took a great delight in entertaining many of the world's greatest cricketers at his Buckinghamshire home. There he gathered around him, amid a considerable library, many books on cricket: 'I sometimes think,' he once said, 'that the deepest and most enduring pleasure is to read about cricket'. His devotion to literature reflected itself in his many and beautifully phrased writings on the game, capturing at once the spirit of Broadhalfpenny Down or the modern Test arena. He readily contributed forewords to many cricket books and found great pleasure in writing the engagingly Elian essay for *The Game of Cricket* in 1955. He contributed, too, with his habitual felicity of expression, to *Wisden* and other cricket journals, always with an eloquent grace that made one aware how much he was adding to the literature of the game.

Birkett was generally acknowledged as the best after-dinner speaker in London. He was the greatest of all 'catches' for dinner organizers, and many were the audiences he captivated in the latter years of his life with the rhythmic beauty of his diction and his exquisitely apt choice of language. He was an indispensable adornment to the dinners given by the Cricket Writers' Club, when he welcomed touring sides to England with a sincerity and charm that never failed to impress them. At his happiest, perhaps, when speaking of his native Lancashire and her immortal players, he was able to see merit in cricketers the world over, not least those on the village green. At the time of his death he was the President of The Cricket Society, in whose affairs he had always taken the keenest interest. He had been the principal speaker at the winter luncheon of The Society only two weeks before he died.

IRVING ROSENWATER

BLACKHAM, John McCarthy (1853–1932)

Victoria 1874–75 to 1894–95 (Captain 1882–83 to 1897–98). Australia: in Australia 1876–77, 1878–79, 1881–82, 1882–83, 1884–85 (Captain), 1886–87, 1887–88, 1891–92 (Captain), 1894–95 (Captain); in England 1880, 1882, 1884, 1886, 1888, 1890, 1893 (Captain).

'Old Jack' Blackham, with his short beard, glinting dark eyes, and small cap perched on the back of his head, was a wicket-keeping pioneer. In the first of all Tests, at Melbourne, there was some objection to his being chosen as wicket-keeper instead of Murdoch, but he soon silenced doubts, and accompanied David Gregory's team to England in 1878. The cool, workmanlike way in which he took Spofforth (then at his fastest) impressed everybody; he had no long-stop, and was called 'the prince of wicket-keepers', though Pilling is said to have been before him in both respects. Whatever the truth of this, Blackham's gathering of the ball and whipping off the bails in one motion were widely acclaimed. He played in the First Test in England, he and Lyttelton both giving a masterly display behind the stumps. He came to England with the first 8 touring teams, giving away very few byes, and having 60 victims in Test Matches – 24 stumped and 36 caught. He was a useful, if unorthodox, batsman, and put on 154 for the 9th wicket with S. E. Gregory at Sydney in 1894, his share being 74. This was his last Test Match. He captained Australia at home in 1891–92, and also in England in 1893. He may have found the responsibility excessive: in the dressing-room he would stride up and down, hands clenched and chin on chest, but there was no sign of nerves out in the field. Modern stumpers would criticize the stance shown in some photographs, with feet splayed out, but he remains a memorable figure.

G. D. MARTINEAU

CAREER FIGURES

	INNS	NO	RUNS	HS	AVGE	100S
Batting	442	61	6398	109	16·79	1

Bowling 2 wkts at 69·00 W/k: ct 272; st 179 Total 451

Test Record (35)

	INNS	NO	RUNS	HS	AVGE	100S
Batting	62	11	800	74	15·68	–

W/k: ct 36; st 24 Total 60

BLAND, Kenneth Colin (1938–)

Pretoria Boys HS. Rhodesia 1956–57, 1968–69, Eastern Province 1969–70, 1970–71. Orange Free State 1972–73, 1973–74. South Africa: in South Africa 1961–62, 1964–65, 1966–67; in England 1965; in Australia 1963–64; in New Zealand 1963–64.

Few players have been so brilliant in the field that they drew spectators especially to see them; Colin Bland was such a cricketer. A Rhodesian, Bland built up an impressive batting record for South Africa in 21 Tests over 5 years from 1961, but he is remembered mainly as the 'Golden Eagle' who swooped on many a hapless victim. He reached a peak in England in 1965 with the running out of Ken Barrington and Jim Parks in the First Test at Lord's. Parks was unlucky, the ball passing between his legs to hit the stumps, but Barrington's dismissal was a classic effort. Batting at the Pavilion End, with his score on 91, Barrington played wide of mid-on and called for what seemed a safe single. Bland, running to his left from midwicket and thus having to throw away from his body, hit the stumps side-on. It was the turning point of the tour and the series, which South Africa won 1–0.

Bland saved many runs through his speed and the incredible accuracy of his throwing, which he was sometimes called on to demonstrate to crowds before play. In addition, his mere presence caused batsmen to turn down apparently safe runs for fear that he would perform a miracle. As a batsman he ranked only slightly behind his country's best players. A magnificent driver of the ball and frequent hitter of the straight 6, he played 2 match-saving innings against England – 144 not out after South Africa had followed on against M. J. K. Smith's team in the Second Test at the Wanderers in 1964, and 127 at the Oval in 1965. Bland's career ended tragically at the Wanderers in the First Test against Australia in 1966. His left knee collapsed as he chased a ball to the fence and he crashed into the rails, badly damaging the leg.

TREVOR BISSEKER

CAREER FIGURES

	INNS	NO	RUNS	HS	AVGE	100S
Batting	219	28	7208	197	37·73	13

Bowling 43 wkts at 35·16 Ct 51

Test Record (21)

	INNS	NO	RUNS	HS	AVGE	100S
Batting	39	5	1669	144*	49·08	3

Bowling 2 wkts at 62·50 Ct 10

BLIGH, Hon Ivo Francis Walter (later 8th Earl of Darnley) (1859–1927)

Eton 1876–1877. Cambridge Univ 1878–1881 (Captain 1881). Kent 1877–1883; President 1892, 1902. England: in Australia 1882–83 (Captain). President MCC 1900.

Ivo Bligh was captain of the first side that went to Australia to recover the Ashes; as of the 3 Tests originally arranged he won 2 and lost 1, some hold that he succeeded; as he lost a 4th, which was arranged later, others maintain that he failed. He was primarily a forward player and a fine driver and was a good fielder whether in the deep or at point. His career was terminated by ill-health.

R. L. ARROWSMITH

BLYTHE, Colin (1879–1917)

Kent 1899–1914. England: in England 1905, 1907, 1909; in Australia 1901–02, 1907–08; in South Africa 1905–06, 1909–10.

Colin, or, as he was generally called, 'Charlie' Blythe was, like John Small of Hambledon, devoted to his violin: his left-arm slow bowling reflected the sensitive touch and the sense of rhythm of a musician, and to watch his mastery of flight and spin was an aesthetic experience. The left arm came from behind his back in a long and graceful arc, and his fingers whipped the ball into life whether in the orthodox break from leg or in a late inswerve. He bowled consistently to a full length and could be driven on a true wicket, but given any real help from the pitch he set batsmen a most formidable problem. He got a wicket with the 1st ball he ever bowled for Kent in 1899, and in his 16 seasons took 2,506 wickets for 16·8 each, over 100 in every season except his first and 1901. In 1909 he took 215 wickets for 14 each, and between that year and 1914 he was never below 3rd in the regular English bowling averages, and headed them in the last three. He took 10 or more wickets in a match 70 times, 13 or more wickets 15 times, and bowled unchanged through both completed innings in 5 matches. In 1907 against Northants he took 17 wickets in a single day, all 10 for 30 in the 1st innings, and 7 for 18 in the 2nd.

Colin Blythe: bowler and violinist.

In 19 Test Matches between 1901 and 1909 he took exactly 100 wickets at an average of 18; his 15 for 99 in 38 overs won the match at Leeds which was decisive in the rubber against the strong South African side of 1907. And 2 years later, at Birmingham, when he and Hirst bowled virtually unchanged through the match, he took 11 for 102; on both occasions the strain on his sensitive temperament brought him to the verge of a complete breakdown. Loved and respected by all his colleagues, the death of Blythe in action in France brought widespread sorrow, expressed in the memorial erected by his county club on the Canterbury ground.

H. S. ALTHAM

CAREER FIGURES

	INNS	NO	RUNS	HS	AVGE	100S
Batting	587	137	4440	82*	9·87	–

Bowling 2506 wkts at 16.81 Ct 206

Test Record (19)

	INNS	NO	RUNS	HS	AVGE	100S
Batting	31	12	183	27	9·63	–

Bowling 100 wkts at 18·63 Ct 6

BOOTH, Brian Charles (1933–)

Bathurst HS. New South Wales 1954–55 to 1968–69 (Captain 1965–66 to 1967–68). Australia: in Australia 1962–63 to 1965–66 consecutively (Captain 1965–66); in England 1961, 1964; in West Indies 1965–66; in India 1964–65; in Pakistan 1964–65.

For a while in the early 1960s Brian Booth was about the most successful of Australia's batsmen just as he was certainly the most stylish and, with Harvey and O'Neill, the most enjoyable to watch. A tall, upstanding man with a natural grace of movement, his bat flowed freely through a rigidly vertical plane. Within 3 years he made in Test Matches 5 hundreds – of which he was probably most proud of one at Port of Spain where he and the left-handed R. M. Cowper withstood with stout hearts a torrid onslaught by Hall and (especially) Griffith in a stand of 228 which, temporarily at least, did much to restore Australia's waning spirits.

He was vice-captain to Simpson on the tour to England of 1964, and, deputizing for Simpson, led Australia against England in 1965–66 at Sydney in his 29th and, as it proved, last Test. As it happened England, under M. J. K. Smith, won handsomely, and as they came in from the field after bowling out Australia a second time, Booth was waiting at the dressing-room door to shake his victors' hands one by one. It does not say a great deal perhaps for the spirit that has too often since permeated Anglo-Australian Tests that this little gesture of sportsmanship should have stuck so clearly in one's mind. A schoolmaster by profession, Booth was in all respects an ornament to the game.

E. W. SWANTON

CAREER FIGURES

	INNS	NO	RUNS	HS	AVGE	100S
Batting	283	35	11265	214*	45·42	26

Bowling 16 wkts at 59.75 Ct 116

Test Record (29)

	INNS	NO	RUNS	HS	AVGE	100S
Batting	48	6	1773	169	42·21	5

Bowling 3 wkts at 48·66 Ct 17

BOSANQUET, Bernard James Tindal (1877–1936)

Eton 1896. Oxford Univ 1898–1900. Middlesex 1898–1919. England: in England 1905; in Australia 1903–04.

Bosanquet will always be remembered as the inventor of the googly, still in Australia called 'the Bosie'. A tall, strong man, who threw the hammer for Oxford and was a versatile games-player, he was originally an orthodox fast-medium bowler, but developed the googly playing 'twisty-grab' on the billiard table and tried it at Lord's in 1900, his earliest victim being Coe stumped off a 4-bouncer. Though his length was irregular, he had two great days in Tests, taking 6 for 51 at Sydney and 8 for 107 at Nottingham. After 1905 he abandoned regular county cricket and his career as an effective bowler ceased, but he remained, what he always had been, a fine forcing bat, good on both sides of the wicket, who could produce his best form however short he was of first-class practice. In 1911, on his first appearance for 3 years, he made 103 for the Gentlemen at Scarborough in 75 minutes off, amongst others, Barnes. Sir Pelham Warner rightly called him 'a great and original cricketer'.

R. L. ARROWSMITH

CAREER FIGURES

	INNS	NO	RUNS	HS	AVGE	100S
Batting	382	32	11696	214	33·41	21

Bowling 629 wkts at 23·80 Ct 191

Test Record (7)

	INNS	NO	RUNS	HS	AVGE	100S
Batting	14	3	147	27	13·36	

Bowling 25 wkts at 24·16 Ct 9

Ian Botham: an exciting talent.

BOTHAM, Ian Terrence (1955–)

Buckler's Mead Secondary Modern Sch. Somerset 1974– . England: in England 1977, 1978, 1979; in Australia 1978–79, 1979–80; in India 1979–80; in New Zealand 1977–78.

Ian Botham enjoyed the acclaim of being England's leading all-rounder within 5 years of his first-class debut for Somerset in 1974. Just as eye-catching as his statistical achievements were the strength and enthusiasm which he took into every game; when he was not powering to the crease on his run-up to bowl at a very lively fast-medium, he was crouching aggressively in a close-catching position or, with the bat, swinging strongly through the classic arcs. There were times when his youthful exuberance reduced the efficiency of his play. More than once he started a bouncer war against a batsman who was known to be a suspect hooker; yet his bowling was never quite fast enough to escape unnecessary punishment, nor did the wicket always fall in the end.

But Botham quickly developed the subtleties of the full-length away-swinger and later the in-swinger. Initially, the taking of 5 wickets in a Test match innings became his hallmark. Then in 1978 at Lord's he produced an amazing all-round performance against Pakistan. His 8 for 34 in Pakistan's 2nd innings were the best figures by an England bowler since Jim Laker's 9–37 and 10–53 at Old Trafford in 1956. No England player had ever added a hundred to such a bowling feat, but Ian Botham scored 108 in the 1st innings of the same match, his 2nd hundred in successive Test innings. By the beginning of 1980 he had taken 5 wickets in an innings no fewer than 14 times in his first 25 Test Matches, and made a hundred against a full Australian side at Melbourne, and surpassed his all-round performance against Pakistan at Lord's with an innings of 114 and 13 wickets for 106 runs in the same match against India at Bombay. All of which he did by demonstrating the finest attacking qualities of youth. No one, either during or immediately after the rival attraction of WSC, when many Test players forsook established cricket for contracts with Kerry Packer in Australia, did as much to sustain the appeal of English cricket.

TONY LEWIS

BOYCOTT, Geoffrey (1940–)

Hemsworth GS. Yorkshire 1962– (Captain 1971–1978). Northern Transvaal 1971–72. England: in England 1964–1974 consecutively, 1977, 1978, 1979; in Australia 1965–66, 1970–71, 1978–79, 1979–80; in South Africa 1964–65; in West Indies 1967–68, 1973–74; in New Zealand 1965–66, 1977–78 (Captain); in India 1979–80; in Pakistan 1977–78.

There can never have been a more dedicated cricketer than Geoffrey Boycott. Were his mind not so completely wrapped up in cricket, he might, ironically, have achieved more of the prizes he so covets and which have so far eluded him. Admirable though it may be to be so single-minded, in Boycott's case it could have proved a hindrance to ambition.

As an accumulator of runs he ranks very high. Coming into the Yorkshire side in 1962, when he was 22, he was playing for England within a couple of years, and already, both at home and abroad, compiling, with clinical efficiency, a great stockpile of runs. In 1971, by which time he was launched upon a controversial captaincy of his native Yorkshire, he became the 1st Englishman ever to average 100 runs an innings over a full season. The previous winter, he had been on the point of breaking Walter Hammond's record aggregate for an Australian tour when he suffered a broken wrist. It was impossible not to marvel at his powers of concentration.

Nothing would stop him, it seemed, from passing one milestone after another. But that was not to be. Both his batting and his attitudes became increasingly introspective. Occasionally, in his earlier days, he had shown himself to possess every stroke in the book. His own reason for not airing them more often was that whether for Yorkshire or England he carried the main burden of the batting, and so, very often, he did.

Boycott longed for the England captaincy, but, when he might have had it, Denness, Greig, and then Brearley, were all preferred to him. Such was his disappointment at this that between 1974 and 1977 he could not bring himself to play for England. Everyone was deprived by this, not least Boycott himself, as was shown when, upon returning to Test cricket against Greg Chappell's Australian side, he did so with successive scores of 107, 80 not out and 191. This last innings provided him with his finest hour. It was played at Headingley, before many of his staunchest supporters, and it was his 100th

Geoffrey Boycott: looking for the gap.

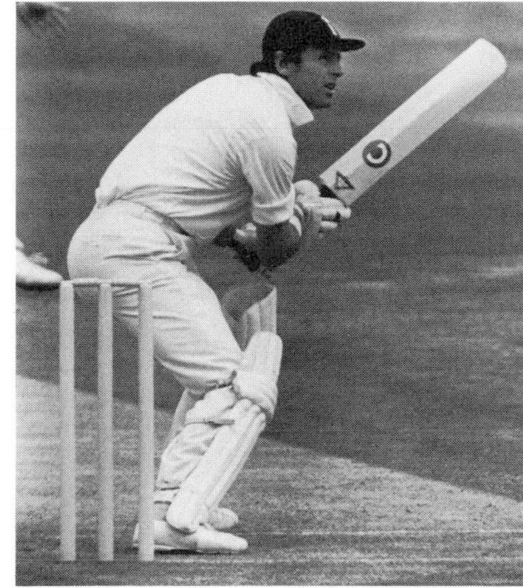

first-class hundred. Sadly, barely a year later he had been ousted from the captaincy of Yorkshire. More happily the second phase of his Test career continued to bring him further personal success, not least in Australia in 1979–80.

Boycott's idea of bliss might be to bat all night (so long as it was not for Mr Packer), having batted all day. Even in the nets his attention to detail never falters. His special glory is the back-foot force, square of the wicket on the off-side. Many cricketers owe him much. He has had his detractors, but his admirers outnumber them. A reliable fielder, an in-swing bowler with some useful victims to his name and a Yorkshireman through and through, Boycott has been one of the most talked-about cricketers of the last 30 years.

JOHN WOODCOCK

BRADMAN, Sir Donald George
(1908–)

Bowral Intermediate HS. New South Wales 1927–28 to 1933–34. South Australia 1935–36 to 1948–49 (Captain 1935–36 to 1947–48). Australia: in Australia 1928–29, 1930–31, 1931–32, 1932–33, 1936–37 (Captain), 1946–47 (Captain), 1947–48 (Captain); in England 1930, 1934, 1938 (Captain), 1948 (Captain). Selector 1936–71 (except 1952 and 1953). Chairman Australian Board of Control. Knighted 1949.

Bradman's birthplace, on 27 August 1908, was Cootamundra, New South Wales, but from the age of 2 his boyhood was spent in Bowral, some 80 miles from Sydney. There he revealed precocious skill in games and athletics and through the elaborate organization of Australian sport he was filtered into Grade and State cricket.

His 1st Sheffield Shield match, for New South Wales in 1927, brought him a score of 118. Through the remainder of his first-class career, extending over 21 years, he was to average a hundred for every 3 innings he played, creating standards of performance beyond earlier contemplation. At the time of his retirement in 1948 he had made 117 centuries, 29 of them in Test matches. His highest score was 452 not out, he had played 6 innings of over 300 runs and 37 of over 200.

Bradman's 1st Test match was a chastening experience, but 20-year-old Australians of his resolution and ability are only deflected, not deterred, and on restoration to the national team for the Third Test of the 1928–29 series he established his position with a century. Australian selectors never doubted again.

Don Bradman as a prodigy on his first tour of England.

Reputation preceded him to England for the tour of 1930, but his warmest admirers could not have contemplated the success that garlanded his way. The programme began at Worcester, where Bradman scored 236; at its end his aggregate was 2,960 and his average 98·66. In the Headingley Test, batting at No. 3, he was 309 not out at the end of the 1st day and he reached 334 before dismissal on the 2nd morning. In the Lord's Test his score was 254, at the Oval 252.

From 1930 to his retirement in 1948, after a 4th tour of England, Bradman dominated the batting of the world. After a 2nd tour of England no less impressive than the 1st, though beset by injury and ending in dangerous illness, he became Australia's captain and never lost a rubber. In leadership he displayed the same shrewd judgment, the same unflagging concentration, the same flexible resolve that were characteristics of his own contributions at the crease. By its very efficiency Bradman's batsmanship implied a ruthless self-containment, but his batting was never coldly mechanical in the sense of lacking co-operative purpose. His great scores were invariably compiled to fit the framework of the match and attuned to the circumstances of the occasion.

A keen eye and exceptional powers of co-ordination gave him the initial advantage in his command over all types of bowling. His inspiration was confidence in his own ability. Only on the untrustworthy pitch was he prepared to concede equal rights for bowlers. Beneath the calculated devastation lay a rich seam of creative batsmanship, vigorous in execution, astonishing in certainty. The timing of on-drive, cut and hook caught the breath in wonder and the footwork dazzled.

The pinnacle Bradman attained was bound to be lonely. As a public figure of immense significance he could scarcely hope for existence as a private person. In cricket and in business he lived in limelight. After playing retirement he undertook administrative responsibility, becoming a selector and a powerful influence in cricket politics. He thought shrewdly, wrote convincingly and spoke fluently, justifying all the implications of knighthood for services rendered to cricket.

J. M. KILBURN

CAREER FIGURES

	INNS	NO	RUNS	HS	AVGE	100S
Batting	338	43	28067	452*	95·14	117

Bowling 36 wkts at 37·97 Ct (including w/k) 131; st 1 Total 132

Test Record (52)

	INNS	NO	RUNS	HS	AVGE	100S
Batting	80	10	6996	334	99·94	29

Bowling 2 wkts at 36·00 Ct 32

BRAUND, Leonard Charles (1875–1955)

Surrey 1896–1898. Somerset 1899–1920. England: in England 1902, 1907; in Australia 1901–02, 1903–04, 1907–08.

'Len' Braund was one of the great all-round cricketers in a great period of English cricket. Surprisingly discarded by Surrey, he threw in his lot with Somerset, and whilst qualifying for them in 1899 played innings of 125 (for W. G. Grace's XI) and 82 (for Somerset) against the Australians. Few cricketers can have established themselves with such early decision as he did in his first 3 regular seasons (1901, 1902 and 1903) in which he made – in all first-class games – 4,444 runs and took 426 wickets. Of these 1902 was the highlight, when he took 172 wickets, and made 141 for the Players against the Gentlemen at Lord's. No one then had more cause to respect him than Yorkshire, champions though they were at that time expected to be as if by prescriptive right. In 1901 he took 10 wickets against them at Taunton, and at Leeds, when his county went in 238 behind, his 107 and 4 for 41 carried them to one of the most astonishing victories of the year. In 1902 his 15 wickets for 71 demolished the champions at Sheffield, and next year he took 10 wickets at Taunton, again to confound every layer of odds. He played in 20 Tests against Australia and in 3 against South Africa, scoring hundreds at Adelaide and Sydney in the 1901–02 and 1903–04 tours respectively, and another at Lord's against South Africa in 1907.

Lithe and athletic, cheerful but determined, Len Braund was an outstanding figure in Somerset's predominantly amateur, colourful and incalculable side, and in an era of all-round players he was in the very top rank. Sound in defence and an attractive stroke-player, he welcomed a challenge; he bowled his leg-breaks rather faster than most, was sometimes expensive, but on his day combined accuracy and stamina with formidable turn and lift; he was a slip-fielder of the very highest class. A later generation will recall him as an umpire and a coach, and surely not least in his closing years as he sat watching a Test Match from his wheelchair beside the pavilion at Lord's – he had lost both his legs – still indomitably cheerful, happy to remember and talk about the past, but generous in his appreciation of the players who had succeeded him.

H. S. ALTHAM

CAREER FIGURES

	INNS	NO	RUNS	HS	AVGE	100S
Batting	752	57	17801	257*	25·61	25

Bowling 1113 wkts at 27·30 Ct 547

Test Record (23)

	INNS	NO	RUNS	HS	AVGE	100S
Batting	41	3	987	104	25·97	3

Bowling 47 wkts at 38·51 Ct 39

BREARLEY, John Michael, OBE
(1942–)

City of London Sch 1956–1960 (Captain 1959–1960). Cambridge Univ 1961–1964 (Captain 1963–1964). Middlesex 1961– (Captain 1971–). England: in England 1976, 1977 (Captain), 1978 (Captain), 1979 (Captain); in Australia 1976–77, 1978–79 (Captain), 1979–80 (Captain); in India 1976–77, 1979–80 (Captain); in Pakistan 1977–78 (Captain).

The story of Mike Brearley's cricket career explodes several popular fallacies. To have led successively his university, county and country is not, of course, unique, though, over the century of Test cricket the triple

Mike Brearley: distinctive stance and wearing one of the early helmets. Note the hands far apart, not according to the text-book.

honour has rarely been achieved: N. W. D. Yardley, M. C. Cowdrey, E. R. Dexter, M. J. K. Smith and A. R. Lewis are the only other men to qualify over an English Test Series – unless you add H. D. G. Leveson Gower whose pre-First World War MCC Team to South Africa was far from being representative. To have led Oxford or Cambridge in these specialist days and also achieved high academic distinction is at least extremely unusual. Brearley emphasized the point by taking a 1st in Classics and a good 2nd in Moral Sciences, scoring in his 4 years more runs (4,310) than have ever been made for Cambridge, before or since.

After touring with scant success with MCC in South Africa in 1964–65, he played little first-class cricket for five years; though he gave an inkling of his capability as a leader during this period by taking an MCC under-25 side to Pakistan in 1966–67 and scooping all the honours both on the field and off.

The challenge of leading a county team when the chance came with Middlesex in 1971 appealed to the psychologist in him, and though success after an undistinguished period did not come at once his side reached both the knock-out finals at Lord's in 1975, won the Championship in 1976, and in 1977 took both the Gillette Cup and a half-share in the Championship. Coincidentally with these things he began to be thought of, in his middle thirties, as the batsman close to the England XI who had first aroused such hopes 10 years earlier. Graduating as vice-captain to Greig on the Indian tour of 1976–77, he was appointed England captain in 1977 when the extent of Greig's involvement with Kerry Packer became known.

This last phase of an unusual story contains the most important contradiction of accepted theories in that he retained the job over many Test Matches, though in purely cricket terms he has been barely worth his place. It says much for his character that at critical moments he has gritted his teeth and come up with a valuable innings, to save both the selectors' faces and his own.

It has never been exactly the case that a candidate for the captaincy of England must first be an automatic member of the side. The fact is that in these post-amateur days, with more and more depending on the result (not least in financial terms to the players), the demands on leadership are greater than ever. Human as well as tactical understanding is called for, the ability to communicate with all concerned and especially with one's own side.

In two books written in company with an able games-journalist, strangely enough American by birth, Dudley Doust, Brearley has given us a privileged glimpse into the dressing-rooms of the late 1970s. He grasped his chance of power with mature assurance, and led an England side deficient in batting class but adequate in bowling to 15 victories in his first 6 Test Series. The technical key lay in a general fielding excellence which in the memory of the oldest and crustiest has never been equalled.

E. W. SWANTON

BRIGGS, John (1862–1902)

Queen Mary GS, Walsall. Lancashire 1879–1900. England: in England 1886, 1888, 1893, 1896, 1899; in Australia 1884–85, 1886–87, 1887–88, 1891–92, 1894–95, 1897–98; in South Africa 1888–89.

'Johnny' Briggs, one of the finest all-rounders of his day, was dogged by ill health for most of his short life, being subject to epilepsy. A little man, full of quips and resilient as a rubber ball, he was tried for Lancashire at 16, scored his 1st hundred 4 years later, and, on his 1st visit to Australia in 1884, made 121 in the First Test at Melbourne. The following summer, his left-handed, slow-medium bowling – with two skips and a bound – came into its own. As his bowling advanced, his batting – apt to suffer from injudicious slashes – appeared to decline. In the Second Test, at Lord's, in 1886, his 11 wickets for 74, together with a great innings by Shrewsbury, achieved an innings victory, and he had 6 for 58 at the Oval. In 1888, he took 160 wickets (average 10), 12 being against Australia, and, with Aubrey Smith's side in South Africa the following winter, he achieved a slaughter, taking, at Cape Town, 7 for 17 and 8 for 11. On his 4th tour to Australia, in 1891–92, he did the hat-trick at Adelaide, sealing belated victory with 12 for 136. He won the Oval Test of 1893 with 10 wickets for 148. His final trip to Australia (1897–98) proved him no longer the bowler he had been, and, on his last appearance for England at Leeds, in 1899, his life-long enemy struck him down.

A brave return to the Lancashire team seemed to show that he could bowl as well as ever, but it was the last fling, and he died at 39. He was a sad loss, both as a cricketer and a personality, a man with a clownish sense of fun who once answered 'Monkey' Hornby's charge of insobriety by an exhibition of bicycle trick-riding; a rare cricketing character as well as a bowler of genius.

G. D. MARTINEAU

CAREER FIGURES

	INNS	NO	RUNS	HS	AVGE	100S
Batting	821	54	14002	186	18·25	10

Bowling 2212 wkts at 15·95 Ct 259

Test Record (33)

	INNS	NO	RUNS	HS	AVGE	100S
Batting	50	5	815	121	18·11	1

Bowling 118 wkts at 17·74 Ct 12

BROWN, David John (1942–)

Warwickshire 1961– (Captain 1975–1977). England: in England 1965–1970; in Australia 1965–66; in West Indies 1967–68; in New Zealand 1965–66; in Pakistan 1968–69.

David Brown was an important member of the Warwickshire team for almost two decades, from his debut in 1961. Born in Walsall, he quickly became one of the most respected fast-medium bowlers in the country and it was no coincidence that he was at the peak of his powers when Warwickshire enjoyed the most successful period in their history, which included the County Championship once and the Gillette Cup twice.

Though not an out-and-out fast bowler, Brown's control and movement made him a force in English conditions; on days when batsmen reigned, his big-hearted approach to the job set a fine example to his team-mates. He first appeared for England in 1964 and in 1968 achieved his best Test match bowling figures of 5 for 42 against Australia at Lord's.

His stamina and willingness to work were also qualities which made him an invaluable tourist. Towards the end of his career, injury began to reduce his effectiveness, but he captained the county with a degree of success and, as a dignified and approachable cricketer, was always mindful of the game at large.

To this end, he was an ideal choice to succeed Peter Walker as Chairman of the Cricketers' Association. His benefit, in 1973, was more than twice as big as any other for a Warwickshire player, an indication of the esteem he enjoyed within the county and elsewhere.

MICHAEL CAREY

Freddie Brown leading out his MCC side up-country, Australia 1950–51.

BROWN, Frederick Richard, MBE (1910–)

Leys Sch 1926–1929 (Captain 1928–1929). Cambridge Univ 1930–1931. Surrey 1931–1948. Northamptonshire 1949–1953 (Captain). England: in England 1931, 1932, 1937, 1949 (Captain), 1950 (Captain), 1951 (Captain), 1953; in Australia 1932–33, 1950–51 (Captain); in New Zealand 1932–33, 1950–51 (Captain). Selector 1951–1953 (Chairman 1953). Manager MCC in South Africa

1956–57; in Australia and New Zealand 1958–59. President MCC 1971–1972. Chairman Cricket Council 1974–79. Chairman National Cricket Association 1977– .

Freddie Brown enjoyed every minute of his two astonishing cricket careers. He had no time for those who did not give the game everything they had to give. To him cricket was the greatest challenge in the world and what fun he made it. He was primarily a leg-spin bowler, slightly quicker than average, but he was also a tremendous hitter of the ball who delighted in using the open spaces behind the bowler. He was, as well, a wonderfully active and nimble fielder for a man of such powerful build.

Brown was born in Lima, Peru. In his prep-school days he came under the influence of Aubrey Faulkner, who persuaded him to bowl leg-breaks and googlies. From the Leys School he got into the Cambridge side as a freshman, and within three years of leaving school he played for Surrey and England and gained selection to tour Australia with D. R. Jardine's MCC side. Although he did not play in any of the Tests he was to represent England 6 times before the Second World War. Brown had a tough war and was captured at Tobruk. He returned 4½ stone lighter with little thought of playing Test cricket again. In 1949 he took over the captaincy of Northamptonshire and gave that county's cricket a shot in the arm. His second cricket career had begun. In the same season England twice made him their captain against New Zealand but few considered him a likely candidate for the Australian tour in 1950–51. A superb hard-hit century in the Gentlemen v Players match of 1950 altered that and in his 40th year he set off as the leader of the side to Australia.

By his heroic personal example he blended his team into a force to be reckoned with. He bowled at medium-pace with great success and played some fine innings. His inspiration brought victory at last to England in the Fifth Test Match at Melbourne. There has never been a more popular captain with the Australians. To them he was a veritable John Bull with his fine physique, his pipe and an ever cheerful countenance. Before he left the country an Australian vendor of lettuces was offering his wares with 'hearts as big as Freddie Brown's'. He captained England again in the home series against South Africa in 1951 and played against Australia once more in 1953.

He took MCC teams to South Africa and Australia as manager in addition to managing private tours to East Africa. As President of MCC in 1971–1972, and Chairman of the Cricket Council and the National Cricket Association, Freddie Brown has continued to give to the game much of the vigour and enjoyment and forthrightness he displayed as a player.

E. D. R. EAGAR

CAREER FIGURES

	INNS	NO	RUNS	HS	AVGE	100S
Batting	534	49	13303	212	27·43	22

Bowling 1219 wkts at 26·19 Ct 208

Test Record (22)

	INNS	NO	RUNS	HS	AVGE	100S
Batting	30	1	734	79	25·31	

Bowling 45 wkts at 31·06 Ct 22

BULLER, John Sidney, MBE (1909–1970)

Yorkshire 1930. Worcestershire 1935–1946. First-class Umpire 1951–1970; Test Umpire 1956–1970.

Apprenticed to Yorkshire, Sid Buller moved to Worcestershire where he soon established himself as the regular wicket-keeper until the war intervened. He played a full season in 1946 and after 4 years as official coach he turned his hand to umpiring. Given his first Test Match in 1956, he was to stand in 33 Tests, and together with his colleague C. S. Elliott did much to lift the standard and status of umpires. He will be remembered for his readiness to take on unpleasant tasks, as in the case of having to call the South African fast bowler, Griffin, for throwing in the Lord's Test in 1960. He played his part quietly and unobtrusively, yet he was fearless in speaking out whenever he saw the spirit of the game offended. He was awarded the MBE in 1965 and a Winston Churchill Travelling Fellowship to tour Australia, a fitting reward for a lifetime of service to the game. In his later years, he was increasingly beset with ill health. Standing in a match at Edgbaston between Warwickshire and Nottinghamshire, during a hold up for rain, he collapsed and died. It was a tragic loss to the game for he was still in harness and the senior member of the Test Match panel of umpires.

COLIN COWDREY

CAREER FIGURES

	INNS	NO	RUNS	HS	AVGE	100S
Batting	171	44	1746	64	13·75	

W/k: ct 175; st 59 Total 234

BURGE, Peter John Parnell (1932–)

Brisbane GS. Queensland 1952–53 to 1967–68 (Captain 1960–61 to 1967–68). Australia: in Australia 1954–55, 1958–59, 1960–61, 1962–63, 1963–64, 1965–66; in England 1956, 1961, 1964; in South Africa 1957–58; in West Indies 1954–55; in India 1956–57, 1959–60, 1964–65; in Pakistan 1959–60, 1964–65.

Peter Burge, a tall, strong, right-handed batsman with an ideal temperament, was a singularly tough Australian batsman. A surprise selection at a young age, he toured West Indies in 1955, with his father as manager of the team. He came first to England in 1956, but it was not until 1961 that he became a fully established top-class Test player. At Lord's, when Australia needed only 69 for victory, Burge came to the wicket with the score 19 for 4, and Statham and Trueman at their best. Burge's onslaught at a tense moment won the day. It was a typical Burge innings (of 181) at the Oval in 1961 which destroyed England's chance of winning. A big run-getter for Queensland, his highest score was 283 against New South Wales in 1963–64. In England in 1964 he scored 160 at Headingley, which turned the match and gave Australia the victory needed to keep the Ashes. Strong in defence, he was at his best attacking the bowling, when, unlike most Australian batsmen, he preferred to play off the front foot.

COLIN COWDREY

CAREER FIGURES

	INNS	NO	RUNS	HS	AVGE	100S
Batting	354	46	14640	283	47·68	38

Bowling 1 for 129 Ct (incl w/k) 166; st 4 Total 170

Test Record (42)

	INNS	NO	RUNS	HS	AVGE	100S
Batting	68	8	2290	181	38·16	4

Ct 23

BURGESS, Mark Gordon (1944–)

Auckland GS. Auckland 1966–67– . New Zealand: in New Zealand 1967–68, 1968–69, 1970–71, 1972–73, 1973–74, 1975–76, 1976–77, 1977–78, (Captain), 1978–79 (Captain); in England 1969, 1973, 1978 (Captain); in West Indies 1971–72; in India 1969–70, 1976–77; in India 1969–70, 1976–77; in Pakistan 1969–70, 1976–77.

Mark Burgess has the distinction of having represented his country at both cricket and association football. His greatest day was 15 February 1978, when he left the Basin Reserve at Wellington at the head of the 1st New Zealand team ever to have beaten England in a full Test. It was the peak of a distinguished career. He had shown much promise at Auckland Grammar School and the game was in his blood. His father, G. C. Burgess, was an Auckland player, a noted national administrator, and manager of the 1969 New Zealand to England, India and Pakistan.

Burgess has delighted spectators at home and abroad with his free and fluent batting. His contribution to New Zealand cricket has been immense. The first of his 5 Test hundreds was memorable. In 1969 New Zealand went to Dacca for the final Test against Pakistan one up. But with nearly 5 hours left of the last day, New Zealand, 8 wickets down, led by only 84. Then Burgess, partnered by R. S. Cunis, launched a brilliant assault. They stayed together for 2 hours for 96 runs, to save the match and give New Zealand its first Test rubber. A swift and strong fieldsman in front of the wicket for many years, Burgess was a popular captain, and as an attacking batsman a warm favourite with New Zealand crowds.

R. T. BRITTENDEN

Mark Burgess: New Zealand's captain when they first beat England.

CALTHORPE, Hon Frederick Somerset Gough (1892–1935)

Repton 1909–1911. Cambridge Univ. 1912–1914, 1919. Sussex 1911–1912. Warwickshire 1919–1930 (Captain 1920–1929). England: in West Indies 1929–30 (Captain).

'Freddy' Calthorpe, a man with an attractive and happy nature, played cricket in tune with his character. A free-scoring batsman and fine medium-paced bowler, he won a blue as a freshman from Repton. He was still in France with the RAF when an invitation to captain Cambridge failed to reach him. He came back to play for Cambridge again, however, and then joined Warwickshire, being appointed captain in 1920. He promptly accomplished the double. In the winter of 1922–23 he toured Australia and New Zealand under MacLaren. He took 54 wickets, hitting 110 against New South Wales, and taking 6 wickets for 53 in the last New Zealand match. For the next 2 seasons he virtually led his county's batting, and it was now that he became peculiarly associated with the Folkestone Festival. In 1925–26 he captained MCC in the West Indies, though without achieving anything particular himself. He took another MCC team to the West Indies in 1929–30 before handing over the captaincy of Warwickshire to R. E. S. Wyatt. He played little first-class cricket afterwards; he was already far from well, but his death at 43 was a sad blow. Memory sees him in a Faulkner Cricket School net, seeking to mend his faults: a good-length ball on the off was slammed towards cover, but with Calthorpe's ringing laugh recognizing that bat and foot had been far apart, Aubrey Faulkner just turned away with a smile.

G. D. MARTINEAU

CAREER FIGURES

	INNS	NO	RUNS	HS	AVGE	100S
Batting	576	52	12596	209	24·03	13

Bowling 782 wkts at 29·90 Ct 214

Test Record (4)

	INNS	NO	RUNS	HS	AVGE	100S
Batting	7	0	129	49	18·42	

Bowling 1 wkt for 91 Ct 3

CAMERON, Horace Brakenridge (1905–1935)

Hilton, Natal and Jeppe HS, Johannesburg. Transvaal 1924–25 South Africa: in South Africa 1927–28, 1930–31; in England 1929, 1935; in Australia 1931–32 (Captain); in New Zealand 1931–32 (Captain).

'Jock' Cameron kept wicket for South Africa from 1927 until shortly before his death in 1935. During this time England had an outstanding wicket-keeper/batsman in Ames, and Australia another in Oldfield; which was the leader of this trio is largely a matter of opinion, but Cameron's claims would find a large body of supporters amongst contemporary players. Cameron learnt his craft on the matting wickets of South Africa which, despite their advantage of consistency, presented problems of their own. On them he was particularly adept in taking the fastish, sharply-turning off-breaks of Nupen, a very awkward bowler seen from behind the stumps. A man of quiet but noticeably determined character, his form was as consistent as the pitches upon which he was bred. The writer cannot recall any day or match when he relaxed, or dropped below his habitual high standard. Cameron was a sound, stalwart batsman who, in the middle of the order, could readily adapt his tactics to the needs of the situation. His moments of aggression were spectacular, as when he hit Verity for 30 in one over at Sheffield in 1935.

At Lord's in 1929 he received a tremendous blow on the head from a ball bowled by Larwood which rose unexpectedly from a good length. His nerve was apparently unaffected by this catastrophe but its effects were possibly more lasting than he would admit. He died in 1935 at the early age of 30, but his place is assured and high amongst the number of exceptional wicket-keeping batsmen South Africa has produced.

IAN PEEBLES

CAREER FIGURES

	INNS	NO	RUNS	HS	AVGE	100S
Batting	161	17	5396	182	37·47	11

Bowling 0–13 W/k: ct 155; st 69 Total 224

Test Record (26)

	INNS	NO	RUNS	HS	AVGE	100S
Batting	45	4	1239	90	30·21	

W/k: ct 39; st 12 Total 51

CARDUS, Sir Neville, CBE (1889–1975)

The lasting achievement of Neville Cardus is that, in company with Bernard Darwin, he made writing about sport into a popular art. For many who have never entered a cricket-ground, cricket and Cardus are synonymous. He even managed to be born in a street called Summer Place, in the Manchester suburb of Rusholme. Poor and self-educated, he played street cricket and saved pocket-money to go to Old Trafford. He had several menial jobs before becoming assistant cricket coach at Shrewsbury School in 1912. In 1916 he became secretary to C. P. Scott, editor of the *Manchester Guardian*, and a year later joined the paper as a reporter, serving it, apart from the 1939–47 period in Australia, until the day of his death.

After an illness in 1919 he was sent, as part of his recuperation, to report Lancashire's matches. Abandoning the stereotyped sports-reporter's jargon, he wrote, under the pseudonym 'Cricketer', what were in effect stylish essays, illuminated by telling and memorable phrases, on what he saw, even on what he did not see. Within 3 years Grant Richards had published a selection of Cardus's writings (*A Cricketer's Book*) and over the next 20 years others followed, all now regarded as classics: *Days in the Sun, The Summer Game, Good Days* and *Australian Summer*. The frequent occurrence of musical metaphors and similes in these writings – of which in later years, when his style became sparer and flavoured with irony, he pretended to be rather ashamed as his 'purple period' – betrayed his other passion and occupation. He was a sensitive music critic, but only one of many; it was as a writer on cricket – relishing its humour, drama and humanity – that he achieved greatness (and I shall be in trouble in the Elysian Fields for that judgment). He took full advantage of the gallery of characters in Lancashire and Yorkshire cricket between the wars and in doing so has been accused of sometimes wandering from the strict path of truth. He did not deny the charge. About remarks attributed to such as Dick Tyldesley he said: 'To realize the truth of his Lancashire nature and being, it simply *had* to be said. Whether he himself said it, or whether I put the words into his mouth for him, matters nothing . . .' In the process he immortalized these players and probably himself. The flavour of Cardus the man is there for posterity in his autobiographies.

Something of the music-halls he loved lingered about him. In boyhood he was stage-struck with the idea of being a famous writer; he achieved his ambition and remained slightly surprised that he was paid for enjoying himself. He was a wonderful talker. Holding court behind the Warner Stand at Lord's or at the Garrick Club, he flowed on – and woe betide the apostate interrupter: a bony forefinger would warningly probe the offender's lapel. He was a romantic, in life as in prose: he was made CBE in 1964 and knighted in 1967, but the honour he cherished most was having been President of Lancashire County Cricket Club at Old Trafford in 1970–1971, 70 years after he had paid sixpence to sit on a hard bench and begin a lifetime's hero-worship of A. C. MacLaren.

MICHAEL KENNEDY

CARR, Arthur William (1893–1963)

Eton. Sherborne 1909–1911. Nottinghamshire 1910–1934 (Captain 1919–1934). England in England 1926 (Captain), 1929 (Captain); in South Africa 1922–23. Selector 1928.

Carr was a fine, attacking batsman, a splendid field near the wicket and a strong and inspiring, if provocative, captain. In 1925, his best season, he must surely, had there been Tests, have been picked, whether captain or not. Tate was then the greatest bowler in the world. Carr averaged 61 against him for 9 innings, which included 104 in 2 hours and 124 in 70 minutes. Altogether that year he made 2,338 runs with an average of 51·95. There have been few fiercer straight-drivers, especially off the quicker bowlers. Aggression was indeed the keynote to his character. He was the centre of many rows, only some of which ever reached the papers. In 1926 he was jettisoned from the captaincy for the last Test almost exactly as Chapman was 4 years later. Yet difficult though he could be, he had many devoted friends, not least among the Notts pros, and it was his uncompromising but not always wise support of Larwood in the Body-line controversy that brought his career to a premature close.

R. L. ARROWSMITH

CAREER FIGURES

	INNS	NO	RUNS	HS	AVGE	100S
Batting	709	42	21051	206	31·61	45

Bowling 31 wkts at 37·10 Ct (incl w/k) 393; st 1

Test Record (11)

	INNS	NO	RUNS	HS	AVGE	100S
Batting	13	1	237	63	19·75	

Ct 3

CARR, Donald Bryce (1926–)

Repton 1942–1944 (Captain 1944). Oxford Univ 1949–1951 (Captain 1950). Derbyshire 1946–1963 (Captain 1955–1962). England: in India 1951–52 (Captain). Manager MCC in South Africa 1964–65; in India and Pakistan 1972–73; in West Indies 1973–74. Assistant Secretary MCC 1962–73. Secretary TCCB 1973– . Secretary Cricket Council 1974– .

Donald Carr made his debut in first-class cricket the year after he left school, in the 'Victory Test Match' against Australia at Lord's in 1945. After completing his National Service he failed to get a blue as a freshman but played in the University Match in the following 3 years. He became assistant secretary to Derbyshire in 1953 and secretary in 1960. He captained Oxford in 1950 and was elected captain of Derbyshire in 1955, which post he held until his appointment as assistant secretary of MCC in September 1962. Donald Carr was a fine batsman, particularly strong on the on-side. A good hooker of the ball, he was at his best against fast bowling. In 1959 he set up a Derbyshire record by scoring 2,292 runs in the season. In 1951–52 he was vice-captain of the MCC side in India and Pakistan. He played 2 Test Matches in India and captained England in the Fifth Test Match. He also captained the MCC 'A' side in Pakistan in 1955–56.

After moving to the secretariat at Lord's he managed the full MCC side to South Africa in 1964–65, India, Sri Lanka and Pakistan in 1972–73 and West Indies in 1973–74. In 1968 he became the first secretary of the newly formed Test and County Cricket Board. Carr was a great close-to-the-wicket fielder, a splendid captain and as captain and manager he commanded both loyalty and affection.

E. D. R. EAGAR

CAREER FIGURES

	INNS	NO	RUNS	HS	AVGE	100S
Batting	745	72	19257	170	28·61	24

Bowling 328 wkts at 34·74 Ct 501

Test Record (2)

	INNS	NO	RUNS	HS	AVGE	100S
Batting	4	0	135	76	33·75	

Bowling 2 wkts at 70·00

CHALLENOR, George (1888–1947)

Barbados 1905–1930. West Indies: in England 1928.

Challenor in the 1923 West Indies tour to England made 1,556 runs and was 3rd, to Hendren and Mead, in the English averages. Some English players will remember the batsman who for nearly 20 years regularly welcomed them with the same brilliant hundred. Not only was he unmistakably in the same class as the 'Three Ws' (one cannot reasonably say less, or more); he was the originator of the great tradition of Barbados, that is to say of West Indian, batting. At 18 he visited England with the 1906 team and returned to Barbados to become a superb example of the Golden Age. His strokemaking dazzled in 1923. Not accidentally. Nowhere in the world of those days was more brilliant batting practised than in Barbados around the First World War. An MCC team to the West Indies included Razor Smith, Humphreys, A. E. Relf and S. G. Smith; Challenor scored 118 and 109. In 1920 in 2 successive club finals Challenor made 261, and 204 and 133. Bets would be laid as to whether he would hit the 1st ball for 6. In 1926 for All-West Indies v MCC in British Guiana he hit Root for 6 over cover's head in the 1st over. No bowling ever bothered him. He had all the strokes, but he was essentially an off-side batsman. He did not hook but to the short fast ball he moved back and away and slashed, sometimes over the head of point or cover. He came to England again with the 1928 team, but bowlers had then developed the ball that began on the wicket and ended outside the leg-stump. Challenor was 40 and did not have the youthful energy to develop a new attack.

Yet he had already done enough to establish a tradition which lasts to this day. One of George Headley's most significant memories is of Challenor playing one of his last innings for Barbados in 1930, and demonstrating to Derek Sealy (then a boy of 18), batting at the other end, how to play Voce and Rhodes on a wet wicket. Sealy went on to become one of the great batsmen of the West Indies. As a master of Combermere School he influenced Frank Worrell, and Worrell more than any other player shaped the approach of modern West Indies batsmen. The history of West Indies maturity is unintelligible unless it begins with the batting of George Challenor.

C. L. R. JAMES

CAREER FIGURES

	INNS	NO	RUNS	HS	AVGE	100S
Batting	160	9	5822	237*	38·55	15

Bowling 54 wkts at 28·87

Test Record (3)

	INNS	NO	RUNS	HS	AVGE	100S
Batting	6	0	101	46	16·83	

'Chandra': spinner of genius, who numbered polio among his conquests.

CHANDRASEKHAR, Bhagwat Subramanya (1945–)

Bangapore Nat HS. India: in India 1963–64, 1964–65, 1966–67, 1972–73, 1974–75, 1976–77, 1978–79; in England 1967, 1971, 1974, 1979; in Australia 1967–68, 1977–78; in West Indies 1975–76; in New Zealand 1975–76; in Pakistan 1978–79.

Bhagwat Chandrasekhar is often referred to as India's freak bowler, a term which 'Chandra' resents. The only freak thing about him has been the ups and downs that he has suffered, though he was always regarded as an integral part of India's supreme 3-man spin attack. Yet, either through injury or his own failings, he was never a certainty for inclusion until the summer of 1971 when he destroyed England in an inspired spell between lunch and tea to finish with 6 for 38. It was a performance as devastating as the 7 for 157 in 1964 against Bobby Simpson's team on a true wicket at Brabourne stadium.

Chandra's long, flapping, polio-affected bowling arm has enabled him to whip the ball away at medium pace, with a googly as the master ball. His figures speak for themselves. There is a strange ambivalence about his bowling. He could be 0 for 70 at lunch, and yet finish the day with a major haul, to the delight of his captain and followers. With a stronger batting side, Chandra might have enjoyed the permanency in the Indian team which he truly deserved. A likeable character, he is apt to hum a film song as he runs up to bowl.

K. N. PRABHU

CHAPMAN, Arthur Percy Frank (1900–1961)

Oakham 1914. Uppingham 1916–1919 (Captain 1918–1919). Cambridge Univ 1920–1922. Kent 1924–1938 (Captain 1931–1936). England: in England 1924, 1926 (Captain), 1928 (Captain), 1930 (Captain); in Australia 1924–25, 1928–29 (Captain); in South Africa 1930–31 (Captain).

If the cricket world had the taste of the prize-ring for flamboyant titles Percy Chapman might well have been known as the 'Golden Boy' of the post-First-War decade. A remarkable schoolboy cricketer at Uppingham, he got his blue as a freshman at Cambridge, succeeded brilliantly for Kent, and toured Australia with A. E. R. Gilligan in 1924–25. In 1926 he deposed A. W. Carr as captain of England at the Oval in the final and decisive Test Match in which he regained the Ashes after a lengthy run of Australian supremacy. There followed an overwhelming triumph in the series of 1928–29, at which point Chapman's prestige as a captain of England stood higher than that of any predecessor. The home series of 1930 brought the first portents of decline. Although he batted with considerable success his tactics met with the selectors' disapproval and he was, in turn, replaced by R. E. S. Wyatt as captain. There was a certain irony in the fact that it was again for the crucial Oval Test Match that England once more deposed a reigning captain, and that this time Chapman was destined to fill the role of the dispossessed. He took the MCC side to South Africa in the following autumn, but the era of triumph had in truth ended with the announcement of his replacement in 1930.

No cricketer has been better endowed to fulfil the part he was to play in restoring the confidence and quality of English cricket in the 1920s. Over 6 feet tall, with a mass of curly blond hair, his presence was towering yet cherubic. He radiated a debonair gaiety which immediately captured the imagination of a public yearning for the inspiration of a colourful hero after a period of drab depression in every sporting field. It was noteworthy that, in the less fortunate years ahead, wherever he went he was instantly recognized and applauded by countless of his fellow countrymen, whether followers of cricket or not.

Chapman was a free-hitting left-handed batsman. He loved to loft the ball high into the deep, occasionally with surprising results. The writer recalls a couple of front-footed drives played on matting, aimed at the vicious spin of Nupen, which resulted in 2 towering sixes over third man's head. This extraordinary spectacle was typical of the fresh and original flavour of his play. As a close fielder Chapman was unexcelled. A great reach terminated in 2 enormous hands, the surprising softness of which lent them a prehensile quality. An unusual speed of reflex in so large a man gave him a great span in the gully where he made an almost impassable barrier. As a captain Chapman was not of the subtle or intellectual school of tacticians. He had none the less a shrewd, practical instinct for the game; and he was a leader in whose cheerful wake men followed with a smile. He won or lost with equally good-natured grace.

IAN PEEBLES

CAREER FIGURES

	INNS	NO	RUNS	HS	AVGE	100S
Batting	554	44	16309	260	31·97	27

Bowling 22 wkts at 41·18 Ct 356

Test Record (26)

	INNS	NO	RUNS	HS	AVGE	100S
Batting	36	4	925	121	28·90	1

Bowling 0 wkts for 20 Ct 32

CHAPPELL, Gregory Stephen, MBE (1948–)

Prince Alfred Coll, Adelaide. South Australia 1966–67 to 1972–73. Somerset 1968–1969. Queensland 1973–74 – (Captain). Australia: in Australia 1970–71, 1972–73 to 1976–77 consecutively, 1979–80 (Captain 1975–76, 1976–77, 1979–80); in England 1972, 1975, 1977 (Captain); in West Indies 1972–73; in New Zealand 1973–74, 1976–77 (Captain). WSC.

In addition to being one of the most accomplished batsmen Australia has produced since the Second World War, and some, with reason, would rate him the finest, Greg Chappell is technically the most correct. Everything about him is right – his upright stance, high backlift and full follow-through are copybook and he is an elegant strokemaker with an extensive repertoire of shots. Like all the great players, he has the ability to score runs off good length bowling and to dominate an international attack. On his last England tour, when the problems of captaining a sub-standard team and the Packer situation did not help, he failed to do as well as expected but the gulf between him at the crease and any of his colleagues remained as large as between a club and a good county cricketer. He was able to make batting appear easy, even against what was a formidable England bowling line-up.

Greg Chappell: a natural stance, though apparently covering middle-and-off.

How did Greg compare with his elder brother, Ian? Although Greg had greater ability and style than Ian, many opponents prized Ian's wicket more, because of Ian's character and the fact that he had to be literally blasted out, whereas Greg would occasionally contribute to his own dismissal. The most enchanting of all Greg's strokes is his on-drive off his front foot, which is also one of the most difficult shots to play. A high percentage of his runs are produced by straight-bat shots off either foot, when the ball, although struck on the rise, is still kept on the ground. In addition to ability as an attacking batsman, he possesses a splendidly organized defence. The time he spent with Somerset, combined with his sound technique, allows him to adapt to different conditions with greater ease than most Australians. He is a master batsman and a perfect model.

TREVOR BAILEY

CHAPPELL, Ian Michael (1943–)

Prince Alfred Coll, Adelaide. South Australia 1961–62 to 1975–76 (Captain 1970–71 to 1975–76). Lancashire 1963. Australia: in Australia 1964–65, 1965–66, 1967–68, 1968–69, 1970–71, 1972–73 (Captain), 1973–74 (Captain), 1974–75 (Captain), 1975–76, 1979–80; in England 1968, 1972 (Captain), 1975 (Captain); in South Africa 1966–67, 1969–70; in West Indies 1972–73 (Captain); in New Zealand 1973–74 (Captain); in India 1969–70. WSC.

Any successful captain of a cricketing country occupies a substantial place in the game's story. Of his first 30 Tests, Ian Chappell won 15 and lost only 5; the first 2 when he was thrown in at the deep end by the Australian selectors with only half a side following the dismissal of Bill Lawry at the end of the home series against Ray Illingworth's victorious England team. Chappell needs to be considered as a batsman, as a captain and as an influence in his own generation.

He was born into cricket's purple as the grandson of Victor Richardson, the captain of South Australia and of Australia in the 1930s, a man squeezed out of his position by the recruitment of Don Bradman to Adelaide from Sydney by the then powers of South Australian cricket. Ian Chappell and his two brothers, Greg and Trevor, were born to cricket but it fell to the eldest, Ian, to blaze the trail. Thus there is a ruggedness about his batting which is absent from that of his brother Greg, who on pitches as far apart as Adelaide and Taunton developed that degree of elegance which has earned him his reputation as a giant among batsmen. For many judges, however, Ian has proved the more durable player, an everlasting fighter, a man

Ian Chappell: a great competitor.

less prone to loss of form than his obviously more talented brother. His skill as a leg-spinner was less important in the bits and pieces of his cricket than the example which he set to the Australian close catchers as an adhesive first slip.

In his captaincy he revealed a cricket brain as shrewd as that of his grandfather. Furthermore he became the leader of his own generation of Australian cricketers and held on to that influential role even after he had given up the captaincy to his brother. The style which he set was not, to say the least, universally admired. Whilst he was captain a new technique was introduced to Test cricket to which Australians gave the name of 'sledging' – the collective verbal abuse of opposing batsmen. Sledging is short for sledge-hammering and when Bobby Simpson resumed the Australian captaincy after the Packer revolution, the removal of this stain on Australian sportsmanship became a priority.

By then Ian Chappell, a captain with real support amongst his players, had carried his isolation from the Australian cricket establishment to the point of separation. With the enthusiastic support of Tony Greig, England's captain, and the co-operation of Richie Benaud, a former captain of Australia and one of Ian Chappell's foremost admirers, an alternative form of cricket was established under the Packer umbrella and given the name of World Series Cricket.

Thereafter he dedicated himself to recovering his reputation as both player and captain. Like many other positive influences he has been branded as both saint and sinner. If, as I think, history will find him to have been one of cricket's barbarians, that will be all the sadder because of his memorable excellence as a batsman.

ROBIN MARLAR

Having lost a hand in the First World War, Frank Chester turned as a young man to umpiring and was acclaimed the best ever.

CHESTER, Frank (1895–1957)

Worcestershire 1912–1914. First-class Umpire 1922–1955; Test Umpire 1924–1955.

Chester was the most famous umpire of the century; but for the loss of a hand in the First World War he might have been one of the most famous players. Instead he was an umpire in his physical prime, with all his faculties at their peak; he regarded it not as a retirement job, but as his life's work and applied to it a shrewd brain and a forceful character. When he was first appointed at 26, the average age of his contemporaries was well over 50. He set new standards and raised the whole conception of what an umpire should be. He umpired in 48 Tests. For Worcestershire, when his career ended at 18, he had already made 4 hundreds and done useful work as an off-spinner. Playing very straight, he had a sound defence, but could hit as well; in 1914 he hit J. W. H. T. Douglas for 4 sixes while making 178 not out. He was widely regarded as a coming England player.

R. L. ARROWSMITH

CAREER FIGURES

	INNS	NO	RUNS	HS	AVGE	100S
Batting	92	18	1773	178*	23·95	4

Bowling 81 wkts at 31·61 Ct 25

CLARKE, William (1798–1856)

Nottinghamshire 1835–1855. Founder and Captain of All-England XI 1846–1856.

'Old Clarke', as he was called, was the founder and autocrat of the All-England XI. As such he had an incalculable effect on the course of cricket. His under-arm bowling, after round-arm had become established, captured an average of 340 wickets annually from 1847 to 1853, by varied length, flight, pace, observation and field-placing. His famous touring team, rendered practicable by railways, popularized cricket by exhibiting the skill of numerous first-class cricketers to many who had never seen such prowess. Subsequently, this opened the way to overseas tours and to the Test Match era. He founded the Trent Bridge ground, having acquired the inn by his 2nd marriage in 1838.

A man of solemn, deceptively parsonic expression under his tall hat, he would trot to the crease, bend back his elbow at the last moment, and deliver the ball from the maximum height possible in under-arm, with a vicious rise from the pitch and a baffling spin. His various remarks – 'We shall 'ave a haccident sir, in a minute'; 'Stand there for the Harrow drive'; 'I have summed them up, and they are worth (so much)' – are familiar to cricket history, as are his snubs to young braggarts and doting parents. To cap everything, Clarke had lost an eye early in life. Yet, at past 50, he bowled unchanged with John Wisden through the Gentlemen's 2 innings, taking 12 wickets and dismissing them for 42 and 58. It was Wisden who led the revolt against Clarke's tight-fisted and dictatorial ways, and founded the United England XI with other dissidents. After Clarke died, having taken a wicket with his last ball, the match between these rival teams became the chief attraction of the season. An equal number from either side formed the first overseas touring team. Not long before his death, Clarke, leading his team to Bristol, presented Mrs Grace with a book of *Practical Hints on Cricket*. Few cricketers have had a wider influence on the game.

G. D. MARTINEAU

CLAY, John Charles (1898–1973)

Winchester 1915–1916. Glamorgan 1921–1949 (Captain 1924–1927, 1929, 1946). England: in England 1935. Selector 1947, 1948.

John Clay was an off-spin bowler in the classical mould, and for his endeavours both on and off the field must be acclaimed one of the masters of Glamorgan cricket. Born in Monmouthshire, he played for Glamorgan in the county's initial season in first-class cricket (1921) and was still bowling for them when past 50 years of age. He was one of the pillars of the county in their dark days, his slow off-breaks bringing him over 1,300 wickets in his first-class career; his 176 wickets for Glamorgan in 1937 is still a county record. He had a tempting length but rarely wilted under punishment, and his lean frame (he stood over 6 feet) and flowing action personified Welsh cricket over 3 decades. As a batsman he was not negligible – many fifties and 2 hundreds came his way. As a captain he commanded great loyalty. A serene demeanour behind a cool tactical brain made him of great value as a selector.

IRVING ROSENWATER

CAREER FIGURES

	INNS	NO	RUNS	HS	AVGE	100S
Batting	554	90	7186	101*	15·49	1

Bowling 1315 wkts at 19·77 Ct 176

Test Record (1)

Did not bat in his only Test; took 0 wkts for 75; and made 1 catch.

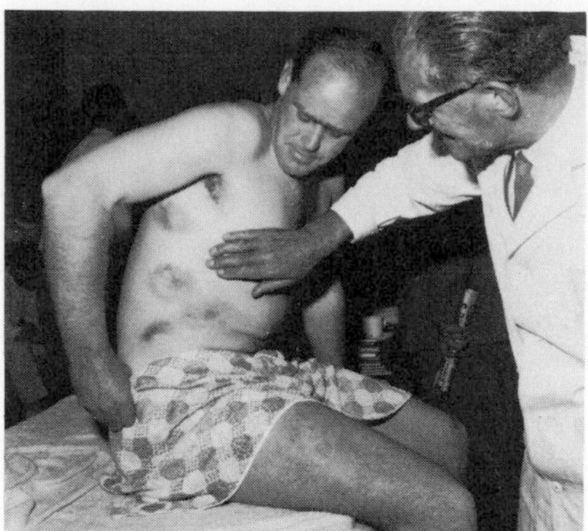

Brian Close: an intrepid cricketer, as evidenced by these bruises suffered while batting against Hall and Griffith at Lord's in 1963.

CLOSE, Dennis Brian, CBE (1931–)

Aireborough GS. Yorkshire 1949–1970 (Captain 1963–1970). Somerset 1971–1977 (Captain 1972–1977). England: in England 1949, 1955, 1957, 1959, 1961, 1963, 1966 (Captain), 1967 (Captain), 1976; in Australia 1950. Selector 1979.

The career of Brian Close had its disappointments, indeed its ironies, though he was not quite so unlucky as he claims in his autobiography *I Don't Bruise Easily*, a title only true in the physical sense. Not in his stars alone do his misfortunes lie. He was not an unsuccessful cricketer, but one who never reached the heights predicted and possible. In a long career, he scored just under 35,000 runs, and took – mostly in his earlier years – nearly 1,200 wickets. He was a redoubtable fielder in the dangerous positions: a man of immense bravery. It is said, with some foundation, that he once, from short-leg headed a fully hit hook to the wicket-keeper, crying out 'Catch it' as he fell. He never flinched from a fast bowler. His best-remembered innings in Tests were played against Hall and Griffith in 1963, and Holding and Roberts when in 1976, aged 45, he was brought back to show the young men how to do it.

When he first played for England, he was a young man himself, 18½ in fact, the youngest English Test player. That was in 1949, his 1st season with Yorkshire, when he achieved the double. He became captain of Yorkshire in 1963, and led them to 4 Championships in 7 years, and a Gillette Cup. He was summarily sacked at the end of the 1970 season. He spent the rest of his career, peacefully on the whole, with Somerset, whom he also captained, and although he never quite managed to win them anything, he left a strong young side behind him. His successful captaincy of England ended when he was censured for wasting time in a Yorkshire match at Edgbaston, and stubbornly refused to apologize for it. Otherwise he might have been the England captain for a long time – or then again, not; something else could have cropped up. Controversy clung to Close, and he did not reject it.

He was a left-handed batsman, very handsome when he was going well, though often criticized for over-using the sweep, especially – and possibly unjustly – in the Fourth Test against Australia at Old Trafford in 1961. He bowled mostly off-spinners right-handed. He retired (he said so, but one can never be sure with such a chap) at the end of the 1977 season.

ALAN GIBSON

CAREER FIGURES

	INNS	NO	RUNS	HS	AVGE	100S
Batting	1217	169	34833	198	33·23	52

Bowling 1167 wkts at 26·42 Ct 810

Test Record (22)

	INNS	NO	RUNS	HS	AVGE	100S
Batting	37	2	887	70	25·34	

Bowling 18 wkts at 29·55 Ct 24

COBHAM, 10th Viscount (Charles John Lyttelton), KG, PC, GCMG, GCVO, TD (1909–1977)

Eton. Worcestershire 1932–1948 (Captain 1936–1939). Vice-Captain of MCC in New Zealand and Australia 1935–36. President of MCC 1954–1955; Treasurer 1963–1964.

Though he did splendid work as captain of Worcestershire, the climax of Lord Cobham's career came when in 1961, towards the end of his term as a brilliantly successful and much loved Governor-General of New Zealand, he captained his own side against MCC at Auckland. His age, his figure and his lack of practice would alike have excused a failure; instead he made 44 in 21 minutes, delighting not only the huge crowd on the ground but innumerable friends all over the world.

A member of a famous cricketing family, he might be supposed to have inherited his skill, yet at Eton he was nowhere near the XI and for some years afterwards was only a respectable club cricketer. But by study and practice he improved his technique, and courage and common sense did the rest. For Worcestershire – as Hon C. J. Lyttelton – he constantly got runs when they were wanted. His highest score was 162 against Leicestershire at Loughborough in 1938, but probably more meritorious was his 48 in 35 minutes on a bad wicket, which enabled the county to beat Yorkshire in 1936 for the first time since 1909, and 50 and 35 as an opener against the 1938 Australians. In between he took an occasional wicket with orthodox medium pace and an even more occasional one with a most unorthodox slow ball which he called his 'flipper'. Later the same wisdom, humanity and humour which endeared him to the New Zealanders made him invaluable on committees, and he was a tower of strength not only to MCC but also to I Zingari, Butterflies and Free Foresters. He narrowly missed a golf blue at Cambridge and in his prime was almost the longest hitter in the world.

R. L. ARROWSMITH

CAREER FIGURES

	INNS	NO	RUNS	HS	AVGE	100S
Batting	171	14	3181	162	20·26	1

Bowling 32 wkts at 41·19 Ct 51

COLLINS, Herbert Leslie (1889–1959)

New South Wales 1909–10 to 1925–26 (Captain 1919–20 to 1925–26). Australian Imperial Forces side 1919 (Captain). Australia: in Australia 1920–21, 1924–25 (Captain); in England 1921, 1926 (Captain); in South Africa 1921–22 (Captain).

Collins was a shrewd and highly respected captain and a successful opening bat, who scored a hundred in his 1st Test and in that series made 557 runs in 9 innings. He was an unobtrusive cricketer who aroused no enthusiasm among the spectators and who is, after 50 years, almost forgotten, but he was most valuable to his side. Though handicapped by ill-health, he was a dour fighter, always at his best when things were at their worst; in 1921 his 40 in 5 hours at Manchester saved Australia from possible defeat. He would deliberately farm the most difficult bowling to protect an inexperienced or less confident partner, and by these means helped Ponsford to a hundred in his 1st Test innings. A small slightly built man, he was a fine field and a thorough cricketer; in 1919 in England, finding his side short of bowling, he turned to and took a hundred wickets with innocent-looking left-hand slows. Thereafter, Australia being well supplied, he rarely bowled.

H. L. Collins: known as 'Horseshoe' because of his luck in the toss.

R. L. ARROWSMITH

CAREER FIGURES

	INNS	NO	RUNS	HS	AVGE	100S
Batting	256	10	9921	282	40·32	32

Bowling 180 wkts at 21·51 Ct 113

Test Record (19)

	INNS	NO	RUNS	HS	AVGE	100S
Batting	31	1	1352	203	45·06	4

Bowling 4 wkts at 63·00 Ct 13

COMPTON, Denis Charles Scott, CBE (1918–)

Bell Lane Sch, Hendon. Middlesex 1936–1958 (Captain (joint) 1951–1952). England: in England 1937–1956 consecutively; in Australia 1946–47, 1950–51, 1954–55; in South Africa 1948–49, 1956–57; in West Indies 1953–54; in New Zealand 1946–47, 1950–51.

Denis Compton, as one of the greatest artists the game has known, made a strangely plebeian start by being born at Hendon on 23 May 1918. He should, in the light of future events, have been borne down from Valhalla on a silver cloud. Certainly he must rank as one of the greatest entertainers cricket has ever produced. Cavalier in approach with a showman's flair and a genius for the game, he poured out his skill to a captivated public. Untutored yet basically sound he improvized his way to 38,942 runs, including 122 hundreds. When he could spare the time he took 622 wickets and when he was looking he took 415 catches. In Test cricket he averaged over 50, playing in 78 matches and scoring 5,807 runs. Figures pay the scantest justice to the pleasure given by him round the entire cricket-speaking world.

He made his debut in 1936 and up to the outbreak of war he was merely giving a gentle foretaste of things to come. R. W. V. Robins, the Middlesex captain, recognized that we had a rare genius in our midst and he gave him full rein. After the war, and particularly in 1947, his cricket reached a breathtaking maturity. He broke every record with the bat, scoring 18 hundreds in a total of 3,816 runs for the season. All bowling came alike and went in the same way. The South African Test attack that year was torn to ribbons. A year later an old football injury to his knee flared up and his mobility was impaired, not before he had scored 300 in 3 hours at Benoni in South Africa in 1948–49. Some of the old dash left his play but he fought a long battle against his disability. His worst time was in Australia in 1950–51 when he averaged under 10 for the series. He was appointed joint captain of Middlesex in 1951–52 but his gifts proved too personal to be communicated to others.

The technique of his batting had a poetic quality mixed in with the spirit of the eternal schoolboy. A twirl of the bat, a toss of the unruly mane supposed to be kept in place by the advertised unguent, and a smell of challenge in the air. His most publicized shot was the sweep which he played perilously late and to whichever ball took his fancy. His most pleasing stroke was the cover drive, placed exquisitely and tantalizingly out of the reach of fielders. He would often compel off-spinners to feed this particular shot by manoeuvring their line of flight into just the right place. By a combination of wrist and timing he could make nonsense of any defensive field. A good hooker and cutter, he never really hit well straight. If he ever read the coaching book he must have been holding it upside down. He was never tied to his crease and he loved to do battle with the best wrist-spin bowlers. The only uncertainty about his batting was his running between the wickets. The air at Lord's was sometimes heavy with call and counter-call. He ran his brother Leslie out in his benefit match. He

Denis Compton coming in at Hastings in 1947 having scored his 17th hundred, thus bettering J. B. Hobbs's 16 in 1925. Later he got an 18th for luck.

was the only player to call his partner for a single and wish him good luck at the same time. The crowd was kept in delicious suspense throughout.

Apart from his genius with the bat, he was an accomplished left-hand bowler. He graduated naturally from the orthodox to chinamen and googlies. Capable on his day of baffling the best, he had Bradman mesmerized for a spell at Leeds in 1948. His fielding was rather dependent on the phases of the moon. If the signs were right he could catch and stop everything in sight but he was prone to lose interest during a long, hard day. Punctuality for the start of play was not his strongest point. Any lapse of concentration could be forgiven in a man who added such lustre to the game. He had a fan club of film-star proportions; his good looks and natural charm brought him friends all round the world. A prince of players who must command a place in the XI of the greatest cricketers ever.

JOHN WARR

CAREER FIGURES

	INNS	NO	RUNS	HS	AVGE	100S
Batting	839	88	38942	300	51·85	122

Bowling 622 wkts at 32·27 Ct 415

Test Record (78)

	INNS	NO	RUNS	HS	AVGE	100S
Batting	131	15	5807	278	50·06	17

Bowling 25 wkts at 56·40 Ct 49

CONGDON, Bevan Ernest, OBE (1938–)

Motueka District HS. Central Districts 1960–61 to 1970–71. Wellington 1971–72. Otago 1972–73 to 1973–74. Canterbury 1974–75– . New Zealand: in New Zealand 1964–65, 1965–66, 1967–68, 1970–71, 1972–73 (Captain), 1973–74 (Captain), 1974–75 (Captain), 1975–76, 1976–77, 1977–78; in England 1965, 1969, 1973 (Captain), 1978; in Australia 1973–74 (Captain); in West Indies 1971–72 (Captain); in India 1964–65, 1969–70; in Pakistan 1964–65, 1969–70.

If Congdon had been born in Sydney, he might not have been regarded as exceptional. With the lean look of the cartoon Australian went the fighting qualities which long distinguished men in green caps. He was 26 before he entered international cricket but on retiring, at 40, he held New Zealand records in Test runs and appearances. Born in a country area, his cricket at first wore a rustic look. But he realized he needed a tighter technique and went from strength to strength. His development as a bowler was on similar lines. In the West Indies in 1971–72 he saw there was a need for a batsman who could fill a 5th bowling place and so he became a useful medium-pace seamer. In the Second Test at Port of Spain Congdon scored 166 and 82; and followed this with 126, 61 not out, 11 and 58. In the First Test in England in 1973 he was run out for 9. In the 2nd innings New Zealand faced the daunting task of scoring 479. Struck on the head late on the 3rd day, Congdon batted for most of the 4th to score 176 and help his side to a brave 440. At Lord's he contributed 175 to a record 551 for 9. So in 6 consecutive overseas Tests he had made 864 at an average of 108. He finished with 3,448 runs from 61 Tests.

R. T. BRITTENDEN

Learie Constantine: genius at work.

CONSTANTINE, Baron (Sir Learie Nicholas Constantine), MBE (1902–1971)

Trinidad. West Indies: in West Indies 1929–30, 1934–35; in England 1928, 1933, 1939; in Australia 1930–31. Knighted 1962; created a Life Peer 1969.

Learie Constantine was one of the most dynamic figures cricket has ever known. Whether batting, bowling or fielding he was always the centre of attraction. He was a dazzling and unorthodox hitter who was unlikely to take much more than an hour over a hundred. He was a dangerous fast bowler who adapted himself shrewdly to advancing years and on his last tour of England bowled, and bowled successfully, every variation of medium pace, with an occasional fast ball. He was perhaps the greatest fielder of all time. Those who remember him will always believe that by anticipation and cat-like activity he brought off catches which the second-best, whoever he may have been, could never have reached. Whether bowling or fielding he applied to cricket that acute brain which after his retirement won him great respect in the political world and brought him a knighthood and a Life Peerage.

Though he had his moments in Test Matches – notably when at the Oval in 1939 he followed an analysis of 5 for 75 by making 78 out of 103 in 55 minutes on the last morning – his most spectacular feat was against Middlesex at Lord's in 1928. After making 86 in just an hour, he took 7 for 57 and then settled the match with 103 in an hour. No wonder crowds flocked to see him play whether in first-class cricket or in the league. Some of his hits were stupendous. In the match at Lord's already quoted, he hit a ball of G. O. Allen's over cover's head far up into the Grand Stand and played back to Hearne with such force that the ball, after breaking the bowler's finger, crashed into the pavilion rails and ricocheted among the seats. At Lord's, too, in 1933 he hit a high full-pitch from M. J. C. Allom virtually over his shoulder for six just to the left of the press box at fine-leg; while at Canterbury in 1928 he carried the tree that stands inside the playing area.

Where does he rank among the great? As a fieldsman probably top, as a draw for the public among the first. It is a fascinating problem to consider whether any Test side in history could have afforded to leave him out.

R. L. ARROWSMITH

CAREER FIGURES

	INNS	NO	RUNS	HS	AVGE	100S
Batting	194	11	4451	133	24·32	5

Bowling 424 wkts at 20·60 Ct 133

Test Record (18)

	INNS	NO	RUNS	HS	AVGE	100S
Batting	33	0	635	90	19·24	

Bowling 58 wkts at 30·10 Ct 28

COWDREY, Michael Colin, CBE (1932–)

Tonbridge 1946–1950 (Captain 1949–1950). Kent 1950–1976 (Captain 1954–1971). Oxford Univ 1952–1954 (Captain 1954). England: in England 1955–68 consecutively (Captain 1959, 1960, 1961, 1962, 1966, 1968), 1970, 1971; in Australia 1954–55, 1958–59, 1962–63, 1965–66, 1970–71, 1974–75; in South Africa 1956–57; in West Indies 1959–60 (Captain), 1967–68 (Captain); in New Zealand 1954–55, 1958–59, 1962–63, 1965–66, 1970–71; in India 1963–64; in Pakistan 1968–69 (Captain).

Cowdrey was long one of the world's greatest bats, yet had he given full play to his natural abilities he could have been even greater. An Oxford batsman years ago, leaving Lord's dressing-room at 87 for 5 to face a formidable Cambridge attack, remarked 'I can't think how they have the face to come to Lord's with bowling like this', and proceeded to smite them hip to thigh. It was this spirit, often not an amiable quality, that Cowdrey lacked. He could not believe that he was a far greater player than most of the bowlers he faced and too often he let them dictate to him when he should have been dictating to them. His natural gifts were wonderful and his technique irreproachable: no bat could be straighter or closer to the leg and he could force the ball with equal ease off the front foot or the back. He was a master of that neglected stroke, the straight drive. On his legs and legstump few have ever excelled him.

An infant phenomenon, the youngest player ever to appear in a school match at Lord's, he was unlucky not to play for England while still at Oxford. In the winter after he went down, his method and consistency alike with Hutton's side in Australia created a great impression; he made a splendid hundred in the Third Test and 2 in one match against New South Wales. After that he was virtually a certainty for England. Of his Test innings, none is better remembered than the 154 at Birmingham in 1957, when he and May, by putting on 411 in 8 hours 20

Colin Cowdrey in perhaps his finest Test innings, against Australia at Melbourne in 1954–55. He scored 102 out of England's 1st innings total of 191. He is seen here driving Lindwall.

minutes, not only deprived the West Indians of an apparently certain victory, but scotched the menace of Ramadhin for the season. Three years later he again saved England with 155 against South Africa at the Oval, a magnificent exhibition of strokeplay. It would be impossible to recount all his great innings, but there are none one would sooner have watched than his 2 hundreds for Kent against the Australians at Canterbury in 1961, or his 151 not out in the corresponding match in 1975, which brought Kent their 1st win against the Australians since 1899. That was Cowdrey at his best, Cowdrey whom, with his majestic poise, his perfect balance and sense of timing and his full range of strokes, it seemed quite impossible that any bowler should keep quiet. He was a great slip and at school was a formidable leg-spinner, but leg-spin and change bowling being alike out of fashion, he abandoned the art.

It is sad that he never, as he might occasionally have expected to do, captained England in Australia and typical that, at the very end of his career, he should go out there at a moment's notice to face Lillee and Thomson. It was too much to hope that, at his age and without practice, he would score heavily, but his average on a losing side was a tribute alike to his skill and his unselfishness.

R. L. ARROWSMITH

CAREER FIGURES

	INNS	NO	RUNS	HS	AVGE	100S
Batting	1130	134	42719	307	42·89	107

Bowling 65 wkts at 51·21 Ct 638

Test Record (114)

	INNS	NO	RUNS	HS	AVGE	100S
Batting	188	15	7624	182	44·06	22

Bowling 0 wkts for 104 runs Ct 120

CRAWFORD, John Neville (1886–1963)

Repton 1902–1905 (Captain 1905). Surrey 1904–21. South Australia 1909–1914. England: in England 1907; in Australia 1907–08; in South Africa 1905–06.

Crawford was born at Cane Hill, Surrey. In 1904, when not yet 18, he was invited to play for Surrey, which he did during the summer holidays. When he went back to school he was top of the county's bowling averages. He was a prodigy at Repton where, in 4 seasons, he scored 2,098 runs and took 244 wickets. After leaving school he played for Surrey until 1909, when he quarrelled with the county club and went to Australia to join the teaching staff of St Peter's College, Adelaide. Thus at the age of 22 he was lost to English cricket.

He had represented England in 5 Tests in Australia, 5 in South Africa (as a member of P. F. Warner's team of 1905–06) and twice v South Africa in England in 1907. On paper his Test Match record gives no idea of Crawford's talents. In Australia, on the shirt-front wickets of 1907–08 (he was only 21 years old), he took, in the Test Matches, 30 wickets, average 24·73. His victims included Victor Trumper (3 times), M. A. Noble (3 times), Warwick Armstrong (5 times) and Hill (twice). Seldom has a bowler had a haul of such individual richness. Crawford played often for South Australia, performing amazing all-round deeds. When the conquering England XI of 1911–12 was in Australia, an 'Australian XI' played against the side, at Brisbane. Crawford, not qualified now to appear either for England or Australia in an authentic Test Match, scored 110 in as many minutes from the attack of S. F. Barnes, Frank Foster, Wilfred Rhodes, J. W. Hearne and Frank Woolley.

He played first-class cricket in England for only 4 full seasons, twice achieving the double of 1,000 runs and 100 wickets, the first time under the age of 20. His break with Surrey must be regarded as a sad deprivation of fame and pleasure to himself, and a grievous loss to the annals of English cricket. He was classically sound in method as a batsman, an upright stance and a straight swing of the bat, the feet firmly and quickly positioned. He shared his brother Vivian's power to drive straight with a strength and easy rhythm equalled in more recent times by E. R. Dexter. He was beautifully built physically, with fine shoulders, in height about 5 feet 10 inches. He was one of the first top-grade cricketers to play in glasses. As a bowler his pace varied from medium to really quick. He ran to deliver in easy swinging strides, and as the right arm came over his left side and shoulder were classically forward. He could swing the new ball away from the bat; but his best trick was a breakback – which Clem Hill assured me Crawford could 'bring back' inches on the fast flawless wickets of Adelaide. As H. S. Altham, who was a contemporary at Repton, has written: 'Crawford wore his flannels so naturally that he might have been born in them'.

NEVILLE CARDUS

CAREER FIGURES

	INNS	NO	RUNS	HS	AVGE	100S
Batting	322	33	9470	232	32·76	11

Bowling 815 wkts at 20·66

Test Record (12)

	INNS	NO	RUNS	HS	AVGE	100S
Batting	23	2	469	74	22·33	

Bowling 39 wkts at 29·48 Ct 13

DARLING, Hon Joseph, CBE (1870–1946)

Prince Alfred Coll, Adelaide. South Australia 1893–94 to 1907–08 (Captain 1898–99 to 1906–07). Australia: in Australia 1894–95, 1897–98, 1901–02 (Captain); in England 1896, 1899 (Captain), 1902 (Captain), 1905 (Captain); in South Africa 1902–03 (Captain).

Son of a father who did more than any man to create the Adelaide Oval, Joe Darling made 252 on it for his school, St Peter's, when still under 15, and became one of the outstanding figures in Australian cricket. A compact, determined batsman, and fine field at mid-off, it was as captain that he made his greatest impact. Of the 31 games he played against England between 1894 and 1905, he captained in 18, leading his side to victory in 3 rubbers, most sensationally in 1902 when his own 51 and 37 played a decisive part in their historic 3-run win at Old Trafford. His highest aggregate on tour was 1,768 in 1905, but his finest batting was seen against Stoddart's team in 1897–98, when he made 3 hundreds in Test Matches, the highest 178 in Adelaide, and averaged 67 for the series. A stocky, moustachioed figure, his authority as captain was unquestioned. His life aggregate of runs was 10,637, and he made 21 hundreds.

H. S. ALTHAM

CAREER FIGURES

	INNS	NO	RUNS	HS	AVGE	100S
Batting	334	25	10637	210	34·42	21

Bowling 1–55

Test Record (34)

	INNS	NO	RUNS	HS	AVGE	100S
Batting	60	2	1657	178	28·56	3

Ct 27

Alan Davidson: a match-winner, as batsman, bowler and fielder.

DAVIDSON, Alan Keith, OBE (1929–)

Gosford HS. New South Wales 1949–50 to 1962–63. Australia: in Australia 1954–55, 1958–59, 1960–61, 1962–63; in England 1953, 1956, 1961; in South Africa 1957–58; in India 1956–57, 1959–60; in Pakistan 1956–57, 1959–60.

Alan Keith Davidson – 'Davo' to his friends – maintained the highest standards and traditions of the Australian all-round cricketer between 1949 and 1963. He played for Australia 44 times, starting against England in 1953, and finishing against them 10 years later. Meanwhile he scored 1,328 Test runs and took 186 Test wickets, and no numerical scale can convey the value of his superb fielding.

Davidson was born in Lisarow, in New South Wales. He was a successful schoolboy cricketer, but at that stage bowled left-handed 'chinamen' on the pattern of Fleetwood-Smith. In turning to fast bowling at a later date he almost reversed the case of his predecessor, who turned from fast right to slow left. On introduction to State cricket in 1949, Davidson was immediately successful against rival sides depleted, in some cases, by the then current Australian tour in South Africa. Grasping this opportunity, he progressed rapidly and came to England in 1953. In that year he played in all 5 Tests, but was still, as a bowler, in a supporting role to the great fast trio, Lindwall, Miller and Johnston. On their decline he became the undisputed leader of the Australian attack, having fair claims to being the best new-ball bowler in the world by the time May's team reached Australia in 1958–59.

A very powerful man of 6 feet and great girth, Davidson bowled genuinely fast without quite equalling the pace of Lindwall or Miller. He ran a lively 15 yards, a modest distance in current times, culminating in a strong, wheeling action. His delivery lacked classical grace, as he made less use of his right arm than the purist would demand, but gave an impression of immense resilient strength. The new ball he could move very late in the air, and off the pitch in either direction. As a batsman, Davidson made full use of his great physique. Two hits off successive balls from Cowdrey at Sydney remain in the observer's mind as amongst the most exhilarating of their type ever played – a steeple-high pull which dropped vertically on the roof of the stand, and a straight drive which hit the enclosing wall of the Hill, still on the ascent. In the field his ability to move immediately and astonishingly fast enabled him to bring off many spectacular catches near the wicket, whilst in the deep he was just as sure, and a fine thrower. Relatively few distinguished Australian players play prominent parts in administration after retirement, but Davidson has risen to be President of the NSW Cricket Association.

IAN PEEBLES

CAREER FIGURES

	INNS	NO	RUNS	HS	AVGE	100S
Batting	246	39	6804	129	32·86	9

Bowling 672 wkts at 20·91 Ct 142

Test Record (44)

	INNS	NO	RUNS	HS	AVGE	100S
Batting	61	7	1328	80	24·59	–

Bowling 186 wkts at 20·53 Ct 42

DEMPSTER, Charles Stewart (1903–1974)

Wellington 1921–22. Leicestershire 1935–1939 (Captain 1936–1938). Warwickshire 1946. New Zealand: in New Zealand 1929–30, 1931–32, 1932–33; in England 1931.

As an opening batsman, Dempster was one of the finest New Zealand ever produced, and a brilliant fieldsman. At 17, he played for Wellington and later was so successful in 'unofficial Tests' against England, as well as against a team sent over by the Melbourne Club, that his place in the 'official' New Zealand team was assured. In 1929–30 he scored 136 in the Second Test, joining Mills in a 1st-wicket stand of 276. In the series he averaged 82. In 1931 he started his 2nd visit to England with 212 against Essex, and helped to save New Zealand in the Second Test with a fine 120. He made 7 hundreds that year. When England toured New Zealand in 1932–33, he alone proved capable of dealing with Bowes. A business trip to England in 1933 was combined with Lancashire League cricket before he qualified for Leicestershire, for whom he scored many hundreds (3 in succession in 1936), usually standing high in the English first-class averages. He captained the county for 3 seasons, and then handed over to M. St J. Packe. His best was now past, but, having a business appointment in Birmingham after the Second World War, he appeared in a few matches for Warwickshire in 1946, though without distinction.

G. D. MARTINEAU

CAREER FIGURES

	INNS	NO	RUNS	HS	AVGE	100S
Batting	306	36	12145	212	44·98	35

Bowling 8 wkts at 37·50 Ct 94 (incl. w/k); st 2 Total 96

Test Record (10)

	INNS	NO	RUNS	HS	AVGE	100S
Batting	15	4	723	136	65·72	2

Bowling 0 wkts for 10 Ct 2

DENNESS, Michael Henry (1940–)

Ayr Academy. Scotland 1959–1961. Kent 1962–1976 (Captain 1972–1976). Essex 1977– . England: in England 1969, 1974 (Captain), 1975 (Captain); in Australia 1974–75 (Captain); in West Indies 1973–74 (Captain); in New Zealand 1974–75 (Captain); in India 1972–73; in Pakistan 1972–73.

Mike Denness had the unenviable task in 1973 of taking over from Ray Illingworth as England's captain. Illingworth's players – you could almost call them his disciples – regretted his going. It should not be forgotten, however, that whereas under Illingworth England, in 1973, had been beaten hollow at home by West Indies, Denness, with the most difficult of assignments and his place to earn as a batsman, emerged from the Caribbean that following winter with a halved series. What he had achieved in 1973–74 he could not repeat in 1974–75 against an Australian side with Lillee and Thomson at the height of their powers.

Denness was 18 when he came down from Scotland to take his chance with Kent. At Ayr Academy he had shown exceptional promise, as a fly-half at rugby football as well as a cricketer, and in England he soon made a name for himself as a fine, quick-footed player of spin bowling. Against fast bowling he was less at ease, though it had to be genuinely fast to find him out. His own batting record while captaining England is indicative of this. Against the Indian spinners in 1974, for example, he made 2 Test hundreds; then, when Thomson missed the last Test in Australia in 1974–75 and Lillee broke down after bowling only 6 overs, Denness, who earlier had dropped himself from the Fourth Test, scored 188; while against New Zealand's medium-pacers, after moving on from Australia, his scores in the 2 Test Matches were 181 and 59 not out. When among the runs he had an attractive, flowing style, and as a fielder, especially away from the bat, he was in the very highest class.

An ill-fated decision to put Australia in to bat, at Edgbaston in 1975, hastened the end of Denness's Test captaincy. He accepted the setback defiantly yet with good grace, as was his way, until Kent, too, decided to appoint another captain. That was in 1976, after Denness, in the 5 preceding seasons, had led them to victory in all the one-day competitions. In 1977, feeling a little hard done by, he moved to Essex, there to play a significant part at an exciting time.

JOHN WOODCOCK

DEXTER, Edward Ralph (1935–)

Radley 1950–1953 (Captain 1953). Cambridge Univ 1956–1958 (Captain 1958). Sussex 1957–1968 (Captain 1960–1965). England: in England 1958–1965 consecutively (Captain 1962, 1963, 1964), 1968; in Australia 1958–59, 1962–63 (Captain); in West Indies 1959–60; in New Zealand 1958–59, 1962–63 (Captain); in India 1961–62 (Captain); in Pakistan 1961–62 (Captain).

Years ago Fry wrote of MacLaren, 'like all the great batsmen he always attacked the bowling'. Dexter was one of the few England players since the Second World War who have measured up to this criterion. An innings by him took one back to the golden age of cricket. Above all he could show, as in his splendid innings of 70 against the West Indies at Lord's in 1963, that fast bowlers are just as vulnerable to attack as slow. Curiously, he first made his mark in representative cricket as a bowler, taking 5 for 8 and 3 for 47 for the Gentlemen in 1957 – a remarkable performance for one hitherto regarded as a rather mild change. Often handicapped by injury, he remained in fact a dangerous, lively, quickish bowler, with a great knack in breaking partnerships: he might profitably have put himself on more.

Though he made a praiseworthy 52 in his 1st Test in 1958, he was slow to establish himself in that class. As an emergency replacement late on the next Australian tour he was a failure, and, after making 141 in a Test in New Zealand, he did little against India in England. He really came to the front in the West Indies in 1959–60, heading the Test averages and making 2 hundreds. Later his outstanding innings were the 180 with which he saved the Birmingham Test against Australia in 1961 and the even more remarkable 174 in 8 hours which again saved England against Australia at Manchester in 1964.

Indeed it was sad that so great an attacking player was forced so often to save matches rather than to win them and it is a tribute to his character that he was able to school himself to do so. On the other hand when he was playing his natural game he too often got out not to an extra-good ball or a good stroke that just failed to come off but to a bad stroke for which he was probably cursing himself the moment he had played it. In his early days his fielding was often criticized, sometimes unfairly. Later he became a fine, aggressive field, always eager for a chance of getting a wicket. Whatever he was doing, he looked what he was – a great natural games-player.

In 1965 he broke a leg and resigned the captaincy of Sussex and it seemed that his serious career had come to an end. But 3 years later he was persuaded to return and in his first innings for Sussex made 203 not out against Kent, scoring his 2nd hundred in 103 minutes. On the strength of this he was picked for the last 2 Tests. It was not to be expected that with so little practice he would do full justice to his ability, but he did enough to show what a tragedy his early retirement was.

His cricketing days over he turned his hand to many things, among them flying his family to Australia in his own light aeroplane to report an MCC tour; surprising even the best professionals by the power and majesty with which he could hit a golf ball; and becoming a useful summarizer of the Test Match scene on television.

R. L. ARROWSMITH

CAREER FIGURES

	INNS	NO	RUNS	HS	AVGE	100S
Batting	565	48	21093	205	40·79	51

Bowling 419 wkts at 29·90 Ct 230

Test Record (62)

	INNS	NO	RUNS	HS	AVGE	100S
Batting	102	8	4502	205	47·89	9

Bowling 66 wkts at 34·93 Ct 29

d'OLIVEIRA, Basil Lewis, OBE (1931–)

St Joseph's Sch, Cape Town. Commonwealth Tours 1961–62, 1962–63, 1963–64. Worcestershire 1964–1979. England: in England 1966 to 1972 consecutively; in Australia 1970–71; in West Indies 1967–68; in New Zealand 1970–71; in Pakistan 1968–69.

Basil d'Oliveira's cricketing story will go down as one of the epics of the game – even without the 'political cricket ball' episode recorded in detail elsewhere in this volume. For it is the tale of the 'nice guy', the poor Cape Coloured cricketer who, as a bewildered but determined and talented young man, made his way to England – with fares paid by the public subscription of his Cape Town admirers – to achieve fame and fortune as an England player. Very often as the story is told, too little is made of the 80 hundreds he scored in his early years of non-white cricket in South Africa. Certainly he did not meet too many class players, but I am sure that the timing and lightning reflexes needed to build so many big innings on the underprepared wickets he met week after week in those formative days were the sure foundation of much that came later. Add the qualities of quiet unflappability in moments of stress, an incredible capacity for concentration, and an insatiable ambition to succeed and you have the real essence of d'Oliveira and his saga of success.

Even so, the speed of his progress was astonishing. From the break that brought him to England in 1960 on a first season trial contract of £450 as professional with Middleton in the Central Lancashire League, it took him just 5 years to become an outstanding county player with Worcestershire and only one year more to establish himself in the England side at 35 years of age. He crossed both frontiers with real style. When he stepped up from League cricket he hit hundreds in each of his first 2 County Championship games – both against Essex – and had 6 hundreds and 7 other innings of over 50 in a first full county season that saw Worcestershire retain the Championship for the second successive year. When he achieved what he thought was the impossible the following year by being picked for England against West Indies he played with such calm maturity that only Tom Graveney and Colin Milburn bettered his average of 48·66 from 4 Tests. He went on to play 48 times for England, scored 2,792 Test runs, and averaged 40·46. Along the way he hit 2 hundreds against Australia, one each against the Rest of the World, Pakistan, India and New Zealand, and took 47, often crucial, breakthrough wickets with his accurate medium-paced seamers.

Basil d'Oliveira: ambassador extraordinary – in Israel.

With one of the shortest back-lifts in the first class game d'Oliveira's timing and power, especially off the back foot, were tremendous. And the tougher the situation the harder he hit. To illustrate the point he hit 8 fours and 4 sixes – one a magnificent straight drive off a startled Wes Hall – in a brilliant 88 in the West Indies Test at Leeds in 1966.

CRAWFORD WHITE

CAREER FIGURES

	INNS	NO	RUNS	HS	AVGE	100S
Batting	542	83	18154	227	39·55	42

Bowling 531 wkts at 27·35 Ct 207

Test Record (44)

	INNS	NO	RUNS	HS	AVGE	100S
Batting	70	8	2484	158	40·06	5

Bowling 47 wkts at 39·55 Ct 29

DONNELLY, Martin Paterson (1917–)

New Plymouth Boys' HS, and Canterbury Univ. Wellington 1936–37. Oxford Univ 1946–1947 (Captain 1947). Middlesex 1946. Warwickshire 1948–1950. New Zealand: in England 1937, 1949.

C. B. Fry, asked which of the left-handers of his day he would rate superior to Martin Donnelly, replied unhesitatingly 'not one'. Under pressure he admitted that Clem Hill and Woolley 'were also rather good'. Further he would not go. Nobody who watched cricket in the Parks in 1946–1947 would quarrel with this appraisal. In his youth Donnelly had toured England with the New Zealanders in 1937. In 1945 he had scored a hundred at Lord's for the Dominions v England. He had already a reputation when he first appeared for Oxford. His deeds in the Parks are legendary. His hundred against Cambridge in 1946 must be one of the greatest innings ever played in the Varsity Match. Next year he made 162 (more than half the total) for the Gentlemen; in 1949 he completed the cycle with 206 for New Zealand in the Lord's Test Match. In his last 2 innings in England that year he was undefeated in a great match at Scarborough won by New Zealand 2 minutes from time. While at Oxford he also won a rugby football blue and was capped once for England.

Bare figures can give no idea of the electric atmosphere in the Parks when that short, sturdy figure went in to bat. A lucky spectator might have half an hour to spare between, say, a lecture at Keble and a tutorial in Parks Road. In that half-hour he might well see Donnelly hit 9 boundaries, each from a different stroke. Most exquisite of all would be the late cut and the straight drive; there would be an on-drive, a square leg-hit, a devastating hook, perhaps a rustic pull worthy of George Hirst. There was not a stroke of which Donnelly was not the master. If Oxford were fielding, the spectator's eyes would turn to cover-point. There have been great covers in cricket's history – Royle, Jessop, S. E. Gregory, Hobbs, John Gunn – but few greater than Donnelly. He was equally brilliant in anticipation, in pick-up and in throw. Equable of temper, modest, friendly and possessing a great gift of fun, Martin Donnelly was as popular off the field as on it. His cricket career was short: memories of it will endure.

Martin Donnelly: on his way to a hundred for Oxford at Lord's.

GERALD BRODRIBB

CAREER FIGURES

	INNS	NO	RUNS	HS	AVGE	100S
Batting	221	26	9250	208*	47·44	23

Bowling 43 wkts at 39·14 Ct 75

Test Record (7)

	INNS	NO	RUNS	HS	AVGE	100S
Batting	12	1	582	206	52·90	1

Bowling 0 wkts for 20 Ct 7

DOUGLAS, John William Henry Tyler (1882–1930)

Felsted 1898–1901 (Captain 1901). Essex 1901–1928 (Captain 1911–1928). England: in England 1912, 1921, 1924; in Australia 1911–12, 1920–21 (Captain), 1924–25; in South Africa 1913–14 (Captain). Selector 1928.

Nicknamed by a wise-cracking Australian 'Johnny Won't Hit Today' because of his tendency at times to carry defence to the extreme, John Douglas was drowned along with his father at the age of 48 when the ship in which they were passengers was in a collision in thick fog in the Kattegat. Almost certainly Douglas could have saved himself, but he went down to save his father and was not seen again.

During his 28 years in first-class cricket Douglas experienced the giddy heights of outstanding success and the bitter depths of heart-breaking failure. He brought back the Ashes from Australia in 1911–12 when he took over the captaincy from Sir Pelham Warner who had fallen ill on arrival. He led a highly successful England team to South Africa in 1913–14. After the war he was appointed captain of the 1920–21 side to Australia. He lost all 5 Tests. When the Australians came to England in the following summer he retained the captaincy for the first 2 Tests, both of which were lost. He then played for England under both the Hon L. H. Tennyson and A. E. R. Gilligan. The late swing which caused the best of opening batsmen to regard his bowling so highly was still there, but his 'nip' was inevitably less apparent.

Douglas was nearly 6 feet in height, powerfully built with classical features and a mass of shining black hair which was always parted immaculately down the centre. He had bushy eyebrows, piercing blue eyes and a square jaw that had determination and guts written all over it. Stripped, he had the physique of a champion boxer which indeed he was for he won the Olympic middle-weight title in 1908 in a historic bout with 'Snowy' Baker. He also played association football for the Corinthians and Casuals and gained an AFA international cap. Douglas was a born leader. He was a good captain, if quick-tempered and dictatorial. Under his rugged exterior was a kindliness and a generous nature that only his intimate friends were permitted to see.

CHARLES BRAY

CAREER FIGURES

	INNS	NO	RUNS	HS	AVGE	100S
Batting	1035	156	24531	210*	27·89	26

Bowling 1894 wkts at 23·32

Test Record (23)

	INNS	NO	RUNS	HS	AVGE	100S
Batting	35	2	962	119	29·15	1

Bowling 45 wkts at 33·02 Ct 9

DOWLING, Graham Thorne (1937–)

St Andrew's Coll, Christchurch. Canterbury 1958–59. New Zealand: in New Zealand 1962–63, 1963–64, 1964–65, 1967–68 (Captain), 1968–69 (Captain), 1970–71 (Captain); in England 1965, 1969 (Captain); in South Africa 1961–62; in West Indies 1971–72 (Captain); in India 1964–65, 1969–70 (Captain); in Pakistan 1964–65, 1969–70 (Captain).

A lean, athletic, right-handed batsman, Graham Dowling is the most successful of New Zealand Test captains. He led his country for 4 of its Test victories, one more than J. R. Reid. And he was New Zealand's captain in Pakistan in 1969 when for the 1st time they won a Test series. A product of St Andrew's College, Christchurch, Dowling showed much promise as a rugby three-quarter, but he concentrated on cricket.

His batting was based on a sound defence and a determined approach to the game, but he could attack with the best and was a superb fieldsman, especially in the close catching positions. He scored more than 9,000 runs in first-class cricket, including 16 hundreds, and he had a particularly productive summer in 1967–68, when he set national records with his aggregate of 968 and a Test innings of 239 against India at Christchurch. Both have since been surpassed by Glenn Turner. Dowling scored 3 hundreds and made 2,306 runs in his 39 Tests. He will be remembered not only for his performances but also for the courage and selflessness he brought to his cricket and his captaincy. He is now a member of the New Zealand Board of Control and was manager of the New Zealand Prudential Cup team to England in 1979.

R. T. BRITTENDEN

CAREER FIGURES

	INNS	NO	RUNS	HS	AVGE	100S
Batting	282	13	9399	239	34·94	16

Bowling 9 wkts at 41·00 Ct 112

Test Record (39)

	INNS	NO	RUNS	HS	AVGE	100S
Batting	77	3	2306	239	31·16	3

Bowling 1 wkt for 19 Ct 23

DUCKWORTH, George (1901–1966)

Warrington GS. Lancashire 1923–1938. England: in England 1924, 1928, 1929, 1930, 1935, 1936; in Australia 1928–29; in South Africa 1930–31; in New Zealand 1932–33. Manager Commonwealth sides in India 1949–50, 1950–51, 1953–54. Scorer and baggage-master MCC sides in Australia 1954–55, 1958–59; South Africa 1956–57.

George Duckworth, born at Warrington, first played for Lancashire in 1923 and was the county's regular wicket-keeper until 1937. Also he was wicket-keeper for England in 24 Test Matches, 5 against Australia in England in 1930 and 5 in Australia. At his best he was likened to Strudwick for swiftness of execution; but his methods and vocalism were much more demonstrative. Duckworth's appeal was less a question than a statement of fact in his favour; and it was uttered in a triumphant cock-crow, his right glove going affirmatively on high.

He was in his element for the county of his birth during the years of 1926–1928 when Lancashire won the Championship thrice consecutively. He kept wicket to the pace of E. A. McDonald, bringing off wonderful leg-side catches. He stood reasonably far back, never hindering the slips, and always actively and offensively present. He was a 'creative' wicket-keeper, not merely a passive accessory to the bowler's act, but on the attack from behind the stumps as directly, almost, and as aggressively, as the bowler himself. Duckworth had that anticipatory vigilance which prevents a batsman from attempting strokes safely ventured on, given a wicket-keeper who is content to 'wait and see'. He went after catches not considered catches at all by ordinary pragmatical observers. And because he was not always able to snap up the definitely elusive chance he was frequently thought to have missed one or two. In the Oval Test Match of 1930, against Australia, he missed Woodfull when 6 and Ponsford when 23 and 45; whereupon Woodfull proceeded to score 54 and Ponsford 110. At least 2 of these potential 'chances' were rendered actual by Duckworth's astonishing agility and foresight.

George Duckworth in active retirement as major-domo on one of his several tours.

In his most prosperous season, 1928, he caught 77 and stumped 30, a record then surpassed only by one other wicket-keeper, L. E. G. Ames. These figures barely indicate Duckworth's omnipresent hostility, his general rapid accuracy, or the number of times he, on average, appealed hour by hour. He was a keen, fine sportsman, a Lancashire 'character' through and through, a wise, knowledgeable judge of the game, and a man of intelligent views and philosophy, off the field as well as on it. After the Second World War his commonsense and irrepressible humour were valuable assets to several MCC touring sides, whom he accompanied as scorer and baggage-master, guide, philosopher and friend.

NEVILLE CARDUS

CAREER FIGURES

	INNS	NO	RUNS	HS	AVGE	100S
Batting	544	195	4932	75	14·13	–

Bowling 0–73 W/k: ct 751; st 339 Total 1090

Test Record (24)

	INNS	NO	RUNS	HS	AVGE	100S
Batting	28	12	234	39*	14·62	–

W/k: ct 45; st 15 Total 60

DULEEPSINHJI, Kumar Shri (1905–1959)

Cheltenham 1921–1923 (Captain 1923). Cambridge Univ 1925–1928. Sussex 1924–1932. England: in England 1929, 1930, 1931; in New Zealand 1929–30.

In the all too few years of his cricket life in England before a breakdown in health drove him out of the game, the effortless ease and brilliance of 'Duleep's' batting, and the charming friendliness and modesty of his spirit, captured the hearts of all who watched or came to know him. With 'Ranji' as a devoted uncle, Charles Fry as his guardian when he came to England, and Aubrey Faulkner as occasional coach, he could not have been better guided, but from the start there was no mistaking his exceptional promise.

In his 3 years in the Cheltenham XI he made 1,119 runs, took 124 wickets with flighted leg-breaks and, playing for the representative Public School side at Lord's, was hailed in *Wisden* as a batsman of outstanding class. In the following May, he made 120 and 43 for MCC against Cambridge, a significant prelude to what was to come. Given his blue after his 3rd match as a freshman, he made 932 runs for the University and a fine 75 against Oxford. Though ill-health only allowed him to play 5 innings in 1927 – one of them 254 not out, the highest of any University player at Fenner's – his total aggregate for Cambridge was 2,333.

Qualifying for Sussex by residence in 1926, his record for his 6 seasons with that county (he played no match for them in 1927), could compare with Ranji's and Fry's. In all matches of the seasons of 1929–1931 he made, with an average of 55, 7,791 runs, more than any other batsman in England, and 29 hundreds; of these the highest was the 333 against Northants with which, on the 1st day of the 1st home match of 1930, he inaugurated the new score-board at Hove. But perhaps even more memorable were his 3 doubles of 115 and 246 against Kent in 1929, and, in 1930, 116 and 102 not out against Middlesex, and 125 and 103 not out for the Gentlemen at Lord's; those were the years when 'Tich' Freeman was carrying all before him, but at Hastings and Lord's Duleep 'tore him to shreds'. Of his 12 hundreds in 1931, 4 were in consecutive innings. Of his 19 innings in Test Matches, by far the best remembered will always be the first he ever played against Australia when he scored 173 at Lord's; he also made a hundred against New Zealand in each of the series he played against them.

Lithe and quick on his feet, with the ability to sight the ball just that fraction earlier which is the mark of greatness, Duleep combined a basically sound defence with fascinating facility and variety of stroke play, rivalling his uncle alike in late cutting, leg glancing and in driving power. As captain of Sussex in his last two seasons, his tactical intuition and selfless thought for others won him unstinted loyalty and respect. A magnificent slip, he made 252 catches. In 1950 he was appointed Indian High Commissioner in Australia, and on his return Chairman of the All Indian Council of Sports. Nothing meant more to him than the campaign he led to help the boy cricketers of his country.

H. S. ALTHAM

CAREER FIGURES

	INNS	NO	RUNS	HS	AVGE	100S
Batting	333	23	15485	333	49·95	50

Bowling 28 wkts at 48·04 Ct 252

Test Record (12)

	INNS	NO	RUNS	HS	AVGE	100S
Batting	19	2	995	173	58·52	3

Bowling 0 wkts for 7 Ct 10

EDINBURGH, Duke of (HRH The Prince Philip) (1921–)

Gordonstoun (Captain 1938). President MCC 1949–50 and 1974–1975; Committee 1950–1953.

The only member of the Royal Family in this century who has taken more than an official interest in cricket, Prince Philip was a useful medium-pace right hand off-spinner, a good field and a hard hitting right-hand bat. For many years his cricket was confined almost entirely to an annual match on behalf of the National Playing Fields Association, in which he himself whenever possible captained one side. The series began in 1949 and later was played at Arundel, the opposition being captained by the Duke of Norfolk. In these matches he often showed that, given the opportunities, he would have been well up to the standard of good club cricket. As it was, he collected a wicket and a dozen runs against Hampshire and a splendid 22 against the Duke of Beaufort's XI. But (alas!) cricket takes time, whereas polo and four-in-hand driving takes relatively little. It says much for his enthusiasm that, despite his many other commitments, he found time to visit Lord's and carry out his duties during his years as President. He is the only man in this century who, except during the wars, has had 2 terms as President.

R. L. ARROWSMITH

John Edrich: shoulders and arms of great strength.

EDRICH, John Hugh, MBE (1937–)

Brackendale Sch, Norwich. Combined Services 1956. Surrey 1958–1978 (Captain 1973–1977). England: in England 1963–1976, except 1973; in Australia 1965–66, 1970–71, 1974–75 (Captain); in West Indies 1967–68; in New Zealand 1965–66, 1970–71, 1974–75; in India 1963–64; in Pakistan 1968–69.

Edrich's actual deeds with a bat in his hand are the straightforward measure of his efficiency as a cricketer. He was not a natural athlete, being a virtual non-bowler and possessed of no more than a modest throwing arm. He had, it is true, a safe enough pair of hands, and developed into something of a specialist gully fielder, but I doubt whether he won many fielding prizes in his long career. No – it was his batting, pure and simple, for which selectors regularly picked him. Even his occasional periods as captain showed him in no exceptional light.

I can hardly remember a time when 'young John', so called to differentiate him from the older Bill (his cousin) of Middlesex, did not open the batting. Stocky and determined, he would walk out to bat as though it was the only position he had ever contemplated and it certainly suited his style of play. Movement of his feet was never greater than was absolutely necessary to achieve the required result. There was no more than a minor flourish of the bat as, from a somewhat tense stance, he planted it solidly in the path of the ball. Most left-handers have a natural swing which makes them strong on the leg-side and good square cutters. John Edrich bore no resemblance to this breed at all, keeping the bat firmly perpendicular and adroitly tucking the ball away off his legs rather than swinging at it. Amongst his greatest attributes were a sound knowledge of what to leave alone, a shrewd eye for the well-placed single and a penchant for anything pitching around leg stump. Strong in the forearm, he was no mean hitter of the ball through the covers or even over them when the occasion allowed; but he should be remembered most for his obdurate performances against dangerously fast bowling, even though his natural technique was not specially well suited to dealing with it or to taking personal avoiding action. He took some severe blows on the hands during his career, some of which required major surgery, including bone grafts on damaged knuckles. He took the most direct blow on the head (unhelmeted) I ever saw, from the South African fast-bowler, Peter Pollock, at Lord's in 1965; he remains one of the few batsmen to live through such an experience and emerge with his nerve almost wholly intact.

No greater tribute to these sterling qualities was ever paid than his recall to the England team against the West Indian fast bowlers in 1976 at the age of 38. He and Brian Close survived one of the most torrid evening sessions against the lifting ball ever seen at Old Trafford. They were battered, bruised, even slightly bewildered, but they were not intimidated. I watched one of Edrich's most attractive innings on the television, in black-and-white in those days, from my hospital bed in 1965. It was a triple-hundred at Headingley, against a not entirely incapable New Zealand attack, compiled with a power and certainty of timing that even Bradman might have envied. Unfortunately such occasions were rare; the onlooker usually had to make do with less fluent offerings.

It always surprised me, in view of his limited footwork (he never to my recollection took a step down the pitch to anybody), how well he played the spinners, but the scores are there to prove he did, a fair number of them against us at Sussex. Later on in his Test career, Edrich seemed to have difficulty warming up, his 2nd-innings record being infinitely better than his 1st. It was as though his true qualities were not switched on until the situation became desperate, particularly against his favourite Australian opponents. He should be remembered, perhaps, like wartime bomber pilots, as someone who faced a lot of flak and lived to let someone else tell the tale.

TED DEXTER

CAREER FIGURES

	INNS	NO	RUNS	HS	AVGE	100S
Batting	979	104	39790	310*	45·47	103

Bowling 0 wkts for 53 runs Ct 311

Test Record (77)

	INNS	NO	RUNS	HS	AVGE	100S
Batting	127	9	5138	310*	43·54	12

Bowling 0 wkts for 23 runs Ct 43

EDRICH, William John, DFC (1916–)

Brackendale Sch, Norwich. Middlesex 1937–1958 (Captain 1951–1957). England: in England 1938, 1946–1950 consecutively, 1953, 1954; in Australia 1946–47, 1954–55; in South Africa 1938–39; in New Zealand 1946–47.

Bill Edrich was born at Lingwood in Norfolk. His career started in his native county, but his great cricket talent soon took him to Lord's and from there to all the great cricket grounds round the world. He came first to the front in

W. J. Edrich: he knew no fear.

1938 when, having by this time qualified for Middlesex, he scored 1,000 runs before the end of May. He had been awarded his cap in 1937, and he remained devoted to Middlesex throughout his first-class career. He captained them from 1953 to 1957, after 2 years of joint captaincy with Denis Compton. A professional cricketer at the outset, he changed his status after a distinguished war record, and so played for both the Gentlemen and the Players.

He will be remembered on the international scene for his great courage and determination. A fearless hooker with a sound defence, his game was always lifted in adverse circumstances. His skill on bad wickets in Australia endeared him to the crowds there. Judged from the highest standards his batting was very bottom-handed and not pretty to watch. Sometimes his rustic origins were obvious. His favourite shots were the pulled drive, the hook and the late cut. Watchfulness and grit were the keynotes, with most of the runs accruing on the on-side. His bowling was explosive and tearaway. Operating from a short run he was capable of great speed in short bursts. In addition he was a slip fielder and, therefore, always 'in the game'.

The zenith of his career came in 1947. Middlesex won the Championship and he contributed 3,539 runs to the first-class scene. That season at both county and international level all bowling was put to the sword. Edrich and Compton spent practically the whole summer at the crease. He never quite recaptured that form again, and in his last two seasons he was a pale shadow of that gay cavalier. As a captain he showed great intuition with his timing of declarations. Close finishes became a Middlesex speciality, and he fully maintained the county tradition for bright play. It is hard to find a single word to summarize any cricketer, but in Edrich's case it would be 'guts'. Relishing a scrap, he never gave up in any game until the last entry was made in the scorebook. The same was so when, upon leaving Middlesex in 1958, he returned to Norfolk, for whom he played with undiminished vigour and considerable success until he was 55.

JOHN WARR

CAREER FIGURES

	INNS	NO	RUNS	HS	AVGE	100S
Batting	964	92	36965	267*	42·39	86

Bowling 479 wkts at 33·31 Ct 526

Test Record (39)

	INNS	NO	RUNS	HS	AVGE	100S
Batting	63	2	2440	219	40·00	6

Bowling 41 wkts at 41·29 Ct 39

EMMETT, Tom (1841–1904)

Yorkshire 1866–1888 (Captain 1878–1882). England: in Australia 1876–77, 1878–79, 1881–82. Coach at Rugby 1888–1898; to Leicestershire 1898–1904.

Emmett was a magnificent fast left-hand bowler who could pitch on the leg-stump and hit the off. An occasional ball came with his arm. More often he varied it with one outside the off-stump and it was this that beguiled him into bowling more wides than any other famous bowler. He remained a fine, crafty bowler long after his pace had gone. He was a good left-hand bat and one of the greatest and best-loved characters in the cricket world. In later life he made a notable reputation as coach at Rugby.

R. L. ARROWSMITH

CAREER FIGURES

	INNS	NO	RUNS	HS	AVGE	100S
Batting	700	90	9051	104	14·84	1

Bowling 1582 wkts at 13·36 Ct 269

Test Record (7)

	INNS	NO	RUNS	HS	AVGE	100S
Batting	13	1	160	48	13·33	–

Bowling 9 wkts at 31·35 Ct 9

EVANS, Thomas Godfrey, CBE (1920–)

Kent Coll, Canterbury. Kent 1939–1959 and 1967. England: in England 1946–1959 consecutively; in Australia 1946–47, 1950–51, 1954–55, 1958–59; in South Africa 1948–49, 1956–57; in West Indies 1947–48, 1953–54; in New Zealand 1946–47, 1950–51, 1954–55.

Evans was the outstanding wicket-keeper of his day. He was so far ahead of all his rivals that there was no second, and, as soon as the first signs appeared that his supremacy was waning, he retired from the game. Yet even so his exact position among the great, with whom clearly he must be ranked, is not easy to determine. One of the hallmarks of the great 'keepers had always been their quietness and absence of fuss. They made the whole thing look so easy that only an expert could see how great they were: the man in the street merely saw that they never had an off-day and hardly ever made an obvious mistake. Evans was the opposite of this. He was never quiet for a moment, never out of the picture, always darting this way and that and hurling himself to bring off apparently impossible catches. No wonder the public loved him and almost idolized him. Doubtless with his astonishing quickness he made catches which no other man could have reached, but doubtless, too, much of what he did would have been done equally well without attracting any attention at all. Probably no wicket-keeper and very few players of any kind have done so much to keep a game alive and to get the best out of their bowlers and fieldsmen. Bedser, for instance, is admitted to have bowled far better to Evans standing up than to lesser 'keepers standing back.

Godfrey Evans: Morris misses a ball from Bedser and Evans makes another brilliant leg-side take, Melbourne 1950–51.

In an age when wicket-keepers were turning into long-stops, Evans by his own example showed them for the pedestrian practitioners that they were. In an age when cricket was in danger of becoming not only a business, but a dreary business, he did all that one man could do to keep it a game. Indeed, had he taken it a trifle more seriously, he could have been one of the best bats of his day. Very quick on his feet, in times when most batsmen were anchored to their crease, he had a wonderful eye and was no respecter of persons. Significantly 2 of his comparatively few hundreds were made in Test Matches, and at Lord's in 1952 he failed by only 2 runs to complete one before lunch. Significantly, too, in a crisis at Adelaide in 1947 he stayed in for 95 minutes without scoring. But too often he took his batting as a joke or even played to the gallery, and he cannot rank, as otherwise he might have done, with Ames or Cameron.

R. L. ARROWSMITH

CAREER FIGURES

	INNS	NO	RUNS	HS	AVGE	100S
Batting	753	52	14882	144	21·22	7

Bowling 2 wkts at 122·50 W/k: ct 811; st 249 Total 1060

Test Record (91)

	INNS	NO	RUNS	HS	AVGE	100S
Batting	133	14	2439	104	20·49	2

W/k: ct 173; st 46 Total 219

FARNES, Kenneth (1911–1941)

Royal Liberty Sch, Romford. Cambridge Univ 1931–1933. Essex 1930–1939. England: in England 1934, 1938; in Australia 1936–37; in South Africa 1938–39; in West Indies 1934–35.

Farnes, with considerable height and high action, bowled sometimes 'as fast as any man ever bowled'. Such an occasion was the Gentlemen and Players match of 1938, Farnes having just previously been dropped from the Test side. In his 1st over, containing 2 wickets, his speed was truly ferocious, and the 8 for 43 in the Players' 1st innings which paved the way for their defeat was rated the best piece of fast bowling seen in the match since Arthur Fielder took all 10 wickets at Lord's in 1906. Farnes first appeared for

Essex against Kent at the age of 19, and took 5 wickets for 36. He and H. D. Read became the fastest pair in England, and on occasion he was liable to be intimidating. Farnes often bowled on unresponsive pitches against powerful batting, but he played for England against Australia, the West Indies and South Africa, the last occasion being the 'timeless Test', so that his analyses seldom did him justice. He did the hat-trick against Nottinghamshire at Clacton in the last match but one before the Second World War, in which he was killed.

G. D. MARTINEAU

CAREER FIGURES

	INNS	NO	RUNS	HS	AVGE	100S
Batting	199	58	1178	97*	8·35	–

Bowling 720 wkts at 20·55 Ct 84

Test Record (15)

	INNS	NO	RUNS	HS	AVGE	100S
Batting	17	5	58	20	4·83	–

Bowling 60 wkts at 28·65 Ct 1

FAULKNER, George Aubrey, DSO
(1881–1930)

Transvaal 1902–03, 1913–14. South Africa: in South Africa 1905–06, 1909–10; in England 1907, 1912, 1924; in Australia 1910–11.

Aubrey Faulkner, South Africa's greatest all-rounder, was one of the major figures in a revolutionary period of his country's cricket. The googly had been invented by Bosanquet at the turn of the century and had, from the hand of its inventor, some success, although rather by reason of its novelty than its intrinsic quality. The South African spinners developed it to a weapon of great potency on their own matting pitches and created something of a sensation in the wet English season of 1907. Vogler was generally regarded as the best of a formidable quartet, but many judges thought that Faulkner on his day was equally dangerous. He bowled with a fine, lively wheeling action at slow-medium pace with a fierce spin, concealing his googly adroitly, and whipping in a fast yorker with the minimum of warning. Catching England on a helpful pitch at Headingley in 1907 he took 6 wickets for 17, the best of many outstanding bowling performances.

As a batsman Faulkner was in the solid, rather than dashing mould, but great strength of wrist and forearm gave his strokes a decisive and powerful aspect. Bred on matting, he was a particularly able hooker and cutter. On visiting Australia in 1910–11, he devoted himself almost exclusively to batting, with resounding success in the Tests. At Melbourne he scored 204, and at Adelaide 115. His return to England in 1912, for the Triangular Tournament, was less successful for, with his fellows, he found Barnes an insurmountable obstacle in another season of soft wickets. What was virtually his last bow was happily his greatest all-round feat. For A. C. MacLaren's team at Eastbourne in 1921 he scored 153 and took 6 wickets to help defeat the hitherto invincible Australians. Faulkner had always been a thoughtful cricketer with a keen analytical flair for the techniques of the game. On retirement from active play he employed these talents by opening the Faulkner School of Cricket. His principles were sound and he was a tireless instructor, patient with the humble and enthusiastic wherever he scented promise. Many distinguished cricketers benefited from his coaching but E. T. Killick, whom he guided from an early age, was generally regarded as the perfect model of Faulkner orthodoxy. Faulkner was a man of restless highly-strung temperament. He died, tragically, by his own hand in 1930.

IAN PEEBLES

CAREER FIGURES

	INNS	NO	RUNS	HS	AVGE	100S
Batting	199	23	6392	204	36·31	13

Bowling 449 wkts at 17·42 Ct 94

Test Record (25)

	INNS	NO	RUNS	HS	AVGE	100S
Batting	47	4	1754	204	40·79	4

Bowling 82 wkts at 26·58 Ct 20

FENDER, Percy George Herbert
(1892–)

St Paul's 1908–1910. Sussex 1910–1913. Surrey 1914 and 1920–1935 (Captain 1920–1931). England: in England 1921, 1924, 1929; in Australia 1920–21; in South Africa 1922–23.

When Surrey emerged from the First World War, it was to find that they possessed a fine all-rounder and, after 1920, an exceptionally able captain. Fender had already proved a valuable addition to the bowling in 1914, but, as a batsman, he also hit with exceptional power, and picked up wonderful catches in the slips. In 1920 he hit gloriously for the defeated Gentlemen – 3 sixes and 5 fours in a memorable 50 – and, with 113 not out, he partnered Peach in making 171 in 42 minutes against Northamptonshire, reaching his own hundred in the record time of 35 minutes. In 1922, against Hampshire at the Oval, his 185 included 3 sixes, 3 fives and 25 fours. His 137 against Kent took 90 minutes and sixes and fours again abounded. Yet, though Surrey's batting strength was formidable, the bowling was then the reverse and Fender, himself the 'best change bowler in England', needed all his guile to make the most of slender resources. He had bowled as successfully as any Englishman in Australia in 1920–21, but his 12 wickets were expensive, and in South Africa, on matting, his best was 4 for 29 at Cape Town in January 1923. 'Tall, dark, with twinkling ferocious glasses', Dudley Carew remembered him.

G. D. MARTINEAU

P. G. H. Fender, in 1980 England's senior living Test cricketer and in the '20s a famous captain of Surrey.

CAREER FIGURES

	INNS	NO	RUNS	HS	AVGE	100S
Batting	783	69	19034	185	26·65	21

Bowling 1894 wkts at 25·05 Ct 558

Test Record (13)

	INNS	NO	RUNS	HS	AVGE	100S
Batting	21	1	380	60	19·00	–

Bowling 29 wkts at 40·86 Ct 14

FERGUSON, William Henry, BEM
(1880–1957)

From 1905 to 1957 no major cricket team toured England, Australia, South Africa or New Zealand, without 'Fergie' as scorer and baggage-master. The length of the unique career this short, slightly-built man created for himself in cricket was extraordinary; his claim that he never lost a piece of luggage on 43 tours was miraculous.

Ferguson was a clerk in a Sydney office when he pretended to need treatment from his dentist, M. A. Noble, the Test player, and lobbied him about scoring for the Australian side about to leave for England under Darling. He got the job and continued to accompany Test teams all the year round until an accident prevented him completing the 1957 tour to England by West Indies.

All told Ferguson scored in 208 Test Matches and travelled over 600,000 miles with touring sides, predominantly in the days before regular air travel. His scorebooks were wonderfully neat and he was the first to keep diagrams of a batsman's strokes. These were used by several famous captains when they planned their field-placing tactics. Reproductions of some of the most famous of these scoring charts were a feature of his autobiography, *Mr Cricket*.

RICHARD STREETON

FINGLETON, John Henry Webb, OBE
(1908–)

New South Wales 1930–31 to 1939–40. Australia: in Australia 1931–32, 1932–33, 1936–37; in England 1938; in South Africa 1935–36.

In the pages of *Wisden*, Jack Fingleton is remembered for having scored 4 successive Test hundreds – 3 of them in South Africa in 1935–36, followed by one against England at Brisbane in 1936–37. Statisticians will also recall that he was concerned in a 6th-wicket partnership of 346 with Bradman in the same season at Melbourne. He was noted in Australia for possessing a strong defence and high courage, as he showed when facing England's attack in 1932–33. Though not judged to be an attractive batsman of the McCabe type, he was able on occasion to hit hard and score fast. He played many fine innings apart from those for which he is best known and regularly helped both New South

Jack Fingleton: 4 successive Test hundreds.

Wales and Australia by giving them a good start. A superb fieldsman, he moved fast to gather the ball and return it was a smooth, rhythmical movement which was characteristically Australian.

These are the attributes of a memorable cricketer. Yet, besides all this, he has become something which is rarer in his country – a cricket-writer of scholarly style, not simply a racy reporter, relying on pithy colloquialisms. His writing may be judged by books such as *Brightly Fades the Don*, *The Ashes Crown the Year*, *The Greatest Test of All*. Here, indeed, we have an unusual combination: at once a cricketer of high international quality and a literary critic, free from vulgarity or bias, whose fair-minded good humour was echoed in his BBC commentaries.

G. D. MARTINEAU

CAREER FIGURES

	INNS	NO	RUNS	HS	AVGE	100S
Batting	166	13	6816	167	44·54	22

Bowling 2 wkts at 27·00 Ct (incl. w/k) 82; st 4

Test Record (18)

	INNS	NO	RUNS	HS	AVGE	100S
Batting	29	1	1189	136	42·46	5

Ct 13

FLETCHER, Keith William Robert
(1944–)

Comberton Village Coll. Essex 1962– (Captain 1974–). England: in England 1968–1975; in Australia 1970–71, 1974–75, 1976–77; in West Indies 1973–74; in New Zealand 1970–71, 1974–75; in India 1972–73, 1976–77; in Pakistan 1968–69, 1972–73.

From the moment when, as a wee 14-year-old, he bridged the considerable gap dividing public school from village school cricket and earned a place in the Young Amateurs of Essex, it was obvious that Keith Fletcher was destined to become an international cricketer. A shy, small, country lad, he joined the county staff, where he was christened 'the Gnome' as a young teenager. Keith was always encouraged to play his wide range of spectacular strokes, which included driving seamers off the back foot over extra cover, and depositing off-spinners into the crowd. He made his first appearance for Essex at 17. A year later he had established himself as a first team regular with exciting runs, not just the promise to justify his place. The manner in which he dealt with the West Indian pair, Hall and Griffith, showed that, in addition to character, he possessed that extra something which divides the potentially great from the highly competent.

Although nearly 3,000 runs in 52 Tests with an average of over 40 are highly respectable figures and far better than most, Keith seldom did himself full justice when representing England. His batting, though valuable, was often laboured, so that it was hard to believe what a brilliant strokemaker he could be. He lost and dropped many of his strokes, even in domestic cricket, when he became, first the mainstay, and, later, the captain of Essex. Throughout his international career, too, England were usually struggling for runs. Fletcher has also been, on several occasions, the victim of circumstances, as when, on tour, he continued to play although injured, or, as when he was preferred in his 1st Test to Phil Sharpe at Headingley and then failed to hold 3 stinging chances at slip – something which the Yorkshire crowd have never allowed him to forget – or, finally, as when he fell a shell-shock victim to Lillee and Thomson. As Mike Brearley has so often remarked, Keith possesses an exceptional knowledge of the game. In using it he has shown himself a shrewd, tactical, rather self-effacing skipper.

TREVOR BAILEY

CAREER FIGURES

	INNS	NO	RUNS	HS	AVGE	100S
Batting	263	17	6548	305*	26·72	7

Bowling 717 wkts at 20·75 Ct 119

Test Record (11)

	INNS	NO	RUNS	HS	AVGE	100S
Batting	15	1	330	71	23·57	–

Bowling 45 wkts at 20·57 Ct 11

FOSTER, Frank Rowbotham
(1889–1958)

Warwickshire 1908–1914 (Captain 1911–1914). England: in England 1912; in Australia 1911–12.

Foster will always be remembered as Barnes's partner in one of the greatest bowling combinations England has ever had, and as the man who won Warwickshire the Championship in 1911, thus taking it for the only time in 60 years outside the 'Big Six'. Left-handed, with a short run and a beautifully easy action, he was, if only fast-medium through the air, fast off the ground, with an occasional very fast ball. Sometimes the ball would straighten out; usually it came with his arm and the batsman would find himself playing constantly in a hurry and, if he was late with his stroke, being hit on the legs. To a right-hander he had 6 men on the leg and was thus one of the pioneers of leg-theory, and years afterwards was consulted by Jardine before the 'Body-line' tour, though he himself disapproved of Body-line. In his Test series in Australia he headed the averages with 32 wickets for 21·62. A right-handed batsman, he was a natural hitter who did not worry too much about technique; he is one of the select body who have made over 300 in a county match. He was a fine slip. For Warwickshire in 1911 he made 1,383 runs and took 116 wickets and this, combined with Field's bowling and his own inspiring captaincy, raised the side from 14th in 1910 to Champions. His career was finished by a crash on a motor-cycle early in the First World War.

R. L. ARROWSMITH

FOSTER, Reginald Erskine (1878–1914)

Malvern 1893–1896 (Captain 1896). Oxford 1897–1900 (Captain 1900). Worcestershire 1899–1912 (Captain 1901). England: in England 1907 (Captain); in Australia 1903–04.

Reginald Erskine Foster, most gifted of a most gifted family of cricketers, had a brilliant but pathetically short life and career. He died of diabetes at the age of 36. At Malvern his batting showed a natural skill, but was hardly prophetic of his rapid development into a player described by C. B. Fry as one who used a bat quicker than anybody of his period, excepting K. S. Ranjitsinhji. At Oxford he won his blue as a freshman and played 4 times at Lord's. His brilliant 171 in 1900 was the record individual innings in the University Match up to that date. Ten days later, for the Gentlemen v Players at Lord's, he scored 102 not out and 136 in the same match.

After 1901, apart from the winter of 1903–04, he could spare little time for first-class cricket and was more or less out of the game when the Australians visited England in 1905 and 1909. He was obliged to refuse the captaincy of the MCC team for Australia in 1907–08, but was free to lead England against South Africa in England in 1907. During his only rubber against Australia, in Australia in 1903–04, he achieved the then record individual Test score of 287, at Sydney. Cricketers who saw his cutting at Sydney that day agreed that it was incomparable for rapidity, certainty of touch and effortlessness.

Foster was regarded without question as one of the three or four really great batsmen of the early 1900s. The advent in his period of the swerve and the googly put no break or burden on his style, which was as delightful to the eye as any batsmanship could be. Against the googlies of Vogler, Faulkner, Gordon White and Schwarz, at Kennington Oval in 1907, he scored a rapier-like 51 for England against South Africa. The remarkable fact about Foster's cricket is that he was able to return, after a considerable absence, to top-class cricket and at once find touch and form. In 1910 he could turn out once for Worcestershire but scored 133 – against Yorkshire. In 1901, when he was free to go to the wicket 44 times, his aggregate of runs was 2,128, average 50·66. He was also one of the most swift and fluent of slip fielders; and at association football he played three times for England against Wales, once each against Scotland and Ireland. He was, if ever there was one, on or off the field, a 'thoroughbred'.

NEVILLE CARDUS

CAREER FIGURES

	INNS	NO	RUNS	HS	AVGE	100S
Batting	234	17	9076	287	41·82	22

Bowling 25 wkts at 46·16 Ct 175

Test Record (8)

	INNS	NO	RUNS	HS	AVGE	100S
Batting	14	1	602	287	46·30	1

Ct 13

FREDERICKS, Roy Clifton (1942–)

New Amsterdam Technical Coll. Guyana 1963–64– . Glamorgan 1971–1973. West Indies: in West Indies 1970–71, 1971–72, 1972–73, 1973–74, 1975–76, 1976–77; in England 1969, 1973, 1976; in Australia 1968–69, 1975–76; in New Zealand 1968–69; in India 1974–75; in Pakistan 1974–75. WSC.

Roy Fredericks is one of a small group of diminutive batsmen to have succeeded at the highest level. The 5 feet 4 inches tall Guyanan first caught the public eye with scores of 127 and 115 against Barbados in the 1967 Shell Series in the West Indies. Both innings were full of the wristy cutting and explosive hooking which were to become his trademark in the cricket stadia of the world. Paradoxically, it was a slow, rearguard 57, for Guyana against the 1968 MCC touring team, in his birthplace, Georgetown, which clinched his selection in the West Indian team which toured Australia in 1968–69. There he averaged 33·87 in the series. He was the only batsman on the short tour of England in 1969 to score over 1,000 runs, and in the 1971–72 series against New Zealand in West Indies, Fredericks again had the highest aggregate of the home players, 487 runs in the 5 Tests.

Between 1971 and 1973 he spent 3 years with Glamorgan, earning his county cap in his first game by scoring 145 and taking 5 wickets against Nottinghamshire. Fredericks was one of Mr Packer's first signings, but after one season in Australia he announced his retirement from international cricket. He will be best remembered as an important member of the West Indian side that won the Prudential World Cup in 1975 and for the Jekyll and Hyde nature of his batting. His 150 against England in the Second Test at Edgbaston in 1973 took him 8½ hours and saved his side from defeat; in Perth, in 1975, his 169 against Thomson and Lillee in their prime was a brilliant exhibition of sustained hitting.

PETER WALKER

FREEMAN, Alfred Percy (1888–1965)

Kent 1914–1936. England: in England 1928, 1929; in Australia 1924–25; in South Africa 1927–28.

At his most robust 'Tich' Freeman was just 5 feet 2 inches tall. He had appeared for Kent before the First World War but it was not until the resumption that he established and maintained his pre-eminence amongst English spin bowlers. He may periodically have been eclipsed by a rival practitioner but, over the span of his post-First War career his record is unexcelled. His total of 3,776 wickets is only exceeded by Wilfred Rhodes. In 1928 Freeman took 304 wickets in the English season, and, in 1933, reached 298. Altogether he took over 200 wickets 8 times, and over 100 17 times, in a career lasting from 1914 to 1936.

Freeman's hands were in proportion to his size and therefore very small; but this did not prevent him getting a very firm, wide-fingered grip on the ball which he spun sharply from the leg. He also bowled a top-spinner which he used freely to destroy the weaker of the opposition. His googly was a good if not particularly venomous ball, fairly well concealed. Freeman invariably hitched up his trousers as a warning signal, ran about 5 yards and delivered the ball with a neat, rotary action, which gave the impression of a spring snapping. He was meticulously accurate for a bowler of his type, and could maintain his accuracy over very long periods. He was at all times a most interesting bowler. Freeman played for England 12 times, but only twice against Australia. It was maintained in some quarters that he was not a great bowler against great batsmen, and prone to be discouraged by them. This is open to doubt for he fought some fine duels with Bradman, and did as well as anyone, except Tate, in his 2 Australian appearances in 1924–25. Though not required in the Tests of 1928–29 he bowled with much success also for A. P. F. Chapman's team against the Australian states. He retired in 1936 to a house picturesquely named 'Dunbowlin'.

IAN PEEBLES

CAREER FIGURES

	INNS	NO	RUNS	HS	AVGE	100S
Batting	716	194	4964	66	9·51	–

Bowling 3776 wkts at 18·42 Ct 236

Test Record (12)

	INNS	NO	RUNS	HS	AVGE	100S
Batting	16	5	154	50*	14·00	–

Bowling 66 wkts at 25·86 Ct 4

FRY, Charles Burgess (1872–1956)

Repton 1888–1891 (Captain 1890–1891). Oxford Univ 1892–1895 (Captain 1894). Surrey 1891. Sussex 1894–1908 (Captain 1904–1908). Hampshire 1909–1921. England: in England 1899, 1902, 1905, 1907, 1909, 1912 (Captain); in South Africa 1895–96. Selector 1909, 1912.

Fry was beyond all doubt the greatest all-round athlete, and one of the most gifted men, that ever played cricket for England. So good a classicist as to be placed senior to F. E. Smith on the scholarship roll to Wadham College, Oxford; he held for 21 years the world record for the long jump, played association football for England, and after appearing for Southampton in the final of the FA Cup on a Saturday in April, 1902, made 82 on the following Monday at the Oval for London County against Surrey. Four years in each of the Repton and Oxford XIs, and captain of both, he made a hundred in the University Match of 1894, in which year, after taking part in one match on a birth qualification for Surrey in 1891, he began playing regularly for Sussex. He continued to do so until, on taking over the command of the TS *Mercury* on the Hamble in 1909, he transferred his support to Hampshire. His last season in first-class cricket was 1921 when, even though now in his 50th year, he still batted well enough to be invited to play for England, but declined on the ground that he did not feel in full form.

Fry's life aggregate was 30,886 runs, with an average of 50. In 6 seasons he topped the English batting averages, averaging over 70 in 4 of them. He hit 94 hundreds, 13 of them in 1901, his greatest season, when he made 6 hundreds in succession, and totalled 3,147 runs. Of these hundreds 16 were 200s, and none more impressive than the 232 not out for the Gentlemen at Lord's in 1903, the highest score ever made for them there against the Players. In Test cricket his form was rather uneven, but he made 2 hundreds of majestic authority at the Oval, the first against the Australians in 1905, and the second 2 years later on a none-too-easy wicket against the famous quartet of South African spin bowlers whom most English batsmen had found unnervingly formidable. In the Triangular Tournament of 1912, he captained England in the 6 Tests against Australia and South Africa and was never on the losing side.

As a versatile sportsman C. B. Fry outdid all-comers: more than a hint here of his strength of mind and body.

He was pre-eminently a back player and a driver, who got more of his runs on the on than on the off side. His batting never revealed itself as an art, but rather as the scientific exposition of technique, mastered by the concentrated application of a first-class mind, and a fit and tireless body. The two books which he produced in collaboration with G. W. Beldam, *Great Batsmen* and *Great Bowlers and Fielders*, preserve at once in their action photographs an incomparable gallery of great contemporary players, and in their text a masterly analysis of the mechanics of the game. An arresting personality, and a brilliant conversationalist, Fry could, alike in form and in feature, have stepped straight out of the frieze of the Parthenon.

H. S. ALTHAM

CAREER FIGURES

	INNS	NO	RUNS	HS	AVGE	100S
Batting	658	43	30886	258*	50·22	94

Bowling 165 wkts at 28·58 Ct 244

Test Record (26)

	INNS	NO	RUNS	HS	AVGE	100S
Batting	41	3	1223	144	32·18	2

Bowling 0 wkts for 3 runs Ct 17

GAVASKAR, Sunil Manohar (1949–)

St Xavier's HS, and Bombay Univ. India: in India 1972–73, 1974–75, 1976–77, 1978–79, 1979–80, (Captain 1978–79, 1979–80); in England 1971, 1974, 1979; in Australia 1977–78; in West Indies 1970–71, 1975–76; in New Zealand 1975–76 (Captain); in Pakistan 1978–79.

Not since the two Vijays, Merchant and Hazare, made their mammoth scores in the Ranji Trophy during the Second World War, has an Indian batsman been as prolific as Sunil Gavaskar. His aggregate of 774 (average 154·80) in his 1st series in the West Indies in 1970–71, was the launching of a Test career which has included hundreds against England, Australia, Pakistan and New Zealand as well as West Indies, and 1,000 Test runs 3 times in a calendar year.

Blessed with a sound technique, Gavaskar has a Boycott-like determination to soldier on. These are the chief factors of his fabulous – to Indian eyes – career. He relies mainly on his percentage stroke, the drive. Yet, as he builds an innings, he hooks and cuts with the very best. His short stature makes him marginally vulnerable to the rising ball just short of a length, but it is a relative weakness.

Like most Bombay batsmen, Gavaskar made his mark in school cricket. His record score of 327 in University cricket, set in 1970, stood till 1978–79. Short and stocky, he prefers to field at slip, where he has been safe and smart. A public relations officer in a textile firm, he is a shrewd judge of men and has made the most of his opportunities. The image he projects in India is comparable to that of Denis Compton when he was associated with a hair cream in the postwar years. Gavaskar, too, is an idol in his own country where he has acted in a film.

K. N. PRABHU

GEARY, George (1893–)

Leicestershire 1912–1938. England: in England 1924, 1926, 1929, 1930, 1934; in Australia 1928–29; in South Africa 1927–28.

Geary was a fine all-round bowler of fast medium pace with a nice rhythm, and a poker-straight right arm which gave him a good command of spin and seam, allied to an unfailing accuracy. He would use the new ball to advantage and, on hard wickets, would plug away at a good length all day long without conceding a point. When the pitch gave him any help he became a most dangerous and hostile spinner. His stock ball was the off-break; but this he varied with an exceptionally well-concealed 'cutter' which went a sufficient amount the other way. This versatility made him a useful bowler in all conditions so that he was as successful abroad as in his own country. He was at his best on the faster of the matting wickets in South Africa where the great Herbie Taylor was so impressed that he likened Geary at Johannesburg to Barnes, the highest tribute he could accord to any bowler.

Having 'done his bit' for King and country George Geary returned to his chosen profession in 1919. As the mainstay of a moderate Leicester team it was an arduous one. A large, strong, cheerful man, he was admirably fitted for the job. Geary played for England in 14 Test Matches and 11 times took a 100 wickets in an English season. He was a most popular and loyal member of every side in which he played, a staunch and most engaging companion. These qualities he brought to his subsequent post as coach at Charterhouse, a position in which he revealed a shrewd judgment. When an old companion called upon him, Geary announced he was going to show him an England player and escorted him to a nearby net. The 14-year-old occupant was Peter May.

IAN PEEBLES

CAREER FIGURES

	INNS	NO	RUNS	HS	AVGE	100S
Batting	820	138	13504	122	19·80	8

Bowling 2063 wkts at 20·03 Ct 451

Test Record (14)

	INNS	NO	RUNS	HS	AVGE	100S
Batting	20	4	249	66	15·56	–

Bowling 46 wkts at 29·41 Ct 13

GIBBS, Lancelot Richard (1934–)

Standard HS, Georgetown. Guyana 1953–54 to 1975–76. Warwickshire 1967–1973. South Australia 1969–70. West Indies: in West Indies 1957–58, 1961–62, 1964–65, 1967–68, 1970–71, 1971–72, 1972–73, 1973–74; in England 1963, 1966, 1969, 1973; in Australia 1960–61, 1968–69, 1975–76; in New Zealand 1968–69; in India 1958–59, 1966–67, 1974–75; in Pakistan 1958–59, 1974–75; Rest of the World in England 1970.

Lance Gibbs's debut in first-class cricket hardly gave a clue to the outstanding career he was to enjoy. As a raw, gangling 19-year-old he was picked for British Guiana (as it then was) against the touring MCC side in 1954. His figures of 2 for 126 were unimpressive yet by the time he retired from first-class cricket at the end of the West Indian tour of Australia in 1976 his tally of 312 Test wickets was a world record. He stands 2nd only to Sobers (93) in number of appearances for West Indies and he will be rated by many of those who saw him during his 22 years in the first-class game as arguably the finest hard-wicket off-spinner of all time.

Gibbs played for Warwickshire between 1967–73 and in 1971 was one of only 6 bowlers in the country to get 100 wickets. In doing so he enabled Warwickshire to finish with the same number of points as Surrey, though they were runners-up for the title. Gibbs was an artist when it came to subtle variations in flight; he was also a considerable spinner of the ball, which, on the hard-baked West Indian pitches, he had to be to get any response. As a result, the middle knuckle of the index finger on his bowling hand became grotesquely enlarged. Gibbs was an impatient opponent. A 5 pace run-up full of bounce and energy – a contemporary once described his action as the nearest thing to a human grasshopper he had seen – he was a predatory hunter of batsmen. If he had a weakness it was a long-held reluctance to bowl around the wicket; an obvious advantage in the United Kingdom where turning pitches make lbw decisions virtually impossible to achieve for a bowler of his type operating from over the wicket. Besides his Test and County careers, Gibbs had a spell with Burnley in the Lancashire league and with Whitburn in the Durham league. He also played for South Australia in the Sheffield Shield in 1969–70.

In Test matches he took 10 wickets in a match twice and 5 wickets in an innings no fewer than 18 times. After being left out of the West Indian team against Australia on the 1960–61 tour for the first 2 Tests he removed 3 batsmen in 4 balls at Sydney in the Third and followed that with a hat trick at Adelaide in the fourth. A genuine No. 11 batsman, he was, however, one of the best of the postwar gully fieldsmen.

PETER WALKER

CAREER FIGURES

	INNS	NO	RUNS	HS	AVGE	100S
Batting	352	150	1729	43	8·55	–

Bowling 1024 wkts at 27·22 Ct 203

Test Record (79)

	INNS	NO	RUNS	HS	AVGE	100S
Batting	109	39	488	25	6·97	–

Bowling 309 wkts at 29·09 Ct 52.

GIFFEN, George (1859–1927)

South Australia 1880–81 to 1902–03 (Captain 1886–87 to 1897–98). Australia: in Australia 1881–82, 1882–83, 1884–85, 1891–92, 1894–95 (Captain); in England 1882, 1884, 1886, 1893, 1896.

A great all-rounder, often termed 'the "W.G." of Australia', George Giffen played in 31 Tests, scoring in them 1,238 runs, and taking 103 wickets. On the 1886 tour to England he headed both the batting and bowling averages but his most successful Test season was 1894–95 when, captaining the side in 4 of the 5 matches, his 161 and 41 and 8 wickets in the First Test at Sydney, and his 8 for 40 later in the series at Sydney, were 2 of the outstanding performances in that dramatic rubber in which he scored 475 runs and took 34 wickets. A determined and aggressive batsman, and a slow-medium bowler of great accuracy and subtle variation of flight, he scored in all first-class matches 11,757 runs and took 1,022 wickets. Still playing for South Australia in 1902–03 when nearly 42, he made 81 and 97 not out, and took 15 wickets in a match against Victoria. A respected figure wherever the game was played in Australia, he devoted much time in his later years to coaching young cricketers.

H. S. ALTHAM

CAREER FIGURES

	INNS	NO	RUNS	HS	AVGE	100S
Batting	421	24	11757	271	29·61	18

Bowling 1022 wkts at 21·31

Test Record (31)

	INNS	NO	RUNS	HS	AVGE	100S
Batting	53	0	1238	161	23·35	1

Bowling 103 wkts at 27·09 Ct 24

GILLIGAN, Arthur Edward Robert (1894–1976)

Dulwich 1911–1914 (Captain 1913–1914). Cambridge Univ 1919–1920. Surrey 1919. Sussex 1920–1932 (Captain 1922–1929). England: in England 1924 (Captain): in Australia 1924–25 (Captain); in South Africa 1922–23. Selector 1926. President MCC 1967–68. Patron Sussex 1973–1976.

Arthur Gilligan was the captain under whom England at last won a Test against Australia after the First World War – our 1st in 14 matches. He made Sussex into an immensely popular side and one of the most brilliant fielding sides in England. For a few years, while his health lasted, he was a really fast bowler who was accurate and bowled at the stumps or for catches in the slips. He was a courageous batsman, usually in the lower half of the order (his 1st hundred in first-class cricket was made at No. 11), who was always most likely to make runs when they were most needed and who believed that bowlers, especially quick bowlers, were made to be hit. As a mid-off he ranks with the greatest.

Endlessly cheerful and an indefatigable trier, he was always aggressive and he got the best out of his men; there was never a more popular captain. In one way his Australian tour must have been frustrating. In the previous June he had taken 6 for 7 and 5 for 83 against South Africa and with Tate had bowled them out for 30. A few weeks later he was badly hit over the heart while batting and was told by the doctors he must never bowl fast again. Needless to say, he disregarded the advice, but they were right and, try as he would, he was never thereafter a bowler of Test class. He was one of three brothers who gained distinction at the game.

R. L. ARROWSMITH

CAREER FIGURES

	INNS	NO	RUNS	HS	AVGE	100S
Batting	510	55	9140	144	20·08	12

Bowling 868 wkts at 23·20 Ct 160

Test Record (11)

	INNS	NO	RUNS	HS	AVGE	100S
Batting	16	3	209	39*	16·07	–

Bowling 36 wkts at 29·05 Ct 3

GODDARD, John Douglas Claude (1919–)

Harrison Coll, and Lodge Sch, Barbados. West Indies: in West Indies 1947–48 (Captain); in England 1950 (Captain), 1957 (Captain); in Australia 1951–52 (Captain); in New Zealand 1951–52 (Captain), 1955–56; in India 1948–49 (Captain).

John Goddard will have to his eternal credit that he led the devastating West Indies team in England in 1950. He had previously led West Indies successfully in India in 1948–49. In England in 1950 he not only let his batsmen and his bowlers have their heads; he himself repeatedly brought off the boldest and most difficult catches, could make runs and take wickets if they were needed (not out 58 and 4 for 25 in 17·4 overs in the Oval Test). Things did not go well in Australia in 1951–52 and Goddard has borne what probably is an unfair share of responsibility for this: of the 'three Ws' and Ramadhin and Valentine, who had been the mainstay of the 1950 tour, only Valentine maintained his 1950 form. Sent to New Zealand in 1955 as player-manager, with a team composed mainly of juniors, Goddard consistently batted well and in 4 Test innings was not out 3 times. He is, and has been for years, an active partner in a family business in Barbados.

C. L. R. JAMES

CAREER FIGURES

	INNS	NO	RUNS	HS	AVGE	100S
Batting	145	32	3769	218*	33·35	5

Bowling 146 wkts at 26·33

Test Record (27)

	INNS	NO	RUNS	HS	AVGE	100S
Batting	39	11	859	83*	30·67	

Bowling 33 wkts at 31.81 Ct 22

GODDARD, Thomas William John (1900–1966)

Gloucestershire 1922–1927 and 1929–1952. England: in England 1930, 1937, 1939: in South Africa 1938–39.

Goddard was a fine off-spinner, born from his own point of view some years too early. He was 35 when the new lbw Law gave encouragement to bowlers who attacked the leg and nearing 50 when off-spin began to replace leg-spin in Tests. Had he been 15 years younger, he would doubtlessly have played many more times for England. He was originally a fast bowler, but in 6 seasons his 153 wickets cost 34 runs each and, when he left Gloucestershire at the end of 1927, most people thought that an undistinguished career had ended. In fact he spent 1928 at Lord's, learning to bowl off-breaks and, returning to Gloucestershire, took in 1929 184 wickets for 16 runs each. When he retired, he had taken 2,979. Standing 6 feet 3 inches, a big man with enormous hands, he could turn the ball sharply, came fast off the pitch and was a master of flight; moreover, bowling as he did round the wicket, he dismissed many batsmen with one that kept straight on towards the slips.

R. L. ARROWSMITH

CAREER FIGURES

	INNS	NO	RUNS	HS	AVGE	100S
Batting	775	218	5234	71	9·40	–

Bowling 2979 wkts at 19·84 Ct 313

Test Record (8)

	INNS	NO	RUNS	HS	AVGE	100S
Batting	5	3	13	8	6·50	–

Bowling 22 wkts at 26·72 Ct 3

GODDARD, Trevor Leslie (1931–)

Durban HS. Natal 1952–53 to 1965–66 and 1968–69, 1969–70. North East Transvaal 1966–67 to 1967–68. South Africa: in South Africa 1956–57, 1957–58, 1964–65 (Captain), 1966–67, 1969–70; in England 1955, 1960; in Australia 1963–64 (Captain); in New Zealand 1963–64 (Captain).

Trevor Goddard, left-handed whether batting or bowling, and an outstanding close-to-the-wicket catcher, was a fine all-round cricketer. Touring England first in 1955, he scored 1,163 runs and took 60 wickets. He was a back-foot player and a rugged fighter. In 1957–58 against Australia at Johannesburg he scored 90 out of 176. He soon became an automatic choice for South Africa, opening the innings, and a first-change bowler in support of the spearhead. In scoring 56 against Australia at Cape Town he carried his bat through an innings of 99. In 1959–60 he scored 200 for Natal against Rhodesia and took 6 for 3, including the hat-trick, against Border at East London. Vice-captain in England in 1960, he was again successful with 1,377 runs and 73 wickets, scoring 99 in the Fifth Test at the Oval. With the introduction of the leg-side restriction of fielders

Trevor Goddard: the best Test record of all South African all-rounders.

Goddard's bowling became less of a force. But he developed into a skilful leader. He played a captain's part in the drawn series against Australia in 1963–64 and captained South Africa against England in South Africa in 1964–65.

COLIN COWDREY

CAREER FIGURES

	INNS	NO	RUNS	HS	AVGE	100S
Batting	293	19	11203	222	40·88	26

Bowling 525 wkts at 21·51 Ct 172

Test Record (41)

	INNS	NO	RUNS	HS	AVGE	100S
Batting	78	5	2516	112	34·46	1

Bowling 123 wkts at 26·22 Ct 48

GOMEZ, Gerald Ethridge (1919–)

Queen's Royal Coll. Trinidad. West Indies: in West Indies 1947–48 (Captain), 1952–53, 1953–54; in England 1939, 1950; in Australia 1951–52; in New Zealand 1951–52; in India 1948–49.

Gomez was a West Indian all-rounder whose career began with a trip to England in 1939 when he was not yet 20. While still at school he had been coached by the Australian Arthur Richardson. He made useful runs but failed in Tests and in first-class matches did not bowl one ball. Returning home he took his full share in the heavy scoring of the time. He helped Stollmeyer to reach within 11 runs of the then world record (445) for the 3rd wicket.

It was in England in 1950, and very much in Australia in 1951–52, that Gomez attained a high status as an all-rounder. He made 1,000 runs, was always dependable as a middle-order batsman in the Tests and, apart from Ramadhin and Valentine, was the most valuable bowler on the side, taking 55 wickets. In Australia he surpassed himself. Alone among the West Indians who had been such successes in England in 1950, Gomez in match after match mastered the Australian bowling. In his own bowling he was almost as successful. He increased his pace to fast-medium, moving the ball in the air, and in one innings took 7 Australian Test wickets. He also developed the habit of taking apparently impossible catches near the wicket. Altogether, when one considers the odds he had to contend with, his all-round play in Australia was among the most effective ever shown there by any visitor. In international cricket he never approached the same form again though he was always a player whom the opposing side had to watch.

In 1957 he was an effective broadcaster of the Test Matches of the West Indies against England and he was manager of the history – making team in Australia in 1960–61. Gomez for years has been an active partner in a substantial commercial business in the West Indies.

C. L. R. JAMES

CAREER FIGURES

	INNS	NO	RUNS	HS	AVGE	100S
Batting	182	27	6764	216*	43·63	14

Bowling 200 wkts at 25·26

Test Record (29)

	INNS	NO	RUNS	HS	AVGE	100S
Batting	46	5	1243	101	30·31	1

Bowling 58 wkts at 27·41 Ct 18

GOWER, David Ivon (1957–)

King's Sch, Canterbury 1972–1974 (Captain 1974). London Univ. Leicestershire 1975– . England: in England 1978, 1979; in Australia, 1978–79, 1979–80; in India 1979–80.

When he was 21 David Gower was being hailed as the reincarnation of Frank Woolley. Heady stuff, perhaps, but those lucky enough to see both of these majestic batsmen in spate recognized in the young man that rare quality of style which had established the older man, then still alive, as a yardstick for comparison, generation upon generation. This style has much to do with left-handedness. It comes from years of practice at stroking on the off-side balls from right-handed bowlers which slant across the face of the bat's swing. To make contact as frequently as Gower does indicates the gift of eye, a sureness of touch and confidence in success which creates an aesthetic satisfaction in those who watch. It is hard to combine watchfulness with stroke-play, and it may be that when the verdict on his whole career comes to be written that the quality of his Test runs rather than their quantity will need to be recorded, as indeed was the case with Woolley.

Gower arrived in English cricket when a player such as he was badly needed. As a fledgling county player he had skill in abundance. Ray Illingworth, his Leicestershire captain, refused to have him rushed into the Test arena, even though the sight of a single stroke separated him from the pack of contenders. When he was finally chosen, first in one- and then in 5-day matches, he showed that he was well able to bridge the gap between county and Test cricket, the gap into which many hopefuls plunge to oblivion. Quickly he made a place his own: so much so that by the age of 22 his was the one unchallenged name in England's top 5 batsmen. None the less at such a tender age he had much to learn. Against a shrewd bowler with a well-set field Gower looked vulnerable early in an innings. He was lucky on his 1st tour of Australia that the opposing captain, Yallop, was poorly versed in cricketing lore; less lucky on his 2nd when Australia were led by Greg Chappell. At times Gower moves with joints apparently so stiff that one wonders at his capacity to play across the full width of the crease. There is also a sleepiness, a vagueness, about his approach which seems a strange bedfellow with the exuberant self-expression which makes him a talkative member of the dressing-room. As a Test batsman David Gower made a better beginning than almost anyone in the 1970s; by the end of 1979, though, he still had a long way to go to fulfil his exceptional promise.

David Gower hooking his second ball in Test cricket nonchalantly for four.

ROBIN MARLAR

GRACE, Dr Edward Mills (1841–1911)

Gloucestershire 1868–1896; Secretary 1871–1909. England: in England 1880; in Australia 1863–64.

E. M. Grace – 'The Coroner' – had an influence on cricket second only to that of his brother W.G. In his youth excessive deference was paid to orthodoxy. For every ball there was a 'correct' stroke and batsmen were rated not so much by their runs as by their style. E.M. saw no sense in this. He made it his business to put the ball by whatever means where the field was not. Being a cricket genius he was wonderfully successful and the lesson he taught has never been wholly forgotten. Ever since then an ability to find the gaps has been regarded as one of the tests of a great batsman. E.M. was also a dangerous bowler, whether of lobs or in his earlier days round-arm, and the greatest point his contemporaries had ever seen. His most famous feat was to score 192 not out and take 10 wickets in an innings for the MCC at Canterbury in 1862. He remained a menace in club cricket into extreme old age and the stories of him are legion; he is one of the immortal characters and despite all his idiosyncrasies was much loved.

E. M. Grace: 7 years older than 'W.G.', 'The Coroner' was in many respects a law unto himself.

R. L. ARROWSMITH

CAREER FIGURES

	INNS	NO	RUNS	HS	AVGE	100S
Batting	555	18	10025	192*	18·67	5

Bowling 305 wkts at 20·38 Ct (incl w/k) 366; st 1

Test Record (1)

	INNS	NO	RUNS	HS	AVGE	100S
Batting	2	0	36	36	18·00	–

Ct 1

GRACE, Dr William Gilbert (1848–1915)

Gloucestershire 1868–1899 (Captain 1870–1898). London County 1900–1904 (Captain throughout). England: in England 1880, 1882, 1884, 1886, 1888 (Captain), 1890 (Captain), 1893 (Captain), 1896 (Captain), 1899 (Captain); in Australia 1873–74, 1891–92 (Captain). Selector 1899.

For nearly 40 years W. G. Grace – 'W.G.', 'the Champion', 'the Old Man' – bestrode the world of cricket like a Colossus. Some later players have surpassed his figures: no one has by prowess and personality alike so long and so indisputably dominated the field; indeed it has been said that he was for years, with W. E. Gladstone, the best known of all Englishmen. The youngest but one of 5 brothers, of whom his elder, 'E.M.', for some years enjoyed almost equal fame, he was from childhood enthusiastically coached by an uncle, and critically watched by his mother, in the garden of the family home near Bristol.

Tall and strong for his age, no boy has ever made so early and decisive an entry into cricket of the top class. He was only just 15 when he made 32 against an All-England XI; two years later he took 13 wickets for the Gentlemen v the Players of the South, and went in 1st for the Gentlemen at Lord's, and he was only just 18 when for England against Surrey at the Oval he scored 224 not out – and, incidentally, during the match was allowed by his captain to slip off to the Crystal Palace and run in, and win, the quarter-mile hurdles championship.

For the next 30 years he dominated the game, nowhere more sensationally than in the Gentlemen v Players matches at Lord's, the Oval and Prince's. In the 35 years before his first appearance in it the Gentlemen had only won 7 times; of their next 50 matches they won 31 and only lost 7. Over 41 years he made 6,008 runs for them, including 15 hundreds, and took 271 wickets. His 2 greatest seasons were 1871 and 1876: in the 1st of these, in which he made 10 hundreds, his aggregate, quite unprecedented, was 2,739 and his average 78, with the 34 of that great batsman Richard Daft *proxime accessit*. The season of 1876, in which he scored 2,622 runs, will always be remembered for the fantastic climax of his 3 consecutive innings played between 11 and 18 August – 344 against Kent, 177 against Notts and 318 not out against Yorkshire; he finished it in September by making 400 not out against XXII of Grimsby, all 22 fielding, and on a rather grassy and slow outfield. Four years later in the first home Test Match against Australia he celebrated the occasion typically with a score of 152; his 170 at the Oval in 1886, the highest of 3 hundreds which he inflicted on the tourists that year, was for 35 years a record for a home Test Match.

With the dawn of the 1890s it was generally agreed that even the 'Old Man' was proving human, and that his batting was not quite what it was, a delusion which in 1895 he proceeded to shatter with sensational and characteristic vehemence. Opening the season with 103 against Sussex at Lord's, he made a week later his 100th hundred to the tune of 288 against Somerset; on 23–25 May he scored 257 and 73 not out against Kent, being on the field for every ball of the match and, needing 153 runs on 30 May to be the 1st batsman ever to make 1,000 runs in May, he triumphantly crossed the Rubicon with 169. Five more hundreds helped him to an aggregate of 2,346, the highest by any batsman that season, and the 3rd best in his own career: all this when he was 47 years old. Inevitably the rest of the story had to be something of an anti-climax, but he was still opening for England in his 51st year, only retiring then from Test Match cricket because 'the ground was getting a bit too far away'. His long connexion with Gloucester had ended rather sadly in 1899, and his last years of cricket were associated with London County, for whom he made 166 on the day after his 56th birthday. Two years later, on his 58th birthday, he made what was virtually his final and dramatic exit with a score of 74 for the Gentlemen against the Players.

Those who played with 'W.G.' never found it easy in retrospect to analyze his batting, so forthright and uncomplicated did it seem; but all agreed that no one sighted the ball and assessed its length earlier, or timed it more truly; that he was equally at home off the front or the back foot, playing every ball on its merits with 'a bat that seemed all middle', and a concentration that was inexhaustible. 'The faster they bowl the better I like them,' he used to say, and let us never forget how many of the great scores of his early years were made against bowlers who still today could only be rated as genuinely fast, and on wickets that would be condemned as impossible.

As a bowler 'W.G.' belonged to the 'high, home and easy' school of a much earlier day; with a round-arm action he varied skilfully the arc of his slows, worked them in from leg, and was a magnificent catcher of the hardest drives hit back at him. With his massive frame, dark hair and ever lively eyes surmounted by his MCC cap, 'W.G.' was a compelling and authoritative focus wherever he appeared: physically tireless he played each game with inexhaustible zest, could at times argue with asperity, but had the kindest of hearts. When he died, England paused for a moment in the breathless business of war to mourn the passing of a national figure.

H. S. ALTHAM

CAREER FIGURES

	INNS	NO	RUNS	HS	AVGE	100S
Batting	1493	105	54896	344	39·55	126

Bowling 2876 wkts at 17·92 Ct 877

Test Record (22)

	INNS	NO	RUNS	HS	AVGE	100S
Batting	36	2	1098	170	32·29	2

Bowling 9 wkts at 26·22 Ct 39

GRAVENEY, Thomas William, OBE (1927–)

Newcastle Royal GS, and Bristol GS. Gloucestershire 1948–1960 (Captain 1959–1960); Worcestershire 1961–1970 (Captain 1968–1970); Queensland 1969–70 to 1970–71. England: in England 1951–1958 consecutively, 1962, 1966–1969 consecutively (Captain 1968); in Australia 1954–55, 1958–59, 1962–63; in West Indies 1953–54, 1967–68; in New Zealand 1954–55, 1958–59; in India 1951–52; in Pakistan 1968–69.

Tom Graveney was a master-craftsman with a rich array of graceful, elegant strokes. He was a safe close fielder, usually at slip, and a useful leg-spin bowler. His most successful season was 1956 when he scored 2,397 runs. He scored more than 1,000 runs in a season 22 times and 100 in each innings of a match on 4 occasions. He has scored more runs than any other postwar player and more than a hundred hundreds. For Gloucestershire against Essex in 1956, he scored 100 out of 153 and 67 out of 107, more than half his team's total in each innings. In the same year against Glamorgan he scored 200 out of 298. His 231 against British Guiana in a partnership of 402 with W. Watson for the 4th wicket is a record for any wicket for MCC abroad. There was a period in the early part of his career when he failed to do himself justice in Test cricket. If there was a slight chink against the fastest bowling he nevertheless displayed complete mastery of all the varying conditions of English cricket. In later years, on his return to the England side, he had matured into a complete batsman, playing several sterling knocks for his country.

A Northumbrian by birth he faced a difficult choice between golf and cricket when he left Bristol Grammar School. Happily, 1948 saw him hitting his maiden hundred in his first season for Gloucestershire. By 1951 he had developed into a fine player, topping 2,000 runs with 8 hundreds, winning an England cap against South Africa and enjoying a successful tour of India and Pakistan. He made plenty of runs on his 3 tours of Australia and New Zealand, but apart from a superb 2-hour hundred in the Fifth Test at Sydney in 1954–55, after the rubber had been decided, success in Test cricket proved to be elusive. Returning from Australia in 1955, he was given one more chance as an opening batsman against South Africa, but was then discarded until 1957. He came back against the West Indies to make his highest Test score, 258, at Trent Bridge, and a magnificent 164 at the Oval on a turning wicket. He had broken through, it seemed, but on returning from Australia in 1959 he was overlooked again until 1962. He came back with a vengeance against Pakistan with 97 in the First Test and 153 in the Second Test at Lord's.

Having left Gloucestershire in 1960, when he lost the captaincy there, he moved to Worcestershire in 1961, there to finish his career on a high note. In 1964 he helped Worcestershire to their first-ever Championship; from 1968–70 he captained them, and after his 40th birthday he made his last and most triumphant return to the England side. No one who saw them will easily forget his 96 at Lord's against the full pace of the West Indies attack in 1966 or his memorable hundred at Port of Spain in 1968. Of Tom Graveney's very rare skill as a batsman there is no possible doubt.

COLIN COWDREY

CAREER FIGURES

	INNS	NO	RUNS	HS	AVGE	100S
Batting	1223	159	47793	258	44·91	122

Bowling 80 wkts at 37·96 Ct 551

Test Record (79)

	INNS	NO	RUNS	HS	AVGE	100S
Batting	123	13	4882	258	44·38	11

Bowling 1 wkt for 167 Ct 80

GREENIDGE, Cuthbert Gordon (1951–)

St Peter's Sch, Barbados. Hampshire 1970– . Barbados. West Indies: in West Indies 1976–1977, 1977–78; in England 1976; in Australia 1975–76; in India 1974–75. WSC

It is hard to credit that many people in the history of cricket, far less an opening batsman, have hit the ball more savagely than Gordon Greenidge, a Barbadian who with his parents came to live in Berkshire, aged 14; played for England Schoolboys at 16; joined Hampshire the next season (1968); but chose West Indies for his Test career. One can only speculate on the difference it might have made to England's batting if, having been sounded by the selectors in 1972, he had gone on to play for his adopted country; but he was in no doubt where his heart lay and won the first of many Test caps in 1974 after 2 seasons with Barbados during the English winters.

In his early years, Greenidge's main ambition sometimes appeared to be to knock the cover off the ball – perhaps to avoid being outshone by the artistic Barry Richards, his county opening partner. Though more consistent than a batsman of that type could expect to be on English pitches, Greenidge's reputation was founded more on an ability to butcher attacks than on reliability – indeed, most of his contemporaries thought he would have been a still more dangerous player had he not tried to hit the ball so hard.

Not tall, but very strongly built, sheer brute force was certainly a factor in his batting: mainly in so far as it enabled him to go on hooking, cutting and driving off either foot for longer and with greater power than anyone could think of except for Sobers, and, before him, Weekes and Bradman. The 1970s were littered with examples of Greenidge's devastation, notably his 273 not out against the 1974 Pakistanis at Eastbourne, described by Barry Richards as his conception of a perfect innings because for $4\frac{1}{4}$ hours every bad ball went for six (13) or four (31); and the fact that by the end of the decade he held the record score in all 3 English one-day competitions. But growing maturity and the acceptance of greater responsibility following

Richards's retirement, modified Greenidge's philosophy and by the late 1970s he had shown signs of becoming one of the soundest as well as the most exciting batsmen in the world.

JOHN THICKNESSE

GREGORY, Jack Morrison (1895–1973)

New South Wales 1920–21 to 1928–29. Australia: in Australia 1920–21, 1924–25, 1928–29; in England 1921, 1926; in South Africa 1921–22.

For the 3 years following the First World War, J. M. Gregory was certainly the most spectacular, and perhaps the greatest, all-round cricketer in the world. His tempestuous fast bowling, rugged aggressive batting and predatory slip fielding made him something of a cricketing one-man band. Born of a famous cricketing family, Gregory found himself in 1918 as a soldier of the AIF, billeted at Lord's where he soon came to the notice of P. F. Warner, who unhesitatingly predicted the great career before him. A man of immense physique, well over 6 feet tall, Gregory in 1919 was an enormous force still in the development stage. The pace of his bowling impressed all, and an early lack of control was extremely disconcerting, to all but the stoutest heart. By the following year he had advanced to his greatest powers, his dynamic all-round cricket doing much to shatter an optimistic, but scarcely resuscitated, England.

His partnership with E. A. McDonald, founded during the Third Test of this series, was to become one of the legendary associations of the game. His run to the wicket was in the nature of a charge at the full gallop, ending in a joyous leap of about 3 yards, and a beautiful full high sweep of the arm. It seems that this awe-inspiring performance made his actual speed difficult to assess, for contemporary estimates vary over a considerable margin. Sir Jack Hobbs, for instance, did not consider him in the fastest category, whilst his partner, Herbert Sutcliffe, has coupled Gregory with Larwood as the quickest in his experience.

Gregory batted left-handed with the same whole-hearted gusto, swinging the bat lustily with powerful hands, unprotected by batting-gloves. In the 1920–21 series he averaged over 70 against England, scoring a hundred at Sydney. Without ever quite reproducing this form he remained, in later years, a great asset to his side's batting for he was a correct and judicious striker in times of need. As a slip fielder Gregory was unexcelled. His great reach and exceptional agility enabled him to cover a large area which he increased by a shrewd sense of anticipation. The latter talent was said to lead him occasionally astray, but it also achieved some dazzling results especially in conjunction with Mailey's leg-breaks and googlies. Almost invariably bare-headed, towering, tanned and powerfully lithe, he was a conspicuous and dominating personality wherever he played.

IAN PEEBLES

J. M. Gregory: fast bowler, hitter and brilliant slip, one of the greatest all-rounders.

CAREER FIGURES

	INNS	NO	RUNS	HS	AVGE	100S
Batting	173	18	5661	152	36·52	13

Bowling 504 wkts at 20·99 Ct 192

Test Record (24)

	INNS	NO	RUNS	HS	AVGE	100S
Batting	34	3	1146	119	36·96	2

Bowling 85 wkts at 31·15 Ct 37

GREGORY, Sydney Edward (1870–1929)

New South Wales 1889–90 to 1912–13 (Captain 1894–95 to 1911–12). Australia: in Australia 1891–92, 1894–95, 1897–98, 1901–02, 1903–04, 1907–08, 1911–12; in England 1890, 1893, 1896, 1899, 1902, 1905, 1909, 1912 (Captain); in South Africa 1902–03.

Syd Gregory, who has been described as 'book-perfect in his technique', was not a giant in stature, but he played more innings against England than any other Australian of his day, and thus may be regarded as the most distinguished of a great cricketing family. In Sheffield Shield matches, he did much to keep New South Wales supreme from the first. His earliest great achievement in Test Matches was to score 201 at Sydney in 1894–95, putting on 154 with Blackham for the 9th wicket – and yet the match was lost. Much later, in 1909, he and Bardsley made an opening stand of 180 at Kennington Oval. In 1912, when there was a rift in Australian cricket, greatly weakening the team, he came to England as captain in the Triangular Tests. He also played 3 matches against South Africa in 1902, but did not prosper on matting against Llewellyn and Kotze. Four hundreds in Test Matches may not seem an impressive record in our times, but the fame of Syd Gregory, with his curling moustache and text-book style, does not depend on statistics. He was a magnificent cover-point.

G. D. MARTINEAU

CAREER FIGURES

	INNS	NO	RUNS	HS	AVGE	100S
Batting	592	55	15303	201	28·49	25

Bowling 2 wkts at 197·00 Ct 194

Test Record (58)

	INNS	NO	RUNS	HS	AVGE	100S
Batting	100	7	2282	201	24·53	4

Bowling 0 wkt for 33 Ct 25

Tony Greig: Sussex sweater, MCC cap, and the stance he adopted in mid-career.

GREIG, Anthony William (1946–)

Queen's Coll, Queenstown. Border 1965–66 to 1969–70. Eastern Province 1970–71 to 1971–72. Sussex 1966–1978 (Captain 1973–1977). England: in England 1970, 1972–1977 consecutively (Captain 1975, 1976); in Australia 1974–75, 1976–77 (Captain); in West Indies 1973–74; in New Zealand 1974–75; in India 1972–73; 1976–77 (Captain); in Pakistan 1972–73. WSC.

From the moment that Tony Greig returned to the pavilion at Hove in May 1967, having saved Sussex from collapse against a strong Lancashire attack with a splendid innings of 156 in his 1st county match, it was plain that a prodigy had arrived. He was only 20, almost 6 feet 8 inches tall. With his fair good looks and an engaging manner, Greig was the South African-born son of a Scots father with a distinguished RAF record who had been sent to South Africa to train pilots during the Second World War and had stayed on there. Such were Tony Greig's credentials for the place in the England XI which came his way 3 years later during the Rest of the World series. Thus began a Test career which brought in all 61 caps and reached its climax when he led England in the Centenary Test at Melbourne in March 1977.

At this point Greig, aged just 30, had reached a position of responsibility and respect in English cricket that has been granted to few. Given the captaincy when Australia were very much in the ascendant after the first home Test of 1975, he had checked the trend largely by dint of his own personality and performance. Though England succumbed to the West Indian fast bowlers in 1976 Greig's leadership was not in question. The following winter he won a Test series in India 3–1 and in so doing appeared to confirm his own maturity both on the field and off. Where all emerged with credit from the phenomenal Centenary Test England's recovery seemed to reflect especially the courage and belligerence of their captain.

One way and another the game at this point had reached a high peak of prosperity, both from the financial angle and in terms of public interest. No one grudged the high income that the top players, and in particular the England captain, were beginning to earn. Then, out of the clearest of blue skies, came the revelation of Kerry Packer's secret intrusion into the cricket world wherein Greig, while England's captain, had played a crucial recruiting part. In the past Greig had done and said certain misguided, headstrong things. His reign of 4 years as Sussex captain had promised much and achieved very little. This latest activity was seen as a betrayal of trust, from which inevitably followed his loss of both the England and Sussex captaincies. In July 1978, just over 11 years after his first triumphal appearance and following a TCCB suspension imposed for a breach of discipline, Sussex agreed to Greig's request to be released from his contract. The continued presence of the idol with feet of clay had become an embarrassment to all.

There was, however, an aspect of Greig's life with which all in close touch had long been familiar but which was unknown to the world at large until it was disclosed, after Greig's departure, in Henry Blofeld's *The Packer Affair*. The fact that he was an epileptic explained and condoned (to this writer at least) not a little. His battle against such a handicap surely commanded sympathy.

When the damage that he and some of his contemporaries have done to the game is assessed, his merits as an all-round cricketer also deserve to be remembered. Within the space of 4 years he scored 8 hundreds for England. While averaging all but 40 with the bat he took 152 Test wickets at a shade over 30 a time and made 89 catches. He was a magnificent fielder anywhere and, in Test parlance, a valuable 5th bowler of fast-medium pace, tireless and determined. In the West Indies he turned all too briefly to slow-medium off-spin and with 13 wickets at Port of Spain enabled England to gain a narrow victory and against all prediction square the rubber. He was a batsman of high courage who used his physical advantages to the full, and never more so than at Brisbane in 1974–75 when in an innings of 110 on a pitch of uneven bounce he confronted the great speed of Lillee and Thomson for 5 hours and saved his side from otherwise certain humiliation.

E. W. SWANTON

GRIFFITH, Stewart Cathie, CBE, DFC, TD (1914–)

Dulwich 1930–1933. Cambridge Univ 1935. Surrey 1934. Sussex 1937–1954 (Captain 1946). England: in South Africa 1948–49; in West Indies 1947–48. Secretary Sussex 1946–1950. Secretary MCC 1962–1974; President 1979–80.

'Billy' Griffith, as he is known to all cricketers, was 4 years in the Dulwich XI, during which time by resolute and at times powerful batting he made over 1,300 runs and, after winning considerable fame as a fielder, kept wicket impressively in the last two. Tried in 3 games for Cambridge in 1934, in one of which he made 85, he got his blue next year. He served with distinction as a glider pilot in the Airborne Division, and it was as a Lieutenant-Colonel, and with the DFC, that he kept wicket for England in all 5 'Victory' Tests against Australia in 1945. Appointed that winter as secretary of Sussex he also captained the county in 1946, and played regularly for the next 3 years.

'Billy' Griffith, forgetting the cares of office.

Selected as player and assistant manager for the MCC team which G. O. Allen led to the West Indies in the winter of 1947–48, and pressed into service as an opening batsman in the Second Test at Port of Spain, he made cricket history by scoring in it his 1st hundred in first-class cricket, a resolute innings of 140 that lasted 6 hours, and incidentally was the highest score for that side in any match of the tour. A year later he went with the MCC team to South Africa, and kept so well as to replace Evans in the last 2 Test Matches.

Appointed in 1952 assistant secretary to MCC, in which office he was primarily responsible to the Secretary for the organization of the club's cricket activities, he succeeded Ronny Aird as Secretary of MCC on 1 October 1962. Not only the club but the game of cricket were indeed fortunate in having at the focus of its administration for 12 eventful years a man of his experience, personality and complete devotion.

H. S. ALTHAM

CAREER FIGURES

	INNS	NO	RUNS	HS	AVGE	100S
Batting	338	43	4846	140	16·42	3

Bowling 0 wkts for 23 W/k: ct 327; st 80 Total 407

Test Record (3)

	INNS	NO	RUNS	HS	AVGE	100S
Batting	5	0	157	140	31·40	1

W/k: ct 5

GRIMMETT, Clarence Victor (1891–1980)

Mount Cook Boys' Sch, Wellington. Wellington 1911–12 to 1913–14. Victoria 1918–19 to 1923–24. South Australia 1924–25 to 1940–41. Australia: in Australia 1924–25, 1928–29, 1930–31, 1931–32, 1932–33; in England 1926, 1930, 1934; in South Africa 1935–36.

Clarence Victor Grimmett was one of the great slow leg-break bowlers, and a particularly bright link in the chain of Australian wrist spinners which ran unbroken from Hordern in 1911 until the outbreak of the Second World War. As a Test Match bowler Grimmett's career overlapped that of Mailey, and lasted well into O'Reilly's reign. Between 1925 and 1936 he took 216 wickets for Australia at 24 apiece.

Grimmett was a New Zealander by birth and, his action being inelegant to the casual observer, and his methods subtle, he took some time to convince a sceptical world of his true worth. Originally he played for Victoria, but migrated to South Australia, whence he graduated in 1926 to the Australian XI. His start as an international bowler, at the age of 33, was sensational. England, having won a match against Australia for the 1st time in 15 years, at Melbourne, took the field at Sydney with high hopes. These were shattered by Grimmett, who, only latterly aided by rain, took 11 wickets for 82 runs. His appearance in England the following year created some surprise. A small, prematurely bald figure, he embarked on each assault with a little lamb-like skip, trundled diagonally to the crease, and swung a bony arm a little above shoulder high. His 13 wickets in the series cost him 31 runs apiece but, an ardent student of his craft, each over brought him experience of English conditions he was to ponder and put to untold advantage. When he returned in 1930 he was a complete bowler, the centrepiece of his country's attack.

His stock ball was the leg-break, amply spun, and launched over a great range of pace and flight, ever with complete control of length and direction. His googly was a more modest affair, clearly discernible and used mostly for tactical purposes. His top-spinner was, on the other hand, a wicket-taking weapon, delivered rather faster and tending to dip late in its flight. It was also a strong deterrent to quick-footed batsmen. He scarcely ever bowled a loose ball, and opposing strikers must have reflected that, for a man born on Christmas Day, he was sparing with his presents. For those who love the art of bowling it was, as Professor Moriarty said to Sherlock Holmes, 'an intellectual treat', to watch him in action. So great was his own love for the game that, at 70, he still had an occasional bowl in his garden, but was heard to say that he had lost some of his pace from the pitch.

IAN PEEBLES

CAREER FIGURES

	INNS	NO	RUNS	HS	AVGE	100S
Batting	321	54	4720	71*	17·67	–

Bowling 1424 wkts at 22·28 ct 139

Test Record (37)

	INNS	NO	RUNS	HS	AVGE	100S
Batting	50	10	557	50	13·92	–

Bowling 216 wkts at 24·21 ct 17

Clarrie Grimmett: 34 when he first played for Australia, yet in 37 Tests he took 216 wickets.

GROUT, Arthur Theodore Wallace MBE (1927–1968)

State HS, Brisbane. Queensland 1946–47 to 1965–66. Australia: in Australia 1958–59, 1960–61, 1962–63, 1963–64, 1965–66; in England 1961, 1964; in South Africa 1957–58; in West Indies 1964–65; in India 1959–60, 1964–65; in Pakistan 1959–60, 1964–65.

Wally Grout, who died sadly young, was one of Australia's greatest wicket-keepers. Not as neat as Oldfield, perhaps, or as quick as Tallon, he was, none the less, wonderfully reliable and took many spectacular catches standing back to fast bowling. He twice had 8 victims in a Test Match and his 6 victims in a Test innings, all caught, against South Africa at Johannesburg in 1957–58, remained as a joint record until beaten by Wasim Bari in 1979. Grout still holds the world record for catches taken in one innings – 8 for Queensland against Western Australia at Brisbane in 1959–60. His daughter became a respected umpire of men's cricket.

JOHN WOODCOCK

CAREER FIGURES

	INNS	NO	RUNS	HS	AVGE	100S
Batting	253	24	5168	119	22·57	4

Bowling 3 wkts at 38·33. W/k: ct 473; st 114; Total 587

Test Record (51)

	INNS	NO	RUNS	HS	AVGE	100S
Batting	67	8	890	74	15·08	

W/k: ct 163; st 24; Total 187

GUNN, George (1879–1958)

Nottinghamshire 1902–1932. England: in England 1909; in Australia 1907–08, 1911–12; in West Indies 1929–30.

George Gunn was a great batsman of original character. A nephew of William Gunn, his style as a batsman had sound classic foundations, but his mind and nature were whimsical, so that one day he would play an innings correct in every movement and principle, and next day put into performance strokes which might seem entirely unorthodox. He could cut a ball square from the leg-stump. He liked to walk out to the fastest bowling, walk to the pitch of it leisurely. 'If I stayed in crease for it,' he argued, 'me being not tall would have to play dangerously high up. So I go where I can get near and over it!' By amazing eyesight and judgment he frequently demoralized fast bowlers by his peripatetic methods.

If his team needed runs or patient defence, Gunn had the talent to stay in with the watchful and reliant straight bat of Arthur Shrewsbury. If his side were securely placed he proceeded to jazz the eternal verities of batsmanship. Yet all that he fantastically and humorously did with his bat was thoroughly logical, stylish and, apparently, easy. In his career, extending from 1902 to 1932, he scored 35,208 runs, average 35·96, with 62 hundreds. A third of his innings he probably got out by his own sweet will. For England his record was 1,120 runs in 28 completed innings, average 40.

He was first given his chance in a Test match because, during the MCC tour in Australia of 1907–08, he happened to be there for reasons of health. The England captain fell ill, so Gunn was called in as a reserve. He scored 119 and 74 in his 1st Test match, then, in the following 4 games added 15, 0, 65, 11, 13, 43, 122 and 0. He explained to me that during his innings of 119 at Sydney, he was unable really to concentrate on the Australian bowling because a band played after lunch and the cornet was never quite in tune.

If Gunn had been born with a strict economical mind – as batsman – he would not have been statistically surpassed by many. He mingled classic forward play, left foot over for a cover-drive beautifully poised with the more modern back to the stumps method, right pad in front level with left, if the spin be quick and subtle. At the age of 48 he scored 100 and 110 in the same game v Warwickshire. He celebrated his 50th birthday with an innings of 164 v Worcestershire. He announced to his friends before the event that he would do something of the kind, and invited them to come and see it. He goes down in cricket's annals as an incalculable genius, a batsman of very rare personal skill, and of infinite wit and caprice.

NEVILLE CARDUS

CAREER FIGURES

	INNS	NO	RUNS	HS	AVGE	100S
Batting	1061	82	35208	220	35·96	62

Bowling 66 wkts at 35·61 Ct 472

Test Record (15)

	INNS	NO	RUNS	HS	AVGE	100S
Batting	29	1	1120	122*	40·00	2

Bowling 0 wkts for 8 Ct 15

GUPTE, Subhas W. Pandhrinath (1929–)

Bombay Univ. Bombay. Bengal. India: in India 1951–52, 1952–53, 1955–56, 1956–57, 1958–59, 1960–61, 1961–62; in England 1959; in West Indies 1952–53; in Pakistan 1954–55.

At the peak of his career 'Fergie' Gupte was considered the finest leg-break and googly bowler in the world. He was able to turn the ball on the plumbest of wickets, though he often suffered from weaknesses in the field. He narrowly missed the tour to England in 1952, but soon afterwards he established his reputation in the West Indies when he took 27 wickets in a series. A little man, he made a clever use of flight, but in England in 1959 he was not the menace he was expected to be: his 17 Test wickets cost 34·64 each. Nevertheless, at the time that he retired, only Mankad exceeded his 149 wickets for India. He took 9 Test wickets in an innings against West Indies at Kanpur in 1958–59 and 4 years earlier had become the 1st Indian bowler to take all 10 wickets in an innings in a first-class match. He was never afraid of hard work and gave of his best whatever the conditions.

IRVING ROSENWATER

CAREER FIGURES

	INNS	NO	RUNS	HS	AVGE	100S
Batting	125	31	782	47	8·32	–

Bowling 535 wkts at 23·78

Test Record (36)

	INNS	NO	RUNS	HS	AVGE	100S
Batting	42	13	183	21	6·31	–

Bowling 149 wkts at 29·55 Ct 14

Richard Hadlee: a New Zealand match-winner.

HADLEE, Richard John (1951–)

Christchurch Boys' HS. Canterbury 1971–72– . Nottinghamshire 1978– . New Zealand: in New Zealand 1972–73, 1973–74, 1975–76, 1976–77, 1977–78, 1978–79; in England 1973, 1978; in Australia 1973–74; in India 1976–77; in Pakistan 1976–77.

It is infrequent that a famous father has an even more famous son. Walter Hadlee was a fine Test batsman, a successful captain and an outstanding administrator; but his 4th son, Richard, as a fast right-hand bowler has written his name in even larger letters in New Zealand records. In his 3rd first-class match, he did the hat-trick. In his 4th Test, he gave New Zealand a moral victory over Australia. In his 6th, his match figures of 7 for 130 helped New Zealand beat Australia. Against India in 1975–76 he took 11 for 58, a New Zealand Test record. When England was defeated in 1977–78, Hadlee took 10 for 100. Against Pakistan in 1978–79 he became the 4th New Zealander with 100 Test wickets. The most exciting of some notable Test innings was his 81 against Australia in 1976–77. He came in at 31 for 5, with Lillee very fast on a lively pitch. But he straight-drove the Australian for 6 and reached 50 from 43 balls. Richard Hadlee seems certain to set a Test record future New Zealand bowlers will find a distant target.

R. T. BRITTENDEN

HADLEE, Walter Arnold, OBE (1915–)

Christchurch Boys' HS. Canterbury. Otago. New Zealand: in New Zealand 1945–46 (Captain), 1946–47 (Captain), 1950–51 (Captain); in England 1937, 1949 (Captain). Manager 1965. Selector.

Hadlee was a courageous and enterprising batsman, who played cricket in the sporting manner associated with his country. Under M. L. Page, in 1937, he scored an aggressive 93 in the Second Test against England before treading on his wicket. In 1946, against the visiting Australians, he hit 198 out of 347 for Otago, and, against Hammond's team, at Christchurch in 1947, New Zealand having been put in 1st in very cold weather, he opened with 116, in which he drove superbly. His chief mark, however, was as a captain, particularly of his popular and successful 1949 side to England, and later as an administrator. He made a commanding President of the New Zealand Cricket Council at the time of the Packer intrusion.

Two of his sons, Dayle and Richard, have opened the bowling for New Zealand, and a 3rd, Barry, was a member of the New Zealand side to come to England for the Prudential Cup in 1975.

JOHN WOODCOCK

CAREER FIGURES

	INNS	NO	RUNS	HS	AVGE	100S
Batting	202	17	7421	198	40·11	17

Bowling 6 wkts at 49·17 Ct 69

Test Record (11)

	INNS	NO	RUNS	HS	AVGE	100S
Batting	19	1	543	116	30·16	1

Ct 11

HAIGH, Schofield (1871–1921)

Yorkshire 1895–1913. England: in England 1905, 1909, 1912; in South Africa 1898–99, 1905–06.

The name of Schofield Haigh will always be associated with those of Hirst and Rhodes as the bowlers of Lord Hawke's great Yorkshire XI who won 4 Championships in 5 years. A quick-medium-paced bowler with a delivery stride as long as the sweep of his bowling arm was smooth, he could, given any help from the pitch, turn the ball back from the off with devastating penetration. In 11 seasons he took over 100 wickets, in 5 of them heading the bowling averages and in 3 taking more wickets than any other bowler. Most strikingly did he do so in 1905 and 1906, in which he totalled 342 wickets for less than 14 each; he did 5 hat-tricks, and 7 times took 8 wickets in an innings. A sturdy and determined batsman, he made 85 in a 9th-wicket partnership of 192 with Hirst against Surrey in 1898, and over 1,000 runs in 1904. A man of sterling character, humour and natural friendliness, his early death brought sorrow to all who knew him, not least at Winchester College where he had gone as coach in 1914.

H. S. ALTHAM

CAREER FIGURES

	INNS	NO	RUNS	HS	AVGE	100S
Batting	747	119	11715	159	18·65	4

Bowling 2012 wkts at 15·94 Ct 297

Test Record (11)

	INNS	NO	RUNS	HS	AVGE	100S
Batting	18	3	113	25	7·53	–

Bowling 24 wkts at 25·91 Ct 8

HALL, Wesley Winfield (1937–)

Combermere Sch. Barbados 1955–56 to 1966–67 and 1970–71. Trinidad 1966–67 to 1969–70. Queensland 1961–62. West Indies: in West Indies 1959–60, 1961–62, 1964–65, 1967–68; in England 1963, 1966; in Australia 1960–61, 1968–69; in New Zealand 1968–69; in India 1958–59, 1966–67; in Pakistan 1958–59.

Wesley Hall: 'never a hint of malice.'

The odd thing about Wesley Hall's fast bowling – and it was definitely fast – was that a crack on the thigh never hurt quite so much from him as from others of his kind. I suppose it was psychological to the extent that there was never a hint of malice in the man or in his bowling. Forgiveness for a painful blow, even on the most delicate part of one's anatomy, was instantaneous because the ball, one knew, had been delivered without the least intent to do bodily harm: and when once I managed an effective bumper in retaliation at Port-of-Spain, reducing the great man to his knees, he never held that against me either. He had something of the natural comic about him and his wholehearted efforts for his team told you all you needed to know about his character.

He was certainly enormously fast on those occasions when the rhythm of his run-up matched its overall speed and general physical abandon. It needed no great stretch of the imagination occasionally to conceive of a situation where his whirling arms would actually tie themselves into a rubbery knot, although photographs show clearly that his was the classical action during the most important moments of delivery. His stamina became legendary after he had bowled throughout England's 2nd innings at Lord's in 1963 – a matter of 40 overs, taking 4 wickets for 93 runs – but I had seen similar toughness earlier in the West Indies in our 1959–60 tour when he bowled uncomplainingly at full speed despite a number of fearful-looking blisters on his feet.

I first played against him at Cambridge in 1957 when, as a 19-year-old, he ambled in off a shortish run and generated no more pace than you might expect from any loose-limbed youngster. It was the famous tied-Test tour to Australia which cast him in his new role as express bowler and those who played him then, Simpson, McDonald and company, still vouch for his fiery speed from that lengthy, hurtling approach to the stumps. His natural ball was the away-swinger to the right-hander and his arm was high enough to ensure him a fair proportion of 'nip-backers'. Accuracy was not normally his forte; he preferred all-out attack to pick up wickets even when conditions were against him. His batting, catching and ground fielding were all cast in a similar mould, demonstrating certain natural abilities in each department but giving no hint that he ever worked hard to improve them. He bowled in Test cricket for the last time in England in 1966 when his pace was not what it had been, though the heart was still in the same place. It was around this time that he suffered severe physical injury to his legs in a car crash, although, given the opportunity, he was still not beyond limping up to the stumps with a new ball in his hand and the light of battle in his eyes.

TED DEXTER

CAREER FIGURES

	INNS	NO	RUNS	HS	AVGE	100S
Batting	210	38	2635	102*	15·31	1

Bowling 529 wkts at 26·22 Ct 58

Test Record (48)

	INNS	NO	RUNS	HS	AVGE	100S
Batting	66	14	818	50*	15·73	–

Bowling 192 wkts at 26·38 Ct 11

HAMMOND, Walter Reginald (1903–1965)

Portsmouth GS and Cirencester GS. Gloucestershire 1920–1925 and 1927–1951 (Captain 1939–1946). England: in England 1928–1939 consecutively (Captain 1938, 1939), 1946 (Captain); in Australia 1928–29, 1932–33, 1936–37, 1946–47 (Captain); in South Africa 1927–28, 1930–31, 1938–39 (Captain); in West Indies 1934–35; in New Zealand 1932–33, 1946–47 (Captain).

Walter Hammond was one of the greatest cricketers ever to do honour to the game. Born at Dover, he was taken as a child to Malta; then at the age of 11 his family came back to England but not to Kent. Hammond attended as a youth the Cirencester Grammar School and so came to play for Gloucestershire. Naturally enough, the Kent CCC tried to win him back to his native county but in vain.

Like every classical exponent in any art or calling he could have been described a 'romantic' in his early period. When first he attracted public attention he did so by batsmanship which was extremely daring and brilliant. In his prime, his style ripened to an almost statuesque nobility, easy and powerful of stroke-play but absolutely correct in its observance of first principles. In 1927, on a sunny Whitsun Friday at Old Trafford, Hammond at the age of 24 put to the sword a Lancashire attack which included the most lithe and fearsome of fast bowlers of his day, E. A. McDonald. In 3 hours he scored 187, having begun the morning by driving McDonald for 5 fours from the first 5 balls sent down. During this wonderful innings Hammond repeatedly hooked McDonald. In his maturity Hammond seldom employed the hook. Under the command of D. R. Jardine he settled down to a responsible and monumental position in the England XI. He put vain things behind him and, as a batsman, played majestically within the confines of his great skill. Against Australia at Lord's in 1938, England in the first innings lost the wickets of Hutton, Edrich and Barnett for 31,

Wally Hammond: one of the great batsmen.

all overwhelmed by the fast-rising bowling of McCormick. Hammond walked to the wicket in this moment of crisis with impressive sureness of tread, his blue handkerchief just visible outside his right hip pocket. He destroyed the onslaughts of McCormick with a regal authority. From the back foot he crashed ball after ball to the off-side boundary with a superbly timed propulsion of forearms and wrists. In 6 hours he scored 240, with 32 fours. As he came back to the pavilion the whole of the vast crowd at Lord's stood up for him.

He came first to prominent recognition when he was chosen to join the MCC team visiting the West Indies in 1925–26, where he scored 733 runs, average 45·81. With the world of cricket at his feet he caught some germ in the West Indies and was unable to play at all the summer of 1926. He came back to the game refreshed indeed, scoring 1,000 runs in May 1927, including that wonderful innings at Old Trafford. In this season of his restoration his runs amounted to 2,969, average 69·04. He had already, in his early twenties, made secure his position in the company of the permanent adornments of cricket as batsman of the blue blood, as a clever lissome bowler, especially with a new ball, and as a slip fieldsman swift, omnipresent, and lovely to see.

In 1927–28, in South Africa, he took part in the 1st of his 85 Test Matches for England, scoring 321 in the rubber, highest innings 90, average 40·12, with 15 wickets, average 26, thrown in. His first engagements against Australia, as a member of A. P. F. Chapman's team in 1928–29, established a new currency in Test Match individual expenditure of runs. (Bradman had not yet begun to disburse his vast thousands.)

All the cricket world wondered at Hammond's sequence of scores against Australia: 44, 28, 251, 200, 32 (run out), 119 and 177 (in the same Test Match), 38 and 16 – total 905, average 113·12. The flawless Australian wickets, on which Test Matches were played to a finish, encouraged disciplined batsmanship. The impulsive dashing front-footed young Hammond of Gloucestershire was changed to Hammond of England, classic and statesmanlike. He became essentially a player from the back foot. His right arm acted like some sort of flexible iron piston, punching the ball to the off-side with thrilling yet regal strength. He scored 9 hundreds against Australia, 6 against South Africa, 4 against New Zealand; and 167 hundreds in all. He was England's captain v Australia in England in 1938, and in Australia in 1946–47. As evidence of his superb slip-fielding, he in one season held 78 catches. His place in the Permanent National Gallery of Cricketers is safe – not as a painting but as a nobly looming sculpture.

NEVILLE CARDUS

CAREER FIGURES

	INNS	NO	RUNS	HS	AVGE	100S
Batting	1005	104	50551	336*	56·10	167

Bowling 732 wkts at 30·58 Ct 819

Test Record (85)

	INNS	NO	RUNS	HS	AVGE	100S
Batting	140	16	7249	336*	58·45	22

Bowling 83 wkts at 37·80 Ct 110

HANIF MOHAMMAD (1934–)

Suid Madarasa Sch., Karachi. Karachi. PIA Pakistan: in Pakistan 1954–55, 1955–56, 1956–57, 1958–59, 1959–60, 1961–62, 1964–65 (Captain), 1968–69, 1969–70; in England 1954, 1962, 1967 (Captain); in Australia 1964–65 (Captain); in West Indies 1957–58; in New Zealand 1964–65 (Captain); in India 1952–53, 1960–61.

The tiny little figure of Hanif Mohammad became a run-machine second only to Don Bradman. Starting at the age of 16, he was playing Test cricket a year later. His rock-like defence made him one of the hardest batsmen to bowl out in modern cricket, especially in his own country. Although he could play every stroke in the book and hit the ball very hard indeed, he liked to cruise relentlessly on in a steady rhythm. With a world record score of 499 for Karachi v Bahawalpur in January 1959, he was run out off the last ball of the day going for his 500th run, after a stay of 640 minutes. He played the longest innings in first-class cricket, 337 runs in 970 minutes for Pakistan v West Indies in Barbados in 1957–58. At Dacca in 1962 he scored 2 hundreds in the Test Match for Pakistan against England. Put together, the feats of Hanif and his 3 Test-playing brothers, Mushtaq, Sadiq and Wazir, form the backbone of Pakistan's first 25 years of Test cricket.

COLIN COWDREY

CAREER FIGURES

	INNS	NO	RUNS	HS	AVGE	100S
Batting	371	45	17059	499	52·32	55

Bowling 53 wkts at 28·58 Ct (incl w/k) 177; st 12

Test Record (55)

	INNS	NO	RUNS	HS	AVGE	100S
Batting	97	8	3915	337	43·98	12

Bowling 1 wkt for 95 Ct 40

HARDSTAFF, Joseph, Jr (1911–)

Nottinghamshire 1930–1955. Auckland. England: in England 1935–1939 consecutively, 1946, 1948; in Australia 1936–37, 1946–47; in West Indies 1947–48.

'Young Joe' Hardstaff batted in an easy, polished style, approved, no doubt, by his famous father, who sometimes watched as umpire. Interrupted by the Second World War, by which time his 215 partnership with Hutton at Kennington Oval in 1938 had revealed both attacking and defensive qualities, he played some notable innings after it, including 205 not out against India in 1946, and there is no doubt that he would have been well up among those batsmen with a hundred hundreds to their credit but for the lost years of the Second War.

G. D. MARTINEAU

CAREER FIGURES

	INNS	NO	RUNS	HS	AVGE	100S
Batting	812	94	31847	266	44·35	83

Bowling 36 wkts at 59·50 Ct 122

Test Record (23)

	INNS	NO	RUNS	HS	AVGE	100S
Batting	38	3	1636	205*	46·74	4

Ct 9

HARRIS, 4th Lord (George Robert Canning), GCSI, GCIE (1851–1932)

Eton 1868–1870 (Captain 1870). Oxford Univ 1871–1872, 1874. Kent 1870–1911 (Captain 1875–1889); President 1875; Secretary 1875–1880. England: in England 1880 (Captain), 1884 (Captain); in Australia 1878–79 (Captain). President MCC 1895; Trustee 1906–1916; Hon Treasurer 1916–1932.

It is arguable that Lord Harris is the greatest figure in cricket history except 'W.G.'. No man has exercised so strong an influence on the cricket world so long or so wisely and it is unlikely that, in more democratic days, any man will do so again. This influence was due primarily not to his eminence as a player, considerable though that was, nor to his title, but to his masterful personality, to the acknowledged soundness of his judgment, whether on the practical side of cricket or on its organization and finance, and to his unimpeachable fairness. He was a scrupulously just man. He might be and often was feared – indeed he was a formidable figure – but no one could fail to respect him and by those who knew him well and by the many whom he had helped in some difficulty or crisis he was deeply loved. He was a staunch friend and supporter of the professionals. Strong though his own views were, he never tried to impose them upon a meeting: he was an ideal chairman, not suffering fools gladly, but giving everyone his fair say and prepared to modify his own opinions if occasion arose.

He had himself been for years in the front rank as a forcing batsman, who was especially severe on fast bowling; he was a brilliant field and a useful change bowler. When over 70 he could still make runs in good club cricket. He had his first net at Lord's in 1862 and played his last game there in 1929 and was 79 when he last played at Eton. To him more than anybody else was due the revival of Kent cricket after years of depression, and to the end of his life he was the controlling influence in it. He collected and captained the side for the 1st Test Match in England and but for him the match might never have been played. He fearlessly opposed unfair bowling and in 1885 persuaded Kent to cancel their return match with Lancashire, two of whose bowlers, Nash and Crossland, threw unashamedly. He himself jettisoned from the Kent side at this period 2 promising and much-needed fast bowlers whose actions were not above suspicion.

He was no less prominent at Lord's than in Kent: he once said, 'My whole life has pivoted on Lord's.' Among the various offices he held, he was for some years chairman of the Finance and Cricket Sub-Committees and, though it might seem to some that he got his own way too often, they were generally compelled in the end to admit that his way had been right. Under no circumstances would he tolerate any breach of the laws of cricket and he insisted that they were 'Laws' and not 'Rules'. 'Rules,' he said, 'are made to be broken, laws are made to be kept.' He was responsible for 2 valuable contributions to cricket literature, as editor of the admirable *History of Kent County Cricket* and joint-editor of *Lord's and the MCC*, and also wrote his own reminiscences, *A Few Short Runs*. Prominent latterly in the City, he had earlier been successively Under-Secretary for India, Under-Secretary for War and Governor of Bombay.

R. L. ARROWSMITH

CAREER FIGURES

	INNS	NO	RUNS	HS	AVGE	100S
Batting	393	23	9873	176	26·68	10

Bowling 75 wkts

Test Record (4)

	INNS	NO	RUNS	HS	AVGE	100S
Batting	6	1	145	52	29·00	–

Bowling 0 wkts for 29 Ct 2

HARVEY, Robert Neil, MBE (1928–)

Collingwood Tech Sch. Victoria 1946–47 to 1956–57 (Captain 1956–57). New South Wales 1958–59 to 1962–63. Australia: in Australia 1947–48, 1950–51, 1951–52, 1952–53, 1954–55, 1958–59, 1960–61, 1962–63; in England 1948, 1953, 1956, 1961 (Captain); in South Africa 1949–50, 1957–58; in West Indies 1954–55; in India 1956–57, 1959–60; in Pakistan 1956–57, 1959–60. Selector.

In 15 years, between 1948 and 1963, Harvey played in more Test Matches than any other Australian, scored more runs in Tests than all but Sir Donald Bradman, and was headed by only that great batsman in Australian Test hundreds and average. That having been said, it may be added that the last thing Harvey was ever interested in was statistics. Tell him that he was ·02 behind in the tour averages and he would look at you in amazement; provide a challenge for him with the bat and he would accept it faster than you could sight his twinkling feet dancing down the pitch. I saw Harvey play some wonderful innings over the years – a double-hundred against South Africa, 90-odd not out in Sydney when Tyson and Statham were sweeping all before them, a double-hundred in a Sheffield Shield match in Sydney, but the batting that really sticks in one's memory was in a series of matches where his top score was a mere 69. This was in 1956 in England, on pitches that called for the use of superb technique to keep out Laker and Lock, and Harvey played with just that technique. In those innings watchers could see the meaning of the word 'batsmanship'. It was brinkmanship too, I suppose; the tenure of life on those pitches being insecure.

Like most who have possessed beautiful footwork at the crease Harvey was small of stature, but there was nothing small about his batting. Opposition bowlers used to claim he was vulnerable outside the off-stump, and the very qualification tells its own story. He himself agreed that he was dismissed more by bowlers operating outside the off-stump than in any other way. His explanation of it was simple. 'If they want to bowl out there, they can,' he would say. 'I could let 'em pass but what would be the fun of that – I'd rather have a go and take a bit of a chance.' Spectators might well offer a sigh of gratitude that this was his philosophy, for he gave them more value over the years than most other Australian cricketers. He offended the purists occasionally by falling away slightly as he square-cut the fast bowlers like a bullet to the off-side fence, and he made the bowlers shudder as he danced down the pitch to balls an ordinary batsman would have played defensively.

In the time I played against him in Australian cricket he was the most difficult batsman in the game to bowl to, a fact that will no doubt be borne out by others who encountered him after he moved in 1957 to New South Wales. There were often arguments in Australia to decide whether Davidson or Harvey was the better fieldsman. There can never really be an answer to this for both were superb, but cricket watchers will have their picture of Harvey in the covers, on the boundary or even in the slips – small and dapper, swooping on the ball and flicking it back to the 'keeper with a minimum of effort inches from the top of the bails.

RICHIE BENAUD

Neil Harvey: only 5 feet 6 inches tall, but a marvellous natural player.

CAREER FIGURES

	INNS	NO	RUNS	HS	AVGE	100S
Batting	461	35	21699	231*	50·93	67

Bowling 30 wkts at 36·86 Ct 229

Test Record (79)

	INNS	NO	RUNS	HS	AVGE	100S
Batting	137	10	6149	205	48·41	21

Bowling 3 wkts at 40·00 Ct 64

HASSETT, Arthur Lindsay, MBE (1913–)

Geelong Coll. Victoria 1933–34 to 1952–53 (Captain 1946–47 to 1952–53). Australia: in Australia 1946–47, 1947–48, 1950–51 (Captain), 1951–52 (Captain), 1952–53 (Captain); in England 1938, 1948, 1953 (Captain); in South Africa 1949–50 (Captain); in New Zealand 1945–46.

Hassett was a great batsman, a faultless field and a captain who missed little and controlled his team with a minimum of fuss. Yet he is in danger of being underrated, partly because like others of his contemporaries he was overshadowed by Bradman, partly because those who saw him after the war are apt to think of him as a solid, defensive player and not as the glorious attacking batsman he was by nature. Australian players age younger than English and it almost seemed that, resuming cricket at 32 after a long gap, he had lost the confidence to play his strokes. Certainly he seldom showed them in Tests. Standing only 5 feet 6 inches, he was one of the most brilliant batsmen of his size the world has seen. Nor was it only the small man's strokes he possessed, the hook, the cut, the quick-footed drive: he could force the good length ball in front of the wicket and never get underneath it. Even at his most defensive, he was always perfectly balanced and always made batting look easy. The number of runs he made was astonishing; when he retired, only Bradman among Australians had scored more hundreds. Yet perhaps he never played better than at Headingley in 1938, when Australia, wanting 105, had lost 4 for 61 and Hassett's 33 won the match. Since his retirement he has kept in touch with the game, and his many followers have kept in touch with him, through his Test Match commentaries in Australia.

R. L. ARROWSMITH

CAREER FIGURES

	INNS	NO	RUNS	HS	AVGE	100S
Batting	322	32	16890	232	58·24	59

Bowling 18 wkts at 39·05 Ct 170

Test Record (43)

	INNS	NO	RUNS	HS	AVGE	100S
Batting	69	3	3073	198*	46·56	10

Bowling 0 wkts for 78 Ct 30

HAWKE, 7th Lord (Martin Bladen) (1860–1938)

Eton 1878–1879. Cambrige Univ 1882–1883, 1885 (Captain). Yorkshire 1881–1910 (Captain 1883–1910); President 1898–1938. Captain of 10th English team in Australia 1887–88. England: in South Africa 1895–96 (Captain), 1898–99 (Captain). Selector 1899–1909, 1933. President of MCC 1914–1919; Trustee 1916–1938; Treasurer 1932–1938.

Lord Hawke was a good enough bat to play for the Gentlemen, a famous captain of Yorkshire and a great power at Lord's. By taking innumerable sides abroad he did much to foster a love of cricket in many parts of the world. But above all he deserves to be remembered for what he did for the 'pros'. In his early days many of them had short careers and few had long lives. Though there were honourable exceptions, they were as a whole improvident, often given to drink, and easily distinguished from amateurs on the field by their shabby appearance. Lord Hawke insisted on discipline and neatness and dismissed summarily two whose behaviour fell below the standards he set. Moreover, he gave them the financial stability they had lacked. He instituted winter pay. He abolished the pernicious system of talent money and substituted a system of marks awarded by himself, and he persuaded the committee to retain and invest for a player two-thirds of his benefit money instead of handing it all to him to spend as he wished. It was no wonder that, despite his strictness, the pros held him in great affection. Nor was it only the pros: invitations to join his touring sides were greatly coveted. As a bat he was a fine off-side player, who on his good days looked worth many more runs in a season than he normally got. Yorkshire were Champions 8 times under his captaincy.

R. L. ARROWSMITH

CAREER FIGURES

	INNS	NO	RUNS	HS	AVGE	100S
Batting	920	105	16506	166	20·25	13

Bowling 0 for 16 Ct 209

Test Record (5)

	INNS	NO	RUNS	HS	AVGE	100S
Batting	8	1	55	30	7·85	–

Ct 3

HAYWARD, Thomas Walter
(1871–1939)

Surrey 1893–1914. England: in England 1896, 1899, 1902, 1905, 1907, 1909; in Australia 1897–98, 1901–02, 1903–04; in South Africa 1895–96.

Tom Hayward, who died at Cambridge, his birthplace, in July 1939, was amongst the most precisely technical and most prolific batsmen of any time in the annals of cricket. He played in 29 Test Matches against Australia, including 3 tours to Australia; also he played 6 times against South Africa. But in Hayward's career Test Matches were, compared with today, rare events. The standard of English county cricket, all-round, was probably higher then than it has ever been since. Hayward was the 1st batsman following W. G. Grace to score a hundred hundreds. Twenty seasons consecutively he reached 1,000 runs. In 1904 he totalled 3,170, average 54·65, and in 1906, 3,518, average 66·37. He completed 1,000 runs before the end of May in 1900. Hayward and Hobbs, before 1914, scored a hundred for Surrey's 1st wicket 40 times. In 1907 these two Cambridge-born batsmen scored a century for Surrey's 1st wicket 4 times in one week. Thrice Hayward scored 2 hundreds in the same match; in 1906 he actually performed this double feat twice in 6 days – 144 not out, and 100 v Nottinghamshire at Trent Bridge; and 143 and 125 v Leicestershire at Leicester. In 1898 he played his most prosperous innings of 315 not out v Lancashire at Kennington Oval. In 1906 he scored 13 hundreds in the season. He was one of the Players' XI v the Gentlemen in 33 matches, scoring 2,535 runs, average beyond 46.

In 1899, at Old Trafford, he scored a hundred for England v Australia in a challenging period. In the same rubber he and F. S. Jackson put on 185 for England's 1st wicket, Hayward 137. Curiously enough Hayward, having made 2 hundreds in this rubber of 1899 never again reached a hundred against Australia. His fielding was not a strong point. But while Hayward is sure of a lasting place among England's great batsmen, it is not generally well known that he enjoyed profitable seasons as a medium-pace off-break bowler. In 1897 he took 114 wickets at 18·18 each besides scoring 1,368 runs. Twice in 1899 he did the hat-trick.

Still, it is as a classic batsman that Hayward is remembered. He came from a classic cricket family – son of Daniel Hayward and nephew of Thomas Hayward, who in the 1860s was renowned as the finest professional batsman anywhere. Tom Hayward, subject of this memoir, was tallish and well built. His bat was scrupulously put to the line of the ball. His patience and watchfulness have not been excelled even by Sir Leonard Hutton. Yet Hayward was no mere passive resister. On a turning pitch against Gloucestershire at Bristol, in 1906, he scored 100 not out in a total of 127 for three, with 50 in 55 minutes out of 60. On a firm wicket his driving could be devastating to the attack. He was, with 'Bobby' Abel, Surrey personified. Only Sir Jack Hobbs has worn the chocolate-coloured cap as symbolically, as worthily, as Tom Hayward wore it.

NEVILLE CARDUS

CAREER FIGURES

	INNS	NO	RUNS	HS	AVGE	100S
Batting	1138	96	43551	315*	41·79	104

Bowling 481 wkts at 22·96 Ct 487

Test Record (35)

	INNS	NO	RUNS	HS	AVGE	100S
Batting	60	2	1999	137	34·46	3

Bowling 14 wkts at 36·71 Ct 19

HAZARE, Vijay Samuel (1915–)

Sangli High Sch. Maharashtra 1934–35. Central India 1935–36. Baroda 1941–42 to 1960–61 (Captain 1950–51 to 1955–56). India: in India 1948–49, 1951–52 (Captain) 1952–53; in England 1946, 1952 (Captain); in Australia 1947–48; in West Indies 1952–53 (Captain).

Hazare was a conscientious, if not successful, captain of India for 3 crowded years in the early 1950s. One of the most prolific scorers in India's history, Hazare was a right-hander gifted with interminable concentration who could, however, in rare moods play as attractively as most. Though he played against MCC at Poona in 1933–34 and toured England with the Rajputana side in 1938, it was not until the war that he gained real prominence. He scored 316 not out for Maharashtra in 1939–40 and an incredible 309 for The Rest v Hindus at Bombay in 1943–44 – out of an innings total of 387. In 1947–48 he made 116 and 145 in the Adelaide Test against Australia, and was a partner (with Gul Mahomed) in the highest partnership ever recorded in first-class cricket – 577 for the 4th wicket v Holkar in 1946–47. He was also a capable medium-pace bowler who took exactly 100 wickets on his 2 post-war tours of England. He played league cricket in Lancashire for Rawtenstall and Royton.

IRVING ROSENWATER

CAREER FIGURES

	INNS	NO	RUNS	HS	AVGE	100S
Batting	366	46	18569	316*	58·02	57

Bowling 565 wkts at 24·83

Test Record (30)

	INNS	NO	RUNS	HS	AVGE	100S
Batting	52	6	2192	164*	47·65	7

Bowling 20 wkts at 61·00 Ct 11

HEADLEY, George Alphonso, MBE
(1909–)

Jamaica 1927–28 to 1953–54. West Indies: in West Indies 1929–30, 1934–35, 1947–48 (Captain); in England 1933, 1939; in Australia 1930–31; in India 1948–49.

Between 1929 and 1939 Headley never failed in a series of Tests. In the interval between the wars only the computing Bradman surpasses his figures. And there are considerations which no mechanical calculations can adequately register. For almost the whole of his career Headley, going in 1st wicket down, knew that if he failed to score or merely to stay, it was problematical whether his side would reach 150.

He was born in 1909 in Panama where there is a substantial West Indian community, originating from the numerous West Indians who went there at the beginning of the century to help build the Panama Canal. His early game was rounders. The national language of Panama is Spanish and in 1919 his mother took him to Jamaica where she was born, so that he might go to an English school. There he was introduced to cricket and soccer, and took to cricket, sometimes playing without stopping for meals, with home-made bats and balls. At school he used man-size bats so he held the handle with one hand and the blade with the other. He was devoted to cricket, watching visiting cricketers like Ernest Tyldesley and Percy Holmes, and working his way up. Yet he had his ticket ready to leave for the United States to study dentistry. There was, however, a long delay in getting his passport from Panama and an English team arrived before the passport. Headley was chosen and not yet 19 years of age made 78 in the 1st match and 211 in the 2nd. Gradually he came to know that he would prefer to stay and play cricket rather than go to the United States to study a profession.

George Headley: 'The black Bradman', batting against England at the Oval in 1939. Wood at the wicket, Hammond at slip.

In 1929–30 the MCC sent a team to the West Indies to play 4 Test Matches. In the First Test in Barbados Headley made 176, and scored a hundred in each innings of the last Test at Georgetown. He went to Australia in 1930–31, began brilliantly and, after a period in which the Australian concentration on his leg-stump bothered him, mastered the Australian attack to such a degree that Grimmett considered him the finest on-side player he ever bowled against. Headley came to England in 1933 and again in 1939. He was master of the English bowling, achieving a remarkable climax to a remarkable career by making a hundred in each innings of the 1939 Test at Lord's.

He was essentially a back-foot player but made all the strokes and except when overburdened with responsibility always attacked bowlers. His record on wickets affected by rain is notable even for a great batsman. He bowled leg-breaks with great assiduity whenever he got the chance and fielded finely anywhere. After the war he played odd games in one or two series but was never his old self. He continued for years, however, to be a notable performer in League cricket in England.

C. L. R. JAMES

CAREER FIGURES

	INNS	NO	RUNS	HS	AVGE	100S
Batting	164	22	9921	344*	69·86	33

Bowling 51 wkts at 36·11

Test Record (22)

	INNS	NO	RUNS	HS	AVGE	100S
Batting	40	4	2190	270*	60·83	10

Bowling 0 wkts for 230 Ct 14

HEARNE, John Thomas (1867–1944)

Middlesex 1888–1923. England: in England 1896, 1899; in Australia 1897–98; in South Africa 1891–92.

Born in Buckinghamshire, J. T. Hearne first played for Middlesex against the Australians in 1888, and then, qualifying by residence, began in 1890 24 years of regular, devoted and distinguished service to his county. This culminated in his election to the County Committee in 1920, in those days an almost unprecedented honour for a professional player, and a tribute to his charming personality and uncompromising standards. A bowler of lively medium pace, with a run-up and delivery of classic rhythm, Hearne was a model of accuracy, able to turn the ball back on any wicket, and with deadly effect on one that helped him; he could also move it away with the arm. In 15 seasons he took over 100 wickets; in 3 of them over 200, 257 in 1896 being the highest, and including 56 in all the games he played that summer against the Australians. In his 12 Tests he made history at Headingley in 1899 with a hat-trick that accounted for Hill, Gregory and Noble. His life aggregate of 3,061 wickets is the 4th highest yet achieved. A useful batsman, especially at need, he made over 7,000 runs. After his retirement from county cricket he was for some years a most respected and successful coach to Oxford University.

H. S. ALTHAM

CAREER FIGURES

	INNS	NO	RUNS	HS	AVGE	100S
Batting	919	318	7205	71	11·99	–

Bowling 3061 wkts at 17·75 Ct 421

Test Record (12)

	INNS	NO	RUNS	HS	AVGE	100S
Batting	18	4	126	40	9·00	–

Bowling 49 wkts at 22·08 Ct 4

HEARNE, John William (1891–1965)

Middlesex 1909–1936. England: in England 1912, 1921, 1924, 1926; in Australia 1911–12, 1920–21, 1924–25; in South Africa 1913–14.

J. W. Hearne's record proclaims him for what he was, an all-round cricketer of the highest class. Five times he did the double (making 2,000 on three of those occasions). Another 14 times he made 1,000 runs. Though the First World War came when his promise was at its height he made, in all, 96 hundreds. Yet, impressive as Hearne's figures are, they would have been much more so had he not suffered throughout his career from indifferent health and frequent accidents. He started his career as a ground-boy at Lord's – selling score-cards, cleaning up and so on. In those days the senior professionals on the ground staff were in no hurry to part with their 'know-how' to the youngsters treading on their heels. He was more or less self-taught and was very individualistic in all departments of the game. Everything he did was neat and effortless, perhaps elegant is the correct word.

He was at times accused of being a slow scorer. This was true on dead wickets, but on fast wickets he kept pace and outpaced reputedly fast scorers. He was able to do so because he moved farther across to the off than the majority and scored off deliveries that were normally left alone. As a googly bowler in the period 1911–1914 he was outstanding. His leg-break had the ideal trajectory, slightly up when leaving the hand and dipping at the end – not slow enough to be easily got at down the wicket, very sharply spun. On a turning wicket he had 2 slips and a close gully. When the occasion demanded, he was cheerfully prepared to sacrifice his wicket to push the score along – a none too common virtue. He and 'Patsy' Hendren formed for Middlesex one of the most famous partnerships in the history of county cricket.

NIGEL HAIG

CAREER FIGURES

	INNS	NO	RUNS	HS	AVGE	100S
Batting	1025	116	37252	285*	40·98	96

Bowling 1839 wkts at 24·43 Ct 349

Test Record (24)

	INNS	NO	RUNS	HS	AVGE	100S
Batting	36	5	806	114	26·00	1

Bowling 30 wkts at 48·73 Ct 13

HENDREN, Elias Henry (1889–1962)

Middlesex 1907–1937. England: in England 1921, 1924, 1926, 1928, 1929, 1930, 1934; in Australia 1920–21, 1924–25, 1928–29; in South Africa 1930–31; in West Indies 1929–30, 1934–35.

Patsy Hendren going out to bat in his last season, aged 48, partnered by Denis Compton, aged 19.

'Patsy' Hendren was largely a self-taught cricketer. He laid the foundations of a great and wonderfully comprehensive career as a boy on Turnham Green where, in recognition of his services as a fielder, he was allowed to practise with the local club. On graduating to Lord's his early days were moderately successful, his outstanding talent being his speed and sureness of hand in the deep field. It was on the resumption of cricket in 1919 that he really established himself in county cricket. His batting and fielding ensured his selection for the tour of Australia the following year but, for some years, a totally unaccountable nervousness seemed to assail him in Test Matches. In consequence it was not until the latter half of the 1920s that he did himself full justice in this highest class. Thereafter his record was consistently magnificent.

Hendren was a shortish, solidly built man of immense strength. He stood at the wicket with a slight crouch, a sharply protruding rump proclaiming his resolution. The speed of foot which made him a fine footballer served him well against slow bowlers and he was unexcelled amongst English batsmen against speed. With his power of forearm and wrist he was the finest hooker of the short ball in this country. For this stroke he would position himself just inside the line of the ball, which he thus could place precisely over a wide arc. He always hooked square rather than to the less controllable and more dangerous area of fine leg. All the other strokes he had at his command, reinforced by a strong and orthodox defence. His record in plain figures makes extraordinary reading. He made 170 hundreds, a number only exceeded by Sir Jack Hobbs. He scored 57,611 runs, an aggregate again only bettered by the 'Master' and by Frank Woolley. It is a happy reflection that each of the 3 leading makers of runs should have been such very attractive batsmen, each in his own highly individual and strongly contrasting style. In the vast total of runs achieved by this great trio there can have been very few obtained by dull or inelegant play.

Apart from his great ability as a player, Hendren was a most outstanding personality in his own right. With his slightly comical cast of countenance, twinkling and friendly eye, Hendren had an unequalled quality for endearing himself to every crowd wherever he went. On his appearance the IZ Tent at Canterbury and the Hill at Sydney would in their somewhat differing ways spontaneously and equally express their affection. In the West Indies his personality, his tremendous batting and a talent for innocent and really comical buffoonery evoked a response nigh to delirium. He made a duck in his 1st match for Middlesex, and a duck in his last, a memory which gave him as much pleasure as that of his 170 hundreds.

IAN PEEBLES

CAREER FIGURES

	INNS	NO	RUNS	HS	AVGE	100S
Batting	1300	166	57611	301*	50·80	170

Bowling 47 wkts at 54·77 Ct 755

Test Record (51)

	INNS	NO	RUNS	HS	AVGE	100S
Batting	83	9	3525	205*	47·63	7

Bowling 1 wkt for 31 Ct 33

HILL, Clement (1877–1945)

South Australia 1892–93 to 1922–23 (Captain 1901–02 to 1922–23). Australia: in Australia 1897–98, 1901–02, 1903–04, 1907–08, 1910–11 (Captain), 1911–12 (Captain); in England 1896, 1899, 1902, 1905; in South Africa 1902–03.

Many regard Hill as the greatest of all left-handers. He had an ugly stance, with the bat held very low, but, as soon as he started to move, any awkwardness vanished. He was probably strongest on the leg, but was very quick on his feet, could drive to the off or straight and was a tremendous cutter. Indeed he had all the strokes and, like most great batsmen, was merciless to anything short. Few could hit fast bowling as he did. His instinct was to attack, but he was a born fighter and could defend, if need arose, as obstinately as anyone. He normally came in 1st-wicket down. Perhaps his greatest innings was 188 against England at Melbourne in 1897–98, when he was still under 21. Coming together at 58 for 6, he and Trumble added 165 – a stand which won the match. When he retired, he had the finest Test record of any Australian batsman, better even than Trumper's. He was also one of the greatest of out-fields and a man who was universally popular.

R. L. ARROWSMITH

Clem Hill: Australia's prime left-hander in the 'Golden Age'.

CAREER FIGURES

	INNS	NO	RUNS	HS	AVGE	100S
Batting	417	21	17216	365*	43·47	45

Bowling 10 wkts at 32·30

Test Record (49)

	INNS	NO	RUNS	HS	AVGE	100S
Batting	89	2	3412	191	39·21	7

Ct 33

HIRST, George Herbert (1871–1954)

Yorkshire 1891–1929. England: in England 1899, 1902, 1905, 1907, 1909; in Australia 1897–98, 1903–04.

Even if life figures of 36,323 runs and 2,739 wickets were not enough to establish Hirst's playing stature, it would be signed and sealed for all time by his 2,385 runs and 208 wickets in the season of 1906, an unparalleled record, and one, as we may hazard, highly unlikely ever to be equalled. In 19 seasons he made over 1,000 runs, in 15 he took over 100 wickets, and in 14 he did both, a feat only surpassed by his life-long friend, Wilfred Rhodes.

Originally a straightforward faster than medium left-hand bowler, with a lively run and pace off the pitch, it was in 1901 that he learnt how to swing the ball, in and devastatingly late, and passed at once from the good to the great. The natural corollary of 3 close leg-fields was the first example of a pattern destined to become all too familiar. Given the right wind or a heavy atmosphere, he could make the ball 'come in like a boomerang' and, with help from the wicket, could straighten it back. A magnificent and dauntless fielder, generally at mid-off, he made 550 catches, many of them off full drives. If the overall figures of his 24 Tests are comparatively modest, at least two can never be forgotten: the first at Birmingham when he and Rhodes bowled the Australians out for 36 (in their next match against Yorkshire he, 5 for 9, and Jackson, did the same for 23); the second, the historic Oval game of 1902 when, with an unbeaten 58, he rescued England from a desperate position in the 4th innings, and with Rhodes made those famous 15 runs for the last wicket.

George Hirst will always be remembered as one of the outstanding personalities in cricket history. Born at Kirkheaton, he combined the toughness of fibre and loyalty traditionally typical of his county with a sense of humour, kindliness, interest in and influence over the young, that made him in his playing days a natural leader, and after his retirement a coach, who commanded in full measure, and for 18 years, the respect and affection of all Eton cricketers.

H. S. ALTHAM

CAREER FIGURES

	INNS	NO	RUNS	HS	AVGE	100S
Batting	1215	151	36323	341	34·13	60

Bowling 2739 wkts at 18·72 Ct 550

Test Record (24)

	INNS	NO	RUNS	HS	AVGE	100S
Batting	38	3	790	85	22·57	–

Bowling 59 wkts at 30·00 Ct 18

HOBBS, Sir John Berry (1882–1963)

Surrey 1905–1934. England: in England 1909, 1912, 1921, 1924, 1926, 1928, 1929, 1930; in Australia 1907–08, 1911–12, 1920–21, 1924–25, 1928–29; in South Africa 1909–10, 1913–14. Knighted 1953.

'Jack Hobbs', as he will be remembered by all cricketers, was born in Cambridge, but, influenced by his boyhood contact with and admiration for Tom Hayward, qualified by residence for Surrey; and in April 1905 made 88 in his 1st match for that county against a Gentlemen of England XI captained by 'W.G.'. A fortnight later he made 155 against Essex in his 1st Championship match and was at once given his county cap by Lord Dalmeny, a sensational start to what was to prove a historic cricket career. Many records stand to his name: his aggregate of 61,237; his total of 197 hundreds – and it may well surprise the modern generation to know that 98 of them were made after he attained the age of 40; the highest score (316 not out) ever made in a first-class match at Lord's; the highest score (266 not out at Scarborough) in the Gentlemen v Players match; his 16 hundreds and aggregate of 4,052 runs in that fixture; his 12 hundreds against Australia; and, until D. C. S. Compton passed it in 1947, his 16 hundreds (10 of them in his 1st 12 matches) in the season of 1925 when, at the age of 42, he made 3,024 runs with an average of 70. In 14 Test series in which he played for England, beginning in 1907 and ending in 1930, he totalled 5,410 runs, averaging 56; of these 2,493 runs, including 9 hundreds, were made in Australia. Establishing himself at once as an opening batsman, he took part in 166 1st-wicket partnerships of over a hundred, of which 28 exceeded 200; the highest of these was his 428, against Oxford, with Sandham who succeeded Hayward as his regular Surrey partner, but the most memorable was the 323 with Wilfred Rhodes at Melbourne in the 1911–12 tour. In all he shared in 23 partnerships of over a hundred in Test Matches, 8 of them with Rhodes and 15 with Sutcliffe.

In batting technique Hobbs bridged in undisputed supremacy what may be termed the classic with the more 'modern' and sophisticated age. Like all great batsmen he sighted the ball very early, and moved into the stroke of his choice with fascinating ease and poise. In the decade before the First World War he consistently dictated to the bowler in terms of what seemed at once art and adventure; after it, against the increasing problems of seam and spin bowling, that dictation was more deliberate and cumulative, based on mastery of back play but still coloured by variety and beauty of attacking strokes, whether the cut, the drive or the hook. Most clearly was it revealed in the challenge of a really difficult wicket, formidable bowling, the crisis of a match; as when at the Oval in

Jack Hobbs: off to make a hundred and happy in his work.

1926, and at Melbourne in 1929, with Sutcliffe as his partner and on wickets of what seemed limitless treachery, he led England from the prospect of inevitable defeat into the sunshine of victory. A magnificent field in the covers, and a master of the art of luring batsmen into a run by superficial lethargy, he ran out 15 batsmen on the 1911–12 Australian tour.

As 'W.G.' was for all cricketers 'The Champion', so Hobbs was known by all his own generation as 'The Master'. But it is not only for his prowess on the field that he will be remembered with such admiration and affection by all who knew him. A man of natural dignity, with at the same time an engaging twinkle that revealed a charming and constant sense of humour, utterly unspoilt by success and always prepared to help others, especially the young, he soon became and remained throughout his playing days an ideal support for any touring captain, and the embodiment of the highest standards and values in the game. A service held in his memory on 20 February 1964 filled Southwark Cathedral.

H. S. ALTHAM

CAREER FIGURES

	INNS	NO	RUNS	HS	AVGE	100S
Batting	1315	106	61237	316*	50·65	197

Bowling 108 wkts at 24·89 Ct 332

Test Record (61)

	INNS	NO	RUNS	HS	AVGE	100S
Batting	102	7	5410	211	56·94	15

Bowling 1 wkt for 165 Ct 17

HOLMES, Percy (1886–1971)

Yorkshire 1913–1933. England: in England 1921, 1932; in South Africa 1927–28.

Holmes is remembered as Sutcliffe's partner in one of the historic opening pairs and especially in the record opening stand of 555 at Leyton in 1932, but few of his contemporaries doubted that, given the opportunities, he would have made his mark in Tests. Technically he was probably Sutcliffe's equal, possibly his superior, but he was by instinct an attacker and lacked the unwearying concentration and complete imperturbability which made Sutcliffe unique. Quick and light on his feet, he was a particularly good hooker and cutter and a fine field.

R. L. ARROWSMITH

CAREER FIGURES

	INNS	NO	RUNS	HS	AVGE	100S
Batting	810	84	30574	315*	42·11	67

Bowling 2 wkts at 91·50 Ct 342

Test Record (7)

	INNS	NO	RUNS	HS	AVGE	100S
Batting	14	1	357	88	27·46	–

Ct 3

HOME OF THE HIRSEL, Baron (Sir Alexander Frederick Douglas-Home, formerly 14th Earl of Home), KT, PC (1903–)

Eton 1921–22. Middlesex 1924–25. MCC in South America 1926–27. President of MCC 1966–67.

Lord Home of the Hirsel (formerly Sir Alec Douglas-Home) is the only British Prime Minister to have been a first-class cricketer. The eldest son of the 13th Earl of Home, he played 2 years – as Lord Dunglass – against Harrow at Lord's. He was a useful batsman and fast-medium bowler whose serious cricket was restricted by his entry into politics. Against Harrow at Lord's in 1922 he made 66, the highest score for Eton. Later that season he played for Lord's Schools v The Rest. He appeared in occasional first-class matches between 1924 and 1927, playing for Oxford without getting a blue, and also for Middlesex. He was elected an Oxford Harlequin in 1925, and in 1926–27 toured South America with MCC under P. F. Warner, playing in the Argentine, Chile, Peru and Uruguay. His highest score in first-class cricket was 37 not out for Free Foresters v Oxford University at Oxford in 1924. Both before and after the Second World War he often represented Lords and Commons.

IRVING ROSENWATER

HORNBY, Albert Neilson (1847–1925)

Harrow 1864–1865. Lancashire 1867–1899 (Captain 1880–1893, 1897–1898). England: in England 1882 (Captain), 1884 (Captain); in Australia 1878–79. President Lancashire 1894–1916.

'Monkey' Hornby, one of 2 men who have captained England both at rugby football and cricket, was a brilliant attacking batsman, a fast and expert runner between the wickets and a splendid field. He and Barlow, a stonewaller, made a notable Lancashire opening pair, immortalized by Francis Thompson, 'O my Hornby and my Barlow long ago'.

R. L. ARROWSMITH

CAREER FIGURES

	INNS	NO	RUNS	HS	AVGE	100S
Batting	710	41	16108	188	24·08	16

Bowling 11 wkts at 23·45 Ct 312

Test Record (3)

	INNS	NO	RUNS	HS	AVGE	100S
Batting	6	0	21	9	3·50	–

Bowling 1 wkt for 0 runs

HUNTE, Conrad Cleophas (1932–)

Alleyne Secondary Sch, Barbados. Barbados from 1950–51. West Indies: in West Indies 1957–58, 1959–60, 1961–62, 1964–65; in England 1963, 1966; in Australia 1960–61; in India 1958–59, 1966–67; in Pakistan 1958–59.

Conrad Hunte was born in humble surroundings, the eldest of 9 children, in the rural parish of St Andrew, Barbados. From his early childhood he showed more interest in cricket than in his school work. At that time, opportunities for cricketers were few and far between, but he came to notice in 1951 when he scored 137 when opening for the Barbados Cricket League against the Barbados Cricket Association. Having gone on to represent Barbados with distinction, he journeyed to England, where, assisted by Worrell and Weekes, he obtained a professional contract in 1957 for Enfield in the Lancashire League. He was unfortunate, because of a telegram going astray, to miss the West Indies tour of England that year.

On his 1st appearance for West Indies, in January 1958, he scored 142 against Pakistan, going in 1st with Kanhai, the first of his 13 opening partners for West Indies. As West Indies' most consistent and reliable opening batsman during the late 1950s and through the 1960s, he represented West Indies in 44 Tests, scored 3,245 runs, including 8 hundreds, for an average of 45·06 and a highest score of 260.

During the 1960–61 West Indies' tour of Australia he was introduced to Moral Re-Armament by James Coulter, an Australian journalist. On his return to England, he met T. C. ('Dickie') Dodds, the former Essex cricketer, Dr Buchman, the founder, and Peter Howard, a leader of MRA, and became deeply committed to the movement. He thus found the fulfilment in life that he felt had previously been lacking. He believed that, through his cricket, he was being given the opportunity to be a Christian ambassador, not only for the West Indies, but for the coloured and oppressed people of the world.

Hunte was hurt and desperately disappointed at being passed over for the West Indies captaincy when Frank Worrell retired in 1963. He later apologized to Sobers, his new skipper, for harbouring thoughts of resentment, and gave him his full support. Hunte's record for West Indies is an impressive one. It fails, all the same, to record the true value of the great contribution he has made, on and off the field, to cricket in general, and West Indies cricket in particular. Many people talk about Christianity, Conrad Hunte lives it.

PETER SHORT

CAREER FIGURES

	INNS	NO	RUNS	HS	AVGE	100S
Batting	222	19	8916	263	43·92	16

Bowling 17 wkts at 37·88 Ct (incl w/k) 69; st 1

Test Record (44)

	INNS	NO	RUNS	HS	AVGE	100S
Batting	78	6	3245	260	45·06	8

Bowling 2 wkts at 55·00 Ct 16

HUTTON, Sir Leonard (1916–)

Pudsey Sch. Yorkshire 1934–1955. England: in England 1937, 1938, 1939, 1946–54 consecutively (Captain 1952–54); in Australia 1946–47, 1950–51, 1954–55 (Captain); in South Africa 1938–39, 1948–49; in West Indies 1947–48, 1953–54 (Captain); in New Zealand 1950–51, 1954–55 (Captain). Knighted 1956. Selector 1975, 1976.

Sir Leonard Hutton will always be remembered as the maker of the record score in England v Australia Test Matches, 364, at the Oval in 1938, and as the 1st professional to be regularly appointed captain of England. He was also the 1st professional to be elected to membership of the MCC before his career had finished and the 2nd to be knighted for services to cricket. He is one of the few who have made a hundred in their 1st Test innings against Australia; one of the select band, too, who have made over a hundred hundreds in first-class cricket. He holds the record for the number of runs made in a month – 1,294 in June 1949.

After this it is almost superfluous to say that he was a great batsman, how great one only realizes when one considers the handicaps under which he laboured for much of his career. The Second World War cost him 6 of his best years and after it his left arm was permanently shorter and weaker than his right. For years against Australia he was in an unreliable batting side struggling against overwhelming opposition and later was subjected to the strain of being captain – always greater for the professional who has not been brought up to it than for the amateur who has. Yet against Australia he made 2,423 runs with an average of 54·46 and in the 1950–51 series, which we lost 1–4, his average of 88·83 was 50 ahead of the next Englishman and 45 ahead of the first Australian. It is easy to belittle his record score – the perfect Oval wicket, the weakness of the Australian bowling except O'Reilly (what an exception!) and the 13 hours it took. Yet it is like *Paradise Lost* – easy enough to criticize, but still, when the critics have said their worst, a stupendous work. Indeed 'work' is the right word and most of us would rather have seen that 37 at Sydney in 1946, made out of 49 in 24 minutes before lunch, and ended even more unluckily than Woolley's 41 at Lord's in 1930, with which it is often compared.

Len Hutton: controlled off-drive, eyes following the ball.

More controversial is his influence on a younger generation of batsmen. He was almost the 1st great player who habitually, at least after the war, played slow bowling from the crease, and he was himself for this reason relatively vulnerable to the off-spinner. Many copied him, which was a pity. Apart from his batting he was a splendid field close in and a fair leg-spinner of the type who seldom produces a startling analysis but who, shrewdly used, often gets a valuable wicket or two – a type in fact now sadly extinct.

R. L. ARROWSMITH

CAREER FIGURES

	INNS	NO	RUNS	HS	AVGE	100S
Batting	814	91	40140	364	55·51	129

Bowling 173 wkts at 29·42 Ct 396

Test Record (79)

	INNS	NO	RUNS	HS	AVGE	100S
Batting	138	15	6971	364	56·67	19

Bowling 3 wkts at 77·33 Ct 57

ILLINGWORTH, Raymond, CBE (1932–)

Wesley Street Secondary Modern Sch, Farsley. Yorkshire 1951–1968. Leicestershire 1969–1978 (Captain). Team Manager Yorkshire 1979– . England: in England 1958–1962 consecutively, 1965–1973 consecutively (Captain 1969–1973); in Australia 1962–63, 1970–71 (Captain); in West Indies 1959–60; in New Zealand 1962–63, 1970–71 (Captain).

Ray Illingworth, over a career that began with the county of his birth at the age of 19 and ended, as a player, with Leicestershire when he had turned 46, was the very embodiment of a modern Yorkshire cricketer. With Leicestershire indeed: and it is one of the stranger quirks of cricket history that it was in those last 10 of his 28 playing seasons, as one of the many expatriate Yorkshiremen, that he consummated his reputation as an all-rounder of high achievement and a formidable captain both of Leicestershire and England.

As one of only 9 all-rounders who have made 20,000 runs and taken 2,000 wickets, Illingworth's record speaks for itself: likewise his tally for England of 2,312 runs and 133 wickets with his off-spinners. Yet it is as a successful captain that he will be chiefly remembered. When he moved to Leicestershire as their captain in 1969 they had filled only a modest role in the English summer scene, though in his 2nd and last year as captain in 1967 Tony Lock had brought them to 3rd in the Championship and there was a bright young player-turned-secretary of Illingworth's own age, Mike Turner, in whom the county had shown their confidence. Turner and Leicestershire made a shrewd assessment when they put their trust in Illingworth, and so did the Test selectors when early in his first summer they suddenly had to find another captain of England to replace Colin Cowdrey, who tore an Achilles tendon and was plainly out of action for a long time. This was Illingworth's crucial piece of luck since Cowdrey was firmly in the saddle while he, now 37, could look back on 30 Test appearances of no great account spread over 13 series.

Ray Illingworth: bowlers need to concentrate too.

From the start Illingworth showed qualities that secured his position, at least as far as home Tests were concerned. Never previously having made more than 50 he chose the Lord's Test against West Indies in 1969 to rescue England's cause with an innings of 113 full of good driving and forward play. In 1970, against the immensely strong Rest of the World side in the Test series improvized when the South African tour was cancelled, he averaged 52 and emerged for a brief spell as England's most reliable batsman. Thus came the ultimate honour of leading the 15th MCC team to Australia, and the recovery of the Ashes. It was only a pity that at times on the field England were guilty of an undue aggression which the Cricket Council subsequently saw fit to rebuke. At home Illingworth continued to lead England for the next 3 summers, successively beating Pakistan and losing to India in 1971, retaining the Ashes in an admirable drawn series against Australia in 1972, and in 1973 beating New Zealand before falling decisively to the West Indies.

By this time Leicestershire had begun to taste the fruits of success and won the 1st of 2 victories at Lord's in the Benson & Hedges Cup. There were 2 wins also in the John

Player Sunday League, plus the culminating honour of the Championship. In 1975, aged 43, Illingworth enjoyed the dual triumph of Championship and B. & H.

Illingworth's years with Leicestershire were a barren time for his native county whose ranks he had left on the straight issue of playing terms. The offer of the new post of manager of Yorkshire must have been accepted by him with special relish when, after the 1978 season, he felt the time had come to retire. For his roots extend deep into West Riding soil, in Pudsey where he was born and lives. With Farsley, close by, he learned the grammar and the logic of cricket in the hard school of the Bradford League. It was the general respect for the knowledge and judgment thus acquired that was the basis of his success as a leader.

E. W. SWANTON

CAREER FIGURES

	INNS	NO	RUNS	HS	AVGE	100S
Batting	1051	207	23977	162	28·40	22

Bowling 2031 wkts at 19·93 Ct 432

Test Record (61)

	INNS	NO	RUNS	HS	AVGE	100S
Batting	90	11	1836	113	23·64	2

Bowling 122 wkts at 31·20 Ct 45

INSOLE, Douglas John, CBE (1926–)

Sir George Monoux GS. Cambridge Univ 1947–1949 (Captain 1949). Essex 1947–1963 (Jt Captain 1950, Captain 1951–60). England: in England 1950, 1955, 1956, 1957: in South Africa 1956–57. Selector 1959–1968 (Chairman 1965–1968). Manager England Tour to Australia 1978–79. Chairman TCCB 1975–1978.

'Doug' Insole, a batsman somewhat unprepossessing perhaps in style but full of resolution and combative spirit, is one of a select handful to have scored 25,000 runs since the Second World War. Going up to Cambridge from Sir George Monoux Grammar School, he got a blue as a freshman, and in his 3rd year led his side to a famous victory at Lord's. Evidence of Insole's powers as a captain led Essex to utilize his services in this capacity directly he came down. After sharing the job for one summer with T. N. Pearce he shouldered it for 10 years, bringing the side from the bottom of the Championship to a regular position in the top half. In 1955 he became the 1st amateur to score 2,000 runs in a season for Essex. Several openings failed to bring him a regular place in the England XI at home. But on his only tour abroad, to South Africa in 1956–57, when he was vice-captain to P. B. H. May, he played in all 5 Tests and headed the batting averages, scoring one of only 3 English hundreds in the series. He was a fine all-round fielder and latterly developed into a very good slip.

Despite an active business life no contemporary can match the scope of his services to cricket. Ten years as a selector included the last 4 as Chairman. He has had several spells of duty on the MCC Committee and over several momentous years was Chairman of the Test and County Cricket Board. Most recently he managed the successful 1978–79 tour to Australia.

He was also a first-rate association football player who captained Cambridge and won a FA Amateur Cup Finalist's medal with Corinthian Casuals. He is the author of *Cricket from the Middle* and *Batting*, both published in 1960.

E. W. SWANTON

CAREER FIGURES

	INNS	NO	RUNS	HS	AVGE	100S
Batting	743	72	25237	219*	37·61	54

Bowling 138 wkts at 33·95 Ct (including w/k) 363; st 6

Test Record (9)

	INNS	NO	RUNS	HS	AVGE	100S
Batting	17	2	408	110*	27·20	1

Ct 8

INTIKHAB ALAM (1941–)

Church Mission Sch, Karachi. Karachi 1957–58. PIA. Surrey 1969– . Pakistan: in Pakistan 1959–60, 1961–62, 1964–65, 1968–69, 1969–70 (Captain), 1972–73, 1974–75 (Captain), 1976–77; in England 1962, 1967, 1971 (Captain), 1974 (Captain); in Australia 1964–65, 1972–73 (Captain); in West Indies 1976–77; in New Zealand 1964–65, 1972–73 (Captain); in India 1960–61. Rest of the World in England 1970.

The drier historians in years ahead will note that Intikhab Alam was the 1st man to reach 1,000 runs and 100 wickets in Test matches for Pakistan, and that he was captain in New Zealand in 1972–73 when they won their 1st series overseas. What should also be remembered is the cheerfulness, thought and capacity for hard work that Intikhab brought to his cricket. He remained in the top echelon of leg-spin and googly bowlers as their numbers dwindled; among late-order hitters his forceful, front-foot driving had more power than most; and for a burly man he was a deceptively good fieldsman. Wrist spinners need an equable temperament; Intikhab's helped to sustain both him and the teams he captained amid disappointments on the field and political buffetings off it.

Intikhab was 16 when he first played for Karachi in 1957–58; 2 years later he dismissed the Australian, C. C. McDonald, with his first ball in Test cricket. He joined Surrey in 1969 after 3 years in Scottish cricket. He twice led Pakistan on tours of England: in 1971 he took 104 wickets, 72 with the tourists and the rest to help Surrey win the Championship. In 1974 his Pakistan side became the first unbeaten touring team since the 1948 Australians. His only Test hundred was an aggressive 138 against England at Hyderabad in 1972–73; better remembered perhaps is the 9th wicket stand of 190 he shared with Asif Iqbal against England at the Oval in 1967.

RICHARD STREETON

JACKSON, Rt Hon Sir Francis Stanley, GCSI, GCIE (1870–1947)

Harrow 1887–1889 (Captain 1889). Cambridge Univ 1890–1893 (Captain 1892, 1893). Yorkshire 1890–1907. England: in England 1893, 1896, 1899, 1902, 1905 (Captain). President MCC 1921. President Yorkshire 1939–1947. Selector (Chairman 1934).

F. S. Jackson ('Jacker' to all his generation) was in natural ability, personality and, above all, in his genius for rising to an occasion, a great cricketer. He was only 15 when, in 1887, he played for Harrow at Lord's; in the next year his 80 runs and 11 wickets, and in 1889 his 68, top score of the match, and 5 wickets carried his side to 2 resounding victories. He was 4 years in the Cambridge XI, captaining it in his 3rd, 1892 (in which he topped both the batting and bowling averages), and being captain again – a rare honour – in 1893. He first played for the county of his birth, Yorkshire, in the year after he left school, and continued to do so until 1907, though the claims of business only allowed him one full season of county cricket, 1898, in which he made 1,566 runs and took 104 wickets: even so his overall figures for the county were over 10,000 runs and 500 wickets.

F. S. Jackson: Spy's mild impression of a great and singularly determined cricketer

It will, however, always be his performances in home Tests against Australia – he never played for England overseas – that constitute his unquestionable claim to greatness. In his last year as an undergraduate, 1893, he made 91 and 103 in his first 2 of these games, and thereafter he was an automatic choice. In 1899 he made 73 at Lord's when England had lost 6 for 66, and at the Oval 118, sharing with Tom Hayward an opening stand of 185. In the famous '3-run' Test at Old Trafford in 1902 he again redeemed a dreadful English start with a masterly innings of 128, and at the Oval held up a threatened landslide, and paved the way for Jessop's dramatic counter-attack. But it was when he captained England in 1905 that he dominated the series with scores of 82 not out, 144 not out, 113 and 76, an average of 70 for 492 runs, and 13 wickets for 15 apiece, the best figures of any English bowler.

As a batsman Jackson was fully armed: he was a beautiful timer, driving on both sides of the wicket and cutting with grace and power; but behind his stroke-play was at once a classically sound defence, basically off the back foot, and a temperament and judgment raised to their highest power by any challenge. Bowling genuine medium-pace with a model run up and action, he was, with his power to turn the ball from the off and his subtle variation of pace, always a good, and at times a great, bowler. An astute captain, he had in high measure the power to inspire others to believe in themselves and to enjoy their cricket. President of MCC in 1921 and later of Yorkshire, chairman of selectors in 1934, Tory member for the Howdenshire division of Yorkshire from 1915 to 1926, Jackson subsequently became Governor of Bengal, where he reacted to an attempt on his life with the same imperturbable assurance as he had always shown in any crisis on the cricket field.

H. S. ALTHAM

CAREER FIGURES

	INNS	NO	RUNS	HS	AVGE	100S
Batting	500	35	15824	160	34·03	31

Bowling 774 wkts at 20·40 Ct 191

Test Record (20)

	INNS	NO	RUNS	HS	AVGE	100S
Batting	33	4	1415	144*	48·79	5

Bowling 24 wkts at 33·29 Ct 10

JARDINE, Douglas Robert (1900–1958)

Winchester 1917–1919 (Captain 1919). Oxford Univ 1920–21, 1923. Surrey 1921–1933 (Captain 1932–1933). England: in England 1928, 1931 (Captain), 1932 (Captain), 1933 (Captain); in Australia 1928–29, 1932–33 (Captain); in New Zealand 1932–33 (Captain); in India 1933–34 (Captain).

Born in Bombay, the son of M. R. Jardine who made 140 in the University Match of 1892, Douglas Jardine, as a boy, owed much to the early coaching of the headmaster of his preparatory school, Horris Hill, the famous Oxford bowler A. H. Evans. Three years in the Winchester XI, he celebrated his captaincy in 1919 by scoring 997 runs, the highest aggregate by any Wykehamist until the Nawab of Pataudi beat it 37 years later. Averaging that season over 2 hours for each innings he played, his batting revealed a soundness of method and a maturity of judgment that stamped him as already of a different stature from 'just a good school cricketer'. Four years in the Oxford XI, though owing to an injury he was little seen in 1922, he played no outstanding innings in the University Match. He first played for Surrey at the end of the Oxford season in 1921, and continued to do so – so far as the claims of business allowed – until 1933, captaining them in the last 2 years. In 1927 he made 5 hundreds, 3 of them in succession, and ended at the top of the English batting table with an average of 91, a position which he maintained next year though his average dropped to 87. But it was in representative games that his greatness stood most clearly revealed.

All passion spent: a portrait of D. R. Jardine shortly before his death at 57.

On his 1st tour to Australia with Chapman's MCC side he shared in a 3rd-wicket partnership of 262 with Hammond in the Adelaide Test, and made successive hundreds in his 1st 3 innings. But it was with his next tour and captaincy in Australia in 1932–33 that his name will always be associated in cricket history. For it, and perhaps especially to meet the menace of Bradman's batting, he devised, and on it he directed, the Body-line bowling tactics which were to go near to alienating a continent, and which MCC in 1934 were to legislate out of the game. But the moral courage with which, amid formidable hostility, he stuck to his convictions throughout the tour cemented his team's loyalty to him as surely as the unflinching century which next summer at Old Trafford he made against the West Indies' fast bowlers, employing the same tactics, revealed his physical courage.

Tall and angular, with the head of a Highland chieftain, invariably surmounted by a Harlequin cap, Jardine was an arresting figure on the field; a back player of the highest class, and particularly strong in on-side strokes, he reinforced a classic method with an unfaltering will. Alike in tactical skill and in personality, he must rank as one of the great captains: if he demanded much of his men, he never failed to give to them and to the game all that he had himself.

H. S. ALTHAM

CAREER FIGURES

	INNS	NO	RUNS	HS	AVGE	100S
Batting	378	61	14848	214*	46·84	35

Bowling 48 wkts at 31·10 Ct 187

Test Record (22)

	INNS	NO	RUNS	HS	AVGE	100S
Batting	33	6	1296	127	48·00	1

Bowling 0 wkts for 10 Ct 26

JESSOP, Gilbert Laird (1874–1955)

Cheltenham GS 1885–1889. Cambridge Univ 1896–1899 (Captain 1899). Gloucestershire 1894–1914 (Captain 1900–1912). England: in England 1899, 1902, 1905, 1907, 1909, 1912; in Australia 1901–02.

No man in history has combined so consistent a capacity for the devastating hitting of a cricket ball with such brilliance in stopping and throwing it in the field as Gilbert Jessop. In his great years he was for the spectator the most consistently exciting figure in the game, and to declare an innings against him was to tempt Providence. In 5 innings of over 200, the highest 286 against Sussex in 1903, he maintained a scoring rate of only just under 100 runs an hour, whilst in the Hastings Festival of 1907 he made 191 in an hour and a half. For the Gentlemen against the Players in 1913 he scored at the Oval 81 in 70 minutes, and 107 in under 2 hours, and at Lord's 63 off 58 balls. But the most famous of all his innings was in the Oval Test Match against Australia in 1902; when he went in to bat in the last innings England had lost 5 wickets for 48 in pursuit of a target of 273. In 75 minutes on none too easy a pitch, and against bowling of the highest class, he hit 104 runs and so made it possible for the last pair, Hirst and Rhodes, to fight England home.

A short, compact figure, Jessop had great strength in his hands and in his exceptionally long arms. Sighting the ball very early from a crouched stance he would, by his unsurpassed quickness of foot, dictate to the bowler by stroke-play of such variety that 'length' and the setting of the field seemed both to lose their meaning. His drives and pulls left the bat 'as if they had been fired', he was a magnificent cutter, and with all his unorthodoxy no one watched the ball more closely or was more balanced in execution. The same resources of physique and concentration made him perhaps the greatest fielder and thrower there has ever been: he could stand 10 or 15 yards deeper than anyone else in the covers and still save one, and throw down either wicket with unerring accuracy. If perhaps not a good enough fast bowler to justify his opening the England attack, as he did in his 1st Test Match at Lord's in 1899, he took 104 wickets next year as well as scoring over 2,000 runs. His natural friendliness and modesty endeared him to all with whom he played.

H. S. ALTHAM

CAREER FIGURES

	INNS	NO	RUNS	HS	AVGE	100S
Batting	855	37	26698	286	32·63	53

Bowling 873 wkts at 22·79 Ct 463

Test Record (18)

	INNS	NO	RUNS	HS	AVGE	100S
Batting	26	0	569	104	21·88	1

Bowling 10 wkts at 35·40 Ct 11

JOHNSON, Ian William, OBE (1918–)

Wesley Coll, Melbourne. Victoria 1935–36 to 1955–56 (Captain 1953–54 to 1955–56). Australia: in Australia 1946–47, 1947–48, 1950–51, 1951–52, 1952–53, 1954–55 (Captain); in England 1948, 1956 (Captain); in South Africa 1949–50; in West Indies 1954–55 (Captain); in New Zealand 1945–46; in India 1956–57 (Captain); in Pakistan 1956–57 (Captain).

Ian Johnson was the slowest bowler of recent Test Match cricket and one of the few successful off-spin bowlers to come out of Australia. His 6 for 42 in 30 overs against England at Sydney in 1946–47 saw the start of a successful career. Bradman hardly used him in England in 1948 and he was left at home in 1953, but returned as captain in 1956.

He was at his best bowling into the breeze, where his unusual action produced a natural, teasing flight, which floated the ball deceptively in the air. He was not quick enough to make use of wet wickets, and of his 109 Test wickets, only 13 were taken in England. More at home on harder, faster pitches, he took 79 wickets in South Africa in 1949–50 and his 7 for 44 against West Indies at Georgetown in 1955 ensured victory for his side. He was a useful middle-order batsman and a very good slip fielder. He took over the

Australian captaincy from Lindsay Hassett at a time when England were developing into a powerful side. An astute leader and a fine ambassador for cricket, he was victorious against West Indies, India and Pakistan, but lost 2 series against England. On retirement he became secretary of the Melbourne Cricket Club.

COLIN COWDREY

CAREER FIGURES

	INNS	NO	RUNS	HS	AVGE	100S
Batting	243	29	4905	132*	22·92	2

Bowling 619 wkts at 23·31 Ct 138

Test Record (45)

	INNS	NO	RUNS	HS	AVGE	100S
Batting	66	12	1000	77	18·51	–

Bowling 109 wkts at 29·19 Ct 30

JOHNSTON, William Arras (1922–)

Colac HS. Victoria 1945–46 to 1954–55. Australia: in Australia 1947–48, 1950–51, 1951–52, 1952–53, 1954–55; in England 1948, 1953; in South Africa 1949–50; in West Indies 1954–55.

Beginning as a slow spinner with an occasional faster ball, 'Bill' Johnston will be remembered as a great medium-fast swing bowler with a dangerous slower ball. With a 10-pace run-up, dipping his head in curious fashion before gearing himself to deliver from his full height, he always bowled over the wicket. He could swing the ball late either way, yet it was the disconcerting lift he could extract from the most lifeless wicket that made him such a fearsome proposition. For 7 years he was the vital link in the Australian attack. Bradman used him as the foil for his spearhead of Lindwall and Miller. In 1948 he was the only Australian bowler to take a hundred wickets, and became the leading Australian wicket-taker in 3 consecutive series. A damaged knee, which restricted him severely in England in 1953, did much to bring about Australia's defeat in this series. He was leading wicket-taker once again against England in Australia in 1954–55. As a bowler, courageous, skilful and hostile, but quietly philosophical and always good-humoured, he made the ideal tourist, the perfect competitor. Now a resident of Adelaide he has had the pleasure of watching his son playing for South Australia.

COLIN COWDREY

CAREER FIGURES

	INNS	NO	RUNS	HS	AVGE	100S
Batting	162	73	1129	38	12·68	–

Bowling 554 wkts at 23·35 Ct 52

Test Record (40)

	INNS	NO	RUNS	HS	AVGE	100S
Batting	49	25	273	29	11·37	–

Bowling 160 wkts at 23·91 Ct 16

KALLICHARRAN, Alvin Isaac (1949–)

Port Mourant Comp Inst, Berbice. Guyana 1966–67– . Warwickshire 1971– . Queensland 1977–78. West Indies: in West Indies 1971–72, 1972–73, 1973–74, 1975–76, 1976–77, 1977–78 (Captain); in England 1973, 1976; in Australia

Alvin Kallicharran: on tip-toe to get on top of a hook.

1975–76, 1979–80; in India 1974–75, 1978–79 (Captain); in Pakistan 1974–75.

Born at Port Mourant, in the sugar country of Berbice along the east coast of Guyana, Alvin Kallicharran maintains a rich cricketing tradition. For this is the nursery from which those three other great West Indian Test players – Kanhai, Solomon and Butcher – all came. Only 5 feet 4 inches in height, many insist that 'Kalli' is Kanhai through the looking glass – a left-handed image of one of the most immaculate cricketers of our time. The same instinct for the game, the same ease of style and timing, and the same talent for tall scoring at the highest level.

Graduating into the Guyana Shell Shield side from the Guyana Schools XI in 1966 the dapper Kallicharran faithfully followed the Kanhai trail. To the extent, even, that after making the West Indies side in 1971 – starting with successive hundreds against New Zealand – he joined his mentor with Warwickshire. More recently Kallicharran made a further succession to Kanhai as West Indies captain, this during the schism of World Series Cricket. As with Kanhai so with Kallicharran, a hundred is a thing of great joy that makes a difficult game look easy.

CRAWFORD WHITE

KANHAI, Rohan Babulal (1935–)

Port Mourant Sch, Berbice. British Guiana from 1954–55. Western Australia 1961–62. Tasmania 1969–70. Warwickshire 1968–1977. West Indies: in West Indies 1957–58, 1959–60, 1961–62, 1964–65, 1967–68, 1970–71, 1972–73 (Captain), 1973–74 (Captain); in England 1957, 1963, 1966, 1973 (Captain); in Australia 1960–61, 1968–69; in India 1958–59, 1966–67; in Pakistan 1958–59. WSC. Rest of the World in England 1970.

In full flow Rohan Kanhai came nearer to batting like Don Bradman than anyone else since Bradman retired; nearer even than Everton Weekes, who was built on similar lines, or Vivian Richards, who, though no less exciting, resorts more often to violence.

If, as I think, Kanhai had a genius for batting, why, you may ask, was he not more consistent? How come, that whereas Bradman scored 29 hundreds in 80 Test innings, Kanhai scored only 15 in 137? The answer to that is that Kanhai was less responsible than Bradman, or, to put it another way, that he bothered less. Often, even in Test Matches, Kanhai got himself out, sometimes through indifference, sometimes through arrogance, sometimes through impatience, sometimes through boredom. But when he was trying, what a batsman he was!

Even now, one is seldom in Melbourne for long without reference being made to the innings of 252 which Kanhai played there in 1960, for the West Indians against Victoria. On that same wonderfully eventful tour, at Adelaide, having decided it was time a West Indian, other than Clyde Walcott, scored 2 hundreds in a Test Match against Australia, Kanhai did so. His 117 in the 1st innings and 115 in the 2nd came at almost a run a minute. There was about him an audacity that was breathtaking. Yet when he wanted, he could be a fiend to get out.

Coming first to England chiefly as a part-time wicket-keeper, in 1957, he returned many times, either to play for West Indies, or in one of the leagues, or, finally, for Warwickshire. He was a beautiful fieldsman, as safe at slip as he was swift in the covers. Always neatly dressed, his sleeves buttoned at the cuffs, his bat a very part of him, Kanhai was moody one day, magnificent the next, and never remotely dull. Sometimes, for the hell of it, he would swing himself off his feet, trying to hit a bowler out of sight. He might do it as soon as he came in. But for that, and that sort of thing, he would have captained West Indies more than 13 times in his 79 Tests.

JOHN WOODCOCK

Rohan Kanhai: prematurely grey, but still a brilliant player at 40. Vanburn Holder in the background.

CAREER FIGURES

	INNS	NO	RUNS	HS	AVGE	100S
Batting	663	82	28639	256	49·29	83

Bowling 18 wkts at 55·11 Ct (incl. w/k) 315; st 7

Test Record (79)

	INNS	NO	RUNS	HS	AVGE	100S
Batting	137	6	6227	256	47·53	15

Bowling 0 wkt for 85 Ct 50

KARDAR, Abdul Hafeez (1925–)

Islamia Coll, Lahore, and Punjab Univ. Northern India 1943–44 to 1946–47 Oxford Univ 1947–1949. Warwickshire 1948–1950. Pakistan: in Pakistan 1954–55 (Captain), 1955–56 (Captain), 1956–57 (Captain); in England 1954 (Captain); in West Indies 1957–58 (Captain); in India 1952–53 (Captain). For India in England 1946.

A product of Punjab University, Kardar first played for Northern India during the Second World War and toured England with the Indian side in 1946, under the name of Abdul Hafeez. He remained in England to read philosophy at Oxford, playing 3 times in the University Match and once for the Gentlemen at Lord's. It is for his services to cricket in Pakistan, however, that he will be remembered. As captain in the first 23 Tests played by Pakistan, he quickly led his country to a position of respect in the cricket world. He was a competent left-hand batsman and slow left-arm bowler who achieved no startling performances in Test cricket, but he successfully steered Pakistan, then virtually an unknown team, through their initial tour of England in 1954.

After his playing days, as a powerful President of the Pakistan Board of Control, he was responsible for reorganizing domestic cricket in Pakistan to advance it from a purely inter-provincial structure. He represented Pakistan several times at ICC meetings at Lord's, and was a forceful protagonist of barring the bouncer in the first World Cup tournament in 1975.

IRVING ROSENWATER

CAREER FIGURES

	INNS	NO	RUNS	HS	AVGE	100S
Batting	262	33	6814	173	29·75	8

Bowling 344 wkts at 24·55 Ct 108

Test Record (26)

	INNS	NO	RUNS	HS	AVGE	100S
Batting	42	3	927	93	23·76	–

Bowling 21 wkts at 45·42 Ct 16

KENNEDY, Alexander Stuart (1891–1959)

Hampshire 1907–1936. England: in South Africa 1922–23.

Though only selected for one England tour, when he headed the Test averages in South Africa with 31 wickets for 19 each, Alec Kennedy was for many years one of the most dedicated and successful bowlers in county cricket. His pace was a subtly varied medium, his length a model of consistency, his stamina inexhaustible, and his greatest asset a mastery of the leg-cutter which would swing in late and then straighten back. His total bag of 2,874 wickets is the 7th highest recorded: 744 of them came in 4 successive seasons, 1920–1923; he took over a hundred wickets 15 times, did 3 hat-tricks, and in 1927 took all 10 for 37 in the Gentlemen's 1st innings at the Oval. A sound and resolute batsman, he achieved the double 5 times, outstandingly with 1,129 runs and 205 wickets in 1922, a feat shared with only 3 others in history. In 1921 he carried his bat right through the Hampshire innings v Notts for 152.

H. S. ALTHAM

CAREER FIGURES

	INNS	NO	RUNS	HS	AVGE	100S
Batting	1025	130	16586	163*	18·53	10

Bowling 2874 wkts at 21·24 Ct 527

Test Record (5)

	INNS	NO	RUNS	HS	AVGE	100S
Batting	8	2	93	41*	15·50	–

Bowling 31 wkts at 19·32 Ct 5

KENYON, Donald (1924–)

Audnam Senior Sch, and Brierley Hill Tech Sch. Worcestershire 1946–1967 (Captain 1959–1967). England: in England 1953, 1955: in India 1951–52. Selector 1965–1972.

Don Kenyon was born in Staffordshire and had a trial for Worcestershire in 1939, but owing to the Second World War the start of his career was delayed until 1946. He was given his county cap in 1947 and went on to score more runs and make more hundreds than any other Worcestershire cricketer. He was a fine craftsman with a shrewd cricket brain. His 8 Test appearances brought him only one good score, but for Worcestershire he played many very fine innings, including one of 259 against Yorkshire in 1956 and 122 against the 1953 Australians. There is no doubt about his permanent and honoured place in the history of his county. Elected captain in 1959, he led Worcestershire to 2nd place in the Championship in 1962. In 1963 they were runners-up in the Gillette Cup Competition and in 1964 Champion County for the 1st time in their history. It was a popular triumph, both for the county and their able captain.

E. D. R. EAGAR

CAREER FIGURES

	INNS	NO	RUNS	HS	AVGE	100S
Batting	1159	59	37002	259	33·63	74

Bowling 1 wkt for 187 Ct 327

Test Record (8)

	INNS	NO	RUNS	HS	AVGE	100S
Batting	15	0	192	87	12·80	–

Ct 5

KIPPAX, Alan Falconer (1897–1972)

New South Wales 1918–19 to 1935–36 (Captain 1926–27 to 1933–34). Australia: in Australia 1924–25, 1928–29, 1930–31, 1931–32, 1932–33; in England 1930, 1934.

There are a select few among Australian batsmen around whom a special aura seems to hang in the eyes of their countrymen, and among this small company Alan Kippax is generally accorded a place. In cold figures he is bettered by many, respectable though his Test record is. No doubt it would have been more impressive had Australia been more often pressed for runs when he went in. He spent countless hours with his pads on watching Bradman, Woodfull and Ponsford. What endeared him was the polish and freedom of his strokeplay, allied as it was to a charm of manner which was as evident from the ring as his elegant, classical style. He was even mentioned in the same breath as Victor Trumper.

Kippax was 31 when he established his place in the Australian XI against the MCC team of 1928–29. He came twice with success to England on the tours of 1930 and 1934 without quite matching his feats over 20 years with New South Wales which he 3 times led to the Sheffield Shield and for which he had a career average of 70. His most remarkable exploit was perhaps the last-wicket partnership of 307 for NSW against Victoria with Hal Hooker, afterwards a popular broadcaster. The latter stood firm, making 62, while Kippax took his total to 260 not out, the score rising from 113 for 9 to 420. This was and still is a world record for the 10th wicket.

Alan Kippax, the supreme stylist.

E. W. SWANTON

CAREER FIGURES

	INNS	NO	RUNS	HS	AVGE	100S
Batting	254	33	12747	315*	57·69	43

Bowling 21 wkts at 52·52 Ct 70

Test Record (22)

	INNS	NO	RUNS	HS	AVGE	100S
Batting	34	1	1192	146	36·12	2

Bowling 0 wkts for 19 Ct 13

KNIGHT, Donald John (1894–1960)

Malvern 1909–1913 (Captain 1912–1913). Oxford Univ 1914, 1919. Surrey 1911–1937. England: in England 1921.

Donald Knight will always be remembered by his contemporaries as, for all too few years, a young amateur batsman of high distinction. Chosen to open the innings for Malvern in the 1st match of his 1st summer term, he was 5 years in the XI, captained it in 1912 and 1913, made a hundred in each innings against the Old Malvernians in his last season, and averaged over those 5 years 47 for an aggregate of 2,860. First tried for Surrey 2nd XI when only 15 years old, he made 50 in a county game in the August before he left Malvern, and a few days after leaving played a splendid innings of 90 against Notts in the Bank Holiday match at the Oval. He had only 2 years at Oxford, 1914 and 1919, but his scores of 64 in his Freshman's year, the highest in the game, and 35 and 78 in the match of 1919 were decisive in carrying Oxford to victory. The rest of the latter season was one of continuous triumph: on his 1st appearance for the Gentlemen at Lord's he made 71 and 124 and, replacing Sandham as Hobbs' opening partner, topped the Surrey averages with 58, making 4 hundreds for them, 2 of them in the same match against Yorkshire.

For those 2 months the classic soundness, balance and certainty of his batting provided a highlight in postwar cricket. After a dreadful blow to his head when fielding at short-leg in 1920 he was never the same, and, though he played in the first 2 Tests in 1921, making the highest English score of 38 at Trent Bridge, he dropped out of the regular first-class game at the end of the season, but made occasional appearances in later years. A modest and lovable man, for whom nothing was too much trouble in the service of the young, generations of boys at Westminster, the staff of which he joined in 1920, owe him a great debt, not only for his devoted coaching in the game he loved, but in a wider field for the example of his personality.

H. S. ALTHAM

CAREER FIGURES

	INNS	NO	RUNS	HS	AVGE	100S
Batting	215	13	6231	156*	30·84	13

Bowling 1 for 25 Ct 74

Test Record (2)

	INNS	NO	RUNS	HS	AVGE	100S
Batting	4	0	54	38	13·50	–

Ct 1

KNOTT, Alan Philip Eric (1946–)

Northumberland Heath Secondary Sch. Kent 1964–1977, 1979– . Tasmania 1969–70. England: in England 1967–1977 consecutively; in Australia 1970–71, 1974–75, 1976–77; in West Indies 1967–68, 1973–74; in New Zealand 1970–71, 1974–75; in India 1972–73, 1976–77; in Pakistan 1968–69, 1972–73. WSC.

For the greater part of his career, Alan Knott has deserved to be recognized (but as a wicket-keeper seldom is) as one of the best all-rounders in Test cricket. Small, perky, alert as a cat, he is unmistakable from the farthest corner of a ground, whether crouching low beside the stumps, or poised wide-eyed in front of them, handle of the bat thrust forward, as alive to possibilities of misadventure as a boy playing French cricket on a bumpy lawn. His fanaticism for health and fitness, manifest on the field by endless little exercises during breaks of play, and off it by faddiness in what he eats, stems from fear of losing his agility – someone told him once his knee-joints had too little play in them. There is never any need to ask if Alan Knott has eaten: the pile of banana-skins and orange peel, flanked by a milky glass or two, tells all.

Alan Knott: 'Mr Punch'.

Spectators are occasionally irritated by his calisthenics, unselfconscious as they are. But there are no complaints from bowlers: standing up or back, diving right or left or forward, the sight of his muscly little frame flying through the air, ball in glove, has become universally familiar. Through amazingly quick reflexes, backed up by powerful gymnastic springs, he takes catches that seem impossible. His reflexes and anticipation also make him a perfect partner for Derek Underwood on drying pitches, where he never looks flurried or surprised no matter how erratic the bounce and turn might be.

His batting is highly personal, but through determination and ferocious concentration, frequently effective. At the crease, with his bony nose and chin pointing at the bowler, he looks more like 'Mr Punch' than ever – and with bat held well away from body in a very open stance, not much like a batsman.

The originality of his attacking strokes, especially the sweep (which he plays with equal skill from well outside the off-stump or from off his legs) tends to obscure his straightness in defence. His magnificent judgment of line, plus good footwork, experience and concentration, and ability to attack or defend according to the position of a match, have made him in his time the ideal No. 7 in an England side that was often short of runs.

JOHN THICKNESSE

KORTRIGHT, Charles Jesse (1871–1952)

Tonbridge 1887–1888. Essex 1889–1907 (Captain 1903).

Traditionally Kortright was the fastest bowler that ever lived. In fact it is impossible to compare the speed of bowlers of widely different generations. One can only say that Kortright was undoubtedly very fast and that few who played him ever thought anyone faster. But one who could take 7 for 73 against the Players at Lord's and bowl out Surrey (at one time his analysis read 6 for 4) and Yorkshire in their Championship years had more than mere pace. He was a fine bowler – tall, with a long springy run and a fearsome yorker; moreover he bowled at the stumps. Contemporary with Lockwood and Richardson, he never played for England, but in 1899, with Richardson past his best and Lockwood injured, he would almost certainly have done so had he not been incapacitated himself. He was a fine slip and a useful forcing batsman who made a couple of hundreds for Essex and kept his place in the side when his bowling had left him; in 1898 he nearly saved the Gentlemen at Lord's with a fighting innings of 46.

R. L. ARROWSMITH

Speed in repose: many reckoned C. J. Kortright of Essex the fastest bowler they ever saw.

CAREER FIGURES

	INNS	NO	RUNS	HS	AVGE	100S
Batting	271	21	4404	131	17·61	2

Bowling 489 wkts at 21·04 Ct 186

LACEY, Sir Francis Eden (1859–1946)

Sherborne 1876–78 (Captain 1878). Cambridge Univ 1882. Dorset 1878. Hampshire 1879–97 (Captain 1888–89); President 1927–28. Secretary of MCC 1898–1926; Trustee 1926–46. Knighted 1926.

A great Secretary of the MCC, Sir Francis Lacey was the first man knighted for services to cricket. He exercised far stricter control than his predecessors, inaugurated many important reforms and set the finances on a sound footing. He had been a fine forcing batsman and his 323 not out for Hampshire against Norfolk in 1887 was the highest innings ever played up to that time in a county match. It is still the highest in a minor-county match. He also kept goal for Cambridge at association football.

R. L. ARROWSMITH

LAKER, James Charles (1922–)

Salts HS, Saltaire. Surrey 1946–1959. Essex 1962–1964. England: in England 1948–58 consecutively; in Australia 1958–59; in South Africa 1956–57; in West Indies 1947–48, 1953–54.

A Yorkshire exile, who started with Surrey and finished with Essex, Jim Laker was perhaps the best off-spin bowler the game has seen. Tall and strong, with big hands and a high action, he was the perfect model for an aspiring slow-bowler. Capable of long, accurate spells on good wickets, he could flight the ball deceptively, yet given any assistance from the wicket he had the extra pace and spin to be almost unplayable.

Coming to the forefront in 1947 with 66 wickets for Surrey, his promise was rewarded with a tour to West Indies. He was the leading wicket-taker in the series, but against the strong Australian side of 1948 he came in for heavy punishment. This failure seemed to cost him dearly at the hands of the selectors,

Jim Laker, in his prime, bowling against Australia in 1956.

in spite of continuing success for Surrey. Apart from a tour to West Indies in 1953–54, he was not to find a regular place in the England side until 1956. In 1950, his best season, he took 166 wickets, which included the remarkable figures of 8 for 2 in the Test Trial at Bradford. By 1956 he was a mature, experienced campaigner, who was quick to take advantage of the rain-affected wickets, tailor-made for his skill. At the Oval for Surrey against the Australians he took 10 for 88. In the 1st innings of the Old Trafford Test a month later he went one better with 10 for 53 and in the 2nd innings he took 9 for 37, becoming the only bowler to take 19 wickets in a first-class match. He went on to take 46 wickets in the series, a new record. He took 4 hat-tricks and was a more than useful lower-order batsman with two first-class hundreds under his belt and a good close fielder.

By now, of course, he was universally recognized as the best spin bowler in the world. Both in South Africa (1956–57) and Australia (1958–59) he attracted great interest and attention and met with fair success, though he never again bowled with the same historically devastating effect of 1956 in England. Leaving Surrey in 1959, still with plenty of bowling in him, he became specially registered for Essex in 1962 and appeared for them on and off for 3 seasons. An outspoken autobiography (*Over to Me*) got him into trouble, both at the Oval and Lord's, but in time all that was forgotten and for some years now, with his own brand of television commentary, he has once again been a figure to be reckoned with.

COLIN COWDREY

CAREER FIGURES

	INNS	NO	RUNS	HS	AVGE	100S
Batting	548	108	7304	113	16·60	2

Bowling 1944 wkts at 18·40 Ct 269

Test Record (46)

	INNS	NO	RUNS	HS	AVGE	100S
Batting	63	15	676	63	14·08	–

Bowling 193 wkts at 21·24 Ct 12

LANGRIDGE, John George, MBE (1910–)

Newick Village Sch. Sussex 1928–55. First-class Umpire 1956– . Test Match Umpire 1960–1963.

A wonderfully consistent opening batsman and a great slip, Langridge made 1,000 runs in a season 17 times and 2,000 11 times. When he was 39 he only just missed his 1,000 runs in May. In his last season he held 69 catches. With a two-eyed stance, he was particularly strong on the leg and dealt well with the short ball, but did not always do justice to the strokes he possessed. But for the Second World War he would have gone to India with MCC in 1939–40. He is younger brother of the all-rounder and Sussex captain (1950–52), James Langridge. A much respected first-class umpire since 1956, John has the distinction, perhaps unique, of being involved in first-class cricket on the field of play for over 50 years consecutively.

R. L. ARROWSMITH

CAREER FIGURES

	INNS	NO	RUNS	HS	AVGE	100S
Batting	984	66	34380	250*	37·45	76

Bowling 44 wkts at 42·00 Ct 786

LARWOOD, Harold (1904–)

Nottinghamshire 1924–1938. England: in England 1926, 1928, 1929, 1930, 1931; in Australia 1928–29, 1932–33.

No contemporary cricketer believes that there was ever a faster bowler than Harold Larwood. Those who stood in the slips to him at Melbourne in January 1933 are convinced to this day that they saw the fastest spell ever delivered by man. R. W. V. Robins who, whilst receiving the gentle closing overs of an inevitable drawn game, remarked that 'Lol was flighting the ball very well this season', knew beyond doubt that the next ball, which brought his innings to an abrupt and explosive end, was the fastest single delivery of all time.

Larwood first appeared for Nottinghamshire in 1924 as a fair, blue-eyed youth of about medium-height and neat but not outstandingly robust build. It was natural that he should make an immediate impression for all the ingredients of the champion were already apparent. He ran about 18 yards, accelerating with controlled rhythmical strides, on the last of which his shoulders opened with a long swing of his fully extended arms. His right hand described a great arc starting from near the calf of his leg and, at full pressure, his knuckles would touch the pitch on his follow through. Co-ordination was perfect so that the whole concerted effort was applied to the moment of delivery. Here was the model action which not only generated abnormal pace but gave a measure of control and accuracy unsurpassed by any bowler of this type. During his 3rd season in first-class cricket he played for England against Australia at Lord's and the Oval with a good measure of success. With A. P. F. Chapman in Australia in 1928–29 he made a wonderful start in the series but, with physical and nervous strain, fell away in the later matches. His indifferent showing in the home series of 1930 can be wholly attributed to the feather-bed pitches upon which it was played. These, apart from rare and brief intervals when lubricated by a drop of rain, were especially stultifying to fast bowlers.

In 1932–33 Larwood found himself the central figure in the great 'Body-line' controversy. The consensus of opinion is that this method of bowling to a packed leg-side was not in the best interests of cricket but at least it served to demonstrate Larwood's greatness. Bowling at immense pace his short-pitched balls skidded disconcertingly on the rock-hard pitches, and he could at will produce the lightning straight half-volley or yorker to shatter the unsettled receiver. No other bowler could have equalled his effectiveness in the use of these somewhat ruthless tactics. Ironically this triumph destroyed its hero, for as the result of constant pounding he received an injury to his left foot from which he never recovered. For a few succeeding seasons he played as a fast-medium bowler from a short run but was the merest shadow of his true self. Larwood is, as he was in his days of fame and glory, a quiet, unassuming man, whose interests centre more on his family life than the game of cricket and its attendant publicity. It is a happy ending to an occasionally painful and bitter story that Larwood settled happily in Australia with his five daughters.

IAN PEEBLES

CAREER FIGURES

	INNS	NO	RUNS	HS	AVGE	100S
Batting	438	72	7290	102*	17·19	3

Bowling 1427 wkts at 17·51 Ct 236

Test Record (21)

	INNS	NO	RUNS	HS	AVGE	100S
Batting	28	3	485	98	19·40	–

Bowling 78 wkts at 28·35 Ct 15

LAWRY, William Morris (1937–)

Preston Tech Inst, Melbourne. Victoria 1955–56 to 1970–71 (Captain 1961–62 to 1970–71). Australia: in Australia 1962–63, 1963–64, 1964–65, 1965–66, 1967–68, 1968–69 (Captain), 1970–71 (Captain); in England 1961, 1964, 1968 (Captain); in South Africa 1966–67, 1969–70 (Captain); in West Indies 1964–65; in India 1964–65, 1969–70 (Captain); in Pakistan 1964–65.

'Bill' Lawry came to England in 1961 as a comparatively unknown opening batsman and scored 2,019 runs on the tour. He was an automatic selection for Australia for 10 years, the mainstay of their batting. He was a tall and slender left-handed batsman, using a short back-lift and showing infinite patience and exceptional powers of concentration. He was a fast outfielder with a good arm. Predominantly on-side at first, he came to develop a wider range of strokes, though tending to be tied down by good slow

Bill Lawry: a real battler.

bowling. In 1961 he scored match-winning hundreds at Lord's and Old Trafford and 3 fine Test hundreds against South Africa in Australia in 1963–64. Taking over the Victorian captaincy from C. C. McDonald in 1962, he led his State to victory in the Sheffield Shield in 1962–63. He captained the Australian team to England in 1968, a level series of 1 Test match each, retaining the Ashes and himself topping the Test averages with 270 runs and 135 in the final Test at the Oval. He led Australia through Ceylon and India in 1970 and straight on to a gruelling 4-Test Series in South Africa, losing all 4 by depressingly wide margins.

After captaining a losing series against England in 1970–71, and going through a disappointing spell with the bat, he was replaced in the last match at Sydney by Ian Chappell. The performance of his life must remain the 6 hours 10 minutes he spent at the crease against England at Lord's in 1961, scoring 130 out of 238 against the hostile fast bowling of Statham and Trueman on a fiery wicket. By way of relaxation he was a pigeon-fancier.

COLIN COWDREY

CAREER FIGURES

	INNS	NO	RUNS	HS	AVGE	100S
Batting	417	49	18734	266	50·90	50

Bowling 5 wkts at 37·60 Ct 121

Test Record (67)

	INNS	NO	RUNS	HS	AVGE	100S
Batting	123	12	5234	210	47·15	13

Bowling 0 wkts for 6 Ct 30

LEVESON GOWER, Sir Henry Dudley Gresham (1873–1954)

Winchester 1890–1892 (Captain 1892). Oxford Univ 1893–1896 (Captain 1896). Surrey 1895–1920 (Captain 1908–1910). England: in South Africa 1909–10 (Captain). President Surrey 1929–1939. Selector 1909, 1924 (Chairman), 1928–30 (Chairman). Knighted 1953.

Henry, or, as he was invariably called, 'Shrimp' Leveson Gower was for nearly 60 years a considerable personality in English cricket. Short and of slight physique, but with a fine eye and supple wrists, he was a particularly good cutter, but his greatest asset was his invariably cheerful and resolute temperament which revelled in a crisis. Along with this went a sense of humour and a natural friendliness which helped all those who played under him to enjoy the game and get the best out of themselves.

He was 3 years in the Winchester XI, captaining it in his last, 1892, when in a famous victory over Eton he made 16 and 83, and took 8 for 43 – he bowled slow-medium and could make the ball 'drift'. Four years in the Oxford XI (1893–96), he led his side to a great win in the last year when, set to make 330 in the 4th innings, they won by 5 wickets. He captained Surrey in 1908–10 when the county finished 3rd, 5th and 2nd in the Championship, and became its President in 1929; he twice went with an MCC side to South Africa, captaining the team in 1909–10. Four times chairman of the Board of Control Selection Committee, he played a major part for half-a-century in running the Scarborough Cricket Festival, and in 1953 was knighted for his services to the game.

H. S. ALTHAM

CAREER FIGURES

	INNS	NO	RUNS	HS	AVGE	100S
Batting	400	78	7635	155	23·71	3

Bowling 46 wkts at 29·96 Ct 103

Test Record (3)

	INNS	NO	RUNS	HS	AVGE	100S
Batting	6	2	95	31	23·75	–

Ct 1

LEWIS, Anthony Robert (1938–)

Neath County GS. Glamorgan 1955–1974 (Captain 1967–1972). Cambridge Univ 1960–1962 (Captain 1962). England: in England 1973; in India 1972–73 (Captain); in Pakistan 1972–73 (Captain).

Tony Lewis was a batsman of grace and quality whose first-class career from 1955 to 1974 was often hampered by injury and whose method required truer pitches than were regularly forthcoming in that era. While still at Neath Grammar School he played for Glamorgan and, after National Service, was 3 years in the Cambridge XI, captain in 1962. As a freshman in 1959 he was full-back at Twickenham. His best-remembered innings of those days is probably the elegant 95 in the 2nd innings of the 1960 University match. His rugby football career ended with a knee injury but he began a successful career in journalism and television by writing about the game. He acted briefly as assistant secretary of Glamorgan and became captain in 1967, holding the captaincy for 6 years during which Glamorgan, in 1969, won their 2nd County Championship.

During the 1960s Lewis played many fine innings, notably one of 223 against Kent at Gravesend in 1966. In that year he made 2,052 runs for Glamorgan but he was not consistent enough to be picked for a Test match at home, though he was the nominated 12th man for the Oval Test of 1966. He had clear qualifications as a touring captain and, having taken an MCC side to Asia in 1969–70, he led England on a major tour to India, Sri Lanka and Pakistan in 1972–73 with success as both player and captain. He played a big part in winning the First Test against India, making 70 not out in the last innings, and he scored 125 in the Fourth Test in Kanpur. After the 8 Tests of that tour he played only once more for England, against New Zealand at Trent Bridge in 1973, and he retired after the 1974 season, having scored 20,495 runs in first-class cricket and averaged 32·42.

MICHAEL MELFORD

CAREER FIGURES

	INNS	NO	RUNS	HS	AVGE	100S
Batting	708	76	20495	223	32·42	30

Bowling 6 wkts at 72·00 Ct 193

Test Record (9)

	INNS	NO	RUNS	HS	AVGE	100S
Batting	16	2	457	125	32·64	1

LEYLAND, Maurice (1900–67)

Yorkshire 1920–1947. England: in England 1928, 1929, 1930, 1933, 1934, 1935, 1936, 1938; in Australia 1928–29, 1932–33, 1936–37; in South Africa 1930–31; in West Indies 1934–35.

There have been many cricketers who have exemplified the fighting spirit of their native Yorkshire, but none more happily than the left-handed Maurice Leyland. He loved a battle and he waged it invincibly, always with

Maurice Leyland, steady of eye, firm of purpose in the course of making his 187 – the 6th, the last and the highest of his hundreds against Australia – the Oval 1938.

the utmost good humour. He made a hundred in his 1st Test match against Australia in 1928–29 and another 6 thereafter. He also made 2 against South Africa. A very powerful man, deep in the chest and broad in the beam, Leyland made no claims to elegance. He stood rather wide of the block, holding the bat well up the handle, and all his movements were weighty and decided. Strokes he had in plenty with a taste for hitting powerful skimming shots in front of the wicket. If no particular bowlers impressed him unduly there were many in their ranks who quailed at the recollection, or in anticipation, of that heavy flailing blade.

But even dispirited opponents could appreciate his never failing wit, occasionally at its happiest when he was himself hard pressed. Twenty minutes before the close of a stifling day at Melbourne he had completed a hard won hundred, but England still required over 300 runs for victory. When a newly arrived partner ran him clean off his feet and out of breath he protested. 'Take it easy lad,' he gasped. 'We can't get *all* these roons tonight.' His sallies, verbal or with the bat, were alike in being robust and to the point, but never unkind.

His services to his country and his county were prodigious. He scored 33,660 runs in all, including 80 hundreds, but the true worth of the many runs he made is hard to assess, for so many were made when desperately needed, a state of affairs which he relished with the confidence of a stout-hearted but unconceited man. He bowled left-hand 'chinamen', which, it can at least be said, were considerably better than they looked. Amongst several distinguished clients was Sir Donald Bradman, whom he described as being 'Tired out b Leyland'. In a career lasting from 1920 to 1948 he was an outstanding personality in his profession. Subsequently, as Yorkshire's coach, he was a constant source of encouragement and strength.

IAN PEEBLES

CAREER FIGURES

	INNS	NO	RUNS	HS	AVGE	100S
Batting	932	101	33660	263	40·50	80

Bowling 466 wkts at 29·29 Ct 245

Test Record (41)

	INNS	NO	RUNS	HS	AVGE	100S
Batting	65	5	2764	187	46·06	9

Bowling 6 wkts at 97·50 Ct 13

LILLEE, Dennis Keith (1949–)

Belmont HS, Perth. Western Australia 1969–70– . Australia: in Australia 1970–71, 1972–73, 1974–75, 1975–76, 1976–77, 1979–80; in England 1972, 1975; in West Indies 1972–73; in New Zealand 1976–77. WSC.

No player in recent years has epitomized as unmistakably as Dennis Lillee the all-round skill and the air of latent savagery inbred in world-class fast bowlers. Originally a tearaway, he acquired guile and variation. To his fearsome physical presence was added mastery of the bouncer, the yorker, balls that swerved or cut either way, and clever changes of pace. In addition to all these problems, batsmen often had to cope with verbal barrages. Truly there were few more testing experiences during the mid-1970s than facing Lillee in full flight – with new ball or old.

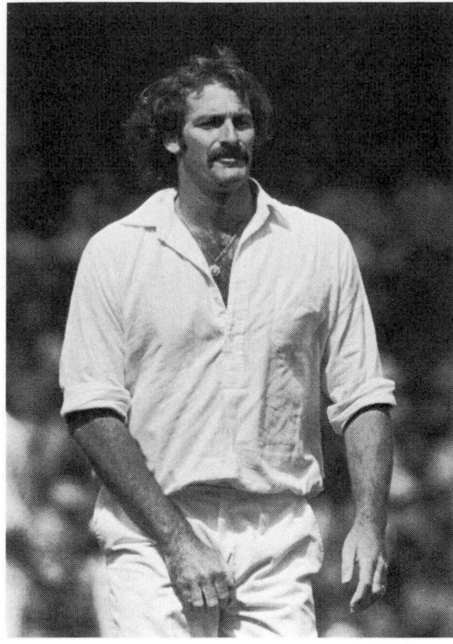

Dennis Lillee: a study in power and hostile intent.

Yet it seemed, soon after a spectacular showing against the Rest of the World (8 for 29 at Perth) and during the 1972 tour of England (a record 31 Test wickets), that his career would be short-lived, for stress fractures of the lower spine threatened to end his playing days at 23. The story of his iron-willed recovery is one of the most inspiring in the history of sport. He returned to torment England in the 1974–75 series, taking 25 wickets and, with his comrade-in-assault, Jeff Thomson, who took 33 wickets, striking fear into all hearts. In the 1975 series Lillee was easily the leading wicket-taker, helping to retain the Ashes with 21 wickets and showing the British public a previously unrevealed grace and maturity. His mended back held up to the strains of taking a further 27 Test wickets when West Indies were demolished in Australia, and a year later, in 1976–77, he was in magnificent form at home against Pakistan (21 wickets in 3 Tests), in New Zealand (11 wickets in the Auckland Test), and in the Centenary Test against England at Melbourne, a match which he effectively saved for his country by taking 6 for 26 in the 1st innings and 5 for 139 off 34·4 8-ball overs in the second.

Then, within weeks, came the news that he was among the first batch of players to join WSC (where he was to evoke similar frenzied crowd support from a new kind of audience).

DAVID FRITH

LILLEY, Arthur Frederick Augustus (1866–1929)

Warwickshire 1888–1911. England: in England 1896, 1899, 1902, 1905, 1907, 1909; in Australia 1901–02, 1903–04.

The greatest tribute to Lilley as a wicket-keeper is that for 13 years he was only once omitted when available from an England side, though his contemporaries included 7 or 8 other 'keepers of Test class. Some of these may have been more brilliant, but none was more reliable: Lilley's quiet method was a model. Moreover, he was a fine forcing bat, with an average of over 20 in Tests, and a man whose advice successive captains greatly valued.

R. L. ARROWSMITH

CAREER FIGURES

	INNS	NO	RUNS	HS	AVGE	100S
Batting	639	46	15597	171	26·30	16

Bowling 41 wkts at 36·22 W/k: ct 709; st 190 Total 899

Test Record (35)

	INNS	NO	RUNS	HS	AVGE	100S
Batting	52	8	903	84	20·52	–

Bowling 1 wkt for 23 W/k: ct 70; st 22 Total 92

LILLYWHITE, James, Jr (1842–1929)

Sussex 1862–1883. England: in Australia 1876–77 (Captain).

James Lillywhite, nephew of the *'non-pareil'*, and cousin of 3 famous brethren, goes down to history as England's 1st Test captain. With his left-handed, medium-paced bowling, he came into the Sussex side at 20, and did not miss a match for the county for 20 consecutive seasons. For some 15 years he was often chosen for the Players, and helped to beat the Gentlemen in his 1st match with 8 for 29. In 1868, he went with Willsher's team to America. As a left-handed batsman, he was less noted, but he scored hundreds against Hampshire and Middlesex in his early days. His bowling was more reliable, and he took all 10 wickets in an innings for South v North at Canterbury in 1872. He had his first experience of Australian conditions with W.G.'s team in 1873. His bowling provided a course of instruction for a country team in South Australia: 13 wickets for 7 runs in 84 balls. Three years later Lillywhite took his own side on a pioneering tour which is well described in Alfred Shaw's *Cricket Reminiscences*. The first 2 Tests in the long saga were enacted at Melbourne, and the way was clear for the sending of the first Australian team to England in 1878.

That tour was the extent of Lillywhite's achievement as a Test Match player, but, in a managerial capacity, he did more, helping Conway to arrange matches on the Australian visit to England in 1878, and accompanying four more teams to Australia, where he sometimes acted as umpire. He was once consulted about the action of the South Australian bowler, Whitridge, who had been no-balled by a Victorian umpire, and his verdict in the bowler's favour was unquestionably accepted. Not a great cricketer, but a notable initiator, organizer and wise counsellor, he served the game off the field as much as by his cunning in action.

G. D. MARTINEAU

LINDWALL, Raymond Russell, MBE (1921–)

Darlinghurst Marist Brothers Coll. New South Wales 1945–46 to 1953–54. Queensland 1954–55 to 1959–60 (Captain 1955–56 to 1959–60). Australia: in Australia 1946–47, 1947–48, 1950–51, 1951–52, 1954–55, 1958–59; in England 1948, 1953, 1956; in South Africa 1949–50; in West Indies 1954–55; in New Zealand 1945–46; in India 1956–57 (Captain); 1959–60; in Pakistan 1956–57, 1959–60.

Ray Lindwall was born in Mascot (Sydney) and started his career in the red-hot crucible of New South Wales cricket, finishing it in the more gentle climate of Queensland. He played in 61 Test Matches and took 228 wickets for 23·03 each. He also averaged over

Ray Lindwall: a perfect natural rhythm.

20 with the bat, scoring 2 Test hundreds. Most of his cricket was played at the highest level, on the best wickets against the finest opposition. He was never presented with easy problems to solve. England was probably the country which saw his skill in fullest flower. He relished the atmosphere here which gave the ball a chance to swing in the air. He tried his hand at League cricket and that forced him to develop the in-swinger. He found that he had to hit the wicket because slip catches were out of the question.

He was essentially a bowler's bowler. An incredibly smooth run-up followed by a beautiful action where only the arm was lower than perfection decreed. The acceleration to the crease and the twinkling feet lent the illusion of his being pulled in on wheels by a hidden wire. When Lindwall bowled the first ball in a Test Match anywhere in the world the tension round the ground was electric. Twelve times he took 5 wickets or more in an innings in a Test Match. In 1948 in an England starved of the sight of a really great fast bowler he was given a tumultuous reception. Nor did his ability end with the ball. He was a fine forcing batsman and a more than useful fielder. His technique was based on supreme control coupled with an artistic change of pace. He was sparing in his use of the bouncer but it was lethal when it came. Mainly an out-swinger, he seldom wasted a ball. Having seen him operating in a net with an experimental smaller ball, the organizers gave up the project. They realized that batting would become impossible against such movement in the air and off the wicket. Temperamentally less dynamic than Miller, he tended to seek less of the limelight. His skill was not extrovert but something for the connoisseur to savour. I suppose if one were granted one last wish in cricket it would be the sight of Ray Lindwall opening the bowling in a Test Match from the Nursery End at Lord's.

JOHN WARR

CAREER FIGURES

	INNS	NO	RUNS	HS	AVGE	100S
Batting	268	39	5017	134*	21·90	5

Bowling 794 wkts at 21·33 Ct 118

Test Record (61)

	INNS	NO	RUNS	HS	AVGE	100S
Batting	84	13	1502	118	21·15	2

Bowling 228 wkts at 23·03 Ct 26

LLOYD, Clive Hubert (1944–)

Chatham HS, Georgetown. Guyana 1963–64– . Lancashire 1968– . West Indies: in West Indies 1967–68, 1970–71, 1971–72, 1972–73, 1973–74, 1975–76 (Captain), 1976–77 (Captain), 1977–78 (Captain); in England 1969, 1973, 1976 (Captain); in Australia 1968–69, 1975–76 (Captain), 1979–80 (Captain); in New Zealand 1968–69; in India 1966–67, 1974–75 (Captain); in Pakistan 1974–75 (Captain); Rest of the World in England 1970. WSC.

'I've never seen a man look less like a cricketer,' said one experienced judge, when, in 1969 or thereabouts, the tall, bespectacled Guyanan slouched into his ken. That was before he had seen him play. But we had had warning that here was the next great West Indian batsman. Clive Lloyd, born in 1944, had first played for the West Indies in 1966, and made 82 and 78 not out on his debut against India. He followed this with hundreds on his 1st appearance against England, and then Australia. He bats left-handed, bowls right at medium pace, and fields ambidextrously. His fielding, especially in the covers, has been almost as outstanding as his batting.

I think it was John Woodcock, in an analogy often borrowed, who first compared Lloyd in the field with one of the great cats – the silent, shadowy lurking; then the sudden, overwhelming pounce. Constantine had fielded in the covers like this: 'I worked very hard for half-an-hour, and then just strolled around for the rest of the day, *because they wouldn't come*'. As for his batting, Lloyd is remembered mostly as a big-hitter. After he joined Lancashire in 1969, he soon became the idol of the one-day crowds, and not only on home grounds. Opponents felt that if they got him out cheaply they would win the match; and if they did not, at least they would have some fun.

But it would be a pity if he was remembered only as a hitter. I cannot think of any left-hander of recent years, save Sobers himself, with so wide and commanding a range of strokes. Because of his size, he could look clumsy when out of touch, and perhaps he was out of touch rather more often than a batsman of such exceptional quality should have been. He was often tempted to take risks and sometimes yielded to Oscar Wilde's view that the best way to get rid of temptation is to yield to it. After such indiscretions, he would return to the pavilion with shaking head, bowed shoulders, a picture of self-reproach, the old lion whose leap has unexpectedly missed the deer. But soon there would be another sinister slinking in the undergrowth. As captain of the West Indies, while he commanded great personal respect, a failure at times to install discipline in his team must be held against him.

ALAN GIBSON

Clive Lloyd in full cry.

Tony Lock: that lethal left arm.

LOCK, Graham Anthony Richard (1929–)

Limpsfield Sch. Surrey 1946–1963. Western Australia 1962–63 to 1970–71 (Captain 1963–64 to 1970–71). Leicestershire 1965–1967 (Captain 1966–1967). England: in England 1952, 1953, 1955, 1956, 1957, 1958, 1961, 1962, 1963; in Australia 1958–59; in South Africa 1956–57; in West Indies 1953–54, 1967–68; in New Zealand 1958–59; in India 1961–62; in Pakistan 1961–62.

Starting as a slow left-arm bowler with a generous flight, Tony Lock did not command a regular place in the Surrey side until 1949. On the slow turning wickets at the Oval during their great Championship-winning run, he altered his technique and bowled faster. In doing so he became the most dangerous attacking slow left-arm bowler in the world. He played a vital part in the Oval Test of 1953 when England recovered the Ashes, but was never quite so successful overseas. By 1956 he had taken 1,000 wickets at the age of 26. His best performance was 16 wickets for 83 against Kent in 1956, which included 10 for 54.

Although no-balled for throwing in England in 1952 and in both a Test and colony match in the West Indies in 1954, Lock went on bowling at the faster pace, and in much the same style until the end of the MCC Australasian tour of 1958–59. Then, it is said on the evidence of a film showing his bowling which he saw in New Zealand, he decided, on his own volition, to put an end to controversy by returning to his slower style. Very soon his experience brought him to the top again.

He was a much better batsman than his figures reveal, capable of producing every stroke, and the most obdurate defence when it was needed. He also held 830 catches, including 8 in a match against Warwickshire at the Oval in 1957. But figures alone cannot portray the facility with which he took catches at backward short-leg to the slow bowlers, or fast. Some of the catches off his own bowling had to be seen to be believed. Whether batting, bowling or fielding, he gave everything he had to his captain with a boyish enthusiasm. Surprisingly omitted from the MCC tour of Australia in 1962–63, he played for Western Australia that season. He returned to play for Surrey and England in 1963 before emigrating to Perth where first as player-coach then as captain of Western Australia, he began perhaps the most exciting period of his career.

He was appointed captain of Western Australia and Leicestershire, commuting at the end of each season, following the sun. He forged the beginnings of Leicestershire's triumphant run, led Western Australia to victory in the Sheffield Shield, and in the process became the most successful slow left-arm bowler ever to play in Australia.

COLIN COWDREY

CAREER FIGURES

	INNS	NO	RUNS	HS	AVGE	100S
Batting	812	161	10342	89	15·88	–

Bowling 2844 wkts at 19·23 Ct 830

Test Record (49)

	INNS	NO	RUNS	HS	AVGE	100S
Batting	63	9	742	89	13·74	–

Bowling 174 wkts at 25·58 Ct 59

LOCKWOOD, William Henry (1868–1932)

Nottinghamshire 1886. Surrey 1889–1904. England: in England 1893, 1899, 1902; in Australia 1894–95.

W. H. Lockwood was one of the most formidable fast bowlers of the 1900s, his name being for ever linked with Tom Richardson's of Surrey. He was a perfect foil to Richardson. Ranjitsinhji held the opinion that Lockwood was, for him, the more likely of the two bowlers to get him out. 'Tom was faster and as honest as the day with his break-back and always trying. But Lockwood could never be taken for granted. And he had a cleverly disguised slow ball.' Lockwood's bowling would seem sometimes to sulk. Batsmen would then be taken off their guard, as though reclining at ease on the sunny slopes of Vesuvius. Then Lockwood erupted. He bowled with a high, perfectly poised action from a run not too long. His right arm nearly brushed his right ear.

He played for Surrey from 1889 to 1904, and 7 times he took 100 wickets in a season. Twice, in 1899 and 1900, he performed the double. He scored a hundred for the Players v the Gentlemen at Lord's in 1902; and in the same game took nine wickets at less than 12 runs each. His figures present Lockwood not only as the great bowler of general fame but also as an all-round player of more than usual calibre. At Old Trafford in 1902, he achieved one of the most decisive fast-bowling onslaughts in all cricket's history. This was in the famous Test Match which England lost by 3 runs. On the 1st day Victor Trumper scored a hundred before lunch on a turf so soft that Lockwood could not bowl at all, because of slippery grass, until Australia's score had reached 129 for none. (Wickets were not covered then.) As soon as Lockwood could get a foothold he swept the Australian batsmen aside comprehensively – 6 for 48. Next innings he overwhelmed Trumper, Hill and Duff for 10 runs only – then Fred Tate dropped his fatal and immortal catch. Three times Lockwood performed the hat-trick in his career; and against Warwickshire at the Oval in 1894 he took four wickets in four balls. He was that sort of suddenly and violently destructive bowler.

Curiously, he failed completely during his one visit to Australia, with A. E. Stoddart's team in the terrifically hot season of 1894–95. He was a 'rough diamond' and a character. Years after his retirement to Nottingham the Notts County CC sent out scouts one Saturday afternoon to 'spot' talent. Two experts saw in the distance a bowler running to bowl beautifully. 'Let's see who he is,' they said, 'with that action he's bound to be good.' When the scouts got closer to the scene they discovered that the bowler was W. H. Lockwood, now aged 50, playing club cricket again, with pages of history behind him.

NEVILLE CARDUS

CAREER FIGURES

	INNS	NO	RUNS	HS	AVGE	100S
Batting	531	45	10673	165	21·96	15

Bowling 1376 wkts at 18·34 Ct 133

Test Record (12)

	INNS	NO	RUNS	HS	AVGE	100S
Batting	16	3	231	52*	17·76	–

Bowling 43 wkts at 20·55 Ct 4

George Lohmann: a match-winning cricketer, and supreme on his day.

LOHMANN, George Alfred (1865–1901)

Surrey 1884–1896. Western Province 1895–1897. England: in England 1886, 1888, 1890, 1896; in Australia 1886–87, 1887–88, 1891–92; in South Africa 1895–96.

Lohmann was one of the greatest match-winners in cricket history and so live a wire that he burnt himself out in less than ten years. 'W.G.' and Fry both regarded him as the finest medium-paced bowler they had played; and these two spanned together almost 60 years. He was a subtle master of flight and variation of pace; though he had a natural tendency to dip in the air, an occasional one would come farther up than the batsman expected. He could turn both ways and got many wickets with balls that came straight through. He was always experimenting, always attacking and yet his length never suffered. He was a forcing bat, a wonderful player for a crisis, and one of the most brilliant slips there has ever been. His health broke down in 1892, and he was never the same man again.

R. L. ARROWSMITH

CAREER FIGURES

	INNS	NO	RUNS	HS	AVGE	100S
Batting	427	39	7247	115	18·68	2

Bowling 1805 wkts at 13·91 Ct 334

Test Record (18)

	INNS	NO	RUNS	HS	AVGE	100S
Batting	26	2	213	62*	8·87	–

Bowling 112 wkts at 10·75 Ct 28

LOWRY, Thomas Coleman (1898–1976)

Christ's Coll, Christchurch, NZ. Auckland. Wellington. Hawkes's Bay. Cambridge Univ 1923–1924 (Captain 1924). Somerset 1921–1924. New Zealand: in New Zealand 1929–30 (Captain); in England 1931 (Captain). Manager 1937.

Tom Towry, born in Wellington, New Zealand, played for Cambridge in the University Matches of 1923 and 1924, being a victorious captain on the 2nd occasion. During his stay in England, Lowry played with some success for Somerset. It was said that he made his choice because of the name of his birth-place, and that a benevolent authority cast a blind eye on the fact that the Wellingtons concerned were several thousand miles apart.

On his return to New Zealand, Lowry was appointed to captain his country against the visiting MCC team in 1929–30. Although beaten in the First Test, New Zealand drew the remaining 3. In 1931 Lowry captained New Zealand in England. At Lord's his side gave the home side, under Jardine, a real fright but lost the only match to be decided, at the Oval. Lowry was an effective rather than an elegant cricketer. A large, powerful man he batted with a short back lift, but urged the ball in front of the wicket with massive thrusts and pushes. He kept wicket with unspectacular efficiency. He was a fine captain – shrewd, firm and courageous. Lowry's two sisters married A. P. F. Chapman and R. H. B. Bettington to form a truly impressive triumvirate-in-law. After retirement he managed the 1937 New Zealand side to England with a characteristically easy command, and in the course of nature attained the Presidency of the New Zealand Cricket Council.

IAN PEEBLES

CAREER FIGURES

	INNS	NO	RUNS	HS	AVGE	100S
Batting	322	20	9421	181	31·19	18

Bowling 49 wkts at 27·02 W/k: ct 188; st 49 Total 237

Test Record (7)

	INNS	NO	RUNS	HS	AVGE	100S
Batting	8	0	223	80	27·87	–

Bowling 0 wkts for 5 Ct 8

LYTTELTON, Rt Hon Alfred, KC (1857–1913)

Eton 1872–1875 (Captain 1875). Cambridge Univ 1876–1879 (Captain 1879). Middlesex 1877–1887. England: in England 1880, 1882, 1884. President MCC 1898.

Alfred Lyttelton was a glorious batsman, to whom was applied the phrase 'the champagne of cricket' and a great wicket-keeper. Like Blackham, but unlike his predecessors, he stood up without a long-stop. Yet curiously his best-remembered performance is his 4 for 19 in the 1884 Oval Test when he bowled lobs, with his pads on, after the recognized bowlers had failed. A great tennis player, a soccer international, a rackets and athletics blue, he could play any game, and later had a distinguished political career.

R. L. ARROWSMITH

CAREER FIGURES

	INNS	NO	RUNS	HS	AVGE	100S
Batting	171	12	4429	181	27·85	7

Bowling 4 wkts at 43·00 W/k: ct 135; st 71 Total 206

Test Record (4)

	INNS	NO	RUNS	HS	AVGE	100S
Batting	7	1	94	31	15·66	–

Bowling 4 wkts at 4·75 Ct 2

McCABE, Stanley Joseph (1910–1968)

St Joseph's Coll, Sydney. New South Wales 1928–29 to 1941–42 (Captain 1936–37 to 1941–42). Australia: in Australia 1930–31, 1931–32, 1932–33, 1936–37; in England 1930, 1934, 1938; in South Africa 1935–36.

In relation to the vast field of cricket records the truly historic individual innings, which lives in the imagination of those who saw or read of it, is comparatively infrequent. It fell to Stan McCabe to play 3 such innings in the short span of 6 years. At Sydney in 1932–33 he rallied a side nonplussed by the full fury of Larwood, with 187 not out. In South Africa, in 1935–36, he scored 189, again not out, and in 1938 at Trent Bridge he scored 232. A large proportion of each of the sallies against England was played with no more than the fragile and very final support of a vulnerable tail. At Nottingham Bradman exhorted his team not to miss a ball of this batting for, he said, never again would they see the like.

McCabe came to England for the first time in 1930, to average 35 in the Test Matches and top the bowling with 8 wickets at 27. From this start he developed into a superb attacking batsman, generally batting for Australia at No 4, immediately after Bradman. In his prime McCabe was of medium size, well-knit, strong and extremely agile. His stance was nicely balanced, and the bat came down from exactly over the middle stump. McCabe was a fine player of all types of bowling but excelled against pace. Perfect reflexes, and the fact that his weight was evenly distributed on either foot, enabled him, when faced by the greatest fast bowlers of his day, to drive the over-pitched ball without losing the ability to position himself for the hook when necessary, a talent confined to the highest class of batsman. A cheerful and convivial temperament was reflected in his play which, in all circumstances, had a daring and cavalier gaiety. In an era of heavy scoring he was indifferent to the records so frequently established and broken by more statistically-minded contemporaries. It took the challenge of adversity to stimulate his powers to the full. He was a respectable, if not overwhelming, bowler at fast-medium, producing, by way of surprise, an occasional googly of remarkable pace. This ball beset Hammond at the Oval in 1930, an event which did much to determine the result of the match and, with it, the series. He fielded magnificently in any position. In his later career McCabe suffered, somewhat ironically, from his feet, an affliction which shortened his span. Latterly he was a popular and successful dealer in sporting goods in Sydney.

IAN PEEBLES

Stan McCabe, hooking Doug Wright during his brilliant innings of 232 for Australia at Trent Bridge in 1938.

CAREER FIGURES

	INNS	NO	RUNS	HS	AVGE	100S
Batting	262	20	11951	240	49·39	29

Bowling 159 wkts at 33·73 Ct 137

Test Record (39)

	INNS	NO	RUNS	HS	AVGE	100S
Batting	62	5	2748	232	48·21	6

Bowling 36 wkts at 42·86 Ct 41

MACARTNEY, Charles George (1886–1958)

New South Wales 1905–06 to 1926–27. Australia 1907–08, 1910–11, 1911–12, 1920–21; in England 1909, 1912, 1921, 1926; in South Africa 1921–22.

Macartney was one of the most audacious and brilliant batsmen in the annals of Australian cricket. He was less courtly in his strokeplay than Trumper, whose most masterful innings had a certain effortless charm, almost persuading the attacking bowlers that they were enjoying themselves as he toyed with them. Macartney, perfect of technique, nonetheless used his bat with an unmistakable pugnacity. Sir Donald Bradman annihilated all bowlers as though he were merely performing the day's work, driving, cutting, hooking and pulling with a deadly efficiency which he was setting into motion impersonally, like a man in calm control of a wonderful machine. Macartney slaughtered bowling quite rapaciously. If he was obliged to bat through a maiden over he looked annoyed with himself at the end of it; and he would gnaw at his glove. He had the born cricketer's appearance, square-shouldered, not tall, in fact under medium height. His forearms were formidably strong, his chin was aggressive and his eyes perpetually alive.

C. G. Macartney, successor to Trumper, forerunner to Bradman.

When first he played for Australia in the season of 1907–08, his place in the batting order fluctuated from No. 1 to No. 8, and it was as an all-round player that he retained his place in the team. Even 2 years later, on his 1st visit to England in 1909, he scarcely hinted in Test Matches of his great batsmanship to come. But in the Headingley game of the same rubber he took 11 wickets for 85 with his slow-medium left-hand spinners. (He batted right-hand.) And at Edgbaston in the First Test Match of this rubber, he dismissed MacLaren, Fry and Hobbs for next to nothing – MacLaren b Macartney 5, Fry b Macartney 0, Hobbs lbw b Macartney 0. He scored 7 Test hundreds, 5 against England (3 in consecutive Tests in England in 1926), and 2 against South Africa. He could not take part in the Australian rubbers against England of 1911–12 and 1924–25. And in Australia, in 1920–21, also against England, ill-health intervened after the First Test of the rubber, until the Fifth, when he achieved a blinding 170 in 4 hours. His figures are proof of his rare skill. At Lord's in 1926 England declared on the 3rd and last afternoon of the Test against Australia. Woodfull at once was accounted for; Macartney, in 1st-wicket down, immediately received a really nasty ball from Maurice Tate, and crashed it to the off railings, a really bad-tempered stroke. Macartney scored a hundred and pulled Australia through to a draw. At close of play I asked him about the ball from Tate at his innings' beginning. 'As soon as I saw it,' said Macartney, 'I knew that either me or Maurice was for it. So it had to be Maurice.' At Trent Bridge in 1921 against Nottinghamshire, Macartney scored 345 in just under 4 hours. At Headingley in 1926 A. W. Carr won the toss and sent Australia to the wicket first. He missed Macartney off the 5th ball of Tate's 1st over. Then Macartney reached a hundred before lunch.

Nothing could daunt him. Before the start of a Lord's Test Match he came down to breakfast in a London hotel, looked through the window at the June sunshine and said 'Lovely day. Cripes I feel sorry for any poor cove who's got to bowl at me today'. He was swift-footed and, like every great batsman, saw the ball quickly and played with a split-second or so to spare. The Australian crowds rightly and unanimously called him 'The Governor-General'.

NEVILLE CARDUS

CAREER FIGURES

	INNS	NO	RUNS	HS	AVGE	100S
Batting	360	32	15020	345	45·79	49

Bowling 419 wkts at 20·91 Ct 100

Test Record (35)

	INNS	NO	RUNS	HS	AVGE	100S
Batting	55	4	2131	170	41·78	7

Bowling 45 wkts at 27·55 Ct 17

McDONALD, Colin Campbell (1928–)

Scotch Coll, Melbourne. Victoria 1947–48 to 1962–63 (Captain 1958–59 to 1962–63). Australia: in Australia 1951–52, 1952–53, 1954–55, 1958–59, 1960–61; in England 1956, 1961; in South Africa 1957–58; in West Indies 1954–55; in India 1956–57, 1959–60; in Pakistan 1956–57, 1959–60.

Using a short back-lift, very strong off the back foot and a good judge of the swinging ball, Colin McDonald was a fine opening batsman for Victoria and Australia. He scored 2 double-hundreds in Shield cricket for Victoria, whom he captained on the retirement of Ian Johnson in 1958. He enjoyed a triumphant series against South Africa in 1952–53, scoring 437 runs in the series, including a magnificent 154 in the Fourth Test Match at Adelaide. Nothing would go right for him in England in 1953, but he returned successfully in 1956 and 1961. His opening stand of 137 with J. W. Burke on the 1st day of the Lord's Test Match in 1956 set his side on the way to a comfortable victory. In the 1958–59 series against England, he became the leading Australian batsman with 519 runs at an average of 64, with 170 in the Fourth Test Match at Adelaide, his highest score in Test cricket. His last series was against the West Indies in Australia where he bore the brunt of Wesley Hall's speed with great courage. He scored 337 runs in the series with a valuable contribution of 91 in the vital Fifth Test Match which decided the rubber for Australia.

COLIN COWDREY

CAREER FIGURES

	INNS	NO	RUNS	HS	AVGE	100S
Batting	307	26	11375	229	40·48	24

Bowling 3 wkts at 64·00 Ct (including w/k) 53; st 2

Test Record (47)

	INNS	NO	RUNS	HS	AVGE	100S
Batting	83	4	3107	170	39·32	5

Bowling 0 wkts for 3 runs Ct 14

McDONALD, Edgar Arthur (1892–1937)

Charles Street Sch, Launceston. Tasmania 1909–10 to 1910–11. Victoria 1911–12 to 1921–22. Lancashire 1924–1931. Australia; in Australia 1920–21; in England 1921; in South Africa 1921–22.

Although one of the greatest fast-bowlers of all time 'Ted' McDonald's international career was confined to 8 matches for Australia against England and 3 against South Africa. That his span was so short was due to circumstance, for the quality of his bowling was not only superlative, but also remarkably lasting. McDonald, a Tasmanian by birth, appeared as early as 1911 for Victoria, but principally as a batsman. It was not until the series of 1920–21 that he was picked, for the last 3 matches, as partner to the all-conquering Gregory. He took only 6 expensive wickets, but his remarkable talent was clear to see, and underlined by the disproportionate number of times he beat the bat. This promise came to full fruition almost as soon as he bowled his first over on English pitches. McDonald made the perfect counterpart to the rumbustious Gregory. He was certainly one of the most graceful bowlers of modern times and, as an athletic performance, his action has not been excelled in any field. A tall, perfectly proportioned man, he ran a relaxed high-stepping run of 16 yards going into, and through, his delivery without pause or strain. His feet left little mark even on soft ground, so perfect was his balance and co-ordination. His smoothly generated pace was difficult to assess especially when contrasted with that of his leaping, thundering partner – but it was tremendous. So shrewd a judge as D. R. Jardine observed that all the fastest bowlers attained a common maximum speed, but that McDonald's fastest *ball* perceptibly exceeded it. In addition to his pace he had complete control and could move the ball either way. He had a taste for slowing to medium-pace off-breaks on soft wickets, but this was a side-line and unimpressive compared to the normal performance.

In 1922 McDonald went to the Nelson Club, thence qualified for Lancashire and so was lost to Australia. His greatest performances for his adopted county were when there was urgent need. This was typical of a curiously detached, and somewhat taciturn, nature. He had no interest in bowling out inferior batsmen for the sake of compiling records. When catches went astray, which they were inclined to do in abundance, he was never to say an impatient word, nor betray a flicker of expression on a face cast in Red Indian mould. Confronted by Hobbs and Gunn he would attack unceasingly, and when H. J. Enthoven faced him at Old Trafford, having made a hundred against him at Lord's, he was greeted with a burst which onlookers considered the fastest bowling they had ever seen in this country. When 38 he clean bowled Bradman for 9.

His end, in 1937, was strange and tragic. Having run off the road, after colliding with another car, he emerged unhurt and went to help the other motorist. As he was doing so a passing car knocked him down and killed him. So departed a remarkable and, in some ways, unique figure.

IAN PEEBLES

CAREER FIGURES

	INNS	NO	RUNS	HS	AVGE	100S
Batting	302	47	2663	100*	10·44	1

Bowling 1395 wkts at 20·76 Ct 98

Test Record (11)

	INNS	NO	RUNS	HS	AVGE	100S
Batting	12	5	116	36	16·57	–

Bowling 43 wkts at 33·27 Ct 3

McGLEW, Derrick John (1929–)

Maritzburg Coll, and Natal Univ. Natal 1947–48 to 1966–67 (Captain 1951–52 to 1966–67). South Africa: in South Africa 1953–54, 1956–57, 1957–58 (Captain), 1961–62 (Captain); in England 1951, 1955 (Captain), 1960 (Captain); in Australia 1952–53; in New Zealand 1952–53.

This diminutive figure was one of the most tenacious batsmen in the game, a brilliant fielder in the covers and a generally astute leader. He showed astonishing powers of concentration. Forcing strokeplay was a luxury he denied himself. He appeared to set his nose to the grindstone, as if dedicated to the task of batting for ever. Consequently, he has been concerned in many dour rearguard actions, none more so than against England at Trent Bridge in 1955 where he scored 68 in 5 hours in the 1st innings and 51 in 4 hours in the 2nd. In 1957–58 he recorded the 2nd slowest Test hundred ever made (545 minutes) against Australia at Durban. In 1952–53 he hit his highest score, 255 not out against New Zealand, a Test record for South Africa. During the 1957–58 season he scored 953 runs, at that time the highest aggregate by a South African batsman. He topped 1,000 runs on each of his 3 visits to England, scoring 1,871 runs in 1955.

COLIN COWDREY

CAREER FIGURES

	INNS	NO	RUNS	HS	AVGE	100S
Batting	299	34	12170	255*	45·92	27

Bowling 35 wkts at 27·40 Ct 76

Test Record (34)

	INNS	NO	RUNS	HS	AVGE	100S
Batting	64	6	2440	255*	42·06	7

Bowling 0 wkts for 23 Ct 18

Jackie McGlew: great powers of concentration.

MacGREGOR, Gregor (1869–1919)

Uppingham 1886–1887. Cambridge Univ 1888–1891 (Captain 1891). Middlesex 1892–1907 (Captain 1899–1907). England: in England 1890, 1893; in Australia 1891–92.

To a generation accustomed to seeing wicket-keepers consistently standing back even to medium-paced bowling, the spectacle of G. MacGregor in his light-blue cap invariably standing up to the formidable pace of S. M. J. Woods in their 4 years' association for Cambridge would today surely excite wonder to the point of incredulity. Cool determination and unostentatious dexterity combined to make him an outstanding wicket-keeper; a batsman always liable to produce runs at a crisis, quiet authority was the keynote of his successful captaincy of Cambridge and subsequently of Middlesex whom, succeeding A. J. Webbe in 1899, he led to the Championship in 1903. He kept wicket for England in 4 Tests at home and in Australia with Lord Sheffield's team in 1891–92. As a three-quarter and full-back in rugby football he won at least equal distinction, playing 2 years for Cambridge and winning 13 international caps for Scotland.

H. S. ALTHAM

CAREER FIGURES

	INNS	NO	RUNS	HS	AVGE	100S
Batting	412	58	6381	141	18·02	3

W/k: ct 410; st 150 Total 560

Test Record (8)

	INNS	NO	RUNS	HS	AVGE	100S
Batting	11	3	96	31	12·00	–

W/k: ct 14; st 3 Total 17

McKENZIE, Graham Douglas (1941–)

John Curtain HS, Fremantle. Western Australia 1959–60 to 1973–74. Leicestershire 1969–1975. Australia: in Australia 1962–63, 1963–64, 1964–65, 1965–66, 1967–68, 1968–69 1970–71; in England 1961, 1964, 1968; in South Africa 1966–67, 1969–70; in West Indies 1964–65; in India 1964–65, 1969–70; in Pakistan 1964–65. Rest of the World in England 1970.

Graham McKenzie, with a superb physique, shared the Australian opening attack against England with Alan Davidson in 1961 and 1962–63, and himself became the spearhead in 1964. Each season saw an improvement in his batting until he was considered a genuine all-rounder. In the Australian victory at Lord's in 1961, he took 5 wickets in each innings, but made an even greater contribution with the bat, since he was at the crease whilst the last 2 Australian wickets put on 149 runs – a margin which sealed the match for Australia. In the Old Trafford Test Match, Davidson and McKenzie put on 98 for the last wicket. In the Third Test Match against South Africa in 1963–64 he contributed 76. He was a fine away-swinger when the conditions were right, at his best on good wickets using his full height and immense strength to combine fast-bowling with a deceptive change of pace. He had the knack of unsettling the greatest players, even when they were well set. Despite losing his impact at Test level, he enjoyed 7 successful years leading the Leicestershire attack.

COLIN COWDREY

CAREER FIGURES

	INNS	NO	RUNS	HS	AVGE	100S
Batting	471	108	5662	76	15·59	–

Bowling 1218 wkts at 26·98 Ct 200

Test Record (60)

	INNS	NO	RUNS	HS	AVGE	100S
Batting	89	12	945	76	12·27	–

Bowling 246 wkts at 29·78 Ct 34

MacLAREN, Archibald Campbell (1871–1944)

Harrow 1887–1890 (Captain 1890). Lancashire 1890–1914 (Captain 1894–1896, 1899–1907). England: in England 1896, 1899 (Captain), 1902 (Captain), 1905, 1909 (Captain); in Australia 1894–95, 1897–98 (Captain), 1901–02 (Captain).

By virtue alike of his batsmanship and personality A. C. ('Archie') MacLaren was one of the outstanding cricket figures of his generation. Gaining his colours at Harrow when only 15, he scored 55 and 67 in the great match against Eton, and 3 years later, as captain, made 76 against them out of a total of 133 by batting of a mature command hardly to be associated with school cricket. In the August of that year he was asked to play for his native Lancashire, and in his 1st innings for them against Sussex at Hove he made 108. In 1894 he became county captain and celebrated the following year by making 424 against Somerset at Taunton, thereby annexing from 'W.G.' a record (344) that had stood for 19 years, and which was to remain until W. H. Ponsford beat it nearly 30 years later. That winter he went with Stoddart's team on the 1st of his 3 tours to Australia: in these he made 2,696 runs, with an average of over 50, and 12 hundreds, 7 of them at Sydney, by batting so masterly that he was hailed as perhaps the greatest batsman yet seen there.

When W.G. retired from international cricket after the First Test against Australia in 1899, MacLaren, though he had not yet that year played in a first-class match, was nominated to succeed him as captain, and when at Lord's England followed on hopelessly in arrears, he carried his bat, on a crumbling pitch, for 88 of the best runs that perhaps he ever made. In 1905, under Jackson's captaincy, he made 140 against Australia at Trent Bridge. Perhaps nothing in his cricket became him more than the leaving of it. In his 50th year, 1921, he raised and captained an amateur side that in August at Eastbourne defeated by 28 runs Warwick Armstrong's hitherto invincible team. When in the winter of 1922 he took a team of his own to Australia, he could still make 50 on his favourite Sydney ground, and with 200 not out and 5 slip catches in a match in New Zealand could cut down to scale men half his age. With a handsome face and figure, a high back-lift, a command of strokes all round the wicket, and a general air of proconsular authority, MacLaren at the crease was an outstanding reflection of what has been called 'the golden age of batting'. As a captain no one would question his stature or tactical acumen, but he was no consultant and rather lacked the gift of making others believe in, and so make the best of, themselves.

H. S. ALTHAM

CAREER FIGURES

	INNS	NO	RUNS	HS	AVGE	100S
Batting	699	52	22022	424	34·03	47

Bowling 1 wkt for 274 Ct 445

Test Record (35)

	INNS	NO	RUNS	HS	AVGE	100S
Batting	61	4	1931	140	33·87	5

Ct 29

McLEAN, Roy Alastair (1930–)

Hilton Coll, Natal. Natal 1949–50 to 1964–65. South Africa: in South Africa 1953–54, 1956–57, 1957–58, 1961–62, 1964–65; in England 1951, 1955, 1960; in Australia 1952–53; in New Zealand 1952–53.

Like Norman O'Neill of Australia, Roy McLean was a superb stroke-maker, a cutter and hooker of tremendous power. He toured England 3 times, scoring 1,448 runs in 1955 and 1,516 in 1960. He collected his 1st Test hundred against New Zealand in 1953–54, and the Second Test Match at Lord's in 1955 saw his 1st against England. On a lively wicket against Statham and Trueman at their best he scored 142 in 3½ hours. Chasing hard for victory in the Third Test Match at Old Trafford, McLean took charge, scoring 50 out of 72 in 50 minutes, and South Africa won with a few minutes to spare. He had 2 more hundreds against England – his 109 in the Fourth Test at Old Trafford, 1960, being completed in 2¼ hours – and also made his highest score in England, 207 against Worcestershire in under 4 hours. Whenever he was at the crease, the cricket was never dull. He was also a beautiful and versatile fielder.

COLIN COWDREY

CAREER FIGURES

	INNS	NO	RUNS	HS	AVGE	100S
Batting	318	20	10969	207	36·80	22

Bowling 2 wkts at 52·00 Ct 147

Test Record (40)

	INNS	NO	RUNS	HS	AVGE	100S
Batting	73	3	2120	142	30·28	5

Bowling 0 wkts for 1 run Ct 23

MAHMOOD, Fazal (1927–)

Islamia Coll, Lahore. Northern India. Pakistan: in Pakistan 1954–55, 1955–56, 1956–57, 1958–59 (Captain), 1959–60 (Captain), 1961–62; in England 1954, 1962; in West Indies 1957–58; in India 1952–53, 1960–61 (Captain).

Fazal Mahmood began his first-class career in the Ranji Trophy Tournament when he was 17. In 1946 he narrowly missed selection for the Indian team to tour England. After partition, his fine bowling in 1951 helped Pakistan to beat MCC at Karachi and did much to earn his country Test Match status. He played in 34 Test Matches, 10 of them as captain. He had magnificent stamina, being able to bowl for hours on end to a nagging persistent length at just above medium pace with a regular movement from leg. His bowling at the Oval in 1954 was mainly instrumental in Pakistan's surprise victory over England; and there were times on matting pitches in Pakistan when he was virtually unplayable.

E. D. R. EAGAR

CAREER FIGURES

	INNS	NO	RUNS	HS	AVGE	100S
Batting	143	32	2593	100*	23·36	1

Bowling 459 wkts at 18·93

Test Record (34)

	INNS	NO	RUNS	HS	AVGE	100S
Batting	50	6	620	60	14·09	–

Bowling 139 wkts at 24·70 Ct 11

Arthur Mailey: artist, author, bowler, wit.

MAILEY, Arthur Alfred (1886–1967)

New South Wales 1912–13 to 1929–30. Australia: in Australia 1920–21, 1924–25; in England 1921, 1926; in South Africa 1921–22.

Arthur Mailey was one of the great leg-spin and googly bowlers, a member of the triumphant Australian teams of the 1920s. He won distinction also as a cartoonist and writer, who contributed for nearly 40 years to newspapers in his own and other Test-playing countries. He is the author of an autobiography, *Ten For 66 and All That*, which is expressive of a highly individual whimsicality that was never absent either from his own play or from his journalism. As a 'character', and as a bowler with exceptional power of spin, Mailey has a place in cricket all his own. When Mailey wrapped his abnormally strong fingers round a cricket ball he had one predominant object in mind – to spin it nigh to bursting point. Cartoonist and artist by profession, philosopher and wit by temperament, it is impossible to imagine him practising the straightforward sobrieties of seam, or off-spin. To bamboozle the would-be striker with great leaping twist was his heart's delight but, if the occasional but inevitable inaccuracy resulted in his being hit for 6, his pleasure was undiminished. His philosophy he expounded when rebuked by an Australia manager for revealing his secrets to the writer. 'Bowling is an art,' he retorted, 'And as such international.'

The enormous spin was the product of an ideal leg-break bowler's action. Mailey ran a few springy paces at an angle to the wicket, curled his wrist up in the region of his hip-pocket, and flipped the ball out with nicely co-ordinated movement of arm, wrist and fingers. He was a dangerous bowler in the air as well as off the pitch, for the fast-revolving ball dropped steeply at the end of its flight. The batsman who made any misjudgment of length was in poor case to combat the sharp break in either direction. Mailey played 21 times for Australia and took 99 wickets. That they cost 33 runs apiece is neither here nor there. In 1920–21 he took 36 wickets in the series, an Australian record. In latter times he turned his attention to landscape painting.

IAN PEEBLES

CAREER FIGURES

	INNS	NO	RUNS	HS	AVGE	100S
Batting	182	62	1556	66	12·97	–

Bowling 779 wkts at 24·10 Ct 153

Test Record (21)

	INNS	NO	RUNS	HS	AVGE	100S
Batting	29	9	222	46*	11·10	–

Bowling 99 wkts at 33·91 Ct 14

MAJID Jahangir Khan (1946–)

St Anthony's Sch, Lahore, Aitchison Coll, Lahore, and Punjab Univ. Lahore PIA. Glamorgan 1968–1976 (Captain 1973–1976). Cambridge Univ 1970–1972 (Captain 1971–1972). Queensland 1973–74. Pakistan: in Pakistan 1964–65, 1968–69, 1972–73 (Captain), 1974–75, 1976–77; in England 1967, 1971, 1974; in Australia 1972–73, 1976–77; in West Indies 1976–77; in New Zealand 1972–73. WSC

Majid Khan, son of Jahangir Khan the former Cambridge and India fast-medium bowler, demonstrated exceptional talents at an early age. His progress as a batsman and fast bowler, though not, he will confess, as an academic, at Aitchison College in Lahore and then at Punjab University, was astonishing, even allowing for the Pakistani habit of producing young prodigies.

He made his first-class debut while still at school, in 1961–62, and scored 111 not out as well as taking 6 for 67 against Khairpur Division. He was 18 years and 26 days old when he played his 1st Test against Australia in Karachi, which made him the 9th youngest Test cricketer in history. His early impact was as a hostile bowler, but his action was considered illegal by some, especially when he bowled his frequent bouncers. He was content to turn to off-spin, concentrating on his batting technique which is as sound as his stroke-making is lavish and superb to watch. He also became an excellent slip-fielder.

On tour with Pakistan in 1967, he scored 147 in 89 minutes against Glamorgan at Swansea which immediately recommended him to that county. He became a Glamorgan player in 1968: whereupon Glamorgan rose from 14th place to 3rd and, in 1969, won the County Championship. It was in the match against Worcestershire at Cardiff which brought the Championship back to Wales after an interval of 21 years that Majid played what he, and all who witnessed it, consider to be his finest innings. On a broken wicket, on which the ball turned sharply and lifted, he danced down the pitch time and again and stroked a brilliant 156, the innings which, without question, won the match.

Majid was made captain of Glamorgan in 1973. He resigned the leadership and left the club in 1976. In 1973 he also led Pakistan in 3 Tests against the touring MCC. By that time he had established himself as one of the world's leading batsmen. His career was limited between 1970 and 1972 while he was an undergraduate at Cambridge University though he left many memories at Fenner's of his superb batting and thoughtful captaincy. In 1977, World Series Cricket in Australia lost no time in signing him for their Rest of the World squad, but he declared himself disillusioned by the artificial nature of the competition as well as by the abundance of fast bowling.

TONY LEWIS

MANJREKAR, Vijay Laxman (1931–)

King George Sch, Bombay. Bombay. Bengal. Andra. Uttar Pradesh. India: in India 1951–52, 1952–53, 1955–56, 1956–57, 1958–59, 1960–61, 1961–62, 1963–64, 1964–65; in England 1952, 1959; in West Indies 1952–53, 1961–62; in Pakistan 1954–55.

A correct and accomplished right-hander, Manjrekar made his debut in first-class cricket as a schoolboy, having scored prolifically in the All-India Schools' Tournament. A fine strokeplayer, especially sound against fast bowling, he came to the fore with a fine 133 in his 1st Test innings in England in 1952, and exceeded 1,000 runs on the tour. That innings of 133 (at Headingley) marked his maiden hundred in the first-class game. In 1959 he was dogged by injury and ill-health, though he hit a faultless 204 not out at Oxford. A professional, he was also able to keep wicket and was an occasional off-break bowler. He played for Castleton Moor in the Central Lancashire League (1956–1958), scoring 1,456 runs in his first year at the phenomenal average of 161·77.

IRVING ROSENWATER

CAREER FIGURES

	INNS	NO	RUNS	HS	AVGE	100S
Batting	295	38	12832	283	49·92	36

Bowling 20 wkts at 31·80

Test Record (55)

	INNS	NO	RUNS	HS	AVGE	100S
Batting	92	10	3208	189*	39·12	7

Bowling 1 wkt for 44 Ct (incl. w/k) 19; st 2

MANKAD, Mulvantrai Himmatlal (1917–1978)

Nawanagar HS. Western India. Nawanagar. Maharashtra. Gujerat (Captain). Bengal. Bombay. Rajasthan (Captain). India: in India 1948–49, 1951–52, 1952–53, 1955–56, 1956–57, 1958–59 (Captain); in England 1946, 1952; in Australia 1947–48; in West Indies 1952–53; in Pakistan 1954–55 (Captain).

The finest all-round cricketer India has produced, 'Vinoo' Mankad was a batsman who could open the innings or bat elsewhere as the situation decreed and a slow left-arm bowler who perplexed many a Test batsman in the years after the Second World War. Coached by A. F. Wensley, he made a great impression when Lord Tennyson's team toured India in 1937–38, but the war prevented his Test debut until 1946. That year he became the only Indian ever to perform the double on a tour of England. On his only visit to Australia he scored centuries in both the Melbourne Tests and in all games on the tour took more than twice as many wickets as any other Indian. He completed the Test double of 1,000 runs and 100 wickets in only 23 games. In the Lord's Test of 1952, with no previous first-class match practice that season, he scored 72 and 184 against England and bowled 97 overs for 5 wickets, but even so could not save his side from defeat. He took part in the record opening partnership in Test cricket, of 413 with P. Roy against New Zealand in 1955–56, when he himself scored 231 – the highest-ever for India. He also held 33 catches in Tests – another record for India at the time that he retired. His son, Ashok, also played Test Cricket for India.

IRVING ROSENWATER

CAREER FIGURES

	INNS	NO	RUNS	HS	AVGE	100S
Batting	359	26	11554	231	34·69	26

Bowling 781 wkts at 24·53 Ct 190

Test Record (44)

	INNS	NO	RUNS	HS	AVGE	100S
Batting	72	5	2109	231	31·47	5

Bowling 162 wkts at 32·32 Ct 33

MANN, Francis George, DSO, MC (1917–)

Eton 1934–1936 (Captain 1936). Cambridge Univ 1938–1939. Middlesex 1937–1954 (Captain 1948–1949). England: in England 1949 (Captain); in South Africa 1948–49 (Captain). Chairman TCCB 1978– .

George Mann, elder son of F.T. and brother of J.P., followed his father in the captaincy of Middlesex and England. In both capacities he showed a rare power of leadership which was reflected in happy and successful sides. In 1948–49 his MCC team beat South Africa in that country by the only 2 Tests decided; the following summer Middlesex under him shared the Championship with Yorkshire. A free bat by nature, and in particular a strong driver – when making 49 in less than 30 minutes against New Zealand at Headingley he hit a vast straight 6 which all but carried the football stand before bouncing on to the field behind – he usually showed up best in a crisis. His 136 not out for England at Port Elizabeth was made when the tide was running strongly South Africa's way. In 1950 he was favourite to take MCC to Australia when the claims of business won the day. After that he played little more first-class cricket. After long service on the Committee of MCC and latterly as Chairman of Middlesex he was elected in 1978 to the chairmanship of the TCCB. With the cricket world in a turmoil those who knew him best were thankful that he was at hand to fill a post of such importance and responsibility.

E. W. SWANTON

CAREER FIGURES

	INNS	NO	RUNS	HS	AVGE	100S
Batting	262	17	6350	136*	25·92	7

Bowling 3 wkts at 129·67 Ct 72

Test Record (7)

	INNS	NO	RUNS	HS	AVGE	100S
Batting	12	2	376	136*	37·60	1

Ct 3

MANN, Francis Thomas (1888–1964)

Malvern 1904–1907 (Captain 1907). Cambridge 1909–1911. Middlesex 1909–1931 (Captain 1921–1928); President 1947–1949. England: in South Africa 1922–23 (Captain). Selector 1930.

Mann was a born leader, an immensely popular captain both of Middlesex and of England, and one of the biggest hitters of this century. Further, he was a highly capable batsman, ready always to adapt himself to the needs of the moment. The worse the situation the better he played. He did not always score fast: his highest innings, 194 v Warwickshire in 1926, took 5 hours. But when he did open his shoulders the results were so startling that little else is remembered, and his powers of defence are now forgotten. He once hit Macaulay into the wind at Lord's: the ball finished against the wall on the farther side of the practice ground. In 1924 he lifted 2 consecutive balls from Rhodes on to the roof of the Lord's pavilion, one striking the parapet at the back full-pitch. Against Notts in 1921 he received 20 balls and scored 53 in 19 minutes. A great outfield before the First War, after it he was an exceptionally safe mid-off. His son, F. G. Mann, also captained Middlesex and England.

R. L. ARROWSMITH

CAREER FIGURES

	INNS	NO	RUNS	HS	AVGE	100S
Batting	612	47	13237	194	23·43	9

Bowling 3 wkts at 83·00 Ct 176

Test Record (5)

	INNS	NO	RUNS	HS	AVGE	100S
Batting	9	1	281	84	35·12	–

Ct 4

MARSH, Rodney William (1947–)

Armadale HS, Perth, and Univ of Western Australia. Western Australia 1968–69– . Australia: in Australia 1970–71, 1972–73, 1973–74, 1974–75, 1975–76, 1976–77, 1979–80; in England 1972, 1975, 1977; in West Indies 1972–73; in New Zealand 1973–74; in Pakistan 1976–77. WSC.

Few wicket-keepers improved more drastically in basic skill after reaching Test level than Rodney Marsh, whose 52 consecutive matches for Australia from 1970 to 1977 were only halted when he signed for World Series Cricket. By then Marsh, with 190 catches and 8 stumpings, was unrecognizable in terms of technique from when he first played against England. A swarthy West Australian, Marsh still looked a clumsy, ungainly figure as he stood many yards back to Lillee and Thomson, diving for balls sprayed wide, jumping for bouncers and lumbering up to the wicket for fielding returns. Match by match, however, he had become sounder; his work close to the stumps improved and he reduced his weight. In appearance he is strong rather than athletic, but his acquired efficiency has brought a high ratio of success. In an era of raucous appeals, Marsh exuded Australian belligerence. A bandit moustache and shaggy hair, protruding from under his cap, strengthened this impression. His combative streak, though, only occasionally outran discretion. Forceful left-handed batting has brought Marsh the distinction of Test Hundreds, including the first by a specialist Australian wicket-keeper and another in the Centenary Test of 1977 in Melbourne.

RICHARD STREETON

MARSHALL, Roy Edwin (1930–)

Lodge Sch, Barbados. Barbados 1945–46 to 1953–54. Hampshire 1953–1972 (Captain 1966–1970). West Indies: in Australia 1951–52; in New Zealand 1951–52.

Roy Marshall made his first-class debut for Barbados in 1946 when he was not yet 16. Three years later he was making big scores for them and in 1950 he was selected to tour England. Although not playing in the Test Matches he made over 1,000 runs at an average of 40. In 1951–52 he toured Australia and New Zealand and played in 2 Test Matches in each country. In 1953 he came to Hampshire and by 1955 he was qualified to play for them in the County Championship. From 1966 until 1970 he was to captain them.

It is hardly possible to overestimate his contribution to county cricket and to Hampshire in particular. His batting was one of the more thrilling experiences of the 1950s and 1960s. Had he been born an Englishman he must have been an automatic Test selection. His policy was to dictate to the bowler before the bowler could dictate to him. That was why he liked to open the innings. Occasionally his aggression brought about his downfall, but more often spectators were able to glory in the power of his cutting, in his driving through the covers and his magnificent hitting wide of mid-on. To add to which Marshall had a wide knowledge of the tactics and history of the game.

E. D. R. EAGAR

CAREER FIGURES

	INNS	NO	RUNS	HS	AVGE	100S
Batting	1053	59	35725	228*	35·94	68

Bowling 176 wkts at 28·93 Ct 293

Test Record (4)

	INNS	NO	RUNS	HS	AVGE	100S
Batting	7	0	143	30	20·42	–

Bowling 0 wkts for 15 Ct 1

MAY, Peter Barker Howard (1929–)

Charterhouse 1944–1947 (Captain 1947). Cambridge Univ 1950–1952. Surrey 1950–1963 (Captain 1957–1962). England: in England 1951–1959 consecutively (Captain 1955–1959), 1961 (Captain); in Australia 1954–55, 1958–59 (Captain); in South Africa 1956–57 (Captain); in West Indies 1953–54, 1959–60 (Captain); in New Zealand 1954–55, 1958–59 (Captain). Selector 1965–1968.

Peter May stands as one of the finest English batsmen in memory. Slightly unorthodox in his grip of the bat (according to the purists) he nevertheless was never anything but straight in defence, while his attacking strokes covered the area from slip to fine-leg. He was especially strong on the on-side and woe betide any bowler who chose to bowl at this particular angle for he would be dispatched through mid-on and mid-wicket with an ease that bespoke perfect timing and precision. May played his 1st Test Match at the age of 21 and celebrated it by hitting a hundred against South Africa; no mean feat against an attack of McCarthy, Chubb, Athol Rowan and Mann, with England chasing a total of 538. This was the beginning of a career wherein he rescued England from disaster time after time when their batting was confirming opposition hopes of brittleness. He first played against Australia in 1953, his introduction (in the

Peter May who carried many an England innings.

game between Hassett's team and Surrey) being a memorable one. The central figure was not May but Lindwall who bowled him an over that has gone down in cricket history.

The moral effect of Lindwall's *tour de force* – wherein with both varieties of late swing and movement off the pitch he repeatedly beat the bat – was probably chiefly responsible for limiting May's appearance in the series to the First Test and the last. At the Oval his batting was a substantial factor in England's victory, and from that moment until his premature retirement he was the chief thorn in Australia's flesh. Statistics matter little with a player of his qualities and long after one had forgotten the fact that he made over 4,000 runs in Test cricket, the dynamic batting he produced in the Australian XI match in Sydney in 1958 will come back to mind. Between lunch and tea on the 3rd day he made his 2nd hundred of the match with batting that can rarely have been bettered by an English player anywhere in the world. He led England 41 times (35 of them consecutively). This intensive captaincy took in only 6 years of his cricket life, which was then cut short by illness. This necessitated an early return from West Indies in 1959–60, after which he only played spasmodically for his country. English cricket was the poorer when he gave up playing, though since his retirement he has been closely and helpfully associated with the administration of the game, both at Lord's and the Oval.

May was a fine player as well as being an extremely pleasant one; a cricketer of sensitive nature who could be as hard as nails on the field without ever slipping from the peak of sportsmanship. I would put him at the top of the English captaincy tree during my time, ahead even of the victorious Hutton in 1954–55.

RICHIE BENAUD

CAREER FIGURES

	INNS	NO	RUNS	HS	AVGE	100S
Batting	618	77	27592	285*	51·00	85

Bowling 0 wkt for 49 Ct 282

Test Record (66)

	INNS	NO	RUNS	HS	AVGE	100S
Batting	106	9	4537	285*	46·77	13

Ct 42

MEAD, Charles Philip (1887–1958)

Hampshire 1905–1936. England: in England 1921; in Australia 1911–12, 1928–29; in South Africa 1913–14, 1922–23.

Purely in the terms of efficiency Philip Mead could claim to be the leading English left-handed batsman of the century. As a player he lacked the dashing grace of Woolley, or the dominant personality of Leyland, but as a technician, especially in defence, was the superior of either, and excelled by very few batsmen of any denomination. That he played for England no more than 17 times is strange, and possibly due to a certain inertia in the field.

It was curious, in the fact that he made 153 hundreds, that he was always affected by a great nervousness on reaching the 90s, an idiosyncrasy which caused his partners an equal anxiety. He was a batsman of unvarying routine in that between each ball he would glance round the field, pluck his cap as if in salutation and shuffle his feet into a somewhat crouching stance. Thence, a large heavily built man, he would move deliberately into a wide range of strokes. These were sound, safe and unspectacular so that the general impression was one of slow and stolid progress. This was deceptive, for he was constantly on the move, and he never missed a loose ball. He was equipped to deal with all types of bowling in all conditions, pace, spin and swing coming alike to him. Dealing with the last form of attack he was adept at the late removal of the bat from the flight of the swerving ball. Mead toured Australia twice, in 1911–12 and 1928–29, an interval so remarkably long that on the 2nd tour he was greeted by an admirer as his own son. Coming into the disastrous 1921 series for the last 2 matches he was only once out in scoring 229 runs. Mead's interest was entirely centred on his batting, and he could seldom be induced to bowl his presentable slow left-handers. In latter years he became totally blind, an affliction he bore with admirable fortitude.

IAN PEEBLES

CAREER FIGURES

	INNS	NO	RUNS	HS	AVGE	100S
Batting	1340	185	55061	280*	47·67	153

Bowling 227 wkts at 34·46 Ct 668

Test Record (17)

	INNS	NO	RUNS	HS	AVGE	100S
Batting	26	2	1185	182*	49·37	4

Ct 4

MELVILLE, Alan (1910–)

Michaelhouse Sch, Natal. Oxford Univ 1930–1933 (Captain 1931–32). Natal 1928–29 to 1929–30. Transvaal 1936–37 to 1948–49. Sussex 1932–1936 (Captain 1934–1935). South Africa: in South Africa 1938–39 (Captain), 1948–49; in England 1947 (Captain).

Alan Melville is one of the names which raises a nostalgic echo with the players and watchers of the 1930s, for his cricket had a grace and style that set it apart. Arriving at Oxford from Natal, never having played on a turf wicket, he announced himself brilliantly with 132 not out in the Freshmen's Match, 78 run out against Kent and 118 against Yorkshire in his first 3 innings in the Parks. In University cricket he developed into a batsman of a classical upright method with a particular partiality towards fast bowling. His driving and hooking in an innings of 114 for Sussex against the West Indies fast bowlers of 1933 (made in 2½ hours) was a classic in its day. At Oxford he also showed a cool shrewdness in leadership which prepared him in turn for the captaincy of Sussex and later of South Africa. In his time Sussex, runners-up for 3 years, came as near as they have ever done to winning the County Championship.

Melville was appointed captain of South Africa immediately on his return there in 1938. With innings of 78 and 103 he played a prominent part in the 'Timeless Test' that ended the 1938–39 series, and when the war ended, continuing as captain, brought his sequence to 4 successive Test hundreds by scoring, in 1947, 189 and 104 not out at Trent Bridge and 117 at Lord's. Losing much weight in that hot and rigidly rationed summer he found this superb early form impossible to maintain. His record, however, in Test and other cricket speaks for itself. After his retirement he served for many years as a Test selector.

E. W. SWANTON

CAREER FIGURES

	INNS	NO	RUNS	HS	AVGE	100S
Batting	295	15	10598	189	37·85	25

Bowling 132 wkts 29·99 Ct 156

Test Record (11)

	INNS	NO	RUNS	HS	AVGE	100S
Batting	19	2	894	189	52·58	4

Ct 8

MENZIES, Rt Hon Sir Robert Gordon, KT, CH, QC (1894–1978)

Cricket has been something between a fond pastime and a passion to eminent men in many walks of life; but it would be impossible to name one who in modern times has given such a warm and unstinted patronage to the game as Sir Robert Menzies, the former Prime Minister of Australia – or exacted in return such respect and affection from all sorts and conditions of cricketers. Sir Robert's interest in the game, though he scarcely played it, went back at least to the Body-line troubles of 1932–33, when, as a young barrister, his advice on the tactics of their protest to MCC was sought by the Australian Board of Control, but, unfortunately, not accepted.

He spoke and wrote with equal charm and obvious enjoyment on cricket, both at dinners and in many forewords requested by impor-

Old friends – Bob Menzies and Lindsay Hassett.

tunate authors. There are extended references to the game in his 2 volumes of memoirs *Afternoon Light* and *The Measure of the Years*. Not least he was a generous host to cricketers, notably in the matches he instituted at Canberra between the Prime Minister's XI and successive touring teams to Australia. As Lord Warden of the Cinque Ports he was a regular visitor to the Canterbury Week, and was President of Kent in 1969. He was President briefly also of the Forty Club, until illness compelled his resignation. In a less eventful and demanding age one likes to think he might well have made history by becoming the first Australian to be nominated as President of MCC.

E. W. SWANTON

MERCHANT, Vijay Madhavji (1911–)

Sydenham Coll. Bombay. Hindus 1929–30 to 1945–46. Bombay 1933–34 to 1951–52. India: in India 1933–34, 1951–52; in England 1936, 1946.

A sound, consistent batsman, Merchant, touring England in 1936, scored 114 in the Old Trafford Test, achieving a record 1st-wicket stand (203) with Mushtaq Ali. Ten years later (when he sometimes led the team) he was pre-eminent among the Indians, scoring nearly twice as heavily as any other. At home, in 1943–44, he played his highest innings – 359 not out for Bombay against Maharashtra. During 1941–42 he had scored 4 hundreds in succession. When England toured India in 1951–52, he and Hazare put on 211 for the the 3rd wicket at Delhi. For calm, patience and confidence, he had few superiors. Dudley Carew, watching him in 1946, remarked that he thought of him as a batsman who would play in a representative World XI. It was a disappointment to Vijay Merchant that he never led India in an 'official' Test series. As an administrator and selector, though, especially in his native Bombay, he remained for many years an influential figure.

G. D. MARTINEAU

CAREER FIGURES

	INNS	NO	RUNS	HS	AVGE	100S
Batting	221	44	12876	359*	72·74	43

Bowling 68 wkts at 30·97

Test Record (10)

	INNS	NO	RUNS	HS	AVGE	100S
Batting	18	0	859	154	47·72	3

Bowling 0 wkt for 40 Ct 7

MILBURN, Colin (1941–)

Northamptonshire 1960–1974. Western Australia 1966–67. England: in England 1966, 1967, 1968; in Pakistan 1968–69.

No greater tribulation befell English cricket in the 25 years after the Second World War than the motor-car accident in which Colin Milburn lost his left eye on 23 May 1969. At a time when county cricket was beginning to emerge from a colourless decade through the change of rule allowing overseas players into the game by immediate registration, and the inception of the John Player League, the Falstaffian Milburn was the only English cricketer who could match the likes of Sobers and Clive Lloyd in crowd appeal. Jovial and rotund (5 feet 9 inches and 18 stone), with short thick legs and arms, his batting had a simplicity even the most casual onlooker could identify with and understand. It consisted of hitting the bad balls as hard as possible and stopping or leaving anything he did not fancy. But the resemblance to the village blacksmith, enhanced by his appearance, was only superficial. For in defence he was essentially orthodox, with a long forward stroke to kill the turning ball, while the lusty power of his leg-side hitting, notably with the hook, tended to obscure the pure timing of his cover-drives. A high proportion of his many sixes came in the wide-mid-on/midwicket area, but they were mainly hit straight-batted.

Like many another youngster who joined Northamptonshire, Milburn came from the north-east – Burnopfield, 7 miles from Newcastle, where his father, Jack, was a professional in the Tyneside Senior League. Milburn junior was opening the batting and bowling for Burnopfield by the time he was 13, and at 18, in his only innings for County Durham, scored 101 against the Indian tourists. He signed for Northamptonshire in 1960, was capped in 1963, and 3 years later played his 1st Test against Sobers's West Indians, clubbing 94 in 2½ hours after England had followed on 317 behind. At Lord's he made 126 not out; but partly through the cautiousness of the selectors and partly through the limitations of his fielding (though he was a quick-armed short-leg) he played only 7 more – out of 22 – before his accident, making a 2nd hundred in his last, in Pakistan, at the end of a tour for which he was not even originally selected.

Among his famous innings was one of 243 for West Australia against Queensland, of which 181 came in two hours between lunch and tea, and a fearless attacking 83 against Australia's McKenzie on a flying pitch at Lord's. It was typical of his pluck that, despite his disability, he came back to play 25 more first-class matches for Northants in 1973 and 1974; but in 35 innings his top score was 57 and he reluctantly gave up the unequal struggle.

JOHN THICKNESSE

CAREER FIGURES

	INNS	NO	RUNS	HS	AVGE	100S
Batting	435	34	13262	243	33·07	23

Bowling 99 wkts at 32·03 Ct 226

Test Record (9)

	INNS	NO	RUNS	HS	AVGE	100S
Batting	16	2	654	139	46·71	2

Ct 7

MILLER, Keith Ross, MBE (1919–)

Melbourne HS. Victoria 1937–38 to 1946–47. New South Wales 1947–48 to 1955–56 (Captain 1949–50 to 1955–56). Notts 1959. Australia: in Australia 1946–47, 1947–48, 1950–51, 1951–52, 1952–53, 1954–55; in England 1948, 1953, 1956; in South Africa 1949–50; in West Indies 1954–55; in New Zealand 1945–46; in Pakistan 1956–57.

Keith Miller was born appropriately in the same city and in the same month as the Melbourne Cup, on 28 November 1919. He started his career with Victoria in 1937–38 and scored 181 against Tasmania in his 1st match. He exploded on the scene and the ability to startle and surprise stayed with him

Keith Miller: the beau ideal.

through his whole career. After flying service in the RAAF during the Second War, he left Melbourne for Sydney and New South Wales in 1947–48. He had first attracted attention in England by his brilliant play in the Victory Tests in 1945. When he scored 185 in 165 minutes at Lord's for a Dominions' XI, the pavilion came under a sustained barrage.

Bradman, however, saw this dynamic athlete more as a great natural bowler. In 1948 he back-pedalled on Miller's batting ability and used him as the spearhead with Lindwall. Miller responded to the challenge and gave the English batsmen a warm time. His action was a model of co-ordination. The arm was classically high and the ball was banged down from the full 6 feet of his height. The run-up varied with the time of day and the bowler's state of health. Bouncers were a constant part of the diet. If the crowd showed its displeasure, he always doubled the ration. In fact he was the supreme extrovert, sensing and playing with the emotions of the spectators. He would gesture, shake his head, point to heaven and generally keep everyone informed of his feelings. In the meantime he was capable of producing bursts of great fast bowling in sufficient strength to break any batting side. He could move the ball both ways off the wicket. Crowds loved him because he communicated and made them part of the show. Considering his great talents he was slightly disappointing with the bat. A powerful driver and delicate late-cutter he never really rose to the heights at crisis time. On wet wickets in England his technique looked almost ludicrous; falling about, all pad and no bat. As a fielder he had a touch of intuitive genius. Some sixth sense seemed to impel him into strange positions where a catch would follow shortly afterwards. He was a Cavalier in a world of Roundheads, a man of moods who could seize a game by the throat. He could never be dull. Everything he touched seemed to ignite. If he had ever heard of the word humdrum he never showed it.

JOHN WARR

CAREER FIGURES

	INNS	NO	RUNS	HS	AVGE	100S
Batting	326	36	14183	281*	48·90	41

Bowling 497 wkts at 22·30 Ct 136

Test Record (55)

	INNS	NO	RUNS	HS	AVGE	100S
Batting	87	7	2958	147	36·97	7

Bowling 170 wkts at 22·97 Ct 38

MILTON, Clement Arthur (1928–)

Cotham GS. Gloucestershire 1948–1974 (Captain 1968). England: in England 1958, 1959; in Australia 1958–59.

Arthur Milton played first-class cricket between 1948 and 1974 and his achievements during that time can stand comparison with those of any Gloucestershire batsman apart from Grace and Hammond. Of middle height and sparely built, he was a games player of unusual talents, winning a full English association football cap on the right wing against Austria at Wembley in 1952 as well as representing his country at cricket on 6 occasions.

He played pace and spin bowling with equal certainty and was successful both as an opener and in the middle of the order. His method was simple and correct, his defence being based on extreme watchfulness and the ability to play the ball late; this, allied to patience and quick reflexes, made him one of the most effective players of his time on difficult pitches. He was not a particularly powerful striker of the ball but his skill in placing meant that he obtained full value for his attacking strokes. His liking for the cut and pull and a particular facility off his legs gave him a marked preference for the back foot, though at times he drove firmly on either side of the wicket.

His skill in recognizing the quick single was uncanny. At first, as his partner, I found difficulty in believing that runs existed where he saw them, but I soon learnt to trust his judgment totally and thereafter I found that the constant availability of runs from defensive strokes took much of the pressure out of batting. With his speed and remarkable co-ordination of hand and eye he was a superb fielder in any position; Gloucestershire's traditional reliance on spin bowling meant that he spent much of his time close to the bat. Mostly at short leg and slip he took over 750 catches. Having retired from cricket he retained his keen interest in greyhound racing, in which field he could be a bookmaker's nightmare, and played occasional golf to a low handicap without practice or apparent effort.

DAVID GREEN

CAREER FIGURES

	INNS	NO	RUNS	HS	AVGE	100S
Batting	1078	125	32150	170	33·73	56

Bowling 79 wkts at 45·94 Ct 759

Test Record (6)

	INNS	NO	RUNS	HS	AVGE	100S
Batting	9	1	204	104*	25·50	1

Bowling 0 wkts for 12 Ct 5

MITCHELL, Bruce (1909–)

St John's Coll, Johannesburg. Transvaal 1925–26 to 1949–50. South Africa: in South Africa 1930–31, 1935–36, 1938–39, 1948–49; in England 1929, 1935, 1947; in Australia 1931–32; in New Zealand 1931–32.

Mitchell first played for South Africa at the age of 20 on his first tour of England in 1929. His experience of turf wickets was practically nil, yet he scored more runs in first-class games than any other member of the side. He soon became recognized as one of the classical opening batsmen of his age, with a temperament for the big occasion and a defensive skill that served South Africa nobly. For all his patience, he played with a graceful style and his footwork could rarely be faulted. At Cape Town in 1930–31 he shared in the existing South Africa Test record for the 1st wicket (260 with I. J. Siedle) and altogether took part in 24 century partnerships for his country. One of his great triumphs was at Lord's in 1935, when South Africa won a Test Match in England for the 1st time, and he contributed a chanceless 164 not out in 5½ hours. He was a regular choice for South Africa until 1949. At the Oval in 1947 further fame came his way when he scored a hundred in each innings against England – 120 and 189 not out – being on the field for the entire match with the exception of 12 balls. He was then 38. That season was a triumph for him, with over 2,000 runs and 8 hundreds. He was also a fine slip fieldsman.

IRVING ROSENWATER

CAREER FIGURES

	INNS	NO	RUNS	HS	AVGE	100S
Batting	281	30	11395	195	45·39	30

Bowling 249 wkts at 25·63 Ct 229

Test Record (42)

	INNS	NO	RUNS	HS	AVGE	100S
Batting	80	9	3471	189*	48·88	8

Bowling 27 wkts at 51·11 Ct 56

MORRIS, Arthur Robert, MBE (1922–)

Newcastle HS, and Canterbury HS, Sydney. New South Wales 1940–41 to 1954–55 (Captain 1947–48 to 1954–55). Australia: in Australia 1946–47, 1947–48, 1950–51, 1951–52 (Captain), 1952–53, 1954–55; in England 1948, 1953; in South Africa 1949–50; in West Indies 1954–55.

There have been few more elegant left-handed batsmen than Arthur Morris, who after hitting a hundred in each innings of his 1st first-class match went on to become one of the greatest opening batsmen Australia produced. Though an opening batsman he was at his most brilliant when facing spin, and with footwork that has never been bettered, he would sidle yards down the pitch to disturb the bowler's length. Morris was 24 years of age when he played his first Test against England in Brisbane. Nine years later he played his 46th and last. I never heard colleague or opponent say a harsh word about him – an achievement that in high-pressure cricket days does not come easily. For a while he figured with Keith Miller in a controversy that surrounded the New South Wales and Australian captaincy, when the State selectors chose Miller whilst the Australian selectors made Morris vice-captain of the Test team. Eventually the matter was resolved and Miller went to England as vice-captain to Ian Johnson in 1956, having already superseded Morris on the earlier 1955 tour to the West Indies. Through this and other setbacks, Morris remained perfectly poised and pleasant, as always sticking to his often-spoken theory that 'cricket is a game to be enjoyed'.

The most triumphal of his seasons was that of 1948 in England where he was in command against bowlers of all types and paces. When Laker was found wanting at Headingley (in 1948, not 1956), it was Morris who led the 2nd innings onslaught on him after Harvey, in the 1st, had put together his 1st hundred against England. In the Australian 2nd

Arthur Morris: a prolific opening batsman.

innings, Morris (182) and Bradman (173 not out) drove Australia to a remarkable victory which clinched the rubber. Morris made 696 runs in the 1948 series, heading the averages with 87. A certain fallibility against the swinging ball around the leg-stump, brilliantly exploited by Bedser, later restricted his consistency in Test cricket. He remained, however, a tremendously heavy scorer in State cricket. A career average of 65 in the Sheffield Shield places him near the top of a list of New South Wales batsmen since the game was first played in Australia.

In 1963, 8 years after retirement, he went on a short Commonwealth tour of India and South Africa, and his batting at Bombay was so magnificent that Indian players found themselves applauding his commanding strokeplay. Norman O'Neill, himself no mean strokemaker when going, raced into the dressing-room on this occasion to retrieve 2 other Australians who were resting. 'Come and watch this,' he said excitedly, 'you'll never see a better batsman than this fellow.' A nice and well-merited tribute from the new generation to the one before. In recent years, as one of the rare cricketing members of the Sydney Cricket Ground Trust, he has held a place in the corridors of power.

RICHIE BENAUD

CAREER FIGURES

	INNS	NO	RUNS	HS	AVGE	100S
Batting	250	15	12614	290	53·67	46

Bowling 12 wkts at 49·33 Ct 69

Test Record (46)

	INNS	NO	RUNS	HS	AVGE	100S
Batting	79	3	3533	206	46·48	12

Bowling 2 wkts at 25·00 Ct 15

MURDOCH, William Lloyd (1855–1911)

Sydney Univ. New South Wales 1876–77 to 1889–90 (Captain 1878–79 to 1889–90). Sussex 1893–1899 (Captain throughout). London County 1899–1904. Australia: in Australia 1876–77, 1878–79, 1881–82 (Captain). 1882–83 (Captain), 1884–85 (Captain); in England 1880 (Captain),

1882 (Captain), 1884 (Captain), 1890 (Captain). England: in South Africa 1891–92.

Murdoch, the first Australian batsman to rank with England's best, besides having a good style and plenty of strokes, possessed the footwork required for difficult pitches. His career is in many ways unique. Originally considered as wicket-keeper for Australia, he played as a batsman. He captained Australia in the 1st Test Match in England, scoring 153 not out in the 2nd innings, led his side to victory at the Oval on the next visit in 1882 and was the 1st to score a double-hundred in Tests (211 in 1884). Victorian-born, he made 321 for New South Wales against Victoria, and, having ended his Australian career in 1890, kept wicket for England against South Africa at Cape Town in 1892. He then played for Sussex, captained the county from 1893 to 1899 (dividing the honour with Ranji in the latter year), with a highest score of 226. He had previously made 286 not out for the Australians against Sussex. He next joined London County, and continued to make runs till the club's dissolution in 1904, the year he made 140 for the Gentlemen at the Oval. Finally, he died of a stroke at Melbourne while watching a Test Match against South Africa.

G. D. MARTINEAU

CAREER FIGURES

	INNS	NO	RUNS	HS	AVGE	100S
Batting	684	48	17070	321	26·83	20

Bowling 10 wkts at 43·00 Ct (inc. w/k) 213; st 25

Test Record (19) (Australia and England)

	INNS	NO	RUNS	HS	AVGE	100S
Batting	34	5	908	211	31·31	2

Ct (incl. w/k) 13; st 2

MURRAY, Deryck Lance (1943–)

Queen's Royal Coll, Port of Spain, and Nottingham Univ. Trinidad 1960–61– . Cambridge Univ 1965–1966 (Captain 1966). Nottinghamshire 1966–1969. Warwickshire 1972–1975. West Indies: in West Indies 1967–68, 1972–73, 1973–74, 1975–76, 1976–77, 1977–78; in England 1963, 1973, 1976; in Australia 1975–76, 1979–80; in India 1974–75; in Pakistan 1974–75. Rest of the World in England 1970. WSC.

Deryck Murray's talents as a wicket-keeper and part-time leg-spinner were nurtured in a cricketing family in Port of Spain, Trinidad. His father, Lance, played for the island as a leg-spinner and he later contributed greatly to the administration of Trinidad and West Indian cricket. His uncle, Sonny, was synonymous with the famous Queen's Park Club as secretary. The Murray household was no more than a mile from Queen's Park Oval itself. Even so, Deryck Murray's elevation to international cricket was a surprise. He was only 20; just out of Queen's Royal College, when he was chosen to tour England with Sir Frank Worrell's side in 1963. He kept wicket in all 5 Tests and set a record for his country of 24 dismissals in a series.

A most promising career was fragmented when, in 1964, he entered Jesus College Cambridge. He won blues for 2 years, captaining the University in 1966. At the same time he registered for Nottinghamshire. He proved his independence hereabouts by opting out of cricket for 3 seasons to obtain from Nottingham University a business study degree. Once back in the West Indies side in 1973 he remained there, his poise and neatness contrasting markedly with the usually exuberant Caribbean attitudes. Deryck Murray has long been vice-captain of his country; not surprising, because he is a man of much charm and humour who has also displayed the purpose to be a prime mover in the formation and organization of the West Indies Players' Association.

TONY LEWIS

MURRAY, John Thomas MBE (1935–)

St John's C of E Sch, London, Middlesex 1952–1975. England: in England 1961, 1962, 1966, 1967; in Australia 1962–63; in South Africa 1964–65; in New Zealand 1962–63, 1965–66; in India 1961–62; in Pakistan 1961–62. Selector 1977–1978.

Blessed with a superb physique, John Murray, immaculate and always the stylist, was a wicket-keeper of the highest quality, and a fine batsman too. His all-round play made him first choice for England against Australia in 1961. Playing in all 5 Test Matches that year, he did well enough to take over the position relinquished by Godfrey Evans. With exceptional agility he brought off some spectacular diving catches. But injury, both in India with MCC the following winter and again in Australia in 1962–63, deprived him of his regular place. As a batsman he was technically correct and strong on the off-side. Six times he scored 1,000 runs in a season, achieving a wicket-keeper's double in 1957 with 1,025 runs and 104 dismissals (82 caught, 22 stumped). (Only L. E. G. Ames had previously done this.) Over his career he produced some fine innings when runs were needed. His hundred for the Rest of the World in Barbados showed courage and technique against the fastest bowlers, as did his one Test hundred against West Indies in 1966. He served Middlesex with great loyalty over a long span; his 1,527 victims constitute an all-time wicket-keeping record.

COLIN COWDREY

CAREER FIGURES

	INNS	NO	RUNS	HS	AVGE	100S
Batting	936	136	18872	142	23·59	16

Bowling 6 wkts at 40·50 W/k: ct 1270; st 257 Total 1527

Test Record (21)

	INNS	NO	RUNS	HS	AVGE	100S
Batting	28	5	506	112	22·00	1

W/k: ct 52; st 3 Total 55

MUSHTAQ MOHAMMAD (1943–)

Christian Mission HS Karachi. Karachi Whites. PIA. Northamptonshire 1964–1977 (Captain 1975 to 1977). Pakistan: in Pakistan 1958–59, 1961–62, 1968–69, 1969–70, 1972–73, 1974–75, 1976–77 (Captain), 1978–79 (Captain); in England 1962, 1967, 1971, 1974; in Australia 1972–73, 1976–77 (Captain); in West Indies 1976–77 (Captain); in New Zealand 1972–73; in India 1960–61, Rest of the World in England 1970. WSC.

Acceptance as an outstanding all-rounder came early for Mushtaq Mohammad, 4th of the 5 Mohammad brothers who have contributed so much to Pakistan's short cricket history. It seems unlikely that one aspect of Mushtaq's career will disappear from record books: he is the youngest man ever to have played first-class cricket (13 years 41 days); or to have appeared in a Test (15 years, 124 days); or to have scored a Test hundred (17 years, 82 days). Nobody has ever had reservations about Mushtaq's ability, even if his cricket has had its variable moods. A compact, muscular man, with thick forearms, he is an exciting strokemaker, by inclination, but one who does not spurn responsibility when a match has to be saved. His inbred gifts of eye, footwork and timing enable him to play most of the strokes, including the unorthodox ones. His leg-breaks and googlies are tidier in length than most and would have earned more headlines in days when such skills were more fashionable. Mushtaq's seniority took him, eventually, to the captaincy of both Northamptonshire, whom he joined in 1964, and Pakistan; but like other naturally gifted players he seldom found the role easy. He joined World Series Cricket in 1977, leaving Northamptonshire soon afterwards.

RICHARD STREETON

NOBLE, Montague Alfred (1873–1940)

Sydney Univ. New South Wales 1893–94 to 1919–20 (Captain 1902–03 to 1909–10). Australia: in Australia 1897–98, 1901–02, 1903–04 (Captain), 1907–08 (Captain); in England 1899, 1902, 1905, 1909 (Captain); in South Africa 1902–03.

M. A. Noble was one of the greatest all-round Australian cricketers in the game's history. In his period which extended roughly from 1899 to 1909 he played in 42 Test matches, 39 against England and 3 against South Africa, scoring 1,997 runs and taking 121 wickets. Only 2 other cricketers during that period did the double in Test cricket, George Giffen and Wilfred Rhodes. Also he was, as captain, as thoughtful and judicious a technician as any before his day or since. Born in Sydney on 28 January 1873, he looked the typical 'Cornstalk', tall, keen-faced and shaven – most cricketers of the early 1900s wore moustaches. His first rubber in England, in 1899, at once announced his quality. Favoured by a dry summer he came out 2nd in the Test Match lists for Australia. His innings of 60 not out and 89 saved Australia from defeat at Manchester. He defended for 8½ hours in all.

'Monty' Noble: one of the great figures in Australian cricket, on the field and off.

He was a cricketer whose very movement and attitude on the field of play expressed his character. His batting was as studious as his medium-paced bowling. His stance at the wicket, though beautifully positioned and relaxed, hands gripping the blade's middle, suggested great mental concentration. He made use of his height but did not risk the free uplift of the bat more or less fashionable among some of his contemporaries. He watched the ball intently, almost to the last split-second. Any boy watching him at the wicket could be sure of learning what it was wise – and unwise (by deduction) – not to do. In his career altogether he scored 37 hundreds, including 284 v Sussex at Hove in 1902, 281 for New South Wales v Victoria at Melbourne in 1905–06, and 5 other double-hundreds, all in Australian State cricket.

His bowling consisted of off-spin combined with accuracy of pitch, and cunning variation of pace and flight. In addition he exploited a late-swing – this at a time when only one and the same ball was available by law during the longest of a team's innings. But his chief asset, as a bowler, was changeful and precise length. In a way, though right-arm, he bowled rather in the manner of, a shade more quickly than, J. C. White. Sir Pelham Warner said that Noble was one of the most astute of all Australian captains.

His temperament inclined him towards the more scientific aspects of cricket; and on the field of play he often seemed to be working-out in his inner consciousness some problem not to be discerned even on the horizon of average mentality. As a fieldsman he stood at the old-time place of point, where he could be quite brilliantly alert, and where he could see what was going on not only on the surface of an opening batsman's innings but within the mind of him. 'I always,' said A. C. MacLaren, 'tried to anticipate Monty's moves.' High praise indeed!

NEVILLE CARDUS

CAREER FIGURES

	INNS	NO	RUNS	HS	AVGE	100S
Batting	378	34	14034	284	40·79	37

Bowling 627 wkts at 23·04 Ct 189

Test Record (42)

	INNS	NO	RUNS	HS	AVGE	100S
Batting	73	7	1997	133	30·25	1

Bowling 121 wkts at 25·00 Ct 26

NORFOLK, 16th Duke of KG, PC, GCVO, GBE, TD (1908–75)

President of Sussex 1933 and 1949–74. President of MCC 1955–56. Manager of MCC in Australia 1962–63.

Before he was chosen to manage the English side in Australia – a choice which proved brilliantly successful – the Duke of Norfolk was chiefly known to the cricket public for the sides which he raised to play touring teams from overseas on his beautiful ground at Arundel and his matches there against Prince Philip's XI in aid of the National Playing Fields' Association. His popularity had been convincingly shown when, after he had resigned the Presidency of Sussex in 1950 during the bitter controversy over the captaincy of the county side, he was a few weeks later unanimously re-elected at a meeting of almost a thousand people. A charming host,

'Heads, Your Grace'. The Duke of Norfolk tosses; the Duke of Edinburgh calls.

he successfully maintained in club matches at Arundel the spirit of country-house cricket, playing himself and by his own obvious enjoyment greatly increasing the enjoyment of his guests. Since his death, thanks to the kindness of his successor and the enthusiasm and indefatigable efforts of Lavinia, Duchess of Norfolk, the Friends of Arundel Castle Cricket Club have been formed and there is more cricket at the castle than ever before.

R. L. ARROWSMITH

NOURSE, Arthur Dudley (1910–)

Natal 1931–32 to 1952–53. South Africa: in South Africa 1935–36, 1938–39, 1948–49 (Captain), 1949–50 (Captain); in England 1935, 1947, 1951 (Captain).

Dudley Nourse played in 34 Test Matches. Between them he and his father, Dave Nourse, played for South Africa 79 times. Dudley Nourse was a strong and gifted right-

A. D. Nourse, jr: a Test average of 53.

hand batsman with all the strokes. He could also fight bravely and stubbornly when the occasion demanded. His innings of 208 in the First Test at Trent Bridge in 1951, made with a broken thumb, was largely responsible for South Africa's victory. He batted throughout in pain. All through his career he was one of the mainstays of his country's batting. Dudley Nourse captained South Africa in 3 series, 2 against England in 1948–49 and 1951 and 1 against Australia in 1949–50.

E. D. R. EAGAR

CAREER FIGURES

	INNS	NO	RUNS	HS	AVGE	100S
Batting	269	27	12472	260*	51·53	41

Bowling 0 wkt for 124 Ct 134

Test Record (34)

	INNS	NO	RUNS	HS	AVGE	100S
Batting	62	7	2960	231	53·81	9

Bowling 0 wkt for 9 Ct 12

NOURSE, Arthur William (1878–1948)

Mansfield Road Boys' HS Durban. Natal 1896–97 to 1924–25. Transvaal 1925–26 to 1926–27. Western Province 1927–28 to 1935–36. South Africa: in South Africa 1902–03, 1905–06, 1909–10, 1913–14, 1921–22, 1922–23; in England 1907, 1912, 1924; in Australia 1910–11.

'Dave' Nourse, a left-hander of rock-like stability and nerve, was South Africa's first great batsman. He made 72 when first facing Australia in 1902–03, 93 not out in gaining the 1st victory over England in 1905–06, 62 out of 140 at Lord's in 1907, 92 out of 205 against Australia at Melbourne in 1910–11, 42 out of 93 at Kennington Oval in 1912, and, in 1921–22, 64 and 111 against Australia at Johannesburg. He also made 304 not out for Natal against Transvaal in 1919–20. His son stands higher statistically, but his achievements were founded on the paternal rock.

G. D. MARTINEAU

CAREER FIGURES

	INNS	NO	RUNS	HS	AVGE	100S
Batting	371	39	14216	304*	42·81	38

Bowling 305 wkts at 23·36 Ct 173

Test Record (45)

	INNS	NO	RUNS	HS	AVGE	100S
Batting	83	8	2234	111	29·78	1

Bowling 41 wkts at 37·87 Ct 43

OLD, Christopher Middleton (1948–)

Acklam Hall GS, Middlesbrough. Yorkshire 1966– . England: in England 1970, 1973–1978 consecutively; in Australia 1974–75, 1976–77, 1978–79; in West Indies 1973–74; in New Zealand 1974–75, 1977–78; in India 1972–73, 1976–77; in Pakistan 1972–73, 1977–78.

Following a national institution into a county XI as demanding as Yorkshire is the hardest of tasks. Happily, along with intolerance of failure can there be found supportiveness. Thus if there is real talent in a young player the hard-bitten benches of Park Avenue and Headingley are swift to recognize it. When the time came for Wilfred Rhodes to step down as his own half-century began to loom

Yorkshire launched Hedley Verity who became, like Rhodes, the unrivalled left-arm bowler not only in Yorkshire but in all England. When Fred Trueman, the most natural fast bowler of them all, began to miss the high notes it was time to find his successor as the blaster in the Yorkshire attack. The choice fell on Chris Old and for years he had to live down the comparison with the Fiery Fred of the 1950s.

Old had arrived at the nets as a left-handed batsman. He was the youngest of 3 games-playing brothers. Besides playing as an all-rounder in the Durham team which became the first Minor County to win a Gillette Cup-tie (at Yorkshire's expense), Alan Old, the middle brother, gave the family a rare distinction by playing at fly-half for England, whilst Chris, the baby of the family, was playing cricket for England in the West Indies. By then Yorkshiremen had accepted Chris Old for what he was: not a fast bowler like Fred but one of the finest fast-medium bowlers of his generation and on his day a huge hitter of the ball with as safe a pair of hands as you could find between Middlesbrough, his home town, and the Truemans' seat at Maltby Main. Chris Old's action is a rhythmic model for the young. An accelerating run, not too long, and a delivery without strain. As he matured he developed that priceless gift of knowing where the ball was going, the prelude to accuracy. From that base comes the possibility of a wicket, and then several more, or of containment.

At times Old moved the ball so much that important batsmen were not good enough to play him. I see him now coming down the hill at Headingley, devastating on a first morning at Adelaide, keeping his side in the game under a hot sun in Bridgetown or Bombay. Yet, paradoxically, this talent for any Test tempo played but fitfully. His fine frame, capable of taking 9 wickets and hitting a hundred in a Roses match, was so susceptible to injury that others made Test appearances which were his by right of prior performance. In the early 1970s he was much troubled by his knees; later his shoulder went. In India his rib muscles tore; in Australia his groin. Like a fine instrument the rhythms could not be found unless Old's body was in tune. As he enters his thirties, with all the honours in the game behind him, Chris Old seems to be looking for more from his life. The game will miss his sane and sensible approach, his quietness in the hurly-burly, the quiet of a countryman. Deep down this is the very essence of his spirit.

ROBIN MARLAR

OLDFIELD, William Albert Stanley, MBE (1894–1976)

Cleveland Street Sch, Sydney. New South Wales 1919–20 to 1937–38 (Captain 1925–26 to 1934–35). Australia: in Australia 1920–21, 1924–25, 1928–29, 1930–31, 1931–32, 1932–33, 1936–37; in England 1921, 1926, 1930, 1934; in South Africa 1921–22, 1935–36.

'Bert' Oldfield, one of the cleverest and most stylish wicket-keepers of his period (1919–1938) played for Australia in 54 Test Matches, held 78 catches and had 52 stumpings. At Melbourne, in February 1925, he stumped Hobbs, Woolley, Chapman and Whysall; and in the same innings caught A. E. R. Gilligan. Against England, in all matches, he allowed on average only 1 bye every 68 runs scored. Also he could bat more than usefully in quite an elegant manner. In Test Matches he scored 1,427 runs, average 22·65. As a man and cricketer alike, he possessed a certain manner of composure and deliberate poise. He never addressed an appeal to the umpire in a raucous, or even demanding tone of voice. He did his work behind the stumps stealthily and courteously. A sudden swoop, the flash of a bail – then we would see Oldfield turning politely to the umpire as though addressing him reluctantly but on a strict point of order: 'How was that?' Almost a request for information. To the batsman given out Oldfield would seem to say 'I am so sorry, but what could I do in the circumstances? Law 23, you know. Better luck – perhaps, in the next innings.' He stooped low as the bowler began to run, heels firmly on the ground. To fast bowling he stood where he could take the ball breast-high. To medium-paced or slow bowling he stood some two feet behind the wickets, so that he could reach the bails without having to step forward. He was, in fact, a studious 'keeper, always bringing observation to re-inforce natural-born intuitions and a superb muscular response.

Like other great artists of his calling, Oldfield was fortunate to play cricket during an epoch of fast pitches and of great spin-bowlers, such as Mailey, O'Reilly and Grimmett. He was always the gentleman, he might well have kept wicket in the gloves in which he was married. None of his victims could ever feel aggrieved as Oldfield performed his happy, necessary dispatch. In retirement, too, Oldfield was an unfailingly courteous and delightful companion.

NEVILLE CARDUS

CAREER FIGURES

	INNS	NO	RUNS	HS	AVGE	100S
Batting	315	57	6135	137	23·77	6

W/k: ct 390; st 263 Total 653

Test Record (54)

	INNS	NO	RUNS	HS	AVGE	100S
Batting	80	17	1427	65*	22·65	–

W/k: ct 78; st 52 Total 130

O'NEILL, Norman Clifford (1937–)

Kogarah Intermediate HS. New South Wales 1955–56 to 1966–67. Australia: in Australia 1958–59, 1960–61, 1962–63, 1963–64; in England 1961, 1964; in West Indies 1965–66; in India 1959–60, 1964–65; in Pakistan 1959–60.

Heralded as 'the new Don Bradman', Norman O'Neill became at the end of his 1st season, 1957–58, the 3rd Australian cricketer ever to score 1,000 runs in the Sheffield Shield. Against Victoria at Melbourne he scored 175 in just over 3 hours, drowning this performance with 233 in 4 hours at Sydney in the return match. Chosen for the Combined XI against MCC at Perth in 1958–59, his presence attracted enormous crowds and the sort of publicity which had surrounded Bradman a generation before.

Under such a fierce spotlight it was to O'Neill's credit that he batted with impressive consistency in the 1958–59 series against England. He had, even so, to wait until his 10th Test Match for his 1st Test hundred, 117 at the Oval in 1961. On this, his

Norman O'Neill: in the late 1950s, the 'white hope' of Australia.

1st tour of England, he came close to 2,000 runs and had a splendid Test record. With such a fearful reputation to live up to, it is hardly surprising that at times he found the going hard. In 1961–62 he lost his confidence completely and there were serious doubts expressed as to his future. Starting badly in 1962–63, he chose the New South Wales match against MCC to confound his critics with a memorable innings of 143 in 3 hours and he scored 100 in the Fourth Test Match at Adelaide. He was immensely successful in India and Pakistan with a Test hundred against Pakistan at Lahore and 2 hundreds against India at Bombay and Calcutta. In the tied Test Match against West Indies at Brisbane in 1960 he made his highest Test score, 181. His highest score in all first-class cricket was 284 against the President's XI at Ahmedabad in 1959–60.

Figures cannot relay the brilliance of the spectacle when Norman O'Neill was going well. Always a nervous starter, anxious to display his range of stroke, he was a back-foot player of the highest class, as powerful as anyone since Bradman. Quick on his feet to the spinners, a very fast runner between the wickets, the scoreboard was always moving whilst he was at the crease. A great batsman, the best Australian fielder and thrower of his generation and a wrist-spinner who broke many a Test partnership, Norman O'Neill made for cricket entertainment at the highest level. Since his retirement he has moved west to Perth where he runs a successful cricket school. He has a son who has played first-class cricket in Australia and Lancashire League cricket in England.

COLIN COWDREY

CAREER FIGURES

	INNS	NO	RUNS	HS	AVGE	100S
Batting	306	34	13859	284	50·95	45

Bowling 99 wkts at 41·01 Ct 99

Test Record (42)

	INNS	NO	RUNS	HS	AVGE	100S
Batting	69	8	2779	181	45·55	6

Bowling 17 wkts at 39·23 Ct 21

W. J. O'Reilly: the smile on the face of the tiger.

O'REILLY, William Joseph (1905–)

St Patrick's Coll, Goulburn. New South Wales 1927–28 to 1945–46 (Captain 1940–41 to 1945–46). Australia: in Australia 1931–32, 1932–33, 1936–37; in England 1934, 1938; in South Africa 1935–36; in New Zealand 1945–46.

'Bill' O'Reilly played for Australia from 1931–32, when he bowled against South Africa, until the outbreak of the war. In that time he took 144 wickets at 22 apiece, and established himself as the greatest spin bowler of his era. His name is inevitably bracketed with that of Barnes but, apart from the fact that each was over 6 feet tall and bowled leg-breaks of superlative quality, there is little physical resemblance. They were, however, at one in their relentless hostility to all batsmen. O'Reilly's run-up and action was a glorious rampage of flailing arms and legs. The actual delivery did little to please the purist as he inclined to stoop and, showing his chest to the receiver, made only limited use of his left arm. But the sweep of his right arm was full and rhythmical, whilst the general gusto of the performance made it very difficult to gauge his pace from his hand. Being a man of strong views he wisely ignored the misguided, who, early on, tried to mould him to more orthodox lines. There were also pundits who pointed out that he merely rolled his leg-break and sought to teach him to spin it. They received a characteristic and forceful reply which, in time, they had the doubtful pleasure of digesting, along with their own words.

O'Reilly bowled practically every known ball, but his stock delivery was his rolling leg-break which tended for the most part to come straight on. The googly he spun sharply and every ball he bowled had an abnormal bouncing quality. His pace was such that few batsmen could move out to the pitch of the ball, and his accuracy was unfailing. On a good Australian wicket C. J. Barnett, a devastating strokeplayer, was instructed by G. O. Allen to 'chase' O'Reilly in the interests of the side, a mandate he readily obeyed. After a few hazardous assaults it was clear to all that such tactics must lead even the great to early disaster and, in the case of the less gifted, must be immediately suicidal. There is no hypocrisy in O'Reilly's attitude to his job, and any scoring-stroke was greeted by a testy demand for the immediate return of the ball rather than a congratulatory word. Full well did he deserve his sobriquet of 'Tiger', but equally the more affectionate address of 'Big Bill'. With Grimmett in support this was the finest leg-spin combination of modern times. O'Reilly was originally a schoolmaster, but later turned to other pursuits, including journalism. His writings have the same honest, forthright quality which made him such a doughty unrelenting opponent. But no man of good sense ever resented the scorching blast of his enthusiasm as it emanated from the warmth of a very big heart.

IAN PEEBLES

CAREER FIGURES

	INNS	NO	RUNS	HS	AVGE	100S
Batting	167	41	1655	56*	13·13	–

Bowling 774 wkts at 16·60 Ct 65

Test Record (27)

	INNS	NO	RUNS	HS	AVGE	100S
Batting	39	7	410	56*	12·81	–

Bowling 144 wkts at 22·59 Ct 7

PARDON, Sydney Herbert (1855–1925)

Editor of *Wisden* 1890–1925.

Sydney Pardon was editor of *Wisden's Cricketers' Almanack* for 35 years, from 1890 until 20 November 1925, on which date he died suddenly, some 2 months after his 70th birthday. He was a typical English gentleman, late-Victorian and ripe Edwardian, aristocratic of countenance, with a curving moustache, heavily lidded eyes, delicate fingers and a voice which he seldom, if ever, raised. He was not tall, and not in the least difficult to know, despite his exclusive tastes and perfect manners. He knew cricket thoroughly, mainly as an essential part of the English and London scene in summer. Pardon would never presume in his writing to go deeply into fine points of technique; but he insisted on style. He waged a relentless war against bowlers whose actions even faintly hinted of a throw. He watched the game from the Press Box at Lord's through small ivory-ornamented opera glasses, through which, the evening of the same day, he would look at Jean de Reszke or Destinn, at the Royal Opera House, Covent Garden. He was always proud to tell his friends that he had contributed special articles to *The Times* on music, the theatre, cricket and racing. One Derby Day he came down from the Press Box at Lord's into the pavilion to learn the winner of the race. After inspecting the tape he bit his fingernails. 'Dear me,' he murmured, 'won by an outsider, a non-thoroughbred. I'm deeply thankful I didn't accidentally back it.'

His biographies and reports of matches in *Wisden* remain unsurpassed for concentration and civilized observation and expression. When first I went to Lord's as a cricket-writer, he led me to the Press Box and introduced me to his colleagues – some dozen at most. They bowed to me; it was rather like a social function. 'You will,' he said to me, 'first sit there' – indicating a seat on the back row – 'but, in the course of time, I am confident you will graduate.' It was years before the honour of sitting next to him came my way. He was of his period, unique and inimitable.

NEVILLE CARDUS

PARKER, Charles Warrington Leonard (1882–1959)

Gloucestershire 1903–1935. England: in England 1921.

It is one of the stranger quirks of cricket history that the man who has taken more wickets (3,278) than any other bar Rhodes and Freeman, should have played only once for England. Unusual, too, was the fact that a left-arm bowler so gifted, introduced to Gloucestershire by W. G. Grace and playing first at the age of 20 in 1905, should not have come to the front until he was 35. From 1920 to his retirement aged 50 in 1935 he took 100 wickets in 16 successive seasons, 5 times exceeding 200. With his high action and acute power of spin his pace when the ball bit was fully slow-medium. In such conditions he was a sore test to the best, with Goddard's off-spin in contrast from the other end, Hammond to do the slip catching and the whole operation under the aggressive leadership of Bev Lyon.

Like many an artist before and since Parker needed handling, and he was never averse from speaking his mind. By all reports he did so before the England v Australia Test at Headingley in 1926, when, after rain, A. W. Carr adopted the contradictory course of putting Australia in and leaving Parker out. As late as 1930 he was summoned to the Oval Test and again discarded. This time however he had swift revenge for directly after Australia had won and so regained the Ashes they found themselves locked in a deadly struggle at Bristol where on a turning wicket and, thanks to Parker's 7 for 54 in the 2nd innings, the game ended in a tie.

E. W. SWANTON

CAREER FIGURES

	INNS	NO	RUNS	HS	AVGE	100S
Batting	954	195	7951	82	10·48	–

Bowling 3278 wkts at 19·47 Ct 235

Test Record (1)

	INNS	NO	RUNS	HS	AVGE	100S
Batting	1	1	3	3*	–	–

Bowling 2 wkts at 16·00

PARKS, James Michael (1931–)

Hove County GS. Sussex 1949–1972 (Captain 1967–1968). Somerset 1973–1976. England: in England 1954, 1960, 1963, 1964, 1965, 1966; in Australia 1965–66; in South Africa 1964–65; in West Indies 1959–60, 1967–68; in New Zealand 1965–66; in India 1963–64.

The son of a famous father, Jim Parks had the distinction of playing for England as a batsman in 1954, little realizing that 10 years later he would be England's wicket-keeper. He was always a brilliant strokemaker, especially quick on his feet to slow bowling, scoring more than 2,300 runs both in 1955 and 1959. Having toured Pakistan in 1955–56, he was then chosen to tour South Africa in 1956–57, but had to return home after the first match because of illness. Injury to the regular Sussex wicket-keeper resulted in Parks donning the gloves for the first time to help out in the emergency, and in 1959 he became the regular county wicket-keeper.

His best years behind the stumps were 1959 and 1961, with 93 victims each season. By happy chance, he was coaching in Trinidad during the MCC tour of West Indies, 1959–60, when an urgent replacement was needed. Seizing his opportunity, he kept wicket well and scored a courageous, match-saving 101 not out in the 2nd innings of the final Test. Although he toured New Zealand in 1960–61, it was not until the injury to John Murray in 1963 that opportunity came his way again. Although, judged by the highest standards, he may not have looked the part, he was a much safer and more efficient wicket-keeper than many realized. It was disappointing that he did not do himself justice with the bat in Test cricket for he could be such a destroyer of all bowling and his performances in one-day cricket were prolific. He became Sussex captain in 1967, but lack of form and ill-health forced him to relinquish the post the following year.

In 1973, he retired after 25 years with the county. A move to Somerset gave him a second career, in which he continued to score and keep wicket well. He retired in 1977, hopeful that his son registered with Hampshire would keep the family line going on.

COLIN COWDREY

CAREER FIGURES

	INNS	NO	RUNS	HS	AVGE	100S
Batting	1227	172	36673	205*	34·76	51

Bowling 51 wkts at 43·82 W/k: ct 1089; st 93 Total 1182

Test Record (46)

	INNS	NO	RUNS	HS	AVGE	100S
Batting	68	7	1962	108*	32·16	2

Bowling 1 wkt for 51 W/k: ct 103 (including 2 catches in 3 Tests when not keeping wicket); st 11 Total 114

PATAUDI, Iftikhar Ali, Nawab of (1910–1952)

Chief's Coll, Lahore. Oxford Univ 1929–1931. Worcestershire 1932–1938. England: in England 1934; in Australia 1932–33. India: in England 1946 (Captain).

One of the most gifted batsmen of his generation, Pataudi held the unique distinction of having played for both England and India in a Test Match. Coached by Frank Woolley when he came to England as a boy of 16, he won his blue in 1929, when Oxford owed almost everything in their drawn match at Lord's to his 2 dominating innings of 106 and 84. Two years later he made 4 hundreds on the University tour, and after an exhausting day in the field at Lord's cheered his colleagues in the dressing-room by assuring them that Ratcliffe's record score of 201 for Cambridge would not last 24 hours. This promise he made good with an unbeaten 238, an innings in which classic method was illuminated by natural brilliance. Next season, in a memorable partnership with Duleepsinhji, he made 165 for the Gentlemen at Lord's, and in the following winter made a hundred in his 1st Test Match against Australia on 'Jardine's Tour'. For Worcestershire in the next 2 seasons he scored heavily – 3 double-hundreds in 1933, and an average of 91 next year – but then went back to India, only to return on short visits in 1937 and 1938 and as captain of the Indian team that came to England in 1946.

Pataudi was a player of great natural gifts, quick to sight the ball and to move his feet, but his fluent strokeplay had a firm basis alike in judicious patience and basically correct technique. He died from a heart attack when in the saddle playing polo.

H. S. ALTHAM

CAREER FIGURES

	INNS	NO	RUNS	HS	AVGE	100S
Batting	204	24	8750	238*	48·61	29

Bowling 15 wkts at 35·27 Ct 56

Test Record (6) (England and India)

	INNS	NO	RUNS	HS	AVGE	100S
Batting	10	0	199	102	19·90	1

PATAUDI, Mansur Ali, Nawab of (1941–)

Winchester 1956–1959 (Captain 1959). Oxford Univ 1960–1961, 1963 (Captain 1961, 1963). Sussex 1957–1970. India: in India 1961–62, 1963–64 (Captain), 1964–65 (Captain), 1966–67 (Captain), 1969–70 (Captain), 1972–73, 1974–75 (Captain), in England 1967 (Captain); in Australia 1967–68 (Captain); in West Indies 1961–62 (Captain); in New Zealand 1967–68 (Captain).

In his 4 years in his school XI, Pataudi totalled 2,036, the highest by any Wykehamist, scoring 1,068 in his last season with an average of 71, and in August making 52 for Sussex against the champion county, Yorkshire. Winning his blue as a freshman, he made 131 in the drawn University match of 1960, and next summer, with 3 matches still to come, needed only 92 more runs to surpass his father's record aggregate for an Oxford season of 1,307, when tragic damage to an eye in a motor accident at Hove ended his cricket for that season.

Though the sight of that eye was permanently affected, he fought his way back with great courage and so successfully as to be picked in the last 3 Test Matches for India against the MCC touring team of 1961–62, making a hundred in the Fifth at Madras. Returning to captain Oxford in 1963, he made over 800 runs for the University, and 51 in their drawn game at Lord's. Soon afterwards he was leading India against England in India and scoring 203 not out in the Fourth Test in New Delhi. All told he captained India 22 times, in England, Australia, New Zealand and India. He was never more brilliant than against Australia at Melbourne in 1968, when, with a badly strained leg, he scored 75 and 85.

A natural ball-games player of compact physique and great speed of reaction and footwork, Pataudi's batting, even as a boy, against good bowling, could be authoritative in the versatility and wonderful timing of his strokeplay; as a fielder he was in the very highest class. The determination with which he came back into cricket after his accident witnessed alike to his courage and to his devotion to the game.

H. S. ALTHAM

CAREER FIGURES

	INNS	NO	RUNS	HS	AVGE	100S
Batting	500	41	15425	203*	33·60	28

Bowling 10 wkts at 77·60 Ct 207

Test Record (46)

	INNS	NO	RUNS	HS	AVGE	100S
Batting	83	3	2793	203*	34·91	6

Bowling 1 wkt for 88 Ct 27

The Nawab of Pataudi (or as he is now known Mansur Ali Khan) led India in 40 Tests, with almost no sight in his right eye.

PAYNTER, Edward (1901–1978)

Clayton-le-Moors Secondary Sch. Lancashire 1926–1939. England: in England 1931, 1932, 1937, 1938, 1939; in Australia 1932–33; in South Africa 1938–39; in New Zealand 1932–33.

Paynter was a good county batsman and a great Test Match one. Against Australia in Tests he averaged 84·42. He began with 77 in a crisis. In his next Test he rose from his sickbed to save the side with a historic innings of 83. At Nottingham in 1938 he made 216 not out, adding 206 in a record 5th-wicket stand with Compton. At Lord's, coming in at 31 for 3, he made 99 and helped Hammond to put on 222, another record. It was perhaps typical that at the Oval, the scoreboard reading 546 for 3, he did not score. His omission from the 1934 Tests and from Allen's team in Australia seems almost incredible. He was a left-hander, the natural counter to the leg-spin on which Australia then largely relied, and, being very quick on his feet, was by nature an attacker, but could defend doggedly when necessary. In South Africa in 1938–39, his Test average was 81 and for all Tests throughout his career 59. He was a glorious fieldsman and thrower, and at Lord's in 1938 kept wicket competently when Ames was injured.

R. L. ARROWSMITH

CAREER FIGURES

	INNS	NO	RUNS	HS	AVGE	100S
Batting	533	58	20075	322	42·26	45

Bowling 30 wkts at 45·70 Ct 156

Test Record (20)

	INNS	NO	RUNS	HS	AVGE	100S
Batting	31	5	1540	243	59·23	4

Ct 7

PEEBLES, Ian Alexander Ross (1908–1980)

Glasgow Acad 1922–1924. Oxford Univ 1930. Middlesex 1928–1948 (Captain 1939). Scotland 1937. England: in England 1930, 1931; in South Africa 1927–28, 1930–31.

For a brief period in and around 1930, at a time, moreover, when England was richer in leg-spin and googly bowling than it ever was or has been since, Ian Peebles was rated by the best judges (including the Test selectors) as the finest of the bunch. Tall and with a smooth, flowing run-up culminating in a high delivery he posed a dual problem of flight and break which kept the best batsmen at full stretch, ever watchful for the enticing ball that asks to be driven and proves not to be quite 'there'.

A son of the manse, Peebles was sufficiently confident of his talents to come down from Scotland on a brief holiday to the Aubrey Faulkner School of Cricket. He was promptly offered the secretaryship of the School by the great South African all-rounder, and was soon spotted by Plum Warner who was so impressed that he engineered a place for him on the strong but not representative MCC team to South Africa in 1927–28. Peebles took 34 wickets on the South African mat, and in 1929 came to the front with 107 wickets for Middlesex – this was the year when for the only time in history 3 amateurs took 100 wickets for the same county, the other two being R. W. V. Robins and N. Haig.

In the 1930 University Match, though Oxford went down to catastrophic defeat and the chances missed off him reputedly went into double figures, Peebles took 13 wickets for 237 in 81 overs. A fortnight later, in the Fourth Test, came the classic duel at Old Trafford with Bradman, who had been carrying all before him. On a slow but not vicious turner Peebles had him first missed at 1st slip, then caught at 2nd for 14. Though Bradman resumed his conquering way in the concluding Test at the Oval, Peebles was called upon for 71 overs, his 6 for 204 contrasting with the meagre returns of the rest, notably Larwood and Tate whose 2 wickets, 1 apiece, cost 285.

A successful tour to South Africa with MCC immediately followed, and he was England's best bowler in 1931 against New Zealand. But the long winter days and months of bowling at Faulkner's School as a teenager, followed by several thousand overs in his early 20s, caused a muscular weakness of the shoulder the effect of which was to take the fizz out of the leg-break. At the School he had taught himself to bowl left-arm, occasionally to relieve the strain. With the googly now his chief weapon, he remained a bowler to be reckoned with up to the Second World War, during which he sustained the almost total loss of his right eye. In 1939, succeeding Robins as captain, he brought Middlesex in (for the 4th successive year) as Championship runners-up, relishing most without a doubt the last-wicket stand at Canterbury with Jim Smith which enabled the latter to make his one and only hundred – in 81 minutes.

After the war he brought to a wider audience the wit and gift of anecdote which had long entertained his fellow-cricketers. Cricket correspondent erstwhile of *The Sunday Times*, for whom he toured Australia twice and also West Indies, he later contributed to *The Observer* and *The Guardian*. Though by trade a wine merchant, he found time to write a dozen books, of which the best perhaps is the autobiographical *Spinner's Yarn* which in 1977 won the Cricket Society's Literary Award.

E. W. SWANTON

CAREER FIGURES

	INNS	NO	RUNS	HS	AVGE	100S
Batting	330	101	2213	58	9·66	–

Bowling 923 wkts at 21·38 Ct 174

Test Record (13)

	INNS	NO	RUNS	HS	AVGE	100S
Batting	17	8	98	26	10·88	–

Bowling 45 wkts at 30·91 Ct 5

PEEL, Robert (1857–1941)

Yorkshire 1882–1897. England: in England 1888, 1890, 1893, 1896; in Australia 1884–85, 1887–88, 1891–92, 1894–95.

One of Yorkshire's famous left-hand slow bowlers, Peel was also a batsman to be reckoned with. He exceeded 100 wickets 9 times in 16 seasons, and did the double in the last but one, twice failing to do so by only a few runs. He helped Yorkshire to beat the Australians in 1888, and that year at Sydney, dismissed them for 42. His 7 for 31 at Old Trafford ensured another English victory. His highest score in a Test was 83, but at Sydney, in 1894–95, his 6 for 67 gained a thrilling 10-run triumph after England had followed on. His last Test was at Kennington Oval in 1896, when he took 6 for 23 in the 2nd innings, dismissing Australia for 44. In that year he made his highest score – 210 not out, in partnership with Lord Hawke (166) – against Warwickshire. The 8th-wicket stand produced 292. It was all the sadder that his career with the county should have concluded with a celebration, which, being continued in a singular performance on the cricket field, brought about his dismissal from the side.

G. D. MARTINEAU

CAREER FIGURES

	INNS	NO	RUNS	HS	AVGE	100S
Batting	689	66	12135	210*	19·46	7

Bowling 1754 wkts at 16·21 Ct 215

Test Record (20)

	INNS	NO	RUNS	HS	AVGE	100S
Batting	33	4	427	83	14·72	–

Bowling 102 wkts at 16·81 Ct 17

PERKS, Reginald Thomas David (1911–1977)

Worcestershire 1930–1955. England: in England 1939; in South Africa 1938–39.

Reg Perks bowled right-arm fast-medium with good control. He could move the ball into and away from the bat and was never easy to get away. During his long and honourable career he took more wickets for his county than any other bowler. No less than 16 times he accomplished the feat of taking 100 wickets in a season and twice did the hat-trick. As a left-handed batsman he was a good hitter of the ball who liked to chance his arm. Perks only played in 2 Test Matches just before the Second World War including the last prewar Test, against West Indies in 1939. If it had not been for the war he might well have gone down in history as something more than the great and loyal county cricketer that he was.

E. D. R. EAGAR

CAREER FIGURES

	INNS	NO	RUNS	HS	AVGE	100S
Batting	884	150	8956	75	12·20	

Bowling 2233 wkts at 24·07 Ct 244

Test Record (2)

	INNS	NO	RUNS	HS	AVGE	100S
Batting	2	2	3	2*	–	–

Bowling 11 wkts at 32·27 Ct 1

PHILLIPS, James (1851–1930)

Victoria 1885–86 to 1895–96. Middlesex 1890–1898. Canterbury 1898–99. Test Umpire 1884–85 to 1905–06.

Though he was a useful batsman and a good medium-pace bowler, to most people Phillips will always be the umpire who put a temporary end to throwing. For years, despite the efforts of Lord Harris, there had been flagrant throwers in first-class cricket. Phillips began by no-balling Ernest Jones in a Test Match in Australia in 1897–98, and next summer no-balled C. B. Fry in England. Other umpires followed suit and finally, in 1901, Phillips himself no-balled Arthur Mold 16 times in an innings. That was virtually the end, and for 50 years throwing ceased to be a problem.

R. L. ARROWSMITH

CAREER FIGURES

	INNS	NO	RUNS	HS	AVGE	100S
Batting	203	58	1826	110*	12·59	1

Bowling 355 wkts at 20.00 Ct 50

POLLOCK, Peter Maclean (1941–)

Grey HS, Port Elizabeth. Eastern Province 1958–59 to 1971–72. South Africa: in South Africa 1961–62, 1964–65, 1966–67, 1969–70; in England 1965; in Australia 1963–64; in New Zealand 1963–64. Rest of the World in England 1970.

Peter Pollock, a genuinely fast bowler in his prime, was one of the talented players who raised South African cricket in the 1960s to perhaps its highest peak. In 1969–70, in the last series before South Africa were forced out of Test cricket, Australia were beaten 4 times in 4 matches by huge margins and Pollock, with a formidable young partner in Mike Procter, took 15 wickets at 17 apiece.

Peter Pollock: 116 wickets in 28 Tests.

He had by then cut his pace since his earlier successes which began against New Zealand in Durban in 1961–62 when his match figures were 9 for 99. He took 25 wickets in the series in Australia 2 years later, but his most memorable feats were the 5 for 53 and 5 for 34 which helped South Africa to win the Trent Bridge Test and, as it proved, the series in England in 1965. His younger brother, Graeme, made 125 in the same match.

Peter Pollock stood nearly 6 feet 3 inches and bowled with a good rhythmic action after one of the longer runs up to the wicket. He took 116 Test wickets at 24 apiece. He was a competent batsman whose positioning at No. 10 illustrated South Africa's great depth of batting at that time. It was often said, not entirely frivolously, that Graeme Pollock, a somewhat uncertain starter, should ideally have had his brother to play the first 20 minutes of an innings for him.

MICHAEL MELFORD

CAREER FIGURES

	INNS	NO	RUNS	HS	AVGE	100S
Batting	177	44	3028	79	22·76	–

Bowling 485 wkts at 21·89 Ct 67

Test Record (28)

	INNS	NO	RUNS	HS	AVGE	100S
Batting	41	13	607	75*	21·67	–

Bowling 116 wkts at 24·18 Ct 9

POLLOCK, Robert Graeme (1944–)

Grey HS, Port Elizabeth. Eastern Province 1960–61– . South Africa: in South Africa 1964–65, 1966–67, 1969–70; in England 1965; in Australia 1963–64; in New Zealand 1963–64. Rest of the World in England 1970.

If his Test career had been allowed to run its normal course there is no telling how high Graeme Pollock might by now have ranked as a batsman in world estimation. As it was, political events cut short his Test career at the age of 26, by which time he had made already 3 hundreds against England, 5 against Australia, and convinced all who had eyes to see that here was a young batsman worthy to be accounted in the highest class.

Pollock lost no time in announcing his promise as a tall, exceptionally gifted left-handed bat. Before his 17th birthday he became the youngest man to score a hundred in the Currie Cup. Two years later he was the youngest South African to score a double first-class hundred. His 20th birthday came at the end of a tour to Australia and New Zealand, which brought him 1,111 runs, an average in the 50s and a half-share in a stand of 341 for the 3rd wicket with E. J. Barlow in the Adelaide Test Match.

The innings which stamped itself so indelibly upon all who saw it on television or who were lucky enough (as was the writer) to watch it in the flesh, was his 125 against England at Trent Bridge in 1965. When Pollock was taking his bearings on the 1st morning, the South African effort was poised between success and failure. Soon the board showed 80 for 5. Without straining after effect, using the classic strokes of his type, and especially those on the off-side off the front foot, Pollock now batted with a quintessence of timing and fluent power. He made 125 out of 160 in 2 hours 20 minutes, and if ever one innings stamped its maker among the great this was it.

Graeme Pollock: the lofted on-drive, a perfect example.

In the last Test series yet played by South Africa, when the Australians toured the Republic with such scant success in 1969–70, he made at Durban the South African record Test score of 274, and in the 4 Tests averaged 73. Since then he has, inevitably, scored heavily in the Currie Cup, but, of course, he has been playing below his true level. Who knows what the spur of top-rank competition might not have produced?

E. W. SWANTON

PONSFORD, William Harold (1900–)

Alfred Crescent Sch, Melbourne. Victoria 1920–21 to 1933–34. Australia: in Australia 1924–25, 1928–29, 1930–31, 1931–32, 1932–33; in England 1926, 1930, 1934.

The names Woodfull and Ponsford are inseparably linked in cricket history and represent one of the most successful Australian opening partnerships in both Test Match and Sheffield Shield cricket. Seldom can 2 partners have had such close understanding, almost identical records and yet been so different in method. Ponsford made his 1st appearance for Victoria against MCC in 1920, but after a meagre batting success did not reappear until the season 1922–23, after he had broken MacLaren's record by making 429 against Tasmania. In 1924–25 he played in the First Test against England at Sydney and, having survived a hazardous first meeting with Tate, made 110. In the Second Test at Melbourne he made 128 but this was the last hundred he scored against England in Australia. His first trip to this country in 1926 brought him little success in the series, but on his return to Sheffield Shield cricket he had a remarkable run the the following year. In December 1927 he scored 1,146 runs in 5 innings, breaking his own record with 437 against Queensland. This did not presage success against Chapman's side of 1928–29, for Larwood, having dismissed him twice for paltry scores in the First Test, put him out for good with a broken finger in the Second. 1930 brought him full success in England but once again, in 1932–33, Larwood's speed prematurely halted his progress, and he was dropped from the Australian side. In 1934 his career ended gloriously when he averaged 94 in Test Matches, whereupon he announced his retirement at the early age of 34.

This variable record reflects fairly closely the general estimate of Ponsford's abilities. He was a truly great player of spin, but suspect against the highest class of fast bowling. He was a particularly good player on slow English wickets, the bane of so many overseas batsmen, a talent largely attributable to the good use he made of his top, or left hand. A squarely-built man with wide pads always in close adjacency to the bat he gave the bowler the impression of an impassable barrier. His movements had a ponderous air, but his footwork was sharp and precise so that in defence he was always perfectly positioned to push the ball between the field. He had a wealth of strokes all round the wicket but was specially strong around the leg stump, placing the ball through any available gap, and continually harassing the defenders. At the wicket a temperament prone to anxiety gave him a somewhat taciturn air which belied an amiable and friendly disposition. He was for some years a popular and efficient assistant secretary to the Melbourne Cricket Club.

IAN PEEBLES

CAREER FIGURES

	INNS	NO	RUNS	HS	AVGE	100S
Batting	235	23	13819	437	65·18	47

Bowling 0 wkt for 41 Ct 71

Test Record (29)

	INNS	NO	RUNS	HS	AVGE	100S
Batting	48	4	2122	266	48·22	7

Ct 21

PRASANNA, Erapalli Anatharao Srinivasa (1940–)

National Coll, Bangalore. Mysore 1961–62– . India: in India 1961–62, 1966–67, 1969–70, 1972–73, 1974–75, 1976–77; in England 1967, 1974; in Australia 1967–68, 1977–78; in West Indies 1961–62, 1970–71, 1975–76; in New Zealand 1967–68, 1975–76; in Pakistan 1978–79.

E. A. S. Prasanna, a master of flight.

Prasanna belonged to the magic circle of spinners who helped Indian cricket to the top in the early 1970s. Yet his best years were when he virtually had to go it alone, on the true, fast wickets of Australia in 1967–68. From that tour he returned with 25 wickets and his reputation made. Ian Chappell considers him to be the best of his type he has ever played. When Bedi arrived on the scene, and India's close-in fielding improved dramatically, Prasanna joined in to play a major role in victory over Australia at Delhi in 1969–70 and in an earlier series against New Zealand.

With the ability to make the ball hum and drift like a 'yo-yo', Prasanna's mastery of flight and spin raised his particular type of bowling to a fine art. With Chandrasekhar in support, he captained Karnataka to 2 rare triumphs in the Ranji Trophy. His main challenger, Venkataraghavan, was also an engineer by profession; Prasanna's flight and variety, however, were an aesthetic delight.

K. N. PRABHU

PRESTON, Hubert (1868–1960)

Editor of *Wisden* 1944–1951.

A journalist of the old school, Hubert Preston joined the Pardon brothers at their cricket reporting agency in Fleet Street in 1895, thus beginning an association with *Wisden* that was to last for more than half-a-century. After the First World War – in which he served in the East Surrey Regiment – he became a partner, and was a familiar and courteous figure on cricket grounds throughout the country. Most players of note counted him as a friend and his criticism was always fair and constructive. He was a meticulous writer who could be vivid within a few words. He was editor of *Wisden* between 1944 and 1951, when he was succeeded by his son, Norman. In youth he played cricket for Brixton Wanderers, and at Lord's he performed the hat-trick for the Press against the Authors.

IRVING ROSENWATER

PROCTER, Michael John (1946–)

Hilton Coll, Natal. Gloucestershire 1965– (Captain 1977–). Natal 1965–66 to 1968–69 and 1976–77– . Western Province 1969–70. Rhodesia 1970–71. South Africa: in South Africa 1966–67, 1969–70. Rest of the World in England 1970. WSC.

Of all the post-1945 importations into English cricket, none has become so popular with the natives, none has identified himself so whole-heartedly with his adopted county, as Michael Procter. Not a naturally forthcoming man – Gloucestershire people at first mistook his diffidence for dourness, his shyness for sullenness – he gradually became as much a part of the scene of the Severn and Cotswolds as ever he had been of the Veld. 'Our Mike', they say of him in Gloucestershire, as they used to say 'Our Tom' in Goddard's time, and 'Our Walter' when Hammond was king.

Procter is an all-rounder; a fast bowler, at one time, just before Lillee, probably the fastest in the world; a batsman not quite so good as Barry Richards, but a harder trier than Richards when the pressure is on. Sometimes he has been too hard a trier to make sense. After taking a long time to recover from a knee injury (he had to be content with knocking them over with off-spinners during his convalescence), he decided that he might turn a Gillette Cup semi-final if he put in a few overs at high speed. He tried, and the knee bust. This was an occasion when the game was not worth the candle, even though he had a score or two to settle at Old Trafford. But that is the man, and I expect he would do it again.

Procter played 7 times for South Africa, and 5 times for the Rest of the World in 1970. In, say, 1975, when he was at his peak, he would have been the obvious choice to lead an Earth XI in the Galactic Championships. It would not have occurred to any of his team to ask what colour his captain happened to be, nor would it have crossed the captain's mind to enquire about the pigmentation blend of his team. It was not always thus: cricket has been a civilizing influence upon Procter, but so has Procter been a civilizing influence on cricket.

His batting style is classical. His bowling, however fearsome, and though he denies it, is mostly done off the wrong foot. That he has sustained such an action for so long with such success is an astonishing testimony to his strength.

ALAN GIBSON

QUAIFE, William (known as W. G. Quaife) (1872–1951)

Sussex 1891. Warwickshire 1893–1928. Griqualand West 1912–13. England: in England 1899; in Australia 1901–02.

This diminutive all-rounder, coming from Sussex, was one of those who seemed to go on for ever. A model batsman, a slow leg-break bowler and one of the finest cover fieldsmen, he was perhaps the smallest man who ever played for England against Australia. Only once did his batting come off in a Test Match, at Adelaide in January 1902, when he made 68 and 44. Twenty-four times did he make 1,000 runs, always showing perfect balance, footwork and control; and it was characteristic of the man that his last innings for Warwickshire at the age of 56 produced his 72nd hundred.

G. D. MARTINEAU

CAREER FIGURES

	INNS	NO	RUNS	HS	AVGE	100S
Batting	1203	185	36012	255*	35·38	72

Bowling 931 wkts at 27·38 Ct (incl. w/k) 347; st 1

Test Record (7)

	INNS	NO	RUNS	HS	AVGE	100S
Batting	13	1	228	68	19·00	–

Bowling 0 wkt for 6 Ct 4

RAIT KERR, Col Rowan Scrope, CBE, DSO, MC (1891–1961)

Rugby 1908–1909. Secretary MCC 1936–1952.

Colonel Rait Kerr was once described by Sir Pelham Warner as 'the ablest secretary the MCC have ever possessed'. On his 2 appearances for Rugby v Marlborough at Lord's he scored a half-century each year and as an Army batsman he scored many runs both in England and in India. In the summer of 1936 he assumed the secretaryship of MCC and brought to Lord's rich qualities that stemmed from a penetrating and agile mind. He had a deep knowledge of the structure of the modern game and made an exhaustive study of the laws of cricket, upon which he published the definitive work in 1950. Apart from the cares of administration he showed a sympathy for the literature, prints and paintings of cricket. His daughter, Miss Diana Rait Kerr, was curator of the MCC museum and library at Lord's from 1946 until she retired in 1968.

IRVING ROSENWATER

RAMADHIN, Sonny (1929–)

Canadian Mission Sch, Duncan Village, Trinidad. Trinidad from 1949–50. Lancashire 1964–65. West Indies: in West Indies 1952–53, 1953–54, 1954–55, 1959–60; in England 1950, 1957; in Australia 1951–52, 1960–61; in New Zealand 1951–52, 1955–56; in India 1958–59; in Pakistan 1958–59.

The South African googly bowlers who came to England in 1907 marked a new stage in slow bowling. Since that revolutionary tour nothing in slow bowling has so gripped the attention and wonder of the world of cricket as the performance of Valentine and Ramadhin for West Indies in the summer of 1950. Whereas the great slow bowlers have usually taken a decade or more to mature, each was barely 20 years of age when the season started. In 1934 Grimmett and O'Reilly had dominated English batting. O'Reilly was 29, Grimmett was already 42 – and ever since 1914 the master slow bowlers have taken 10 years to mature.

A friendless orphan, 'Sonny' Ramadhin was helped, as a budding cricketer and otherwise, by a Barbadian inter-colonial cricketer living in Trinidad. Two trial games were the only first-class matches before his selection for England, and John Goddard and Jeffrey Stollmeyer should be remembered for

'Sonny' Ramadhin: leg-break or off-break? The mystery the batsman had to solve.

one of the boldest and most successful adventures in the history of cricket selection. Ramadhin in a one-day trial match against Indian Gymkhana took 5 for 9; in the 2nd match against Yorkshire he took 4 for 30 and up to the last game at Scarborough, when he took 10 wickets for 85, he and his partner were never mastered by any line of English batsmen.

What exactly was his degree of skill as compared to the great masters of slow bowling? It is, of course, difficult to state. But he had the unique virtue, impeccable length; he turned the ball from the off, but, though no googly bowler, he bowled a leg-break or one that straightened. Walcott, who kept wicket to him all through the season, has admitted that to the end he could not tell which way Ramadhin would turn the ball.

Ramadhin went to Australia and in the First Test at Brisbane completely mystified the Australian batsmen. But afterwards, under a planned and determined assault by Miller, he did not live up to expectations. Against India in the West Indies Ramadhin again was disappointing but he had a faculty of recovery and against the formidable array of batsmen in the 1953–54 MCC side he bowled a maiden over in every 3 and took 23 wickets, far more than anyone else on either side. Against Australia in the West Indies he failed badly. But when he came to England again in 1957, he bowled at times as devastatingly as ever. He had, however, what proved to be a traumatic experience in the First Test at Edgbaston. In the 1st innings he seemed as mystifying as in 1950; in the 2nd innings, May and Cowdrey faced him with a planned resolution and put on 411 runs. In addition Ramadhin was over-bowled. He never recovered and in the remaining Tests of the season he was singularly innocuous. He started well in Australia in 1960–61 but when he wavered, another off-spinner, Gibbs, supplanted him and he dropped out of the West Indies side. Kent aimed to make him one of their professionals but it was Lancashire for whom he played a little in the mid-1960s and for whom he showed much of his old skill. Finally, before retiring to keep a public house in the North of England, he had several successful seasons with Lincolnshire.

C. L. R. JAMES

CAREER FIGURES

	INNS	NO	RUNS	HS	AVGE	100S
Batting	191	65	1106	44	8·77	–

Bowling 758 wkts at 20·24 Ct 38

Test Record (43)

	INNS	NO	RUNS	HS	AVGE	100S
Batting	58	14	361	44	8·20	–

Bowling 158 wkts at 28·98 Ct 9

RANDALL, Derek William (1951–)

Frederick Milner Secondary Modern Sch, Retford. Nottinghamshire 1972– . England: in England 1977, 1979; in Australia 1976–77, 1978–79, 1979–80; in New Zealand 1977–78; in India 1976–77; in Pakistan 1977–78.

There is a radio programme which seems to have been running as long as the BBC itself called *Desert Island Discs* during which composers and opera singers, generals and novelists are invited to pick first 8, and then one, favourite gramophone record with which to be shipwrecked. During his turn Derek Randall chose a cheerful singalong chorus: 'The sun has got his hat on, Hip Hip Hip Hooray: the sun has got his hat on and he's coming out to play'. Here he comes now, this imp that strayed across the border from Lincolnshire to Nottinghamshire, to Retford, a declining railway town that he has put back on the map. If we are at Lord's he has turned round to make sure that the gate is shut; if this is Sydney he's hopping, skipping and jumping to the wicket, miming shots as he goes. As far as Australian bowlers are concerned he is like a bunsen burner under a retort. Their blood boils and they start to steam.

Wise old heads see him jumping up and down from dressing room benches and tables, hear him talking to himself in the nets – 'Come on, Arkle, Come on' – and shake in wondrous disbelief. Is this the heir to 'obbs, 'ammond and 'utton? *Vive l' ingenu.* Maddening he may be, a desperate fellow to captain in a side whose batting is as brittle as ricepaper. Yet at his best Derek Randall can rival the strokemakers of the West Indies. Nor is this all. Hardly an innings passes when he does not contrive a run-out or disturb a batsman with a near-miss. He is the finest England cover-point since Hobbs. And Hutton, Hutton of all people his temperamental antithesis has said he is worth playing for England for his fielding alone.

It is impossible to assess his contribution to a team. As I write this, he is now the outfield star of the best England fielding side in history. How will he change, this joker? Will he for ever need to feel the bat hard on the ball at the start of his innings? What will happen when his eye goes? Or when his appetite for the cheers, for the affection that only a clown can command, begins to wane? He needs to be skippered. Who can do it but Brearley? What will become of him? Oh God of cricket, let it be good, for he has given much to your game.

ROBIN MARLAR

RANJITSINHJI, HH the Maharajah Jam Sahib of Nawanagar (1872–1933)

Rajkumar Coll, India. Cambridge Univ 1893. Sussex 1895–1920 (Captain 1899–1903). England: in England 1896, 1899, 1902; in Australia 1897–98.

K. S. Ranjitsinhji (from 1907 Maharajah the Jam Sahib of Nawanagar) bridged the turn of the century with batsmanship as brilliant as the game has ever known. Coming up to Cambridge with little cricket background, he did not get a blue until his last year, 1893; but 2 years later at Lord's and in his 1st match for Sussex he made 77 not out and 150, and never looked back. In 1896 he beat W.G.'s record with an aggregate of 2,780, made 62 and 154 not out in his 1st Test Match against Australia, and scored 100 and 125 not out against Yorkshire in a single day. For A. E. Stoddart's team in 1897–98, he made 189 in his 1st innings in Australia, and 175 in his 1st Test Match there. Then in 1899 and 1900 he dominated English cricket with aggregates of 3,159 and 3,065, the latter including 5 scores of over 200; of these perhaps the greatest was his 202 against Middlesex, made in 3 hours when all his partners could total no more than 70. His highest score was the 285 not out which he made against Somerset at Taunton in 1901, the more remarkable because he had been up all the previous night – fishing. He captained Sussex for 5 years, 1899–1903, and in his last full season with them, 1904, again made over 2,000 and headed the English averages. In all he made 72 hundreds and 24,692 runs.

'Ranji's' impact upon batting technique was historic: with him, even against the fastest bowling, the back stroke replaced 'bridge-building' forward play as the basis of defence; in late-cutting and leg deflection he opened new vistas of timing and adventure, and he would flash down the wicket to drive with murderous severity. His bat seemed a scimitar, and his execution the expression not so much of art as of oriental magic. A man of basic loyalties and sense of duty, he did valuable service on the Indian Council of Princes and in the League of Nations where, as on the cricket field, his modesty, natural dignity and unfailing kindness won him both affection and respect.

H. S. ALTHAM

CAREER FIGURES

	INNS	NO	RUNS	HS	AVGE	100S
Batting	500	62	24692	285*	56·37	72

Bowling 133 wkts at 34·59 Ct 234

Test Record (15)

	INNS	NO	RUNS	HS	AVGE	100S
Batting	26	4	989	175	44·95	2

Bowling 1 wkt for 39 Ct 13

REDPATH, Ian Ritchie, MBE (1941–)

Geelong Coll. Victoria 1961–62 to 1975–76 (Captain 1967–68 to 1974–75). Australia: in Australia 1963–64, 1965–66, 1967–68, 1968–69, 1970–71, 1972–73, 1974–75, 1975–76; in England 1964, 1968; in South Africa 1966–67, 1969–70; in West Indies 1972–73; in New Zealand 1973–74; in India 1964–65, 1969–70; in Pakistan 1964–65. WSC.

Ian Redpath belongs to that host of cricketers whose worth, while not unrecognized by spectators, is most fully admired by their team mates – and opponents. Tall, spare, angular, long-necked, wide-stanced, there was nothing smooth or elegant about his batting; it may indeed have been his very awkwardness that made him such a favourite. 'Redder' he was to Australian crowds, and nobody watching him cannily settling down to bat could doubt that here was a man giving of his best. Redpath did not so much build an innings as slowly melt into his surroundings, so that after a time opponents tended to treat him like a dully-aching tooth – inconvenient and better out than in, but tolerable provided he did not get above himself.

Whatever his appearance, however – and with daylight showing between bat and well-spread feet there was a suggestion in his stance of an old man leaning on his walking stick – he was a brilliant negotiator of fast bowling with a particular aptitude for what bridge-players call 'avoidance play'. One seldom saw him caught in the slips or at the wicket from a ball wide enough to leave alone, while on the leg-side he had a habit of hollowing his back to dodge the riser. But he was not afraid of being hurt and often accepted a hit rather than risk giving a catch off a high defensive stroke. He was adept at the angled strokes past gulley and off his legs and on-drove solidly. But the lasting impression of a Redpath innings was not the shots he played. It was his doggedness, unpretentious courage and adhesiveness.

Quick reflexes and safe hands enabled him to take 83 catches in 66 Tests – a high success rate for other than a 1st-slip fielder – and he was still as lean as when he had played his last Test 3 years earlier when he came out of retirement to sign for WSC in 1977. By rupturing an achilles tendon in a warm-up game, he enabled Kerry Packer to demonstrate one of the main attractions of his cricket from the players' point of view – contractual protection against injury.

JOHN THICKNESSE

REID, John Richard, OBE (1928–)

Hutt Valley HS. Wellington from 1947–48 (Captain 1951–52). Otago 1956–57. New Zealand: in New Zealand 1950–51, 1951–52, 1952–53, 1954–55, 1955–56 (Captain), 1958–59 (Captain), 1962–63 (Captain), 1963–64 (Captain), 1964–65 (Captain); in England 1949, 1958 (Captain), 1965 (Captain); in South Africa 1953–54, 1961–62 (Captain); in India 1955–56, 1964–65 (Captain); in Pakistan 1955–56, 1964–65 (Captain).

John Reid is one of the 2 best all-round cricketers ever produced by New Zealand. Only Bev Congdon runs him close. Reid played in 58 Test Matches, batting, bowling, fielding and sometimes keeping wicket with the flair of the natural player and the strength of an Olympic weight-lifter. From 1958 until 1965 he captained them, better and more patiently as it dawned on him that few cricketers of whatever nationality were possessed of such a talent as his. While on tour of South Africa in 1953–54 he became the 1st cricketer ever to score 1,000 runs and take 50 wickets in a season. Eight years later, also in South Africa, he broke every batting record, including even Denis Compton's aggregate on the MCC tour of 1948–49.

JOHN WOODCOCK

John Reid: a great New Zealand cricketer

CAREER FIGURES

	INNS	NO	RUNS	HS	AVGE	100S
Batting	418	28	16128	296	41·35	39

Bowling 466 wkts at 22·60 Ct (incl. w/k) 229; st 7

Test Record (58)

	INNS	NO	RUNS	HS	AVGE	100S
Batting	108	5	3428	142	33·28	6

Bowling 85 wkts at 33·35 W/k: ct 43; st 1 Total 44

RHODES, Wilfred (1877–1973)

Yorkshire 1898–1930. England: in England 1899, 1902, 1905, 1909, 1912, 1921, 1926; in Australia 1903–04, 1907–08, 1911–12, 1920–21; in South Africa 1909–10, 1913–14; in West Indies 1929–30.

On sheer weight of figures Wilfred Rhodes has perhaps as strong a claim as any cricketer to be bracketed with 'W.G.'. Only 10 batsmen exceed his aggregate of 39,802 runs, and no bowler approaches his total of 4,187 wickets – indeed, only 3 others have exceeded 3,000. Only Hirst is within 6 of his 16 doubles of 1,000 runs and 100 wickets in the same season, and only Freeman and Shackleton within 7 of his 23 years of taking 100 wickets.

Appearing first for Yorkshire in 1898, he lost no time in making his mark, taking 13 wickets for 48 against Somerset in his 2nd match and next year bowling unchanged through a match with F. S. Jackson for an analysis of 15 for 56; indeed no bowler has ever asserted his authority with anything that can compare with his 154 wickets in his opening summer, and his 1,251 in his first 5 years. Of these 261 fell to him in 1900, a very wet season; but to confound the carpers who prophesied that he would find it a very different story in a dry one, he took only 10 less in the halycon summer of 1901. For 5 years he took a lowly place in the Yorkshire order but, not out at the end of more than a quarter of the innings he played, his batting potential was obvious, and his 6th year saw the first of 20 successive seasons in which he totalled over 1,000 runs, the last of them in 1926 when he was 48 years old. First capped for England in 1899, he had a wonderful day at Birmingham in 1902 when he and Hirst dismissed the subsequently triumphant Australian side for 36, and his analysis was 7 for 17; but perhaps even more impressive was his 15 wickets for 124 in the Melbourne Test 2 winters later. By 1909 batting had become his primary role, and his 1st opening Test partnership with Hobbs at Johannesburg in 1909–10 produced 159 runs, but was surpassed by their 221 together in the last at Cape Town; even this faded beside their 323 at Melbourne 2 years later, still the highest ever made against Australia.

After the First World War, refusing heavy pressure to go into League cricket, Rhodes returned to the Yorkshire side and astonished everybody by the recovery of his bowling form to the tune of 325 wickets in 1919 and 1920. He was still taking 100 wickets in his 51st year, but the day that probably gave him most pleasure to remember was the last of the Oval Test in 1926, when, recalled to play against Australia at the age of 48, he took 4 for 44 in 20 overs to win the rubber for England. His last match was at Scarborough in 1930, and appropriately he took a wicket with the last ball he bowled. As a batsman Wilfred Rhodes was Yorkshire through and through, dedicated, combative, tenacious. His defence was eminently sound, and he commanded a variety of strokes on both sides of the wicket.

But his batting can be termed almost pedestrian compared with the classic art of his slow left-hand bowling: an action of balanced economy but beautiful rhythm was the basis for supreme control of both length and direction; he could turn the ball on wickets that gave no help, and on those that did its bite and lift were deadly. His greatest gift lay in his power to torment, and sooner or later – so often sooner – fatally seduce the batsman with subtle variations of arc and flight. 'Here no man stood beside him, the laurel was all his own'.

H. S. ALTHAM

CAREER FIGURES

	INNS	NO	RUNS	HS	AVGE	100S
Batting	1528	237	39802	267*	30·83	58

Bowling 4187 wkts at 16·71 Ct 708

Test Record (58)

	INNS	NO	RUNS	HS	AVGE	100S
Batting	98	21	2325	179	30·19	2

Bowling 127 wkts at 26·96 Ct 60

RICHARDS, Barry Anderson (1945–)

Durban HS. Natal 1964–65 to 1975–76 (Captain 1973–74). Glos 1965. Hampshire 1968–1978. South Australia 1970–71. South Africa: in South Africa 1969–70. Rest of the World in England 1970. WSC.

Barry Richards was for some years, around 1970 to 1975, the best batsman in the world. He was one of those whose career would have taken a different course, had it not been for the cricketing breach with South Africa. The new career which he adopted – he was the first of the really high-class *caballeros* to roam the world – brought him much more money than an ordinary Test career would have done. Whether he is better pleased with this outcome it is hard to say. Many men who feel deeply take care to conceal their feelings; others appear unemotional because they have no deep emotions.

Richards was born at Durban in 1945. He was captain of the South African Schools side which toured England in 1963. In 1964 he played for Natal; in 1965 he had a season with Gloucestershire, not qualified for the county and so playing 2nd XI cricket. M. J. Procter was his colleague in this adventure. They decided that county cricket had insufficient appeal for them and went back to South Africa. Richards returned, now to Hampshire, in 1968, and left them in 1978, soon after he had signed for Mr Packer.

He played 4 matches for South Africa against Australia, and 5 matches for the Rest

Barry Richards: in the mid-1970s the best batsman in the world. Here his genius is shown as he cover drives a ball from outside the leg stump, (note the position of Engineer's gloves.)

of the World against England. Although he scored heavily for Hampshire, his heart was never in the 3-day game, which seemed to him the worst of both worlds. Some of his most dramatically beautiful innings have been in limited-over matches. He also played, fruitfully, for South Australia. He became a kind of cricketing Wallenstein, and he fell (at least from grace) because, as was said of Wallenstein, no man could divine his motives, and he has no country of his own. He is fair, tall, athletic, and there can have been few batsmen who were better technically, with so comprehensive a range of handsome strokes.

ALAN GIBSON

Vivian Richards: after another hundred in the heat.

RICHARDS, Isaac Vivian Alexander (1952–)

Antigua GS. Leeward Islands 1971–72. Combined Islands 1971–72– . Somerset 1974– . Queensland 1976–77. West Indies: in West Indies 1975–76, 1976–77, 1977–78; in England 1976; in Australia 1975–76; in India 1974–75; in Pakistan 1974–75. WSC.

Vivian Richards became, probably, the best batsman in the world as Barry Richards passed his peak. He was certainly the best of the West Indies batsmen, in his prime. Enthusiasts declare that he is the best of *all* West Indian batsmen there have ever been, but enthusiasts do say these things, and anyone who saw Headley, and the 'three Ws' (I am counting Sobers as an all-rounder), will have reservations. Somerset pulled off a notable stroke of business when they persuaded him to join them in 1974. That was only 22 years after he had been born, in Antigua. He had already played for the Combined Islands but not, then, for the West Indies. He has subsequently played for Queensland, and for Packer. He holds the record for the number of Test runs in a calendar year: 1710 in 11 Tests in 1976. Of these, 829 were scored in 4 Tests against England.

Richards has an element of unpredictability in his masterful strokeplay which is a special delight, not only to the Sunday sloghunters but to the connoisseur. A fast bowler, tired of trying to plug the gaps on the off-side, will switch his field and bowl a full length outside the leg stump. Richards will step away and hit him for six over extra-cover. I have seen this happen more than once. Yet the foundations of his play are classical. He also bowls a bit, little off-breaks and sometimes little seamers.

As a young man he sometimes wavered: not exactly in concentration, more in the clarity of his own intent. He has found responsibility weighing upon him, because he is always anxious to do the best for his side. Thus in 1978, when Somerset (who had never won anything) had the chance of winning 2 competitions in 2 days, he played too cautiously on the Saturday in the Gillette Cup; and then, over-reacting, too dashingly on the Sunday in the John Player. Barry Richards, if placed in a similar position for Hampshire, would have played his natural game each time, and probably won at least one, simply because he did not care so much about the result. Even so, the 2 Richardses played a single-wicket match at the end of that season and Vivian won.

ALAN GIBSON

CAREER FIGURES

	INNS	NO	RUNS	HS	AVGE	100S
Batting	794	41	26055	185	34·60	44

Bowling 11 wkts at 45·36 Ct 220

Test Record (34)

	INNS	NO	RUNS	HS	AVGE	100S
Batting	56	1	2061	126	37·47	5

Bowling 3 wkts at 16·00 Ct 6

RICHARDSON, Peter Edward (1931–)

Cathedral Sch, Hereford. Worcestershire 1949–1958 (Captain 1956–1958). Kent 1959–1965. England: in England 1956, 1957, 1958, 1963; in Australia 1958–59; in South Africa 1956–57; in New Zealand 1958–59; in India 1961–62; in Pakistan 1961–62.

Peter Richardson, a left-hand batsman from Hereford, was the eldest of 3 brothers to play county cricket. In 1953, only his 2nd full season with Worcestershire, he scored 2,294 runs. Three years later, after establishing his claims on the MCC 'A' tour of Pakistan, he returned home to lead his county side and open the England innings in all 5 Tests against Australia. In his 1st Test against Australia he scored 81 and 73, going on to 1,000 runs in fewer innings than any other Englishman in the history of Test cricket.

A lean spell in Australia in 1958–59 preceded his move from Worcestershire to Kent. This marked an immediate return to form, earning a tour of India and Pakistan in 1961–62, but only one subsequent appearance for England in England against West Indies in 1963. Kent were the richer for his skill. He scored 2,110 runs in all matches for them in 1963 and a hundred in each innings against the Australians at Canterbury in 1964. Short of stature, very strong in the forearm, achieving everything with the minimum back-lift, he built an innings upon watchful defence and the quick single. In later years he opened out, developing various attacking strokes of his own improvization. He became a member of the Kent Committee in 1979.

COLIN COWDREY

RICHARDSON, Thomas (1870–1912)

Surrey 1892–1904. Somerset 1905. England: in England 1893, 1896; in Australia 1894–95, 1897–98.

It is not difficult to make the claim on Tom Richardson's behalf that he was one of the greatest of fast bowlers. He looked the part: tall, splendidly built and proportioned, with a long – not too long – striding run culminating in a beautifully poised leap, left shoulder and side pointing down the wicket; the right arm swinging over, then finishing near or behind the left hip. The sweep of his arm and hand across the line of flight towards the left, and the swing of the upper part of the body in the same direction, produced the famous break-back which Richardson could perform on the hardest, fastest grounds.

It should be borne in mind that in Richardson's day only one ball was available to the fielding side throughout the longest innings. Moreover, Richardson did the bulk of his bowling on the flawless surface of the Kennington Oval wicket in the period of Sam Apted and his weighty, manually pulled roller. Flawless surface – but with pace. In 1894–95 Richardson sent down 3,554 balls in Australia, taking 69 wickets at 23·42 runs each; and after his haul of 273 wickets at home in 1897 he went to Australia again, bowled at last to his knees. W. H. Lockwood, Richardson's fast bowler foil and colleague for Surrey, said, when asked to measure himself against Richardson, 'I wasn't in the same street'. At Manchester, in the Test Match between England and Australia of 1896, Richardson bowled 68 5-ball overs in Australia's 1st innings of 412. On the 3rd and concluding day Australia needed 125 to win, England having had to follow-on. Richardson all but won the match. For 3 hours he attacked magnificently, taking 6 wickets before Australia scraped home. A catch was missed off him at the crisis.

Richardson was a good-natured soul, fond of a pot of ale at the end of a day's bowling. He was born at Byfleet and died at, of all places (and tragically), St Jean d'Arvey at the age of 41. His first-class seasons extended from 1892 to 1905 inclusive. He actually left Surrey at the end to play for Somerset; but he was then getting heavy and sluggish. In his prime he presented as handsome a sight as was ever seen in a cricket field: dark, black-haired, black-moustached, and he had twinkling gypsy eyes. When he came up to the wicket to release the ball he called to mind a great wave of the sea about to break. Strudwick standing yards back, would sometimes take the ball shoulder high. But Richardson never deliberately 'bounced'. If the pitch was nasty and he hit a batsman he was the first to run and rub the bruise. It was hard to believe that with so large a heart and such a noble physique he could have taken his own life, and it has recently been established that he did not.

NEVILLE CARDUS

CAREER FIGURES

	INNS	NO	RUNS	HS	AVGE	100S
Batting	481	124	3445	69	9·65	–

Bowling 2105 wkts at 18·42 Ct 127

Test Record (14)

	INNS	NO	RUNS	HS	AVGE	100S
Batting	24	8	177	25*	11·06	–

Bowling 88 wkts at 25·22 Ct 5

V. Y. Richardson: famous as gamesplayer, commentator and grandfather of the Chappells.

RICHARDSON, Victor York
(1894–1969)

Kyre Coll (now Scotch Coll), Adelaide. South Australia 1919–20 to 1937–38 (Captain 1921–22 to 1936–37). Australia: in Australia 1924–25, 1928–29, 1932–33; in England 1930; in South Africa 1935–36 (Captain).

Richardson was a great batsman in Sheffield Shield cricket who never quite reached the top rank in Test Matches, though he achieved some fine performances, notably an innings of 138 at Melbourne in 1924–25, and batted bravely against Jardine's team. Holding the bat rather low, he had an awkward stance, but could drive well on both sides of the wicket, was good off his legs and a beautiful hooker: in 1928–29 he created a sensation by hooking Larwood for 6 in the course of an innings of 231 for South Australia. His great weakness was outside the off-stump to anything that lifted or went away a little, and this probably explains his modest Test record. A great all-round games player, he was, even by Australian standards, a magnificent field, especially at mid-off, though in fact he could field anywhere. Endlessly cheerful, he was a lively, enterprising and unorthodox captain. Indeed in many ways he did not conform to the ordinary type of Australian cricketer and at times seemed to have more in common with an English amateur of the old school. He was grandfather of the Chappell brothers.

R. L. ARROWSMITH

CAREER FIGURES

	INNS	NO	RUNS	HS	AVGE	100S
Batting	297	12	10727	231	37·63	27

Bowling 8 wkts at 66·50

Test Record (19)

	INNS	NO	RUNS	HS	AVGE	100S
Batting	30	0	706	138	23·53	1

Ct 24

ROBERTS, Anderson Montgomery Everton (1951–)

Princess Margaret Sch, Antigua. Leeward Islands 1969–70. Combined Islands 1970–71– . Hampshire 1973–1978. New South Wales 1976–77. West Indies: in West Indies 1973–74, 1975–76, 1976–77, 1977–78; in England 1976; in Australia 1975–76, 1979–80; in India 1974–75; in Pakistan 1974–75. WSC.

Anderson Roberts of the West Indies, Hampshire, New South Wales and World Series Cricket, was born in Antigua in 1951, and would be by far that island's best cricketer had not Vivian Richards been born there the following year, thus reopening the question. Of all aspects of cricket, the speed of fast bowlers in their various epochs is the hardest to judge: even among their contemporaries we constantly encounter widely differing opinions. But we would be safe in placing Roberts among the half-dozen fastest since the Second World War. He took his 100th wicket in Test cricket after only 2 years, 144 days. That was in 1976, 3 years after he first played for Hampshire for whom he was occasionally devastating. He also had a knack of looking quite a formidable batsman at critical moments, as the Pakistanis discovered in the World Cup in 1975.

Roberts has been accused of bowling too many bouncers. Certainly he had nothing to be proud of in the Manchester Test of 1976, when he and Holding subjected Close and Edrich to a cruel bombardment ('Our fellows got carried away', said Clive Lloyd, in one of the less laudable remarks made by a fielding captain). But I never thought him one of the worst offenders. Perhaps because he was so very fast his bouncers commanded more public attention than those of others. He is a cheerful man in a quiet way, with a taste for what American novelists used to call homespun philosophy, and well enough liked among cricketers.

ALAN GIBSON

Andy Roberts: every hint of menace.

ROBERTSON, John David Benbow
(1917–)

Arlington Park Coll, London. Middlesex 1937–59. England: in England 1947, 1949; in West Indies 1947–48; in India 1951–52.

I shared 6 pegs in a corner of the Middlesex dressing room for 10 years with Sid Brown, our opening bat; and he once asked me, as he selected a pair of clean socks from my cricket bag, and complained of shrinkage, 'Who do I remind you of?' (This question had nothing to do with pinching socks . . . It referred to his partner Jack Robertson who reminded everyone of J. W. Hearne.) He'd had enough of it. My reply was 'No one, you are unique.' Strangely enough this quite pleased him. Certainly in bearing, neatness of style and general 'trim', J.D.R. greatly resembled J.W.H. Why, J.W. himself the doyen of Middlesex batsmen, who flourished from 1909–1936, and later was senior coach to the county, would look pleasantly satisfied at this allusion – in itself a compliment.

Jack Robertson had, in plenty, balance and timing, those essentials of defensive forward and back play, in addition to the strictest self-discipline outside the off stump. He was a great late-cutter and possessed a self-composure which was most reassuring to his partners. He played 11 times for England, but one innings we particularly remember in Middlesex was his 331, made in a day at Worcester in 1949.

In his youth Jack Robertson opened the innings with his father for Turnham Green, and received coaching at the Acton Cricket School, which was run by that great coach, confidant and friend of young players, Jack Durston. Jack Robertson emulates him in many ways now, as lecturer and coach to the school in connexion with the Middlesex Centenary Youth Trust.

J. A. YOUNG

CAREER FIGURES

	INNS	NO	RUNS	HS	AVGE	100S
Batting	897	46	31914	331*	37·50	67

Bowling 73 wkts at 34·74 Ct 340

Test Record (11)

	INNS	NO	RUNS	HS	AVGE	100S
Batting	21	2	881	133	46·36	2

Bowling 2 wkts at 29·00 Ct 6

ROBINS, Robert Walter Vivian
(1906–1968)

Highgate 1922–1925 (Captain 1925). Cambridge Univ 1926–1928. Middlesex 1925–1950 (Captain 1935–1938, 1946–1947, 1950). England: in England 1929–1933 consecutively, 1935, 1936, 1937 (Captain); in Australia 1936–37. Selector 1946–1948, 1962–1964 (Chairman).

Walter Robins, born in Stafford, promised cricketing distinction at Highgate School and Cambridge University, and subsequent achievement as a Middlesex all-rounder carried him into the England team on 19 occasions, with a tour of Australia in 1936–37. After outstanding success in school cricket, Robins was awarded a blue as a freshman in 1926 and in a 3rd appearance against Oxford he made a hundred at Lord's, also taking 8 wickets in the same match. In 1929, his 1st full season for Middlesex, he scored 1,134 runs and took 162 wickets and began his Test career. Robins held the Middlesex captaincy from 1935 to 1938 and again in 1946, 1947 and 1950, leading the county to aggressive challenge for the Championship, which they won in 1947. In 1937, when Middlesex and Yorkshire were in the keenest of Championship rivalry, Robins instigated an end-of-season challenge match between the 2 counties. The September encounter roused public

R. W. V. Robins: a fine illustration of the off-drive.

interest, raised money for cricket charities, but was only grudgingly approved by conservative authority on grounds that it might lead to a revival of stake-money cricket.

Robins brought a quality of eager antagonism to all his cricket. His batsmanship was founded on enterprising footwork and his Test hundred against South Africa at Old Trafford in 1935 was completed in little more than 2 hours, although it had to be constructed under threat of an England collapse. His fielding, notably in the covers and to his own bowling, was equally energetic and accomplished, and as a right-arm bowler of leg-break and googly he was irrepressibly adventurous and experimental.

As administrator, he sought the same enterprising approach as he had shown on the field, encouraging innovation and accepting the need for change in outlook to suit changing times. He gave secretarial service to Middlesex, sat on MCC committees and was a member of the 1961 Cricket Enquiry. He was an England selector for 6 years and he won high regard as Manager of MCC in West Indies on the 1959–60 tour.

J. M. KILBURN

CAREER FIGURES

	INNS	NO	RUNS	HS	AVGE	100S
Batting	565	39	13884	140	26·40	11

Bowling 969 wkts at 23·30 Ct 220

Test Record (19)

	INNS	NO	RUNS	HS	AVGE	100S
Batting	27	4	612	108	26·60	1

Bowling 64 wkts at 27·46 Ct 12

ROWE, Lawrence George (1949–)

Greenwich Primary Sch, Kingston. Jamaica 1968–69– . Derbyshire 1974. West Indies: in West Indies 1971–72, 1972–73, 1973–74, 1975–76; in England 1976; in Australia 1975–76. WSC.

Few, if any, contemporary batsmen are harder to categorize than Lawrence Rowe. Exploding on the international scene with 2 hundreds in his 1st Test – 214 and 100 not out against New Zealand – a unique achievement unlikely to be emulated, and adding 3 more in his next 15 Test innings, including a stunning 302 off England, nothing seemed more certain in the mid 1970s than that West Indies had discovered another great batsman in the dynasty founded by George Headley in the 1930s. Yet, by the turn of the decade, the stocky Rowe, while continuing to look a great player shackled, had been overtaken by Richards, and arguably Greenidge and Kallicharran, in the Caribbean firmament and no longer commanded an automatic place in the West Indian side. His ability was so manifest, however, it was impossible to rule out a renaissance in the 1980s.

It was a peculiarity of Rowe's career that it was not until his 5th season in first-class cricket he managed a hundred outside Jamaica, where he made all his first 10. Indeed, the contrast between his performances at Sabina Park and on other grounds was so bizarre that doubts were being voiced about his temperament when, in March 1974, he squashed them as emphatically as possible with his 302 against Denness's team in Bridgetown. Cool, compact and perfectly balanced, Rowe never played an ugly stroke. But his execution was so brilliant that he hit a 6 and 36 fours in 140 overs. Up till that match, he had scored 514 in 4 completed Test innings in Jamaica and 139 in 8 in the other islands.

At his best Rowe presented desperate problems for new-ball bowlers, especially on the true, slow pitches of the Caribbean on which it often looked impossible to draw him forward in defence. His first move was inevitably back, from where he played unhurriedly even balls of fuller than good length. But he saw the ball so early he was able to switch swiftly to attack, driving to the sightscreen off the front foot if it was just a fraction more pitched up. The method made him vulnerable in England. But, though failing to make a hundred yet again, he still topped Derbyshire's averages with 36·5 in his only county championship season, 1974.

JOHN THICKNESSE

SANDHAM, Andrew (1890–)

Surrey 1911–1937. England: in England 1921, 1924; in Australia 1924–25; in South Africa 1922–23; in West Indies 1929–30.

Sandham is remembered as Hobbs's opening partner for Surrey, and there is a danger that people may forget what a good player he was in his own right; yet the figures are there for all to see – 41,283 runs for an average of 45 and 107 hundreds. There have been many more brilliant and spectacular players; there can have been few who played so sensibly and efficiently within their limitations. A small, well-proportioned man, he was a great cutter, a great player off his legs and a good hooker. He was quick on his feet and, if runs were wanted quickly, was unlikely to be kept quiet by the slower bowlers. Contemporary with Hobbs and Sutcliffe, he had few chances for England and many of his finest innings for Surrey were played with Hobbs at the other end attracting all the attention. He was a splendid outfield in the days when, with the Oval boundaries not shortened, a deep fielder there could save or could lose hundreds of runs in a season. Had luck favoured him, he might have been remembered among the great.

R. L. ARROWSMITH

CAREER FIGURES

	INNS	NO	RUNS	HS	AVGE	100S
Batting	1000	79	41283	325	44·82	107

Bowling 18 wkts at 31·11 Ct 159

Test Record (14)

	INNS	NO	RUNS	HS	AVGE	100S
Batting	23	0	879	325	38·21	2

Ct 4

SHACKLETON, Derek (1924–)

Roomfield Senior Sch, Todmorden. Hampshire 1948–1969. England: in England 1950, 1951, 1963; in India 1951–52.

Derek Shackleton was born in Todmorden, and came to Hampshire as a batsman who could bowl temperamental leg-spinners. A shortage of opening bowlers on the staff brought about the discovery of possibilities in his medium-pace bowling. He played 16 matches in 1948 taking 21 wickets for an average of just under 30, but he had learnt a lot. In 20 of the next 21 years he took over 100 wickets, often bowling more overs in a season than anyone else. His stamina was incredible and he kept himself very fit. Early in his career he would make the ball come in to the batsman; later his main weapon was the one that left the bat very late. He had a splendid easy action and always appeared to be bowling within himself. Only Alec Kennedy (in 23 seasons) has taken more wickets and bowled more overs for Hampshire. It brought great pleasure to his many admirers when he was recalled by the England selectors for 4 Tests against West Indies in 1963. His career coincided with that of Alec Bedser and on the latter's retirement England looked for real pace. Thus Shackleton played for his country only 3 times before 1963: in 1950 against West Indies, 1951 against South Africa and in India in 1951–52. On the rare occasions that he bowled a long hop it was difficult to know whether the batsman or those who were watching were more surprised.

E. D. R. EAGAR

CAREER FIGURES

	INNS	NO	RUNS	HS	AVGE	100S
Batting	852	197	9561	87*	14·59	–

Bowling 2857 wkts at 18·65 Ct 223

Test Record (7)

	INNS	NO	RUNS	HS	AVGE	100S
Batting	13	7	113	42	18·83	–

Bowling 18 wkts at 42·66 Ct 1

SHAW, Alfred (1842–1907)

Nottinghamshire 1864–1887. Sussex 1894–1895. England: in England 1880; in Australia 1876–77, 1881–82 (Captain).

Shaw was the greatest English bowler of his time and the ideal of what a medium-pace bowler should be. His length is proverbial and the proportion of maidens he bowled in an age rich in attacking batsmen almost incredible. With a beautifully easy action, the arm barely above the shoulder, he had flight and spin and that artistry which has been missing from so many bowlers who possessed all the other gifts; ball after ball looked the same, yet no 2 balls ever were precisely the same. There could be no clearer proof of his greatness than the success which attended him when after 7 years' interval he returned, a heavy, middle-aged man, to bowl out a new generation for Sussex – a success terminated only when his legs finally collapsed under the strain. Originally an all-rounder, he never wholly lost his batting and was always a fine slip. In later years several famous players owed much to his coaching.

R. L. ARROWSMITH

CAREER FIGURES

	INNS	NO	RUNS	HS	AVGE	100S
Batting	630	101	6585	88	12·83	–

Bowling 2027 wkts at 12·12 Ct 364

Test Record (7)

	INNS	NO	RUNS	HS	AVGE	100S
Batting	12	1	111	40	10·09	–

Bowling 12 wkts at 23·75 Ct 4

SHEPPARD, Rt Rev David Stuart (Bishop of Liverpool) (1929–)

Sherborne 1946–1947. Cambridge Univ 1950–1952 (Captain 1952). Sussex 1947–1962 (Captain 1953). England: in England 1950, 1952, 1954 (Captain), 1956, 1957, 1962; in Australia 1950–51, 1962–63; in New Zealand 1950–51, 1962–63.

With less natural ability than most great players, it says much for David Sheppard's application and determination that he won the highest honours in the game. Outstanding at Sherborne in 1947, he made his debut for Sussex in the school holidays. In 1949 a good spell for Sussex, including 204 against Glamorgan, gave promise of all that was to come. His 1,000 runs for Cambridge in 1950 included 2 remarkable opening partnerships with J. G. Dewes – 343 against the West Indies and 349 against Sussex, both University records. Selected for the final Test against West Indies at the Oval, he toured Australia and New Zealand that winter, playing in 2 Test Matches. Examinations delayed his start in 1951, but he finished the season with 2,104 runs, more than 1,000 of them in 11 matches for Sussex. Cambridge captain in 1952, he made a hundred in the University Match and scored more runs than any other undergraduate had done previously in a University season. Playing in the last 2 Test Matches against India, he scored his maiden Test hundred at the Oval, topping the first-class averages with 2,262 runs. To beat Worcestershire against the clock he made 239 not out, his highest score in first-class cricket. His superb close fielding, inspiring leadership and consistent batting (2,270 runs) in the season, helped to take Sussex from 13th position to 2nd in the table in 1953. Although he was reading for holy orders, an illness to Hutton in 1954 brought him an unexpected invitation to captain England in the Third and Fourth Test Matches. In 1956, now ordained, he was recalled for the Fourth Test Match and made his 1st hundred against Australia as the 1st priest to play in Test cricket. He played in 2 Tests against West Indies in 1957, but made only rare appearances in first-class cricket during the next 4 seasons.

David Sheppard: on the field appealing, and off the field, signing.

Returning to cricket again in 1962, he made a hundred for the Gentlemen at Lord's, played in the last 2 Test Matches against Pakistan and was selected for his second MCC tour of Australia and New Zealand. A glorious 113 in the 2nd innings of the Third Test Match at Melbourne in 1963 contributed to England's only victory of the series. His Test career came to a close against New Zealand at Auckland in 1963. As a batsman, tall and especially powerful on the off-side, with amazing powers of concentration, Sheppard was an imposing personality. Throughout the tour of Australia, in 1962–63, he won universal admiration, not only for his skill as a cricketer, but as much for the zeal and sincerity of his vocation. From the Mayflower Family Centre, where he was Warden both before and after this 2nd visit to Australia, he went to Woolwich as a Suffragan Bishop, and he was still in his early 40s when he became Bishop of Liverpool.

COLIN COWDREY

CAREER FIGURES

	INNS	NO	RUNS	HS	AVGE	100S
Batting	395	31	15838	239*	43·51	45

Bowling 2 wkts at 44·00 Ct 195

Test Record (22)

	INNS	NO	RUNS	HS	AVGE	100S
Batting	33	2	1172	119	37·80	3

Ct 12

SHEPHERD, Donald John (1927–)

Glamorgan 1950–1972.

Summer after summer from 1950 to 1972, Don Shepherd sent down over 1,000 overs for Glamorgan. He was respected for his accuracy on good pitches as much as for his menace on any surface which helped his medium-fast off-cutters. His run-up was a rhythmical lope ending in a high delivery, sideways to the batsman, straight from the text-book. He cared for his action and it was probably the ease of it which took him through a long, hard career with scarcely an injury.

Shepherd first joined Glamorgan after an apprenticeship on the Lord's Ground staff. He started out as a fast bowler, talented enough to take 100 wickets in that mode in 1952 and to win a county cap. However, his consistency and wicket-taking ability rose sharply in 1956 when he turned to off-cutters. He ended that season with 177 wickets, average 15·36.

Why did Don Shepherd not win selection for England? He was certainly a good enough bowler, but for a long time it was thought that he could only be effective on the inferior wickets which were being produced at Swansea and Cardiff. His consistency year after year eventually proved the lie to that theory, but then, also, he did not fit the classic role of slow off-spinner. This, more than anything else, probably persuaded Test selectors to bypass him. Professional batsmen always express surprise at his omission, saying that 'Shep', as he was known everywhere in the game, was simply a very fine bowler who missed out at the top because his style was so much his own. If he belonged to a breed it was a small one, including, during his playing days, Bob Appleyard and the left-arm Derek Underwood.

Shepherd's outfielding was of a high standard; he had a wonderful arm and held over 200 catches. His tail-end batting was lusty for many years. He once hit 26 runs off an over by Derbyshire's Edwin Smith. Against an Australian touring side at Swansea he struck 51 runs from 11 scoring shots. Later in his career he applied himself more defensively to partnerships calculated to madden any attack, fast or slow.

Perhaps Shepherd's greatest value to Glamorgan and to cricket as a whole was the pride he had in his profession. It made him a perfect senior professional and his influence in this role throughout the 1960s was delightfully rewarded by the winning of the County Championship in 1969. Shepherd was then 42 years old; he took the wicket which sealed Glamorgan's 1st Championship win for 21 years, and at that precise moment became the 1st Glamorgan cricketer to enter the hallowed company of those who have taken 2,000 first-class wickets.

TONY LEWIS

CAREER FIGURES

	INNS	NO	RUNS	HS	AVGE	100S
Batting	837	248	5696	73	9·67	–

Bowling 2218 wkts at 21·32 Ct 251

SHREWSBURY, Arthur (1856–1903)

People's Coll, Nottingham. Nottinghamshire 1875–1902. England: in England 1884, 1886, 1890, 1893; in Australia 1881–82, 1884–85 (Captain), 1886–87 (Captain), 1887–88.

The classic tribute to Shrewsbury's cricket stature is surely to be found in W.G.'s traditional answer to the question which of his contemporaries he rated highest as a batsman – 'Give me Arthur'. An aggregate of 26,439 runs and 59 hundreds of which 10 were double-hundreds hardly reflects his greatness; this was predominantly revealed by his mastery on turning wickets, basically by back play. No one has ever made more use of the ground between the creases, watched the ball more closely or played it later. In 23 Tests he averaged 35, making a historic 164 on a difficult wicket at Lord's in 1886, and dominating the rubber of 1893 with successive scores of 106 not out, also on a turning pitch, 81 and 66. In the winters of 1884–85 and 1887–88 he captained sides to Australia, winning 5 out of the 7 Tests played. His most successful season was 1887, when he made 8 hundreds and averaged 78 for 1,653 runs. His name will always be associated with that of William Gunn, with whom the highest of their many partnerships was their 398 for the 2nd wicket against Sussex in 1890; 9 years later he made 391 for the 1st wicket with A. O. Jones.

H. S. ALTHAM

CAREER FIGURES

	INNS	NO	RUNS	HS	AVGE	100S
Batting	811	90	26439	267	36·67	59

Bowling 0 wkt for 2 Ct 317

Test Record (23)

	INNS	NO	RUNS	HS	AVGE	100S
Batting	40	4	1277	164	35·47	3

Bowling 0 wkt for 2 Ct 29

SIMPSON, Robert Baddeley, AM (1936–)

Marrickville High Sch, Sydney. New South Wales 1952–53 to 1977–78 (Captain 1962–63 to 1967–68, 1977–78). Western Australia 1956–57 to 1960–61 (Captain 1960–61). Australia: in Australia 1958–59, 1960–61, 1962–63, 1963–64 (Captain), 1964–65 (Captain), 1965–66 (Captain), 1967–68 (Captain), 1977–78 (Captain); in England 1961, 1964 (Captain); in South Africa 1957–58, 1966–67 (Captain); in West Indies 1964–65 (Captain), 1977–78 (Captain); in India 1964–65 (Captain); in Pakistan 1964–65 (Captain).

Playing first for New South Wales at the youthful age of 16, Bobby Simpson matured slowly into a solid opening batsman, the best slip-fielder since W. R. Hammond, a useful leg-break bowler and a shrewd captain. He took over the Australian captaincy relinquished by Benaud in 1964, leading the team successfully to England, India and Pakistan. Scoring 98 on his 1st appearance against MCC for New South Wales in 1954–55, he toured South Africa in 1957–58, but could not find his feet. He moved to Western Australia in 1957 and, although he was overlooked for a while, a season in the Lancashire League helped him considerably and the dividends accrued in 1959–60. At one point he had amassed 902 runs at an average of 300, which included 236 not out against New South Wales and 230 not out against Queensland. His prolific scoring continued on a short tour of New Zealand. In spite of scoring close on 2,000 runs with 6 hundreds in England in 1961, nothing would go right for him in the Test Matches.

Bobby Simpson batting in West Indies during his 2nd career.

On his return, he rejoined New South Wales, now a fully recognized opening batsman, with an automatic Test place. He scored 400 runs against England in 1962–63, with 3 hundreds against MCC outside Test Matches. In 1963–64 he scored 800 in 4 innings for New South Wales including 359 against Queensland. With his innings of 247 not out against Western Australia he holds the unusual distinction of making the highest score both for and against the State. Surprisingly, it was not until the Fourth Test Match at Old Trafford in 1964, his 30th appearance for Australia, that he collected his maiden Test hundred. He crowned it by batting for nearly 2 days to finish with 311. As a bowler he would certainly have been given more opportunities but for the skill and stamina of Benaud.

In 1965–66 Simpson captained Australia in 3 Tests against England, scoring 355 runs with 225 in the Fourth Test at Adelaide. He led Australia in South Africa in 1966–67. Whilst his team went down by 3 Tests to 1, he himself enjoyed a good tour – 1,344 runs with a highest score of 243 against North East Transvaal in Pretoria and a memorable 153 in the Second Test Match in Cape Town. It was to be his last major season until the advent of World Series Cricket saw him stepping out of retirement to captain a team of raw youngsters – Thomson apart – against India in 1977. He batted well enough, and bowled his share of overs too, for the selectors to invite him to take the side to West Indies. Predictably, the Australian team were no match for West Indies, though Simpson's courageous leadership will long be remembered. After that it was something of a surprise when he was discarded for Yallop in the series against England of 1978–79.

COLIN COWDREY

CAREER FIGURES

	INNS	NO	RUNS	HS	AVGE	100S
Batting	436	62	21029	359	56·22	60

Bowling 349 wkts at 38·07 Ct 384

Test Record (62)

	INNS	NO	RUNS	HS	AVGE	100S
Batting	111	7	4869	311	46·81	10

Bowling 71 wkts at 42·26 Ct 110

SIMPSON, Reginald Thomas (1920–)

Nottingham HS. Nottinghamshire 1946–1963 (Captain 1951–1960). England: in England 1949–1954 consecutively; in Australia 1950–51, 1954–55; in South Africa 1948–49; in New Zealand 1950–51, 1954–55.

Rumours of 'Reg' Simpson's talents preceded him from India, for it was whilst serving with the RAF in 1944–1945 that he made his debut in first-class cricket. Many counties would have welcomed him, but he naturally turned to the county in which he was born and educated. In 1946 he made his debut for Nottinghamshire and was given his cap. He took over the captaincy in 1951 and by his example made them one of the most attractive batting sides to watch.

Reg Simpson: rolling the wrists.

Simpson was a beautiful striker of the ball and a glorious fielder. He played 27 times for England and shares the 1st-wicket record partnership against New Zealand (with Sir Leonard Hutton) and against West Indies (with C. Washbrook). His most famous innings was his 156 not out in the Fifth Test at Melbourne in 1950–51. It was largely owing to this that England gained their 1st victory over Australia after the Second World War.

E. D. R. EAGAR

CAREER FIGURES

	INNS	NO	RUNS	HS	AVGE	100S
Batting	852	55	30546	259	38·32	64

Bowling 59 wkts at 37·74 Ct 189

Test Record (27)

	INNS	NO	RUNS	HS	AVGE	100S
Batting	45	3	1401	156*	33·35	4

Bowling 2 wkts at 11·00 Ct 5

SMITH, Cedric Ivan James (1906–1979)

Middlesex 1934–1939. England: in England 1937; in West Indies 1934–35.

During the 6 seasons following his qualifying for Middlesex from Wiltshire in 1934 until the onset of the Second World War, Jim Smith made a short but startling impact on the game. Smith was something of a giant, 6 feet 4 inches in height and with a frame to match. He was primarily a bowler, exemplary in direction and with an awkward lift, in pace fast-medium. But if that was his stock-in-trade, he is recalled chiefly as a hitter guaranteed to empty every bar during his brief but sometimes productive and, for the opposition, demoralizing tenure of the crease. The phrase is used advisedly since he offered a fast-footed stroke to every ball bowled. Moreover it was the same stroke made with a vast heave of the shoulders in the direction of mid-wicket. As contact was made with every part of the bat, including even the back, the ball flew off in unpredictable directions to the confusion of the fielders and amid general hilarity. If he middled the ball truly and on the up it was not a question of the ball clearing the boundary but, on the smaller grounds, whether it would ever be seen again.

Wisden records two instances of fast scoring by him. In June 1938 he made 69 against Sussex at Lord's in 20 minutes, and 10 days later 66 in 18 minutes, the first 50 of them in 11 minutes. But his biggest triumph came a few weeks before the Second War at Canterbury when he and his captain, Ian Peebles, scored 116 together for the last wicket. Smith's 101 in 81 minutes included 7 sixes, some of them still spoken of with awe by those present. It would only have added to the pleasure of the hero of the hour if he heard his innings written off by the arch-pundit, Gerry Weigall, maybe with a twinkle in his eye, as 'A travesty of the game, sir!'

E. W. SWANTON

CAREER FIGURES

	INNS	NO	RUNS	HS	AVGE	100S
Batting	304	31	4007	101*	14·68	1

Bowling 845 wkts at 19·25 Ct 95

Test Record (5)

	INNS	NO	RUNS	HS	AVGE	100S
Batting	10	0	102	27	10·20	–

Bowling 15 wkts at 26·20 Ct 1

SMITH, Michael John Knight, OBE (1933–)

Stamford Sch 1946–1951 (Captain 1949–1951). Oxford Univ 1954–1956 (Captain 1956). Leicestershire 1951–1955. Warwickshire 1956–1975 (Captain 1957–1967). England: in England 1958, 1959, 1960, 1961, 1965 (Captain), 1966 (Captain), 1972; in Australia 1965–66 (Captain); in South Africa 1964–65 (Captain); in West Indies 1959–60; in New Zealand 1965–66 (Captain); in India; 1961–62, 1963–64 (Captain); in Pakistan 1961–62.

Mike Smith was an outstanding schoolboy cricketer at Stamford who played for Leicestershire in the school holidays of 1951. After National Service, his 3 years in the Oxford side were memorable for his scores in the University Match – 201 not out in 1954, 104 in 1955 and 117 in 1956 (as Captain). Moreover, Smith's aggregate of 477 for the 3 matches surpassed the previous best (457), by the Nawab of Patuadi. In 1956 Smith left Leicestershire to captain Warwickshire, with whom he scored 2,000 runs for 5 consecutive seasons, with 3,000 in 1959. He challenged Hutton's record of 1,294 for the month of June 1949, with 1,209 in July 1959.

For so prodigious a run-getter he had a chequered Test career. Starting as an opening batsman against New Zealand, he scored his maiden Test hundred batting at No. 4 against India in 1959. But perhaps the best innings of his career was his hundred in the Second Test Match against West Indies in Trinidad in 1959–1960. Three times he was dismissed in the 90s in Test Matches. In his earlier years, he could look rather an uncertain starter, susceptible to the yorker at the start of an innings. But once set, he was a difficult man to bowl to, especially punishing on the on-side where he hit in the air and found the gaps with great skill. A brilliant short-leg fielder, he set up a new Warwickshire record of 52 catches in a season. It was soon apparent that he was a good touring captain and, as a result of his successes in India and South Africa, he was selected to lead England to Australia in 1965–66. 1966 was his last season as Warwickshire's captain and he retired, or so it seemed, only to be persuaded to come back in the 1970s under A. C. Smith's captaincy, batting well enough to earn an England cap against Australia in 1972.

His quiet, unflappable temperament masked a wry sense of humour and an astute cricket brain. He will be remembered as one of the most likeable of cricket's characters, and as an exceptional all-round games-player. As a rugby international he played fly-half for England – he was thus a double cap, an increasingly rare breed.

COLIN COWDREY

CAREER FIGURES

	INNS	NO	RUNS	HS	AVGE	100S
Batting	1091	139	39832	204	41·84	69

Bowling 5 wkts at 61·00 Ct 593

Test Record (50)

	INNS	NO	RUNS	HS	AVGE	100S
Batting	78	6	2278	121	31·63	3

Bowling 1 wkt for 128 Ct 53

SMITH, O'Neill Gordon (1933–1959)

Kingston Coll. Jamaica 1954–55 to 1957–58. West Indies: in West Indies 1954–55, 1957–58; in England 1957; in New Zealand 1955–56; in India 1958–59; in Pakistan 1958–59.

'Collie' Smith was a noteworthy example of the maxim of Napoleon that in battle the morale was to the material as 3 to 1. Not that Smith was not gifted as a cricketer. Hardly a big man, he was one of the hardest hitters in the game; at Nottingham in 1957 he sent Statham straight into the pavilion off the back foot. He was one of those who would field brilliantly anywhere. His bowling never received the appreciation due to it. He was an off-spin bowler with a mastery of awkward flight that seemed able to deceive any batsman at any stage of his innings. Good judges have believed that in time (and with encouragement) he would have become the main slow spin bowler of a Test side.

Smith walked into big cricket with a hundred for Jamaica against the Australian touring side in the West Indies in 1954–55, followed by a hundred in the First Test. Coming to England in 1957, in the 1st innings of the First Test he was the sheet-anchor of the West Indian batting with a score of 161. More astonishingly, when West Indies were in real trouble at Nottingham, Smith again held the fort with a score of 168. His batting did not otherwise live up to these quite substantial examples of courage and skill. But Smith was a young man, of high moral character and great charm, with obviously a great future still before him. There was therefore a universal sense of tragic loss when in 1959, a League cricketer in England, he was killed in a motor accident.

C. L. R. JAMES

CAREER FIGURES

	INNS	NO	RUNS	HS	AVGE	100S
Batting	112	12	4031	169	40·31	10

Bowling 121 wkts at 31·02

Test Record (26)

	INNS	NO	RUNS	HS	AVGE	100S
Batting	42	0	1331	168	31·69	4

Bowling 48 wkts at 33·85 Ct 9.

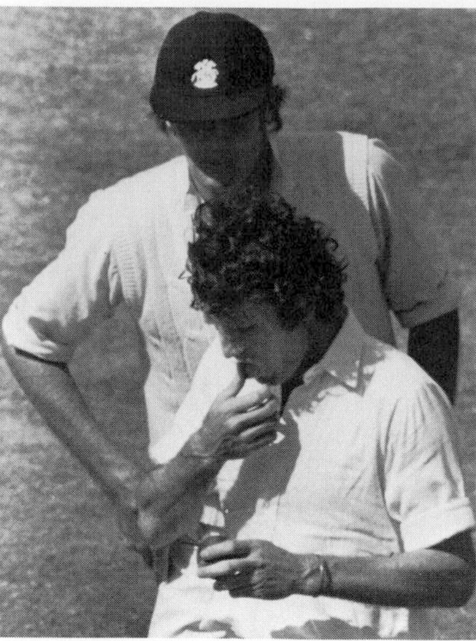

John Snow: 'an interesting character . . .'

SNOW, John Augustine (1941–)

Christ's Hospital 1958–1959. Sussex 1961–1977. England: in England 1965–1973, 1975, 1976; in Australia 1970–71; in West Indies 1967–68; in Pakistan 1968–69. WSC.

John Snow was England's most formidable and successful fast bowler in the period between Trueman and Statham, on the one hand, and the arrival of Willis and Hendrick in the mid-1970s on the other. He was, unquestionably, a better bowler for England than he was for Sussex, by whom he was once dropped for not trying. An interesting character, if not ostensibly a particularly sympathetic one, he published an autobiography, *Cricket Rebel* (1976), which, though often bitter in tone, had constructive things to say; and also two volumes of poems. He made his debut for Sussex in 1961, received his cap in 1964, and played his last match in 1977. In 1974 his benefit realized over £18,000. Although constantly in trouble with Sussex he produced over the years numerous devastating performances for them, including 8 for 87 against Middlesex at Lord's in 1975. At Hove he could be lethal when the mood was on him, but as often as not he was innocuous, slouching about on the boundary with a look of total disinterest. He was, nevertheless, a good deep fielder with a strong arm and as his bowling declined he developed into a useful batsman, sometimes going in first. At the Oval in 1966 he shared a last-wicket stand of 128 with Higgs against the West Indies.

Snow had a beautifully easy and controlled bowling method, slanting the ball into the batsman but also cutting it sharply off the pitch. His arm was generally high, his action completed on the run and rather straighter on than the classical 'whippy'. His pace was short of the fastest, but despite, for a fast bowler, a slim build, he was aggressive, got life and lift out of most pitches, and had a dangerous bouncer. When he was in business he was always doing something interesting with the ball, varying pace and angle, and at his best he was deadly. Bowling apparently well within himself he had great command of length, though he was unusually generous with no-balls.

Snow's first Tests were against New Zealand and South Africa in 1965 and by the end of the 1973 season, by which time he had played in 47 Test matches, he had taken the 4th most Test wickets of any English bowler. Only Trueman, Statham and Bedser were above him. He ended his Test career with 202 wickets at an average of 26·66, appearing in 49 Tests in all. His greatest triumphs were under Cowdrey in the West Indies and under Illingworth in Australia in 1970–71, when he bowled quite superbly, taking 31 Test wickets at 22·83 apiece, 26 of these coming in the first 4 Tests. He was the mainstay of the attack and with Boycott and Edrich largely responsible for England's victory. His batting average in that series was 23·50.

ALAN ROSS

CAREER FIGURES

	INNS	NO	RUNS	HS	AVGE	100S
Batting	451	110	4832	73*	14·17	–

Bowling 1174 wkts at 22·72 Ct 125

Test Record (49)

	INNS	NO	RUNS	HS	AVGE	100S
Batting	71	14	772	73	13·54	–

Bowling 202 wkts at 26·66 Ct 16

SOBERS, Sir Garfield St Aubrun
(1936–)

Bay Street Sch, Barbados. Barbados from 1952–53. South Australia 1961–62 to 1963–64. Nottinghamshire 1968–1974 (Captain 1968–1971, 1973). West Indies: in West Indies 1953–54, 1954–55, 1957–58, 1959–60, 1961–62, 1964–65 (Captain), 1967–68 (Captain), 1970–71 (Captain), 1971–72 (Captain), 1973–74; in England 1957, 1963, 1966 (Captain), 1969 (Captain), 1973; in Australia 1960–61, 1968–69 (Captain); in New Zealand 1955–56, 1968–69 (Captain); in India 1958–59, 1966–67 (Captain); in Pakistan 1958–59. Rest of the World in England 1970 (Captain).

Few, if any, who had the pleasure and privilege of watching Garfield Sobers from start to finish of his career will allow that an all-round cricketer of such skill and attainments has ever been seen. Beginning as an orthodox slow left-arm bowler with pretensions as a left-handed bat he was first chosen for the West Indies at the age of 17. Four years later he made the record Test score of 365 not out against Pakistan, and was now adding to his virtuosity with chinamen and googlies. When for 3 seasons early in the 1960s he assisted South Australia, he turned his hand to speed and became just about the most deadly new-ball bowler in the world. It was not out of the common to see him using the 3 separate styles in the same session of play. As a young man he was fast and agile anywhere in the field. Eventually he was to be found in any of the close-catching positions where his sleight-of-hand was on a par with all else that he did.

By the time he came first to England in 1957 his batting was already on a footing with that of the 3 famous 'Ws'. Like that of these fellow-Barbadians his play had about it a naturalness and freedom of stroke that told of perfect wickets allied to a long tradition of fine batting to follow. He had a full repertoire, played from a generous pick-up and with a long follow-through, his partiality being for the off and straight drive. If a weakness can be hinted at in such a paragon it lay perhaps in his reluctance to move his feet early in an innings: thus he could be beaten by late swing or by high-class spin. Once he was in he exercised a command that demoralized all but the best. In his approach to batting he was remarkably similar to Frank Woolley, who in his latter days could never see enough of him.

It was the first 4 winters of the 1960s which perhaps completed Sobers's cricket education. First, with Frank Worrell's side in 1960–61, he had a hero's part in one of the best of all Test series. In the following seasons for South Australia he did what has never otherwise been accomplished, making 1,000 runs and taking 50 wickets in the 10 Sheffield Shield matches. A year later he did the same again. When Worrell retired, Sobers was the natural successor as captain. With his old leader as manager he responded by leading West Indies to their first victory in a series against Australia. This was the start of a record run of 39 Tests as captain, wherein his example on the field never faltered, the only criticism to be heard being that he was inclined to err on the side of generosity. At Port of Spain against England in 1967–68 he declared and lost, thereby as it turned out losing the rubber – and great was the commotion.

In 1968 he came to England at the head of the overseas invasion of county cricket to lead Notts, who had been in low water for a long time. The effect was immediate and he spent 7 seasons (apart from Test calls) as the mainspring of the side. But the accumulation of almost perpetual cricket summer and winter was taking its toll both physically and mentally. Like Denis Compton before him, he developed a knee which often made playing a burden. At Lord's in 1973 he gave England a last taste of his powers, helping West Indies to their largest-ever win with his 28th Test hundred, in all the 26th for his country. Only Sir Donald Bradman with 29 betters this and even he cannot match Sobers's aggregate: nor can any but 3 exceed his tally in all Tests (including the Rest of the World Matches in 1970) of 256 wickets, nor any but Cowdrey either his 98 Test appearances or his 117 catches. Such figures demonstrate the authority he wielded over the 20 years of his career. But the true measure of his influence must take account of a sportsmanship and an unselfishness that were never questioned, an example second to none. C. L. R. James in our 1st edition called him 'this superb product of the modern age'. When shall we see another?

E. W. SWANTON

CAREER FIGURES

	INNS	NO	RUNS	HS	AVGE	100S
Batting	609	93	28315	365*	54·87	86

Bowling 1043 wkts at 27·74 Ct 407

Test Record (93)

	INNS	NO	RUNS	HS	AVGE	100S
Batting	160	21	8032	365*	57·78	26

Bowling 235 wkts at 34·03 Ct 109

SOUTHERTON, Sydney James
(1874–1935)

Editor of *Wisden* 1934–1935.

Few men could have been more thoroughly steeped in cricket than Sydney Southerton. The son of James Southerton, the famous bowler, after acting as scorer to the Australian touring team to England of 1893 he spent his working life with the Pardon brothers, Sydney and Edgar, in the Cricket Reporting Agency. He duly succeeded his old friend Charles Stewart Caine as Editor of *Wisden*, but after 2 years in office died suddenly, after proposing the toast of Cricket at a dinner of the Ferrets CC at the Oval. Though his editorship was so short it has a special claim to remembrance for his fair and forthright analysis of the Body-line tour of Australia in 1932–33. He knew the conditions (having accompanied A. P. F. Chapman's MCC tour 4 years earlier), he knew the chief protagonists at close quarters, above all he knew the game. His article in the 1934 edition pricked the English cricket conscience and brought opinion round to a dispassionate view of the issues involved, rather as the denunciations of throwing by his predecessor, Sydney Pardon, had done more than 30 years earlier.

E. W. SWANTON

SPOFFORTH, Frederick Robert
(1853–1926)

New South Wales 1874–75 to 1887–88. Derbyshire 1889–1891. Australia: in Australia 1876–77, 1878–79, 1881–82, 1882–83, 1884–85, 1886–87; in England 1882, 1884, 1886.

If by the time of Spofforth's first tour in England, 1878, 'W.G.' had for some years been universally accepted as 'The Champion', the Australian lost no time in staking his claim to be called 'The Demon'. Of Yorkshire stock but born in Sydney, he first played for New South Wales in 1874, and for Australia in the 2nd of all Test Matches at Melbourne at the end of March 1877. But it was on 27 May next year, and appropriately at Lord's, that he made his first and indelible impact on cricket history when the tourists in their blue-and-white caps routed a strong MCC side, captained by 'W.G.', by 9 wickets

F. R. Spofforth: first of the great Australian bowlers; a splendid example of looking behind the left shoulder.

in a single day. In the 1st innings, Spofforth took 6 wickets for 4 runs in 23 balls, including the hat-trick; and in the 2nd, 5 for 16. Seven months later he played in the only Test Match of Lord Harris's tour at Melbourne, where his 13 wickets for 110 and another hat-trick were decisive in Australia's victory. But his greatest claim to immortality was surely made in the historic setting of the 'Ashes' Test Match at the Oval in 1882. Set 85 to win in their last innings England had reached 51 for 2, with W.G. 32 not out, when Spofforth, crossing over to the pavilion end, began his last demonic spell in which in 11 overs he took 5 wickets for 12 runs, and brought his analysis for the match to 14 wickets for 90: no wonder, when Australia won by 7 runs he was carried into the pavilion.

On that tour he took 188 wickets for 12 apiece; and on his next, 2 years later, 218 at the same cost, including 7 for 30 against an England XI at Birmingham, and a hat-trick against the South at the Oval. Handicapped by an injury to his bowling hand on the 1886 tour, he still easily headed the Test Match averages, and his overall record for the 18 Tests in which he played against England was 94 wickets for 18 each. After settling in England he played occasionally for Derbyshire and consistently for several seasons for Hampstead, for which club in 1894 he took 200 wickets for just over 2,000 runs, including all 10 for the 2nd year running against Marlow at a cost of 14. But no figures in bowling history can compare with his overall record for 1878 and 1880: admittedly they include the games in Australia that preceded and followed visits to England and, in 1878, a short tour in America, but 763 wickets (391 in England) and 714 (326 in England) for just about 6 runs a wicket surely defy argument.

Originally Spofforth, modelling himself on Tarrant, relied on pure speed, but he soon subordinated this to accuracy, subtle variation of pace and break-back; given any help in the pitch he could turn the ball the width of the wicket, his fast yorker was devastating, and no bowler had ever clean-bowled so high a proportion of his victims. Six feet two inches tall, his run-up, less than 10 yards long, culminated in a formidable leap in the pre-delivery stride and a full follow through; true to his sobriquet, there was about it all a machiavellian malignity. In 1881 he rode 400 miles to play in a minor match in Australia, and then took all 20 wickets – all clean-bowled.

H. S. ALTHAM

CAREER FIGURES

	INNS	NO	RUNS	HS	AVGE	100S
Batting	236	41	1928	56	9·88	–

Bowling 853 wkts at 14·95 Ct 83

Test Record (18)

	INNS	NO	RUNS	HS	AVGE	100S
Batting	29	6	217	50	9·43	–

Bowling 94 wkts at 18·41 Ct 11

SPOONER, Reginald Herbert
(1880–1961)

Marlborough 1897–1899 (Captain 1899). Lancashire 1899–1921. England: in England 1905, 1909, 1912. Selector 1921.

R. H. Spooner, one of the most handsome-looking batsmen of the great amateur domination of English batsmanship, played for Lancashire against Middlesex at Lord's in 1899, while still a boy at Marlborough. Before this match of his baptism, J. T. Tyldesley, kindest of professional batsmen, as well as among the greatest, took the boy aside and gave him fatherly advice, especially warning him against Albert Trott's slow ball. 'He hides it artfully, so watch out.' Spooner opened the Lancashire innings and scored 44. Tyldesley was bowled for a single by Trott's slow ball. Next innings Tyldesley again spoke to young Spooner, and again referred to Trott's slow ball. 'You did well yesterday, sonny, but don't take Albert Trott for granted.' And next innings, while Spooner was scoring an immaculate, effortless 83, Tyldesley was again clean bowled by Trott's slow ball, this time for none.

In 1903 he announced his pedigree class by an innings of 247 at Trent Bridge against Nottinghamshire. At once the connoisseurs of cricket ranked him alongside L. C. H. Palairet as a stylist – a term used in those days frequently, and as a compliment. He was, in fact, one of the first cricketers to find the answer to the googly, the new weapon perfected by Vogler, Gordon White and R. O. Schwarz. In 1912 at Lord's Spooner scored 119 for England v South Africa, and the attack included Aubrey Faulkner, Pegler and Schwarz, 3 of the cleverest of all 'back of the hand' spinners. Fieldsmen at cover-point have, at close of play, returned to the pavilion with fingers blackened and swollen after an innings by Spooner. He could also drive the fastest bowling straight. At Kennington Oval in 1911, during an innings of 224, he drove Hitch of Surrey – who was, to say the least, as fast as, say, Statham – so straight and powerfully that Hitch had to leap into the air, to save his shins. He treated the fury of 'Tibby' Cotter the same way at Kennington Oval for England v Australia in 1905, scoring 79, following a first innings of 0, clean bowled, middle-stump sent flying yards, by Cotter, a ball which Spooner told me he never saw against the dark background of the Oval pavilion.

He was a correct player, without a hint of academic formalism. He put a bloom on the orthodox. His driving had a beautiful swing and follow-through, but there seemed no physical effort in it. The timing, and hence the rhythm, were perfect. Unlike most of the stylists of his period he usually defended from a shortish back-lift of the bat, yet here again, without restriction or angularity.

Three years of war between 1899–1902, then the war of 1914–1918, sadly shortened his seasons. In any case he had work to do. He was perhaps at his very best in 1904. Lancashire were champion county that year, undefeated and, at the wicket and in the field, brilliant, with MacLaren, Spooner and J. T. Tyldesley the first 3 batsmen in the order. No other cricket XI anywhere, or at any time, has known 3 such superb and diverse stroke-players at an innings' outset. At Liverpool in 1903 v Gloucestershire, MacLaren and Spooner scored 200 for Lancashire's 1st wicket in 2 hours. Spooner enjoyed an equally handsome and prosperous season in 1911, scoring 2,312 runs, average 51·37. He was asked to captain the MCC England team in Australia in 1920–21, but was unable to accept because of an injury. He also had to decline an invitation to go to Australia in 1911–12. He played for England 10 times between 1905 and 1912. A succession of 5 single-figure innings v Australia in 1912 were the consequence of terribly wet wickets. Yet in the same Triangular Tournament, against the spinners of South Africa, his average was 60. He was in the Gentlemen's XI v the Players 17 times, and had a hundred at Lord's in 1906, and another at the Oval, in 1911. As a cover-point he was the acme of grace, as swift and accurate as he was lovely to see. He also played rugby football for England v Wales at Swansea in 1903.

NEVILLE CARDUS

CAREER FIGURES

	INNS	NO	RUNS	HS	AVGE	100S
Batting	393	16	13681	247	36·28	31

Bowling 6 wkts at 97·00 Ct 141

Test Record (10)

	INNS	NO	RUNS	HS	AVGE	100S
Batting	15	0	481	119	32·06	1

Ct 4

STACKPOLE, Keith Raymond, MBE
(1940–)

Christian Brothers Coll, Clifton Hill, Melbourne. Victoria 1959–60 to 1973–74 (Captain 1972–73 to 1973–74). Australia: in Australia 1965–66, 1968–69, 1970–71, 1972–73, 1973–74; in England 1972; in South Africa 1966–67, 1969–70; in West Indies 1972–73; in New Zealand 1973–74; in India 1969–70.

England's bowlers in the first 2 Ashes series of the 1970s would undoubtedly have plumped for Keith Stackpole if invited to nominate the luckiest Australian batsman. He certainly seemed to get away with more than his share of chances in the slips – and at Brisbane one notorious run-out early in a knock of 207 – while amassing 1,112 at an average in the 50s. But as a pugnacious opening batsman, very powerful on the cut and hook and always ready to pounce on the short ball, he could justly claim to have made his own luck to a great extent: like Sobers, when he edged the ball he edged it hard. There was a straight-forwardness about Stackpole's game that, allied to his fresh-faced, boyish looks, made him a favourite with crowds wherever he played.

He was 25, and a middle-order batsman, when he won his first cap against M. J. K. Smith's England side of 1965–66, one of 4 changes Australia made after being beaten by an innings in the Third Test at Sydney. At Adelaide they reversed the result, Stackpole playing a full part with an innings of 43 and the wickets of Cowdrey and Smith with his leg-spin. His bowling fell off as his batting developed, but his catching, mostly at 2nd slip, made him an asset in the field.

As an inveterate back-foot player, there were doubts about his ability to succeed when, aged 31, he made his only tour of England as Ian Chappell's vice captain in 1972. In the event (with the co-operation of the England slips) he headed the averages, with 5 50s and a hundred at Trent Bridge. Seven months later, by making 152 against West Indies in Jamaica, he joined Harvey and Simpson as the only Australians to make Test hundreds in 5 different countries.

JOHN THICKNESSE

CAREER FIGURES

	INNS	NO	RUNS	HS	AVGE	100S
Batting	279	22	10100	207	39·29	22

Bowling 148 wkts at 39·28 Ct 166

Test Record (43)

	INNS	NO	RUNS	HS	AVGE	100S
Batting	80	5	2807	207	37·42	7

Bowling 15 wkts at 66·73 Ct 47

STATHAM, John Brian, CBE (1930–)

Manchester Central GS. Lancashire 1950–1968 (Captain 1965–1967). England: in England 1951, 1953–1963 consecutively; in Australia 1954–55, 1958–59, 1962–63; in South Africa 1956–57; in West Indies 1953–54, 1959–60; in New Zealand 1950–51, 1954–55; in India 1951–52.

Brian Statham, of Lancashire and England, was a part of 2 fast-bowling partnerships which in a 9-year span, and each in their turn, allowed England constantly to recover from the problems provided by a Test batting line-up that often fell far short in performance of its strength on paper. First, with Frank Tyson, Statham ripped through the Australian sides of 1954–55, and then, when Tyson retired, he joined with Trueman in providing a fast attack fit to rank with most that have operated in Test cricket over the years.

Tyson was fast and variable; Statham was straight and honest. Trueman, when he began, was fast and variable too, but later he was to pick up the subtleties of the craft and became a fine bowler, as distinct from a good fast bowler. Statham, though, was always the catalyst with these two, and in fact was the one most feared over the period by opposition batsmen – not in the physical sense but in the matter of wicket-taking, for his superb accuracy and movement off the seam left little margin for error. 1954–55 was his greatest season against Australia, and Melbourne and Sydney were his greatest matches.

His speed at this time was not much less than that of Tyson, and his accuracy and probing length such that never could the slightest liberty be taken. This was a great factor in the success of Tyson at the other end. His 252 Test wickets and 2,260 first-class wickets came to him through sheer hard work. At the end of any long stint in the field, Statham would take off his boots and look sorrowfully at his feet – the feet that had carried him to and from his bowling mark for anything up to 30 gruelling overs.

In some ways Statham was an unusual fast bowler. He was for instance the only one in my memory to whom histrionics did not come easily. When he beat the bat or found the edge there was no arm-waving or muttering, as one ran thankfully to the other end, but rather a sad shake of the head, and if it was a really bad stroke an admonishing look to go with it. I doubt whether his bowling action would have pleased the old school despite the fact that in delivery he was smooth as silk, almost bringing both feet together and delivering with an arm that was always brushing against his right ear. Movement of the ball in the air was not one of his strongest points, but off the pitch not even Miller and Lindwall could deviate more. I suspect that watching Lindwall on his 1st tour in Australia may have taught him that length, direction and variation of pace were the requirements of the fast bowler who was to stay in the game a long time. These lessons he always exemplified in all the time he was in the England side.

RICHIE BENAUD

CAREER FIGURES

	INNS	NO	RUNS	HS	AVGE	100S
Batting	647	145	5424	62	10·80	–

Bowling 2260 wkts at 16·36 Ct 230

Test Record (70)

	INNS	NO	RUNS	HS	AVGE	100S
Batting	87	28	675	38	11·44	–

Bowling 252 wkts at 24·84 Ct 28

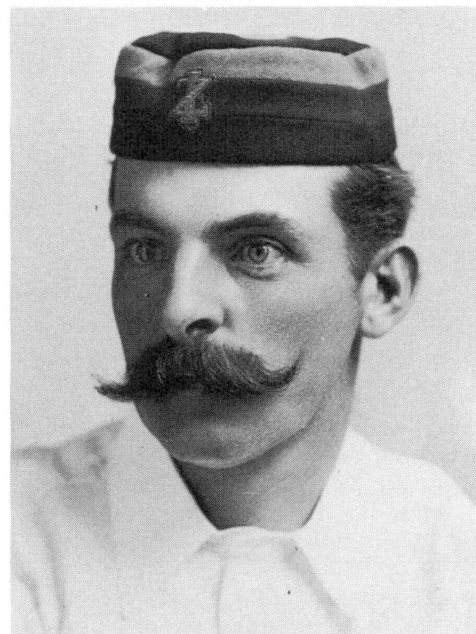

A. G. Steel: a great all-rounder.

STEEL, Alan Gibson, KC (1858–1914)

Marlborough 1874–1877 (Captain 1876–1877). Cambridge Univ 1878–1881 (Captain 1880). Lancashire 1877–1893. England: in England 1880, 1882, 1884, 1886 (Captain), 1888 (Captain); in Australia 1882–83. President MCC 1902.

A Lancastrian born and bred, A. G. Steel was for some years second only in stature as an all-round cricketer to 'W.G.' himself. Four years in the Marlborough XI, which he captained in 1876 and 1877, it was said that before he left school he was worth his place in an England side. Next year at Cambridge he achieved a record that no freshman in history rivals: heading both average tables for that famous side which won all its matches and beat the Australians by an innings, he finished the season top of the English bowling table with 164 wickets for 9 apiece. In his 4 years for Cambridge – he was captain in 1880 – he took in all 198 wickets for the University, 38 of them for 9 each in the University Match. Of his 18 matches for the Gentlemen the most sensational was in 1879 at the Oval when he and his great contemporary and Oxford rival, A. H. Evans, bowled unchanged through both innings: his figures were 9 for 43. A year after leaving Cambridge he went with Ivo Bligh's team that recovered the Ashes from Australia; for it he took more wickets than any other bowler, and made 135 not out in the Sydney Test Match; two summers later he played a splendid innings of 148 in the Test Match at Lord's. His work as a barrister made regular cricket for his county impossible, but he would turn out when he could, and Yorkshire in particular came to realize how his natural genius for the game could dispense with practice.

Only 5 feet 8 inches high, but strong and quick on his feet and with a wonderful eye, Steel's attacking instinct and wide repertoire of strokes could at its best dominate any bowling with easy authority. But his fame rests more surely on his slow bowling. Consistently accurate, able to turn the ball either way, bowling to a full length with subtle variations of pace, it was his leg spin – then an almost forgotten phenomenon in cricket – that so often reduced the best batsmen to harassed impotence. A most popular and able man, he took an active part in the councils of the game at Lord's, and his chapter on bowling in the *Badminton* book is a classic.

H. S. ALTHAM

CAREER FIGURES

	INNS	NO	RUNS	HS	AVGE	100S
Batting	262	23	7004	171	29·31	7

Bowling 788 wkts at 14·80 Ct 138

Test Record (13)

	INNS	NO	RUNS	HS	AVGE	100S
Batting	20	3	600	148	35·29	2

Bowling 29 wkts at 20·86 Ct 5

STEPHENSON, Heathfield Harman (1833–1896)

Surrey 1853–1871. Players 1857–1869. England: in America 1859; in Australia (Captain) 1861–62.

H. H. Stephenson was born before round-arm bowling was legalized. He played against Alfred Mynn and W. G. Grace and lived to know of the artistry of 'Ranji' and Fry. His playing days saw the game transformed from the medieval era of spotted shirts and flannel caps, when no bowler's hand could be higher than his shoulder, to the modern age of the County Championship and international rivalry.

His claims to fame were many. He visited America in 1859 with the first team ever to leave England on a cricket tour, and in 1861–62 he captained the 1st English side to play in Australia. He had already represented Surrey and the Players with much success – apart from showing his skill as a huntsman in the winter – and William Clarke was quick to gain his services for the All-England XI. Standing 6 feet in height and with a long reach, he was a fine leg-hitter. A popular man, with a fringe of beard, he was nicknamed 'Spurgeon' from the black frock-coat that he wore off the field. As a bowler, one of his contemporaries called him 'a genius'. He was fast, and of the round-arm school, with a pronounced break-back, and for some seasons was one of the most difficult bowlers in England to play. His talents were not confined to batting and bowling. When Lockyer was not present, he proved himself a splendid wicket-keeper – one of the first to stand up to the stumps.

Stephenson's greatest renown, however, came as an outstanding coach at Uppingham between 1872 and 1896. A universal favourite with boys and masters alike, he helped produce such players as A. P. Lucas, D. Q.

Steel, W. S. Patterson, G. MacGregor, G. R. Bardswell and C. E. M. Wilson. He was a benevolent tyrant and the severest of purists, but many of his happiest years were spent at the school. Uppinghamians have for ever been grateful for the foundations he laid. Apart from the historic honour of leading the 1st cricket team from England to Australia, it is at Uppingham that the real fame of 'H.H.' lies.

IRVING ROSENWATER

STEVENS, Greville Thomas Scott
(1901–1970)

Univ Coll Sch 1916–1919 (Captain 1918–1919). Oxford Univ 1920–1923 (Captain 1922). Middlesex 1919–1932. England: in England 1926; in South Africa 1922–23, 1927–28 (Captain); in West Indies 1929–30.

Had circumstances permitted Stevens to play regularly for Middlesex, after coming down from Oxford, he would have been an even more outstanding amateur all-rounder than he was. That he was exceptionally gifted is proved by the fact that, in 1926, when twice selected to play for England v Australia, he had only played 7 times for Middlesex. He first hit the headlines in 1919 by scoring 466 not out for Beta v Lambda in a UCS House match at Neasden. In the same year he became the 1st and only schoolboy in modern times to play for the Gentlemen v Players at Lord's. Amongst many fine innings, the most notable were 182 for Oxford v West Indies and 122 going in first for the Gentlemen at Lord's, both in 1923. In 1924, batting for the Gentlemen at No. 3, he scored 42 not out on a very difficult pitch. Going in 1st in 1925 for the Gentlemen at Lord's he scored 75 and 129; but without doubt the highlight of his career with the bat was an innings of 149 made against the Australians of 1926, their full Test side; going in 1st he gave no chance whilst batting for 5 hours.

As a 'googly' bowler he was amongst the best of his time, not as accurate as C. S. Marriott or I. A. R. Peebles, nor did he spin the ball as viciously as R. W. V. Robins, but he had one invaluable asset. Even the best players failed to see the difference between his 'top-spinner' and his 'googly' – he also had a well-disguised fast straight delivery, which snatched victory for Middlesex from the jaws of defeat by Yorkshire at Bradford in 1920. He was a remarkably safe catcher anywhere near the wicket, but on one occasion he sinned in the grand manner, by dropping 5 catches before the luncheon interval – he started by dropping a 'sitter' from Jack Hobbs and finished by missing Wilfred Rhodes off the 3rd, 4th and 5th deliveries of one over, fielding in the gully – a unique achievement in the history of first-class cricket, and worthy of inclusion in *Wisden* amongst 'Other Hat-Tricks'. The game when this occurred was Gentlemen v Players at Scarborough in 1920.

NIGEL HAIG

CAREER FIGURES

	INNS	NO	RUNS	HS	AVGE	100S
Batting	387	36	10376	182	29·56	12

Bowling 684 wkts at 26·85 Ct 216

Test Record (10)

	INNS	NO	RUNS	HS	AVGE	100S
Batting	17	0	263	69	15·47	

Bowling 20 wkts at 32·40 Ct 9

A. E. Stoddart, an all-rounder who gained 10 caps for England on the rugby field.

STODDART, Andrew Ernest
(1863–1915)

St John's Coll Sch, London. Middlesex 1885–1900 (Captain 1898). England: in England 1893 (Captain), 1896; in Australia 1887–88, 1891–92, 1894–95 (Captain), 1897–98 (Captain).

First appearing for Middlesex in 1885, few men can have made a more impressive exit than Stoddart, when in his last innings for his county in J. T. Hearne's benefit match against Somerset at Lord's in 1900 he made 221. Stoddart took part in 4 tours to Australia: with G. F. Vernon's side in 1887–88, with Lord Sheffield's in 1891–92 and with the 2 teams which he himself organized and captained in 1894–95 and 1897–98. On the first of these he scored 285 in a match against XVIII Melbourne juniors, the highest score ever made by an Englishman in Australia until R. E. Foster beat it 16 years later. On the 1st of his own tours, he made 173 in the Melbourne Test, led his side to victory in the decisive 5th game of the rubber and averaged over 40 for the tour. In 5 Tests in England his highest score was 83 at the Oval in 1893; this was his finest season, in which he scored over 2,000 runs, made a hundred in each innings, 195 not out and 124, for Middlesex against Notts, and shared with 'W.G.' in 3 opening partnerships of over 100 against the Australians. In the Centenary Match at Lord's in 1887 he and Arthur Shrewsbury made 266 for England against MCC.

When not playing for Middlesex Stoddart made nearly 14,000 runs for Hampstead, including an innings of 485 against the Stoics in 1886, then the highest score made by any batsman. With his handsome features, athletic body and attacking spirit, Stoddart coming out to open an innings would quicken the pulse as readily at Lord's as his three-quarter play often did on rugby football grounds, on which he gained 10 international caps.

H. S. ALTHAM

CAREER FIGURES

	INNS	NO	RUNS	HS	AVGE	100S
Batting	537	16	16738	221	32·12	26

Bowling 278 wkts at 23·63 Ct 260

Test Record (16)

	INNS	NO	RUNS	HS	AVGE	100S
Batting	30	2	996	173	35·57	2

Bowling 2 wkts at 47·00 Ct 6

STOLLMEYER, Jeffrey Baxter
(1921–)

Trinidad 1938–39 to 1954–55. West Indies: in West Indies 1947–48, 1952–53 (Captain), 1953–54 (Captain), 1954–55 (Captain); in England 1939, 1950; in Australia 1951–52 (Captain); in New Zealand 1951–52; in India 1948–49.

A mere statement of J. B. Stollmeyer's achievements in big cricket will surprise all except the most knowledgeable. He is one of the few who has shared in a partnership of 300 for the 1st wicket, v Sussex at Hove in 1950. His stand for the 3rd wicket in Trinidad in 1946–47 is only 22 short of the world record. In that game he made 324. He made his 2,000 runs in Tests. He made his 4 Test hundreds. He captained the West Indies with more than average success. To which may be added an unusually sober and balanced judgment of West Indian players and their opponents, as he has shown in his years as a selector and administrator.

Stollmeyer came to England at the age of 18 with the 1939 team. He was more than a useful junior, averaging 26 in the Tests. On his return home he played his role in the period of mammoth scoring characteristic of West Indian cricketers, cut off as they were from international cricket during the Second World War. In England in 1950 he was overshadowed by the 'three Ws'; yet Stollmeyer and Rae, who opened the innings for the West Indies, shared 1st-wicket stands of 52, 32, 37, 48, 77, 103 (to win by 10 wickets) and 72 in the 4 Tests. Thus a firm foundation (sometimes even more) was laid for the brilliant batsmen who followed. Stollmeyer played the finest innings of his career in the Fifth Test in Australia in 1951–52, showing calm defence and brilliant strokes against a very powerful attack when wickets were

J. B. Stollmeyer: elegant batsman and a suave negotiator.

falling around him. He had done the same for 78 in England on a terrible pitch at Manchester in 1950. Always batting well, he led West Indies in 1952 and to a draw against the powerful English side of 1953–54. Ill-health prevented him from leading his side, except in one or two games, against Australia in the West Indies. An elegant stylist in the orthodox tradition, but in the modern style strong on the on-side, Stollmeyer was coached by Arthur Richardson, the Australian, when still a boy at school in Trinidad.

C. L. R. JAMES

CAREER FIGURES

	INNS	NO	RUNS	HS	AVGE	100S
Batting	194	16	7942	324	44·61	14

Bowling 55 wkts at 45·12 Ct 95

Test Record (32)

	INNS	NO	RUNS	HS	AVGE	100S
Batting	56	5	2159	160	42·33	4

Bowling 13 wkts at 39·00 Ct 20

STRUDWICK, Herbert (1880–1970)

Surrey 1902–1927. England: in England 1921, 1924, 1926; in Australia 1911–12, 1920–21, 1924–25; in South Africa 1909–10, 1913–14.

Strudwick was the wicket-keeper Oldfield admired most. There could be no finer tribute; many regard Oldfield himself as the greatest of all. Figures applied to 'keepers are especially fallacious: they can take only such chances as are offered. Yet Strudwick's bag of 1,493 – a record for 40 years – is amazing. In his day Surrey had few spinners and he kept mainly to quick bowlers. Huish and Ames, who both broke so many records, kept largely to spinners. When Strudwick in his 1st full season got 91 wickets, then easily a record, the leading Surrey bowlers were all fast. Yet he was 41 before he kept in a Test in England, first Lilley being preferred to him and then E. J. Smith. Both were far better bats, and Smith was expert at taking the very difficult bowling of Foster. Of all 'keepers before Evans, Strudwick was the quickest on his feet. He stood up to all but the really fast. His quiet, unobtrusive methods were a model and no one was more consistent. Nor was anyone more popular or respected. His playing days over, he spent some quietly happy years as Surrey's scorer.

R. L. ARROWSMITH

CAREER FIGURES

	INNS	NO	RUNS	HS	AVGE	100S
Batting	835	243	6445	93	10·89	–

Bowling 1 wkt for 102 W/k: ct 1235; st 258 Total 1493

Test Record (28)

	INNS	NO	RUNS	HS	AVGE	100S
Batting	42	13	230	24	7·93	–

W/k: ct 60; st 12 Total 72

SUTCLIFFE, Bert (1923–)

Takapuna GS. Auckland 1941–42. Otago. Northern Districts. New Zealand: in New Zealand 1946–47, 1950–51, 1951–52 (Captain), 1952–53, 1954–55, 1955–56, 1958–59; in England 1949, 1958, 1965; in South Africa 1953–54; in India 1955–56, 1964–65; in Pakistan 1955–56, 1964–65.

Bert Sutcliffe leaning into the stroke.

One of the most productive and cultured batsmen in New Zealand's history, Sutcliffe's left-handed strokeplay was characterized by adventure and artistry. He burst into prominence with scores of 197 and 128 in the same match against MCC at Dunedin in 1946–47, and thereafter his record flowered into magnificence. No New Zealander had scored more runs or hundreds when he retired and no left-hander in the world has made a higher score than his 385 against Canterbury in 1952–53. Three years before he scored 355 against Auckland, while in 1955–56 in a Test at New Delhi he made the then record score for New Zealand – 230 not out. In England in 1949 he scored 2,627 runs (average 59·70) – another New Zealand record – and for the fourth time in his career hit a century in each innings of a match, with 243 and 100 not out v Essex at Southend. A man of conspicuous modesty, he has given much to New Zealand cricket as a player, coach and mentor.

IRVING ROSENWATER

CAREER FIGURES

	INNS	NO	RUNS	HS	AVGE	100S
Batting	405	39	17283	385	47·22	44

Bowling 86 wkts at 37·95 Ct (incl w/k) 157; st 1

Test Record (42)

	INNS	NO	RUNS	HS	AVGE	100S
Batting	76	8	2727	230*	40·10	5

Bowling 4 wkts at 86.00 Ct 20

SUTCLIFFE, Herbert (1894–1978)

Pudsey Sch. Yorkshire 1919–1939. England: in England 1924, 1926, 1928–1935 consecutively; in Australia 1924–25, 1928–29, 1932–33; in South Africa 1927–28; in New Zealand 1932–33. Selector 1959–1961.

Herbert Sutcliffe first played for Yorkshire at the mature age of 24. This was due to his service in the First World War, during which he was commissioned in the Sherwood Foresters. So immediate was his success that, after one season's play, *Wisden* selected him as one of the 'Five Cricketers of the Year'. For some time there was a degree of speculation as to whether he or his fellow Yorkshireman, P. Holmes, would succeed as partner to Hobbs, but by 1924 Sutcliffe had eclipsed all rivals. It was soon apparent that, technically and temperamentally, England had acquired an opening batsman of altogether exceptional calibre. A successful series against South Africa in 1924 was followed by a triumphant tour of Australia in 1924–25. Sutcliffe made a hundred on his 1st Test Match appearance in Australia and sustained this form so consistently that, on retirement from international cricket in 1935, he averaged 60·73, the highest figure reached by an English batsman. His association with Hobbs is judged, by results and all-round efficiency in all conditions, the greatest of all English first-wicket partnerships and will probably never be excelled. There lay between the two an extraordinary understanding, manifested in their perfect and unhesitating judgment of the short single.

There was none of the polished elegance of Hobbs about the batting of Sutcliffe. He was essentially a practical batsman, with a superb judgment of length, pace and direction. He stood with the face of the bat very open, and presented its full width to the ball on all occasions. He made few classical strokes, but hit the ball firmly off the forward stroke, and cut and hooked efficiently. He was a splendid runner, who always came when called, however lowly the caller. Where he was unexcelled was in the courage, determination and concentration he brought to the job in hand. Never flustered, and certainly never intimidated, he was at his best on the big or testing occasion. It is notable that his Test Match figures exceed those he recorded in lesser matches. For Yorkshire he and Holmes were a splendid partnership sharing the then world record of 555 for the 1st wicket made against Essex at Leyton in 1932. These strong qualities brought Sutcliffe success in realms beyond that of cricket, and he became a very capable and successful business man, using the foundations laid during his active days in the field.

IAN PEEBLES

Herbert Sutcliffe: immaculate as ever.

CAREER FIGURES

	INNS	NO	RUNS	HS	AVGE	100S
Batting	1088	123	50138	313	51·95	149

Bowling 14 wkts at 40·21 Ct 473

Test Record (54)

	INNS	NO	RUNS	HS	AVGE	100S
Batting	84	9	4555	194	60·73	16

Ct 23

TALLON, Donald (1916–)

North Bundaberg State Sch. Queensland 1933–34 to 1953–54 (Captain 1946–47 to 1950–51). Australia: in Australia 1946–47, 1947–48, 1950–51; in England 1948, 1953; in New Zealand 1945–46.

Don Tallon did not begin his Test career until after the Second War, there having been criticism at his omission from the 1938 side which toured England. In the 1938–39 Australian season which followed he equalled the record set up by E. Pooley in 1868 by helping to dismiss 12 batsmen (9 caught and 3 stumped) for Queensland against NSW. In the same season he accomplished the rare feat of dismissing 7 batsmen (3 caught and 4 stumped) in an innings for his State against Victoria. Tallon was one of the quickest and most brilliant stumpers in the history of the game. After the war he was to play in 21 Test Matches and proved himself a very valuable middle-order batsman in addition to his great skill behind the stumps.

E. D. R. EAGAR

CAREER FIGURES

	INNS	NO	RUNS	HS	AVGE	100S
Batting	228	21	6034	193	29·14	9

Bowling 0–202 W/k: ct 303; st 129 Total 432

Test Record (21)

	INNS	NO	RUNS	HS	AVGE	100S
Batting	26	3	394	92	17·13	–

W/k: ct 50; st 8 Total 58

TATE, Maurice William (1895–1956)

Sussex 1912–1937. England: in England 1924, 1926, 1928, 1929, 1930, 1931, 1935; in Australia 1924–25, 1928–29; in South Africa 1930–31; in New Zealand 1932–33.

During his first few seasons for Sussex, Maurice Tate closely followed the methods of his father, who bowled slow-medium off-breaks, interspersed by an occasional fast ball. It was Ernest Tyldesley who, defeated by a fast ball, and recognizing its merits, advised the young man to abandon his off-breaks and concentrate on pace. The resulting transition was instantaneous and startling. From the humble role of a county change, Tate advanced overnight to become the greatest fast-medium bowler of his era.

He was a big man with heavy shoulders and powerful thighs. His large feet delighted the cartoonists, and gave him a rolling, rustic gait. But when he turned on his mark, which he invariably and unusually did in a clockwise direction, all was grace and co-ordination. There was no point in his action upon which the purist could quibble. He ran up briskly, a distance of about 8 yards. At the crease he started his swing leaning well back on his right leg with a fully extended left arm. The bend of his back and roll of his shoulders brought his right arm catapulting over with a smooth elasticity which gave an impression of immense momentum. The pace of the ball through the air was short of being genuinely fast but, on hitting the pitch with a resounding thump, it appeared to fly on with redoubled velocity. Whether this is scientifically possible or not, the fact remains that, notably in Australia, his slips stood considerably deeper than they did to the accredited fast bowlers.

His technique was simple. He placed the ball with the seam between, and parallel to, his first 2 fingers and let fly. His late swerve from the leg had the rare merit that the ball could be aimed to hit the stumps. Occasionally he would bring the ball back from outside the off stump to hit the middle or leg like a bullet. By nature Tate was a genial and loquacious man. A taste for small talk, combined with an elaborately confidential air and a tendency to malapropism, disarmed friend and foe alike. Amongst a myriad of heart-warming memories there occur at random his description of the Jam Sahib in oriental regalia as looking like 'a veritable Hindoo', and the moment of chagrin at a third unsuccessful lbw appeal when, in his astonishment, he 'stood there nude'. That he was a very serviceable batsman who, on occasions, opened the innings for his county and 12 times scored 1,000 runs in a season, is often overlooked. But this was a small matter in comparison with the glory of Tate in his opening overs at Hove on a green wicket, freshened by a slight sea haze. Uneasy was the captain who had won the toss and decided to bat.

IAN PEEBLES

CAREER FIGURES

	INNS	NO	RUNS	HS	AVGE	100S
Batting	970	102	21717	203	25·02	23

Bowling 2784 wkts at 18·16 Ct 206

Test Record (39)

	INNS	NO	RUNS	HS	AVGE	100S
Batting	52	5	1198	100*	25·48	1

Bowling 155 wkts at 26·16 Ct 11

TAYFIELD, Hugh Joseph (1928–)

Durban HS. Natal 1945–46 to 1955–56. Rhodesia 1947–48 to 1948–49. Transvaal 1956–57 to 1962–63. South Africa: in South Africa 1949–50, 1953–54, 1956–57, 1957–58; in England 1955, 1960; in Australia 1952–53; in New Zealand 1952–53.

For one decade that saw South African cricket revel in unaccustomed glory, Hugh Tayfield was in the top flight of the world's off-spin bowlers. He succeeded Athol Rowan in South Africa's side, and by a mixture of personal ability and judicious handling by his captains, he achieved a psychological ascendancy over most of the world's leading batsmen. He was aided perhaps by the fashion of the age – especially among English players – of not using the feet to spin bowling: but on any assessment he was an extremely able bowler.

A nephew of S. H. Martin, of Worcestershire, he was only 17 when he first played for Natal. An analysis of 7 for 23 against Australia at Kingsmead in 1949–50 presaged things to come, and 3 years later – after the memorable tour of Cheetham's side in Australia – his reputation was secure: his off-breaks, always accurate and persistent, captured 30 wickets in the 5 Tests, although he broke his finger in the Third. He held sway for several years thereafter, and he took his 100th Test wicket in England in 1955 after only 22 Tests. South Africa's captains took pains to shield him from punishment – a policy which, with careful field placing, paid happy dividends. He could certainly be hit for four – and even for six – but not many batsmen got the chance to do it too often. He acquired the nickname 'Toey' from his habit of stubbing his toe into the ground before bowling a ball or receiving one. Perhaps it was all part of his mesmerism.

Hugh Tayfield: one of the great exponents of flighted spin.

IRVING ROSENWATER

CAREER FIGURES

	INNS	NO	RUNS	HS	AVGE	100S
Batting	259	47	3668	77	17·30	–

Bowling 864 wkts at 21·86 Ct 150

Test Record (37)

	INNS	NO	RUNS	HS	AVGE	100S
Batting	60	9	862	75	16·90	–

Bowling 170 wkts at 25·91 Ct 26

TAYLOR, Herbert Wilfred, MC (1889–1973)

Michaelhouse Sch, Durban. Natal 1909–10 to 1923–24. Transvaal 1925–26 to 1935–36. South Africa: in South Africa 1913–14 (Captain), 1921–22 (Captain), 1922–23 (Captain), 1927–28, 1930–31; in England 1912, 1924 (Captain), 1929; in Australia 1931–32; in New Zealand 1931–32.

Each cricketing country has contributed one or more players to the ranks of the immortals, a somewhat grandiose term for those who will always be remembered for their quite exceptional ability. 'Herbie' Taylor certainly takes his place, although not without reservations. In his native environment, on matting pitches, he was unquestionably of these immortals but on turf, although a very fine player, he did not quite achieve a comparable mastery.

For a man of original, and occasionally somewhat eccentric, theories on the practice of the game he was, paradoxically, the perfect model of orthodox technique. The foundation of his strokeplay was a free and absolutely perpendicular back-lift. Although of no more than average height, his nimble footwork more than compensated for any lack of reach. On the back stroke his feet were within inches of the stumps, whilst he played forward to the maximum of his stride. His accurate judgment of length utilized this commanding range to best advantage so that he was seldom forced into a hurried stroke. He employed all the accepted scoring shots, and played them with the same text-book perfection. He was, in fact, the ideal model for all aspiring batsmen. His supremacy on matting wickets he demonstrated against the most exacting yardstick of all time, the bowling of Barnes, who found these pitches an ideal medium for his own particular genius. Thus, in 1913–14, Taylor averaged 50 in the series against England whilst his colleagues could offer no more than token resistance. In 3 tours of England he met with varied success, and it is possible that the very precision of his methods, so perfectly attuned to the consistency of matting, was beset by the lesser predictability of turf. Of his 7 hundreds for South Africa, 6 were made in his own country. The writer recalls Taylor as a generous and, to a struggling young cricketer, very helpful opponent.

IAN PEEBLES

CAREER FIGURES

	INNS	NO	RUNS	HS	AVGE	100S
Batting	340	27	13105	250*	41·87	30

Bowling 22 wkts at 25·45 Ct 75

Test Record (42)

	INNS	NO	RUNS	HS	AVGE	100S
Batting	76	4	2936	176	40·77	7

Bowling 5 wkts at 31·20 Ct 19

TAYLOR, Robert William (1941–)

St Peter's Secondary Modern Sch, Stoke. Derbyshire 1961– (Captain 1975 and part of 1976). England: in England 1978, 1979; in Australia 1978–79, 1979–80; in New Zealand 1970–71, 1977–78; in India 1979–80; in Pakistan 1977–78.

In Australia there have never been more than 6 first-class wicket-keepers regularly in the public eye. The succession has been more regular than most other features of cricket. From Blackham to Kelly in the distant days, and then more recently from Tallon to Langley, and Jarman to Marsh. In England, where there are 17 'keepers, and then some, the understudy role is a familiar form of disappointment for these specialists. When Ames was available there was seldom a place for Duckworth. For almost a decade Taylor played second fiddle to Alan Knott, one of the game's greatest all-rounders, a fitness fanatic, a fixture in the England side and one who was 5 years younger. Ironically Taylor is only the 3rd Derbyshire 'keeper, after Harry Elliott and Dawkes, in more than 60 years. It took Packer to change the England cast: suddenly Taylor, who had travelled the world hopefully, arrived as the senior member of Brearley's XI.

For years he had been the acknowledged master of his craft in the eyes of his peers. Alan Knott has always thought Taylor the better all-round 'keeper. Neat and unspectacular, he seldom misses chances. Taylor typically has always set himself the highest standards.

Universally loved – a gentleman – Bob Taylor lives in a house called Hambledon in his native Staffordshire in the building of which he played a major part, doubtless bringing the same care to the task as he does to that of maintaining his kit. In 15 busy years he used only 2 pairs of his blue-backed gloves and one of those was then stolen. His stature reached its highest pinnacle in the 5th and clinching Test against Australia at Adelaide in 1979 when England, as usual desperately short of runs, were put into a position from which they could win by a Derbyshire stand of 135 for the 7th wicket between Miller and Taylor. When he had made 97, 3 runs short of his first-ever hundred, Taylor was caught at the wicket off Hogg out of sorts and bowling off a short run. Tough old cricket-writers, their pens pickled in acid, were close to tears. That hundred would have been a fitting reward for a man who has borne misfortune with such style that he earned himself the nickname of 'Chat' because of his unremitting skill in making conversation during the social round of half-a-dozen tours in which he knew that he was no more than a spare. His long career has been in the very best tradition of cricket in England.

ROBIN MARLAR

TENNYSON, 3rd Baron (Lionel Hallam Tennyson) (1889–1951)

Eton 1907–1908. Hampshire 1913–1935 (Captain 1919–1933). England: in England 1921 (Captain); in South Africa 1913–14.

Lionel Tennyson, the 3rd Baron of that ilk, originally was a fast bowler and heavy hitter in the lower rungs of the Eton batting order. These roles were well attuned to his lusty physique and sanguine temperament but, when it became apparent that his bowling would never carry him to the highest cricketing circles, he concentrated upon batting with very considerable success. He first appeared for Hampshire in 1913 and did well enough to be selected for the South African tour of 1913–14, playing in all 5 Test Matches and averaging 16. Surviving a couple of war wounds he took over the captaincy of his county in 1919 and led it until his virtual retirement in 1933. In 1920 a friend, after due consideration, laid 1,000 to 1 against his captaining England. It was an expensive view.

Brought into a depressed England side at Lord's in 1921 he attacked the Australian fast bowlers with such gusto that the selectors saw in him the inspiring figure to resuscitate England's flagging spirits, and appointed him captain for the next match at Leeds. His heroic one-handed batting, after an injury in the field, did much to restore England's shattered prestige, and he went on to fight 2 very honourable draws in the Fourth and Fifth Tests. This brief period was his span as a Test Match cricketer but he continued to play, in various roles, until the Second World War. Tennyson was a large, heavy man of immense strength who loved to hit the ball off his front foot. He was not a very good player of slow bowling, a fact he readily and petulantly recognized, but against all faster types he was a dangerous and indomitable opponent.

In an age when there was still a fair wealth of individuality, Tennyson was an outsize personality. He was something of a throwback to the age of the Regency buck. Great and endearing were his conceits, the more so that disaster seemed to mingle incessantly with triumph in a boisterous, whole-hearted career. Wherever cricketers gather his name is sure to arise as the centre of some epic in which those ingredients predominate. Whatever the scene he was never known to pass unnoticed, and perhaps the aptest comment upon an extremely engaging presence was made by a contemporary who observed that, when he entered the room, everyone smiled.

IAN PEEBLES

CAREER FIGURES

	INNS	NO	RUNS	HS	AVGE	100S
Batting	759	38	16828	217	23·33	19

Bowling 55 wkts at 54·11 Ct 178

Test Record (9)

	INNS	NO	RUNS	HS	AVGE	100S
Batting	12	1	345	74*	31·36	–

Bowling 0 wkt for 1 Ct 6

Jeff Thomson: 'Get out of my way'.

THOMSON, Jeffrey Robert (1950–)

Condell Park and Punchbowl Boys' HS, Sydney. New South Wales 1972–73 to 1973–74. Queensland 1974–75– . Australia: in Australia 1972–73, 1974–75, 1975–76, 1976–77, 1977–78, 1979–80; in England 1975, 1977; in West Indies 1977–78.

Most batsmen who have had the experience of facing Jeff Thomson on a quick pitch would agree that 'shattering' is an apposite adjective to describe his bowling: a ball from him is always liable to behave like a grenade and explode. His outstanding success as a world-class fast bowler has stemmed from 2 main factors. First, there is his sheer speed through the air, which makes the normal 'quickie' seem fast-medium by comparison. As was once the case with Frank Tyson, this has enabled him not only to capture wickets with full tosses, half-volleys and long hops, but also to get away with many erratic deliveries. Secondly, unlike Tyson, Jeff has the ability to make the odd ball lift unpleasantly from only fractionally short of a good length. When a bowler of his pace drops one short, a batsman is prepared for it to rise at least chest high, and if he is a good batsman this should not worry him. What, however, is disconcerting, and can prove fatal, is to be struck on the gloves, or in the ribs by a ball which he expects to play comfortably off the backfoot.

Thomson's rare speed is largely derived from very powerful arm, shoulder and back muscles, combined with what is close to the old-fashioned slinger's action. It is this action, in which his left shoulder moves further round than most bowlers, and his braced left leg hammers into the ground, which causes the occasional ball to lift, or to cut back viciously off the seam. It also accounts for sudden lapses in line and length, when his timing is marginally out. He is essentially a shock bowler with a very high striking rate in terms of wickets taken against overs bowled. Although at present he uses a lengthy, ambling run-up, Thomson should be able to achieve great pace from a comparatively few paces. With Dennis Lillee he made an ideal and contrasting pair: Dennis, the artist; Jeff, the slugger, with the knock-out punch.

TREVOR BAILEY

THORNTON, Charles Inglis
(1850–1929)

Eton 1866–68 (Captain 1968). Cambridge Univ 1869–1872 (Captain 1872). Kent 1867–1872. Middlesex 1875–1885.

Thornton's contemporaries were unanimous that he hit the ball harder and hit more balls farther than any other man. While still at school he carried the old pavilion at Lord's and his measured hits include six of over 150 yards. At Scarborough in 1886 for the Gentlemen v I Zingari, he made 107 in 29 hits, sending 8 balls out of the ground for six: in his day over the ropes counted four only. Once against Merchant Taylors he lost 7 balls. But the man who could average 29 in those days on his 18 appearances for Kent must have been a fine bat, not a mere slogger. He used his feet to all types of bowling, never wore pads, thinking they cramped his movements, and seldom wore gloves. He was a magnificent field. For his services to the Scarborough Festival over 50 years he received the Freedom of the Borough.

R. L. ARROWSMITH

CAREER FIGURES

	INNS	NO	RUNS	HS	AVGE	100S
Batting	374	16	6928	124	19·35	5

Bowling 47 wkts at 20·13 Ct 119

TITMUS, Frederick John, MBE (1932–)

William Ellis Sch, Highgate. Middlesex 1949–1976 (Captain 1965–68) and 1979. Surrey 1978. England: in England 1955, 1962–1967 consecutively; in Australia 1962–63, 1965–66, 1974–75; in South Africa 1964–65; in West Indies 1967–68; in New Zealand 1962–63; in India 1963–64.

Fred Titmus played his 1st game for Middlesex at the age of 16 in 1949; but it was in 1953, having completed 2 years of National Service, that he swept to prominence among an already rich field of off-spinners in the country. He took 105 wickets and won his county cap. During the 1950s, 1960s and early 1970s cricket followers at Lord's will remember him as part of the permanent scenery, twirling his off-spin, helped by the slope, from his favourite Pavilion end. His brief run-up to the stumps began with a tripping footstep, reached the fulcrum with a hop, and then he pivoted with the sharp coordination of wrist, shoulder and hip of the classic off-spin. Such a conscientious study of the basics of bowling began on the Lord's groundstaff. Over the years his art expanded to include a finely disguised faster ball, which brought into the act his wicket-keeper, John Murray, for many stumpings; and also the gently drifting away-swinger.

Fred Titmus: the off-spinner's pivot.

Titmus's first Tests were played in 1955 against South Africa. In 1962–63 in Australia, as one of 3 off-spinners – Illingworth and Allen were the others – he captured 21 Test wickets and averaged 36·40 with the bat. His career took a dramatic turn in the West Indies in 1967–68, when, as a result of a boating accident, he lost 4 toes on his left foot. His Test career was thought to be ended, and even his county career was in jeopardy. The success story was completed in 1974, 6 years later, when, at the age of 42, his name was again on England's list for Australia. He played in 4 Tests.

Fred Titmus was appointed Middlesex captain in 1965, but resigned during the season of 1968. After leaving Middlesex in 1976 he had 2 seasons as Surrey's coach at the Oval, which ended discontentedly. He even took a first-class wicket for Surrey and another 3 for Middlesex in 1979 by when he had become a country postmaster and a school coach.

TONY LEWIS

CAREER FIGURES

	INNS	NO	RUNS	HS	AVGE	100S
Batting	1135	204	21564	137*	23·16	6

Bowling 2815 wkts at 22·34 Ct 472

Test Record (53)

	INNS	NO	RUNS	HS	AVGE	100S
Batting	76	11	1449	84*	22·59	–

Bowling 153 wkts at 32·22 Ct 35

TOONE, Sir Frederick Charles
(1868–1930)

Secretary Yorkshire CCC 1903–1930. Manager of MCC in Australia 1920–21, 1924–25, 1928–29.

One of the few men to be knighted for administrative services to cricket, Toone achieved a high reputation as an organizer. On being appointed to the secretaryship of Yorkshire in 1903, he quickly exerted a great influence over the county's affairs. He organized every detail in the county office, effected great improvements on the county's grounds and, not least, worked indefatigably in ensuring the success of players' benefits. He had, too, a fine grasp of controversial questions and was an effective voice in many meetings at Lord's. Charm, tact and firmness resulted in his managing – with great success – the 3 MCC tours to Australia of the 1920s. He also edited the *Yorkshire Year Book*, and during his secretaryship, which he held until his death, the Yorkshire membership was more than doubled.

IRVING ROSENWATER

TROTT, Albert Edwin (1873–1914)

Victoria 1893–94 to 1895–96. Middlesex 1898–1910. England: in South Africa 1898–99. Australia: in Australia 1894–95.

There have been few greater natural cricketers than Albert Trott. His stock ball was medium with a low delivery and a sharp off-break, but he had a natural swerve from leg and no two balls were ever the same. His fast ball was very fast and his changes of pace were wonderfully concealed. Now he would raise his arm high, now he would hold the ball back in the air, sometimes he bowled slow leg-breaks. At times indeed this love of experiment made him unnecessarily expensive. As a bat, he was a really good player until his famous hit over the pavilion at Lord's in 1899 gave him a mania for vast carries and he degenerated into a slogger. Possessed of enormous hands, he was a wonderful catcher, especially in the slips or to his own bowling. One feat will always be remembered: in his benefit he took four wickets in four balls and later in the same innings did the hat-trick. Inexplicably omitted from the 1896 Australian side, he was thereafter, as an Australian playing for an English county, ineligible for Tests against Australia. He was brother of G. H. S. Trott.

R. L. ARROWSMITH

CAREER FIGURES

	INNS	NO	RUNS	HS	AVGE	100S
Batting	602	53	10696	164	19·48	8

Bowling 1674 wkts at 21·09 Ct 449

Test Record (5)

	INNS	NO	RUNS	HS	AVGE	100S
Batting	9	3	228	85*	38·00	–

Bowling 26 wkts at 15·00 Ct 4

TROTT, George Henry Stevens
(1866–1917)

Victoria 1885–86 to 1907–08 (Captain 1892–93 to 1903–04). Australia: in Australia 1891–92, 1894–95, 1897–98 (Captain); in England 1888, 1890, 1893, 1896 (Captain).

Harry Trott was a great captain who at a time when Australian teams desperately needed discipline secured it without *enforcing* it and without making an enemy. A supreme tactician, he once created a sensation by opening the bowling in a Test with his own leg-breaks, normally regarded as a change, and having 'W.G.' and Stoddart stumped almost immediately. Combining great driving powers with impenetrable back play, he was a splendid bat in a crisis. He was also a fine field at point.

R. L. ARROWSMITH

CAREER FIGURES

	INNS	NO	RUNS	HS	AVGE	100S
Batting	393	19	8797	186	23·52	9

Bowling 386 wkts at 25·12 Ct 183

Test Record (24)

	INNS	NO	RUNS	HS	AVGE	100S
Batting	42	0	921	143	21·92	1

Bowling 29 wkts at 35·13 Ct 21

TRUEMAN, Frederick Sewards (1931–)

Maltby Mod Sch. Yorkshire 1949–1968. England: in England 1952, 1953, 1955–1965 consecutively; in Australia 1958–59, 1962–63; in West Indies 1953–54, 1959–60; in New Zealand 1958–59, 1962–63.

Freddie Trueman was born – some would say quarried – at Stainton in Yorkshire on 6 February 1931. Thirty-three years later, on 15th August at the Oval, he became the first man in the history of cricket to take 300 wickets in Test Matches. He was asked if he thought the feat would ever be repeated. Characteristically he replied, 'Aye, but whoever does it will be bloody tired.' This comment reveals the essence of the man. A touch of belligerence, a hint of humility, a pinch of roughness and an over-riding sense of humour: a Yorkshireman from the ends of his unruly hair to the tips of his pigeon-toes who felt controversy at his elbow throughout his career.

His debut was in 1949 and he was capped for Yorkshire in 1951. He did a spell of National Service in the RAF which somewhat retarded his cricket development. In his early days his natural hostility earned him the nickname 'Fiery Fred'. From the first his run-up was curving and long but nicely modulated. The final stride had a pronounced drag which caused some difficulties later when the front-foot rule was introduced. The arm was high and the movement of the ball was predominantly away from the bat. Allied to this was a burning desire to see all batsmen back in the pavilion as rapidly as possible. He found his early Test opponents, India, easy meat. They retreated and he chased them remorselessly. Overseas he found wickets harder to come by and he was not an automatic selection for all tours. Tyson and Statham brought back the Ashes from Australia in 1954–55. His forthright views and colourful language did not always find favour with the selectors either.

Fred Trueman: after a day's work.

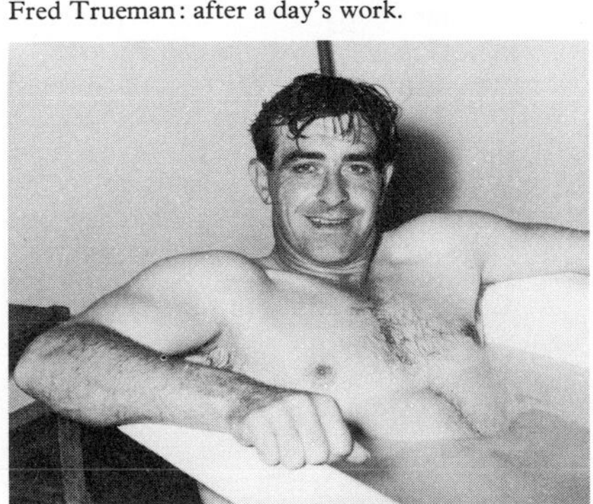

However, control of temperament came with maturity. A boundary off his bowling did not always signal a bouncer next ball and the yorker was introduced as a potent weapon. He learnt that sheer pace was only one facet of the job. The advent of full television coverage of Test Matches made him a national figure. Every glower and gesture marked him down as 'a great character' in the game. He played for laughs on occasions and found them easy to get. His cricketing skill did not end with the ball. His batting could be demoralizing for any fielding side, but his concentration frequently cracked under the pressure to please the crowd. A safe catcher and a brilliant ambidextrous thrower, he made life very easy for his captain to place him advantageously in the field. One of his most endearing personal traits is a fantastic memory for any game in which he has played. He can almost recite his 307 Test wickets victim by victim. Not the least of his gifts is a pungent turn of phrase. In recent years radio and television audiences, in England and Australia, have found him an informative observer. Cricket and the Anglo-Saxon tongue have been enriched by his presence.

JOHN WARR

CAREER FIGURES

	INNS	NO	RUNS	HS	AVGE	100S
Batting	713	120	9231	104	15·56	3

Bowling 2304 wkts at 18·29 Ct 438

Test Record (67)

	INNS	NO	RUNS	HS	AVGE	100S
Batting	85	14	981	39*	13·81	–

Bowling 307 wkts at 21·57 Ct 64

TRUMBLE, Hugh (1867–1938)

Victoria 1887–88 to 1903–04 (Captain 1899–1900 to 1903–04). Australia: in Australia 1894–95, 1897–98, 1901–02 (Captain), 1903–04; in England 1890, 1893, 1896, 1899, 1902. Secretary Melbourne CC 1911–1938.

Trumble was one of the greatest medium-pace bowlers because to his physical ability he added an unusually shrewd cricket brain. A tall man, with a high action, he kept an impeccable length, even on the hardest wickets, doing a little each way, and, if the ball was turning, he was formidable indeed. He would attack not only a batsman's weakness but his strength, knowing that there is no more insidious trap than to tempt a man to play his favourite stroke once too often. He was a master in the art of adapting his field to the batsman and the wicket. Like many Australians he retired while still in his prime and in his last Test innings (it was also his last first-class match) took 7 for 28. In all Australia–England Tests he took 141 wickets, easily a record for either side. He was a good enough bat to make 1,000 runs on a tour of England and was one of the finest slips of his day. After his retirement he was a much-loved secretary of the Melbourne Club.

R. L. ARROWSMITH

CAREER FIGURES

	INNS	NO	RUNS	HS	AVGE	100S
Batting	344	67	5395	107	19·47	3

Bowling 929 wkts at 18·46 Ct 329

Test Record (32)

	INNS	NO	RUNS	HS	AVGE	100S
Batting	57	14	851	70	19·79	–

Bowling 141 wkts at 21·78 Ct 45

Victor Trumper: the unrivalled Australian hero of the Golden Age. Note the generous back-lift and the open face of the bat.

TRUMPER, Victor Thomas (1877–1915)

New South Wales 1894–95 to 1913–14 (Captain 1907–08 to 1913–14). Australia: in Australia 1901–02, 1903–04, 1907–08, 1910–11, 1911–12; in England 1899, 1902, 1905, 1909; in South Africa 1902–03.

The name Trumper has still for all who saw him bat a magic of its own. He first gained fame in his own country by his initial hundred, 292 not out, for NSW v Tasmania in 1898–99, and in England the following summer by his 135 not out at Lord's in only his 2nd Test Match; but it was in 1902 that he established himself beyond question as among the very first of contemporary batsmen when, in a deplorably wet summer, he made 2,570 runs and 11 hundreds.

The greatest of these was in the 1st innings of the historic Test Match at Manchester which Australia eventually won by 3 runs: the wicket was soft with rain and, with the sun coming out, a formidable English attack had been enjoined by their captain, 'Keep Victor quiet till the ball really starts turning'; at lunch the Australian score was 173 for 1, and Trumper was out for 104. Eighteen months later in Australia he made 185 not out in the First Test against P. F. Warner's side, and in the Second, on an 'impossible' Melbourne wicket, scored 74 superlative runs out of a total of 122. Seven years later he dominated the series against the South African visitors, averaging 94 with a total of 661 runs, and, touring New Zealand in the winter of 1913 just before he was struck down by his fatal illness, he scored 1,246 in 15 innings, including a contribution of 293 made in 3 hours in a partnership of 433 for the 8th wicket with Arthur Sims.

But the measure of Trumper's genius is not to be found in any figures: it was essentially qualitative rather than quantitative, revealed in terms of spontaneous art rather than in an acquired technique. He had the lissome and co-ordinated body of a natural athlete; like all great batsmen he seemed to sight the ball almost as soon as it left the bowler's hand, and he moved into his strokes with effortless and perfectly balanced ease. There was no limit to their range, or flaw in their fluency or timing: the better the bowling, the more difficult the wicket, the more likely was his genius to rise to the challenge. To it and the man behind it no better tribute could be paid than Sir Pelham Warner's words: 'He was as modest as he was magnificent: batting seemed to be just part of himself'.

H. S. ALTHAM

CAREER FIGURES

	INNS	NO	RUNS	HS	AVGE	100S
Batting	401	21	16939	300*	44·57	42

Bowling 64 wkts at 31·73 Ct 171

Test Record (48)

	INNS	NO	RUNS	HS	AVGE	100S
Batting	89	8	3163	214*	39·04	8

Bowling 8 wkts at 37·62 Ct 31

TURNER, Charles Thomas Biass (1862–1944)

New South Wales 1882–83 to 1896–97. Australia: in Australia 1886–87, 1887–88, 1891–92, 1894–95; in England: 1888, 1890, 1893.

Turner succeeded Spofforth as Australia's star bowler and many of their contemporaries thought him the better of the two. According to 'W.G.', Turner, though only fast-medium, came off the ground quicker than any bowler he had played except George Freeman, and Sir Stanley Jackson called him the best medium-paced bowler he had ever met. With a curiously full-fronted action and a rather low delivery, he none the less made the ball lift sharply, varied his off-break with one which moved a bit from leg and had a deadly yorker. No Australian has approached his 283 wickets in 1888 in first-class matches and he has the finest Test record, too, of any Australian bowler. Nor has any other bowler taken 100 wickets in an Australian first-class season. He was also a very useful bat.

R. L. ARROWSMITH

CAREER FIGURES

	INNS	NO	RUNS	HS	AVGE	100S
Batting	259	13	3855	103	15·67	1

Bowling 992 wkts at 14·26 Ct 84

Test Record (17)

	INNS	NO	RUNS	HS	AVGE	100S
Batting	32	4	323	29	11·53	–

Bowling 101 wkts at 16·53 Ct 8

TURNER, Glenn Maitland (1947–)

Otago Boys' HS, Dunedin. Otago 1964–65 to 1975–76. Northern Districts 1976–77– . Worcestershire 1967– . New Zealand: in New Zealand 1968–69, 1970–71, 1972–73, 1973–74, 1974–75, 1975–76 (Captain), 1976–77 (Captain); in England 1969, 1973; in Australia 1973–74; in West Indies 1971–72; in India 1969–70, 1976–77 (Captain); in Pakistan 1969–70, 1976–77 (Captain).

At Northampton on 31 May 1973, Dunedin-born Glenn Turner became only the 8th man in the history of first-class cricket in England to score 1,000 runs before the end of May. He remains, and, with the restructuring of the modern game, is likely to continue as the only man since the Second World War to climb this batting Everest. Consistency is Turner's password. Between 24 April and 31 May he played in 11 matches and had 18 innings occupying 35 hours 42 minutes. They were: 41, 153 not out, 143, 85, 7, 8, 17 not out, 81, 13, 53, 44, 153 not out, 3, 2, 66 not out, 30, 10 not out, and 111 not out – 1,018 runs at an average of 78·30. Not surprisingly he headed the English averages that year, the only man to score over 2,000 runs (2,416), at an average of 67·11.

This was a vintage period for Turner. The year before, in West Indies, he and Congdon had held off the opposition. In the Kingston Test Turner batted throughout the innings for 223 not out. In the same series he occupied the crease for 705 minutes at Georgetown in making 259. But there is another side to Turner. At Swansea in 1977 he made 141 in Worcestershire's total of 169 against Glamorgan. This represented 83·63% of his side's runs – a world record. He is one of only 15 batsmen to have scored 2 hundreds in a match on 4 or more occasions. Turner has one of the soundest defensive techniques in the modern game and plays with an unusually straight bat. The demands of fast scoring imposed by limited-over cricket helped transform him from a safety-first player into a free-scoring opener fit to be compared with the best of all time.

PETER WALKER

TYLDESLEY, Ernest (1889–1962)

Salford Sch of Tech. Lancashire 1909–1936. England: in England 1921, 1924, 1926, 1928; in Australia 1928–29; in South Africa 1927–28.

Ernest Tyldesley was one of the finest batsmen ever to play for Lancashire. Ernest, like his famous brother, J.T., was born at Roe Green near Manchester. He learned to play, also like his brother, at the Roe Green cricket field, coached by J.T. from whom he inherited a slightly cross-bat. J. T. Tyldesley used to argue that a straight bat is of use only to a straight ball, and it is not worth while just pushing forward! J.T. frequently insisted that Ernest was technically his superior. The truth is, though, that J.T. had a touch of genius.

Ernest Tyldesley's experiences as an England player were peculiar. He first played for England v Australia, at Trent Bridge, in 1921, against the menacing fast attack of Gregory and McDonald. He scored 0 and 7, bowled off his cheekbone by Gregory in his 2nd innings and knocked out. He was not recalled to the England XI until the Fourth Test Match of this same 1921 rubber, when he scored a truly brilliant 78 not out. In the following Test Match, at Kennington Oval, his contribution was a cultivated 39, after which the England Selection Committee (apart from one match in 1924) ignored him until 1926. Then, in the Fourth Test Match v Australia, at Old Trafford, he scored 81, only to be dropped for the concluding game of the rubber. Two years afterwards he was taken to Australia, one of A. P. F. Chapman's victorious team, but was trusted with 1 Test Match only, in which he scored 31 and 21. Never again was he picked to play for England v Australia. So, over a period of 8 years and a few months, Tyldesley was thought, by the various England Selection Committees, good enough to be given only 5 matches against Australia, in which he averaged 42·83. In South Africa, in the Test Matches of the 1927–28 rubber, he topped the England batting averages – 520 runs, average 65. In 1928 Tyldesley in county cricket in England amassed 3,024 runs, average 79. In his career he reached a hundred 102 times, twice getting 2 hundreds in one and the same match.

His batsmanship was like the man himself, courteous yet shrewd. Even while he put an attack to the sword, he never suggested violence or brutality. His was the batsmanship of good manners. He commanded a late cut of great charm, a graceful lean over the ball and a modest but purposeful flick of the wrists. George Duckworth's story of Tyldesley's last weeks is typical of a Lancashire man of unobtrusive but sterling character. Duckworth visited him at his home during his last days. 'And how are you, Ernest?' 'Well,' replied Ernest, 'I was at specialist's yesterday and he says my eyes are going, and I've pretty bad pains in my thighs and my chest is giving me jip.' Then, after a pause, he added, 'Mind you, George, there's nothin' the matter with me, tha knows.' The county of the Red Rose will remember and revere him as long as they remember brother 'J.T.'.

NEVILLE CARDUS

CAREER FIGURES

	INNS	NO	RUNS	HS	AVGE	100S
Batting	961	106	38874	256*	45·46	102

Bowling 6 wkts at 57·67 Ct 295

Test Record (14)

	INNS	NO	RUNS	HS	AVGE	100S
Batting	20	2	990	122	55·00	3

Bowling 0 wkt for 2 runs Ct 2

TYLDESLEY, John Thomas (1873–1930)

Lancashire 1895–1923. England: in England 1899, 1902, 1905, 1907, 1909; in Australia 1901–02, 1903–04; in South Africa 1898–99.

From 1902 to 1909 J. T. Tyldesley, one of the greatest of Lancashire batsmen, was an automatic choice to bat 1st wicket down for England. Round about 1902 he was the only professional player who could keep his place in the England XI on the strength of his batting alone, though his brilliant fielding, notably at 3rd man and deep long-on, no doubt also added to this indispensability. As we sum up his skill and character, we must keep in mind the important fact that of the 31 Test Matches he played in, 19 were confined to a 3-day limit in this country, during a period when wickets were not protected from rain, and marl was freely used, to the advan-

J. T. Tyldesley: at the turn of the century the only professional to command a Test place as a batsman.

tage of a school of spin bowlers not since equalled in resource.

In 1901 the wicket at Old Trafford was so fiery during May and half of June that it was a danger to skull and thorax. Playing half his innings at Old Trafford that season, Tyldesley's summer total came to no less than 3,041 runs, average 55·29, a performance, considering the circumstances, seldom equalled by a batsman of Tyldesley's rapid strokeplay. He was very quick on his feet, less than middle height but square of shoulder, with strong flexible wrists. He was superb against fast bowling; also he was one of the first to show how to cope with the googly, brought to a truly dangerous stage of its development by the South Africans of 1907. On 13 occasions he scored a double hundred, his highest innings 295 not out v Kent, at Old Trafford in 1906. He was nearing his 46th birthday, in 1919, when he scored 272 v Derbyshire at Chesterfield, in 5 hours. He scored 3 hundreds against Australia, and one against South Africa.

His Test Match statistical record grotesquely underrates Tyldesley's quality as a batsman of international rank, especially his performance against odds and in difficult wicket conditions. At Melbourne, in January 1904, his innings of 62, out of England's total of 103 against Australia, during P. F. Warner's campaign which recovered the Ashes for England, was then regarded almost as of unprecedented skill in hot sunshine on Melbourne's notoriously vicious turf after rain. Hugh Trumble took 5 wickets for 34 in England's innings. He afterwards, many years later, assured me that though the ball now reared shoulder high from a length, now squatted and turned, Tyldesley scarcely made a mishit. 'His footwork was marvellous,' said Trumble. His 1st hundred for England against Australia, at Birmingham in 1902, was another instance of Tyldesley's psychological and technical resource in a dire situation. England had lost MacLaren, Fry and Ranjitsinhji for 35 before Tyldesley got to work in an innings of finely mingled aggression and resistance.

For all his swift play of strokes, broadsword square-cuts and leaping drives, he commanded a sound defence. He seldom was so far forward that he could do little but push. He was a convincing example of the Ranjitsinhji–Fry precept – 'Play back or drive.' The only batsman of my time whom I could mention to give some idea of what J. T. Tyldesley was like is Charles Macartney. And I include Tyldesley in the company of the finest professional cricketer-gentlemen I have ever known – among the others being Sir Jack Hobbs, George Gunn, George Hirst, Ernest Tyldesley, Andy Sandham and Jack Robertson.

NEVILLE CARDUS

CAREER FIGURES

	INNS	NO	RUNS	HS	AVGE	100S
Batting	994	62	37897	295*	40·66	86

Bowling 3 wkts at 70·33 Ct 314

Test Record (31)

	INNS	NO	RUNS	HS	AVGE	100S
Batting	55	1	1661	138	30·75	4

Ct 16

TYSON, Frank Holmes (1930–)

Queen Elizabeth GS, Middleton, and Durham Univ. Northamptonshire 1952–1960. England: in England 1954, 1955, 1956; in Australia 1954–55, 1958–59; in South Africa 1956–57; in New Zealand 1954–55, 1958–59.

Frank Tyson, born in Lancashire on 6 June 1930, was invited to trials at Old Trafford, but he reached the first-class ranks after residential qualification for Northamptonshire. His 1st full season in 1954 brought him to national prominence with selection for England in the final Test against Pakistan and an MCC invitation to tour Australia and New Zealand in the side captained by Hutton.

On that tour he touched the zenith of his fast bowling. His achievement lay in creating, with Statham, one of the most effective fast bowling partnerships in all cricket history.

Frank Tyson: taken when he was the fastest bowler in the world.

After a discouraging early experience and a revision of technique, Tyson took 10 wickets in the Second Test at Sydney, which England won; at Melbourne, in the Third Test, he had the memorable figures of 7 for 27 in the 2nd Australian innings. Tyson's bowling confirmed the England authority that brought triumph in the rubber.

Tyson left Australia in 1955 with a worldwide reputation and the designation of 'Typhoon'. The severe physical demands imposed by quest for exceptional speed from a somewhat ungainly action virtually precluded the possibility of a long career. Injuries limited his appearance in both county and international cricket and, though he made a second tour of Australia in 1958–59, the dramatic splendour of the first proved beyond recapture.

With a total of 766 first-class wickets to his name, Tyson retired from professional cricket to take up an appointment in Melbourne as a schoolmaster, on academic qualifications from Durham University. He was subsequently drawn back into cricket involvement as coach and organizer in the Victorian Cricket Association and as a television commentator.

Tyson was an impressive bowler essentially in the speed he commanded and the resolution he expressed in run-up and delivery. His best pace was nothing short of startling to batsmen and spectators alike. He represented an elemental force obscuring the details of technique and the highest tribute he received was the gasp of incredulity frequently emitted by the crowd as the ball passed from his hand to the distant wicket-keeper. For Northamptonshire his effectiveness was reduced by the type of pitch commonly produced at the county headquarters and he took only 509 wickets in the Championship, but in the favourable conditions of his triumphs he stood in the highest ranks of fast bowling.

J. M. KILBURN

CAREER FIGURES

	INNS	NO	RUNS	HS	AVGE	100S
Batting	316	76	4103	82	17·09	–

Bowling 766 wkts at 20·92 Ct 86

Test Record (17)

	INNS	NO	RUNS	HS	AVGE	100S
Batting	24	3	230	37*	10·95	–

Bowling 76 wkts at 18·56 Ct 4

UMRIGAR, Pahlan Ratanji (1926–)

Bharda New HS, and Bombay Univ. Parsees 1944–45. Bombay 1946–47. Gujerat 1950–51. India: in India 1948–49, 1951–52, 1952–53, 1955–56 (Captain), 1956–57 (Captain), 1958–59 (Captain), 1959–60, 1960–61, 1961–62; in England 1952, 1959; in West Indies 1952–53, 1961–62; in Pakistan 1954–55.

A tall, powerful right-hander, especially strong in front of the wicket, 'Polly' Umrigar captained Bombay University and scored a hundred for Indian Universities against the touring West Indians in 1948–49. By the middle 1950s he had become the sheet-anchor of India's batting and, until surpassed by S. M. Gavaskar in 1978, had scored more Test runs for India than any other batsman. His 59 Test appearances were also a record for India for a time. He scored 3 double-hundreds in England in both 1952 and 1959, making well over 1,000 runs on each tour. He proved himself a shrewd captain when he led Bombay to 5 successive Ranji Trophy victories, beginning in 1958–59. He was a brilliant fielder and good bowler of off-breaks on a helpful wicket. He played League cricket in Lancashire for Werneth, Church and Oldham, and also, after retiring from active cricket managed and selected Indian teams.

IRVING ROSENWATER

CAREER FIGURES

	INNS	NO	RUNS	HS	AVGE	100S
Batting	350	41	16155	252*	52·28	47

Bowling 306 wkts at 25·86 Ct 218

Test Record (59)

	INNS	NO	RUNS	HS	AVGE	100S
Batting	94	8	3631	223	42·22	12

Bowling 35 wkts at 42·08 Ct 33

UNDERWOOD, Derek Leslie (1945–)

Beckenham and Penge GS. Kent 1963– . England: in England 1966–1977; in Australia 1970–71, 1974–75, 1976–77, 1979–80; in West Indies 1973–74; in New Zealand 1970–71, 1974–75; in India 1972–73, 1976–77, 1979–80; in Pakistan 1968–69, 1972–73. WSC.

Derek Underwood was a teenage prodigy of the 1960s who played his 1st game for Kent at the age of 17 and who, by the end of that season, had taken over a hundred wickets with a wholly individual style of left-arm spin bowling. Cricket is used to seeing such startling overtures unfulfilled, and although his wickets had cost only 19·55 runs each, there were experienced judges who thought his run-up too long, his trajectory too flat, and that the sharp turn extracted at near medium-pace would disappear on better wickets than those which Kent had played on that year. Derek Underwood not only answered those sceptics, but, year after year, remorsely taught them the lesson that individuality works, and that a good bowler with rhythm and a natural action will always take wickets.

His Test debut was in 1966. In 1968 he took 7 Australian wickets for 50 to win the final Test at the Oval, thereby levelling the series. On MCC's tour of New Zealand in 1970–71, now 25 years old, he collected his 1,000th first-class wicket; only the gilded names of Rhodes and Lohmann had reached the target at a younger age.

In his loyal and sensitive way Derek Underwood has often heeded advice. Throughout the 1970s he worked hard to produce a much slower variety of delivery, aimed classically at the off-stump and outside, rather than at middle-and-leg, his happier, quicker approach. In 1977, having taken 265 Test wickets and only rarely forfeited his England place, he shocked the cricket world by signing a 3-year contract with World Series Cricket in Australia. More than 2 years passed before he was back in the England side and once again chasing Lance Gibbs's record of 312 Test wickets.

TONY LEWIS

VALENTINE, Alfred Lewis (1930–)

St Catherine's Sch, Speightstown. Jamaica from 1949–50. West Indies: in West Indies 1952–53, 1953–54, 1954–55, 1957–58, 1961–62; in England 1950, 1957; in Australia 1951–52, 1960–61; in New Zealand 1951–52, 1955–56.

Alf Valentine: he came from nowhere to bowl England out.

Valentine, who was coached in Jamaica by Mercer, of Sussex and Glamorgan, and taught by him the value of spin, was accepted as, at his best, the finest slow left-arm spin bowler seen since the end of the Second World War. In 4 Test Matches in England in 1950, he took 33 wickets and dismissed Hutton 3 times in Tests when that batsman seemed to have reached the forbidding stage of being set for a long innings. In Australia he was perhaps the only player of the 1951–52 team who lived up to, if he did not increase, his reputation. Against India in the West Indies, Valentine maintained his skill undiminished. However, against the MCC in the West Indies in 1953–54, whereas Ramadhin was quite successful, Valentine failed; and it was their double failure that more than anything else eased the way for the decisive Australian victory in the West Indies in 1955. In England in 1957 Valentine was never the bowler he had been; he suffered from ill-health and when he seemed to have caught his best form at last (6 for 8 v Leicestershire), and to be set for the Oval Test, he broke a bone in his nose.

Valentine reached his 100 wickets in Tests with remarkable speed, but he was not selected to go to India in 1958–59 and did not play against England in 1959–60. His career in big cricket seemed over, but that was far from the case. His length, spin and experience took him to Australia again in 1960–61, and his bowling was always valuable and on occasion dangerous there. In each innings of the Third Test he took 4 wickets and had 3 for 60 in the last innings of the Fifth Test. Worrell insisted that Valentine, still the best left-hand spin bowler in the West Indies, should be on the side to England in 1963. The ubiquitous Sobers never allowed room for another left-arm spinner and Valentine therefore had very little to do. But Valentine was not only a quiet man of great popularity and wisdom in the lore of tours, but always bowled with enough to show that there was a capable and experienced replacement to hand if accident befell either Sobers or Gibbs. His pretensions as a batsman may be gauged by the fact that in 3 tours of England he never once reached double figures.

C. L. R. JAMES

CAREER FIGURES

	INNS	NO	RUNS	HS	AVGE	100S
Batting	138	46	454	24*	4·93	–

Bowling 471 wkts at 26·00 Ct 44

Test Record (36)

	INNS	NO	RUNS	HS	AVGE	100S
Batting	51	21	141	14	4·70	–

Bowling 139 wkts at 30·32 Ct 13

VAN DER MERWE, Peter Laurence (1937–)

St Andrew's Coll, Grahamstown, and Univ of Cape Town. Western Province from 1957–58. Eastern Province 1966–67. South Africa: in South Africa 1964–65, 1966–67 (Captain); in England 1965 (Captain); in Australia 1963–64; in New Zealand 1963–64.

Peter van der Merwe ranks with Jack Cheetham as the best of modern South African captains. He led the Springboks in 2 series – in England in 1965 and against Australia at home in 1966–67 – and each time he won. Van der Merwe was not a brilliant cricketer, though he was good enough to play for Eastern Province and Western Province for many years. But his leadership qualities were soon apparent, and it was as a captain that he made his name. He compensated for his limitations as a middle-order batsman with a determination and grit which marked all his efforts, and through practice and fitness he became one of the best fieldsmen of his day. A tall man, he was a safe catcher and threw so well that few risks were taken against him when the ball ran near mid-off.

He was fortunate to have under him in England in 1965 the nucleus of the great South African teams which departed international cricket with such a flourish against the Australians in 1966–67 and 1970. When they went out to field at Lord's in the First Test, not one of the players had ever set foot on the ground before, yet Van der Merwe welded them into a match-winning combination whose particular strength was their belief in themselves. A quiet, meticulous leader, he inspired his players through his personality and drive rather than by his own example. He was a deep thinker and a good analyst whose careful planning frequently surprised more experienced opponents. He was also well liked, another reason why his players responded so readily to him.

TREVOR BISSEKER

CAREER FIGURES

	INNS	NO	RUNS	HS	AVGE	100S
Batting	152	12	4087	128	29·19	4

Bowling 82 wkts at 25·82 Ct 72

Test Record (15)

	INNS	NO	RUNS	HS	AVGE	100S
Batting	23	2	533	76	25·38	–

Bowling 1 wkt for 22 Ct 11

VAN RYNEVELD, Clive Berrange (1928–)

Diocesan Coll, Cape Town. Western Province 1946–47 to 1957–58. Oxford Univ 1948–1950 (Captain 1949). South Africa: in South Africa 1953–54, 1956–57 (Captain), 1957–58 (Captain); in England 1951.

Like Alan Melville before him, van Ryneveld, after profiting from the experience of a season's leadership at Oxford, was subsequently appointed captain of South Africa. Van Ryneveld's cricket was affected in his earlier years by the claims on his academic time of rugby football; judged by his performances for Oxford, and for England in 1948–49, he was one of the best centre three-quarters, if not the best, possessed by any country in the postwar decade. His cricket was brought to an end, at the top level, without ever having really matured, by his entry into South African politics. Shortly after the Australian series of 1957–58, he entered Parliament as a Progressive, the party pledged to oppose apartheid.

Going up to Oxford from Diocesan College, Rondebosch (known as Bishop's), he gained a double blue as a freshman, and quickly established himself as a correct, watchful batsman, a dangerous leg-spin and googly bowler and a magnificent fielder. He was a great natural prospect. Back home, while working as a barrister, before his active participation in politics, he led South Africa in the fight-back that enabled them to draw the 1956–57 series against England after being 2 down. The following year when Australia were the visitors, he was less successful.

E. W. SWANTON

CAREER FIGURES

	INNS	NO	RUNS	HS	AVGE	100S
Batting	173	12	4872	150	30·26	4

Bowling 206 wkts at 30·25 Ct 72

Test Record (19)

	INNS	NO	RUNS	HS	AVGE	100S
Batting	33	6	724	83	26·81	–

Bowling 17 wkts at 39·47 Ct 14

VENKATARAGHAVAN, Srinivasaraghavan (1946–)

Vivekananda Coll, Madras. Madras 1963–64. Derbyshire 1973–1975. India: in India 1964–65, 1966–67, 1969–70, 1972–73, 1974–75, 1976–77, 1978–79, 1979–80; in England 1967, 1971, 1974, 1979 (Captain); in Australia 1977–78; in West Indies 1970–71, 1975–76; in New Zealand 1975–76.

Srinivasaraghavan Venkataraghavan, universally known, to the relief of copy-takers and compositors, as Venkat, was one of India's quartet of famous spin bowlers who between them took the best part of 1,000 wickets in Tests. An offspinner of exceptional accuracy and durability, it was at once a stroke of luck and a misfortune for him to be inseparably linked with Bedi (slow left-arm), Chandrasekhar (right-hand wrist-spin) and Prasanna (off-spin); it meant that while he benefited, when he played, from being a member of the strongest spin attack in the world, he could only be certain of his place in the team when he was its captain, in England in 1975 (World Cup) and in England again in 1979.

His direct rival was the stocky Prasanna, 5 years his senior, whose bustling, quick-armed action made him the equal of Bedi in deceptiveness of flight, and it was a tribute to Venkat's consistency, as well as his superior batting and fielding, that he was preferred as often as he was. On the one occasion they played throughout a series, against Lawry's Australians in India in 1969–70, Prasanna overshadowed him; but Venkat deservedly acquired the reputation of being the steadier under fire, and on 2 high-scoring tours of West Indies he played 8 Tests against Prasanna's 4.

Venkat, tallish and very slim, made a great start when as an 18-year-old he headed India's averages against New Zealand with 21 wickets at 19·0, including 8 for 72 in his 4th Test. Though he seldom approached those figures again, his high, fluid, well-balanced action functioned so smoothly that throughout a career lasting the best part of 2 decades, his Test overs cost well under 2½ runs each.

JOHN THICKNESSE

VERITY, Hedley (1905–1943)

Yeadon and Guisley Sec Schs. Yorkshire 1930–1939. England: in England 1931, 1933–1939 consecutively; in Australia 1932–33, 1936–37; in South Africa 1938–39; in New Zealand 1932–33; in India 1933–34.

Hedley Verity was one of the most skilful left-arm spin bowlers in cricket's history; and he followed in the great Yorkshire tradition of Peate, Peel and Rhodes. Not until he had gone beyond his 25th birthday could he be sure of a place in the Yorkshire XI; for Rhodes did not renounce his arts until 1930. Verity was not really a disciple, conscious or not, of Peel and Rhodes, because each of these classical masters was truly slow of pace, with a variation now and again of a slightly quicker ball. Verity deployed his skill from the basis of a pace falling little below medium. When first he played at Lord's for Yorkshire, Maurice Leyland asked me, 'What do you think of our new fast bowler?' – a humorous reference to Verity. His action was thoroughbred: a run-up of upright easy balance and a high circling arm. On a turf at all responsive, after sun and rain, his spin had an abrupt angularity, turn and 'lift', not surpassed by any other spinner of his day, excepting, possibly, Charles Parker of Gloucestershire.

Verity quickly established his position in the game. His 2nd season with Yorkshire saw the team Champions; and he headed the bowling averages with 138 wickets at 12·34 each. But a year before this, in the summer of his debut, he had taken 13 for 83 against Hampshire at Bournemouth. In his 2nd season he took all 10 wickets in an innings v Warwickshire, and in his 3rd he had 10 for 10 v Nottinghamshire at Leeds, the most economical such analysis in history. He went through his initiation to Yorkshire cricket modestly and quietly, despite these imposing performances. In those years a young Yorkshire cricketer had no choice but to be seen and not heard in the great company of Rhodes, Robinson, Macaulay and the rest. After Verity had spun 13 Hampshire batsmen out at Bournemouth, in 1930, he was taken aside, and to task, by Emmott Robinson, who told him, 'You let one slip down leg-side, long hop it were. Tha' should have had 7 for 22. Keep 'em up whatever you do.'

His art expressed the man himself, unassertive yet persuasive of speech, a student of the game, and life, with not too many words but enough seriousness of thought. He preferred to go to work on a flawless Australian wicket against Bradman than revel in a 'sticky' pitch where the batsmen could set him few problems at all. Verity could keep Bradman occasionally quiet on the best Australian wickets. He survives comparison with the greatest exponents of his craft. Maybe on good pitches his bowling did not put the questions to batsmen which they had to answer when faced with the curving, hovering flights of Rhodes or Blythe. On his day, though, Verity was irresistible, as at Lord's on 25 June 1934 when, between noon and late afternoon, he routed the Australians, including Bradman, by taking 14 wickets for 80 runs. His record for the short 10 years of his career was nearly beyond comparison: 40 Test Matches and 144 wickets at 24·37 runs each; 1,956 wickets in all his brief days in the sun at 14·87 each. In each of his 9 full English seasons he accounted for, on average, 180 wickets. In consecutive summers, 1935, 1936 and 1937, he took 200 wickets. He topped the country's bowling averages in his 1st and last (1939) seasons, and was never in lower than 5th place.

Hedley Verity: in the classical mould, bowling for the Champion County against The Rest, at the Oval 1935.

Also he could bat usefully, with a graceful if often not formidable forward stroke. He actually went in 1st for England v Australia at Adelaide during the 1936–37 rubber, and with Charles Barnett shared in 1st wicket partnerships of 53 and 45. In 1936, when he devoured 216 wickets, he found time and opportunity to amass 855 runs.

His last words, as he fell wounded in action for England on the field of war were 'Keep going'. It was his simple, unaffected, modest motto throughout his life. He died of wounds in an Italian prisoner-of-war camp, aged 38.

NEVILLE CARDUS

CAREER FIGURES

	INNS	NO	RUNS	HS	AVGE	100S
Batting	415	106	5603	101	18·13	1

Bowling 1956 wkts at 14·87 Ct 264

Test Record (40)

	INNS	NO	RUNS	HS	AVGE	100S
Batting	44	12	669	66*	20·90	–

Bowling 144 wkts at 24·37 Ct 30

VILJOEN, Kenneth George (1910–1974)

Kimberley Boys' HS. Griqualand West. Orange Free State. Transvaal. South Africa: in South Africa 1930–31, 1935–36, 1938–39, 1948–49; in England 1935, 1947; in Australia 1931–32; in New Zealand 1931–32. President South African Cricket Association 1962–63, 1964–65.

A stylish right-hander, Viljoen headed the averages for the South Africans in England in 1935, when he scored 124 in the Test at Old Trafford and gained a reputation as a brilliant out-fielder. His maiden hundred in first-class cricket was the highest of his career and established the record innings for Griqualand West – 215 v Western Province at Kimberley in 1929–30. Always orthodox, he was the only South African to score a Test hundred in Australia in 1931–32, and played 27 Tests in all. In England in 1947 he again exceeded 1,000 runs and made 201 v Sussex at Hove. He achieved a reputation as a firm disciplinarian rather on the rugby football model as manager of the South African sides that toured Australia and New Zealand in 1952–53 and 1963–64 and England in 1955.

IRVING ROSENWATER

CAREER FIGURES

	INNS	NO	RUNS	HS	AVGE	100S
Batting	209	25	7964	215	43·28	23

Bowling 29 wkts at 24·90 Ct 49

Test Record (27)

	INNS	NO	RUNS	HS	AVGE	100S
Batting	50	2	1365	124	28·43	2

Bowling 0 wkts for 23 Ct 5

VISWANATH, Gundappa Ranganath (1949–)

Fort HS, and Bangalore Univ. Mysore 1968–69– . India: in India 1969–70, 1972–73, 1974–75, 1976–77, 1978–79, 1979–80; in England 1971, 1974, 1979; in Australia 1977–78; in West Indies 1970–71, 1975–76; in New Zealand 1975–76; in Pakistan 1978–79.

Gundappa Viswanath: wrists of steel and flashing eyes.

In 1969 a young Bangalore batsman made his Test debut against Lawry's Australian side at Kanpur. In India's 2nd innings of 312 for 7, his 137 had most to do with earning India a draw. This was Gundappa Viswanath, who thus gave notice that he was to become one of the next major Indian batsmen. Since 1971 he and his brother-in-law, Sunil Gavaskar, have, through a decade of high pace, defined the 2 distinct strains of Indian batsmanship.

While Gavaskar draws his inspiration from the Bombay school of Vijay Merchant, which manifests itself in immaculate defence allied to great concentration, Viswanath belongs to the more stylish school of Vijay Hazare, which, being gentle and philosophical, is more representative of southern India. 'Vishy's' achievements are the more remarkable for the fact that he is only 5 feet 2 inches tall. He failed to make his school team because his master thought that good batsmen needed more inches.

The rise of Gavaskar has tended to overshadow Viswanath's worth to the Indian side, though against England in 1971 it was the latter's 68 which kept India in the Second Test at Lord's, while his 33 at the Oval had a good deal to do with India making the 173 they needed to win their 1st Test victory on English soil. After, for him, a moderate series in England in 1974, he demonstrated his match-winning capabilities against Clive Lloyd's West Indians in India in 1974–75. After the pace of Roberts and the batting of Richards and Kallicharran had given West Indies victories by wide margins in the 1st 2 Tests, Viswanath came into the picture, his 52 and 139 at Calcutta and 97 not out in Madras, out of an Indian total of 190, helping to construct 2 narrow victories.

In India's famous victory over West Indies at Port of Spain in 1976, when they scored 406 to win the Third Test Match, Viswanath's 112 ensured that the later batsmen had a task they could cope with. Since then he has played with splendid consistency, getting out too often between 50 and 100 perhaps, but still forming with Gavaskar a partnership which has brought as much happiness and relief to India as any in their Test history.

MIHIR BOSE

VOCE, William (1909–)

Nottinghamshire 1927–1952. England: in England 1931, 1932, 1936, 1937, 1946; in Australia 1932–33, 1936–37, 1946–47; in South Africa 1930–31; in West Indies 1929–30; in New Zealand 1932–33.

Voce was a great fast left-hand bowler who might under firmer and wiser direction have been greater. Throughout his career he was a centre of controversy. Should he bowl slow or fast? Over the wicket or round? To a leg-trap or to a full array of slips? Above all, should he bowl Body-line? It was this dispute which lost him his chance of playing for England v Australia in this country, as he must surely have done otherwise in 1934. But, despite his value as a foil to Larwood in 1932–33, he reached his greatest height under G. O. Allen in Australia 4 years later, when his bowling in the first 2 Test Matches nearly won the rubber. Relying mainly on the ball that left the batsman, he had for those 2 matches the astonishing figures of 17 wickets for 133 runs.

Very strong, he had a beautiful action and

Bill Voce: Harold Larwood's henchman.

that long, loose arm, so characteristic of left-handers, which made him also a glorious thrower. He was a magnificent field and developed into an effective bat who made several hundreds for his county. It is sad proof of the havoc which 6 years of war is bound to wreak on a country's cricket that Voce should still have been required for England in 1946. The outward semblance of the great bowler and the action were still there, the greatness had gone.

R. L. ARROWSMITH

CAREER FIGURES

	INNS	NO	RUNS	HS	AVGE	100S
Batting	525	130	7583	129	19·19	4

Bowling 1558 wkts at 23·08 Ct 280

Test Record (27)

	INNS	NO	RUNS	HS	AVGE	100S
Batting	38	15	308	66	13·39	–

Bowling 98 wkts at 27·88 Ct 15

VOGLER, Albert Ernest Edward (1876–1946)

Natal 1903–04. Transvaal 1904–05, 1909–10. Eastern Province 1905–06, 1906–07. Middlesex 1906. South Africa: in South Africa 1905–06, 1909–10; in England 1907; in Australia 1910–11.

Vogler was the greatest of the South African googly bowlers. He came very fast off the ground, varied his flight and pace, and had a deadly slow yorker. His googly was the hardest to detect and was almost impossible to tell from his top-spinner. With the new ball he could bowl orthodox fast-medium swingers. In 1907 he was, next to Barnes, the finest bowler in the world. He was besides a useful hard-hitting batsman and a good field.

R. L. ARROWSMITH

CAREER FIGURES

	INNS	NO	RUNS	HS	AVGE	100S
Batting	137	19	2375	103	20·13	1

Bowling 401 wkts at 18·14 Ct 83

Test Record (15)

	INNS	NO	RUNS	HS	AVGE	100S
Batting	26	6	340	65	17·00	–

Bowling 64 wkts at 22·73 Ct 20

WADEKAR, Ajit Laxman (1941–)

Chabildas Lallubhai Boys' Sch, and Bombay Univ. Bombay from 1958–59. India: in India 1966–67, 1969–70, 1972–73 (Captain); in England 1967, 1971 (Captain), 1974 (Captain); in Australia 1967–68; in West Indies 1970–71 (Captain); in New Zealand 1967–68.

Ajit Wadekar had the distinction of being the 1st Indian to win 3 Test series, 2 of them abroad, in succession. He was a typical product of Bombay. He learnt the hard way, being in and out of the Bombay team in the 1950s and having to wait till 1967 before making good his Test place with 67 against Hall and Griffith in the Fifth Test at Madras. Wadekar impressed the critics on his first visit to England in 1967, when E. W. Swanton wrote in the *Daily Telegraph* that his 70 in the Edgbaston Test 'on a badly worn pitch was played with the judgment of a truly high-class batsman'. It was in England that he adopted the double-eyed stance, limiting his freedom of strokeplay; after a lean season against West Indies in 1971 he reverted to his old style to make an ideal No. 3. As a captain he was defensive without being negative and splendidly successful. A first-class slip fielder, he held 44 catches in 37 Tests and finished with 2,113 runs from 71 Test innings (average 31·07) and with 4,388 (average 60·94) in the Ranji Trophy.

K. N. PRABHU

CAREER FIGURES

	INNS	NO	RUNS	HS	AVGE	100S
Batting	358	33	15377	323	47·31	36

Bowling 21 wkts at 43·23 Ct 270

Test Record (37)

	INNS	NO	RUNS	HS	AVGE	100S
Batting	71	3	2113	143	31·07	1

Bowling 0 wkts for 55 Ct 46

WALCOTT, Clyde Leopold, OBE (1926–)

Combermere Sch, and Harrison Coll, Barbados. Barbados 1941–42 to 1953–54. British Guiana 1954–55 to 1963–64. West Indies: in West Indies 1947–48, 1952–53, 1953–54, 1954–55, 1957–58, 1959–60; in England 1950, 1957; in Australia 1951–52; in New Zealand 1951–52; in India 1948–49.

Walcott stands 6 feet 2 inches with the breadth and weight to correspond. Yet in 1950 in England he was the regular West Indies wicket-keeper, and later took everything that came within his enormous reach at slip. He was just 16 and a Harrison College boy when he first played for Barbados. When he and Worrell made 574 together, Walcott made 314 not out. Against England in the West Indies in 1947–48 only his wicket-keeping kept him in the Test side. He established himself as a batsman against India in India in 1948–49, and in 1950, though somewhat overshadowed by Weekes and Worrell, he added the dimension needed to construct the 'W' triumvirate. He made 7 hundreds, including a great 168 not out at a critical time in the Test at Lord's, and when Weekes and Worrell seemed to tire near the end, he took over the brunt of the batting.

Clyde Walcott: the delayed drive.

In Australia Walcott seemed to be troubled by the fast bowling of Lindwall and Miller. Against India in the West Indies he scored heavily. But it was in the West Indies, against England in 1953–54 and Australia in 1955, that Walcott assumed an unrivalled supremacy. Against England he scored 698 runs with hundreds in 3 Tests, against Australia 827 runs in 10 completed innings: he scored 5 hundreds (twice a hundred in each innings) and this against Lindwall, Miller, Benaud and Archer.

He dominated the scene when at the wicket. Crouching low in his stance, he stood straight to play. Off either foot he bombarded fielders from mid-on to cover. Anything short, however fast, he hooked to the on-boundary not getting quite behind but with great strength of wrist and forearm. He missed no opportunity to cut square and even flicked the straight length ball past mid-on.

He was an outstanding figure in the English Leagues. He started the 1957 season in England in splendid form, but injured himself in the First Test when scoring 90. Never afterwards on that tour did he recapture form and though he ended the season with good figures his past achievements and commanding style when he did make runs left a feeling of some massive piece of machinery gone wrong. In the West Indies against Pakistan in 1957–58, Walcott seemed to have recovered himself, scoring a brilliant 145 for West Indies at Georgetown. Since retirement he has managed several West Indies sides, a commanding figure; and had an important job in a public relations office in a large Guyanan firm.

C. L. R. JAMES

CAREER FIGURES

	INNS	NO	RUNS	HS	AVGE	100S
Batting	238	29	11820	314*	56·55	40

Bowling 35 wkts at 36·25 Ct 175 (incl w/k); st 33

Test Record (44)

	INNS	NO	RUNS	HS	AVGE	100S
Batting	74	7	3798	220	56·68	15

Bowling 11 wkts at 37·09 W/k: ct 53; st 11 Total 64

WALKER, Maxwell Henry Norman (1948–)

Friends' Sch, Hobart, and Royal Melbourne Inst of Technology. Victoria 1968–69– . Australia: in Australia 1972–73 to 1976–77 consecutively; in England 1975, 1977; in West Indies 1972–73; in New Zealand 1973–74, 1976–77. WSC.

Max Walker is one of the few Tasmanians to have played for Australia, though it was primarily with the idea of furthering his career as an Australian Rules footballer that he moved to Melbourne as a young man. A 6 feet 4 inch, heavily-built fast-medium seamer who bowled off the wrong foot, he forced his way into the Victoria side in 1971–72 and next season, with 39 wickets, went on to win the 1st 2 of his 32 Test caps, heading Australia's averages against Pakistan. However, he truly made a name for himself in the second half of that season, stepping into the breach created by Lillee's back injury on Australia's tour to West Indies to take 26 Test wickets at 20·73. The magnificence of that performance is best shown by comparing his figures with those of West Indies' most successful fast bowler, Keith Boyce, whose 9 wickets cost nearly 40 runs each in a series which Australia won 2–0. From then until 1977, when he joined WSC, Walker was a fixture, usually in support of Lillee and Thomson.

Big-boned and jovial, Walker arrived at the crease in 13 powerful strides and propelled the ball at a brisk pace amid a whirl of arms and legs. His stock ball was the in-swinger. But he also possessed a dangerous leg-cutter and this, allied to a superb command of line just outside off-stump led to many catches in the slips or at the wicket. Because of his stamina and heart, though, he was equally valuable as a stock bowler on days when the batsmen were on top. No captain need worry where his next over was coming from when he had Walker on the side and perhaps no performance better epitomized the big man's qualities than at Melbourne in 1974–75, when, after England had reached 507 for 4, he took 5 wickets for 17 to finish with 8 for 143 at the end of an innings lasting 700 minutes.

JOHN THICKNESSE

WALTERS, Cyril Frederick (1905–)

Neath County Sch. Glamorgan 1923–1928. Worcestershire 1930–1935 (Captain 1931–1935); Secretary 1928–1935. England: in England 1933, 1934 (Captain); in India 1933–34.

Walters was one of the most beautiful stroke-players in Test cricket since 1914. Slightly built, he had glorious wrists and all he lacked was the urge to pile up runs. In his 9 innings as an opener against Australia in 1934 he was only twice out under 30, yet never exceeded 82. This is wonderful consistency, especially for one who would begin hitting fours with a full old-fashioned swing in the 1st over. Yet a Test player should not get out so often when he is well set and on top of the bowling. There was about his batting a touch of that casualness which sometimes appeared in his fielding, and it is perhaps significant that in 1935 he retired not only from first-class cricket but from almost all contact with the game. Still, at his best, he was worth going a long way to see.

R. L. ARROWSMITH

CAREER FIGURES

	INNS	NO	RUNS	HS	AVGE	100S
Batting	427	32	12145	226	30·74	21

Bowling 5 wkts at 76·00 Ct 95

Test Record (11)

	INNS	NO	RUNS	HS	AVGE	100S
Batting	18	3	784	102	52·26	1

Ct 6

WALTERS, Kevin Douglas, MBE (1945–)

Dundog HS. New South Wales 1962–63– (Captain 1968–69, 1973–74 to 1975–76). Australia: in Australia 1965–66, 1967–68, 1968–69, 1970–71, 1972–73, 1973–74, 1974–75, 1976–77; in England 1968, 1972, 1975, 1977; in South Africa 1969–70; in West Indies 1972–73; in New Zealand 1973–74, 1976–77; in India 1969–70. WSC.

In his native Australia, and most other cricketing countries, Doug Walters was a brilliant batsman, an unconventional and speedy acquirer of runs. No sooner had he burst on to the international scene with a string of spectacular innings, this small, dapper, jaunty man than he became the darling of the Sydney fans. His appeal stemmed not only from the fact that he was a quality entertainer, but because he was one of them who remained unaffected by his success, liked a convivial drink and invariably lit up a fag on entering the dressing room. Doug's main roles for Australia were either to press home a sound start with a spectacular assault, or to lead a dashing counter attack after a collapse. He was feared by opposing sides, who knew that, if he stayed any time at the crease, the runs had to come. In a very short time he was able to change the whole course of a game. He was a born match-winner.

The Walters style was essentially flamboyant; his strokes, including his own speciality, 'the come-to-attention shot', when he clicked his 2 heels together with both feet facing the bowler and whipped the ball to the mid-wicket boundary, were often unorthodox. Not surprisingly with methods which depended so much upon eye, timing and reflexes he was far happier on pitches with a true bounce, and most of his best innings were played before he was 30, which is when many more correct players are reaching their prime. In England, where seamers reign supreme, Doug was noticeably less successful. Almost unbelievably for a player of his calibre, he failed to score a Test hundred during 4 tours to England. His failure to adapt to local conditions stemmed basically from an unsound defensive technique, combined with a tendency to play too square and across the line. This also explains his uncertainty against extreme pace and why he so frequently holed out in the gully, falling to the most obvious of traps. In addition to his exciting batting, Doug Walters was a very useful 'away-floater', with a knack of ending long stands, and a superb cover point with a lovely arm.

TREVOR BAILEY

Johnny Wardle: a constant thorn in South Africa's side. Here he has Trevor Goddard caught at the wicket by McIntyre at Headingley in 1955. Goddard and McGlew (the non-striker) had made 176 for South Africa's 1st wicket.

WARDLE, John Henry (1923–)

Wath-on Dearne GS. Yorkshire 1946–1958. England: in England 1950, 1951, 1953–1957 consecutively; in Australia 1954–55; in South Africa 1956–57; in West Indies 1947–48, 1953–54; in New Zealand 1954–55.

Wardle came to first-class cricket when Yorkshire were rebuilding after the Second World War. He continued the line of the county's slow left-arm bowlers and brought to his heritage manifest powers of spin, a strong physique and unbounded enthusiasm. His outstanding virtues proved to be also disadvantages in the development of his career. Spin sometimes took precedence over the need for basic accuracies and on occasions he neglected opportunities presented by circumstances. Yorkshire teams in the 1950s contained much individual playing talent but lacked a thread to bind together some ill-assorted temperaments. Dressing-room disaffection inevitably became reflected in attitudes and performances on the field. The common interest was too frequently obscured by the personal concern. Wardle was not a silent witness in an uncomfortable atmosphere.

In 1958, when he was established at international level, having been particularly successful in South Africa in 1956–57, where he took a record 90 wickets, mostly out of the back of the hand, and had just been chosen for a second tour of Australia, Yorkshire quietly announced that his county engagement was not to be renewed. The immediate consequence was a sensation of cricket. Wardle subscribed his name to scathing newspaper comment on his county captain, colleagues and committee. Yorkshire dismissed him forthwith and the England authorities withdrew the tour invitation. After brief journalistic exploitation, Wardle passed into Minor Counties cricket.

His breach with Yorkshire was healed over when, in the 1970s, he rendered coaching services acknowledged by election to honorary life-membership of the County Club. Thirty-five when he had last played for them he was left with any amount of rich cricket in him.

J. M. KILBURN

CAREER FIGURES

	INNS	NO	RUNS	HS	AVGE	100S
Batting	525	71	7318	79	16·11	–

Bowling 1842 wkts at 18·95 Ct 257

Test Record (28)

	INNS	NO	RUNS	HS	AVGE	100S
Batting	41	8	653	66	19·78	–

Bowling 102 wkts at 20·39 Ct 12

WARNER, Sir Pelham Francis, MBE (1873–1963)

Rugby 1889–1892 (Captain 1892). Oxford Univ 1895–1896. Middlesex 1894–1920 (Captain 1908–1920). England: in England 1909, 1912; in Australia 1903–04 (Captain), 1911–12 (Captain); in South Africa 1905–06 (Captain). Joint Manager in Australia 1932–33. Selector 1905, 1926, 1931, 1932, 1935–1938 (Chairman each year except 1905). Deputy Secretary MCC 1939–1945; Trustee 1946–1961; President 1950–51; Life Vice-President 1961. President of Middlesex 1937–1946.

Few men have performed greater or more varied services to cricket than 'Plum' Warner. He represented England as a batsman in this country in the golden age of batting. He was a notable captain of England in Australia and took many lesser sides abroad. For years he was one of the most consistent bats in county cricket and he was an outstanding captain of Middlesex, who led them to a sensational Championship in his final season and himself

Sir Pelham Warner going out to bat against Surrey in his last triumphant season.

by his batting saved the side in the decisive game, his last county match. He was a member of the committee at Lord's off and on for almost 60 years, and during the Second War did much of the secretarial work there. His services were fittingly honoured when he was elected President in 1950 and again when 2 years before his death he became the first life Vice-President in the history of the club. A more permanent memorial is the Warner Stand. He served constantly as a selector and was joint manager on a particularly difficult tour in Australia. He founded and for many years edited *The Cricketer* and was from 1921 to 1932 cricket correspondent of *The Morning Post*. He wrote or edited some 20 books on cricket: charmingly written, they form between them an invaluable addition to the history and literature of the game.

He had innumerable friends of all ages and on a crowded day at Lord's would greet the humblest and most obscure with the same transparently sincere pleasure and interest as the most eminent. He lived for cricket, yet it was by no means his only interest. He was, as his books and conversation showed, a well-read man, with the instincts of a scholar, and delighted particularly in military and naval history. By keenness and practice he turned himself from a good county batsman into almost a great one, and his performances are the more remarkable when it is remembered that for years he was grievously handicapped by ill-health. Never spectacular, he was a wonderfully neat and efficient bat, beautifully balanced, a fine back player when the ball was turning, very good off his legs and also an expert cutter. It was a tribute to his technique and his courage alike that one physically so frail should have been especially good against fast bowling. A fighter himself, he was a courageous and inspiring captain, who got the best out of his men and was a shrewd tactician as well. No man can have deserved more thoroughly the knighthood bestowed on him in 1937 for all that he had done for the game.

R. L. ARROWSMITH

CAREER FIGURES

	INNS	NO	RUNS	HS	AVGE	100S
Batting	875	76	29028	244	36·33	60

Bowling 15 wkts at 42·40 Ct 187

Test Record (15)

	INNS	NO	RUNS	HS	AVGE	100S
Batting	28	2	622	132*	23·92	1

Ct 3

WARR, John James (1927–)

Ealing County GS. Cambridge Univ 1949–1952 (Captain 1951). Middlesex 1949–1960 (Captain 1958–1960). England: in Australia 1950–51.

John Warr, or 'J.J.' as he became widely known during a career stretching well beyond the boundaries of the cricket field, earned playing recognition in inverse ratio to his prowess. From Ealing County Grammar School and service in the Navy, he played 4 years for Cambridge and after 2 of them, when he was captain-elect of the University and had only played in the vacation for Middlesex, he was included in the MCC team which toured Australia and New Zealand in 1950–51.

He played in 2 Test matches on that tour in a weakened bowling side, but as competition increased was never considered for Test cricket subsequently, though he became a fast-medium bowler of guile and formidable out-swing, capable of defeating the best batsmen. His partnership with Alan Moss won Middlesex many matches in the 1950s and, as a shrewd judge of the game, he led them up to 3rd place in the County Championship in the 3 years of his captaincy which ended in 1960. He took 956 wickets (average 22·79), including 116 at 18·17, 9 for 65 against Kent at Lord's and a hat-trick against Leicestershire at Loughborough, all in 1956.

After retiring he was a member of MCC's 1961 Committee of Enquiry into first-class cricket, served for some years on the Middlesex committee and wrote with characteristic humour until 1970 for the *Sunday Telegraph* on cricket and other sporting affairs. Throughout his years in first-class cricket he had been renowned as a speaker of great wit and after his retirement, when he became a prominent figure in the London discount market, he was one of the most popular after-dinner speakers of the day. His interests extended to racing and, having served on the Tattersalls Committee and as a steward at Windsor, he was elected a member of the Jockey Club in 1977.

John Warr: a late out-swinger and a rare wit.

MICHAEL MELFORD

CAREER FIGURES

	INNS	NO	RUNS	HS	AVGE	100S
Batting	544	191	3838	54*	11·46	–

Bowling 956 wkts at 22·79 Ct 116

Test Record (2)

	INNS	NO	RUNS	HS	AVGE	100S
Batting	4	0	4	4	1·00	–

Bowling 1 wkt for 281

WASHBROOK, Cyril (1914–)

Clitheroe GS, and Bridgnorth GS. Lancashire 1933–1959 (Captain 1954–1959). England: in England 1937, 1946–1950 consecutively, 1956; in Australia 1946–47, 1950–51; in South Africa 1948–49; in New Zealand 1946–47, 1950–51. Selector 1956–1957, 1971–1972.

Cyril Washbrook's career in first-class cricket began in 1933 and continued until 1959. He was educated at Clitheroe Grammar School, later at Bridgnorth Grammar School; and he always carried himself with a jauntiness of pouter-like chest and stride which Richard Tyldesley might well have called 'well-off-like'. He looked at once a cricketer, with the born cricketer's shoulders; and he wore his flannels like a cricketer. His determined chin and mouth told of the right, tough Lancastrian stuff in his bones. He needed all of it to begin with, his 1st season bringing him only 419 runs, average 26·18. Next year, 1934, he was asked to play for Lancashire only 6 times. The season after, though, he firmly announced he had come to stay. Although the Hitler war ripped years from his career, there began soon after it the Hutton-Washbrook opening partnership which served England so well.

Washbrook always put character as well as strong technique into his innings. He would hook daringly sometimes, even in a Test Match, and his square cutting was incisive and beautifully timed. At bay he could reveal untiring patience, a quite Spartan self-denial. He and Hutton were called on to withstand the fearsome pace of Lindwall and Miller. Despite this, at Leeds in 1948 they put on 168 in England's first innings and 129 in the 2nd. But Washbrook's finest hour was destined to come after he and most of us had imagined that Test cricket had seen the last of him.

After England had lost the Second Test Match to Australia at Lord's in 1956, he was recalled to the team, at the age of 41. A retrograde step, spoke the critics, confession of weakness. Washbrook did not open England's innings in this Test Match of his recall. He had, even so, to face a dire challenge. England had lost 3 wickets for 17 when he walked to the wicket. But with the calmness of experience and mastery, Washbrook took charge, taking care for a while of Peter May before sharing with him a 4th-wicket partnership of 187. This was an innings of vintage, of ripeness.

Washbrook was a swift and accurate cover point. As Lancashire's captain he insisted on discipline, but never more than that which he imposed upon himself.

NEVILLE CARDUS

CAREER FIGURES

	INNS	NO	RUNS	HS	AVGE	100S
Batting	906	107	34101	251*	42·67	76

Bowling 7 wkts at 44·14 Ct 207

Test Record (37)

	INNS	NO	RUNS	HS	AVGE	100S
Batting	66	6	2569	195	42·81	6

Bowling 1 wkt for 33 Ct 12

WATSON, William (1920–)

Paddock Council Sch, Huddersfield. Yorkshire 1939–1957. Leicestershire 1958–1964 (Captain 1958–1961). England: in England 1951, 1952, 1953, 1955, 1956, 1958; in Australia 1958–59; in West Indies 1953–54; in New Zealand 1958–59. Selector 1962–1964.

More graceful batsmen than Willie Watson are few and far between. He made batting look easy and seemed to have all the time in the world to play his shots. He was a beautiful runner between the wickets and moved, in the field, like the athlete he was. Watson first played for Yorkshire in 1939 and gained his cap in 1947. During his career he played 23 Test Matches, being selected first for the whole series against South Africa in 1951. His 1st appearance against Australia, at Lord's in 1953, is probably his finest and best-remembered innings. He made 109 and, with T. E. Bailey, saved the match for England against all the odds. In 1958 Watson became captain and assistant secretary of Leicestershire. After retirement he settled in Johannesburg where he became the chief sports administrator at the famous Wanderers' Club.

Watson was a kind and shrewd cricketer who was always willing to help young ones. He became a Test selector in 1962. He was also an international association footballer who won 4 caps for England and was selected for the Rio World Cup side in 1950.

E. D. R. EAGAR

CAREER FIGURES

	INNS	NO	RUNS	HS	AVGE	100S
Batting	753	109	25670	257	39·86	55

Bowling 0 wkts for 127 Ct 293

Test Record (23)

	INNS	NO	RUNS	HS	AVGE	100S
Batting	37	3	879	116	25·85	2

Ct 8

WEEKES, Everton de Courcy, OBE (1925–)

St Leonard's Sch, Bridgetown. Barbados 1944–45 to 1963–64. West Indies: in West Indies 1947–48, 1952–53, 1953–54, 1954–55, 1957–58; in England 1950, 1957; in Australia 1951–52; in New Zealand 1951–52, 1955–56; in India 1948–49.

Everton Weekes: a lovely piece of cricket.

Weekes was a batsman who for long periods attacked all bowlers in the same relentless manner as did Bradman and for long periods with not dissimilar success. In 1947–48 only a hundred in the last Test kept Weekes in the side for India in 1948–49. In India he added 4 Test hundreds in succession and missed a 6th only by being run out at 90. In England in 1950 the first 5 times he reached a hundred he went on to 200, once to 300, and was notably successful in Tests. He failed in Australia, but in the West Indies, against India, England and Australia, Weekes scored his hundreds, double-hundreds and narrowly missed a hundred in each innings of one Test against Australia. Sent to New Zealand with a team of juniors, Weekes hit 5 hundreds in his 1st 5 innings and 6 out of a total of 10. Despite this consistency Weekes showed that he was also the most dazzling stroke-player who had ever visited New Zealand.

He excelled in fierce cuts and hooks off the fastest bowlers and drove powerfully off either foot. He was not orthodox but would stand back to hit the length ball to the off or to the on. A defensive stroke often seemed a last improvization to a ball which he had vainly planned to force away. In 1957 in England, suffering from sinus trouble, he did not continue his unbroken run of success but at Lord's he made an audacious 90, said by many to be the nearest approach yet seen to Bradman of the 1930s. Weekes recovered runs, if not form, in the West Indies against Pakistan the next year. With keen appreciation of the demands his style made upon him, he retired from Test cricket, but continued to play for Barbados, captaining the side with notable skill and scoring many runs. He was for years a brilliant field either close in or anywhere. His record as a League cricketer is second to none and on Commonwealth tours in Africa and elsewhere he again won the immense popularity which he enjoyed as a League cricketer and later as a cricket coach in Barbados. He was also, when his playing days were over, an international bridge player.

C. L. R. JAMES

CAREER FIGURES

	INNS	NO	RUNS	HS	AVGE	100S
Batting	241	24	12010	304*	55·34	36

Bowling 17 wkts at 43·00 Ct (incl w/k) 125; st 1

Test Record (48)

	INNS	NO	RUNS	HS	AVGE	100S
Batting	81	5	4455	207	58·61	15

Bowling 1 wkt for 77 Ct 49

WELLARD, Arthur William (1902–)

Old Bexley Sch. Somerset 1927–1950. England: in England 1937, 1938.

Wellard was a valuable all-rounder, but is remembered largely as a hitter of sixes. In 1936, before the days of artificially shortened boundaries, he hit 72; 5 of them off consecutive balls in one over from Armstrong of Derbyshire. In 1938 he again hit 5 consecutively off Woolley and was missed on the boundary off the 6th ball of the over. In the 1938 Lord's Test he hit McCabe into the grandstand.

Still he was no rustic slogger, but a serious batsman with a respectable defence. He was, moreover, a fine field near the wicket and a good fast bowler with a fierce break-back, who was prepared to bowl medium-paced off-spinners as a variety. Three times he made 1,000 runs and took 100 wickets in a season. Born and bred in Kent, he played several times against Kent Club and Ground, but rumour has it that, when he inquired about the possibility of being taken on the staff, he was told he had much better go and be a policeman. The story will seem improbable only to those who have never tried to judge young cricketers.

R. L. ARROWSMITH

CAREER FIGURES

	INNS	NO	RUNS	HS	AVGE	100S
Batting	679	45	12515	112	19·73	2

Bowling 1614 wkts at 24·35 Ct 375

Test Record (2)

	INNS	NO	RUNS	HS	AVGE	100S
Batting	4	0	47	38	11·75	–

Bowling 7 wkts at 33·85 Ct 2

WHITE, John Cornish (1891–1961)

Taunton Sch. Somerset 1909–1937 (Captain 1927–1931). England: in England 1921, 1928, 1929 (Captain), 1930; in Australia 1928–29; in South Africa 1930–31. Selector 1929–1930.

'Farmer' White, who played for his native county of Somerset for 28 years and in 15 Test Matches, was a unique slow left-handed bowler. Unlike most of his ilk he spun the ball but little, relying on a great variety of flight and constant well-concealed changes of pace. His action was simple and economical, a few easy paces leading to a smooth unhurried swing of the fully extended left arm. This endowed the whole performance with a deceptive simplicity, whilst achieving a wonderful degree of accuracy. Accomplished players found him difficult to attack, only Bradman really chasing him, and that on the easiest of Lord's wickets in 1930. White was one of the outstanding successes in the triumphant Australian tour of 1928–29. On the fast pitches then prevalent he was able to pitch the ball appreciably shorter, and thus had fuller scope for his tricks of flight and trajectory. At Brisbane he rounded off the Australian innings with 4 wickets for 7 runs. As a very presentable batsman, he twice achieved the double.

He was appropriately known as 'Farmer' White for, not only was this his profession, but in presence and character he epitomized the popular idea of the West Country yeoman. Middle-sized and sturdy, his apple cheeks and bright blue eyes radiated well-being. He was a man of singularly attractive character, imperturbable and cheerful in all circumstances. When the day was done he loved a game of poker which he played as he bowled, with a fine bland shrewdness.

IAN PEEBLES

CAREER FIGURES

	INNS	NO	RUNS	HS	AVGE	100S
Batting	765	102	12202	192	18·40	6

Bowling 2356 wkts at 18·57 Ct 423

Test Record (15)

	INNS	NO	RUNS	HS	AVGE	100S
Batting	22	9	239	29	18·38	–

Bowling 49 wkts at 32·26 Ct 6

Bob Willis bowling in the Centenary Test Match, Melbourne 1977.

WILLIS, Robert George Dylan (1949–)

Guildford Royal GS. Surrey 1969–1971. Warwickshire 1972– (Captain 1980). England: In England 1973, 1974, 1976, 1977, 1978, 1979; in Australia 1970–71, 1974–75, 1976–77, 1978–79, 1979–80; in West Indies 1973–74; in New Zealand 1970–71, 1977–78; in India 1976–77, 1979–80; in Pakistan 1977–78.

Bob Willis took over from John Snow as England's key fast bowler half way through the 1970s. His potential was shown at the age of 21 when he went as a late reinforcement to join the 1970–71 MCC side in Australia and played in the last 4 Tests; but his progress was hindered by injury, the pounding of his giant frame through an awkward bowling action damaging both knees to such an extent that only surgery gave him hope of carrying on.

His comeback season was 1976: that winter he took 20 wickets in 5 Tests in India, traditionally the graveyard of fast bowlers. In 1977 he triumphed with 27 wickets, a record for an England fast bowler in a home series against Australia, and further successes came that winter in Pakistan and New Zealand, and again against those same opponents during their reciprocal visits to England in 1978. Then came the 6-Test series in Australia, and Willis, though looking worn towards the end of the season, added 20 more inexpensive wickets to his already imposing Test tally. His was a major contribution, as bowling spearhead and vice-captain, to England's decisive reversal of the 1974–75 debacle at the hands of Lillee and Thomson. An obstinate tail-end batsman, he managed even to average three-quarters of an hour at the crease during the Test matches. His determination and physical courage, aided by hypnotherapy and a wry humour, are renowned and admired, as is his record.

DAVID FRITH

WILSON, Evelyn Rockley (1879–1957)

Rugby 1895–1897 (Captain 1897). Cambridge Univ 1899–1902 (Captain 1902). Yorkshire 1899–1923. England: in Australia 1920–21.

Rockley Wilson was an England bowler, a famous coach and a great character, with an unsurpassed knowledge of cricket, much of whose unique collection of cricketana is now at Lord's. An all-rounder at Cambridge, he scored 117 not out and 70 on a bad wicket in his 1st first-class match and went on, like his brother Clement, to make a hundred against Oxford. Becoming a master at Winchester, where he ran the cricket for years, he played no more first-class cricket till 1913, but from then till 1923 assisted Yorkshire regularly in August. After the war he abandoned serious batting, but bowled so successfully that he headed the first-class averages and played for England in Australia.

At the time he was one of the most accurate bowlers in the world; with a somewhat low action, he had a deceptive flight and a bias from leg rather than a genuine leg-break, combined with one difficult to detect which came back slightly from the off. He came through a little quicker than expected. He was a sound defensive bat, particularly good on the on-side but with an effective cut. He believed firmly in the importance of length and of the straight bat, which he always declared to be 'far better than the lion heart'.

His conversation, enriched and illustrated by innumerable anecdotes, was an unending delight, and he always knew to whom he had told a particular story before. He is constantly imitated still – the slightly nervous manner, with a good deal of fidgeting and fingering of the tie, the unmistakable tone and cadence of the voice, the characteristic use of 'Sir' to those whom he did not know well, often years younger than himself, and the equally characteristic use of 'really'; 'Usually gets duck really: if there's a second innings, gets double duck'. But no imitation can do justice to the richness of the original, based as it was on a wide knowledge and an astonishing memory. A brilliant scholar as a boy, he devoted to the history and practice of games in general and cricket in particular, and to the study of those who played them, talents which might have earned high academic honours. He wrote all too little on the game and it is ironical that some articles he sent to the *Daily Express* from Australia should have led to players being forbidden to contribute to the Press while on tour.

R. L. ARROWSMITH

CAREER FIGURES

	INNS	NO	RUNS	HS	AVGE	100S
Batting	168	27	3121	142	22·13	4

Bowling 397 wkts at 18·32 Ct 104

Test Record (1)

	INNS	NO	RUNS	HS	AVGE	100S
Batting	2	0	10	5	5·00	–

Bowling 3 wkts at 12·00

WISDEN, John (1826–1884)

Sussex 1845–1863. All-England XI and United England XI. All-England Team to North America 1859.

Wisden, a midget in size, was a fast off-break bowler. He played both for Sussex and the All-England and United England XIs, having founded the latter. During a business engagement at Leamington in 1850, he played for North v South, and took all 10 2nd innings wickets, clean bowled. He made hard-hitting hundreds against Kent and Yorkshire, but, as a bowler, he averaged 225 wickets annually for 12 years, with 455 in 1851. Against a Canadian and United States XXII, he took 6 wickets in 6 balls. For all this, Wisden's *Cricketers' Almanack* (first issued in 1864) remains his most enduring memorial.

G. D. MARTINEAU

WOODFULL, William Maldon, OBE (1897–1965)

Victoria 1921–22 to 1933–34 (Captain 1926–27 to 1933–34). Australia: in Australia 1928–29, 1930–31 (Captain), 1931–32 (Captain), 1932–33 (Captain); in England 1926, 1930 (Captain), 1934 (Captain).

William Maldon Woodfull took his middle name from the Victorian town in which he was born. His first contact with English cricketers was at Ballarat, where he played against the MCC team of 1920–21. Next year he was included in his State team. There was nothing dramatic about his early years, they were solidly and steadily successful. When Gilligan arrived in Australia in 1924–25 he found the great Victorian duet, Woodfull and Ponsford, well established in their State side, but Woodfull failed to get a place in the Australian team. Both, however, came to England in 1926, where Woodfull was considerably the more successful. When Collins and Bardsley had gone, Woodfull and Ponsford became the recognized international openers. Woodfull succeeded Ryder as captain in 1930, and twice won the series in England. He was at the centre of the Bodyline controversy in 1932–33, both as captain and, in the more physical sense, as the recipient of several severe blows. He was amongst those who strongly denounced this form of attack.

Woodfull was an altogether remarkable batsman. What small preparatory movement of the bat he made was almost vertical, so that his strokes had an air of the guillotine. Despite this lack of momentum he could strike the ball firmly in front of the wicket. Elsewhere he had a good variety of pushing and deflecting strokes. His defence was such that he was almost impossible to bowl out on the fast, true wickets of his own country, where he was affectionately known as 'the worm-killer'. Woodfull was a quiet, determined man who, a schoolmaster in private life, brought a habitual consideration and sense of responsibility to his duties as captain. He was always to be found where things were most dangerous, and always sought to interpose himself between his team and the most menacing bowler. In the field he was a firm, patient and unspectacular leader, who enjoyed the fullest affection and confidence of his team. He retired after his successful tour of England in 1934, having played for Australia in every match for 7 successive series, including one each against South Africa and the West Indies.

IAN PEEBLES

CAREER FIGURES

	INNS	NO	RUNS	HS	AVGE	100S
Batting	245	39	13392	284	65·00	49

Bowling 1 wkt for 24 Ct 77

Test Record (35)

	INNS	NO	RUNS	HS	AVGE	100S
Batting	54	4	2300	161	46·00	7

Ct 7

WOODS, Samuel Moses James (1867–1931)

Brighton Coll 1885–86. Cambridge Univ 1888–1891 (Captain 1890). Somerset 1886–1910 (Captain 1894–1906); Secretary 1894–1923. England: in South Africa 1895–96. Australia: in England 1888.

Sam Woods was a wonderful natural games-player, a great fast bowler, a famous captain of Somerset and a rare character, beloved by people of all ages and classes throughout the whole county. Enormously strong, he was really fast and accurate, with a deadly yorker and an equally deadly slow ball. Sir Pelham Warner calls him 'the most artistic and subtle fast bowler there has ever been'. His record of 36 wickets for 8 runs each in the University Match has never been surpassed, and in 1894 he and F. S. Jackson bowled unchanged through both innings for the Gentlemen at Lord's. After 1893 his bowling went off rapidly, but his batting improved proportionately and by 1900 it was as a batsman that he captained the Gentlemen. He was a fine hitter and an indomitable fighter, who could defend stubbornly at a crisis. He was also a great mid-off. As a rugby football forward, too, he is among the immortals.

R. L. ARROWSMITH

CAREER FIGURES

	INNS	NO	RUNS	HS	AVGE	100S
Batting	690	35	15352	215	23·43	19

Bowling 1040 wkts at 20·82 Ct 282

Test Record (6) (Australia and England)

	INNS	NO	RUNS	HS	AVGE	100S
Batting	10	0	154	53	15·40	–

Bowling 10 wkts at 25·00 Ct 5

Frank Woolley: 'when you bowled to him there weren't enough fielders; when you wrote about him there weren't enough words' (R. C. Robertson-Glasgow).

WOOLLEY, Frank Edward (1887–1978)

Kent 1906–1938. England: in England 1909, 1912, 1921, 1924, 1926, 1929 to 1932 consecutively, 1934; in Australia 1911–12, 1920–21, 1924–25; in South Africa 1909–10, 1913–14, 1922–23; in New Zealand 1929–30.

Frank Woolley played for Kent from 1906 to 1938, and for England from 1909 to 1934, and the evidence for his claim to a place in a very narrow top bracket of great all-round cricketers is indisputable. In all first-class cricket he scored 58,969 runs, an aggregate 2nd only to Hobbs's, and took 2,068 wickets. In 4 of the 13 seasons in which he made 2,000 runs – his highest aggregate was 3,352 in 1928 – he also took 100 wickets, a feat which no other cricketer has achieved more than twice: only 'W.G.' can match his 1,000 runs in 28 seasons, in 8 of which he took 100 wickets. If his total of 145 hundreds is but 6th in that table, only Hammond of those above him bowled seriously at all. Of those hundreds, the 305 not out which he made in 210 minutes against Tasmania on the 1911–12 MCC tour remained for more than 50 years the highest score ever made by an Englishman in Australia. As early as his 4th season he played the major part with A. Fielder in what is still the record partnership for the last wicket in county cricket, and 20 years later, in 1929, he made 4 hundreds in successive innings. As a bowler his most successful seasons were 1920, 1921 and 1922 in which he took 515 wickets.

For a player of his outstanding gifts his record in the 64 Tests in which he played is curiously uneven. Though he made 5 hundreds, the first of them, 133 not out at Sydney and decisive to the rubber of 1911–12, and the last, 154 against the South Africans at Manchester in 1929, it is likely that none will be so long remembered as the magnificent 95 and 93 with which, in a lost cause but with almost negligent majesty, he defied the formidable Australian attack at Lord's in 1921. As a bowler his greatest impact was made at the Oval, where on turning pitches in the 2 matches of the Triangular Tournament he took 6 South African wickets for 65 and 10 Australian for 49.

Born and bred in Tonbridge, Frank Woolley absorbed as a boy, and reflected as a player, much of the life and colour which a succession of gifted amateurs for long made synonymous with Kent cricket. With his tall and graceful figure, his quiet air and unhurried movements, he brought to the cricket field as a batsman an unmistakable air of majestic, almost casual, command. With his great gift for timing, and long reach, he would with fascinating ease and power drive off the back foot what to other men was good-length bowling: to watch him in full vein was at once an excitement and an artistic delight.

His left-hand slow bowling was equally graceful, and though he lacked Rhodes's subtlety of flight, his height, accuracy and power of spin made him, on any wicket that helped him at all, truly formidable. An outstanding slip field with a long reach, and large prehensile hands, he made in all 1,015 catches, still a record. Throughout his long career Frank Woolley never failed to be a focus of attention and esteem, and, wherever he played, he seemed to evoke for all who knew it the setting of the tents and trees of his own Canterbury ground.

H. S. ALTHAM

CAREER FIGURES

	INNS	NO	RUNS	HS	AVGE	100S
Batting	1532	85	58969	305*	40·75	145

Bowling 2068 wkts at 19·85 Ct 1015

Test Record (64)

	INNS	NO	RUNS	HS	AVGE	100S
Batting	98	7	3283	154	36·07	5

Bowling 83 wkts at 33·91 Ct 64

WORRELL, Sir Frank Mortimer Maglinne (1924–1967)

Combermere Sch, and Manchester Univ. Barbados 1941–42 to 1945–46. Jamaica 1947–48 to 1961–62. West Indies: in West Indies 1947–48, 1952–53, 1953–54, 1954–55, 1959–60, 1961–62 (Captain); in England 1950, 1957, 1963 (Captain); in Australia 1951–52, 1960–61 (Captain); in New Zealand 1951–52. Knighted 1964.

When Worrell first played for Barbados in 1942 as a slow-left-arm bowler he was 18 years of age and had never yet seen a first-class game. In 1943, going in as night-watchman, he carried out his bat for 64 and soon was opening the innings. During the war years, just as Challenor and his circle had done, Worrell, Walcott and John Goddard carried local cricket to a high pitch. In 1943–44 Worrell and Goddard made an unbroken 502 v Trinidad. Worrell, then 19 years of age, made 308 not out. In 1946–47 Worrell and Walcott added 574 runs – in another unbroken stand – against Trinidad. Against the MCC Test side in 1947–48

Frank Worrell: during his 191 not out against England at Trent Bridge, 1957.

Worrell enhanced his reputation: already he had been engaged to play in English league cricket. He did not go with the West Indies team to India in 1948–49, but he did go there with a Commonwealth side in 1949–50 and averaged over 97 in 10 unofficial Test innings. Worrell was therefore a seasoned cricketer in England in 1950. No praise was thought too high for his batting, which reached its peak in a wonderful innings of 261 against England at Nottingham. By this time Worrell, as Sobers was to do, was bowling a fast-medium which at times could be distinctly fast. In Australia in 1951–52 Worrell was perhaps the only batsman whose form approached what Australia had been led to expect. In one Test innings this batsman took 7 wickets. In the West Indies, against India, England and Australia, he was not consistent. In England in 1957 he seemed to find form again. He saved West Indies at Trent Bridge by playing right through the innings for 191 not out. At Leeds his fast-medium bowling took 7 England wickets in an innings.

Worrell was a strictly orthodox player – he confessed that he was unable to hit across the line even if he thought he should. His strength lay in quick judgment of the flight and rapid placing of himself in position in order to put the ball away with exquisite timing. His late-cutting was one of the finest strokes in the game. He dominated League cricket; in India in a Commonwealth team he won a reputation as captain, deputizing for an unfit Ames. He entered Manchester University to study sociology, but played well for West Indies v England in 1959–60. Then, in 1960, Worrell, as captain for the Australian tour, led his team in such dynamic cricket as Australia had not seen within living memory. His batting bloomed once again as in his earliest days and, returning to slow bowling, he could keep runs down and get valuable wickets. In 1963 in England the West Indies team, as in Australia, made all lovers of the game aware that modern technique did not inherently inhibit exciting play. Worrell, not the player he had been, was no passenger with either bat or ball.

But it was his leadership, in matter and manner, which marked him as the most remarkable captain of the age. His knighthood in 1964 was universally acclaimed. Before his tragically early death, from leukaemia, at the age of 42, he had become launched on what had all the makings of a distinguished career within the University of the West Indies.

C. L. R. JAMES

CAREER FIGURES

	INNS	NO	RUNS	HS	AVGE	100S
Batting	326	49	15025	308*	54·24	39

Bowling 349 wkts at 29·00 Ct 137

Test Record (51)

	INNS	NO	RUNS	HS	AVGE	100S
Batting	87	9	3860	261	49·48	9

Bowling 69 wkts at 38·72 Ct 43

Doug Wright: always philosophical, sometimes unplayable.

WRIGHT, Douglas Vivian Parson

(1914–)

Kent 1932–1957 (Captain 1954–1956). England: in England 1938, 1939, 1946–1950 consecutively; in Australia 1946–47, 1950–51; in New Zealand 1946–47, 1950–51. Coach at Charterhouse 1959–1971.

Wright remains unique. Nobody judging by figures could divine why he constantly represented England. Against Australia his 48 wickets cost 42·72 runs each, and, although his 7 hat-tricks in first-class cricket are a record, his final figures suggest simply a good county bowler. Nowhere in cricket history is there so great a disparity between reputation and results. Yet for years there was no bowler against whom the greatest bats felt less secure, however well set. It was this feeling that he might bowl any batsman neck and crop at any moment that kept him in Test cricket. Against Australia he achieved one outstanding performance – 7 for 105 at Sydney in 1946–47, a match which, had Bradman been caught off him for 2 in the 2nd innings, he might have won for England, just as for a brief spell he looked like winning the Leeds Test in 1938.

With a long springy run, which sometimes got out of control and led to no-balls, and a high action, he bowled considerably faster than earlier leg-breakers. He was never master of the top-spinner which got Freeman so many wickets: it was the quick, good-length leg-break that batsmen feared. But this turned so much and lifted so sharply that it constantly missed not only the edge of the bat, but the stumps too. Perhaps no bowler has ever beaten so many batsmen without getting them out. He was a useful tail-end bat and a good field. Totally unspoiled by success, he was later a much-loved and most effective coach at Charterhouse.

R. L. ARROWSMITH

CAREER FIGURES

	INNS	NO	RUNS	HS	AVGE	100S
Batting	703	225	5903	84*	12·34	–

Bowling 2056 wkts at 23·98 Ct 165

Test Record (34)

	INNS	NO	RUNS	HS	AVGE	100S
Batting	39	13	289	45	11·11	–

Bowling 108 wkts at 39·11 Ct 10

WYATT, Robert Elliott Storey

(1901–)

King Henry VIII Sch, Coventry. Warwickshire 1923–1939 (Captain 1930–1937). Worcestershire 1946–1951 (Captain 1949–1951). England: in England 1929, 1930 (Captain), 1933–1935 (Captain), 1936; in Australia 1932–33, 1936–37; in South Africa 1927–28, 1930–31; in West Indies 1929–30, 1934–35 (Captain); in New Zealand 1932–33 (Captain). Selector 1949–1953 (Chairman 1950).

Wyatt was for some years indispensable to England at a time when English cricket was strong. He was a good cricketer who by perseverance, commonsense and character made himself into a great one. Essentially he was a sound batsman, whose function was to lend solidity to the middle of the order, but he was adaptable and always ready to go in first if required, or, if runs were wanted quickly, to use a full range of strokes in getting them. At Lord's in 1934 the Players set the Gentlemen 232 to make in 170 minutes. Wyatt and Walters opened and scored 121 in the 1st hour. The match was won with half-an-hour to spare and Wyatt's share was 104 not out. But such fireworks were exceptional: 'solid', 'dependable' – these are the adjectives that spring to one's mind and they are borne out by his Test record against Australia, an average of 33 and a highest score of 78. Twice only in Tests did he make a hundred, each time against South Africa, at Manchester in 1929 and at Nottingham in 1935.

But his cricket by no means ended with his batting: he was a fine outfield and bowled medium-pace away-swingers and off-breaks which, if in Tests used only as an occasional change, brought him many useful wickets in county cricket. Indeed in early days he was regarded as an all-rounder. As an England captain he was perhaps unlucky. Inevitably he had to stand comparison with his contemporaries, Chapman and Jardine, who were, in their totally different ways, two of the greatest in cricket history. If he lacked the dynamic personality of the one and the coldly logical brain of the other, well who did not? Few selections have roused fiercer feelings or have been more generally condemned after the event than when he superseded Chapman as captain for the last Test in 1930. But none of the feeling was personal: he has always

R. E. S. Wyatt: few cricketers have had a wider knowledge of cricket, or a greater affection for it.

been one of the most popular of men. He has strong and independent views on cricket and is a shrewd judge of the game.

R. L. ARROWSMITH

CAREER FIGURES

	INNS	NO	RUNS	HS	AVGE	100S
Batting	1142	157	39470	232	40·07	85

Bowling 902 wkts at 32·38 Ct (incl. w/k) 417; st 1

Test Record (40)

	INNS	NO	RUNS	HS	AVGE	100S
Batting	64	6	1839	149	31·70	2

Bowling 18 wkts at 35·66 Ct 16

YARDLEY, Norman Walter Dransfield (1915–)

St Peter's Sch, York 1930–1934 (Captain 1933–1934). Cambridge Univ 1935–1938 (Captain 1938). Yorkshire 1936–1955 (Captain 1948–1955). England: in England 1947, 1948, 1950 (Captain each year); in Australia 1946–47; in South Africa 1938–39; in New Zealand 1946–47. Selector 1951–1954 (Chairman 1951–1952).

Yardley was a sensible, reliable, practical cricketer who did valuable, if unspectacular, service for England both as a player and as captain during lean and difficult years. After he retired he became well known as a broadcaster on cricket. Unlike many famous players, he did himself full justice in the University Match, making 90 in 1936 and 101 in 1937, and in 1939 he was clearly established as one of England's coming cricketers. After being wounded in the Second World War he went as vice-captain of Hammond's side to Australia, where he batted most consistently, while his bowling created quite a sensation. Barely regarded up till then as a change in the Yorkshire side, he dismissed Bradman thrice running and headed the Test averages, as he did in England the following year. The comment of a famous old Yorkshire cricketer was, 'One has to play for England now to get a bowl'.

Medium-pace right-hand, he bowled at the wicket, was not afraid to pitch the ball up and came through rather quicker than the batsman expected. He was a notable breaker of partnerships. As a batsman, he was primarily an on-side player: even his off-side strokes tended to go more to the fieldsman's right than expected. But he had strokes all round and was by inclination an attacking player. His highest Test innings was 99 against South Africa at Nottingham. He was also, as befitted a natural games-player who had won a distinction at squash and hockey, a good and versatile field.

R. L. ARROWSMITH

CAREER FIGURES

	INNS	NO	RUNS	HS	AVGE	100S
Batting	658	75	18173	183*	31·17	27

Bowling 279 wkts at 30·48 Ct (incl w/k) 325; st 1

Test Record (20)

	INNS	NO	RUNS	HS	AVGE	100S
Batting	34	2	812	99	25·37	–

Bowling 21 wkts at 33·66 Ct 14

ZAHEER ABBAS, Syed (1947–)

Jahangir Road Secondary Sch, Karachi, and Karachi Univ. Karachi Whites 1965–66. PIA. Gloucestershire 1972– . Pakistan: in Pakistan 1969–70, 1972–73, 1974–75, 1976–77, 1978–79; in England 1971, 1974; in Australia 1972–73, 1976–77; in West Indies 1976–77; in New Zealand 1972–73; in India: 1979–80.

Zaheer Abbas belongs to that select band of batsmen incapable of a boring innings. He is a deceptive player because, while being one of the most prolific batsmen of the 1970s, he possesses none of the obvious characteristics of the committed run-getter. About 6 feet tall, of willowy build, he has the sympathetic air of a doctor putting a patient at ease, as, from a relaxed and slightly open stance, he gazes enquiringly down the pitch at the approaching bowler. A high, circular and apparently rather loose back-lift adds to the illusion that one is watching a man more likely to waft a languid 35 than 150 or 200.

Until getting to know him, many bowlers must have been taken in by his exterior. Tempted by the backlift many tried to slip a yorker past him. It was then they discovered how quickly he moves the bat. Just as they were preparing to celebrate his wicket, the ball would be sent scudding to the boundary as strong and pliant wrists whipped the blade through half a circle. Zaheer had no formal coaching as a boy. But having modelled himself on Tom Graveney and Colin Cowdrey, whom he watched as a young man in Karachi, it was only to be expected that the off-side would be his magnet. Beautiful timer that he is, his ability to angle straight balls either side of extra-cover is what sets him apart from other batsmen of his generation. He has scoring strokes all round the wicket, including a solid hook which enables him to stand his ground against fast bowling. Allied to high concentration and, for a man of such gentle nature, an unexpectedly ruthless appetite for runs, his gifts combined to bring him nearly 70 first-class hundreds in the 1970s and, despite a disappointing Test record, a reputation as one of the best dozen batsmen in the game.

JOHN THICKNESSE

Part IV
International Cricket

Test Series will be found alphabetically in this Part but with the senior country according to the date of admission to Test status named first. Other entries are interpolated alphabetically among them.

Aborigines

IRVING ROSENWATER

Several Australian aborigines have in earlier days taken part in State cricket, the most recent being E. Gilbert, of Queensland, who despite a dubious action made a name for himself as a fast bowler. He was no-balled for throwing in 1931–32. After H. Larwood had passed his peak Gilbert was considered the fastest bowler in the world, and is one of the few men who have dismissed Don Bradman for a duck. Most of the aborigines who made their mark were fast bowlers, but the best of them, Mullagh, was one of the best Victorian batsmen when Lord Harris's team visited Australia in 1878–79.

The aboriginal connexion with cricket is remembered for the tour in 1868 of the first team ever to visit England from overseas. This expedition was conceived by W. R. Hayman of Lake Wallace, near Edenhope, Victoria. He organized the collection and coaching of natives in this area, and after prolonged preparation brought the best of them to England under his managership. They were captained by Charles Lawrence, of Surrey, who had stayed on in Australia as a coach after taking part in the first tour there of an English team, that of 1861–62, which was sponsored by Messrs Spiers and Pond and led by H. H. Stephenson. This aboriginal team played 47 matches in England, winning 14, losing 14 and drawing 19. Though beaten by MCC at Lord's they led on 1st innings, Mullagh making 75.

When the games were over the aborigines entertained the crowds with various athletic feats including throwing the boomerang. Altogether they made a very favourable impression, and it was said that when the first Australian team proper landed in England 10 years later some were both surprised and disappointed that they were not black.

This Aboriginal group was taken in 1863 in Australia and includes most of those who later that year undertook the 1st tour of any Australian side to England. They had been coached by T. W. Wills from Edenhope, Victoria. The star player was Johnny Mullagh who in England took 261 wickets and made 1,177 runs, including 75 against MCC at Lord's. At back: King Cole, Tarpot, T. W. Wills, Mullagh and Dick-a-dick; sitting: Jellico, Peter, Red Cap, Harry Rose, Bullocky and Cuzens.

The names of this team are perpetuated as follows on a monument to their memory at Edenhope: Charles Lawrence (captain), Mullagh, Dick-a-Dick, Twopenny, Red Cap, Mosquito, King Cole, Peter, Cuzens, Tiger, Jim Crow, Bullocky, Dumas, Sundown.

Australia v South Africa

LOUIS DUFFUS AND MICHAEL OWEN-SMITH

One of the biggest fillips given to the spread of international cricket around the turn of the century was the enterprise displayed by the enthusiastic South Africans who in 1902 invited the Australian team to visit them on their way home from England. In those days the gesture was tantamount to asking Kreisler to play in a suburban orchestra. The Australians were already masters in the game. They had just won their series 2–1 against England. South Africa were still being outplayed by modest opposition. In the next 60 years they could rarely excel the prowess of their neighbours across the Indian Ocean. South Africa had to wait until 1966 for their 1st victory over Australia on home soil. This tour marked a change of fortune, with South Africa winning successive home series 3–1 and 4–0 against Australia, having managed to win only 4 Tests hitherto.

The team of 1902 included such giants as J. Darling, the captain, V. T. Trumper, M. A. Noble, W. W. Armstrong, C. Hill, R. A. Duff and H. Trumble. They were the first fully representative side of any country to visit South Africa. Darling's team won 2 of their 3 Tests, each of which was played over 3 days; the other was drawn. This, the 1st match ever played between the two countries, took place at Johannesburg in October 1902. The South Africans excelled themselves by scoring 454 in the 1st innings. Their unexpected success was primarily due to 97 from the opening batsman, L. J. Tancred, and 90 by C. B. Llewellyn, who had a triumph as an all-rounder. The left-hander, A. D. Nourse, at No. 8 made 72 in his 1st Test and E. A. Halliwell, who is often regarded as the country's finest wicket-keeper, 57 at No. 9.

There was a further surprise when Australia were dismissed for 296, Llewellyn taking 6 for 92. With a lead of 158 South Africa were in a strong position but their hopes of victory were dispelled when in the follow-on the left-hander, Hill, played a splendid innings of 142. They were able to declare at 372 for 7 and a draw became inevitable.

Again Australia had to produce a 2nd innings recovery in the Second Test, which was also played at Johannesburg. This time it was followed up by devastating bowling by Saunders who took 7 for 34 in dismissing South Africa for 85. Australia won handsomely in the end by 159 runs. The rubber was decided at Cape Town where Darling's team confirmed their superiority in a win by 10 wickets. Llewellyn crowned his exceptional displays by taking 6 for 97 which gave him 25 wickets with an average of 17·92 for the series. In scoring 104 Sinclair gained fame by hitting 6 sixes.

When the 1st tour of Australia by a South African team was undertaken in the summer of 1910–11 the series was extended to 5 matches. Australia was still a team of many renowned batsmen – Trumper, Bardsley, Armstrong and Macartney – but it was chiefly due to two bowlers, W. J. Whitty and A. Cotter, that they won the rubber by 4 games to 1. South Africa went on the tour without a fast bowler and found that their famous googly bowlers were not so effective on Australian pitches as they had been on matting. In the First Test at Sydney they were severely punished. The captain, Hill, who made top score of 191, put on 224 in the astonishing time of 120 minutes for the 2nd wicket with Bardsley who made 132. Australia ended the 1st day 494 for 6, the most runs ever made on a Test 1st day. Not only were the South Africans then flummoxed by the fast bowling of Cotter and Whitty but rain presented them with a sticky wicket and overwhelming defeat was inevitable. G. A. Faulkner began the series that was to bring him most distinction in his career by scoring 62 and 43.

Australia won the Second Test at Melbourne by 89 runs as the result of a remarkable anti-climax. Faulkner played the innings of his life, scoring 204, and South Africa reached 506 for a lead of 158. Trumper wiped this off with an opening innings of 159, but when the whole side were out for 327 South Africa were left in a priceless position from which to achieve their first victory. They had to make only 170 but were tumbled out for a mere 80. Whitty bowled magnificently to take 6 for 17 but it was an inexplicable failure.

Their initial triumph against Australia came in the next match at Adelaide after 6 days of hard play. The batsmen of both sides ran riot and 1,646 runs were scored, the most then ever made in a Test Match. Winning the toss for the 1st time, South Africa ran up a total of 482, with centuries by J. W. Zulch (105) and Snooke (103). The peerless batting of Trumper, who hit a superb and chanceless 214 not out, brought the Australians to within 17 runs of their opponents. A close finish seemed likely when South Africa were dismissed for 360. Left to make 378 the Australians scored steadily but after an absorbing struggle wanted 86 when the last pair, Cotter and Whitty, started their partnership. They were still only 39 runs short when Schwarz held a catch from Whitty, and South Africa had beaten Australia for the 1st time.

As if to prove that the victory was not a true reflection of the cricket capabilities of the two countries Australia won the rubber with an overwhelming victory in the Fourth Test at Melbourne by 530 runs. Sherwell did not profit from putting them in to bat for they scored 328 to South Africa's 205, while the full might of the Australian batting was let loose in a 2nd innings of 578. Again in the final Test at Sydney Sherwell put Australia in to bat, and once more the move proved disastrous. Macartney, whose lack of form had caused his omission from the Fourth Test, came back with a flourish and played a brilliant opening innings of 137, out of a total of 364. Schwarz accomplished his country's best bowling of the series in taking 6 for 47 but the batsmen, except for Faulkner, found trouble in playing the Australian googly bowler Dr H. V. Hordern and were all out for 160. In a last attempt to redeem themselves they rallied to make 401 when they followed on, with a splendid 150 by Zulch and 92 from the unfailing Faulkner, but Australia easily made the required 198 and won by 7 wickets. Faulkner established a record with a total of 732 runs (average 73) but, while he scored twice as heavily as the next South African batsman, Australia had 4 players, topped by Trumper (661 – average 94), who had averages of more than 50.

The next meeting between the two countries arose from South Africa's initiative in proposing the Triangular Tournament in England in 1912. The undertaking was not a success, partly because of bad weather and partly because South Africa were so much weaker than the other two competitors. Because of differences between the Board of Control and some of the players Australia were not represented by their strongest team but they were good enough to defeat South Africa in 2 of their 3 Tests. The Third was washed out by rain. The First match at Manchester provided a sensation when T. J. Matthews accomplished the hat-trick in both South African innings – a unique feat by a cricketer of quite ordinary talents who did little of note either before or afterwards.

When hostilities ceased, the formation of the Australian Imperial Forces XI led to a quick revival of their cricket and established their marked superiority for several years. On their way home from England for demobilization they called at South Africa and played a series of matches including two representative games. Both were unofficial, but they served to demonstrate the unequal strengths of the two countries.

When one considers the great names in the team of 1902 it might be a subject for debate to say that the side of 1921–22 was the most accomplished to visit South Africa from Australia, but they were patently a combination of immense talent. Again their tour followed a highly successful season in England where they had won the rubber 3–0. Sustaining an injury on the sea voyage, the gigantic Armstrong could not appear on fields where he had played 19 years before and the captaincy was undertaken by H. L. Collins. With Taylor back as captain, South Africa showed an improvement in their batting but, not surprisingly, their bowlers were overshadowed by an attack which began with J. M. Gregory and E. A. McDonald, with A. A. Mailey, J. Ryder, H. L. Hendry and Collins to follow. Moreover, the Australian bowlers were supported by some superlative fielding, contributed by Gregory, C. E. Pellew and Hendry in the slips and by Taylor, T. J. E. Andrews and W. Bardsley in the outfield.

The Tests, still played on matting pitches, were extended to 4 days and resulted in 1 victory to Australia with 2 games drawn. Time alone prevented the Australians from winning the first game in Durban, where Gregory virtually carried on where he had left off 2 years previously by taking 8 wickets, scoring 57 runs and holding 5 catches in the slips. The wizardry of Macartney in scoring 116 preceded a late declaration, and without any individual distinction the South Africans managed to play out time. None who saw it has ever forgotten the extraordinary Second Test in Johannesburg where again a draw was the result. Australia scored 450, with Collins (203) for the 2nd time in 2 tours reaching a double-hundred, while Gregory hit, in 70 minutes, the fastest Test hundred ever. South Africa fared badly before the famous bowling combination of Gregory and McDonald, and, being all out for 243, followed on. Two wickets had fallen for 44 when Taylor (80) and C. N. Frank added 105. Then followed the present record 4th-wicket partnership of 206 between Frank and Nourse. The frail and slightly built Frank, who had been badly gassed during the war, in a remarkable defensive innings that lasted 8½ hours went on to score 152. Nourse (111) made the only Test hundred of his career. From facing defeat South Africa rose to a prospect of victory, but their attempts to force runs were thwarted by the shrewd bowling of Collins wide of the off-stump. They declared at 472 for 8, leaving Australia to make 266. The final innings had barely started when rain washed out play. The Australians at last established their obvious superiority by winning the Third Test at Cape Town by 10 wickets, needing only 1 run to win in the 4th innings. Ryder surpassed himself with a score of 142 and ended the series with the top average of 111.

There was an interval of 21 years between the South Africans' 1st and 2nd tours of Australia, and the series which took place in 1931–32 revealed a widening of the gap between their respective standards. Led by the wicket-keeper, H. B. Cameron, the South Africans were unlucky in meeting treacherous, sticky pitches in 2 of the 5 Tests, but the winning of all 5 games by Australia with great ease was a just indication of the merits of the sides. It was the early heyday of Bradman, whose remarkable innings in the 4 Tests in which he batted was the feature of the tour. The South Africans contributed to his success by missing Bradman twice early in the First Test at Brisbane. As it was, he beat Trumper's record of 214 not out and went on to total 226.

Another hundred by Bradman (112) with 127 from K. E. Rigg led to another innings victory at Sydney, the chief destroyer being Grimmett who took 8 for 72. South Africa's best hope of success appeared at Melbourne, where fine bowling by the fast bowler, A. J. Bell, had Woodfull's team out for 198. With K. G. Viljoen (111) scoring the only hundred for his country in the series they made 358 to gain a 1st-innings lead of 160. Australia made a shattering recovery by scoring 554 (Bradman 167, Woodfull 161). Wanting 395 to win, the South Africans were again checked by Grimmett (6 for 92), and could total only 225. Although Grimmett accounted for 7 batsmen in each innings in the Fourth Test at Adelaide, the South Africans gave their best display of batting in scoring 308 and 274. But their feats were dwarfed by the irresistible onslaught of Bradman, who made 299 not out, his last partner being run out while they were attempting the 300th run. The big total of 513 was not enough for an innings victory but Australia won by 10 wickets. It was in this match that W. J. O'Reilly entered Test cricket.

The final game at Melbourne was a freak. The wet black clay (pitches in Australia were not then covered) provided a surface like treacle and in an hour and a half South Africa were put out for 36. Australia made 153, then bowled out their visitors. The aggregate of 234 is still the lowest in Test history – but what perhaps hurt the South African bowlers was that, because he had injured himself fielding, Bradman, their tormentor, did not bat. Ironmonger took 6 for 18, O'Reilly 3 for 19 and Grimmett did not bowl in the match. In 4 games, however, he had 33 wickets to Ironmonger's 31. Bradman had the phenomenal average of 201·50 from a record aggregate of 806 runs.

Although Australia did not win all 5 Tests – 1 was drawn because of rain – they again outclassed their opponents in 1935–36 when they undertook their first full-scale tour of South Africa and raised the number of Test matches to five. Bradman was not available, and it was just as well, for the play might have been farcically one-sided. As it was McCabe (420 – average 84·00), Fingleton (478 – average 79·66) and W. A. Brown (417 – average 59·57) dominated batting that was always adequate, while in bowling the combination of Grimmett and O'Reilly swept through the country like a veld fire. Grimmett took no fewer than 44 wickets (average 14) while O'Reilly's total was 27 (17). V. Y. Richardson led the team with enterprise, and except in one instance continually cramped the batsmen by setting 2 'suicide' fielders in the leg-trap for O'Reilly.

The exception arose in the Second Test at Johannesburg – the drawn game, and the one in which South Africa provided their best display. Grimmett, O'Reilly and the fast bowler E. L. McCormick had the South Africans out for 157 and Australia were comfortably ahead with 250. The event that followed is an epic in South African history, for against 2 of the game's finest bowlers Nourse scored a brilliant 231 out of a total of 491. No other batsman made more than 45. Nourse's innings was at that time the highest by a South African in Tests. Even so Australia had a glimpse of victory when a magnificent 189 not out by McCabe had lifted the total to 274 for 2, at which point a storm washed out play. That was virtually the end of the competitive side of the series as Australia won each of the remaining matches by an innings. Fingleton scored 3 successive Test hundreds.

When A. L. Hassett captained the side in South Africa 14 years later in 1949–50, the story of their overwhelming superiority was repeated, except in one Test which they won through a glorious recovery. South African cricket was at a low level and the series again ended 4–0, with one match drawn. The greatest individual distinction fell to the 21-year-old left-hander, R. N. Harvey, who scored 660 runs at an average of 132·00. An injury to W. A. Johnston resulted in K. R. Miller joining the team after being mysteriously omitted from the original selection. The glorious recovery took place in the Third Test at Durban. South Africa scored 311 after a typically determined 143 by Rowan and then dismissed Australia on a turning pitch for 75, the lowest score ever made against South Africa. The hero was the off-spinner, Tayfield, who entered the series only because A. M. B. Rowan was injured. He took 7 for 23 in 8·4 overs. Nourse, after a weekend's cogitation, did not force the follow-on, a timid decision he must have grievously regretted ever since. The South Africans batted poorly in their 2nd innings for 99, but even so left Australia to make 336 in the last innings on a doubtful pitch. This they accomplished through one of cricket's epic innings – 151 not out scored in 5½ hours by Harvey. He batted with exceptional skill and judgment and did not give a chance. Australia won by 5 wickets with 25 minutes to spare. In the final match Australia scored their biggest victory against South Africa – by an innings and 259 runs – at Port Elizabeth. After Durban it was not surprising.

Neil Harvey was the particular scourge of South Africa's bowlers, taking 8 hundreds off them in consecutive series, 4 in each. Here he is in course of making 190 at Sydney. The wicket-keeper is John Waite, non-striker Colin McDonald.

Following another interval of 21 years, South Africa visited Australia for the 3rd time in 1952–53 and despite unpropitious circumstances accomplished their biggest triumph in Tests between the 2 countries. Eight of their leading players were not available for the tour. The bowling was thought to be the weakest ever to leave their shores and they had a new captain with no international experience in J. E. Cheetham. Their chances seemed forlorn, yet by developing inspired team-work and becoming the most brilliant fielding side ever to represent South Africa they won 2 Tests in a series for the first time and shared the rubber. Signs of a decline in Australian supremacy, the absence of Miller and Lindwall from the Fifth Test, and the unexpected retirement of the unorthodox spin bowler, J. Iverson, contributed to their success but it was a meritorious achievement none the less.

The First Test at Brisbane gave a glimpse of their possibilities for after dismissing Australia for 280 and 277 they made 221 and 153 for 2 in their 2nd innings. At this stage they required 183 for victory. They failed by 96 runs mainly because of the match-winning bowling of Lindwall. Though the climax was disappointing the course of the game was, however, not discouraging. Striking performances by W. R. Endean and Tayfield, who were to become South Africa's heroes of the series, dominated a victory at Melbourne by 82 runs. The decisive feat came when Endean scored a chanceless 162 not out in 7½ hours in South Africa's 2nd innings of 338. Australia had to score 373 in 8 hours but were put out for 290 with 2½ hours to spare. Tayfield, with figures of 6 for 84 and 7 for 81, became the first South African to take 13 wickets in a Test. He was supported by some remarkable catches, one of which was taken by Endean with one hand upstretched as a hit from Miller (52) was sailing over the boundary.

It was the magnificent bowling of Lindwall and Miller that gave Australia a lead of 2–1 in the Third Test at Sydney. They accounted for 13 wickets in South Africa's 173 and 232. Harvey, who had a wonderful season, scored 190 in 6 hours in Australia's 443. Injuries affected both sides in the drawn match at Adelaide. Tayfield played with a broken thumb, and Australia must surely have won the game and the rubber, but for both Lindwall and Miller breaking down. They were unable to bowl in South Africa's 2nd innings. The captain, A. L. Hassett, surpassed himself in an innings of 163, McDonald batted splendidly for 154 and Harvey recorded the season's fastest hundred in 106 minutes.

The fighting qualities of the South Africans were revealed at their best in their memorable victory by 6 wickets at Melbourne. Their cause seemed hopeless when a demoralizing 520 was registered against them in the 1st innings. Harvey crowned his triumphs with his 1st Test double-hundred of 205 after Morris had sportingly sacrificed his wicket to his new partner in a run out when his score was 99. South Africa replied with 435 – 85 runs behind. The turning point of the match followed when E. R. H. Fuller bowled Harvey for 7 and Australia succumbed for 209. Fuller finished with 5 for 66. Good fortune, including a chance given by McLean, who hit a dashing 76 not out, before he had scored, favoured the South Africans and they made a winning 297 for 4. Harvey eclipsed the record 806 of Bradman by scoring 834 (average 92·66).

After their success in Australia, and the sharing of the rubber with England at home, the South Africans were well equipped to break the bogey of Australian invincibility in South Africa when I. D. Craig led the 1957–58 team overseas. That they were not able to do so was due to the growth of the mania for defensive play and the adoption of strategy that did not make the best use of their resources. The upshot was that for the 5th time an Australian team toured the country without suffering a defeat, the series being won by 3–0. The Australians by contrast made clever use of talent which did not match that of their predecessors. This was particularly apparent in the batting of K. D. Mackay who more than once thwarted South Africa's hopes of success. He had an average of 125·00. They did, however, develop in R. Benaud an outstanding all-rounder, with A. K. Davidson little behind him. The bowling of these two was consistently the cause of South Africa's downfall. L. Kline, a left-arm wrist-spinner, accomplished the hat-trick in the Second Test at Cape Town and, for South Africa, McGlew made the 2nd slowest Test hundred in 545 minutes at Durban.

South Africa went once more to Australia in 1963–64 under the shadow of their exit from what was still called the Imperial Cricket Conference, and with the memory of the tragic tour to England of 1960 not far behind them. It was therefore a source of great encouragement that they managed to draw the series – as had Cheetham's side before them – and furthermore emerge with most of the moral honours thereof. Rain helped to produce a draw – with South Africa never in danger – at Brisbane, but at the New Year they were beaten at Melbourne by 8 wickets. The draw that followed at Sydney showed South Africa's new attacking spirit in a welcome light. To get within 83 of victory with 5 wickets in hand after being set 409 in the 4th innings gave a fillip to South African spirits which was reflected in a 10-wicket victory at Adelaide, their 595 there being the highest total made by either side at that time against the other. South Africa held the upper hand throughout the Fifth Test at Sydney, but were baulked by the Australian tail. In the end they needed only another 85 to win the series with all 10 wickets left.

According to the relative standards of the 2 countries in the past the South African team captained by Trevor Goddard accomplished a meritorious performance. Outside the Test series they were the 1st overseas team in 31 years to defeat New South Wales, and of 14 first-class matches they won 5, lost 3 and drew 6. They scored more runs, hit more centuries (19), broke more records, dropped more catches, and in general scored at a faster rate than any of their 3 predecessors. They drew the largest crowds, aggregating 500,000, of any South African team in Australia and made the biggest profit – an estimated £5,000.

Their aggressive batting proved to be the commanding strength of the team. Their bowling was adequate and might have been distinguished but for their enduring spate of missed catches. The ground fielding, except for the magnificent work of Colin Bland, did not match the high quality attained by the previous side captained by Cheetham. The most notable feature in the South Africans' cricket was the development of several young attacking batsmen of whom the 19-year-old left-hander, Graeme Pollock, and the bespectacled Eddie Barlow excelled themselves and became the drawcards of the season. Two other batsmen who matured into first-class Test cricketers were Bland and Denis Lindsay, the reserve wicket-keeper to Waite. Pollock and Barlow reached the height of their powers in the Fourth Test when their 341 for the 3rd wicket became South Africa's highest partnership for any wicket against any country. In scoring 201 Barlow joined G. A. Faulkner (204) and Dudley Nourse (231) as the 3rd South African to score a double Test hundred against Australia. Pollock made 175 and the first 200 of their stand came at a rate of 84 runs an hour.

Barlow left his homeland as a dashing, unorthodox, hard-hitting batsman with a penchant for slashing fours over the heads of slips. In Australia he acquired refinements which not only made him the most consistent batsman in the team but the most daring and most likely to score off good-length bowling. His aggregate of 1,523 runs was only 11 short of Faulkner's unsurpassed 1,534 in Australia in 1910–11. Perhaps even more valuable to the team than Barlow's prolific scoring was the abounding confidence and aggressive manner in which he set the initial tempo of an innings. Pollock captured the imagination of Australian spectators not only through his readiness to attack but through the power and placing of his strokes. He obtained 2 Test hundreds and 3 in other first-class matches, his gem being his chanceless 175 in the Fourth Test.

LEFT Day of days! After 64 years South Africa have beaten Australia in a Test at home. The scene is Johannesburg, the date Christmas, 1966, and the celebrants are (*from the left*) Dumbrill, Barlow, Lindsay and Graeme Pollock.

RIGHT Keith Stackpole earns 4 for a hook as Ali Bacher, South Africa's future captain, takes avoiding action. Johannesburg, 1967.

When Australia, under the captaincy of R. B. Simpson, arrived in South Africa in the summer of 1966–67, there were high hopes of the home side finally breaking the invincibility of Australian teams on African soil. The Springboks, during the 4 previous years, had drawn an away series with Australia, lost 1–0 at home and won 1–0 away against England, and produced modern-day stars of the calibre of R.G. and P. M. Pollock, K. C. Bland, E. J. Barlow and J. D. Lindsay. The popular feeling was given greater confidence when first Transvaal and then a South African invitation XI lowered the tourists' colours. However, nobody expected South Africa to win by such a decisive 3–1 margin with the Fourth Test drawn very much in South Africa's favour.

Apart from the Second Test at Newlands, the Australian batting failed badly and their bowling attack was one of the weakest to visit this country, being carried by G. D. McKenzie, who took twice as many wickets as any other bowler. The series was dominated by Lindsay, who took 24 catches, and established a record of 606 runs, including 3 hundreds, for a wicket-keeper-batsman in an international series. T. L. Goddard, making a return to Test cricket, set a record of 26 wickets for a South African in a series against Australia and M. J. Procter made an impressive debut with 15 wickets in 3 Tests.

The First Test at the Wanderers was remarkable in that at the end of the 1st day, after winning the toss, Australia were in complete control with 9 wickets in hand and a deficit on the 1st innings of less than 100. Yet they lost the match by 233 runs. A combination of brilliant batting, headed by Lindsay's 182 and 90 from R. G. Pollock, aided by appalling fielding enabled South Africa to make their highest ever Test score of 620 in the 2nd innings. Australia then fell apart against the persistent attack of Goddard (6 for 53) to give South Africa her first victory on home soil against Australia at Test level in 64 years. Australia turned the tables in the Second Test at Newlands. They won the toss and hundreds from Simpson and K. R. Stackpole enabled them to reach 542. Not even a brilliant double-hundred by Pollock, who was hampered by a hamstring injury, could save the follow-on, and when Simpson bowled Pollock for 4 in the 2nd innings, he struck a psychological blow from which the Springboks never recovered.

In the Third Test at Kingsmead Australia quickly gained the initiative to have South Africa 94 for 6. However, Lindsay's 2nd hundred proved to be the turning point of the series. The home team finished with 300 and finally won by 8 wickets after Australia had been forced to follow on. Procter had an outstanding First Test with match figures of 7 for 98.

The remainder of the series became increasingly one-sided as the Australian batsmen were unable to master the South African fast attack. The pattern in the Fourth Test at the Wanderers was almost identical to Durban except that this time Australia won the toss and batted first. Twice in the match their batting collapsed woefully before rain rescued them in the final session, and, in between, South Africa recovered from a bad start thanks to another Lindsay century. Procter enhanced his rising reputation with a further 6 wickets. In the Fifth Test at Port Elizabeth the Australians were sent in first and once again failed to reach 200 in their 1st innings. With Pollock this time scoring a hundred on his home ground, the game took the inevitable course and the South Africans won comfortably with 7 wickets in hand.

The 1970 Australian tour of South Africa for a 4-match series was an occasion of exhilaration and despair. The exhilaration was provided by a clean sweep of the series with ever-increasing margins of success and the knowledge that South Africa had a team capable of taking on and beating the best in the world. The despair was not apparent at the time but this was to be South Africa's final Test series before isolation on political grounds plunged some of the world's greatest players into the wilderness of internal competition with occasional forays of the top players into England's County Championship.

The 1970 Springboks' strength lay with their immense batting line-up headed by B. A. Richards, playing in his only Test series, R. G. Pollock, E. J. Barlow, B. L. Irvine and J. D. Lindsay, and the shock opening bowling attack provided by P. M. Pollock and M. J. Procter. The latter took 26 wickets in only 4 Tests to equal the record set by T. L. Goddard in the previous series. The Australians, following successful tours of England, the West Indies and India, had every reason to be confident but in the end they were humiliated, 452 being the smallest total they had to chase in any of the 4 Tests in the final innings.

One of the biggest disappointments for the Australians was the loss of form of McKenzie, the opening bowler, who took 1 wicket in the series. This meant that A. N. Connolly had to carry the pace attack single-handed and his performance in taking 20 wickets while his team was being outclassed was no mean achievement. The unorthodox spinner J. W. Gleeson provided the main support, taking 19 wickets. However, the real failure lay with the batsmen and the captain W. M. Lawry and his assistant, I. M. Chappell, having their worst-ever series. Chappell managed only 92 runs in 8 innings. Other experienced Test batsmen such as I. R. Redpath and K. D. Walters were also well below their best.

The closest match was the First Test when South Africa, under a new captain, Ali Bacher, scored an historic first victory

M. J. Procter flat out off the wrong foot: just as he reached his youthful potential cricket isolation came to South Africa.

over Australia at Newlands. The writing was already on the wall for the visitors with Pollock and Procter between them taking 10 wickets on the slowest Test pitch in the country, and they only managed 164 in their 1st innings. This debacle against accurate fast bowling and a century by Barlow ensured South Africa's victory by 170 runs. Thereafter the series became more and more one-sided, South Africa's winning margin in the remaining Tests being an innings and 129 runs and finally 323 runs.

The pattern was the same in virtually every Test. Lucky with all 4 tosses, South Africa, batting first each time, made good scores with which Australia could not compete. There were many highlights for the South Africans. Richards, by scoring 94 in the opening session of the Second Test at Kingsmead, almost became the 4th batsman and the 1st non-Australian to score a hundred before lunch on the opening day of a Test match – he went on to make a flawless 140 and shared a hundred stand in an hour with Pollock. There was Pollock's record-breaking 274 – the highest Test score by a South African – in the same innings as South Africa made their highest ever Test total of 622 for 9 declared. There were further hundreds in the Third and Fourth Tests for Barlow, Richards and Irvine; and, above all, there was the sight of Procter and P. M. Pollock ripping the heart out of one Australian innings after another. In the final innings of the series Pollock was indisposed but it made no difference as Procter carried the attack virtually single-handed to finish with 6 for 73.

South Africa lacked only an established spin bowler. They certainly had the batsmen, faster bowlers and fielders to challenge the world. But it was a challenge that they were denied by forces beyond their control.

AUSTRALIA V SOUTH AFRICA

			RESULT	CAPTAINS
1902–03	1 Johannesburg	SA 454, 101–4; A 296, 372–7D	Drawn	J. Darling, H. M. Taberer
	2 Johannesburg	A 175, 309; SA 240, 85	A 159 runs	J. Darling, J. N. Anderson
	3 Cape Town	A 252, 59–0; SA 85, 225	A 10 wkts	J. Darling, E. A. Halliwell
1910–11	1 Sydney	A 528; SA 174, 240	A inns 114	C. Hill, P. W. Sherwell
	2 Melbourne	A 348, 327; SA 506, 80	A 89 runs	C. Hill, P. W. Sherwell
	3 Adelaid	SA 482, 360; A. 465, 339	SA 38 runs	C. Hill, P. W. Sherwell
	4 Melbourne	A 328, 578; SA 205, 171	A 530 runs	C. Hill, P. W. Sherwell
	5 Sydney	A 364, 198–3; SA 160, 401	A 7 wkts	C. Hill, P. W. Sherwell
1912	1 Old Trafford	A 448; SA 265, 95	A inns 88	S. E. Gregory, F. Mitchell
	2 Lord's	SA 263, 173 A 390, 48–0	A 10 wkts	S. E. Gregory, F. Mitchell
	3 Trent Bridge	SA 329; A 219	Drawn	S. E. Gregory, L. Tancred
1921–22	1 Durban	A 299, 324–7D; SA 232, 184–7	Drawn	H. L. Collins, H. W. Taylor
	2 Johannesburg	A 450, 7–0; SA 243, 472–8D	Drawn	H. L. Collins, H. W. Taylor
	3 Cape Town	SA 180, 216; A 396, 1–0	A 10 wkts	H. L. Collins, H. W. Taylor
1931–32	1 Brisbane	A 450; SA 170, 117	A inns 163	W. M. Woodfull, H. B. Cameron
	2 Sydney	SA 153, 161; A 469	A inns 155	W. M. Woodfull, H. B. Cameron
	3 Melbourne	A 198, 554; SA 358, 225	A 169 runs	W. M. Woodfull, H. B. Cameron
	4 Adelaide	SA 308, 274; A 513, 73–0	A 10 wkts	W. M. Woodfull, H. B. Cameron
	5 Melbourne	SA 36, 45; A 153	A inns 72	W. M. Woodfull, H. B. Cameron
1935–36	1 Durban	SA 248, 282; A 429, 102–1	A 9 wkts	V. Y. Richardson, H. F. Wade
	2 Johannesburg	SA 157, 491; A 250, 274–2	Drawn	V. Y. Richardson, H. F. Wade
	3 Cape Town	A 362–8D; SA 102, 182	A inns 78	V. Y. Richardson, H. F. Wade
	4 Johannesburg	SA 157, 98; A 439	A inns 184	V. Y. Richardson, H. F. Wade
	5 Durban	SA 222, 227; A 455	A inns 6	V. Y. Richardson, H. F. Wade
1949–50	1 Johannesburg	A 413; SA 137, 191	A inns 85	A. L. Hassett, A. D. Nourse
	2 Cape Town	A 526–7D, 87–2; SA 278, 333	A 8 wkts	A. L. Hassett, A. D. Nourse
	3 Durban	SA 311, 99; A 75, 336–5	A 5 wkts	A. L. Hassett, A. D. Nourse
	4 Johannesburg	A 465–8D, 259–2; SA 352	Drawn	A. L. Hassett, A. D. Nourse
	5 Port Elizabeth	A 549–7D; SA 158, 132	A inns 259	A. L. Hassett, A. D. Nourse
1952–53	1 Brisbane	A 280, 277; SA 221, 240	A 96 runs	A. L. Hassett, J. E. Cheetham
	2 Melbourne	SA 227, 388; A 243, 290	SA 82 runs	A. L. Hassett, J. E. Cheetham
	3 Sydney	SA 173, 232; A 443	A inns 38	A. L. Hassett, J. E. Cheetham
	4 Adelaide	A 530, 233–3D; SA 387, 177–6	Drawn	A. L. Hassett, J. E. Cheetham
	5 Melbourne	A 520, 209; SA 435, 297–4	SA 6 wkts	A. L. Hassett, J. E. Cheetham
1957–58	1 Johannesburg	SA 470–9D, 201; A 368, 162–3	Drawn	I. D. Craig, D. J. McGlew
	2 Cape Town	A 449; SA 209, 99	A inns 141	I. D. Craig, C. B. van Ryneveld
	3 Durban	A 163, 292–7; SA 384	Drawn	I. D. Craig, C. B. van Ryneveld
	4 Johannesburg	A 401, 1–0; SA 203, 198	A 10 wkts	I. D. Craig, C. B. van Ryneveld
	5 Port Elizabeth	SA 214, 144; A 291, 68–2	A 8 wkts	I. D. Craig, C. B. van Ryneveld

1963–64	1 Brisbane	A 435, 144–1D; SA 346, 13–1	Drawn	R. Benaud, T. L. Goddard
	2 Melbourne	SA 274, 306; A 447, 136–2	A 8 wkts	R. B. Simpson, T. L. Goddard
	3 Sydney	A 260, 450–9D; SA 302, 326–5	Drawn	R. B. Simpson, T. L. Goddard
	4 Adelaide	A 345, 331; SA 595, 82–0	SA 10 wkts	R. B. Simpson, T. L. Goddard
	5 Sydney	A 311, 270; SA 411, 76–0	Drawn	R. B. Simpson, T. L. Goddard
1966–67	1 Johannesburg	SA 199, 620; A 325, 261	SA 233 runs	R. B. Simpson, P. L. van der Merwe
	2 Cape Town	A 542, 180–4; SA 353, 367	A 6 wkts	R. B. Simpson, P. L. van der Merwe
	3 Durban	SA 300, 185–2; A 147, 334	SA 8 wkts	R. B. Simpson, P. L. van der Merwe
	4 Johannesburg	A 143, 148–8; SA 332–9D	Drawn	R. B. Simpson, P. L. van der Merwe
	5 Port Elizabeth	A 173, 278; SA 276, 179–3	SA 7 wkts	R. B. Simpson, P. L. van der Merwe
1969–70	1 Cape Town	SA 382, 232; A 164, 280	SA 170 runs	W. M. Lawry, A. Bacher
	2 Durban	SA 622–9D; A 157, 336	SA inns 129 runs	W. M. Lawry, A. Bacher
	3 Johannesburg	SA 279, 408; A 202, 178	SA 307 runs	W. M. Lawry, A. Bacher
	4 Port Elizabeth	SA 311, 470–8D; A 212, 246	SA 323 runs	W. M. Lawry, A. Bacher

CAPTAINS (Australia)	TESTS	WON	LOST	DRAWN
J. Darling	3	2		1
C. Hill	5	4	1	
S. E. Gregory	3	2		1
H. L. Collins	3	1		2
W. M. Woodfull	5	5		
V. Y. Richardson	5	4		1
A. L. Hassett	10	6	2	2
I. D. Craig	5	3		2
R. Benaud	1			1
R. B. Simpson	9	2	4	3
W. M. Lawry	4		4	
	53	29	11	13

CAPTAINS (South Africa)	TESTS	WON	LOST	DRAWN
H. M. Taberer	1			1
J. H. Anderson	1		1	
E. A. Halliwell	1		1	
P. W. Sherwell	5	1	4	
F. Mitchell	2		2	
L. J. Tancred	1			1
H. W. Taylor	3		1	2
H. B. Cameron	5		5	
H. F. Wade	5		4	1
A. D. Nourse Jr	5		4	1
J. E. Cheetham	5	2	2	1
D. J. McGlew	1			1
C. B. van Ryneveld	4		3	1
T. L. Goddard	5	1	1	3
P. L. van der Merwe	5	3	1	1
A. Bacher	4	4		
	53	11	29	13

HIGHEST INNINGS TOTALS

Australia in Australia, 578, Melbourne 1910–11
Australia in South Africa, 549–7D, Port Elizabeth 1949–50
South Africa in Australia, 595, Adelaide 1963–64
South Africa in South Africa, 622–9, Durban 1969–70

LOWEST INNINGS TOTALS

Australia in Australia, 153, Melbourne 1931–32
Australia in South Africa, 75, Durban 1949–50
South Africa in Australia, 36, Melbourne 1931–32
South Africa in South Africa {85, Johannesburg 1902–03; 85, Cape Town 1902–03}

HIGHEST INDIVIDUAL INNINGS

Australia in Australia, 299*, D. G. Bradman, Adelaide 1931–32
Australia in South Africa, 203, H. L. Collins, Johannesburg 1921–22
South Africa in Australia, 204, G. A. Faulkner, Melbourne 1910–11
South Africa in South Africa, 274, R. G. Pollock, Durban 1969–70

HIGHEST AGGREGATE OF RUNS IN A SERIES

Australia in Australia, 834, R. N. Harvey 1952–53
Australia in South Africa, 660, R. N. Harvey 1949–50
South Africa in Australia, 732, G. A. Faulkner 1910–11
South Africa in South Africa, 606, D. T. Lindsay 1966–67

BEST INNINGS BOWLING FIGURES

Australia in Australia, 7–83, C. V. Grimmett, Adelaide 1931–32
Australia in South Africa, 7–34, J. V. Saunders, Johannesburg 1902–03
South Africa in Australia, 7–81, H. J. Tayfield, Melbourne 1952–53
South Africa in South Africa, 7–23, H. J. Tayfield, Durban 1949–50

BEST MATCH BOWLING FIGURES

Australia in Australia, 14–199, C. V. Grimmett, Adelaide 1931–32
Australia in South Africa, 13–173, C. V. Grimmett, Durban 1935–36
South Africa in Australia, 13–165, H. J. Tayfield, Melbourne 1952–53
South Africa in South Africa, 10–116, C. B. Llewellyn, Johannesburg 1902–03

HIGHEST WICKET AGGREGATE IN A SERIES

Australia in Australia, 37, W. J. Whitty 1910–11
Australia in South Africa, 44, C. V. Grimmett 1935–36
South Africa in Australia, 30, H. J. Tayfield 1952–53
South Africa in South Africa, 26 {T. L. Goddard 1966–67; M. J. Procter 1969–70}

RECORD WICKET PARTNERSHIPS – AUSTRALIA

1 J. H. Fingleton and W. A. Brown, 233, Cape Town 1935–36
2 C. C. McDonald and A. L. Hassett, 275, Adelaide 1952–53
3 W. Bardsley and C. Kelleway, 242, Lord's 1912
4 R. N. Harvey and K. R. Miller, 168, Sydney 1952–53
5 W. W. Armstrong and V. T. Trumper, 143, Melbourne 1910–11
6 C. Kelleway and V. S. Ransford, 107, Melbourne 1910–11
7 R. Benaud and G. D. McKenzie, 160, Sydney 1963–64
8 A. G. Chipperfield and C. V. Grimmett, 83, Durban 1935–36
9 {D. G. Bradman and W. J. O'Reilly, 78, Adelaide 1931–32; K. Mackay and I. Meckiff, 78, Johannesburg 1957–58}
10 V. S. Ransford and W. J. Whitty, 82, Melbourne 1910–11

RECORD WICKET PARTNERSHIPS – SOUTH AFRICA

1 D. J. McGlew and T. L. Goddard, 176, Johannesburg 1957–58
2 L. J. Tancred and C. B. Llewellyn, 173, Johannesburg 1902–03
3 E. J. Barlow and R. G. Pollock, 341, Adelaide 1963–64
4 C. N. Frank and A. W. Nourse, 206, Johannesburg 1957–58
5 J. H. B. Waite and W. R. Endean, 129, Johannesburg 1957–58
6 R. G. Pollock and H. R. Lance, 200, Durban 1969–70
7 D. T. Lindsay and P. L. van der Merwe, 221, Johannesburg 1966–67
8 A. W. Nourse and E. A. Halliwell, 124, Johannesburg 1902–03
9 R. G. Pollock and P. M. Pollock, 85, Cape Town 1966–67
10 S. J. Pegler and L. A. Stricker, 53, Adelaide 1910–11

Australia v West Indies

C. L. R. JAMES AND TONY COZIER

Individual West Indians played Australians at cricket before the First World War. In 1909 H. B. G. Austin played for MCC v Australia and made 24 on a wet wicket. In August 1913, an Australian team was touring the United States and played a match against coloured West Indians in New York. The West Indians lost by an innings falling before C. G. Macartney who took 7 for 7 and 7 for 6. But Richard Ollivierre, who had played well for West Indies in England in 1906 and against MCC in 1912–13 in the West Indies, took 7 for 57 and had H. L. Collins, Warren Bardsley and J. N. Crawford for 0.

Macartney saw the West Indies in England in 1928, thought their cricket was much better than it looked and was active in getting a West Indian team invited to Australia in 1930–31. The West Indies team in Australia was not equal to the task. That must be said without equivocation and only this will allow certain extenuating considerations to be noted. These could have mitigated but not prevented the almost continuous failures. They were nevertheless not negligible and they are a part of West Indian cricket history and cricket history as a whole. First the team was haphazardly put together. Some of them met each other and the captain, Jack Grant, for the first time at Cristobal Colon on the journey out. Grant was a Cambridge blue. The vice-captain was Birkett, another young player, a Barbadian living in Trinidad who had not played in any of the 1930 Tests.

The West Indies had heard that Australian wickets were fast. Therefore, in addition to their three fast bowlers, Constantine, Francis and Griffith, they chose another fast-medium bowler, Edwin St Hill. The wickets turned out to be so slow that J. M. Gregory, the famous fast bowler, told Constantine that if he had been given such wickets to bowl on he would have played tennis. This was not malice aforethought and more than mere ill-luck. Long before the tour was over the West Indies recognized that they should have brought the veteran googly bowler, C. R. Browne, who bowled finely for years after, was a great master of the game and had developed remarkable hitting powers. With the needed spin bowlers so lacking, the left-hander, Martin, one of the batsmen of the side, had to be called upon to do a deal of bowling. He was near 40 and his batting was affected.

It is a tradition in West Indies cricket that, in 1928, Sutcliffe said, after the Lord's match, that he had never played better fast bowling than the combined attack of Constantine, Francis and Griffith. What ruined the West Indies attack was notoriously bad slip fielding. When catches are constantly missed off them fast bowlers get into the habit of bowling at the stumps. They may get away with this against a county team, but that is a bad preparation for a line of Test batsmen. The West Indies in the 1930 side had strengthened their slip fielding; they were eager to pose their fast bowling on fast wickets against the Bradman who had scored so heavily in England in 1930. To conclude this fascinating episode in the West Indian tradition, West Indians claim that in his whole career Bradman never met such a trio of fast bowlers as West Indies had ready for him in 1930–31. West Indians further compare the heavy scoring of English batsmen against Australia in England in 1934 and the complete failure of some of those same batsmen in the West Indies in 1935–36.

Alas! The first 4 Test Matches were a martyrdom. Australia won the 1st by 10 wickets, the next 3 by an innings and over 100, 1 by over 200 runs. All the Australian batsmen came off, Bradman and McCabe earning the unstinting admiration of their visitors by their style of attacking the bowling from the moment they came in until they got out. West Indies batsmen except Headley could not manage Grimmett and Ironmonger. Headley, who had begun the tour brilliantly, was for a while bothered by the concentration on his leg-stump, but he mastered this attack and in the thousand runs he made for the season attacked the Australian bowling with a vigour equal to that of the great Australian batsmen. In the last 2 games of the tour M. A. Noble and rain came to the help of the West Indians. Noble personally went to the New South Wales groundsman and asked him to prepare the fastest wickets possible. West Indies then beat a powerful New South Wales side, Constantine not only showing his usual good all-round form but being at his all-round best.

The 1st West Indies team to tour Australia in 1930–31 contained much talent but was unversed in cricket at Test level. Back row: G. A. Headley, C. A. Roach, E. A. C. Hunte, F. I. deCaires, O. C. Scott, O. S. Wight, I. Barrow and E. L. St Hill; sitting: H. C. Griffith, L. N. Constantine, J. E. Seheult (assistant manager), G. C. Grant (captain), R. H. Mallett (manager), L. S. Birkett, F. R. Martin, E. L. Bartlett and G. Francis; on ground: J. E. D. Sealey.

In the final Test Headley made a hundred which drew warm approval from the Australians on the field. Martin batted soundly, if slowly, for another hundred and West Indies reached 350 for 6. In addition to a faster wicket (Griffith bowled Bradman for a duck), rain came to their assistance and they won the match by 30 runs. Grant had not only steadily improved in his handling of the side but his watchful batting in all games now reached a climax with two fine innings. All Australia was happy that the side had won a victory. Yet more than 20 years were to pass before the next meeting.

After the war Australia quickly established an unchallengeable supremacy over England and, after West Indies' triumphal English tour in 1950, West Indies in Australia (1951–52) seemed to herald a battle of the giants. This was from all sides a most disappointing and, in many respects, quite inexplicable tour. Many features to this day defy the journalistic or historical commentator and perhaps only the players, if they, can throw a revealing light. To mention only a few, Walcott and Weekes failed against Miller and Lindwall on the fast Australian wickets. Yet 4 years later on equally fast or even faster wickets they repeatedly scored so brilliantly against the same bowlers that Lindwall has been quoted as saying that the only better batsmen than Walcott and Weekes he had seen were Bradman and McCabe. West Indies nearly won the First Test; won the Third Test, a tough match; had Australia 222 for 9 in the equally hard-fought Fourth Test, and allowed Nos. 9 and 11 to make the 38 runs required for victory. West Indies then beat a very powerful Victoria side containing 7 Test players by making 297 for 6 wickets. Then, having to get 416 to win the last Test, began the last day having 112 for 2 and a line of batsmen to come, yet collapsed for 213. Valentine consolidated his reputation as the best left-hand spinner seen since the war, and the best bowler on the side. Yet his 24 wickets took him 218.1 overs and cost 28.79 runs each. Worrell the batsman had 17 wickets for 19.35 runs each in 89.1 overs. Gomez had even better figures, 18 wickets in 104.2 overs at 14.22 runs each.

The West Indies batting wilted before Lindwall and Miller. Yet Lindwall's 21 wickets cost 23.04 runs each, Miller's 20 wickets, at 19·9 each, were little better than Worrell or Gomez. Later, after a review of the facts, we shall venture some observations by cricketers of experience qualified to make them. West Indies had one first-class match before the Tests began, against Queensland, and lost it by 10 wickets. Ramadhin, Valentine and Worrell did not play and Queensland began with 455. Gomez with 3 for 54 and 34 run out and 97 not out established himself as the sheet-anchor of the side, a position he never lost. Australia scrambled home in the First Test by 3 wickets. In a small scoring match Valentine took 5 for 99 in the 1st innings and Ramadhin 5 for 90 in the 2nd. But even in the 1st innings Ramadhin tied up all the batsmen for all to see.

Goddard thus received every encouragement to believe that his 2 slow bowlers could repeat their triumph in England in 1950. In the final innings Gomez and Worrell, whose future figures as opening bowlers no one had any reason to expect, had bowled only 5 overs for 14 runs, Gomez taking a wicket. Goddard rubbed the ball on the ground to get off the shine and thus prepare for Ramadhin and Valentine who bowled unchanged to the end, 40 overs each. West Indies batting had failed, Gomez made 22 and 55, and Weekes whose play in the nets had confirmed his great reputation in the eyes of A. G. Moyes, made 70 in his finest, most aggressive style: he was only once to get near that form again. In the Second Test at Sydney their 1st innings score was 362, another of the lesser batsmen, Christiani, making a very brilliant 76. Worrell with 64 and Walcott with 60 also seemed to know how to deal with Lindwall, Miller and Johnston. But Miller who did not get a wicket had by now made a shrewd psychological estimate. Impressed as was everybody by Ramadhin's spin, Miller decided that the only way to deal with this dangerous bowler and to stay the havoc he might wreak was to attack him and keep on attacking him. This he proceeded to do with great success, and with Hassett putting his head down over every ball Australia reached 517. This time Weekes alone of the recognized batsmen could deal with Lindwall, Miller and Johnston, and Australia had only 136 to make.

The West Indies team now seemed to go to pieces. It bowed to South Australia by 227 runs and lost even to Western Australia by 1 wicket. The tour, so eagerly anticipated, threatened to end in pitiful failure but the side came alive again to win the Third Test by 6 wickets. In dismissing Australia for 82 Worrell took 6 wickets. Set 233 to win in a small scoring match, Gomez who had made 54 and 41 in the Second Test now made 46 not out. In the Fourth Test which followed directly, West Indies led on the 1st innings by 56 runs, Worrell despite painful injuries batting finely for 108. Gomez who had made 37 in the 1st innings made 52 in the 2nd and, in a match still of mournful memory in the West Indies, Australia, having to make 260 to win, had 9 wickets down for 222. In the previous Test, Ring, a dangerous hitter, had hit 67 run out. Again he went boldly for the West Indies attack. West Indies lost control and, with Ring 32 not out and Bill Johnston 7 not out, Australia made the series safe. West Indies in the last Test simply could not deal with the bouncers first of Miller and then of Lindwall. Stollmeyer who had batted with steady if not outstanding consistency all through the season now made a superb hundred, playing Lindwall and Miller with calm defiance interspersed with brilliant strokes. Gomez for once failed with the bat, but he took 10 wickets in the match, 7 for 55 in the first innings. Not even Miller exceeded him in all-round value to his side, in addition to which he took some brilliant catches.

It will have been noticed how, besides winning one match, West Indies in two approached within measurable distance of the dramatic games of 1960–61 which lay 9 years ahead. If they had won the matches at Brisbane and Melbourne it would have surprised nobody. Let two West Indians who knew their countrymen's cricket well and played in Australia have the last word. After watching the Australians in England in 1948 and the West Indians of 1950, Constantine's opinion was that if he or George Headley with their experience had gone to Australia with the team it could not possibly have lost the series. Headley himself was moved to one of his rare, almost unique, explosions over cricket at the inability of West Indies batsmen to deal with the short balls of Miller and Lindwall. That they could was proved in the West Indies a few years later. Somehow, somewhy, the team could not make the best of itself.

If one can venture an explanation, Test cricket in Australia (this is Barnett's written opinion) is unbelievably tough, the Australians are eagle-eyed, alert in spotting weaknesses, and relentless in pursuing them. Fine players though the West Indians were, English cricket in 1950 had not tested them sternly enough. Their opponents, recognizing their strong possibilities, never gave them the chance, even in State matches, to acquire that moral confidence in which individuals not only do themselves justice but rise to heights. Nevertheless one can risk saying that, despite the failure to repeat the brilliant success of 1950, in the experience of 1951–52 could be seen early gleams of what was to blaze 10 years later.

At last the Australians visited the West Indies. The 1955 Australian tour in the West Indies, lasting from March until June, was a tour full of events which captured headlines. In fact, few recent tours have had such striking achievements, from which such misleading conclusions could be drawn. Australia's score of 758 for 8 declared in the Fifth Test was the highest score Australia had ever made in Tests. Never before had 21 hundreds been scored in a Test series and never since, Australia leading with 12 and West Indies only 3 behind. Walcott scored 5 hundreds, twice scoring a hundred in each innings; and this against Miller, Lindwall, Benaud and that fine bowler, Archer. One other record is quite a feat of batsmanship, which many records are not. In the Fourth Test, following on a score of 668 by Australia, West Indies were 146 for 6. Atkinson, batting at No. 7, and Depeiza, batting at No. 8, then came together and put on 41 before the close of play. Next day the two batted all day to take the score ultimately to 494. This stand of 348 for the 7th wicket surpassed all others for that wicket not only in Tests but in any first-class cricket. Other records are too numerous to mention, particularly in regard to the fact that, of these makers and breakers of records, the Australians were soundly thrashed by England in 1956 and the West Indies in the same place received a similar drubbing in 1957.

Australia, like West Indies in 1951–52, had only one first-class match against Jamaica before the First Test. By hard practice systematically organized, Australia were ready and won the First Test by 9 wickets. 'Collie' Smith who had made a hundred in the Jamaica match made 44 in the 1st innings and, sent in 1st wicket down, made 104 in the 2nd. In the Second Test Walcott, who had made a hundred in the First, and Weekes hit free but well-controlled hundreds. In reply, McDonald, Morris and Harvey opened Australia's innings with a hundred each and Australia made 600 for 9 declared. The 2nd West Indies wicket fell at 103, still over 100 behind. But Walcott and Weekes got together again, Walcott scored another hundred and, to the grievous disappointment of his fellow-countrymen, Weekes was left at 87 not out. The match was drawn.

Not so the next one. Wickets fell to the spinners, Benaud, Sobers and Ian Johnson. The highest total was Australia's 257 but Australia lost only 3 wickets in making the 133 needed for victory. In a small-scoring match Weekes made 81, Walcott 73 and Worrell 56. The Fourth Test Match was the one in which Atkinson and Depeiza twice saved their side. In their 2nd innings Australia made only 249 and were 119 for 6, Atkinson taking 5 for 56, bowling 36 overs. West Indies in their 2nd innings were 207 for 6 when Atkinson, 20 not out, and Depeiza, 11 not out, played out time. In this match this redoubtable pair quite overshadowed the fact that Miller and Lindwall opened the bowling and both made hundreds, a rare occurence in first-class cricket. In the Fifth Test West Indies seemed to begin well with 357, the unfailing Walcott scoring 155. But Australian batsmen made 5 hundreds, Harvey getting 204 to average over 100 per innings. Walcott finished with yet another hundred and West Indies again reached 300 to lose by an innings and 82 runs.

Coming events cast their shadows before them. For the British Guianan Kanhai, with his mentor Walcott as partner, batted noticeably well. The deeds of Sobers without being spectacular underlined his teenage promise. Atkinson took most wickets (13) and was first in the averages with 35.30. Where Valentine and Ramadhin took only 5 wickets, each bowling nearly 150 overs, Sobers with 93.5 overs took 6 wickets and followed Atkinson's 35.30 with 35.50. For Barbados he opened the innings and hit Miller for a startling succession of fours. Here was a great cricketer in the making. Both with bat and with ball he was being shaped early in a hard school. Ramadhin, Valentine, 'Collie' Smith, Kanhai all had these early disciplines. The small number of first-class players in the West Indies is not always a handicap.

The tour of West Indies to Australia in 1960–61 will be remembered as the beginning of a new epoch, rather a regeneration of Test cricket. That the West Indies players provided the initial impetus and maintained it is certain; not to be forgotten or ignored is the fact that Benaud, the Australian captain, responded to Worrell's challenge from the First Test to the very last. He seemed to accept the fact that the gauntlet was not thrown down to an Australian team, but to a certain type of cricket which had overtaken the Test game. The tour began indifferently for West Indies, apart from the Victoria match wherein Kanhai struck the first great chord with a chanceless 252 and Ramadhin's bowling ensured a wholesale victory. So the First Test was approached with no great expectation.

The tied Test between Australia and West Indies at Brisbane, 14 December 1960. Solomon's throw-in hits the stumps. Meckiff is run out and West Indian jubilation has begun. In 850 Tests this is the only tie.

In this now historic match West Indies batted first and Sobers hit one of the finest hundreds ever seen in Australia. To 453 Australia replied with 505, O'Neill contributing 181. West Indies with 284 gave Australia 233 to make. Hall wrecked the early Australian batting and Australia were 6 for 92. Benaud and Davidson, however, went fearlessly for the runs and, with half an hour to go, needed only 27. Solomon threw out Davidson and when the last over from Hall began 6 runs were needed. Benaud, attempting a hit which could win the match at one stroke, was caught at the wicket off the second ball. Hunte saved a 3rd run which would have given Australia the match, and made a superb throw from deep square-leg which enabled Alexander, the wicket-keeper, to run out Grout. The scores still level, Kline came in to attempt the winning run off the last ball but one. Aiming at a single stump, Solomon from square-leg hit the wicket. The match was not only a tie in figures. Magnificent cricket had been played by both sides and henceforth the ball was at their feet. They kept it moving.

West Indies lost the next Test at Melbourne by 7 wickets. They had the worst of what was not a very bad wicket. But Kanhai dominated the bowling for 84, Hunte reinforced the impression he had made at Sydney by another fine hundred. Needing only 67 to win, Australia lost 3 wickets.

Sixty-five thousand people had come to see West Indies follow on 167 behind in the Second Test. Now West Indies showed what they could do by winning the Third Test by 222 runs. Sobers made 168 and in the second half of his innings let the spectators see what they had heard of at Brisbane. A newcomer for batting, however, now firmly established himself. Alexander, the wicket-keeper, known so far as only a batsman of sound defence and courage, had made 60 in the First Test at a critical moment and had followed it up with 72 in the Second Test, begun when the score was 99 for 5. Now Alexander hit a chanceless hundred to give Australia 464 to win. This Test also marked the emergence of a new feature in the West Indies attack. Lance Gibbs with his slightly faster than slow off-spinners had done well in India. Now he replaced Ramadhin. He had 3 wickets in the 1st innings and on the 5th day in a spell of 27 balls took 4 wickets for 2 runs, his victims including Harvey and O'Neill.

The next 2 Tests were to show that the drama of the tie in the First Test was not in any way accidental. Kanhai fulfilled all expectations by making a hundred in each innings at Adelaide, needing little more than even time to score the runs. Alexander, now a fully accredited Test batsman, scored 63 not out and 87 not out. Worrell made 71 and 53. Davidson, all through the season in his finest form, was absent through illness, but West Indies batting was obviously able to deal with anything that Australia could bring against it. Gibbs did the hat-trick in the 1st innings and in the 2nd Hall had Favell for 4 and Simpson for 3. All seemed over when, needing 460 to win, 9 Australian wickets had fallen for 207. But for well over an hour Mackay and Kline defied the West Indies bowling. Against all odds they saved the game for Australia.

The final Test, at Melbourne, provided yet another game of tense competitiveness. West Indies batted steadily and well without glamour for 292 and 321. Sobers batted well again, so did Alexander with 73, and Hall with 21 in both innings continued to show that he could make runs when they were badly needed. West Indies seemed to have lost the game when, having to make 258, Australia were 248 for 7. Then came some of the dramatic events which this tour so regularly produced. Australia reached 254 for 7; from a ball by Valentine a bail fell and confusion followed as to whether the batsman was bowled or not. After consultation between the umpires the decision went to Australia who won by 2 wickets. The vast crowd swarmed on to the Melbourne field to mark the end of as fine a series as had been seen in Australia or anywhere else for many, many years.

When Australia returned for their 2nd tour of the West Indies in 1965, several of those involved in the magnificent series four years earlier had passed into retirement. Benaud, Burge, Davidson, Harvey, Mackay and McDonald – all of whom had played significant parts then – had to be replaced and Australia, now under the captaincy of Simpson, was unquestionably weaker. The West Indies on the other hand, had won fresh laurels in the intervening years. Worrell had retired but had only done so satisfied that the team which he had taken over in Australia was united into a spirited, all-round combination with no serious deficiencies. He had been at the helm as India was defeated in all 5 Tests in the Caribbean in 1962 and England outplayed 3–1 in England in 1963. He handed the mantle of leadership over to the genius, Sobers, but reassuringly remained close in the background as manager.

In contrast to the individual losses suffered by the Australians, the West Indies had made several important gains. Hall, who had been so restricted by lack of adequate support in the 1960–61 series, had been joined by Charlie Griffith, a fellow Barbadian, massively built, immensely strong and with pace almost comparable with Hall's. His stock-in-trade were the fast bowler's two most potent deliveries, the bouncer and the yorker, with which he had laid waste English batsmen in 1963: 31 wickets in the Tests, over 100 in all first-class games. They made a formidable pair, effectively supported by Sobers's fast-medium over the wicket, left-arm swing. When spin was necessary, Gibbs, who had confirmed the potential he first showed in Australia, and Sobers, either orthodox or unorthodox, provided it.

Charlie Griffith (West Indies 1959–68) was a formidable partner for W. W. Hall. Ready here to unleash, his arm looks straight enough, but it was at times suspect.

As for batting, Butcher, a surprise omission from the touring team for the 1960–61 series, had come into his own while the stylish Nurse now finally cemented his place in the XI. Even the perennial problem of a reliable opening pair was settled, if only temporarily, by the success of Bryan Davis as Hunte's new partner. With Kanhai and Sobers at the height of their careers and the impeccable Hendriks behind the wicket, it was as strong and well-balanced a side as the West Indies had ever had.

The Australians, in the process of rebuilding, could not boast such individual brilliance. Yet, in Simpson and Lawry, they possessed an effective opening partnership which might have been expected to blunt the hostility of Hall and Griffith. O'Neill began with a great reputation, an uninhibited striker of the ball with a fine record, while Booth, tall and elegant, and the left-handed Cowper completed batting of real worth. Of their bowlers, McKenzie carried all the credentials needed to be an outstanding successor to Lindwall, while Hawke, for all the awkwardness of his delivery, could be a difficult proposition at fast-medium. Philpott, it was hoped, would expose supposed West Indian frailty against leg-spin.

As it turned out, West Indian strength prevailed and the series was virtually decided in the home team's favour by the end of the third Test when they held a 2–0 lead. The Australians showed characteristic spirit in scoring heavily in the drawn Fourth Test and in conclusively winning the Fifth but there could be no doubt that the first triumph by the West Indies in a series against Australia was deserved.

Unfortunately, the atmosphere throughout was sullied by the allegation made in the international and local press during the course of the First Test by the former Australian captain, Richie Benaud, that Griffith's action was illegal. It was a view shared, if not publicly expressed, by most of the Australian players and they became so obsessed by it that it proved detrimental to their play. As far as the West Indian public was concerned, there was reason to question the motive for raising the issue at this particular point. It was pertinent that Benaud had expressed no qualms about Griffith's action during the 1963 tour of England which he watched throughout. It proved a highly emotive issue and was never far below the surface.

Fast bowling was the decisive factor in the First Test on the fast and true Sabina Park pitch. Hall took 9 wickets, 5 in the 1st innings and 4 in the 2nd, and Griffith 4 crucial ones as the West Indies recorded their first victory over Australia on home soil. Hunte's 81 in the West Indies' 2nd innings was the highest individual score in the match and Booth was the only Australian to muster a half-century.

The Second Test was condemned to the dullness of a high-scoring draw by Queen's Park Oval's sluggish pitch which frustrated both bowlers and stroke-making batsmen with its lack of pace and bounce. Simpson's decision to field 1st on winning the toss was more a tribute to Hall and Griffith than anything else, and the West Indies duly batted into the 2nd day for 429, the highlight of which was Butcher's first hundred in the Caribbean. Cowper and Booth responded with hundreds in a 4th-wicket partnership of 225, Australia totalled 516 and the West Indies used the final day for batting practice.

Until now, the Australians had encountered contrasting conditions at the 2 Test grounds – Sabina hard, fast and reliably true; Queen's Park so slow it had riled both captains into a consensus that it should be dug up and relaid. They now journeyed to Georgetown where, they had been led to believe, the Bourda pitch would be a batsman's paradise. They found it anything but. The West Indies won the toss in the Third Test and, with it, the match. They reached 201 for 2 on the 1st day which was adequate for, thereafter, the pitch became increasingly responsive to spin. After that opening day, 38 wickets fell for 657 runs. There were 2 rest days, Good Friday and Easter Day, so the pitch had that much longer to last than usual, yet it was clear from the Thursday that there was no way it would.

The basis of a West Indian 1st innings total of 355 was Kanhai's 89. None of the other 3 innings passed 180, Australia falling for 179 and 144 to lose by 212 runs. The admirable Hawke, often bowling round the wicket, took 10 wickets in the match but the vital bowling performance was Gibbs's. The off-spinner had 9 for 80 in the match, including 6 for 29 in the 2nd innings.

Australian faith in the quality of West Indian pitches was restored in Barbados where head groundsman Jimmy Bowen prepared two beauties for the island game and the Test. In the former, Simpson, O'Neill and Thomas all scored hundreds against an attack including Hall, Griffith, Sobers and White of the Test Side; in the latter, Simpson and Lawry compensated fully for their earlier failures with an opening partnership of 382, both recording double-hundreds (the first time the feat had been achieved by the openers in the same innings of a Test). Cowper also utilized the opportunity and recorded his 2nd hundred of the series, Simpson allowing the innings to reach 650 for 6 before declaring midway through the 3rd day of a 6 day match. To keep Australia's interest alive in the rubber, victory was imperative, but West Indian batsmen, too, were keen to join in the bonanza provided for them by the pitch.

In 8 previous Tests spread over 4 series, the stylish Nurse had not made a hundred. Now he became the 3rd batsman in the match to pass a double. Kanhai got 129 during a 200-run 3rd-wicket stand and the threat of a follow-on, Australia's main hope, was comfortably avoided. Despite Simpson's tempting 2nd innings declaration, victory for either side was never, realistically, 'on'.

Within a week of achieving this signal triumph over Australia and claiming the Frank Worrell Trophy, the West Indies were being beaten by 10 wickets inside 3 days in the final Test at Queen's Park. Perhaps Sobers's team allowed itself to unwind too soon after the high tension of the first 4 Tests. Perhaps the Australians had, finally, found their true form. Whatever the reasons, the West Indies were well and truly beaten, mainly because of inept batting which could total only 224, of which Kanhai made 121, and 131, through which Hunte batted for an undefeated 60. It was a disappointing way to end a series which had generated great international interest and controversy and it rather spoiled claims that this West Indian side had been the strongest ever.

The tour to Australia in 1968–69 proved a sad and definite final chapter to one of the greatest eras West Indian cricket has known. Such a demise had been predictable for some time. The glorious days of the early 1960s were fewer and further between in India in 1966–67 and in the West Indies against England in 1967–68 only the phenomenal all-round talents of Sobers camouflaged the fact that the moment of truth was at hand.

Certainly the selectors did not recognize it for they stuck to the old faithfuls in choosing the 17 for the tour, 9 of them over the age of 30 with the average age of the group just over 29. Almost inevitably it proved a handicap against opponents who were not only younger and fitter but who were at the start, not the end, of their careers. The West Indians of that year had already created their reputations, the youthful Australians were anxious to make theirs. Many of them did, principally because their opponents' bowling, fielding and general attitude lacked the youthful zeal which had been the hallmark of earlier successes. Hall and Griffith were no longer the menace they had been in 1965 and were seldom fit together so that Gibbs and Sobers found themselves in the unaccustomed roles of stock bowlers. The trouble was accentuated by a staggering spate of dropped catches, no fewer – by Sobers's estimation – than 34 in the 5 Tests.

In the circumstances, Lawry, now captain in succession to Simpson, Ian Chappell and Walters did almost as they pleased. Lawry determined to erase the indignities he and his colleagues had suffered 3 years earlier, scored a double-hundred in the Second Test and singles in the First and Fifth; Chappell took 5 hundreds off the West Indies in various matches, including 2 in the Tests, and Walters plundered 699 runs in the 4 Tests he played, including the then-unique feat of scoring a single and a double-hundred in the same Test, the Fifth.

Australia passed 500 an innings in each of the final 4 Tests and it was a depressing sight as a once-great West Indian side visibly disintegrated in the swift course of 3 months. There was, in fact, a most encouraging start to the series for Sobers's men for they won the First Test at Brisbane by 125 runs. It is true that they owed that victory primarily to the toss, the loss of which committed Australia to batting last on a pitch which favoured spin throughout. Yet it was not only this factor which proved decisive for there was some excellent batting and fielding.

A 2nd-wicket partnership of 165 between Carew, the left-handed Trinidadian who was to prove the most consistent batsman in the series, and Kanhai, who was caught at long on for 94, was the basis of a 1st innings total of 296. Australia appeared certain to lead that by a substantial amount when Lawry and Chappell were scoring their first hundreds of the series in a 2nd wicket partnership of 217. Sobers then speculated, as he had often done, and brought on Lloyd who dismissed both to start an amazing collapse which provided the West Indies with a narrow lead. A brilliant hundred by Lloyd, in his 1st Test in Australia, and Carew's second important innings of the match left Australia far too many to get and Sobers, with his best analysis in Test cricket, 6 for 73, and Gibbs duly clinched the decision with their contrasting finger-spin.

The result was deceptive. Brisbane's conditions merely concealed West Indian problems and weaknesses for a time. They were soon highlighted at Melbourne and Sydney where Australia won massively to take the lead in the series. In the Second Test, the West Indies struggled in miserable weather on Boxing Day after being sent in and collapsed for 200 to McKenzie's pace and movement which earned him 8 for 71. Lawry's 205 and Chappell's 165 provided Australia with a 310 advantage which was ample enough for victory by an innings and 30.

Lance Gibbs in his 79th and last Test, at Melbourne in 1976, took his 309th wicket for his country, the highest bag in history. R. C. Parish, chairman of the Australian Board, makes a suitable presentation.

In the Third Test, which followed immediately, the pattern was similar. The West Indies batted disappointingly for 264, Australia built up a lead this time of 283 (Walters 118) and only Butcher's 2nd innings hundred saved the West Indies yet another innings loss.

For almost 3 days the fortunes of the Fourth Test at Adelaide followed those of the preceding 2 with an uncanny preciseness. The West Indian batsmen failed to use the opportunity of batting first on an ideal pitch and were out for 276, Sobers playing like a man inspired for 110 out of 154 made while he was at the crease in 132 minutes. Australia yet again replied massively with 533, of which Walters top-scored with 110. However, Sobers's side demonstrated that its spirit was not broken yet. All down the line, everyone fought doggedly and got runs – Butcher 118, Carew 90, Kanhai 80, Holford 80, Sobers 52. By the time the innings ended, early on the final day, the total of 616 was the highest by the West Indies against Australia and the target to win for the home team was 360 in 5¾ hours.

The task was steep, but the Australians approached it so positively that they entered the final hour and the minimum 15 overs requiring a mere 62 with 7 wickets standing. Inexplicably, they panicked. There were no fewer than 4 run outs (one, Redpath, done by the bowler, Griffith, backing up) several loose shots and the West Indies found themselves with 26 deliveries in which to remove the last pair to square the series. Amidst excitement reminiscent of so many of the matches on the 1960–61 tour, Sheahan and the No. 11 Connolly, held fast to claim the draw.

Australia, therefore, entered the final Test needing no more than a draw to clinch the rubber and regain the Worrell Trophy. In fact, Australia won in the most emphatic fashion and the Trophy was theirs long before the final ball was bowled. It might well have been different but for the continuing epidemic of dropped catches in the West Indian camp. Sobers won the toss and chose to field first, whereupon Hall, in his last Test in Australia, and Sobers himself reduced Australia to 51 for 3. By then 2 slip catches had been missed and, later, Lawry and Walters also benefited by fielding lapses.

The West Indies paid dearly for their mistakes. Walters scored 242 and Lawry 151, adding a record 336 for the 4th wicket, and the final total was 619. The West Indies responded weakly with 279, a deficit of 340. Lawry, conscious of his team's position and of the opposition's second innings batting at Adelaide, decided against the follow-on, batted again and declared to leave the West Indies 735 to win. Redpath fittingly ended a series in which he had batted fluently and consistently with his 1st hundred while Walters entered the record books with his 103. Sobers and Nurse saved some face for their team with sparkling hundreds at a time when there was obviously only one possible result, but they merely delayed the moment of revenge.

Australia returned to the West Indies for their 3rd tour in 1973 this time under Ian Chappell, in buoyant mood. Against all expectations, the Ashes series in England the previous summer had been shared 2–2 and all 3 Tests against a competent Pakistan team in the following Australian season had been won. Greg Chappell, tall and classically upright, had joined his brother, Walters, Stackpole and Redpath to constitute a formidable batting order while Lillee, menacingly fast and accurate, and Massie, a master of swing, represented a new ball combination which had demoralized the best English and Pakistani batting. Ian Chappell, in less than 2 years in the position, had earned a considerable reputation as a skipper.

In contrast, West Indian cricket was in a state of melancholy. Of the 26 previous Tests they had played, the West Indies had won only 2 and the loss to India and failure to dispose of New Zealand in the 2 previous home seasons were depressing experiences. Sobers, his fitness and his interest waning after nearly 20 years of continuous top-class cricket, had surrendered the captaincy and Kanhai, the young petrel of the 1960s but now the greying elder statesman, was appointed in his stead.

Kanhai's was a difficult, almost impossible, task made no easier by the furore caused when the selectors refused to select Sobers. The great left-hander had undergone surgery for the removal of a cartilage the previous summer and, at his own request, was not considered for the First Test. When he was omitted from the Second, he declared that he was ready, willing and able to join the fray.

The selectors and the West Indies Board were wary, asking Sobers, who had had no first-class practice to produce a doctor's certificate clearing him and thereby touched off Sobers's indignation and his supporters' anger. Neither selectors nor Sobers yielded and, whether the submission of a Barbadian parliamentarian that Sobers on one leg was better than most players on two was valid or not, the West Indies were left to soldier on without an individual who had carried their hopes on his shoulders many times in the past.

Australia, for its part, had to do without Lillee and Massie for the entire series. The former suffered a severe back injury which threatened his career and played only 1 Test, in which he took no wicket; the latter simply lost his ability to wobble the ball in the air and was dropped. In their absence, Walker, a strongly-built Tasmanian who bowled fast-medium from a peculiar, wrong-footed delivery, and Hammond, a hard-working fast bowler from Adelaide, proved more than adequate replacements. Walker bowled 100 more overs in the Tests than any of his team-mates and took 26 wickets at 20 each, a record by an Australian bowler in the Caribbean.

The first 2 Tests were inconclusive draws in which neither team held any advantage. In the First at Sabina Park the 2nd innings of the match was not completed until midway through the 4th day by which time a draw was inevitable. Foster, a native of Kingston, delighted his home crowd with the 1st hundred of the series which was quickly followed by one from Stackpole on the other side. Even in this game, so dominated by batsmen, those bowlers who were to hold most sway in the series gave ample forewarning of their intentions. Walker took 6 wickets and Hammond 4; Gibbs, after a period in the wilderness, claimed the first 4 of his eventual 26 in the 5 Tests.

At Kensington Oval, in the Second, the West Indies had the satisfaction of a 1st innings lead but the pitch was as faultless at the end as it was at the beginning and a decision was out of the question. Greg Chappell, in the 1st innings, and Ian Chappell and Walters, in the 2nd innings, were Australian hundred-makers. Kanhai scored 105 and Fredericks 98 for the West Indies.

The series, therefore, was in need of an impetus when the Third Test started at the Queen's Park Oval. It received this through an unforgettable match in which fortunes constantly fluctuated and at the end of which a mere 44 runs separated the teams. The West Indies were unlucky in losing one of their premier batsmen, Rowe, through a badly twisted ankle on the 1st day which prevented him batting in either innings. Even so, the advantage appeared theirs at lunch on the final day when 66 were required with 5 wickets standing. Kallicharran, then 91, and the in-form Foster were in occupation, but Chappell then claimed an overdue new ball, Kallicharran touched Walker's first ball with it to the wicket-keeper and a terminal collapse set in.

The match had built to its tremendous climax hour after hour, day after day. Walters's 112, in Australia's 1st innings of 332, was the innings of the series, unleashing a volley of magnificent shots and bludgeoning exactly 100 between lunch and tea. It was batting which entirely contrasted with that from anyone else in the match, for strokeplay was always at a premium on a slow, turning pitch. The West Indies fell 52 short on 1st innings but Gibbs, with 5 wickets, ensured that Australia did not build an impregnable advantage in their second innings. Kallicharran's diligent application carried the

Australia v West Indies 1975–76: Vivian Richards is superbly caught by Gilmour for a duck off Lillee. Redpath and the Chappell brothers are the other slips, Marsh behind the wicket.

West Indies to within sight of a great victory, but the Australians, bowling and fielding tenaciously, would not be denied.

The Fourth Test at Georgetown produced similarly tense and close cricket for 3 days. The West Indies ended the 1st day at 269 for 3 – and yet lost by 10 wickets. They contrived to do so through a remarkable 2nd innings collapse in which they were all out for 109 to the persistent accuracy of Walker and Hammond. Lloyd's 178, in fact, had yielded the West Indies a 1st innings lead of 25 despite Ian Chappell's 1st innings hundred for Australia and a real battle was in prospect when the 2nd innings debacle occurred.

The series was, therefore, decided even before the final Test at the Queen's Park Oval and, as a result, the match was shunned by the public to an extraordinary degree. Whereas 90,000 had watched the 5 days of the enthralling Third Test there, only a 10th of that turned out to see the final rites of the series. On some days barely 1,000 were present in the emptiness of a ground capable of holding 28,000. The cricket was seldom of true Test standard and the West Indies just held on for a draw.

No rubber between the teams excited quite as much interest as the 5th West Indian tour of Australia, organized as a substitute for an abandoned South African visit. The two sides were recognized as the strongest in contemporary cricket and had contested a magnificent final in the game's 1st World Cup at Lord's the previous summer. The West Indies had won that match, continuing to prosper under the captaincy of Lloyd who had been appointed in succession to Kanhai in 1974. Australia had completed successive home and away triumphs in Ashes series against England, including a 4–1 triumph in Australia the previous season.

Early indications suggested that the contest would fulfil all expectations. Australia won the First Test by 8 wickets. The West Indies responded magnificently by levelling matters in the Second through an innings victory. Thereafter, West Indian fortunes declined rapidly and disappointingly and the result was one-sided anti-climax, the Australians comfortably winning the last 4 Tests of a 6-match series. Disappointment was no stranger to West Indian sides in Australia but none of its predecessors had suffered it so acutely as this one. It was undone by a number of factors, all with a familiar ring. As had been the case many times in the past, Australia possessed a pair of very fast bowlers, Lillee and Thomson, well supported in the field. They were a constant threat mastered only briefly in the Perth Test when the West Indies totalled 585. As if this worry was not enough, the West Indies were plagued by injury, lack of form of leading players, faulty catching and questionable umpiring. It was a combination which, long before the end, had broken their spirit.

Statistics, so often misleading, revealed much on this occasion. Lillee, Thomson and the youthful left-arm fast-medium Gilmour shared 76 of the 110 West Indian wickets; the dreaded hook shot was fatal to 14 West Indian batsmen and wicket-keeper Marsh claimed a record-equalling 26 catches; 5 West Indian batsmen were forced to retire hurt at one time or another after being struck and there was only one West Indian opening partnership in excess of 50.

In many respects, the First was the best of the 6 Tests and the margin of Australia's victory, by 8 wickets, was deceptive. The West Indies lost it in the 1st session in which they contrived to lose 6 wickets for 125. From that point it was always an uphill struggle for them. Greg Chappell celebrated his 1st Test as captain in succession to his brother with hundreds in each innings. Rowe and Kallicharran scored 2nd innings hundreds for the West Indies, the former in his 1st Test innings outside the Caribbean, and while they were together in a partnership of 198 a West Indian victory was possible. However, a target of 219 for Australia proved too little.

The Second Test will always be remembered for some breathtaking West Indian batting and fast bowling which yielded them an innings and 87 runs win. The left-handed Fredericks attacked from start to finish during 3½ hours for 169, hitting a six and 27 fours, and Lloyd included a six and 22 fours in 149 as the West Indies dwarfed Australia's 1st innings 329 (Ian Chappell 156) with 585. Roberts then bowled at fearsome pace to take 7 for 54 as Australia capitulated for 169.

The public was thoroughly captivated by the position of the series and more than 85,000 spectators were present for the start of the Third Test at Melbourne. As at Brisbane, the West Indies were beaten because of a 1st innings collapse against the fast bowling. Cosier, in his 1st Test, and Redpath yielded a healthy Australian advantage with hundreds and, in spite of an excellent 102 from Lloyd, the West Indies only just avoided an innings defeat.

The turning point in the series came in the West Indies' 2nd innings of the Fourth Test at Sydney. Until then, the teams had fought an engaging struggle for 1st innings honours, Greg Chappell's undefeated 182 earning his team a lead of 50. It appeared inconsequential on a still true pitch but Thomson emphasised the value of sheer pace, dismissing 6 batsmen as the West Indies fell for 128. At that point the match and the series were as good as over.

The West Indies patently had no heart for the remaining 2

Tests at Adelaide and Melbourne and lost them by 190 runs and 165 runs, Australia declaring their 2nd innings each time. There was, however, one important gain for them as Vivian Richards finally fulfilled the obvious potential he had shown since entering Test cricket a year earlier. Promoted to open the batting he ended the series with scores of 30, 101, 50 and 98 – the beginning of a string of exceptional scores which, finally, brought him a record 1,730 runs during the 12 months of 1976.

There was another satisfying individual West Indian performance amidst the disappointment. In the final Test, Gibbs dismissed Redpath to pass Trueman's overall record of 307 Test wickets for his country, a historic feat after 19 years and 78 Tests. It was Gibbs's last appearance for the West Indies and, for the 3rd time, he had been on a losing side in Australia.

The series in the Caribbean in early 1978 was a chaotic and disagreeable exercise, cruelly affected by the contentious controversy caused by the formation of World Series Cricket some months earlier. It was marred by a split between the West Indies Board and many of the players, which led to a complete reorganization of the team midway through the rubber, by heated and emotional arguments over the issue, by crowd boycotts, by a riot and by the unrepresentative standard of the cricket.

The inauguration of World Series Cricket was felt by Australia and the West Indies more than by any other Test playing country. Two dozen of the leading Australian players of the day had been recruited by its agents who had also signed an entire West Indian contingent of 15. While the Australian Board remained adamant that none of those who had defected to the rival camp would be considered for official Test selection, the West Indies Board adopted a more liberal attitude, stating that it would choose its team from all those players who were available.

This meant that, initially, the teams were mismatched. The West Indies, except for the absence of Holding through injury, were at full strength for the first 2 Tests. The Australians, on the other hand, comprised mainly young and inexperienced individuals under the captaincy of the veteran Simpson, recalled to the international scene after an absence of 10 years as a result of the unusual circumstances.

The outcome was predictable. The West Indies, consisting mostly of WSC players, overwhelmed their unfortunate opponents inside 3 days in both the first 2 Tests – by an innings and 106 runs at the Queen's Park Oval and by 9 wickets at Kensington. The Australians were undone principally by fast bowling. In the First Test, they fell for 90 and 209 as Roberts took 7 wickets, Garner 5 and Croft 4; in the Second, they totalled 250 and 178 with Garner getting 8 wickets and Roberts and Croft 5 each. The West Indian batting was not particularly distinguished either, except for a hundred by Kallicharran in the First Test and 3 consecutive half-centuries by the stylish new opener, Haynes. But it hardly mattered.

By now, it was becoming clear that the Board and those players with WSC contracts were at loggerheads. The Board was anxious to have some commitment from its players as to their availability for a tour to India and Sri Lanka later in the year and issued a deadline of 23 March for an answer. When none was forthcoming from the WSC group, the selectors, needing to blood new men for the forthcoming Indian tour, nominated a team which excluded 3 WSC players – Murray, who was also secretary of the Players' Association, and Haynes and Austin, who had signed for WSC during the Second Test.

Complaining that there had been no clear principles in the selection, Lloyd resigned as captain and at the last moment was joined, en bloc, by his WSC colleagues. Shockwaves reverberated throughout the Caribbean and the Board was widely vilified. Groups were organized in Trinidad and Jamaica to boycott the final 2 Tests to be played there, a campaign which proved generally successful.

The West Indies, therefore, were forced at the very last moment possible to reconstitute their team, replacing Lloyd with Kallicharran as captain and including no fewer than 6 new caps in the Third Test team. There was, at least, one beneficial side-effect from the episode. The contest was now more evenly balanced and the Third and Fourth Tests produced 2 keenly fought matches, Australia winning the former and the West Indies the latter to regain the Worrell Trophy.

In the Third, neither team batted with any merit in their 1st innings. In their 2nd, however, the West Indies amassed 439 with maiden hundreds from the Jamaican opener, Williams, playing his 1st Test, and the left-handed Gomes. Australia required a demanding 362 to win, lost 3 for 22 and yet still got home by 3 wickets, thanks to a stand of 251 between the left-handed West Australians, Wood and Serjeant, both of whom scored hundreds.

The West Indian triumph in the Fourth Test at Port of Spain, achieved before crowds seldom bigger than 3,000 on any day, was achieved by the spin of Parry and Jumadeen on a worn pitch. There had been nothing in it in the first 3 innings before the Australians finally collapsed to an abysmal 94.

R. B. Simpson, 10 years after his retirement, stepped into the breach for Australia when the Test team was raided by K. Packer. Here, at Port of Spain in 1978, the signs of strain are showing after losing a vital toss in the First Test Match. A few weeks later, Clive Lloyd, on the eve of the Third Test, walked out of the West Indian team, which he was due to lead, taking all the other WSC players with him.

This is one of several versions of helmet or visor designed to protect batsmen from the short, fast bowling to which they became increasingly subjected in the 1970s, to the detriment of the game in all respects. Try as they would, administrators failed to obtain the co-operation of the captains; nor were umpires willing to apply the clear provisions of the Unfair Play Law. This, in fact, is G. N. Yallop batting for Australia against West Indies in 1977–78, wearing the 1st helmet ever seen in a Test Match.

Australia would surely have won the final Test, which it dominated throughout, had the crowd not reacted to an umpiring decision by throwing bottles and other missiles on to the ground. Toohey batted brilliantly for 122 and 97, and hundreds by Gomes, in the 1st innings, and Kallicharran, in the 2nd, averted complete West Indian collapses. However, when the 9th West Indian wicket fell, 6 overs and 2 balls of the match remained, ample time for the visitors to notch a consolation victory. The crowd interference denied them their opportunity and, when the West Indian Board endeavoured to have the time made up on an unscheduled 6th day, Umpire Ralph Gosein determined that there was no such provision in the conditions of play and refused to take the field. It was the final melancholy chapter in a very sad series.

AUSTRALIA V WEST INDIES

Season	Test	Scores	Result	Captains
1930–31	1 Adelaide	WI 296, 249; A 376, 172–0	A 10 wkts	W. M. Woodfull, G. C. Grant
	2 Sydney	A 369; WI 107, 90	A inns 172	W. M. Woodfull, G. C. Grant
	3 Brisbane	A 558; WI 193, 148	A inns 217	W. M. Woodfull, G. C. Grant
	4 Melbourne	WI 99, 107; A 328–8D	A inns 122	W. M. Woodfull, G. C. Grant
	5 Sydney	WI 350–6D, 124–5D; A 224, 220	WI 30 runs	W. M. Woodfull, G. C. Grant
1951–52	1 Brisbane	WI 216, 245; A 226, 236–7	A 3 wkts	A. L. Hasset, J. D. C. Goddard
	2 Sydney	WI 362, 290; A 517, 137–3	A 7 wkts	A. L. Hassett, J. D. C. Goddard
	3 Adelaide	A 82, 255; WI 105, 233–4	WI 6 wkts	A. R. Morris, J. D. C. Goddard
	4 Melbourne	WI 272, 203; A 216, 260–9	A 1 wkt	A. L. Hassett, J. D. C. Goddard
	5 Sydney	A 116, 377; WI 78, 213	A 202 runs	A. L. Hassett, J. B. Stollmeyer
1954–55	1 Kingston	A 515–9D, 20–1; WI 259, 275	A 9 wkts	I. W. Johnson, D. S. Atkinson
	2 Trinidad	WI 382, 273–4; A 600–9D	Drawn	I. W. Johnson, J. B. Stollmeyer
	3 Georgetown	WI 182, 207; A 257, 133–2	A 8 wkts	I. W. Johnson, J. B. Stollmeyer
	4 Barbados	A 668, 249; WI 510, 234–6	Drawn	I. W. Johnson, D. S. Atkinson
	5 Kingston	WI 357, 319; A 758–8D	A inns 82	I. W. Johnson, D. S. Atkinson
1960–61	1 Brisbane	WI 453, 284; A 505, 232	Tie	R. Benaud, F. M. Worrell
	2 Melbourne	A 348, 70–3; WI 181, 233	A 7 wkts	R. Benaud, F. M. Worrell
	3 Sydney	WI 339, 326; A 202, 241	WI 222 runs	R. Benaud, F. M. Worrell
	4 Adelaide	WI 393, 432–6D; A 366, 273–9	Drawn	R. Benaud, F. M. Worrell
	5 Melbourne	WI 292, 321; A 356, 258–8	A 2 wkts	R. Benaud, F. M. Worrell
1964–65	1 Kingston	WI 239, 373; A 217, 216	WI 179 runs	R. B. Simpson, G. S. Sobers
	2 Trinidad	WI 429, 386; A 516	Drawn	R. B. Simpson, G. S. Sobers
	3 Georgetown	WI 355, 180; A 179, 144	WI 212 runs	R. B. Simpson, G. S. Sobers
	4 Barbados	A 650–6D, 175–4D; WI 573, 242–5	Drawn	R. B. Simpson, G. S. Sobers
	5 Trinidad	WI 224, 131; A 294, 63–0	A 10 wkts	R. B. Simpson, G. S. Sobers
1968–69	1 Brisbane	WI 296, 353; A 284, 240	WI 125 runs	W. M. Lawry, G. S. Sobers
	2 Melbourne	WI 200, 280; A 510	A inns 30 runs	W. M. Lawry, G. S. Sobers
	3 Sydney	WI 264, 324; A 547, 42–0	A 10 wkts	W. M. Lawry, G. S. Sobers
	4 Adelaide	WI 276, 616; A 533, 339–9	Drawn	W. M. Lawry, G. S. Sobers
	5 Sydney	A 619, 394–8D; WI 279, 352	A 382 runs	W. M. Lawry, G. S. Sobers
1972–73	1 Kingston	A 428–7D, 260–2D; WI 428, 67–3	Drawn	I. M. Chappell, R. B. Kanhai
	2 Barbados	A 324, 300–2D; WI 391, 36–0	Drawn	I. M. Chappell, R. B. Kanhai
	3 Trinidad	A 332, 281; WI 280, 289	A 44 runs	I. M. Chappell, R. B. Kanhai
	4 Georgetown	WI 366, 109; A 341, 135–0	A 10 wkts	I. M. Chappell, R. B. Kanhai
	5 Trinidad	A 419–8D, 218–7D; WI 319, 135–5	Drawn	I. M. Chappell, R. B. Kanhai
1975–76	1 Brisbane	WI 214, 370; A 366, 219–2	A 8 wkts	G. S. Chappell, C. H. Lloyd
	2 Perth	A 329, 169; WI 585	WI inns 87 runs	G. S. Chappell, C. H. Lloyd
	3 Melbourne	WI 224, 312; A 485, 55–2	A 8 wkts	G. S. Chappell, C. H. Lloyd
	4 Sydney	WI 355, 128; A 405, 82–3	A 7 wkts	G. S. Chappell, C. H. Lloyd
	5 Adelaide	A 418, 345–7D; WI 274, 299	A 190 runs	G. S. Chappell, C. H. Lloyd
	6 Melbourne	A 351, 300–3D WI 160, 326	A 165 runs	G. S. Chappell, C. H. Lloyd
1977–78	1 Trinidad	A 90, 209; WI 405	WI inns 106 runs	R. B. Simpson, C. H. Lloyd
	2 Barbados	A 250, 178; WI 288, 141–1	WI 9 wkts	R. B. Simpson, C. H. Lloyd
	3 Georgetown	WI 205, 439; A 286, 362–7	A 3 wkts	R. B. Simpson, A. I. Kallicharran
	4 Trinidad	WI 292, 290; A 290, 94	WI 198 runs	R. B. Simpson, A. I. Kallicharran
	5 Kingston	A 343, 305–3D; WI 280, 258–9	Drawn	R. B. Simpson, A. I. Kallicharran

CAPTAINS (Australia)	TESTS	WON	LOST	DRAWN	TIE
W. M. Woodfull	5	4	1		
A. L. Hassett	4	4			
A. R. Morris	1		1		
I. W. Johnson	5	3		2	
R. Benaud	5	2	1	1	1
R. B. Simpson	10	2	5	3	
W. M. Lawry	5	3	1	1	
I. M. Chappell	5	2		3	
G. S. Chappell	6	5	1		
	46	25	10	10	1

CAPTAINS (West Indies)	TESTS	WON	LOST	DRAWN	TIE
G. C. Grant	5	1	4		
J. D. C. Goddard	4	1	3		
J. B. Stollmeyer	3		2	1	
D. S. Atkinson	3		2	1	
F. M. Worrell	5	1	2	1	1
G. S. Sobers	10	3	4	3	
R. B. Kanhai	5		2	3	
C. H. Lloyd	8	3	5		
A. I. Kallicharran	3	1	1	1	
	46	10	25	10	1

HIGHEST INNINGS TOTALS

Australia in Australia, 619, Sydney 1968–69
Australia in West Indies, 758–8D, Kingston 1954–55
West Indies in Australia, 616, Adelaide 1968–69
West Indies in West Indies, 573, Barbados 1964–65

LOWEST INNINGS TOTALS

Australia in Australia, 82, Adelaide 1951–52
Australia in West Indies, 90, Trinidad 1977–78
West Indies in Australia, 78, Sydney 1951–52
West Indies in West Indies, 109, Georgetown 1972–73

HIGHEST INDIVIDUAL INNINGS

Australia in Australia, 242, K. D. Walters, Sydney 1968–69
Australia in West Indies, 210, W. M. Lawry, Barbados 1964–65
West Indies in Australia, 169, R. C. Fredericks, Perth 1975–76
West Indies in West Indies, 219, D. S. Atkinson, Barbados 1954–55

HIGHEST AGGREGATE OF RUNS IN A SERIES

Australia in Australia, 702, G. S. Chappell 1975–76
Australia in West Indies, 650, R. N. Harvey 1954–55
West Indies in Australia, 503, R. B. Kanhai 1960–61
West Indies in West Indies, 827, C. L. Walcott 1954–55

BEST INNINGS BOWLING FIGURES

Australia in Australia, 7–23, H. Ironmonger, Melbourne 1930–31
Australia in West Indies, 7–44, I. W. Johnson, Georgetown 1954–55
West Indies in Australia, 7–54, A. M. E. Roberts, Perth 1975–76
West Indies in West Indies, 6–46, G. C. Griffith, Trinidad 1964–65

BEST MATCH BOWLING FIGURES

Australia in Australia, 11–79 H. Ironmonger, Melbourne 1930–31
Australia in West Indies, 10–115 N. J. N. Hawke, Georgetown 1964–65
West Indies in Australia, 10–113 G. E. Gomez, Sydney 1951–52
West Indies in West Indies, 9–80 L. R. Gibbs, Georgetown 1964–65

HIGHEST WICKET AGGREGATE IN A SERIES

Australia in Australia { 33 C. V. Grimmett 1930–31; 33 A. K. Davidson 1960–61 }
Australia in West Indies, 26 M. H. N. Walker 1972–73
West Indies in Australia { 24 A. L. Valentine 1951–52; 24 L. R. Gibbs 1968–69 }
West Indies in West Indies, 26 L. R. Gibbs 1968–69

RECORD WICKET PARTNERSHIPS – AUSTRALIA

1 W. M. Lawry and R. B. Simpson, 382, Barbados 1964–65
2 W. M. Lawry and I. M. Chappell, 298, Melbourne 1968–69
3 C. C. McDonald and R. N. Harvey, 295, Kingston 1954–55
4 W. M. Lawry and K. D. Walters, 336, Sydney 1968–69
5 K. R. Miller and R. G. Archer, 220, Kingston 1954–55
6 K. R. Miller and R. G. Archer, 206, Barbados 1954–55
7 A. K. Davidson and R. Benaud, 134, Brisbane 1960–61
8 R. Benaud and I. W. Johnson, 137, Kingston 1954–55
9 K. D. Mackay and J. W. Martin, 97, Melbourne 1960–61
10 J. W. Gleeson and A. N. Connolly, 73, Sydney 1968–69

RECORD WICKET PARTNERSHIPS – WEST INDIES

1 C. C. Hunte and B. A. Davis, 145, Barbados 1964–65
2 M. C. Carew and R. B. Kanhai, 165, Brisbane 1968–69
3 C. L. Walcott and E. D. Weekes, 242, Trinidad 1954–55
4 L. G. Rowe and A. I. Kallicharran, 198, Brisbane 1975–76
5 R. B. Kanhai and M. L. C. Foster, 210, Kingston 1972–73
6 R. B. Kanhai and D. L. Murray, 165, Barbados 1972–73
7 D. S. Atkinson and C. C. Depeiza, 347, Barbados 1954–55
8 F. C. M. Alexander and L. R. Gibbs, 74, Sydney 1960–61
9 D. A. J. Holford and J. L. Hendriks, 122, Adelaide 1968–69
10 K. D. Boyce and L. R. Gibbs, 37, Perth 1975–76

Australia v New Zealand

REX ALSTON

The 1st ever Test between these two neighbouring countries was played in early 1946 in New Zealand only a few months after VJ day. Australia, led by W. A. Brown, won by an innings and 103 runs, having taken a side of overwhelming strength, including W. J. O'Reilly, S. G. Barnes and K. R. Miller, and New Zealand made 42 and 54, only W. M. Wallace reaching double figures in each innings. It was upwards of 20 years before an Australian 'B' team played ten matches in New Zealand, who won 1 'Test' match by 159 runs, the other 3 being drawn.

In 1967–68 a New Zealand team toured Australia for the first time since 1925–26. It was part-educational and no Tests were played. Another Australia 'B' team played 3 drawn representative matches in New Zealand in 1969–70. Persistent rain spoilt the tour, but S. C. Trimble, the captain, made the most runs, including 213 in one representative game. T. J. Jenner took the most wickets, and for New Zealand the captain, B. E. Congdon, made a hundred.

After these spasmodic preliminaries New Zealand undertook their first-ever full tour in Australia in 1973–74. They lost 2 and drew 1 of the 3 Tests. Their best batsman G. M. Turner was injured, but J. F. M. Morrison and J. M. Parker both scored Test hundreds and K. J. Wadsworth showed himself a promising wicket-keeper/batsman. The Hadlee brothers, R. J. and D. R., were the best of a weak bowling side. For Australia K. D. Walters was the leading batsman and R. W. Marsh and K. J. Stackpole made hundreds in Tests. The best bowlers were the spinners K. J. O'Keeffe and A. A. Mallett. But for 2 days' rain at Sydney, New Zealand would almost certainly have won the Second Test – it is unnecessary to stress what such a victory would have done for their ambitions and their morale.

In the same year, in a return series in New Zealand, each side won 1 match and the 3rd was drawn. New Zealand's victory by 5 wickets was the 1st ever against Australia, Turner making two hundreds, the Hadlees sharing 12 wickets. Turner averaged 100 in the 3 Tests. In the first the Chappell brothers, I. M. and G. S., each scored hundreds in each innings for Australia, and G. S. Chappell set the record for the most runs in a Test Match by scoring 380 (247 not out and 133) to beat the 375 (325 and 50) by A. Sandham at Kingston in 1929–30.

In 1976–77 Australia played 2 Tests in New Zealand, winning 1 and drawing the other. In the drawn game Walters made 250 for Australia, and G. J. Gilmour 101, and Congdon's 107 not out for New Zealand achieved the draw. In Australia's victory, D. K. Lillee took 11 wickets and R. J. Hadlee, the fast bowling son of W. A., the former Test captain, was the best New Zealand batsman, making 44 and 81.

G. M. Turner, for New Zealand at Christchurch in 1973/74, scored 101 and 110 not out, so enabling his country to beat Australia for the 1st time.

AUSTRALIA V NEW ZEALAND

		RESULT		CAPTAINS
1945–46	1 Wellington	NZ 42,54; A 199–8D	A Inns 103 runs	W. A. Brown, W. A. Hadlee
1973–74	1 Melbourne	A462–8D; NZ 237, 200	A Inns 25 runs	I. M. Chappell, B. E. Congdon
	2 Sydney	NZ 312, 305–9D; A 162, 30–2	Drawn	I. M. Chappell, B. E. Congdon
	3 Adelaide	A 477; NZ 218, 202	A Inns 57 runs	I. M. Chappell, B. E. Congdon
1973–74	1 Wellington	A 511–6D, 460–8; NZ 484	Drawn	I. M. Chappell, B. E. Congdon
	2 Christchurch	A 223, 259; NZ 255, 230–5	NZ 5 wkts	I. M. Chappell, B. E. Congdon
	3 Auckland	A 221, 346; NZ 112, 158	A 297 runs	I. M. Chappell, B. E. Congdon
1976–77	1 Christchurch	A 552, 154–4D; NZ 357, 293–8	Drawn	G. S. Chappell, G. M. Turner
	2 Auckland	NZ 229, 175; A 377, 28–0	A 10 wkts	G. S. Chappell, G. M. Turner

CAPTAINS (Australia)	TESTS	WON	LOST	DRAWN
W. A. Brown	1	1		
I. M. Chappell	6	3	1	2
G. S. Chappell	2	1		1
	9	5	1	3

CAPTAINS (New Zealand)	TESTS	WON	LOST	DRAWN
W. A. Hadlee	1		1	
B. E. Congdon	6	1	3	2
G. M. Turner	2		1	1
	9	1	5	3

HIGHEST INNINGS TOTAL

Australia in Australia, 477, Adelaide 1973–74
Australia in New Zealand, 552, Christchurch 1976–77
New Zealand in Australia, 312, Sydney 1973–74
New Zealand in New Zealand, 484, Wellington 1973–74

LOWEST INNINGS TOTAL

Australia in Australia, 162, Sydney 1973–74
Australia in New Zealand, 221, Auckland 1976–77
New Zealand in Australia, 200, Melbourne 1973–74
New Zealand in New Zealand, 42, Wellington 1945–46

HIGHEST INDIVIDUAL INNINGS

Australia in Australia, 132, R. W. Marsh, Adelaide 1973–74
Australia in New Zealand, 250, K. D. Walters, Christchurch 1976–77
New Zealand in Australia, 117, J. F. M. Morrison, Sydney 1973–74
New Zealand in New Zealand, 132, B. E. Congdon, Wellington 1976–77

HIGHEST AGGREGATE OF RUNS IN A SERIES

Australia in Australia, 214, K. D. Walters 1973–74
Australia in New Zealand, 449, G. S. Chappell 1973–74
New Zealand in Australia, 249, J. F. M. Morrison 1973–74
New Zealand in New Zealand, 403, G. M. Turner 1973–74

BEST INNINGS BOWLING FIGURES

Australia in Australia, 5–58, G. Dymock, Adelaide 1973–74
Australia in New Zealand, 6–72, D. K. Lillee, Auckland 1976–77
New Zealand in Australia, 5–148, D. R. O'Sullivan, Adelaide 1973–74
New Zealand in New Zealand, 6–40, J. Cowie, Wellington 1945–46

BEST MATCH BOWLING FIGURES

Australia in Australia, 7–102, G. Dymock, Adelaide 1973–74
Australia in New Zealand, 11–123, D. K. Lillee, Auckland 1976–77
New Zealand in Australia, 6–49, R. J. Hadlee, Sydney 1973–74
New Zealand in New Zealand, 9–166, B. E. Congdon, Auckland 1976–77

HIGHEST WICKET AGGREGATE IN A SERIES

Australia in Australia, 11, K. J. O'Keeffe 1973–74
Australia in New Zealand, 15, D. K. Lillee 1976–77
New Zealand in Australia, 8, D. R. Hadlee 1973–74
New Zealand in New Zealand, 17, R. O. Collinge 1973–74

RECORD WICKET PARTNERSHIPS – AUSTRALIA

1 K. R. Stackpole and A. P. Sheahan, 75, Melbourne 1973–74
2 I. R. Redpath and I. M. Chappell, 141, Wellington 1973–74
3 I. M. Chappell and G. S. Chappell, 264, Wellington 1973–74
4 I. R. Redpath and I. C. Davis, 106, Christchurch 1973–74
5 G. J. Cosier and K. D. Walters, 93, Christchurch 1976–77
6 I. R. Redpath and R. W. Marsh, 87, Auckland 1973–74
7 K. D. Walters and G. J. Gilmour, 217, Christchurch 1976–77
8 G. J. Gilmour and K. J. O'Keeffe, 93, Auckland 1976–77
9 K. D. Walters and D. K. Lillee, 50, Christchurch 1976–77
10 K. D. Walters and M. H. N. Walker, 48, Christchurch 1976–77

RECORD WICKET PARTNERSHIPS – NEW ZEALAND

1 G. M. Turner and J. M. Parker, 107, Auckland 1973–74
2 G. M. Turner and J. F. M. Morrison, 108, Wellington 1973–74
3 B. E. Congdon and J. M. Parker, 58, Christchurch 1976–77
4 B. E. Congdon and B. F. Hastings, 229, Wellington 1973–74
5 J. M. Parker and J. V. Coney, 80, Sydney 1973–74
6 M. G. Burgess and R. J. Hadlee, 105, Auckland 1976–77
7 K. J. Wadsworth and D. R. Hadlee, 66, Adelaide 1973–74
8 M. G. Burgess and H. J. Howarth, 42, Christchurch 1976–77
9 H. J. Howarth and D. R. Hadlee, 73, Christchurch 1976–77
10 H. J. Howarth and M. G. Webb, 47, Wellington 1973–74

Australia v India

REX ALSTON AND D. J. RUTNAGUR

India's first visit to Australia, in 1947–48, was not a notable success, though the tourists fared better than anticipated after four of the originally selected party dropped out. Vijay Merchant, who had had a distinguished tour of England the year before, was appointed Test captain for the first time but withdrew on grounds of health, as did Rusi Modi. Mushtaq Ali, Merchant's famous opening partner, also declined to go. As for the bowling, that was weakened by the loss of Fazal Mahmood (the team was picked before partition became a political reality). Australia, on the eve of their famous England tour of 1948 and as strong a side as at any time in their history, won 4 of the 5 Tests, needing to bat only once on each occasion.

India held the upper hand in the one Test in which the weather prevented a decision. India were unlucky with the toss, Bradman winning it 4 times, and twice in the series they were caught on a sticky pitch. The Australian Board had suggested covering pitches, but Amarnath declined, appreciating that a drying pitch represented India's best hope of beating the much stronger Australians. His gamble looked like succeeding in the Second Test at Sydney, but rain intervened decisively when India, after dismissing Australia for 107, led by 142 runs, with 3 second-innings wickets in hand. The high spot of the tour for the Indians was the beating at Sydney of an Australian XI, which included Brown, Bradman, Miller, Harvey, Hamence, Loxton, Dooland and Johnston – this in spite of an innings of 172 from Bradman.

Amarnath, then 36, had a fine tour. He made 5 hundreds against State sides and aggregated over 1,000 runs, too few of them in the Test matches. He was effective with the ball as well, taking 30 wickets. As in England the year before, Mankad proved an outstanding all-rounder. He took the most wickets and, opening the innings, made 2 Test hundreds. Hazare, at Adelaide, became the first Indian to score 2 separate hundreds in a Test match. Phadkar, picked mainly as a pace bowler, also scored a hundred at Adelaide. For Australia, Bradman aggregated 715 runs, including 4 hundreds. Hassett, Morris and Barnes each scored hundreds and in the Fifth Test Neil Harvey announced his arrival on the international scene with an outstanding innings of 153. Lindwall was the most successful Australian bowler.

Australia, with Ian Johnson captaining, returned the visit in 1956, on their way back from England, winning 2 of the 3 Tests and drawing the other. The bowling of Benaud, in the 1st innings, and Lindwall, in the 2nd, gave them a win in the First Test; the tranquil Brabourne pitch enabled India to force a draw in the Second, in spite of being 282 behind on the 1st innings, and Australia won a low-scoring Third Test in which spinners on both sides exploited an unusual Calcutta pitch.

Australia, led by Benaud, undertook their first full tour of India in 1959–60. It was during this visit that India scored their first-ever win over Australia, in the Second Test at Kanpur, after Australia had won the First at New Delhi, with the spin of Benaud and Kline forcing home the advantage given to Australia by a superb Harvey hundred.

The pitch at Kanpur, where India won, was a crumbler and India had the advantage of winning the toss. Although Jasu Patel, an off-spinner, took 9 wickets, Australia took a 1st-innings lead of 67. But India, batting with great determination in their 2nd innings, left Australia 225 to win and routed them for 105, Patel taking 5 more wickets to bring his tally for the match to 14. For Australia, Alan Davidson took 12 for 124, most of them with spin. The Australian batting was in its element again in the Third Test, played on a plumb Bombay pitch. Harvey made 102, O'Neill 163 and the match was drawn. Nari Contractor contributed a staunch 108 to India's 1st innings. Davidson and Benaud bowled very well to give Australia an innings win at Madras in the Fourth Test and were denied at Calcutta, in the Fifth Test, only by a dogged stand between Jaisimha and Kenny (who had to have a tooth extracted in mid-innings).

Australia encountered strong resistance in 1964 when they stopped off for a 3-Test series on their way home from England. Thanks to a magnificent unbeaten hundred by Pataudi, India led by 65 runs in the 1st innings of the opening Test at Madras. Australia, however, batted tenaciously enough in their second innings to give them a convincing win. McKenzie took 10 wickets in the match and, for India, Nadkarni took 11. India had their revenge at Bombay, chasing runs to win by 2 wickets in a thrilling finish. This was the Australians' first encounter with Chandrasekhar, who took 4 wickets in each innings. The Indians, who had never before raced the clock to win a Test match, were steered towards their target by Borde and Manjrekar, who had been kept back in the order to deal with the tension of the final assault. McKenzie, Connolly and Veivers bowled determinedly, but not without avail, to stop India from winning. The Third Test, at Calcutta, which started on a damp pitch – with India sending Australia in – could have been another close match had rain not washed out the last 2 days' play. The series was thus left drawn.

Although India went to Australia in 1967–68 with much the same side that had proved such good opposition in their last home series, Australia won all 4 Tests. India's batting was adventurous and entertaining, but never consistent. Without bowlers of genuine pace, their attack was ill-suited to Australian conditions and their shortcomings were shown up in a harsh light until the fielding started to improve, midway through the tour. The Test series was a triumph for Prasanna, who took 25 wickets in the 4 games. Surti bowled left-arm in two styles – seam up and orthodox spin – to pick up 15 wickets. A pugnacious batsman, he was also high up in the batting averages. India finished the series looking a better side than when they started and one of the reasons for this was that the captain, the Nawab of Pataudi, missed the early matches because of a persistent hamstring injury. His first appearance in a first-class match on the tour was not until the Second Test, when, although still handicapped, he played 2 unforgettable innings of 75 and 85. Wadekar scored 99 in the 2nd innings of that Test match but India were still beaten by an innings.

Two down in the series, India were joined in Brisbane by Jaisimha, who had been sent out to reinforce the side. Only hours off the plane, he scored 74 and 101 in the Third Test and nearly won it for India, who needed 389 in the 4th innings and failed by only 39 runs to make them. While Jaisimha's 101 was the only hundred for India in the series, there were 5 for Australia, Simpson and Cowper getting 2 apiece and Ian Chappell one. Three bowlers, Simpson, Cowper and McKenzie, took 13 wickets each and shared the top place among Australian wicket-takers. McKenzie would have been out in front, but he was rested after the first 2 Tests. He was the match-winner in the Second Test, taking 7 for 66 in the 1st innings and 3 for 85 in the 2nd.

The Indian spinners, Prasanna, in particular, and Bedi, were at their peak during a home series in 1969–70. Prasanna took 26 wickets and Bedi 21, and although there is no doubt that they bowled in masterly fashion the pitches were prepared to suit them. Australia's chief spinner, Ashley Mallett, was the highest wicket-taker on either side with a tally of 28. Australia won the series 3–1, their superior batting tipping the scales in their favour. India's selectors gave their side's batting little chance to settle down. They were in haste to introduce fresh blood and made drastic changes after Australia had won the First Test. However, the inclusion of 20-year-old Gundappa Viswanath in the Second Test not only paid immediate dividends – he scored a hundred on debut – but proved a splendid long-term investment. Ian Chappell's expertise in playing spin bowling stood Australia in good stead. But for his 103, Australia would have been hopelessly outplayed in the one Test they lost, the Third at Delhi, and his 99 shaped Australia's win in the Fourth, at Calcutta. The robust batting of Keith Stackpole while making 103 proved vital in the First Test and Doug Walters's 102, coupled with Ian Redpath's 63 in the 2nd innings, swung the balance in the final Test.

The 3rd Indian visit to Australia, in 1977–78, was memorable for more reasons than one. It coincided with the season in which Kerry Packer launched his World Series Cricket. Australia were deprived of their best players and still managed to win the series, 3–2. So lively was the cricket played during the Test matches and the series followed such an interesting course that traditional cricket was able to meet the challenge of the counter-attraction. This was in spite of World Series Cricket arranging their major fixtures, the so-called 'Supertests', to coincide with the Test matches. On the television front, the Test series, broadcast by the Australian Broadcasting Commission, had the beating of its rival on the Packer Channel 9. Cricket-lovers sat spellbound before their sets as the First Test at Brisbane came to the boil after repeated fluctuations of fortune. Australia eventually won by 22 runs. The Second Test, at Perth, produced 1,478 runs in 5 days and still ended decisively, again in a hectic finish, with Australia winning by 2 wickets. With Chandrasekhar in devastating form and taking 6 wickets in each innings, India won the Third

Bhagwat Chandrasekhar's day of glory at Melbourne, where his 12 wickets for 104 enabled India to beat Australia in 1977–78 by 222 runs. Stricken with polio of the right shoulder, Chandra yet bowled right-arm and threw left.

Test at Melbourne comfortably and took the Fourth, at Sydney, by an even more convincing margin. So the sides went to Adelaide for the final Test at 2-all and it provided a fitting climax. India, left with 492 to make in the 4th innings, failed by only 47 runs, despite making a poor start.

Credit for leading a relatively inexperienced Australian side to victory against well-tried opposition went to Bobby Simpson who, at 41, staged a comeback after almost a decade's retirement from first-class cricket. His batting was as vital to Australia as his leadership, which was not limited to providing inspiration and making shrewd tactical judgments. He restored to the Australian team old-fashioned virtues which have made the game of cricket synonymous with a high code of conduct and sportsmanship. Simpson's opposite number, Bishen Bedi, also strove to uphold the image of traditional cricket. Simpson, scoring 539 runs, and Peter Toohey, who played with uncommon skill and confidence for a newcomer to Test cricket, formed the backbone of the Australian batting, although Graham Yallop weighed in with an innings of 121 in the final Test. Wayne Clarke, at fast medium, was Australia's most effective bowler, while Jeff Thomson, who had reversed an earlier decision to join WSC, took 22 wickets.

The Indian batting, so feeble against England the previous winter and traditionally suspect against pace, stood up better than expected. Viswanath, although he failed to make a hundred, was the most productive, with an aggregate of 473 runs. Gavaskar was next with 450, including a hundred in each of the first 3 Tests. Chauhan proved a game opening partner for Gavaskar, and Amarnath often batted with courage and determination. Kirmani not only kept wicket brilliantly, but more than once made runs in a crisis. Dilip Vengsarkar also developed well. Bedi was the outstanding bowler, taking 31 wickets and making a contribution in every Test but the last. Chandrasekhar did not come into his own until the Third Test, but finished the series with 28 wickets, thus making amends for a moderate performance on his 1st tour of Australia 10 years earlier.

AUSTRALIA V INDIA

			RESULT	CAPTAINS
1947–48	1 Brisbane	A 382–8D; Ind 58, 98	A Inns 226	D. G. Bradman, L. Amarnath
	2 Sydney	Ind 188, 61–7; A 107	Drawn	D. G. Bradman, L. Amarnath
	3 Melbourne	A 394, 255–4D; Ind 291–9D, 125	A 233 runs	D. G. Bradman, L. Amarnath
	4 Adelaide	A 674; Ind 381, 277	A Inns 16	D. G. Bradman, L. Amarnath
	5 Melbourne	A 575–8D; Ind 331, 67	A Inns 177	D. G. Bradman, L. Amarnath
1956–57	1 Madras	Ind 161, 153; A 319	A Inns 5	I. W. Johnson, P. R. Umrigar
	2 Bombay	Ind 251, 250–5; A 523–7D	Drawn	R. Lindwall, P. R. Umrigar
	3 Calcutta	A 177, 189–9D; Ind 136, 136	A 94 runs	I. W. Johnson, P. R. Umrigar
1959–60	1 New Delhi	Ind 135, 206; A 468	A Inns 127	R. Benaud, G. S. Ramchand
	2 Kanpur	Ind 152, 291; A 219, 105	Ind 119 runs	R. Benaud, G. S. Ramchand
	3 Bombay	Ind 289, 226–5D; A 387–8D, 34–1	Drawn	R. Benaud, G. S. Ramchand
	4 Madras	A 342; Ind 149, 138	A Inns 55	R. Benaud, G. S. Ramchand
	5 Calcutta	Ind 194, 339; A 331, 121–2	Drawn	R. Benaud, G. S. Ramchand
1964–65	1 Madras	A 211, 397; Ind 276, 193	A 139 runs	R. B. Simpson, Nawab of Pataudi
	2 Bombay	A 320, 274; Ind 341, 256–8	Ind 2 wkts	R. B. Simpson, Nawab of Pataudi
	3 Calcutta	A 174, 143–1; Ind 235	Drawn	R. B. Simpson, Nawab of Pataudi
1967–68	1 Adelaide	A 335, 369; Ind 307, 251	A 146 runs	R. B. Simpson, C. G. Borde
	2 Melbourne	Ind 173, 352; A 529	A Inns 4 runs	R. B. Simpson, Nawab of Pataudi
	3 Brisbane	A 379, 294; Ind 279, 355	A 39 runs	W. M. Lawry, Nawab of Pataudi
	4 Sydney	A 317, 292; Ind 268, 197	A 144 runs	W. M. Lawry, Nawab of Pataudi
1969–70	1 Bombay	Ind 271, 137; A 345, 67–2	A 8 wkts	W. M. Lawry, Nawab of Pataudi
	2 Kanpur	Ind 320, 312–7D; A 348, 95–0	Drawn	W. M. Lawry, Nawab of Pataudi
	3 Delhi	A 296, 107; Ind 223, 181–3	Ind 7 wkts	W. M. Lawry, Nawab of Pataudi
	4 Calcutta	Ind 212, 161; A 335, 42–0	A 10 wkts	W. M. Lawry, Nawab of Pataudi
	5 Madras	A 258, 153; Ind 163, 171	A 77 runs	W. M. Lawry, Nawab of Pataudi
1977–78	1 Brisbane	A 166, 327; Ind 153, 324	A 16 runs	R. B. Simpson, B. S. Bedi
	2 Perth	Ind 402, 330–9D; A 394, 342–8	A 2 wkts	R. B. Simpson, B. S. Bedi
	3 Melbourne	Ind 256, 343; A 213, 164	Ind 222 runs	R. B. Simpson, B. S. Bedi
	4 Sydney	A 131, 263; Ind 396–8D	Ind inns 2 runs	R. B. Simpson, B. S. Bedi
	5 Adelaide	A 505, 256; Ind 269, 445	A 47 runs	R. B. Simpson, B. S. Bedi

CAPTAINS (Australia)	TESTS	WON	LOST	DRAWN
D. G. Bradman	5	4		1
I. W. Johnson	2	2		
R. R. Lindwall	1			1
R. Benaud	5	2	1	2
R. B. Simpson	10	6	3	1
W. M. Lawry	7	5	1	1
	30	19	5	6

CAPTAINS (India)	TESTS	WON	LOST	DRAWN
L. Amarnath	5		4	1
P. R. Umrigar	3		2	1
G. S. Ramchand	5	1	2	2
Nawab of Pataudi	11	2	7	2
C. G. Borde	1		1	
B. S. Bedi	5	2	3	
	30	5	19	6

HIGHEST INNINGS TOTALS

Australia in Australia, 674, Adelaide 1947–48
Australia in India, 523–7D, Bombay 1956–57
India in Australia, 445, Adelaide 1977–78
India in India, 341, Bombay 1964–65

LOWEST INNINGS TOTALS

Australia in Australia, 107, Sydney 1947–48
Australia in India, 105, Kanpur 1959–60
India in Australia, 58, Brisbane 1947–48
India in India, 135, New Delhi 1959–60

HIGHEST INDIVIDUAL INNINGS

Australia in Australia, 201, D. G. Bradman, Adelaide 1947–48
Australia in India, 163, N. O'Neill, Bombay 1959–60
India in Australia, 145, V. S. Hazare, Adelaide 1947–48
India in India, 137, G. R. Vishwanath, Kanpur 1969–70

HIGHEST AGGREGATE OF RUNS IN A SERIES

Australia in Australia, 715, D. G. Bradman 1947–48
Australia in India, 376, N. C. O'Neill 1959–60
India in Australia, 473, G. R. Vishwanath 1977–78
India in India, 438, N. J. Contractor 1959–60

BEST INNINGS BOWLING FIGURES

Australia in Australia, 7–38, R. R. Lindwall, Adelaide 1947–48
Australia in India, 7–43, R. R. Lindwall, Madras 1956–57
India in Australia, 6–55, Abid Ali, Auckland 1967–68
India in India, 9–69, J. Patel, Kanpur 1959–60

BEST MATCH BOWLING FIGURES

Australia in Australia, 11–31, E. R. H. Toshack, Brisbane 1947–48
Australia in India, 12–124, A. K. Davidson, Kanpur 1959–60
India in Australia, 12–104, B. S. Chandrasekhar, Melbourne 1977–78
India in India, 14–124, J. Patel, Kanpur 1959–60

HIGHEST WICKET AGGREGATE IN A SERIES

Australia in Australia, 28, W. M. Clark 1977–78
Australia in India 29, R. Benaud 1959–60; 29, A. K. Davidson 1959–60
India in Australia, 31, B. S. Bedi 1977–78
India in India, 26, E. A. S. Prasanna 1969–70

RECORD WICKET PARTNERSHIPS – AUSTRALIA

1 W. M. Lawry and R. B. Simpson, 191, Melbourne 1967–68
2 S. G. Barnes and D. G. Bradman, 236, Adelaide 1947–48
3 R. N. Harvey and N. C. O'Neill, 207, Bombay 1959–60
4 R. N. Harvey and S. J. E. Loxton, 159, Melbourne 1947–48
5 A. R. Morris and D. G. Bradman, 223*, Melbourne 1947–48
6 T. R. Veivers and B. N. Jarman, 151, Bombay 1964–65
7 T. R. Veivers and J. W. Martin, 64, Madras 1964–65
8 T. R. Veivers and G. D. McKenzie, 73, Madras 1964–65
9 I. W. Johnson and P. Crawford, 87, Madras 1956–57
10 J. R. Thomson and A. G. Hurst, 50, Brisbane 1977–78

RECORD WICKET PARTNERSHIPS – INDIA

1 V. Mankad and C. T. Sarwate, 124, Melbourne 1947–48
2 S. M. Gavaskar and M. Amarnath, 193, Perth 1977–78
3 N. J. Contractor and A. A. Baig, 133, Bombay 1959–60
4 A. V. Mankad and Nawab of Pataudi, 146, Bombay 1969–70
5 A. A. Baig and R. B. Kenny, 109, Bombay 1959–60
6 V. S. Hazare and D. G. Phadkar, 188, Adelaide 1947–48
7 V. S. Hazare and H. R. Adhikari, 132, Adelaide 1947–48
8 Nawab of Pataudi and R. F. Surti, 74, Melbourne 1967–68
9 Nawab of Pataudi and R. B. Desai, 54, Melbourne 1967–68
10 C. G. Borde and B. S. Chandrasekar, 40, Calcutta 1964–65

Australia v Pakistan

REX ALSTON

On a matting pitch so slow that only 95 runs could be prized out of it on the 1st day – a record in terms of tardy scoring – Pakistan won their first-ever Test against Australia in 1956 at Karachi by 9 wickets. The Australians, after a strenuous tour of England, were bowled out for 80 by Fazal Mahmood (6 for 34) and Khan Mohammad (4 for 43). A partnership of 104 for the 6th wicket between Wazir Mohammad and A. H. Kardar was mainly responsible for Pakistan leading by 119, but though the 3 all-rounders R. Benaud, R. G. Archer and A. K. Davidson all made useful scores in Australia's 2nd innings, Fazal (7 for 80) and Khan (3 for 69) again bowled dangerously, and Pakistan needed only 69 for a remarkable victory. Fazal (13 for 114) with his extreme accuracy and ability to cut the ball either way off the seam was a highly formidable proposition at this time, as England had already discovered.

In 1959 Australia made another short visit and won a 3-match rubber 2–0. In the First Test on matting at Dacca (now in Bangladesh), Benaud and Davidson each took 4 wickets, and Pakistan were out for 200, of which Hanif Mohammad made 66 and D. Sharpe 56. Beautiful batting by R. N. Harvey (96) and fine hitting by wicket-keeper A. T. W. Grout (66 not out) gave Australia a lead of only 25, Fazal taking 5 for 71. Pakistan then made 134, K. D. Mackay taking 6 for 42 with off-spinners, and Australia won by 8 wickets. In the Second Test at Lahore only Hanif (49) could cope with the speed of the left-arm pair, Davidson and I. Meckiff, and the spin of Benaud and L. Kline, and Pakistan made only 146. With Fazal absent Australia scored easily, N. C. O'Neill making his 1st Test hundred (134), and Benaud declared at 391 for 9. Pakistan made a great fight in their 2nd innings, Saeed Ahmed (166), Imtiaz Ahmed (54), Shuja-ud-Din (45) showing great concentration, but Kline (7 for 75) exploited a wearing wicket. Australia, set to make 122, won by 7 wickets, Harvey, O'Neill and Benaud all batting aggressively.

With the rubber decided, the Third Test at Karachi, on the same sort of lifeless pitch as that of 3 years before, ended in a desperately tedious draw. The match was notable only, perhaps, for a visit by Dwight D. Eisenhower, then President of the United States. Since Pakistan spent all day making 104 for 5, one wonders what he made of this British and Commonwealth game.

In the series, Harvey for Australia scored the most runs (273) and Benaud (18 wickets) and Davidson (12) were the most dangerous bowlers. For Pakistan, beaten at home for the first time, Saeed (334) and Hanif (304) made the most runs, whilst Fazal was in a class by himself as a bowler.

In 1964, Australia, after a tour of England, drew the only Test match at Karachi. Pakistan led by 62 runs on the 1st innings, after an opening partnership of 249 by K. Ibadulla (166) and Abdul Kadir, G. D. MacKenzie taking 6 for 69. For Australia the captain, R. B. Simpson, made 153. Pakistan declared again at 279 for 8, but Simpson made another century (115) to draw the match with ease.

Pakistan toured Australia for the first time in 1972–73 but lost all 3 Tests after hard-fought games. Sadiq Mohammad, Mushtaq Mohammad and Majid Khan made the most runs, and Sarfraz Nawaz and Saleem Altaf, both fast-medium, took the most wickets. The Chappells headed the Australian batting, and M. H. N. Walker, A. A. Mallett and D. K. Lillee took the most wickets.

In 1976–77 Pakistan had their 1st win in Australia by 8 wickets in a drawn 3-match series. Asif Iqbal made 120 and Imran Khan took 6 wickets in each innings. In a high scoring series Zaheer Abbas, Asif and Sadiq made hundreds for

Imran Khan. In the Third Test at Sydney, January 1977, his figures of 6 for 63 in the 1st innings and 12 for 165 in the match set new records for Pakistan in Australia; and were decisive in Pakistan gaining their 1st Test win in Australia.

Pakistan, and the Chappell brothers, A. P. Sheahan, J. Benaud, I. R. Redpath and R. W. Marsh for Australia, for whom D. K. Lillee took 21 wickets.

After a 3-match tour in New Zealand, Pakistan played 2 Tests in Australia in 1979. They won by 71 runs at Melbourne and Australia won by 7 wickets in Perth. Pakistan's team was composed almost entirely of 'Packer' players, so Australia's victory was a notable triumph for their young side. At Melbourne, Pakistan led on the 1st innings by 28, R. J. Hogg and Imran each taking 4 wickets. Majid (108) and Zaheer (59) had good support by the middle order in Pakistan's 2nd innings of 353 for 9 declared, and Australia, needing 382 to win, replied bravely, reaching 304 for 3 after a fine partnership between A. R. Border (105) and K. J. Hughes (84). On the 5th day Sarfraz was inspired, taking the last 7 wickets for 1 run, and his figures – 9 for 86 in 35 overs – were a record for a visiting player to Australia.

Javed Miandad saved Pakistan at Perth, making 129 not out out of 277. Australia in reply led by 50, Border (85) and R. Darling (75) doing best. Pakistan lost their first 4 wickets for 86 in their 2nd innings, but Asif with a superb 134 not out rescued them so that Australia needed 236 to win. Darling (76) and Border (66 not out) saw that they got them with seven wickets to spare. Outstanding for Australia were the fast-medium A. Hurst, who took 9 for 155 at Perth, and the left-handed Border whose scores included 105, 85 and 66 not out. For Pakistan Javed, Majid and Asif made hundreds, and Sarfraz was in a class by himself as a bowler. From these two significant matches it was Australia who, in the circumstances, had best reason to be pleased with themselves.

AUSTRALIA V PAKISTAN

			RESULT	CAPTAINS
1956–57	1 Karachi	A 80, 187; Pak 199, 69–1	Pak 9 wkts	I. W. Johnson, A. H. Kardar
1959–60	1 Dacca	Pak 200, 134; A 225, 112–2	A 8 wkts	R. Benaud, F. Mahmood
	2 Lahore	Pak 146, 366; A 391–9D, 123–3	A 7 wkts	R. Benaud, I. Ahmed
	3 Karachi	Pak 287, 194–8D; A 257, 83–2	Drawn	R. Benaud, F. Mahmood
1964–65	1 Karachi	Pak 414, 279–8D; A 352, 227–2	Drawn	R. B. Simpson, Hanif Mohammad
1964–65	1 Melbourne	Pak 287, 326; A 448, 88–2	Drawn	R. B. Simpson, Hanif Mohammad
1972–73	1 Adelaide	Pak 257, 214; A 585	A Inns 114 runs	I. M. Chappell, Intikhab Alam
	2 Melbourne	A 441–5D, 425; Pak 574–8D, 200	A 92 runs	I. M. Chappell, Intikhab Alam
	3 Sydney	A 334, 184; Pak 360, 106	A 52 runs	I. M. Chappell, Intikhab Alam
1976–77	1 Adelaide	Pak 272, 466; A 454, 261–6	Drawn	G. S. Chappell, Mushtaq Mohammad
	2 Melbourne	A 517–8D, 315–8D; Pak 333, 151	A 348 runs	G. S. Chappell, Mushtaq Mohammad
	3 Sydney	A 211, 180; Pak 360, 32–2	Pak 8 wkts	G. S. Chappell, Mushtaq Mohammad
1978–79	1 Melbourne	Pak 196, 353–9D; A 168, 310	Pak 71 runs	G. N. Yallop, Mushtaq Mohammad
	2 Perth	Pak 277, 285; A 327, 236–3	A 7 wkts	K. J. Hughes, Mushtaq Mohammad

CAPTAINS (Australia)	TESTS	WON	LOST	DRAWN
I. W. Johnson	1		1	
R. Benaud	3	2		1
R. B. Simpson	2			2
I. M. Chappell	3	3		
G. S. Chappell	3	1	1	1
G. N. Yallop	1		1	
K. J. Hughes	1	1		
	14	7	3	4

CAPTAINS (Pakistan)	TESTS	WON	LOST	DRAWN
A. H. Kardar	1	1		
Fazal Mahmood	2		1	1
Imtiaz Ahmed	1		1	
Hanif Mohammad	2			2
Intikhab Alam	3		3	
Mushtaq Mohammad	5	2	2	1
	14	3	7	4

HIGHEST INNINGS TOTAL

Australia in Australia, 585, Adelaide 1972–73
Australia in Pakistan, 391–9D, Lahore 1959–60
Pakistan in Australia, 574–8D, Melbourne 1972–73
Pakistan in Pakistan, 414, Karachi 1964–65

LOWEST INNINGS TOTAL

Australia in Australia, 180, Sydney 1976–77
Australia in Pakistan, 80, Karachi 1956–57
Pakistan in Australia, 106, Sydney 1972–73
Pakistan in Pakistan, 134, Dacca 1959–60

HIGHEST INDIVIDUAL INNINGS

Australia in Australia, 196, I. M. Chappell, Adelaide 1972–73
Australia in Pakistan, 153, R. B. Simpson, Karachi 1964–65
Pakistan in Australia, 158, Majid Khan, Melbourne 1972–73
Pakistan in Pakistan { 166, Saeed Ahmed, Lahore 1959–60; 166, K. Ibadulla, Karachi 1964–65 }

HIGHEST AGGREGATE OF RUNS IN A SERIES

Australia in Australia, 343, G. S. Chappell 1976–77
Australia in Pakistan, 273, R. N. Harvey 1959–60
Pakistan in Australia, 343, Zaheer Abbas 1976–77
Pakistan in Pakistan, 334, Saeed Ahmed 1959–60

BEST INNINGS BOWLING FIGURES

Australia in Australia, 8–59, A. A. Mallett, Adelaide 1972–73
Australia in Pakistan, 7–75, L. F. Kline, Lahore 1959–60
Pakistan in Australia, 9–86, Sarfraz Nawaz, Melbourne, 1978–79
Pakistan in Pakistan, 7–80, Fazal Mahmood, Karachi 1956–57

BEST MATCH BOWLING FIGURES

Australia in Australia, 10–135, D. K. Lillee, Melbourne 1976–77
Australia in Pakistan, 8–90, L. F. Kline, Lahore 1959–60
Pakistan in Australia, 12–165, Imran Khan, Sydney 1976–77
Pakistan in Pakistan, 13–114, Fazal Mahmood, Karachi 1956–57

HIGHEST WICKET AGGREGATE IN A SERIES

Australia in Australia, 21, D. K. Lillee 1976–77
Australia in Pakistan, 18, R. Benaud 1959–60
Pakistan in Australia, 18, Imran Khan 1976–77
Pakistan in Pakistan, 13, Fazal Mahmood 1956–57

RECORD WICKET PARTNERSHIPS – AUSTRALIA

1 I. C. Davis and A. Turner, 134, Melbourne 1976–77
2 A. P. Sheahan and J. Benaud, 233, Melbourne 1972–73
3 R. B. Simpson and P. J. P. Burge, 116, Karachi 1964–65
4 A. M. Hilditch and K. M. Hughes, 177, Melbourne 1978–79
5 G. S. Chappell and G. J. Cosier, 171, Melbourne 1976–77
6 R. M. Cowper and T. R. Veivers, 139, Melbourne 1964–65
7 R. W. Marsh and K. J. O'Keeffe, 120, Adelaide 1972–73
8 G. J. Cosier and K. J. O'Keeffe, 117, Melbourne 1976–77
9 J. R. Watkins and R. A. L. Massie, 83, Sydney 1972–73
10 G. J. Cosier and D. K. Lillee, 87, Sydney 1976–77

RECORD WICKET PARTNERSHIPS – PAKISTAN

1 K. Ibadulla and Abdul Kadir, 249, Karachi 1964–65
2 Sadiq Mohammad and Majid Khan, 195, Melbourne 1972–73
3 Saeed Ahmed and Shuja-ud-Din, 169, Lahore 1959–60
4 Javed Burki and Hanif Mohammad, 84, Melbourne 1964–65
5 Mushtaq Mohammad and Asif Iqbal, 139, Sydney 1972–73
6 Asif Iqbal and Javed Miandad, 115, Sydney 1976–77
7 Intikhab Alam and Wasim Bari, 104, Adelaide 1972–73
8 Asif Iqbal and Saleem Altaf, 56, Sydney 1972–73
9 Intikhab Alam and Afaq Hussain, 56, Melbourne 1964–65
10 Asif Iqbal and Iqbal Qasim, 87, Adelaide 1976–77

Body-line

E. W. SWANTON

'Body-line' was a pejorative term coined by Australian journalists to describe the fast leg-theory bowling adopted extensively by H. Larwood, and to a lesser degree by W. Voce and W. E. Bowes, on the tour of D. R. Jardine's MCC team of 1932–33. It was brought into world-wide notice on 18th January 1933, in the first of the telegrams that passed between the Australian Board of Control and MCC, as follows:

Body-line bowling has assumed such proportions as to menace the best interests of the game, making protection of the body by the batsmen the main consideration. This is causing intensely bitter feelings between the players as well as injury. In our opinion it is unsportsmanlike. Unless stopped at once it is likely to upset the friendly relations existing between Australia and England.

The bowling chiefly objected to was that of Larwood, who, after the shine had left the new ball, directed his attack on the general line of the batsmen's body with an attendant ring of close leg-side fielders plus one, or on occasions two, on the boundary. Larwood's great speed, combined, as it was, with unusual accuracy, and a short length, made the protection of his person a batsman's first consideration. The difficulty in this was that from a defensive back-stroke the ball was apt to carry to the short legs. A hook stroke was possible in theory, and in at least one innings S. J. McCabe (187 not out in the First Test at Sydney) exploited it with great brilliance and courage. The margin of error, however, was extremely small, with a dangerous blow on the head, either direct or from a glancing hit, an ever-present possibility.

The first telegram was sent by the Australian Board towards the end of the Third Test at Adelaide, described by Sydney Southerton in *Wisden* as 'probably the most unpleasant ever played'. He added, 'altogether the whole atmosphere was a disgrace to cricket'. Woodfull and Oldfield were both hit by Larwood, and the resentment of the crowd at the English bowling methods was such that a large force of police stood in reserve behind the main stand. The particular fear concerned the crowd's reaction if Bradman, the popular idol, should have been hit. This Test formed the climax of the bitterest quarrel between countries in the history of cricket, but in days before general air travel, and the sending of film by air, considerable time elapsed before the Committee of MCC were able to appreciate the true picture of events. Naturally resenting the implications made against their team, they replied:

We, Marylebone Cricket Club, deplore your cable. We deprecate your opinion that there has been unsportsmanlike play. We have fullest confidence in captain, team and managers and are convinced that they would do nothing to infringe either the Laws of Cricket or the spirit of the game. We have no evidence that our confidence has been misplaced. Much as we regret accidents to Woodfull and Oldfield, we understand that in neither case was the bowler to blame.

If the Australian Board of Control wish to propose a new Law or Rule, it shall receive our careful consideration in due course.

We hope the situation is not now as serious as your cable would seem to indicate, but if it is such as to jeopardise the good relations between English and Australian cricketers and you consider it desirable to cancel remainder of programme we would consent, but with great reluctance.

While further cables were exchanged the tour continued, Larwood using the same methods, and England, thanks largely to the trepidation he inspired (though G. O. Allen, bowling fast to an orthodox field, was also successful), winning the rubber by 4 games to 1.

On the team's return MCC called to Lord's the captain, Jardine, the two managers, P. F. Warner and R. C. N. Palairet, and the two bowlers concerned, Larwood and Voce. Warner argued strongly against this form of bowling. But neither R. E. S. Wyatt, the vice-captain, who had disapproved of what was being done, nor Allen, the other fast bowler, who had himself refused his captain's request to follow Larwood's methods, was called in evidence. Nor was H. Sutcliffe, the senior professional. The full significance of the English tactics in Australia therefore took time to sink in at Lord's. But in the following summer (1933) in a Test at Old Trafford the West Indians, L. N. Constantine and E. A. Martindale, gave England a taste of their own medicine, and E. W. Clark replied in kind. The wicket was much slower than those in Australia and the methods accordingly less effective. Nevertheless W. R. Hammond was injured, and gradually responsible opinion hardened against what the Australians had called 'Body-line'. Southerton in a fully documented article in the 1934 *Wisden* crystallized the objections to it thus:

For myself, I hope that we shall never see fast leg-theory bowling as used during the last tour in Australia exploited in this country. I think that (1) it is definitely dangerous; (2) it creates ill-feeling between the rival teams; (3) it invites reprisals; (4) it has a bad influence on our great game of cricket; (5) it eliminates practically all the best strokes in batting.

DOWNING-ST. TALK ON BODY-LINE

.C.C. LEADERS AT THE DOMINIONS OFFICE

ATTORNEY-GENERAL ALSO PRESENT

R. J. H. THOMAS. LORD LEWISHAM.

EST MATCH INCIDENTS

NSIDE INFORMATION FOR MR. THOMAS

SPECIAL "DAILY MAIL" NEWS

LEADING MEMBERS OF THE M.C.C. VISITED THE DOMINIONS OFFICE, DOWNING-STREET, YESTERDAY, AND MET MR. J. H. THOMAS, SECRETARY FOR THE DOMINIONS.

M.C.C. TEAM DEMAND

"UNSPORTSMANLIKE" MUST BE WITHDRAWN

LEG THEORY

Cable Of Protest Sent To M.C.C.

"THE ADVERTISER" HAS RADIO PHONE TALK WITH GILLIGAN

Former English Captain Says Methods Do Not Savor Of Fairness

OLDFIELD RECOVERING FROM HEAD BLOW

About the time that A. E. R. Gilligan, captain of the M.C.C. team in Australia in 1924-5, was telling "The Advertiser," in a special interview by radiophone last night, that leg theory bowling should be controlled by giving the umpires power to say whether it was fair or unfair play, it was learned that the Board of Control, after a special meeting at the Adelaide Oval yesterday, had cabled an emphatic protest to the M.C.C. against such tactics. The message is reported to have set

A. E. R. GIL

RYDER TESTS IN D

Former Captain Views

TALK OF NO MORE TESTS

The Star
No. 14022 LONDON, SATURDAY, MAY 6, 1933. ONE PENNY.

HOBBS CONDEMNS 'BODY-LINE.'

Evenin
To-morrow's Weather—
No. 33,932 LONDON,

JARDINE BREA SILENCE

"Body-line Bowling" a Te Coined to Explain Defe

CONTROL BOARD "FAILED CONTROL THEMSELVES"

Mr. D. R. Jardine, captain of the M.C.C. side regained the Ashes from the Australians durin most contentious tour in cricket history, has at broken his silence.

EVENING NEWS, Thursday, Feb. 16, 1933.

The Evening News
LARGEST EVENING NET SALE IN THE WORLD
No. 15,950 Fifty-second Year LONDON: THURSDAY, FEBRUARY 16, 1933 ONE PENNY

NGLAND WIN THE "ASHES" BY SIX WICKETS

"The Men Were Splendid!" Says P. F. Warner : His Praise of Jardine

AYNTER'S WINNING HIT A GLORIOUS SIX

eyland's Great Innings of 86: Rain Falls Five Minutes After the Finish

ARDINE QUOTES KIPLING

rner's Revelation: "I Went Away When Leyland Was Out ... But Came Back"

GLAND won the Ashes at Brisbane to-day, in the Fourth Test Match, by six wickets. Paynter scored the ing hit, a six, and the long-threatening rain fell five tes after stumps were drawn!

eyland had a splendid innings of 86. He was at the wicket for s and 42 minutes, but yesterday, of course, he was obeying the 's order of "Caution."

nd this is what the two captains said about it, according to r, at a reception attended by both teams, presided over by Sir Wilson, Governor of Queensland:

D. R. JARDINE

It was a great match, but

his chance at winning the toss, and that half his correspond-

Jardine and Woodfull

The Final Scores

AUSTRALIA.—First Innings

V. Y. Richardson, st Ames, b Hammond	83
W. M. Woodfull, b Mitchell	67
D. G. Bradman, b Larwood	76
S. J. McCabe, c Jardine, b Allen	20
W. H. Ponsford, b Larwood	19
L. Darling, c Ames, b Allen	17
E. H. Bromley, c Verity, b Larwood	26
H. S. Love, lbw, b Mitchell	5
T. Wall, not out	6
W. J. O'Reilly, c Hammond, b Larwood	6
H. Ironmonger, st Ames, b Hammond	8
Extras (b 5, l-b 1, n-b 1)	7
Total	340

FALL OF THE WICKETS

1	2	3	4	5	6	7	8	9	10
133	200	233	264	267	292	315	317	329	340

BOWLING ANALYSIS

	O.	M.	R.	W.
Larwood	31	7	101	4
Allen	24	4	83	2
Hammond	23	5	61	2
Mitchell	16	5	49	2
Verity	27	12	39	0

AUSTRALIA.—Second Innings

W. M. Woodfull, c Hammond, b Mitchell	19
V. Y. Richardson, c Jardine, b Verity	32
D. G. Bradman, c Mitchell, b Larwood	24
W. H. Ponsford, c Larwood, b Allen	0
S. J. McCabe, b Verity	22
L. Darling, run out	39
E. H. Bromley, c Hammond, b Allen	7
H. S. Love, lbw, b Larwood	3
T. Wall, c Jardine, b Allen	2
W. J. O'Reilly, b Larwood	4
H. Ironmonger, not out	0
Extras (b 13, l-b 9, n-b 1)	23
Total	175

FALL OF THE WICKETS

1	2	3	4	5	6	7	8	9	10
46	79	81	91	136	163	169	169	171	175

BOWLING ANALYSIS

	O.	M.	R.	W.
Larwood	17.3	3	49	3
Allen	17	3	44	3
Hammond	10	4	18	0
Verity	19	6	30	2
Mitchell	5	0	11	1

ENGLAND.—First Innings

D. R. Jardine, c Love, b O'Reilly	46
Sutcliffe, lbw, b O'Reilly	86
Hammond, b McCabe	20
R. E. S. Wyatt, c Love, b Ironmonger	12
Leyland, c Bradman, b O'Reilly	12
G. O. Allen, c Love, b Wall	13
Ames, c Darling, b Ironmonger	17
Paynter, c Richardson, b Ironmonger	83
Larwood, b McCabe	23
Verity, not out	23
Mitchell, lbw, b O'Reilly	0
Extras (b 6, l-b 12, n-b 3)	21
Total	356

FALL OF THE WICKETS

1	2	3	4	5	6	7	8	9	10
114	157	165	188	198	216	225	264	356	356

BOWLING ANALYSIS

	O.	M.	R.	W.
Wall	33	6	66	1
O'Reilly	67.4	26	120	4
Ironmonger	43	19	69	3
McCabe	23	7	40	2
Bromley	10	4	19	0
Bradman	7	1	17	0
Darling	2	0	4	0

ENGLAND.—Second Innings

D. R. Jardine, lbw, b Ironmonger	24
Sutcliffe, c Darling, b Wall	2
Leyland, c McCabe, b O'Reilly	86
Hammond, c Bromley, b Ironmonger	14
Ames, not out	14
Paynter, not out	14
Extras (b 2, l-b 4, n-b 2, w 1)	9
Total (4 wkts)	163

FALL OF THE WICKETS

1	2	3	4
5	78	118	138

BOWLING ANALYSIS

	O.	M.	R.	W.
Wall	7	1	17	1
O'Reilly	30	11	65	1
Ironmonger	35	13	47	2
McCabe	7.4	2	25	0

LEG THEORY IN LONDON

Defence Of Bov

WIDE APPEAL BETTER SPIR

Australian Board P Case

After the 1933 season the MCC Committee passed the following resolution:

That any form of bowling which is obviously a direct attack by the bowler upon the batsman would be an offence against the spirit of the game.

This was accepted by the county captains at a meeting at Lord's, and affirmed by the Imperial Cricket Conference, representing all the Test-playing countries, in July 1934. As, however, there were certain circumstances in 1934 involving Larwood and Voce, playing for Notts under the captaincy of A. W. Carr, MCC in the following winter further ruled:

That the type of bowling regarded as a direct attack by the bowler upon the batsman and therefore unfair consists in persistent and systematic bowling of fast short-pitched balls at the batsman standing clear of his wicket.

They assured the umpires of full support if they took action under the law relating to Unfair Play, and a note was subsequently added to the law specifying what was Direct Attack. So long as there is fast bowling, and the winning and losing of Test Matches matters much to many people, the safeguard of the law will be necessary to prevent a repetition, on a lesser scale no doubt, of what happened in Australia in 1932–33. It is sufficient here to add that though umpires have cautioned several bowlers none has ever found it necessary to apply the ultimate remedy, which is to order the fielding captain to take off the offending bowler for the rest of the innings.

To this day tactics expressed by the phrase remain a slur on cricket and on the traditional conception of English sportsmanship.

The d'Oliveira Affair

DAVID FRITH

In the autumn of 1968 cricket suddenly found itself embroiled in a bitter and far-reaching disputation. It was politically-inspired and bred a chain-reaction that culminated in South Africa's expulsion from the international game, a step which almost certainly expedited the movement towards racial integration in sport in that country. By 1979 South Africa had a non-racial cricket administration, and an ICC fact-finding party had paid a visit to assess whether there had been a complete abandonment of discrimination, which development would entitle, though perhaps not guarantee, South Africa's readmission to Test cricket.

The central figure in the 1968 contention was Basil Lewis d'Oliveira, a Coloured all-rounder from Cape Town, already approaching his 37th birthday (though confessing only to 33 years at the time). Denied – by the apartheid policy of the South African Government – any opportunity of playing first-class cricket in the land of his birth, he ventured to England in 1960 to play in the Central Lancashire League. His performances in primitive conditions in his home country had been prodigious, but he was now compelled to modify and refine his game. This he succeeded in doing to such an extent that in 1965, by which time Worcestershire had seen fit to engage him, he scored 6 hundreds and a 99 for the county, helping substantially towards their retention of the Championship. In the following season he was chosen to play for England.

By the start of the Australian tour of England in 1968, d'Oliveira had played in 14 Test matches, though with only moderate success in West Indies during the previous winter. Despite an 87 not out in the opening Test against Australia he was discarded, and it was not until 10 weeks later that his name appeared again on a Test scorecard. Even then it was by default, since Roger Prideaux had been forced to withdraw from the original team for the final Test at the Oval.

There followed a bewildering sequence of events. D'Oliveira grasped his chance dramatically, scoring 158 to ensure England's sizable first-innings total and then taking a vital wicket to initiate a winning breakthrough on the exciting final afternoon. His passionate hopes of touring South Africa with MCC seemed about to be fulfilled.

On the day following the Test, after d'Oliveira had completed a further hundred for his county, the touring team was announced, and d'Oliveira's name was not included. It was accepted by most that the selectors, believing he would be no more successful as a bowler in South Africa than he had been in West Indies, had chosen the team strictly on merit; but there was also an area of assumption that his omission was in deference to South Africa's racial policy: his inclusion might have created local embarrassment and even disruption during the tour.

The voice of protest was widely heard, and came loudest from certain Members of Parliament and members of MCC (some of whom resigned). A former England captain, the Rev David Sheppard, was outspoken and assumed leadership of what became known as 'The Sheppard Group' whose steering committee requested a special meeting with MCC. The news that d'Oliveira would cover the tour for the *News of the World* did not help – particularly in South Africa – to calm a furious situation.

Then, within 3 weeks of his sensational omission, d'Oliveira was in the team. All-rounder Tom Cartwright had failed a fitness test and Worcestershire's coloured South African was called up as replacement. His personal despair turned in an instant to jubilation; but, as he later wrote, he knew then that the tour would probably not take place. In time it was revealed that South Africa's Prime Minister, B. J. Vorster, had told Lord Cobham, who was on a business visit to the Republic,

'Body-line': an impression from cuttings and pictures.

D. R. Jardine's MCC team of 1932–33 gave the theory a modified exposure before the Test series. Woodfull playing for an Australian XI was hit over the heart by Larwood (No. 4).

Don Bradman, for whose benefit the tactics were chiefly devised, was unfit for the First Test which England won. Applauded all the way to the wicket in the Second Test at Melbourne he (rightly) anticipated a bouncer first ball from Bowes, moved too far across his wicket and dragged the ball into his stumps. He walked back, after his 1st duck in Test cricket, in awesome silence (No. 2).

The full leg-trap of 6 here deployed at Adelaide. Anti-clockwise the short-legs are: Leyland, Allen (in white hat), Jardine, Sutcliffe, Voce and Hammond. Larwood is the bowler; Wyatt on the off-side. Ames was the 'keeper, with Paynter and Verity on the boundary. Woodfull ducks under a bouncer. When the ball rose between waist and shoulder the difficulty lay in playing it down short of the fielders (No. 3).

The climax of feeling came in the Third Test at Adelaide. Oldfield is here struck on the head by Larwood. Woodfull was also struck twice, while carrying his bat through the 2nd innings. The exchange of cables began at this point (No. 1).

The innings that started it all – the dust begins to fly as d'Oliveira scores 158 at the Oval in 1968.

that d'Oliveira would not be acceptable as a member of the MCC touring team. This was in March 1968. In July d'Oliveira had received a most lucrative offer to coach in South Africa for 5 or even 10 years, conditional upon his being unavailable for the forthcoming tour. In the face of repeated and increasingly eager overtures, d'Oliveira declined the offer – which, the businessman concerned insisted, was not backed by outside influences.

The instinctive fears of d'Oliveira and others that the tour might be cancelled were hardened by a speech at Bloemfontein by the South African Prime Minister on September 17. Mr Vorster said: 'It's not the MCC team. It's the team of the anti-apartheid movement. We are not prepared to accept a team thrust upon us . . .'.

MCC secretary S. C. Griffith made it clear that 'if the chosen team is not acceptable to South Africa, the MCC will call off the tour.' A week later, after a meeting at Lord's with South African Cricket Association officials Jack Cheetham and Arthur Coy, MCC announced that the tour was cancelled, a unanimous decision reached after it had been made clear that the team would not be acceptable, for reasons beyond the control of the SACA. The controversy raged on. MCC at the request of critical members were obliged to hold a special general meeting on 5 December 1968 at Church House, Westminster, when 3 votes of censure on the committee were heavily defeated. The president, Ronald Aird, paid tribute to the 'great dignity which Basil d'Oliveira has maintained throughout the whole business'. That dignity was displayed in spite of tremendous emotional strain, and was rewarded in part with the OBE in the 1969 Queen's Birthday Honours.

By 1970 d'Oliveira was again on the verge of playing Test cricket for England against the all-white South African team. But the break in relations begun in late 1968 was rendered complete less than 2 years later when the Cricket Council, after striving to the limit to stage the 1970 South African tour of England, were requested by the British Government to cancel the visit.

Opposition to sporting contact with South Africa had swelled, one of the principal dissidents being a South African-born student, Peter Hain, who launched a 'Stop the Seventy Tour' committee. The 1969–70 Springbok rugby tour of Britain was disrupted by demonstrators, and it was all too apparent that a cricket tour would be even easier to undermine. The cost of protection to facilities and personnel would be enormous – more than the game could withstand. The 1970 Cricket Fund was set up, approved by the Cricket Council – which had in the previous year become the game's first duly constituted governing body – with a target of £200,000; but South Africa's banishment moved inexorably nearer. Thirteen African countries threatened to withdraw from the Commonwealth Games in Edinburgh if the cricket tour went ahead, and world sport stopped to think when in May 1970 South Africa was expelled from the Olympic movement.

Though aware of the threat to law and order and of the inevitable serious repercussions, the Cricket Council, holding to its belief that more would be achieved by maintaining 'bridges' to South Africa, had stated on 19 May that the tour would proceed. However, the SACA were told pointedly that no further tours after 1970 would be agreed to, in either direction, until such time as South Africa chose its teams on a multi-racial basis. All 14 players chosen for the 1970 tour, under the leadership of Dr Ali Bacher, were now prepared to travel to England.

Then the British Government stepped in. Taking into account the likely impact on race relations in Britain and effect throughout the Commonwealth, and mindful of the huge diversion of police manpower that would be necessary, on 21 May the Home Secretary, James Callaghan, requested the Cricket Council to withdraw the invitation to the SACA. This the Council did immediately, 'with deep regret'.

South Africa's cricket isolation was now absolute, and Basil d'Oliveira, the man described by South African Prime Minister Vorster as 'a political cricket ball' and now moving well into the veteran class, was left to play county cricket in England with continued success throughout the 1970s and to take his total of Test appearances for England to 44 – not one of them against his native land, where he had known only denial.

England v Australia

The Beginning to 1930

I. A. R. PEEBLES

It would be extremely gratifying to the researcher into cricket history to establish a material connexion between the fact that Australia was discovered by a Yorkshireman, and the enthusiasm and self-confidence of Australian cricket. But the plain truth is that, however flexible and generous the imagination of the interpreter, he must content himself with the reflection that the coincidence is an apt and happy one, and nothing more. When, in 1770, Captain James Cook sailed into Botany Bay cricket was a well-established pastime in his native land, but his biographers offer no evidence that he was actively, or academically, interested in the subject. Indeed, although Leeds had met Sheffield in a match 5 years previously, the game was then much more popular in the South.

With the early development of Australian cricket dealt with elsewhere in this volume, the period we are concerned with started in the late 1870s. In March and April of 1878 an all professional side played 2 matches against Australia in Melbourne, losing the 1st and winning the 2nd. The visitors were in no way representative of England's full strength but these encounters are generally recognized as the first 2 official Test Matches. In January the following year Lord Harris led a side which played and lost a match against Australia, again at

Melbourne. A dispute concerning the running out of Murdoch, the Australian captain, led to a brawl, the crowd rushed on to the field and Lord Harris was assaulted in the resulting free-for-all.

An attack on the person of an English nobleman seems to have made more impression on the home press than the outcome of the match, for A. G. Steel, writing in the *Badminton Book of 1890* says the doings of the teams in Australia, although reported in the press, did not interest the cricketing community at home. The event to which can be attributed this sudden awakening is, of course, the extraordinary match at Lord's in which the first visiting Australian team defeated a very strong MCC side in the astonishing time of $4\frac{1}{2}$ hours. In the ranks of the defeated were several of England's leading players captained by 'W.G.' himself, and for the first time it was apparent that victory over the full strength of England was within the compass of the Australians. This possibility, due almost entirely to the strength of their bowling – for the batting was rough and ready – was soon to be realized.

On 6 September 1880, at the Oval, 'W.G.', as was appropriate, opened this great and enduring sporting series by winning the toss and making 152. When Australia were all out for 149 to England's 420, it seemed that Goliath had for once crushed David but the Australians revealed that resilient power of recovery which has characterized their play ever since. Their captain bettered 'W.G.' by 1 run in making 153 and they eventually set England 57 to win and caused some anxiety by getting 5 of them out before admitting defeat.

The period is particularly interesting as being the genesis of Test Match cricket; but what strikes the reader is the frequency of the meetings, although the number of international matches on each trip was usually limited to 4 or less. Australian teams came to this country in 1882, 1884, 1886 and 1888, and English teams visited Australia in 1881–82, 1882–83 and 1884–85. When one considers the times and conditions of travel, over the seas and in Australia at that time, this is an astonishing programme. It was as though the initial excitement had touched off a bingo-like craze.

The historic Test Match played at the Oval in August 1882 remains one of the most dramatic that has ever taken place in England. The English batting led by 'W.G.' was so well graduated that Steel batted number 9, with A. N. Hornby next in. Australia could not match this array, but Bannerman took a deal of shifting, and there were several robust strikers, including the gigantic Bonnor. But, as Steel pointed out, rain-spoilt wickets can do a lot to narrow the gap between the correct, methodical player and the really determined slogger. In the event rain was a potent factor. The bowling was a very different matter. The left-handed Peate opened for England with Ulyett, and they were supported by Barlow, Steel, W. Barnes and Studd, which made a very fair attack. All put together, nonetheless, could not match the splendid technique and crusading fire of the Australian trio, Spofforth, Garrett and Boyle. And, as rain lessened the disparity between the respective batting strengths, so it tended to increase the margin of Australian superiority in the field. All 3 of their bowlers were deadly performers when the ball bit the turf.

Spofforth is one of the true immortals of cricket. His name has the legendary quality of 'Lumpy' Stevens, Old Clarke, Alfred Mynn and Sydney Barnes, largely because, like them, he was not only a great craftsman, but also an explorer and inventor. The cinema camera not being available to give posterity an accurate picture, the present age must depend upon the copious writings and the splendid photographs of Beldam, taken in later years, in forming their impression of 'The Demon'. From these one would surmise that he must have, to some extent, resembled his successor, E. A. McDonald. There would appear to be a close similarity in the extreme elasticity of action, the reserve of great pace and its variation, the ability to fetch the ball back off the seam on hard wickets, and spin it back on soft. For Beldam's benefit Spofforth also demonstrated a leg-break, but contemporaries make no mention of this, although he certainly made the occasional ball 'go with his arm'. His fast ball was undoubtedly very fast and, as every ball was delivered with the concentrated hostility common to Barnes and O'Reilly, he induced a feeling of awe in all but the stoutest breasts. The Hon Edward Lyttelton, a man of picturesque phrase, described how he faced him, gloveless on a 'bouncy' pitch. 'I give you my word,' he said, 'that for several overs I stood on the brink of the tomb.'

His colleagues, Garrett and Boyle, although they have not been illuminated in the same vivid colours, were far from being just honest toilers. Boyle, whose portraits reveal an athletic looking man of ample beard and beady eye, was a medium-paced right-hander who could turn the ball either way. He was of further assistance to Spofforth by fielding magnificently at short-leg right on the bat, a strange reflection on all the talk of 'modern' field placings. Garrett was a lawyer, and although he lacked the versatility of his companions, he bowled rather above medium-pace, with off-spin and all the precision to be expected from one of his profession.

The Oval Test of 1882 has been graphically described by many writers, notably H. S. Altham in *A History of Cricket*. Every cricketer is familiar with the breathless tension of the final innings with Spofforth's fury overwhelming the English batsmen, when victory seemed so close that few of them can have expected to bat again. That a spectator gnawed through the handle of his umbrella during this time is not improbable, but that another fell dead is a picturesque but unsubstantiated story.

An attempt to rescue the freshly created Ashes was made in the following Australian summer by a team under the captaincy of the Hon Ivo Bligh. It was scarcely fully representative of England, but the fine all-round cricket of Steel, the batting of W. W. Read and a good steady attack were sufficient to win the Second and Third Tests, after losing the First at Melbourne and, subsequently, the Fourth and last at Sydney. The Australian batting was beginning to assume a more orthodox look, possibly as a result of English contact and influence. Scoring on the improving Australian pitches, except when weather intervened, was comparatively high and it was not until the Third Test, at Sydney, that Spofforth produced another of his really devastating performances. Even so his 7 for 44 in England's 2nd innings was bettered by Barlow who, in reply, took 7 for 40 to win the match for England. The Fourth Test was not in the original fixture list so that England had in fact won the rubber. In after years it has been customary

The Hon Ivo Bligh's team of 1882–83, the first to go in search of the Ashes, the legend having been published by *Punch* after England's defeat by 7 runs at the Oval in 1882.

to include this 'extra' match in the series, and so record it as a draw; but this is incorrect.

Scarcely had the Englishmen departed when W. L. Murdoch was once again hot on their trail. Massie and Horan, upon whom so much depended, did not make the trip; but H. J. H. Scott had a most successful first visit, averaging 73 in the 3 Test Matches. Garrett, the patient and crafty solicitor, had dropped out, but Palmer proved a most adequate successor. His medium-paced spinners, reinforced by a shrewdly delivered yorker, accounted for 14 England wickets, and this was the prelude to an outstanding career. At Manchester, England's batsmen in the 1st innings on a soft wicket mustered 95. The position would have been very much worse but for a very fine innings of 43 by Shrewsbury, whose mastery of back play, and skilful use of his pads, put him ahead of all his contemporaries. Australia, thanks to McDonnell, Murdoch and Midwinter, just failed to double this score. Grace, in an unusually defensive role, ensured that England escaped with a draw. At Lord's, England, with a hundred from the redoubtable Steel, won by an innings and 5 runs. An interesting sidelight on the spirit of the times is provided by the memory of W. L. Murdoch fielding 'sub' for England and catching Scott. The Oval match saw the highest scoring to date, Australia making 551 and England replying with 346 and 85 for 2. Murdoch made 211 and Scott and McDonnell 102 and 103 respectively. When England had lost 8 wickets for 181, Read came in to join the rock-like Scotton, who, starting with Grace, had then reached 53. The pair added 151 in a couple of hours, of which Read made 117. An intriguing feature of the score sheet is that 'W.G.' was run out. If Scotton was the culprit his nerve was apparently unshaken but, remembering the perfection of the wicket, one doubts whether many of his side were in the dressing-room to greet their returning leader. The entire England side bowled, their wicket-keeper, Lyttelton, being by far the most successful.

The shuttle service was maintained when Shrewsbury set off in the autumn to play 5 Test Matches during the Australian season. His side was all professional, and a strong one, but the tour was marred by dispute and squabble about money between certain Australian players, first with Shaw, the joint touring manager, and later with their own authorities. Coming at a time when many of the older stalwarts were naturally on the decline, these unseemly disturbances did much to precipitate a decline in Australian cricket which lasted until the close of the decade. Shrewsbury's professionals, with a strong batting side, won 4 out of the 5 Tests. The Third was lost when, following some violent and erratic weather, Australia added 80 for the last wicket of their first innings. Peel had the astonishing bag of 321 wickets for all matches.

In May 1886, Scott brought to England a team organized for the first time by an official body, the Melbourne Cricket Club. It was early seen to be an ill-starred venture. Bad weather restricted its success to but a single victory in May and in the following month a hard drive from Lord Harris's bat put Spofforth out of action for a prolonged period with an injury to his hand. In July, Bonnor was also incapacitated. The First Test at Manchester was perhaps their most successful match for only Barlow's steady resistance in both innings got England home by no more than 4 wickets. At Lord's a splendid 164 by Shrewsbury put England in an overwhelming position when the rain came, Briggs taking advantage of this change of fortune with 11 wickets for 74 runs. The Oval was an even heavier reverse for here 'W.G.' made 170 out of 434, and then watched Lohmann shoot the opposition out for 68 and 149. At least Giffen again proved himself Australia's greatest all-rounder, heading both batting and bowling averages for the tour. It was Spofforth's last trip, but not farewell. He returned to settle in England and die, a very rich man, years later.

1886–87 saw the arrival of Arthur Shrewsbury's 2nd side in Australia. In the 2 Tests, both played at Sydney, the Australians were in a considerable state of disarray, but lost the First by the modest margin of 13 runs, and the Second by 71. That they ran the tourists so close was entirely due to one of the hopeful signs which illuminated a dark age. In the midst of depression Australia turned out a pair of bowlers, Turner and Ferris, whose deeds were to bear comparison with any other complementary bowlers before or since. In these their first 2 matches, they took 35 wickets between them for 404 runs, putting England out for 45 on first acquaintance. As their record would argue, they were not only individually fine bowlers, but they were admirably matched. Turner, despite a rather full-fronted action, got tremendous life from the pitch with his sharply spun medium-paced off-breaks and, to a generation which used its legs purely for purposes of locomotion, was unplayable on broken wickets. Ferris was a left-hander, lively in pace, and could turn the ball either way. Had there been an adequate batting side in support Australia would have been a formidable proposition at this time. As things stood, Test Matches were kept to low levels of scoring; but Australia won only 1 match during the span of this remarkable partnership.

In February 1888, W. W. Read, leading a very strong English side, defeated Australia at Sydney by 126 runs. In this match Turner and Ferris took 18 wickets for 190 runs, but Lohmann and Peel did even better, with 19 for 110. Australia by force and enterprise in soft, wet weather, won the Lord's Test of 1888 by 61 runs, Turner and Ferris once again dominating the scene. Both at the Oval and at Manchester they were crushed by an innings. So ended the wars of the 1880s, at which point one may pause briefly to consider the period as a whole.

It was a crowded, eventful and in some ways a haphazard, time. There can be no doubt that the participants in those privately organized tours richly earned such rewards as came their way. The sea passage between the countries was lengthy and ships far from luxurious. Internal travel was rough and ready in Australia and accommodation variable but never particularly plush. The party was small, with no great reserve for injury, and programmes were enormous, many matches being against odds of up to XXIIs. In a young country crowds were hearty and demonstrative, so incidents, such as the assault on Lord Harris, could not have been wholly unexpected.

The 1890s were a decade of much change and development in England v Australia cricket. By its end had come the existing pattern of 5-match series, the establishment of the Board of Control for Test cricket, and the selection of the teams entrusted to a committee appointed for the purpose. In the practical field the first problem to be encountered was a serious decline in public interest in Australia. The waning powers and successes of their sides in the late 1880s had a discouraging effect on a sporting fraternity, as yet comparatively small, whose enthusiasms were prodigious but volatile. Lord Sheffield, one of the great enthusiasts, determined to counter this with a generous and practical step. He not only financed a strong side, but persuaded W. G. Grace to lead it. This tour proved to be the spring-board which finally set Australian cricket on its prosperous course. In the first 2 Tests, played at Melbourne and Sydney, Australia won by 54 and 72 runs. Their success was due in the main to much improved batting led by Bannerman and Lyons, who averaged 33 and 47 in the series. This advance in the power of the batting in relation to the previous domination of the bowlers was to be one of the sustained features of the period. That England won the final match at Adelaide by an innings did little to lessen the new wave of enthusiasm. Australia had retasted blood and found it stimulating. The following tour of England under Blackham was less of a triumph than anticipated. England won the only completed match at the Oval which, strangely enough, was devoted to the Benefit of J. M. Read, who was not included in the England side. The Australian batting was adequate but the bowling was ineffective, with a declining Turner at a disadvantage in a dry season. There was no fast bowler to counter England's wealth of pace supplied by Richardson, Lockwood and Mold.

In 1894–95 A. E. Stoddart led a side which played 5 Tests, winning 3 and losing 2. Fortunes varied dramatically, the pattern being set by the first match at Sydney. England were compelled to follow on, and recovered bravely from a seemingly hopeless position. Even so, Australia wanted but 177 to win, but were so dilatory in their pursuit of this modest total that rain eventually brought about their defeat by 10 runs. England won by 94 runs at Melbourne, but were overwhelmed in the Adelaide heat. Weather again played a large part in an English defeat in the Fourth Test at Sydney, but England ran out winners in the last match by 6 wickets, a margin which belied the closeness of the fight. Both sides contained some established and some emergent players of distinction. Australia had the Trotts and George Giffen, whilst Ernest Jones had given a fleeting glimpse of the pace that was soon to astonish all England.

In addition to this stimulating spectacle of Jones at full blast, 1896 saw the addition of several illustrious names on both sides. Australia's batting disintegrated on a perfect Lord's wicket against Richardson and Lohmann, so that 2nd innings hundreds by Trott and Gregory could only lessen the margin of defeat to 6 wickets. Clem Hill started his career against England with 1 and 5, but F. S. Jackson got off with a stylish 44 on the other side. At Manchester, Australia's early advantage looked like ensuring an easy win but the newly arrived Ranjitsinhji scored 154 not out in his 2nd innings. Richardson complemented this effort with such a tremendous spell of sustained fast bowling that Australia just got home by 3 wickets. They were still 3-match series in England, and the home side ended with a win at the Oval. The weather ensured a very low scoring match, with Peel and Hearne on one side and Trumble's flight and off-spin on the other.

In 1897 A. E. Stoddart set out for Australia on a second quest for the Ashes. He had assembled a very strong team in which the best amateur batting was blended with top professional bowling headed by Richardson, Hirst, Hearne and Briggs. They were soundly trounced by a fine Australian side led by G. H. S. Trott. Centuries by MacLaren and Ranjitsinhji paved the way for a 9 wicket win at Sydney in December but, with the New Year, 4 heavy defeats were sustained in a row. Australia won the Second and Third matches by an innings, and the other 2 by 8 and 6 wickets. This was a very well-knit side, 7 batsmen averaging over 36, and the bowling shared between half-a-dozen from the pace of Jones to Trott's leg-breaks.

W.G.'s last Test, Trent Bridge 1902. Back row: R. G. Barlow (umpire), T. W. Hayward, G. H. Hirst, W. Gunn, J. T. Hearne, W. Storer, W. Brockwell and V. A. Titchmarsh (umpire); middle row: C. B. Fry, K. S. Ranjitsinhji, W. G. Grace, F. S. Jackson; on ground: W. Rhodes and J. T. Tyldesley.

The Australians of 1902 won a classic series 2–1 with 2 drawn. Back row: J. J. Kelly, J. V. Saunders, H. Trumble, W. W. Armstrong, M. A. Noble, W. P. Howell and Major Wardill (manager); sitting: C. Hill, R. A. Duff, J. Darling (captain), V. T. Trumper and E. Jones; on ground: A. J. Hopkins, H. Carter and S. E. Gregory.

When Australia came to England in 1899 only one match, the Second at Lord's, was decided, England going down by 10 wickets. The series was notable in other ways. England sadly bade farewell to 'W.G.' as a Test Match cricketer after he had had an indifferent opening match. By way of compensation, admittedly at high cost to England's prospects, the country was introduced to the glories of Victor Trumper. He also failed in the first match but a splendid 135 not out, a score equalled by Clem Hill, led the way to Australia's decisive win. Possibly here was established the legend which exists to this day giving Trumper a unique place in cricket history.

The 1890s had been a decade studded with illustrious England names, MacLaren, Ranjitsinhji and Jackson appearing midway to carry the torch into the next century. Blackham and Trott had led Australia in the initial surge forward. Now Darling commanded a wealth of batting and a fine bowling side, with Trumble, Noble and Howell to follow the violence of Jones's initial assault.

If the 1890s were the start of the Golden Age there was sufficient overspill of treasure to make the following period an equally fascinating one in international affairs. It lasted until 1914, and started immediately with A. C. MacLaren's visit to Australia in 1901. Australia had a fine nucleus of young players, with a more experienced core. England had an array of batsmen, but the great Yorkshiremen, Hirst and Rhodes, were debarred by the committee from joining the party. The unexpected selection, and surely the most successful gamble in cricket history, was the inclusion of S. F. Barnes, a little-known bowler from the Lancashire League. Within a matter of months the Australians were acclaiming him as the best bowler yet received from England. Unfortunately Barnes had knee trouble which ended his triumphal progress midway through the Third Test, at which point he had taken 19 wickets at 17 runs apiece. Thus deprived, MacLaren ran out a loser by 4 matches to 1, a result which might at least have been more even but for this misfortune. For Australia Noble and Trumble bowled splendidly, and Hill and Trumper led a wonderful younger school of batsmen.

The season of 1902 was a very wet one in England, frequently producing the peculiarly local conditions which bedevil visiting players from warmer climes. But Darling had some fine counters to these difficulties in the dashing attack of Trumper and Hill, and the all-round skill and craft of Noble, supported by a young Armstrong. Trumble, Noble and Saunders were a good trio on wet or damaged wickets. England had also good reason for optimism, much enhanced when

LEFT R. E. Foster: the most famous of the illustrious Worcestershire brotherhood. Aged 24, and in his 1st Test Match, he made 287 against Australia at Sydney. This remained the highest score by either side against the other until D. G. Bradman made his 334 at Headingley in 1930.

RIGHT An early action-photograph shows A. C. MacLaren on-driving C. E. MacLeod in the Lord's Test of 1905.

Hirst and Rhodes bowled Australia out for 36 at Birmingham in the First Test. Rain, by way of evening the balance of fortune, then saved Australia, and later limited play in the Lord's Test to just over an hour and a half. The Third was played at Sheffield, and some fine bowling by Barnes was outweighed by a century by Hill which carried Australia to victory by 143 runs. The last 2 matches are still vividly remembered because of the closeness of the finishes, and their somewhat dramatic circumstances. At Manchester poor Fred Tate got a shooter from Saunders with 4 runs wanted to win. At the Oval the Yorkshire fibre of Hirst and Rhodes secured the 15 runs required for victory by 1 wicket. The picturesque 'get them in singles' legend has since, and rather sadly, been discredited.

At this point in history MCC were persuaded by friend and foe alike to undertake the responsibility for English sides to Australia. They would play henceforth under their colours. P. F. Warner set off with the good wishes, if not the complete confidence, of his fellow countrymen. A good captain and splendid tactician, Warner won the first 2 matches decisively, lost the Third, won the Fourth and lost the last. Foster with 287 in the First Test broke all records, but there was plenty of batting in support with Tyldesley, Hayward and their captain. Hirst and Braund gave fine all-round strength, and Bosanquet's googlies were a great novelty.

When Darling brought his side in 1905 the English ascendancy was further heightened. The hosts won the only 2 matches to be completed, the First at Nottingham and the Fourth at Manchester. England at full strength in this season were a very powerful side; but the result of the series was in a large measure due to the astonishing performance of the Hon F. S. Jackson, the newly appointed captain. Jackson was certainly one of the brave, and never has fortune smiled more benignly on one of her chosen. He won the toss 5 more times in a row, and headed both batting and bowling averages. The batting at his command comprised most of Warner's team and was now augmented by Fry and Spooner, and he had a large array of bowlers even without calling on Barnes. In the face of this combination of material strength and unvarying *bonne chance* Darling deployed his forces courageously but, with Trumper and Hill out of form, and no more than a serviceable bowling side, he never came within sight of victory.

Neither Jackson nor Fry was available when MCC collected the next touring side in 1907. By way of compensation Barnes was ready and willing, and a young man named Hobbs was expectantly regarded. Results were, from the tourists' point of view, disappointing. Beaten in the opening match, England got home by 1 wicket in the Second at Melbourne, but lost the next 3, all but the last decisively. The margin might have been more severe had not George Gunn been in Australia for his health. Recruited for the First Test he made a magnificent hundred, and remained to become a mainstay of the batting.

That Field-Marshal of cricket captains, M. A. Noble, brought the side of 1909 and was victorious by 2 matches to 1. England, aided by some timely rain, got off to a good start at Birmingham, where Hirst and Blythe twice ran through the opposition, taking all 20 wickets between them. At Lord's, Australia returned the compliment by 9 wickets, one less than the margin of the previous match. At Leeds, Australia won by 126 runs, and the 2 remaining draws were rather to their advantage. On paper there seems, if anything, a preponderance of talent on the English side but the selectors apparently suffered from some lack of confidence and came in for some forthright criticism. A series of sweeping changes introduced 25 players for England in the 5 matches. It is also true that, whilst Noble was a great captain, MacLaren was a fine tactician, but a notoriously unfortunate leader.

The stage was now set for possibly the most dramatic series to be seen in the entire history of these fixtures. P. F. Warner was again appointed captain of one of the strongest all-round teams yet mustered to tour Australia. It was a bitter blow when he was struck down by illness, and unable to take the field in any of the Tests; Douglas took over, and chose to open the bowling in the First Test at Sydney. How far this decision contributed to his side's defeat by 146 runs is impossible to say, but an ensuing conference urged that he must give preference to Barnes. Thus one of the immortal partnerships was born, and a powerful Australian batting side was harassed unceasingly by Barnes's impeccable fast-medium swing and spin at one end, and the vicious left-handed pace of Foster at the other. A long, well-graded batting order, led by Hobbs and Rhodes, exploited or paved the way towards the situation constantly created by this superb attack, according to the sequence of events. At Melbourne in the Fourth match Hobbs and Rhodes put up 323 for the 1st wicket in answer to Australia's modest 191. Although beaten 4 to 1 Australia were a fine side, little inferior in batting to their opponents. The bowling was not of the same calibre, but Hordern had the remarkable record, on a losing side, of 32 wickets for 24 runs apiece, and impressed Warner as one of the best googly bowlers he had ever seen, a view he never had reason to alter.

In contrast to the magnificent play throughout this series the final encounter before the First World War was the most indifferent of the century so far. The 3 matches were integrated into the 'Triangular Tournament', a fine conception but, in practice, a great disappointment. For this debacle the weather was largely to blame, but there were other inherent causes of failure. Australian cricket was for the moment bedevilled by

S. F. Barnes, usually rated the finest of all bowlers, discussing, in his later years, the arts of spin with Ian Peebles, author of this article and himself a Test cricketer.

domestic disputes, so that 6 of those chosen declined the Australian Board's invitation to tour. The Australians of 1912 were capable of annihilating a South African team, also far below ordinary standards, but against England lost the only match to be completed. At the Oval they went down by 244 runs, partly in deference once again to Barnes, Hobbs and Rhodes, but chiefly in the face of Woolley who, in a low-scoring match, contributed 62 and took 10 wickets for 49 runs.

Thus ended one of the best epochs in England and Australian cricket. In the long war years many great names were lost to the international scene. In 1915 Victor Trumper died. Clem Hill had played his last match in 1911–12. Cotter was killed in action and Hordern, fairly senior in his great season, called it a day. The giants of the early days of the century were already mostly in retirement. On the English side Blythe was killed. Fry and Spooner were both approached to play against Australia in postwar years, but, without regular practice, declined. Barnes preserved his magical skill for many years, but was never again seen in a Test Match. By the end of the Triangular Tournament England and Australia had met 93 times. England had won 39 to Australia's 35, and 19 matches had been drawn.

When the 'War to end Wars' had subsided there was, as at the conclusion of its successor, an immense urge in every man to get back quickly to the things he loved. The first shots in the renewed battle of England v Australia cricket were fired in 1919 by the Australian Imperial Forces team which played the counties, the Gentlemen and other assorted sides. The team lost only 4 matches, and contained several cricketers who were destined for greater deeds. Kelleway was already established but Collins, Pellew and Oldfield were on the threshold. The most remarkable cricketer of all was J. M. Gregory, of the famous cricketing family. P. F. Warner saw him at Lord's, where he was billeted, and, with that unerring eye for the stuff of which cricketers are made, pronounced him a Test player. Here then was the nucleus of a good Australian team to come but, at that moment, no one foresaw quite how good.

Indeed English supporters were strongly optimistic when Douglas led forth his team at Sydney in December 1920. The result of this match was a rude shock, for England, in losing by 377 runs, were clearly outplayed. So they were to be for the most part in losing the next 4 Tests, the heaviest defeat ever suffered by either side. Armstrong, now a colossus, and an all-round one at that, had a fine batting side with Bardsley and Macartney in their prime. Gregory's pace was as great as it had been in England, but he was now a mature bowler. Mailey, hitherto unknown to English batsmen, amazed them with the power of his spin. Later McDonald joined the hunt, and another bowling partnership was born, its span as ephemeral and its legend as lasting as that of Barnes and Foster. Hobbs played magnificently and Douglas, tormented into grotesque attitudes by Mailey, fought with all his lion heart; but nothing could stay the tide.

When Armstrong arrived on the same boat with the defeated MCC there were high hopes that England would successfully assert herself on her native soil. The First Test at Nottingham roughly quelled any such aspirations. Gregory's pace was even more devastating than in his own country, and McDonald was seen to be the classical and ideal complement on English pitches. Lord's ran to much the same pattern, England saved from total humiliation by Woolley's 2 superb innings of over 90 apiece. The change of captaincy, when Tennyson took over from Douglas, brought no immediate change of fortune. At Leeds, Hobbs returned from absence due to injury, but was removed for an emergency operation for appendicitis and in fact played no Test innings that summer. Tennyson split a hand, but batted bravely only to see his side again losers by 219 runs. Manchester saw a fine reassertion of English batting, but a stonewall marathon by Collins saved Australia any embarrassment in what had become a 2-day match. The Oval was evenly contested, but ended in a near-farcical draw. It was apparent that England, at a low ebb, had struck one of the great Australian sides of all time.

An easy passage against a weak South African team in 1924 raised great hopes of success against Australia when Gilligan took his side there in 1924–25. Of the giants of 1921, Armstrong was retired, and McDonald had settled in England, whilst the fierce flame of Gregory's youth was on the wane. Even so Australian resilience was equal to crushing the visitors by 4 matches to 1. England by way of consolation could point to the magnificent bowling of Tate, who tried the finest Australian batsmen far beyond even the evidence of his record of 38 wickets at 23 apiece. Equally encouraging was the batting of Sutcliffe, who had joined Hobbs to make England's greatest opening partnership.

The Australian side which came to defend the Ashes under H. L. Collins in 1926 was composed of veterans, some clearly in decline, plus the new discoveries Woodfull, Ponsford and Grimmett. It had the appearance of a moderate side and, with Grimmett not yet at his greatest, a very ordinary bowling one. England had made steady progress and hopes again ran high. But there was little to argue any English advantage in the first 4 matches. The First was obliterated by the weather. Lord's,

The great Australian team of 1921. Back row: W. Bardsley, J. Ryder, H. L. Hendry, J. M. Gregory, E. R. Mayne, T. J. E. Andrews and Sydney Smith (manager); sitting: A. A. Mailey, E. A. McDonald, H. L. Collins, W. W. Armstrong (captain), C. G. Macartney, H. Carter and J. M. Taylor; on ground: C. E. Pellew and W. A. Oldfield.

Leeds and Manchester were chiefly notable for the scintillating stroke-play of Macartney, who made a hundred in each. The Oval match turned out to be one of the most notable and eventful Tests of all time. Even the preliminaries had a slightly bizarre air: the captain was deposed, Chapman succeeding Carr; Wilfred Rhodes was recalled at the age of 49 – he had played for England before his captain had been born; George Brown of Hampshire, a great success of 1921, was originally appointed to keep wicket (which he seldom did for his county), but withdrew owing to an injury to his thumb. Chapman won the toss and England, having batted most of the day for 280, did well to dispose of four Australians for 60 runs in the last session. Next day some lusty strokes from Gregory and a stout defence from Collins brought their side a lead of 22. This was discounted by Hobbs and Sutcliffe before the close of play.

A thunderstorm broke overnight and the English batsmen were faced with a very different proposition the next morning. Collins had 4 spinners to exploit the helpful conditions and his tactics have since come in for a certain amount of criticism; but what in fact dominated the situation was the superb batsmanship of Hobbs and Sutcliffe, and their shrewd judgment in deceiving the Australian captain into persevering with Richardson's off-spin which they considered to be the least of the threats with which they were faced. By lunchtime the score was 161 and the openers still in command. This virtually decided the match for, with Australia set 415 to make on the last innings, further rain had added to the difficulties of an already damaged pitch. England's victory by 289 runs won them a series for the first time since the triumph of 1912. The veteran Wilfred Rhodes took in all 6 wickets for 79, and the apprentice Larwood 6 for 116.

Chapman's star waxed greatly and 1928–29 saw his full triumph. Heading a magnificent side he despatched Australia by four matches to one. Larwood's pace decided the early course of events, but Tate was still a force, and White the ideal slow bowler for Australian conditions. Hammond's full power and majesty routed an Australian attack which lacked pace of any quality. Only in the last match did Australia, introducing a number of younger players, assert herself, but this passed without making any great impression. Australians were optimistic, saying they had a young batsman who would emulate Trumper. His name was Jackson.

When Woodfull arrived in 1930 he was received by comfortably confident opposition. At Worcester, in the first match of the tour, Bradman showed his appreciation of English turf with a double-hundred. His first 3 innings yielded 500 runs and cost him his wicket but once. Jackson, a sick man, could not get started and McCabe was having a meagre time. It was not until the series got under way that the cricket world gradually realized that this young man Bradman had inaugurated a new era and somewhat reinterpreted the old saw that 'bowlers win matches'. Never before had an individual batsman so consistently given bowlers the opportunity of winning matches by the speed and extent of his scoring. In 1930 the matches were extended to 4 days, and the pitches achieved an approach to perfection never excelled. In these conditions Bradman struck international cricket like a tornado. He was supported by an immensely powerful batting side which accompanied him at a very respectable pace.

At Nottingham, Tate and Robins bowled Australia out for 144 in the 1st innings and so made possible a win by 93 runs, a result which though welcome occasioned no great surprise. At Lord's, Bradman swept along in devastating form to score 254, and see his colleagues well on the way to the record total of 729 for 6 wickets. A courageous English 2nd innings led by a hundred from Chapman gave his side sufficient material to cause Australia a moment's dismay on a wearing wicket; but the issue was soon resolved. At Leeds, Bradman scored 309 not out on the 1st day, which meant England were thenceforth preoccupied in saving the match. At Manchester, rain

Test cricket with a smile: Maurice Tate and England's captain, Percy Chapman, going out to bat against Australia at Headingley, 1930.

prevented even a 1st innings decision, and England went to the Oval all square. For the 3rd home series in a row England made a change of captaincy. This time Chapman was the dispossessed, and Wyatt took over. This match was much in character with the run of the series. England scored over 400 against a tight Australian attack, to be overwhelmed by the crushing strength of Australia's batting. Bradman again dominated the scene with 232, and the innings reached just short of 700. Rain came to complete England's discomfort and the Ashes remained with Australia.

Thus ended nearly 60 years of cricket played between England and Australia. The record now showed that England had won 46 matches to Australia's 49, with 27 drawn. The fixture had become one of the great events in the British sporting calendar, commanding intense interest in many people not normally much concerned with cricket. From casual and somewhat haphazard beginnings the whole business of touring cricket sides had become a highly organized affair. MCC and the Australian Board of Control raised and financed the sides to play abroad, where in the early days private enterprise had reigned supreme. The home side was now selected by an officially appointed committee, so was protected from local whim and prejudice. Physically the visiting sides were very much better off, for transport and accommodation, although basically the same, were much improved. Travellers were still, of course, wholly dependent on ships for overseas travel, and trains, once arrived at their main destination. A crossing from Perth to Melbourne took several days and, owing to the differing State gauges, several changes of trains.

The game itself had seen few changes in the law, the only ones of major consequence being the alterations in the over from 4 balls to 5 in 1889, and thence to 6 in 1900. The 8-ball over was introduced in Australia in 1918. The follow-on was made optional in 1900. The techniques of batting, bowling and field placing had advanced steadily. Australian batting in the 1880s was, for the most part, fairly rough and ready, but the great improvement in their home pitches towards the end of the decade made possible the wide range of strokeplay characteristic of antipodean batsmen from then on. Bowlers were, conversely, faced with much increased problems, and they too had soon acquired the basic qualities still necessary for success on hard, fast, unyielding pitches. To do anything more than survive the Australian bowler needed one or more of the qualities of extreme accuracy, abnormal spin or exceptional pace, allied to patience and ingenuity. The greatest Australian bowlers in fact have tended to belong to one or other end of the scale. Whilst the names of Jones, Cotter, McDonald, Gregory, Lindwall and Lillee come readily to mind at one end with O'Reilly, Hordern, Mailey, Grimmett and Benaud at the other, no *great* bowler of fast-medium pace has emerged, apart perhaps from Davidson. Excepting Ironmonger, a unique type, no great orthodox slow left-hander has so far represented Australia. In passing, Spofforth and his contemporaries are omitted from the list, as they played prior to the advent of the marble-smooth pitches composed of Bulli and Merri Creek soils.

It is possible to see equally strong but differing trends in the English methods and usages over the years, also deriving from native conditions. Brought up on pitches of much greater variation the English batsman inclines, in the broadest sense, to be sounder in technique but less prolific in stroke play. Generally speaking the Australian batsman will attempt to hit his way out of trouble, where his English counterpart prefers to dig in. In a more individual sense it has always struck the writer that, where the Australian batsman always seeks to score from a defensive stroke, the English batsman makes a clear distinction between defence and attack. It is unwise to cite genius in seeking to support a generalization of this nature, but it is to some extent evident when contrasting Hobbs with Bradman. Perhaps a clearer example would be the superb but opposing methods of Ponsford and Sutcliffe. English bowling, born of pitches seldom approaching the pace of Sydney or Melbourne, has, similarly developed certain characteristics. Thus England can challenge Australian pace with Larwood, Richardson, Lockwood and others, but has produced no leg-spin to compare with the aforementioned Australian dynasty. On the other hand, during the period with which we are concerned, England produced several slow left-armers of the highest calibre in Rhodes, Blythe and White. Also in the middle category as regards speed, where Australia is almost unrepresented, Barnes and Tate reigned supreme. Foster, from contemporary accounts, comes fairly near this bracket being, like Tate, remarkable for his pace *from* the pitch.

The benefits of climate, baseball training and a lighter domestic programme were all reflected in the superiority of the Australian fielding, in every instance within the writer's experience. It is not unreasonable to conclude that this superiority prevailed over the whole period, as it has in every series since – until, under the influence of limited-over cricket, England has become second to none. How agreeable to end this review on such a satisfactory note.

1932–1979

RAY ROBINSON

In today's world of telecasts and radio via satellite, cricket followers can scarcely realize how misunderstandings and recriminations came close to breaking off MCC's 1932–33 series in Australia, as summarized under the heading BODY-LINE (*qv*). The England captain, D. R. Jardine, devised a combination of fast bowling and field-placing to curb a high-scoring band of batsmen, notably Bradman. The insatiable Australian's average after 9 Tests against England exceeded 100. How explosive a mixture Jardine compounded can be judged from happenings today, when skilful batsmen, some wearing helmets or skullcaps, cannot hide aversion to less-frequent bouncers, though only 2 catch-awaiting fieldsmen behind square dot the leg-side acres.

No doubt anxiety about the high risk of injury ahead contributed to Bradman's run-down state, which caused a doctor to advise him to rest a fortnight instead of playing in the First Test at Sydney. Larwood and Voce there set the pattern for the series by capturing 4 wickets for 87 before Australia's boldest hooker, McCabe, 187 not out, and Victor Richardson, 49, made the only substantial partnership, 129, in Australia's 360. Larwood was in the middle of a burst in which he took 3 wickets for 7 runs when McCabe faced him to begin what many survivors of the occasion regard as the greatest innings played in Australia. It required the highest blend of courage and daring for more than 4 hours. At an average of 47 an hour the graceful right-hander scored 187 while 7 partners made fewer than 90. Most of his 25 fours were hooks between midwicket and square-leg.

Sutcliffe began his last series in Australia by batting $7\frac{1}{4}$ hours for 194. Fourth out at 423, he shared hundred stands with his first 3 partners, Wyatt, 38, Hammond, 112, and the Nawab of Pataudi, 102. Beginning the 2nd innings 164 behind, Australia never recovered from seeing Larwood bowl the captain, Woodfull, for 0 and Voce skittle Ponsford for 2. Before he bowled Kippax, 19, with a sudden straight ball Larwood had 8 leg-side fieldsmen. Larwood, with 5 wickets in each innings, and Voce captured 16 out of 20 wickets. England's overwhelming victory by 10 wickets after losing the toss rattled Australia's selectors perhaps more than the white-faced batsmen. The line-up was regrouped by promoting the determined Fingleton to go in first with Woodfull and adding a dogged left-hander, O'Brien, in the hope that these 3 defensive players would wear the sharpest edge off Larwood and Voce's hostility before they could get at the recovered Bradman, lowered a place to No. 4.

Melbourne's wicket for Bradman's first Test encounter with the new tactics looked different from any strip English players had seen there. England's bowlers no sooner began operations than it became evident that the dead surface was drawing the fangs of the fast men. This time there were 4 of them, as Bowes replaced Verity, leaving no slow bowler. Two were out for 67 when 64,000 cheered Bradman to the wicket, only to be shocked when Bowes skittled him first ball with a bouncer. A hasty step outside the off-stump and a flurried hook dragged the ball down into the stumps. After nearly 4 hours for 83, Fingleton came out with only 3 fours but a dozen bruises on ribs, thigh, arms and hands. Expectations that England would go far ahead of Australia's 228 were upset when Wall and Grimmett helped O'Reilly bowl their side to a lead of 59, only to see their batsmen all out again for 191. With nerves under intense pressure before a New Year crowd of 68,000, Bradman re-established himself with 103 not out in the last 3 hours of the innings. This hundred, his most courageous in Tests, was to be the last made against English bowling in the series. O'Reilly and Ironmonger's turn made 251 a target beyond England. The losing margin was 111 when O'Reilly got his tenth victim in the match.

Fielding as England's first 4 wickets tumbled for 30 in the Third Test at Adelaide, Australia's batsmen were grateful that Jardine had won the toss for the first time, as the Adelaide wicket was abnormally lively. Resistance by Wyatt, 78, the left-handers Leyland, 83, and Paynter, 77, enabled a recovery to 341. Incidents which caused the simmering dispute to boil over began on the 2nd day of a match which *Wisden* calls probably the most unpleasant ever played, adding 'the whole atmosphere was a disgrace to cricket'. Larwood was bowling to his normal new-ball slip field when the last ball of his 2nd over struck Woodfull over the heart. The captain took minutes to recover. Before he faced Larwood's next ball Jardine waved fielders across to pack a leg-trap with men ready for a catch from a bat defending the body from a succession of rearing balls. The sight turned the noisy crowd into a raving mob, booing Larwood's every step as he ran to bowl. Amid the din the coarsest epithets were shouted at Jardine and Larwood. How envenoming Jardine's tactics were could be judged from a cricketer of Woodfull's character responding to a sympathizing MCC manager with reproachful words about two teams being out there and only one playing cricket. This was the second severe blow over the heart suffered by Woodfull against Larwood, the first having been in the match between an Australian XI and MCC.

Uproar broke out again on the 3rd day when the Adelaide crowd saw Oldfield's head being bathed as he lay on the ground after his attempt to hook edged a Larwood bumper against his right temple. Oldfield took no further part as batsman or wicket-keeper in that Test or the next. Sitting beside the scorers, one of England's reserves, Tate, said to W. H. Ferguson; 'I'm getting out of here. Somebody is going to get seriously hurt and that will start a riot.' Before Australia went down by 338 runs, clamorous controversy prevented proper recognition of Ponsford's skilful 85, in which he took 10 blows from Larwood on his back and side; Allen's fine bowling in both innings; Bradman's hectic 66 and stoical resistance by Woodfull, who hung on 4 hours in carrying his bat for 73 not out of Australia's 193.

Two noughts in Adelaide had brought the selectors' axe down on Fingleton, so in Brisbane in the Fourth Test Woodfull had his 3rd opening partner, Richardson. As the 1st wicket's dismal sequence so far had been 22, 2, 29, 1, 1 and 3, the resolute pair astonished their countrymen by scoring 133, profiting by the wicket's ease. In exhausting heat, the tiring Larwood bowled 20 overs without a wicket, and by evening Bradman reached 71 of Australia's 251 for three. With their two greatest batsmen, Bradman and Ponsford, together for the second hot day, I thought this the most favourable opportunity Australia ever had to overcome Larwood and thereby blunt the lance which was winning the Ashes for England. Instead, Bradman attempted a cross-bat cover-slash and had his leg stump flattened. After ducking 5 bouncers Ponsford was bowled behind his legs by a short ball that kept low. So in 4 stirring overs Larwood reimposed his mastery in a way that virtually decided the series. Next to Larwood's right arm, England owed most to Paynter's grit. When tonsilitis put the little Lancashire left-hander in hospital with a temperature of 102 it looked as if England would have to bat one short. Despite Sutcliffe's 114 opening partnership with Jardine, England were 124 behind with 6 out when the crowd stared unbelievingly at Paynter trudging in. On Jardine's orders, Voce had taken clothes to hospital and smuggled Eddie out. Pick-me-ups of egg and brandy at the wicket helped Paynter hang on for 90 minutes. Reappearing from hospital next morning he went on to score 83. In the 2nd innings Paynter finished off the match with a 6, to bring England victory by 6 wickets. Thus at Brisbane the Ashes were lost and won.

In Sydney, Larwood opened what was to be his last Test by taking the first 3 wickets for 14. L. S. Darling, a dashing left-hander playing his 2nd Test, top-scored with 85. Until this match, England's bowlers had been supported by good catching, but 14 turfed chances enabled Australia to reach their highest total of the series, 435. For the 4th time, England headed Australia's 1st innings, this time by 19. With 101 full of grand driving, Hammond made himself the only man on either side to score 2 hundreds in the rubber. Larwood, piqued by being sent in as night-watchman, made his highest Test score next day, 98. By contrast with the hoots and abuse hurled at his short-pitched bowling, Larwood's batting was applauded. Ready to acclaim his hundred, the crowd seemed sorry as 2¼ hours of hitting ended with an on-drive lodging in Ironmonger's hands. In his last encounter with Larwood, Bradman's audacious unorthodoxy stirred the crowd to rapturous shouts. Often, outside the leg-stump, he played breathtaking slashes through the little guarded off-side. Strokes of genius they were, the more piquant for being fraught with hazard. He was attempting one when he was hit for the only time in the series – a blow on the left arm. Larwood's left foot was troubling him (an X-ray later showed a broken bone) but he continued to bowl in short spells until he saw Bradman, 71, hit over an attempted drive against Verity at the other end. Following his famous foe from the field, the great bowler limped out of Test cricket. England's 4–1 rubber triumph was sealed by a 6 by Hammond which bounced into a bar, finishing the series in an atmosphere more cordial than had been known on the field.

Bradman could justly claim that he scored most runs, 396, for Australia (11 more than McCabe) and passed 50 four times in four Tests. To take this as evidence that he withstood Body-line best would be to disregard that three-fifths of his total came from bowlers who did not resort to it. More than 70% of his runs were made off bowlers other than Larwood. No great perception was needed to see who came from this stormy season happiest, Bradman or Jardine, Larwood and Company. They were fully satisfied at getting rid of him quickly, and almost halving his average, by harrying him into methods that dismayed his fellow-batsmen – some of whom (notably Woodfull) faced more balls from the terrorizing trio. Hobbs, who had called their bowling 'terrifying', made this compassionate comment: 'Bradman was not going to be hit . . . He has my sympathy.' With his legion on the leg-side, Larwood captured 33 wickets in 5 Tests. He reaped his wickets twice as quickly for less than half the cost of his 31 wickets in his previous 10 Tests against Australia. Together, Larwood, Voce and Bowes shared 49 victims. As Allen – refusing to use a packed leg-field – took 21 wickets, 4 fast bowlers captured 71 wickets out of the 99 which fell – an astonishing proportion then, though it would not be so today.

Qualms persisted among Australia's batsmen as they began the 1934 tour of Britain feeling uncertain whether county captains would eschew the tactics they wanted outlawed. Doubtless this anxiety delayed Bradman's full recovery from a run-down condition. In the first half of the tour he repeatedly played venturesome strokes at reputable bowling, as if to show England's bowlers they could hope to get him out without resorting to extreme tactics. Repercussions from the Body-line tour persuaded Jardine to write rather than to play, while Larwood declared that he would refuse to play against the Australians because political influence had been used to make the selection of England's team suitable to them.

When a broken thumb prevented Wyatt's becoming captain, Worcestershire's skipper, Walters, in his first Test against Australia, was called on to lead England at Trent Bridge. Woodfull's winning of the toss helped Australia to victory without benefit of a Bradman hundred. The choice of Farnes to take Larwood's place as spearhead paid instantly as the 6 foot 4 inch Essex fast bowler's 10 wickets in his first Test included only one tail-ender. He had Australia's two most successful batsmen caught in each innings – McCabe for a quick-time 65 and 88 and Chipperfield for 99 and 4.

O'Reilly and Grimmett, whose like has not since been seen, snared all England's wickets except one in this Test. They wove the first loops of a net that was to enmesh 53 out of 71 wickets in the series. Deceptive flight and pace changes, as well as varied spin, so played on the nerves of England's batsmen that Woodfull seemed reluctant to take them off while their fingers retained the power to drag off their sweaters and grip the ball. The pair spun along 4,381 balls out of 6,721 in the rubber, leaving the lightest duty I have ever seen fall to a Test team's supporting bowlers. Mostly they worked tandem. O'Reilly, 6 foot 3½ and hefty enough to carry his gnome-like accomplice under one arm, performed his hobgoblin trickery with the wind at his broad back. Over-cautiously, Woodfull at Trent Bridge waited until 379 ahead before closing, leaving the pair 4¾ hours in which to bowl out the enemy on a dusty pitch.

They managed it, but England were only 10 minutes from drawing the match when O'Reilly trapped the last man lbw at 141, to bring victory by 238.

As a guard shielded his right thumb, Wyatt spun the coin with his left at Lord's, where toss and weather enabled England to square the series with victory by an innings. Walters's attractive 82 was the closest his long-swinging bat brought him to a hundred in a rubber in which he passed 40 seven times. In a 6th-wicket of 129 with Ames (120), Leyland made 109, the first of his three in the rubber. The sturdy Yorkshireman's unshakeable temperament and obdurate left-handedness enabled him to counter O'Reilly with an effectiveness no right-hander could rival. Replying to 440, the Australians were relieved that Farnes could not bowl his fastest because of a strained heel tendon. Their Saturday night total was 192 for 2. Weekend rain then so drastically changed the pitch that they lost 18 wickets in a day, following on 156 behind and being bundled out for 118. Fourteen of the 18 wickets fell to Verity, making his match total 15. With the ball denting the softened pitch, the tall left-hander successfully strove to make the Australians play at every ball. Their uneasiness was heightened by Hammond's closeness at gully to snap up catches from the bat's shoulder. One such catch removed Woodfull, 43, fifth out in the follow-on. A cross-hit by Bradman, 13, was skied so near the wicket that Ames's gloves waited for the catch.

By contrast, on the Manchester wicket for the Third Test of 1934 only 20 wickets fell in the four days while bowlers were paying out 1,307 runs. Though England made 627 for 9 in their 1st innings, Australia saved the follow-on with their last pair together, and thus the match.

Though Wyatt won the toss at Leeds, Australia's spinners found enough in the pitch to put England out for 200. So far, the highest of Bradman's 5 innings had been 36, but much of his old confidence and concentration returned as he made England pay for going into the Test with only one fast bowler, Bowes. In 5 hours Bradman and Ponsford put on 388 for the 4th wicket before the Victorian, 181, trod on his wicket after pulling Verity to the fence. Though 184 of Bradman's 304, his 2nd triple-hundred at Leeds, came in boundaries, all but 7 hours' batting so tired him that fellow-players undressed him and lifted him to the massage table. Curtailing the last day by 5½ hours, rain denied the Australians a chance to force victory.

Next time Bradman joined Ponsford in the middle they excelled their Leeds 388 with 451 for the 2nd wicket at the rate of 86 an hour on a plumb Oval pitch. Each partner in this Test record fell to a bouncer. Hooking at Bowes, Bradman was caught for 244. Ponsford stayed 7½ hours for 266 until, with his post-Body-line habit of turning his back on bumpers, his bat brushed his bails off. Judged by fellow-players to be their country's 2 greatest batsmen of the past half-century, the pair enabled Australia to total 701 in 10 hours. Never was the need to hold chances and turn half-chances into catches emphasized more than in their mammoth stands. At Leeds, Bradman was let off in the 50s and 70s and at the Oval, Ponsford's 200 contained 5 chances – difficult, but the kind that a Harvey or a Lock often brought off. The only consolation for England's bowlers in their Oval ordeal was that it was Ponsford's last Test, so they would not again have to tackle a pair with such a boundless appetite for runs and the strokes and concentration to appease it. Remembering no doubt many things, Woodfull despite a lead of 380 on 1st innings declined to enforce the follow-on, Australia winning by the grotesque margin of 562 runs.

Woodfull is the only Australian captain who has twice regained the Ashes in England – each time on his birthday, 22 August. Essentially practical, he possessed in rare degree the faculty of winning his team's loyal support. Before becoming headmaster of Melbourne High School he led Australia 25 times.

Bradman began his captaincy in Australia in 1936–37 by losing his first toss to 'Gubby' Allen in a series wherein only one Test was rainless. On wickets unsheltered except for foothold covers one of the most exciting rubbers ever played was watched by the largest crowds (960,794) ever to attend a series in any country. Allen had the dual task of grappling with tour captaincy's trials and handling the touchy situation left by the Body-line row. Though it was impossible to erase sour memories, his frank and sportsmanlike air restored good feeling. The happier atmosphere solved the problem of barracking by bringing it back to normal proportions – noisy but no longer savagely abusive. Seven of Allen's 17 players had long stretches on the casualty list. A wrist injury kept Wyatt out of 3 Tests and a finger broken at fielding practice prevented Robins producing his best. In the First Test at Brisbane the fastest bowler since Larwood, McCormick, made England 20 for 3 before lumbago sent him off after his only 8 overs in the match. Bruised on the shoulder before he scored, Leyland made 126, his 4th hundred in 5 consecutive Tests against Australia. With 100 as Australia's opening batsman, Fingleton made himself the 1st player to score 4 hundreds in consecutive Test innings, having begun the sequence in South Africa. In his greatest triumph against Australia, Voce captured 6 for 41 on an easy pitch. Struggling to combat the brawny left-hander's sharp in-swing, the Australians fell easier victims to length balls he ran away. Their troubles, as they dropped 124 behind, were similar to those which Davidson created for batsmen a quarter of a century later. Chosen to profit by English batsmen's inadequate footwork against spin, the newest of 3 leg-spinners, Ward, replied with 6 wickets in the 2nd innings. Australia's concern at being left 381 to get was shown by 6 appeals against dull light in 12 balls, to which they lost the 1 wicket for 3 runs. They could have saved their breath because rain in the night made the pitch so sticky that Allen and Voce bundled them out in a dozen overs for 58.

Hammond's 231 not out in Sydney, his 3rd Test double-hundred in Australia, took him nearly 8 hours, largely because of defensive bowling around his leg-stump. With 426 up for 6 wickets when rain fell, Allen wisely lost no time in getting the Australians on to a soft pitch. Making the ball jump, Voce took 3 wickets in 4 balls, including Bradman's for his second consecutive 0. A total of 80 – swollen by O'Reilly's left-hand hitting of three sixes in 37 not out – left England 346 ahead. By ordering a follow-on, Allen provoked intense debate, because the wicket rolled out well, but his decision was in the best tradition of what I call gainful generalship. All his bowlers were fresh (only Voce had bowled even 8 overs) and, but for a grassed chance from Bradman at 22, England's victory by an innings would have come a lot sooner.

Two up, with 3 to go, England lost the toss in Melbourne but sent back 6 Australians for 181 before rain ended the first day. A saturated pitch turned the match topsy-turvy, arousing almost delirious excitement among crowds that totalled 350,534 and broke all records. With the ball rearing, 9 were out for 200 when Bradman's closure put England on the most treacherous gluepot wicket I have seen. Though length balls leapt at their chests, or sometimes skidded past their shins, Hammond and Leyland astonished us with a 3rd wicket stand of 42. The pair showed that pluck and skill could make sticky-wicket batting a science on turf which most batsmen would write off as unplayable. Though struck as high as the throat, Hammond made a wondrous 32, lasting 81 minutes where luck was needed to survive a single over. Failing light spared the Australians having to bat more than a few minutes of the day's last half-hour and only one of the tail-enders who opened the innings got out. Sunday intervened, enabling the wicket to recover. A Monday crowd of 87,798 saw the beginning of a Bradman-Fingleton partnership, 346, which still stands as a 6th-wicket record for any country. Fingleton's 136, his 5th Test hundred, took 6½ hours, with an average of a boundary an hour. Batting an hour longer, Bradman hit 22 4s in 270. This

This classic action photograph shows G. O. Allen bowling to Stan McCabe in the Adelaide Test of 1936–37.

was the highest score by an Australian captain, until exceeded by Simpson at Old Trafford in 1964. England were left hopelessly behind (688) and there was no disgrace in the 4th innings of 323, containing the best strokeplay Leyland ever showed an Australian crowd.

With Farnes adding sting to the attack, England again took the early honours in the Fourth Test by dismissing Australia for 288 on one of Adelaide's most comfortable wickets. Fleetwood-Smith, after a finger injury, and McCormick, recovered from lumbago, had joined O'Reilly, bringing Australia's bowling to a higher level. The googly left-hander prevented England from gaining a bigger lead than 42 by trapping Barnett lbw for 129 and having Leyland caught at slip for less than half his customary century. Verity, as stop-gap, joined Barnett in England's best opening stands of the series, 53 and 45.

Another Bradman double-hundred, 212, again lifted Australia into a winning position but this time patience was more evident than power. As if remembering the cramping of Hammond in Sydney, Allen set fields so deep that only 14 of Don's strokes in 7¼ hours got through to the boundaries. For the only time in his 12 Test double-hundreds he was kept below 30 runs an hour. A new all-rounder, Ross Gregory, helped in a 135 stand before being run out for 50. Needing 392 in the last innings, England could not cope with Fleetwood-Smith's perplexing wrist-spin, unequalled by any bowler, since the First World War. His 6 wickets, making 10 in the match, included Hammond, 39, with a perfect ball that drifted out to create a gap, then turned back through it. The problems his matchless spin presented were heightened by the then new law allowing batsmen to be lbw to balls turning in from the off.

With the Ashes still in dispute Australia in the final Test won the toss and assisted by several fielding lapses piled up 604. Spared at 11, McCabe helped add 249 with Bradman in a 3rd-wicket stand at 92 an hour. For the 3rd consecutive time Bradman played a match-winning part with 169 in 3½ hours. Badcock, 118, added 161 with Gregory to take Australia to 507 before the 5th wicket fell. Hardstaff made the best score, 83, for England, who had to follow on 365 behind. Though winning his 3rd consecutive toss was a matter of luck, Bradman owed nothing to fortune in his 270, 212 and 169 which did so much to make Australia the 1st team in Test history to recover from 2-down to win a rubber. Record crowds at this series showed that Australian customers preferred the dramatic changes always possible on wickets open to the weather. Such excitements cannot be repeated since MCC yielded in 1954 to the Australian Board's pressure for full covering.

English batsmen were entitled to feel relief in 1938 when Bradman and his 2 co-selectors broke up the O'Reilly-Grimmett combination which had proved decisive on English wickets 4 years earlier. Though one of the greatest solo performers – he was chief match-winner at Leeds in Australia's only win – O'Reilly plainly missed his artful companion as he toiled on and on. Fleetwood-Smith's support was fitful and only at Lord's did McCormick do himself justice after the unsettling experience of being no-balled 35 times in 20 overs in his opening match at Worcester. Both England's opening batsmen, Barnett and the budding Hutton, led off with hundreds after Hammond, now an amateur, gained first use of a Trent Bridge wicket crammed with runs. When the strokeful Barnett drove and cut his way to 99 out of 169 the Australians fielded like terriers to prevent his becoming the first Englishman to make a hundred before lunch, as Trumper, Macartney and Bradman had done. The 3rd century-maker of the innings, Paynter, whom Compton, 102, joined in a 5th-wicket stand of 206, amassed 216 not out at the rate of 40 an hour before Hammond closed at 658 for 8.

More than 500 behind with half their wickets down, the Australians seemed doomed until McCabe rallied them with 232. His captain classed this as the greatest innings ever played. In less then 4 hours 232 runs streamed from McCabe's bat while 7 partners fell for 58. Not one slogging stroke detracted from the artistry of his batting. Though it did not avert a follow-on, McCabe's magnificence brought the task of avoiding defeat within the Australian's compass. In the 2nd innings Brown stayed 5½ hours for 133 and Bradman, defending all the last day, 6 hours for 144 not out.

After McCormick's speed had rushed Hutton, Barnett and Edrich out for 31 at Lord's, Hammond took over the role of rescuer, making light of a bruising blow on the elbow and a strained leg muscle. In support of his superb drives – one split Chipperfield's finger – England's champion used a wider range of strokes than in his three double centuries in Australia. His 240 out of 494 was the highest score by an England captain until May's 285 not out against West Indies 19 years later. For half Hammond's 6-hour innings his partner was Paynter, 99, in a stand of 222.

Opening for Australia, Brown carried his bat, one of the straightest, for 206 through an innings of 422 in 6½ hours. None of the batsmen except Hassett (56) stayed with him long and it took O'Reilly (42) in an 8th-wicket stand to avert a follow-on. Hammond's closure at 242 for 8 left Australia 314 behind with 165 minutes to bat – long enough for Bradman to make 102 not out in the 2nd draw of the series.

The Test listed for Old Trafford (like that of 1890) was abandoned without a ball bowled. The pitch for the Fourth Test at Headingley responded enough to bowlers to produce the most exciting match of the series. Only the world's two finest batsmen mastered the bowling – Hammond for 76 of

Walter Hammond, leading England for the 1st time, goes out to toss with Don Bradman in 1938 at Trent Bridge.

England v Australia at the Oval, 1938. Hutton sweeps O'Reilly early in his great innings of 364.

England's 223 and Bradman for 103 of Australia's 242 in poor light, the dimmest in which Australia ever batted. Their captain instructed them not to appeal, because he estimated they would make more runs in the gloom on a dry wicket than they would after the threatening rain fell. Wicket-keeper B. A. Barnett, a night-watchman who hardly noticed the dawn, was the only other player to pass 50 in the innings. The biggest partnership of the match, 60 by C. J. Barnett and Edrich, brought England well back into the game but the middle batsmen found O'Reilly almost unplayable. His dismissal of Hardstaff and Hammond with successive balls began a rattle of 8 wickets for 50. Getting 105 to win was a struggle which Bradman could not bear to watch as Hassett boldly lifted the ball over fieldsmen. But Australia got home by 5 wickets.

Hutton, recovered from an injury which kept him out at Headingley, signalled his return at the Oval with an unprecedented Test innings of 364. This stands as a monument to his unsurpassed concentration and to his orderly correctness of style. His innings formed the spinal column of England's colossal total, 903 for 7 (declared), Test history's only instance of a side exceeding 850. Australia's miscasting of 2 medium-pace all-rounders as an opening attack – Bradman seemed to gamble on winning the toss for the 1st time in England – gave Hutton an opening to make the most of a pitch that bowlers found heart-breaking. Classic drives and precise cuts brought most of Hutton's 35 boundary hits in his patient progression. If Hutton's mien seemed thoughtful, he had the bowlers thinking harder, but to no avail. With stamina belying his pale face and slim figure, he carried on for 13 hours and nearly 20 minutes – vigil outlasted only by Hanif Mohammed's 16 hours 39 minutes in saving Pakistan in Barbados in 1958. Hutton's 364 stood almost 20 years as the world Test record until Sobers' 365 not out in 10 hours 8 minutes against Pakistan at Kingston. Sir Leonard is still the only man in Test cricket who has stayed in while 770 runs have been scored. It was calculated that he ran 6 miles and made 211 scoring shots with play so impregnable that he allowed only 1 chance off 836 balls: at 40 Fleetwood-Smith might have had him stumped.

All reality left the match when, with England 887 for 7, Bradman when bowling chipped an ankle bone in a pothole. Fieldsmen carried him off (Fingleton was already disabled) and he took no further part in the tour. Two men short when Hammond closed at 903 for 7, the Australians batted under instructions that they must avoid having to bowl again in the timeless Test. O'Reilly had lost a stone weight in 85 overs, Fleetwood-Smith was jaded after 87 overs and the team still had 6 matches to play to complete the tour. Out for 201 and 123, they lost the Test by the widest-ever margin, an innings and 579.

The Australian Board were eager for an MCC tour as soon as possible after the war ended and prevailed on MCC to send a team a year sooner than was intended. Gratefully, larger crowds attended in 1946–47 than on any tour since. They enjoyed much eventful cricket, though England, with a somewhat makeshift attack, did no better than draw 2 of the 5 Tests played under a time-limit of 6 5-hour days. Hammond, worried by fibrositis and inability to succeed in Tests, was not a happy touring captain and caused surprise by often travelling by road separately from his team. The series brought England's first collision with Lindwall and Miller, an outstanding pair of fast bowlers heading a ready-made attack containing almost every known style of bowling – so strong that such spinners as Tribe and Dooland were not given permanent places. Backed by fine fielding, and Tallon's brilliant 'keeping, the bowlers out-gunned England. Costly chances were dropped off Wright and Bedser and worse leather-chasing was averted only by 2 of the batsmen, Yardley and Edrich, surpassing themselves as bowlers. Though eager to play, Bradman looked far from well when he won the toss in the First Test – and thereby the match. His movements were perceptibly slower – a legacy from the fibrositis which had caused his discharge from the Army in 1941. Yet the 38-year-old captain steeled himself to play a comeback innings of 187 in $5\frac{1}{4}$ hours, a triumph of willpower.

After an hour's struggle for 28 he chopped with diagonal bat at an off-side yorker from Voce and the ball flew chest-high into Ikin's hands at 2nd slip. The fieldsmen stared when Bradman stood his ground, then appealed for a catch. In believing that the bat jammed the ball down on to the ground before it rose, Don was in a minority of the nearest witnesses on the field but that minority included the umpire. There was a belief in the English camp that, had Bradman gone for 28, it could have persuaded him that he was unwise to try to continue in Test cricket. He added 159 and his 3rd-wicket stand with Hassett (128) put on 276. McCool, dropped at 1, got within 5 of a hundred in his first Test innings before Australia wound up on the 3rd day with 645.

Thunderstorms on the 3rd and 4th evenings doomed England to bat twice on sticky wickets where the ball cut such capers that much courage and skill were needed to make totals of 141 and 172. The second storm, the fiercest I have seen in Australia, tore sheets of iron from the grandstand roof. Miller's experience with the Australian Services in England enabled him to capture 9 wickets with fast-medium break-backs. Nine more fell to the left-handed Toshack who, having difficulty in amending his habitual dry-wicket length and direction, was taken to the wicket before the last day by his captain, who pointed out the exact spot where the ball should be pitched.

Though chicken-pox spared their having to face Lindwall in the Second Test, few batsmen in England's 255 produced the footwork needed to counter McCool's turn from leg and I. W. Johnson's off-breaks. Crease-bound defence to balls pitched well up suited Johnson's tossed flight so admirably that he took 6 for 42 in his first bowl in a Test. On a stormy Saturday, Barnes and Johnson angered the crowd by making 8 appeals against the light in 11 minutes. No sign of goodwill anywhere at this stage of the goodwill tour! This stalling saved Australia losing more than Morris's wicket, and the granting of the last appeal enabled Bradman to rest a strained leg for Monday. The pitch rolled out well enough to allow the captain (batting No. 6 with his leg strapped) to join Barnes in a stand of 405, still the highest in any Test played Down Under. Accelerating to a run a minute before falling lbw, Bradman, 234 in $6\frac{3}{4}$ hours, trudged off and remarked: 'There's runs out there, if only a man had legs.' Barnes, who had legs as well as a larynx, made exactly the same score but they took him $10\frac{3}{4}$ hours, the longest stay by any batsman on an Australian wicket. Bradman's closure at 659 for 8, a record against England in Australia, left Hammond's men 404 to get to avoid an innings loss. The indomitable Edrich, the only Englishman in the match to cope confidently with spin bowling, fought it out for more than five hours for 119 of the total 371.

In Melbourne, despite 37-year-old Voce's breakdown with a leg strain, 6 wickets went for 192 before McCool (104 not out) played the finest innings of his career. England had hopes of heading Australia's 365 until Edrich was adjudged lbw for 89 when the umpire failed to notice a snick. Australia's lead of 14 looked less narrow when Morris made 155 – 1st of 3 consecutive Test centuries by the quick-footed left-hand opener. Lindwall's power-driven hundred and Tallon's stroke-rich 92 clapped on 154 at the scorching rate of 106 an hour before Wright ended a stand he had been unlucky not to break earlier. England, 550 behind, saw through the last 7 hours, thanks largely to Washbrook's 112 and to Yardley, who had a double of 61, 53 not out and 5 wickets.

In a heat-wave that touched 105 degrees, on an Adelaide wicket to suit, a batsman of each side made a hundred in each innings of a drawn match – Compton, 147 and 103 not out and Morris, 122 and 124 not out. By bowling the last 3 men in 4 balls, Lindwall ended England's 1st innings at 460. Bedser skittled Bradman, 0, with what the great batsman acknowledged to be the finest ball ever to take his wicket. Yet Australia went 27 ahead, thanks to Miller's glorious 141 not out with batting of a quality he was unable to repeat as he was given more and more bowling. England did not make the most of Hutton and Washbrook's feat of hundred opening stands in each innings. While his longest 2nd innings partner, Evans, stayed 97 minutes before his first run, Compton often declined singles to keep the strike. In his determination to counter such tactics Bradman appeared to think more of spreading fieldsmen around the outfield than pressing to get more wickets; some fielders trotted outward alongside rolling balls from Compton's bat. In an atmosphere hardly chummy, Hammond's riposte on the last day was to close England's innings one ball after lunch. Needing 314 to win, Australia would have had to score 7 runs an over, and never threatened to do so.

Taking over in the last Test at Sydney from an injured Hammond, Yardley began his captaincy by winning the toss. This helped England to lead for the first time. Despite his shortened left arm, a bout of tonsilitis and Lindwall at his most fearsome, Hutton batted all day with Yorkshire tenacity for 122 not out, only to be lost to England for the rest of the match when he was admitted to hospital. Lindwall bowled with pace enough to knock Compton's bat from his grasp. Most of his 7 victims were beaten neck and crop on a good wicket. Hostility: a little too much; I thought his and Miller's bumpers got close to the borderline of intimidation. Wright answered by taking 7 wickets with the most penetrative leg-spin bowling Australians have faced from an Englishman for more than half a century. So difficult were Wright's rising leg-breaks and 'wrong-'uns' that only one right-hander (Barnes, 71) passed 30 in Australia's 253. Without Hutton, England left Australia 214 to get on the last afternoon, when Bedser's leg-cutters were, if anything, more troublesome and equally as unlucky as the leg turn of Wright. When Bradman, 2, edged a lifting leg-break chest-high, Edrich, of all people, dropped the most important slip catch of his career. With Hassett's help, Bradman (63) added 98 but the Australians were not out of danger. The captain sent word to Miller that the only hope was to hit out. No message ever had a readier recipient and the mettlesome all-rounder's drives helped win the match by 5 wickets 6 minutes before time.

The bowling Bradman brought to England in the almost invincible 1948 side was strong enough, in all conscience – probably the most formidable force to land in the British Isles since 1066. Containing the world's 2 fastest bowlers, Lindwall and Miller, and the versatile left-hander W. A. Johnston – backed by 3 kinds of spin – this attack became more incisive through a rule change that allowed new balls after 55 six-ball overs instead of after 200 runs. On an average, Australia called for a new ball before 130 runs were on the board. Twice it was taken before 90. Bradman could not resist the temptation to choke England's scoring with defensive field-placings while awaiting the next new ball. There was no fast bowler in postwar Britain. England's mainstay, Bedser, and his changing supporters were up against run-making resources so great that one of Australia's finest English-wicket batsmen, Brown, was squeezed out of 3 Tests. The Australians are the only touring side to attract 520,000 to 5 Tests in Britain. Showers that caused Lindwall to pull a groin muscle in the First Test kept livening the Trent Bridge wicket for Miller and Johnston to bustle England out in 4 hours for 165. Australia went ahead with only 3 out. In desperation, Yardley resorted to leg-theory. Annoyance showed in the way Bradman sometimes leaned on his bat, with legs crossed, ignoring the leg-side balls. His rate for his 18th Test hundred against England was 28 an hour.

For a new ball next morning Bedser set a 3-man leg-trap, with Hutton slightly backward of square. Trying to force an in-swinger from outside his off-stump through this field Bradman did not middle the swerving ball. It flew to Hutton for a chest-high catch that set a pattern for the season's encounters with the Australian captain. As recipient of several of Young's 11 consecutive maiden overs, Hassett took nearly 6 hours for 137. Though England were 344 behind, Hutton batted so confidently that he scored 14 off one over from Miller. Nettled, the fast bowler hurled down 4 short balls in his next over, one of which struck the ducking batsman's left shoulder – a signal for a storm of hooting. Before the next day's play a Notts official admonished the crowd and asked for more rational behaviour. In the worst light I have ever seen play continue, Compton saved England from an innings defeat with one of the most courageous and resourceful hundreds in Test history. For his 184, his timely highest against Australia, he had to make 10 starts in $6\frac{1}{2}$ hours, spread over 3 interrupted days. Hutton's catching of Bradman, 0, gave Bedser the captain's wicket twice in 16 deliveries with new balls. Rainclouds threatened as Hassett and Barnes hastily hit off 98 runs to win.

Bradman's only toss win in 9 Tests in England brought first use of a Lord's greentop on which Morris gave a taste of his quality with 105 of Australia's 350. For the 3rd time running, Hutton caught Bradman off Bedser's in-dipper (in the 2nd innings it was to be a slip catch off a leg-cutter). Lindwall had most to do with England's dismissal for 215. Johnston shared the new ball with him only after the captain had tried to give it to Miller, who had previously reported a ricked side after his exertions at Trent Bridge. Barnes was the first Australian since

The Australians of 1948, the only ones to return undefeated in any match. Back row: W. H. Ferguson (scorer), D. Tallon, D. T. Ring, I. W. Johnson, R. R. Lindwall, R. A. Saggers, W. A. Johnston, S. J. E. Loxton, K. R. Miller, E. R. H. Toshack and K. O. E. Johnson (manager); sitting: A. R. Morris, C. L. McCool, A. L. Hassett, D. G. Bradman, W. A. Brown, S. G. Barnes, R. A. Hamence and R. N. Harvey.

1905 to have his wife watching him make a hundred in England. With a hopeless leeway of 595, England fell to Lindwall, Johnston and Toshack (5 for 40) for 186.

Defeat by 409 hardly disturbed England's selectors more than Hutton's unbalanced flicking at rising off-balls, as if the fast attack had broken his nerve. Unaware that he was disabled by a paralyzing blow on the hip joint, they dropped him from the Third Test, to the astonishment of Australia's bowlers, who regarded him as England's soundest batsman, though less challenging to their sway than Compton.

At Old Trafford for the first time in the series England led handsomely on 1st innings and went on to such an advantageous position that the Australians, or some of them, unashamedly welcomed downpours that washed out the match. The game was marked by another epic innings by Compton after England won the toss. Hearing the umpire call a short-pitched waist-high ball from Lindwall, Compton tried to hook it but edged it up into his face. Knees buckling, he was helped off, bleeding from a gash between the eyes. Less than 3½ hours after two stitches closed the wound, Compton reappeared when England's 5th wicket fell at 119 . . . to face Lindwall. His gameness was rewarded with 145 not out, in which he had to keep out the most menacing over the fast bowler ever let loose in Britain. Fielding at forward short-leg about 8 yards from the bat when Pollard swung at off-spinner Johnson, the fearless Barnes was felled by a blow on the left ribs. Despite a bruise the size of a soup-plate, he tried to bat next day but collapsed. Barnes was sent back to Manchester Infirmary and was still unfit for the next Test. England with 2 days to go and 7 wickets in hand led by 316 before the weather let Australia off the hook.

On the Headingley wicket, which has so often rewarded spin, England went into the Fourth Test without Wright or Hollies or a regular left-arm spinner to support Laker. This deficiency helped Bradman, on his favourite English ground, and Morris to lift Australia to the most remarkable victory in Test annals. Restored to his place, Hutton joined Washbrook in stands of 168 and 129. Washbrook's 143 was the best innings I saw him play. Sent in as night-watchman, Bedser made a 3-hour stand of 155 with Edrich, 111. After 'Big Al' had played through a new ball, the realization that he needed only 21 for a Test century cramped him into giving a return catch off the kind of ball he had been driving for fours. This wicket, at 423, began a counter-attack in which Australia captured the last eight for 73. Bedser and Pollard had 3 Australians out for 68 before Harvey's scintillating 112, his 1st Test innings against England. The 19-year-old left-hander clapped on 121 with Miller and 105 with Loxton, whose 93 included 5 sixes. Australia, 38 behind, tried to keep runs down but England were 403 ahead when Yardley declared after 2 overs on the last day; as captain of the batting side he used a heavy roller, no doubt with expectation of later effects. On a dusty surface the batsmen would have done well to last until tea had Wright been playing, yet Morris, 182, his most influential innings, and Bradman, 173 not out, enabled Australia to set a record by making 404 in a 4th Test innings to win. Granted that 8 catching or stumping chances were missed, a rate of almost 90 an hour in such conditions tells of spirited batting which, against long odds, brought rich rewards.

On his greatest day abroad, Lindwall, in the Fifth Test, with the rubber decided, took 6 for 20 with 99 balls at the Oval in bundling England out for 52, their lowest total on a home ground. On a wicket made in wet weather all the batsmen looked suspicious and only Hutton, 30, overcame this enough to hit a boundary. Morris's 196 put Australia well on the way towards an innings victory. Clinching this, Lindwall and Johnston each finished with 27 wickets in the series. In his last Test innings Bradman fell, 2nd ball, for 0, edging in Hollies' undetected googly. This personal disappointment was far outweighed by the satisfaction he derived from his team's being the 1st to win 4 Tests in England (they were the 1st to play 5-day Tests there) and the first to achieve his long-standing ambition to go through a tour of Britain unbeaten.

A croaking plea for cancellation of the 1950–51 tour of Australia was heard as F. R. Brown, 3rd choice for captain, sailed with his team. Primarily because of his indomitable spirit, I rank Brown as England's most inspiring skipper for many a day – one who could play to win when others saw no silver lining, and who set an example in carrying the fight to the enemy. These qualities became so widely known that a Sydney barrowman stimulated sales by calling, 'Fine lettuce . . . ninepence . . . 'earts as big as Freddie Brown's!' Adverse luck of toss and thunderstorms failed to depress the massive all-rounder when his bowlers got rid of Australia for 228 at Brisbane, only for England to be trapped on turf so sticky that 20 wickets tumbled in a day for 130. By closing at 68 for 7 – 160 behind – to get Australia in on the mudheap, Brown took a calculated risk. In an hour the crash of 7 wickets for 32 impelled Hassett to close, leaving the Englishmen 68 minutes to negotiate on a still difficult, but improving wicket that evening, if they were to have a chance to win next day; in the last quarter of an hour two unguarded strokes and an incongruous run out made England 30 for 6, leaving too many (163) for the last 4 wickets to get. Yet Hutton made 62 not out with the most glorious strokeplay he ever showed Australians, who from that day ranked him highest of all English batsmen of his time.

On a sweating Melbourne wicket in the Second Test Bedser and Bailey so harried the Australians that they totalled only 194. With Lindwall and Miller fiery, Australia's bowlers struck back to prevent England getting more than 3 ahead. After topping the score with a plucky 62 – despite unhappy moments against bouncers – Brown took 4 wickets in Australia's 2nd innings. Two diving catches by Bailey in the gully and Washbrook's running out of Harvey helped keep Australia down to 181. Failure to balance strokeplay with defence lost England, needing only 179, the chance to square the rubber.

Sydney saw an astonishing slip catch and a paralyzing over by Miller illustrate the mercurial all-rounder's ability suddenly to change the course of a match. At 128 for 1 wicket Miller removed Hutton, 62, and Compton, 0, in 4 deliveries with an old ball. With his best batting against Australia, Brown, 79, topped England's score for the 2nd consecutive Test but the innings ended for 290. A ball from Lindwall which fractured Bailey's right thumb and a groin injury to Wright reduced England to three bowlers, Bedser, Brown and Warr. Their manful efforts could not prevent Australia totalling 426, but defensive fields so slowed the scoring that Miller, despite his power, was kept to 24 an hour for his 145 not out. On the last day, Iverson, with his folded-down finger grip, not only spun awkardly from the off but, for the only time in the series, got response with his leg-break. The big bowler's reward: 6 for 27 off 156 balls. England, 123, went down by an innings.

On a paceless Adelaide pitch Morris overcame his fallibility by making 206 out of Australia's 371. First in, Morris was last out, bowled by Tattersall, who had been flown out with Statham as replacements. Nobody could stay long with Hutton as he carried his bat for 156 while England, 272, fell 99 behind. Hassett allowed Burke to complete a hundred in his first Test before closing 502 ahead. Such a total was unattainable in the 4th innings, in which England batted without their captain, whose left knee and shoulder were badly injured in a traffic accident.

Though sore from his injuries, Brown joined Bedser in a medium-pace attack to such effect that 3 wickets fell to him without a run in the last Test at Melbourne. The 15-stone pair dismissed Australia for 217. As had happened with Hutton in Brisbane, arrival of England's last man was a signal for Simpson to unleash his full range of strokes without waiting for poor balls. Lindwall was never treated so roughly as when Simpson was making 64 out of 74 in an hour. In helping himself to a 31st birthday present of 156 not out, the erect Notts right-hander put England 103 ahead. Turning a ball from Hassett's leg-stump to take the off-bail, Wright spun England within sight of victory, which the indefatigable Bedser brought close by capturing 10 wickets in the match. Fittingly, Hutton and Compton were at the wicket when the Yorkshireman made the hit that brought the long-awaited result which formed the title of E. W. Swanton's book and film, *Elusive Victory*. The win by 8 wickets made England the first side to beat Australia in 26 Tests. History slipped one cog in repeating itself, as it took England 15 postwar Tests to lower Australia's colours, one more than the number required after the First World War. The captain was deeply moved by the Australian crowd's generous acclamation of the underdog's success. Bedser was the first Englishman since Larwood's day to take 30 wickets in a series in Australia. He, Wright, Brown and Bailey, owed much to Evans's brilliant wicket-keeping.

R. T. Simpson hooks Lindwall during his 156 not out, the innings of his life, v Australia at Melbourne in 1950–51, so paving the way for the victory which had eluded England over the postwar span of 14 Tests. Tallon keeping wicket.

England owed it chiefly to Bedser and his assistants that the 1953 series was still open to be won in the Final Test, the only one finished in a closely fought rubber. The English batsmen averaged only 33 an hour, three-quarters of the Australians' rate. Leading the most dazzling fielding side Australia ever sent, Hassett, for the first time against England, strung 9 men – all except cover – in catching positions round the bat.

In the First Test at Trent Bridge Bedser's 7 in each innings deserved to give England the match. With 2 days to go they needed 187 to win with 9 wickets standing but rain prevented more than 2 hours' play on the last 2 days. With a true captain's selflessness, Hassett took up the burden of opening the innings in the remaining Tests. He made 104 at Lord's, aided by a couple of chances but troubled by cramp. Seldom have Australian bowlers had to contend at both ends with batting of the quality of Hutton's 168 stand with Graveney. The polished pair helped England to lead, 372 to 346. After Miller's conscientious 109 and Lindwall's fastest 50, England needed 343 to win, 80 more than their highest winning 4th innings at home. On the final day Hassett's bowlers had six hours to clean up the last 7 wickets for under 322. Watson's calm concentration never wavered and Bailey almost revelled in a situation suiting his ice-cold batting technique. Making 109 in his 1st Test against Australia, Watson kept the bowlers out for $5\frac{3}{4}$ hours. The sober left-hander and Bailey, 71, prevented a wicket falling for more than $4\frac{1}{4}$ hours while they put on 163. Their epic rearguard action enabled England to see out a trying day.

Between showers at Old Trafford, Harvey took frequent risks in making 122. The best stand in Australia's 318 was the left-hander's 173 with Hole, the surest slip-catcher in the series. England's 276 left Australia 42 ahead with only an hour to go in a rain-ruined match. There could be no result, yet, with the ball turning and lifting, England's capture of 8 wickets for 35 did nothing to enhance confidence for future innings on pitches aiding finger-spin.

By sending England in at Leeds, Hassett made himself the only Australian captain who has dared to do this on English soil in 70 years. His judgment was confirmed when Lindwall and 3 supporting fast bowlers, Miller, Davidson and Archer, bundled England out for 167. Lindwall shot out the mainstays, Hutton and Compton, for 0 each. Australia held the initiative throughout the match and Bedser, Bailey and Lock did well to limit them to a lead of 99. A race for 177 in the 4th innings, at 92 an hour, required the Australians to average 5·25 runs an over. Their response was 111 for 3 wickets off 21 overs in the next 70 minutes, thanks chiefly to the daring of left-handers Morris and Harvey. Challengingly, Hutton had chosen Lock to open the bowling with Bedser, and Morris hit 14 off the left-hand spinner's 1st over. Australia needed 66 in the last 45

Coronation Ashes: the England team which beat Australia by 8 wickets at the Oval in August 1953. Back row: T. E. Bailey, P. B. H. May, T. W. Graveney, J. C. Laker, G. A. R. Lock, J. H. Wardle (12th man) and F. S. Trueman; sitting: W. J. Edrich, A. V. Bedser, L. Hutton (captain), D. C. S. Compton and T. G. Evans.

minutes to win when Hutton shut the gate by placing 6 on-side fielders for Bailey to wheel along 6 overs well outside the leg-stump for 9 runs, while Bedser, as if tireless, kept the other end tight with the last 6 of his 17 overs unchanged. His opponents never forgave Bailey for stringing out one over to 7 minutes.

Hassett's 5th consecutive toss win was nullified at the Oval by humidity which suited the swing of Bedser and Trueman, followed by a lunch-break shower. For the first time since the war England had a fast bowler to answer the Australian battery and to end 8 years of one-way traffic by letting fly a few bumpers. Despite 2 dropped chances, Trueman captured 4 wickets in the dismissal of Australia for 275. Hutton, as usual, was the backbone of England's answer, yet they led only by 31 on 1st innings. However they had the finger-spinners Australia lacked, and on the 3rd afternoon Laker and Lock beckoned victory close, sharing the credit of Australia's dismissal for 162.

Refusing to recognize that defeat was a foregone conclusion, Australia's bowlers and fieldsmen made Edrich, Hutton, May and Compton fight more than 3½ hours for the 132 runs that won the match by 8 wickets. Lindwall bowled fast for 75 minutes in an 11-over stretch, yet after lunch saddled up again for 8 overs of leg-theory. Johnston, in the absence of a regular spinner, twisted along 23 consecutive overs between 11.30 and 2.50 pm on the last day – enough to make even Bedser sympathetic. After Compton's winning hit 15,000 overjoyed people massed in front of the pavilion to do spontaneous honour to the men who after 20 long years had regained the Ashes.

Lifting the record from 24 to 39 Australian wickets in a series at home, Bedser made his tally 69 victims in two consecutive rubbers against Australia. Nearest to this come Laker's 61 wickets in the 1956 and 1958–59 series. Hassett led home a team which had made itself highly popular, and with the substantial consolation of a profit close to £100,000, a figure no other visiting team has approached.

Although Trueman was not in the 1954–55 team to Australia, Tyson and Statham fulfilled Hutton's wish for a two-edged fast attack. His experience against Lindwall and Miller from 1948 to 1951 gave him unrivalled first-hand knowledge of a batsman's feelings when facing bumper-spiced speed from both ends. England's selectors had not allowed transient form to dissuade them from recognizing the potentialities of Tyson, 24, and Cowdrey, 20, a batsman of exceptional talent. Disasters in the First Test at Brisbane left England one down, crushed by an innings and 154. In sending Australia in, Hutton was influenced by the desire that his all-pace attack should have the benefit of the wicket's first-day lift, but the pitch was browner than the nearby greentop from which Queensland's bowling had bounced awkwardly. Though the Test pitch was quieter, Morris's arm bore several bruises from Tyson before he was halfway to his 153. He and Harvey, 162, were dropped, and I counted 11 chances and half-chances – 7 off Bedser – as Australia piled up 601 for 8 before Johnson's closure at lunch on the third day. Despite Bailey's best batting against Australia for 88 in 4¼ hours, England were out for 190 and 257 with more than a day to spare. Brisbane having shown that Bedser, though unlucky, had not regained normal zip after shingles, Hutton and his co-selectors took a momentous step at Sydney by standing down the Test recordholder. On a pitch favouring the faster bowlers throughout, Australia led England in first innings by 74. At 55 for 3, Cowdrey joined May in a fateful stand with only Edrich due next before an unduly long tail. Together they made 116, May going on to one of the most admirable of his 13 Test hundreds.

Tyson and Statham then saved everybody's faces by bowling their side to victory by 38 runs in a breathless finish to a Test more exciting than any England has since played Down Under. As Harvey, in his most stirring innings on a home ground, counter-attacked the pair for 92 not out, schoolboys leaned over the fence to beckon his strokes to the boundary. With a strong, cold wind as ally, Tyson took 16 wickets with 148 balls of swifter velocity than the Australians had known, though countrymen of Miller and Lindwall. While he thundered into 8 eight-ball overs with an old ball, Statham poured his last reserves of energy into his 6 overs 'up the cellar steps' into a vicious headwind.

With the rubber squared, Tyson and Statham so dominated the Melbourne Test that Bedser was not even missed. After Cowdrey's mature 102 in a total of 191 Australia looked like falling behind until a plucky rally by wicket-keeper Maddocks and his recovered captain, Johnson, put them 40 ahead. A blistering wind all Sunday parched everything in Melbourne, from gardens to throats, except the wicket. Instead of widening, cracks from which some balls had kept low on Saturday were narrower on Monday when boot-sprigs sank into softer turf. All signs supported a report that the wicket had been watered in breach of Law 10. Embarrassed officials issued a denial. Fortunately for Melbourne's good name, Hutton thought the illicit hosing helped his team. Driving grandly in England's 2nd innings, 279, May got within 9 of another hundred. By the 4th day, Tuesday, all effects of Sunday's visitation had evaporated and Australia crashed for 111. Unnerved by shooters and kickers from the cracked surface, they were helpless as Tyson and Statham's annihilating speed routed the last 8 wickets for 34. The pair shared 31 of 40 Australian wickets at Sydney and Melbourne, where England's 4 main match-winners were all under 25. Nine weeks after the Brisbane drubbing the revitalized Englishmen's 3rd win in a row clinched the Ashes at Adelaide Oval, where Tyson and Statham finished off the shaken Australians.

For the first time in Australia, rain at Sydney washed out 3 days of a Test, leaving 13 hours 10 minutes for play. No Australian captain sending opponents in was ever given the about-turn more promptly than by Graveney's 111 in $2\frac{1}{2}$ hours, made with elegant power as spontaneous as the most abundant congratulations I ever saw a batting craftsman receive from the entire fielding side. The speed of Graveney's 182 stand with May, 79, helped give Hutton the opportunity to declare, and on the last afternoon to order a follow-on. Taunted by Wardle's wrist-spin, which took 8 out of 16 wickets, the low-ebb Australians were saved by time from a 4th loss. One aspect of Hutton's efficient captaincy sometimes annoyed watching crowds – tactics which once lowered England's bowling rate to 54 8-ball overs in a 5-hour day. This item apart, Hutton thoroughly earned the distinction of being the only English captain in more than 30 years to retain the Ashes after winning them in England.

Confidence regained by Australian batsmen in the West Indies did not carry them far against Laker and Lock on English pitches suiting spin in 1956. Inopportune rain, loss of 4 tosses and injuries to leading bowlers contributed to the poorest tour record by Australians abroad since the First World War. A ruinous defeat by Surrey, gave England's captain, May, and his co-selectors a strategical advantage which was reversed only once – on a grassy Lord's pitch suiting Australia's hard-wicket attack. On this strip, vice-captain Miller took 10 wickets – for the only time in his magnificent Test career – wicket-keeper Langley set a record with 9 dismissals and Benaud made his highest score against England, 97. Instead of the feat of a lifetime, Laker's 10 wickets for Surrey in the 1st innings proved to be a forerunner of deeds beyond achievement by the deadliest old-timers in days before dandelions were banished from pitches: 10 wickets in a Test innings, 19 in the match, 30 in two consecutive Tests, 46 in a series, at the trifling cost of 9 runs each. On Leeds and Manchester wickets where England scored well until past lunch on the 2nd day – May, Richardson and Sheppard made hundreds – the Australians on the same afternoon found the great off-spinner virtually unplayable. His finger-spin, matchless and remorseless, dwarfed all else in the series, but the players who hardly missed a catch close-up in his 4-man leg-trap deserve to be remembered – Lock, May, Sheppard, Graveney, Trueman and Oakman.

No Australian reached a hundred in the series. I rank Harvey's batsmanship for 69 at Leeds his most skilful ever. McDonald's back-to-the-wall 89 at Old Trafford involved 7 starts in $5\frac{1}{2}$ hours. They were unable to prevent innings wins which gave England the rubber, 2–1. The Australians, dissatisfied with the quick crumbling of the Leeds pitch, questioned that pure mischance changed the Old Trafford wicket's character from the grassy, dark-soiled strip of their match against Lancashire to the shaven, reddish Test track on which they were out for 84 and, after rain, 205.

The bowling May took to Australia in 1958–59 could hardly have looked more formidable – Tyson, Trueman, Statham, Loader and Bailey for pace, Laker and Lock for spin. Yet England were vanquished 4–0. This startling reversal of 1956 form derived primarily from the dramatic 11th-hour emergence of Benaud as a captain with a rare capacity to influence the course of matches. Catching May on the wrong foot when England batted first on a dubious Brisbane wicket, Benaud, abetted by Bailey whose 68 in $7\frac{1}{2}$ hours beat all records for slowness in England's 2nd innings, grabbed the initiative and held it throughout the rubber, except for the last two days of the Sydney Test. A troublesome injury list, which caused MCC to fly Dexter and Mortimore out as reinforcements, culminated in Statham and Loader being disabled in a road accident before the Fifth Test. By contrast with May's faultless handling of England's bowlers and fieldsmen in his

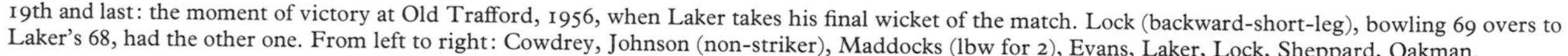
19th and last: the moment of victory at Old Trafford, 1956, when Laker takes his final wicket of the match. Lock (backward-short-leg), bowling 69 overs to Laker's 68, had the other one. From left to right: Cowdrey, Johnson (non-striker), Maddocks (lbw for 2), Evans, Laker, Lock, Sheppard, Oakman.

own country, his captaincy in Australia showed too much concern with saving runs, too little with getting wickets. Promotion of Bailey to No. 3 in the 2nd innings at Brisbane presented the initiative to Australia and pushed England's 3 best batsmen lower down the list. Bailey did not score off 388 of the 428 balls he received and seemed to put a blight on his partners. After Cowdrey, 28, was given out to a controversial catch at short-leg, re-runs of television film failed to confirm opinions either way. It took O'Neill, playing his 1st Test, to prove that strokes could still be played. His 71 not out off 122 balls swept Australia to victory by 8 wickets.

With 3 wickets in one over of unanswerable swing, Davidson gained a quick advantage for Australia in the Second Test in Melbourne. Averting a hat-trick on his 29th birthday, May scored 113. Bailey, with 48 penitently well made, and Cowdrey, 44, helped the captain in stands of 85 and 108. Statham's capital bowling for 7 wickets on a plumb pitch kept England well in the game but Harvey, giving his wide range of attractive strokes full rein for 167, enabled Australia to reach 308, 49 ahead. Three hours later the Englishmen were all out for 87, probably the worst let-down batsmen ever gave England on a good wicket. Superlative catching was one reason; Davidson, Harvey, Grout and Burke turned a number of half-chances into wickets. Another reason was that 6 of the Englishmen who fell to Meckiff's speed and lively lift were hardly happy at being victims of deliveries that began with a bent arm and finished with a pronounced wrist-whip. Taking 9 wickets in this Test, the 6 foot 2 inch left-hander became the chief central figure in a throwing controversy. He finished the rubber with 17 of the 97 English wickets lost.

More sublime catching limited England to 219 in Sydney. Though Australia went 138 ahead, Laker and Lock shared 9 wickets, leaving the batsmen concerned about how difficult their spin might be on the 6th day. This anxiety became obvious in England's 2nd innings as May and Cowdrey's 182 stand developed. On the 5th afternoon Benaud abruptly forsook his customary positive captaincy by having Davidson bowl leg-theory. May's closure left 150 to be chased in 110 minutes to win, but the Australians did not attempt the 6 runs an over required and concentrated on keeping Laker and Lock out in a drawn game.

When swelling of Laker's arthritic forefinger left May with 4 bowlers of pace and one spinner in Adelaide he put Australia in first, to give his attack whatever life the new wicket possessed. The pitch never aided bowlers with the lift seen in MCC's match against South Australia 5 weeks earlier. Only 1 wicket (Burke, 66) fell all day. With the Saturday temperature in the high 90s, England's bowlers managed only 51 overs – a new low for a full day – and were further discouraged when Evans broke a recently mended finger. The consistent McDonald, 149 at Saturday's lunch, retired hurt with a pulled thigh muscle and had 35 hours' rest before resuming, with a substitute runner, to make 170 of Australia's 476. To avert defeat, with Evans a casualty, England tried to bat out most of the remaining 17¾ hours. Cowdrey, 84 in one innings, and May, 37 and 59, each hung on more than 4 hours, but for steadfast resistance under constant pressure the outstanding man was Graveney (41 and 53 not out) for a total of 8 hours. Benaud, Lindwall and the 6 foot 4 inch Rorke (who with his long drag made other fast bowlers look no longer swift) made England's aim unattainable and Australia won by 10 wickets.

Given 4 fast bowlers, Benaud did as May had done – sent the opposition in – and a moistish Melbourne wicket yielded much livelier bounce than Adelaide. Quick bowlers took 6 cheap wickets in England's 205. Left-hander Peter Richardson's 68 was the only half-century by an English opening batsman in the series. By contrast, McDonald scored his 2nd hundred – the first Australian since the Bradman era to top 500 in a rubber against England. England's heaviest scorer, May (405), had the going made harder when he unselfishly moved up to No. 3, which often allowed the Australians to tackle the world's best batsman in the 2nd over. For the only time in the series, 100 runs in a session were raised by Benaud, 64, and hard-hooking Grout, 74. Victory by 9 wickets brought Australia the rubber, 4–0.

It was the only time since 1890 that England had gone through a rubber without an innings reaching 300. Opening failures helped Benaud's methods of keeping more fieldsmen in catching positions, while his bowlers averaged seven balls an hour more than England's. Fielders aided in the dismissal of two-thirds of England's batsmen, compared with only half Australia's wickets. Benaud's batsmen scored 5 runs per 100 balls faster. Benaud (31 wickets) was the first since Mailey in 1920–21 to take 30 English wickets in a series in his own country.

Benaud carried his go-ahead captaincy into the 1961 tour of Britain, risking losses with daring declarations against MCC and counties. Cowdrey's Birmingham toss win lost its value when showers kept stimulating the wicket. Australia had only 2 front-rank bowlers, Davidson and Benaud, and the captain's right shoulder was creaking from torn fibres. Up from the second rank stepped – or shambled – Mackay, with medium-pace swing and cut which took 3 wickets in 4 balls. The shocked Englishmen fell back on defence and made only 195. On a wicket that rolled out invitingly, Harvey and O'Neill responded with the choicest stroke-play an English crowd had seen from Australians for a dozen years. Off 37 overs they hit 146, before Statham caused O'Neill, 82, to play on. Harvey's delightful 114 came off 190 balls. With his highest and riskiest score against England, 64, Mackay helped Australia to average 60 an hour over a total of 516 for 9, declared. Few hundreds have filled such a yawning gap as left-hand opener Subba Row's 112 in his First Test against Australia and Dexter's upstanding 180 on a last-day pitch that gave no help to any kind of bowler. Dexter so dominated a stand with Barrington that more than two-thirds of the 161 runs came from his masterful bat. Before he was stumped trying to lift Simpson's leg-break on to some distant fairway, Dexter hit 31 fours.

With Benaud out of the Lord's Test, visiting hospital daily, there was no certainty that Australia's deputy captain, Harvey, would have the other half of the bowling, Davidson, in match trim. Back trouble kept recurring. May, after a groin strain, was found fit to resume as batsman but Cowdrey continued as captain for this Test and again won the toss. England were all out, 206, on a day when 12 wickets tumbled as batsmen's hands, arms and bodies were frequently struck by balls kicking from a ridge. I recall having expressed the fear that before the Test was over the Nursery End might be renamed the Surgery End. Playing the innings of his life for the only hundred of the match, Lawry made light of a bruised thumb. His height, 6 feet 2 inches, was a help but, after being winded by Trueman, he fell over backwards dodging one of Statham's bouncers. This failed to shake the imperturbable left-hander, whose nerve stood the dual test of saving his ribs and seeing shorter partners suffer disabling bruises. Lofty tailenders, McKenzie (on his 20th birthday) and Misson helped limping Mackay, 54, put Australia 134 ahead. After England's batting had struggled a second time Australia needed only 69 but England still hoped, as wickets toppled to Statham and Trueman, flinging every ounce into 10 overs each. They would have had 5 for 33 had a difficult leg-side chance stuck as the diving Lock's elbow struck the ground. Forceful in the crisis, Burge finished the match with 2 hooked boundaries and walked off with a cluster of 5 bruises, resembling linked Olympic rings, on his right thigh. In 4 days, 21 of 35 wickets had fallen at the Nursery End and surveyors confirmed the existence of high points and a depression in that part of the pitch.

Insufficient watering-in of a late dressing was blamed for a piebald green-and-white Headingley pitch on which, after the ridgemanship at Lord's, the teams tried their hands at patchmanship. At this art the Englishmen were superior.

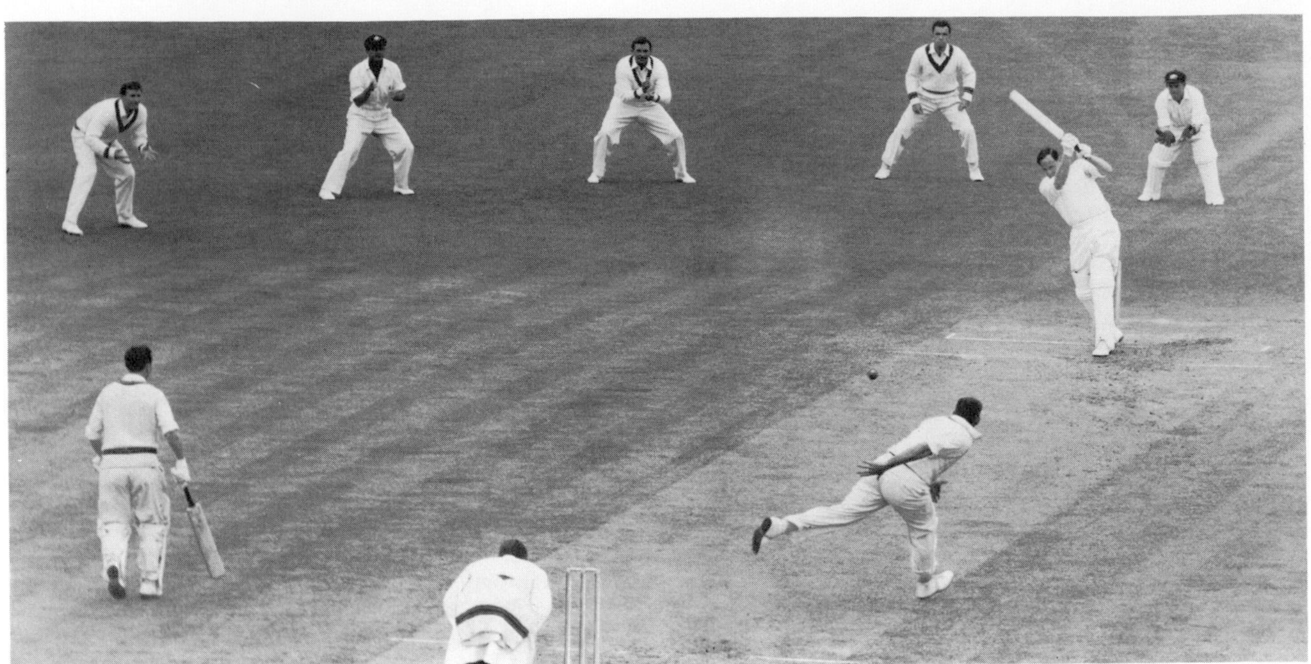

A battle of giants, 1961: May straight-drives Davidson for 4, watched by 5 famous Australians, McKenzie, Mackay, Benaud, Simpson and Grout.

Trueman was outstanding with 11 wickets for 88 in a match wherein only 2 batsmen on each side reached 50. His 6 overs with the 2nd new ball captured five for 16 as, with Jackson, he sent Australia's score spinning dizzily from 187 for 2 to all out 237. Going round the wicket, Davidson cut the ball disconcertingly in taking 5 wickets but Cowdrey grappled skilfully with the conditions. Surviving chances at 22 and 70 he reached 93. Lock's bold 30 off 13 balls from Benaud helped England to lead by 62 – a winning advantage if Australia could be routed in the 2nd innings. Trueman attended to that. In the most sensational burst in Test annals the black-maned Yorkshireman fired out 5 for 0 with 24 off-cutters. Harvey's batsmanship as he made 73 and 53 almost made the pitch look playable but 18 wickets crashed on the 3rd day, ending the match 2 days ahead of time.

A Test Match that will be remembered when most others are forgotten began at Manchester with 4 English bowlers of pace dismissing Australia for 190 – the 4th time the side bowling first fared better than the toss-winners. Statham began the inroads with cut and bounce that took 5 of the first 7 wickets on a well-greased pitch kept juicy by showers. Among the 5 were Lawry, top-scorer with 74, and Booth, 46 in his 1st Test. May signalled his return to commanding form by making 95 before Simpson alertly apprehended a slip catch deflected by Grout's glove. Pullar's highest innings against Australia, 63, and Barrington's 78 helped gain England's longest first-innings lead of the series, 177. Missed more than once Lawry escaped to make 102 and take part with Simpson in the only hundred opening partnership of the rubber. O'Neill's confident 67 showed no after-effects of his first innings bruising.

Twice on the last enthralling day the match appeared to be in England's grip, only to be wrenched away dramatically, first by Australia's greatest-ever left-hand all-rounder, Davidson, and later by his right-hand confederate, Benaud. By taking 3 for 0 in 15 balls, Allen's off-spin brought in the last man, McKenzie, with Australia only 157 ahead. The tail-ender shaped so gingerly at Allen that Davidson took over that end and hit 20 off an over. To save more punishment May took Allen off. That was what the Australians wanted. McKenzie made 32 and helped Davidson, 77 not out, hit up 98 for the last wicket.

England were set 256 to win at 66 an hour. In the crisis neither side shirked the issue. Dexter's imperious 76, at almost a run a minute, brought the crowd to their feet and the bowlers to the last shot in their locker. Benaud staked all on going round-the-wicket to right-handers for the first time, aiming for more awkward turn from boot-scrapes, yet knowing that every off-line ball was likely to be hit to the leg boundary. Dexter's daring had reduced England's task to 106 in 106 minutes when Grout caught his attempted square-cut off a lifting leg-break. May's swing missed a leg-side ball that broke behind his knee to the top of the leg-stump. These 2 wickets in 3 balls were the 4th turning-point in a gripping day. In 9 overs Benaud captured 6 for 22 – his greatest match-winning feat in England, at a time when it was desperately needed to retain the Ashes. When Davidson hit Statham's wicket at 201 Australia had won a rousing match with 20 minutes to spare. Thus after many exciting shifts of fortune Australia retained the Ashes.

Remembering boot-marks more than dropped chances, England went into the Oval Test without Trueman, leading wicket-taker in the series. Though their 256 was the highest opening innings of the rubber, no Englishman produced strokes with the power and confidence of O'Neill's 117, his 1st Test hundred off English bowling, and Burge's 181, his 1st in any Test. After Australia led by 238, the fall of 4 batsmen for 90 left England in a plight demanding a rearguard stand to rival Watson and Bailey's 1953 epic. The men were at hand. Subba Row's 137 outlasted Watson's vigil by almost an hour, despite a groin strain that necessitated a runner. Barrington's stay for 83 outdid Bailey's by nearly half-an-hour. Mackay swung the ball remarkably throughout a marathon of 68 overs in the 2nd innings and took 7 wickets in the match. For Englishmen to survive Davidson and Benaud yet fall to the bent-kneed Queenslander was rather like being run down by a scooter while avoiding a train. With 21 wickets, Grout made himself the 1st wicket-keeper to have taken 20 wickets in each of 2 series against England, yet he was no surer than Murray, whose 18 wickets are the most by an English 'keeper in a home rubber.

Dexter, leading MCC in Australia in 1962–63, set his side an exhilarating example as a stroke-maker. An average of 39 runs per 100 balls (though one fewer than the Australian's and 6 fewer than the 1961 West Indians') was, even so, England's highest rate in Australia for 38 years. If both sides failed to recapture the spirit of Old Trafford it was primarily because English bowlers' lower delivery rate in the early Tests, and some restrictive field-settings, caused an adverse reaction in Australia's strategy.

As quick consolation for loss of the Brisbane toss, Trueman's belligerent bowling removed Lawry and O'Neill in the 1st hour. Booth, wristily stylish, survived a stumping chance off Titmus at 21 to pull the innings around with his 1st Test hundred. In England's answer to Australia's 404, Dexter hit over a ball from Benaud at 70. Australia's captain snared 6 of the first 8 batsmen, including top-scorers Barrington, 78, and Parfitt, 80, each of whom battled determinedly for about 4 hours. After Simpson and Lawry's 136 for the 1st wicket, Harvey and O'Neill's lively half-centuries helped raise the highest one-day total of the series, 346. They enabled Benaud to declare, leaving a 6 hour day to get England out. After Pullar and Sheppard's only century opening of the series, the target was 75 an hour when Dexter strode in at 114. With the confidence that sets a great player apart, he made two-thirds of the runs while he was in until, when 99, an over-daring stroke at McKenzie cost his wicket. England finished with 6 out, 100 runs short, after averaging 3·33 runs an over.

At Melbourne England never looked back from the time Coldwell took 2 of the first 3 wickets and Trueman the 1st of the 8 he was to capture in the match. Dexter and Cowdrey after a poor start rallied their side with a 175 stand, England's highest of the series. Dexter, 93, narrowly missed a hundred for the 3rd time but Cowdrey went on patiently to 113, the highest of his 5 hundreds against Australia. In a tense struggle for a lead, Graveney's batting against Benaud and Davidson could not have been surpassed. Harvey ran him out for 41 but England led by 15. This margin looked larger when, with consecutive balls, Trueman dismissed Simpson and O'Neill, 0, out-fielder Pullar's throw ran out Harvey, 10, and Dexter skidded a shooter through Lawry who, in his 2nd half-century of the match, hardly averaged 1 run an over. Leg-theory so cramped Booth that his 103 took 2¼ hours longer than his Brisbane 112. He was last out at 248, leaving England needing 234.

After a sprawling leg-side catch which Jarman – or any other wicket-keeper – is unlikely ever to better, Dexter answered the problem of fading light by marching in himself to face a rampant McKenzie and Davidson with a new ball. With Sheppard, he saw England through that evening and next day the 2nd wicket stand took England halfway to their goal. For the most significant innings of his life, Sheppard summoned up such form that his half-century came 20 minutes quicker than his skipper's. Australia's last hope of a breakthrough slid by when chances from Dexter (44) and Cowdrey (7) did not stick in usually reliable hands. Sheppard, 113, was run out seeking the winning run, and Cowdrey's undefeated 58 sealed victory.

Davidson's peerless left hand, backed by Simpson's sterling all-round play, enabled Australia to square the rubber in 3½ days after losing the toss in Sydney. With masterly control of late in-swing Davidson made top-class batsmen play down the wrong line more often than any other bowler I have seen on Australian turf. Titmus's flighty off-spin snared 7 Australians and Simpson's leg-breaks and wrong 'uns 5 Englishmen in an innings. Most males in the Australian population knew how to hit Titmus out of the attack but the selectors kept filling the Australian XI with the minority who did not. The Middlesex off-spinner's hard-to-drive length tantalized even the nimblest batsmen and his clever use of the breeze to drift away made leg shots so risky that 14 of his 21 wickets in the rubber fell to attempts to score to the on-side. Simpson's bowling success was coupled with 91, 34 not out and three consecutive slip catches which began the ruination of England's second innings for 104. In his First Test, Shepherd, a burly left-hander, hit up 71 not out. England were unlucky that Murray should have severely injured his right shoulder diving to catch Lawry. Hemmed in by 9 fieldsmen in a 6-yard radius, Murray batted one-handed for 74 minutes before attempting to score and stayed 100 minutes to be 3 not out when Australia won by 8 wickets.

The highest 1st-day tally of the series, 322 for 5, rewarded Australia for averaging 4 runs an over on an excellent Adelaide wicket. The bowlers suffered from Harvey's free-stroking response to having been dropped three times before 30. O'Neill joined in the highest and most sparkling stand of the rubber, 194 at 5 an over. O'Neill's chanceless back-to-form hundred was the quickest of the series (169 minutes); Harvey's 154 was his 21st.

As Dexter bowled 23 overs in Australia's 393 – dismissing both century-makers and Benaud – the captain wisely lowered himself in the batting order, obtaining 2½ hours' rest. Davidson pulled a hamstring after 3½ hours – a mishap that profoundly affected his captain's tactics. In Davidson's absence McKenzie bore the burden on young but broad shoulders, and excelled his previous best bowling at Lord's in 1961, also for 5 wickets. After Barrington, 63, and Dexter, 61, England were best served by Titmus, 59 not out, who, as in every Test, put his head down and played the ball on its merits. Half a day lost because of rain lessened the chance of either side forcing a win.

Thanks chiefly to their most consistent pair, Simpson, 71, and Booth, 77, Australia's lead of 62 grew to 326 by 12.20 pm on the last day. A closure at that point could have made England begin half-an-hour before lunch, needing 326 at 5 runs an over or almost 73 an hour. By not hitting out to get England to the wicket then, Benaud clearly believed that, without Davidson, Australia's weakened attack could not dismiss them in 4½ hours on a good wicket. Absence of a gesture left a sour taste with the 22,000 last-day crowd. Benaud's image as an enterprising skipper suffered. Barrington, never in doubt for 132, and Graveney, 36, carried England to 223 with 6 wickets still standing.

Widespread assumptions that Dexter would stake all on going for a win to regain the Ashes at Sydney proved to be unfounded when England occupied the crease 9½ hours for 321. Their 2·33 runs an over sagged below the average Anglo-Australian Test rate (3·5 an over), and left the match under a shadow from which it never emerged. Preoccupation with how to get through Davidson's new-ball bowling made their approach defensive. A dead wicket discouraged driving, a patchy centre took pace off shots and only half the slow outfield was mown daily. In such frustrating conditions the batsmen remained more conscious of the risks than the rewards of strokes and Australia's fielding seemed almost impenetrable, headed by Harvey, whose 6 catches in his last Test equalled the record for other than wicket-keepers. Even Dexter hardly averaged 21 an hour for his 47. Barrington's 2nd consecutive hundred, 101 in 5½ hours, was notable chiefly for his grafting concentration against the 344 balls he received out of 624 bowled while he was in.

By the time the Australians batted, they seemed hardly in a mood to accept having the onus of brightening the game passed to them. Burge's 103 took 7 minutes longer than Barrington's 101. Yet, thanks to O'Neill and Benaud's vigour, Australia equalled England's 321 off 112 fewer balls. With off-spinners Titmus and Allen doing most of the bowling England achieved 15 eight-ball overs an hour, outdoing Australia's bowlers for the first time. Illingworth, as Sheppard's stop-gap partner, helped put up 40 for the 1st wicket – England's best opening since the First Test. How the strategic approach had altered since the Third Test was emphasized when Benaud overcame his distaste for 5 man on-side fields by placing such a restrictive setting for Davidson, who bowled half-pace cutters on the leg and middle stumps. This change of front helped keep England's second innings down to 34 an hour. Tactical clockwork is in need of a brisk winding-up when the first 23 hours of a Test are dawdled away before an attempt to win is crowded into part of the last 7 hours.

Dexter's declaration at lunch on the last day left 4 hours to get the Australians out. They needed 241 at 60 an hour to win but did not attempt such a dizzy acceleration on so sluggish a pitch where the run rate of the match had been 38 an hour. By taking 4 wickets for 70, Trueman and Allen scared the Australians enough to make Benaud direct Lawry and Burge to stay in. When the pair cautiously played out time, making Australia 152 for 4, about half the crowd hooted them from the field, especially Lawry for his dolefully dutiful 4 hours at 11 runs an hour. Dexter, entering the last Test with the rubber squared, had no wish to risk going home as loser of the series. Benaud, as holder of the Ashes, was this time unwilling to take a risk that might involve losing them. The upshot was that the attendance total at the 5 Tests was 30,000 below that of the previous English tour, and a series containing much enterprising cricket ended in anti-climax.

Only one of the rain-plagued 1964 Tests in England was finished – Australia's win at Headingley – but, appreciating the finest weather and wicket of the series, batsmen showed Old Trafford what could be achieved by unremitting concentration when conditions were heavily in their favour.

England had the better of the half-Tests which rain permitted at Trent Bridge and Lord's, and began with 268 at Headingley. Losing 7 for 178, the Australians were underdogs, unmistakably. Soon afterwards, Dexter made the bowling change which turned out to be the most ill-fated of his career: his replacement of 2 deeply respected spinners, Titmus and Gifford, with new-ball bowlers Trueman and Flavell. The change was no mere whim, as it aimed to take advantage of Hawke's lack of batting experience against a new ball. So far so good – but not for long. Dexter could hardly have foreseen that Burge and his partner would slam 42 runs off 7 inaccurate overs. He persisted with speed for 15 overs, which yielded 63 runs, before recalling Titmus. With masterful muscularity, Burge took control in the innings of his life. Seldom has such hooking and square-cutting been seen as for many of the 24 boundaries in his magnificent 160. In $5\frac{1}{4}$ hours the massive Queenslander's batting changed the course of the match. Burge made his 160 out of 211 added for the last 3 wickets before he was last out, caught near the boundary. Hawke and Grout, each 37, helped the 8th and 9th wickets to double the score, and Australia, 121 ahead, went on to win by 7 wickets.

Simpson turned his only toss win of the series to such profit on a flawless wicket at Old Trafford that he made sure of the Ashes by insuring Australia against defeat. On the way, the captain and Lawry (106 not out) set a 1st-wicket record for Australia and Simpson scored his 1st Test hundred. He had to wait 30 Tests for it and the fieldsmen had to wait 12 hours 40 minutes while he played the longest innings Englishmen ever endured. After 2 days he was 265 and Australia 570 for 4 wickets, though many contended that a more urgent run-rate and a declaration would have advanced Australia's cause more. Simpson's 311 is the highest score ever made by a Test captain and ranks 2nd to Bradman's 334 as the tallest innings for Australia. The Australians batted an hour into the 3rd day before Simpson's closure at 656 for 8. There was more than tit-for-tat in England's response. A sterner Dexter kept his head down as never before for 8 hours, making 174 with self-discipline more characteristic of Barrington, his partner in a 3rd-wicket stand of 246. Barrington stayed $11\frac{1}{2}$ hours in piling up 256, the 3rd highest innings ever played for England against Australia. He kept out 623 balls before falling low to McKenzie, whose 7 wickets came from impressive bowling on such a perfect pitch. Unchanged on the last day, off-spinner Veivers finished with 95·1 overs in the innings. England's 611 took 36 overs longer than Australia's 656 – no surprise by a side that had only a draw to play for. This is the only time anywhere around the globe that 600 or more has been answered by a like total. Dexter and his men could take pride in that, as proof of their determination not to allow the Australians to emerge from the unfinished match confident that they were the stronger side.

A rain curtain blotted out the Oval, but not before Cowdrey was hugged by Trueman on holding the slip catch which helped the resilient Yorkshireman to become the first man to take 300 Test wickets. I rank this as the greatest of all records as, in addition to talent and skill, it calls for physical strain and stamina exceeding anything demanded of batsmen. The 300 wickets took this colourful cricketer 13 years, 65 Tests and the sweat of 14,850 balls, delivered with much turbulence, marked truculence and accompanied by cuss-words beyond count.

McKenzie, hardest-worked bowler of the series, was rewarded with 29 wickets, equalling Grimmett's record for an Australian touring England. Simpson, finest slip-catcher of his generation – and, I believe, all generations – kept up his marvellous average of 2 catches a Test. In his purposeful captaincy he won his players' full confidence. The element which neither side could defeat was the rain.

In Australia in 1965–66 Simpson gave full credit to captain Mike Smith when, for the first time he had known, both sides stuck through a tour to a policy of playing bright cricket without jeopardy to either side's chance of winning. Hassett said other teams from England may have been better technically but none had tried so hard to make the game as interesting as possible. A broken wrist and chickenpox kept Simpson out of 2 Tests in which Booth led the side. Lawry, in the First Test at Brisbane, was not halfway toward his 166 when 19-year-old Doug Walters joined him for a debut of 155. Leg-spinner Philpott's 5 wickets enabled Booth to order a follow-on, but a rained-off Saturday prevented a finish. Each side had a leg-spinner and 2 off-spinners. At Melbourne hundreds by Edrich and Cowdrey put England 200 ahead on 1st innings, but Walters, with his second hundred, partnered Burge, 120, in a stand of 199. Time prevented a finish to a very high-scoring match.

Barber tanned 185 at Sydney off the first 67 overs of the match, still unequalled for an opening batsman's dictation to Test bowlers. Backing up Barber and Edrich, 103, David Brown's pace and Titmus's flighty off-spin put Australia down by an innings and 93. Returning to lead Australia at Adelaide, Simpson had most to do with the 4-day victory which levelled the series. He and Lawry in an opening stand of 244 passed England's score on their own, Simpson going on to a monumental 235. Opening bowlers McKenzie and Hawke shared 13 wickets in an innings win.

With an on-drive for his 2nd 6 in the final Test at Melbourne on a blameless pitch, Barrington hoisted a rousing 100 off 122 balls in England's opening score of 485. At the end of the 3rd day Australia were 333 for 3 with the left-handed Cowper not out for 159. Rain prevented any play on the 4th day, thus killing the game; but on the last Cowper batted on correct and tireless to make 307, the highest Test score and, spread over 12 hours, the longest innings ever played in Australia. As an exercise in patience and restraint Cowper's innings could not be faulted. Thus, through no fault of the players, another MCC tour ended in anti-climax. The long and short of it was that the batting of both sides was much stronger than the bowling.

Lawry brought the Australians to England in 1968, and it was his somewhat uncharacteristic seizure of the initiative in the 1st over after lunch on the 1st day of the First Test at Old Trafford which put Australia in winning gear. His attack on Pocock, the off-spinner, playing in his 1st home Test, including 2 sixes, made Cowdrey take him off. After Lawry and Walters had made 144 together Sheahan and Ian Chappell took the score on to 319 for 4 off the 1st day's 108 overs. When their opponents scored at only half that rate Sir Learie Constantine said England put the Test to sleep. The advantage carried Australia through to win by 159, though Pocock spun out 6 in the second innings. Out-fielding as well as out-batting England, the Australians held every catch.

With showers imminent at Lord's, Cowdrey promoted Milburn from No 6 to No 3. The best hooker and back-foot driver in the country entered in the 4th over and suffered many bruises in making 83; he was the unrivalled prizewinner for the innings of the match. Barrington also was at his best for 61 in England's 351 for 7. Brown, winner of the bowling prize, Snow and Knight sank Australia on a rain-softened pitch for 78, their worst score in England since 65 at the Oval in 1912. Rain, reducing the playing time by 15 hours, denied England the chance to win after Australia's follow-on reached 127 for 4.

On his way to his 21st Test hundred when England won the toss in the Third Test, Cowdrey needed a runner after tearing his left hamstring. Immobility prevented his giving more of the strike to Graveney (96). Cowdrey's inflexible pursuit of 409 in 9½ hours, after rain had prevented play on the 1st day, caused F. R. Brown to criticize a rate of 2·3 runs an over by a team, one down, having limited time for a win. Australia, 222, saved a follow-on and were set 330 to get in 373 minutes at 3 runs an over. Brown's criticism was borne out when rain washed out the last afternoon.

With Lawry (broken finger) and Cowdrey out of action, Jarman won the toss from Graveney at Headingley. With 92 out of 152, Redpath launched Australia towards 315. Connolly's best reward, 5 wickets, kept England 13 runs behind. Australia were 250 ahead by tea on the 4th day but, instead of hitting out to get England in before the close, they shut down in the last hour. By batting into the last day they used up time their bowlers would have needed to put Australia 2-up in the series. Set 325 to get in barely 5 hours, England still had 6 wickets standing at the end.

Edrich's chanceless 164 in 461 minutes at the Oval in the last Test made him 1st to exceed 500 in a home series since Compton in 1948. An admirable 158 by d'Oliveira (returning after having been dropped) helped England to reach 494. Lawry's reply took nearly as long but it was harder going because of bootmarks outside his off-stump. He was dropped at 58 and 84 off Snow before Knott caught him for 135 after 441 minutes. The gates were closed on the 2nd and 3rd days. England's 170 lead was built on to set Australia 362 to win at 54 an hour. A storm on the 5th morning looked like preventing a finish until scores of volunteers from the crowd helped the ground staff mop up the arena. After d'Oliveira had broken the only stand of the innings, Underwood, 7 for 50, took the last 4 wickets in 27 balls, finishing with Inverarity, lbw after a skilful resistance lasting 4 hours. England won with 5 minutes to spare and so shared the rubber. *Wisden* complimented the Australians on averaging 20 overs an hour when England were pressing for runs.

And so to the momentous series of 1970–71. Beginning with 6 in the first innings Snow's fast bowling dominated it. His 31 wickets were the most since Larwood's 32 in 1933. Illingworth's side was the first since the Second World War to score 7 Test hundreds. Boycott made 2 of them and figured in 6 century stands. He is the only visitor to reach 1,000 runs in first-class games before New Year.

Stackpole, 207, and Walters, 112, were the century makers in a drawn Test at Brisbane of which England had just the better. In the first Test played by England at Perth umpire Rowan warned Snow after Walters ducked 3 consecutive bouncers. Hundreds by Luckhurst, 131, and Edrich, 154, were answered by Redpath, 171, and Greg Chappell, an auspicious 108 in his 1st Test, likewise drawn. Boycott, 142, and Snow's 7 wickets in the 2nd innings in Sydney brought victory by 299. Lack of urgency in Lawry's captaincy after Australia led by 100 in Melbourne undermined his position. At his bowlers' wish, Illingworth spared Australia having to follow-on in Adelaide, where Stackpole, 136, and Ian Chappell, 109, celebrated the reprieve with a 2nd wicket stand of 262. Thereupon Australia for the first time in 70 years dropped their captain.

The Oval, 1968: the last day of the Fifth Test against Australia, when the spectators helped to dry up after a cloudburst. England won by 226 runs, Underwood taking the last of his 7 Australian wickets with 5 minutes left.

Winning his first toss, Ian Chappell got England out for 184 in the deciding Test at Sydney, Australia leading on first innings by 60. After Snow had felled Jenner, batting 9th, with a bouncer and Rowan had cautioned him, barrackers on the 2nd afternoon threw beercans on the field. Illingworth led his team off, but the umpires (whom Illingworth had not consulted) had them back on again in 7 minutes. Australia's hopes of making

Ashes-winners, 1970–71. Back row: B. L. d'Oliveira, K. Shuttleworth, G. C. A. Saulez (scorer), D. Wilson and P. Lever; second row: A. P. E. Knott, K. W. R. Fletcher, B. W. Luckhurst, D. L. Underwood, J. H. Hampshire, R. W. Taylor and A. Ward; front row: B. W. Thomas (assistant manager), J. A. Snow, M. C. Cowdrey, R. Illingworth (captain), J. H. Edrich, G. Boycott and D. G. Clark (manager).

223 to win, and so keeping the Ashes, faded when Knott stumped Greg Chappell off Illingworth, who with Underwood had the final say in an unduly contentious series.

Australia's morale touched rock bottom at Old Trafford in 1972, for they had suffered 7 defeats in 11 Tests and failed to win any. On a pitch suiting seamers Greig top-scored in both innings, 57 out of 249 and 62 of 249. Against Arnold's late swing Australia made only 142. Lillee and Snow took 8 wickets each and Lillee's 6 in the 2nd innings were his side's only encouragement. Eight were out for 147 when Marsh began a defiant onslaught for 91, his highest outside Australia. Though England won by an innings, 4 towering sixes from Marsh lifted his team's mood from its lowest point.

At Lord's in his 1st Test, Massie's 16 wickets, setting an Australian record, were the closest anyone has got to Laker's 19 and Barnes's 17. Massie baffled England with either-way swing of full length and control of line. Half his victims were dismissed from around the wicket. Lillee's speed kept batsmen under pressure in their innings of 272 and 116. Greg Chappell's 131 was the only outstanding Australian innings of the series, scored off 302 balls in 373 minutes against Snow, Price, Greig, d'Oliveira, Illingworth and Gifford. This Lord's win ended Australia's longest unsuccessful stretch against England, 11 Tests in all.

The most consistent scorer, Stackpole, made 114 at Trent Bridge, where Australia led by 126. Against Massie, Lillee and Colley, no Englishman reached 40 in the 1st innings, and, in the 2nd, Luckhurst's 96 was his side's top score for the series. Opening the 2nd innings, Ross Edwards played his finest innings, 70 not out. Ian Chappell's closure left England needing a record 4th innings, 451, in 10 hours, which would have meant 5 an over. On a dead pitch only 4 wickets fell in 148 overs.

A fungus affected the Headingley wicket. It took spin on the 1st day and the match ended on the 3rd. Though off-spinner Mallett took 5 wickets England went 117 ahead. No one could stay with Sheahan, 41 not out, in the 2nd innings, which totalled 136. Australian criticism of the pitch was deepened because it coincided with Underwood's 1st match of the series. The left-hander's 10 for 82 enabled England to win by 9 wickets. An inquiry was held into the sub-standard wicket – not the first of its kind on this ground.

Lillee's 10 wickets at the Oval where Australia arrived 1–2 down in the rubber were the chief factors in a victory which was the prelude to 4 successful years. In reply to 234, the Chappells made a 201 3rd-wicket stand, the 1st time brothers had scored centuries together in one Test. Ian, 113, hit 20 fours in 243 minutes and Greg, 118, 20 in 331 minutes. They had a hand in 5 century stands in the series. It was Illingworth's 4th loss in 26 Tests. For the first time in 5 series no Englishman reached 100. Four Australians, Stackpole, the Chappells and Sheahan, had higher averages than England's top batsman, Greig. On his 1st tour Lillee set an Australian record of 31 wickets in a series in England, as did Marsh's 23 victims behind the stumps; Snow's 24 were his most in a home series. The last day was the first telecast direct to Australia. 383,395 people paid £261,231 to watch the five Tests, a record for one series.

The 1974–75 series opened as usual at Brisbane where, retaliating for Willis and Peter Lever's bouncers to tail enders in the First Test, Lillee and Thomson assailed batsmen at great speed which on a pitch of unpredictable bounce broke hands, cracked ribs and inflicted many bruises. Batsmen, alarmed by the danger of injury, became shell-shocked.

Fall of the first 4 wickets for 57 to the fast attack reduced England's chance of approaching 309 until Greig answered savage speed with swashbuckling slashes over fieldsmen's heads. He challenged the bowlers with taunting gestures, such as patting the middle of a blade raised combatively. Greig's defiant 110, containing 15 fours, reduced the leeway to 44, but Thomson swept through the 2nd innings to bring Australia in by 166. Nine wickets in his 1st Test against England started him toward 33, most by an Australian fast bowler in a series at home. At the University of Western Australia his speed was timed at 92 miles an hour and a year later at 99·6 mph.

Following Greig's example with daring square-cuts, Knott, in the Perth Test, was one of only 2 Englishmen to reach a half-century. Titmus made a defiant 61, and Cowdrey, summoned following England's crop of injuries in Brisbane as a white hope from the depths of an English winter, and stepping almost straight from the aeroplane, managed 22 and 41. Edwards, 115, and Walters, 103, enabled Australia to win by 9 wickets. Only Walters raised a hundred with a 6 off a day's last ball.

The 1st of the 2 Melbourne Tests, unlike any of the other 5 in the series, was evenly contested, toe to toe, from first to last, as may be deduced from the extraordinary scoring pattern: England 242 and 244; Australia 241 and 238 for 8. This was the one time in the series when Amiss (and this on a pitch that no one quite trusted), in his 2nd innings, punished Lillee and Thomson with a succession of fine strokes. England were reduced to 4 bowlers when Hendrick in his 3rd over of the match tore a hamstring. Greig, with 6 wickets as well as a

Dennis Lillee: getting up steam. Jeff Thomson: the batsman's view.

crucial 60 in the 2nd innings, revelled in the extra responsibility. It was anyone's game to the last over, indeed to the last 4 balls when, with Australia's No. 10 arriving and 11 to get all 4 results were technically possible.

Denness, England's captain, who had led the side well but had had no batting success, stood down from the Fourth Test at Sydney where the pattern of Australian superiority reasserted itself. Edrich, leading England, made 83 for once out despite a sickening blow in the ribs at the start of his 2nd innings. He did his staunch best, and with Willis and Arnold as his partners the last 2 wickets lasted 2½ hours before Australia, for whom Redpath and Greg Chappell made hundreds, won the game and recaptured the Ashes with 5 overs to spare.

Australia gained their 4th victory at Adelaide without much difficulty, England failing once more against the fast bowling. That this was the beginning and end of the difference between the sides was evidenced at Melbourne in the last Test when, with Thomson away hurt and Lillee damaging himself after 6 overs, England made 529 and won by an innings and 4 runs. Fletcher (146) and Denness (188) by admirable batting made 192 together, the latter's score being the highest ever made by an England captain in Australia. Some excellent swing bowling by Peter Lever (6 for 38) on the 1st day gave England an advantage that was never threatened.

A few months later at Edgbaston, Denness's policy of sending in the side with the 2 fastest bowlers was designed to spare batsmen having to face them on a fresh pitch, but untimely rain presented Lillee, Thomson and the medium-fast Walker with a surface on which they bowled England, 101 and 173, to defeat by an innings and 85.

After England's defeat at Edgbaston Denness was replaced by Greig, who, although not by nature defensive, made a cautious start in the Second Test at Lord's. After Edrich had scored 175 in 9 hours in England's 2nd innings (they led by 47 runs on the 1st), the Australians thought it a compliment to their batting when Greig waited until England's lead crept to 483 before declaring. That left them 5 hours in which they scored 339 for 4 off 100 overs. At Headingley Australia promoted wicket-keeper Marsh as opener with McCosker, to make room for left-arm swinger Gilmour. Although the all-rounder's 9 wickets in the match seemed to justify this selection, it was not repeated at the Oval. Bowling England to a lead of 159, the slow left-armer Edmonds in his 1st Test took 3 of his 5 wickets in 7 balls. Leading old players of both sides criticized Greig for letting England's 2nd innings run right through to give a lead of 444. With McCosker 96 not out, the last 7 Australian wickets needed 225 on the 5th day. The match, however, was abandoned when the pitch was damaged in a campaign to free a bank robber (who incidentally, a year after release, was convicted of another armed robbery). Though 1 down, England gave avoidance of a second defeat priority over the chance to level the series.

At the Oval, in the Fourth and last Test (the number in this extra series dictated by the 1st Prudential World Cup) McCosker made his 1st Test hundred, 110. After the longest innings of his life, 440 minutes, Ian Chappell showed his disappointment when caught at 192. After dismissal for 191, England's follow-on became a desperate struggle to avoid a 2nd defeat. Woolmer batted 392 minutes for England's slowest-ever Test 100 and England stayed in from Friday to Wednesday afternoon, 14 hours 50 minutes. At Lord's 121,000 paid a world record gate, £125,000.

Melbourne's Centenary Test earned unprecedented attention and emphasized cricket's place as a pioneer in international sport. The match was the brainchild of Melbourne vice-president, Hans Ebeling, who had been an opening bowler in the Oval Test of 1934. The Centenary occasion spilt over even on to benches in factories, which made everything from ashtrays to T-shirts for sale as souvenirs.

David Hookes, batting in the Centenary Test from which he emerged as a cricketer of the highest promise.

When Greig sent Australia in, 120 ex-player guests from the 2 countries saw John Lever, Willis, Old and Underwood dismiss their team for 138. Their concern was matched by the dismay of 65 English Test cricketers at the sight of Lillee and Walker demolishing England for 95. Captain Greg Chappell's 40 was the only innings lasting 2 hours on the first 2 days. These low skirmishes left time for the match to develop in ways that brought the best out of the players and enthralled crowds totalling 247,875. The new left-hander David Hookes compelled attention by hitting Greig for four off the last 5 balls he received. Australia's livelier 53 per 100 balls (4·3 an over) challenged England to score similarly in the fourth innings.

When Marsh was 83 (he scored 110 not out in Australia's second innings), a figure suggestive of a part-wrapped mummy walked gingerly in, accompanied by a runner. It was McCosker, peering past a bandage around his wired jaw, broken by the ball with which Willis had bowled him in the 1st innings. Among the 67 balls McCosker faced were 4 bouncers, none of them from England's best bowler, Old (7 for 143 in the match). McCosker's plucky stay of 85 minutes had much to do with enabling Marsh to make the 1st hundred by an Australian wicket-keeper against England.

When Australia set England 463 to win, Derek Randall, making the most of chances at 42 and 146, formed the spinal column of a grand attempt that piled up 417, 11 runs more than the highest 4th innings to win any Test. With his distinctive shuffle to the line of the ball, and his irrepressible court-jester ways, he spangled his 174 with 21 fours, which skimmed over the outfield as smoothly as The Queen's Rolls-Royce. When bowler Greg Chappell's appeal for a snicked catch at 161 was upheld, Marsh called that the ball had not carried to his gloves; the departing batsman did not hear, so the captain recalled him. Randall's brisk rate – 53 per 100 balls – enabled England to average 3·71 an over.

Loss of wickets failed to chill England's glowing attempt to win until Lillee captured the last wicket (Knott), 45 short – by an extraordinary fluke exactly the same margin as Australia had won by in 1877. Compelling the fall of 11 wickets, Lillee, much like a scorpion among silkworms, made the difference between sides otherwise evenly matched.

Contentions about Kerry Packer's raid stirred up choppy seas for the 1977 Australian side to England, but it would strain credulity to accept opinions that it was the main cause of the team's foundering. Premature disclosure in mid-May of the signing of a dozen of the side dismayed the captain who had hoped at least to become embarked on the series before it became known that he and 11 of the others had secretly contracted to switch to World Series Cricket in the next summer Down Under. The tourists' team-spirit impressed Boycott, who said he had never played against an Australian

History at Headingley: Geoffrey Boycott in the Fourth Test of 1977 v Australia on-drives Greg Chappell for the 4 that takes him to his 100th hundred.

side that tried harder. When they were bowling and fielding all the players were encouraging each other and egging each other on.

Both captains thought there was little between the teams. Surer catching put the Englishmen in front. The First Test was drawn with little advantage to either side. As English victories in the next 3 Tests regained the Ashes mounting confidence lifted their form while loss of it eroded their opponents' catching and batting. It was like 1958–59 in reverse, accentuated this time by the number of players lacking experience in England. Once England's captain, Mike Brearley, found he held the selectors' faith for more than one Test his intelligent generalship's pressure against Australia's batsmen intensified.

With level-eyed scrutiny, Woolmer pulled England round from early losses in both innings of the First Test at Lord's with 79 and 120. Serjeant's sound 81 was the highest debut at Lord's since H. Graham's 107 not out in 1893. With a reshaped run-up Willis prevented Australia from getting more than 80 ahead. He finished with 9 wickets.

Entering in the 1st over at Old Trafford, Greg Chappell earned an ovation by hitting 15 fours and a six in making Australia's only hundred of the series, 112, while 7 partners contributed a mere 76. After 3 years of self-imposed exile, Boycott was brought back for the Third Test, after England had easily won the Second, and mustered 492 runs and figured in 3 century stands. Had McCosker held Boycott's edge at 20 off Pascoe, England, at Trent Bridge, would have been 6 down for 82, a springboard from which Australia might have squared the rubber with 2 Tests to go. As it was, Knott, with his 2nd hundred against Australia (135), gave his side a strong advantage on 1st innings, and England won again by 7 wickets. In his first 14 overs in Test cricket, Botham took 5 wickets, seaming either way – something that caused Chappell to predict a distinguished career. Boycott followed 107 and 80 not out at Trent Bridge with an innings perhaps beyond even his most sanguine dreams, for in front of his own Headingley crowd he reached his 100th hundred in first-class cricket, and went on to make 191. England's 3rd win in a row (something that had not happened since 1886) was gained by an innings and 85 runs on the 4th afternoon. Thomson, Pascoe, Walker and Bright bore the dropping of many catches with undismayed spirit. Compared with the bowler of the series, Willis, having his best rubber, 27 wickets, average 19, Thomson's 23 cost 6 runs more each and for each wicket he required 15 more balls. Yet his quickest balls were still the world's swiftest of the year and their steeper bounce the most fearsome. The Post Office answered 22,556,000 calls for Test scores, another English record.

Assertions that bowlers win matches passed unquestioned in 1978–79, when England again visited Australia. Even in days when pitches lay open to every raindrop no team ever lost all its wickets for under 200 9 times out of 12. From the first 'seaming' morning in Brisbane England had bowlers to probe into an inexperienced team's faults in technique and flaws in concentration. Brearley was a peerlessly observant skipper, whose direction of the bowlers and placing of fieldsmen for each opponent made Australia's new captain look like a learner feeling his way. Yallop, the only batsman to score 2 hundreds confessed that the Englishmen seemed able to concentrate longer. Three players chosen for special awards after England's 5–1 triumph were bowlers Hendrick, Botham and Miller, the last 2 with all-round qualifications.

After scoring 129 in the 2nd innings of the First Test Hughes, by his impulsiveness, rather let himself and his side down. At least twice the Englishmen confessed to relief at being spared when Hughes, a very gifted batsman, had them 'on toast'. Skilful bowling, led by Hendrick, drove Toohey from the heights of his 81 not out in the Second Test at Perth to

The England side which toured Australia in 1978–79 and retained the Ashes, winning the series 5–1. Back row: R. W. Tolchard, D. W. Randall, J. K. Lever, G. A. Gooch, J. E. Emburey, I. T. Botham, P. H. Edmonds, G. Miller, D. I. Gower, C. T. Radley and G. C. A. Saulez (scorer); sitting: B. W. Thomas (physiotherapist), M. Hendrick, R. W. Taylor, R. G. D. Willis, J. M. Brearley (captain), D. J. Insole (manager), G. Boycott, C. M. Old and K. F. Barrington (assistant manager).

an increasing lack of confidence and eventual rejection. Wood's opening 100 in Melbourne set Australia up, but he was involved in 5 out of 10 ruinous run-outs. Most of the 10 betrayed failure to observe elementary team-work. The bowlers' rout of England for 143 and 179 at Melbourne, in the Third Test, levered Australia through to their only win.

Darling's best innings of the series, 91, enabled Australia to lead by 141 in Sydney but 6 dropped catches helped the deliberation of Brearley's ringcraft to pull England through. Randall there batted 9½ self-disciplined hours for 150, the highest innings of the series. As Geoff Miller and John Emburey's off-spin undermined Australia for 111, Border, in his second Test, solidly completed 105 in the match without dismissal.

The comeback from a desperate position reaffirmed Brearley's status as one of England's most successful captains. As outstanding batsman and fieldsman, Gower carried off most runs in the series, made the finest century and ended with the highest average.

In his first international season, Hogg's pace, line and length earned an unprecedented string of records, headed by 41 wickets in 6 Tests, average 12. He and Hurst, often equally fast, were repeatedly let down by their batsmen. It reflected credit on these bowlers as on leg-spinner Higgs and the left-arm Dymock when Brearley said afterwards that 5 of the Tests could have gone the opposite way on the last day, and manager Doug Insole attributed the results as much to fortune as to comparative strength. Be that as it may, England in successive series, one with Packer players engaged and one without, had won 8 Tests, drawn 2, and lost 1 – a state of affairs, so far as they were concerned, quite without parallel.

From obscurity to fame inside a season: Rodney Hogg took 41 wickets for Australia against England in 1978–79.

ENGLAND V AUSTRALIA

			RESULT	CAPTAINS
1876–77	1 Melbourne	A 245, 104; E 196, 108	A 45 runs	J. Lillywhite, D. W. Gregory
	2 Melbourne	A 122, 259; E 261, 122–6	E 4 wkts	J. Lillywhite, D. W. Gregory
1878–79	1 Melbourne	E 113, 160; A 256, 19–0	A 10 wkts	Lord Harris, D. W. Gregory
1880	1 Oval	E 420, 57–5; A 149, 327	E 5 wkts	Lord Harris, W. L. Murdoch
1881–82	1 Melbourne	E 294, 308; A 320, 127–3	Drawn	A. Shaw, W. L. Murdoch
	2 Sydney	E 133, 232; A 197, 169–5	A 5 wkts	A. Shaw, W. L. Murdoch
	3 Sydney	E 188, 134; A 260, 66–4	A 6 wkts	A. Shaw, W. L. Murdoch
	4 Melbourne	E 309, 234–2; A 300	Drawn	A. Shaw, W. L. Murdoch
1882	1 Oval	A 63, 122; E 101, 77	A 7 runs	A. N. Hornby, W. L. Murdoch
1882–83	1 Melbourne	A 291, 58–1; E 177, 169	A 9 wkts	Hon Ivo Bligh, W. L. Murdoch
	2 Melbourne	E 294; A 114, 153	E inns 27 runs	Hon Ivo Bligh, W. L. Murdoch
	3 Sydney	E 247, 123; A 218, 83	E 69 runs	Hon Ivo Bligh, W. L. Murdoch
	4 Sydney	E 263, 197; A 262, 199–6	A 4 wkts	Hon Ivo Bligh, W. L. Murdoch
1884	1 Old Trafford	E 95, 180–9; A 182	Drawn	A. N. Hornby, W. L. Murdoch
	2 Lord's	A 229, 145; E 379	E inns 5 runs	Lord Harris, W. L. Murdoch
	3 Oval	A 551; E 346, 85–2	Drawn	Lord Harris, W. L. Murdoch
1884–85	1 Adelaide	A 243, 191; E 369, 67–2	E 8 wkts	A. Shrewsbury, W. L. Murdoch
	2 Melbourne	E 401, 7–0; A 279, 126	E 10 wkts	A. Shrewsbury, T. Horan
	3 Sydney	A 181, 165; E 133, 207	A 6 runs	A. Shrewsbury, H. H. Massie
	4 Sydney	E 269, 77; A 309, 40–2	A 8 wkts	A. Shrewsbury, J. M. Blackham
	5 Melbourne	A 163, 125; E 386	E inns 98 runs	A. Shrewsbury, T. Horan
1886	1 Old Trafford	A 205, 123; E 223, 107–6	E 4 wkts	A. G. Steel, H. J. H. Scott
	2 Lord's	E 353; A 121, 126	E inns 106 runs	A. G. Steel, H. J. H. Scott
	3 Oval	E 434; A 68, 149	E inns 217 runs	A. G. Steel, H. J. H. Scott
1886–87	1 Sydney	E 45, 184; A 119, 97	E 13 runs	A. Shrewsbury, P. S. McDonnell
	2 Sydney	E 151, 154; A 84, 150	E 71 runs	A. Shrewsbury, P. S. McDonnell
1887–88	1 Sydney	E 113, 137; A 42, 82	E 126 runs	W. W. Read, P. S. McDonnell
1888	1 Lord's	A 116, 60; E 53, 62	A 61 runs	A. G. Steel, P. S. McDonnell
	2 Oval	A 80, 100; E 317	E inns 137 runs	W. G. Grace, P. S. McDonnell
	3 Old Trafford	E 172; A 81, 70	E inns 21 runs	W. G. Grace, P. S. McDonnell
1890	1 Lord's	A 132, 176; E 173, 137–3	E 7 wkts	W. G. Grace, W. L. Murdoch
	2 Oval	A 92, 102; E 100, 95–8	E 2 wkts	W. G. Grace, W. L. Murdoch
1891–92	1 Melbourne	A 240, 236; E 264, 158	A 54 runs	W. G. Grace, J. M. Blackham
	2 Sydney	A 145, 391; E 307, 157	A 72 runs	W. G. Grace, J. M. Blackham
	3 Adelaide	E 499; A 100, 169	E inns 230 runs	W. G. Grace, J. M. Blackham
1893	1 Lord's	E 334, 234–8D; A 269	Drawn	A. E. Stoddart, J. M. Blackham
	2 Oval	E 483; A 91, 349	E inns 43 runs	W. G. Grace, J. M. Blackham
	3 Old Trafford	A 204, 236; E 243, 118–4	Drawn	W. G. Grace, J. M. Blackham
1894–95	1 Sydney	A 586, 166; E 325, 437	E 10 runs	A. E. Stoddart, J. M. Blackham
	2 Melbourne	E 75, 475; A 123, 333	E 94 runs	A. E. Stoddart, G. Giffen
	3 Adelaide	A 238, 411; E 124, 143	A 382 runs	A. E. Stoddart, G. Giffen
	4 Sydney	A 284; E 65, 72	A inns 147 runs	A. E. Stoddart, G. Giffen
	5 Melbourne	A 414, 267; E 385, 298–4	E 6 wkts	A. E. Stoddart, G. Giffen
1896	1 Lord's	A 53, 347; E 292, 111–4	E 6 wkts	W. G. Grace, G. H. S. Trott
	2 Old Trafford	A 412, 125–7; E 231, 305	A 3 wkts	W. G. Grace, G. H. S. Trott
	3 Oval	E 145, 84; A 119, 44	E 66 runs	W. G. Grace, G. H. S. Trott
1897–98	1 Sydney	E 551, 96–1; A 237, 408	E 9 wkts	A. C. MacLaren, G. H. S. Trott
	2 Melbourne	A 520; E 315, 150	A inns 55 runs	A. C. MacLaren, G. H. S. Trott

	3 Adelaide	A 573; E 278, 282	A inns 13 runs	A. E. Stoddart, G. H. S. Trott
	4 Melbourne	A 323, 115–2; E 174, 263	A 8 wkts	A. E. Stoddart, G. H. S. Trott
	5 Sydney	E 335, 178; A 239, 276–4	A 6 wkts	A. C. MacLaren, G. H. S. Trott
1899	1 Trent Bridge	A 252, 230–8D; E 193, 155–7	Drawn	W. G. Grace, J. Darling
	2 Lord's	E 206, 240; A 421, 28–0	A 10 wkts	A. C. MacLaren, J. Darling
	3 Headingley	A 172, 224; E 220, 19–0	Drawn	A. C. MacLaren, J. Darling
	4 Old Trafford	E 372, 94–3; A 196, 346–7D	Drawn	A. C. MacLaren, J. Darling
	5 Oval	E 576; A 352, 254–5	Drawn	A. C. MacLaren, J. Darling
1901–02	1 Sydney	E 464; A 168, 172	E inns 124 runs	A. C. MacLaren, J. Darling
	2 Melbourne	A 112, 353; E 61, 175	A 229 runs	A. C. MacLaren, J. Darling
	3 Adelaide	E 388, 247; A 321, 315–6	A 4 wkts	A. C. MacLaren, J. Darling
	4 Sydney	E 317, 99; A 299, 121–3	A 7 wkts	A. C. MacLaren, H. Trumble
	5 Melbourne	A 144, 255; E 189, 178	A 32 runs	A. C. MacLaren, H. Trumble
1902	1 Edgbaston	E 376–9D; A 36, 46–2	Drawn	A. C. MacLaren, J. Darling
	2 Lord's	E 102–2; A –	Drawn	A. C. MacLaren, J. Darling
	3 Sheffield	A 194, 289; E 145, 195	A 143 runs	A. C. MacLaren, J. Darling
	4 Old Trafford	A 299, 86; E 262, 120	A 3 runs	A. C. MacLaren, J. Darling
	5 Oval	A 324, 121; E 183, 263–9	E 1 wkt	A. C. MacLaren, J. Darling
1903–04	1 Sydney	A 285, 485; E 577, 194–5	E 5 wkts	P. F. Warner, M. A. Noble
	2 Melbourne	E 315, 103; A 122, 111	E 185 runs	P. F. Warner, M. A. Noble
	3 Adelaide	A 388, 351; E 245, 278	A 216 runs	P. F. Warner, M. A. Noble
	4 Sydney	E 249, 210; A 131, 171	E 157 runs	P. F. Warner, M. A. Noble
	5 Melbourne	A 247, 133; E 61, 101	A 218 runs	P. F. Warner, M. A. Noble
1905	1 Trent Bridge	E 196, 426–5D; A 221, 188	E 213 runs	F. S. Jackson, J. Darling
	2 Lord's	E 282, 151–5; A 181	Drawn	F. S. Jackson, J. Darling
	3 Headingley	E 301, 295–5D; A 195, 224–7	Drawn	F. S. Jackson, J. Darling
	4 Old Trafford	E 446; A 197, 169	E inns 80 runs	F. S. Jackson, J. Darling
	5 Oval	E 430, 261–6D; A 363, 124–4	Drawn	F. S. Jackson, J. Darling
1907–08	1 Sydney	E 273, 300; A 300, 275–8	A 2 wkts	F. L. Fane, M. A. Noble
	2 Melbourne	A 266, 397; E 382, 282–9D	E 1 wkt	F. L. Fane, M. A. Noble
	3 Adelaide	A 285, 506; E 363, 183	A 245 runs	F. L. Fane, M. A. Noble
	4 Melbourne	A 214, 385; E 105, 186	A 308 runs	A. O. Jones, M. A. Noble
	5 Sydney	A 137, 422; E 281, 229	A 49 runs	A. O. Jones, M. A. Noble
1909	1 Edgbaston	A 74, 151; E 121, 105–0	E 10 wkts	A. C. MacLaren, M. A. Noble
	2 Lord's	E 269, 121; A 350, 41–1	A 9 wkts	A. C. MacLaren, M. A. Noble
	3 Headingley	A 188, 207; E 182, 87	A 126 runs	A. C. MacLaren, M. A. Noble
	4 Old Trafford	A 147, 279–9D; E 119, 108–3	Drawn	A. C. MacLaren, M. A. Noble
	5 Oval	A 325, 339–5D; E 352, 104–3	Drawn	A. C. MacLaren, M. A. Noble
1911–12	1 Sydney	A 447, 308; E 318, 291	A 146 runs	J. W. H. T. Douglas, C. Hill
	2 Melbourne	A 184, 299; E 265, 219–2	E 8 wkts	J. W. H. T. Douglas, C. Hill
	3 Adelaide	A 133, 476; E 501, 112–3	E 7 wkts	J. W. H. T. Douglas, C. Hill
	4 Melbourne	A 191, 173; E 589	E inns 225	J. W. H. T. Douglas, C. Hill
	5 Sydney	E 324, 214; A 176, 292	E 70 runs	J. W. H. T. Douglas, C. Hill
1912	1 Lord's	E 310–7D; A 282–7	Drawn	C. B. Fry, S. E. Gregory
	2 Old Trafford	E 203; A 14–0	Drawn	C. B. Fry, S. E. Gregory
	3 Oval	E 245, 175; A 111, 65	E 244 runs	C. B. Fry, S. E. Gregory
1920–21	1 Sydney	A 267, 581; E 190, 281	A 377 runs	J. W. H. T. Douglas, W. W. Armstrong
	2 Melbourne	A 499; E 251, 157	A inns 91 runs	J. W. H. T. Douglas, W. W. Armstrong
	3 Adelaide	A 354, 582; E 447, 370	A 119 runs	J. W. H. T. Douglas, W. W. Armstrong
	4 Melbourne	E 284, 315; A 389, 211–2	A 8 wkts	J. W. H. T. Douglas, W. W. Armstrong
	5 Sydney	E 204, 280; A 392, 93–1	A 9 wkts	J. W. H. T. Douglas, W. W. Armstrong
1921	1 Trent Bridge	E 112, 147; A 232, 30–0	A 10 wkts	J. W. H. T. Douglas, W. W. Armstrong
	2 Lord's	E 187, 283; A 342, 131–2	A 8 wkts	J. W. H. T. Douglas, W. W. Armstrong
	3 Headingley	A 407, 273–7D; E 259, 202	A 219 runs	L. H. Tennyson, W. W. Armstrong
	4 Old Trafford	E 362–4D, 44–1; A 175	Drawn	L. H. Tennyson, W. W. Armstrong
	5 Oval	E 403–8D, 244–2; A 389	Drawn	L. H. Tennyson, W. W. Armstrong
1924–25	1 Sydney	A 450, 452; E 298, 411	A 193 runs	A. E. R. Gilligan, H. L. Collins
	2 Melbourne	A 600, 250; E 479, 290	A 81 runs	A. E. R. Gilligan, H. L. Collins
	3 Adelaide	A 489, 250; E 365, 363	A 11 runs	A. E. R. Gilligan, H. L. Collins
	4 Melbourne	E 548; A 269, 250	E inns 29 runs	A. E. R. Gilligan, H. L. Collins
	5 Sydney	A 295, 325; E 167, 146	A 307 runs	A. E. R. Gilligan, H. L. Collins
1926	1 Trent Bridge	E 32–0; A –	Drawn	A. W. Carr, H. L. Collins
	2 Lord's	A 383, 194–5; E 475–3D	Drawn	A. W. Carr, H. L. Collins
	3 Headingley	A 494; E 294, 254–3	Drawn	A. W. Carr, W. Bardsley
	4 Old Trafford	A 335; E 305–5	Drawn	A. W. Carr, W. Bardsley
	5 Oval	E 280, 436; A 302, 125	E 289 runs	A. P. F. Chapman, H. L. Collins
1928–29	1 Brisbane	E 521, 342–8D; A 122, 66	E 675 runs	A. P. F. Chapman, J. Ryder
	2 Sydney	A 253, 397; E 636, 16–2	E 8 wkts	A. P. F. Chapman, J. Ryder
	3 Melbourne	A 397, 351; E 417, 332–7	E 3 wkts	A. P. F. Chapman, J. Ryder
	4 Adelaide	E 334, 383; A 369, 336	E 12 runs	A. P. F. Chapman, J. Ryder
	5 Melbourne	E 519, 257; A 491, 287–5	A 5 wkts	J. C. White, J. Ryder
1930	1 Trent Bridge	E 270, 302; A 144, 335	E 93 runs	A. P. F. Chapman, W. M. Woodfull
	2 Lord's	E 425, 375; A 729–6D, 72–3	A 7 wkts	A. P. F. Chapman, W. M. Woodfull
	3 Headingley	A 566; E 391, 95–3	Drawn	A. P. F. Chapman, W. M. Woodfull
	4 Old Trafford	A 345; E 251–8	Drawn	A. P. F. Chapman, W. M. Woodfull
	5 Oval	E 405, 251; A 695	A inns 39 runs	R. E. S. Wyatt, W. M. Woodfull
1932–33	1 Sydney	A 360, 164; E 524, 1–0	E 10 wkts	D. R. Jardine, W. M. Woodfull
	2 Melbourne	A 228, 191; E 169, 139	A 111 runs	D. R. Jardine, W. M. Woodfull
	3 Adelaide	E 341, 412; A 222, 193	E 338 runs	D. R. Jardine, W. M. Woodfull

	4 Brisbane	A 340, 175; E 356, 162–4	E 6 wkts	D. R. Jardine, W. M. Woodfull
	5 Sydney	A 435, 182; E 454, 168–2	E 8 wkts	D. R. Jardine, W. M. Woodfull
1934	1 Trent Bridge	A 374, 273–8D; E 268, 141	A 238 runs	C. F. Walters, W. M. Woodfull
	2 Lord's	E 440; A 284, 118	E inns 38 runs	R. E. S. Wyatt, W. M. Woodfull
	3 Old Trafford	E 627–9D, 123–0D; A 491, 66–1	Drawn	R. E. S. Wyatt, W. M. Woodfull
	4 Headingley	E 200, 229–6; A 584	Drawn	R. E. S. Wyatt, W. M. Woodfull
	5 Oval	A 701, 327; E 321, 145	A 562 runs	R. E. S. Wyatt, W. M. Woodfull
1936–37	1 Brisbane	E 358, 256; A 234, 58	E 322 runs	G. O. Allen, D. G. Bradman
	2 Sydney	E 426–6D; A 80, 324	E inns 22 runs	G. O. Allen, D. G. Bradman
	3 Melbourne	A 200–9D, 564; E 76–9D, 323	A 365 runs	G. O. Allen, D. G. Bradman
	4 Adelaide	A 288, 433; E 330, 243	A 148 runs	G. O. Allen, D. G. Bradman
	5 Melbourne	A 604; E 239, 165	A inns 200 runs	G. O. Allen, D. G. Bradman
1938	1 Trent Bridge	E 658–8D; A 411, 427–6	Drawn	W. R. Hammond, D. G. Bradman
	2 Lord's	E 494, 242–8D; A 422, 204–6	Drawn	W. R. Hammond, D. G. Bradman
	3 Headingley	E 223, 123; A 242, 107–5	A 5 wkts	W. R. Hammond, D. G. Bradman
	4 Old Trafford	No Play		
	5 Oval	E 903–7D; A 201, 123	E inns 579 runs	W. R. Hammond, D. G. Bradman
1946–47	1 Brisbane	A 645; E 141, 172	A inns 332 runs	W. R. Hammond, D. G. Bradman
	2 Sydney	E 255, 371; A 659–8D	A inns 33 runs	W. R. Hammond, D. G. Bradman
	3 Melbourne	A 365, 536; E 351, 310–7	Drawn	W. R. Hammond, D. G. Bradman
	4 Adelaide	E 460, 340–8D; A 487, 215–1	Drawn	W. R. Hammond, D. G. Bradman
	5 Sydney	E 280, 186; A 253, 214–5	A 5 wkts	N. W. D. Yardley, D. G. Bradman
1948	1 Trent Bridge	E 165, 441; A 509, 98–2	A 8 wkts	N. W. D. Yardley, D. G. Bradman
	2 Lord's	A 350, 460–7D; E 215, 186	A 409 runs	N. W. D. Yardley, D. G. Bradman
	3 Old Trafford	E 363, 174–3D; A 221, 92–1	Drawn	N. W. D. Yardley, D. G. Bradman
	4 Headingley	E 496, 365–8D; A 458, 404–3	A 7 wkts	N. W. D. Yardley, D. G. Bradman
	5 Oval	E 52, 188; A 389	A inns 149 runs	N. W. D. Yardley, D. G. Bradman
1950–51	1 Brisbane	A 228, 32–7D; E 68–7D, 122	A 70 runs	F. R. Brown, A. L. Hassett
	2 Melbourne	A 194, 181; E 197, 150	A 28 runs	F. R. Brown, A. L. Hassett
	3 Sydney	E 290, 123; A 426	A inns 13 runs	F. R. Brown, A. L. Hassett
	4 Adelaide	A 371, 403–8D; E 272, 228	A 274 runs	F. R. Brown, A. L. Hassett
	5 Melbourne	A 217, 197; E 320, 95–2	E 8 wkts	F. R. Brown, A. L. Hassett
1953	1 Trent Bridge	A 249, 123; E 144, 120–1	Drawn	L. Hutton, A. L. Hassett
	2 Lord's	A 346, 368; E 372, 282–7	Drawn	L. Hutton, A. L. Hassett
	3 Old Trafford	A 318, 35–8; E 276	Drawn	L. Hutton, A. L. Hassett
	4 Headingley	E 167, 275; A 266, 147–4	Drawn	L. Hutton, A. L. Hassett
	5 Oval	A 275, 162; E 306, 132–2	E 8 wkts	L. Hutton, A. L. Hassett
1954–55	1 Brisbane	A 601–8D; E 190, 257	A inns 154 runs	L. Hutton, I. W. Johnson
	2 Sydney	E 154, 296; A 228, 184	E 38 runs	L. Hutton, A. R. Morris
	3 Melbourne	E 191, 279; A 231, 111	E 128 runs	L. Hutton, I. W. Johnson
	4 Adelaide	A 323, 111; E 341, 97–5	E 5 wkts	L. Hutton, I. W. Johnson
	5 Sydney	E 371–7D; A 221, 118–6	Drawn	L. Hutton, I. W. Johnson
1956	1 Trent Bridge	E 217–8D, 188–3D; A 149, 120–3	Drawn	P. B. H. May, I. W. Johnson
	2 Lord's	A 285, 257; E 171, 186	A 185 runs	P. B. H. May, I. W. Johnson
	3 Headingley	E 325; A 143, 140	E inns 42 runs	P. B. H. May, I. W. Johnson
	4 Old Trafford	E 459; A 84, 205	E inns 170 runs	P. B. H. May, I. W. Johnson
	5 Oval	E 247, 182–3D; A 202, 27–5	Drawn	P. B. H. May, I. W. Johnson
1958–59	1 Brisbane	E 134, 198; A 186, 147–2	A 8 wkts	P. B. H. May, R. Benaud
	2 Melbourne	E 259, 87; A 308, 42–2	A 8 wkts	P. B. H. May, R. Benaud
	3 Sydney	E 219, 287–7D; A 357, 54–2	Drawn	P. B. H. May, R. Benaud
	4 Adelaide	A 476, 36–0; E 240, 270	A 10 wkts	P. B. H. May, R. Benaud
	5 Melbourne	E 205, 214; A 351, 69–1	A 9 wkts	P. B. H. May, R. Benaud
1961	1 Edgbaston	E 195, 401–4; A 516–9D	Drawn	M. C. Cowdrey, R. Benaud
	2 Lord's	E 206, 202; A 340, 71–5	A 5 wkts	M. C. Cowdrey, R. N. Harvey
	3 Headingley	A 237, 120; E 299, 62–2	E 8 wkts	P. B. H. May, R. Benaud
	4 Old Trafford	A 190, 432; E 367, 201	A 54 runs	P. B. H. May, R. Benaud
	5 Oval	E 256, 370–8; A 494	Drawn	P. B. H. May, R. Benaud
1962–63	1 Brisbane	A 404, 362–4D; E 389, 278–6	Drawn	E. R. Dexter, R. Benaud
	2 Melbourne	A 316, 248; E 331, 237–3	E 7 wkts	E. R. Dexter, R. Benaud
	3 Sydney	E 279, 104; A 319, 67–2	A 8 wkts	E. R. Dexter, R. Benaud
	4 Adelaide	A 393, 293; E 331, 223–4	Drawn	E. R. Dexter, R. Benaud
	5 Sydney	E 321, 268–8D; A 349, 152–4	Drawn	E. R. Dexter, R. Benaud
1964	1 Trent Bridge	E 216–8D, 193–9D; A 168, 40–2	Drawn	E. R. Dexter, R. B. Simpson
	2 Lord's	A 176, 168–4; E 246	Drawn	E. R. Dexter, R. B. Simpson
	3 Headingley	E 268, 229 A 389, 111–3	A 7 wkts	E. R. Dexter, R. B. Simpson
	4 Old Trafford	A 656–8D, 4–0; E 611	Drawn	E. R. Dexter, R. B. Simpson
	5 Oval	E 182, 381–4; A 379	Drawn	E. R. Dexter, R. B. Simpson
1965–66	1 Brisbane	A 443–6D; E 280, 186–3	Drawn	M. J. K. Smith, B. C. Booth
	2 Melbourne	A 358, 426; E 558, 5–0	Drawn	M. J. K. Smith, R. B. Simpson
	3 Sydney	E 488; A 221, 174	E inns 93 runs	M. J. K. Smith, R. B. Simpson
	4 Adelaide	E 241, 266; A 516	A inns 9 runs	M. J. K. Smith, B. C. Booth
	5 Melbourne	E 485–9D; 69–3; A 543–8D	Drawn	M. J. K. Smith, R. B. Simpson
1968	1 Old Trafford	A 357, 220; E 165, 253	A 159 runs	M. C. Cowdrey, W. M. Lawry
	2 Lord's	E 351–7D; A 78, 127–4	Drawn	M. C. Cowdrey, W. M. Lawry
	3 Edgbaston	E 409, 142–3D; A 222, 68–1	Drawn	M. C. Cowdrey, W. M. Lawry
	4 Headingley	A 315, 312; E 302, 230–4	Drawn	T. W. Graveney, B. N. Jarman
	5 Oval	E 494, 181; A 324, 125	E 226 runs	M. C. Cowdrey, W. M. Lawry
1970–71	1 Brisbane	A 433, 214; E 464, 39–1	Drawn	R. Illingworth, W. M. Lawry
	2 Perth	E 397, 287–6D; A 440, 100–3	Drawn	R. Illingworth, W. M. Lawry

	3 Melbourne	No play		
	4 Sydney	E 332, 319–5D; A 236, 116	E 299 runs	R. Illingworth, W. M. Lawry
	5 Melbourne	A 493–9D, 169–4D; E 392, 161–0	Drawn	R. Illingworth, W. M. Lawry
	6 Adelaide	E 470, 233–4D; A 235, 328–3	Drawn	R. Illingworth, W. M. Lawry
	7 Sydney	E 184, 302; A 264, 160	E 62 runs	R. Illingworth, I. M. Chappell
1972	1 Old Trafford	E 249, 234; A 142, 252	E 89 runs	R. Illingworth, I. M. Chappell
	2 Lord's	E 272, 116; A 308, 81–2	A 8 wkts	R. Illingworth, I. M. Chappell
	3 Trent Bridge	A 315, 324–4D; E 189, 290–4	Drawn	R. Illingworth, I. M. Chappell
	4 Headingley	A 146, 136; E 263, 21–1	E 9 wkts	R. Illingworth, I. M. Chappell
	5 Oval	E 284, 356; A 399, 242–5	A 5 wkts	R. Illingworth, I. M. Chappell
1974–75	1 Brisbane	A 309, 288–5D; E 265, 166	A 166 runs	M. H. Denness, I. M. Chappell
	2 Perth	E 208, 293; A 481, 23–1	A 9 wkts	M. H. Denness, I. M. Chappell
	3 Melbourne	E 242, 244; A 241, 238–8	Drawn	M. H. Denness, I. M. Chappell
	4 Sydney	A 405, 289–4D; E 295, 228	A 171 runs	J. H. Edrich, I. M. Chappell
	5 Adelaide	A 304, 272–5D; E 172, 241	A 163 runs	M. H. Denness, I. M. Chappell
	6 Melbourne	A 152, 373; E 529	E inns 4 runs	M. H. Denness, I. M. Chappell
1975	1 Edgbaston	A 359; E 101, 173	A inns 85 runs	M. H. Denness, I. M. Chappell
	2 Lord's	E 315, 436–7D; A 268, 329–3	Drawn	A. W. Greig, I. M. Chappell
	3 Headingley	E 288, 291; A 135, 220–3	Drawn	A. W. Greig, I. M. Chappell
	4 Oval	A 532–9D, 40–2; E 191, 538	Drawn	A. W. Greig, I. M. Chappell
1976–77	1 Melbourne	A 138, 419–9D; E 95, 417	A 45 runs	A. W. Greig, G. S. Chappell
1977	1 Lord's	E 216, 305; A 296, 114–6	Drawn	J. M. Brearley, G. S. Chappell
	2 Old Trafford	A 297, 218; E 437, 82–1	E 9 wkts	J. M. Brearley, G. S. Chappell
	3 Trent Bridge	A 243, 309; E 364, 189–3	E 7 wkts	J. M. Brearley, G. S. Chappell
	4 Headingley	E 436; A 103, 248	E inns 85 runs	J. M. Brearley, G. S. Chappell
	5 Oval	E 214, 57–2; A 385	Drawn	J. M. Brearley, G. S. Chappell
1978–79	1 Brisbane	A 116, 339; E 286, 170–3	E 7 wkts	J. M. Brearley, G. N. Yallop
	2 Perth	E 309, 208; A 190, 161	E 166 runs	J. M. Brearley, G. N. Yallop
	3 Melbourne	A 258, 167; E 143, 179	A 103 runs	J. M. Brearley, G. N. Yallop
	4 Sydney	E 152, 346; A 294, 111	E 93 runs	J. M. Brearley, G. N. Yallop
	5 Adelaide	E 169, 360; A 164, 160	E 205 runs	J. M. Brearley, G. N. Yallop
	6 Sydney	A 198, 143; E 308, 35–1	E 9 wkts	J. M. Brearley, G. N. Yallop

CAPTAINS (England)	TESTS	WON	LOST	DRAWN
J. Lillywhite	2	1	1	
Lord Harris	4	2	1	1
A. Shaw	4		2	2
A. N. Hornby	2		1	1
Hon Ivo Bligh	4	2	2	
A. Shrewsbury	7	5	2	
A. G. Steel	4	3	1	
W. W. Read	1	1		
W. G. Grace	13	8	3	2
A. E. Stoddart	8	3	4	1
A. C. MacLaren	22	4	11	7
P. F. Warner	5	3	2	
F. S. Jackson	5	2		3
F. L. Fane	3	1	2	
A. O. Jones	2		2	
J. W. H. T. Douglas	12	4	8	
C. B. Fry	3	1		2
L. H. Tennyson	3		1	2
A. E. R. Gilligan	5	1	4	
A. W. Carr	4			4
A. P. F. Chapman	9	6	1	2
J. C. White	1		1	
R. E. S. Wyatt	5	1	2	2
D. R. Jardine	5	4	1	
C. F. Walters	1		1	
G. O. Allen	5	2	3	
W. R. Hammond	8	1	3	4
N. W. D. Yardley	6		5	1
F. R. Brown	5	1	4	
L. Hutton	10	4	1	5
P. B. H. May	13	3	6	4
M. C. Cowdrey	6	1	2	3
E. R. Dexter	10	1	2	7
M. J. K. Smith	5	1	1	3
T. W. Graveney	1			1
R. Illingworth	11	4	2	5
M. H. Denness	6	1	4	1
J. H. Edrich	1		1	
A. W. Greig	4		1	3
J. M. Brearley	11	8	1	2
	236	79	89	68

CAPTAINS (Australia)	TESTS	WON	LOST	DRAWN
D. W. Gregory	3	2	1	
W. L. Murdoch	16	5	7	4
T. Horan	2		2	
H. H. Massie	1	1		
J. M. Blackham	8	3	3	2
H. J. H. Scott	3		3	
P. S. McDonnell	6	1	5	
G. Giffen	4	2	2	
G. H. S. Trott	8	5	3	
J. Darling	18	5	4	9
H. Trumble	2	2		
M. A. Noble	15	8	5	2
C. Hill	5	1	4	
S. E. Gregory	3		1	2
W. W. Armstrong	10	8		2
H. L. Collins	8	4	2	2
W. Bardsley	2			2
J. Ryder	5	1	4	
W. M. Woodfull	15	5	6	4
D. G. Bradman	19	11	3	5
A. L. Hassett	10	4	2	4
I. W. Johnson	9	2	4	3
A. R. Morris	1		1	
R. Benaud	14	6	2	6
R. N. Harvey	1	1		
R. B. Simpson	8	2		6
B. C. Booth	2		1	1
W. M. Lawry	9	1	2	6
B. N. Jarman	1			1
I. M. Chappell	16	7	4	5
G. S. Chappell	6	1	3	2
G. N. Yallop	6	1	5	
	236	89	79	68

HIGHEST INNINGS TOTALS

England in England, 903–7D, Oval 1938
England in Australia, 636, Sydney 1928–29
Australia in England, 729–6D, Lord's 1930
Australia in Australia, 659–8D Sydney 1946–47

LOWEST INNINGS TOTALS

England in England, 52, Oval 1948
England in Australia, 45, Sydney 1886–87
Australia in England, 36, Edgbaston 1902
Australia in Australia, 42, Sydney 1887–88

HIGHEST INDIVIDUAL INNINGS

England in England, 364, L. Hutton, Oval 1938
England in Australia, 287, R. E. Foster, Sydney 1903–04
Australia in England, 334, D. G. Bradman, Headingley 1930
Australia in Australia, 307, R. M. Cowper, Sydney 1965–66

HIGHEST AGGREGATE OF RUNS IN A SERIES

England in England, 562, D. C. S. Compton 1948
England in Australia, 905, W. R. Hammond 1928–29
Australia in England, 974, D. G. Bradman 1930
Australia in Australia, 810, D. G. Bradman 1936–37

BEST INNINGS BOWLING FIGURES

England in England, 10–53, J. C. Laker, Old Trafford 1956
England in Australia, 8–35, G. A. Lohmann, Sydney 1886–87
Australia in England, 8–31, F. Laver, Old Trafford 1909
Australia in Australia, 9–121, A. A. Mailey, Melbourne 1920–21

BEST MATCH BOWLING FIGURES

England in England, 19–90, J. C. Laker, Old Trafford 1956
England in Australia, 15–124, W. Rhodes, Melbourne 1903–04
Australia in England, 16–137, R. A. L. Massie, Lord's 1972
Australia in Australia, 13–77, M. A. Noble, Melbourne 1901–02

HIGHEST WICKET AGGREGATE IN A SERIES

England in England, 46, J. C. Laker 1956
England in Australia, 44, I. T. Botham 1978–79
Australia in England, 31, D. K. Lillee 1972
Australia in Australia, 41, R. M. Hogg 1978–79

RECORD WICKET PARTNERSHIPS – ENGLAND

1 J. B. Hobbs and W. Rhodes, 323, Melbourne 1911–12
2 L. Hutton and M. Leyland, 382, Oval 1938
3 W. R. Hammond and D. R. Jardine, 262, Adelaide 1928–29
4 W. R. Hammond and E. Paynter, 222, Lord's 1938
5 E. Paynter and D. C. S. Compton, 206, Trent Bridge 1938
6 { L. Hutton and J. Hardstaff, Jr, 215, Oval 1938
G. Boycott and A. P. E. Knott, 215, Trent Bridge 1977 }
7 F. E. Woolley and J. Vine, 143, Sydney 1911–12
8 E. H. Hendren and H. Larwood, 124, Brisbane 1928–29
9 W. H. Scotton and W. W. Read, 151, Oval 1884
10 R. E. Foster and W. Rhodes, 130, Sydney 1903–04

RECORD WICKET PARTNERSHIPS – AUSTRALIA

1 W. M. Lawry and R. B. Simpson, 244, Adelaide 1965–66
2 W. H. Ponsford and D. G. Bradman, 451, Oval 1934
3 D. G. Bradman and A. L. Hassett, 276, Brisbane 1946–47
4 W. H. Ponsford and D. G. Bradman, 388, Headingley 1934
5 S. G. Barnes and D. G. Bradman, 405, Sydney 1946–47
6 J. H. Fingleton and D. G. Bradman, 346, Melbourne 1936–37
7 C. Hill and H. Trumble, 165, Melbourne 1897–98
8 C. Hill and R. J. Hartigan, 243, Adelaide 1907–08
9 S. E. Gregory and J. M. Blackham, 154, Sydney 1894–95
10 J. M. Taylor and A. A. Mailey, 127, Sydney 1924–25

England v South Africa

LOUIS DUFFUS AND MICHAEL OWEN-SMITH

England for many years nurtured Test cricket against South Africa with tolerant restraint, rather like an indulgent parent spending summer after summer bowling under-arm on the garden lawn to an eager son. It is only because of the generous attitude of authority that the 102 games played between the 2 countries since they first met in the 1888–89 season are all designated as 'Test Matches'. Of the 58 matches held in South Africa only 20 – from 1938–39 onwards – were contested by teams that were fully representative of English cricket. Before 1939 South Africa had won 11 out of their 12 Test victories at home. South African teams visited England on 3 occasions, in 1894, 1901 and 1904 before they were accorded Test Match status.

The 1st Test, played on a matting pitch, took place at St George's Park, Port Elizabeth – still the ground for international matches – on 12 and 13 March 1889. The 2 matches of the series were the climax to the 1st cricket tour ever undertaken to South Africa. The pioneers were Major Wharton's team, captained by C. A. Smith (later to become known as Sir Aubrey Smith, the film actor). The Tests were the only matches in which the visiting side, regarded as of average county standard, played against as few as 11 opponents. England won the First Test easily by 8 wickets. Only A. B. Tancred and O. R. Dunell, the 1st captain of South Africa, aged 33, made double figures in South Africa's 1st innings of 84. In the Second Test, played at Cape Town, the bowling of Briggs who had the signal double achievement of taking 7 for 17 and 8 for 11, overwhelmed the colonists. England's win by an innings and 202 runs with a moderate team suggested that it would be many years before it was necessary to send out a full-strength side and this, of course, proved to be true.

When W. W. Read captained the 2nd English team in South Africa in 1891–92 the only Test, played at Cape Town, where England won by an innings and 189 runs, had some strange aspects. Read's side included two Australians, W. L. Murdoch and J. J. Ferris, who had played in Tests against England, while F. Hearne, who had represented England in the First Test against South Africa in 1889, was now in the home team captained by W. H. Milton. Wood, who scored 134 not out for England as No. 8 batsman, recorded his 1st and only first-class hundred.

Lord Hawke's 1st touring team of 1895–96 also scored easy victories – 2 by an innings – in the 3 Tests played at Port Elizabeth, Johannesburg (the 1st in this town) and Cape Town. For the first time the young pupil challenged the teacher when Lord Hawke's 2nd team of 1898–99 won the First Test at Johannesburg by no more than 32 runs. In the Second and final Test at Cape Town – won by England by 210 runs – the hero was J. H. Sinclair who scored South Africa's 1st Test hundred (106) and took 6 for 26 in England's 1st innings of 92.

The 1st official MCC team to South Africa in 1905–06, led by P. F. Warner, marked the beginning of a period, producing the country's most accomplished cricketers until the 2 post-Second World War eras. Partly it was due to the success with which R. O. Schwarz, G. A. Faulkner, G. C. White and A. E. Vogler had adopted googly bowling which they learned from its inventor, B. J. T. Bosanquet, on their tour to England in 1904.

Amid unbridled excitement from 10,000 spectators South Africa recorded their 1st victory in Test cricket, by 1 wicket, when A. D. Nourse (senior) and the 25-year-old captain, P. W. Sherwell, scored 48 for the last wicket at Johannesburg. In the unique circumstances of being represented in all 5 Tests by the same 11 players, South Africa won 4 of the 5 matches and lost 1. The strength and consistency of South Africa's batting on matting pitches was conspicuous throughout the series.

In 1907 on their 4th visit to England in 13 years South Africa played Test Matches in England for the 1st time. England won

ABOVE Aubrey Faulkner, whose all-round talents, as much as anything, brought South Africa to Test status. After the First World War he founded the 1st Indoor Cricket School at Hammersmith, London.
LEFT J. H. Sinclair, a South African all-rounder of high potential and fine physique in the early years of the century. Once, while batting at Harrogate, he is said to have knocked a cabby off his perch.

1 with 2 drawn, but South Africa were saved from defeat when rain washed out the 3rd day of the First Test at Lord's. Features of the series were Sherwell's magnificent innings of 115 in just over 100 minutes in the follow-on at Lord's; England's dismissal for their lowest-ever score against South Africa of 76 at Leeds, where they nevertheless won by 53 runs; and the bowling feat of Faulkner who took 6 for 17 in the same innings. The South African batsmen, who were not accustomed to turf pitches, were inconsistent, but the general success of the tour – achieved largely by their googly bowlers – led in 1912 to the staging of the Triangular Tournament.

In the meantime, South Africa, under the captaincy of S. J. Snooke, continued to do well at home and against H. D. G. Leveson Gower's side of 1909–10 won 3 and lost 2 of the Test Matches. The series was significant for the inauguration of the famous Hobbs-Rhodes opening partnership, for the feats of the last of the underhand lob bowlers, G. H. Simpson-Hayward, who took the highest number of wickets (23) for England, and the performances of Vogler and Faulkner.

By 1912 the first brief heyday of South African cricket had drawn to a close. It was largely because their standard fell well below that of England and Australia, and because of a wet summer, that the triangular experiment was not a success. England won their 3 matches against South Africa by substantial margins, and the great Sydney Barnes took 34 wickets. The MCC team of 1913–14, led by J. W. H. T. Douglas, struck South Africa in the midst of their lean years and overwhelmed them. The series was overshadowed by the bowling of Barnes and the lone outstanding South African batting of H. W. Taylor. Playing in only 4 matches Barnes took 49 wickets – including 17 in the Second Test at Johannesburg. In Tests Taylor played innings of 109, 93 and 70 against Barnes and, representing Natal in the provincial match, the only English defeat of the tour, made 91 and 100. His batting against Barnes has gone down in history as a classic of its kind.

Tests between the 2 countries were resumed after the First World War on a happy note, for, although the side captained by F. T. Mann in South Africa in 1922–23 was almost the strongest that could be picked, the series was evenly contested. Taylor was again the dominant South African figure, supported by Nourse and J. M. Blanckenberg, but new players in R. H. Catterall, A. E. Hall and E. P. Nupen gave the team good balance. The outstanding feat for South Africa was the victory in the First Test, thanks to a magnificent 176 by Taylor. Since the teams were 1-all after the Fourth Test, the deciding game in Durban was played to a finish, and owing to rain lasted 6 days. It is often referred to as 'Russell's Match', for in it the Essex professional scored hundreds in each innings. England won by 109 runs, although Taylor scored 102 – his 3rd hundred of the series – and finished with an aggregate of 582 and average of 64, the best figures for either side.

Despite South Africa's good showing their next series in England in 1924 has been described as their most tragic overseas experience. England won the first 3 matches, 2 by an innings and 18 runs and 1 by 9 wickets, and the remaining 2 were drawn. This was the season in which South Africa for the 2nd time in their history were dismissed for 30. They were bowled out in 45 minutes in the First Test at Birmingham by Tate and Gilligan after England, put in to bat, had scored 438. One of the few bright spots for South Africa was the batting of Catterall who scored 2 hundreds and a 95 for 471 runs at an average of 67 – outstanding for a team that was outplayed. The series ended Taylor's captaincy in 18 Tests, a number no one has exceeded.

It was indicative of England's enduring strength that the team led by Captain R. T. Stanyforth in 1927–28 excluded such renowned players as Hobbs, Hendren, Tate, Larwood, Jardine and Chapman. Yet they shared the rubber with 2 victories to each side. England suffered a severe handicap when Geary, who had taken 12 wickets for 130 in the First Test, broke down in the Second and missed the remaining Tests. The season was notable for South Africa's recovery after being 2 down with 2 to play, a recovery which created a reputation for daring for the new captain, H. G. Deane. He won all 5 tosses and 3 times put England in to bat.

In the Fifth Test in Durban Deane again sent England in to bat and the visitors collapsed against the pace of Bissett (7 for 29) in their 2nd innings after trailing by 50 on the 1st. Needing only 69 runs for victory South Africa won by 8 wickets. Especially pleasing was the growth of enterprise in the South African batting through the series with Deane and H. B. Cameron adding 89 in 47 minutes for the 6th wicket in the Fourth Test and Catterall (119) and Cameron 53, including 4, 4, 4, 6 off successive balls from Freeman, 136 for the 5th wicket in 90 minutes. Bissett took 25 wickets in the series.

South Africans were always conscious of the fact that their status could not be regarded highly until they had won a victory in England against the full strength of the country. The one-sidedness of the series was not destined to change in the happy summer of 1929, for England won the rubber 2–0, but wise policy in choosing the South African team brought success measurably nearer. They had not yet played a Test Match on a turf pitch at home. But, profiting by the lessons of the calamitous visit of 1924, they sent Deane abroad with an extremely young side of whom only Deane, Taylor and Catterall had previously played in England. It was to be an educational trip and it resulted in launching the distinguished careers of B. Mitchell, H. G. Owen-Smith and E. L. Dalton, and in providing zestful joyous cricket marked by excellence in fielding.

South Africa gained an even draw in the First Test at Birmingham, with Catterall and Mitchell providing opening partnerships of 119 and 171. This was Mitchell's Test debut, as it was K. S. Duleepsinhji's for England. The Second Test at Lord's was also drawn but this time very much in England's favour, although South Africa gained a lead on the 1st innings. At Headingley England won by 5 wickets, scoring 328 and 186 for 5 against South Africa's 236 and 275. They must have won far more easily but for a memorable display by South Africa's youngest batsman, the 20-year-old Owen-Smith, who at No. 7 scored 129 – 102 of them on the last morning. He is the only South African in the select list of 13 to have made a hundred before lunch. The last-wicket partnership of 103 between Owen-Smith and A. J. Bell remains a South African record.

In the Fourth Test at Old Trafford, England gave a display more in keeping with their superior experience and talent when they won by an innings and 32 runs and with it took the rubber. Rain made the pitch particularly favourable for Freeman, who took 7 for 71 and 5 for 100, while a superb 3rd-wicket partnership of 245, scored in 165 minutes by Woolley (154) and Wyatt (113), enabled England to declare at 427 for 7 on the 1st day.

It became a characteristic of the young South Africans' cricket for them to recover from setbacks and in the final match, a draw at the Oval, they excelled themselves. Dismissing England for 258 they increased their highest total against England to 492 for 8 declared. Taylor (121) and Deane (93) added a record 215 for the 4th wicket. Any hope that their first innings lead of 234 might presage victory was quickly dispelled by the overwhelming response of England's top batsmen. Sutcliffe, who had scored 104 in the 1st innings, achieved the unprecedented feat of scoring a hundred in each innings of a Test for the 2nd time in his career. For South Africa the 40-year-old Taylor accomplished the leading performance of scoring 221 for an average of 55.25.

The 1930–31 season, in which A. P. F. Chapman led the team to the Union, was an eventful one for South Africa. It coincided with some striking changes of personnel, the playing of the 1st Test Match on a grass pitch (at Cape Town) and with their winning the rubber for the 3rd time at home. The victory came in the only match played to a conclusion, the First Test in Johannesburg.

This was the last series in which any matting pitches were used, and it brought both triumph and disappointment to Nupen, the last great matting-wicket bowler. Before the season started Deane announced his retirement and Nupen was made captain for the First Test in Johannesburg. It was the only time he captained South Africa. His bowling, with which he took 5 for 63 and 6 for 87, was the deciding factor in an exciting game which South Africa won by 28 runs. Responding to public pressure, Deane came back to captain South Africa for the next 2 matches before withdrawing; Cameron then led the side for the remaining 2. It was certainly a season when odd things happened. Time saved England from defeat in the Cape Town match on the turf pitch. Exceeding 500 for the 1st time against England, South Africa scored 513 for 8 declared against 7 bowlers. Mitchell (123) and I. J. Siedle (141) established the present 1st-wicket record of 260, after which Taylor scored a brilliant 117.

Rain washed out a full day of the match in Durban, and it was drawn, with England the more impressive team. England held the whip-hand in the Fourth Test at Johannesburg after splendidly consistent batting had raised the total to 442. A 4th successive draw brought the series to a close. Hammond stood out in the series with 517 runs (average 64), while Nupen took 21 wickets at the low cost of 19 each for South Africa.

At Cape Town in 1930–31, 6 Test captains took part in the Second Test: (*from the left*) H. G. Deane (SA), A. P. F. Chapman (E), H. W. Taylor (SA), J. C. White (E), E. P. Nupen (SA) and R. E. S. Wyatt (E). The match was the 1st Test to be played in South Africa on grass.

For the last time South African Tests were confined to 3 days when the side under H. F. Wade visited England in 1935 and after 28 years won their 1st Test in England. Again, one match decided the rubber. England had the better of 2 of the 4 drawn games, but in their victory by 157 runs at Lord's South Africa won handsomely on merit. It was felt that the introduction of turf pitches in their home country contributed to their success. Four members of the touring team won notable distinctions in their triumph at Lord's. Mitchell scored 30 and 164 not out; E. A. B. Rowan, who made 40 and 44, virtually rose from a hospital bed to play; Cameron hit a thrilling 90 (including 58 in half-an-hour and 3 sixes), and X. C. Balaskas, a leg-break and googly bowler of Greek origin, took 9 for 103. He outdid the England slow bowlers on a spinners' wicket. It was a good summer for batsmen, Mitchell heading the series with 488 runs and an average of 69.

After 10 official tours ranging over 50 years England for the 1st time sent their strongest available team to South Africa in 1938–39. It was also the 1st series played entirely on turf pitches, and was conspicuous for the heavy scoring on both sides and for the fabulous unfinished 'timeless Test' which extended over 10 playing days, one of which was lost to rain. The team, led by W. R. Hammond, won the Third Test, and thus 3 times in succession 1 game decided the rubber.

England won the Third Test in Durban by an innings and 13 runs in 3 days with the left-handed Paynter making 243 – the highest score in Tests between the countries. The fast bowling of K. Farnes (7 for 109) was the dominating factor in South Africa's dismissal for 103 and 353 in reply to England's total of 469 for 4 declared.

The 'timeless Test', also played in Durban, was a freak of cricket history. The most incredible feat to those who were not on the spot was the fact that after South Africa had scored 530 and 481, England, who had made 316 in their first innings, were left to score 696 for victory and actually reached 654 for 5. At this point the 10th day was terminated by rain, after which – irony of ironies – England had to catch their ship home. The game lasted the length it did because at the end of the 3rd and 7th days heavy rain fell overnight. The Playing Conditions permitted the heavy roller to be used twice on each following morning and the pitch was thus completely remade. Something like 50 records accrued from the match. They included such things as the using of 12 new balls while 1981 runs were scored.

It was 8 years before the 2 countries met again. Because of the war South Africa were represented by their oldest team in many years in England's glorious summer of 1947. England were not strong in bowling but the unprecedented and prolific scoring of Compton and Edrich gave them mastery of the series, 3–0, after a remarkable recovery in the First Test.

This game at Trent Bridge was one of the most tantalizing ever experienced by a South African team. They surpassed themselves by scoring 533, at that time their highest total against England, then dismissed England for 208. With 4 wickets down for 170 in England's 2nd innings, South Africa were well placed for victory. Then Yardley was dropped at 51, and went on to make 99 and to put on 237 for the 5th wicket with Compton, who scored a priceless 163. Evans hit a thrilling 74 in 75 minutes, while a last-wicket stand by J. W. Martin and E. Hollies not only added 51 but clipped a precious 48 minutes off South Africa's batting time. Left to make 227 in 140 minutes, they scored 166 for 1. The captain, Melville (189 and 104 not out), most elegant of batsmen, who had made 103 in the 2nd innings of the 'timeless Test', became the 1st South

African to score a Test hundred in each innings, and, with Nourse (149), put on 319, the existing record, for the 3rd wicket. But after this golden chance had eluded them South Africa were never quite the same team.

England won the Second Test at Lord's by 10 wickets, Melville (117) scoring his 4th successive Test hundred, and at Old Trafford their winning margin was 7 wickets. The forceful batting of Edrich and Compton proved decisive on both occasions while Nourse's 2nd innings at Manchester of 115 on a difficult, drying pitch was one of his most accomplished displays in Test cricket. Victory by 10 wickets gave England the rubber at Headingley. In the drawn game at the Oval, South Africa, after a declaration by Yardley, came within 28 runs of victory with 3 wickets to fall. Mitchell, who was off the field for only 15 minutes of the entire game, won the double distinction of scoring hundreds in each innings (120 and 189 not out) and achieved South Africa's highest aggregate in Tests by surpassing Taylor's 2,936. Edrich finished the series with an average of 110 from 552 runs and Compton scored no fewer than 753 runs with an average of 94.

By adventurous batting and splendid fielding F. G. Mann's team in South Africa in 1948–49 won the rubber with exhilarating victories in the First and Fifth Tests. On the final day of the initial Durban match, one of the three most exciting Tests ever played in South Africa, England had to score 128 in 135 minutes. Eight runs were needed with 8 wickets down when Tuckett bowled the last over, with Bedser and Gladwin batting. One run was wanted when Gladwin, who had walked to the wicket with his historic remark, 'Cometh the hour, cometh the man', faced the last ball. It ricocheted off his thigh and the pair scampered to a breathtaking victory.

The plumb pitch at Ellis Park, Johannesburg, a temporary ground where the Second Test was played, proved a heart-breaking ordeal for bowlers. In England's 608, Hutton (158) and Washbrook (195) established what was then a world's record Test opening partnership of 359, and Compton scored an entertaining 114. In South Africa's 2nd innings – they trailed by 293 on the 1st – Rowan batted 6 hours for a match-saving 156 not out; this after hearing he had been dropped for the Third Test. Slow scoring by South Africa squandered their chance of exploiting their 48-run lead on the 1st innings at Cape Town. Another declaration by England left the onus on South Africa to score 376 at the daunting rate of 85 an hour in the drawn Fourth Test in Johannesburg. Hutton, Watkins and Nourse scored hundreds. In a thrilling climax to the series, England accepted Nourse's challenge to score 172 in 95 minutes at Port Elizabeth and won by 3 wickets with 1 over to go. Mann made 136 not out in England's 1st innings and W. W. Wade a maiden Test hundred for South Africa. Nourse (76) and Hutton (64) led the respective batting averages, while spin bowlers, 'Tufty' Mann of South Africa and Jenkins, had the best bowling figures.

In 1951, after 16 years, South Africa won their 2nd Test Match in England. The victory came as a result of an epic, courageous innings by Nourse who scored a record 208 at Nottingham after batting for 9¼ hours with a fractured thumb. But it did not prevent England from winning the rubber by 3 matches to 1. This was another excellent summer, and was conspicuous for the splendid bowling of Bedser, who took 30 wickets in the series, the batting of Hutton, Compton, R. T. Simpson and E. A. B. Rowan, the impressive debut of P. B. H. May and the admirable bowling of the 40-year-old G. W. A. Chubb, whose 21 wickets were the most taken for South Africa.

Nourse's great innings at Trent Bridge gave his side a lead of 64. When Bedser (6 for 37) skittled out South Africa for 121 England needed only 186 to win. On a turning wicket against the tight spin bowling of A. M. B. Rowan (5 for 68) and Mann (4 for 24), well handled by E. A. B. Rowan in the absence of Nourse, they could muster only 114 and South Africa won by 71. For the 1st time the Tests were extended to 5 days, but only 3 were necessary for England to win by 10 wickets at Lord's. England were better able to adapt themselves to wet conditions at Old Trafford where the outstanding bowling of Bedser (12 for 112) gave them victory by 9 wickets. By contrast there was a spate of scoring at Headingley. In South Africa's 538 – their existing record total against England – E. A. B. Rowan made 236 in 9½ hours. Hutton's 100, scored in 5 hours, launched England on the way to their total of 505 and May in his 1st Test hit a delightful 138.

Although the match at the Oval ended in 3 days, with England winning by 4 wickets, the more even balance between batting and bowling provided absorbing cricket. There was an exciting chance that South Africa might win and thus share the rubber. To score 50 on this pitch that gave so much encouragement to bowlers was a major achievement and was accomplished only twice – by E. A. B. Rowan (55) and by Compton (73). Laker had a match analysis of 10 for 119. The match will be remembered for the Hutton incident. A ball from Rowan popped up off his glove as he attempted a sweep. As the wicket-keeper, W. R. Endean, lunged forward desperately for a catch Hutton flicked the ball away with the back of his bat and was given out for 'obstruction'.

The international programme produced the rare occurrence of 2 successive series in England, for South Africa returned in 1955. At their zenith of 66 years of Test history, led by J. E. Cheetham, who had to hand over the reins to D. J. McGlew in their 2 victories, they were a superlative fielding side and supplied a thrilling climax to the season by winning the Third and Fourth Tests after they had lost the 1st 2. It was the 1st time they had won 2 tests in England, for whom May, in his first series as captain, had the distinction of leading the side to a 3–2 victory.

England won easily by an innings and 5 runs in 4 days at Nottingham and were victorious by 71 runs at Lord's, after trailing by 171 on the 1st innings. P. S. Heine, in his 1st Test, took 5 for 60 and R. A. McLean made a spectacular 142, but South Africa failed in their 2nd innings after being set only 183 to win. At Old Trafford, South Africa saved the rubber by scoring a victory by 3 wickets in a breathless finish 5 minutes from time. Hundreds were scored by Compton (158), May (117), McGlew (104), J. H. B. Waite (113) and P. L. Winslow (108). Winslow reached his 1st first-class hundred by hitting a straight 6 over the sight-screen and into the practice ground. At Headingley it was the turn of South Africa to make an inspiring 2nd innings recovery with McGlew scoring 133 and 116 not out. The left-hander, T. L. Goddard, attacking the leg-stump, took 5 for 69 in 62 overs in England's 2nd innings. South Africa won decisively by 224 runs, H. J. Tayfield, the off-spinner, due to become his country's biggest wicket-taker, having a match analysis of 9 for 164.

The spin bowling of Lock (9 for 101) and Laker (7 for 84) dominated the exciting final game at the Oval. England won by 92 runs. Tayfield had a remarkable spell of 53.4 overs in which he bowled unchanged for 5 hours to take 5 for 60.

Tayfield reached his greatest heights in the next series played in South Africa in 1956–57. He took 37 wickets in the 5 Tests (average 17.18) and thus surpassed by 1 the record held for 46 years by Vogler. It was a summer of unprecedented slow scoring which did enduring harm to the public following the game. The saving grace of the series was the competitive aspect which led to South Africa sharing the rubber after being 2 down with 2 to play. The batting was generally of a low and laborious standard with May, the captain, and Compton singularly out of form. Because of injury McGlew captained South Africa in only one Test, his place being taken by the former Oxford captain, C. B. van Ryneveld.

Batting for 8 hours and 8 minutes in the First Test, on the new Wanderers' ground, P. E. Richardson scored what was then the slowest hundred in Test history. In the Second Test at Cape Town Endean was given out 'handled the ball' – the 1st batsman in Test history to suffer this fate. A ball from Wardle spun off his pad and was dropping near the stumps when the batsman caught it. On the last day of the Fourth Test in Johannesburg England needed only 85 runs with 8 wickets in hand in order to win the rubber. Victory seemed assured at 147 for 2 when Tayfield achieved his greatest single-innings performance. Bowling unchanged for 5 hours he took 9 for 113, and South Africa won by 17 runs. Tayfield's match figures of 13 for 192 are unsurpassed by a bowler representing South Africa.

Unfortunately the newly laid pitch at Port Elizabeth fell far below requirements and in the final Test discounted stroke-play. The ball scarcely ever came stump-high. The two outstanding feats were Tyson's 6 for 40, obtained from a run of 5 yards, and Tayfield's 2nd innings 6 for 78, which gave South Africa victory by 58 runs. Taking the tour as a whole, Wardle with 90 wickets, 26 of them in 4 Tests, bowling mostly out of the back of the hand, was in a class of his own.

Coming as it did after the glories of 1955, the series of 1960 was the most depressing in which the two countries ever engaged. England were by far the superior team and won the 1st 3 Tests easily. The remaining 2 were drawn. Attendances fell to an unprecedentedly low level, and gloom was cast over the South Africans when the young fast bowler, G. Griffin, was banned from bowling after the Second Test by the South African Cricket Association after he had repeatedly been penalized for throwing. Fast bowlers were the central figures of the season for Statham, who took 27 wickets, and Trueman (25), met with conspicuous success; while Adcock (26) excelled himself and was the one South African to come out of the series with high distinction. For the first time in England the tour showed a financial loss.

Adcock took 8 for 119 in the opening match at Birmingham where South Africa went down by 100 runs. Rain affected the match at Lord's where great bowling by Statham, whose 11 for 97, was the best performance of his career, was the climax to a victory by an innings and 73 runs. An atmosphere of drama marked the end of Griffin's bowling. He was 'called' for throwing 5 times on the 1st day, thus becoming the 1st bowler penalized for this offence in a Test in England. Then on the 2nd day, after further no-balling, he became the first South African to perform the hat-trick in a Test. In an exhibition game which followed the early termination of the Test he was no-balled 4 times in succession and had to finish the over by bowling underhand.

The rubber was decided at Nottingham where South Africa were beaten by 8 wickets. In the 2nd innings, McGlew, the captain, was run out after he had collided with the bowler, Moss, who was trying to field the ball. As McGlew scampered on, a direct throw by Statham struck the stumps. The England captain, M. C. Cowdrey, tried to recall McGlew, but after consultation the umpires upheld their decision on the grounds that the obstruction had been unintentional. No play was possible on the first 2 days at Old Trafford where England held the upper hand in the draw. McLean (109) recorded his side's only hundred of the series. Although Cowdrey won the toss for the 5th time at the Oval, South Africa appeared to have gained a winning position when, having dismissed England for 155, they scored 419. A magnificent opening stand of 290 – the highest for England in England – by Pullar (175) and Cowdrey (155) however completely transformed the position.

The 1964–65 tour by M. J. K. Smith's MCC team provided another disappointing series for South Africa. Following a drawn series in Australia and the arrival of outstanding Test players such as R. G. Pollock, E. J. Barlow, K. C. Bland and J. D. Lindsay to join established men such as Goddard and P. M. Pollock, the South African prospects were bright. England, although strong in batting with K. F. Barrington

End of an era: this MCC side of M. J. K. Smith's to South Africa in 1964–65 was the last to tour there before the trouble over the choice of Basil d'Oliveira brought the series to a halt. Back row: P. H. Parfitt, J. T. Murray, J. M. Brearley, G. Boycott and R. N. S. Hobbs; middle row: R. I. A. Nicholas (physiotherapist), J. S. E. Price, N. I. Thomson, D. J. Brown, R. W. Barber, T. W. Cartwright and M. McLennan (baggage master); front row: D. A. Allen, K. F. Barrington, D. B. Carr (manager), M. J. K. Smith (captain), E. R. Dexter (vice-captain), F. J. Titmus and J. M. Parks.

topping the averages in the Tests at 101.60, had a limited fast attack. The 2 off-spinners, D. A. Allen and F. J. Titmus, claimed 35 of the 69 wickets to fall to bowlers.

England took their chances in the First Test at Durban to win by an innings and 104 runs. This victory was sufficient to decide the series. England's win was inevitable when they won the toss, declared at 485 for 5, and exploited a pitch that helped the spinners from the 2nd day. The match was over in less than 4 days with G. Boycott and R. W. Barber sharing an opening stand of 120, Barrington and J. M. Parks compiling undefeated hundreds, and Titmus and Allen taking 5 wickets each in an innings.

Bland, who had scored the only South African 50 at Durban, saved South Africa with an undefeated 2nd innings hundred in the Second Test at Johannesburg. The pattern of the First Test was repeated. Smith won the toss, Barrington – his 2nd successive in Tests – and Dexter scored hundreds, Allen and Titmus mesmerized the South African batsmen, and there was a 2nd follow-on – this time 214 runs in arrears – before Bland saved the match.

Thereafter the series became a battle of batting attrition as England held grimly on to their lead and South Africa lacked the drive and above all the enterprise to chase victory. The Third Test at Newlands, apart from completely uninspiring batting, produced 2 controversial decisions. Barlow, who had made 41 after South Africa won the toss, stood his ground when P. H. Parfitt appealed for a slip catch off Titmus, and went on to make 138. Then Barrington 'walked' in the England 1st innings when 49, after the umpire failed to respond to an appeal for a catch behind the wicket.

In the Fourth Test at Johannesburg Smith surprised by sending South Africa in to bat. Barlow and Goddard, the captain, responded with a century opening stand and England could have been in trouble when the pitch helped the spinners following rain. However, South Africa missed vital chances – in particular Parfitt, who took out his bat for 122. The other feat was Goddard's performance in scoring his maiden Test hundred in his 62nd innings. By the Fifth Test at Port Elizabeth injuries had left England's attack in a sorry state and they had to borrow K. E. Palmer, who was coaching in South Africa. Barlow and Goddard shared another hundred stand and Graeme Pollock made a distinguished hundred in front of his home crowd. A resolute hundred by Boycott meant that England trailed by no more than 67 runs. The two 1st innings having consumed most of the first 4 days, a draw was inevitable before rain came on the last.

The 1965 side to visit England, under the captaincy of P. L. van der Merwe, heralded the most successful era in the history of South African cricket. They emulated their predecessors of 1935 in winning a Test series in England by the same 1–0 margin, although, this time, only 3 matches were played. This side did have its weaknesses – notably an opening partner with the bat for Barlow and an opening partner with the ball for P. M. Pollock – but produced a brand of exciting and entertaining cricket that drew huge crowds in sharp contrast to the dismal series of 1960. In addition they arrived in England midway through the season, having to find form quickly while the home players already had a 3-match series against New Zealand behind them, and to beat England under these conditions was a signal achievement.

South Africa went into the First Test at Lord's as slight underdogs. This was a fascinating contest as first one side and then the other held sway. South Africa, after winning the toss, collapsed on the 1st day to 178 for 7. Yet in the end England were close to defeat, with 7 wickets down for 145 and J. H. Edrich retired hurt, having been set the target of 191 in 235 minutes. Another turning point was the brilliant run out of Barrington (91) with a direct throw that helped restrict England's 1st innings lead to 58. Bland's ability to pick up the ball and throw down the stumps virtually in one movement became a feature of the tour. No finer fielding in the covers has been seen in England than his. He was also South Africa's top scorer in the match with 70. R. Dumbrill took 7 wickets.

Two players have seldom dominated a match to the same extent as the brothers P. M. and R. G. Pollock did the Second Test at Trent Bridge. South Africa again won the toss and began poorly, but Graeme made a brilliant 125 out of a total of 160 while he was at the crease in 2¼ hours. It was one of the classic Test innings. Van der Merwe (38) was the next highest scorer in a total of 269. T. W. Cartwright, exploiting overcast conditions, took 6 for 94 and it was England's bad luck that he broke his right thumb and was unable to bowl in the 2nd innings. Cowdrey replied with a hundred for England, but the rest of the batting was swept aside by Peter Pollock, who took 5 wickets in each innings and had match figures of 10 for 87, until Parfitt produced a fighting innings of 86 that threatened to turn the game. He was finally bowled with the new ball by Pollock and South Africa had won by 94 runs.

England made a great effort to level the series at the Oval. They put South Africa in to bat and there were only 6 runs between the 2 sides on the 1st innings. The feature was the recall of Statham, who took 5 wickets in the innings, with Pollock replying in equal measure for South Africa. A 2nd innings hundred by Bland seemed to put the visitors on top but England, set to score 399 in 7 hours, had reached 308 for 4 before rain washed out the prospect of a thrilling finish to an enthralling series.

ENGLAND V SOUTH AFRICA

			RESULT	CAPTAINS
1888–89	1 Port Elizabeth	SA 84, 129; E 148, 67–2	E 8 wkts	C. A. Smith, O. R. Dunell
	2 Cape Town	E 292; SA 47, 43	E Inns 202 runs	M. P. Bowden, W. H. Milton
1891–92	1 Cape Town	SA 97, 83; E 369	E Inns 189 runs	W. W. Read, W. H. Milton
1895–96	1 Port Elizabeth	E 185, 226; SA 93, 30	E 288 runs	Sir T. C. O'Brien, E. A. Halliwell
	2 Johannesburg	E 482; SA 151, 134	E Inns 197 runs	Lord Hawke, E. A. Halliwell
	3 Cape Town	SA 115, 117; E 265	E Inns 33 runs	Lord Hawke, A. Richards
1898–99	1 Johannesburg	E 145, 237; SA 251, 99	E 32 runs	Lord Hawke, M. Bissett
	2 Cape Town	E 92, 330; SA 177, 35	E 210 runs	Lord Hawke, M. Bissett
1905–06	1 Johannesburg	E 184, 190; SA 91, 287–9	SA 1 wkt	P. F. Warner, P. W. Sherwell
	2 Johannesburg	E 148, 160; SA 277, 34–1	SA 9 wkts	P. F. Warner, P. W. Sherwell
	3 Johannesburg	SA 385, 349–5D; E 295, 196	SA 243 runs	P. F. Warner, P. W. Sherwell
	4 Cape Town	SA 218, 138; E 198, 160–6	E 4 wkts	P. F. Warner, P. W. Sherwell
	5 Cape Town	E 187, 130; SA 333	SA Inns 16 runs	P. F. Warner, P. W. Sherwell
1907	1 Lord's	E 428; SA 140, 185–3	Drawn	R. E. Foster, P. W. Sherwell
	2 Headingley	E 76, 162; SA 110, 75	E 53 runs	R. E. Foster, P. W. Sherwell
	3 Oval	E 295, 138; SA 178, 159–5	Drawn	R. E. Foster, P. W. Sherwell
1909–10	1 Johannesburg	SA 208, 345; E 310, 224	SA 19 runs	H. D. G. Leveson Gower, S. J. Snooke
	2 Durban	SA 199, 347; E 199, 252	SA 95 runs	H. D. G. Leveson Gower, S. J. Snooke
	3 Johannesburg	SA 305, 237; E 322, 221–7	E 3 wkts	H. D. G. Leveson Gower, S. J. Snooke
	4 Cape Town	E 203, 178; SA 207, 175–6	SA 4 wkts	F. L. Fane, S. J. Snooke
	5 Cape Town	E 417, 16–1; SA 103, 327	E 9 wkts	F. L. Fane, S. J. Snooke
1912	1 Lord's	SA 58, 217; E 337	E Inns 62 runs	C. B. Fry, F. Mitchell
	2 Headingley	E 242, 238; SA 147, 159	E 174 runs	C. B. Fry, L. Tancred
	3 Oval	SA 95, 93; E 176, 14–0	E 10 wkts	C. B. Fry, L. Tancred
1913–14	1 Durban	SA 182, 111; E 450	E Inns 157 runs	J. W. H. T. Douglas, H. W. Taylor
	2 Johannesburg	SA 160, 231; E 403	E Inns 12 runs	J. W. H. T. Douglas, H. W. Taylor
	3 Johannesburg	E 238, 308; SA 151, 304	E 91 runs	J. W. H. T. Douglas, H. W. Taylor
	4 Durban	SA 170, 305–9D; E 163, 154–5	Drawn	J. W. H. T. Douglas, H. W. Taylor
	5 Port Elizabeth	SA 193, 228; E 411, 11–0	E 10 wkts	J. W. H. T. Douglas, H. W. Taylor
1922–23	1 Johannesburg	SA 148, 420; E 182, 218	SA 168 runs	F. T. Mann, H. W. Taylor
	2 Cape Town	SA 113, 242; E 183, 173–9	E 1 wkt	F. T. Mann, H. W. Taylor
	3 Durban	E 428, 11–1; SA 368	Drawn	F. T. Mann, H. W. Taylor
	4 Johannesburg	E 244, 376–6D; SA 295, 247–4	Drawn	F. T. Mann, H. W. Taylor
	5 Durban	E 281, 241; SA 179, 234	E 109 runs	F. T. Mann, H. W. Taylor
1924	1 Edgbaston	E 438; SA 30, 390	E Inns 18 runs	A. E. R. Gilligan, H. W. Taylor
	2 Lord's	SA 273, 240; E 531–2D	E Inns 18 runs	A. E. R. Gilligan, H. W. Taylor
	3 Headingley	E 396, 60–1; SA 132, 323	E 9 wkts	A. E. R. Gilligan, H. W. Taylor
	4 Old Trafford	SA 116–4; E –	Drawn	J. W. H. T. Douglas, H. W. Taylor
	5 Oval	SA 342; E 421–8	Drawn	A. E. R. Gilligan, H. W. Taylor
1927–28	1 Johannesburg	SA 196, 170; E 313, 57–0	E 10 wkts	R. T. Stanyforth, H. G. Deane
	2 Cape Town	E 133, 428; SA 250, 224	E 87 runs	R. T. Stanyforth, H. G. Deane
	3 Durban	SA 246, 464–8D; E 430, 132–2	Drawn	R. T. Stanyforth, H. G. Deane
	4 Johannesburg	E 265, 215; SA 328, 156–6	SA 4 wkts	R. T. Stanyforth, H. G. Deane
	5 Durban	E 282, 118; SA 332–7D, 69–2	SA 8 wkts	G. T. S. Stevens, H. G. Deane

1929	1 Edgbaston	E 245, 308–4D; SA 250, 171–1	Drawn	J. C. White, H. G. Deane
	2 Lord's	E 302, 312–8D; SA 322, 90–5	Drawn	J. C. White, H. G. Deane
	3 Headingley	SA 236, 275; E 328, 186–5	E 5 wkts	J. C. White, H. G. Deane
	4 Old Trafford	E 427–7D; SA 130, 265	E Inns 32	A. W. Carr, H. G. Deane
	5 Oval	E 258, 264–1; SA 492–8D	Drawn	A. W. Carr, H. G. Deane
1930–31	1 Johannesburg	SA 126, 306; E 193, 211	SA 28 runs	A. P. F. Chapman, E. P. Nupen
	2 Cape Town	SA 513–8D; E 350, 252–9	Drawn	A. P. F. Chapman, H. G. Deane
	3 Durban	SA 177, 145–8; E 223–1D	Drawn	A. P. F. Chapman, H. G. Deane
	4 Johannesburg	E 442, 169–9D; SA 295, 280–7	Drawn	A. P. F. Chapman, H. B. Cameron
	5 Durban	SA 252, 219–7D; E 230, 72–4	Drawn	A. P. F. Chapman, H. B. Cameron
1935	1 Trent Bridge	E 384–7D; SA 220, 17–1	Drawn	R. E. S. Wyatt, H. F. Wade
	2 Lord's	SA 228, 278–7D; E 198, 151	SA 157 runs	R. E. S. Wyatt, H. F. Wade
	3 Headingley	E 216, 294–7D; SA 171, 194–5	Drawn	R. E. S. Wyatt, H. F. Wade
	4 Old Trafford	E 357, 231–6D; SA 318, 169–2	Drawn	R. E. S. Wyatt, H. F. Wade
	5 Oval	SA 476, 287–6; E 534–6D	Drawn	R. E. S. Wyatt, H. F. Wade
1938–39	1 Johannesburg	E 422, 291–4D; SA 390, 108–1	Drawn	W. R. Hammond, A. Melville
	2 Cape Town	E 559–9D; SA 286, 201–2	Drawn	W. R. Hammond, A. Melville
	3 Durban	E 469–4D; SA 103, 353	E Inns 13 runs	W. R. Hammond, A. Melville
	4 Johannesburg	E 215, 203–4; SA 349–8D	Drawn	W. R. Hammond, A. Melville
	5 Durban	SA 530, 481; E 316, 654–5	Drawn	W. R. Hammond, A. Melville
1947	1 Trent Bridge	SA 533, 166–1; E 208, 551	Drawn	N. W. D. Yardley, A. Melville
	2 Lord's	E 554–8D, 26–0; SA 327, 252	E 10 wkts	N. W. D. Yardley, A. Melville
	3 Old Trafford	SA 339, 267; E 478, 130–3	E 7 wkts	N. W. D. Yardley, A. Melville
	4 Headingley	SA 175, 184; E 317–7D, 47–0	E 10 wkts	N. W. D. Yardley, A. Melville
	5 Oval	E 427, 325–6D; SA 302, 423–7	Drawn	N. W. D. Yardley, A. Melville
1948–49	1 Durban	SA 161, 219; E 253, 128–8	E 2 wkts	F. G. Mann, A. D. Nourse
	2 Johannesburg	E 608; SA 315, 270–2	Drawn	F. G. Mann, A. D. Nourse
	3 Cape Town	E 308, 276–3D; SA 356, 142–4	Drawn	F. G. Mann, A. D. Nourse
	4 Johannesburg	E 379, 253–7D; SA 257–9D, 194–4	Drawn	F. G. Mann, A. D. Nourse
	5 Port Elizabeth	SA 379, 187–3D; E 395, 174–7	E 3 wkts	F. G. Mann, A. D. Nourse
1951	1 Trent Bridge	SA 483–9D, 121; E 419–9D, 114	SA 71 runs	F. R. Brown, A. D. Nourse
	2 Lord's	E 311, 16–0; SA 115, 211	E 10 wkts	F. R. Brown, A. D. Nourse
	3 Old Trafford	SA 158, 191; E 211, 142–1	E 9 wkts	F. R. Brown, A. D. Nourse
	4 Headingley	SA 538, 87–0; E 505	Drawn	F. R. Brown, A. D. Nourse
	5 Oval	SA 202, 154; E 194, 164–6	E 4 wkts	F. R. Brown, A. D. Nourse
1955	1 Trent Bridge	E 334; SA 181, 148	E Inns 5	P. B. H. May, J. E. Cheetham
	2 Lord's	E 133, 353; SA 304, 111	E 71 runs	P. B. H. May, J. E. Cheetham
	3 Old Trafford	E 284, 381; SA 521–8D, 145–7	SA 3 wkts	P. B. H. May, D. J. McGlew
	4 Headingley	SA 171, 500; E 191, 256	SA 224 runs	P. B. H. May, D. J. McGlew
	5 Oval	E 151, 204; SA 112, 151	E 92 runs	P. B. H. May, J. E. Cheetham
1956–57	1 Johannesburg	E 268, 150; SA 215, 72	E 131 runs	P. B. H. May, C. B. van Ryneveld
	2 Cape Town	E 369, 220–6D; SA 205, 72	E 312 runs	P. B. H. May, D. J. McGlew
	3 Durban	E 218, 254; SA 283, 142–6	Drawn	P. B. H. May, C. B. van Ryneveld
	4 Johannesburg	SA 340, 142; E 251, 214	SA 17 runs	P. B. H. May, C. B. van Ryneveld
	5 Port Elizabeth	SA 164, 134; E 110, 130	SA 58 runs	P. B. H. May, C. B. van Ryneveld
1960	1 Edgbaston	E 292, 203; SA 186, 209	E 100 runs	M. C. Cowdrey, D. J. McGlew
	2 Lord's	E 362–8D; SA 152, 137	E Inns 73 runs	M. C. Cowdrey, D. J. McGlew
	3 Trent Bridge	E 287, 49–2; SA 88, 247	E 8 wkts	M. C. Cowdrey, D. J. McGlew
	4 Old Trafford	E 260, 153–7D; SA 229, 46–0	Drawn	M. C. Cowdrey, D. J. McGlew
	5 Oval	E 155, 479–9D; SA 419, 97–4	Drawn	M. C. Cowdrey, D. J. McGlew
1964–65	1 Durban	E 485–5D; SA 155, 226	E Inns 104 runs	M. J. K. Smith, T. L. Goddard
	2 Johannesburg	E 531; SA 317, 336–6	Drawn	M. J. K. Smith, T. L. Goddard
	3 Cape Town	SA 501–7D, 346; E 442, 15–0	Drawn	M. J. K. Smith, T. L. Goddard
	4 Johannesburg	SA 390–6D, 307–3D; E 384, 153–6	Drawn	M. J. K. Smith, T. L. Goddard
	5 Port Elizabeth	SA 502, 178–4D; E 435, 29–1	Drawn	M. J. K. Smith, T. L. Goddard
1965	1 Lord's	SA 280, 248; E 338, 145–7	Drawn	M. J. K. Smith, P. L. van der Merwe
	2 Trent Bridge	SA 269, 289; E 240, 224	SA 94 runs	M. J. K. Smith, P. L. van der Merwe
	3 Oval	SA 208, 392; E 202, 308–4	Drawn	M. J. K. Smith, P. L. van der Merwe

CAPTAINS (England)	TESTS	WON	LOST	DRAWN
C. A. Smith	1	1		
M. P. Bowden	1	1		
W. W. Read	1	1		
Sir T. C. O'Brien	1	1		
Lord Hawke	4	4		
P. F. Warner	5	1	4	
R. E. Foster	3	1		2
H. D. G. Leveson Gower	3	1	2	
F. L. Fane	2	1	1	
C. B. Fry	3	3		
J. W. H. T. Douglas	6	4		2
F. T. Mann	5	2	1	2
A. E. R. Gilligan	4	3		1
R. T. Stanyforth	4	2	1	1
G. T. S. Stevens	1		1	
J. C. White	3	1		2
A. W. Carr	2	1		1
A. P. F. Chapman	5		1	4
R. E. S. Wyatt	5		1	4
W. R. Hammond	5	1		4
N. W. D. Yardley	5	3		2
F. G. Mann	5	2		3
F. R. Brown	5	3	1	1
P. B. H. May	10	5	4	1
M. C. Cowdrey	5	3		2
M. J. K. Smith	8	1	1	6
	102	46	18	38

CAPTAINS (South Africa)	TESTS	WON	LOST	DRAWN
O. R. Dunell	1		1	
W. H. Milton	2		2	
E. A. Halliwell	2		2	
A. Richards	1		1	
M. Bissett	2		2	
P. W. Sherwell	8	4	2	2
S. J. Snooke	5	3	2	
F. Mitchell	1		1	
L. J. Tancred	2		2	
H. W. Taylor	15	1	9	5
H. G. Deane	12	2	4	6
E. P. Nupen	1	1		
H. B. Cameron	2			2
H. F. Wade	5	1		4
A. Melville	10		4	6
A. D. Nourse (jr)	10	1	5	4
J. E. Cheetham	3		3	
D. J. McGlew	8	2	4	2
C. B. van Ryneveld	4	2	1	1
T. L. Goddard	5		1	4
P. L. van der Merwe	3	1		2
	102	18	46	38

HIGHEST INNINGS TOTALS

England in England, 554–8D, Lord's 1947
England in South Africa, 654–5, Durban 1938–39
South Africa in England, 538, Headingley 1951
South Africa in South Africa, 530, Durban 1938–39

LOWEST INNINGS TOTALS

England in England, 76, Headingley 1907
England in South Africa, 92, Cape Town 1898–99
South Africa in England, 30, Birmingham 1924
South Africa in South Africa, 30, Port Elizabeth 1895–96

HIGHEST INDIVIDUAL INNINGS

England in England, 211, J. B. Hobbs, Lord's 1924
England in South Africa, 243, E. Paynter, Durban 1934–39
South Africa in England, 236, E. A. Rowan, Headingley 1951
South Africa in South Africa, 176, H. W. Taylor, Johannesburg 1922–23

HIGHEST AGGREGATE RUNS IN A SERIES

England in England, 753, D. C. S. Compton 1947
England in South Africa, 653, E. Paynter 1938–39
South Africa in England, 621, A. D. Nourse (jr) 1947
South Africa in South Africa, 582, H. W. Taylor 1922–23

BEST INNINGS BOWLING FIGURES

England in England, 8–29, S. F. Barnes, Oval 1912
England in South Africa, 9–28, G. A. Lohmann, Johannesburg 1895–96
South Africa in England, 7–65, S. J. Pegler, Lord's 1912
South Africa in South Africa, 9–113, H. J. Tayfield, Johannesburg 1956–57

BEST MATCH BOWLING FIGURES

England in England, 15–99, C. Blythe, Headingley 1907
England in South Africa, 17–159, S. F. Barnes, Johannesburg 1913–14
South Africa in England, 10–87, P. M. Pollock, Trent Bridge 1965
South Africa in South Africa, 13–192, H. J. Tayfield, Johannesburg 1956–57

HIGHEST WICKET AGGREGATE IN A SERIES

England in England, 34, S. F. Barnes 1912
England in South Africa, 49, S. F. Barnes 1913–14
South Africa in England, { 26, H. J. Tayfield 1955; 26, N. A. T. Adcock 1960 }
South Africa in South Africa, 37, H. J. Tayfield 1956–57

RECORD WICKET PARTNERSHIPS—ENGLAND

1 L. Hutton and C. Washbrook, 359, Johannesburg 1948–49
2 P. A. Gibb and W. J. Edrich, 280, Durban 1938–39
3 W. J. Edrich and D. C. S. Compton, 370, Lord's 1947
4 W. R. Hammond and L. E. G. Ames, 197, Cape Town 1938–39
5 D. C. S. Compton and N. W. D. Yardley, 237, Trent Bridge 1947
6 K. F. Barrington and J. M. Parks, 206*, Durham 1964–65
7 J. W. H. T. Douglas and M. C. Bird, 115, Durban 1913–14
8 C. W. Wright and H. R. Bromley-Davenport, 154, Johannesburg 1895–96
9 H. Wood and J. T. Hearne, 71, Cape Town 1891–92
10 C. A. G. Russell and A. E. R. Gilligan, 92, Durban 1922–23

RECORD WICKET PARTNERSHIPS—SOUTH AFRICA

1 I. J. Siedle and B. Mitchell, 260, Cape Town 1930–31
2 E. A. B. Rowan and C. B. van Ryneveld, 198, Headingley 1951
3 A. Melville and A. D. Nourse (jr), 319, Trent Bridge 1947
4 H. W. Taylor and H. G. Deane, 214, Oval 1929
5 A. J. Pithey and J. H. B. Waite, 157, Johannesburg 1964–65
6 J. H. B. Waite and P. L. Winslow, 171, Old Trafford 1955
7 H. G. Deane and E. P. Nupen, 123, Durban 1927–28
8 B. Mitchell and L. Tuckett, 109*, Oval 1947
9 E. L. Dalton and A. B. C. Langton, 137, Oval 1935
10 H. G. Owen-Smith and A. J. Bell, 103, Headingley 1929

England v West Indies

J. B. STOLLMEYER AND HENRY BLOFELD

West Indies' introduction to Test cricket came with their tour of England in 1928. Five years earlier they had toured England not unsuccessfully, winning 12 matches. Some of the same players came again in 1928, among them G. Challenor and L. N. Constantine, but Challenor, now 40, averaged 27 instead of 51 and the team as a whole was weaker. Led by R. K. Nunes, they lost all 3 Test Matches to England by an innings, but even in heavy defeat made a considerable impact on English cricket with their acrobatic fielding and with the fiery fast bowling of Constantine, Francis and Griffith.

At Lord's they were bowled out largely by the English spinners, Freeman and Jupp, after England had made 401 (E. Tyldesley 122). At Old Trafford Freeman was again the main obstacle to West Indian progress, for in 51.4 overs he took 10 wickets in the 2 innings for 93. He took 6 more wickets at the Oval when the English captain, A. P. F. Chapman, undermined the West Indian 1st innings by 4 superb slip catches. Slip-catching, or the lack of it, off the fast bowlers had been one of the West Indian weaknesses in the field, failure with the bat against high-class spin another. Nunes was not faultless behind the wicket and Constantine, though a great success overall with his 107 wickets, 1,381 runs and brilliant fielding, did little in the Test Matches. The widely-held view was that West Indies had been given Test status prematurely, though their ability on their own hard pitches was not in doubt.

This ability was put to the test 18 months later when the Hon F. S. G. Calthorpe took an MCC side to the Caribbean to play a rubber of 4. Something of England's resources in this era can be assessed from the fact that another MCC team was playing a Test series of 4 in New Zealand that winter under A. H. H. Gilligan, and that of the 21 cricketers who took part in the Test series against Australia the following summer only

West Indian pioneers, to England in 1906, who, wrote *Wisden*, 'failed to make any strong appeal to the public.' L. S. Constantine, father of Learie, was only able to make the trip because of well-wishers 'passing the hat round' on the quay. Back row: T. C. Learmond, J. J. Cameron, C. K. Bancroft and C. S. Morrison; middle row: S. G. Smith, L. S. Constantine, P. A. Goodman and R. Ollivierre; front row: G. Challenor, O. H. Layne, J. E. Parker, H. B. G. Austin (captain), R. H. Mallett (manager) and C. P. Cumberbatch.

5 were called upon for either of these tours. Calthorpe's tour is mostly remembered for the batting of Hendren, who, at the age of 40, averaged 126 for all matches, 115 in Test Matches and on 4 occasions played innings of over 200 undefeated. Yet the runs he made were a mere fraction of the friends he won by his warmth and sense of fun. For all his popularity throughout the rest of the cricket world, it was West Indies which took him most to heart.

England, unrepresentative as they were, halved the 1929–30 rubber of 4, and would have won it but for what seems retrospectively a preposterous decision by Calthorpe which cost them victory in the last match. It must be remembered, though, that until the 1950s the West Indies were handicapped in home Tests both by shortage of money, which restricted travel, and by the young West Indies Board's decision, for reasons of harmony, generally to name a captain belonging to the colony wherein the Test was played. Thus only the 2 leading batsmen, George Headley and C. A. Roach, played in all 4 matches and of the West Indian side which had won its first-ever Test at Georgetown only 3 travelled the thousand miles to Kingston, Jamaica, for the one following.

The Georgetown victory owed most to Roach, who made a double-hundred, to Headley, who had a hundred in each innings, and to Constantine, who took 9 wickets. At Kingston Andrew Sandham batted 10 hours for the then record Test score of 325 (duly eclipsed by Bradman a few months later), and England amassed 849 before bowling out the weary West Indies for 286. In theory the game was to be played to a finish – the only possible justification for Calthorpe batting again with a lead of 563. However the seasonal rains were due, Headley made 223, his 4th hundred of the series, and there were still 5 wickets standing – with 428 needed to win – when the weather closed in. On the 8th and 9th days no play was possible, after which the MCC side had to board the boat for home.

West Indies' next visit to England in 1933 showed a little improvement on that of 1928. They profited from a fine, warm summer; they were led by the young Cambridge blue G. C. Grant; they had one batsman, Headley, who made over 2,000 runs at an average of 66 and was now a great player by any standards, and they had one fine fast bowler, Martindale. But Constantine, playing for Nelson in the Lancashire League, was only released for the Second of the 3 Test Matches; Francis, now 35, was also in the League and in his one Test was markedly slower; and the rest of Grant's team proved of a standard well below that of Headley and Martindale. Thus England won the First and Third Tests at Lord's and the Oval, each by an innings. At Lord's West Indies were bowled out for 97 and 172, R. W. V. Robins taking 6 for 32 in the 1st innings. West Indian limitation against spin was again illustrated at the Oval where C. S. Marriott, in his only Test Match, took 11 for 96.

In between these 2 defeats, West Indies led England by 1 run on 1st innings in a drawn match at Old Trafford. Barrow (105) and Headley (169) made hundreds for West Indies and Jardine (127) for England, but the match is mostly remembered as the only occasion in a Test Match in England when fast leg theory was employed. On an easy-paced pitch Martindale and Constantine with a strong leg field bowled short and fast. Jardine withstood the fierce attack for 5 hours, but the docility of the pitch made this form of bowling a little less menacing and less effective than it had been in Australia.

The team which MCC sent to West Indies at the end of 1934 was still not the strongest which England could field. Amongst others it lacked Sutcliffe, C. F. Walters, Woolley, G. O. Allen, Verity and Bowes of those who had recently played against Australia; and it lost the rubber 2–1. The times when England could afford to go to the Caribbean below strength were passing. England were captained by Wyatt and began with a win by 4 wickets in an extraordinary match in Barbados. The pitch was wet for much of the 3 days which the match lasted and the captains, Grant and Wyatt, were understandably reluctant to bat while it was at its worst. Thus the West Indies 1st innings of 102, after being put in, was the only one of the 4 to be finished. England, at 81 for 5 were not ill placed at the end of the 1st day, but play did not begin until after tea on the 2nd day and in 3 balls Hylton removed Hammond, who had made 43 on the previous evening, and E. R. T. Holmes. Wyatt at once declared, but Grant countered this move by sending in his more expendable batsmen first.

That night it rained heavily again and when play started at 3.30 next day West Indies continued on a wicked drying pitch. Three wickets, including that of Headley for 0, were lost for 18 runs before tea, when Grant, staking everything on getting England in and out before the pitch dried out, declared, leaving England needing only 73 runs to win. At one time it seemed that this bold move might just succeed, for England were 48 for 6. But Wyatt, too, had reserved his batting and Hammond and Wyatt himself were still left. An assault, mostly

An early photograph of Learie Constantine making a model straight hit: West Indies v Essex at Leyton, 1928.

by Hammond, on Martindale and Hylton brought the remaining 25 runs needed in 24 balls and the match was won.

The rest of the series was less remarkable though it was only in the last available minutes that West Indies won the Second Test in Trinidad by 217 runs. Constantine had much to do with the victory, making 121 runs in the match and taking 5 wickets. Leyland was adjudged lbw to the 5th ball of what must have been the last over. The Third Test in British Guiana ended in an unspectacular draw of which England had slightly the better. These were only 4-day Tests but there was time enough for West Indies to win the last, and thus the rubber, by an innings and 161 runs at Kingston. A brilliant innings of 270 not out by Headley helped West Indies to a score of 535 for 7 declared. Wyatt, opening the England innings, was then struck on the jaw by a rising ball from Martindale, suffering a compound fracture. Ames made 126 in the 1st innings, but soon after lunch on the 4th day England had gone down before Constantine and Martindale who had 13 wickets between them.

The West Indies tour of England in 1939 was led by R. S. Grant (younger brother of G.C.). There was much controversy in the West Indies over the selection of the team and criticism was both carping and outspoken. One press comment attributed to a former captain of British Guiana read as follows:

> The treatment meted out to this colony (British Guiana) in the selection of the West Indies team to tour England is so scandalously inequitable that I find it difficult to bring myself to view it in any light other than as a glaring example of bigotry and insularism.

This type of comment is less prevalent today, in the West Indies, than it was in prewar days, but insular prejudices are not dead yet.

It was true that in 1939 several very good cricketers were left at home. C. A. Merry, who was the best batsman in Trinidad at the time; R. J. Christiani of British Guiana, then a promising wicket-keeper-batsman; and R. Tang Choon, a Chinese cricketer of great ability and personality, one of the finest West Indian players never to gain a Test place, were among those omitted. L. G. Hylton was originally excluded from the side but subsequently joined the team following a public subscription in his home colony, Jamaica. It was unfortunate that Barrow, who had played so well in England in 1933 but who had been living in the United States and consequently had been playing little cricket, was selected as the No. 1 wicket-keeper. It did not take long to discover that he had completely lost form. By a lucky coincidence, however, the talented all-rounder, Sealy, proved to be a fine substitute. Though he was not chosen even as 2nd wicket-keeper, he kept in 2 of the 3 Tests. Another player, J. H. Cameron, who had been a schoolboy bowling prodigy in England and then a Cambridge blue some years before, was selected as a googly bowler. It was only when the team arrived that it was discovered that he was no longer bowling googlies but off-spinners. This type of error was likely to occur when players were gathered from such diverse sources. Several of the players met each other for the first time at the team's London hotel. This happened regularly in the tours before the Second World War.

The West Indies, considering the strength of England at the time, acquitted themselves better on their visit of 1939 than previously. Headley underlined his pre-eminence by scoring 2 hundreds in the Lord's Test wherein J. B. Stollmeyer, at 18 the youngest West Indian to be capped bar Sealy, in his 1st Test, made 59. The new English generation distinguished themselves (Hutton 196, Compton 120) and England won their only victory in the series with 30 minutes to spare. On a soft pitch at Old Trafford the West Indies drew a rain-affected match though they might have been pressed hard if Hammond's captaincy had been rather more enterprising.

The last Test in England before the Second World War saw some sparkling cricket at the Oval, though a finish never seemed likely. In their only innings the West Indies really came of age by scoring 498. V. H. Stollmeyer, elder brother of J.B., made 96 in his one and, as it proved, only Test while K. H. Weekes (no relation to Everton) in his 2nd and last Test scored 137 in 2¼ hours. Conny for his part signed off his Test career with a breathtaking 79 after having taken 5 wickets.

With war looming close the West Indian captain after this game was advised to take his team home. Very reluctantly they set sail on the SS *Montrose* from Greenock to Montreal where they arrived on 3 September 1939. The next ship of the same line to sail on the transatlantic run was the ill-fated *Athenia* which was sunk. The captain was strongly criticized for taking his team home and received one or two derogatory cables from the counties whose fixtures had not been fulfilled. The safety of his team was, however, surely his first consideration, and subsequent events showed the decision to have been a wise one.

During the war West Indies cricket was kept alive by goodwill tournaments played regularly between Trinidad, Barbados and British Guiana. Jamaica had Trinidad and Barbados teams to visit her shores in 1946 and 1947, so all was set to meet G. O. Allen's MCC side of 1947–48. Several batting stars had emerged, as was soon to be evident. It has been the misfortune of many MCC touring teams coming out to the West Indies to play against Barbados before they have found their land-legs and accustomed themselves to the sun and glare of the tropics. To play against the full strength of Barbados, though it is an island only 21 miles by 14, is akin to playing against New South Wales in Australia. In the same decade it has produced Worrell, Weekes, Walcott, Sobers, Hall, Goddard, the 2 Atkinsons, Nurse, Lashley, Hunte, G. Carew, Roy and Norman Marshall, King, C. Smith and Allan – all players who have represented their country, most of them with great distinction. It is sometimes doubtful which is the stronger team – West Indies or Barbados.

After 18 months of solid cricket starting in April 1946, the front-line England players were mostly rested in preparation for the Australians' arrival the following summer. Allen's side, of problematical strength, found themselves subjected to a murderous assault on landing in Barbados. This was a shock from which they never fully recovered. A cruel succession of injuries also afflicted the side throughout the tour. Headley led a strong West Indies combination in the Barbados Test, though as yet only 3 of these names meant anything to English readers: Stollmeyer, Walcott, Weekes, Worrell, Gomez and Goddard. The English bowlers, hit all over the place by Barbados in the previous game, seemed as yet unsure of themselves under the conditions. Coming from an English winter, they were certainly not yet fighting fit. Nevertheless, Headley took a cautious attitude during the course of the game after winning the toss and establishing a 1st-innings lead. The game was made more interesting by the fact that rain fell on each night. As the wickets in those days were uncovered, the bowlers, particularly spinners, were highly effective. Laker, on his 1st tour, looked most useful under the conditions. Allen, the England captain, had a leg-muscle injury which prevented him from playing, the team being led by Cranston, who lost the toss. West Indies batted all day for 244 for 3. After overnight rain the last 7 wickets fell for 52 runs mostly to Laker who had 7 for 103 and had bowled splendidly in his 1st Test.

Up to a point, the makeshift England side did well enough, but after Christiani had had the misfortune to be lbw for 99, an easy catch dropped allowed Foffy Williams to run riot with 28 off the first 6 balls he received and 79 in an hour altogether. The West Indies were scenting certain victory when more tropical rain brought the game to an end.

In the Second Test at Trinidad, played on the easy-paced jute mat, Stollmeyer, who was to have been captain, gave place to Gomez, and England had their first sight of the 3rd of what was to become the famous trinity of Walcott, Weekes and Worrell. The first 2 had given a taste of their mettle in Barbados but Worrell, also a native of that same small island, had been unfit. With a classic 97 he made his mark at the first attempt. But he was not the only one. First, S. C. Griffith, MCC's player-manager and reserve wicket-keeper to Godfrey Evans, opened the innings – in the absence of 3 accredited batsmen – and made history in his 1st Test by getting his maiden first-class hundred – a sterling 140 made in 6 hours. For West Indies 2 likewise new openers, Ganteaume and Carew, each made hundreds: Ganteaume (in the only Test he ever played) contributed a quiet, sober effort; Carew's was a dashing affair matching the trilby hat that he wore at a rakish angle. Ferguson, the leg-spinner, with 11 for 229, was the only bowler who seemed suited by the mat, and England escaped once more, and not without honour.

Hutton had joined Allen's stricken team by the Third Test at Georgetown and had his first view of Worrell, who took out his bat for 131. Rain, as in Barbados, took a hand again, encouraging Goddard, the 3rd West Indian captain in 3 matches, to declare at 297 for 8. The effect of the roller eased the wicket a bit and Hutton and Robertson scored 48 without loss, but when Goddard came on himself he was able to turn the ball sharply and, bowling to 3 short-legs, he quickly broke the back of the England batting. It took only the 1st over of the 3rd day to bring the innings to an end for 111. Goddard had taken 5 for 31. England followed on and fought back gamely in difficult circumstances. Eventually the West Indies needed 78 to win, and when they lost 3 for 26 the issue was still open. Walcott, however, batted magnificently on a hateful wicket and steered his side to victory while Gomez was dying a hundred deaths at the other end.

For the Fourth Test Goddard retained the captaincy, Headley, who was originally chosen, being still unable to play. Following on his victory in this Test Goddard was to become West Indies' captain for the next 4 years. Weekes was only retained because of Headley's absence, and this last chance enabled him to score the 1st of 4 successive Test hundreds. In answer to England's 227 West Indies, after a moderate start, scored 490. Weekes, dropped early at the wicket, and surviving several moments of discomfort, finally found his true form and showed something of what the future promised for him with a dashing innings of 141. In England's 2nd innings, a sound innings by Hutton (60) and then a pedestrian but valuable effort from Place (107) indicated that the game might be saved, but against the tail the tall fast bowler, Hines Johnson, repeated his 1st-innings performance, finishing with a match analysis of 10 for 96. Thus MCC went through the tour without a single victory, while the West Indies had served notice on the cricket world of great things to come.

It was with a feeling of supreme confidence that the West Indies set out for their tour of England in 1950. A tour of India had further established the class of the batting, and all that remained to be seen so far as this department was concerned was whether the batsmen could adapt themselves to English conditions. The fielding of such a young team could be expected to be of a high standard and Walcott had proved himself a tremendous power as a wicket-keeper-batsman. He was certainly two players in one. The bowling, however, could prove more of a problem. The fast bowler, Johnson, at 40, was unlikely to withstand the rigours of such a strenuous tour, and Jones and Pierre at this stage of their careers seemed to lack the devil of top-class fast bowlers.

Two unknowns, Ramadhin and Valentine, both 19-year-olds, had been included as spin-bowlers, neither of them having had much first-class experience. Indeed the former had played in only 2 first-class matches and the latter had just come through a series between Jamaica and Trinidad with an analysis of 2 for 151. Nevertheless, the talent was manifest. The team finally selected was J. D. Goddard (captain), E. D. Weekes, C. L. Walcott, F. M. Worrell, R. E. Marshall and C. B. Williams (Barbados); J. B. Stollmeyer, G. E. Gomez, K. B. Trestrail, P. E. Jones, L. R. Pierre and S. Ramadhin (Trinidad); A. F. Rae, H. H. Johnson and A. L. Valentine (Jamaica); and R. J. Christiani (BG).

The Old Trafford wicket prepared for the First Test appeared to be likely to crumble quickly, and give the two young West Indians something encouraging to bowl on. Ramadhin's wristy finger-spin caused damage. On a wicket where he could get the ball to turn to any extent, county batsmen were virtually guessing which was his leg-spinner. He was truly an enigma. The pitch, to put it mildly, appeared to be underprepared. The England selectors, indeed, decided to leave out their best stock bowler, A. V. Bedser. By lunch on the 1st day England were 88 for 5, and Valentine was already turning the ball between 6 inches and a foot, with undue lift as well. Then came Evans and Bailey in an adventurous stand which was primarily responsible for England winning the match. Valentine bowled too short and too much on the off-stump, a pardonable error in one so inexperienced, and Goddard failed to stop Evans's main run-getting shot. These two added 161, Evans scoring 104, his maiden hundred in first-class cricket, mainly by cuts. Bailey, using the sweep-shot to advantage, was not out with 82 when England were all out for 312. Valentine had bowled 50 overs for figures of 8 for 104. It was not unnatural that the West Indies batsmen should be at sea in the circumstances to the spinners, Berry and Hollies. Stollmeyer (43) and Weekes (52) played best but West Indies could score only 215. England made 288 in her 2nd innings. In the absence of Johnson, Walcott opened the bowling and Christiani kept wicket. Edrich fought well for 71; Hutton, nursing an injured hand, made 43 and Laker 40. The 386 set West Indies was clearly miles out of reach. Only Stollmeyer (78) played adequately under the difficult conditions, and West Indies lost what they considered a highly unsatisfactory match by 202 runs.

Lord's was the scene of the historic Second Test. This was the 1st Test ever to be won by the West Indies in England and the margin of defeat, 326 runs, left no doubt as to which was the better team under normal cricket conditions. On the 1st day West Indies scored 320 for 7, greatly enthusing the experts by the quality and attraction of their play. Hutton and Washbrook scored 62 for England's 1st wicket, but thereafter no one could cope successfully with the spin of Ramadhin and Valentine and the innings totalled only 151. In the 2nd innings England were still in the game until Gomez joined Walcott with the score at 199 for 5. These two, playing sensibly and well, then added 211 for the 6th wicket and put the match firmly in the grip of the West Indies. Walcott treated the crowd to a masterly exhibition of driving in front of the wicket off both front and back foot. He went on to score 168 not out, only one less than Headley's then record Test score for West Indies v England in England.

Goddard declared at 425 for 6, leaving England to make 601 to win in the 2 days left for play. Valentine soon bowled Hutton with one which came 'up the hill' with the arm, and although Washbrook in a grim rearguard action scored 114, West Indies won the game shortly after lunch on the final day. Ramadhin had bowled splendidly and had a match analysis of 11 for 152. He was ably supported by Valentine who took 7 for 127. Between them they bowled 143 overs in the innings (231 in the match) and, at one stage, Washbrook stayed for 66 minutes at one end batting against Ramadhin, who eventually won the duel by bowling him comprehensively. 'Ram and Val' promptly became the heroes of a popular calypso which was being played and sung by the happy West Indian throng serenading their heroes the moment the game ended. The West Indies' triumph had been largely theirs.

At Trent Bridge, where the Third Test was played, England fielded a weak batting side, with Hutton unfit in addition to

Compton whom the West Indies had not yet seen since he was recovering from a knee operation. Gimblett, brought to Trent Bridge to play if Hutton was not available, developed a boil on his neck and could not take part. West Indies won the match by 10 wickets, after bowling England out on the 1st day for 223. The 2nd day produced a batting feast, and those who saw Weekes and Worrell add 241 will never forget the manner in which these two players dominated the English bowling. When on the 3rd day the Worrell-Weekes partnership was broken, having added 283, Worrell had scored 261 and broken all Test records for a West Indian batsman in England. It was a truly masterful innings. Weekes finished with 129 and the innings closed for 558. England started the uphill battle well, Simpson and Washbrook taking the score to 212 before the 1st wicket fell. Washbrook went for 102, Simpson for 94. England fought hard, but the odds were too great and the West Indies got the 103 needed to win without losing a wicket.

Great now was the West Indians' confidence and tough the task tackled by F. R. Brown, who having now been appointed MCC's captain in Australia in the coming winter naturally took over the captaincy for the last Test at the Oval. England lost the toss and West Indies were soon building hugely. Hundreds from Rae and Worrell and good support from Gomez and Goddard helped the score to reach 503. Wright, brought into the England team for the 1st time in the series, took 5 for 141. It was left to Hutton to show his class and value to the England batting. He carried his bat through the innings for a monumental 202. Compton, playing also for the 1st time in the series, struggled for 44 before he was run out by his illustrious partner. The wicket was badly affected by rain, and it became a question whether England could save the follow-on. Had they done so they might conceivably – to home eyes anyway – have turned the tables. But they failed by 10, and the 2nd innings on a most unpleasant surface was a debacle. Thus, and deservedly, the West Indies at the 4th time of asking beat England in England.

The stormy MCC tour of the West Indies in 1953–54 began on the sunny island of Bermuda. MCC spent some days there acclimatizing before proceeding to Jamaica for the 1st first-class fixture. The first signs of trouble and friction developed in Jamaica, some of the MCC players disagreeing openly with umpires' decisions. Verbal battles ensued between the crowds and Trueman. It appeared also as though it was the policy of some of the touring party not to fraternize with their West Indian counterparts. Such was the background to a gripping, if somewhat bitter, series in which strategy and tactics were sometimes overplayed and the latter carried to a point where the line drawn between them and sharp practice was hardly discernible. In retrospect, it was not a series which would bear repetition.

The West Indies XI for the First Test was widely criticized on the grounds that 5 Jamaicans were selected, but the proof of the pudding was in the eating, for the West Indians won the game, a thriller in many ways, by 140 runs. England's initial mistake was in their team selection. No doubt influenced by previous wickets in Jamaica and the appearance of the Test strip, Hutton played 4 fast bowlers and both Laker and Wardle were left out. The error was soon obvious after they lost the toss and the wicket proved to be easy paced. West Indies scored a remarkably level 417, the runs taking until shortly before lunch on the 3rd day to compile while England bowled at the rate of 14 overs per hour. England's reply was disastrous, 170 all out; their destroyers the old firm of Ramadhin and Valentine. Stollmeyer did not enforce the follow-on, a decision which did not meet with the favour of the crowd, and he was in for some anxious moments as England fought a fine rearguard action. Bailey bowled on or outside the leg stump to a leg-field and held up West Indies who declared at 209 for 6 on the morning of the 5th day. Set to make 457 in the 4th innings, England were well placed at 227 for 2 at the end of the 5th day, with only Hutton (56) and Watson (116) out. The lunch score was 282 for 3 but then came a remarkable collapse before the fast bowling of Kentish, and England were out for 316. Kentish's figures were 29-11-49-5, but he was 38 and was not selected for another game in the series.

The pattern of the Second Test was not dissimilar to the First, and again the finish came shortly after lunch on the 5th day. Walcott played a magnificent innings of 220, his highest Test score. Pairaudeau (71) and Atkinson (53) helped the total along to 383. Then came another sorry batting performance by England. The ball hit the bat not vice-versa and England on a plumb wicket and with a fast outfield scored 181 off 150.5 overs. Ramadhin's figures were 4 for 50 in 53 overs and Valentine's 3 for 61 in 51 overs. England's 2nd innings was less abject than the 1st, but this defeat was as comprehensive as the first.

The Third Test in British Guiana marked the turn of events in the series. England at last brought in Wardle, while West Indies took the field without a fast bowler. Thus the home selectors went to the other extreme vis-a-vis England in the First Test. It was a regrettable decision. England won the toss and, led by a magnificent 169 by Hutton supported by Compton (64), Bailey (49) and Wardle (38), made 435. When West Indies batted Statham's initial overs were devastating. He broke the crust of the West Indies batting, taking the first 3 wickets for 16 runs. The West Indies never really recovered, though Weekes scored 94 and an 8th-wicket partnership between McWatt and an injured Holt added 99 before the former was run out attempting a rash 2nd run. Though the decision was a formality it was too great a disappointment for the crowd to take, and there occurred the first of the bottle-throwing interruptions which have become such an ugly feature of the game in the Caribbean. West Indies followed on, but made only 256, leaving England 73 to win. West Indies won the toss on the mild jute mat of Port of Spain and put together 681 for 8 declared, the 'three Ws' all making hundreds. Statham soon injured himself while running up to bowl and took no further part in the match, or the series. England replied with 537, narrowly saving the follow-on. On the final day, when it became certain that neither side could win, the cricket was played in a light-hearted vein.

So it was all to play for in the last Test at Kingston where Bailey, in the best performance of his career, took 7 for 34 on the 1st day with only the minimum of freshness in the pitch to help him. Against a paltry West Indian total of 139, Hutton followed with one of his finest innings: 205 out of 414. Wardle helped him to add 105 for the 7th wicket, after which England never looked like losing their grip. For the West Indies the rubber's extraordinary change of fortune was hard to bear especially since the demeanour of the England side had not always endeared itself. The one consolation lay in the appearance of a 17-year-old Barbadian left-hander named Sobers who with slow spin took 4 for 75 and made 40 for once out – an auspicious portent of greatness to come.

West Indies, again under J. D. Goddard, went to England in 1957 in an atmosphere which their more sensible followers realized at the time was one of over-optimism. The glories of 1950, the presence in the side of the main architects of that famous victory and the arrival of some new players of undoubted promise tended to blind many enthusiastic West Indian supporters to the facts. These were that the 'three Ws' were not quite the force of their younger days, the young players such as Kanhai, O. G. Smith and Sobers were still developing and England, with such bowlers to call on as Trueman, Statham, Loader, Bailey, Laker and Lock, were a strong experienced side very hard to beat in their own country. Much also depended on whether Ramadhin and Valentine could bemuse this generation of English batsmen as they had done their predecessors, but this was decided at Edgbaston in the First Test, in its after-effects one of the most conclusive of all time.

On the 1st day it seemed that Ramadhin might be going to continue where he had left off in 1950, for on a slightly damp pitch he took 7 wickets for 49 in 31 overs and bowled England out for 186. The First Test at Edgbaston for 28 years was attended by perfect weather, and during the next 2 days the West Indies batsmen took their chance. 'Collie' Smith, who was to die so tragically 2 years later in a motor accident not far away, made 161 in his 1st innings against England. He added 190 in 5 hours for the 6th wicket with Worrell (81) and batted nearly 7 hours. England batted again 288 behind, and by the close of the 3rd day Ramadhin had taken the first 2 wickets.

This, as it turned out, was the limit of West Indian success not only in the match but in the series. For on the Monday morning the England captain, May, and Cowdrey came together in the highest of all English Test partnerships, a matter of 411 made by the utmost application over 8¼ hours. May, who took out his bat for a matchless 285, did not declare until England were 295 runs on and only 2 hours and 20 minutes remained. As it proved, Laker and Lock, on a pitch now taking a little spin, would have bowled out demoralized opponents with only a little more time, for West Indies were 72 for 7 at the end. But May and Cowdrey, playing Ramadhin almost entirely off the front foot, had worn him down and killed his menace so completely that, after his initial 7 for 49, he took only another 7 wickets for 498 in the whole series. It was a valid criticism directed against Goddard that he himself had helped to exorcize Ramadhin's magic by 'bowling him into the ground', and for nearly all the time with a defensive field at that. His 98 overs is the record number bowled in a Test innings – long before the end he could scarcely get his arm over.

England went on to win at Lord's, Leeds and the Oval, each time by an innings. On a fast pitch at Lord's, Bailey took 7 wickets for 44 on the 1st day when the grass was at its freshest. England, helped by dropped catches, replied to West Indies' 127 with 424 (Cowdrey 152) and although Weekes, despite many body blows and with a cracked bone in a finger, then played a brilliant innings of 90, West Indies were beaten by an innings and 36 runs on the 3rd day. A plumb pitch and more hot weather at Trent Bridge helped West Indies to draw the Third Test after following on. England made 619 for 6 declared (Graveney 258, Richardson 126 and May 104). Worrell then batted throughout the 9½ hours of the West Indian 1st innings, making 191 out of 372. In the follow-on Smith saved his side and underlined his promise by another hundred, this time 168.

At Leeds, West Indies went down in 3 days again, this time by an innings and 5 runs. Loader, 6 for 36, finished off their 1st innings of 142 with a hat-trick and, after May, Cowdrey and the Rev D. S. Sheppard had all played innings in the 60s, West Indies were bowled out again for 132.

The last Test of 1957 was played at the Oval on a pitch pinkish in colour and prone to dust from the start. England, with all the moral mastery by now batted well on it, Richardson making 107 and Graveney a magnificent 164. Laker and Lock then bowled West Indies out for 89 and 86, their lowest scores against England. It was a dismal end to an unlucky tour in which injuries to Weekes and Walcott and the immaturity of the fast bowlers, Gilchrist and Hall – Hall did not play in a Test Match – and the captain's own poor form at the age of 38 had prevented the full potential of the side from being developed.

The England side which went to West Indies at the end of 1959 had lost most of the bowlers who had contributed so much to the successes of the 1950s and had fallen from grace in Australia a year before. Trueman and Statham remained, and they took 21 and 10 wickets respectively. Of these, Trueman took 5 and Statham 3 in the innings which decided the rubber in the Second Test at Port of Spain. England's victory in the rubber – their 1st in 5 trips to the Caribbean – was the more remarkable because their captain and the leading batsman, May, was never fit and, after suffering considerable pain without revealing the fact to his team, had to surrender the captaincy to Cowdrey after the Third Test. Alexander captained West Indies, following his successful leadership of the West Indies in India.

Only the Second Test was finished and there were occasions when it seemed that West Indies, for whom Sobers scored 709 runs at an average of 101·28, might, with more enterprise, have gained the initiative. There was much slow batting in the First Test at Barbados, and after England had made 482 (Barrington 128, Dexter 136 not out) West Indies replied with 563 for 8 declared in 51 overs more. To the general surprise England scored the faster in the series as a whole. The 226 of Sobers and the 197 not out of Worrell were the 2 longest innings ever played against England, lasting 10 hours and 47 minutes and 11 hours and 20 minutes respectively. Their stand of 399 for the 4th wicket lasted 9½ hours.

England's win by 256 runs in Trinidad occurred in one of the most extraordinary matches in Test history. The excitement in the crowd grew until on the 3rd afternoon, when West Indies had collapsed in their 1st innings against Trueman and Statham, there was a sudden eruption of bottle-throwing. The crowd (which had been packed over-tight) invaded the playing area, and, since there was no practicable way of clearing the field, play was abandoned for the day. That night apologies were tendered with much fervour to the MCC side, on whose behalf they were sympathetically accepted by the manager, R. W. V. Robins. The last 3 days' play took place in peace and quiet. In England's 1st innings of 382, Barrington had made 121 and M. J. K. Smith 108 against much short bowling which brought cautions from the umpires to both Hall and Watson. Trueman and Statham returned the bumpers at the start of the West Indian innings, but they ended there and it was good honest fast bowling and poor batting which had West Indies out for 112. The follow-on was not enforced and England had 10 hours on the last 2 days to bowl West Indies out again. Kanhai made 110 but the innings ended with nearly 2 hours to spare.

There was an exciting and fluctuating Third Test in Jamaica in which Cowdrey made 114 and 97, the 2nd innings being one of his most brilliant for England. West Indies passed England's disappointing 277 with only 2 wickets down but when Sobers was out for 147, McMorris for 73 and Nurse for 70, they collapsed and led by only 76 runs. England's 305 in the 2nd innings left West Indies to make 230 in just over 4 hours, but the pitch had worn a little and they finished 55 short with 4 wickets standing.

A classic defensive stroke against a fast bowler: Dexter v Hall in the Third Test, Kingston, Jamaica 1959–60.

On an easy-paced pitch in British Guiana England had no difficulty in earning a draw after Sobers had made 145 and West Indies had declared 107 ahead. Subba Row and Dexter made hundreds in the 2nd innings of an unexciting match. By the time of the Fifth Test at Port of Spain England were further weakened by the return home of Statham; and Parks, who was coaching in the Caribbean, was called in to keep wicket and strengthen the batting, which he did by making 101 not out in the 2nd innings at a time when England were in some difficulty. From 148 for 6 a stand of 197 between Parks and Smith took England to safety. With England one up in the rubber no declaration was forthcoming and a series of hostile fast bowling and mixed excitement and stagnation ended with a 4th draw.

By the time Worrell, aged 38 (as Goddard had been 6 years earlier), brought a team of talented players many years his junior to England in 1963, the promise of the young West Indians of a few years before had been fulfilled and English cricket, now without May, had entered one of its leaner phases. In a wet summer the Tests were almost completely spared the rain. West Indies, who won a memorable series 3–1, were clearly the better side throughout in almost every way, but England succeeded in hanging on and playing a worthy, if minor, part in a rubber which lifted the reputation of West Indian cricket sky-high. It was not done through consistently brilliant batting as in 1950, for the mainstay of the more important innings was usually the patient Hunte. There were short periods of spectacular batting, as when Kanhai, Butcher and Sobers were extending a substantial 1st innings lead at Leeds, and when Kanhai was making a gay 77 on the last day at the Oval. But England scored the faster overall and Dexter's 70 in 81 minutes at Lord's against the fiery fast bowling of Hall and Griffith is no doubt the innings by which the Tests will be most clearly remembered.

The attraction of Worrell's West Indian team stemmed, therefore, not especially from dashing batting but from the variety of their bowling, their capacity in the field for making everything they did entertaining and from the noisy participation of their immigrant followers who gave the scene an atmosphere entirely new to English cricket. Since 1950, when West Indians in England had last had anything about which to cheer, their numbers had multiplied many times and whole sections of the Test grounds were occupied by West Indian faces: shouting, waving West Indian cricket-lovers. One more factor contributed to the success of the series. Just as in Australia in 1960–61 a tie in the First Test at Brisbane had sparked off the series, so now an equally thrilling match at Lord's in the Second Test brought interest to a high pitch.

West Indies, with rather the better of the pitch, which took spin by the 3rd day, had won the First Test at Old Trafford by 10 wickets. Hunte made 182, Kanhai 90 and Worrell 74 not out in West Indies 501 for 6 declared. England were then bowled out for 205 and 296, mostly by the off-spinner, Gibbs, with Sobers in support. At Lord's England, by some poor cricket and obscure tactics, allowed West Indies to make 391 in the 1st innings in conditions by no means unhelpful to the fast bowling. Dexter's 70, an innings of 80 by Barrington and 52 not out by Titmus enabled England to come within 4 runs of this early on the 3rd day. For the rest of that day England, captained by Cowdrey, in the absence of Dexter who had suffered a strain, gave an entirely different exhibition of out-cricket. At 104 for 5 West Indies were perilously placed, but Butcher established himself, Worrell made a useful 33 that night and though the last 5 wickets fell for 15 in 6 overs on Monday morning to Trueman and Shackleton, West Indies had been able to leave England to make 234. Butcher had made a priceless 133, his 6th-wicket stand with Worrell adding 110. England had nearly 2 days to make the runs – or so it seemed. In fact, after Cowdrey had suffered a broken arm at the hands of Hall while England were making 116 for 3, rain stopped play for the day. More rain next day meant that England with 6 sound wickets remaining needed a further 118 in 200 minutes. The two West Indian fast bowlers, Hall and Griffith, with astonishing stamina and frequent recourse to the bumper, bowled all but 5 of the overs at rather less than 15 an hour. Every run was bitterly disputed, but only 15 runs were needed with 19 minutes left when Close, who had stood up to the fast bowling magnificently in the innings of his life, was 8th out for 70. From the last over 8 were needed. The first 3 balls yielded 2. Shackleton, slow to start, was run out from the 4th, whereupon Allen, with his captain, arm in plaster, now at the non-striker's end, had no option but to stay put.

The series was still further stimulated by being levelled at Edgbaston where the pitch stayed damp almost throughout and England, in conditions suiting them, won by 217 runs. On the last day Trueman took 7 wickets for 44 and West Indies were bowled out for 91. It did not take long, however, for West Indies to confirm which was the better side. At Leeds they made 397 (Sobers 102, Kanhai 92). By now it was the newcomer Griffith, not the more experienced Hall, who was doing the most damage to the English batting with his variations of pace and his lightning yorker most accurately produced. He took 6 for 36 in the 1st innings and shared with Gibbs and Sobers the final destruction which brought England down by 221 runs.

At the Oval the margin was 8 wickets, but until the last day England had apparently had a shade the better of a duel between fast bowlers. Griffith took 6 for 71, but Trueman and Statham each took 3 wickets and helped to earn England a 1st innings lead of 29. England were then bowled out by Hall, Griffith and Sobers for 223 which left West Indies to make 253 to win. On a good pitch, however, Hunte made 108 not out, his partners, Rodriguez, Kanhai, in particular, and Butcher joined him in some of the best batting of the series and the runs were made with great ease and amid unprecedented scenes of West Indian jubilation.

Thus ended one of the most successful Test series for years and one which swiftly led to a reorganization of the international tours programme. England's proposal of the double tours principle to the ICC meant that instead of waiting 8 years for their next visit West Indies might return in 3.

The series between the two countries between 1965 and 1980 reflected the disintegration of Frank Worrell's marvellous side and the subsequent period of rebuilding. Once again it was remarkable how soon replacements were found: the West Indies showed that it has an almost limitless supply of exciting young players. At the end of 1973 when the West Indies beat England 2–0 in a 3 match series in England it looked as if a side to compare with Worrell's had been thrown up in only 10 years. But in the next 3 years the side changed again and the likes of Roberts, Holding, Richards, Daniel and Gordon Greenidge appeared and formed maybe the most formidable West Indies side yet seen.

The West Indies returned to the Caribbean in 1963 with as well-balanced a side as they can ever have had – that of Clive Lloyd has been, ideally, top heavy with fast bowling – but Frank Worrell now retired from Test cricket and the captaincy passed to Gary Sobers. Worrell's steadying influence on the excitable characters he had under him had been at least as important in his 5 years of captaincy as his immense tactical skill. When the side came again to England, in 1966, Sobers himself was at the height of his powers in his 4 different roles, and the batting with Butcher, Kanhai, Nurse and Hunte in addition to Sobers spoke for itself. Yet they were not quite the same irresistible bowling side for Hall and Griffith were getting no younger, although it was not until the last Test that this became fully apparent.

England's own cricket in 1966 was in some disarray. They called upon 23 players for the 5 matches in this series and no less than 3 captains, M. J. K. Smith, Cowdrey and Close. The

West Indies made an impressive start, winning the First Test in 3 days by an innings and 40 runs and England might have been forgiven for thinking that nothing had changed in 3 years. Sobers scored 161 in this match and strode through the series in the most remarkable way, taking 20 wickets and scoring 722 runs in the 5 Test Matches. In this First Test he was certainly lucky to win the toss and bat first on a pitch which had only recently been prepared and gave a good deal of help to the spin of Gibbs and Sobers himself on the 2nd and 3rd days.

Cowdrey took over from M. J. K. Smith for the Second Test and for 3 days England had the better of the match before being finally thwarted by Sobers. England gained a 1st innings lead of 86 and had taken 5 West Indies' 2nd innings wickets for 95 when Sobers was joined by his young cousin, David Holford. They stayed together for $5\frac{1}{4}$ hours adding 274, a record for the West Indies 6th wicket against England, and saved the match. This was the game in which Tom Graveney made a successful return to Test cricket, scoring 96 in England's 1st innings. The next 2 Tests were both won convincingly by the West Indies with Butcher making 209 not out in the 2nd innings at Trent Bridge on a glorious pitch and Sobers (174) and Nurse (137) making hundreds in the Fourth at Headingley. Graveney apart, the England batting had been extremely inconsistent.

The West Indies, therefore, came to the Oval with an unassailable 3–0 lead. Close now succeeded Cowdrey and presided over one of the most astonishing turn-arounds in the history of Test cricket for England won this match by an innings and 34 runs. The West Indies probably relaxed to some extent knowing that the series was theirs, but England's victory was still as impressive as it was unlikely. They made 6 changes for the match: Higgs, in fact, was the only England player to take part in all 5 Tests. The West Indies were first dismissed for 268 with Kanhai making his only hundred of the series and then the pattern of England's recent batting continued. They had lost 7 wickets for 166 when Murray joined Graveney; these two proceeded to put on 217 for the 8th wicket, and then Snow and Higgs added 128 for the last. England's lead was 259 and the West Indies who were by then demoralized, were bowled out a 2nd time for 225.

When England went to the West Indies in 1967–68 Cowdrey was once again captain of the side for Close had lost his place for disciplinary reasons following the notorious incident at Edgbaston in August 1967, when he was accused, and convicted, of time-wasting in Yorkshire's match with Warwickshire. By now time had made further inroads into the West Indies side. Hall and Griffith were some way past their best and the infallible West Indies batting was now curiously inconsistent. But batting replacements were quickly at hand, for this series saw the emergence of Clive Lloyd, who had toured India 2 years before, as a Test batsman. Although Cowdrey had several times held the England captaincy, it had never before been for long and this time in the West Indies he proved perhaps for the first time that the job was his as of right. His captaincy played a major part in England's victory by the only Test finished.

The West Indies came close to losing both the 1st two Tests. In the 1st, at Port of Spain, only a resolute 9th-wicket stand between Sobers and Hall which endured for just over 2 hours on the last day prevented England from winning. They had led the West Indies by 205 on the 1st innings in spite of an exciting 118 from Lloyd in his 1st Test in the West Indies. England's fast bowlers, Snow, Brown and Jones, showed at once that they were a more formidable combination than their West Indies counterparts while Cowdrey and Graveney scored hundreds. Graveney's innings must remain to anyone who saw it as one of the most technically beautiful hundreds ever to have been made in Test cricket.

In the Second Test at Kingston on a newly laid pitch at Sabina Park which had a hopelessly uneven bounce England batted 1st and gained a 1st innings lead of 233 and when Parks caught Butcher down the leg-side off d'Oliveira, West Indies were 204 for 5 in their 2nd innings and the match was as good as lost. At this point the crowd were unable to contain their disappointment any longer and one section of it on the public side of the ground opposite the pavilion began to throw bottles on to the playing area. The game was held up and soon other sections of the crowd joined in and eventually the police, in conflict with their orders, used tear-gas to disperse the rioters. When play was eventually resumed that evening, Sobers went on to complete a wonderful hundred and by then much of the impetus had gone out of the English performance. When Sobers declared England were left to score 159 to win on a deteriorating pitch which underlined the brilliance of Sobers's own innings. It had been decided that the 75 minutes which had been lost to the riot would be made up on an unscheduled 6th day and when the end came England were more perilously close to defeat than the score of 68 for 4 may suggest.

The Third Test, in Barbados, ended in an uneventful draw with Butcher and Lloyd making runs for the West Indies and Edrich and Boycott for England, and the pitch was excellent until the end. The Fourth Test in Trinidad also looked to be heading towards a high-scoring draw when Sobers made a declaration which will never be forgotten in the cricketing West Indies. Batting first, the West Indies had made 526 for 7 declared, Nurse and Kanhai each getting hundreds, and England had replied with 414, Cowdrey making 148. Then, when the West Indies had reached 92 for 2 in their 2nd innings, Sobers declared asking England to score 215 in 165 minutes – admittedly a fast rate for the series as a whole with its fast bowlers and their long run-ups. But Hall had been dropped for the match and Griffith had hurt his leg which left only Sobers to bowl fast, and he was forced to share the new ball with Gibbs. England were given a good start by Boycott and Edrich, Cowdrey batted magnificently for 71 and Boycott, pacing his innings perfectly, was 80 not out when England won with 3 minutes to spare.

As there was only one match between the 2 sides, the last Test, in Georgetown, was lengthened to 6 days in accordance with the tour regulations and England somehow hung on for a draw in an unforgettably exciting finish with their last pair of Knott and Jones together. Brilliant batting by Kanhai (150) and Sobers (152) had taken the West Indies to an invincible position on a pitch which, like most at Bourda, took spin increasingly as the match wore on. In England's 2nd innings Gibbs took 6 for 60 in 40 overs, but the West Indies were frustrated first by Cowdrey and then by Knott.

It was the turn of the West Indies to come to England for a short tour of 3 Tests in 1969 immediately after their disastrous tour of Australia. By now the side of the early 1960s had finally disintegrated. Hall, Griffith, Nurse, Hunte and Kanhai, although he was to return, had all gone. They were still captained by Sobers who was no longer quite the all-commanding figure he had been formerly. The West Indies, however, were unlucky in that this was an extremely wet first half of the summer. They lost the series 2–0, although if Sobers had won the toss in the First Test and West Indies had batted while the pitch was good, this match might have gone the other way; as might the Third if Sobers himself had not thrown away his wicket (quite uncharacteristically) in the 2nd innings before he had scored. As it was, the West Indies lost by only 30 runs.

This year, 1969, was probably the unhappiest for the West Indies in the recent past. The new players such as Camacho, Edward, Fredericks, Charlie Davis, Findlay, Irving and Grayson Shillingford and Foster could not fill the eminent gaps which had been left although the tour gave them useful experience.

When the West Indies returned to England in 1973 the captaincy had passed from Sobers to Kanhai. In the intervening 4 years the rebuilding process had continued apace and once again they had a pretty formidable side. Lloyd, Fredericks, Kallicharran and Julien, in addition to Kanhai and Sobers – who was available only for the Tests, being under contract to Nottinghamshire – made a strong batting line-up; while Sobers, Gibbs, Boyce, Julien and Holder completed a nicely balanced attack. This series came at a time when England were having problems with their batting which even Illingworth's astute leadership could not paper over, and the West Indies won the 3 match series 2–0.

In the First, a hundred by Lloyd assured the West Indies of a big 1st innings score which was to prove decisive in spite of 2 good innings from Boycott and a hundred in his 1st Test Match by Hayes of Lancashire. The Second Test was drawn with Lloyd and Fredericks both playing big innings for the West Indies. The Third, at Lord's, was memorable for a marvellous batting display by the West Indies. Both Kanhai and Sobers made 150 and they could hardly have finished their Test careers in England more handsomely. Later on Julien hit a powerful hundred and a total of 652 for 8 was far beyond England in spite of 2 determined innings by Fletcher.

During the Third Test Match, which was played at Lord's, Illingworth was dropped from the England captaincy and Denness was appointed in his place to take MCC to the Caribbean that winter, 1973–74. This was another series very much in keeping with the recent tradition of the Wisden Trophy for which the 2 sides play. Amazingly England managed to draw the 5-Test rubber 1–1 against the same side which had beaten them so convincingly in England less than 6 months earlier. The West Indies temperament which tends to live in the extremes, together with the wonderful form of Greig and Amiss, were the main contributory factors to this result. The West Indies won the First Test by 7 wickets after putting England in to bat on a damp pitch and bowling them out for 131. Even so, the West Indies, who gained a 1st innings lead of 261, were made to work hard, for Amiss and Boycott then put on 209 for the 1st wicket in England's 2nd innings, Amiss making 174. In the end, Gibbs, as he has so often done at Queen's Park Oval, Port of Spain, went through the rest of the innings finishing with 6 for 108 and the West Indies were left with a simple task in the 4th innings. England had an extraordinary escape in the Second Test. After the West Indies had built up a 1st innings lead of 230 at Kingston, England were saved by an astonishing innings of 262 not out by Amiss and managed to draw the match. Already there were signs that the West Indies attack, which had beaten England so convincingly in England, was no longer quite so formidable, and there were injury problems. Julien and Boyce never found their previous consistency.

The Oval 1973: West Indies celebrate their 1st victory over England for 9 Test Matches.

The Third Test was not dissimilar from the Second and England survived because of splendid hundreds from Greig and Fletcher. But this match in Bridgetown will be longest remembered for Lawrence Rowe's innings of 302, the highest individual score by a West Indian against England. In this same match, his last, as it proved, before his home crowd, Sobers made a duck. The Fourth Test in Georgetown was spoilt by rain but not before Amiss again and Greig had made hundreds and Greig had caused the West Indies batsmen some anxious moments with the newly-discovered off-breaks which were to prove so decisive in the final Test of the series at Port of Spain.

This was a match which was won for England by two outstanding personal performances. Greig took 13 wickets for 156 with his off-breaks and Boycott played innings of 99 and 112. He was probably not quite at his best but his application and his concentration never wavered in either knock. After winning the toss England were dismissed for 267. The West Indies then achieved a 1st innings lead of 38, largely through an invaluable but cautious 123 by Rowe, although Greig took 8 for 86 with his off-breaks, which were the best figures by an Englishman against the West Indies. England scored 263 in their 2nd innings after again being held together by Boycott and the West Indies with plenty of time were left to make 226 to win. After Fredericks and Rowe had put on 63 for the 1st wicket, Greig again cast his spell and took 5 more wickets. In the end the West Indies lost by 25 runs and so had to be content with a drawn series. This was Gary Sobers's last Test and, in the 2nd innings, just as he looked as if he would win the match, he drove over a ball from Underwood and was bowled. Greig's bowling was slow–medium in pace, and his great height gave him unusual bounce. The degree of his success was as extraordinary as the fact that he never persevered in this style.

By the time the two sides met again in England in 1976 the West Indies had again changed considerably and now had a side with a battery of fast bowlers who must have been as hostile as any there have ever been. In a 5-match series they won 3–0. In Holding, Roberts and Daniel they had discovered the successors to Hall and Griffith, and in Richards and Greenidge they had found 2 batsmen to stand comparison with any of their former stars. In spite of the lack of spin bowling, it would be a brave man who would dispute that Lloyd's side was the most formidable in the history of West Indies cricket.

Richards gave the West Indies a great start to the series at Trent Bridge when he made 232, but the pitch was too good and England had no trouble in holding on for a draw. For this match the England selectors recalled Brian Close at the age of 45 to try and combat the West Indian fast bowlers. The Second Test at Lord's was also drawn, and with Richards unable to play because of an injury, the West Indies batting was made to seem vulnerable. They were saved by an innings of 138 by Fredericks in their 2nd innings having been set to score 323 in 5 hours.

The might of the West Indies fast bowling could not be held back any longer at Old Trafford, but their batsmen struggled at the start of the match and only a brilliant 134 out of a total of 211 from Greenidge saved them on the 1st day. Then Roberts, Holding and Daniel dismissed England in 33 overs for 71, after which their batsmen underlined this considerable advantage. Greenidge made his 2nd hundred of the match, Richards his 2nd of the series and England needed 552 to win. It was now that Roberts and Holding unleashed an unnecessary and unpleasant barrage of bouncers at Close and Edrich in the last 80 minutes of the Saturday which unhappily the umpires, Alley and Budd, chose to ignore. If ever there was a situation when fast bowlers needed warning against intimidation this was it. Somehow these two elderly batsmen survived the

RIGHT Joy unconfined: the Oval, 1976. Holding has just bowled Greig. From left to right: King, Richards, Holding, Murray (back), Fredericks and Lloyd.

LEFT Vivian Richards in the course of making 291 against England in 1976, when he averaged 118 in 4 Tests and was acclaimed the most brilliant West Indian batsman since the prime of Gary Sobers. Alan Knott is keeping wicket.

session. They might well have found survival harder if the ball had been pitched further up. It was a piece of cricket which reflected little credit on the West Indies. The 3 fast bowlers again shared all 10 wickets between them as England were bowled out for 126.

The West Indies' margin of victory in the Fourth Test at Headingley was only 55 runs and, although their fast bowlers again proved the decisive factor, England came out of the match with considerable kudos. Greenidge and Fredericks both made hundreds, putting on 192 for the 1st wicket in the 1st innings. Greig and Knott then replied with hundreds for England whereupon Willis, Snow and Ward got the West Indies out for 196 in their 2nd innings and England needed 260 to win. Woolmer, Willey and Greig all batted splendidly but no one else reached double figures and so West Indies made sure of the rubber.

They went on to win the final Test at the Oval by 231 runs in a manner which left no one in any doubt about their overall superiority. First they made 687 for 8 declared with Richards reaching 291. England replied with 435, thanks largely to Amiss who showed that he had, at least temporarily, conquered his weakness against fast bowling by moving over to the off stump as the ball was delivered. Amiss made a wonderfully brave 203. In the West Indies 2nd innings Fredericks and Greenidge put on an unbeaten 182 for the 1st wicket before the declaration and England's batting was again destroyed by the fast bowlers, Holding being the most successful.

The next time the 2 countries met was in the Prudential World Cup final at Lord's in 1979. By then the formation of Kerry Packer's World Series Cricket had split the cricket world in two. Most of the West Indies side that day had played for WSC. The West Indies batted 1st and made 286 for 9 thanks to a fine innings of 138 not out by Richards and to some magnificent hitting by King, who made 86. England, who had not welcomed back any of their Packer players, were given a good but slow start by Brearley and Boycott, and once again the West Indies were taken to victory by their fast bowlers. Although Holding and Roberts were playing, Joel Garner was the most successful with 5 wickets. At the time of writing it is difficult to imagine that any side will defeat the West Indies for a year or two.

ENGLAND V WEST INDIES

			RESULT	CAPTAINS
1928	1 Lord's	E 401; WI 177, 166	E Inns 58 runs	A. P. F. Chapman, R. K. Nunes
	2 Old Trafford	WI 206, 115; E 351	E Inns 30 runs	A. P. F. Chapman, R. K. Nunes
	3 Oval	WI 238, 129; E 438	E Inns 71 runs	A. P. F. Chapman, R. K. Nunes
1929–30	1 Barbados	WI 369, 384; E 467, 167–3	Drawn	F. S. G. Calthorpe, E. L. G. Hoad
	2 Trinidad	E 208, 425–8D; WI 254, 212	E 167 runs	F. S. G. Calthorpe, N. Betancourt
	3 Georgetown	WI 471, 290; E 145, 327	WI 289 runs	F. S. G. Calthorpe, M. P. Fernandes
	4 Kingston	E 849, 272–9D; WI 286, 408–5	Drawn	F. S. G. Calthorpe, R. K. Nunes
1933	1 Lord's	E 296; WI 97, 172	E Inns 27 runs	D. R. Jardine, G. C. Grant
	2 Old Trafford	WI 375, 225; E 374	Drawn	D. R. Jardine, G. C. Grant
	3 Oval	E 312; WI 100, 195	E Inns 17 runs	R. E. S. Wyatt, G. C. Grant
1934–35	1 Barbados	WI 102, 51–6D; E 81–7D, 75–6	E 4 wkts	R. E. S. Wyatt, G. C. Grant
	2 Trinidad	WI 302, 280–6D; E 258, 107	WI 217 runs	R. E. S. Wyatt, G. C. Grant
	3 Georgetown	E 226, 160–6D; WI 184, 104–5	Drawn	R. E. S. Wyatt, G. C. Grant
	4 Kingston	WI 535–7D; E 271, 103	WI Inns 161 runs	R. E. S. Wyatt, G. C. Grant
1939	1 Lord's	WI 277, 225; E 404–5D, 100–2	E 8 wkts	W. R. Hammond, R. S. Grant
	2 Old Trafford	E 164–7D, 128–6D; WI 133, 43–4	Drawn	W. R. Hammond, R. S. Grant
	3 Oval	E 352, 366–3; WI 498	Drawn	W. R. Hammond, R. S. Grant
1947–48	1 Barbados	WI 296, 351–9D; E 253, 86–4	Drawn	K. Cranston, G. A. Headley
	2 Trinidad	E 362, 275; WI 497, 72–3	Drawn	G. O. Allen, G. E. Gomez
	3 Georgetown	WI 297–8D; 78–3; E 111, 263	WI 7 wkts	G. O. Allen, J. D. C. Goddard
	4 Kingston	E 227, 336; WI 490, 76–0	WI 10 wkts	G. O. Allen, J. D. C. Goddard
1950	1 Old Trafford	E 312, 288; WI 215, 183	E 202 runs	N. W. D. Yardley, J. D. C. Goddard
	2 Lord's	WI 326, 425–6D; E 151, 274	WI 326 runs	N. W. D. Yardley, J. D. C. Goddard
	3 Trent Bridge	E 223, 436; WI 588, 103–0	WI 10 wkts	N. W. D. Yardley, J. D. C. Goddard
	4 Oval	WI 503; E 344, 103	WI Inns 56 runs	F. R. Brown, J. D. C. Goddard

1953–54	1 Kingston	WI 417, 209–6D; E 170, 316	WI 140 runs	L. Hutton, J. B. Stollmeyer
	2 Barbados	WI 383, 292–2D; E 181, 313	WI 181 runs	L. Hutton, J. B. Stollmeyer
	3 Georgetown	E 435, 75–1; WI 251, 256	E 9 wkts	L. Hutton, J. B. Stollmeyer
	4 Port of Spain	WI 681–8D, 212–4D; E 537, 98–3	Drawn	L. Hutton, J. B. Stollmeyer
	5 Kingston	WI 139, 346; E 414, 72–1	E 9 wkts	L. Hutton, J. B. Stollmeyer
1957	1 Edgbaston	E 186, 583–4D; WI 474, 72–7	Drawn	P. B. H. May, J. D. C. Goddard
	2 Lord's	WI 127, 261; E 424	E Inns 36 runs	P. B. H. May, J. D. C. Goddard
	3 Trent Bridge	E 619–6D, 64–1; WI 372, 367	Drawn	P. B. H. May, J. D. C. Goddard
	4 Headingley	WI 142, 132; E 279	E Inns 5 runs	P. B. H. May, J. D. C. Goddard
	5 Oval	E 412; WI 89, 86	E Inns 237 runs	P. B. H. May, J. D. C. Goddard
1959–60	1 Barbados	E 482, 71–0; WI 563–8D	Drawn	P. B. H. May, F. C. M. Alexander
	2 Trinidad	E 382, 230–9D; WI 112, 244	E 256 runs	P. B. H. May, F. C. M. Alexander
	3 Kingston	E 277, 305; WI 353, 175–6	Drawn	P. B. H. May, F. C. M. Alexander
	4 Georgetown	E 295, 334–8; WI 402–8D	Drawn	M. C. Cowdrey, F. C. M. Alexander
	5 Trinidad	E 393, 350–7D; WI 338–8D, 209–5	Drawn	M. C. Cowdrey, F. C. M. Alexander
1963	1 Old Trafford	WI 501–6D, 1–0; E 205, 296	WI 10 wkts	E. R. Dexter, F. M. Worrell
	2 Lord's	WI 301, 229; E 297, 228–9	Drawn	E. R. Dexter, F. M. Worrell
	3 Edgbaston	E 216, 278–9D; WI 186, 91	E 217 runs	E. R. Dexter, F. M. Worrell
	4 Headingley	WI 397, 229; E 174, 231	WI 221 runs	E. R. Dexter, F. M. Worrell
	5 Oval	E 275, 223; WI 246, 255–2	WI 8 wkts	E. R. Dexter, F. M. Worrell
1966	1 Old Trafford	WI 484; E 167, 277	WI Inns 40 runs	M. J. K. Smith, G. S. Sobers
	2 Lord's	WI 269, 369–5D; E 355, 197–4	Drawn	M. C. Cowdrey, G. S. Sobers
	3 Trent Bridge	WI 235, 482–5D; E 325, 253	WI 139 runs	M. C. Cowdrey, G. S. Sobers
	4 Headingley	WI 500–9D; E 240, 205	WI Inns 55 runs	M. C. Cowdrey, G. S. Sobers
	5 Oval	WI 268, 225; E 527	E Inns 34 runs	D. B. Close, G. S. Sobers
1967–68	1 Trinidad	E 568; WI 363, 243–8	Drawn	M. C. Cowdrey, G. S. Sobers
	2 Kingston	E 376, 68–8; WI 143, 391–9D	Drawn	M. C. Cowdrey, G. S. Sobers
	3 Barbados	WI 349, 284–6; E 449	Drawn	M. C. Cowdrey, G. S. Sobers
	4 Trinidad	WI 526–7D, 92–2D; E 404, 215–3	E 7 wkts	M. C. Cowdrey, G. S. Sobers
	5 Georgetown	WI 414, 264; E 371, 206–9	Drawn	M. C. Cowdrey, G. S. Sobers
1969	1 Old Trafford	E 413, 12–0; WI 147, 275	E 10 wkts	R. Illingworth, G. S. Sobers
	2 Lord's	WI 380, 295–9D; E 344, 295–7	Drawn	R. Illingworth, G. S. Sobers
	3 Headingley	E 223, 240; WI 161, 272	E 30 runs	R. Illingworth, G. S. Sobers
1973	1 Oval	WI 415, 255; E 257, 255	WI 158 runs	R. Illingworth, R. B. Kanhai
	2 Edgbaston	WI 327, 302; E 305, 182–2	Drawn	R. Illingworth, R. B. Kanhai
	3 Lord's	WI 652–8D; E 233, 193	WI Inns 226 runs	R. Illingworth, R. B. Kanhai
1973–74	1 Trinidad	E 131, 392; WI 392, 132–3	WI 7 wkts	M. H. Denness, R. B. Kanhai
	2 Kingston	E 353, 432–9; WI 583–9D	Drawn	M. H. Denness, R. B. Kanhai
	3 Barbados	E 395, 277–7; WI 596–8D	Drawn	M. H. Denness, R. B. Kanhai
	4 Georgetown	E 448; WI 198–4	Drawn	M. H. Denness, R. B. Kanhai
	5 Trinidad	E 267, 263; WI 305, 199	E 26 runs	M. H. Denness, R. B. Kanhai
1976	1 Trent Bridge	WI 494, 176–5D; E 332, 156–2	Drawn	A. W. Greig, C. H. Lloyd
	2 Lord's	E 250, 254; WI 182, 241–6	Drawn	A. W. Greig, C. H. Lloyd
	3 Old Trafford	WI 211, 411–5D; E 71, 126	WI 425 runs	A. W. Greig, C. H. Lloyd
	4 Headingley	WI 450, 196; E 387, 204	WI 55 runs	A. W. Greig, C. H. Lloyd
	5 Oval	WI 687–8D, 182–0D; E 435, 203	WI 231 runs	A. W. Greig, C. H. Lloyd

CAPTAINS (England)	TESTS	WON	LOST	DRAWN
A. P. F. Chapman	3	3		
F. S. G. Calthorpe	4	1	1	2
D. R. Jardine	2	1		1
R. E. S. Wyatt	5	2	2	1
W. R. Hammond	3	1		2
K. Cranston	1			1
G. O. Allen	3		2	1
N. W. D. Yardley	3	1	2	
F. R. Brown	1		1	
L. Hutton	5	2	2	1
P. B. H. May	8	4		4
M. C. Cowdrey	10	1	2	7
E. R. Dexter	5	1	3	1
M. J. K. Smith	1		1	
D. B. Close	1	1		
R. Illingworth	6	2	2	2
M. H. Denness	5	1	1	3
A. W. Greig	5		3	2
	71	21	22	28

CAPTAINS (West Indies)	TESTS	WON	LOST	DRAWN
R. K. Nunes	4		3	1
E. L. G. Hoad	1			1
N. Betancourt	1		1	
M. D. Fernandes	1	1		
G. C. Grant	7	2	3	2
R. S. Grant	3		1	2
G. A. Headley	1			1
G. E. Gomez	1			1
J. D. C. Goddard	11	5	4	2
J. B. Stollmeyer	5	2	2	1
F. C. M. Alexander	5		1	4
F. M. Worrell	5	3	1	1
G. S. Sobers	13	3	4	6
R. B. Kanhai	8	3	1	4
C. H. Lloyd	5	3		2
	71	22	21	28

HIGHEST INNINGS TOTAL

England in England, 619–6D, Trent Bridge 1957
England in West Indies, 849, Kingston 1929–30
West Indies in England, 687–8D, Oval 1976
West Indies in West Indies, 681–8D, Trinidad 1953–54

LOWEST INNINGS TOTAL

England in England, 71, Old Trafford 1976
England in West Indies, 103, Kingston 1934–35
West Indies in England, 86, Oval 1957
West Indies in West Indies, 102, Barbados 1934–35

HIGHEST INDIVIDUAL INNINGS

England in England, 285*, P. B. H. May, Edgbaston 1957
England in West Indies, 325, A. Sandham, Kingston 1929–30
West Indies in England, 291, I. V. A. Richards, Oval 1976
West Indies in West Indies, 302, L. G. Rowe, Barbados 1973–74

HIGHEST AGGREGATE OR RUNS IN A SERIES

England in England, 489, P. B. H. May 1957
England in West Indies, 693, E. H. Hendren 1929–30
West Indies in England, 829, I. V. A. Richards 1976
West Indies in West Indies, 709, G. S. Sobers 1959–60

BEST INNINGS BOWLING FIGURES

England in England, {7–44 T. E. Bailey, Lord's 1957; 7–44 F. S. Trueman, Edgbaston 1963}
England in West Indies, 8–86 A. W. Greig, Trinidad 1973–74
West Indies in England, 8–92 M. A. Holding, Oval 1976
West Indies in West Indies, 7–69 W. W. Hall, Kingston 1959–60

BEST MATCH BOWLING FIGURES

England in England, 12–119, F. S. Trueman, Edgbaston 1963
England in West Indies, 13–156, A. W. Greig, Trinidad 1973–74
West Indies in England, 14–149, M. A. Holding, Oval 1976
West Indies in West Indies, 11–229, W. Ferguson, Trinidad 1947–48

HIGHEST WICKET AGGREGATE IN A SERIES

England in England, 34, F. S. Trueman 1963
England in West Indies, 27, J. A. Snow 1967–68
West Indies in England, 33, A. L. Valentine 1950
West Indies in West Indies, {23, W. Ferguson 1947–48; 23, S. Ramadhin 1953–54}

RECORD WICKET PARTNERSHIPS—ENGLAND

1 C. Washbrook and R. T. Simpson, 212, Trent Bridge 1950
2 P. E. Richardson and T. W. Graveney, 266, Trent Bridge 1957
3 L. Hutton and W. R. Hammond, 264, Oval 1939
4 P. B. H. May and M. C. Cowdrey, 411, Edgbaston 1957
5 C. Milburn and T. W. Graveney, 130*, Lord's 1966
6 A. W. Greig and A. P. E. Knott, 163, Barbados 1973–74
7 M. J. K. Smith and J. M. Parks, 197, Trinidad 1959–60
8 T. W. Graveney and J. T. Murray, 217, Oval 1966
9 G. A. R. Lock and P. I. Pocock, 109, Georgetown 1967–68
10 K. Higgs and J. A. Snow, 128, Oval 1966

RECORD WICKET PARTNERSHIPS—WEST INDIES

1 R. C. Fredericks and L. G. Rowe, 206, Kingston 1973–74
2 L. G. Rowe and A. I. Kallicharran, 249, Barbados 1973–74
3 E. D. Weekes and F. M. Worrell, 338, Trinidad 1953–54
4 G. S. Sobers and F. M. Worrell, 399, Barbados 1959–60
5 S. M. Nurse and G. S. Sobers, 265, Headingley 1966
6 G. S. Sobers and D. A. J. Holford, 274*, Lord's 1966
7 G. S. Sobers and B. D. Julien, 155*, Lord's 1973 (231 runs were added for this wicket in 2 separate partnerships. G. S. Sobers retired ill and was replaced by K. D. Boyce when 155 had been added)
8 C. A. McWatt and J. K. Holt, 99, Georgetown 1953–54
9 G. S. Sobers and W. W. Hall, 63*, Trinidad 1967–68
10 F. M. Worrell and S. Ramadhin, 55, Trent Bridge 1957

England v New Zealand

R. T. BRITTENDEN

In Victorian times, etiquette demanded that social visits should be returned. But it was no lack of courtesy which saw 63 years pass between the first visit of an English team to New Zealand in 1864 and New Zealand's first tour of England. It was not a desperate lack of playing strength which delayed the venture so long, but a dismal lack of money. The New Zealand Cricket Council was formed in 1894, but when the invitation came to tour England in 1927, a private company had to be floated to finance the trip. There were 11,407 shares, each of £1. Not unexpectedly, the shareholders had little return.

But they did New Zealand cricket signal service, for the New Zealanders, with breezy batting, won 7 and lost 5 of the first-class matches. This minor success led to Test status for the matches in New Zealand in 1929–30. It was not a full strength MCC side but in bleak conditions it won the First Test at Christchurch by 8 wickets. New Zealand was in confusion against the fast bowling of Allom and Nichols, Maurice Allom (a future MCC President) taking 4 wickets in 5 balls, including a hat-trick. No one else in Test History has ever taken 4 in 5.

New Zealand began the Second Test with a record partnership of 276. Mills, a slim and elegant left-hander, scored 117. Dempster, short, bow-legged, but a splendid batsman, made 136. On his tours of England in 1927 and 1931 Dempster totalled 3,208 runs at 55·3. Later he captained Leicestershire, scoring 17 hundreds and making 4,516 at 46·6. England, 120 behind, had little trouble in saving the Second Test. Rain ruined the other two, although there were fine batting performances from Duleepsinhji, Bowley and Legge.

New Zealand was in England again in 1931, with a Lord's Test on the programme. Dempster started the tour brilliantly – 783 in 11 innings at 111·8. At Lord's he scored 53, but New Zealand fell to the spin of Peebles and Robins for 224. England lost 7 for 190 before Ames and Allen made 246 for the 8th wicket – a record – and England led by 230. Mills was out 2nd ball, but Dempster, with 120, gave another fine display. Weir, Page and Blunt took New Zealand to a proud declaration at 469 for 9. The match was drawn, but New Zealand's performance was good enough for 2 more Tests to be added to the itinerary. England won easily at the Oval and the Third was ruined by rain.

Weather helped New Zealand to 2 drawn Tests in 1932–33 against Jardine's powerful side. At Christchurch Hammond was in his most masterful form in scoring 227. He was even more dynamic at Auckland, with a Test record 336 not out in 319 minutes – 34 fours and 10 sixes. This visit by MCC following their Australian tour started a regular 4-year pattern which extended until, but not including, 1978–79.

The best prewar New Zealand batsman was C. S. Dempster, here in the course of making 120 v England at Lord's 1931.

England looked much stronger at home in 1937. New Zealand struggled to a draw in the First Test but had a distinct chance at Old Trafford. England led by 77, then spirited bowling by the strongly built Cowie had the home team at 75 for 7. Ames batted calmly; Brown produced ferocious hitting, but he was dropped 4 times in making 57. England reached 187 and New Zealand needed 265 in 4 hours. The catching lapses had kept England in on a deteriorating pitch and although Vivian and Moloney started with a brisk 50, Goddard was able to turn his off-breaks abruptly. He ran through the side, although the 19-year-old Donnelly fought tenaciously for 37 not out. The Third Test, interrupted by rain, was drawn. (It marked Compton's 1st appearance for England.)

Two features distinguished the first postwar Test in 1946–47 at Christchurch. It was the first time a day was added to a Test after it had started; the 3rd day was washed out, and the extra day also rained off. And it was Hammond's last Test. He made it memorable with a superb slip catch and 79 majestic runs. In his 1st Test for New Zealand, the left-handed Sutcliffe scored 58 and helped Hadlee (116) in an opening stand of 133. A week earlier Sutcliffe had scored 197 and 128 for Otago against MCC and had thus become the 1st to score 2 hundreds in a first appearance against a first-class touring side.

The 1949 New Zealand team in England is remembered for the splendour of its batting. It won 13 major matches and lost only 1, on a rain-affected pitch at Oxford. It drew its 4 3-day Tests, admittedly against England bowling recuperating after the war. Sutcliffe scored 2,627 runs on tour, a figure exceeded only by Sir Donald Bradman. Seven others made more than 1,000 and the left-arm spinner, Burtt, took 128 wickets. At 37, Cowie's fast-medium bowling was still most effective. In his 8 Tests against England, he took 39 wickets at 24 runs each. The Tests were high-scoring and usually fast-scoring, and there was seldom prospect of a result. Eight hundreds were scored for England, 2 for New Zealand. Highlights were Hutton's 206 in the Fourth Test, Simpson's Third Test 103, when he made his last 53 runs in 27 minutes; and for New Zealand, Donnelly's 206 at Lord's when, on the 3rd morning, he made 80 in 90 minutes.

There was a dreadfully dead pitch and slow scoring at Christchurch in 1950–51. New Zealand, batting to tea on the 2nd day, made 417 for 8. England's innings continued until about half-an-hour before the end of the match – 550 in 12½ hours. Bailey took 4½ hours to reach 50 and only an hour more for his 1st Test hundred. But the bowlers were in command at Wellington. Wright and Tattersall were dominant, but if England won a low-scoring match by 6 wickets, it had only 14 minutes to spare.

Hutton's team in 1954–55 enjoyed 2 easy victories. At Dunedin, New Zealand set records for slow scoring. It had achieved the dignity of 5-day Tests for the 1st time, and on the 1st day, limited to 4½ hours, it made 125. Sutcliffe hit 3 sixes in his 74, but batted 271 minutes; Rabone was 3 hours over 18. England won by 8 wickets.

At Auckland, New Zealand batted over 5 hours for 200, Reid all defiance for 73. There were 30,000 spectators on the 2nd day, when England went to 148 for 4 in uncertain light and on a damp pitch. On the 3rd morning England struggled to 183 for 7 and there was the dazzling prospect of a 1st New Zealand victory. The situation persuaded a Christchurch man to leave his office and set off by air for Auckland, some 600 miles away. He was about halfway there when the match ended. After conceding a lead of 46 New Zealand was dismissed, in 104 minutes, for 26, still the lowest score in Test cricket. The dynamic fast bowling of Tyson and Statham, the probing skills of Appleyard, brought about this extraordinary collapse.

New Zealand went to England in 1958 to play a 5-Test series for the first time. It was an unhappy tour in that success was so hard to come by. It was a very young side, but the main problems were wet weather, the splendid spin bowling of Lock and Laker, and the masterful batting of May. In 8 completed innings on tour, May scored 777 against the New Zealanders. Batting for Surrey on a fiery pitch, he scored 165 when no one else passed 25; the New Zealanders reckoned it to be the finest innings they had seen. During the Tests, Lock took 34 wickets for 254, Laker 17 for 173, and although the tourists had started well in their 3-day games, their Test scores were 94 and 137, 47 and 74, 67 and 129, 267 and 85, 161 and 91 for 3. England won the first 4 easily, and the Fifth was drawn.

New Zealand suffered a further heavy defeat at Christchurch in 1958–59. Dexter scored his 1st Test hundred in lordly style, and on a crumbling pitch, Lock took 11 for 84; Trueman captured his 100th Test wicket. Auckland suffered from the tail-end of a hurricane, the last 2 days being washed out. Dexter was England's captain in 1962–63 when his side easily won all 3 Tests. Barrington, Parfitt and Knight scored hundreds in a massive 562 for 7 at Auckland, Parfitt and Knight setting an England record with 240 for the 7th wicket. New Zealand fought hard but followed on 304 behind. Larter and Illingworth disposed of a demoralized side. England won at Wellington by an innings, Cowdrey making an unbeaten hundred and adding 161 for the 9th wicket with A. C. Smith – another record. New Zealand did a little better at Christchurch, where Reid's grimly defensive batting brought him 74, then 100 of 150 from the bat. In taking 7 1st innings wickets Trueman broke Statham's England record of 239 Test wickets.

In this depressing period, New Zealand lost all 3 Tests in England in 1965, the first of the short tours. In bitterly cold weather at Edgbaston, England made 435, with Barrington taking 375 minutes to reach his hundred. New Zealand collapsed for 116 but fought back so well that the match went into its 5th day. Seven players scored 40 or more, the best being the 19-year-old Pollard with 81 not out. At Lord's it was a similar pattern. After being 132 behind, New Zealand made a spirited 347, but England won by 7 wickets. New Zealand was then overwhelmed at Leeds. Edrich, batting almost 9 hours, scored 310 not out and set a new record for boundaries in Test cricket: 52 fours and 5 sixes. He was with Barrington while 369 were scored in 339 minutes for the 2nd wicket. This innings came in the middle of a golden spell for Edrich in which he could not go wrong. New Zealand succumbed to Larter and Illingworth for 193 and were then dismissed for 166. In his last Test Reid scored 54 in the 1st innings and again Pollard distinguished himself, with 33 (run out) and 53. Titmus had an extraordinary over on the 4th afternoon – 4 wickets in 6 balls, without a hat-trick.

There was rather more competition in the 1965–66 series in New Zealand, although England very nearly won the First Test. Twice England lost top batsmen cheaply, twice M. J. K. Smith and Parfitt rescued the side. Allen also batted well but, with Congdon scoring a hundred, New Zealand had a narrow lead. When set a target of 197 in 140 minutes, the home team batted wretchedly. Eight fell for 32, mostly to Higgs, before Pollard and Cunis held out for the last 35 minutes. In this match Cowdrey held his 100th Test catch, standing just where Hammond had been when he reached 100 catches in Tests. England had the better of a cold, wet Second Test. Cowdrey scored handsomely, Motz hit hard for New Zealand – 22, including 3 sixes, off an over by Allen. The final match was closely fought. Sinclair scored a hundred in under 3 hours and England, after being 120 for 1, were out for 222, 74 behind. England had to make 204 in 272 minutes on a pitch taking spin. Edrich had withdrawn after the 1st day to undergo an appendicitis operation and Brown was injured. But New Zealand pursued a defensive policy, bowling seamers for far too long. At tea England were 84 for 3 – in effect, 5 – but a draw was accomplished in some comfort.

The left-arm bowling of Underwood dominated the 1969 Tests in England. The batsmen were subservient and, when the pitches gave him some help, he was merciless. At Lord's England made 190 and New Zealand reached 76 for 1. Underwood and Illingworth then took control; Underwood ended the match with 11 for 70. Turner became the 1st New Zealander and the youngest player to bat through a Test innings. He made 43 not out in 255 minutes. At Trent Bridge Congdon and Hastings scored 150 for the 2nd wicket but Sharpe and Edrich did better – 246 for the 2nd wicket. Rain interfered and the game was drawn. Underwood was again the demon king at the Oval. He took 12 for 101 as England won by 8 wickets. There was so much rain that, although only 759 runs were scored, the match went into the 5th afternoon.

It was Underwood again at Christchurch in 1970–71. On a dreadful pitch he had the ball turning and lifting or scuttling low as he took 6 for 12, then 6 for 85. England won by 8 wickets, d'Oliveira making a brilliant hundred in difficult circumstances. New Zealand, on the eve of its best period in Test cricket, won an honourable draw at Auckland. Indeed, England had to defend dourly to save the match. England made 321, Knott scoring his 1st Test hundred, but he was missed 3 times off the spinner, Shrimpton. Burgess batted beautifully for 104 as New Zealand went to 313 for 7. At 67 for 4 England was in trouble, but an injured Cowdrey defended steadily and Knott, batting 5 hours, fell only 4 short of a 2nd hundred.

New Zealand produced two of its finest performances on the 1973 tour of England. At Nottingham England made 250 and New Zealand were bowled out by Snow, Arnold and Greig, in helpful conditions, for 97. Extras, 20, top-scored. England, 24 for 4 in their 2nd innings, owed a fine recovery to Amiss and Greig, each of whom made hundreds. They scored 210 together, Greig driving with particular power and certainty. New Zealand had the near-impossible task of making 479. Both opening batsmen were out at 16 but the captain, Congdon, led a superb, sustained recovery. With Hastings, he added 52 for the 3rd wicket; with Burgess, 62 for the 4th. The principal partnership was between Congdon and Pollard, who scored 177 for the 5th wicket. Late on the 3rd evening Congdon was struck on the face by a ball from Snow, but he batted nearly all the 4th day to reach 176 in 410 minutes of courageous cricket. Pollard and Wadsworth fought on, and just before lunch on the 5th day New Zealand passed 400, still with 5 wickets in hand. Then Roope held a spectacular tumbling catch to dismiss Wadsworth after the pair had added 95, and Pollard went a few runs later, after making 116 in 435 minutes. The tail-enders tried hard but succumbed, chiefly to Greig, and England won a remarkable match by 38 runs. This brave performance put a fresh face on New Zealand cricket in the eyes of the English public.

In 1973 Bev Congdon, the New Zealand captain, made 176 and 175 in successive Tests against England at Trent Bridge and Lord's.

New Zealand came even closer to victory at Lord's. England was dismissed for 253 whereupon New Zealand made their record Test score, 551 for 9. Congdon this time scored 175, there were hundreds from Pollard and Burgess, an attractive 86 by Hastings, and New Zealand led by a massive 298. Boycott, Amiss, Roope and Fletcher fought strongly in England's 2nd innings but, with 130 minutes remaining, England led by only 70, and the 8th wicket fell. In the same over Arnold was missed, a difficult chance to the wicket-keeper. The thin thread by which New Zealand held control was snapped. Fletcher went on to the attack and, with vigorous hitting, reached 178 to take his side to safety. The left-arm spinner Howarth bowled 70 overs with sustained accuracy to take 4 wickets.

After these two epic struggles, the Third Test was anti-climactic. New Zealand made 276 and then bowled very inefficiently on a damp pitch. Failure to keep the ball up allowed England to make 419 and then Arnold provided the New Zealanders with an object lesson. The side was out for 142. Turner, who opened, was last out, for 81. Earlier that summer he had become the 1st for 35 years to score 1,000 runs before June.

It was all England again at Auckland in 1974–75. After the openers had gone quickly, Edrich and Denness added 117. Then Denness shared a brilliant partnership of 266 with Fletcher, a 4th-wicket record in these matches. Denness made 181 in 330 minutes and Fletcher went on to 216 in 420 minutes. At the end of the 3rd day New Zealand were 285 for 5 mainly through Parker's 121. Batting was difficult on the 4th day and New Zealand slid to 326 all out, Greig becoming only the 4th England player with 2,000 runs and 100 wickets in Tests. New Zealand struggled for survival and 9 were down at close of play. On the last morning the No. 11 batsman, Chatfield, was hit on the head by a bouncer and nearly lost his life. The MCC physiotherapist, Bernard Thomas, gave Chatfield mouth-to-mouth resuscitation. He said Chatfield's heart had stopped beating for several seconds. This unhappy incident hastened legislation to protect tail-end batsmen from bouncers.

Rain spoiled the Christchurch Test, but there was time for Turner to score 98 in New Zealand's 342 and for Amiss to make 164 not out in splendid style as England went to 272 for 2.

When Boycott, deputizing for the injured Brearley, brought the 1977–78 team to tour, New Zealand rejoiced, nationwide, at its greatest cricket triumph. The defeat of Australia 4 years earlier had been a splendid success, but the major goal, a victory over England, had been awaited for almost 50 years. There was erratic bounce at the Basin Reserve, Wellington, and New Zealand made only 228. Despite Boycott staying in 442 minutes for 77, England trailed by 13 runs, with Richard Hadlee giving a spirited display of fast bowling. England's powerful fast attack had New Zealand out for 123 and England needed only 137. But the tall left-hander Collinge whipped away 3 batsmen, including Boycott, and Richard Hadlee then struck swiftly. The bowlers were supported by catching of a standard rarely achieved by a New Zealand team, and by vigorous encouragement from ecstatic spectators. Life stood still, throughout the country, as the nation listened, or watched this spectacular collapse on television. Even the hotel trade came to a standstill in New Zealand, a remarkable happening. At the end of the 4th day England were an incredible 53 for 8. Rain delayed play for 40 minutes on the last morning but Hadlee soon had the last 2 wickets, the final one through an athletic gully catch by Howarth. Hadlee took 6 wickets, 10 in the match, and became a national hero.

England won the Second Test convincingly, Botham batting purposefully for a hundred and taking 8 wickets in a match England dominated after the 1st hour. When England was seeking quick runs in the 2nd innings, Randall, over-eager in his backing-up, was run out at the bowler's end by

Chatfield, an incident which pleased few. New Zealand started slowly in Auckland and was in almost 10 hours for 315. Howarth scored his 1st Test hundred. England laboured too – 13½ hours for 429. Radley took over 8 hours to score a hundred. There were many interruptions through showers and bad light and, although the game took 6 days, a result never seemed likely. Howarth scored a 2nd hundred, an attractive display, but the pitch never gave the bowlers much encouragement.

New Zealand went to England in 1978 with high hopes of another good performance but were under persistent pressure from England's strong attack. England also fielded much better. New Zealand lacked support for Richard Hadlee who bowled ably, although handicapped by injury in the 1st 2 of the Test series sponsored by Cornhill Insurance.

At the Oval Congdon set a New Zealand record by appearing in his 59th Test. At 130 for 1, New Zealand held a strong hand. Howarth fell only 6 short of a 3rd consecutive hundred against England. However Willis ran through the lower order and after Gower had made a delightful 1st Test hundred England led by 45. Indiscreet shots contributed largely to a poor New Zealand 2nd innings and England won by 7 wickets, after aggressive batting by Gooch to defeat the threat of rain.

England was fortunate to reach 429 at Trent Bridge. The bowlers, particularly Hadlee, beat the bat repeatedly on the first morning and Boycott survived a straightforward chance at 2. He went on to 131. Botham wrecked the New Zealand innings with fiery bowling and New Zealand never looked likely to recover, losing by an innings and 119. New Zealand had a chance at Lord's. After Howarth had scored a 4-hour hundred New Zealand totalled 329 and led by 50, Hadlee having bowled most effectively. This triumph was short-lived. Bowling of violent hostility by Willis and Botham had New Zealand 37 for 7 by the end of a Saturday on which 15 wickets fell for 151 runs. England needed only 118. Hadlee removed Boycott and Radley with successive balls, at 14, but Gower and Gooch were untroubled in adding 70, England winning by 7 wickets.

ENGLAND V NEW ZEALAND

			RESULT	CAPTAINS
1929	1 Christchurch	NZ 112, 131; E 181, 66–2	E 8 wkts	A. H. H. Gilligan, T. C. Lowry
	2 Wellington	NZ 440, 164–4D; E 320, 107–4	Drawn	A. H. H. Gilligan, T. C. Lowry
	3 Auckland	E 330–4D; NZ 96–1	Drawn	A. H. H. Gilligan, T. C. Lowry
	4 Auckland	E 540, 22–3; NZ 387	Drawn	A. H. H. Gilligan, T. C. Lowry
1931	1 Lord's	NZ 224, 469–9D; E 454, 146–5	Drawn	D. R. Jardine, T. C. Lowry
	2 Oval	E 416–4D; NZ 193, 197	E Inns 26 runs	D. R. Jardine, T. C. Lowry
	3 Old Trafford	E 224–3; NZ –	Drawn	D. R. Jardine, T. C. Lowry
1932–33	1 Christchurch	E 560–8D; NZ 223, 35–0	Drawn	D. R. Jardine, M. L. Page
	2 Auckland	NZ 158, 16–0; E 548–7D	Drawn	R. E. S. Wyatt, M. L. Page
1937	1 Lord's	E 424, 226–4D; NZ 295, 175–8	Drawn	R. W. V. Robins, M. L. Page
	2 Old Trafford	E 358–9D, 187; NZ 281, 134	E 130 runs	R. W. V. Robins, M. L. Page
	3 Oval	NZ 249, 187; E 254–7D, 31–1	Drawn	R. W. V. Robins, M. L. Page
1946–47	1 Christchurch	NZ 345–9D; E 265–7D	Drawn	W. R. Hammond, W. Hadlee
1949	1 Headingley	E 372, 267–4D; NZ 341, 195–2	Drawn	F. G. Mann, W. A. Hadlee
	2 Lord's	E 313–9D, 306–5; NZ 484	Drawn	F. G. Mann, W. A. Hadlee
	3 Old Trafford	NZ 293, 348–7; E 440–9D	Drawn	F. R. Brown, W. A. Hadlee
	4 Oval	NZ 345, 308–9D; E 482	Drawn	F. R. Brown, W. A. Hadlee
1950–51	1 Christchurch	NZ 417–8D, 46–3; E 550	Drawn	F. R. Brown, W. A. Hadlee
	2 Wellington	NZ 125, 189; E 227, 91–4	E 6 wkts	F. R. Brown, W. A. Hadlee
1954–55	1 Dunedin	NZ 125, 132; E 209–8D, 49–2	E 8 wkts	L. Hutton, G. O. Rabone
	2 Auckland	NZ 200, 26; E 246	E Inns 20 runs	L. Hutton, G. O. Rabone
1958	1 Edgbaston	E 221, 215–6D; NZ 94, 137	E 205 runs	P. B. H. May, J. R. Reid
	2 Lord's	E 269; NZ 47, 74	E Inns 148 runs	P. B. H. May, J. R. Reid
	3 Headingley	NZ 67, 129; E 267–2D	E Inns 71 runs	P. B. H. May, J. R. Reid
	4 Old Trafford	NZ 267, 85; E 365–9D	E Inns 13 runs	P. B. H. May, J. R. Reid
	5 Oval	NZ 161, 91–3; E 219–9D	Drawn	P. B. H. May, J. R. Reid
1958–59	1 Christchurch	E 374; NZ 142, 133	E Inns 99 runs	P. B. H. May, J. R. Reid
	2 Auckland	NZ 181; E 311–7	Drawn	P. B. H. May, J. R. Reid
1962–63	1 Auckland	E 562–7D; NZ 258, 89	E Inns 215 runs	E. R. Dexter, J. R. Reid
	2 Wellington	NZ 194, 187; E 428–8D	E Inns 47 runs	E. R. Dexter, J. R. Reid
	3 Christchurch	NZ 266, 159; E 253, 173–3	E 7 wkts	E. R. Dexter, J. R. Reid
1965	1 Edgbaston	E 435, 96–1; NZ 116, 413	E 9 wkts	M. J. K. Smith, J. R. Reid
	2 Lord's	NZ 175, 347; E 307, 218–3	E 7 wkts	M. J. K. Smith, J. R. Reid
	3 Headingley	E 546–4; NZ 193, 166	E Inns 187 runs	M. J. K. Smith, J. R. Reid
1965–66	1 Christchurch	E 342, 201–5D; NZ 347, 48–8	Drawn	M. J. K. Smith, M. E. Chapple
	2 Dunedin	NZ 192, 147–9; E 254–8D	Drawn	M. J. K. Smith, B. W. Sinclair
	3 Auckland	NZ 296, 129; E 222, 159–4	Drawn	M. J. K. Smith, B. W. Sinclair
1969	1 Lord's	E 190, 340; NZ 169, 131	E 230 runs	R. Illingworth, G. T. Dowling
	2 Trent Bridge	NZ 294, 66–1; E 451–8D	Drawn	R. Illingworth, G. T. Dowling
	3 Oval	NZ 150, 229; E 242, 138–2	E 8 wkts	R. Illingworth, G. T. Dowling
1970–71	1 Christchurch	NZ 65, 254; E 231, 89–2	E 8 wkts	R. Illingworth, G. T. Dowling
	2 Auckland	E 321, 237; NZ 313–7D, 40–0	Drawn	R. Illingworth, G. T. Dowling
1973	1 Trent Bridge	E 250, 325–8D; NZ 97, 440	E 38 runs	R. Illingworth, B. E. Congdon
	2 Lord's	E 253, 463–9; NZ 551–9D	Drawn	R. Illingworth, B. E. Congdon
	3 Headingley	NZ 276, 142; E 419	E Inns 1 run	R. Illingworth, B. E. Congdon
1974–75	1 Auckland	E 593–6D; NZ 326, 184	E Inns 83 runs	M. H. Denness, B. E. Congdon
	2 Christchurch	NZ 342; E 272–2	Drawn	M. H. Denness, B. E. Congdon
1977–78	1 Wellington	NZ 228, 123; E 215, 64	NZ 72 runs	G. Boycott, M. G. Burgess
	2 Christchurch	E 418, 96–4D; NZ 235, 105	E 174 runs	G. Boycott, M. G. Burgess
	3 Auckland	NZ 315, 382–8; E 429	Drawn	G. Boycott, M. G. Burgess
1978	1 Oval	NZ 234, 182; E 279, 138–3	E 7 wkts	J. M. Brearley, M. G. Burgess
(CORNHILL	2 Trent Bridge	E 429; NZ 120, 190	E Inns 119 runs	J. M. Brearley, M. G. Burgess
SERIES)	3 Lord's	NZ 339, 67; E 289, 118–3	E 7 wkts	J. M. Brearley, M. G. Burgess

CAPTAINS (England)	TESTS	WON	LOST	DRAWN
A. H. H. Gilligan	4	1		3
D. R. Jardine	4	1		3
R. E. S. Wyatt	1			1
R. W. V. Robins	3	1		2
W. R. Hammond	1			1
F. G. Mann	2			2
F. R. Brown	4	1		3
L. Hutton	2	2		
P. B. H. May	7	5		2
E. R. Dexter	3	3		
M. J. K. Smith	6	3		3
R. Illingworth	8	5		3
M. H. Denness	2	1		1
G. Boycott	3	1	1	1
J. M. Brearley	3	3		
	53	27	1	25

CAPTAINS (New Zealand)	TESTS	WON	LOST	DRAWN
T. C. Lowry	7		2	5
M. L. Page	5		1	4
W. A. Hadlee	7		1	6
G. O. Rabone	2		2	
J. R. Reid	13		11	2
B. W. Sinclair	2			2
M. E. Chapple	1			1
G. T. Dowling	5		3	2
B. E. Congdon	5		3	2
M. G. Burgess	6	1	4	1
	53	1	27	25

HIGHEST INNINGS TOTAL

England in England, 546–4D, Headingley 1965
England in New Zealand, 593–6D, Auckland 1974–75
New Zealand in England, 551–9D, Lord's 1973
New Zealand in New Zealand, 440, Wellington 1929–30

LOWEST INNINGS TOTAL

England in England, 187, Old Trafford 1937
England in New Zealand, 64, Wellington 1977–78
New Zealand in England, 47, Lord's 1958
New Zealand in New Zealand, 26, Auckland 1954–55

HIGHEST INDIVIDUAL INNINGS

England in England, 310*, J. H. Edrich, Headingley 1965
England in New Zealand, 336*, W. R. Hammond, Auckland 1932–33
New Zealand in England, 206, M. P. Donnelly, Lord's 1949
New Zealand in New Zealand, 136, C. S. Dempster, Wellington 1929–30

HIGHEST AGGREGATE OF RUNS IN A SERIES

England in England, 469, L. Hutton 1949
England in New Zealand, 563, W. R. Hammond 1932–33
New Zealand in England, 462, M. P. Donnelly 1949
New Zealand in New Zealand, 341, C. S. Dempster 1929–30

BEST INNINGS BOWLING FIGURES

England in England, 7–32, D. L. Underwood, Lord's 1969
England in New Zealand, 7–75, F. S. Trueman, Christchurch 1962–63
New Zealand in England, 6–67, J. A. Cowie, Old Trafford 1937
New Zealand in New Zealand, 6–26, R. J. Hadlee, Wellington 1977–78

BEST MATCH BOWLING FIGURES

England in England, 12–101, D. L. Underwood, Oval 1969
England in New Zealand, 12–97, D. L. Underwood, Christchurch 1970–71
New Zealand in England, 10–140, J. A. Cowie, Old Trafford 1937
New Zealand in New Zealand, 10–100, R. J. Hadlee, Wellington 1977–78

HIGHEST WICKET AGGREGATE IN A SERIES

England in England, 34, G. A. R. Lock 1958
England in New Zealand, { 17, K. Higgs 1965–66; 17, D. L. Underwood 1970–71; 17, I. T. Botham 1977–78 }
New Zealand in England, 20, A. R. MacGibbon 1958
New Zealand in New Zealand, { 15, R. O. Collinge 1977–78; 15, R. J. Hadlee 1977–78 }

RECORD WICKET PARTNERSHIPS—ENGLAND

1 L. Hutton and R. T. Simpson, 147, Oval 1949
2 J. H. Edrich and K. F. Barrington, 369, Headingley 1965
3 J. Hardstaff, jr, and W. R. Hammond, 245, Lord's 1937
4 M. H. Denness and K. W. R. Fletcher, 266, Auckland 1974–75
5 W. R. Hammond and L. E. G. Ames, 242, Christchurch 1932–33
6 B. R. Knight and P. H. Parfitt, 240, Auckland 1962–63
7 A. P. E. Knott and P. Lever, 149, Auckland 1962–63
8 L. E. G. Ames and G. O. Allen, 246, Lord's 1931
9 M. C. Cowdrey and A. C. Smith, 163*, Wellington 1962–63
10 A. P. E. Knott and N. Gifford, 59, Trent Bridge 1973

RECORD WICKET PARTNERSHIPS—NEW ZEALAND

1 C. S. Dempster and J. W. E. Mills, 276, Wellington 1929–30
2 B. Sutcliffe and J. R. Reid, 131, Christchurch 1950–51
3 B. E. Congdon and B. F. Hastings, 190, Lord's 1973
4 M. L. Page and R. C. Blunt, 142, Lord's 1931
5 B. E. Congdon and V. Pollard, 177, Trent Bridge 1973
6 M. G. Burgess and V. Pollard, 117, Lord's 1973
7 B. Sutcliffe and V. Pollard, 104, Edgbaston 1965
8 D. A. R. Moloney and A. W. Roberts, 104, Lord's 1937
9 J. A. Cowie and T. B. Burtt, 64, Christchurch 1946–47
10 F. L. H. Mooney and J. A. Cowie, 57, Headingley 1949

England v India

LESLIE SMITH

Test Matches between England and India are of comparatively modern origin, although games between the two countries date back to before the turn of the century. Not until the Indian tour of England in 1932 was the 1st Test arranged between the two countries and then it was just a single match. Six of the 7 Indian victories have come in their own country against English teams below full strength. Two of them occurred during the tour in 1961–62 when, for the 1st time, they won a series against England. They also gained 2 victories to England's 1 in 1972–73. The solitary success in England came at the Oval in 1971 and was enough to give them the series.

The best of the batsmen when India were granted Test status was C. K. Nayudu, and he earned high praise for his handling of the side during the one Test in 1932. Played at Lord's in late June, the match ended shortly after 4 o'clock on the 3rd afternoon with England victorious by 158 runs.

In 1933–34 D. R. Jardine took a strong side to India for the 1st series of Tests there. England won 2 games with 1 drawn. Apart from Jardine, England possessed entertaining and successful batsmen in C. F. Walters, B. H. Valentine, A. H. Bakewell, and a strong all-round element which included M. S. Nichols, James Langridge, L. F. Townsend and H. Verity. E. W. Clark was always a menacing fast bowler. The Indian discovery was Amarnath, an all-rounder who was to figure a little later in one of the most controversial incidents in cricket. C. K. Nayudu played a number of fine innings and

C. K. Nayudu, a highly-gifted cricketer and the mainstay of India when they entered the Test arena in the 1930s.

V. M. Merchant and Mushtaq Ali, India's opening pair in the 1936 Tests against England, put on 203 together at Old Trafford in 2½ hours of a day in which were scored the record aggregate of 588 runs.

Dilawar Hussain, a large, heavy wicket-keeper, proved a stubborn batsman who could also hit hard at times. England won the First Test at Bombay by 9 wickets soon after lunch on the 4th day, their bowling being too strong. England found nothing wrong with the pitch, running up 438, with Valentine scoring 136, Walters 78 and Jardine 60. Jardine and Valentine added 145 for the 5th wicket. India did well in their 2nd innings, mainly through Amarnath and C. K. Nayudu, who after the loss of 2 wickets cheaply, added 186. Amarnath, on his Test debut, made 118, the 1st hundred for India against England. England needed only 40 to win. Playing for India were Wazir Ali and V. M. Merchant who were to become 2 of their country's best batsmen.

The Second Test at Calcutta was drawn, but England again held the upper hand, India being forced to follow on. The ball lifted nastily at times and several batsmen received bad blows. Dilawar Hussain was struck on the back of his head and had to retire. But he recovered, and by scoring 116 in the match helped to avert defeat. England had to fight on the first day when the pace of Nissar and the accuracy and swing of Amar Singh caused trouble. England drove home their superiority at Madras, winning by 202 runs. They were a little fortunate to bat 1st for the pitch crumbled towards the end, but they left little doubt that they were too good for India. An opening stand of 111 between Bakewell and Walters gave England a good start, but 4 wickets fell cheaply before Jardine and Verity rescued them. Verity found the pitch so suitable for his left-hand spin that he took 7 for 49 in a total of 145. The left-handed spinners, Langridge and Verity, took all the wickets.

The visit to England in 1936 was a sad disappointment to India, who had been hoping to show some improvement. They won no more than 4 of the 28 first-class matches, but played a little above themselves in the Tests when Amar Singh, Jahangir Khan (the Cambridge blue) and Dilawar Hussain were available. The weather was against them, being cold and wet for most of the season. But the tour was doomed almost from the start because of internal difficulties which led to Amarnath being ordered home a week before the First Test. Amarnath had shown himself to be one of the big personalities of the side in batting and bowling. Shortly before he left for India he had hit a hundred in each innings against Essex. The captain, the Maharaj Kumar of Vizianagram, and his manager decided on this severe disciplinary action. Opinions were divided about the rights and wrongs of the case and some years later Armanath not only regained his Test place, but became India's captain, both in Australia and at home. There is little doubt that about this time, and for a number of years afterwards, Indian cricket was held back by jealousies, both among players and officials and, only naturally, team-work suffered.

C. K. Nayudu again toured, but could not produce his top form, the leading batsman being Merchant, who enjoyed a fine season, averaging over 51. Mushtaq Ali, a tall, handsome and sparkling personality, excited crowds with his unorthodox batting. He made an excellent contrast to the more correct Merchant and they shared many splendid stands, including 203 in the Manchester Test and 215 against Minor Counties.

England won the First Test at Lord's by 9 wickets, although surprisingly behind on 1st innings. Following a good deal of rain, G. O. Allen sent India in to bat and himself played a major part in dismissing them for 147 by taking 5 for 35. India made 62 before losing a wicket, but were out in a further 85 minutes. England found conditions just as difficult and with Amar Singh making the ball swing they were 41 for 5 before Leyland and James Langridge, two left-handers, added 55. Artificial drying of the pitch was tried for the 1st time in a Test. At first the ball kicked and rose at different heights, but later the pitch became easier. India, 13 ahead, could never recover from the shock of losing 4 wickets for 28. England needed 107 to win and, after losing a wicket without a run scored, hit off the remainder without further loss. Gimblett, on his Test debut, played a good innings when conditions were at their best for batting.

The Second Test was a complete contrast, with batsmen on top for the most part. Several fine innings were played, notably by Hammond, Merchant and Mushtaq. Winning the toss, India were disappointing on an easy Manchester pitch and England established a mastery when Hammond and Fagg added 134 for the 2nd wicket. On his return to the England side, Hammond was in tremendous form and his 167 came in just over 3 hours. Worthington helped Hammond add 127 in 75 minutes. Robins and Verity rubbed it in with 138 in 70 minutes and England declared at 571 for 8, having averaged 91 runs an hour. India, 368 behind, appeared to be facing an impossible task, but Merchant and Mushtaq showed their skill with a stand of 203 in 2½ hours, Mushtaq making 112 in that time. The more careful Merchant stayed 4¼ hours for 114. India easily saved the game, finishing with 390 for 5.

England were back on top again at the Oval, winning by 9 wickets. They batted 1st and reached 422 before the 4th wicket fell. Hammond, again at his majestic best, scored 217 and Worthington obtained 128, this pair adding 266.

England should have sent a team to India in 1939–40, but the war prevented the tour taking place and the next series of matches was delayed until 1946. This was the last of the joint sides before the partition of India and Pakistan, but despite the tensions at home the team worked well together and did better than either the 1932 or 1936 sides, winning 11 games and losing only 4 of the 29 first-class matches, in another poor summer. England won the Test series 1–0 with 2 games drawn. In actual fact India hoped to do better, for while cricket continued in their country during the war, there was not a great deal in England. The Nawab of Pataudi led the side in which Amarnath and Mankad bowled splendidly in the Tests, only to be let down by poor fielding. Pataudi came out of almost complete retirement for the tour and, never in the best of health, failed to show anything like his previous skill. Hazare impressed with his soundness, but in general the side was not good enough to worry England overmuch.

A highlight of the tour was a stand of 249 for the last wicket against Surrey at the Oval, an English record for that wicket. Sarwate and Banerjee were the heroes and they became the first Nos 10 and 11 to score a hundred apiece in one innings. In the same match C. S. Nayudu, a leg-break bowler, did the hat-trick.

England won the First Test at Lord's by 10 wickets, the match being over at lunch-time on the 3rd day. India, at one point 87 for 6, improved and reached 200. A. V. Bedser caused the breakdown, taking 7 for 49 on his Test debut. England lost Hutton, Compton, Hammond and Washbrook cheaply. On the Monday, with the pitch faster, Hardstaff was in brilliant form. Gibb gave him sound support in a stand of 182. England reached 428 with Hardstaff batting 5¼ hours for 205 not out. Following a long bowling spell, Mankad opened the innings when India went in 228 behind and he helped Merchant start with 67. On the last morning India were 66 behind with 6 wickets left, but Bedser and Wright caused a collapse which left England with a light task. In the match Bedser took 11 for 145. So keen were the public to watch cricket after the war that the gates had to be closed on each of the 1st 2 days with about 30,000 inside.

India saved the Second Test at Manchester with their last pair together, Sohoni and Hindlekar staying for the final 13 minutes. Merchant and Mushtaq repeated their success on the same ground 10 years earlier, opening with a stand of 124 against the 7 bowlers tried. Pataudi changed his batting order to maintain the bright scoring with disastrous results. Hafeez and Mankad were out to successive balls and in a deadly spell Pollard took 4 for 7. India were set to get 278 to win. A comfortable English victory looked likely when India were 5 for 3, but Hazare and Modi added 74. After tea Bedser had a fine spell of 6 overs, taking 4 wickets and England would have won but for 2 dropped catches at the wicket when the last pair were together. Bedser again took 11 wickets in the match, beginning his Test career with 22 for 238 in his 1st 2 games. The Oval Test was ruined by the weather, the match being abandoned at lunch-time on the last day.

The MCC team of 1951–52 lacked May, Hutton, Bedser, Evans and others, and was a good deal below full strength. N. D. Howard, of Lancashire, captained the side, but late in the tour developed pleurisy. Graveney and Watkins were easily the most successful England batsmen, but the bowlers did little. India, on their easy pitches, were a strong batting side and in Mankad they possessed the most successful bowler. This clever slow left-hander took 34 wickets in the series – a great performance. England did fairly well to share the rubber, each side winning once with 3 games drawn. India threw away a good chance of winning the First Test at Delhi by over-cautious tactics and weak catching. India lost 2 wickets for 64 before Merchant and Hazare added 211, but too slowly, considering India were ahead with 8 wickets in hand. Merchant made 154 and Hazare 164 not out, batting 8½ hours. When India declared at 418 for 6 England were 215 behind with 2 days left. At 116 for 3 they were struggling, but Watkins and Carr saved the match with a stand of 158 in 5 hours. Watkins stayed 9 hours for 138 not out, an innings of intense concentration.

After a month's visit to Pakistan, England played the Second Test at Bombay and did much better, although the match was drawn. India reached 485 for 9 before Hazare declared. Roy and Hazare added 187 for the 3rd wicket. Roy batted 5½ hours for 140 and Hazare completed his 2nd hundred in successive Test innings before retiring hurt with a cut on his forehead in attempting a hook. He was never the same player again in the series. England batted consistently, with Graveney always the dominating figure. He held out for 8¼ hours, scoring 175. Best support came from Watkins in a stand of 148. India's lead was restricted to 29. Seven hours were left, but in a dramatic last half-hour on the 4th day India lost 4 wickets and were only 71 ahead. Three more wickets fell for the addition of 46 and they were 88 for 7. Their strong tail pulled them through and England eventually needed 238 in 100 minutes, a task too much for them. Graveney was on the field for 24¾ hours out of a possible 27.

A dull, lifeless pitch led to dreary cricket at Calcutta, where the Third Test was drawn. England made certain of not losing the series when they won the Fourth Test at Kanpur by 8 wickets. The pitch gave considerable aid to spin and England were more experienced all round in such conditions.

India won the Fifth Test at Madras by an innings and 8 runs with a day left and shared the series. This was the 1st Test victory in their history and was gained emphatically. Mankad had a personal triumph with 12 wickets for 108 runs; his 8 for 55 in the 1st innings on an unresponsive pitch being a splendid effort. India batted solidly. Roy made 111, Phadkar and Umrigar added 104 for the 6th wicket and Umrigar and Gopinath put on 93 in 80 minutes. Umrigar finished with 130 not out. England, 191 behind, were soon in trouble and despite another good innings from Robertson, the match was over before tea on the 4th day.

India visited England the same summer, 1952, with bright prospects, but finished with a poor record, 4 victories coming in first-class matches. Although they lost only 5, they were outplayed in the Tests. Three of the 4 were lost and the other drawn. They just could not cope with the speed of Trueman and the swing of Bedser. No longer did they have Merchant, Mankad, Amarnath and Mushtaq. Three of them could have toured. Merchant was unfit, but Amarnath and Mushtaq were omitted and Mankad left out because of a difference of opinion with his Board, played League cricket in England. He was brought in for 3 Tests when Haslingden released him on request. He had a wonderful match at Lord's and showed how valuable he would have been if playing for the side regularly. Hazare was too shy and modest to establish himself as a personality in the role of captain. Manjrekar and Hazare were the leading batsmen. Umrigar, fine outside Tests, did little when it mattered and another failure was Roy, the opening batsman, who did not score in 5 of his 7 Test innings.

The First Test at Headingley, which England won by 7 wickets, will always be remembered for the worst start to an innings in the history of Test cricket. Batting in their 2nd innings India, inside a few moments, found themselves with the remarkable score of 0 runs for 4 wickets. (At Brisbane in 1950, England had taken 3 Australian wickets without a run on the board). Until this dramatic collapse India had done fairly well. Hutton, who broke a long-standing tradition by being appointed captain of England when a professional, lost the toss but on an easy-paced pitch, despite their caution, India were 42 for 3. Manjrekar and Hazare changed the situation by adding 222. An overnight downpour changed the conditions and on a difficult pitch Laker took the last 4 wickets in 9 balls. Ghulam Ahmed, also an off-spinner, carried on the success of bowlers and England lost Hutton, Simpson, May and Compton for 92. Graveney and Watkins, the successes of the tour of India a few months earlier, led a recovery. Even so, England's lead of 41 did not look very good considering they had to bat last. About half-an-hour later the match looked almost over. Trueman took 3 wickets in his first 14 balls and Bedser another and when Umrigar left, India were 26 for 5. Hazare stopped the rot and with Phadkar added 105. Three more wickets fell at 143 and England needed 125 to win. They struggled all the way taking 2½ hours over the runs and losing 3 wickets.

Not even England's triumph by 8 wickets at Lord's could take away the glory from Mankad. In the match he scored 256 runs and bowled 97 overs, taking 5 for 231. England scored 537; India followed on, 302 behind, and lost 2 wickets for 59. Then Mankad and Hazare added 211. Mankad's 184 was made out of 270 in 4½ hours. Despite this India had no prospects of avoiding defeat and England needed only 77 to win.

England's success at Old Trafford was even more emphatic, India being defeated by an innings and 207 runs. Magnificent fast bowling by Trueman, supported by great close catching, virtually decided the match when India went in for their 1st innings. England batted first, but in dismal conditions made a

A field-day at Old Trafford: on 19 July 1952, England on a damp pitch bowled out India twice in the day – something that had not happened in a Test in England for half-a-century. Trueman (8 for 31) has bowled here to P. Roy. England held 14 chances and missed none.

slow start. Cricket was limited to 3¾ hours and the showers persisted on the 2nd day. Hutton made a careful 104, May a good 69 and Evans a bright 71 out of 84 in 70 minutes. The England innings went into the 3rd morning, but India's lasted very little time.

Bowling downwind at the top of his speed on a greasy pitch, Trueman took 8 for 31. India were out for 58 and they followed on 289 behind. They did little better, being disposed of for 82. This time Bedser and Lock did the damage and the last 8 wickets fell for 27. They were dismissed twice in a day. The weather ruined the Fourth Test at the Oval, only 10½ hours being played out of a possible 30.

India had another poor tour in 1959, winning 6 times and losing 11 of the 33 first-class games. For the first time England won all 5 Tests in a series. On this occasion India had no excuse for the weather was fine for most of the summer. In general they had a negative approach to the game, lacked a top-class opening batsman and a genuine fast bowler and fielded weakly. Also their captain, D. K. Gaekwad, did not possess the personality to bring enthusiasm to a struggling team. Manjrekar, the one man who looked capable of getting runs consistently, suffered from knee trouble and he did not play again after the Lord's Test. He had to have a knee-cap removed. Umrigar was once more powerful against lesser sides but not in the Tests, except that he did score a hundred at Manchester. A. A. Baig, the Oxford blue, replaced Manjrekar and he brought a different approach to the play, being prepared to produce attractive, attacking strokes.

England won the First Test at Nottingham by an innings and 59 runs with a day to spare. They began by losing 3 wickets for 60 but finished the 1st day with 358 for 6. May, the captain, made 106 and Barrington helped him add 125 for the 4th wicket. Evans hit 73 off 73 balls received. England batted a further hour next day and reached 422. India were never happy against Trueman, Statham and Moss. At tea they were 79 for 1, but a little later a heavy storm arrived and this proved their undoing. On the 3rd day India collapsed. Borde fractured the little finger on his left hand and this handicapped them, but there was no real excuse for a total of 206. They followed on 216 behind and despite a solid effort by Roy they again disappointed.

It took England only 3 days to win at Lord's, although India put up a slightly better fight before losing by 8 wickets. Roy led the side, as Gaekwad was unfit, and he won the toss and gave his side first use of a lively pitch. The ball rose awkwardly at times and Contractor, despite a cracked rib, battled determinedly for 81. The leg-breaks of Greenhough caused a breakdown. He took 5 for 12 in 31 balls and in a total of 168 the last 7 wickets went for 24. But India fought back well. England were 50 for 3 overnight and ran into more trouble next day. Against lively bowling by Desai and Surendranath they were 80 for 6. Barrington and the tail-enders remedied the situation. India, 58 behind, lost 2 wickets without scoring and were 42 for 4 before Manjrekar and Kripal Singh added 89. England needed 108 to win, which they scored for the loss of 2 wickets.

The Third Test, at Headingley, again lasted only 3 days, England winning by an innings and 173 runs. India were again outplayed and were struggling from the first day when, on a slow pitch, they were dismissed for 161. Parkhouse, recalled to the England side after an absence of 9 years, shared an opening stand of 146 with Pullar. With Cowdrey and Barrington adding 193 for the 4th wicket, England finished the 2nd day with 408 for 4. They declared with 8 wickets down for 483, Cowdrey hitting 4 sixes and 14 fours while scoring 160. India were 322 behind and with the ball starting to turn they had no chance.

The only match in the series which went to 5 days was the Fourth Test at Old Trafford where England won by 171 runs. This was largely due to Cowdrey's decision not to enforce the follow-on even before the India 1st innings was completed and before the start of the 3rd day. A heavy atmosphere helped bowlers when England went in first but poor catching enabled them to run up a total of 490. By the close India were 127 for 6, only Borde, with 75, saving them from rout, and England led by 282. India made a better fight when they set about their enormous task of scoring 548 to win. Contractor and Baig added 109 for the 2nd wicket, but later Baig was struck on the temple by a ball from Rhodes and retired. He resumed next day and completed a hundred in his 1st Test and Umrigar made 118, but after that India broke down and England had plenty in hand.

Another innings victory came to England at the Oval, the match ending just before lunch on the 4th day. On a perfect pitch India were 74 for 7 but the tail improved things slightly and they reached 140. England led by 221. India made 194, Nadkarni batting 4 hours for 76 but he was alone in his resistance.

Having narrowly avoided the loss of the rubber on their previous visit to India, England continued to find it difficult to win matches when they went there again in 1961–62. The first 3 Tests were drawn, but India won the last 2 and so, for the 1st time, beat England in a series. India were perhaps a little fortunate to win the toss 4 times out of 5 and in the last 2 Tests this had an important bearing on the result for the pitches steadily took spin, but there was little doubt they deserved their success. The strength of their batting, particularly in the middle, was something that the England bowlers could not master. England were without Statham and Trueman, besides

Cowdrey and one or two other top-class players. Early on, the batting was reliable, with Dexter and Barrington in fine form, but later it fell away. Dexter won the toss for the only time at Bombay and England ran up 500 for 8 before declaring. Richardson and Pullar, left-handed opening batsmen, began with a stand of 159, Barrington made 151 not out and Dexter 85. India were not well placed at 173 for 4. Borde and Durani changed the situation by adding 142, but England led by 110. The batting was not really fast enough for the situation and, when the declaration came, India made no attempt to score 295 at 72 an hour.

England received a shock at Kanpur, being forced to follow on for the first time against India, but in the end they saved the game easily. The pitch was dead and big totals seemed likely from the first. No play was possible because of rain on the last 2 days of the match at Delhi and another draw resulted. Even before the weather changed no other result seemed possible: only 13 wickets fell on the 1st 3 days. The young Nawab of Pataudi gained his 1st Test honour, following his father who had previously appeared for England and India.

India won the Fourth Test at Calcutta by 187 runs. India made 380 after half the side had gone for 194. Despite a good innings by Richardson, England were always struggling and India, 168 ahead, steadily built a strong position. England never looked like getting the 421 needed to win.

At Madras the pattern was the same as in the Fourth Test, India batting first on a pitch taking increasing spin and making the most of it. They showed welcome enterprise on the 1st day despite the fact that only a draw was needed to give them the rubber. Pataudi hit a dashing hundred and India totalled 428. England disappointed and despite a last wicket stand of 55 between Millman and D. R. Smith were 147 behind. Good bowling by Lock (6 for 65) prevented India getting too much on top, but England, needing 338, began poorly and never recovered. The match was over just after lunch on the 5th day, India winning by 128 runs.

The enthusiasm for cricket in India evidenced by the huge crowds led to MCC's sending another team in 1963–64, this time captained by M. J. K. Smith and with a programme lasting less than 2 months, in which 5 Test matches and 5 other matches were played. The tour was well led and administered, the experience of 2 years before being invaluable. It lacked some half-dozen players from the most recent England sides, but was strengthened after the Second Test by the arrival, as replacements, of M. C. Cowdrey and P. H. Parfitt. Cowdrey, playing his 1st innings since breaking an arm 7 months before, made 107 at Calcutta and later 151 at Delhi. Parfitt made 121 in the last Test at Kanpur. Both at Madras and Bombay, where the First and Second Tests were played, England were reduced by stomach ailments and injury to a state in which they could only hope to live to fight another day.

At Calcutta a stronger England side started well on the most lively pitch encountered in India and had 9 Indian wickets down for 190. But from then on the match was allowed to slip away through a combination of an easing of the pitch, ill-luck with the weather on the 3rd day and batting which had yet to find confidence and purpose. On the dead clay pitches of New Delhi and Kanpur there could be little hope of anything but a draw, although a much-improved, better-balanced England held, on paper, a strong position at Kanpur. Having won the toss for the 5th time in 5 matches, the Nawab of Pataudi put England in. They made 559 for 8 declared, Knight as well as Parfitt making a hundred, and having taken a wicket on the 2nd night had 3 days left to take 19 wickets. Though they made India follow on, there was never any real likelihood on this pitch that they could do more.

The India tour of England in 1967 was disastrous for them. They lost all 3 Tests, suffered badly from injuries and, as had happened so often in the past, had to spend a lot of time in the pavilion because of bad weather. When they did play the pitches were often wet and unsuitable to them. A remarkable recovery by India marked the First Test at Headingley although it did not save them. England, with 246 from Boycott and a hundred from d'Oliveira, reached 550 for 4 declared. Despite his massive score Boycott was omitted from the next Test for lack of enterprise. He and d'Oliveira added 252 for the 4th wicket. India failed in their 1st innings but, following on 386 behind, ran up 510, Pataudi (148), Wadekar (91) and Engineer (87) leading the way. England had no trouble scoring the 125 needed, winning by 6 wickets.

At Lord's India were outclassed, losing by an innings and 124 with a day and a half to spare. Their batting collapsed twice whereas England reached 386, Graveney scoring 151 with 2 sixes and 25 fours. On a rain-damaged pitch Illingworth took 6 for 24 in India's 2nd innings. England were just as superior at Edgbaston, winning with 2 days left by 132 runs on a pitch which helped spin for most of the match. Although England led by 206 on the 1st innings Close did not enforce the follow-on and India, out for 92 in their 1st innings, had little hope of scoring 410 to win.

In complete contrast the next series proved a triumph for India who, for the 1st time, won a Test in England. That was enough to give them the 1971 series for the other 2 games were drawn. The powerful spin combination of Chandrasekhar, Bedi, Venkataraghavan and Prasanna was the highlight. Between them they captured 197 of the 244 wickets taken in first-class matches on the tour. Another important factor was the much-improved fielding inspired by the captain, Wadekar.

Rain after tea on the last day upset the chance of a thrilling finish at Lord's. With 2 wickets left India needed 38 to win. England, 71 for 5 at one stage, recovered through Knott (67) and Snow (73). Wadekar and Viswanath batted well for India who led England's 304 by 9 and eventually needed 183 for victory. An incident in the match led to Snow being left out of the Second Test. After bowling he collided with Gavaskar, who was going for a run, knocked him over and was subsequently told to apologize.

At Old Trafford Peter Lever enjoyed a fine all-round match. He scored 88 not out in England's first innings of 386 (Illingworth 107) and took 5 for 70 in India's total of 212. Illingworth and Lever put on 168 for the 8th wicket. After a 2nd innings hundred for England by Luckhurst, India needed 420 to win, but no play was possible on the 5th day. India won

Another for Bedi, India's most prolific wicket-taker: at Calcutta, in 1976–77, Solkar catches Brearley at short-leg for 5.

at the Oval by 4 wickets, despite a 1st innings of 355 by England. India replied with 284, but devastating bowling by Chandrasekhar (6 for 38) dismissed England for 101. Steady batting enabled India to obtain the 173 needed. This was India's 1st Test triumph in England after 26 abortive attempts.

India maintained their supremacy in their own country in 1972–73, winning the 5-match series 2–1. Rather surprisingly England triumphed in the First Test, but only rarely looked capable of repeating the performance. A 1st innings failure cost India the match at Delhi. Against good swing bowling by Arnold (6 for 45) they were dismissed for 173. An even better effort came from Chandrasekhar, whose 8 for 79 included 4 wickets in 8 balls, but England led by 27. India were 103 for 5 before Solkar and Engineer added 103. Needing 207 England were 107 for 4, but A. R. Lewis, the new captain, and Greig added 101 to clinch victory.

India levelled the series in a close game at Calcutta, winning by 28 runs in a low-scoring match. Chandrasekhar was again prominent with 5 for 65 in England's 1st innings and 4 for 42 when they went in to get 192 to win. At Madras India won by 4 wickets but had something of a scare when going in to get 86 to win. Chandrasekhar (6 for 90) prevented England getting on top in the 1st innings and India's consistent batting brought them a lead of 74. Bedi and Prasanna each took 4 wickets when England were out for 159 a second time. India lost 6 wickets hitting off the runs. England were on top at the end of the drawn game at Kanpur. India again batted consistently in their total of 357 but England, with Lewis scoring 125, led by 40. India, at one stage 39 for 4, were rescued by Viswanath's 75 not out and finished at 186 for 6. The Bombay Test was always heading for a draw, both sides topping 400 in the 1st innings. Engineer (121) and Wadekar put on 192 for India's 2nd wicket and Viswanath followed with 113. For England, Fletcher and Greig hit hundreds and added 254 for the 5th wicket. India made a token declaration at 244 for 5 and England replied with 67 for 2. Chandrasekhar finished with 35 wickets, the highest for an Indian bowler in a Test series.

Another experience of bad weather in England cost India dearly in 1974, all 3 Tests being lost. England found most of the answers to India's spin attack and in conditions suitable to their type of bowling always worried a suspect batting side. The First Test at Old Trafford went to England by 113 runs. In bitterly cold weather, and with heavy showers at times, India had an unhappy match; only a 101 by Gavaskar and a lively 70 by Abid Ali saved them from complete rout. A mere 3 men reached double figures. Fletcher hit 123 not out in the 1st innings and Edrich made a hundred in England's 2nd innings. India, needing 296, were out for 182. The margin at Lord's was a massive innings and 285. England ran up 629 with Amiss scoring 188, Denness 118, Greig 106 and Edrich 96. Amiss and Edrich added 221 for the 2nd wicket; Denness and Greig 205 for the 5th. Bedi had the remarkable bowling figures of 6 for 226 in 64·2 overs. India reached a reasonable 302 but following on 327 behind were dismissed in 77 minutes for 42, their lowest Test score. They had no answer to the swing of Old and Arnold in a heavy atmosphere. India's batting again failed at Edgbaston. They were out for 165 and 216 and England won by an innings and 78 in a little over 2½ days' actual playing time. In England's total of 459 for 2, D. Lloyd made 214 not out and shared stands of 157 for the 1st wicket with Amiss and 211 for the second wicket with Denness (100).

England confirmed their improvement in 1976–77 by taking the series 3–1. It was the first time in 5 tours of India since the Second World War that they had managed this. Good bowling, high-class fielding and splendid captaincy by Greig were the main reasons for the triumph. England clinched matters with big wins in each of the first 3 Tests. They won at Delhi by an innings and 25, J. K. Lever playing an important role with 7 for 46 in India's first innings and 53 with the bat. England made 381, Amiss scoring 179. He and Knott put on 101 for the 6th wicket. India collapsed against Lever's swing, followed on 259 behind and this time failed against the spin of Underwood and Greig. India's batting again let them down at Calcutta, their totals of 155 and 181 enabling England to win by 10 wickets. Willis caused the 1st innings breakdown with 5 for 27. At one point 90 for 4 England recovered through a 5th wicket stand of 142 between Greig (103) and Tolchard.

No batting improvement by India came at Madras, totals of 164 and 83 being completely inadequate, and England won by 200 runs. This was the liveliest pitch of the series and England's bowlers exploited it well. With the series settled, India at last found some form, winning at Bangalore by 140 runs. They made the most of batting first on a pitch that deteriorated. Chandrasekhar took 7 for 76 in England's 1st innings of 195 and Bedi 6 for 71 when England went in to get 318 to win.

The drawn Bombay Test was the most even of the series. Gavaskar scored 108 in India's 1st innings of 338. Amiss and Brearley began with 146, but, despite a 76 by Greig, England were 21 behind. Underwood prevented India taking control and England, needing 214 in just over 4 hours, found the task beyond them on a difficult pitch and lost 7 for 152, to bring the series to an end.

The 1979 4-match Cornhill-sponsored series began ill for India with defeat at Edgbaston by an innings and 83 runs. When, at the start of the Second Test, they were dismissed for 96, a one-sided contest seemed certain, but by the end of the series India had made a considerable advance. Indeed, they all but pulled off a dramatic victory in the final Test. By their solitary success at Edgbaston, England took the rubber, the remaining 3 games being drawn.

India, captained by Venkataraghavan, found their spin attack, on which they had relied for many years, on the decline, but in Kapil Dev they possessed one of the best fast-medium bowlers in their history. His control of line and length plus his ability to move the ball either way made him a formidable foe.

Tony Greig reached the summit of his cricket career, in terms both of leadership and performance, when at Madras in January 1977 he won the Third Test against India and with it the rubber. Within 2 months, while still England's captain, in the Centenary Test at Melbourne he had pledged his future to Kerry Packer and had begun to seek recruits among his own players. Ironically, it is two of those who soon became most implacably opposed to the WSC system – Chris Old and John Lever – who are here bearing him aloft.

Unfortunately for India he received little support. In batting Gavaskar confirmed his position as one of the best players in the world and his double-hundred at the Oval was an innings of the highest class. Viswanath often brought his experience to bear and Vengsarkar, who hit a hundred at Lord's, was the best of the younger batsmen.

England's lowest total of the series was 270 and they were rarely in difficulty with the bat. Botham again excelled as an all-rounder; Gower began brilliantly with 200 not out at Edgbaston, but faded, and Boycott was as solid as ever. The Yorkshireman played a typically sound innings on the opening day of the series, taking 5½ hours over his hundred. He went on to make 155, but this was surpassed by Gower who batted 6 hours before Brearley declared at 633 for 5, England's highest total for 40 years and the best against India. The 4th-wicket stand between Boycott and Gower produced 191. Gower and Miller added 165, a record for England's 6th wicket against India. Kapil Dev took all 5 England wickets. A disheartened India followed on 336 behind and after an opening stand of 124 between Gavaskar and Chauhan they collapsed badly.

India fought gallantly and saved the game at Lord's after being 323 behind on 1st innings. Botham (5 for 35) was mainly responsible for India being out for 96. England batted consistently for their big lead, but could not force a breakthrough again. Viswanath and Vengsarkar each hit a century and put on 210 for the 3rd wicket, batting almost the entire last day.

The weather restricted cricket to 2 days at Headingley, the highlight being a fine, attacking innings of 137 by Botham. At the Oval India again had to fight back after trailing by 103 on 1st innings. Boycott made 125 in England's 2nd innings which Brearley declared at 334 for 8, setting India to get 438 in a little over 8 hours. Gavaskar and Chauhan began with 213 in almost 5¼ hours. Gavaskar's 221, the highest for India against England, was a truly great innings. Both sides went all out for victory until the closing minutes and India finished 9 short of their target with 2 wickets left after one of the best-fought Tests seen in England for many years.

If anyone doubted the high place Sunil Gavaskar had reached among the world's batsmen, his innings of 221 against England at the Oval, in September 1979, gave the clearest possible proof. Needing 438 to win, India got to within 9 – thanks chiefly to Gavaskar – a remarkable achievement.

ENGLAND V INDIA

			RESULT	CAPTAINS
1932	1 Lord's	E 259, 275–8D; Ind 189, 187	E 158 runs	D. R. Jardine, C. K. Nayudu
1933–34	1 Bombay	Ind 219, 258; E 438, 40–1	E 9 wkts	D. R. Jardine, C. K. Nayudu
	2 Calcutta	E 403, 7–2; Ind 247, 237	Drawn	D. R. Jardine, C. K. Nayudu
	3 Madras	E 335, 261–7D; Ind 145, 249	E 202 runs	D. R. Jardine, C. K. Nayudu
1936	1 Lord's	Ind 147, 93; E 134, 108–1	E 9 wkts	G. O. Allen, Vizianagram
	2 Old Trafford	Ind 203, 390–5; E 571–8D	Drawn	G. O. Allen, Vizianagram
	3 Oval	E 471–8D, 64–1; Ind 222, 312	E 9 wkts	G. O. Allen, Vizianagram
1946	1 Lord's	Ind 200, 275; E 428, 48–0	E 10 wkts	W. R. Hammond, Nawab of Pataudi
	2 Old Trafford	E 294, 153–5D; Ind 170, 152–9	Drawn	W. R. Hammond, Nawab of Pataudi
	3 Oval	Ind 331; E 95–3	Drawn	W. R. Hammond, Nawab of Pataudi
1951–52	1 New Delhi	E 203, 368–6; Ind 418–6D	Drawn	N. D. Howard, V. S. Hazare
	2 Bombay	Ind 485–9D, 208; E 456, 55–2	Drawn	N. D. Howard, V. S. Hazare
	3 Calcutta	E 342, 252–5D; Ind 344, 103–0	Drawn	N. D. Howard, V. S. Hazare
	4 Kanpur	Ind 121, 157; E 203, 76–2	E 8 wkts	N. D. Howard, V. S. Hazare
	5 Madras	E 266, 183; Ind 457–9D	Ind Inns 8 runs	D. B. Carr, V. S. Hazare
1952	1 Headingley	Ind 293, 165; E 334, 128–3	E 7 wkts	L. Hutton, V. S. Hazare
	2 Lord's	Ind 235, 378; E 537, 79–2	E 8 wkts	L. Hutton, V. S. Hazare
	3 Old Trafford	E 347–9D; Ind 58, 82	E Inns 207 runs	L. Hutton, V. S. Hazare
	4 Oval	E 326–6D; Ind 98	Drawn	L. Hutton, V. S. Hazare
1959	1 Trent Bridge	E 422; Ind 206, 157	E Inns 59 runs	P. B. H. May, D. K. Gaekwad
	2 Lord's	Ind 168, 165; E 226, 108–2	E 8 wkts	P. B. H. May, P. Roy
	3 Headingley	Ind 161, 149; E 483–8D	E Inns 173 runs	P. B. H. May, D. K. Gaekwad
	4 Old Trafford	E 490, 265–8D; Ind 208, 376	E 171 runs	M. C. Cowdrey, D. K. Gaekwad
	5 Oval	Ind 140, 194; E 361	E Inns 27 runs	M. C. Cowdrey, D. K. Gaekwad
1961–62	1 Bombay	E 500–8D, 184–5D; Ind 390, 180–5	Drawn	E. R. Dexter, N. J. Contractor
	2 Kanpur	Ind 467–8D; E 244, 497–5	Drawn	E. R. Dexter, N. J. Contractor
	3 New Delhi	Ind 466; E 256–3	Drawn	E. R. Dexter, N. J. Contractor
	4 Calcutta	Ind 380, 252; E 212, 233	Ind 187 runs	E. R. Dexter, N. J. Contractor
	5 Madras	Ind 428, 190; E 281, 209	Ind 128 runs	E. R. Dexter, N. J. Contractor
1963–64	1 Madras	Ind 457–7D, 152–9D; E 317, 241–5	Drawn	M. J. K. Smith, Nawab of Pataudi
	2 Bombay	Ind 300, 249–8D; E 233, 206–3	Drawn	M. J. K. Smith, Nawab of Pataudi

	3 Calcutta	Ind 241, 300–7D; E 267, 145–2	Drawn	M. J. K. Smith, Nawab of Pataudi
	4 New Delhi	Ind 344, 463–4; E 451	Drawn	M. J. K. Smith, Nawab of Pataudi
	5 Kanpur	E 559–8D; Ind 266, 347–3	Drawn	M. J. K. Smith, Nawab of Pataudi
1967	1 Headingley	E 550–4D, 126–4; Ind 164, 510	E 6 wkts	D. B. Close, Nawab of Pataudi
	2 Lord's	Ind 152, 110; E 386	E Inns 124 runs	D. B. Close, Nawab of Pataudi
	3 Edgbaston	E 298, 203; Ind 92, 277	E 132 runs	D. B. Close, Nawab of Pataudi
1971	1 Lord's	E 304, 191; Ind 313, 145–8	Drawn	R. Illingworth, A. L. Wadekar
	2 Old Trafford	E 386, 245–3D; Ind 212, 65–3	Drawn	R. Illingworth, A. L. Wadekar
	3 Oval	E 355, 101; Ind 284, 174–6	Ind 4 wkts	R. Illingworth, A. L. Wadekar
1972–73	1 Delhi	Ind 173, 233; E 200, 208–4	E 6 wkts	A. R. Lewis, A. L. Wadekar
	2 Calcutta	Ind 210, 155; E 174, 163	Ind 28 runs	A. R. Lewis, A. L. Wadekar
	3 Madras	E 242, 159; Ind 316, 86–6	Ind 4 wkts	A. R. Lewis, A. L. Wadekar
	4 Kanpur	Ind 357, 186–6; E 397	Drawn	A. R. Lewis, A. L. Wadekar
	5 Bombay	Ind 448, 244–5D; E 480, 67–2	Drawn	A. R. Lewis, A. L. Wadekar
1974	1 Old Trafford	E 328–9D, 213–3D; Ind 246, 182	E 113 runs	M. H. Denness, A. L. Wadekar
	2 Lord's	E 629; Ind 302, 42	E Inns 285 runs	M. H. Denness, A. L. Wadekar
	3 Edgbaston	Ind 165, 216; E 459–2D	E Inns 78 runs	M. H. Denness, A. L. Wadekar
1976–77	1 Delhi	E 381; Ind 122, 234	E Inns 25 runs	A. W. Greig, B. S. Bedi
	2 Calcutta	Ind 155, 181; E 321, 16–0	E 10 wkts	A. W. Greig, B. S. Bedi
	3 Madras	E 262, 185–9D; Ind 164, 83	E 200 runs	A. W. Greig, B. S. Bedi
	4 Bangalore	Ind 253, 259–9D; E 195, 177	Ind 140 runs	A. W. Greig, B. S. Bedi
	5 Bombay	Ind 338, 192; E 317, 152–7	Drawn	A. W. Greig, B. S. Bedi
1979	1 Edgbaston	E 633–5D; Ind 297, 253	E Inns 83 runs	J. M. Brearley, S. Venkataraghavan
	2 Lord's	Ind 96, 318–4; E 419–9D	Drawn	J. M. Brearley, S. Venkataraghavan
(CORNHILL	3 Headingley	E 270; Ind 223–6	Drawn	J. M. Brearley, S. Venkataraghavan
SERIES)	4 Oval	E 305, 334–8D; Ind 202, 429–8	Drawn	J. M. Brearley, S. Venkataraghavan

CAPTAINS (England)	TESTS	WON	LOST	DRAWN
D. R. Jardine	4	3		1
G. O. Allen	3	2		1
W. R. Hammond	3	1		2
N. D. Howard	4	1		3
D. B. Carr	1		1	
L. Hutton	4	3		1
P. B. H. May	3	3		
M. C. Cowdrey	2	2		
E. R. Dexter	5		2	3
M. J. K. Smith	5			5
D. B. Close	3	3		
R. Illingworth	3		1	2
A. R. Lewis	5	1	2	2
M. H. Denness	3	3		
A. W. Greig	5	3	1	1
J. M. Brearley	4	1		3
	57	26	7	24

CAPTAINS (India)	TESTS	WON	LOST	DRAWN
C. K. Nayudu	4		3	1
Maharaj of Vizianagram	3		2	1
Nawab of Pataudi (sr)	3		1	2
V. S. Hazare	9	1	4	4
D. K. Gaekwad	4		4	
P. Roy	1		1	
N. J. Contractor	5	2		3
Nawab of Pataudi (jr)	8		3	5
A. L. Wadekar	11	3	4	4
B. S. Bedi	5	1	3	1
S. Venkataraghavan	4		1	3
	57	7	26	24

HIGHEST INNINGS TOTALS

England in England, 633–5D, Edgbaston 1979
England in India, 559–8D, Kanpur 1963–64
India in England, 510, Headingley 1967
India in India, 485–9D, Bombay 1951–52

LOWEST INNINGS TOTALS

England in England, 101, Oval 1971
England in India, 159, Madras 1972–73
India in England, 42, Lord's 1974
India in India, 83, Madras 1976–77

HIGHEST INDIVIDUAL INNINGS

England in England, 246*, G. Boycott, Headingley 1967
England in India, 179, D. L. Amiss, Delhi 1976–77
India in England, 221, S. M. Gavaskar, Oval 1979
India in India, 203*, Nawab of Pataudi (jr), Delhi 1963–64

HIGHEST AGGREGATE OF RUNS IN A SERIES

England in England, 399, L. Hutton 1952
England in India, 594, K. F. Barrington 1961–62
India in England, 542, S. M. Gavaskar 1979
India in India, 586, V. L. Manjrekar 1961–62

BEST INNINGS BOWLING FIGURES

England in England, 8–31, F. S. Trueman, Old Trafford 1952
England in India, 7–46, J. K. Lever, Delhi 1976–77
India in England, 6–35, Amar Singh, Lord's 1936
India in India, 8–55, V. Mankad, Madras 1951–52

BEST MATCH BOWLING FIGURES

England in England, 11–93, A. V. Bedser, Old Trafford 1946
England in India, 11–153, H. Verity, Madras 1933–34
India in England, 8–114, B. S. Chandrasekhar, Oval 1967
India in India, 12–108, V. Mankad, Madras 1951–52

HIGHEST WICKET AGGREGATE IN A SERIES

England in England, 29, F. S. Trueman 1952
England in India, 29, D. L. Underwood 1976–77
India in England, 17, S. P. Gupte 1959
India in India, 35, B. S. Chandrasekhar 1972–73

RECORD WICKET PARTNERSHIPS – ENGLAND

1 P. E. Richardson and G. Pullar, 159, Old Trafford 1961–62
2 D. L. Amiss and J. H. Edrich, 221, Lord's 1974
3 R. Subba Row and M. J. K. Smith, 169, Oval 1959
4 W. R. Hammond and T. S. Worthington, 266, Oval 1936
5 K. W. R. Fletcher and A. W. Greig, 254, Bombay 1972–73
6 D. Gower and G. Miller, 165*, Edgbaston 1979
7 A. P. E. Knott and R. A. Hutton, 103, Oval 1971
8 R. Illingworth and P. Lever, 168, Old Trafford 1971
9 K. W. R. Fletcher and N. Gifford, 83, Madras 1972–73
10 J. T. Murray and R. N. S. Hobbs, 57, Edgbaston 1967

RECORD WICKET PARTNERSHIPS – INDIA

1 S. M. Gavaskar and C. P. S. Chauhan, 213, Oval 1979
2 F. M. Engineer and A. L. Wadekar, 192, Bombay 1972–73
3 { V. M. Merchant and V. S. Hazare, 211, Delhi 1951–52
V. Mankad and V. S. Hazare, 211, Lord's 1952 }
4 V. S. Hazare and V. L. Manjrekar, 222, Headingley 1952
5 Nawab of Pataudi (jr) and C. G. Borde, 190*, Delhi 1963–64
6 V. S. Hazare and D. G. Phadkar, 105, Headingley 1952
7 S. A. Durani and C. G. Borde, 153, Bombay 1963–64
8 R. G. Nadkarni and F. M. Engineer, 101, Madras 1961–62
9 G. S. Ramchand and S. G. Shinde, 54, Lord's 1952
10 R. G. Nadkarni and B. S. Chandrasekhar, 51, Calcutta 1963–64

England v Pakistan

LESLIE SMITH

Pakistan, the newest of the Test-playing countries, has met England 30 times since 1954, winning only 1 match, losing 11 and drawing 18. The intense national spirit and pride in the early days when Pakistan were striving to establish themselves as a nation led to a determination to succeed. Also, the pitches they played on, usually matting, helped bowlers and produced results. Later Pakistan turned to all-turf pitches in their Test centres and these were often too dead to permit good stroke making or penetrative bowling. The side fell away for a time, but in recent years many exciting batsmen have emerged although, with the odd exception, the bowling has not been strong enough to bring full reward. The early teams were fortunate to have as their captain Abdul Hafeez Kardar who had wide experience of England, first with the All-India side which toured there in 1946 and subsequently with Warwickshire. His ability as leader and his skill as a left-handed all-rounder were important factors in the growth of Pakistan cricket. They were also lucky to possess capable fast and fast-medium bowlers in Fazal Mahmood, Khan Mohammad and Mahmood Hussain, who would have held their own in most company. Also in at the start were Hanif Mohammad, a pocket-size batsman of tremendous concentration who developed into one of the leading players in the world, and Imtiaz Ahmed, a wicket-keeper-batsman of high quality.

The English players first met the Pakistanis during the MCC tour of 1951–52, but no official Tests were played then. Pakistan had yet to be admitted to the Imperial Cricket Conference, but the events of that tour played an important part in getting them included. An exciting game on the mat at Karachi led to Pakistan winning by 4 wickets with 35 minutes to spare.

Pakistan had earned their right to be included among the Test nations and soon they were embarking on tours abroad. In 1954 they visited England and their success did much towards inspiring their own people back home. Only 3 matches were lost throughout the tour. Among their 9 victories was the all-important Fourth Test which levelled the series, each side winning once with 2 games drawn. Imtiaz, behind the stumps, set a new record for a touring wicket-keeper, claiming 86 victims (including 6 catches made when not keeping wicket). Fazal's 20 Test wickets, at an average of 20·40, was a fine effort, but the batting was weak, the best being that of Hanif with an average of 22·62.

The First Test at Lord's was upset by the weather, only a little more than 8 hours' cricket being possible in the 5 days. The first 3 days were blank and play started at 3.45 on the 4th afternoon. Pakistan were outclassed in the Second Test at Nottingham, England winning by an innings and 129 runs. With Hutton unfit, Sheppard took over the captaincy. Pakistan failed in their 1st innings when Appleyard on his 1st Test appearance dismissed Hanif with his 2nd ball and in a deadly spell took 4 for 6 in 26 balls. At his most adventurous, Compton made 278, and his 2nd hundred took only 80 minutes. When England declared at 558 for 6, Pakistan were 401 behind. With Hanif and Alim scoring 59 together the total runs for the day were 496 for the fall of 4 wickets. Rain restricted play on the 3rd day but when play was possible the ball did many awkward things and the game ended just before lunch on the Monday. The weather was again unkind at Old Trafford when the Third Test was drawn with less than 11 hours' play possible. At the Oval Pakistan were desperately placed but the weather in this wettest of all summers eventually came to their rescue. Because of rain, play did not start until 2.30 pm on the 1st day and Pakistan at one point 51 for 7 reached 133. Just before noon on the 2nd day a 10-minute cloudburst flooded the ground and prevented further cricket. England went through a nasty experience on the 3rd morning, Fazal and Mahmood making the ball kick. England were out for 130, 3 behind. On a drying pitch Pakistan were 82 for 8 but again the late batsmen rallied them, the last 2 wickets doubling the total. Wardle took 7 for 56. England needed 168 to win. When the 3rd wicket fell only 59 were needed, but Evans, Graveney and Compton left in quick succession and on the last morning 43 more were required with 4 wickets left. The match was over in less than an hour.

Not until 1961–62 was the next series of Tests played between the 2 countries and then only 3 games took place. This was part of the MCC tour of India, Pakistan and Ceylon, and because

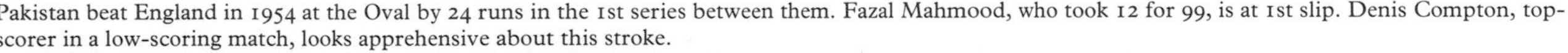

Pakistan beat England in 1954 at the Oval by 24 runs in the 1st series between them. Fazal Mahmood, who took 12 for 99, is at 1st slip. Denis Compton, top-scorer in a low-scoring match, looks apprehensive about this stroke.

India had to visit West Indies a curious arrangement was made. The First Test between Pakistan and England was played at Lahore. Then came the entire tour of India, including 5 Tests, before the Englishmen returned for two more Tests in Pakistan. Winning the First and drawing the next 2, England won the series. They were just a little too good but did not have a great deal in hand. The Pakistan bowling had lost its sting and the batting lacked adventure.

The best of the games was the First Test at Lahore which England won by 5 wickets with 35 minutes to spare. Pakistan declared at 387 for 9, Burki having made 138. England also began shakily, recovering through a 3rd wicket stand of 192 between Barrington and M. J. K. Smith. Pakistan led by 7, but were put on the defensive by losing their first 3 wickets for 33. Despite a last-wicket stand of 52 against them, England unexpectedly needed only 208 to win at just under a run a minute. The 5th wicket fell with 100 needed, but Dexter and Barber settled the issue with an unbroken stand of 101 in 85 minutes.

A lot of dull cricket took place on a slow pitch at Dacca. Hanif, scoring 111 and 104, became the 1st Pakistan batsman to obtain a hundred in each innings of a Test. England were on top for most of the Third Test at Karachi but with the pitch becoming easier as the game went along they had to be content with a draw.

The Pakistan team which visited England in 1962 was heavily outplayed in the Tests and did little better in the outside matches. The lack of penetration in attack was a big handicap and the batting was seldom convincing. The team also suffered through the cold dismal weather for most of the tour and through injuries. Mushtaq Mohammad, one of the few successes of the party, did better than his brother Hanif, who was worried by a groin strain throughout. Burki, the captain, had a difficult time maintaining enthusiasm among a side which so rarely had the encouragement of a victory. England won 4 of the Tests and were on top in the other which, with the help of the weather, Pakistan drew.

England showed how superior they were by winning the First Test at Edgbaston by an innings and 24 runs. England ran up a total of 544 for 5, declaring at lunchtime on the second day, Cowdrey, returning as opening batsman, made 159, sharing stands of 166 with Dexter and 107 with Graveney. Pakistan began badly and, despite a stand of 78 between Hanif and Mushtaq, were out for 246. Following on 298 behind they continued to run into trouble and the match ended just after lunch on the 4th day.

At Lord's the game was over with 2 days to spare, England winning by 9 wickets. Burki decided to bat on a lively pitch in a heavy atmosphere and Pakistan were dismissed for 100, 45 minutes after lunch. Trueman, making the most of the conditions, took 6 for 31. The pitch eased and England went ahead with only one man out. Pakistan, 270 behind, were rushing to defeat when the 4th wicket fell at 77, but there followed a splendid stand of 197 between Burki and the left-handed Nasim-ul-Ghani. Each made 101, Nasim obtaining the 1st hundred of his career. Coldwell, the Worcestershire fast-medium bowler had figures of 9 for 110 on his Test debut. England, needing 86 to win, hit the last 50 in 20 minutes.

The Third Test at Headingley also ended in 3 days. Put in to bat England were 194 for 6 at the close of the 1st day. Poor Pakistan fielding enabled them to make a complete recovery. Parfitt made 119 and England reached 428. By the close Pakistan were 73 for 3 and on the 3rd day they lost 17 wickets. The remaining 7 in the first innings went down for 58 in an hour and a half. In the follow-on Pakistan were dismissed for 180 and England won by an innings and 117.

Pakistan were again outplayed at Trent Bridge, but this time saved the game. Sheppard, after a long absence, returned to open the England innings. Fazal, flown out a few days before the match, reinforced Pakistan. For the 2nd time running Burki put England in to bat. Before a ball could be bowled rain interfered and nothing could be done on the 1st day. Play began on time next morning and Sheppard and Dexter put on 161 for the 2nd wicket. Then Graveney and Parfitt added 184. Graveney made 114 and Parfitt obtained his 3rd hundred of the series, scoring 101 not out before the declaration came at 428 for 5. Fazal showed remarkable stamina, bowling for 7 of the 7½ hours the innings lasted. Pakistan again failed with the bat and followed on 209 behind. At 78 for 3 they looked well beaten but Mushtaq and Saeed rescued them with a stand of 107 and just before the close Mushtaq completed a hard-fought hundred. England were back to another of their easy victories in the Fifth Test at the Oval, winning by 10 wickets on the 4th day. Dexter won the toss and England were given a fine send off by Sheppard and Cowdrey who made 117 together. A magnificent stand of 248 in 165 minutes followed from Cowdrey and Dexter. Cowdrey made 182 and Dexter 172, England reaching 406 for 2 by the close of the 1st day. They declared at 480 for 5. Dexter's fierce hitting brought him 5 sixes and 18 fours. Imtiaz and Mushtaq made 82 for Pakistan's 2nd wicket, but the last 8 went for 90 and they were out for 183. Larter, the tall Northamptonshire fast bowler, made an impressive debut with 5 for 57 on a slow easy pitch. Imtiaz and Mushtaq again did well when Pakistan followed on 297 behind, sharing a stand of 137, but only 45 minutes were needed to end the match on the 4th morning, England being set to get 27 to win.

Like India, who shared the 1967 English season, Pakistan for their 3rd successive visit found the weather far from helpful to them and they were unable to show their best form. On the credit side was the rise of Majid Khan as an aggressive batsman and the emergence of Wasim Bari as a fine wicket-keeper. A remarkable innings by Majid came against Glamorgan, 147 not out in 89 minutes including 13 sixes. He subsequently joined that county. In Tests their most successful effort was at Lord's. With 148 from Barrington, England reached 369; but Hanif batted 9 hours for 187 not out and Pakistan were only 15 behind. Eventually set to get 257 at 73 an hour, Pakistan settled for a draw.

England won the Second Test at Trent Bridge by 10 wickets despite almost 2 days being lost because of bad weather. Saeed played 2 defiant innings, but Pakistan were out for 140 and 114. Barrington scored 109 not out in almost 7 hours on a difficult pitch and England led by 112 on the 1st innings. Barrington hit his 3rd successive Test hundred (142) at the Oval where England won by 8 wickets in 4 days. Arnold's swing worried Pakistan in the 1st innings of 216, but England built a total of 440. At 53 for 7 Pakistan looked doomed to an innings defeat, but Asif Iqbal produced a tremendous display, scoring 146 in just over 3 hours, and with Intikhab put on 190 for the 8th wicket.

The England tour of Pakistan in 1968–69 was ill-fated. It had been arranged in place of England's cancelled visit to South Africa. The political situation in Pakistan at the time was unsettled and this left its mark on the cricket, rioting and general rowdiness causing stoppages at Lahore and Dacca. The upheavals came to a climax at Karachi where a riot led to the tour being abandoned early on the 3rd day of the Test. The cricket naturally suffered and the 3 Tests were drawn. The Lahore game was very close. England made 306 (Cowdrey 100) and 225 for 9 declared after being 58 for 5 at one time. Pakistan, dismissed for 209 the 1st time, reached 203 for 5 when set to get 323 in 5 hours. At Dacca batsmen generally struggled. Pakistan were out for 246 and England led by 28 thanks to 114 not out by d'Oliveira. Pakistan made a token declaration at 195 for 6 and England replied with 33 for no wicket. Only England batted at Karachi, running up 502 for 7. Milburn and Graveney hit hundreds and Knott was foiled by the riot when only 4 short of that figure.

The Pakistan team in England in 1971 showed plenty of skill although they lost the 3-match series 1–0 with 2 games drawn. Intikhab Alam, with his knowledge of English conditions, was a good leader and Zaheer Abbas came to the fore as a world-class batsman. Sadiq Mohammad, the youngest of 5 famous cricketing brothers including Hanif and Mushtaq, also showed his ability. Zaheer dominated the drawn game at Edgbaston with a superb 274 in a total of 608 for 7 declared. He and Mushtaq (100) put on 291 for the 2nd wicket and Asif also hit a hundred. Although Knott scored 116 and d'Oliveira 73, England followed on for the 1st time against Pakistan 255 behind. Luckhurst's 108 not out saved them, but they were still 26 behind with 5 wickets left at the close, rain having prevented play until after 5 pm on the last day.

The Lord's game was also drawn, rain taking 17 hours and 20 minutes out of the match. Boycott scored 121 not out in England's 1st innings of 241 for 2 declared. Pakistan replied with 148 and England made 117 without loss. A thrilling match at Headingley brought England victory by 25 runs and with it the rubber. Boycott played another solid innings of 112, but England's 316 was headed by 34, Zaheer, Wasim and Mushtaq playing useful innings. Dismissing England for 264, Pakistan needed 231. They began badly at 65 for 4, recovered to 160 for 5, but Peter Lever finished the match with 3 wickets in 4 balls.

All 3 Tests in Pakistan in 1972–73 were drawn, batsmen generally having much the better of the argument. Amiss (112) and Denness gave England a good start to the series at Lahore with an opening stand of 105 and the total reached 355. Pakistan, with Sadiq scoring 119 and Asif an attacking 102, led by 67. England had a few anxious moments, but recovered to 306 for 7 declared and Pakistan batted out time. The totals at Hyderabad were even higher. Amiss was again prominent with 158 as England ran up 487, but this was surpassed by Pakistan's 569 for 9 declared. Mushtaq (157) and Asif added 153 for the 5th wicket and Intikhab hit his 1st Test hundred, his 138 including 4 sixes and 15 fours. England were in danger at 77 for 5, but Greig and Knott saved the match with a stand of 112 for the 6th wicket.

Another riot and invasion of the pitch marred the Karachi match which was abandoned 45 minutes early because of a dust storm. The Test was remarkable for the number of hundreds just missed. For Pakistan Majid and Mushtaq each made 99 and Sadiq 83. For England Amiss scored 99 and Lewis 88.

Zaheer Abbas batting during one of his 2 double-hundreds against England.

Geoffrey Boycott led England for the 1st time at Karachi in 1977–78, following J. M. Brearley's withdrawal from the tour with a broken arm.

Spin bowlers at last found some help in Pakistan's 2nd innings. Declaring at 445 for 6 the 1st time, they were then out for 199, Gifford and Birkenshaw each taking 5 wickets in the innings. England scored 386 and 30 for 1 when set to get 259.

For the 2nd successive time a 3-match series between the countries in 1974 ended without a definite result. Pakistan were unbeaten in 17 first-class matches in England and produced some splendid performances, notably in the Oval Test when they amassed a total of 600. A thrilling First Test at Headingley ended disappointingly with no play on the last day. England then needed 44 to win with 4 wickets left. England, out for 183, were 102 behind on 1st innings, but came back by dismissing Pakistan for 179. Needing 282 to win, they were 22 for 2, but mainly through Edrich and Fletcher reached 174 before the 4th wicket fell. Rain leaked through the covers at Lord's and brought an official protest of neglect from the Pakistan authorities. MCC pointed out the difficulties caused by the Lord's slope in bad weather. No play was possible on the last day with England well on top. Pakistan began with 71 for the 1st wicket before the weather changed and they declared at 130 for 9. England were 118 for 6 but the last 4 wickets added 152. Mushtaq resisted for $4\frac{1}{4}$ hours for 76, but Underwood worried all the others, taking 8 for 51 to add to his 5 for 20 in the 1st innings. England needed only 87 to win and made 27 without loss when more rain came. Zaheer played another of his big innings at the Oval, 240 in a total of 600 for 7 declared. He and Mushtaq added 172 for the 3rd wicket. England countered with 545, Amiss (183) and Fletcher (122) being their mainstays. Fletcher's hundred in 7 hours and 40 minutes, was the slowest 100 in first-class matches in England. Only 2 hours remained when the 3rd innings began, Pakistan scoring 94 for 4.

England were vastly superior when Pakistan toured in 1978, winning the 1st 2 Tests with an innings to spare. The Third Test was restricted to little more than 10 hours. At Edgbaston Old took 7 for 50 including 4 wickets in one over and Pakistan were dismissed for 164. With hundreds from Radley and Botham, England led by 288 and despite a good innings by Sadiq, Pakistan again failed, losing by an innings and 57 with a day to spare. Botham accomplished a splendid all-round performance at Lord's where England won by an innings and 120 runs in less than 13 hours' playing time. He scored 108 in the England innings of 364, and in Pakistan's 2nd innings took 8 for 34 in conditions which helped his controlled swing. Willis and Edmonds caused Pakistan's 1st innings failure and they followed on 259 behind. The match at Headingley was ruined by the weather. The valuable Cornhill Insurance patronage of Tests in England began with this series.

ENGLAND V PAKISTAN

			RESULT	CAPTAINS
1954	1 Lord's	Pak 87, 121–3; E 117–9D	Drawn	L. Hutton, A. H. Kardar
	2 Trent Bridge	Pak 157, 272; E 558–6D	E inns 129 runs	D. S. Sheppard, A. H. Kardar
	3 Old Trafford	E 359–8D; Pak 90, 25–4	Drawn	D. S. Sheppard, A. H. Kardar
	4 Oval	Pak 133, 164; E 130, 143	Pak 24 runs	L. Hutton, A. H. Kardar
1961–62	1 Lahore	Pak 387–9D, 200; E 380, 209–5	E 5 wkts	E. R. Dexter, Imtiaz Ahmed
	2 Dacca	Pak 393–7D, 216; E 439, 38–0	Drawn	E. R. Dexter, Imtiaz Ahmed
	3 Karachi	Pak 253, 404–8; E 507	Drawn	E. R. Dexter, Imtiaz Ahmed
1962	1 Edgbaston	E 544–5D; Pak 246, 274	E inns 24 runs	E. R. Dexter, J. Burki
	2 Lord's	Pak 100, 355; E 370, 86–1	E 9 wkts	E. R. Dexter, J. Burki
	3 Headingley	E 428; Pak 131, 180	E inns 117 runs	M. C. Cowdrey, J. Burki
	4 Trent Bridge	E 428–5D; Pak 219, 216–6	Drawn	E. R. Dexter, J. Burki
	5 Oval	E 480–5D, 27–0; Pak 183, 323	E 10 wkts	E. R. Dexter, J. Burki
1967	1 Lord's	E 369, 241–9D; Pak 354, 88–3	Drawn	D. B. Close, Hanif Mohammad
	2 Trent Bridge	Pak 140, 114; E 252–8D, 3–0	E 10 wkts	D. B. Close, Hanif Mohammad
	3 Oval	Pak 216, 255; E 440, 34–2	E 8 wkts	D. B. Close, Hanif Mohammad
1968–69	1 Lahore	E 306, 225–9D; Pak 209, 203–5	Drawn	M. C. Cowdrey, Saeed Ahmed
	2 Dacca	Pak 246, 195–6D; E 274, 33–0	Drawn	M. C. Cowdrey, Saeed Ahmed
	3 Karachi	E 502–7; Pak	Drawn	M. C. Cowdrey, Saeed Ahmed
1971	1 Edgbaston	Pak 608–7D; E 353, 229–5	Drawn	R. Illingworth, Intikhab Alam
	2 Lord's	E 241–2D, 117–0; Pak 148	Drawn	R. Illingworth, Intikhab Alam
	3 Headingley	E 316, 264; Pak 350, 205	E 25 runs	R. Illingworth, Intikhab Alam
1972–73	1 Lahore	E 355, 306–7D; Pak 422, 124–3	Drawn	A. R. Lewis, Majid Khan
	2 Hyderabad	E 487, 218–6; Pak 569–9D	Drawn	A. R. Lewis, Majid Khan
	3 Karachi	Pak 445–6D, 199; E 183, 238–6	Drawn	A. R. Lewis, Majid Khan
1974	1 Headingley	Pak 285, 179; E 183, 238–6	Drawn	M. H. Denness, Intikhab Alam
	2 Lord's	Pak 130–9D, 226; E 270, 27–0	Drawn	M. H. Denness, Intikhab Alam
	3 Oval	Pak 600–7D, 94–4; E 545	Drawn	M. H. Denness, Intikhab Alam
1977–78	1 Lahore	Pak 407–9D, 106–3; E 288	Drawn	J. M. Brearley, Wasim Bari
	2 Hyderabad	Pak 275, 259–4D; E 191, 186–1	Drawn	J. M. Brearley, Wasim Bari
	3 Karachi	E 266, 222–5; Pak 281	Drawn	G. Boycott, Wasim Bari
1978	1 Edgbaston	Pak 164, 231; E 452–8D	E inns 57 runs	J. M. Brearley, Wasim Bari
(CORNHILL	2 Lord's	E 364; Pak 105, 139	E inns 120 runs	J. M. Brearley, Wasim Bari
SERIES)	3 Headingley	Pak 201; E 119–7	Drawn	J. M. Brearley, Wasim Bari

CAPTAINS (England)	TESTS	WON	LOST	DRAWN
L. Hutton	2		1	1
D. S. Sheppard	2	1		1
E. R. Dexter	7	4		3
M. C. Cowdrey	4	1		3
D. B. Close	3	2		1
R. Illingworth	3	1		2
A. R. Lewis	3			3
M. H. Denness	3			3
J. M. Brearley	5	2		3
G. Boycott	1			1
	33	11	1	21

CAPTAINS (Pakistan)	TESTS	WON	LOST	DRAWN
A. H. Kardar	4	1	1	2
Imtiaz Ahmed	3		1	2
J. Burki	5		4	1
Hanif Mohammad	3		2	1
Saees Ahmed	3			3
Intikhab Alam	6		1	5
Majid J. Khan	3			3
Wasim Bari	6		2	4
	33	1	11	21

HIGHEST INNINGS TOTAL

England in England, 558–6D, Trent Bridge 1954
England in Pakistan, 507, Karachi 1961–62
Pakistan in England, 608–7D, Edgbaston 1971
Pakistan in Pakistan, 569–9D, Hyderabad 1972–73

LOWEST INNINGS TOTAL

England in England, 130, Oval 1954
England in Pakistan, 191, Hyderabad 1977–78
Pakistan in England, 87, Lord's 1954
Pakistan in Pakistan, 199, Karachi 1972–73

HIGHEST INDIVIDUAL INNINGS

England in England, 278, D. C. S. Compton, Trent Bridge 1954
England in Pakistan, 205, E. R. Dexter, Karachi 1961–62
Pakistan in England, 274, Zaheer Abbas, Edgbaston 1971
Pakistan in Pakistan, 157, Mushtaq Mohammad, Hyderabad 1972–73

HIGHEST AGGREGATE OF RUNS IN A SERIES

England in England, 453, D. C. S. Compton 1954
England in Pakistan, 406, D. L. Amiss 1972–73
Pakistan in England, 401, Mushtaq Mohammad 1962
Pakistan in Pakistan, 407, Hanif Mohammad 1961–62

BEST INNINGS BOWLING FIGURES

England in England, 8–34, I. T. Botham, Lord's 1978
England in Pakistan, 7–66, P. H. Edmonds, Karachi 1977–78
Pakistan in England, 6–46, Fazal Mahmood, Oval 1954
Pakistan in Pakistan, 6–44, Abdul Qadir, Hyderabad 1977–78

BEST MATCH BOWLING FIGURES

England in England, 13–71, D. L. Underwood, Lord's 1974
England in Pakistan, 8–225, G. A. R. Lock, Dacca 1961–62
Pakistan in England, 12–99, Fazal Mahmood, Oval 1954
Pakistan in Pakistan, 7–181, Intikhab Alam, Hyderabad 1972–73

HIGHEST WICKET AGGREGATE IN A SERIES

England in England, 22, F. S. Trueman 1962
England in Pakistan, 13, D. A. Allen 1961–62
Pakistan in England, 20, Fazal Mahmood 1954
Pakistan in Pakistan, 15, Intikhab Alam 1972–73

RECORD WICKET PARTNERSHIPS – ENGLAND

1 G. Pullar and R. W. Barber, 198, Dacca 1961–62
2 M. C. Cowdrey and E. R. Dexter, 248, Oval 1962
3 K. F. Barrington and T. W. Graveney, 201, Lord's 1967
4 E. R. Dexter and P. H. Parfitt, 188, Karachi 1961–62
5 D. C. S. Compton and T. E. Bailey, 192, Trent Bridge 1954
6 P. H. Parfitt and D. A. Allen, 153*, Edgbaston 1962
7 A. P. E. Knott and P. Lever, 159, Edgbaston 1971

8 P. H. Parfitt and D. A. Allen, 99, Headingley 1962
9 T. W. Graveney and F. S. Trueman, 76, Lord's 1962
10 D. L. Underwood and P. I. Pocock, 55, Hyderabad 1972–73

RECORD WICKET PARTNERSHIPS – PAKISTAN

1 Hanif Mohammad and Alim Uddin, 122, Dacca 1961–62
2 Zaheer Abbas and Mushtaq Mohammad, 291, Edgbaston 1971
3 Mudassar Nazar and Haroon Rashid, 180, Lahore 1977–78
4 Javed Burki and Mushtaq Mohammad, 153, Lahore 1961–62
5 Javed Burki and Nasim-ul-Ghani, 197, Lord's 1962
6 Mushtaq Mohammad and Intikhab Alam, 145, Hyderabad 1972–73
7 Saeed Ahmed and Nasim-ul-Ghani, 51, Trent Bridge 1962
8 Hanif Mohammad and Asif Iqbal, 130, Lord's 1967
9 Asif Iqbal and Intikhab Alam, 190, Oval 1967
10 Sarfraz Nawaz and Asif Masood, 62, Headingley 1974

England v Rest of the World

E. W. SWANTON

One of the consequences of the late cancellation, at the British Government's urgent request, of the South African tour of England in 1970 was that at the last moment the authorities had to face the prospect of a season without a Test series. From several angles such a state of affairs was undesirable. First, MCC were due to fly to Australia in the autumn, and the selectors could only have been handicapped if they had had to choose their team on purely domestic evidence. The loss of revenue from the series and from television was a factor at a time when the finances of cricket had scarcely yet begun to reap great revenue sponsorship. Also the game would have had nothing to put into the shop window, so to speak, against the powerful rivalry of the Football World Cup and then the Commonwealth Games in Edinburgh.

It was in this unique context that the TCCB devised a series of 5 matches between England and the Rest of the World. They found a patron in Guinness, the brewers, prepared to step into the breach. It was announced that England caps would be given and that the matches would be accorded the dignity of unofficial Test status. Within a few weeks a team had been mustered which compared with almost any side ever to have come to England. It included 5 of the South Africans who had been turned back, and about the most formidable 5 at that, Barlow, the brothers Pollock, Procter and Richards; 5 eminent West Indians, whom the counties holding their contracts released as required, Sobers, Gibbs, Lloyd, Kanhai and Murray; Intikhab Alam and Mushtaq from Pakistan; and McKenzie from Australia. There were several other Test cricketers in England who would have been available if required.

Gary Sobers was appointed captain and was given 2 English selectors whose names might be thought a complete guarantee of their disinterested labours, Les Ames and Freddie Brown. From the start this trio were determined that their side would maintain the highest degree of effort associated with Test cricket, and one gathered that before the First Test the captain addressed his team in such a way as to command without further prompting a zest on their part which never slackened. Whether or not it was the cricketers' way of disassociating themselves utterly from politics, the fact was that both Sobers's co-selectors went out of their way to say afterwards that the spirit in the dressing-room of this side of assorted races was as happy as any they had known.

The only thing that was at first a disappointment was the gates. The uncertainty about the South African tour had prevented advance sales. There was a short time only to publicize the matches, while by a malign chance the dates earmarked for the Lord's Test – always the most fruitful by far in cash terms – coincided with the General Election. As it turned out neither Cowdrey nor Boycott wished to be considered for the First Test on grounds of lack of form, while Edrich was hurt. It was thus a singularly weak batting side which confronted the might of the Rest and were brushed aside for 127, wherein the 63 of Illingworth, the captain, stuck out like a ray of light. In the 2nd innings, Illingworth, helped now by d'Oliveira and Luckhurst, did even better, with 94, but in between times the Rest had run up a little matter of 546. Sobers's contribution to the occasion was 8 for 64 in the match and 183 runs.

The change of fortune after England had been beaten by an innings and 80 was a surprise of the first order. After the 1st 3 innings had been level-pegging with scores a little under 300 each, England at Trent Bridge made 284 for 2 to win the match thanks to a determined 113 by Luckhurst, well supported by Cowdrey and Fletcher. Yet it was Illingworth who had previously held the side together with 97. Greig in his 1st Test took 7 wickets.

Only 16,000 saw this admirable English performance, after which the gates picked up to 30,000 at Edgbaston. 43,500 at Headingley, and rather more at the Oval, so that apart from other considerations the venture made a profit of £43,000. While there was no doubting which was the stronger side there was nothing to be in the least ashamed of in England's last 3 performances, the Rest having to make 141 for 5 to win the Third Test, 226 for 8 the Fourth, and 287 for 6 the Fifth. Both these last 2 games might have gone the other way, and the England selectors must have emerged in the knowledge of a well-knit, well-led side – this whether for the Australian tour they went back to Cowdrey, the senior man, or stuck (as they did) to Illingworth, who had certainly repaid their trust with a vengeance. Not often has England been called upon to cope with a batting order of such a calibre, reading from 1 to 7: Barlow, B. A. Richards, Kanhai, R. G. Pollock, Lloyd, Sobers and Procter.

Since 1970 there has been much unseemly and surely small-minded squabbling over the status of this series, organized as

The Rest of the World team, which played a series of 5 Tests against England in 1970. Back row: Basharat Hassan (Kenya), Intikhab Alam (Pakistan), M. J. Procter (South Africa), R. G. Pollock (South Africa), C. H. Lloyd (West Indies), G. D. McKenzie (Australia), B. A. Richards (South Africa) and F. M. Engineer (India); sitting: R. B. Kanhai (West indies), E. J. Barlow (South Africa), G. S. Sobers (captain, West Indies) and L. R. Gibbs (West Indies).

These two great left-handers, Gary Sobers and Graeme Pollock, have just scored 88 in an hour together for the Rest of the World against England in the Fifth Test at the Oval.

has been described and contested with the utmost rigour as well as a higher level of skill than had been seen, save perhaps from such sides as the 1948 Australians or the West Indies of 1963. *Wisden* has very properly given the individual figures separately as befits a one-off occasion belonging to no regular series. Certain countries have persuaded a majority of the ICC to declare that the games should not rate as Tests – to which the polite answer is that they remain, as they were billed originally, *unofficial* Tests.

TESTS	WON BY ENGLAND	WON BY REST	DRAWN
5	1	4	–

HIGHEST INNINGS TOTAL
England, 409, Edgbaston
Rest of the World, 563–9D, Edgbaston

LOWEST INNINGS TOTAL
England, 127, Lord's
Rest of the World, 276, Trent Bridge

HIGHEST INDIVIDUAL INNINGS
England, 157, G. Boycott, Oval
Rest of the World, 183, G. S. Sobers, Lord's

HIGHEST AGGREGATE OF RUNS IN THE SERIES
England, 476, R. Illingworth
Rest of the World, 588, G. S. Sobers

BEST INNINGS BOWLING FIGURES
England, 7–83, P. Lever, Oval
Rest of the World, 7–64, E. J. Barlow, Headingley

BEST MATCH BOWLING FIGURES
England, 7–106, B. L. d'Oliveira, Trent Bridge
Rest of the World, 12–142, E. J. Barlow, Headingley

HIGHEST WICKET AGGREGATE IN THE SERIES
England, 19, J. A. Snow
Rest of the World, 21, G. S. Sobers

India v Pakistan

REX ALSTON AND D. J. RUTNAGUR

Pakistan opened her career as the youngest member of the Imperial Cricket Conference by touring India in 1952, and although winning only 1 of the 5 Tests and drawing 2, her performances showed considerable promise for the future. The leading batsmen were Nazar and the 17-year-old Hanif, whilst Waqar Hassan proved steady in a crisis and scored the most runs – 357. Pakistan's most successful bowlers were Fazal and Mahmood Hussain, both fast-medium. India had many more experienced players, including V. S. Hazare and P. R. Umrigar, and though their seam bowlers were not of the same class as Fazal and Mahmood, their spin bowlers V. Mankad, S. P. Gupte and Ghulam Ahmed were vastly superior.

India won the First Test at New Delhi by an innings and 70 runs. Having made 372, with top scores from H. R. Adhikari, not out 81, and Hazare, 76, they bowled out Pakistan for 150 and 152. Only Hanif reached 50 in either innings, the Pakistan batsmen being quite unable to cope with Mankad, who took 13 wickets for 131.

Pakistan had their revenge in the Second Test at Lucknow, winning by an innings and 43 runs. Hazare, Adhikari and Mankad could not play, and India were bowled out for 106, Fazal taking 5 for 52. Pakistan then made 331, Nazar carrying his bat for 124. In their 2nd innings L. Amarnath defended stoutly, but Fazal (7 for 42) won the match with a fine display of accurate bowling. Three weeks later the teams met again at Bombay, and this time India won by 10 wickets. A. H. Kardar, the Pakistan captain, won the toss for the 1st time and batted, though sun following early morning dew made the wicket awkward. Pakistan lost their 1st 6 wickets for 60 before a determined partnership between Waqar and Fazal added 83, and they finally totalled 186.

Amarnath, medium-pace, and Mankad took 7 wickets between them, and leg-spinner S. P. Gupte took the last 2. India then made 387 for 4 declared, a partnership of 183 for the 4th wicket between Hazare (not out 146) and Umrigar (102) completely dominating the Pakistan bowlers. Pakistan did better in their 2nd innings, Hanif making 96 of a total of 242. Mankad took 5 for 72, and India easily scored the 42 needed for victory. The Fourth Test at Madras was drawn, rain preventing any play on the last 2 days. This was unfortunate for Pakistan who made 344 and had taken 6 Indian wickets for 175 when the rain intervened. Kardar played a captain's innings of 79 and had excellent support from Zulfiqar (63 not out), the latter, with Amir Elahi (47), putting on 104 for the last wicket. For India, Umrigar made 62.

Pakistan had to win the Fifth Test at Calcutta to share the rubber and they made a fine start, Nazar and Hanif putting on 94 for the 1st wicket, after having been sent in to bat. But only Imtiaz consolidated this advantage and Pakistan were all out for 257. India then batted remarkably consistently, everyone reaching double figures, and D. H. Shodhan (No. 8) making 110. They were finally all out for 397, Mahmood and Fazal taking 7 wickets between them. In their 2nd innings, Pakistan, 140 behind, had lost 4 wickets before clearing off the deficit, but a stubborn innings of 97 by Waqar, supported by Fazal saved the day. They were able to make a token declaration at 236 for 7, after which India made 28 for no wicket.

Two years later in 1954–55 India became the first visiting side to tour Pakistan, but unfortunately both sides concentrated so sternly on avoiding defeat that all 5 Test Matches were drawn. Such a state of affairs had never happened in cricket before. So defensive was the batting and so negative the bowling to deep

'Polly' Umrigar's 12 Test hundreds for India include 5 against Pakistan. He has also been a popular team manager.

set fields that throughout the series barely 30 runs were scored in the hour. The Pakistan fast–medium bowlers Khan, Fazal and Mahmood took 51 of the 58 wickets which fell to the bowlers, whereas once more India relied largely on spinners Gupte and Mankad, their captain. The leading batsmen for Pakistan were Alim-ud-Din and Hanif; for India, Umrigar and V. L. Manjrekar. Kardar won the toss for Pakistan in 4 matches and each time they led on the first innings, but the teams were so evenly matched that the advantage counted for little.

In the First Test at Dacca, Pakistan made 257 and India replied with 148. Pakistan's 2nd innings realized 158, but India had no difficulty in saving the day, P. Roy and Manjrekar putting on 130 for the 3rd wicket before stumps were drawn. The Second Test took place at Bahawalpur, and the scoring was so slow that not even 3 innings were completed. India made 235 and Pakistan replied with 312 for 9 declared, Hanif (142) and Alim putting on 127 for the 1st wicket. In their second innings India scored 209 for 5, Roy making 77 and Manjrekar 59. Could dullness go further?

Well, the Third Test was played at Lahore, and Pakistan led by 77 on the 1st innings after a typically unenterprising display by both sides. The middle order Pakistanis, Maqsood (99), Kardar, Wazir and Imtiaz, batted steadily. For India Umrigar was top scorer with 78. Pakistan declared their 2nd innings closed with 5 down for 136, and India replied with 74 for 2. The scoring in the Fourth Test at Peshawar was slower than ever, only 638 being scored in 4 days. Pakistan made 188 and 182, whilst India, thanks to a hundred by Umrigar, made 245 and 23 for 1. Any hopes of a result in the Fifth Test at Karachi were abandoned when a heavy thunderstorm stopped play on the third day. Pakistan (162) led India (145) by 17 runs. A more determined effort in their 2nd innings enabled Pakistan to declare with 5 wickets down for 241, Alim scoring 103 not out and Kardar 93, and India then made 69 for 2. So the sterile saga ground to a close.

Pakistan made their 2nd tour of India in 1960–61 and 5 more were added to the 7 consecutive draws which the 2 countries had already played. Fazal Mahmood, the Pakistan captain, won the toss and batted 1st in the 1st 4 Tests. Pakistan, therefore, were able to control the tempo and style of play, but they again appeared more intent on avoiding defeat than in taking risks for victory. India were willing collaborators in this policy, and the result was another tedious series in which Pakistan averaged 35 per hundred balls and India 39. So slow was the play that on only 11 out of 25 days were 200 runs or more scored. Nine hundreds were made in the series, Saeed (2), Hanif, Mushtaq and Imtiaz for Pakistan, and Umrigar (3) and Borde for India. In the First Test at Bombay, Pakistan made 350, Hanif (160) and Saeed (121) putting on 246 for the 2nd wicket. India replied with 449 for 9 declared, Manjrekar, Desai and Contractor being the chief contributors. In their 2nd innings Pakistan made 166 for 4. In the Second Test at Kanpur Pakistan made 335, but again India took the lead, Umrigar making 115 and M. L. Jaisimha 99 out of a total of 404. Pakistan then played out time with 140 for 3.

In the Third Test at Calcutta rain helped towards the 3rd stalemate, but Pakistan were on top for most of the game. Having scored 301 in their 1st innings, Fazal (5 for 26) bowled India out for 180. Pakistan then made 146 for 3 declared but India had no difficulty in saving the game, scoring 127 for 4. The Fourth Test at Madras saw Pakistan make their biggest total of the tour, 448 for 8 declared, of which Imtiaz made 135 and Saeed 103. But again India went one better, making 539 for 9 declared, Borde making 177 not out, Umrigar 117 and Contractor 81. Pakistan then made 59 for no wicket.

At last in the Fifth Test at New Delhi India batted first, Umrigar (112) and Contractor (92) being the chief contributors to a total of 463. Pakistan replied with 286, Mushtaq making 101. For the first time in the series the follow-on was enforced, and India might well have won but for a last-wicket stand of 38 between Mahmood and Mohammad Farooq. India then scored 16 for no wicket in the 4th innings, a mere 58 runs from glory.

Two wars and the resulting acrimony kept the two neighbouring countries from playing each other again for 17 years. Their rivalry was resumed in 1978 with a 3-Test series in which Pakistan proved vastly superior. The opening Test, played on a bland, bald pitch at Faisalabad, produced a high-scoring draw. Zaheer Abbas and Javed Miandad made 176 and 154, respectively, for Pakistan in a total of 503 for 8 declared, to which India replied with 462 for 9 declared, including 145 by Viswanath. The match was almost 4 days old before the 2nd innings began and the outcome, inevitably, was a draw, the 13th in consecutive matches between India and Pakistan. Asif Iqbal added himself to the list of century-makers before the match petered out.

Pakistan had India's strengths and weaknesses sized up during the First Test and ruthlessly exploited their shortcomings in the next 2, both of which they won by 8 wickets. In both instances, they had to chase runs at breakneck speed in the final innings, but the margin left no doubt that Pakistan were stronger in every department of the game. For the Second Test at Lahore, the pitch was the fastest and greenest ever seen in Pakistan. India were put in and bundled out for

Zaheer Abbas and Asif Iqbal run for cover after Pakistan's 8-wicket victory over India at Lahore in 1978. This was the 1st Test series between them since 1961, and the 1st result following 13 successive draws.

199, with Imran Khan and Sarfraz Nawaz taking 4 wickets apiece. Pakistan replied with 539 for 6 declared, including an unbeaten 235 not out by Zaheer Abbas. India started off with an opening partnership of 192 by Gavaskar and Chauhan, and made a huge score in the 2nd innings, but they could not prolong their resistance long enough to foil Pakistan, an inspired, highly-professional team.

In the final Test at Karachi, Pakistan had a more daunting chase. They required 164 in the final 95 minutes and got home by dint of a spectacular partnership of 97 between Asif Iqbal and Javed Miandad and a volatile 31 not out by Imran. For India, Gavaskar made a hundred in each innings, but without avail. Again, India were undermined by the pace of Imran and Sarfraz, who bowled more than their fair share of short-pitched deliveries. By the standards he had set up in the 2 previous Tests (176, 96, 235 not out, 34 not out), Zaheer Abbas had a lean match, scoring only 42, but Miandad made a hundred in Pakistan's 1st innings of 481 for 9 declared.

INDIA V PAKISTAN

			RESULT	CAPTAINS
1952–53	1 New Delhi	Ind 372; Pak 150, 152	Ind Inns 70 runs	L. Amarnath, A. H. Kardar
	2 Lucknow	Ind 106, 182; Pak 331	Pak Inns 43 runs	L. Amarnath, A. H. Kardar
	3 Bombay	Pak 186, 242; Ind 387–4D, 45–0	Ind 10 wkts	L. Amarnath, A. H. Kardar
	4 Madras	Pak 344; Ind 175–6	Drawn	L. Amarnath, A. H. Kardar
	5 Calcutta	Pak 257, 236–7D; Ind 397, 28–0	Drawn	L. Amarnath, A. H. Kardar
1954–55	1 Dacca	Pak 257, 158; Ind 148, 147–2	Drawn	V. Mankad, A. H. Kardar
	2 Bahawalpur	Ind 235, 209–5; Pak 312–9D	Drawn	V. Mankad, A. H. Kardar
	3 Lahore	Pak 328, 136–5D; Ind 251, 74–2	Drawn	V. Mankad, A. H. Kardar
	4 Peshawar	Pak 188, 182; Ind 245, 23–1	Drawn	V. Mankad, A. H. Kardar
	5 Karachi	Pak 162, 241–5D; Ind 145, 69–2	Drawn	V. Mankad, A. H. Kardar
1960–61	1 Bombay	Pak 350, 166–4; Ind 449–9D	Drawn	N. J. Contractor, Fazal Mahmood
	2 Kanpur	Pak 335, 140–3; Ind 404	Drawn	N. J. Contractor, Fazal Mahmood
	3 Calcutta	Pak 301, 146–3D; Ind 180, 127–4	Drawn	N. J. Contractor, Fazal Mahmood
	4 Madras	Pak 448–8D, 59–0; Ind 539–9D	Drawn	N. J. Contractor, Fazal Mahmood
	5 New Delhi	Ind 463, 16–0; Pak 286, 250	Drawn	N. J. Contractor, Fazal Mahmood
1978–79	1 Faisalabad	Pak 503–8D, 264–4D; Ind 462–9D, 43–0	Drawn	B. S. Bedi, Mushtaq Mohammad
	2 Lahore	Ind 199, 465; Pak 539–6D, 128–2	Pak 8 wkts	B. S. Bedi, Mushtaq Mohammad
	3 Karachi	Ind 344, 300; Pak 481–9D, 164–2	Pak 8 wkts	B. S. Bedi, Mushtaq Mohammad

CAPTAINS (India)	TESTS	WON	LOST	DRAWN
L. Amarnath	5	2	1	2
V. Mankad	5			5
N. J. Contractor	5			5
B. S. Bedi	3		2	1
	18	2	3	13

CAPTAINS (Pakistan)	TESTS	WON	LOST	DRAWN
A. H. Kardar	10	1	2	7
Fazal Mahmood	5			5
Mushtaq Mohammad	3	2		1
	18	3	2	13

HIGHEST INNINGS TOTAL

India in India, 539–9D, Madras 1960–61
India in Pakistan, 465, Lahore 1978–79
Pakistan in India, 448–8D, Madras 1960–61
Pakistan in Pakistan, 539–6D, Lahore 1978–79

LOWEST INNINGS TOTAL

India in India, 106, Lucknow 1952–53
India in Pakistan, 145, Karachi 1954–55
Pakistan in India, 150, Delhi 1952–53
Pakistan in Pakistan, 158, Dacca 1954–55

HIGHEST INDIVIDUAL INNINGS

India in India, 177*, C. G. Borde, Madras 1960–61
India in Pakistan, 145, G. R. Viswanath, Faisalabad 1978–79
Pakistan in India, 160, Hanif Mohammad, Bombay 1960–61
Pakistan in Pakistan, 235*, Zaheer Abbas, Lahore 1978–79

HIGHEST AGGREGATE OF RUNS IN A SERIES

India in India, 382, P. R. Umrigar 1960–61
India in Pakistan, 447, S. M. Gavaskar 1978–79
Pakistan in India, 460, Saeed Ahmed 1960–61
Pakistan in Pakistan, 583, Zaheer Abbas 1978–79

BEST INNINGS BOWLING FIGURES

India in India, 8–52, V. Mankad, Delhi 1952–53
India in Pakistan, 6–49, G. S. Ramchand, Karachi 1954–55
Pakistan in India, 7–42, Fazal Mahmood, Lucknow 1952–53
Pakistan in Pakistan, 6–67, Mahmood Hussain, Dacca 1954–55

BEST MATCH BOWLING FIGURES

India in India, 13–131, V. Mankad, Delhi 1952–53
India in Pakistan, 7–76, G. S. Ramchand, Karachi 1954–55
Pakistan in India, 12–94, Fazal Mahmood, Lucknow 1952–53
Pakistan in Pakistan, 9–159, Sarfraz Nawaz, Karachi 1978–79

HIGHEST WICKET AGGREGATE IN A SERIES

India in India, 25, V. Mankad 1952–53
India in Pakistan, 21, S. P. Gupte 1954–55
Pakistan in India, 20, Fazal Mahmood 1952–53
Pakistan in Pakistan, 22, Khan Mohammad 1954–55

RECORD WICKET PARTNERSHIPS—INDIA

1 S. M. Gavaskar and C. P. S. Chauhan, 192, Lahore 1978–79
2 S. M. Gavaskar and M. Amarnath, 117, Karachi 1978–79
3 P. Roy and V. L. Manjrekar, 130*, Dacca 1954–55
4 V. S. Hazare and P. R. Umrigar, 183, Bombay 1952–53
5 P. R. Umrigar and C. G. Borde, 177, Madras 1960–61
6 C. G. Borde and R. G. Nadkarni, 82, Bombay 1960–61
7 D. G. Phadkar and D. H. Shodhan, 86, Calcutta 1952–53
8 K. D. Ghavri and Kapil Dev, 84, Karachi 1978–79
9 P. G. Joshi and R. B. Desai, 149, Bombay 1960–61
10 H. R. Adhikari and Ghulam Ahmed, 109, Delhi 1952–53

RECORD WICKET PARTNERSHIPS—PAKISTAN

1 Hanif Mohammad and Imtiaz Ahmed, 162, Madras 1960–61
2 Hanif Mohammad and Saeed Ahmed, 246, Bombay 1960–61
3 Zaheer Abbas and Asif Iqbal, 166, Faisalabad 1978–79
4 Zaheer Abbas and Javed Miandad, 255, Faisalabad 1978–79
5 Alim Uddin and A. H. Kardar, 155, Karachi 1954–55
6 Zaheer Abbas and Mushtaq Mohammad, 169, Lahore 1978–79
7 Mushtaq Mohammad and Intikhab Alam, 88, Calcutta 1961–62
8 Nazar Mohammad and Zulfiqar Ahmed, 63, Lucknow 1952–53
9 Mushtaq Mohammad and Iqbal Qasim, 39, Karachi 1978–79
10 Zulfiqar Ahmed and Amir Ilahi, 104, Madras 1952–53

International Cricket Conference

H. S. ALTHAM AND E. W. SWANTON

The first meeting of the then Imperial Cricket Conference took place at Lord's on 15 July 1909, and to it there was an interesting and little known background. In December 1907, MCC had received a letter from Sir (then Mr) Abe Bailey of South Africa, suggesting a scheme for an 'Imperial Cricket Contest', to be staged in England during the summer of 1909 between that country, his own and Australia. It took Australia and the countries a while to digest this imaginative idea. However, a year later the Secretary of MCC was instructed to prepare the way for a meeting in the following summer of a British Colonial Cricket Conference to discuss arrangements under which matches between England, Australia and South Africa might be held, each country to nominate two representatives, and the chair to be taken by the President of MCC.

It is not known whether the secretary substituted 'Imperial' for 'British Colonial' in the official invitation, or whether the body so rechristened itself, but it was under this historic title that the minutes record its first 2 meetings on 15 and 20 July 1909. The chair at the first was taken by Lord Chesterfield, the MCC President, but at the second by Lord Harris, deputizing for him. Australia was represented by Mr P. A. McAlister and Mr L. O. S. Poidevin, and South Africa by Mr G. W. Hillyard at the 1st and by Mr Abe Bailey at the 2nd, supported in each case by Mr H. D. G. Leveson Gower. At these meetings the principle of triangular contests was approved; also that one should be staged in 1912, and that the term 'Test Matches' should be confined to games between the 3 countries concerned. Agreement was also reached on the machinery for the appointment of umpires, the hours of play and the principles of qualification – birth, or continuous residence in a country for 4 years, provided that no man who had represented one country should ever play for another without the former's consent.

Nothing more of importance is recorded until the 2 meetings in 1912: at the first of these, in April, it was agreed that visiting teams should receive half the gross gate admissions, *i.e.* 1s per head, and a panel of 6 named umpires for the 9 Tests was accepted. At the second Australia opposed the continuation of 'Triangular Tests'; it is well to remember in this context that, owing to internal dissensions, their touring side was very far from representative, the weather very poor, and the gates disappointing, especially in the Tests between the visiting sides.

Little can the representatives who attended this important meeting in 1912 have imagined that more than 50 years would pass before any renewal of such a Triangular Contest on a Test Match level was again considered, and that it would even be 9 years before the Conference itself met again. When it did, in June 1921, the chair was taken again by Lord Harris, whose long experience and wise counsel never failed to command respect; Sydney Smith, destined to become the doyen of Australian administrators, then first represented that country; P. F. Warner and H. D. G. Leveson Gower South Africa, and W. Morrison attended on behalf of Jamaica. The only outstanding business recorded in the 2 meetings that year was an agreement on the 8-ball over as operative in Australia only, and a request from South Africa that consideration should be given to playing Test Matches in England to a finish.

Much more surprising than this 9-year war gap were the 5 blank years that followed before, in 1926, the Conference met again. But when it did, its coverage had been substantially widened, with representatives welcomed from the West Indies, India and New Zealand, the latter led by Sir (then Mr) Arthur Sims, to whom his country's cricket was to owe so much for so long. Again there were 2 meetings in which the main decisions were that 'MCC may of its own initiative, and shall on request of any two Governing Bodies, summon a meeting of the Conference', and that Governing Bodies should be entitled to send two representatives.

At their next meeting, in 1929, the Conference expressed the hope that the preparation of turf wickets would be extended in all countries where climate and conditions permitted; a proposal by Australia that in any series in which either side after 4 Test Matches only led by 1, the final game should be played to a finish, was defeated and a project aired for a double visit by New Zealand and India in 1931, each side to meet an 'England XI and each other'. In 1930 the 'larger wicket' was accepted. England proposed, but unavailingly, a time limit for Test Matches in Australia. Though the Conference was now meeting yearly, its business was confined to such routine matters as the programme for future tours, until in 1934, under the Presidency of Lord Cromer, it tackled the formidable aftermath of the 'Body-line' tour of 1932–33, and unanimously passed the following resolution:

> That this Conference affirms the principle laid down by MCC that any form of bowling which is obviously a direct attack on the batsman would be an offence against the spirit of the game. It is further of opinion that the controlling Bodies of cricket should not promote or countenance such forms of bowling.

Two years later (1936) all countries accepted the new 'experimental' lbw law, and Lord Cobham, presiding for MCC, felt obliged to warn the other delegates of the strain imposed upon England's players by the ever-increasing programme of tours.

The first major issue after the war arose in 1948 following Pakistan's decision to set up its own Board of Control: it was agreed that India by herself should remain a member 'provisionally for 2 years', and the hope was expressed that she might be able to organize a combined team representing both countries. Two years later her 'official membership' was unanimously confirmed, and in 1952 on her proposal, seconded by MCC, Pakistan was invited to join the Conference.

In 1956 a proposal was tabled to substitute the word 'Commonwealth' for 'Imperial' in the title of the Conference: in a free-spoken but friendly discussion opinion on this was found to be divided, and in the end no vote was taken. But 2 years later an important constitutional decision was reached. In 1930 the Conference had agreed that England, Australia and South Africa should each have 2 votes, and other members 1. In 1950 a proposal by the West Indies for equal voting powers met with no support, and in 1952 a similar proposal by India had been resisted; but in 1958, on the motion of South Africa, agreement was reached that in future each member should have 1 vote but that 'no alteration or addition to the rules of the Conference should be made except by a majority vote which must carry the support of 2 "Foundation Members"'. The same year saw the first discussion of what was to prove an increasingly urgent problem, the writing or broadcasting by players about tours upon which they were, or had recently been, engaged. It was agreed that a uniform ruling might be difficult, but that representatives should stress to their Boards the dangers they saw in irresponsible and sensational reporting.

In welcoming the delegates to Lord's in 1959 on the occasion of the 50th anniversary of the first Conference, the President of MCC, from the chair, expressed his conviction, warmly endorsed by all present, that its meetings had served not only to promote the welfare of cricket, but to strengthen the fellowship of the Commonwealth. Two problems that were to confront them in that year and in those that have followed were both put to the test.

In 1960 all countries supported the 'playing regulations' current in England to stop 'time wasting', and in 1961 the Conference agreed that some form of limitation in the number of leg-side fielders was in principle desirable for the reason that 'it would discourage "bouncers", and make for better and brighter cricket'; but when in 1963 this was again debated, the West Indies found themselves unable to support such legislation. At the same meeting the majority of delegates expressed themselves in favour of the complete covering of wickets, but agreed that the decision should always rest with the home country; Mr (later Sir) Frank Worrell broke new and interesting ground with his suggestion that consideration should be given to limiting the length of a bowler's run. MCC were also asked to examine, especially in its financial implications, a proposal from Pakistan for the foundation of a Junior Section of the ICC to help the game in minor cricket countries not necessarily confined to the Commonwealth. This, it was felt, might best be done on a zonal basis, but though all countries were sympathetic to the aim, several felt that their administrative responsibilities were already as heavy as they could expect to carry.

These, however, were issues of but minor importance compared with two with which the Conference in the years 1959–1963 found itself primarily occupied. The first of these concerned Law 26 in its two aspects of 'drag' and 'throwing'. At the 1959 Conference MCC expressed their concern at the increasing violation of the law by drag, and their hope that all countries would consider carrying out experiments in terms of the front foot landing behind the popping crease. To this all except Australia expressed support. Next year, after a long debate, it was unanimously agreed that all countries should consider the adoption of the front-foot principle as an experiment starting not before September 1962. When this was again debated in that year Australia and the West Indies were still sceptical, but it was hoped that all Boards would begin to experiment not later than 1963–64.

If the problem of drag had thus been recognized as of importance, that of 'throwing' was at once more vital and potentially explosive. It had first been raised at the 1959 Conference by G. O. Allen. MCC, he then stated, had in the spring of 1958 warned all English first-class umpires of the growing number of what they considered to be suspect actions, but no bowler had in fact been called that season. A year later, on the initiative of MCC, endorsed by the Advisory CCC, the umpires had agreed on a list of bowlers whose action they considered doubtful, and these names were passed confidentially to the countries concerned who undertook to warn the bowlers. The umpires had been unanimous that the law, as it stood, was clear and had accepted the urgent duty of calling any action with which they were not 'perfectly satisfied', whether the bowler concerned had been 'listed' or not. Mr A. H. Coy, South Africa, emphasized the danger of schoolboys imitating suspect actions, and the Conference unanimously agreed that each country should do everything possible to eliminate throwing from the game.

When the debate was resumed a year later, it was in a tension initiated by the considerable Press comment on the action of some Australian bowlers during the MCC tour there in the preceding winter, complicated by the disputed evidence of the high-speed camera, and brought to a climax by the no-balling of the South African, Griffin, in the recent Lord's Test in June. With a number of overseas delegates flying over especially for it, this Conference of 1960 was unprecedentedly representative, including as it did the Presidents of the Boards of Australia, South Africa and the West Indies, reinforced by Sir Donald Bradman, HH the Gaekwar of Baroda, for India, and the High Commissioner for Pakistan. At the end of a long discussion, animated but basically co-operative and free from rancour, the Conference unanimously reaffirmed their determination to eliminate throwing from the game, and accepted the following experimental definition of a throw:

The 1960 meeting, which thrashed out the great throwing controversy, was the most momentous in the history of what was still called the Imperial Cricket Conference. Its chairman was H. S. Altham, the reigning president of MCC, seen here in a relaxed moment with Sir Donald Bradman and G. O. Allen on his left, G. W. A. Chubb and R. E. Foster Bowley, the South African representatives, on his right.

> A ball shall be deemed to have been thrown if, in the opinion of either umpire, the bowling arm, having been bent at the elbow, whether the wrist is backward of the elbow or not, is suddenly straightened immediately prior to the instant of delivery. The bowler shall, nevertheless, be at liberty to use the wrist freely in the delivery action.

That winter agreement was reached between MCC and Australia on a 'moratorium' in which English umpires were instructed not to 'call', prior to the First Test Match in 1961, any Australian bowler about whose delivery they were not happy, but to report it to MCC and the Australian team manager.

Overlapping the issues of Law 26 the Conference found themselves in 1961 facing a very different and much wider problem. By the South African Government's decision, taken on 31 May, to withdraw from the Commonwealth, that country had, by constitution, ceased to be a member of the Imperial Conference; they were, however, by general consent represented at this meeting by an 'observer', R. E. Foster Bowley. In a written statement, read by the chairman, Mr Foster Bowley emphasized that though his Association considered it unwise for fear of political repercussions in their own country to support inter-racial games there, there was no question in their own constitution of any colour bar, and they would welcome invitations to tour in India, Pakistan and the West Indies. In the discussions that followed, and that were resumed in the next 2 years, it became clear that no such invitations could in existing circumstances be expected, and that the countries concerned felt that South Africa's claim to equal treatment in a programme of future tours should be reconsidered. At the same time delegates fully supported the view expressed by the MCC President, Sir William Worsley, that their supreme concern must be with the welfare of cricket wherever it was played, and that it was, and should remain, open to any member country to visit or receive visits from any other country they liked.

To some extent associated with South Africa's changed status, but certainly stimulated by the sensational cricket of their Australian and English visits, came a request from the West Indies to the 1963 Conference for a reconsideration of the accepted tour programme with a view to their returning to England before 1971. MCC gave assurance that they would be happy to receive more frequent visits from all countries, but saw the only possibility of this to lie in some system of doubled tours: the Conference unanimously asked MCC to examine such a scheme, especially in its financial implications, and submit a memorandum to all countries. This they did, and their proposals were accepted by all countries to cover the experimental period of 1965 to 1968. Under these, there would be 2 double tours, South Africa and New Zealand visiting England in 1965, and India and Pakistan in 1967; each would play 3 Test Matches, one of them at Lord's, and 14 other 3-day matches. Australia's regular full season visits would not be affected.

Such, in necessarily very compressed outline, is the story of the Imperial Cricket Conference for the early period of its history. But when much of its detail is forgotten, those privileged to attend it will surely remember the spirit which has consistently prevailed at its debates. Inevitably there have been differences of domestic angle, and outspoken expressions of opposing views, but always underlying them there has been a singleness of basic purpose, the welfare of cricket and a feeling of essential unity, strengthened by many personal friendships, and tested and cemented over the passing years. Of that unity there is, hard by the committee-room at Lord's in which the Conference always meets, a visible and lasting symbol in the Memorial Gallery dedicated to all cricketers who gave their lives in the 2 World Wars, and enriched by the gifts of pictures of cricket grounds from almost every country in which the game is played.

Until the eruption of the Packer affair on a shocked and startled cricket world in 1977, the most important of the ICC's activities between 1965 and 1980 were the admission of associate members, thus broadening the Conference to admit any country where cricket is fully established, and the setting-up of the World Cups of 1975 and 1979. The former decision involved a change of title which was, in any event, overdue. Since entry was by no means to be confined to countries within the Commonwealth the obvious manoeuvre was to replace the word 'Imperial' with 'International'. This occurred at the 1965 meeting under the chairmanship of R. H. Twining, the first elections being of the United States, Ceylon and Fiji. The healthy expansion of the associate idea, which culminated in the participation of most of the associates in 1979 in their own preliminary competition to decide which two should join the 6 Test-playing countries in the Prudential Cup proper, will assuredly be followed up when the next World Cup comes round though whether the associates trust another English May, which this first time was horridly cold and wet, or whether they find another earlier venue in the sun, is always likely to be a matter of debate. The growth of the associate membership idea is described by Philip Snow in the continuation of this article. He represented Fiji, one of the original trio, along with John Marder and Gamini Goonesena.

An item from the 1966 meeting, and a follow-up 2 years later, illustrates well enough the limitations implicit in ICC being in essence a consultative body. It meets normally only once a year, and recommendations by one country can merely be passed on for consideration to their home authority, with no great likelihood of any unanimity of view. It was in 1963 that Frank Worrell, at that time captain of the West Indies whose fast bowlers, like those elsewhere in the world, were taking an inordinate time to bowl an over, suggested that consideration should be given to limiting the length of the bowler's run-up. Not till 1966 did ICC announce that there was 'no support for limiting the run-up'. The following year, by which time Worrell was dead, the delegates agreed to continue to encourage young bowlers to limit their run-up so that eventually this would be general, and no legislation would be necessary. The effect of this pious hope, as was to be expected, was precisely nil. The report of the ICC meeting of 1967 sounds a plaintive note which still echoes down the years:

> Finally the Conference decided that representatives should convey to their boards the view that delegates should be given the power to make decisions and not to be compelled to refer back recommendations to their boards.

The truth is that no ruling body is anxious to dilute its own autonomy save perhaps when an issue of the gravity of the WSC incursion demands a unified stand, and even then a solid front cannot be guaranteed, as will be seen.

Year after year the Conference exercised itself over such matters as the definition of a throw, the over-use of the pads,

Lord's 1971. One of the first ICC meetings after the decision to elect Associate Members.
Standing: S. C. Griffith (Secretary MCC), H. Grijseels (Holland), D. G. Steptoe (Denmark), E. W. Miles (Ceylon), T. A. Pearce (Hong Kong), C. O. Oates (East Africa), Masud Salahuddin (Pakistan), D. King (Canada), P. A. Snow (Fiji), J. R. Gardiner (U.S.A.), Prof M. V. Chandgadkar (India), C. G. A. Paris (United Kingdom), D. G. Clark (New Zealand).
Sitting: F. R. Brown (President Designate of MCC), T. N. Pearce (West Indies), I. A. Khan (Pakistan), B. A. Barnett (Australia), Sir Cyril Hawker (President of MCC), A. N. Ghose (India), Sir Denis Blundell (New Zealand), G. O. Allen (United Kingdom), P. D. B. Short (West Indies).

the front foot experiment as the antidote to 'drag', and, not least, the over-use of the bouncer, less politely defined as intimidation. But unanimity was hard to come by. The limitation of leg-side fielders to 5 has long been advocated by Australia, with some support from New Zealand, the clear object being to rectify the balance as between leg-side and off-side play. But this has never got through, though the new Law provides that no more than 2 fielders shall station themselves behind the popping-crease on the leg-side.

In 1970 a move to vary the venue of the Conference was discussed and defeated, and a motion unanimously passed expressing gratitude to MCC for its immense service to cricket. As always, therefore, MCC continue to provide the President of the day as Chairman of the ICC, the Secretariat to administer it, and Lord's pavilion to house it.

The possibility of South Africa being readmitted to the Conference has been regularly discussed in view of steps being taken in that country to integrate their cricketers of all races, both on the field and off. It was decided in 1978 (by 13 votes to 7 with 2 abstentions) that a fact-finding delegation from ICC should examine the situation in South Africa under the aegis of the new multi-racial South African Cricket Union. It returned giving an encouraging picture, but ICC contented itself with 'noting' the report.

The activities of the ICC which resulted in the litigation of the autumn of 1977, wherein the Judge ruled against the governing bodies imposing a ban on the Packer players on the grounds of 'restraint of trade', is covered in the article on WSC cricket (*qv*). On the face of it, both the ICC and TCCB were badly advised, and the result put these bodies both financially and morally at a serious disadvantage.

In the 2 Australian winters following the High Court judgment the chairmen of the ICC, David Clark in 1977–78, and Charles Palmer following, travelled far and wide to maintain contact with all the member-countries in the effort to find a practical formula for bringing to a close a confrontation primarily concerning the Australian Cricket Board and their rival promoter but, of course, having the most serious implications throughout International cricket and beyond. During the England tour of Australia in 1978–79 these two, with J. A. Bailey, the ICC secretary, established a working relationship with Kerry Packer in Sydney which they were hopeful of bearing fruit. It was at this delicate point that the Australian Board, which had been the most hostile element in the situation *vis-à-vis* the Packer organization, suddenly changed their ground and presented the other Test countries at the 1979 ICC with a situation which, however unsatisfactory it might seem to them, was, realistically speaking and in the light of the resources available, irreversible. What the deal portends for the future of the game – and especially its very nature, threatened as it is by the power of such formidable commercial interests – only time will tell.

ICC: Growth of the Associate Membership Idea

By revolutionary, or rather imaginatively evolutionary, decision in 1965 the 6 Test-playing countries of the ICC elected Ceylon, Fiji and United States of America to join them as associate members. Gamini Goonesena, Philip Snow and John Marder, representing these three countries, were welcomed at the 1st Conference and encouraged to offer views on any subjects, Test cricket apart. Ideas on increasing cricket's appeal, at a time when there were few or no subsidies from sponsors who had little to attract them, were specially listened to. One suggestion, from Fiji in 1966, that there should be a single new ball per innings so as to give slow bowlers a fresh breath of life remains on the agenda 13 years later.

The Secretary of ICC, S. C. Griffith, had applied his energy and discretion to obtaining the admission of the new countries against opposition in some quarters over a few years up to 1965. The next year, 1966, saw the election of Bermuda, Denmark, East Africa and the Netherlands. Then, in 1967 Malaysia; 1968 Canada; 1969 Gibraltar and Hong Kong; 1973 Papua New Guinea; 1974 Argentina, Israel (whose nomination caused the walk-out of A. H. Kardar of Pakistan) and Singapore; in 1976 West Africa; 1978 Bangladesh. Possible future candidates (who are required to meet criteria of quantity and quality of players) might be Brazil, New Hebrides and Tonga.

Until 1971 associate members were not entitled to vote: since then they have a single vote each (inevitably not on Test cricket) and are rightly, of course, not in a position to outvote the major countries with their 2 votes each. They make suggestions on the Laws, often giving views where legislation can be important at the lower levels. Fiji had proposed in 1966 that coaching aid in grants or personnel was where the major countries might make a most effective contribution to world cricket. When the member countries decided to set up a committee to promote this idea, associate members were included on it. A coaching fund was set up and associate members (as well as a country not even in the ICC – Sweden) have been variously helped, sometimes centrally, mostly by members under whose sphere of assistance the countries, with a view to the extension, encouragement and improvement of cricket throughout the world and the organization of minor tours have been divided:

England: Holland, Denmark, Canada, Argentina, Gibraltar, Israel
Australia: Malaysia, Hong Kong, Papua New Guinea
West Indies: Bermuda, USA
India: Sri Lanka, East Africa, Singapore
New Zealand: Fiji.

Associate members have similarly been on committees organizing the 1st World Cup competition, examining advertising, and other questions. Without associate country representation on the ICC, it is doubtful whether 2 non-Test-playing countries would have been able to participate in the 1st World Cup competition in 1975. There was little advance warning of it but Sri Lanka and East Africa found themselves available. When plans for the next World Cup competition quickly followed on the first, all the associate countries hoped to be in a position to be considered. To decide the 2 to join the Test countries, the associate members resolved to run their own preliminary competition.

How this developed is described in the article on the Associate Members Competition (*qv*). There it will be seen how far the countries outside the Test-playing ones have moved since those first days of the ICC. With the detailed help of the Midlands Club Cricket Conference in many vital directions, a grant from the ICC and separate obtaining of sponsors (a daunting task and tremendous outlay for countries travelling from the other side of the world, Malaysia, Singapore, Papua New Guinea and Fiji), it was organized by a management committee of the representatives of USA (chairman, secretary and donor of what has been called the ICC Trophy, J. R. Gardiner), Holland, Fiji, Sri Lanka, Gibraltar and Argentina. Hong Kong could not meet the residence qualification rule. West Africa applied after the closing date, and Gibraltar had to withdraw. But 14 of the 17 countries competed in the Midlands in 1979, with Sri Lanka and Canada going through to join the Test countries in the Prudential Cup Competition. The countries outside the Test-playing ones have moved far since those first days of the ICC in the mid-1960s.

PHILIP SNOW

New Zealand v India

REX ALSTON AND D. J. RUTNAGUR

India beat New Zealand 2–0 in the first-ever series between the 2 countries. There was no question of India's superiority in the 2 Test matches they won. In fact the only match during the rubber in which New Zealand made the running even briefly was the Fourth, at Calcutta, and even then India's recovery, after trailing by 204 runs, was so complete that New Zealand finished on the receiving end.

The leg-spin of Subash Gupte, who took 34 wickets (average 19·67) in the series, and their superior batting were principal factors in India's marked superiority. Vinoo Mankad made 2 double-hundreds; in scoring the 2nd he took part, with Pankaj Roy, in an opening partnership of 413, a 1st-wicket record for Test Cricket. Although New Zealand's tour party contained a variety of bowlers, they relied heavily on pace and their quicker bowlers found conditions trying everywhere except at Calcutta, where they bundled India out for 132 in their 1st innings. Bert Sutcliffe, regarded as one of the outstanding batsmen of his time, aggregated 611 runs in the series, including an unbeaten 230 in the Third Test and a hundred in the First. Guy weighed in with some good scores, a hundred in the First Test being the most prominent; and John Reid was consistently attractive.

Vinoo Mankad, India's leading all-round cricketer, made 2,109 runs and took 162 Test wickets. He scored 2 Test double-hundreds on New Zealand's 1st visit to India in 1955–56.

New Zealand, on their way to England in 1965 broke their journey to play another 4-Test series in India. Again, India were rather the stronger side, though they won only the last Test and that in a race against time. There were situations in the Second and Third Tests from which New Zealand might well have won. The Second Test at Calcutta was Bruce Taylor's match. He was not meant to play in it until just before the toss, his inclusion being brought about by B. W. Sinclair's sudden illness. Batting at No. 8, Taylor scored a belligerent 105 and assisted in a 7th-wicket stand of 133 with Sutcliffe, who made 151. Reid made an unforgettable 82 (at one stage hitting 4 sixes in ten balls) and New Zealand, in their 1st innings, declared at 462 for 9. With Taylor striking at India with the ball as well, and taking 5 for 62, India would have been hopelessly outplayed had New Zealand held their catches. Pataudi, who sustained India's innings and made 153, was allowed 3 early escapes.

The Third Test, at Bombay, also produced some fascinating twists of fortune. After shooting India out for 88 and forcing them to follow on 209 runs behind, New Zealand were so heavily outplayed that they nearly lost. Sardesai led India's rescue operation with 200 not out, and Hanumant Singh and Borde batted handsomely for 75 and 109 respectively. Only 150 minutes were left when New Zealand went in again. Taking a draw for granted, they batted in relaxed fashion and ran into such trouble that they had only 2 wickets left at the end.

At Delhi, in the final Test, the pitch was in league with the spinners right from the start. Venkataraghavan having run rampant and taken 8 for 72, India took a 1st innings lead of 203, with Sardesai and Pataudi making hundreds. New Zealand resisted bravely in the 2nd innings, but not for quite long enough. Left with 70 to win in an hour India got them with 13 minutes to spare.

India's 1st visit to New Zealand, in 1967–68, was an extension of a tour to Australia on which they had not fared particularly well. Far from discouraged by that they played purposeful, entertaining cricket to beat New Zealand 3–1 in a 4-Test series which yielded a worthwhile financial profit. New Zealand had the consolation of gaining their first-ever win over India in the second Test played at Christchurch. There, Pataudi, deceived by the greenness of the pitch, put New Zealand in and paid dearly. Dowling made 239; New Zealand totalled 502 and never looked back. Except at Christchurch and Dunedin, where the series opened, the pitches took spin to India's advantage. E. A. S. Prasanna, who had been the leading wicket-taker in the Australian series as well, captured 24 wickets in the series and the two left-arm spinners, Nadkarni and Bedi, benefited. The series was marred by controversy over the action of G. A. Bartlett, New Zealand's most successful bowler in the one Test match they won.

In 1969, New Zealand again combined a visit to India with a tour of England and were unlucky not to win the three-match rubber. The 2 sides went 1–1 to Hyderabad for the final Test, which turned out to be one of the lowest-scoring Tests ever played in India. Even so, it was left unfinished because of rain, a disagreement on the playing conditions and, not least, due to the time consumed by crowd disturbances. Morally, New Zealand were winners of that final Test. The opening match of the series, at Bombay, had been won by India, an inevitable victory once the Nawab of Pataudi had won the toss on an underprepared pitch. The groundsman had had only 3 days to get it ready, the Test having been earmarked for Ahmedabad where there was political unrest. The pitch at Nagpur for the Second Test had also been amenable to spin. So apparent were its qualities that New Zealand left out Bruce Taylor and played every available spinner. Hedley Howarth took 9 wickets in the match and New Zealand won by 167 runs.

India's 2nd visit to New Zealand followed 8 years after their 1st in 1976. Although the Tests were played in midsummer, the weather was often too cold and wet for the Indians. The period of acclimatization was short, but India won the First Test by 8 wickets, played on a spinner's pitch at Auckland. New Zealand dropped more chances than they took, Gavaskar (leading the side in the absence of Bedi, who was injured) and Surinder Amarnath (in his maiden Test) both being reprieved several times while scoring hundreds. Prasanna and Chandrasekhar spread havoc in both the New Zealanders' innings so that India had no cause to miss Bedi. India were hard put to it to defend their lead. New Zealand, having been denied by the weather in the Second Test at Christchurch, won the Third at Wellington by an innings and 33 runs. India batted poorly against the pace of Richard Hadlee, who took 11 wickets in the match.

Later that same year New Zealand paid a return visit to India. They played the First Test at Bombay, during a heatwave, and lost; they held out for a draw in the Second at

Kanpur, but were heavily beaten again in the Third at Madras, in which rain played a part. Losing the toss for the 3rd time in the series at Madras, New Zealand were condemned to batting last on a sub-standard pitch. New Zealand were poorly equipped for the tour, several of their key players being unavailable, Bev Congdon and Hedley Howarth among them. Their long-standing wicket-keeper, Ken Wadsworth, was included in the party, but died before the tour began. On many occasions during the series New Zealand complained bitterly about the umpiring, not always without reason.

NEW ZEALAND V INDIA

			RESULT	CAPTAINS
1955–56	1 Hyderabad	Ind 498–4D; NZ 326, 212–2	Drawn	H. B. Cave, Ghulam Ahmed
	2 Bombay	Ind 421–8D; NZ 258, 136	Ind Inns 27 runs	H. B. Cave, P. R. Umrigar
	3 New Delhi	NZ 450–2D, 112–1; Ind 531–7D	Drawn	H. B. Cave, P. R. Umrigar
	4 Calcutta	Ind 132, 438–7D; NZ 336, 75–6	Drawn	H. B. Cave, P. R. Umrigar
	5 Madras	Ind 537–3D; NZ 209, 219	Ind Inns 109 runs	H. B. Cave, P. R. Umrigar
1964–65	1 Madras	Ind 397, 199–2D; NZ 315, 62–0	Drawn	J. R. Reid, Nawab of Pataudi
	2 Calcutta	NZ 462–9D, 191–9D; Ind 380, 92–3	Drawn	J. R. Reid, Nawab of Pataudi
	3 Bombay	NZ 297, 80–8; Ind 88, 463–5D	Drawn	J. R. Reid, Nawab of Pataudi
	4 Delhi	NZ 262, 272; Ind 465–8D, 73–3	Ind 7 wkts	J. R. Reid, Nawab of Pataudi
1967–68	1 Dunedin	NZ 350, 208; Ind 359, 200–5	Ind 5 wkts	B. W. Sinclair, Nawab of Pataudi
	2 Christchurch	NZ 502, 88–4; Ind 288, 301	NZ 6 wkts	G. T. Dowling, Nawab of Pataudi
	3 Wellington	NZ 186, 199; Ind 327, 59–2	Ind 8 wkts	G. T. Dowling, Nawab of Pataudi
	4 Auckland	Ind 252, 261–5D; NZ 140, 101	Ind 272 runs	G. T. Dowling, Nawab of Pataudi
1969–70	1 Bombay	Ind 156, 260; NZ 229, 127	Ind 60 runs	G. T. Dowling, Nawab of Pataudi
	2 Nagpur	NZ 319, 214; Ind 257, 109	NZ 167 runs	G. T. Dowling, Nawab of Pataudi
	3 Hyderabad	NZ 181, 175–8D; Ind 89, 76–7	Drawn	G. T. Dowling, Nawab of Pataudi
1975–76	1 Auckland	NZ 266, 215; Ind 414, 71–2	Ind 8 wkts	G. M. Turner, S. M. Gavaskar
	2 Christchurch	Ind 270, 255–6; NZ 403	Drawn	G. M. Turner, B. S. Bedi
	3 Wellington	Ind 220, 81; NZ 334	NZ Inns 33 runs	G. M. Turner, B. S. Bedi
1976–77	1 Bombay	Ind 399, 202–4D; NZ 298, 141	Ind 162 runs	G. M. Turner, B. S. Bedi
	2 Kanpur	Ind 524–9D, 208–2D; NZ 350, 193–7	Drawn	G. M. Turner, B. S. Bedi
	3 Madras	Ind 298, 201–5D; NZ 140, 143	Ind 216 runs	G. M. Turner, B. S. Bedi

CAPTAINS (New Zealand)	TESTS	WON	LOST	DRAWN
H. B. Cave	5		2	3
J. R. Reid	4		1	3
B. W. Sinclair	1		1	
G. T. Dowling	6	2	3	1
G. M. Turner	6	1	3	2
	22	3	10	9

CAPTAINS (India)	TESTS	WON	LOST	DRAWN
Ghulam Ahmed	1			1
P. R. Umrigar	4	2		2
Nawab of Pataudi	11	5	2	4
S. M. Gavaskar	1	1		
B. S. Bedi	5	2	1	2
	22	10	3	9

HIGHEST INNINGS TOTAL

New Zealand in New Zealand, 502, Christchurch 1967–68
New Zealand in India, 462–9D, Calcutta 1964–65
India in New Zealand, 414, Auckland 1975–76
India in India, 537–3D, Madras 1955–56

LOWEST INNINGS TOTAL

New Zealand in New Zealand, 101, Auckland 1967–68
New Zealand in India, 127, Bombay 1968–69
India in New Zealand, 81, Wellington 1975–76
India in India, 88, Bombay 1964–65

HIGHEST INDIVIDUAL INNINGS

New Zealand in New Zealand, 239, G. T. Dowling, Christchurch 1967–68
New Zealand in India, 230*, B. Sutcliffe, Delhi 1955–56
India in New Zealand, 143, A. L. Wadekar, Wellington 1967–68
India in India, 231, V. Mankad, Madras 1955–56

HIGHEST AGGREGATE OF RUNS IN A SERIES

New Zealand in New Zealand, 471, G. T. Dowling 1967–68
New Zealand in India, 611, B. Sutcliffe 1955–56
India in New Zealand, 330, A. L. Wadekar 1967–68
India in India, 526, V. Mankad 1955–56

BEST INNINGS BOWLING FIGURES

New Zealand in New Zealand, 7–23, R. J. Hadlee, Wellington 1975–76
New Zealand in India, 5–34, H. J. Howarth, Nagpur 1969–70
India in New Zealand, 8–76, E. A. S. Prasanna, Auckland 1975–76
India in India, 8–72, S. Venkataraghavan, Delhi 1964–65

BEST MATCH BOWLING FIGURES

New Zealand in New Zealand, 11–58, R. J. Hadlee, Wellington 1975–76
New Zealand in India, 9–100, H. J. Howarth, Nagpur 1969–70
India in New Zealand, 11–140, E. A. S. Prasanna, Auckland 1975–76
India in India, 12–152, S. Venkataraghavan, Delhi 1964–65

HIGHEST WICKET AGGREGATE IN A SERIES

New Zealand in New Zealand, 15, R. C. Motz 1967–68
New Zealand in India, 15, B. R. Taylor 1964–65
India in New Zealand, 24, E. A. S. Prasanna 1967–68
India in India, 34, S. P. Gupte 1955–56

RECORD WICKET PARTNERSHIPS—NEW ZEALAND

1 B. A. G. Murray and G. T. Dowling, 126, Christchurch 1967–68
2 G. T. Dowling and B. E. Congdon, 155, Dunedin 1967–68
3 B. Sutcliffe and J. R. Reid, 222*, Delhi 1955–56
4 G. T. Dowling and M. G. Burgess, 103, Christchurch 1967–68
5 G. T. Dowling and K. Thomson, 119, Christchurch 1967–68
6 J. W. Guy and A. R. MacGibbon, 87, Hyderabad 1955–56
7 B. Sutcliffe and B. R. Taylor, 163, Calcutta 1964–65
8 V. Pollard and G. E. Vivian, 81, Calcutta 1964–65
9 M. G. Burgess and J. C. Alabaster, 69, Dunedin 1967–68
10 J. T. Ward and R. O. Collinge, 61, Madras 1964–65

RECORD WICKET PARTNERSHIPS—INDIA

1 V. Mankad and P. Roy, 413, Madras 1955–56
2 S. M. Gavaskar and S. Amarnath, 204, Auckland 1975–76
3 P. R. Umrigar and V. L. Manjrekar, 238, Hyderabad 1955–56
4 P. R. Umrigar and A. G. Kripal Singh, 171, Hyderabad 1955–56
5 V. L. Manjrekar and G. S. Ramchand, 127, Delhi 1955–56
6 D. N. Sardesai and Hanumant Singh, 193*, Bombay 1964–65
7 B. P. Patel and S. M. H. Kirmani, 116, Wellington 1975–76
8 R. G. Nadkarni and F. M. Engineer, 143, Madras 1961–62
9 S. M. H. Kirmani and B. S. Bedi, 105, Bombay 1976–77
10 R. B. Desai and B. S. Bedi, 57, Dunedin 1967–68

New Zealand v Pakistan

REX ALSTON

To New Zealand fell the distinction of being the 1st country, in 1955–56, to tour the new state of Pakistan, who signalized the occasion by winning the 3-Test series 2–0. S. N. McGregor, N. S. Harford, A. R. MacGibbon, J. R. Reid and H. B. Cave were the most effective bowlers. For Pakistan, Imtiaz Ahmed, Waqar Hassan and Hanif Mohammad all made big scores, whilst A. H. Kardar, their captain, Zulfiqar Ahmed and Khan Mohammad took the most wickets. In the First Test the off-spin of Zulfiqar (11 wickets in 2 innings) and the slow left-arm of Kadar proved too much for New Zealand.

In the Second Test a hundred by McGregor and 93 from Harford saw New Zealand to 348. Pakistan lost their first 6 wickets for 111, but a partnership between Waqar (189) and Imtiaz (209) put on 308 for the 7th wicket and they totalled 561. New Zealand fought back with 328 but, despite a steady 4 for 38 by Reid, Pakistan won. New Zealand just saved the Third Test. Fazal and Khan shot them out for 70, Hanif made 103 out of Pakistan's total of 195 for 6 declared, and New Zealand were 69 for 6 in their 2nd innings at the close.

In 1964–65 a 3-match series in New Zealand was drawn. For New Zealand, Reid (97) played the best innings and R. O. Collinge took most wickets (15). For Pakistan, Hanif made the only 100 (not out) and Asif Iqbal took the most wickets. In 1969, in Pakistan, New Zealand won their 1st victory against them by 5 wickets. In the series G. M. Turner and M. G. Burgess made hundreds; spinners H. J. Howarth and V. Pollard excelled. For Pakistan, spinners Pervez Sajjad and Intikhab Alam were the best. Pakistan in New Zealand won 1 match and drew 2 on their next confrontation. Mushtaq Mohammad, Sadiq Mohammad, Majid Khan and Asif all made hundreds and spinners Intikhab and Mushtaq bowled successfully. For New Zealand, Turner and B. F. Hastings were the leading batsmen and B. R. Taylor and Howarth the best bowlers. The class of the best Pakistani batsmen told. Again in 1976 New Zealand lost 2–0 in Pakistan, where Javed Miandad, Mushtaq, Asif, Majid and Sadiq all made hundreds, and Sarfraz Nawaz, Imran Khan and Intikhab were the leading bowlers. For New Zealand R. J. Hadlee took the most wickets and wicket-keeper batsman W. K. Lees and Burgess both made hundreds.

In 1979 Pakistan, with a full complement of 6 Packer players, toured New Zealand, winning 1 and drawing 2 Tests. In the First Test New Zealand led by 19 on the 1st innings, Javed making 81 while Hadlee took 5 for 62. For New Zealand B. A. Edgar made 129 and Hadlee 42, Mushtaq taking 4 for 61. Javed (160) again dominated Pakistan's 2nd innings, and Talat Ali made 61. New Zealand then collapsed on a worn pitch to the spinners Mushtaq (5 for 59) and Wasim Raja (4 for 78) and lost by 128 runs.

Javed Miandad in his 1st Test series in 1976–77 made 504 runs against New Zealand in Pakistan, averaging 126.

The other 2 Tests were drawn through rain. In the Second, Pakistan made 360 (Asif 104 not out, Raja 74, Hadlee 4 for 101). New Zealand led by 42 (G. Howarth 114, J. Wright 88, J. V. Coney 69, Imran Khan 5 for 106). In Pakistan's reply, Javed again excelled with 119 out of 234 for 3. In the Third Test New Zealand made 254 (Coney 82), Wasim Bari taking 7 catches behind the stumps. Pakistan established a long lead making 359 (Zaheer Abbas 135, Hadlee 5 for 104). Batting again 105 behind, New Zealand made 281 for 8 (M. G. Burgess 71, Coney 49, W. K. Lees 45 not out), after which rain ended play. Pakistan domination now stands at 7 victories and 1 defeat in the series – New Zealand have fought gamely but in vain.

NEW ZEALAND V PAKISTAN

			RESULT	CAPTAINS
1955–56	1 Karachi	NZ 164, 124; Pak 289	Pak Inns 1 run	H. B. Cave, A. H. Kardar
	2 Lahore	NZ 348, 328; Pak 561, 117–6	Pak 4 wkts	H. B. Cave, A. H. Kardar
	3 Dacca	NZ 70, 69–6; Pak 195–6D	Drawn	H. B. Cave, A. H. Kardar
1964–65	1 Wellington	NZ 266, 179–7D; Pak 187, 140–7	Drawn	J. R. Reid, Hanif Mohammad
	2 Auckland	Pak 226, 207; NZ 214, 166–7	Drawn	J. R. Reid, Hanif Mohammad
	3 Christchurch	Pak 206, 309–8D; NZ 202, 223–5	Drawn	J. R. Reid, Hanif Mohammad
1964–65	1 Rawalpindi	NZ 175, 79; Pak 318	Pak Inns 64 runs	J. R. Reid, Hanif Mohammad
	2 Lahore	Pak 385–7D, 194–8D; NZ 482–6D	Drawn	J. R. Reid, Hanif Mohammad
	3 Karachi	NZ 285, 223; Pak 307–8D, 202–2	Pak 8 wkts	J. R. Reid, Hanif Mohammad
1969–70	1 Karachi	Pak 220, 283–8D; NZ 274, 112–5	Drawn	G. T. Dowling, Intikhab Alam
	2 Lahore	Pak 114, 208; NZ 241, 82–5	NZ 5 wkts	G. T. Dowling, Intikhab Alam
	3 Dacca	NZ 273, 200; Pak 290–7D, 51–4	Drawn	G. T. Dowling, Intikhab Alam
1972–73	1 Wellington	Pak 357, 290–6D; NZ 325, 78–3	Drawn	B. E. Congdon, Intikhab Alam

	2 Dunedin	Pak 507–6D; NZ 156, 185	Pak Inns 166 runs	B. E. Congdon, Intikhab Alam
	3 Auckland	Pak 402, 271; NZ 402, 92–3	Drawn	B. E. Congdon, Intikhab Alam
1976–77	1 Lahore	Pak 417, 105–4; NZ 157, 360	Pak 6 wkts	G. M. Turner, Mushtaq Mohammad
	2 Hyderabad	Pak 473–8D, 4–0; NZ 219, 254	Pak 10 wkts	G. M. Turner, Mushtaq Mohammad
	3 Karachi	Pak 565–9D, 290–5D; NZ 468, 262–7	Drawn	J. M. Parker, Mushtaq Mohammad
1978–79	1 Christchurch	Pak 271, 323–6D; NZ 290, 176	Pak 128 runs	M. G. Burgess, Mushtaq Mohammad
	2 Napier	Pak 360, 234–3D; NZ 402	Drawn	M. G. Burgess, Mushtaq Mohammad
	3 Auckland	NZ 254, 281–8D; Pak 359, 8–0	Drawn	M. G. Burgess, Mushtaq Mohammad

CAPTAINS (New Zealand)	TESTS	WON	LOST	DRAWN
H. B. Cave	3		2	1
J. R. Reid	6		2	4
G. T. Dowling	3	1		2
B. E. Congdon	3		1	2
G. M. Turner	2		2	
J. M. Parker	1			1
M. G. Burgess	3		1	2
	21	1	8	12

CAPTAINS (Pakistan)	TESTS	WON	LOST	DRAWN
A. H. Kardar	3	2		1
Hanif Mohammad	6	2		4
Intikhab Alam	6	1	1	4
Mushtaq Mohammad	6	3		3
	21	8	1	12

HIGHEST INNINGS TOTAL

New Zealand in New Zealand, { 402, Auckland 1972–73; 402, Napier 1978–79 }
New Zealand in Pakistan, 482–6D, Lahore 1964–65
Pakistan in New Zealand, 507–6D, Dunedin 1972–73
Pakistan in Pakistan, 565–9D, Karachi 1976–77

LOWEST INNINGS TOTAL

New Zealand in New Zealand, 156, Dunedin 1972–73
New Zealand in Pakistan, 70, Dacca 1955–56
Pakistan in New Zealand, 187, Wellington 1964–65
Pakistan in Pakistan, 114, Lahore 1969–70

HIGHEST INDIVIDUAL INNINGS

New Zealand in New Zealand, 129, B. A. Edgar, Christchurch 1978–79
New Zealand in Pakistan, 152, W. K. Lees, Karachi 1976–77
Pakistan in New Zealand, 201, Mushtaq Mohammad, Dunedin 1972–73
Pakistan in Pakistan, 209, Imtiaz Ahmed, Lahore 1955–56

HIGHEST AGGREGATE OF RUNS IN A SERIES

New Zealand in New Zealand, 242, J. V. Coney 1978–79
New Zealand in Pakistan, 296, J. R. Reid 1964–65
Pakistan in New Zealand, 366, Sadiq Mohammad 1972–73
Pakistan in Pakistan, 504, Javed Miandad 1976–77

BEST INNINGS BOWLING FIGURES

New Zealand in New Zealand, 5–35, F. J. Cameron, Auckland 1964–65
New Zealand in Pakistan, 5–80, H. J. Howarth, Karachi 1969–70
Pakistan in New Zealand, 7–52, Intikhab Alam, Dunedin 1972–73
Pakistan in Pakistan, 7–74, Pervez Sajjid, Lahore 1969–70

BEST MATCH BOWLING FIGURES

New Zealand in New Zealand, 9–70, F. J. Cameron, Auckland 1964–65
New Zealand in Pakistan, 7–140, H. J. Howarth, Karachi 1969–70
Pakistan in New Zealand, 11–130, Intikhab Alam, Dunedin 1972–73
Pakistan in Pakistan, 11–79, Zulfiqar Ahmed, Karachi 1955–56

HIGHEST WICKET AGGREGATE IN A SERIES

New Zealand in New Zealand, 18, R. J. Hadlee 1978–79
New Zealand in Pakistan, 16, H. J. Howarth 1969–70
Pakistan in New Zealand, { 18, Asif Iqbal 1964–65; 18, Intikhab Alam 1972–73 }
Pakistan in Pakistan, 22, Pervez Sajjid 1969–70

RECORD WICKET PARTNERSHIPS—NEW ZEALAND

1 R. E. Redmond and G. M. Turner, 159, Auckland 1972–73
2 J. G. Wright and G. P. Howarth, 195, Napier 1978–79
3 B. W. Sinclair and J. R. Reid, 178, Lahore 1964–65
4 B. F. Hastings and M. G. Burgess, 128, Wellington 1972–73
5 M. G. Burgess and R. W. Anderson, 183, Lahore 1976–77
6 M. G. Burgess and W. K. Lees, 91, Karachi 1976–77
7 W. K. Lees and R. J. Hadlee, 185, Karachi 1976–77
8 B. W. Yuile and D. R. Hadlee, 100, Karachi 1969–70
9 M. G. Burgess and R. S. Cunis, 96, Dacca 1969–70
10 B. F. Hastings and R. O. Collinge, 151, Auckland 1972–73

RECORD WICKET PARTNERSHIPS—PAKISTAN

1 Sadiq Mohammad and Majid Khan, 147, Karachi 1976–77
2 Mohammad Ilyas and Saeed Ahmed, 114, Rawalpindi 1964–65
3 Sadiq Mohammad and Majid Khan, 171, Wellington 1972–73
4 Mushtaq Mohammad and Asif Iqbal, 350, Dunedin 1972–73
5 Javed Miandad and Asif Iqbal, 281, Lahore 1976–77
6 Hanif Mohammad and Majid Khan, 217, Lahore 1964–65
7 Waqar Hassan and Imtiaz Ahmed, 308, Lahore 1955–56
8 Asif Iqbal and Imran Khan, 72, Lahore 1976–77
9 Intikhab Alam and Arif Butt, 52, Auckland 1964–65
10 Salah-ud-Din and Mohammad Farooq, 65, Rawalpindi 1964–65

South Africa v New Zealand

LOUIS DUFFUS AND MICHAEL OWEN-SMITH

South Africa's traditional opponents on the football field tried conclusions at cricket at the earliest possible moment after New Zealand had attained Test status. In 1931–32 South Africa called in after their tour of Australia. Yet in the next 30 years there followed only 4 series, 2 of 2 Tests in New Zealand and 2 of 5 in South Africa.

The 1st Test between the 2 countries took place in Christchurch in late February 1932. New Zealand, led by M. L. Page, started the historic game indifferently by losing 3 wickets for 38 runs, but a 4th-wicket stand of 90 by G. L. Weir and A. W. Roberts preceded steady scoring by the middle batsmen, of whom F. T. Badcock made top score of 64. The innings closed at 293 with the leg-spin bowler Q. McMillan having the best bowling figures of 4 for 61. A 1st-wicket partnership of 196 by J. A. J. Christy (103) and B. Mitchell (113) gave South Africa the foundation for a substantial lead on the 1st innings. New Zealand had to score 158 to avoid an innings defeat, but were dismissed for 146 and South Africa won by an innings and 12 runs.

The outcome was closer in the Second Test which was played at Wellington. Had not the New Zealand batting fallen off rather unexpectedly in their 2nd innings, South Africa could not have won by 8 wickets. The man of the match for New Zealand was the youthful H. G. Vivian, who became the first of 6 New Zealanders to score a hundred against South Africa.

Batting 1st, New Zealand seemed to have made themselves safe from defeat by scoring 364. There was every chance of their gaining a 1st innings lead when South Africa lost 6 wickets for 257. But X. C. Balaskas and the left-hander C. L. Vincent put on 105 for the 7th wicket – the former making 122 not out, his only Test hundred – and South Africa finished with a total of 410. New Zealand could manage only 193 in their 2nd innings with N. A. Quinn, a left-hander, taking 4 for 37 in 24 overs and South Africa, needing 148 for victory, lost Mitchell and Christy in reaching their target.

There is little need to stress the advantage enjoyed by a side battle-trained in a 5-Test series in Australia. Next time it was the side captained by J. E. Cheetham in 1952–53 that went on to New Zealand from Australia, New Zealand being led by W. M. Wallace. The Tests were now extended to 4 days and as a consequence the scoring tempo tended to slacken. The first Test played at Wellington, where South Africa won by an innings and 180 runs, is remembered most for the remarkable innings of 255 not out played by D. J. McGlew and the 7th-wicket partnership of 246, between McGlew and A. R. A. Murray, which was then a world Test record. South Africa batted for all but 2 hours of the 1st 2 days and declared at 524 for 8. After the enterprising left-hander, B. Sutcliffe, had fallen to a brilliant catch by McGlew for 62, the New Zealanders sought refuge in stubborn defence, but were all out for 172. By a coincidence New Zealand were dismissed for the same total in the 2nd innings.

The 1st Test between the 2 countries to be played at Auckland was drawn. On a lively pitch it took South Africa the best part of 2 days to score 377. In the process Endean (116) achieved his 2nd Test hundred and by putting on 130 for the 5th wicket with Cheetham, after 4 wickets had fallen for 139, ensured that South Africa would reach a safe total. New Zealand, avoiding the follow-on with 2 wickets in hand, replied with 245, but South Africa showed no inclination to try to win the match. Cheetham delayed his declaration until South Africa had 200 for 5, leaving New Zealand to play out the last 90 minutes.

Now in 1953–54 came a more ambitious venture, the 1st full-scale tour of South Africa, with G. O. Rabone leading New Zealand. In the First Test in Durban, Cheetham won the toss, New Zealand missed catches and R. A. McLean went on to score his 1st Test hundred. Cheetham was able to declare early in the afternoon of the 2nd day at 437 for 9. The New Zealand 1st innings was dominated by the patient display of Rabone. He scored his 1st Test hundred (107) after batting close on 6 hours. New Zealand were all out for 230 and were made to follow on. They required 207 to avoid an innings defeat, but were dismissed for 149, giving South Africa victory by an innings and 58 runs. The game was a triumph for H. J. Tayfield, whose match analysis of 9 for 97 was the best in Tests between the 2 countries. In New Zealand's 2nd innings N. A. T. Adcock took his first wickets in Test cricket.

The Second Test in Johannesburg was the outstanding match of the series. The Test was played on the international rugby field at Ellis Park, where the fiery pitch favoured the fast bowlers, particularly Adcock. The New Zealanders gave their best exhibition of cricket against South Africa and, in spite of 7 missed chances, dismissed South Africa for 271. Trying to avoid his 3rd ball from Adcock, the left-hander, Sutcliffe, was struck a blow on the head and fell to the ground. Later Miller sustained a blow in the ribs when facing Adcock. Both he and Sutcliffe were taken to hospital but returned to continue their innings. Miller was soon bowled, and with the total 82 for 6, Sutcliffe came on to the field with a bandage round his head and a big pad of cotton wool over his ear. After facing 2 balls he hit D. E. J. Ironside for 6. When Adcock returned to the attack, Sutcliffe slashed him for 4 through the covers. In one of the most spectacular innings played against South Africa he proceeded to hit 7 sixes, 6 off Tayfield – including 3 in one over – and was left undefeated with an heroic 80 scored in 98 minutes. In a day of drama and heroism New Zealand scored 187 and then dismissed 3 South African batsmen for 35. They were all out for 148, so that New Zealand had to score 233 to win. But in an anti-climax they were dismissed for 100, giving South Africa victory by 132 runs.

At Cape Town New Zealand retaliated by scoring 505, their highest total in 25 years of Test history. They were aided by 10 missed chances. South Africa batted defensively, McGlew scoring 86 in 4½ hours, but had lost 7 wickets for 204 when a partnership between Cheetham, who made his highest Test score, a forceful 89, and Tayfield added 95 that saved them from threatening defeat. South Africa were all out for 326 and in a follow-on made 159 for 3.

Before the Fourth Test in Johannesburg the New Zealanders suffered a severe blow when Rabone fractured a bone in his foot while batting in a provincial match against Border. Sutcliffe took over the captaincy and put South Africa in to bat on a pitch that had lost its fire of the First Test. South Africa laboured to a total of 243, then virtually decided the rubber when they dismissed their opponents in 3 hours for 79. Tayfield had the remarkable analysis of 6 for 13. In the follow-on New Zealand reached 188, with Adcock taking 5 for 45, and were defeated by 9 wickets.

The slow scoring which characterized the series was broken at the 11th hour by South Africa. They were left to make 212 in 225 minutes on the final day of the Fifth Test in Port Elizabeth and hit off the runs for the loss of 5 wickets with 40 minutes to spare. It was the 1st time South Africa had won a Test series anywhere by 4–0. The wicket-keeper, J. H. B. Waite, established a world record by taking 23 wickets in the series, while Adcock in his first Test series finished with 24 wickets.

The 1961–62 visit to South Africa was the most successful tour New Zealand have undertaken. For the 1st time they won a Test match abroad and, by achieving a 2nd victory in the last game of the series, shared the rubber. The matches were a signal triumph for the captain, J. R. Reid, who led both the batting and bowling averages for his team.

South African cricket was going through a stage of transition, and in the First Test at Durban the side included no fewer than 7 new caps. They won narrowly by 30 runs, largely due to their captain, McGlew, carrying his bat for 127 in the 1st innings of 292, and the outstanding bowling of P. M. Pollock, who in the absence of Adcock took 9 for 99 in the game, an unprecedented feat by a South African fast bowler in his 1st Test.

J. R. Reid, whose sterling all-round qualities were the backbone of the New Zealand sides of the 1950s and 1960s. He led that of 1961–62 to a drawn series in South Africa.

The Second Test in Johannesburg was spoilt on the 1st day when 4¾ hours' play was lost because of rain. The draw was in favour of South Africa who scored 322 and 178 for 6 declared against New Zealand's 223 and 165 for 4. Waite scored a masterly 101, while G. B. Lawrence's 8 for 53 was the best performance on paper by a South African fast bowler in 73 years of Test cricket.

The slow Cape Town pitch which closely resembled their home conditions provided the scene for the New Zealanders' historic success. Both in batting and bowling they outplayed South Africa and levelled the series at one-all through a handsome victory by 72 runs. The South African bowler, S. F. Burke, had the unusual experience of taking 6 for 128 and 5 for 68 in his 1st Test and not playing again because of the return of Adcock for the last 2 matches.

The sharp contrast between the Cape Town and Johannesburg pitches enabled South Africa to turn the tables completely in the Fourth Test. P. S. Heine, who had dropped out of cricket for a while, was brought back to partner Adcock for the 1st time for 4 years, but it was again Lawrence who dominated the bowling. South Africa won by an innings and 51 to lead the series 2–1. A demoralizing 1st-wicket stand of 134 by McGlew (120) and Barlow (67) set South Africa off on a batting spree and they reached the match-winning total of 464. Back under coastal conditions at Port Elizabeth, New Zealand crowned their memorable tour by winning an exciting final match by 40 runs and thus sharing the rubber. Once again it was their cheap dismissal of South Africa in their first innings for 190, the same total they had made in losing at Cape Town, which clinched the victory. In his last Test innings before retiring McGlew was run out for 26, but he ended the series with the highest average (60·85) of either side. Lawrence took 28 wickets, a record for a South African fast bowler, and Waite regained the world wicket-keeping record of 26 dismissals. Alabaster equalled MacGibbon's total of 22 wickets against South Africa. By their wisdom and zeal in the use of inferior resources, and the rich all-round skill of Reid, New Zealand reached an exhilarating pinnacle in their cricket.

At Port Elizabeth in 1961–62 for South Africa v New Zealand John Waite made his 26th wicket-keeping dismissal in a Test series – a record at the time. Waite, who made 4 Test hundreds, was a stylist both as batsman and wicket-keeper.

South Africa visited New Zealand for the 3rd time in 1963–64, at the end of their exciting tour of Australia. The 3 Tests – at Wellington, Dunedin and Auckland – were all drawn, though in every case a further 30 minutes' play might well have seen South Africa win. South African highlights included Barlow's 92 in the First Test; D. B. Pithey's 6 for 58 in the Second; and Barlow and Goddard's opening stand of 115, followed by Bland's delightful 83, in the Third. For New Zealand Reid took 6 for 60 in the Second Test and B. W. Sinclair scored a maiden Test hundred in the Third. Despite the drawn series, the South Africans had shown themselves the stronger side and left a notable impression in New Zealand as attacking and purposeful cricketers. But the start at Wellington had been threatened – a portent, as it turned out, of things to come.

SOUTH AFRICA V NEW ZEALAND

			RESULT	CAPTAINS
1931–32	1 Christchurch	NZ 293, 146; SA 451	SA Inns 12 runs	H. B. Cameron, M. L. Page
	2 Wellington	NZ 364, 193; SA 410, 150–2	SA 8 wkts	H. B. Cameron, M. L. Page
1952–53	1 Wellington	SA 524–8D; NZ 172, 172	SA Inns 180 runs	J. E. Cheetham, W. M. Wallace
	2 Auckland	SA 377, 200–5D; NZ 245, 31–2	Drawn	J. E. Cheetham, W. M. Wallace
1953–54	1 Durban	SA 437–9D; NZ 230, 149	SA Inns 58 runs	J. E. Cheetham, G. O. Rabone
	2 Johannesburg	SA 271, 148; NZ 187, 100	SA 132 runs	J. E. Cheetham, G. O. Rabone
	3 Cape Town	NZ 505; SA 326, 159–3	Drawn	J. E. Cheetham, G. O. Rabone
	4 Johannesburg	SA 243, 25–1; NZ 79, 188	SA 9 wkts	J. E. Cheetham, B. Sutcliffe
	5 Port Elizabeth	NZ 226, 222; SA 237, 215–5	SA 5 wkts	J. E. Cheetham, B. Sutcliffe
1961–62	1 Durban	SA 292, 149; NZ 245, 166	SA 30 runs	D. J. McGlew, J. R. Reid
	2 Johannesburg	SA 322, 178–6D; NZ 223, 165–4	Drawn	D. J. McGlew, J. R. Reid
	3 Cape Town	NZ 385, 212–9D; SA 190, 335	NZ 72 runs	D. J. McGlew, J. R. Reid
	4 Johannesburg	NZ 164, 249; SA 464	SA Inns 51 runs	D. J. McGlew, J. R. Reid
	5 Port Elizabeth	NZ 275, 228; SA 190, 273	NZ 40 runs	D. J. McGlew, J. R. Reid
1963–64	1 Wellington	SA 302, 218–2D; NZ 253, 138–6	Drawn	T. L. Goddard, J. R. Reid
	2 Dunedin	NZ 149, 138; SA 223, 42–3	Drawn	T. L. Goddard, J. R. Reid
	3 Auckland	SA 371, 200–5D; NZ 263, 191–8	Drawn	T. L. Goddard, J. R. Reid

CAPTAINS (South Africa)	TESTS	WON	LOST	DRAWN
H. B. Cameron	2	2		
J. E. Cheetham	7	5		2
D. J. McGlew	5	2	2	1
T. L. Goddard	3			3
	17	9	2	6

CAPTAINS (New Zealand)	TESTS	WON	LOST	DRAWN
M. L. Page	2		2	
W. M. Wallace	2		1	1
G. O. Rabone	3		2	1
B. Sutcliffe	2		2	
J. R. Reid	8	2	2	4
	17	2	9	6

HIGHEST INNINGS TOTAL

South Africa in South Africa, 464, Johannesburg 1961–62
South Africa in New Zealand, 524–8D, Wellington 1952–53
New Zealand in South Africa, 505, Cape Town 1953–54
New Zealand in New Zealand, 364, Wellington 1931–32

LOWEST INNINGS TOTAL

South Africa in South Africa, 148, Johannesburg 1953–54
South Africa in New Zealand, 223, Dunedin 1963–64
New Zealand in South Africa, 79, Johannesburg 1953–54
New Zealand in New Zealand, 138, Dunedin 1963–64

HIGHEST INDIVIDUAL INNINGS

South Africa in South Africa, 127*, D. J. McGlew, Durban 1961–62

South Africa in New Zealand, 255*, D. J. McGlew, Wellington 1952–53
New Zealand in South Africa, 142, J. R. Reid, Johannesburg 1961–62
New Zealand in New Zealand, 138, B. W. Sinclair, Auckland 1963–64

HIGHEST AGGREGATE OF RUNS IN A SERIES

South Africa in South Africa, 426, D. J. McGlew 1961–62
South Africa in New Zealand, 323, D. J. McGlew 1952–53
New Zealand in South Africa, 546, J. R. Reid 1961–62
New Zealand in New Zealand, 264, B. W. Sinclair 1963–64

BEST INNINGS BOWLING FIGURES

South Africa in South Africa, 8–53, G. B. Lawrence, Johannesburg 1961–62
South Africa in New Zealand, 6–47, P. M. Pollock, Wellington 1963–64
New Zealand in South Africa, 6–68, G. O. Rabone, Cape Town 1953–54
New Zealand in New Zealand, 6–60, J. R. Reid, Dunedin 1963–64

BEST MATCH BOWLING FIGURES

South Africa in South Africa, 11–196, S. F. Burke, Cape Town 1961–62
South Africa in New Zealand, 9–127, Q. McMillan, Christchurch 1931–32
New Zealand in South Africa, 8–180, J. C. Alabaster, Cape Town 1961–62
New Zealand in New Zealand, 7–142, R. W. Blair, Auckland 1963–64

HIGHEST WICKET AGGREGATE IN A SERIES

South Africa in South Africa, 28, G. B. Lawrence, 1961–62
South Africa in New Zealand, 16, Q. McMillan, 1931–32
New Zealand in South Africa, { 22, A. R. MacGibbon, 1953–54; 22, J. C. Alabaster, 1961–62 }
New Zealand in New Zealand, { 12, R. W. Blair 1963–64; 12, J. R. Reid 1963–64 }

RECORD WICKET PARTNERSHIPS—SOUTH AFRICA

1 J. A. J. Christy and B. Mitchell, 196, Christchurch 1931–32
2 J. A. J. Christy and H. B. Cameron, 76, Wellington 1931–2
3 D. J. McGlew and R. A. McLean, 112, Johannesburg 1961–62
4 D. J. McGlew and R. A. McLean, 135, Durban 1953–54
5 W. R. Endean and J. E. Cheetham, 130, Auckland 1952–53
6 E. L. Dalton and D. P. B. Morkel, 79, Christchurch 1931–32
7 D. J. McGlew and A. R. A. Murray, 246, Wellington 1952–53
8 J. E. Cheetham and H. J. Tayfield, 95, Cape Town 1953–54
9 P. M. Pollock and N. A. T. Adcock, 60, Port Elizabeth 1961–62
10 P. N. F. Mansell and E. R. H. Fuller, 37, Auckland 1952–53

RECORD WICKET PARTNERSHIPS—NEW ZEALAND

1 G. O. Rabone and M. E. Chapple, 126, Cape Town 1953–54
2 S. N. McGregor and J. T. Sparling, 44, Cape Town 1961–62
3 M. E. Chapple and B. Sutcliffe, 94, Cape Town 1953–54
4 B. W. Sinclair and S. N. McGregor, 171, Auckland 1963–64
5 J. R. Reid and J. E. F. Beck, 174, Cape Town 1953–54
6 H. G. Vivian and F. T. Badcock, 100, Wellington 1931–32
7 J. R. Reid and G. A. Bartlett, 84, Johannesburg 1961–62
8 P. G. Z. Harris and G. A. Bartlett, 73, Durban 1961–62
9 C. F. W. Alcott and I. B. Cromb, 69, Wellington 1931–32
10 A. E. Dick and F. J. Cameron, 49*, Cape Town 1961–62

Test Selectors

D. J. INSOLE

The 1st officially appointed English Selectors, in the august persons of Lord Hawke, Dr W. G. Grace and H. W. Bainbridge, began in 1899 the highly controversial process which has since provided a permanent 'Aunt Sally' for cricket opinion, informed and otherwise, and which will remain an open target for as long as interest in cricket remains alive. Prior to this date, England teams had been selected by the club on whose ground a match was to be fought out, and it is not entirely unreasonable to suppose that the players were chosen with at least half an eye on their crowd-pulling potential, with perhaps some 'local' bias. At the turn of the century, and indeed until 1928, Test series in England were played at 2- and 3-yearly intervals because India, West Indies, New Zealand and Pakistan had not entered upon the Test Match scene. The appointment of a Selection Committee was not, therefore, an annual event, and the duties of individual Selectors were not as onerous as they have since become.

Until 1969, when a major reorganization of administration took place, and the Test and County Cricket Board was established, there were two Selection Committees in England – one for Tests played at home, the other for overseas tours. The 'home' Selectors were appointed by the Board of Control, a body comprising representatives of the Counties and of MCC. For tours abroad, the Selectors were appointed by MCC, under whose auspices all official overseas tours were formerly made.

Today, the Selectors appointed by the Test and County Cricket Board, together with their chosen captain, select teams both for Tests at home and for those played overseas, where the team representing cricket in the UK is now called 'England' and not 'MCC', as was the case until 1977. For overseas tours, the Selectors are augmented by the Chairman of the Cricket Council, the governing body of cricket in the UK, which may disapprove of selections on other than purely 'cricketing' grounds, if it so wishes.

The selectors of the MCC team to South Africa in 1922–23: (from the left) F. T. Mann (captain), H. D. G. Leveson Gower, J. W. H. T. Douglas and P. F. Warner.

The Board of Control in 1899 appointed a Selection Committee of 3 who, having chosen a captain, were to co-opt him as a member. In fact their 1st choice as captain was Dr W. G. Grace, then 50 years of age, who was one of the appointed 3. However, after leading the England team in the First Test of the series against Australia, the Doctor decided to retire from Test cricket, and A. C. MacLaren was appointed in his place. The pattern of the choice of Selectors remained constant, with 3 distinguished amateur players or administrators in command, until 1926 when the appointed committee under the chairmanship of P. F. Warner was instructed to co-opt 2 professionals, one from the north and one from the south. Their choice fell on Jack Hobbs and Wilfred Rhodes, and it would be hard to imagine 2 more shrewd judges of a player. Then, in 1938, it was decided to increase the number of Selectors to 4, including 2 captains of county teams, so that for the Australian series of that year A. B. Sellers of Yorkshire and M. J. Turnbull of Glamorgan joined their illustrious seniors, Sir Pelham Warner and P. A. Perrin, on the committee.

Immediately after the war, in 1946, a committee of 3, with the captain co-opted, was again considered sufficient, but in 1949 the number was once more increased to 4, and in 1950 Leslie Ames became the 1st of a continuing series of 'professional' cricketers to be appointed, as distinct from co-opted. From that time, the appointment of what were once known as 'professional' as distinct from 'amateur' cricketers has become the rule rather than the exception. Cyril Washbrook, Tom Dollery, Herbert Sutcliffe, Alec Bedser and Willie Watson were among those who served as Selectors in the days prior to the abolition of 'amateur' status and from the late 1960s committees comprised solely of former 'professionals' have become commonplace.

Within the obvious limits of the nominations received from the counties, the modern committee is chosen to give as wide a geographical coverage as possible, so that it is feasible for its members to attend selected county matches in any part of the country, although any 'playing' members are clearly confined to the games in which they are taking part. The manner in which the Selectors set about their duties has differed over the years, but the now established procedure is for the chairman to call the first meeting just prior to the start of the season. Various points of policy are considered at this meeting, but the most important item on the agenda is the drawing up of the list of players who will be under review in the early weeks of the season. The list will be augmented from time to time as promising newcomers make their mark, but the Selectors arrange between them to watch each of the players mentioned at least twice before the team for the First Test Match is chosen. Other topics for discussion will almost always include an assessment of strengths and weaknesses highlighted during the previous season, or perhaps during a winter tour, the merits of various candidates for the captaincy, and the broad lines of policy to be followed during the season. The next meeting is usually held during the MCC match against the tourists at Lord's, when several prospective England players are invariably on view. At this stage it is possible to make an initial assessment of current form, and the opportunity is often taken to select the captain for the First Test Match, so that he can join in any preliminary discussion, and also make himself available to be present when the Test team is chosen.

Prior to the introduction of the John Player League in 1968, it was usual for the Committee to meet on the Sunday before a Test Match, but this procedure is now seldom feasible because of the involvement of the captain in a county match on that day. Meetings are often held on the Friday preceding a Test Match at a place which suits the travel plans of the majority. Test Matches apart there is, in modern times, the probability that one-day internationals will be played against the touring side, and these involve additional meetings and the consideration of rather different techniques when selecting the England team. In consequence, the task of the modern Selector is even more difficult than ever before.

Before settling down to the business of choosing individual players, the Selectors will talk over any lessons to be learned from previous matches, and discuss matters of tactics and general policy with the captain. There is no preconceived or regular order of selecting the side, although it is usual to begin with the batsmen. Whether a start is made on batsmen or bowlers, however, the balance of the team will necessitate switching from one to the other. The selection of the 1st 6, 7 or even 8 names is seldom very much of a problem, but the choice of the remaining few is often the cause of very lengthy discussion and, dare one say it, argument. The considerations are often quite fundamental, and even mundane, but they are none the less vital for that.

Whether to select a newcomer in form or stick to an established player temporarily out of touch; whether in particular circumstances to include an extra bowler of pace; whether to go for the inconsistent aggressive player or the sound run-getter; whether to choose an average batsman who is a good slip-fielder or the good player who is only an average fielder. There is nothing mystical about these or many other problems which arise, but they can cause differences of opinion, especially in the middle of a tough series. The captain has, of course, a special part to play in all this, and I will say something about his position later on.

One further consideration for the Selectors is that they are required to act as the trustees of the spirit, in addition to and as distinct from the laws of cricket, and refrain from choosing any player whose fairness is in any way in question. The responsibility accepted by the Selectors once the side has been chosen has varied, but certain obligations are more or less statutory. Unless there is some very strong reason for his absence, a Selector is expected to be on hand on the 1st morning of a Test, when in fact the final selection has to be made on those occasions when more than 11 names have been announced. He is required to watch the whole of the 1st 3 Test Matches in a series and some part – the first 2 days at least – of the remainder.

In recent years it has become the custom, and a very sound one, to appoint one Selector as 'manager' for each Test Match. In this capacity he undertakes a number of chores, such as allocating hotel accommodation, arranging transport to and from the ground each day, making sure that good net wickets and net bowlers are available for practice on the day prior to the match and on each morning, organizing fielding practice and perhaps net practice on the captain's behalf – in fact leaving the captain free to think exclusively about the game in hand.

Apart from attending Test Matches, non-playing Selectors watch county fixtures every week-end, and at other times as frequently as business and other commitments will allow. One of the major frustrations in the life of a Selector is to arrive at a county ground after a 3-hour journey on a Saturday morning in the hope of seeing an opening batsman only to find that the wrong team is in the field, and likely to remain there all day. Basically, of course, every Selector prefers to trust his own judgment of the ability of a player, but there are occasions, like that instanced above, when the opinions of county captains are extremely valuable – not merely in helping to assess the technical capabilities of a player but also, equally important, in the matter of the contribution he makes to team spirit, and his reaction to varying circumstances. Temperament and character are vital considerations in judging potential England cricketers, and there have been many instances of omissions from touring parties of players who must have appeared on their records in county cricket to be certain of selection. The morale of a touring side can be lowered very substantially by the discontent caused by one troublemaker.

The role of the captain in choosing the side is a vital one in as much as it is clearly wrong to select any player who is completely unacceptable to him, especially when the Selectors have laid down a general policy which the captain has been asked to follow. One England captain in particular, A. C. MacLaren, is known to have been almost continuously at loggerheads with his fellow Selectors, and on one famous occasion during the Australian series in 1902 is alleged to have thrust open the dressing-room door on the 1st morning of the match, cast a critical eye around the assembled players and shouted 'My God, look what they've given me this time!' Not, perhaps, an opening calculated to instil any very great confidence into the side, and, of course, not typical of England

D. J. Insole, author of this article, takes the chair at the Lord's meeting which chose the 1965–66 MCC team to Australia, of which M. J. K. Smith (on Insole's right) had already been made captain. The other Test selectors, D. Kenyon, A. V. Bedser and P. B. H. May, are joined by G. O. Allen, F. R. Brown and S. C. Griffith (secretary) representing MCC.

captains as a whole. In general, Selection Committee meetings are fairly harmonious. Once the team is chosen, the Selectors leave the tactical approach to a match in the hands of the captain and although they are always available to give assistance, they have rarely interfered, in modern times anyway, with the captain's conduct of affairs.

In days of yore there was a good deal more direction of the pattern of play by the Selectors, as is indicated by a particular incident during the 1921 series against Australia. Nigel Haig was obliged to go in to bat shortly after his captain, J. W. H. T. Douglas, had been dismissed by a very lengthy long hop and was not feeling any too pleased with himself. Haig was confronted on leaving the dressing-room by the Selectors, who told him to try to force the pace, in contradiction of the captain's instructions. Anxious to get his brief right, Haig put his head round the dressing-room door and said to his very dejected captain: 'Johnny, the Selectors are telling me to have a go. What shall I do?' One may be forgiven for believing that this was largely a rhetorical question, and Haig was neither surprised nor abashed by the answer. Clearly, having been given the responsibility, the captain must be allowed to stand or fall by his own decisions.

The Selector has to become philosophical about criticism or his life becomes intolerable. He is, of course, often in possession of information which must remain confidential and which is, therefore, denied to both press and public. It is both good sense and elementary 'public relations' to give as much background information as possible, but personal details affecting widely acclaimed players are frequently not for general consumption, and the Selection Committee must be prepared to suffer in silence criticism based on an unavoidable ignorance of the facts of the case.

Feelings about Selectors have often run high in this country, and as long ago as 1909 the committee of that year, Lord Hawke, C. B. Fry and H. D. G. Leveson Gower were accused in *Bailey's Magazine* of having 'betrayed England to Australia', while *Wisden* reported that one of their decisions 'touched the confines of lunacy'. Strong words, but there have been stronger since, and if they are occasionally unduly hard on Selectors whose knowledge and experience are overwhelmingly greater than that of some of their critics, they are at least in some way indicative of the significance of cricket in English life and of the importance attached to the task of selection.

In recent years the most controversial issue concerned with the selection of a Test team was the initial omission and subsequent inclusion, due to the withdrawal of another player, of Basil d'Oliveira from the MCC side to tour South Africa in 1968–69. In the event, the South African government refused to accept d'Oliveira as a member of the touring party, and the tour was cancelled. The original outcry arose because, in the final Test in the home series against Australia in 1968, d'Oliveira scored 158 and was considered by many people to be an automatic choice for the tour. The Selectors thought otherwise and the omission brought with it charges of racial discrimination against the Selectors of the MCC team.

The most inspired selections of the postwar era occurred in the mid-1950s. First, there was the choice for the tour of Australia in 1954–55 of Colin Cowdrey and Frank Tyson, 2 young players, completely untried at Test level, whose contribution to the retention of the Ashes by England, as it turned out, was absolutely vital. Then, soon afterwards, the recall of two veterans, Cyril Washbrook and Denis Compton; and a 'part-time' player, the Rev David Sheppard, effectively rescued England's batting in the home series against Australia in 1956 when the Ashes were retained after an early setback.

As a general rule, the Selector can only plough conscientiously along, pinning his faith in his convictions and those of his colleagues and hoping that his assessment of players is borne out by events on the field. There is no recognized set of qualifications for the Selector, and men with eccentric ideas can, if their opinions are adequately controlled, contribute in no small way to the deliberations of a committee. Basically, however, Selectors should have played Test Cricket and, therefore, be aware of the strains and stresses which affect the players; they must of course be dedicated to cricket in order to want to spend all their leisure time watching; they must be tolerant of the varied views of their colleagues about a game which, perhaps more than any other, inspires definite opinions; and they must be prepared to risk unpopularity by making decisions which run counter to the popular view.

A committee is often as good as its chairman – not because the chairman imposes his views on his colleagues, but because he must evaluate their opinions and provide the balance required to produce an effective team. Four pre-eminent cricketers – Lord Hawke, Sir Pelham Warner, G. O. Allen and Alec Bedser – have between them served as chairman on over 30 Selection Committees, and all have rendered very distinguished service to the game. Lord Hawke was, of course, captain of Yorkshire and a very influential figure in the world of cricket, especially perhaps in the 1st decade of this century. Sir Pelham Warner's reputation was made sufficiently recently for his great efforts on behalf of cricket to be widely recognized and appreciated. His judgment of players and his obvious love and enthusiasm for cricket throughout all its phases endeared him to young players, who so often find themselves compared pointedly and unfavourable with the 'old masters'.

G. O. Allen was chairman of the Selectors for 7 consecutive seasons beginning in 1955, and he established a high standard of devotion to duty both in the time which he gave to his task and in the dedicated manner in which he carried it out. Alec Bedser first became a Selector in 1962, and was made chairman in 1969, succeeding D. J. Insole. He is the longest-serving Selector and his service to the game in which he had such a distinguished playing career has been invaluable. The increasing amount of time involved in the selection process, particularly in the case of the Chairman, was acknowledged in 1979 when Alec Bedser received from the TCCB a lump sum of £2,500 for the season, and his fellow-selectors the sum of £20 for each day spent on selection duties, in recognition of their labours.

English cricket has been fortunate in the calibre of the players and administrators who have been able to give their time and energy to the selection of Test teams. Yet whoever may be called upon to serve in the future can rest assured that, like all his predecessors, he will never satisfy everybody.

TEST SELECTORS

1899 Lord Hawke, H. W. Bainbridge, W. G. Grace
1902 Lord Hawke, H. W. Bainbridge, G. MacGregor
1905 Lord Hawke, J. A. Dixon, P. F. Warner
1907 Lord Hawke, H. K. Foster, C. H. B. Marsham
1909 Lord Hawke, C. B. Fry, H. D. G. Leveson Gower
1912 J. Shuter, H. K. Foster, C. B. Fry
1921 H. K. Foster, J. Daniell, R. H. Spooner
1924 H. D. G. Leveson Gower, J. Daniell, J. Sharp
1926 P. F. Warner, A. E. R. Gilligan, P. A. Perrin (J. B. Hobbs and W. Rhodes were co-opted)
1928 H. D. G. Leveson Gower, A. W. Carr, J. W. H. T. Douglas
1929 H. D. G. Leveson Gower, N. E. Haig, J. C. White
1930 H. D. G. Leveson Gower, F. T. Mann, J. C. White
1931, 1932 P. F. Warner, T. A. Higson, P. A. Perrin
1933 Lord Hawke, T. A. Higson, P. A. Perrin
1934 Hon F. S. Jackson, T. A. Higson, P. A. Perrin
1935, 1936 P. F. Warner, T. A. Higson, P. A. Perrin
1937 Sir Pelham Warner, T. A. Higson, P. A. Perrin (E. R. T. Holmes was co-opted)
1938 Sir Pelham Warner, P. A. Perrin, A. B. Sellers, M. J. L. Turnbull
1939 P. A. Perrin, A. J. Holmes, A. B. Sellers, M. J. Turnbull
1946 Sir F. S. Jackson, A. J. Holmes, R. W. V. Robins, A. B. Sellers
1947, 1948 A. J. Holmes, J. C. Clay, R. W. V. Robins
1949 A. J. Holmes, T. N. Pearce, R. W. V. Robins, A. B. Sellers
1950 R. E. S. Wyatt, L. E. G. Ames, T. N. Pearce, A. B. Sellers
1951, 1952 N. W. D. Yardley, L. E. G. Ames, F. R. Brown, R. E. S. Wyatt
1953 F. R. Brown, L. E. G. Ames, R. E. S. Wyatt, N. W. D. Yardley
1954 H. S. Altham, L. E. G. Ames, R. W. V. Robins, R. E. S. Wyatt
1955 G. O. Allen, L. E. G. Ames, A. B. Sellers, W. Wooller
1956 G. O. Allen, L. E. G. Ames, C. Washbrook, W. Wooller
1957 G. O. Allen, H. E. Dollery, C. Washbrook, W. Wooller
1958 G. O. Allen, L. E. G. Ames, H. E. Dollery, W. Wooller
1959, 1960, 1961 G. O. Allen, D. J. Insole, H. Sutcliffe, W. Wooller
1962, 1963, 1964 R. W. V. Robins, A. V. Bedser, D. J. Insole, W. Watson
1965, 1966, 1967, 1968 D. J. Insole, A. V. Bedser, D. Kenyon, P. B. H. May
1969, 1970 A. V. Bedser, D. Kenyon, A. C. Smith, W. H. H. Sutcliffe
1971, 1972 A. V. Bedser, D. Kenyon, A. C. Smith, C. Washbrook
1973 A. V. Bedser, A. C. Smith, B. Taylor, O. S. Wheatley
1974 A. V. Bedser, J. D. Bond, B. Taylor, O. S. Wheatley
1975, 1976 A. V. Bedser, K. F. Barrington, C. S. Elliott, Sir Leonard Hutton
1977, 1978 A. V. Bedser, K. F. Barrington, C. S. Elliott, J. T. Murray
1979 A. V. Bedser, K. F. Barrington, D. B. Close, C. S. Elliott

West Indies v New Zealand

REX ALSTON

West Indies first visited New Zealand from Australia in 1952, when they had just proved themselves a match for the best. It was scarcely surprising, therefore, that things went very much their way. The First Test was won by West Indies by 5 wickets and the Second advantageously drawn. West Indies led by 51 and, needing 139 to win, they lost 5 wickets for 99, but F. M. Worrell and G. E. Gomez saw them through. The spinners, S. Ramadhin and A. L. Valentine, troubled all the New Zealand batsmen. In the drawn Test, J. B. Stollmeyer (152), Worrell (100) and Walcott (115) all made hundreds and A. F. Rae made 99 in a total of 546 for 6 declared. New Zealand struggled to 160 against Ramadhin and Valentine, V. J. Scott resisting staunchly for 84, but rain then ruined the match.

In 1956, in New Zealand, West Indies, with a side somewhat below their best, in order to try out a few youngsters, won the 1st 3 Tests easily and New Zealand the Fourth. E. D. Weekes made a hundred in each of the 1st 3 Tests, Worrell and Walcott did not tour, and Ramadhin took 9 wickets in the First Test and 6 in the Second. New Zealand's win in the Fourth Test by 190 runs was their first-ever against West Indies. They led by 110 after 84 from J. R. Reid and accurate fast-medium bowling by A. R. MacGibbon and H. B. Cave (4 wickets each). New Zealand then declared at 157 for 9, D. Atkinson taking 7 for 53,

At Kingston, Jamaica, his home town, Lawrence Rowe in 1971–72 against New Zealand became the only man who in his 1st Test Match has made a double-hundred and a hundred (214 and 100 not out).

but West Indies, needing 268, lost their 1st 6 wickets for 22 and were all out for 77, Cave taking 4 for 21.

In 1968–69 West Indies played 3 Tests in New Zealand, each side winning 1 match and the Third was drawn. After losing the First Test by 5 wickets, New Zealand won the Second by 6 wickets. In the First Test B. R. Taylor played an extraordinary innings of 124 in under 2 hours. In the Third Test B. F. Hastings (117 not out) saved the day. In the series, Taylor, Hastings, B. E. Congdon and G. T. Dowling all made over 200 runs, and fast bowler R. C. Motz took the most wickets (15). The West Indies batsman S. M. Nurse played 2 tremendous innings of 168, which won the First Test, and 258 out of 417 in the drawn match. Nurse totalled 558 in the 3 Tests and R. M. Edwards, a white fast bowler from Barbados, took 15 wickets.

New Zealand drew 5 Tests in West Indies in 1971–72. The batting was too strong for weak bowling, but New Zealand excelled in the field. For the West Indies, L. G. Rowe, C. A. Davis and R. C. Fredericks all batted impressively, and V. A. Holder, G. S. Sobers and Inshan Ali shared the most wickets. For New Zealand, G. M. Turner made 672 runs including 2 double hundreds. Congdon made 531, and the fast-medium bowler Taylor took 27 wickets. To take on the West Indies on their own pitches, and emerge unscathed, was an achievement the measure of which is apparent when the early New Zealand Tests are considered.

WEST INDIES V NEW ZEALAND

			RESULT	CAPTAINS
1951–52	1 Christchurch	NZ 236, 189; WI 287, 142–5	WI 5 wkts	J. D. C. Goddard, B. Sutcliffe
	2 Auckland	WI 546–6D; NZ 160, 17–1	Drawn	J. D. C. Goddard, B. Sutcliffe
1955–56	1 Dunedin	NZ 74, 208; WI 353	WI Inns 71 runs	D. S. Atkinson, H. B. Cave
	2 Christchurch	WI 386; NZ 158, 164	WI Inns 64 runs	D. S. Atkinson, J. R. Reid
	3 Wellington	WI 404, 13–1; NZ 208, 208	WI 9 wkts	D. S. Atkinson, J. R. Reid
	4 Auckland	NZ 255, 157–9D; WI 145, 77	NZ 190 runs	D. S. Atkinson, J. R. Reid
1968–69	1 Auckland	NZ 323, 297–8D; WI 276, 348–5	WI 5 wkts	G. S. Sobers, G. T. Dowling
	2 Wellington	WI 297, 148; NZ 282, 166–4	NZ 6 wkts	G. S. Sobers, G. T. Dowling
	3 Christchurch	WI 417; NZ 217, 367–6	Drawn	G. S. Sobers, G. T. Dowling
1971–72	1 Kingston	WI 508–4D, 218–3D; NZ 386, 236–6	Drawn	G. S. Sobers, G. T. Dowling
	2 Trinidad	NZ 348, 288–3D; WI 341, 121–5	Drawn	G. S. Sobers, G. T. Dowling
	3 Barbados	WI 133, 564–8; NZ 422	Drawn	G. S. Sobers, B. E. Congdon
	4 Georgetown	WI 365–7D, 86–0; NZ 543–3D	Drawn	G. S. Sobers, B. E. Congdon
	5 Trinidad	WI 368, 194; NZ 162, 253–7	Drawn	G. S. Sobers, B. E. Congdon

CAPTAINS (West Indies)	TESTS	WON	LOST	DRAWN
J. D. C. Goddard	2	1		1
D. S. Atkinson	4	3	1	
G. S. Sobers	8	1	1	6
	14	5	2	7

CAPTAINS (New Zealand)	TESTS	WON	LOST	DRAWN
B. Sutcliffe	2		1	1
H. B. Cave	1		1	
J. R. Reid	3	1	2	
G. T. Dowling	5	1	1	3
B. E. Congdon	3			3
	14	2	5	7

HIGHEST INNINGS TOTAL

West Indies in West Indies, 564–8D, Barbados 1971–72
West Indies in New Zealand, 546–6D, Auckland 1951–52
New Zealand in West Indies, 543–3D, Georgetown 1971–72
New Zealand in New Zealand, 367–6, Christchurch 1968–69

LOWEST INNINGS TOTAL

West Indies in West Indies, 133, Barbados 1971–72
West Indies in New Zealand, 77, Auckland 1955–56
New Zealand in West Indies, 162, Trinidad 1971–72
New Zealand in New Zealand, 74, Dunedin 1955–56

HIGHEST INDIVIDUAL INNINGS

West Indies in West Indies, 214, L. G. Rowe, Kingston 1971–72
West Indies in New Zealand, 258, S. M. Nurse, Christchurch 1968–69
New Zealand in West Indies, 259, G. M. Turner, Georgetown 1971–72
New Zealand in New Zealand, 124, B. R. Taylor, Auckland 1968–69

HIGHEST AGGREGATE OF RUNS IN A SERIES

West Indies in West Indies, 487, R. C. Fredericks 1971–72
West Indies in New Zealand, 558, S. M. Nurse 1968–69
New Zealand in West Indies, 672, G. M. Turner 1971–72
New Zealand in New Zealand, 239, B. F. Hastings 1968–69

BEST INNINGS BOWLING FIGURES

West Indies in West Indies, 5–59, Inshan Ali, Trinidad 1971–72
West Indies in New Zealand, 7–53, D. S. Atkinson, Auckland 1955–56
New Zealand in West Indies, 7–74, B. R. Taylor, Barbados 1971–72
New Zealand in New Zealand, 6–69, R. C. Motz, Wellington 1968–69

BEST MATCH BOWLING FIGURES

West Indies in West Indies, 7–158, Inshan Ali, Trinidad 1971–72
West Indies in New Zealand, 9–81, S. Ramadhin, Dunedin 1955–56
New Zealand in West Indies, 9–182, B. R. Taylor, Barbados 1971–72
New Zealand in New Zealand, 8–43, H. B. Cave, Auckland 1955–56

HIGHEST WICKET AGGREGATE IN A SERIES

West Indies in West Indies, 12, V. A. Holder 1971–72
West Indies in New Zealand, 20, S. Ramadhin 1955–56
New Zealand in West Indies, 27, B. R. Taylor 1971–72
New Zealand in New Zealand, 17, R. C. Motz 1968–69

RECORD WICKET PARTNERSHIPS—WEST INDIES

1 J. B. Stollmeyer and A. F. Rae, 197, Auckland 1951–52
2 R. C. Fredericks and L. G. Rowe, 269, Kingston 1971–72
3 S. M. Nurse and B. F. Butcher, 174, Auckland 1968–69
4 E. D. Weekes and O. G. Smith, 162, Dunedin 1955–56
5 F. M. Worrell and C. L. Walcott, 189, Auckland 1951–52
6 C. A. Davis and G. S. Sobers, 254, Barbados 1971–72
7 D. S. Atkinson and J. D. C. Goddard, 143, Christchurch 1955–56
8 J. D. C. Goddard and S. Ramadhin, 75, Dunedin 1955–56
9 D. A. J. Holford and V. A. Holder, 56, Trinidad 1971–72
10 T. M. Findlay and G. C. Shillingford, 31, Barbados 1971–72

RECORD WICKET PARTNERSHIPS—NEW ZEALAND

1 G. M. Turner and T. W. Jarvis, 387, Georgetown 1971–72
2 G. M. Turner and B. E. Congdon, 139, Trinidad 1971–72
3 B. F. Hastings and V. Pollard, 75, Christchurch 1968–69
4 B. E. Congdon and B. F. Hastings, 175, Barbados 1971–72
5 B. F. Hastings and V. Pollard, 110, Christchurch 1968–69
6 G. M. Turner and K. J. Wadsworth, 220, Kingston 1971–72
7 J. E. F. Beck and A. M. Moir, 90, Dunedin 1955–56
8 B. E. Congdon and R. S. Cunis, 136, Trinidad 1971–72
9 F. L. H. Mooney and D. D. Beard, 50, Christchurch 1951–52
10 B. E. Congdon and J. C. Alabaster, 41, Trinidad 1971–72

West Indies v India

J. B. STOLLMEYER AND D. J. RUTNAGUR

At their first opportunity after the Second World War the West Indies gave an indication of their strength when MCC were able to send them in 1947–48 a side lacking too many of their best. As a result the 1st tour of India, in 1948–49, by a West Indies team was welcomed by both countries. The West Indian team was: J. D. Goddard (captain), J. B. Stollmeyer (vice-captain), E. D. Weekes, C. L. Walcott, G. M. Carew, A. F. Rae, G. A. Headley, K. Rickards, F. J. Cameron, W. Ferguson, P. E. Jones, J. Trim, D. Atkinson, C. A. McWatt, G. E. Gomez and R. J. Christiani.

This tour took place only months after the partition of India and the country was still largely in a state of flux. The West Indians did very little in the way of air travel, and this only when they insisted that they could not continue in such prolonged discomfort as they were experiencing in the trains. It was perforce very much an austerity tour with journeys frequently lasting 1½ days and one from Delhi to Poona 2½. It was certainly a 'pioneer' tour, the last of its kind after the war. India's cricket, like West Indies', had been built up during the war years, during which several outstanding players had come to the fore. Besides L. Amarnath, V. Merchant and Mushtaq Ali of the prewar era, there were V. S. Hazare, V. Mankad, R. S. Modi and D. G. Phadkar, who had emerged as outstanding players during and since the war. It looked as though many runs would be scored and so they were. Eventually 4 Tests were drawn and one, at Madras, won by West Indies by an innings.

On this tour Weekes, particularly, and Walcott established themselves as batsmen in the very front rank. It gave everyone infinite pleasure to watch Weekes in full flight. He had a tremendous tour and the distinction of creating a world record in scoring 5 consecutive Test hundreds, the first being against England at Kingston, followed by 128 at Delhi, 194 at Bombay, 162 and 101 at Calcutta. But for an unfortunate run-out decision at Madras in which the batsmen appeared to lose the benefit of the doubt, in a close finish, he would surely have got the 6th, for he had scored 90 and was going great guns.

One of the features of the series was the fact that in the 1st 3 Tests West Indies scored heavily and quickly in the 1st innings, but were still unable to clinch the match, even after twice enforcing the follow-on. This may be attributed first to the lasting qualities of most Indian wickets; secondly to the general lack of penetration of the West Indies' attack; and thirdly to the tenacity of some of the Indian batsmen particularly Hazare, Modi and Adhikari. The 1st 2 Tests at Delhi and Bombay were drawn, West Indies scoring over 600 in each of the 1st innings after winning the toss. At Delhi, besides Weekes's hundred, 3-figure innings came also from Walcott (152), Christiani (107) and Gomez (101): it was the maiden Test hundred for all 3. Adhikari was the hero of the day for India and scored 114 not out and 29 not out in the match. The repetitive chant of the spectators on the final day of the game between the overs, as Adhikari played India to safety, of 'Well-played -Ad-hi-ka-ri', is an everlasting memory of an interesting game, another feature of which was that the ball had to be changed no fewer than 6 times during the course of the 1st innings.

The Bombay wicket, well prepared, is a batsman's paradise and so it proved to be in the Second Test. West Indies won the toss and scored 629 for 6. But again their bowling under the conditions was inadequate to bowl India out twice. They were dismissed for 273 in the 1st innings but in the second Hazare and Modi, eschewing most if not all of their attacking shots, hung on tenaciously to see India through, both scoring hundreds.

At Calcutta a most interesting game which went first one way and then the other was finally drawn. Weekes had another amazing double of 162 and 101, and Walcott with 54 and 108 was again in the runs. West Indies left India 431 to make in 410 minutes in the last innings and at the end of the match India were 325 for 3. For India, Mushtaq, who scored a hundred in the 2nd innings, Hazare and Modi were consistent and played well in both innings. This was a better game of cricket if only because the Eden Gardens wicket gave the bowlers a little more help.

The Madras wicket where the Fourth Test was played was distinctly faster than any of the wickets previously played on in India, and West Indies included both fast bowlers, Trim and Jones, for the 1st time in the series. It was these 2 bowlers, who took 13 wickets between them, and consistent batting which produced a very convincing win for West Indies by an innings and 193 runs. None of the Indian batsmen was happy when Jones and Trim warmed to their work and it was obvious that India had made a tactical error by encouraging Phadkar to bowl bumpers at the West Indies batsmen; Jones and Trim who were much faster were able to give far more than the West Indies got. Goddard won the toss for the 4th time in succession and West Indies scored 582, Rae (109) and Stollmeyer (160) the faithful opening pair putting on 239 for the 1st wicket.

On arriving at the Brabourne Stadium in Bombay for the last Test, the West Indies were surprised to find that the pitch on which the match was to be played could hardly be discerned from the rest of the square. It was obviously underprepared and in the next 5 days it provided absorbing cricket and a tremendous finish. Goddard again won the toss, making it 5 straight, and West Indies batted. This time, though, it was an uphill fight, for the quicker bowlers got some life and the spinners Ghulam and Mankad were both able to turn.

On the last day the game was beautifully poised with India needing 271 runs with 7 wickets in hand and 330 minutes playing time left. The game swung first one way and then the other, and for the hour before and the whole period after tea, it was anybody's match, including the clock's, which eventually prevailed. The last over was highly nerve-wracking yet somewhat pathetic, and ended in a dramatic anti-climax, if such a contradiction in terms exists. Jones bowled it to Phadkar who was in with Ghulam. Thirteen runs were needed. The other Indian batsman to come, Sen, had a dislocated shoulder and was unable to bat. The last ball fell due and 6 were still needed with Ghulam facing. But it was never bowled. The umpire lifted the bails and the players came in. He had apparently miscounted. So ended this strange but stimulating tour.

The 1st visit in January 1953 of an Indian team to the West Indies was anticipated enthusiastically, especially in Trinidad and British Guiana where East Indians – originally introduced as indentured labour for the Sugar Estates – abound, and comprise nearly half the population. India under Hazare brought a team strong in all-rounders and in spin bowling and they proved a magnificent fielding side, especially on the ground. India won the toss in the First Test at Port of Spain and batted on the jute-matting wicket. By careful if unenterprising cricket they scored 417. The West Indies reply was

438, of which Weekes's contribution was 207. He was ably supported by Pairaudeau who, in his Test debut, made 115. The combination of Gupte (7 for 162) and Mankad kept all the other batsmen in check. India batted even more cautiously in the 2nd innings; their 294 coming at an average of 2 runs per over. Umrigar with 69 was again top scorer while Phadkar (65) and Apte (52) gave him chief support. West Indies had less than 3 hours to score the 274 needed to win and no attempt was made to get the runs. Rae (63) and Stollmeyer (76) were unseparated at the close.

On a slow wicket at Barbados in the Second Test, West Indies batted 1st and scored 296, owing much to Walcott who made 98. India fared worse and were 43 short of the West Indies total, thanks to Valentine who found his best form and, for a change, to some help from the wicket. When West Indies batted again, Phadkar (5 for 64) bowled in his best form and, with the wicket rather uncertain, West Indies could only reach 228, Stollmeyer (54) batting well. India were then left 272 to get, but with the ball keeping low and Ramadhin pushing his off-spinners through they could only reach 129 and West Indies won by 142 runs.

The Third Test began a week later in Trinidad. India played carefully in her 1st innings for 279. Weekes with another classic innings of 161 was responsible for more than half his side's total of 315. It was a disappointing score, but Gupte bowled at his best and some of the other Indian bowlers adopted negative leg-side tactics to keep the run-scoring rate in check. In the 2nd innings India did better, scoring 362 for 7 before declaring and setting West Indies the task of scoring 327 in 165 minutes. Apte, with considerable application, determination and not a little luck, compiled 163 not out. The game, as dull a Test Match as ever there was, petered out into a draw, West Indies being 192 for 2 at the end. Stollmeyer finished with 104 not out.

The Test Match in British Guiana was ruined by rain. India, winning the toss, had batted and scored 182 for 6 on the first day. After heavy rains over the weekend, water had leaked through the tarpaulins and the wicket was affected. Accordingly the captains agreed to suspend play until after lunch. But heavy rains fell during the lunch interval and the umpires finally called off play for the day. But the large crowd which had waited patiently all day for play to begin, much of the time in brilliant sunshine, threatened to become hostile and the umpires were persuaded by the West Indies Board officials after consultation with the captains and the manager of the Indian team to continue play between 4.30 pm and 5.30 pm. That the ground was unfit there was no doubt, and the Laws were transgressed. Small wonder that a note was received subsequently from Lord's to the effect that 'the game must not be subject to mob rule'.

The final Test of the series was played at Kingston. West Indies preferred Scott, who had done well in the Colony game, to Ramadhin, and Christiani and Gomez returned for Miller and Wight. India batted first and made 312, Roy (85) and Umrigar (117) doing best. West Indies made 576 and the Kingston crowd had the privilege of seeing the 'three Ws' each get hundreds, a phenomenon they were due to repeat against England a year later at Port of Spain. Worrell, who had had a comparatively lean series, came into his own with 237, while Weekes (109) and Walcott (118) maintained their remarkable consistency. Between them, Mankad and Gupte took all 10 wickets for 408 runs, a highly curious statistic. India made 444 in their 2nd innings, thanks to a plucky 150 by Roy and a classic 118 from Manjrekar.

West Indies eventually needed 181 in 135 minutes but, losing Pairaudeau and Stollmeyer, reverted to defence, thus winning the series by the only game finished. Too much of the cricket played was defensive. The bowling of Gupte, however, the superb ground fielding of the Indian team, and the magnificence of Weekes and Walcott, were the highlights of an otherwise pedestrian series.

West Indies went to India a 2nd time in 1958–59 and won the rubber 3–0 under the captaincy of F. C. M. Alexander. Though they were subsequently beaten 2–1 in Pakistan, their fast bowlers, Hall and Gilchrist, taking 56 wickets between them, were too fast and too fierce for the Indian batsmen. To win 3 Test Matches on Indian pitches is a remarkable feat, but the free use of the bouncer and the 'beamer' meant that the tour is not one of pleasant memories in India. Gilchrist, in fact, was sent home on disciplinary grounds before the team moved on to Pakistan.

Cricket in India proved to have made big advances in its administration since the previous West Indian tour of 10 years before, but it was a transitional period on the playing side. This showed in the fact of 24 players being used in the series, of whom 12 only played once. There were 4 different captains – Ghulam Ahmed, P. R. Umrigar, V. Mankad and H. R. Adhikari. Gupte bowled over 300 overs and took 22 wickets at 42 apiece. No other Indian took more than 5 and, not for the last time, India were beaten through lack of fast bowling and the ability to play fast bowling.

The docility of the Bombay pitch enabled India to draw the First Test after they had spent most of the 5 days struggling against the odds. Sobers made 142 not out in the 2nd innings, and Alexander's declaration left his bowlers over 1½ days to dismiss India, who needed 399 to win. Yet the match was comfortably saved, largely by Roy, who batted nearly 7½ hours for 90.

At Kanpur, in the Second Test, the 1st innings finished level at 222, but Sobers then played another fine innings before being run out for 198, and Hall, who took 11 wickets in the match, drove the advantage home on the last day for West Indies to win by 203 runs. West Indies won even more comfortably at Calcutta by an innings and 336 runs. Kanhai's 1st Test hundred eventually grew to 256, the highest for West Indies against India. Butcher made 103, Sobers 106 not out and, having declared at 614 for 5, West Indies bowled India out for 124 and 154, 15 of the wickets being taken by Gilchrist and Hall. In the Fourth Test at Madras, Butcher made 142 and Kanhai 99 in the 1st innings, Hall and Gilchrist took half the wickets, and West Indies won by 295 runs.

It was not until the Fifth Test at New Delhi that India provided any real opposition. Adhikari, aged 39, was brought back as captain and India, batting 1st for the 1st time in the series, scored 415. Borde, whose all-round performance had been one of the more encouraging Indian developments, made 109 and 96, Contractor 92. Once again, however, there were no bowlers to contain the West Indian batsmen on the sluggish pitch and Hunte made 92, Holt 123, O. G. Smith 100 and Solomon 100 not out. Solomon, only 3 times out, averaged 117 in the series. Borde's 2nd innings of 96 enabled India to save the game.

India brought a better side to West Indies in 1962, though a combination of ill-luck and their usual lack of fast bowling led to a defeat by the maximum score of 5–0. They had just beaten E. R. Dexter's England side 2–0 in India, but within 3 weeks were in Trinidad, having come through the cold of an English winter, and proved prone to injury as well as staleness. They fielded well, the young Nawab of Pataudi being a valuable asset in this department, and they were well captained by Contractor until the lamentable accident during the match against Barbados between the Second and Third Tests. The left-handed Contractor, opening the innings, was hit over the right ear by a short ball from Griffith. His skull was fractured and for some days there were fears for his life, but an emergency brain operation was performed. A brain surgeon was flown from Trinidad and after a 2nd operation Contractor started on a slow recovery. Though the Second Test at Kingston proved to be his last, he was well enough to captain West Zone against MCC 2 years later.

The First Test at Port of Spain was a fair indication of later trends. India batted with spirit in the first innings but as the match progressed lost their grip and were beaten by 10 wickets. India began the Second Test in Jamaica by making 395 (Borde, 93, Nadkarni 78 not out) with a briskness which has not always characterized their batting at home. But West Indies made 631 for 8 declared (McMorris 125, Kanhai 138 and Sobers 153) before Hall, 6 for 49, bowled India out in the 2nd innings with help from Gibbs and Sobers. West Indies thus won by an innings and 18 runs.

In the Third Test at Barbados, which followed much the same pattern, India were captained for the 1st time by Pataudi, who, at 21 and 2 months, became the youngest of all Test captains. There was a grim 3rd day when the West Indies, already ahead, made only 164 for the loss of 4 wickets. But the Indian collapse on the last day from 158 for 2 to 187 all out allowed West Indies to win comfortably by an innings and 30 runs, Gibbs taking the last 8 wickets for 6 runs. With the rubber already decided, the West Indies maintained their superiority in the last 2 Tests. India did their best but were decisively outgunned.

Heavy restrictions on the outflow of foreign currency from India curtailed the 1966–67 series to just 3 Tests. West Indies won it 2–0 but the gap between the sides had narrowed since they last met 4 years earlier. This was mainly because West Indies' 2 great fast bowlers, Wes Hall and Charlie Griffith, had not quite recovered from the strain of an exacting tour of England during the previous summer. Age too was catching up with them. Another prominent weakness of that West Indies team, led by Gary Sobers, was at the top of its batting order, where Conrad Hunte had no reliable partner.

West Indies prevailed by 6 wickets in the First Test at Bombay, where they had not before been able to force a result. This Test made for the first confrontation between the West Indies batsmen and Chandrasekhar, the freak wrist-spinner India had unearthed 2 years earlier. He took 7 wickets for 157 runs in the 1st innings and West Indies would not have scored as many as 421 and gone 125 runs ahead but for India's errors in the field. India, who batted 1st, were dealt some early shocks by Hall and Griffith, but were rallied by a hundred from Borde, with support from his captain, Pataudi and Durani India's batsmen scored more evenly in the 2nd innings and totalled 316, leaving West Indies to make 191 on a pitch that was taking spin. Gibbs and Holford had taken 7 wickets in the Indian 2nd innings. In the circumstances, the issue looked wide open when West Indies lost 4 wickets before reaching the halfway mark. But Sobers and the newcomer Clive Lloyd, who had already scored 50 and 82 respectively in the 1st innings, cracked India's resistance and, shortly after lunch on the last day, put on the victors' seal.

The Second Test at Calcutta marked the start of Bishen Bedi's long Test career. Only just turned 20, Bedi at once looked the part of a world-class spinner and, in a high-scoring innings, took the wickets of Lloyd and Basil Butcher for 92 runs in 36 overs. But India had little else to celebrate. The Eden Gardens pitch, under-prepared and never likely to last the distance, wore more rapidly through being trampled on by stampeding crowds during a violent riot on the second morning. The incident was provoked by police excesses. The ground authorities had sold tickets for many more seats than existed. The stands got so overcrowded that some spectators scaled, or were even hurled over the wire-netting fence. This triggered off the worst riots ever witnessed at a Test Match. The day's play was abandoned, and the players on both sides, understandably apprehensive, were reluctant to continue the match. After prolonged negotiations, in which Sir Frank Worrell (who was in India on a goodwill visit) took part, the match was resumed after a 2-day break. Lance Gibbs and Sobers, bowling spin, encountered little resistance and West Indies won by an innings and 45 runs to clinch the series.

India nearly gained a consolation win in the final Test at Madras, where, after a 13-year exile, Test cricket had come back to its traditional venue, Chepauk. India batted first and got off to a great start, with Engineer getting within 6 runs of becoming the first Indian to score a hundred before lunch. He duly got his hundred after the break and Borde also played his 2nd 3-figure innings of the series. India put up a total of 404, which West Indies matched, thanks mainly to Kanhai and Sobers. India again batted purposefully and scored 323. The pitch was now yielding spin in increasing measure and India would surely have won had they not reprieved Sobers twice before he had reached double-figures. He went on to make 74 and West Indies saved the match with 3 wickets to spare. Griffith, using his pads and even his body, at times, to protect his wicket, stayed in with Sobers for the last 90 minutes.

After 23 Tests against the West Indies, of which they had lost 12 and won none, India, playing under a new captain in Ajit Wadekar, scored their first-ever win over them at Queen's Park Oval, Trinidad, in the Second Test of the 1971 series. That maiden win, completed with a day to spare, also clinched the series, for the other 4 Tests were all drawn. India's win came abruptly and after a dramatic swing in fortunes. But it could not be described as a fluke, for India had also held the upper hand in the previous Test, at Kingston, and in the one following, at Georgetown. India were also in a winning position in the drawn final Test, a 6-day match, in Trinidad. At Bridgetown, however, the West Indies had India cornered, but allowed them to escape through indifferent out-cricket.

India's superiority over the whole series reflected their all-round strength and shrewd tactical planning in which the side's senior member, M. L. Jaisimha, was a great aid to the new captain. For all his experience, Sobers was often outwitted. But it is equally true to say that luck ran very strongly in India's favour. Even an injury to Viswanath, on the eve of the start of the tour, worked to their advantage, for Dilip Sardesai, who took Viswanath's place in the opening game, proved the backbone of their batting.

It was during this rubber that Sunil Manohar Gavaskar, then only 21 and just down from university, proclaimed his genius to the world, scoring 774 runs in his maiden series, and that despite missing the First Test because of an infected finger. In the final Test, he performed the then unique feat of scoring a hundred and a double-hundred in the same match (Rowe and Greg Chappell have done so since). Viswanath, who had made his mark against the Australians 2 years earlier, did not recover from his injury until the Third Test and did not really do himself justice. But Sardesai, who was virtually the last man to win selection in the tour party, showed the way, batting with tremendous authority from the start of the tour to the finish. A double-hundred by him in the First Test rescued

When India surprised the West Indians by beating them 1–0 in a full series in the Caribbean in 1970–71, D. N. Sardesai made 3 hundreds and averaged 80. He is seen here batting against Sobers during his 150 at Bridgetown.

India, who were put in on a damp, 2-paced pitch at Sabina Park, from a desperate situation and placed them in a position of such strength that India were able to force the West Indies to follow on (for the 1st time ever). Sardesai's 112 was also the main batting contribution to India's historic win in the Second Test although Gavaskar, making his debut, played his part with innings of 65 and 67 not out. India would doubtless have lost their lead in the series had Sardesai not come up with another hundred in the Fourth Test, at Bridgetown.

India's spinners, Bedi, Prasanna and Venkat were all at their peak at the time. At the Queen's Park Oval, they found the pitch most amenable to their skills. But they were such masters of their craft that they also confounded the majority of the West Indian batsmen on pitches less responsive to spin. Venkataraghavan was the outstanding bowler, with 22 wickets, but Bedi and Prasanna were rarely in the background. Salim Durani, playing his last series abroad, took only 3 wickets, but the capture of 2 of them (those of Lloyd and Sobers) in quick succession ensured India's win in the dramatic Second Test by 7 wickets.

Sobers and Kanhai, both massive scorers against India during the past 4 series, had faded from the scene before the West Indies met India again, in 1974–75. But new batting stars had emerged in Gordon Greenidge and Vivian Richards and, in the 3 years since the 2 countries last met, Alvin Kallicharran had established himself as a batsman of true Test class. Their bowling too was immeasurably strengthened by the discovery of Anderson Roberts. India's morale at the start of the series was desperately low. They had just come back from England after a 3–0 beating and their star bowler, Bishen Bedi, was made the scapegoat for the debacle and stood down on very flimsy disciplinary grounds. Wadekar, captain of the beaten touring side in England, had retired from Test cricket and, with Bedi's career under a cloud, there was no obvious captain. So the Nawab of Pataudi was persuaded to come out of retirement and take charge. But he was injured during the First Test and did not play again until the Third, which also marked the reinstatement of Bedi.

Although West Indies had to cope with the pitch at its worst during a rain-affected First Test, at Bangalore, they won it by 26 runs. Greenidge, playing in his maiden Test, just missed a hundred in the 1st innings, but duly got it in the 2nd. Kallicharran and Lloyd both scored hundreds (124 and 165), the latter at such speed that his bowlers had more than enough time to bowl out India, who were batting 2 men short – Engineer having joined Pataudi on the injured list.

Pending Pataudi's recovery, Gavaskar was appointed captain for the Second Test. But in an intervening Ranji Trophy match he fractured a finger and finally the choice fell on Venkataraghavan. He won the toss, but little else went right for the caretaker captain. Vivian Richards, when only on 12 at the time, was appealed against for a catch at the wicket and was quite prepared to go when the umpire ruled in his favour. He went on to make 192. Boyce then joined Richards in the pitiless persecution of a dispirited Indian attack. Gibbs put the Indian batting to flight in the 2nd innings, a wet pitch adding to the problems of survival.

So one-sided were the 1st 2 Tests that the whole series looked like fizzling out without India offering opposition worth the name. But the tide changed with the Third Test, in which India were still without Gavaskar, but stronger for the return of Bedi. India scored their first-ever win over the West Indies on home soil and they owed it in large measure to the guts and flair of Viswanath, who was top scorer in both innings, with 52 and 139. The only other score of over 50 in either innings was 61 by Engineer who, opening the innings, batted with uncharacteristic patience. At the same time, West Indies contributed to their own downfall. Over-confidence, bred by the easy win in the First Test, led to erratic batting. Their 1st innings would have been an utter disaster but for a hundred from Fredericks, and he too was dropped before he had scored.

West Indies' over-confidence in this Test match turned to despair and diffidence during the Fourth, at Madras, which India won by a hundred runs, with a day to spare, and that despite Roberts (7 for 64) ripping the heart out of their 1st innings. India were bowled out for only 190, of which Viswanath made 97 not out. Considering the nature of the pitch and the fire with which Roberts bowled, it was perhaps the greatest innings of Viswanath's career.

The Chepauk pitch at Madras started to take spin early and Prasanna and Bedi, both taking 7 wickets in the match, used it to the fullest. But West Indies, who had gone into the match with only one specialist spinner, Lance Gibbs, continued to depend heavily on Roberts, even in the 2nd innings. He followed up his 7 for 64 with 5 for 57, but India made 256 and left West Indies to get 254 in the final innings. In scoring 51 before being run out, Kallicharran again showed what a master he is in playing on a poor pitch.

The rubber now depended on the final Test at Bombay and West Indies were so apprehensive about the pitch at the new Wankhede Stadium that they would probably have panicked and lost had the coin not fallen in their favour. They had protested frantically about the pitch even before a ball was bowled and their manager, former Test captain F. C. M. Alexander, took close-up photographs of some of its bare patches. He must have cast the roll of film into the Arabian Sea by the end of West Indies' innings; for they declared at 604 for 6, the captain, Lloyd, whose tactics had often been questionable, redeeming all in a tremendous innings of 242. The Indians still made a brave fight of the Test, replying with 406. But the West Indies, brimming with confidence once more, brought the power of their batting to bear in their 2nd innings, scored 205 for 5 in quick time and left their bowlers 7 hours to bowl India out again. Vanburn Holder, who had had little luck in the previous Tests, bowled India to their doom. By the standards he had set up in the earlier Tests, Roberts had a lean match, but he produced some spells at a fearsome pace, even on this lifeless pitch, and he sealed India's fate by removing Gavaskar (who had made 86 in the 1st innings) for 0.

The next series was played in the West Indies in 1976. It closely followed the contours of the dramatic 3–2 rubber in India of only a year before. While the West Indies went into it almost directly after a severe trouncing at the hands of Australia, India had arrived in the Caribbean straight from the wet, cold and slow pitches of New Zealand. Before they settled to the changed conditions, they were a Test down in a 4-match series, having been routed in only 3 days at the Kensington Oval in Barbados, which had seen the Indians at their worst on every tour. But India nearly levelled the score in the Second Test at the Queen's Park Oval in Trinidad, where they always get fervent support from the East Indian community and where the pitch is always so amenable to their spinners.

If India did not win this Test, after dismissing the West Indies for 241 and themselves scoring 402 for 5 and declaring, it was because they dropped many catches on the last day. West Indies, though, did not save the Test by much. Gavaskar made 156, his 3rd hundred in consecutive Tests on that ground, and while India were rushing along to declare, Brijesh Patel, a dangerous batsman on a slow wicket, batted brilliantly for 115 not out.

This series was unique (at least since the 1880s in Australia) in that 2 consecutive Tests were played on the same ground. Bourda, in Georgetown, where the Third Test was to have been played, was under flood after days of torrential rain. The Indians made a perfunctory trip to the territory, where the match against Guyana was abandoned even before the tourists arrived there, and returned to Trinidad, where hurried preparations were made to stage the Third Test. The change of ground fully suited the Indians, who grasped their chance to score a historic win. It was historic because they became only the 2nd team ever to score more than 400 runs in the 4th innings to win a Test match. And winning was by no means a struggle. They prevailed with 6 wickets in hand.

West Indies clinched the issue in the Fourth Test on a Sabina Park pitch that added to the lethal nature of a West Indian pace attack comprising Holding, Daniel, Julien and Holder. The 1st 3 days produced highly combative cricket and yet the 6-day Test finished very abruptly, with the last 2 days unused. India, batting 1st, did not lose their 1st wicket until just before tea at 136. Then the West Indian fast bowlers resorted to intimidatory bowling in increasing measure, but the Indians did not succumb readily. The 2nd new ball started their troubles. Mohinder Amarnath, who made a game 39, and Viswanath were both caught at backward short-leg, off the glove. The ball from Holding that dismissed Viswanath broke his left hand. The tall Aunshuman Gaekwad, who made 81 and stood his ground for more than a day, taking umpteen blows on his chest and on his arms, was ultimately felled by a ball that struck him over the ear and put him in hospital for a prolonged stay. Patel was another who had to retire hurt, after being struck over the mouth, although he could be said to have invited injury by ducking into a ball through misjudgment. But he too had been put through the softening-up process. Bedi closed the innings at the fall of the 6th wicket rather than risk injury to himself and Chandrasekhar, the two main bowlers.

It was obvious by then that none of the 3 injured batsmen would be able to bat in the 2nd innings and yet the Indians did not allow these problems to daunt them. Fredericks and Rowe started off the West Indies with an opening partnership of 105, but the Indians fought back resiliently, through Bedi and Chandrasekhar, and when West Indies were 217 for 6, a 1st-innings lead for India seemed in prospect. But a late partnership between Holding and Holder eventually put West Indies 85 runs in front. From then on, India merely went through the motions, although Amarnath again made a brave 59 in India's second innings, in which only 6 men batted. Bedi and Chandrasekhar too had gone on the injured list, having been struck over their hands in the field. The final Test of an otherwise fascinating series ended on a sour and bitter note, and when, 2 days later, the Indians walked towards their homebound plane at Kingston's Manley airport, many of them wrapped in bandages, they resembled the flight from Moscow.

The 1978–79 series in India, the 1st of 6 Tests between the 2 countries, was a happier series, although the least distinguished of the 9 rubbers played between them. This was mainly due to the fact that the West Indies players engaged by World Series Cricket were not available for the tour. Still, India, for whom Gavaskar scored as heavily as on his first encounter with the West Indians, managed to win only 1 of the 6 Tests. Gavaskar aggregated 732 runs in the series, including a double-hundred in the First Test and 2 separate hundreds in the Third. The West Indies, for their runs, depended heavily on Kallicharran, their captain, and Larry Gomes. None of the others batted with any consistency, but Faoud Bacchus scored a brilliant double-hundred in the final Test. The bowling of both sides looked inadequate to produce decisive results. But India were very near winning the Third Test, at Calcutta, and were in a strong position in the Fourth, at Delhi, which was severely disrupted by rain. The final Test was also rain-affected and the Second, at Bangalore, lost the last day due to rioting. The disturbance, however, had its roots in politics and was totally unconnected with the cricket.

The one Test that finished was the Fourth, at Madras, played on a fast pitch that yielded extravagant bounce. West Indies, with their superior power in the department of pace bowling, should have won it. But they dropped more chances than they took, and their bowlers got a bit over-excited at getting so much help from the pitch and bowled much too short. In a sense it was delayed retribution for the deplorable happenings at Sabina Park of the previous tour.

WEST INDIES V INDIA

			RESULT	CAPTAINS
1948–49	1 New Delhi	WI 631; Ind 454, 220–6	Drawn	J. D. C. Goddard, L. Amarnath
	2 Bombay	WI 629–6D; Ind 273, 333–3	Drawn	J. D. C. Goddard, L. Amarnath
	3 Calcutta	WI 366, 336–9D; Ind 272, 325–3	Drawn	J. D. C. Goddard, L. Amarnath
	4 Madras	WI 582; Ind 245, 144	WI inns 193 runs	J. D. C. Goddard, L. Amarnath
	5 Bombay	WI 286, 267; Ind 193, 355–8	Drawn	J. D. C. Goddard, L. Amarnath
1952–53	1 Trinidad	Ind 417, 294; WI 438, 142–0	Drawn	J. B. Stollmeyer, V. S. Hazare
	2 Barbados	WI 296, 228; Ind 253, 129	WI 142 runs	J. B. Stollmeyer, V. S. Hazare
	3 Trinidad	Ind 279, 362–7D; WI 315, 192–2	Drawn	J. B. Stollmeyer, V. S. Hazare
	4 Georgetown	Ind 262, 190–5; WI 364	Drawn	J. B. Stollmeyer, V. S. Hazare
	5 Kingston	Ind 312, 444; WI 576, 92–4	Drawn	J. B. Stollmeyer, V. S. Hazare
1958–59	1 Bombay	WI 227, 323–4D; Ind 152, 289–5	Drawn	F. C. M. Alexander, P. R. Umrigar
	2 Kanpur	WI 222, 443–7D; Ind 222, 240	WI 203 runs	F. C. M. Alexander, Ghulam Ahmed
	3 Calcutta	WI 614–5D; Ind 124, 154	WI inns 336 runs	F. C. M. Alexander, Ghulam Ahmed
	4 Madras	WI 500, 168–5D; Ind 222, 151	WI 295 runs	F. C. M. Alexander, V. Mankad
	5 New Delhi	Ind 415, 275; WI 644–8D	Drawn	F. C. M. Alexander, H. R. Adhikari
1961–62	1 Trinidad	Ind 203, 98; WI 289, 15–0	WI 10 wkts	F. M. Worrell, N. J. Contractor
	2 Kingston	Ind 395, 218; WI 631–8D	WI inns 18 runs	F. M. Worrell, N. J. Contractor
	3 Barbados	Ind 258, 187; WI 475	WI inns 30 runs	F. M. Worrell, Nawab of Pataudi
	4 Trinidad	WI 444–9D, 176–3; Ind 197, 422	WI 7 wkts	F. M. Worrell, Nawab of Pataudi
	5 Kingston	WI 253, 283; Ind 178, 235	WI 123 runs	F. M. Worrell, Nawab of Pataudi
1966–67	1 Bombay	Ind 296, 316; WI 421, 192–4	WI 6 wkts	G. S. Sobers, Nawab of Pataudi
	2 Calcutta	WI 390; Ind 167, 178	WI inns 45 runs	G. S. Sobers, Nawab of Pataudi
	3 Madras	Ind 404, 323; WI 406, 270–7	Drawn	G. S. Sobers, Nawab of Pataudi
1970–71	1 Kingston	Ind 387; WI 217, 385–5	Drawn	G. S. Sobers, A. L. Wadekar
	2 Trinidad	WI 214, 261; Ind 352, 125–3	Ind 7 wkts	G. S. Sobers, A. L. Wadekar
	3 Georgetown	WI 363, 307–3D; Ind 376, 123–0	Drawn	G. S. Sobers, A. L. Wadekar
	4 Barbados	WI 501–5D, 180–6D; Ind 347, 221–5	Drawn	G. S. Sobers, A. L. Wadekar
	5 Trinidad	Ind 360, 427; WI 526, 165–8	Drawn	G. S. Sobers, A. L. Wadekar
1974–75	1 Bangalore	WI 289, 356–6D; Ind 260, 118	WI 267 runs	C. H. Lloyd, Nawab of Pataudi
	2 Delhi	Ind 220, 256; WI 493	WI inns 17 runs	C. H. Lloyd, S. Venkataraghavan
	3 Calcutta	Ind 233, 316; WI 240, 224	Ind 85 runs	C. H. Lloyd, Nawab of Pataudi
	4 Madras	Ind 190, 256; WI 192, 154	Ind 100 runs	C. H. Lloyd, Nawab of Pataudi
	5 Bombay	WI 604–6D, 205–3D; Ind 406, 202	WI 201 runs	C. H. Lloyd, Nawab of Pataudi

1975–76	1 Barbados	Ind 177, 214; WI 488–9D	WI inns 97 runs	C. H. Lloyd, B. S. Bedi
	2 Trinidad	WI 241, 215–8; Ind 402–5D	Drawn	C. H. Lloyd, B. S. Bedi
	3 Trinidad	WI 359, 271–6D; Ind 228, 406–4	Ind 6 wkts	C. H. Lloyd, B. S. Bedi
	4 Kingston	Ind 306–6D, 97; WI 391, 13–0	WI 10 wkts	C. H. Lloyd, B. S. Bedi
1978–79	1 Bombay	Ind 424, 224–2; WI 493	Drawn	C. H. Lloyd, B. S. Bedi
	2 Bangalore	WI 437, 200–8; Ind 371	Drawn	A. I. Kallicharran, S. M. Gavaskar
	3 Calcutta	Ind 300, 361–1D; WI 327, 197–9	Drawn	A. I. Kallicharran, S. M. Gavaskar
	4 Madras	WI 228, 151; Ind 255, 125–7	Ind 3 wkts	A. I. Kallicharran, S. M. Gavaskar
	5 Delhi	Ind 566–8D; WI 172, 179–3	Drawn	A. I. Kallicharran, S. M. Gavaskar
	6 Kanpur	Ind 644–7D; WI 452–8	Drawn	A. I. Kallicharran, S. M. Gavaskar

CAPTAINS (West Indies)	TESTS	WON	LOST	DRAWN
J. D. C. Goddard	5	1		4
J. B. Stollmeyer	5	1		4
F. C. M. Alexander	5	3		2
F. M. Worrell	5	5		
G. S. Sobers	8	2	1	5
C. H. Lloyd	9	5	3	1
A. I. Kallicharran	6		1	5
	43	17	5	21

CAPTAINS (India)	TESTS	WON	LOST	DRAWN
L. Amarnath	5		1	4
V. S. Hazare	5		1	4
P. R. Umrigar	1			1
Ghulam Ahmed	2		2	
V. Mankad	1		1	
H. R. Adhikari	1			1
N. J. Contractor	2		2	
Nawab of Pataudi	10	2	7	1
A. L. Wadekar	5	1		4
S. Venkataraghavan	1		1	
B. S. Bedi	4	1	2	1
S. M. Gavaskar	6	1		5
	43	5	17	21

HIGHEST INNINGS TOTAL

West Indies in West Indies, 631–8D, Kingston 1961–62
West Indies in India, 644–8D, Delhi 1958–59
India in West Indies, 444, Kingston 1952–53
India in India, 644–7D, Kanpur 1978–79

LOWEST INNINGS TOTAL

West Indies in West Indies, 214, Trinidad 1970–71
West Indies in India, 151, Madras 1978–79
India in West Indies, 97, Kingston 1975–76
India in India, 118, Bangalore 1974–75

HIGHEST INDIVIDUAL INNINGS

West Indies in West Indies, 237, F. M. Worrell, Kingston 1952–53
West Indies in India, 256, R. B. Kanhai, Calcutta 1958–59
India in West Indies, 220, S. M. Gavaskar, Trinidad 1970–71
India in India, 205, S..M. Gavaskar, Bombay 1978–79

HIGHEST AGGREGATE OF RUNS IN A SERIES

West Indies in West Indies, 716, E. D. Weekes 1952–53
West Indies in India, 779, E. D. Weekes 1948–49
India in West Indies, 774, S. M. Gavaskar 1970–71
India in India, 732, S. M. Gavaskar 1978–79

BEST INNINGS BOWLING FIGURES

West Indies in West Indies, 9–95, J. Noreiga, Trinidad 1970–71
West Indies in India, 7–64, A. M. E. Roberts, Madras 1974–75
India in West Indies, 7–162, S. P. Gupte, Trinidad 1952–53
India in India, 9–102, S. P. Gupte, Kanpur 1958–59

BEST MATCH BOWLING FIGURES

West Indies in West Indies, 9–128, W. W. Hall, Kingston 1961–62
West Indies in India, 12–121, A. M. E. Roberts, Madras 1974–75
India in West Indies, 8–126, B. S. Bedi, Trinidad 1975–76
India in India, 11–235, B. S. Chandrasekar, Bombay 1966–67

HIGHEST WICKET AGGREGATE IN A SERIES

West Indies in West Indies, 28, A. L. Valentine 1952–53
West Indies in India, 32, A. M. E. Roberts 1974–75
India in West Indies, 27, S. P. Gupte 1952–53
India in India, {27, S. P. Gupte 1958–59; 27, K. D. Ghavri 1978–79}

RECORD WICKET PARTNERSHIPS – WEST INDIES

1 J. B. Stollmeyer and A. F. Rae, 239, Madras 1948–49
2 E. D. A. McMorris and R. B. Kanhai, 255, Kingston 1961–62
3 I. V. A. Richards and A. I. Kallicharran, 220, Barbados 1975–76
4 C. L. Walcott and G. E. Gomez, 267, Delhi 1948–49
5 E. D. Weekes and B. H. Pairaudeau, 219, Trinidad 1952–53
6 C. H. Lloyd and D. L. Murray, 250, Bombay 1974–75
7 G. S. Sobers and I. Mendonca, 127, Kingston 1961–62
8 I. V. A. Richards and K. D. Boyce, 124, Delhi 1974–75
9 R. J. Christiani and D. S. Atkinson, 106, Delhi 1948–49
10 F. M. Worrell and W. W. Hall, 98, Trinidad 1961–62

RECORD WICKET PARTNERSHIPS – INDIA

1 S. M. Gavaskar and C. P. S. Chauhan, 153, Bombay 1978–79
2 S. M. Gavaskar and D. B. Vengsarkar, 344, Calcutta 1978–79
3 M. Amarnath and G. R. Viswanath, 159, Trinidad 1975–76
4 G. R. Viswanath and A. D. Gaekwad, 172, Kanpur 1978–79
5 S. M. Gavaskar and B. P. Patel, 204, Trinidad 1975–76
6 D. N. Sardesai and E. D. Solkar, 137, Kingston 1970–71
7 D. N. Sardesi and E. D. Solkar, 186, Barbados 1970–71
8 R. D. Nadkarni and F. M. Engineer, 94, Kingston 1961–62
9 D. N. Sardesai and E. A. S. Prasanna, 122, Kingston 1970–71
10 D. N. Sardesai and B. S. Bedi, 62, Barbados 1970–71

West Indies v Pakistan

REX ALSTON

Pakistan, after their admission to the Test ranks, were not slow to spread their wings. By 1958 they were trying conclusions in the Caribbean, where West Indies beat them 3–1 with 1 draw. In the First Test at Barbados, Hanif Mohammad saved the match by batting for over 16 hours (easily the longest innings in history) to make 337, thus saving the day after Pakistan had been bowled out for 106 in reply to the West Indian total of 579 for 9 declared. In the Third Test, Sobers scored his 1st Test hundred and went on to set up a world record of 365 not out. He followed this with a hundred in each innings in the Fourth Test. After Sobers, the most prolific run-maker was C. C. Hunte, who scored a hundred in his First Test and made 260 whilst Sobers was piling up his record score. For Pakistan Saeed Ahmed proved himself a beautiful strokemaker, whilst Wazir, brother of Hanif, batted with great skill and determination. Others who made useful contributions were the

Hanif Mohammad at Kingston in 1957–58 saved the 1st Test between West Indies and Pakistan by batting for 16 hours and 10 minutes – the longest innings in history – for 337, then the 2nd-highest Test score. Pakistan had followed on 473 behind.

captain, A. H. Kardar, and wicket-keeper Imtiaz Ahmed. Pakistan had difficulty in coping with the speed of R. Gilchrist, but fortunately for them he had no satisfactory partner, and much of the bowling burden fell on the shoulders of the 2 off-spinners, O. G. Smith and L. R. Gibbs. Fazal Mahmood bore the brunt of the Pakistan bowling, whilst a 16-year-old slow left-hander, Nasim-ul-Ghani, took 19 wickets.

In the First Test, Hunte (142) and Weekes (197) were the chief contributors to the total of 579. Gilchrist and Smith bowled Pakistan out for 106 and in the follow-on, 473 behind, Hanif on the flawless Bridgetown pitch performed his monumental feat. With useful contributions from Imtiaz (91) and Saeed (65), the side totalled 657 for 8 declared. The score looked better for Pakistan in the Second Test, though West Indies won at Port of Spain by 120 runs. Good batting by Sobers, Weekes and R. B. Kanhai gave West Indies a total of 325, to which Pakistan replied with 282, Wallis Mathias, Fazal and Mahmood Hussain adding 132 for the last 3 wickets. Fine bowling by Fazal and Nasim confined the West Indies to 312 in their 2nd innings, Sobers being top scorer with 80, but despite 81 from Hanif and 64 from Saeed, Pakistan were bowled out by Gilchrist, Sobers and Gibbs for 235. West Indies won the Third Test at Kingston by an innings and 174 runs. Following Pakistan's total of 328, West Indies made 790 for 3 declared, of which Hunte and Sobers put on 446 for the 2nd wicket and Sobers, ultimately (in $10\frac{1}{4}$ hours), his 365 not out. It is only fair to record that Nasim, Kardar and Mahmood were all injured, which left Pakistan with only 2 fit bowlers. The only wicket-taker was Fazal, with 2 for 247 in 85·2 overs. (I wonder if anyone dared to console Fazal with the thought that on a certain immortal occasion at the Oval in 1938 Fleetwood-Smith, the Australian, bowling 2 overs more, emerged with 1 for 298.) Only 9 Pakistanis were fit to bat in their 2nd innings, the feature of which was a determined 106 by Wazir, and they were finally out for 288.

More high scoring was seen in the Fourth Test at Georgetown, which West Indies won by 8 wickets, thus clinching the rubber. Saeed made his 1st Test hundred (150) and Pakistan totalled 408. West Indies led by only 2 runs, due to hundreds by Sobers (125) and C. L. Walcott (145), Nasim taking 5 for 116. In their 2nd innings Pakistan made 318, Wazir making 97 not out and Gibbs taking 5 for 80, but the Pakistan bowlers, with Fazal injured, were unable to contain the brilliant batting of Hunte (114) and Sobers (109 not out).

Pakistan won a consolation victory by an innings and 1 run in the Fifth Test at Port of Spain. Fazal, with 6 for 83, bowled brilliantly and West Indies could only total 268, Smith being top scorer with 86. Pakistan then made 496 – Wazir (189) and Saeed (97). Fortunately for them, Gilchrist sprained an ankle and could only bowl 7 overs. When West Indies batted again the pitch helped spin, and after a 1st-wicket partnership of 71 between Hunte and Kanhai, only Walcott (62) dealt effectively with Nasim who took 6 for 67.

A year later the teams met again in a rubber of 3 in Pakistan where the West Indies lost the 1st 2 Tests, then won the Third overwhelmingly. In the First Test at Karachi, Fazal sent West Indies in on a matting wicket and only B. F. Butcher and, to a lesser degree, J. K. Holt and Kanhai resisted the medium-pace of Fazal and the slow left-arm spin of Nasim, each taking four for 35. Pakistan replied with 304 (Hanif 103, Saeed 78), and though West Indies did better in their 2nd innings, Butcher and J. S. Solomon being the chief contributors to their total of 245, Pakistan knocked off the 88 needed for victory without losing a wicket.

Pakistan won the Second Test in the east at Dacca after F. C. M. Alexander, West Indies' captain and wicket-keeper, had sent them in. Wesley Hall took 4 of the first 5 wickets for 22, but a steadfast 64 by Mathias, with support from the tail, took Pakistan to 145. West Indies were then shot out for 76 by Fazal (6 for 34) and Nasim (3 for 4), the last 6 batsmen all failing to score. In their 2nd innings, Mathias was again the backbone for Pakistan, making 45 out of 144, which left West Indies 214 to win. But Fazal (6 for 66) again bowled magnificently, and though Sobers made 45 and Smith 39, a good burst by Mahmood Hussain (4 for 48) gave Pakistan their second victory, and with it, the rubber.

By winning the Third Test at Lahore, West Indies administered Pakistan's 1st Test defeat at home. A brilliant innings by Kanhai of 217, with good support from Sobers and Solomon, enabled West Indies to score 469. Pakistan made a good start, Imtiaz and Wazar Hassan each batting steadily, but the speed of Hall was too much for the rest and they were all out for 209, Hall finishing off the innings with a hat-trick. Following on, Pakistan were skittled out for 104 on a sticky wicket by S. Ramadhin and Gibbs. Pakistan had the worst of the pitch, rain interfering with both their innings. Mushtaq Mahommad, at 15 years 124 days, here became the youngest-ever Test cricketer.

After a 15-year gap in the series, West Indies, in conjunction with an Indian tour, played 2 drawn matches in Pakistan in 1974–75. Fine batting by both sides produced hundreds for Pakistan by Mushtaq Mohammad, Majid Khan and Wasim Raja, and for West Indies by A. I. Kallicharran, B. D. Julien and L. Baichan. In the First Test at Lahore Sarfraz Nawaz took 6 for 89 and A. Roberts in the match 9 for 187. A political riot in Karachi probably prevented a West Indian victory in the Second Test.

In 1976–77 West Indies at home beat Pakistan by the odd match. After 2 draws and a West Indies win by 6 wickets, Pakistan levelled the series with a win by 266, only to lose the final by 140. Pakistan's win was a triumph for their captain Mushtaq, who made 121 and 56 and took 5 for 28 and 3 for 69.

For the West Indies C. G. Greenidge and R. C. Fredericks were the star batsmen, and C. H. Lloyd made one fine hundred. The leading bowlers were two hitherto unknowns, both fast – C. Croft (33 wickets including 8 for 29 in the Second Test) and J. Garner (25). For Pakistan Majid, Mushtaq, Asif and Raja all made hundreds and the fast bowlers, Imran Khan (25 wickets) and Sarfraz (16), were the most successful. Having played 3 Tests at home again in New Zealand and 3 in Australia before this tour, the Pakistanis could be excused for feeling somewhat jaded by the end of the season.

WEST INDIES V PAKISTAN

			RESULT	CAPTAINS
1957–58	1 Barbados	WI 579–9D, 28–0; Pak 106, 657–8D	Drawn	F. C. M. Alexander, A. H. Kardar
	2 Trinidad	WI 325, 312; Pak 282, 235	WI 120 runs	F. C. M. Alexander, A. H. Kardar
	3 Kingston	Pak 328, 288; WI 790–3D	WI Inns 174 runs	F. C. M. Alexander, A. H. Kardar
	4 Georgetown	Pak 408, 318; WI 410, 317–2	WI 8 wkts	F. C. M. Alexander, A. H. Kardar
	5 Trinidad	WI 268, 227; Pak 496	Pak inns 1 run	F. C. M. Alexander, A. H. Kardar
1958–59	1 Karachi	WI 146, 245; Pak 304, 88–0	Pak 10 wkts	F. C. M. Alexander, Fazal Mahmood
	2 Dacca	Pak 145, 144; WI 76, 172	Pak 41 runs	F. C. M. Alexander, Fazal Mahmood
	3 Lahore	WI 469; Pak 209, 104	WI inns 156	F. C. M. Alexander, Fazal Mahmood
1974–75	1 Lahore	Pak 199, 373–7D; WI 214, 258–4	Drawn	C. H. Lloyd, Intikhab Alam
	2 Karachi	Pak 406–8D, 256; WI 493, 1–0	Drawn	C. H. Lloyd, Intikhab Alam
1976–77	1 Barbados	Pak 435, 291; WI 421, 251–9	Drawn	C. H. Lloyd, Mushtaq Mohammad
	2 Trinidad	Pak 180, 340; WI 316, 206–4	WI 6 wkts	C. H. Lloyd, Mushtaq Mohammad
	3 Georgetown	Pak 194, 540; WI 448, 154–1	Drawn	C. H. Lloyd, Mushtaq Mohammad
	4 Trinidad	Pak 341, 301–9D; WI 154, 222	Pak 266 runs	C. H. Lloyd, Mushtaq Mohammad
	5 Kingston	WI 280, 359; Pak 198, 301	WI 140 runs	C. H. Lloyd, Mushtaq Mohammad

CAPTAINS (West Indies)	TESTS	WON	LOST	DRAWN
F. C. M. Alexander	8	4	3	1
C. H. Lloyd	7	2	1	4
	15	6	4	5

CAPTAINS (Pakistan)	TESTS	WON	LOST	DRAWN
A. H. Kardar	5	1	3	1
Fazal Mahmood	3	2	1	
Intikhab Alam	2			2
Mushtaq Mohammad	5	1	2	2
	15	4	6	5

HIGHEST INNINGS TOTAL

West Indies in West Indies, 790–3D, Kingston 1957–58
West Indies in Pakistan, 492, Karachi 1974–75
Pakistan in West Indies, 657–8D, Barbados 1957–58
Pakistan in Pakistan, 406–8D, Karachi 1974–75

LOWEST INNINGS TOTAL

West Indies in West Indies, 154, Trinidad 1976–77
West Indies in Pakistan, 76, Dacca 1958–59
Pakistan in West Indies, 106, Barbados 1957–58
Pakistan in Pakistan, 104, Lahore 1958–59

HIGHEST INDIVIDUAL INNINGS

West Indies in West Indies, 365*, G. S. Sobers, Kingston 1957–58
West Indies in Pakistan, 217, R. B. Kanhai, Lahore 1958–59
Pakistan in West Indies, 337, Hanif Mohammad, Barbados 1957–58
Pakistan in Pakistan, 123, Mushtaq Mohammad, Lahore 1974–75

HIGHEST AGGREGATE OF RUNS IN A SERIES

West Indies in West Indies, 824, G. S. Sobers 1957–58
West Indies in Pakistan, 274, R. B. Kanhai 1958–59
Pakistan in West Indies, 628, Hanif Mohammad 1957–58
Pakistan in Pakistan, 199, Saeed Ahmed 1958–59

BEST INNINGS BOWLING FIGURES

West Indies in West Indies, 8–29, C. E. H. Croft, Trinidad 1976–77
West Indies in Pakistan, 5–66, A. M. E. Roberts, Lahore 1974–75
Pakistan in West Indies, 6–67, Nazim-ul-Ghani, Trinidad 1957–58
Pakistan in Pakistan, 6–34, Fazal Mahmood, Dacca 1958–59

BEST MATCH BOWLING FIGURES

West Indies in West Indies, 9–95, C. E. H. Croft, Trinidad 1976–77
West Indies in Pakistan, 9–187, A. M. E. Roberts, Lahore 1974–75
Pakistan in West Indies, 8–97, Mushtaq Mohammad, Trinidad 1976–77
Pakistan in Pakistan, 12–100, Fazal Mahmood, Dacca 1958–59

HIGHEST WICKET AGGREGATE IN A SERIES

West Indies in West Indies, 33, C. E. H. Croft 1976–77
West Indies in Pakistan, 16, W. W. Hall 1958–59
Pakistan in West Indies, 25, Imran Khan 1976–77
Pakistan in Pakistan, 21, Fazal Mahmood 1958–59

RECORD WICKET PARTNERSHIPS – WEST INDIES

1 R. C. Fredericks and C. G. Greenidge, 182, Kingston 1976–77
2 C. C. Hunte and G. S. Sobers, 446, Kingston 1957–58
3 R. B. Kanhai and G. S. Sobers, 162, Lahore 1958–59
4 G. S. Sobers and C. L. Walcott, 188*, Kingston 1957–58
5 E. D. Weekes and O. G. Smith, 185, Barbados 1957–58
6 C. H. Lloyd and D. L. Murray, 151, Barbados 1976–77
7 C. H. Lloyd and J. Garner, 70, Barbados 1976–77
8 B. D. Julien and V. A. Holder, 50, Karachi 1974–75
9 J. Garner and C. E. H. Croft, 46, Trinidad 1976–77
10 A. M. E. Roberts and C. E. H. Croft, 26, Georgetown 1976–77

RECORD WICKET PARTNERSHIPS – PAKISTAN

1 Majid Khan and Zaheer Abbas, 159, Georgetown 1976–77
2 Hanif Mohammad and Saeed Ahmed, 178, Karachi 1958–59
3 Saeed Ahmed and Wazir Mohammad, 169, Trinidad 1957–58
4 Wazir Mohammad and Hanif Mohammad, 154, Trinidad 1957–58
5 Mushtaq Mohammad and Asif Iqbal, 87, Kingston 1976–77
6 Wazir Mohammad and A. H. Kardar, 166, Kingston 1957–58
7 Wasim Raja and Wasim Bari, 128, Karachi 1974–75
8 Imran Khan and Sarfraz Nawaz, 73, Trinidad 1976–77
9 Wasim Raja and Sarfraz Nawaz, 73, Barbados 1976–77
10 Wasim Raja and Wasim Bari, 133, Barbados 1976–77

Women's Cricket Overseas

NETTA RHEINBERG

Australia

The first public women's cricket match in Australia is said to have been played in 1874. Certainly there was an Inter-Colonial match in 1891, and early in the present century the Victorian Ladies' Cricket Association organized a number of highly enterprising inter-State tours between Tasmania, New South Wales and themselves. The Gregory family, D.W. and S.E., were a great influence and remained so until the First World War. In 1931, Victoria, New South Wales and Queensland banded together to form the Australian Women's Cricket Council. It was later resolved to affiliate with the Women's Cricket Association in England, and matches were arranged annually between the 3 member states. Three years later, with less than £1 in the bank, the Council courageously invited an England team to tour Australia. Australia adopted the 6-ball over for the tour and this has been adhered to in international matches ever since, together with England's use

of the 5 oz ball. In 1928, at the same time as the New South Wales Association was founded, the Pioneer Victorian Ladies' Cricket Association was formed, its membership comprising earlier players whose help in fostering women cricketers throughout Australia remains active still.

New South Wales produced some first-class players, among them being Betty Wilson, who was certainly the finest player of her day, 1948–1959, and, in the opinion of some, the most brilliant player ever. Victoria also had its stars, a very early one being Rosalie Deane, who, in 1891, received the singular honour of being the 1st woman cricketer to be recorded in *Wisden* for scoring a hundred in each innings, playing for the Inter-Colonial Club against the Sydney Club. Later, Peggy Antonio, an outstanding leg-spin bowler, was a world beater.

Queensland, West Australia and South Australia eventually joined the Council. The 1st inter-State tournament was held in 1931 and has become an annual event.

Owing to financial problems the exchange of visits between Australia and England for Test series were few and far between. Australia toured England in 1937, 1951, 1963 and 1976 and England's visits to Australia took place in 1933–1934, 1948–1949, 1957–1958 and 1968–1969. Australia also took part in the World Cup in England in 1973. There was also an exchange of visits between Australia and New Zealand, and the opportunity was taken whenever possible to play other countries on the way to and from England.

Australia have not yet been successful in obtaining sponsorship for women's cricket and there were many players in the Australian team for the 1976 tour of England who were absent at the annual Inter-State tournament the following January. They were recovering financially from that tour, for which each player paid about £1,000 for the privilege of representing her country. Some financial assistance is given by the Federal Government for which due acknowledgement is given, but such is the problem of funds that the number of Test matches in any international series is dependent on the money in the kitty. The Australian WCC celebrates its Golden Jubilee in 1980–1981 and is hoping to stage, as part of the anniversary, the 3rd World Cup competition.

Women's cricket in Australia remains strong and active. The average age of players is lower than formerly and there is a wealth of young talent in the ranks. Despite the financial difficulties and the fact that women's cricket is not a spectator sport in Australia, the future should be assured.

New Zealand

The administrators of the game in Auckland first put women's cricket on an organized basis in 1928 and founded the Auckland Association. Auckland was followed within the next 4 years by Christchurch, Otago and Wellington, by which time the prospect of a coming tour by England helped to close the ranks and pave the way for the founding of the New Zealand Women's Cricket Council in 1934. Thereafter 3 further Provinces affiliated, namely Wanganui, Nelson and Southland. Prior to 1928, not one single public reference to women's cricket in New Zealand has been traced, though the game may well have been played by women members of families settled from overseas.

The 1935 tour by England established the game and provided public support, finally sweeping away the derision and ridicule to which women playing cricket were first subjected. In 1938 the 1st New Zealand overseas tour took place, in response to an invitation from New South Wales who were celebrating their 150th anniversary, but war intervened and it was not until 1948 that further international games could be arranged. In that year the Australian visit provided a strong stimulus and, followed by England's visit in 1949, renewed badly-needed public support. An invitation to tour England for the 1st time in 1954 was accepted, and by 1960 women's cricket in New Zealand was thriving.

Further progress both in administration and standards has been made in latter years, mainly due to the efforts in fostering youth cricket and the financial help forthcoming from the Rothman's Sports Foundation and the New Zealand Sports Council. In 1976 a New Zealand XI visited India, the fares being met by the hostess country, heralded as a unique event. A return visit from India a few months later was badly affected by rain. The Indian team took part in New Zealand's inter-provincial tournament, but again, owing to bad weather, it became impossible to finish most of the matches.

En route to India for the 2nd World Cup competition in 1977–1978 New Zealand played 2 games in Australia, winning 1 and losing the other; on their return they took part in a Test series against Australia on their home ground, which they lost by 1 match.

One of the results of the hard work carried out in recent years for youth cricket is that women's cricket continues to thrive in New Zealand. In the late 1970s an internal tour of the country by an Under-23 team was introduced. These tours have been very successful in building up the strength and experience of younger players, the best of whom have already been included in the national team.

South Africa

The South Africa and Rhodesia Women's Cricket Association was officially formed in 1952, although 7 of the provinces were

OPPOSITE A group of State teams who took part in cricket week, Wellington, January 1950. Back row: Canterbury; middle row: Otago; front row: Auckland; Wellington in black blazers.

RIGHT 'A Dutch XI' going out to field at the Groenendaal Club, The Hague. This team includes 4 members of 'The Dutch XI'; namely, Saw Panders, Corry Nagel (2nd and 3rd from left), Hennie de Ruiter (5th from left), and Erna Bruynesteyn (8th from left). The captain is Mrs Reinders (with glasses).

playing, without a central organization, before that date. In Western Province women played cricket at the beginning of this century, but one of the first clubs, the Peninsula Ladies' Cricket Club, was not founded until 1932 when it was affiliated to the WCA in England. From then until the Second World War, when it ceased, women played cricket fairly regularly. The formation of the Association in 1949, was the outcome of valuable help given by well-known men cricketers, particularly Eric Rowan, who chaired the steering committee and was a selector for the inter-provincial competition held in 1952–1953.

The 1960–1961 England tour and Test series aroused interest and attracted women playing cricket. More recently South African women's cricket has suffered the same unfortunate isolation as men's cricket. An England visit arranged in 1968 was cancelled, though a Dutch team substituted, and in 1972 a New Zealand visit took place, thus helping to maintain the interest. The 5 South African players selected for the World Cup International XI in 1973 were forced to withdraw for political reasons and there have been no official international encounters for 18 years. A private English team raised from club players has visited South Africa 3 times in recent years which has helped maintain cricketing relationships. On the last occasion, the English players undertook to coach coloured players at Paarl, resulting in the formation of an additional club in that area. The Provincial women's teams are picked on merit, regardless of colour.

Due to the lack of international opposition there is a struggle to maintain standards though that is eased by the renewal of encouragement and help from men cricketers. If and when the situation returns to normal South Africa will surely provide strong opposition.

Holland

Women first played cricket in Holland in 1930; the main organization, the Nederlandse-Dames Cricket Bond, was founded in 1934. Three clubs playing league cricket were then in existence, the number rising to 5 by 1937. During 1936 and 1937 there was an exchange of visits between Dutch and English clubs as well as a brief tour by the Australian touring team.

Not surprisingly there was no cricket during the Second World War, and by 1947 only 2 clubs had been reformed; but great efforts were made and 5 clubs were playing again by 1951, followed by a 6th 2 years later. Naturally the clubs took time to re-establish themselves after the war. In the 1950s, however, there were fairly regular visits between Holland and England, the highlight being a short official WCA tour in connexion with the Nederland-Dames Cricket Bond Silver Jubilee in 1959.

Interest in the game for women decreased in the 1960s, owing to a lack of responsible administration. Despite various efforts new members were not forthcoming. However, in 1968, a Dutch XI was raised for an enjoyable visit to South Africa during which much was learned, though all the matches lost. In 1974, helped by their men colleagues, a new committee was formed and the interest revived. Two qualified England players coached the Dutch in the late 1970s by when the WCA Annual Cricket Week at Colwall never lacked its intake of Dutch players.

Although the Nederlandse-Dames Cricket Bond is a small association its members are very enthusiastic and have succeeded in obtaining sponsorship in a small way, a large Dutch banking group offering a prize for the woman cricketer of the year. This recognition and the fact that 3 Dutch players have recently been awarded the NCA elementary coaching certificate point to an encouraging future.

West Indies

Although women had played cricket on a casual basis in several of the islands for many years, Jamaica pioneered the game officially in 1966, helped by Johnny Wongsam, cricketer, coach and umpire. Six teams took part in a league competition and in 1967 a Jamaican XI visited Trinidad, resulting in the formation of the Trinidad and Tobago WCA. Ten clubs, 6 in the North and 4 in the South, competed in league and knock-out competitions. In both islands the game for women was sponsored by companies who gave their names to the teams.

In 1970 and 1971 English teams visited Jamaica, the matches, including unofficial Tests, being watched by thousands. The Jamaican XI had been coached by Jackie Hendriks and the standard was good. Interest continued to grow in the other islands; in 1971 Guyana visited Trinidad and the latter also started a secondary schools league for girls. By 1973 Barbados had joined in, followed the year after by Grenada, where 30 teams were in existence by 1975. The 4-islands tournament, staged in Trinidad and with Barbados, Grenada and Jamaica as the guests, marked the birth of the Caribbean Women's Cricket Federation, whose West Indies women's team visited England in 1979 for their 1st Test series.

West Indian women cricketers have shown much enterprise in arranging various tours, one of which, to India in 1976, proved highly successful, a local newsagency reporting that some 70,000 people watched the Fourth Test Match which India won. Six Tests were played and the honours remained even.

A group of Indian women cricketers at the National Coaching Camp at Chail Cricket Ground, May–June 1975. At 7,500 feet, Chail is the highest cricket ground in the world.

First President and founder member of the Caribbean Women's Cricket Federation was Monica Taylor, who also captained the first Jamaican team. Guyana joined the Federation in 1977, by when a 5-island tournament took place biennially, each one in a different island.

India

Except as a compulsory sport at one school, cricket for women did not exist in India until the 1960s when enthusiasm suddenly spread in Madras, Bombay, Delhi and Calcutta, under the influence of the gradual growth of freedom for women. Delhi had already held tournaments, but the other zones were very inexperienced when the 1st National Women's Championship was held in Poona in 1973. It coincided with the founding of the Women's Cricket Association of India. The Association had a male secretary, Mahendra Sharma, of Lucknow, at whose invitation an Australian Under-25 XI became the 1st overseas team to visit India, in 1975. Enormous crowds attended the matches which provided a spectacle never seen before. The Indian teams came mostly from State Colleges, and the players made up in enthusiasm what they lacked in experience.

The unexpected financial success of this tour enabled India to pay the air fares of the New Zealanders, who had accepted the invitation to tour India in 1976. West Indies paid India a visit in 1977, and in the same year India toured New Zealand. Despite bad weather it was noticeable that the standard of cricket played by the Indian team on this tour of New Zealand had improved considerably; they registered several wins against the Provinces in one-day matches. The financial success of their home tours enabled India to stage the second World Cup Competition in 1977–1978, involving India, Australia, England and New Zealand.

Ireland

Women played cricket in Ireland after the Second World War, when there was an active association, the Leinster Women's Cricket Union, consisting of 3 clubs and 3 schools. In Northern Ireland 5 clubs played League cricket, and a Union was formed. Women cricketers continued to play now and again until 1957, when both Unions found difficulty in keeping their associations alive, though neither disbanded completely. A few Irish cricketers take the opportunity of attending the WCA week at Colwall each year, thus keeping the interest alive, and more recently enthusiasm has increased especially in Southern Ireland. The Tyler Cup final for women's clubs held in Dublin in 1977 attracted a larger crowd than the men's final. The winning team, Clontarf Ladies, included an 11-year-old who won an award for her performance.

Denmark

There are 4 clubs in the women's section of the Akademisk Boldklub of Copenhagen, which has 2,300 members playing football, cricket, handball and tennis.

Canada

Before the Second World War, when one or two teams of students and schoolgirls from Harrogate College and Cheltenham Ladies' College played demonstration matches in Montreal and Toronto, it was forecast, albeit wrongly, that this would start an enthusiasm among Canadian women for the game. There was an attempt in 1958 by Eileen Stevens, a South African who emigrated to Vancouver, to organize the game and this met with some success, a few matches being played at Vancouver. The game was still being played in 1959, but when Eileen Stevens left the country at the end of that season no one emerged to continue her work for women's cricket in Canada.

Papua New Guinea

A women's team from Papua New Guinea attended the Australian Inter-State Tournament in 1975. Their cricket is sponsored by firms and breweries. It is of a primitive kind, played barefoot on concrete wickets, though in Australia the players felt it advisable to protect their feet from the large ball. At home the Papuan women use the smaller one.

New Caledonia

In the capital city of Noumea more than 10 teams play a primitive kind of cricket started by English missionaries in the 19th century. Although the laws and conditions of play are curious, the game is definitely recognizable as cricket.

England Test Records

RESULTS	WON	LOST	DRAWN
v Australia	5	3	16
v New Zealand	5		8
v South Africa	1		3
v West Indies	2		1
	13	3	28

CAPTAINS

1934–35 B. Archdale (Kent) v Australia & New Zealand, Away
1937 M. Hide (Surrey) v Australia, Home
1948–49 M. Hide (Surrey) v Australia & New Zealand, Away
1951 M. Hide (Surrey) v Australia, Home
1954 M. Hide (Surrey) v New Zealand, Home
1957 M. Duggan (Middlesex) v New Zealand, Away
1958 M. Duggan (Middlesex) v Australia, Away
1960–61 H. Sharpe (Middlesex) v South Africa, Away
1963 M. Duggan (Middlesex) v Australia, Home
1966 R. Heyhoe (Staffs) v New Zealand, Home
1968–69 R. Heyhoe (Staffs) v Australia & New Zealand, Away
1976 R. Heyhoe-Flint (Staffs) v Australia, Home
1979 S. Goatman (Kent) v West Indies, Home

HIGHEST SCORES

For 503 v New Zealand at Christchurch 1935
Against 379 by Australia at the Oval 1976

LOWEST SCORES

For 35 v Australia at St Kilda CG, Melbourne 1958
Against 38 by Australia at St Kilda CG, Melbourne 1958

HIGHEST INDIVIDUAL INNINGS

For 179 R. Heyhoe-Flint v Australia at the Oval 1976
Against 155 P. McKelvey for New Zealand at Wellington 1969

CARRYING BAT THROUGH INNINGS

C. Robinson 96 (188) v Australia 1958
E. Bakewell 112* (164) v West Indies 1979

MOST RUNS IN ONE SERIES

E. Bakewell, 412 v New Zealand 1969
R. Heyhoe-Flint, 350 v Australia 1976

MOST RUNS IN TESTS

R. Heyhoe-Flint, 1,842 in 15 Tests
E. Bakewell, 1,246 in 15 Tests

MOST HUNDREDS IN TESTS

E. Bakewell 4
R. Heyhoe-Flint 3

MOST WICKETS IN ONE SERIES

J. Greenwood, 23 v West Indies 1979
M. Maclagan, 20 v Australia 1934
M. Duggan, 20 v Australia 1951

MOST WICKETS IN TESTS

M. Duggan, 77 in 17 Tests
M. Maclagan, 60 in 14 Tests
E. Bakewell, 53 in 12 Tests

WICKET-KEEPERS – MOST DISMISSALS IN ONE SERIES

S. Hodges, 16 v Australia 1969

WICKET-KEEPERS – MOST DISMISSALS IN TESTS

S. Hodges, 28 in 8 Tests

RECORD WICKET PARTNERSHIPS

1 E. Bakewell and L. Thomas, 164, v Australia, Edgbaston 1976
2 M. Hide and E. Snowball, 235, v New Zealand, Christchurch 1935
3 E. Barker and R. Heyhoe, 137, v Australia, Melbourne 1968
4 A. Ratcliffe and R. Heyhoe, 85, v South Africa, Johannesburg 1960
5 C. Robinson and R. Westbrook, 119, v Australia, Adelaide 1958
6 A. Ratcliffe and A. Sanders, 77, v South Africa, Johannesburg 1960
7 B. Birch and O. Marshall, 57, v Australia, Perth 1958
8 J. Moorhouse and L. Clifford, 76, v New Zealand 1966
9 S. Brown and D. Macfarlane, 48, v Australia, Edgbaston 1963
10 E. Barker and H. Hegarty, 78, v Australia, Adelaide 1958

World Series Cricket

The Packer Intrusion

TREVOR MACDONALD

In its short and turbulent existence, nothing about Kerry Packer's World Series Cricket was quite so extraordinary as the secrecy of its conception and the high drama of its birth. Looking back now, it is terribly easy to understand how the international cricket authorities were wrong-footed from the start. Accustomed by tradition to the manners of the well-ordered Tennysonian world 'where faction seldom rises head', and where the power of the administration derives quietly from 'precedent to precedent', the respective governing bodies had immediately been forced on to the defensive. Initiative had been wrested from them. They lost their composure. They were obliged to react, instead of assuming their customary command. In shaping the first frantic response to Mr Packer's challenge, costly mistakes were inevitably made. Such alas are the consequences of revolution.

The visible beginnings of the Packer revolution occurred in early May 1977 with the announcement by an Australian national magazine that 35 of the world's best cricketers had signed lucrative contracts of between 1 and 3 years to play a series of one-day games during the Australian summer of that year. It was envisaged at the time of announcement that the entire programme of matches would last 54 days. The package had been arranged by J.P. Sport and Television Corporation Ltd, proprietors of Channel 9, one of Australia's 5 television stations. The magazine which broke the story and Channel 9 are part of the Kerry Packer business empire.

J.P. Sport were not new to sports promotion. They had acquired considerable expertise 'merchandizing' sportsmen like Australian tennis star John Newcombe. The tie-up with Channel 9 was simple and meant to be effective. Sporting promotions could be arranged with the assurance of prime-time television coverage. In a country where sport was a vital ingredient of the national life, there were rich pickings for the promoters, large viewing figures for Channel 9 and generous rewards for sportsmen who allowed themselves to be 'merchandized': commercial interests and sporting prowess fused by electronics. The arrangement seemed a classic of its kind.

J.P. Sport and the Packer business empire had converged on the game of cricket from different routes. J.P. Sport were a go-ahead sporting agency seeking to exploit as many financial avenues as possible for the sporting personalities on its books; Dennis Lillee was a client. The idea of employing well-known sporting stars to promote products or projects well outside their field is not uncommon in Australia where the big names in sport are revered. J.P. Sport were simply cashing in on the popularity of their clients. In Mr Packer, J.P. Sport found not only the owner of a television station, but someone who was keen on sport and took a great interest in Channel 9's coverage of major sporting events. Rumour had it that he had run foul of one television governing authority and some commercial television station managers by trying to deal *unilaterally* with the Russians over coverage of the 1980 Olympics. More successfully negotiated were his plans to attract the world's top golfers to the Australian Open. He commissioned his friend Jack Nicklaus to redesign a suitable course and committed more cameras to the coverage of the Open than had ever been done before.

A conversation with J.P. Sport about finding more work for 'clients' occurred only a short time after Mr Packer had been sharply rebuffed by the Australian Cricket Board. Mr Packer had been anxious to televise cricket on Channel 9. He had gone to the Australian Board with the offer of a great deal of money in exchange for the rights to televise exclusively matches played under the auspicies of the Australian Board. Two problems stood in the way of the Board, as they saw it. They had always awarded the rights to the state-owned Australian Broadcasting Commission. They also claimed that they were worried about the *principle* of 'exclusive rights'.

Having always operated in the belief that no deal is impossible if one makes a big enough offer ('Come on! We're all harlots – what's your price?' he apparently asked the Board), Mr Packer saw the Board's refusal to grant Channel 9 the rights as a deliberate snub. He was convinced that he was being shut out by a collusion of establishment interests. WSC was conceived in Mr Packer's anger at the Australian Board and in J.P. Sport's interest to find work for star clients. Both concerns were to find willing allies in a number of senior Australian Test players, this despite the fact that the Board had already established, early in the 1976–77 Australian season, a cricket sub-committee comprising senior Board members and the State Captains (respectively Greg Chappell, Doug Walters, Richie Robinson, Ashley Woodcock and Rodney Marsh) with the stated object of providing closer relationship with the players and involving them more in the running of the game, especially in regard to financial benefit to them from team sponsorships.

The swift upshot of the formation of this cricket sub-committee was that the Board, by January 1977, had arranged contracts which would bring in to a Test player fulfilling the 1977 Australian programme the equivalent of £12,000. (A players' retirement scheme had also been running for several years, and it has to be remembered that Australian cricketers all have regular employment outside the game.) This new important sub-committee of Board administrators and players had agreed in its original terms of reference – no doubt as a mere formality – that the Board should continue to be the sole Australian promoter of all matches involving teams from overseas. On 10 March 1977, 2 days before the Centenary Test, a further meeting of the cricket sub-committee confirmed the division of the substantial Benson & Hedges sponsorship and accepted the consequent obligations.

Greg Chappell meanwhile had had time to insert in a book under his name about to be published, *The 100th Summer*, a reference to how cricketers' rewards had 'increased dramatically in a comparatively short time . . . Cash endorsements are flowing as never before, and the Test team is now sponsored for three years. It's hardly surprising that Australia leads the way in providing a far better deal for the cricketers.' Yet some at least of the 5 State captains concerned had by then already signed Packer contracts which would prevent them carrying out the obligations of the official sponsorship.

The Board, in fact, had no inkling of the players' secret activities until the story broke in the press on 9 May, 2 months later. Only then did they know that 4 of the players on their Committee, Chappell, captain of Australia, Marsh, Robinson and Walters had changed camps. In these circumstances was not the Board's bitterness understandable?

The other group of players was headed by Tony Greig, who only a few months before had led England in India, and was England captain in the memorable Centenary Test Match against Australia in Melbourne at the end of the Indian tour. Much later it was to be revealed that it was during that Centenary Test match that several players had been secretly approached to join Mr Packer's rival cricket venture. Tony Greig, having given his promise to Mr Packer to act with the utmost discretion, had assumed the role of chief liaison officer between Mr Packer and the players.

Greig himself had first met Mr Packer on the recommendation of his Australian agent, Bruce Francis, to talk about the possibility of finding work with Channel 9. At that meeting, the idea of promoting a rival cricket series was discussed, and Tony Greig's practical views on the subject were of considerable interest. Although he was still England captain, Greig entertained the philosophy of a rival cricket venture and the money it offered, and was so impressed by what he had been told of Mr Packer's plans that he had undertaken to try to persuade other players to join the venture. The Melbourne Centenary Test was not only an obvious starting point, but a heaven-sent opportunity for meeting with and talking to players. After that game Greig went to the West Indies, again on Mr Packer's behalf, to talk to players there. It was to become an enduring point against the conduct of Tony Greig that, having found himself getting into a new venture on the ground floor, as it were, he saw the chance of a small fortune in Mr Packer's employ, and proceeded to do his new master's bidding – in spite of his moral obligations to English cricket.

The Packer approach, whether it came from the man himself, J.P. Sport or recruiting agent Tony Greig, was essentially the same. Players were offered the prospect of earning sums of money far greater than they had thought possible in the traditional game. Contracts were proffered for signatures there and then; and, to make sure there was no breach of vital confidentiality, the signed documents were then retained by the contracting agent. Some players accepted part-payment at the introductory meeting. One thing was impressed on those who signed and those who asked for time to think over Mr Packer's proposition. Confidentiality was essential. There was to be absolute secrecy. Even though three members of the Test and County Cricket Board had a very cordial meeting with a man from Mr Packer's organization who had on the same day been talking to potential recruits to the Packer cause, the cricket authorities never heard a whisper about the plans for WSC.

The list of players persuaded to join was impressive. Asif Iqbal, Imran Khan and Mustaq Mohammed from Pakistan; Eddie Barlow, Mike Procter, Barry Richards and Graeme Pollock from South Africa; Knott, Underwood and Snow teamed up with Tony Greig and that England contingent was later to be joined by Bob Woolmer and Dennis Amiss. From the West Indies came Vivian Richards, Clive Lloyd, Michael Holding, Andy Roberts and Deryck Murray. In the weeks that followed all the other big West Indian names were to be added.

The news of Mr Packer's rival series exploded on the cricket world like a bombshell. The governing bodies of international cricket plunged into lengthy crisis meetings. Two things were immediately clear. Mr Packer's matches in the Australian summer of that year were in direct conflict with England's winter tour of Pakistan and New Zealand. Greig, Knott and Underwood had ruled themselves out of that tour. It was similarly obvious that the Australian Test team India would face in Australia in 1977–78 would bear no resemblance to the Australian party in England that summer. Mr Packer's agents had seen to that. All but 4 of the 1977 Australian touring party had been signed up.

Of more immediate concern was the England v Australia Test series about to begin. Forty-eight hours after the first news of Mr Packer's rival series, the Cricket Council met in emergency session in London. To no one's surprise it decided to relieve Greig of the England captaincy. Having by this time discovered the role Greig had played in secretly recruiting players from the traditional game on Mr Packer's behalf, the Chairman stated the Cricket Council's reasons with exemplary restraint. 'The captaincy of the England team', said F. R. Brown, 'involves close liaison with the selectors in the management, selection and development of England players for the future and clearly Tony Greig is unlikely to undertake this as his stated intention is to be contracted elsewhere during the next three winters'.

In the weeks that followed, the governing Council of England cricket came to regard the sacking of Greig as England captain as one of the easiest decisions it had to take in a turbulent period. Greig could not feign surprise. 'When I got into this,' he stated, 'I knew I was putting my captaincy on the line. The only redeeming factor is that I have sacrificed cricket's most coveted job for a cause which I believe could be in the interests of cricket the world over'.

Greig's decision to join Packer and to impugn the honour of the England captaincy by encouraging other players to join was seen by many commentators as nothing short of treason. He was accused of 'disembowelling' world cricket and of 'succumbing to a sickening temptation'. John Woodcock, the respected cricket correspondent of *The Times*, a most gentle man, delivered the most memorably brutal comment on Greig's 'defection'. 'What has to be remembered', Woodcock wrote, 'is that Greig is English only by adoption, which is not the same as being English through and through'.

Greig and his England 'Packer recruits' were not barred from playing in the home series against Australia. Had the English Selectors taken such a step, the Australians might have been left with no other course of action but the recall of their entire touring party. That summer, the Australian dressing-room was not a happy place. The players had gone behind the backs of their controlling Board and were obviously at odds with their team manager on the tour, Len Maddocks, himself a Board member. Not surprisingly their cricket suffered. The Jubilee Test ended in a draw. Australia were beaten by 9 wickets at Old Trafford and by 7 wickets at Trent Bridge. At Headingley they were mauled by an innings and 285 runs, surrendering the Ashes without so much as a whimper. They threatened to make a comeback in the Oval Test when Mick Malone took 5 wickets for 53 in England's first innings, but the English weather had taken a controlling hand in the game and the final Test ended in a draw. It was England's most conclusive home victory in history over Australia.

The Test Matches had taken place against a background of endless meetings by the international cricket authorities. Rumours ran wild about players, umpires and groundsmen who had been approached by or signed with Mr Packer's agents. Mr Packer, portrayed by most of the sporting press as a rapacious promoter shrewdly bartering the skills of professional cricketers in the undignified marketplace of commercial television, even rated an editorial in *The Times*.

The International Cricket Conference decided to invite Mr Packer to meet their representatives at Lord's. Their invitation might have conveyed the impression that they were well in command of the situation. 'Mr Kerry Packer is advised that should he wish to discuss his plans . . . a meeting will be arranged.' In fact the boot was clearly on the other foot. The Test Match playing countries were desperately anxious to discover what Mr Packer wanted in exchange for a promise not to further endanger the international structure of the game.

On the afternoon of 23 June 1977, Mr Packer and three colleagues, Richie Benaud, David McNicoll and Lynton Taylor, met members of the International Cricket Conference at Lord's. At first the meeting promised well, the ICC offering some amendment of the agreed Australia v India programme, and to grant the 1977–78 Packer activities first-class status provided they did not exceed 6 weeks. After an interval for reflection the Packer party returned to the Committee-room, indicated they might accept the ICC compromise but then threw in a fresh demand for exclusive television rights. There came the sticking point.

The Australian Board representatives, whose response to Mr Packer's approach on the television matter had started the whole affair, were in no mood to compromise with a man they saw first as an upstart and later as an adversary. In rejecting Mr Packer's offer to buy the rights to televise exclusively 'Official' cricket in Australia, the Board argued that it was against the principle of exclusive rights. In effect they were rather happy with their cosy relationship with the Australian Broadcasting Commission and had felt there was little Mr Packer could do in retaliation. At the Lord's meeting, although moderate voices were raised, the Australian hard line won the day. For his part, Mr Packer felt he had been the injured party. He had been prepared perhaps to make some small concessions like adjusting his dates to help the official game, but considered in the main that he held all the cards and would teach the intransigent Australian Board a lesson. In that first flush of the Packer affair the Australian Board and the brash Mr Packer were two immovable objects.

By the time of ICC's Annual Meeting a month later most of its members were in belligerent mood. Delegates talked in almost militaristic terms about declaring 'open war' on Mr Packer's scheme, of 'nipping it in the bud'. The ICC Chairman said that 'wars are not won by appeasement'. It was a mood brought on by a feeling that they had been betrayed by the players. There was the tendency to see the 'defection' to Mr Packer as a breach of trust to be punished. The rival Packer series was viewed with contempt, not as competition to be fought. This was the prevailing mood which led to the protracted High Court battle between the cricket authorities and Mr Packer's players. When he met the ICC delegates at Lord's, Mr Packer had indicated that he was prepared to fight to protect his players from victimization. The 26 July meeting took very little heed of that warning. By that time both sides were set on a collision course.

The 26 July meeting reaffirmed the views of Test-playing countries at their 14 June meeting, in which it had been agreed that the structure of cricket worldwide could be 'severely damaged' by the type of promotion proposed by Mr Packer and his associates. It went on to say that following the breakdown of negotiations with Mr Packer, the ICC were determined to continue to promote international fixtures and to oppose 'to the maximum extent the series of exhibition matches' arranged for the Australian summer of 1977. The ICC statement made it clear that Mr Packer's matches would neither have first-class status, nor appear in official records. In order to give effect to these views, the statement went on, the ICC passed unanimously a change in its rules relating to qualifications for Test matches:

> No player who after 1 October 1977 has played or has made himself available to play in a match previously disapproved by the Conference shall thereafter be eligible to play in any Test match.

Member countries were urged to apply the same sanctions at first-class and domestic levels.

In effect, players who had signed Packer contracts were being given until 1 October to withdraw from those contracts, or face a ban from Test and County cricket. Thus by what was referred to as a 'guidance resolution' and by strong recommendations the international cricket authorities had given the full force of their consent to a ban at Test and first-class levels. That ICC resolution was a grave mistake.

The West Indies representatives at the 26 July meeting had warned their colleagues that the courts might seriously challenge the legality of such a ban. The West Indians were even more worried about the retroactive element in the proposed ban. Why not, argued Jeffrey Stollmeyer and Allan Rae, take action against players 'as and when they became unavailable?' The ICC press statement after the meeting made no mention of the West Indies' reservations, but they were

Kerry Packer and Tony Greig outside the Law Courts in London, September 1977.

soundly based. The proposed ban was not only in danger of being challenged in the courts as representing an illegal restraint of trade, but by setting a date by which players should withdraw from their Packer contracts or face the consequences, there was the strongest suggestion that players were being induced to break their contracts. That would clearly be illegal.

On the major question of 'restraint of trade', the law was clear. There had been ample precedent. In 1966, for example, the Jockey Club refused to grant a trainer's licence to one Florence Nagle, although they had in the past granted licences to menservants in her employ. In ruling against the Jockey Club and in favour of Florence Nagle, the Master of the Rolls, Lord Denning put the issue beyond doubt:

> The common law of England has for centuries recognised that a man has a right to work at his trade or profession, without being unjustifiably excluded from it. He is not to be shut out from it at the whim of those having governance of it.

The international cricket authorities had fallen into the trap of allowing their annoyance at what some players had done to govern their method of dealing with the problem. Far more composed would have been the simple device of not selecting Packer players, instead of the sledgehammer method of banning them and taking action which might be construed as inducing them to break their contracts. But such was the mood of those controversial summer days in 1977. Even as the High Court began its sitting in London to hear the Packer players' case against the ban, the West Australian CA in Perth announced a total ban on Ross Edwards, Bruce Laird, Dennis Lillee, Mick Malone and Rodney Marsh.

The Packer High Court case began in late September. It had been expected to last for 2 or 3 weeks; in fact it lasted for nearly 7. The cricket authorities told Mr Justice Slade about the precarious state of the game's finances, explained why they found it difficult if not impossible to pay players more, and attempted to justify their proposed bans by asserting that it was in the best interests of the game to ensure that top players were not creamed off by private promoters paying big money. The authorities emphasized that their responsibilities extended to all players, not only the famous capable of attracting lucrative contracts. If they allowed top players to desert the traditional game at will, they argued, traditional cricket, which gets most of its money from people paying at the gates, would suffer. The authorities denied that their proposed bans were 'punitive' and stressed that they had always been concerned to act within the law. They told the High Court they saw no way in which Mr Packer's cricket could benefit the game as a whole.

Counsel for the Packer players told the High Court that from the moment Mr Packer's plans became known, the ICC and TCCB had used every weapon at their disposal to fight what they clearly felt was 'thoroughly unwelcome competition'. There had been, said counsel for the Packer players, statements at ICC meetings like 'wars are not won by appeasement', and 'siege situations'. In prosecuting the war, the authorities saw fit to introduce provisions which were plainly 'dictatorial and penal and an infringement of the liberty of the individual'. They did this, counsel maintained, 'to persuade players to break their contracts, to penalize those who did not and to prevent others who might be tempted to sign to play with Mr Packer's troupe'. Counsel said that references during the hearing by TCCB Chairman Doug Insole to 'authorized cricket', and by ICC/MCC Secretary Jack Bailey who talked of ICC rules as 'legislation', indicated their belief that they had an authority more appropriately possessed by a sovereign state. Counsel contended that the prosecution of war against Packer players led the authorities to infringe common law, both with regard to restraint of trade and inducement to breaches of contracts. 'We suggest it is now for the court in its traditional role to protect the individual and his property'.

Giving judgment, Mr Justice Slade agreed with the Counsel for the Packer players. The international cricket authorities were roundly condemned for their proposed ban on Packer-contracted players. Mr Justice Slade said in his judgment he appreciated that the structure and finances of Test cricket were vulnerable. And he sympathized with the view expressed by the authorities' witnesses that anything which was likely to prejudice the attraction and profitability of Test cricket must concern the organizers. But he concluded that a challenge from some private promoter was bound to come sooner or later. Mr Justice Slade expressed surprise that it had not happened before.

The judge saw the force of criticism directed at Tony Greig for his role in the Packer affair, but he added:

> A professional cricketer needs to make his living as much as any other professional man. It is straining the concept of loyalty too far for the authorities to expect him to enter into a self-denying ordinance not to play cricket for a private promoter during the winter months merely because the matches promoted could detract from the future profits of the authorities, who were not themselves willing or in a position to offer him employment over the winter or guarantee him employment in the future.

Mr Justice Slade concluded that the players concerned, with the possible exception of Tony Greig, could not be justifiably criticized on moral grounds for having entered into contracts with WSC in conditions of secrecy. 'The defendants' [meaning the cricket authorities] subsequent actions made it abundantly clear that had they been informed in advance of the WSC project, they would have done their utmost to prevent it taking root and prevent the players involved from enjoying the advantages offered by WSC'.

A WSC match before a day-time attendance at Victoria Football League Park, Melbourne.

Mr Justice Slade ended his judgment against the cricket authorities by saying that they had acted without regard to the fact that WSC had contractual rights with the players concerned and were entitled to the protection of the law. The judge believed that the cricket authorities had acted in good faith and in what they considered the best interests of the game. That, however, had not been enough to justify the bans they had proposed.

The High Court decision was a shattering blow to the cricket authorities. Above everything else they had to find a quarter-of-a-million pounds to pay the costs of the action against them. And the reaction among some county officials showed just how widely opinion about Packer players was split, even among the most famous clubs in the country. The Sussex Club Secretary saw the verdict as no occasion for universal sorrow. 'We do not believe', he said, 'that our members would have been at all happy if the careers of our three great players, Greig, Snow and Imran Khan, had ended in a ban. It is not for us to comment on the court decision, but we are relieved that we can plan our team for the next year'.

Mike Turner of Leicestershire declared disappointment at the verdict. He felt it could have a far-reaching effect on the game. Gloucestershire's club treasurer said he was 'tickled pink' that Procter and Zaheer would not be banned from playing for the club because of their Packer associations. The Hampshire captain, without wishing to comment on the High Court verdict, seemed sure it represented 'good news for Hampshire cricket'.

Nowhere did the verdict cause more delight than at the hotel in Melbourne which WSC had made its headquarters in preparation for its 1st match. Tony Greig talked expansively about 'getting round the table and working out a compromise'. Ian Chappell and Mike Procter shared a joke about the money the ICC would have to find to pay the costs of the High Court action.

One of the pitches artificially grown in greenhouses being lowered into position for a WSC match at the VFL Park outside Melbourne.

But there were more serious matters ahead. The thought of litigation had enveloped the Packer camp. At a press conference before the first Packer game, Richie Benaud, the cricket brain behind WSC, announced that Packer cricket would *not* be played under what were generally known as the 'Rules [*sic*] of Cricket'. Those 'rules' he pointed out were the copyright of the MCC.

There were to be other innovations for Packer cricket. In the first place, having been denied the use of some established grounds, Mr Packer was forced to turn showgrounds and trotting parks into cricket grounds. Not all were suitable. His organizers hit upon a novel way of preparing wickets. They were grown in hot-houses in huge concrete trays and dropped into place in the ground at the appropriate time. There were also to be night games under floodlights with white cricket balls. The emphasis was to be on entertaining cricket – and there were rules governing the placing of defensive fields at the start of each game. The games were also to be made a television spectacle (the real idea of the early evening start to the night fixtures) and more cameras than had been used before were deployed to cover the matches. The games were to be heavily promoted on television.

WSC had 3 teams – a West Indies team, an Australian team and Rest of the World team made up of England, Pakistan and South African players. Fixtures were built around these teams. There were bonus payments for winning teams so that maximum effort from players was assured. The WSC organizers placed a great deal of emphasis on what they called 'professionalism'. Players were given lectures on what the word meant and were expected to allow themselves to be used to promote the sale of hamburgers and washing machines.

The one hitch in the proceedings in that first year of Packer cricket was that several key people in the organization knew very little about the game and even less about its administration. So, although Mr Packer had been led to believe that from the start his matches would draw mammoth crowds, many games in that 1st year were played before merely a handful of spectators. Some of the cricket was attractive enough. The composition of the teams meant that there was almost continual pace attack, lots of television pictures of batsmen bobbing and weaving, hard-hitting and spectacular fielding. The serious flaw seemed to be that the results of matches did not really seem to matter after a time, except to the team winning the bonus money.

The organizers of WSC had also been hoping that the official Australia v India series would be a massive 'switch-off'. But the official Test matches were keenly contested and in the bars up and down the country, faced with the choice of watching WSC or the official Tests, Packer cricket invariably came second.

During that first year although Channel 9 claimed good television ratings a great deal of money had to be pumped into WSC. No money was made at the gates and the several television cameras seemed to be avoiding having to show the yawning spaces in vast football grounds where the matches were played.

The cricket authorities continued to say that they were hoping eventually to reach some compromise with Mr Packer, but the poor crowd response to the Packer first summer put no real pressure on them to do so. English cricket had taken steps to ensure that players needed for Test matches were available, and to combat Packer cricket a great deal of new sponsorship money began to flow into the game. Suddenly Test cricketers and even umpires were given hefty increases. Although his first year's games had failed to win the universal admiration of the Australian population, the effects of Mr Packer's entry into the game were already beginning to be felt.

West Indies in pink, Australians in yellow and girls in attendance.

If the authorities were proceeding on the sound and realistic basis that any 'deal' with Mr Packer's WSC should be carefully thought out – not rushed into, securing a truce only for its own sake – the English professional Cricketers' Association, which comprised all the players contracted to the county clubs, were not given the opportunity for such quiet reflection. The Association was usually to be found in the thick of any speculation about starting new talks with Mr Packer, or clearing away any obstacles in the way of a possible compromise. One interesting aside is that the involvement of the Cricketers' Association occurred very much with the blessing of the cricket administrators, who felt their fingers burnt somewhat by a few of Mr Justice Slade's remarks. Never again would the cricket authorities lay themselves open to the charge of 'dictating' the way the game is run.

The Association had tried to get both sides together well before the declarations of 'open war'. But when they saw Mr Packer he seemed convinced that they were merely another arm of the cricket establishment. The Association felt it should represent the interest of all its members, including those who had joined WSC.

The stirring words of Mr Justice Slade about a professional cricketer's right to work failed to impress some club officials and players. Some clubs saw the continued presence in domestic competitions of players who had sought the safer ground of financial security by bargaining the long-term interests of the traditional game as a divisive element to be resisted at all costs. The courts may have ruled that it was improper to try to ban Packer players but it never said anything about renewing their contracts. So ran the argument. There were numerous whispers of dressing-room conflicts between players on both sides of the dispute.

Ironically, the atmosphere became most poisonous in the dressing-rooms of the West Indies Test players. It was perhaps a little tough on West Indian Board officials who had done their best to represent the very special interests of their players to discover that they (the officials) were being regarded by the players as avowed enemies. It was this mood which precipitated the walk-out by Packer players in the West Indies team when the Board omitted one of their number for a Test match against the touring Australian team. The Australians had come to the West Indies under the captaincy of Bobby Simpson who had been recalled by the selectors to fill the gap by the sudden departure of virtually the entire Australian Test team. Two up in the series, the West Indies Board attempted to make 3 changes in the team with a view to selecting players for the forthcoming tour to India for which the Packer players would not be available. There was a row, culminating in a last-minute walk-out by the captain, Clive Lloyd, followed by his WSC colleagues. The timing of this unprecedented manoeuvre in Guyana, on the South American mainland, meant that the West Indies were only able to get a fresh and untried team together in the nick of time from the Caribbean Islands in order to fulfil the fixture.

There was more than a suspicion that the players had the full backing of Mr Packer in their action in walking out on the Board. Alvin Kallicharran, the West Indian and Warwickshire left-hander, took over the leadership against Bobby Simpson's Australians in the Guyana Test Match, led the team for the remainder of the series and took the 'new' West Indies team to India as well.

In England, county players faced several practical problems. With the TCCB intent on keeping a low profile, the Cricketers' Association found itself once more in the firing line. One major consideration was the security of players who had been chosen to fill those vacancies caused by their colleagues who had joined WSC. Court ruling or not, the 'replacements' were not prepared to be brushed aside when the 'sinners' were welcomed back to the fold. The attitude of the players in the England team on tour in Pakistan in 1977–78 was not insignificant in this regard. When it was learnt that WSC had released 3 Pakistani players to play for their country against the England touring team, the England players revolted. Apparently, over the head of their administrators on tour, some England players threatened not to play. In the event the players released by Mr Packer flew to Pakistan but were not selected and the threatened strike was averted.

At home the Players' Association was being called on increasingly to deal with situations not far removed from the one involving the England players in Pakistan. The Association remained convinced that 'fighting' Mr Packer was not in the long-term interests of the game or its members. When Mr Packer's representatives asked to be allowed to talk to the players at an Association meeting, an invitation was promptly extended. WSC were also thinking of ending the 'open war'. There were 2 reasons for this. In the first place, Mr Packer was very keen for these players to continue to keep in the cricket-loving public's eye with performances in the internationally publicized county game. Secondly, it was never Mr Packer's intention, he said, to lead a band of star players in perpetual rebellion against the traditional authorities. Hence the desire of Mr Packer's emissaries to convince the English county players of the 'good faith' of WSC. There were no open fights at the resulting Association meetings. The most contentious resolutions by the anti-Packer groups were defused or deferred.

For its part, the ICC had always committed itself from the outset to seeking a broad agreement which could be assured of the full-hearted consent of all the Test-playing countries. The mere logistics of sticking to that commitment meant that progress towards a settlement of the Packer dispute was always going to be slow and at times barely discernible. ICC representatives journeyed to the West Indies and to the Indian sub-continent. There were long barren periods when it looked for all the world as though there would never be an end to the dispute.

England prepared to tour Australia in defence of the Ashes and Mr Packer's second year was about to begin. Everything about this second time round was to be different from the first. The Packer cricket organization had become more streamlined and the promotion of matches, with a plethora of gimmicks, cricket sets, sweat-shirts, indoor cricket games and every variety of giveaway, had become something of a minor industry. There were competitions and advertisements on commercial radio and in the national press. All this was backed up by some of the most skilfully produced television commercials ever seen in Australia. No effort was to be spared to get the message across to the paying fans this time. This was to be WSC's 'make or break' year. And WSC had one crucial advantage. Channel 9, an entire television network, seems to have been placed at the disposal of a team of producers whose job it was to sell WSC to Australia.

In its inaugural year, WSC had sought to widen the market of potential paying customers and television viewers. A programme of 'country matches' took players to places in the Australian outback where international cricketers had seldom, if ever, gone before. To keep alive the interest of the players making these pilgrimages to out of the way places with questionable cricket grounds, the visiting teams competed for a 'Country Cup'. Whatever inconvenience the players may have experienced, the country folk lapped it up. To them it seemed that Mr Packer cared. This at least is how the 'success' of the country matches was represented on Channel 9's glossily-produced promotion programmes before the start of the 2nd year of WSC.

In the second year's programme of matches, WSC commentators went one step further in widening the interest of the game. There has generally been a tendency (one is sure it is not policy) to treat cricket as a feast for the aficionados only, for the purists, those who have always loved and understood the game. The Packer approach was to be radically different. Advertising, for the night games in particular, was aimed at whole families. Reference in a broadcast to an 'in-swinger' or a 'googly' was invariably accompanied by a televisual illustration of how that kind of delivery was expected to deceive the batsman. It was a brilliant idea. It gave rise during the Australian summer of 1978–79 to people saying they were not terribly keen on cricket but that they 'watched WSC'.

For the Australian Board, the consequences of this 'Packer approach' to marketing cricket were serious. While their attendances dropped automatically in comparison to those of the previous England tour, 50,000 people shouting and applauding filled the Sydney Cricket Ground (which Mr Packer had in his 2nd year been given permission to use) to see the first limited-over one-day WSC game under floodlights. (50,000 was the accepted figure, but admission by the evening was through open turnstiles – the paid attendance was never revealed.) The lights which changed the landscape of that part of Sydney were an engineering feat in themselves, and the advertising men were not above urging people, even those not interested in the game itself, to come and see the new lights.

Sydney was undoubtedly the high watermark. But there were also good crowds in Melbourne and Brisbane. When it was clear that Mike Brearley's England team would demolish the less-experienced team under Graham Yallop, Australian supporters were only too eager to identify with Ian Chappell's 'Packer' Australians, battling it out in one-day games against the well-known West Indians, or against Tony Greig and his 'World' team. Australian crowds are very apt quickly to desert losers, and the Board, for the first time, lost heavily on an Ashes tour. The Board said weakly they would have to consider staging night matches, and Mr Packer caught the public mood when he offered a large sum of money if the Board

Sydney Cricket Ground floodlit for a WSC match. The ball is white, the sight-screens black. On the right the new Brewongle stand is being built.

When WSC ventured abroad, rioting interrupted play in the West Indies several times. The most serious disturbance took place at Georgetown, Guyana, where spectators, angered by delay because of rain and the absence of information, hurled seats and debris onto the ground, and ransacked the pavilion, destroying Georgetown CC records.

would agree to an Australian team including his players, meeting Mike Brearley's England team in a 'deciding' fixture.

And yet, despite all this, the speed with which the Australian Board sued for peace caused international consternation. Throughout that Australian summer ICC officials had twice visited Australia to negotiate with Mr Packer and his team ways of ending the conflict that had so terribly divided the game. Despite the lukewarm attitude towards them of the Australian Board, the talks made modest progress in a civil atmosphere, although both sides were extremely cautious about raising too many false hopes. Both sides saw as the major problem the attitude of the Australian officials, who on the surface at least remained obdurate defenders of 'fair dinkum' cricket. With the West Indies, India and Pakistan clamouring for an agreement to end the dispute and with English officials cast in the role of 'honest brokers' the possibility was raised of the Australian Board holding out so long that the ICC could be disastrously split.

Then, almost as suddenly as the news of Mr Packer's rival series had burst upon an unsuspecting world, came news from Australia that the cricket authorities there had struck a multi-million dollar deal with Mr Packer giving him in effect, now that their existing ABC television contract had run out, everything he had ever wanted. The Australian Board went further. It had always been agreed among the ICC members that no individual country would contract a unilateral agreement with WSC. Yet the Australian Board's agreement was reached with the utmost haste and to the embarrassment of some member-countries. Part of the agreement, for example, allowed Mr Packer to insist on the cancellation of a planned visit by India in 1979–80, to accommodate instead the admittedly more attractive proposition of a series of Test matches and one-day fixtures involving Australia, England and the West Indies.

Always with an eye to their own interests, the Australians had agreed to put off the Indian invitation. The agreement gave the Australian Board an unspecified amount of Packer money, and it gave Mr Packer (quite contrary to the position of cricket sponsors and patrons elsewhere in the world) a strong voice in the running as well as the televising of cricket in that country. In view of what had always been regarded as Australian intransigence in dealing with Mr Packer, their capitulation was more than a little surprising. The sight of Mr Packer and the Australian Board Chairman, Bob Parrish, cooing delightedly in accord was not one for weak stomachs.

There were ominous grumblings when the ICC convened in London to 'ratify' the deal. Member countries had been forced to wait for several days before Mr Parrish and his colleagues finally turned up to explain just what had been agreed. More in relief that the potentially disastrous conflict had been resolved than in admiration for the *volte face* of the Australians, the ICC accepted in principle if not in detail the deal worked out by the Australian Board. Several questions remained unanswered and in the end the ICC Secretary, Jack Bailey, admitted that unresolved issues simply had to be left to the 'goodwill' of the Australians. It was a far cry from the days when the Australian Board were shouting for Mr Packer's head on a silver salver.

There remained one test of the strength of the agreement. Mr Packer had consistently demanded visible proof that his players would not be victimized after any compromise. The announcement in early September 1979 that England for their tour of Australia had recalled Derek Underwood, a Packer player, in place of Phil Edmonds, the man who had filled Underwood's place with distinction, was the first visible sign that, at a formal level at least, the war maybe was really ending.

CHRONOLOGY

1977	
24 April	South Africa's *Sunday Times* states that 4 South African Cricketers have signed 'lucrative contracts'
11 May	Australia's *Bulletin*, a 97-year-old magazine owned by Australian Consolidated Press (Chairman Kerry Packer) announces that 35 cricketers have been signed for 3 years
13 May	The Cricket Council announces that A. W. Greig would not be considered for the England captaincy
15 May	South Africa supports ICC
26 May	TCCB instructs selection committee to pick England's team on merit
14 June	Emergency meeting of ICC – Agreement to meet Packer
23 June	Breakdown of talks between ICC and Packer
15 July	Test and County Cricket Board meets at Lord's
23 July	Packer threatens legal action against ICC
24 July	Dates of Packer matches announced
26 July	ICC meets
2 August	Packer states that he will apply for an injunction and damages in the High Court
4 August	Mr Justice Slynn rejects applications for injunction, but accepts undertaking by TCCB not to ban Packer players until dispute has been tried in court
5 September	The Professional Cricketers' Association vote to reopen negotiations with Packer and to ban county cricketers from playing in his series
26 September	High Court hearing before Mr Justice Slade opens in London
7 November	Hearing concluded
16 November	First WSC trial match: over 5,000 present – no admission charge
25 November	TCCB announce postponement of decision concerning an appeal until 6 January
2 December	First 'Super Test'
1978	
17 January	Strike by England players in Pakistan averted
31 January	Sussex relieve Greig of captaincy
2 February	It is announced that ICC and TCCB will not appeal against High Court judgment
25–26 July	ICC reject WSC proposals
1979	
24 April	Australian Cricket Board give Packer exclusive Television rights for 3 years
30 May	10-year agreement signed between Packer and the Australian Cricket Board
28–29 June	ICC approve agreement between Packer and the Australian Cricket Board
30 June	TCCB announce maximum of 11 one-day matches in Australia and the non-acceptance of 'abnormal conditions'

Part V
English Counties and Universities

The County Championship

E. W. SWANTON

THERE WAS no formal institution of the County Championship, which for many years existed only to the extent of tables occasionally published in the press. As early as 1837 there was a reference in a Maidstone newspaper to a game between Kent and Notts being for a county championship, apparently on the specious grounds that both had already beaten Sussex. These three and also Surrey, were playing one another with some regularity in the middle of the century. Middlesex, Yorkshire and Lancashire, each boasted some sort of county club by the early 1860s, while most of the other 'major' counties of today had founded organizations distinctly earlier than this, though several failed to last and were ultimately reformed. The generally accepted date for the start of the Championship is 1873 since in the preceding winter of that year, at the instigation of Surrey, all the leading counties except Notts met in London and agreed a few basic rules, the chief of which were that: (1) a cricketer should not play for more than one county in the same season; (2) a qualifying period of 2 years' *bona fide* residence should be imposed on any man anxious to change his allegiance; and (3) in case of dispute MCC should be asked to arbitrate. Surrey provided both the President and the Secretary at these meetings, and Gloucestershire were represented by a 24-year-old who was already being talked about, by name W. G. Grace. The idea of a Championship or League was all somewhat haphazard, and it is noteworthy that whereas John Wisden was in the early years reduced to add substance to his publication by information not remotely connected with cricket the *Almanack* did not publish its first county table until 1888.

The 9 counties involved in 1873, and for the 14 years following, were Derbyshire, Gloucestershire, Kent, Lancashire, Middlesex, Notts, Surrey, Sussex and Yorkshire. At this point Derbyshire fell from favour at the instigation, if you please, of the *Sporting Press* in London, the other counties apparently conniving on the grounds that they had won only 1 match in 4 years. That, incidentally, was one win more than was achieved (with a much bigger fixture-list) by Northants in 4 years in the 1930s. Somerset slipped in, in Derbyshire's place, in 1891, but the great year when the Championship took off, as it were, if that be the phrase, for it was decided by the county captains and secretaries, was 1895.

The Trophy presented by the Lord's Taverners which the Duke of Edinburgh in his capacity as 'Twelfth Man' annually presents to the Champion County at Buckingham Palace.

In that year Essex, Hampshire, Leicestershire and Warwickshire were brought into the fold and Derbyshire permitted to return. So there were now 14 contestants, with the later addition of Worcestershire in 1899 and Northants in 1905. Glamorgan entered in 1921, and there at 17 the number still stands, though it should be mentioned that overtures were also made in 1921 to Bucks, who declined because of a shortage of playing facilities – and maybe sufficient areas of population. Year in, year out between the wars not only Bucks but Norfolk also were at least as good a side as those who habitually finished at the foot of the table.

Throughout history MCC have only concerned themselves with affairs outside their own spheres of control (and notably, of course, in the matter of the laws) when earnestly pressed. Retrospectively it seems to have been a pity that they did not resolve the power vacuum within county cricket earlier than they did. As it was, it was all but a century later when the late Rowland Bowen made the derivation and early doings of the counties a special interest. It was two carefully-documented articles by him in the *Wisdens* of 1959 and 1960 that led the *Almanack* in its centenary year and thereafter to publish a list of Champions dating from a decade before the previously-accepted date of 1873.

Since it could lead to confusion for one publication to give one starting date and the other another, the names of the usually-accepted 'winners' are listed, for what they are worth, and the aggregate Championship results calculated, from 1864. On the other hand the competition's enhanced status in the public mind coincided with the enlargement of 1895, and it is accordingly from this date that the annual placings are given in the table overleaf.

Methods of Scoring

CHRONOLOGY

1895–1909 1 point for a win; 1 point deducted for a loss; drawn games not counted. Greater proportionate number of points in finished games decided.

1910 Percentage of wins to matches played.

1911–1914 5 points for a win; 3 points for 1st innings lead; 1 point for losing on 1st innings. Final placings decided by taking percentage of points obtained to possible points in matches played.

1919 Percentage of wins to matches played.

1920–1923 5 points for a win; 2 points for 1st innings lead in drawn match. Order decided by percentage of points obtained to points possible.

1924–1926 5 points for a win; 3 for 1st innings lead in drawn match; 1 point for team behind on 1st innings in drawn match. Order decided by percentage of points obtained to points possible.

1927–1928 8 points for a win; 5 points for a win on 1st innings in drawn game; 3 points for a team behind on 1st innings in drawn game; 4 points each for all other games. Order decided by percentage of points obtained to points possible.

1929–1930 Each County to play 28 matches; no percentages. Points only to decide placings in the table. Points awarded as in 1927–1928.

1931–1932 15 points for a win; 7½ points for a tie; 5 points for 1st innings lead in a drawn game; 3 points for losing 1st innings in a drawn game; 4 points for all other games.

Counties to play 28 matches and points to decide placings.

1933–1937 Same points system as previously with the addition of an award of 10 points for a win on the 1st innings and 3 points for the other team where there was no play on the first 2 days.

Each County to play a minimum of 24 matches. Order decided by a percentage of points obtained to points possible.

1938–1939 12 points for a win; 6 points each for a tie; 4 points for a win on 1st innings in match either lost or drawn; 2 points each if scores level on 1st innings; 8 points for a win on 1st innings in match where there is no play on first 2 days.

1946–1948 12 points for a win (6 each for a tie); 4 points for a 1st innings lead where game is lost or drawn; 2 points each for tie on 1st innings; 8 points for 1st innings win in game where there is no play on first 2 days.

Each County to play 26 matches. Points obtained to decide placings.

1949 Same as above except for matches ending in a tie. 8 points were now awarded to the side leading on the 1st innings and 4 to the side behind.

1950–1952 Same points system, but each County to play 28 matches.

1953–1956 Scoring in a tied match reduced to 6 points each.

1957–1959 An award of 2 bonus points was made to the side leading on the 1st innings if they had scored at a faster rate (runs per over) than the opposition.

Points to decide the Championship, but if two Counties finished level the Championship would be decided first by most wins and, if still equal, by bonus points.

1960–1962 Counties were now allowed to play 32 matches if they so desired. The final placings now to be decided from the average number of points obtained from each match.

1963–1966 10 points for a win; 2 points for a win on 1st innings in match lost or drawn; 5 points each in the case of a tie.

Each County to play 28 matches. Points only to decide.

1967 8 points for a win; 4 points for a win on 1st innings, 2 if equal, but if a drawn match with the 1st innings of the side batting 2nd not completed, only that side shall score 2 points; 2 points each in a drawn match plus any points scored in 1st innings, points only awarded for a drawn match provided a result has been achieved in the 1st innings.

1968 Bonus points were introduced and, as in 1966, 10 points were awarded for a win, 5 points for a tie and 5 for a draw. 1st innings points were only awarded for performances in the 1st 85 overs of each 1st innings and retained whatever the result of the match.

(i) For each 25 runs above 150 runs scored in the 1st 85 overs by the batting side – 1 point, *i.e.* 175 runs – 1 point; 200 runs – 2 points; 225 runs – 3 points and so on.

(ii) For each two wickets taken by the fielding side in the 1st 85 overs – 1 point *i.e.* 2 wickets – 1 point; 4 wickets 2 points; 6 wickets – 3 points; 8 wickets – 4 points; 10 wickets – 5 points.

CHAMPION COUNTY SINCE 1864

1864	Surrey
1865	Notts
1866	Middlesex
1867	Yorkshire
1868	Notts
1869	Notts / Yorkshire
1870	Yorkshire
1871	Notts
1872	Notts
1873	Gloucestershire / Notts
1874	Gloucestershire
1875	Notts
1876	Gloucestershire
1877	Gloucestershire
1878	Undecided
1879	Notts / Lancashire
1880	Notts
1881	Lancashire
1882	Notts / Lancashire
1883	Notts
1884	Notts
1885	Notts
1886	Notts
1887	Surrey
1888	Surrey
1889	Surrey / Lancashire / Notts
1890	Surrey
1891	Surrey
1892	Surrey
1893	Yorkshire
1894	Surrey
1895	Surrey
1896	Yorkshire
1897	Lancashire
1898	Yorkshire
1899	Surrey
1900	Yorkshire
1901	Yorkshire
1902	Yorkshire
1903	Middlesex
1904	Lancashire
1905	Yorkshire
1906	Kent
1907	Notts
1908	Yorkshire
1909	Kent
1910	Kent
1911	Warwickshire
1912	Yorkshire
1913	Kent
1914	Surrey
1919	Yorkshire
1920	Middlesex
1921	Middlesex
1922	Yorkshire
1923	Yorkshire
1924	Yorkshire
1925	Yorkshire
1926	Lancashire
1927	Lancashire
1928	Lancashire
1929	Notts
1930	Lancashire
1931	Yorkshire
1932	Yorkshire
1933	Yorkshire
1934	Lancashire
1935	Yorkshire
1936	Derbyshire
1937	Yorkshire
1938	Yorkshire
1939	Yorkshire
1946	Yorkshire
1947	Middlesex
1948	Glamorgan
1949	Middlesex / Yorkshire
1950	Lancashire / Surrey
1951	Warwickshire
1952	Surrey
1953	Surrey
1954	Surrey
1955	Surrey
1956	Surrey
1957	Surrey
1958	Surrey
1959	Yorkshire
1960	Yorkshire
1961	Hampshire
1962	Yorkshire
1963	Yorkshire
1964	Worcestershire
1965	Worcestershire
1966	Yorkshire
1967	Yorkshire
1968	Yorkshire
1969	Glamorgan
1970	Kent
1971	Surrey
1972	Warwickshire
1973	Hampshire
1974	Worcestershire
1975	Leicestershire
1976	Middlesex
1977	Middlesex / Kent
1978	Kent
1979	Essex

CHAMPIONSHIP WINS

County	Wins	Shared
Yorkshire	31	2(=)
Surrey	18	2(=)
Notts	12	5(=)
Lancashire	8	4(=)
Kent	6	1(=)
Middlesex	6	2(=)
Gloucestershire	3	1(=)
Warwickshire	3	
Worcestershire	3	
Glamorgan	2	
Hampshire	2	
Derbyshire	1	
Essex	1	
Leicestershire	1	

AGGREGATE RESULTS 1864–1979

COUNTY	YEARS OF PLAY	PLAYED	WON	LOST	TIED	DRAWN
Derbyshire	1871–87, 1895–1979	1863	464	710	–	689
Essex	1895–1979	1825	495	555	5	770
Glamorgan	1921–1979	1355	309	480	–	566
Gloucestershire	1870–1979	2105	643	793	1	668
Hampshire	1875–85, 1895–1979	1912	499	672	4	737
Kent	1864–1979	2215	839	687	2	687
Lancashire	1865–1979	2295	892	460	3	940
Leicestershire	1895–1979	1791	373	713	1	704
Middlesex	1864–1979	2000	749	525	5	721
Northamptonshire	1905–1979	1558	371	582	2	603
Nottinghamshire	1864–1979	2132	646	568	–	918
Somerset	1891–1979	1809	435	772	3	599
Surrey	1864–1979	2370	965	517	4	884
Sussex	1864–1979	2273	648	801	4	820
Warwickshire	1895–1979	1804	488	531	1	784
Worcestershire	1899–1979	1746	429	644	1	672
Yorkshire	1864–1979	2402	1148	383	2	869
Cambridgeshire	1864–69, 1871	19	8	8	–	3
		33474	10401	10401	38	12634

COUNTIES PLACINGS, 1895–1979

	DERBYSHIRE	ESSEX	GLAMORGAN	GLOUCESTERSHIRE	HAMPSHIRE	KENT	LANCASHIRE	LEICESTERSHIRE	MIDDLESEX	NORTHAMPTONSHIRE	NOTTINGHAMSHIRE	SOMERSET	SURREY	SUSSEX	WARWICKSHIRE	WORCESTERSHIRE	YORKSHIRE
1895	5	9		4	10	14	2	12	6		12	8	1	11	6		3
1896	7	5		10	8	9	2	13	3		6	11	4	14	12		1
1897	14	3		5	9	12	1	13	8		10	11	2	6	7		4
1898	9	5		3	12	7	6	13	2		8	13	4	9	9		1
1899	15	6		9	10	8	4	13	2		10	13	1	5	7	12	3
1900	13	10		7	15	3	2	14	7		5	11	7	3	6	12	1
1901	15	10		14	7	7	3	12	2		9	12	6	4	5	11	1
1902	10	13		14	15	7	5	11	12		3	7	4	2	6	9	1
1903	12	8		13	14	8	4	14	1		5	10	11	2	7	6	3
1904	10	14		9	15	3	1	7	4		5	12	11	6	7	13	2
1905	14	12		8	16	6	2	5	11	13	10	15	4	3	7	8	1
1906	16	7		9	8	1	4	15	11	11	5	11	3	10	6	14	2
1907	16	7		10	12	8	6	11	5	15	1	14	4	13	9	2	2
1908	14	11		10	9	2	7	13	4	15	8	16	3	5	12	6	1
1909	15	14		16	8	1	2	13	6	7	10	11	5	4	12	8	3
1910	15	11		12	6	1	4	10	3	9	5	16	2	7	14	13	8
1911	14	6		12	11	2	4	15	3	10	8	16	5	13	1	9	7
1912	12	15		11	6	3	4	13	5	2	8	14	7	10	9	16	1
1913	13	15		9	10	1	8	14	6	4	5	16	3	7	11	12	2
1914	12	8		16	5	3	11	13	2	9	10	15	1	6	7	14	4
1915–18																	
1919	9	14		8	7	2	5	9	13	12	3	5	4	11	15		1
1920	16	9		8	11	5	2	13	1	14	7	10	3	6	12	15	4
1921	12	15	17	7	6	4	5	11	1	13	8	10	2	9	16	14	3
1922	11	8	16	13	6	4	5	14	7	15	2	10	3	9	12	17	1
1923	10	13	16	11	7	5	3	14	8	17	2	9	4	6	12	15	1
1924	17	15	13	6	12	5	4	11	2	16	6	8	3	10	9	14	1
1925	14	7	17	10	9	5	3	12	6	11	4	15	2	13	8	16	1
1926	11	9	8	15	7	3	1	13	6	16	4	14	5	10	12	17	2
1927	5	8	15	12	13	4	1	7	9	16	2	14	6	10	11	17	3
1928	10	16	15	5	12	2	1	9	8	13	3	14	6	7	11	17	4
1929	7	12	17	4	11	8	2	9	6	13	1	15	10	4	14	16	2
1930	9	6	11	2	13	5	1	12	16	17	4	13	8	7	15	10	3
1931	7	10	15	2	12	3	6	16	11	17	5	13	8	4	9	14	1
1932	10	14	15	13	8	3	6	12	10	16	4	7	5	2	9	17	1
1933	6	4	16	10	14	3	5	17	12	13	8	11	9	2	7	15	1
1934	3	8	13	7	14	5	1	12	10	17	9	15	11	2	4	16	5
1935	2	9	13	15	16	10	4	6	3	17	5	14	11	7	8	12	1
1936	1	9	16	4	10	8	11	15	2	17	5	7	6	14	13	12	3
1937	3	6	7	4	14	12	9	16	2	17	10	13	8	5	11	15	1
1938	5	6	16	10	14	9	4	15	2	17	12	7	3	8	13	11	1
1939	9	4	13	3	15	5	6	17	2	16	12	14	8	10	11	7	1
1940–45																	
1946	15	8	6	5	10	6	3	11	2	16	13	4	11	17	14	8	1
1947	5	11	9	2	16	4	3	14	1	17	11	11	6	9	15	7	7
1948	6	13	1	8	9	15	5	11	3	17	14	12	2	16	7	10	4
1949	15	9	8	7	16	13	11	17	1	6	11	9	5	13	4	3	1
1950	5	17	11	7	12	9	1	16	14	10	15	7	1	13	4	6	3
1951	11	8	5	12	9	16	3	15	7	13	17	14	6	10	1	4	2
1952	4	10	7	9	12	15	3	6	5	8	16	17	1	13	10	14	2
1953	6	12	10	6	14	16	3	3	5	11	8	17	1	2	9	15	12
1954	3	15	4	13	14	11	10	16	7	7	5	17	1	9	6	11	2
1955	8	14	16	12	3	13	9	6	5	7	11	17	1	4	9	15	2
1956	12	11	13	3	6	16	2	17	5	4	8	15	1	9	14	9	7
1957	4	5	9	12	13	14	6	17	7	2	15	8	1	9	11	16	3
1958	5	6	15	14	2	8	7	12	10	4	17	3	1	13	16	9	11
1959	7	9	6	2	8	13	5	16	10	11	17	12	3	15	4	14	1
1960	5	6	11	8	12	10	2	17	3	9	16	14	7	4	15	13	1
1961	7	6	14	5	1	11	13	9	3	16	17	10	15	8	12	4	2
1962	7	9	14	4	10	11	16	17	13	8	15	6	5	12	3	2	1
1963	17	12	2	8	10	13	15	16	6	7	9	3	11	4	4	14	1
1964	12	10	11	17	13	7	14	16	6	3	15	8	4	9	2	1	5
1965	9	15	3	10	12	5	13	14	6	2	17	7	8	16	11	1	4
1966	9	16	14	15	11	4	12	8	12	5	17	3	7	10	6	2	1
1967	6	15	14	17	12	2	11	3	7	9	16	8	4	13	10	5	1
1968	8	14	3	16	5	2	6	9	10	13	4	12	15	17	11	7	1
1969	16	6	1	2	5	10	15	14	11	9	8	17	3	7	4	12	13
1970	7	12	2	17	10	1	3	15	16	14	11	13	5	9	7	6	4
1971	17	10	16	8	9	4	3	5	6	14	12	7	1	11	2	15	13
1972	17	5	13	3	9	2	15	6	8	4	14	11	12	16	1	7	10
1973	16	8	11	5	1	4	12	9	13	3	17	10	2	15	7	6	14
1974	17	12	16	14	2	10	8	4	6	3	15	5	6	13	9	1	10
1975	15	7	9	16	3	5	4	1	11	8	13	12	6	17	14	10	2
1976	15	6	17	3	12	14	16	4	1	2	13	7	9	10	5	11	8
1977	7	6	14	3	11	1	16	5	1	9	17	4	14	8	10	13	12
1978	14	2	13	10	8	1	12	6	3	17	7	5	16	9	11	15	4
1979	16	1	17	10	12	5	13	6	13	11	9	8	3	4	15	2	7

If play starts when less than 8 hours playing time remains and a one-innings match is played, no first-innings points shall be scored. The side winning on the one innings to score 10 points.

1969 The matches played were reduced from 28 to 24 by each County.

1972 The matches played were further reduced to 20 per County.

1973 Bonus points amended to include an additional point for a team scoring 75 runs within the first 25 overs, and additional point for 150 within the first 50 overs.

1974 First innings to be limited to 100 overs by the side batting first. Should the side batting first be dismissed inside this limit, the overs remaining would be added to the innings of the side batting second. Bonus points in the first innings to be won thus: Batting – 150 runs 1 point; 200 runs, 2; 250, 3; 300 runs 4. Bowling – 3 wickets, 1 point; 5 wickets, 2; 7 wickets 3; 9 wickets 4.

1977 Points for a win increased to 12, including one innings matches. Counties to play 22 matches each.

Schweppes' Sponsorship

In 1977 the County Championship, which had long ceased to be financially viable, was sponsored by Schweppes for an initial 3-year period. The sum involved was about £360,000. As home Test series and all other competitions had commercial backing the new sponsorship was a logical development. Both clubs and players benefited. Some of the burden of the counties in promoting a costly and poorly-supported competition – though still the backbone of first-class cricket – was eased, and prize money for players was put up. Initially £4,000 went to the champions, £2,500 to the runners-up, and £1,250 for the 3rd-placed team. Every win was worth £100 and every bonus point £5. The first year of the sponsorship coincided with an exciting 3-way race between Middlesex, Kent and Gloucestershire which was not settled until 9 September, the last day of the season. The title was shared by Middlesex and Kent – the 1st joint championship since 1950. In 1978 the competition for the first time was called 'The Schweppes Championship' and the prize money was increased. Kent, as champions, took £8,000, Essex, runners-up, £2,500, and Middlesex (3rd), £1,250. Bonus money from wins and bonus points ranged from £1,930 to Kent, to £685 to Northants. Essex took the top prize in 1979.

Sponsorship gave a new impetus and strength to the oldest of the competitions which too often in modern cricket has been obliged to take a back seat. Yet none of the more glamorous occasions would be possible without the Championship, which over the full season remains the ultimate test of strength.

ALEX BANNISTER

Benefits

MICHAEL CAREY

An ancient custom ordains that a cricketer (pre-1962 – 'professional') be given a benefit by his club or county after a reasonable length of service. The average period is 10 years after the award of a county cap. It is essential to the award that it be *ex gratia*, uncontracted. It was on this ground that in a test case regarding the liability of a benefit to tax (Seymour v Reed, 1927) the late Lord (then Sir John) Simon decided in the cricketer's favour. The late Lord Harris was active in organizing opinion to this effect.

In 1978, a remarkable story passed along the well-used grapevine of gossip that provides a fascinating aspect of the county cricket circuit. The gist of it was that a cricketer, well-known and respected without having achieved Test status, had been offered a substantial sum of money by a businessman in exchange for his benefit fund. The amount was said to be approaching 6 figures. In return, the businessman and his acolytes would administer the fund under the player's name and pocket the proceeds – tax free, of course.

The tale may well be apocryphal, not least in the fanciful sum of money bandied about, but if, in fact, it were to happen one of these days, no one in close contact with the game would be unduly surprised. Cricketer's benefits and testimonials in the 1970s have emerged as big business indeed.

Thoughtfully planned, often up to 2 years in advance, slickly organized and with a mixture of sponsorship, gimmickry and imagination that frequently stretches over the boundaries of cricket, they have advanced beyond recognition from the days when the old-time professional would have a bucket passed among the crowd and hope for the best.

Nowadays, indeed, some players make as much from a single collection (or raffle) in this fashion as an earlier beneficiary might have acquired in an entire season, especially from a full house for a match in one of the one-day competitions at, say, Canterbury or Old Trafford. Kent, in fact, provide an excellent example of what is possible nowadays at the wealthier end of the county spectrum. Several of their players have received benefits of £20,000 and more in recent seasons, though one wonders, in these inflated days, if George Hirst, who collected an astonishing £3,703 in 1904, was not far better off.

Some of Kent's beneficiaries were Test players: Luckhurst (£18,231), Knott (£27,037), Denness (£19,219), Underwood (£24,114), etc. But in 1977 J. N. Graham, who never aspired to be anything more than an honest county bowler, topped the lot with a figure of some £38,000. More than that, Graham provides an insight to the behind-the-scenes workings of the modern benefit by revealing that his personal expenditure needed to raise that sum – postage, printing, telephone calls, purchase of prizes, etc – was a staggering figure approaching £40,000. In all, therefore, Graham turned over a massive £80,000 or so from the Kentish public that year.

Only a player with a county of traditional wealthy patronage and consistently good support, such as Kent, dare commit himself so deeply. Graham readily recalls many a sleepless night, especially before the season started and the benefit wagon began to roll, pondering the enormity of his debts. 'Fortunately, I had a sympathetic bank manager and a lot of trustworthy friends, with items like telephone bills and postage stamps running well into four figures, the fund was well into July or August before it was in credit,' he recalls.

Like any other realistic professional, Graham saw his benefit season as a once-in-a-lifetime opportunity to hit the financial jackpot and provide security for his family, hence his willingness to take financial risks and work, day in, day out, for 18 months. Thus he visited some 700 public houses (rather more than even the thirstiest county cricketer manages in a year), as well as organizing the usual autographed cricket bats, brochures, golf and cricket matches and dinners and the sundry other items dreamed up by modern players to raise funds. As it happened Graham was unfit most of the season – which allowed him all the more time for benefit activities.

It all seems a far cry from the days of Hirst and company. But benefits have always thrown up contrasting stories and statistics right from the beginning. In the early days a benefit meant simply a benefit match, against opposition of the beneficiary's choice, and there were numerous examples of players finishing scantily rewarded or even out of pocket, since match expenses were deducted first. There is no better example than that of Somerset's Bertie Buse, whose match was over in a day. His reply, when asked if he would like another benefit some day, is now a cricketing classic: 'No thanks, I can't afford one.'

Before the First World War, 7 cricketers had benefits exceeding £2,000, excellent reward in those days. But there were others who received much less, notably Webb of Hampshire, who collected the modest sum of £150 from his benefit match against Surrey, despite an innings of 162 not out. Not every cricketer has been in such prime form in his benefit season. On the contrary, such are their demands off the field that many of them have struggled and even lost their place. 'Oh, well, it's his benefit year,' has become a commonplace explanation for a run of mediocrity.

Nowadays, most players are given testimonial funds, with events throughout the calendar year (beyond, in one notorious case of recent seasons). There have also been exceptions to the 10-year 'rule', notably in the case of some overseas players. Some long-serving players have actually had more than one testimonial with the same county. Others, like Ray Illingworth, have profited by moving on and enjoying playing success elsewhere: a benefit of £6,604 with Yorkshire in 1965; a testimonial of some £40,000 with Leicestershire 13 years later. Let us not forget, either, that a handful of luckless players who played county cricket for 10 or more years, but with two or more clubs, never qualified for a benefit or testimonial with any of them.

Between the wars, money was scarce and benefits did not advance much. Only 7 cricketers obtained more than £2,500, with Roy Kilner, of Yorkshire, heading the list with £4,016. In 1934, Yorkshire's Maurice Leyland received £3,648, over £1,000 more than Gloucestershire raised for Walter Hammond. Phil Mead, whose total of more than 55,000 runs has been bettered by only 3 players, earned just £1,095 from his 1st benefit in 1920. A collection after completing his 100th hundred in 1927 produced £382 and a second benefit in 1930 realized £640.

Even Leslie Ames, the Kent and England wicket-keeper, received only £1,265 in 1937. One wondered, as he assisted in running the fund for Kent's John Shepherd in 1979, what he thought of all the modern sponsorship and razzmatazz – especially Shepherd's pizza-eating contest. But remember again the changing values. One former player of my acquaintance, now a respected scorer, took barely a four figure sum from his pre-war benefit but it was enough to buy a house, a car and start a thriving antique business.

After the Second World War, benefits increased as the problems of pre-war England – depression, unemployment and general shortage of money – disappeared. The country, too, was hungry for sport. A memorial match for the dependants of the late Hedley Verity produced £8,233, more than double any pre-war sum. Bill Bowes (to whom the writer is indebted for his researches into this subject for the 1st edition of this book) received a similar sum for his labours with Yorkshire, but it was across the other side of the Pennines, where they share a reputation for looking after 't'brass', that the benefit came into its own. Lancashire's Cyril Washbrook caused a stir by being granted his county's 2nd match against the Australian tourists for his benefit in 1948, the first Lancashire professional to be so rewarded, and the £4,270 2s 9d he received from a gross gate of £8,648 helped to swell his fund to the then undreamed of sum of £14,000.

The astute, forward-thinking Washbrook, one of the first players and administrators to foresee Sunday cricket in England, introduced many innovations now taken for granted. He formed a committee to take the pressure of the benefit off his shoulders. Show-business personalities like Wilfred Pickles staged money-raising concerts for him. A special tie was designed (ties were later outlawed because of possible tax problems). 'No benefit could have been better organized,' Washbrook wrote later in his autobiography. Even that was called *Cricket – the Silver Lining*.

Before the days when a combination of inflation and high-powered organization put all previous figures in the shade the county of Lancashire, having given Cyril Washbrook the 2nd match against the 1948 Australians, subscribed £14,000 and this stood as the record sum for 23 years.

Washbrook's ideas caught on and all over the country benefit records were broken, though, curiously, a glamorous, crowd-pulling batsman like Denis Compton fell nearly £2,000 below Washbrook's figure the following year. Maybe Denis just wasn't organized! Leslie Ames enjoyed a second benefit with Kent, making another £4,336, Yorkshire produced more than £9,000 for Len Hutton – again, it does not stand comparison with Washbrook – and even the less-prosperous counties were able to give their long-serving players nice little nest eggs. Glamorgan raised almost £4,000 for Gilbert Parkhouse – Emrys Davies had received a mere £688 before the war – and the droll Charlie Harris, of Notts, had a record sum of £3,500.

Cricketers throughout the country now no longer left their benefits and testimonials to the vagaries of the weather and the generosity of the public. They began to organize. It was now possible to take out a 'Pluvius' insurance against rain. In certain cases, if the requisite amount of rain fell late in the day, after the crowd had paid admission, a lucky individual could collect both match receipts and an insurance pay-off.

The £3,000 benefit became commonplace. Derbyshire's Leslie Jackson, having collected £2,940 in 1957 when he became the first player with that county to risk a benefit for 30 years, shared another £2,902 just 5 years later when he took a joint testimonial with the wicket-keeper George Dawkes. In 1959, Derbyshire even gave their long-serving secretary Will Taylor a testimonial, while in 1968 Harold Rhodes picked up an unprecedented £8,495, largely because of many donations from outside the county from cricket enthusiasts who sympathized with Rhodes's problems during the long drawn-out throwing controversy.

In 1961, Brian Statham, the Lancashire and England fast bowler, topped everyone except his distinguished Lancashire predecessor with a benefit that made £13,047, but by now the benefit match system was beginning to be replaced in some cases by the testimonial fund or, in counties like Lancashire and Yorkshire, an endowment assurance scheme. In the past, some counties had withheld part of a player's benefit money until his playing days were over. It was not unknown for a cricketer to drink, gamble or simply give the money away. In the 1970s I knew one cricketer who gambled most of his away on the Hong Kong stock exchange – and he was a Yorkshireman, too.

Under the new system, a player was included in the scheme on the award of his county cap. After 10 years' service, a player would be considered for a testimonial, instead of a benefit, and in the meantime the assurance benefits would have grown enough to be larger than any average gate takings at a match. Any player finishing before the age of 40 had the option of continuing the payments or receiving a paid-up policy. The idea became so popular that even 'middle-distance' players who had completed 4 or 5 years of service voted to join in.

Any young man fortunate enough to make a living as a county cricketer nowadays may have the best of two well-rewarded worlds. Salaries are now much more realistic, so much so that a cricketer with one of the more 'fashionable' counties who goes on to reach Test status could, even in these inflationary times, become well-heeled indeed by the time he reaches his mid-thirties. Many cricketers have used their benefit or testimonial money to launch themselves on successful second careers in business. I know of one man who bought himself a share in a chic restaurant, another who acquired a holiday cottage in a lovely, remote part of England.

Indeed, many benefits reached such large proportions towards the end of the 1970s that a note of caution crept in. Players were warned on no account to devise schemes that could be construed as trading and, therefore, attract the attention of the taxman. Cricket has always needed its work-horses – the less gifted, the less rewarded players – without whom the county game simply could not function. It is because of them that the tradition of allowing a spectator to dip into his pocket to show his appreciation will continue to be an integral part of the game, no matter what other changes take place.

County Organization

WILFRED WOOLLER

There are 17 first-class county cricket clubs and no two have exactly similar requirements or organizations although in recent years a more even pattern of administration has emerged. Obviously the clubs which stage Test Matches, Lancashire, Yorkshire, Notts, Surrey and Warwickshire need a larger administration, ground staff, and more highly rateable spectator facilities than those other counties who do not. The formation of county clubs began in the first half of the 19th century, Sussex for example being formed in 1839 and by the 1860s the basis of the formation of the major clubs, Surrey, Nottingham, Yorkshire, Lancashire, Kent and Middlesex had been laid. The last county to be granted first-class status in 1921 was Glamorgan, although as a minor county organization it was formed in 1884.

There are counties who own their own grounds, for example, Lancashire (Old Trafford), Nottingham (Trent Bridge), Warwickshire (Edgbaston), Sussex (Hove), right up to the most recent who have acquired their own ground, Leicester (Grace Road) and the last, Essex (Chelmsford); there are counties who have permanent exclusive use of the grounds, Surrey (Oval); there are counties that share a permanent ground, Middlesex (Lord's), and counties who have a variety of forms of tenure on grounds on which they play like Glamorgan who share with clubs at St Helens, Swansea, and Sophia Gardens (Cardiff), and Yorkshire whose headquarters is a club ground (Headingley) but who also play on other grounds.

Since the advent of limited-over cricket which started with the Gillette Cup in 1963 and was further developed through the Benson & Hedges and John Player League competitions there has been a tendency for all counties to make occasional use of additional club ground facilities where generous spectator sport is anticipated. In broad principle, however, the high cost of developing a county ground and encouraging high membership support has led counties to develop in the main on either one or two major grounds for the bulk of their fixture list. One might note for example that more than £1 million has been spent on the development of Edgbaston since the last war and the most progressive county of the modern era, Leicestershire, raised and spent some £250,000 during 1978 and 1979 in the further development of their headquarters ground, Grace Road, which a decade or so before warranted the title 'Graceless' ground. In the 1950s PEP, a semi-political economic survey group, prophesied the termination of first-class county cricket in its present form; defeated by shortage of finance. In my *Glamorgan Year Book* editorial I stated that they had omitted one vital factor, the goodwill of supporters who will always find a way to survive.

To understand the structure of a first-class county, and the county committee, which is the governing body, and wholly responsible for the affairs and property of each county, one must appreciate that each county is a non-profit-distributing organization, technically owned by its members. In theory, if a county was disbanded its assets would be realized and the money divided among the current members of the club. One should also bear in mind that the distant beginnings were very small, based on the amateur principle, and thereafter tended to grow like Topsy, varying administrative patterns to evolutionary changes.

Since a county club is technically owned by its members it follows that the committee will be elected by them and this is the custom. Annually members vote for and finally confirm at the annual general meeting a committee according to the custom of the club. It follows that committees were composed originally of the more leisured classes and were very broadly based in a variety of different districts to represent the members and supporters of the county. A widely-based county like Glamorgan spreads support across three major South Wales counties and inevitably began with a committee membership representing areas from Monmouth to Carmarthen and a massive committee of 36. This has become 24. This would not be likely in a county as compact as Northants, but one can never tell. Hampshire for example had a committee 30 strong, Worcester 57 (since cut to 27 in 1975). Lancashire on the other hand, centred mainly on Old Trafford, was very much more compact and businesslike. Old Trafford is a massive business structure.

The officials of the county, president, chairman are normally selected by the committee, the appointments being subject to the approval of the annual general meeting. Other honorary officials include the treasurer, the solicitor, physician and occasionally honorary secretary, although this post has fallen greatly into disuse. It has been replaced by the contract secretary who is a paid official answerable to his committee, and serving all sub-committees.

Since the war there has been a steady reorganization of top county administration of first-class cricket, the TCCB staff being housed at the headquarters of MCC at Lord's. The Test and County Cricket Board has increasingly divorced itself from the influence of MCC and governs most of the affairs of first-class cricket although there is close liaison on cricket matters with MCC who have a strong guiding influence.

Each county has two representatives at the TCCB meetings held biannually at Lord's, summer and autumn, as a regular feature, and at other times when occasion requires. Each county has one vote and may submit such propositions and recommendations as it thinks fit to the TCCB. The Cricket Council, comprising delegates from the TCCB, MCC and also the National Cricket Association (*qv*), is however the supreme governing body of English cricket, and all decisions of broad international significance affecting the whole game are subject to their approval. In practice the control of first-class cricket is firmly in the hands of the first-class counties, but minor counties and the Universities (Oxford and Cambridge) also have a modest say within the TCCB.

The county committee these days is drawn from men in all walks of life and increasingly from businessmen, many of whom have been involved with cricket as an enthusiast or player. The work is entirely honorary and save under exceptional circumstances no expenses are paid. The reward is service to the game which has given them pleasure. Active, intelligent committee men are an asset beyond price.

Under the control of a general county committee, and with the ability to co-opt for special requirements, there are a number of sub-committees. Finance is one of prime importance as it monitors the income and expenditure of the county. Membership is one of the major income committees. The Cricket committee handles the object of the whole exercise, the playing staff and the cricket activities. Marketing, promotion or under whatever heading it goes by deals with the income derived from sponsorship. A Supporters' Club which might be directly controlled by the county committee or indirectly associated, is responsible for all forms of income arising from lotteries, football pools and ancillary incomes on the sales side including publications. The ground committee handles all matters connected with the administration of the ground, ground staff, facilities, and catering on the ground. Each county has its own particular emphasis on the importance of its committees. The committees' prime task is to produce and finance a worthy county team.

At the top end of the scale is a county like Surrey whose annual expenditure is £340,000, against which its income under broad headings, marketing (advertising, local sponsorship, etc) is £150,000, membership revenue is £95,000, gate receipts £25,000, TCCB revenue (Test Match, sponsorship, etc, receipts) £80,000. This is in contrast to one of the smaller counties that may not own the ground but rents ground facilities and therefore has neither access to increased revenue nor a capacity for such expenditure, but who may control the activities of the club on a budget of £150,000 per annum (pre-war £9,000). Surrey employ a permanent administrative staff of around 14 plus 3 on maintenance and 4 on the ground under the direct control of the secretary. He has below him an assistant, and an executive assistant. Members of the staff are directly answerable for various sub-committees, finance, marketing, membership, ground, office and, in addition, the head groundsman, cricket manager and general cricket administration.

At the other end of the scale, Glamorgan, after the reorganization following an extraordinary general meeting in 1978, are operating on committee responsibility with an administrative secretary controlling the office and running the general administration, grounds and gates, etc. Committee men are responsible for each sub-committee activity. Glamorgan have in addition appointed a coach-manager responsible under the chairman for the cricket administration. I do not like the system. An expert in control is essential under modern conditions.

The county which has most fully met the complicated modern requirements of the first-class game with its problems of staff, overseas players, sponsorship, supporters' club finance, and development, is in my view, Leicestershire. The county is controlled by 8 elected committee men plus a president, chairman and treasurer. The county was fortunate in its chairman elected in 1963, C. H. Palmer, who was not only a former player of quality, but also a former county secretary, and therefore in both capacities understood the exact requirements of the modern county. In 1969, Mike Turner, a fine administrator, was made a secretary-manager with full executive authority. The executive meet monthly to review progress. This bold policy has paid rich dividends. The result has been a restructure of Leicestershire cricket, first under Tony Lock, an inspired choice as captain and organizer of the county cricket side, and then Ray Illingworth, two of the finest thinkers in the game. The result of this has been the most successful playing era in the history of the Leicestershire club. Alive to the financial possibilities came the development of the ancillary income on the promotion side. The formation of income-bearing schemes like the 200 Club and the football pools are under the control of the secretary and committee but have a separate promoter; a lottery manager operates a separate unit to take advantage of the new Betting and Lottery Act and the 25p lottery. The success has been unquestionable and as a result Leicestershire has been the only county to make a profit in ten successive years. Seen against this background of recent years when many counties have made a financial loss, this is good government.

Secretaries old style and new – Wilfred Wooller, who for so many years combined the secretaryship and captaincy of Glamorgan, and F. M. Turner, the young secretary-manager of Leicestershire.

The lifeblood of the county is, of course, membership and most counties have a membership committee and approach this problem in much the same way. From time to time a county may employ a commercial promotions firm to lead a membership drive and this has proved financially rewarding in the second year. The ultimate basis of success in this profitable department depends in the final analysis on the quality of the cricket that the county is playing, the facilities which they can offer their members on the grounds on which they play, and the service they can offer. Members approved the wider variety of competition, better facilities and identification with their county. Membership varies today within the 5,000 to over 18,000 range and income between £35,000 and £90,000. Membership fees rate between £10 and £20 per annum with various categories. County administration services them. This contrasts with as few as 2,500 for the smaller county pre-war. Test Match counties offer an advantage to their members in Test Match privileges on their own grounds. Recently, however, a modest membership charge has been made to augment the central TCCB fund. This may be an additional charge to a member or a gross liability accepted by the county.

The average county contracted playing staff on a basic salary is approximately 20 per county but this number may be as low as 16/17 or as high as 25/26. Since the difference between amateur and professional was abolished nearly two decades ago and all players became cricketers, there are no amateurs playing in the first-class game in the sense of the amateur of yesteryear. The England captain, Mike Brearley, for example, has high rewards from cricket, and in 1978 enjoyed a benefit of over £25,000. A benefit is usually awarded to a county player after approximately 10 years.

All county players have to be officially registered whether they are contracted paid players, or players who may be used only on an occasional match basis. As many as 40/50 may be registered. The list is held at TCCB headquarters, and no player may take part in any official competition game unless his registration is properly lodged and approved. Certain counties challenged recently the validity of control of the registration rules on certain players who desired, against their counties' wishes, to move from one county to another. It was discovered, regrettably, that the provisions of what might be termed 'a gentleman's agreement' between counties did not hold good in a court of law. This has necessitated a totally new form of contract in which, broadly speaking, players must be offered and sign for a specified playing period usually 1–2 or 3 years, to be agreed. If the contract period elapses a player may move to another county. Freedom of movement is not, however, yet absolute because there is a measure of control by the registration committee of the TCCB, which is a subcommittee on which committee members of county cricket clubs serve. There is no doubt that the system now presents many problems for the county administration. There will always be the awkward player and the acquisitive county who wish to marry mutual activities for personal benefit, to the disadvantage of their fellow-players and counties. Subject to the normal safeguards, a contracted player is absolutely under the control of his elected county from approximately 1 April to mid September.

A decade ago with the full authority and support of first-class cricket administration there was formed a players' union, the Cricketers' Association. This body has since had a great bearing on the terms of contract of first-class players, who are all members of the union. In the summer meeting of 1978, the TCCB agreed to recommend to counties the Cricketers' Association request for a basic minimum annual wage for capped players of £4,000 for the 1979 season; for an uncapped player of £1,500 up to 21 years of age and £2,500 afterwards. The working contract is for the period of the home first-class county season which, broadly speaking, starts on 1 April and ends approximately in the second week in September. Adjustments for future inflation are envisaged.

This basic wage is however by no means the whole remuneration that goes to the county cricketer. Each competition, Schweppes, John Player, Benson & Hedges and Gillette has its own form of bonus and prize-money for team and individual performance. Test Cricket has Cornhill and Prudential sponsorship. Progress to the finals is financially very productive for players and county. Each county has, in addition, its own particular bonus schemes which in many cases are based on individual performance during the season and payable at the end of the season in September. A particular success in a competition also attracts additional bonuses from the county concerned. It would probably be accurate to say that the average capped first-class county player in the season 1979 would have averaged at least £5,000 per annum taxable income. All expenses, of course, are covered by the counties concerned and that includes travel, hotel, subsistence and agreed mileage rates where cars or other forms of transport are concerned.

Counties release players for Test cricket without any obligation and usually paying their basic wages into the bargain. A fee of £600 per player from TCCB funds is paid to the county for each player released. Players who achieve Test status benefit by a considerable increase in their income. Test match pay is £1,200 per game. If in addition a man is selected to go on an overseas tour a further sum of around £5,000 could be earned. In addition there are many promotional bonuses to be won. A Test match cricketer is therefore today in a very high income bracket and inevitably in surtax levels.

In broad principle, counties endeavour to attract and train the promising young players within their county orbit, but for a variety of reasons it is not possible or even practical for certain counties to draw their cricketers entirely from within their borders. For example, it is absurd to compare the nursery of a county like Northants with Yorkshire, with its vast background of competitive league and club cricket. However in the context of their catchment areas counties have their own winter and summer training schedules often based on one or more indoor cricket schools which are serviced by trained staff and which coach a wide range of enthusiasts. The use of the Indoor School is invaluable in the winter and the uncertain weather in this country. In 1977 MCC opened the biggest and the most up-to-date Indoor School at the Nursery side of Lord's. Glamorgan first built one at Neath in 1952 and all the young Welsh cricketers who later became prominent members of the first team were trained in that West Wales School.

In theory no county is permitted to approach any player who is on the registered list of another county, and there is nothing to prevent a county having a very big list of registered players. However a good deal of discreet searching through the cricketing talent of other counties does go on and where a player is not registered by a county it is not difficult to get authority from the county of his birth for a trial and subsequent employment on the staff. In this way a number of players move from their native area to other counties, and it could be seen from a study of many of the smaller counties that a very substantial proportion of their players were born in other counties with a much stronger cricket club background.

I come now to the difficult question of the registration of overseas players. It was found simpler and cheaper by a number of counties to go overseas to acquire a ready-made player than to undertake the expensive development at home of a young player with no guarantee of success at the end. This led to an overbalance of overseas players in county sides and inevitably a deterioration of the England team standard at national level. The TCCB have controlled the number of overseas players in each county side who are ineligible for England to 2. In 1981 this 2 will be reduced to one.

The biggest advance in the last decade or so in the development of coaching has been made by the advanced coaching scheme first promoted by MCC which has its own advanced certificate which most first-class players now take at some stage of their playing career. Great stress has been laid on the benefits of group coaching which was devised and perfected by the MCC Youth Cricket Association. The whole basis of this form of coaching has been broadened to take in any interested individuals and in particular schoolmasters who handle the boys at their school. There is no doubt that the growth of the big comprehensive school system has militated against the development of cricket at school level. Attention to the skills of cricket are often simply not there, nor are the facilities. Counties, through their own branches of the National Cricket Association, further coaching schemes for youth and, not least, for sons of members in the Christmas and Easter holidays. Many young players gain their first real insight into the technicalities of the game at the county training headquarters. Helping individual schools' cricket is also done wherever practicable. Glamorgan, which makes use of the Neath school and the Sports Council Recreational Centre at Cardiff, has nets for juniors and senior boys ranging from the 12, 13, 14 mark up to 18 on 4 nights a week from January up to the start of the season. Trained coaches are in charge and any particularly enterprising or promising youth is invited for special training in the county nets. This is common county practice.

The Supporters' Club in its modern form came into being in most counties in the early 1950s at a time when revenue from the post-war spectator boom was falling rapidly, and costs were rising fast. It was initially based on a shilling-a-week football pool, a mild gambling innovation which had caught public imagination. Leicester, Worcester, Glamorgan and Warwickshire, in that order, were first in the field in 1951–52. Eventually most counties in one form or another developed the Supporters' Club.

After a while the football pool lost favour with the public and the character of money raising changed. The 200 members club, and major raffles, were substituted and after recent changes in the Betting and Lottery Act, there came the big prize (25p ticket) new lottery, which when operated successfully, is now the biggest money-raiser. Leicester, ever efficient, quickly added to their separate Supporters' Club, a lottery organization under expert management. Glamorgan, who concentrated very successfully on a fully-staffed Supporters' Club organization controlled by a supporters committee, and a full-time organizer and staff, have also profited. There is a wide variety of this form of activity pursued with varying degrees of success. Warwickshire have raised the greatest aggregate sum – it must aggregate between 1 and 2 million pounds.

The major new development in money-raising in the last decade or so has come in the field of promotions. The TCCB, the counties' governing body, set up a separate department with expert management to deal with all sponsorship at national level. This includes also income ranging from television to the main sponsored competitions, and any other money-raising idea at national level.

This expertise in 1979 brought in a gross revenue of £1,400,000, based on approximately £700,000 from Test cricket, £357,000 from the Gillette Cup, £238,000 from Benson and Hedges, and £120,000 from the John Player League (the county retains its own gates direct in this competition). From the gross source each county can expect approximately £55,000 and those with Test Match grounds, with their greater financial commitment, between £73,000/£78,000. Pre-war a couple of thousand pounds was the return per county, and smaller counties needed even that for survival.

Counties have in addition set up their own promotion sub-committees and those that are a little more progressive have engaged their own expert in a managerial capacity to project their interests. Evidence demonstrates that this is wise finance and produces a far superior revenue than when left to amateur sub-committee control. There is a wide range of income promotions. Ground advertising around the perimeter, where grounds are owned by the county, can bring in between £10,000 and £25,000 per annum. Potential television coverage is important. Individual match sponsorship is widespread and ranges from fees charged of upwards of £100 per day with entertainment provided for the sponsors. Warwickshire have constructed executive suites which are hired through the season by business firms who use them for entertaining. The suites are serviced by highly efficient catering services. A wide variety of other forms of sponsorship has also been developed. Local television also brings in income and in this respect Glamorgan, who are fortunate to have a separate Welsh network, can hope for around £5,000 per annum.

Counties with spacious ground facilities have also realized that it is inefficient management to allow them to lie unproductive during the fallow months. Warwickshire early established a magnificent dining and entertaining suite, and Lancashire soon followed the trend at Old Trafford. These centres of entertainment have been profitably occupied throughout the winter – and the asset of excellent car parking facilities at a well known sporting headquarters is invaluable.

The age of the benevolent, general factotum secretary of yesteryear, often a retired serving officer working long hours for peanuts, has gone. The more efficient counties have employed a top-class executive secretary which is in my view vital in these complex modern conditions. County expenditure ranges from £150,000 per annum in the smaller clubs to upwards of £350,000 per annum at Test Match county level. Several counties have reported heavy losses both in 1978 and 1979. Leicestershire, however, who streamlined their committee to board-room efficiency have made a profit for ten successive years. No other county has achieved this record.

It will be seen from the foregoing that there is a wide variety of approach to the administration of the 17 first class counties, but whatever the size and complexity at the administrative level at the head is the secretary. His problems are many and complex, ranging over a variety of sub-committees, controlling promotion, membership, ground organization, catering, playing staff and coaching, Supporters' Club activities, team travel and hotel arrangements in a crowded summer season. It is a 7-day-a-week job in the playing season but in the winter he can relax down to an average 5-day week with, of course, a substantial amount of night work involving committees, club dinners, and promotional schemes. It is only in recent years that a number of counties have begun to realize the importance of this position, and even now few award a salary commensurate with the responsibility and activity required.

I am never tired of reminding committee men, often experts in their particular line of business, that the object of the county exercise is to put 11 players in the field worthy of the county – a difficult and expensive exercise. The rewards of a quality shop window to display first-class cricket at county and Test level is a demanding and thoroughly worthwhile job.

The Cricketers' Association

M. J. SMITH

The current importance and standing of the Cricketers' Association in English cricket owes much to the manner of its conduct since its inauguration in 1968 as the brainchild of that poet, fast bowler and man of ideas, Fred Rumsey. It has slowly, but surely, pressed its claims for a worthwhile voice in most aspects of the game, and, happily, although a potentially powerful force, it is a relatively conservative and non-radical group. The CA has a proud record of achievement in its short history and can rightly claim to have significantly improved player involvement and career prospects for its 300 or so members by careful negotiation with a somewhat prickly governing body of English first-class cricket.

Radical changes in our British society only succeed, it seems, if the problem has really reached rock bottom. This certainly applied to the foundation of the Cricketers' Association. In the middle-1960s cricket was generally thought by outsiders to be in danger of dying as a major spectator sport. The John Player Sunday League was still a pipe dream; the Gillette Cup was rather grudgingly accepted as vital to the finances of the clubs but viewed by many administrators as 'certainly not good for real cricket'. The finances of county clubs and the wages they paid to their players were at an all-time low in value. The players had no official avenues through which collectively to air their views and grievances. It was a classical situation for Rumsey to exploit and inspire the formation of an association.

The Middlesex Club was no exception to that pattern but it took an embarrassing rebuff from the then President of the club, following a request for a wage review, to underline the need for more team-work off the field. In fact, the off-hand treatment of those senior England cricketers was just the fuel needed for the Middlesex branch of the CA to take off. One can imagine many similar experiences happening in county clubs all over the country. The birth of the CA was not without its labour pains. The 'establishment' did not clutch it immediately to its bosom in its early days. Within a year or two, however, the wiser heads at Lord's realized the logic and inevitability of such an association, and by 1973 had actually granted a small percentage of television and radio fees to help with the CA's administrative costs.

Membership of the association was much less than 100% for more than 3 years after its foundation. The Association was viewed from several widely differing viewpoints by the players (apathy being one) and these varied attitudes just served to remind one how many different types of characters are to be found playing county cricket. It took a crisis or two and much lobbying by enthusiasts to achieve a near 100% membership by the mid-1970s and there are still one or two players who choose to resign from time to time.

Much of the important work of the CA takes place during the winter months while many of its members are sunning themselves on overseas cricket grounds and beaches. A dozen or so cricketers, some past but mostly present, converge on the National Liberal Club in Westminster for the monthly executive meeting. The executive is made up of a representative from each county, an elected chairman, an appointed secretary and the President of the Association. There have also been several people co-opted on to this executive for their special knowledge in fields where the CA needs advice on such matters as finance and the Law. The monthly meeting usually takes the form of an extended working lunch and lasts from 11am until late afternoon. The CA had, and still has, an impressive list of officers. However, with due respect to chairmen and secretaries, past and present, the guiding light has undoubtedly been the longest-standing President, John Arlott.

John's democratic views and diplomatic eloquence has been a steadying influence in some tight corners. He is much respected and admired by all connected with first-class cricket and his influence and wise counsel has greatly speeded the acceptance of, and growth to maturity by the association. He is, as every cricket-lover knows, a keen historian and a great raconteur. What perhaps is not fully appreciated is his great affection for the game and particularly the players and his enormous, entirely honorary, efforts to improve their lot, as President of the Association.

John Arlott's most important contribution, however, was the role he and the association's officers played in the recent confrontation between the International Cricket Conference and World Series Cricket. His repeated efforts to keep the CA neutral in this crisis was wise counsel indeed. Although opinions and attitudes within the membership of the CA were very varied during the Packer affair, two successive AGM's proved that compromise was the wish of the majority of the members. By the time of the April 1979 AGM, recognition of the good and the bad side of WSC's activities was clearer in members' minds, thanks largely to John Arlott's clear minded, sometimes passionate eloquence. A motion was moved for the association to urge, and almost demand, a dialogue between the two promoters, which would hopefully enable all players to play Test cricket again and tour with national teams. It seemed, however, that most members acknowledged the short-term good WSC had done for their living standards. The majority appeared to feel that the promotion of a limited season by WSC was the ideal situation for the well-being and the prosperity of the professional game. Competition between employers was thought to be healthy. It is cricket history now what the outcome of the 'agreement' was and I believe the CA, led by John Arlott, played a substantial and sensible part in helping to arrive at a solution.

Several other notable achievements have been made by the association over the years. Not only do they give financial backing and legal advice, when thought by the executive to be justified, to players in disputes with their club, but they now have a representative on the sub-committees concerning the registration of players and discipline, and are consulted on relevant matters by the Test and County Cricket Board's Chairman's Advisory Committee. A pension scheme and minimum wage agreement were also big steps in the right direction to help cricket attract the sort of talent to hold its own with the other professional sports. With such capable and respected administrators as David Brown, the Warwickshire and England fast bowler, as chairman, and Jack Bannister, also of Warwickshire, as secretary, not to mention John Arlott, cricket as a career looks to be in safe and orthodox hands.

David Brown, the Warwickshire and England fast bowler, formerly captain of the county, for whom he still plays, is Chairman of the Cricketers' Association. All first-class players now belong to the Association which enjoys a close working relationship with the TCCB.

The Lawrence Trophy

BRIAN THORNTON

Within the memory of many old or elderly cricket followers, the late Sir Walter Lawrence was the forerunner of the modern breed of sponsors. His Lawrence Trophy, first awarded in 1934, was presented to the batsman who scored the fastest hundred in county cricket. With the trophy went a prize of £100. Frank Woolley was the first winner, and from its inception the award became something of a household word to all those interested in cricket. Other pre-war winners were Leslie Ames, who won it twice, Harold Gimblett, Joe Hardstaff and Hugh Bartlett.

Sir Walter, on whose private ground at Hyde Hall, near Sawbridgeworth in Hertfordshire, much excellent club cricket was played between the wars, died in 1939, and with the onset of war the Trophy naturally went into abeyance.

It was not until 1966 that the directors of Walter Lawrence & Son Ltd, the family building contracting company, which had been established by Sir Walter's father in 1871, decided to re-introduce the trophy. It was then awarded to the English batsman who scored the fastest hundred in Test cricket in a calendar year, based on the number of balls received. With the trophy went a cash prize of £250. The first winner under these conditions was Ken Barrington, followed by Basil d'Oliveira, Tom Graveney, Colin Milburn and Geoff Boycott.

Gordon Greenidge holding the Walter Lawrence Trophy which he won in 1978 by scoring a hundred in 82 minutes.

In 1971 the donors of the Award reverted to its original purpose, to reward the scorer of the fastest hundred of the season in first-class cricket. The recent winners under the old criteria have been:

1971 B. Davison (Leicestershire)
1972 Majid Khan (Glamorgan)
1973 Asif Iqbal (Kent)
1974 G. S. Sobers (Notts)
1975 R. N. S. Hobbs (Essex)
1976 A. P. E. Knott (Kent)
1977 C. M. Old (Yorkshire)
1978 C. G. Greenidge (Hampshire)
1979 M. J. Procter (Gloucestershire)

The First-Class Counties

Derbyshire

MAJOR D. J. CARR AND MICHAEL CAREY

Foundation 1870
Colours Chocolate, Amber and Pale Blue
Badge Rose and Crown
Champions 1936

Cricket was presumably being played in Derbyshire before Bonnie Prince Charlie and his Highlanders reached Derby in 1745, as the game was referred to in the *Derby Mercury* of that year. It was certainly played seriously enough 30 years later when one William Waterfall was found guilty of manslaughter at Derby Assizes, having killed George Twigg in a cricket match at Bakewell. Soon after 1800, matches were common throughout the county. Money was usually at stake and winning was often more important than the methods employed. In one match in 1825, the Langley team needed 4 runs to win against Derby Old Club with 8 wickets down. At this stage the Langley umpire called 'no ball' after the batsman had played on. The Derby umpire countered by giving him out from square-leg, the incident being referred to the Marylebone club for adjudication.

The first match at the County Ground, Derby, was played in 1863, but there was not enough support to launch a county club until Derbyshire had beaten MCC at Lord's 7 years later. The county was founded at a meeting at the Guildhall, Derby, on 4 November 1870, largely due to Walter Boden, who became honorary secretary for 12 years. Derbyshire patently owed much to Boden's energy and enthusiasm, and he was later rewarded with the Presidency. Suitable opponents were difficult to find at first and only Lancashire would play the newcomers on level terms for the first 3 seasons. The opening match was played at Old Trafford in 1871 and resulted in a great victory. Lancashire were dismissed for 25, to this day their lowest score in county cricket. Two years later, Nottinghamshire were dismissed for 14 at Wirksworth, though the story goes that a generous patron of the club, a well-known wine merchant, held open house for Nottinghamshire before their innings.

In these formative years, the county's fortunes ebbed and flowed. With 3 victories and 1 draw in 1874, Derbyshire were considered champions, for in those days the team losing fewest matches took the title in the opinion of some authorities. With so few fixtures, Derbyshire clearly had an advantage and later Gloucestershire were named as champions. Three years later, after the departure of established players like Sugg, Shacklock and Docker and the death on the football field of Cropper, results deteriorated and Derbyshire for 7 seasons lost their first-class status.

The club also faced a financial struggle, partly due to the fraudulent activities of the assistant secretary, S. Richardson. His misdeeds were exposed by none other than F. R. Spofforth, the 'Demon' himself, who took a business appointment in the county after marrying a local girl and during his unfortunately brief stay at Derby devoted his spare time to close scrutiny of the club's accounts. Richardson disappeared to Madrid where he became Court tailor to the King of Spain. Spofforth, although not then qualified, was allowed by Yorkshire to play against them, a gesture he repaid by taking 15 wickets in the match. Derby County Football Club, who shared the ground at the Race Course, suffered similar financial loss at Richardson's hands.

On his hurried departure, W. Barclay Delacombe became the county's first paid secretary, holding the post for 20 years. His successor was W. T. Taylor, whose 51 years in the post was a record for a cricket administrator. His involvement and interest in the club continued until his death in 1976. In 1887, W. Storer appeared; he was the first of a succession of long-serving wicket-keepers and the first professional to score two centuries in a first-class match. He and his successor, J. Humphries, both played for England, as did H. Elliott, who kept wicket for 27 years, and of course, latterly, the great R. W. Taylor. It is remarkable that in Elliott, G. O. Dawkes and Taylor, Derbyshire have had only 3 regular wicket-keepers since the First World War.

At last, in 1894, Derbyshire were permitted to return to the fold and first-class cricket was again seen at Derby; the following year they finished 5th in the Championship, then consisting of 14 counties. Chatterton, the first Derbyshire player to be chosen for England, was still at his best as a batsman, while Davidson was reaching his prime as an all-rounder. From 1897, however, until the First World War, the county entered another period of decline, partly due to a shortage of quality bowlers, a situation unknown before or since.

The beautiful ground at Queen's Park, Chesterfield, overlooked by the crooked spire, was used for the first time in 1898. Such was the enthusiasm that the number of matches played there was gradually increased, until in recent years it has become as important a centre as Derby.

In 1904, the county won a remarkable victory against Essex who, batting first at Chesterfield, made 597 in little more than 6 hours. Perrin's 343 not out contained 68 fours, still the largest number ever hit in an innings. And for what meagre reward! Derbyshire replied with 548, the West Indian Olivierre making 229. On the last day Essex were dismissed for 97, leaving Derbyshire to make 147, which they did for the loss of 1 wicket. Around this time, one Derbyshire player was sentenced to a term of imprisonment after a public-house fracas, but on appeal from the club the magistrates suspended the sentence until the season was over.

Derbyshire, County Champions 1936. Back row: H. Elliott, L. F. Townsend, W. H. Copson, H. Parker (scorer), A. V. Pope, D. Smith and C. S. Elliott; sitting: H. Storer, T. S. Worthington, A. W. Richardson, T. B. Mitchell and A. E. Alderman.

In 1920, Derbyshire experienced the most humiliating season ever suffered by any county team, losing 17 out of 18 matches; the other game was abandoned without a ball being bowled. G. M. Buckston, a former Cambridge blue, later to do the club good service as Chairman, agreed to take over this wretched side for one year at the age of 40 and Bestwick, a fast bowler who had been dismissed by the club for intemperance, returned at the age of 45 to take 147 wickets, including all 10 against Glamorgan. The following year G. R. Jackson became captain and, by personal example and high-class leadership, raised the standard of cricket to a level previously unseen in the county. In 1927, his skill as a captain earned him an invitation to take the MCC side to South Africa, but he was unable to accept.

Jackson's leadership undoubtedly laid the foundation of Derbyshire's most prosperous era and, under another fine captain in A. W. Richardson, they began to assemble the team which became county champions for the only time in 1936, having been 3rd and 2nd the two previous years. For a county with a small staff and ever-present financial problems, this was a magnificent achievement. Among those who emerged during this period were a number who were to win Test recognition: D. Smith, the most prolific scorer the county has ever had and later the club coach; Mitchell, the leg-spinner; Copson, of the fiery head and pace to match; two fine all-rounders in G. H. Pope and L. F. Townsend; and T. S. Worthington, who once scored a hundred in an hour against Nottinghamshire and remains the only Derbyshire player to reach a century for England in Test cricket, though Taylor ran him agonizingly close in Adelaide in January 1979.

Others like H. Storer, widely regarded as technically the most complete Derbyshire batsman of the time, Alderman and C. S. Elliott, later to become a Test umpire and selector, were also on the scene as, of course, was H. Elliott, the wicket-keeper. After the Second World War, Smith and P. Vaulkhard shared a record partnership of 328 against Nottinghamshire, which was beaten when J. D. Eggar, a Repton schoolmaster, and C. S. Elliott put on 349 against the same opponents the following year. In the same

D. B. Carr was captain successively of Repton, Oxford, Derbyshire and (once as a deputy) England. He led a happy county side for 8 summers before becoming assistant secretary of MCC in 1962. P. B. H. May at slip.

season, a remarkable innings victory was achieved over Somerset in a single day, G. H. Pope taking 13 wickets for 50.

From 1951, the side was led by G. L. Willatt and the famous partnership of Gladwin and Jackson made Derbyshire's the most feared opening attack in the game. Both played for England, though why Jackson made only 2 appearances, and those 12 years apart, remains one of the game's unsolved mysteries. Batting, however, was invariably made to seem a dour and difficult art, which was later summed up memorably by Willatt thus: 'Like the Spanish sailors in the Armada, they are regarded as subordinates, an inferior race with a secondary role. Not much is expected of them and not much is forthcoming.'

There were, and happily still are exceptions. Not every Derbyshire recruit from other counties has been as successful as Hamer, a Yorkshireman with a cherubic countenance and scant regard for new ball bowling. D. B. Carr, who followed Willatt as captain and led the side for 16 years, had an elegant repertoire of strokes not easily associated with the county's gritty image of those days. He is the only player to make 2,000 runs in a season for the county and the one Derbyshire man to lead his country in a Test match. He also served as secretary and assistant secretary before taking up administrative posts at Lord's.

The 1960s and 1970s were to include some of the most traumatic years in the county's history, with the club's playing performances reaching their nadir when they were Championship wooden-spoonists 3 times in 4 seasons from 1971. Additionally, Derbyshire started to attract more than their share of controversy, starting when H. J. Rhodes, their fast bowler and the son of the former leg-spinner A. E. G. Rhodes, was no-balled for throwing, most notably by J. S. Buller, the Test umpire, in the county's game against the South Africans in 1965.

The dispute over the fairness of Rhodes's action was to rage for years. There were many remarkable episodes, on and off the field. Film cameramen, official and otherwise, became a familiar sight wherever the county were playing. One opposing player made his point by walking out to bat wearing a motor cyclist's crash helmet. Various medical tests and X-rays eventually led to the diagnosis that Rhodes had a 'hyper-extension' of his elbow which in turn gave an 'optical illusion' of his arm straightening prior to delivery. His action was officially pronounced fair at Lord's but he never added to his 2 Test appearances, prior to the furore, and ended his career an embittered man.

Without becoming the force they were in the immediate post-war years, Derbyshire remained a respected side and maintained their uncanny knack of unearthing medium-fast bowlers of the highest quality, two more of whom, M. Hendrick and A. Ward, were to win Test recognition. In 1967, too, the county discovered that rarity, a local-born spin bowler, in Swarbrook, who, at 16 years of age, became the youngest player ever to appear for them.

In 1969, the side dropped to 16th place in the Championship but, with their fast bowling armoury strengthened by F. E. Rumsey of Somerset, who joined as Public Relations officer but also played in one-day games, they were beaten finalists in the Gillette Cup. This year also saw the retirement of D. C. Morgan, who had succeeded C. Lee as captain. Morgan was the most successful all-rounder in Derbyshire's history and one of only 10 players ever to score 15,000 runs, take 1,000 wickets and hold 500 catches. Despite this, he never once did the double, nor was he selected for England.

Another all-rounder, I. R. Buxton, followed Morgan at the helm and in 1970, the county's centenary year, led them to 7th place in the Championship and third in the John Player League, helped by some refreshing stroke-play by C. P. Wilkins, a South African who was Derbyshire's first overseas player (of modern times). The following year, with a record loss of £15,000 and last place in the championship, was dismal indeed and it was hereabouts that the club seemed to be drifting aimlessly. Communication between the administration and dressing room was hazy, leadership was uncertain, both on and off the field, and policies of both team selection and recruitment of new players were sometimes hard to follow. Several players were dismissed, only to be re-engaged, often with much success, a year or two later. In addition, the club were slow to grasp the rapidly developing need for sponsorship and better public relations and much of the cricket was drab and purposeless.

Controversy still stalked them, too. In one game, Derbyshire declared behind and followed on, rather than concede bowling bonus points. In another, the prospect of acquiring a sponsors' motor-car for an individual batting performance was placed before trying to win the match, which ended with acrimony all round and another blow to the club's image. In 1973, J. B. Bolus, who had taken over the captaincy on arrival from Nottinghamshire, was obliged to dismiss Ward from the field at Chesterfield for refusing to bowl against Yorkshire, an incident unprecedented in modern times and only the third known case of its kind in the history of the game. The bowler later apologized for his behaviour. He also announced his retirement, returned to Derby and moved on to Leicestershire in 1976, but stayed with that county for only two seasons and a great cricketing talent remained sadly unfulfilled.

Two more overseas players, Venkataraghavan and L. G. Rowe, came and went and no better evidence concerning the county's search for stability was provided than the fact that they used as many as 17 different opening pairs in the 1974 season. Under the captaincy of wicket-keeper Taylor, the side improved enough to win 5 Championship matches in 1975, as many as in the 4 previous seasons, but they also suffered one of the biggest defeats in history, losing by an innings and 348 runs to Lancashire in a match interrupted by snow (in June).

Taylor handed over the leadership to the South African all-rounder E. J. Barlow midway through the following season, in order to concentrate on the skills which enabled him to take over from Knott as the England wicket-keeper. Barlow introduced a rigorous training programme and a much more purposeful attitude to the county's cricket. This, plus the arrival of two more overseas players in J. G. Wright from New Zealand and P. N. Kirsten from South Africa and the development of several home-bred players, led to a long-awaited resurgence in fortunes.

Even then, Derbyshire's aptitude for producing the unusual did not desert them and in 1978 they wrote another piece of cricketing history. In the game against Glamorgan, Russell, wearing one of the protective helmets which had come into increasingly common usage that year, was struck by a fierce blow from Nash. Despite his protection, Russell still fractured a cheekbone but the ball lodged temporarily in the helmet's visor and the umpires had to decide whether technically a catch had been made. They ruled 'dead ball', a decision subsequently upheld by the TCCB.

In Barlow's last season, 1978, Derbyshire were beaten finalists in the Benson and Hedges Cup final, having never previously progressed beyond their zone. At the end of that season, Hendrick, Miller and Taylor were selected for the tour of Australia, the first time the county had had so many representatives on a major tour. D. S. Steele, the Northamptonshire and England batsman, joined the county in 1979 to take over the captaincy, but soon resigned. His successor was Geoff Miller, who became at 26 the youngest county captain. With D. A. Har-

Derbyshire 1978: Benson & Hedges Cup finalists in a season of fluctuating fortunes. Back row: D. A. Harrison (secretary), J. M. H. Graham-Brown, A. J. Borrington, C. J. Tunnicliffe, H. Cartwright, F. W. Swarbrook, P. N. Kirsten and C. Beardmore (scorer); sitting: A. Hill, P. E. Russell, E. J. Barlow (captain), R. W. Taylor, M. Hendrick and G. Miller.

Bob Taylor, Geoff Miller and Mike Hendrick: the 1st three Derbyshire players to appear simultaneously for England.

rison, who had become secretary on the retirement of D. J. Carr, handling the club's administrative affairs with vigour, Derbyshire appeared to have the resources to suggest they were entering their most prosperous period since the Second World War, if not in their history.

CAPTAINS

1871–75	S. Richardson
1876–83	R. P. Smith
1884	L. C. Docker
1885–6	E. A. J. Maynard
1887	E. A. J. Maynard and W. Chatterton
1894–98	S. H. Evershed
1899–1901	S. H. Wood
1902–03	A. E. Lawton
1904–05	A. E. Lawton and E. M. Ashcroft
1906	A. E. Lawton and L. G. Wright
1907	L. G. Wright
1908	A. E. Lawton and R. B. Rickman
1909	A. E. Lawton
1910–12	J. Chapman
1913–14	R. R. C. Baggallay
1919	R. R. C. Baggallay and J. Chapman
1920	J. Chapman and L. Oliver
1921	G. M. Buckston
1922–30	G. R. Jackson
1931–36	A. W. Richardson
1937–39	R. H. R. Buckston
1946	G. F. Hodgkinson
1947–48	E. J. Gothard
1949	D. A. Skinner
1950	P. Vaulkhard
1951–54	G. L. Willatt
1955–62	D. B. Carr
1963–64	C. Lee
1965–69	D. C. Morgan
1970–72	I. R. Buxton
1973–75	J. B. Bolus
1975–76	R. W. Taylor
1976–78	E. J. Barlow
1979	D. S. Steele and G. Miller

HIGHEST TOTALS

For 645 v Hants, Derby 1898
Against 662 by Yorks, Chesterfield 1898

LOWEST TOTALS

For 16 v Notts, Trent Bridge 1879
Against 23 by Hants, Burton-on-Trent 1958

HIGHEST INDIVIDUAL INNINGS

For 274 G. Davidson v Lancs, Old Trafford 1896
Against 343* P. A. Perrin for Essex, Chesterfield 1904

HUNDRED ON DEBUT

A. J. Harvey-Walker, 100* v Oxford University, Burton-on-Trent 1971

MOST RUNS

In a season 2,165 D. B. Carr 1959
In a career 20,516 D. Smith 1927–1952

INDIVIDUAL INNINGS OF 250 AND OVER

G. Davidson, 274 v Lancs, Old Trafford 1896
P. Vaulkhard, 264 v Notts, Trent Bridge 1946

MOST HUNDREDS

In a season 6 L. F. Townsend 1933
In a career 30 D. Smith 1927–1952

RECORD WICKET PARTNERSHIPS

1 H. Storer and J. Bowden, 322 v Essex, Derby 1929
2 C. S. Elliott and J. D. Eggar, 349 v Notts, Trent Bridge 1947
3 J. M. Kelly and D. B. Carr, 246 v Leics, Chesterfield 1957
4 D. Smith and P. Vaulkhard, 328 v Notts, Trent Bridge 1946
5 C. P. Wilkins and I. R. Buxton, 203 v Lancs, Old Trafford 1971
6 G. M. Lee and T. S. Worthington, 212 v Essex, Chesterfield 1932
7 G. H. Pope and A. E. G. Rhodes, 241* v Hants, Portsmouth 1948
8 A. H. M. Jackson and W. Carter, 182 v Leics, Leicester 1922
9 J. Chapman and A. Warren, 283 v Warwicks, Blackwell 1910
10 J. Humphries and J. Horsley, 93 v Lancs, Derby 1914

MOST WICKETS

In a match 17–103 W. Mycroft v Hampshire, Southampton 1876
In a season 168 T. B. Mitchell 1935
In a career 1,670 H. L. Jackson 1947–1963

ALL 10 WICKETS IN AN INNINGS

W. Bestwick v Glamorgan, Cardiff 1921
T. B. Mitchell v Leics, Leicester 1935

HAT-TRICKS

A. E. G. Rhodes 4 (5 in all matches)
W. H. Copson 3
H. L. Jackson 2
G. Davidson 2
C. Gladwin 1 (2 in all matches)
I. R. Buxton, W. Cropper, F. Davidson, H. Evans, E. J. Gothard, J. Horsley, J. J. Hulme, J. Marlow, J. Platts, G. H. Pope, H. J. Rhodes, L. F. Townsend 1 each

WICKET-KEEPING – MOST DISMISSALS

In an innings 7 R. W. Taylor (2)
In a match 10 H. Elliott and R. W. Taylor
In a season 90 H. Elliott 1935
In a career 1,183 H. Elliott 1920–1947

COUNTY CAPS AWARDED SINCE 1946

1946	J. D. Eggar, C. Gladwin, G. F. Hodgkinson, P. Vaulkhard
1947	G. O. Dawkes, E. J. Gothard, E. A. Marsh, A. C. Revill
1949	H. L. Jackson, D. A. Skinner
1950	A. Hamer, G. L. Willatt
1951	D. B. Carr, J. Kelly, D. C. Morgan, R. Sale
1954	E. Smith
1956	C. Lee
1958	H. L. Johnson, H. J. Rhodes
1961	R. Berry, I. W. Hall
1962	I. R. Buxton, W. F. Oates, R. W. Taylor
1963	A. B. Jackson, G. W. Richardson
1964	M. H. Page
1967	T. J. P. Eyre
1968	P. J. K. Gibbs, J. F. Harvey, D. H. K. Smith
1969	A. Ward
1970	C. P. Wilkins
1972	J. B. Bolus, M. Hendrick
1973	S. Venkataraghavan
1975	P. E. Russell, F. W. Swarbrook
1976	E. J. Barlow, A. Hill, G. Miller
1977	A. J. Borrington, C. J. Tunnicliffe, J. G. Wright
1978	H. Cartwright
1979	D. S. Steele

Essex

D. J. INSOLE

Foundation 1876
Colours Blue, Gold and Red
Badge 3 Scimitars, with 'Essex' below
Champions 1979

Followers of Essex cricket are accustomed to expect the extraordinary. To defeat the Champions and lose to the wooden-spoonists has been a regular rather than a rare occurrence for Essex, and for over 100 years the team was never consistent enough to win anything. Then, in 1979, remarkable as always, Essex won not only the County Championship but also the Benson and Hedges Cup and, in so doing, sustained the club's reputation for enterprising cricket played in the right spirit.

The county gained first-class status in 1894 when, captained by A. P. Lucas, it won only 1 of 12 non-Championship matches played. In 1895, however, the team finished 8th in the table under the leadership of H. G. Owen and since that time, despite an unimpressive statistical record until it struck gold in 1979, the club has provided more than its fair share of personalities, quite apart from making a substantial contribution to the spirit and camaraderie of cricket.

In early days all county matches were played at Leyton, a suburb of East London then almost rural in character. Essex have only recently begun to achieve financial stability. At the start they were considerably indebted to C. E. Green, the President, who for many years guaranteed the bank overdraft on the purchase of the Leyton ground. In the 4 seasons following their first appearance in Championship cricket, Essex finished 5th, 3rd, 5th and then 6th in the table, and so became a power in the land. Outstanding memories of 1897 include two wins against Yorkshire, by one run and three wickets. In 1899 the great achievement was a victory by 126 runs against the Australian tourists.

Heroes of these pioneering days were a number of players with honoured places in the history of both Essex and England cricket. Of the bowlers perhaps C. J. Kortright, W. Mead, H. Young and F. G. Bull are the best known. Kortright is still regarded by many who have had the opportunity of watching and playing cricket over many years as being the fastest bowler of all time. Tall and athletic, he bowled as fast as he could, straight at the stumps, without consciously using either the seam or the shine on the ball. Of the 319 wickets he took between 1895 and 1898, 226 were clean bowled. Walter Mead, a short, slightly built man, was the first Essex bowler to take 100 wickets, which he did with a mixture of off- and leg-spin. He twice took 17 wickets in a match, played for England against Australia in 1899, and took over 1,900 wickets in his career. H. 'Sailor' Young was a completely natural left-arm bowler who established his reputation by very nearly demoralizing the Australians in 1899, later became a Test umpire and was in every sense a 'character'.

The outstanding Essex batsmen in the early years were P. A. Perrin, C. P. McGahey and H. Carpenter. Perrin is acknowledged to have been a great player of fast bowling, if rather less proficient against spin. He scored nearly 30,000 runs in first-class cricket, and made 66 hundreds, without ever being invited to play for England. His most noted innings was 343 not out in the first innings of a match against Derby which Essex somehow contrived to lose. Perrin had a long career as an administrator, and served for 10 years as an England selector, being chairman in 1939.

C. P. McGahey was a tower of strength in the early years. He played twice for England, scored over 20,000 runs in his career, and captained the county side from 1907 until 1910. J. W. H. T. Douglas first played for Essex in 1901, and embarked on a distinguished career for the county and for England. From 1911 until 1928 he captained Essex and in 1911–12 went with MCC to Australia, where he deputized for P. F. Warner, the captain, who became ill. Douglas, who played 23 times for England, was captain in South Africa in 1913–14, and in Australia in 1920–21. He was a great fast-medium bowler and a courageous but often pedestrian batsman. A stern disciplinarian, he was greatly respected as a player and as a man. Other prominent Essex personalities of similar vintage include F. L. Fane, a neat opening batsman who played 14 times for England and captained Essex from 1904 until 1906, and Canon F. H. Gillingham, who first played for the county in 1903 and made irregular but welcome appearances over the next 25 years. A fine attacking batsman, he was outstanding as a fielder and his influence on Essex cricket was lively and stimulating.

The years immediately following the First World War were not particularly prosperous for Essex cricket. There were occasional good performances, as one would expect from a county which could regularly include players of the calibre of A. C. Russell, Jack Freeman, Perrin and Douglas, and had assistance from G. M. Louden, Hubert Ashton and Frank Gilligan, but the overall record was dismal, and in 1924 there was a financial crisis which necessitated a public appeal for £1,000. Even at this time, however, there were encouraging signs of better times to come, as young professionals like Jack O'Connor, L. C. Eastman and M. S. Nichols began to establish themselves. Throughout these post-war years the outstanding Essex batsman was A. C. ('Jack') Russell, a brilliant opening batsman who in a distinguished career scored over 27,000 runs and made 71 hundreds. Russell played 10 times for England, and was the 1st English batsman to score 2 hundreds in a Test Match – against South Africa at Durban in 1922–23.

Hubert Ashton (who was knighted in 1956) was President of MCC in 1960, and was for many years a guiding light in Essex cricket. A fine batsman and magnificent fieldsman, Hubert Ashton seemed in 1921 to be on the brink of a brilliant future in the game, but he decided to put his business career first, and in consequence was lost to cricket for some years.

In 1925 the fortunes of the county improved, and 7th position in the table was encouraging. O'Connor scored over 1,000 runs and Nichols took 51 wickets for 23 runs apiece. By now the club was playing an increasing number of fixtures away from Leyton, and Chelmsford joined Colchester, Ilford and Southend as 'provincial' venues. It was clear, however, that a major change in the make-up of the team was imminent, with Douglas, Perrin and Freeman, of the regular players, approaching the point of retirement. Jack Freeman, a very competent wicket-keeper, left the game in a blaze of glory by scoring nearly 2,000 runs in the season of his retirement in 1926. The county finished 9th in 1926 and 8th in 1927, and although the cricket lacked neither character nor entertainment value, with an occasional appearance from L. G. Crawley enlivening the scene, the side was barely holding its own. In 1928 came a drop to 16th and at the end of this season both P. A. Perrin and J. W. H. T. Douglas retired.

The year 1929 saw the first appearance for Essex of T. N. Pearce, Peter Smith and T. H. Wade and, under the captaincy of H. M. Morris, the fortunes of the side improved somewhat. M. S. Nichols became the first Essex professional to complete the 'double'; Jack O'Connor, by this time one of the most consistent players in the country, played for England against South Africa, and the county rose 4 places in the table. Four years later, in 1933, came the move from the headquarters at Leyton. D. R. Wilcox, a young Cambridge blue and schoolmaster, and Pearce, an established and attractive batsman, jointly assumed the captaincy and took the side to 4th place in the table. Nichols did the 'double' as usual, Peter Smith took 100 wickets with his leg-spinners and in August that magnificent fast bowler Kenneth Farnes came into the side to add fire at the psychological moment.

The shift in 1933 from Leyton appears in retrospect to have been the only and obvious way of attracting greater support for the county club, but at the time it was a courageous move which was by no means certain to succeed. Westcliff, Clacton and Brentwood were added to the existing centres, and what has become known as the 'Essex circus' was effectively begun. From 1934 until 1967 when the Chelmsford ground was purchased, Essex played all their matches on 'club' grounds and carried all the equipment necessary for the establishment of a first-class cricket ground from venue to venue. In 1935, Essex finished 9th in the table, one place lower than in the previous year. Nichols was in magnificent form, however, and apart from playing in 4 Tests against South Africa he had the lion's share of the credit for an amazing win over Yorkshire, the county champions, at Huddersfield, by an innings and 204 at one o'clock on the 2nd day.

At this time, Essex were able to call on a formidable selection of fast and fastish bowlers including Nichols, Farnes, H. D. Read, Stephenson and Ray Smith, and it was these 5, together with Peter Smith, who were largely responsible for the marked improvement in the playing fortunes of the side in the seasons 1937–1939. M. S. Nichols, almost universally known as 'Nick', bowled at fast-medium pace and moved the ball into and away from the bat whenever the pitch offered the slightest assistance. In his career he took 1,834 wickets for 21 apiece, played for England 14 times and was the first to the double in 5 consecutive seasons – 1935 to 1939. A left-handed bat, he was effective rather than scintillating, but he had a fine temperament, and never ran from a fight. Kenneth Farnes, 6 feet 5 inches in height, was an Essex colt who won a blue at Cambridge and returned to teach in the county. A genuinely fast bowler who made the ball move in to the bat, he was fearsome whenever there was any lift in the wicket. Farnes played for England 15 times and in all took 690 wickets for 21 runs apiece.

H. D. Read and J. W. A. Stephenson were two more outstanding amateurs. Read was tall, well-built, ungainly, erratic, very fast, and on his day devastating. Stephenson was a lively medium-paced bowler whose enthusiasm for cricket made him a joy to watch in the field. He had an excellent record in Gentlemen v Players matches, including 9 for 46 in 1936. It is a remarkable fact that 2 Essex bowlers, Farnes and Stephenson, between them took 39 of the 47 Players' wickets that fell in the seasons 1936, 1938 and 1939.

The years immediately prior to the war were noteworthy in the history of Essex cricket. In 1937 the side rose to 6th place, and maintained this position in 1938, when Farnes appeared in all the Tests against Australia that season, while 4 players, Farnes, Stephenson, Nichols and Peter Smith played in the Gentlemen v Players match at Lord's. In 1939 Essex came very near to winning the Championship, although eventually having to be satisfied with fourth place. It would be difficult to convince any follower of Essex cricket that his team was not destined to head the table in 1940, and for a few years thereafter. The mainstay of the county's batting for some 15 years up to the war was Jack O'Connor, who scored over 1,000 runs in 15 consecutive seasons. Short, light on his feet and adventurous, O'Connor was a superb player of slow bowling who played 4 times for England. In his career he scored nearly 29,000 runs and made 72 hundreds. He was also a very useful leg-spin bowler who took 599 first-class wickets.

The war deprived Essex cricket of several of its best and most entertaining players. Kenneth Farnes and Claude Ashton, both in the RAF, were killed on active service, while Laurie Eastman, a sparkling all-round cricketer, died after a bombing raid. Nichols and O'Connor retired from first-class cricket.

The county began the post-war programme unobtrusively, finishing 8th in 1946. Peter Smith, whose leg-spin bowling was outstanding, played for England against India and was selected for the tour in Australia; 'Sonny' Avery, a neat opening batsman who was particularly strong on the on-side, scored runs in a Test trial; Trevor Bailey made his first appearance in county cricket with immediate effect; T. C. ('Dicky') Dodds, an amateur leg-spin bowler who soon became a professional opening bat, looked promising; Ray Smith bowled over 1,000 overs and hit lustily; D. R. Wilcox and H. P. Crabtree, appearing occasionally, topped the averages; and Tom Pearce scored more runs than anybody else. Attendances were large, membership grew steadily, and enthusiasm everywhere was unbounded. In 1947 the side dropped three places to finish in 11th position. T. N. Pearce had a batting average of

England's first post-war all-rounder – Trevor Bailey, here cocked at the start of the delivery stride. In 1959 he scored 2,000 runs and took 100 wickets – the only man to have done so since 1937.

nearly 50, but only Peter Smith had a bowling average of less than 30. No fewer than 8 Essex batsmen scored over 1,000 runs in the season. Against Derbyshire at Chesterfield in 1947 Vigar and Peter Smith, who scored 163 batting at No. 11, together added 218 in 140 minutes for the last wicket. A record membership figure was reached in 1948, while 1949 saw some playing improvement, with Trevor Bailey doing the double, being selected for the 4 Tests against New Zealand and taking all 10 wickets against Lancashire at Clacton. K. C. Preston, a young fast bowler, looked promising, and D. J. Insole struck a productive patch when he joined the side after the University Match.

In 1950, unexpectedly, the county plumbed the depths and finished bottom. Bailey was out of the attack for long periods with muscle trouble, while the batting was generally inconsistent. Following the inquest at the end of the season, several professional contracts were not renewed and D. J. Insole was appointed captain. Tom Pearce also ended a playing career which had stretched over a period of 22 years, during which time he had been joint captain with Denys Wilcox from 1933 until 1939, and skipper in his own right since 1946. He was an entertaining, slightly unorthodox and usually free-scoring batsman, who was imperturbable, and as captain was never happier than when things were ticking over quietly, so that he could stroll from first slip to first slip passing the time of day with batsmen and umpires. On relinquishing the captaincy he became chairman of the Executive Committee, and later succeeded Sir Hubert Ashton as President.

1951 saw a change of tempo in Essex cricket and a rise to 8th place in the table. The approach became more aggressive, and with Ray Smith, Dodds and R. Horsfall in good form, Essex supporters found plenty of entertainment. Insole became the first Essex amateur to score over 2,000 runs in a season, and Bailey had a fine season with the ball. This year saw the retirement of Peter Smith, one of the most outstanding cricketers ever to have played for Essex. He took 1,611 wickets for the county – more than any other bowler – and scored some 10,000 runs. A fine leg-spinner, brilliant on his day, Peter Smith was a somewhat temperamental cricketer, but he was a very useful all-rounder.

In 1952, Essex membership topped 5,000 for the first time. The batting was enterprising and forceful, the side won the trophy awarded for the fastest-scoring team in the Championship, and both Ray Smith and Bailey completed the double. The following year was again marked by plenty of runs made quickly, resulting in the retention of the fast-scoring trophy, but a drop of 2 places to 12th. Bailey topped the batting averages, but conceded 1st place among the bowlers to J. A. Bailey, a tall medium-paced bowler, subsequently Secretary of MCC, who played only in August but who took 25 wickets for 13 apiece. A series of indifferent performances in 1954 saw Essex end up in 15th position. A. V. Avery and F. H. Vigar retired from first-class cricket. Both were competent cricketers, but Avery had a touch of class which might have taken him into the top flight had he been more inclined to apply himself.

There was very little improvement in 1955, although some of the younger players, notably G. Barker and B. Taylor, showed signs of promise; and L. H. R. Ralph, a medium-paced bowler, produced some useful performances. Insole had the highest aggregate of runs in the country and scored 9 hundreds. Things looked up somewhat in 1956, and if Insole and Bailey again bore the brunt of the batting, recruits of promise were forthcoming in B. R. Knight and M. J. Bear, the latter a magnificent fielder. Taylor's wicket-keeping earned him a tour to South Africa with MCC.

Ray Smith retired at the end of the 1956 season, after making the winning hit against Yorkshire in his last home match. It would be difficult to imagine a more whole-hearted performer than Smith, who took 1,350 wickets, scored over 12,000 runs, completed the double on 3 occasions and 3 times in 5 seasons scored the fastest hundred of the year in English cricket. A quite prodigious swinger of the ball, he often bowled off-spinners when the shine was gone. Paul Gibb went into retirement in the same year, having given the club 6 seasons of excellent service, both behind the stumps and with the bat. In 1957 Essex went up to 5th place in the table, thanks to a series of excellent all-round performances. The fielding was lively and the catching a class above anything achieved previously. In the course of this season 3 counties, Leicestershire, Warwickshire and Lancashire, were dismissed for their lowest-ever totals against Essex. The revival continued in 1958 when consistently accurate bowling from Bailey, Preston and Ralph was supplemented to good effect on the many wet wickets by that of two young off-spinners, A. Hurd and P. J. Phelan. Barker had a good year with the bat, but only Insole of the others averaged over 30.

For the first 6 weeks of the 1959 season Essex led the field, but then five pointless weeks – literally and metaphorically – killed any Championship hopes. As it was, the county finished 9th. Insole and Bailey were in good form with the bat, and behind them six up-and-coming players made useful contributions. One of them, Barry Knight, took 100 wickets and headed the Essex bowling averages in county games. Dicky Dodds retired at the end of the 1959 season. Unpredictable and unreliable he may have been, but he was a great entertainer. A ferocious hooker and a fine driver of fast bowling, Dodds scored over 19,000 runs and made 17 hundreds in first-class cricket.

In maintaining the position in 1960 Essex played some entertaining cricket, and many of the younger players confirmed their promise. In the winter of 1960–61 Insole an-

Essex had a good season with this side in 1951. Back row: H. Dalton (masseur), W. Greensmith, R. Horsfall, F. Rist, F. Vigar, T. C. Dodds and K. Preston; sitting: R. Smith, T. P. B. Smith, D. J. Insole (captain), T. E. Bailey and A. V. Avery.

D. J. Insole, captain, chairman of Essex, former TCCB chairman and England tour manager, has since his undergraduate days contrived to bear many of cricket's burdens as well as making a successful business career.

nounced his retirement from the captaincy, and his place was taken by Trevor Bailey. The season of 1961 saw Essex once again 6th. The start of the 1962 season found Essex short of recognized players, although the special registration of J. C. Laker, who played as an amateur for about half the season, made a big difference to the attack. Knight did the double for the first time and went to Australia with MCC. By beating Pakistan, Essex became the first county team to defeat every touring side. The season marked the debut of Keith Fletcher. In 1963 there was a further decline to 12th place in the Championship and a defeat by Lancashire in the 1st round of the newly instituted Gillette Cup. In 1964 Essex beat the Australians and rose two places to 10th in the Championship. Ken Preston, a great club servant whose career as a fast bowler was wrecked by a serious injury in 1949, but who developed his skill as a seam bowler to such good effect, announced his retirement, and this was Jim Laker's last season, also.

In 1965 the County narrowly avoided finishing last and there was little about which to enthuse although Stuart Turner and Keith Boyce, a young Barbadian all-rounder, both joined the staff. The following season was no better. Because the responsibility of being both secretary and captain was too great, Trevor Bailey relinquished the former post, but unfortunately he was injured early in the season and could not find his usual form. Knight, too, had a disappointing season, but Keith Fletcher began to blossom. Two events of 1966 were significant. The County Club purchased the Chelmsford Ground, with the aid of a generous loan from the Warwickshire Supporters Association, and Essex was the first county in which Championship cricket was staged on a Sunday – at Ilford in May.

In 1967 Brian Taylor became captain. It was an important year in the Club's history. A series of fairly substantial financial losses over previous years had brought about a serious situation, and stringent economies were introduced. The playing staff was reduced to 12, and Taylor's first year as captain saw him leading a young side which for the first time on a regular basis included 4 outstanding young players in John Lever, Keith Boyce, Ray East and David Acfield. Taylor did not have the services of Barry Knight, who joined Leicestershire. Knight who joined the staff at the age of 17 was a very good all-rounder whose fast-medium bowling could be devastating and who was a superb player of slow bowling, even if his technique against the quicker variety was often suspect. The team rose one place to 15th in the table, but Trevor Bailey played very little and he retired at the end of the season after 21 years with the county. He was a tower of strength in the Essex side and, for much of the time, in the England team, during that period. Statistically his performances are chronicled elsewhere, but he was a skilful and underrated fast-medium bowler who could be devastating when conditions suited him and who bowled accurately and thoughtfully at other times. His batting was correct, obdurate and sometimes unnecessarily pedestrian, but he was a great man in a crisis and a formidable fighter.

The years between 1967 and 1973 saw Brian Taylor leading a small, young and extremely fit band of cricketers who provided magnificent entertainment and who achieved no little success. Gordon Barker gave Taylor his experienced support in the early days of the latter's captaincy and Lee Irvine, a left-hander from South Africa, reinforced the batting in 1968 and 1969, but encouraging performances came from the new and younger players – Fletcher, Boyce, Lever, Hobbs, Turner, East, Edmeades, Acfield and so on. A handsome profit and improved performances in 1968 were followed by a marked improvement in 1969, when Essex finished 3rd in the inaugural year of the John Player League; 6th in the County Championship; and reached the 3rd round of the Gillette Cup.

In 1970, now without Irvine, Essex achieved 4th place in the John Player League, and 12th place in the Championship was a worthy performance in the circumstances. In 1971 Essex came very near to winning something. They were 2nd in the John Player League and narrowly defeated by Lancashire, the eventual winners, in a 3rd-round Gillette Cup match which broke several local hearts. Bruce Francis, from New South Wales, had a fine first season and Fletcher and Lever were outstanding. Gordon Barker did not have many playing opportunities and retired at the end of the season having given Essex 17 years of yeoman and highly original service as an opening batsman of courage, character and flair.

Performances in 1972 were maintained, and 5th place in the Championship and 3rd in the John Player League were evidence of a new consistency. Fletcher had an outstanding season with the bat, being well supported by Edmeades and Keith Pont, a young hard-hitting player. Boyce and Lever excelled as opening bowlers. In 1973, however, Essex lost Boyce during the West Indies tour and Fletcher appeared regularly for England, playing in only 10 games in the Championship in which the side finished a creditable 8th. At the end of the season Brian Taylor retired. He first played for Essex in 1949, and at one stage appeared in 301 consecutive Championship matches. He gave magnificent service to the County and his approach to the game was, and is, exemplary: a spirited and hard-hitting left-hand bat; a competent wicket-keeper; a great team man, and a courageous captain.

Keith Fletcher's first season as captain, in 1974, was not, by recent standards, successful; its most hopeful features were the emerging talents of Gooch and Hardie and a heartening debut by Ken McEwan, a young South African who replaced Francis, the opening bat, who had returned to Australia at the end of the previous season. Things came right in 1975, with vastly improved performances, but Robin Hobbs left at the end of the season after many years of entertaining and accomplished service as leg-spinner, superb fieldsman and, occasionally, dynamic batsman.

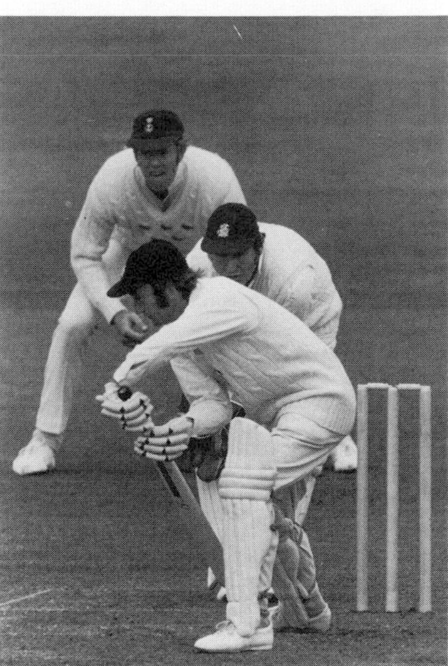

Keith Fletcher, the captain who 'did it at last', has played in 56 Tests and scored 7 hundreds: a particularly good player of spin bowling.

The club's Centenary Year, 1976, almost produced the trophy which had eluded Essex for 100 years – but not quite. Second place in the John Player League was in the end the best the side could achieve. A notable development, arising from a major fund-raising effort, was the construction of a new indoor school on the ground at Chelmsford, where a substantial development programme over recent years has transformed an open field into a first-class ground.

The enforced retirement of Keith Boyce in 1977 made the team's performances in that year – 2nd in the John Player League and 6th in the Championship – appear feats of heroism. Michael Denness joined the staff on leaving Kent, and had a satisfactory season, but the loss of Boyce, through injury, was a heavy blow. His retirement marked the end of an outstandingly successful career in which the Barbadian had been a major attraction for spectators throughout the country. There can seldom have been a more whole-hearted or a more entertaining all-round cricketer than Keith Boyce.

The season of 1978 was the most frustrating yet for followers of Essex cricket. Defeat by Somerset in the semi-final of the Gillette Cup with the scores level was sustained in the best match of the season, but cruel luck with weather was a major factor in the county's finishing as runners-up in the Championship. McEwan, Fletcher and Gooch, who regained his place in the England team, all batted well, while Lever, East and Norbert Phillip, a West Indian replacement for Boyce, were successful bowlers. Gooch and Lever were both selected for the England tour of Australia

Essex's first: in 1979 Essex broke the drought of a century by 'winning something' – the Benson & Hedges Cup – which was followed a month later by the County Championship. Keith Fletcher, their captain, surrounded by his team bears the Cup modestly aloft.

with Insole, former captain and chairman, as manager of the team.

The Essex tradition for playing attractive cricket has been successfully maintained in recent years, and an increase in staff after the stringent economies of the mid-1960s is encouraging the emergence of many good young players. The club has, as a result of careful husbandry, built up its assets and is on a sound financial footing. Essex would not be far from the top of the tree if cricket could be measured in terms of entertainment, and now that they have won both the County Championship and the Benson & Hedges into the bargain it is reasonable to hope that in the 1980s interest within the county will reach fresh heights.

CAPTAINS

1894	A. P. Lucas
1895–1900	H. G. Owen
1901	H. G. Owen and A. P. Lucas
1902	H. G. Owen
1903	C. J. Kortright
1904–06	F. L. Fane
1907–10	C. P. McGahey
1911–28	J. W. H. T. Douglas
1929–32	H. M. Morris
1933–38	T. N. Pearce and D. R. Wilcox
1939	D. R. Wilcox, F. St. G. Unwin and J. W. A. Stephenson
1946–49	T. N. Pearce
1950	T. N. Pearce and D. J. Insole
1951–60	D. J. Insole
1961–66	T. E. Bailey
1967–73	B. Taylor
1974–	K. W. R. Fletcher

HIGHEST TOTALS

For 692 v Somerset, Taunton 1895
Against 803–4D by Kent, Brentwood 1934

LOWEST TOTALS

For 30 v Yorks, Leyton 1901
Against 31 by Derby, Derby 1914
31 by Yorks, Huddersfield 1935

HIGHEST INDIVIDUAL INNINGS

For 343* P. A. Perrin v Derby, Chesterfield 1904
Against 332 W. H. Ashdown for Kent, Brentwood 1934

MOST RUNS

In a season 2,308 J. O'Connor 1934
In a career 29,162 P. A. Perrin 1896–1928

MOST HUNDREDS

In a season 9 { H. O'Connor 1934; D. J. Insole 1955 }
In a career 71 J. O'Connor 1921–1939

INDIVIDUAL INNINGS OF 250 AND OVER

P. A. Perrin, 343* v Derby, Chesterfield 1904
C. P. McGahey, 277 v Derby, Leyton 1905
J. R. Freeman, 286 v Northants, Northampton 1921
A. C. Russell, 273 v Northants, Leyton 1921

HUNDRED ON DEBUT

G. Barker 107* v Canadians, Clacton 1954
A. W. Lilley 100* v Notts, Trent Bridge 1978

RECORD WICKET PARTNERSHIPS

1 A. V. Avery and T. C. Dodds, 270 v Surrey, Oval 1946
2 G. A. Gooch and K. S. McEwan, 321 v Northants, Ilford 1978
3 P. A. Gibb and R. Horsfall, 343 v Kent, Blackheath 1951
4 A. V. Avery and R. Horsfall, 298 v Worcester, Clacton 1948
5 J. O'Connor and C. T. Ashton, 287 v Surrey, Brentwood 1934
6 { J. O'Connor and J. W. H. T. Douglas, 206 v Gloucester, Cheltenham 1923; B. R. Knight and R. A. G. Luckin, 206 v Middlesex, Brentwood 1962 }
7 J. W. H. T. Douglas and J. R. Freeman, 261 v Lancs, Leyton 1914
8 D. R. Wilcox and R. M. Taylor, 263 v Warwicks, Southend 1946
9 J. W. H. T. Douglas and S. N. Hare, 251 v Derby, Leyton 1921
10 F. H. Vigar and T. P. B. Smith, 218 v Derby, Chesterfield 1947

MOST WICKETS

In a match 17–119 W. Mead v Hants, Southampton 1895
In a season 172 T. P. B. Smith 1957
In a career 1,611 T. P. B. Smith 1929–1951

ALL 10 WICKETS IN AN INNINGS

H. Picket v Leicester, Leyton 1895
T. E. Bailey v Lancs, Clacton 1949

HAT-TRICKS

J. W. H. T. Douglas 2 (3 in all matches) T. E. Bailey, K. D. Boyce, P. Cousens, R. E. East, K. Farnes, A. B. Hipkin, G. M. Louden, M. S. Nichols, J. O'Connor, H. D. Read, P. Toone, B. Tremlin, S. Turner, H. Young 1 each

WICKET-KEEPING – MOST DISMISSALS

In an innings	6	T. M. Russell (2)
		K. L. Gibson
		F. W. Gilligan
		T. H. Wade
		B. Taylor
In a match	9	K. L. Gibson
In a season	91	B. Taylor 1962
In a career	766	B. Taylor 1949–1964

COUNTY CAPS AWARDED SINCE 1946

1946	H. P. Crabtree, T. C. Dodds R. F. T. Paterson, F. H. Vigar
1947	T. E. Bailey, L. S. Clark, S. J. Cray
1948	R. Horsfall, F. Rist
1949	D. J. Insole, G. R. Pullinger
1951	P. A. Gibb, K. C. Preston
1952	W. T. Greensmith
1954	J. A. Bailey
1955	G. Barker
1956	B. Taylor
1957	L. H. R. Ralph
1958	M. J. Bear
1959	B. R. Knight, L. H. Savill
1960	G. J. Smith
1963	K. W. R. Fletcher
1964	R. N. S. Hobbs, P. J. Phelan
1965	B. E. A. Edmeades
1967	K. D. Boyce, R. E. East
1968	B. L. Irvine
1970	D. L. Acfield, J. K. Lever, G. J. Saville, S. Turner, B. Ward
1971	B. C. Francis
1974	B. R. Hardie, K. S. McEwan
1975	G. A. Gooch, N. Smith
1976	K. R. Pont
1977	M. H. Denness
1978	N. Phillip

Glamorgan

WILFRED WOOLLER

Foundation 1888
Badge Gold Daffodil
Colours Blue and Gold
Champions 1948, 1969

Glamorgan County Cricket Club was formed on 6 July 1888 at Cardiff. It attained first-class status in 1921, the 17th and last county to do so. At minor county level it was strong but at top first-class its weakness was promptly exposed. First-class cricket in Wales may be grouped conveniently into three phases. The first irresistible fling of youth, immaturity and inexperience in its first decade was characterized by the curt initial comment by *Wisden* that Glamorgan's entry into first-class cricket was not justified by results.

This first period, when the county was served by a wide range of indifferent amateurs, endured until 1930 by which time M. J. Turnbull was firmly entrenched as captain and secretary. The second era under Turnbull introduced method, sanity and efficiency. It had like the first period many financial problems and troubled times, but a more workmanlike approach was reflected in a modestly-better playing record. The third period came after the Second World War when Glamorgan reached maturity, with money to jingle, a far better playing record, and a coaching programme of merit and diversity. Unfortunately during the last decade it has lost its cricket way once again.

The first period opened with much pomp and civic ceremony under the captaincy of N. V. H. Riches when, in the first match at Cardiff Arms Park in May 1921, the county beat Sussex. They were not, however, to win again until July when Worcestershire were defeated at Swansea; a neat equality of victory between rival cities east and west of Wales but a poor record overall. Riches, a fine bat, scored 1,005 runs at an average of 41 in that first summer of 1921, but he was 38. Nash, who took 90 wickets at 17·5 runs apiece, and Creber, another fine spinner, were both 47 years of age. The team contained a permutation of 8 amateurs supported by the 3 professionals Nash, Creber and Bates. It is interesting to note that J. C. Clay, aged 23, bowling extremely fast or slow as the whim took him, collected 41 first-class wickets in his first season. The honour of scoring the first hundred went to W. Spiller the Welsh international three-quarter who, given the time, could have made his mark in first-class cricket. As a member of the Glamorgan constabulary, Spiller could play only during holidays and off-duty periods.

In 1923 the tradition began of playing the touring side at August Bank Holiday, simply because Glamorgan was the odd county out in 17 and the others had their lucrative traditional fixtures. The custom started auspiciously with the defeat of the West Indies. The international flavour quickly caught Welsh cricket imagination and resulted in excellent support. For many years Glamorgan's results against touring teams remained outstanding.

A year later Dai Davies became the first of the native-born Welsh professionals. F. Ryan, an unconventional Irish American who had hitch-hiked from Hampshire, was the leading spin bowler with 120 wickets, and Turnbull, a schoolboy from Downside, made his mark at the age of 17. Glamorgan cricket has always had an element of the unpredictable. In 1926 supporters feared the worst, but under Clay they were actually contenders for the Championship until the last few matches ended in disaster and brought them back to 8th in the table. This was the highest position held until 1937 when, under Turnbull, Glamorgan finished 7th. Bell and Bates were the first regular opening pair. C. F. Walters in 13 matches averaged 34 and recorded his first hundred, but a year later left Glamorgan to become secretary of Worcestershire. It was from Worcestershire that he won his Test cap. Jack Mercer was the star opening bowler and performed with rare skill and stamina right up to the Second World War.

In 1927 Glamorgan upset form and Notts with an innings victory in the last game of the season, thereby depriving them of the Championship and presenting it by a decimal point to Lancashire. In 1929 the South Africans were defeated at Pontypridd and Trevor

One of the great all-round sportsmen between the wars, Maurice Turnbull captained Cambridge and Glamorgan, and played cricket for England, rugby football and hockey for Wales. He was later killed in action, aged 33.

Every promised as an outstanding wicket-keeper until his career was cut short by blindness. Turnbull was selected for the MCC tour to New Zealand and Australia and gained the first Test cap to be won by a Glamorgan player against New Zealand at Christchurch.

Turnbull was elected captain in 1930 and a year later secretary and under his inspired leadership the second phase established the county on sounder business lines and produced a more constructive playing policy. Bates, Bell, Dai Davies, Emrys Davies (at the start of a long and estimable all-round career), Dyson, his opening partner, Mercer, Ryan, Hills, Every were the established players, with the amateurs Clay, T. Arnott, Riches and J. T. Morgan available from time to time. In the last match of the 1932 season Glamorgan, always capable of upsetting form, hit 502 off a Notts attack containing Larwood and Voce, who, that winter, were to bowl out Australia in the Body-line tour.

By the mid-1930s the team had a more settled look and certainly possessed a very aggressive middle-order batsman in Cyril Smart who hit a then world record of 32 runs off a 6-ball over by G. Hill (Hampshire) at Cardiff in 1935. Another mild sensation came that year when Glamorgan, following on 259 runs behind the South Africans at Cardiff, lost their first 9 wickets on the last day for 114. Thereupon Smart was joined by D. W. Hughes, playing his first match, and the pair added 131 at a furious pace to save the match.

Benefits brought no great reward in Wales, and in 1935 Dai Davies's realized only £659. Emrys Davies at this stage became the first Glamorgan player to perform the double, while Clay belatedly gained a cap for England against South Africa at the Oval. Mercer in 1936 achieved another county record by taking all 10 Worcestershire wickets in an innings. J. W. Hitch, former Surrey Test bowler, was appointed coach – another innovation.

In the best season to date, 1937, 13 matches out of 30 were won outright and the county finished 7th. The recipe for success was the regular appearance of Clay, one of the finest off-spinners that I have ever seen. In 1937 he took the county record total of 176 wickets at 17·34. A. D. G. Matthews played in 7 matches, having returned to Glamorgan from Northants, and, selected for the Third Test v New Zealand at the Oval, became the first Glamorgan professional to play for England. In 1939 I came to work in Cardiff and played my first games for the county, collecting a maiden hundred and 7 wickets at Cardiff against the West Indies who were defeated. This side was a good, sound combination lacking one good all-rounder to challenge at the top of the table.

In 1946 Glamorgan regrouped like the other counties, finding their players from various parts of the world returning from war action. Clay captained the side and opened well by giving Yorkshire a hard struggle, and beating Lancashire at Old Trafford. The experts thought this to be something of a fluke, I remember. Yet Glamorgan won 10 matches and finished 6th, their highest place in the Championship to date. Public support was excellent and over August Bank Holiday 48,500 paid £4,850 to watch the game against the Indians. The season saw the initial development of Allan Watkins, a young professional from Usk; Dyson and Davies still opened the innings; and Clay, bowling superbly, played regularly. In 1947 I took over the captaincy and also became secretary of the club. The side was strengthened by B. L. Muncer, the Middlesex all-rounder. Normally a leg-spin bowler he also bowled off-breaks with skill, and realizing that our line of attack was now to be developed on to the leg-side, I asked him to concentrate on off-spin. In this medium he became one of the outstanding bowlers of the next few seasons.

It was the theory of concentrating on leg-side attack and training fielders specially for this purpose that brought a totally unexpected success in 1948 with the first County Championship victory for Glamorgan – or, indeed, for any of the smaller counties to that date. It was, I believe rightly, said that neither the batting nor the bowling merited Championship honours but the fielding and field-placing certainly did. By 1948 I had trained Watkins, Clift and myself, supported by Dyson, in the leg trap and between us we took 120 catches. We had also a top-class first slip in W. G. A. Parkhouse, who had started his career as an opening bat by making a thousand runs. Haydn Davies was a splendid 'keeper and Clay, at the age of 50, was able to complete his career with a dream realized. In his career, which had run like a silver thread through Glamorgan's history from its start in 1921, he took 1,292 wickets and scored 6,895 runs.

The 13 players who brought victory to Wales were W. Wooller (captain), J. C. Clay, S. Trick, W. E. Jones, E. Davies, A. J. Watkins, B. L. Muncer, W. G. A. Parkhouse, P. Clift, J. T. Eaglestone, J. E. Pleass, H. G. Davies and N. G. Hever. Nine of them were born in Wales and Stan Trick, a very fine medium-pace left-arm bowler, could only play at Swansea where his success was remarkable.

Glamorgan fortunes varied after that epic year of 1948 because the leg-side theory had been quickly accepted by other counties and the advantage was thereby lost. A few years later Glamorgan made use of a wicket-keeper standing back to medium-pace bowling, particularly that of Shepherd, on the theory that stumpings were few and far between at this pace but the thick edges came often. A wicket-keeper standing back was an extra slip on both sides of the wicket. Davies needed

Glamorgan, County Champions 1948. Back row: W. E. Jones, P. B. Clift, J. Pleass, A. J. Watkins, W. H. Griffiths, B. L. Muncer, N. G. Hever, W. G. A. Parkhouse and J. T. Eaglestone; sitting: H. Davies, E. Davies, W. Wooller (captain), A. Dyson and G. Lavis.

courage to carry out my instructions and he was subject to some derision, but in the end results paid and it was interesting to note that these tactics were eventually used at Test level.

In the period after the Second War Glamorgan trod pastures new. An immediate post-war Appeal launched by Mr H. Merrett, later president of the club, raised £11,000 and by 1950 Glamorgan had acquired liquid assets of nearly £30,000 – a remarkable change from the position pre-war. The county embarked on a new and broader coaching scheme under George Lavis, the former player. This was subsequently taken over by his great friend Phil Clift, and it has produced very many fine Welsh-born players. In 1952, following the lead of Leicestershire, Glamorgan, after a stormy committee meeting had debated the moral issue, started a Supporters' Club and ran football pools. These were to succeed beyond the dreams of avarice and, true to policy, coaching schemes were spread far and wide throughout South Wales and a new indoor school opened at Neath.

It was at the Cardiff indoor school that J. E. McConnon, who was formerly bowling fast-medium for Newport, was trained as an off-spinner. He revealed considerable ability with his high, flighted delivery from a height of 6 feet 2 inches. His style contrasted perfectly with the flatter trajectory of Muncer. In 1951 McConnon's hat-trick at Swansea led to a brilliant victory over the South Africans. Glamorgan were the only county to defeat them on that tour. Parkhouse and Watkins both represented England, the latter having an excellent tour with MCC in India. McConnon also visited India as a member of a Commonwealth side and went to Australia with MCC but was handicapped by an injury suffered early on the tour.

In 1954 Watkins and I both reached the double of 1,000 runs and 100 wickets, a target hitherto only achieved with Glamorgan by Emrys Davies and Muncer. In this year Muncer netted £3,500 from his benefit. The playing record at this period was modest, partly because of an unlucky run with injuries. However, Shepherd, who had been failing as a fast-medium opening bowler, began to concentrate on off-breaks. After two years of concentrated work at the indoor nets he achieved great success. In his changed style he was to take more wickets than any other Glamorgan bowler.

In 1957 Shepherd captured 168 wickets, just falling short of Clay's record. Parkhouse, fluent as always, was the mainstay of the batting and young players such as A. R. Lewis, Alan Jones and P. Walker were coming into orbit. (At this time I was appointed an England Test selector – a position I held for 7 years. Clay and Turnbull had been Selectors before me.)

Internal problems began to split the county in 1958–59. It was a traumatic period. After my resignation, the members demanded a Special General Meeting of the club. I was coming to the end of my career as a captain and was only prepared to continue with the club as secretary on a full-time basis. The committee were not amenable to this idea. There followed an Extraordinary General Meeting which ousted the committee. A new one was elected and I accepted a permanent administrative appointment. During my next (and final) season I was fortunate to find O. S. Wheatley, the former Cambridge and Warwickshire player, willing to take over the captaincy. Glamorgan lost my playing services together with those of Watkins and McConnon, which took 3 all-rounders from the side, but Walker, who had played well for England against South Africa, was steadily improving his batting technique, bowling with some skill at medium-pace, and had also developed into the most brilliant close-to-the-wicket fielder in the country.

Wheatley, the captain who followed me in 1961, had been outstanding for Cambridge. Tall and well-built, he had also bowled with success for Warwickshire when the occasion permitted. He welcomed the challenge of captaining a county side and promptly moved to South Wales to take up a business appointment. There he has subsequently stayed, having married a Welsh girl and set up his home in the Principality. He proved to be a bowler of considerable stature and might well have played for England had competition been less severe at the time. He was a skilful captain of a different mould from myself taking his troops over the top with a cheerful smile and an amusing wisecrack.

Wheatley captained Glamorgan for 6 years from 1961–66 inclusively and played periodically for another couple of years under Lewis. There were four poor and two very good years. In 1963 Glamorgan finished 2nd to Yorkshire in the County Championship, winning 11 of 28 matches. That they lost 8 games was simply due to the fact that Wheatley was a captain who always took a chance and liked to make a good game of cricket by declaring. Bernard Hedges had established himself with that remarkably sound technical batsman, Alan Jones, who was to continue to the time of writing opening the batting for Glamorgan with reliable consistency.

Tony Lewis, who had shown his flair for captaincy at Cambridge, was a superb craftsman at No. 3 and Alan Rees, J. Pressdee, at his best in adversity, were among other players to make their mark. Parkhouse was just tailing off his long career but Walker had developed into a fine all-rounder. The attack aided by some excellent fielding produced the good results. Pressdee and Shepherd, a combination of left-arm and right-arm spin comparable with any in England, each took 100 wickets that season; Wheatley got 94, and I. J. Jones, who had now come on to the scene as the only really fast bowler that Glamorgan has ever produced, was at times very effective with 58. This side produced two more Welsh players for England – Lewis, captain of England in India and Pakistan, and Jeff Jones, who made a high reputation in a number of Test games particularly in the West Indies and Australia. Jones, left-arm over the wic-

Captain successively of Cambridge, Glamorgan and England (1972–73), Tony Lewis is uniquely distinguished. His cricket gave premature place to journalism and broadcasting when, in 1974, a long-endured knee injury became increasingly restrictive. Thus his potential as a Test leader had not been fully utilized.

ket, later suffered an elbow injury which finished his career. This was a tragedy for Jones, Glamorgan and England.

In 1965 Glamorgan finished 3rd in the Championship and it was a neck-and-neck race between Worcester, Northants and Glamorgan right up to the last couple of matches. The Championship was eventually won by Worcestershire, with Northants 2nd and Glamorgan 3rd, only 12 points separating the 3. The match which probably prevented Glamorgan winning the Championship was played at Cardiff in the first week of August against Northants who eventually won by 18 runs. Up to the last day Northants were in trouble and at one stage were 32 for 6 with a lead of only 39. Jim Watts and Crump stayed under difficulties and Glamorgan were left with 139 to get on the 3rd day, a comparatively easy task. A heavy storm, however, affected the wicket before the match resumed, and the Northants bowlers won a close game. There were two milestones of note: Walker topped 400 catches, the record for Glamorgan, and Don Shepherd 1,500 wickets.

The 1964 season produced yet another distinction for Glamorgan against touring sides. Over the August Bank Holiday before a very large crowd Glamorgan defeated the Australians for the first time in a low-scoring match. Glamorgan batted first and scored 197. A shower then stirred the wicket to life and before the close of play on Saturday Shepherd and Pressdee had dropped 6 Australian wickets for 39. Though the wicket became easier Australia never recovered against Glamorgan's spin attack and brilliant catching.

Lewis, a former Neath schoolboy, was the captain to follow Wheatley. Leading Cambridge with rare promise, he had been groomed as a future Glamorgan player and captain. He was a batsman of high skill and a delightful technique which was an artistic pleasure to watch. As a captain he was in a different mould again from Wheatley, quieter, more thoughtful of detail, and always conscious of the wide variety of problems in handling a first-class county both on and off the field.

After a slow start in 1967 with team-building necessary because Pressdee had unexpectedly left for South Africa, and David Evans, a consistently fine wicket-keeper who followed Davies, had given way to Eifion Jones – 3rd of 3 very fine post war 'keepers – Glamorgan began to show some form in 1968. They moved up to 3rd in the Championship. The team had been strengthened by the West Indian batsman, Bryan Davis, and a young Pakistan star, Majid Khan. Roger Davis was establishing himself as the new opening partner to Alan Jones and Cordle and Nash had joined the medium-fast bowling attack.

The highlight of that season was another famous victory over the Australians at Swansea by 59 runs. Glamorgan was skippered, in the absence of Lewis through injury, by Shepherd and they won with a mixture of fast and spin bowling on an excellent batting wicket. The incident that turned the match was on the 3rd day of the Australian 2nd innings when Sheahan, in full control, was brilliantly caught and bowled by Walker for 137.

In 1969, 21 years after Glamorgan had won the 1948 Championship, Lewis led Glamorgan to another Championship success. The county were undefeated in 24 games – the last county to achieve as much was Lancashire who were unbeaten in 1930. Glamorgan were a well-equipped team of all-rounders with a superb batting spearhead in Majid. Those who saw his 156 in the defeat of Worcestershire in the first week of September at Cardiff which settled the Championship, will not forget the power and grace of his innings. The team had many bits-and-pieces players capable of helping to win a match. Roger Davis bowled off-spin, Bryan Davis could always be relied upon to get runs under pressure, Walker with bat, ball or fielding was a match-winner, the bowlers, Cordle and Nash, could get fast runs when required and in Shepherd – now boosting his aggregate to 2,000 wickets – and Wheatley Glamorgan had two fine attacking bowlers.

Glamorgan when they won the 2nd of their Championships in 1969 were the 1st county since 1930 to go through the season unbeaten. Back row: E. Jones, B. A. Davis, M. A. Nash, D. L. Williams, R. C. Davis and Majid Khan; sitting: A. E. Cordle, P. M. Walker, A. R. Lewis (captain), D. J. Shepherd, A. Jones.

The following year Kent took the Championship from Glamorgan, who finished 2nd, and that was the last season, apart from their reaching the Gillette Final in 1977, in which Glamorgan had any real claim to distinction. That year, too, Glamorgan made a first-ever overseas tour to the West Indies under Phil Clift, the coach and organizer. One cannot pay too high a tribute to Clift for his long service to the county as player, coach and administrator. He has been directly responsible for a vast number of fine young Welsh players making a first-class impact.

In 1971 things began to go wrong. Bryan Davis decided to remain in the West Indies and was replaced by Roy Fredericks, an exhilarating opening bat, but never as capable as his predecessor of getting runs when most required. Lewis injured a shoulder in May and never recovered, and then was troubled by an old football injury to his knee. The chairman of the selectors, Mr Tom Taylor, a former player, who had had a great deal to do with the fashioning of the team and spent many hours with me discussing tactics, died suddenly. The Glamorgan Cricket Committee was now chaired by a leader without the benefit of playing experience and the whole structure of the cricket began to disintegrate. After a difficult season in 1972. Lewis decided to call it a day, and in 1973 Majid Khan was elected captain.

Majid had spent 3 of his playing years with Glamorgan at Cambridge where he took a degree and captained the University with splendid success. The committee's decision to make him captain of Glamorgan was, in retrospect, a mistake. The claims of Peter Walker were, on reflection, superior. Majid was one of the most exciting batsmen I have seen, a fielder of personality and a bowler of merit when he wished, but he was no captain of a side which needed restructuring and properly drilling in the way they should play. The team fell back to the lower half of the table from which it has never recovered. The opening batsman, the Test cricketer Fredericks, was replaced by a wildly erratic fast bowler, Gregory Armstrong, who was not successful, and a far better player who was not persevered with, Collis King. He in turn was replaced by a South African, Peter Swart, a very sound performer with bat and ball. At the end of 1979 he returned to league cricket and Javed Miandad, of Pakistan and Sussex, was engaged.

By 1974 the members again demanded an Extraordinary General Meeting because of the playing record of the club. That season Majid resigned as captain and 3 other players refused to take up their contracts. Roger Davis resigned immediately. Alan Jones took over the captaincy during August. It was a difficult situation which on this evidence of reorganization the members accepted. Wheatley became chairman of the club and the general committee was restructured.

After the season of unrest the committee decided to make Alan Jones captain in 1977. In my view this was an error. Jones has been one of the most consistent performers as an opening bat that Glamorgan has had, as loyal a team-man as I have met, and in the season

1979 reached a career aggregate of 30,000 runs – a record for the county. He had been in service for 23 years, but it was unfair to put the onus of captaining and developing a poor side on to his shoulders. Jones did however have one lucky break by taking the side into the Gillette Cup final in 1977 when Glamorgan lost to Middlesex. It was a great occasion for Welsh supporters who turned up in thousands, and Lord's was filled with cheering Welshmen who thoroughly enjoyed the day at headquarters.

A number of young Glamorgan players of promise were, however, emerging: John Hopkins, an opening bat of quality, Mike Llewellyn, the strong-hitting left-hander, G. Richards, a batsman who bowls off-spin, Arthur Francis, a bat and fine fielder, and a medium-fast left-arm bowler, Alan Watkins, among others. It was no doubt hoped by the committee that the appointment of the former England, Warwickshire and Somerset bowler, Tom Cartwright would develop their talents when he came to play with the side in 1977. Subsequently he has been made chief coach and, surprisingly, team manager in addition, with full control. This again, in my view, is a mistake. Yet another was made in 1979 in the appointment of Robin Hobbs, the former Essex and England leg-spin bowler, as captain in place of Jones. Leg-spin bowling has never been a profitable feature on Welsh wickets and Hobbs had also been out of the game for three years and had very little experience of captaincy.

In 1977 I reached the age of retirement and duly handed over the secretaryship to Phil Clift. The county now had £150,000 in Stock Exchange investments and various large fixed assets. The playing expertise, however, I did not like. Glamorgan have been importing more players than I believe desirable for a Welsh-based county and it is not bringing success. In the last decade the highest position they have achieved in the County Championship was 9th in 1975, when they won 7 games. This is double what they have won in any of the other recent seasons. They have never been higher than 8th in the John Player Sunday League. In the Benson & Hedges they have reached the quarter-finals twice and only once the Gillette Cup final. It is a very uninspiring record.

CAPTAINS

1921	N. V. H Riches
1922–23	T. A. L. Whittington
1924–27	J. C. Clay
1928	T. Arnott
1929	J. C. Clay and N. V. H. Riches
1930–39	M. J. Turnbull
1946	J. C. Clay
1947–60	W. Wooller
1961–66	O. S. Wheatley
1967–72	A. R. Lewis
1973	M. J. Khan
1974	M. J. Khan and A. Jones
1975	M. J. Khan
1976	M. J. Khan and A. Jones
1977–78	A. Jones
1979	R. N. S. Hobbs

HIGHEST TOTALS

For 587–8D v Derby, Cardiff 1951
Against 653–6D by Gloucester, Bristol 1928

LOWEST TOTALS

For 22 v Lancs, Liverpool 1924
Against 33 by Leics, Ebbw Vale 1965

HIGHEST INDIVIDUAL INNINGS

For 287* E. Davies v Gloucester, Newport 1939
Against 302* W. R. Hammond for Gloucester, Bristol 1934

MOST RUNS

In a season 2,071 W. G. A. Parkhouse 1959
In a career 28,921 A. Jones 1957–1979

MOST HUNDREDS

In a season 7 W. G. A. Parkhouse 1950
In a career 44 A. Jones 1957–1979

INDIVIDUAL INNINGS OF 250 AND OVER

R. Duckfield, 280* v Surrey, Oval 1936
E. Davies, 287* v Gloucester, Newport 1939

HUNDRED ON DEBUT

F. B. Pinch, 138* v Worcester, Swansea 1921

RECORD WICKET PARTNERSHIPS

1 A. Jones and R. C. Fredericks, 330 v Northants, Swansea 1972
2 A. Jones and A. R. Lewis, 238 v Sussex, Hastings 1962
3 E. Davies and W. E. Jones, 313 v Essex, Brentwood 1948
4 G. Lavis and C. Smart, 263 v Worcester, Cardiff 1934
5 M. Robinson and S. W. Montgomery, 264 v Hants, Bournemouth 1949
6 W. E. Jones and B. L. Muncer, 230 v Worcester, Worcester 1953
7 W. Wooller and W. E. Jones, 195* v Lancs, Liverpool 1947
8 D. Davies and J. J. Hills, 202 v Sussex, Eastbourne 1928
9 J. J. Hills and J. C. Clay, 203* v Worcester, Swansea 1929
10 C. Smart and W. D. Hughes, 131* v South Africans, Cardiff 1935

MOST WICKETS

In a match 17–212 J. C. Clay v Worcester Swansea 1937
In a season 176 J. C. Clay 1937
In a career 2,174 D. J. Shepherd 1950–1972

ALL 10 WICKETS IN AN INNINGS

J. Mercer v Worcester, Worcester 1936

HAT-TRICKS

T. Arnott, E. Davies, I. J. Jones, M. J. Khan, J. E. McConnon, J. Mercer, D. J. Shepherd, O. S. Wheatley, 1 each

WICKET-KEEPING – MOST DISMISSALS

In an innings 7 E. W. Jones
In a match 8 H. G. Davies
8 E. W. Jones
In a season 94 E. W. Jones 1970
In a career 782 H. G. Davies 1935–1958

COUNTY CAPS AWARDED SINCE 1946

1946	W. E. Jones, A. Porter, M. Robinson
1947	B. L. Muncer, A. J. Watkins
1948	P. B. Clift, J. Eaglestone, N. G. Hever W. G. A. Parkhouse
1951	J. E. McConnon
1952	J. E. Pleass, D. J. Shepherd
1954	B. Hedges
1955	J. Pressdee
1956	L. N. Devereux
1958	P. M. Walker
1959	D. L. Evans
1960	J. B. Evans, A. R. Lewis
1961	D. Ward, O. S. Wheatley
1962	A. Jones
1963	A. Rees
1965	I. J. Jones, E. Lewis
1967	A. E. Cordle, E. W. Jones
1968	M. J. Khan
1969	B. A. Davis, R. C. Davis, M. A. Nash
1971	R. C. Fredericks, D. L. Williams
1973	J. W. Solanky
1974	L. W. Hill
1976	G. Richards
1977	J. A. Hopkins, M. J. Llewellyn
1979	R. C. Ontong, P. D. Swart

Gloucestershire

JOHN ARLOTT

Foundation 1870
Colours Blue, Brown, Sky Blue, Green and Red
Badge Bristol Coat of Arms
Champions 1873 (=), 1874, 1876, 1877

Gloucestershire's place in the memory of cricket is that of the county of two of the greatest batsmen the world has ever known – W. G. Grace and Walter Hammond – a tradition of aggressive stroke-play and a remarkable sequence of outstanding slow bowlers. Since the Second World War the side has held an average position in the Championship narrowly in the upper half of the table. Gloucestershire's finest period of success was in the 9 seasons from 1873 to 1881, when they were 3 times outright Champions, once bracketed 1st with Notts and 3 times 2nd. The earliest possible known link between Gloucestershire and cricket is somewhat tenuous. In 1709 William Goldwin was appointed Master of Bristol Grammar School. Three years previously Goldwin had published *Musae Juveniles*, a book of poems in Latin, one of which, entitled *In Certamen Pilae*, was the famous ode to cricket. On safer ground, *The Weekly Journal* dated 20 September 1729, contained –

Gloucester, September 15th: On Monday, the 22nd inst., will be played in the Town-Ham of this City, by 11 men of a side, a game of cricket, for upwards of 20 guineas.

The first well-known cricketer from Gloucestershire was H. R. Kingscote, a tall, hard-hitting batsman who, in 1827 when he was only 24, was made President of MCC; Kingscote played for the Gentlemen against the Players from 1825 to 1834 and in an 'England' team of that period, but there are no records of his playing in any match of importance in his native county.

Recent research indicates that on 3 November 1863, a club was founded called The Cheltenham and County of Gloucester Cricket Club. It was wound up on 14 March 1871, and Lord Fitzhardinge, who had been its President, became a vice-president – the Duke of Beaufort was President – of the new county club which had been founded, largely by the Grace family, in Bristol. The date of the foundation of the present county club has never been clearly established as taking place in 1870 or 1871, but certainly a Gloucestershire team with the 3 Grace brothers – W.G., E.M. and G.F. – played in 1870. Dr Henry Mills Grace (1808–1871), a Bristol man, had played cricket in the district for many years before 1845. He founded the Mangotsfield Cricket Club, which was later amalgamated into the West Gloucestershire Club. In 1854 Dr H. M. Grace, his wife's brother, Alfred Pocock, and the eldest of Dr Grace's 5 sons, Henry, all played for the West Gloucestershire Club against Clarke's All-England XI.

In the next year E. M. Grace, still a small boy, took his place in the team for this, the major match of the year in the county. The Gloucestershire club grew up around Dr H. M. Grace and his 5 sons – Henry (b. 1833), Alfred (1840), Edward Mills (1841), William Gilbert (1848) and George Frederick (1850) – and with considerable support from their mother. E.M., W.G. and G.F. were all in the Gloucestershire team which, in 1868, for the first time, played MCC and Ground at Lord's; they took between them 17 MCC wickets – the other 3 batsmen were run out; E.M. made the highest score of the match and Gloucestershire won by 134 runs. This result might well have precipitated the formation of a regular county club earlier than it did.

By 1870 the younger players had matured to produce a playing strength quite remarkable for any county club in its first season. Five matches were played that year – 2 each against Surrey and Glamorgan and 1 against MCC – and all were won. W. G. Grace, who had already made his mark in the cricket world (he scored over 1,000 runs in 1869) was elected captain, a post he held for 29 seasons. In the first game, against Glamorgan at Bristol, W. G. Grace scored 197, G.F. took 9 wickets and E.M. 7; Gloucestershire won by an innings and 268. But the Grace brothers were by no means alone: Frank Townsend made 105; and other regular players were T. G. Matthews (201 v Surrey in the next year); R. F. Miles, earliest of the county's long succession of left-arm slow bowlers; C. S. Gordon who sometimes opened the innings; J. A. Bush, wicket-keeper; C. R. Filgate and G. Strachan, both all-rounders. MCC were beaten by an innings and 88 on an awkward wicket; W.G. scored 172 of the Gloucester total of 276; no other batsman in the match except C. S. Gordon made more than 30; Miles took 5 for 34 in the 1st innings, 3 for 44 in the 2nd. In 1871, 4 of the Grace brothers – all but Alfred – played in the side that beat Surrey by an innings at the Oval.

So, when the fully organized County Championship began in 1873, the Gloucestershire team had played 17 matches in the 3 preceding seasons, had won 11, drawn 4 and lost 2. Their Championship season consisted of home and out matches against Surrey, Sussex and Yorkshire; they beat Surrey at the Oval and Sussex at Brighton and drew the returns in Gloucestershire, and then beat Yorkshire twice. W.G. averaged 57, Frank Townsend 43; Miles took 12 Yorkshire wickets and G.F. scored 165 not out against them at Clifton. So the side went strongly on; invariably the 3 Grace brothers and Frank Townsend were in the first 4 places in the final batting averages and they did a fair amount of the bowling between them; but Miles was still from time to time a match-winner – especially against Yorkshire – and in 1877 the Australian professional Midwinter became Gloucestershire's first regular professional player. Soon E. M. Grace dropped down the batting order and a cousin of the Graces, W. R. Gilbert, opened the innings with W.G. – and the 2 of them bowled unchanged throughout the 2 innings of Lancashire at Clifton in 1878.

Despite the quality of his team-mates, in the public mind W.G. *was* Gloucestershire. But, as Ashley-Cooper's analysis shows, he played considerably less than half his first-class innings, and made many less than half his runs, for Gloucestershire; though he did take almost half his wickets for them. In his time the County Championship, in which half a dozen matches could constitute a county's matches for a season, did not dominate the domestic game as it does now. According to Ashley-Cooper's figures, W.G. played 618 innings for Gloucestershire but 224 for MCC, 151 for Gentlemen v Players, 137 for the South, 103 for London County, and even 37 for the Gentlemen of the South, as well as in many other 'invented' teams like 'Non-smokers', 'Single', and 'Over-thirty'. In the 1870s he had the energy to exploit his mighty gifts and in 1871 he became the 1st batsman to score over 2,000 runs in a season: actually 2,739 in only 39 innings. He took 79 wickets, as well. Little wonder that Gloucestershire, for a decade, were so strong that, even as an XI of amateurs, they could beat Yorkshire and Surrey sides full of the leading professionals of the day. In 1876 and 1877 they won the Championship without losing a match. They met a full England side at the Oval in both 1877 and 1878 and won the first match by 5 wickets. But for W.G. we might think of E.M. – 'The Coroner' – as the Eminent Victorian of cricket. A strong batsman, artful bowler of lobs and round-arm, fearless fieldsman at point, he was a fine player. His work did not allow him so much time as W.G. for cricket but Ashley-Cooper calculated that between 1851 and 1910, in all classes of cricket, he made 75,762 runs and took 11,906 wickets. When the 1st Test Match was played in England (1880) 3 Grace brothers, W.G., E.M. and G.F., were all in the England team. W.G. and E.M. opened the English batting; W.G. scored 152 in the 1st innings. G.F. caught Bonnor off a stroke which went so high that the batsmen had started on their 3rd run before the ball came down; but he made a 'pair' and, 6 weeks later, not yet 30, he was dead.

Gloucestershire were never quite such a good side after his death. Only once again – 1881, when they were 2nd – did they finish in the first 3 under W.G.'s captaincy which endured until 1898. They were bottom of the Championship tables of 1891, 1893 and 1894. For 13 seasons between 1882 and 1894, they lost more Championship matches than they won. One of the happier occasions of 1893 was the match with the Australians when W.G., E.M. (now 51) and W.G. Jnr. were all in the Gloucester team that played the Australians; but young W.G. had little of his father's skill and never succeeded in holding a place in the county side.

Yet there were some accesses of strength in this period. William Woof – the second of their slow left-arm bowlers – came into the side in 1878 and, having taken 100 wickets in 1884 and 1885, he took the post of professional at Cheltenham College and was not available to the county until August in subsequent summers. Fred Roberts, left-arm, and one of the few consistently successful pace bowlers who played for Gloucester, came into the side; he was over-bowled but showed remarkable endurance. A few years later Jack Board began his long career as a professional wicket-keeper.

During the darkest days of 1893 and 1894 – at the bottom of the table with only 5 matches won out of thirty-two – Gloucestershire brought in 2 men who were to develop into match-winning all-rounders. The first (1893) was C. L. Townsend, son of Frank and, incidentally, father of David Townsend who opened the England innings in the West Indies in 1935. His first impact was as a right-arm leg-break bowler who, at the age of 16, spun the ball so prodigiously that even the most experienced players found him baffling to play. His unique hat-trick of 3 batsmen all stumped (by W. H. Brain) from consecutive balls was performed in only his 2nd county match. As a boy of 18, he was unable to play more than one match before late July 1895, yet, by the end of the season, he had taken 131 wickets at an average of 13. He developed, too, as a left-hand bat. Perhaps because he was physically slight, he rarely seemed to be in form as both batsman and bowler except in his great season, 1899, when he scored 2,440 runs (average 51) as well as taking 101 wickets; that year he was picked for England against Australia at Lord's and the Oval. He was already a considerable cricketer by the time he was 23 but after that season, 1900, his solicitor's practice rarely left him free to play

G. L. Jessop on the prowl: his nickname 'The Croucher', deriving from his stance at the crease, also fits his electric movements in the covers.

county cricket. Gilbert Jessop, who came into the side for a few matches in 1894, was to become the most consistently brilliant and fast-scoring batsman in cricket history; he was also a useful fast bowler, and one of the two or three great cover-points. Year in, year out, in some hard seasons from 1894 to 1914, he served Gloucester wonderfully as both player and captain.

As the century moved into its '90s and W. G. Grace into his 40s, it seemed inevitable that the Old Man must fade. Yet 1895, the year he was 47, proved perhaps his greatest of all: he made 1,000 runs in May – in fact between the 9th and 30th of that month – and averaged 50·85 for Gloucester who, with 8 wins from 18 matches, moved to 4th place among the counties. The next year they dropped back to 10th (and were bowled out for the lowest total in their history – 17 – by the Australians, at Cheltenham; W.G. was top scorer of the innings with 9). Yet the development of the young batsmen and the varied attack of Jessop, Roberts, Townsend and W.G. carried them up to 5th (1897) and 3rd (1898). Something like the old glory seemed to be returning: W.G. averaged 47; 4 more batsmen over 30 and another 4 more than 20; Townsend took 130 wickets and Jessop 41. 1899 seemed full of promise: in the 1st 5 matches the side, without Gilbert Jessop, lost to Yorkshire, and to Middlesex; but Kent and Sussex were both well beaten and yet another slow left-arm discovery, Arthur Paish, had taken 35 wickets. Then, suddenly, W. G. Grace announced his resignation from the captaincy, and that he proposed to sever all connection with the county club. There was a cross-fire of statement and argument but, whatever the rights or wrongs of the affair, W. G. Grace never played another match for Gloucestershire. It was said at the time that W.G. was unduly autocratic, but surely that had always been the case. He was now beginning his 30th season as captain and some felt it was time for a change. A firmer fact is that he had undoubtedly accepted the management of the London County team at the Crystal Palace, and had said that he proposed to combine that duty with the captaincy of Gloucestershire. In the end it was agreed that no grudges would be borne. W.G. left Gloucestershire and spent the rest of his life in and around London.

Major Walter Troup took over the captaincy. He was a dogged batsman who, most unusually, switched from left-handed to right-handed after a broken collar-bone was badly set by a ship's surgeon. Fortunately for the county, Charles Townsend batted magnificently; 7 centuries and an average of 56 made him the sheet anchor of the batting which, surprisingly after the consistency of the previous season, developed an embarrassing tail. Paish took 125 wickets for the county and Townsend 72, while Jessop's batting developed, though his bowling went back. The shortness of the batting proved conclusive and, with only 5 wins in 20 matches, Gloucester were 9th in the final county table. When Troup returned to his Army duties, Jessop became captain for 1900 and remained in office until 1912. Jessop was the mainspring of the side for that season: he scored over 2,000 runs and took more than 100 wickets, an all-round performance only previously equalled in all cricket by W.G. (1876) and, in the previous year, C. L. Townsend. Nine wins to 7 defeats left Gloucestershire 7th. But then came the grim years: Townsend could no longer play regularly and he was quite irreplaceable. Gloucester were bottom but one in 1901 and 1902; 13th in 1903; a part recovery – 9th, 8th, 9th – but then another drop, to the bottom of the Championship in 1909, and little improvement when C. O. H. Sewell took over from Jessop for 1913 (9th) and 1914 (bottom).

Yet slowly a group of professionals grew up who were to give the county many years of faithful, competent, and sometimes outstanding, service. Harry Huggins played from 1901 to 1921; Percy Mills 1902–1929; George Dennett 1903–1926; Charles Parker 1905–1935; Alf Dipper 1908–1932; Harry Smith 1912–1935. Those 6 men played, between them, for 147 years. Harry Huggins was a game, if not always economical, bowler of medium-pace, right-arm spinners. Percy Mills was a tidy, medium-pace, stock bowler: his 823 wickets for Gloucestershire were taken at an average of 25·20.

George Dennett, yet another of the Gloucestershire slow left-arm bowlers, was one of the unlucky cricketers. He took more wickets – 2,147 – than any other bowler who was never picked for a Test Match. His method was so different from that of Parker that there was no sameness about their combination. He was a flighty but precise bowler.

Charles Parker was recommended to Gloucester by W. G. Grace – surely a worthy peace-offering. Although he is described as a slow left-arm bowler, he was appreciably faster than most of his type – of about Underwood's pace. From 1919 onwards he settled down as a bowler of tight length and extremely sharp spin, deficient, perhaps, in flight by comparison with the great, and not always steady in face of punishment. Yet on his day, with even a little response from the pitch, he was utterly deadly. Only two bowlers – Wilfred Rhodes and 'Tich' Freeman – have taken more wickets in first-class cricket than Parker's 3,278. He was obviously unfortunate only to play once for England. In his benefit match, for Gloucester against Yorkshire (1922), he took 9 for 36 and, at one point, hit the stumps with each of 5 consecutive balls; but the 2nd was a no ball. When the ball turned, the combination of Hammond at slip and Parker's bowling was feared throughout the other 16 counties. Dipper was an obdurate, faithful opening batsman. His method was careful, with little back-lift and good late adjustment against the swinging ball: his great value to his side was his reliability in the lean years of the batting. After 2 seasons in reserve to Jack Board, Harry Smith took over as the Gloucestershire wicket-keeper in 1914, kept regularly until he fell ill in 1932 and played again in 1935. He kept wicket tidily, could bat usefully and played for England in a single Test – v West Indies in 1928.

Although these developing professionals were in the side, Gloucestershire cricket immediately after the First World War reverted to an amateur character reminiscent of the 1870s. It was not so successful, and for 10 years they were only 3 times in the upper half of the Championship table (7th, 1921; 6th 1924; 5th 1928). Like the first decade of the century, however, those years produced a great potential in F. J. Seabrook, the loyal Bernard Bloodworth, Walter Hammond, B. H. Lyon, T. W. Goddard, W. L. Neale, R. A. Sinfield, E. J. Stephens and C. J. Barnett. Walter Hammond took time to find his feet, but from the middle of the 1920s until 1946 there was not a county in England that did not face Gloucestershire with trepidation. Hammond must be bracketed with W. G. Grace, Victor Trumper, Sir Jack Hobbs and Sir Donald Bradman at the peak of batsmanship. Yet none of the other 4 could match him in his quality as bowler and fieldsman. This was a glorious cricketer, fit to lift any team to the heights. Tom Goddard was, originally, a rather erratic fast bowler. But, after a spell on the staff at Lord's, he returned to Gloucestershire as an off-break bowler of precise length and sharp spin, to join the few men who have taken more than 2,000 wickets in first-class cricket. Billy Neale was a steady batsman, churning out his 1,000-plus runs a season. Reg Sinfield was an all-rounder good enough to play for England and worth his place in any county team for either his steady batting or his accurate off-spin bowling. E. J. Stephens was a useful middle-order batsman overshadowed by Charles Barnett who played as an amateur until he was satisfied that he had the ability to make a mark in the first-class game. He was one of the most militant

A comparatively rare action shot of Walter Hammond, the great straight and off-side strokemaker, who used also not infrequently to open his shoulders for the leg-side hit.

opening batsman modern cricket has ever known and, brilliant in hooking, cutting and driving, he could open the innings in a Test with an unusual and effective aggression.

To this gathering talent, with its valuable blend of experience and young brilliance, there came, in 1929, one of the finest of modern captains – Beverley Lyon. He was an accomplished batsman, good enough to make his 1,000 runs a season even while he adjusted his method to attack or defence as the state of the game demanded. He was happy, too, in acquiring Cecil Dacre, the New Zealand Test player, a superb striker of the ball, to emphasize the side's aggression in its batting. The full-strength XI of the B. H. Lyon period in Gloucestershire was – A. E. Dipper, R. A. Sinfield, W. R. Hammond, B. H. Lyon, H. Smith, C. C. Dacre, F. J. Seabrook, W. L. Neale, C. J. Barnett, C. Parker and T. W. Goddard. Its weakness lay in pace bowling. None of the 'pure' fast bowlers with whom the county constantly experimented was good enough to deserve a regular place. So Hammond and Barnett were employed, as some opposing counties suggested, to 'wear the shine off' for the spinners, Parker, Goddard and Sinfield. Nevertheless, on a fast pitch, Hammond could be a match-winner and Barnett could make the new ball move about at medium pace. One of Beverley Lyon's first moves was to turn Goddard from a tentative to an attacking bowler by setting an aggressive field for him, and the side, its fielding sharpened, at once began a magnificent period. In 1929 Gloucestershire were 4th in the Championship. In 1930 they were 2nd to Lancashire; but they won 13 matches – 3 more than any other side in the competition. Moreover, they were without Hammond – playing in Tests or injured – for 12 matches, Parker for 9 and B. H. Lyon for 6. They were never beaten when those three were present. The next year they were again 2nd when B. H. Lyon upset some of the more old-

In August 1930 Gloucestershire fought a historic tie at Bristol against the Australians, whom no county had beaten since 1912. These cheerful faces suggest that a party is imminent. Back row: R. G. Ford (12th man), B. S. Bloodworth (scorer) and A. E. Dipper; third row: E. J. Stevens, C. C. Dacre, R. A. Sinfield and W. R. Hammond; second row: W. L. Neale, C. J. Barnett, H. Smith; front row: C. W. L. Parker, B. H. Lyon (captain), F. J. Seabrook and T. W. Goddard. Parker had 10 wickets, Goddard 7, and Hammond made 89.

fashioned thinkers in the game by the unorthodox methods he employed to conjure finishes out of games which would otherwise have been spoilt by rain.

Gloucestershire's greatest match in the B. H. Lyon era was against the 1930 Australians. Gloucester were put out for 72; the Australians made 157 (Ponsford 51, Bradman 42; Goddard 5 for 52). The Gloucester 2nd innings of 202 (Hammond 89; Hornibrook 5 for 49) left Australia 118 to win and Jackson and McCabe made 59 – half of them – for the 1st wicket. Then Parker struck a length on to a worn spot and, after a hard chance from Grimmett had been dropped, Australia reached 115 for 9; Parker (7 for 54) and Goddard bowled 3 maiden overs with the scores level before Hornibrook was lbw to Goddard in scenes of excitement as great as anything known in the time of the Graces: the result was a tie. Lyon resigned the captaincy to attend to his business at the end of the 1934 season. Still, before the Second World War began, the side was 4th under D. A. C. Page (1936) and B. O. Allen (1937) and 3rd in the 1st year of Hammond's captaincy (1939). The major forces of these years were Hammond, Barnett, Sinfield and Goddard with Crapp, the dour left-hander, Emmett – brilliant strokemaker – Wilson, the wicket-keeper, and Scott and Lambert, the seam bowlers, as the rising young players.

Gloucestershire's main problem since the Second World War has been the pitch on their county ground at Bristol which proved depressingly slow. The best efforts have been made to improve it with no fortune apart from an early period when a sand dressing made it a spin bowler's dream. The county's two good seasons of the early period were 1947 and 1959, when they finished 2nd in the Championship table. The team of 1947, under B. O. Allen, virtually lost the Championship in the match at Cheltenham which Middlesex, the eventual Champions, won by 68 runs. The side of that year was well balanced. Charles Barnett, Jack Crapp, George Emmett, Andy Wilson, the wicket-keeper, and Basil Allen all made over 1,000 runs in Championship matches; Goddard took 206 wickets and the latest in the line of the county's slow left-arm bowlers, Sam Cook, 120; there was, too, some useful seam-bowling, when needed, from Charles Barnett, Colin Scott and George Lambert.

Succeeding years saw the emergence of Tom Graveney, one of the most handsome batsmen of post-war years, who most unhappily left Gloucestershire and joined Worcestershire when the captaincy was given to C. T. M. Pugh after the 1960 season; Arthur Milton, an accomplished back-foot player and superb close fieldsman; two off-spinners of different types, John Mortimore, accurate and resourceful, and David Allen, flighty and with considerable spin. Martin Young, coming from Worcestershire, opened the innings capably, latterly with the developing Ron Nicholls. After Andy Wilson, another of the county's long-serving wicket-keepers, retired in 1956, the post passed to Barry Meyer. Cook gave nearly 20 years' service from 1946, an accurate and patient slow left-arm bowler.

The weakness was generally in the middle-order batting. Still, in 1959, under Tom Graveney, the bowling of Allen, Cook, Mortimore, Brown and Smith – who in that order in the averages took 448 Championship wickets between them – concealed most of the flaws. Also, Young, Graveney, Milton, Mortimore, Allen, Nicholls and Brown all scored over 500 runs, and Gloucestershire were 2nd in the table to Yorkshire by only 18 points. J. K. Graveney became captain in 1963 after considerable dissensions within Gloucestershire cricket, taking over a side strong in bowling but lacking in batting pedigree by the high standards of the past.

There followed 6 unsuccessful seasons under Ken Graveney, John Mortimore and Arthur Milton. Without Tom Graveney, Milton and Nicholls had too great a weight of batting to carry, just as Smith lacked support with the new ball. Twice – in 1964 and 1967 – they were bottom in the Championship. In 1968, when Mike Procter returning from South Africa, and David Green from Lancashire, joined the team, they finished bottom but one of the table.

In 1969 Tony Brown was made captain and Gloucestershire embarked on the most successful decade in their history since the early days of W. G. Grace. Reinforced, for one important season, by Geoff Pullar from Lancashire, although they did not win the Championship, they were once runners-up, 3 times third; and twice in contention for the title until the last; and they won both the Gillette Cup and, in 1977, when Procter succeeded Brown, the Benson & Hedges Cup.

Brown, a capable, straightforward batsman, resourceful medium-pace bowler, fine close fieldsman, thoughtful and determined captain, was a considerable force in the side. As the two Test spinners, David Allen and John Mortimore – genuine all-rounders at county level – began to age after long service, Procter became a match-winning bowler. When free of the injuries probably produced by his unorthodox action, he was extremely fast. He could bowl slower off-breaks capably; was a superb strokeplayer; a sharp

Tony Brown, now Gloucestershire's secretary, ended a long drought when he led the county to victory in the 1973 Gillette Cup. Back row: A. Avery (scorer), Zaheer Abbas, M. S. T. Dunstan, J. H. Shackleton, R. D. V. Knight, D. A. Graveney, J. Davey, D. R. Shepherd, Sadiq Mohammed; front row: R. B. Nicholls, M. J. Procter, A. S. Brown (captain), J. B. Mortimore and R. Swetman.

M. J. Procter, the South African all-rounder, has been the mainstay and inspiration of Gloucestershire throughout the 1970s.

fieldsman, and a captain capable of turning a match and lifting a side. His early hat-trick against Hampshire probably won the Benson & Hedges Cup in 1977. Smith, Meyer and Allen retired in 1971, but the two Pakistanis, Zaheer Abbas, a brilliant stroke-maker, and Sadiq Mohammad, a dogged opener who could bowl left-arm spin, partly balanced the deficit. David Shepherd and Roger Knight reinforced the batting; Jack Davey, David Graveney and Tony Brown the bowling. The side, though, was never at a genuine peak of performance without Procter, who must rank with the most dynamic of the county's players. Milton's retirement in 1974 after 26 seasons saw the end of the immediate post-war strength. In 1976 Tony Brown became county secretary and the Phoenix Assurance Company took over the Bristol Ground and appear to have guaranteed its continued use for county cricket. Brian Brain, recruited from Worcestershire as a short-term pace bowler; Stovold, a useful batsman who could keep wicket; Andy Brassington, a highly talented wicket-keeper; John Childs – like David Graveney a slow left-arm spinner; and Philip Bainbridge, a young batsman from Stoke-on-Trent, offered Procter encouraging support; but the county went into the 1980s anxious for fresh talent.

CAPTAINS

1871–98	W. G. Grace
1899	W. G. Grace and W. Troup
1900–12	G. L. Jessop
1913–14	C. O. H. Sewell
1919–21	F. G. Robinson
1922–23	P. F. C. Williams
1924–26	D. C. Robinson
1927–28	W. H. Rowlands
1929–34	B. H. Lyon
1935–36	D. A. C. Page
1937–38	B. O. Allen
1939–46	W. R. Hammond
1947–50	B. O. Allen
1951–52	Sir D. T. L. Bailey
1953–54	J. F. Crapp
1955–58	G. M. Emmett
1959–60	T. W. Graveney
1961–62	C. T. M. Pugh
1963–64	J. K. R. Graveney
1965–67	J. B. Mortimore
1968	C. A. Milton
1969–76	A. S. Brown
1977–	M. J. Procter

HIGHEST TOTALS

For 653–6D v Glamorgan, Bristol 1928
Against 774–7D by Australians, Bristol 1948

LOWEST TOTALS

For 17 v Australians, Cheltenham 1896
Against 12 by Northants, Gloucester 1907

HIGHEST INDIVIDUAL INNINGS

For 318* W. G. Grace v Yorkshire, Cheltenham 1876
Against 296 A. O. Jones for Notts, Trent Bridge 1903

MOST RUNS

In a season 2,860 W. R. Hammond 1933
In a career 33,664 W. R. Hammond 1920–1951

MOST HUNDREDS

In a season 13 W. R. Hammond 1938
In a career 113 W. R. Hammond 1920–1951

INDIVIDUAL INNINGS OF 250 AND OVER

W. G. Grace, 318 v Yorks, Cheltenham 1876
W. G. Grace, 288 v Somerset, Bristol 1895
W. G. Grace, 257 v Kent, Gravesend 1895
W. G. Grace, 301 v Sussex, Bristol 1896
G. L. Jessop, 286 v Sussex, Hove 1903
A. E. Dipper, 252* v Glamorgan, Cheltenham 1923
W. R. Hammond, 250* v Lancs, Old Trafford 1925
W. R. Hammond, 264 v Lancs, Liverpool 1932
W. R. Hammond, 264 v West Indians, Bristol 1933
W. R. Hammond, 290 v Kent, Tunbridge Wells 1934
W. R. Hammond, 265* v Worcester, Dudley 1934
W. R. Hammond, 302* v Glamorgan, Bristol 1934
W. R. Hammond, 252 v Leicester, Leicester 1935
W. R. Hammond, 317 v Notts, Gloucester 1936
W. R. Hammond, 271 v Lancs, Bristol 1938
W. R. Hammond, 302 v Glamorgan, Newport 1939

HUNDRED ON DEBUT

D. R. Shepherd, 108 v Oxford University, Oxford 1965

RECORD WICKET PARTNERSHIPS

1 D. M. Young and R. B. Nicholls, 395 v Oxford University, Oxford 1962
2 T. W. Graveney and C. T. M. Pugh, 256 v Derby, Chesterfield 1960
3 W. R. Hammond and B. H. Lyon, 336 v Leicester, Leicester 1933
4 W. R. Hammond and W. L. Neale, 321 v Leicester, Gloucester 1937
5 W. G. Grace and W. O. Moberley, 261 v Yorks, Cheltenham 1876
6 G. L. Jessop and J. H. Board, 320 v Sussex, Hove 1902
7 W. G. Grace and E. L. Thomas, 248 v Sussex, Hove 1896
8 W. R. Hammond and A. E. Wilson, 239 v Lancs, Bristol 1938
9 W. G. Grace and S. A. P. Kitcat, 193 v Sussex, Bristol 1896
10 W. R. Gouldsworthy and J. G. Bessant, 131 v Somerset, Bristol 1923

MOST WICKETS

In a match 17–56 C. W. L. Parker v Essex, Gloucester 1925
In a season 222 T. W. J. Goddard 1937 and 1947
In a career 3,171 C. W. L. Parker 1903–1935

ALL 10 WICKETS IN AN INNINGS

G. Dennett v Essex, Bristol 1906
C. W. L. Parker v Somerset, Bristol 1921
T. W. J. Goddard v Worcester, Cheltenham 1937
J. K. R. Graveney v Derby, Chesterfield 1949

HAT-TRICKS

C. W. L. Parker 6
T. W. J. Goddard 4 (6 in all matches)
M. J. Procter 4
G. Dennett 2
D. G. A'Court, A. S. Brown, J. Davey, J. H. Huggins, P. T. Mills, C. L. Townsend, G. G. M. Wiltshire 1 each

WICKET-KEEPING

In an innings	6 B. J. Meyer
	6 H. Smith
	6 A. E. Wilson
In a match	10 A. E. Wilson
In a season	74 B. J. Meyer
In a career	1013 J. H. Board 1891–1914

COUNTY CAPS AWARDED SINCE 1946

1946	C. Cook
1948	T. W. Graveney
1949	Sir D. T. L. Bailey, J. K. R. Graveney, C. A. Milton
1950	D. M. Young
1954	F. P. McHugh, J. B. Mortimore, B. D. Wells
1955	P. Rochford
1957	A. S. Brown, D. G. Hawkins, R. B. Nicholls, D. R. Smith
1958	B. J. Meyer
1959	D. A. Allen
1961	D. G. A'Court, D. Carpenter, C. T. M. Pugh
1965	S. E. J. Russell, A. R. Windows
1968	D. M. Green, M. J. Procter
1969	D. R. Shepherd
1970	M. Bissex
1971	J. Davey, R. D. V. Knight
1972	R. Swetman
1973	Sadiq Mohammad
1975	Zaheer Abbas
1976	D. A. Graveney, A. W. Stovold
1977	B. M. Brain, J. H. Childs, A. J. Hignell
1978	A. J. Brassington
1979	J. C. Foat

Hampshire

JOHN WOODCOCK

Foundation 1863
Colours Blue, Gold and White
Badge Tudor Rose and Crown
Champions 1961, 1973

If Hambledon in Hampshire was not the birthplace of the game, as popular misconception sometimes has it, it was there, in the 1760s, that the first great cricket side came into being. Through the writings of John Nyren we have a charming insight into those days on Broadhalfpenny Down when the Hambledon Club was the very focus of the game. Two centuries later, in 1961, Hampshire won the County Championship for the first time. Nyren was not alone in writing with rich distinction of the Hambledon era. The Rev James Pycroft and Arthur Haygarth each did so, and the reminiscences of the Rev John Mitford are delightful.

By 1793 Hambledon had played its last match. Some years earlier a Hampshire County Club had begun to take its place. In 1788 3 matches were played against Surrey; in 1790 Hampshire played for the first time at Lord's, winning there against both Kent and England. The first recorded meeting of the Hampshire County Cricket Club was in 1795. It was followed by a period of varying fortunes. With Lord Frederick Beauclerk playing as a 'given man' in 1805, and making 68 and 129 not out, Hampshire again beat England at Lord's. In 1806 and 1807 there were further victories over England. It was not, however, until 1863, at a meeting held in Southampton, that the county club was constitutionally and reliably formed, under the chairmanship of Mr Thomas Chamberlayne and the patronage of Sir Frederick Bathurst. The appointment of Mr Clement Booth as captain and secretary in 1875 was the final stabilizing factor. He strengthened the fixture list and set Hampshire on the road to first-class status and with it a place in the County Championship.

In 1884 Hampshire made 645 against Somerset; in 1885, at the opening of the new ground in Southampton, which still survives today, they were skittled by George Lohmann, the great Surrey bowler. In 1887 Col James Fellowes was succeeded as secretary by Dr Russell Bencraft, the man to whom, in the view of that great Hampshireman, H. S. Altham, the county owes perhaps its greatest debt. Through the 1880s F. E. Lacey, his great work as Secretary of MCC due soon to begin, was Hampshire's outstanding cricketer. E. G. Wynyard, a young soldier, emerged as a most promising batsman, and in 1893 A. J. L. Hill began a long and valuable career with the county. In May 1894, MCC decided that Hampshire's matches against Derbyshire, Essex, Leicestershire and Warwickshire should be regarded as first-class.

A sweeping victory against Sussex in August 1894, in the midst of a run of 5 victories in their last 6 matches, clinched their Championship status. Their first Championship match, against Somerset in 1895, was won by 11 runs, and not long afterwards Yorkshire were beaten at Sheffield. Of 16 matches in 1895, 6 were won. Harry Baldwin, who had joined the club as a ground bowler in 1888, was, with T. Soar, the chief wicket-taker. The batting relied mainly upon Wynyard and Hill, Wynyard's selection against Australia in the last Test Match of 1896 came after he had made 268 for Hampshire against Yorkshire at Southampton. In 1897 and 1898 the falling away of Baldwin and Soar took its toll.

Although one of the weakest bowling sides in the Championship in 1899, Hampshire possessed in R. M. Poore a batsman whose exploits had the country by the ears. In 16 innings between 12 June and 12 August Poore scored 1,399 runs for an average of 116. Hard, strong and handsome, he was a magnificent driver. To the present generation he would have epitomized the 'old school' – left heel cocked, stance upright, left hand ungloved and bat 'at the ready'. He and Wynyard, when they were in form, made Hampshire a force to be reckoned with. For some years the nucleus of the side was composed of amateurs, one of the most notable of them being the all-rounder, C. B. Llewellyn, from South Africa. Being amateurs their availability was unreliable and Hampshire's fortunes varied accordingly. As in earlier days the established professionals bore the brunt of the bowling.

Between 1900 and 1906 Hampshire were almost permanently at the foot of the Championship. Only the tenacity of Russell Bencraft kept them going. The tide turned in 1906, a season which began badly but ended with a string of victories. Eighth place in the Championship brought encouragement to no one more than E. M. Sprot, captain through some depressing years. In the side by now was Philip Mead, an exile from the Oval and destined to become one of the county's greatest cricketers. When, within the next 2 years, Mead was joined by Jack Newman, Alec Kennedy and George Brown, Hampshire had a core of fine cricketers who were to play together until the early 1930s. With the arrival of C. B. Fry to take charge of the training ship *Mercury*, on the Hamble, they acquired another of confirmed greatness, and by 1910, with 10 victories in 24 games, they had risen to 6th place in the Championship. In 1912 Hampshire beat the Australians by 8 wickets, a feat not repeated by an English county until Surrey won at the Oval in 1956. At the end of that season Dr Bencraft, by then President of the club, described this as the best Hampshire team he had seen in an experience going back to the 1870s. The leading players were all in wonderful form. In 1913 the Hon Lionel Tennyson, later Lord Tennyson, a genial, Regency character, who cared little for his own reputation or anyone else's, had a successful introduction to the side; in 1914, when war broke out, Hampshire's 5th position in the Championship was the best they had ever achieved.

The attack was varied and accurate, and the batting not undistinguished. Mead was regularly near the top of the English averages, and Newman and Kennedy were both performing the double or getting very near to it. No one has ever made more runs in county cricket than Mead did for Hampshire (48,892), and in all first-class cricket only Sir Jack Hobbs, E. Hendren and F. E. Woolley have larger aggregates than Hampshire's great left-hander. With inexhaustible patience Mead pursued his methodical and acquisitive way. Though seldom a fast scorer he was seldom slow. Kennedy and Newman constituted the main force of Hampshire's bowling for a quarter of a century. Kennedy was of medium pace, varying in-swingers and leg-cutters in a way that was less fashionable then than it is now. Newman was of a more slender build. Everyone who knew him talked of his modesty. Although he never played for England he was a great off-break bowler, and at medium pace with the new ball he could also be highly effective. No county ever had a more loyal, hard-working or reliable pair. Often they bowled unchanged throughout an innings; twice they did so throughout a match. Kennedy took 2,874 wickets and made 16,586 runs; Newman made 15,333 runs and took 2,032 wickets. To this day there are homes in Hampshire where they are household names.

So Hampshire resumed their cricket after the First World War with the makings of one of the best sides in the Championship. Much better indeed than their record suggests.

Philip Mead (*right*), holder of every Hampshire batting record, a rock of strength for 30 years, with Hon L.H. (later Lord) Tennyson, his captain for half that time. They made runs together for England as well as their county.

Between 1920 and 1930 their average position was a disappointing 11th. From 1919 until 1933 Tennyson was the captain. As a tactician he was impulsive, as a man gay and wholehearted. Facing fast bowling there was no more fearless batsman, as he showed in 1921 against Australia at Leeds, when, as England's captain, he made 63 and 36 with one hand badly bruised. Mead soon picked up the pre-war threads. Between 1919 and 1929 he only twice averaged less than 50 for the county; seven times he averaged over 60, and twice, in 1921 and 1928, he made over 3,000 runs. Chosen for the Fourth Test Match in 1921, after England's batsmen had been routed by Gregory and McDonald, Mead made 47; at the Oval in the Fifth Test Match he scored 182 not out.

In 1922, Hampshire gained one of the most famous of all victories. Replying to Warwickshire's 1st innings total of 223 they were dismissed for 15. Following on 208 behind, Hampshire lost their 6th 2nd-innings wicket at 186. But stands of 85 for the 7th wicket, 177 for the 9th between Brown and Walter Livesey, the wicket-keeper, and 70 for the last between Livesey and Stuart Boyes, left Warwickshire needing 304 to win. Whereupon Hampshire bowled them out for 158 and won by 155 runs. At the end of that season Mead, Newman, Kennedy and Livesey all toured South Africa with MCC. Yet in 1924 only 1 of their first 10 matches was won, and in 1926 not a single victory was gained after the end of July.

By 1930 the old order was beginning to change. In Hampshire's closing match of the season, Mead, Brown, Kennedy and Newman took the field for the last time together. Livesey, a stalwart since 1913, had already given up. In the winter of 1930–31 Newman fell ill and retired. Mead was now 43, Brown 42 and Kennedy 39. Younger men, with Johnny Arnold the most promising of them, began to take their places. For over 20 years Brown had been one of the most arresting and popular figures in the game. Strong yet gentle, forthright yet generous, kind yet manly, and marvellously versatile, he scored 25,649 runs, took over 600 wickets, and in the same Test Match against Australia was chosen both to keep wicket and go in 1st. Brown was a great natural cricketer – in fact a legendary one. The highest score of his career (232 not out) won a match against Yorkshire; his bowling had much to do with Hampshire's great victory over the Australians in 1912. He was, as John Arlott said of him, 'a combative man, yet one with full capacity for the relish of life and humour'.

Through the 1930s Hampshire were again one of the weaker counties. They managed 8th position in 1932, but they were generally fighting to keep away from the bottom of the table. By 1933 N. McCorkell, W. L. Creese, A. E. Pothecary and O. W. Herman, as well as Arnold, had established themselves. G. Hill was soon to do so. The feature of 1933 was Mead's remarkable batting at the age of 46, his average being 68·83. In 1934 the captaincy passed from Tennyson to W. G. L. F. Lowndes, an Oxford blue and a gifted all-rounder. Lowndes led the side for 2 years, and is remembered for a dashing hundred against the Australians. At the end of 1934 Kennedy retired, followed, in 1936, by Mead.

Hampshire's best players hereabouts were of county rather than possible Test Match standard, the one exception being Arnold. From 1929 until 1950 Arnold scored 21,831 runs for Hampshire and was for many years under consideration for the England side. His 1 cap was gained, in fact, against New Zealand in 1931. Quick-footed and adaptable as a batsman, superb in the covers, and an international association footballer, Arnold was an exceptional games-player.

McCorkell, Hampshire's wicket-keeper for 19 years, was a neat and effective cricketer, good enough to be chosen to tour India in 1937–38. R. H. Moore, an amateur from Bournemouth, was capable of brilliant things: his 316 not out, against Warwickshire in 1937, is still the highest individual score made for Hampshire. The medium-paced bowling of Herman, Pothecary's left-handed batting and the all-round ability of Creese were now constant factors in the side. Herman, tall and easy-going, took over 1,000 wickets; Pothecary and Creese each scored over 9,000 runs. Creese also took 401 wickets. When war broke out in 1939 Hampshire were 15th in the Championship. When, 7 years later, first-class cricket was resumed, the nucleus of the side was still there. Common to the pre- and post-war teams were McCorkell, J. Bailey, Arnold, Herman, G. E. M. Heath and Hill.

In getting the club going again after the Second War the inspiring presence of H. S. Altham and the irrepressible keenness, both as captain and secretary, of E. D. R. Eagar, were the key factors. To these two belong the main credit for Hampshire's last 30 years having been their most successful since the Hambledon days. As an attacking batsman Harry Altham played 24 times for Hampshire after the First World War; as a cricket historian he had no peer. He was President and Treasurer of MCC, and for many years President of Hampshire. Desmond Eagar was a former Oxford blue, who had played cricket for Gloucestershire before the Second War and took Hampshire to his heart immediately after it. His infectious enthusiasm struck everyone who met him. As captain in 1946 he took over a side with unstable batting and somewhat ponderous fielding. C. J. Knott, an off-spinner later to become Chairman of the club, took 100 wickets in this first year of peace and played for the Gentlemen against the Players. Hampshire finished a respectable 10th. Sixteenth place in 1947, however, confirmed the prevailing weaknesses: the batting needed strengthening and the bowling was short of an opening pair. It was now that Hampshire were joined by a young batsman from Todmorden in Yorkshire, who was to become not a great run-getter but a bowler more prodigious in his feats of endurance and skill even than Kennedy and Newman. His name – Derek Shackleton.

Derek Shackleton: 2 half-volleys a season, one full toss, and in a career 2,857 wickets.

1948 was a much better year. Jim Bailey completed a double composed of stubborn batting and slow, guileful left-arm bowling. Shackleton was already showing form as a bowler and Herman and Hill had some good figures. Knott again took 100 wickets. By 1949 Shackleton's advance was being described by Eagar as the best thing to have happened to Hampshire cricket since the war. In 1950 'Shack' played for England against West Indies, the first of his 7 widely-scattered caps, and was joined in the county side by V. H. D. Cannings, a Hampshire man by birth who had had a season or two with Warwickshire. This was to prove an important capture. The aim in 1950 was to give youth its chance, a policy that was continued in 1951 when Hampshire enjoyed their most successful season since the Second War.

Shackleton and Cannings were already one of the best opening attacks in the country, both craftsmen at using the seam. Leo Harrison, who had been on the ground staff since before the Second War, and J. R. Gray did encouragingly well with the bat, and N. H. Rogers had a fine season, making 1,971 runs for an average of 41·06. Not least by his own example, Eagar had made Hampshire into a splendid fielding side. In 1951 A. C. D. Ingleby-Mackenzie, who was to succeed Eagar as captain in 1958 and lead Hampshire to the Championship in 1961, had a good first year. With Gray developing into a useful opening partner for Rogers, things in the early 1950s were really looking up.

The acquisition of Roy Marshall in 1953, to become eligible to play in Championship matches in 1955, underwrote the future. A Barbadian, Marshall had toured England with the successful West Indian side of 1950, and in 1953 he was still only 22. He was destined, as a Hampshire batsman, to spread untold pleasure round the grounds of England. Also in 1953 Henry Horton was registered from Worcestershire, and he, too, was to become a pillar of the side. Marshall threw the bat at the ball without, as it were, letting go of the handle. Horton, on the other hand, had at the wicket an ungainly crouch, though there emerged from behind it one of the straightest and most obdurate bats in England. When, in 1955, Marshall became a regular member of the team, Hampshire scaled heights which they had not previously reached in the Championship. Until then 5th place in 1914 was the best they had done. Now they were 3rd. It was their Diamond Jubilee year and they celebrated it with 16 victories. The fine weather and the style of their cricket sent Hampshire's attendance figures to their highest level since 1947. Marshall's cavalier batting gave the team the confidence they needed. There was a fortunate lack of injuries, the fielding was brilliant and under the kindly eye of Arthur Holt, the county coach, Mike Barnard, Mervyn Burden, Peter Sainsbury and Malcolm Heath (son of G.E.M.) were all coming on well.

If 1956 brought a fall of three places, there was no decline in optimism. In 1957 Eagar retired, having for 12 years, in the words of *Wisden*, 'inspired those he led by personal example'. Thirteenth position was a nasty fall from the 2 preceding years, but Eagar handed down to his successor, Colin Ingleby-Mackenzie, a side with one great bowler in Shackleton, one great batsman in Marshall, one great fielder in Sainsbury, several professionals of real proficiency and, above all, an understanding and enjoyment of the game. In the 7 years of Ingleby-Mackenzie's captaincy Hampshire finished 3rd, 6th, 12th, 1st, 10th, 10th and 12th. The new captain, himself a dashing left-handed batsman, brought to his job more than a touch of the charm, the love of a gamble and the tactical ingeniousness of Lord

Roy Marshall, for 20 years one of the great entertainers in county cricket, comes in at Southampton in his last innings before retirement in 1972: 69 not out.

Tennyson. In his 1st year (1958) Marshall and Shackleton were both in tremendous form. Heath took 100 wickets for the first time and Gray's game was raised by Marshall's example to a new level. Marshall and Gray were to open the innings together, to consistently good effect, until 1963. In 1959, when Marshall and Shackleton were two of *Wisden's* Five Cricketers of the Year, Hampshire played entertaining cricket. Batting was their strength, slow bowling their weakness. Horton had a fine year, making 2,428 runs. Marshall was little behind him and Gray exceeded 2,000 runs for the 1st time in his career. With 83 dismissals Harrison broke Livesey's wicket-keeping record for the county. At the end of the season Cannings left to become coach at Eton College, after giving 10 years of yeoman service to Hampshire. There appeared, not in his place but as a promising youngster, a genuinely fast bowler in D. W. White, who was to play a leading part in Hampshire's final assault on the Championship.

It was on the first day of September 1961 that the title was finally won. Danny Livingstone, a West Indian from Antigua in his 1st full year with Hampshire, caught R. W. Taylor of Derbyshire in the long-field at Bournemouth and for the 1st time in 66 years Hampshire were champions. There were memorable scenes at the culmination of one of the most exciting campaigns for many years. In mid-season a three-cornered fight developed between Hampshire, Middlesex and Yorkshire. Hampshire eventually moved into the lead on 1 August, after which they were never caught. They won 19 of their 32 matches, 5 of them in a row during the last few vital weeks.

The experimental law which applied at the time and ruled out the follow-on put a premium on well-timed declarations on the last day. In this Ingleby-Mackenzie excelled. The fact that 10 victories came from declarations speaks for itself. The popularity of the Hampshire captain with other captains, and of his side with other sides, was a factor in their being offered favourable terms by opposing teams. After years of dominance and mastery Yorkshire were never so generously treated. It could also be said of Ingleby-Mackenzie that he maintained his side's enthusiasm by the example of his own – this although his fielding strategy, especially his dependence upon Shackleton, was often, sometimes necessarily, defensive. Individually, Marshall, Horton and Gray passed 2,000 runs in all matches. On his day no one in the world could make batting look easier than Marshall. Sainsbury and Livingstone each had a good season, and Shackleton, in his 13th year with the county, took 153 wickets.

Although grey by now, Shackleton remained a master-craftsman. He could still bowl all day. His approach to the wicket was as light as a feather, his length almost unassailable. Inswingers, outswingers, faster, slower, higher, lower – Shackleton was always changing, rarely perceptibly, the accent of his attack. On a green wicket he could be virtually unplayable. Ingleby-Mackenzie used him to influence the course of almost every game. White, too, with 121 wickets (he was chosen to tour India with MCC in the winter of 1961/62), decided a number of matches with his explosive bursts of speed. The following 14 players appeared in 12 matches or more in 1961: A. C. D. Ingleby-Mackenzie, R. E. Marshall, D. O. Baldry, H. M. Barnard, M. D. Burden, J. R. Gray, L. Harrison, M. Heath, H. Horton, D. A. Livingstone, P. J. Sainsbury, D. Shackleton, D. W. White and A. Wassell.

Colin Ingleby-Mackenzie, who brought Hampshire to their 1st Championship in 1961, congratulates Richard Gilliat when he too led a Championship-winning team.

Several disappointing seasons followed. Although, in 1965 at Middlesborough, Shackleton, White and Bob Cottam bowled out Yorkshire for 23 (the lowest total in their history) Hampshire were not in the 1st 6 again until 1968. With the retirement of Ingleby-Mackenzie in 1965, Marshall succeeded to the captaincy. Faithfully, and annually, until his own retirement in 1968, Shackleton took his 100 wickets; but until the arrival of Barry Richards from South Africa and of Gordon Greenidge the side struggled for runs. 'Hampshire without Shackleton will be like Blackpool without its tower', wrote *Wisden* when Shackleton hung up his boots. In each of 20 seasons he had taken 100 wickets, a record surpassed only by Wilfred Rhodes.

Just as Marshall had brought a rare talent to Hampshire in the 1940s, so did Richards in 1968. At his best and keenest Richards was the best batsman in the world. When his heart was in the job – sometimes even when it was not – he could bat with a mastery that no one can ever have surpassed. If the cover drive was his special glory, he played every stroke with an arrogance, a certainty and a flourish that sometimes had his opponents shaking their heads in disbelief. Richards was a marvellous player. It could be said that he found batting too easy for his own good. That and the English county game, although it was this that made his name and fame, reduced him all too soon to boredom. Before it did so, though, he helped Hampshire to their second title in 1973.

The bowling of Shackleton, White and Cottam, allied to Richards's batting, took them to 5th place in 1968. This was the second of two excellent years for Cottam, a lively medium-pacer who cut the ball off the pitch and really 'dug it in'. In 1969 Richard Gilliat, another Oxford blue, scored 5 Championship hundreds, including the fastest of the season. A left-hander, with a natural sense of timing and a wide range of leg-side strokes, Gilliat had 10 years with Hampshire, in which, between 1971 and 1978, he led them twice to the John Player League, as well as to 1st and 2nd places in the Championship.

Although he was Barbadian-born and went on to play for West Indies, Greenidge learnt most of his cricket first as a boy in Berkshire and then with Hampshire. When he (with driving and hooking of astonishing ferocity) and Richards were batting together, at the start of a Hampshire innings, watchers were treated to many memorable displays. From 1974 until 1978 Hampshire also had the services of one of the world's fastest bowlers, the Antiguan Anderson Roberts. With these 3 in the team, plus the estimable Sainsbury and several promising youngsters, of whom Jesty and Turner were the first to make a mark, Hampshire really did have a side to be reckoned with.

Even so, their 2nd Championship victory was unexpected. It came with Roberts not yet eligible for Championship matches, and it was a triumph as much for an unsung attack as for Richards and Greenidge. At the start of the season the bookmakers were laying 50 to 1 against Hampshire winning the title. An attack of Sainsbury, Mike Taylor (an important acquisition from Nottinghamshire), David O'Sullivan (an orthodox left-arm spinner, who played for New Zealand), Tom Mottram and Bob Herman (son of O.W.) looked scarcely strong enough; but a conspicuously happy atmosphere (Richards's disenchantment had yet to set in) was worth many points, and with a late run of 6 wins in 7 matches Hampshire got home by 31 points from Surrey, the runners-up.

Peter Sainsbury: 'seldom allowed a match to go by without making a contribution.'

The 1975 team that won the John Player League. Much the same side won the 1973 County Championship and, deprived of Richards and Roberts, the JPL again in 1978. Back row: R. V. Lewis, A. J. Murtagh, R. S. Herman, J. M. Rice, J. W. Southern, A. M. E. Roberts, C. G. Greenidge and N. G. Cowley; sitting: T. E. Jesty, P. J. Sainsbury, R. M. C. Gilliat (captain), B. A. Richards and G. R. Stephenson.

With Roberts available for Championship matches in 1974 Hampshire's retention of their title was a reasonable expection. In the event Roberts took 111 wickets and only the weather prevented it. But for losing 5 whole days play in their last 3 matches Hampshire would almost certainly have won again. Instead, Worcestershire, finding a succession of fine days while Hampshire languished in the pavilion, finished 2 points ahead of them. Victory in the John Player League and 3rd place in the Championship made a fair return in 1975, and in 1978, rather out of the blue, came a 2nd Sunday League title.

This last success was achieved after Richards and Roberts had both left the county with their contracts unexpired. With six weeks of the season still to go they grew tired of the daily grind; nor was Roberts as fit as he had been. The retirement, at the end of 1978, of Gilliat, and the loss the year before, also through retirement, of Sainsbury, left the new captain, wicket-keeper Bob Stephenson (specially registered from Derbyshire in 1969), with the task of rebuilding the side.

No one better epitomized the loyalty and hard work that went into Hampshire's successes of the 1960s and 1970s than Peter Sainsbury on the field, and, of course, Desmond Eagar off it. Whether nudging the ball away through the on-side, or fielding it like a flycatcher round the corner, or bowling with geometric accuracy, Sainsbury seldom allowed a match to go by without making a contribution. And when Eagar died while on holiday in September 1977, at the age of 59, he had seen the labours of a lifetime bear fruition.

CAPTAINS

1895	H. W. R. Bencraft
1896–99	E. G. Wynyard
1900–02	C. Robson
1903–14	E. M. Sprot
1919–33	Hon L. H. Tennyson
1934–35	W. G. L. F. Lowndes
1936–37	R. H. Moore
1938	C. G. A. Paris
1939	G. R. Taylor
1946–57	E. D. R. Eagar
1958–65	A. C. D. Ingleby-Mackenzie
1966–70	R. E. Marshall
1971–78	R. M. C. Gilliat
1979–	G. R. Stephenson

HIGHEST TOTALS

For 672–7D v Somerset, Taunton 1899
Against 742 by Surrey, Oval 1909

LOWEST TOTALS

For 15 v Warwicks, Edgbaston 1922
Against 23 by Yorks, Middlesborough 1965

HIGHEST INDIVIDUAL INNINGS

For 316 R. H. Moore v Warwicks, Bournemouth 1937
Against 302* P. Holmes for Yorks, Portsmouth 1920

MOST RUNS

In a season 2,854 C. P. Mead 1928
In a career 48,892 C. P. Mead 1905–1936

MOST HUNDREDS

In a season 12 C. P. Mead 1928
In a career 138 C. P. Mead 1905–1936

INDIVIDUAL INNINGS OF 250 AND OVER

E. G. Wynyard, 268 v Yorks, Southampton 1896
R. M. Poore, 304 v Somerset, Taunton 1899
C. B. Fry, 258* v Gloucester, Southampton 1911
C. P. Mead, 280* v Notts, Southampton 1921
R. H. Moore, 316 v Warwicks, Bournemouth 1937
C. G. Greenidge, 259 v Sussex, Southampton 1975

HUNDRED ON DEBUT

No instance

RECORD WICKET PARTNERSHIPS

1 R. E. Marshall and J. R. Gray, 249 v Middlesex, Portsmouth 1960
2 G. Brown and E. I. M. Barrett, 321 v Gloucester, Southampton 1920
3 C. P. Mead and G. Brown, 344 v Yorks, Portsmouth 1927
4 R. E. Marshall and D. A. Livingstone, 263 v Middlesex, Lord's 1970
5 G. Hill and D. F. Walker, 235 v Sussex, Portsmouth 1937
6 R. M. Poore and E. G. Wynyard, 411 v Somerset, Taunton 1899
7 G. Brown and C. H. Abercrombie, 325 v Essex, Leyton 1913
8 C. P. Mead and C. P. Brutton, 178 v Worcester, Bournemouth 1925
9 D. A. Livingstone and A. T. Castell, 230 v Surrey, Southampton 1962
10 A. Bowell and W. H. Livesey, 192 v Worcester, Bournemouth 1921

MOST WICKETS

In a match 16–88 J. A. Newman v Somerset, Weston 1927
In a season 190 A. S. Kennedy, 1922
In a career 2,669 D. Shackleton 1948–1969

HAT-TRICKS

A. S. Kennedy 3
G. S. Boyes, D. W. White 2
T. A. Dean, O. W. Herman, J. W. Holder, J. A. Newman 1 each

WICKET-KEEPING – MOST DISMISSALS

In an innings	6 B. S. V. Timms 6 G. R. Stephenson
In a match	9 W. H. Livesey
In a season	83 L. Harrison 1959
In a career	685 N. McCorkell 1932–1951

COUNTY CAPS AWARDED SINCE 1946

1946	E. D. R. Eagar, A. G. Holt
1947	N. H. Rogers
1948	G. Dawson
1949	V. J. Ransom, D. Shackleton, C. Walker
1950	V. H. D. Cannings
1951	J. R. Gray, L. Harrison
1952	A. W. H. Rayment
1953	D. E. Blake
1954	J. R. Bridger, R. Dare
1955	H. M. Barnard, M. D. Burden, H. Horton, R. E. Marshall, P. J. Sainsbury
1957	M. Heath, A. C. D. Ingleby-Mackenzie
1959	D. O. Baldry
1960	D. W. White
1961	D. A. Livingstone
1963	B. S. V. Timms, A. Wassell
1965	R. M. H. Cottam
1967	B. L. Reed
1968	B. A. Richards
1969	R. M. C. Gilliat, G. R. Stephenson
1970	D. R. Turner
1971	T. E. Jesty
1972	C. G. Greenidge, R. S. Herman
1973	M. N. S. Taylor
1974	A. M. E. Roberts
1975	J. M. Rice
1978	N. G. Cowley, J. W. Southern
1979	K. Stevenson

Kent

R. L. ARROWSMITH AND E. W. SWANTON

Foundation 1870
Colours Blue and White
Badge White Horse on a Red Ground
Champions 1906, 1909, 1910, 1913, 1970, 1977 (=), 1978

For 250 years the history of Kent cricket is really the history of cricket. Of the scanty references to the game in the 17th century many come from Kent. When in the early eighteenth century we first find county matches, 'there was no greater draw to a cricket match than the announcement that the opponents were coming out of Kent.' Later in the century under the patronage of Sir Horace Mann, Kent were the chief rivals to Hambledon. At the beginning of the 19th century, though matches were few, two Kent men, John Willes and G. T. Knight, were largely responsible for the establishment of round-arm bowling, and then between 1834 and 1850 we have the great days of 'the good old Kent XI' when

with five such mighty cricketers 'twas but natural to win
As Felix, Wenman, Hillyer, Fuller Pilch and Alfred Mynn.

All this is chronicled elsewhere in this book and we may take up the tale in 1850, but first we must glance briefly at the formation of the county club. The first attempt to found one was at Town Malling in 1835 by Thomas Selby and Silas Norton. It was they who persuaded Fuller Pilch to qualify for Kent and for 5 years most of the home matches were played at Malling. But the place was too small for the venture to pay and in 1842 during the 1st Canterbury Week the Beverley Club was reconstituted as the Kent Cricket Club. This too was soon in financial difficulties and moreover was thought to be interested solely in the Week, and in 1859 a new County Club was formed at Maidstone, not ostensibly in rivalry to the existing one but to supplement its efforts. It was impossible that this diarchy should prosper. Overtures were made for an amalgamation with Canterbury and at last in 1870 these were successful and the two clubs were merged into what has ever since been the Kent County Cricket Club.

The financial troubles of these years were accentuated by a grave decline in the standard of Kent cricket; it was indeed 50 years before the county regained its old prestige. The great players of the old Kent XI left only one worthy successor, Edgar Willsher, a wonderfully accurate fast left-hander, who was for years one of the best bowlers in England and is now remembered for the part he played in legalizing overarm bowling. One other professional, George Bennett, occasionally represented the Players, but was not more than a useful county all-rounder. Moreover, though plenty of good amateurs were qualified, the University and school ones preferred club and country-house cricket and made, at most, an occasional appearance in the Week. Honourable exceptions were C. I. Thornton, traditionally the biggest of all hitters, W. Yardley, whom his contemporaries put second only to W.G. as a bat, and that immortal character, C. A. Absolom, who could play 'every stroke that was not in the books and very few that were' and was always collecting runs and wickets and fielding tirelessly anywhere, even if his breakfast had been a quart of beer and a pint of gooseberries and he had walked 12 miles carrying his bag. Others who deserve mention are G. M. Kelson, a useful all-rounder, Bob Lipscomb, a good fast bowler, and W. South Norton, who was a moderate cricketer but toiled unselfishly for years as captain and secretary.

A landmark was the appointment of Lord Harris as captain in 1875. For nearly 60 years he *was* Kent cricket. In the earlier part of that time he was captain and for a while secretary: he was one of the leading batsmen of the day and a fine field. Then, after 5 years as Governor of Bombay, he watched over the county's cricket from behind the scenes and no important decision was taken without his concurrence. He ruled the players, amateurs and professionals alike, with a rod of iron and, if he disapproved of them, left nothing unsaid, but this was accepted because they recognized his absolute fairness and knew that if trouble arose he would prove their best friend.

One of Lord Harris's acts was to revive the Band of Brothers, which over the years has done so much for amateur cricket in the county, and he soon made an invitation to play, what it has ever since remained, something to be refused only if it was impossible to accept. Nevertheless most of the amateurs had their livings to earn and there was never a sufficient nucleus of good pros to make the side consistently successful. Of amateurs one should mention 3 who played for England in the county, Frank Penn, a fine bat, Stanley Christopherson, a fast bowler, and E. F. S. Tylecote, a notable bat and wicket-keeper: Ivo Bligh, who took the side out to recover the Ashes in 1882: M. C. Kemp, for years the county's sole reliable wicket-keeper, but available only in August: 2 good slow left-handers who had very short careers, Alfred Penn and C. M. Cunliffe: the Rev W. Rashleigh, a beautiful stylist, invited by Stoddart to Australia in 1894–95: and 2 batsmen who excelled on turning wickets, W. H. Patterson, a splendid back player who scored largely on the leg-side, and Frank Marchant, a brilliant hitter. Later, in the 1890s, came W. M. Bradley, a really fast bowler and a great trier, who did good work for England in 1899, and two who had much to do with the side's later successes, J. R. Mason and C. J. Burnup. Mason was a splendid attacking bat, a good fast-medium bowler and a great slip: moreover many regarded him as the best captain they ever played under. He went with Stoddart to Australia in 1897, but never played in a Test in England. Burnup was a sound opening bat, who could master the turning ball but could also score fast when wanted, and, as befitted a soccer international, a great outfield.

For professionals the side relied for years on the Hearnes – 3 brothers, George and Alec, both good all-rounders who represented the Players, and Frank, a neat bat and beautiful field, and 2 cousins, Herbert and Walter, whose careers were curtailed by injury, Walter's when he was just reaching the top as a medium-pace bowler. Besides these Jimmy Wootton was a good slow left-hander and Walter Wright, imported from Notts, a medium pace left-hander with a natural swerve. Only one Kent pro in this period played for England, 'Nutty' Martin, a slow left-hander who was unlucky to be contemporary with 2 far better ones, Peel and Briggs, but who, on his one appearance against Australia, at the Oval in 1890, took 12 for 102.

One feature of this period was the success of the county against the Australians. Between 1884 and 1899 out of seven matches Kent won five and lost two. After the 1884 victory the enthusiasm was so great that Lord Harris was carried round the ground. Forty-seven years later the whole side and their scorer were still alive.

The real turning point in Kent cricket was the foundation of the Tonbridge nursery in 1897. Perhaps full justice has never been done to this astonishing institution. By 1914 it had supplied the county with Blythe, Humphreys, Fielder, Seymour, Fairservice, Hardinge, Hubble, Woolley, Preston, Jennings, Collins and Freeman, all of whom had got, or were destined to get, caps. Besides these it had produced Murrell for Middlesex, Vincett for Sussex, Badcock for Hampshire and Haywood and Claude Woolley for Northants, while Hickmott later played for Lancashire. The coach, Captain McCanlis, had been a moderate player in the county side in the dim days of the 1860s and 1870s. Like some other great coaches, he owed his success rather to the enthusiasm and affection he inspired than to the technical advice he imparted. As one of his pupils said years afterwards, 'We were all so keen to please him.'

As a result of the nursery, Kent soon had for the first time a nucleus of good professionals on whom to rely: no longer did everything depend on whether certain amateurs were available. How much this meant was shown in 1906, when at last the county won the Championship. Though the batting of this side was largely amateur, the bowling was, apart from Mason, wholly professional. There have certainly been greater bowling sides, but perhaps no county has ever had a

Kent 1906: County Champions for the first time. Back row: E. Humphreys, F. E. Woolley, F. H. Huish, J. Seymour and W. Hearne (scorer); sitting: A. Fielder, R. N. R. Blaker, C. H. B. Marsham (captain), J. R. Mason, K. L. Hutchings; on ground: J. C. Hubble, W. J. Fairservice.

more brilliant batting and fielding side. Certainly no county fast bowler has ever had such a combination to bowl to as Huish behind the wicket with Mason, Seymour and Hutchings in the slips. But as one of the side said long afterwards, 'We had so many people who could field anywhere.'

The batting averages were headed by Burnup, but the batsman who is best remembered now is K. L. Hutchings, who came 2nd. Tremendously strong and a wonderful driver, he hit the ball, according to Denton and Hirst (and few could have been better qualified to judge), harder than any player in their time. He was, too, a great all-round field with an astonishingly powerful throw, which came almost wholly from the wrist. At Canterbury once for a bet he threw 6 balls consecutively without a run into the top of the pavilion from the far wicket and then, taking a run, threw one over. Though he did brilliant things at times for some years, he was never again consistently as successful as in 1906. The other amateur batsmen were Mason, R. N. R. Blaker, a hitter who could score about as fast as Jessop and was also a wonderful field, E. W. Dillon, a very consistent left-hander, and C. H. B. Marsham, the captain. The professional bats were Humphreys and Seymour.

Humphreys was a splendid player of slow bowling, who really enjoyed batting on a turning wicket; he was also a good slow left-hander, overshadowed by Blythe and Woolley, and a fine mid-on. A great coach, he did splendid work later at Uppingham and in the West Indies and finally, for almost 20 years, in charge of the Kent nursery. Seymour was always a joy to watch: few batsmen had more strokes and, though he was never really sound enough to be a candidate for the highest honours, he could follow the ball closely when it was turning and at times would make the best bowling look pretty simple stuff while his colleagues were helpless.

The great bowlers of the side were Blythe and Fielder. Fielder's best-remembered performance was to take in this year all 10 wickets for the Players at Lord's: many have forgotten that he once took 24 wickets in a Test series in Australia. As a fast bowler he ranks just behind the great, but in 1906 and for some years after he was a formidable county bowler.

To those who remember him Blythe will always seem the model of what a slow left-hander should be. With all the natural gifts, including a beautiful action, he could be almost unplayable if the wicket helped him, but it was on plumb wickets that he really rose above others of his type: his control of length, his flight and subtle variation of pace enabled him still to attack, instead of becoming, like most slow left-handers under those circumstances, mainly defensive. Of a temperament so sensitive that latterly he was forbidden by the doctors to play in Test Matches, he delighted in accepting a challenge to his skill and of all slow bowlers was the least likely to be hit off his length. At Dover in 1910 Llewellyn, of Hampshire, scored 91 in an hour, including 5 sixes off Blythe. As ball after ball soared out of the ground, Blythe stood there, lost in admiration, applauding as heartily as any of the crowd, 'Oh, well hit, Charles! Well hit, Charles!' When the war came in 1914, he refused to recognize cricket as a man's job and cut the last match to join up: he was killed in action 3 years later. Blythe and Fielder habitually took the new ball for Kent, as they continued to do till 1914. In 1906 they were followed by Humphreys and at least one of Mason, Woolley and Fairservice. Fairservice was unlucky: a medium-pace off-spinner with a model action, he was condemned until late in his career to act as a hack bowler on plumb wickets and, when there was a chance that he might enjoy himself, to see the ball tossed to Blythe and Woolley.

1906 was Woolley's 1st season, and perhaps no beginner has ever done so much and yet failed to secure a regular place: that alone speaks volumes for the strength of the side. In his 1st match, against Lancashire, he scored 64. He followed it with 6 for 39 against Somerset, 72 (easily the highest score) and 23 not out at a crisis against Surrey, as well as 8 wickets, and 116 and 6 for 46 against Hampshire. Yet no room could be found for him in Canterbury Week. Until he was 35, Woolley ranked as a slow left-hander only behind the very great. As a batsman he was unique and had no more fervent admirers than those who bowled at him. No one has made batting look easier or bowlers more inept. Most great batsmen who have retained their skill into middle age have adapted their methods to advancing years: W.G. and Hobbs are notable examples. Woolley made no such concessions. He batted in 1938 just as he had batted in 1914. That he could do so successfully was a tribute as much to the straightness of his bat as to his wonderful physical gifts. Perhaps only L. C. H. Palairet and R. H. Spooner have ever rivalled him for beauty of execution.

Huish, the wicket-keeper for so many years, was in the highest class, whether standing back to Fielder or standing up to the others and, helped by an unrivalled battery of slow spinners, had by the time he retired broken almost every wicket-keeping record.

The great days continued up to 1914. Kent won the Championship in 1909, 1910 and 1913, and in 1911 were only a fraction behind Warwickshire, whom they had not played and would probably have beaten. Meanwhile the structure of the side had changed: in 1913 only 3 amateurs played any considerable part – Dillon, the captain, A. P. Day, who played in 10 matches, and D. W. Carr, who was available only in August. Carr had a remarkable career. For many years a good club cricketer, he was impressed by the early googly bowlers and took up the art himself with such success that, after playing for Kent for the first time in 1909 at the age of 37 against Oxford, his next match was for the Gentlemen at Lord's and by mid-August he had played for England. A schoolmaster by profession, he continued for the next 4 years to come into the side during the holidays and to be, when the wicket helped him, such a terror to batsmen that they were tempted to face Blythe rather than him.

A. P. Day was one of 3 Malvernian brothers who played for Kent. The year after he left school he made 1,000 runs for the county and later developed into a dangerous fast-medium bowler. A sounder player when the ball was turning than most Malvernians, he came very near to playing for England. Yet it may be doubted whether he was a better bat than his elder brother, S.H., who actually made a hundred for the county the year before he left school. He, too, could play on a turning wicket and was a particularly fine cutter; over 22 years he made many runs for Kent and the experts are unanimous in placing him high among the batsmen of his day.

Two professionals of the pre-1914 era remain to be mentioned. Hardinge was an opener whom a weakness against fast bowling just excluded from the top class, though he did play once for England. Against slow and medium-paced bowling he had few superiors. In the brilliant but slightly unsound batting sides of those days his job was to act as sheet-anchor and he was often regarded as slow: actually he was a beautiful off-driver and cutter and a fine leg-hitter and was always sent in in his usual place when runs were wanted quickly. He was, moreover, a very safe outfield and a slow left-hander with a wonderful knack of tempting stolid batsmen into a fatal indiscretion. Hubble, who succeeded Huish as wicket-keeper after the First World War, had established himself in the side as a batsman for some years before it. Though he made few large scores, he was a remarkably consistent player and, unlike some of his colleagues, was at his best against fast bowling.

One game may be quoted to illustrate the remarkable versatility and striking power of the Kent XIs of the golden years. At noon on the 3rd day against Warwickshire at Tonbridge in 1913 Kent finished their first innings 130 runs behind. By 3.30 they had won by six wickets. Blythe and Woolley had bowled Warwickshire out in 45 minutes for 16, and on a wicket that was still far from easy Woolley had scored 76 in 80 minutes.

After the First World War Kent were never quite so strong again. It is true that in 1919 a few more minutes against Middlesex at Lord's would have given them the Championship, but it would have been a lucky win, and after that, though for years they were among the top few and were a menace to the best sides, they never had the consistency of champions. The popular view is that the bowling was not strong enough;

'Tich' Freeman, whose leg-spinners and googlies brought him 3,776 wickets, nearly all of them for Kent and taken in the 17 seasons between 1920 and 1936 (when, aged 48, he retired). In 1928 his bag was 304.

and, indeed, after Woolley's great bowling days ended, their only match-winner, except when C. S. Marriott was available in August, was Freeman. But Freeman took so many wickets himself that, with such help as Collins, Wright, Woolley and Hardinge or later Ashdown, Watt and Todd could afford, opponents were usually got out somehow. It was not the draws that put Kent just outside the Championship class: year after year they won their full share of matches. It was the matches they lost. Thus in 1921 they won 16, but lost 7; in 1923 they won 15, but lost 9. Again they lost 8 matches in 1929, 7 in 1930, 7 in 1931 and 8 in 1933, and it is bad batting that actually loses matches.

The truth is that they never after the First World War had quite the nucleus of solid professional batting that they had before it and, though perhaps no county has ever possessed a greater number of brilliant amateurs, few of them were available early in the season, and the side would often go up north in May or June to face Yorkshire and Lancashire on slow wickets with several young and inexperienced batsmen who under such circumstances were quite out of their depth. Moreover, even later in the season the batting, overwhelmingly strong on paper and wonderfully attractive to watch, was more liable to sudden collapses, especially against fast bowling, than a champion county can afford to be.

Of the side's attitude to batting no better example could be found than the match with Surrey at the Oval in 1922. Kent were 392 runs down on the 1st innings, and began the last day at 82 for one with J. L. Bryan out and only a draw to play for. In the first 80 minutes Hardinge and Seymour added 153, of which Seymour made 98. Woolley followed with a hundred in 101 minutes, described by *The Times* as a sedate innings, and at the close of play the score was 557 for 7. Better remembered is the match against Gloucestershire at Dover in 1937 when the 219 runs required to win were scored in 71 minutes. But throughout this period, as before 1914, attack was the keynote of Kent batting. When G. J. Bryan, in the year he left Wellington, celebrated his first appearance for Kent with a century, he completed his 50 with a six and his hundred with another. When at Maidstone 7 years later A. P. F. Chapman faced McDonald with the score-board reading 70 for 5, he did not attempt to retrieve the situation by grim defence: he made 260 in 3 hours.

Despite his successes in higher grades of cricket, this innings was probably the greatest of Chapman's career. No doubt he is remembered more for what he did for England than for what he did for Kent, more too for his captaincy and personality and his wonderful catching than for his batting. As time went on, more and more strokes were played with the head in the air and the foot farther from the ball than the books recommend, but in his earlier years at least he was a great batsman in his own right. Nor was there any lack of other entertaining bats; even if one did not see these two, one was sure of entertainment in plenty. In the 1920s there were still on occasions A. P. Day, who had a wonderful season in 1921, and C. S. Hurst, who, after 10 years' absence from county cricket, made 3 hundreds in a month in 1922. Then there were A. F. Bickmore, L. P. Hedges, the three Bryans, C. P. Johnstone, C. H. Knott and A. J. Evans; a little later came G. B. Legge, B. H. Valentine, A. M. Crawley, I. Akers Douglas, J. G. W. Davies and F. G. H. Chalk, almost all brilliant attacking batsmen and almost all equally brilliant fields. Of these one can only deal briefly with one or two.

Kent war casualties: K. L. Hutchings (*left*), dashing bat and fielder was killed in 1916; F. G. H. Chalk, who had proved himself an ideal county captain, in 1943. He had recently won the DFC.

J. L. Bryan was sounder than most left-handers and less vulnerable outside the off-stump, but he was far from a slow scorer and in particular was a devastating exponent of the pulled-drive over or wide of mid-on. He went to Australia in a side overweighted with opening bats and never got a chance in a Test Match. But perhaps the most remarkable, though certainly not the most graceful, among these amateurs was C. H. Knott. With a scarcely perceptible back-lift, he hit the ball harder than almost anyone in England. In club cricket his scoring feats were phenomenal and he was well capable of stepping into the Kent side without any match practice and making hay of reputable bowlers. In 1930 at Tonbridge he made 73 in just under half an hour against Warwickshire, his innings being almost exactly bisected by lunch. In 1928 after a lean period he was left out against the West Indians at Canterbury and Kent lost by an innings. The West Indians proceeded to Eastbourne, where Knott for the Harlequins against them made 261 not out – almost as much as the whole Kent side had got in their 2 innings put together.

Valentine, luckier than most in being able to play regularly, was a singularly gifted games player and, by the time the Second War came, had added to his natural fast-wicket strokes the power to play under difficult conditions. He returned to captain the side after the war. The professional batsmen immediately after the First War were Woolley, Hardinge and Seymour, and they were gradually reinforced or replaced by Ashdown, Todd and Fagg, three beautiful all-round stroke players who never perhaps wholly fulfilled their promise, though Fagg played for England. Yet if they were slightly disappointing, the same could not be said of Ames. Very quick on his feet, he was yards down the wicket to slow bowlers, who must have found him very difficult to bowl to, while he was regarded as one of the finest players of fast bowling in his generation. As a wicket-keeper, he never caught the eye like his successor Godfrey Evans, and one can sense a disposition among critics to damn him with faint praise. Yet on the Body-line tour he is said to have missed only one catch in the Tests and that barely possible, and the records in *Wisden* bear testimony to what he could do for spin bowlers. He deserves to rank with such great all-rounders as Hirst, Rhodes and Woolley.

In wicket-keeping between the wars Kent were indeed well served. From 1919 to 1926 the stock 'keeper was Hubble, but he had constantly to give way to the brilliant, if slightly uncertain, G. E. C. Wood, who kept for England against South Africa in 1924, and was twice asked to go to Australia. In Ames's time, W. H. V. Levett was probably the best second-string wicket-keeper any couny has ever had.

There remains the bowling and that, for most of the period, was Freeman. Figures in cricket do not prove much, but they do show that, simply as a wicket-taker in county cricket, 'Tich' Freeman has never been approached. To a few of the leading batsmen, largely of the quick-footed type such as Duleepsinhji, Hendren and Hammond, he was money for jam. To the ordinary good county players he was always a menace and to the rank and file of moderate or inexperienced batsmen he was sudden death. When the Australians came to Canterbury in 1930, few of them having played him in this country before, their leading batsmen, including Bradman, were all at sea. In the 2nd innings Bradman, after a shaky start, made 205 not out and no doubt from then on would have been his master. Freeman relied mainly on the leg-break, pitched on the leg or middle-and-leg, where the batsmen had to play it, and a top-spinner which was perhaps his most formidable weapon, especially as these two varieties, an intentional one, for which he altered his grip, possible to spot though difficult, and one which was simply a leg-break which failed to take the spin. Moreover, he was as accurate as most off-spinners. After Woolley ceased to bowl seriously, Freeman had only one helper of real class, C. S. Marriott, a slow right-hander with an action so bizarre that it reduced crowds who had not seen him before to helpless laughter. One of the worst bats and fields in cricket history, he was a fine enough bowler to play for England in spite of it; indeed some batsmen, given the choice, preferred to face Freeman.

Useful work was also done in the 1920s by 2 fast-medium bowlers – Charlie Wright, whose cheerfulness was proof against any number of dropped catches, and Collins, whose great feat was to take all ten wickets against Notts in 1922. A man of huge physical strength, who could lift a pavilion chair by the top bar parallel to the ground between his teeth, he was the clumsiest and ugliest of cricketers, but would quite unaccountably now and then bowl out the best sides and had an extraordinary knack of getting runs by sheer determination when they were wanted. In the 1930s the faster bowling was supplied by Watt, who was also a fine field and a cheerful hitter, and Todd.

The great bowling find of the 1930s was Doug Wright, a leg-break bowler of the modern medium-pace variety. In county cricket his record does not approach Freeman's; his far quicker leg-break constantly beat both bat and stumps. But for years there was probably no one against whom the greatest batsmen in the world felt less secure, even when well set, and as long as he was in the England side, what old Clarke used to call 'an accident' seemed a possibility at any moment. He has to his credit an unequalled number of hat-tricks.

It would be difficult to find a clearer example of a span of cricket history comprising two halves of strongly contrasting quality than that of Kent since the Second World War. The first 2 years of post-war adjustment were negotiated with reasonable success under the ever-cheerful leadership of Bryan Valentine, who with Ames, Fagg, Wright, Todd, and, when available, J. G. W. Davies of the old guard, made as useful a nucleus as many another county could command. Moreover there arrived a 'keeper more than up to the traditional Kent standard in Evans. Ridgway, too, established himself as a sturdy fast bowler not far short of top pace. Such was the backbone of a side made up by a small professional staff of no outstanding quality and reinforced from time to time in the Kent tradition by such amateurs as H. A. Pawson, who like his father led Oxford as well as playing for Kent, A. C. Shirreff and J. W. Martin, whose bowling was once used to open the England attack.

Les Ames, Arthur Fagg and Leslie Todd soldiered on, giving stability to the batting, until well into their 40s, but of these only Fagg had survived when Colin Cowdrey, as an 18-year-old from Tonbridge, began to show his promise in 1951. Then for 3 years Cowdrey was available only after the University Match, while on coming down from Oxford he was needed regularly by England. Kent, for the first and only time in their history until the recruitment of a trio of distinguished overseas cricketers in the late 1960s, began to look everywhere for imports. The results were unrewarding both in results and the attraction of the cricket.

There was the brilliance of Godfrey Evans to admire, though he could not regularly repeat his England form in county cricket, the spinning genius of Doug Wright, and the class of Cowdrey. Wilson, a left-handed bat of sound method, Dixon as an all-rounder, Phebey and Leary from South Africa, as batsmen, Dovey as a stock bowler, became steadfast cricketers of county standard. Yet Kent continued to languish. Whereas in 60 years they had been only four times lower than 9th in the table, between 1948 and 1963 their average position in the championship was fourth from the bottom.

Kent's faithful supporters – or at least those of them old enough to make comparisons – though they continued to support Canterbury and the other old-established Weeks in good numbers, sighed for the days of Woolley, the patron saint, who had set the mood and the pace of the XI for so long. One of the remaining links with times past went when Ames, following a moment of rare sentiment at Canterbury where he became the only wicket-keeper in history to reach a hundred hundreds, was forced into retirement by back trouble.

The beginnings of Kent's revival, though it was all but a decade before it came to full fruition, date from 1957 when Cowdrey was appointed captain and Ames became manager. Later the latter assumed the double responsibility of Secretary-Manager with a correspondingly wider responsibility. Together these illustrious players formed a working partnership which gradually led to an improvement both in morale and performance.

Peter Richardson, already a Test player, came in 1960 from Worcestershire to improve

Colin Cowdrey, Frank Woolley and Leslie Ames made 354 first-class hundreds between them, and 225 appearances for England – an immortal Kentish trio.

the batting while Halfyard as a stock bowler gave willing, tireless service. But both of these had passed on by 1967 when there began the sequence of success which at the moment of writing still retains its momentum.

A new generation had now emerged, Knott as a wicket-keeper-batsman in the class of Evans and Ames, Underwood as a slow-medium left-armer *sui generis*, Luckhurst and Denness as a 1st-wicket partnership equal to any in the country. Following the deliberate opening of the doors to overseas cricketers by the new policy of immediate county registration John Shepherd, an all-rounder of high potential, had been recruited from Barbados, the Pakistani Asif Iqbal, already the hero of a famous Test hundred against England, following in 1968.

In 1967 came not only the winning of the Gillette Cup but, more significantly, 2nd place in the Championship to Yorkshire, the difference between them being the result of their meeting in the Canterbury Week when

Derek Underwood, the foundation of the Kent XI since his boyhood. His eye is on the good length spot.

the strength of both sides was greatly weakened by Test calls. This was the first of many occasions when Kent had to endure the absence not only of their captain but of their brilliant young wicket-keeper and the irreplaceable Underwood. Yorkshire and Kent again headed the Championship in that order in 1968. Two years later, in the Club's centenary season, after a grotesquely poor start which found them bottom of the table at the beginning of July, Kent defied all probability by carrying off the title. Cowdrey at this joyful moment determined the shape of the side for the future by capping 3 promising young men, all Kentish-bred, Johnson, Ealham and Woolmer.

The side thus rejuvenated were clearly well-equipped for the limited-over competitions, the rewards from which tended now to threaten the century-old prestige of the Championship itself. Julien, a cricketer from Trinidad of great potential (though, as it proved, inadequate strength of purpose), was recruited in 1971, adding another all-rounder to a list already containing Shepherd, Woolmer, Johnson and Asif. Thus the batting, with Alan Knott at No. 7 good enough to make hundreds in Test Matches, extended almost to the foot of the order while the bowling, sustained by wonderfully good fielding, was adequate for containment though with no sharp cutting edge unless Underwood was able to extract something from the wicket. Granted a little help he was a match-winner in any company in any of the game's forms old and new. The one-day honours followed closely on one another: Gillette Cup 1974 (and narrow losers of a great final to Lancashire in 1972); Benson and Hedges Cup 1973, 1976 and 1978; John Player League 1972, 1973 and 1976.

Cowdrey, after announcing his wish to vacate the captaincy at the end of the 1971 season, began it in great form only to be afflicted with pneumonia which brought his summer's cricket to a particularly untimely end. Yet he could look back on a 15 years' lease of the captaincy equalled only by Lord Harris and a happy transition from poverty to riches. When he had started it was a signal event if Kent won a match: in 1971 they beat Yorkshire of all counties four times, twice in the Championship by an innings. Cowdrey when he handed over to Michael Denness had, however, 4 years of service yet to run, culminating in his recall to the colours in Australia to help Denness's own stricken MCC side in 1974–75. His hundred hundreds safely achieved, he signed off with 5 more in the summer of 1975, the only regret being perhaps that he could not quite last to take the field with his promising son, Christopher.

Denness's reign of five years from 1972–76 was one of consistent success in the one-day field. There was substance perhaps in the contention that he was a better Test than county captain, yet no one could improve upon his example in the field nor upon Kent's out-cricket generally in the limited-over game.

The story of Kent's cricket in the following 3 years was clouded more than that of most counties by the advent of the Packer threat since 3 of the key men, Underwood, Knott and Asif, the new captain, and also Julien, who was not retained after the end of the season, were named in the original signings when the cat was let out of the bag in May

1977, while Woolmer joined them in September. Asif brought to the leadership that summer much of the flair that marked all he did on the cricket field, Kent jumping from 14th to a half share of the championship with Middlesex.

Once the Committee decided in the winter of 1977 that they must reluctantly part with their Packer signatories after the end of the 1978 season another captaincy change was a logical sequel. Thus Alan Ealham, whose forcing batting and magnificent fielding had long been a popular feature of Kent's cricket, succeeded to the job, and it said much for him and his whole side that the strong political overtones off the field, including a reversal by the newly-appointed Committee of the decision of their predecessors in regard to the Packer men, were not allowed to enter the dressing-room. In July Kent won the Benson and Hedges yet again while, more importantly and helped substantially by the fact that for the first summer since 1909 they were not called upon to supply a single man to the England XI, they went one better than the year before by winning the Championship outright. As usual Underwood's bowling was a crucial factor.

By now Chris Tavaré, after showing high promise as a batsman at Oxford, had established himself not only with Kent but as a possible for higher things, while Paul Downton, like Tavaré a product of Sevenoaks School – following the extraordinary succession of fine wicket-keepers produced by the county – was chosen, though only 20, for the England tour of Pakistan and New Zealand. Charles Rowe, Kevin Jarvis and Richard Hills won their caps, and the former, along with Graham Dilley when included, gave to the attack a measure of speed it has too often lacked.

All in all Kent enter the 1980s richly blessed, with a talented team in which every man, apart from Shepherd and Asif, learned his cricket in the county, a membership of 8,500 which has never been exceeded, and a management well versed in the technique, so necessary in these days, of turning the great enthusiasm for the game in this corner of England to the best financial advantage.

CAPTAINS

1870	W. S. Norton
1871–89	Lord Harris
1890–93	F. Marchant and W. H. Patterson
1894–97	F. Marchant
1898–1902	J. R. Mason
1903	C. J. Burnup
1904–08	C. H. B. Marsham
1909–13	E. W. Dillon
1914–23	L. H. W. Troughton
1924–26	W. S. Cornwallis
1927	A. J. Evans
1928–30	G. B. Legge
1931–36	A. P. F. Chapman
1937	R. T. Bryan and B. H. Valentine
1938–39	F. G. H. Chalk
1946–48	B. H. Valentine
1949–51	D. G. Clark
1952–53	W. Murray-Wood
1954–56	D. V. P. Wright
1957–71	M. C. Cowdrey
1972–76	M. H. Denness
1977	Asif Iqbal
1978–	A. G. E. Ealham

HIGHEST TOTALS

For 803–4D v Essex, Brentwood 1934
Against 676 by Australians, Canterbury 1921

LOWEST TOTALS

For 18 v Sussex, Gravesend 1867
Against 16 by Warwicks, Tonbridge 1913

HIGHEST INDIVIDUAL INNINGS

For 332 W. H. Ashdown v Essex, Brentwood 1934
Against 344 W. G. Grace for MCC, Canterbury 1876

MOST RUNS

In a season 2,894 F. E. Woolley 1928
In a career 48,483 F. E. Woolley 1906–1938

MOST HUNDREDS

In a season 10 F. E. Woolley 1928 and 1934
In a career 112 F. E. Woolley 1906–1938

INDIVIDUAL INNINGS OF 250 AND OVER

F. E. Woolley, 270 v Middlesex, Canterbury 1923
A. P. F. Chapman, 260 v Lancs, Maidstone 1927
H. T. W. Hardinge, 263* v Gloucester, Gloucester 1928
L. E. G. Ames, 295 v Gloucester, Folkestone 1933
W. H. Ashdown, 332 v Essex, Brentwood 1934
W. H. Ashdown, 305* v Derby, Dover 1935
A. E. Fagg, 257 v Hants, Southampton 1936
A. E. Fagg, 269* v Notts, Trent Bridge 1953
M. C. Cowdrey, 250 v Essex, Blackheath 1959

HUNDRED ON DEBUT

S. H. Day, 101* v Gloucester, Cheltenham 1897
G. J. Bryan, 124 v Notts, Trent Bridge 1920
A. J. Evans, 102 v Northants, Northampton 1921
A. L. Hilder, 103* v Essex, Gravesend 1924
P. Hearn, 124 v Warwicks, Gillingham 1947
N. R. Taylor, 110 v Sri Lankans, Canterbury 1979

RECORD WICKET PARTNERSHIPS

1 A. E. Fagg and P. R. Sunnucks, 283 v Essex, Colchester 1938
2 W. H. Ashdown and F. E. Woolley, 352 v Essex, Brentwood 1934
3 A. Hearne and J. R. Mason, 321* v Notts, Trent Bridge 1899
4 H. T. W. Hardinge and A. P. F. Chapman, 297 v Hants, Southampton 1926
5 F. E. Woolley and L. E. G. Ames, 277 v New Zealanders, Canterbury 1931
6 A. P. F. Chapman and G. B. Legge, 284 v Lancs, Maidstone 1927
7 A. P. Day and E. Humphreys, 248 v Somerset, Taunton 1908
8 A. L. Hilder and C. Wright, 157 v Essex, Gravesend 1924
9 B. R. Edrich and F. Ridgway, 161 v Sussex, Tunbridge Wells 1949
10 F. E. Woolley and A. Fielder, 235 v Worcester, Stourbridge 1909

MOST WICKETS

In a match 17–48 C. Blythe v Northants, Northampton 1907
In a season 262 A. P. Freeman 1933
In a career 3,359 A. P. Freeman 1914–1936

ALL 10 WICKETS IN AN INNINGS

E. Hinkly v England, Lord's 1848
C. Blythe v Northants, Northampton 1907
G. C. Collins v Notts, Dover 1922
A. P. Freeman v Lancs, Maidstone 1929
A. P. Freeman v Essex, Southend 1930
A. P. Freeman v Lancs, Old Trafford 1931

HAT-TRICKS

D. V. P. Wright 6 (7 in all matches)
W. M. Bradley 3
A. P. Freeman 2 (3 in all matches)
C. Blythe, D. J. Halfyard, F. Ridgway 2
G. C. Hearne 1 (2 in all matches)
F. Martin 1 (2 in all matches)
D. M. Sayer 1 (2 in all matches)
D. L. Underwood 1 (2 in all matches)
W. F. Best, A. Hearne, W. Hearne, C. Lewis, J. Wells, F. E. Woolley, C. Wright 1 each

WICKET-KEEPING – MOST DISMISSALS

In an innings	6	A. P. E. Knott (5)
		L. E. G. Ames (2)
		W. H. V. Levett (2)
		J. C. Hubble
		F. H. Huish
		D. Nicholls
In a match	10	F. H. Huish
		J. C. Hubble
In a season	116	L. E. G. Ames 1929
In a career	1,248	F. H. Huish 1895–1914

COUNTY CAPS AWARDED SINCE 1946

1946	T. G. Evans, R. R. Dovey, J. W. Martin, H. A. Pawson
1947	N. W. Harding, P. Hearn, F. Ridgway
1948	E. E. Crush
1949	D. G. Clark, B. R. Edrich, A. W. H. Mallett
1951	M. C. Cowdrey, W. Murray-Wood
1952	R. Mayes, A. H. Phebey, A. C. Shirreff
1953	G. Smith
1954	J. Pettiford, R. C. Wilson
1955	J. M. Allan
1956	D. G. Ufton
1957	D. J. Halfyard, S. C. Leary, J. C. T. Page, J. F. Pretlove
1960	A. L. Dixon, P. E. Richardson
1961	A. Brown, P. H. Jones
1962	A. W. Catt, D. M. Sayer
1963	B. W. Luckhurst
1964	M. H. Denness, D. L. Underwood
1965	A. P. E. Knott, J. W. Prodger
1966	J. C. J. Dye
1967	J. N. Graham, J. N. Shepherd
1968	Asif Iqbal
1969	D. Nicholls
1970	A. G. E. Ealham, G. W. Johnson, R. A. Woolmer
1972	B. D. Julien
1977	R. W. Hills, K. B. S. Jarvis, C. J. C. Rowe
1978	C. J. Tavare
1979	C. S. Cowdrey, P. R. Downton

Kent in 1978 were winners of the first Schweppes County Championship and the Benson and Hedges Cup. Back row: C. Lewis (scorer), B. W. Luckhurst, N. J. Kemp, C. J. C. Rowe, R. W. Hills, K. B. S. Jarvis, C. J. Tavare, P. R. Downton, G. S. Clinton, J. C. T. Page (manager); front row: R. A. Woolmer, D. Nicholls, D. L. Underwood, A. G. E. Ealham (captain), G. W. Johnson, J. N. Shepherd, Asif Iqbal.

Lancashire

J. M. KILBURN

Foundation 1864
Colours Red, Green and Blue
Badge Red Rose
Champions 1879 (=), 1881, 1882 (=), 1889 (=), 1897, 1904, 1926, 1927, 1928, 1930, 1934, 1950 (=)

Manchester cannot claim the thought that originated county cricket for England, but Manchester ideas and endeavour were directly responsible for the formation of Lancashire County Cricket Club in 1864. The decisive resolutions were approved in January and in the summer months Lancashire took the field. The first inter-county engagements were home and away with Middlesex in 1865 and by the time playing qualifications had been instituted in 1873 Lancashire had half-a-dozen county opponents on their fixture list.

The early Lancashire teams were predominantly amateur but peripatetic professionals were engaged for specific occasions and the Yorkshireman Roger Iddison scored the 1st Lancashire hundred in 1866. F. R. Reynolds, ground manager and playing professional at Old Trafford, established himself in a Lancashire association that lasted, in various capacities, for more than 40 years and covered developments that must have been beyond his most optimistic anticipations. As a young man, Reynolds knew the Rowleys and the Hornbys, whose forceful characters in committee and on the field were revealed as the county club was built and consolidated in reputation. A. B. Rowley was a founder-member of the club and President from 1874 to 1880. Edmund Rowley was captain until 1880. A. N. Hornby played over the period from 1867 to 1899 and was captain for 11 seasons, President for 23 years. His brothers were enthusiastic players and his son, an enterprising batsman and a brilliant close-in fielder, led the side in later years.

Equally significant among the founding fathers was S. H. Swire, player in the early years and honorary secretary until 1905. His involvements included the purchasing of Old Trafford, the amalgamation of the Manchester and Lancashire clubs and the building programme that provided a new pavilion in 1895.

A fusion of amateur and professional talent carried the club through a healthy childhood in the field. The professional playing strength was represented by R. G. Barlow, A. Watson and W. McIntyre and the amateur quality was reinforced by the appearances of Vernon Royle and A. G. Steel. Character was crystallized in the immortal association of Hornby and Barlow, 'the Boss' and happy henchman. Hornby was a powerful and energetic batsman, a fearless fielder and a forthright, not to say dictatorial, leader. He was impetuous in performance and warm-hearted in personal relations. 'He runs you out', maintained his professionals, 'and then gives you a sovereign'. Amid the alarums and excursions Hornby scored over 10,000 Lancashire runs. Barlow's aggregate was smaller because time was against him. Three-day matches limited the scope of a batsman whose principle was survival for its own sake. He carried his bat through an innings 12 times; and he stayed 2½ hours for 5 not out at Trent Bridge in 1882.

Barlow was also a patient and accurate left-arm bowler, but the early Lancashire attack contained more exciting and controversial resources. Watson, Crossland and Mold achieved both fast-bowling success and the unwelcome distinction of questionable legality of their actions and after Steel's slow leg-breaks came the activity of Johnnny Briggs. Briggs first played county cricket in 1879, before his 17th birthday, on the recommendation of Barlow. The talent was obvious and the enthusiasm was boundless. Briggs made his mark as batsman and fielder and then became a slow left-arm bowler of the highest quality, taking over 2,000 wickets in a career that gave him taste of all the major bowling feats. He took 100 wickets in a season 11 times, he took all 10 wickets in an innings – against Worcestershire in 1900 – he did the hat-trick for England against Australia, and against South Africa at Cape Town he returned match figures of 15 wickets for 28 runs. All his cricket was eager and purposeful. He enjoyed it and, by sad irony, his jollity turned to mental disorder. He died at the age of 39.

Lancashire's 1st Champions: the team of 1881. Back row: G. Nash, J. Crossland, G. Smith (umpire), R. Pilling, A. Watson; sitting: A. G. Steel, Rev V. P. F. A. Royle, A. N. Hornby (captain) and A. Appleby; on ground: W. Robinson, R. G. Barlow, O. P. Lancashire and J. Briggs.

Briggs and Mold made Lancashire a powerful side in the 1890s, when they were 2nd in the Championship 5 times in 7 seasons before finishing at the top in 1897. The batting was uneven, heavily dependent on the form of Albert Ward and A. C. MacLaren. Ward was an import from Yorkshire and reached international level both at home and overseas, but his merits tended to be obscured in the shadow of MacLaren playing in the same side. MacLaren took the eye and commanded the attention. With a schoolboy reputation from Harrow, MacLaren joined Lancashire in 1890 and in his 1st match against Sussex at Brighton he made a century. That introductory innings was characteristic in confidence of approach, majesty of manner and standard of technical accomplishment. MacLaren never ceased to be a force in cricket until he had captained his last side and played his last innings. Growth in authority no doubt led to dictatorial exhibitions and at various times in his career he entangled himself in untenable positions, but of the splendour of his own batting and the shrewdness of his cricketing observation there has been no query. He met bowling challenge with immediate counter challenge and scorned innings of mere accumulation. His 424 against Somerset in 1895 was made at a rate of 54 runs an hour in the course of a three-day match. He saw greatness in the bowling of S. F. Barnes without requiring statistical evidence. He said he could raise a side to beat the 1921 Australians and he did. At the age of 51 he led an MCC team to New Zealand and set an example with an innings of 200 not out.

To match Old Trafford's development as a cricketing estate Lancashire found brilliant batting. MacLaren's regal flourish was augmented by the grace of R. H. Spooner and the superb craftsmanship of J. T. Tyldesley. Bowlers meeting Lancashire were threatened, charmed and bewildered.

Spooner played only 170 matches for his county but he left an indelible impression of flowing off-side batsmanship. He was gifted in the art of games, an international in cricket and football, but games were his recreation only and he could not make himself available for England on tour.

John T. Tyldesley was a cricket professional of the highest standing. He scored 31,941 runs for his county and 37,897 in a career that included 31 appearances for England. In maturity he accepted senior responsibilities in the dressing room with unfailing loyalty and with playing days behind him he gave ungrudging service as an encouraging coach. His youthful batsmanship ranked with the most attractive of the time. He was probably unexcelled, even by Victor Trumper, in ability to score readily and safely on difficult pitches. Small of stature, with dazzling footwork, he would cut and hook where less gifted players were stumbling in anxious defence and in easier conditions his off-driving was more uninhibited and powerful than most. As a fieldsman in the deep he was equally accomplished and enthusiastic. Lancashire will always be content for their cricket to be personified in Johnny Tyldesley.

From 1900 to 1914 Lancashire won the Championship only once – in 1904 when they went through their programme without defeat – but they were invariably among the leaders and they contributed enormously to the cricketing character of the period. Their lack, for Championship success, was bowling strength. S. F. Barnes was engaged after the departure of Mold and Briggs and he played regularly in 1902 and 1903, but Barnes, masterly in Test cricket and phenomenal in minor cricket, was only moderately successful in county routine. He took 82 wickets in one season and 103 in the other but he was a hard bargainer on his own behalf and terms of further contract could not be agreed.

Only in Dean's left-arm swing and spin could Lancashire find professional consistency to complement the fire and energy displayed over a decade by Walter Brearley. From 1902 to 1911 Brearley swirled through cricket as a tempest of fast bowling and lively personality. A well-balanced action preceded by a short run-up enabled him to maintain pace through the longest day and extract response from the most placid pitch. All batsmen were his natural enemies, but the best batsmen and the special occasion gave him added spur. He averaged 7 wickets a match in his appearances at Lord's for the Gentlemen against the Players and for Lancashire against Yorkshire he took 125 wickets in 14 games.

Lancashire cricket could not have grown true to strain without occasional controversy bursting from opinion firmly held and uninhibitedly expressed. In 1896 Yorkshire were threatened with suspension of fixtures following an accusation of discourtesy. In 1907 heated exchanges with Middlesex developed from MacLaren's refusal to continue a match at Lord's because he insisted that spectators had damaged the pitch. In 1905 Brearley bowled full tosses at the Gloucestershire batsmen, Jessop and Board, after dressing-room differences. In 1913 a domestic quarrel became public property and resulted in fundamental administrative reorganization. At one time MacLaren indicated an intention to leave Lancashire for Hampshire and Brearley's imminent resignation was almost an annual proclamation.

Lancashire also offered more constructive ideas to cricket. They proposed the new ball at 200 runs; they sponsored changes in the championship reckoning; they recommended the Saturday start; they protested against excessive preparation of pitches and followed words with deeds at Old Trafford.

Controversy and constructive proposal continued in the Lancashire story in the period between the wars. The 1919 championship was organized on a two-day basis at Lancashire's instigation and Lancashire, under the persuasion of necessity, were innovators in the artificial drying of turf. They also maintained their policy of attracting players, promising or established, into their ranks on a basis of cricketing qualification before birth certificate.

Outstanding importations of the 1920s were Cecil Parkin, born in Durham, and the Australian E. A. McDonald. From 1919 to 1921 Parkin's county appearances were restricted by his league commitments, but his quality was rated at international level and when he became fully available to Lancashire 4 seasons brought him over 700 wickets. McDonald qualified by residence in 1924 and with his advent the most effective of all Lancashire sides was constructed. McDonald had already made his reputation as a Test match bowler for Australia and Lancashire took him as a public attraction and an immeasurable strengthening of their team.

E. A. McDonald, of Australia and Lancashire, the great fast bowler – saturnine of feature but with just a hint of warmth! Joining the county aged 32, he took 1,053 wickets between 1924 and 1931, and had a full share in 4 Championships.

McDonald was a genuinely fast bowler with a beautiful action in the classical mould. He was effective by skill and devastating under inspiration. Parkin and McDonald were together for only one full season, Parkin dropping out early in 1926, and the leading bowlers of 3 successive Championship years under the captaincy of Leonard Green were McDonald and Richard Tyldesley. McDonald burst through the first defences of opponents with his thrilling speed, though he was so masterly in control that he could turn readily to medium-pace off-breaks. Tyldesley, huge in frame, placid in disposition, challenged by alluring flight, endless patience and leg-spin of actuality or implication.

Lancashire were champions in 1926, 1927 and 1928. In these seasons McDonald took 484 wickets in Championship matches, Tyldesley 303. Under the protection of this authority, Iddon, Hopwood and Sibbles had the chance to learn a bowling craft for exploitation in years to follow. Treasure uncovered by the bowlers was safely locked away by the batsmen. Lancashire, once famous for their scoring rate, grew notorious for cautious approach. Makepeace, Hallows and Watson set the pace and a standard of impressive aggregates. Iddon and Hopwood noted the principles and Paynter, arriving later, inhaled the resolution without assuming the hairshirt.

Ernest Tyldesley, Frank Watson, Charlie Hallows, Richard Tyldesley and Harry Makepeace: household names in Lancashire's great Championship days of the 1920s.

One batsman outranged all others in ability and achievement. Ernest Tyldesley, younger brother to John by 16 years, had come into the side in 1909 but his most prolific scoring came with his maturity in which polished technique and thoughtful adaptation combined to create astonishing consistency. For Lancashire alone he scored 34,222 runs and 91 hundreds. His county aggregate exceeded 2,000 in 5 seasons and 1,000 18 times. Ernest Tyldesley's batting expressed his character in calmness and resolution and his gentle single placed wide of mid-on was as typical as his superbly timed hook. His sense of service never faltered in the ideal illustration of a professional career. He played in 5 Championship winning sides, for Lancashire were top again in 1930 and 1934.

The same satisfaction was enjoyed by Richard, the Tyldesley of a different family, and by George Duckworth, a wicket-keeper whose ability and personality added colour to the county and international cricket of his time. Pilling, the 'prince of wicket-keepers' in an earlier generation, conducted his executions in speed and stealth. Duckworth was acrobatic and emphatic of gesture and appeal, a positive contributor to aggressive spirit in the field.

Lancashire, 1934, Championship winners with this team. Back row: C. Washbrook, J. L. Hopwood, J. Iddon, F. Booth, R. Pollard, L. Parkinson and N. Oldfield; sitting: E. Paynter, E. Tyldesley, P. T. Eckersley (captain), W. H. L. Lister and G. Duckworth.

Winston Place and Cyril Washbrook launching Lancashire's innings after the Second War.

With the gradual disintegration of a formidable side Lancashire experienced mixed fortunes through the later 1930s. They found the successors to departed leaders but on a rather lower level of attainment and only Paynter, the eager batsman of indomitable spirit, wrote his name in capital letters on England pages. Paynter played 293 innings for Lancashire; two of them alone would have assured his name in memory. At Bradford in 1932 he hit 5 sixes and 17 fours in an innings of 152 against Yorkshire and at Hove in 1937 he needed only 5 hours to score 322 against Sussex, hitting 3 sixes and 39 fours.

The Second World War virtually ended Paynter's appearances and made severe inroads into the career of Cyril Washbrook who was on the fringe of international cricket by 1939. The war also imperilled Old Trafford itself. Bomb craters scarred the turf and pavilion, stands and the groundsman's house were severely damaged. There was loss of life.

Cricket returned; Old Trafford was repaired; Washbrook played for England and captained Lancashire. The return of the game drew attendance of over 70,000 to the three-day 'Victory Test' of 1945. The ground renovation fund received world-wide response and applications for county membership overflowed into a waiting list. Reconstruction of the ground proved easier than reconstruction of a powerful team. Washbrook fulfilled all expectations with a 1946 average of 74 and he, Pollard and Ikin were chosen to tour Australia. They were joined at international level by K. Cranston, a gifted player of cricket and hockey who captained Lancashire for 2 seasons, but the side as a whole lacked critical resources for championship success.

By banning the heavy roller and deliberately preparing spin-bowling wickets Lancashire helped Tattersall to 153 wickets with off-breaks in 1950 but other bowling was unduly flattered and Washbrook was left in virtual isolation of batting accomplishment. Playing visitors to Old Trafford were aggrieved. Sussex, defeated in a single day, made formal complaint that the pitch provided was unsuitable for first-class cricket.

Through the 1950s Lancashire's Championship record ranged from the praiseworthy to the disastrous, with correspondingly wide variations in public support. The administrators were called on at various times to defend their policies. Importation of players had always been challenged as a principle but the practice continued through the periods of debate. Lancashire consistently offered high reward, both financial and fraternal, for loyalty by adoption and faithful service by the native. Wages were good and benefits exceptional by the standards of the time.

Pollard and Ikin were typical in the measure of service rendered and appreciation accorded. Pollard's advance as a fast-medium right-arm bowler was delayed by the war, but he took over 1,000 wickets for Lancashire and played for England at home and overseas. Ikin was a left-handed batsman of resolute approach, a right-arm bowler of leg-break and googly and a short-leg fieldsman of exceptional skill and daring.

Pollard and Ikin were succeeded in Lancashire and England favour by J. B. Statham, whose fast bowling startled Yorkshire in their first meeting with him in 1950. Statham's talent was not advertised in his appearance. His nickname of 'whippet' specified slim build and smooth approach and no fast bowler could have seemed less menacing to the unwary. The illusion was completed with modest droop of the shoulders behind a belated bat. Most of his successes had to be twice-earned, for he was notoriously unlucky in missing the stumps or the edge of the bat and the consistency of his length and direction probably added to his own labour. He was a fast bowler of uncommonly equable temperament and inevitably he was called upon for more than his share of bowling.

Lancashire's cricket has known wide variation of fortune in recent decades and consequently wide fluctuation in self-esteem. Some miserable Championship performances have been mingled with exciting successes in the one-day forms of county cricket. Administrative enterprise in management of the cricket and of the ground facilities has brought controversial changes in outlook and practices. One-day competition brought a surge of public interest and sponsorship permitted financial benefits to players, but Lancashire have discovered the disadvantage as well as the satisfactions of the new outlook on cricket presentation. Support tends to wax and wane with competitive success. Lancashire winning a trophy have rapturous encouragement; Lancashire failing in immediate endeavour find loyalties fickle. The attenuated forms of cricket no more develop a deep-rooted interest in cricket than they develop first-class cricketers.

Last over by Brian Statham (1950–1968), Lancashire's highest-ever wicket-taker (1,816) and best-ever trier. He bowls to Brian Close.

In recent years Lancashire have not hesitated to speculate in attempt to accumulate. They acquired exciting cricketers in the West Indian Clive Lloyd, and the Indian Farokh Engineer. They have transformed Old Trafford amenities to attract commercial usage. In their relations with players and public they have moved into the market-place of modern sport, perhaps – in common with some other countries – at the expense of traditional ideals. The image of Old Trafford as a stately home of cricket, peopled by an aristocracy of cricketers, has been overlaid by a presentation directed towards survival in harsher economic environment.

Through all their periods of triumph and disappointment Lancashire have never been a negligible influence in cricket. Their great players have been among the world's greatest, Old Trafford has always been a 'desirable residence' and the county outlook has never failed to exhibit enterprise and optimism.

Lancashire in 1975, one of the county's Gillette Cup-winning years. Back row: F. C. Hayes, B. W. Reidy, B. Wood, A. Kennedy, R. M. Ratcliffe, J. Simmons, P. G. Lee and J. Abrahams; sitting: D. P. Hughes, P. Lever, D. Lloyd (captain), C. H. Lloyd and F. M. Engineer.

CAPTAINS

1866–79 E. B. Rowley
1880–91 A. N. Hornby
1892–93 A. N. Hornby and S. M. Crosfield
1894–96 A. C. MacLaren
1897–98 A. N. Hornby
1899 A. C. MacLaren and G. R. Bardswell
1900–07 A. C. MacLaren
1908–14 A. H. Hornby
1919–22 M. N. Kenyon
1923–25 J. Sharp
1926–28 L. Green
1929–35 P. T. Eckersley
1936–39 W. H. L. Lister
1946 J. A. Fallows
1947–48 K. Cranston
1949–53 N. D. Howard
1954–59 C. Washbrook
1960–61 R. W. Barber
1962 J. Blackledge
1963–64 K. Grieves
1965–67 J. B. Statham
1968–72 J. D. Bond
1973–77 D. Lloyd
1978– F. C. Hayes

HIGHEST TOTALS

For 801 v Somerset, Taunton 1895
Against 634 by Surrey, Oval 1898

LOWEST TOTALS

25 v Derby, Old Trafford 1871
22 by Glamorgan, Liverpool 1924

HIGHEST INDIVIDUAL INNINGS

For 424 A. C. MacLaren v Somerset, Taunton 1895
Against 315* T. Hayward for Surrey, Oval 1898

MOST RUNS

In a season 2,633 J. T. Tyldesley 1901
In a career 34,222 E. Tyldesley 1909–1936

MOST HUNDREDS

In a season 11 C. Hallows 1928
In a career 91 E. Tyldesley 1909–1936

INDIVIDUAL INNINGS OF 250 AND OVER

A. C. MacLaren, 424 v Somerset, Taunton 1895
J. T. Tyldesley, 250 v Notts, Trent Bridge 1905
J. T. Tyldesley, 295* v Kent, Old Trafford 1906
J. T. Tyldesley, 253 v Kent, Canterbury 1914
J. T. Tyldesley, 272 v Derby, Chesterfield 1919
F. Watson, 300* v Surrey, Old Trafford 1928
E. Tyldesley, 256 v Warwicks, Old Trafford 1930
E. Paynter, 266 v Essex, Old Trafford 1937
E. Paynter, 322 v Sussex, Hove 1937
E. Paynter, 291 v Hants, Southampton 1938
W. Place, 266* v Oxford University, Oxford 1947
C. Washbrook, 251* v Surrey, Old Trafford 1947

HUNDRED ON DEBUT

J. Ricketts, 195* v Surrey, Oval 1867
A. C. MacLaren, 108 v Sussex, Hove 1890
R. Whitehead, 131* v Notts, Old Trafford 1908

RECORD WICKET PARTNERSHIPS

1 A. C. MacLaren and R. H. Spooner, 368 v Gloucester, Liverpool 1903
2 F. Watson and E. Tyldesley, 371 v Surrey, Old Trafford 1928
3 E. Paynter and N. Oldfield, 306 v Hants, Southampton 1938
4 A. C. MacLaren and J. T. Tyldesley, 324 v Notts, Trent Bridge 1904
5 B. Wood and A. Kennedy, 249 v Warwicks, Edgbaston 1975
6 J. Iddon and H. R. W. Butterworth, 278 v Sussex, Old Trafford 1932
7 A. H. Hornby and J. Sharp, 245 v Leicester, Old Trafford 1912
8 J. Lyon and R. M. Ratcliffe, 158 v Warwicks, Old Trafford 1979
9 L. O. S. Poidevin and A. Kermode, 142 v Sussex, Eastbourne 1907
10 J. Briggs and R. Pilling, 173 v Surrey, Liverpool 1885

MOST WICKETS

In a match 17–91 H. Dean v Yorks, Liverpool 1913
In a season 198 E. A. McDonald 1925
In a career 1,816 J. B. Statham 1950–1968

ALL 10 WICKETS IN AN INNINGS

W. Hickton v Hampshire, Old Trafford 1870
J. Briggs v Worcester, Old Trafford 1900
R. Berry v Worcester, Blackpool 1953

HAT-TRICKS

R. G. Barlow, E. A. McDonald 3
K. Higgs, J. B. Statham 2 (3 in all matches)
A. Mold, R. Pollard, J. Tyldesley 2
W. Brearley, J. Bullough, J. Crossland, W. R. Gregson, J. T. Ikin, A. Kermode, P. Lever, F. W. Moore, J. Simmons, R. Tattersall, R. K. Tyldesley, R. Whitehead, L. L. Wilkinson 1 each

WICKET-KEEPING – MOST DISMISSALS

In an innings 7 W. Farrimond
In a match 9 G. Clayton
In a season 97 G. Duckworth 1928
In a career 921 G. Duckworth 1923–1938

COUNTY CAPS AWARDED SINCE 1946

1946 T. L. Brierley, G. A. Edrich, J. A. Fallows, J. T. Ikin, B. P. King, E. Price, A. Wharton
1947 K. Cranston, R. G. Garlick, B. J. Howard
1948 E. H. Edrich, N. D. Howard
1949 P. Greenwood, K. Grieves
1950 A. T. Barlow, R. Berry, M. J. Hilton, J. B. Statham, R. Tattersall
1951 A. Wilson
1952 J. G. Lomax
1953 F. D. Parr
1956 J. Dyson, T. Greenhough, J. Jordan, C. S. Smith
1958 R. W. Barber, P. T. Marner, G. Pullar
1959 K. Higgs
1960 G. Clayton
1961 J. D. Bond, B. J. Booth, R. Collins
1962 J. F. Blackledge, D. M. Green, C. Hilton
1963 R. Bennett
1964 S. Ramadhin
1965 K. Goodwin, P. Lever, H. Pilling
1966 D. R. Worsley
1967 G. Atkinson, J. Savage
1968 F. M. Engineer, D. Lloyd, K. Shuttleworth, B. Wood
1969 C. H. Lloyd, J. Sullivan
1970 D. P. Hughes
1971 J. Simmons, K. L. Snellgrove
1972 F. C. Hayes, P. G. Lee
1975 A. Kennedy, J. Lyon
1976 R. M. Ratcliffe

Leicestershire

E. E. SNOW

Foundation 1873
Colours Dark Green and Scarlet
Badge Gold Running Fox on Green Ground
Champions 1975

Leicestershire is one of the earliest of counties to have become interested in cricket. The probable reasons for this are interesting to consider. The game began as a recreation for rural and town craftsmen, and in Leicester and surrounding villages artisans did not work in organized factories, but were engaged on hosiery piece-work undertaken in their own homes in their own time. Thus, as in neighbouring Nottingham and Sheffield, they were able to find the time to watch and play cricket. Also, Leicestershire is the foxhunting county *par excellence*, and the gentry either residing in the county or visiting it for the hunting must have helped to spread the game. Then there was the influence of the 9th Earl of Winchilsea, one of the chief founders of MCC, who lived at Burley-on-the-Hill, near Oakham, only a few miles over the border. The first reference to cricket in the county is in 1744 when a game took place at Barrow-on-Soar. By the 1780s, the Leicester teams were, for all intents and purposes, representative of the county, and met Nottinghamshire on several occasions. In 1791, Leicestershire played MCC for the first time, when at Burley a strong visiting XI won by an innings and 41 runs.

St Margaret's Pasture is the first known Leicester ground (it is still used as a recreation ground), but this was very inadequate and a great step forward was reached in 1825, when the Wharf Street ground was opened. For the next 35 years some of the principal matches in England were staged on this ground. The first and most important representative match took place in 1836, when the South beat the North by 218 runs; this game was made memorable by the performance of Alfred Mynn, who scored 21 and 125 undefeated in both innings, but was so badly battered by the fast bowling that it was feared for a time that his right leg would have to be amputated.

In this era Leicestershire cricket was fortunate in having the services of some of the leading amateur players of the day; amongst these were T. C. Goodrich, a very good slow bowler, the Rev R. T. King, the greatest of all 'points' and a first-class bat, the Rev E. Elmhirst, the best amateur wicket-keeper of his day, the Rev A. Payne and his twin brother A.F., the Rev J. Bradshaw and R. Cheslyn. The number of clergy may seem large, but is not surprising in a county famous for its sporting parsons. Probably the most prominent Leicestershire professional during this period was Dakin who played for the Players at Lord's in 1851. The end of this period, in 1860, was notable for the 1st performance for Leicestershire of R. A. H. Mitchell at the age of 17; he captained Oxford University for 3 years, and was the greatest amateur batsman in England until W. G. Grace came to power. Unfortunately for Leicestershire, Mitchell became a master at Eton in 1866, and subsequently made but few appearances in first-class cricket.

Following the closure of the Wharf Street ground in 1860, owing to building operations, there was a sad decline in Leicestershire cricket, which was all the more regrettable as this period was a critical one in the development of county cricket. For a time the only matches arranged took place on private grounds in the county, and later on at Victoria Park in Leicester. The notable touring sides such as All-England, United All-England and the United South of England XIs played matches in the district against the usual odds. In spite of the lack of proper headquarters, the Leicestershire Cricket Association was formed in 1873, mainly through the efforts of Charles Marriott and Edward Holmes, and home and away matches were arranged with MCC, both of which Leicestershire won. In 1874 XXII of the district played All-England at Victoria Park, but by this time the importance of these touring sides was declining; in the same year the county beat MCC at Victoria Park thanks to the bowling of F. Randon and good batting by C. Marriott, R. A. H. Mitchell and Panter. In 1875, 2 matches were arranged with Lancashire, the home game being drawn and the return at Manchester lost. At Lord's MCC again lost, this time by 66 runs.

After the keenness shown in previous years, the almost blank season of 1877 was disappointing, but the knowledge that a fine new ground was being laid out at Aylestone was comforting to the loyal supporters of the game. The Grace Road ground of 12 acres was opened in 1878, and new life given to the game in the district. In July the Australians played Leicestershire who were the 1st county to make arrangements with them and guarantee a lump sum for playing. In 1879, the county club was reformed on the lines we know today, and soon figured prominently in the second-class championship. C. Marriott was an outstanding batsman and one of the most prominent members of the club at this time; Rylott and Parnham were two more than useful left-handed bowlers who also appeared on many occasions for MCC. By this time the county club had adopted the running fox as its badge, and the colours of green and scarlet – thus combining green fields with hunting 'pink'.

The season of 1888 was outstanding as the Australians were beaten for the 1st time in the club's history, and Leicestershire finished at the top of the second-class counties. C. E. de Trafford, who was a fast-footed hitter, made his debut in this year and captained the side from 1890 to 1906 inclusive; he was largely responsible for Leicestershire's promotion to the ranks of the first-class counties in 1895, although the games played in 1894 were ranked as first-class. At this time the county was fortunate to have a good bowling side in which Pougher and Woodcock were particularly outstanding. Pougher was top of the English bowling averages in 1894, and will always be remembered for his sensational bowling for MCC against the Australians in 1896, when he and J. T. Hearne dismissed the tourists for 18, Pougher taking 5 wickets for no runs. He bowled medium-pace off-breaks with an occasional leg-break; also a useful bat, he was the first Leicestershire player to score 1,000 runs in one season. The home game against Sussex in 1900 was one of the most remarkable ever played, for, in the course of 3 full days' cricket, 1,295 runs were scored and only 16 wickets lowered. Leicestershire declared at 609 for 8 wickets, and Sussex replied with 686 for 8, Ranjitsinhji scoring 275.

These first few years had brought only moderate support and success, but the bold move of laying out a new ground nearer the centre of Leicester was undertaken, and the Aylestone Road ground was opened in 1901. In 1902 (although with only one win and several draws), from the end of May until well into July, Leicestershire were at the head of the Championship table, but unfortunately fell to below halfway; in 1904, the 7th position was reached and in the next year even better results were obtained, when the side finished 5th in the table.

The attractive displays of the side during these years – the first Golden Age of Leicestershire cricket – were not equalled until some 70 years later. C. E. de Trafford, V. F. S. Crawford (who had formerly played for Surrey under a residential qualification), Jayes and Gill were hitters of character and quality, Knight and J. H. King were first-class batsmen with orthodox styles, and C. J. B. Wood always provided a solid foundation. Wood carried his bat through the innings on 17 occasions, a record he shared with W. G. Grace, and in 1911 against Yorkshire carried his bat through the 2 innings for 107 and 117, a feat without parallel in first-class cricket. Crawford, one of the hardest hitters of all time, was a member of a famous cricketing family; his brothers were J.N., who played for England and Surrey, and R.T. who also played for his native county, Leicestershire. Knight wrote a fine book *The Complete Cricketer*, published in 1906; this effort was almost entirely his own work, and must be considered a rarity for a professional, particularly of this era. A rare character, it is said he used to read Greek and Latin during the intervals, and that, before batting, he always prayed for divine aid and guidance at the wicket. He and J. H. King played for England against Australia. King was a good all-round left-hand player, and for the Players v Gentlemen at Lord's in 1904, scored a hundred in each innings, although only taking part in the game as a substitute. With his slow accurate bowling he took 8 wickets for 17 runs against Yorkshire at Leicester in 1911, including 7 for no runs in 20 balls. He maintained his form for many years and at the age of 52 scored 205 v Hampshire; he also performed the 'double' in 1912.

There were also other useful batsmen such as Whitehead and Coe, the latter making the club's highest individual score, 252 not out against Northamptonshire in 1914. Coe became the official scorer for the club in 1931 and continued until the season of 1950. W. W. Odell was an amateur fastish-medium bowler with swing, who appeared many times for the Gentlemen against the Players. Jayes, an uncle of Astill, was a fine fast bowler, and would have made a big name for himself had he not suffered from ill health. He was chosen to play for England v Australia at Lord's in 1909, but for some unaccountable reason was omitted at the last minute, and England took the field on a hard wicket without a fast bowler. In 1906, Leicestershire scored 701 for 4 wickets against Worcestershire, with Whitehead and Wood making 380 for the 1st wicket, which until 1979 remained the highest stand for any wicket by Leicestershire. A total of 1,425 runs was scored in this match for the loss of only 16 wickets, which aggregate had only been exceeded twice previously in first-class cricket in England. In 1907 Sir Arthur Hazlerigg took over the captaincy and Leicestershire cricket owed much to his devotion and leadership. When the season of 1908 opened with a match against Warwickshire at Leicester, the experiment was made of starting play on a Saturday, a step which was generally adopted in county cricket in later years. J. Shields took over the captaincy in 1911, when only one game was won and eighteen lost. However, Jayes only played twice and V. F. S. Crawford had left the country for Ceylon where he became a tea planter and one of the most successful batsmen in Ceylon's history. Astill's form suffered a temporary set-back and the brunt of the bowling was borne by King and W. Shipman, a fast bowler.

George Geary, a sharp medium-pacer of subtle skills and tireless stamina gave equally high value, in turn, to Leicestershire, to England (as a member of two Ashes-winning sides), and to Charterhouse. Over a span of 13 post-war summers he coached many fine cricketers there – with Peter May topping the list.

The last years before the outbreak of the First World War saw the development of Astill and Geary, who later became two of the most outstanding figures in the game. Astill was one of the greatest players never to be chosen to play against Australia, although he played for England against South Africa and the West Indies, and altogether in first-class games scored 22,731 runs and took 2,432 wickets, doing the double 9 times. Geary appeared for England on many occasions, against Australia and South Africa, and his totals in first-class cricket were 13,504 runs and 2,063 wickets. Fortunately, only W. W. Odell among Leicestershire players was killed in the First World War, although W. N. Riley lost a leg; but new blood was sadly needed when play was resumed in 1919. However, under the successive leadership of A. T. Sharp, Major G. H. S. Fowke and E. W. Dawson, new players developed. Skelding, the fastest English bowler of his time, who later became a famous and well-loved umpire, Alan Shipman (brother of W.) and Haydon Smith supplied the speed, Geary with his great pace off the wicket and deadly going-away ball was always dangerous and Astill supplied subtle spin and flight. Further variety was added by Snary, one of the most accurate bowlers of his generation (conceding only 29 runs for every 100 balls bowled), and the left-handed Bale. Sidwell, probably the best Leicestershire wicket-keeper of all time, was consistent, and also scored many runs. A. T. Sharp was in splendid form in the early years after the First War, and was one of the best amateur bats in the country, but it was a pity he could not spare more time for county cricket. Major Fowke was 41 years old when he took over the captaincy in 1922, but for the next 3 years never spared himself. His charming personality and staunch determination helped to build up a very useful side. Following the successful season of 1927, when the side finished 7th, Dawson, Astill and Geary were chosen for the MCC South African tour; this is the largest representation Leicestershire ever had on MCC touring sides.

An extraordinary incident took place in a minor-counties match with Staffordshire at Aylestone Road in 1928; the visitors made no attempt to take the first-innings lead, so G. B. F. Rudd, the 2nd XI captain, proceeded to bowl an over which yielded 14 wides, and as 47 byes were also registered, Staffordshire were compelled to take the lead. S. F. Barnes was one of the batsmen concerned in the incident. This state of affairs helped to secure an alteration to the percentage system in the County and Minor Counties Championships. In 1932, the captaincy was given to C. W. C. Packe, but as he was unable to play regularly, it was shared by no fewer than 6 amateurs during the season. H. A. Smith, Snary and Marlow had by now graduated permanently from the Minor Counties side to become very useful bowlers indeed. In 1933, the side occupied the bottom place alone for the first time, although in 1898 the position had been shared with Somerset, and in 1903 with Hampshire. Curiously enough, bowling was the chief weakness, and probably this was due to Geary's not being quite fit. Armstrong, consistent as ever, totalled 2,113 and Berry 1,931 runs, averaging 43 and 37 respectively. Corrall was badly injured in the Lancashire match, when he sustained a fractured skull, and Sidwell returned to keep wicket after a year's retirement. A welcome improvement was made in 1934 thanks to good bowling by Smith, Astill, Marlow and Shipman. Armstrong had another splendid season with an average of 42·52 for 1,701 runs. A. G. Hazlerigg (now Lord Hazlerigg) had accepted the captaincy following the resignation of Dawson, and proved a popular and successful leader. W. K. Beisiegel took over later in the season, and had the satisfaction of leading the side to victory over Yorkshire. Corrall recovered from his accident, and returned to keep wicket as well as ever.

The 1935 season was outstanding, and Leicestershire reached the 6th position in the table, and 11 matches were won – then a record in the club's history. Not a little of the credit was due to the captaincy of Astill, who was the first professional to be appointed to the regular captaincy of any county side this century. Another reason for the side's success was the bowling partnership of Geary and Smith: they bowled unchanged for many innings. C. S. Dempster, the great New Zealand batsman, who was a member of Sir Julien Cahn's team and probably the best batsman ever to play for the county, captained the side in 1936, 1937 and 1938: his brilliant batting and fielding were an inspiration to the team. No one in the 1930s hit the ball harder on the off-side, his footwork to slow bowling being extremely quick, and his fielding was a joy to witness. At the end of 1938, George Geary severed his connexion with Leicestershire, when he was appointed coach to Charterhouse School. In what was to prove to be the last season before the Second World War, Leicestershire had a disastrous time, and the side sadly lacked experienced players. One of the brightest features of the season was the magnificent wicket-keeping of 19-year-old Dawkes, who left the county after the Second War to join Derbyshire.

When the war finished, the club's lease was not renewed as the electricity generating station required more land for extensions, and soon two huge cooling towers were built on the old practice end. Although this ground had been progressively improved for some years before the war, it had acquired a bad reputation because of the nuisance caused by smuts dropping from the adjoining chimneys. George Headley is reputed to have tasted them under the impression that they were black snow. So a hunt for a new home took place, and eventually the Leicester Education Committee offered the use of the old Grace Road ground when it was not required by the school to whom it belonged. This restricted use proved a severe handicap to the club who were not able to provide good amenities for the players or public. As no amateur was available, Berry was appointed captain in 1946 – the first professional captain of the county since Astill in 1935. Although lacking good fast bowlers, the side was useful; Berry (the only Leicestershire player to score over 30,000 runs in first-class cricket), Tompkin, Prentice and Watson (G.S.) batted well, but the real mainstay of the side were Jackson and Walsh, two Australian all-rounders who had appeared occasionally before the war when members of Sir Julien Cahn's team. Jackson only performed the double once, in 1955, but in 3 other years only fell short by two or three wickets. Walsh, one of the finest left-handed googly bowlers of all time, and a hard hitter, obtained the double in 1952.

Leicestershire 1936, the year that C. S. Dempster, the great New Zealand batsman took over the captaincy from W. E. Astill, the first professional regularly to captain a county side this century: back row: P. Corrall, N. F. Armstrong, F. T. Prentice, S. Coe (scorer), G. S. Watson, A. W. Shipman and H. C. Graham; front row: H. A. Smith, W. E. Astill, C. S. Dempster (captain), G. Geary and L. G. Berry.

C. H. Palmer came to Leicestershire from Worcestershire in 1950 and was appointed captain and secretary for the next seven years. He began the task of rebuilding Leicestershire cricket. In 1952, the side finished 6th in the table. In the following year, it reached joint 3rd, and in fact, in late August, was top for a short time; but, erratic as ever, Leicestershire slumped to 16th next season. But again in 1955 they rose to 6th place with very much the same side, although M. J. K. Smith (later transferred to Warwickshire and to play for England at cricket and rugby football), Hallam, Spencer and Boshier were beginning their first-class careers. The season of 1956 had a tragic ending, for Tompkin, who had a poor season, died in September at the early age of 37; a fine driver, particularly of fast bowling, he had toured Pakistan with MCC in 1955–56. Jackson left at the end of the season and Walsh retired from first-class cricket, but later became coach and 2nd XI captain. During this period Palmer had given yeoman service with his stylish batting and steady medium-pace bowling; he played once for England v West Indies and scored two distinguished hundreds for the Gentlemen at Lord's. His outstanding bowling performance was a sensational 8 wickets for 7 runs against Surrey at Grace Road in 1955 – and he only put himself on to bowl to allow a change of ends!

Palmer retired at the end of 1957, but fortunately the club was able to engage W. Watson, the former Yorkshire player, as captain for 1958. This appointment appeared to give this great batsman a new lease of life: before he retired at the end of 1962 he had again represented England both at home and abroad and was undoubtedly the best left-handed batsman in England, at the age of 42. He is one of the few men who have represented their country at cricket and association football. Watson was vice-captain of the MCC team which toured New Zealand in 1961 and was appointed a Test selector in 1962.

However, the erratic course continued in spite of some fine individual performances, chiefly by Watson and Hallam with the bat and by Boshier, Savage and Spencer, who in 1961 each took over 100 wickets. The side, however, was unbalanced as there was not a good left-handed bowler available. Following the improved season of 1961, it was again disappointing to find the county, under the new leadership of the Cambridge blue, D.

After a notable career with Surrey and England as left-arm bowler and magnificent close fielder, Tony Lock surprised the cricket world by inspiring first Leicestershire and then Western Australia as their captain.

Kirby, finishing bottom of the table in 1962. Apart from fine batting by Watson and Hallam, the brightest feature of the season was the form shown by J. Van Geloven, who, for the first time in his career performed the double.

Hallam was the obvious successor when Kirby resigned the captaincy after only one season but during his first spell of 3 years' leadership success still eluded the side. Leicestershire, like all small counties, have to import established players and 1965 saw the advent of Tony Lock but, owing to prior league engagements, he was only able to appear in 8 mid-week games. This was also the season in which Roger Tolchard made his debut and he was destined to play an important part in Leicestershire's future; he was to exceed the Leicestershire wicket-keepers' record – previously held by Sidwell – in 1978.

The year 1966 was probably the first turning point in the club's fortunes for not only did Lock's captaincy bring a more determined and confident approach which generated greater success but, at long last, the Grace Road ground belonged to the club. A splendid new pavilion was built and this, and other improvements, made the amenities worthy of a first-class club. Next season the side reached the highest position – equal 2nd with Kent – that Leicestershire had held in the first-class history of the club. On 4 July they went to the top of the table for the 1st time since 1953. Lock's enthusiastic example inspired the side, which won 10 games; he took 128 wickets which even improved on his previous season's total of 109. Birkenshaw also did well with 111; 5 batsmen reached their 1,000 runs and no side found them easy to beat. Unfortunately, Lock did not return from Australia in 1968 and, at short notice, Hallam took over once again but the side slipped down to ninth position.

If 1966 had been a turning point for the club the season of 1969 was an even greater milestone. Michael Turner, who had been Secretary since 1960, was appointed Secretary-Manager and developed into one of the ablest and most imaginative administrators in the game. His cheerful personality has been largely responsible for attracting star players to the county and, in 1969, he persuaded Ray Illingworth to join Leicestershire. This partnership proved very successful for the next 9 years. Illingworth was one of the greatest leaders and tacticians of modern times and he had great triumphs as captain of England and Leicestershire. Unfortunately for the county he missed many games through Test calls whilst Knight was absent for 7 games so that the final position of 14th in 1969 was disappointing. The following season was also unrewarding, mainly due to Illingworth and McKenzie, who had also joined Leicestershire in 1969, being absent for representative games and Knight's failure to return from Australia.

The long awaited improvement arrived in 1971 when 6 wins and only 2 defeats took the side to 5th position in the Championship whilst in the John Player League the side was 4th. The Rhodesian, Brian Davison, scored the fastest hundred in Leicestershire's annals – 100 in 68 minutes – and this gained him the coveted Lawrence Trophy (*qv*).

The last 6 years of Illingworth's leadership were the real Golden Age of Leicestershire cricket. During this period the club's successes both on the field and financially were unrivalled by any other county. The first moment of triumph came in 1972 when, at Lord's, Leicestershire won their 1st major trophy by beating Yorkshire in the Benson & Hedges Cup Final. They also finished 6th in the Championship and were runners-up in the John Player League. Birkenshaw and Tolchard deserved their inclusion in MCC's party which toured India and Pakistan. The glorious summer of 1973 was comparatively disappointing, but Illingworth only appeared in 8 Championship matches. Most prominent amongst the batsmen was Davison who has been consistently brilliant over several seasons and now stands second to C. S. Dempster in the Leicestershire career batting averages. For the first time Illingworth, no longer captain of England, was ever-present in 1974 and the season produced great results. Winners of the John Player League, finalists in the Benson & Hedges Cup, fourth in the Championship and quarter-finalists in the Gillette Cup. This is the only trophy not yet won and it is rather ironic as this competition followed the pattern of the Midland KO Cup inaugurated by Leicestershire in 1962. The batting was very strong and the brunt of the bowling was borne by McKenzie, Illingworth, Birkenshaw and the newcomer, McVicker.

Although the 3 previous seasons had been vintage years there can be no doubt that 1975 was the greatest in the club's long history; winners of the Benson & Hedges Cup in July, the Under-25 Competition in August followed by the greatest prize of all, the County Championship for the 1st time. To complete this triumphal season the Australians were beaten for the 1st time since 1888. Magnificent cricket fit to match the glorious weather was the result of all-round team effort under the superb leadership of Illingworth. The side batted down to the last man. Davison had a splendid season; Dudleston, Steele and Balderstone each scored over 1,000 runs, whilst Illingworth just missed by 3 and Tolchard by 27. Match-saving innings also came from McVicker and McKenzie at crucial moments. By comparison the bowling was steady but with only moderate averages. Two young players made their debut in 1975, P. B. Clift, the Rhodesian all-rounder, and D. I. Gower, whose progress was phenomenal; before the age of 22 he had played in 12 Tests and gained almost every possible honour.

No trophies were won in 1976 but to be 4th in the Championship, joint runners-up in the John Player League and quarter-finalists in the Benson & Hedges Cup was no mean feat. Davison was again in great form but Balderstone, who played in 2 Tests against the West Indies, was the only other to reach 1,000. The bowling was evenly shared by Clift, Higgs, Balderstone, McVicker, P. Booth and Birkenshaw. Tolchard again received well-deserved recognition when he toured India, Sri Lanka and Australia to play in 4 Tests in India – as a batsman and excellent fieldsman. Next season, 1977, was mainly cold and wet and the side suffered through injuries to Clift, Dudleston, Gower and Tolchard at critical periods, but the John Player League was again won, 5th place achieved in the Championship and a semi-final place obtained in the Gillette Cup. Ray Illingworth's benefit fund pro-

Leicestershire's team in 1975, the best year in their history, when they won both the County Championship and the Benson & Hedges Cup. Back row: R. W. Tolchard, B. Dudleston, D. I. Gower, J. C. Balderstone, B. F. Davison and J. F. Steele; sitting: J. Birkenshaw, K. Higgs, R. Illingworth (captain), G. D. McKenzie and N. M. McVicker.

duced a Leicestershire record of over £38,000.

Leicestershire celebrated, in 1978, their Centenary since the club was reformed. The year, like the weather, was disappointing although the side finished equal top on points in the John Player League. David Gower made his debut in Test Cricket with great success, and it was no surprise when he was chosen for the England tour of Australia in 1978–79. He headed the England Test averages and scored more runs in the Tests than any player on either side. Most important of all was the attractive stroke play he invariably produced together with his magnificent fielding. Tolchard also went as reserve wicket-keeper and showed such fine form with the bat that he would probably have challenged for a place in the later Tests had he not suffered a serious face injury at Newcastle which prevented him from playing again on the tour.

Fortunately the Centenary Appeal Fund was very successful and enabled a large rebuilding programme to be undertaken. This included a new dining room, enlarged Members' Long Room and indoor school; these and other planned improvements should result in representative games being staged at Grace Road in the next few years. The playing future augurs well as the many young players such as Briers, Taylor, P. Booth, Parsons and Schepens should mature to support Gower and the older established men.

CAPTAINS

1879–85	C. Marriott
1886–89	H. T. Arnall-Thompson
1890–1906	C. E. de Trafford
1907–10	Sir A. Hazlerigg
1911–13	J. Shields
1914–20	C. J. B. Wood
1921	A. T. Sharp
1922–27	G. H. S. Fowke
1928–29	E. W. Dawson
1930	J. A. F. M. P. de Lisle
1931–33	E. W. Dawson
1934	A. G. Hazlerigg
1935	W. E. Astill
1936–38	C. S. Dempster
1939	M. St. J. Packe
1946–48	G. L. Berry
1949	S. J. Symington
1950–57	C. H. Palmer
1958–61	W. Watson
1962	D. Kirby
1963–65	M. R. Hallam
1966–67	G. A. R. Lock
1968	M. R. Hallam
1969–78	R. Illingworth
1979	K. Higgs

HIGHEST TOTALS

For 701–4D v Worcester, Worcester 1906
Against 739–7D by Notts, Trent Bridge 1903

LOWEST TOTALS

For 25 v Kent, Leicester 1912
Against 24 by Glamorgan, Leicester 1971

HIGHEST INDIVIDUAL INNINGS

For S. Coe, 252* v Northants, Leicester 1914
Against G. H. Hirst, 341 for Yorks, Leicester 1905

MOST RUNS

In a season 2,446 G. L. Berry 1937
In a career 30,143 G. L. Berry 1924–1951

MOST HUNDREDS

In a season 7 G. L. Berry 1937
W. Watson 1959
In a career 45 G. L. Berry 1924–1951

INDIVIDUAL INNINGS OF 250 AND OVER

S. Coe 252* v Northants, Leicester 1914

HUNDRED ON DEBUT

No instance

RECORD WICKET PARTNERSHIPS

1 B. Dudleston and J. F. Steele, 390 v Derby, Leicester 1979
2 W. Watson and A. Wharton, 287 v Lancs, Leicester 1961
3 W. Watson and A. Wharton, 316* v Somerset, Taunton 1961
4 C. S. Dempster and G. S. Watson, 270 v Yorks, Hull 1937
5 N. E. Briers and R. W. Tolchard, 233 v Somerset, Leicester 1979
6 A. T. Sharp and G. H. S. Fowke, 262 v Derby, Chesterfield 1911
7 B. Dudleston and J. Birkenshaw, 206 v Kent, Canterbury 1969
8 M. R. Hallam and C. T. Spencer, 164 v Essex, Leicester 1964
9 W. W. Odell and R. T. Crawford, 160 v Worcester, Leicester 1902
10 R. Illingworth and K. Higgs, 228 v Northants, Leicester 1977

MOST WICKETS

In a match 16–96 G. Geary v Glamorgan, Pontypridd 1929
In a season 170 J. E. Walsh 1948
In a career 2,130 W. E. Astill 1906–1939

ALL 10 WICKETS IN AN INNINGS

G. Geary v Glamorgan, Pontypridd 1929

HAT-TRICKS

J. Birkenshaw 2
V. E. Jackson 2
T. Jayes 2
J. H. King 2
G. A. R. Lock 1 (4 in all matches)
W. E. Benskin, K. Higgs, W. W. Odell 1 (2 in all matches)
J. C. Balderstone, P. B. Clift, J. Cotton, G. Geary, R. Illingworth, V. S. Munden, J. Savage, W. Shipman, K. Shuttleworth, J. E. Walsh 1 each

WICKET-KEEPING – MOST DISMISSALS

In an innings 6 P. Corrall (2)
R. W. Tolchard
In a match 10 P. Corrall
In a season 85 J. Firth 1952
In a career 726 R. W. Tolchard 1965–1979

COUNTY CAPS AWARDED SINCE 1946

1946	V. E. Jackson, G. Lester, M. Tompkin, J. E. Walsh
1949	G. Evans, S. J. Symington
1950	C. H. Palmer
1951	J. Firth, V. S. Munden, G. A. Smithson
1952	C. T. Spencer
1953	T. J. Goodwin
1954	M. R. Hallam
1955	M. J. K. Smith
1958	B. S. Boshier, A. C. Revill, J. Savage, W. Watson
1959	J. Van Geloven
1960	H. D. Bird
1961	L. R. Gardner, R. Julien, A. Wharton
1962	D. Kirby
1963	S. Jayasinghe, C. C. Inman
1964	B. J. Booth
1965	J. Birkenshaw, J. Cotton, G. A. R. Lock, P. T. Marner
1966	M. E. J. C. Norman, R. W. Tolchard
1968	B. R. Knight
1969	B. Dudleston, R. Illingworth, G. D. McKenzie
1971	B. F. Davison, J. F. Steele
1972	K. Higgs
1973	J. C. Balderstone
1974	N. M. McVicker
1976	P. Booth, P. B. Clift
1977	D. I. Gower, K. Shuttleworth, A. Ward

Middlesex

MICHAEL MELFORD

Foundation 1864
Colours Blue
Badge Three Seaxes
Champions 1866, 1903, 1920, 1921, 1947, 1949 (=), 1976, 1977 (=)

Records exist of a side bearing the name of Middlesex playing in 1850, but it was not until 2 February 1864 that the county club was formed at a meeting at the London Tavern in Bishopsgate. Preliminary work had already been done by Messrs John and V. E. Walker, C. Gordon, C. Hillyard and W. Nicholson, who had rented a ground in Islington from a Mr Norris who ran a hotel in the Cattle Market. From this group, which reconnoitred the ground one afternoon in November 1863, came Middlesex's first administrators, for John Walker and Gordon became vice-presidents, Nicholson the honorary treasurer, Hillyard the first honorary secretary and the brothers Walker the joint captains.

The service of the numerous Walker brothers to Middlesex cricket was to continue until 1922 when R.D. died at the age of 80. He was then President and his death ended a family association with a cricket club which can have had few parallels. V.E. had been captain until 1872, and honorary secretary as well for a time. He was succeeded as captain for 12 seasons by I.D., who was to die much lamented in his early 50s. In 1898 V.E., after a spell as treasurer, succeeded the Earl of Stafford as President, an office to which R.D. succeeded in 1906 when his brother died. Thus, when Middlesex won the Championship in 1920, their President was a man who had played for them in 1866 when they were first considered Champions by the somewhat controversial reckoning of the time and who, with 3 of his brothers, had played in the first match which the club ever played, in June 1864.

Most of the outstanding feats in the early records of Middlesex cricket were performed by the Walkers of Harrow and Southgate, and V.E. was responsible for some of the most remarkable. He was considered the greatest amateur lob bowler of his day, operating round the wicket with a measure of leg-spin, and he fielded superbly to his own bowling.

A record which still stands was set up in the 1st season of 1864, for in their 4th match Middlesex were bowled out by MCC at Lord's for 20. However, on the cricketing side, the club's first years were generally successful. The 1st 2 matches against Bucks and Sussex were won, and both score-cards show the name of Hearne which was destined to appear many times in Middlesex sides in the next seventy years. Tom Hearne played for Bucks in the first match but a week later made 50 for Middlesex and shared the Sussex wickets with V. E. Walker. These 2 great all-rounders were largely responsible for the successes of 1866.

Off the field the club prospered less and, after disagreements with the landlord, Middlesex gave up the ground at Islington after the season of 1868. They turned down repeated offers by MCC to accommodate them at Lord's, though the finances were in need of every possible help, and went without a ground in 1869. For 1870 they hired the running ground at Lillie Bridge, West Brompton, but the surface there proved unsuitable for cricket even before a dry summer made it worse. For three years Middlesex played just 2 matches a year against Surrey and it was only in 1871 that Lillie Bridge was used for the home match. At a General Meeting earlier in that year it had been suggested that the interest in London was not big enough to justify the existence of a 3rd first-class club beside MCC and Surrey and a meeting attended by only 13 members decided to carry on only by one vote. That year, however, there was an increase in membership and ambitions grew. With more gate money than could be taken at the distant West Brompton ground, more good professional talent could be engaged, though the emphasis here was on quality, for Middlesex until the 1930s was predominantly amateur. Until 1900 it was rare for more than 3 professionals to be in the side.

In 1872, therefore, Middlesex moved to Prince's in Hans Place, Kensington. This brought solvency and, resisting another proposal to move again to Alexandra Park and another invitation from MCC in 1875, Middlesex settled down at Prince's until the end of the 1876 season. Then, after a disagreement with Messrs Prince, an Extraordinary General Meeting considered a new invitation from Mr. Henry Perkins, secretary of MCC. There was still strong opposition from the captain, I. D. Walker, but he eventually gave way. His opposition stemmed from doubts about the financial wisdom of the move and not from any apprehension about the fiery Lord's pitches, for there and elsewhere both he and R.D. scorned the use of pads.

MCC's keenness for Middlesex to play at Lord's was doubtless prompted by the fact that there were now not enough big matches outside county cricket to keep the ground in regular and profitable use. At first Middlesex paid nothing, but in 1885 they began to make donations to MCC and in 1899 a firm financial arrangement was reached.

In the 1880s the lack of bowling was acute but the batting was amateur batting at its grandest, consisting as it did of such as I. D. Walker, A. J. Webbe, the Lytteltons, the Studds, the Fords, Sir Timothy O'Brien and A. E. Stoddart. Nor was there any sign of decline as Middlesex entered the 1890s. The problem, inevitable with so many amateurs, of not being able to field a regular side remained; and Middlesex's record on paper suffered perhaps from the fact that they met only the stronger counties – Kent, Surrey, Gloucestershire, Notts and Yorkshire were played twice each until 1888 when Lancashire were added, Sussex and Somerset following 3 years later. But the younger generation of Stoddart, F. G. J. Ford and O'Brien were even more prolific than their seniors. Stoddart played first in 1885 at the age of 22 and made his 1st hundred for Middlesex at Gravesend in 1886, the year of his 485 for Hampstead against the Stoics. He was absent in Australia in 1888 as a member of the British rugby touring team, taking over the captaincy after R. L. Seddon's tragic death through drowning in the Hunter River. But he returned and in 1893 made a hundred in each innings against Notts, the 1st time this feat had been performed at Lord's since Lambert had done it in 1817. Like O'Brien, he was a powerful driver, in some contrast, perhaps, to the more willowy Ford whose timing and swing of the bat earned the same lyrical eulogies as those of Frank Woolley a generation or two later.

A. J. Webbe, whose span of service to Middlesex as player, captain, honorary secretary and president stretched from 1875 to 1926.

Though Stoddart captained England in Australia in 1894–95 and again 3 years later, the Middlesex captain, succeeding I. D. Walker in 1885, was A. J. Webbe whose heyday as a batsman was 1887. In August of that year, at the age of 32, he made 192 and 243 against Kent and Yorkshire respectively, carrying his bat through the innings in each case. He continued as an inspiring captain until 1898 and in 1900 became honorary secretary. He had first played for Middlesex in 1875. He was secretary until after the First World War, President from 1922 to 1936, retiring 61 years after he had first played for Middlesex.

In the later years of Webbe's captaincy there were two important developments. One was the increased stature of P. F. Warner who had played a few not very productive innings for Middlesex during his 3 years at Oxford. Now he played throughout the 1897 season and made 916 runs. The other was the gradual improvement in the bowling which had its origin in the arrival in 1888 of J. T. Hearne. Born in Bucks, he had been a professional bowler at a private school in Middlesex and was not an instant success. But by 1891 he was playing the prodigious part in Middlesex affairs which he was to sustain, sometimes with little support, until 1914. With his easy action, immaculate command of length and ability to move the ball either way off the pitch at medium pace, he took over 3,000 wickets in that period. His best year was 1896 when he took 118 wickets for Middlesex and 257 in all. By then, however, he was not quite alone, for J. T. Rawlin had established himself rather late in life – he was 31 when he first played for Middlesex in 1889 – as a bowler of above medium pace able to swing the ball more than was customary at the time. When they were joined by the redoubtable Albert Trott, Middlesex's bowling carried a new menace.

Trott had played with success for Australia against Stoddart's team of 1894–95, but he was not selected to come to England in 1896. He came, however, on his own account and, after 2 years' qualification, provided the extra drive, expertise and consistency which Middlesex needed to lift them from the middle reaches of the Championship table. In his 2nd and 3rd seasons he took over 200 wickets and scored over 1,000 runs and though he was known latterly more as a mighty hitter than as a regular source of runs, he was for a long time that rarity among cricketers – a 'match-winner'. In 1897 Middlesex did not win a match until mid-August. In the following season, Trott's first, they finished 2nd to Yorkshire, Trott and Hearne taking 102 and 125 wickets respectively. No other bowler in the side took more than 18. They were 2nd again in 1899 and in 1901.

Middlesex started the new century under the captaincy of Gregor MacGregor who was still unsurpassed among amateur wicket-keepers. The problems of a Middlesex captain did not change. Hearne, Rawlin and Trott were the only professionals, and the amateurs were only irregularly available. When they did play, they were more noted for their dash and brilliance than for their soundness and consistency.

The word 'cosmopolitan', which used to be often used in connexion with Middlesex cricket, was seldom more apt than in the first years of the century. Warner had been born in the West Indies. G. W. Beldam was of French descent, B. J. T. Bosanquet a Huguenot. R. O. Schwarz's family came from Silesia. Ahsan-ul-Hak was an Afridi. W. P. Robertson had been born in Peru, Lord Dalmeny in Scotland, Rawlin in Yorkshire, Trott in Australia and Hearne in Bucks. It was the more remarkable, therefore, that the Championship should have been won in one of the wettest English summers on record, that of 1903. MacGregor was unable to play until July of that year but under Warner Middlesex made an excellent start to the season, the acting captain beginning with hundreds against both Gloucestershire and Somerset. In spite of the wet wickets, Beldam, C. M. Wells and Warner all averaged over 40, Bosanquet, J. Douglas and L. J. Moon also made plenty of runs and Wells, Beldam and Bosanquet lent variety to the bowling, taking some of the weight off Hearne and Trott. The fielding was of a high standard.

This proved to be an isolated year of triumph and the only other ventures into the higher realms of the Championship in the next decade were in 1910 and 1911 when third place was reached. These 2 seasons were a remarkable Indian summer for Hearne who had in recent seasons been taking only around 50 wickets a season for Middlesex. In 1910, aged 43, he took 116 and headed the first-class averages. In 1911 the tally was 108.

As the skill of Trott and J. T. Hearne had begun to diminish, another great Australian cricketer had come to Middlesex. F. A. Tarrant, having done his 2 years' qualification, first played in 1905 and for 10 seasons averaged 1,200 runs a year for Middlesex and 100 wickets. This astonishing record was achieved by left-arm slow-medium bowling which made the most of a bad wicket and by batting founded on soundness and confidence. Trott remained with Middlesex until 1910 and it was during the last less successful period of his career that he performed one of the feats for which he is best remembered. Early in the second innings of his benefit match against Somerset in May 1907, he took the wickets of Lewis, E. S. M. Poyntz, S. M. J. Woods and Robson in 4 successive balls, the 1st lbw, the last 3 bowled. After Tarrant had taken a wicket, Trott wrote his name in the record books for all time by finishing off the innings with a second hat-trick.

By the time Trott dropped out, a new side was being built under the enthusiastic and devoted captaincy of Warner. Warner himself was a wonderfully consistent opening batsman of superb temperament and he was fortunate to have two more all-rounders of the very highest class to support him, for Tarrant and J. W. Hearne – 'Young Jack' to distinguish him from his namesake – became an even more successful all-round combination than Trott and J. T. Hearne had been. Though in later years J. W. Hearne was known mainly as a correct, well-organized but rather frail partner for the sturdy Hendren with the irrepressible humour, he was also a leg-break and googly bowler, slow-medium in pace and particularly successful in his early days before the First World War. He was chosen to tour Australia in 1911–12 before he was 21 whereas Hendren, 2 years older, was still developing when, after he had played 6 seasons for Middlesex, the war came.

In 1912 E. L. Kidd and J. Douglas temporarily took over the captaincy when Warner was prevented from playing by ill health, but the captain returned to make 3 hundreds in 1913 when the all-round partnership of Tarrant and J. W. Hearne was reaching extraordinary heights. That year they each performed the double for Middlesex with runs and wickets to spare. In 1914 they did even better. Hearne, averaging 74 and making 8 hundreds, scored 2,021 runs for the county and took 114 wickets. Tarrant scored 1,743 runs and took 131 wickets. Hendren, improving all the time, now averaged 37, and nothing seemed more certain than that soon the Championship would come to Lord's again. In fact, it was almost won in 1914, for Middlesex were unbeaten until Kent won at Maidstone in late July and they suffered only one other narrow defeat when, a week after the outbreak of war, they had difficulty in raising a side to play Yorkshire at Sheffield. They lost there by 2 wickets, and in November the MCC Committee declared Surrey, who had had to cancel their last 2 matches, to be the Champions.

Tarrant was only 32 and J. W. Hearne only 23 when they walked off the field at Lord's after the last match of 1914. An unparalleled partnership of all-round skill was at the peak of its achievement. But they never played together for Middlesex again.

When, after 4 lost summers, the 1919 season of two-day Championship matches began, Middlesex could call on the bulk of the batting which had served them so well just before the war. Hendren, now 30, continued his steady improvement, averaging nearly 60, and was now clearly one of the leading batsmen in the country. That he should remain so for another 18 seasons was more than anyone can then have hoped. Warner, J. W. Hearne and H. W. Lee were back, and to the group of young amateurs who had played with varying frequency before the war – F. T. Mann, N. Haig, G. E. V. Crutchley, E. L. Kidd, the Hon C. N. Bruce (later Lord Aberdare), R. H. Twining and S. H. Saville – was now added an 18-year-old schoolboy, G. T. S. Stevens, who was already an accomplished batsman and leg-break bowler. The

'Plum' Warner's triumphal farewell after the great Middlesex victory over Surrey in 1920 which won them the Championship.

bowling, however, was very thin. J. T. Hearne had retired, J.W. was hampered by a damaged finger, Tarrant had gone. The larder seemed bare and only a wild optimist could have foreseen that a year later Middlesex would be Champions – to the joy of almost everyone, for after the 1920 season P. F. Warner, now 46, was retiring.

The batting had class, consistency and depth. Hearne and Hendren averaged 54 and 69 over the 22 matches of 1920. Each made 5 hundreds in the Championship, as did Lee. The fielding was excellent. The bowling found a new unforeseen strength from various quarters. Hearne, fit again, took 123 wickets, Stevens 46 in the 12 matches for which he was available. The most unexpected development, however, was the improvement of F. J. Durston, a tall fast bowler who in 4 matches in 1919 had taken only 5 wickets at 74 apiece. Now he took 111 at 20 apiece. Lee and Haig completed an attack whose main strength was the leg-break and googly bowling of Hearne and Stevens.

At the end of July 1920, few can have thought of Middlesex as possible Champions. Then, beginning at Hove where Stevens took 13 Sussex wickets for 60 over the Bank Holiday week-end, they won their last 9 matches. Haig's 7 for 33 in the 1st innings and Hearne's 8 for 26 in the 2nd enabled them to scramble home at Canterbury by 5 runs. They won by only 4 runs at Bradford when Yorkshire's last pair, E. R. Wilson and Waddington, made 53 of the 58 needed to win before Stevens bowled Waddington. Some less agonizing victories followed, and then only Surrey, their last opponents, stood between them and the Championship.

Middlesex began this famous match at Lord's by losing 5 wickets for 109 and although Warner (70) and Stevens (53) repaired this, Warner batted for $4\frac{1}{2}$ hours and the score that evening was only 253 for 8. Next day the innings ended for 268, whereupon Sandham batted brilliantly to make 167 not out and Surrey declared at 341 for 9 in time for Middlesex to have 40 minutes' batting. Next day, amid intense excitement, C. H. L. Skeet, an Oxford blue of that year, made his only hundred for Middlesex. Lee made one, too, in an opening stand of 208 and Warner was able to declare leaving Surrey to score 244 in 3 hours. They made a good start, but the middle batting ran into trouble against Stevens and, with 40 minutes to spare, Warner was carried shoulder-high from the field with Middlesex the winners by 55 runs.

F. T. Mann's captaincy began with the winning of another Championship in 1921. Nothing could quite have equalled the finish of 1920, but again the last match with Surrey at Lord's was decisive and this time Surrey would have been Champions if they had won. This 2nd Championship success differed from the 1st in that this time Middlesex led the field from the start and in that the medium-paced Haig, who did the double, replaced Hearne as the main wicket-taker with Durston. It was also to Middlesex's advantage in the final match that Surrey, who had been without Hobbs for many weeks, could be Champions only through an outright win.

For a day and a half Surrey made the running, scoring 269 and bowling out Middlesex for 132. At 115 for 2 in their 2nd innings, they had the Championship well in their sights, but their last 8 wickets fell for 69, mostly to Haig, and Middlesex had just over a day's play in which to make 322. R. H. Twining, who 43 years later was to become President of MCC, played an innings of 132 which was probably his finest for Middlesex; Hearne made 106; and Middlesex won comfortably by 6 wickets. There followed a modest period of 13 years which was relieved only by a near miss in 1924. Towards the end of that season Middlesex needed to beat Gloucestershire at Bristol to be almost sure of the Championship and when Haig and Durston had bowled the opposition out for 31 in 23 overs, all seemed well. But Hammond, dropped several times, played a magnificent second innings of 174 not out, Parker did the hat-trick in each innings and Yorkshire became Champions with Middlesex 2nd.

Until 1929 Middlesex occupied the middle of the Championship, but some lean years followed. The tradition of much respected captains was maintained through F. T. Mann (1921–1928) and N. Haig (1929–1934) – H. J. Enthoven sharing the captaincy during the last 2 years – but they could not overcome the lack of penetrative bowling, particularly fast bowling, and the inconsistency inseparable

'Young Jack' Hearne (distinguishing him from his cousin 'J.T.') was an ornament in every sense to Lord's where, beginning as a ground-boy, he formed a long never-to-be-forgotten batting association with Pat Hendren, and also took nearly 2,000 wickets.

from an unsettled side. The store of talented amateurs was as rich as ever – G. O. Allen, R. W. V. Robins, Enthoven, R. H. Bettington, E. T. Killick and I. A. R. Peebles began to play during the 1920s; but young amateurs were finding it increasingly difficult to play regularly and many were available for no more than 5 or 6 matches a year. The quality of Middlesex sides, therefore, varied greatly from match to match, especially as by the early 1930s the fast bowling of Allen and the leg-spin of Robins and Peebles were often required for England.

Hearne and Hendren went on until 1935 and 1937 respectively, carrying between them the weight of countless innings. Hearne had lost little of his talent but suffered frequently from ill-health. Hendren was so little touched by the passing years that, in his 40th year, he scored 2,574 runs and 12 hundreds for Middlesex. Six years later, in 1934, he was still being picked for England. The quick-footed belligerence of his batting and the humour and warmth of his personality had long before then won him a special place in English cricket. To meet the shortages of the early 1930s several not unsuccessful improvizations were made. W. F. Price, the wicket-keeper, was promoted from No. 11 to open the innings and in 1934 made over 1,200 runs. Durston in his later years took many wickets as an off-spinner. But the 1920s and early 1930s were mostly a period of increasing hardship interspersed with moments of brilliance, usually involving Hendren or Mann with his mighty driving.

One such was at Trent Bridge in 1925 when Middlesex made 502 for 6 in the 4th innings to beat Notts by 4 wickets. After Stevens, Lee and Hearne had been out for 60, Bruce made 103 and the match ended with an unbroken 7th-wicket stand of 271 in $3\frac{1}{4}$ hours between Hendren (206 not out) and Mann (101 not out). This was the climax of a fortnight in which Hendren scored 869 runs in 6 innings. In 1923, the first 4 batsmen, H. L. Dales, 103, Lee, 107, Hearne, 232, and Hendren, 177 not out, made hundreds in a score of 642 for 4 against Hampshire at Southampton. In 1929, Allen, though arriving late and missing the new ball, took all 10 Lancashire wickets for 40 at Lord's, a wonderful piece of fast bowling on a good pitch. Eight of his victims were bowled, one stumped and one caught at the wicket. In 1930, Enthoven, batting no. 7 in one of the stronger sides, made 102 out of a last-wicket stand of 107 with Price against Sussex at Lord's – and scored another hundred in the 2nd innings.

In 1934, the year before Robins succeeded to the captaincy, there were signs of better times ahead, for J. Smith, a big fast-bowler from Wiltshire and one of the most prodigious hitters of all time, took 139 wickets at 17 apiece. He and J. M. Sims, who had recently changed from medium pace to leg-spin, played a big part in raising Middlesex to 3rd and 2nd place in Robins's first 2 years. The new leader was himself a vast asset to the side with bat and ball.

Middlesex – captained in 1939 by Peebles – remained in 2nd place until the Second War, but there was a new significance about their success from 1937 onwards, for it was achieved with a fresh generation of batsmen such as few counties have been able to introduce at the same time. W. J. Edrich had come from Norfolk, J. D. Robertson and S. M. Brown, the future opening pair, had worked their way up through the 2nd XI; and, most momentous of all, at Whitsun, 1936, an 18-year-old boy, D. C. S. Compton, had come in as a replacement against Sussex, batting No. 11. A week later he was making 87 against Northants, 3 weeks later 100 not out, also against Northants. He exceeded 1,000 runs before the end of the season. Fourteen months on his extraordinary fluency of stroke was already such that, on being sent in one evening against Worcestershire to make runs quickly, he left the field 43 minutes later with his score 80 not out. In 1937 Hendren retired aged 48. He made 103 of his best runs in his last match at Lord's against Surrey and was accorded an ovation which nobody present will forget.

It seemed certain that this young side would soon do still better, but history was to repeat itself in a singular way. For the second time war broke out as a period of plenty for Middlesex was developing. Once again years were lost which might have been great ones. Once again the Championship was won in the second year after the war ended. Once again a second success followed, though this time it was in the form of a half-share, and it was 2 years later; and just as Warner had retired after the 1920 victory, leaving the next to Mann, so Robins retired after 1947, handing on to Mann's son, F. G. Mann, a captain in the finest Middlesex traditions.

In the wet of 1946 Middlesex again finished 2nd to Yorkshire but in the next gloriously sunny summer of 1947 they won with a brand of cricket which did much to revive public interest in the game after the war. The bowling largely depended on Sims and the left-arm spinner, J. A. Young, and on L. H. Gray, a fast-medium bowler of over 30. But Denis Compton and Bill Edrich made their mountain of runs so quickly that the bowlers had time on their side and runs to spare. In the Championship, Compton and Robertson each made 11 hundreds, Edrich 8 and Brown 3. For Middlesex alone, they made respectively 2,467, 2,328, 2,650 and 1,990; and if any more runs were needed there was no shortage from Mann, A. Thompson, L. H. Compton, the wicket-keeper, Sims and A. Fairbairn, who made hundreds in 2 of his 4 matches.

The vital match against Gloucestershire, who were lying 2nd, was played at Cheltenham in August during a Test Match which deprived Middlesex of Compton and Robertson. The ball turned from the start, and Middlesex, helped by batting 1st, won a close and exciting game in 2 days by 68 runs through more adaptable batting and the spin of Sims, Young and H. P. Sharp. The year ended with victory over the Rest at the Oval by 9 wickets. Compton made 246, Edrich 180, but a small cloud had crept over the horizon, for Compton retired during his innings with the knee trouble which was to haunt the rest of his career.

It can be argued that Middlesex were also the best side in 1948 when Glamorgan won, but they lacked the reserves to replace Compton, Edrich and Young during Test Matches and finished 3rd. Early in that season Compton (252), and Edrich (168), gave one of their most devastating exhibitions, scoring 424 against Somerset at Lord's in an unbroken 3rd-wicket stand

Middlesex County Champions 1947. Back row: P. I. Bedford, A. Thompson, L. H. Gray, L. H. Compton, J. D. Robertson, S. M. Brown and J. A. Young; sitting: W. J. Edrich, F. G. Mann, R. W. V. Robins (captain), J. M. Sims and D. C. S. Compton.

lasting only 4 hours. The pitch was well up towards the grandstand, but their feat of scoring 209 in 70 minutes after tea, during which period Compton made 139, must rank high in the records of big hitting. A year later Robertson, in another remarkable piece of batting, made 331 not out in a day at Worcester. In 1949, another dry year, Middlesex were joint Champions with Yorkshire, though only a memorable 3-wicket victory over Derbyshire at Lord's in the last match earned them their half-share. On a lifting pitch Middlesex's young fast bowler, J. J. Warr, had taken 5 for 36 in Derbyshire's 2nd innings and their chances of making 193 against 3 hostile and experienced fast bowlers in Copson, Gladwin and Jackson seemed slim, the more so when they lost 5 wickets for 36. Compton's 97 not out which followed was one of his great innings and Robins's 50, at the age of 43, could only have been played in these circumstances by an exceptional cricketer.

After F. G. Mann's retirement that autumn, Robins, taking over for the 3rd time, returned for one more year, after which the captaincy was shared by Edrich and Compton, an arrangement never likely to produce superlative results. Edrich later took full charge as Compton's knee restricted him increasingly. Neither was as prolific now, and though Edrich revealed a happy knack for producing a good game of cricket, Middlesex's days at the top had passed. After a sharp drop to 14th in 1950, much of which Compton spent in hospital, they hovered for 7 years between 5th and 7th before descending to 10th in 1958 and 1959.

By then, however, Warr had succeeded Edrich and was developing a team of young players with considerable all-round ability. The fast bowler, A. Moss, F. J. Titmus and D. Bennett had all established themselves in the side at an early age, followed in the middle 1950s by the wicket-keeper, J. T. Murray. P. H. Parfitt, W. E. Russell, R. A. Gale and R. W. Hooker came soon afterwards, nearly all of them batsmen who could bowl. Their development as batsmen was delayed by the 2-year national service in operation at the time and by the fast but grassy and unreliable pitches in vogue at Lord's in the late 1950s. But on these pitches Moss and Warr were a formidable pair of fast bowlers, Moss moving the ball mostly into the bat, Warr away from it, and in 1960, Warr's last year, Middlesex were 3rd, with hopes of glory dawning again. Though they were 3rd again, playing some good cricket, in 1961, the 1st of P. I. Bedford's 2 years of captaincy, these hopes were not fulfilled either then or in 1963 or 1964 under C. D. Drybrough. The 16 players of MCC's team to South Africa in 1964–65 included 5 – Titmus, Murray, Parfitt, J. M. Brearley and J. S. E. Price – from Middlesex, but they were part of a team at home which played below its potential.

The fielding, from the early days of Warr's captaincy, was exceptionally agile but the batting during the heyday of Warr and Moss was not good enough and by the time the batsmen were reaching their best, batting down to No. 9 or 10 with little drop in quality, Warr had retired and Moss was troubled by injury. In 1955 Titmus had taken 158 wickets for Middlesex, 4 more than Trott's record of 1900, and in 7 seasons he did the double, the sequence ending only because when he became a regular member of the England side his opportunities decreased. In 1964 he was still only 31 and, as a batsman who seldom failed in a crisis and an off-spin bowler of great variety, he had a record of service to Middlesex of which the Trotts, Hearnes, Tarrants and other all-rounders of the past would not have been ashamed. Fred Titmus was to be a member of another championship-winning side in 1976, 27 years after he played for the 1949 side aged 16. But, before that, Middlesex passed through one of the more dismal periods in their history.

Another victim for Fred Titmus (*above*). Titmus took a record 2,344 wickets for Middlesex. (*Right*) The batsman is Hampshire (Yorkshire); Murray keeps wicket and Parfitt and Russell are the fielders.

Short of fast bowling, except for odd seasons when Price was fit and in form, they relied mainly on Titmus and the medium-paced Hooker. The importing of an Australian Test bowler, the fast-medium Alan Connolly, had little success in 1969 and 1970. Despite the consistency of Parfitt, the batting became less and less positive and there were problems of captaincy as well. In August 1968 Titmus, who had been appointed in 1965, resigned and Peter Parfitt took over for the last 6 matches and for the next 2 seasons. In 1970, however, Middlesex had the worst year in their history, finishing 16th in the Championship with the same number of points as Gloucestershire who were bottom. Nor had they had any success in the limited-over competitions now being introduced.

In 1971 Mike Brearley returned to captain the side after an interrupted career in which his promise as an undergraduate at Cambridge had not been fulfilled. He had not played at all in 1966 or 1967 while in the United States and only a few matches in other seasons. He did not make a Championship 100 for Middlesex until 1973, but gradually under his leadership the side was strengthened and the next few seasons were ones of rising hopes and changing faces. Some older players, such as M. J. Smith and Clive Radley, began to play better than ever before. Titmus still took 85 wickets in 1974. But young players began to appear from the side presided over by the coach Don Bennett which had won the Under-25 competition three years running.

The rewards began to come in 1975 when Middlesex reached both limited-over finals at Lord's, though without winning either. By now the side was a good blend of youth and experience. Brearley himself now averaged 50 and to the consistency of Smith and Radley was added the occasional match-winning brilliance of Norman Featherstone from South Africa. The bowling had gained in variety with the arrival of Philippe Edmonds from Cambridge and could depend on the tireless fast-medium accuracy of Mike Selvey.

In 1976 the Championship was won outright for the first time since 1947 and once again, as in 1947 and 1921, in an abormally dry summer. The batting was given an extra vigour by the left-handed Graham Barlow in an *annus mirabilis*. Young players in their teens such as Michael Gatting and Ian Gould played their part and a 35-year-old member of the committee, Michael Sturt, kept wicket in August with high success when all other candidates were injured or unavailable. On the dry turning pitches of that month his 'keeping to the off-spin of Titmus and Featherstone, and the left-arm spin of Edmonds, did much to keep Middlesex on top. Another important part was played by Allan Jones who, at a lively fast-medium, far exceeded anything he had done previously for Somerset or Sussex. He was in fact the biggest wicket-taker of the season with 69.

With the arrival of the young and genuinely fast West Indian bowler Wayne Daniel, Middlesex seemed to have a side strong and varied enough to win a lot more in the next few years. In 1977 they did win the Gillette Cup and in a remarkable finish shared the Schweppes County Championship with Kent, after Gloucestershire had led into the last day. Their strength at this time was such that, in August 1977, they were able to inflict a singularly humiliating defeat on the old enemy Surrey. After rain had limited the first 2 days' play to only 5 overs, Middlesex bowled Surrey out for 49 on a wet pitch, batted for one ball before declaring, bowled Surrey out again for 89 and made the 139 needed for victory for the loss of only 1 wicket.

But by 1978 they were losing Brearley, Edmonds, Radley and Emburey to Test matches and, with the reserves hard pressed to cope with some poor pitches at Lord's, there was a pause in the run of success.

CAPTAINS

1864–72	V. E. Walker
1873–84	I. D. Walker
1885–97	A. J. Webbe
1898	A. J. Webbe and A. E. Stoddart
1899–1907	G. MacGregor
1908–20	P. F. Warner
1921–28	F. T. Mann
1929–32	N. E. Haig
1933–34	N. E. Haig and H. J. Enthoven
1935–38	R. W. V. Robins
1939	I. A. R. Peebles

Middlesex, County Champions in 1976 for the first time since 1947, in the flush of victory: R. O. Butcher, M. W. W. Selvey, J. M. Brearley (captain), P. H. Edmonds, G. D. Barlow.

1946–47 R. W. V. Robins
1948–49 F. G. Mann
1950 R. W. V. Robins
1951–52 W. J. Edrich and D. C. S. Compton
1953–57 W. J. Edrich
1958–60 J. J. Warr
1961–62 P. I. Bedford
1963–64 C. D. Drybrough
1965–67 F. J. Titmus
1968–70 P. H. Parfitt
1971– J. M. Brearley

HIGHEST TOTALS

For 642–3D v Hants, Southampton 1923
Against 665 by West Indians, Lord's 1939

LOWEST TOTALS

For 20 v MCC, Lord's 1864
Against 31 by Gloucester, Bristol 1924

HIGHEST INDIVIDUAL INNINGS

For 331* J. D. Robertson v Worcester, Worcester 1949
Against 316* J. B. Hobbs for Surrey, Lord's 1926

MOST RUNS

In a season 2,650 W. J. Edrich
In a career 40,302 E. H. Hendren

MOST HUNDREDS

In a season 13 D. C. S. Compton 1947
In a career 119 E. H. Hendren 1907–1938

INDIVIDUAL INNINGS OF 250 AND OVER

F. A. Tarrant, 250* v Essex, Leyton 1914
E. H. Hendren, 277* v Kent, Lord's 1922
J. W. Hearne, 285* v Essex, Leyton 1929
E. H. Hendren, 301* v Worcester, Dudley 1933
W. J. Edrich, 257 v Leicester, Leicester 1947
W. J. Edrich, 267* v Northants, Northampton 1947
D. C. S. Compton, 252* v Somerset, Lord's 1948
J. D. B. Robertson, 331* v Worcester, Worcester 1949

HUNDRED ON DEBUT

A. Fairbairn, 108 v Somerset, Taunton 1947
E. A. Clark, 100* v Cambridge University, Cambridge 1959

RECORD WICKET PARTNERSHIPS

1 W. E. Russell and M. J. Harris, 312 v Pakistanis, Lord's 1967
2 F. A. Tarrant and J. W. Hearne, 380 v Lancs, Lord's 1914
3 W. J. Edrich and D. C. S. Compton, 424* v Somerset, Lord's 1948
4 J. W. Hearne and E. H. Hendren, 325 v Hants, Lord's 1919
5 R. S. Lucas and T. C. O'Brien, 338 v Sussex, Hove 1895
6 C. T. Radley and F. J. Titmus, 227 v South Africans, Lord's 1965
7 E. H. Hendren and F. T. Mann, 271* v Notts, Trent Bridge 1925
8 M. H. C. Doll and H. R. Murrell, 182* v Notts, Lord's 1913
9 E. H. Hendren and F. J. Durston, 160* v Essex, Leyton 1927
10 R. W. Nicholls and W. Roche, 230 v Kent, Lord's 1899

MOST WICKETS

In a match 16–114 G. Burton v Yorks, Sheffield 1888
16–114 J. T. Hearne v Lancs, Old Trafford 1898
In a season 158 F. J. Titmus 1955
In a career 2,346 F. J. Titmus 1949–1979

ALL TEN WICKETS IN AN INNINGS

V. E. Walker v Lancs, Old Trafford 1865
G. Burton v Surrey, Oval 1888
A. E. Trott v Somerset, Taunton 1900
G. O. Allen v Lancs, Lord's 1929

HAT-TRICKS

F. A. Tarrant 4 (5 in all matches)
J. T. Hearne 3 (4 in all matches)
J. W. Hearne 3
F. J. Durston, R. W. V. Robins, A. E. Trott, J. A. Young 2 each
H. J. Enthoven 1 (2 in all matches)
C. D. Drybrough, S. M. Haslip, T. Hearne, A. E. Moss, I. A. R. Peebles, J. M. Sims, C. I. J. Smith, F. J. Titmus, J. J. Warr 1 each

WICKET-KEEPING – MOST DISMISSALS

In an innings 7 W. F. F. Price
In a match 9 M. Turner
9 J. T. Murray
In a season 99 J. T. Murray
In a career 1,223 J. T. Murray 1952–1975

COUNTY CAPS AWARDED SINCE 1946

1946 J. P. Mann, A. Thompson, J. A. Young
1947 L. H. Compton, A. Fairbairn
1948 P. I. Bedford, J. G. Dewes, E. A. Ingram, H. P. Sharp
1949 J. J. Warr
1951 R. Routledge
1952 D. Bennett, W. Knightley-Smith, A. E. Moss
1953 F. J. Titmus
1955 G. P. S. Delisle
1956 J. T. Murray
1957 R. A. Gale, R. J. Hurst, A. C. Walton
1959 R. W. Hooker, W. E. Russell
1960 P. H. Parfitt
1961 P. I. Bedford, E. A. Clark
1962 C. D. Drybrough
1963 J. S. E. Price, R. A. White
1964 J. M. Brearley
1965 D. A. Bick
1967 M. J. Harris, C. T. Radley, M. J. Smith, M. O. C. Sturt
1968 H. C. Latchman
1969 A. N. Connolly, R. S. Herman
1971 N. G. Featherstone, K. V. Jones
1973 D. A. Marriott, M. W. W. Selvey
1974 P. H. Edmonds
1976 G. D. Barlow, A. A. Jones
1977 W. W. Daniel, J. E. Emburey, M. W. Gatting, I. J. Gould
1979 R. O. Butcher

Northamptonshire

JOHN ARLOTT AND ALEX BANNISTER

Foundation 1878
Colours Maroon
Badge Tudor Rose

The history of Northants as a first-class county falls into 3 phases. From 1905, when they entered the Championship, until 1914 they were a fair average county, taking time to find their feet but, in 1912 and 1913, especially, a hard side to beat. Then came a long period, from the 1919 restart to 1948 when Northants were the chopping block of the other counties: in those 24 seasons they never held a single-figure position in the Championship table; 10 times they were bottom, 6 times bottom-but-one. Finally, beginning with the captaincy of F. R. Brown (1949) and in a state of financial security the club had never known before, there began an era of the businesslike approach. Many of the better players were imported from other counties, or even other countries, but they drew the crowds, won matches and gave Northants cricket a new and altogether more expert appearance.

'Eleven Gentlemen of Northamptonshire' took the field at least twice in 1741, and there was a club in the town of Northampton as early as 1775. There probably was some kind of county team in 1820 but no county club is known to have been formed before 1843. The present club, which grew more or less naturally out of the Northampton Town Club – although Peterborough was for long a stronger centre of the game in the county – dates from 1878. It made its way slowly and played its first match on the present county ground at Northampton in May 1886, against Surrey Club and Ground who won by 6 wickets. The Minor Counties Competition of 1896 was a rather ramshackle affair. Four of the entrants of the previous season did not play enough matches to qualify and Northants were one of the 4 who made up a competition quorum of 7; they won 2 matches, lost 2, drew 4 and finished 4th. In all their matches for the season, G. J. Thompson, 18-years-old, who had just left Wellingborough Grammar School, scored 416 runs (at 21·17) and took 61 wickets (average 18·34).

George Thompson was born in Northampton; he was a fast-medium bowler who, in modern terms, 'cut' the ball off a good length and made it lift awkwardly from any lively or worn pitch. His batting was competent: he had a sound defence but could hit hard at need. Strongly built and hardy, he was the best player Northamptonshire has ever produced, and he had a more important effect on his county's cricket even than W. G. Grace on Gloucestershire's. *Wisden* wrote, in 1906:

George Joseph Thompson stands in an almost unique position among the professional cricketers of the present day, inasmuch as he has brought a new county to the front. But for his bowling it is quite safe to say that Northamptonshire would not in 1905 have been given a place among the first-class teams. . . . Thompson, to a greater extent than all the other members of the eleven put together, rendered the promotion possible.

As a Minor Counties player, Thompson was chosen for the Players against the Gentlemen at Scarborough (1900) when he scored a hundred, and for 'An England Eleven' against the 1902 Australians, when he took 8 for 88 which won him his place in Lord Hawke's team to New Zealand that winter. He was, too, the 1st Northants player to appear for England in a Test against Australia (1909) and the 1st professional ever to captain that county (1913). A wound in the First World War virtually ended his cricket career and without him Northants entered on a long run of failure. In first-class cricket he scored 12,018 runs and took 1,591 wickets. W. H. Kingston and C. J. T. Pool were both valuable amateur batsmen in the side that had such a fine run in the Minor Counties Competition, but it was the bowling partnership of Thompson and William East (both of whom also made runs) which carried the side through to 1914. Between 1905 and the outbreak of war, East, an accurate, medium-pace bowler who spun the ball a little, took 493 wickets for Northants in first-class matches and made a fine foil for Thompson.

One of the major surprises of the pre-1914 years in the Championship was the performance of Northants in finishing so closely 2nd to Yorkshire in the table of 1912. Of their 18 matches, they won 10 and lost only 1 to Warwickshire. They were fortunate in being able to maintain a regular XI which was – G. A. T. Vials (captain), W. H. Denton, R. Haywood, W. East, G. J. Thompson, S. G. Smith, J. S. Denton, J. Seymour, F. Walden, W. Wills and W. A. Buswell. C. N. Woolley was the reserve and only those 12 players appeared in Championship matches. *Wisden's* comment was, 'Constant association gave the eleven a fighting power that was out of all proportion to the individual talent.' The main strength lay in the bowling. S. G. Smith, an all-rounder who came over with the 1906 West Indian team, took 84 wickets, bowling slow left-arm; Thompson had 106, East 41 and W. 'Bumper' Wells, the fastest of the 4, 44: they accounted for all but 16 of the wickets taken by Northants bowlers, and all had averages below 20. Vials, J. S. Denton, East, Smith, Seymour and Thompson had batting averages of more than 20. 1912 remained for long the enviable, almost unbelievable and most successful season in the history of Northants. They finished 4th in 1913 and if 9th position in 1914 was something of an anti-climax, the side was still a useful one. When cricket began again in 1919 Smith had settled in New Zealand, East was ill. Neither played again. Thompson was wounded and virtually finished. The 3 Denton brothers could only muster a dozen matches between them, which was especially galling in the case of J.S. whose 3 innings of the season were 70, 30 not out and 56 not out and he took 10 wickets. For the 1st time Northants were bottom of the Championship table: they were desperately short of truly first-class cricketers. Off the field, Stephen Schilizzi gave much-needed financial help and a local man, Alfred Cockerill, bought the present county ground and presented it to the club.

V. W. C. Jupp was persuaded to join Northants from Sussex as secretary and player: he can hardly have imagined the roughness or the length of the furrow he was to plough. Vallance Jupp was a stocky, aggressive, bustling cricketer: he spun his not particularly slow off-breaks sharply and occasionally made one run away; he batted briskly and would put his hands to anything. He remained Secretary until 1932; became qualified by residence in 1924; captained the county from 1927 (when he was joint captain with J. M. Fitzroy) until 1931 and, in his career, achieved the rare all-round feat of scoring over 10,000 runs and taking over 1,000 wickets; he played in 8 Tests for England. From time to time Jupp, E. W. Clark, also an England player and a magnificent left-arm fast bowler on his day, the accurate A. E. Thomas and Wells, who bowled gamely on, could put a side out cheaply.

But the batting was woefully weak. The amateurs W. W. Timms, H. F. Bagnall and A. P. R. Hawtin all at times contributed good runs but R. Haywood, C. N. Woolley, 'Fanny' Walden (also a football player with Tottenham Hotspur), J. E. Timms (1925–1949) and Ben Bellamy the wicket-keeper were almost the sole professional props of the batting until A. H. Bakewell came into the side in 1928. An obviously gifted batsman with brilliant strokes and fine assurance, Bakewell was also a fine short-leg fieldsman. He was picked for England in 6 Tests between 1931 and 1935 and, though he did not make his position secure, his batting was still increasing in command when, in 1936, while he was still only 27, he was so badly injured in a motoring accident that he was never able to play cricket again. A. W. Snowden, from Peterborough, showed great promise; he was only 17 when he first played for the county and he rapidly settled down as Bakewell's opening partner; but he went into business and could play little after 1935. Jupp was ageing; disputes, injuries and Test selection kept Clark – by far the county's most effective bowler – often out of the side and from May 1935 to May 1939 Northants did not win a match. Jackie Timms, a neat, brave batsman; K. C. James, the wicket-keeper from New Zealand; another New Zealand Test player, Bill Merritt, the leg-break bowler who qualified in 1938; 2 reliable opening bowlers in Reg Partridge and Austin Matthews; Dennis Brookes, the stylish opening batsman from Yorkshire; Jupp and 3 captains – W. C. Brown, G. B. Cuthbertson and R. P. Nelson – held the side together during those hard times when Northants were bottom of the Championship for 5 consecutive years and only improved to 16th in 1939.

When Northants mustered their forces for post-war cricket R. P. Nelson, who had seemed a natural captain, had been killed by enemy action; James had retired; Matthews had joined Glamorgan; E. W. Clark, though still capable of bursts at high speed, was 44, Jackie Timms 38. P. E. Murray-Willis was captain for 1946, Arthur Childs-Clarke for the next 2 years. The West Indian leg-spinner, C. B. Clarke, gave immense help when he could play; Dennis Brookes and Percy Davis batted loyally and Broderick emerged as an all-rounder. Sixteenth in 1946, bottom in 1947 and 1948, it seemed that the pre-war pattern of Northants cricket was to be repeated.

The next year, however, Northants entered on a plateau of prosperity beyond the dreams of their men of the inter-war years. Their Supporters' Club and the local firm of British-Timken at last put them on a financial footing which would enable them to recruit the best players. At the same time, F. R. Brown, the Test all-rounder formerly with Surrey, took over the captaincy. He inherited some capable players in Broderick, slow left-arm, who had completed the double in the previous season; Albert Nutter, experienced medium-paced bowler, and Norman Oldfield, Test batsman, both from Lancashire; Dennis Brookes, a cool, mature opening bat; and 4 products of the ground staff in the brothers Eddie and Percy Davis and Bill Barron as batsmen, and a young left-arm pace bowler, Bob Clarke. Two rather similar-looking Yorkshiremen – both hard hitters – in Desmond Barrick and Fred Jakeman, were specially registered. Ten Championship matches were won, good enough for 6th position – the highest the county had known for 36 years.

Northants had for 30 years been everyone's chopping-block when F. R. Brown took over the leadership (and then the England captaincy) in 1949.

1950 – 10th; 1951 – 13th; 1952 – 8th; 1953 – 11th: that was the side's record under Freddie Brown. It would have been poor enough by the standards of most counties but even the worst of those positions was better than Northants had known since 1933. Brown, a strong captain and a capable all-rounder, seemed also to rehabilitate himself as a cricketer: he had virtually finished with the game when he agreed to join Northants, yet, within his 1st season with his new county, 38 years old and 12 years after he had last played in a Test, he captained England against New Zealand. This was a fillip not only for Brown but for cricket in Northants. There probably was some friction before he gave up the captaincy in 1953. Such a revitalizing as he had achieved was not brought about without some plain speaking and violent upheavals. But he had done the job and, if he ruffled some feathers in the process, that may have cleared those feathers of some very old dust; in any case, Northants cricket must be eternally grateful to F. R. Brown. Certainly he had the advantage of a financial position none of his predecessors had known, but he used it well.

Dennis Brookes, an elder statesman among professional batsmen, now took over. At the end of 1954, Frank Tyson and Keith Andrew became the 1st Northants professionals ever chosen for an MCC tour of Australia. Under Brookes, the team was 7th in 1954, their best position since 1913. That year Jack Manning, an orthodox left-arm spinner from Australia, took 116 wickets; Livingston, Brookes, Barrick, Tribe, Reynolds and Arnold all scored over 1,000 runs in Championship matches; and Northants beat the Champions – Surrey – twice. 1957 recalled 1912: Northants won 15 matches, more than they had ever done in a single season, and ended as runners-up. Mick Allen, from Bedford, had an effective season as a slow left-arm bowler. Fellows-Smith, the

Northamptonshire 1957, runners-up in the County Championship: back row: J. S. Manning, B. Reynolds, R. Subba Row, H. R. A. Kelleher, F. H. Tyson, M. H. J. Allen and D. R. Muscott (scorer); front row: K. V. Andrew, D. W. Barrick, D. Brookes (captain), L. Livingston and G. E. Tribe.

Colin Milburn: with his weight behind the ball. White hope for all too short a time.

South African, played some valuable innings and Kelleher, from Surrey, opened the bowling with Tyson. It was the last year of Brookes's captaincy.

Raman Subba Row became captain for 1958 when he himself was top of the batting in aggregate and average; a knee injury had taken Livingston from the side but Dennis Brookes and Peter Arnold scored over 1,000 runs and 2 players developed on the staff, Brian Reynolds and Albert Lightfoot, fell only a few short of 1,000. A bad month of August and some untidy fielding weakened Northants' challenge for the Championship which was strong in mid-season. After that year there was something of a slump: 1959 – 11th; 1960 – 9th; 1961 – 16th; then, when Subba Row retired, the captaincy passed to Keith Andrew: 1962 – 8th; 1963 – 7th; 1964 – 3rd. The retirement of Tribe, Tyson, Manning and Brookes inside 3 years was obviously not a problem to be lightly solved. But the development of Reynolds, Norman and Lightfoot, plus Roger Prideaux from Kent and Colin Milburn, a young heavyweight from Durham with immense potential, promised to solve Northants' batting problems for many years to come. David Larter, considered a fine fast-bowling prospect, went far towards making good the loss of Tyson, and Brian Crump proved a considerable asset as an all-rounder. Northants now awaited the development of the Watts brothers as all-rounders and of at least two of their young spin bowlers before they could consider themselves adequately equipped to return to the top of the Championship.

Yet since 1949, the entire attitude towards cricket in Northants had undergone a change. The county ground, with its new buildings and equipment, was altogether different: it was no longer a backwater of cricket but a modern centre of the game, solvent, up to date, progressive. The debt owed to secretary Ken Turner as fund raiser, team-builder and general factotum could scarcely be exaggerated. From his appointment in 1958, after 9 years as assistant secretary, his activities ranged from the recruitment of such distinguished overseas players as Mushtaq Mohammad, Bishen Bedi and Sarfraz Nawaz to running discotheques and rock concerts at the club's Indoor School.

By sound planning and hard work a peak was reached in 1976 when Northants beat Lancashire in the final of the Gillette Cup – the first success in any competition in the county's history – and also finished 2nd to Middlesex in the County Championship. Yet within a year, for a variety of reasons, one of the most powerful sides in England broke up. Mushtaq resigned the captaincy with 4 matches still to be played, and Northants faced their centenary season also without Virgin, a competent opening batsman from Somerset tantalizingly close to Test class, Bishen Bedi and the left-arm quick bowler Dye. Cottam, another able pace bowler, had gone in 1976. In 13 seasons Mushtaq, a Packer recruit, scored almost 16,000 runs, took 550 wickets with his leg-breaks and googlies, and his fielding matched his other skills. With Mushtaq and Bedi at their best, Northants had match-winning spinners.

A centenary season was no time for rebuilding. Sadly in 1978 Jim Watts, the former captain now pressed back into service, suffered the loss of his wife after missing several matches through illness and injury. The Pakistani, Sarfraz was unavailable until mid-June. Northants finished bottom for the first time since 1948, and the record of only 2 victories was the worst since 1947. At the end of the season, Steele, a long-serving stalwart to whome England had successfully turned in 1975, also left to captain Derbyshire. Some consolation was found in the continued progress of Wayne Larkins, an opening batsman of exciting potential, evidence of Cook's promise both as batsman and leader, and the good form of the South African batsman, Allan Lamb.

What heights Northants might have scaled a decade earlier but for Milburn's tragic motor accident on the evening after victory over the West Indies for the second successive tour, is a matter for conjecture. Colin Milburn's rich and thrilling talent, which had taken him to the fastest century of the season both in 1966 and 1967, was emerging into full flower. Though he made a brave attempt to return as a middle-order batsman and medium pace bowler four years later, despite being almost completely blinded in his left eye, it is not hard to imagine the impact of a Northants with Milburn at his peak supporting a bowling array of Cottam, Dye, Bedi, Mushtaq and Willey.

The crash which in 1969 cost Milburn his left eye and impaired the sight of the other cut short a brilliant career, robbed the English game at large of its most colourful character, and was an incalculable blow to Northants and England. In the same season Steele broke an arm, and for the next 2 years Northants were 14th, their lowest position since 1961. The 1970 season limped to a depressing end without a victory in the last 2 months, and in 1971 Sussex gained Prideaux's services, and Northants no longer had the experience of the reliable opener Reynolds, Lightfoot and the bowler Kettle.

With a greatly improved attack in 1972, Northants jumped 10 places to 4th, their best position in 7 years. Dye, released by Kent, took 75 wickets with his fast left-arm over the wicket, Mushtaq 52, Cottam 41 and Bedi 62, and altogether 77 bonus bowling points were won. Mushtaq also averaged 60 with the bat and Steele 50. Not surprisingly Northants were 3rd a year later, and only three late defeats robbed them of 2nd place. Mushtaq again shone, and Willey, one of several on the staff from the north-east, an area never neglected by the club, began to live up to the promise he had shown when making his debut and scoring 78 against Cambridge at the age of 16 years 5 months. When Steele and Willey played for England in 1976 it was the first time Northants had provided 2 representatives in a Test since Tyson and Andrew at Brisbane in 1954.

Willey's outstanding batting in one-day cricket at last made Northants a team to be reckoned with in the single innings competitions. After his third knee operation in 4 years Willey was twice 'Man of the Match' in the Gillette Cup, including the final for an innings of 65, and hit 3 hundreds in the John Player League. He also scored 3 in the Championship, including 227 against Somerset.

The bowling strength gave many opportunities to Sharp, who was top of the national wicket-keepers' table. He had no easy task in following Andrew and Johnson, two gifted wicket-keepers, and his improving ability was also reflected in pugnacious batting. Northants also reached the quarter-finals of both the Gillette and Benson & Hedges Cups in 1977, but the 40-over John Player League brought few challenges. By 1979 their highest-ever position was a modest 4th.

Perhaps the biggest disappointment to Northants was to be beaten to the Championship post in the Diamond Jubilee season of 1965. Worcestershire came from nowhere to win 10 of their last 11 matches and head the table for the 1st and only time in the summer on 31 August. In the final run-in Northants had lost the crucial game at Worcester on 20 August, and rain interfered with their one remaining fixture at home to Gloucestershire.

Team work rather than individual brilliance was the key to the results obtained by a side well led by Andrew. Only Reynolds, his opening partner Norman, later to move to Leicestershire, Milburn and Steele scored hundreds that summer, but Crump took 112 wickets and scored 784 runs, and his cousin, Steele, a deadly fielder close to the wicket, 40 catches. Crump's standing as an all-rounder suffered from his increasing work-load as a bowler, but in 14 loyal seasons he hit 8,000 runs and took 800 wickets.

Northants have always been obliged to search far and wide for talent, and an interesting reinforcement in the mid-1960s was Sully, from Somerset, a tall off-spinner who had several notable performances. No county could boast of a more formidable opening batting pair at the time of Milburn and Prideaux. In 1966 Prideaux scored 6 hundreds.

Inconsistency around this period cost Northants many points. Lacking penetrative bowling they slumped to the lower half of the table. On the plus side was the arrival of the burly left-handed South African batsman, Ackerman. But it needed the acquisition of seasoned bowlers to restore pride and fortune in the early 1970s. Twice 3rd, and only 16 points behind Middlesex in the halcyon summer of 1976, Northants were a side which for sheer professionalism, consistency and varied skills few could equal.

Northamptonshire 1976, triumphant after winning the Gillette Cup, as well as being runners-up in the County Championship. Left to right: D. S. Steele, Sarfraz Nawaz, B. S. Bedi, R. T. Virgin, Mushtaq Mohammad (captain), A. Hodgson, T. J. Yardley (12th man), P. Willey (man of the match), W. Larkins, G. Sharp, J. C. J. Dye, G. Cook.

CAPTAINS

1905–06	T. Horton
1907	E. M. Crosse
1908–10	T. E. Manning
1911–12	G. A. T. Vials
1913	G. A. T. Vials and S. G. Smith
1914	S. G. Smith
1919	J. N. Beasley
1920–21	R. O. Raven
1922	C. H. Tyler
1923–24	A. H. Bull
1925–26	J. M. Fitzroy
1927	J. M. Fitzroy and V. W. C. Jupp
1928–31	V. W. C. Jupp
1932–35	W. C. Brown
1936–37	G. B. Cuthbertson
1938–39	R. P. Nelson
1946	P. E. Murray-Willis
1947–48	A. W. Childs-Clarke
1949–53	F. R. Brown
1954–57	D. Brookes
1958–61	R. Subba Row
1962–66	K. V. Andrew
1967–70	R. M. Prideaux
1971–74	P. J. Watts
1975	R. T. Virgin and Mushtaq Mohammad
1976–77	Mushtaq Mohammad
1978–	P. J. Watts

HIGHEST TOTALS

For 557–6D v Sussex, Hove 1914
Against 670–9D by Sussex, Hove 1921

LOWEST TOTALS

For 12 v Gloucester, Gloucester 1907
Against 43 by Leicester, Peterborough 1968

HIGHEST INDIVIDUAL INNINGS

For 300 R. Subba Row v Surrey, Oval 1958
Against 333 K. S. Duleepsinhji for Sussex, Hove 1930

MOST RUNS

In a season 2,198 D. Brookes 1952
In a career 28,980 D. Brookes 1934–1959

MOST HUNDREDS

In a season 8 R. Haywood 1921
In a career 67 D. Brookes 1934–1959

INDIVIDUAL INNINGS OF 250 AND OVER

A. H. Bakewell, 257 v Glamorgan, Swansea 1933
D. Brookes, 257 v Gloucester, Bristol 1949
F. Jakeman, 258* v Essex, Northampton 1951
R. Subba Row, 300 v Surrey, Oval 1958

HUNDRED ON DEBUT

No instance

RECORD WICKET PARTNERSHIPS

1 N. Oldfield and V. H. Broderick, 361 v Scotland, Peterborough 1953
2 L. Livingston and D. W. Barrick, 299* v Sussex, Northampton 1953
3 L. Livingston and F. Jakeman, 320 v South Africans, Northampton 1951
4 R. T. Virgin and P. Willey, 370 v Somerset, Northampton 1976
5 D. Brookes and D. W. Barrick, 347 v Essex, Northampton 1952
6 R. Subba Row and A. Lightfoot, 376 v Surrey, Oval 1958
7 W. W. Timms and F. A. Walden, 229 v Warwicks, Northampton 1926
8 F. R. Brown and A. E. Nutter, 155 v Glamorgan, Northampton 1952
9 R. Subba Row and S. Starkie, 156 v Lancs, Northampton 1955
10 B. Bellamy and J. V. Murdin, 148 v Glamorgan, Northampton 1925

MOST WICKETS

In a match 15–31 G. E. Tribe v Yorks, Northampton 1958
In a season 175 G. E. Tribe 1955
In a career 1,097 E. E. Clark 1922–1947

ALL 10 WICKETS IN AN INNINGS

V. W. C. Jupp v Kent, Tunbridge Wells 1932

HAT-TRICKS

V. W. C. Jupp 2 (5 in all matches)
M. R. Dilley, S. G. Smith 2 each
E. W. Clark, J. V. Murdin, R. J. Partridge, H. Sully, A. E. Thomas, G. J. Thompson, W. Wells, C. N. Woolley, G. Wooster 1 each

WICKET-KEEPING – MOST DISMISSALS

In an innings 7 K. V. Andrew
In a match 10 L. A. Johnson (2)
In a season 89 K. V. Andrew 1962
In a career 810 K. V. Andrew, 1953–1966

COUNTY CAPS AWARDED SINCE 1946

1946	W. Barron, P. E. Murray-Willis
1947	V. H. Broderick, A. W. Childs-Clarke, C. B. Clarke, K. Fiddling, J. Webster
1948	A. E. Nutter, N. Oldfield
1949	F. R. Brown, R. W. Clarke, R. G. Garlick
1950	T. L. Livingston
1951	F. Jakeman
1952	D. W. Barrick, G. E. Tribe
1953	E. Davis
1954	K. V. Andrew, S. Starkie, F. H. Tyson
1955	P. Arnold, R. Subba Row
1956	J. S. Manning, B. L. Reynolds
1957	M. J. H. Allen
1960	L. A. Johnson, M. E. J. C. Norman
1961	A. Lightfoot, J. D. F. Larter
1962	B. S. Crump, R. M. Prideaux, P. D. Watts, P. J. Watts
1963	C. Milburn
1964	M. E. Scott
1965	D. S. Steele
1966	H. Sully
1967	Mushtaq Mohammad
1969	H. M. Ackerman
1971	P. Willey
1972	B. S. Bedi, R. M. H. Cottam, J. C. J. Dye
1973	G. Sharp
1974	R. T. Virgin
1975	G. Cook, Sarfraz Nawaz
1976	A. Hodgson, W. Larkins
1978	B. J. Griffiths, A. J. Lamb, T. M. Lamb, T. J. Yardley
1979	R. G. Williams

Nottinghamshire

PETER WYNNE-THOMAS

Foundation 1841
Colours Green and Gold
Badge County Badge of Nottinghamshire
Champions 1865, 1868, 1869 (=), 1871, 1872, 1873 (=), 1875, 1879 (=), 1880, 1882 (=), 1883, 1884, 1885, 1886, 1889 (=), 1907, 1929

In its progress northwards, the game of cricket probably reached Nottinghamshire in the early years of the 18th century, though the 1st recorded match by a Nottingham team did not take place until 1771. The venue was the racecourse on The Forest, where on 26 and 27 August, the Nottingham Club played Sheffield. The standard of play at the time was well below that of the famous Southern teams, but in 1791, the Hon Charles Churchill, who was stationed in Nottingham, was so impressed by the Nottingham cricketers that he organized an XI-a-side match against MCC. The game took place on King's Meadow on 29 and 30 August and unfortunately proved a disaster for the local side; so much so that Nottingham did not venture to challenge another Southern club until 1817. This time the locals were more cautious and XXII of the Town played William Lambert's England XI. Amid great excitement – the crowd was estimated at 15,000 – Nottingham won by 30 runs. The match was repeated the following year with the home side again victorious, this time by 14 wickets. The main architects of the success were George Smith, Peter Bramley, Humphrey Hopkin, Joe Dennis, the wicket-keeper, and Thomas Warsop, the renowned slow bowler.

The Nottingham Club did not follow up its triumph over the next decade and was largely to confine its matches to games against Sheffield, Leicester and its other immediate neighbours. By 1834 however it had become quite plain that Nottingham cricket was altogether stronger than the other clubs north of the Thames. Both Cambridge and Sheffield were beaten by an innings that season and therefore the Nottingham Old Club, as the principal side in the county was called, arranged home and away games with Sussex for 1835. These 2 matches are generally regarded as the starting point of Nottinghamshire inter-county cricket, since the 'Old Club' was, to all intents and purposes, the county side. Sussex were beaten in both matches and it would be fair to say that as a result Nottinghamshire could claim to be the equal of any county in England.

The leading light in the cricketing fraternity of Nottingham at this time was William Clarke and his Bell Inn in the Market Place was the unofficial headquarters of the 'Old Club'. In 1838, he moved to the Trent Bridge Inn and laid out a cricket ground in the meadow next to his new home. He had little difficulty in persuading the Nottingham cricketers to quit The Forest and move to his new ground and on 27 and 28 July 1840 Sussex played Nottingham in the 1st county contest staged on the turf of Trent Bridge Cricket Ground. Apart from Clarke, who was notable for his under-arm bowling, the leading members of the Nottingham side were the elegant batsman, Joe Guy, the left-handed all-rounder Billy Good, Sam Redgate, who was for a brief period the most feared fast bowler in the county, and Thomas Barker, another all-rounder.

The first meeting to set up a bona fide county cricket club in Nottinghamshire was held in the spring of 1841, when T. B. Charlton was appointed Secretary. County cricket seemed to be progressing well during the early 1840s, but in 1846 William Clarke's interest switched from purely Notts cricket to cricket on a national scale and he formed the All England XI, which comprised the best professionals in the country, and spent the season touring the British Isles. Clarke took with him all the best Nottingham men and as a result Notts county cricket became all but moribund. There were no matches in 1846, 1847, 1849 or 1850, but in 1851 Notts did raise a side to play Surrey – the 1st time these 2 counties met.

The following year, Charley Brown, the eccentric county wicket-keeper, re-formed the County Club and due to his efforts and those of John Thornton and John Johnson, inter-county contests once more became frequent events. William Clarke died in 1856 and though his successor as manager of the All England XI was George Parr, who combined this office with the captaincy of Notts, the vogue of All England XI matches gradually waned, as the novelty wore off.

In the winter of 1859–60, the chief organizers of the Notts County matches decided to form a committee to run the affairs of the County Club. The prime mover in the innovation was the secretary, John Johnson. The committee's first step to improve the county team was the holding of a Colts trial. Twenty-two young players were picked to oppose the county in a two-day game at Easter. This idea was most successful and the annual Notts Colts Match opened the season at Trent Bridge every year, weather permitting, until 1907.

The sporting press started the fashion of picking a 'Champion County' at the close of the 1864 season and by virtue of winning 6 out of 7 games, Notts were acclaimed champions in 1865. A typical Notts team of that time consisted of George Parr, the leading batsman and captain; Brampton, Richard Daft, William Oscroft and Bignall as the other batsmen; Biddulph, the wicket-keeper; Wootton and Jackson as fast bowlers; Grundy and Tinley as all-rounders; and young Alfred Shaw, later the most famous of all bowlers, but now mainly playing as a batsman. Some idea of the quality of the team may be gauged from the fact that all 11 represented the Players v the Gentlemen at Lord's.

Through the 1860s and 1870s the county remained, by and large, the best in the country. Daft succeeded Parr both as the best professional batsman in England and as Notts captain, Fred Morley and Jemmy Shaw took over the bowling from Wootton and Jackson. In the mid-1870s arose Arthur Shrewsbury, the Nottingham batsman who was rivalled only by W. G. Grace himself. First playing for Notts in 1875, Shrewsbury was at the height of his career in 1887, with an average of 78. He was a master of back play with great concentration and superb confidence. W.G. remarked to a chairman of selectors, 'Give me Arthur – and you and your committee can pick the rest.' If Shrewsbury was a good little one, then William Gunn was a good big 'un. He was a natural hitter, but on Shrewsbury's insistence, curbed this instinct, and scored his runs mostly from the orthodox forward shot at the rate of 25 runs an hour, the last part of the innings being played as methodically as the first.

Notts and the Gunns are synonymous: William, uncle of George and John, formed with Arthur Shrewsbury one of the earliest of the famous opening partnerships.

The strike of Notts professionals in 1881, including the captain, was not without its effects, for it gave young Attewell a place in the XI for which he might have grown tired of waiting and gone elsewhere. It settled once and for all time the responsibility for the management and well-being of the club firmly in the committee's hands. It underlined the importance of an amateur captain of the side, and this they found in J. A. Dixon, who was succeeded by A. O. Jones. These two soon altered the dull state of affairs at Trent Bridge. J. A. Dixon was a member of the Notts County XI from 1882 to 1905, captain and a member of the committee from 1895 till his death. Apart from cricket, at which he excelled as an all-rounder and as a vigilant commander, he was a sagacious man of affairs, a faithful citizen, a philanthropist, a wise magistrate and a true friend. A. O. Jones, one of the best fielders ever to step on a cricket ground, came into the side 10 years after J. A. Dixon. Stanley Jackson played him in the Cambridge side for his fielding alone; for Notts he caught over 500 catches.

Jones and Iremonger, a fine pair of opening bats, made a hundred without loss on 25 occasions but it is Jones's all-round keenness, his vigilance and his team spirit that are best remembered. Alas, he died in his early 40s, during the First World War. J. Iremonger had a great influence for good on all cricketers who were fortunate to meet him. He was a natural off-spin bowler and made himself into a very reliable opening bat. He was also the best coach and teacher of cricket of his time –

England players came to him to be put right, as well as preparatory schoolboys with all the years before them. 'It were all one' to Jimmy. He played for Nottinghamshire from 1897 to 1914.

There were great characters in the Notts side of those pre-1914 days. The world had changed from the days of Scotton and Shrewsbury. Society was throwing off its mid-Victorian smugness and self-satisfaction. This breath of fresh air pervaded the cricket grounds. It was an age of great batting, the Golden Age of the amateur, with his free style and natural ability. No more natural player has ever taken stance than George Gunn, who first played for Notts in 1901. He scored over 30,000 runs, and it is doubtful if he was ever off balance or ever made an ugly hurried shot for one of them, unless he wished for reasons of his own to give his wicket away. John Gunn, his elder brother, was a left-hand bat, solid and reliable, and an untiring and accurate left-arm bowler. Notts held both in affection and latterly in veneration, but it has always been felt that in spite of their magnificent records for Notts and England, they never got their full recognition at Lord's. Hardstaff, Sr (or 'Hotstuff' as he was known), was, with Payton, the strength of the middle batting. He was the father of young Joe, who made such a name for himself before and after the Second World War. The best bowlers were Wass and Hallam who between them virtually won the Championship for the county in 1907, Wass with his fast leg-breaks and Hallam with his off-breaks. John Gunn bowled occasionally so that Wass could change ends with Hallam. Wass was what was known in those days as a bit of a rough diamond, but woe betide anyone who presumed to call him 'Topsy', his nick-name, unless they knew him very well. Hallam was a smaller man of lighter build. Throughout all this period, the bow-legged Tom Oates, in his skeleton pads, kept wicket in leather gloves as the Greeks kept the Pass at Thermopylae. Alletson from Welbeck was a remarkable hard hitter, who has passed into cricket history for his 189 in 90 minutes one May day at Hove. A. O. Jones said that he would always play Alletson in all future games if only he would hit, but after this one great feat, overwhelmed by the enormity of his offence, he hardly ever opened his shoulders to the bowling again, and alas, had to be dropped from the side.

For the first 16 years in the inter-war period, Notts were always well placed in the County Championship, which they won in 1929. The side in the early 1920s was a strong batting side, led by Arthur Carr, W. Whysall, Walker, George and John Gunn, Payton and Hardstaff (Sr). The opening bowlers were burly Fred Barratt and 'long John' Matthews, with that great off-break bowler Sam Staples and left-hander John Gunn as first change. 'Tich' Richmond, season after season, took his 100 wickets. Carr was one of those captains in county cricket who knew the value of the leg-break and googly bowler, and, what is also important, when and how to use him. Iremonger, the county coach, demanded a high standard, and Walter Marshall, the groundsman, a character, created cricket pitches at Trent Bridge which were very fast and very true, the backcloth for great fast bowlers.

In the mid-1920s, a boy from Nuncargate named Harold Larwood appeared. He played 1 match in 1925 and was so carefully nursed and encouraged by Carr and Iremonger that in 1927 he headed the bowling averages with 100 wickets for 17 runs. Larwood was of medium height and lissom build, but with a fine pair of shoulders and long arms and hands. His pace and accuracy were due to his rhythmical run to the wicket, which he started slowly, and his action when delivering the ball was dynamic. Bill Voce as a young and somewhat overgrown boy walked from Hucknall to Trent Bridge in hope of a trial in the nets. He was tall and well built and with an easy action could make his left-arm fast bowling swing in the air in a most devastating manner. Ben Lilley, who had replaced Tom Oates as wicket-keeper, did noble work behind the stumps, and there was no gambit of this varied attack with which he could not cope.

Such a combination must sooner or later win a Championship, but it is surprising that they did not win more often. A tragic 3rd day at Swansea, when after a night's heavy rain they were skittled out by Glamorgan, then bottom of the table, lost them the palm in 1927. They were runners-up in 1922, 1923, 1927, and always fighting for a place with the top few in the 1920s and early 1930s. Notts then were a fine side forcefully led by A. W. Carr. The story of the acrimonious Body-line controversy which led to his retirement is told elsewhere. Larwood also gave up first-class cricket, and Nottinghamshire cricket suffered an upset from which recovery was difficult. G. F. H. Heane and S. D. Rhodes took over joint-leadership in 1935, then Heane alone held the captaincy until the Second World War and continued after. A good right-hand bowler and a forceful left-hand bat, he was a forthright character around whom a new side was built. One of the young players of that pre-war era was Walter Keeton, who replaced Whysall as an opening bat. He had a wealth of strokes and scored freely all round the wicket. He was a master at making runs against time in the last innings of a match. Joe Hardstaff, the son of 'Hotstuff', had the stamp of a class cricketer in all he did. His run-getting was prodigious and he scored quickly. He made the quickest hundred of the season in 1937 and was 2nd in the batting averages. Also of that time, C. B. Harris, an opening bat and off-spin bowler, gave the side solidity and his hearers delight for he was a born comedian. Butler, with his windmill action, and Jepson with an orthodox round delivery, were a pair of opening bowlers, hard worked, but always giving of their best. Butler was particularly dangerous with a new ball and these two carried the tradition of Morley and Shaw, Hallam and Wass, Larwood and Voce, well into the 1950s. Hardstaff, Harris, Butler, Jepson were all on active service in various parts of the world in the war, but they returned in 1946 to be the mainstay of Nottinghamshire cricket for several years afterwards.

Harold Larwood, in action and repose, smallish in frame and mechanically perfect. It was the left foot that at last 'went' under the strain.

Notts, the 1929 Champions. Back row: W. R. D. Payton, H. Larwood, W. Walker, F. Barratt, W. Voce, B. Lilley, G. V. Gunn and J. Carlin (scorer); sitting: S. J. Staples, G. Gunn, A. W. Carr (captain), W. W. Whysall and A. Staples.

There had been no intake of young players to the ground staffs, and Nottinghamshire (like Derbyshire) were affected by the changed conditions in the mining areas and the improved status of the colliers. Hitherto, men with cricket ability had been ever-ready to seize the opportunity of escape from the darkness and hard grind of the coalface; nobody glories in fresh air and sunshine more than the miner, and to play cricket and be paid for it – well, nothing could be better. Now conditions in the pits were vastly different and improving all the time; mechanization

'Young Joe' Hardstaff (to distinguish him from his greatly-respected father, also Joe and also of Notts and England) was one of the most elegant and attractive batsmen both before and after the Second World War.

was working wonders in removing the sweat and hard labour from the winning of coal, and miners were rightly among the best paid of manual workers. Pre-war, it used to be said in Nottingham that the county coach had only to whistle down the pit shaft and up came a bowler. Today, the club cannot offer a financial reward big enough to induce a collier to forsake the pit. Since the war only one ex-miner (F. W. Stocks) has been capped by Notts, whereas between the wars the team rarely took the field with less than 6. Small wonder, therefore, that since 1950 the club has finished 4 times in bottom place. How are the mighty fallen!

It could be argued that in 1946 Notts were in no worse state than other counties for most of the pre-war players were available and everyone was looking forward with pleasurable anticipation to the release from the RAF of a young man of whom much had been heard. During the war R. T. ('Reg') Simpson was engaged on flying duties with Transport Command and whilst serving in India had his first experience of top-grade cricket. Returning to England in 1946 with a great reputation as a batsman, he went straight into the side and delighted the spectators with his polished stroke-play and brilliant fielding. To see Simpson and Hardstaff together at the wicket was a delight to the eye; no other county had two such stylists – 'all ease and elegance', and spectators were treated to the top quality of batsmanship. Keeton was also in splendid form and making a lot of runs and in 1949 he and Simpson put on 318 for the 1st wicket against Lancashire at Old Trafford. In this same year Cyril Poole was awarded his cap; an aggressive left-hand batsman with a punishing pull and scorching off-drive, he was always at his best when chasing quick runs. Who will ever forget that wonderful exhibition of hitting with which he and Simpson regaled the crowd at Trent Bridge in 1949 when they scored 251 against Leicestershire in an unbroken 2nd-wicket match-winning stand? They reached 100 in 40 minutes, 200 in 75 minutes and 251 in 97 minutes!

At the end of the 1950 season, W. A. Sime, who had succeeded G. F. H. Heane in 1947, resigned the captaincy because of the increasing demands of his practice as a barrister, and Reg Simpson assumed command. It was an unenviable task, coincident with the worst period of Nottinghamshire cricket, but Simpson brought to it qualities of tenacity and determination which carried him undaunted through all the vicissitudes of the next 10 years; to his great credit he was always ready and willing to issue or accept a challenge in order to keep a game alive and, within the side's limitations, to play attractive cricket.

In 1951, Notts finished bottom of the table and next to the bottom in 1952; an unprecedented situation demanded drastic action, and the committee decided to break with tradition and go outside the county to secure a badly needed top-class bowler. In fact, they went outside the country and engaged Bruce Dooland, the Australian leg-spin and googly bowler. Thus, amid the encircling gloom, there burst on the Trent Bridge scene in 1953 a kindly light which for a while dispersed the prevailing despondency. The team jumped to 8th place in the table and in 1954 advanced to 5th position; this remarkable improvement was due, in large measure, to the many outstanding performances of Dooland and the tonic effect they had on the side, for Notts acquired a 'new look' and a winning team's confidence. Hardstaff and opening bowlers Butler and Jepson of pre-war days were still playing well, Reg Simpson was in excellent form, other batsmen were Poole, Giles and Clay, and all-rounders Stocks and Gamini Goonesena, with wicket-keeper Meads, made up the side. Stocks, a left-hand bat and right-arm off-spinner was a sound and useful player who had made a spectacular debut in first-class cricket by scoring a hundred in his 1st innings and taking a wicket with his 1st ball – a feat unique in cricket history. He also set up a county record by scoring 171 against the Australians. Goonesena (from Ceylon) first played for Notts in 1952; he went up to Cambridge, was awarded his blue in 1954, captained the side in 1957, and had the distinction of scoring 211 in the University Match of that year. A leg-spin bowler of ability, he learned much from Dooland and had some good performances with the ball. He achieved the double in 1955 and 1957.

The brief occupancy of 5th place in the table in 1954 coincided with Dooland's finest year, for he took 196 wickets and scored 1,012 runs. He had a remarkable match against Essex taking 16 wickets for 83 runs and created a new Notts record of 181 wickets in a season, beating Len Richmond's 169 wickets in 1922; Richmond, who was present at Trent Bridge at the time, was so overcome with emotion that tears streamed down his cheeks. Around this time the wind of change began to sweep through the counties (Yorkshire excepted) and cricket entered upon a new era. Clubs began to throw their nets wider than their own boundaries in order to recruit players and strengthen their teams. With the retirement of Hardstaff (scorer of 83 centuries and close on 32,000 runs) and the urgent need of a fast bowler, Notts entered the common market for players and engaged A. K. Walker, a left-arm fast-medium bowler from Australia, K. Smales, off-spinner from Yorkshire, and Maurice Hill, a young batsman of promise from Lincolnshire. These 3 along with new wicket-keeper, Geoffrey Millman from Bedfordshire, had scarcely been welded into the side when Dooland dropped a bombshell by announcing that he would be returning to his native Australia, when his contract ran out at the end of the 1957 season. The club made every effort to retain his services for a further period and were hopeful of so doing right up to the end; however, Dooland and his wife wanted their children to be educated in Australia and so the decision to return home was made. To lose such a fine cricketer at the peak of his power – he was only 33 – was a crippling blow to Notts and a sad loss to English county cricket; leg-spin bowlers were few, and one of his excellence rare indeed. In 5 years of first-class cricket in this country he took 5 or more wickets in an innings 73 times and altogether captured 808 wickets and scored 5,175 runs – a truly magnificent contribution to the game.

The 5 years after Dooland's departure were mostly a time of lamentation and woe; thrice bottom of the table and twice just a little more successful. During this period 5 capped bowlers retired from the game – Walker, Smales, Harvey, Goonesena and great-hearted Jepson – leaving a gap desperately hard to fill. Walker returned to Australia leaving a notable performance in the record book, for in 1956, against Leicestershire, he took a wicket with the last ball of the 1st innings and then achieved a unique hat-trick with the first 3 balls of the 2nd innings. Smales, in his brief career, had the distinction in 1956 of taking all 10 Gloucestershire wickets for 66 runs, a feat which deserved a better fate, for Notts lost the match by 9 wickets. Only one other Notts player has taken all 10 wickets in an innings; the great William Clarke in 1845. Despite the importation of an experienced off-spinner, B. D. ('Bomber') Wells from Gloucestershire, and the steady improvement of J. Cotton, a young Notts-born fast bowler, the paucity of the bowling resources was obvious; in addition, apart from the evergreen Simpson and Poole, the team lacked batsmen of experience, though Norman Hill, a left-hander from the Duke of Portland's estate at Welbeck, proved a sound opener and dependable run getter.

At the end of the 1960 season Simpson relinquished the captaincy to the professional Clay and renounced full-time cricket in order to devote more time to the increasing claims of his business appointment with the well-known Nottingham firm of bat manufacturers. Fortunately for the club he continued to play in most of the home games and in 1962, as if to prove he was no spent force at 42, headed the batting averages for the whole country. Furthermore, he set the seal on a brilliant career by completing 30,000 runs in first-class cricket. Of Notts batsmen, only George Gunn and Joe Hardstaff (Jr) had previously reached this aggregate. He played in 27 Test Matches (a Notts record equalled only by Voce) and his finest innings was undoubtedly his 156 not out at Melbourne in 1951 which helped England to win her first post-war Test victory over Australia and was a masterly effort against the fast bowling of Lindwall and Miller. He made his highest score on this tour of Australia, 259 for MCC against New South Wales. For his county he exceeded 200 on 9 occasions. Simpson will always be remembered as a superb player of fast bowling, making his strokes with consummate artistry, and when the bumpers came hurtling at him he would, as R. C. Robertson-Glasgow once so graphically put it, 'bow his black head with the cool grace of a Spanish grandee'.

In 1963 Notts moved up to 9th position in the table, the highest since the Dooland era. Bolus, the new opening batsman, had a remarkably good season, scoring 2,427 runs. He made six centuries including two against Yorkshire, his former county. On this form he was selected for the Fourth and Fifth Tests against the West Indies and for the MCC tour of India. The success of Bolus had a tonic effect on the whole team; of the bowlers, Davison and Wells finished with 111 and 97 wickets respectively. Sad to relate, this welcome improvement was not maintained and 1964 proved to be a most disappointing season; though the side was mostly the same in personnel, the quality of performance fell far below that of the previous year. The batting let the side down badly in 1965 – not a single player could manage to average 30 runs per innings and only Smedley, the young colt from Yorkshire, exceeded 25. The attack was a 2-man affair, the fast bowlers, Forbes from Jamaica and A. J. Corran, the Oxford blue; the latter, however, decided to emigrate to Australia at the close of the season and another who left Trent Bridge was 'Bomber' Wells, the off-spinner who had done so well in his first seasons with the county, but was now apparently bowled out.

Millman announced his intention of leaving first-class cricket in the autumn and thereby left the county without either a captain or a wicket-keeper. The county persuaded the former Surrey and England 'keeper, Swetman to take Millman's place behind the stumps and as a double-insurance signed the West Indian keeper, D. L. Murray, who was studying at Cambridge. Norman Hill took over the captain's reins, but the team remained at the foot of the Championship. Another importation was that of Bob White, the Middlesex batsman, though he became increasingly used as an off-spinner and his batting powers faded away.

1967 saw a slight improvement in the playing record, but a dramatic change was effected in 1968. This was the 1st season of the 'instant' qualification system in county cricket and Notts managed the scoop of the summer by signing the great West Indian captain and all-rounder Garfield Sobers. He scored 1,570 runs (average 44·85) and took 83 wickets (average 22·67) and the county made a spectacular improvement going up to 4th place in the Championship. Sadly such success was of a temporary nature. Sobers was absent for half 1969 and although M. J. Harris was brought in from Middlesex to partner Bolus in opening the batting, the bowling was rather weak – Forbes was not the force he had been and only Stead's deliveries really had much bite. Halfyard, the old Kent player, who in recent years had been an umpire, was specially registered but could do little more than keep the runs down.

It was hoped that Sobers, who was badly missed in 1969, would make all the difference in 1970, but he was spirited away to captain the Rest of the World, missing 10 matches. When he did appear, he batted brilliantly, but his bowling had grown stale and it was a bowler that Notts desperately required. Both Forbes and Stead suffered injuries and no one elsewhere was very effective. The first half of 1971 was even more of a disaster, but happily the county improved a little during July and August. It was a great year for Harris, who by hitting 9 hundreds equalled the county record. White's off-spinners proved most successful, but there was not much to be said for the rest. The following season found the county still struggling, Sobers was often away injured, Harris had a poor year with the bat and the only glimmer of hope came from 3 youngsters – Derek Randall, Paul Todd and Nirmal Nanan. For a welcome change Randall and Todd represented local talent. The committee decided on change and both Bolus and Taylor left at the end of the year. The drastic measures had no immediate effect on the results and, although Randall received much favourable comment, the bowling was feeble; even Stead, who had fought valiantly for years, failed to take 50 championship wickets. At the ground itself, the redevelopment programme under the guidance of the President, Frank Gregory, was under way, thus improving the financial prospects if not the playing ones.

Sobers left after the 1974 season. To the surprise of some, J. D. Bond, the former Lancashire captain, was engaged as player-manager, but the plan back-fired and within weeks the members demanded and got an extraordinary general meeting to enquire into the lack of playing success. It was plain that the team was in dire need of new bowlers.

In place of the internationally-famous Sobers, Notts imported an unknown Transvaal player, Clive Rice, for 1975. He has proved in his 4 seasons with the club to be a valuable asset and succeeded Smedley as captain during the 1979 season. By 1976, Derek Randall had matured and was producing runs in his inimitable style. The county had also, at long last, unearthed a local born bowler who seemed more than just promising – Kevin Cooper – and the era of vast importations appeared to be fading. For some inexplicable reason both Randall and Harris utterly failed in 1977 and although Rice played exceptionally well, he could not make up for this lack of runs and the county fell back to 17th in the county table.

1978 began with controversy surrounding Rice's signing for World Series Cricket. He had been selected to captain the county, but was dismissed from the club when his agreement to play for Kerry Packer became known. Happily the affair was settled amicably and Rice was reinstated – though not as captain. Notts had hastily signed Richard Hadlee, the New Zealand fast bowler, when it was thought that Rice would not play and the happy outcome was that the county suddenly possessed the most effective opening attack in decades. With Randall and Harris also back among the runs, the club produced its best cricket for almost 10 years.

Derek Randall, of Notts, one of the characters of cricket in the 1970s, is no slave to the orthodox. An idea where this ball pitched can be judged from the position of the wicket-keeper's gloves.

CAPTAIN

1859–70	G. Parr
1871–80	R. Daft
1881–82	W. Oscroft
1883–86	A. Shaw
1887–88	M. Sherwin
1889–99	J. A. Dixon
1900–12	A. O. Jones
1913	A. O. Jones and G. O. Gauld
1914	A. O. Jones
1919–34	A. W. Carr
1935	G. F. H. Heane and S. D. Rhodes
1936–46	G. F. H. Heane
1947–50	W. A. Sime
1951–60	R. T. Simpson
1961	J. D. Clay
1962	A. J. Corran
1963–65	G. Millman
1966–67	N. W. Hill
1968–71	G. S. Sobers
1972	J. B. Bolus
1973	G. S. Sobers
1974	J. D. Bond
1975–78	M. J. Smedley
1979	M. J. Smedley and C. E. B. Rice

HIGHEST TOTALS

For 739–7D v Leicester, Trent Bridge 1903
Against 706–4D by Surrey, Trent Bridge 1947

LOWEST TOTALS

For 13 v Yorks, Trent Bridge 1901
Against 16 by Derby, Trent Bridge 1879
16 by Surrey, Oval 1880

HIGHEST INDIVIDUAL INNINGS

For 312* W. W. Keeton v Middlesex, Oval 1939
Against 345 C. G. Macartney for Australians, Trent Bridge 1921

MOST RUNS

In a season 2,620 W. W. Whysall 1929
In a career 31,592 G. Gunn 1902–1932

MOST HUNDREDS

In a season 9 W. W. Whysall 1928
M. J. Harris 1971
In a career 65 J. Hardstaff, jr 1930–1955

INDIVIDUAL INNINGS OF 250 AND OVER

A. Shrewsbury, 267 v Middlesex, Trent Bridge 1887
A. Shrewsbury, 267 v Sussex, Trent Bridge 1890
J. A. Dixon, 268* v Sussex, Trent Bridge 1897
A. O. Jones, 250 v Gloucester, Bristol 1899
W. Gunn, 273 v Derby, Derby 1901
A. O. Jones, 296 v Gloucester, Trent Bridge 1903
J. R. Gunn, 294 v Leicester, Trent Bridge 1903
J. Iremonger, 272 v Kent, Trent Bridge 1904
A. O. Jones, 274 v Essex, Leyton 1905
W. W. Keeton, 261 v Gloucester, Trent Bridge 1934
J. Hardstaff, jr, 266 v Leicester, Leicester 1937
W. W. Keeton, 312* v Middlesex, Oval 1939

HUNDRED ON DEBUT

F. W. Stocks 114 v Kent, Trent Bridge 1946
K. R. Miller 102* v Cambridge University, Trent Bridge 1959

RECORD WICKET PARTNERSHIPS

1 A. O. Jones and A. Shrewsbury, 391 v Gloucester, Bristol 1899
2 W. Gunn and A. Shrewsbury, 398 v Sussex, Trent Bridge 1890
3 J. R. Gunn and W. Gunn, 369 v Leicester, Trent Bridge 1903
4 A. O. Jones and J. R. Gunn, 361 v Essex, Leyton 1905
5 A. Shrewsbury and W. Gunn, 266 v Sussex, Hove 1884
6 H. Winrow and P. F. Harvey, 303* v Derby, Trent Bridge 1947
7 M. J. Smedley and R. A. White, 204 v Surrey, Oval 1967
8 G. F. H. Heane and R. Winrow, 220 v Somerset, Trent Bridge 1933
9 W. McIntyre and G. Wootton, 167 v Kent, Trent Bridge 1869
10 E. B. Alletson and W. Riley 152 v Sussex, Hove 1911

MOST WICKETS

In a match 17–89 F. C. L. Matthews v Northants, Trent Bridge 1923
In a season 181 B. Dooland 1954
In a career 1,653 T. Wass 1896–1920

ALL 10 WICKETS IN AN INNINGS

J. C. Shaw v England, Eastwood 1870
K. Smales v Gloucester, Stroud 1956

HAT-TRICKS

H. J. Butler 3
A. Shaw 3 (2 in same match)
J. R. Gunn and H. Larwood 2 each
C. E. Dench, J. A. Dixon, W. Flowers
A. W. Hallam, T. L. Richmond, F. Shacklock, K. Smales, B. Stead, M. N. S. Taylor, A. K. Walker, T. Wass 1 each

WICKET-KEEPING – MOST DISMISSALS

In an innings 6 E. A. Meads (2)
T. W. Oates (2)
B. Lilley (1)
G. Millman (1)
In a match 10 T. W. Oates
In a season 85 G. Millman 1961
In a career 958 T. W. Oates 1897–1925

COUNTY CAPS AWARDED SINCE 1946

1946 E. A. Meads, T. B. Reddick, R. T. Simpson, F. W. Stocks
1947 W. A. Sime, H. Winrow
1949 P. F. Harvey, C. J. Poole
1951 R. J. Giles
1952 J. D. Clay
1953 B. Dooland
1954 E. J. Martin, E. J. Rowe
1955 G. Goonesena, K. Smales
1956 A. K. Walker
1957 G. Millman
1959 N. W. Hill
1960 J. Cotton, J. D. Springall, B. D. Wells
1961 M. Hill
1962 A. J. Corran, I. Davison, H. M. Winfield
1963 J. B. Bolus
1965 C. Forbes, H. I. Moore
1966 M. J. Smedley, R. Swetman, R. A. White
1967 D. L. Murray, M. N. S. Taylor
1968 D. J. Halfyard, G. S. Sobers
1969 B. Stead
1970 M. J. Harris, B. Hassan
1971 D. A. Pullan
1973 D. W. Randall
1974 J. D. Bond, P. A. Wilkinson
1975 P. D. Johnson, H. C. Latchman, C. E. B. Rice, W. Taylor
1977 D. R. Doshi, P. A. Todd
1978 R. J. Hadlee

Somerset

ERIC HILL

Foundation 1875
Colours Black, white and maroon
Badge Wessex Wyvern

Much of cricket's fascination lies in the unexpected and, if surprise is the yardstick of success, Somerset must be among the most successful clubs in the land. The most unlikely records and paradoxes decorate the diverting story of this county of rolling acres and small population, and through them runs an endearing thread of rich, earthy West Country humour. Indeed future generations will look back on the pinnacle year of 1979 with the sort of wry chuckle never far from the lips of many of the memorable early characters. In May a legal, but unhappily ill-judged, use of the rules brought widespread and bitter condemnation from the cricket world, ending in expulsion from the Benson & Hedges Cup for 'bringing the game into disrepute'. In September the same year the same cricket world echoed with warm and approving congratulation as Somerset – the last of the first-class counties never to have won a title – broke the spell in marvellous style with 2 trophies in 2 days. The happy Somerset flair of drawing to herself fine cricketers and rich characters from all over the world has greatly enhanced the worth of the locally-born heroes, and although results have rarely been startlingly good, a splendid reputation for enterprising cricket has grown, coupled with the delightful trick of often toppling the great ones against all known odds. It all started in 1825 when one of the oldest clubs, Lansdown (Bath) was formed. It is still going strongly, associated closely with the county's progress. In 1861, XXII of Lansdown beat an All-England XI and 2 years later, a 14-year-old made a 'pair' in the corresponding match. Thirty-two years later, W. G. Grace, for it was he, reached his 100th first-class hundred – against Somerset. In 1925 J. B. Hobbs made a hundred in each innings at Taunton to equal, then to exceed, Grace's record of 126 hundreds.

A team called the Gentlemen of Somerset held a meeting at Sidmouth, in Devon, and initiated the Somerset paradoxes by deciding to start a county team, stipulating that there should be no county ground. That was on 18 August 1875, and precisely 100 years later I. V. A. Richards, the West Indian batting genius, marked the Centenary with a hundred against Gloucestershire, the 'old foe', at Taunton. In 1886 the club took a 19-year lease on the Athletic Ground at Taunton, and 10 years later acquired the leasehold for £2,000. It became one of the pleasantest headquarters grounds and was to be the scene for some superb cricket from many of the greatest performers.

The year 1886 was momentous for another reason. Samuel Moses James Woods first played for Somerset in his last year at Brighton College and soon became a legend. Sir Pelham Warner wrote: 'The name of Sammy Woods is famous for all time in the annals of cricket'. He played for England in South Africa (1895), for Australia against England in 1888, and but for injury would have played for England in Australia in 1902 when S. F. Barnes was hurt. Born in Sydney, Australia, his magnificent fast bowling, big hitting, inspiring captaincy and salty anecdote, besides earning him the sobriquet 'Great-heart' established the essence and character of the years spanning Somerset's emergence as a first-class county in 1891. Woods was the first of the long and honourable line of Somerset all-rounders and the achievements in the early years created many of the precedents that can be followed like precious threads of quality through the Somerset story. H. T. Hewett set a standard of bold captaincy and sturdy batting rewardingly present in many of his successors. The slow left-arm bowling arts passed with much success from E. J. Tyler to B. Cranfield and J. C. White and through the line. The graceful, positive batting of L. C. H. Palairet gave an example of skill and dedication which was to be followed, with fascinating and wide variations in styles, through a long and distinguished list. Always there has been a tradition of long service and loyalty from the professionals, starting with Tyler and G. B. Nichols, the first of the fast bowlers. Wicket-keeping has also been a Somerset forte, paired with stout batting. A. E. Newton, said to have given Woods a wicket with his 1st ball for Somerset (a brilliant leg-side stumping) added another strand of real quality to the traditions. While the main fibres of quality were so bright, however, much of the supporting talent has been considerably less so. A recurring theme was the unavailability of many talented amateurs and not until the 1930s was an acceptably large and capable nucleus of professionals engaged.

The legendary S.M.J. ('Sammy') Woods: Australian by birth, Somerset by mutual adoption, supreme stalwart of the early days.

Although Somerset won all their matches in 1890, the scepticism which delayed their first-class entry at first seemed justified. On his 26th birthday George Lohmann bowled them to a heavy defeat at the Oval. Lancashire won at Taunton by 9 wickets. However, the doubts were stilled at Maidstone, where Woods steered them to victory over Kent, who were unbeaten at the time. Four other victories followed, notably over Yorkshire and the champions, Surrey. With 50 minutes left and Surrey's 4th-wicket pair coasting quietly to a draw, Woods erupted. He and Nichols ripped through, and with an over (5 balls) left, the last pair stood between Somerset and victory. Two high full tosses from Woods set the scene for the yorker which hit the middle stump for a famous success by 131 runs. Even better followed, for in 1892 an extremely well-balanced Somerset came 3rd to Surrey and Notts. Tyler took 15 for 96 while beating Notts and Palairet, scoring perhaps the most famous of his 27 hundreds, helped Hewett to produce an opening stand of 346 in 3½ hours against the powerful Yorkshire attack.

Successes dwindled in the absence of more bowling support (Woods writes of himself, Tyler and Nichols as being 'bowled silly') but there were some great days. In 1895 Palairet's hundred and Tyler's 14 wickets beat Yorkshire at Taunton by 29 runs and Tyler's all 10 for 49 brought a brilliant win over the champions, Surrey. Rather more typical of the period, however, were the innings of 601 by Essex and 801 by Lancashire in successive Taunton defeats. A. C. MacLaren made a record 424 in the latter match, in 470 minutes, with a six and 64 fours.

It was the turn of the century which established Somerset as the 'Team of Surprises'. From 1900 to 1902 Yorkshire won 3 Championships, losing only 2 matches, both to Somerset, who ended up 11th, 13th and 7th the while. Somerset beat them again in 1903. The most famous was the 1901 match at Leeds which began with Somerset 87 all out, and Yorkshire 325. Palairet and L. C. Braund followed noughts in the first innings with hundreds in the second and Somerset totalled 630. Then the spinners Braund and Cranfield bowled them to triumph by 279 runs. This marked a high point in the immense contribution made by Braund. Joining the county from Surrey in 1899, his opening batting, well-controlled leg breaks, consummate slip catching and overall reliability did much to hold the side together. He took nearly 700 wickets, made over 12,000 runs, played 23 times for England, and took 25 wickets in the 1902 and 1903 victories over Yorkshire. This success was not to be repeated against Yorkshire for another 56 years.

Things became hard as the First World War approached. Four times in 7 seasons, even with fewer fixtures than most, Somerset were bottom. The staunch efforts of the professionals, now A. E. Lewis and E. Robson, gained some support from newcomers of the calibre of J. Daniell and P. R. Johnson, but there was promise coming. Daniell, a forthright captain, with much in common with Woods, notably in the rugby football sphere, led Somerset to 5th in 1919, but until 1924 success was very limited. In that year J. C. W. MacBryan, R. C. Robertson – Glasgow, M. D. Lyon and J. C. White all appeared for the Gentlemen to underline the amateur strength. In a traditional upset in 1922 the champions Middlesex were beaten at Weston-super-Mare with a six in the final over by Robson, then 51 years old. He was promptly given £50 by a delighted supporter. In an honourable career lasting from 1895 to 1923, Robson took over 1,100 wickets and scored over 12,000 runs, bowling all through an innings when 49 and making a hundred the following year.

In 1925 the 46-year-old Daniell made 2 hundreds in the Essex match, but by now the main burden fell on the willing shoulders of John Cornish White, born in West Somerset in 1891. From 1919 to 1932, his dipping flight and remarkable accuracy brought him 100 or more wickets a season. Twice he scored over 1,000 runs and, in all, a marvellous contribution over some 28 years brought Somerset more than 11,000 runs and 2,166 wickets, both at an average of about 18. He played in 15 Test matches and on his triumphant return from a decisive part in retaining the Ashes in 1929, the delighted population dragged his car with ropes back to his home in Combe Florey, and a spontaneous fund raised £1,000 for him.

W. T. Greswell, who was to follow White into the Club Presidency, was one of the very first in-swing bowlers, while J. J. Bridges, another capable seam bowler, took 684 wickets. Nevertheless Somerset were usually in the wrong half of the table. It was the familiar story of too much expected from too few. Gradually the professional staff was built up. W. T. Luckes kept the wicket-keeping traditions high for nearly 25 years; H. L. Hazell, with plenty of time to study White, took 957 wickets with his left-arm slows in 23 years, starting in 1929. W. H. R. Andrews, a lively bowler and batsman, completed 2 doubles before the Second World War, and H. T. F. Buse, an accomplished all-rounder from Bath, added quality. But excellent as they were, they had to give place in purely dramatic terms to two outstanding players and personalities.

Arthur Wellard, a fast bowler and big hitter straight from the Woods mould, joined Somerset from Kent in 1929. He took 131 wickets in his 1st year and soon completed the 1st of his 3 doubles. His classic out-swing action, and no fewer than 500 six hits (in a total of 11,000 runs), made him the schoolboy's dream cricketer. One summer he hit 72 sixes: he took over 1,500 wickets (many of them later on, with off-breaks made possible by his enormous hands) and he accepted many unlikely catches in the close positions. Twice he hit 5 sixes in an over, one of them when completing a double over the 1936 champions, Derbyshire. At Wells, Wellard took 9 wickets in the match and when all appeared lost, hit 7 sixes and 8 fours making 86 out of 102 in under an hour for a famous one-wicket victory.

In 1935 another star rose from West Somerset, which had already produced White and Greswell. Harold Gimblett, a 21-year-old, having made a slight impression at practice, was called on to play against Essex at Frome. He arrived at the ground after a very long walk with his bag, having missed his bus. The result startled the cricket world. Going in with the score at 107 for 6, he showed an astonishing range of strokes and made 123 with 3 sixes and 17 fours, reaching the fastest hundred of the season (63 minutes) in his 1st county innings. Promoted to open the innings

LEFT J. C. ('Farmer') White: 'Whether it was cows or batsmen he had the treatment for the trouble' (R. C. Robertson-Glasgow).

RIGHT On 18 May, 1935 Harold Gimblett, a 20-year-old club cricketer from Watchet, in Somerset, astonished the cricket world by scoring a hundred in 63 minutes against Essex on the 1st day of his 1st county match. In 14 playing seasons (the war intervening) his cheerful approach to batting brought him 21,108 runs – the highest aggregate in Somerset's history.

in 1936 he began wonderfully, won 2 of 3 Test caps, and went on to take most of the Somerset batting records. His 21,000 runs and 49 hundreds included no fewer than 265 sixes, surely a record for a regular opening batsman. What the international scene lost in Wellard (2 Tests) and Gimblett, Somerset most gladly accepted.

J. W. Lee had been a useful all-rounder in the 1930s. His brother F.S., later to become a Test umpire, made a valuable and interesting contrast as an opening batsman with Gimblett. He became, in 1938, the 1st Somerset player to reach 2,000 runs, made 2 hundreds against Worcestershire, being on the field throughout; and another against Surrey in the next match. He totalled over 15,000 runs before retiring in 1947. In 1938 E. F. Longrigg, who had followed White and Ingle to the captaincy, led the team to 10 victories – the highest to date – and although such fine amateurs as H. D. Burrough, R. J. O. Meyer and N. S. Mitchell-Innes could play infrequently, the team was building well, and the scene was set for the record 1946 season.

Longrigg's 1946 team had the experience and quality available to few of his adversaries, with the addition of J. Lawrence, a batsman and googly bowler from Yorkshire, who was to play an important part in the next 10 seasons with over 9,000 runs and 791 wickets. After a depressing May, 12 victories, 4th position in the Championship table, innings victories over the Indians and Middlesex, and 3 consecutive 500 totals at Taunton, made it a memorable year. The cultured batting of M. M. Walford, a triple Oxford blue, was a comfort during several Augusts, but as the opposition recovered from the war, Somerset's hopeful visions faded. Seventh position was attained in 1950 under a Londoner, S. S. Rogers but though the spin bowling, with Hazell, Lawrence and the newly recruited E. P. Robinson from Yorkshire, was strong, young fast bowlers and reliable batsmen proved difficult to find.

For 4 seasons, 1952 to 1955, Somerset were bottom and the decline was marked by outcry from members, led by the late R. A. Roberts, then a young journalist in Taunton, and later the originator of worldwide multi-racial cricket tours. Two special general meetings of members amply demonstrated widespread concern about the club – itself a healthy sign – and club officials, alerted and alarmed, reacted excellently, while the new Supporters' Club gathered strength and made many things possible. New players were brought in from all over the world. P. B. Wight, a delightful stroke maker from British Guiana, made a hundred in his first match (against the 1953 Australians) and up to 1965 made nearly 17,000 runs. Colin McCool, the Australian, who could turn a match with his crackling strokes in an hour, belied his age with some great performances in the 5 years starting in 1956. W. E. Alley joined from Blackpool in 1957 and was to create many records with his lusty batting and acute medium-paced bowling. J. W. McMahon, completing the trio of Australians, brought his dual-purpose slow left arm bowling from Surrey. Two all-rounders proved useful from Lancashire, J. G. Lomax and J. Hilton. B. Lobb, taking 282 wickets in 3 seasons, and K. D. Biddulph were other seam bowlers deeply involved in the resurgence.

A real nursery and 2nd XI was started with most gratifying results. B. A. Langford, who took 26 wickets in his first 3 matches (at Bath in 1953) took nearly 1,400 wickets in a long career of off-breaks; K. E. Palmer achieved Somerset's 1st double for 23 years in 1961, contributed 832 wickets and nearly 8,000 runs in 16 seasons; and G. Atkinson a Yorkshireman, who joined the club at 13 years of age, became a splendid opener with over 14,000 runs in 12 seasons. Alley, coming into county cricket at 38, had two astounding years in 1961–62. At the age of 42 he scored 3,000 runs in a season. A year later the Australian all-rounder scored 1,915 runs and took 112 wickets.

The path away from the early 1950s gloom was neither easy nor short, but there was typical Somerset romance and charm about M. F. Tremlett, the club's first professional captain, leading them to 3rd position in 1958. His first job was office boy at the Taunton Headquarters. His 1st match brought him 8 wickets, and an exciting innings in a breathtaking 1-wicket victory over Middlesex at Lord's in the 1st match of 1947. Somerset beat Middlesex again later in the season before they became champions. Tremlett, over-written and over-coached in the glare of two MCC tours, lost his bowling, but developed his majestic attacking batting and reached 2,000 runs in 1951. Two years later while fielding at Bath he took a terrible blow over the eye which threatened his life, then his eyesight. He came back again splendidly, and left in 1960 with a warm memory of over 15,000 runs, 326 wickets and the contribution of astute captaincy.

Tremlett and H. W. Stephenson had battled through a losing period in the early 1950s, when in 112 games the county lost 66 matches many in 2 days, and won 10. Stephenson came from Durham in 1949, quickly showed wonderful wicket-keeping skills, developed into an effective batsman, and overcame back ailments. He led the side to 6th position in 1962 and to a highly satisfactory 3rd a year later. His career brought over 12,000 runs and over 1,000 dismissals, including 311 stumpings.

A fine crop of new young players now arrived, including Taunton-born R. T. Virgin, who was to enjoy a successful 1970, including hundreds in each of the 3 current competitions in the space of 15 days. M. J. Kitchen from Nailsea, a sturdy left-hander, served the county excellently over a long period. Both made some 15,000 runs. F. E. Rumsey, one of Somerset's fastest bowlers, came from Worcestershire in 1963 and took 520 wickets in 6 seasons. He, Alley, Ken and Roy Palmer, and two other newcomers, G. I. Burgess and P. J. Robinson, fashioned Somerset into a powerful Gillette Cup side. Another useful all-rounder C. R. M. Atkinson, later to become headmaster of Millfield School, led them to the Gillette Cup final in 1967. They lost to Kent, but not by much.

The season of 1968 was notable for two events. R. C. Kerslake, later to be Cricket Chairman and Club Chairman, had an unlucky year as captain; and G. S. Chappell offered his services which were accepted. Chappell later captained Australia (incidentally captaining them on the 1st occasion, in 1977, when Somerset beat them) and added much to the county's standing in his 2 seasons on the staff. He scored the 1st hundred in the John Player League (128 not out against Surrey at Brislington in 1969) and developed his seam bowling, but as resources generally became thinner, Langford, now the veteran player, was captain for 2 years. Somerset sunk to the bottom of the Championship for the 1st time since 1955. In the 1st season of the John Player League, Langford bowled 8 maiden overs against Essex at Yeovil, a record which can only be equalled.

Somerset repaired their playing deficiencies quickly and without public prompting. T. W. Cartwright, from Warwickshire, whose medium-pace accuracy was a byword, became the linchpin of the bowling from 1970 to 1973 before three serious injuries intervened; D. J. S. Taylor, from Surrey, immediately adopted the highest wicket-keeping traditions from Somerset (his third name) besides batting splendidly when asked to open; K. J. O'Keeffe, an Australian leg-spinner, had one excellent season; A. A. Jones, a fast bowler from Sussex, took 291 wickets in 6 seasons to 1975; J. M. Parks ended a great career with England and Sussex with two useful seasons; H. R. Moseley, a Barbadian opening bowler, recommended by Sobers, immediately registered with his skill, stamina and loyalty on starting in 1971. Then came the vital decision, which caused much misgiving in the county, to sign D. B. Close after he left Yorkshire in 1970. He was 40, supposed to dislike one-day cricket, and – it was argued by many – his uncompromising approach was unlikely to endear itself to the gentle Somerset ways. There was also a suspicion he was not fit. In the event the Committee's decision turned out to be inspired.

Close upset a few players and other people at times, but missed hardly any games until 1977, his last season, and he exerted a tremendous influence on the club. His fearless batting and fielding, and steely insistence on making the best of everything going on the field brought a new determination and discipline to a side that was, in any event, promising to be of excellent quality.

Meantime, with Kerslake and Cartwright as chairman and coach, young players were being found and developed. It was interesting to see how many of them were born in Somerset's troubled period around 1950. Such players as B. C. Rose, P. W. Denning, I. T. Botham, P. A. Slocombe, P. M. Roebuck and V. J. Marks were coming along to complement the seasoned experience already there, and after 2 rather quiet years, 1974, under Close, became the best playing year of the Club's history. Continuing strong challenges brought 5th place in the Championship; second position (by 2 points) in the John Player League; and semi-final places in both knock-out competitions.

Ian Botham: a whole-hearted all-round cricketer in the best Somerset tradition.

The year of 1974 was momentous in many ways, echoing and developing many of the old traditions. The vice-chairman, on his own initiative, had brought to England I. V. A. Richards, batsman extraordinary from Antigua. He began a blazing trail of batting brilliance that took him to wonderful achievements for Somerset and West Indies. His 1st innings brought him a Benson & Hedges Gold Award – something like Gimblett's entry into the game – and Ian Botham marked his arrival with a performance of tremendous courage and skill in the Benson & Hedges quarter-final against Hampshire on 12 June. R. J. Clapp's enthusiastic seam bowling brought him 51 wickets in one-day cricket – a record at the time – and D. Breakwell, quickly establishing himself as a highly capable slow bowler and lively batsman, became part of a successful, well-disciplined outfit clearly set for big things.

By now Somerset were among the most powerful and attractive sides and, although spending a year without Richards (he was breaking records against England at the time), they came within a single run of winning the John Player League title after an agonizing match at Cardiff in the heat of 1976. Burgess, a faithful all-rounder since the mid-1960s, was in the thick of this and several other dramatic situations. Other local players were winning their spurs. C. H. Dredge from Frome, who worked himself into a regular place as all-rounder with much dedication, and K. F. Jennings, a medium pacer of Milverton, joined the University players Roebuck and Marks, and Rose and Denning, with splendidly sustained batting, were now firm fixtures in a side steadily developing a strong Somerset theme. Competition for places was severe.

Close, having fought his way back to an England place at 45, 27 years after his 1st Test, honourably retired in 1977 after giving Somerset magnificent value, and his successor, Rose, equipped with a fine side and a will-to-win not often present before the Close era, had a wonderful 1978. In his 1st year he just exceeded Close's 1974 achievements. Removed, a shade unluckily, in a Benson & Hedges semi-final tie, Somerset, ending up 5th in the Championship, faced 2 crucial tests on 2 and 3 September. They had never won a title before, but the prospect of winning 2 titles in 2 days evaporated. Failing to do themselves justice on either occasion, they lost both in one crushingly disappointing week-end. Even so, the reaction of two vast crowds at Lord's and Taunton was astonishing, as they greeted their shattered heroes as if they had won everything in sight. Their reward came in 1979 but not before one traumatic, and almost unprecedented event.

The 1979 season was a few very wet weeks old when Somerset, in a rain-delayed Benson & Hedges cup match at Worcester, won the toss and declared at 1 for no wicket. They had won the other 3 qualifying zone matches, and, fearful that the weather would rob them, conceded the match, thus ensuring enough match points and a high enough 'wicket-taking rate' to gain a quarter-final place. A storm of criticism overtook them and eventually the Test and County Cricket Board expelled them from the competition by a 17–1 majority. After the disappointments of 1978 this could have shattered morale, but Somerset acknowledged their error, took the punishment manfully, and approached the weekend of 8 and 9 September again with the chance – somewhat remote – of winning the Gillette Cup and the John Player League. In the end it was a magnificent team effort to win both. While the West Indians Richards and Garner played leading roles the bulk of the side was home-produced. Playing success, lucky weather, sponsorship and better house-keeping put the club on a better financial footing. The highly-successful 1974 season brought a serious loss of £10,000, but 5 great seasons had accumulated total profits approaching £100,000. Ground developments at Taunton will concentrate more cricket at headquarters in future, leaving, at least for a while, the pleasing rural grounds like Glastonbury, Yeovil, Bristol Imperial and Street. But the Festivals at Bath and Weston-super-Mare will continue as happy and traditional ingredients of Somerset cricket.

Victory at last – Brian Rose the Somerset captain is applauded by his team as he holds the Gillette Cup aloft after their defeat of Northamptonshire in the 1979 Final. Left to right: Rose, P. W. Denning, D. J. S. Taylor, G. I. Burgess, I. V. A. Richards, I. T. Botham, D. Breakwell, P. A. Slocombe.

CAPTAINS

1891–93 H. T. Hewett
1894–1906 S. M. J. Woods
1907 L. C. H. Palairet
1908–12 J. Daniell
1913–14 E. S. M. Poyntz
1919–26 J. Daniell
1927–31 J. C. White
1932–37 R. A. Ingle
1938–46 E. F. Longrigg
1947 R. J. O. Meyer
1948 N. S. Mitchell-Innes, J. W. Seamer and G. E. S. Woodhouse
1949 G. E. S. Woodhouse
1950–52 S. S. Rogers
1953–54 B. G. Brocklehurst
1955 G. G. Tordoff
1956–59 M. F. Tremlett
1960–64 H. W. Stephenson
1965–67 C. R. M. Atkinson
1968 R. C. Kerslake
1969–71 B. A. Langford
1972–77 D. B. Close
1978– B. C. Rose

HIGHEST TOTALS

For 675–9D v Hants, Bath 1924
Against 811 by Surrey, Oval 1899

LOWEST TOTALS

For 25 v Gloucester, Bristol 1947
Against 22 by Gloucester, Bristol 1920

HIGHEST INDIVIDUAL INNINGS

For 310 H. Gimblett v Sussex, Eastbourne 1948
Against 424 A. C. MacLaren for Lancashire, Taunton 1895

MOST RUNS

In a season 2,761 W. E. Alley 1961
In a career 21,142 H. Gimblett 1935–1954

MOST HUNDREDS

In a season 10 W. E. Alley 1961
In a career 49 H. Gimblett 1935–1954

INDIVIDUAL INNINGS OF 250 AND OVER

L. C. H. Palairet, 292 v Hants, Southampton 1896
L. C. Braund, 257* v Worcester, Worcester 1913
M. M. Walford, 264 v Hants, Weston 1947
H. Gimblett, 310 v Sussex, Eastbourne 1948

HUNDRED ON DEBUT

B. L. Bisgood, 116* v Worcester, Worcester 1907
H. Gimblett, 123 v Essex, Frome 1935
P. B. Wight, 109* v Australians, Taunton 1953

RECORD WICKET PARTNERSHIPS

1 H. T. Hewett and L. C. H. Palairet, 346 v Yorks, Taunton 1892
2 J. C. W. MacBryan and M. D. Lyon, 286 v Derby, Buxton 1924
3 G. G. Atkinson and P. B. Wight, 300 v Glamorgan, Bath 1960
4 I. V. A. Richards and P. M. Roebuck, 251 v Surrey, Weston 1977
5 J. C. White and C. C. C. Case, 235 v Gloucester, Taunton 1927
6 W. E. Alley and K. E. Palmer, 265 v Northants, Northampton 1961
7 S. M. J. Woods and V. T. Hill, 240 v Kent, Taunton 1898
8 E. F. Longrigg and C. J. P. Barnwell, 143* v Gloucester, Bristol 1938
9 C. M. H. Greetham and H. W. Stephenson, 183 v Leicester, Weston 1963
10 J. Bridges and H. Gibbs, 143 v Surrey, Weston 1919

MOST WICKETS

In a match 16–83 J. C. White v Worcester, Bath 1919
In a season 169 A. W. Wellard 1938
In a career 2,166 J. C. White 1909–1937

ALL 10 WICKETS IN AN INNINGS

E. J. Tyler v Surrey, Taunton 1895
J. C. White v Worcester, Worcester 1921

HAT-TRICKS

E. Robson 2
W. H. R. Andrews, L. C. Braund, J. Bridges, J. Hilton, J. Lawrence, J. G. Lomax, E. J. Tyler, A. W. Wellard, J. C. White 1 each

WICKET-KEEPING – MOST DISMISSALS

In an innings 6 H. W. Stephenson
G. Clayton
In a match 9 A. E. Newton
H. W. Stephenson
In a season 83 H. W. Stephenson 1949
In a career 1,007 H. W. Stephenson 1948–1964

COUNTY CAPS AWARDED SINCE 1946

1946 F. Castle, G. R. Langdale, J. Lawrence, M. M. Walford
1947 M. Coope, M. F. Tremlett, G. E. S. Woodhouse
1949 E. Hill, S. S. Rogers, H. W. Stephenson
1950 F. L. Angell, E. P. Robinson
1951 J. Redman
1952 G. G. Tordoff
1953 B. G. Brocklehurst, T. A. Hall, C. G. Mitchell, R. Smith
1954 J. G. Lomax, J. W. McMahon, P. B. Wight, Y. Saeed
1955 B. Lobb
1956 C. L. McCool, L. Pickles
1957 W. E. Alley, B. A. Langford, D. R. W. Silk
1958 G. G. Atkinson, K. E. Palmer
1959 K. Biddulph
1960 R. T. Virgin
1961 C. R. M. Atkinson, A. A. Baig
1962 C. Greetham, B. Roe
1963 F. E. Rumsey
1964 P. Eele
1965 G. Clayton
1966 M. J. Kitchen, P. J. Robinson
1968 T. I. Barwell, R. A. Brooks, G. I. Burgess, G. S. Chappell, A. Clarkson, R. C. Kerslake
1969 R. Palmer
1970 T. W. Cartwright
1971 D. B. Close, K. J. O'Keeffe, D. J. S. Taylor
1972 A. A. Jones, H. R. Moseley
1973 P. W. Denning, J. M. Parks
1974 I. V. A. Richards
1975 B. C. Rose
1976 I. T. Botham, D. Breakwell
1978 C. H. Dredge, K. F. Jennings, P. M. Roebuck, P. A. Slocombe
1979 J. Garner, V. J. Marks

Surrey

NORMAN PRESTON

Foundation 1845
Colours Chocolate
Badge Prince of Wales' Feathers
Champions 1864, 1887, 1888, 1889 (=), 1890, 1891, 1892, 1894, 1895, 1899, 1914, 1950 (=), 1952, 1953, 1954, 1955, 1956, 1957, 1958, 1971

The name of Surrey was established in cricket circles long before the formation of the Surrey County Cricket Club in 1845. The game evolved in the meadows and the village greens scores of years earlier. The first known reference appears in a legal document concerning a parcel of land at Guildford in which one John Derrick implies that when at the Free School of Guildford he 'and several of his fellows did run and play there at cricket and other plaies' in about 1550. Kennington Oval, the home of the Surrey County Cricket Club, situated almost in the heart of London, is famed throughout the cricket world. All the great players of the last 130 years have performed there under the shadow of the mighty gas-holder which sprang up even before the land was taken over by the cricketers. The first steps taken towards the formation of the County Cricket Club were in the autumn of 1844. The Montpelier Club had to give up their ground next to the Bee Hive Tavern, Walworth, and their treasurer, Mr W. Baker, an all-round cricketer, approached the Otter family who held the area now known as the Oval on a 99 year lease granted to them by the Duchy of Cornwall in 1835. Baker obtained a lease of 31 years and so the Oval was transformed from a market garden to a cricket ground in the spring of 1845, 10,000 turves being transferred from Tooting Common. The first game undertaken by the Surrey Club – Gentlemen of Surrey v Players of Surrey – was played on 21 and 22 August 1845 and following the match a dinner was held at The Horns, Kennington, presided over by Mr William Ward, previously responsible for the lease of Lord's. The official inauguration took place at the same historic inn in October 1845, when the President was the Hon F. Ponsonby (later the Earl of Bessborough). To him Surrey owe much. After some vicissitudes Surrey steadily advanced and played a leading part in the development of first-class cricket. This was due to a succession of capable secretaries, beginning with John Burrup (1848–55), and his brother, William Burrup, who followed him in office.

Surrey were fortunate, too, in producing many sound captains. F. P. Miller, the first notable leader, reigned from 1851 to 1866 and he had some powerful XIs. G. Brockwell and W. Martingell were the first of the long line of professionals who have served the county so faithfully right up to the present time. Fifty of them have appeared in Tests for England. Among the early players who dominated the scene was W. Caffyn. He went with the second team to Australia in 1863 and remained there as their first professional coach, so obviously Surrey can claim to have figured prominently in nurturing the game in the Southern Hemisphere. Previously another Surrey stalwart, H. H. Stephenson, captained the first team to visit Australia in 1861. In 1852, Surrey for the first time since 1817 met England at Lord's on even terms – XI-a-side – and won by 2 wickets. The victorious side (all Surrey born) were Julius Caesar, J. Chester, G. Brockwell, W. Caffyn, W. Martingell, N. Felix, C. H. Hoare, T. Lockyer, J. Heath, T. Sherman and D. Day. Of these Tom Lockyer was responsible for 249 victims during 17 years with Surrey and he also excelled as an attacking bat and round-arm bowler of goodish pace. His gigantic hands were known as saucepans. By 1858 the first pavilion was erected and three years later Surrey reached their peak for that period when they gained victory over England by 56 runs. Like all counties they experienced lean times although they had fine players in Jupp, the Humphreys, Southerton and Pooley. Nevertheless, as pitches improved at the Oval, runs came more easily and in 1862 the Surrey and Middlesex match yielded 1,042, the first aggregate of more than 1,000 in the history of the game. In 1864 Surrey were the premier county. Southerton, born in Sussex, was the first of the really great slow spin bowlers, although he did not take his 1st wicket in first-class cricket until he was 32. First to capture 4 wickets in 5 balls, against Lancashire at the Oval in 1869, he claimed 13 wickets in the day. He was also the first bowler to take 200 wickets in a season.

The change in Surrey's fortune began on the appointment of John Shuter as captain in 1880. He had already shown his quality as a leader of the Winchester College XI in 1873 and Surrey, under his direction, went from strength to strength. At that time Nottinghamshire, at their zenith, headed the Championship 7 times between 1879 and 1886, being indisputably at the top the last 4 years. In 1887, as *Wisden* states, Surrey regained first position among the counties after an interval of 23 years. Except on slow pitches the team was as good as any county had ever put into the field. Look at the names: J. Shuter, W. W. Read, W. E. Roller, K. J. Key, G. Lohmann, Maurice Read, R. Abel, J. Beaumont, T. Bowley, G. Jones and H. Wood. Over a span of 13 seasons (1887–1899), Surrey finished top 9 times and also shared the title once (1889) when they tied with Lancashire and Nottinghamshire. By then other noted players like Tom Hayward, W. H. Lockwood, W. Brockwell, Tom Richardson and D. L. A. Jephson had arrived.

George Lohmann proved one of the finest all-rounders ever to play for Surrey and England. He was born in June 1865, and the main part of his career covered 8 seasons, 1885 to 1892. No cricketer ever played more wholeheartedly and, if he had not bowled, his batting and fielding (2nd slip) would have gained him a place in any team. His health broke down because he was allowed to do too much and he died in South Africa at the age of 36. Lohmann sometimes opened the batting, yet his bowling brought him most fame. Though his pace varied from fast to medium, his rhythmical action was always the same. In 18 Test Matches he took 112 wickets, at an average of 10·75.

There may have been faster bowlers than Tom Richardson, but for sustained speed over long spells he had no parallel. When Australia wanted 125 to beat England at Old Trafford in 1896, they occupied 3 hours before they won by 3 wickets and it was averred that during that time Richardson did not send down one bad ball. He took 6 wickets and with any real help from the other end England must have won. In 5 English seasons, 1893–1897, Richardson averaged nearly 250 wickets, a total of 1,179, but 2 tours to Australia sapped his strength. In 14 Tests, all against Australia, Richardson took 88 wickets for 25·22 runs each. Bill Lockwood joined Surrey from Nottinghamshire in 1887 at the age of 19 and he became one of the best fast bowlers in the history of the game at a time when George Lohmann and Tom Richardson also flourished. Lockwood did not attempt such a long run as Richardson, nor was he so fast through the air, but he was very quick off the pitch and possessed a deadly off-break as well as a deceptive slow ball. It was no fault of Lockwood when Australia beat England by 3 runs at Old Trafford in 1902, for, in the 2 innings, he took 6 for 48 and 5 for 28. He was also a fine batsman and in the same year at Lord's, besides taking 9 of the Gentlemen's wickets for 106, he made a hundred in a tremendous late stand of 159 with Braund.

William Brockwell played first for Surrey in 1886 when 20 and held a regular place from 1891 to 1902. During his career at the Oval, Surrey won the Championship eight times and tied once. Another fine all-rounder, he made his name as a stylish batsman, sound in back play and a forceful hitter. He headed the English batting in 1894 with an aggregate of 1,491 runs, average 38·23. A splendid fast-medium bowler and superb slip fielder, Brockwell played 7 times for England against Australia. The year of 1872 was particularly notable for Surrey. Mr Charles Alcock began his long reign as secretary till he died in 1907; he was also secretary of the Football Association, 1867–1896. Thanks to his enterprise and foresight not only were the Australians the first overseas team to play at the Oval in 1878, but it was mainly due to him that the 1st Test Match between England and Australia in England took place there in 1880.

It could truthfully be said that batsmen reigned supreme at the Oval for the first half of the 20th century. Of course there were many fine bowlers and bowling feats, but in fine weather the groundsmen did all in their power to provide perfect conditions for batsmen. Sam Apted was groundsman from 1888 until 1911 and it was said that his pitches were so good as to drive even the best bowlers to despair. Probably the strongest team Surrey ever possessed was that captained by K. J. Key in the 1890s. Certainly Stuart Surridge's side, which carried off the Championship 7 years in succession, 1952–1958, proved magnificent in bowling and fielding during a spell when pitches encouraged the bowlers, but the earlier stalwarts were immensely strong in all departments. The unbroken line of talented batsmen who have served Surrey and England to such good purpose down to the era of Peter May, Ken Barrington and John Edrich had already begun. Brockwell enjoyed many

Surrey, winners of the abbreviated Championship of 1914. Back row: J. W. Hitch, H. Strudwick, A. Ducat, T. Rushby, A. Goatly, A. Sandham and W. J. Abel; sitting: P. G. H. Fender, E. G. Hayes, C. T. A. Wilkinson (captain), J. B. Hobbs and W. G. Smith.

big opening partnerships with 'Bobby' Abel, who, known as 'The Guv'nor', began at the Oval in 1881 and played his last match in 1904. Abel remained a popular figure for many years until he died at his home only a few yards away from his favourite ground in 1936 at the age of 79. Very small of stature, he set his fellow professional batsmen an example in emulating the big scores of W. G. Grace.

Abel's 357 not out against Somerset at the Oval in 1899 still stands as the highest innings played by any Surrey cricketer and remains second in county cricket to A. C. MacLaren's 424 for Lancashire against Somerset at Taunton in 1895. Like another little man, Don Bradman, Abel did not always keep his bat straight. He had a very wide range of strokes and while he drove and cut freely he was also a brilliant leg-side player. Abel finished his career with 74 hundreds and an aggregate of 33,124 runs, average 35·35.

Surrey alone can boast 4 batsmen with 100 hundreds to their names – Tom Hayward, Jack Hobbs, Andy Sandham and John Edrich. Hayward, though born at Cambridge, came from a family which for generations lived at Mitcham; his father and grandfather played in the Surrey XI and back in the 1860s his uncle was considered the best professional batsman in the country. Here was a case of hereditary talent and Tom had all the qualities that make a successful run-getter. Tall and strong, Hayward possessed perfect style and the stamina necessary for long days in the field. Indeed, at the outset of his career he too excelled as a bowler and performed the double in 1897. For 20 years in succession, 1895–1914, Hayward scored more than 1,000 runs and his stand of 448 with Abel (193) against Yorkshire at the Oval remains as a record for the English 4th wicket; Hayward's score was 273. Space prevents mention of all the wonderful deeds he accomplished at the crease but one cannot omit his 1,000 runs before the end of May in 1900, nor his 4 three-figure opening stands in one week in 1907 with Hobbs – 106 and 125 against Cambridge University at the Oval, and 147 and 105 against Middlesex at Lord's. Twice in 1899 Hayward performed the hat-trick with medium-paced off-breaks, against Gloucestershire at the Oval and Derbyshire at Chesterfield. Altogether Hayward scored 43,551 runs, average 41·79, and took 481 wickets for 22·94 each. Twice his season's aggregate exceeded 3,000 and his highest innings, 315 not out against Lancashire in 1898, was made at the Oval where he hit 58 of his 104 hundreds.

The beginning of the 20th century found Surrey past their zenith. Indeed, between 1899 and 1950 they won the Championship only once, in 1914, though occasionally they came within a hairbreadth of lifting the title, notably in 1906, 1910, 1920 and 1921. All through that long period of 50 years Surrey possessed a galaxy of batting talent. Reference has already been made to Hayward and Hobbs and there were many other personalities including first-rate amateurs as well as splendid captains, but the great problem was to dismiss the opposition twice in 3 days in fine weather on those adamantine Oval pitches. Even if Surrey could not claim pride of place at the top, their wonderful batting and particularly the presence of Hobbs drew vast crowds wherever they went.

The story of Jack Hobbs is a romance on its own. Like Hayward, he was born in Cambridge and besides modelling his style on Hayward he decided to join Surrey on Hayward's recommendation. Hobbs arrived at the Oval in 1903, spent 2 years qualifying and within a fortnight of playing his 1st first-class match against the Gentlemen of England, captained by W. G. Grace, he was awarded his county cap by Lord Dalmeny (later the Earl of Rosebery), by virtue of a superb innings of 155 against Essex in his 1st Championship match. One example bears testimony to his youthful brilliance. Facing Hampshire at the Oval in 1909, Surrey reached 645 in $5\frac{1}{4}$ hours on the opening day for the loss of 4 wickets; the highest score in one day by a side in the Championship. Hobbs and Hayes put on 371 in $2\frac{3}{4}$ hours and Hobbs, despite the tremendous pace, offered no chance while getting 205. Hayes played brilliantly enough for 276, yet was overshadowed by his dazzling partner.

The years took away none of Hobbs's genius. One of his most memorable seasons was that of 1925. For the first time he made more than 3,000 runs and also for the first time he headed the English batting averages. He eclipsed the largest number of hundreds by any individual, completing three figures 16 times (since surpassed by Compton), but, above everything else, that year was notable for his triumph in passing the highest number of centuries in a career, which then, at 126, stood to the credit of W. G. Grace. That summer Hobbs returned to England after a winter's tour of Australia and, far from being a tired man, he immediately found his most brilliant form. A hundred against Kent at Blackheath on 20 July took him within one of the 'G.O.M.'s' record. Then came a nerve-racking time. The deeds of Hobbs were followed by the whole country. Everyone talked about him and never a day passed without him being sought by photographers and interviewers. No matter how big was his score, or how valuable it was to Surrey, he was said to have 'failed'. He began to look weary as 4 weeks passed without his making a hundred, but on 16 August he scored 101 against Somerset at Taunton and equalled the coveted record. Next day his joy was complete when he beat it with a not-out innings of 101. To end his marvellous summer Hobbs hit 266 not out at Scarborough – the highest innings played in the Gentlemen v Players match which dated back to 1806.

Hobbs carried on for 9 more seasons. If the Oval was his favourite ground – he hit nearly 90 hundreds there – he had a special affection for Lord's, where in 1926 he scored 316 not out for Surrey against Middlesex, which stands as the individual record for Lord's. Hobbs was in his 52nd year when he finally laid down his bat. I can see now the enthusiasm of the Old Trafford crowd when he made the last of his 197 hundreds there in George Duckworth's benefit match. Many people wished that he had plodded on for 3 more and completed 200 hundreds, but while his sight and ability were willing, his legs had had enough. They had carried him round the cricket world for 30 years and helped to produce the biggest aggregate of all time, 61,237 runs, average 50·65. In Surrey the public marked his retirement by contributing so generously to the wrought-iron 'Hobbs Gates' which adorn the main entrance to the Oval that the surplus money was used to erect a brick wall right round the ground.

Hand in hand through the years with Hobbs went that prince of wicket-keepers, Herbert Strudwick. Another product of Mitcham, he began his connexion with Surrey in 1898 and finished in 1958 – 30 years as stumper and 30 years as scorer. In all first-class cricket Strudwick dismissed 1,493 batsmen and he held 1,235 catches.

Albert Craig, 'the Surrey poet', dispensed regular topical verse on Oval happenings – a figure as familiar in his day as Bobby Abel or Tom Hayward.

The 126th: Jack Hobbs at Taunton in 1925 equalled W.G.'s tally of hundreds. Next day in the 2nd innings he went one better.

One of Surrey's main bowlers in the early days of Hobbs was Walter Lees, a Yorkshireman whose benefit at the Oval in 1906 when Yorkshire were the visitors drew 80,000 people. During the 3 days 66,923 sixpences were received at the turnstiles. Lees's best period was between 1903 and 1910 when at faster than medium pace he took 1,031 wickets, 193 of them in 1905. Lees had an easy run-up and a quick action. N. A. Knox, a product of Dulwich College who stood over 6 feet, was considered by his contemporaries as one of the fastest bowlers ever known. He enjoyed 2 seasons of enormous success and bore a big hand in the Gentlemen's victory over the Players at Lord's in 1906 by taking 12 wickets for 183. Sore shins, caused no doubt by the hard Oval ground, cut short his career when he was 26. Another opening bowler was Tom Rushby, a deadly man on a helpful pitch, but never extremely fast. He took all 10 Somerset wickets at Taunton in 1921. Over a long period one of the best slow bowlers was W. C. ('Razor') Smith. On a treacherous Oval pitch in 1909 when Yorkshire were dismissed for 26, Rushby took 5 for 9 and Smith 5 for 12.

About this time Surrey were really powerful. Three fine hitters were the brothers, V. F. S. Crawford and J. N. Crawford, both schoolboy prodigies, and Alan Marshal, an Australian professional. Unfortunately, when Smith was all-powerful, Rushby went for a brief spell into the Lancashire League, and a quarrel with the committee over team selection resulted in J. N. Crawford going away; otherwise Surrey might well have won the Championship in 1910 instead of finishing 2nd to Kent.

So not until 1914 did Surrey regain the title and then Hitch had arrived to help Rushby, and the youthful P. G. H. Fender provided spin support for Smith. Andrew Ducat and Andrew Sandham were two fine batsmen whose full talents were not to be seen until peace came 4 years later. A modest man, small and neat, a supreme stylist, Sandham was content to play second fiddle to Hobbs, yet between 1911 and 1937 he made 41,283 runs (average 44·82) and he comes 11th in the honours list of highest aggregates. Surrey never had a more loyal servant than Sandham who spent 60 years with the club, having been coach and scorer. One innings alone emphasized his greatness: the highest score for any county against the Australians, 219 at the Oval in 1934. Ducat figured in first-class cricket from 1909 to 1931 and was a fine all-round sportsman who played for England at Association football and cricket. All his 52 hundreds were hit for Surrey and he died at the crease, bat in hand, during a war-time match at Lord's in 1942.

One of the pillars of Surrey over a span of nearly 60 years (1895–1955), was H. D. G. Leveson Gower, knighted in 1953 for his services to cricket as player, legislator and Test selector. Known everywhere as 'Shrimp' he found himself referred to as 'the man with the sanguinary name' when he toured America in 1897. Leveson Gower emanated from Winchester and Oxford. He was a capable batsman, excellent cover-point and captained Surrey between 1908 and 1910. M. C. Bird, a commanding figure in stature and ability who first made his name by scoring two hundreds for Harrow in 1907 against Eton, took over the captaincy from Leveson Gower and played many grand innings. In 2 matches for Surrey against the Australians in 1912 he hit 76, 68 and 112.

Two-day matches in 1919 scarcely suited Surrey when cricket returned after the war. The Oval pitches under 'Bosser' Martin's care were as good as ever and Surrey possessed a fine array of batsmen: Hobbs, D. J. Knight, Sandham, Ducat, Shepherd and E. G. Hayes. Hayes, who in a career of 30 years scored 27,318 runs, now turned out as an amateur. J. N. Crawford, too, came back to the fold and in Hobbs's 2nd benefit knocked off 96 with 'The Master' in 32 minutes, Kent being defeated by ten wickets. When Middlesex won the Championship in 1920 and 1921 the issue was clinched each time at Lord's in their final match with Surrey.

In 1921 P. G. H. Fender began his 11-year spell as captain and was at once acclaimed the most astute and boldest leader in the game. When Surrey wanted runs, Fender would appear and shatter the opposition with fearless hitting. The fastest hundred in first-class cricket, made in 35 minutes at Northampton in 1920, stands to his name. A genuine leg-break bowler with cunning variations of flight and length, Fender also held a world bowling record for 45 years. At Lord's in 1927 he took 6 Middlesex wickets in 11 balls for one run. P. I. Pocock, another Surrey man, beat this in 1972 at Eastbourne with 6 Sussex wickets in nine balls and seven in eleven balls – both world records. Six times Fender performed the double. No one who saw him will forget the energy of Hitch, a fast bowler of the highest quality and a magnetic fielder, particularly at short leg. Hitch was capable of holding anything within reach there.

Four amateurs, E. C. Kirk (left-arm fast), J. H. Lockton, G. M. Reay and M. J. C. Allom, in turn reinforced Surrey's opening attack, and then there were Peach, Geary, Sheffield and Sadler, all of brisk pace. New batsmen, Gregory, Barling and Squires appeared before the Fender era closed in 1931. Three Dark blues, D. R. Jardine, E. R. T. Holmes and H. M. Garland-Wells, in turn held the captaincy until the Second World War intervened. Besides the last 3 named, the Universities also gave Surrey F. R. Brown, S. A. Block and R. de W. K. Winlaw, all of Cambridge. It seems strange that throughout this history not only is there a general absence of left-arm bowlers, but until L. B. Fishlock made his first-class debut in 1931 – one of Hobbs's last opening partners – one cannot find a left-handed batsman of any note in the Surrey ranks. The alteration in the lbw law gradually changed the fashion in opening bats and Fishlock led the way in showing how to deal with the growth of in-slant bowling. Four times he hit 2 separate hundreds in a match and altogether made 25,376 runs before he put away his bat in September, 1952. The arrival in 1928 of Alf Gover brought a welcome touch of hostility to the Surrey attack in the years preceding the war. In 1936 and again in 1937 his haul of wickets numbered 200, a feat accomplished by no fast bowler since the days of Tom Richardson, but still the Surrey bowling was not equal to taking the team to the top.

The year 1938 was significant in that two strapping youngsters, the Bedser twins, came for a trial on the recommendation of Alan Peach. The full impact of their engagement was not appreciated until 1946. Immediately after the final Test in 1939 between England and West Indies, the Oval was requisitioned. First a searchlight site, it became a prisoner-of-war camp for parachutists, but none arrived. Seven high explosives hit the vicinity and countless incendiaries. When Surrey began the task of putting the Oval in shape for cricket again in the winter of 1945–46, 40,000 turves were imported from Gravesend.

Surrey celebrated the completion of 100 years at Kennington Oval – on 22 August 1945 – by launching an appeal for £100,000 for purposes of reconstruction. King George VI, patron of the club, gave £100 to the Centenary Appeal and was present with 15,000 of his people on 23 May 1946, when Surrey played Old England. It was truly a festive occasion with the band of the East Surrey Regiment in attendance. So began a new era for Surrey. At first the pitch seemed as heartbreaking as ever for bowlers, but the turf in the outfield, luxuriant in growth, was never the same. The ball did not flash any more to the boundary over a 'concrete' surface and within a few years more consideration was given to the bowlers in the

Surrey, because of the Second War, were obliged to celebrate their centenary a year late – which they did with a memorable match on 23 May 1946, between the county and an Old England XI. King George VI was among the 15,000 spectators who in hot sunshine saw a well-contested match: Surrey 248 for 6 declared, Old England 232 for 5. This is the Old England team. Back row: J. B. Hobbs (umpire), E. R. T. Holmes, M. J. C. Allom, M. W. Tate, E. W. J. Brooks, A. Sandham and H. Strudwick (umpire); sitting: E. Hendren, D. R. Jardine, P. G. H. Fender (captain), H. Sutcliffe and F. E. Woolley; on ground: D. J. Knight and A. P. Freeman. Woolley and Hendren made 102 together, and Hendren and Jardine 108. For many present it was the most sentimental, nostalgic cricket occasion of their lives.

preparation of the pitch, now under the care of H. C. Lock.

Difficulty in finding a captain was Surrey's biggest handicap just after the war. They tried N. H. Bennett who had had no experience of first-class cricket, and although they possessed plenty of fine players, L. B. Fishlock, R. J. Gregory, T. H. Barling, J. F. Parker, H. S. Squires, A. R. Gover, A. V. Bedser, E. A. Bedser and A. J. McIntyre, the absence of talented amateurs was keenly felt.

E. R. T. Holmes led the side again in 1947–1948 and they jumped to 2nd place, and then M. R. Barton, a batsman from Winchester and Oxford, held office for 3 years, 1949–1951. Under him Surrey, in 1950, gained their highest number of Championship victories, 17, since 1906 and shared first place with Lancashire, thus reaching the top for the first time since 1914. This was really a notable season. For the second year running Fishlock scored over 2,000 runs in Championship games, but batsmen generally were not quite so comfortable at the Oval. The faster bowlers made the ball stand up from a good length and spinners found response, particularly after rain.

Some notable personalities were now established in the side. J. C. Laker, a Yorkshireman, was a lucky find. After service in the Middle-East, he was stationed at the War Office in London and Surrey spotted him while he was playing club cricket for Catford. He signed as a professional in 1946 and after only one full season, MCC chose him to tour West Indies in 1947–48. In May 1950, Laker dominated a Test trial at Bradford, 5 miles from his birthplace, Shipley, by taking 8 for 2 on drying turf. The Rest were dismissed for 27, the lowest total at that time for a match of representative class. In due course, he became one of the greatest off-spin bowlers of all time. So, in 1950, Surrey found the attack which paved the way for them to beat all county records, when between 1952 and 1958 they carried off the Championship seven years in succession. Besides Laker, there were A. V. Bedser, two left-arm slow bowlers, G. A. R. Lock and J. W. McMahon (an Australian), and W. S. Surridge, ably supported by J. F. Parker, a very fine all-rounder who believed in getting runs quickly.

In 1952, the Surrey committee made a vital decision. For captain, they had three choices, two Light blues, one of ordinary ability, or W. S. Surridge, born within 2 miles of the Oval and the son of a noted maker of sports goods, particularly cricket equipment. Happily, they went for the man who had already proved his worth to the county, and at once Surridge, with his dynamic drive and personality, wielded his men into a victorious combination. Surridge himself was a lively fast bowler, but nowhere near the highest class, a superb fielder close to the bat and a fearless hitter when runs were wanted. Nothing suited Surridge better than a tense situation. The year of 1950 also marked the introduction of P. B. H. May to county cricket in mid-July as a Cambridge Freshman, and so Surrey already possessed the foundations of a triumphant team.

England often called on Alec Bedser, Laker, May and Lock, and only the brilliant Godfrey Evans kept McIntyre from the Test side. It was while A. V. Bedser was on duty for England in 1952 that Surrey suddenly produced P. J. Loader for 4 matches and he, too, became an indispensable as well as an England bowler. That year Surrey's Championship victories numbered 20. Eric Bedser and Fletcher shouldered the task of opening batsmen in Surridge's 1st season as captain and Constable was a stylish diminutive No. 3 moulded in the Sandham fashion. On occasion, G. J. Whittaker hit sixes of tremendous velocity. T. H. Clark, from Bedfordshire, also gave strength to the batting and, with Eric Bedser, became a regular opener as well as a valuable off-spinner when Laker was not mowing down the opposition. For 5 years Surridge held the captaincy and, for the 1st time in the history of the Championship, the same county won the title – a personal triumph for Surridge. He always maintained he was himself just a club cricketer – he was never picked for the Gentlemen at Lord's. But he expected Surrey to play with one fixed purpose – victory in the shortest possible time.

One of the biggest thrills for Surrey during Surridge's reign was the first visit to the Oval of the Queen, as Patron of the Surrey Club, for the South African match in 1955. Another occurred in May 1956, when Surrey became the 1st county to defeat the Australians for 44 years. Laker took all 10 wickets in the Australians' 1st innings and Constable hit a patient and valuable hundred. At the end Ian Johnson presented his Australian cap to Surridge, his rival captain. That same season Surrey won 23 of their 28 Championship engagements and totalled 284 points. During the period Surridge was captain, Surrey played 170 matches, won 101, drew 42 and lost only 27 – an amazing achievement both by the county and its leader.

The leadership passed automatically to Peter May. Indeed, he had already held the England captaincy for two seasons and under his guidance, as well as through his superb batsmanship, Surrey remained at the top for two more years, although the stress and strain were already evident. Yet even when they surrendered the premier position in 1959, it was only after a terrific struggle. They had to win their last two matches to stay at the top and the issue was settled when Middlesex held them to a draw in the first of these

The 1st of Surrey's 7 successive years as champions, 1952. From the left: G. N. G. Kirby, P. J. Loader, D. G. W. Fletcher, G. A. R. Lock, A. J. McIntyre, J. F. Parker, W. S. Surridge, L. B. Fishlock, E. A. Bedser, A. V. Bedser, Sandy Tait (masseur), P. B. H. May, G. J. Whitaker, B. Constable and T. H. Clark.

engagements. May was absent most of that season and A. V. Bedser, Loader, Lock and Laker all took their wickets at higher cost. With Peter May laid low through illness throughout 1960, A. V. Bedser wound up his wonderful career as deputy-captain in his final season of 1960. Eleven times he took 100 or more wickets in a season and altogether his victims numbered 1,924, at an average of 20·41. Perfect length and variation of swing were his main weapons. Neither Surrey nor England ever had a more loyal cricketer.

Laker and Lock were two of the most gifted slow bowlers of all time in English cricket and each supported the other, often swapping ends. Lock saw Laker twice take all 10 Australian wickets in 1956 – nineteen in the Test match at Old Trafford – and when Laker was absent from the Surrey side in the same season, Lock himself claimed all 10 against Kent at Blackheath. Lock first came to Surrey in 1944 and played for the Colts. He signed as a professional in 1946 before his 17th birthday. In those days he had a tidy action, but in 1952 he unintentionally lowered his arm at some indoor nets and his delivery became suspicious. Twice he changed his action before it was again beyond any question of doubt. He bowled the natural left-hander's leg-break and the one that came on with the arm. As a fielder he was admirable in any position and in the leg-trap was without a peer.

Stewart and Barrington not only reinforced Surrey's batting, but also the close fielding. In 1957 Stewart held 77 catches, only one short of W. R. Hammond's all-time record, and these included 7 in one innings against Northamptonshire, a new record for a fielder other than a wicket-keeper. May's virtual retirement at the end of 1962, when only 32, was a severe blow, as was Lock's emigration to Australia a year later and subsequent transfer to Leicestershire. But the mature advance of Barrington as a batsman was a tremendous comfort to Surrey. Few post-war cricketers have applied themselves with a greater determination to their task and few achieved the consistency against all attacks that Barrington showed: a true professional, his service to Surrey, as well as to England, was immense. Altogether Barrington hit 31,714 runs (average 45·63), including 76 hundreds.

Since 1958 Surrey's batting has been well served, too, by the left-handed J. H. Edrich, of the famous Norfolk family. An opener with much inherited grit, he proved a fine partner for Stewart. Edrich played for England in 77 Tests, excluding 2 against Rest of the World in 1970. A tremendous hitter on his day, in June and July 1965 he played consecutive innings for Surrey and England of 139, 121 not out, 205 not out, 55, 96, 188, 92, 105 and 310 not out, a total of 1,311 runs in 9 innings, 3 times not out. When he retired in 1978, having received the MBE, his first-class record was 39,790 runs (average 45·47), including 103 hundreds. He held the Surrey captaincy between 1973 and 1977.

Stewart himself, apart from his brilliance as a close-to-the-wicket fielder, was an adventurous batsman who scored consistently and attractively and, after 2 seasons as vice-captain, was appointed leader of the side in 1963. In that season D. A. D. Sydenham, as in 1962, took more than 100 wickets as a left-arm fast-medium bowler, and another Surrey-born fast-medium bowler, D. Gibson, also showed good form.

Surrey in 1971, the only year in which the county has won the County Championship since their run of victories in the 1950s. Back row: Jack Hill (scorer), R. D. Jackman, Younis Ahmed, C. E. Waller, R. M. Lewis, R. G. D. Willis, J. M. M. Hooper, G. R. J. Roope, Intikhab Alam and D. R. Owen-Thomas; sitting: L. Skinner, G. G. Arnold, M. J. Edwards, S. J. Storey, M. J. Stewart (captain), A. J. McIntyre, J. H. Edrich, A. Long, P. I. Pocock and G. P. Howarth.

At the end of 1963 Loader, like Lock, went to Western Australia, and Surrey's forces were further depleted by the retirement in 1964 of the long-serving Bernard Constable, never a brilliant but a highly competent batsman who had joined the Oval staff in 1938.

Surrey's fortunes have fluctuated since their great period of the 1950s. They won the County Championship only once more, in 1971. The attack was never the same deadly machine, although G. G. Arnold, superb with the new ball, P. I. Pocock (off-breaks), and Intikhab Alam (leg spin and googlies), performed admirably on occasion, as did R. Harman, left-arm slow, for a short time until he lost his cunning.

In 1966 S. J. Storey became the 1st Surrey player to perform the double since F. R. Brown in 1932. Arnold Long maintained Surrey's long line of efficient wicket-keepers and established a record at Hove in 1964 when he held 11 catches against Sussex. Later, he joined Sussex and began another successful career.

Rising inflation caused much concern behind the scenes. Surrey let slip away to other counties men like R. G. D. Willis, R. D. V. Knight (who returned as captain in 1978), M. W. W. Selvey and J. E. Emburey. A ground development scheme of 1965 fell through in 1975 mainly because the bureaucrats held up planning permission. Meanwhile, Surrey had shown little aptitude for the one-day game first sponsored by Gillette in 1963. They have reached the final only once in that competition, in 1965, when Yorkshire outplayed them at Lord's. They have a very ordinary record in the Sunday John Player League, but under Edrich's shrewd guidance they won the Benson & Hedges Cup in 1974, mastering Leicestershire by 27 runs. They were also beaten finalists in the competition in 1979.

Meantime, 5 talented batsmen in M. J. Edwards, G. R. J. Roope, Younis Ahmed (Pakistan), A. R. Butcher and G. P. Howarth (New Zealand) enjoyed some success and Roope excelled in the slips. R. D. Jackman toiled manfully with the ball, but seemed to waste energy on an abnormally long run-up. Still, Surrey's general weakness was emphasized in 1976 when for the first time for 25 years the county had no representative player on the MCC tour to India, Sri Lanka and Australia (Centenary Test) although the side was chosen by Alec Bedser (Chairman of the Selectors) and Barrington went as manager.

That all was not well with Surrey was further stressed when, in 1977, the secretary, W. H. Sillitoe, resigned and the club went across the Thames to find a coach in F. J. Titmus of Middlesex and England fame. For more than 100 years there had been a chain of former Surrey players willing and able to pass on the gospel: men like A. J. McIntyre, A. Sandham, E. G. Hayes, H. A. Peach, 'Razor' Smith, R. Thompson and M. C. Bird. Titmus, disillusioned, stayed only 2 years and now M. J. Stewart has returned and taken over as Team Manager, with David Gibson as coach. The problem of finding a captain in 1978 to succeed Edrich was solved by persuading R. D. V. Knight, the tall left-handed batsman, to return to the fold, following his sojourn first with Gloucestershire and later with Sussex.

While the Oval remains a Test Match centre, attendances for county matches have dwindled to such an extent that serious thought is being given to staging more matches away from Kennington. At the moment Guildford, the county town, alone has that privilege in the Championship.

CAPTAINS

1846–50	C. H. Hoare
1851–57	F. P. Miller
1858–65	F. Burbidge
1866	E. Dowson
1867	W. J. Collyer
1868	C. T. Calvert
1869–70	S. H. Akroyd
1871	J. C. Gregory
1872–75	G. Strachan
1876	A. Chandler
1877–79	G. Strachan
1880–93	J. Shuter
1894–99	K. J. Key
1900–02	D. L. A. Jephson
1903	L. Walker
1904	No Official appointment
1905–07	Lord Dalmeny
1908–09	H. D. G. Leveson Gower
1910	H. D. G. Leveson Gower and M. C. Bird
1911–13	M. C. Bird
1914–19	C. T. A. Wilkinson
1920	C. T. A. Wilkinson and P. G. H. Fender
1921–31	P. G. H. Fender
1932–33	D. R. Jardine

1934–38 E. R. T. Holmes
1939 H. M. Garland-Wells
1946 N. H. Bennett
1947–48 E. R. T. Holmes
1949–51 M. R. Barton
1952–56 W. S. Surridge
1957–62 P. B. H. May
1963–72 M. J. Stewart
1973–77 J. H. Edrich
1978– R. D. V. Knight

HIGHEST TOTALS

For 811 v Somerset, Oval 1899
Against 705–8D by Sussex, Hastings 1902

LOWEST TOTALS

For 16 v Notts, Oval 1880
Against 15 by MCC, Lord's 1839

HIGHEST INDIVIDUAL INNINGS

For 357* R. Abel v Somerset, Oval 1899
Against 300* F. B. Watson for Lancs, Old Trafford 1928
300 R. Subba Row for Northants, Oval 1958

MOST RUNS

In a season 3,246 T. W. Hayward 1906
In a career 43,703 J. B. Hobbs 1905–1934

MOST HUNDREDS

In a season 13 T. W. Hayward 1906
J. B. Hobbs 1925
In a career 144 J. B. Hobbs 1905–1934

INDIVIDUAL INNINGS OF 250 AND OVER

W. W. Read, 338 v Oxford University, Oval 1888
R. Abel, 250 v Warwicks, Oval 1897
T. W. Hayward, 315* v Lancs, Oval 1898
T. W. Hayward, 273 v Yorks, Oval 1899
R. Abel, 357* v Somerset, Oval 1899
E. G. Hayes, 273* v Derby, Derby 1904
E. G. Hayes, 276 v Hants, Oval 1909
A. Ducat, 306* v Oxford University, Oval 1919
A. Ducat, 271 v Hants, Southampton 1919
A. Ducat, 290* v Essex, Leyton 1921
A. Sandham, 292* v Northants, Oval 1921
J. B. Hobbs, 261 v Oxford University, Oval 1926
J. B. Hobbs, 316* v Middlesex, Lord's 1926
T. F. Shepherd, 277* v Gloucester, Oval 1927
A. Sandham, 282* v Lancs, Old Trafford 1928
T. H. Barling, 269 v Hants, Southampton 1933
L. B. Fishlock, 253 v Leicester, Leicester 1948
J. F. Parker, 255 v New Zealanders, Oval 1949

HUNDRED ON DEBUT

N. Miller, 124 v Sussex, Hove 1899
H. C. Pretty, 124 v Notts, Oval 1899
H. O. Bloomfield, 107* v Northants, Northampton 1921

RECORD WICKET PARTNERSHIPS

1 J. B. Hobbs and A. Sandham, 428 v Oxford University, Oval 1926
2 J. B. Hobbs and E. G. Hayes, 371 v Hants, Oval 1909
3 A. Ducat and E. G. Hayes, 353 v Hants, Southampton 1919
4 R. Abel and T. W. Hayward, 448 v Yorks, Oval 1899
5 J. N. Crawford and F. C. Holland, 308 v Somerset, Oval 1908
6 A. Sandham and H. S. Harrison, 298 v Sussex, Oval 1913
7 T. F. Shepherd and J. W. Hitch, 200 v Kent, Blackheath 1921
8 T. W. Hayward and L. C. Braund, 204 v Lancs, Oval 1898
9 E. R. T. Holmes and E. W. J. Brooks, 168 v Hants, Oval 1936
10 A. Ducat and A. Sandham, 173 v Essex, Leyton 1921

MOST WICKETS

In a match 16–83 G. A. R. Lock v Kent, Blackheath 1956
In a season 250 T. Richardson 1895
In a career 1,775 T. Richardson 1892–1905

ALL 10 WICKETS IN AN INNINGS

T. Richardson v Essex, Oval 1894
T. Rushby v Somerset, Taunton 1921
E. A. Watts v Warwicks, Edgbaston 1939
J. C. Laker v Australians, Oval 1956
G. A. R. Lock v Kent, Blackheath 1956

HAT-TRICKS

T. Richardson 4
J. C. Laker 3 (4 in all matches)
W. H. Lockwood 3
P. G. H. Fender, R. Harman, T. W. Hayward, J. W. Hitch, R. D. Jackman, P. I. Pocock, W. C. Smith 2 each
G. A. R. Lock 1 (4 in all matches)
P. J. Loader 1 (2 in all matches)
G. G. Arnold, A. V. Bedser, W. Brockwell, D. Gibson, A. R. Gover, Intikhab Alam, D. L. A. Jephson, W. S. Lees, H. A. Peach, W. E. Roller, W. C. H. Sadler, T. F. Shepherd, S. J. Storey 1 each

WICKET-KEEPING – MOST DISMISSALS

In an innings 7 A. Long
In a match 11 A. Long
In a season 88 A. J. McIntyre 1949
In a career 1,235 H. Strudwick 1902–1927

COUNTY CAPS AWARDED SINCE 1946

1946 A. V. Bedser, N. H. Bennett, A. J. McIntyre
1947 E. A. Bedser, D. G. W. Fletcher, J. C. Laker
1948 M. R. Barton, J. W. McMahon, W. S. Surridge
1949 G. J. Whittaker
1950 B. Constable, G. A. R. Lock, P. B. H. May
1952 T. H. Clark
1953 P. J. Loader, R. Subba Row
1955 K. F. Barrington, M. J. Stewart
1958 R. Swetman
1959 J. H. Edrich
1960 D. Gibson
1961 A. B. D. Parsons
1962 A. Long, D. A. D. Sydenham, R. A. E. Tindall, M. D. Willett
1964 R. Harman, R. I. Jefferson, S. J. Storey
1966 M. J. Edwards
1967 G. G. Arnold, P. I. Pocock
1968 W. A. Smith
1969 Younis Ahmed, Intikhab Alam, G. R. J. Roope, D. J. S. Taylor
1970 R. D. Jackman
1972 C. E. Waller
1974 G. P. Howarth
1975 A. R. Butcher, L. E. Skinner
1978 R. D. V. Knight, C. J. Richards

Sussex

GEOFFREY BOLTON AND ALAN ROSS

Foundation 1839
Colours Dark Blue, Light Blue and Gold
Badge County arms of Six Martlets

Sussex have never been Champion County. The reason is not far to seek. Ever since the glorious days of Lillywhite, Dean and Wisden (and except for a period to be mentioned later) Sussex has suffered from a chronic weakness in bowling. For a time, in the late 1880s and early 1890s, they were almost entirely dependent for their wickets on the lobs of Walter Humphreys and the off-breaks of Fred Tate. The brothers Jesse and Arthur Hide had their days of triumph, and C. A. Smith was always useful when he could play. But little availed the fine batting of the Cotterills, the Lucases, George Bean, W. Newham, G. Brann – even of Murdoch, Ranjitsinhji and Fry – when the other side could not be got out. Humphreys was the last of the *great* lob bowlers. He played till he was 47 and he took 767 wickets for Sussex – an astonishing record, considering the shortness of the first-class programme. On the only occasions when Sussex beat the Australians (1888) and the South Africans (1894) he took 9 for 40 and 11 for 120 respectively.

When Humphreys retired, Tate (who once took 5 for 1 against Kent) soldiered on without much help until in 1900 Albert Relf returned to his native county. Relf was perhaps the best all-rounder and probably the second-best bowler that Sussex has had in this century. He was a model of accuracy and he never lost his control over spin and flight. In 1920, at the age of 46, he bowled 85 overs against Essex to take 9 wickets for 93. The batsmen Vine and Killick were useful bowlers. George Cox joined the side at roughly the same time and stayed in it for 30 years. After a slow beginning he became a formidable left-hand bowler. In 1905 he was spoken of by some who should have known better as the equal of Rhodes and Blythe. That he never was, but at his best he was a fine bowler and often the Sussex attack depended on him. Other bowlers of the period up to 1914 were Leach, Jupp and N. J. Holloway (all fastish) and Vincett (slow). It was not an attack to inspire terror in the opposition, but it was a good deal more effective than in the early years of the century.

It was not until the famous Australian, W. L. Murdoch, qualified for and took over the captaincy of Sussex in 1893 that Sussex began to achieve very much. Murdoch is generally regarded as one of the greatest of all Australian batsmen – *the* greatest before Trumper. He had made 286 v Sussex in 1882 and 158 in 1890; and now for 6 years he skilfully led a reviving Sussex, handing over to Ranjitsinhji in 1899 a side which, though still weak in bowling, was immensely strong in batting. Few counties, indeed, can ever have had a more forceful batting side than Sussex from 1899 to 1905. In 1901, for example (the year in which Fry scored 13 centuries), the first-class averages were headed by Fry, Brann and Ranji, each with an average of over 70. Six totals of 500 were registered, Fry and Killick each making 200 against Yorkshire; against Somerset the score was 466 for 1 (Ranji 285 not out). In 1900, facing a total of 609 at Leicester, Sussex made 686 (Fry 139, Ranji 275). In 1902 Sussex hit their highest score, 705 for 8, against Surrey (Fry 159, Ranji, 234). Of the other batsmen Vine, Killick, Newham and Relf made many runs (Fry and Vine scored a hundred for the 1st wicket on 33 occasions), but it remained very difficult to get the other sides out. Sussex, indeed, occupied 2nd place in 1902 and 1903, but in 1902 Yorkshire was no less than 45 per cent ahead.

It would be easy to dwell too long on Fry and Ranji. Their joint feats in 8 seasons from 1896–1904 (Ranji was away in 1898) are

Six of the old brigade. At top: C. B. Fry, G. R. Cox, sr, W. L. Murdoch; below: H. Phillips, A. E. Relf and 'Ranji'.

rivalled only by those of Compton and Edrich in 1947, when English bowling was of a lower standard. One thing remains to be said of Ranji: in his ability to make runs on *any* wicket he surpasses all the batsmen of cricket's history, save only W.G., Trumper and Hobbs. There was a match against Middlesex in 1900 when the wicket was ruined by a thunderstorm. Fry made a century before things got really bad; subsequently Killick made 39 and nobody else reached double figures except Ranji, who made 202 in 3 hours. An era ended in 1904, when Ranji became ruler of Nawanagar; but there was a glorious aftermath in 1905. For once the bowling proved adequate (Cox, Relf and Killick did wonders) and, even without Ranji, the batting was unexpectedly strong. Fry averaged 86, Vine had one of his best summers; Relf, Killick and R. A. Young had splendid figures, and Sussex finished 3rd in the Championship.

Thereafter the county fell on comparatively evil days. Fry, so badly injured at Lord's in May 1906 that he played no more that year, was nearing the end of his Sussex career; on two brief visits Ranji, though averaging over 50, was not quite the force that he had been; and for a time Sussex seemed to have lost the spirit of enterprise. But in the last seasons before the First War there was a welcome revival. Jupp and Vincett added variety to the bowling; the captain, H. P. Chaplin, H. L. Wilson, R. B. Heygate, Robert Relf, Jupp and Bowley considerably strengthened the batting, of which Vine and Albert Relf were still the main props.

Unpredictable is the word which best describes Sussex cricket in the years between the wars. A splendid season in 1920, in which Ranji made a few sad appearances, was followed by 2 rather depressing years, when Sussex *might* beat anybody (including Armstrong's Australians) but probably would not. In 1921 they won 13 of their 28 county matches – an excellent record, had they not lost 12. In 1922 they put Yorkshire out for 42 and lost the match with something to spare. But it must be remembered that for some years, until the coming of Duleepsinhji, the batting depended almost entirely on Bowley. For a few seasons Vine, Young and the Relfs strengthened the side in August; Tate and Arthur Gilligan often made runs. But on the whole the batting was undependable, and if Bowley got out early there was nearly always trouble. In 1923 a remarkable thing happened: Tate, almost overnight, became the best bowler in the world. In this and the next 2 seasons he took 652 wickets, enjoying in addition a highly successful tour in Australia. Moreover, Arthur Gilligan developed into a first-class fast bowler, and for a time the two carried all before them. In the course of a fortnight in 1924 they dismissed Surrey for 53, Middlesex for 41 and the South Africans for 30. Despite the terrible weakness of the batting – for Bowley was out of form that year – they might have carried Sussex to the upper reaches of the Championship, had not Gilligan been forced to give up cricket for a time after being knocked out in a Gentlemen v Players match. At this time Sussex had a great reputation as a side that played cricket for enjoyment. This was the spirit inculcated by Arthur Gilligan and it is an element in the greatness of his captaincy. In addition, by example even more than by precept (for he was unequalled as a mid-off), he made Sussex into the finest fielding side in the country, Yorkshire alone aspiring to parity. After captaining the county for longer than anyone since Edwin Napper in the dark ages, he had retired before Sussex reached their peak in 1932–1934; but it was his hand that had built the side.

In the last few years before Hitler's war Sussex had not more than an ordinarily good side. But in 1932 and the 2 succeeding years they touched greatness. In each year they came 2nd in the Championship, and it is worth particular mention that in 1933 and 1934 they beat Yorkshire 3 times running. In 1932 there was a tremendous struggle and at one time it seemed any odds that the Championship would depend on the final match against Yorkshire at Brighton. Most unhappily, Duleepsinhji was seized with the illness which ended his cricket career and, with Bowley also absent, Sussex had lost their chance before the great day came. At no time in its history has Sussex had a more powerful side than between 1928 and 1935.

As a brilliant batsman and fielder, a truly

Maurice Tate: big feet, a big heart and pace off the pitch. In a few months he developed into a great England bowler.

worthy successor of his famous uncle, Duleepsinhji stood out by himself. In 1930 he beat the Sussex record of 285 (scored by Ranji in 1901), making 333 at a run a minute against Northants. Even finer, perhaps, was the 246 which he scored against Kent in 1929 (he had already made a hundred in the 1st innings); these runs were made in $3\frac{1}{4}$ hours, largely off the bowling of Freeman, who took 267 wickets that year. At slip he was partnered by Bowley, a great batsman who did not have the best of luck in selection for Test Matches. Bowley, the critics would say, was too right-handed; but his right hand helped him to more than 50 hundreds and it was in virtually his last year that he made his highest score, 283, in a first wicket stand of 490 with John Langridge.

A. Melville, John Langridge, Harry Parks and Cook were other outstanding batsmen, with the young George Cox (who, but for the war, must have played for England) just coming to the fore. All-rounders of great ability were Jim Parks (who in 1937 made 3,000 runs and took 100 wickets) and James Langridge. Tich Cornford completed a quar-

Sussex in 1931 when 'Duleep' took on the captaincy. Back row: John Langridge, H. E. Hammond, James Langridge and H. W. Parks; sitting: T. E. Cook, M. W. Tate, A. E. R. Gilligan, K. S. Duleepsinhji (captain), E. H. Bowley, A. F. Wensley and W. L. Cornford.

tette of exceptionally competent wicket-keepers (Phillips, Butt and Street were the others) whose line stretches from 1871 to 1939. It was in bowling that Sussex was for once so admirably served. Cox *père* had retired in 1928, full of honours (not many men at the age of 50 have taken 100 wickets in a season). By 1932 Tate had passed his peak, but was still a great bowler: in Bowley's benefit match that year he took 13 Middlesex wickets for 58 (and made 50, going in last but one). Wensley, a bowler of somewhat similar type, had some splendid seasons, eventually giving way to Jim Cornford, who had modelled himself, with partial success, on Tate.

James Langridge's record as a left-hand bowler is a fine one; Jim Parks as an off-spinner and Bowley with leg-breaks completed a very well-varied attack. By 1938, however, Tate, Bowley and Wensley had retired and Sussex bowling was again on the decline. In 1938, when Sussex, because of this decline, were dropping down the Championship table, there was a startling reinforcement to the still powerful batting. H. T. Bartlett, a left-hand hitter of enormous power, had a truly remarkable season, of which the highlights were a century against the Australians made in under an hour and 175 for the Gentlemen at Lord's made in less than 3 hours. Never again did he reach such heights, but his crowded hour of glorious life was unforgettable.

Sussex, the earliest winners of the Gillette Cup, in 1978 brought off a surprise by beating Somerset in the final. Here Arnold Long shows off the Trophy – a typical end-of-season scene.

History has a habit of repeating itself on broad lines, if not in detail. In 1946, as in 1919, Sussex started with a new captain; there were some old hands to get things going again; and the bowling was incredibly weak, weaker now than at any time in the county's existence. As secretary-captain S. C. Griffith (a fine enough wicket-keeper to have been preferred in 2 Test Matches to Godfrey Evans) found the dual job almost too great a strain. Unlucky to occupy the bottom place in 1946 (for victory over Gloucestershire would have averted the ignominy and rain alone prevented that victory), Sussex never rose above 10th place in the next 6 years. Yet in 1953 they shot up from 13th to 2nd, not so very far behind Surrey. How did that happen? Of the old hands mentioned above, the Langridge brothers, Cox and Harry Parks made heaps of runs in the early post-war years. But for a time – and this must be ascribed largely to the weakness of the bowling – the aggressive spirit seemed to have deserted Sussex cricket.

By 1949, however, things had begun to improve. In that year John Langridge had a marvellous season, making nearly 3,000 runs, averaging 60 and scoring 12 centuries; as *all* of these were made for Sussex, he passed C. B. Fry's 1901 record of 11. In this year, too, Sussex began to recapture the spirit of attack in their batting. Cox, it may be said, had never lost it; but now it was fostered chiefly by the 2 young amateurs, D. S. Sheppard and G. H. G. Doggart. It is much to be regretted that neither found time for more than one full season (Sheppard in 1953, Doggart in 1954); but they must be accorded high rank among the amateurs who have played for Sussex. Sheppard, indeed, has a batting average inferior only to those of Ranji, Fry and Duleepsinhji. But the bowling remained too weak and Sussex could not rise in the Championship.

In 1953 James Langridge, who had succeeded Bartlett in the captaincy, decided to retire. What he and his brother John (who retired 2 years later) accomplished for Sussex may conveniently be summarized here. In careers which began in 1924 and 1928 respectively, James scored nearly 29,000 runs and John over 34,000. No other Sussex batsman approaches these totals. James took more wickets than any other bowler except Cox, Maurice Tate and Albert Relf. John caught more catches than any other fieldsman, wicket-keepers excluded; as a slip-field he was at least the equal of Bowley and Duleepsinhji.

When Sheppard took over the captaincy, prospects were improving. In the previous year two new bowlers had come to the fore, R. G. Marlar, an off-spinner, and Ian Thomson, a bowler something on the lines of Tate and one who used both his brain and the seam. In 1953 Thomson, Marlar and the hard-working A. E. James all took 100 wickets (in all matches) and received much help from the left-handed Wood and from Oakman's off-breaks. Sheppard and Cox were in fine form with the bat. Young Jim Parks, Oakman, Suttle and D. V. Smith were developing into first-rate batsmen. Sheppard was an astute and enthusiastic captain and Sussex, losing only 3 matches, fully deserved their position of second to Surrey. This success has not been repeated.

When Marlar's bowling declined, the old state of things recurred; this time it was Thomson on whom Sussex depended to get the opposition out. The batting, consistently useful, received a powerful reinforcement when, in Marlar's last year as captain, E. R. Dexter became regularly available. Dexter, a mighty hitter of the ball and a hostile bowler, took over the captaincy in 1960, and in 1963 led Sussex to victory in the first knock-out competition ever held by the counties. He did the same in 1964, by which time – if the formula for Championship victory had not yet been found by Sussex – they had certainly proved themselves masters of the one-day game.

Indeed, during the next 15 years, it was only their performances in the Gillette Cup that lent Sussex any distinction at all. Even these were variable, but in 1967 they got to the semi-finals before being beaten by Kent and in 1968, 1970 and 1973 they were beaten in the final by Warwickshire, Lancashire and Gloucestershire respectively. After an appalling season in other respects, they confounded everyone by beating a strong Somerset side in the 1978 final by 5 wickets. It looked as if at last the tide was turning, for by then promising young players like Parker, Mendis and Barclay were establishing themselves, and the all-round strength of the side had been increased by imports from overseas: K. C. Wessels from South Africa, a useful opening batsman, Imran Khan, and Javed Miandad from Pakistan, both enterprising batsmen of high quality. In addition, Imran was a decidedly quick opening bowler. From Surrey had come Arnold Long, who took over the wicket-keeping and captaincy from A. W. Greig in 1978, and Geoff Arnold, the former England fast bowler.

Their achievements in the Championship during this period were pretty depressing for anyone who associated Sussex with a particular style and way of playing. They never finished higher than 7th, in 1968 they were bottom, and usually they were not many places above that. They did dismally in the newly-founded Benson & Hedges Cup and in the John Player League they were twice bottom, never rising higher than joint 4th in 1977.

Their captains, after Dexter retired in 1965 – he was one of their great batsmen, though rather more successful for England, whom he captained, than for Sussex – were the Nawab of Pataudi and J. M. Parks (for a season each), M. G. Griffith for 4 seasons, and A. W. Greig for 5. They never played under any of these as a happy or confident side, though they had in J. A. Snow for much of this time one of the outstanding fast bowlers of the period, who appeared 49 times for England between 1965 and 1976, taking 202 Test wickets. During the 1960s, too, J. M. Parks, who took up wicket-keeping and became England's regular wicket-keeper, graced all the county grounds and many overseas Test grounds in Australia, South Africa and West

Indies, with the brilliance of his stroke-play, not least in Gillette Cup matches. Greig, too, produced some splendid all-round performances before in 1978 he threw in his lot with Packer.

But after the removal of Parks from the captaincy in 1968, Sussex never gave the impression of enjoying their cricket. The players seemed at odds with each other and their achievements reflected this divisiveness and general lack of purpose. Neither Griffith, who had a tough job, nor Greig, in their different ways, managed fully to carry the side with them, and neither was among the more shrewd or enterprising of county captains.

There were compensations. Michael Buss was an exciting and successful opening batsman for several seasons before he suddenly lost his form, and he was a useful left-arm bowler at slow-medium. K. G. Suttle, who in 1969 missed his 1st Championship match after 423 consecutive appearances, made great quantities of runs and always fielded brilliantly until the years took their toll. Tony Buss, elder brother of Michael, took over from Thomson as the main seam bowler – in the frequent absences of Snow on Test duty – and he bowled long and well at rather over medium pace. In 1965 and 1966 he took 120 wickets, and in 1967, 113 wickets. P. J. Graves, one of the most brilliant fieldsmen in the country close to the wicket, was an elegant left-hand batsman who came, on several occasions, close to Test selection. But he was frequently hampered by illness and injury, and never fully realized his potential.

Others who made their mark in the late 1960s and early 1970s were Geoffrey Greenidge, an engaging if slightly limited opening batsman from the West Indies, who in 1970 hit 5 Championship hundreds, and L. J. Lenham, another fairly stolid opener, who had one or two admirable seasons without ever developing into quite the strokeplayer he occasionally suggested.

If the batting was generally an affair of stops and starts, alternately exciting and fallible, the bowling, except when Snow was in the mood, was relentlessly humdrum and lacking in variety. J. Spencer came down from Cambridge to give good service at medium-pace, as did D. L. Bates. U. Joshi, a spinner from India who never quite made the grade, gave some useful performances, while J. R. T. Barclay improved steadily as an off-spinner, and C. E. Waller, a left-arm spinner joining the county from Surrey, had his moments. But as an attack it was never quite formidable enough to win many matches for Arnold Long, the wicket-keeper, another transferance from Surrey, who inherited the captaincy from Greig.

In 1972 the Hove ground celebrated its centenary. In recent years, with the levelling of the square and the building of blocks of flats to the north and south, the appearance and atmosphere have changed radically. Sussex cricket has always had something of the sea about it, a mixture of the raffish and the Regency; it has always been a 'family' club, with its Coxes and Tates, Gilligans and Langridges, Parkses, Griffiths and Busses. But it has also produced a fair crop of dashing exotics, players quite outside the general run of county cricketers: Ranji, Duleep, Melville, Bartlett, Dexter, Snow, Greig, not to mention George Cox, Jr, and J. M. Parks. Imran Khan, K. C. Wessels and Garth Le Roux, yet another import, a fast bowler from South Africa, may add to their number. In the next few years Paul Parker, John Barclay, Mendis and Phillipson could help Sussex to altogether better things.

CAPTAINS

1839–46	C. G. Taylor
1847–62	E. Napper
1863	J. H. Hale
1864	J. H. Hale and C. H. Smith
1865–73	C. H. Smith
1874	C. H. Smith and J. M. Cotterill
1875	J. M. Cotterill
1876–78	F. F. J. Greenfield
1879	C. Sharp
1880	R. T. Ellis
1881–82	F. F. J. Greenfield
1883–84	H. Whitfeld
1885	G. N. Wyatt
1886	F. M. Lucas
1887–88	C. A. Smith
1889	W. Newham
1890	C. A. Smith
1891–92	W. Newham
1893–98	W. L. Murdoch
1899	W. L. Murdoch and K. S. Ranjitsinhji
1900–03	K. S. Ranjitsinhji
1904–05	C. B. Fry
1906	C. B. Fry and C. L. A. Smith
1907–08	C. B. Fry
1909	C. L. A. Smith
1910–14	H. P. Chaplin
1919–21	H. L. Wilson
1922–29	A. E. R. Gilligan
1930	A. H. H. Gilligan
1931–32	K. S. Duleepsinhji
1933	R. S. G. Scott
1934–35	A. Melville
1936–39	A. J. Holmes
1946	S. C. Griffith
1947–49	H. T. Bartlett
1950–52	James Langridge
1953	D. S. Sheppard
1954	G. H. G. Doggart
1955–59	R. G. Marlar
1960–65	E. R. Dexter
1966	Nawab of Pataudi
1967	J. M. Parks
1968	J. M. Parks and M. G. Griffith
1969–72	M. G. Griffith
1973–77	A. W. Greig
1978–	A. Long

HIGHEST TOTALS

For 705–8D v Surrey, Hastings 1902
Against 726 by Notts, Trent Bridge 1895

LOWEST TOTALS

For { 19 v Surrey, Godalming 1830
19 v Notts, Hove 1873 }
Against 18 by Kent, Gravesend 1867

HIGHEST INDIVIDUAL INNINGS

For 333 K. S. Duleepsinhji v Northants, Hove 1930
Against 322 E. Paynter for Lancs, Hove 1937

MOST RUNS

In a season 2,850 J. G. Langridge 1949
In a career 34,152 J. G. Langridge 1928–1955

MOST HUNDREDS

In a season 12 J. G. Langridge 1949
In a career 76 J. G. Langridge 1928–1955

INDIVIDUAL INNINGS OF 250 AND OVER

K. S. Ranjitsinhji, 260 v MCC, Lord's 1897
K. S. Ranjitsinhji, 275 v Leicester, Leicester 1900
K. S. Ranjitsinhji, 285* v Somerset, Taunton 1901
R. R. Relf, 272* v Worcester, Eastbourne 1909
E. H. Bowley, 280* v Gloucester, Hove 1929
T. E. Cook, 278 v Hants, Hove 1930
K. S. Duleepsinhji, 333 v Northants, Hove 1930
E. H. Bowley, 283 v Middlesex, Hove 1933
J. G. Langridge, 250* v Glamorgan, Hove 1933

HUNDRED ON DEBUT

L. Winslow, 124 v Gloucester, Hove 1875
A. H. Trevor, 103 v Kent, Hove 1880
F. W. Marlow, 144 v MCC, Lord's 1891
J. G. C. Scott, 137 v Oxford University, Eastbourne 1907
K. A. Higgs, 101 v Worcester, Hove 1920

RECORD WICKET PARTNERSHIPS

1 E. H. Bowley and J. G. Langridge, 490 v Middlesex, Hove 1933
2 E. H. Bowley and M. W. Tate, 385 v Northants, Hove 1921
3 K. S. Ranjitsinhji and E. H. Killick, 298 v Lancs, Hove 1901
4 G. Cox and James Langridge, 326* v Yorks, Headingley 1949
5 J. H. Parks and H. W. Parks, 297 v Hants, Portsmouth 1937
6 K. S. Duleepsinhji and M. W. Tate, 255 v Northants, Hove 1930
7 K. S. Ranjitsinhji and W. Newham, 344 v Essex, Leyton 1902
8 C. L. A. Smith and G. Brann, 229* v Kent, Hove 1902
9 H. W. Parks and A. F. Wensley, 178 v Essex, Horsham 1930
10 G. R. Cox and H. R. Butt, 156 v Cambridge University, Cambridge 1908

MOST WICKETS

In a match 17–106 G. R. Cox v Warwicks, Horsham 1926
In a season 198 M. W. Tate 1925
In a career 2,223 M. W. Tate 1912–1937

ALL 10 WICKETS IN AN INNINGS

C. H. G. Bland v Kent, Tonbridge 1899
N. I. Thomson v Warwicks, Worthing 1964

HAT-TRICKS

V. W. C. Jupp 3 (5 in all matches)
M. W. Tate 2 (3 in all matches)
A. Buss, W. Humphreys 2 each
W. Blackman, P. A. D. Carey, C. H. Ellis, A. E. R. Gilligan, H. E. Hammond, J. B. Hide, James Langridge, A. S. M. Oakman, A. C. S. Pigott, A. E. Relf, D. V. Smith, F. W. Tate, A. F. Wensley 1 each

WICKET-KEEPING – MOST DISMISSALS

In an innings 6 H. R. Butt (3)
R. T. Webb (2)
M. G. Griffith
J. M. Parks
H. Phillips
A. A. Shaw
In a match 10 H. Phillips
In a season 95 G. Street 1923
In a career 1167 H. R. Butt 1890–1912

COUNTY CAPS AWARDED SINCE 1946

1948	P. D. S. Blake
1949	G. H. G. Doggart, J. Oakes, D. S. Sheppard
1950	A. E. James, D. V. Smith, R. T. Webb
1951	A. S. M. Oakman, J. M. Parks
1952	R. G. Marlar, K. G. Suttle
1953	N. I. Thomson
1957	D. L. Bates, L. J. Lenham
1959	E. R. Dexter
1961	R. V. Bell, G. C. Cooper, R. J. Langridge
1963	Nawab of Pataudi, A. Buss
1964	J. A. Snow
1965	T. Gunn
1966	D. J. Foreman
1967	M. A. Buss, A. W. Greig, M. G. Griffith, E. J. Lewis
1969	P. J. Graves
1970	G. A. Greenidge
1971	U. C. Joshi, R. M. Prideaux
1973	J. D. Morley, J. Spencer
1976	J. R. T. Barclay, R. D. V. Knight, A. Long, C. E. Waller
1977	Javed Miandad, K. C. Wessels
1978	Imran Khan
1979	G. G. Arnold, P. W. G. Parker

Warwickshire

ALAN SMITH

Foundation 1882
Colours Dark Blue, Gold and Silver
Badge Bear and Ragged Staff
Champions 1911, 1951, 1972

Six of the most famous of the old time Warwickshire cricketers: E. J. ('Tiger') Smith, W. G. Quaife, F. S. G. Calthorpe, J. H. Parsons, L. A. Bates and H. Howell.

The imposing west wing at Edgbaston is named 'The William Ansell Stand'. This is a just commemoration since not only was Ansell virtually the founder of the Warwickshire County Cricket Club, but he also won for it first-class status in the face of opposition from the established counties. Moreover, he was one of the pioneers who helped to secure the ground in Edgbaston Road, once rough meadow grazing land, to be the home of Warwickshire cricket. He led the movement that was to take Warwickshire cricket out of the control of 'a few gentlemen in and around Warwick', as he put it, and place it in the hands of a coalition committee. This occurred in 1882, which is accepted by the club as the year of its inauguration. From the inaugural meeting the great cricket potential of Birmingham, and other industrial centres, became available for the first time. But it was not all plain sailing. Fixtures were not easily come by; members were slow to join. The picture began to change from the opening of the new ground in 1886 for the membership grew and playing form began to improve, and in 1894 Warwickshire were granted first-class status.

In terms of results Warwickshire achieved little of note during their first 15 or so seasons. In 1910 they finished last but 2, despite the comment in *Wisden* that there had been a departure from the previous lack of enterprise in batting. The man appointed captain in 1911, F. R. Foster, remains to this day perhaps the most intriguing figure in Warwickshire cricket. His career was sadly brief. He began modestly in 1908, but in 1910 took 100 wickets and scored 574 runs. In the Championship season of 1911, for Warwickshire alone, he scored 1,383 runs and took 116 wickets to complete the double – a feat only performed on one other occasion in Warwickshire's history – by Tom Cartwright in 1962. At the end of this marvellous season Foster went with county colleagues 'Tiger' Smith and S. P. Kinneir to Australia, to form a formidable bowling partnership with S. F. Barnes who had himself played one first-class match for Warwickshire, though with uncharacteristic lack of success. Sadly, the First World War ended Foster's career. He was crippled for life in a motor-cycle accident in 1915. Later he became a tragic legend, but his ability and his dashing personality make his memory imperishable.

Wisden demonstrated incredulity at Warwickshire's 1911 Championship success, but having recovered from the shock paid fair tribute to the team. With the ball Foster received wonderful support from Field with 122 wickets. There were also more modest contributions from Quaife and Santall. The batting performances were spread more evenly, Kinneir, Charlesworth and Quaife all scoring 1,000 runs and Smith 800.

During the formative years many able men played their part in the development of the club. G. H. Cartland was chairman for 47 years and its captains included H. W. Bainbridge and J. F. Byrne, as well as the princely Foster. Then there was Dick Lilley, good enough to keep wicket for England on 35 occasions; Pallett and Shilton, bowlers at their best operating in tandem; the diminutive Willy Quaife, who was to play to the age of 56; his brother Walter; Sydney Santall, also the club's first historian; the brothers Frank and George Stephens; the tall and powerful Jack Parsons (later a Canon of the Church); Frank Field, Crowther Charlesworth and Septimus Kinneir. Later, between the wars, a dominant personality at Edgbaston was to be found not on the field, but in the cramped rooms which sufficed as the Secretary's office. R. V. Ryder had succeeded Ansell in 1895 and continued to hold office until 1944. His successor, Leslie Deakins, continued until 1976 so that the present incumbent, Alan Smith, is only the 4th Secretary in nearly 100 years. Deakins held the reins in the years after the Second War, when, thanks to his energies and abilities in very large part, the club assumed greater influence and authority. The modern Edgbaston and its organization is a far cry from the Sundays that Ryder used to recall when he might spend all day in a hansom cab, trying to assemble a side. Edgbaston's 1st Test Match, between England and Australia in that great cricketing year of 1902, was organized without a telephone. Membership during the First World War dwindled to 500, but in 1919 the figure rose to 1,700, and continued through to 1926, after which a fall in gate receipts was attributed by Ryder to greyhound racing opening in Birmingham in 1927.

The county's playing fortunes in the inter-war years fluctuated without ever scaling great heights. Throughout the 1920s, under the Hon F. S. G. Calthorpe, the lack of bowling was a severe handicap, although Calthorpe himself and Harry Howell, who twice toured Australia, often made inroads with the new ball. In no game was this more evident than the celebrated match in 1922 when Hampshire were bowled out for 15, with Howell taking 6 for 7 and Calthorpe 4 for 4. Despite this Hampshire scored 521 in their 2nd innings and won quite comfortably. Throughout Calthorpe's captaincy the Edgbaston story is complicated by an overlapping of generations which could never happen in modern times. It was not until the end of 1928 that Willie Quaife retired at the age of 56. In his final appearance against Derbyshire at Edgbaston he made 115 in 4½ hours. Another who linked the Foster era with the 1920s was 'Tiger' Smith, who began in 1904 and continued playing until 1930. Smith's services to Warwickshire as a coach continued into the 1960s and he remained until his death in 1979 as much a symbol at Edgbaston as the Warwickshire Bear, the more endearing characteristics of which uncompromising animal he possessed to a considerable degree.

R. E. S. Wyatt took over the captaincy in 1930, helping by his ability as an all-round technician to bring the team up to 7th place in 1933, and 4th in 1934, their best since 1911. To support Wyatt with the bat was that apostle of forceful cricket Canon Jack Parsons. The burden of the bowling was borne at a quickish pace by J. H. ('Danny') Mayer and by the left-arm spin of George Paine, who toured West Indies in 1934. Wyatt went to Australia in 1936–37 and scored more runs than anyone else for Warwickshire in 1937, but at the end of the season the committee announced that, whilst they appreciated his captaincy, they had decided to make a change. Under Wyatt's youthful successor, Peter Cranmer, more of the adventure and zest for cricket came to Warwickshire to replace the asceticism of Wyatt, who continued, however, to be a valuable member of the side. For the 2 difficult years in which he continued to hold the captaincy after the Second War, Cranmer led his men with a cheerful disregard for the conventions of the game. Any latter-day successes that Warwickshire have

For 40 years no county outside 'the big six' had won the Championship until in 1951 Warwickshire repeated their 1911 victory. Back row: G. Austin (scorer), D. Taylor, R. Weeks, A. V. Wolton, F. C. Gardner, C. Belam, A. Townsend, R. T. Spooner and E. J. Smith (coach); sitting: C. W. Grove, W. E. Hollies, H. E. Dollery (captain), J. S. Ord and T. L. Pritchard.

had owe no little debt to the attitude encouraged by Cranmer.

The 1930s saw the burgeoning of the talents of Tom Dollery and Eric Hollies. But the best days of these 2 fine cricketers came near the end of their playing careers. They formed the backbone of Cranmer's makeshift team in 1946, with Dollery scoring nearly 2,000 runs and Hollies taking more wickets than anyone else in the country, 184 at an average of 15·60. In 1948 the captaincy was shared between R. H. Maudsley and Dollery, a curious set-up which did not succeed, so that Maudsley asked not to be considered in 1949. Meanwhile, Hollies had procured for himself a niche in cricket history by bowling Bradman 2nd ball for a duck in that great Australian's last Test Match innings at the Oval in 1948. The Championship side was beginning to take shape in 1948. The New Zealander, Tom Pritchard, took 172 wickets, and his partner, Charlie Grove, 60. R. T. Spooner had arrived from Durham to keep wicket and to add a sizeable contribution with the bat. Jimmy Ord and Fred Gardner had settled down and A. Townsend had joined Dollery in one of the best slip combinations in the country. Off the field activities ensured a strong increase in membership, and gate attendances rose in parallel.

In 1949 and 1950 the team was 4th in the Championship. It also had the distinction of being the only county to defeat the West Indians, who so decisively won the 1950 Test series. In 1951 the jig-saw fell into place when Warwickshire – 'an extraordinary team of ordinary cricketers playing purposeful cricket' (to quote Dollery's own words) – led runners-up Yorkshire by no fewer than 42 points. Happily free from injury the 4 main bowlers were remarkably consistent. Pritchard, Grove and Hollies were well established, and a young slow lefthander, R. T. Weeks, ranked with them that season, though thereafter he soon fell away. The team as a whole was settled and the batting positive and reliable. Gardner, Spooner and Ord nearly always ensured a confident start, and Dollery masterminded the proper progress of the innings from No. 5.

Encouraged by the success of the large crowds that followed Warwickshire's success Deakins and his committee set about restoring Test cricket to Edgbaston. It was not an easy task, for not unnaturally the 4 counties, who, with Lord's provided the grounds for the 5 Tests, were reluctant to promote the introduction of a 5th, however superbly equipped, and it was principally the resourcefulness of Leslie Deakins in proposing the rota system now in existence that won the day in 1957. The early 1950s also saw the setting up of the Supporters' Association without whose existence Warwickshire's subsequent history would have been entirely different. Loyally and ably served by the largely unsung husband and wife team of David Blakemore and Winnie Crook, the Supporters' Association has effectively paid for the development of the ground, as well as setting up an Endowment Fund designed to safeguard the future of cricket on the ground.

On the playing side, the magnificence of 1951 was not to be recaptured for more than 20 years. In 1952 the county finished 5th. Dollery gave up the captaincy in 1955 and Hollies was persuaded to take over for one season until M. J. K. Smith could be qualified for 1957. The records of such as Dollery and Hollies must always inspire. All but 1,000 of Dollery's 24,000 runs were scored for Warwickshire, as were all but one of his 50 hundreds. There are few Warwickshire bowling records that Eric Hollies does not hold. He took 2,323 first-class wickets, of which 2,201 were for the county. He has taken the most wickets for Warwickshire in a season (180 in 1946) and has bowled the most overs in a season (1,399 in 1949).

An impressive inconsistency has marked Warwickshire's performances over the years. In 1953, for example, they suffered defeat in a single day by Surrey at the Oval, being bowled out for 45 and 52, but when it came to the return match at Edgbaston they defeated the champions by 140 runs. Later in the same season they secured a moral victory over Lindsay Hassett's Australians. This last game produced by all accounts the finest defensive innings ever seen at Edgbaston. Those present saw an unforgettable duel between Hassett and Hollies on a worn pitch, with Hassett, almost single-handed, saving the day for the Australians.

The first 5 years of Mike Smith's captaincy saw the building of a new team. Throughout his 11 years in office 'M.J.K.' led the side with a cheerful nonchalance which effectively disguised to some onlookers his considerable ability as a leader. Players for England, as well as Warwickshire, liked him greatly, and in 1962, 1963 and 1964 his team went close to rewarding his leadership with tangible success. Third and fourth in the preceding two years, Warwickshire led the table for much of 1964, but were eventually overtaken by Worcestershire. The batting was prolific in the new Gillette Cup competition and went to Lord's for the final full of confidence. Hopes were dashed however in the 1st hour's play on a September morning when the ball swung prodigiously for the Sussex bowlers.

Amongst players now making their mark was the captain's namesake, another former Oxford captain, Alan Smith, who had a brief sojourn as England's wicket-keeper. Bob Barber had arrived from Lancashire, and the Warwickshire air transformed his style of batting so that, particularly in combination with Norman Horner, he became the county's outstanding attacking batsman. Jim Stewart, too, made himself a reputation as a formidable striker of the ball, not just because of his 17 sixes in a match against Lancashire at Blackpool. The leading bowlers throughout the 1960s included the thoughtful and canny Jack Bannister and the long-serving fast bowler David Brown, a model in every sense for aspiring youngsters. From overseas came a Pakistani, Billy Ibadulla, and a West Indian doctor, Rudi Webster. Pre-eminent, however, was Tom Cartwright. After the near-misses in the Championship and the disappointment of the 1964 Gillette Cup final, there was compensation with the Gillette Cup victory of 1966 when Worcestershire were defeated at Lord's.

Mike Smith gave up the captaincy in 1967 to be succeeded by Alan Smith. 'A.C.' had a strong personal wish to bring the Championship back to Edgbaston, and he began in 1968 with the introduction of the 2 West Indian stars, Lance Gibbs and Rohan Kanhai. This year the side was disappointing in the Championship, but again won the Gillette Cup, the new captain distinguishing himself with a match-winning onslaught with the bat just when Sussex had seemed to be taking control in failing light. Hopes for Championship success were seriously dented at the end of

LEFT M. J. K. Smith: a wizard on the on-side, and popular captain of, successively, Oxford, Warwickshire and England.

RIGHT Dennis Amiss was the 1st Warwickshire-born player to score a hundred for England.

1969 when Cartwright announced that he wanted to leave Warwickshire in order to go somewhere where he could establish himself in an ancillary job for the future. It was therefore a matter of some surprise when, in 1971, the team came within a whisker of lifting the Championship title for the 3rd time. When the campaign ended they and Surrey were level on points (255), but Surrey had more outright victories and were thereby declared champions. By 1971 Lance Gibbs had come to terms with local conditions and the special demands of the English county game. Before the season he had promised 100 wickets, and paid that with interest by taking 131, a remarkable figure bearing in mind the number of matches played. Almost single-handed he kept Warwickshire in the hunt.

Responding to this disappointment the team-building continued, the captain flying to West Indies to obtain the services of the as yet little-known Alvin Kallicharran. Bob Willis, dissatisfied with Surrey, took the chance to move to Warwickshire and the club also secured the services of West Indian wicket-keeper, Deryck Murray. Murray's introduction meant that Alan Smith gave up keeping wicket to indulge his first love of bowling, bringing to the scene a somewhat bizarre, whirling action.

1972 became the next golden year in the club's history. The Championship was won by a 36-point margin with the team being undefeated. They also reached the Gillette Final, in which they were defeated by Lancashire, and still found time to reach the semi-final of the new Benson & Hedges Cup Competition. This Championship success was the culmination of efforts made by a great many people and was just reward for those responsible for assembling the side as well as the players themselves. The batting was consistently attractive, positive, and sometimes even violent throughout the season, due to no one more than Rohan Kanhai, who displayed peerless form throughout the campaign and played all his innings according to the needs of the situation. Mike Smith was not far behind and thoroughly deserved his recall to the England team for matches in the series against Australia. The diminutive Kallicharran was another, along with Dennis Amiss, John Jameson and John Whitehouse. Gibbs again looked after the slow bowling almost entirely on his own, and the seamers all chipped in usefully from time to time. Brown, Norman McVicker, Steve Rouse, and Alan Smith all had their moments with the ball. Halfway through the season Bob Willis was deemed to have completed his residential qualification period and the attack received the added impetus of real pace for the second half of the season. Even the fielding, seldom a Warwickshire strong point, matched the general quality of other facets of the game.

The only blot on the year, which included a Gillette final appearance and a Benson & Hedges semi-final appearance, was that barely 13,000 people watched the home matches. It had always been said that the Birmingham public would respond to a winning or an attractive team, but in 1972 when the two elements were put together the response was sadly disappointing.

As the 1911 and 1951 teams declined after their years of triumph, so too did the 1972 team. Alan Smith was succeeded in 1975 by the cheerful and popular David Brown, but there was no one to take the place of Lance Gibbs. After 3 years of honest endeavour Brown handed on the captaincy to Whitehouse, whose early days in charge were far from easy. Throughout the middle and late 1970s there was little to show beyond fairly frequent appearances in the Benson & Hedges semi-final.

The process of rebuilding the team was long drawn out. Warwickshire suffered from the advent of Mr Kerry Packer. Three of its cricketers were approached; Amiss was quick to sign to play for the Australian television magnate; Kallicharran, although signing quickly, just as speedily withdrew; and Willis, who sought the club's advice as to what best to do, stayed with the established game. It was almost inevitable that the team as a whole felt that Amiss, though perfectly entitled to support an organization which threatened their livelihood, should not be able to come back to Warwickshire just as and when it suited him. The majority of the committee took the same view. The club's membership was sharply divided between those who felt Amiss should have been more loyal to club and country and those who felt that he was entitled to maximize on his own potential, and that in any event Warwickshire's batting was such that they could ill afford to dispense with his services. Fortunately, as attitudes shifted in Australia, it became possible at the beginning of the 1979 season happily to reintegrate Amiss into the team.

Throughout the 1960s and 1970s the committee had been successively led by Edmund King and Cyril Goodway, two individuals well fitted to succeed the early pioneers. At no stage did they seek to compromise the potential created by the Supporters' Association's financial success of the 1960s, and Warwickshire's stock and standing within the game was carefully nurtured by them and their Committee colleagues.

As the 1970s drew to a close so Warwickshire faced up to the future with an uncertainty shared by many counties. On the playing side the team contained fewer high quality players than for 2 decades, and fewer also with the crowd-pulling potential so vital as the game became more directly commercial. Of the older players, Whitehouse, Willis, Amiss and Kallicharran all had valuable cricket left in them, although Brown was close to the end of his fine career; the younger element, Geoff Humpage, David Smith, Steve Perryman, Andy Lloyd, and the South African, Anton Ferreira, had the future in their hands.

The club's headquarters at Edgbaston are splendidly appointed, comparing with the best in the world, but even this extensive complex is not always the blessing it may seem to be. As facilities have increased so maintenance costs have soared, so that the Committee needs to remain acutely alert to any future chance of commercial development. On that front Warwickshire introduced their Executive Club in 1975, which has been a conspicuous success. A carefully planned alteration to the top of the William Ansell Stand enabled a luxurious facility to be offered for membership by firms and companies within the area. Demand remains strong and involvement with the business and industrial community, including local sponsorship, has brought welcome revenue. The populace of the great Midlands metropolis in general, however, are harder to please. Whatever the reason, there continues to be a reluctance to take local pride in team and ground, an interest that is essential to sustaining Warwickshire cricket as a prominent feature of the midland community.

CAPTAINS

1894–1901	H. W. Bainbridge
1902	H. W. Bainbridge and T. S. Fishwick
1903–06	J. F. Byrne
1907	J. F. Byrne and T. S. Fishwick
1908–09	A. C. S. Glover
1910	H. J. Goodwin
1911–14	F. R. Foster
1919	G. W. Stephens
1920–29	F. S. G. Calthorpe
1930–37	R. E. S. Wyatt
1938–47	P. Cranmer
1948	H. E. Dollery and R. H. Maudsley
1949–55	H. E. Dollery
1956	W. E. Hollies
1957–67	M. J. K. Smith
1968–74	A. C. Smith
1975–77	D. J. Brown
1978–79	J. Whitehouse

HIGHEST TOTALS

For 657–6D v Hants, Edgbaston 1899
Against 887 by Yorks, Edgbaston 1896

LOWEST TOTALS

For 16 v Kent, Tonbridge 1913
Against 15 by Hants, Edgbaston 1922

HIGHEST INDIVIDUAL INNINGS

For 305* F. R. Foster v Worcester, Dudley 1914
Against 316 R. H. Moore for Hants, Bournemouth 1937

MOST RUNS

In a season 2,417 M. J. K. Smith
In a career 33,862 W. G. Quaife 1894–1928

MOST HUNDREDS

In a season { 8 R. E. S. Wyatt 1937; 8 R. B. Kanhai 1972 }
In a career 71 W. G. Quaife 1894–1928

INDIVIDUAL INNINGS OF 250 AND OVER

W. G. Quaife, 255* v Surrey, Oval 1905
S. Kinneir, 268* v Hants, Edgbaston 1911
F. R. Foster, 305* v Worcester, Dudley 1914
R. B. Kanhai, 253 v Notts, Trent Bridge 1968

HUNDRED ON DEBUT

J. E. Hill, 139* v Notts, Trent Bridge 1894
J. F. Byrne, 100 v Leicester, Edgbaston 1897
H. Venn, 151 v Worcester, Edgbaston 1919
R. B. Kanhai, 119 v Cambridge University, Cambridge 1968
J. Whitehouse, 173 v Oxford University, Oxford 1971

RECORD WICKET PARTNERSHIPS

1 N. F. Horner and K. Ibadulla, 377* v Surrey, Oval 1960
2 J. A. Jameson and R. B. Kanhai, 465* v Gloucester, Edgbaston 1974
3 S. Kinneir and W. G. Quaife, 327 v Lancs, Edgbaston 1901
4 R. B. Kanhai and K. Ibadulla, 402 v Notts, Trent Bridge 1968
5 W. Quaife and W. G. Quaife, 268 v Essex, Leyton 1900
6 H. E. Dollery and J. Buckingham, 220 v Derby, Derby 1938
7 H. E. Dollery and J. S. Ord, 250 v Kent, Maidstone 1953
8 A. J. W. Croom and R. E. S. Wyatt, 228 v Worcester, Dudley 1925
9 G. W. Stephens and A. J. W. Croom, 154 v Derby, Edgbaston 1925
10 F. R. Santall and W. Sanders, 128 v Yorks, Edgbaston 1930

MOST WICKETS

In a match 15–76 S. Hargreave v Surrey, Oval 1903
In a season 180 W. E. Hollies 1946
In a career 2,201 W. E. Hollies 1932–1957

ALL 10 WICKETS IN AN INNINGS

H. Howell v Yorks, Edgbaston 1923
W. E. Hollies v Notts, Edgbaston 1946
J. D. Bannister v Combined Services, Portland Road 1959

HAT-TRICKS

T. L. Pritchard 3
K. R. Dollery, G. A. E. Paine, R. G. D. Willis 2 each
J. D. Bannister, R. W. Barber, T. W. Cartwright, R. Cooke, E. F. Field, D. G. Foster, C. W. Grove, E. E. Hemmings, J. A. Jameson, A. C. Smith, R. G. Thompson 1 each

WICKET-KEEPING – MOST DISMISSALS

In an innings 7 E. J. Smith
In a match 9 E. B. Lewis
In a season 79 J. A. Smart 1932
In a career 800 E. J. Smith 1904–1930

COUNTY CAPS AWARDED SINCE 1946

1946 W. E. Fantham, J. J. Hossell, J. M. A. Marshall, R. H. Maudsley, R. Sale, N. A. Shortland, K. A. Taylor
1947 V. H. D. Cannings, C. W. Grove, T. L. Pritchard, J. R. Thompson
1948 M. P. Donnelly, R. T. Spooner, A. Townsend
1949 F. C. Gardner, A. H. Kardar, A. V. Wolton
1951 R. E. Hitchcock, E. B. Lewis, R. T. Weeks
1953 N. F. Horner
1954 J. D. Bannister, K. R. Dollery
1955 R. G. Thompson
1957 K. Ibadulla, M. J. K. Smith, W. J. Stewart
1958 R. G. Carter, T. W. Cartwright
1959 O. S. Wheatley
1961 W. B. Bridge, A. C. Smith
1962 A. Wright
1963 R. W. Barber, R. V. Webster
1964 D. J. Brown, J. A. Jameson
1965 D. L. Amiss
1966 R. N. Abberley
1968 L. R. Gibbs, R. B. Kanhai
1969 W. Blenkiron
1971 N. M. McVicker, B. S. V. Timms
1972 A. I. Kallicharran, D. L. Murray, R. G. D. Willis
1973 J. Whitehouse
1974 E. E. Hemmings, S. J. Rouse
1976 G. W. Humpage
1977 S. P. Perryman
1978 K. D. Smith

Worcestershire

MICHAEL VOCKINS

Foundation 1865
Colours Dark Green and Black
Badge Three Pears Sable on Shield Argent
Champions 1964, 1965, 1974

Worcestershire stoutly survived many barren and testing years before emerging as one of the most formidable sides in the 1960s and 1970s. Success was elusive, and, apart from being runners-up in the Championship in 1907, and achieving 3rd position in 1949, there was little to show for much effort and dedication.

H. K. Foster was Worcestershire's captain in 12 of the seasons before the First World War and made more than 17,000 runs. A model position early in the pick-up with the wrists about to be cocked.

Since 1971, however, Norman Gifford, a versatile captain, has taken Worcestershire to the County Championship in 1974, the John Player League title in 1971, and to 2 Benson & Hedges Cup finals at Lord's in 1973 and 1976. Gifford followed in the triumphant wake of his predecessor Don Kenyon, who led Worcestershire to their first-ever Championship in 1964. Kenyon retained the title in the following year; he had already gained distinction by reaching the 1st Gillette Cup final in 1963. They were also finalists in the competition in 1966, but Lord's is not a lucky ground for Worcestershire. In 4 finals in the Gillette Cup and the Benson & Hedges Cup they have never won.

To those Worcestershire cricketers and supporters with long memories the modern triumphs would seem miraculous for they would be able to recall times when it was a contradiction of logic that there was a Worcestershire team in first-class cricket at all. In 1914 there was a move to wind up the club. After the First World War the county did not resume first-class cricket until 1920 and of that season *Wisden* says: 'Sorry as one may feel for Worcestershire, there is no getting away from the fact that their return to the Championship was a complete failure'. Those were grey days indeed for the county, which, for 10 seasons, was never out of the bottom 4 of the Championship and in 4 of those seasons they were last of all.

And yet throughout that period, and from the club's earliest years, there was an enthusiasm and zeal to keep first-class cricket alive in this the smallest of the first-class counties. The club was formed officially at a meeting at the Star Hotel, Worcester, on 11 March 1865. There is evidence of Worcestershire teams taking the field some 20 years earlier and, in 1855, with the amalgamation of the city and county clubs, a club was formed which the artisans could join at a cost of 5*s* for which they were 'entitled to use bats and balls and the cricket ground on three nights a week and to have the privilege of playing cricket with the half-guinea members one night a week'.

The club's most rapid progress, apart from the most recent 2 decades, came towards the end of the last century, when P. H. Foley was appointed honorary Secretary of the club. He proved to be a far-sighted and generous official. Together with H. K. Foster he played a large part in founding the Minor Counties Championship in 1895, which Worcestershire then won for the next 3 years. The county was stimulated to seek first-class status, which was granted at the end of 1898 when the requisite number of fixtures were obtained with other first-class counties; some of those counties required £50 guarantees, an insurance required by Sussex until 1902. Paul Foley negotiated with the Dean and Chapter of Worcester Cathedral for a parcel of farm land – 3 fields with a hedge through the middle, and a hay-rick. He appointed Fred Hunt groundsman supreme, and together they turned their plot into the picturesque and renowned County Ground which nestles alongside the Severn under the shadow of Worcester's great Cathedral. It was Foley too who, as the Worcestershire players took the field against Yorkshire in 1899 in their 1st Championship match, was seen with paint brush in hand putting the finishing touches to the sight-screen.

Such dedication and enthusiasm has been matched throughout the club's history by other captains and secretaries, players and committee-men. Indeed there have been times when only unbounded enthusiasm and injections of private funds have kept the county afloat. It is that dedication and zeal which provides the thread between the club's formative years and its later – and therefore sweeter – successes of recent seasons. It is that fine thread of dedication and determination which also allows the Foleys and the Lytteltons, the Fosters, the Roots, Perkses, Jewells, Dowtys, Kenyons and Giffords – and many others besides – justly to bask in the light of the county's successes of more recent seasons.

At the centre of the Worcestershire tapestry lies the cathedral, and among the splendid threads running through it are 2 famous cricketing families, the Lytteltons and the Fosters. In 1867, at Hagley, a Lyttelton family XI defeated Bromsgrove School, and the name has always been closely identified with the club. The late Viscount Cobham, a former Governor-General of New Zealand, who was also President of MCC, captained Worcestershire (as the Hon C. J. Lyttelton) from 1936–1939. The playing record of the Fosters is without parallel in cricket. Seven brothers all played for the county, and as many as 4 of them appeared in one match together. H. K. Foster was captain when the club was given first-class status and two other brothers, R.E. and M.K., followed in his footsteps, the 3 of them covering 26 years of captaincy between them. R.E. was perhaps the brightest star in this firmament but all his brothers were considerable cricketers and, particularly, batsmen. H.K. and W.L. headed the Worcestershire batting in 1892 while they were both at Malvern. While the brothers were in their heyday, the county was colloquially referred to as 'Fostershire'. Three of them, H.K., captain, R.E. and W.L. played in the 1st first-class match against Yorkshire. W.L. and R.E. each scored a hundred in both innings against Hampshire in that 1st season, a record that was not equalled until C. C. Dacre and W. R. Hammond did it, again at New Road, in 1933. R.E. accomplished it 3 times in all. The remaining members of the Foster brotherhood were M.K., B.S., G.N. and N.J.A. Three of them were Oxford blues, R.E. being captain of the University side in 1900.

The Worcestershire story in the years leading to the First World War was one of unremarkable achievement so far as Championship honours were concerned (with the exception of 1907), but of a capacity, which they have never lost, for capturing popular imagination. In 1907, they not only defeated Yorkshire for the 1st time; they achieved the 'double' over them. The part played by the Fosters should not be allowed to obscure other fine material, not all of it, of course, drawn from the the amateur class. Arnold who accompanied R. E. Foster on the 1903–04 Australian tour was a prolific scorer who made 200 not out against Warwickshire in 1909 and took 3 for 70 and 7 for 44 in the same match. But as elsewhere in the spacious days around the turn of the century when country-house cricket typified the gracious living of the aristocrats, it was the amateurs who were the mainstay of Worcestershire cricket. One of the county's prominent amateurs, the Hon C. J. Coventry, went with an England touring side to South Africa in the winter of 1888–89. The list of Worcestershire presidents and vice-presidents at the beginning of the century reads like an extract from *Burke's Peerage*. It included 3 earls, the son of an earl, a viscount, a baron and two baronets.

Another amateur who played for England and who captained Worcestershire in 1911–1912 was G. H. Simpson-Hayward, remembered as one of the last great under-arm bowlers. In the 1907 season, Worcestershire were greatly assisted by the bowling of J. A. Cuffe, an Australian, who took 100 wickets for 18·91 apiece, but it was again the famous Fosters who contributed most. Against Kent at Worcester, the home county scored 567 in the first innings and the family supplied 375 of them (H.K. 123, before retiring; R.E. 174 and G.N. 78). In the following year, M. F. S. Jewell, captain intermittently from 1919 to 1933 and President of the club from 1950 to 1953, made his first appearance against Oxford University, thus beginning an illustrious association with Worcestershire as player and administrator. The First World War ended the playing career of one of Worcestershire's and probably England's most brilliant prospects. In 1913, at the age of 17, Frank Chester scored 698 at an average of 29·08 and took 43 wickets for 25·93, but he lost an arm serving England on another field. Instead of becoming a great batsman – 'Probably no cricketer of 18 had shown such promise since the days of W. G. Grace', *Wisden* wrote of him – he became cricket's most notable umpire, a name to conjure with and a man who was conspicuously no respecter of persons. The county later also produced another umpire of integrity and fearlessness in J. S. Buller, who had previously been a wicket-keeper of more than average ability.

Between the wars, Worcestershire were never far from the bottom of the table, although some of the outstanding cricketers of the day began to appear among their number. They finished last in 1922 and were there again from 1926 to 1928, yet in this period the immortal Fred Root held the stage. Root's performances, with his in-swing, have become legendary. In 1923, he took 165 wickets at 20·21 apiece in county matches alone, his 'bag' including 7 for 31 to help Worcestershire to their 1st victory against neighbouring Warwickshire since 1911. He dismissed Hammond for a 'pair'. In 1928, when Worcestershire cricket was at its nadir, he achieved the double, and in 1931, at the age of 41 and in his last season, bowling against Lancashire, he took 9 for 23, the best performance ever by a Worcestershire bowler.

At the end of 1922, F. L. Bowley, one of the county's most consistent batsmen, who had scored his 1st hundred in 1900, retired from the scene with the biggest aggregate any Worcestershire batsman had produced, as well as the county's highest individual Championship score of 276, scored in a day against Hampshire at Dudley. They must have been frustrating years for the current Foster, M.K., who carried the batting as well as leading the side. When he handed over the captaincy to Jewell in 1926, he still headed the county averages. The division of the captaincy between Foster, C. B. Ponsonby, Jewell and the Hon J. B. Coventry between 1925 and 1930 was unsettling, and there were also several players of note whose services were intermittent. Secretary-players became commonplace for a period in more recent years, but C. F. Walters, who was Secretary of Worcestershire from 1928 to 1935, was one of their exceptional precursors. He and H. H. I. Gibbons put on over a hundred for the 1st wicket 5 times in 1933, the season in which he was chosen to play for England against the West Indies in all 3 Tests. In the winter of that year, Walters went to India with a strong MCC side under D. R. Jardine and scored 284 runs in the 3 Tests, including a hundred in the Third Match. He became one of England's recognized opening batsmen and played in all 5 Tests against Australia in 1934, captaining the side at Trent Bridge when R. E. S. Wyatt was unable to play.

Walters was one of a trio – Maurice Nichol and Gibbons were the others – who each scored over 2,000 runs in 1933. Walters and Nichol passed R. E. Foster's record aggregate and Gibbons outdid them the following season. In 1928, Gibbons, with Root, was chosen to play against the Gentlemen at the Oval, but although he was top scorer then with 84, he was never given a chance to make his mark in the highest grade of cricket. Despite this proliferation in 1933, Worcestershire were 3rd from bottom, and, in the following season, tied for bottom but one. The county suffered a tragic loss in this latter season when Nichol died suddenly in the course of the match with Essex. Another batting luminary, the Nawab of Pataudi, joined the side in 1932, and in the following winter was a member of the England party on the controversial Body-line tour of Australia. The emphasis, in the 4 seasons preceding the Second War, swung from batting, as represented in the galaxy already described, to the bowling of Howorth – who was one of the best all-rounders the club has ever had – Perks, Martin and Jackson, all 4 of whom each took more than 100 wickets in the 1937 season. Martin did not reappear after the war, but the other 3 spanned the years before and after, Jackson and Howorth retiring together at the end of the 1951 season and the universally popular Perks's great services being recognized in 1955 when he became the club's first professional captain.

An ever-cheerful cricketer, Reg Perks, fast-medium in pace and a big swinger of the new ball, with a bag of 2,233 remains Worcestershire's leading wicket-taker. Aged 43 he led the county in his last season.

Another whose distinguished services to the club as a player ended with the war was the Hon C. J. Lyttelton. He captained the side, and went with an MCC team to New Zealand and Australia in 1935, playing in one representative match against New Zealand. A. P. Singleton filled the breach as captain for one season after the war and then, after two seasons on his own, A. F. T. White, the Cambridge blue of 1936, shared the leadership with R. E. S. Wyatt, who had captained Warwickshire before the war but had now transferred to Worcestershire. The club was not the only one to discover that rehabilitation was difficult. For one thing there was no settled captaincy. R. E. Bird succeeded Wyatt in 1952 and was followed for one season, his last before well-earned retirement, by Perks. P. E. Richardson held the position until he relinquished it to Kenyon in 1959. Both Richardson and Kenyon opened for England, and for Worcestershire they constituted a 1st-wicket partnership that had qualities reminiscent of some of the famous opening combinations of the past.

By 1949, Worcestershire had so far achieved stability as to finish 3rd in the table. The previous 3 seasons had been unexceptional. Hugo Yarnold had taken over as wicket-keeper from Buller, whom he was to join later as an umpire; Charles Palmer, subsequently to be captain and secretary of Leicestershire, had made his cheerful presence felt, and Jenkins, a further addition to the county's spinning strength and to England's, had gone to South Africa when Eric Hollies had to stand down. Jenkins, another of Worcestershire's all-rounders – although he was, above all, a leg-spinner – achieved the double in 1949. Howorth had gone on the West Indian tour in 1947, and had also demonstrated his exceptional stamina by playing in every match.

The climb to the heights of the County's first Championship title in 1964 was not done without some disheartening downward slides. A graph of the period, indeed, would be positively Alpine in outline. In 1950, when they were 6th, and in 1951, when they were 4th to Warwickshire in their Championship year, the promise of 1949 was only tenuously held. In the following year, they dropped to 14th, and they could do nothing better to signalize Perks's captaincy in 1955 than finish 3rd from bottom. Perks himself retired at the end of the season, after 27 years with the club. In the last match, he took his 100th wicket for the 16th consecutive time. Lord Cobham, his old captain, wrote on Perks's retirement:

> Seldom in cricket history has a county cricket XI been given such splendid service by a fast bowler as that bestowed on Worcestershire by Reg Perks. Had the war not come at a time when Perks was approaching the height of his powers, one feels that his MCC tour to South Africa in 1938 must have been followed by others. He would have been in his element on the green-top Australian wickets on which Alec Bedser reaped such a rich harvest in 1950–51

On the face of it, to finish 13th in 1960 scarcely denotes resurgence, but, about the middle of July, the side began a succession of 5 victories, and the foundations were laid for an all-out assault on the rest of the counties in the following season. Again they delayed their

Don Kenyon: holder of many Worcestershire records and captain of the Championship-winning sides of 1964 and 1965. Keeping wicket is E. C. Petrie of the 1958 New Zealanders.

effort until late in the season. Later even than in 1960, for it was in the last week of July and the first half of August that they began a run, this time of 7 victories. At the vital period, Kenyon and George Dews went sick, and Flavell was called on a 2nd time by England. Yorkshire – the old enemy – who were lying 2nd at the time, defeated them, as did Hampshire, the eventual champions. Worcestershire finished 4th. Flavell, Coldwell, Gifford and Horton each took over 100 wickets during the season. Without doubt, by 1962, they had the best-balanced side in the country. Graveney's period of qualification had come to an end, and his classic batting had been added to that of Kenyon, the captain, Martin Horton and Dick Richardson, brother of Peter and himself an England player. The spin bowling of Horton, Gifford and Slade, mixed with the pace of Flavell and the deceptive slower ball of Coldwell, blended into the most formidable attack in the country. All these assets, plus the maturing skill of Headley as a batsman, and his excellence alongside Richardson as a close catcher, and, in addition, the valuable medium-pace bowling of Standen, combined to produce the final Championship recipe – after a peculiar lapse from grace in 1963 when, as a consolation, the County appeared in the first-ever Final of the Gillette Cup.

For a small, so-called 'unfashionable' county the flying of the much-prized Championship pennant over the County Ground at the end of the 1964 campaign was the culmination of excellent cricket by an astutely-led and well-balanced team. It was also the culmination of almost a century of ideals, ambition, enthusiasm and very considerable effort. In the darker days, particularly during the 1920s, for the team to find itself in a position even to consider declaring was infrequent, so the pleasure that Don Kenyon and his team provided for their predecessors as well as for themselves and their supporters knew no bounds.

Some fairy tales do come true – and so it must have seemed when, in 1965, the county retained its Championship title in their centenary year. If Paul Foley and his colleagues had earlier provided the foundations, Kenyon and his team now provided a thoroughly professional finish. Sir George Dowty was President during this vital middle part of the 1960s and his drive and inspiration were of considerable importance.

In 1966 the county slipped one place from the summit but proved again they were a difficult side to beat when, for the 2nd time in 4 years, they reached the final of the Gillette Cup. Some counties took considerable time to adjust to the special demands of the one-day competitions, but Worcestershire quickly took to the limited-over games. Since the introduction of the Gillette Cup in 1963, the Benson & Hedges Cup in 1973, and the John Player League in 1970, Worcestershire have proved themselves to be adept at the one-day game. They have appeared in 4 'Cup Finals' at Lord's – even if they have yet to win one – and have won the John Player League title once, in 1971.

In 1969 Kenyon retired and handed over the captaincy to Tom Graveney who, exiled from his native Gloucestershire, had produced his most fruitful form for his new county and had contributed much to their successes. Graveney's reign was a period of transition as R. Booth, another in a long line of stalwart county 'keepers, Flavell, Coldwell, Horton and Standen retired. B. L. d'Oliveira, the Cape Coloured South African who, because of his country's policy of apartheid, had been denied the opportunity to represent South Africa, had now qualified and was making a valuable all-round contribution for Worcestershire and England. By his impeccable dignity in the face of considerable off-the-field problems he gained many friends for himself and the game of cricket. Ormrod was blossoming forth as a batsman in the Graveney mould. Gifford, the left-arm spinner, was among the best of his type and almost unplayable on wickets that offered some assistance, and B. M. Brain, perhaps with insufficient frequency, gradually emerged as a bowler of high class. The county had introduced overseas players. G. M. Turner, from New Zealand, came out of his early defensive cocoon to become a world-class batsman. V. A. Holder, a lively and accurate bowler, was introduced to the county from Barbados by Graveney, and has proved to be an important member of the county and the West Indian pace attack.

Gifford took over the captaincy in 1971 and marked his first season by taking the John Player League title, albeit by the margin of only 0·003 runs per over from Essex. During this latter period Worcestershire seemed to make a habit of close-run things which, if nothing else, indicated an indomitable spirit and certainly provided excitement enough at New Road. Another County Championship win in 1974 was sandwiched between Benson & Hedges Cup Final appearances in 1973 and 1976. In terms of results Gifford's term as county captain bears favourable comparison with that of Kenyon and, together, they have led the county through the most successful and fruitful period of its history. In recent seasons the county has introduced young players to the County game, brightest of whom are Dipak Patel, an England-qualified batsman of the highest promise and a capable off-spinner, and P. A. Neale, a workmanlike batsman of considerable potential. It is hoped that these, and other young players in the county's stable, will provide the continuation of the successes to which the county recently has become accustomed, so that the Championship pennant will again fly out over the New Road Ground.

There has always been a certain caprice amounting to charm in Worcestershire's cricket. They have rarely been without a batsman cast in the classical mould or a bowler of real distinction. Much of the county's charm is attributable to its players and in recent years the Queen has acknowledged the service given to the county and to the game by Graveney (MBE), d'Oliveira (OBE) and Gifford (MBE). Part of Worcestershire's charm lies in the setting of the county headquarters. The ground in New Road has contrived to keep a great deal of the pastoral quality which Foley and groundsman Hunt first encountered 80 years ago. One aspect, looking over to the cathedral, is unsurpassed, and, for many, symbolizes the English county cricket scene. Many a touring cricketer, seeing it for the first time and hearing the tuneful chimes borne on the breeze from the cathedral's carillon must have experienced a new thrill and felt an awareness of the tradition and mystique of the game hitherto not fully appreciated. How appropriate then, that Worcester (until the temporary interruptions of recent years) became the accepted ground for the Tourist's opening game, and no wonder that some of the world's greatest players have responded to its uniquely warm and yet sylvan atmosphere. Bradman in particular responded to this atmosphere with scores of 236, 206, 258 and – his one 'failure' – 107, from 4 visits.

Since 1899 the club had been tenants of the cathedral's Dean and Chapter, and what kindly and benevolent landlords they had proved to be. So conscious were they of Worcestershire's place in the cricketing world that the county's offer to buy the County Ground in 1976 was not resisted. Indeed, following typically friendly discussions, Worcestershire found themselves owners of the County Ground, one of the most attractive in the country (some would say in the world) at a cost of £30,000. To the club officials who, in 1865, paid 16*s* for 'hire of horse and man for two days rolling', or to Foley with his very limited band of professionals, £30,000 would have seemed a vast sum indeed. To the Worcestershire Club in

Tom Graveney, of Gloucestershire and Worcestershire, using his height and reach to play the square-drive. In the background is K. Ibadulla, of Warwickshire and Pakistan.

Worcestershire 1974, County Champions. Back row: K. W. Wilkinson, I. N. Johnson, R. J. Lanchbury, J. Cumbes, J. D. Inchmore, A. P. Pridgeon, C. P. Roberts, J. M. Parker, R. Senghera, A. Shutt and H. G. Wilcock; sitting: G. R. Cass, B. M. Brain, B. L. d'Oliveira, R. G. A. Headley, N. Gifford (captain), J. A. Ormrod, G. M. Turner, V. A. Holder and T. J. Yardley.

1976 it also seemed a very sizeable sum but thanks to the typically splendid generosity of the County's Supporters' Association, aided by donations from county members, the purchase was completed. Over the years the facilities for spectators, and for the players, have been improved, but the county committee has always endeavoured to ensure that the inherent charm of the County Ground is neither lost nor endangered and, in recent years, almost as much thought has been given to the planting of trees, shrubs and flowers as to the provision of new seats. It has been apparent, throughout the life of the club, that the pastoral and pleasing appearance of the County Ground has contributed as much to its attractiveness to spectators as the excellence of the Worcestershire pitch has to the successes of the players. By obtaining the freehold of the County Ground the club has ensured, for many years to come, the future of county cricket at Worcester and commendably it has set the seal on the bold, far-sighted and sympathetic initiatives of Foley and his colleagues and on the dedicated enthusiasm and zeal of all those officials, players, spectators and supporters who, through the ages, have played their part in providing for the success and for the future of the Black Pears county.

CAPTAINS

1899–1900 H. K. Foster
1901 R. E. Foster
1902–10 H. K. Foster
1911–12 G. H. Simpson-Hayward
1913 H. K. Foster
1914 W. H. Taylor
1920–21 M. F. Jewell
1922 W. H. Taylor
1923–25 M. K. Foster
1926 M. F. S. Jewell
1927 C. B. Ponsonby
1928 M. F. S. Jewell
1929 M. F. S. Jewell and Hon J. B. Coventry
1930 Hon J. B. Coventry
1931–35 C. F. Walters
1936–39 Hon C. J. Lyttelton
1946 A. P. Singleton
1947–48 A. F. T. White
1949 A. F. T. White and R. E. S. Wyatt
1950–51 R. E. S. Wyatt
1952–54 R. E. Bird
1955 R. T. D. Perks
1956–58 P. E. Richardson
1959–67 D. Kenyon
1968–70 T. W. Graveney
1971– N. Gifford

HIGHEST TOTALS

For 633 v Warwicks, Worcester 1906
Against 701–4D by Leicester, Worcester 1906

LOWEST TOTALS

For 24 v Yorks, Huddersfield 1903
Against 30 by Hants, Worcester 1903

HIGHEST INDIVIDUAL INNINGS

For 276 F. L. Bowley v Hants, Dudley 1914
Against 331* J. D. B. Robertson for Middlesex, Worcester 1949

MOST RUNS

In a season 2,654 H. H. I. Gibbons 1934
In a career 34,490 D. Kenyon 1946–1967

MOST HUNDREDS

In a season 10 G. M. Turner 1970
In a career 70 D. Kenyon 1946–1967

INDIVIDUAL INNINGS OF 250 AND OVER

F. L. Bowley, 276 v Hants, Dudley 1914
M. Nichol, 262* v Hants, Bournemouth 1930
D. Kenyon, 253* v Leicester, Worcester 1954
D. Kenyon, 259 v Yorks, Kidderminster 1956

HUNDRED ON DEBUT

M. Nichol 104 v West Indians, Worcester 1928

RECORD WICKET PARTNERSHIPS

1 F. L. Bowley and H. K. Foster, 309 v Derby, Derby 1901
2 H. H. I. Gibbons and Nawab of Pataudi, 274 v Kent, Worcester 1933
H. H. I. Gibbons and Nawab of Pataudi, 274 v Glamorgan, Worcester 1934
3 M. J. Horton and T. W. Graveney, 314 v Somerset, Worcester 1962
4 Younis Ahmed and J. A. Ormrod, 281 v Notts, Trent Bridge 1979
5 E. G. Arnold and W. B. Burns, 393 v Warwicks, Edgbaston 1909
6 E. J. O. Hemsley and D. N. Patel, 227 v Oxford University, Oxford 1976
7 H. H. I. Gibbons and R. Howorth, 197 v Surrey, Oval 1938
8 F. Chester and W. H. Taylor, 145* v Essex, Worcester 1914
9 J. A. Cuffe and R. D. Burrows, 181 v Gloucester, Worcester 1907
10 W. B. Burns and G. A. Wilson, 119 v Somerset, Worcester 1906

MOST WICKETS

In a match 15–87 A. J. Conway v Gloucester, Moreton 1914
In a season 207 C. F. Root 1925
In a career 2,143 R. T. D. Perks 1930–1955

ALL 10 WICKETS IN AN INNINGS

No instance (best innings analysis: C. F. Root 9–23 v Lancs, Worcester 1931)

HAT-TRICKS

J. A. Flavell, R. O. Jenkins, G. A. Wilson 3 each
L. J. Coldwell, R. T. D. Perks 2 each
W. B. Burns, R. G. M. Carter, J. A. Cuffe, J. Cumbes, N. Gifford, M. J. Horton, R. Howorth, P. F. Jackson, F. Pearson, C. A. Preece 1 each

WICKET-KEEPING – MOST DISMISSALS

In an innings 7 H. Yarnold
In a match 9 H. Yarnold
In a season 104 H. Yarnold, 1949
In a career 1,015 R. Booth, 1956–1970

COUNTY CAPS AWARDED SINCE 1946

1946 R. E. Bird, A. F. T. White, R. E. S. Wyatt
1947 D. Kenyon, H. Yarnold
1948 L. Outschoorn
1949 M. L. Y. Ainsworth
1950 G. H. Chesterton, G. Dewes
1951 R. G. Broadbent
1952 P. E. Richardson
1955 J. Flavell, M. J. Horton
1956 R. Booth, D. W. Richardson
1957 R. Berry
1959 K. J. Aldridge, L. J. Coldwell, D. B. Pearson
1960 D. N. F. Slade
1961 R. G. A. Headley, N. Gifford
1962 T. W. Graveney, J. A. Standen
1965 R. G. M. Carter, B. L. d'Oliveira
1966 B. M. Brain, J. A. Ormrod
1967 K. Griffith
1968 G. M. Turner
1969 E. J. O. Hemsley
1970 G. R. Casss, V. A. Holder
1972 T. J. Yardley
1974 J. M. Parker
1976 Imran Khan, J. D. Inchmore
1978 J. Cumbes, D. J. Humphries, P. A. Neale

Yorkshire

J. M. KILBURN

Foundation 1863
Colours Dark Blue, Light Blue and Gold
Badge White Rose
Champions 1867, 1869 (=), 1870, 1893, 1896, 1898, 1900, 1901, 1902, 1905, 1908, 1912, 1919, 1922, 1923, 1924, 1925, 1931, 1932, 1933, 1935, 1937, 1938, 1939, 1946, 1949 (=), 1959, 1960, 1962, 1963, 1966, 1967, 1968

Yorkshire cricket has an identity widely recognized, though not universally approved in all aspects. County loyalty has developed a pride that sometimes obscures judgment and presages fall. One element of the pride and contributory to the character is the commitment to select only the native born for the county team, though, ironically, the greatest single influence in Yorkshire cricket was one of the few exceptions permitted to the unwritten rule. Lord Hawke was born in Lincolnshire.

Conceding the few aberrations, Yorkshire have maintained a principle without claiming a hardship. The county is big, the population is to be counted in millions and there has usually been a surplus of player-production for export. Yorkshire's 'closed shop' in cricket has deepened county loyalty and also, perhaps, increased the bitterness when occasional dissension promoted family feud.

Where and by whom cricket was first played in Yorkshire is now beyond discovery, but by the second half of the 18th century the game was sufficiently established to receive note in newspapers. There was organized cricket in Leeds, Doncaster and York, in Selby and Beverley and, from 1771 onwards Sheffield and Nottingham were meeting with teams drawn from a wider range than civic bounds. A Yorkshire county side was in the field 30 years before formation of the county club, opposing Norfolk in the early September of 1833. Its composition was entirely of Sheffield players, 8 professionals and 3 amateurs, and the match was staged on the Hyde Park ground in Sheffield.

The Yorkshire County Cricket Club, constituted in 1863, was essentially a Sheffield foundation, promoted and administered by Sheffield enterprise. Beginnings were unpropitious. Within 2 years the committee found themselves with a players' strike on their hands. The objection of the professionals Anderson, Atkinson, Iddison, Rowbotham and Stephenson was not to terms offered, but against appearance on the field with opponents involved in a long-standing dispute over bowling principles.

Yorkshire fulfilled their 1865 fixtures without the dissentients but played no matches in the following season. George Anderson, a hard-hitting batsman and a highly-respected member of All-England teams, played no more for Yorkshire but the others returned to the county fold and the constituted county club gradually acquired status. The early Yorkshire cricketers could be described as colourful in character as well as by the customary dress of the time, which included striped or spotted shirt and tie, broad leather belt with metal buckle and either the bowler hat or peaked cap with high crown. George Freeman was a fast bowler with a sharp breakback from his shoulder-high delivery and on the rough pitches so frequently encountered he proved himself as unnerving as he was successful. In his 26 county matches spread over 5 seasons Freeman took 194 wickets and won respect from W. G. Grace, who was not given to flattery of fast bowlers by word or deed. Tom Emmett, origin and subject of endless anecdotes, joined Freeman briefly to form such devastating attack that in 1868 the 2 bowled unchanged to dismiss Lancashire for totals of 30 and 34.

Emmett was a left-hander of lively pace and even livelier spirits who claimed distinction for the number of wides in his analyses and for the self-styled 'sostenutor', which pitched on the leg stump and hastened away to hit the off. The records give him 1,217 wickets in 300 matches of varying classification for Yorkshire.

First in a succession of professional captains was Roger Iddison, a noted batsman who took engagements as they came on offer and played for both Yorkshire and Lancashire in the same season of 1867. Lockwood of Lascelles Hall introduced himself in 1868 at the Oval, where his unsophisticated dress and manner raised scorn and sympathy that turned to admiration when he and his uncle, John Thewlis, put on 176 runs for Yorkshire's 1st wicket. Lockwood stayed in the side for 15 years to score nearly 8,000 runs.

In the youth of the county club the talent was individual more than collective. Yorkshire fixtures were too few to be the sole, or even primary, concern of the peripatetic professionals who tended to view each match in isolation and a team as an ephemeral unit. Results were wildly inconsistent. It was not until the 1880s that a succession of disappointing seasons roused public murmuring against the county's cricketing representatives and the county club.

Yorkshire showed poor results but had the services of some remarkable players whose reputation stretched across the country and overseas. Ulyett was a splendid all-rounder, welcome in any team for his skill and happy disposition. Peate's success as a slow left-arm bowler was no less than startling, with an average of 7 wickets a match over 3 successive seasons. Peate was followed by Peel whose career was longer and skill no less. G. P. Harrison flared like a meteor across the sky of fast bowling. William Bates was an all-rounder of international class.

For all their individual splendour Yorkshire as a team were unreliable. They would defeat the strongest opponents and fall to the weakest. The need was for a controlling hand. Lord Hawke, who took over the captaincy in 1883, assumed the necessary authority and formulated the principles on which he ultimately based a county team to be universally respected because of its own self-respect and loyalty.

Lord Hawke never ranked among the great players of cricket, but among influences on the development of the game he must stand with William Clarke, with W. G. Grace and with Thomas Lord. He joined Yorkshire as a Cambridge undergraduate, was captain of the county for 28 years, President from 1898 until his death in 1938, cricketing adventurer and advocate across the world, selector of England teams and sometime President and Treasurer of MCC. His good fortune in life was to pursue a pastime as a vocation. His justification was leaving his limited world a little better than he found it. He claimed privileges of authority but he also accepted responsibilities of office and he returned to cricket even more than he extracted from it.

In the first decade of his Yorkshire captaincy he had to feel his way among playing peers and administrative restrictions. Towards the end of the 1880s Yorkshire cricket had lost public favour. Playing inadequacies led to falling finances and criticism was finally concentrated on the management, which in 1891 issued self-defence in the annual report. By 1893 reorganization had been undertaken. The long Sheffield domination was broken and in the very first season of change Yorkshire won a county championship that was now an actuality though without a legal existence. This championship was incidental rather than directly consequential upon administrative reform but it marked the beginning of a new Yorkshire era. Lord Hawke could now build on his own ideas on the field, in the dressing room and in committee. He became a senior among players and an authority among administrators. He offered a sense of security in a hazardous profession through the introduction of winter pay and concern for physical and financial welfare and he instilled a community pride as old team gave way to new. Magnificence was approaching.

Yorkshire personified: Lord Hawke (captain from 1883 to 1910), with the two immortal all-rounders George Hirst, in umpire's coat, and Wilfred Rhodes, on his last appearance for Yorkshire, at Scarborough in 1930.

Lord Hawke's dearest dream came true with the turn of the century. In 1900, 1901 and 1902 he led Yorkshire to 3 Championships in which one of the most powerful county sides ever constructed played 60 matches and lost only 2. In a firmly-established side Lord Hawke himself rarely missed a match. Brown and Tunnicliffe opened the innings, with David Denton and T. L. Taylor following. Wainwright and Hirst were the all-rounders, Haigh and Rhodes the bowlers and David Hunter was wicketkeeper.

A welcome into this Yorkshire side was always at the disposal of F. S. Jackson, but because of the South African War he missed the seasons of 1900 and 1901, and in 1902 much of his cricket was concentrated on Test matches and other representative occasions. Frank Mitchell played through 1901 to head the batting averages and Ernest Smith brought reinforcement to the fast bowling in the schoolmaster's holidays of 1900 and 1901. Yorkshire's great strength lay in exceptional individual talent expressed as a unity. The team was so powerful and purposeful that in 43 consecutive engagements without defeat, 13 matches were won by an innings and 4 by 10 wickets. Defeat, when it came at Headingley in July 1901, was a sensation of the season, Somerset recovering from a 1st-innings deficit of 238 to win by 279 runs.

Descent from the peaks was inevitable but between 1903 and 1914 Yorkshire won the Championship 3 times and were 3 times runners-up. George Hirst and Wilfred Rhodes remaining, they were never without a player of the highest quality and Denton's attractive batting and peerless fielding formed outstanding features of the cricket in an outstanding cricket era. In 1906 Hirst carried all-round achievement to unparalleled heights by scoring, 2,385 runs and taking 208 wickets. Astonishing figures were not full measure of his greatness. The characteristic that made him a hero everywhere and an idol in his own county was the capacity to succeed in the hours of greatest need.

Wilfred Rhodes is generally supposed to have set bowling aside for batting during the middle part of his career and for England he did devote himself to rising from last to first in the order, sharing records in both places, but only in 1910, 1912 and 1913 did he neglect to take his 100 wickets and in 1909 and 1911 he took over 100 wickets and scored over 2,000 runs. Denton the adventurous reached 2,000 runs 4 times, with 1912 as his zenith of accomplishment because that summer was wet and only he and Hobbs reached the aggregate

Yorkshire 1925: champions for the 4th successive year. Back row: E. Oldroyd, M. Leyland, H. Sutcliffe, G. G. Macaulay, J. T. Bell and W. Ringrose; sitting: E. Robinson, P. Holmes, W. Rhodes, Major A. W. Lupton (captain), A. Dolphin, R. Kilner and A. Waddington.

and average usually returned by leading batsmen in more accommodating conditions. Another side of exceptional resources was under construction when war interrupted to cost Booth his life, Drake his career and delay the development of Holmes, Oldroyd, Dolphin and Roy Kilner. Drake had died before county cricket was resumed, Hirst retired on his 50th birthday in 1921, but in the early 1920s Yorkshire were masters of their world again. In the 4 seasons from 1922 to 1925 they were at the head of the Championship, losing only 6 matches in 122 engagements. In 1925 they were so dominant that they won 25 of their 31 Championship matches.

The basis of success was much as it had been in the earlier triumph; an established team of resolute outlook with exceptional resources in bowling and fielding. Rhodes returned to the craft in which he had no peer, substituting subtlety and experience for the flexibility of youthful muscles. Kilner served as assistant and foil and flourished an enterprising bat when need arose. Waddington, Emmott Robinson and Macaulay formed a vigorous opening attack, Macaulay in due course turning to accurate off-spin. E. R. Wilson came from Winchester to give August relief to the bowlers.

In the batting, Holmes and Sutcliffe earned a world-wide reputation by their consistency and records. Oldroyd was a defensive master to a point of occasional irritation but incalculable value and Leyland fulfilled all the early promise that won him a county cap after unusually brief experience.

Character in the side was as strongly defined as technical accomplishment. The attitude was authoritative to a degree of ruthlessness. Success was a commonplace that no doubt exaggerated reaction to occasional frustration and Yorkshire were inclined to play their cricket with businesslike calculation, ignoring provision for goodwill. They were satisfied to be the most powerful of opponents without claiming to be the most popular.

Lord Hawke's presidential influence and the soothing captaincy of A. W. Lupton and W. A. Worsley reduced the temperature of inter-county relations to normal reading and after pause for readjustment of bowling forces Yorkshire made another leap into dominance of the championship. Through the 1930s they expressed their authority with 7 successes in 9 seasons.

Resurgence began under F. E. Greenwood, who led the 1931 side and was nominal captain in 1932, but the power was preserved and developed by A. B. Sellers, younger son of the Arthur Sellers distinguished as a Yorkshire batsman of the 1890s. Brian Sellers never became a leading batsman in his own team, though he scored hundreds against Kent, Nottinghamshire, Cambridge University and the 1934 Australians, but he made himself an immensely significant figure by his brilliant and courageous fielding and by his dynamic approach to the game. Sellers inherited a formidable Yorkshire side, governed by a committee respected for knowledge of cricket, financial expertise and strong sense of service. Holmes and Sutcliffe ended their partnership in 1933, the year after they had set up the world record of 555 against Essex at Leyton, but Sutcliffe, 8 years younger than partner, still had 29 of his 112 Yorkshire centuries to come.

From the beginning to the end of his career, Sutcliffe's consistency and reliability represented a wonder of cricket. Through 21 seasons his lowest aggregate in Yorkshire matches alone was 1,235 and in all matches he scored over 3,000 runs in 1928, 1931 and 1932. In the 8 successive seasons from 1925 to 1932 his average never fell below 50 and in the wet summer of 1931 he contrived 3,006 runs and an average of 96·96. Throughout his career it seemed that Sutcliffe had only to be given an assignment to accomplish it. No bowling, no pitch, no situation daunted him and the outstanding occasion was invariably a stimulus. In Test matches and at county level in his later years his patience and defence in all conditions were the memorable qualities, but in his greatest period his power of attack was equally remarkable. He hit 10 sixes in an innings at Kettering and at Scarborough he reached a hundred against Essex in 2 hours and then added 94 in 40 minutes, he and Leyland taking 102 runs from 6 successive overs. Sutcliffe's 100th hundred was made against Gloucestershire at Bradford when Yorkshire were seeking victory in a match apparently doomed to be drawn. In less than 2 hours Sutcliffe hit 8 sixes and 8 fours and so gave scope for a last-over win.

Nobody rivalled Sutcliffe in personality in the Yorkshire of the 1930s, but he was not isolated in splendour and he was a wholehearted member of a unified team. His part, with Leyland and Mitchell and Barber, was to provide time and substance for a match-winning attack by Verity and Bowes, supported by Macaulay, Smailes, Ellis Robinson and Turner. Verity's skill as a slow-medium left-hander was recognized before he stepped into the side as Wilfred Rhodes was stepping out. Success was immediate. His first half-season took him to the top of the averages; within 2 years he had twice taken all 10 wickets in an innings and was bowling for England. Between 1930 and 1939 he took 1,558 wickets for Yorkshire.

Bowes was less readily appreciated and served apprenticeship on MCC staff at Lord's before convincing Yorkshire of his exceptional quality. The wet seasons that encouraged Verity were a frustration to ambitious fast bowlers, but Bowes missed no opportunity to learn by tutorial and experiment and he rapidly developed into a new-ball bowler of uncommon liveliness and control. His great height and high action gave disconcerting lift and his command of direction and swing made him a swift eliminator of complacency in opening batsmen. His sense of service was strong and no call on his resources was ever declined, to the consequent admiration and support of his colleagues and affection of the county followers. His bowling function for Yorkshire was essentially to create advantage and he was not often privileged to complete destruction for the benefit of his own analyses, but in one opportunity to bowl unchanged through both innings he took 8 for 18 and 8 for 17 against Northamptonshire.

555 for 1 at Leyton, 1932. P. Holmes (despite lumbago!) 224 not out, H. Sutcliffe 313.

As many as 12 Yorkshire players were awarded England caps between 1930 and 1939 and none presented the county talent and character more plainly than did Maurice Leyland. He made 9 hundreds for England and won respect and affection everywhere for achievement and for his approach to the game.

No one was more contented with cricket as a career, Leyland's enjoyment was made evident in left-hand batting firm in the hour of need, forceful when the occasion warranted; in left-arm bowling always liable to take a wanted wicket with the 'chinaman' and in fielding that ranked him justifiably among all-rounders. Yorkshire were champions in 1931 and in all successive seasons except 1934 and 1936 until the outbreak of the Second World War. There, with a final hasty victory at Hove, the unit disintegrated beyond reassembly.

When county cricket returned in 1946, Sutcliffe, Mitchell and Wood had retired, Verity had died of wounds in Italy, Bowes had spent years as a prisoner-of-war and was, on medical insistence, no longer a fast bowler. Leyland, Barber and Turner played through only one post-war season and Sellers resigned the captaincy in the autumn of 1947.

In 1962 (last year of the amateur), Vic Wilson became the 1st Yorkshire professional ever to lead the county to the Championship. Back row: J. H. Hampshire, W. B. Stott, K. A. Taylor, D. Wilson, M. Ryan, D. E. V. Padgett and P. J. Sharpe; sitting: R. Illingworth, D. B. Close, J. V. Wilson (captain), F. S. Trueman and J. G. Binks.

Yardley's captaincy lasted for 8 seasons but in only one of them could Yorkshire reach the top of the Championship, sharing 1st place with Middlesex in 1949. Yardley was the 1st Yorkshire captain to undertake coincidental responsibilities for England and he was unfortunate in his time of holding both offices. Neither Yorkshire nor England carried the resources for success.

Yorkshire were not, however, to be rated among the weaker counties in the 1950s. They were 2nd in the Championship 5 times and descent to 11th place in 1958 was at least partially due to weather that kept them off the field altogether on no fewer than 24 playing days. They were, however, a disappointment to supporters because they denied their own talents and obscured their own traditions. The contrast in performance and approach between 2 successive generations could not escape notice by even the most myopic of loyalists and members finally expressed discontent in refusal to confirm a proposed increase of subscriptions. Protest was not so much a reaction against financial management as against diminishing reputation in cricket.

Individual playing ability was not lacking. Hutton remained the outstanding batsman of the world until his retirement in 1955 by which time he had made 85 Yorkshire centuries and scored nearly 25,000 Yorkshire runs, though in later seasons his interests lay in national rather than county concerns. For England he made himself ill with cares of captaincy in exceptionally demanding circumstances. For Yorkshire he played in an isolation of technical superiority, as the county's one assurance of logical and masterful batting.

Some unconvincing experiments were made in the rebuilding, but there were also notable introductions. Close and Trueman at the age of 18 were cricketers of infinite prospect. Both had to suffer frustrations of delayed development because of national service, and the intoxication of premature glorification. Appleyard took 200 wickets in his first full season, suffered a breakdown in health, recovered to tour Australia in 1954–55, but was unable to exploit great talent in a long career. Wardle held the spin-bowling world at his command but his skills were not always effectively displayed.

In general the batting was unstable. Easy runs awaiting collection in the seasons immediately following the war raised false standards and without a background of stern experience times of crisis brought exposure. Yorkshire presented some brilliant batting, one player or another enjoyed flashes of form, but the side as a whole could not be relied on for the specific occasion and some bitter defeats had to be acknowledged.

Even harder to bear were indications on the field of dressing-room disharmony. By word and deed Yorkshire lost caste among opponents. Committee and team fell out of sympathy and sickness touched crisis in 1958 after Watson chose migration to Leicestershire and J. R. Burnet had succeeded W. H. H. Sutcliffe, son of Herbert, as captain.

Burnet came to the leadership at the age of 39 from the 2nd XI captaincy and could not have been expected to improve the playing strength, but disrespect for his office was beyond toleration. In late July the dismissal of Wardle brought public acknowledgement of internal dissension, Wardle promptly accepting a newspaper temptation to pass criticism on his captain, colleagues and committee. Yorkshire business thereupon became MCC business and an invitation to tour Australia was withdrawn from Wardle.

In clearer skies after the storm, Yorkshire unexpectedly and dramatically won the Championship of 1959. The side was young and inexperienced and heavily dependent on Trueman for incisive attack through a batsman's summer, but there was welcome eagerness in approach and though the batting was inconsistent it was invariably optimistic and sometimes brilliant. The decisive match exemplified the spirit. In the last Championship fixture, at Hove, Yorkshire knew they had to win to be sure of the title. They were at early disadvantage, recovered through an Illingworth hundred, but seemed imprisoned in a drawn game when Sussex batted into the 3rd afternoon. The final Yorkshire requirement was 205 runs in 75 minutes. Inspired by need and virtually unhampered by Sussex tactics, the batsmen flung themselves into such riotous scoring that the runs were hit off for the loss of 5 wickets with 7 minutes to spare. Stott made 96 in 86 minutes and Padgett 76 in little more than the hour in which 146 runs were plundered.

No more appropriate moment for Burnet to step aside, mission accomplished, could have been devised. Yorkshire adopted a spreading practice among counties of captaincy by professional players. They appointed J. V. Wilson, senior by length of service but so variable in batting form that he had lost his first team place in 1959. Wilson led Yorkshire to Championship success in 1960 and 1962 and retired to leave a vacancy for D. B. Close.

Close found cricketing maturity overnight. The inconsequence that had limited his earlier development disappeared under the challenges of responsibility. During his term of office he became not only an enterprising tactician but also an adult batsman.

Close's 8-year reign began in sunshine but with storm clouds gathering. The cricket revolution was developing and Yorkshire were reluctant participants. Players preferred the three-day form of the game and the committee opposed extension of one-day competitions. Innermost feelings were expressed on the field and Yorkshire were notably more successful in the Championship than in the new interpretations. They won 4 championships in 8 years but had less feeling for other competitions. Even in the Championship Yorkshire were less than dominant. Too many of their victories depended on some exceptional individual performance – an innings by Close himself or a decisive bowling spell by Trueman. The supporting cricket was inconsistent and some of the promising rosebuds never came quite to full bloom. Padgett, Sharpe, Illingworth and Hampshire touched international level with-

Three great Yorkshire batsmen, each with a hundred hundreds: Geoffrey Boycott, Herbert Sutcliffe and Sir Leonard Hutton.

out retaining hold and through the decade only Boycott emerged as a batsman of indisputable quality. Close was a forthright and enterprising captain, with Illingworth an increasingly helpful lieutenant, but the course of cricket in this period of change tended to widen the differences of outlook between the game's players, authorities and followers. Players advanced professional self-interests with the appointment of personal agents and the formation of a representative association. Authorities tried to balance control between independence and expanding sponsorship. Followers were divided between search for sensationalism and satisfaction derived from more lasting values. For Yorkshire the consequences were dramatic. Underlying unease promoted a series of public confrontations and controversies that weakened the county's standing and achievement.

Illingworth, unable to secure a long-term contract, asked for release and moved to Leicestershire. Close, unable to reconcile his beliefs with the committee policy, led his club to public reprimand over behaviour, in a match at Edgbaston in 1967. Differences unresolved, he was relieved of the captaincy in 1970 and his going raised a protest group among members.

The dispersal of such individual forces as Illingworth, Trueman, Close and the wicket-keeper Binks, left Yorkshire with a rebuilding programme under the captaincy of Boycott. It was never completed in that context. Yorkshire passed into a playing period of almost unrelieved disappointment. In 8 seasons none of the 4 established competitions was won and in most of the years no strong challenge was presented. Yorkshire were manifestly among the weaker counties. Year after year spring optimism turned to midsummer resignation. No opponents felt at disadvantage in meeting Yorkshire and nadir was touched when Durham, a Minor County, came into Yorkshire to win.

The new pattern of cricket involving matches extending from the 5-day Test to the half-day Sunday league made development of the young cricketer difficult and slow. Team tended to become squad. Yorkshire's young cricketers lost direction through being over-directed and lost purposefulness in confusion of purpose. For the first time in almost 100 years Yorkshire fell to insignificance in county cricket.

The crown of captaincy rested uneasily on Boycott's head. He sought too much and too dictatorially; he conceded too little for the common good from his own vast store of talent. Yorkshire's poor performance in the 1970s generated much beating of breast and intemperate expression culminating in focus on personality cult. The outcome was a stormy 1978 of internal politics, involving the appointment of Ray Illingworth as team manager, the dismissal of Boycott from the captaincy and a polarization of divergent views that were meat and drink for the Press but made indigestible fare for the convalescence of Yorkshire cricket.

CAPTAINS

1863–70	R. Iddison
1871–75	J. Rowbotham
1876–77	E. Lockwood
1878–82	T. Emmett
1883–1910	Lord Hawke
1911	E. J. Radcliffe
1912–14	Sir A. W. White
1919–21	D. C. F. Burton
1922–24	G. Wilson
1925–27	A. W. Lupton
1928–29	W. A. Worsley
1930	A. T. Barber
1931–32	F. E. Greenwood
1933–47	A. B. Sellers
1948–55	N. W. D. Yardley
1956–57	W. H. H. Sutcliffe
1958–59	J. R. Burnet
1960–62	J. V. Wilson
1963–70	D. B. Close
1971–78	G. Boycott
1979–	J. H. Hampshire

HIGHEST TOTALS

For 887 v Warwicks, Edgbaston 1896
Against 630 by Somerset, Headingley 1901

LOWEST TOTALS

For 23 v Hants, Middlesborough 1965
Against 13 by Notts, Trent Bridge 1901

HIGHEST INDIVIDUAL INNINGS

For 341 G. H. Hirst, v Leicester, Leicester 1905
Against 318* W. G. Grace, for Gloucester, Cheltenham 1876

MOST RUNS

In a season 2,883 H. Sutcliffe 1932
In a career 38,561 H. Sutcliffe 1919–1945

MOST HUNDREDS

In a season 12 H. Sutcliffe 1932
In a career 112 H. Sutcliffe 1919–1945

INDIVIDUAL INNINGS OF 250 AND OVER

J. T. Brown, 311 v Sussex, Sheffield 1897
J. T. Brown, 300 v Derby, Chesterfield 1898
G. H. Hirst, 341 v Leicester, Leicester 1905
P. Holmes, 302* v Hants, Portsmouth 1920
P. Holmes, 277* v Northants, Harrogate 1921
W. Rhodes, 267* v Leicester, Headingley 1921
H. Sutcliffe, 255* v Essex, Southend 1924
P. Holmes, 315* v Middlesex, Lord's 1925
P. Holmes, 275 v Warwicks, Bradford 1928
P. Holmes, 285 v Notts, Trent Bridge 1929
P. Holmes, 250 v Warwicks, Edgbaston 1931
H. Sutcliffe, 313 v Essex, Leyton 1932
H. Sutcliffe, 270 v Essex, Headingley 1932
W. Barber, 255 v Surrey, Sheffield 1935
M. Leyland, 263 v Essex, Hull 1936
L. Hutton, 271* v Derby, Sheffield 1937
L. Hutton, 280* v Hants, Sheffield 1939
L. Hutton, 270* v Hants, Bournemouth 1947
L. Hutton, 269* v Northants, Wellingborough 1949
F. A. Lowson, 259* v Worcester, Worcester 1953
G. Boycott, 260* v Essex, Colchester 1970

HUNDRED ON DEBUT

C. Tyson, 100* v Hants, Southampton 1921

RECORD WICKET PARTNERSHIPS

1 P. Holmes and H. Sutcliffe, 555 v Essex, Leyton 1932
2 W. Barber and M. Leyland, 346 v Middlesex, Sheffield 1932
3 H. Sutcliffe and M. Leyland, 323* v Glamorgan, Huddersfield 1928
4 D. Denton and G. H. Hirst, 312 v Hants, Southampton 1914
5 E. Wainwright and G. H. Hirst, 340 v Surrey, Oval 1899
6 M. Leyland and E. Robinson, 276 v Glamorgan, Swansea 1926
7 D. C. F. Burton and W. Rhodes, 254 v Hants, Dewsbury 1919
8 Lord Hawke and R. Peel, 292 v Warwicks, Edgbaston 1896
9 G. H. Hirst and S. Haigh, 192 v Surrey, Bradford 1898
10 Lord Hawke and D. Hunter, 148 v Kent, Sheffield 1898

MOST WICKETS

In a match 17–91 H. Verity v Essex, Leyton 1933
In a season 240 W. Rhodes 1900
In a career 3,608 W. Rhodes 1898–1930

ALL 10 WICKETS IN AN INNINGS

A. Drake v Somerset, Weston 1914
H. Verity v Warwicks, Headingley 1931
H. Verity v Notts, Headingley 1932
T. F. Smailes v Derby, Sheffield 1939

HAT-TRICKS

G. G. Macaulay, F. S. Trueman 4 each
S. Haigh, D. Wilson 3 each
M. W. Booth, A. Drake, A. Hill, G. H. Hirst, E. Peate, E. Robinson 2 each
R. Appleyard, J. T. Brown, G. A. Cope, A. Coxon, G. Deyes, H. Fisher, W. Fletcher, G. Freeman, H. W. Hart, M. Leyland, J. T. Newstead, R. Peel, W. Rhodes, A. L. Robinson, E. P. Robinson, H. Sedgwick, G. Ulyett, H. Verity, A. Waddington, E. Wainwright 1 each

WICKET-KEEPING – MOST DISMISSALS

In an innings 6 D. Hunter (2)
R. Allen
D. L. Bairstow
J. G. Binks
J. Hunter
In a match 9 D. L. Bairstow 1971
J. Hunter 1887
In a season 108 J. G. Binks 1960
In a career 1,209 D. Hunter 1889–1909

COUNTY CAPS AWARDED SINCE 1946

1946	A. Booth
1947	D. V. Brennan, A. Coxon, G. A. Smithson, J. H. Wardle, W. Watson
1948	R. Aspinall, H. Halliday, E. Lester, J. V. Wilson
1949	D. B. Close, F. A. Lowson
1951	R. Appleyard, F. S. Trueman
1952	W. H. H. Sutcliffe
1955	R. Illingworth
1957	J. G. Binks, W. B. Stott, K. Taylor
1958	J. R. Burnet, D. E. V. Padgett
1959	R. K. Platts
1960	J. B. Bolus, M. J. Cowan, P. J. Sharpe, D. Wilson
1962	M. Ryan
1963	G. Boycott, J. H. Hampshire, A. G. Nicholson
1964	R. A. Hutton
1969	B. Leadbeater, C. M. Old
1970	G. A. Cope
1973	D. L. Bairstow
1974	R. G. Lumb
1976	P. Carrick, A. L. Robinson
1978	G. B. Stevenson

The Universities

Cambridge University

J. G. W. DAVIES

The University Cricket Club was founded soon after the Battle of Waterloo; and upon its origins, whatever the Duke of Wellington may have claimed, the playing fields of Eton exerted a stronger influence than upon that famous victory. At the beginning of the 19th century team games did not have an important place in undergraduate life. Cricket was largely a pursuit of Etonians who had formed a taste for the game at school. The earliest newspaper reports of cricket matches involving undergraduates date from 1755 when the Gentlemen of Eton twice played the Gentlemen of the University. We also know that cricketing talent tended to concentrate in King's College, which by its foundation is closely linked with Eton. Between 1816 and 1820 King's took on the rest of the University 5 times, a situation which modern Cambridge would regard as unexpected, for in the 20th century King's can hardly be said to have fostered an athletic tradition.

It was probably in 1820 that the University Cricket Club was formed. Its affairs were directed by two 'treasurers', Messrs Hannington and Oxenden. For the next 6 years there are records showing annually a trio of 'treasurers' holding office. They played local sides, such as Cambridge Town and Bury. Most of the games took place on Parker's Piece, the great open space near the middle of Cambridge, on which four or five games of cricket can still be seen every Saturday. But at times the UCC played on the 'New Ground' to the north of Parker's Piece. They played in knee-breeches and silk stockings on rough, unscarified wickets. Batsmen and wicket-keepers wore no protective devices such as pads or gloves. A pair of stockings was sometimes rolled down to fortify the ankles against the worst effects of shooters. A painting dated 1842 shows undergraduates playing on Parker's Piece with the old town jail in the background. They are still without gloves or pads, but white trousers have replaced knee-breeches. The players (except extra-cover, whose head is covered by the démodé top hat) are wearing either a kind of Panama hat or 'porkpie' caps. Fixed boundaries were by no means the rule and long hits were run out to their maximum value. Until the 1860s, of course, only round-arm or lobs were permitted. There was no pavilion, but tents were pitched for each day's play. An old score-book in the club's possession speaks of non-playing members having the 'privilege of the Tent'.

The 1st match against Oxford, which was spoiled by bad weather, took place at Lord's in 1827. It seems to have been arranged on the initiative of Herbert Jenner (later Jenner-Fust and President of MCC) and Charles Wordsworth, who had opposed one another at Eton and Harrow respectively and then taken up residence at the rival universities. Although another contest was held 2 years afterwards, there was then a gap of 7 years and it was only from 1838 that the series continued unbroken. Between 1829 and 1850 the 'Varsity match was played at Oxford on 5 occasions (but never at Cambridge) and thenceforward always at Lord's.

From these modest beginnings there evolved a fixture list of growing complexity which, while ostensibly serving as a prelude to the University Match, in fact provides the team with an introduction to the first-class game. In the 1860s the fixture list began to shed its local component, suggesting that the University teams were making their mark at national level. Counties start to appear on the list, though it was not until the Edwardian era that counties occupied the predominant place in the fixtures. But as early as the 1870s the pattern emerges of an initial series of games at Fenner's followed by a 'tour' culminating in the game with Oxford at Lord's.

A developing fixture list, however, called for a ground over which the club would have adequate control. In 1846 F. P. Fenner had leased from Gonville and Caius College a field to the south of Parker's Piece which he deemed suitable for cricket. Two years later he sub-let it to the UCC which from that date never played elsewhere in Cambridge and which has perpetuated Fenner's name wherever cricket is played and understood. It was not until 1856 that a pavilion was erected—an unpretentious wooden structure on the west side of the ground where the scoreboard now stands.

It is an unsatisfactory proposition to be tenant of a property which is used only in the summer months and lies idle in the winter. Fortunately for the club the University Athletic Club, which held most of its events in the winter, was looking for a convenient base. The Athletic Club began to use Fenner's in the early 1860s and in 1865 the cinder track surrounding the playing area, with which so many Cambridge men are familiar, was laid down. The Athletic Club ran on this track until 1959, when a modern track was constructed on the opposite side of the city. The Athletic Club's matches appear to have attracted substantial gates, the proceeds of which were a welcome buttress to the shaky finances of the Cricket Club. In the 1850s and 1860s the club's affairs were still managed by the 'troika' of undergraduate officers established in 1821. By 1867, the first year for which printed rules are extant, these 3 officers had become a President and 2 secretaries. In 1871, however, the club was faced with a situation which could not easily be dealt with by undergraduates alone. Undergraduate institutions often require the services of senior members of the University, not because students are incapable of handling finances effectively, but because, when long-term financial commitments are undertaken, they require greater continuity of attention than can be given by officers who change every year and who are resident in Cambridge only during University terms.

Fenner's leasehold with Caius expired in 1876 and since he had departed from Cambridge 10 years previously, it was not renewed. Caius were thought to be contemplating ways of developing the property which might jeopardize the Cricket Club's use of the ground. It is probable that the College, though sympathetic to the Cricket Club, hesitated to do business with undergraduates on the future of a very desirable site. At the same time, the old pavilion was proving quite inadequate for accommodating the 2 clubs and lacked the amenities which first-class visiting sides were beginning to expect. A major piece of capital equipment must be financed. It was the moment for a father-figure to take over.

He appeared in the ample person of the Rev Arthur Ward, who had established himself during the 1860s as one of the club's most whole-hearted supporters. Quite apart from the conspicuous contribution he made to the growth of the club, Ward is too rich a character to be dismissed in a few sentences. He was the younger brother of W. G. Ward, who played a prominent part in the controversies provoked in Oxford by the Tractarian movement. His father was William Ward, a wealthy merchant and banker, who acquired the freehold of Lord's and whose score of 278 made there in 1820 stood unchallenged for many years as the record for the ground. The young Ward came up to St John's from Eton in 1851 and was appointed captain of the University in 1854. He was reputed to weigh 20 stone as an undergraduate and to have put on a further 8 stones as he matured. According to Lord Hawke, in Ward's prime Charles Studd counted 38 buttons on his waistcoat. In his young days he was sensitive about his girth – so much so that in the year of his captaincy, having received a merciless 'ribbing' from the Lord's crowd during the University's match v MCC, he refused to reappear before them in the Oxford match and confined himself to directing his side's operations from the pavilion.

Two years after leaving Cambridge he became curate of All Saints, the parish adjoining Jesus College, and a few years later Vicar of St Clement's. His parish duties were not so exacting as to prevent him from devoting himself single-mindedly to the club's welfare. He was elected President and treasurer in 1873 and until his death in 1884 he was the dominating figure in the club's affairs. To him must be accorded the principal credit for two important projects – the negotiation of a 35-year lease of the ground from Caius; and the financing and erection of a new and comely pavilion, a famous landmark in the cricket world for nearly a century. He was an indefatigable fund-raiser. The list of subscribers to the Pavilion Fund includes the Prince of Wales and many other notables. Ward is said to have written more than 1,500 letters in his own hand in pursuit of this aim. In 4 years the money was found and the building completed. From this point onwards Ward's attitude to the club became proprietary. His pride in the pavilion was without reserve. Walking sticks had to be left outside for fear that visitors in pointing out names in the teams listed on the walls might scratch the new paint. He acted as Master of Ceremonies at every match. Guests introduced by members were expected to take sherry with him and to receive his approval.

Ward was probably rather obtuse, and quick-witted undergraduates unquestionably pulled his leg, to his great delight. He was also intensely hospitable. Members of both visiting and University teams were regularly entertained to breakfast in his rooms. The menu, which never changed, consisted of eggs, sausages and salmon cutlets, the repast being washed down by Bollinger which, as a concession to the imminent demands of the game, was diluted with Apollinaris. It must have been quite a nasty drink, and even for the unflinching digestive organs of the Victorians an injudicious preparation for a morning's cricket.

Ward's stewardship brought the club's finances to a state of comparative prosperity, for, when in 1892 Caius were approached about selling the freehold of the ground, the Cricket and Athletic Clubs between them were able to muster reserves of £6,000, half the proposed price. Indeed, with the aid of an appeal for funds and a modest mortgage the club felt able also to acquire some of the land surrounding the playing area. In 1895 the whole property was assigned to a company which held it in trust for the constituent clubs. This arrangement endures to the present day. It was in the great days of the Pavilion Fund that Ward permitted the election to life membership (at the usual rates) of a Dandie Dinmont, Hugo, the inseparable companion of Dr Porter, the Master of Peterhouse, who would otherwise have been obliged to leave him outside, for the treasurer considered dogs as dangerous as walking sticks to the amenities of the new building. The same privilege was extended upon Hugo's death to his successor, Rollo. It would be interesting to know whether any other first-class club can lay claim to the election of 2 quadruped life members.

In 1972 this apple of Ward's eye was demolished and replaced by a modern structure at the opposite end of the ground, the architect being Colin Stansfield Smith, the Cambridge fast bowler of the 1950s. Five years later the Club's finances, reduced to a parlous condition by the impact of inflation, were rescued by the University, who assumed responsibility for most of the labour and maintenance costs at Fenner's. Coming at a time when higher education was already feeling the pinch of Government economies, this innovation was deeply appreciated by the Club. The rescue was further reinforced by sponsorship, first by Royal Insurance and then by Schweppes.

1890, a vintage Cambridge side led by the Australian, S. M. J. Woods. Five of them played Test cricket. Back row: D. L. A. Jephson, E. C. Streatfeild, R. N. Douglas, F. S. Jackson, H. Hale and A. J. L. Hill; sitting: C. P. Foley, F. G. J. Ford, S. M. J. Woods, R. C. Gosling and G. MacGregor.

Having summarized its growth as an institution, we can now make an attempt to assess the club's position in first-class cricket. The University clubs tend to be judged by the quality of the individual players they produced rather than by the collective strength of their sides. Good players count for more than good teams. This is because the counties do not see the clubs as potential rivals, but as a transitional area from which talent may come their way later. It remains relatively easy for a good undergraduate to spend the second half of the summer with the ground staff of a county. What is no longer practicable is the easygoing arrangement of 20 years ago whereby, after leaving University, an amateur could play part of each season and so combine professional or business life with participation in the first-class game. Since 1963 the amateur has become extinct. With professional captains (and more recently with professional managers) and with appreciable earnings flowing from sponsored competitions, counties understandably frown on part-time employees. If they want to play for a county, young men must commit themselves to full-time professional status, at any rate for half of each year. Having your cake and eating it has become progressively more unattainable.

Sixty-three Cambridge men have represented England in official Test Matches (the term 'Test Match' dates only from the early 1900s). Only in one period since Test Matches began has there been a dearth in the Cambridge sides of men whose talent took them sooner or later to the highest level of cricket. Curiously enough, this was the Edwardian era, the era often commended as the fairest flowering of amateur cricket. Between 1900 and 1914 only 5 Cambridge blues went on to represent England – and none of them played in more than one series. The great Cambridge names of the period – Stanley Jackson, Jessop, 'Ranji', A. O. Jones – were an earlier undergraduate vintage.

Fourteen members of Cambridge teams who received their blues since 1946 have played in Test Matches – among them Peter May, Bailey, Dexter and Sheppard, all of whom must be assigned to the highest category. The teams in the inter-war years contributed 17 Test Match players, who include Arthur Gilligan, Chapman, Robins, F. R. Brown, Farnes, G. O. Allen, Norman Yardley and 'Duleep'.

In the 19th-century sides there were 27 future England players and there might have been more if Test Matches had been as frequent events as they are today. Besides the 4 notables mentioned above, they include A. G. Steel, Alfred Lyttelton, A. P. Lucas, Charles Studd and S. M. J. Woods. Cambridge names abound in the score-sheets of county matches, though the hard economics of earning a living have often restricted the frequency of their presence. There can seldom have been a Gentlemen v Players match without at least one Light Blue participant.

On the other hand, if University teams are assessed not as nurseries of talent, but for their strength in relation to contemporary first-class sides, a clear estimate is not easy to arrive at. When the formative, locally oriented phase of the club's development was over (the late 1850s would be roughly the conclusion of this phase) the Universities were already two of the best sides in the country. But at this point cricket was not organized in such a way as to exploit to the best advantage the available talent elsewhere. Very few of the county clubs were formed before the 1860s and no exercise approaching a Championship was inaugurated until the 1870s. Conspicuous individual ability shows itself whatever the condition of the game may be. But *collective* strength depends on organization and on the forces of competition and incentive. The creation of a large class of competing professionals by the growth of the County Championship, the commercial incentive involved in attracting a crowd of supporters, the stimulus of international cricket, all combined to widen the range of good sides and to raise standards. It was somewhere in the neighbourhood of 1880 that the Universities had to meet the challenge of well-integrated teams geared to playing together for the whole of each summer. As professional cricket developed, techniques and tactics gained in importance. The things which depend on knowledge, experience and discipline rather than an aptitude became a necessary part of a first-class cricketer's equipment. This makes it a little harder for young men in their introductory years in the advanced game to reach the standard of the professional.

The evolution of this trend can be illustrated by showing for successive decades the results of all Cambridge matches against counties.

PERIOD	WON	LOST	DRAWN	TOTAL
1882–1891	11	12	6	29
1892–1901	13	21	7	41
1902–1911	14	28	11	53
1920–1929	22	17	32	71
1930–1939	15	31	33	79
1950–1959	13	45	62	120
1960–1969	5	67	44	116

The same table converted into percentages is shown below.

PERIOD	WON	LOST	DRAWN	TOTAL
	%	%	%	%
1882–1891	38	40	22	100
1892–1901	32	51	17	100
1902–1911	26	53	21	100
1920–1929	31	24	45	100
1930–1939	40	41	19	100
1950–1959	11	37·5	51·5	100
1960–1969	4	58	38	100

The following conclusions can be drawn from these results. First, up to the First World War it was getting gradually harder for the University to beat counties, but the chances of finishing a match remained roughly the same. Secondly, from 1920 onwards drawn games begin to predominate with a diminishing capacity on the University's part to achieve a win. Thirdly, the chances that a county will actually defeat the University, after declining somewhat after the First World War, reverted in the 1960s to roughly the level of the late Victorian and Edwardian era.

Figures for the decade 1970–79 have not been added to the table shown above because in the 1970s the pattern of the University's fixture list underwent a radical change. Oxford and Cambridge were given the opportunity of participating in the Benson & Hedges competition, most of which is completed in the first half of the season before the University teams disperse. This move implied a reduction in the number of three-day games with counties, but it brought up-to-date the kind of experience offered at the University to the young aspiring cricketer, *i.e.* a blend of the three-day and the one-day game. It also provided a much-needed supplement to the Club's finances, which took a share of the competition's proceeds.

At first Oxford and Cambridge competed independently in alternate years, but after 3 seasons on this basis the solution of an annual entry by a combined Oxford/Cambridge side was adopted. In the first year the Combined Universities won 2 of their 4 'zonal' matches and another in the 2nd year. But success in the one-day game relies greatly on special tactics which only experience can teach. As the counties have mastered these skills the Universities, with much less opportunity to acquire them, have become less likely to beat their opponents.

One decade belies the general trend. In the 5 years following the First World War a brilliant burst of talent coincided with a period in which first-class cricket was recovering from the effects of a 4-year stoppage, a stoppage which was far more pervasive than the reductions in cricket-playing imposed by the Second World War. Of the 22 wins recorded in the decade 1920–1929 all but two were gained before 1926. The 1921 and 1925 sides each beat 5 counties and the 1922 side 4.

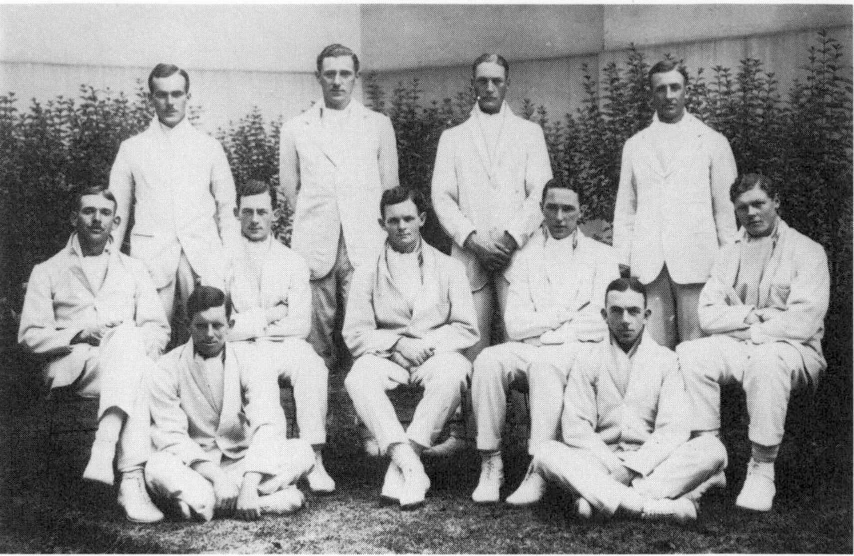

Cambridge 1921, probably the strongest University side of the century. Back row: A. G. Doggart, M. D. Lyon, C. A. F. Fiddian-Green, J. L. Bryan; sitting: C. S. Marriott, H. Ashton, G. Ashton (captain), C. H. Gibson and A. P. F. Chapman; on ground: C. T. Ashton and R. G. Evans.

The increase in drawn games was not peculiar to University cricket but was reflected in all first-class cricket. Improved groundsmanship contributed greatly to the dominion of bat over ball. But techniques and an attitude to the game also entered into it. Wickets were of high quality from the turn of the century, yet before 1914 results were more frequently obtained. Both batsmen and bowlers were less prone to adopt defensive tactics.

It may be argued that counties take their games with the Universities more lightly than their games in the Championship programme and that they do not always field their strongest sides. There is some force in this argument, but it is not my experience that they treat the games so lightly as to throw the match away. And against any relaxation in the rigour of the game must be set the face that a large part of the University's fixtures are played in the opening weeks of the season when conditions are apt to be uncertain, and that inevitably the players are combining their devotion to cricket with preparations to satisfy their examiners. University teams tend to do better on the tour which precedes the 'Varsity match than at Fenner's.

The abiding difficulty of University sides is to produce bowlers who at the age of 19 to 22 are sufficiently penetrating or sufficiently accurate to get a county side out twice. The batting is frequently strong enough to compete successfully, but if it is supported by mediocre bowling, a high proportion of draws will follow. In the years 1948–1952 Cambridge had some of the strongest batting in the country with Dewes, May, Doggart, Sheppard, Insole and Bailey all in residence. None of these sides lost more than 3 games in a season, but none won more than 3. The bowling was not strong enough to finish the matches off. This tendency has been intensified by the perfection – in the batsman's eyes – of the wickets prepared at Fenner's by Cyril Coote, who has been in charge of the ground since 1935. The fact remains that no Cambridge team has beaten more than three counties in a single year since 1925. But this is not to say that they have been unable to extend counties and to give them a good game. Incidentally Cyril Coote retires in 1980 after 44 years of service to the club. There can be no adequate acknowledgement of the contribution he has made during this long period to the well-being of the club, whether as a personality or as an expert in the care of sports fields.

The most effective University teams have been those in which there has been a pair or trio of gifted bowlers supported by a varied change attack. In 1878, possibly the finest XI Cambridge ever produced, there was A. G. Steel and P. H. Morton; in 1882, C. T. Studd, R. C. Ramsay and C. Aubrey Smith; in 1891, Stanley Jackson, S. M. J. Woods and C. M. Wells; in 1906, A. F. Morcom, G. G. Napier and P. R. May; in 1911, M. Falcon, E. L. Kidd and J. F. Ireland; in 1921, C. S. Marriott, C. H. Gibson and A. G. Doggart; in 1923, G. O. Allen, P. A. Wright and F. B. R. Browne; in 1925, R. J. O. Meyer and H. J. Enthoven with S. T. Jagger in support; in 1935, Jahangir Khan and J. H. Cameron. In the 1950s the strongest side was that which included G. Goonesena, O. S. Wheatley and C. S. Smith; in the 1960s that which included R. A. Hutton A. R. Windows and A. J. G. Pearson. In the 1970s the most formidable team had P. H. Edmonds, J. Spencer and R. J. Hadley.

In the post-war period no bowler has approached O. S. Wheatley's remarkable achievement in 1958 of taking 80 wickets in the short University season, most of them on the true batting wickets at Fenner's. This is the largest 'bag' in the history of the Club.

For all-round achievement over a period of time no Cambridge player can match Trevor

Cyril Coote, the Fenner's groundsman for more than 40 years and wise adviser to generations of Cambridge cricketers. He says the best batsman of his time was Peter May.

Bailey's record. He scored 1,000 runs and took 100 wickets 8 times from 1948. The only amateur to obtain the double more often is 'W. G.'. Bailey's showing at the University might not have presaged such a fine record, for, though a very useful member of the side, he was not outstanding. No cricketer added to his own stature so effectively by self-discipline, tactical shrewdness and the capacity to benefit by experience.

From 1869 to 1872 Cambridge had one of the best amateurs in the country in W. Yardley. He scored the 1st hundred recorded in the University match. This was in 'Cobden's Match', the game in 1870 which Cambridge won by 2 runs, F. C. Cobden finishing off the Oxford 2nd innings with a hat-trick. Two years later Yardley scored another hundred at Lord's, a truly remarkable performance on the wickets of those days. He could throw prodigiously with either hand and was a capable actor, playwright and journalist. In 1878 A. G. Steel took 75 wickets in 8 matches for 7·5 runs apiece. On the average he captured a wicket every 15 balls! This astonishing feat was the foundation of the success of Edward Lyttelton's team, which won all its fixtures and defeated the Australians by an innings. Steel may well have been the finest all-rounder Cambridge ever produced.

Few undergraduates have had so fine a record as Charles Studd, who was in residence from 1879–1883. He was one of three brothers who successively captained the University and in this respect share a remarkable record with the Ashton brothers who in turn were captains from 1921–1923. To maintain an average of nearly 40 for over 50 innings on the wickets of that time argues immense ability and concentration. He also took well over 100 wickets for the University. He played 5 times for England against Australia in those years and twice scored 1,000 runs and took 100 wickets in a season. He lacked Steel's brilliance, but he was astonishingly correct and infallible as a batsman and as a bowler tremendously accurate and persevering. As soon as he left Cambridge he embraced a religious life with the same single-mindedness which he had brought to his cricket. He divested himself of all his possessions, never played cricket again and served as a missionary in China, India and Central Africa until his death. His brother, George, who was captain in 1882 and toured Australia the following winter also became a missionary and was later Principal of a theological training college in California. It was in the year of his captaincy that Cambridge defeated the Australians for the last time, Charles Studd making a hundred and taking 5 wickets in their 1st innings.

A few years later the outstanding figure was the redoubtable S. M. J. ('Sam') Woods. He was one of the finest fast bowlers of an era in which fast bowling flourished abundantly. Of Australian origin, though educated in England, he was a man of inexhaustible energy and physical strength with a rumbustious, warm-hearted disposition which made him a conspicuous personality. He took nearly 200 wickets for the University in 4 seasons and was the only regular bowler playing later than 1885 who secured his wickets for less than 15 runs apiece. In 1890 he took all 10 wickets against a strong XI brought to Fenner's by C. I. Thornton, having fortified himself for this feat with a breakfast of hot lobster and audit ale. No other University bowler took 10 wickets in an innings until 1961 when A. J. G. Pearson equalled his performance against Leicester. A famous *tour de force* was the spectacle of Gregor MacGregor standing up to Woods behind the wicket and taking his fastest deliveries with the utmost ease and certainty.

In the 1890s Cambridge had an array of fine batsmen which included Jackson, Jessop, 'Ranji', Frank Mitchell and C. J. Burnup. But they were all put in the shade by Norman Druce, who in four seasons scored nearly 2,500 runs for the University with an average of over 50. No earlier batsman had been so consistently successful. He toured Australia in 1897, but soon afterwards went into the distilling business and played practically no more cricket. In the 1900–1914 period Cambridge were not always so strong, though there was a fine side in 1906 captained by C. H. Eyre, a confident, aggressive batsman. A most successful trio of bowlers, A. F. Morcom, G. G. Napier and P. R. May, were chiefly responsible for the University's successes in the middle of this period. There was also a formidable side in 1911, when three first-rate all-rounders, M. Falcon, J. F. Ireland and E. L. Kidd were in residence simultaneously.

The early 1920s saw Cambridge cricket in its most dazzling flower. It was the point in the 20th century when no county was safe from a beating at the University's hands. Within 3 years there were 3 future captains of England in the side – Arthur Gilligan, Percy Chapman and G. O. Allen; and there must surely have been a 4th if a career in business overseas had not withdrawn him from the game. Hubert Ashton outshone even the gifted players who were his contemporaries. By common consent he was regarded as the most promising amateur batsman of the inter-war years. In 1921 no other player tackled the dreaded Australian openers, Gregory and McDonald, with such courage and certainty. He averaged over 60 in each of the 3 seasons he played. Not even the prolific trio of the 1950–1952 period, Dewes, Sheppard or May, quite succeeded in attaining his figures. He was an excellent captain and a superb fielder close in on the leg-side.

Another casualty to the great British mercantile tradition was C. H. Gibson, one of the opening bowlers in the same side. His reputation was not as high as Ashton's, but discerning judges have rated him as the most gifted of the amateur bowlers playing in the 1920–1940 era. He was of sharp medium pace, moving the ball either way, a 'stock' bowler, if ever there was one. But after two years at Cambridge he went to Argentina, though he played for Sussex in 1926. A few years later that most attractive player, K. S. Duleepsinhji, nephew of 'Ranji', was in the side and after two reasonably successful seasons broke the ground record at Fenner's in 1927 with a score of 254 not out against Middlesex. Almost immediately afterwards his health broke down for the first time and he did not play for the University again that season.

The sides which included such fine batsmen as M. J. Turnbull, E. T. Killick and B. H. Valentine lacked just the extra bowling strength to be really successful, though in one of these years Maurice Allom had an excellent season and took 60 wickets. When the bowling became stronger, with Farnes and F. R. Brown in residence together, the batting was not so formidable. In 1931 when Brown captured 66 wickets, the nearest approach at that time to A. G. Steel's 'bag' in 1878, he probably bowled as well as at any point in his career and made many England players look distinctly small in stature.

In the 1930s the best sides came in the middle years, the strength being derived not from a few stars, but from a high general level of ability. They batted all the way down and had plenty of bowling, with Jahangir Khan, J. H. Cameron, W. Wooller and J. M. Brocklebank as the most effective quartet. In the next three years, though P. A. Gibb and J. R. Thompson had fine records as batsmen, virtually no matches were won because of a dearth of bowlers.

After the Second World War, Cambridge cricket climbed painfully back to first-class standards. By 1949 there was a reasonably good side which D. J. Insole led to a well-deserved, but unexpected, victory in the 'Varsity match. There followed the 3 years of prolific run-getting (but no great success against Oxford) when Dewes, Doggart, Sheppard and May made hay in the Fenner's sunshine. Few will forget the University's match against West Indies when 1,324 runs were scored for the loss of 7 wickets.

G. H. G. Doggart went down from Cambridge in 1950 with 5 blues – for cricket, association football, rackets, fives and squash – and a Test cap. He was captain of 4 of these games.

The sides in the middle of the 1950–1960 decade which included Goonesena, Dexter, C. S. Smith, Wheatley and R. W. Barber, though they did not beat many counties, could unquestionably give them a keen tussle. After this the sides began to lack all-round strength, though C. B. Howland's team in 1960 beat three counties. These sides were again hard put to it to find adequate bowlers, but there were batsmen of high calibre in A. R. Lewis and R. M. Prideaux. They were succeeded in the 1962–64 period by a group of players whose claim to first-class status can scarcely be challenged. In J. M. Brearley they had one of the most promising young batsmen in the country. He was selected for Gentlemen v Players as a freshman, exceeded the record aggregate scored for Cambridge by any one batsman and was the first man to be elected captain of the club twice since F. S. Jackson in 1893. Supported by players of the ability of E. J. Craig, R. C. White, R. A. Hutton, A. R. Windows and R. C. Kerslake, Brearley led teams which bear comparison with vintage years. it took him 12 years to occupy a similar position at international level, but in the end he has done so with real distinction.

The sides in the late 1960s were mediocre, but with the 1970s there was another upturn, largely stimulated by the arrival of Majid

P. H. Edmonds, captain in 1973, is the latest in the roll of Cambridge cricketers capped for England.

Khan, who, despite his youth, was already a Test player. He averaged over 50 in each of his 3 seasons and played a number of truly memorable innings, including a 200 in the 'Varsity match. His example (like Brearley, he was twice elected captain) helped to bring on players as promising as D. R. Owen-Thomas and R. D. V. Knight. Having P. H. Edmonds and J. Spencer among his bowlers, 3 counties were beaten and the Pakistani tourists routed during his captaincy.

Since then there have been some gifted batsmen – P. M. Roebuck of Somerset, P. W. G. Parker of Sussex (who scored 215 against Essex as a Freshman), A. J. Hignell of Gloucester and M. K. Fosh of Essex – but until 1979 the bowling was thin. In 1979 under I. A. Greig, brother of the redoubtable Tony, Cambridge began to bowl county sides out again and finished with an innings victory over Oxford.

Anyone who speculates on the future of University cricket cannot rid himself of certain misgivings. First, competition for admission, already intense and governed pretty strictly by academic attainment which has kept out players who even 20 years ago would have found the doors open, is likely to intensify further as the effects of admitting women to men's Colleges without commensurate expansion make themselves felt. On the other hand, the development of national coaching schemes and the growth of representative youth cricket has done something to offset the limitations imposed on cricket in schools by the retiming of summer exams and the rearrangement of the dates for summer terms. But these reforms have also brought young players closer to the county clubs who are closely involved in youth cricket. One hopes that the counties will encourage youngsters capable of winning a place at Oxford or Cambridge to make this their aim rather than to plump for an immediate place on their ground staff. In University sides they can get more experience of playing in first-class company than by spending the same years in the County 2nd XI.

Oxford University

GEOFFREY BOLTON AND ALAN GIBSON

Most cricket clubs – I Zingari, for example, or the Free Foresters – have a real birthday; one day they are not, the next they are challenging one another to battle. Some, however, and of them the OUCC is perhaps the most prominent, 'just growed'. Yet it was not without pride of ancestry, as one may say that its forefathers were the Bullingdon Club and the Magdalen Club. In the south of England will be found many a village green on which cricket has been played for hundreds of years; but you will search in vain for Cowley Marsh, the cradle of Oxford University cricket. This was an enormous common stretching from the Cowley end of Magdalen Bridge right up to the foot of Shotover Hill. At the northern end was the ground of the Bullingdon Club, said by William Lillywhite to have the finest turf on which he ever played. Brasenose and St John's had grounds somewhere near, but it was not until Cowley Marsh was split up and sold in small lots that most of the colleges were able to own a ground.

The ground of the Magdalen Club was about a mile from Magdalen Bridge. It acquired its name from the Magdalen Choir School, whose boys used to play there until their headmaster, the Rev H. Jenkins, handed over to the University the ground which he had annexed.

The constitution of the Magdalen Club was curious. The government consisted of 3 stewards, none of whom was responsible for any particular office and all of whom had a prescribed right both to play in any match and to captain the side. It was quite normal, therefore, to find more than one man placing the field or changing the bowling, and there must have been a number of 'incidents' – as when all three stewards (history has suppressed their names) were fined 10*s*. for not turning up to a match. Irresponsibility could go further: in 1839, for example, the year of Cambridge's 1st victory, only 10 Oxford men appeared at Lord's. One can only guess that each of the stewards had left it to the other two to produce the 11th man. This haphazard state of affairs lasted till 1862. By now the University owned their ground and it was realized that there must be a properly constituted club. A committee of undergraduates was formed, a report and recommendations were made, and it was decided to appoint annually a captain, a secretary and a treasurer. The right to wear the dark blue cap was conceded by the OUBC in 1863.

When we speak of Cowley Marsh, it is to be remembered that the operative word was *marsh*. Frequently the ground was so flooded that play was impracticable. Indeed, one of the games against Cambridge had to be played on the Bullingdon ground. Moreover, the other chief sport at Oxford in the early part of last century was horse-racing, much of which took place on Cowley Marsh: it is easy to imagine the state of the outfield in wet weather. It was in the 1860s that the question of a move to the Parks was first mooted; but by then many of the colleges had bought grounds near the University's ground and they were unwilling to move. The dons, too, feared that such a step would involve a multiplicity of pavilions and pitches all over the Parks. It was not until the 1870s that Dr Evans, Master of Pembroke, urged Professor Case – the famous Tommy Case, later principal of Corpus – to take energetic steps to stir the dons to action. Case needed little persuading; he had powerful backing, including that of Dr Benjamin Jowett, and it was not long before a perpetual lease of 10 acres in the Parks was granted to the OUCC.

Since 1881 this has been the club's home ground. When the Australians are over, matches with them have often been played on the Christ Church ground in order that gate money might be taken; in 1900 Sussex were met there for the same reason, it being expected that C. B. Fry and Ranjitsinhji would be playing; and once the New College ground was borrowed for a match with the South Africans; for the first time in 1964 the fixture against the Australians was held at the Parks. Otherwise, all Oxford matches are played on the ground which is considered by many to be the most beautiful in England.

On the hearts of all those of either University who care what happens when Oxford meet Cambridge the name of Charles Wordsworth should be engraved; for it was he who 'invented' both the Cricket Match and the Boat Race. His father was Master of Trinity, Cambridge, a fact which at least made liaison possible. But for an undergraduate in his 2nd year, in days when trains, telephones and taxis were unknown, to arrange for the Universities to meet at Lord's and to get both sides there was a feat that could fairly be described as staggering. That was in 1827. Two years later Wordsworth was at it again. This time he arranged for the Boat Race to be rowed *two days* before the Cricket Match took place, and himself took part in both (and Oxford won both), but his hands were so sore from rowing that he could scarcely hold his bat.

After 1829 there was an interval and little is known about Oxford cricket in the next 6 years except for a few matches against the MCC. It is interesting to note that Wordsworth and Price continued to play for Oxford long after they must normally have gone down. Then Mr Pycroft of Trinity (later the Rev James Pycroft, prolific author of works on cricket) took it on himself – or so he says – to restart the matches with Cambridge, which, except for 1838, 1915–1918, 1940–1945, have gone on ever since. It is from about this time that names destined to be famous in cricket history begin to appear in University cricket.

In the years before 1870 two names lead all the rest in the story of Oxford cricket. C. D. B. Marsham, a son of the warden of Merton, not to be confused with his elder brother, Charles, appeared for the Harlequins against the University *before he had matriculated* and took 11 wickets. Later he invariably played for the Harlequins and for his county, Oxfordshire, when they opposed the University, even when he was the Oxford captain. Yet (in 5 years) he took more wickets for the University than anyone has taken since, except F. H. E. Cunliffe and R. H. Bettington. His bag against Cambridge was 40 wickets at less than 9 apiece. Subsequently he played for the Gentlemen for some years. he bowled fast-medium round-arm and in those days, when round-arm bowling was often very expensive in the matter of wides, he had a name for accuracy of pitch. No less famous is the name of R. A. H. Mitchell. He was in the team from 1862–1865 and *three times* led Oxford to victory at Lord's. He was by far the best batsman yet produced by either University. In 6 completed innings against Cambridge he made 254 runs – a wonderful record for the notoriously difficult Lord's ground of that day. Mitchell was for 30 years in charge of cricket at Eton, and among the famous Oxford cricketers whom he produced were C. J. Ottaway, S. E. Butler, Lord Harris, B. J. T. Bosanquet, F. H. E. Cunliffe, C. C. and H. C. Pilkington, and Lord George Scott. Cambridge may also thank him for the Lytteltons, the Studds and many others.

It may be said that in the last decade before the move to the Parks Oxford cricket came to maturity and proved itself worthy of a better home than Cowley Marsh could offer. The debut of W. G. Grace in 1864 and the visits of the Australians, who came in alternate years from 1878 to 1890, gave an enormous fillip to cricket, not least at the Universities, where men of international standard now began to appear. At Oxford the first of these was C. J. Ottaway, who has been called 'the greatest exponent of ball games ever known at Oxford or Cambridge'. C. B. Fry and Alfred Lyttelton might dispute this title, but Ottaway was a quadruple blue (cricket, soccer, athletics, tennis) and represented Oxford at rackets also for 4 victorious years. He was an international association football player and, but for his premature death, would surely have played in the early Test Matches. He captained Oxford in 1873, that great year when the record read: played 5, won 5. Lord Harris, A. J. Webbe and E. F. S. Tylecote were the Oxford internationals of this period. The first two are among those who must always be remembered in cricket.

Among the other notable players of these years was S. E. Butler, who in 1871, just before the 'Varsity Match, took 8 MCC wickets for 25 with his fast bowling; he followed this by taking eleven Cambridge wickets on the 1st day of the 'Varsity Match, though Oxford had batted first. Then there was A. W. Ridley, a good batsman, a masterly captain and a very useful lob bowler; W. H. Game, the first to score a hundred for Oxford v Cambridge; V. F. Royle, reputedly the model for all cover-points, as Game was for deep fieldsmen; F. M. Buckland, who in 1877 had a batting average of 88 and took 17 wickets at 8 apiece; and A. H. Evans, who for 4 years was almost the only Oxford bowler whom Cambridge feared. A particular feature of the 1870s – it is mentioned again and again in *Wisden* – was the magnificence of the Oxford fielding, especially compared with that of Cambridge. So often, particularly in the 1920s, has the boot been on the other foot that this fact is worth recalling.

The period from 1870 to 1914 was the heyday of amateur cricket and is often called the Golden Age. It was an age in which University cricket played a great part and the University Match was one of the events of the London season. Though less well equipped with all-rounders than Cambridge (between 1878 and 1893 the Cantabs had A. G. Steel, C. T. Studd, S. M. J. Woods and F. S. Jackson), Oxford had many splendid seasons. Between 1870 and 1899 they won 14 of the 30 'Varsity Matches and drew 2 – a creditable record in view of the strong opposition.

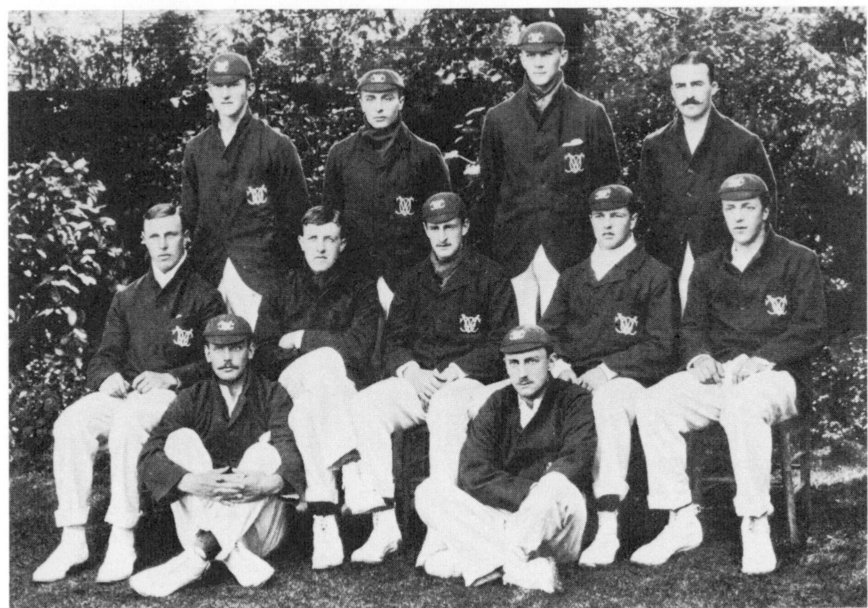

R. E. Foster's side of 1900 was the last at either University to end the season unbeaten. (He made 171 against Cambridge and averaged 77.) Back row: C. D. Fisher, J. W. F. Crawfurd, H. White and H. C. Pilkington; sitting: H. Martyn, F. H. B. Champain, R. E. Foster, F. P. Knox and B. J. T. Bosanquet; on ground: R. E. More and C. H. B. Marsham.

There were some fine Oxford sides in the 1880s, one reputed the finest of them all. That was the side of 1884, captained by M. C. Kemp, who for many years afterwards, until his death in 1951, was the inspiration behind Harrow cricket. He was the best captain since Mitchell and he was followed by one but little his inferior, H. V. Page. Special mention must be made of the 1884 side. They played 8 matches and won 7 of them, losing only to the Gentlemen by 31 runs. Their victims were Cambridge, the Australians (no other Oxford side has accomplished this feat), Surrey, MCC (twice) and Lancashire (twice). Yet the highest score made by Oxford this year was 251. This speaks volumes for the consistency of the batsmen and for the effectiveness of the bowling. In fact, only 6 bowlers were used altogether. Far and away the best was the fast bowler, H. O. Whitby, with 53 wickets at 15 each. Kemp headed the batting averages and kept wicket brilliantly.

The Australians were a formidable side. Two years previously they had won the Ashes in perhaps the most famous of all Test Matches; now, with virtually the same side, including those deadly bowlers Spofforth and Boyle, they came to Oxford fresh from the rout of an almost-England side at Sheffield Park. They were put out for 148, Whitby bowling 41 overs for 82 runs and 8 wickets. Oxford, thanks to Page, O'Brien and K. J. Key, had a lead of 61. E. W. Bastard then got rid of Bannerman and Murdoch for 0 apiece and Oxford had but 110 to make. Thanks to Kemp (63 not out) the runs were obtained for the loss of 3 wickets. The scenes in Oxford that night were comparable to those that occurred after Waterloo.

In 1886 Page captained another memorable team, one whose fame rests on two achievements: a near-win against the Australians (but Spofforth took 15 wickets for 36) and the rout of a Cambridge side who were expected to win easily. They had but 2 bowlers, Whitby and A. H. J. Cochrane – though E. H. Buckland suddenly found himself in an inspired burst at Lord's – and the batting depended too much on Key and Page. But Key was an outstanding 'Varsity Match player. When he went down in 1887 he had set up at least 4 Oxford records, 2 of which still stand. In 1886 he took part with W. Rashleigh in an opening stand of 243 against Cambridge, and in 1887 he made 281 v Middlesex at Chiswick, a score which no other Oxford batsman has yet reached.

After 1887 Oxford fell away; they had a series of weak sides and at Lord's they had to face both Woods and Jackson. But they recovered in 1892 and in the rest of that decade they had some of the finest batsmen and fieldsmen ever known. To that period belong M. R. Jardine, L. C. H. Palairet, C. B. Fry, H. K. and R. E. Foster, G. J. Mordaunt, P. F. Warner, G. O. Smith, F. H. B. Champain, F. L. Fane and B. J. T. Bosanquet. H. Martyn, who kept wicket in 1899–1900, was perhaps the best of all Oxford wicket-keepers. The bowling was not so strong, but F. H. E. Cunliffe (fastish left-hand), Bosanquet (a fast bowler in those days), G. F. H. Berkeley (slow left), J. C. Hartley (leg-breaks) and J. B. Wood (lobs) were often very effective. Cunliffe and Berkeley were rather more than that, the former taking 180 wickets in his 4 years, while Berkeley went nearer than anyone else to beating Cambridge in Woods's days. Of the batsmen mentioned above, 3 are among the greatest of all time. Palairet played only twice for England, but for sheer grace he has never been surpassed, and Woods used to say that he was the hardest driver in England. R. E. Foster had an all too brief career, into which he packed some astonishing feats: the record score against Cambridge, followed immediately by a hundred in each innings for the Gentlemen, the record score in Test Matches against Australia and the captaincy of England v South Africa – all by the time he was 30. He played little thereafter, but could always be relied on for runs when he did appear.

So much has been written of Fry that there

is nothing new to say; one of the greatest of all athletes, he was also a supreme judge of games, especially of cricket. Ever to be remembered is the fact that, on a Saturday in April 1902, he played for Southampton in the Cup Final; on the following Monday – still in April – he played for W. G. against Surrey and made 82.

In is not usually to be expected that an undergraduate should prove his greatness as a captain so early in life. Mitchell, Kemp and Page had done so: in 1896 H. D. G. Leveson Gower added himself to the list. Not only was he shrewd and imperturbable; he had also the supreme ability to make runs when runs were badly wanted. Oxford had a very good side that year, losing but two matches, but they had to struggle at Lord's and Leveson Gower played a great game in the last innings. Moreover, he had kept G. O. Smith in the side after meaning to drop him – and Smith's 2nd innings is a part of cricket history.

The year 1900 marks in a sense the end of an era. Oxford were undefeated that year, and this is the very last time that a University side could made such a boast. They had 7 first-class batsmen, with Martyn to keep wicket; but they had only one real bowler, Bosanquet, and he failed at Lord's. Foster had an incredible season: he scored 930 runs with an average of 77 and made 5 hundreds, of which the highest were 171 in 3 hours against Cambridge, and 169 v London County in the Parks. In the course of this innings he hit W. G. for 4 consecutive sixes. The best of the Oxford victories was that over Sussex on a very bad Christ Church wicket.

From 1901 to 1914 Oxford for the most part fared indifferently. Only 5 of the 14 'Varsity Matches were won and, on the whole, it was not an age of great cricketers in the Parks. But there were some brilliant exceptions: first of all, there was Oxford's greatest all-rounder to date, W. H. B. Evans, the 1st Oxonian to make 1,000 runs and take 100 wickets for the University (H. V. Page missed this distinction by a few wickets). Evans was a batsman of the authentic Malvern style, not much inferior to R. E. Foster; he was a fast bowler of more than average ability and an excellent slip. J. E. Raphael was perhaps the best Oxford batsman of this period. He could play a solid, defensive game if necessary, but he once made 111 in 50 minutes v Worcester; and when he scored 201 v Yorkshire in 1904 (Hirst, Rhodes and Haigh were bowling), his 2nd hundred came in an hour. A. J. Evans, son of A. H. and cousin of W. H. B., was a beautiful batsman and an effective bowler, but was not very consistent. G. N. Foster and D. J. Knight carried on the Malvern tradition at Oxford.

There were 2 outstanding bowlers. H. A. Gilbert, fastish right-hand, bowled unchanged through the 'Varsity Match of 1907. In 1909 he took 8 for 71 against the Australians, bowling Trumper and Macartney, and was in reserve for the Edgbaston Test Match. P. R. Le Couteur was a leg-break and googly bowler, whose equal had not been seen at Oxford. On the strength of his remarkable innings against Cambridge in 1910 he could be rated an all-rounder, but in fact he made only 700 runs in his University career. In 1910 and 1911 he was a superb bowler, keeping his best performances in both years for the great match.

In 1914 Oxford had a good side; in 1915 they would have had a great one, starting the season with 8 or 9 blues. But when the curtain rose again, cricket, though this was not at once apparent, had suffered as profound a change as had the rest of our life.

In 1919 and 1920 it seemed likely, however, that cricket at Oxford would flourish as never before. The pre-war blues, M. Howell, D. J. Knight and F. C. G. Naumann, led Oxford to an unexpected win at Lord's. Then, after their departure, the 1920 side – like its counterpart at Cambridge – was studded with fine cricketers and future internationals. It was the first year of those great all-rounders G. T. S. Stevens and R. H. Bettington; the captain was F. W. Gilligan, of high repute among amateur wicket-keepers, and D. R. Jardine was the best of a very good lot of batsmen. Much success was enjoyed by this side, but heavy rain entirely ruined the 'Varsity Match.

From 1921 to 1936 Oxford had a poor time of it, at any rate as regards success against Cambridge. In those 16 seasons only 2 'Varsity Matches were won. One which should have been won was wantonly thrown away, 6 were drawn (one heroically), but only in one of these did Oxford seem likely to have been the ultimate winner. Stevens and Bettington finished triumphantly in 1923, but they were never replaced. For one season I. A. R. Peebles did wonders, but the bowling support he received was negligible, and at Lord's it was something worse than that. Yet there were great batsmen in those years, none greater than the Nawab of Pataudi, who in 1931 surpassed even the feats of R. E. Foster. He scored over 1,300 runs with an average of 93, making 6 hundreds, including the record score of 238 not out against Cambridge. Other fine batsmen were A. M. Crawley and E. R. T. Holmes; there were also N. S. Mitchell-Innes, who made over 3,000 runs for Oxford, R. C. M. Kimpton, A. Melville, B. W. Hone, H. G. Owen-Smith, F. G. H. Chalk and D. C. H. Townsend. There was no lack of entertainment in the Parks, but nearly always there was the lurking fear that the bowling would not be strong enough. There were wicket-keepers of high class in I. A. W. Gilliat, G. E. B. Abell, E. T. Benson and P. C. Oldfield, but the fielding all too often fell below the standard expected of a University side. Cambridge were as much on top in this department as Oxford had been sixty and seventy years earlier.

In 1937 there was a reversal of fortune, under the forceful captaincy of A. P. Singleton. More matches were won than ever before and the game was played with more dash and determination than had been seen in the Parks for years. The batting was strong and the fielding excellent; the bowling was often expensive, but D. H. Macindoe and R. F. H. Darwall-Smith made a fine opening pair. There were some remarkable feats of fast scoring: Mitchell-Innes on his first appearance of the season made 137 v Leicester in under 2 hours, and in the 2nd innings put on 163 with Kimpton in exactly 1 hour; J. N. Grover made a hundred before lunch in the University Match; and this match was finished by M. R. Barton and Kimpton scoring 68 in half an hour.

Some emphasis has been laid on this year because it was the first of a period of Oxford domination. It is true that things went awry the next year and that the 'Varsity Match was barely saved; but Oxford were building up a formidable side which enjoyed great success in 1939 and might, in 1940, have developed into one of the finest University teams of all time. The star batsman was J. M. Lomas (a Carthusian), who made 90 in each of his 'Varsity Matches and could, given life and health, have been an England cricketer. There were other fine batsmen and the bowling was good and varied. The prospects in July 1939, seemed to be bright indeed.

LEFT G. T. S. Stevens, captain of Oxford in 1922, one of the best all-round cricketers of the 1920s, was in the Ashes-winning side at the Oval in 1926.

RIGHT A. M. Crawley (Oxford 1927–1930) was one of the best University batsmen between the wars before enjoying a varied and successful career in politics, television and as an author.

After Hitler's war the Oxford domination continued for 6 years. In that period only one University Match was lost, and that loss was due less to the superiority of Cambridge than to a mixture of muddled thinking off the field and bad running on it. Even so, 1949 cannot be called an unsuccessful year, for Oxford were the only team to beat the New Zealanders and their other victims included Yorkshire and Middlesex, who finished the season as joint champions. To revert to 1946: two old blues returned and they were joined by M. P. Donnelly, whom some would call the greatest of all Oxford batsmen. In his 2 seasons at Oxford Donnelly made 2,400 runs with an average of 65; he scored 9 hundreds, including a truly glorious innings against Cambridge; and he was as good a fieldsman as could be found in all England. Small wonder that in those years the crowds in the Parks were the largest ever known there.

Notable cricketers in those early post-war years were H. A. Pawson (whose father had captained Oxford in 1910), W. G. Keighley and H. E. Webb as batsmen, P. A. Whitcombe as a bowler and A. H. Kardar and C. B. Van Ryneveld as all-rounders. Kardar is the only Oxonian to have scored 1,000 runs and taken 100 wickets for the University in three seasons. A little later there were other fine batsmen in M. B. Hofmeyr, D. B. Carr, P. D. S. Blake and B. Boobbyer, but of bowlers there was a shortage. R. V. Divecha, the Indian Test player, was easily the best; he bowled in two styles – orthodox in-swingers to start with, off-breaks when the shine was off the ball. Backed by superb fielding – the Oxford side of 1951 can scarcely have been surpassed in this respect – Divecha fairly won the University Match of that year. It was an unexpected triumph and it was the last for a long time.

After 1951 Oxford cricket entered a long and dark tunnel. It is sadly to be recorded that from 1952 until 1955 Oxford won not a single match (though only time saved Cambridge in 1954) and that in the seasons 1952–1957 they won but 6 matches out of 88 and lost 41. The trouble, as so often, was lack of bowlers. In M. C. Cowdrey and M. J. K. Smith, Oxford had 2 batsmen fit to rank with the best (both made 3,000 runs in 3 seasons and Smith scored a century at Lord's in each year). There were other good batsmen, such as C. C. P. Williams, A. C. Walton and J. P. Fellows-Smith, and J. M. Allan was a most useful all-rounder. But a glance at the bowling averages will reveal the terrible weakness of Oxford in the most important department of the game. The fielding, too, fell away.

After a bad beating in 1957, Oxford improved in 1958, under the thoughtful leadership of J. A. Bailey. They might not have lost to Cambridge, but for an injury to the captain on the last day. In 1959, under A. C. Smith's captaincy, they won at Lord's emphatically (and 5 other matches as well). Two men from the east, Javed Burki and Abbas Ali Baig, strengthened and brightened the batting. In 1960 they were joined by a third, another Nawab of Pataudi. The 1960 Cambridge match (A. C. Smith captain again) would probably have been won, but for the weather. D. M. Green, who later played successfully for Lancashire and Gloucestershire, and nearly for England, was another formidable batsman of this time.

Many say that the second Pataudi was an even better batsman than his father, but this can never be decided, because his eyesight was damaged in a motor-car accident shortly before the match of 1961, when he was captain. There was, partly in consequence, a dismal draw. In 1962 Oxford did rather better in another draw, but had no win that season.

Indeed, from 1960 to 1978 Oxford won only twice against Cambridge, which, small consolation though it is, was twice as many as Cambridge won against Oxford. All the rest were drawn. This has been a dismal period in the history of the University Match. The blame cannot be put on the English climate, though it has sometimes been unusually unkind. There has been a lack of challenge and chivalry, which, apart from other changing social circumstances, has done much to reduce the public appeal of the match. The reporter for *The Times* in 1978 suggested that it would do better if transferred to somewhere like Bletchley (where, incidentally, there is a very good cricket club, which would give it a hearty welcome).

Abbas Ali Baig at Old Trafford in 1959 scored 112 for India as an Oxford undergraduate. Aged 20 he is the youngest Indian Test centurion. He was one of the chief figures in Oxford's revival during his time.

Lest you think too much has been made of this run of draws, consider that from 1827 to 1898, of the 64 matches played, 2 were drawn. From 1899 to 1959, of 51 matches, 19 were drawn – only a little more than a third. So the 19 matches from 1960 to 1978 produced nearly half the total number of draws.

Oxford's wins came under R. M. C. Gilliat, in 1966, by an innings; and V. J. Marks, 10 years later. Gilliat subsequently confirmed himself, with Hampshire, as a good captain – good enough to be mentioned occasionally as a possibility for the England job. His Oxford side also beat Lancashire. Marks was also a player who had the ability to play for a county, and possibly to lead one. He was captain again in 1977, but the 1976 win over Cambridge was his only first-class victory. Perhaps his best moment came in 1978, when a brave, attacking innings at a critical time put Oxford in what should have been a commanding position – but for the rain.

The defeat in this period – and it was by an innings – came in 1972. This would have been a poor side at its best, even had it reached its best, though it won a county match, after a generous declaration by the Warwickshire captain, not altogether surprising since he was A. C. Smith. The Oxford captain, P. C. H. Jones, did what he could with what he had. Of the joint Oxford/Cambridge side which played the Australians (for to this the Universities were now reduced), only 3 were Oxonians. P. C. H. Jones was a Rhodesian. Extraordinarily, Oxford had Rhodesian captains in 6 consecutive seasons. There had been G. N. S. Ridley in 1967; he was a capable left-arm spinner, and his side had a thumping win against Somerset, who were visiting the Parks for the first time in 45 years. He was followed, in 1968 and 1969, by F. S. Goldstein, one of the best of Oxford's post-war batsmen. Both his University matches at least had tense finishes. His 1969 side beat Kent by a wicket, one of the odder results, since Kent had lost only 4 wickets in the match, and scored 560 runs.

Then came M. St J. Burton in 1970, and B. May in 1971, before Jones. Burton was an off-spinner, very useful when he was pitching it. May was a batsman who looked better than his averages. Burton did not win a first-class match, but May did, against Derbyshire on tour, playing the important innings himself on the last afternoon. The improved form of Oxford in 1971 was aided by the appointment of a coach, Jim Stewart, who got on with the lads well.

The Rhodesian era ended in 1973, but the captain's name was still Jones, though the initials were now A.K.C. Keith Jones came from Solihull and was not an outstanding cricketer but a hard-working one and a leader. In his year Oxfor beat Warwickshire, for the 2nd year running, and also won a Benson & Hedges match against Northamptonshire. This was at the time when the Universities participated in the competition separately and alternately. He scored 82 against Northamptonshire, which pretty well won the match. The Lord's match, however, was dull and slow.

Keith Jones had the advantage of Imran Khan playing in his side (he had been turned down for admission to Cambridge) and Imran was captain in 1974. He was a player capable of winning a University match almost by himself, and Oxford, with a win in the Parks against Northamptonshire (Imran scoring 170 and taking 7 wickets) were strong favourites. Imran won the toss and put Cambridge in, and that was the last adventurous thing that happened. Upon 3 fine days, 37 wickets fell, less than a thousand runs were scored, and Oxford, needing in the last innings 205 in 260 minutes, and only 31 in the last 8 overs, still with 3 wickets in hand, miserably declined to try.

V. J. Marks, an all-rounder who in 1976 led Oxford to their first victory at Lord's in 10 years.

Well, nothing could have been worse than that, and things have got a little better since. In 1975, under T. R. Glover (a famous name and initials, but as a batsman the word for him would be 'persevering') Oxford did not win a first-class match, but the Combined Universities – Glover captain – beat Worcestershire at Cambridge in the Benson & Hedges, and Northamptonshire at Oxford. These were resounding wins, but neither so good as the day in 1976 when, with Marks captain, they beat Yorkshire by 7 wickets at Barnsley.

Of recent Oxford batsmen, Tavaré and Pathmanathan have been of Test class. The men of quality still come along from time to time. There are also still the men of honest endeavour, such as Wingfield-Digby, who won his first Blue in 1971 and his last in 1977 (it takes a long time to become a parson nowadays). He was no flier, but he managed to take nearly a hundred wickets for the University, and was a comforting reminder of the zeal which – the occasional shining star apart – has maintained Oxford University cricket.

University Match

MICHAEL MELFORD

As the oldest first-class fixture, first played in 1827 and then in unbroken sequence – war years excepted – since 1838, the University Match has a distinction sometimes forgotten in the second half of the 20th century, though Oxford and Cambridge are still producing

Test cricketers. The glamour of the occasion may have been dimmed by counter-attractions and changed standards, the two Universities may have their cricket impaired by increased academic demands and unsympathetic admissions-tutors, but Cambridge especially have plenty of players whom the first-class counties are glad to take on their staffs in the vacation.

Yet it is a different world from that of 1827, and even from the 1930s and immediate post-war years, when this was still one of the big matches of the year at Lord's and a major social occasion.

The first match was played at Lord's, but it was not until 1851 that the University match settled down there for good. The nearest that it came to moving was in 1979, when, if Lord's had been unavailable because Middlesex were drawn at home in the Benson & Hedges Cup semi-final, Oxford and Cambridge, by their own wish, would have played each other at Arundel.

The fixture was started through the enterprise of Charles Wordsworth whose versatility was such that when he captained Oxford for the 2nd time 2 years later he batted with hands blistered from rowing in the University boat. The first match was drawn and so, because of rain, was that of 1844. It was another 44 years before there was another draw and it was 1899 before the next, which began a sequence of 3. In the early days bad pitches seem often to have given the bowlers a big advantage – not until 1870 was the first individual 100 made by W. Yardley. He made another 2 years later and no one else made 2 100s in the University match until H. J. Enthoven did so in successive years in the mid-1920s.

One other reason for the absence of draws was an agreement to play on until a result was achieved, as existed in Cobden's Match in 1870. Yardley made his 100 after Cambridge, 28 runs behind on 1st innings, had been 40 for 5 in the 2nd. Though 9 batsmen mustered only 31 runs between them, his stand with J. W. Dale meant that Oxford had to score 179 to win. At 7.30 they needed only 4 runs and had 3 wickets in hand. F. C. Cobden then bowled the over which brought him immortality. An over was then of 4 balls and, after conceding a run off his 1st ball, he finished the match with his last three balls to give Cambridge victory by 2 runs.

In the 1870s each side won 5 times. In 1875 it was Cambridge who lost their last three wickets abruptly, leaving Oxford the winners by 6 runs. The margins of 2 runs and 6 runs in these 2 matches remain the narrowest in the history of the University Match.

In between these 2 stirring contests, in 1871, S. E. Butler, a fast bowler operating on a rough pitch, took all 10 Cambridge wickets for 38 runs, followed by 5 in the 2nd innings. Twelve were bowled. No one else has taken all 10 wickets in over 150 years of this match.

The Cambridge side of 1878 is considered one of the strongest they have ever fielded. They beat the 1st Australian touring team by an innings and Oxford by 238 runs. At Lord's their outstanding player was a freshman from Marlborough, A. G. Steel, who made 44 not out and then, with accurate leg-spin, took 13 wickets for 73.

Alfred Lyttelton, who played in that match, was one of 6 of his name to play for Cambridge through the years. The 3 Studd brothers were in the sides of 1881 and 1882 and were captains in successive years but Oxford produced one of their strongest sides in 1884, beating the Australians and then Cambridge.

Yardley in his day had been second only to W. G. Grace as a batsman and players of the highest class were to be found in both sides in the 1880s. In 1889 the fast bowling of the redoubtable freshman S. M. J. Woods took 11 for 82 and started Cambridge on a run of three successive wins.

In 1900 R. E. Foster, the middle of three Foster brothers to play for Oxford, scored 170 which was the highest yet made in the match but was exceeded in 1904 by J. F. Marsh's 172 not out for Cambridge. It was to be another 27 years before this record was beaten – and then by 2 batsmen in the same match. There was an easy win for Oxford in 1910 when an Australian Rhodes Scholar P. R. Le Couteur made 160 and took 11 for 66. Two years later Cambridge won by 3 wickets, a match in which G. E. V. Crutchley, who was suffering from measles, scored 99 not out for Oxford.

Though Oxford won in 1919 and by an innings in 1923 when a thunderstorm put Cambridge at the mercy of 2 spinners, G. T. S. Stevens and R. H. Bettington, Cambridge fielded some immensely talented sides in the 1920s. The Ashtons and A. P. F. Chapman overlapped G. O. Allen, who, as a freshman, took 9 for 78 in the match. H. J. Enthoven made his 2 100s and in 1928 R. W. V. Robins scored 53 and 101 not out and took 8 wickets. That match had an exciting ending, for, with $1\frac{3}{4}$ hours left, Oxford, reduced to 114 for 7 by Robins and T. C. Longfield, seemed certain to lose. However, C. K. Hill-Wood batted through to the end, first with H. M. Garland-Wells and for the last half-hour with the No. 11, E. T. Benson.

In 1930 Oxford, again with only a draw in prospect, succumbed ignominiously in just over 2 hours in the last innings. Earlier in the day Cambridge had themselves been in some danger but had been rescued by E. T. Killick's fine 136. Their declaration, 306 ahead, left Oxford with only $2\frac{1}{2}$ hours batting. Oxford's bowling had relied largely on Ian Peebles who in 80 overs took 13 wickets, but their batting, beginning with A. M. Crawley, D. N. Moore and the Nawab of Pataudi and with Alan Melville at No. 6, looked far stronger. In the event they lost their last 7 wickets in under an hour.

Oxford put this straight in 1931, the year in which the previous highest individual innings was twice surpassed. A. T. Ratcliffe made 201 for Cambridge, but next day the Nawab of Pataudi countered with a brilliant innings of 238 not out. On the last day Cambridge were bowled out for 122 and Oxford won by 8 wickets. Both sides were well stocked with good players during the rest of the 1930s, among them F. G. H. Chalk, the Australian R. C. M. Kimpton, and N. S. Mitchell-Innes at Oxford; F. R. Brown, N. W. D. Yardley and P. A. Gibb at Cambridge. They won

The teams in the 1936 University Match, 5 of whom either were or became Test cricketers. They include 10 future county captains. Back row: J. N. Grover, N. W. D. Yardley, M. M. Walford, A. F. T. White, B. H. Belle, J. M. Brocklebank, M. R. Barton, W. Wooller, J. H. Dyson and R. P. Nelson; sitting: J. H. Cameron, J. W. Seamer, M. Tindall, N. S. Mitchell-Innes, H. T. Bartlett, A. P. Singleton, M. Jahangir Khan and R. F. H. Darwall-Smith; on ground: J. H. Pawle, P. A. Gibb, M. H. Matthews and W. Murray-Wood.

twice apiece. The most memorable match was the last of the era when in 1939 Cambridge, who might have followed on but were not asked to do so, were left to make 430 on the last day.

When they were 249 for 8 the match seemed almost over but P. J. Dickinson played a historic innings of 100, the 1st hundred in the match by a Cambridge freshman since 1887. With J. Webster, who at No. 10 had been elevated in the order since the 1st innings, he put on 95 in 95 minutes. Webster carried on in a last wicket stand of 40 and made 60 himself before he was bowled and Oxford had won by 45 runs a match often to be recalled with pleasure in the years before the fixture was resumed in 1946.

After the Second World War, as after the First, there were many fine players at both Universities, the outstanding being the New Zealander, Martin Donnelly, who had first come to England aged 19 as a member of the New Zealand touring team of 1937. His innings of 142 when Oxford won in 1946 was a classic which he followed with another of similar calibre for the Gentlemen a year later.

In 1939 the start of the University match had been switched to a Saturday which brought the first day's attendance slightly up – to 9,000. But if there had been a match in 1940 it would have reverted to Monday. In 1968, when the Oxford captain F. S. Goldstein, a Rhodesian, launched the match with a magnificent innings of 155 in the first 3½ hours, the total attendance for 3 days was 2,033 and it continued to decrease irrespective of the cricket played. In the television era interest in big events was fostered in most sports to the detriment of smaller events.

There were players such as Trevor Bailey and Douglas Insole at Cambridge in the 1940s and Bailey was employing all his defensive ability, later to become so well known, to save the 1948 match, when it rained. In the early 1950s Cambridge had outstanding sides containing Peter May, David Sheppard, Hubert Doggart, John Dewes, John Warr, Raman Subba Row, all of whom played for England, and F. C. M. Alexander who later captained West Indies. Yet in 1951, Oxford, with some talented games-playing South Africans, Murray Hofmeyr and Clive Van Ryneveld, as well as the Indian R. V. Divecha and Donald Carr, were still strong enough to win an unexpected victory by 21 runs over one of the most powerful Cambridge sides of all.

Colin Cowdrey played in his 1st University match in 1952 and made a splendid hundred in 1953, though in that year the 12 wickets of the Cambridge captain Robin Marlar, and Dennis Silk's 116 not out in the last innings, won Cambridge the match by 2 wickets. Silk made another hundred in the 1954 match, but in that year M. J. K. Smith, then a freshman, scored 201 not out for Oxford and followed it with a hundred in each of the next 2 years to become the only batsman to make 3 centuries in the University Match.

Good players continued to appear, among them the subsequent captains of Pakistan and India, Javed Burki and the young Nawab of Pataudi at Oxford, and 3 future England captains E. R. Dexter, A. R. Lewis and J. M. Brearley at Cambridge. However, when Cambridge won an overwhelming victory in 1979 it was only the 9th match not drawn in the last 30 and only the 3rd in the last 20. Year after year the match was marred by bad weather. Generally, too, the bowling was not strong enough to upset the batting on a good Lord's pitch. But the draws also derived from a preoccupation with not losing, especially in years when one side was obviously stronger than the other.

E. R. Dexter, Cambridge captain in 1958, playing at Lord's against Oxford, for whom A. C. Smith, captain in 1959–1960, is keeping wicket. The latter inspired a revival in Oxford cricket, his 1959 side beating Cambridge – and 4 counties into the bargain.

After the surprising win in 1951, Oxford won only 3 times in the next 27 years – in 1959 when David Sayer and Andrew Corran, fast and fast-medium respectively, took 15 wickets and again in 1966 and 1976. Each time they had exceptional captains, in A. C. Smith (Warwickshire) Richard Gilliat (Hampshire) and Victor Marks (Somerset), but also a fuller larder than usual of good players.

In the 1970s, the standards at both Universities rose under captains of the calibre of Marks and Alastair Hignell, but Cambridge's resources were better equipped to sustain them. Oxford had been so short of good-class English players in the years after Gilliat that they were captained for 6 successive years by Rhodesians. After the resurgence of the 1970s, they slipped back again and the heavy defeat at Lord's in 1979 reflected their overall weakness that season.

Three of Cambridge's 5 victories in 30 years were won in the 1950s, the first by Silk's innings, the others in 1957 and 1958 by sides including Ted Dexter. His 58 and 6 wickets in 1958 were his main contribution and, like Peter May a few years earlier, his great career included little success in the University Match.

Cambridge's win in 1957 by an innings and 186 runs was their biggest ever in the match and was won by a very good side captained by Gamini Goonesena from Ceylon. Though mainly a leg-spinner – he took 5 for 32 in this match – Goonesena made 211, the highest in the match by a Cambridge batsman, and shared in a 7th-wicket stand of 289 with G. W. Cook (111 not out), which is the highest for any wicket by either side in the match.

Goonesena's side included R. W. Barber, later to open the innings for England with success; Ian McLachlan, later 12th man for Australia; a good fast bowler, C. S. Smith; and O. S. Wheatley of Warwickshire and Glamorgan, whose 5 wickets for 15 were mainly responsible for bowling Oxford out for 92 on the 1st day.

Cambridge's win in 1972 under Majid Khan, later captain of Pakistan, was also by an innings and achieved so comfortably that the future England left-arm spinner Philippe Edmonds was not required to bowl a ball in the match.

First match 1827 Results: Cambridge University won 52, Oxford University won 45, 38 drawn

CAPTAINS SINCE 1946

OXFORD

1946	D. H. Macindoe
1947	M. P. Donnelly
1948	H. A. Pawson
1949	C. B. Van Ryneveld
1950	D. B. Carr
1951	M. B. Hofmeyr
1952	P. D. S. Blake
1953	A. L. Dowding
1954	M. C. Cowdrey
1955	C. C. P. Williams
1956	M. J. K. Smith
1957	A. C. Walton
1958	J. A. Bailey
1959, 1960	A. C. Smith
1961*, 1962	C. D. Drybrough
1963	Nawab of Pataudi
1964	D. R. Worsley
1965	J. D. Martin
1966	R. M. C. Gilliat
1967	G. N. S. Ridley
1968, 1969	F. S. Goldstein
1970	M. St. J. Burton
1971	B. May
1972	P. C. H. Jones
1973	A. K.C. Jones
1974	Imran Khan
1975	T. R. Glover
1976, 1977	V. J. Marks
1978	J. A. Claughton
1979	S. M. Clements

*Nawab of Pataudi appointed captain, unable to play owing to car accident

CAMBRIDGE

1946	P. E. Bodkin
1947	G. L. Willatt
1948	J. M. Mills
1949	D. J. Insole
1950	G. H. G. Doggart
1951	J. J. Warr
1952	D. S. Sheppard
1953	R. G. Marlar
1954	M. H. Bushby
1955	D. R. W. Silk
1956	M. E. L. Melluish
1957	G. Goonesena
1958	E. R. Dexter
1959	D. J. Green
1960	C. B. Howland
1961	D. Kirby
1962	A. R. Lewis
1963, 1964	J. M. Brearley
1965	R. C. White
1966	D. L. Murray
1967	S. G. Russell
1968	G. A. Cottrell
1969, 1970	A. M. Jorden
1971, 1972	Majid Khan
1973	P. H. Edmonds
1974	W. Snowden
1975	C. J. Aworth
1976	T. J. Murrills
1977, 1978	A. J. Hignell
1979	I. A. Greig

HIGHEST TOTALS

503 by Oxford 1900
432–9D by Cambridge 1936

LOWEST TOTALS

32 by Oxford 1878
39 by Cambridge 1858

HIGHEST INDIVIDUAL INNINGS

238* Nawab of Pataudi (Oxford) 1931
211 G. Goonesena (Cambridge) 1957

MOST RUNS IN THE MATCHES

M. J. K. Smith (Oxford) 477

MOST HUNDREDS IN THE MATCHES

M. J. K. Smith (Oxford) 3 1954–56

RECORD WICKET PARTNERSHIPS

1 K. J. Key and W. Rashleigh, 243, Oxford 1886
2 W. G. Keighley and H. A. Pawson, 226, Oxford 1947
3 A. T. Barber and E. R. T. Holmes, 183, Oxford 1927
4 D. C. H. Townsend and F. G. H. Chalk, 230, Oxford 1934
5 J. E. Raphael and E. L. Wright, 191, Oxford 1905
6 M. R. Jardine and V. T. Hill, 178, Oxford 1892
7 G. Goonesena and G. W. Cook, 289, Cambridge 1957
8 H. E. Webb and A. W. H. Mallett, 112, Oxford 1948
9 J. F. Marsh and F. J. V. Hopley, 97*, Cambridge 1905
10 W. J. H. Curwen and E. G. Martin, 90, Oxford 1906

ALL 10 WICKETS IN AN INNINGS

S. E. Butler (Oxford) 1871

HAT-TRICKS

F. C. Cobden, J. F. Ireland, R. G. H. Lowe, P. H. Martin, A. G. Steel 1 each (all of Cambridge)

UAU Cricket

REX HAZELDINE

The author traces the growth of cricket in the Universities (other than Oxford and Cambridge) of which there are 37 throughout England and Wales at which the game is now played.

It was as long ago as the First World War that a feeling grew up within the Universities and University Colleges of the north, midlands and Wales that some form of association was necessary to promote and improve the development of the various sports played within those Universities. In 1919 a body was constituted entitled 'The Inter-Varsity Athletic Board of England and Wales' and after many manipulations during the 1920s the Universities Athletic Union, or the UAU as it is usually called, was inaugurated in 1930. Thus the foundation was laid for the Universities to strive for and attain the high standard of performance in sport which they have achieved today. So emerged an association which now controls all sports in 37 Universities throughout England and Wales, although contact is also maintained with Oxford, Cambridge and London, which are non-affiliated Universities.

The Universities Athletic Union promotes championships for the Universities in membership and lays down strict terms and conditions for all sports. The Universities are grouped geographically into 4 divisions: East, West, South and Wales, and as far as the form of the cricket championship is concerned, each University must play each other member of the same division. Two points are awarded for a win and the 2 Universities with the highest number of points in each division proceed to the quarter-finals, semi-finals and final which are played on a knock-out basis. All matches including the final consist of one innings per team and are restricted to 60 overs each side. There are, of course, various provisions for matches affected by light or weather conditions.

These championship games are very keenly contested through all the stages up to and including the final. Since 1959 Loughborough have won the championship on no less than 7 occasions, the next being Manchester with 4 wins.

At national level UAU regularly play MCC and also have a long-standing fixture with Kent 2nd XI and in the past have included the Middlesex and Yorkshire 2nd XIs in the list. Usually these games are played in the early part of the season and at a time when county players are seeking match practice. These matches are always popular with the counties as the fieldsmen are usually young, fit athletes and the bowling is keen. The game accordingly provides very useful match practice. Consequently the county sides are frequently strengthened substantially by the inclusion of 1st XI players. Representative games are played also against British Colleges and British Polytechnics with an annual game between English Universities and Welsh Universities.

It would be a lapse if mention is not made of the British Universities Sports Federation (BUSF) Cricket Tournament played each year. The participants in this are teams representing Cambridge, Oxford, London, UAU, Irish, Scottish and Welsh Universities. The UAU have twice won this tournament.

The UAU fixture list also included a representative game against the Pakistan Touring side. This was a 2-day match at Colwyn Bay and, although they lost, the student side was certainly not disgraced. In all these games the cricket is played keenly and gives the UAU cricketer a vast and professional expertise in very competitive cricket. There is a genuine ambition by the students who are selected for the representative games to do well and so qualify to play in higher level cricket. This is as important as the enlargement of the experience gained and certainly is of inestimable benefit to their own University teams by the standard they set.

The UAU organize coaching courses each year, usually at Lilleshall and Bisham Abbey, and these are attended by some 50 to 60 students. In conjuction with the National Cricket Association, these courses are directed by members of the UAU Cricket Committee, some of whom are qualified NCA Advanced Coaches. The Committee, who are all members of various Universities, are also UAU team selectors, so there is an unambiguous relevance between the coaching and team selection and a direct link with the NCA. On the courses coaching is given by the NCA Advanced and National Coaches on all aspects and techniques of the game. New players, mainly 18-year old freshmen who show an aptitude for the game, are chosen for one of these courses. In addition many Universities manage to provide cricket coaches from their own resources, but there is prevalent amongst Universities the view that the amount of quality and suitable coaching could with advantage be increased everywhere.

All Universities have regular fixtures with local clubs and many of these include schools. Many enter a team in the local league. A number either lend or hire their facilities to local clubs and schools, particularly indoor nets in the winter, and there are several Universities which establish a basis for local coaching arrangements. Almost all cricketers are in the 18 to 22 age group (roughly one third being under 19 years old) and because of this fact provide an effective bridge at a high level between junior and senior cricket. This is a vital factor in bringing on highly promising cricketers in an orderly fashion and it prepares them for the more rigorous cut and thrust of county and Test cricket.

These Universities also form an invaluable link with Youth cricket through their postgraduate courses, most of which include cricket as one of the sports. Postgraduate students taking this course thereby are able to enter the teaching profession well qualified to coach schoolboys.

Of course the Universities have the usual problems of team selection such as injuries and other absences experienced by all cricket teams. But there are two additional problems at Universities which are fundamental. The first is the acute shortness of the playing period which cannot obviously begin until some date in April but must finish before the end of July. Superimposed on this, is that this period covers the time leading up to and during examinations. By its very nature cricket is a sport which demands time. Hence the choice of a team, both at University or representative level, can be exacting and difficult. Students consider it an honour to play but this does promote at times a conflict between their academic work and the game of cricket.

The game, whether played against local clubs or schools or for the Universities at representative level, is played at a high standard. In consequence the playing facilities and equipment must also be equally good. Cricket is one of the more expensive sports to run and it does mean some financial commitments and sacrifices on the part of the Universities and the students who are keen, indeed anxious, to succeed at the game. Amongst this considerable force can be included many household names who have joined the select band who have played for their country or their respective counties.

Loughborough has made a particularly strong contribution to first-class cricket because, in addition to Graham Barlow (Middlesex and England), Andy Stovold (Gloucestershire), Tony Borrington (Derbyshire), Trevor Tunnicliffe (Nottinghamshire), Tom Mottram (Hampshire), Paul Phillipson (Sussex), Peter Booth (Leicestershire) and Bob Clapp (Somerset) are all products of that College and now University.

Durham cricket too has proved very strong over the past decade, having produced such players for first-class cricket as Tony Good, Paul Allott and Graeme Fowler to Lancashire, Gehan Mendis to Sussex and Steve Henderson to Worcestershire. Frank Hayes (England and Lancashire) was a product of Sheffield University, but players of this calibre have been spread throughout other Universities with such names springing to mind as Ian Hall (Birmingham University) with Derbyshire, John Whitehouse (Bristol University) captain of Warwickshire (1978 and 1979) and Peter Whiteley from the same University with the Yorkshire team. Mike Selvey (Manchester University) plays for Middlesex, and is an England Test player. But not only are this country's players catered for, Deryck Murray, the West Indies wicket-keeper, captained the UAU when he was at Nottingham University.

The Captain of UAU Cricket in 1978, David Partridge (Bradford University), is a Gloucestershire cricketer, and the 1979 captain, Paul Downton (Exeter University), was chosen as reserve wicket-keeper for the 1977–78 England tour of Australia and has been awarded his Kent cap. All these have played in representative games for the UAU. This is not by any means a complete list of names but the quality of each player is an indication of the prevailing standard of cricket through which he has passed during this part of his career.

The UAU Cricket Championship has been dominated mainly during recent times by 4 Universities, Loughborough, Manchester (winners in 1978 and 1979), Southampton and Durham, but a very pleasing trend is growing right across the board. Whereas previously some Universities were considered to be easy opponents, this picture is now changing with cricket growing stronger with increasing competition from these Universities.

The record over the years shows clearly the marked contribution which the Universities have made to senior cricket in this country but it must be added that the organization of the UAU, which now fosters cricket at 37 Universities, has fulfilled a much-needed want in the development of the skills and tactics of the game.

Minor Counties Cricket Association

R. A. C. FORRESTER

At the suggestion of Worcestershire, not then a first-class county, a meeting was held in March 1895 at the Queen's Hotel Birmingham, at which the Minor Counties Cricket Association was formed. The Rules provide that all counties not in the first-class (as classified by MCC, later the TCCB) and the 2nd XIs of first-class counties are eligible to join the Association upon payment of an annual subscription and are entitled to compete in the Second Division of the County Championship (the Minor Counties competition). This is subject to every county arranging out and home 2-day matches with at least 4 other counties. In the 1970s the average number of such opponents is 5 and the total has seldom exceeded 8. The competition began in 1895, Worcestershire being the winners in each of the first 4 years, and has continued until the present time (except during the 2 World Wars).

The first Chairman was C. Pigg (Herts) and, after 4 men had held office for short periods, R. H. Mallett (Durham) was in the chair from 1909 to 1931, K. C. Raikes (Monmouth) 1932–1939, W. B. Franklin (Bucks) 1945–1957, H. R. Neate (Bedford) 1958–1964 and R. A. C. Forrester (Wilts) since then. There was no president until 1937, when R. H. Mallett was elected; to be followed by Sir Pelham Warner, W. B. Franklin and Sir Cyril Hawker, who has been in office since 1969. The early secretarial duties were principally carried out by R. H. Mallett and Dr J. Earl Norman (Herts), who were followed by R. C. Campbell (Devon) from 1927 to 1944, Frank Crompton (Bedford) 1944–1970 and latterly Laurance Hancock (Staffs).

MCCA had 3 representatives on the former Advisory County Cricket Committee and 2 on the Test Match Board of Control. Since the reorganization of 1968, it has had 1 representative on the Cricket Council and 2 on the TCCB, all with full voting powers. It has also one representative on several of the TCCB Committees, the NCA and National Playing Fields Association.

Minor county cricketers have to be qualified by the same rules as those affecting first-class cricketers and have to comply with the same code of discipline. Umpires, who have to be nominated by first- or second-class counties, are elected by the Minor County captains at a meeting chaired by the Secretary of TCCB and the selectors have before them the reports from each match of the previous season. Reports upon the condition of pitches and number of overs bowled per hour are sent to the Secretary of MCCA after each match.

After the formation of the 2nd XIs competition in 1959 many first-class counties withdrew their 2nd XIs from the Minor Counties' competition so that by 1979 only Lancashire and Somerset remained. The championship has been won 23 times by 2nd XIs, Lancashire winning 7 times and Yorkshire 5. Of the Minor Counties, Bucks have won 8 times, Staffordshire and Durham each 6 times and Norfolk 4; but Cornwall, Cumberland, Dorset and Northumberland have not yet succeeded. Devon won for the 1st time in 1978. During its long history there have been several methods of organizing the competition, but during the last 50 years each county has had freedom of choice of opponents, although usually the opposition comes from the same geographical area in order to save expense.

The present award of points is 10 for a win, or win in a 1 innings match played on the 2nd day when there has been no play on the 1st; 3 points for a 1st-innings lead determined by the result after each side has bowled not more than 55 overs; and 2 points when there is no result. Seven hours are allocated for play each day.

Since 1964 the 1st 5 minor counties in the championship table of the preceding year have competed in the Gillette Cup competition. By the end of the 1978 season, 3 victories over first-class counties had been achieved, Durham beating Yorkshire, Lincolnshire beating Glamorgan and Hertfordshire beating Essex. Only Cumberland have so far not gained a place in the Cup in one or more years. Keen competition for the first 5 places has brought life to the Minor Counties Championship.

Since 1972 MCCA has had 2 teams in the Benson & Hedges Cup competition. One is selected from the 9 northern counties and the other from the 10 southern. No match has yet been won, but a very close finish against Leicestershire in 1978 resulted in the MCCA XI receiving the 'Team of the Week' award from the sponsors, the first time a losing side had received it. For many years MCCA has played the overseas side touring in England and when 3 days are allotted the match is first-class. The Selection Committee's policy of recent years has built up an experienced team, which has been well led first by F. W. Millett for several years, and then for the last 5 years by D. Bailey, both from Cheshire.

The Australians were beaten at Sunderland in 1977 and the New Zealanders at Torquay in 1978, both after sporting declarations which underestimated the ability of Minor County batsmen to score over 200 in the 4th innings of the matches. In January 1978 a fully representative team, under the cap-

C. G. Howard, Honorary Treasurer of MCCA, was successively Secretary of Lancashire and Surrey, and in 1954–55 managed Leonard Hutton's successful MCC tour to Australia and New Zealand.

taincy of D. Bailey and the management of C. G. Howard (now the honorary Treasurer of MCCA after his Secretaryship of Surrey) successfully and happily toured Kenya, the 1st overseas tour MCCA have attempted.

During the 84 years of the Minor Counties competition Worcestershire, Northamptonshire and Glamorgan have been promoted to the first-class. There have been a number of cricketers who, first playing for a minor county, have later played for England, among these being a famous captain A. P. F. Chapman and H. E. Dollery (Berks) and W. J. Edrich (Norfolk). Many cricketers have been transferred from minor to first-class counties and some have returned after the end of their first-class careers. There have also been players of first-class ability who have played all their county cricket for a minor county, among them being M. Falcon (Norfolk); W. B. Franklin and F. Edwards (Bucks); B. W. Hone (later Sir Brian) formerly of South Australia and captain of Oxford, and G. S. Butler, both for Wiltshire. Ben Barnett, a former Australian Test Match wicket-keeper, was captain of Bucks for several years.

MOST RUNS IN A SEASON

1212 A. F. Brazier, Surrey II 1949
1097 K. F. Barrington, Surrey II 1952
1068 R. M. James, Berkshire 1962
1067 R. C. E. Pratt, Surrey II 1952
1031 E. G. Witherden, Norfolk 1959
1025 M. M. Walford, Dorset 1955
1024 J. T. Ikin, Staffordshire 1961
1015 N. V. H. Riches, Glamorgan 1911
1011 C. Lever, Bucks 1964

RECORD WICKET PARTNERSHIPS

1 D. F. Walker and H. E. Theobold, 323, Norfolk v Northumberland, Norwich 1939
2 T. H. Clark and A. F. Brazier, 388*, Surrey II v Sussex II, Oval 1949
3 R. Harris and J. W. Murphy, 329, Cornwall v Berkshire, Camborne 1954
4 J. L. Swann and A. W. Thompson, 293, Middlesex II v Surrey II, Oval 1952
5 J. A. Sutton and G. C. Hardstaff, 271*, Cheshire v Shropshire, Northwich 1969
6 D. J. Carnill and L. Bateman, 333*, Hertfordshire v Norfolk, Norwich 1953
7 H. S. Harrison and W. C. Smith, 274, Surrey II v Bucks, Reigate 1908
8 L. Horridge and W. Farrimond, 243, Lancashire II v Yorkshire II, Old Trafford 1930
9 H. L. Hever and F. Phillips, 195, Kent II v Surrey II, Oval 1927
10 G. Rogers and F. Whiting, 185, Cornwall v Dorset, Camborne 1931

MOST WICKETS IN A MATCH

18–100 N. W. Harding, Kent II v Wiltshire, Swindon 1937
17–65 D. J. Laitt, Oxfordshire v Somerset II, Taunton 1970
17–74 H. E. White, Hertfordshire v Bedfordshire, St Albans 1909
17–82 S. F. Barnes, Staffordshire v Durham, South Shields 1911

MOST WICKETS IN A SEASON

119 S. F. Barnes, Staffordshire 1906
104 F. Edwards, Bucks 1923
103 H. Creber, Glamorgan 1906
103 M. J. Hilton, Lancashire II 1949
100 G. J. Thompson, Northants 1902
100 H. Creber, Glamorgan 1905

ALL 10 WICKETS IN AN INNINGS (FOR UNDER 30 RUNS)

G. J.W. Platt, 10–15 Surrey II v Dorset, Dorchester 1908
M. E. Ashenden, 10–15 Bedfordshire v Shropshire, Luton 1958
C. G. Perkins, 10–23 Suffolk v Hertfordshire, Felixstowe 1960
G. R. Langdale, 10–25 Berkshire v Dorset, Reading 1953
S. F. Barnes, 10–26 Staffordshire v Yorkshire II, Wakefield 1907
F. Whiting, 10–26 Cornwall v Wiltshire, Trowbridge 1921
M. G. Kilvington, 10–26 Dorset v Cornwall, Wadebridge 1969
D. J. Halfyard, 10–29 Cornwall v Dorset, Penzance 1974

CHAMPIONS SINCE 1946

1946 Suffolk
1947 Yorkshire II
1948 Lancashire II
1949 Lancashire II
1950 Surrey II
1951 Kent II
1952 Bucks
1953 Berkshire
1954 Surrey II
1955 Surrey II
1956 Kent II
1957 Yorkshire II
1958 Yorkshire II
1959 Warwickshire II
1960 Lancashire II
1961 Somerset II
1962 Warwickshire II
1963 Cambridgeshire
1964 Lancashire II
1965 Somerset II
1966 Lincolnshire
1967 Cheshire
1968 Yorkshire II
1969 Bucks
1970 Bedfordshire
1971 Yorkshire II
1972 Bedfordshire
1973 Shropshire
1974 Oxfordshire
1975 Hertfordshire
1976 Durham
1977 Suffolk
1978 Devon
1979 Suffolk

HIGHEST TOTALS

621 Surrey II v Devon, Oval 1928
550-5D Surrey II v Norfolk, Oval 1925
540 Glamorgan v Devon, Exeter 1907

LOWEST TOTALS

14 Cheshire v Staffordshire, Stoke on Trent 1909
15 Kent II v Bucks, Bletchley 1925
19 Denbighshire v Staffordshire, Porthill 1930
19 Bedfordshire v Cambridgeshire, Chatteris 1971

HIGHEST INDIVIDUAL INNINGS

282 E. Garnett, Berkshire v Wiltshire, Reading 1908
254 H. E. Morgan, Glamorgan v Monmouthshire, Cardiff 1901
253* G. J. Whittaker, Surrey II v Gloucestershire II, Oval 1950
253 A. Booth, Lancashire II v Lincolnshire, Grimsby 1950
252 J. A. Deed, Kent II v Surrey II, Oval 1924

SECOND ELEVEN CHAMPIONSHIP PLACINGS 1959–1979

	DERBYSHIRE	ESSEX	GLAMORGAN	GLOUCESTERSHIRE	HAMPSHIRE	KENT	LANCASHIRE	LEICESTERSHIRE	MIDDLESEX	NORTHAMPTONSHIRE	NOTTINGHAMSHIRE	SOMERSET	SURREY	SUSSEX	WARWICKSHIRE	WORCESTERSHIRE	YORKSHIRE	GLOUCESTERSHIRE AND SOMERSET
1959	15	16	8	1	12	13	4	14	3	2	17	11	9	6	5	10	7	*
1960	5	2	4	12	10	6	13	9	8	1	17	16	3	15	11	7	14	*
1961	10	3	5	*	9	1	13	2	8	6	14	16	12	15	7	4	11	*
1962	15	13	9	7	6	3	10	8	12	14	16	11	2	4	5	1	*	*
1963	14	6	5	10	15	4	12	16	9	2	11	13	3	8	7	1	*	*
1964	11	6	5	16	8	14	1	3	13	4	15	12	7	9	10	2	*	*
1965	14	5	1	2	15	9	11	6	16	10	4	3	13	8	12	7	*	*
1966	15	14	6	11	4	10	7	13	5	16	3	2	1	8	9	12	*	*
1967	11	15	2	*	1	4	8	12	13	3	9	*	7	6	14	5	*	10
1968	4	15	6	*	3	7	13	5	9	10	11	*	1	2	8	14	*	12
1969	7	13	6	9	8	1	12	4	3	5	11	*	2	14	10	15	*	*
1970	13	6	7	2	3	1	8	5	15	10	12	*	4	14	9	11	*	*
1971	14	*	13	4	1	3	12	9	8	2	5	*	7	10	6	11	*	*
1972	10	9	15	14	6	11	12	7	5	4	1	*	2	13	3	8	*	*
1973	12	1	2	14	13	7	10	5	6	11	9	*	3	4	8	15	*	*
1974	9	2	11	14	6	10	5	15	1	8	7	*	3	4	12	13	*	*
1975	*	13	11	9	8	10	7	2	5	14	15	16	1	3	6	12	4	*
1976	*	6	8	12	11	1	14	9	4	3	7	13	10	2	15	16	5	*
1977	6	15	14	9	3	2	4	10	7	13	12	16	17	5	8	11	1	*
1978	16	2	12	17	6	13	3	7	14	15	8	10	11	1	4	9	5	*
1979	15	9	8	10	11	5	6	14	2	17	7	16	13	4	1	12	3	*

CHAMPIONSHIP WINNERS

1959 Gloucester II
1960 Northants II
1961 Kent II
1962 Worcester II
1963 Worcester II
1964 Lancashire II
1965 Glamorgan II
1966 Surrey II
1967 Hampshire II
1968 Surrey II
1969 Kent II
1970 Kent II
1971 Hampshire II
1972 Notts II
1973 Essex II
1974 Middlesex II
1975 Surrey II
1976 Kent II
1977 Yorkshire II
1978 Sussex II
1979 Warwicks II

MINOR COUNTIES PLACINGS 1895–1979

	BEDFORDSHIRE	BERKSHIRE	BUCKS	CAMBRIDGESHIRE	CARMARTHENSHIRE	CHESHIRE	CORNWALL	CUMBERLAND	DENBIGHSHIRE	DERBY II	DEVON	DORSET	DURHAM	ESSEX II	GLAMORGAN	GLAMORGAN II	GLOUCESTER II	HAMPSHIRE II	HERTFORDSHIRE	KENT II	LANCASHIRE II	LEICESTER II	LINCOLNSHIRE	MIDDLESEX II	MONMOUTHSHIRE	NORFOLK	NORTHAMPTONSHIRE	NORTHAMPTONSHIRE II	NORTHUMBERLAND	NOTTS II	OXFORDSHIRE	SHROPSHIRE	SOMERSET II	STAFFORDSHIRE	SUFFOLK	SURREY II	SUSSEX II	WARWICKSHIRE II	WILTSHIRE	WORCESTERSHIRE	WORCESTERSHIRE II	YORKSHIRE II
1895	4	*	*	*	*	*	*	*	*	*	*	*	2	*	*	*	*	*	6	*	*	*	*	*	*	1	*	*	*	*	5	*	*	7	*	*	*	*	*	3	*	*
1896	*	6	2	*	*	*	*	*	*	*	*	*	*	*	*	*	*	*	3	*	*	*	*	*	*	*	4	*	5	*	7	*	*	*	*	*	*	*	*	1	*	*
1897	*	8	4	*	*	*	*	*	*	*	*	*	3	*	2	*	*	*	10	*	*	*	*	*	*	6	9	*	7	*	*	*	*	*	*	*	*	*	5	1	*	*
1898	*	2	2	6	*	*	*	*	*	*	*	*	*	*	4	*	*	*	9	*	*	*	*	*	*	4	2	*	*	*	*	*	*	*	*	*	*	*	8	1	*	*
1899	*	10	1	11	*	*	*	*	*	*	*	*	7	*	3	*	*	*	6	*	*	*	*	*	*	5	1	*	8	*	*	*	*	*	*	3	*	*	9	*	*	*
1900	8	10	4	11	*	*	*	*	*	*	*	*	1	*	1	*	*	*	11	*	*	*	*	*	*	11	1	*	4	*	6	*	*	11	*	9	*	*	6	*	*	*
1901	14	14	3	5	*	*	*	*	*	*	14	*	1	*	5	*	*	*	11	*	*	*	*	*	12	14	4	*	12	*	7	*	*	10	*	2	*	*	9	*	*	7
1902	12	14	6	*	*	*	*	*	*	*	9	16	8	*	4	*	*	*	7	*	*	*	*	*	13	*	3	*	15	*	9	*	*	5	*	2	*	*	1	*	*	9
1903	4	13	10	10	*	*	*	*	*	*	16	17	2	*	4	*	*	*	8	*	*	*	*	*	7	*	1	*	4	*	15	*	*	14	*	8	*	*	3	*	*	10
1904	9	18	10	10	*	*	19	*	*	*	10	20	4	*	3	*	*	*	6	*	*	*	*	*	15	16	1	*	10	*	8	*	*	7	14	17	*	*	2	*	*	5
1905	7	17	8	13	*	*	17	*	*	*	3	14	5	*	8	*	*	*	12	*	*	*	*	*	2	1	*	*	14	*	17	*	*	10	10	14	*	*	4	*	*	6
1906	3	4	15	15	*	*	17	*	*	*	2	12	8	*	8	*	*	*	7	*	19	*	*	*	11	8	*	*	20	*	17	*	*	1	14	4	*	*	13	*	*	6
1907	13	9	18	16	*	*	17	*	*	*	8	13	10	*	2	*	*	*	3	*	1	*	15	*	19	6	*	*	19	*	*	*	*	5	11	3	*	*	6	*	21	12
1908	9	17	16	20	21	*	17	*	*	*	5	14	8	*	2	*	*	*	3	*	17	*	12	*	5	14	*	*	12	*	*	*	*	1	9	5	*	*	3	*	*	11
1909	11	22	17	16	21	20	17	*	*	*	6	10	12	*	2	*	*	*	9	*	*	*	3	*	12	14	*	*	19	3	*	*	*	7	15	5	*	*	1	*	*	7
1910	17	2	21	21	12	19	17	*	*	*	14	16	11	*	3	*	*	*	12	*	*	*	10	*	4	1	*	*	8	14	*	*	*	9	4	6	*	*	20	*	*	7
1911	7	3	15	10	21	19	18	*	*	*	17	13	6	*	5	*	*	*	9	4	*	*	14	*	7	16	*	*	11	*	*	*	*	1	12	2	*	*	20	*	*	*
1912	18	15	4	16	*	20	8	*	*	*	8	13	6	*	10	*	*	*	5	11	*	*	11	*	16	2	*	*	6	*	*	*	*	2	19	3	*	*	14	*	*	*
1913	8	10	16	16	*	15	14	*	*	*	13	10	5	*	2	*	*	*	3	19	*	*	7	*	12	1	*	*	6	*	*	*	*	4	20	9	*	*	16	*	*	*
1914	17	17	8	16	*	12	11	*	*	*	3	21	13	19	6	*	*	*	2	5	*	*	8	*	14	6	*	*	15	*	*	*	*	1	20	8	*	*	4	*	*	*
1920	12	2	4	*	*	7	*	*	*	*	8	16	11	15	6	*	*	*	9	2	*	*	*	*	*	5	*	*	13	*	*	*	*	1	*	14	*	*	10	*	*	*
1921	18	2	8	19	*	3	13	*	*	*	6	14	15	*	*	*	*	*	11	7	17	*	*	*	16	4	*	*	12	*	*	*	*	1	*	10	*	*	9	*	*	5
1922	16	3	1	20	*	8	13	*	*	*	6	4	10	*	*	*	*	*	11	5	7	*	*	*	15	2	*	*	14	*	18	*	*	12	*	19	*	*	17	*	*	9
1923	8	6	1	20	*	12	14	*	*	*	13	3	17	*	*	*	*	*	7	8	11	*	*	*	18	16	*	*	3	*	18	*	*	5	*	2	*	*	14	*	*	10
1924	19	1	4	23	*	11	16	*	*	*	9	10	20	*	*	*	·	*	5	8	11	11	22	*	21	6	*	*	2	17	18	*	*	6	*	15	*	*	3	*	*	14
1925	22	7	1	16	*	23	9	*	*	*	17	10	13	*	*	*	*	*	4	7	3	5	20	*	21	6	*	*	2	18	14	*	*	10	*	12	*	*	18	*	*	15
1926	16	12	2	18	*	14	17	*	*	*	2	11	1	*	*	*	*	*	13	10	8	6	22	*	23	20	*	*	19	21	2	*	*	7	*	5	*	*	14	*	*	9
1927	19	8	3	17	*	23	10	*	*	*	5	13	4	*	*	*	*	*	9	22	16	17	21	*	10	12	*	*	15	2	14	*	*	1	*	6	*	*	6	*	*	20
1928	17	1	5	18	*	22	7	*	*	*	15	19	3	*	*	*	*	*	8	14	2	20	9	*	23	9	*	*	11	16	11	*	*	4	*	6	*	*	11	*	*	21
1929	18	13	2	23	*	10	21	*	*	*	14	7	11	*	*	*	*	*	8	9	4	20	16	*	22	15	*	*	11	19	1	*	*	5	*	3	*	*	17	*	*	6
1930	12	12	4	11	*	9	10	*	23	*	17	17	1	*	*	*	*	*	7	15	3	*	16	*	22	19	*	*	21	14	5	*	*	7	*	2	*	*	6	*	*	20
1931	12	14	3	17	*	19	17	*	25	*	23	14	5	*	*	*	*	*	13	11	4	1	20	*	24	10	*	*	21	21	8	*	*	7	*	2	*	14	9	*	*	6
1932	23	2	1	9	*	20	21	*	*	*	15	5	7	*	*	*	*	*	11	8	16	12	22	*	19	17	*	*	10	*	18	*	*	4	*	6	*	14	13	*	*	3
1933	22	4	15	8	*	10	18	*	23	*	20	12	10	*	*	*	*	*	5	13	6	*	19	*	21	1	*	*	16	*	14	*	*	16	*	7	*	8	2	*	*	3
1934	21	11	16	6	*	11	20	*	23	*	8	7	4	*	*	*	*	*	10	18	1	*	11	*	22	3	*	*	15	*	5	*	*	14	19	2	*	*	16	*	*	8
1935	21	17	9	14	*	4	23	*	24	*	10	12	7	*	*	15	*	*	2	20	5	*	19	1	*	3	*	*	6	*	12	*	*	16	11	8	*	*	22	*	*	18
1936	16	19	20	6	*	18	22	*	*	*	15	12	21	*	*	8	*	*	1	16	3	*	19	5	*	2	*	*	14	*	11	*	*	6	23	9	*	*	4	*	*	13
1937	4	17	7	21	*	19	22	*	*	*	17	6	16	*	*	9	*	*	3	12	1	*	14	8	*	10	*	*	4	*	11	*	*	15	23	2	*	*	20	*	*	13
1938	14	21	1	11	*	20	4	*	*	*	13	17	5	*	*	*	12	*	6	15	2	*	17	9	*	8	*	*	17	*	15	*	*	10	23	3	*	*	22	*	*	7
1939	15	21	4	13	*	5	9	*	*	*	14	6	18	*	*	*	22	*	10	12	2	*	19	*	*	7	*	*	16	*	20	*	*	11	3	1	*	*	17	*	*	8
1946	7	17	1	15	*	10	8	*	*	*	12	8	12	*	*	*	*	*	6	*	11	*	16	*	*	26	*	*	18	*	5	*	*	4	2	*	*	*	*	*	*	3
1947	7	10	13	11	*	20	20	20	*	*	12	16	7	*	*	*	17	*	14	9	3	*	22	*	*	18	*	*	23	19	6	*	*	4	5	1	*	*	14	*	*	2
1948	2	8	23	27	*	25	22	*	*	21	17	5	16	7	*	26	11	*	13	12	1	*	9	*	*	24	*	*	18	28	6	*	*	15	14	10	18	*	20	*	3	4
1949	10	13	6	23	*	31	29	*	*	25	33	14	16	15	*	28	5	3	7	22	1	*	26	12	*	27	*	*	20	21	2	*	*	3	19	8	18	11	30	*	17	9
1950	2	25	12	29	*	17	32	*	*	17	14	16	22	5	*	4	28	11	7	13	9	*	6	27	*	30	*	20	25	21	15	*	*	10	19	1	23	3	24	*	31	8
1951	25	15	9	23	*	20	18	*	*	27	19	14	4	26	*	*	*	16	13	1	2	*	24	5	*	28	*	11	17	22	7	*	*	9	3	6	29	21	30	*	12	8
1952	19	4	1	9	*	27	26	*	*	*	14	15	10	22	*	*	*	24	11	2	5	*	21	7	*	18	*	23	13	25	17	*	*	8	15	3	*	6	19	*	*	12
1953	18	1	2	19	*	22	4	*	*	*	10	22	26	14	*	*	*	*	16	9	3	*	12	4	*	15	*	12	7	20	24	*	*	10	21	6	*	7	25	*	*	16
1954	10	33	2	24	*	13	17	*	*	*	4	18	5	9	*	*	*	*	25	8	11	*	20	22	*	20	*	16	6	3	6	*	*	14	15	1	*	12	26	*	*	18
1955	5	24	12	16	*	29	21	30	*	25	23	17	3	18	*	*	*	*	6	7	10	26	27	8	*	11	*	9	2	20	19	*	4	13	22	1	*	14	28	*	*	15
1956	24	11	7	4	*	30	22	26	*	21	23	19	14	28	*	*	*	*	15	1	8	16	16	9	*	29	*	12	2	3	27	*	5	16	24	9	*	13	20	*	*	6
1957	29	4	19	9	*	27	25	30	*	32	17	13	15	22	*	*	14	*	7	23	8	10	25	6	*	28	*	12	21	11	16	30	3	18	5	24	*	2	20	*	*	1
1958	5	23	12	13	*	32	27	30	*	29	17	21	21	3	*	*	11	*	20	23	4	28	23	10	*	26	*	7	19	14	2	30	6	8	15	18	*	9	15	*	*	1
1959	13	25	13	4	*	26	26	28	*	*	11	3	19	17	*	*	16	*	6	*	2	23	22	*	*	7	*	12	21	10	20	24	9	18	15	*	*	1	7	*	*	5
1960	14	12	3	15	*	6	23	20	*	*	9	24	18	*	*	*	*	*	20	*	1	*	10	*	*	2	*	*	19	22	7	13	8	16	4	*	*	17	11	*	*	5
1961	13	5	4	14	*	6	22	23	*	*	17	16	15	*	*	*	*	*	9	*	11	*	19	*	*	20	*	*	21	*	2	12	1	7	10	*	-	8	18	*	*	3
1962	15	12	9	21	*	16	22	23	*	*	17	11	7	*	*	*	*	*	4	*	2	*	6	*	*	8	*	*	19	*	20	18	5	13	14	*	*	1	9	*	*	3
1963	11	9	16	1	*	8	17	23	*	*	13	20	5	*	*	*	*	*	3	*	5	*	10	*	*	19	*	*	22	*	15	20	4	18	14	*	*	5	2	*	*	11
1964	18	8	7	3	*	13	14	23	*	*	11	21	9	*	*	*	*	*	19	*	1	*	15	*	*	9	*	*	24	*	16	21	12	17	20	*	*	6	2	*	*	5
1965	15	8	11	17	*	5	16	23	*	*	19	17	10	*	*	*	*	*	8	*	12	*	3	*	*	21	*	*	13	*	15	22	1	20	7	*	*	4	14	*	*	6
1966	7	14	22	4	*	12	21	23	*	*	13	19	9	*	*	*	*	*	16	*	6	*	1	*	*	11	*	*	17	*	8	24	2	17	15	*	*	5	19	*	*	10
1967	7	12	14	13	*	1	16	20	*	*	14	4	6	*	*	*	*	*	10	*	9	*	11	*	*	5	*	*	22	*	19	22	3	18	16	*	*	2	20	*	*	8
1968	14	16	3	11	*	11	15	21	*	*	2	8	9	*	*	*	*	*	6	*	20	*	18	*	*	4	*	*	7	*	18	17	*	11	22	*	*	10	5	*	*	1
1969	2	16	1	20	*	13	3	18	*	*	9	11	19	*	*	*	*	*	12	*	10	*	15	*	*	5	*	*	8	*	5	21	22	7	17	*	*	*	13	*	*	4
1970	1	15	8	22	*	14	20	13	*	*	11	17	10	*	*	*	*	*	5	*	16	*	2	*	*	12	*	*	4	*	5	19	5	3	21	*	*	*	18	*	*	9
1971	18	15	7	4	*	9	21	20	*	*	19	13	2	*	*	*	*	*	7	*	10	*	16	*	*	22	*	*	17	*	6	12	2	11	14	*	*	*	5	*	*	1
1972	1	11	10	13	*	7	22	14	*	*	14	5	4	*	*	*	*	*	12	*	14	*	8	*	*	20	*	*	14	*	19	14	9	3	21	*	*	*	6	*	*	2
1973	19	16	4	14	*	17	21	22	*	*	8	9	7	*	*	*	*		5	*	3	*	6	*	*	18	*	*	15	*	10	1	2	20	13	*	*	*	10	*	*	12
1974	19	14	7	3	*	9	2	22	*	*	16	21	11	*	*	*	*	*	10	*	6	*	17	*	*	14	*	*	18	*	1	13	8	4	11	*	*	*	20	*	*	5
1975	10	2	12	18	*	21	15	8	*	*	16	17	13	*	*	*	*	*	1	*	11	*	5	*	*	20	*	*	7	*	14	3	19	4	5	*	*	*	9	*	*	*
1976	5	8	11	21	*	15	2	16	*	*	13	18	1	*	*	*	*	*	2	*	16	*	7	*	*	18	*	*	4	*	12	9	9	13	6	*	*	*	20	*	*	*
1977	10	15	6	21	*	13	17	19	*	*	4	9	2	*	*	*	*	*	7	*	18	*	14	*	*	12	*	*	11	*	20	3	8	5	1	*	*	*	16	*	*	*
1978	8	5	4	17	*	11	20	21	*	*	1	7	2	*	*	*	*	*	13	*	6	*	14	*	*	12	*	*	18	*	19	9	14	14	3	*	*	*	10	*	*	*
1979	17	16	12	18	*	20	5	21	*	*	4	14	2	*	*	*	*	*	6	*	11	1	10	*	*	8	*	*	13	*	3	7	19	15	1	*	*	*	9	*	*	*

The Minor Counties side which made history by beating the Australian tourists in 1977. Back row: N. A. Riddell (Durham), B. G. Collins (Herts), J. S. Wilkinson (Durham), P. N. Gill (Staffs), R. Entwistle (Cumberland) and M. D. Nurton (Oxford); sitting P. J. Kippax (Durham), F. E. Collyer (Herts), R. A. C. Forrester (chairman), D. Bailey (captain, Cheshire), R. C. Kerslake (Somerset II) and D. I. Yeabsley (Devon).

Bedfordshire

Foundation 1899

Bedfordshire first competed in the Minor Counties Championship in 1895, four years before the county club was officially formed. They returned to the competition in 1900 and have played in it ever since. The years from 1903 to 1906 were successful ones. H. R. Orr was captain, and others to do well were B. L. Peel, R. W. Rice, G. E. Wharmby and T. Brown. There followed a lean period lasting until and beyond the First World War; when, in 1937, Bedfordshire finished in the first half of the table it was for the first time that many could remember.

Between the wars Bedfordshire had no fewer than 8 captains. Such frequent changes made for an unsettled side and led to poor results. H. Grierson, founder of the Forty Club, was the first captain after the First World War, followed by W. E. King, D. Turnbull, Rex Alston (the BBC commentator), E. D. Dynes, F. Rawlins, W. A. Sime (later captain of Nottinghamshire), and R. de W. K. Winlaw. Outstanding players of this period were H. Holdstock. R. V. Ward, C. Dilley, E. Page, A. B. Poole and A. Haywood. In 1926 F. Crompton became the Secretary of Bedfordshire. In this and other capacities he gave wonderful service to the county for 50 years.

Under Winlaw Bedfordshire achieved 4th place in 1937 and a good side was built up. J. A. R. Oliver, G. L. B. August and J. G. Owen, all of whom were to make important contributions for many years, started their careers under Winlaw and, although many of the pre-war side were missing when cricket was resumed in 1946, the county was still strong. A. B. Poole became captain in 1946, his side being runners-up in 1948 and 1950. Poole retired in 1951, having played for Bedfordshire for 27 years. He was succeeded by Oliver, who was captain until 1961 and had also served the county for 27 years when he retired in 1961. After 1950 Bedfordshire slipped down the table, this being a period when many of their players were attracted into first-class cricket, in which at one time more than a complete Bedfordshire team was playing. This was the era of B. E. Disbury, A. G. Coomb, N. S. Gunn, R. D. Lowings, I. Davison and M. Ashenden, as well as August and Owen; and also G. Millman, the only Bedfordshire cricketer ever to have played for his country.

In 1962 J. Smith took over the captaincy, which he retained for 14 years. An excellent side was gradually built up under Smith, with players no longer leaving for the first-class game as they had in the 1950s. In 1969 Bedfordshire were runners-up again, and then, in 1970, they won the Championship for the first time. They were champions again in 1972, this time beating Yorkshire in the Challenge Match, the only minor county ever to have defeated the 2nd XI of a first-class county in one of these challenge matches. Smith and G. M. Jarrett made a formidable pair of spin bowlers, excellently supported by T. G. A. Morley and W. J. Bushby as seam bowlers. The batting strength came from R. Cox, T. K. Rosier, M. E. Gear, W. Chamberlain, D. J. F. Hoare and N. S. Cooley. By 1976 K. V. Jones, formerly of Middlesex, was captain and another period of transition was under way.

Berkshire

Foundation 1858

Berkshire won the Minor Counties competition in 1924, 1928 and 1953, and have been runners-up 6 times. There have been a number of Test and first-class cricketers who started their careers in Berkshire, including A. P. F. Chapman, J. H. Human, R. H. C. Human, H. E. Dollery, P. B. H. May, K. F. Barrington and G. R. J. Roope.

Success came slowly in the Minor Counties' Championship, but in 1906 Berkshire were 4th with G. G. M. Bennett scoring 853 runs, which remained a county record until 1962. In 1910 and 1911 Berkshire headed the Southern Section of the table. W. Y. Woodburn succeeded to the captaincy after the First World War and in the next 12 years, under him, Berkshire won the Championship twice and were second three times. Other outstanding players at that time, besides Woodburn and Bennett, were R. R. Relf, formerly of Sussex, and Percy Chapman. The Human brothers and Tom Dollery also played for Berkshire in the early 1930s.

D. W. Stokes took on the captaincy in 1937 and kept it until 1953 when the Championship was won again. J. A. Mence was captain in 1954. He was followed by G. R. Langdale (an outstanding bowler who took 71 wickets in 1953) and then by A. T. Davis, who built up an experienced side which qualified for the Gillette Cup in 1965 and 1966. In 1962 R. M. James won the Wilfred Rhodes Trophy for the outstanding Minor Counties' cricketer, scoring 1,068 runs in 17 innings (which included 3 noughts). A bleak period followed until 1975 when Berkshire were runners-up under F. W. Neate, who had succeeded Davis as captain in 1971. The improvement continued under M. D. Mence, who led the county to 5th place and another Gillette Cup qualification in 1978.

An attractive feature of Berkshire cricket has been the outstanding loyalty of many individuals. The first name which springs to mind is H. L. Lewis, who played from 1924 to 1946 and was Secretary from 1947 to 1973 – 50 years of dedicated service. Others in recent years are the Mences (father and son, both captain); the Neates (father and two sons); and Davis and P. A. Simpkins, who had 21 and 18 years as players respectively. The schoolboys' side, the Berkshire Bantams, have contributed many players to the county side.

Buckinghamshire

Foundation 1891

The club was formed in 1891 and christened 'Bucks County Cricket Club,' the familiar county abbreviation being preferred. It was mainly through the interest of the Rothschild family that this club was launched, though there had been a county organization since 1864. The 1st President was Baron Rothschild and the county still enjoys the hospitality of his family. A Championship match is played at Ascott Park each year.

Bucks first competed in the Championship in 1896, finishing 2nd to Worcestershire. There was only limited success in the years prior to 1914 although the Championship was shared with Northamptonshire in 1899. Since then the county have won the Championship another 7 times – more often than any other county. The late Lord Rosebery (then Lord Dalmeny) won a Bucks cap as an Eton schoolboy in 1899 – he went on to become a successful captain of Surrey. In the very early years the good cricketers in the side included C. R. H. Gresson, P. J. de Paravicini and the professional, Matt Wright, the coach at Eton

Bucks in their heyday: W. B. Franklin, captain and wicket-keeper, with some of his side at Ascott Park in 1931. Others (from the left) are J. H. L. Aubrey-Fletcher, L. G. Baker, A. G. Skinner, R. H. Rutter, B. O. Byass and Frank Edwards.

who performed prodigious feats with bat and ball.

E. H. D. Sewell took over the captaincy in 1908, becoming secretary as well in 1911, the year in which Walter Franklin first played. Sewell handed over the captaincy to Franklin in 1919 and persuaded Frank Edwards, who afterwards became a famous coach at Uppingham to come and qualify for Bucks after demobilization. From then until 1939 Bucks were a very powerful side, equal in strength to a number of first-class counties. An invitation to join the senior division in 1921 was declined owing to the lack of the necessary playing facilities within the county. Franklin and Edwards are the two names that will for ever be linked with Bucks cricket. Not only was Franklin a first-rate captain; he was also an outstanding wicket-keeper. In 1926, H. L. Collins rated him one of the best in England. He was also a capable batsman, his record of runs for the county being exceeded only in 1977 by John Turner.

Edwards's record for Bucks is unequalled. In 19 seasons (1921–1939) he took 1,073 wickets for an average of 10.83; in 1932, in only 9 matches, he took 104 wickets for just under ten runs apiece. He is one of only six bowlers (S. F. Barnes was another) to take 100 wickets or more in a Minor Counties' Championship season. The Championship was won 5 times between 1922 and 1938, Edwards and Franklin being helped during this time by such good players as P. W. le Gros, W. Jackson, R. H. J. Brooke, A. G. Skinner, A. W. Payne, W. E. Hazelton and R. H. Rutter. When the Championship was won in 1932, Bucks won all 10 of its matches, 5 of them by an innings.

A number of distinguished players have captained the side. Apart from Franklin (for a record 22 seasons), there was de Paravicini (1899–1907); B. A. Barnett, who had kept wicket for Australia; Oliver Battcock (one of Bucks's finest bowlers), Peter Stoddart, David Johns (a most successful all-rounder), John Slack, Chris Parry, David Mackintosh and Brian Poll. Others to have enhanced the county's reputation are Leslie Baker, Vic Lund, Sir John Aubrey-Fletcher, Jack O'Connor and Claude Taylor.

Then there are more who have played a prominent part in Bucks' cricket such as Alfred Hughes, Fred Harris, Norman Butler, David Janes, Colin Lever, Ron Hooker (after a successful career with Middlesex), John Turner, Bill Atkins (an outstanding cover point), Chris Pickett, Don Rickard, Ray Bond, Ray Bailey and Peter Gooch. Lever's record will give an idea of his great all-round ability. In 1964 he scored 1,011 runs, which won him the Wilfred Rhodes Trophy, and in 1970, with a bowling average of 8.52, he won the Frank Edwards Trophy. Bucks have also had some success in the Gillette Cup competition.

PAUL SLATTER

Cambridgeshire

Foundation 1844

The Cambridgeshire club grew out of the Cambridge town club which was playing competition cricket in 1818. In 1832 a team from Cambridge beat MCC at Lord's by 6 wickets, but the Cambridgeshire club really came into existence in 1844. T. Hayward, uncle of the great Surrey batsman, was a stalwart of the early days, as was William Buttress, reputedly one of the greatest of all leg-break bowlers. During the first half of the 19th century the home ground, for the county, town and university XIs, was Parker's Piece and Cambridgeshire were one of the strongest counties in England. The present county club, founded in 1891, competed in the Minor Counties Competition for the first time in 1898. George Watts, D. Hayward, Jack Hobbs and W. Hitch all played before the First World War, the last 3 quickly progressing to first-class cricket. Sammy Ling was also a splendid batsman and captain.

Between the wars Cyril Coote, a legendary figure at Fenners where he was groundsman and constant adviser, made a profound impression as a batsman, as did C. J. Smith as a bowler. H. W. F. Taylor was 2nd in the Minor Counties batting averages in 1938. After the Second War, Maurice Crouch and Coote, captains for 17 years between them, made many runs. Wickets, though, were harder to come by. The most consistent bowler was R. A. Taylor, who once took 7 wickets in an innings. The 1950s and 1960s produced a good crop of batsmen: R. A. Gautney, T. S. Hale and D. H. R. Fairey among them. J. H. Wardle, the former Yorkshire and England bowler, engaged in 1963, took 55 wickets that year and contributed decisively to Cambridgeshire winning their 1st Championship.

Recently the county has drawn on the talents of some distinguished university players. F. C. M. Alexander, who later captained the West Indies, and J. M. Brearley have both given their assistance.

R. A. TAYLOR

Cheshire

Foundation 1894

Having first entered the Minor Counties competition in 1909, Cheshire did not achieve much success until they finished 7th in 1920 and 3rd in 1921. This was their most successful season until suddenly they won the Championship in 1967.

The most notable players between the wars were W. E. Jones and W. E. Bates with the bat; all-rounders F. W. Dennis, L. N. Jones and J. Cook; and H. Wilson and J. Bartley with the ball. Vernon Hope was captain for 15 years during this period.

After the Second War, Cheshire had a difficult time until the early 1960s. Since then there has been considerable improvement under 3 successive captains – B. M. Lowe, F. W. Millett and J. A. Sutton. Millett led the side to the Championship and to 3 appearances in the Gillette Cup, besides. J. A. Sutton, R. M. O. Cooke, D. Cox and P. A. C. Kelly, in addition to Millett, scored many runs. Prominent as wicket-takers during these latter years have been Millett, Sutton and D. J. Smith.

Cornwall

Foundation 1895

Cornwall's successes in the Minor Counties Championship have not matched their unfailing enthusiasm. Only once before the First World War did they finish in the top half of the table. They were 4th in 1938 and again in 1953; and in 1974, with the arrival of the peripatetic Dave Halfyard, who had already played for Kent, Nottinghamshire, Durham and Northumberland, they were runners-up to Oxfordshire.

The best of their early batsmen was H. Tresawna, whose most prolific season was 1909 when he scored 508 runs. Between 1906 and 1932, by when he was past the age of 60, F. Whiting took 888 wickets. He and Halfyard both took 10 wickets in an innings for Cornwall, Whiting with 10 for 26 against Wiltshire in 1921 and Halfyard 10 for 29 against Dorset in 1974.

In 1925 C. Shaw Baker scored 756 runs, one of several good seasons he enjoyed around that time; in the 1930s G. Rogers was the leading run-getter. After the Second War the same could be said for R. F. Hosking and then, in the 1960s, of G. R. Harvey. Jesse Lawry (who kept wicket a time or two for the representative Minor Counties side), Peter Kendall, Roger Hosen, Eric Willcock, Chris Chaplin, Mike Trenwith, Brian Read, Alan Lawrence, David Toseland and Brian Laity are other stalwarts to have kept the flag flying beyond the River Tamar. Remember, too, Arthur Lugg, for 37 years honorary Secretary of the club, and Jack Crapp, Test cricketer, Test umpire and Cornish born.

Cumberland

Foundation 1853

Early records are non-existent, but there is reference to a Cumberland county team playing in 1853. Official records record a meeting held in January 1884, though it was not until April 1948 that the present club was formed. It was called the 'Cumberland and Westmorland CCC', the Westmorland being dropped from the title on admission to the Minor Counties Association in 1955.

Before 1955 matches were played against neighbouring counties on both sides of the Border and clubs from the North Lancashire League. Among the highlights of the club's existence have been matches against official touring teams, among them the Australians of 1921, the West Indians of 1950 and the South Africans of 1955.

Following admission to the Minor Counties Championship the side was strengthened by the signing of various professionals, including H. Halliday (formerly of Yorkshire), G. A. Edrich (formerly of Lancashire), P. N. Broughton and R. Entwhistle. It is not easy to run a Minor Counties side in so thinly populated a county; but the officials and committee members, with a small core of helpers, keep the flag flying. In 1975 Cumberland missed qualifying for the Gillette Cup competition by only 0·23 of a point.

NORMAN WISE

Devon

Foundation 1901

Devon entered the Minor Counties Championship in 1901 but did not win it, despite near misses, until 1978. Some outstanding players from the early days were T. C. G. Sandford (for 35 years master-in-charge of Marlborough cricket), R. G. Cruwys, F. H. Carroll and the professionals, Light and Ashton. After the First World War the captain was J. H. Amory. Another to figure prominently at that time was J. F. Shelley, who was President for 30 years until 1962. The bowling of Amory and T. Jennings and the batting of S. W. Fielding were largely contributory to Devon's 3rd position in 1926. The decade before the Second War saw the county usually in the lower half of the table, despite the efforts of such as R. G. Seldon, W. W. Hoare, C. E. S. and J. H. Poynder, W. T. French and the professional, H. C. Lock, later to win fame as groundsman at the Oval.

Since the Second War Devon have been runners-up twice and champions in 1978. Notable players during the period were N. H. Humphries, H. D. Fairclough, D. H. Cole, G. Trump and B. Matthews, all of whom captained the side. Another who has made an impressive contribution is D. I. Yeabsley. Devonians to have played for England are George Emmett of Gloucestershire, Len Coldwell of Worcestershire and Roger Tolchard of Leicestershire; while others who have graduated to the first-class game are D. Shepherd, J. Davey, J. Swinburne, J. Childs and A. Allin.

Devon have had 2 winners of the Wilfred Rhodes Trophy in D. H. Cole and J. R. Tolliday. The former also captained the Minor Counties, who, on several occasions, have played touring sides at Torquay. There has certainly been a recent upsurge of interest in the game within the county, one important factor in this having been an enthusiastically-run Cricket Association which has done much to foster youth cricket.

Dorset

Foundation 1896

The early years of Dorset's fortunes in the Minor Counties competition – which was entered in 1902 – were not successful, but in the 1920s and 1930s the side usually gave a good account of itself. Well-known players in those years were the Rev W. V. Jephson (who took Dorset to 4th in the Championship in 1922, and 3rd in 1923), M. B. Elderton (who looked after Sherborne cricket for 30 years and captained the county from 1926 to 1938), A. M. Harrison, who succeeded Elderton in the captaincy, W. Knight, M. Taylor, R. D. Buck and R. G. Tindall.

Dorset were soon in action after the Second War, and have had their customary good, and not so good, seasons. The captains since then have been W. Lancashire (1947–1952) G. C. Tovey (1952–1953), D. J. W. Bridge (1954–1967), M. Hardwicke (1968–1972), D. M. Daniels (1972–1975) and D. R. Hayward from 1976. Leading batsmen during these seasons were M. M. Walford, G. W. L. Courteney, W. L. Creese, G. E. S. Woodhouse, D. E. Lawes, J. Baker, D. M. Daniels and R. Lewis. The wickets were taken mostly by E. J. Swann, F. King, W. L. Creese, R. R. Dovey, D. J. W. Bridge, D. C. P. R. Jowett, J. Baker, D. R. Hayward and C. Allen. Dorset has always been well-served by wicket-keepers, amongst whom have been H. G. Hunt, C. Roper, H. W. Stephenson and M. E. Beall, and by all-rounders such as C. M. G. Hunter, J. Baker and D. R. Hayward.

D. J. W. BRIDGE

Durham

Foundation 1895

If Durham's most widely-heralded achievement is their victory over Yorkshire in the 1st round of the Gillette Cup in 1973, it is only one of many that stamps them as having been among the best of the minor counties. They have won the Championship 6 times, and come within a few runs of beating both Nottinghamshire and Worcestershire, as well as Yorkshire, in the Gillette Cup.

Founder members of the Minor Counties competition, Durham were champions 3 times in their early years. They won next in 1926 and then again in 1930. Before the First World War R. Bousfield and E. W. Elliott were among the leading batsmen, with G. Turnbull and Morris, a professional as faithful as he was effective, the chief wicket-takers. Denis Hendren, brother of Patsy and much later a Test umpire, played for Durham, as, though only very occasionally, did A. G. Doggart, a fine all-round games-player. M. Nichol, L. H. Weight, J. Carr and J. Cook had as much as anyone to do with the winning of the title in 1925; the same could be said of Carr, S. Ellis, A. L. Howell, H. Gibbon and C. L. Adamson in 1930.

Since the Second War Durham have either given to, or taken from, the first-class game some well-known players. H. W. Stephenson (Somerset), R. T. Spooner (Warwickshire), Colin Milburn (Northamptonshire) and P. Willey (Northamptonshire) all came from there; while A. Coxon (Yorkshire), R. Aspinall (Yorkshire), D. J. Halfyard (Kent), K. D. Biddulph (Somerset), D. R. O'Sullivan (New Zealand and Hampshire), Mohinder Amarnath (India) and Wasim Raja (Pakistan) have all served as professionals for the county. R. B. Proud had some good years as batsman and captain before and after the Second War. So, since 1955, have D. W. Hardy, H. J. Bailey and B. R. Lander. In 1955 H. D. Bell had a particularly good season with the ball.

Recent years have been among Durham's most consistently successful. Besides winning the Championship in 1976 they were runners-up in 1977, 1978 and 1979. R. Inglis has been an outstanding batsman, Peter Romaines made a match-saving hundred in the 1979 Challenge Match, Alan Old has been a good all-rounder, and in 1978 N. A. Riddell won the Wilfred Rhodes Trophy for leading the Minor Counties batting averages. In the great victory over Yorkshire at Harrogate in 1973, Lander, with 5 wickets for 15 runs, took the main bowling honours, before S. Greenwood and Inglis made sure that Yorkshire's total of 135 was safely passed. When the 2 sides met again in the Gillette Cup, in 1979, Yorkshire avenged the defeat of 1973, though only by the skin of their teeth.

Hertfordshire

Foundation 1895

As founder members of the Minor Counties competition, Hertfordshire were one of the 7 counties to compete in 1895, since when they have met with a fair degree of success. The Championship has been won twice, in 1936 and 1975, and over the years a number of outstanding minor county cricketers have been produced.

Before the First World War the county relied largely on their 3 professionals, White, Coleman and Golding, the first two as all-rounders and the third with the bat. In 1906, C. H. Titchmarch had the first of many good seasons as a batsman, which continued until 1930 when he died. In 1906 Titchmarsh scored 796 runs, Golding 749 and White 610, and in addition Coleman took 89 wickets and White 85. Another outstanding professional to appear before the First World War was F. Burton, who remained a consistent wicket-taker until the early 1930s. After the First World War Titchmarsh and Burton were the mainstays of the side; in the winter of 1922–23 the former toured New Zealand and Australia under the captaincy of A. C. MacLaren. In 1924 R. J. O. Meyer, a Cambridge blue later to play for Somerset, scored 463 runs and took 51 wickets for Hertfordshire. In 1926 Titchmarsh scored 890 runs in the season, then a record for the county and one which included an innings of 218 against Norfolk at Norwich. In E. Roberts Herfordshire found a splendid substitute for Burton. In 1935 F. C. De Saram, a talented Oxford blue, who made a hundred against the Australians, beat Titchmarsh's record with an aggregate of 904 runs; in 1936, when Hertfordshire won the championship, Roberts took a record 97 wickets.

P. G. T. Kingsley, the Oxford captain of 1930, was captain after the Second War, although he no longer scored as many runs as he had in the 1930s. At this time the batting lacked an outstanding player, though in 1951 T. W. Tyrwhitt-Drake, who had by then taken on the captaincy, scored 847 runs and continued for several seasons as a leading scorer. R. C. V. L. Marques succeeded to the captaincy in 1956 and over the next few years the success of the side again rested more with the team as a whole than with one or two individuals. It was when Frank Collyer was appointed captain in 1972 that Hertfordshire experienced their most successful period, winning the Championship in 1975 and coming 2nd in 1976 when they also reached the 3rd round of the Gillette Cup with a famous victory over Essex. The outstanding players hereabouts were B. G. Collins, A. R. Garofall, D. G. Ottley, A. J. Burridge and R. Johns.

Lincolnshire

Foundation 1870

Although the 1st Lincolnshire County Cricket Club was not formed until 1853, the Louth Club (1822) collected the leading players around to challenge the Norwich club (representing Norfolk) to an inter-county match in 1828 at East Dereham. Winning easily, Lincolnshire fixed a return for the following year at Louth and Lincs once again won by an innings. The next games under the auspices of Lincs were less happily contested in 1835 and 1836. In the latter year, Lincs left the field of play and refused to continue in a dispute over the Laws of the game. But, alas, history records no more.

After the initial club became defunct a 2nd came into being in 1870 to 1874 when leading clubs like the Harrow Wanderers and the Free Foresters figured among the opposition. Another attempt to establish a sound county club was made in 1880 but it was not until 1888 that a 4th club was put on to a better footing.

An attempt to obtain a county ground (Lincoln Lindum) was also made, but failed and it was 1906 before a 5th and lasting club was established. Entry was given to the Northern section of the Minor Counties competition where they met Lancashire, Staffordshire, Northumberland, Yorkshire and Durham in their first season.

In 1909 the club, transferred to the Eastern Region, won this easily, but met their Waterloo in playing Wiltshire in a challenge match for the crown. The county was not accepted back into the Minor Counties competition until 1924. Only once until the Second War did the county finish in the top ten, and upon resumption, except for 1948 and 1950, had to wait until the early 1960s to make their presence felt. After finishing 6th in 1962 they jumped to 3rd 3 years later, then finally took the Championship in 1966.

Four years later, 1970, an appearance was made in a championship challenge to Bedford's supremacy, but in a rain-ruined match Lincs were unable to force a win, and had to be content with second place. The Gillette Cup has been quite a fillip to interest. Since 1966 the county has made seven appearances in the Gillette Cup, winning twice (Northumberland 1971 and Glamorgan 1974). By inflicting defeat upon Glamorgan, the county became only the second Minor County to beat a first-class side.

K. TRUSHELL

Norfolk

Foundation 1827

Only 4 years after its foundation, the Norfolk Club was described in the *New Sporting Magazine* as 'now the next club to the Marylebone' and indeed the Minute Book and Scorebook for that period, which are still in existence, bear ample testimony to the healthy state of the club at the time.

The subsequent loss of Fuller Pilch to Kent, and the sudden death of the President, Lord Suffield, weakened the Club to such an extent that from 1848 to 1862 and from 1870 to 1877 it went out of existence; but from 1877 to this day it has enjoyed a continuous span of over 100 years, and in 1977 celebrated, with a Dinner, the 150th anniversary of the original foundation, and the centenary of the present club. 1881 saw the advent of the Norwich Cricket Week which, apart from interruptions by the 2 World Wars, has continued to this day. In 1885 against MCC a 1st-wicket partnership of 241 between the brothers L. K. Jarvis (181) and C. J. E. Jarvis (130) enabled Norfolk to set a record of 695 for an innings total at Lords.

The beginning of the Minor Counties Championship in 1895 brought immediate success to Norfolk, the title being shared with Durham and Worcestershire. A major factor in Norfolk's strength at this time was the bowling of their professional, Charlie Shore, who had joined the club in 1890. Five times in 6 seasons from 1895 he exceeded 50 wickets, and in 1897 he achieved innings figures of 10 for 50 against Durham at Lakenham.

The Rev G. B. Raikes led the team to the Championship in 1905 and again in 1910, while M. Falcon, who was captain from 1912 to 1946, helped them win the title in 1913. In the 1910 Challenge Match against Berkshire G. A. Stevens, who must be considered second only to Falcon in service to Norfolk, scored the County's 1st double-hundred.

Between the wars the Championship was never won, yet this was perhaps Norfolk's strongest period, with a galaxy of blues and future first-class players in their ranks. Falcon himself; D. C. and R. C. Rought-Rought of Cambridge; G. R. R. Colman, D. F. Walker, T. G. L. Ballance and M. R. Barton of Oxford; and the brothers W. J., G. A. and E. H. Edrich all helped to ensure that Norfolk were seldom far from the top of the table; indeed for nearly 5 years in the 1930s they were undefeated in Championship matches.

The end of the Second War saw Norfolk struggle to regain their strength. War casualties, *anno domini* and departures to first-class counties necessitated a search for new talent. In the 8 seasons to 1953, C. S. R. Boswell and P. G. Walmsley as bowlers, N. H. Moore as a batsman would all have graced the pre-war XIs. Promising players in P. H. Parfitt, A. J. Corran, J. H. Edrich and later C. T. Radley then emerged, only to move to first-class counties and it was not until 1959, when W. J. Edrich returned from Middlesex to captain his native county, that a period of prosperity ensued. In that year E. G. Witherden, formerly of Kent, established a record aggregate of 1,031 runs in 10 matches, and the following season saw Norfolk take top place in the table, only to lose the Challenge Match to Lancashire II. Edrich led the side with tremendous flair, bringing on players such as T. I. Moore, W. Rose, D. G. Pilch and F. L. Q. Handley. Acquisitions from outside who made an impact included R. V. Bell, G. J. Saville and R. I. Jefferson.

Upon the eventual retirement of Edrich in 1971 another period of transition ensued, in which Ken Taylor, once of Yorkshire, was prominent.

D. J. M. ARMSTRONG

LEFT Michael Falcon (1888–1976), a bowler verging on greatness and for many years the lynch-pin of Norfolk cricket.

RIGHT Henry Blofeld, the well-known cricket-writer and Test Match broadcaster, played for Norfolk as well as Eton and Cambridge. He covered the Minor Counties for our 1st edition.

Northumberland

Foundation 1896

Northumberland finished 1st in the Minor Counties Championship in 1924 and 1925; in 1955 and 1956 they were 2nd, and in 1970 and 1976 they were high enough – 4th each time – to qualify for the Gillette Cup competition. They have also had long periods when they have languished low in the table.

In their early years they were short of bowling. F. G. H. Clayton, however, F. W. Gillespie, and Marshall, the professional, were consistent batsmen. After the First World War some lean years came to an end with the success of G. Milne and W. Hetherton, both professionals, who took 274 wickets between them in 1924 and 1925, the years of victory. The 1930s were thin, though through no fault of W. G. McKay and J. B. Bruce, the mainstays of the batting, and 2 left-hand spinners, H. Robson and Arthur Booth, who took plenty of wickets.

Northumberland's fortunes after the Second War followed a similar pattern to the 1920s. After two or three poor seasons the team developed into a well-balanced combination under the captaincy of L. E. Liddell, a prolific hitter, G. Walton, K. D. Smith and R. W. Smithson, and a strong opening attack of K. J. Earl and L. McGibbon. H. B. Henderson, the wicket-keeper, had the remarkable record of playing in 255 successive matches. The 1960s were less successful than the 1970s. J. M. Crawhall, who led the side from 1969 until 1977, scored over 6,000 runs

Northumberland 1976. Back row: H. Jude (scorer), K. Norton, K. Pearson, P. C. Graham, B. D. Parsons (team chairman), P. J. Kippax, Asif Masood, G. Dodds and R. W. Smithson (honorary secretary); sitting: A. S. Thompson, J. Thewlis, J. M. Crawhall, J. S. Oswald (chairman), M. Youll, A. A. Johnson and W. Robson.

for the county. In 1978 M. Youll, the new captain, scored 889 runs, the highest aggregate in the championship that year. In over 20 years K. Norton, a left-arm spinner, took nearly 600 wickets. Northumberland engages a full-time professional, these in recent years having included J. Van Geloven, Asif Masood and I. W. Callen.

Oxfordshire

Foundation 1779

Oxfordshire celebrated its bicentenary in 1979, its 1st recorded match having taken place in 1779 against Berkshire on Cowley Marsh, Oxford, for £20 a side. In 1895, when the Minor Counties Competition was founded, Oxfordshire was one of the first 7 counties to join, but it was not until 1929 that they won the Championship, though in 1926 they had finished as runners-up. In 1929 the XI was one of the strongest ever fielded by the county with such as J. Arnold (later of Hampshire), H. Walker, L. Rogers and F. Hartley all scoring between 400 and 600 runs, and C. Walters and J. Rogers (later of Gloucestershire) taking more than 50 wickets. Although during the next decade Oxfordshire had some experienced players – C. Walters, W. W. Inge, J. P. O'Shea, A. P. D. Montgomery, W. G. Kalaugher, S. C. B. Lee, to name but a few – they fell to within 3 of the bottom of the Championship table in 1939.

In 1945, when the Championship was resuscitated, the then Mayor of Oxford, Councillor R. P. Capel, called a public meeting in the Town Hall to inaugurate the revival of the activities of the county club. Within a dozen years, Oxfordshire thrice challenged for the championship, but lost respectively to Lancashire II, Yorkshire II and Somerset II. Now, and later, a number of their players were selected for the representative Minor Counties XI against touring sides: these included J. F. Mendl, G. F. Betts, L. E. G. Hemming, D. J. Laitt, E. J. Lane Fox, G. N. S. Ridley and M. D. Nurton. Nurton toured Kenya with the MCCA side in 1978 and has been a regular member of the Minor Counties (South) XI in the Benson & Hedges Competition.

The 1974 Oxfordshire team which won the Minor Counties Championship. Back row: M. F. D. Lloyd, A. Crossley, R. Evans, R. Busby, D. Locke, S. R. Porter and J. Potter; sitting: P. Garner, M. D. Nurton, P. B. Smith (captain), N. Harper and B. Jeffries.

Post-war Captains have been W. W. Inge, succeeded by J. E. Bush (Oxford Blue) in 1956 and by D. Banton in 1962, but it was under P. B. Smith, who assumed the captaincy in 1971, that the County repeated its success of 1929 and defeated Cornwall to win the Championship in 1974 for a second time. For this success Oxfordshire relied heavily upon Nurton, M. F. D. Lloyd and P. J. Garner with the bat and upon B. R. Jeffries, Smith and R. N. Busby with the ball.

After this, the side slumped for a few seasons, but recovered under the new captain, Nurton, who took over from Smith in 1978 and achieved Gillette Cup qualification status in 1979 for the 5th time. Main contributors to this run of success were Laitt and Banton who between them took nearly 1,250 wickets.

L. B. FREWER

Shropshire

Foundation 1850

Shropshire has one of the oldest county clubs in the country, its records dating back to the middle of the 19th century. It was not until March 1951, however, that a Shropshire Cricket Association was formed, and it was 1957 before they were elected to the Minor Counties Championship. G. V. Othen was appointed captain in 1970, a position he held until becoming chairman of the club in 1977.

After a period in the lower reaches of the table, considerable improvement was achieved: from 12th position in 1971, Shropshire became champions in 1973; in 1975 and 1977 they finished third. In 1976 they gave Yorkshire a hard fight in the first round of the Gillette Cup, as they did Surrey in 1978. Shropshire have been fortunate in the enthusiasm of their officials.

H. BOTFIELD

Staffordshire

Foundation 1871

Staffordshire were one of the 7 clubs to play in the 1st Minor Counties Championship in 1895, though they took no further part until 1901 when the competition was officially recognized by MCC. Apart from a bad year in 1903 they finished around the middle of the table until, in 1906, they won the Championship. There followed an extraordinarily successful period between that year and 1927 when the title was won 6 times.

This tremendous run depended largely on the feats of one man, the legendary S. F. Barnes. Barnes played for Staffordshire from 1904 to 1934, between the ages of 31 and 61. Until the First World War he played frequently for England, and during these 30 years, which for him involved 22 seasons (he did not play between 1919 and 1924), he bowled 5,457·3 overs for Staffordshire and took 1,441 wickets at an average of 8·15 per wicket. In addition to this he scored several hundreds for the county, his most remarkable being in a match against Durham at South Shields in 1911 when he made 136 before going on to take 17 wickets in the match for 83 runs. Against Cheshire at Stoke in 1909 he had a match analysis of 14 wickets for 13 runs.

Since the county's success in 1927 the Championship has eluded them, although

John Ikin made his debut with Staffordshire at the age of 16 alongside Sydney Barnes, then 61, and went on to play Staffordshire and Lancashire League cricket before becoming a Lancashire and England player.

they have often been well positioned in the table and have taken part in the Gillette Cup competition in 5 seasons. After Sydney Barnes, the most notable all-rounder for Staffordshire has been Aaron Lockett, a great stalwart of the team between the two world wars. Lockett's bowling figures for the county were: 3,774 overs, 1,052 maidens, 8,565 runs, 633 wickets. He was also an aggressive batsman of considerable ability and a magnificent slip-fielder.

Following Bernard Meakin's retirement from the captaincy, which he held from 1911 to 1921, a number of players held the office for short terms until Dennis Haynes, a war-time Cambridge blue, had it from 1949 to 1957. Haynes was followed by John Ikin, who had left Staffordshire for Lancashire in 1938. Ikin held the office for 10 years, creating in 1961 a record for the county with an aggregate of 1,024 runs. Ikin was followed in 1968 by Douglas Henson (1968–1973) and in 1974 David Hancock took over from Henson. By 1978 David Hancock had created 2 records for Staffordshire, having played regularly for the county for 21 consecutive years (1958–1978) and scored over 8,000 runs.

In 1947 Staffordshire players occupied the first 3 places in the Minor Counties' bowling averages: Fred Taylor, Stanley Crump and Bert Shardlow; while in 1956 Staffordshire players took four of the first 9 places in the Minor Counties' batting averages. In 1974 Keith Stride took 5 wickets for 0 runs in a spell of 8 balls against Shropshire at Shrewsbury; in 1975 he took 8 for 13 against Lincolnshire at Longton. Other players who have given notable service include Nasim-ul-Ghani, the Pakistan all-rounder; Peter Gill; John Moore, a hard hitting middle order batsman and a brilliant fielder; Michael Ikin (son of John) and Tom Pearsall, a left-handed opening batsman.

A Staffordshire match that will be remembered for a long time by those fortunate enough to be present was in the second round of the Gillette Cup played at Stone in July 1978 against Sussex. Sussex batted 1st and scored 221 for 6 in their 60 overs. When Staffordshire batted they lost 2 quick wickets, but a 3rd-wicket partnership between David Hancock and Nasim-ul-Ghani put on 140 runs in 99 minutes so that when the last over started Staffordshire needed 11 runs to win a remarkable match. Alas! only 8 were scored, and Sussex won by two runs!

L. W. HANCOCK

Suffolk

Foundation 1864

Suffolk joined the Minor Counties Championship in 1904. They were involved in the competition, without a great deal of success, until the start of the First World War, under the captaincy of H. F. Fox, P. W. Cobbold, H. L. Wilson and H. Bassett. Following the war they lacked the support to resume Championship cricket until 1934, and it was not until the arrival of Philip Mead from Hampshire in 1938 that their fortunes really began to look up. From holding the wooden spoon in 1938 they leapt to 3rd place the following summer when Mead scored 883 runs in 14 innings.

Suffolk reached their first peak just after the Second War. Led by Adam Powell they carried off the Minor Counties' title in 1946 for the first time. Cyril Perkins, a slow left-armer who had played for Northamptonshire, and Brian Belle, who captained the side from 1948 to 1953 and scored 4,459 runs before he retired in 1960, were well to the fore.

Although Suffolk found it hard going in the 1950s and 1960s, when Martin Corke had a lengthy spell as captain, there were bright spots, such as the emergence of David Larter who went on to play for England. Personalities included Norman Stevens, Herbert Hargreaves, Dick Mayes, Ian Prior, Wally Duckham, Cliff Piper and Richard English, but only when R. E. Cunnell took over the side did they climb to the top again. After twice finishing 6th they won the title for the 2nd time in 1977, came 3rd in 1978 and won again in 1979.

A well-balanced team was given an extra boost by the leg-break and googly bowling of Robin Hobbs (until his surprising departure for Glamorgan) and the left-arm spin of Peter Jones. Tony Warrington became the most prolific of all Suffolk run-makers and Richard Robinson's hitting was comparable with that of David Henley-Welch 25 years previously. Wicket-keeper Stuart Westley won the Wilfred Rhodes batting trophy in 1977 and Colin Rutherford, Roger Howlett and Simon Clements, who scored 800 runs at an average of 50 in 1978, were also key players. Having finished 3rd in the Minor Counties Championship in 1978 Suffolk qualified for the Gillette Cup of 1979, when, after beating Buckinghamshire in the 1st round, they lost by only 2 wickets to Sussex, at Hove, in the 2nd. Victory in the 1979 Championship owed most to Timur Mohammad, a Pakistani, whose double of 179 and 80 in the Challenge Match against Durham made sure of their finishing 1st.

Wiltshire

Foundation 1881

After the first 4 years of the Minor Counties Championship (these were dominated by Worcestershire) Wiltshire and Northamptonshire came to the fore, Wiltshire winning the title for the first time in 1902. This was Wiltshire's most successful period: in 1903 a report described A. M. Miller's side as 'the equal of any first-class county.' Miller, who had toured South Africa in 1896, was captain from then until 1920. In the early 1900s runs were scored with great consistency by C. H. Ransome, W. S. Medlicott and J. E. Stevens, while Jesse Smith, Smart and Miller, the captain, shared the bowling honours. In 1903 Smith took 103 wickets in 16 games. The Championship was won again in 1909, when C. S. and R. W. Awdry and S. R. Nicholson

Suffolk today and yesterday: some of the Suffolk team which won the Minor Counties Championship in 1946 hold the flag which their successors flew to another Championship victory in 1977. Centre-back are the respective captains in the Challenge Match at Ipswich, B. R. Lander (Durham) and R. E. Cunnell (Suffolk) with some of their players. The old brigade in front are: M. Corke, B. H. Belle, G. C. Perkins, H. Hargreaves, N. Stevens, H. L. Porter and W. Duckham.

Wiltshire v Buckinghamshire, 1974. The two teams and officials, with the captains, B. H. White (Wiltshire) and D. Mackintosh (Buckinghamshire), in the centre of the kneeling players.

scored most of the runs, and Arthur Newman and Mitchell took most of the wickets.

After the First World War a new side had to be formed, but, under the leadership of R. W. Awdry, the splendid all-round cricket of Newman took the county to 3rd place in 1924. This was followed by a lean period until, in 1933, Wiltshire were denied 2nd place, and with it the right to challenge Norfolk for the title, only by an error in the allocation of points which was not uncovered until October. The success of this side was largely due to the excellent bowling of Bill Smith and his brother Jim (both sons of Jesse), supported by C. E. and A. L. Awdry, sons of C. S. Jim Smith left for Middlesex at the end of the 1933 season.

With W. Lovell Hewitt leading the side from 1935 until 1946, the county had only 3 captains during its first 50 years in the Championship. Between the wars the best of the batsmen were G. S. Butler, who played throughout that time, and B. W. Hone, of South Australia and Oxford, who, when a Marlborough master, played during the last 4 years. Butler made 74 and Hone 124 in a drawn match against the West Indian touring side in 1939. A. E. Lloyd also played several brilliant innings, including one of 196 against Surrey 2nd XI at the Oval in 1937.

After the Second War, Wiltshire met with little success for some years. However, in 1953, with J. Hurn succeeding to the captaincy, a new era dawned, due in no small measure to the batting of J. R. Thompson, the Cambridge captain-designate of 1940, who had played for Warwickshire. Thompson was on the staff at Marlborough, a regular source of Wiltshire players. In the 1950s A. G. Marshall, player and coach, did well with the ball. It was largely due to his bowling, as well as that of J. H. Merryweather and M. H. Martin, and the all-round skill of A. M. Smith, I. R. Lomax and P. Hough, that Wiltshire were 2nd in the championship in both 1963 and 1964. Lomax, Merryweather, Smith and Marshall all played for the Minor Counties, Marshall at different times taking 7 Pakistani and 5 Australian wickets in one innings of a match.

In more recent years, Wiltshire have mostly been in the middle of the championship table. B. H. White became captain in 1968 and then the county's leading run-getter. W. A. Smith, after a few seasons with Surrey, came and played under his birth qualification, and David Turner, born in Chippenham, had a year in the side before joining Hampshire. R. A. C. Forrester, who became the county's honorary secretary in 1929, held the post for 35 years until his election in 1964 as chairman of the Minor Counties' Cricket Association.

J. C. GREENWOOD

Part VI
The Limited-Over Game

A Not-So-Quiet Revolution

E. W. SWANTON

IT WILL be difficult for younger readers of this book to realize how different was the face of cricket – and especially of English cricket – before the introduction in 1963 of the first limited-over competition contested by first-class cricketers, the Gillette Cup. Until the counties – without over-much enthusiasm in some cases – accepted the idea of a limited-over match, to be finished in one day, weather permitting, they had been content to restrict themselves to the one ancient competition, the County Championship. Nor would they have countenanced any change had it not been for the drop in public interest in Test as well as county cricket which at the latter end of the 1950s began to put at risk the well-being, and even the existence, of the weaker brethren. Championship gates had dropped from all but 2,000,000 in 1950 to 700,000 in 1963 – and they were due to fall to 500,000 only 3 years later.

It was the committee set up by MCC in 1956, under the chairmanship of H. S. Altham, to look into the decline in gates and the general tempo of the game which first proposed a Knock-Out competition. The idea took much digesting, but with the overall financial position deteriorating the plunge was eventually taken. The Gillette being a success from the start, it was not long before other limited-over schemes were considered. Hence came the Sunday afternoon John Player League in 1969 and the Benson & Hedges Cup in 1972.

But if limited-over cricket, spiced by the arrival of overseas celebrities, proved popular at county level, why should it not be extended in both directions, to international cricket on the one hand (granted the necessary sponsorship) and club cricket on the other? Accordingly in 1972 there sprang up the Prudential Trophy, consisting of three 55-over matches between England and the touring Australians. After further games in the following 2 years involving England and their Test opponents came the great adventure of the 1975 Prudential World Cup. In other countries limited-over cricket was launched likewise, though with fewer overs because of limited hours of daylight. Generally speaking, the greater number of overs the better – if you like, the less artificial – the game.

Club cricket in the south changed course, as Frank Dolman tells us in these pages, at the end of the 1960s, though not without a stiff rearguard action by the old stalwarts of the Club Cricket Conference who treasured as a holy tablet rule 2 of their constitution naming as a prime object the fostering of club cricket 'on non-competitive lines'. As it happened, I had a hand in setting-up the first 2 limited-over knock-out competitions of any consequence because of my connexion with *The Cricketer*. The first, started in 1967, was the *Cricketer* Cup for invited Old Boy teams.

Two years later came what was at first known as the *Cricketer* National Club Knock-out with prizes given by D. H. Robins, and is now the John Haig Trophy, contested under the auspices of the NCA. When 350 clubs applied from all over the country it was decided to admit at first 256 instead of the intended limit of 128. Championships, leagues and cups from this point proliferated apace among clubs everywhere, most though not all contested on a limited-over basis. Not least came the Village Championship which has dwarfed all others in size and geographical scope.

There are still, of course, many clubs, mostly of the wandering kind, who continue to play what is often generalized as 'friendly cricket', or, as the Australians have it, 'social cricket'. Fixture lists have had to be amended or even transformed according to the dictates of particular competitions. Cricket in the south of England in fact has become regimented, just as it has long been in the north and midlands. Sponsorship, in common with other features of the limited-over game at higher levels, has come to the clubs in various forms and eased financial stresses.

Naturally the introduction of limited-overs has been a boon in some respects, detrimental to the traditional concept of cricket in others. It is not too far from the truth to say there is no better fun than the best of it nor anything more boring than the worst. If the side batting first makes such a score as to put it altogether out of range, or if either side suffers an abject collapse, interest and enjoyment wane rapidly. In an early Cup game an old pundit who hadn't quite got the hang of it remarked to the hilarity of his companions: 'looks as though we'll have to play for a draw.' But there is no playing for draws and thereby an interesting and sometimes very exciting element in cricket has been lost.

That, however, is almost a detail compared with the fundamental alteration in the object of the game as it concerns the bowler. No longer is his prime job to get the batsman out so much as to deny him runs. It will probably be of more value to his side to take 0 for 20 in 10 overs than 3 for 45. Equally, the self-discipline needed to build an innings against good attacking bowling is less of an asset than a readiness to play risky strokes from the start against a field that is very soon flung far and wide in defence.

Perhaps the most adverse aspect of limited-over cricket is the discouragement it brings to slow bowlers. It is not that accurate slow bowling is not likely to be of value but that the opportunities of the slow bowler to learn his subtle and exacting craft are so greatly reduced. The arts of spin are not come by without regular practice – and, one might add, a knowledgeable and understanding captain. Slow bowlers take longer to develop than the other types and modern cricket is increasingly a young man's game. Thus the dice are loaded in favour of just-short-of-a-length medium-pace, the dullest type of all. That variety in attack which has always been the spice of cricket is less often to be seen.

There is however one major gain, especially from the point of view of the spectator, whatever class of cricket he is watching, and that is the quality of the fielding. The saving of runs being the prime requisite, a captain calls for a very high degree of athleticism and throwing power. Physical fitness has become almost the first priority, to the detriment sometimes of technique. The modern county cricketer is apt to spend as much time in the gymnasium before the season starts as in the nets. When Hobbs, Woolley and Hammond were batting for England there was no doubt which department of the game gave the most pleasure: equally obviously the England of today are seen to most advantage in the field.

The effect of the new fixture pattern on modern batting technique is a vexed subject. Alec Bedser, the long-serving chairman of the England selectors, was wont to remark very frequently that the new competitions induced bad habits in batsmen: hence, he thought, a drop in the standard. In particular the deliberate angled stroke through the vacant slips area led to a failure to get behind the line of fast bowling in first-class and Test cricket. Though there was substance in this theory it could be argued that the many overseas players in county cricket, and the West Indians in particular, did not seem to be similarly infected.

Being on record as having given the warmest possible welcome to the Gillette from the start I would not wish to be thought of as having deserted from the ranks. Limited-over cricket in England has not only proved a financial necessity but has given a vast deal of pleasure to a wider public both present at the games and, of course, watching on television. It has surely given a sensible county player the opportunity of increasing the range of his stroke-play. A decade or more ago there were county batsmen whose slowness was a byword. There are very few such today.

The amount of limited-over cricket, however, needs careful control by authority. Otherwise it may submerge the orthodox match, be it of one day or three or five, and the true essence of cricket would evaporate beyond recall. One thinks in particular at the moment of writing of Australia which, despite the restraining hand of the International Cricket Conference and certain modifications made in consequence, is embarked on a wholly unbalanced programme of limited-over International matches designed to attract big TV audiences and also apt to bring in the louder, more demonstrative and more ignorant spectator. Such a programme can only be detrimental to Test cricket which, at its best, is still the highest expression of the game and the guardian of its standards.

One way and another the spread of the limited-over game at all levels has revolutionized cricket within the last decade and more, and it has been a not-so-quiet revolution at that. In England, though partisanship at times has grown too fierce to be funny, cricket still attracts for the most part the sort of spectator who would wish, and would deserve, to be called a sportsman. With so much at stake there were fears before the 2nd Prudential World Cup that players or spectators or both might let their feelings run away with them. But at none of the matches was there a hint of trouble, while in the Final the Lord's crowd, as usual, lived up to their high reputation.

Without being complacent we can be confident that the TCCB, with the co-operation of the Cricketers' Association, can keep the English game on the right lines. As to the new partnership between the Australian Cricket Board and the Packer promoting organizations, one can but hope.

International

The Prudential Cup

TWO WORLD TITLES TO WEST INDIES

MICHAEL BREARLEY

The massive power of the West Indies, captained each time by Clive Lloyd, enabled them to win the first 2 Prudential World Cups, in 1975 and 1979. The 2 Finals at Lord's followed a similar pattern. West Indies were put in to bat, lost early wickets (they were 55 for 3 in 1975, 99 for 4 in 1979), but the individual brilliance of Lloyd and Rohan Kanhai, Vivian Richards and Collis King, saw them to huge totals in the 290s. Australia, in 1975, and England, in 1979, both batted well up to a point, but Australia needed a last-wicket stand of 41 to take them within 17 of their target, and England after falling increasingly behind the required rate succumbed dramatically to the amazing Joel Garner.

In 1975, West Indies found themselves in easily the tougher group. Apart from Sri Lanka their other opponents in the qualifying matches were Australia and Pakistan. Only 2 sides of the 4 would go through to the semi-finals, so that 1 defeat could mean elimination from the competition. Lloyd's team could hardly have come closer to defeat than in their 2nd match, against Pakistan at Edgbaston. Several of the talented Pakistan batsmen played well for them to score 266 for 7 in their 60 overs. In reply, only Lloyd of the main batsmen made a score, and West Indies slumped to 166 for 8. When Sarfraz Nawaz took his 4th wicket the score was 203–9, with 14 overs remaining. But Andy Roberts and Deryck Murray played marvellously and they scrambled home with 2 balls to spare. That defeat cooked Pakistan's goose, as they had already lost to Australia at Headingley, where Ross Edwards scored 80 not out in a total of 278 for 7. Then Dennis Lillee took 5 for 34 to bring victory by 73 runs.

These 2 rounds ensured that Australia and West Indies would be in the semi-finals, but their match at the Oval was important as a rehearsal between the 2 most powerful sides for a probable final, and to decide the pairings in the semi-finals; for the winners the reward would be a match against New Zealand, while the losers would have to take on England at Headingley. Lloyd won the toss and, on a cloudy morning, put Australia in to bat. The ball swung, and only a fighting 6th wicket stand between Edwards and Rodney Marsh allowed Australia to reach the relative respectability of 192. The West Indies response was crushingly brilliant. Roy Fredericks cut and hooked his way to 58, and Alvin Kallicharran savaged a surprised Lillee, scoring 35 runs off the last 10 balls he received from him. An excited crowd cheered a West Indies victory by 7 wickets with the large margin of 14 overs to spare. Australia learned from this match. In the final itself, on an equally easy-paced pitch, their bowlers rarely bowled short against batsmen so quick to hook and pull.

Meanwhile, in the other group, England were having things very much their own way. Indeed, it may well have been a handicap to have had so little opposition in these early games, as the team had hardly been stretched either bowling or batting. It is only under the pressure of hard-fought games that a side learns its strengths and the range of its resources. As it was their opponents were East Africa (a much weaker team than Sri Lanka, who surpassed themselves to score 276 for 6 against Australia), India, whose experience of one-day cricket was minimal, and New Zealand, a competent but ordinary side. Dennis Amiss and Keith Fletcher played exceptionally well in the 3 matches and the bowling was excellent.

Up to this point most pitches in this hot summer had favoured the batsmen, and scores had been high. The semi-final at Headingley, however, was played on a grassy pitch and in overcast conditions. Australia won the toss, and Gary Gilmour exploited the conditions perfectly. Bowling left-arm over the wicket at a lively pace, he swung the ball sharply either way. His 6 victims were in the first 7 in the order, and all were completely beaten, mainly by in-swing. He took 6 for 14 and England were all out for 93. Despite having had to bat in more difficult conditions, England nearly won the game. John Snow had both Chappells lbw, Chris Old took 3 wickets, and Australia were soon 39 for 6. But it was Gilmour's match. Playing their shots, he and Doug Walters took their side to victory in only 28 overs. On the same day, West Indies were having little difficulty in defeating New Zealand by 5 wickets at the Oval. Geoff Howarth scored 51 out of a total of 158; then Gordon Greenidge and Kallicharran played well for the favourites to win by 5 wickets with almost 20 overs to spare.

And so to the Final, a match that fully lived up to expectations at the end of a fortnight of almost uniquely perfect weather. The pitch was as benign as the day, so that Gilmour, for example, fresh from his success at Headingley, found himself being driven over mid-off by Lloyd. Despite this he came back with 4 late wickets to finish with 5 for 48. But it was a batsman's match, almost from the start. Fredericks's dismissal was remarkable; in the act of hooking Lillee for 6 he dislodged a bail. Greenidge and Kallicharran were more genuinely dismissed, so when Kanhai joined Lloyd at 55 for 3, the West Indies' position was precarious. These two, however, made few mistakes. Lloyd faced only 82 balls while scoring 100, a fantastically powerful innings. Ian Chappell's team were scattered around the outfield, and the ball still raced past them. There was a period in the second Final when I knew just how helpless Chappell must have felt. Kanhai was more restrained; but even in defence he is an elegant and correct player. When Lloyd was eventually out, caught low down on the leg-side by Marsh, a big total was virtually certain; the Australians may even have been relieved that it did not exceed 300.

Australia made batting look almost simple. The pitch was now at its best. I have never seen fast bowlers driven so frequently or played with such ease. The scorecard, in a way, gives an indication of this, for what defeated Australia was only the pressure of keeping up the required rate against brilliant fielding. Remarkably, Richards twice hit the stumps direct from side-on to run out Turner and Greg Chappell and also ran Ian Chappell out with his throw to Lloyd. Three of the first 4 wickets went in this way, and Richards, who had not got going with the bat, had made his decisive mark on the competition.

After tea, I went and sat in the sun at the Nursery End with Peter Walker; the crowd, with its majority of West Indians, was immensely happy and good-natured. It was a wonderful day. Australia lost wickets and fell further behind the run-rate. When Lillee joined Jeff Thomson, the cause was almost lost and hundreds of us went and sat by the boundary rope to wait for the end. Thomson drove Vanburn Holder in the air to Kallicharran at cover; the match must be over... We picked up sandals and picnic baskets, beer cans and scorecards, and ran on to the field. Few of the spectators had seen Umpire Tom Spencer's arm, and none had heard his no-ball call. Meanwhile Kallicharran shied at the stumps and missed; the ball raced down towards the Tavern and disappeared in another wave of spectators advancing from that quarter. Lillee and Thomson hared between the wickets. Eventually the ball was retrieved, the spectators shamefacedly but good-humouredly retreated, and Umpire Spencer, pragmatically, but with disregard for the letter of the law, 'awarded' the batsmen 3 runs. A few minutes later, at 8.45, with the shadows well over the square, the match was over. It had been a miraculous day, in cricketing terms: perfect weather, perfect pitch and a superb game.

The success of the 1975 competition made a repeat mandatory. There were voices advocating India or other countries as the venue, but only the long midsummer English days would allow 120 overs in a day. Recent developments in illumination might allow a future World Cup to take place in other countries. The

Clive Lloyd accepts the Prudential Cup from the Duke of Edinburgh, President of MCC in 1975, after a great final against Australia.

1975 Prudential Cup was the occasion on which one-day international cricket fully came of age. The appeal of limited-overs cricket had become established at county level in the 1960s, but one-day internationals, although a part of tour programmes since the early 70s, had not really become fully accepted by public and players. The matches were felt to be very much secondary to the Tests; the success of a tour was measured by cricketing performance in Tests, and the one-day matches sometimes seemed a laborious encumbrance. Now the 'World Cup', condensed into a 15-day period, with all the glamour of self-contained competition, gave these matches unprecedented appeal.

Also a younger generation of cricketers, brought up from the start on a diet containing liberal portions of limited-over cricket, relishes this form of it. They do not, so much as their elders, regard it as a second-best introduced solely for entertainment. The adrenalin flows, the fielding is spectacular and athletic, and the running between the wickets dynamic. Many batsmen have discovered a wider range of strokes because of the demands of this game. And 60 overs each side is long enough to enable a team to attack early on, and for slow bowlers to have an important role to play. The Prudential Insurance Company, who had also sponsored earlier internationals, now realized that they were on to a winner, and arrangements were soon made for 1979.

Meanwhile, another more abrasive sponsor had thrown an Australian spanner in the works. At one time it seemed unlikely that any of the World Series cricketers could be involved in the Prudential Cup, or that, if they were, others might boycott the competition. West Indies and Pakistan, though, decided to pick their full-strength sides, so that 10 of the West Indies party of 14 players and 8 of the Pakistan team had played for Packer a few months before. India and New Zealand had been, so far, unaffected; England and Australia did not consider their World Series men. In the few weeks before the World Cup the news emerged that reconciliation was likely, and by the time it started the atmosphere was, if not rosy, at least less prickly than for 2 years. The side most affected was, of course, Australia, though their players had twice beaten England in one-day internationals at Melbourne in February, and a month later had drawn with the full Pakistan team in a 2-match Test series.

This time there was a little more seeding. Australia and West Indies, the previous finalists, were placed in different halves of the draw, each with one ICC Associate team. The Associates

Line-up for the 1979 Prudential Cup: the captains in front, B. Warnapura (Sri Lanka), Asif Iqbal (Pakistan), C. H. Lloyd (West Indies), J. M. Brearley (England), K. J. Hughes (Australia), M. G. Burgess (New Zealand), S. Venkataraghavan (India) and B. M. Mauricette (vice-captain of Canada).

were now to fight for the right to play in the competition proper rather than being appointed as in 1975. So, more democratically, Canada emerged from this rain-spoilt mini-cup by beating Bermuda in a play-off; Sri Lanka, not surprisingly, won the other place. New Zealand and India again found themselves together in Group 'B' with West Indies and Sri Lanka, while England were this time in the more difficult group with Pakistan, Australia and Canada.

It was a good Prudential Cup for England. We won all 4 matches to reach the Final, where we worried the West Indies at several stages of the match before the last decisive chapter. Twelve of our 14 players had been on the recent tour of Australia, and the other 2 had spent the winter in Sydney. Someone remarked, when we got together less than 48 hours before the first match, that it was like the tour starting again, a feeling strengthened by the fact that our first encounter was against the same Australian side, now captained by Kim Hughes. We put them in to bat hoping to take advantage of the slight damp in the pitch, but Darling and Andy Hilditch played well; a lunch score of 97 for 1 should have led to a total of more than 200, but our accurate bowling, together with some rash running between the wickets, produced a collapse. We needed only 160 to win. For 4 overs Rodney Hogg produced, for the only time in England, his pace of the previous winter, and at 5 for 2 we were in danger. Graham Gooch, however, looked in complete control from the start, and together we took the score beyond 100. We won by 6 wickets. This was the start of Gooch's emergence as an international batsman of class. Perhaps I overestimated Australia as a one-day side; certainly they had a depressing time, losing easily to Pakistan after Hogg had withdrawn because of illness; Alan Hurst, too, hurt himself during the match so that they were reduced to bowling Graham Yallop, who had stood in as a 'keeper at Sydney, against Javed Miandad and Asif Iqbal.

Our 2nd match was against Canada; having won this we were certain of a place in the semi-finals as Pakistan had beaten Australia. But the losers of the England v Pakistan match would have to meet West Indies in the semi-final. The conditions at Headingley suited our bowlers perfectly. The ball moved off the seam and the bounce was irregular. Fortunately for us, Sarfraz was unfit; unfortunately Asif won the toss and put us in to bat. We struggled, inevitably, against Imran Khan and Sikander Bakht; but, what was more disappointing, we lost 3 key wickets to Majid Khan whose 12 overs cost only 27 runs. In reply Mike Hendrick had a field-day. Often he beats the bat repeatedly without finding the edge; now he had a fairer share of luck, but his figures of 4 for 15 did not flatter him. Asif however, played an excellent innings and took Pakistan from 31 for 6 to the brink of victory. Geoff Boycott had already bowled well for us against Australia; now as the overs remaining to our front line bowlers ebbed away he did an invaluable job. With less than 4 overs remaining, after an absorbingly tight match, Sikander was well caught by Hendrick at deep mid-off, and we had won the match by 14 runs.

Meanwhile West Indies had won comfortably against India, had been rained off against Sri Lanka, and now beat New Zealand. New Zealand put up a good fight. As we were to find out at Old Trafford, they used their limited bowling resources

Zaheer Abbas is caught and bowled G. J. Cosier for 16 but Pakistan in 1979 were too strong in batting for Australia and beat them by 89 runs.

Greenidge run out by Randall in the 1979 final – an illustration of the brilliant out-cricket that brought England to Lord's.

intelligently. Knowing that they had only one real attacking bowler in Richard Hadlee, they set the field deep for their other bowlers from an early stage. They accepted 3 or 4 singles an over, but hoped to cut off the boundaries and drive the batsmen to desperate shots. West Indies, batting on a good pitch at Trent Bridge, needed a late burst from Lloyd to reach 241, and though the margin was wider than the score suggests, won by only 32 runs. Poor India, still inexperienced in one-day cricket, were defeated by the talented Sri Lanka team who went on to a successful tour against the counties.

For the semi-final we played an extra batsman, relying on Boycott and Gooch to bowl 12 overs between them. As it turned out we needed the batsmen, for a middle order collapse left Derek Randall, batting at No 7, in with the tail. His 43 not out and his outstanding fielding – he ran out 2 of their main batsmen – enabled us to win another close game, this time by 9 runs. For New Zealand, John Wright, Bruce Edgar, Bob Cairns and Richard Hadlee had played well throughout the competition, and though their bowling was below Test standard they made the best possible use of it.

In the other semi-final, Greenidge, the most successful batsman in the competition, led the favourites to a huge score of 293. In reply Majid and Zaheer Abbas played superbly to take the score to 176 for 1, but in the end the power and pace of Mike Holding and the others, together with Richards's shrewd off-breaks, was too much. Gradually the required run rate increased. Pakistan did themselves credit. They lacked the ability to attack with the ball after the initial burst, but their depth and skill of batting, together with the shrewd use of Majid and Asif as bowlers, made them one of the top 3 sides in the competition.

For the final we were without Bob Willis, while West Indies were able to field the side that had played in every match. Willis had limped off in the semi-final with a recurrence of a knee injury – not as bad as was feared, but he could not be risked in the last match. The injury may well have been crucial. For when we had West Indies 55 for 3, and then 99 for 4, we were unable to keep attacking. The drawback of playing spinners in one-day cricket is not so much the fear that they may be more expensive than seam bowlers, as the probability that a pitch prepared for a one-day match will not take spin. Yet the ball may well seam, swing and bounce for the quicker bowlers. Phil Edmonds, who replaced Willis, bowled very well, and in the end it was our policy of playing the extra batsman – so successful at Old Trafford – that proved costly, as 12 overs of Boycott, Gooch and Wayne Larkins went for 86 runs. Two brilliant innings were played. Vivian Richards, who must have been within a hair's breadth of being lbw 2nd ball, scored 135 not out, despite being below his best for his first 50. King played an extraordinary innings of 86. The eventual total of 286 was very high. Like Australia in 1975 and Pakistan 3 days before, we were well placed at various points. At tea, after 25 overs, the score was 79 for 0; we all reckoned that this was a good start, a better score than, say, 95 for 3. At this point my inclination was for us to have a real 'go', setting a target of 6 runs an over from the start. I regret being talked out of this in favour of a more modest target. In fact Boycott and I scored 50 runs from the next 13 overs. Now 7 runs an over were needed, and though Gooch and Randall kept up with that demanding rate, it would have been remarkable if we could have won the match. Still, when Gooch was out, we were in much the same position as Pakistan had been. Our collapse, however, was more dramatic. Garner, who stands 6 feet 9 inches, is the only fast bowler whose hand, when he delivers the ball, comes from above the sightboards at the Nursery End; he bowled fast and straight, and right up to the batsman, and kept hitting the stumps. We must give credit to him and the others – Holding, Croft and Roberts.

The match-winners: coming together at 99 for 4 Vivian Richards (138 not out) and Collis King made 139 together in 21 overs, of which King's share was 86.

There have probably been better Test teams than this West Indies one, for they lack high quality spinners. But I cannot imagine that, in the history of the game, there has been a side better equipped for one-day cricket. In fact their closest rivals were probably the winners of the 1975 World Cup!

CUP FINAL RESULTS

1975 West Indies beat Australia by 17 runs
1979 West Indies beat England by 92 runs

HIGHEST TOTAL

334–4 England v India, Lord's 1975

HIGHEST TOTAL BATTING SECOND

276–4 Sri Lanka v Australia, Oval 1975

LOWEST TOTAL

45 Canada v England, Old Trafford 1979

HIGHEST MATCH AGGREGATE

604 Australia (328–5) v Sri Lanka (276–4), Oval 1975

LOWEST MATCH AGGREGATE

91 Canada (45) v England (46–1), Old Trafford 1979

BIGGEST VICTORIES

10 wickets India beat East Africa, Headingley 1975
202 runs England beat India, Lord's 1975

NARROWEST VICTORIES

1 wicket West Indies beat Pakistan, (with 2 balls to spare), Edgbaston 1975
9 runs England beat New Zealand, Old Trafford 1979

HIGHEST INDIVIDUAL SCORE

171* G. M. Turner, New Zealand v East Africa, Edgbaston 1975

HUNDRED BEFORE LUNCH

A. Turner (101), Australia v West Indies, Oval 1975

HIGHEST BATTING AGGREGATE

333 (average 166·50) G. M. Turner, New Zealand, 1975

HIGHEST PARTNERSHIP FOR EACH WICKET

1 R. B. McCosker and A. Turner, 182, Australia v Sri Lanka, Oval 1975
2 D. L. Amiss and K. W. R. Fletcher, 176, England v India, Lord's 1975
3 G. M. Turner and J. M. Parker, 149, New Zealand v East Africa, Edgbaston 1975
4 R. B. Kanhai and C. H. Lloyd, 149, West Indies v Australia, Lord's 1975
5 I. V. A. Richards and C. L. King, 139, West Indies v England, Lord's 1979
6 R. Edwards and R. W. Marsh, 99, Australia v West Indies, Oval 1975
7 K. D. Walters and G. J. Gilmour, 55*, Australia v England, Headingley 1975
8 D. R. Hadlee and B. J. McKechnie, 48, New Zealand v England, Trent Bridge 1975
9 S. Abid Ali and S. Venkataraghavan, 60, India v New Zealand, Old Trafford 1975
10 D. L. Murrary and A. M. E. Roberts, 64*, West Indies v Pakistan, Edgbaston 1975

BEST BOWLING

6–14 G. J. Gilmour, Australia v England, Headingley 1975

HIGHEST BOWLING AGGREGATE

11 (average 5·63) G. J. Gilmour, Australia, 1975

MOST ECONOMICAL BOWLING

12–8–6–1 B. S. Bedi, India v East Africa, Headingley 1975

MOST EXPENSIVE BOWLING

11–1–83–0 K. D. Ghavri, India v England, Lord's 1975

WICKET-KEEPING – MOST DISMISSALS

4 D. L. Murray, West Indies v Sri Lanka, Old Trafford 1975

FIELDING – MOST CATCHES

3 C. H. Lloyd, West Indies v Sri Lanka, Old Trafford 1975

PRUDENTIAL CUP NATIONAL RECORDS

Australia

Highest Total 328–5 v Sri Lanka, Oval 1975
Lowest Total 159–9 v England, Lord's 1979
Highest Score 101 A. Turner v Sri Lanka, Oval 1975
Best Bowling 6–14 G. J. Gilmour v England, Headingley 1975
Highest Aggregates:
Batting 201 A. Turner 1975
Bowling 11 G. J. Gilmour 1975

Canada

Highest Total 139–9 v Pakistan, Headingley 1979
Lowest Total 45 v England, Old Trafford 1979
Highest Score 45 G. R. Sealy v Pakistan, Headingley 1979
Best Bowling 2–27 C. C. Henry v Australia, Edgbaston 1979
Highest Aggregates:
Batting 73 G. R. Sealy 1979
Bowling 3 J. N. Valentine 1979

England

Highest Total 334–4 v India, Lord's 1975
Lowest Total 93 v Australia, Headingley 1975
Highest Score 137 D. L. Amiss v India, Lord's 1975
Best Bowling 4–8 C. M. Old v Canada, Old Trafford 1979
Highest Aggregate:
Batting 243 D. L. Amiss 1975
Bowling 10 M. Hendrick 1979

East Africa

Highest Total 128–8 v New Zealand Edgbaston 1975
Lowest Total 94 v England, Edgbaston 1975
Highest Score 45 Frasat Ali v New Zealand, Edgbaston 1975
Best Bowling 3–63 Zulfiqar Ali v England Edgbaston 1975
Highest Aggregates:
Batting 57 Frasat Ali 1975
Bowling 4 Zulfiqar Ali 1975

India

Highest Total 230 v New Zealand, Old Trafford 1975
Lowest Total 132–3 v England, Lord's 1975
Highest Score 75 G. R. Viswanath v West Indies, Edgbaston 1979
Best Bowling 3–15 Madan Lal v East Africa, Headingley 1975
Highest Aggregates:
Batting 113 S. M. Gavaskar, 1975
Bowling 6 S. Abid Ali, 1975

New Zealand

Highest Total 309–5 v East Africa, Edgbaston 1975
Lowest Total 158 v West Indies, Oval 1975
Highest Score 171* G. M. Turner v East Africa, Edgbaston 1975
Best Bowling 3–21 D. R. Hadlee v East Africa, Edgbaston 1975
Highest Aggregates:
Batting 333 G. M. Turner 1975
Bowling 9 B. J. McKechnie 1979

Pakistan

Highest Total 330–6 v Sri Lanka, Trent Bridge 1975
Lowest Total 151 v England, Headingley 1979
Highest Score 97 Zaheer Abbas v Sri Lanka, Trent Bridge 1975
Best Bowling 4–44 Sarfraz Nawaz v West Indies, Edgbaston 1975
Highest Aggregates:
Batting 209 Majid Khan 1975
Bowling 9 Asif Iqbal 1979

Sri Lanka

Highest Total 276–4 v Australia, Oval 1975
Lowest Total 86 v West Indies, Old Trafford 1975
Highest Score 67 S. R. de S. Wettimuny v India, Old Trafford 1979
Best Bowling 3–29 D. S. de Silva v India, Old Trafford 1979
Highest Aggregates:
Batting 83 S. R. de S. Wettimuny 1979
Bowling 4 D. S. de Silva

West Indies
Highest Total 293–6 v Pakistan, Oval 1979
Lowest Total 244–7 v New Zealand, Trent Bridge 1979
Highest Score 138* I. V. A. Richards v England, Lord's 1979
Best Bowling 5–38 J. Garner v England, Lord's 1979
Highest Aggregates:
Batting 253 C. G. Greenidge, 1979
Bowling 10 K. D. Boyce, 1975
10 B. D. Julien, 1975

TOTAL ATTENDANCES		TOTAL TAKINGS
1975	117,809	£188,598
1979	132, 768	£359,717

The ICC Trophy

ENTHUSIASM SURVIVES A WATERY BAPTISM

PHILIP SNOW

The 1979 competition was the first organized for a significant number of non-Test Match countries. A hope that something on these lines could be achieved was expressed broadly by A. Hunt, Bermuda's representative on ICC in 1967, and when B. G. Brocklehurst expounded ideas which led to the Prudential sponsorship and first 'world' competition in 1975, associate countries set about planning for participation in a preliminary competition in England in 1979.

As it was evident that there would not be Prudential backing for associate members competing to see which two could qualify for the Prudential-sponsored tournament, the associate members set up their own management committee. This consisted of the USA representative, J. R. Gardiner, who undertook to be secretary as well as chairman and designed and donated what has been called the ICC Trophy; the Holland representative, P. A. Snow, and the Argentina representative, R. V. C. Robins, as joint honorary treasurers; together with the representative of Sri Lanka, A. Pinto, and Gibraltar, J. Buzaglo.

This committee had many meetings, including a conjoint one with Midlands Club Conference representatives, without whose detailed cooperation in many vital directions (selection of grounds, appointment of umpires and match managers and fixtures for inter-country and friendly club matches, hotels, publicity, transport, for the concentration of matches within 40 miles of Birmingham) the competition might not have been possible.

The TCCB having given limited financial support and there being virtually no sources of income within England, it was the responsibility of each country to obtain sponsors for their total expenses – a daunting task and tremendous outlay for countries travelling from the other side of the world, notably Malaysia, Singapore, Papua New Guinea and Fiji. Hong Kong could not meet the residence qualification rule, West Africa applied after the closing date, and Gibraltar, regrettably having to withdraw late, had its fixtures taken over by Wales (excluding Glamorgan) on condition that as Wales are not in the ICC they could not gain points.

With 14 of the 17 associate members taking part, a larger number than had been thought likely in the management committee's most optimistic reckoning, and having added Wales, J. R. Gardiner and his assistant, Mary Rose Chesterson, immersed themselves in the execution of heavy detailed work in the Isle of Man and Birmingham offices. Two factors, the Midlands and May, neither renowned for sun in combination, had originally caused hesitancy in the management committee's mind. The warm welcomes and efficient arrangements on the Midlands grounds by their officials with their fine facilities helped to make memorable what were in some cases first visits to England by the national overseas teams. It will be seen that, even so, Round III, with fears becoming realistic for the remaining Rounds, almost wrecked the competition as such, which was short enough, spread as it was intermittently over 16 days.

Most teams reaching England before mid-May were able to prepare on unfamiliar turf wickets: one or two arrived as the weather broke, making it the wettest, coldest May since 1722. They consequently remained inexperienced on grass, compared with Holland, Denmark (and Wales). As 5 teams were to meet each other within 3 groups, a theoretical maximum of 4 matches only could be played by any country. In fact, a mere 3 matches within the Competition were played, except by Canada and Bangladesh, to whom the weather allowed 4, apart, of course, from the semi-finalists and finalists. Fiji and Papua New Guinea travelled 24,000 and 20,000 miles respectively for their 2 or 3 competition matches. Countries occupied the remaining (dry) dates with friendly practice matches against Midlands clubs.

It was recognized that the final tables, so affected either by no play or play in conditions not tolerated in, for instance, county matches, would have to be treated with reservations in discerning the main Competition aim – the relative order of strengths of non-Test-playing countries. These were the final tables:-

	WON	LOST	NO RESULT	POINTS	SCORING RATE
GROUP I					
Bermuda	3	0	1	14	4·06
East Africa	2	1	1	10	2·26
Papua New Guinea	1	1	2	8	2·87
Singapore	1	2	1	6	2·15
Argentina	0	3	1	2	2·19
GROUP II					
Denmark	4	0	0	16	2·74
Canada	3	1	0	12	3·09
Bangladesh	2	2	0	8	2·67
Fiji	0	3	1	2	2·63
Malaysia	0	3	1	2	2·54
GROUP III					
Sri Lanka	2	1*	1	10	3·82
USA	2	1	1	10	3·06
Holland	1	2	1	6	2·73
Israel	1*	3	0	4*	2·11
(Wales)	(2)	(1)	(1)	(0)	(3·50)

* = from forfeiture

They evoke comment:

(a) Estimates of strength from results have to be related to the matches being limited to 60 overs.
(b) Scoring rate had to be much in teams' minds: Bermuda's was conspicuous.
(c) Papua New Guinea were unfortunate in 2 of their 4 matches being inconclusive.
(d) All matches being played within 40 miles of Birmingham, Canada were lucky to win (and Bangladesh unlucky in losing) when no other countries in that round could play.
(e) Denmark was the only country to win all 4 matches.
(f) Performances were inevitably low-key in the often inhibiting conditions.
(g) Because of their Government's late refusal to allow Sri Lanka to play Israel, with whom diplomatic relations had chilled years before, and the consequent forfeiture by Sri Lanka of 4 points (to Israel's gain), Sri Lanka had to show their strength in their only 2 matches.

ABOVE J. R. Gardiner, the USA representative on the ICC, organized the Associates competition and donated 'The ICC Trophy', which was won by Sri Lanka.

This unusual stroke by Peni Dekai of Fiji went for 6 in the match between Fiji and Bangladesh at Water Orton.

The progress to final positions was:

ROUND I

Group I

(a) Argentina v Singapore provided one of the closest of finishes. Argentina's 153 for 9 was controlled by the leg-breaks of L. P. Y. K. Sen who took 5 for 54 but D. A. Culley scored 34 not out. With only 4 balls to spare, Singapore obtained 155 for 9, largely through G. S. Heng (40 not out) and S. N. Houghton (32 not out): A. G. Morris, a young seam bowler, took 4 for 29 for Argentina.
(b) Papua New Guinea obtained 161 for 8 v East Africa, A. Leka scoring 51 not out, when rain prevented further play: each team gained 2 points.

Group II

(a) In hail and wind the Canada v Malaysia match was contested over 2 days. For Canada's 185 for 9, 1 of its 9 West Indians, C. A. Marshall, scored 78, supported by 2 other West Indians, G. R. Sealey (38) and F. A. Dennis (28). Malaysia's captain, R. Ratnalingam, took 3 for 21. Another West Indian, J. C. Vaughan (4 for 33), and Marshall (3 for 16) kept Malaysia to 141 (Mahinder Singh 35 not out).
(b) Under jet-lag and lacking practice on turf, Fiji were unprepared for the 28-yard run of the opening Denmark bowler, Ole Mortensen, as fast as any County bowler and with turf experience. He went straight through his 12 overs, taking 4 for 15. Against Fiji's 89, Henrik Mortensen (no relation) made the win a convincing one by 8 wickets with his 52 not out.

Group III

(a) USA were 31 for 6 against Israel, but their 44-year-old Indian captain and correct left-hand bat, A. Lashkari, with 44, helped take his team to 126. For Israel R. Reuben took 4 for 37 and M. Jacob 3 for 27 but their batting, despite B. Kampol's 24 not out, could only reach 85.
(b) In a contentious match Wales obtained 170 for 7 (J. Hopkins 71) against Holland. With no play possible on the second day Holland, having made 59 for 2 at a lower run-rate, were declared to have lost.

ROUND II

Group I

(a) Argentina scored 147 against East Africa; G. W. A. Ferguson batted with impressive correctness for 44, supported by R. E. Villamil (31). East Africa's experienced Zulfiqar Ali took 3 for 13. East Africa lost 5 wickets in passing Argentina's score. A. Rehman, the wicket-keeper, scored 37 and N. P. Thakkar 44 not out. Argentina's best bowler was P. R. Stocks (3 for 18).
(b) Bermuda found Papua New Guinea's 90 (L. Ao, the wicket-keeper, made 25) against W. Trott, left-arm fast, 3 for 23, and C. Wade, slow right, 3 for 16, not difficult to pass. Bermuda lost only 3 wickets, L. Thomas making 27.

Group II

(a) Bangladesh were 54 for 8 against Fiji but recovered to reach 103. M. K. Isimeli, a flighting left-armer, took 3 for 14. Fiji attempted too high a scoring rate unnecessarily: mis-timing the off-spin of S. A. Haq, whose 7 for 23 was the best analysis of the competition, they lost by 21 runs.
(b) For Denmark against Malaysia, Ole Mortensen was again menacing (5 maidens and 3 wickets in his first 12 overs). Against Malaysia's 156 Denmark only lost 3 wickets. Henrik Mortensen for the 2nd successive match batted formidably for 55 not out. Carsten Morild (43 years old), who had taken 3 for 32, had an excellent match in obtaining 66 not out.

Group III

(a) Holland restricted Israel to 105, D. Moss (39) and S. B. Periman (27) with R. van Weelde taking 3 for 32. They then obtained the runs for the loss of 2 wickets, A. Bakker scoring 60 not out and M. Flohil 29.
(b) Against Sri Lanka, USA, through a West Indian, W. B. Stuger (48) and the wicket-keeper, K. R. Khan (one of 6 Pakistanis in an otherwise largely West Indian contingent), made 44, scored 168. Sri Lanka's batting strength ensured a win by 6 wickets – R. L. Dias 76 not out and B. Warnapura 36.

ROUND III

Group I

(a) Argentina v Papua New Guinea: with Argentina 85 for 4, the match was abandoned and points shared.
(b) Bermuda v Singapore: match abandoned without a ball bowled.

Group II

(a) Canada were most lucky in their match against Bangladesh. It was the only game played in Round III although not more than 40 miles from any of the other matches. Canada made 190 for 8 (Dennis 61) and their West Indian captain, G. E. Brisbane, hit 34, J. S. Badsha at medium pace taking 4 for 17. In Bangladesh's 141, A. S. M. R. Hassan scored 34, whilst the tall, ever-active West Indian all-rounder, Vaughan, took 3 for 28.
(b) Fiji v Malaysia: match abandoned without a ball bowled.

Group III

(a) Holland v USA: match abandoned without a ball bowled.
(b) Wales v Sri Lanka: match abandoned without a ball bowled.

ROUND IV

Group I

(a) Bermuda had an overwhelming win over Argentina, dismissing them for 81 (a left-armer, C. Parfitt, taking 3 for 16) and obtaining 85 for 1 (W. A. Reid 43 not out and L. E. Thomas 36 not out).
(b) Singapore's 131 for 9 was insufficient to stretch East Africa who passed it with the loss of 5 wickets.

Group II

(a) Malaysia scored 114 against Bangladesh, for whom D. Zaman took 4 for 23. Bangladesh won by 7 wickets, Badsha scoring 39.
(b) In a low-scoring match Denmark made 118, the Canadian M. P. Stead taking 4 for 16 and H. Mortensen again among the runs with 36. Canada could only reach 72, Carsten Morild taking 4 for 12.

Group III

(a) Sri Lanka compiled, for this competition, a high score in obtaining 212 for 8 (R. D. Mendis, the wicket-keeper and a prolific as well as adventurous batsman, making 51). Van Weelde took 3 for 22 at a considerable pace. In Holland's 167 for 8 Bakker made a creditable 74.
(b) For Wales v Israel, Hopkins scored 92 and G. Edwards, 67 in Wales's 234 for 5. Israel responded with 143 for 9.

ROUND V

Group I

(a) Bermuda defeated East Africa with maximum ease. Against their opponents' 94 for 9 (E. G. James 3 for 23, Trott 3 for 8), Bermuda, largely through Reid's 59 not out, scored 100 for 1.
(b) Papua New Guinea won comfortably against Singapore, their innings of 174 being countered by only 87.

Sri Lanka won the ICC Associates final at Worcester by 60 runs after making 324 for 8. Duleep Mendis, who scored 66, was their 'Man of the Match'.

Group II

(a) The Bangladesh v Denmark match was very close. Denmark made 164 for 8, K. Kristensen making an invaluable 74. Bangladesh finished only 9 short.

(b) Reasonable scores were reached by both Canada and Fiji. Canada's 209 for 6 was achieved mainly by Dennis's 48 and Vaughan's powerful straight-driving for 64, which turned the game for Canada after a shaky start. Fiji reached 153 (C. A. C. Browne 34).

Group III

(a) Israel v Sri Lanka: Sri Lanka withdrew; 4 points were allotted to Israel.

(b) For USA, Lashkari scored 73 and Stuger 37 against Wales in a total of 190 (S. Carey 3 for 19). Khan's 5 for 17 was largely responsible for an 8 run win: G. Ellis scored 56.

SEMI-FINALS

(a) Bermuda, expected to beat Canada, scored 181 (J. Tucker 49, G. A. Brown 34) and when Canada were 62 for 5 this looked certain. But Canada's West Indian vice-captain, B. M. Mauricette, made 72 in strong style, supported by the Pakistani T. Javed's 47 not out, helping Canada to obtain a surprising 4-wicket victory.

(b) Sri Lanka showed their extra class by electing in the semi-final against Denmark to obtain the competition's highest score: 318 for 8 – Dias (88), Mendis (68), Warnapura (34), A. P. B. Tennekoon (45). D. S. de Silva scored 41 and using leg-cutters took 3 for 20 which, with Warnapura's 3 for 22 and S. P. Pasqual's 3 for 7, virtually decided Denmark's total of 110, Kristensen alone, with 34, showing resistance.

FINAL

Sri Lanka again produced a large total for a 60-over match in defeating Canada. Their batting, always stronger than their bowling, achieved 324 for 8 – Mendis 66, Dias 44, D. S. de Silva 39 not out, Pasqual 39, R. S. Madugalle 33, and the wicket-keeper S. A. Jayasinghe 64. Canada nevertheless reached 264 for 5, the dependable Vaughan hitting 80 not out and Marshall 55.

These two teams in the fortnight between the semi-finals and final had the experience of playing the Test countries in the Prudential Cup Competition where Sri Lanka distinguished themselves by beating India.

For those seeking to settle the fundamental question as to the next strongest 2 teams in 1979 after the 6 Test countries and Sri Lanka, it would have helped if countries had also played those, or most of those, which had been placed in different groups. As it was, only three such matches between ICC countries took place; Bermuda defeated Bangladesh by 8 wickets, whilst Fiji beat USA by 83 runs (dismissing USA for 55, the lowest in a match between ICC countries) and also defeated Argentina by 6 wickets. Any future competition, it has now been agreed, should arrange for all countries to meet each other.

The Prudential Trophy

ALEX BANNISTER

Started in 1972 the 55-over international tournament for the Prudential Trophy provides a lively, competitive and financially rewarding diversion from the sterner stuff of five-day Test Matches. It owes its origins to a 40-over (8-ball) match arranged to compensate the public of Melbourne for the loss by rain of the Third Test with England in 1971. The size of the crowd, estimated at 46,000, alerted the authorities in England to the possibilities of single-innings internationals organized on a series basis. In 1972 accordingly a new competition, consisting of 3 matches against the touring Australians and sponsored by Prudential, was launched in preference to a Sixth Test. Aggregate attendances of 51,000 at Old Trafford, Lord's and Edgbaston produced receipts of £46,000 to add to a guarantee of £30,000. The backing was increased later to £110,000 over a 2-year period with the bulk earmarked for the Test and County Cricket Board. A balance is reserved for prize money for teams and individual performances including awards for Man of the Match and Man of the Series. The 1st series was excitingly won by England after a 2-wicket victory in the final match at Edgbaston, and the success of the new venture was assured. Except for the 2 Prudential Cup years, the Trophy has since become an integral part of every season, and continues to flourish.

Playing conditions are broadly on Gillette Cup lines, with attacking batting, tight bowling and spectacular fielding

England had won the first 2 Prudential Trophy matches against Australia in 1977 before the 3rd at the Oval ended, at 8.15 pm, in heavy rain and against a blinding low sun.

concentrated into the standard hours of play between 10.45 am and 7.15 pm. To obtain a result in a day – which is half the appeal of one-day cricket – umpires are given much latitude. At the Oval in 1977 Australia won at 8.15 pm with 2 wickets and 10 balls to spare with England's fielders drenched to the skin and squelching through pools of water. Normally play would have been unthinkable during a comparable downpour. Provision is made for a 2nd day, and in the 1st 9 series of the competition only once – at Old Trafford in 1973 – was it impossible to achieve a result.

Each bowler is limited to 11 overs, and with cash and prestige at stake tactics have grown increasingly sophisticated. Captains and players need to be aware of every changing tactical requirement as one over can dramatically change a situation, and a careless period can mean the difference between victory and defeat. High demands are placed on team discipline and individual initiative. Batsmen need to tread a difficult path between aggression and prudence, bowlers have to be accurate and bowl to their fields, and field-placing is crucial. The regulations are obliged to cover all conceivable eventualities. For example, if there is a tie the result stands unless it is necessary to declare a winner for the series. From there the winner is (a) the side losing the lesser number of wickets; or (b) if both sides are all out, the side with the higher overall scoring rate (runs per over), or, if a result still cannot be achieved, by the side with the higher scoring rate in the 1st 30 overs.

As befits the Prudential Cup champions, the West Indies have shown their dominant strength in the Trophy. In 5 matches they have lost only once to England, and that by 1 wicket at Headingley in 1973, while in 1976 they won by margins of 6 wickets, 36 runs and 50 runs. The disparity between the sides was shown in the prize money distribution. The West Indies took £5,150, and England's 14-man party shared £200. In the series Richards had scores of 119 not out out of a total of 207 for 3 at Scarborough, 97 at Lord's, including a record 50 off 42 balls, and 0 at Edgbaston. To compensate for Richards's final failure, Clive Lloyd also took 50 off 42 balls. The nearest an England player has come to emulating such fast scoring was Knott's 50 in 47 balls bowled by Australia at Lord's in 1972, when Colley conceded 72 runs in his allotted 11 overs. He had 1 maiden. Despite Colley's extravagant punishment Australia managed to win by 5 wickets, thanks to a 4th-wicket stand of 103 by Greg Chappell and Sheahan.

Greg Chappell's stature as an all-rounder is demonstrated by two of the most outstanding performances in the competition – a top score of 125 not out at the Oval and 5 for 20 in the same 1977 series at Edgbaston where the conditions were ideal for his medium-paced bowling. Cosier was even better with 5 for 18 and England were put out for 171 in 53·5 overs. Lever, however, replied with 4 for 2 in 15 balls and Australia, dismissed for 70 in only 25·2 overs, lost by 101 runs. Australia were beaten 2–1 in both series, and Amiss scored 2 of his 3 hundreds in the Trophy against them. His 103 in the inaugural match not only set up England's 6-wicket victory, but reinstated him at top level after disappointing results in major Tests. Radley and Randall also used Trophy games to show their mettle. Amiss made 108 at the Oval in 1977, and 100 off New Zealand at Swansea in 1973. New Zealand had won the Australian one-day competition twice in the previous 4 years, but their competent bowling could not contain Amiss, who made 46 of the 1st 52 off the bat with Boycott as his partner, and went on to 100 out of 135 in 39 overs.

Perhaps the most dazzling innings of all was played by Majid Khan at Trent Bridge in 1974. From the 1st ball he attacked without mercy, and with Sadiq Mohammad the 1st wicket put on 113 in only 18·2 overs against the bowling of Willis, Lever, Old, Underwood and Greig. Majid reached 100 off 88 balls and scored 109 in 31 overs. England, who had made a healthy 244 for 4 in 50 overs (reduced by a late start) with David Lloyd scoring 116 not out, were swept aside and defeated by 7 wickets. Worse was to come for England in the 2nd match at Edgbaston. No play was possible on the 1st day, and a late start on the 2nd meant the overs were cut to 32. Put in to bat in damp and difficult conditions England were 28 for 7 after 17 overs, and limped to 81 for 9 on the strength of 40 by the 9th pair, Taylor and Underwood. Majid, this time, fell to Arnold without scoring, but Zaheer Abbas, another brilliant strokemaker, hit 57 not out and Pakistan won by 8 wickets. By then the bowlers had lost the advantage of the conditions. England gained a measure of revenge in 1978, overwhelming a weakened Pakistan by 132 runs and 94 runs. Gower made 114 not out at the Oval. In the 1st match at Old Trafford Sarfraz Nawaz, with 1 for 13 in his 11 overs, almost equalled the record of the West Indian Gibbs, who had 1 for 12 at the Oval in 1973.

Majid Khan during his dazzling innings of 109 in 31 overs at Trent Bridge in 1974.

At full strength Pakistan have presented stiff opposition, but India, perhaps because of an emphasis on spin in attack, have never quite come to terms with single-innings cricket. Yet they managed a total of 265 in an aggregate of 531 runs at Headingley in 1974. England's 266 for 6 on that occasion was bettered at Old Trafford in 1978 with 278–5 against New Zealand. Radley made 117 not out, and Cairns, who had taken 5 for 28, including 4 for 5 in a 9-ball spell, now conceded 84 in his 11 overs. His response was to slog 60 out of the last 67 runs, pull Edmonds for 4 sixes, and earn New Zealand's Man of the Match award. Cairns's fluctuating experiences provided one perfect reason for the charm and appeal of the competition.

ENGLAND

Won 12   Lost 8   Drawn 1

HIGHEST TOTALS

For 278–5 v New Zealand, Old Trafford 1978
Against 265 by India, Headingley 1974

LOWEST TOTALS

For 81–9 v Pakistan, Edgbaston 1974
Against 70 by Australia, Edgbaston 1977

HIGHEST INDIVIDUAL INNINGS

For 117* C. T. Radley v New Zealand, Old Trafford 1978
Against 125* G. S. Chappell for Australia, Oval 1977

BEST BOWLING

For 4–15 R. G. D. Willis v Pakistan, Old Trafford 1978
Against 5–18 G. J. Cosier for Australia, Edgbaston 1977

AUSTRALIA

Won 2   Lost 4

HIGHEST TOTALS

For 246–8 Oval 1977
Against 242 Oval 1977

LOWEST TOTALS

For 70 Edgbaston 1977
Against 171 Edgbaston 1977

HIGHEST INDIVIDUAL INNINGS

For 125* G. S. Chappell, Oval 1977
Against 108 D. L. Amiss, Oval 1977

BEST BOWLING

For 5–18 G. J. Cosier, Edgbaston 1977
Against 4–27 G. G. Arnold, Edgbaston 1972

WEST INDIES

Won 4 Lost 1

HIGHEST TOTALS

For 223–9 Edgbaston 1976
Against 202–8 Scarborough 1976

LOWEST TOTALS

For 181 Headingley 1973
Against 173 Edgbaston 1976

HIGHEST INDIVIDUAL INNINGS

For 119* I. V. A. Richards, Scarborough 1976
Against 88 D. W. Randall, Lord's 1976

BEST BOWLING

For 5–50 V. A. Holder, Edgbaston 1976
Against 3–27 D. L. Underwood, Lord's 1976

NEW ZEALAND

Lost 3 Drawn 1

HIGHEST TOTALS

For 187–8, Scarborough 1978
Against 278–5, Old Trafford 1978

LOWEST TOTALS

For 152, Old Trafford 1978
Against 159–3, Swansea 1973

HIGHEST INDIVIDUAL INNINGS

For 60 B. L. Cairns, Old Trafford 1978
Against 117* C. T. Radley, Old Trafford 1978

BEST BOWLING

For 5–28 B. L. Cairns, Scarborough 1978
Against 4–32 J. A. Snow, Swansea 1973

INDIA

Lost 2

HIGHEST TOTALS

For 265 Headingley 1974
Against 266–6 Headingley 1974

LOWEST TOTALS

For 171 Oval 1974
Against 172–4 Oval 1974

HIGHEST INDIVIDUAL INNINGS

For 82 B. P. Patel, Headingley 1974
Against 90 J. H. Edrich, Headingley 1974

BEST BOWLING

For 2–31 E. D. Solkar, Headingley 1974
Against 3–36 C. M. Old, Oval 1974

PAKISTAN

Won 2 Lost 2

HIGHEST TOTALS

For 246–3 Trent Bridge 1974
Against 248–6 Oval 1978

LOWEST TOTALS

For 84–2 Edgbaston 1974
Against 81–9 Edgbaston 1974

HIGHEST INDIVIDUAL INNINGS

For 109 Majid Khan, Trent Bridge 1974
Against 116* D. Lloyd, Trent Bridge 1974

BEST BOWLING

For 3–56 Sikander Bakht, Old Trafford 1978
Against 4–15 R. G. D. Willis, Old Trafford 1978

County Competitions

The Benson & Hedges Cup

CHRISTOPHER MARTIN-JENKINS

From the outset a most generous sponsorship, the Benson & Hedges competition was worth £130,000 to British cricket in 1979, the year in which it may fairly be said to have established itself finally as a worthwhile tournament. More than £27,000 of this money was distributed in prizes to players. Like the League Cup in Association Football, the Benson & Hedges Cup suffered at first because it was the second of county cricket's knock-out competitions, in a playing sense the poor relation of the earlier Gillette Cup, feeling its way uneasily in the first rainy weeks of the English season and seldom firing the imagination of any but the most partisan spectators on Cup Final day. Then, on 21 July 1979, Essex defeated Surrey at Lord's by 35 runs in a truly memorable game which produced 545 runs on an ideal pitch in 7½ hours of magnificent entertainment. Like the little girl in the nursery rhyme, limited-over cricket tends either to be very good or horrid: this was one-day cricket at its excellent best, with Graham Gooch scoring 120, a majestic innings on a sunlit stage before a full house.

The problem facing the TCCB when they accepted Benson & Hedges as the latest of their sponsors in 1972 was how to devise a new limited-over knockout cup which would be different enough from the Gillette Cup to make an impact and which would fit into an already busy calendar. The solution was to allow 55 overs per innings instead of 60, and to start the competition with a league from which eight qualifiers would emerge to play a knock-out tournament. To save travel and expense, the league was divided into 4 zones and, to round up the numbers, the 17 first-class counties were joined by a university team and by 2 representative teams from the minor counties, roughly entitled either north and south or east and west. Initially Oxford and Cambridge played in alternate years, but since 1975 they have joined forces to play as the Combined Universities. It is a remarkable fact that whereas giant-killing acts by lesser clubs in football cups are perennial occurrences, neither the minor counties nor a university side has ever qualified for the quarter-finals of the Benson & Hedges. The minor counties did not win a single match between 1972 and 1979. The universities fared rather better, Oxford defeating Northamptonshire in the 1st year; and the combined Oxford and Cambridge team beating Worcestershire and Northamptonshire in 1975 and Yorkshire in 1976, by a remarkable performance at Barnsley. Amongst the victorious undergraduate side on that occasion were Peter Roebuck and Victor Marks of Somerset, Christopher Tavaré of Kent and Paul Parker of Sussex, all of whom have performed with considerable distinction in county cricket since. On the day, however, the hero was the Cambridge opening batsman from Sri Lanka, G. Pathmanathan, whose aggressive 52 included a disrespectful assault on the England fast bowler, Chris Old. In

RIGHT An early-season meeting between Glamorgan and Gloucestershire in the qualifying rounds of the Benson & Hedges Cup; Swansea 1979. In the background an oil tanker enters Swansea Harbour.

LEFT A model stroke in a splendid innings. Graham Gooch was made Man of the Match for his 120 in the Benson & Hedges Cup final of 1979 which gave Essex their first major success. C. J. Richards, of Surrey, is the wicket-keeper.

1980 Scotland entered the competition for the first time, replacing one of the Minor County sides.

For various reasons the zonal rounds of the Benson & Hedges Cup were unsatisfactory, until, in 1980, the timing of them was put forward from the very start of the season to the 2nd and 3rd weeks of May, so that the league part of the competition might be condensed considerably. Hitherto, there had been an unfortunate reduction in County Championship matches early in the season, making it difficult for cricketers to get into form and for selectors to pick Test sides on the evidence of a surfeit of one-day matches. Moreover, the weather was frequently cruel to the Benson & Hedges Cup, and matches often lingered into 2nd and 3rd days in gloomy conditions before inevitably sparse crowds. The whole point of limited-over cricket from many a spectator's viewpoint, namely to see a match finished in one day, was lost.

The knock-out rounds, played later in the summer, have been very different. At once they drew large crowds, seemed to be blessed with better weather and often produced good and exciting cricket, with the teams knowing that they needed only to win 2 games to be sure of a place in a cup final at Lord's and an even chance of winning one of the season's main trophies and a large financial prize. (By 1979 the original prize of £2,500 had risen to £6,500).

The extra competition, indeed, has had the admirable effect of turning some traditional underdogs into 'top teams'. Thus Leicestershire's win in 1972 was the 1st major success in their history, although, under Ray Illingworth's astute captaincy, it was by no means their last. Again, in 1977, Gloucestershire's victory under Mike Procter marked the end of a long, barren era and was a well deserved success for a side who always played their cricket in the right spirit. Exactly the same might be said of Essex in 1979 when their maiden success in the Benson & Hedges Cup was soon followed by a memorable one in the County Championship.

Until the spectacular Essex win, a total of 200 had been reached only 3 times in 14 innings in the final, and until Surrey's spirited attempt to score 291 to win, it had seemed, quite illogically, that a score of 200 was the kiss of death for the side batting second. When Kent scored 236 in 1976, a total based on an opening partnership of 110 by Graham Johnson and Bob Woolmer, Worcestershire could reply with only 193 despite a remarkable 50 by Basil d'Oliveira, batting almost on one leg because of a severely pulled hamstring. The following year Kent themselves found Gloucestershire's 237 for 6 (Andy Stovold, a handsome 71, Zaheer Abbas, a typically elegant 70) too much for them. Worcestershire had failed in similar fashion in 1974, going down by 39 runs, again at the hands of Kent, although at one point in an excellent match it had looked as though the experienced pair of d'Oliveira and Norman Gifford might deny Mike Denness the first of 3 Benson & Hedges Cup Winners' medals. Denness captained Kent to success both in 1973 and 1976, as well as in other limited-over competitions, but, having changed counties, he was just an experienced NCO when Essex defeated Surrey in 1979. He set that splendid match going with a series of perfectly timed strokes off his legs and through the covers.

Several other cricketers will look back at the Benson & Hedges with special affection in days to come, including Gordon Greenidge who hit 173 not out in 55 overs at Amersham in 1973, and Wayne Daniel who twice took 7 wickets for Middlesex in 1978. Barry Wood, the rugged little Lancashire opening batsman, who also makes a speciality of dangerous spells of medium-paced swing bowling and brilliant diving catches in the gully, has collected no fewer than 10 'Gold Awards' as the outstanding player in a match. The long-time stalwart of Surrey and England cricket, John Edrich, has 9 such mementos of individual success in a team game. Edrich also had the satisfaction of leading his county to victory in a final – in 1974 when, by skilful manipulation of some very accurate bowlers on a disappointingly slow and lifeless pitch, he successfully defended against Leicestershire an apparently inadequate Surrey total of 170.

Edrich was in the commentary box when Surrey returned to Lord's 5 years later, although it might well have been Somerset, not Surrey, whom Essex met that day. Somerset had won the first 3 matches in their Zone, and only a couple of unlikely results could have deprived them of a place in the quarter finals when their final zonal match, against Worcestershire, began. To the amazement of everyone, Somerset's captain, Brian Rose, declared after one over at a score of 1 for 0, so permitting Worcestershire to win the match, which lasted in all less than 20 minutes, by 10 wickets. A small crowd who had waited patiently in rainy conditions for the game to start, was incensed and so were most followers of the game. Rose took his decision because the points-scoring system decreed that if two or more teams finished equal at the top of a Zone, the final positions would be determined on the faster rate of taking wickets in all qualifying matches, calculated by dividing wickets taken into balls bowled. By declaring at once Somerset ensured that their wicket-taking rate could not be overtaken by their nearest rivals, Worcestershire and Glamorgan. In the event the county's ill-conceived and uncharacteristic gamesmanship back-fired, because at a special meeting of the

TCCB it was decreed that they should be expelled from the competition for 1979 and that Glamorgan should take their place in the quarter-finals. Somerset, entirely repentant, concurred in the decision, accepting that though they had played this rule of the competition according to the letter they had acted quite contrary to its spirit, and also to the interests of sponsors, spectators and other county clubs. The lesson was learned. Somerset quickly put the unhappy business behind them and it was soon made unlawful for captains to declare.

One final word about the Benson & Hedges Cup from the viewpoint of a professional reporter: the sponsors have been blessed with the support of a public relations company, West & Nally, who have looked after the needs of journalists and broadcasters with a consideration seldom before shown in cricket. There is no easier way, of course, to persuade a journalist to attach the sponsor's name to a new cricket competition in the prescribed manner, than to give him a glass of beer and a ham sandwich at lunchtime (the tastes of most are quite satisfied by humble fare such as this), but it is pleasant to be made welcome, and by supplying useful statistical material the sponsors have made themselves doubly useful to the press. It has been friendly persuasion of an entirely honest nature which has not prevented journalists from criticizing the competition where necessary. The Benson & Hedges Cup, partly because its organizers (the TCCB) have learned from early mistakes, has become an acceptable and worthwhile, if not yet indispensable, part of the British cricket season.

CUP FINAL RESULTS

1972 Leicestershire beat Yorkshire by 5 wickets
1973 Kent beat Worcestershire by 39 runs
1974 Surrey beat Leicestershire by 27 runs
1975 Leicestershire beat Middlesex by 5 wickets
1976 Kent beat Worcestershire by 43 runs
1977 Gloucestershire beat Kent by 64 runs
1978 Kent beat Derbyshire by 6 wickets
1979 Essex beat Surrey by 35 runs

HIGHEST TOTALS IN THE FINAL

290 for 6 Essex v Surrey 1979
255 Surrey v Essex 1979

LOWEST TOTALS IN THE FINAL

136 Yorkshire v Leicestershire 1972
143 Leicestershire v Surrey 1974

HIGHEST INDIVIDUAL INNINGS IN THE FINAL

120 G. A. Gooch, Essex v Surrey 1979
83 M. J. Smith, Middlesex v Leicestershire 1975

BEST BOWLING FIGURES IN THE FINAL

4–10 K. Higgs, Leicestershire v Surrey 1974
4–20 N. M. McVicker, Leicestershire v Middlesex 1975

HIGHEST TOTALS IN THE COMPETITION

350–3 Essex v Combined Universities, Chelmsford 1979
327–4 Leicestershire v Warwickshire, Coventry 1972

LOWEST TOTALS IN THE COMPETITION

61 Sussex v Middlesex, Hove 1978
62 Gloucestershire v Hampshire, Bristol 1975

HIGHEST INDIVIDUAL INNINGS IN THE COMPETITION

173* C. G. Greenidge, Hampshire v Minor Counties (South), Amersham 1973
158* B. F. Davison, Leicestershire v Warwickshire, Coventry 1972

BEST BOWLING IN THE COMPETITION

7–12 W. W. Daniel, Middlesex v Minor Counties (East), Ipswich 1978
6–8 N. Gifford, Worcestershire v Minor Counties (South), High Wycombe 1979

HAT-TRICKS

K. Higgs, A. A. Jones, G. D. McKenzie, M. J. Procter 1 each

The Fenner Trophy

SIDNEY B. HAINSWORTH

In a cricketing world which is tightly packed with one-day matches and the crowds that go with them, it was a pleasure in 1979 to have the 9-year-old 'Fenner' Trophy matches contested so well and so competitively at Scarborough. For this thanks go to Mike Procter and Gloucestershire, to Glamorgan and to Leicestershire, who narrowly won the Final against Yorkshire – 222 runs to 216. Almost every county side has now appeared in this competition with, by custom, Yorkshire present every year; this time they were led by John Hampshire and guided by that most wise and experienced cricketer, Raymond Illingworth. The 4 'Men of the Match' were Richard Lumb, who had to face a most ferocious opening attack by Procter, and was selected by Tony Lewis on the 1st day; Eifion Jones from Glamorgan on the 2nd day when Bill Bowes said 'I always appreciated a good stumper'; and P. B. Clift on the 3rd day, 'a most promising young player in the Leicestershire side', according to Sir Leonard Hutton.

The 'Fenner' is a great social occasion for the cricketers and their wives and families and supporters. In 1979 they were entertained by the then Scarborough President, Joe Palmer, who is also the chairman of the sponsoring company which, it is said, has a great liking for cricketers. So indeed it has. There was some splendid cricket in 1979 over the 3 days, with almost 500 runs scored on the first day match between Yorkshire and Gloucestershire. Glamorgan played well on the 2nd day but found the Leicestershire bowlers much too accurate for their batsmen when facing a total of 191. On the final day, the turning point came when Richard Lumb, after making 17, was most unfortunately run out, the ball being driven hard back to the bowler who deflected it on to the wicket. Only a breezy partnership between Stevenson and Old brought Yorkshire, in a most thrilling finish, within sight of victory, which they just missed to a fine competitive Leicestershire side.

We find that cricketers like playing at Scarborough because the place is full of present and past cricketers, the crowd at the 'Fenner' is quiet, knowledgeable and well-mannered and there is no fuss – just cricket. This good atmosphere is mostly due to the players. At luncheon and tea intervals the ground is covered by boys and their fathers playing cricket just as they do on the Maidan at Calcutta and Queen's Park at Port of Spain, and, for that matter, at Canterbury. Lastly let me add a line of thanks to Waid Wood who has just retired as Chairman of Scarborough after 22 years' magnificent service in keeping this grand Cricket Festival of the North unspoiled and in good shape.

It is the Fenner Trophy, competed for by Yorkshire and 3 other selected counties, which keeps the Scarborough Festival viable. K. Higgs receives the cup in 1979 from S. B. Hainsworth, the Chairman of J. H. Fenner, of Hull.

CUP FINAL RESULTS

1971 Kent beat Lancashire by 66 runs
1972 Yorkshire beat Lancashire by 60 runs
1973 Kent beat Yorkshire by 28 runs
1974 Yorkshire beat Warwickshire by 7 wickets
1975 Hampshire beat Yorkshire by 7 wickets
1976 Hampshire beat Yorkshire by 32 runs
1977 Hampshire beat Essex by 44 runs
1978 Northamptonshire beat Yorkshire by 8 wickets
1979 Leicestershire beat Yorkshire by 9 runs
Derbyshire are the only county not to have competed for this trophy; Sussex lost to Yorkshire on the toss of a coin in 1976

The Gillette Cup

GORDON ROSS

The Gillette Cup was inaugurated in 1963 with the sole purpose of supplementing county finances, which had reached a disturbing level, gates having declined steadily from the years of the postwar boom. The introduction of a one-day knock-out competition had met with substantial opposition on the grounds that the revenue from just one day's cricket, especially in bad weather if teams were required to stay for a 2nd or even a 3rd day in order to achieve a result, would make the competition uneconomical, and it was this conviction which prompted discussion on the possibility of interesting a commercial concern in the proposition.

That company was The Gillette Safety Razor Company, and it is interesting that in the early correspondence the word 'sponsorship' was not mentioned. Gillette agreed to underwrite the competition against loss to the tune of £6,500 (£100,000 in 1979), and this block grant was put into a central pool with all other sources of revenue, and divided up amongst the counties, each getting one slice of the cake for each match in which it played. The title of the competition in 1963 was 'The First-Class Counties Knock-out Competition for the Gillette Cup', a thoroughly unwieldy mouthful, which was not surprisingly contracted by the media to 'KO Cup'. In 1964 it was renamed 'The Gillette Cup'. Also abandoned in 1964 was the cautious move, in order to save expense, of visiting teams being put up in private houses, usually the houses of home committee members, instead of in hotels.

The playing conditions for the competition were the same as for first-class matches in the United Kingdom with certain amendments tailored to a one-day knock-out competition. The matches consisted of one innings per side and each innings was limited to 65 overs (this was reduced to 60 overs in 1964 because of the number of twilight finishes in 1963). No bowler was allowed to bowl more than 15 overs (subsequently reduced to 13, and then to 12). The pitch was to be completely covered throughout the match. The matches were not to be accorded first-class status – nor have they been since, despite the remarkable development in one-day cricket and the intensity of the various competitions.

In order to facilitate the draw and give the competition an even number of counties, it was necessary to reduce 17 counties to 16 and the method used was for the 2 counties at the bottom of the County Championship table in 1962 to play off for the right of a place in the 16. The 2 counties concerned were Lancashire and Leicestershire, and so the 1st Gillette Cup match was played at Old Trafford on 1 May 1963. Gillette, whose block grant was going into a central pool, were anxious to be seen to be doing something for the players involved as well as for the game of cricket and they – and their advisers – were the first to conceive and introduce the idea of 'Man of the Match'.

This move was not without its critics, because it was felt by many that it was a sheer impossibility to decide, in the context of any game, whether 51 not out was more valuable in the overall result than, shall we say, 4 wickets for 32. Gillette believed that the best answer to this lay in the appointment of England Test cricketers to make the decision since their ability to judge, and their integrity, could not be questioned. The idea of the Man of the Match award has since been used in almost every sport in many parts of the world, to confirm Gillette's belief that the principle would work, and would also generate very considerable interest. The judge in the first match at Old Trafford was Frank Woolley, one of the greatest left-handers of his, or indeed, any other generation.

The 1st winners of the Gillette Cup were Sussex who beat Worcestershire at Lord's by 14 runs. Left to right: L. J. Lenham, J. M. Parks, A. S. M. Oakman, G. C. Cooper, E. R. Dexter (captain), R. J. Langridge, K. G. Suttle, A. Buss, N. I. Thomson, D. L. Bates and J. A. Snow.

The Man of the Match received £50 (now £100) and a Gold medal, worth £14 in 1963, and now valued at £150. Latterly, a tie was struck, and all Man of the Match winners throughout the competition were presented with one. In having the Cup designed, Gillette were anxious to depart from traditional ideas so as to be in keeping with a new competition, but without discarding the essential characteristics of the game of cricket. The cup is of sterling silver and 9-carat gold and stands on a rosewood plinth. On the foot of the cup are the crests of the seventeen First-Class Counties with the Minor County crests on the plinth. The stem is surrounded by a stylized cluster of willow leaves representing the traditional association between the willow tree and cricket; the modelled figure of Father Time based on the famous weather vane at Lord's surmounts the cup.

Although the first match at Old Trafford was disrupted by rain and took two days to complete before a mere handful of spectators – Peter Marner being the first-ever Man of the Match – the competition met with surprising success in its first season, and drew a full-house to Lord's for the final between Sussex and Worcestershire on 7 September. The admission charge was 7*s*. 6*d*. (in 1979 it was £4.50*p*.) The Cup brought to cricket a new dimension and certainly a new type of spectator. It was said that many Sussex people who came to the 1st Cup Final were not necessarily cricket enthusiasts, but they were partisans, supporting their county in a Cup Final. Peter Wilson, Fleet Street's leading sports columnist, caught the mood of cricket's changing face when he wrote:

> If there has ever been a triumphant sporting experiment, the knock-out cricket Cup for the Gillette Trophy was that experiment. A year ago, anyone suggesting that on a cold, damp September Saturday afternoon, Lord's, the temple of tradition, could be transformed into a reasonable replica of Wembley on ITS Cup Final day, would have been sent post haste to the nearest psychiatrist's couch. Yet that's what happened – a sell-out with rosettes, singing, cheers, jeers and counter-

cheers. Plus a hark-a-way on a Worcestershire hunting horn when England and Sussex captain, Ted Dexter, was dismissed by a fine diving slip catch by Broadbent. This may not have been cricket to the purists, but by golly it was just the stuff the doctor ordered. And I am sure Dr W. G. Grace would have been one of the doctors concurring. It's sufficient to say that the Gillette Cup may well in future years assume the status of such established 'Cups' as even the FA, the Rugby League or, stretching the imagination, the Davis or the Canada Cup. And if I may slightly amend the sponsor's well-known slogan; 'Good evenings end with Gillette.'

One very significant feature of this first Final was that the Man of the Match award was won by a spin bowler – Norman Gifford – because there had been an almost unanimous decision by county captains to leave out their spin bowlers for this type of cricket, and introduce perpetual seam bowling to the detriment of the game itself. The error of their ways was seen as time went on. There has also been a great tendency on the part of captains winning the toss to put the opposition in (a fatal decision in 2 Cup Finals), and although some captains still prefer to set themselves a batting target rather than a bowling one, in the main a side winning the toss now bats.

The instantaneous success of the competition prompted a number of cricket clubs to seek admission, among them the Lancashire League, the Universities, the Services and the Minor Counties. But it was pointed out that the aims of the competition were financially to benefit the 17 county clubs, and, in the end, 5 Minor Counties (the top five in 1963) were admitted in 1964, only because Gillette agreed to put in some more money. Otherwise, said the Counties, the slices of cake will be smaller. Even so, the Minor Counties were not to receive rewards equal to those of the first-class Counties, and, in any event, were unlikely to progress through many rounds. In fact, it was felt unlikely that a Minor County would ever beat a first-class county. This view remained intact until 1973 when Durham became the 1st Minor County to defeat a first-class county, and, surprisingly to most followers of traditional cricket, that county was Yorkshire. They were beaten at Harrogate by 5 wickets. Once the ice was broken, 2 more Minor County successes followed. Lincolnshire beat Glamorgan at Swansea by 6 wickets in 1974, and then Hertfordshire created a distinguished Minor County triumvirate when they beat Essex at Hitchin in 1976.

In the 1965 Gillette Cup final Geoffrey Boycott for Yorkshire against Surrey made a sparkling 146 – an innings still vividly remembered and often cited.

The spirit of the Gillette, symbolized in 1967 by these Somerset supporters with their pitchforks and barrels of cider.

The 2 principal protagonists throughout the 17 years of the competition (1963–1979) have been Lancashire and Sussex, each having appeared in 6 Cup Finals, Lancashire winning 4 of them, and Sussex 3; moreover, Lancashire were involved in a Gillette Cup match which has now become a cricket legend to take its place in the folklore of the game alongside the great matches of all time. It was a semi-final in 1971 between Lancashire and Gloucestershire at Old Trafford when a crowd of 23,520 paid £9,738 to watch one of the longest days in cricket history. Play began at 11 o'clock, and an hour's play was lost at lunchtime because of rain. The finish, with the lights on in the pavilion and beaming out from Warwick Road station, was finally achieved amid frenzied excitement at 8.50 pm. Television viewers had no possible conception of just how dark it really was because modern science is able to improve the quality of the picture.

Play continued in what has since become known as 'The Lamplight Match' because Bond, the Lancashire captain, who was batting, felt it impossible to deprive such a crowd of a finish, even though he well knew that it could produce Lancashire's downfall. The reverse happened in one of the most remarkable pieces of cricket imaginable. With quick bowlers in action at the other end, Lancashire's only chance seemed to be to try and take runs off an over from John Mortimore, Gloucestershire's spinner. Bond told David Hughes to do what he could against Mortimore. Hughes replied 'If I can see them, skipper, I think I can hit 'em.' Battle then commenced, and Hughes saw them all right. He hit Mortimore for 4–6–2–2–4–6, clean calculated blows that would have done credit to any batsman of any generation in perfect light. In darkness, it was little short of a miracle. All that was required of Bond was to push a single for victory. Old Trafford erupted; the crowd swarmed across the field, engulfing the escaping players. It was just as if an armistice had been signed; for Mortimore, perhaps it had.

But if Lancashire had walked a tightrope in this match, they were to do so again in the final, when Kent appeared to be coasting to victory. Asif, batting supremely well, was 89 not out and virtually taking the Lancashire attack apart. He thumped a ball from Simmons over mid-off's head and the crowd were scanning a point on the pavilion rails where they imagined the ball would strike – and even splinter the

The 2 Lancastrian Lloyds confer shortly before taking their side to a 7-wicket victory over Middlesex in the 1975 final – their 4th triumph in the competition, an unrivalled record. Clive Lloyd's 73 not out won him the 'Man of the Match' award and was one of his many outstanding performances in the Gillette Cup. Brearley and Gomes are the Middlesex players.

woodwork. But somehow – and even he hardly knows how – the Lancashire captain took off to hold an astonishing catch in mid-air. Lancashire had contrived a victory for the 2nd year in succession, having beaten Sussex in the 1970 final. They were back at Lord's in 1972 to bring off a hat-trick of Cup Final successes in successive years. They missed in 1973, but were then back at Lord's for another 3 years in succession, though without achieving similar success. They were beaten by Kent in 1974 in the only final which could not be started and finished on the Saturday (it was played on the Monday); they then beat Middlesex in 1975 and lost to Northamptonshire in 1976. So in 7 golden years, Lancashire had appeared in the Gillette Final 6 times and won 4.

Sussex's 6 Finals have been spread much more evenly over the 17 years. Inspired by Dexter's liking for a challenge they won the Cup in the first 2 years of the competition in 1963 and 1964, and although they appeared at Lord's again at intermittent intervals – in 1968, 1970 and 1973, they did not win another Final until in 1978 they became the 2nd county to win 3 finals. Three other counties, Warwickshire, Yorkshire and Kent have each won 2 finals; 4 Counties have been successful once – Gloucestershire, Northamptonshire, Middlesex and Somerset. Four counties have appeared in a final without winning – Worcestershire (twice), Surrey, Derbyshire and Glamorgan, and 4 have yet to enjoy the atmosphere of a final – Essex, Hampshire, Leicestershire and Nottinghamshire.

It has been a great testimony to the law-makers that so few amendments have been necessary to the original laws which were created for the first season in 1963. Although close-to-the-wicket fielders, especially in the slips, have become few and far between in this type of cricket, fears that field-placing could make a mockery of the game, with almost the entire field placed round the boundary's edge, have happily not been realized, although there have certainly been isolated incidents which have caused caustic comment. In fact when the Gillette Cup was launched in South Africa very severe restrictions were imposed on field-placing. They tied a captain's hands almost completely in limiting the number of fielders who could be placed more than a certain distance from the bat. The Gillette Cup was discontinued in South Africa when Gillette felt that the new sponsorship fee asked by the South African Cricket Board was not realistic. The Cup was also discontinued in West Indies after a 2-year trial period although Gillette were well conscious of the problems confronting them when the Competition was launched in the Caribbean.

The Cup still thrives in Australia and New Zealand as well, of course, as in the United Kingdom, where its history has been liberally sprinkled with outstanding cricket. Eighty hundreds have been scored – 11 in the record year of 1975. Four hat-tricks have been performed; a hundred in a shade over an hour and a quarter; 3 double-hundred partnerships; and some of the most desperate finishes in cricket's history. The purists may still argue that this is not cricket as we have known it, and, in limiting the number of overs that a bowler is allowed to bowl, this is true. But it has unquestionably brought into the game a totally different attitude to fielding, and has made it almost as exciting as batting or bowling. This, inevitably, has brushed off on three- and in five-day cricket, and has done nothing but good. Gone are the days when an aging player can be hidden; there are no hiding places in one-day cricket. Gillette, by their foresight, created the hatchery from which first-class cricket in this country has gathered financial stability. Gillette's suppression in the early years of blatant commercialism, gave cricket the much-needed confidence in sponsorship, and has since allowed the game to open the flood-gates to many willing customers in the sponsorship field. Henry Garnett, Gillette's far-seeing Chairman in 1963, is quoted as having said that if cricket is ever obliged to sell its whole soul to sponsorship it will lose an integral part of itself. Perhaps it has, but it has gained something, too.

CUP FINAL RESULTS

1963 Sussex beat Worcestershire by 14 runs
1964 Sussex beat Warwickshire by 8 wickets
1965 Yorkshire beat Surrey by 175 runs
1966 Warwickshire beat Worcestershire by 5 wickets
1967 Kent beat Somerset by 32 runs
1968 Warwickshire beat Sussex by 4 wickets
1969 Yorkshire beat Derbyshire by 69 runs
1970 Lancashire beat Sussex by 6 wickets
1971 Lancashire beat Kent by 24 runs
1972 Lancashire beat Warwickshire by 4 wickets
1973 Gloucestershire beat Sussex by 40 runs
1974 Kent beat Lancashire by 4 wickets
1975 Lancashire beat Middlesex by 7 wickets
1976 Northamptonshire beat Lancashire by 4 wickets
1977 Middlesex beat Glamorgan by 5 wickets
1978 Sussex beat Somerset by 5 wickets
1979 Somerset beat Northamptonshire by 45 runs

HIGHEST TOTALS IN THE FINAL

317–4 Yorkshire v Surrey 1965
269–8 Somerset v Northamptonshire 1979

LOWEST TOTALS IN THE FINAL

118 Lancashire v Kent 1974
127 Warwickshire v Sussex 1964

HIGHEST INDIVIDUAL INNINGS IN THE FINAL

146 G. Boycott, Yorkshire v Surrey 1965
126 C. H. Lloyd, Lancashire v Warwickshire 1972

BEST BOWLING FIGURES IN THE FINAL

6–29 J. Garner, Somerset v Northamptonshire 1979
5–29 R. Illingworth, Yorkshire v Surrey 1965

HIGHEST TOTALS IN THE COMPETITION

371–4 Hampshire v Glamorgan, Southampton 1975
330–4 Somerset v Glamorgan, Cardiff 1978

LOWEST TOTALS IN THE COMPETITION

41 Cambridgeshire v Buckinghamshire, Cambridge 1972
41 Middlesex v Essex, Westcliff 1972
41 Shropshire v Essex, Wellington 1974

HIGHEST INDIVIDUAL INNINGS IN THE COMPETITION

177 C. G. Greenidge, Hampshire v Glamorgan, Southampton 1975
146 G. Boycott, Yorkshire v Surrey, Lord's 1965

BEST BOWLING FIGURES IN THE COMPETITION

7–15 A. L. Dixon, Kent v Surrey, Oval 1967
7–30 P. J. Sainsbury, Hampshire v Norfolk, Southampton 1965

HAT-TRICKS

R. N. S. Hobbs, J. D. F. Larter, N. M. McVicker, D. A. D. Sydenham 1 each

The John Player League

PETER WALKER

If imitation is the sincerest form of flattery then the John Player League, like all other limited-over competitions, must pay homage to the Gillette Cup, the original form of this kind of cricket which began in the United Kingdom in 1963. But it was not until 1969 that first-class cricket in England felt ready for a further addition to the season and even then it needed an outside prod to get it off the ground. The John Player League – it gets its name from the international cigarette company of the same name based in Nottingham – was spawned from a highly successful private promotion sponsored ironically by a rival cigarette giant, Rothmans. Calling themselves 'the Cavaliers', great players from the past from all parts of the world got together on Sundays to play against professional county sides, often in aid of that county's current beneficiary. Although nothing was at stake, these games proved an enormous success both from the point of view of attendance at the ground and of the television audience watching at home. The Advisory County Committee were not slow to see the potential although it took them 3 years to act. As all first-class cricketers were registered with 'the Advisory' part of their terms of employment prevented them from playing in matches outside their jurisdiction without consent. The formation of the John Player League effectively froze the Cavaliers out. Without the benefit of television coverage, and denied quality opposition, they disbanded the following season.

Three things are exclusive to the John Player League. Unlike other limited-over cricket, it is on a league basis, not knock-out; it is played exclusively on a Sunday and the whole competition is televised, ball by ball, from start to finish, one match being featured each weekend. Due to the Sunday Observance Laws in the United Kingdom play cannot begin before 2 pm and the rules have been tailored to meet the dual demands of obtaining a result in an afternoon's play (at 40 overs per side it is the shortest form of limited-over cricket at first-class level), and providing the most spectacular form of cricket for the television audience at home. This varies between 2 and 3 million each Sunday. It is broadcast exclusively on the BBC 2 transmitter and for the first two-thirds of the season the cameras cover all the 17 first-class counties at least once. In the run-in to the end of the season the league leaders understandably take precedence. The playing conditions for the competition are the same as in first-class cricket except for:

Duration: Matches will consist of 1 innings per side. Each innings is limited to 40 overs. If the team fielding 1st fails to bowl 40 overs by 4.10 pm the over in progress shall be completed. The innings of the team batting second shall be limited to the same number of overs. If bad weather delays the start of the 1st innings or suspends the length of either innings, the number of overs will be re-arranged so that each side bats for the same number of overs.

Bowling: No bowler may bowl more than 8 overs and the length of a bowler's run up is limited to 15 yards measured from the wicket.

Result: (i) A result can be achieved only if both teams have batted for at least 10 overs, unless one team has been all out in less than 10 overs or unless the team batting second score enough runs to win in less than 10 overs. All other matches in which one or both teams have not had an opportunity of batting for a minimum of 10 overs shall be declared 'no result' matches.

(ii) In matches in which both teams have had an opportunity of batting for the agreed number of overs (*ie* 40 overs each, in an uninterrupted match, or a lesser number of overs in an interrupted match), the team scoring the higher number of runs shall be the winner. If the scores are equal, the result shall be a 'tie' and no account shall be taken of the number of wickets which have fallen.

(iii) If the team batting second has not had the opportunity to complete the agreed number of overs and has neither been all out, nor has passed its opponents score, the following shall apply:

a) If the match is abandoned before 6.40 pm, the result shall be decided on the average run rate throughout both innings.

b) If due to suspension of play, the number of overs in the innings of the side batting second has to be revised, their target score shall be calculated by multiplying the reduced number of overs by the average runs per over by the side batting 1st.

(iv) In the event of the team batting 1st being all out in less than their full quota of overs, the calculation of their average run rate shall be based on the full quota of overs to which they would have been entitled and not the number of overs in which they were dismissed.

Points: Winning team gets 4 points. In the event of a tie each side gets two points. In a no result match each side gets two points. In the event of 2 or more teams finishing in 1st position with an equal number of points, their final positions will be decided on (i) the most wins; or, if still equal (ii) the most away wins; or, if still equal (iii) the higher run rate throughout the season. Teams finishing equal 2nd or 3rd shall be considered as such and share the prize money.

Keith Boyce of Essex, a dangerous all-rounder in limited-over cricket.

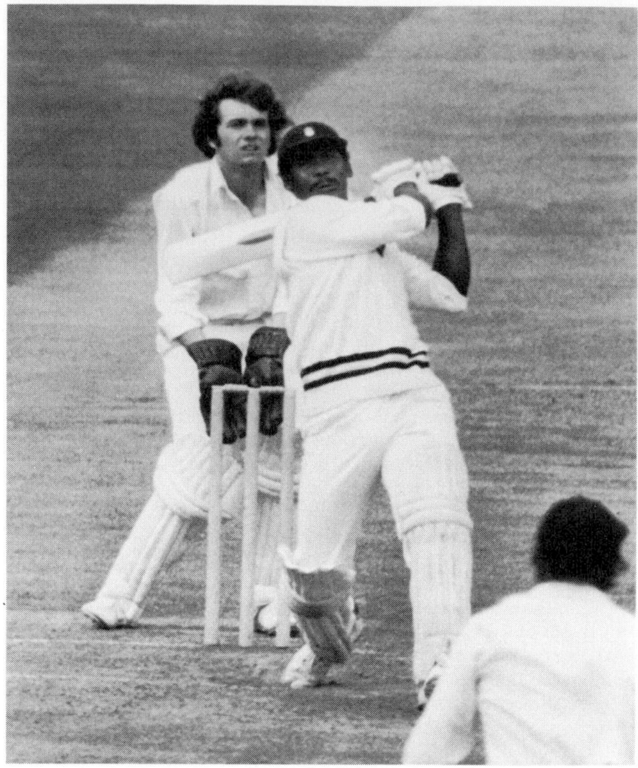

The one-day champion: Gordon Greenidge in 1979 held the individual innings record in all 3 limited-over competitions – 177 in the Gillette, 173 not out in the Benson & Hedges and 163 not out in the John Player League. Here he is hitting one of the 10 sixes in the last of these innings, for Hampshire against Warwickshire at Edgbaston in 1979. C. Maynard is the wicket-keeper.

That prize money has steadily increased from £9,550 (1st £1,000) in 1969 to £28,920 (1st £5,500) in 1979, while the total sponsorship going into the League has grown from £65,000 in the 1st year to £140,000 in 1979.

The John Player League is not without its critics. They lament the abbreviation of the fast bowler's run-up which frequently neutralizes much of his speed and they also complain about the heavy emphasis on defensive field-placings from the first ball of a match. Spin bowlers, too, have had a thin time of it in the crash-wallop atmosphere of a 40-over-game. However, tactically, the game has evolved a great deal from its early beginnings when batsmen tried to hit every ball out of the ground! Now there is an awareness that the first 5 batsmen must absorb most of the overs leaving the slogging to the tail-enders. The game is much more scientific and 'real' than 10 years ago. On the plus side the John Player League has unquestionably had a marked effect on fielding and throwing standards as well as running between the wickets. Occasionally, too, it has transformed a stodgy player into a stroke-maker of true class – Glenn Turner of Worcestershire and New Zealand is a prime example of this. What also cannot be doubted is that it has established a permanent place in the cricket programme in the United Kingdom.

WINNERS	POINTS	RUNNERS-UP	POINTS
1969 Lancashire	49	Hampshire	49
1970 Lancashire	53	Kent	48
1971 Worcestershire	44	Essex	44
1972 Kent	45	Leicestershire	44
1973 Kent	50	Yorkshire	44
1974 Leicestershire	54	Somerset	52
1975 Hampshire	52	Worcestershire	50
1976 Kent	40	Essex	40
1977 Leicestershire	52	Essex	52
1978 Hampshire	48	Somerset	48
1979 Somerset	50	Kent	48

HIGHEST TOTALS

307–4 Worcestershire v Derbyshire, Worcester 1975
288–6 Sussex v Middlesex, Hove 1969

LOWEST TOTALS

23 Middlesex v Yorkshire 1974
36 Leicestershire v Sussex 1973

HIGHEST INDIVIDUAL INNINGS

163* C. G. Greenidge, Hampshire v Warwickshire, Edgbaston 1979
155* B. A. Richards, Hampshire v Yorkshire, Hull 1970

BEST BOWLING FIGURES

8–26 K. D. Boyce, Essex v Lancashire, Old Trafford 1971
7–15 R. A. Hutton, Yorkshire v Worcestershire, Headingley 1969

HAT-TRICKS

W. Blenkiron, K. D. Boyce, A. Buss, A. E. Cordle, A. Hodgson, G. D. McKenzie, M. A. Nash, R. Palmer, J. M. Rice, C. J. Tunnicliffe, A. Ward, R. G. D. Willis 1 each

Clubs and Villages

The Cricketer Cup

A. S. R. WINLAW

The *Cricketer* Cup, a knock-out competition (55 overs) for the old boys of 32 public schools, was started in 1967. It was the post-prandial idea of Henry Lewis (Shrewsbury) and Tony Winlaw (Harrow), who received the generous support of *The Cricketer* when it came to the launching of the event. For the first 2 years 16 clubs took part – Bradfield Waifs, Charterhouse Friars, Eton Ramblers, Harrow Wanderers, Old Malvernians, Marlborough Blues, Radley Rangers, Repton Pilgrims, Rugby Meteors, Sherborne Pilgrims, Shrewsbury Saracens, Old Tonbridgians, Uppingham Rovers, Old Wellingtonians, Old Westminsters and Old Wykehamists. Repton and Malvern were the first 2 winners.

In 1969 the entry was increased by invitation to 32 with the addition of Old Amplefordians, Old Blundellians, Old Brightonians, Old Cheltonians, Old Cliftonians, Downside Wanderers, Old Alleynians, Felsted Robins, Haileybury Hermits, Old Cholmelians (Highgate), Lancing Rovers, Old Merchant Taylors, Oundle Rovers, St Edward's Martyrs, Stowe Templars and Old Whitgiftians. In that year the finalists were 2 of the new entrants, Brighton and Stowe, with Brighton winning by 156 runs. The Surrey batsman A. B. D. Parsons was top scorer for Brighton with 68. Stowe were dismissed for 57, M. Rowland taking 6 for 18.

The first year, 1967, produced cricket of the highest quality, so setting the standard of competitive play to follow. In the 1st round of 1967, P. B. H. May showed the way. England's former captain scored 113 not out in Charterhouse's winning total of 158 for 3 against Harrow Wanderers and shared in an unbeaten partnership with the Hampshire captain, R. M. C. Gilliat. Perhaps the most renowned of all school XIs was Repton's in 1905, captained by J. N. Crawford. It was appropriate, therefore, that Repton were the first team to win the *Cricketer* Cup. Led by D. B. Carr they beat Radley, captained by E. R. Dexter, by 96 runs. R. A. Hutton scored 69 out of Repton's winning total of 240 for 8, and although Dexter made 80 not out for Radley they were dismissed for 144.

In the 2nd year there was one memorable 1st round match between Harrow and Radley. After splendid batting by Dexter (75) and the 1956 Oxford captain A. C. Walton (64), Radley looked set for a comfortable success. They came to the last over needing only 3 to win, with 3 wickets in hand. But an 'unknown' Harrovian, R. Woolley, who had been nowhere near the school XI, took Radley's last 3 wickets in the 6 remaining balls. The scores were level on 207, but Harrow, having lost the fewer wickets, were the winners. Harrow went on to lose to Malvern in the final by 5 wickets.

Since then the competition has been dominated by Malvern, Tonbridge, Charterhouse and Winchester. Malvern were champions again in 1975, with the evergreen G. H. Chesterton (Oxford and Worcestershire) much to the fore. Chesterton played a major part with his (by now) slow-medium in-swing bowling. In another Oxford blue, A. R. Duff, Malvern had a successful all-rounder. In 1970 they scored 333 for 3 against Eton, a total surpassed 2 years later by Repton's 351 for 5 against Clifton, of which P. N. Gill made 194.

Until 1970 Tonbridge failed to get beyond the 1st round. From then on they have been the most successful side, winning the cup in 1971, 1972, 1976 and 1979, and being runners-up in 1970 and 1973. At various times M. C. Cowdrey has raised the tone of their batting, as, in the early years, did R. M. Prideaux. One of Tonbridge's Oxford blues, D. P. Toft, became the 1st batsman to score 2 *Cricketer* Cup hundreds. R. M. K. Gracey and N. Heroys have been noted stalwarts.

Tonbridge were beaten in the 1970 final by a Winchester team that included G. H. G. Doggart, P. A. Whitcombe and B. L. Reed. In an earlier round Winchester's leading batsman had been the Nawab of Pataudi. Winchester won the cup for a 2nd time in 1974 on faster scoring rate in a rain-affected match against Dulwich, one notable feature of which was a brilliant slip catch by T. E. Bailey for Dulwich. Tonbridge also lost the 1973 final in an exciting finish against Rugby, who, having been outplayed for most of the day, came from behind to win. Tonbridge scored 217; Rugby, in reply, were 140 for 5 with fewer than 9 overs left. But in 29 balls and 25 minutes D. A. C. Marshall turned the tables with a blistering 56 not out, Rugby winning in the end with 2 overs to spare.

Shrewsbury, whose previous record had been undistinguished, won convincingly in 1977, beating Oundle in the final by 9 wickets. This was due mainly to the all-round play of N. E. J. Pocock, who took 4 for 17 in Oundle's innings of 117 and then scored 96 not out. In 1978 and again in 1979 Pocock scored a 1st-round hundred. Having run into Pocock in prime form in 1977 Oundle were beaten again in the final of 1978 by Charterhouse, also by 9 wickets. After Oundle had scored 212 for 6 (D. C. Holliday 86 not out), E. J. Craig (Cambridge and Lancashire) made 80 not out and J. M. M. Hooper 68 not out for Charterhouse.

The final of this popular competition is played at Burton Court, Chelsea, by permission of the Guards' Cricket Club. It is generously sponsored by the celebrated champagne firm of Moët & Chandon, whose product helps to make the final a particularly happy occasion. Each year Moët & Chandon entertain the winners at their château at Epernay, which is an additional inducement to win cricket's equivalent of the Halford Hewitt (golf) or the Arthur Dunn (association football).

THE FINALS AT BURTON COURT

1967 Repton beat Radley by 96 runs
1968 Malvern beat Harrow by 5 wkts

Burton Court, Chelsea, home of the Guards CC, is the ideal ground for the *Cricketer* Cup final. It has been played there since this Old Boys' knock-out competition began in 1967.

1969 Brighton beat Stowe by 156 runs
1970 Winchester beat Tonbridge by 94 runs
1971 Tonbridge beat Charterhouse on scoring rate
1972 Tonbridge beat Malvern by 114 runs
1973 Rugby beat Tonbridge by 5 wkts
1974 Winchester beat Dulwich on scoring rate
1975 Malvern beat Harrow by 97 runs
1976 Tonbridge beat Blundells by 140 runs
1977 Shrewsbury beat Oundle by 9 wkts
1978 Charterhouse beat Oundle by 9 wkts
1979 Tonbridge beat Uppingham by 5 runs

The National Club Cricket Championship

F. L. J. DOLMAN

Following the inauguration in 1967 of the *Cricketer* Cup for Old Boys' clubs and the Kemp's Cup (now the Bertie Joel Cup) for clubs in the Club Cricket Conference area, a national tournament on similar lines was launched in 1969 by Derrick Robins. The 256 competing clubs were grouped into regions, with the regional winners entering a non-geographical phase in the closing rounds.

The competition, at first known as the National Club Knock-out, played for the Derrick Robins Trophy, has proved very popular, necessitating preliminary rounds in September between clubs competing for vacancies in the following season. Since clear winners must emerge in each round, games are played on a limited-over basis, 45 being allotted to each side, with a maximum of 8 for any bowler. Consistent success is normally attainable, therefore, only by clubs boasting six economical bowlers.

Hampstead, who had won the Kemp's Cup in 1967 and 1968, were also the 1st winners of the Derrick Robins Trophy in 1969. They were followed by Cheltenham in 1970; Blackheath in 1971; Scarborough in 1972; Wolverhampton in 1973; Sunbury in 1974; and York in 1975.

On the emigration of Derrick Robins to South Africa the organization of the competition passed to the National Cricket Association and it is now played for the John Haig Trophy. Scarborough won again in 1976 and 1979, Southgate in 1977 and Cheltenham in 1978. Over 500 clubs now enter.

RESULTS OF FINALS

1969 Hampstead beat Finchley by 7 wkts
1970 Cheltenham beat Stockport by 3 wkts
1971 Blackheath beat Ealing by 8 wkts
1972 Scarborough beat Brentham by 6 wkts
1973 Wolverhampton beat Maidstone by 5 wkts
1974 Sunbury beat Tunbridge Wells by 7 wkts
1975 York beat Blackpool by 6 wkts
1976 Scarborough beat Dulwich by 5 wkts
1977 Southgate beat Bowdon by 6 wkts
1978 Cheltenham beat Bishop's Stortford by 15 runs
1979 Scarborough beat Reading by 2 wkts

The National Village Championship

HON FINDLAY REA

This competition was researched and set up by Ben Brocklehurst, Managing Director of *The Cricketer*, and came to life in 1972 thanks to the good offices of Michael Henderson, Managing Director of John Haig & Co, who for 6 years provided generous sponsorship. After a gap of one year, in which *The Cricketer* footed the bill, the sponsorship was enthusiastically taken up by the brewers, Whitbread & Co, for a minimum of 3 years. The competition got off to a good start with almost 800 entries drawn from all parts of the country, and has remained at about that level ever since. Some 10,000 cricketers play in the competition each year and it is estimated that the aggregate attendance at all matches approaches 90,000. In the early rounds the entrants are divided into 32 groups, based on county boundaries, and in the 2nd half of the season the 32 county winners play a knock-out competition until the last 2 meet in the final at Lord's at the end of August amid scenes of great enthusiasm and noisy partisanship.

Elderly MCC members, who retain a concept of village cricket as a blacksmith in braces hitting every ball hard and high, to land, through the vicar's hands, at the aptly-named cow-shot corner, are annually astonished at the standard of cricket displayed. Naturally the finalists tend to come from the more sophisticated sides, but the rigidly enforced conditions of entry, of which the 2 most important limit the size of a village to 2,500 inhabitants and specify that all players must have played at least 8 recent matches for the club, ensure that only genuine village clubs and genuine village players can enter the competition. No doubt primitive conditions still exist, but teams from those remote areas welcome the opportunity of meeting and playing against better sides. However, the vast majority of village clubs in the 1970s are well organized and enthusiastic entities. Many of them have made major ground improvements and funds are raised in a variety of imaginative ways by a series of winter social activities in a pavilion possibly built by the members with their own hands. This new sports centre becomes the focal point of the village. For such clubs 'the Whitbread' offers a unique opportunity to widen their horizons and their fixture-list since many contacts first made in this competition develop into regular fixtures in following seasons.

With 9 rounds to be completed before the final, the competition usually has to start in April. Thereafter a round is scheduled for alternate Sundays throughout the season. Wet Sundays can, and do, cause difficulties but various ingenious tie-breaking devices are included in the rules, so that an artificial result can be obtained when necessary. In the last resort a match may have to be settled by the toss of a coin, in order to maintain the time schedule. In the early rounds there is inevitably an occasional hollow victory. Did not one Welsh side travel 100 miles across country to bowl the opposition out for 12? The visitors then scored 13 for 0 in 7 balls and travelled 100 miles home again. In the later rounds, clubs who have exceeded their survival expectations sometimes have difficulties with inescapable league obligations, but most difficulties are overcome by determination and ingenuity such as a 9 am start to clear the decks in time for an afternoon league match.

Grandstand, village style: the scene at Troon for their semi-final match against Linton Park in 1972, the 1st year of the Haig National Village Cricket Championship. Troon went on to beat Astwood Park in the final at Lord's.

Lord's 1979: the two teams, East Bierley and Ynysygerwn, arrive for the final of the Samuel Whitbread Village Cricket Championship in two brewers' drays drawn by Shire horses. East Bierley won by 92 runs with a record total for the competition of 216 for 4.

With a competition of this size, ranging from Scotland to Cornwall, much of the organization and administration has to be left to the good sense and goodwill of the competitors, and by and large this works well; only rarely is *The Cricketer*, as competition organizer, called upon to make a judgment of Solomon, perhaps from a distance of 400 miles, between 2 factually-conflicting versions of a disagreement which usually concerns an allegedly unqualified player.

Although each innings is limited to 40 overs, there have been 6 totals of over 300, and three individuals have exceeded 200 in an innings. Trevor Botting of Balcombe in Sussex hit 20 sixes in his 206, and in another match he made 127 and took the first 7 wickets for 15 runs before running out of overs. Botting is one of only 4 players to have made 3 separate hundreds, the others being B. Carter of Troon (Cornwall), D. Gallagher of Fenns Bank (Shropshire) and R. McQueen of Aston Rowant (Oxfordshire). Although bowlers are limited to 9 overs in each innings, I. Enters of Alfriston in Sussex and J. Bobbin of Mulbarton in Norfolk have each taken 9 wickets, while A. Hudson of Bitteswell in Leicester had taken 8 for 4 when his captain dropped a catch to rob him of a record analysis.

There has been only one representative match and in this, in 1976, a selected village side trounced the full Surrey County XI with its 7 Test players, by 6 wickets. This was largely due to the inspiring captaincy and batting of Terry Carter of Troon, and the fact that Surrey failed to realize the strength of the opposition until too late. Troon, near Camborne in Cornwall, has proved to be much the most successful village side, with an almost unbroken run in the county sector, and three outright wins in the competition. Among several talented players of all generations, the Carter brothers, Barry and Terry, have been outstanding, and it was noticeable that when they were away temporarily overseas in 1978, Troon failed to win the Cornish group for only the 2nd time. Gowerton of Glamorgan had a successful run for a few years until their population outgrew the arbitrary village limit. Collingham (Notts) showed a remarkable consistency in reaching the last eight 6 times in 7 years. Bomarsund, who won in 1974, have been almost equally dominant in Northumberland.

The influence of the family has been much in evidence throughout the years of the competition and at Lord's in 1975 the Isleham (Cambridgeshire) team included 3 Houghton brothers as well as pairs of Collens and Sheldrakes. To end on a note expressive of the spirit of village cricket, in Wiltshire Mrs Amor and Mrs May have, between them, given 82 years of tea service to their husbands, sons, grandsons and others, in the Spye Park Pavilion.

CHAMPIONSHIP FINAL – RESULTS

1972 Troon beat Astwood Bank by 7 wkts
1973 Troon beat Gowerton by 12 runs
1974 Bomarsund beat Collingham by 3 wkts
1975 Gowerton beat Isleham by 6 wkts
1976 Troon beat Sessay by 18 runs
1977 Cookley beat Lindal Moor by 29 runs
1978 Linton Park beat Toft by 4 wkts
1979 East Bierley beat Ynysygerwn by 92 runs

HIGHEST TOTALS IN THE FINAL

216–4 East Bierley v Ynysygerwn 1979
176–3 Troon v Gowerton 1973

LOWEST TOTALS IN THE FINAL

95 Sessay v Troon 1976
109 Collingham v Bomarsund 1974

HIGHEST INDIVIDUAL INNINGS IN THE FINAL

79* T. Carter, Troon v Astwood Bank 1972
70* T. Carter, Troon v Gowerton 1973

BEST BOWLING FIGURES IN THE FINAL

6–24 R. Coulson, Cookley v Lindal Moor 1977
5–25 P. Johns, Troon v Astwood Bank 1972

HIGHEST TOTALS IN THE CHAMPIONSHIP

331–6 Canon Frome v Flyford Flavell 1978
318–5 Sutton-on-the-Hill v Hilton 1972

LOWEST TOTALS IN THE CHAMPIONSHIP

6 Marston St Lawrence v Abthorpe 1978
7 Little Eaton v Quardon 1976

BEST BOWLING IN THE CHAMPIONSHIP

9–14 I. Enters, Alfriston v Selmeston 1977
9–14 J. Dunlop, Goldsithney v Madron 1979

HIGHEST INDIVIDUAL INNINGS IN THE CHAMPIONSHIP

214 M. Hopkins, Cookley v Woolhope Wayfarers 1978
206 T. Botting, Balcombe v Chiddingfold 1977

Cricket Indoors

A. W. P. FLEMING

The successful introduction and development of Indoor Cricket in its present form of six-a-side has provided cricketers of all ages and abilities with the opportunity to play competitive cricket during the winter months. The game has caught on remarkably quickly for the North-West-Shropshire Indoor Cricket League, pioneers of the idea, were not formed until September 1970. Yet 7 years later a competition administered by the NCA through their County Associations attracted about 750 clubs, who competed for the Wrigley Trophy in the Indoor Six-a-Side Club Cricket Championships. In 1978, the number of entries exceeded 1,000, the semi-finals and final being played in April 1979 in the MCC Indoor School at Lord's.

As one senior and well-respected coach remarked after his first six-a-side game: 'There's a lot of cricket in it.' Indeed there is. A newcomer to the game will soon appreciate that the axioms of line and length for bowlers and of good basic technique for batsmen are as important in the indoor game as they are in conventional cricket. Ground fielding, in halls with good lighting and a flat playing surface, is often quite spectacular. Successful batting demands judicious placement of the ball and a high standard of calling and running between the wickets. Good captaincy is also important. With fewer fielders to deploy, intelligent field management is of the essence.

The dimensions of the playing area are, naturally, elastic according to the space available. The ideal is 120′ × 75′ with a height not less than 20′. As the bowling is usually from one end of the hall only, the netting protecting vulnerable points may be a permanent installation.

A conventional pitch located centrally along the length of the playing area needs to allow the bowler a reasonable run-up and the wicket-keeper an adequate distance from the wicket. In general, the ball used for six-a-side is of the 'traditional' leather type, although a purpose-made indoor ball may be obtained through the NCA and is considered by many competition organisers to be less destructive, in so far as lights and windows are concerned. The boundary wall referred to in the Playing Regulations which follow is the wall behind the bowler. At halls where the boundary wall is permanently sited at one end of the playing area, the batsmen change ends at the completion of each over.

The Playing Regulations listed below are reprinted by kind permission of the Wrigley Cricket Foundation (*qv*):-

LAWS

The Laws of Cricket shall apply together with the experimental rules and conditions laid down by the National Cricket Association for the preceding cricket season, with the exception of the following playing regulations:

1 Teams shall consist of 6 players each.
2 Each match shall consist of 1 innings per team.
3 Each innings shall consist of a maximum of 12 six-ball overs.
4 No bowler shall bowl more than 3 overs. (In the case of a bowler becoming incapacitated, the over shall be completed by a bowler who has not bowled 3 overs even if he bowled the preceding over.)
5 There shall be a 10 minute interval between innings.
6 Two batsmen shall be at the wicket at all times during an innings. In the event of a team losing 5 wickets within the permitted 12 overs, the last man shall continue batting with the 5th man out remaining at the wicket as a runner.
7 When a batsman reaches a personal total of 25, he shall retire but may return to the crease in the event of his side being dismissed within the 12 overs. Retired batsmen must return in the order of their retirement and take the place of the retiring or dismissed batsman. Two 'live' batsmen shall be at the wicket until such time as the 5th wicket has fallen.
8 If, in the opinion of the umpire, negative or short-pitched bowling becomes persistent, he shall call and signal 'No ball.'
9 The Laws relating to 'Wides' shall be strictly interpreted by the umpire.

RESULTS

The team scoring the most runs in its innings shall be the winner. If the scores of both teams are equal, then the team losing the fewer wickets shall be the winner. If the teams are still equal, then each member of both teams shall bowl one ball (overarm): the team hitting the stumps the greater number of times shall be the winner.

SCORING

The scoring for Indoor Cricket shall be as follows:

1 A ball struck to hit the boundary wall behind the bowler without touching the floor or any other wall or ceiling shall count 6 runs. If, however, the ball touches the floor but does not touch any of the other walls or the ceiling and hits the boundary wall, then it shall count as 4 runs.
2 A ball struck to hit the ceiling or one or more of the side or back walls shall count as 1 run, even if the ball subsequently hits the boundary wall. Two additional runs shall be scored if the batsmen complete a run. (If the ball is struck to hit the ceiling or side or back wall and a batsman is then run out 1 run shall be scored.)
3 Two runs shall be scored if the striker plays the ball and it does not hit a wall direct and the batsmen complete a run.
4 A Bye shall count as 1 run if the ball hits a wall; a leg-bye shall count as 1 run if the ball hits a wall. In each case if the batsmen complete a run 2 additional runs shall be scored.
5 Two Byes or 2 leg-byes shall be scored if the batsmen complete a run without the ball hitting a wall.
6 No Ball.
   (a) If the batsmen do not run when a No Ball is called, a penalty of 1 run shall be credited under extras. This shall apply even though the ball hits the ceiling, a side or a back wall.
   (b) If the batsman does not strike the ball and completes a run, 2 runs shall be credited under extras. This shall apply whether or not the ball hits the ceiling, a side or a back wall.
   (c) If a striker hits a No Ball the number of runs resulting, as specified in Rules 1, 2 and 3 above, shall be added to his score but not the penalty in addition.
7 Wide
   (a) If a Wide ball is called, a penalty of 1 run shall be credited under extras even though the ball hits the ceiling, a side or a back wall.
   (b) Two runs shall be credited under extras for every run completed by the batsmen but not the penalty in addition. This shall apply whether or not the ball hits the ceiling, a side or a back wall.
8 An overthrow hitting any wall shall count as 1 run to the batsman. (The batsmen shall not change ends.)
9 No runs shall be scored if a batsman is out caught off the walls or ceiling.

METHODS OF DISMISSAL

Apart from the normal methods of dismissal contained in the Laws of Cricket, the following variations shall apply:

(a) The batsman shall be given out if the ball is caught by a fieldsman after the ball has hit the ceiling, the netting or any wall except directly from the boundary wall, provided the ball has not touched the floor.
(b) The last not-out batsman shall be given out if the non-striker running with him is run out.
(c) The batsman or the non-striker shall be given out if the ball rebounds from a wall or ceiling and hits a wicket without being touched by a fieldsman.

Part VII
Grounds of the World

Test Match Grounds in England

J. M. KILBURN

The Oval

BY CHRONOLOGICAL measurement the Oval comes first among English Test Match grounds. There, in 1880, England played Australia, a September climax to the tour led by W. L. Murdoch. This Test (which was not so designated at the time) was an improvization created by C. W. Alcock, the Surrey secretary, who persuaded Lord Harris and W. G. Grace to raise a representative England side, and who compensated Sussex for giving up their fixture with the tourists. Alcock judged the public fancy shrewdly. The match attracted 40,000 spectators and established the appeal of the Oval for major occasions in cricket.

Kennington Oval was a market garden enclosed by a straggling hedge when it came within cricketing consideration in 1844. The Montpelier CC took a lease of it and with turf from Tooting Common prepared 4 of the 10 acres for their club games. Neither Montpelier nor the subsequent Surrey County Club found immediate satisfaction in the amenities provided and residents in the neighbourhood were equally disturbed by the poultry shows, athletics meetings and exhibitions that were staged between cricket matches. By 1854 Surrey were prepared to abandon the Oval and the ground landlords, the Duchy of Cornwall, were preparing the way to sell for building purposes. This way was cut off by the intervention of the Prince Consort and a new leasehold was arranged with Surrey club trustees. The ground has been held under cricket authority ever since, though it has been made available to many other forms of sport.

Both rugby and association football have been played there to a degree of distinction reaching international matches and cup finals. There was once a racquets court attached to the tavern and a roller-skating rink at the Vauxhall end, but, naturally, the cricketing leaseholders concentrated their primary attention on amenities for cricket. The first 2-storey pavilion was extended in 1858 to include a clubroom with dressing-rooms behind and in 1890 another dressing-room was added with the uncommon luxury of a bath. Profits from the 1882 Test, the game originating the Ashes, were ploughed back to

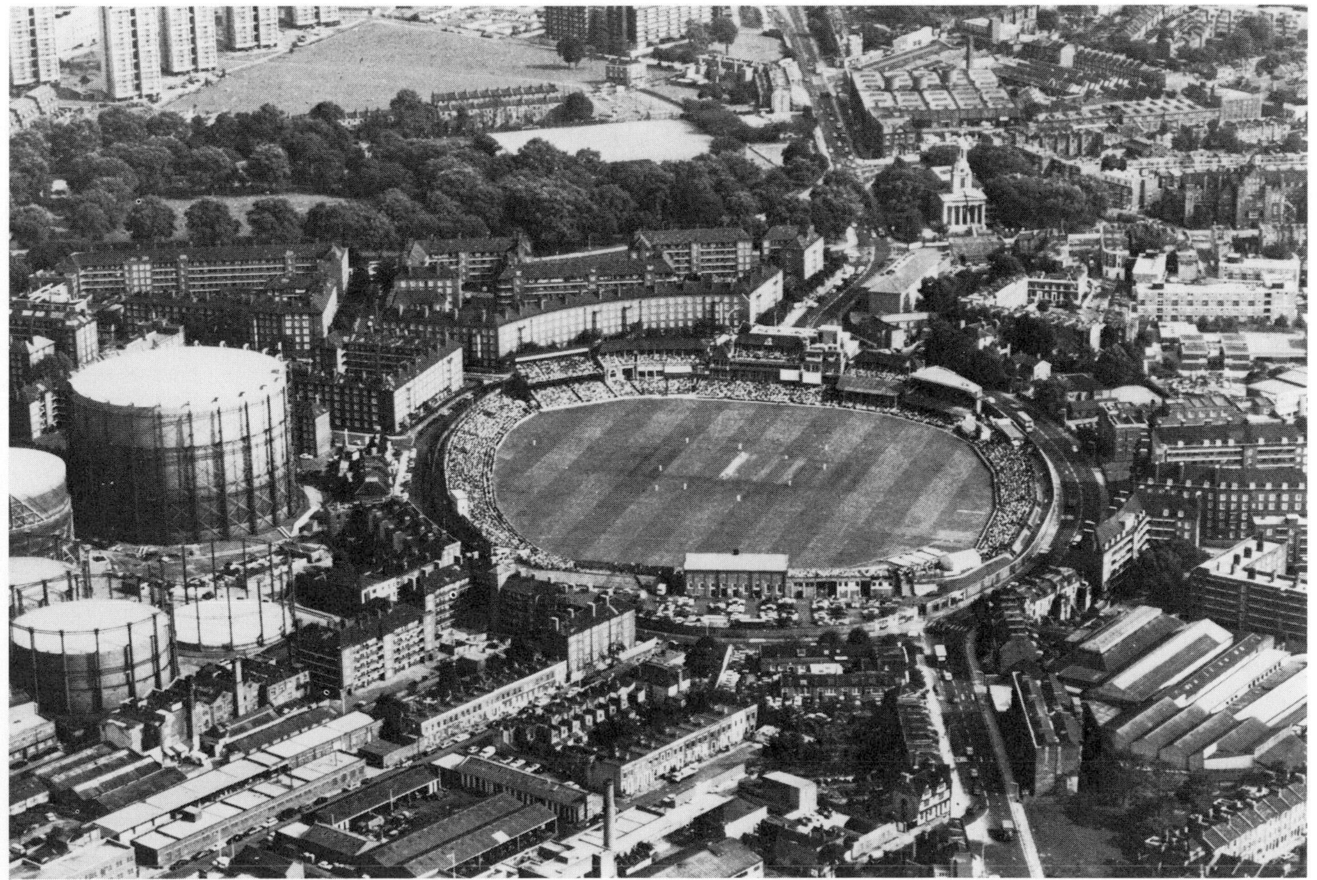

The Oval: an aerial view, giving an idea of the ground's metropolitan setting. Scene of the first Test Match in England, in 1880.

provide roofing for the stand adjoining the pavilion, but the most comprehensive building development was undertaken after the renewal of lease in 1896. Surrey then agreed to spend £10,000 on improvements. The rebuilding accomplished cost them nearly 4 times as much and brought the pavilion and main stands close to their present size and appearance. From the open space with the straggling hedge in a setting of parkland the Oval has become a breathing space in an agglomeration of bricks and mortar. Gasholders instead of the tower of Kennington Church catch the roving eye between overs. The Oval has changed appearance without losing favour, changed its character without losing individuality. It is a cricket ground of the workaday world, most conveniently approached by the public transport of bus and tube. No lawn or flower-bed relieves the harsh practicality of its pathways and courtyards; no tree offers shade for picnic lunch. Encircling traffic, less intrusive since the abolition of the clanging tramcar, prohibits restful contemplation; tall buildings reflect the glare and heat of summer days. Oval crowds are warm-hearted in the traditional surge across the turf at the conclusion of the final Test.

The members' entrance is graced by a tribute. The main gates, put up in 1934 as finishing touch to a new enclosing wall, are the Hobbs Gates, 'In Honour of a Great Surrey and England Cricketer'. They open, rather reluctantly, for admission is by hard-won privilege, to a courtyard bounded by tavern, east stand and outer wall which serves as car-park for players and officials. The pavilion block indicates its time of origin in appearance and design. It is massive, elaborate and enduring. Planning is round a ground floor Long Room which looks out on to the front seating and the field of play. To the east of the Long Room are administrative offices, to the west is a reading-room. Back stairways lead to an upper-floor refreshment-room and the dressing-rooms, which have balconies for players' appearances on state occasions. Behind the pavilion the modernized tavern provides banqueting facilities for winter and summer use. East and west alongside the pavilion are the main stands, roofed and multi-storied. They look down the pitch, the view foreshortened from the higher seats but inevitably distant because of the size of ground, which is big enough for 5 all run to have been commonplace before boundaries were restricted. Long ago Anderson and Carpenter ran 8, without overthrows, for one of Anderson's full-blooded drives.

Pavilion and stands provide the Oval's main architectural feature but they do not give the ground its individuality. This is to be found in the open terracing that curves along the eastern and western sides of the huge arena, merging finally into the smaller stands behind the bowler at the Vauxhall end. This terracing seats the bulk of the crowd on great occasions. They must shiver in the cold, scorch in the heat, soak in the characteristic thunderstorms of late summer. They must try to follow the ball from mid-wicket against the disturbing background of their kin on the opposite terracing and they must endure from interval to interval, for peregrination with the play kept in sight is virtually impossible. Oval crowds are long-suffering and wonderfully responsive. They come prepared for elation, boredom and discomfort and display the appropriate reaction to all moods. No cricketer plays at the Oval without a sense of place, though some may have been thought lacking in a sense of time. The first timeless Test in England was played at the Oval and in 1938 England batted to the tea interval of the 3rd day after winning the toss to take first innings on an everlasting monument to a groundsman named Martin.

His successor, H. C. Lock, was presented with a vastly different prospect 7 years later. No first-class cricket ground was so ill-treated as the Oval during the Second War. In 1939 it was commandeered and prepared as a camp for prisoners of war. Wire-netting cages were spread across the turf, supported by hundreds of poles set in concrete bases. Prisoners never came, not one, but the weeds did. Untended grass grew long and rank, seeded and changed texture. Neglect fell upon terracing and buildings and in 1940 and years succeeding the bombs fell. The pavilion escaped with superficial damage but the west wall became little more than rubble and there were craters at the Vauxhall end. Searchlight and gun-site scarred the outfield and when cricket came to be considered again an Army 'assault course' was among the debris requiring preparatory clearance. A miracle of rehabilitation was accomplished in little more than 6 months. Levelling and returfing was completed in time for the 1946 season and quietly and persistently the Oval struggled back to the routine of cricket. The first Test in England was played there; if ever there is a last no more appropriate ground could be found for it, with the evening flocks of pigeons and sparrows 'star-scattered on the grass' to watch the closing overs.

Today the scene is bespangled with advertising signs, an indication of the cripplingly heavy burden to be borne by the Metropolitan grounds. Since the Second War the Oval has been completely seated and ladies admitted to membership. Cricket lovers flocked there between 1952 and 1958 when Surrey won the County Championship 7 years in succession. Now only Test matches tax the ground's capacity.

Through the 1970s ways and means were extensively sought for turning the Oval into a leisure centre. An important development within the Surrey club was the formation of a marketing committee with its own professional staff. Large sums were raised through commercial activities and fund-raising schemes to combat the effects of the changing pattern of leisure. A Test Match crowd today, when West Indies are playing, sounds as much like Barbados as Battersea. Whether the huge playing area can be retained remains to be seen. It must be doubtful.

Lord's

Lord's takes the Second Test of rubbers in England mainly for reasons of social custom and obligation. Late June is traditionally the climax of London's summer 'season'. Sporting events crowd upon the metropolis. The hats and the frocks challenge belief and strawberries and cream fill the luncheon dishes. Lord's forms a background with Ascot and Wimbledon for the social scene. Its Test Match is high noon in the cricketing year. Lord's above all other grounds in the world is representative of cricket. It is outranged in size, in beauty, even in age, but it is incomparable in renown. It is onomatopoeic. In cold fact the designation has plebeian origin. Lord's is Lord's simply because of Thomas Lord, a Yorkshireman who sought his fortune in London and was financially encouraged to open a private cricket ground on a site in Dorset Square in 1789. There he drew revenue from cricket, athletics, pigeon-shooting and even a ballon ascent until the prospect of increased rental drove him northwards. His second venture, called North Bank, was comparatively unsuccessful and it was with some relief that the lessee found himself dispossessed when plans were approved to cut the Regent's Canal across his territory. Lord moved again, moving the original turf from Dorset Square, and found his final field in St John's Wood.

Jubilee Test, England v Australia, 1977: a panoramic view of Lord's.

His essential patronage was always the long-established MCC and in 1825 his patrons purchased his leasehold and left Lord to untroubled retirement in Hampshire. William Ward, the MCC member who had bought Lord's leasehold transferred the tenancy to his bailiff, John Henry Dark, in 1835 and under Dark's enterprising management amenities were steadily developed. Trees were planted, a bowling green and a garden were constructed, buildings were extended and real (or royal) tennis and racquets courts were built. In 1866, having missed an earlier opportunity, MCC came into freehold possession of the ground that meant so much to them. They were in debt at the time but they had complete faith in the future and were unhesitant in spending on pavilion improvements and ground drainage.

The Lord's of today has a Main Gate that is undistinguished in itself, being overshadowed by the back of the Mound Stand. This entrance lost any attraction it had when it became a hole in a wall rather than a gateway to a cricket ground after the building of the Mound Stand in 1899–1900. Construction of the Mound involved demolition of tennis and racquets courts which were rebuilt behind the pavilion. The Main Gate, however, is still the appropriate entrance for a newcomer to Lord's. A few strides through the tunnel between Tavern and Mound stands, a few steps beyond the bookstall bring a full view of splendour: immediately in front of the field, backed by the Grandstand topped by the Father Time weather-vane; to the right the Mound Stand running into the unroofed stands at the Nursery end; to the left 'Q' Stand and the Warner Stand flanking the great and gracious block of the pavilion.

In the chill and emptiness of winter a first sight of Lord's would be impressive. On a summer's morning, the seating filled and the field prepared for play, the picture checks the breath and clutches at the heart. There are few days from May to September without a match at Lord's and there is no day in the year without the feel of cricket. Lord's is history modelled in turf and building. In the pavilion or on the grass at the boundary edge Lord's offers participation in the brotherhood of cricket. There idolator and iconoclast are touched by the magic of a game. They have visited a cricket ground and involved themselves in an institution. [*See also*: 'Lord's and MCC'].

Trent Bridge: opened by William Clarke in 1838. The first hundred was scored there by 'W.G.' in 1871; the first Test Match staged there was in 1899, between England and Australia. Here the same two sides are meeting each other in 1972.

Trent Bridge

Journeying southward from Nottingham the traveller must cross the River Trent. A river crossing, by ford or bridge, invariably demands a pause, and a pause in English travel usually calls for an inn. The hostess of the Trent Bridge Inn in 1837 married another Nottingham innkeeper, William Clarke, and discovered that she had exchanged one form of widowhood for another. William Clarke, devoted as he may have been to the widow Chapman at Trent Bridge Inn, was also a cricketer. He enclosed the field attached to the inn and combined pleasure and profit in the presentation of cricket. From his acumen, enterprise and persistence grew one of the great Test Match centres. Clarke's fame and fortune were based essentially on his foundation and management of the itinerant All-England XI, but he shrewdly brought more and more matches of national significance to his own ground. By 1842 he had lured an England XI led by Fuller Pilch to meet Nottinghamshire at Trent Bridge and by the time of his death in 1856 he had, at least, established his field as a headquarters for the cricket of his county.

Nottinghamshire cricket and the Trent Bridge ground developed happily together, in cause and effect, through the 19th century. 'Fiddler' Walker prepared some of the most trustworthy pitches in the land; Arthur Shrewsbury, among many others, made some of the most assured runs. Amenities were increased to meet growing demands; 1871 brought a new pavilion (on the north side of the ground) and the 1880s saw new stands and an enclosing wall and a larger inn to replace the Clarkes' old home.

Trent Bridge today would be beyond recognition by 'Old William' yet in its appearance may be traced virtually the whole story of its growth. The Trent Bridge Inn still serves travellers and cricket-followers at the corner nearest to the bridge. Cattle-pen and thorn hedge of ancient time have long since disappeared, but refreshment can be taken where once spectators watched from elm-tree shade. Until 1976, when it was swept away in a gale, one famous elm linked past and present. In its heyday it was a target so frequently found by the leg-hitting of a Nottinghamshire immortal that it became known as George Parr's tree.

When Parr died, in 1891, a branch of this tree went with him to the grave and another branch, in the form of a bat, stands among the pavilion treasures. Trent Bridge illustrates its history in pavilion pictures and mementoes and in its comprehensive library. The Long Room is a museum and exhibits overflow into stairways and refreshment-rooms of the pavilion. A wet day at Trent Bridge is not a wasted day of cricket. The pavilion looks down the wicket, providing an ideal view of play from the upper storey, though sometimes disturbing play by its very presence behind the bowler's arm. Dressing-rooms, at two levels, with little balconies for use by the players, are at the western end of the building and at the other end are president's room, library and committee dining-room. Their windows look out to the splendid spaciousness of the playing area. Six acres of turf are too much for any one cricket match, but the spread permits row upon row of spectators on the grass, augmenting the seating accommodation to a ground capacity of some 35,000. Within the members' enclosure supplementary stands run east and west of the pavilion, with the new secretarial offices and six recently built squash courts (two with glass backs) now filling this area behind it. Access to all this is by a gateway of intrinsic significance, for it honours the memory of J. A. Dixon, who was Nottinghamshire captain from 1889 to 1899 and a leading administrator for nearly forty years. Stands completely enclose the western and northern bounds of the playing area and to the east the turf stretches away to open terracing whose value is essentially for Test Match occasions. On county days cars can be taken on to the grass of this practice-net area and temporary seating is provided up to the boundary edge. In the north-eastern corner the biggest scoreboard on any English ground winks its comprehensive information of current batting and bowling figures in the Australian manner.

The outstanding impression given by Trent Bridge is of spaciousness. Some of the pathways behind the stands narrow to bottlenecks, but there is strolling space near the Dixon Gates, strolling space beside the Trent Bridge Inn, strolling space on the eastern turf. Most of the seating is unroofed, necessitating flurries of movement when the showers fall, but eliminating that domination of the playing field so inescapable in the greatest stadiums of sport. At Trent Bridge, with the boundaries marked by lines and flags, even Test Matches maintain a suggestion of cricket played on a smooth meadow beside a river bank.

Old Trafford

In 1856 the Manchester CC were evicted from their ground on the Chester Road in the district of Old Trafford on the civic insistence that the site was required for an Art Treasures Exhibition. Less than a mile away they found 8 acres of 'good, level, sandy land', with a pavilion 'well adapted to the purposes for which it will be used', having 'an excellent wine cellar'. From this acquisition has grown the extensive headquarters of Lancashire cricket, superb stage for Test Matches since 1884, a ground of delight in its playing characteristic and splendour in its accommodation; a palace of cricket, scarred by war and enshrined by tradition; a name to be respected and an experience to be enjoyed – with occasional meteorological misgiving. Old Trafford has sustained that early belief in suitability for its purpose. For players the amenities are satisfying to a degree of luxury; the turf is smooth and kind to the feet, the light is peculiarly soft and clear. Dressing-room accommodation is ample and private and nets are available on the practice ground. For spectators access is easy and car-parking facilities are exceptionally convenient; there is seating for 20,000 apart from improvisation on the grass and in unlikely corners; there is generous provision for obtaining refreshment and there is comfortable sight of score-board and clock from any viewpoint.

Test Match grounds are the cathedrals of cricket and in the ecclesiastical custom the building of Old Trafford is always to be regarded as incomplete. No year passes without development or plan for development. Three pavilions have been built and none left through its lifetime without extension. Stands and terracing have been remodelled; administrators and groundsmen rehoused; the pitches have undergone positive violence of experiment; and necessity has mothered invention in the protection and drying of turf.

Old Trafford is impressive from any viewpoint but perhaps most alluring of all from the open stand in the south-western corner. As the pitch runs east-west this is not the most favoured place for watching play but it offers splendid prospect of the ground itself. To the right stretch the southern roofed stands and beyond them the open terraces backed by handy turnstiles for invaders through Warwick Road railway station. To the left the seating runs to the enclosure of the Ladies' Stand and refreshment-rooms, topped by the wind-swept and sometimes wind-rocked Press box. A great curve of embankment covers the north-western corner, extending to the main block of a pavilion left unsymmetrical since renovation after war-damage, but proudly standing guard over the turf spreading from the foot of its enclosure steps.

The Old Trafford pavilion has a conventional Long Room at its ground-floor level, dressing-rooms and committee-rooms on the first floor and a roof balcony with covered seats for members. The supplementary amenities are extensive and sufficiently complicated to demand direction signs. Up the stairs and down the stairs, along the corridors and round the corners run the routes of exploration, leading to exhilarating views of the field from wide window or open balcony. The players coming down the pavilion steps through the crowded enclosure stirred Neville Cardus to his concept of 'white waterfall' that lingers among cricket's loveliest phrases. Down these steps have come the greatest of the cricketing nations, many to illustrate their greatness. In 1902 the Test Match brought a golden beginning with Victor Trumper's century before lunch and fantastic ending with Australian victory by three runs. In 1934 the Test was laboriously drawn, but contained the immortal over in which O'Reilly dismissed – on a flawless pitch – Walters, Wyatt and Hammond in four successive balls. Ranjitsinhji's 154 not out made magic in 1896 and forty years later Hammond's 167 against India earned gratitude from the devastated opponents who proclaimed themselves privileged to have been means and witness to it. Old Trafford was Hammond's rose-garden, as Sydney Cricket Ground was his commercial estate; at Old Trafford, against McDonald, Hammond announced himself in the royal succesion. Lancastrians are reputedly level-headed in their approach to cricket, as to any aspect of business or pleasure, and they rightly favour their own. Lancashire players have received the biggest benefits known in their time; a county match, not a Test, drew the biggest crowd Old Trafford (or any other ground in England) has ever known. Yet Old Trafford echoes rare sentiment. No cricketing tribute was more deeply moving than the farewell accorded J. B, Hobbs in the year of his retirement. He played in Duckworth's benefit match and after scoring a 1st innings century he was given an ovation lasting all the way from the wicket to the boundary edge. As the gate of the pavilion enclosure was opened for the departing 'Master' the thunder of applause turned spontaneously to song and Jack Hobbs climbed the steps through the ranks of standing members to the strains of *Auld Lang Syne* as a chorus taken up all round the ground.

Five years later Old Trafford was no longer a cricket ground. On the outbreak of war in 1939 it was requisitioned by the Army and after Dunkirk became a transit camp in which weary soldiers took brief rest in the pavilion, in the stands, on the terraces, almost anywhere they could stretch themselves in sleep. 1940 and 1941 brought severe air-raid damage. A sentry at the main gate was killed; the pavilion and the groundsman's house were battered and craters appeared in the playing area. The Army eventually gave way to the Ministry of Supply who filled car parks and practice ground with stores. Old Trafford's own furnishings from the the endangered pavilion and dining-rooms had to be buried in bank vaults or removed to rural areas for safe keeping. With the return of cricket Old Trafford's turf was smoothed and Old Trafford's accommodation was repaired or rebuilt. Man-power from the Services and prisoners of war helped the restoration and a public appeal for building funds brought response from many parts of the world. The pavilion was not entirely rebuilt but gained dressing-rooms, committee-rooms and general refurbishing. Stands in the south-western corner changed appearance and size and in the south-eastern corner neater terracing has been constructed from a once rather dusty embankment. Colour has come to the monotony of concrete and timber, secretarial offices have been built near the main gate and Old Trafford's plans still stretch far ahead with the self-confidence of assured position and esteem in the world of cricket.

Old Trafford: the home of Lancashire cricket, where England are playing West Indies and Pat Pocock is bowling to Clive Lloyd.

Edgbaston

In Birmingham's pleasant suburb of Edgbaston the reorganized Warwickshire County Cricket Club of 1884 took lease of a 'meadow of rough grazing land at a fair and reasonable rental, without harrowing conditions'. The rough grazing land has become one of the most attractive stretches of cricketing turf in the world and administrative enthusiasm and enterprise have developed the ground into a distinguished stadium. Harrowing conditions of leasehold and ownership may have been escaped but cricket at Edgbaston has rarely known a carefree existence. Until recent experience of supplementary income, cash has always had to be counted with extreme care and the somewhat inexplicable indifference towards cricket of Birmingham's enormous population has invariably left Edgbaston offering more accommodation than was apparently required.

The merits of the ground were recognized nationally in 1902 when England played Australia in the First Test of the rubber. The cricket was historic, for after England had declared at 376 for 9 wickets Australia were

Edgbaston: fully equipped and beautifully maintained.

dismissed for 36, but the financial features were sensational and disastrous for Warwickshire. The secretary of the time – R. V. Ryder, whose time, indeed, extended over 50 years – was besieged on the first morning by members seeking admission by payment of overdue subscriptions. On the third morning, with Australia in the follow-on, the ground was under water. Gatemen and police were sent away in an effort to reduce match expenses, but afternoon sunshine brought hordes of the optimistic to the gates and the barriers were stormed. Token cricket had to be offered for an evening hour but Warwickshire, having spent £1,500 in additional stand accommodation for their Test, received no more than £750 when the final proceeds were distributed. Before the Second World War Edgbaston cricket, played within easy reach of a million people, carried an air of rurality. There was room and to spare on the field and around. Players came from a rambling pavilion, spectators could choose benches round the boundary, shelter in a 2 tier stand or could watch the game from refreshment tables in a grassy enclosure.

Metamorphosis came after the Second War when an era of income from outside cricket was opened. Capital investment was eagerly undertaken and a new Edgbaston of steel and brick and concrete and paved pathways came under construction. No cricket ground in England can now claim to be better equipped in provision for play and for watching. The field is encircled by terraced embankment, some of it roofed and all of it easily entered by stairways from the bank. From any vantage point the prospect is impressive and supplementary amenities are in the category of luxurious. Members and players have a handsome dining-room in the west wing of the pavilion suite, which is revenue producing from social activities in the winter. Ladies have their own stand accommodation and refreshment facilities. Cricket practice can be taken indoors, on grass or on artificial pitches. The enormous car parks on the western and northern sides have not yet been overtaxed. Groundsmen and secretarial staff are housed within the bounds of the property and there still remains room for a small practice ground in the north-western corner.

Only the pavilion remains as reminder of Edgbaston's earlier unsophistication. Its red roofing, almost hidden in the cluttering improvisations of publicity demands, stands scarcely shoulder-high among towering neighbours, but its ageing façade covers innumerable interior renovations and no doubt an office or committee-room within contains the blue print for a mightier construction. Edgbaston acknowledges history and personal service and generosity in names. Gates, score-boards and stands record appreciation and serve as memorials. The outlook is towards tomorrow.

Headingley

Headingley is a sporting estate of divided interests with accommodation for matches at the highest level. The cricket ground stages Test Matches, the football ground takes international Rugby League occasions. Management of the property is vested in the Leeds Cricket, Football and Athletic Club, but the Yorkshire CCC hold a long lease on the cricket ground and have administrative headquarters there in a building put up in 1963. For cricket – as, indeed, for football – Headingley is handsomely appointed in major aspects, though inadequate in provision for the details of spectatorial comfort. The main stand, facing like Janus two ways towards the separate cricket and football fields, presents an admirable view of play, but its cavernous interior draws the public to refreshment by necessity rather than by any intrinsic appeal. This stand, stretching along the southern boundary of the cricket field, offers the only covered accommodation available to cricket spectators except in the

Headingley: the view from the football stand, the new pavilion on the *right*.

members' stand. To the west is the great terraced embankment of open seating that is the primary public favour. The northern end includes a terraced enclosure behind the bowler's arm, backed by a grassy mound and a row of trees planted to cut off intrusion by surrounding houses. The eastern curve of the field has changed appearance with the demolition of a winter practice shed of white-washed brick to make way for county offices and players' dressing-rooms. Behind this building and the neighbouring enclosure is the club's bowling-green.

Headingley has in some measure developed from mishap. Fire destroyed an old stand to hasten building of the new; fire brought alteration to the original pavilion structure now the members stand. The deep embankments and the concentration of roofed building to the south leaves Headingley with a pleasantly open atmosphere and the old paved cycling track encircling the turf increases the sense of spaciousness, but players find sighting the ball as difficult as they would against a darker background. There are no sight-screens. When P. B. H. May came to the wicket in his first Test Match he failed to sight the first ball bowled to him and, plunging speculatively forward, edged a boundary down the leg side. He stayed to make a hundred. Fieldsmen are also occasionally disconcerted not only by 'losing' the ball against spectators or trees but by the general north to south slope of the playing area which makes judgment of speed more difficult and pursuit sometimes unexpectedly ineffective.

Headingley has made dramatic interpretation of some of its Test Match fare. In 1899 Briggs, the Lancashire bowler, collapsed and had to leave the match. In 1921 Hobbs was persuaded from the field for an urgent operation. In 1926 Macartney scored a century before lunch on the first day and in 1930 so did Bradman, who also stayed to make over 300 in the day. In 1934 a memorable thunderstorm flooded the ground when England were close to defeat. In 1948 Australia scored 404 for 3 wickets in the 4th innings. Bradman played only in Test Matches at Headingley. In six innings he scored 963 runs for an average of 192·60 and was accorded not only honorary life membership of Yorkshire 'to mark appreciation of the pleasure given to spectators in Yorkshire and at Headingley in particular', but also the most stirring public acclaim, by his own reckoning, of his whole career. Yet all Headingley's remarkable cricket and adventurous by-products have left the ground still without any marked quality and character. The touch of sentiment so strongly impressed upon other great grounds has seldom fallen significantly upon the Headingley atmosphere. Headingley gives no obvious cause for either affection or dislike. It is efficiently designed and administered for the presentation of cricket but it contains no treasures of picture or memento, no plaque or memorial gate. It has the commercial rather than the domestic appeal. Time, perhaps, will bring its heart to be worn on its sleeve.

Test Grounds Abroad

R. A. ROBERTS AND JOHN WOODCOCK

England is the home of cricket, but the homes of cricket know no frontiers. Their origins and progress provide an important slice in the social history and development of the British Empire. The ways and habits of Empire builders die hard. Just as the Romans gave us baths, the British gave cricket to the world. If the habit – cricket not bathing – has worn thin in some parts, it has become institutional elsewhere. Except in Canada with its climatic hazards, cricket has become a major sport in all parts of the world under direct and sustained British influence in the last century or more.

Australia

Australia soon established herself as the natural venue for international contests. It follows then that the great grounds should have traditions and histories almost as long, and certainly as eventful, as those of the most famous in England itself. Sydney may be poles apart from Lord's in distance and also appearance, but it is its closest rival in eminence.

SYDNEY

Until floodlighting was installed there in 1978, which required the erection of 6 huge towers (240 feet high), Sydney, in the opinion of most cricket travellers and countless players, was considered the finest of all Australian grounds, indeed, by many, the finest cricket ground in the world. The floodlighting was considered necessary by vote of the SCG Trustees (political appointees) as a means towards 'making ends meet'. With the introduction, at the same time, of World Series Cricket to the ground, the playing facilities also declined, due to the square having to be used for more days' cricket than ever before. During the Australian season of 1978–79 good pitches were scarce at the SCG. The ground, even so, has not lost all its character – not by any means. Some of the old Edwardian dignity remains in the turreted and pinnacled architecture of the pavilion and the ladies' stand. To the left of the pavilion are the Noble and Bradman stands, named, as is the custom in Australia, after famous cricketing figures and providing an uninterupted view of the whole wide sweep of the playing area.

The Sydney Hill, one of cricket's best known landmarks, is a testimony to the far-sightedness of the Trustees. While the ground developments are mostly in step with the present and future, they have ensured that the Hill keeps faith with the traditions of the past. It is a large grassy slope which the Trustees have preserved, resistant to overtures to convert it into another grand stand. Yet behind the Hill is one of the biggest electrically operated scoreboards in the world. The Hill provided Sir Jack Hobbs with one of his richest memories in a treasure-house of cricket experience. On his 46th birthday, during the 1928–29 tour, he was called to the pickets and handed, on behalf of the Hillites, a birthday gift. Sometimes they are less kind on the Hill, a traditional habitat of the barracker. Well stocked for his day's cricket with pies, prawns and iced beer, his piercing but mostly good-natured shafts of wit and advice penetrate deep into the heart of otherwise formal occasions.

Sydney cricket ground had rather stormy early days: in the year after it was opened in 1878 there was a riot on the ground when Lord Harris's touring team played against New South Wales. Lord Harris believed that betting was responsible but also, at the centre of the dispute, were the NSW objections to the decision of a Victorian umpire accompanying the touring side. This threatened a rift in Anglo-Australian cricket relations but happily the breach was soon healed and since then, of course, the Sydney ground has borne

Sydney: before the pylons were planted, with the Hill on the *left* and the pavilion on the *far right*.

Melbourne: a bird's-eye view of the modern ground. It was here on 11 February 1961, that 90,800 people, a record for a single day's play, watched Australia playing West Indies.

witness to many memorable matches. Its wicket, especially in the days of bulli soil, has been well disposed towards batsmen and Sir Donald Bradman made his highest score of 452 not out there against Queensland in 1929–30. A. C. MacLaren and W. R. Hammond scored many runs at Sydney. The bowlers, however, have also had their days. G. Giffen, the great Australian all-rounder, once took all 10 wickets there at a cost of 66 runs, and T. W. Wall, the South Australian fast bowler, did even better with 10 for 36 in 1932–33. The West Indies have reason to remember Sydney with special satisfaction. Two of their first 3 Test wins in Australia (in 1930–31 and thirty years later) were gained at Sydney. England have also gained more wins there than on any other Australian ground – 20 out of 46 – up to the 1978–79 tour.

MELBOURNE

The Melbourne Cricket Ground (or MCG) is the largest in the world. So vast is it (capacity 130,000) that it was the venue for the 1956 Olympic Games. Crowds of well over 100,000 are commonplace there for the grand finals of the Australian Rules football season, the governing passion during the winter of sportsmen in the southern States. The world-record cricket aggregates and attendances have also been set up at Melbourne. On the Saturday of the Fifth Test between Australia and West Indies in 1961 the play was watched by nearly 91,000 people.

The Melbourne Cricket Club was founded in the 1830s and moved to the present site in Jolimont or Yarra Park in 1853. Flower-beds and shrubs have, in the course of time, had to give way to massive blocks of concrete, but the ground is still set in pleasant surroundings and a stroll from the Windsor Hotel, where for many years the teams stayed, through Fitzroy Gardens, past Captain Cook's cottage, is a tree-lined route the whole way to the ground. The first English team to play in Australia in 1862 planted elm trees in Yarra Park and the first Test between Australia and England was played at Melbourne in 1877. In the early days of tours between the two countries, the Melbourne Cricket Club were responsible for the arrangements in Australia. It is a curiosity of cricket that the two clubs directly responsible for making the sport into the world-wide activity it is to-day should bear the same initials – MCC.

It was at Melbourne in 1926–27 that Victoria made the highest ever score of 1,107 – though the scales of justice were smartly tipped the other way by their opponents, New South Wales, only a month later when, in Sydney, Victoria were dismissed for 35. In these days of covering, rain-affected pitches in Australia are rare; but at one time a Melbourne 'sticky' was regarded as the most spiteful of all. South Africa, for example, were bowled out for 36 and 45 there in a Test Match in 1931–32. In earlier days, back in 1879, F. R. Spofforth performed the 'hat-trick' against England, while 4 years later W. Bates retaliated with one against Australia. In recent years the amenities at Melbourne under the secretaryship of Ian Johnson, the former Australian Test captain, have been raised to a very high level. They now make an important social contribution to the life and times of Melbourne as a city. For touring sides, however, one snag remains: on match days there is no adjoining subsidiary ground on which nets and open practice can be organized.

ADELAIDE

If Sydney is the best-equipped cricket ground and Melbourne the largest, Adelaide qualifies as one of the most beautiful in the world and certainly without rival within Australia. Like Sydney and Melbourne it is set in parkland, but the background is much more imposing. One side is flanked by a pair of large and airy stands which extend in a generous sweep the full length of this very long ground. From the centre of the Giffen Grandstand, the position is side on to the play, but the background view is without parallel in Australia and only equalled by the views at Newlands, in Cape Town, and Queen's Park, Port of Spain. To the left of the Adelaide ground, the spire of St Peter's Cathedral rises nobly above a score-board that is big even by Australian standards. The Cathedral sets off the scene, just as at Worcester, but here that is not all. Away to the north the Lofty Mountains stretch up into the shimmering blue of the Australian sky.

All cricket grounds in Australia are known as ovals, but only Adelaide is designated as such by authority. It is understood that a former Surrey member, resident in the colony when the Adelaide ground came into being in

The Adelaide Oval: only half a mile from the city centre.

the 1860s, proposed it should be called 'The Oval'. One criticism of the Adelaide ground must be that it is too elongated for cricket. The straight boundaries are unreasonably long and those square to the wicket unusually short. Batsmen, however, have enjoyed themselves more there even than on other Australian grounds: Compton, Morris, Hazare and Kanhai have each made two centuries in the same Test Match at Adelaide since the war.

Bradman made his 1st first-class century there in 1927, so it was perhaps appropriate that he should have chosen ultimately to settle in Adelaide and is now regarded and respected as the presiding authority of the game in the 'Queen city of the South'. Adelaide has staged fewer than half the Test Matches of Sydney and Melbourne, yet has a capacity of well over 40,000. The reason for this is that Sydney and Melbourne, with their larger populations, alternately have two Test Matches during a 5-match or 6-match series.

BRISBANE

The first Test was not played at Brisbane until 1928–29 and this was at the Exhibition ground. Subsequently, the Queensland Cricket Association and Test Matches moved to Woolloongabba, an Aboriginal word more conveniently shortened to 'The Gabba'. Test Matches have often had an aura of drama around them at Brisbane. England won the first 3 Tests they played there and lost the next 4. Brisbane is subjected to thunderstorms of a tropical intensity which, in the days of uncovered pitches, affected drastically the course of Test Matches. If matches between Australia and England have been dramatic, they have been nothing compared with the astonishing game between Australia and West Indies in 1960–61. The Brisbane tie, the first in the history of Test cricket, is now commonly regarded as the greatest match ever played. I will never forget the atmosphere at the end of it. Everyone was delirious with excitement and there was the unique feeling of general satisfaction at the result of a Test Match.

No one would pretend that 'The Gabba' is the prettiest ground in the world. At one time it had a rather stark appearance with its old-fashioned stand and corrugated iron roof and bare spaces around other parts of the field, encased, in the Australian tradition, by its white picket boundary fence. In recent years, however, facilities have been vastly improved. The dressing-rooms and Press box above are now among the most modern in the world and afford a splendid vantage point. Some fine new stands, a lavish cricketers' club, a smooth outfield and a new practice area go towards making it one of Australia's best-equipped rather than most primitive grounds, as it was until the late 1950s. There is also a greyhound track, well-maintained and profitably used. No one had more to do with these recent developments than Mr Clem Jones, for some time the Lord Mayor of Brisbane and a catalystic and controversial figure in the sporting life of the city.

PERTH

With the addition of Perth to the rota, during the MCC tour of 1970–71, Australia gained another fine Test ground. Since the Second World War cricket in Western Australia had been making steady strides. They won their first Sheffield Shield, as full members, in 1967–68, and went on to dominate the competition in the 1970s. The WACA (pronounced 'Wacker'), as the ground is called, is the most spacious in Australia. Crowds of more than 15,000 are rare, but as the population of so prosperous a state grows so will the ground and the attendances.

The Perth pitch is generally reckoned to be the fastest and truest in the world – a delight to batsmen (the season 1978–79 proved an exception) and a joy to fast bowlers. The 'Fremantle Doctor', the name given to the cooling breeze which blows up in the middle of the day off the near-by Swan River, provides off-spin bowlers with something to harness, bowling either with or against it. When the 'Doctor' overdoes it the ground can become bitterly cold. As a rule, though, Perth's climate is ideal for cricket, and the light crystal-clear. The ground is barely more than a mile from the city centre, and for those wanting an evening's racing when the cricket is finished there is a trotting track the other side of the fence. For many years touring sides to Australia, having left their ocean liner in Fremantle, opened their programme in Perth. Now, more often, they fly straight to one of the Eastern States and visit Perth later in the tour for a Test Match.

South Africa

There are four South African Test grounds, Cape Town, Johannesburg (where 2 Tests of a 5-match series are held), Port Elizabeth and Durban.

CAPE TOWN

The Newlands ground at the Cape, dominated by the great mass of Table Mountain, is one of the wonders of the cricket world. With its magical changing hues of blue and grey, the mountain provides an incomparable backcloth, yet even without it Newlands is handsomely appointed with its generous fringe of trees and lovely Cape skies.

Newlands was made available for cricket in 1888 just in time for the first visit by a touring team to South Africa. That was Major R. G.

Perth: the ground of the Western Australia Cricket Association, known colloquially as the 'Wacker', which was put on the Test rota in 1970. The playing area is unusually large, the light particularly good, and most afternoons the heat of the day is tempered by the arrival of the 'Fremantle Doctor', the strong breeze that blows off the sea.

Newlands, Cape Town: Peter May leading MCC into the field in 1956, on one of the world's loveliest grounds. The view from under the oaks, with a shoulder of Table Mountain in the background.

Warton's team, led by C. A. (later Sir Aubrey) Smith. Most of their matches were played against odds but in the closing days two games were played on level terms against South Africa and these were subsequently regarded as Tests. The second of these was played at Newlands where the England left-arm spin bowler, Briggs, distinguished himself with 15 wickets in the match for only 28 runs. 14 of his victims were clean bowled, and as the other was leg before wicket, he required no help from his colleagues in achieving this truly remarkable analysis.

For many years Cape Town was an unlucky ground for South Africa. Of the first 20 Test Matches they played there they won only 2 and lost 14. But when one thinks of Newlands, it is not of records and feats on the field; it is of cricket played in perfect surroundings and with the Western Province Cricket Club as ideal hosts.

JOHANNESBURG

The Wanderers' Stadium in Johannesburg with its capacity of 36,000 is at once the newest and the largest ground in South Africa. The Wanderers' is one of the most famous amateur sports clubs in the world, and Test Matches were played on their original ground in the heart of Johannesburg from the turn of the century. After the Second World War, railway development absorbed the original ground and international matches were played for some years at Ellis Park, the centre of Transvaal rugby football. The new Wanderers' rose within the precincts of the club's golf course at Kent Park. It is strictly contemporary in design and while it gives admirable viewing facilities and seating for a very large number of people, the fact that it affords so little shade accommodation from the fierce rays of the African sun is a defect. Most of the ground is surrounded by a latticework of tiered wooden uncovered seating. At one end, however, is a huge aluminium stand of unique design, the covering being on the cantilever principle so that spectators underneath have an uninterrupted view of the game.

The new ground was opened in time for the MCC tour of 1956–57. A year later the gates had to be closed at a Test Match for the first time in the history of South African cricket with an official attendance on Boxing Day of the First Test against Australia of 36,057. It was also at the new Wanderers' ground, on 28 December 1966, that South Africa beat Australia in South Africa for the first time, after 64 years of trying. After losing their first 5 first innings wickets, on the first morning, for 41 runs, they won by 233 runs, having made 620 in their 2nd innings.

PORT ELIZABETH

There are two other Test Match centres in South Africa, at Port Elizabeth and Durban, the Port Elizabeth ground being the oldest in the country. The club was formed in 1843 and the first Test Match against England was played there in 1889. Most of the accommodation at the ground is contained in a fine spacious stand that extends the whole length of one side of it. The pitch is usually very slow, the weather very windy and the hospitality very lavish.

DURBAN

At Kingsmead, Durban, there long existed the charming ceremony of planting trees by cricketers to commemorate outstanding performances achieved on the ground. One finds, during a stroll at the back of the old wooden stand, trees bearing the names of Paynter (who made 243 in a Test Match there), Nourse, Hammond, Voce, Verity, Fingleton and many others.

Durban's most famous match was the timeless Test of 1938–39. One person not too distressed by those seemingly endless proceedings was the General Editor of this book. Engaged upon broadcasting the match for the BBC he was being paid on a daily basis. The match was terminated on the 10th day when the MCC players had to leave to catch their ship home, ironically when England, needing almost 700 to win, were within sight of victory. An aggregate of 1,981 runs were scored for the loss of 35 wickets.

West Indies

Each of the four chief homes of cricket in the West Indies is a regular Test centre: Barbados, Trinidad, Guyana and Jamaica. Generally it is Queen's Park, Port of Spain, Trinidad, which takes 2 Tests out of the 5.

BARBADOS

No account of the cricket grounds of the world would be complete without reference to Kensington Oval at Bridgetown. Much West Indian cricket history has been centred around this island, no longer than the Isle of

Johannesburg: the new Wanderers, the third ground in the city on which Test cricket has been played. This picture was taken in 1956, when crowds were segregated; the non-white section can be clearly seen towards the *top left-hand corner*.

Wight, yet most productive of all centres of great players – an island of waving sugar canes and golden beaches where one is for ever within sound of the sea. When R. Slade Lucas's team toured the West Indies in 1895, the home of the Pickwick Cricket Club at Kensington became established as the chief centre of the game. The first Test was played in Barbados in 1930. A main stand on the ground is named after George Challenor, one of the great early figures of West Indian cricket. The capacity of the ground as a whole is no more than 10,000, but this is increased somewhat by the West Indian habit of erecting pirate stands outside the area. People with property adjoining the cricket fields find a profitable little sideline with makeshift seating accommodation, other perches and even trees – anywhere, in fact where an enthusiast is prepared to deposit himself at a price less than he would have to pay at the gate.

The Kensington ground on a big match day is a sight to remember, with its background of swaying palms and its excited clusters of knowledgeable, dusky onlookers themselves perhaps the most typical of the West Indian crowds. It is in the order of things that the wickets should be fast and true. Among the notable scoring feats here, Pakistan's Hanif Mohammad made 337 in the longest innings – 999 minutes – in the history of Test cricket in 1957–58; F. M. Worrell who, with the other 2 'Ws' was born close to the ground, has played several of his longest innings at Kensington, including 308 not out against Trinidad in 1943–44 when he joined with another famous Barbadian, John Goddard, in an unbroken 4th wicket stand of 502. Worrell and Sobers, yet another of the outstanding personalities Barbados has given to cricket, batted for more than 2 days in another vast partnership in a Test Match against England in 1959–60. Yet the Barbados turf can be as treacherous as Melbourne's when affected by rain. Although Barbados themselves have hit three totals of over 700 there, Trinidad were bowled out for 16 in 1941–42 when J. E. D. Sealy took 8 of their wickets for 8 runs.

Barbadians take their cricket seriously. One local character, affectionately known as King Dial, a local dandy, used to wear a fresh suit of the most striking appearance each day of a big match. With his cane and straw hat, and coats of many colours, he timed his entrance to the ground during the first over of play with the skill of a vaudeville artist and the crowd on the popular side, with their unfailing good humour, duly accorded him a 'kingly' welcome. It all adds to the gaiety and good fun that is a traditional part of the West Indian scene.

Not until 1979 when Kerry Packer took his cricket 'circus' to Barbados was there a riot at Kensington. One of a series of WSC matches had to be abandoned when some of the players and then the crowd over reacted to an umpiring decision.

Port of Spain: the largest and most beautiful of the West Indian grounds, with a Test Match in progress between West Indies and Australia.

TRINIDAD

The Queen's Park ground at Port of Spain is not only the most commodious and best-appointed of West Indian grounds, it is also the most attractive, beautifully situated adjacent to the open parkland in the centre of the city known as the Savannah and in the lee of foothills heavy with luxuriant tropical vegetation. On the sky-line, mauve and mountainous, climbs the Northern Range. For many years cricket at Queen's Park was played on the mat, even when in the other main centres the wickets were turf. First the pitch was of coconut fibre, but in 1935 a jute mat was substituted and on that no Test Match reached a definite conclusion. Turf, however, was introduced in the mid-1950s and although the wicket generally continues to favour the batsman, as is the general rule in the West Indies, it was here that Statham and Trueman bowled England to the victory that decided the 1959–60 series. The extraordinary thing about England's bowling success was that the pitch looked dry and grassless and yet Statham kept making the ball move off the seam as though he were bowling on 'green' turf. He beat the hapless Butcher 8 or 9 balls in succession. Statham himself was unable to account for the phenomenon, saying in his usual modest way, 'It was just one of those days.'

Mention of this occasion impels some word about the crowd scenes that marred it when play was brought to a premature close on the evening of the second day. Overcrowding, betting and the strength of the local rum were probably more active ingredients in the trouble than disappointment at the unexpected course of the game. What the sympathetic spectator will remember perhaps most vividly is the dismay, amounting to intense grief, that was shown by the more responsible citizens – and especially by the officers of the Queen's Park Club – at the disorders that had brought their ground and island into disrepute. For a while the large-scale invasion of the field, following the throwing of bottles on to it, had ugly possibilities; but the good sense of the majority prevailed, and order and good relations were restored as swiftly as they had been put in jeopardy. The first explosion of this kind had taken place during a Test Match in Georgetown in 1953–54. Others were to follow in Kingston and finally in Bridgetown. They show how the red-hot fervour for cricket in the Caribbean carries its own dangers.

GUYANA

Much West Indian history has been made on the superb Bourda wicket in the midst of the trim ground with its old-fashioned wooden pavilion set up on stilts in the Dutch style characteristic of this town of wide streets and parallel dykes. Georgetown is actually built below the level of the sea, buttressed against the waters of the Atlantic by a long sea wall.

The first Test in Georgetown was the occasion of West Indies' first win over England. That was in 1929–30 and the great George Headley gave special quality to the match by making a century in each innings, while Roach also distinguished himself with an innings of 209. In the England attack were 2 famous left-arm bowlers, or at least one already famous and the other destined to become so. Rhodes who was almost 52 and Voce who was 20. England were beaten again at Georgetown in the first series after the war. The ground's recent history has been tarnished by crowd trouble. The first of the large-scale West Indian cricket riots erupted at the Bourda Oval when McWatt, the West Indian wicket-keeper, was given run-out against Len Hutton's England side in the 3rd Test in 1953–54. Because of political troubles in Guyana a Test Match between West Indies and India had to be switched from Georgetown in 1962, and in 1979 over £50,000 worth of damage was done when a large crowd became wild with irritation, the reason being that they felt the two sides representing World Series Cricket were being dilatory in starting play following heavy rain. If this trend continued it was feared that Georgetown's future as a Test centre would be in danger.

JAMAICA

The largest of the West Indian islands, Jamaica has a number of fine grounds. First-class matches have been played both at Sabina Park and Melbourne Park in Kingston itself, a bare mile or so apart. Sabina, however, is the Test Match centre. History was made there in 1957–58 when Sobers surpassed Hutton's world-record Test score by making 365 not out against Pakistan. The excitement of the big occasion is perhaps more noticeable here than on any other ground in the world. Space is so limited that the straight boundaries are no more than 60 yards from the pitch. The crowd appears to sit on top of the players.

Sabina Park, Kingston, Jamaica: taken from the press box this photograph shows Wes Hall, at a distance of only 6 or 7 yards, tucking in his shirt before bowling to Boycott at the start of the Second Test Match between England and West Indies in 1967–68. Umpire Douglas Sang Hue looks round to see what is happening. With the stands forming the boundaries, the ground has the atmosphere of a cockpit.

When Hall, the West Indies fast bowler, arrived at the turning point in his long walk back to his bowling mark, he seemed to be within touching distance of the sightscreen.

In this veritable cockpit of excitement, full of dust and noise and tension, many great innings have been played and there has been some memorable bowling. Two Jamaican batsmen have been responsible for many of the innings, the legendary George Headley and Lawrence Rowe. There have also, sadly, been some tragic occasions, with the crowd deciding to take matters into their own hands. They did it when England were playing West Indies in 1967–68 and again when Australia were playing there in 1978. A game of cricket one moment has brought out the riot squad with their tear gas the next.

India

India's Test centres are Bombay, Calcutta, Madras, Delhi, Kanpur and Bangalore, although Hyderabad and Nagpur have also staged the occasional Test. Eden Gardens in Calcutta is India's most spacious ground, but the game's spiritual home, as is soon apparent to any visiting side, is Bombay.

BOMBAY

Test cricket has been played on 3 different grounds in Bombay. The first was the Bombay Gymkhana, set in one corner of a large common, called the Esplanade Maidan, situated in the heart of Bombay's commercial centre. This was where India played her first home Test Match, against England in 1933–34. The Gymkhana was picturesque. Its excellent pitches made for good cricket and there was an attractive pavilion with a mock-tudor facade. But by the time Test cricket was resumed after the Second World War Bombay boasted the magnificent Cricket Club of India, incorporating the Brabourne Stadium, erected on ground reclaimed from the Arabian Sea.

The Brabourne Stadium was the brainchild of Anthony Stanislaus De Mello, a flamboyant, far-sighted man. The whole Brabourne complex, named after the then Governor of Bombay, was years ahead of its time. Residential, and with every sporting amenity, it was seen in India as being the MCC of the sub-continent. With a capacity of 40,000 it possessed a glorious Test Match atmosphere. Unfortunately, though, the pitches were so slow (due, perhaps, to their being founded on reclaimed land) that a high proportion of matches played there were drawn.

The last of Brabourne's 15 Tests was against England in 1973–74, by when there raged a serious disagreement between the Bombay Cricket Association and the Cricket Club of India over the allocation of seats. The larger proportion of the profits went to the club, a private institution, while the Association, which bore the rising costs of running the game within the territory as well as of staging the Test Match, got little.

After fruitless negotiations over several years the Bombay Cricket Association built its own ground, the Wankhede, only a mile away from the Brabourne Stadium. Considering the over-crowding that exists in Bombay, and this particular area is certainly no exception, the building of a second stadium, duplicating the first, seemed to many an appalling extravagence. The Wankhede staged its first Test during the 1974–75 tour by West Indies. A functional ground it lacks the character of Brabourne, but being more modern it provides better spectator facilities, and it allows the local Cricket Association to earn its due revenue.

CALCUTTA

Eden Gardens in Calcutta, situated on the banks of the Hooghly River, has a history as old as that of the East India Company. It was originally the property of the Calcutta Cricket Club and is one of the oldest grounds in the world being used for Test cricket. Its lease was transferred to the National Cricket Club at the end of the Raj. Like the Bombay Gymkhana ground it used to be enclosed by improvized stands on big occasions. Now it is a huge concrete bowl with a capacity of over 70,000, the biggest, apart from Melbourne, of any in the world. Being so near the river the pitches can be green, and the humid air, mingled with the smoke from the funnels of passing ships, can be an aid to swing bowling.

Eden Gardens, Calcutta: a vast concrete stadium, capacity 80,000. It is almost always full for a Test Match, even when, as here, the day holds little promise of much play. This was taken during the second Test Match between England and India in January 1977. India, facing imminent defeat overnight, lost within an hour of the start.

Madras: the Chepauk Ground, recently transformed into a major stadium.

MADRAS

The Chepauk ground in Madras is India's best-appointed and best-administered ground. Its site was once part of the grounds of the palace of the Nawabs of Arcot. The East India Company caused its ownership to pass to the Madras Cricket Club, formed in 1861. Then, when the club's lease expired in the early 1960s, the Government of the time passed it on to the Tamil Nadu Cricket Association, who constructed a stadium, naming it after its President and veteran cricket administrator, Mr M. A. Chidambaram. While the Association waited to acquire the lease Test Matches were staged for some years at the municipally-owned Madras Corporation Stadium. This was between 1953 and 1956. Chepauk (the Chidambaram Stadium to give it its new official title) has always provided good pitches, except for a few years when they were too much in the spinner's favour. Chepauk has produced more finishes than any other Test ground.

DELHI

Ferozshah Kotla is the name of Delhi's Test ground. Placed on the borders of New Delhi and Old Delhi it has a flavour of the Moghul Empire. Headquarters of the Delhi and District Cricket Association the ground is poorly equipped and its administration has yet to catch up with the times. Were it not for its being in India's capital city, and Delhi's only ground of any substance, its Test status might have been in some jeopardy.

KANPUR

Green Park, Kanpur, was accorded Test status during the MCC tour of 1951–52. Some of the earlier Tests there were played on jute matting. Surprising though it may seem, Green Park is a fitting name, the outfield being well-watered and lush. Its clay pitches, however, are invariably shaved to the roots, leading to cricket so slow and heavily weighted in the batsman's favour that it tends sometimes to seem almost meaningless. There was one notorious exception to this, in 1959–60, when Australia, short of spinners, were routed on a seriously underprepared pitch.

BANGALORE

The most junior of India's Test grounds, Bangalore, staged its first Test in 1974–75. The playing area is in keeping with Bangalore's reputation as India's Garden City. Situated in Bangalore's cantonment area, on what was once the parade ground of the British garrison, it may be some years before the money is forthcoming to put to the stadium its finishing touches

D. J. RUTNAGUR

Pakistan

Since the partition of the Indian subcontinent in 1947, Test cricket has been played in 6 cities in Pakistan – Lahore, where the offices of the Board of Control for Cricket in Pakistan (the BCCP) are situated, Karachi, Hyderabad, Bahawalpur, Peshawar and Rawalpindi. In Lahore it was played on the Gymkhana ground until 1959, since when it has moved to the Gaddafi Stadium.

LAHORE

First at the Gymkhana ground and then at the Gaddafi Stadium there have been some excellent turf wickets in Lahore. The Gymkhana ground was charming. Vijay Hazare, the Indian batsman who knew it well, was much reminded of it when he played in the Parks at Oxford. It was tree-lined and peaceful, but it has not been used for Test cricket since India played there in 1965. The Gaddafi Stadium, named after the Libyan leader, is a vast concrete bowl, capable of holding 50,000 people. The pitch is either very slow or green enough to be of some help to seam bowlers, according, some might say, to the forte of the opposition. Stoppages are frequent, due more often to crowd troubles than unsettled weather. In the off-season international hockey festivals are staged on the ground. Bernard Flack, the Edgbaston groundsman, was flown out to Lahore in 1976 to advise the ground authorities there as to how best to quicken up their pitches, though the fruits of his visit were not immediately evident.

KARACHI

This is another huge concrete stadium, ringed mostly by uncovered terraces but made more colourful by the chamianas which divide them. Until the 1960s the pitches were of matting, the ground being too arid (it is on the fringe of the Sind Desert) to support grass. With improved watering a turf square has been laid, though the pitches there are of the texture more of baked mud than turf. On the Karachi mat Fazal Mahmood, Pakistan's great leg-cutter, could be virtually unplayable; on the turf most matches are drawn, batsmen being hard to dislodge as the pitch gets ever slower

The National Stadium is 10 miles from the city centre and like the Gaddafi Stadium it is a regular centre of crowd troubles. The MCC tour of 1968–69 ended with the early abandonment of the last Test Match in Karachi, which happened when England, in their first innings, were 502 for 7 and Knott was 96 not out. Dust can also be a hazard.

HYDERABAD

Hyderabad is some 120 miles from Karachi, north across the Sind Desert. Ornamental buildings overlook the ground, which has a bare and parched outfield and a typically slow Pakistani pitch. When Pakistan are in the ascendant good crowds attend. Schoolgirls have been known to scream with enthusiasm, whether in approval of Pakistan's ten wicket victory over New Zealand in 1977 or Abdul Qadir's bowling when he was taking 6 England wickets for only 44 runs in 1978.

Lahore: the Gaddafi Stadium, one of the world's largest playing areas, seen through the eyes of the press.

BAHAWALPUR

This is a delightful tree-lined ground on which Pakistan played one of their earliest Tests, against India in 1955. It was developed in the days of the Raj and has been well maintained by responsible local support. What stands there are are erected only for big matches and provide limited accommodation. Even so, large and enthusiastic crowds, often containing women in purdah, enjoy the play, which takes place usually in beautiful weather.

PESHAWAR

At Peshawar, as at Bahawalpur, Pakistan met India in the first series ever played between the two countries. A neat, square-shaped ground, no distance from the Khyber Pass, it has a pitch which tends to give encouragement to spin bowling. Lovely days are followed during the cricket season by crisp nights. It was at Peshawar, playing for MCC Under-25 against North Zone in 1966–67, that Mike Brearley scored 312 not out, the highest first-class score ever made by an Englishman on the Indian sub-continent.

RAWALPINDI

Rawalpindi's first Test Match, and their only one before 1980, was between Pakistan and New Zealand in 1965. Pakistan won it by an innings and 64 runs. It is a pleasant ground, though scarcely substantial enough for a modern, well-attended Test Match. When an England touring team plays there they can expect more patriotic support than elsewhere in Pakistan, due to the proximity, in Islamabad, of the British Embassy.

New Zealand

WELLINGTON

The ground at Wellington was originally a lake, which in the mid-19th century, the town-planners intended to turn into an inner harbour. An earthquake in 1853, however, turned the lake into a swamp, whereupon the cricketers asked permission for it to be converted into a cricket ground since their own had been lost. The request was granted and in 1868 a match was played there between Wellington and HMS *Falcon*. The Basin Reserve, as the ground is now called, is within comfortable reach of shops and docks. Bowlers find it one of the windiest in the world and the wind they find disconcertingly changeable. When New Zealand gained their historic first victory over England there in 1978, after 50 years of trying, Richard Hadlee, who took 10 English wickets, had the help of a strong, gusting wind, which blew southerly one day and northerly the next.

The highest score ever made by a South African in a Test Match, until Graeme Pollock's 274 against Australia at Durban in 1970, was Jackie McGlew's 255 against New Zealand at Wellington in 1953. Also at Wellington, New Zealand were dismissed for 42 and 54 in the first Test Match against Australia. That was in 1946. When next the two sides played there New Zealand made 484, their highest score against Australia.

When large-scale improvements were being undertaken at the 'Basin' in 1979 the Test Match against Pakistan, which was due to have been played there, was switched to Napier, a seaside resort 200 miles north-east

Wellington, New Zealand: the Basin Reserve, which owes its name to the fact that it was an anchorage before Wellington's last major earthquake.

of Wellington, which thus became the 50th ground on which Test cricket had been staged. Unlike the grounds at Christchurch, Auckland and Dunedin, the Basin Reserve is not used for rugby football. Soccer, however, is played there.

CHRISTCHURCH

The oldest of New Zealand's Test grounds is Lancaster Park in Christchurch. It has a background of hills and an affectionate place among New Zealand cricketers as being the scene of their first victory over Australia. None of the many rugby internationals played there has produced more excitement than New Zealand's five wicket victory over Ian Chappell's team in 1974. With a hundred in each innings Gleen Turner was New Zealand's particular hero.

The first defeat of an English team in New Zealand was also at Lancaster Park. That was in the New Year of 1906–07, when an MCC side, after a rough sea crossing from Wellington, lost to Canterbury by seven wickets. Cricket had started at Lancaster Park in 1882. In 1891, for the meeting of Canterbury and Otago, each side was given the choice of a pitch when their turn came to bat. Now a large, mostly modern stand spans one half of the ground, an open terrace the other. The city, of streams and spires, elms and parks, has an air of easy contentment.

AUCKLAND

Auckland's Eden Park attracts the largest cricket crowds in New Zealand – upwards of 30,000 can be expected for a day's play in an important Test Match. Large stands enclose the rectangular playing area, the unusual feature of which is a pitch placed diagonally from one corner to another. At large expense the rooms and offices have recently been splendidly modernized, more because of the ground's rugby than its cricket connexion.

New Zealand's first-ever Test victory came at Eden Park – in March 1956, over a West Indian side that included Weekes, Sobers, Colne Smith, Ramadhin and Valentine. 'The day will be remembered,' wrote R. T. Brittenden, 'not for the victory itself, so much as the proof that it could be done and for the inspiration it gave the nation's cricketing youth.'

DUNEDIN

Carisbrook at Dunedin is another football field-cum-cricket ground. From the road climbing away from it (known as the Scotsman's Grandstand) spectators get a free bird's-eye view of play. Drivers of passing trains blow their whistles as they pass. Carisbrook is a friendly place, more practical than scenic; more beautiful by far is the countryside surrounding the city. Otago is the home province; for many years Bert Sutcliffe was their proud possession.

County Grounds of England

J. M. KILBURN AND NORMAN DE MESQUITA

Travelling the counties in search of cricket can be an experience for only the few. Players enjoy it, of course, and the more peripatetic writers, and there is evidence of commercial necessity and sporting interest happily coincident in the occasional sight of familiar faces far from home. Holidays have long been conditioned by cricketing concern, and the labour of love that is selectorial duty frequently demands exploration of the wilder first-class territory, but for most cricketers a season spent in following the game through its habitat must remain a dream unfulfilled, a prospect enchanged by the distance of impracticality. One summer could not complete a survey of the county grounds with county cricket being played, because, apart from complications imposed by the fixture list, some counties do not allot matches to all their grounds every year. A general tendency during the development of county cricket as a public entertainment was towards concentration. Major grounds became county club headquarters and were used for the majority of home matches as a justification for overhead costs and for administrative convenience.

The most recent trends have brought divergence of principle. Some county sides have become nomadic within their own boundary; others have developed amenities of headquarters to a high degree of efficiency and attraction. When Essex lost Leyton in 1933, after nearly 50 years of occupation, they chose to spread their cricket across the county, arranging home engagements as far as possible in weekly festivals. By ingenious improvization and organization they transported not only players but also the trappings of presentation – scoreboard, printing press, seating, secretarial offices and boundary boards. From seaside to inland centre, from public park to private club, the cavalcade of cricket moved down the lanes to the financial benefit of the county club and for wider spread of public interest in the game. In Warwickshire the concentration upon headquarters has brought remarkable development to the Edgbaston ground. There an enormous income derived from sources outside cricket has been devoted to the construction of a stadium to accommodate the major occasions of cricket in positive luxury and so designed to produce revenue from its own amenities. Warwickshire county cricket lives well on Edgbaston's catering facilities.

The broad division of cricketing counties into categories of the concentrated and the diversified points no clear way to prosperity. Where county cricket is taken to several grounds the basis of financial comfort is an adequate membership, as in Yorkshire. Where an elaborate headquarters must be maintained the requirement is accessibility, as exemplified by the Oval, Old Trafford and Edgbaston. Centralized counties are finding advantage from the development of their properties towards a spread of overheads throughout the year. Winter revenue from social functions augments and sometimes exceeds the summer takings from gate-money. Nomadic counties are turning towards the presentation of first-class cricket as a holiday attraction. Matches at seaside resorts, or 'weeks' given a special significance, have become more profitable than routine engagements even in the larger centres of population. A pilgrimage of country cricket would include industrial areas as well as parkland, sophistication and the bucolic. It would step from south to north, from sea to city, and it would illustrate a nation's life in bricks and mortar, wood and stone and in personal characteristics and attitudes. Cricket itself is conditioned by environment, coloured in some degree by setting.

The ideal expedition would presumably be designed to touch climax at Lord's for a late June Test Match, leaving the greater part of exploration for the homeward way when summer suns are warmer and the season finally declines into the cheerful farewells of festival. Opening is for the West Country, where tours traditionally begin and the promise of harvest is offered in the orchard blossom that lights and scents the way to WORCESTER. There the county cricket ground is happily sited on the bank of Severn. Sometimes, in the wetter winters, it rests beneath the Severn, for the flooding river has often drowned the field to renew vitality in the turf and to create a legend of the floating heavy roller. More authentic are recollections of swimming from the pavilion steps and rowing-boat propelled across the pitch. The old pavilion was perched on stilts and the new accommodation for players and administrative staff is discreetly elevated, giving not only safety from the winter inundation but vantage point for one of cricket's loveliest scenes. From the pavilion or pavilion enclosure the smooth turf stretches towards the hidden river, trees marking the limits of the ground, and the trees themselves are topped by the warm brown stone of the cathedral where John, the unloved King of England, lies entombed.

Worcester has developed the amenities of first-class cricket without dispersing an impression of cricket as a meadow game. There are deck-chairs at the boundary edge and trees to give shade to the strolling spectator pausing in peregrination. Play can be watched from a parked car; and in the kinder summers play is often interrupted by blinding reflection from the windscreens of parked cars. Worcester offers formal lunch from the dining room or scope for the picnic basket and, of course, fruit stall or ale bar for the simpler improvisation. Press box and scoreboard are products of recent affluence and, as building extends, the representation of a cricketing headquarters grows more marked. Worcestershire cricket has a home of dignity

Worcester: Bradman batting on the ground where he scored 236 (1930), 206 (1934), 258 (1938) and 107 (1948).

at the Worcester ground. Dignity is matched by convenience and encouragement. The Worcester ground is readily accessible from the city centre; now, if anything, rather noisily so with New Road having become part of a one-way system. It offers cricket for the spare hour of the business day, cricket for a pause on the homeward way, cricket as conclusion to marketing. To players it offers uncommon attraction. Worcester has an atmosphere of cricket; it is a natural setting for the game as distinct from an improvisation imposed by urban or exotic exigencies. Given this water meadow at the side of the Severn what more appropriate than some summer game upon its inviting turf; a game to be enjoyed in the freshness of morning, the warmth of afternoon and the cool of evening when the sun is falling behind the Malvern Hills? Worcestershire stay contentedly and comfortably in Worcester for the bulk of their home engagements, but occasional expeditions are made to DUDLEY, KIDDERMINSTER and STOURBRIDGE where amenities are less evident but where local enthusiasm justifies the experience of comparative inadequacies, once in a while.

Westwards from Worcestershire the road of cricket runs into Wales. Glamorgan have won the County Championship and made their cricket a regional if not a nationalistic concern of summer, yet cricket in Cardiff and Swansea and in the townships of the valleys still breathes a slightly alien air. It remains an adjunct to the sporting life more than an essential. Speak of Wilfred Wooller and the response will be: 'He was one of the great three-quarters, man, for Cardiff and for Wales; he played cricket, too.' Cricket is a young brother in the family of sport in Wales.

The St Helen's ground at SWANSEA has an awkward size and an awkward shape and an awkward arrangement of seating for the presentation of cricket, but it has the virtues of fresh air and adequate light. Beyond the football stand and across the Mumbles road and railway stretches the seaway of the Bristol Channel to give a sniff of salt and a surge of hope for seam bowling in the evening air.

The pavilion tops a high embankment which forms the members' enclosure and from the top of the pavilion the distant cricket must compete for attention with the passing ships at sea. St Helen's is a fine-weather ground; there is no comfort and little shelter when cold winds blow or damp mist swirls, but when the sun shines it warms and burns to make play a pleasure and watching a relaxation. There is scope for perambulation across the turf at the football end and time for reconsideration as batsmen coming and going make the longest journey in first-class cricket. Dismissal first ball at Swansea involves a fair day's exercise.

St Helen's is not a ground for accurate spectatorial assessment of playing detail. Pavilion and the greater part of the terraced enclosure are not behind the bowler's arm and are, in any case, vastly distant from the pitch. When Trueman found his first success as a medium-fast, 'off-cutting' bowler there was some bewilderment among observers, professional and uncommitted. Results indicated off-breaks, but the technicalities of bowling action were difficult to discern and some curious conclusions were overheard in the club-room and appeared in print. The orthodox and the traditional are most readily appreciated at Swansea. Seating on the football side of the cricket area is temporary and uncomfortable. Opposite, the embankment accommodation has been extended and improved, but a view from square-leg is a strain on day-long concentration and when playing hours are abnormal the declining sun can become an embarrassment. Swansea spectators are not easily dismayed. Their enthusiasm is readily roused, their appreciation is uninhibited and the Swansea hospitality is generous and persistent.

It is difficult to stray far from rugby football in Wales, but cricket in CARDIFF has deserted the old Arms Park for a relatively new venue at Sofia Gardens. Although only a short distance from the old venue, the move has brought a change of atmosphere in Cardiff cricket. The new ground is adjacent to (at times part of) a modern sports centre and boasts a modern and attractive dressing room block which also houses the dining room. Sofia Gardens is an open ground with the eastern side of the playing area adjacent to a number of rugby pitches. The south side is bounded by the River Taff, but the river is hidden from view by a line of trees and there is also a low, covered stand, press box and commentary box in front of the river. This affords the press and the radio commentator a good line of vision, not the necessary height. From scaffolding at the ground's northern end cameras and commentators, on behalf of BBC Wales, provide the sort of coverage to Glamorgan cricket which must make supporters of the other 16 counties envious.

Cardiff and St Helen's, Swansea, provide the substance in Glamorgan cricket, the sophistication of the first-class, but rougher gardens must also be cultivated to raise county interest. Matches are taken to NEATH and to NEWPORT, to LLANELLI and PONTYPRIDD, to the steel works at MARGAM and to EBBW VALE. These are unpretentious grounds, welcoming a county occasion as highlight of the season, with temporary accommodation and amenities added to the standing provision for club cricket. They ask fine weather for

St Helen's, Swansea: the scene of some famous Welsh victories, both at cricket and rugby.

spectatorial comfort and the simpler issues of play for spectatorial appeal, yet they are well attended and there would be no grave misinterpretation of the meaning in Glamorgan cricket were the observer allowed only experience of these outposts.

Bath: a lovely setting, a good crowd and a middle stump flying.

By crow's flight or its mechanical equivalent Somerset offers the shortest cricketing journey from South Wales, but it is passage into a contrasting cricketing world. Somerset could put forward some rather questionable claim to first-class status as far back as 1881, though they were not generally accepted in the highest estate until 10 years later, but the dignities of history have never been a grave Somerset concern. Their cricket grew inevitably from the challenge of a fine day and a field and someone wanting to make a match. Somerset is predominantly an agricultural county, the towns are market towns and there is no enormous agglomeration of people to serve as a ready source of income from the presentation of sport. The first county committee resolved that there should be no county cricket ground, but in changed circumstances Taunton became headquarters and so remains for administration, though the home fixture list is still spread from the seaside resort of Weston-super-Mare through the ruralities to the spa of Bath.

Expeditions to the smaller grounds may not have been altogether beneficial to Somerset finances or to the match records, but they have produced some cricket to remember. The ground at Wells has little in the way of accommodation but it was an inspiration to A. W. Wellard, who, in 1936 and again in 1938, hit sixes from 5 successive balls. The first onslaught was against Derbyshire, Armstrong the bowler. The second was against Kent, Woolley bowling. In this match Wellard, scoring 57 and 37, hit 11 sixes in all and in the whole game no fewer than 24 sixes were recorded. This was only second best at Wells. In 1937 the Somerset v Hampshire match provided 35 sixes. Wellard showered his sixes over all the Somerset grounds, large and small. Bath, Taunton and Weston-super-Mare demanded the greatest resource in losing the ball altogether.

At TAUNTON there is a long, high carry over a guardian palisade at the north end, opposite the pavilion, and behind the pavilion the property within the boundary wall contains car-park and practice pitches. Taunton is not a strikingly beautiful ground but it forms a pleasant setting for county cricket and it carries a West Country flavour, insubstantial by definition but impressive in experience. It is a fine-weather ground, for though there is some covered accommodation at the pavilion end most of the seating is open to sun and wind (and rain which is considered imminent when view of the Quantock Hills has disappeared). In sunshine and with a crowd of no more than 5,000 or 6,000 it is a delightful setting for cricket experience. The pavilion is unpretentious and could be counted inconvenient in its layout with dressing-rooms at the back, but it looks as though it grew from its environment and it tells the Somerset story in the pictures on the dining-room walls. The balcony gives an ideal view of play from behind the bowler's arm and there is admirable viewing, too, from the stands to its right and left.

The charm of the ground, however, must be sought from the less exalted seating which looks towards the pavilion and beyond for a backcloth of trees and the tower of St James's Church. Here, in the sun-trap of the tall hoarding, faces glisten, limbs stretch, children chatter and their elders pass somnolent opinion upon the course of play and the prospect of harvest. When the benches harden, or the sun burns beyond toleration, a stroll to the western corner brings opportunity for refreshment and a cooling pause beneath the shade of trees. On the greater occasions comfort is lost in overcrowding. In compensation, there is no problem of arrival and departure. The ground is close to Taunton's main streets and hotels and bus station. Under pressure even the players can catch a train leaving 20 minutes after drawing of stumps.

BATH has the same convenience of situation. The ground is the bottom of the bowl in which the ancient city lies. In very warm weather it is stifling and in very wet weather it is muddy. It is a cricket ground within grounds and therefore at one and the same time small but spacious. There is plenty of room for spectators, but little comfortable accommodation, because the seating is mainly an improvisation of benches and canvas chairs. Marquees serve for refreshments and as seclusion for Press and scorecard printer and the privileged spectators. The pavilion is more decorative than commodious and the pitch has been known to make third days superfluous. Bath can be the most soporific of cities but its cricket presentations are usually colourful and lively. In August Somerset spend a week or sometimes more at WESTON-SUPER-MARE where the ground is again a festival improvisation of tenting and temporary stands. The first county venture there was in 1914 when consideration of the amenities apparently failed to include the quality of the pitch, for Drake and Booth of Yorkshire bowled unchanged through the match and in the 2nd Somerset innings Drake took all 10 wickets in 9 overs.

Somerset and Gloucestershire have BRISTOL as a meeting point in county cricket in more senses than one. Both play home matches in the city. Somerset take occasional games to the pleasant Wills' ground in the southern outskirts; Gloucestershire have their headquarters towards the northerly suburb of Filton. The Gloucestershire ground at Ashley Down is an old home of county cricket. It was first used in 1888 when Gloucestershire's W. G. ruled the empire of batting he had virtually created. It provided hundreds for the 'Old Man', centuries for Jessop and hundreds for Hammond. It has been setting for all the great cricketers down the years and magnet for Gloucestershire's following through dark days and splendid. The county ground at Bristol is an essential pause in any cricketing pilgrimage. It is not easily discovered by the stranger. From the city centre a long climb up the Gloucester Road may be undertaken by public transport, leaving a short walk to either of the principal entrances. The playing area is bigger than current requirements demand and there is an immediate sense of light and spaciousness. Spectators have room to move and to breathe and cricket can be watched in perambulation. Wickets are pitched almost east-west and the pavilion and members' enclosure take morning sunshine in their siting at the western side of the ground. The pavilion lacks architectural distinction and has the inconvenience of dressing-rooms from which play cannot be seen. These dressing-rooms are also at first-floor level, leaving awkward flights of steps to be negotiated by anxious in-going batsmen; those departing have more time for care and can tread warily. Bristol's ground would not claim to be ideal for county cricket, but its faults are mainly of longevity and the improvizations of successive generations and the interwoven atmosphere of Gloucestershire greatness adds to the sense of character without which no ground can be enduringly impressive. A most comforting event for Gloucestershire supporters in recent years has in fact been the acquisition of the Bristol ground by a commercial concern, which has spent a lot of money on ground improvements and expressed its intention to spend more, in an attempt to make the ground a worthy headquarters for Gloucestershire cricket.

Two or three matches are played each season on the Wagon Works ground, at GLOUCESTER, somewhat awkward of access from the city centre and much less accommodating for crowds. Here the majority of spectators must endure backless benches and brave cold wind or scorching sun in extremes

Cheltenham: the only school ground still used regularly for first-class cricket. This photograph was taken in 1955, during the Cheltenham Week, and shows Gloucestershire playing the South Africans, Arthur Milton batting.

of weather, unless fortune gives tented shelter or convenient parking place for motor-car.

At CHELTENHAM an August festival of three matches has long been a happy feature of the Gloucestershire programme. The setting is the College ground, attractive in itself, with the school buildings and trees as its borders, and given adequacy for first-class occasions by marquees and temporary stands. The Cheltenham College cricket field has to cope with more than one match at the same time during term and has space to spare when Gloucestershire make their August visit. Spectatorial amenities are inevitably limited and in poor weather positive discomfort can scarcely be avoided. Sometimes it can find compensation in the marvels of the play. In one Cheltenham week W. R. Hammond played 2 matches as, rather than for, Gloucestershire. In the first he scored 2 separate hundreds, 139 and 143, against Surrey and when Surrey were batting he took 1 wicket and 10 slip catches. In the 2nd, against Worcestershire, he batted once to score 80; in the 1st Worcestershire innings he took 9 wickets, in the 2nd he took 6.

The beauties of the Midlands seem particularly dependent upon the eye – and mood – of the beholder, for the forest of Arden and 'the rolling green fields of the cream of the shires' make one picture to balance the 'sodden and unkind' of another. Whatever the reaction, exploration must be undertaken on a cricketing journey because the Midlands are more than a bridge between North and South; they have cricketing history and character and quality of their own.

The great grounds of the Midlands are TRENT BRIDGE and EDGBASTON, settings for cricket at its higher level (*see* 'Test Match Grounds in England', above), but both Nottinghamshire and Warwickshire take occasional home matches away from their headquarters to satisfy local interests and spread the blessing of cricket at county standard. Once or twice a year Nottinghamshire slip away to WORKSOP, the busy market town of the Dukeries, where the local cricket and association football clubs share the same ground. The overlap of playing areas means a rough outfield for cricketers and an open touchline for footballers, but for both games the ground enjoys benefit of handy situation within a minute's walk of the main street. The only shelter for cricket spectators is in the football stands which are too far from the pitch for popular viewpoint, but an embankment behind one sightscreen and bench seating or standing room behind the other offer the bulk of the crowd a sense of participation and an opportunity to appreciate the accomplishments of bowling. The pavilion, sited at square-leg, has small dressing-rooms and a small enclosure, and catering facilities for players and public have to be augmented for the major occasions.

An inevitable drawback of any country ground is the lack of adequate spectator accommodation. For a works ground, NEWARK has a good wicket and a well cared for outfield but, as at Worksop, the well informed spectator knows he has to get there early to gain a good vantage point.

Warwickshire's second centre of population is COVENTRY where county cricket is played on Courtaulds' ground. The surroundings are industrial and the cricketing amenities unextravagant, but public interest usually touches the crowd capacity of the ground. The playing area leaves rather short boundaries on either side of the wicket, but both pitch and outfield have been given careful attention with the requirements of first-class cricket in mind, and Warwickshire and their visitors are assured of warm welcome from the boundary edge and in the social and recreational club that is the essential building on the ground.

While Middlesex and Surrey toy with the idea of taking cricket to the remoter parts of their respective counties, Leicestershire have decided, in recent years, to put all their eggs in one basket – Grace Road in LEICESTER. A great deal of money has been spent at Grace Road and it is now as well appointed as any non-Test ground. The county has, in fact, achieved much under the aggressive and imaginative leadership of Mike Turner. Mr Turner was the first of the cricket managers and his modern approach to the marketing and presentation of first-class cricket has led to a great improvement in the fortunes of Leicestershire, both on and off the field.

It cannot be a coincidence that all Leicestershire's successes in the major cricketing competitions have come during the 1970s: 1 County Championship, 2 Benson and Hedges Cups and 2 John Player Leagues, all in the span of 6 years. Success has bred success and the profit made seems to have been intelligently used to make Grace Road a ground of which to be proud. It is sad that such names as Ashby-de-la-Zouch and Loughborough no longer appear in the fixture list, but there can be no doubting the justification of the county's policy. Grace Road has had a chequered history. It was formerly owned by the Civic Authority, who used it as a schools sports ground. It used to be possible, from the roof of the pavilion, to discern the markings of both football and hockey pitches on the outfield. But it is now the county's own property and they have made the fullest use of it for some years. It has its drawbacks, the main one being inaccessibility.

From Leicestershire to Derbyshire is a step from plain to Pennines, a move from Midlands to North. Derbyshire cricketers come from both field and factory, from mine and machine-shop, and to capture a county following the fixtures are spread from industrial centres to holiday resorts. Derby and Chesterfield take most of the home matches, but Buxton, Ilkeston and Burton-on-Trent (which is in Staffordshire) are brought into the list. Buxton wears a festival air, with bunting in the town and tenting on the small ground. Ilkeston offers the spaciousness of a public recreation ground. Burton carries the encouraging atmosphere of its principal industrial product.

CHESTERFIELD serves best to typify the county's cricket and the county's self-presentation. There, in Queen's Park, miner and mechanic have a 'meadow game' at hand in appropriate setting. Queen's Park raises no problem of accessibility and the cricket ground is charmingly sited on a slope that runs down to a little valley with the town buildings perched on the opposite rise. The park itself contains more than the almost-circular cricket ground. There are walks beside a boating lake; there is grassy space for general recreation, serving as a car-park for county-cricket occasions; there is a bandstand; there are greenhouses and flowers; there are trees. The general slope of the ground is from south to north, with the pavilion behind the bowler's arm at the southern end. Dressing-rooms are small and there is little indoor accommodation for spectators, but it is fronted by terracing that descends to the encircling track at field level. To the left of the pavilion, facing the field, the enclosure terracing runs back into the shade of trees and the embankment is graced by hedge and rockeries.

Beyond the members' enclosure, to the west, the recreation field ends in a grassy slope making a natural embankment for the cricket spectators who prefer room for movement to a nearer view of play from the temporary seating at the boundary edge. At the top of this embankment are the refreshment marquees serving players and public. At its lower, northern end trees separate the cricket field from a boating lake and tubular-scaffolding stands aid the view up-wicket.

Chesterfield: one of Derbyshire's two main grounds, Derby being the other. In the background, All Saints' Church with its crooked spire; behind the stumps, Bob Taylor.

The main public entrance is in the south-eastern corner, nearest the town, and from there the visitor, turning left, can work a way behind temporary seating towards the score-board and pavilion enclosure.

Only by wholesale change of character could this Chesterfield ground give comfortable housing to crowds of more than some 12,000. More have been accommodated, but not to the complete satisfaction of all, for unless the advantages of mobility augment the attractions of the play some of the delight in cricket at Queen's Park is inevitably lost. The typical Chesterfield spectator no doubt appreciates the intrinsic satisfactions of the setting, but unless the cricket also pleases there is usually sharp comment and uninhibited expression. Chesterfield crowds have a clear conception of their wants and a proper relish for the discomfiture of opponents – particularly Yorkshire. There is, of course, some iron in the soul; at Chesterfield John Tunnicliffe and J. T. Brown once began a match with a partnership of 554.

DERBY is the headquarters of Derbyshire county cricket. There the official practices and about half the home matches are played on a ground within grounds, part of the old racecourse on Nottingham Road. For many years the cricketers were modestly self-contained in a small pavilion and the playing area had open boundaries from which longing eyes were lifted towards the distant mountain of the unused racecourse grandstand. When decision was made, Mahomet moved. The pavilion was abandoned, its balcony re-erected as a members' stand, and the whole playing area was reconstituted to make the racecourse grandstand available to cricket spectators. Cricket officials now have their offices and players their changing-rooms in the buildings that were once the jockeys' quarters. There is no pavilion or pavilion enclosure in the accepted sense and consequently the appearance of the ground, as well as the amentities, must lack the finishing touches of traditional appearance. Though there cannot be claim that every prospect pleases some of the recent building has satisfied long-felt wants and received general approval. A new score-board has been put up and the indoor practice-shed, close to the dressing-rooms, has more than justified construction by its popularity as a training school and its usefulness when outdoor cricket could not be contemplated.

One unfortunate aspect of the ground, since the rearrangement, is that the wicket now runs east-west instead of north-south. This can lead to the unusual reason for stoppage of play, 'good light': towards the end of the season, with the sun low in the western sky, the batsmen find it difficult to see.

Lancashire and Yorkshire, so similar in their cricketing approach and ambitions, have different schemes of presentation. Lancashire are proud possessors of OLD TRAFFORD (*see above*). Yorkshire have no land of their own, though they have recently acquired a long lease of the cricket section of the HEADINGLEY (*see above*) grounds and have invested in bricks and mortar and steel and concrete there. From Old Trafford Lancashire venture occasionally to the lawns of Aigburth in LIVERPOOL and to Stanley Park in BLACKPOOL and they have made experimental visits elsewhere, but home is essentially and enviably Old Trafford. Yorkshire have no more than 4 matches on any of the grounds on which they play and the season's allocations are an annual committee problem.

To satisfy a large and far-flung membership Yorkshire must spread their favours. They go from southern boundary to northern, from seaside to spa, into all three Ridings. Only chance and the course of the Championship decides where the most significant match of the season shall be played, for opponents may find themselves in Middlesbrough one year and in Sheffield the next. Scarborough provides the best returns in the holiday months and Bradford asks a fixture in the August week known as Bowling Tide.

It is nearly a decade since cricket was last played at Bramall Lane, SHEFFIELD, but it is impossible to ignore the place in any summary of Yorkshire cricketing grounds. It was the original home of Yorkshire cricket, since being leased for 99 years from the Duke of Norfolk in 1855 – on condition that 'matches be conducted in a respectable manner'. In recent years it was hardly an attractive ground, surrounded by terraced houses and with the not-too-distant prospect of Sheffield United Football Club with its grandstand and floodlight pylons. The encroachment of football brought about the demise of this historic ground as a venue for Yorkshire cricket.

So what to do for Yorkshire cricket without the use of Bramall Lane? They lighted on a solution that has caused their new Sheffield ground to become something very unusual in county cricket – a ground that has played host to two different first class counties. Abeydale Park is the home of Sheffield United Lawn Tennis Club and is also the venue for several leading squash tournaments. In common with so many of the country's leading tennis clubs, the advance of squash as both a participation and spectator sport has seen a shift of emphasis. There are not many grounds that can boast to have played host to two first-class counties. But the ever-increasing spread of Sheffield means that much of what is now part of the city was, at one time, within the boundaries of Derbyshire. Derbyshire played a few matches at Abbeydale Park shortly after the Second War, until the development of Chesterfield and Derby. There has been some criticism of the playing surface at Abbeydale Park: a certain West Indian fast bowler quite recently gave Yorkshire a torrid time, leading to the retirement of three of their batsmen with damaged fingers. But the pitches are now acceptable and Yorkshire cricket has once again found a suitable home in Sheffield.

Acklam Park, MIDDLESBOROUGH, accommodates both cricket and rugby-union football, though not on the same turf, and clubhouse amenities are jointly enjoyed. The pavilion is small – sharing this defect with the numbers on the score-board – and its seating is to be numbered in tens rather than hundreds. For county matches tubular-scaffolding stands, tarpaulin-roofed, provide enclosure accommodation and presidential and civic marquees brighten the boundary edge and give shelter to the few. There is no cover for the general public and the embankment providing the bulk of spectatorial accommodation has the backless seating that becomes a trial in a full day's watching. Nevertheless, Middlesbrough spectators do welcome the sight of county cricket, do take risks of the weather, and year by year the amenities of the ground are being improved.

Anlaby Road, HULL, has one covered stand, built of brick and concrete to replace the wooden shelter lost during the Second World War. This looks down the wicket and is therefore better placed for watching than the 2-storey pavilion, sited at square-leg and fronted by a small terraced enclosure. Embankments for public seating are not extensive, but Anlaby Road is a bigger ground than it looks and even a sprawling crowd soon begins to count in thousands. They are inclined to be fatalistic thousands, for when county cricket is due in Hull some meteorological marvel seems the rule rather than the exception. Extremes of heat or cold, of drought or rain, of gale or fragrance from the fish-dock are apparently inevitable; once there was a match abandoned without a ball bowled, the decision unhesitatingly taken on the second morning.

Yorkshire's HARROGATE match is a concession to members resident in Nidderdale, Wensleydale and Swaledale and an escape from industrial setting in the West Riding. The ground is unpretentious, with a low wooden stand providing the only cover for spectators and a grassed embankment offering an attraction for the unconcentrated in fine weather. The permanent seating round the boundary rails is simple and in the pavilion enclosure augmented by canvas chairs. In the absence of surrounding trees or tall buildings the light is good and a slope helps the drainage of the playing area. Harrogate gives Yorkshire their nearest approach to garden-party cricket in their home championship programme.

SCARBOROUGH attracts holiday crowds, but with the full convenience of commercial presentation. Nowhere in England are more cricketing advantages concentrated in one ground. Access is simplicity itself and the property must carry an enormous potential value as building land. Playing conditions in the clear seaside air and on beautiful turf are an inspiration, though sighting the ball against a background of spectators is not always easy. Accommodation is adequate for all but the most demanding of occasions and if the virtue of size were extended another would be lost by taking away the watchers' sense of participation. In nearly every seat the spectator is above ground level and both the embankment and the open stands are steeply tiered, giving the field itself as partial background to the play, which is always easier on the eyes than trying to follow the ball from ground level.

The Scarborough ground is attractive from the moment of entry through the main gateway on North Marine Road. From that viewpoint the open embankment, constructed when the playing area was first cut out from a sloping field, stretches down to the boundary edge. To the right the pathway runs to the red-brick pavilion set across the north-eastern corner and looking towards the pitch from the angle of mid-off or fine-leg. Modernization has brought the pavilion, with its small railed enclosure at ground level, to a high degree of comfort. Dressing-rooms are on the ground floor, giving easy access to the field. The first floor carries an open balcony with two or three rows of coveted seats and a dining-room with wide windows looking on the field of play. Secretarial offices, committee-room and a club lounge complete the first-floor accommodation. To the right of the pavilion and running the length of the northern boundary is an uncovered concrete stand rising to the height of the pavilion balcony. An ideally situated scorers' and Press box is built into this stand and the main score-board is perched on the corner. The western side of the ground was originally levelled by material excavated from the eastern embankment and is the most open area of the property. There, at festival time, the marquees are pitched in the corner opposite the pavilion and there, facing the embankment, is the stand most recently built. To the south the space between playing area and surrounding wall is narrow and is made over to a roofed enclosure carrying rows of seats that increase in number as the slope rises towards the embankment. Behind this enclosure the ground is overlooked by the high Victorian houses of Trafalgar Square, their towering roof-tops a perpetual challenge to hitters of sixes. For a whole day's cricket or a stolen hour Scarborough is an uncommonly attractive ground to spectators and the end-of-season festival is a famed farewell to the cricketers' summer.

Park Avenue, BRADFORD, has some of Scarborough's appeal in less salubrious setting. It is big enough to provide adequate scope for first-class cricket and small enough to give spectators a close association with the play. Park Avenue, once on the outskirts of Bradford and still shielded from urban encirclement by a public park on one side and railway cutting on another, was designed and constructed as a sports centre. There is a ground for cricket and a ground for football, separated by a stand that primarily serves the football club but makes a backing to the cricket field and contains in a narrow balcony an admirable vantage point immediately alongside the sightscreen. The cricket field is roughly square, with wickets pitched more or less north-south on an almost indiscernible table levelled from the slight fall of the land towards the north. The higher, southern end contains the principal accommodation for spectators.

It is dominated by a 2-storey pavilion set above a steeply rising enclosure, which is itself above the level of the turf and separated from it by a 6-foot-high boundary wall, marking the last steep step. Dressing-rooms, administrative offices and a dining-room that is also equipped as a winter practice-shed are on the upper floor, where the only disadvantage of the balcony is its sunlessness through the cricketing hours. To left and right of the pavilion the mound has been used for terraced enclosures, uncovered, which gradually decrease in depth towards the side-view terraces. These terraces, backed by roadways, are a limiting factor in provision for the biggest crowds, but their comfort has been increased by recent renovation and additional building and they offer the ground's best service to sun worshippers. Park Avenue is a neatly fashioned ground, strictly business-like in its appeal for cricket, and to show its best face needs the smartening of fresh paint, tidy terracing and well-preserved pathways. The dust of its environment and the litter of occasions past soon leave it looking forlorn in emptiness.

Though there is a separation of many miles Yorkshire could, without absurd stretch of imagination, consider themselves in home surroundings at NORTHAMPTON. Parallels cannot be drawn too closely, but the Northampton environment is industrial, the

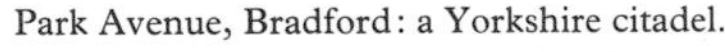
Park Avenue, Bradford: a Yorkshire citadel.

Northampton ground accommodates both cricket and football and the developments and improvizations of different generations remain evident. Northampton's ground is in an eastern suburb and was originally laid out, from ploughland, by the Northamptonshire County Cricket and Recreation Grounds Co Ltd in 1885. Representative Northamptonshire matches had been staged for many years earlier on the Northampton racecourse, but difficulties of enclosure prevented any development there and the county cricket club moved to the new quarters in 1886. They struck early association with Yorkshire. The first coach was Tom Emmett and the groundsman, who had served on the racecourse, was Alfred Stockwin of Sheffield. Stockwin was a forceful character, greatly plagued by the public rights over the racecourse, where he once pulled the driver from a brewer's dray that had been transgressing on pitch preparation and, confessing some satisfaction from the consequent fisticuffs, suggested a pay-rise for supplementary duties.

Stockwin, himself a useful medium-pace bowler, prepared his wickets with sympathy for batsmen and remained head groundsman at the Northampton county ground until his collapse and death in the pavilion in 1922. Later care has been bestowed by another Yorkshireman, R. Johnson, who became groundsman in 1930 and continued the tradition of Stockwin, to the advantage of yet another Yorkshireman, Dennis Brookes. Brookes, Northamptonshire's opening batsman for 20 years and professional captain, scored over 30,000 runs in first-class cricket.

The principles of the Ground Company's intent are to be seen in the layout at Northampton. The 8½ acres contain a joint cricket and association-football area, tennis courts, bowling green and the inn that was a usual feature of 19th-century sports promotion. The extent and plan of the grounds can be appreciated from the balcony of the cricket pavilion, situated at the southern end and looking down the line of the pitches. Directly opposite lies the football stand, too distant to be of service to cricket spectators, who ring the boundary on bench seating or in parked cars across the open touchline of the football pitch. Flanking the stand and behind the football goals are terraced embankments, one open, one covered, which, again, are of little attraction to the cricket spectator because of their remoteness from play. For cricket the accommodation offers a choice of open or covered seating. There is an old stand on the western side of the ground, giving a square-leg view of play, and a new stand close to the pavilion, on its left, looking more or less down the wicket. This new members' stand, seating some 600, is the upper section of the building put up in 1958 as an indoor cricket school, splendidly equipped and augmented by changing facilities. In summer the 'winter shed' becomes a dining-room with glass frontage giving sight of the play. Behind this attractive and useful building of dual purpose are the lawn tennis courts, flanking the pathway from the members' entrance.

The pavilion, with a small tiered enclosure, has merit more in historical association than in modern amenity, but for the peripatetically inclined there is space for strolling along the northern boundary, where seats are set out or cars can be parked either at playing level or on a little slope beside the scoreboard. Where the boundary line turns inwards towards completion of an irregular circle, the grounds broaden to include the bowling green, duly fenced and hedged about. The Northampton county ground cannot claim striking beauty of either setting or construction. The approaches are urban though the surrounding houses and nearby factories are not oppressive and there are some trees for the eye's refreshment. The stands serving football are serviceable rather than impressive, but they do not obtrude upon cricketing occasions. Some of the pathways are discouragingly dusty but circumnavigation on turf is possible. Circumstances, in fact, tend to colour the prevailing impression. Dreariness of a dull, damp day can become sparkle under fresh paint and the solace of sunshine. Northampton has cricketing appeal in its heart. Northamptonshire home matches are also taken to the small club grounds of KETTERING, PETERBOROUGH and RUSHDEN.

Just as Leicestershire has tasted success since its administration moved into the 20th century, so Essex, in 1979, won something, after more than 100 years of waiting. There, though less nomadic than they were, the game is still taken to Colchester, Ilford and Southend. With the majority of games now being played at Chelmsford, Essex cricket can no longer be termed a travelling 'circus'. The change started in the 1960s when Essex were near to financial disaster. Warwickshire came to the rescue (as they did for several counties thanks to their Supporters Association and its profitable football pool) and gave Essex an interest-free loan to allow them to develop the County Ground at CHELMSFORD. At last, Essex could develop a real home and much has been done during the past decade to improve it.

The offices, bar and dressing rooms take up the western side of the ground with a semi-permanent marquee alongside, in which the players and public have lunch and tea. In the south-west corner, a number of private boxes with a balcony and bar above make up the Arbours and the renting of these boxes is a valuable source of extra income for the county. The hospital still has an uninterrupted view from the eastern side of the ground, but seats and more permanent stand accommodation are increasing at the river end and Chelmsford will soon be able to accommodate as many people as want to watch cricket there in more comfort than hitherto.

COLCHESTER boasts 2 grounds which have been used by Essex: Castle Park and The Garrison. The Garrison is high on a hill, very flat and very exposed and with a press tent that fulfilled all the conditions of an Essex press tent in the bad old days – facing the prevailing wind and situated in such a way that it was impossible to see the scoreboard without leaving your seat. Perhaps, or perhaps not, because Boycott twice scored a double-hundred there, Essex have now gone back down the hill to Castle Park, a more attractive, tree-lined ground which boasts a new pavilion.

ILFORD is a public park and has both the advantages and disadvantages of such. It has a good outfield and is able to accommodate large crowds. LEYTON, unfortunately, has ceased to occupy a place in the Essex fixture list. Although never a beautiful ground, Leyton occupies an important place in cricket history. It was there in 1932 that Sutcliffe and Holmes made 555 for Yorkshire's first wicket; it was Leyton that allowed the game to be brought to metropolitan Essex.

SOUTHEND (Southchurch Park) has recently regained favour, at the expense of Westcliff (Chalkwell Park). The main reason is the ability to accommodate larger crowds at Southend than at Westcliff and this is particularly important on Sundays. Southchurch Park is a pleasant ground with some terraced seating, 2 pavilions, a clock that has been known to go backwards and a boating lake within easy reach.

The cricket of the Channel counties, Kent, Sussex and Hampshire, stretches far back into the misty unrecorded and a modern pilgrimage is offered fascinating caravanserai for pause upon a leisurely way. The home of the Hambledon Men on Broadhalfpenny Down no longer draws Hampshire crowds to Grand Matches when 'half the county would be present – the multitude forming a complete and dense circle round the green'; when punch was 6*d.* a bottle and ale was 2*d.* a pint; when 'tich and turn' urged on the scampering batsmen. yet Hampshire cricket still carries some salt of the sea, some breath of the downland breeze into more sophisticated settings at Southampton, Portsmouth and Bournemouth. They go, too, to Basingstoke and the delightfully-named May's Bounty.

SOUTHAMPTON is county headquarters. Terracing on all sides of the playing area serves the general cricket public, whose comforts will increase as permanent building develops under demand and the scope of financial resources. Members and players have their corner near the north-western entrance, which leads past the groundsman's house to a car-park adjoining the practice ground. A general pavilion, social rooms and the administrative offices, with a nearby ladies' pavilion, look across the field to give a third-man or long-on view of the pitch, facing such easterly wind as might be unkind enough to chill the early-season cricket, but catching at least the morning sunshine. Southampton's ground, like Southampton itself, is Hampshire's commercial centre.

PORTSMOUTH wears uniform. County cricket and rugby football are welcomed to the United Services ground as civilians are welcomed aboard or entertained in barracks on open days. The cricket field is made circular by some encroachment upon the football pitch, for which the permanent covered stands to north and east were primarily designed. Benches provide much of the public seating accommodation, but their hardship is eased by scope for strolling on the grass and varying the viewpoint from square-leg to sightscreen. The basic classification of commercial cricket grounds and recreational is this possibility of perambulation. Movement loses money; enclosure compels concentration. The full life of spectatorship includes experience, in frequent alternation, of both. Portsmouth is essentially a stroller's ground. There is a small steep-tiered enclosure, with refreshment facilities handily placed, almost behind the bowler's arm at the northern end, and the small pavilion, with ground-floor dining-room and bar, has tiny balconies, but there is no completely satisfactory vantage point for a whole day's play. The foot and fancy free would spend an hour on a seat in front of the pavilion, looking upon the cricket from third-man or long-on. Enclosures on the western side provide a change of angle and a comparison between wood and canvas as a form of seating. When a batting partnership seems firmly established and the course of cricket as assured as ever it can be in such a 'funny game', half an eye at least can be turned to the lawn-tennis courts laid out to the south of the cricket field.

For holidays Hampshire cricket still moves westward to BOURNEMOUTH. Dean Park is a delightful little ground, bewilderingly secreted from the uninitiated by surrounding residential property, but, once discovered, a joy from pitching of wickets to close of play on sunny days. In poor weather it is forlorn as the sandy bathing beaches that form another Bournemouth attraction, for its appeal is the appeal of green foliage against blue sky, of white tenting and bright flags flying, of picnic basket and unfenced boundary. Dean Park is another ground best suited to the strolling spectator. From the main and only public entrance the pavilion is on the left, small and more picturesque than practical, with the visitors' dressing-room at the rear and the greater part of the ground floor occupied by a licensed bar that also serves as miniature Long Room. There is an upper-storey secretarial office and committee balcony and the pavilion enclosure is stepped from building level to the turf, but only the early arrivals have the chance to establish squatters' rights near the players.

Another members' enclosure, partly covered, lies to the left of the pavilion, flanked by the wooden groundsman's quarters which serve also as an umpires' room and Press box – with the most excruciatingly uncomfortable seats in all first-class cricket. To the right of the pavilion, members are given raised platform on a tubular-scaffolding stand, which fronts the marquees serving as dining-rooms. Circumnavigating with the port, there are minor corrals with standing space and handy refreshment tents between members' reservations and the northern sightscreen. From there the various club and municipal marquees show their backs to the boundary hedges of surrounding gardens and their inviting frontages of canvas chairs in roped seclusion stretch to the edge of the playing area. From these marquees looking towards the pavilion the cricketing scene is enchanting; from the pavilion looking towards the marquees it offers equal benediction and delectable prospect for close of play. The most open section of the ground is the public seating, by backless wooden benches, on the eastern side, where trees and high garden hedges provide the only shade for the sunburned or the soporofic. As the space narrows towards the southern sightscreen refreshment tents flutter their invitations to the most popular public seating which lies to the left of the southern sightscreen. Down the years Dean Park has staged some stern and dramatic cricket. The Hampshire season usually ends there, sometimes with Championship issues to be determined, as when Hampshire themselves won their first title there in 1961.

Sussex cricket has sea air and the wide sweep of the Downs in its nature. Hove is the county headquarters and for occasional change home matches are taken along the coast to Eastbourne, Hastings or Worthing. Inland, Horsham has known first-class cricket for a period of more than 100 years on the little ground beside the church, and Chichester sometimes takes a match, but all the characteristics of the county's cricketing attraction can be savoured at Hove, and there the financial returns are greatest.

The long cricketing history of Sussex and particularly its early 19th-century distinction is closely linked with Brighton and HOVE. The first county matches were played in Ireland's Gardens in the northern outskirts of Brighton; William Lillywhite's ground was nearer the centre of the town but had to be abandoned to building requirements, and in 1848 Sussex county cricket came within sight and sound of the sea on the Brunswick ground. By 1872 another move had been compelled, Sussex finding a barley field upon which to build their headquarters. They reaped the barley, levelled the field and laid the Brunswick turf and have been adding amenities ever since. The Hove ground, a few hundred yards from the sea front, has southern entrance gates flanked by an hotel. The entry opens on to small lawns and flower beds but without immediate prospect of the playing area and the pathways run to the back of an embankment and covered stand or behind the main score-board and the pavilion. Levelling of the old barley field was not carried to a point of mathematical precision. The ground still follows the general line of its site and has a fall of some 20 feet from north to south. The slope is not without advantages; it permits ready drainage and it adds to the individuality of appearance. It also introduces a curiosity of play. Fast bowlers usually relish bowling downhill but at Hove they sometimes find the experience disconcerting because of the change from the steeper slope of the outfield to the comparative level of the square. Rhythm in the run-up is easily lost and, other factors permitting, it is often more comfortable and profitable to accept the apparently harder course of bowling 'up the cellar steps'.

Bowling is usually arduous labour at either end, for in fine weather the normal Hove pitch is notoriously fast and true. Morning and evening are the times for batting collapses when the cooler damp air of sea coast helps the ball to swing. Maurice Tate knew both morning glory and sunset touch when he played for Sussex. Hove wickets are pitched north-south and the pavilion is on the western side, permitting excellent batting visibility against the northern sightscreen. Watching is not difficult from any point of the ground. Though the pavilion view is from square-leg, the distance is not excessive and innumerable levels of seating from roof-top to enclosure steps help to create that desirable impression of being involved in the play instead of remotely detached from it.

The pavilion building has little architectural distinction and every possible inconvenience for movement but, like an over-furnished and unskilfully planned house, it contrives to carry a homely atmosphere. It is full of improvizations in stairways and rooms. It needs time and perhaps a guide for adequate exploration and no more than half its rooms offer a glimpse of play – and that invariably of the non-striker's end at the moment of observation. The compensations are in unexpected discovery of an old picture of score-card or trophy, for the Hove pavilion, without a Long Room, is a treasure-house of Sussex cricketing history. Hove has the inherent virtues of headquarters in established catering facilities, permanent paving, printing machinery for score-cards, but it also retains an air of emphasis upon cricket as a holiday concern. The playing area is unfenced and becomes playground and promenade during intervals. County matches are part of summer's routine yet contrive to be holiday occasions, more significant in themselves than as a championship concern. Somehow Sussex sunburn seems deeper than most on arms and faces, Sussex caps more faded from their original blue.

Attractions of the EASTBOURNE ground begin with its name. The significance of The Saffrons is not evident all the summer and the justification has no doubt diminished under urban development, but the cricket ground still shows trees that were rooted before the first wickets were pitched. The Saffrons, some distance from the Eastbourne sea front, is a recreation ground catering for cricket, football and bowls. Cricket field and football pitch overlap to a slight extent, but the football stand is too far from the cricket pitch to serve cricket spectators, who must find their shade beneath tree or awning nearer the

Hove: the county headquarters of Sussex with the sea in the distance and the indoor school at the far end. The photograph draws attention to two important sources of income, ground-parking and deck chairs.

boundary edge. On the eastern, football side the boundary is open and play can be watched from bench seating or peripatetically, with scope for that 'longing, lingering look behind' on the way to the gate when cricket is still in progress. In 1921 a professional spectator, reluctantly departing, permitted himself that pause for 'one more over'.

One more over became 2, 2 became 3 and, as the balance of advantage swung, Mr Neville Cardus stayed not only another hour but another day to see the dramatic first defeat of Armstrong's Australians in a match that ranks high among the improbabilities of history and highest in sensations of The Saffrons. The ground is not, in fact, sympathetic to the sensational in its setting and construction. Surrounding trees and guardian hills, marquees and deck-chairs, encourage a little folding of the hands during the warmer afternoons and in fine weather batsmen find the ball inclined to keep low, thus discouraging the more adventurous strokes. The Saffrons is essentially a fine-weather ground. Trees drip and marquees look mournful in the rain, but, then, the only tolerable cricket grounds in wet weather are those with amenities to draw attention away from the window.

At HASTINGS the consolation for interrupted or abandoned play is ease of departure. The little ground with an oblong playing area is handily situated in the town and has the guardian castle as backcloth and improvised embankment. An end of season festival, dating back to 1887 though with breaks in continuity, and county matches since 1895 have given Hastings occasion to build some permanent amenities into the ground. There is terracing and there are stands and refreshment rooms to represent basic accommodation, though for completion the ground needs the finery of club tents, deck-chair enclosures and gay bunting. Hastings, like Hove, has the seaside atmosphere that sometimes adds awkwardness to first-morning batting, but the short boundaries to leg and off encourage ready scoring and captains tend to overestimate their advantage in making declarations.

From Hastings the step across a county border into Kent is easily made and in Kent as in Sussex and Surrey the story of cricket runs back far into the mists of time. Cricket was a game of the Weald before the Armada sailed into the Channel; it was probably a boys' game and a countryman's game until the Royalist supporters retreated to their estates and there became interested and involved in a recreation which they eventually took back to the capital city and, by their patronage, helped to develop into a national concern. The Kent cricket of today has discarded the shepherd's smock and the knee-breeches of its origins. It is as modern as the hour in outlook and enterprise, but the influence remains in the setting of some of its beautiful grounds. Kent cricket at Maidstone is cricket on a ground in parkland of wooded slopes; Kent cricket at Folkestone has sight of sea and hills; Kent cricket at Tunbridge Wells has the natural flavour of cricket where cricket could be expected as a pastime.

Mote Park at MAIDSTONE offers a playing area at the foot of an embankment on which spectators can stand or stretch themselves. They can descend to the playing level by steps at the northern end or they can sit on the terracing to the south. They can use their motorcars for armchair or picnic-base, or crowd the small stand and pavilion enclosure. In any circumstances of fine weather they can scarcely fail to find delight.

The oldest 'Week' – Canterbury, dating from 1841, changes little. The ancient lime (*left centre*) flourishes still within the boundary.

At TUNBRIDGE WELLS there is rather more sense of enclosure, though the Nevill ground has room for more than specific cricketing requirements. The southern Nevill gate leads to the permanent buildings of ladies' stand, pavilion and public stand and the tiny pigeon-loft Press box that challenges constitution with climb up a circular stairway. On north and east the boundary is ringed by temporary seating, with space to move behind. To the west club tents provide comfort for the favoured and add to the attractions of the scene for all.

Kent cricket was in being before the CANTERBURY Week, but the two devotions married so happily that the one without the other is scarcely conceivable. The Canterbury Week is now established as an early-August feature of the home programme and the touring team in England also are always taken to the county headquarters. In the first Canterbury Weeks, which originated in cricket by day and amateur theatricals by night, the matches were played on the Beverley ground, adjoining the cavalry barracks. In 1847 the cricket moved to the present St Lawrence ground, named from its one-time ownership by the neighbouring St Lawrence hospital. The St Lawrence ground is easily discovered by taking the old Dover road out of Canterbury. Its gateway leads into a field bigger than the needs of cricket, but happily preserving the sense of yesterday in spaciousness and scattered trees. Near the Dover road entrance is the Kent club's war memorial and space permits a carriageway to run round the playing area behind the buildings and the seating.

Much that Felix and the first 'Old Stagers' knew has changed, yet the departed returning would not find their Canterbury playground entirely strange. Where once the spectator could ride his horse to the boundary edge he can still watch play from a motor-car and all the permanent buildings of pavilion and stands still leave the trees and the tents as dominating features of the festal scene. Wickets are pitched north-west and south-east with the pavilion and the covered two-tier stands facing south-east. Opposite them the ground is open immediately to the left of the sight-screen, with a motor bank behind the bench seating. In the southern corner, the 'Iron' Stand has given way to the Leslie Ames Stand which has a large scoreboard embodied within it and boasts a number of private boxes which contain lunch and tea parties during playing days. Following the sun, there is public seating, with a square-leg view of play and a tree for shade or shelter, to the boundary edge and, behind, another bank for parked cars. Behind all this accommodation, the ground stretches away to the hospital property with room for refreshment tents and a tea lawn and the office buildings of the club.

Circumnavigation during play necessitates passing behind the principal stands and the pavilion, which are fenced off from the field but are shallow enough to avoid any impression of undue remoteness from events at the crease. Open seating stretches from the privileged enclosures half-way round the Dover road side of the playing area and from that point to the south-eastern sightscreen are ranged the tents, each flying gay colours of identification and offering their hospitality of soft seating, soft drinks (if so preferred), though not the most enviable viewpoint for watching play. There is, indeed, an obstruction to the view, for in this corner a famous tree stands sentinel over the cricket. Without the tents, without the trees, without the imprint of history, the St Lawrence ground might be an undistinguished cricket field; pleasant enough, adequate for its occasional county service, but comparatively unremarkable in its own right. Adorned for festival, seen in the light of its associations, coloured by the tints of generations gone, it is spiritual home for the cricket of Kent and appropriate shrine for a pilgrimage of the county grounds.

The University Grounds

The Parks

It was in 1881, when the Queen Empress Victoria and her Empire seemed ensconced for ever, that the Oxford University Cricket Club first played on that most lovely ground, the Parks, which always reminds me of the old Greek poet's lines about 'the plane whispering love to the elm in the beautiful season of Spring'. Moreover, the ordinary spectator can watch free; the OUCC member pays but a small subscription. The Oxford v Cambridge match is no longer a big draw or occasion at Lord's. The Press, examinations and public ignorance have ruined it between them; but as from Fenner's at Cambridge University, so from the Parks at Oxford, have come, and still do come, cricketers and leaders of cricket who have made history in the game at its highest level.

Our own Oxford teams of 1920 and 1923 were good enough to hold and often to beat any county team in England. There was Douglas Jardine, a classical batsman, who combined a kindly wit with Cromwellian determination. It was he who quelled Bradman in his prime, and Australian cricket in that 1932–33 tour, and caused a raging controversy that reached Cabinet level; there was G. T. S. Stevens, who, with the Australian R. H. Bettington, formed a leg-spin-cum-googly attack which unhooked some of England's best batsmen. Stevens, also a fine batsman, went on to play for England before business foreclosed on him; there was C. H. L. Skeet, an outfielder to rank with C. E. Pellew of Australia. Above all, there were conversations and friendships such as last, in fact or memory or both, for a lifetime.

I suppose that the greatest batsmen in the Parks during the latter years of the last century were, in order of time, C. B. Fry and R. E. Foster. Fry's contribution to cricket, numerical and literary, is part of cricket history. R. E. Foster was one of the famous Malvern brotherhood. In the Sydney Test of 1903 he gave the Australian spectators a Christmas present of 287 runs. Those who saw it say that the second half of the innings could hardly be surpassed for brilliance. Four times he played against Cambridge at Lord's, reserving a notable century for his last year, and, till then, finding some difficulty with the bowling of one G. L. Jessop.

Jessop's two innings of 59 and and 68 in a heavily losing match for MCC in the Parks are still talked of by those who saw them. That was in 1913. A little earlier, Oxford had the sometimes absent-minded services of that master of medium-paced skill and variety in bowling, Humphrey A. Gilbert, from Charterhouse. Gilbert was fond of bowling, and even fonder of ornithology and fishing. But he remained in the memory of that fine cricketer-golfer, his slip-fielder, C. V. L. Hooman, as the bowler of one of the most unplayable balls ever delivered. It swerved from leg, pitched on the middle-off, and knocked out the leg stump of the great Victor Trumper. This miracle was performed on the Christ Church ground; but the Parks must have the reflected glory.

I suppose these beautiful Parks were also the scene of one of the greatest catches ever made. It was in mid-May, 1928. A. M. Crawley, a batsman of England class, who could never afterwards afford time for regular appearances with Kent, had reached 55 against the West Indians, when he fiercely hooked a short ball from O. C. Scott. It seemed to be about to fly over the long-leg boundary, when L. N. Constantine, running in almost Olympic style, leapt high in the air and caught the ball plumb in the palm of his right hand.

Somehow, it seems to be the *batsmen* who are most remembered: D. J. Knight's perfection of style and timing, E. R. T. Holmes's driving, the great and exciting skill of two Nawabs of Pataudi. Others crowd into the mind: N. S. Mitchell-Innes, like Ted Dexter also a masterly golfer; M. C. Cowdrey, that variable and enigmatic genius; A. H. Kardar, a graceful and talented left-hand all-rounder from Pakistan; A. A. Baig, a brilliant if sometimes over-daring stroke-player from India; and, perhaps, the greatest of them *all*, Martin P. Donnelly, that left-hander from New Zealand who must have been picked early in any contemporary World XI.

Like another left-hander, the late Percy Chapman of Cambridge and England, Donnelly did the great 'batting hat-trick' at Lord's, 206 v England in a Test, 162 not out for Gentlemen v Players, 142 for Oxford v Cambridge, an innings so wonderfully made that it set a new standard for university batting. In the summers of 1946 and 1947 Parks Road was invariably full of hurrying undergraduates when it was learned that Martin Donnelly was at or on his way to the wicket.

But the Parks cannot be described merely in terms of cricketing fame or achievement. For over 80 years it has been a refuge for the connoisseur of the beloved game. The cricket is watched in the quietude of unexpressed but deep enjoyment. There is no barracking. Generations of dons have sat in the pavilion seats; some, perhaps, when they ought to have been writing books or correcting essays. The standing spectators are a more mobile company: undergraduates of either sex, often with lecture-notes under their arm; schoolboys, snatching 'a fearful joy', perhaps when their presence is expected elsewhere; all sorts and creeds; all joined in one worship, one pleasure.

But, in case you may be comparing all this to 'the island valley of Avilion, where falls not hail, nor rain, nor any snow, nor even wind blows loudly', let me add that there are few colder cricket grounds than the Parks in a north-east wind. My own memory recalls, still with abhorrence, my first match for Oxford, against Warwickshire, in a wind so piercing that even an Eskimo would have longed for two pairs of combinations under his flannels. I took no wickets, and a very fast drive on the chest-bone at mid-off; a miss that my kindly captain, Frank Gilligan, at once excused. I did my best to make up for these failures with 2 not out and 13 not out at number 10 in the order.

To continue, unashamedly, on a personal note, it was in my third match, against Essex, that I received a nickname that stuck. C. P. McGahey, the Essex opening batsman, a tough but benevolent character, then in his 50th year, had reached the middle 20s in the 2nd innings when he missed one from me and was bowled. The cricketers' dressing-room in the Parks is subterranean, so that those in it can follow the match by hearsay only. When McGahey walked down to it, it seems that his

The Parks, Oxford: old men remember.

captain, the great J. W. H. T. Douglas, asked him 'How were you out, Charlie?' To which came the answer 'I was bowled by an old —— I thought was dead 2,000 years ago, called Robinson Crusoe.'

'I would we were boys as of old, in the field, by the fold.' What wouldn't I give to have my years at Oxford over again; without the radio, without all things nuclear; when all was laughter and friendship, and a ghastly war was just over, and all the geese were swans; when the sun seemed always to shine. I still like to recall the powerful presence of my last captain, Dr R. H. Bettington, of Sydney, and his voice shouting 'take a spell'; an expression which he used equally for bowler about to try his luck and for one who had tried it in vain. May all who play cricket in the Parks love it as much as we did.

R. C. ROBERTSON-GLASGOW

Since that was written, there have been changes. The Parks remains a beautiful ground, yet it has, and will have for many years – at least for those with long memories – a gap-toothed look: the consequence of Dutch elm disease. You still do not have to pay to go in, but, reasonably enough, you have to pay for a seat, and even if you stand, you will be confronted, politely, by a contributions box. In 1978 the box was sometimes carried by the Oxford coach, Arthur Milton, looking as pink and youthful as any undergraduate. 'I think it's a bit hard', he would say disarmingly, 'having to preach the sermon *and* take the collection'.

There is not often much money in the box, because it is not often that there are many people present. It is customary to put this down to the increased demands of the examiners, but this is not, in my view, an adequate explanation. Certainly examinations account for the University XI being below strength in term. A man facing his final schools can hardly be expected to make a public display of staying away from his books. But are your potential undergraduate spectators so devoted to academic duty, so passionately set on a good degree, that they cannot spare the time to watch for an hour or two, say around lunchtime or in the early evening? Of course not. Look at all the other extra-curricular activities they undertake. The truth is, they have simply lost interest.

One thing which could be done to mitigate this is to improve the facilities; or, to be specific, the refreshment facilities. The beer-tent at the Parks, when it happens to be open, is a small, poky, seatless affair. There is no clubhouse. Compare this with Fenner's, with the famous institution of Tolley's Tent, and, in recent years, a capacious and comfortable clubhouse/pavilion. The financial difficulties of doing anything comparable in the Parks are no doubt considerable, but certainly Fenner's does far more to make its members and spectators comfortable, and this is one reason why more people watch Cambridge, at home, then watch Oxford. (Much the same applies to rugby matches).

However, the news is not all of gloom. Although a win over a county is rare, Oxford continues to produce cricketers of quality, and also cricketers who enjoy their game (though you could not be too sure of the second part when P. J. K. Gibbs or T. R. Glover were in a sombre mood). Most of any University side would make competent county cricketers, if they chose to make cricket their profession. That's the rub: *if they chose to make it their profession*. Not many do, and nowadays county cricket has no room for the promising youngster who is not prepared to commit himself, unless the promise is exceptional.

But the quality is still there, and so is the free entrance, provided you do not mind standing up, and provided you have the courage to outface the innocent, compelling eyes of Arthur Milton, or his successor, Colin Milburn, or whoever the coach may be.

ALAN GIBSON

Fenner's

Fenner's: in the days when Cambridge were a match for any county side.

Fenner's with its surrounding trees must by any standard be one of the most beatiful cricket grounds in England, in spite of the recent additions of buildings adjacent to it: some would also consider Trent Bridge, the pre-war Oval and Fenner's the best batting wickets in the country.

It has been the home of Cambridge University cricket since 1848. For the most part cricket in Cambridge had till then been played on a few college grounds and on that large open space known as Parker's Piece. Here many famous cricketers, including Tom Hayward, K. S. Ranjitsinhji and Sir Jack Hobbs, played a good deal of their early cricket. Parker's Piece had the disadvantage of being very public, with several matches going on simultaneously (as at present), though there was no suggestion that the pitches were not good. The desire for greater privacy moved such cricketers as the Earl of Stanford and Lord Darnley among others to give support to finding a new ground. This was soon found not much more than a hundred yards away by F. P. Fenner, for some time connected with Cambridge cricket and the first man in *Wisden's* list of players who have taken 17 wickets in a match (for Cambridge Town v the University in 1844). Fenner had found two fields and leased them from Caius College, and then prepared his ground to be ready for play in May 1846 and to be known as 'Fenner's Cricket Ground'.

Fenner sold this ground to the University Cricket Club in 1848, since when it has been the club's home; after various vicissitudes the freehold was acquired from Caius in 1894 for £17,500 raised by appeal, the ground (containing now in all 10½ acres) being shared by the University Cricket and Athletics Clubs. The latter used Fenner's until the late 1950s; the track around the ground measured some 600 yards, and down one side it was easy to run a straight 100 yards. This gives some idea of the size of the Fenner's ground, but it can hardly have been a very satisfactory arrangement for the athletes in the summer terms.

The first pavilion, a low wooden structure, was built in 1856; it was replaced in 1877 thanks to the activity of the Rev A. R. Ward who had become Vicar of St Clement's after a curacy at All Saints'. He was a former Cambridge cricket captain, and became President and Treasurer in 1873. He raised the money by personal appeal (among the contributors was Edward VII, who had had a special wicket reserved for him at Fenner's while up at Trinity).

This pavilion, which many will remember, remained for nearly a century; it was a friendly place with a happy atmosphere about it. It suffered severe damage from bombs dropped on the University Lawn Tennis Club, which owned land next to the cricket field, and at the opposite corner near Mortimer Road. The pavilion was repaired and renovated by the generosity of the widow of G. D. Kemp-Welch, captain in 1931, who had been killed when the Guards' Chapel was bombed. Indeed many who have revisited the ground in recent years have found it something of a shock to find flats where the familiar pavilion used to be. Its successor is what may be termed a functional building on the opposite site of the ground; fortunately it has retained in its Long Room the panels containing the names of every team to have played against Oxford since the first University match.

It would be invidious to pick out names from the many illustrious players who represented Cambridge in the University match, and their biographies may be found elsewhere in this book. The number of England captains included on the panels is particularly striking.

Fenner's has only had three groundsmen, Walter Watts, who served for 40 years, Dan Hayward for nearly 30 years and Cyril Coote, who happily still fills the post which he took over in 1936. He was one of the best players to appear for Cambridgeshire but suffered from a game leg, permanently stiff at the knee-joint, since childhood: there are those who think that but for this he would have played for England for many years. He is a fine judge of the game, and has meant a great deal to successive generations of undergraduates.

It is to his skill and experience that Fenner's owes so much of its reputation as an ideal batsman's wicket: indeed N. W. D. Yardley, who captained both Cambridge and England, has advanced the view that while such conditions certainly increased the confidence of young batsmen they might in some cases develop over-confidence: thus he considers that while Fenner's is a wonderful training ground for the development of strokes, the further arts and techniques of batting can only be learned through later experience.

The match against the West Indies in 1950 produced 1324 runs for the loss of 7 wickets: Cambridge scored 594 for 4, with an opening partnership of 343 by D. S. Sheppard and J. G. Dewes (and this against the bowling of Ramadhin at his very best), and the West Indies replied with 730 for 3.

This is a supreme example of the triumph of bat over ball and perhaps justifies Yardley's view that from the bowler's point of view Fenner's could well be described as a nightmare; none the less he maintained that provided bowlers have the intelligence and the will to succeed it must be an ideal training ground.

In latter years Fenner's has been used by the University Cricket Club, Association Football Club, Hockey Club and Lawn Tennis Club, the Athletics Club having moved to its own ground in Milton Road.

The Cricket Club's finances, even with help from TCCB, have always been an anxiety. Unlike the Parks at Oxford, Fenner's is an enclosed ground with paying entrances when required. These are only used today for a few important matches, but collections are taken on the ground from time to time, usually by the players. The ground is often quite full at lunch-time and during the last hour of the evening's play. The Cricket Club has recently taken the initiative in attracting sponsorship on a national level (Royal Insurance and Schweppes), together with sponsorship on a smaller scale from local firms. Recent treasurers have however had a hard struggle to put the finances on a sound basis.

In 1959 the University had set up an Athletics Syndicate to ensure that its needs in the field of sport were properly provided for, and as funds became available the University was able to accept more and more responsibility for sport. Finally, in 1976, the University assumed full financial responsibility for the maintenance of the ground and the employment of the regular ground staff and a Committee of Management of Fenner's was set up accordingly. Thus the future of Fenner's, so far as its upkeep is concerned, looks secure: a more difficult problem may arise from the social changes which may affect cricket at the University. The immediate question is whether Cambridge can attract and the colleges will admit men good enough and willing to play first-class cricket.

J. F. BURNET

The Groundsman

W. H. BOWLES

1 Evolution and present status

Whisper the word 'cricket' and somewhere in the mental pictures evoked is the turf on which the game is played. From the early days grass has been so much a part of its magic that one wonders whether cricket would have had the same appeal if any other playing surface had been universally adopted. The very title of a report published by MCC and the National Playing Fields Association – *Cricket on Non-Turf Pitches* – implies an apology for the suggestion that alternatives are possible.

Certainly they are unthinkable to the enthusiast so long as he can play on grass – grass with its recuperative properties and varying reactions to rain, wind and sun. He would only agree to the use of alternatives rather than forego his game altogether. In the beginning, in any case, grass would have been the only surface to hand. Good agricultural sward, cropped by sheep, or even rabbits, would have been chosen so that the ball ran as true as possible. The field would have been selected because its natural turf met these requirements, and in old paintings and prints it is evident that these fields were an integral part of the landscape, with the countryside seeming to flow through the game itself. Trees and thickets obtruded on the outfield; irregularities of terrain appeared almost on the wicket itself. In contrast the modern pitch is often imposed on the landscape and does not so easily blend with its surroundings. Even on the traditional village green a century or so of levelling and tidying has produced a purposeful playing area unlike the casual field of the early cricketers. This may not be so satisfactory from the aesthetic point of view, but is a testimony to the years of effort which groundsmanship – whether paid or unpaid – has given to improving these surfaces.

'The history of cricket is one long battle between batsman and bowler, the groundsman holding the ring', says Neville Cardus in *English Cricket*, and many of the changes which have occurred in the techniques of playing the game are attributable to the surface on which it takes place. Faster and over-arm bowling called for better wickets. This gave the wicket-keeper greater scope to improve his methods. Smoother turf favoured batsmen which in turn encouraged the bowlers to vary their deliveries. Some of the changes in the Laws of Cricket have been made for these reasons. Yet the provider of the turf, the groundsman, is seldom a public name. In the beginning there were no recognized groundsmen. The activities of turfing and draining were understood and may have been performed by landscape gardeners who were fully competent long before cricket came to be played in an organized way. Other techniques were apparently known – the 1820 version of the Laws of Cricket says that 'it shall not be lawful for either Party during a match, without the consent of the other, to alter the Ground by rolling, watering, covering, mowing or beating'. The same Laws give the 'away' team the choice of pitching a wicket within 30 yards of a centre fixed by the adversaries. This would have entailed, in theory, the maintenance of a cricket table of about 2,800 sq. yd. against the average present-day club square of 25 × 25 yd. or 625 sq. yd. The latter is kept in condition with the aid of modern equipment. The standard which would have been possible on the old circle of 2,800 sq. yd. with the limited equipment of that time would have been very low.

In the various histories of cricket the bad turf and the dangerous wickets thus produced are recurring themes. At Lord's, for example, the practices of keeping grass down by weekly flocks of sheep, of cutting creases with knives and allowing the public to play on the ground on non-match days produced wickets which were frequently criticized. On the other hand, the apparent care devoted to the centre of the ground, where even a scythe was not allowed (this was before the mower was available), and small boys were employed to pick out the rough stalks of grass, indicates that the need for a true playing surface was soon recognized. Nevertheless John Lillywhite was able to say that a pitch at Lord's 'only resembled a billiard table in one respect and that was in the pockets', Pooley refers to cracks in the ground which would take the fingers. At this time many village greens or county club grounds were considered superior to Lord's. Generally, however, grounds were rough, and pebbles or gravel were sometimes discovered on the wicket.

Maintenance of grounds in the first half of the nineteenth century seems often to have been the responsibility of the ground proprietor who may have even owned or rented the ground. He would have employed casual labour to perform the various aspects of groundsmanship as then practised. One of the earliest groundsmen, as such, was David Jordan, engaged by MCC in 1864 at 25*s.* a week. During his 10 years wickets were still unsatisfactory and there was even a fatal accident in 1870, but some improvement was noticed after Percy (Peter) Pearce joined Lord's from the Sussex ground at Hove. On 27 June 1876, the *Standard* wrote: 'Time was when a good wicket at Lord's was the exception but now, happily, thanks to Pearce, the *groundman*, the playing portion of the arena is in faultless condition.' Pearce seems to have been an early example of the good, practical type of groundsman who was observant, who experimented, and who studied the soil and other aspects of the turf. He gained a reputation and laid down several grounds. His opinions were eagerly sought. In 1898 he was succeeded by T. A. Hearne, a member of a family of groundsmen and cricketers who laid several first-class grounds in the London area. Pearce, Hearne, Sam Apted of the Oval and some of their contemporaries were now producing pitches of high quality, lacking any element of danger to the batsmen and wicket-keepers. The term 'batsman's paradise' began to be talked about during the early 20th century.

The term 'groundsman' (with the 's') dates from 1886 and it is from about this period that the numbers employed began to increase. Apart from the top-flight men on the main pitches, however – the Pearces, the Apteds, the Hearnes – they were regarded as little more than labourers. But through the years their importance has grown and more men have joined their ranks. There are three main reasons for the change:

(a) increase in numbers of sports grounds;
(b) availability and variety of 'aids' to help in ground maintenance;
(c) the intensive use to which all grounds are now put.

As the game spread in popularity from the early enthusiasts, from the village greens and the private houses, cricket clubs were formed by the leisured classes and gentry of the mid-19th century. This did not necessarily mean that much money was put into the game to encourage men to specialize in groundwork for firms to develop researches into turf culture. It was not, perhaps, until professional men – from banks and business houses – began to form their clubs towards the end of the last century that more money began to be available. Later came the works' clubs to join the growing numbers. Many of these date from the immediate post-First World War period. These have brought much more money, some of it provided by the managements of the firms themselves, and this has promoted greater interest by manufacturers of equipment and materials.

There has also been the trend towards providing schools with grass playing areas instead of asphalt. Local authorities have given more facilities for games. There has therefore been a need for men to maintain the many separate sports grounds thus created. Groundsmen have grown in numbers and status in line with the great social forces of democratization and state welfare. The growth of population has had the inevitable effect of increasing the demand for sports facilities.

The first of the aids for ground maintenance was the mower, the idea for which dates from 1830, when Edwin Budding of Stroud, Gloucestershire, patented a machine based on that used for shearing nap off cloth. The mass-produced heavy iron roller came in about 1870, though rolling had been practised with wooden or stone rollers for many years hitherto. Several fine grounds were damaged by wrong use of the heavy roller. Thus rollers and mowers, with harrows, were the only mechanical aids available to the groundsman at the end of the nineteenth century. Even so, the techniques of wicket preparation practised in some quarters were such that in 1901 MCC sent out a circular to county clubs which said:

It is undesirable, in the interests of cricket, that the wickets should be prepared artificially (*i.e.* in any way other than by water and the roller, except when patching is necessary).

Natural fertilizers were, of course, understood, but only a limited range of artificial manures, most of which were organic in origin, were available. These were frequently misused. Chemical fertilizers were hardly known. Worm-killers were not introduced until 1905.

Until motor-driven machinery became reliable and within financial reach of clubs, horses were a familiar sight on sports grounds and complementary to the groundsman. Flat-footed animals were desirable because they would not normally mark the turf, but leather boots were available for fitting to animals where this risk existed. Such boots and horse-drawn machinery are included in a 1939 catalogue of sports-ground equipment, with a testimonial from W. G. Grace still being quoted. The selection and training of suitable horses was difficult. Pulling a mower demanded a constant effort from the animal, for it was not like a normal load which required less tractive effort once movement had started. Certain hazards existed when horses were used. Sometimes they got loose and galloped across pitches. Always there was the inconvenience of the animal's natural functions happening on a critical part of the square. Considerable disfigurement could result if the roller was being drawn at the time. The groundsman therefore needed to know his horses as well as his ground and arrange preventive action if disaster threatened.

Up to the First World War the situation then on most grounds was largely one where horse-drawn and hand-mowers were being used with occasional assistance from the expert wielder of the scythe who could produce a better finish than the hand-machine and could even go over a piece of grass after such a machine and still improve the finish. Such a procedure was particularly applied to bowling greens. Weed-killing was a laborious chore and fertilisers were not properly understood. Many grounds were over-rolled and under-fed. Manual labour was easy to come by, cheap and widely used. The groundsman worked all the week, looking forward to the Saturday – usually the one day on which his ground was used. At this time Sunday games (except golf) were frowned upon. Moreover, many groundsman were employed only in the summer, until the advent of winter games and the using of grounds throughout all playing seasons provided them with a full-time occupation.

In 1914 gang-mowers were patented in America in the name of *Worthington*. They came into general use by the 1920s, for pulling by horses or petrol-driven motors and solving the economic problem of keeping grass short on large sports grounds. Lawn-sands, to assist in weed-killing, were also available by then. Aeration was recognized in 1930 as a necessary part of soil conditioning, and equipment could be purchased from about 1935 to help in this function. Hand-spiking with forks was practised, and still continues to this day. A mechanised spiking-machine has been on the market since about 1950 and will treat the same area in 2 hours as one man with a fork would take two weeks to do.

So we come to the present day, when the groundsman is no longer bothered with weeds as a major problem. Selective weed-killers (discovered about 1938 and marketed after the Second War) are an effortless way of disposing of unwanted plant life especially when the liquid is distributed mechanically. He sees gang-mowers rapidly dealing with his out-fields and one man covering 60 acres in a day rather than 6 acres as when a horse was

Ancient and modern: *left* Fred Hunt (with dog), a famous maker of pitches at Worcester with his staff and horse-drawn roller; *right* Bernard Flack of Edgbaston (on the right), one of today's leading groundsmen with the paraphernalia of his craft.

used. Harrows, aerators, cultivators, brushes, rejuvenators – all drawn by the ubiquitous tractor – allow for maximum maintenance with minimum man-power. A wide variety of precision-built mowers are available for wicket-preparation. A remedy is available for most pests and diseases. The soil can be analysed and the requisite fertilisers, trace elements and organic matter recommended to put matters right. Distribution of these substances and seeding can also be effected mechanically. Add remote-control watering-apparatus to his long list of aids, and the lot of the modern groundsman will appear a happy one by comparison with his predecessors.

Is he, however, that much 'happier'? The answer generally is yes, but inevitably with some reservations. The increase in mechanical and other aids has been accompanied by a decline in the labour force for two main reasons: the cost of employing manual labour and the difficulty of obtaining men in competition with other employers, most of whom can offer better wages. Coupled with this is the more intensive use now demanded of most sports grounds where games are played on all days of the week, winter and summer. Turf is being made to do more work.

Despite all the labour-saving devices the best wickets of today are probably no better than the best wickets of previous days. The general standard of pitches, however, is much better than it was. Whereas the 100 acre fully-used sports ground of 50 years ago would have required 25 men and 6 horses to maintain, the same area, with up-to-date machinery in use, can be managed with only 10 men, with pitches of a better all-round standard and more matches being played per week.

In 1934 the National Association of Groundsmen (now the Institute of Groundsmanship), was formed by eleven groundsmen meeting in 'The London Stone', Cannon Street. This modest beginning was an attempt to raise the status of groundsmen and to improve standards of sports-ground maintenance. By the end of that year there were 95 members of the Association and, apart from the hiatus caused by the Second War, it has grown steadily to a large organization which has a countrywide network of branches. The Institute is not a trade union, but it is true to say that sports clubs nowadays work in close co-operation with the Institute in various directions; for its own part, it has in its 45 years' existence done much to improve groundsmen's rate of pay and conditions of service. As a national body it has attracted notice from various authorities since 1936, when the Club Cricket Conference invited officials of NAG to explain its objects. It now maintains good relations with all types of sporting organizations, giving help and advice or recommending suitable staff as required. Contact has also been kept with organizations having grass as a common interest such as the Institute of Park Administration, the National Playing Fields Association, the Greenkeepers' Association and the many firms interested in research into the problems of turf culture.

One of the aims of the Institute is to disseminate information about the latest developments in ground-work. This is done by courses, meetings, lectures and publications. It has naturally involved liaison with manufacturers of sports-ground equipment, with biologists and with any organization interested in the production of materials used to promote the growth of grass, and the needs of sports grounds. An event promoted by the NAG is the Annual Exhibition held at Motspur Park. The first of these was in 1937 at Hurlingham at a time when the tempo of invention and improvement of equipment and materials was beginning to increase, and it can be claimed that the contact between the trade and the groundsman, encouraged by this exhibition and other demonstrations sponsored by the Institute, has resulted in further improvements to the aids supplied for turf culture. A system of examinations has also been instituted to provide a set of standards of knowledge required by groundsmen. National Certificates classes 1, 2 and 3 are awarded.

In conclusion it is worth considering the qualities and mental attitudes which can be expected from the good, modern head-groundsman. It is inevitable that he will have a sense of dedication to his job. Ground work does not attract the same material rewards as employment in industry, and there must be other satisfactions to be gained. Living on the ground he cannot be so conscious of the clock as some workers. He must be as competent a manager as any industrial executive. With equipment under his control worth many thousands of pounds and a staff under him he must plan the work, co-ordinate the activities of both men and machines and motivate the staff to give of their best. The latter activity, as in so many other walks of life, is an important one, especially in full employment conditions when it is not possible to pick and choose men. The groundsman must be constantly aware of his total responsibility for the area of land under his charge. For him it is a case of 'the game must go on', as often as modern requirements dictate and at all costs.

2 Doing the job

In the eyes of a groundsman the cricket field is an area of conflict in two senses. To the players and spectators it is the game itself which provides the conflict, to the groundsman the conflict occurs between his purpose of supplying a satisfactory playing surface and the various defects of soil, grasses and so on. The requirements in a pitch are the first thing to establish. A balance between a pitch which causes danger to players and an unresponsive surface which completely inhibits the bowler's attempts to use his skill is clearly desirable. A durable square which will either allow for a match of a few days or several matches on consecutive days, and one which will not become unusable after sudden modest climatic changes such as a summer storm, but will react naturally to such changes, is also to be aimed at. Assuming that the level of the pitch and a playing direction as near possible north–south have been achieved, there remain the two constituents, soil and grass. Soil is important for two reasons – firstly because it contributes to the liveliness, durability and drainage of the pitch, and secondly because it provides most of the requirements for growing turf. Grass is important because in conjunction with the soil it causes the ball to react according to the impetus given by the bowler. The main efforts of a groundsman are devoted to correcting deficiencies and combating various hazards affecting these two constituents.

Men and methods at Brisbane: *above* the Woolloongabba ground was the last on which a scythe was used for the final cut; *below* Clem Jones, a regular Pooh-Bah, was a former Lord Mayor, Queensland member of the Australian Cricket Board, and (in 1974–75) temporary curator. The result was one of the most treacherous pitches in modern history.

SOIL

Construction
Neither the light, sandy type of soil nor the heavy, clay type is any use where a cricket square is concerned: the former will crumble quickly and hold insufficient water moisture, and the latter will not drain and will dry to a rock-like consistency, possibly cracking. Something in between is desirable. It is possible, out of the playing season, to stiffen light soils and lighten heavy soils by the application of suitable soil to make a satisfactory balance. Spiking should precede dressings, and both dressing and ground surface should be moist when the former is applied. Harrowing and brushing will help to 'work' the dressing into the area. This procedure may be necessary over several winters as too heavy an application will result in a false top-layer of soil which will not react in tune with the basic soil beneath. If a square fails to drain properly after several such treatments a large-scale operation involving reconstruction of the square on a porous bed (*e.g.* clinker) will be necessary.

Aeration
All turf will benefit from aeration, but the cricket square in particular requires this treatment exclusively, especially in the winter. Even judicious rolling compacts the soil during the summer. It would be unwise to open up the square during the playing season unless there is a long interval between matches. The use of aerating machines or hand forking is therefore needed out of season so that air, water and plant food can reach the grass roots.

Fertilization
The essential constant mowing of a cricket square removes the reserves of food in the soil and these must be replaced by applying fertilisers of various kinds. They fall broadly into two types, organic and inorganic; the former mostly slow-acting and the latter more rapid in action. This means applying at the proper time of the year – autumn/winter for the slow-acting, spring for the faster types. There are many kinds of fertiliser now available and the subject cannot be dealt with exhaustively in a short essay. It is often advisable to submit a plug of soil to a reputable soil-testing organization for analysis and to rectify deficiencies according to the report and advice. Soil will benefit from the use of harrows and scarifiers to provide surface aeration and remove or distribute debris.

Worms
Worm-casts are undesirable as they produce a lumpy soil surface which is likely to cake and encourages the growth of coarser grasses. Suitable worm-killers or irritants should therefore be used to clear the cricket square.

GRASS

Seed Mixture
There is a great variety of grass seed available. It is divided into 2 main classes, fine and coarse. All sorts have different characteristics, and each favours a different soil and climatic condition. A mixture of grasses in the correct proportion is necessary to give the best results. Nowadays it is advisable for the groundsman to specify his requirement and a reputable seed merchant will supply the necessary mixture.

Turfing
Certain worn areas at the crease and behind the wicket can only be renovated successfully by returfing at the end of the season.

Mowing
This process continues throughout most of the year. Starting with a 'long' cut and working gradually to a 'close' cut will promote a flat growth of each grass plant, free of harsh, stalky matter.

Brushing and Raking
Use of appropriate equipment for these operations pulls out stalky matter, removes rubbish and surface roots and causes grass to stand more upright prior to mowing.

Weed-killing
Selective weed-killers are now available to deal with any variety of weed including clover. These should be used carefully in accordance with the manufacturer's directions. It is not advisable to spray the square during the playing season but spot treatment is permissible.

Diseases and Pests
Here again many proprietary mixtures are available and once the trouble has been identified the remedy should be applied according to the instructions.

Watering
Water is absorbed both through the roots and the leaves. It also makes the soil plastic when applied correctly before preparation for cricket.

A MONTHLY SCHEDULE

Success in ground work often depends more on what *was* done in previous months than on what is being done. The following suggested programme applies specially to grounds used solely for cricket. Certain variations occur in the case of grounds used for winter games as well.

January Finish any turfing if the weather is not too bad. If dry, brush and harrow surface. Mow very lightly if there has been growth. Check all machines and send away for renovation if necessary.
February Similar to January. Aeration. Roll lightly if frost has loosened the surface.
March Resist the temptation to mow other than very lightly lest a late frost should damage growth. Clear worms on any warm or humid days. Apply treatment for turf diseases and insects. Give application of quick-acting fertiliser.
April Mowing becomes progressively closer. If gang-mowers are used frequently perfect quality outfields are possible. Aerating equipment to be used extensively, as very little aeration will be possible during the playing season. Brush and harrow. Light rolling on the square. Weed-killing *en masse* or spot weeding as required. Seed sowing where needed.
May Remove early morning dews on square by brushing. Frequent mowing preceded by harrowing and brushing when possible.
June Mowing, watering and rolling as necessary. Selective weed-killing.
July Proceed as for June.
August As for June and July according to requirements of matches and weather.
September With the closing down of play the square should be thoroughly raked to remove old grass and debris. Seeding and dressing proceeds. Deep aeration is essential to counteract the compactness of the playing season.
October Application of autumn fertilizers. Aeration – worm-killing – dressings.
November Turfing, re-levelling and as for previous two months if winter weather is not too advanced.
December As for November.

PREPARING A WICKET

The year's work has the aim of supplying satisfactory pitches during the playing season. Detail of the actual procedure which is carried out immediately before the day of a match is as follows. About one week previously the site should be lightly brushed and a 16-inch wide, top-quality mechanized mower adjusted to give its lowest cut. Let the mower travel once up and once down covering about 9 inches in all and ensuring a clean-cut pitch free from irregular mowing. After this the area should be watered if weather conditions require. When the water has sunk in, the strip should be inspected and any indentations lifted with a fine-pronged fork all round (or even a knife if the area is small) and trodden back towards the centre. After this the roller should be used if surface moisture has disappeared. Should the roller be a heavy one the pitch should be allowed longer to dry out. Rolling should, in any case, be stopped if water stands on the surface. This is indicated by dark patches appearing on the pitch. Rolling should not continue once a reasonable surface has been obtained on the first day. Thereafter, until the match, the pitch should be brushed and cut every other day. The amount of watering prior to a match depends on the type of pitch needed. If a fast pitch is the aim, water should be withheld for at least a week beforehand. An easy-paced wicket should be watered to within three or four days. The heaviest roller may be used once surface water has disappeared. It may be used on subsequent days if needed but not if conditions are set for a fast pitch or crumbling or dust may occur.

With careful examination and attention it will be possible to reconstitute a pitch so that it may quickly be used again. The first operation in a chain of treatments is a good sweeping to remove dislodged grass, soil, roots, etc. A good watering should follow and any indentations should be forked up as described in 'wicket preparation'. Considerable damage is inevitable in the areas used by batsmen, bowlers and wicket-keepers. Some of these can be forked and seed worked into the surface and covered by a layer of fine soil, then pressed down. Light watering will soon produce a healthy mat of grass to rehabilitate worn spots. Sprouted seed can be used if available. Bowlers' foot marks are sometimes deep enough to necessitate re-turfing. In this case regular watering must ensue to prevent shrinking. Failing this, filling depressions with fine soil, well rolled, is a temporary expedient which will restore a safe surface.

Part VIII
Other United Kingdom Cricket

The National Cricket Association

J. D. ROBSON

All cricket in the United Kingdom below the first and second class is under the aegis of The National Cricket Association. It is appropriate therefore that an article outlining the achievements and hopes for this young body by the Chairman of the NCA should introduce this part. He has chosen a novel story to illustrate its practical value.

THE BATSMAN peered down the wicket as the bowler turned to start his run. Slowly and deliberately the bowler prepared for his supreme effort. He glided into movement gradually gathering momentum until he reached the stumps and exploded into a blur of action. The batsman almost instinctively decided this was the ball to hit. The bat swung and with a beautiful resounding clunk made contact. As the ball lifted into the air and headed into space the batsman gave a cry of horror. The ball was heading for Mrs Miller's garden. The spectators tensed as they automatically calculated the path of the ball. Suddenly the tension was released, the ball hit the top of the net 40 feet high and the six was achieved.

Why should the hitting of a six cause so much concern? Simply, the householder had served an injunction on the Lintz Cricket Club to prevent them from playing since she was unable to enjoy her garden when any game was in progress. The club contested the action and with great efforts raised the £3,000 necessary. They lost. Disaster faced this small village club. They were strong members of the NCA and through their county association (Durham) received the support of the national body. The case was then presented to the Cricket Council who gave unanimous support and bore the cost of the appeal. Fortunately the appeal succeeded and Lintz Cricket Club will play on their ground for many years to come. Membership of NCA means something to Lintz Cricket Club. Ten years previously there was no forum for the recreational game to discuss its problems or organize itself – NCA has changed all that.

Perhaps the easiest way to explain NCA is to quote several of cricket's personalities. For instance 'Gubby' Allen – 'NCA has a grave responsibility. In its hands lies the future of the game.' This comment outlines the basic philosophy of the organization. Its first priority is to achieve greater involvement. As many boys as possible must be able to participate, or be introduced to cricket. It is easy to understand the difficulties facing

Keith Andrew, the NCA Director of Coaching.

schools – inadequate facilities, examination pressures, changing social habits, short summer term, etc., and clubs must be encouraged to offer their facilities to young players. NCA does this by promoting various competitions and coaching courses which are open to all members. Keith Andrew, Director of Coaching, has said 'My job is not only to encourage greater involvement but to ensure that the standards achieved by young players are the best possible at both local and national level'. To this end, much energy is directed to improving the quality and number of good coaches at youth level, as well as making the Advanced Coaching Award the most coveted in the game. Many first-class players and prominent amateurs consider the course a most stimulating experience. Don Wilson, former Yorkshire and England bowler, now Head Coach at the MCC Indoor School, commented: 'It was one of the most strenuous, interesting and enjoyable weeks of my cricket life'. Plans are afoot to have national and regional refresher courses to upgrade our coaching ideas. TCCB are well aware of the importance of NCA and have recently agreed a development plan to stimulate regional activity. Cedric Rhoades, Chairman of Lancashire, says quite candidly 'NCA must succeed or cricket will fail. The recreational game is the base of the pyramid with Test cricket at the top. The stronger the base the better the game.'

The NCA is also deeply involved in grant aid and has lately been able to channel funds for coaching courses, junior equipment and non-turf wickets to many clubs. They work closely with the Lord's Taverners without whom cricket would be infinitely poorer. The amount of support this organization gives to cricket is amazing. We are unable to express adequately our appreciation of their efforts.

Freddie Brown, President of NCA as well as a former captain of England, remarked 'I have had many wonderful experiences in this game but tonight is special. To see so many young boys from different countries enjoying each other's company, discussing cricket and making friendships which will last for life is worth all the effort.' The occasion was the Youth Festival at Charterhouse in 1977 when Canada, Holland, Denmark, Ireland and England competed. NCA organized the event, again with support from the Lord's Taverners.

Many players throughout the land have benefited from the excellent insurance scheme which has expanded beyond our initial expectations. Lately NCA has been able to develop aspects of the game because of the generosity of sponsors who perhaps do not consider commercial returns as the first criteria for support. The Wrigley Trophy is available to the indoor six-a-side contingent who have shown a deep dedication to the game. John Arnold, Managing Director of Wrigley's says 'We have been delighted by the performances of the cricketers and the efforts of the organizers who have produced a worthwhile competition'. In 1979 the Commercial Union Insurance Company sponsored a national Under-16 competition with surprising results. Competition was extremely keen and the final week an outstanding success. The back-up from the company was unusual and most refreshing. Vernon Bryan of the Commercial Union commented 'Delighted – every penny was well spent. We will help again.' Add to these the Under-13 Lord's Taverners' Festival at Sherborne and our activities may be seen as truly national.

We would hope that MCC will continue to pursue a positive educational role in cricket. Our relationship has produced courses at the Indoor School at Lord's as well as an agreement by them to finance posters for school and club purposes. There are many new and exciting developments planned and our growing membership will benefit without doubt. NCA will increasingly be seen as a necessary institution by all lovers of the game – and especially by club cricketers everywhere.

Ireland's finest hour: Londonderry 1969, when they dismissed a casual West Indian side for 25 and beat them by 9 wickets. Goodwin, the Irish captain took 5 for 6, and O'Riordan 4 for 18. Back row: M. Stott (umpire), M. L. C. Foster (WI), I. Anderson (I), V. A. Holder (WI, 12th man), J. N. Shepherd (WI), G. A. Duffy (I), G. A. Shillingford (WI), L. P. Hughes (I), T. M. Findlay (WI), A. J. O'Riordan (I), P. Roberts (WI), A. Trickett (umpire); seated: P. D. Blair (WI), P. J. Dineen (I), M. C. Carew (WI), D. R. Pigot (I), C. L. Walcott (WI), D. E. Goodwin (I, captain), B. F. Butcher (WI, captain), M. S. Reith (I), C. H. Lloyd (WI), J. Harrison (I), G. S. Camacho (WI).

Ireland

STANLEY BERGIN AND DEREK SCOTT

To gain a true picture of the history of cricket in Ireland it is necessary to relate the game to the political and social life of the country in the 18th century. It is from there that one must start to gain insight into its beginning, growth, decline and current revival. At that time the British ruled the country and whatever cricket was played in Ireland was confined essentially to the military, the gentry and members of the viceregal or Chief Secretary's staff and household. Hence the first cricket match in Ireland of which there is any record took place in the Phoenix Park in 1792 between teams styled The Garrison and All-Ireland, although the latter is a misnomer. Captain of the Garrison team was Lt-Col Lennox, later to return to Ireland as Lord Lieutenant, and leading the All-Ireland team was the Secretary of War, Major Hobart. The historic game developed from a friendly discussion which led to 1,000 guineas being wagered on the result, and the records show that the Garrison team won by an innings and 94 runs.

Such challenge matches were common enough then, but the Irish themselves cannot have shown any major interest in the game, for one passes into the 1820s before there are signs of an Irish club being formed. By an odd twist of fate, the first of these sprang up in Ballinasloe, Carlow and Kilkenny, present-day strongholds of the national games of hurling and gaelic football. Dublin University, on whose picturesque ground the vast majority of home representative matches were played until 1963, could field a team in 1827, although the actual cricket club was not formed until 1842. Before that, the Phoenix Club, which has produced some of Ireland's greatest players, including J. C. Boucher, comes into the general picture of expansion. Again there is a link with the military. When the cricket club moved to its present setting in the Phoenix Park, it was urged that permission to play there would confer great benefits upon the officers of the garrison.

Numerically, the strongest northern club of today is North of Ireland CC which was founded in 1859, under the patronage of the Lord-Lieutenant of Ireland. The club has always been noted for its enterprise, and the ground is among the best-equipped in the country. A strong All-England team played NICC early in the club's career and the star of the home side was C. E. Stelfox. His equal in more modern times would be J. S. Pollock, a fine forcing batsman and an excellent cover-fielder. An interesting feature of Pollock's international career is the fact that his only hundred was that scored against Scotland in 1951 at College Park, Dublin. His father, W. Pollock, also hit a hundred against the Scots in 1922 at Glasgow. In Derry in 1963 the ICU were hosts to the Scottish side in the first representative match to be played there. This change from Dublin and Belfast, normal centres for representative cricket, is in recognition of the work being done in the north-west of the country to promote the game. In those parts the outstanding players in the past decade have been the slow left-arm bowler, S. S. J. Huey, who headed the English first-class bowling averages in 1954 for those who had taken 10 or more wickets in the season. His average was 6·92, the outstanding feature being his performance against MCC in Dublin when he took 6 for 49 and 8 for 48, thus enabling Ireland to gain an exciting win. In this context, it is interesting to note that 'Jimmy' Boucher headed the English averages in 1931, 1937 and again in 1948.

The second North-West player of renown is O. D. Colhoun, the wicket-keeper, who holds a record number of caps and victims.

While cricket was progressing in northern parts, the southern scene was improving. Again the military dominated the scene, with teams in Fermoy, Cork, Spike Island, Ballincollig and at the Naval Training Depot in Ringaskiddy. Teams also sprang up in Midleton, Douglas, Clonakilty and Castlemartyr, while in Cork city itself there was quite a flourishing fraternity.

Nowadays the Cork County CC is regarded as the hub around which cricket in the south of Ireland rotates. In recent years particularly they have expanded their programme and have acted as hosts to several county teams, including Glamorgan and Somerset. Their efforts to keep the game flourishing exemplify difficulties which face most clubs, especially in provincial Ireland. Cork, one of the great strongholds of gaelic football and hurling, is a relaxing city, and until the formation of the Munster Cricket Union in the 1950s, the cricket played there was equally relaxing. Most visiting teams found it difficult to fathom the rather peculiar timing of intervals. Breaks for tea and drinks were seldom kept to the official limits; nor was the rolling of the wicket. Yet nothing can detract from the enjoyment of playing cricket in Cork, even if the game is now played along more official lines. Hospitality abounds and the standard of cricket has improved in post-war years. The province of Munster has produced several internationals in the past decade, most notable among these being N. C. Mahony, a very shrewd captain, P. J. Dineen and J. F. Short. The name of P. W. G. Stuart-French is also very closely associated with the game in Cork. He captained the Munster side at the age of 62.

In W. P. Hone's book, *Cricket in Ireland*, the story is told that W. G. Grace saw Stuart-French play in Cork and was so impressed by his batting that he invited him to England to play for London County. It is recalled, too, that Stuart-French, having made 50 against the formidable Surrey bowler, Lockwood, was presented by Grace with a bat, for which the Irishman had to pay. In later life Stuart-French was appointed private secretary to the Governor of the Windward Islands and played a lot of cricket with MCC. Also from the south of Ireland came Sir Timothy O'Brien who had the unusual distinction of playing both for Ireland and England.

Some junior clubs have gone out of existence in the past 20 years. This points to the economic difficulties which beset Irish cricket, both at club and international level. The ICU has overcome this problem to some extent by establishing an associate-membership scheme, without which it would be extremely difficult not only to provide funds for defraying players' expenses for annual visits to Scotland and Lord's, in turn, but also to cover the cost of inviting leading touring and English county teams to Ireland.

Such difficulties did not present themselves in the old days when cricket was a much more leisurely affair.

A much wealthier class played the game in the last century, so that it was possible in 1879 to send a team to the United States. The sponsors of the trip were the St George's Club of New York, the Irish side being captained by N. Hone, a family name very closely associated with cricket in Ireland. By all accounts it was a highly successful tour, during which the Irish players travelled on to Philadelphia and later to Canada. Subsequent tours were undertaken, and it is not without significance that the records show that for the 1892 trip a dispute among the Dublin clubs resulted in the team being less representative than it should have been.

Cricket at that time was not on any organized footing in the country and although many of the most famous names in the game appear quite regularly in the records, the Irish Cricket Union, as it is known today, did not come into being until 1923. This followed on a meeting between representatives of the Leinster Union and the Northern Union in July of that year. A Leinster representative at this meeting was R. H. Lambert who, in a career stretching from his first appearance in 1893 to his retirement in 1930, proved his ability with bat and ball. The family tradition was carried on by N. H. Lambert, a son of R. H. Lambert, who played for Ireland in 21 games between 1931 and 1947.

The dominating figures in the Irish team of that period were, however, J. C. Boucher and E. A. Ingram. Contemporaries at Belvedere College, Dublin, Boucher and Ingram became one of Ireland's greatest bowling combinations. Each was first capped while still at school, and they played together in the Irish side for almost 25 years, in which time they had outstanding figures with bat and ball against some of the strongest teams to be sent to Ireland. Ingram, concentrating mainly on accuracy and length, was the less spectacular of the two. In his youth, his lean frame brought him the name 'chicken' which stayed all through his career, in spite of the fact that he could safely have shed much weight with the advancing years. Bowling his mixture of medium leg-breaks and top-spinners, Ingram was ever economical and among his many fine achievements was that against Australia in the two-day game in Dublin in 1938. Although the public were disappointed at the absence of Bradman, they caught more than a glimpse of the batting powers of McCabe, Fingleton, Badcock and Barnes, but Ingram had one magnificent bowling spell in which he took 5 wickets in 7 overs for 29 runs.

Another lasting memory of that game was the batting of E. D. R. Shearer. Gifted with a keen eye and nimble feet, Shearer's batting technique was probably never seen to better purpose than that afternoon when for more than two hours he defied the wiles of no less a bowler than O'Reilly. Like Ingram, who played a good deal of his cricket in London and had occasional games for Middlesex, Shearer enjoyed the experience of two years in London, which from a cricket point of view was time well spent. Had he remained in England, it is quite probable that he, too, would have reached county standard, a comment certainly applicable to Boucher. Although his somewhat ungainly and lengthy run-up to the wicket caused a good deal of adverse comment, Boucher could afford to ignore that type of criticism. During an international career extending from 1929 to 1954, he took 307 wickets at an average of 15·73 per wicket, an astonishing record. His best season was 1937 when he set up a record total of 44 wickets. While many of his best figures have been achieved against Scotland, county and touring teams have gone away with high respect for his medium-paced off-breaks.

In 1937 Boucher captained Ireland in a memorable game against New Zealand, a proposed 3-day game being completed in one. Rain affected the wicket at Rathmines and this was to neither side's liking, as can be seen from the scores: Ireland 79 and 30; New Zealand 64 and 46 for 2. The villain of the piece was the fast bowler, Cowie, who took 6 wickets for 3 runs. Boucher, with his off-breaks, had 7 for 13. The 1938 season marked the end of a notable career in cricket when T. G. McVeagh, one of the country's most versatile sportsmen, left the representative scene. An unorthodox, keen-eyed left-hander, McVeagh scored over 1,000 runs in 21 matches for Ireland and his 102 not out against the West Indies at College Park in 1928 is still spoken of by those fortunate enough to have seen it. McVeagh also represented Ireland at lawn tennis, squash rackets and hockey.

Stanley Bergin retired from all cricket at the start of the 1966 season. To his name he had then the record number of runs (2,524) for Ireland. He was only 38 and four years later he died, aged 42. Sadly he saw only the start of an Irish cricket resurgence.

A. J. O'Riordan, the only player to have scored 2000 runs and taken 200 wickets for Ireland, signing autographs when captain of Ireland in 1976.

The Guinness Cup began in 1966. It is an Interprovincial Tournament of 6 teams drawn from different areas and all playing each other. This has been a great help to harassed Irish selectors. In 1969 an identical tournament at Under-19 level (sponsored by Esso) got under way and an Under-15 tournament (sponsored by Smurfit) started in 1976. In 1969 D. E. Goodwin took over the Irish captaincy and revitalized the team. In that very year came the famous dismissal of West Indies for 25 at Sion Mills (they were 12 for 9!). As the 1970s rolled on, commercial sponsorship allowed more and better representative fixtures. A series of matches against Holland and Denmark was begun; a tour to the USA and Canada was embarked on in 1973; the West Indies came in 1976; Australia in 1977; and Surrey in 1978 and 1979. A 10-day tour to England in 1977 saw the defeat of Sussex at Pagham, the county being bowled out twice. The culmination came in 1980 when Ireland gained admission to the Gillette Cup.

Ireland now have a seat on the Cricket Council. The TCCB has played a vastly encouraging part with increased annual financial grants. The NCA has taken the 4 Irish Provincial Unions under its wing and, through the Wrigley and McAlpine Trusts, put money into the Irish club scene. Because of this and new Government Sports grants in both North and South youth cricket has increased and prospered. Under-19 Irish teams have played in tournaments in The Hague and Toronto, and at Charterhouse School. Piped BBC television and live coverage of representative matches by Irish Television have brought the game to areas where it was previously almost unknown. In the Midlands and South-East there has been a strong revival and there are now over 130 clubs scattered throughout the land. The Provincial Unions are well organized and there is a vast amount of competitive cricket played annually at both adult and youth level. Increased finance also allowed a massive coaching scheme to begin and grow. By 1979 there were 10 Irish coaches with the Advanced Coaching Certificate and over 60 with the Primary Certificate. N. C. Mahony, a former Irish captain, was in charge of this most important and expanding aspect of the game.

There have been four outstanding Irish players in the last decade. A. J. O'Riordan, who won 72 caps between 1958 and 1977 and is the only player to score 2,000 runs and take 200 wickets for Ireland; I. J. Anderson, a brilliant stroke player; O. D. Colhoun, the wicket-keeper, whose record has been mentioned earlier, and the current captain, J. D. Monteith, a slow left-armer, who looks on course to surpass J. C. Boucher's 307 wickets in 60 matches. Two powerful clubs dominated the domestic scene in the 1970s, Waringstown in the North and Phoenix in Dublin. The latter celebrated their 150th anniversary in 1980.

CAPTAINS SINCE THE SECOND WAR		MATCHES
1946–47	E. D. R. Shearer	9
1947	G. M. Crothers	1
1948–51	N. C. Mahony	6

1950–52	E. A. Ingram	8
1951–55	J. S. Pollock	10
1956–61	L. Warke	18
1959–62	S. F. Bergin	2
1960–66	S. S. J. Huey	5
1961–77	A. J. O'Riordan	28
1964–66	D. M. Pratt	6
1967	W. R. Hunter	3
1968	I. J. Anderson	5
1969–72	D. E. Goodwin	19
1974–75	A. J. Linehan	6
1976–79	J. D. Monteith	14

HIGHEST TOTALS

For 462 v Mr W. H. Laverton's XI, Westbury 1893
Against 489 by Scotland, Paisley 1954

LOWEST TOTALS

For 24 v MCC, College Park, Dublin 1871
Against 25 by West Indies, Sion Mills 1969

HIGHEST INDIVIDUAL INNINGS

For 198* I. J. Anderson v A. Canadian XI, Toronto 1973
Against 239* N. V. H. Riches for Wales, Ormeau, Belfast 1926

MOST RUNS

In a season 490 J. F. Short 1979
In a career 2,902 I. J. Anderson 1966–1979

MOST HUNDREDS

In a season 2 I. J. Anderson (in same match) 1976
In a career 6 I. J. Anderson 1966–1979

HUNDRED ON DEBUT

H. G. H. Mulholland 149 v Scotland, Hamilton Crescent, Glasgow 1911
M. C. Parry 124 v Scotland, College Park, Dublin 1925
S. J. Edgar 103 v MCC, Sion Mills 1934
J. R. Gill 106 v MCC, Rathmines 1948

RECORD WICKET PARTNERSHIPS

1 N. Hone and D. N. Trotter 161 v MCC, Lord's 1879
2 P. F. Quinlan and R. H. Lambert 149 v Scotland, Edinburgh (Grange CC) 1913
3 Sir T. C. O'Brien and R. H. Lambert 170 v Oxford University, Oxford 1902
4 I. J. Anderson and A. J. O'Riordan 222 v Scotland, Hamilton Crescent, Glasgow 1976
5 J. Harrison and A. J. O'Riordan 175 v Denmark, Castle Avenue, Dublin 1973
6 A. D. Comyn and W. D. Hamilton 201 v I. Zingari, Phoenix CC Dublin 1896
7 W. Hone, sr and W. S. Ashton 150 v Zingari, Viceregal, Dublin 1868
8 T. G. McVeagh and P. A. Thornton 106 v West Indies, College Park, Dublin 1928
9 J. W. Hynes and W. D. Hamilton 96 v Gentlemen of Canada, Rathmines 1887
10 W. R. King and W. Sproule 84 v Wales, Cardiff 1923

MOST WICKETS

In an innings 9 A. Samuels v I Zingari, Phoenix CC Dublin 1859 (the innings total was 92)
9–26 F. Fee v Scotland, College Park, Dublin 1957
In a match 14–97 S. S. J. Huey v MCC, College Park, Dublin 1954
In a season 47 J. D. Monteith 1971
In a career 307 J. C. Boucher 1929–1954

HAT-TRICK

T. H. Hanna (on debut)

WICKET-KEEPING – MOST DISMISSALS

In an innings 5 O. D. Colhoun
C. R. Cuffe
In a match 7 O. D. Colhoun
In a season 23 O. D. Colhoun
In a career 190 O. D. Colhoun 1959–1979
(Colhoun played 87 out of a possible 88 matches before retiring in mid-1979)

Scotland

N. G. R. MAIR

It has been said that cricket is something the English – not being a naturally religious people – invented in order to give themselves some idea of the eternal. The Scots, a naturally God-fearing people, have down the centuries always had a clear conception of eternity, but it is arguable that until they had fielded throughout a Scottish summer day, they had no clear notion of damnation. The weather more than any other factor has retarded the growth of cricket north of the border and has also conditioned the type of cricket played. Manchester has demonstrated that a generous rainfall is not incompatible with an enthusiasm for cricket and, in any case, rain interferes with cricket in Scotland much less than is generally supposed. But in Scotland there are fewer genuine cricketing days than there are in England, fewer days when the sun has real warmth and there is no keen wind to make the removal of a sweater an act of bravado. The weather, too, is mainly responsible for the fact that though there are numerous good, true wickets in Scotland, very few have the pace which enables a batsman to play his shots and which encourages the authentic fast bowler and the back of the hand spinner. With the ball so seldom coming on to the bat, there is a regrettable but understandable tendency for seam bowlers to predominate, particularly in league cricket – as always, to the detriment of the game as a spectacle.

Yet, despite such apparently alien conditions, cricket has been part of the Scottish summer for nigh on 200 years. The Cathcart family group painted by David Allan has, as a background, the first known cricket match in Scotland on the estate of the Earl of Cathcart at Shaw Park, Alloa, on 3 September 1785. A. M. C. Thorburn, the official historian of the Scottish Cricket Union and a veritable perambulating comptometer of cricket facts and figures, considers that the '45 Rebellion probably played its part in popularising the game by bringing the army into Scotland and, certainly, the game appears early in the various garrison towns. Thorburn believes that in the 18th century cricket in Scotland was played, for the most part, by gentlemen of position and leisure and by Army officers, and rather as a means of gambling than as a source of exercise. There is evidence of cricket at the old High School, Edinburgh, as early as 1817 and, not long afterwards, class matches between the High School and Edinburgh Academy were played on Bruntsfield Links. Scorebooks still exist as mute testimony to such battles as that at Grove Street, Edinburgh, in 1849, between an All England XI containing names like Wisden, Parr, Clarke and Box against a Scottish team prudently provided with 22 players.

The Scottish Cricket Union did not come into existence until 1909, though the Scottish XI had been playing representative matches since 1865. In those early days Scotland were a force to be reckoned with and, on 29 July 1882, in an unofficial exhibition match, Scotland bowled out Australia for 122, having themselves made 167, to record an historic victory. Even as late as 1909, Scotland had Australia in dire straits, when time unkindly ran out (Scotland 93 and 230, Australia 121 and 147 for 7). Though occasional Scottish representative matches provided the better players in the country with a worthwhile incentive and valuable experience, the lack of regular first-class county cricket in Scotland, the absence of a counterpart to Glamorgan in Wales, was a grave handicap in a land where golf was the national summer sport, and football of a kind was played all the year round. The heroes of boyhood were seldom cricketing heroes and only the local cricketers provided an outlet for youth's infinite capacity for imitation and emulation. The advent of television has brought first-class cricket into innumerable homes where, previously, it was thought of only as another idiosyncrasy of the Sassenach and, at every level, the game in Scotland now reflects, for better or worse, the tactics, techniques, attitudes and mannerisms of the leading figures in contemporary first-class cricket.

Moreover, though the number of representative matches which Scotland can play each season is limited by the availability of suitable opposition and by the amount of time that the players can afford away from their work, the Scottish Cricket Union have long set about ensuring that there are a handful of Scottish representative matches each season. In the postwar years, the selection committee have generally shown a ready appreciation of the importance to a successful policy of

Scotland v Australians, at Raeburn Park, 1909. Back row: R. Attewell (umpire), Bailey, H. D. Keigwin, W. Bardsley, G. K. Chalmers, J. A. O'Connor, T. A. Bowie, A. J. Hopkins, Ringrose, W. S. MacKenzie (umpire); seated: V. Trumper, B. L. Peel, P. A. M'Alister, R. J. Hartigan, M. R. Dickson (captain), M. A. Noble (captain), R. G. Tait, Broadbent and W. J. Whitty; front row: A. Cotter, A. Lindsay, C. G. Macartney, Joe Anderson and W. Carkeek.

continuity and consistency. The more gifted among Scotland's Saturday afternoon cricketers have always been able to play the shots, but rarely to put together an innings amid the greater tension and different tempo of first-class cricket. There is also in first-class cricket a greater need for the bowler to bowl to his field and, in truth, a greater emphasis on scientific field-setting. Such skills cannot be learned overnight, but by giving the majority of their chosen players an extended run in the Scottish side, the selectors did their best to build a team with enough confidence to set about raising their game to meet the sterner demands imposed by those who live and have their being in first-class cricket.

It must be conceded that, outside of the Benson & Hedges Cup, Scotland's representative programme is not particularly exacting, that not all their more illustrious opponents are at full stretch in matches of this nature and that sometimes the matches are of only two days' duration. Nevertheless, there was predictably much satisfaction when, in 1959, the selectors were rewarded with a first-ever win over an English county, namely Warwickshire, and then, in 1961, with their first victory, since the formation of the Scottish Cricket Union, over MCC. In the annual international matches with Ireland, Scotland have a perilous lead, having won 17 to the enemy's 16, with 23 drawn.

Obedient to Samuel Johnson's dictum that 'much may be made of a Scotsman if he be caught young', the Scottish Cricket Union have progressed from sponsoring group-coaching courses under the auspices of the visiting H. P. Crabtree to the point where they now have a full-time national coach in David Wilson, albeit his brief does admittedly stretch into the north of England. Group coaching was never without its critics and, undeniably, it has its limitations. Probably it is unnecessary in boarding schools such as Fettes, Merchiston, Loretto, Glenalmond and Strathallan, or in a day school such as the Edinburgh Academy, for in such schools cricket is played on most days of the week under the tuition of an often encouragingly knowledgeable staff. But in a country not only sadly lacking in cricketing fathers to guide the embryo cricketer along the right lines but in which few schools boast a professional and where the proportion of schoolmasters with a cricket background is liable to be infinitesimal, it is almost the only way to bring the game to the vast bulk of the school population. The Scottish Cricket Union are increasingly anxious that the clubs should play a major role in fostering the game among the young and Wilson, a former schoolmaster himself and once a player on the Warwickshire staff at Edgbaston, has ambitious plans in that direction. The Scottish climate being what it is, and skilled groundsmen a problem not only in terms of expense, artificial wickets, and not necessarily only for practice, have an obvious part to play. Those few indoor cricket nets Scotland possesses at such locations as the Inverclyde Sports Centre, Largs, Hamilton Crescent, home of West of Scotland, and Myreside, where the Watsonians play, must be invaluable if imaginatively utilized.

Among native-born Scots, M. H. Denness, the Rev J. Aitchison and, in a much earlier generation, J. Kerr, rank as the outstanding batsmen produced on this side of the border. Kerr, whose international career spanned the years 1913 to 1933, played considerably fewer innings for Scotland than Aitchison, but he was at all times equally prolific, his 5 hundreds including a memorable 147 against the formidable Australian side of 1921. In addition, he made for his club, Greenock, a total of 21,558 runs, which still stands as a Scottish record, though A. M. Zuill of Stenhousemuir is closing fast. Aitchison, probably because of his unorthodox grip, allowed the right hand to dominate many of his shots more than the purists advocate, but, particularly in his prime, he saw the ball so early, his footwork was so swift and sure and he owned such astonishing powers of concentration that he quickly established himself as the main bulwark of the Scottish batting. R. H. E. Chisholm, a dour and determined opening batsman, is the only other to have amassed more than 3,000 runs for Scotland but he made 3,175 runs in 137 innings, whereas Aitchison collected 3,669 from 119.

Maybe it should be taken as confirmation of Tennyson's contention that 'more things are wrought by prayer than this world dreams of', but there is no gainsaying the fact that Aitchison's achievement in numbering among his major innings hundreds against both Lancashire and Yorkshire and against South Africa and Australia was quite remarkable for a practising minister with such relatively limited experience of first-class cricket. By his example, Aitchison demonstrated to the other members of the Scottish team that each ball must be played on merit, and he always had that ability noted in Herbert Sutcliffe to forget about the ball before; nor was he ever afraid to ride his luck. Few anecdotes from the realm of Scottish cricket have had a wider airing than the true story of how one perspiring England bowler, as Aitchison proceeded unruffled to his 50, exclaimed indignantly, and with a fine disregard for the independence of the Presbyterian Church of Scotland, 'With your luck, you ought to be b— Archbishop of Canterbury'.

Denness, who first played for Scotland in 1959, as a schoolboy, always had a look of class. A member of an unbeaten Ayr Academy 1st XV which also included Ian Ure, a future Scotland centre-half, and Ian McLauchlan, the 'Mighty Mouse' of rugby fame, Denness at one time had his sights on a rugby cap. Though his cricket commitments put paid to that ambition, he always had in his favour the fact that, in addition to being a most attractive batsman, he was a glorious mover in the field blessed with lovely hands. His problems against extreme pace, accentuated by the uneven bounce of so many pitches on his tour of Australia when Lillee and Thomson often appeared close to unplayable, possibly had their origin in an instinctive movement of the rear foot which was less than classical and the extent of which, when he happened to see a television recording of himself in action during that tour Down Under, considerably took him aback. Nor perhaps did captaincy come easily to him. Yet his haul of trophies in his reign as captain of Kent, before moving on to Essex to join the elite band of those who have won the County Championship under more than one flag, would be the envy of many another, while his England career was put in a perspective which would surprise many by E. W. Swanton: 'Of the 19 matches played by England under his captaincy in a little over 2 years, 6 were won, 5 lost and 8 drawn. Of the 6 wins, 4 were by an innings and in each of these 4 he made a hundred.'

Controversial figure though he was during his time as England's captain, Denness achieved an unprecedented amount for a player who did not leave Scotland until he was out of his teens. Today he finds himself alongside another Scot in the Essex team in the person of B. R. Hardie, who has already established himself as a decidedly useful member of the 1979 County Champions' batting order. Within even so brief a consideration of celebrated Scottish batsmen, mention must also be made of the legendary L. M. Balfour-Melville, who made 73 against Australia in 1882, yet was still good enough to make 91 against Ireland in 1909. And that despite having found time, among other sporting accomplishments, to play rugby for Scotland, win the Scottish long jump title and the Scottish Lawn Tennis championship and beat the immortal John Ball in the final of the Amateur golf championship at St Andrew's in 1895.

Since they were never subjected to the stamina-sapping demands of first-class cricket, it is logical enough that so many of Scotland's leading bowlers have come from the ranks of the all-rounder, a species seldom scarce in the more humble sphere of club cricket. Among the all-rounders who have represented Scotland, 5 stand out. W. A. Edward, a born leader of men and an unqualified success as captain of Scotland, played 41 times for his country, making over 1,000 runs and taking over 50 wickets. W. Nichol, an orthodox slow left-arm bowler and an eminently sound left-handed batsman, was a natural cricketer who might well have attained the game's highest honours had he played his cricket in England; a player with his own niche in the Scottish game and, incidentally, a central figure in that engaging tale of the works cricket match played on a bumpy pitch in the fading light of the evening. White flannels and equipment were notably scarce and when, at the fall of a wicket, the next batsman took guard, Willie Nichol, as umpire, felt constrained to suggest that he was somewhat ill-advised to wear his one pad on his rear leg. 'Och, Willie,' said the batsman, apologetically, 'I thought I was batting at the other end.'

J. M. Allan, a slow left-arm bowler relying on length and flight rather than power of spin, took a record 171 wickets for his native land and, in his own individual way, played some important innings as might be expected of a batsman who, in county cricket, had once made a hundred in each innings against Frank Tyson. Of Oxford, Kent and Warwickshire, Allan played for the Gentlemen against the Players at Lord's and was also invited to tour Pakistan with the MCC 'A' team in 1955–56. Owing to the imminence of his university examinations, Allan had to decline but, as the selectors chose in his place one G. A. R. Lock, Allan at least had the consolation of being left with an excellent story with which to impress his descendants. D. Barr maybe batted only intermittently in his best vein for Scotland, but he frequently used the new ball to much effect, taking 5 for 51 against New Zealand at Selkirk in 1958 and 5 for 43 against India in 1959. A fierce and aggressive cricketer, Barr had, in the vogue word, 'colour'. Once when a batsman had 3 times in succession edged Barr's out-swinger past a

G. F. Goddard, an experienced all-rounder and captain of Scotland on the eve of their entry in 1980 into the Benson & Hedges Cup.

somewhat portly gentleman fielding in the gully, Barr was asked by his captain if he would like gully squarer. 'Not squarer – younger' was the terse retort.

Scotland's captain, George Goddard, who toured West Africa with MCC, is now just a tantalizing 15 runs short of joining Allan and Barr as the only players to have done the double for Scotland, Goddard's match of matches being against MCC at Titwood in 1973 when he made 113 and took 11 wickets, including all 8 to fall in MCC's 1st innings. An off-spinner with a sense of humour, Goddard in the summer of 1979 noted thoughtfully that the only player in the whole of Scottish cricket to have adopted those protective helmets now so much in evidence in the uppermost echelons is the gentleman called upon to field at short-leg to Goddard's own bowling. From the same club, Heriot's FP, H. K. More has also been on tour with MCC, in his case to Bangladesh. A prolific batsman and a beautiful fielder, More was also a good enough wicket-keeper to be invited in that capacity to the Scarborough Festival to play for T. N. Pearce's XI and, indeed, he stands second in the wicket-keeping statistics in a Scotland cap only to the former Scotland captain, Perthshire's J. Brown, who took 112 catches and had 34 stumpings. Holder of a record 85 caps, Brown – who took 7 wickets in an innings, catching 4 and stumping 3, against Ireland in 1957 – also figured at the Scarborough Festival, twice playing for the Gentlemen against the Players. Indisputably the finest wicket-keeper to come out of Scotland, Brown was unobtrusive and usually unspectacular, yet ceaselessly vigilant and effective.

Among the specialist bowlers as distinct from the genuine all-rounders, R. W. Sievwright plied his left-arm spin between 1912 and 1930, capturing 81 wickets at an average cost of 23·7; W. K. Laidlaw, a leg-break and googly bowler of the front rank, took 97 wickets in the years between 1936 and 1953 at a cost per wicket of 23·6; A. D. Baxter, the Middlesex fast bowler, whose Scotland appearances embraced the years 1929 to 1938, had 75 wickets at an average of 23·2; and the lofty G. W. Youngson, with swing and off-break, marked up 81 wickets between 1947 and 1955. Though the Second World War cruelly curtailed his representative career, R. S. Hodge gained considerable prominence as a fast bowler within and without Scotland by taking 5 for 82 for the Under-33s against the Over-33s at Lord's in 1945. In recent years, E. R. Thompson, a medium-fast bowler who achieved his effects mainly off the seam, emulated J. M. Allan, D. Barr and G. F. Goddard in taking more than a hundred wickets for Scotland; while still among the brisker bowlers, two others deserving of a passing salute are Jack Clark and Frank Robertson.

The Scottish selectors include in their field of selection players qualified for Scotland only by residence. Into this category fall such men as S. G. Sismey, the Australian wicket-keeper, who played for Scotland in 1952; and a host of Englishmen, including B. G. W. Atkinson of Middlesex, who was reckoned by many to be the best batsman in Scotland between the First World War and the Second, and G. L. Willatt who, in the 1950s, made many runs for Scotland as a neat and watchful left-hand bat and also exerted a lasting influence through the experience of the English arena he brought to the captaincy. As a general rule, Scotsmen playing their cricket outside Scotland have not interested the Scottish selectors, although such fine cricketers as C. S. Dempster of New Zealand, P. A. Gibb of Cambridge University, Yorkshire and England, and I. A. R. Peebles of Middlesex and England, who was at school at Glasgow Academy, have worn Scotland's colours.

The summer of 1980 was to have its own special significance in the annals of Scottish cricket from the moment it was revealed that Scotland were to take their first step into the county firmament on a competitive footing by playing in the Benson & Hedges Cup. No one was under any illusions because, aside from the fact that Scotland had often been better off for players, the test was likely to be a lot more severe than it had frequently been in the time-honoured friendly matches, even in the days when those Scotland engagements counted in the first-class averages. As G. F. Goddard, Scotland's captain, observed when the news broke, 'The English counties know only too well that odd things can happen in a one-day match and they certainly won't want any slip-up in a competition carrying both money and prestige.'

M. H. Denness and B. R. Hardie would, of course, be playing for Essex in defence of the trophy. Against that, the selectors included in the provisional 21 strong squad B. K. Kunderan and B. E. A. Edmeades who were deemed eligible on a residential qualification being, if one can use such a term since the coming of open cricket, the professionals of, respectively, Drumpellier and Clydesdale. Another focal point was the inclusion of the former Scotland centre-forward, D. A. C. Ford, which was taken as an indication that the selectors were properly worried as to how the Scottish fielding was going to come out of the comparison with the standards now prevalent in one-day cricket in England. However, what really made the headlines on the morning the squad became public was that D. B. Close, the former England captain, had been appointed Scotland's manager for the Benson & Hedges Cup with the sole say in the final selection.

The majority of clubs compete in one of Scotland's cricket leagues, of which the 6 most notable are the Scottish Counties Championship, the D. M. Hall Championship, the Blacklock Farries League, the Ryden and Partners League and the North of Scotland League, while among the various cup competitions the players mostly give pride of place to the Shish Mahal Trophy, an event spanning the country geographically. The nomenclature of these assorted competitions is an indication of the growth of sponsorship even at this level, the D. M. Hall being formerly the Western Union, the Ryden and Partners the old East League, and the Blacklock Farries League until recently the Border League.

The days when a Perthshire v Forfarshire match drew crowds of 10,000 to the North Inch, Perth, are perhaps gone for ever, and attendances on the grounds of what used to be the Western Union have declined alarmingly in the postwar era. Yet, some clubs still manage to employ a professional. Many of the most celebrated names in cricket's storied lore have played in that capacity in Scotland; men such as Rohan Kanhai and Wilfred Rhodes, the latter of whom was always thereafter referred to in the Scottish papers as 'the old Gala player'. Among individual performances in club cricket must be noted N. L. Stevenson's 1,749 wickets, on behalf of Carlton; the 1,623 wickets of W. Anderson of Dunfermline; the 10 hundreds of Kanhai, Aberdeenshire's West Indian professional, in 1959; and the 4 successive hundreds in 1892 of T. Anderson of West Scotland who earned sporting immortality by playing for Scotland at rugby and cricket, while still at school at Merchiston Castle. J. S. Carrick's 419 not out for West of Scotland against Priory Park in 1885 is the highest individual innings recorded by a Scottish cricketer. In 1868 Arbroath United were dismissed for 2 by Aberdeen, which was yet twice as many as Kinross made in 1896 against Edinvale of Auchtermuchty, which scarcely springs to mind among the acknowledged citadels of cricket.

The fact that no team from Scotland competed in the English county Championship gave to the cricket world an image of Scotland as a non-cricketing country even though club cricket had flourished in Scotland for over a hundred years. On grounds such as Edinburgh Academicals' Raeburn Place, where the 1st rugby international between Scotland and England was played, and West of Scotland's Hamilton Crescent, site of the first Scotland v England association football match, the shades of old cricket heroes mingle with the ghosts of the early days of rugby and association football in Scotland.

Today, even in winter, audiences gather in Scottish cities to listen with respect – even reverence – to the great names of cricket, brought north by the Cricket Society of Scotland, which was founded in 1952. The cricket addict is no less besotted for living in Caledonia stern and wild rather than some land of sleepy sunshine, and the pleasure derived from the game is often no less intense. At times, of course, that pleasure can be a little oblique, as witness that morning when Ralf Laing was batting for Scotland at Old Trafford with Colin Croft at his fastest and most lethal. Eventually Laing was hit on the head and no sooner had he recovered than Croft split his bat asunder. Scotland's captain, the aforesaid George Goddard, chose to take out the replacement bat himself because of the opportunity it afforded to whisper words of encouragement to Laing on the job he was doing for the land of Bruce and Wallace.

Ralf Laing looked up in mock bitterness. 'And to think,' he said ruefully, 'that when I left home yesterday, the wife said, "There you are away again for another three days just to enjoy yourself!"'.

CAPTAINS SINCE THE SECOND WAR

1946	W. Clark
1947–1949	W. K. Laidlaw
1949–50	G. L. Willatt
1950–1955	W. A. Edwards
1956–59	S. H. Cosh
1960	J. M. Allan and R. H. E. Chisholm
1961–1973	J. Brown
1974–1979	G. F. Goddard
1977	D. E. R. Stewart

HIGHEST TOTALS

For 489 v Ireland, Paisley 1954
Against 576–6D by MCC, Lord's 1922

LOWEST TOTALS

For 32 v Ireland, Dublin 1910
Against 25 by Ireland, Dublin 1965

HIGHEST INDIVIDUAL INNINGS

For 190* J. Aitchison v Ireland, Dublin 1959
Against 223* J. V. Wilson for Yorkshire, Scarborough 1951

MOST RUNS

In a career 3,669 J. Aitchison 1947–1963

MOST HUNDREDS

In a season 2 B. R. Hardie (in same match) 1971
In a career 7 J. Aitchison 1949–1963

HUNDRED ON DEBUT

W. Nicholson 101 v Ireland, Dublin 1929

RECORD WICKET PARTNERSHIPS

1 J. Kerr and I. T. Parker 203 v Ireland, Glenpark, Greenock 1926
2 J. R. Laing and T. B. Racionzer 177 v MCC, Titwood, Glasgow 1977
3 J. Aitchison and J. A. S. Taylor 178 v Yorkshire, Hamilton Crescent, Glasgow 1952
4 R. H. E. Chisholm and J. Aitchison 125 v Middlesex, Raeburn Place, Edinburgh 1962
5 B. R. Hardie and J. M. Allan 134 v Warwickshire, Edgbaston 1970
6 A. K. McTavish and B. R. Tod 190 v Ireland, Raeburn Place, Edinburgh 1936
7 J. D. Henderson and W. A. Edward 176 v Ireland, Perth 1950
8 J. D. Henderson and W. A. Edward 187 v Ireland, Titwood, Glasgow 1954
9 J. Kerr and W. L. Fraser 67 v Ireland, Raeburn Place, Edinburgh 1913
10 W. H. Thorburn and D. Chapel 86 v Ireland, Perth 1909

MOST WICKETS

In an innings 8–34 G. F. Goddard v Ireland, Greenock 1972
In a match 12–98 W. Nichol v Ireland, Glasgow 1948
In a season 26 R. W. Sievwright 1912
A. D. Baxter 1932
In a career 171 J. M. Allan 1953–1972

WICKET-KEEPING – MOST DISMISSALS

In an innings 7 J. Brown
In a match 9 A. Steele
In a season 17 A. Steele 1977
In a career 146 J. Brown 1953–1973

Wales

TONY LEWIS

Glamorgan County Cricket Club's belated entry into first-class cricket and its early struggles for survival, together with an almost total absence of Welsh cricket literature, rather belie the fact that the game was being played at Swansea in 1780, during the reign of George III. Regrettably even the finest achievements die if not recorded. But this was never to be, and any history of Welsh club cricket must of necessity lack the colour of early events and personalities.

Despite the early beginnings at Swansea, cricket was not a game of the people in the 18th or early 19th century. Its spread from the south of England was closely interwoven with the social history of the Principality, and in particular with the ideals of the Welsh landed gentry. This loosely-defined, landed class, despite the natural geographical obstacles to communication, looked to England for education, business, social and political contact, constantly mimicking the habits and pleasures of the corresponding classes over the border, and pressing on the long process of Anglicization. Cricket came along with these pleasures and spread downwards through the social strata. In the 19th century the country gentleman joined forces in county teams, not truly representative at first, for in an agricultural community only the landowners could possibly find time to play.

There was mention of the Monmouthshire team in 1823 and of their first official match on 10 August 1825. Breconshire first took the field in the same year, followed by Pembrokeshire in July 1830. Membership of such teams remained quite exclusive for some time – Montgomeryshire, who played first in September 1853, restricted membership to country gentlemen, while Carmarthenshire in 1860 specifically excluded tradesmen – but the pleasures of the summer game could not elude the working man for long. Both the ambitious squire, seeking political and social recognition in London, and the genuine cricket-loving gentleman, for different reasons, saw to it that his household could field a team to face any challenge, and that his patronage extended to the village where he allowed or encouraged wickets to be pitched on the green. The Army in those days was also a very effective propagator of the cricket skills.

The game by the 1840s was well in the hands of the common people. The Dolgellau CC was founded in 1841, and in 1846, in the south, Ynysygerwn and Maesteg Town formed the very clubs which exist and thrive to this day. By 1848 the Swansea Club had laid down an initial expenditure of £2,000 and transformed a sandbank in the bay into what was by 1900 the finest athletic ground in Wales or the west of England – St Helens. There were few players in rural areas as the wheels of Industrial Revolution were grinding throughout the south Welsh valleys, urban communities sprang up and quickly adopted cricket as their summer relaxation. In *The Cambrian*, on 23 June 1848, appeared an illuminating account of the way in which cricket had lured the working people. It reported that an early cricket club had been formed in Merthyr and that members, who numbered 26, fixed their practices to begin at 5·30 am on the mornings of Mondays and Fridays. Cardiff, Swansea, Cadoxton, Neath, Merthyr, Llanelli, Maesteg, Bridgend, Penarth and Newport were among the more active clubs, thus establishing the strong southern bias to the game in Wales.

Cricket has been played in North Wales for over a century, Bangor being the oldest club. Other leading clubs in the Principality are Treaddur Bay and Bodedern in Anglesey; Bangor and Llandudno in Caernarvonshire; Colwyn Bay, Wrexham, Bersham and Gresford in Denbighshire; St Asaph, Northop Hall and Shotton in Flintshire; Bala, Dolgellau and Towyn in Merionethshire; and Welshpool and Newtown in Montgomeryshire. Undoubtedly, the leading club in North Wales in postwar years has been Colwyn Bay, who during the years 1939 to 1945 raised £12,000 for charity and since the war have extended their ground, which was originally built by Wilfred Wooller's grandfather. Many of the world's greatest cricketers have played on the ground in the Festival. Another club which comes to mind is Conway, whose enthusiasm and hard work have produced a new ground in the centre of the borough, and the game there is now flourishing. Marchwiel Hall, where the McAlpine family had a private ground – and where A. J. McAlpine has been prominent in the game for so many years – has for a long time run a delightful cricket week. An abundance of personalities have made their marks on the northern game; ex-Rydalians include the Rev A. J. Costain, H. R. W. Butterworth, Alan Ratcliffe (who made 201 for Cambridge in the 1931 University Match), W. H. H. Sutcliffe and Wilfred Wooller. R. W. Barber learnt his various skills at Ruthin School, and R. H. Moore, the former Hampshire captain, came to North Wales in 1947 and led Colwyn Bay for some years.

However, it was in the south that the real pioneer work was done, and in 1881 a particularly ambitious fixture was organized. It was played on 20 August at Swansea between the Gentlemen and Players of South Wales. But despite lofty ideals the game was reported as follows:

> It must be admitted that cricket in South Wales is in a backward state and at the present time there is very little chance of any marked improvement taking place and the old adage 'that the nearer we get to London the better the cricket' has recently been verified.

This must have been a disappointing state of affairs for the patrons of the game, who allowed their land to be used by their dependants, for scarcely a club existed which did not depend on the goodwill of the landowner. The Marquess of Bute in Cardiff, Lord Windsor in St Fagans, the Earl of Jersey in Briton Ferry and Sir J. D. Llewellyn in Ynysygerwn, were among those who not only gave their permission for the game to be played on their land but even financed it.

There was no short cut to improvement and in the 1860s, as today, the students of the game must watch the best players in action, talk with them and play against the strongest opposition whenever possible. It was to meet these needs that the South Wales Club was formed in 1859 by Captain George Homfray. The club had an active membership of about 30 and a fixture list of some 5 or 6 matches.

Emrys Davies, one of the most respected figures in Welsh sport and the product of League cricket in the Llanelli-Port Talbot area. After long and distinguished service to Glamorgan he became a first-class umpire.

There were no great signs of activity, but there was a most significant feature in the club's annual tour to London which included contests against MCC at Lord's and the Gentlemen of Surrey at the Oval. In the early days of its existence the club was extremely 'cosmopolitan'. In 1868 Dr W. G. Grace came to Neath as a member of the United South of England XI and 'bagged a pair' or, as the record so delightfully puts it – 'He was "ciphered" by a professional named Howitt'. In 1864 he played for the South Wales Club. He was simply following the example of his brothers, Henry and 'E.M.', who had sought out a stronger local club side than West Gloucestershire. 'W.G.. turned out for the South Wales Club just before the age of 16, and in a match against the Gentlemen of Surrey at the Oval scored 5 and 38, as well as taking 5 for 86.

Unfortunately for Wales, but fortunately for Gloucestershire and England, the connexion of the Graces with the South Wales Club ceased after the season of 1865. The great Doctor in his book *Cricket* (1891) says of his Welsh team-mates:

> They gave me a bat, which I have today and I am very proud of. The handle and the blade are of one piece of wood: it was the only one to be had on the ground at the end of the innings; however, I value it for the reason that it marks the date of the beginning of my long scores.

After the loss of the Graces, the club lived a quiet life for the remainder of its days until 1888. Native talent was encouraged, however, and by the end of its days an array of Joneses, Lewises, Davieses, Morgans and Evanses was well prepared for the adventures of the Glamorgan County Cricket Club which was ushered in without fanfares in 1888.

From this point up to the beginning of the First World War the game flourished; more teams were formed, many of them engaging professionals from English clubs. Among the well-known professionals of the period were Arthur Webb of Hants, Howitt, Harry Creber, Silverlock, Tremlin of Essex, Briggs, Hirst, Bates, Trevor Preece, Holsinger, Hacker, Arundale, Baker, Bell, Stone and that redoubtable Derbyshire fast bowler, Billy Bestwick. These experienced players greatly improved the game in Wales, preparing better wickets and insisting that practice wickets should be as good as those on the square. The turn of the century witnessed a new trend in the form of competitive cricket. Cricket clubs, particularly those run by steelworks and coalmines, began to explore the possibilities of the league system. Welfare clubs set up by the steelworks between Port Talbot and Llanelli fielded two teams of ages up to 17 and 19 and formed the best-known and most successful league. Glamorgan were certain that the league would produce a rich reserve of talent and indeed Emrys Davies, Glamorgan's stalwart opening batsman, emerged out of such humble but highly competitive conditions. Smaller leagues were organized and – as characteristic of a religiously non-conformist nation – the Chapel teams and Chapel leagues were in evidence in every town.

The senior clubs had sat back carefully viewing the experiments of these younger clubs but after the war they returned to Wales unanimous in their support for the game and for the more competitive set-up. In 1921 was initiated the Glamorgan League, which suddenly, for no obvious reason, fell through. Yet it was felt that those concerned were working along the right lines. In 1926, after hard work in preparation by J. D. D. Davies of Neath and Huw Baxter of Swansea, the South Wales and Monmouthshire League was formed. The game became more highly organized, particular emphasis being placed on neutral umpires and prompt starts.

The players themselves aimed at higher standards and constantly looked to the examples of professionals – Emery, Butler, Gange, Nash, Chandler, Tuan James, W. D. Davies, Ryan, Tomlinson, Cyril Smart, Jim Jones, Spencer, Kingston, Pitchford, Powell, Reed, E. C. Jones and Creber, who continued to play for Swansea when he was well into his sixties. Thereafter, different leagues appeared and disappeared or have been adjusted to meet changing needs throughout Wales.

Most recently, the administrators of the 1970s sought a stronger identity for Wales by launching a national amateur cricket side which plays internationals v England, Ireland and Scotland, and by setting up governing bodies in order to qualify for government grant aid. The Welsh Schools Cricket Association established full international matches, too, at Senior and Junior levels. Senior League cricket thrives in all parts of Wales. The Welsh Cricket Conference and the Morgannwg League are quickly catching up in size and importance on the South Wales Cricket Association. For umpires, regular examinations take place in North and South.

Perhaps the most important happening in Welsh club cricket was the formation in 1969 of the Welsh Cricket Association. It was made in the likeness of the National Cricket Association at Lord's; it gave the game a central administration which qualified for government grant through the Sports Council for Wales. Affiliations to it came slowly but ten years later about 500 clubs and leagues had joined. A Mid-Wales Cricket Association was formed to link with the South and North. Welsh cricket was now at least more organized than ever before.

The South Wales League made history by playing a short tour of Australia in 1977–78 and in 1979 Wales itself was invited to take part in the ICC Trophy competition in which 15 of the minor cricket-playing countries battled out for the Trophy and places in the Prudential World Cup proper. Wales replaced Gibraltar who withdrew at the last moment, but because they did not hold individual membership of ICC, they were not permitted to progress in the competition. It was excellent experience and gave Welsh representative cricket prominence.

Finally, it ought to be pointed out that in spite of governmental reorganization of the counties involving changes of names, cricket was still played in the 1970s under the old associations, Pembrokeshire, Carmarthenshire, Merionethshire, Denbighshire and so on. The 1970s were certainly the years when new ideas were embraced, but neither were the traditions and hard struggles of the past easily forgotten.

The Services

The Defence Services

GROUP-CAPT W. R. FORD

By virtue of their seniority and tradition, when mention is made of Navy or Army cricket, sailors, soldiers and club cricketers tend to recall long-fought games between famous regiments, ships and corps – some played in strange and outlandish spots in the world – others played on well-known, well established grounds surrounded by tradition. On the other hand, airmen tend to dwell more on the part played by the RAF in the upward surge of interest in Service cricket in the latter part of the Second World War and the immediately following years.

In the 19th century, and even earlier, the Royal Navy were carrying out great missionary work as F. S. Ashley-Cooper makes clear in a chapter entitled 'A Girdle round the Earth' in his well-known work *Cricket Highways and Byways.* In fact the honour of the first reference to cricket outside England falls to the Royal Navy when a naval padre in HMS *Assistance* refers, in his diary, to the playing of 'Krickett' at Antioch in May 1676.

Cricket and the Army have long marched together. The Honourable Artillery Company, raised originally as a bodyguard of archers for Queen Elizabeth I, owned, and still owns, the famous cricket ground at Finsbury. The earliest match recorded there took place in 1731 but even then it was described as the 'old ground' so it is probable that cricket was played there by soldiers many years before. In 1803–04 officers of British regiments stationed in Sydney are reported to have introduced the game to Australia. In 1810 Crawford's 'Light Division' played cricket at Lisbon and in 1841 the Duke of Wellington issued an order that a cricket ground was to be made as an adjunct to every military barrack.

The Royal Air Force, the youngest Service arm, has had little time to develop 'grass roots' in station and squadron cricket – the airmen's equivalent of regimental cricket. Early RAF cricket was nurtured and developed mainly through the existence of RAF Halton and Uxbridge, both of which were fortunate to possess good cricket grounds and to be commanded by a series of dedicated and experienced cricketers.

The 1st official inter-service match took place between the Royal Navy and Army in 1908 at Lord's. Except for the war years these games have since been played every year; at Lord's until 1952; from 1953 until 1972 at either Lord's or a service station; and now in the form of a 3-day festival at a service station.

The RAF entered the lists in 1919 with a match against the Army at the Oval. The 2 services played again at the Oval in 1920 but the matches were then discontinued until 1928 at the request of the RAF, to allow them to build up the game within their service. The 1st RAF v Navy game was played in 1920 and this fixture has continued uninterrupted except for the war years ever since.

With their superiority in numbers and strong, well-established basis of regimental and corps cricket, the Army were the dominating force up until the Second World War. Royal Navy had their highspots from time to time, for example in 1914 the Royal Navy and Army match was selected as the 2nd match in MCC's Centenary Week celebrations at Lord's and the sailors enjoyed themselves to the full in beating the soldiers by 170 runs. They have, however, tended to take a rather detached view, or one might say adopted a nautical approach to the game, compared with the other two services, at least up until the Second World War. There is no doubt that the Royal Navy prided itself on its 'all-amateur' side (the Navy's team in 1942 was selected by the Sports Control Board through Admiralty Fleet Orders which resulted in a team with no wicket-keeper and a lot of unsophisticated bowlers).

During the Second World War, and immediately afterwards, cricket in the services started to become a rather more serious business. The RAF played a larger part in this development than either of the other 2 services. On 19 May 1941 they formed a War Emergency Cricket Committee as a small body of 'available and suitable representatives' to choose teams to represent the RAF against selected opponents. As a result a 1st match was played at Lord's on 2 June 1941 against the Rest of England which was lost, despite the strength of the RAF side, by 8 wickets in a one-day, 2 innings match.

The introduction of National Service affected Inter-Service cricket to a marked degree, especially RAF cricket as life in that service appeared to attract a very high proportion of young professionals. Undoubtedly this was to the advantage of cricket generally as it enabled some future county and England players to gain valuable experience (especially in 3-day cricket) during 2 vital years of their development. There was an additional bonus – this period, without doubt, enabled the services to develop their regulars at a higher level of cricket, to improve their fixture lists and to continue to occupy a niche in the world of cricket.

Since 1966 Inter-Service matches have been played on a limited-over basis, which has led to some exciting finishes. The adoption of the limited-over game has seen a change in each service's fixture list. Now each service plays the majority of its matches against county 2nd XIs, and within the context of the one-day game, has resulted in much keener fielding in particular. All 3 services still maintain fixtures against such sides as Incogniti, Free Foresters and Civil Service, but of necessity in a programme of some 14 or 15 matches many club fixtures have had to be dropped. After a period of Royal Navy and Royal Air Force domination with the introduction of the limited-over matches, the Army have since 1972 won 12 out of their 14 Inter-Services matches.

The Army playing the Australians on the Officers' Club ground at Aldershot in 1934.

The first 2 official matches for which the services produced a combined side were remarkable. In 1910 at Aldershot the Royal Navy and the Army in a 2-day game took on the combined strength of Oxford and Cambridge Universities and won convincingly against a very strong side by 6 wickets. The following year the match was extended to 3 days and played at Portsmouth. The services in a remarkably high-scoring game again triumphed by 6 wickets. Although there was agitation to move this match to Lord's, it failed to gain the favour of the authorities and was in fact dropped altogether, and it was not until 1920 that the next combined side was put into the field – a tri-service side for the first time – calling itself Navy, Army and RAF against a Gentlemen of England XI in a 2-day match played at Lord's.

The first time the Combined Services played a touring side was in 1921 against Armstrong's Australians at Portsmouth. The Australians won this match with minutes to spare, but if the wicket had not broken up in the last innings J. M. Gregory might not have been so effective. In 1924 the Combined Services took on the touring South Africans in a 3-day match at Portsmouth. Dismissing the South Africans for 182 (Capt T. O. Jameson 4 for 33) they ran up a total of 418, of which that great batsman G. J. Bryan scored 229, the highest score against the South Africans during the tour. However, the tourists came back with a 2nd innings of 420 (Jameson 7 for 152) and the Combined Services had to be content with a draw.

During the Second World War the only 2 Combined Services games in England recorded in *Wisden* were against the London Counties in 1942, which was lost by 3 wickets, and a drawn match against Northamptonshire in 1944.

In November 1944, an Inter-Services Cricket Committee was formed as a temporary body under the chairmanship of Major-General T. N. F. Wilson, with the following terms of reference:

(a) To co-ordinate Service matches under existing war conditions.
(b) To co-ordinate matters common to all Service sides.
(c) To legislate for Services cricket in the release period.

In November 1945, the name of this committee was changed to Combined Services Cricket Committee. It was established as a permanent body, still under the chairmanship of Major-General Wilson, and constituted one service authority with which the civilian cricket authorities could deal on matters of common interest. The Combined Services team was recognized as a major side for inclusion in fixtures against touring sides, and its matches were regarded as first-class when they fulfilled the normal conditions for such games.

The one constant Combined Services match since 1946, and still played at Lord's, has been that against the Public Schools (later the England Young Cricketers and presently the National Association of Young Cricketers). The other two standard Combined Services fixtures are against Oxford and Cambridge and these matches have usually been closely contested. The Combined Services' record against touring sides is disappointing and reads as follows:

v India	1946 drawn; 1952 lost
v South Africa	1947 lost; 1951 and 1960 both drawn
v New Zealand	1949 lost
v South African Fezela XI	1961 lost
v Australia	1953 lost
v Pakistan	1954 drawn
v Canadians	1954 drawn

The record against the counties is not an impressive one either, bearing in mind the fact that most counties often rested their best players. There is no doubt, however, that a great deal of latent talent is still available in the 3 services, but owing to lack of opportunities for practice it is not easily developed.

Over the years, the services have produced some wonderful cricketing characters and many very good cricketers who would hold their place in the highest company. The 'regulars' were, of course, augmented by significant numbers of 'hostilities only' servicemen in both wars who, in times of peace, regularly represented their counties and countries at the highest levels of the game.

Hampshire benefited greatly from Army players in the latter part of the 19th century, notably from R. M. Poore, who in 1899 averaged 91·23 for the county with a highest score of 304. In the same year he scored the winning goal for his regiment in the Inter-Regimental polo finals at Hurlingham; won the title 'Best Man at Arms in England' and scored 3 hundreds in succession for Hampshire – indeed a modern Corinthian.

J. G. Greig, also Army and Hampshire, got 1,000 runs in his first season (1901) in first-class cricket. E. G. Wynyard, whilst still serving, played in 3 Tests for England, captained the MCC side to New Zealand in 1906–07 and helped out the Secretariat at Lord's during the season.

During this period the Navy can cite Midshipman R. L. B. Cunliffe, who took 8 Army wickets in 1914 in the MCC's Centenary celebrations at Lord's, and subsequently played a prominent part in Navy cricket for many years; rugby internationals C. H. Abercrombie of Scotland and G. H. D. O. Lyon, the England full-back, were both hard hitting Naval batsmen, the latter a good bowler as well.

J. W. A. Stephenson, of the Army and Essex, came nearer to Test selection than any other modern Services cricketer.

In between the wars, Naval cricket was enriched by such characters as R. A. D. Brooks, Royal Marines, who captained the side most ably for many years and who subsequently became Governor of Victoria; R. J. Shaw, a most unorthodox opening bat; K. A. Sellar, who played for Sussex, was an England full-back and a fine front-foot player.

For the Army during these inter-war years, who can forget J. W. A. Stephenson (Essex) and C. W. C. Packe (Leicestershire) both of whom captained their counties, although the former had to retire to do so. Stephenson was probably the best bowler and perhaps also one of the greatest characters the Army has ever had. His 9 for 46 in the Gentlemen v Players match in 1936 was a memorable feat – he was unlucky not to tour Australia that winter with G. O. Allen's side.

Non-regular first-class Army players are legion – to name a few, A. C. Wilkinson, an Oxford blue of 1913, a good bat and an outstanding soldier in both World Wars; 'Buns' Cartwright; Fowler of Fowler's match fame; F. E. Hugonin and R. T. Stanyforth, wicket-keepers – the latter playing for England in 4 Test Matches against South Africa in 1927–28. The outstanding batsman of this period was R. E. H. Hudson, an England player if his military duties had permitted. He, along with C. P. Hamilton, a fellow 'gunner', were an Army opening partnership respected at all levels of the game.

For the RAF before 1939, mention must be made of R. E. G. Fulljames who took 12 Army wickets for 109 in the 1928 Inter-Service match; A. J. Holmes, later to captain Sussex and become a Test Selector; R. P. H. Utley (who became Father Utley of Ampleforth) and C. B. Cooke, both of them class seam bowlers; E. C. Hudleston (later Sir Edmund Hudleston, commander of Allied Air Forces Central Europe) and B. E. Baker (Sir Brian Baker, in later years to organize one of the longest cricket tours on record), both more than useful wicket-keepers; and lastly Sir Douglas Bader, an excellent all-round ball-games player whose later exploits in the Second World War achieved world-wide fame.

With the advent of National Service many more famous names in cricket today came into service cricket. No fewer than 26 'Test players to be' represented their respective services. The 'regulars' nevertheless were not outdone and there were many who fully held their own and maintained the essential nature of service cricket. Two outstanding service cricketers who played during their National Service period and for a number of years afterwards who must be mentioned were A. C. Shirreff (Cambridge, Hants and Kent), who captained the RAF in their 1st first-class match, against Worcestershire in 1946, and J. H. G. Deighton (Lancashire), a bowler of the highest class, who as captain of the 1964 Army side completed his 13th season of Army cricket, a record only equalled by A. C. Wilkinson.

The pattern for the future of representative service cricket seems to lie in the limited-over game against county 2nd XIs, with the Combined Services playing traditional 3-day matches with Oxford and Cambridge and a limited-over match against the Young Cricketers at Lord's. Such a pattern fits in with the present-day complexity and turbulence of service life. Nevertheless at regimental and unit level the dedicated service cricketer, with a bat and ball in his kit as priority items of equipment, will continue to play cricket at the 'drop of a hat'.

A. C. Shirreff, of Cambridge and Kent, did much for RAF and Combined Services cricket.

The Civil Service Cricket Association

SIR RICHARD HAYWARD

At the time of the foundation in 1922 there was a sprinkling of Civil Servants playing for the first-class counties. C. S. Hurst was one of them. He scored hundreds for Kent and was the 1st Secretary of the Association. Other county players in those early days included A. E. S. Rippon of Somerset, C. T. A. Wilkinson, captain of Surrey 1914 to 1920, and W. T. Cook, also of Surrey. One representative match was played in the 1st season.

Sir Richard Hayward, President of the Civil Service Cricket Association since 1966 and of the Association of Kent Cricket Clubs since 1970.

The Royal Navy were the opponents; Rippon scored 129 and the Civil Service won. The following season MCC and the Royal Air Force joined with the Royal Navy to complete the 3 representative matches played annually. After the Second World War, the Army replaced MCC as opponents; games with the Defence Services have continued as the highlights of the Association's activity.

For a brief period the Civil Service team played against some of the world's greatest cricketers. In 1926 they played the Australian touring side; in 1927 it was New Zealand and in 1929 the West Indies. In 1932 very welcome visitors came from South America. J. H. Evans, later Sir John and the Association's President for 10 years, shared a partnership of 140 runs with J. C. Heaslip.

Representative Civil Service cricket is different from what it was before the Second World War. There are no players from the County Championship to call on. The last was George Langdale who was capped for both Somerset and Derbyshire and also Norfolk and Berkshire. To meet the requirements of the Defence Services the two-day matches have been replaced by one-day matches played under limited-over conditions with restrictions on the number of overs allowed to any one bowler.

The Civil Service side has in recent years included many Minor County cricketers, some of whom have played in the Benson & Hedges and Gillette competitions. Scotland's national side has fielded one or two Service players. Many of the remaining representative players have played for the 2nd XIs of the first-class counties. All of them have played regularly in first-class club cricket, mainly in the major leagues.

In addition to the representative matches, the Association annually organizes a knockout competition for a shield donated in 1922 by Sir Noel Curtis-Bennett; it attracts an entry of about 60 teams drawn from various parts of the United Kingdom representing Government Departments or areas of the Civil Service Sports Council.

This brief account would be incomplete if it did not record that, quite apart from the Association's direct involvement in cricket, there are over 300 Civil Service teams playing cricket every week. The Association has been fortunate, as it approaches its Diamond Jubilee, in having officers of great dedication, two of whom have given quite exceptional service. A. R. Farlam spanned the 1930s and late 1940s and E. J. King recently completed 30 years in office.

CAPTAINS SINCE THE SECOND WORLD WAR

1946–48	J. C. Heaslip	1961–62	R. Sewell
1949–56	G. R. Langdale	1963–75	I. E. Moir
1956–57	L. H. Sixworth	1976–78	R. A. Bowles
1958	D. H. Cole	1979	R. N. Golds
1959–60	S. Smith		

Club Cricket

Resident Clubs

STEVE WHITING

If there is one institution that reaches out to every border in the vast world of cricket, if there is one arm of the game that embraces, or has at some time embraced, every player from the Test tyro to the most humble amateur, then that institution is the club game. From club cricket sprang the leagues. From club cricket sprang the counties – and their players. From club cricket sprang even the Tests – and their players too. With well over 2,000 clubs affiliated to the Club Cricket Conference in the South East of England alone, the half-day Saturday and Sunday game is so much the biggest single constituent of our sport that a complete survey of it would make *War and Peace* look like an 'O' Level essay.

Where would one start? Not by picking the best and strongest clubs, for the gods of cricket distribute their favours with such prodigality that even the entry of nearly all the major clubs into the various leagues has failed to establish any recognizable hierarchy. One of the joys of club cricket is that all players are free agents. They come and go as their jobs, their lives and their moods take them. Last year's champions can be this year's wooden spoonists – or the other way round. Dulwich continually propped up the Surrey Championship in the first years after its formation in 1968, yet won it in 1974, 1975 and 1976; while Mitcham were champions 4 times in the 1970s, yet also managed to finish bottom in the same decade.

In the 1920s and 1930s there were few stronger teams than ALEXANDRA PARK, whose fame spread far and wide along with the television signals that emanated from the mast that towered over their ground from the roof of nearby Alexandra Palace. Those were the days of L. W. Newman, who joined the club in 1923, and C. S. Davies, who arrived 2 years later. These two are said to have opened the Park's innings on 626 occasions without ever running each other out. Newman made over 80,000 runs, obtaining his 250th hundred in his 62nd year. Davies, with over 64,000 runs, including 126 hundreds, also took 5,000 wickets for the club. Eighty times they put on over 100 for the 1st wicket and 12 times they passed the 200 mark – with a highest stand of 276 against South Hampstead. Yet Davies is one of only 3 Park players ever to have figured in county cricket – and that was for Warwickshire in the 1930s. One has to wonder how many club players would have gone into the first-class game but for the paucity of the pay – until recent years, anyway. Alexandra Park may never see the like of those days again. If their ground, set in the midst of the old 'Frying Pan' – the 'Ally Pally' racecourse – is less likely than some to attract new players, they are not alone in their problem.

South of the river similar events were befalling MERTON, a club which either fathered or fostered England players like J. N. Crawford, L. B. Fishlock, P. I. Pocock and, of course, Sir John Berry Hobbs. Thirty years ago their meetings with Mitcham on The Green, where cricket has been played for more than 250 years, aroused a fanaticism among the local populace comparable in its intensity, if not in its size, only to Spurs v Arsenal or Liverpool v Everton.

Since then Merton have declined and MITCHAM, founder members of the Surrey Championship under captain Pat Batty, have gone from strength to strength as befits a club whose records date back to 1707 and which played a prominent part in the formation of Surrey County Cricket Club. C. H. Hoare, of Rugby and Oxford, the 1st Surrey captain, was a Mitcham man. So were Tom Richardson, Herbert Strudwick and Andrew Sandham, while young all-rounder David Smith is the club's latest contribution to the Oval. D. J. Halfyard and H. R. A. Kelleher also played on Mitcham's Green, where batsmen cross the road from the old 'Cricketers' pub when they go in and have the chance to end their misery under the wheels of a London Transport double-decker bus should they be so unlucky as to fall first ball. Yet none of them

The Southgate team which beat Bowdon at Lord's in the 1977 final of the National Club Championship. Back row: R. J. Hailey, R. J. Ashby, D. Douglas, A. Wyatt, R. G. Musson, N. B. Bishop (12th man) and C. S. Rowe; kneeling: P. Brown, M. C. Smethers, C. J. Payne (captain), R. L. Johns and M. T. Dunn.

will ever occupy the hearts of the old gentlemen around Mitcham Green in the same way as one Eaton Ohio Swaby, a West Indian fast bowler whose age is the subject of a 'D' notice but makes no secret of the fact that he took over 1,000 wickets for Mitcham before slipping down the road to Sutton a couple of years ago. His pace and accuracy, allied to the left-arm swing of D. A. Marriott, another West Indian, who played for both Surrey and Middlesex, was what made Mitcham *the* Surrey side of the 1970s.

So, if achievement is not to be the yardstick by which we judge the clubs, can we do it by age? If that alone were the criterion, would Hambledon be the all-time champions of England? If they were, then Mitcham would have to be right in there alongside them. Or are there clubs even older? Not every club can say, with the BLUEMANTLE'S CLUB, from Tunbridge Wells, that their records were unavailable since they were destroyed by militant suffragettes in April 1913. Or were the miscreants the first of cricket women's libbers? Would they have been placated if they had known that, some years later, Miss Molly Hide, captain of the England women's team, was to play regularly for Middleton, in Sussex, and that, in 1943, she was to be that club's leading catcher?

No such problems exist for LEWES PRIORY, the Sussex club founded in 1831 but boasting a history that surely makes them one of the oldest cricket establishments in the world. The 2nd earliest recorded match took place there in 1694, followed in 1730 by a game between the 2nd Duke of Richmond's XI and Sir William Gage's XI. The earliest roots of the Priory Cricket Club can be traced back as far as 1763 when the Gentlemen of Lewes played Uckfield and Ifield on Spital Hill (or Race Hill) for a considerable sum. All the earliest games were played on this hill which, some 6 centuries before, had been the scene of the bloodiest fighting in the Battle of Lewes in 1165. In 1793 Lewes played Brighton for a handsome silver cup and lost by 45 notches. In 1831 local brewer Mr J. Langford bought 10 acres of the grounds of Lewes Priory from the Earl of Chichester and that ground, or the 'Dripping Pan', as it became known, was the club's home for 135 years. The club moved to the Stanley Turner Ground, on the western edges of the town, in 1937 – a state of affairs spoiled only slightly in recent years by the building of the Lewes by-pass which has cut across one corner. Since 1938 two Lewes players have represented Sussex – Don Smith and Peter Laker, who is now cricket correspondent of the *Daily Mirror*.

While we are still in Sussex, the influence of the Duke of Richmond's family can be seen again in the history of CHICHESTER PRIORY Cricket Club who leased their ground from him on their formation in May 1851. The influence of England captains (both male and female) can be seen at MIDDLETON where Miss Hide was not the only leader of her country to appear. Colts cricket records at that club reveal the name of a promising young J. M. Brearley, while A. G. Doggart, the Cambridge Blue and father of another Middleton player, G. H. G. Doggart, of Cambridge, Sussex and England, also appeared. Then M. G. Griffith, son of S. C. ('Billy') Griffith, continued the Cambridge–Sussex connexion, as well as that between father and son. Middleton, indeed, has a remarkable record of father and son cricketers. Besides the Griffith and Doggart families, the Neligans, the Langmeads and the Brearleys all had Middleton connexions. Other prominent members whose sons played for the club were: M. A. Pugh, N. C. Fuente, J. Lock, G. Schneerson, J. O'Gorman, A. Gover, J. K. Mathews, P. C. Rushton, D. N. Moore and B. Lush, one of whose two cricketing sons, Peter, is now public relations manager of the Test and County Cricket Board.

Since the formation of the Sussex League, in 1971, a number of clubs, notably HORSHAM, HASTINGS, THREE BRIDGES, led by former Sussex bowler John Denman, and BRIGHTON AND HOVE, have held sway. The standard of the Sussex League, which has provided cricket at various times for Tony Greig (Brighton and Hove), John Edrich and John Snow (East Grinstead) and many other first-class players, is steadily improving. Yet club cricket in the county has a quality of comradeship and friendliness, even though allied to acceptable aggression, found in few other areas. And this is typified by one club, and one man. The club is the BRIGHTON BRUNSWICK Cricket Club and the man is H. A. ('Ossie') Osborne. The Brunswick are a midweek team who draw their players from all the top clubs in Sussex, and sometimes from even further afield. Formed in 1870, they once owned the Hove County Ground and still play their home matches there. Their annual tour to Devon, where they regularly play Exmouth, Exeter University, Exeter, Torquay, Paignton and the Devon Cricket Association, is the highlight of the many hundreds of tours that descend regularly on that western county. And none of it would have been possible without the efforts of 'Ossie' Osborne, an expatriate Londoner now living in Hove, who never allowed the loss of one eye in a childhood illness either to dampen his love of life or to curtail his career as a top-class amateur cricketer and footballer.

Chichester Priory CC: a remarkable group photographed in 1863 in front of the club refreshment room which is still in use. On the extreme *left* with hands clasped is the Rev C. H. Hutchinson, whose son Philip played for South Africa in their first 2 Test Matches against England. Next to him with one hand in his pocket is Harry Foster the father of the Worcestershire brothers. Smoking a pipe is Wyatt Gibbs who played for Sussex. Hatless next to him is Archibald Lewin Smith, a Cambridge rowing blue who later became Master of the Rolls and President of MCC. Seated with the cricket bat is Jimmy Dean and next to him James Lillywhite, who captained England in the first 2 Test Matches against Australia.

Many players in Devon have good reason to remember, look forward to, and be grateful for, the annual visits of Brighton Brunswick. One of them is Barry Matthews, captain of both TORQUAY, probably the leading club in Devon, and the county team that won the Minor Counties Championship in 1978. Torquay, founded in 1851, have come a long way since their early days as a country-house side, playing almost exclusively 2-day matches up to the outbreak of the First World War. They moved to their present ground almost on the sea front in 1925 and now field 5 teams, many of their players being holidaymakers who somehow cannot drag themselves home. Between the wars the outstanding cricketer for Torquay was G. S. Butler, of Marlborough and Wiltshire. He was captain for 25 years, both before and after the Second World War. In the early 1930s the club recruited a young player named G. M. Emmett, who went on to play for Devon, Gloucestershire and England. Emmett had 4 brothers, all of whom played for the club. Other prominent players before the last war were V. H. Riddell, the Cambridge wicket-keeper in 1926, and slow bowlers R. Hicks and F. S. Campling. Since the war, J. E. Dickinson, D. L. Haines, D. H. Cole, J. A. Bonner and D. Post have all given the club fine service. Torquay have also provided Devon with many other fine players including, apart from Matthews, G. Walen, Ray Tolchard (brother of Roger Tolchard), D. Traylor, H. Edwards, M. Goodrich, and V. Hosking.

Our trip to the West Country would not be complete without mention of the DEVON DUMPLINGS, a 350-member club formed by Col. J. H. Fellowes in 1902 at the suggestion of three undergraduates of Exeter College, Oxford. Many of the Devon team, both past and present, are Dumplings, though few have made more impact than R. G. Seldon, who led Devon for many years. In 1929, playing for the Dumplings against Somerset Stragglers, Seldon took all 10 wickets – 7 of them clean bowled – and made 100 not out. There were 3 Dumplings in the Devon side that beat Durham in the Challenge Match in 1978 to take the Minor Counties title for the 1st time. Most of the Dumplings' home fixtures are played at the Devon County

Devon Dumplings v Devon and Dorset Regiment at the County Ground, Exeter, 1961: Back row: Rev R. T. Venn (umpire), F. Davey, M. A. Sutton, R. G. Pitts, J. Avent, D. A. Gilchrist, A. H. Holladay, S. S. Rogers, A. R. Fyler, P. R. B. Freeland, A. L. McEntyre, G. M. Bennett, P. D. W. Daniel and W. A. Wood (umpire); middle row: C. W. Lowton, W. N. Hayes, P. B. E. Acland, G. N. B. Spencer, M. N. Ford (President DDCC), E. A. E. Tremlett, H. E. Garnham; front row: M. Hare, N. Cony, M. E. C. Drew and L. M. Taylor.

Ground at Pennsylvania, which is also the home of Exeter Cricket Club, founded in 1824 and therefore the 2nd oldest club in the county.

Further west and north we come to the cricket-loving area of Bristol, where few clubs fail to lay some sort of claim to an affiliation to Dr W. G. Grace. One such club is DOWNEND, who were founded in 1893 by the Vicar of Downend, the Rev J. W. Dann, who happened to be a brother-in-law of the great Doctor. In 1922 Mrs Dann, the Doctor's sister, opened the W. G. Grace Memorial Ground where the club still play.

The STAPLETON Club, just outside Bristol, claim Dr Grace as their captain back in 1867 at the precocious age of just 19. Many Gloucestershire players have appeared for Stapleton, the most recent being J. F. Crapp, C. A. Milton, D. R. Smith, who joined when he was 11 years old, and D. A. Allen, who arrived at the ripe old age of 12. In 1965 South African Mike Procter played for Stapleton while qualifying for Gloucestershire, heading both the batting and the bowling averages.

Only the KNOWLE club, the largest in the Bristol area, seem to have no connexions with Dr Grace, even though they predate him by a few years. Perhaps their most famous player was A. A. Lilley, the Warwickshire and England wicket-keeper at the turn of the century, who captained the club for 2 seasons on his retirement to the West Country.

Further west still, and across the Severn Bridge, League cricket in the shape of the semi-professional South Wales and Monmouthshire competition, has long vied with traditional clubs like Barry Athletic, Newport, Cardiff and Wilf Wooller's old team, St Fagans. CARDIFF, who have produced players like Jimmy Pleass, Peter Gatehouse, David Lewis and many others for Glamorgan, as well as Wales Rugby international Alun Priday, are probably the most consistent.

But the most English must surely be the SOUTH WALES HUNTS CC, whose membership is confined to landowners and subscribers and supporters of one of the foxhound packs in South Wales. I Zingari, Eton Ramblers, Harrow Wanderers, Downside Wanderers and the Welsh Brigade figure among the visitors to their RRW ground at Cwrt-y-Gollen.

Coming east again on our way back to London we pass Thames Valley clubs like HIGH WYCOMBE, who recently gave West Indian left hander Wilfred Slack to the Middlesex staff. Then come READING, where another West Indian, fast bowler Jeff Jones, played a large part in taking them to the final of the John Haig Trophy last summer, only to lose to Brian Close's Scarborough XI.

Go past DATCHET, who for 25 years were skippered by O. G. Battcock, a medium-paced bowler whose greatest claim to fame, apart from many years as a stalwart of Buckinghamshire, and more wickets taken than any club bowler of this century, was the ability to expel air from his lungs at the beginning of every run-up with a force that frightened batsmen and fielders alike, and you are back in London, which is really where it all started. There you find EALING, perhaps (after Hampstead north of the river and Beckenham south of it) the strongest of all clubs in the years before and after the Second World War. Their superb brick pavilion at Corfton Road was opened in 1900 by Dr Grace's London County side – perhaps to make up for the hundred he made against them a year earlier. In 1913 Gilbert Jessop scored 116 in 58 minutes for Ealing against The Wanderers and even earlier, in 1875, MCC were bowled out for 7 – still the lowest total in the history of that august body. Mention of those great names reminds one of the number of high class players who regularly grace club cricket – and many of them long before they have lost their full powers.

BECKENHAM, once turned out against their ancient rivals, BLACKHEATH (another club of great traditions) a team every member of which had played first-class cricket. Ronnie Bryan, a captain of Kent, was a wonderful servant of Beckenham, as were the Atkinson brothers of HAMPSTEAD, N.S.M. and B.G.W. But these were only two of a galaxy of fine Hampstead cricketers.

The selection of former ADDISCOMBE batsman Alan Butcher to play for England in the final Test against India at the Oval last summer meant he joined Raman Subba Row (Old Whitgiftians), Graeme Pollock (Sutton), Geoff Howarth and David Hookes (Dulwich), Roy Swetman (Banstead), Russell Endean (Malden Wanderers) and John Emburey (Honor Oak) amongst the Test players to have appeared in that league.

HONOR OAK is one of a cluster of south-east London clubs enjoying long associations with each other who in the interwar years produced several county players of distinction. Honor Oak had J. H. Lockton and W. T. Cook of Surrey, and FOREST HILL an admirable all-rounder, A. Jeacocke, also of Surrey, who made 8 first-class hundreds. Another Surrey cricketer, G. M. Reay, did good service for BEDDINGTON, for whom played more recently in their earlier years P. J. Loader (Surrey and England), A. Long (Surrey and Sussex) and the indestructible Dave Halfyard, who before reluctantly turning to umpiring assisted, over a long bowling career, Kent, Notts, Durham, Northumberland and Cornwall. A little farther afield SUTTON can boast a distinguished membership going back to 1861, since when they have played on their present ground in Cheam Road. D. J. Knight, of Surrey and England, was their most famous player, and E. J. Henderson and C. Thain are names never to be forgotten.

Honor Oak's near neighbours on Dulwich Common are STREATHAM HOLLINGTONIANS, until 1977 just plain Streatham. Has any club had a greater servant than Neville Miller, who revitalized Streatham in 1921 when he per-

R. T. Bryan, the middle one of the brotherhood who hailed from Beckenham and played for Kent. Ronnie Bryan captained both club and county and was an enthusiastic coach of the young – including Derek Underwood.

Tony Levick was captain of The Mote and is now the chairman of the club and honorary treasurer of Kent CCC.

suaded Streatham RFC to join them in buying a ground in Frant Road, where they stayed until 1977? Miller, who played for Surrey before the First World War, was captain of Streatham from 1908 to 1934. In that time he scored 36,182 runs at an average of 48 and took 1,518 wickets at 15 runs apiece in a career which lasted 42 years.

Over the border from Honor Oak we come into Kent – and the home of many more great clubs. SEVENOAKS VINE were formed as long ago as 1734. There is evidence in the *Grub Street Journal* of London playing Sevenoaks at Kennington Common in 1731. The historic Vine ground, situated in the centre of the town, was presented by the 3rd Duke of Dorset in 1773. The club captain in 1937, and after the succeeding war, was D. C. G. Raikes, the Oxford and Gloucestershire wicket-keeper. His successor behind the stumps was G. C. Downton, father of Paul Downton, the young Kent 'keeper who went with England to Pakistan and New Zealand in 1977–78.

Much younger, but no less distinguished, are THE MOTE, formed in 1857, who number amongst their postwar captains D. G. Clark, lately President of MCC, and Kent fast bowler D. M. Sayer.

Cricket has been played at Linton, home of the 1978 village knockout champions LINTON PARK, since Sir Horatio Mann patronized many great matches in the early years of the 18th century. Linton passed by marriage from the Manns to the Cornwallis family, whose present head, captain of Kent in the mid-1920s, recalls playing in the village side with his father and 3 brothers before the First World War. (Lord Cornwallis is, at the time of writing, 87). The backbone of Linton in those days was the Peach family, one of whom, Tom, the head keeper and kennel huntsman, was once backed for £10 to beat the great J. T. Hearne at single-wicket at Linton – and did so. Another Peach, Charlie, played for Kent, and Alan with much distinction in the 1920s for Surrey. Two grandsons of Tom Peach are among the mainstays of Linton today, and it was one of them, Nigel Thirkell, who had most to do with the victory over Toft, from Cheshire, in the village final.

Meanwhile the famous village green at MEOPHAM has ample claim to be one of the most ancient haunts of the game. At least it can claim that 'The Cricketers' Inn', which stands alongside the ground and was so named in 1735, is the oldest pub in the land with known cricketing connexions. At the time the inn was in the hands of the Romney family, one of whose number, Valentine Romney, was captain of Kent in the epic 1744 encounter with All England.

The BANK sides – Bank of England, Lloyds, Midland, Barclays and Private Banks, function on grounds both north and south of the River Thames. But only Essex sides function solely on the North. BRENTWOOD, founded in 1881, have produced two distinguished Essex cricketers in J. A. Cutmore and M. J. Bear. BUCKHURST HILL, started in 1864, have brought on W. T. Greensmith, A. W. Durley, L. Savill and S. Turner since the war, as well as Jack Bailey, currently secretary of MCC. Trevor Bailey is a regular stalwart for WESTCLIFF while their neighbours, LEIGH-ON-SEA, are skippered by former Essex player K. W. Wallace, who is a former captain of the county 2nd XI.

Few Essex clubs, however, can match the output of ILFORD, whose 1st Test player was Sussex bowler Ian Thomson, who played 5 times against South Africa in 1964, followed by current Test stars Graham Gooch and John Lever. LOUGHTON, who won the Trumans Essex League in 1970 and celebrated their centenary in 1979, have really had 2 vintage spells. The first came in 1895 when one John Blows took 115 wickets at a cost of only 4·78 each, and the second was in 1924 when J. W. Marston accounted for 150 batsmen at an average of 8·36.

So that is how it has been for the best part of 250 years. Club cricket has been played for many reasons – but always for enjoyment – as in the case of the HOME PARK club in Windsor, who once made it a rule that they had to run every time the ball was played to a fielder with a beard. All went well until they played a team made up of artists from Chelsea!

But I merely ask you at this time to spare a thought for four Surrey clubs whose long and chequered histories count for nought as they seek fresh fields to conquer. OATLANDS PARK, ESHER, and WIMBLEDON, under their captain Chris Brown, son of Freddie Brown, will be conducting their first campaigns after being elected to the Surrey Championship. And FARNHAM, who will be filling one of the places vacated by them in the Surrey Cricketers' League, may yet look back longingly to the days long gone when 'Silver Billy' Beldham and Surrey batsman Julius Caesar performed miracles under the shadow of the castle.

Wandering Clubs

E. W. SWANTON

The wide and diverse array of wandering clubs is an army that no man can number, for they neither acknowledge nor need any formal affiliation either to any other body or to one another. In each case the genesis is the same: a few kindred spirits meet and decide that they would like to band together to play cricket. From a common beginning the resultant clubs have taken widely different forms. Some have become large and prestigious, others purposely restricted to a limited company of friends. Some such clubs, once the playing days of the originators come to an end, quietly fade away. All in some degree are selective, the ambition being to form a happy, homogeneous whole.

From the days of the earliest wandering clubs in the middle of the last century they have always fulfilled a useful and often a very valuable part in the body politic of cricket. The older of the peripatetic clubs set high standards both in the quality and the manner of their playing the game, and accordingly were much sought after to provide opposition to schools and university teams (and in the case of the Free Foresters the University XIs themselves), and Service sides, and clubs with grounds of their own, especially those whose fixtures included a home Week. In the heyday of country-house cricket (*qv*) wandering clubs found a congenial, not to say luxurious habitat. Many gave a stimulus to the game by touring, both at home and abroad.

They provided an outlet to Service cricketers, undergraduates, schoolmasters and many others who were either unable or unwilling to tie themselves down to regular appearance for a single club; also to old blues

Farnham, Surrey, CC where 'Silver Billy' Beldham played all but 200 years ago. The club is a prosperous one today.

Yellowhammers Jubilee: at Heathfield Park in 1969 the Yellowhammers, supported by several older members, played a match in celebration of their 1st on the same ground 60 years earlier. Back row: A. P. B. Roberts, E. St J. Brice, R. S. Franks, P. Pettman, A. C. Burnett, R. F. Eliot, A. Murray, J. Farrar, C. Murray and M. W. Smith; sitting: C. Marzetti, A. L. Hilder, W. C. W. Brice (President), C. H. Knott, F. H. Knott; on ground: R. M. K. Gracey, S. F. Hills, R. M. H. Marriott and P. M. Robinson.

and other first-class cricketers when unavailable or unrequired for their counties. In general one might say that the wandering clubs have tended to keep old friends in touch both with the game and with one another and so contributed in a distinctive way to the fellowship of cricket.

The oldest of the wandering clubs is I ZINGARI, which originated on 5 July 1845 when W. P. Bolland took a side to Harrow. Dining together in London afterwards several of those who had taken part decided to form a club. At that time all clubs employed professional bowlers. The founders of IZ however (J. L. Baldwin, Sir Spencer Ponsonby-Fane and the Hon F. Ponsonby, afterwards Lord Bessborough) decided that they would not do so, and therefore at a stroke brought the game into better balance by encouraging amateur bowling. The 20 friends whom they invited to join I Zingari – the name, by the way, which has puzzled many generations, is merely The Gypsies in Italian – included several keen amateur actors who already took part in the theatricals which formed a central part in the institution started in 1842 which soon became famous as the Canterbury Week. Hence derived the Old Stagers, the oldest amateur theatrical company in the world, just as Canterbury is the forerunner of all Cricket Weeks. A play or plays by the Old Stagers has been performed during Canterbury Week for more than 130 years, those of war excluded, and during it the OS wear the ancient colours of black, red and gold. They symbolized when IZ was formed an ascent 'out of darkness, through fire, into light', the correct thing being therefore for members to wear the gold uppermost.

The active membership of IZ has always been small and the fixture-list accordingly confined to about 30 days' cricket. The sides are generally young, and it is no longer safe, as R. L. Arrowsmith, the custodian of the records, has remarked, to obey the old dictum: 'I always run on principle to anyone wearing an IZ cap.'

Partly through custom perhaps, partly for reasons of geography and climate, the wandering club idea has not caught on widely overseas, but an offshoot, IZ AUSTRALIA, flourishes there, playing mostly at Camden Park, a private estate some 60 miles from Sydney, and providing what is a rarity in Australia, keen but non-competitive cricket. There is also a branch of Incogniti fulfilling a similar function in Western Australia.

Dealing first with what may be termed the 'open' wandering clubs with no special affiliations, next in seniority would seem to be the FREE FORESTERS, which originated in the Forest of Arden and was in the first place confined to members drawn from the midland counties. The colours of crimson, green and white were adopted, combined with a badge consisting of a loosely-tied Hastings knot and a motto, 'United though Untied'. This indicated that members might play against the club, unlike those of IZ, whose rule on this matter was only recently suspended. From their foundation in 1856 the Foresters soon became a largish club undertaking a correspondingly ambitious fixture-list including first-class matches against Oxford and Cambridge and a variety of tours, at home and abroad. Despite the competing claims of league cricket FF still fulfil 100 days' cricket a year, the officers of the club forming a body of 20 headed by the President, Gen Sir Reginald Hewetson.

Six years junior to the Foresters came INCOGNITI – unknown only to the unknown. They, too, have a wide membership and 125 annual fixtures including schools such as Dulwich, Highgate and St Paul's, and among clubs Beckenham, Wimbledon and Oatlands Park, all first played more than a century ago. The 'Incog' colours of purple, yellow and black have flown as far afield as USA (three times), Canada, Germany, Holland and Denmark. Their links with the Services are particularly strong and tours a speciality. One name must be mentioned in this brief note, that of Oliver Battcock, an Incog legend who played every season from 1927 until his death in 1970, with career figures for the club alone – he was also the patriarch of Datchet – of 2,204 wickets at 13 runs each. As the President, Brig W. M. E. White, remarks, he was a splendid bowler – the best the writer ever played outside the ranks of first-class cricketers, and the superior of many of them.

Another club safely past its centenary is the NONDESCRIPTS, who with a strong Hampstead and north London flavour have always restricted their playing membership to 75. For countless years their colours of dark blue and claret stripes divided by a narrow stripe of pink, along with the mascot of a wooden image of a pelican, have been seen on the Devon tour. When R. D. Crump presided at the centenary dinner he did so with the impeccable credentials of having served as secretary 50 years before.

Between the beginning of the century and the First World War were founded at least 3 more itinerant clubs still to the fore, the FROGS (1903), YELLOWHAMMERS (1909) and CRYPTICS (1910). Faithful service, as always, is the hallmark of them all. Edgar Tregoning, founder of the Frogs, served 53 years until his death while Sir Ronald Prain has recently handed over to his son, Graham, after more than 50 years of work. The President, David Fasken, a blue of the early 1950s, still plays in a few at least of the club's 30 matches. The Yellowhammers were founded by Leonard Marzetti when a Tonbridge boy for the benefit of a few school friends. The Tonbridge influence is still strong, with W. C. W. Brice as president and several of the *Cricketer* Cup team as regular players, but the field has widened though membership still seeks only to fulfil a smallish fixture-list. Between the

Cryptics in Portugal when the new Sports Club was opened in Oporto in 1968. Back row: E. Tinkler, A. G. Cochrane, A. H. Lycett, E. E. Greenhalgh; sitting: O. J. Wait, R. B. Hadlee, E. F. Jarrett, J. O. E. Steele, H. J. Fawcus, J. P. Haynes, G. J. Allen and P. N. G. Mountford.

Henry Grierson, founder of the Forty Club, which now has a world-wide membership of 3500. His was the idea and he its focal point and inspiration.

wars C. H. Knott and A. L. Hilder were probably the two best cricketers to play regularly for any club, but the Yellowhammers have usually fielded strong sides well sprinkled with county players.

The CRYPTICS have always been a focus for schoolmasters. In 1910 they were founded at Oxford by a future one, J. G. Fawcus, whose son has followed him successively as secretary and now president. There are a thousand Cryptics, active and otherwise, so that when the Jubilee was celebrated in style at Oxford under C. B. Blackshaw's presidency and inspiration there was no difficulty in finding 7 Cryptic sides to compete simultaneously against 7 long-standing opponents. Southern, Northern and Scottish tours during the summer holidays conclude the Cryptics' season.

Among the wandering clubs of postwar origin are the BUCCANEERS, who since 1930 have been very largely beholden to their founder, Geoffrey Moore. He has been their secretary and father-figure from that day to this. Mr Moore makes no secret of his antipathy to league cricket and successfully guides a still-thriving club almost as an article of faith. Qualification is by invitation, and the title is reinforced by a tie of scimitars to encourage its wearers to adopt a swashbuckling air at the crease. Contemporary in foundation are the ROMANY whose beginning was unusual in that they were founded by the then *Daily Telegraph* cricket correspondent, Col Philip Trevor at the ripe age of 66. Born at a time when Sunday cricket was less prevalent than it afterwards became, the Romany multiplied exceedingly and soon could turn out something near a first-class side. Their present virility is attested by tours at 5-year intervals to South Africa and even one as far afield as Sri Lanka.

Having founded the ARABS, in 1935, the writer is the last man to evaluate their qualities. A taste for touring before the war (our initial flight to Jersey was the first by a cricket team as such) was followed after the war by expeditions to the Rhine Army and BAFO in Germany, to Yorkshire and Lancashire, to Kent and Sussex (which forms the present annual tour), and 3 ambitious ventures overseas, 2 to Barbados and the last in January 1980 to Kenya. Mark Faber heads a strong dark blue element among the present players, among whose predecessors have been such distinguished cricketers as G. O. Allen, H. T. Bartlett, Ian Peebles, J. M. Brocklebank, Colin Ingleby-Mackenzie, Tony Lewis and the legendary R. C. Robertson-Glasgow.

Last in the field, among the better-known, and very far from least is the FORTY CLUB, which was founded in 1936 by a ripe sportsman of singular character and charm, Henry Grierson, with the object of bringing amateur and professional cricketers together when county days were done. With 3,500 members spread all over the world the Forty has far exceeded its first intention though a long programme of matches is undertaken. Its annual dinners, which have drawn upwards of 1,000 when the club's Patron, the Duke of Edinburgh, attends, are famous occasions usually marked by a high standard of speaking. The Presidents have included Sir Pelham Warner, Sir Jack Hobbs, G. O. Allen and Herbert Sutcliffe: the whole institution is a memorial to a sporting character straight from the Golden Age.

The wandering clubs so far mentioned – a selection only, need it be said, from among many more – were formed without any binding connexion. With those which follow, unfortunately at even briefer length, it is otherwise. There are, for instance, LORDS AND COMMONS which, while never encumbered with a formal club, have played together, men of all ranks and political shades, since 1850. The late Lord Ebbisham was a vigorous figure for many years in parliamentary cricket circles, and the scorebooks are alive with such distinguished names as Dunglass (now Home), Harris, Jackson, Eckersley, Crawley, Wakefield and others. In the nature of things most games are played within reasonable nearness to Big Ben.

It is not a bit surprising that the close affinity between cricket and the arts is reflected on the field. There used indeed to be two clubs of which it was said that the THESPIDS consisted of cricketers trying to be actors, the STAGE of actors trying to be cricketers. The Thespids of happy memory are no more, but the Stage, founded in 1930, continues to flourish, having gravitated for a quarter of a century around the ample form of Garry Marsh. 'Rotund, amiable, shrewd – not always up to the intricacies of cricket tactics but shrewd in his handling of some of the team's younger members who were not exactly afraid to display their histrionic talents on the field – he had an easy charm and a generous nature.' What captain could hope for a better testimonial than this little cameo by Gavin Doyle?

The oldest of the many county wandering clubs is the BAND OF BROTHERS who since 1858 have fortified Kent cricket and, from its inception 12 years later, the Kent CCC in particular. BB, as it is usually called, has one unique feature. It has always accepted social as well as cricketing members, and this element of men of distinction resident in the county has given it a special status and influence. The title, by the way, derives not from Shakespeare's *Henry V* but from the resemblance being jokingly remarked on between a photograph of the original Brethren and the Christy Minstrels who had a famous song called 'The Band of Brothers'.

As one proceeds clockwise round the coast one finds in uninterrupted progression the MARTLETS of Sussex, the HOGS of Hampshire, the RANGERS of Dorset, and the DUMPLINGS of Devon, all with reputations for good cricket and ample hospitality to the procession of touring sides which drift their way in the summer months. Turning north there come the SOMERSET STRAGGLERS, the GLOUCESTERSHIRE GYPSIES, followed by several old-established ones with the once-innocent label of GENTLEMEN: those of Worcestershire, for instance, and Shropshire, Leicestershire, Lincolnshire, and Cheshire, not to say Yorkshire itself. The activities and ambitions of these and other county-oriented clubs naturally vary greatly, but it would be fair to say that all have had a stimulating effect on cricket in their own locality, and in the early, struggling days especially their members stood by the county clubs both in financial terms and in services rendered.

Lastly come the wandering clubs connected with Oxford and Cambridge and those many Old Boy clubs deriving from the public schools. Everyone knows of the Oxford HARLEQUINS because of their cap of dark blue, maroon and buff, surely the most distinctive in cricket and many would say the prettiest. The most active days of the Harlequins, as of

Lords and Commons at Westminster School, 1976: John Farr, MP, Robert Hicks, MP, Neil Macfarlane, MP, Nicholas Scott, MP, John Watkinson, MP, Sir Charles Mott-Radclyffe and Geoffrey Pattie, MP.

their Cambridge counterparts, the QUIDNUNCS – each confined to blues or those who came close – lie in the past, but both in recent years have shown signs that they are keen to keep alive their ancient and honourable names. The OXFORD AUTHENTICS and CAMBRIDGE CRUSADERS likewise are still active though they can no longer recruit undergraduates of acceptable quality in the old numbers – this for reasons of college selection beyond the scope of this book.

ETON RAMBLERS are both the senior old boy club by foundation and, with 70 days' cricket a year and 1,400 members, also the most active. Ladies are said to have assisted, at their inception in 1862, in the choice of their beautiful, though complicated colours of magenta, violet and green, with gold lines. The qualification for membership has always been keenness rather than a high degree of skill – otherwise 150 Ramblers could hardly take the field, as they do, each season. As Sir John Hogg, his successor in office writes: 'No record of the club would be complete without a mention of the late President, G. H. M. ("Buns") Cartwright, who served the club both on and off the field, with devotion, with assiduity, with humour, and occasionally with acerbity, as honorary secretary from 1919 to 1954, and as President from 1954 until his death in 1976.'

The BUTTERFLIES, originally confined to old Rugbeians, also dates from 1862. It soon opened its doors to men from Eton, Charterhouse, Harrow, Winchester and Westminster. Out of a membership of 4,000 there are, or have been, 37 England cricketers, while 450 Butterflies have played first-class cricket. Twenty have been MCC Presidents. More even than most, presumably, the Butterflies need to recruit good match-managers since on the face of it the loyalty of their members must be divided.

UPPINGHAM ROVERS, begun only a year later, is unique among old boy clubs in that it is highly selective, a 1st XI colour being by no means a passport. They have a long and distinguished history which is attested by the many heavy and carefully compiled record books which accompany them to every match.

HARROW WANDERERS by contrast are inclusive rather than exclusive and with a long fixture-list to match. Yet they once took the field, wonderful to relate, with 7 who had played for the Gentlemen at Lord's. More important, the Wanderers have for many years ensured good coaching for the school by generous financial help. As might be expected OLD WYKEHAMISTS were another school early in the field (1874), the membership almost confined to former members of the XI, quaintly known as Lord's because until 1855 they played there. Their recent doings, like those of such other sides of high repute,

G. H. M. ('Buns') Cartwright served Eton Ramblers first as honorary Secretary then as President for nearly 60 years.

REPTONIANS, MALVERNIANS, RUGBY METEORS, CHARTERHOUSE FRIARS, OUNDLE ROVERS, and, especially, TONBRIDGIANS may be found in the article on the *Cricketer* Cup. The list, need it be said, is very far from being exhausted, but this perhaps is as good a final note as any to end on.

League Cricket

We present the League Cricket of the North and Midlands in two parts: the first, by John Kay, taking events to 1964 and the second, bringing the story up to date, by M. H. Stevenson. When reading this shortened version of Mr Kay's very thorough coverage up to that point it should be borne in mind that a few details have changed: some clubs, for instance, have since switched from one league to another; 'now' and 'today' mean 1964. Mr Stevenson follows with a thorough picture – and a generally encouraging one – of the happenings of the last 15 years and the prospect for the future.

Frank Dolman contributes an article on the recent arrival of League Cricket in the South.

The North and Midlands: The Story to 1964

JOHN KAY

League cricket is an essential part of our summer game. It has long been a feature of the sports calendar in the north of England, in the Midlands and in Wales. Throughout the counties of Yorkshire, Lancashire, Warwickshire, Worcestershire and Staffordshire the leagues have been responsible for the training and encouragement of many eminent county cricketers.

There are two major differences between league cricket and club cricket. Leagues encourage professionalism. Some leagues allow it to become a dominant feature; others prefer a modest scale of paid help. Many leagues are all-amateur but they flavour their sport with competitive interest. Spectator appeal is part and parcel of league cricket and with it is the necessity to award points and trophies. The club cricketer plays primarily for his own enjoyment but his league counterpart is always conscious of the crowd element.

I am sure that at the turn of the century when professionalism in league cricket first became fashionable the main purpose was to employ experienced players to pass on their knowledge and skill to the younger generation. In brief the professional's main duty was to organize and encourage net practice; prepare worthwhile pitches; and generally serve the club to the best of his ability. At one stage 2 professionals were permissible and in Yorkshire the Bradford League permits 4 professionals in each side. But paid assistance is optional and not compulsory as in the major Lancashire leagues. The ideal league professionals were retired county cricketers; men of proven ability and reputation who could please the crowds by their prowess as well as coaching efficiently at the club nets. This kind of professionalism was undoubtedly good for the game. It did not handicap the amateur because it was an accepted principle that the professional batted and bowled only when it was absolutely necessary. Those were the happy, carefree days of league cricket when individual performances counted for less than team triumphs.

There followed, in the early 1920s, a demand for more and more high-quality professionals and although the Bradford League quickly realized inflation was in the air, the warning was ignored in Lancashire and a feverish race began to procure the best possible players. Barnes was wooed from the first-class game and Parkin left Lancashire to dazzle the Central Lancashire League crowds at Rochdale. Nelson brought McDonald back to England after he had thrilled the country with his superb performances under Warwick Armstrong's Australians. The cotton trade was booming and wealthy mill-owners were prepared to subsidize the engagement of the big-name players. The professional became a star instead of a club servant and soon the search for new men spread wider overseas. The West Indies toured England and such great cricketers as Constantine, Headley, Martindale and Achong became the natural target for the Lancashire league clubs. They proved exciting and attractive entertainers in the cotton towns and villages where rivalry was keen and competition fierce.

Rivalry between the leagues and the teams became keener than ever but few realized that in commercializing league cricket they were destroying something precious in sport. Bigger crowds brought increasing responsibility to players and officials. The amateur who failed felt the excessive criticism of the crowd. The professional who failed became the target of disgruntled spectators. A losing team saw its support dwindle. It was easy to travel a few miles to watch a winning team. Enterprise was carried too far and good cricket was not enough. It had to be winning cricket and the search for professionals intensified. The Second World War halted the race, but once Hitler had been beaten the league clubs of Lancashire turned again to the overseas stars.

Great players of the calibre of Lindwall, McCool and Dooland of Australia, Worrell, Walcott, Weekes and Ramadhin of the West Indies, vied with Mankad, Hazare and Gupte of India and Reid of New Zealand. The glamour of big names and spectacular performances by first-class cricketers playing out of their class tended to blind the Saturday-afternoon watchers to the real purpose of cricket – a balanced struggle between bat and ball. Teams became known more for the prowess of their professional than for the all-round ability of the side but in Lancashire the danger was ignored. Yorkshire had long since forsaken professionalism on a big scale. In the Midlands the Birmingham League tried it but soon discarded it and in the Staffordshire League the accent still remained on amateurism. A gradual falling-off in crowd support was at first attributed to indifferent weather but the sporting public were plainly becoming more and more selective. It was easier to travel and the 5-day week gave families a chance to have two days together. Saturday joined Sunday as a day without work and the family car became more important than ever. Yet take away professionalism and league cricket becomes club cricket played for points and Championship honours. By a strange twist of circumstance the coming of amateur leagues to the south has made the club game throughout the country more akin.

LANCASHIRE AND CHESHIRE

Lancashire and Cheshire boast the biggest league cricket concentration in the country and in the admirable handbook of the Lancashire Cricket Federation over 30 different leagues and associations are listed. The body was formed in 1947 to advise upon and debate the various problems that are always cropping up in cricket. In its short space of life the Federation has already done much to smooth out the rough patches that come to all sporting bodies. One of their biggest successes was in fighting the famous 'six hit' case on behalf of the Cheetham Cricket Club who were sued by an elderly lady struck by a cricket ball while standing outside her house adjoining the club ground. With the help of the National Club Cricket Association, with which the Federation was associated, and with legal advice from redoubtable sources, the case was presented to the House of Lords where the judgment given in the Court of Appeal was overruled and a precedent established for future mishaps of a similar nature.

Pride of place in any 'catalogue' of the various leagues in the country must be awarded to the world-famous Lancashire League, founded in 1890. Of the 14 clubs now in membership, 13 were founder members, and Rishton were only admitted less than a month after the formation. The 14 clubs are: Accrington, Bacup, Burnley, Church, Colne, East Lancs, Enfield, Haslingden, Lowerhouse, Nelson, Ramsbottom, Rawtenstall, Rishton and Todmorden. They represent a 20-square-mile radius of east Lancashire centred on the big industrial towns of Blackburn, Accrington and Burnley and inspiring a degree of local partisanship that has to be experienced to be believed. It is this very spirit of local rivalry that makes league cricket the game it is.

Keenness has always been a cherished league tradition, but the League has been fortunate in the selection of its officials and the clubs wise in their nomination of 2 representatives who form the governing body along with a president, chairman, honorary secretary and honorary treasurer. This League Committee meets monthly, with headquarters in Accrington, and matters of emergency are dealt with by a small Executive Committee consisting mainly of leading officials and long-serving club representatives. Its rules have been drawn up and revised with the one aim of fair play for all and, although there have been occasions when bitterness has crept into debate and majority decisions have been unpopular, the conduct of the League is a model for all cricketing bodies to emulate. The League is strict in its application of all rules, including its amateur qualification rules which call for 3 essentials: birth, residence or business, and there is no short-cut to these aims.

The success or failure of a club financially is governed first by membership; secondly by gate receipts; and finally by outside efforts which down the years have varied between the old-fashioned bazaar and barn dance to bingo and football pools. The winter is by no means a close season for officials. Often it is the time when finance counts most and balancing the annual budget of a Lancashire League club calls for considerable skill and determination. At one time clubs were permitted 2 professionals but for most of the present century the rule has been for one paid player per club. Collections for amateurs are permissible and so are talent-money awards for performances of merit.

Overseas professionals who can claim club and League records include R. B. Simpson, the Australian batsman, who hit 1,444 runs for Accrington in 1959 and had a remarkable run of 11 successive half-centuries; C. G. Pepper, the Australian all-rounder, who is one of only 2 players to hit 1,000 runs and capture 100 wickets in a season; J. M. Blanckenberg, of South Africa, hit 949 runs for East Lancashire in 1929, but by far the most prolific scorers have been the West Indians led by L. N. Constantine at Nelson in the 1930s.

The 1,000 runs (precisely) he hit in 1933 constitute a Nelson club record. In later years other West Indians in Weekes, Walcott, Hunte, Nurse and Butcher have all established themselves as prolific scorers in Saturday-afternoon cricket. Likewise in the bowling records one finds few to compare with the devastating Gilchrist and Hall who, in recent seasons, carried first Bacup and then Accrington to championship successes: and the feats of Griffith for Burnley in 1964, when he broke all records by capturing 144 wickets and ensuring his club the championship with a highest-ever total of 70 points, will surely become legend.

The Central Lancashire League was formed in 1892 under the title of the South-East Lancashire Cricket League; it was approved by 9 founder members at a meeting in Rochdale which has remained the headquarters of the League ever since. The first President of the League was the Rev J. R. Napier, vicar of Walsden, who had previously played with Marlborough and Lancashire. The 9 founder club members were: Heywood, Littleborough, Milnrow, Oldham, Radcliffe, Royton, Walsden, Bury and Todmorden. Darwen, Dukinfield, Glossop, Longsight, Moorside and Stalybridge were also quickly enrolled but left for other spheres at various times. Rochdale came into the League in 1893, Middleton in 1895 and Crompton in 1896, and in the 20th century Werneth, Walsden and Castleton Moor threw in their lot as did Ashton in 1928 after a brief 'innings' a few years earlier. In 1937 the

Eric Windle and Learie Constantine open the innings for Nelson in a Lancashire League match in the boom days of League cricket when it was every young batsman's dream to open alongside the immortal West Indian all-rounder.

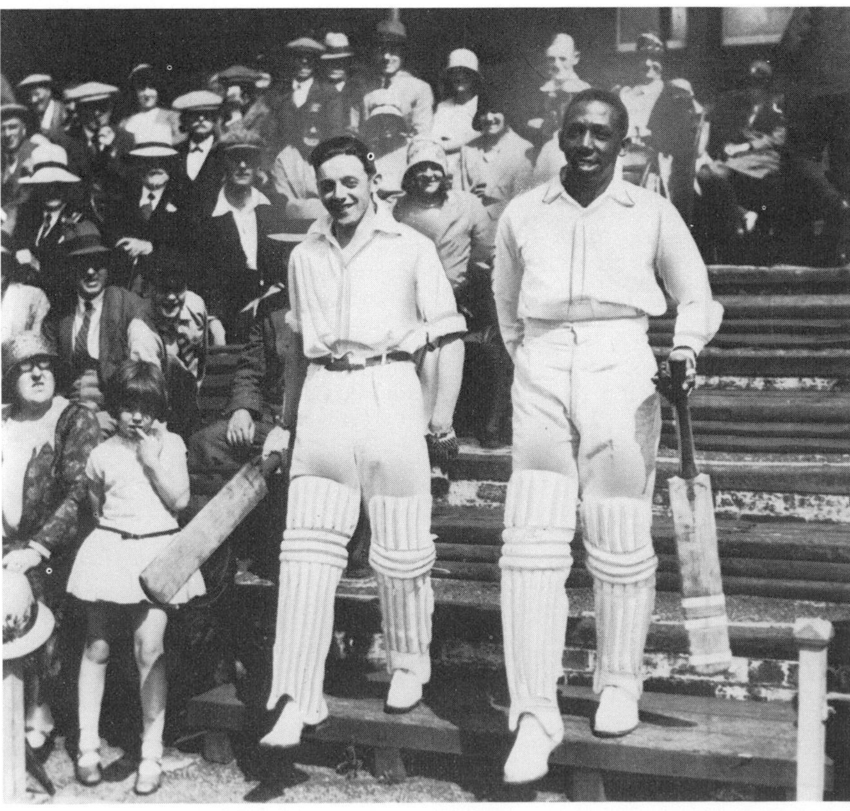

Sydney Barnes has a League cricket record never to be surpassed in the Lancashire, Central Lancashire and Staffordshire Leagues – he was undoubtedly the best League bowler of all time.

League brought its complement up to the present 14 clubs by permitting the re-entry of Radcliffe and the debut of Stockport.

Professionalism has always been a prominent feature of the League and at one time each club was permitted 2 paid players. The present trend is for one professional and there have been repeated attempts to make the signing of such players optional instead of compulsory. Terms are generally more modest than in the Lancashire League but many famous players played in the CLL and the League has also provided young professionals for the county. It has sent, in recent times, M. J. Hilton, J. B. Statham, P. Marner, J. Dyson, G. Clayton, G. Pullar and J. D. Bond to Old Trafford where they have won Lancashire, and in some cases, England caps. In addition K. V. Andrew and F. H. Tyson went to Northamptonshire and J. Hilton and J. G. Lomax migrated from Old Trafford to Somerset. It is also a proud boast of the League that the late Hedley Verity came to Yorkshire's attention when a professional at Middleton in the late 1920s. The League's records are somewhat sketchy but immeasurable delight has been given throughout the years by both amateurs and professionals. Foremost among the latter was Gary Sobers, who was the pride of Radcliffe.

Sobers was on the brink of completing a fabulous double of 1,000 runs and 100 wickets for the 3rd successive season in 1962 when a knee injury forced his retirement in early August. Sobers had then already taken 100 wickets and needed only 96 more runs for a 4-figure batting aggregate. He must surely rank as one of the most attractive cricketers to play in the League, but famous names adorn what records are available. Among them is the immortal S. F. Barnes who played for Rochdale and Castleton Moor; the mercurial L. N. Constantine and the stylish C. J. Barnett were also Rochdale professionals of note. So, too, was C. G. Pepper, the big-hitting batsman and canny spin-bowler from Australia, while at Heywood G. H. Pope, of Derbyshire and England, and J. R. Reid, New Zealand's powerful all-rounder and captain, proved match-winning professionals. Mankad's days at Castleton Moor are still talked about and it was often said that the Indian was always in action with the Moor for whom he opened the batting and the bowling and seldom knew what a double failure meant. Phadkar, Gupte, Hazare and Manjrekar were other Indian cricketers who played Central Lancashire League cricket with great distinction and Australia has also been represented by Tribe, Livingstone and Pepper. Alongside these 'big name' players have been some extremely talented amateurs and E. Kay, of Middleton, hit over 10,000 runs in a career stretching from 1925 to 1954.

The Bolton area of Lancashire has always been a prolific nursery for the county team and although the Bolton League was founded comparatively recently, in 1930, league cricket has flourished in the district since 1888 when the Bolton and District Cricket Association was established. The Bolton League is an offshoot of the older association which is still going strong, as will be realized later when tribute is paid to one of the oldest cricketing bodies in the country. In all but its approach to professionalism the Bolton League is fit to be compared with any in the county and its contribution to first-class cricket through its recruits to Old Trafford is part of Lancashire's history. The famous Tyldesley family, Harry, James, William and Richard – but not the unrelated Ernest and John T. – were all products of the Bolton area and so, too, were Hallows, Farrimond, Pollard, Wilkinson and Tattersall. All these 5 players won England caps at one time or another and there were other Boltonians who distinguished themselves at Old Trafford and elsewhere without reaching England status. Wicket-keeper Barlow stands out as a chirpy little cricketer, brimful of keenness and ability.

The League has at present 12 member clubs. They are: Astley Bridge, Bradshaw, Eagley, Egerton, Farnworth, Heaton, Horwich RMI, Kearsley, Little Lever, Tonge, Walkden and Westhoughton, and all are situated within a 6-mile radius of Bolton Town Hall.

Founded in 1952 after a breakaway from the Ribblesdale League the Northern League caters for clubs in a much wider area beginning with Leyland in the south, taking in the coastal clubs of St Anne's, Blackpool, Fleetwood and Morecambe, and reaching up into the Furness area and into Cumberland with Kendal and Netherfield. The League President is Sir Donald Bradman. The League permits one professional per club and some world-famous players have graced the ranks of a League whose matches are of five hours' duration. Blackpool can claim most championship honours with 6 First Division successes and several Second Division titles to their credit in the first 12 years of the League's existence. The Slater Cup, a knock-out competition inaugurated in 1953, has been eagerly contested with Darwen taking the trophy 3 times and Blackpool and Furness twice. Rohan Kanhai, the West Indies Test batsman, showed outstanding skill in 1962 when he scored 1,165 runs for Blackpool, but he did not reach the record of W. E. Alley, who also played with Blackpool when in the Northern League. Alley hit 1,345 runs in the 1953 season and had an average of 149·44 because he was so seldom dismissed.

There are several leagues in Lancashire that also embrace clubs in other counties and one of the oldest of these is the Saddleworth and District League which includes in its membership clubs from Lancashire, Yorkshire and Cheshire. It was founded in 1898 and serves a rural area around Oldham. At present the League is 14 clubs strong and they are: Micklehurst, Hollinwood, Greenfield, Flowery Field (what a glorious name for a cricket club!), English Steel, Friarmere, Stayley, Austerlands, Heyside, Moorside, Uppermill, Delph and Dobcross, Saddleworth and Droylsden. Professionalism is practised on a modest and optional scale. Most of the paid recruits stem from the amateur ranks of the Lancashire and Central Lancashire Leagues where any outstanding performer is a ready-made target for these village clubs.

Founded in 1946 after the closure of the South-East Lancashire League the North-Western League caters for clubs from towns, villages and workshops and provides keen and competitive cricket with professionals permissible but not compulsory. Present membership of the League stands at 15 clubs: Avro, Anglo-West Indian Sports, Higher Blackley, Denton West, Greenmount, Woodhouses, Woodbank, East Lancashire Paper Mill, Thornham, East Levenshulme, Oldhams, Fieldhouse, Lancashire Steel, Newton Heath and Heymain Recreation.

It is the proud boast of the Bolton and District Cricket Association that they are the oldest cricketing body in the two counties. Founded in 1888 at a meeting in the Coffee Tavern in Bradshawgate, Bolton, the Association began with twenty-four clubs. In the 1920s the number had grown to 84 in various divisions but a fall-away in the 1930s was primarily due to the encroachment of the builder and consequent loss of grounds. Several more clubs failed to weather the difficult years of the Second War and the earlier loss of twelve clubs who broke away to form the Bolton Cricket League in 1930 reduced the ranks still more. Nevertheless 48 teams still compete in the Association's five sections on Saturday afternoons and some famous players have

W. E. ('Bill') Alley, the Australian who afterwards played with success for Somerset and became a Test umpire, was a formidable all-rounder for Blackpool in the 1950s.

learned the game and prospered in Association matches. Albert Ward, Walter Brearley and J. T. Tyldesley are 3 Lancashire County 'immortals' who went from Association clubs to Old Trafford to grace the first-class game.

Founded in 1893 the Ribblesdale League now consists of 12 clubs in its senior division and 8 in its junior section and it caters for a keen cricketing community around the Blackburn and Clitheroe area of Lancashire. A dispute some years ago resulted in the breakaway of some of the strongest clubs, but the Ribblesdale League now features the following 12 senior clubs: Barnoldswick, Baxenden, Blackburn Northern, Clitheroe, Earby, Great Harwood, Padiham, Read, Ribblesdale Wanderers, Settle, Whalley and Rolls-Royce and it will be observed that 2 of the clubs, Earby and Settle, are 'foreigners' from Yorkshire.

The Lancashire and Cheshire League includes one club from Derbyshire, Glossop, an old-established and once distinguished cricketing body notable for the patronage of the famous Hill-Wood family and the appearance of the Derbyshire bowling pair of Cadman and Bestwick. There are now 14 clubs in the League and the standard of cricket is jealously guarded with professionalism practised modestly and by demand instead of command. Several all-amateur sides flourish and hold their own with clubs who enjoy paid assistance. The present 14 clubs are: Bollington, Cheetham, Denton, Denton St Lawrence, Dukinfield, Glossop, Longsight, Marple, Norden, Prestwich, Stalybridge, Stand, Swinton and Unsworth; and although most of the clubs are within easy distance of Manchester, the League's area is scattered.

So much for the major leagues of the two counties. There are many other admirable organizations that provide cricket that enthralls and pleases year after year in spite of all the difficulties that now beset the Saturday-afternoon clubs. Most of the all-amateur leagues manage to keep going despite repeated battles by clubs to preserve grounds from the builders and town-planners. Many have fallen by the wayside but many more survive and among the leagues catering for clubs from workshops, churches, chapels, towns and the even bigger industrial area of Lancashire and Cheshire are: the Accrington and District Cricket League, the Bury and District Amateur Cricket League, the Chorley and District Amateur Cricket League, the Darwen Cricket League, the Denton and District Cricket League, the Fylde Cricket League, the Manchester Amateur Cricket League, the North-East Lancashire Amateur League, the North Lancashire and District Cricket League, the Oldham and Ashton District Cricket League, the North Manchester Cricket League, The Palace (Blackpool) Shield Competition, the Preston and District Cricket League, the South Lancashire Cricket League, the Southport and District Cricket League, the West Lancashire Cricket League and the West Manchester Cricket League. There are, also, several other leagues who provide for the specialized portion of the public who work Saturdays but still get in some cricket in midweek. Foremost among these highly esteemed leagues are: the Manchester and District Wednesday League, the Lancashire Wednesday League and the Rochdale Mid-week League.

There are other spheres of cricket. Some of them provide excellent sport for teams from adjoining counties and two examples of such enterprise and enthusiasm are the recently formed Derbyshire and Cheshire Cricket League and the older-established High Peak League from which the newer league broke away some years ago. One hesitates to describe the formidable Manchester and District Association or the equally powerful Liverpool Competition as 'leagues' in the accepted sense of the title but both provide high-class cricket for amateurs in wide areas and under top-quality conditions. There are honours at stake in both and the Manchester Association now boasts a fiercely contested competition for senior and junior clubs. Similarly the recently formed Cheshire Cricket Association (1957) is rapidly becoming a fertile training ground and there is no real lack of opportunity for both the player and the spectator in Lancashire and Cheshire where rivalry is keen and tradition respected.

MIDLANDS

League cricket in the Midlands is not confined to the Birmingham and District League and the North Staffordshire and District League. The Birmingham League claims to be the oldest league. Founded in 1888 it had been functioning for several years under the title of the Birmingham Cricket Association. The North Staffordshire League was founded one year later. In addition, there was formed in the winter of 1962–63 the North Staffordshire and South Cheshire League, which drew many North Staffordshire clubs into its jurisdiction: the old North Staffordshire and District League, however, continued to operate. County cricket, particularly Warwickshire, Worcestershire and Staffordshire, has benefited considerably from the influence and efforts of the players and administrators of the two leagues.

Ever since 1889 when the North Staffordshire League was formed it has been providing excellent Saturday-afternoon cricket and attracting good crowds around the Stoke area. In fact the League included 3 Cheshire and one Derbyshire club until, in the winter of 1962–63, a serious difference of opinion on the question of promotion and relegation resulted in the migration of all the Section 'A' members: Bignall End, Crewe LMR, Great Chell, Knypersley, Leek, Longton, Nantwich, Newcastle and Hartshill, Norton, Porthill Park, Sneyd and Stone, to the new league. Nevertheless the original League carries on and maintains an attractive brand of cricket. The League has always been closely linked with the Staffordshire County Cricket Club and has 2 representatives on the committee of the Minor County organization which has often fielded a team composed entirely of players from League clubs.

Past England players Charles Barnett, Cliff Gladwin and Jim Laker, have all played in the League. In 1962 one of the most successful professionals was Trevor Goddard, the South African all-rounder. The League has certainly gained an international flavour. On the other hand, the League has also produced its own outstanding players. The great S. F. Barnes was a League discovery as were at least 3 other England cricketers, J. T. Ikin, K. Higgs and D. S. Steele.

Worker for cricket: J. D. Scholfield has been secretary of the League Cricket Conference since its inception in 1962 – and has served North Staffordshire League and County Cricket for more than 20 years.

Founded in 1962–63 after a breakaway from the North Staffordshire and District League over the principle of promotion and relegation, the North Staffordshire and South Cheshire League, under the presidency of J. S. Heath, has produced evidence of keenly competitive matches and a high class of player.

There are innumerable leagues operating in the Birmingham area and all contribute to the ultimate good of several county clubs. The Midlands Club Cricket Conference is possibly the biggest body of all, incorporating some 400 clubs, but the major league is undoubtedly the Birmingham and District League, founded in 1888. The League's aim is simple but all-embracing. It is to promote the best interests of local cricket consistent with loyalty to county cricket.

In recent years the League has consisted of 10 clubs: Aston Unity, Dudley, Kidderminster, Mitchells and Butlers, Moseley, Old Hill, Smethwick, Stourbridge, Walsall and West Bromwich Dartmouth, and, in addition to its championship awards for 1st and 2nd XIs, the League also organizes a popular Knock-out Challenge Cup Competition with the final embracing 2 legs, home and away.

Among the other leagues in the Midland area which provide excellent cricket for the public and playing opportunities for thousands of cricketers are the Birmingham Public Parks Cricket Association, the Birmingham Works Cricket Association, the Midland Works and Business Houses League, the Birmingham Youth Council League (sponsored, incidentally, by the local educational authorities), the West Bromwich and District League, the Coventry Works Sports Association, the Kidderminster and District League and the Smethwick and District League. There are others who combine to create and maintain interest in our great summer game in an area that has now happily re-established itself once again with Edgbaston as a Test Match venue. The Warwickshire county ground, rebuilt on superb lines, is once again recognized as the focal point of tremendous cricketing interest at all levels. The various leagues of the area have and will continue to play their full part in maintaining the Midlands' contribution to the game.

NORTH-EAST

Three major leagues and several junior ones comprise the Saturday-afternoon scene in the North-East. The accent on professionalism is, perhaps, not so internationally flavoured as in Lancashire but most cricketing countries of the world have sent representatives to an area embracing Yorkshire, Durham and Northumberland. Yorkshire has enjoyed the services of many fine players produced in the North-East and numerous others have migrated to other counties. The 2 minor counties, Northumberland and Durham, are particularly well catered for and the leagues of the area provide not only players but ground facilities for second-class matches and a steady flow of administrators.

Founded in 1893 the North Yorkshire and South Durham League enjoys the reputation of being the major league in the area. At present the League comprises some 24 clubs playing in 2 divisions with 14 clubs in the 'A' Section and the other 10 comprising the 'B' Section along with the 2nd XIs of some of the more senior clubs. Matches are of 5 hours' duration and there are rigid rules regarding the playing and registering of professionals and the status of the amateur player. In addition to its major tournaments the League also plays 2 knock-out competitions for the Kerridge Cup (seniors) and the Haith Cup (juniors). In 1964 the clubs in membership were: Barnard Castle, Bishop Auckland, Blackhall, Castle Eden, Darlington, Darlington RA, Great Ayton, Guisborough, Marske, Marton, Middlesbrough, Normanby Hall, Northallerton, Norton, Preston, Redcar, Saltburn, Seaton Carew, Stockton, Stokesley, Synthonia, Thornaby, West Hartlepool and Yarm.

A growing number of players from the League have migrated to first-class cricket including several England cricketers, amateur and professional – E. W. Clark, of Northamptonshire, was a Darlington RA product, and C. H. Parkin, the Lancashire and England bowler, learned his cricket with Norton. M. F. Tremlett (Darlington RA), H. W. Stephenson (Stockton and Synthonia), M. M. Walford (Norton) and H. L. Hazell (Synthonia) became Somerset players; and W. V. Fox (Middlesbrough) along with G. W. Brook (Stockton) became Worcestershire stalwarts. Warwickshire have found the League a profitable 'nursery' and among their several recruits have been R. T. Spooner (Norton) and A. Townsend (Thornaby).

Ever since its formation in 1902 the Durham Senior Cricket League has played its part in maintaining and encouraging the game in the North-East. It permits professionalism; it achieves good cricket, keen and closely contested matches, and a spirit of comradeship. The 14 clubs now in membership are: Boldon, Burnmoor, Chester-le-Street, Durham City, Eppleton, Gateshead Fell, Hordon Colliery Welfare, N. Durham, Philadelphia, Seaham Harbour, South Shields, Sunderland, Wearmouth Collieries and Whitburn. There are no stringent League rules to impede the registration of amateur players although no player is permitted to turn out for more than one club in any given season unless special consideration and official sanction is granted. An amateur, in the opinion of the League Committee, shall be a cricketer who receives no remuneration over and above his actual out-of-pocket expenses although he may also be recompensed within reason for loss of wages when engaged in officially recognized matches. He shall not, in contrast to most other leagues, be permitted the luxury of a collection or talent money for meritorious performances.

A subsidiary competition, on knock-out lines, is played for the *Sunderland Echo* Bowl and this tournament embodies a time limit of an agreed number of overs. It enables the players to provide excellent entertainment on summer evenings when work is finished and relaxation is sought.

For 30 years or more the Northumberland League has been providing the major Saturday-afternoon cricket for the Tyneside area of England and the success of the Northumberland County Club in the Minor Counties Competition is closely linked with an organization that plays in 5 divisions and awards 5 points for an outright victory. Professionalism is permitted, but, with the exception of the county club, most engagements are of a modest character with the accent upon coaching ability rather than playing performances.

There were 30 clubs in membership of the League in 1964 and they represent a wide cross-section of the cricketing community in the North-East ranging from the county club itself to business organizations like the North-Eastern Electricity Recreation Club, Government departments, town and village clubs and the University of Durham Medical School. The standard compares very favourably with the other leagues in the North-East.

Among the professionals of note playing with the county club since 1946 have been W. E. Phillipson (Lancashire), T. S. Worthington (Derbyshire and England), L. F. Townsend (Derbyshire and England) and J. Oakes (Sussex).

WALES

League cricket in Wales is practised on a large scale but, outside the Principality itself, it appears to receive little publicity. Two major bodies are responsible for the organization of the Saturday-afternoon game, the South Wales and Monmouthshire Cricket Association and the North Wales Cricket Association. The Glamorganshire County Cricket Club has every reason to be proud of the contribution the South Wales and Monmouthshire Association makes in the provision of facilities for the young players and the maintenance of cricketing interest among spectators in the hills and the valleys around Cardiff and Swansea. In addition the county club recruits most of its young professionals from the Association and sends out several of its senior professionals as players and coaches.

Founded in 1926 the Association now comprises 4 divisions and since 1960 promotion and relegation issues have tended to increase the interest among both players and spectators.

In 1964 the Association (in 4 divisions) was comprised of: Grovesend Works, Gowerton, Hills Plymouth, Maesteg, Maesteg Celtic, Neath, Pontardulais, Pontyberem, Swansea, SCW (Port Talbot), Ammanford, BP (Llandarcy), Briton Ferry Town, Briton Ferry Steelworks, Clydach, Daffen Welfare, Llanelly, Llangennech, Pontardawe, RT and Baldwins (Landore), Hendy, Cam Gears, Mumbles, Metal Box (Neath), Skewen, Trostre, Ynystawe, Ynysygerwyn, Elba, Ffynnone, Mond Nickel, Morriston, Pontyneathvaughan, Tumle Welfare and Ystradgynlais.

The North Wales Cricket Association is the parent body for 6 cricketing counties. Its member clubs embrace Anglesey, Caernarvonshire, Denbighshire, Flintshire, Merionethshire and Montgomeryshire and they total some 120 cricketing organizations from which the various county sides are selected for an annual competition for the Challenge Cup presented by W. S. Romaine, of Prestatyn.

In the past the Association has played 2-day games against the full Lancashire side and, with the aid of a guest star or two, the North Walians have generally managed to do a little more than hold their own among first-class cricketers at all times. Herbert Sutcliffe was once a regular visitor to the Colwyn Bay Festival and he often led teams packed with top-class players. During the war years the Colwyn Bay Club staged many a match of international standing in aid of the Red Cross and other charities. One of the stalwarts of the home club was R. H. Moore, the old Hampshire captain, who led the Colwyn Bay Club for several years. Moore, of course, was only one of many notable North Wales cricketers, and, in A. Cassley, Colwyn Bay had a professional of great talent. A hard-hitting batsman and a canny leg-spinner, Cassley was also a good coach and groundsman and in a sphere where the general trend is to keep professionalism in the background he earned the respect and admiration of thousands. The emphasis in his case, and in many other North Wales clubs, was upon background work at the nets and in the preparation of wickets with a little aid with bat and ball when required in matches.

YORKSHIRE

League cricket in Yorkshire, like that in Lancashire and Cheshire, is a keenly competitive game with professionalism long-established but modestly practised these days. There are 6 major leagues in the county and many more of smaller and perhaps humbler origins that still contribute significantly, based on the fervent desire of all Yorkshire cricketers to achieve selection for their county.

More is generally known about the Bradford Cricket League than any other Yorkshire cricketing organization and this, in part, may well be due to the League's former policy of engaging professionals of world-wide reputation – especially in the two World War periods. Founded in 1903 the League caters, as its name implies, for the Bradford area and most of the clubs are situated within a few miles or so of the wool city's centre. Such a

Eddie Paynter of Lancashire and England: all punch and grit. He gave fine service on both sides of the Pennines, to Enfield and Keighley.

formation leads to keen and fierce local competition and it is typical of the Yorkshire fondness for the game that it believes in rewarding winning cricket with promotion from one division to another. Likewise it demotes the unsuccessful clubs and this constant striving to better or save oneself leads to some exacting and exciting cricket on a Saturday afternoon. The League at present consists of 24 clubs, 12 in the First Division and a similar number in the Second Division. This entails 6 league matches in each section every Saturday to provide a programme that attracts fair and knowledgeable crowds without quite retaining the numbers and enthusiasm of past years. The 24 constituent clubs in 1964 were: Baildon, Bankfoot, Bingley, Bowling Old Lane, Bradford, Brighouse, East Brierley, Eccleshill, Farsley, Great Horton, Hartshead Moor, Idle, Keighley, Laisterdyke, Lidgett Green, Lightcliffe, Pudsey St Lawrence, Queensbury, Saltaire, Salts, Spen Victoria, Undercliffe, Windhill and Yeadon. The oldest of all these is the Bradford Club itself, which can trace its beginnings back to 1823 and, of course, its ground at Park Avenue is one of the county's major enclosures as well as providing one of county cricket's most interesting and sporting pitches. Redoubtable deeds have been performed in cricket at all levels in Bradford but if you were to ask the stranger to name a Bradford League club he would probably plump for Pudsey St Lawrence and tell you that Herbert Sutcliffe and Len Hutton both learned the game there. So, too, did countless other top-class cricketers and there is hardly a club in the Bradford League whose followers cannot point to some Yorkshire player, past or present, and proudly proclaim: 'He was one of us'.

Eddie Paynter's prowess for Keighley is acknowledged by the *Handbook* which credits him with 14 centuries and 61 half-centuries between 1940 and 1948, and when it comes to bowling, another former Lancashire and England player takes the major award. S. F. Barnes took 122 wickets for Saltaire in 1922 and his average of 4·10 per victim represents far and away the most deadly bowling ever in a sphere that has known most of the game's foremost bowlers. Barnes has still more claim to Bradford League immortality. In 1915 he took 5 Baildon Green wickets with successive deliveries when playing for Saltaire and the next best return in this direction brings to notice 3 more internationally redoubtable cricketers in L. N. Constantine (Windhill), Emmott Robinson (Eccleshill) and T. W. Goddard (Keighley). All had 4 wickets in 4 balls at various times. Barnes also captured all ten wickets for a remarkable 14 runs when Saltaire met Baildon Green in 1915 and so, too, did the redoubtable Cecil Parkin for Undercliffe against Baildon Green in 1917, at a cost of one extra run, but neither Barnes nor Parkin could match the deadliness of T. A. Jacques in 1933. Playing for Saltaire in a match against Bankfoot, Jacques, a fast bowler who made several appearances for Yorkshire in first-class cricket, claimed figures of 10 for 25 and hit the wicket every time.

Glancing through the list of meritorious performances as listed in the admirable *League Handbook*, one comes across many other famous cricketing names, among them J. V. Wilson, Yorkshire's 1st officially appointed professional captain this century, F. A. Lowson, H. Halliday (Yorkshire), W. Place and C. Washbrook (Lancashire), W. W. Keeton and G. Gunn (Notts), G. H. Pope (Derbyshire), and, of course, innumerable other Yorkshire players of days long since gone and of more recent heritage.

Ever since its formation in 1891 the Huddersfield League has enjoyed and held the highest esteem of all Yorkshire and England cricket lovers. On and off the field the League has set an example of sportsmanship and enterprise that has served the game admirably. Famous players by the dozen have learned their trade with member clubs and if Wilfred Rhodes and George Hirst are cited as typifying the quality of the Huddersfield League cricketers it must not be thought that these two magnificent masters of cricket stand alone. There were many others and although the Huddersfield Club ground at Fartown does not now stage a first-class match the League's sphere of influence and its contribution to Yorkshire and English cricket has been of paramount importance. It will undoubtedly continue to be a source of much strength in the changing days and years ahead, for Huddersfield and its surrounding districts are still as cricket-conscious as ever. The League now has 2 divisions with promotion and relegation and its knock-out competition for the Sykes Cup has produced some memorable matches. The constituent clubs in recent years have been: Almondbury, Broad Oak, Hall Bower, Holmfirth, Huddersfield, Kirkburton, Lascelles Hall, Lockwood, Meltham, Rastrick, Thongsbridge, Armitage Bridge, Bradley Mills, Dalton, Elland, Golcar, Honley, Linthwaite, Marsden, Paddock, Primrose Hill, Shepley and Slaithwaite.

Alec Lodge has served the Huddersfield League all his life. A player and official of Lascelles Hall for 30 years, he was League president for 10 years and a member of the Council for 43. He concentrates chiefly now on the juniors.

Thirteen clubs constitute the Yorkshire Cricket League which is a competitive section of the more widely known and broadly scattered Yorkshire Council and in 1964 the members included: Barnsley, Castleford, Doncaster Town, Halifax, Harrogate, Hull, Leeds, Rotherham Town, Scarborough, Sheffield Collegiate, Sheffield United and York. At a glance one can see a close relationship with the Yorkshire County Cricket Club for Harrogate, Hull, Leeds, Scarborough and Sheffield Collegiate all place their grounds at the county's disposal for county or Test Match fixtures. Most of the other club grounds are venues for Yorkshire 2nd XI matches and there is the closest affinity between the first-class and the League administrations.

Catering for clubs from the various districts along with works organizations and other bodies the Leeds and District League has been in existence for over 80 years and has done much good work in creating cricketing interest, maintaining it, and in the provision of facilities for good sport. Formed in 2 sections with 10 clubs in the 'A' Division and 8 in the 'B' Division the League plays time-limit cricket with a span of 94 6-ball overs and an interval break of 15 minutes in each match. Clubs forming the League's two divisions are: Carlton, Gildersome, Hunslet, Nelson, Lofthouse, Pudsey Britannia, Whitkirk, Woodhouse, Yorkshire Copper Works, Clayton Sports, Colton, East Leeds, Garforth, Highbury Works, Kirkstall Educational, Leeds City Police, LICS, Whitehall Printeries and Rothwell.

1965–1980

M. H. STEVENSON

Since John Kay wrote of the Leagues he knew so well as long ago as 1964, cricket has suffered its fair share of trauma; some of the wounds have been self-inflicted; some, like thunder from a clear sky, have been the more daunting because of their unpredictability. Nevertheless the game as a whole is in a vastly stronger and more secure position than it was in the 1950s and early 1960s and this strength is manifest even more clearly at club level than in county and Test cricket.

Cricket may be moving in attitudes and ethos towards association football, a fact that is demonstrated by the pronouncements of Mr Cedric Rhoades, the Lancashire chairman, in answer to criticisms that undue stress had been laid on the club's finances at the expense of its cricket. His reply claimed that in the event of the arrival of a transfer system in cricket, Lancashire would be well able to afford to buy the best players whereas certain other counties would not. This sort of situation has long obtained in the major Leagues but the degree of stability and continuity in League cricket is such that some

League officials seemed mildly surprised that any updating process for a publication of this kind was necessary after a mere fifteen years.

Despite a generally optimistic tone, replies to my enquiries have contained a number of disturbing comments. Gamesmanship is believed in some quarters to be more rife than it was; punctuality with regard to starting matches is not always what it should be; players are too often unwilling to accept demotion and a fight back to the 1st team, preferring to take home their bat and give up the game; discipline generally seems to be more of a problem than used to be the case; rising costs of professionals, labour and equipment are still a problem but enterprising fund-raising and the advent of sponsorship have done much to ease the burden.

A characteristic setting for one of the smaller league clubs in Yorkshire – Linthwaite CC.

YORKSHIRE

The general health of the game in the leagues is, however, confirmed by David Douglas, President of the Yorkshire League and a magnificent, punishing left-hand bat in his day, who between 1952 and 1961 played for Hull, Scarborough and Castleford, captaining the last two. He played in 6 championship-winning sides and in those 9 years was only 9 times on the losing side. 'Ten years ago I was full of pessimism because good youngsters simply were not coming through and making the grade; more recently I have changed my mind completely and travelling round as I do (I make it one of my duties to visit every league ground at least once a season) it does my heart good to see so many young players of undoubted ability.'

The remarkable amateur strength of the Yorkshire League, which does not seem to have varied all that much over the years, makes it an appropriate starting point. Tempted perhaps by the fact that the League plays so many of its matches on county grounds, Bradford Cricket Club recently transferred its allegiance from the Bradford League to the Yorkshire League to bring the number of clubs up to thirteen. Starting in 1979 a bonus points system was introduced for the first time. A batting point is earned at 125, 150, 175 and 200, representing a maximum of 4 points, while bowling points are gained at the fall of the 3rd, 7th, 9th and 10th wickets. Players' reactions to this innovation have been unanimously favourable as the tame draws, so often a depressing feature of League cricket, have been largely eliminated; the precise result of a match now is often not known until the last ball has been bowled.

There are clear signs that the Yorkshire League is governed with intelligence and imagination; an example is the institution of captains' meetings at least once a month at which views and criticisms flow freely. David Douglas was responsible for this crucial development in the hope that club committees would have the opportunity of noting and often acting upon the opinions of their players. The vision to diagnose a deficiency in the set-up and to rectify it was also apparent in the formation during 1972 of the Ridings League in which the 2nd XIs of all Yorkshire League clubs (apart from Scarborough) participate. The basic idea of this League is to encourage young players to join the major town clubs and a pleasing improvement in standard of the Ridings League has been noted.

Having played a couple of seasons for York in the Yorkshire League, I do not need convincing of its quality. To those who do, it might be interesting to point to the fact that in the National Club Knock-out, Scarborough have won the trophy 3 times and York once and that every year that the competition has been held a Yorkshire League club has been prominent, usually up to the quarter-finals or beyond.

There have been few more consistent or prolific run-getters in the Yorkshire League than Peter Chadwick, whom the 1st edn records as achieving a superb aggregate and average in 1959; how impressive then to note that 10 years later he was able to excel himself with: 14 innings; 9 not outs; 686 runs; average 137·20. In 1970 Leeds players R. G. Lumb and P. J. Kippax distinguished themselves by taking 1st and 2nd places in the League batting averages as did York batsmen P. Jackson and A. Backhouse in 1977, while York bowlers J. Taylor and P. Keel took 1st and 2nd places in the bowling averages.

Like the Yorkshire League, the Bradford League seems to its many members and devotees as stable and untouchable as MCC or the Bank of England. There have been no changes in the administration of the League though the playing rules were amended in 1966 by the statutory two-thirds majority of the clubs. The points system was altered, giving 5 points for a win, 3 points to a side scoring most runs in a drawn game (provided that the side batting second had an equal or greater number of overs than the side batting first), 2 points were gained when the scores were equal and 1 point for a draw, the above modifications being intended to encourage brighter cricket. The Bradford League will welcome a new club in 1980 as Bradford Cricket Club's departure has allowed the entry of Hanging Heaton from the Central Section of the Yorkshire Council; much has been done in recent years further to encourage the development of youngsters. Most clubs have Under-17 teams playing in a Wednesday League and an Under-14 League has been added to play on Sunday mornings.

E. W. Sharpe, the League Secretary, writes of an age-old problem where keenness and enthusiasm abound. 'There seems to be any amount of interest in the game, the only problem being the shortage of Sundays, as there are so many competitions taking place these days that on occasions two or three representative games are taking place on the same day. This brings players into conflict as to where their loyalties lie. Administratively this is becoming a nightmare but it proves that cricket is thriving in the area.' A recent tragedy in the League, the death of Mike Fearnley in June 1979 during a match between his own club Farsley and East Bierley, highlighted his unique contribution as the holder of the record aggregate of wickets (1,324).

Outstanding among performances that span a considerable number of years must be that of Denis Bateson of Saltaire, who between 1942 and 1975 scored over 10,000 runs and became only the 8th bowler to take over 1,000 wickets in league matches: it would be hard to equal Bingley's record in 1969; their 1st XI won the First Division of the Bradford League and the Priestley Cup while their 2nd XI won the League's Second Division and the Priestley Shield. A more recent triumph for Bingley is the emergence of their talented captain, Neil Hartley, who made such an encouraging start for the county in 1979. In 1978 two more records were set in the Bradford League. Mark Dalton of Undercliffe received a collection of £52, and in the Undercliffe match against Pudsey St Lawrence a record gate receipt of £217 was taken.

LANCASHIRE

Stability based on a modus operandi which has stood the test of time is also the order of the day in (arguably) the world's most famous cricket league, the Lancashire League. J. Clarke, the League Secretary and a most fluent correspondent, airs a problem that is now unknown in corporate clubs: 'All clubs are better off financially mainly due to the support from their social clubs. From a purely personal point of view my feelings on this matter are mixed. Whilst appreciating that this keeps local cricket alive, I feel that, as with all forms of sponsorship, there is an inherent danger that the sponsors, in this instance the social clubs, will forget that their original purpose was to support cricket and in due course the tail will try to wag the dog.'

Almost incredibly there have been no changes with regard to constituent clubs since 1897 and the crucial sphere of junior cricket has never been healthier. Nearly all clubs now run Under-18, Under-15 and Under-13 sides, as well as 1st and 2nd XIs in which extreme keenness on the one hand is contrasted with the worrying tendency referred to earlier, of young players giving up the game in the face of adversity. The Lancashire League over the years has been able to acquire a dazzling galaxy of professionals, that is until the opening of county cricket to overseas players in 1968; on the other hand the Packer intrusion, which has caused so many headaches in other quarters, clearly benefited the Leagues. During the 1978 season players were recalled by the Indian Board of Control before they had completed their club contracts in order to enter a training camp prior to the beginning of a Test series. Predictably, the players in question were penalized in accordance with League rules for breach of contract; towards the end of the 1979 season, the Australian Board recalled Peter Sleep for medical tests prior to a tour of India.

The League feels strongly that there should be a good deal more give and take in this sort of clash of interests; if a player is selected for a tour, his ability is presumably not in doubt and his club commitments virtually guarantee he will be in good shape physically. The crux of the matter, of course, is that a spell in the Leagues and especially the Lancashire League is very often a significant step towards a successful international career. It would be both intelligent and beneficial for international boards to try harder to meet the Leagues at least half way with regard to the sort of problem mentioned above.

Doubtless League cricket can produce boredom and frustration, but at its best rich entertainment can be the result; few better cricketing weekends could be cited than East Lancashire's two matches in mid-June 1978. On the Saturday they reached 231 for 3 against Burnley, with Alan Border's six carrying him to a superb hundred off the last ball of the innings; though Burnley won the match with their last pair at the wicket. On the following day, Border contributed 179 not out from his side's total of 290 for 4 in a Worsley Cup match against Rawtenstall. To lose a 2nd match, having batted so well, in successive days, seemed desperately bad luck, but Peter Wood, Brian Manning and Abid Ali (119 not out) batted so magnificently that Rawtenstall won by 7 wickets.

Enfield had never won the Worsley Cup, and when they were defeated in the 1977 final by Haslingden it must have seemed that the gods were against them. But they found themselves in the final again in the following year, this time facing Rawtenstall and Abid Ali; Enfield batted 1st, reaching 219 for 6, and the Rawtenstall innings closed at 212 for 9, 3 wickets having fallen in the final over from which the losers had required 18 runs for victory. The sort of lifelong devotion to club and League which is such an integral part of league cricket in the north can readily be illustrated by the utter joy of 91 year-old W. C. Lockett, who had served Enfield for most of his life in virtually every capacity that one can imagine. After the 1977 defeat Billy Lockett was reported to have said that the defeat had put years on to his life.

Sadly, he was one of three great Lancashire League cricketers who died early in 1979. The excellently-produced *League Handbook* pays generous tribute to Eddie Paynter, Jim Smith and Billy Lockett: 'Eddie Paynter started his career with Enfield, moved on to achieve fame with Lancashire and England and resumed his service with Enfield when in his fifties and showed no signs that his ability had abated with the years. 'Big Jim' Smith, after an outstanding career with Middlesex, played as professional with East Lancs from 1945–48 and later as an amateur. Mr Lockett started his career with Enfield as a player and on retirement . . . served as secretary, league representative, committee member and scorer. All three gentlemen were a credit not only to the clubs they served but to the game of cricket in general and we shall remember them all with abiding affection.'

Though Billy Lockett was not there to see it, the 1979 Worsley Cup final was also a considerable triumph for his beloved club. Burnley, whose current prominence is largely due to the high standard of their amateurs, were League champions for the second successive year and clearly started as favourites. They batted 1st and reached 133 at Dill Hall Lane on a thoroughly difficult wicket which was soft on top, guaranteeing help for the spinners, and a variable bounce. Mudassar Nazir had failed for Burnley and if Madan Lal had done so for Enfield the result would probably have been reversed, but a characterful innings of 29 from Keith Windle and Lal's 48 saw Enfield to their 2nd successive cup victory.

It has sometimes been suggested that one of the weaknesses of League cricket is that the better players stay on too long in the game to allow adequate opportunities to the next generation. It is hard to support this argument when considering the record of Church's Jack Houldsworth, who at the age of 43 (fairly mature it must be conceded, for a pace bowler) took his 900th league wicket to establish a new club record.

Unquestionably the Lancashire League has been devotedly served by its administrators. In 1935 Jack Isherwood became assistant secretary of the League and, after holding varied office in the intervening years, became President in 1974, a position that he has occupied with distinction ever since. Problems come and go; fining, disciplining and the occasional cause célèbre are more evidence of an institution's vitality than of its unsoundness. So it is with the Lancashire League. It is not that a state of perfection exists but rather that, when difficulties make themselves apparent, the average northern town seems to possess interested and forceful people who are dedicated to putting things right. The AGM of Colne CC was firmly informed by the two Wharton brothers, Alan (the former Lancashire and England all-rounder) and Colin, that the club was in a far from healthy position. Alan Wharton's text was based on the idea that '. . . the club ran because 20 fools did the work all the year round.' His brother, Colin, took up the assault: 'I blame the town itself. It just does not have enough interest to earn Lancashire League cricket.' This criticism certainly needed answering when one considers the fact that the population of Colne was around 20,000 and the gates at League matches were only 10 pounds or so larger than at far smaller places like Church or Lowerhouse.

On the same evening that the Wharton brothers were going into battle, Bacup Cricket Club was also holding its AGM. A loss on the playing side of £3,172 was reported for the 1978 season, largely offset by donations from supporting organisations of £2,250. The decision was taken to set up a contingency fund to guard against any future emergencies that might occur.

The two examples cited above, far from suggesting weakness or decadence in the League, seem to me to represent involvement and foresight, qualities upon which the soundness and success of the Lancashire League has been squarely based over the years. These comments on the Lancashire League end with a note of caution; their neighbours, the Central Lancashire League, are experiencing a far more worrying phase in their long history. This was the League in which John Kay and his brother Edwin, the present League Secretary, learnt and played their cricket. In his annual report in November 1978, Edwin Kay concerns himself with what he regards as the decline in the fortunes of the CLL. He struck a chord with every club secretary when he referred to the vast expenditure necessary in the day-to-day running of a club: 'It must give great cause for concern that next summer cricket bats will be retailed at £34 and balls will cost £25. Professionals, even those recruited from the amateur ranks, are demanding four figure fees and good groundsmen are difficult to come across and are demanding similar fees.'

Time and again the mooted notion of a merger with the Lancashire League is heard, so that 2 divisions with promotion and relegation could be formed, but it has met with a consistently adverse response; every match played in the Lancashire League is a local Derby for geographical reasons alone and this built-in element of local rivalry does not operate to quite the same extent in the CLL which caters for clubs as dispersed and different in character and background as Walsden on the Yorkshire border, Stockport

Joel Garner of West Indies, the 'Big Bird' who helped Littleborough in the Central Lancashire League.

in Cheshire and Radcliffe on the outskirts of Bolton. Nostalgia will direct the gaze backwards at the days when the CLL possessed among its professionals some of the world's greatest cricketers, Cec Pepper, Vinoo Mankad and George Tribe among them; and Littleborough's recent successes, largely due to their West Indian fast bowler, Joel Garner, seem to confirm the need for gladiators to bring back the crowds, but that notion, of course, merely brings the wheel full circle to the desperate and pressing financial problems stressed by Edwin Kay.

As far as dominance by a particular club is concerned, the CLL has been able to share its honours with liberality. Only Heywood has won the championship 4 times in the past 15 years and just last summer Oldham, aided by their talented Australian professional, John Buchanan, finished as champions for the 1st time since 1957; they had only one Wood Cup to their credit (1943) so that their double of championship and Wood Cup in 1979 was the more remarkable.

Edwin Kay, who has virtually devoted a lifetime to the CLL, must, however, be allowed the last word: 'I can't find anyone in the League to agree with me but I think that the future of the League lies in amateurism.'

THE MIDLANDS

Perhaps oldest League in the world, the Birmingham and District League has changed its members in recent years through the addition of Duport and the Warwickshire County Cricket Club which was admitted to the League along with Worcestershire in 1975. Worcestershire withdrew a year later but Warwickshire greatly appreciate the excellent, competitive cricket that gives extra opportunity of gaining experience to its good young players. In 1977 a Third Division was pioneered by 8 clubs and, in addition to the Saturday afternoon competition which since 1973 has had a maximum 55-over limit on the 1st innings, the league has successfully run a 16 eight-ball-over evening Challenge Cup competition.

The league competes in the Inter-League Conference Trophy which it won in 1972. Most clubs are very actively involved in promoting youth cricket and many clubs compete in the Under-13 and Under-15 NCA youth competitions and in the Under-16 Alpine Soft Drinks competition, organized by the Midlands Club Cricket Conference. In 1979 the Warwickshire county side ended as champions of the First Division, Walsall headed the Second Division and Moseley the Third. Aston Unity won the Challenge Cup.

Easily the two most spectacular feats of recent years in the Birmingham and District League have been achieved by batsmen. In 1975 Graham Yallop, the 1978–79 Australian captain, scored a record 1,152 runs at an average of 128.00 while playing for Walsall; this record only stood for 3 years as Doug Slade, the former Worcestershire all-rounder, playing for West Bromwich Dartmouth, scored 1,407 at an average of 117.25 in 1978.

A little further north, the North Staffordshire and South Cheshire League, founded through a rift in the North Staffordshire and District Cricket League in 1962, has experienced the departure of both the international professionals and the crowds; but small changes in the points system, a bonus point for the team batting at the faster rate and an extra half hour's play have gone some way towards avoiding the many stalemates of former years. At the 1978 AGM a motion to extend the League, either through the addition of 2 clubs to the existing membership or by forming a Second Division with a view to a return to a system of promotion and relegation, was narrowly defeated; in 1979, however, following lengthy discussion there was unanimous support in favour of advertising for additional clubs.

Although insufficient clubs applied for there to be any real chance of forming a Second Division, 2 new clubs were added, Little Stoke and Stafford; it is hoped that a Second Division may still be formed in the future and the first major development in the League since its inception has resulted in fourteen clubs entering a period of entrenchment. As so often in league cricket, different clubs have dominated league championship and cup competitions, with Longton as champions 6 times and Stone, League champions in 1979, winning the Talbot Cup 5 times since 1965. Founder secretary of the North Staffordshire and South Cheshire League was Doug Schofield, who was previously secretary of the North Staffordshire and District League. One of his happiest moments will doubtless be of the new League's victory in the Inter-League Knockout associated with the League Cricket Conference of which Doug Schofield was also Secretary. The League's 4 professionals on that occasion were: D. F. Cox (Surrey), captain; Gary Sobers, Wes Hall and Nasim-ul-Ghani. The league have won this competition on 3 other occasions since, including 1979, under the captaincy of M. J. Ikin, son of the Staffordshire, Lancashire and England batsman, J. T. Ikin.

The North Staffordshire and District Cricket League has continued to flourish, following the redistribution of the county's resources 17 years ago, welcoming new clubs, Hanford and Crewe PW into the League at the start of the 1978 season. The same year saw the introduction of overs-cricket for the first time in the League's history, a development which seems to have met with general approval owing to a marked increase in the number of definite results. The revolution in Staffordshire League cricket that occurred in 1962 was the prelude to a formidable period of command by Cheadle, who up to 1978 had finished as League champions 9 times; the fact that bowling (and not batting) wins matches seems to be illustrated by the fact that only once, in 1976, has a Cheadle player (D. Croft, 707 runs, average 47.1) headed the League batting averages whereas a Cheadle bowler has 7 times finished top of the averages, with Russell Flower, the Warwickshire slow left-hander, achieving this feat in 1970, 1971 and 1974.

The Kidsgrove and District Junior League continues to provide excellent cricket in its own right and to serve as an impressively fertile source of talent for higher spheres. Those who are unconvinced of the service that League cricket can provide to the game as a whole might be interested to note the list of distinguished products of the Kidsgrove and District Junior Cricket League: K. Higgs (Meakins) Lancashire, Leicestershire and England; R. W. Taylor (Bignall End) Derbyshire and England; P. J. K. Gibbs (Norton) Derbyshire; J. F. Steele (Sneyd) Leicestershire; A. R. Barker (Burslem) Worcestershire; K. W. Wilkinson (Longston) Worcestershire; A. Brassington (Sneyd) Gloucestershire; J. M. Ward (Bignall End) Derbyshire; B. S. Crump (Sneyd) Northamptonshire; P. Bainbridge (Sneyd) Gloucestershire; K. Barnett (Leek) Derbyshire.

THE NORTH-EAST

The Test successes of the Indian slow left-hander, Dilip Doshi, will not have come as a surprise to members of the County Club, Northumberland, for whom he performed with such distinction in 1979; he reserved his most spectacular feat for the Cup match in which he took all 10 wickets against Darlington. A new team of only 2 years' standing in the Northumberland League, Ashington Workshops, was the winner of the Wilson Cup in 1979, but Bomarsund, who were recent winners of the National Village Championship, were the League champions; their most successful batsman, Dore Dreyer, was able to amass over 700 runs in 1978 and over 600 last season. No side has dominated either the cup or the championship since 1965 and generally the League seems to be thriving. J. E. Smith, the League Secretary and Treasurer, however, sounds a warning note: 'The day-to-day financial problems of the League are not too worrying but the Inter-League Knock-out has been a real headache. Last season we had to play away at Nottingham and Shropshire and made a loss of £254.'

Mr H. Trenholm, Secretary of the North Yorkshire and South Durham Cricket League, is adamant that there is greater keenness than ever among the youngsters, though they seem to expect the clubs to arrange transport, however near the opposing ground may be. The finances of the league are better than ever owing to increased subscriptions and a system of fines imposed for results that are sent in late. All the clubs are also very sound financially, and in 1979 14 of the Division 'A' clubs had professionals, only 3 of whom were overseas players.

Since its formation as long ago as 1893 the league has been controlled by a representative from each club, but in 1972 its constitution was altered and it is now governed by a management committee of 8 representatives from the clubs, with the full committee only sitting at the AGM. Mr Trenholm also stressed the age-old search, experienced by so many Leagues, for the best possible playing conditions: 'During the years we have tried various forms of awarding points, from 2 points for a win and 1 for a draw to 3 for a win, all on a basis of 5 hours' cricket; we then tried overs-cricket for a year and for the past 5 seasons we have used a system of 20 points for a win, 4 for a draw, 1 point being registered for every 25 runs scored over 75 in the first 45 overs of an innings and 1 point for every 2 wickets taken. During the current season (1979) we made this rule applicable to the first 55 and not 45 overs; in addition, the side batting first must declare after 55 overs. These bonus points are only added in the case of a drawn match or for a losing team. 'We have 16 clubs in Division "A"; 24 in Division "B", comprising 16 2nd XIs and 8 1st XIs. There are 19 clubs in Division "C" in addition to a reserve league which plays on Wednesday evenings. We do not apply promotion and relegation in any of these competitions.'

The strength and enterprise of the North Yorkshire and South Durham Cricket League is also apparent in the multiplicity of the cup competitions that flourish. There are 6 different cups, competed for at various levels from Division 'A' down to the juniors. The 1978 season was remarkable for the spectacular feats of Irving Shillingford, the West Indian Test player, who scored 1,258 runs, including 6 hundreds; in 1975 the League won the Steiner Cup and in 1979 the North Yorkshire and South Durham Cricket League won the John Smith's Trophy, which is contested by all the Yorkshire leagues.

Colin Orr, in his 19th year as secretary of the Durham Senior League, writes with a commendable mixture of shrewd business awareness and optimistic enthusiasm: 'Clubs pay £30 annually to the League and they all have bars. None of them would stay solvent if they relied on gate receipts. Attendances are sadly low but there is a big press following. The ever-increasing cost of equipment has forced the league to dispense with Grade A English balls and the sanctioned ball is now manufactured in India. There has been no change in the constitution of the League since 1961.'

In 1977 the League celebrated its 75th birthday with a visit to Chester-le-Street of the full Yorkshire side which beat Durham by 9 wickets in front of a huge crowd. Philadelphia were champions that year, their 4th success in 5 years and they have also won the championship in the past 2 years, a performance without parallel in the league's history. Their triumphs have been to a considerable extent due to the superb form of the former Leics all-rounder, Stephen Greensword, who, in 1977, set up a new League record with an aggregate of 1,274; this total has been surpassed by Eppleton's Australian professional, Steve Small, who in 1979, his 1st year in the league, reached a total of 1284.

Philadelphia's only setback in the last 7 years was in 1976 when David O'Sullivan, the New Zealand slow left-hander, helped Eppleton to the championship; the League is becoming increasingly attractive to overseas players and 2 more, Wasim Raja and Lance Cairns, joined Chester-le-Street and Whitburn respectively in 1979. In fact Wasim Raja failed by only 40 runs and 5 wickets to become the 1st Durham Senior League player to do the double. The League programme at present comprises 20 Saturday games, 4 on Sundays and 2 on Bank Holidays, making 26 matches. Traditionally the Durham Senior League has always favoured time cricket but a limitation of 55 overs was introduced in 1979 in order to counter negative and defensive thinking by sides batting first. Cup competitions proliferate and on this subject Mr Orr issues a word of caution: 'There are so many midweek knock-out competitions that opportunity for net practice has been seriously reduced. Some clubs who have not contracted their professionals to coach would be well advised to spend some of their surplus money on qualified coaches.'

OTHER LEAGUES

It must not be interpreted as a slight that Leagues of the quality and vitality of, for example, the Bassetlaw and District League and the Northern League, the excellence of which are common knowledge among cricketers, have not been mentioned earlier: the Huddersfield League likewise with its rich history and present prosperity under the guidance of such men as Alec Lodge and the evergreen Eddie Leadbeater. During the past 15 years, new Leagues have been formed in a variety of areas, including the Home Counties, the Midlands, North Wales and Lancashire and Cheshire; at the end of 1974 11 Cheshire clubs resigned from the Manchester and District Cricket Association to form the basis of the new Cheshire County League. This cataclysm naturally caused ripples of concern and controversy, bringing problems especially to the Manchester Association and the Cheshire Cricket Association. A wholesale reorganization of both was essential but the former at least is now as lively as ever with St Helens perhaps the outstanding side, having won 5 championships since 1966. A sad absentee, following the 1979 season, from the Manchester Association will be Broughton, who have been forced to withdraw mainly because of conflict with the Rugby Club with which they share facilities. Broughton CC was founded in 1823 and both W. G. Grace and A. C. MacLaren played on their ground.

The Cheshire Cricket Association, according to their Secretary Stan Woodward, are under considerable pressure: 'We are losing clubs to the Merseyside Competition and the Lancashire and Cheshire League as well as the new Cheshire County League. Probably more will defect. Some clubs have joined in their places but frankly they are of inferior quality.'

The Lancashire and Cheshire League also experienced a shake-up in 1973 when 10 additional clubs were admitted and, the following year, Marple resigned in favour of the Cheshire County League. Two impressive highlights were an unbeaten 190 from John Holder of Norden in 1975 and 3 years later an aggregate for the season of 1195 at an average of 85·36 from Jim Allen of Denton.

The Merseyside and Liverpool Competitions, the latter surely providing some of the best purely amateur cricket in the land, continue to flourish and, to the north, the Northern Cricket League has recently been dominated by Lancaster, who have won the championship for the last 4 years to equal Blackpool's record of 4 successive wins in the 1960s. Kendal have an outstanding record in the Cumbria Cup (now known as the Mageean Cup) which they won in 1977 and 1978 after finishing as runners-up in 1976. A junior division of the Northern League was formed in 1975 and now 9 of the 12 senior League clubs participate. Blackpool run 3 junior sides and Darwen run no fewer than 5 teams, ranging from Under-13 to Under-18.

C. S. Elliott, the Test umpire and selector, began his cricket in the Bassetlaw and District League before starting his county career with Derbyshire.

Eddie Leadbeater, the old Yorkshire leg-spinner, aged 52, topped the Huddersfield League bowling averages in 1979. Playing for Almondbury he had 67 wickets at 10 runs apiece.

The North Lancashire and District League discovered a new hero in 1978 when the amateur, George McMeekin, of Millom scored 973 runs from 22 innings, the highest aggregate ever recorded in the league from amateur or professional; 4 clubs have emerged as outstanding in recent times: Furness, Whitehaven, Millom and Lindal, who were beaten finalists in the National Village Championship at Lord's in 1977.

One of the youngest leagues of all is the South Cheshire Cricket Alliance, which was established in 1976 owing to dissatisfaction with the fact that the Cheshire Cricket Club Conference was run on a percentage and not a league basis. Rupert Rigby, the secretary of the alliance, seems to fear the dangers of inbreeding but is nevertheless hopeful with regard to the future: 'There are cup competitions for both 1st and 2nd XIs and the general feeling is that, for a League that is still in relative adolescence, a good start has been made. The Alliance is looking to improve itself, however, and is wondering whether it should attract new members or perhaps merge with another League. It is commonly felt that the same dozen clubs should not play one another year in and year out.'

Generally the degree of vitality and intensity in the sphere of League cricket would astound those whose only interest is in the international and county game. The Leagues have proved the most productive nursery of talent in the land and any League is justly proud of those cricketers that it sends out to earn renown in an infinitely wider sphere than that of their origins, a fact George Langdale makes in the introduction to his well-produced *History of the Bassetlaw and District Cricket League (1904–1978)*. He chronicles how the league grew '... from modest beginnings to its present position as one of the largest and strongest leagues in the country,

Aigburth with Lancashire playing. The home of the famous Liverpool CC.

having produced no fewer than 3 members of the successful England team in Australia in 1978–79: Mike Hendrick, Geoff Miller and Derek Randall, to say nothing of one of the men who helped to select the side, Charlie Elliott.' He continues: '*Wisden 1979* includes "Three more studies in greatness" by Basil Easterbrook, who chooses two Bassetlaw League players, Bill Copson and Kenneth Farnes, in the three.'

Pride in club, league, county and country is implied if not overtly stated in this passage and if one's last comment concerns an overseas player it is in the devout hope that cricket may help to develop tolerance and understanding; to build bridges, not to erect barriers. On 15 June 1979, 14-year-old Paul Johnson of Balderstone, in hitting 16 sixes in a Nottinghamshire schools match, had beaten a record held for 16 years by New Zealander John Reid with 15 sixes. The very next day, representing Micklehurst in the Saddleworth League in a match against Newton Heath, Omar Henry, a Cape-Coloured South African, scored 243 in an amazing innings which included 23 sixes. It would be pleasant to be there when that record falls.

The South

F. L. J. DOLMAN

Prior to the Second World War, apart from one or two cup competitions played mostly on midweek evenings and by minor clubs, there was no infringement in London or the home counties of the Club Cricket Conference rule stating conditions of membership which, with certain well-defined exceptions, precluded participation in competitive cricket.

The first indication given to the Conference Council that there might be a demand for League cricket in some quarters came from Surrey in the late 1950s, when Jimmy Walker, who had been a representative of that county on the Council and President in 1951, stated that his club, Malden Wanderers, wished to see a league formed of the stronger clubs in his county. This was not given very serious consideration at the time, as it seemed to have little support. However, in the mid-1960s it became clear that the demand was growing, although still principally from Surrey, and an unofficial approach was made to two of the Conference officers, the Chairman and Secretary at that time, by some Surrey cricketers led by Raman Subba Row, of Old Whitgiftians, who produced convincing evidence that there was a sufficient number of big clubs in Surrey ready and anxious to form a league. It has always been an implicit principle of the Conference Council that its function was to serve the member clubs, not to govern arbitrarily or to dictate to them, but it was clear that, under the existing rules, clubs forming a league could not remain in membership.

The officers concerned realized that, if the desires of the League-minded clubs were to be met, the first step must be to obtain the agreement of the Council to a change in the rules governing competitions. Finally, after much protracted heart-searching the 1968 AGM accepted competitive cricket by a big majority. The conditions under which approval could be given to the entry of a club into a competition included a safeguard against the risk of clubs losing fixtures at short notice through regular opponents entering a league, which would probably involve a number of new Saturday fixtures, with the inevitable dropping of some old ones.

The Surrey Clubs Championship became the 1st League to be approved by the Conference and became operative in 1968. The clubs concerned had been playing each other regularly for some years, so no disruption of fixtures was involved. Another competition of a rather different nature was started in the same year but this was composed of nearly all the clubs in Hertfordshire merely agreeing to the award of points when they met each other. In 1970 the Essex Senior Competition was instituted on rather similar lines to the Hertfordshire one and, in 1971, 4 more leagues run on normal lines were introduced. These were the Kent League, the Sussex League, the Surrey County Cricket League and the Surrey Cricketers League. The first two of these were, and have remained, the strongest leagues in their respective counties, just as the Surrey Clubs Championship is still recognised as the strongest in that county.

From that time the number of approved leagues expanded rapidly. The Middlesex County Cricket League, in operation from 1972, was the counterpart of the Kent and Sussex Leagues and the Surrey Championship. Inevitably the 16 or so strongest clubs in the Essex Senior Competition and the Hertfordshire Cricket Competition broke away to form the Essex Cricket League and the Hertfordshire League respectively, the former in 1973 and the latter in 1974. By this time there were 23 leagues in London and the home counties and others were springing up further afield, as in Devon and round Oxford.

An annual meeting convened by the Club Cricket Conference, known as the 'League Forum', had become established as a means of exchanging information about the various special regulations in use by the leagues and their effectiveness. These embraced such matters as playing a fixed number of overs, sometimes for each side and sometimes the total for the match. The system of awarding points also varied from League to League, most, where the fixed overs did not operate, designed to put a premium on winning, while some Leagues awarded points in a drawn game according to the assessed chances of the clubs at the close of play. Discussion in the Forum has always been lively but all Leagues have tended to maintain the superiority of their own systems. Useful discussions have also taken place on the regulations governing the Club Cricket Conference Inter-League Cup Competition, started in 1975 and gaining in size and popularity each year. It is now sponsored by Trumans and was entered by 35 leagues in 1979, when the Southern League were successful. The winners prior to that year were Kent (twice), Essex and Middlesex County.

Sponsorship has now become a valuable feature of the leagues and, in addition to Trumans, who sponsor 6 leagues as well as the Inter-League Cup, there are Benson & Hedges, the *Berkshire Mercury*, Greene King, Kingsford, Lillywhite Frowd, Morrant and Slazengers, providing much appreciated assistance of a practical kind.

In the early days, several bodies were formed professing direct opposition to competitive cricket. These included Ilford and District Cricket Association, North East Hants Association of Cricket Clubs, Romford and District Cricket Association and Sussex Free Cricket Association, but opposition has gradually died away and, although in the hearts of some of the older generation there may remain some nostalgic regrets for the passing of the old order, nearly all players of the present day accept Leagues as an essential part of the game.

Raman Subba Row, the Test cricketer and TCCB administrator, was an early protagonist of League cricket in the South.

School and Junior Cricket

Growth of An Idea

G. H. G. DOGGART

It will be news to many that the coaching of boys and young men on a national scale, and also the organization of representative junior cricket except for the few chosen for the annual games at Lord's between Lord's Schools and the Rest, is a wholly postwar development. H. S. Altham, writing on the MCC Youth Cricket Association in the 1st edition of this book, described how the idea came to fruition.

He told us how at the end of a General Committee of MCC early in 1948, G. O. Allen confronted his colleagues with the question, 'What has MCC ever done to help the boys of this country as a whole over their cricket?' There followed a still, serried silence as the inevitable answer dawned on those present. Once realized, the challenge was accepted, but it was clear from the start that MCC would need support on the widest possible front. The first step was to present the problem to the counties at that year's November meeting of the Advisory County Cricket Committee. At their unanimous request MCC agreed to set up a body for the following purposes:

(1) To examine the problems concerned with the learning and playing of cricket by the youth of the country between the ages of eleven and the time of their entry into National Service.

(2) To consider how best to foster their enthusiasm for our national game by providing them with wider opportunities for reaping its benefits.

Harry Altham was not one to let the grass grow under his feet. The relevant education authorities and other bodies such as the CCPR and the NPFA, as well as county delegates from the recently-formed National Club Cricket Association, and representatives from the English, the Welsh, and the Women's Cricket Associations and the Scottish Cricket Union joined a cluster of MCC members in an Enquiry Committee. From its deliberations the MCC Youth Cricket Association was launched and got to work.

The challenge clearly demanded some basic new thinking. The plain fact was that cricketers had for 200 years or more thought of coaching in terms highly unrealistic to the problem now envisaged: a coach with considerable playing experience, 3 or 4 boys, and a good net wicket – how far removed from the 'facts of life' prevailing for the vast majority of children in their initiation to the game – a hard-surfaced school playground, a 'games period' of some 40 minutes, 20 or 30 small boys, and a schoolmaster, for whom even the basic techniques might, as for his pupils, be almost a closed book, faced with the duty of 'teaching cricket'.

This, then, was the problem, not only what to teach, but how to teach it collectively and individually, that faced the initial three-day conference that met at Lilleshall in November 1951. Of the more than 70 representatives from nearly every county, a number of them Test Match players, who attended it, hardly any had ever heard of 'group coaching', and the majority, when they did, viewed the idea with apprehensive suspicion. How fortunate they were, then, to have in H. P. Crabtree, subsequently appointed MCC Coaching Adviser for Youth, one who could speak with the authority alike of a county cricketer and of an organizer and lecturer in physical education, with a wide experience of group coaching in various fields of sport.

At the end of 3 long days of co-operative debate the conference had not only accepted wholeheartedly this new coaching project as both necessary and practicable, but had reached agreement on basic techniques in all departments of the game. In the following spring many of the same delegates returned for the first full course in group coaching, and then went back to their counties to inaugurate the long process of training of those in their area who wished to learn and practise it.

This, then, was the beginning of an operation that was to develop with most encouraging momentum. Each autumn the MCC YCA held an Advanced Coaching Course, terminating in an examination for the Advanced Coaching Certificate for which the candidates had to satisfy the examiners in practical tests of their ability to instruct a group in the skills of the game, to conduct a net, to lecture, and finally to pass, on a minimum 70% basis, a 2-hour paper covering the whole field of coaching, including not only technique but tactics, organization and personal approach.

There were soon over 300 holders of these Advanced Certificates who went back to their county areas, there to conduct coaching courses organized by the area Youth Association for schoolmasters, youth leaders, indeed anyone who wanted to help the young with their cricket.

There were also MCC Youth Coaching Certificates to be competed for by those short of 'the Advanced'. The response all round was remarkable, it being reckoned that by the mid-1960s 15,000 men had attended one or more of the courses. A variety of coaching aids were also produced, notably the *MCC Cricket Coaching Book* (now in its 12th reprinting); *Cricket – How to Play* (excerpts from which appear in the GLOSSARY of this edition); wall-charts, illustrating the basic techniques; and a series of films and film strips in colour.

Harry Altham ended his article with a passionate defence of coaching, quoting, in powerful support, William Beldham, W. G., Sir Pelham Warner, Denis Compton, Peter May, Colin Cowdrey, Ted Dexter and Sir Donald Bradman, and stressing the basic principles which aspiring young batsmen must master and 'which in fact all the great players have observed far more than they have disregarded.' In the final paragraph he evokes the spirit of the game in words which reflect his own simple but highly articulate belief that the rewards that cricket unfailingly brings its devotees are boundless. He writes:

> Enough of means and mechanisms. What of the ultimate end which the MCC YCA pursues? It is to help all boys who want to play cricket to play it better and so enjoy it more, and to get from it the rich dividends which it can surely yield – recreation for the spirit no less than for the body, comradeship that transcends combat, and memories that will anchor his loyalty to cricket when his own playing days are done.

The reorganization of cricket administration in 1968 included the disbanding of the MCC Youth Cricket Association, whose pioneering work will surely stand the test of time, and the transfer of its work to the recently formed NCA.

There are 5 main ways in which the NCA fulfils its responsibilities in the field of Junior Cricket, the subject of this article. First comes the development of coaching, and in particular of the original coaching scheme, now extended on a national basis, and operated by 6 National Coaches. These are currently Keith Andrew, Director of Coaching, based at Lord's; Bob Carter, Midlands/West, based at Worcester; Graham Saville, Midlands/East based at Chelmsford; L. J. Lenham, South, based at Hove; David Wilson, Scotland, based at Edinburgh; and a new coach shortly to be appointed for the North, based at Old Trafford. Apart from these coaches running courses all over the country and giving national sides the benefit of their professional expertise, they are responsible for the working of the 3 main coaching awards: the Teaching Award; the Coaching Award; and the Advanced Coaching Award. The Proficiency Award Scheme, launched in 1973 in order to stimulate interest amongst youngsters, is another example of NCA's initiative, which, in passing, would have been impossible without support from the Wrigley Cricket Foundation, the Lord's Taverners and the H. S. Altham and A. J. McAlpine Trusts.

Secondly, there is the organization of representative sides at home and abroad. Pride of place must go to the exciting series between 1970 and 1978 in which matches have been played every 2 years between the England Young Cricketers and the West Indies Young Cricketers; they were sponsored first by the Frank Worrell Memorial Fund, and for the past 2 series by Agatha Christie Ltd. A Young England team, sponsored by Wilkinson Sword, has been to Australia, and an NCA Youth team has taken part in a festival in Canada. Already full England players have had their first taste of representative cricket on these tours. There is no substitute for the experience gained and their importance can hardly be overestimated.

Thirdly, the NCA fosters the promotion and encouragement of competitions at all levels, indoors as well as outdoors, at both Club and School level. Two competitions for those of Junior and Youth age are of particular importance, the Lord's Taverners *Cricketer* Colts Trophy for Schools (the Esso Competition, as it was called at its outset in 1973) which attracts an entry of 1,400 schools; and, reflecting the wider role that

MASTERS AT WORK 1 Note the balance and follow-through of this on-drive which brought Don Bradman the 100th run of his 100th 100; 2 The finish of Len Hutton's off-drive shows how the left leg and the arms have followed the line of the stroke; 3 The off-drive as depicted by Gary Sobers. Note the full follow-through; 4 Ray Illingworth off-spinning round the wicket – everything perfect; 5 Another perfect follow-through, this time by John Snow; 6 Again, the perfect position after delivery by Derek Underwood. See how in these action-shots the eyes are glued to the ball.

clubs are now playing in the encouragement of young players, the successful Lord's Taverners NCA Under-13 and Under-15 Competitions. One exciting innovation is the Under-16 County Championship sponsored by Commercial Union.

Fourthly, must be remembered the provision of improved facilities, of which pitches should undoubtedly take pride of place. The work of the NCA, and of Peter Dury in particular, in developing non-turf pitches to a fine art – or should it be a fine science? – should not go unrecorded.

Fifth, and last, is the support given by NCA to those national bodies concerned with Junior Cricket which are affiliated to it, ESCA and NAYC, whose activities are described in the articles following this.

English Schools Cricket Association

C. J. COOPER

ESCA, as it is generally called, is the governing body for Schools' Cricket in England. It embraces all types of schools, both from the independent and state sectors of education. It holds charitable status, and aims to foster the mental, moral and physical development of schoolboys through the medium of cricket, and to improve the standard of schoolboy cricket throughout the country. Membership of the Association is open to all properly constituted Schools County Cricket Associations.

Six counties were present at the inaugural meeting in 1948 at the 'Jolly Blacksmith' in Twickenham. Now every county has its own organization and runs competitions at all age levels from Under-19 to Under-11. For the purposes of age qualification the relevant date is 1 September of the year prior to the current season.

The most important Inter-Schools Competition is the Lord's Taverners *Cricketer* Colts Trophy for Schools, in which over 1,400 schools take part. County Competitions are run at Under-14, the winners taking part in the National Competition the following year at Under-15. Winning schools have included Morpeth Grammar School, Winchester College, Radley College, Stamford School and Queen Elizabeth's School, Blackburn.

The main Under-15 annual event is the Junior Festival, when the best schoolboy cricketers at this age play in a Quadrangular Regional Tournament between North, South, West and Midlands Schools. This is staged each year by a County Association, which helps to raise the necessary finance aided by the Lord's Taverners. Festivals have taken place in Lincolnshire, Lancashire, Norfolk, Northumberland, Avon, Kent, Berkshire, Warwickshire and Leicestershire. After the Regional matches a Representative match is played against the President's XI, and internationals against the Welsh Schools and the Scottish Union Colts.

The peak of the Under-19 programme is the Schools Week at Lords. The full England team, under the title of 'MCC Schools', plays the NAYC in a 2-day game. This is followed by a one-day game between the NCA Youth XI and the Combined Services. Opponents in this country have included the Indian Schools, Australian and West Indies Young Cricketers and Canadian Colts.

At all age levels the most important matches played are inter-county. These are generally one-day matches and not limited over. This helps to maintain the true values of the game.

Much pioneering work is being done at Primary (Under-11) level. Helped financially by the Lord's Taverners, a number of inter-schools festivals, based on the Rules for Junior Cricket (eight-a-side), are held in various parts of the country.

Countless coaching courses are held from school to national level throughout the year. At Christmas 4 national courses (Under-15 and Under-19) are held regionally. At Easter 2 selective courses, the Under-15 Wrigley and the Under-19 Lord's Taverners take place, usually at Crystal Palace and Pocklington School.

In order to help the growth of the game, particularly in the comprehensive schools, the Association has produced a pamphlet on *The Use of Artificial Wickets*. An *Annual Handbook* is produced, and for a period of 20 years up to 1976, Bob Baker edited *Cricket Spotlight*, the proceeds of which went to ESCA.

G. H. G. Doggart is President of the Association; his predecessors were H. S. Altham, Desmond Eagar and F. R. Brown. Charles Hansford, who received the MBE for his work, was the 1st Chairman and held continuous office, mostly as Secretary, until 1978, when he was elected 'Founder Member' of the Association.

The National Association of Young Cricketers

J. G. OVERY

The National Association of Young Cricketers had its inaugural meeting at Lord's on 10 January 1963. At this, representatives from 14 counties were present. The Association was created by members of the National Club Cricket Association who were concerned by the lack of interest shown generally by any organization, other than schools, for the promotion and development of youth cricket; at that time there were no national cricket organizations who could or were prepared to deal with those leaving school. At this meeting a constitution was approved, the 1st officers elected being – Chairman, Harry Harper (Warwickshire); Vice-Chairman, J. G. Overy (Kent); honorary Secretary/Treasurer, W. E. Lindsey. An Executive Committee of five members was also elected.

The aims and objects set out in the Constitution were to promote and encourage the activities of young cricketers, to provide coaching facilities and operate courses to endeavour to improve the standard of play and encourage the promotion and playing of matches at county representative level on a national basis. All very basic ideals and principles, but at that time no effort was being made to achieve these ideals and the NAYC dedicated itself to embrace all young cricketers under the age of 19, not only schoolboys but those who had left to join commerce and industry, who, without encouragement, were being lost to the game. In 1964 by kind permission of the Warwickshire CCC, the first 2-day match was played, North v South, on the County ground, Edgbaston, and this match has become an annual and indeed a traditional event of the Association. In that year also, 22 counties were members of the Association and the first *Year Book* was published, modest in production but it was felt informative and projecting the image of the new Association.

The next landmark was in 1965 when Lord Stafford consented to become the 1st President. There is little doubt that in tandem with Harry Harper he contributed much to the success of the NAYC. In 1967 Harry Harper retired, his place as Chairman being taken by J. G. Overy who still holds that office. In 1969, the inter-county matches played by the members of the Association were given a competitive edge when Mrs Hilda Overy, wife of the Chairman, presented a trophy to be competed for by the counties. The first trophy winners were Warwickshire.

The inter-County NAYC Trophy being presented by Mrs J. G. Overy, the Chairman's wife and donor, to E. Shilton, captain of Warwickshire, the first winners, in 1969.

It was appropriate that in 1970 the MCC recognized the active and constructive part the NAYC were playing and in conjunction with the North v South fixture, on the 3rd day the NAYC National team played MCC and this has been an annual fixture. By now 30 counties were in membership.

In 1973 perhaps the most significant event of NAYC took place, when the 1st week's Cricket Festival was staged at Cambridge, the boys being accommodated in the colleges and the matches played on the college grounds. Six counties took part, and so successful was this venture that another Festival was staged at Oxford to run concurrently with Cambridge. These 2 Festivals are without doubt the largest organized in the United Kingdom today. Twenty counties are currently participating and a whole week's sport is enjoyed by around 280 young cricketers. The Association received a seal of approval when it was invited by MCC to play a 2-day match against MCC Schools at Lord's. This fixture is now an annual event and on the 3rd day a combined team selected from NAYC and MCC Schools plays a match against the Combined Services – making 3 wonderful days' cricket at headquarters for these fortunate young cricketers.

During its short existence it can fairly be claimed that the NAYC has made a profound contribution to cricket at all levels. The national Under-19 side play all the overseas Under-19 touring teams and contribute players to the Young England side. In 1980 there are 35 counties affiliated to the NAYC, and it is sufficient tribute to the success of this organization and its contribution to cricket to name the players who are currently in the England team who have played for the NAYC national side: Geoff Miller, Graham Gooch, David Gower, Graham Dilley, David Bairstow and Derek Randall. Others who have played and have made their mark at national and county level are R. A. Woolmer, G. A. Cope, A. J. Borrington, J. Corrall, R. G. Lumb, H. J. Tunnicliffe, R. Elms, P. Denning, K. Pont, J. R. T. Barclay, P. Topley, J. Graham-Brown, W. Hare, H. Cartwright, G. S. Clinton, D. A. Graveney, A. W. Stovold, B. Gardom, D. Kayum, A. J. Hignell, G. Mendis and M. W. Gatting.

For the future, it is hoped to develop the Festivals in other parts of the country, coaching courses are being planned, the traditional matches will be continued and the Association will play its part in not only finding more county and England players; but, as is more important, will, we hope, continue to give young players greater opportunities to play top-class cricket and generally improve their performance in playing the great game.

School Records

GERALD BRODRIBB

First-class cricketers have generally shown notable promise when still at school, and this survey records a selection of some of the outstanding performances of schoolboy cricketers in England. Any attempt at comparison is pointless, since much depends on whether the school has provided the press with information, how long the boy stayed at school, what quality of opposition he encountered, and the length of the fixture list. For many years the annual figures in *Wisden* tended to come mostly from independent schools, but the formation in 1948 of the English Schools Cricket Association did much to encourage cricket in other schools, and by 1965 boys from ESCA appeared in representative school teams at Lord's. Now the England Young Cricketers XI is made up almost equally by players from Headmasters' Conference and non-Conference Schools, and the current England team provides much evidence of the value of the present system of promoting young cricketers.

Every school has a cricketing hero linked with its name, and many of these appear below; if the emphasis appears to be on batting, that is because bowling records are more difficult to establish, let alone those for wicket-keeping and fielding. An obvious start is a list of the highest individual scores made in inter-school matches:

278	J. L. Guise, Winchester v Eton 1921
249	C. G. Boddington, Rugby v Clifton 1915
240	P. J. Sharpe, Worksop v Wrekin 1955
229	G. O. Smith, Charterhouse v Westminster 1892
229*	N. E. Partridge, Malvern v Repton 1918
228	H. T. Bartlett, Dulwich v Mill Hill 1933
226	C. Palmer, Uppingham v Haileybury 1904
224*	D. F. Walker, Uppingham v Shrewsbury 1932
222*	I. P. Campbell, Canford v Marlborough 1946
220	C. H. Knott, Tonbridge v Lancing 1919
215	I. P. Campbell, Canford v Downside 1945
214	P. H. Latham, Malvern v Rossall 1891

If all double-hundreds are counted, and not only those in inter-school matches, it seems that only 3 batsmen have scored more than one. These are I. P. Campbell with scores of 237, 222 not out and 215, H. T. Bartlett with scores of 228 and 204 and J. Howell (Repton) with scores of 202 and 200. For comparison, the following match aggregates may be of interest:

309 (184* and 125) R. A. A. Holt, Harrow v Charterhouse 1938
286 (8 and 278) J. L. Guise, Winchester v Eton 1921
286 (95 and 191) R. E. H. Hudson, Haileybury v Uppingham 1922
274 (176 and 98) G. E. Hewan, Marlborough v Rugby 1935
268 (215 and 53*) I. P. Campbell, Canford v Downside 1945
267 (69 and 198) R. H. Spooner, Marlborough v Rugby 1899

To reach 1,000 runs in a school season is a target achieved about 50 times in the last 100 years. I. P. Campbell (Canford 1945–46), E. J. Craig (Charterhouse 1959–60), and P. D. Johnson (Nottingham High School 1968–69) seem to be the only ones to have twice achieved this. Craig's run of consecutive scores in 1960 of 146 not out, 62 not out, 95 not out, 152, 102 and 173 not out is probably without equal. Aggregate records depend much on the number of matches played, as this list of the largest aggregates will show:

1904 H. C. Tebbutt (The Leys) 24–0–1443–154–60·1
1901 J. E. Raphael (Merchant Taylors) 26–6–1397–175*–69·8
1897 V. F. S. Crawford (Whitgift) 21–3–1340–201*–74·8
1925 M. J. Turnbull (Downside) 16–2–1323–164–94·5
1946 I. P. Campbell (Canford) 14–3–1277–237–116·0
1955 P. J. Sharpe (Worksop) 16–5–1251–240–113·7
1938 N. M. Mischler (St Paul's) 16–2–1218–221*–87·0

The list of 1,000-run makers who later became well known includes: F. H. Knott (Tonbridge, 1910), L. P. Hedges (Tonbridge, 1919), D. R. Wilcox (Dulwich, 1929), D. N. Moore (Shrewsbury, 1929), C. R. Maxwell (Brighton, 1931), P. J. Dickinson (K. C. S., Wimbledon, 1937), M. C. Cowdrey (Tonbridge, 1950), R. W. Barber (Ruthin, 1953), the Nawab of Pataudi (Winchester, 1959), J. M. Brearley (City of London, 1959), R. A. Hutton (Repton, 1961), M. G. Griffith (Marlborough, 1961) and C. J. Tavaré (Sevenoaks, 1973).

Some have shown a remarkable consistency from an early age as is shown by these figures of those who amassed over 2,500 runs in a school career with an average of over 50 – a notable record:

I. P. Campbell (Canford) 1943–46 50–9–2595–237–63·3
E. J. Craig (Charterhouse) 1957–60 55–10–2803–173*62·2
G. W. Cook (Dulwich) 1951–55 75–21–3258–144–60·3
P. J. Dickinson (KCS) 1934–8 76–17–3518–173*–59·8
Nawab of Pataudi (Winchester) 1956–59 67–15–2956–127*–56·8
D. N. Moore (Shrewsbury) 1925–29 60–9–2879–193·56·4
H. T. Bartlett (Dulwich) 1929–33 67–12–2783–228–50·5
M. J. Turnbull (Downside) 1921–25 61–6–2776–184–50·4

Some of those mentioned played for their school for many seasons. P. D. Johnson is said to have played for 8 seasons without missing a match and in these he scored 3,502 runs and took 473 wickets. J. H. Cameron (Taunton) played for 7 years in which he took 425 wickets. V. F. S. Crawford (Whitgift) in 6 seasons scored 4,130 runs and took 472 wickets. Other prolific wicket-takers include: D. C. Kingsley (Beaumont, 1944–47) with 251 wickets; E. K. Scott (Clifton, 1933–37) with 244; J. N. Crawford (Repton, 1902–05) with 224; M. C. Cowdrey (Tonbridge 1946–50) with 216; G. R. Bardswell (Uppingham, 1889–93) with 205. Others who took over 185 wickets include: C. L. Townsend (Clifton, 1892–94), E. M. Dowson (Harrow, 1895–99), G. T. S. Stevens (UCS, 1916–19), F. R. Brown (The Leys, 1926–29), A. G. Steel (Marlborough, 1874–77) and A. E. R. Gilligan (Dulwich, 1911–14). V. F. S. Crawford took 117 wickets in the season of 1894; J. H. Cameron took 108 wickets in 1929; as also did R. W. Barber (Ruthin) in 1953. The record of J. H. G. Deighton (Denstone) with 83 wickets at 4·7 runs each in 1938 is notable.

The best innings analyses in schools' representative matches would seem to be:

J. H. Cameron 10–32 for The Rest v Lord's Schools 1932
E. P. Hewetson (Shrewsbury) 9–33 for The Rest v Lord's Schools 1920
J. R. T. Barclay (Eton) 9–37 for Public Schools v ESCA 1970

The question is sometimes asked, 'Who was the greatest of all schoolboy cricketers?', and the answer must concern what was achieved in first-class cricket while they were still school cricketers. J. N. Crawford was probably the best ever, since in August 1904, after term was over, he took 44 wickets for Surrey and was virtually top of the first-class averages. In 1905, after another good season at Repton and further games for Surrey in August, he went on tour with MCC to South Africa that same winter and played with success in the 5 Tests. C. L. Townsend (Clifton) first appeared for Gloucester in 1893 when aged 16, and 2 years later he took as many as 94 wickets in the August of 1895, which is still the greatest number of wickets ever taken in a month of first-class cricket. A. G. Steel is said to have never bowled better than in his last year at Marlborough in 1877.

C. L. Townsend, one of the most brilliant schoolboy cricketers.

In 1919 G. T. S. Stevens, of University College School, played for the Gentlemen v the Players at Lord's while still at school. G. J. Bryan (Wellington) was only 17½ when he scored 124 v Notts on his debut for Kent in 1920. S. H. Day (Malvern) also scored a century on his debut for Kent in 1897. Others who achieved great success in first-class cricket while still virtually schoolboys include A. C. MacLaren (Harrow), R. H. Spooner (Marlborough), J. R. Mason (Winchester), D. R. Wilcox (Dulwich), P. F. Judge (St Paul's), A. Ratcliffe (Rydal), and P. I. Bedford (Woodhouse GS).

Among other outstanding schoolboy cricketers not yet mentioned are P. B. H. May (Charterhouse), K. S. Duleepsinhji (Cheltenham), T. E. Bailey (Dulwich), I. A. R. Peebles (Glasgow Academy), R. J. O. Meyer (Haileybury), R. W. V. Robins (Highgate), D. J. Knight and E. R. T. Holmes (Malvern), K. Farnes (Royal Liberty School, Romford), E. T. Killick (St Paul's), N. W. D. Yardley (St Peter's, York), A. W. Carr and D. S. Sheppard (Sherborne), M. J. K. Smith (Stamford), K. L. Hutchings and L. P. Hedges (Tonbridge), and C. H. Taylor (Westminster).

Though this survey is concerned with individual records, I cannot omit the unparalleled performance of the Repton XI of 1908: during the holidays 4 of the team played in county cricket, another was invited to do so, and 2 more played for their county 2nd XIs. One who played successfully for Surrey was H. S. Altham, who in later years did more than anyone to foster school cricket; any such survey should recall his honoured name.

Aldenham School

Foundation 1597

SCHOOL OPPONENTS: Felsted; Bishops Stortford; Berkhamsted; Highgate; Oratory; Merchant Taylors; Mill Hill; King Williams, Isle of Man; Liverpool College; King's School, Chester.

Aldenham can boast a number of splendid cricketers from between the wars, who later did well in the first-class game. These include T. C. Longfield (Cambridge and Kent), R. G. Hunt (Cambridge and Sussex), E. D. R Shearer and J. P. Blake. Later there came D. E. Blake (Hampshire), J. A. Cockett (Cambridge 1951), and J. G. Dewes (Cambridge and Middlesex), who played 5 times for England.

After the Second World War, the 1947 XI was successful, due mainly to the opening bowling of J. N. Sainsbury (49 wickets) and A. S. Heywood-Jones (39 wickets). The latter in his 3 years in the XI took 121 wickets. Aldenham had one of their most talented batsmen in the 1957 captain, A. R. Day. Other good batsmen were P. K. Smith, M. J. H. Johnston, S. C. Lewis and G. D. P. Scott.

Alleyn's School

Foundation 1887

Alleyn's produced its first notable cricketer in W. M. Bradley, who played for Kent between 1895 and 1899 and twice for England against Australia in 1899. A fast bowler, he helped the Gentlemen beat the Players when taking 5 of their 2nd-innings wickets. Bradley apart, Alleyn's cricket seems for a long time to have been notable mostly for its quantity and enthusiasm. By 1914 the school fixture list included many present-day opponents like St Dunstan's and Emanuel. H. H. Farthing scored several hundreds for the school, averaging 86·9 in 1915.

Without reaching great heights the school had many good teams between the wars and produced a notable post-1945 trio in M. J. Stewart (Surrey and England), J. F. Pretlove (Cambridge and Kent) and M. J. Edwards (Surrey). With Stewart and Pretlove in the team between 1947 and 1951 the school was particularly strong. Edwards captained the side for 3 years, 1957–1959, and has recently done much to strengthen the Alleyn's Old Boys' side.

In 1966 and 1967 the school was undefeated. A. P. L. Williams scored 3 hundreds in his 4 years in the XI (1964–1967), with an aggregate of 650 runs in 1967. In that year the wicket-keeper L. E. Smith played for the English Schools. In more recent years Alleyn's has generally lacked reliable batsmen and results have suffered. Exceptions to this were R. L. T. Davis between 1969 and 1972, when the school twice won the London Schools Cup, and C. R. Bangay, who scored 4 hundreds against schools in 1976 and also captained Surrey Young Cricketers.

Ampleforth College

Foundation 1802

SCHOOL OPPONENTS: Durham; Bootham; St Peter's, York; Sedbergh; Worksop; North Yorkshire Schools; Denstone; Stonyhurst; Blundells; Oundle; Uppingham; Pocklington.

The tradition of good cricket at Ampleforth has become established in the last 50 years, and has been based on cultured batsmanship, supported by a consistently high standard of wicket-keeping. The bowling and fielding has often been of insufficient strength to get out stubborn opponents, and the best seasons at Ampleforth have been those when the bowling was strong. The 1947 XI with C. J. M. Kenny and G. A. Robertson; 1949, with J. F. Murphy, P. A. Mitchell and M. J. Tate; and the 1961 side, with T. A. L. Huskinson and R. H. Jackson, are examples of this.

The most successful of those bowling partnerships was the one between Kenny and Robertson. In his 3 years in the side (1945–1947) Kenny took 96 wickets at 9 runs apiece, while Robertson took 135 wickets at 11·3.

Batting of a classical mould is a characteristic of Ampleforth cricket, and the rather moderate figures achieved by even the best batsmen since the Second World War can be partially explained by the bad weather, which does not blend to advantage with the playing fields which are on clay. Ampleforth owe much to Father Peter Utley. He was the most distinguished cricketer to come from Ampleforth, playing for Hampshire, and then returning as a monk to run the cricket from 1936 to 1955. Two of the leading batsmen at Ampleforth before the Second World War were C. F. Grieve, the Oxford and Scotland full-back and stand-off half, and J. A. Waddilove. Grieve played in the XI for 5 years and scored 2,344 runs, including four hundreds. Waddilove was a most attractive batsman and

The Ampleforth 1st XI ground with St Cuthbert's House, the Monastery and the Abbey in the background.

probably the best wicket-keeper Ampleforth have had. He, like Utley, returned to the Ampleforth staff, and it is largely through his coaching that the standard of wicket-keeping has been so high.

In the 1970s the bowling was generally good and the fielding of a high order. W. M. Reichwald was a successful captain in 1970 and led the XI to a record 9 victories with his left-arm spin, and J. P. Pearce (1972–1975) completed his career with 141 wickets. In 1976–1977 F. O'Connor, bowling inswingers, dismissed 91 batsmen at 8·9, including 2 figures, within one week, of 7 for 2 runs and 7 for 5 runs. In these two years, 6 of the regular opponents were dismissed for under 60.

Bedford School

Foundation 1552

SCHOOL OPPONENTS: The Leys; Haileybury; Tonbridge; Stowe; St Edward's, Oxford; Felsted; Bedford Modern; Oundle; Uppingham.

Although Bedford has long been famous as a rugby school its reputation as a cricket school has been strengthened consistently since the Second World War. B. E. Disbury for Kent, W. A. Sime, Captain of Notts 1947–50, and M. J. H. Allen, Northants, are examples of cricketers who made an impact with their counties. A large number of Bedfordians have also played representative schoolboy cricket, competing in the Southern Schools v The Rest trial at Lord's and then the Lord's Schools and, more recently, MCC Schools teams. Such players as P. H. Spray, J. H. Mytton, A. L. O. Green, M. I. McLaren, I. G. Peck and R. J. Boyd-Moss all distinguished themselves at these levels.

In earlier days H. V. Baumgartner played for South Africa against England in 1913, the brothers R. and F. M. Joyce did good service with Leicestershire, while B. L. Peel played for Scotland. E. H. D. Sewell, well known as a writer on cricket and rugby, played for Essex and was later coach to Surrey at the Oval. W. B. Weighell (1866, 1868 and 1869) and H. Grierson (1911) gained blues at Cambridge; and Henry Grierson will be particularly remembered as the founder of the famous XL Club.

Berkhamsted School

Foundation 1541

SCHOOL OPPONENTS: Haberdashers' Aske's; Aldenham; Bishop's Stortford; St Alban's; Brentwood; Abingdon; Framlingham; Kimbolton; Magdalen College School; St Lawrence, Ramsgate; Colchester Royal GS.

The best known cricketer to emerge from Berkhamsted is D. C. Morgan, who captained Derbyshire (1965–1969) and, in his first-class career of 20 years, scored over 15,000 runs and took over 1,000 wickets. At school he was a formidable bowler, taking 165 wickets in his 4 seasons – 1944–1947. C. H. Abercrombie, who made 165 for Hampshire against Essex in 1913, in a partnership of 325 for the 7th wicket – still the county's record – was killed in the First World War. Many Minor County cricketers have come from Berkhamsted, two of the most distinguished being R. G. Simons and P. Isherwood.

It was the appointment of A. V. Pope (Derbyshire) as the professional in 1957 which marked the start of better wickets and a marked improvement in the standard of the school's batting. In 1959, 10 matches were won, with C. Meager taking a record 53 wickets. In the early 1960s there was good batting by P. S. Young and B. J. Keeling, with the latter scoring 1,999 runs in his 4 seasons. There was also good bowling by M. I. Player, M. P. Bulpitt and C. Wright. Keeling and Player both played for Hertfordshire whilst still at school. Then followed the first Berkhamsted blues, with R. A. Niven (1968–1969 and 1973) and A. N. Campbell (1970) playing for Oxford. In 1971 there was good bowling by D. R. J. Arnold and J. A. R. Kirkcaldie, with the latter playing in the Schools' matches at Lord's. This was the middle of an undefeated record of 5 years. In 1977 a Festival was started with Framlingham, Kimbolton and St Lawrence, Ramsgate.

Bishop's Stortford College

Foundation 1868

SCHOOL OPPONENTS: Berkhamsted; Aldenham; Forest; Felsted; Chigwell; Perse; Brentwood; Kimbolton; Bedford Modern; Leys; Framlingham.

The finest cricketer produced by Bishop's Stortford was C. H. Titchmarsh. He played for, and remained loyal to, Hertfordshire all his days, though he would have been welcomed with open arms by any first-class county. Titchmarsh first played for Herts in 1906, but his skill did not mature until later. In 1929 – the year before his death – when 48, he still averaged more than 50 for his county. In 1922–23 he went to Australia and New Zealand with A. C. MacLaren's MCC team.

The best Bishop's Stortford side was that of 1914, which included V. R. Price, who captained Oxford in 1921, and A. G. Doggart, of Cambridge and Sussex, father of G.H.G., and even better known in the world of association football. Good results were achieved in the 1970s, notably so in 1974 and 1975 under the captaincy of the two Tee brothers. In 1974 Bishop's Stortford, with 9 victories, won more matches than ever recorded since the First World War, followed by 8 wins in 1975. T. S. Smith took 61 wickets (average 7·63) in 1972, which were the best figures since 1904, and then 5 years later A. Bentall, with 637 runs, achieved the highest batting aggregate since D. F. Cock in 1933.

Blundell's School

Foundation 1604

SCHOOL OPPONENTS: Taunton; Downside; Sherborne; Clifton; Canford; King's Taunton; Plymouth; Ampleforth; Oundle; Uppingham.

The first cricketer from Blundell's to make his mark on the first-class scene was C. T. A. Wilkinson, a fine all-rounder who led Surrey to their somewhat hollow Championship in 1914, and was again captain in the first 2 years after the First World War. Wilkinson was still playing good cricket for Beckenham in his sixties. Following him were S. G. U. Considine, who played for Somerset in the holidays after leaving school, and E. T. Benson, a fine wicket-keeper, who won an Oxford blue in 1928 and 1929, played for the Gentlemen at Lord's in 1929, and toured New Zealand and Australia in 1929–30.

Since the Second World War, R. J. Morris, who was one of the school's best all-rounders, got a Cambridge blue as a batsman in 1949, and F. J. Davis, a slow left-arm bowler, was a successful member of the 1963 Oxford side. His brother, R. C. Davis, first played for Glamorgan as a schoolboy in 1964, and then regular county cricket until 1976. He was prominent as a batsman, had his success as an off-spin bowler, and held many catches at short-leg. R. C. Davis and V. J. Marks are Blundell's two leading cricketers since the Second World War. Marks captained Oxford in 1976 and 1977, and plays for Somerset. In 1969 Blundells set up a 4-school festival with Ampleforth, Oundle and Uppingham.

An end-of-term festival at Blundell's, showing the teams of Ampleforth, Oundle, Uppingham and the home school.

Bradfield College

Foundation 1850

SCHOOL OPPONENTS: Charterhouse; Westminster; Sherborne; Canford; Stowe; St Edward's, Oxford; Eton; Winchester; Radley; Wellington.

Bradfield have generally reached a high cricket standard even though they have not produced many outstanding players. Their peak was perhaps reached in 1962, under M. D. Mence's captaincy. Mence played for Warwickshire in the holidays after leaving school, having just taken 8 wickets for 34 runs for the Public Schools against Combined Services at Lord's. It was against Radley in 1863 that the first game at Bradfield is recorded.

In 1930 I. A. W. Gilliat, the Oxford wicket-keeper of 1925, took over as master-in-charge, and considerable developments were made in the organization of Bradfield's cricket. Bradfield had a very good season in 1939, when the school had such players as B. G. Brocklehurst, who captained Somerset after the Second World War; B. C. Elgood, a Cambridge blue in 1948; and R. S. Kingsford, who captained Sussex 2nd XI. During the war years Bradfield had a splendid all-rounder in P. E. Bodkin, who captained Cambridge in 1946. In 1962 Mence played a remarkable part in the school's success. A left-hand bat and right-arm fast-medium bowler, Mence broke both the batting and bowling records with 846 runs and 84 wickets. He also played the highest innings ever made by a Bradfield boy, 160 against Westminster. Bradfield had an even more accomplished batsman in the 1964 captain, G. R. J. Roope, who joined the Surrey staff the week after leaving school, and played in one county match that summer. He won his county cap in 1969, and first played for England in 1972.

Bradfield cricket has continued to prosper following the impetus provided by the enthusiasm of M. R. Ricketts as master-in-charge, and the list of matches is now stronger than ever. There have been no outstanding players of the Mence and Roope calibre recently, but mention must be made of the impact of R. E. T. Jennings and D. P. Manners, who opened the bowling so successfully in 1973, and of the leadership and batting of M. C. J. Nicholas, who subsequently joined the Hampshire staff. 1976 marked the golden jubilee of the Pit ground at Bradfield – one of the most beautiful of school arenas. Surrounded by banks, meadows and the River Pang, its conception is attributed to Gerald Hough, a College master who later became Secretary of Kent.

Brighton College

Foundation 1845

SCHOOL OPPONENTS: KCS Wimbledon; Ardingly; Whitgift; Lancing; Epsom; Hurstpierpoint; Christ's Hospital; Cranleigh; Eastbourne.

The most famous cricketer produced by Brighton is S. M. J. Woods, who played 3 times for Australia against England in 1888, and 3 times for England against South Africa in 1895. With his fast bowling he took no fewer than 36 Oxford wickets in his 4 University matches. Two well-known amateur wicket-keepers of the 1930s came from Brighton – W. H. V. Levett of Kent, who toured India with MCC in 1933–34, and C. R. Maxwell, who played in turn for Nottinghamshire, Middlesex and Worcestershire.

After the Second World War, two Brightonians played regular first-class cricket, R. F. T. Paterson appearing for Essex and A. B. D. Parsons winning a Cambridge blue in 1954 and 1955 and going on to play for Surrey. Parsons was an outstanding batsman at Brighton and had the distinction of being captain for 3 years (1951–1953). The standard at Brighton was at its highest in the 1950s, with the XIs of 1952, 1956 and 1959 being undefeated. In 1960 the team achieved the record number of 11 victories. In 1970 C. J. Terleski scored 4 consecutive hundreds.

Canford School

Foundation 1923

SCHOOL OPPONENTS: King's Bruton; King's Taunton; Downside; Bradfield; Blundell's; Sherborne; Taunton; Bryanston.

The most notable cricketer in Canford's history is I. P. Campbell, who played for Oxford in 1949 and 1950. Campbell was chiefly responsible for Canford's most memorable victory, when, in 1946, they beat Marlborough by 212 runs. It was remarkable

Few schools can match the setting at Canford.

for the fact that in 100 minutes before lunch Canford scored 223 for the loss of 5 wickets, of which Campbell made 150. He was not out 222 when Canford eventually declared at 329 for 5. Campbell had an outstanding school record, scoring a thousand runs twice – 1,027 in 1945 and 1,277 (at an average of 116) in 1946. A gifted player of several games, he scarcely did his talents justice as a cricketer after leaving school.

In 1979 the school record partnership was made by P. B. Taylor (169) and A. D. Walker (109 not out) with 301 runs for the 1st wicket against Blundell's. A notable feature of recent Canford cricket has been the achievements of the Taylor brothers – Christopher, Graeme and Paul. For 11 years (1970–1980) there has been at least one Taylor in the XI, and during that period they have scored over 3,000 runs and taken more than 200 wickets.

Charterhouse School

Foundation 1609

SCHOOL OPPONENTS: Wellington; Bradfield; Eton; Winchester; Harrow; Westminster.

Charterhouse have one of the fastest and smoothest batting wickets in the country. Since the Second World War there have been some prolific batting feats by Carthusians – not least from the school's most famous cricketer, P. B. H. May. At the beginning of this century Charterhouse had some strong sides, and from 1900 to 1905 each team had 3 players in it who went on to gain blues at Oxford. There were O. T. Norris, W. J. H. Curwen, G. T. Branston, C. A. L. Payne, C. V. L. Hooman, H. A. Gilbert and R. L. L. Braddell. Contemporary with these was J. N. Buchanan, who later played 4 years for Cambridge. With their fine wickets Charterhouse are more renowned for batsmen than bowlers.

In 1911 Charterhouse were captained by J. S. F. Morrison, who became a triple blue at Cambridge. He was captain of the University association football side in 1914, and after gaining his cricket blue, also before the war, returned in 1919 to reorganize and captain the cricket side. In 1919 Charterhouse, for the first time since those magnificent 6 seasons at the turn of the century had 3 future Oxford blues in their side – I. A. W. Gilliat, a wicket-keeper, F. H. Barnard, a batsman, and R. C. Robertson-Glasgow, a fast bowler and one of the most charming writers on the game of cricket. In the 1920s Charterhouse produced J. T. Morgan and G. D. Kemp-Welch, successive captains of Cambridge in 1930 and 1931, and another Cambridge blue, A. G. Powell, who, both before the war and for a long time afterwards, was one of the best amateur wicket-keepers in the country.

The 1930s started badly with hardly a victory over any school opponent in 3 years, but they had 2 especially fine batsmen in T. R. Garnett, later of Somerset, and J. M. Lomas, who played for Oxford in the 2 years before the war, but died tragically in 1945. In his last season, 1933, Garnett scored 5 hundreds and made over 1,000 runs – an aggregate which was not beaten until E. J. Craig made the first of his seasonal thousands in 1959. Lomas was an even better school batsman than Garnett. In 3 successive years he averaged over 50, and in all made more than 2,000 runs.

Peter May came on the scene in 1944 when at the age of 14 he scored his 1st hundred against Harrow. In his last 3 seasons he averaged 54, 64 and 81. Besides the brilliant batting of May, Charterhouse had a powerful team at this time, with A. G. J. Rimell and O. B. Popplewell, who both went on with May to get Cambridge blues, and 2 good school fast bowlers, R. L. Whitby and S. E. A. Kimmins. Although May was Charterhouse's most distinguished batsman, his and all other batting records were broken in 1959 and 1960 by E. J. Craig, an opening batsman who played 3 years for Cambridge and also, 2 years after leaving school, for the Gentlemen at Lord's. In 1959 he scored 1,079 runs, beating the record aggregate of Garnett in 1933. In the following season he surpassed this with 1,106 runs at an average of 92·17. Following Craig, came R. M. C. Gilliat, an attractive batsman who played 3 years in the Representative Schools Match at Lord's, and A. H. Barker, a slow left-arm bowler, who broke all records at Charterhouse by taking over 100 wickets in 3 seasons. Barker and Gilliat, a nephew of I. A. W. Gilliat, went up to Oxford the year after leaving school, and both gained blues as freshmen in the 1964 Oxford side. Gilliat then became a most successful captain of Hampshire. The 1965 captain, J. M. M. Hooper, played a few matches for Surrey, before becoming a leading club batsman, whilst the 1971 captain, A. C. Hamilton, won an Oxford blue. One recent bowler of note was the fast-medium-paced R. P. T. Marshall, who played for Sussex. In the winter of 1976–77 Charterhouse and Westminster – both in their pink colours – enjoyed a tour of Singapore and New Zealand.

Charterhouse at home to Wellington in 1979.

Cheltenham College

Foundation 1841

SCHOOL OPPONENTS: St Edward's, Oxford; Malvern, Repton; Clifton; Marlborough; Haileybury; Shrewsbury; Sherborne.

Until the Second World War, Cheltenham ranked with the very best cricket schools, with K. S. Duleepsinhji, H. V. Page and G. E. C. Wood as their particular stars. But until A. F. Benke, an off-break bowler, played for Cambridge in 1962 Cheltenham had not had a blue since E. D. R. Eagar (later captain and secretary of Hampshire) got one for Oxford in 1939.

The man who had the greatest influence on Cheltenham cricket was H. V. Page. He captained Oxford in 1885 and 1886, played for the Gentlemen and Gloucestershire, and in 1888 returned to Cheltenham where he remained a master until 1923.

The best Cheltenham side is said to be the one of 1896, in which 5 of the team played eventually for their counties. There were some good cricketers at Cheltenham just before the First World War, including G. P. Brooke-Taylor and G. O. Shelmerdine (both Cambridge blues), but the most notable amongst them was G. E. C. Wood, who captained the XI in 1912. One of the best of all amateur wicket-keepers, Wood played for Cambridge both before and after the war, and was captain of the exceptionally powerful University team of 1920. He kept wicket for England against South Africa in the 3 Test Matches of 1924. After the First World War came the most famous of all Cheltenham cricketers, K. S. Duleepsinhji. At school he was not only a superb batsman, but one of the best of Cheltenham's captains and certainly their most brilliant fieldsman.

The Lord's match against Haileybury was terminated in 1967, and no 2-day matches are now played. These have been partly replaced by a 4-schools end-of-term festival. The best of the more recent seasons for Cheltenham was 1972, when an unbeaten XI played very attractive cricket. This coincided with 2 centenaries – an unbeaten 1872 College XI and 100 years of Gloucestershire cricket on the College ground. The 1972 XI was captained by K. D. G. Thomas, a prolific all-rounder with 1,759 runs and 130 wickets between 1969 and 1972. He also captained the Southern Schools in his last year. In 1976 D. N. Brettell won an Oxford blue.

Christ's Hospital

Foundation 1552

SCHOOL OPPONENTS: Tonbridge; Lancing; Eastbourne; Ardingly; Whitgift; Dulwich; St John's, Leatherhead; Epsom; Cranleigh.

Christ's Hospital have provided captains of both Oxford and Cambridge since the Second World War. D. R. W. Silk captained Cambridge in 1955 and later batted with distinction for Somerset; and J. A. Bailey (now Secretary of MCC), a fast bowler, led Oxford in 1958 and also played for Essex. Other good cricketers at Christ's Hospital since the war have been J. J. McInerny and N. P. Thompson; I. P. Morton was an excellent wicket-keeper. The outstanding product to come out of Christ's Hospital is J. A. Snow, of Sussex and England. There were some good XIs in the 1970s, with that of 1973 outstanding and undefeated. Some of the best cricketers of late have been the opening batsman I. M. Swalwell, all-rounder H. P. Holdsworth, and fast bowler Q. P. V. Brown, who in 3 seasons beat the school record with 132 wickets.

City of London School

Foundation 1442

SCHOOL OPPONENTS: Merchant Taylors'; Chigwell; Eltham Forest; Bancroft's; St Dunstan's; Colfe's; Latymer.

The school produced an outstanding cricketer in the England captain J. M. Brearley; an opening batsman and wicket-keeper, he was captain of the XI in 1959 and 1960. The following year he got his blue as a freshman at Cambridge. City of London's other blue was B. J. K. Pryer (Cambridge, 1948). At the beginning of the century P. W. Hale played for Middlesex, and in the 1930s F. C. Hawker – later Sir Cyril Hawker and President of MCC – played with much success for the Old Citizens and Southgate, and appeared for Essex in 1937. S. A. Hattea and S. H. Courtney went on the England Schoolboys tour to Pakistan in 1967–68. Hattea played for MCC Schools, at Lord's, in 1968, and took 4 wickets in 5 balls against the Combined Services.

Clifton College

Foundation 1862

SCHOOL OPPONENTS: Sherborne; Marlborough; Downside; Rugby; Cheltenham; Malvern; Tonbridge; Felsted; Winchester; Eastbourne; Blundell's; Millfield.

The greatest days of Clifton's cricket took place in the 19th century. In 1899 the spotlight settled firmly on the school when A. E. J. Collins, at the age of 13, played his famous innings of 628 not out in a junior house match, the highest score, still, ever made in any class of cricket. The innings was spread over 5 days and occupied 6 hours 50 minutes – a rate of nearly a hundred an hour. After leaving Clifton, Collins joined the Army and played some cricket in India, but was killed in action in 1914. Thirty-one years before Collins's effort, another Cliftonian amassed the highest score then known, E. F. S. Tylecote making 404 not out for the Classical side against the Modern. Tylecote afterwards captained Oxford for 2 years, kept wicket for England against Australia, and was a leading figure in the Gentlemen and Players matches for nearly 20 years.

At the beginning of the 1890s emerged Clifton's greatest cricketer, C. L. Townsend. Before he even entered Clifton, Townsend took 10 wickets for 68 against the school when playing for Knole Park. He got into the XI in his first year, and at the age of 16 played for Gloucestershire and with his leg-breaks took 5 for 70 against the Australians. At 18 he was the best right-hand slow bowler in the country and 4 years later, when he began to 'lose' his bowling, he had become probably the best left-hand batsman. At the turn of the century, A. D. Imlay and R. P. Keigwin were Clifton's best players. In the First World War years, A. F. Bickmore was a fine aggressive opening batsman, and probably no one has been quite so good since. In between the wars, B. O. Allen had considerable success at school and later as captain of Gloucestershire, and after the Second World War, A. R. Windows had 5 years in the XI, played for Gloucestershire while still at Clifton, and was in the Cambridge sides of 1962, 1963 and 1964. Among bowlers, S. B. Morgan took 66 wickets in 1914 at a cost of less than 10 apiece, including 6 for 18 against Tonbridge, who were played at Lord's for the 1st time that year. From 1933 to 1937, E. K. Scott captured 244 wickets with his leg-breaks and top-spinners, and taking his aggressive batting into account was considered by many to be the best Clifton all-rounder since Townsend.

In recent years R. M. Ridley gained an Oxford blue in 1968, and A. C. D. Moylan one at Cambridge in 1977. The severe restriction on Schools' matches at Lord's in 1968 meant that the traditional game against Tonbridge could no longer be played there. It was this cancellation which inspired the master-in-charge at Eastbourne, J. S. W. Lush, to invite Clifton and Tonbridge, and then Felsted and Winchester, to inaugurate one of the first of the end-of-term Schools' Festivals. In 1979 the Clifton team went on a fortnight's tour to Bermuda.

Cranleigh School

Foundation 1865

SCHOOL OPPONENTS: Christ's Hospital; Eastbourne; Brighton; Epsom; St John's, Leatherhead; Lancing.

The school playing fields are on clay and consequently the preparation and maintenance of good wickets is relatively straightforward. There have been many high-scoring games in the past. Since 1946 no blues have been obtained although C. D. White, who played 7 times for Cambridge in 1959–1960, came very close and R. R. C. Wells was 12th man in 1977 and 1978 for Oxford. N. A. Paul, who scored a hundred for the Southern Schools at Lord's in 1951 and later made an appearance for Warwickshire, has been an outstanding all-rounder in club cricket. D. J. Lister, J. W. McDermott and R. P. K. Whitcomb stand out as high-scoring batsmen at school, while R. Bennett, along with Paul, are the pick of the bowlers. In 1974, when all regular school opponents were defeated, R. R. C. Wells and D. A. B. Bugge both played for the Public Schools XI.

Prewar M. A. McCanlis (also a rugby football blue and international) captained Oxford in 1928; while E. W. Swanton played for Middlesex. Eastbourne and Lancing stand out as being the two strongest school fixtures over the postwar period.

Denstone College

Foundation 1868

SCHOOL OPPONENTS: King Edward's, Birmingham; Wrekin; Worksop; Bromsgrove; Trent; Stonyhurst; Ampleforth; Bedford Modern; Ellesmere; Nottingham HS; Oakham; Pocklington; Shrewsbury; Solihull; Warwick.

Denstone have distinguished themselves at cricket rather less than at rugby football. Two of their best cricketers were D. H. Burrow and J. H. G. Deighton, who were contemporaries from 1936 to 1939. Both played for the Public Schools at Lord's, and Deighton, a very steady bowler slightly above medium-pace, later played for Lancashire and captained the Combined Services. Following these two, Denstone had their most successful captain in D. M. Haynes, who went on to captain Cambridge in war-time matches, Staffordshire and the Minor Counties.

Prominent Denstonian cricketers in the past 20 years include the rugby football International A. J. Hignell (Cambridge and Gloucestershire), who in his last school year won the Cricket Society's award for the best batsman of 1973. Two years previously M. Morgan had won this award as the best all-rounder. In 1969 R. L. Short (Cambridge) became the first Denstone cricketer to win a blue.

Downside School

Foundation 1605

SCHOOL OPPONENTS: Canford; Taunton; Blundell's; Sherborne; Clifton; King's, Taunton; Radley; Lancaster Royal GS; Glenalmond; Dulwich.

The outstanding cricketer to have come from Downside is M. J. Turnbull, who had the rare distinction of being an international at 3 major games – cricket for England, and hockey and rugby football for Wales. In his last year it was said that it was unfair to ask boys to bowl at him, and in 1925 he scored the record number of 1,323 runs. He played for Glamorgan in 1924 and 1925 while still at Downside. Then, having played 3 years for Cambridge, of which he was captain in 1929, he shouldered the double burden of the secretaryship and captaincy of his county until the war, in which he was killed. H. E. Watts, who came back in 1948 to run the cricket for 15 years, was another fine all-round sportsman whose 938 runs in 11 innings in 1940 was one of the best batting achievements at Downside. A powerful left-hander, he played for Somerset before leaving school and did so regularly in August until 1953.

Of the earlier players, T. P. Geoghegan, who scored 717 runs at an average of 119 in 1919, was considered by his contemporaries to be a magnificent player, but he died of pneumonia 2 years after leaving Downside. In the 3 years 1957–1959, A. J. G. Pearson, who opened the bowling for Cambridge in 1961–1963, took 111 wickets and R. J. Sadler 107 with his left-arm spinners. The most successful wicket-keeper from Downside has been D. V. Brennan, who kept for Yorkshire after the Second World War, and played in 2 Tests against South Africa in 1951.

Dulwich College

Foundation 1619

SCHOOL OPPONENTS: King's, Canterbury; Epsom; St Paul's; Mill Hill; Christ's Hospital; Bedford; Merchant Taylor's; Tonbridge.

Dulwich, with their large numbers, have always been one of the leading cricket schools. Among the many outstanding cricketers they have produced in modern times may be mentioned the Gilligans – A.E.R., A.H.H. and F.W. – S. C. Griffith and the England all-rounder, T. E. Bailey. At the latter end of the 19th century several famous cricketers were at Dulwich, including C. M. Wells, F. D. Browne, Rev F. H. Gillingham, L. H. W. Troughton and J. Douglas. The 1903 captain was N. A. Knox, later of Surrey and England, whose feats as a schoolboy fast bowler foreshadowed the shattering speed which for a few brief seasons he showed in first-class cricket.

The best of Dulwich cricket belongs to 4 eras. The first, beginning in 1911, belonged to the Gilligan brothers; the second from 1930–1933 was with H. T. Bartlett and Griffith; the third was in 1941–1942, when Bailey and A. W. H. Mallett were in partnership together; and the fourth from 1964 to 1966, with the Surrey batsmen N. J. Cosh and R. D. V. Knight at the helm. The Gilligans were all fine all-rounders. Frank was a batsman and wicket-keeper, Arthur took 78 wickets for under 9 runs apiece and scored over 500 runs in 1914, while in the same year Harold set up a batting record by scoring 190 against Bedford. Arthur and Harold went on to captain England and Sussex and Frank captained Oxford and also played for Essex. Just before Bartlett and Griffith made their mark, Dulwich had been led by a remarkably gifted captain in D. R. Wilcox, afterwards to lead in turn Cambridge and Essex. Wilcox during his last year in the side scored 1,025 runs. In 1931 Bartlett began the 1st of his 3 years as captain, and there has never been a more exciting or dashing left-handed batsman at Dulwich. Griffith was overshadowed by Bartlett, but he played many fine innings during his 4 years in the XI.

Bailey and Mallett began their careers in the side in 1938 and 1939, and went on to create as famous a school legend as Bartlett and Griffith had done 10 years earlier. Both made a pack of runs, but it was as a bowling pair that they brought Dulwich such success. In 1942 they took 122 wickets between them for a cost of just over 6 runs apiece.

Dulwich has produced 12 blues since the Second World War – T. E. Bailey, O. J. Wait, M. H. Bushby, G. W. Cook, C. B. Howland, M. C. Kirkman, R. D. V. Knight, A. R. Dewes at Cambridge; and A. W. H. Mallett, W. M. Mitchell and I. D. F. Coutts at Oxford. Any mention of Dulwich cricket would be incomplete without a mention of the tremendous work done by C. S. ('Father') Marriott, who was master-in-charge for 25 years from 1923 to 1948.

Eastbourne College

Foundation 1867

SCHOOL OPPONENTS: Christ's Hospital; Cranleigh; Brighton; Hurstpierpoint; King's, Canterbury; Lancing; St John's, Leatherhead; Radley; Tonbridge; Clifton; Felsted; Winchester.

The first player of any subsequent fame to come from Eastbourne was H. S. Poyntz, who had a wonderful summer in 1895, scoring over 1,000 runs and taking 94 wickets; he later played for Somerset. One of the best of all Eastbourne sides was in 1917, when they had 3 very successful bowlers in F. B. R. Browne (Cambridge and Sussex), N. C. Macleod and A. R. Morres. In 1964 they had their 1st blue for 42 years when I. G. Thwaites played for Cambridge. In 1970–1971 M. T. Barford also won a Cambridge blue.

In 1969 the Master-in-charge, John Lush, instigated the Eastbourne Festival, a pioneer of Schools' Cricket Festivals. It is played for 5 days, followed by the Southern Schools v The Rest, and by ESCA v Public Schools XI on the Saffrons ground.

Edinburgh Academy

Foundation 1824

SCHOOL OPPONENTS: Fettes; Glenalmond; Loretto; Merchiston; Strathallan; George Watson's; Kelvinside Academy; Daniel Stewart's; Melville; Denstone; Pocklington; Nottingham HS.

Edinburgh Academy has always been amongst the best Scottish cricket schools. During this century the outstanding cricketer at the Academy has probably been B. R. Tod, who made his 1st appearance in the team at the age of 13 and was in the XI for 6 years. Altogether Tod scored 3,568 runs and took 224 wickets. K. W. Marshall scored over 900 runs in 1930, and, in 1935, R. B. Bruce Lockhart captained an unbeaten side. Since the Second World War, the most successful Academy cricketer has been J. M. Allan, captain in 1949–50. In 1949 he took 85 wickets with his left-arm spin bowling, and then, the following year, opened the innings for the Rest against Southern Schools at Lord's. Allan played 4 years for Oxford, and for Kent, Warwickshire and the Gentlemen, and later captained Scotland. In 1972, the XI, under the captaincy of J. Fulton was unbeaten, a feat previously accomplished in 1862, 1935 and 1950.

Emanuel School

Foundation 1595

SCHOOL OPPONENTS: KCS Wimbledon; Tiffin; Eltham; Colfe's, Reigate GS; Trinity, Croydon; Latymer Upper; Alleyn's; Royal GS, Guildford; Kingston GS; Hampton; Royal GS, High Wycombe; Maidstone GS.

Emanuel's best year was probably 1915, when A. E. Titley scored 1,056 runs and took 87 wickets at 6·7 apiece, and the captain, P. G. Page, captured 105 wickets at an average of 6·0. W. S. Surridge, who was captain of the XI in 1935, was a successful captain of Surrey from 1952 to 1956. In recent times the 1962 side was one of the most successful; against Reading School it scored 301 for 4 declared in 150 minutes. P. J. Barker contributed 109 in under even time and V. J. Dodds (who played for the Southern Schools at Lord's) was undefeated for 130.

Emanuel's outstanding player of the late 1960s was P. R. Needham, who took 80 wickets in his final season and played for Surrey Young Cricketers, London Schools and Surrey Schools.

The College field at Eastbourne where the pitches are good despite being used for rugby football in the Michaelmas term.

The Epsom ground where the school are playing Lancing.

Emanuel cricket thrived with the introduction of knock-out competitions in the 1970s. The school won the London Schools Cup (*Cricketer* Trophy) in 1970, and were runners-up in 1971. In 1976 they were joint winners of the *Cricketer* Trophy and also won the Surrey Schools Cup (Alexander Trophy) in a final that produced 488 runs in 80 overs. I. R. Payne, the captain, scored 143 off 74 balls to complete a season's aggregate of 1,144 runs; he also took 79 wickets at 8·68 apiece. Payne captained the London Schools XI and also played for England Schools, for whom he took 8 for 22 in the match at Millfield. Mention should also be made of I. R. Coleman, who scored 821 runs and, in one week in July 1975, scored 453 runs, including an innings of 168. This was surpassed in 1978 when B. R. Hardwick scored 203 not out in a total of 325 for 5 declared against Royal GS High Wycombe. In the same year the school achieved the knock-out 'double' of winning both the London Schools and Surrey Schools Cup Competitions.

Epsom College

Foundation 1853

SCHOOL OPPONENTS: Dulwich; St John's, Leatherhead; Brighton; Lancing; Cranleigh; Christ's Hospital; KCS Wimbledon; St George's.

The first notable cricketers produced by Epsom came to light around 1900 – the brothers Heygate (R.B. and H.J.) of Sussex, and H. C. Pretty, who scored a hundred on his first appearance for Surrey in county cricket. Since the Second World War there have been both good sides and good players. In 1961 Epsom had an outstanding schoolboy cricketer in M. Manasseh, who created an excellent impression with his off-break bowling and sound batting, when playing for the Public Schools XI at Lord's. The fulfilment of Manasseh's potential came in 1964 when his hundred against Cambridge at Lord's made the game safe for Oxford.

Eton College

Foundation 1440

SCHOOL OPPONENTS: Marlborough; Charterhouse; St Paul's; Bradfield; St Edward's, Oxford; Wellington; Winchester; Harrow.

Eton's contribution to the game is seen in many different ways. They have produced fine players like C. I. Thornton, C. T. Studd and G. O. Allen; they have had characters like Lord Hawke and Lord Tennyson; and they have provided such legislators and administrators as Lord Harris, W. Findlay and R. Aird. Eton have had the advantage of being coached and guided by talented and devoted masters and have played their cricket on two of the most picturesque grounds in the country – Agar's Plough and Upper Club. The 1st Eton and Harrow match was played at Lord's in 1805. Eton were unbeaten at Lord's from 1908 until 1939, and after the Second World War they again began to frustrate Harrow until in 1952 Harrow broke the spell with a handsome win by 7 wickets. Since then honours have been fairly evenly divided.

The birth of modern Eton cricket came in the 1860s. In 1860 R. A. H. Mitchell gave a foretaste of his future skill as a player by scoring 70 out of Eton's total of 98 against Harrow. He was asked to play for the Gentlemen that same summer. At Oxford, Mitchell established himself as the best amateur player of his time, and when he returned to Eton in 1866 he adopted an automatic control of the school's cricket which lasted for almost thirty years. C. I. ('Buns') Thornton came on the scene in 1866, and in the Eton and Harrow match of 1868 he made the first of many notable long hits when he struck the ball over the old Lord's pavilion. The influence of Mitchell's coaching was first seen in 1869 when the Eton side was considered one of the best in their history. C. J. Ottaway (Oxford, Kent, Middlesex) scored the 1st hundred against Harrow since E. Bayley's 152 in 1841, and averaged 78 for the season. The great Eton cricketing families of Lyttelton and Studd distinguished the Eton team of the 1870s, and although Harrow had a fine run towards the end of the 19th century, Eton continued to produce many distinguished players, the most notable of them being B. J. T. Bosanquet, the inventor of the googly.

The new century opened with 3 more defeats at Lord's, but in 1903 Eton gained a great victory by an innings and 154 runs. The match was a triumph for C. E. Hatfield, who, bowling slow left-arm, took twelve wickets for under 100 runs. The following year D. C. Boles made 183 and Eton again won by an innings. Then in 1910 came the most famous of all the contests between Eton and Harrow – Fowler's Match. During the First World War Eton had such players as W. G. L. F. Lowndes (Oxford and Hants), C. H. Gibson (Cambridge and Sussex), W. R. Shirley (Cambridge and Hants) and B. S. Hill-Wood (Derbyshire). In 1919 W. W. Hill-Wood (Cambridge and Derbyshire), R. Aird (Cambridge and Hants) and G. O. Allen (Cambridge, Middlesex and England) all made their 1st appearances in the XI. The following season Allen took 9 wickets for 34 against Winchester, and in the 1921 Winchester match Aird scored a hundred.

In 1920 C. M. Wells retired from his duties as master-in-charge, but at the same time George Hirst came from Yorkshire as coach, making a deep mark on Eton cricket almost up to the Second World War.

The scene at Lord's in 1930 for the Eton and Harrow match.

One of Eton's most consistent batsmen between the wars was E. W. Dawson, who later captained Cambridge and Leicestershire, and played for England against South Africa and New Zealand. Dawson scored a hundred in each school match in 1923, including 159 against Harrow, and against Winchester he and F. G. B. Arkwright shared a 2nd wicket partnership of 301. Another fine bat was I. Akers-Douglas, who followed Dawson's hundred with 158 in 1928. Eton's batting at this period was undoubtedly stronger than the bowling, but in 1931 A. G. Pelham (later a Cambridge blue) gave the best bowling performance at Lord's since Fowler's day by taking 11 Harrow wickets for only 44 runs. The two names that Harrow feared most in the 1930s were the opening batsmen, A. W. Allen and N. S. Hotchkin. In 1931 Hotchkin scored 153 and Allen made 112, then the following year at Lord's, Hotchkin hit 109 and 96, and in 1933 he scored 88. Both Allen and Hotchkin went on to play for Cambridge.

In the immediate prewar years the best players were F. G. Mann, who later captained England and Middlesex; his brother J. P. Mann, also of Middlesex; and D. H. Macindoe, the Oxford captain in 1946, who returned to Eton and ran the cricket for 12 years. There were no Eton and Harrow matches at Lord's during the war, but W. G. Keighley, P. D. S. Blake and C. R. D. Rudd, who all got Oxford blues, were 3 notable batsmen produced at Eton during this period. T. Hare scored 103 in 1947, and 2 years later A. C. D. Ingleby-Mackenzie played some fine aggressive innings. R. V. C. Robins (son of R.W.V.) made the 1st of his 4 appearances in the XI in 1950. His success at first came as a leg-break and googly bowler, but in his last season, as captain at Lord's in 1953, he scored 102, and Eton beat Harrow by 10 wickets. In 1955 Eton won an exciting match at Lord's by 38 runs, their wicket-keeper that year being a 15-year-old, H. C. Blofeld. Blofeld might well have gone on to distinguish himself in senior cricket but for a serious crash on his bicycle outside Agar's in the summer of 1957.

More recently few Etonians have been good enough to make the grade in first-class cricket. Viscount Crowhurst's fast-medium bowling got him some games for Northamptonshire 2nd XI, and R. C. Kinkead-Weekes won a blue at Oxford as a wicket-keeper; M. J. J. Faber also won an Oxford blue and played 4 seasons for Sussex. At schoolboy level the batting records of W. G. A. Clegg, R. C. Daniels and V. A. Cazalet were impressive. The captaincy of M. L. Dunning, in 1959, was outstanding. In 1968 J. R. T. Barclay first played for Eton at the age of 14. His slow off-breaks were as effective as Robins's leg-breaks had been nearly 20 years earlier. He was captain in 1970 and 1971, and, with the help of H. M. Wyndham's accurate slow-medium inswingers, Eton beat both Winchester and Harrow in 1971. In the 1970s Eton's cricket declined, the nadir coming in 1975, when the weakest Eton side since 1954 was obliterated by a strong Harrow side. In 1977 the intelligent captaincy of R. H. M. Raison and the solid batting of J. L. Rawlinson, who made over 50 in every match against another school, led to a victory at Lord's – but only after Harrow had declared twice. Since then Harrow have had the best of it.

Felsted School

Foundation 1564

SCHOOL OPPONENTS: Bishop's Stortford; The Leys; Aldenham; Mill Hill; Bedford; St Paul's; Haileybury; Highgate; Ipswich; Clifton; Eastbourne; Tonbridge; Winchester.

It was a Felstedian, William Byrd, of Westover, Virginia, USA, whose diary provided cricket historians with the first record of cricket in America. He was at Felsted from 1684–1689, and on 25 April 1709 he played two-a-side cricket at Jamestown. The 1st Felstedian to play in the University Match was T. S. Curteis, who represented Cambridge in 1864 and 1865. Others to have emulated him are W. J. V. Tomlinson (1923), B. G. M. Cangley (1947) and K. P. A. Mathews (1951), all of Cambridge. But Felsted's greatest cricketer was J. W. H. T. Douglas. He was in the XI for five years from 1897, played for Essex from 1901–1928 (captain from 1911–1928) and in a long Test Match career captained the MCC sides in Australia in 1911–12 and 1920–21. The highest batting average at Felsted remains Cangley's 317 in 1940, when he was only once dismissed.

The highest batting aggregates have been 1,120 runs by C. R. Clark in 1976 (average 74·7) and 895 (including 5 hundreds) by D. M. Matthews in 1935; 872 runs were scored, in 1956, by R. A. G. Luckin, and 830, in 9 completed innings in 1977, by D. R. Pringle – both of whom afterwards played for Essex; and 801 by N. T. Gadsby in 1978. Of the bowlers, J. W. H. T. Douglas took 56 wickets at 15 runs apiece in 1899; N. J. L. Trestrail 51 in 1976; and Pringle 58 and 53 respectively in 1976 and 1977.

At the end of the 1979 season the school had enjoyed 4 unbeaten seasons (1975–1978), winning 33 out of 53 matches against English schools, including two 'Grand Slams' at the Eastbourne Festival against Clifton, Eastbourne, Tonbridge and Winchester in 1976 and 1977.

Fettes College

Foundation 1870

SCHOOL OPPONENTS: Loretto; Merchiston Castle; Edinburgh Academy; Glenalmond; George Watson's; Strathallan; Durham; Daniel Stewart's; Melville College; St Bees.

Fettes have one of the best natural wickets in Scotland and, despite the encroachment of the city's housing and traffic, their ground remains a beautiful country setting surrounded by trees. The professional from 1920 until his death in 1942 was Bob Haywood, of Northants; he was succeeded by Reg Hollingdale, of Sussex, until his retirement in 1975. Under their tuition the cricket has flourished, although a standard has never been reached quite comparable to the school's rugby football. The school has produced many fine players though, of whom M. R. Jardine and K. G. MacLeod were probably the best. Jardine captained Oxford in 1891, while MacLeod, who was in the Cambridge sides of 1908 and 1909, also played for Lancashire. Several Fettesians have represented Scotland, including J. F. Jones, a prolific scorer who was selected while still at school. Since the Second World War alternatives to cricket have been admitted to the summer programme, but it has remained the major game and the overall standard has altered little. It continues to be played in a sturdy and vigorous spirit.

Glasgow Academy

Foundation 1845

The Academy summer term is short by English standards, and cricket accordingly both starts and ends early. Conditions are not always ideal, but morale and wickets are excellent, and there is a strong enthusiasm for the game. The best cricketer to come from the school has been I. A. R. Peebles, who won fame with his leg-breaks for Middlesex, Oxford and England. The early years were distinguished by such well-known Scottish players as A. D. Laird (1907), I. B. Mackinlay, G. B. McGhee and W. N. Walker (1911). In 1922, A. D. Innes, another fine cricketer for Scotland, was captain of the XI, and the 1924 side, which included Peebles, was captained by J. R. W. Orr, who led a Public Schools team that season against a side of Australian Schoolboys touring in Britain. Other notable players at the Academy before the Second World War were G. G. Crerar, J. G. Loudon, J. W. Denholm, J. R. Henderson, L. Shearer and W. D. Hendry. After the war came C. A. B. Campbell, I. F. Colquhoun, R. N. Prentice, W. M. Mann and A. D. Innes, jr.

Fettes v MCC: the school marked their centenary in 1970 by beating the club for the 1st time. Back row: A. W. R. Trantor, H. L. D. McLaren, R. F. Dickinson, G. J. Timm, W. F. E. Forbes, J. G. Cumming and R. Bowman; middle row: R. A. Hollingdale, D. A. Elliott, G. C. Macnaughton, J. N. Sands, M. J. N. Loudon, R. J. B. Hoare, D. J. Lumsden, Lt-Cmdr G. Hughes-Games, J. D. A. Clayton, J. Brown and M. S. Preston; front row: A. C. D. Ingleby-Mackenzie, D. H. Fell, E. W. Swanton, R. A. B. Reid (captain), C. J. R. Whittle, I. D. McIntosh, S. R. G. Pratt, F. A. Jones.

Haileybury

Foundation 1862

SCHOOL OPPONENTS: Tonbridge; Harrow; Uppingham; Bedford; Wellington; Cheltenham; Felsted; Dulwich; Mill Hill; Sherborne; Marlborough.

The success of Haileybury's cricket can be traced back to the appointment as master of Edward Lyttelton in 1890, and then to the arrival of P. H. Latham, a famous Cambridge cricketer, who came as master-in-charge in 1895. In 1893 Cheltenham were played at Lord's for the 1st time, and although Haileybury lost the contest, they then proceeded to dominate the match until 1902. The 6 years from 1897 to 1902 was an outstanding period in Haileybury's history. The Bignell brothers, H.G. and G.N., and S. M. Toyne (later Headmaster of St Peter's, York), all of whom played for Hampshire, E. S. M. Poyntz of Somerset, A. F. Spooner (younger brother of R. H. Spooner), who played for Lancashire, and A. H. C. Fargus, who got a blue at Cambridge and afterwards played for Gloucestershire, were the best-known players. Just before the First World War, Haileybury produced another blue at Cambridge in H. G. Vincent, and during the war one of their best cricketers emerged, F. J. Seabrook. By the time he went up to Cambridge in 1926 he was already an experienced county player with Gloucestershire, and he played 3 years at Lord's, being captain in 1928. He returned to Haileybury in 1931 and for many years successfully ran the cricket. Many of those connected with Haileybury cricket believe the most polished batsman they have ever had was R. E. H. Hudson, who captained the XI in 1922. That season he scored 191 against Uppingham and finished his school career with innings of 90 and 101 against Cheltenham at Lord's. Hudson was a batsman of great gifts whose subsequent cricket was for the Army.

He was succeeded as captain of the XI in 1923 by R. J. O. Meyer, a fine bowler for Cambridge from 1924 to 1926, and later a useful all-rounder for Somerset, whom he captained in 1947. During the Second World War a notable batsman was A. Fairbairn, who in 1947 scored a hundred in each of his first 2 matches for Middlesex. In 1952 D. H. W. Bolton scored 3 separate hundreds and the 1962 captain, M. A. Freedman, was an outstanding batsman. In 1974 Haileybury were unbeaten in school cricket, while in 1978 they beat Harrow for the 1st time in 18 years.

Harrow School

Foundation 1571

SCHOOL OPPONENTS: Malvern; Wellington; Winchester; Haileybury; Charterhouse; Eton.

It is probably true to say that cricket and in particular 'Lord's' is of even more importance to Harrovians than to Etonians, who also have rowing as a major sport in summer. The cricket tradition has been a marked feature of Harrow for upwards of a century. One of the earliest and most famous of all Harrow cricketing names was that of the Walker family, who were the founders of Middlesex cricket. There were 7 brothers, of whom I. D. Walker was the best known. He started the Harrow Wanderers in 1870. When he retired from first-class cricket he devoted all his time to coaching the boys at Harrow. Following shortly after I. D. Walker at Harrow was A. N. Hornby. As a bat Hornby for a while was second only to 'W.G.', and he did for Lancashire almost as much as the Walkers for Middlesex.

In 1872 there appears for the first time the great Harrow name of A. J. Webbe. He was captain of Cambridge in 1877 and 1878, after which he had a long and distinguished career with Middlesex, first as captain, then as secretary and finally as President. The next decade between 1878 and 1903 saw some of Harrow's greatest times. They won 12 times at Lord's against Eton's 3, with 10 draws. The Harrow captain in 1880 was M. C. Kemp, who has been described as 'one of the patron saints and tutors of Harrow cricket, and its most agonized spectator'. Kemp captained Oxford for 2 years, and played for the Gentlemen and Kent as a batsman and wicket-keeper. He returned to Harrow as a master in 1888 and for the next 50 years the school's cricket owed a vast debt to his wisdom and experience. 1887 was a memorable year as marking the first appearance of two of the greatest Harrow cricketers, F. S. Jackson (later Sir Stanley) and A. C. MacLaren.

Another great Harrow cricketer appeared in 1895, E. M. Dowson, who played at Lord's when barely 15 years of age and while still ridiculously small. He ranks with such heroes as J. N. Crawford and A. G. Steel as one of the best schoolboy players of all time. Harrow won a magnificent match in 1900 by 1 wicket, and their side contained 3 future University captains in F. B. Wilson, who captained Cambridge in 1904 and was later known as a humorous and kindly writer for *The Times* on almost every game under the sun; E. W. Mann, who succeeded Wilson as captain of Cambridge; and K. M. Carlisle, who opposed Mann in 1905 as captain of Oxford. M. Falcon, of Cambridge and Norfolk, who was one of the best amateur fast bowlers of his time, now enters the ranks, joined by an equally illustrious player, M. C. Bird. Morice Bird earned eternal fame in the Eton and Harrow match in 1907 by making a hundred not out in the 1st innings and then 131 in the 2nd. He went twice with MCC to South Africa and was a popular captain of Surrey.

Next came the period when Harrow were continually frustrated by Eton at Lord's. After 1908 they did not win again until the last year before the Second World War, in 1939. There were few features of note among Harrow's performances before the First World War, but Geoffrey Wilson, afterwards to appear for Cambridge and Yorkshire, had 2 great years in which, in consecutive innings, he made 173, 65 and 58. Also with Wilson at Harrow was G. R. Jackson, who captained Derbyshire. The surprising part about Harrow's lack of success in the 1920s was that they had so many good players during this period. C. T. Bennett and H. J. Enthoven were both captains of Cambridge, and Enthoven twice scored hundreds against Oxford at Lord's. L. G. Crawley, also of Cambridge and Essex, was a fine aggressive batsman, who would probably have played for England if he had not concentrated on golf. His cousin, A. M. Crawley, who made a large number of runs for Oxford during his 4 years in the team, was a delightfully free stylist. Other blues in the 1920s were P. H. Stewart-Brown, R. E. C. Butterworth and N. M. Ford at Oxford; and H. F. Bagnall at Cambridge. In the 1930s, W. O'B. Lindsay and A. Benn got Oxford blues; and Cambridge were well served by Harrow with A. S. Lawrence, M. Tindall, captain of Cambridge in 1937, J. H. Pawle, M. A. C. P. Kaye, B. D. Carris and P. M. Studd, the 1939 Cambridge captain. Of these Mark Tindall was a wonderful stylist, and returned after the Second World War, as master-in-charge.

Lord's 1939: A. O. L. Lithgow, the Harrow captain, being chaired off after Eton had been beaten for the 1st time since 1908.

Harrow might well have won in 1938, but rain intervened, and a famous Harrow cricketer was heard to have murmured, 'Now I am sure that God is an Old Etonian'. The outstanding batting that year came from R. A. A. Holt, who scored 152 not out v Winchester, 184 not out and 125 v Charterhouse, and finished the season with an average of 101. Then in 1939 the tide and the luck changed at last, and, amid terrific scenes at Lord's, Harrow won by 7 wickets. A. O. L. Lithgow, the captain, made the winning hit over the bowler's head. It was to be another 13 years before Harrow won again at Lord's, but since 1952 they have flourished, both over Eton and other schools. From 1946 to 1978, 70 Harrow matches were won against 24 lost.

In the immediate postwar years one of Harrow's best bowlers was R. G. Marlar, who took 90 wickets with his off-breaks in the two seasons 1948 and 1949. Marlar was afterwards captain of Cambridge and Sussex. A successful all-rounder was A. R. B. Neame, who crowned his 4 years in the XI by doing the hat-trick at Lord's in 1955. There was an outstanding year in 1975: Harrow beat Eton by an innings and 151 runs. This was their easiest victory in the 140 years' history of the fixture at Lord's: M. K. Fosh scored 161 not out, the 1st Harrovian hundred since E. Crutchley's in 1939 and the 3rd highest scored in the match. That season the fast bowler A. C. S. Pigott took 58 wickets, and in his school career he finished with 108 wickets. Fosh went on to win a Cambridge blue and to play for Essex, and Pigott for Sussex. The following year R. M. Tindall (son of Mark Tindall) scored a hundred at Lord's, as, in 1978, did T. M. H. James.

Highgate School

Foundation 1565

SCHOOL OPPONENTS: Aldenham; Merchant Taylors'; King's, Canterbury; Mill Hill; Cranleigh; St Paul's.

Highgate were perhaps at their strongest in the 1920s, when they produced R. W. V. Robins, A. H. Fabian and W. H. Webster. Robins was a Cambridge blue from 1926 to 1928 and captained Middlesex and England. He was followed in the Cambridge side for 3 more years by Fabian, who returned to Highgate in 1934 and ran the cricket until 1959; Webster got his blue in 1932; so for 7 successive years there was a Highgate player in the Cambridge team.

S. S. Rogers captained Somerset after the Second World War, and M. L. Laws kept wicket on occasions for Middlesex. W. Knightley-Smith was a left-hander of immense promise, who led the Public Schools to victory over the Combined Services in 1951 before getting a blue at Cambridge in 1953. C. D. Drybrough was captain of the school XI in 1956 and 1957, and a most prolific scorer during that time. On going up to Oxford, Drybrough developed his left-arm spin bowling and played 3 years at Lord's, captaining Oxford in Pataudi's absence in 1961 and in his own right in 1962; in 1963 and 1964 he led Middlesex. The outstanding Highgate cricketer of the last 20 years was D. L. Hays (captain 1962 and 1963), who won a Cambridge blue and then, as captain of Finchley, became a distinguished club batsman.

King's College School

Foundation 1829

SCHOOL OPPONENTS: Whitgift; Kingston GS; St John's, Leatherhead; King's, Canterbury, UCS; Epsom, Emanuel; Tiffin; St Paul's; St George's, Weybridge.

The best period in KCS Wimbledon's cricket came in the 1930s when they had 2 outstanding players in D. E. Young and P. J. Dickinson. Young was a leg-break bowler, a sound bat and magnificent field, who got his blue at Oxford in 1938. From 1932 to 1936 he made 1,950 runs and took 198 wickets for the school XI. Dickinson started his career in the XI in 1934 at the age of 14 as a wicket-keeper/batsman, but by 1936 he had made himself into a very useful swing bowler, and in 1939 he opened the bowling for Cambridge at Lord's. His fame, though, comes from his batting in the University Match of 1939, when going in at No. 7 he made a hundred in the 2nd innings and only just failed to save and win the match for Cambridge. At KCS he had a fine record, scoring 3,518 runs and taking 111 wickets.

Dickinson's record aggregate still stands, although J. C. Wolters, who was captain in 1958 and 1959, scored 1,982 runs at an average of 42. The record number of wickets in a season is held by W. P. Lipscomb, who back in 1905 took 92 at 8·19 apiece.

In the 5 years from 1964 to 1968 King's lost only one inter-school match. The most distinguished player of this time was D. R. Owen-Thomas, who had 5 years in the XI, starting at the age of 14 in 1963. He made 2,822 runs, including 9 hundreds, and took 133 wickets with innocent-looking off-breaks. At Cambridge Owen-Thomas scored successive hundreds in the University Match in 1971 and 1972. V. G. B. Cushing, who succeeded Owen-Thomas as KCS' captain in 1968, got an Oxford blue in 1973. During the 1978 season M. L. Allcock scored 719 runs, including 160 not out against St Paul's.

King Edward's School

Foundation 1552

King Edward's has provided the Midlands with many excellent cricketers, the two outstanding ones being O. S. Wheatley and A. C. Smith. Wheatley, a fast bowler, took 80 wickets for Cambridge in 1958 – the largest number ever achieved at either University. After 2 full years with Warwickshire, Wheatley moved to Glamorgan whose side he led from 1961 to 1964. A. C. Smith, a genuine all-rounder, captained Oxford for 2 seasons – the first man to do so twice by appointment for more than 60 years. He toured Australia with MCC in 1962–63, and was chosen for 4 of the Tests.

During his 4 years in the team, J. A. Claughton (1972–1975) scored over 2,000 runs, and went on to captain Oxford in 1978.

Lancing College

Foundation 1848

SCHOOL OPPONENTS: Hurstpierpoint; Brighton; Epsom; Ardingly; Eastbourne; Westminster; Tonbridge; Charterhouse; Cranleigh.

The most successful side that Lancing have had was in 1928, when G. A. K. Collins scored 863 runs at an average of 72. Also in that team was E. Cawston (a Cambridge blue in 1932), who the next season scored 966 runs, while the rest of the XI made 1,301 between them. Both Collins and Cawston played for Sussex while still at Lancing. In 1913, G. H. Heslop took 9 wickets for 14 runs against Eastbourne and ran the last man out himself. In 1914 Heslop scored 981 runs including an innings of 223, an average of 89·18. A. L. Hilder was captain of the XI for 3 years, and on his first appearance for Kent in 1924, made 103 not out against Essex.

The first 2 blues after the Second World War were A. C. Burnett (Cambridge, 1949) and C. J. Saunders, a wicket-keeper, who was unlucky to find some stiff competition during his 3 years at Cambridge, but gained a blue at Oxford, where he went up for one year in 1964. The record of 9 wins, held by the 1928 XI, was equalled by the 1976 XI and the 1978 XI came within 1 win of it. These last 2 XIs, plus that of 1969, must be regarded as the best recent batting sides.

The Leys School

Foundation 1875

SCHOOL OPPONENTS: Perse; Bishop's Stortford; St Paul's; Mill Hill; Oundle; Bedford; Felsted; Gresham's; Highgate.

One of the most notable performances in Leysian cricket was the 220 runs scored by N. J. Holloway against MCC in 1908. Holloway (Cambridge 1910–1912) played for Sussex, and also for Gentlemen v Players, whilst his brother, B.H., went on an MCC tour to the West Indies. He was followed by C. A. Fiddian Green, who played for Cambridge (1921–1922), Warwickshire and Worcestershire. A year of glory for The Leys was 1929, when F. R. Brown's team went through the season without defeat. Brown, a future captain of England, had a batting average of 65·4 and a bowling average of 11·2 (60 wickets). He was ably supported by A. F. Skinner (Derbyshire), the older brother of D. A. Skinner, who captained Derbyshire in 1949. Since the Second World War several Leys players have played Minor Counties cricket. Recently T. J. Murrills has captained Cambridge University in 1976; D. H. R. Fairey has captained Cambridgeshire; and I. Craig has played for the Home Counties against India.

Loretto School

Foundation 1827

SCHOOL OPPONENTS: Edinburgh Academy; Merchiston; Glenalmond; Fettes; George Watson's; Royal High School; Strathallan; Stewart's; Melville.

For over 70 years Loretto was one of the 5 schools, later joined by George Watson's, who competed for the unofficial Scottish 'Championship'. Loretto also had an annual fixture against one English school, Rossall, between 1880 and 1912. It is usually thought that the standard of school cricket in Scotland is inferior to that in England, but over the 33 years of this fixture with Rossall the honours remained fairly even. The 1st Lorettonian to play for Scotland was H. N. Tennant in 1865. He was followed by 7 other cricketers before 1900 – the best known being J. G. Walker, who played for Oxford and Middlesex, and represented the Gentlemen in 1887. Later Scottish players included W. Nicholson and A. D. Baxter from 1929 to 1934. Baxter was a fast bowler who played for Lancashire and Middlesex and toured New Zealand with MCC in 1935–36. The most successful schoolboy player was G. L. Hunting, who, in 1910, achieved the very rare feat of scoring 1,000 runs in a season. He later played regularly for Northumberland. Until recently, the 1st XI traditionally wore shorts and red stockings.

Magdalen College School

Foundation 1478

SCHOOL OPPONENTS: St Bartholomew's, Newbury; Dean Close; Berkhamsted; Abingdon; Pangbourne; Bloxham; Oratory; Oxford School; Perse; Newcastle Royal GS; Douai; King Edward's; King's Lynn; Lord Williams, Thame.

Magdalen College School has had a close connexion with Oxford and Oxfordshire cricket. Their 5 blues, T. H. Belcher, S. Pether, J. E. Bush, J. D. Martin and M. F. D. Lloyd (1974), were all at Oxford. Martin, Oxford's 1965 captain, was a fine fast-bowler at school, and in 1961, when he played for the Public Schools at Lord's, he took 60 wickets at 6·08 apiece.

Besides the blues, Magdalen had 2 good school cricketers before the last war in M.

Evans, who in 1923 scored 520 runs (average 74) and took 62 wickets at 8·37 apiece, and G. W. G. Walker, who in 1938 scored 747 runs (average 75) and took 62 wickets at 11·6. Walker also played for the Public Schools at Lord's.

Malvern College

Foundation 1862

SCHOOL OPPONENTS: Cheltenham; Harrow; Rugby; Repton; Clifton; Shrewsbury.

Malvern College was built in a beautiful position on the lower slopes of the Malvern Hills. In 1873 a terrace was cut out of the hill and a cricket pitch made. Then, about 15 years later, the 'Senior Turf' was extended in length and width. Much of this work was done by the boys, and to the present day a custom introduced for the purpose of levelling the turf has been retained, wherein boys walk round the Senior after Sunday evensong. The Senior remains to this day rather on the narrow side, and sixes have never been allowed. The shape of the ground and the perfection of the wickets have had a marked influence on Malvern cricket. Nearly all the notable performers have been batsmen, and spin-bowlers have been few indeed.

C. Toppin, a young Cambridge blue, joined the staff in 1886, and for nearly 40 years he was to be the inspiration which made Malvern cricket. He firmly believed that defence should only be learnt after attack, and attack he would have. C.T.'s influence remained the dominating force which inspired many fine players who left Malvern up to 1924.

By 1891 the tide had turned in Malvern's cricket fortunes. The Toppin era had arrived and with it such fine natural games-players as the 7 Foster brothers and the brothers Day. The eldest of the Fosters was preceded by Malvern's 1st blue, P. H. Latham, who played for Cambridge in the years 1892–1894. Thereafter during the next 20 years there was hardly a season when there was not a Malvernian playing for either Oxford or Cambridge. From 1889 until 1904 there was only one season when there was not a Foster in the Malvern XI. H.K., W.L., R.E., B.S. and G.N. all played more or less regularly for Worcestershire – or 'Fostershire' as it became known – in the early years of the century.

The Rev H. Foster and his 7 sons who all went to Malvern and all played for Worcestershire. Back row: R.E. and B.S.; middle row: W.L. and H.K.; front row: M.K., N.J.A. and G.N.

Contemporary with the early Fosters were W. W. Lowe, G. H. Nevile, C. J. Burnup, G. H. Simpson-Hayward, who played for England as a lob bowler, and S. H. Day. Shortly after these came W. H. B. Evans, a fine all-rounder, who in 1913 was the victim of a flying accident. In the Malvern side of 1901, captained by Evans, were A. P. Day, who might easily have played for England; W. S. Bird, the best of Malvern's wicket-keepers; and G. N. Foster, who was 4 years in the Oxford side.

In the years up to the First World War, H. L. Simms, J. H. Naumann and D. J. Knight were amongst a number of high-class players who came from Malvern. Knight arrived at Malvern with a sound defence, and it is said that he was never able to watch a 1st XI match as a spectator, playing in the XI for 5 years, from the opening game of his 1st summer term and advancing every season to become possibly Malvern's soundest player on all types of wickets. During the First World War G. B. Cuthbertson, C. G. W. Robson, J. A. Deed and N. E. Partridge were the best players, and Partridge (in 1919) had the distinction of being asked to play for the Gentlemen while still at school. In the year after the First World War, G. B. Legge and E. R. T. Holmes, who was later a popular captain of Oxford and Surrey stand out as the finest products of Malvern cricket. Holmes was a most attractive driver, and played rather in the old style made famous by the Foster brothers.

W. H. Bradshaw, R. G. Stainton and R. H. Maudsley all got Oxford blues, while A. H. Brodhurst played for Cambridge at Lord's in 1939. G. H. Chesterton was a remarkably accurate bowler of medium pace who played for Oxford in 1949 and also for Worcestershire. He returned as a master in 1950, and for 15 years ran the cricket with great success.

Since the war 2 Malvernians have emulated Knight in playing 5 years in the XI. R. K. Whiley (1951–1955) played once for Gloucestershire while still at Malvern, but was rather disappointing afterwards; while J. W. T. Wilcox (1955–1959) narrowly missed a blue 3 years running at Cambridge, and afterwards had some success for Essex. One of the best individual performances since the war was by B. A. Richardson in 1962, when he made nearly 800 runs in 16 innings.

In more recent years two other sets of brothers have contributed greatly to Malvern cricket – the 3 Tolchards and the 3 Prices, who between them made nearly 6,000 runs for the school. Roger Tolchard went on to keep wicket for Leicestershire and to win 3 Test caps for England against India in 1977. Jeff Tolchard was a Leicestershire player in some of the county's best years, and the youngest, Raymond Tolchard, made a hundred for Devon in the Minor Counties Challenge Match which won them the Championship in 1978. In the last 20 years there have been some fine school sides – the most successful of them in 1966.

Malvern can claim 13 players who have played in first-class cricket since 1960, including two Tolchards, H. T. Tunnicliffe (Notts), and I. N. Johnson (Worcestershire), who was leading run scorer on the Young England tour of West Indies (1972) and who also took 151 wickets in his 4 years in the Malvern team. D. Bailey played for Lancashire and later followed his brother, H. J. Bailey, as captain of the Minor Counties. A good seam bowler, S. M. Wookey, had the unusual distinction of gaining a blue at both Cambridge and Oxford. An outstanding Minor County cricketer has been C. M. G. Hunter (Dorset), whose bowling in the *Cricketer* Cup has been one of the strengths of Old Malvernian cricket.

Manchester Grammar School

Foundation 1881

The Cricket Club was founded in 1881 and fully established by 1905 when the ground at the Cliff, Lower Broughton, was acquired. From the beginning, the fixture list was not confined to local schools and clubs; before the First World War there was a fixture with King Edward's School, Birmingham at Edgbaston. The removal of the school to Fallowfield in 1931 was beneficial in many ways, especially with regard to games. For the first time in the school's history, playing fields were adjacent to the school. The War Memorial Pavilion was opened in 1956. Since 1949, the 1st XI has gone on tour at Whitsuntide, playing 3 matches against schools, for the most part in the south of England. Many major boarding schools have entertained them and the record is quite creditable; MGS have won more than they have lost. Against Eton in 1956, T. M. Richardson scored 120 not out. His uncle, T. G. Richardson, who was in the 1st XI for 5 seasons in the 1920s, held the record score, 152 not out, until it was beaten in 1976 by G. M. Beckett.

The 1950s produced some fine cricketers. In 1953–1954 Ian Gibson was chosen to play in the Public Schools Matches at Lord's; in 1954 he was accompanied by Geoffrey Edge. Peter Hutson played in the Lord's match in 1956; David Green in 1957 and 1958; and Dennis Woolley in 1959. Gordon McKinna won a cricket blue in 1953, Ian Gibson in 1955–1958, David Green in 1959–1961. David Green later played for Lancashire and Gloucestershire, scoring 107 against an Australian touring side and being one of *Wisden*'s Cricketers of the Year in 1969.

Marlborough College

Foundation 1843

SCHOOL OPPONENTS: Clifton; Winchester; Eton; Wellington; Sherborne; Cheltenham; Rugby; Millfield; Haileybury; Radley.

The first signs of real interest in cricket at Marlborough came some 10 years after their foundation when James Lillywhite was appointed coach. Within 4 years the 1st match against Rugby was arranged, although it did not become an established fixture until 1862, Marlborough being until then hardly good enough. In 1870 came the era of A. G. Steel which served to put Marlborough indelibly on the cricket map. Under Steel's captaincy Marlborough only lost one match in 2 years, and of his skill it need only be said that at 19 he played for the Gentlemen, he headed the first-class bowling averages as a freshman at Cambridge and the following season was 4th in the batting averages.

After Steel, the most illustrious of Marlborough's cricketers is undoubtedly R. H. Spooner, who ranks with the classic stylists of all time. Spooner was a terror to Rugby, averaging 75 against them in 6 innings, including one of 198 which stands as the 2nd highest innings ever played in school cricket at Lord's. The highest, 211 by P. R. Creed in 1892, also goes to the credit of Marlborough. No mention of Marlborough cricket would be complete without word of the brothers, Ashfield – 3 of whom, R.C., L.A. and C. W. R., accomplished the notable feat of scoring hundreds against Rugby.

After the First World War, Marlborough produced their fair share of blues with G. E. B. Abell (Worcestershire), J. W. Seamer (Somerset) and P. M. W. Whitehouse, all at Oxford; and W. K. Harbinson, S. A. Block, who later played for Surrey, J. T. H. Comber, who kept wicket from 1931–1933, and G. E. Hewan, at Cambridge.

Since the Second World War, N. M. Morgan, A. Goodfellow, M. G. Griffith, C. P. Pyemont and N. P. G. Ross have won blues at Cambridge; P. N. B. Sabine, D. R. Walsh and R. LeQ. Savage at Oxford. Griffith, in the XI for 5 years, was a brilliant schoolboy cricketer. In 1961 he scored 1,070 runs at an average of 97·27 and he kept wicket brilliantly. Savage was an outstanding schoolboy bowler, who took 151 wickets in his 3 years in the XI (1972–1974). C. F. Worlidge (1,579 runs); R. B. M. Johnson, who at the age of 15 scored 124 v Rugby in 1967; and R. Williams-Ellis, whose 683 runs in 1974 averaged 45·5, have all done well with the bat. A successful all-rounder was S. J. Lillyman (1,279 runs and 77 wickets). In J. R. Thompson and D. J. Green Marlborough were well served by their masters-in-charge of cricket for 30 years after the Second World War.

Merchant Taylors' School

Foundation 1561

SCHOOL OPPONENTS: City of London; UCS; Mill Hill; Highgate; St Paul's; Dulwich; Aldenham; St Alban's; St John's, Leatherhead.

In 1900 Merchant Taylors' had its 1st blue, J. W. F. Crawfurd (Oxford), and in 1901 they had 2 outstanding batsmen in the XI, J. E. Raphael and T. Dennis. Between them they put on 326 for an unbroken 1st-wicket partnership against Kensington Park CC in the 1st match. In the next game Raphael and Dennis both made hundreds, and at the end of the season each had scored well over 1,000 runs. Merchant Taylors' had an outstanding season in 1977 with 7 victories, which included 2 wins by 10 wickets and 1 by 9 wickets. The leading figure in this triumphant year was the captain, R. Marsden, who at one stage scored 341 runs before being dismissed in a match. He finished the 1977 season with an average of 127.

Merchiston Castle School

Foundation 1833

SCHOOL OPPONENTS: Fettes; Loretto; Glenalmond; Strathallan; George Watson's; Edinburgh Academy.

Merchiston Castle can boast no blues and no first-class players since T. A. L. Whittington, the Glamorgan captain in 1921. Their best batsman in earlier days was T. B. Lyle, who had a magnificent season in 1914, averaging 91 in school matches and scoring 2 hundreds.

The most successful batsman since the Second World War, and probably the most attractive stroke-player from Merchiston, was I. McLauchlan, who in 1956 hit 3 hundreds in a total of 799 runs. An outstanding era of the school's cricket came between 1967 and 1971, when the XI played 42 matches without defeat. The key feature of this success was the opening pair of J. G. Raven and R. G. Swan; in 1969 these 2 amassed 950 runs between them, while in 1970 Raven scored 658 runs and Swan 560. Swan went on to captain Durham University and UAU, and also played for Scotland. R. M. Richards was a successful off-spin bowler in 1971 and 1972, when he took 50 and 55 wickets respectively in school matches alone. More recently J. A. Turnbull was a hard-hitting batsman in 1977 and 1978; and in 1979 N. H. Cairns scored 590 runs.

The Oratory School

Foundation 1859

SCHOOL OPPONENTS: Abingdon; Aldenham; Douai; Leighton Park; Magdalen College School; Pangbourne; Reading.

For more than 40 years The Oratory was one of only 10 public schools to have a regular fixture at Lords (1926–1968). These matches were discounted when the John Player and Benson & Hedges tournaments were introduced. However, The Oratory boys have one of the finest cricket grounds in the country on which to play their matches. As well as games against other schools, there are some strong club fixtures – MCC., XL Club, Berkshire Gentlemen, Emeriti, Old Oratorians, Woodcote CC, etc. The most notable individual achievement in recent years was a 'double hat-trick' by C. J. P. Bragg in 1969 when he took 8 for 10 against Henley GS.

Oundle School

Foundation 1556

SCHOOL OPPONENTS: Bedford; The Leys; Stowe; St Edward's, Oxford; Rugby; Uppingham; Ampleforth; Blundell's; Mill Hill.

The standard of cricket at Oundle improved noticeably in the 1920s, when they had such players as F. E. Greenwood and R. A. Ingle at the school. Greenwood went on to captain Yorkshire when they won the County Championship in 1931, and Ingle was captain of Somerset for several years before the Second World War. In 1928 N. G. Wykes got a blue at Cambridge and also played for Essex. In the first year after the war Oundle had 2 representatives in the Cambridge side – E. R. Conradi and J. M. Mills. Mills played at Lord's for 3 years, and was captain of Cambridge in 1948.

Since then J. H. Minney has played for Northamptonshire, and in recent years an increasing number of boys have gone on to play in Minor County and County 2nd XI cricket, a fact which reflects a particularly successful period over the last few seasons and the generally growing strength of Oundle cricket.

Pocklington School

Foundation 1514

SCHOOL OPPONENTS: Ampleforth; St Peter's, York; Bradford GS; Leeds GS; Hymer's; Ashville; QEGS Wakefield; Bootham; Denstone; Merchant Taylors', Crosby; Sedbergh; Edinburgh Academy; Mount St Mary's.

Pocklington had their 1st blue in 1963 when M. H. Rose won his place as a batsman in the Cambridge side. Pocklington might well have had 2 players in that Cambridge team, for P. D. Briggs, who captained the school XI for 3 years (1957–59), played in more than half the University matches. Rose had played 2 years for the Public Schools at Lord's, in 1960 and 1961. An excellent batsman, C. Johnson played for MCC Schools at Lord's in 1966, and 3 years later made his debut for Yorkshire. Since 1970 the school has built up a strong fixture list and produced a fine record of victories, with an emphasis on aggressive cricket. In 1978 J. D. Guiller scored 969 runs.

Earlier players of note at Pocklington were C. E. Anson, who played for Yorkshire on occasions after the Second World War; and T. F. Smailes, who was capped for Yorkshire in 1934, did the double in 1938, and played for England against India, at Leeds, in 1946.

Radley College

Foundation 1847

SCHOOL OPPONENTS: Abingdon; Bradfield; Eton; Harrow; Malvern; Marlborough; St Edward's, Oxford; Sherborne; Stowe; Wellington.

Radley's 1st recorded match was against Bradfield in 1853, and in the Centenary Match in 1953 Radley won by an innings and 39 runs, E. R. Dexter making 147 and taking 7 wickets. The first outstanding Radley cricketer was W. E. W. Collins, a man of many parts; scholar, essayist, novel-writer, and part-author of *The Annals of the Free Foresters*. Collins, a prodigious hitter of sixes and a somewhat terrifying left-arm fast bowler, graced the Radley XIs of the middle 1860s. Later came 2 Oxford blues, R. H. Moss and L. C. V. Bathurst, the latter probably Radley's best cricketer before Dexter.

The Radley sides of 1921–1923 contained one of the school's finest batsmen, A. E. Blair, who scored 989 runs in 1922 and 1,011 the following season. G. C. A. Adams, who made nearly 2,500 runs during his five years at Radley, later played a few matches for Hampshire. The period 1929–1932 produced some very strong sides, the best player in them possibly being P. I. Van der Gucht, who in 1933 kept wicket and batted with distinction for Gloucestershire. Following him came H. P. Dinwiddy, who like Adams was 5 years in the XI. He scored 2,590 runs, took 104 wickets with his leg-breaks, and captained the 2 most successful sides in 1931 and 1932, which each won 9 of their 10 school matches.

Radley made a slow start after the Second World War, but from 1948 onwards a series of strong sides followed almost continuously for

15 years. Between 1948 and 1954 only one school match was lost out of the 34 played; between 1957 and 1961 Radley were undefeated by any school. 1952 was the '*annus mirabilis*'. Captained for the 2nd year in succession by A. C. Walton (who later captained Oxford), Radley not only went through the season of 16 matches undefeated, but maintained an average of 82 runs an hour throughout the season. Dexter averaged 83 with the bat, and Walton scored over 700 runs. The 1953 side was not so consistent, but Dexter scored 873 runs and also took 44 wickets. After Walton and Dexter, another prominent cricketer in the 1950s was the leg-break bowler A. R. Duff (Oxford and Worcestershire).

In the 1960s Radley produced the Somerset wicket-keeper C. E. P. Carter, and also R. J. A. Thomas, an Oxford blue in 1965, and S. R. Bielby, who played a few matches for Nottinghamshire. The school's fixture list was considerably strengthened in the 1970s, with new matches against Eton, Harrow and Marlborough. In 1972 T. E. Harris scored 817 runs (average 81·7), followed the next season by M. Glover with 955 runs. N. F. M. Popplewell (Cambridge 1977–1979) achieved an outstanding all-rounder's record in 1975, with 720 runs and 60 wickets. In 20 matches, the 1978 team were unbeaten, 8 batsmen recording innings of 50, and the spin bowlers, C. J. Sutton and T. P. Wise, both taking over 50 wickets.

Repton School

Foundation 1557

SCHOOL OPPONENTS: Worksop; Uppingham; Cheltenham; Shrewsbury; Rugby; Malvern.

Repton's cricket success has been unequalled by any other school, except perhaps Eton, Harrow and Winchester. Some of the Repton sides at the beginning of the century were of a legendary quality. Yet it is a moot point whether they were not as strong in the 1880s, when they had Lionel Ford (subsequently headmaster both of Repton and Harrow), a tremendous hitter; Alfred Cochrane (Oxford and the Gentlemen); Francis Ford, the most illustrious cricketer of the family and one of 5 Reptonians who have played for England against Australia; the Palairet brothers – R. C. N. and L. C. H. – and lastly the most gifted games-player of all, C. B. Fry.

At the turn of the century there appeared at Repton one who by all accounts was one of the greatest schoolboy cricketers of any generation. In his 4 years in the XI, J. N. Crawford revived Repton to its old eminence. According to H. S. Altham (who was in his 1st year in the 1905 Repton side when Crawford, as captain, was in his last), 'a medium-paced bowler of beautiful action, great accuracy, and every possible device, a batsman of extraordinary power but classic method, and a magnificent field in any position, he dominated during his last 2 years every school match in which he took part and appeared, what indeed he was, a first-class cricketer playing in a class below him'.

In his 4 years Crawford made more than 2,000 runs for Repton, and took more than 200 wickets. He took nearly a hundred wickets for Surrey as a schoolboy, and the year after leaving he did the double and played for the Gentlemen at Lord's. Contemporary with Crawford were R. A. Young, who played for England in Australia as batsman and wicket-keeper, E. A. Greswell and the Turner brothers.

With all this excellent talent, Repton in 1905 were, of course, unbeaten, but it is the 1908 side, captained by Altham, which earned fame as perhaps the best school XI of all time. In the August holidays Altham (Surrey), W. T. Greswell (Somerset), R. Sale (Derbyshire) and A. T. Sharp (Leicestershire) played for their counties; and A. E. Cardew and J. L. S. Vidler were asked to play for Somerset and Sussex respectively but were unable to accept.

Immediately before the First World War there were 2 more remarkable schoolboy cricketers at Repton – Miles and John Howell, who opened the batting together. Miles Howell went on to captain Oxford and play with distinction for Surrey, but John Howell, who it was generally agreed was an even better batsman, was killed in action in 1915.

After the war came B. H. Valentine, who later captained Kent and played for England, followed by 2 families who made an invaluable contribution to Repton cricket – the Humans and the Mendls. R. H. C. Human (Cambridge and Worcestershire) was captain in 1927 and 1928; J. H. Human, who captained Cambridge in 1934, played for Middlesex, and went on 2 MCC tours, in 1933 and 1935. J. H. Human was in the XI for 5 years, his best season being 1930, when he scored 704 runs at an average of 78. In this year the 3 Mendl brothers – J.F., D.F. and K.J. – appeared in the same side. The first two scored a great number of runs, K.J. being a fast bowler and hard-hitting batsman.

Before the Second World War, Repton had 2 fine left-handed batsmen in G. L. Willatt and R. Sale, who went on to get blues at Cambridge and Oxford; and in 1944 Repton were captained by D. B. Carr. The following year Carr played for England at Lord's in the Victory Test against the Australian Forces side.

Since 1951 the school sides have been consistently strong, with C. B. Fry's grandson, C. A. Fry, who played 3 years for Oxford, and R. A. Hutton, the elder son of the Yorkshire and England batsman, as two notable products. Richard Hutton (Cambridge, Yorkshire and England) was an outstanding schoolboy cricketer with bat and ball, who in his last season (1961) scored 1,036 runs with an average of 74. His younger brother, J. L. Hutton, showed almost equal promise as captain in 1964. The best batsman in the last 15 years was P. N. Gill, who later enjoyed considerable success for Staffordshire.

The match ground at Repton, the nursery of so many distinguished cricketers from C. B. Fry, the Palairets and J. N. Crawford onwards.

Rossall School

Foundation 1844

SCHOOL OPPONENTS: Shrewsbury; Stonyhurst; Sedbergh; Lancaster Royal GS; Manchester GS.

Rossall made a valuable contribution to Lancashire cricket in its early years. One of the first cricketers to emerge from Rossall, A. B. Rowley, who played for the Gentlemen, was prominent in forming the Lancashire County Cricket Club. His younger brother, E. B. Rowley, played for the Gentlemen when only 20, and also for many years for Lancashire. Following the Rowleys was the Rev F. W. Wright, another Lancashire cricketer, who is considered one of the best of all Rossall batsmen. Many others from the new school went on to play for the county at this time, including the Rev V. P. F. A. Royle, an outstanding cover point, and later T. A. Higson, a Test Match selector for a number of years and chairman of Lancashire.

L. V. Harper, F. H. Mugliston and G. B. Davies all got Cambridge blues before the First World War, but in between the wars Rossall produced fewer cricketers of any subsequent note until the Howard brothers – N.D. and B.J. – in 1942. Both the Howards played for Lancashire, and N.D. went on to captain the county and also the MCC team which toured India in 1951–52.

In 1950 Rossall had one of the strongest school sides in the country, with a team which included G. P. Marsland, a brilliant fielder who got a blue at Oxford (1954), and M. E. L. Melluish, who captained Cambridge in 1956 and kept wicket for the Gentlemen at Lord's. R. M. O. Cooke played for Essex in 1973–1975.

Rugby School

Foundation 1567

SCHOOL OPPONENTS: Clifton; Malvern; Uppingham; Repton; Oundle; Marlborough; Shrewsbury; Charterhouse; Warwick; St Edward's, Oxford.

Rugby School v MCC, 1941 – a match held to mark the centenary of the game between the same teams in *Tom Brown's Schooldays*. Among Old Rugbeians in the picture are Sir Pelham Warner and the then secretary of MCC, Lt-Col R. S. Rait Kerr. Others include R. H. Twining, G. O. Allen, R. E. S. Wyatt, C. I. J. Smith and (in uniform) E. R. T. Holmes. The Rugby boys who have won their colours are wearing the traditional (and unique) pale blue shirt.

Rugby is known to most followers of the game as Sir Pelham Warner's school and by the fact that they are unique in wearing light blue shirts. For over a century these were seen at Lord's until the Rugby v Marlborough match was moved to the schools in 1973. Among the ancient Rugby cricketers may be mentioned E. G. Sandford, who played for Oxford and the Gentlemen, as did B. B. Cooper, who was once spoken of in the same breath as 'W.G.'; T. Case, F. H. Bowden-Smith and E. M. Kenney won blues at Oxford; while W. Yardley will be remembered as the scorer of 2 hundreds in the University Matches of 1870 and 1872. C. K. Francis took all 10 wickets in an innings of the Marlborough Match in 1867; and C. F. H. Leslie was one of the best Oxford cricketers of the 1880s. E. R. Wilson (Cambridge, Yorkshire and England) was another outstanding character to come out of Rugby at this time, but before him was the school captain in 1892 – P. F. Warner.

There were some unusually good Rugby sides around 1915–1920, when the brothers J. L. and R. T. Bryan, M. D. and B. H. Lyon, and G. A. Rotherham were contemporaries. M. D. Lyon, in the top flight as a wicket-keeper/batsman, played for Cambridge, Somerset and frequently for the Gentlemen, while his brother Beverley, an Oxford blue in 1922–1923, went on to captain Gloucestershire with much daring and distinction. J. L. Bryan, one of 3 left-handed brothers, went to Australia with MCC in 1924–25, and R. T. Bryan captained Kent. The 1st University Match after the First World War contained 2 Rugbeians, Rotherham and C. P. Johnstone, who afterwards played some fine innings for Kent. Then came E. F. Longrigg (Cambridge and captain of Somerset); K. L. T. Jackson and M. M. Walford (Oxford); D. G. Clark (captain of Kent after the Second World War); and J. R. Bridger, of Hampshire, who was in the XI for 4 years.

Rugby started well after the Second World War, the 1946 and 1947 sides losing only one match between them, but their most successful period was between 1951 and 1954, under the charge of A. W. E. Winlaw. M. A. Eagar, of Oxford and Gloucestershire, was to the fore during this time, and although the sides in the next 10 years were not so strong they included an excellent batsman in J. L. Cuthbertson, who in 1960 scored more than 1,100 runs, beating the record of 1,034 set up by J. G. Pugh in 1921. Cuthbertson played in the 1962–1963 Oxford sides and was succeeded by M. R. J. Guest, who was in the Oxford team for 3 years. J. I. McDowall kept wicket for Cambridge (1965–1966) and played occasionally for Warwickshire. In 1968 Rugby joined Malvern, Shrewsbury and Repton in one of the early Schools Festivals.

Rydal School

Foundation 1885

SCHOOL OPPONENTS: Birkenhead; Ellesmere; King's, Chester; Liverpool College; Merchant Taylors'; Crosby; Stonyhurst; William Hulme's GS.

Rydal first established a name in school cricket in the 1920s, producing players such as A. Ratcliffe (Cambridge and Surrey), who, in 1931, was the 1st player to score a double-hundred in the University Match; H. R. W. Butterworth (Cambridge and Lancashire); G. Elson (Warwickshire); and then, in the 1930s, W. Wooller, the renowned Glamorgan captain (1947–60). The Second World War years nurtured W. H. H. Sutcliffe, who followed his famous father in playing for Yorkshire. A contemporary of Sutcliffe's was M. H. Stevenson (Cambridge and Derbyshire). Numerous Old Rydalians have recently played Minor Counties cricket, among them M. S. R. Byrne and A. J. Byrne for Cheshire; and J. P. Dawson (Shropshire). In 1977 and 1978 A. E. C. Jones, slow left-arm, won caps for Wales at the Under-19 level.

St Edward's School

Foundation 1863

SCHOOL OPPONENTS: Cheltenham; Bradfield; Oundle; Stowe; Radley; Harrow; Rugby; Abingdon; Eton; Bedford.

Throughout its history St Edward's has produced a good supply of fine cricketers, of whom 2 achieved Test Match status: E. G. Wynyard (Army and Hampshire) at the turn of the century, and P. A. Gibb (Cambridge, Yorkshire and Essex) before and after the Second World War. In the earlier period St Edward's also supplied Hampshire with (Sir) Russell Bencraft, E. G. Read and T. H. Page; while overseas, H. M. B. de Labat played a leading part in the promotion of New Zealand cricket.

Other notable players include R. H. J. Brooke, who played for Oxford in 1932 – averaging over 50 and scoring 4 hundreds; P. Cranmer, who captained Warwickshire at cricket and England at rugby football; E. J. H. Dixon, who captained Oxford in 1939; D. Henderson (Oxford, 1950); the international squash-player, J. N. C. Easter (Oxford, 1966–1967); and P. R. Thackeray (Oxford, 1974).

St George's College

SCHOOL OPPONENTS: Ardingly; Douai; St John's, Leatherhead; St Benedict's, Ealing; Whitgift; Epsom; Kingston GS; Stonyhurst; Tiffin; KCS Wimbledon.

Records of cricket exist from the earliest days of St George's. Enthusiasm was helped by the presence of a contingent of pupils from the West Indies. In 1925, E. Grell, from Trinidad, took 75 wickets, and at this time, under the guidance of the Rev J. A. Fawcett, a fine medium-pace bowler, the standard improved rapidly.

The real rise in standard dates from 1945 when the increased number of boys brought a more consistent level and stronger fixtures. P. R. Burns made 701 runs in 1955, and the XI of 1954, including Beckett, Burns and B. V. O'Gorman (now master-in-charge), which won 14 matches, has claims to be the best team. From 1953 to 1955 the school was unbeaten in school matches. In recent years, D. R. Crane, B. K. McCabe, A. T. Scott and S. Clothier have played for the representative Southern and Public Schools. The most famous cricketer to have attended St George's is P. G. H. Fender (1902–1906) who played frequently in the Old Georgians matches in the 1930s.

St John's School

Foundation 1851

SCHOOL OPPONENTS: Eastbourne; Epsom; Cranleigh; KCS, Wimbledon; Whitgift; St George's, Weybridge; Hurstpierpoint; Christ's Hospital.

Founded as a school for the sons of the clergy at St Mark's, Hamilton Terrace, within a few hits of Lord's, it is not surprising that St John's should have a strong cricketing tradition. Shortly after the school moved to Leatherhead in 1872, it produced some useful cricketers, notably T. T. N. Perkins (Cambridge and Kent) and L. T. Driffield (Cambridge and Northants). In 1915 M. D. A. G. Du Pre, batting at No. 4, had the distinction of scoring a hundred before lunch against a strong MCC team. There were some successful sides at St John's in the early 1950s, with only 3 school matches lost between 1951 and 1955. The captain in 1953 was the hard-hitting batsman R. M. James, who, at Cambridge in 1956, became the first freshman to score a hundred against the Australians.

The teams of 1968 to 1970 were particularly good, when the batting was based on the opening partnership of G. A. Law and J. L. Rose. They opened the batting 42 times together, and figured in 7 partnerships of over 100 runs. In recent years the teams of 1975 to 1977, based on the opening bowling of M. A. Arthur and R. J. Golder, have been the most successful.

St Paul's School

Foundation 1509

SCHOOL OPPONENTS: Mill Hill; Dulwich; Eton; The Leys; Felsted; Merchant Taylors'; Highgate; Hampton; Kingston GS; KCS Wimbledon.

St Paul's, without reaching the top ranks among the cricketing schools, have produced some notable players, including 3 Test Match cricketers – R. O. Schwarz, who played 20 times for South Africa between 1905–1912; P. G. H. Fender, a fine all-rounder and for many years an outstanding captain of Surrey; and the Rev E. T. Killick, of Middlesex, a batsman of classical style who while still at Cambridge played twice for England against South Africa in 1929.

Besides these, St Paul's have had several blues, the best of them probably being H. M. Garland-Wells, who was in the Oxford side for 3 years and captained Surrey in 1939. Their latest blue has been F. W. Neate, a hard-hitting batsman who played for Oxford in 1961–1962. In 1970 the XI, under the captaincy of H. J. Masters, achieved a unique feat in Pauline cricket history with an unbeaten record of 11 wins and 8 draws from 19 matches. Following the move to the new school site in 1968 all cricket was played at Osterley. Since 1975, though, the grounds have been at Barnes.

St Peter's School

Foundation 7th century

SCHOOL OPPONENTS: Worksop; Giggleswick; Durham; Leeds GS; Ampleforth; Bradford GS; Sedbergh; Bootham; Pocklington.

St Peter's, York, can claim to be amongst the best cricket schools in the north. In the early days they produced Frank Mitchell, who was in the Cambridge side 4 years (1894–1897), played for Yorkshire from 1894 to 1904, and captained the South African touring teams to England in 1904 and 1912. The inspiration behind St Peter's cricket for so long was the Headmaster, S. M. Toyne. He was in charge of the XI from 1913 to 1936, and during this time St Peter's provided Yorkshire with 2 further county captains in A. B. Sellers and N. W. D. Yardley.

During the 1950s the school's outstanding cricketer was D. Kirby. Although he never quite fulfilled the batting potential he had shown when captain of St Peter's for 3 years, he went on to captain Cambridge in 1961 and Leicestershire the following season. Kirby then returned to St Peter's to join the staff and is currently master-in-charge of cricket. Recently several promising players have emerged. S. P. Coverdale. played for Cambridge (1974–1977) and has occasionally turned out for Yorkshire as their reserve wicket-keeper. D. I. Riley, the school captain in 1977 went on to play for MCC Schools XI, England Young Cricketers XI and Kent 2nd XI. The latest batsman of outstanding talent from St Peter's is R. Collingwood-Gittins, who led an unbeaten 1978 team in school matches.

Sedbergh School

Foundation 1841

Cricket at Sedbergh made a slow start but by 1879 the Giggleswick match had begun. The most famous player of this era was Charles Toppin. He was a prodigious wicket-taker for Cumberland, and later became a great coach at Malvern.

As the facilities were improved, so the standard of play developed until by the late 1930s, under the tuition of J. M. Coldham (Master-in-charge from 1928 to 1949), some very able players were appearing. Outstanding amongst these was N. S. Mitchell-Innes, a hard hitting batsman, who had the rare distinction to be picked for England in 1935, against South Africa, whilst still at Oxford. J. H. Bruce-Lockhart, who later became Headmaster, took 4 for 91 for Cambridge against the Australians in 1909; R. W. Skene was an Oxford blue in 1928; and more recently R. I. Smyth played 3 years for Cambridge, from 1973 to 1975. The centenary of the 1st school match was celebrated in 1979, the occasion being marked by a tour to Trinidad and Tobago.

Sedbergh in the field, with the Cumbrian hill 'Winder' an imposing backdrop.

Sevenoaks School

Foundation 1418

SCHOOL OPPONENTS: Ardingly; Cranbrook; Caterham; Hastings; King's, Rochester; Maidstone; Reigate; Sutton Valence; Tonbridge.

Sevenoaks' cricket has emerged from relative obscurity in the last decade. This development has reflected the dedicated work of A. Hurd (Cambridge and Essex) as Master-in-charge. Apart from producing a series of match-winning teams, Sevenoaks has won some renown in Kent cricketing circles by providing four members of the county staff, starting with J. M. Graham-Brown, who later moved to Derbyshire. More recently C. J. Tavaré gained an Oxford blue and his county performances brought him near the England side. P. R. Downton, the wicket-keeper, was chosen for the MCC tour of Pakistan and New Zealand 1977–78, and G. D. Spelman, a fast bowler and successful school captain (1976–1977), joined the Kent staff.

Sherborne School

Foundation 1550

SCHOOL OPPONENTS: Bradfield; Radley; Clifton; Canford; Blundell's; Marlborough; Cheltenham; Haileybury.

Sherborne played their 1st school match in 1865, against Clifton, the result being a tie. But for a number of years the game was not well established, and it was not until the 1890s that the school became a leading force in West Country cricket. One of the problems was its geographical isolation from the principal public schools in the Midlands and South East. Gradually, however, a strong fixture list was built up which included Dulwich, Tonbridge, Radley and Bradfield, usually 2-day fixtures. Thus, by the early years of the 20th century a strong tradition of cricket had been built up in the school. Travelling problems led to the disappearance of Dulwich and Tonbridge from the fixture list after the Second World War, but already a strong West Country cricket circuit had emerged with schools such as Downside, Blundell's and Marlborough.

One of the strengths (and, paradoxically, also a weakness) of Sherborne cricket has been the exceptionally true nature of the wicket. The clay soil has proved an ideal surface on which to learn the art of batting and has resulted in a succession of technically sound, front foot players. However the lack of bounce and real pace has meant that there has always been a dearth of fast bowlers. It has also meant that an unusually high proportion of matches have ended in draws.

Outstanding among batsmen have been A. W. Carr (1909–1911) and D. S. Sheppard (1946–1947), both of whom went on to captain England. The latter started his school career with 2 'ducks', but in his last year he scored 780 runs at an average of 78·80 – figures not surpassed since 1901. Another was J. A. Nunn, who scored 448 runs in 8 consecutive innings in 1924, and more recently the 1976 captain, T. D. W. Edwards, scored prolifically. On the bowling front, Oxford blues come to mind: D. C. P. R. Jowett (1947–1949), A. R. Wingfield-Digby (1968) and E. D. Fursdon (1969–1971), who also made a hundred in the 1975 University match. But, statistically, the best bowling figures are held by J. G. B. Fish (1975–1977), who in his last year took 49 wickets at 7·02 each.

In addition to the quality of the facilities the remarkable dedication of the cricket staff has had much to do with the strength of Sherborne cricket in the 20th century. E. J. Freeman was professional for 36 years (1911–1947) and D. J. W. Bridge was master-in-charge for 21 years (1956–1977), whilst much of the technical competence of the cricket stems from M. M. Walford, the Oxford and Somerset batsman.

Shrewsbury School

Foundation 1552

SCHOOL OPPONENTS: Rossall, Uppingham, Repton, Malvern.

Shrewsbury cricket for many years ran a poor second to the rowing. The first turning-point came in 1914 when for the 1st time the school beat Uppingham, by 5 wickets, and then defeated Rossall by an innings. The teams were captained by M. C. Dempsey (later Gen Sir Miles Dempsey), who was to play for Sussex, and 3 other members of the side were to become first-class cricketers – H. R. J. Rhys (Glamorgan), L. B. Blaxland (Derbyshire) and H. P. Ward, a batsman and wicket-keeper, who played for Oxford at Lord's in 1919 and 1921.

In 1917, under Ward's captaincy, Shrewsbury had an even more triumphant season than the one in 1914, for they beat Malvern by 3 wickets, Uppingham by 10 wickets and both Repton and Rossall by an innings. The 2 opening bowlers were largely responsible for this success—H. P. Miles, who later played for the Army, took 35 wickets at an average of 7·7, and H. D. Badger who made the occasional appearance as a fast bowler for Yorkshire, took 20 wickets at 8·2 apiece.

After this, Shrewsbury's cricket became firmly established in the highest schools' bracket, and every year except one between 1923 and 1939, a Salopian appeared for Oxford at Lord's. This is a sequence which no school can improve upon, in this century at least. First of these blues was E. P. Hewetson, who for about 2 seasons was one of the fastest bowlers in the country. He played 3 years for Oxford and was followed by two triple blues, J. S. Stephenson and A. T. Barber, D. N. Moore, D. C. G. Raikes, E. A. Barlow, who kept wicket from 1932–1934, A. P. Singleton, who captained Oxford and Worcestershire, and finally in 1939, P. H. Blagg. Besides the University cricketers, D. G. Foster was in the Warwickshire side, and played for the Gentlemen at Lord's as a fast bowler in 1931. Undoubtedly the best cricketer of these was Moore. At Shrewsbury his deeds were prolific. In 1929, his last year, he averaged 100 and made the record score for a Salopian in 3 out of the 4 inter-school matches; *i.e.* 191 v Malvern, 151 not out v Rossall and 122 v Uppingham. Moore was made captain of Oxford in 1931, a distinction that no undergraduate in his second year had gained since the days of P. F. Warner. But though he accomplished a great deal as regards the reform of Oxford cricket during his year of office, he was taken ill at the end of June and could not even see the glorious Oxford victory which he had done so much to bring about. Barber was not such a graceful bat as Moore, but he was the most dogged of fighters, and after captaining Oxford in 1929 he went on to captain Yorkshire the next season.

A. P. ('Sandy') Singleton led Oxford in 1937 and Worcestershire in 1946 and as an all-rounder would probably have played for England if he had not emigrated to Rhodesia. Just before the war Shrewsbury had a fine upstanding batsman in M. L. Y. Ainsworth, who later played for Worcestershire and captained the Royal Navy.

After the Second War the school went through some lean years, particularly in the late-1950s. In 1961 R. H. C. Waters would have kept wicket for Oxford had he not been injured in a car crash just before the University Match. The mid-1960s saw the welcome appearance of a number of talented players including S. K. Jones, N. E. J. Pocock, Hon T. M. Lamb, P. S. Bryan and R. D. N. Topham. Pocock went on to captain the Public Schools and is the present captain of Hampshire. Lamb and Topham got blues; Lamb has since played for Middlesex and Northamptonshire. The school enjoyed outstanding seasons in 1969 and 1970; since 1967 the end of the season has been highlighted by a festival shared with Malvern, Repton and Rugby. The outstanding player of recent years has been N. C. Crawford, who won a Cambridge blue.

At many schools rowing competes with cricket for the boys' attentions. This aerial photograph shows how well Shrewsbury are able to cater for both tastes. It was here that as a young man Sir Neville Cardus was the assistant cricket coach.

Stonyhurst College

Foundation 1593

SCHOOL OPPONENTS: Rossall; Sedbergh; Denstone; Giggleswick; Lancaster Royal GS; Manchester GS; Birkenhead; Ampleforth; Rydal; Wrekin.

The best Stonyhurst side in the present century was possibly the one of 1925. There was plenty of bowling, and 5 of the batsmen averaged over 40 – with T. Christie towering above everyone with an average of 103. In 47 innings for Stonyhurst Christie scored more than 2,000 runs altogether, at an average of over 50. Since the Second World War, Stonyhurst had an excellent batsman in G. P. S. Delisle, who was in the Oxford side in 1955 and 1956, and later played some good innings for Middlesex.

The school suffered a rather depressing series of results in the late 1960s, but in the past few years the standard has risen steadily. In the 2 seasons that the college entered the Taverners' Colts Trophy they were Lancashire champions (1975) and finalists (1976).

Stowe School

Foundation 1923

SCHOOL OPPONENTS: Bradfield; Bedford; Radley; Oundle; St Edward's, Oxford; Dean Close; Mill Hill; Oakham; Repton; Wellington.

Although Stowe has still to produce a cricketer of Test Match standing, several interesting county and university players have emerged in the school's short history. The excellent golfer, J. D. A. Langley, was an outstanding batsman who, between 1934 and 1936, scored nearly 2,000 runs. Langley became Stowe's 1st blue when he played for Cambridge in 1938. In the early 1950s D. M. Cobham took 150 wickets in 3 years. In 1959 Charles Oakes was appointed professional,

The match ground at Stowe, framed in Palladian splendour.

and over the last 21 years, in partnership with 6 different masters-in-charge, he has inspired numerous young cricketers to continue an active interest in the game.

The most successful cricketers to emerge under Oakes's guidance include C. J. R. Black (Middlesex); R. G. L. Cheatle, who played for Sussex when the county won the Gillette Cup in 1978; J. W. O. Allerton, an Oxford blue in 1969; J. Dixey, G. L. Macleod-Smith, R. G. G. Carr and his brother G. D. G. Carr, J. M. Haywood and D. F. C. Thomas. All these played in National Schools' representative matches.

Sutton Valence School

Foundation 1576

SCHOOL OPPONENTS: St Lawrence College, Ramsgate; Dover College; Cranbrook; King's, Rochester; Sevenoaks; St Edmund's, Canterbury; Trinity School, Croydon; St Peter's, York; Kent College; Maidstone GS.

Existing records show that cricket has been an officially sanctioned pastime at Sutton Valence since, at least, as early as 1840. The most famous cricketer to come out of the school is D. W. Carr (Kent and the Gentlemen), one of the first of the googly bowlers, who played for England against Australia in 1909. Before him they had an outstanding schoolboy cricketer, one Cobb, who in 1884 took 106 wickets at just under 4 runs apiece – including 9 for 1 against Tonbridge, and 8 for 22 against King's, Canterbury. In recent years the school has more than held its own on the Kentish circuit. They also maintain a firm link with the Band of Brothers, who use the school ground ('Upper') for several of their matches.

Taunton School

Foundation 1847

SCHOOL OPPONENTS: Downside; Canford; Bryanston; Blundells; Kingswood; Bolton.

One of the best of all amateur slow bowlers, J. C. White, came from Taunton. He will be remembered for his superb control of length and his unique subtleties of flight. White heads a list of 12 cricketers from Taunton who have gone on to play for Somerset. The others are C. G. Deane, L. H. Key, E. S. Goodland, G. B. Newport, A. G. Marshall, L. P. Marshall, J. D. Harcombe, J. H. Cameron, J. Baker, E. Hill and P. J. Eele.

Of these, the Marshall brothers formed a famous partnership before the First World War; A. G. Marshall took 10 wickets in an innings in successive years (1910 and 1911) against Queen's College. The most successful schoolboy cricketer among the Somerset players was Cameron. A leg-break bowler, he took all 10 wickets for the Rest at Lord's in 1932, and in his school career he got 425 wickets at an average of 10·55. Cameron later played a leading part in Cambridge's win over Oxford in 1935, and appeared in 2 Tests for the West Indies against England in 1939. The 2nd Cambridge blue to come from Taunton, L. G. Irvine, was also a leg-break bowler. As a freshman Irvine took 52 wickets in 1926, and the following year 7 wickets in the University Match, but thereafter was less effective.

The best batsman from Taunton since the Second World War has been J. A. Jameson, who in 1959 scored 1,031 runs, which included 163 not out against Kingswood – the highest scored by a Tauntonian against another school. He played that season for the Public Schools at Lord's and later for Warwickshire and England. On his retirement from first-class cricket in 1976 Jameson returned to Taunton to take up the post of professional. His brother, T. E. N. Jameson, became the 3rd Tauntonian to win a blue, at Cambridge, in 1970.

Tonbridge School

Foundation 1553

SCHOOL OPPONENTS: Haileybury; Bedford; Christ's Hospital; Westminster; Dulwich; Lancing; Wellington; Sevenoaks; Clifton; Winchester; Felsted; Eastbourne.

From the earliest days Tonbridge have had the advantage of a wicket which even before school sport was officially 'organized' was apparently a batsman's paradise. The 1880s were great years for Tonbridge, with C. J. Kortright and W. Rashleigh, of Essex and Kent respectively, the brightest ornaments. Rashleigh, reputed to have been the best stylist Tonbridge ever produced, made a hundred for Oxford in the University Match as a freshman, and once for Kent against Middlesex accomplished the astonishing feat of scoring 160 before lunch on the 1st day. The 7 years from 1896 to 1902 can be classified as the Hutchings era. In this period there was no Tonbridge XI which did not contain at least one Hutchings – W.E.C., F.V. or K.L. Kenneth Hutchings, a brilliant fielder, reached the heights of playing for England against Australia, both here and abroad.

Few schoolboys have ever done so much or looked so good as did F. H. Knott in his last year of 1910. He averaged 80, including 6 hundreds, made 155 for the Public Schools at Lord's, and finished the month of August with an average of 36 for Kent. He captained Oxford in 1914. Whichever seasons may be considered Tonbridge's best, there cannot be much dispute that, for an aggregate of 3, 1919–1921 are unbeatable. L. P. Hedges, C. H. Knott, T. E. S. Francis, H. C. A. Gaunt, N. B. Sherwell and E. P. Solbé were all quite exceptional batsmen, and they made their runs so quickly that, although the bowling was not particularly strong, there was nearly always sufficient time to get the enemy out. In 1919 Hedges and Knott shared in a partnership of 396 against Lancing, and 300 against Westminster at Vincent Square. Hedges went on to play some fine cricket for Oxford and Kent, and Sherwell was the soundest of wicket-keepers for Cambridge in 1923–1925, but none of them became quite so good as Knott. Like his brother, C. H. Knott captained Oxford, and for years was an invaluable member of the Kent side in the August holidays. He came back to Tonbridge and was in charge of the cricket for more than 20 years.

The 'Head' at Tonbridge School, an ideal cricket ground with perfect wickets.

Since this golden period Tonbridge has more than held its own, if in a less spectacular manner. The 3 best cricketers before the Second World War were J. G. W. Davies (Kent and Cambridge), who won fame at Fenner's in 1934 by bowling Bradman for his 1st duck in this country; T. A. Crawford (Kent); and J. R. Thompson, an opening bat for Cambridge and Warwickshire, who was prevented by the outbreak of war from captaining Cambridge in 1940.

M. C. Cowdrey arrived at the school in 1946, and promptly got into the XI at the age of 13. He started his career at Lord's that year with scores of 77 and 44 against Clifton and also took 8 wickets with his leg-breaks. For 5 years Cowdrey dominated the Tonbridge scene, scoring 2,894 runs, taking 216 wickets, and finishing his school career by making 126 for the Public Schools at Lord's. He played for Kent in the holidays while still at school, and after leaving spent a full summer in the county side before going up to Oxford.

R. M. Prideaux made 3 Test appearances and in the course of a first-class career with Cambridge, Kent, Northants and Sussex made 41 hundreds. In more recent years there have been 3 Tonbridge blues – D. P. Toft for Oxford in 1966–67, who made 145 at Lord's in 1967; and, for Cambridge, D. R. Aers in 1967 and M. E. Allbrook in 1975–78. Allbrook, C. S. Cowdrey, N. J. Kemp and R. M. Ellison have all represented England Schools in the last 5 years.

At school level the main development has been the replacement of the match at Lord's against Clifton by an end-of-term Festival which has been held at Eastbourne since 1969, involving Eastbourne, Winchester, Felsted, Tonbridge and Clifton. The dominating cricketers since 1965 have been D. R. Aers, with an aggregate of 2,612 runs and 119 wickets between 1962 and 1965; C. S. Cowdrey, with 2,483 runs between 1972 and 1975, including 966 runs at an average of 80 in 1975; J. C. Spurling, with 2,097 runs in only 3 seasons between 1976 and 1978; C. M. Davies, with 152 wickets between 1970 and 1973; N. J. Kemp, with 1,171 runs and 95 wickets between 1973 and 1975; and R. M. Ellison, with 1,476 runs and 103 wickets between 1975 and 1978. The strong links with Kent cricket have been preserved through having R. R. Dovey and A. L. Dixon as professionals during these years, and through the fact that the two Cowdreys and N. J. Kemp have all played for the county in the 1970s. Since 1930 there have only been three different masters-in-charge, giving a sense of continuity which has been an important feature in the success of the various 1st XIs: C. H. Knott, M. H. Bushby and D. R. Walsh.

Uppingham School

Foundation 1584

SCHOOL OPPONENTS: Repton; Shrewsbury; Rugby; Haileybury; Oundle; Oakham; Blundell's; Ampleforth.

As a nursery of first-class players Uppingham ranks little behind Repton as one of the most famous cricket schools. Much of their success can be traced to H. H. Stephenson, who was appointed professional in 1872. Stephenson was unusual among professional cricketers of that time in that he had been appointed captain of the 1st team to tour in Australia, and he could be considered the forerunner of the modern professional captain. At Uppingham Stephenson was both coach and master-in-charge.

The most famous of all Uppingham cricketers is the Kent and England captain A. P. F. Chapman. He first appeared in the school side in 1916, and during his 4 years scored over 2,000 runs. In 1917 he had an average of 111, and he is the only batsman ever to have achieved an average of over 100 for the school. His runs were scored at a rate which can hardly ever have been surpassed by a schoolboy batsman.

F. G. H. Chalk, who captained Oxford and Kent, was in the XI from 1927–1929; and he was followed by D. F. Walker. Walker was in the side 4 years and captain in his last 2. He was a magnificent opening batsman and succeeded Chalk as captain of Oxford in 1935. Unhappily these 2 fine cricketers were both killed in the Second World War. Walker is remembered at Uppingham for his innings of 224 not out which gave the school victory by an innings over Shrewsbury in 1932. That 1932 XI was one of Uppingham's strongest; besides Walker it contained 2 other Oxford blues, N. S. Knight and T. G. L. Ballance, and a Cambridge blue, A. F. T. White, who later captained Worcestershire.

Uppingham had 2 other blues in the 1930s; W. J. Pershke (Oxford) and D. W. Gillespie (Cambridge). During and after the Second World War they had 2 outstanding cricketers in G. A. Wheatley, who kept wicket for Oxford in 1946 and played later for Surrey, and B. Boobbyer who was 4 years in the Oxford team. The 1947 side had a formidable trio of bowlers in T. A. Hall (Derbyshire and Somerset), D. D. Carter and E. J. Wimperis.

The 1960s produced two prolific scorers in D. H. Smith (1962) and W. R. Ward (1968), both of whom amassed 708 runs in a season – a total only surpassed at Uppingham by C. E. M. Wilson who scored 722 in 1893. No other bowler has equalled M. G. Waller's 59 wickets in the 1957 season, the nearest approach being T. G. L. Ballance's 53 in 1934. In more recent years I. R. H. Simpkin has been the most prominent bat with an average of 51·5 in 1976. In 1978 an Uppingham cricketer made more headlines than any since Chapman, when the captain, J. P. Agnew – after taking 37 wickets with an average of 8·13, and captaining the best side for some years – played for Leicestershire in August and won a Whitbread Scholarship to Australia where he also played for the England Under-19 XI.

Wellington College

Foundation 1853

SCHOOL OPPONENTS: Radley; Charterhouse; Harrow; Eton; Marlborough; Bradfield; Haileybury.

Before the Second World War Wellington cricket was often handicapped by the tendency of many of their best players to leave early and enter the Army. There were, however, from time to time some excellent cricketers – notably G. J. V. Weigall (Cambridge), G. F. H. Berkeley (Oxford), G. J. Mordaunt (the Oxford captain in 1895), M. W. Payne, who captained Cambridge in 1907, and E. L. Kidd, the Cambridge captain of 1912.

Between the wars there were 2 outstanding cricketers at Wellington: G. J. Bryan, who made a hundred for Kent in his 1st county match, the summer he left Wellington; and M. J. C. Allom. Allom was a fast bowler who got a blue at Cambridge in 1927 and 1928, was for many years a leading bowler for Surrey, and played in 5 Test Matches for England in New Zealand and South Africa. Allom is the only Wellingtonian to have played cricket for England, although F. T. Badcock, who was at Wellington in the First World War, played 7 times for New Zealand. Shortly after Allom, P. F. Garthwaite won a blue as a leg-break bowler for Oxford in 1929.

R. O'Brien distinguished himself by scoring 146 for Cambridge in the University Match of 1956; D. K. Fasken was a steady medium-pace bowler for Oxford in the years 1953–1955, and D. J. Mordaunt, who has returned to Wellington as a master, played a season for Sussex in 1960.

D. W. Jarrett won blues at both Cambridge and Oxford as a batsman, and P. H. L. Wilson bowls at a lively pace for Surrey. R. I. H. B. Dyer, with 4 years in the XI, broke the aggregate record with 2,287 runs. He obtained many schoolboy honours, including being selected for the England Under-19 Tour of India in 1977–78. A. J. M. Stileman broke the record for the highest number of wickets in a season, in 1971, with 67. In 1979 came the retirement, at the age of 69, of Fred Berry, the professional since 1946. Many generations of cricketers (and non-cricketers) knew and respected Berry's wisdom and humour.

Westminster School

Foundation 1339

SCHOOL OPPONENTS: UCS; Tonbridge; Bradfield; Lancing; Charterhouse; Highgate; Alleyn's.

Westminster cricket started on a huge expanse of marshy land, called Tuttle Fields, stretching from Westminster to Sloane Square, and it was from 15 acres of this land that, in 1810, Dr Vincent, then Dean of Westminster, mapped out the Westminster playing-fields, now known as Vincent Square. There is no more popular or convenient ground for London cricketers than Vincent Square, and although the school's cricket is perhaps no longer the force it was before the Second World War, the opposition remains strong.

When Westminster played Eton on Hounslow Heath in 1796 it was the 1st known match between 2 public schools, and Westminster easily defeated the Etonians by 66 runs. The Charterhouse Match was played for the first time in 1850. In 1882, F. T. Higgins hit 171 not out against Charterhouse, which is still the highest innings by a Westminster boy against Charterhouse, and a score almost unheard of in school cricket at that time.

One of Westminster's best years was 1896, although they surprisingly collapsed and lost the Charterhouse Match. L. J. Moon, of Cambridge and Middlesex; C. D. Fisher, Oxford and Sussex; R. E. More, Oxford and Middlesex; and R. N. R. Blaker, Cambridge and Kent, were all in that side, and Charterhouse were the only team to beat them. These were halcyon days for Westminster, and later G. B. F. Rudd, who was afterwards captain of

The Westminster School ground at Vincent Square. In the background are the Houses of Parliament.

Leicestershire, led 2 of the best sides in 1912 and 1913.

Much of Westminster's success before the First World War was due to the teaching of S. H. Day, the Malvern and Kent batsman. Shortly after the war Day was succeeded as master-in-charge by another great Malvern batsman, D. J. Knight, of Surrey and England. For 18 years young Westminsters were privileged to learn the arts of cricket from one of the best stylists in the game. Knight was followed by his own most gifted pupil, C. H. Taylor. Taylor was in the XI for 4 years, from 1919–1922. In 1922, Taylor and R. G. H. Lowe bowled Charterhouse out for 25, Westminster winning the match before lunch.

Both Taylor and Lowe were later to distinguish themselves in the University Match – Taylor made a hundred for Oxford as a freshman in 1923, and Lowe did the hat-trick for Cambridge in 1926. Taylor was perhaps Westminster's finest batsman, and Lowe was undoubtedly their best all-rounder. It was sad that ill-health prevented Lowe from playing more than a few games for Kent after coming down from Cambridge.

Lowe was followed by another all-rounder of note, W. N. McBride, who went on to get an Oxford blue in 1926 and to play for Hampshire. Westminster's only other blue before the Second World War was M. H. Matthews, son of the Dean of St Paul's, who kept wicket for Oxford in 1936 and 1937, took a First in Greats and was killed in action in 1940. The war interfered with Westminster's cricket perhaps to an even greater extent than that of any other school. Vincent Square was a mass of trenches and barrage balloons, and the school was evacuated and widely disrupted. There was no cricket on Vincent Square again until 1948, and even then it took another 3 years before the wickets were back to the old standard. One successful batsman was C. C. P. Williams, who played for Oxford from 1953–1955, captaining the University in his last year. Williams finished his career at Westminster with a batting average of 75, and his XI in 1951 defeated Charterhouse, as did the 1952 team, under C. J. H. Davies. This was only the 2nd time in this century that 2 successive victories had been achieved over Charterhouse.

There came a notable extension in the old link between Westminster and Charterhouse when, in 1976–1977, they made a combined tour of Singapore and New Zealand. In recent years the outstanding players have been S. S. Surridge, captain for 2 years in 1969 and 1970, P. R. Wilson and T. W. J. Bailey, an all-rounder of much promise.

Whitgift School

Foundation 1596

SCHOOL OPPONENTS: Dulwich; Hurstpierpoint; Brighton; St Dunstan's; KCS, Wimbledon; St John's, Leatherhead; Christ's Hospital; Trinity School of John Whitgift; St George's, Weybridge.

Whitgift had some distinguished cricketers at the turn of the century – notably V. F. S. Crawford, who played for the Gentlemen in 1897 while still at Whitgift; H. H. B. Hawkins (Cambridge 1898–1900); and R. A. Sheppard (Surrey and the Gentlemen). But their best player has been R. Subba Row, the left-handed batsman, who captained the XI in 1950. Subba Row got his blue at Cambridge in 1951, and played at Lord's for 3 years. After 2 seasons with Surrey, he became captain of Northants; before his premature retirement in 1961, he opened the innings for England against India, South Africa, Australia and the West Indies, and he also went on 2 MCC tours.

William Hulme's GS

Foundation 1887

SCHOOL OPPONENTS: Rydal; Bolton; Arnold; Woodhouse Grove; Batley GS; Queen Elizabeth GS; Merchant Taylors', Crosby; Sir John Dean's; Burnley GS; Birkenhead; Stockport GS; Manchester GS; King's, Macclesfield.

A fixture card of the late 19th century indicates that cricket at William Hulme's was played on a very limited basis, in terms of hours of play and quality of fixtures. The game really came into its own under the Headship of Trevor Dennis. During the Second World War and the immediate post-war years, under the guidance of D. M. Williams and C. Morley, cricket at the school flourished. From 1949 to 1951 the XI was rich in talent, with a fearsome fast bowling attack in A. Godson and C. S. Smith, a Cambridge blue (1954–1957) who later opened both the batting and bowling for Lancashire.

The Headship of J. G. Bird (1947–1974) saw an expansion of the fixture list to include Queen Elizabeth's, Wakefield and Rydal, as well as local rivalry with Manchester Grammar School. A. M. Blight, himself a former captain of the XI, ran the cricket from 1965 to 1976, and many school players, such as C. N. Jenkinson, G. Casale and H. F. Lyon, went on to make their mark in the local leagues. A well-established tour to the West Country has provided fixtures with Allhallows, King's Bruton and Haberdashers. The cricket at all levels has been strong; a fact that was well illustrated in 1975 when the gifted Under-15 team reached the quarter-finals of the Esso Colts *Cricketer* Cup. In 1977 William Hulme's had an outstanding captain in J. Beesley, who scored over 700 runs, at an average of 73·00. Beesley captained the team which made a 3-week tour of the Caribbean (St Lucia and Grenada) in 1978.

Winchester College

Foundation 1382

SCHOOL OPPONENTS: Marlborough; Bradfield; Wellington; Harrow; Charterhouse; Eton.

To write of Winchester cricket is to dig at the very roots of the game, for the school was one of the earliest homes of cricket. Certainly the game was played at Eton, Winchester and Westminster in the 17th century. Before 1854, Eton, Harrow and Winchester met each other at Lord's in the 'Triangular Week'. The Headmaster of Winchester, doubting the good effect of the Festival on the young schoolboys, in that year suspended Winchester's participation therein. Since then 'Eton Match' has been played alternately at New Field and Agar's Plough. The XI, however, is still known as 'Lord's'.

The first great cricketer at Winchester was A. J. 'Dandy' Lowth, a minute man who bowled fast left-arm with a 'beautiful action and quick break'. He played for the Gentlemen against the Players while still at school and took 9 wickets in the match. Another figure in the early days at Winchester was William Ward, who not only held the ground record at Lord's for a hundred years with his innings of 278 for MCC against Norfolk in 1820, but also saved Lord's altogether when it seemed certain to fall into the hands of the property speculators.

E. R. Wilson has described the 1890s as the Golden Age of Winchester cricket. In 1891 and 1892 Winchester beat Eton by comfortable margins, and the leading role in the victories was played by J. R. Mason, whose career at Winchester has never been surpassed. In the 1892 Eton Match, Mason made 147 and 71, and took 8 wickets. He was supported by H. D. G. Leveson Gower, who made 83 in the innings and also took 8 wickets for 33 runs with his slow leg-breaks. In 1904

'Meads', Winchester; Eton the visitors.

Winchester beat Eton by 8 wickets, and this side is rated as the best Winchester ever had. The captain, E. L. Wright, Hon C. N. Bruce (later Lord Aberdare), H. Teesdale and J. H. Gordon all went on to gain blues at Oxford.

In 1914, Gilbert, the first of the Ashton brothers, appeared in the XI. He captained the team in 1915; Hubert succeeded him as captain the next season; and Claude led the 1920 side, which won all its school matches, including the Eton Match by 131 runs. All 3 Ashtons later captained Cambridge; Gilbert played for Worcestershire; and the younger two for Essex.

Winchester also beat Eton in 1919, the captain then being no less a personality than D. R. Jardine, a fine batsman at the school, who scored almost 1,000 runs at an average of 70. Besides Jardine and Claude Ashton, the 1919 side also contained other first-class players: R. H. Hill (Middlesex), T. B. Raikes (Oxford), J. E. Frazer (Oxford and Sussex), M. Patten (Oxford) and W. F. Baldock (Somerset). Ten years later came a very fast bowler, H. D. Read (Essex), who was never considered for the XI, but afterwards in 1935 opened for the England bowling against South Africa.

In the inter-war years Winchester was uniquely lucky in the help given to the cricket by two great coaches and authorities on the game, E. R. Wilson and H. S. Altham.

Mention must be made of 'Guise's Match' on Agar's Plough in 1921. In the 1st innings Eton bundled Winchester out for 57, but the 2nd time J. L. Guise made the highest score by a schoolboy in a school match of importance. He was last out (brilliantly run out) for 278 out of a total of 381. Even so, Eton still won the match. Guise captained Oxford in 1925 and played for Middlesex. In 1927 P. G. T. Kingsley and I. D. K. Fleming accomplished prodigious deeds as a 1st-wicket pair. Kingsley, who captained Oxford in 1930, is the only Wykehamist who has played 5 years in the XI. He was captain in 1926 and 1927, and in the last year his partner, Fleming, scored 210 against Eton.

In the 1930s Oxford cricket was especially well served by Winchester. R. S. G. Scott (captain of Sussex) was a blue in 1931; followed by D. C. H. Townsend, who played 3 Tests for England on the West Indies tour of 1934, R. G. Tindall, A. R. Legard, M. R. Barton (captain of Surrey after the war), J. N. Grover, J. D. Eggar, K. B. Scott, R. B. Proud and J. Stanning. H. A. Pawson was captain of Winchester in 1939 and 1940. After the war he captained Oxford and batted with success for Kent. The only Cambridge blue of this period was R. de W. K. Winlaw (Surrey), who captained Winchester in 1930 and 1931, and made 1,817 runs in his 4 years in the XI.

During the Second World War years Winchester had 3 particularly good cricketers in P. A. Whitcombe (a fast bowler for Oxford and Middlesex from 1947–1949); H. E. Webb, who made 145 not out for Oxford in the 1948 University Match; and G. H. G. Doggart. Doggart, who went on to captain Cambridge and Sussex and play in 2 Tests against the West Indies in 1950, later returned to Winchester as a master. Under his charge the cricket from 1955 to 1960 reached a very high standard, the side going 5 years without defeat at the hands of another school. In 1950 M. R. Coulman scored 200 in the 2nd innings of Eton Match. The Nawab of Pataudi made his 1st appearance in the 1956 XI, and for the following 3 years dominated the scene with his magnificent batting. He played for Sussex in 3 seasons while still at Winchester and was captain of the XI in 1959. In his last year (1959) Pataudi broke all records with 1,068 runs and an average of 71. Two other members of the 1959 team went on to get blues: R. I. Jefferson, a fast-medium bowler, played for Cambridge in 1961 and afterwards for Surrey; and N. L. Majendie kept wicket for Oxford in 1962 and 1963.

After Pataudi and Jefferson, the standard rather fell away; the 1960s questioned the discipline of net practice, and the elements did not help. The success of the 1965 XI, under the captaincy of R. J. Priestley, which beat Eton by 119 runs (T. Verity: 12·2–7–20–6) was the prelude to 3 Eton matches ruined by rain. The 1966 captain, R. L. Burchnall, won an Oxford blue, and M. R. S. Nevin did likewise at Cambridge. At the end of the 1960s Winchester had little success; but there was a revival in 1971, under A. N. M. Longmore, a fine wicket-keeper who toured India with MCC Schools. There was a most exciting draw with Eton in 1973, when the captain was a successful all-rounder E. J. W. Jackson (Cambridge 1974–1976). Two years later, Winchester beat Eton by 76 runs. S. J. G. Doggart, son of G. H. G. Doggart, captained the XI for 2 years and in 1979 became the first Wykehamist to score a hundred against Eton since B. L. Reed (sometime of Hampshire) 24 years earlier.

No account of Winchester cricket in the past 20 years would be complete without paying tribute to Hubert Doggart, master-in-charge for 17 years, and the professional, V. Broderick (Northants), who between them have nursed the bowlers towards accuracy in length and batsmen to a sound defence, and everyone to an enjoyment of the game.

The Royal GS, Worcester

Foundation 1291

SCHOOL OPPONENTS: Warwick; King Edward's, Birmingham; King's, Worcester; Monmouth; Solihull; Wolverhampton GS; Royal GS, High Wycombe; Cheltenham GS; King Henry VIII, Coventry; Bablake; KEC, Stourbridge.

In the years between the 2 wars the school produced a number of outstanding players, including G. C. Cox, C. S. Harrison, M. E. White, E. Tinkler, and W. H. N. Shakes-

The teams for Eton v Winchester in 1979: Back row: Umpire, V. Broderick, R. J. Dannreuther, G. N. R. Everett, S. J. Chambers, Winchester scorer, H. G. B. Derrick, S. R. J. Holden, J. P. Boden, A. R. Macdonald-Buchanan, T. W. S. Blake, J. F. T. Hood, Eton scorer, V. H. D. Cannings and Umpire; middle row: A. R. Crocker, A. D. Waddington, C. J. Davis, S. J. G. Doggart, R. J. Compton-Burnett, P. G. G. Dear, D. J. C. Faber, P. J. N. Barker and P. J. G. Burney; front row: J. P. Mead, J. M. M. Holland, A. S. Hoare, N. A. Metaxa and H. T. Rawlinson.

peare, who all went on to play for Worcestershire. Then between 1943 and 1946 R. V. Kings and P. J. Whitcombe regularly knocked off the runs required for victory without the assistance of the other batsmen. P. J. Whitcombe was also a good wicket-keeper who proceeded to Oxford, gaining blues in 1951 and 1952 and later playing for Worcestershire.

In the late 1940s the Thompson twins, J. W. and G. S., dominated proceedings, being followed by another pair of cricketing brothers, N. M. and R. G. Woodcock. The latter's record is particularly outstanding in that altogether he scored 1,950 runs and took 354 wickets at 8·99 runs apiece. R. G. Woodcock also went on to gain a blue at Oxford. The best batsman in the classical mould in the 1960s was K. Griffith (1964–1967), a player of great natural ability with a free straight flow of the bat. He scored 100 not out for the English Schools XI against the Public Schools at Lord's in 1967 and later played for Worcestershire.

J. Elliot, a wicket-keeper, also played occasionally for Worcestershire after leaving RGS. But unlike anything else in the school's history was the appearance in 1972 of Imran Khan, already a Pakistan Test cricketer. He came to Worcester in 1971 and while obtaining the residential qualification to play for Worcestershire completed his 'A' Levels.

Imran Khan proceeded to Oxford and captained the University in 1974. In 1978 T. S. Curtis beat all previous school records – including Imran Khan's – by scoring 769 runs at an average of 109·8, and hit 3 undefeated hundreds. During his school career he scored 2,649 runs and took 106 wickets (average 17·4). He was selected for the National Cricket Association's tour of Canada in 1979.

Worksop College

Foundation 1895

SCHOOL OPPONENTS: St Peter's, York; Repton; Pocklington; Trent; Wrekin; Denstone; Ampleforth.

The outstanding cricketer to come from Worksop has been P. J. Sharpe, the Yorkshire and England batsman. He captained the XI in 1955, and that year made 240 against Wrekin. Sharpe was a member of 3 of Worksop's best teams – beginning in 1953, when only 2 of the 11 matches were lost, and culminating in 1955 when they won 10 out of their 15 matches. Three other cricketers have played first-class cricket in recent years: C. P. Marks for Derbyshire; S. C. Corlett for Oxford and Ireland; and A. J. Good for Lancashire. Good was chosen as the MCC Young Cricketer of the Year in 1971.

Societies and Sundry Institutions

British Colleges Sports Association

DAVID GAUNT

The British Colleges Sports Association was formed in 1970 to foster and develop sport in those colleges having a responsibility for teacher training. That cricket did not feature in the initial list of 'recognized' sports was hardly a surprise. After all, cricket usually had to take a back seat to athletics. Cricket was the slow, inactive game and seemed to be little understood or played by those responsible for the teaching in the colleges.

To sound out the demand for the game in 1972 a knock-out competition was organized for colleges in the south-west. The response was immediate and gratifying. By 1974 a national inter-colleges had been established and Bede College, Durham, were the first winners of a thrilling final. The losers of that first final, St Paul's, Cheltenham, returned the following year and had a decisive win against Carnegie College and in so doing became the first holders of the Warwick Pool Cup, generously donated by the Warwickshire County Cricket Supporters' Association. It was wholly appropriate that the game was watched by that Association's Chairman, Edgar Hiley, and by no less a person than Freddie Brown, chairman of the National Cricket Association. The competition has since gone from strength to strength and now attracts more colleges than any other of the Association's sports or activities. So much for the lack of interest in the game!

In 1975 the 1st representative side took the field under the leadership of Jim Watts, who had given up the Northants captaincy to become a mature first-year student. Nigel Briers and Barry Lloyd were also members of that very first side and are now, of course, making their names with Leicestershire and Glamorgan. Since then the side has included such players as Michael McEvoy (Essex), Philip Bainbridge (Gloucestershire) and Colin Murray, who captained the Young

P. J. Watts, the Northamptonshire captain, led the British Colleges in 1978 on their first major tour, to the Caribbean.

West Indians on their 1974 tour of this country. It was, and is, rare for a student without county 2nd XI or Minor County experience to make the side. Let it be made clear that the Association does not claim to have 'found' or significantly improved these players. They are mentioned merely to indicate the strength of the side. Unfortunately examinations, the short summer term, teaching practices and a variety of 'going down' dates often make it impossible to field the strongest side in any one game.

There was no doubt that by 1976 cricket in the colleges was 'on the up'. How could this be maintained or even improved upon? The answer proved to be an Easter 1978 tour to the Caribbean. There is no doubt that but for the generous support of Agatha Christie Ltd – through Mathew Prichard, its chairman – and of the A. J. McAlpine Cricket Trust the venture would not have been possible. Equally it would not have been possible without the hard work of the students taking part who by various means raised and saved the greater part of the tour costs. Jim Watts led the team which included Philip Bainbridge, Michael McEvoy, Colin Murray, Keith Tomlins and Paul Allott, all of whom had, or have since, played the game at first-class level. Tour highlights included an 8-wickets win against the Barbados Youth XI and a 99-run victory in a 2-day game with the Queen's Park Club in Trinidad.

Once again thanks mainly to the generosity of Agatha Christie Ltd, the team in 1979 undertook a 2nd West Indian tour. This time the captain was Colin Murray, which ensured that adequate local knowledge would be available. As before the side gave a good account of itself. The first game, scheduled for Tobago, was washed out – an unlikely start to a tour in the sunny Caribbean. The 4 games in Trinidad were won with something to spare. It was an inspired piece of organizing by Sonny Murray, that hard-working secretary of the Queen's Park Club, which had the BCSA visiting teams in the south of the island. Few touring teams venture far from Port of Spain and it can only be their loss. The enthusiasm for the game and the hospitality of the people of such places as San Fernando, Claxton Bay, Penal and Rio Claro is second to none.

In Barbados William Bourne had arranged a formidable fixture list and maybe the 'Jolly Roger' cruise had been deliberately planned for the day before the game with the Barbados Youth XI at the Kensington Oval. There defeats in which the students performed most creditably were followed by convincing wins against the YMPC Club and the Office Invitation XI.

Mark Simmons proved a most able deputy after an ankle injury had put Colin Murray out for several games. At one stage or another all members of the party made valuable contributions to the success of the tour. On the field special mention ought to be made of Russell Heritage who was both top-scorer and leading wicket-taker for the tour. His slow left arm bowling gave him 22 wickets at less than 9 apiece. What is absolutely certain is that all came back with a host of happy memories of places visited and friends made.

It is true, I think, to say that the average student training to be a teacher now has a greater awareness of cricket – there can be few who have escaped the eager ticket sellers as tour funds were raised. Certainly there is far more active participation than there was only a few years ago and this is in spite of the very great reduction in the number of students being accepted for teacher training. The number of colleges has dropped alarmingly. Some have closed completely whilst others have merged with other institutions. Consequently it has never been more important that cricket in the teacher training institutions gets all possible help.

If the children in the schools are to be taught the game, and by this I mean class teaching as opposed to the organizing of school teams, it is vital that the average student in the teacher training colleges is sufficiently motivated to want to teach the game when he takes up his teaching appointment. The game must be presented to children in their middle school years in a purposeful and enjoyable way.

Mathew Prichard, chairman of Agatha Christie Ltd, whose patronage has helped to make possible various overseas tours including those of the BCSA and the English and West Indian young cricketers.

To foster and develop an interest in cricket among the future teachers remains the main aim of the BCSA cricket committee. Generous help has been received from such as Agatha Christie Ltd, the A. J. McAlpine Cricket Trust and the Lord's Taverners. Other individuals and firms have helped in a variety of ways and the BCSA is truly grateful. Without financial backing the Association's activities would almost certainly cease.

Sir Julien Cahn's XI

E. W. SWANTON

The team which played under this title from 1926 until the outbreak of the Second World War was a modern cricket phenomenon to which there is no parallel. Sir Julien Cahn (1882–1944) was a millionaire who had inherited the Nottingham Furnishing Company from his father, and in this line of business built up a considerable empire, with a heavy accent on the hire-purchase side. From youth he had had a great fondness for cricket and cricketers, though unblessed with any natural ability in the game. Cahn was in his middle-forties when after several years of running his own side in local Nottinghamshire circles he set about collecting a team full of well-known players to fulfil what soon developed into an ambitious programme both at home and abroad. From 1926 until the war his hospitable nature had full vent. He was a sociable man of much natural kindliness who enjoyed giving people pleasures far beyond their normal scope.

In 1926 he laid out and equipped in the most lavish way a ground at Loughborough Road, West Bridgford, on the outskirts of Nottingham not far from Trent Bridge. Thither came all the major touring teams to England, except the Australians, several of the midland and northern counties, numerous minor counties, and a host of clubs, service sides, and scratch teams from the Leagues. Almost any club of any attainment who fancied the idea of trying their skill against Cahn's hired troops were accorded the chance – along with a standard of comfort in keeping with the whole sumptuous enterprise. By 1929 he had a second ground of comparable quality operating at his home near Loughborough, Stanford Hall, and few summer weekends went by without a 2-day match there. The visiting teams found themselves accommodated in unaccustomed splendour, and if the fine edge of their play may sometimes have been slightly blunted in consequence that was small cause for worry.

Certainly it did not disturb the host who was happy to win his games, whether against the proud or the humble, by the largest conceivable margins. The only qualification that need be made in this respect concerns Cahn's own bowling which was inordinately slow and quite without intrinsic merit, even if marvellous feats of fielding occasionally brought him moments of much-applauded success. He was in fact more useful as a batsman. Fortified by an outsize pair of pads, keeping his bat straight in defence, and generally enjoying the benefit of the minutest doubts in the case of lbw, Cahn could be hard to dislodge. Often his luck extended to the point of his score being credited for leg-byes which the umpire had forgotten to signal.

For most keen cricketers, on his own side as well as the other, it took something from much of the Cahn cricket that it was hopelessly one-sided. In the palmy days of the 1930s it was no rarity to find 3 or 4 Test cricketers in the XI with every other member bar the captain a player of first-class experience. Even on the Cahn wickets, which were the nearest things to perfection in an imperfect world, Test bowlers of the skill of R. W. V. Robins, I. A. R. Peebles, D. P. B. Morkel, R. J. Crisp and T. L. Richmond, were generally too much for the weekend cricketers who formed a good proportion of the opposition. In his painstaking monograph on Sir Julien Cahn's XI, first printed in *The Cricket Quarterly* and afterwards in book form, E. E. Snow gives the following figures for results in Great Britain:

PLAYED	WON	LOST	DRAWN
565	273	16	276

Of all his opponents both at home and overseas, the Frogs had the unique distinction of beating him twice. It might be added that the cause of many of the draws was a declaration that might with perfect safety have been made a long while earlier. Cahn had more relish for the plunder of opposing bowling by his star-studded side than for the thrill of a close-run finish. All in all, Cahn's cricket (which, it was estimated, cost him more than £20,000 a year) gave a vast deal of fun and happiness to a large number of players and spectators over a period of nearly twenty years. Not least was this the case on his tours abroad wherein he stimulated cricket in various unfamiliar places.

There were 6 of these missionary tours, as follows:

1929 Jamaica
1930 Argentine
1932 Denmark
1933 Canada, USA and Bermuda
1937 Ceylon and Malaya
1938–39 New Zealand

Apart from the famous names already mentioned, Sir Julien Cahn's regular players included at various times: R. C. Blunt (New Zealand), C. S. Dempster (New Zealand), H. G. Vivian (New Zealand), P. A. Gibb (England), John Gunn (England), G. F. H. Heane (Notts), H. Mudge (NSW), F. W. H. Nicholas (Essex), T. B. Reddick (Middlesex), J. B. Hall (Notts), S. D. Rhodes (Notts), F. C. W. Newman (Surrey), V. E. Jackson (NSW), J. E. Walsh (NSW), R. E. C. Butterworth (Middlesex), F. J. Seabrook (Gloucestershire), E. P. Solbé (Kent) and P. Vaulkhard (Derbyshire). Save 2 or 3 charity games the activities of Sir Julien Cahn's XI ceased completely on the outbreak of war. On 26 September 1944, Cahn died suddenly in his library, surrounded by the vast and valuable Ashley-Cooper collection of cricket books which he had purchased shortly after his acquisition of Stanford Hall. His house was bought by the Co-operative Union Ltd as a training college. The splendid ground at Loughborough Road was bought by the civic authorities of West Bridgford, and is maintained as a cricket ground.

Charity Cricket

TIM RICE

The 1950s and 1960s were often troubled times for first-class cricket, but during these decades the game began to prove a spectacular fund-raising force at a less exalted level. By 1980 most cricket clubs had attempted at least once to swell their own or some worthy cause's coffers by staging a charity match – many had made such a match an annual fixture. A well-known personality (not necessarily a cricketer) is approached to raise a team of celebrities, which usually includes more than a handful of famous cricketing names, to play against a club on its own ground. If the visiting team contains enough names of sufficient stellar magnitude, and if the club's own advance publicity for the game is efficiently handled, it is possible for a club that will normally attract just a few devoted spectators to its fixtures to be besieged by a crowd of a thousand or more. It may not always be feasible for the club to charge an admission fee (few minor clubs are able, or would want, to prevent anybody stopping by to watch their matches for free), but once the crowds have been lured to the ground, every

The Friends of Arundel Castle CC fulfils a long fixture-list here at Arundel. A charity game in progress, with the 1956 Australians the visitors.

conceivable method of extracting money for the cause is fair game as far as the charity committee is concerned. Autographs are sold, members of the public pay to have their photograph taken with the celebrities, beer tents and food stalls proliferate. Really ambitious organizers have been known to wheel in half a funfair in order to empty the pockets of those who do not love cricket enough to pay for it. The most blatant form of fund-raising, while falling considerably short of demanding with menaces, is for 4 of the players to walk around the boundary with an outstretched blanket, asking the crowd to throw money into it. They usually do.

Charity cricket matches often produce good cricket, even if the result is sometimes arrived at artificially. There are many more tied charity matches than in other forms of cricket. Often charity games provide spectators with a great opportunity to see a great player of the past demonstrate again some of the skills that delighted an earlier generation on the first-class stage. There may still be a chance for cricket lovers to see Colin Cowdrey or Fred Trueman in majestic action before a large crowd in the 1980s, and to help a charity at the same time.

Church Times Cup

JOHN TREVISICK

By sheer good fortune the welcome appearance of this volume coincides with the 30th anniversary of the *Church Times* cricket cup competition, which attracts teams of Anglican clergymen from about 30 of the 49 dioceses in the provinces of Canterbury, York and Wales. The runners-up receive a trophy given by Messrs Charles Farris, the old-established church furnishers.

The competition, which has grown into a giant oak from the acorn implanted by 2 priests serving Berkshire Downland parishes (one, Hugh Pickles of Blewbury, is included in about 10 of the original pioneers still playing), has been promoted over 3 decades by the principal Anglican weekly, and seeing that nearly 400 parsons (plus a few dignitaries), well versed in bossing their own show, are the *dramatis personae*, the competition has been relatively trouble free. From the start the historic Walker Ground at Southgate has provided a worthy setting for the final.

That the Church, with such men as E. T. Killick, F. H. Gillingham, and more recently David Sheppard – to remind us of just a few – has provided a supply of fit persons able to play cricket with the best cannot be gainsaid, and the *Church Times* Cup has proved this to the hilt.

The rules for its limited-over one-innings matches were not compiled by ecclesiastical canonists; they are simple and uncomplicated. The main and unbreakable stipulation is that every player must hold a licence from the bishop of the diocese in which he serves, be he the Dean of Carlisle or the Chaplain of Brixton Prison. Only once has there been an attempt to flout the rule and since it was dealt with firmly there has been no repetition. Teams from the northern province have the edge over their southern brethren; probably this is due to match practice for several (weddings permitting) play high-grade league cricket in Lancashire and Yorkshire. Long before David Sheppard moved to Liverpool as Bishop – he has not been prominent in the Cup Competition anyway – the Merseyside team has been consistently formidable.

Liverpool, constant visitors to Southgate in recent years, won the trophy again in 1978 and in 1979, beating Chichester in the final in both years – but Sheffield had 6 visits in the first 7 years. The Silver Jubilee year, 1975, saw a host of notable performances. Southwark knocked up 1,000 runs and won the cup. Michael Reeve of Chichester was undefeated for 183; in a later innings he increased the record to 194. There were 6 hundreds in all during 1975 and the Bishop of Southwell (Denis Wakeling) might have made it 7 had he not come a cropper for 94.

The Club Cricket Conference

F. L. J. DOLMAN

During the First World War a drive was made by the authorities to use all available space for growing foodstuffs, which led to sports fields being dug up for this purpose, either in the form of allotments or under direct cultivation by local authorities. This put several well-established cricket grounds at risk, with a real possibility that they would never be brought back to their earlier use, and also that munition workers and servicemen home on leave might be deprived of much needed relaxation on the sports field.

In 1915 a meeting of well-known club cricketers was convened by E. A. C. Thomson, a sports journalist, to discuss ways and means of combating the threat, and at this gathering the London Club Cricket Conference was formed. Later, the membership expanded beyond London and the title was changed to London and Southern Counties Club Cricket Conference and, later still, to the Club Cricket Conference, which is the one now in use, generally abbreviated to CCC.

The 1st Annual General Meeting was held in 1916, when Thomson was officially appointed as honorary Secretary; other officers were elected and the 1st Rules approved. One of the most comprehensive objects, which has been retained through the years, was 'to foster amateur cricket', but at that time the words 'on non-competitive lines' were added and, indeed, until as recently as 1968, the emphasis was strongly on non-competitive cricket, with permitted exceptions in the case of inter-university or college, inter-departmental, inter-hospital and other similar tournaments, as a number of cup competitions in this category were already in existence.

The Conference quickly became the biggest association of cricket clubs in the world and has remained so. It was recognized as able to speak for club cricket in the south-east and MCC, then the sole law makers for cricket, approached the CCC Council for the opinion of club cricket before introducing the larger wicket in 1931 and also obtained, through the same channel, the co-operation of a large number of clubs in using the LBW(N) Law during the two experimental years prior to its permanent adoption in 1937.

Shortly after the Second World War a movement was initiated in Sussex to gather as many associations of cricket clubs together as possible to form a national body and this was welcomed by the Conference, who became founder members of the National Club Cricket Association. This organization was supported by MCC and, when it was found that Government grants for sport would only be made to national bodies, and that MCC as a club did not qualify and that the NCCA was also ruled out as representing only club cricket, the two co-operated to form the MCC National Cricket Association, only to find that this failed on the grounds that first-class cricket was not included. And so the Cricket Council came into being, composed of the TCCB, MCC and NCA, which now dropped the prefix MCC.

Another important body that has received wholehearted support from the Conference is the Association of Cricket Umpires, founded in 1953. Prior to this the Conference had done what it could to improve the standard of club umpiring, which was not generally high, but this only amounted to one or two lectures each year given by first-class umpires and it could not be pretended that this was very effective; whereas the training courses carried over 8 evenings in various parts of the country every year by the ACU are certainly more so. The ACU, which has become international in scope, now has some 4,000 members in this country alone.

One of the more spectacular activities of the CCC has been playing representative matches against MCC, the Services and such other bodies as the Civil Service, the Midlands Club Cricket Conference and the United London Banks. In addition, President's XIs, composed largely of players put forward by their clubs, are sent against clubs requesting it on reaching their jubilee or centenary years. Until recently, a match was always played against the first-class tourists visiting this country, including Australia, South Africa, West Indies, India, Pakistan and New Zealand. Other touring sides met have come from Canada, East Africa, Sri Lanka, and, regularly, the Australian Old Collegians, mostly from New South Wales. In January 1971, a representative side was sent to Australia on the invitation of the Australian Old Collegians and this proved so successful in every way that it was repeated in 1975 and 1979, while in 1977 a side went to Barbados, Trinidad and Tobago.

However, the basis of Conference work remains service in any form for the benefit of club cricket. Every year the *Handbook* is issued, containing, *inter alia*, details of principal officers and grounds, with addresses and telephone numbers, of all the 2,200 clubs. The Emergency Fixture Bureau is another invaluable service and in 1978 received 8,739 applications for fixtures, 7,293 of which were successfully met. All this is achieved by a hard working office staff under the direction of the Secretary and a Council composed of members inspired by enthusiasm for the game.

Country-House Cricket

R. L. ARROWSMITH

On 12 August 1858, the newly formed Band of Brothers played their first match. It was at Evington, near Elmstead, on Sir Courtenay Honywood's ground, and their opponents were a side from the Pembertons' house, Torry Hill, near Sittingbourne. The match is not recorded in *Scores & Biographies*, and, were it not that the Band of Brothers became a famous club and have preserved their records, the score could probably have been recovered only by a diligent search through the local newspaper, and perhaps not even then. There had been Honywoods at Evington since the reign of Henry VII; there have been none there for many years now. Signposts still point to Evington, but the house is gone and no casual passer-by would know that a house had ever stood there. The Pembertons indeed still live at Torry Hill, but in a smaller house.

What is true of Evington is true of countless other houses in the British Isles. Taking East and Mid-Kent alone, 80 years ago cricket flourished at the Cornwallises' at Linton, at the Harrises' at Belmont, at the De Launes' at Sharsted and at the Brasseys' at Preston Hall; it flourished at Hothfield, at Boxley, at Chilham Castle and no doubt at many other houses as well. At some of these the ground is still used by the local club, but it is many years since there was country-house cricket at any of them. At most of them there has been none since 1914. The First World War was responsible for the gradual disappearance of many things, but there are few things which it destroyed so suddenly and so completely as country-house cricket. In 1914 there was still plenty to be played; since 1919 there has been hardly any, and the wonder is that there has been any at all and even more that here and there some should still be found. One cannot feel sufficient respect and gratitude for the few who have contrived to keep that little going. Even in 1903 when, out of 56 days' cricket played by I Zingari, 21 appear to have been at country houses, H. D. G. Leveson Gower could write that the great days of country-house cricket were past. He did not suggest that there was any shortage of houses able and willing to stage such matches. It is the difficulty of getting sides that he blames: men had to work harder than they had done in earlier years, there were more counter-attractions such as golf, and the great increase in the amount of first-class cricket made it hard for good amateurs to find time for other matches.

It is indeed difficult for the present generation to realize how disastrous is the wide breach which now exists between first-class and club cricket. In the old days there were in any good club match a number of men with considerable experience of first-class cricket, including usually some who were still playing it, and from playing with these the ordinary club cricketer learned an enormous amount and greatly improved his own cricket. They in their turn brought into first-class cricket much of the cheerfulness and fun to which they were accustomed in club cricket, so that, however keenly a game might be contested, it never degenerated into the grim business that it usually is now. It is difficult to say whether club or first-class cricket has lost more by the change.

Of course the standard of country-house cricket varied enormously. Some of it was little short of the standard of county or at least of 'Varsity cricket, some of it little better than village cricket. In its simplest form the owner of a house collected his own side to play against a local side, a side raised by one of his neighbours or a wandering club. But not infrequently he would act as host to two clubs which played each other. Matches between the Gentlemen of 2 counties were often played on a country-house ground, such members of either side as required it being put up.

Occasionally professionals were included in country-house sides. We find Edward Hickmott playing for Boxley in 1890; George Hearne for Newbold Revel in 1893; and Needham and West for Preston Hall in 1897. At an earlier period a professional was sometimes engaged at a large country house for the season or part of it. James Grundy was for some years with the Earl of Leicester at Holkham; while in 1846 William Lillywhite and his son John were engaged for the holidays by Lord Stamford at Enville Hall. More recently Maurice Read was professional and groundsman at Tichborne Park, from his retirement from the Surrey side in 1895 to his death in 1929, and continued till he was well over 60 to make hundreds there.

The standard of the grounds varied almost as much as the standard of cricket. Some were very good. As far back as the early 1870s, when many county grounds were still pretty rough, it is said that at Lord Manvers's at Thoresby, 'a wicket could have been pitched, and a *good* wicket too, on any portion of the ground', much as many years later a croquet tournament used to be played in August on the outfield of the Head at Tonbridge School. This was exceptional, but most of those houses at which matches were played at all regularly maintained a fair standard of wicket. The chief characteristic may be said to have been a true wicket, but a natural one, not dangerous except perhaps in dry weather with a really fast bowler, but giving the bowler sufficient help to prevent scores from being unduly large – the type of ground on which an average total was 150 to 200 and a 4-innings match could normally be completed without a declaration. The outfield was usually true, but rather grassy and slow, since it did not get as much rolling as a county ground would. A host who was a keen cricketer himself would take an interest in his wicket and there is a charming story of one such who, going in to receive the 1st ball of the innings and seeing it fly, to his dismay, clean over his head off a good length and the next ball follow suit, left his crease to inspect and found the groundsman's false teeth firmly rolled into the pitch!

The umpire was constantly a retainer – a butler, a gardener, a game-keeper – and this has given rise to the usual crop of umpiring stories. After all, few retainers in such circumstances give universal satisfaction to the other side. In Kent for many years it was held that the vicar of a certain parish, keeping wicket with his sexton umpiring at square-leg, met his match only when playing against the local asylum, for whom the doctor always bowled at the end where his head-warder was umpire.

Naturally in this country-house cricket the social side was very important. One Oxford cricketer is quoted as having failed to receive a second invitation to play at Wighill because he lit a cigar while Lord Hawke's port was going round. At some houses, indeed, the social side rather overweighed the cricket. It was put in its due place by the McGaws at St Leonard's Forest, near Horsham. There, there was a strictly male pavilion for the players and a comfortable stand for the ladies on the other side of the ground, to which those whose inclinations went that way or who felt a strong sense of duty to their hospitable hostess could repair; but if you happened to be feeling somnolent after a good lunch, or to have made a duck or even perhaps to agree with Lord Chesterfield in preferring to study men by day and women by night, then you were welcome to stay on the less social side of the ground.

That any of this cricket should now remain is, as has been said before, incredible. Yet Lord Porchester at Highclere, the McAlpines at Marchwiel, the Blofelds at Hoveton, the Rothschilds at Ascott, the Worsleys at Hovingham, Robin Leigh Pemberton at Torry Hill and Captain Hawkins at Everdon, all in varying degrees keep the flag flying, and no doubt there are others. Shorn of much of its old glory this cricket may be, and in particular the large house-parties are of necessity almost a thing of the past, but from 11.30 to 7 on one of these grounds there is little to show that one is not back in pre-1914 days. Probably what a straggler from those times would chiefly notice is that there are

The cricket ground in front of Hovingham Hall which has been used for cricket for over 150 years. Most of the great names of Yorkshire cricket have played there, many of them at the invitation of Sir William Worsley (1890–1973), Captain and President of Yorkshire CCC and President of MCC, 1961–62. This beautiful ground is still in regular use and is the home of the Hovingham CC, champions in 1979 of the York & District Senior League.

cars instead of carriages and that there is a shortage of blazers: at modern prices these are a luxury which few can afford and indeed most of those one sees have been inherited from some retired cricketer. A passable imitation of country-house cricket is provided here and there by some unselfish preparatory schoolmaster who makes use of his school ground (which may well itself have been a country-house ground in the old days) and his ample accommodation to entertain two sides, one of them often his own old boys, in the holidays. To all such, those who are lucky enough to enjoy their hospitality owe a deep debt of gratitude.

The Cricket Society

IRVING ROSENWATER

The Cricket Society, which prides itself on no further adjectival requirement than the definite article, is the largest and most active body of its kind in the cricketing world. With a membership exceeding 2,000 in Britain and overseas, the Society exists to share and extend among its members the wide variety of experiences that cricket offers. There is no qualification for membership, beyond an enthusiasm for the game, either on paper, in debate or at a cricket ground. The overwhelming majority of its members have been distinctly poor performers with bat or ball (and often positively non-performers) but have been none the less welcome for that. They make good spectators and good companions. The declared object of the Society is 'to support the game at all levels wherever it is played, regardless of race, colour or creed'.

Apart from the old Cricketana Society, which was founded in late 1929 and had a brief prosperity in the early 1930s, there was no organization (outside cricket clubs themselves) for enthusiasts to indulge their cricketing fancies until after the Second World War. Then, at a now historic meeting at Great Scotland Yard, London, on 17 November 1945, was founded The Society of Cricket Statisticians (the original name of The Cricket Society). The founder – uniquely distinguished in the entire cricket society movement – was Antony Weigall (1902–1977), a Kent man who lived in Surrey, an accountant of infinite charm and as thoroughly devoted to the game of cricket in his own way as was his distant cousin, Gerry, in his. Until ill-health intervened in his later years, Tony Weigall was a constant attender at Society functions and remained an inspiration to all. Treasurer of the Society until 1952, he was then appropriately created the 1st honorary life member.

The Cricket Society assumed its new name on 6 November 1948, when it became clear that statistics were by no means the sole interest of its members. The new title attracted fresh members, those interested in the literature of the game, in attending meetings and dinners with fellow members – and in playing the game, for whom a then modest Society fixture-list was inaugurated for the following summer. The Society XI, like The Cricket Society itself, has since gone from strength to strength, and now plays about 40 matches each summer and tours abroad. Among the several captains since the first season in 1949, the longest-serving deserve mention – C. S. ('Con') Davies, Geoffrey Nicholson, C. C. W. Box-Grainger and J. M. Kershaw. The 1st overseas tour was to Paris in June 1954, when 2 one-day matches (both drawn) were played against the Standard Athletic Club; and altogether to the end of 1979 there have been 18 playing tours (as well as occasional social tours) embracing Paris, Belgium, Holland, Corfu, Australia, Hong Kong, Barbados, the Channel Islands and Philadelphia.

The regular monthly meetings, however, have formed perhaps the most attractive feature for Society members in the London area. The Cricket Society has always been based in London, and the principal meeting venues have been successively 'The White Swan', off Fleet Street, the Shaftesbury Hotel, the old Tavern at Lord's, the Berners Hotel, the National Liberal Club and the Royal Overseas League, off Piccadilly. Some 10 or 11 meetings are held each year, and the speakers have ranged over the entire spectrum of cricketing activity – Test match captains, county secretaries, coaches, groundsmen, collectors, journalists, curators, publicists, umpires, scorers, committee-men, authors, lady cricketers, and many more. These meetings, where freedom of speech is encouraged in the absence of the press, are notably well attended (especially in winter) and are sometimes accompanied by film shows.

The titular head of The Cricket Society from its beginning has been its President, of whom since 1945 there has been a distinguished succession of men eminent in cricket lore – the Mackinnon of Mackinnon, Hubert Preston, H. S. Altham, Lord Birkett, A. A. Thomson, General Sir Oliver Leese, A. M. Crawley and, from the start of 1976, E. W. Swanton. This list alone embraces an accumulation of learning to give pardonable cause for pride. The Mackinnon of Mackinnon was aged 97 when he assumed office, and the longest-serving President so far was another nonagenarian, Hubert Preston, from 1947 to 1959 – though his record may be broken. The Chairmen of the Society, and daily guiders of its fortunes, have been successively:

1945–46 A. Weigall
1946–47 Capt. J. A. Bayliss
1947–53 G. A. Copinger
1953–60 A. R. Whitaker
1960–65 Dr R. W. Cockshut
1965–66 L. E. S. Gutteridge
1966– C. C. W. Box-Grainger

Christopher Box-Grainger has been in office continuously since August 1966, while Miss Netta Rheinberg, distinguished as a writer and administrator of women's cricket, has been an invaluable vice-chairman over an even longer period. The first honorary secretary was that great enthusiast, S. Canynge Caple; and others who followed him for lengthy spells were C. V. P. Airey, J. D. Lane and E. C. R. Rice. Eric Rice, whose industry is formidable, and who is also Honorary Treasurer of the Council of Cricket Societies, has held the secretaryship of The Cricket Society since 15 April 1965.

The stature of the Society has been much enhanced by its publications and programme of research. An early object was a bibliography of cricket, which, after many years of Trojan effort, not least by G. K. Whitelock, was brought to magnificent fruition in 1977 by E. W. Padwick. The Society's *Journal*, a twice-yearly vehicle for much original research, began under its founder-editor, Irving Rosenwater, in 1961, and has thrived subsequently with a world-wide reputation under the editorships of Cmdr H. Emmet and J. D. Coldham. Statistics continue to fascinate many members, who find outlets in both the *Journal* and internal *News Bulletin*. The Society administers many awards, among them the Most Promising Young Cricketer of the Year, the Wetherell Awards to leading all-rounders, and the annual Silver Jubilee Literary Award, endowed in 1970 by John McG. Edwards of Beaumaris, Victoria. The spring and autumn dinners in London are highly popular, and the standard of speaking notably high.

From small beginnings, The Cricket Society has inspired branches in the West of England (Bath and Bristol), the Midlands (Birmingham and Worcester) and the North-East (Durham and Newcastle-upon-Tyne), as well as independent 'daughter' societies in Rhodesia and Australia. In Australia alone there are seven active branches. The structure is healthy and happy, the officers devoted. The past serves as a sure foundation for a prosperous future.

Cricket Writers Club

J. M. KILBURN

The Cricket Writers Club was formally established at a meeting in Nottingham. It was derived from the Empire Cricket Writers Club which had been created during the 1946–47 MCC tour of Australia when Australian and English journalists and broadcasters covering the tour set up an organization to facilitate their own professional undertakings and to play cricket at the invitation of many schools, clubs and charitable foundations in Australia.

The Cricket Writers Club in England took for its objects the promotion of cricket and cricket writing and opened membership to recognized correspondents of newspapers, agencies, periodicals and radio. Within the first year of its existence the club achieved public distinction and founded a tradition by entertaining, in the spring of 1948, the visiting Australian team to a dinner in London. HRH The Prince Philip was a guest and the BBC broadcast of part of the toast-list proved so captivating that it was allowed to over-run allotted programme time. Annual hospitality to the touring teams thereafter became a feature of club activities and since 1950 a focal point of the functions has been the presentation of a trophy to the 'Young Cricketer of the Year', elected by members. The club has never sought professional status in journalism but, negotiating on behalf of all cricket writers, has been responsible for closer liaison with cricket administration at home and overseas and for a wider understanding of the service cricket writing can render to the first-class game. Press relations on tour, Press accommodation on Test Match grounds and co-operation in many forms have been influenced, and MCC have set up a Press Advisory Committee to consider the problems of cricket presentation to the public.

In recent years the club has allowed its City Hall dinners to the Australian tourists to lapse because of ever-rising costs, but sponsorship in a modest degree is enabling the club to maintain its annual 'Young Cricketer of the Year' award and encourages smaller social gatherings at which overseas cricket writers are always welcomed.

George Cox, President of the Sussex Cricket Society, in his playing days with the county.

To facilitate establishment of the Cricket Writers Club E. W. Swanton, the 1st chairman, was elected to serve for a 2nd successive year but custom has since decreed an annual change and the chairmen since have been: J. M. Kilburn, A. W. Ledbrooke, Bruce Harris, Charles Bray, Neville Cardus, Norman Preston, J. B. Bapty, Brian Johnston, John Kay, R. C. Robertson-Glasgow, Alex Bannister, W. E. Bowes, Michael Melford, Crawford White, Brian Chapman, B. Easterbrook, John Woodcock, Leslie Smith. J. M. Solan, Peter West, John Arlott, Ian Peebles, R. J. Hayter, Richie Benaud, Roy Ullyett, Denis Compton, H. Abel and Tony Pawson.

The Council of Cricket Societies

C. R. YEOMANS

Cricket Societies came into being after the Second World War. The first of them 'arrived' in 1948. But what is a Cricket Society and what is its main function? Members for the most part are fanatical lovers of England's national game. They meet with regularity, generally in the close season, to talk about the game and to listen to speakers at these meetings and at dinners and similar gatherings. Membership is open to anyone who fulfils the role of a cricket lover. At the last count, there were 27 Societies in Great Britain and abroad, the latter including 7 in Australia and one in Rhodesia.

More than half of these are situated north of the Trent; indeed one of the first 2, in 1948, was based in Leeds. Its list of speakers over the years – totalling well over 300 different people – reads like the pages of *Wisden*, coupled with many other celebrities including writers, politicians, actors and musicians. At Wombwell, a village near Barnsley (the 3rd Society to be formed, in 1951), the honorary Secretary, Jack Sokell, brings along not one, but often 2 or 3 speakers on the same evening. The playing of cricket is not uppermost in the minds of Cricket Societies. The most unusual game that is played is probably that on Boxing Day by the Northern. This started in 1949 and has been played at a variety of grounds in Yorkshire ever since. It is always a strictly competitive game and played seriously, with many well-known Yorkshire cricketers having taken part.

The coaching of youngsters plays an important part with several Societies, notably Wombwell, Chesterfield (formed 1963) and, to a lesser degree, the Northern. Both Wombwell and Chesterfield have quite elaborate coaching schemes on which a good deal of money is spent, while the Northern send specially selected boys for coaching at Headingley.

After the formation of the Cricket Society of Scotland (1952), there was a gap until Chesterfield (1963), Sussex (1965) and the West Lancashire, based at Southport (1965) were established. It needs the enthusiasm of one person and a hard-working committee to get any Society off the ground. The late Jim Fleming was the enthusiast for Scotland, and then Frank Robinson saw the way for Chesterfield 11 years later. Now there is scarcely an area of Great Britain where a Cricket Society cannot be found. Total membership among the Societies is about 7,000.

The Invalids

ALEC WAUGH

The account in A. G. Macdonell's *England, Their England* of a match between a rural Kentish village and a team of London Bohemians captained by a poet is one of the classics of cricket literature. The poet was J. C. (Sir John) Squire and his side was called 'The Invalids'. Thinly disguised, the following characters appeared in Macdonell's narrative: the fat wicket-keeper was the publisher, Cecil Palmer. Mr Harcourt, the journalist who spent a great deal of time in the pub, was J. B. Morton (Beachcomber of the *Daily Express*). Major Hawker, the fast bowler, was Reginald Berkeley, the dramatist. Bobby Southcott, the novelist who made an eccentric 50, was based on myself. Many people will tell you that they took part in that historic match, but it was a composite picture. The incidents were taken from a number of different games, at Bridge, at Ditchling and at Fordcombe.

The colours of orange and hospital blue were in broad stripes. Crossed crutches adorned the pocket badge. The caps were striped on the Harrovian pattern. Between the wars a side took the field every Saturday. It continued to play intermittently during the war and for a few years after it. Five tours were staged, one in Devonshire and four in Surrey, where Squire had a house at Bowler's Green. During the winter dinners were held at the Cheshire Cheese. Long clay pipes were smoked and the evenings ended with Squire leading the singing of 'It'll be all the same, all the same, a hundred years from now'. On New Year's Day 1929, Squire arranged a match on Broadhalfpenny Down, and the sun shone for him. There was no committee; there were no elections. There was no entrance fee. There was only one qualification for membership – to be a friend of the captain, and Squire was, in his own phrase, 'a social centipede with a foot in a hundred worlds'. By marriage he was connected with the one-time Surrey captain, C. T. A. Wilkinson, and first-class cricketers now and again turned out for him. Among those better known in other spheres may be mentioned E. N. da C. Andrade, Clifford Bax, Edmund Blunden, M. R. K. Burge (Milward Kennedy), W. A. Darlington, Edward Davison, Geoffrey Dearmer, A. P. Herbert, Joseph Hane, Kenneth Lindsay, Howard Marshall, H. S. Mackintosh, Walter Monckton, Harold Monro, A. D. Peters, Edward Shanks and W. J. Turner.

In 1923 Squire published a chronicle of the club's first four years – a very rare opusculum, printed on hand-made paper and limited to 125 copies. 'You can ask,' he wrote in it, 'the most unlikely, the most aged, decrepit and unpractised of men to play for a scratch team against a village and you will find they are invariably willing. . . . If a man won't play for any other reason he will play for the sake of a pleasant excursion or because of the exceptional opportunity of raising a thirst.' Curious adventures, inevitably, befell a side recruited in that fashion. Macdonell was a satirist, but his account of an Invalids match was scarcely caricature. It really was like that, with the team arriving, 2 short, in driblets at a station bar, with Squire at work 3 miles away at Chiswick on his weekly *Observer* article, and the taxi-driver being enrolled as the 11th man. Squire had no natural aptitude for the game and little knowledge of it; though, of course, he was a theoretician. Once against a good side, on a good wicket, in a half-day game, he opened his attack with his 2nd and 3rd change bowlers. At tea, with the score 165 for 2, he explained his plan: 'I thought I'd get 2 or 3 quick wickets, then loose my good bowlers, when they were fresh, against the tail.' It was contended sometimes that the strategy of his captaincy consisted in the creation of situations when he would be justified in putting himself on to bowl. But I think that he believed in his own bowling. And he did, indeed, quite often get a good batsman out, caught off a careless mishit after three sixes in a row or yorked on the second bounce. But he did not take himself off when he had broken a partnership.

His teams did a great deal of fielding, yet they achieved some notable performances. Fate had bestowed on Squire a gift that it has denied to a number of great cricketers. He was a much loved man and his men gave him better than their best. An earlier Sir John refused to 'march through Coventry' with a bag of riff-raff and the Invalids at the sight of a well-kept field and opponents with impressive blazers vowed 'to save Jack's face for him'. We beat the RAOC at Aldershot and the Lords and Commons at the Oval. The Invalids *were* unique.

The club is still active on the cricket field, and celebrated its 50th anniversary in October 1979 with a dinner, at which the present writer proposed the health of the club.

Lord's Taverners' occasion: Lord Home, in his capacity as an honorary Lord's Taverner, presented Hubert Doggart, President of ESCA, with a cheque for £11,000 for the benefit of boys' cricket. The names clockwise are: Hon Findlay Rea (*The Cricketer*), G. H. G. Doggart (President ESCA), Lord Home of the Hirsel (Patron ESCA), Chris Howland (Chairman Lord's Taverners), Cyril J. Cooper (hon Sec ESCA), Ron Gerard (host), Harry Constantine (*The Cricketer*), Bernard Berrick, Raphael Djanogly, E. W. Swanton (Editorial Director, *The Cricketer*), Capt J. A. R. Swainson, RN (Director, Lord's Taverners).

Lord's Taverners

CAPT J. A. R. SWAINSON RN (RET)

Lord's Taverners is a club and registered charity, formed in 1950 by men closely identified with the stage and at the same time fond of cricket, with the purpose of swelling the coffers of the National Playing Fields Association. The Duke of Edinburgh, who holds the office of Twelfth Man, has written that 'in a light-hearted fit of fervour the Lord's Taverners were born with the hope that they might be able to hand a few pounds to the National Playing Fields Association to help provide good, true pitches and cricket equipment for the young men and boys of these islands'.

The history of Lord's Taverners was explained thus in the *Boundary Book* (1962): 'The Lord's Taverners, often accurately described as "a cheerful collection of cricketers, cricketing actors and acting cricketers", came into being in 1950. In fact, it was during the summer of 1949 that the idea of forming this unique club was born. It is now 13 years since somebody stirred a tankard of ale with a cricket bat and the Lord's Taverners floated to the surface. A small coterie of actors, writers, broadcasters and others discussed the scheme, not only in the famous Tavern at Lord's Cricket Ground, from which the Taverners, of course, take their name, but also in the "Cock" public house in Great Portland Street and "other spas and watering places". Three of those whose dream it was met often to talk it over – actor Martin Boddey (Lord's Taverner Number One), the late Michael Shepley, actor, and the erudite critic and broadcaster Spike Hughes. Other well-known, and unknown, cricket devotees were roped in. The idea was to form a fraternity of cricket-lovers who watched the game from the Tavern at Lord's and who would help raise money for the National Playing Fields Association – in fact, "to give back to cricket some of the pleasure they had derived from it by means of cash grants to small cricket clubs up and down the United Kingdom".

'It is said that if someone stands by the Tavern during the cricket season – with, inevitably a tankard of beer close to hand – he is certain within minutes to meet somebody he knows. This is especially true of the cricket enthusiasts who make up the Lord's Taverners, for Lord's is a mecca for people from the entertainment world – actors, broadcasters, musicians, writers, artists, poets, stage directors, producers, film men – so many of them come from professions where their work starts mostly after close of play. Martin Boddey and his brave band of enthusiasts decided to go ahead with their idea. The inaugural meeting was held in the Circle Bar of the Comedy Theatre, London, on Tuesday 3 July 1950. The name – a flash of inspiration to Boddey on top of a number 74 bus between Kensington and St John's Wood – was accepted by tacit consent and a provisional committee was appointed and drew up some rules.'

Since those small beginnings in 1950 when it was envisaged that this happy group of enthusiasts might hope to raise perhaps £100 a year for the NPFA, the Lord's Taverners have in fact raised nearly £1 million. Sir Pelham Warner – the much-loved 'Plum' Warner – a doyen of British cricket, was invited to become the 1st honorary member. He listened to the story of the formation of the Lord's Taverners: 'Your trouble will not be to get people to join but to keep them out!' he declared, and he has been proved absolutely right. The Lord's Taverners have been inspired by the interest and participation of their Patron and Twelfth Man, HRH The Duke of Edinburgh. When, shortly after the inaugural meeting, Martin Boddey and Captain Jack Broome, RN, were invited to meet Prince Philip at Clarence House to tell him of their aspirations, His Royal Highness listened attentively and suggested that he might do something to help. When, too, it was respectfully put forward that he might consent to become the club's 1st President he replied: 'I could not do that. If I became your President I should expect to chair your meetings and I really haven't the time. But I will be your Patron if you like . . .' The visitors were overjoyed. Before taking their leave, they mentioned that the honorary and honourable position of 'Twelfth Man' had been left vacant. Prince Philip enquired of the significance of the position. He was told that the traditional duties of that indispensable and always keenest member of a cricket side were to carry the bag from the station, 'sub' in the field, bring out the drinks, look after the scorebook, and run for anybody who did not feel like it after lunch . . . 'Exactly what I thought you meant,' he said, and thereupon claimed the right to fill the role.

Since those early days the membership has grown to 800. Over the past 6 years, the Charity has averaged £100,000 per annum which would have warmed the heart of the founder. The Taverners' charitable objectives are threefold:

1 To provide a sporting challenge for youngsters and, in particular, through the playing of team games such as cricket.
2 To provide through the NPFA adventure playgrounds for the underprivileged children and 'help keep them off the streets'.
3 To provide mini-buses for handicapped children to enable them to get out into the fresh air and away from the confines of hospitals and homes. The buses are named 'New Horizons'.

Private Overseas Tours

IRVING ROSENWATER

Prior to the visit of MCC to Australia in 1903–04, all touring teams from England were in some degree 'private' gatherings in that the players did not come under the aegis of the Marylebone Club and their choice was nearly always in the hands of the tour organizer. In many cases matches which were to become known as Test Matches were played and the primary motive of the tour was a profit one. All such ventures naturally assumed a public importance in which national and international reputations were at stake. The genuine conception of a 'private' tour was one which generally encompassed one of the lesser cricket-playing regions of the world and where goodwill – not profit – was the paramount consideration. Such tours would almost invariably have proved disastrous as strictly commercial movements, but as attempts to advance the growth of the game they have been of immense value. The capable amateur has naturally played his part in such expeditions, but most private tours have contained a sprinkling of professionals, according to the needs of the occasion.

The first of the great team-gatherers for private tours was the illustrious captain of Yorkshire, Lord Hawke. A man of great charm and fine presence, he became known as the Odysseus of cricket, for there was no firmer believer in the value that could be derived from cricket visits to distant parts. He chose his players carefully, and this aspect of Lord Hawke's career was something he always looked back upon with the greatest pride. In the 1890s he took teams to India, the United States and Canada, South Africa and the West Indies; and in 1912 the English team that visited the Argentine, though officially bearing the label of MCC, played in the colours of the captain, Lord Hawke.

These teams contained some of the foremost amateurs of the day – P. F. Warner, C. B. Fry, S. M. J. Woods, A. C. MacLaren, Hon F. S. Jackson, A. J. L. Hill, F. Mitchell, C. E. de Trafford and H. D. G. Leveson Gower – all of them, and many more besides, men of high standing in English cricket and admirable ambassadors to further the game abroad. It was Lord Hawke who induced R. Slade Lucas to captain the 1st English side to visit the West Indies (in 1894–95) – the first of a long series of goodwill tours to that delightful part of the world. Lord Hawke himself took a team there in 1896–97, in the same season that Arthur Priestley's side toured, and between them the two teams played in all the major territories as well as in many of the lesser islands, including Antigua, St Kitts, Grenada, St Lucia and St Vincent.

Before the end of the century P. F. Warner had taken 2 teams to America – the chief encounters being at Philadelphia – among those going with him being G. L. Jessop, C. J. Burnup, B. J. T. Bosanquet and 'Shrimp' Leveson Gower; Canada was included in the 2nd visit. K. S. Ranjitsinhji also took a side to the USA and Canada in 1899, and 2 years later B. J. T. Bosanquet repeated the venture. There had been several private tours to North America before that but these teams contained the best-known names. The West Indies continued to attract English visitors and early in 1902 R. A. Bennett's young side, made up in the main of University men, played 19 matches there. An extensive tour was also undertaken to the West Indies by Lord Brackley's team in 1904–05, 2 professionals (E. G. Hayes and G. J. Thompson) accompanying the side.

Private tours abroad became less frequent once MCC began sending official sides around the world, but good club sides were not daunted and the Incogniti more than once sent a team to America, I Zingari went to Egypt, and Free Foresters in 1921 began a series of visits to Holland that only the Second World War interrupted.

On a more ambitious scale were the tours conducted by the Hon Lionel (later Lord) Tennyson, who fell in love with Jamaica after seeing it as a member of an MCC side in the middle 1920s. He took 3 of his own sides there between 1927 and 1932. They were, as it happened, unbeaten. What is more to the point was Tennyson's conspicuous part in raising Jamaican cricket from comparative obscurity to a position of respect. He also induced his friend Julien (later Sir Julien) Cahn (*qv*) to visit Jamaica in 1929, this being the first of 6 overseas tours that this millionaire-philanthropist undertook in the decade before the Second World War. Sir Julien never covered the same itinerary twice. Few private tours – before or since – have been conducted on such lavish lines as his. Tennyson took a final side on tour in 1937–38, this time to India, where friendships were made – notably concerning A. R. Gover – which have lasted to this day. In that same season Sir Theodore Brinckman led a strong side to the Argentine. The regular tours sponsored by H. M. Martineau to Egypt – beginning in 1929 – also contained some prominent names and gave much pleasure to visitors and hosts alike.

Since the Second World War, thanks to the growth of travel by air, a large number of private tours have taken place, involving most of the cricket-playing countries of the world, major and minor. Minor tours – such as visits to Portugal or Denmark – have always been a feature of expeditions abroad, but in recent years so great a mass of activity has sprung up that hardly a cricket-conscious portion of the globe has failed to receive or send a touring team of some sort. On a more exalted plane was the side taken to Jamaica in 1957 by the late Duke of Norfolk – a side including 7 Test cricketers which lost none of its 10 matches. The Caribbean has also attracted 2 sides managed by E. W. Swanton, in 1956 and 1961, both teams being greeted most enthusiastically in all the places visited, which included Tobago, St Kitts and Grenada, as well as the main centres, Barbados, Trinidad and British Guiana.

Barbados was also the destination of two tours by E. W. Swanton's Arabs, captained by A. C. D. Ingleby-Mackenzie in January 1967, and by A. R. Lewis in January 1974. Swanton also took a side on a less well-trodden itinerary in March–April, 1964, when his team, which included G. S. Sobers, R. Benaud and the Nawab of Pataudi, played in Penang, Singapore, Kuala Lumpur, Hong Kong, Kowloon and Bangkok; this Far-Eastern tour ended with a magnificent victory at Calcutta over an Indian XI that was virtually a Test side. Mention might also be made of the all-first-class team taken to East Africa by F. R. Brown towards the end of 1961 and of several visits by a club side – the Romany – to South Africa starting in 1960. The Romany in 1978 even ventured to Sri Lanka.

The Club Cricket Conference, after a long and distinguished history in which it did not concern itself with overseas tours, sent representative sides to Australia in 1971, 1975 and 1979, and to Barbados and Trinidad in 1977. The Minor Counties Cricket Association, too, broke new ground in January 1978, when they sent a team abroad for the first time, playing 6 matches in Kenya. The Midlands Club Cricket Conference has also made successful tours to Australia and the Far East in 1973 and to Australia and Hong Kong in early 1977, with a brief visit to New Zealand on each tour. Indeed, since 1970 a great many private sides, of varying strengths, have travelled abroad to play cricket, distance and expense apparently now setting few insurmountable problems. At a higher playing level have been the several tours of D. H. Robins, who has taken sides to South Africa (4 times), Canada, the West Indies, the Far East and South America. But somewhere, at almost any time, it is now possible to locate a club, school, old boys' or hybrid side on tour.

Derrick Robins's XI

CRAWFORD WHITE

Derrick Robins is a one-man cricket sponsor, a major sporting philanthropist. He started promoting the welfare of young cricketers, with special concentration on the development and encouragement of England players, before even John Player, Benson & Hedges and Cornhill had moved in to make the whole thing big business. Between 1950 and the end of 1979 he financed close on 200 games in England, involving his own sides against touring teams, counties and universities. As important as that, in the last 15 years he has given valuable overseas opportunities to many of England's best young players on carefully planned tours to South Africa, South America, Canada, the Near East and Australia.

Bob Willis, John Lever, John Snow, Brian Close, Phil Edmonds, Mike Hendrick, Derek Randall, David Gower, Frank Hayes, Clive Radley, Graham Roope, Bob Woolmer, Roger Tolchard, David Bairstow, Mike Gatting, John Emburey and many others have benefited from their contacts with Derrick Robins. 'I know it sounds trite,' he says, 'but I have always felt the need to put something back into cricket.' He had the odd game for Warwickshire as a wicket-keeper/batsman. In 4 tours of South Africa he has set out to maintain cricketing links there. In 1973–74 he took the first multi-racial side to the Republic, which included John Shepherd of West Indies and Kent and Younis Ahmed of Pakistan, Surrey and Worcestershire. Whether playing in the African township of Soweto or at the Wanderers ground in Johannesburg, Shepherd was a smiling success. In the following year the South Africans fielded a multi-racial side against the Robins XI, which was then, of itself, something of an event.

For 13 years Robins was Chairman of Coventry City Football Club. Since then, at vast expense to himself, he has been a cricketing benefactor, doing a job along the lines of Sir Julien Cahn before the Second World War and one for which the game's official bodies owe him a singular debt.

Village Cricket

RONALD MASON

Over the origins and context of village cricket the chronicler must hover warily, for its image exists as much in the common imagination as in actuality. It has taken, for better or worse, a recognizable part in the social picture of the patchwork that is English life and custom, and the vision it projects is

Rural pitch-invasion: a game at Hambledon is held up as the Hambledon Hunt passes through. The matting wicket is a wise precaution in this case.

permeated with a native romanticism which often obscures as much as it reveals. The very name of cricket is the ready cause of much sentimental talking and writing; and in this urbanized and mechanistic age a similar danger is known to attend upon the idea of a village. Combine the two ideas, and objectivity is lost – the mind is diverted out of the distracting bustle of our inhuman century into an agrarian haven of leafy repose wherein this patterned pastime, compact of all the Graces, is played out in an idyllic surrounding answering to all nostalgic longings. The picture casts a potent spell, which we have to understand before we can exorcise it and replace it by an assessment of its true toughness and durability. And to do this we have to remind ourselves of its origins.

With the primitive and unresolved mysteries of cricket's birth, the early proscriptions and associations with bear-baitings and other lewdnesses, we are not here concerned. It is sufficient to establish the historical fact that the game as we know it evolved from unidentifiable varieties of country sports as long ago as the 16th century, and that all the evidence concentrates its earliest recognizable manifestations about the Wealden villages of Kent and Surrey. These areas were then, and in their most attractive aspects still are, largely agricultural; their basic communities were scattered steadings and tenantries about a central manor, where the day's labour was long and the day's relaxations simple and unsophisticated, and where the social hierarchies were steep and rigidly defined. The space of turf about which the workpeople's houses clustered became the green on which they and their children played. Later, the masters of the great houses gave personal patronage to these activities, encouraged them and even instituted them on their own account; the history, for example, of the illustrious Sevenoaks Vine Cricket Club, one of the oldest in the country, is intimately bound up with that of their great patrons, the Sackvilles of Knole, and it is misleading to try to understand the one without the other. The cricket that blossomed out at Hambledon in the 1760s, to become the first-class game that we know today, was part village cricket and part country-house cricket – a division of categories that kept its relevance until barely a generation ago. The country houses fostered its delicacy, its leisured grace, its sense of order and tradition; the villages gave it its oaken core of energy, strength and endurance.

All over England, particularly in the south, the village teams retained their primary feudal tradition until almost the day before yesterday. The legendary comic trio of Squire, Parson and Blacksmith have become as rooted in the lore of the country game as Harlequin, Pantaloon and Clown in the pantomime, but like those classical abstractions they mirror a state that was once reality – in certain privileged places, is a living reality still. The teams, and the kind of game they engaged in, showed a clear cross-section of the anomalous society of 18th- and 19th-century England; the regimental blazer of the squire, the college sash or hat-ribbon of the parson, the braces of the blacksmith, were as consistent and appropriate and unchangeable as the individual saints' crosses that combine to make up the Union Jack.

Much of the comedy and the sentiment that surrounds the topic arises from a natural nostalgia for the comic situations attendant upon social inequality. When many otherwise reasonable critics still seriously assert that you can keep Lord's and the Oval, but give them a real old-fashioned village match, there's cricket for you, they are surely honouring not so much the game itself as a romantic projection of their yearning for a happy Garden-State recalling lost innocence and youth. To this illusion the great Nyren helped to contribute with his heartbreaking evocation of the golden joys of Broadhalfpenny long ago; and Dickens with his fantastic Dingley Dell variations upon a theme he but imperfectly understood; and A. G. Macdonell with his vigorous and farcical misrepresentation, crude and hilarious, which enlivened his gay satire *England, Their England* of the 1930s. For clearer illumination it were better to turn to Siegfried Sassoon's Flower Show Match episode in his *Memoirs of a Fox-Hunting Man*, to Edmund Blunden's *Cricket Country* and, first and last of all, to that minor classic *The Cricket Match* by Hugh de Selincourt. For in all of these, and especially the last, are to be found the humour without the farce, the essence without the overflowing sentiment, the game itself without the eyewash, the virtues and the limitations of this characteristic and individual section of cricket.

On picturesqueness there is no need to enlarge; examples of it proliferate all over the picture-books. Bearsted and Meopham in Kent; Brockham Green and Godstone in Surrey; Roehampton and Kew Green like country oases in the suburban desert; Henfield in Sussex whose traditions are traceable at least to 1721 – all of these, which are 7 beautiful settings invidiously representing 70 times 7 thousand and 7 others each as lively and captivating in character, add their quota to the distinctive beauty of this distinctive nation-wide summer amusement. But the south-eastern counties have no monopoly in this, nor have the 17 first-class counties themselves; and the familiar backgrounds of Kentish weald or New Forest birch or Surrey pinewood can be varied a hundred times over with Cornish granite or Lakeland crag or Black Country chimneys. The northernmost cricket club in the British Isles playing regularly home-and-away cricket is reputed to be St Duthus, at Tain in Ross-shire, near the Dornoch Firth, in sight of the Sutherland Hills, and there are no keener village cricketers than the Scots, as single-minded in their enthusiasm as the lesser breeds just south of the Border. In Cornwall and Cumberland, Shropshire and Suffolk and all the counties lying in and around their circle, the country cricketing communities lie thick, as in much of Scotland and a little of Wales, and there are few areas in the length and breadth of the country where the motorist will fail to encounter up to half a dozen matches in progress on a Saturday afternoon's drive.

Available grounds, fields, open spaces, may be inconveniently small or otherwise handicapped; at Coldharbour in Surrey, at Holyport in Berkshire, the main road runs frighteningly close to the pitch; at Jordans in Bucks the charming and hospitable ground boasts a curious hollow crater like a miniature Devil's Punch Bowl within feet of the infielders, and visitors must accept the hazards, and cheerfully do. Wickets may be surprisingly good or predictably unpredictable, outfields ditto only more so; some grounds have devoted and knowledgeable attention, while others, often for unavoidable reasons, virtually no attention at all. Village cricketers play this game for pure enjoyment, and while well aware that much of cricket's pleasure depends on assiduous behind-the-scenes preparation of ground conditions and player alike, have often neither the funds nor the leisure to provide either. The game itself, the Saturday afternoon 2.30 to 7.30 event, which only starts at all as a result of selfless application by organizing officials and committees and their indispensable catering auxiliaries, the lady-helpers, is often, as a

The village scene: Brooksbottom CC, Summerseatt, Lancashire.

result of these complexities, a spectacle of energetic keenness rather than skill.

It is inevitable that its average quality is dependent upon improvization rather than on ordered development of natural resources. In the main, subtleties go by the board. Batsmen find greater reward in cross-batted energy and bold lofty hitting than in organized defence or scientific stroke-play. Bowlers rely usefully on speed rather than on elaborate variations of flight and spin. Good fielding is often at the mercy of a rough ground; captaincy and umpiring often reveal good will rather than knowledge. (These are generalizations, each of which can be contradicted many times over by specific example; also corroborated by as many.) In these circumstances scores are usually small, finishes often unexpectedly thrilling, the action sensational rather than dramatic.

Out of village cricket the great English game evolved all over the globe; its salient qualities have refined with the years to a more general conformity, but its staple virtues of keenness, rivalry and energetic good humour, deployed with skill varying from the formidable to the negligible, are as strong as ever. C. B. Fry once declared that were he compelled to back himself to make a hundred he would choose a county match rather than a village match for the attempt; Edmund Blunden has defined the village touch as the sweetening of science with the love of the sport and the humour of the unpredicted. The conditions which prompted these two penetrating comments still remain.

The Wrigley Cricket Foundation

In 1969, not long after the formation of the National Cricket Association, The Wrigley Company Ltd, chewing-gum manufacturers of Plymouth, began to make funds available to encourage an interest in the playing of cricket by the young and the achieving by them of a greater proficiency and skill in the game. As a result, the Wrigley Cricket Foundation was set up to administer the funds along clear guidelines. One of the more significant ways in which it has worked is to provide grants toward the cost of coaching courses for young people and for the training of coaches. It has provided visual aids of various kinds, such as films and wall charts. It has sponsored, or helped finance, representative youth matches, both at home and abroad. As far as possible, it lends support to activities which have not taken place before or which could not take place without such help.

In 1973 the Foundation lent a substantial sum to the NCA to enable the latter to set up a Proficiency Award Scheme, under which thousands of boys and girls have passed tests in all aspects of cricket and gained badges. A couple of years later, the Foundation underwrote the publication of a *Coaching Handbook*, designed to be used in association with the Proficiency Award Scheme.

One of the more interesting activities of the Foundation to date is the sponsorship of The Wrigley Trophy National Indoor Six-a-Side Club Cricket Championship, which has taken place annually in the spring since 1976. This competition, which is becoming increasingly popular among club sides, is now a well-established feature of the close season. As played, the game was the inspiration of Michael Vockins, Secretary of Worcestershire County Cricket Club, and was conceived as a way of keeping enthusiasts in touch with each other during the winter months. A special composition ball, weighing only 4 oz, is used and ideally the game is played in an enclosed hall about 120 feet long by 75 feet wide by 20 feet high.

Each match consists of 12 overs a side, bowlers being allowed 3 overs each. A stroke to a side wall earns 1 run, 2 more runs being added if the batsmen cross safely. A drive to the wall behind the bowler is worth 4 runs, 6 if the hit is full pitch. To all the normal ways of being out, batsmen have to face the added risk of being caught off walls or ceiling. The game is usually played at a fast pace, but hard hitting does not necessarily succeed as well as good placing and timing.

The competition is open to all clubs affiliated to the NCA through their County Associations. It is run on a county basis until the Regional rounds are reached, when the draw and venues for Regional rounds are made by the NCA Cricket Sub-committee. The semi-finals and final were held at the MCC Indoor Cricket School at Lord's in April 1979, after taking place at other London venues in earlier years.

WINNERS 1976–1979

1976 Durham City (135–0) beat Enville (88) by 47 runs
1977 Scarborough (128–5) beat Headington United (41) by 87 runs
1978 Percy Main (137–5) beat Dunstable Town (94) by 43 runs
1979 Ickenham (117–4) beat Leamington (73) by 44 runs

Women's Cricket

NETTA RHEINBERG

One year after publication of the original agreed code of Laws the first women's cricket match of which the record still exists took place. The *Reading Mercury* reported on 26 July 1745:

> The greatest cricket-match that was ever played in the South part of England was on Friday, the 26th of last month, on Gosden Common, near Guildford, in Surrey, between eleven maids of Bramley and eleven maids of Hambleton, dressed all in white. The Bramley maids had blue ribbons and the Hambleton maids red ribbons on their heads. The Bramley girls got 119 notches and the Hambleton girls 127.

The next game of which the evidence stands was on 13 July 1747 on the renowned Artillery Ground between the women of Charlton and those of Westdean and Chilgrove, Sussex, and thereafter from the middle of the 18th century there are constant press references to women's matches, most of them played in Sussex, Hampshire and Surrey villages. Titles varied, but 'Married v Single' and inter-village contests were predominant. Most of these were rowdy affairs accompanied by off-the-field betting. The stakes also varied. Plumcake, a barrel of ale, a regale of tea and £500 are all mentioned. The village girls who took part in these exhibition games were no less adept than their counterparts are today. In 1745, 'The girls bowled, batted, ran and catched as well as most men could do in that game'; and there are references to 'numerous concourses' of people at matches.

Thirty years after the event at Gosden Common there were signs that 'fashionable' women were also playing the game. No doubt the wonderful feats by players of the Hambledon Club were having their influence on the ladies. One active enthusiast who spread the gospel was the wife of the famous bat and ball maker, John Small. In the 1770s John Collet painted the well-known picture of Miss Wicket and Miss Trigger which shows the former undoubtedly to be 'a lady of quality', and a *Morning Post* of 1777 records a match played between the Countess of Derby and some other fashionable ladies at The Oaks, Surrey. Contrary to the village matches this was played in private and has become noteworthy. One of the players, Miss Elizabeth Ann Burrell, 'got more notches in the first and second innings than any lady in the game', and thereby fascinated the 8th Duke of Hamilton to such an extent that it was a case of love at first sight. He wedded her before the following season, but his enthusiasm for cricket must have waned somewhat in later years, for the marriage ended in divorce.

Another nobleman, John Frederick Sackville, 3rd Duke of Dorset, wrote in the *Ladies' and Gentlemen's Magazine* in 1797 a piece in favour of women playing cricket, opening with the phrase: 'What is life but a game of cricket? and if so, why should not the ladies play it as well as we?' He was the forerunner of many of the gentry who, during the 19th century, gave their womenfolk encouragement to persevere with the game.

In 1811 Thomas Rowlandson, at the age of 55, drew his 'Cricket Match Extraordinary' depicting the match between the women of Hampshire and Surrey. This game was a considerable event arranged by 2 unnamed noblemen for stakes of 500 guineas a side. The players were recorded as being of all ages and sizes and for the 1st time their names were published.

Towards the end of the century, these romping and rural games died out and Victorian girls played privately, though perhaps not so demurely as one might expect. In many country houses cricket was being followed closely by women and it is certain that their influence was felt behind the scenes. It is generally agreed that the introduction of round-arm bowling by John Willes and its eventual official acceptance stemmed directly from his sister, Christina. She helped him at his cricket practice in a barn near their Canterbury home, and finding that she could not deliver the ball satisfactorily under-arm owing to the voluminous fashionable skirt she was wearing, started throwing the ball 'high-handed' or round-arm. Her brother at once recognized the possibilities of this way of bowling, though this new style was not officially accepted by the authorities until 21 years later.

In the latter years of the last century cricket for women flourished in the great country houses and, in 1887, the first club, White Heather, was formed. Its scorebook survives and can be seen at the Cricket Gallery at Lord's. The copperplate inscription inside the cover tells of the decision to start the club owing to the 'large amount of cricket being played at Normanhurst and Eridge, the country seats of the Brassey and Nevill families. There were 8 founders, mostly bearing famous names; but by 1891 the membership had increased to 50.

In 1890 2 teams of women were raised by a Mr Matthews in response to a press advertisement and became the only recorded professional women players. Entitled the 'Original English Lady Cricketers' they travelled up and down the country accompanied by a chaperone, and a manager, playing exhibition matches. No player was permitted to play under her proper name; each was given sixpence a day expense money and provided with uniforms, red for one team, blue for the other. Great crowds flocked to these matches, all played on well-known grounds, but at the end of the season the teams were suddenly disbanded.

Up to now there was still no sign of organized women's cricket, though Edwardian women players raised teams from time to time and matched themselves against their menfolk's village clubs. Cricket had been included in the curriculum of some of the larger public schools for girls since their foundation and after the First World War, which brought with it the steadily growing emancipation of women, the game became generally more popular. Girls expressed the desire to continue to play after leaving school.

The germ of the idea having an official association on the lines of an MCC of women's cricket seemed to have been in the minds of several people at the same time. In 1926 Miss V. M. M. Cox (first honorary Secretary of the Women's Cricket Association), Miss K. Doman, Kent hockey international, and Mrs J. Scott Bowden, also a hockey player and owner of the Park Hotel, Colwall, near Malvern, raised a team of cricketers for a visit to the West Country. This included 4 further hockey internationals: Missess Blaxland, Cattell and Knott of Kent, and Marjorie Pollard of Northants. Mrs Greenstock, sister of the famous Foster brothers, and her 2 daughters were also in the team.

This first combined venture was so successful that it was decided to call an official meeting in the autumn to discuss the founding of an association and in the months before the meeting plans were laid for the setting up of this new national organization. On 4 October 1926 19 people met in London to take this far-reaching step. Twenty others, prevented from attending, gave their support. There was one dissenting letter, but the overwhelming opinion supported the motion formally put by Miss K. Doman 'that a central association for women's cricket be formed', the official title to be 'The Women's Cricket Association'.

The embryo association was fortunate in the appointment of its officers, Mrs N. Heron Maxwell, chairman, and Misses V. M. M. Cox and J. Hatten, joint secretary and treasurer. All three possessed driving force and admirable administrative abilities. They were determined to establish cricket for women as a regular game and to send as soon as possible a national team to Australia.

The game was now open to any woman or girl wishing to play and the decision to hold an annual cricket week at Colwall, near Malvern, where the association had first been suggested, helped much to publicize its existence. Cricket Week has remained a popular annual event and Colwall, a household name to every woman cricketer, has rightly been named 'the cradle of women's cricket'.

By 1929 the time was considered ripe for the 1st public match which was played at Beckenham between London and District and the Rest of England. It was a lively game of a good standard, commented on favourably by the majority of press reporters, and the association's policy in furthering the game for women and girls was vindicated and strengthened. This match was the first of the so-called 'Representative' games and similar matches have been arranged each year between the 22 best players in the country under titles considered most suitable for the occasion. In 1932 another milestone was reached when men's county grounds were made available to women cricketers for their official matches.

At the end of the first 7 years, the increase in membership and improvement in standard called for a reorganization in administration. It was felt that clubs, schools and colleges should form the real backbone of the association and a concerted drive was made to

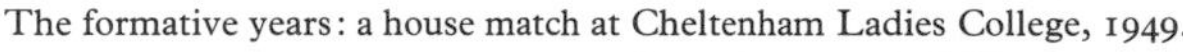
The formative years: a house match at Cheltenham Ladies College, 1949.

Rachael Heyhoe, England's successful captain and leading personality, plays a stroke straight from the coaching manual.

increase these affiliations. At the same time, for ease of organization, the country was divided into 5 territorial associations: East, Midlands, North, South and West, each with its own administration. A territorial match programme was started and from these games and other trials, selectors chose players for the annual 'Representative' match. In 1931 the 1st county associations had emerged and a match was played between Durham and a combined Cheshire and Lancashire XI.

In 1934 an invitation from the Australian Women's Cricket Council to send a touring team to Australia was accepted and the founders' dream came true. The 1st England team to tour Australia and New Zealand sailed from Tilbury on 19 October 1934. Its 16 members all paid their own passages of £80 and purchased their own equipment for the 6 months' tour. Some outstanding players were unable to go, but famous names abounded. The captain was Betty Archdale, of Kent, and the manager was Betty Green, subsequently Mrs Lawson. The two wicket-keepers Betty Snowball and Grace Morgan made a name for themselves and are considered today among the finest of the few outstanding women 'keepers. Molly Hide, later to captain England from 1937–1954, already showed a brilliance which was to shine steadily thereafter, and Myrtle Maclagan, all-rounder, who scored the first century (119) in women's Test cricket at Sydney, achieved a tour average of 63·25 in 9 innings. The team returned unbeaten, winning 2 of the 3 Tests, and on the brief 1st visit to New Zealand they won all 7 matches, including the one Test. This 1st tour was followed in 1937 by a return visit from Australia, memorable for the glorious cricket played by their team. Hazel Pritchard's batting was a revelation; Peggy Antonio showed herself to be a superlative leg-spin bowler; Mollie Flaherty's fast bowling annihilated many county players; but the Test series was drawn.

The financing of tours was difficult. Each touring team found the money for its own fares, while the hostess country bore all expenses of hospitality, entertainment, and travelling on home grounds, but retained all match profits. This procedure remained unchanged for 36 years until 1970 when the first sponsorship came along.

Other financial help came in the early 1960s through a Government Grant Aid scheme which eventually covered administrative costs and by 1971 the Association appointed its 1st full-time salaried official, Miss Anne Sanders, National Development Officer.

In 1970 the Association were fortunate in finding, through Rachael Heyhoe (England captain 1966–1978), a generous sponsor in Jack Hayward, who financed 2 successive tours to the West Indies in 1970 and 1971 and who was responsible in 1973 for backing the 1st World Cup Competition ever to be held in the cricket world. Other sponsorships subsequently became available and these eased the financial burden though they brought with them other problems both of principle and publicity.

A natural development of the exchange of international visits was the formation, in Melbourne in 1958, of the International Women's Cricket Council, to promote international tours and to provide a liaison between countries for discussion on any questions appertaining to the game. Five countries, Australia, New Zealand, South Africa, Holland and England, attended the inaugural meeting. The number of affiliations, with the addition of Barbados, Grenada, India, Jamaica, and Trinidad and Tobago is now ten.

The 1960s brought many changes and innovations. The structure of the WCA was altered, the territorial administrations being replaced by 13 Playing Areas; in order to qualify for necessary grants a Five-Year Development Plan was drawn up. Awards to women of the MCC Advanced Coaching Certificate were made, the 1st recipients being Mary Duggan, England Captain 1957–1963, and her colleague Ruth Westbrook, thus setting the example for many subsequent holders.

1970 started with an unofficial, though pioneer, visit to Jamaica by Rachael Heyhoe and her team, and ended with the Annual General Meeting of the WCA being held in the Long Room at Lord's. The following year an official WCA team captained by Rachael Heyhoe toured the West Indies, consolidating the enthusiasm engendered by the previous visit. At home much work was done to foster the growth of cricket among younger girls and the first Junior England XI was selected and Junior Committees formed.

Seven teams from 5 nations competed in the 1973 World Cup – the absentees being India, who applied too late, and South Africa. Furthermore, the 5 South African players chosen for the International XI were barred owing to political difficulties. The competition was opened officially on 14 June at the Civil Service Ground, Chiswick, by Sir Roger Bannister, Chairman of the Sports Council. For the next $5\frac{1}{2}$ weeks, 21 sixty-over matches were played all over England, all 7 teams playing one another on a league basis. The seeding of Australia and England as the strongest teams proved correct, though New Zealand and the International XI proved dangerous competitors. The final between England and Australia took place at Edgbaston and was a splendid game resulting in a win for England by 92 runs.

The 2nd World Cup Competition was held in 1977–78 in India whose 3-year-old association had made remarkable progress. Unfortunately West Indies and Holland withdrew at the last moment, and a change of management in India caused political innuendos to creep in so that the organization left much to be desired.

The 4th Australian tour of England formed part of the celebrations of the 50th birthday of the WCA. The Test Series was drawn but following the popular trend the fixtures included 3 one-day 60-over matches, England winning 2 and losing 1. The 2nd of these games provided the most memorable event of the Golden Jubilee in that it was played at Lord's on Wednesday 4 August. This falling to women cricketers of the last stronghold of cricket was given wide publicity and the occasion was made fittingly more golden by England's win before a good crowd on a fine summer's day. Another innovation was the sponsoring of the tour by St Ivel, a department of Unigate, which eased greatly the administration and organization.

The dropping of Rachael Heyhoe-Flint as England captain and her replacement by Mary Pilling for the World Cup team to India in 1977 made a considerable impact on both the public and the WCA membership and caused much unrest and split loyalties. The Association was roughly handled by the press, but chose to weather the storm in comparative silence, their only statement being that selectors' decisions must be accepted as final.

In 1979 the WCA welcomed the newly-formed Caribbean Women's Cricket Federation team for its 1st tour of England, another pioneer event in the history of women's cricket. As is now the custom, sponsors helped the event but the WCA carried the main costs. Junior cricket is still being treated as a priority and a Junior team is visiting Holland. Although receiving valuable co-operation from men's cricket, the Women's Cricket Association is controlled entirely by women and has for many years taken its rightful place in the cricketing world.

Women within the hallowed precincts: their first appearance at Lord's, England v Australia, 1976.

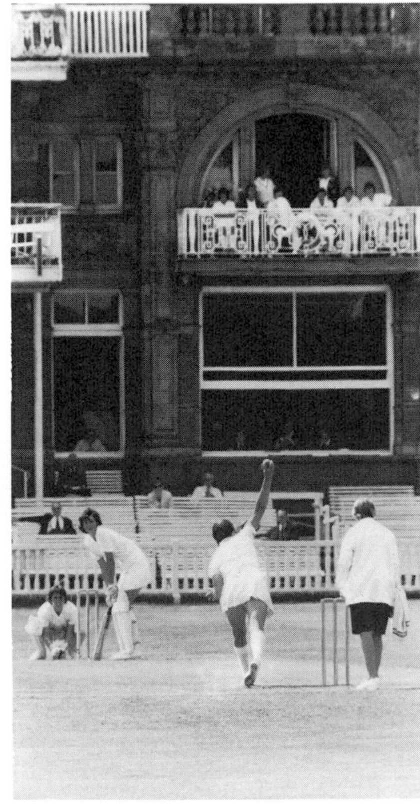

Part IX
A Cricket Treasury

Art

JOHN ARLOTT

THE FIELD of cricket art extends from the masterpiece to completely 'popular' – or folk – art; from Paul Sandby's 'Landscape with Cricket Match in Progress' to naïve Staffordshire figures of cricketers: from a work in which cricket is merely incidental to the unsophisticated jumble of cricketana, important for its subject rather than any 'pure' artistic quality.

In Sandby's superb gouache, and the oil (*c.* 1850) by an unknown artist of 'Cricket Match with a view of Christchurch Priory', the game of cricket is merely an ingredient of the landscape: either would grace any art collection and it would not be quite just to call them 'cricket pictures'. The same applies to a number of 18th- and early-19th-century portraits, usually of youths, shown holding a cricket bat. Essentially these are portraits of the persons; the picture, as a work of art, would not be affected if a riding whip or a fishing rod were substituted for the bat.

Most of the major oil paintings of the game are, in fact, landscapes, the cricketers tiny figures in the broad setting. Among the best are 'Village Cricket' (1855) by John Ritchie, 'A Cricket Match on Parker's Piece, Cambridge' (*c.* 1861: artist unknown), 'A Match between the Army and the Navy at Portsmouth' (?H. Ladbrooke: 1800–1869), 'Kent v Hampshire, 1774', 'The Cricket Match' (?L. R. Boitard, *c.* 1740), 'Gentlemen v Players at Brading, Isle of Wight' (*c.* 1749, attributed to Francis Hayman) and 'A Cricket Match' (George Morland). There are numerous paintings in this style between 1750 and 1850, of varying degrees of excellence; there are also, undoubtedly, a number of copies and some downright forgeries. In recent years some pleasant oil paintings have been made of cricket grounds by Charles Cundall (Lord's and Hastings), Arthur Mailey, the Australian Test cricketer (Sandringham), Col C. T. Burt (Edgbaston), Olive Sharp (Brockton Point, Vancouver) and Mildred Smith Amandoz (Queen's Park Oval, Trinidad).

'Village Cricket' by John Ritchie (1855).

Oil paintings of players exist in fair numbers but it would be hard to describe any of them as great; among the best – most of them hanging in various county pavilions – are W. G. Grace by A. Stuart-Wortley, Len Hutton by Henry Carr (in the possession of Sir Leonard Hutton), A. C. MacLaren, Sir Jack Hobbs, Lord Hawke, Wilfred Rhodes, S. F. Barnes and Denis Compton. There are also some few 'character' paintings in oils, mostly produced about the middle of the last century, which have a genuine cricket feeling.

The most important is that called 'The Scorer' – actually William Davies, who was scorer to Lewes Priory Cricket Club – painted in 1842 by an artist of whom little is known, Thomas Henwood: the study of the old rustic, bespectacled and bearded, wearing a wide-brimmed straw hat and sitting at his table with his book, bottle, glass and churchwarden pipe, has been many times reproduced. James Hayllar was a little later than Henwood and there is, perhaps, a hint of sentimentality about his portrait-studies: nevertheless, his 'Brewer's Drayman, a Cricketer', 'An Old Cricketer' and 'Her First Lesson' have true human – and cricket – sympathy.

In the field of water-colour, crayon and pen-and-ink drawings there have been far more numerous contributions to cricket art. It includes the most historically important item of all cricket art, a single page, 7¾ by 9¾ inches, from the notebook of George Shepheard senior (1770?–1842), himself a cricketer who played for Surrey. The sheet contains 12 water-colour drawings of cricketers of whom 9 are named. Probably executed at a match at Lord's in about 1790, the studies are of Lord Frederick Beauclerk, the Hon Henry Tufton (11th Earl of Thanet), the Hon Charles Lennox (4th Duke of Richmond) and the Hon Edward Bligh – all amateur cricketers of the period – 2 of Thomas Lord, founder of the famous ground, and the only existing action portraits of 3 of the greatest of the Hambledon players, Tom Walker, David Harris and William Beldham. Its survival is surprising and happy; it is now in the possession of MCC and has been reproduced, entire and in detail, many times.

George Belcher's 'Impression of Jack Hobbs', 'Herbert Strudwick' by Frank Eastman, 'The Saffrons Ground, Eastbourne' by G. Prowse, several sketches of county grounds in about 1900 by W. A. Bettesworth, 'The Cricketer' by W. Hunt, 'The Oval in 1849' by C. J. Basébe, 'The Long Room at Lord's' by Dennis Flanders and 'Cricket at Phoenix Park, Dublin' by John Powell provide a good cross-section of this work.

Cricket art, however, has reached most people, and done so most happily, through engravings. The best-known of the early prints is 'Cricket on the Artillery Ground, Finsbury' (1743), engraved on copper by Benoist after a painting by Francis Hayman, one of the series he and Hogarth executed for Vauxhall Gardens. It is said that the wicket-keeper in the scene is, in fact, Hogarth. This print has remained popular for two centuries. Another well-known 18th-century engraving first appeared in *The Sporting Magazine* in 1793 with the title 'Grand Cricket Match played in Lord's Ground, Mary-le-bone, on 20th June and following day between the Earls of Winchilsea and Darnley for 1,000 guineas'. For many years, however, the most widely circulated cricket prints were those – in some cases near-copies of the Hayman engraving – that appeared on the broadsheet, or handkerchief, reproductions of the early codes of laws. Another popular work of the pre-1800 period was the – usually – coloured engraving of John Collet's painting 'Miss Wicket and Miss Trigger'.

In the period of the popularity of aquatints – roughly 1775 to 1825 – some characteristic work was done in that manner on the theme of cricket. In their time most of them were issued in both coloured and uncoloured versions: but nowadays they are generally found coloured, often by a later hand. Two of the best are rather naïve – 'Cricket at White Conduit House: 1784', published by Bowles and Carver, and 'Ireland's Royal Gardens, Brighton', drawn by H. Jones and engraved by G. Hunt, which was one of the plates in Sicklemore's *Views of Brighton* (1827). 'North-east View of the cricket grounds at Darnall, near Sheffield, Yorkshire', after Robert Cruikshank and R. J. Thompson, and Pollard's 'Cricket Match' are genuine cricket pictures; but, in most of the others, like 'Salvadore House Academy, Tooting' (F. Jukes after J. Walker), 'Laytonstone Academy, Essex' (J. Merigot after T. Atkins), 'Rugby School' and 'Hackney School', both by R. Reeve, and those in the Ackermann books, the game is incidental. A famous colour print of the same period is by Thomas Rowlandson – 'Rural Sports' (1811) – of a match between XI women of Hampshire and XI of Surrey. It is drawn in Rowlandson's characteristic fashion, accurately observed, and with robust humour. The cricketer may say it is not *seriously* a cricket picture: the art critic would counter that it is good Rowlandson and that good Rowlandson is by artistic standards very good indeed.

The most popular cricket print of any age was issued by the Brighton publisher and cricketer, W. H. Mason. It is titled 'A CRICKET MATCH between the counties of SUSSEX and KENT, at Brighton'. Announced in 1843, it was first published in 1849 and reprinted from the original copper-plate 30 years later. Each of the 8-guinea subscribers received a 24-page prospectus and key which is now one of the major rarities of cricket-collecting. The title-page of the prospectus described the picture as 'Introducing characteristic portraits of players engaged in the match as well as many Noblemen and Gentlemen, Patrons of the Noble Game of Cricket'. It continued, 'The Portraits are all taken from life by Mr W. Drummond and Mr C. J. Basébe: engraved by G. H. Phillips'. Prices were – prints 3 guineas, proofs 6 guineas, Artists' Proofs (upon Indian paper) 8 guineas. The players represented never appeared together in a Sussex-Kent match, though all of them took part in the fixture between 1849 and 1851. It is, in fact, a fine collection of portraits of 71 of the main figures of the game at that time, and it was finely executed. Despite its popularity it was almost the ruin of the unhappy Mason. During the 30 years the plate lay idle, the picture was constantly 'pirated', copied, misattributed and wrongly described, but it was, meanwhile, becoming the best-known of all cricket prints; and still is to be met with in cricket pavilions all over the world. Though the original – Mason – plate was engraved on copper, its most attractive form probably is the 'pirated' lithograph – found both coloured and uncoloured – by S. Lipschitz. The unmistakable difference between the two versions is that, in the original, there is a central gap between the foreground figures; in the Lipschitz version, with no loss of artistic quality, the gap is closed. The engraved surface of the Mason is 42 by 30 inches; of the Lipschitz, 23½ by 17¾ inches.

The great period of cricket art undoubtedly was the middle of the nineteenth century when the technique of lithography had been mastered. The output of cricket lithographs consists of less than a hundred, of teams and individual players. They are delicate, decorative, and contemporary judges considered the majority to be good likenesses. They continue to appreciate in value. The finest of them – probably the finest of 'pure' cricket art – are 8 lithographs by G. F. Watts. Their titles are 'Play', 'Forward!', 'The Draw', 'The Cut', 'Leg Half-Volley' and 'Leg Volley' – all drawn direct on to the stone by the artist – 'The Bowler' (Alfred Mynn) and 'The Batsman' (Fuller Pilch). 'Felix' (Nicholas Wanostrocht) is said to have been the model for the first 5 of the strokes and the Hon Fred Ponsonby for 'Leg Volley'. Watts's pencil studies for these lithographs – 6 are in the possession of MCC – show, in several cases, the process of Watts's translation of Felix from a left-hand batsman to right hand. They capture balanced movement and a quality of vibrant life quite magnificently.

Three major lithographs of the period are of team-groups. The rarest is 'The Two Elevens of the Town and University of Cambridge in 1847', drawn by Felix (Nicholas Wanostrocht); the other 2 are 'The Eleven of England Selected to contend in the Great Cricket Matches of the North for the year 1847', also by Felix, and 'The United All England Eleven' (*c.* 1852). All of them are carefully made portraits of the players, pleasing in their period fashion. The remainder of the group consists almost entirely of portraits of individual players, most of them by John Corbet Anderson. Virtually the only other artists credited are Felix, C. J. Basébe and W. Drummond. Anderson's warm line and delicate colouring lent itself perfectly to lithography and he invariably drew on the stone himself. The engraved surface of most of his portraits measures about 13 inches high by 9 inches; but the series called 'Sketches at Lord's' consists of 12 portraits, 7 inches high by 5 inches, which were issued in 3 sheets with 4 pictures on each.

Felix published the studies of G. F. Watts, who for a time was an evening pupil at Felix's school, and several others, some of which were from his own drawings, though a lithographer transferred them to stone. Apart from the 2 team groups, his most popular print was one of himself with Alfred Mynn. Felix was a prolific painter and did some work in oils. The 3 editions of his book *Felix on the Bat* were illustrated with different sets of lithographs. There is a considerable collection of his work, mostly in water colour and ranging from self-portraits to views of cricket grounds, in the MCC collection at Lord's. Basébe, who also employed a lithographer, was responsible, too, for the series of 8 sensitive aquatint portraits of players used to illustrate *Lillywhite's Hand Book of Cricket* and they were also sold separately: they now tend to be more rare than the lithos. He and Drummond were, of course, the artists employed by Mason on his 'Sussex and Kent' print.

Most of these lithographs can be come by with fair ease through the better print dealers – perhaps Hankey and Nixon are the least common. A few years ago their price was usually about 10 shillings; nowadays 10 pounds is sometimes asked. Originally they were undoubtedly issued plain – in a uniform sepia or yellowish shade – as well as coloured; now most of the plain prints have been coloured to meet taste and demand.

Immediately upon the heels of the lithographs came an even more widely distributed and popular series of cricket illustrations. No. 1 of *Vanity Fair* was published on 6 November 1868, as 'a weekly show of political, social and literary wares'. On 30 January 1869, it increased its price to 6*d* and included its first 'Full-page cartoon of an entirely novel character printed in chrome-lithography'. For some 30 years *Vanity Fair*, through its weekly cartoon and the – sometimes libellous – prose commentary which accompanied it, was an important ingredient of the British social and political scene. After 1900 its power waned though it continued under its own name until 1913 and some reference books credit it with continuing to exist, after amalgamations and in changed forms, until 1929.

Selection as the subject of the *Vanity Fair* cartoon conferred a stamp of importance – sufficient importance to be publicly praised or attacked – and, since the choice was taken from all fields of activity and from all countries, cricketers were not portrayed very frequently. The first, of course, was W. G. Grace – in the issue of 9 June 1877. Between that date and August 1913, when E. W. Dillon, the captain of Kent, was selected, 31 cricketers were portrayed *as* cricketers in *Vanity Fair* cartoons: a rate of less than one a year. But some 40 celebrities who had also played first-class or major public school cricket, or held high office in the game – such as President of MCC – were included primarily for their eminence in some other field. C. B. Fry, for instance, was drawn as a runner; the Hon Ivo Bligh, after he had become the Earl of Darnley, was shown in a City suit.

Only 2 of the cricketers *qua* cricketers – the Hon Alfred Lyttelton and G. J. Bonnor – were drawn by the earliest and most savage of the *Vanity Fair* cartoonists – 'Ape' (Carlo Pellegrini). Most of them were done by 'Spy' (Sir Leslie Ward), but there were 2 by 'Stuff' and one each by AJS, OWL, WH, Lib and CG. The style of the drawings varies considerably between Ape's mischievously astute exaggerations and the mild near-portraiture of Spy and most of the other later artists. All, though, make gay and colourful contributions to the walls of a cricket pavilion or club. The earlier prints – from the paper's heyday of wide circulation (once even a 'third edition' in a week) – are relatively easy to come by; those *post*-1900 are not quite so simple to find. Once more, prices have risen. *Vanity Fair* cartoons in 1939 cost a shilling; now they are expensive.

Lewis Cage: an engraving by L. Busière after Francis Cotes, RA.

In 1905, the Art Society published, in weekly parts and later in a bound edition, under the title *The Empire's Cricketers*, a series of 48 drawings by A. Chevallier Tayler, with text by G. W. Beldam. The drawings, folio in size, are printed on dark grey paper and make heavy use of chinese white. They are not unpleasant but lack movement and character; nevertheless they enjoyed a period of popularity.

Cricket was sometimes employed as a vehicle of political satire by 19th-century caricaturists. But the first of the popular cricket cartoonists was the man who signed his work 'Rip'. His drawings can be found in the *Evening News Cricket Annual* (1897–1907), his own sporadic volumes called *Kricket Karicatures*, and a number of periodicals. The master of all this kind was Tom Webster who, shortly after the First World War, began to draw for the *Daily Mail* and continued with *Tom Webster's Annual* and for other papers until about 1960. Webster was an original, with a happy sense of humour and an inventive pencil, but he could sting. He spread his attention over most sports but produced some imperishable cricket

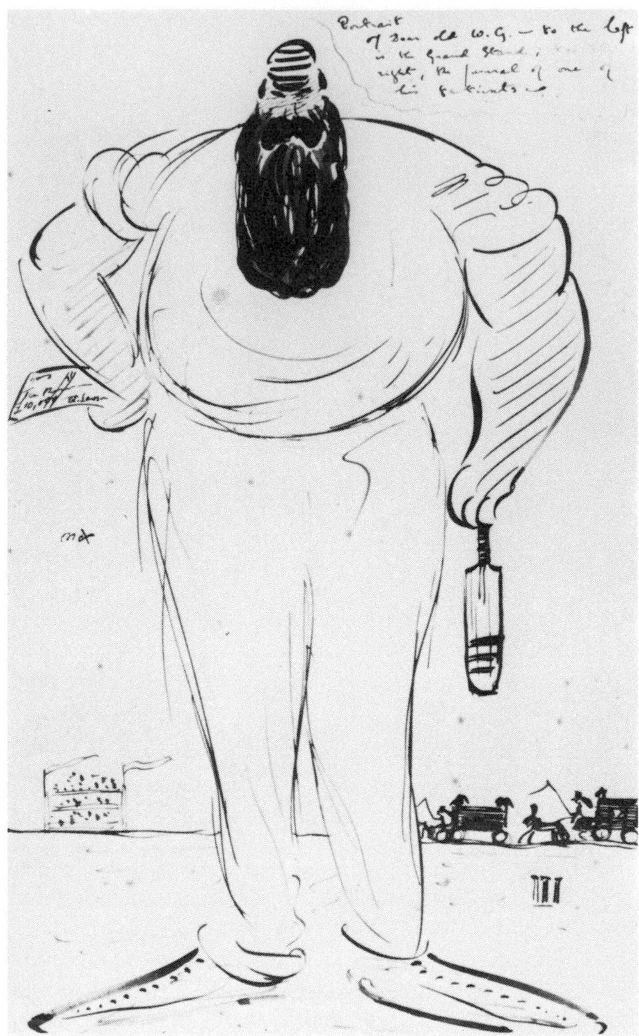

'W.G.' by Max Beerbohm, whose caption reads: 'Portrait of dear old W.G. – to the left is the Grand Stand; to the right the funeral of one of his patients.'

A. A. Mailey: his sketch of Victor Trumper on the hessian walls of his bedroom: from his autobiography, *10 for 66 and all that*.

drawings; his favourite cricket 'characters' – Percy Fender, Patsy Hendren, George Duckworth, Maurice Tate and Jack Hobbs – come sharply back into the memory as Webster drew them.

Arthur Mailey, the New South Wales and Australian Test leg-break bowler, ranged from oil-painting through charcoal portraits to caricature. Between 1920 and 1953 he published some half-dozen booklets of cartoons of cricketers of his time and the well-known separate drawing of Bradman. He illustrated his autobiography *Ten for 66 and All That* with sketches simple, perceptive, evocative and humorous. Roy Ulyett, of the *Daily Express*, who also produces an annual volume of drawings, has followed Webster's method closely, and his 'Fred Trueman' is an awe-inspiringly funny creation.

The term cricketana covers a wide area, of broadsheets, postcards, posters, silver-work, pottery, trophies and other ephemera too varied to list. We may be concerned here largely with items of 'popular' or 'folk' art. Notable in this kind are the 2 large – 13-inch – coloured Staffordshire pottery figures of about 1855, usually said, though not on completely conclusive evidence, to represent Julius Caesar (Surrey) and George Parr (Notts). There is more certainty in describing a smaller figure as Thomas Box and a rather poor piece of modelling as W. G. Grace. There are, too, a number of rather sentimental Staffordshire pieces of children holding bats, or bowling. A Bow china figure of W. G. Grace is more sophisticated and there are numerous plates commemorating Grace's career. One isolated item of some charm is a 'Stevensgraph' of a cricket scene. These small pictures, embroidered in coloured silk, were manufactured by T. Stevens of Coventry and had something of a vogue in the latter part of the 19th-century. From the 1890s onwards many series of cigarette cards and trade cards have been issued, frequently in colour, depicting outstanding cricketers of the day. Since 1948 Miss Mary Mitchell Smith has been responsible for some firmly modelled pottery figures. For some years, too, the Royal Worcester factory made a limited number of bone china plates with a gilt border and reproductions of the signatures of the touring sides, with a special 'Ashes' plate bearing facsimile autographs of the Australian and English teams of 1953.

In 1941 Messrs B. T. Batsford Ltd published *The Noble Game of Cricket*, a large quarto book with a hundred reproductions, some coloured, of famous cricket paintings and prints, almost all of them of considerable significance, from the large collection of Sir Jeremiah Colman. Unfortunately the edition was limited to 150, only 100 of which were for sale, and copies have become hard to find and expensive when found. Happily, in 1955, the same firm produced *The Game of Cricket* with 34 reproductions of major cricket pictures, a distinguished essay by Sir Norman Birkett and notes on the illustrations by Miss Diana Rait Kerr. *Cricket* by Horace G. Hutchinson in the *Country Life* Library of Sport (1903) has 100 plates of sensitively chosen cricket pictures, and is usually described as the best illustrated book of its kind. Green and White, subtitled 'Fenner's Observed', consists of high quality drawings and photographs by 10 students of the Cambridge School of Art.

An exhibition of modern paintings under the title 'Play the Game' at Frost & Reed's Gallery in Bristol in 1976 showed some interesting developments in cricket pictures. Period-primitive portraits and team groups by Gerry Wright had a strong Victorian flavour. Roger Marsh showed some historically sensitive portraits taken from photographs. Strikingly strong, large oils full of action, by Rosemary Taylor, of modern player-groups captured much attention. Outstanding, though, was the work of Laurence Toynbee. He does not by any means confine himself to cricket; though a preponderance of his work is on sporting and outdoor subjects. He would want to be known as a painter with a liking for cricket. Neither is the quality of his work entirely even. He is, though, as highly accomplished a painter as any who has produced any bulk of work on cricket; and he ought to be collected by the cricketing establishments.

The greatest recent advance is among the photographers, inheriting directly from G. W. Beldam, and the Devon-born Australian emigrant, Herbert Fishwick, working with more sophisticated and advanced techniques; Patrick Eagar, Ken Kelly and Bruce Postle have, with high professional skill, illuminated the game in a way that has not been done before with the camera.

For the rest, reference to cricket pictures is largely through catalogues, such as *Catalogue of the Imperial Cricket Memorial Gallery, Lord's; MCC Catalogue 1912; Two Centuries of Cricket Art* (Graves Art Gallery, Sheffield, 1955); *Cricket Exhibition* (National Gallery of British Sport and Pastimes, 1953); and *Catalogue of the collection at 'The Yorker'* (Whitbread & Co Ltd, nd).

Big Hits

GERALD BRODRIBB

Of all memorable cricket feats none gives greater pleasure than the big hit, the super hit which sends the ball soaring out of sight. These rare miracles of timing and power are long remembered and recalled, and though it is sometimes with error and exaggeration it is always with delight. Every cricket ground great or small has its legends of historic hits, and every such hit provokes the question of just how far a cricket ball can be struck hit-to-pitch on level ground. Unfortunately the big hit is often intercepted by some object on its way down, and, even when the ball has landed unimpeded, the exact spot may not have been witnessed, let alone actually marked. We shall never know for certain the greatest distance a ball has been hit. In all first-class cricket there seem to be less than 20 hits which can claim to have been authentically measured, and all but 4 of these belong to the last century.

The oft-quoted record hit of 175 yards made by W. Fellows when practising at Oxford in 1856 is now proved false as a proper measurement, but another hit (also in practice) made by C. I. Thornton on 26 August 1876, on the present ground at Hove, has evidence of being a truly measured hit of some 168 yards. In first-class matches Thornton made at least 6 measured hits of between 132 and 154 yards, and must have a very good claim to be the most frequent producer of the really long hit that the game has ever seen. There are many subtle distinctions between hitters: the man who quite frequently puts the ball over the boundary (and especially the 75 yard one), may score many sixes without producing the really big hit, while other less frequent hitters of sixes may from time to time produce a much longer hit.

When we think of sixes we must remember that up to 1910 6 runs were not generally given for a hit unless the ball was dispatched right out of the ground, not simply its playing area. In a game at Canterbury, for instance, Thornton in 1869 once hit every ball of a 4-ball over well over the ring but earned only 4 runs for each stroke. Gilbert Jessop, an astonishing stroke-player, would in more recent times have accumulated an incredible number of sixes. For example, his 191 runs scored in 90 minutes in a match at Hastings in 1907 included 5 sixes, as well as at least 7 other strokes which since 1910 would have earned him 6 runs. Before I return to the really long hit, let it be put on record that Jessop was the most frequent maker of over-the-boundary hits that the game has ever seen. His nearest rival in this was A. W. Wellard, who was nothing like such a successful run-getter.

To return to Thornton. His enormous hits came from a tremendous full swing of the bat and the impetus with which he went down the wicket to meet the ball. He hit very straight, and that is the direction which produces the longest hits, which to acquire distance must fly rather low and bullet-like similar to a stroke from a brassie at golf. The follow-through must be perfect, and this was the reason for the great hits of Walter Hammond, who made some of his very longest hits in the direction of mid-off. There is no element of slogging about such hits. C. J. Barnett, himself a beautiful hitter, when answering my queries on the matter of big hitting, rejected all across-the-line leg-side hits as quite unworthy of the name of big hits. Thornton added a wonderful eye to his other attributes, as he never bothered to play himself in, making a notable hit even in the first over – and he never wore any pads! Among his many famous hits are over the wall at Fenner's, out of the ground and into the Nackington Road at the far end at Canterbury, right over the old pavilions of both Lord's and the Oval, and over the houses into Trafalgar Square at Scarborough. He must indeed have been 'the prince of long hitters', for he produced the 120-yard hit with ease, and that is a distance which I have regarded as the minimum for qualification as a super hit.

Consider what this 120 yards means: at Lord's the distance from the pavilion-end wicket to the back of the Nursery end cantilever stand is 127 yards; at the Oval the distance from the pavilion-end wicket to the fence at the Vauxhall end is 115 yards; at Hove 138 yards separate the south-end wicket from the wall behind the nets, while the distance from the north-end wicket to the wall behind the low south stand is 120 yards; at Canterbury the distance from the pavilion-end wicket to the hedge on the Nackington Road is 125 yards; at Old Trafford a

Two famous hitters, Arthur Wellard and Freddie Brown, ready for the fray at Scarborough.

ball must be driven 132 yards to reach the boundary wall at the Warwick Road end; at Trent Bridge a drive from the pavilion-end wicket to the edge of the Radcliffe Road must cover 124 yards. These figures should help to give some idea of what a 120-yard hit must be like. It will be obvious that there must have been several hits on these grounds and elsewhere which have carried at least 150 yards.

If Thornton was regarded as the best of all 19th-century hitters, his contemporary rivals would seem to have been J. J. Lyons, G. J. Bonnor and W. J. Ford, but these 3 were all firm-footed hitters who stood and heaved the ball away, often to the leg-side, rather than jumping in wristily to the ball like Thornton. Yet they were all very big hitters, and it is difficult to think of many batsmen at the turn of the century who could hit as they did. Any list of possible rivals would include G. Brann, J. H. Sinclair, of South Africa, the brothers V. F. S. and J. N. Crawford, E. B. Alletson, A. Marshal and K. G. Macleod. Since 1919 the longest hitters would include F. T. Mann, G. F. Earle, Frank Woolley, Col. A. C. Watson, Hammond, F. Barratt, L. N. Constantine, E. R. T. Holmes, F. R. Brown, A. W. Wellard, C. C. Smart, A. E. Watt, Jim Smith, W. Voce, H. T. Bartlett and H. B. Cameron. The post-1945 era would add the names of Jack Oakes, C. Pepper, I. L. Bula of Fiji, W. J. Stewart, G. J. Whittaker, 'Collie' Smith, F. S. Trueman and the 3 Australians, K. R. Miller, R. Benaud and A. K. Davidson. What a pity E. R. Dexter did not attempt the really long hit more frequently.

Though comparison is impossible, there have been some especially well-remembered long hits. Here is a reminder of some of them. Best-known of all is probably that of Albert Trott, who made a drive off M. A. Noble in 1899 which enabled the ball to bounce on the roof of the pavilion at Lord's, and end up somewhere by the tennis court. It was a vast ballooner, but though it went over the pavilion, it had nothing like the potential carry of a hit of Jessop's which once landed on top of the north turret of the pavilion – or of one of F. T. Mann's which hit the back seats on the top tier and was still on the rise. These are largely forgotten, Trott's is remembered because it went over, and this shows the need for some particular target if a hit is to be memorable. Pavilion hits at the Oval have never become famous, but in 1921 T. F. Shepherd hit a ball from Woolley which bounced on the roof and went over – a hit quite as big as Trott's. F. G. Mann and D. B. Close have landed balls on top of the giant football stand at Leeds – a colossal carry – while at Trent Bridge in 1905 Warwick Armstrong hit a ball right over the Press Box into Radcliffe Road. What is more, it was the last ball of the day's play in a Test Match. Also at Trent Bridge was a famous hit by Voce who in 1947 hit a ball which pitched right in the doorway of the Trent Bridge Inn. At Old Trafford (also in a Test Match in 1909) Cotter, the Australian, drove a ball comfortably over the Warwick Road wall (132 yards away), and in a more recent Test Match, in 1955, Paul Winslow, the South African, off-drove a ball to the top-most scaffolding set up for television cameras and thence into the car park, an amazing stroke which enabled him to reach his first and only Test hundred. At Bristol V. F. S. Crawford once hit a ball straight over the top of the pavilion – a unique feat measured at 160 yards. At Hove Robert Relf batting at the south end once drove a ball from Haigh right over the 138-yard-distant wall behind the present nets, while Alletson during his famous 189 is said to have landed a ball on the roof of the old factory at the south end.

In recent years the most notable 6-hitting feat has been Gary Sobers's 6 sixes in an over from M. A. Nash (Glamorgan) at Swansea in 1968. In scoring 226 for Sussex v Warwickshire at Hastings in 1975 A. W. Greig ended with 4 consecutive sixes, the 3rd of which sent the ball into Queen's Road, a unique skimming square-leg hit. Javed Miandad in his 162 v Kent at Canterbury in 1976 made an on-drive which went first bounce into Nackington Road – a carry of some 120 yards. In 1977 Vivian Richards hit 44 sixes in first-class matches – the 8th highest total ever in a season.

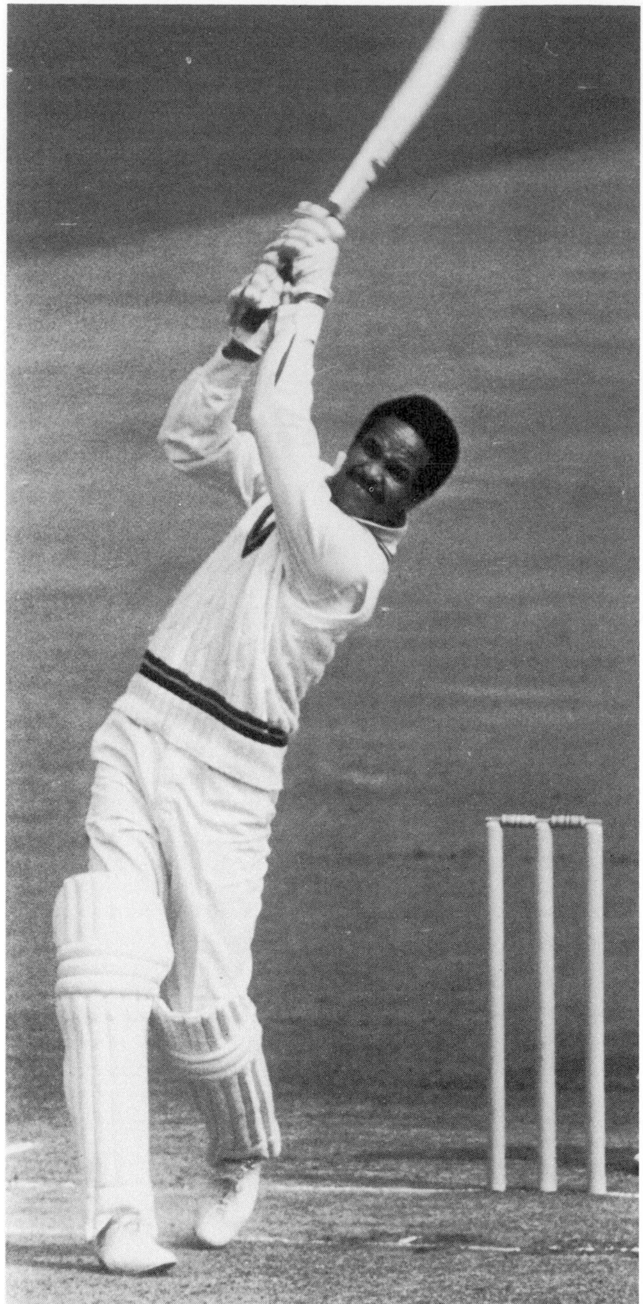

Gary Sobers, who once hit 6 sixes in an over at Swansea, was second to none in power and range of stroke.

Though one-day matches are not deemed first-class, 2 recent hits at Lord's are worth mentioning. In the Gillette Cup Final of 1977 M. J. Llewellyn of Glamorgan made an on-drive off a ball from Emburey which landed the ball in the guttering beside the broadcasting box on the northern pinnacle of the pavilion, and in 1979 D. Bailey, playing for Minor Counties (N) v Middlesex in a Benson and Hedges match drove a ball from P. H. Edmonds straight over the screen, over the stand beyond, and right into the Nursery – a very rare hit.

These are only a few of the famous hits, for every ground has its historic hits; some have been well documented, others, equally big, have had fewer targets to fix them by. There can be no 'top 10' long hits, but I am sure that one of those hitters I have mentioned produced the biggest of all, and that if it had been possible to measure it, it would have reached at least 170 yards.

Books

LEFT Arthur Haygarth, whose labours in compiling *Scores and Biographies*, the standard work for all 'medieval' researchers, were spread over 60 years.

RIGHT H. T. Waghorn (1842–1930), a disciple of Haygarth, worked at the British Museum devoting himself to the study of 18th-century cricket.

Histories

JOHN ARLOTT

Virtually every book written about cricket, from scores and statistics to biographies of players and examinations of technique, is, in essence, historical. Certainly, anyone setting out to write a history of the game in any period would want to find out not only match results and details, but also what manner of men they were who played, and the accepted technical methods of the time. Even the books automatically accepted as histories show a wide disparity. There are those of wide scope – the entire scene; full histories of play in a single country or a single county; club histories varying in size between fat volumes and single sheet fold-overs; results of research within a deliberately limited field; or subject-studies – of the County Championship, the Gentlemen v Players Match, big hitting, specific grounds or the public schools. Inevitably, too, the titles must overlap with reference books.

The basic chronicles of cricket are not generally well known. They fall into two categories: either they are early, exceptionally rare and costly, or they are research, presented in a scholarly fashion, without concern for 'popularity'. The tendency in the writing of history on any subject has always been to copy previous histories. This has happened quite grievously in cricket: too many hastily written books, prepared for a quick-buying, quick-forgetting market, were no more than paraphrases of paraphrases. So the early work of Nyren, Mitford, Pycroft and Box has been repeated, often garbled – and sometimes garbled again. With one great exception – *Scores & Biographies* – it is only in modern times that genuine and original research into early cricket has been carried out, set down and published. The first score-books – of Britcher (of which no complete set is known), Epps and Bentley – are all scarce and proportionately expensive; Bentley (1786–1822) is the most easy to come by, though it is unusual to find it with its two supplements, for 1823 and 1824. Fortunately for the student, if not for the collector, though almost all the early scores are available in the monumental work of scholarship called *Cricket Scores & Biographies*, published in 15 volumes, covering the matches and players of any importance, between 1746 and 1878.

Later discoveries have added to it, but only in an extremely small degree by comparison with the extent of the original. '*S. & B.*', as it is generally called, was the life's work of Arthur Haygarth; the 15th volume – of index and extra, and later, biographies – was compiled by F. S. Ashley-Cooper on the basis of Haygarth's notes.

Wisden (first issued 1864), of course, overlaps *S. & B.* and, between them, they provide a fairly complete record of all first-class matches until recent years, when *Wisden*, for sheer reasons of space, found it impossible to include full scores of overseas matches. Generally, these are available in publications of the countries where the cricket was played but, in the cases of West Indies and Pakistan, this is not so, whence a regrettable gap has occurred, which can only now be filled by some large and ambitious volumes which are not likely to prove an economic publishing venture, but which are reported as being compiled.

The origins of cricket, and all their possible antecedent variations, were explored, so diligently that they can hardly be added to, by P. F. Thomas. He published the result of his studies, under the pen name 'H. P.-T.', between 1923 and 1929, in 6 booklets which were collected under the general title of *Old English Cricket*. Thomas was fortunate in finding the most enthusiastic of all cricket publishers, C. H. Richards, of Nottingham, who, over many years, put out a number of books, largely recondite or of limited appeal, solely out of his enthusiasm for the game. Not many copies of the 'H. P.-T'. studies were printed and, consequently, they are now difficult to obtain. The early match scores not included in *Scores & Biographies* are largely to be found in the books of two painstaking students, H. T. Waghorn and G. B. Buckley. Waghorn, who was employed in the reading room of the British Museum, published his researches in *Cricket Scores, 1730–1773* (Blackwood, 1899) and the now far scarcer *The Dawn of Cricket* (MCC, 1906).

Buckley's two collections were both put out by the Birmingham firm of Cotterell, specializing in cricketana, under the titles *Fresh Light on 18th Century Cricket* and *Fresh Light on Pre-Victorian Cricket*. But his researches, probably the widest and most far reaching – apart from Haygarth's – ever conducted into any game, were continued in volumes of photo-reproduced typescript and manuscript, produced under the aegis of Major Rowland Bowen in 1960. It is probable that even more notes by Buckley still exist unpublished. Two studies by H. F. and A. P. Squire are notable: their titles are *Henfield Cricket and Its Sussex Cradle* and *Pre-Victorian Sussex Cricket*; they explore the press files on early cricket in Sussex with a thoroughness never before devoted to any county.

The definitive history of cricket, unlikely to be rivalled and certainly never superseded for its period, has grown from H. S. Altham's *A History of Cricket*, which began in serial form in *The Cricketer* and appeared as a book in 1926. Subsequent editions were kept up to date with additional chapters by E. W. Swanton; but in 1962 the logical step was taken and the *History* appeared in 2 volumes: Volume 1 – 'From the Beginnings to the First World War', by H. S. Altham and Volume 2 – 'From the First World War to the Present Day', by E. W. Swanton. The 2 books are essentially and inevitably different in character, yet they form an undoubted unity. In the 1st volume, Altham moves from early research to the 'Golden Age' graciously and surely and with an impressive sense of perspective. In the 2nd, Swanton succeeds in compressing the huge, complicated picture of modern cricket – 395 Tests played by 7 countries, compared with 134 by 3 prior to 1914 – with admirable lucidity.

Other writers have used other methods. C. L. R. James in *Beyond a Boundary* may seem to adopt an autobiographical method or to concentrate on West Indian cricket but his work illuminates all cricket, its character and development in arguably the finest piece of literature about this or any other game. Rowland Bowen in *Cricket: A History of Its Growth and Development* aired some unexpected theories; nevertheless, if only for its conscientiously researched and immaculately arranged dates in the history of the game all over the world, his work is of genuine value.

The only other attempt to tackle the subject on a comparable scale was made by Eric Parker in *The History of Cricket* (The Lonsdale Library) in 1950: 672 pages long, it is impressive for its weight of facts and generous illustration. *The Phoenix History of Cricket*, by Roy Webber, is deliberately more concentrated, and more concerned with modern play – a readable introduction to the subject. There are numerous histories of specific periods or aspects of the game, notably *Cricket Between Two Wars* (1919 to 1939), an impressive record of first-hand observation by Sir Pelham Warner; *The County Championship* from 1873 to 1956, an orderly marshalling of facts by Roy Webber; *Cricket: A Social History 1700–1885* by John Ford valuably illustrated a period; and *Maiden Over*, by Nancy Joy, is a record of women's cricket.

The Changing Face of Cricket by A. G. Moyes (1963) perceptively observed a period of flux through Australian eyes. Two totally different yet equally authentic studies of another period are *The Golden Age of Cricket* (1967) by Patrick Morrah; and *The Golden Age of Cricket 1890–1914*, an illuminating and surprising pictorial presentation by David Frith.

Other compartmented English histories are *Cricket in the Leagues* (1970) by John Kay; *The Fast Men*, the first study of fast bowling, by David Frith; and *One-Day Cricket* by Jim Laker.

The Cricket Conspiracy by Derek Humphrey, published by The National Council for Civil Liberties, dealt with the protest which eventually prevented the South African cricket tour of 1970 from taking place.

Two students who have worked patiently and well are Gerald Brodribb and G. D. Martineau. Much patient research must have gone to make Gerald Brodribb's *All Round the Wicket* ('facts and fancies'), *Next Man In*, which is a survey of cricket laws and customs, and the unique *Hit for Six*. Martineau, who wrote with the craftsmanship of a poet, published *They Made Cricket*, a study of the men who shaped the game, *The Field is Full of Shades*, dealing with the very early players, *Bat, Ball, Wicket and All*, a history of cricket equipment, and *The Valiant Stumper*, a history of wicket-keeping.

In the last century, many books combined useful history with instruction or reminiscence: such were *The Cricket Field* by the Rev James Pycroft, which is one of the classics of the game; *The English Game of Cricket*, by Charles Box, somewhat ponderous but the fullest history to its date (1877) and for many years afterwards; and *Annals of Cricket*, by W. W. Read. *Cricket Highways and Byways* is a series of scholarly and pleasant essays from one of the game's most devoted students, F. S. Ashley-Cooper. A book based on the most famous ground provides a much wider view of cricket over a substantial period. *Lord's 1787–1945* was a subject on which Sir Pelham Warnet wrote with immense knowledge and deep feeling; the result is not only the story of the traditional centre of cricket, but of the growth of the game. His work was continued in *Lord's 1946–1970* by Diana Rait Kerr and I. A. R. Peebles.

Australia

Surprisingly enough, Australia completely lacked any sort of solid history – George Giffen's autobiography, *With Bat and Ball*, was the nearest approach – until, in 1959, A. G. Moyes produced his *Australian Cricket: A History*. Informed, firmly written and sound in feeling, it should be kept up to date, but it is not likely to be improved upon, or replaced. *An Illustrated History of Australian Cricket* (1973) by R. S. Whitington provides valuable pictorial reinforcement. *The Paddock That Grew* is subtitled 'The Story of Melbourne Cricket Club' but, in writing it, Keith Dunstan dealt relevantly enough with many aspects of Australian life and of world cricket so that the eventual picture is much broader than the theme would suggest; and it is most handsomely presented. *Cricket Walkabout* (1967) by D. J. Mulvaney is an historically and socially acute study of the Australian aboriginal cricketers tour of 1867–68.

South Africa

The cricket of South Africa is dealt with in 'hard' factual fashion, with a considerable weight of full scores, in 3 volumes, *The History of South African Cricket* (1876 to 1914) and *South African Cricket, 1919 to 1927*, both by M. W. Luckin, and *South African Cricket, 1927 to 1947*, by Louis Duffus. *Cricketers of the Veld* by Louis Duffus is a pleasantly turned, first-hand account of major South African cricket and cricketers from 1929 to 1939.

West Indies

In *West Indies Cricket*, Christopher Nicole has written a full, balanced account of the game in the Caribbean to 1956. In *The West Indies: Fifty years of Test Cricket* (1978) Tony Cozier faithfully recorded the major aspects of the Caribbean game. Other slighter and earlier books are *Big Cricket in West Indies*, 1923 to 1927, by T. S. Birkett, *Inter-Colonial Cricket After the War*, H. R. Harewood (1937), and *West Indies Cricket History*, L. S. Smith (1922).

New Zealand

In two substantial books, largely consisting of match-scores, called *New Zealand Cricket, 1841 to 1914*, and *New Zealand Cricket, 1914 to 1933*, T. W. Reese established records of the game in that country which ought, now, to be continued, perhaps by R. T. Brittenden, who has gone part way towards covering the subsequent period in *New Zealand Cricketers* and *Great Days in New Zealand Cricket*. *New Zealand International Cricket* (1975) by A. H. Carman is a major study, and a model of its kind.

India

There have been many books on cricket in India, but none which approximates to a major history. J. M. Patel's *Stray Thoughts on Indian Cricket* gave a good survey to its date, but that was 1905. After that, the facts lay between a number of books, the best of which probably were *March of Indian Cricket* by Professor Deodhar, *Twelve Years of Ranji Trophy Cricket, 1934 to 1945*, by S. K. Gurunathan, *India – England Cricket Visits, 1911 to 1946*, by S. K. Roy, *India Cricket Cavalcade* by Arbi, W. D. Begg's *Cricket and Cricketers in India*, and *Portrait of Indian Sport* by A. de Mello. The most complete and latest summary is *History of Indian Cricket* (1976) by Edward Docker.

Pakistan

There is, as yet, no serious history of the cricket of the youngest Test-playing country; the nearest approach is *Cricket in Pakistan Annual, 1954*, which is necessarily brief, with so short a story to tell. The two best – though they are both behindhand – studies of the youngest Test playing country are *Twenty years of Pakistan Cricket 1947–67* by

M. H. Maqsood and *Compendium of Pakistan Test Cricket* issued by the Board of Control for Cricket in Pakistan. In *The Cricket Conspiracy* (1977) A. H. Kardar gave his version of dealings between the Pakistan Board of Cricket Control, the Pakistan Sports Board, the Prime Minister and six of their players in 1976; with supporting documents.

The extent and frequency of Test Matches all over the world in modern times is such that even the soundest books that attempt to cover the subject are rendered inadequate in a few years. So the best and most efficient now is the most up-to-date which, as indicated in the section on REFERENCE BOOKS (*qv*), is *The Wisden Book of Test Cricket 1876–77 to 1977–78* by Bill Frindall; with a more concentrated version in *Test Cricket Records from 1877* by James Gibb. Two Test histories of specific periods are *Cricket Decade*, in which J. M. Kilburn writes with his invariable poise and thought on England v Australia Tests from 1946 to 1956, and *The Testing Years*, Gordon Ross's story of English fortunes from 1946 to the peak of holding the Ashes, and beating West Indies, in 1957.

Cricket on all its levels in Ceylon has been most amply recorded by the devoted and prolific S. P. Foenander. His chief book is *Sixty Years of Ceylon Cricket*, published in 1924, but, in at least a dozen others, he has explored various aspects and stories of play in that country. *Sixty Years of Canadian Cricket* by J. E. Hall and R. O. McCulloch is a somewhat surprising book: it appeared in 1895, 572 pages long and, up to then, it was the largest book of cricket history ever published. *A Century of Philadelphia Cricket*, edited by J. A. Lester, is, to all intents and purposes, the history of major cricket in America; with a preface by Christopher Morley and essays by various outstanding American players, it is much better written than most cricket books, and handsomely produced. *The International Series* (1968) by John I. Marder covers the history of matches between the United States of America and Canada from 1844 onwards. *Cricket in the Fiji Islands*, by P. A. Snow, is another book that many a country with a more important sporting history might envy; it is an often exciting story, sympathetically told. Patrick Hone, of the famous Irish literary and cricketing family, wrote *Cricket in Ireland*, a well-made, convivial, sensitive and nostalgic book. Cricket in Scotland is the subject of several volumes, notably the early *Fifty Years' Reminiscences of Scottish Cricket* by D. D. Bone and, more recently, *Play*, by N. L. Stevenson. *The Story of Continental Cricket (1969)* by P. C. G. Labouchere, T. A. J. Provis and Peter S. Hargreaves deals with the game as played in Corfu, Rome, Portugal, Belgium, France, Germany, Switzerland, Eastern Europe, Holland and Denmark.

Most of the English first-class counties have good and fairly up-to-date histories. Derbyshire is perhaps the worst served: *History of the Derbyshire CCC*, by W. J. Piper (2nd edition 1897), is little more than a list of match-scores; *The Rise of Derbyshire Cricket, 1919–1935*, by L. E. Simpson, is smaller, but later, and more imaginatively written. Essex has one fairly short, but sympathetic, account, called *Essex County Cricket*, by Charles Bray (1950). The youngest first-class county has two histories – *Glamorgan CCC, 1921–1947*, by Roy Webber and K. M. Arnott, which has a strong statistical bias, and *Glamorgan*, by J. H. Morgan, which is a reminiscent account from personal observation. It has, too, a statistical record in *Glamorgan County Cricket Club Book of Cricket Records* (1976) by Wayne Thomas. There have been several books about Gloucestershire, but the latest and fullest is *History of the Gloucestershire CCC* by S. Canynge Caple. *Hampshire County Cricket*, by several hands, published in 1957, was the first history of that county and it was continued in the club's handbook for 1962, to include the winning of the County Championship in the previous season. Kent were most admirably served in 1907, when Lord Harris published his *History of Kent County Cricket*, an imposing and authoritative study. It has been continued less fully in four appendices, the first of which, Appendix E, is now impossible to obtain. There had been several slight books on Lancashire before the official *Lancashire County Cricket, 1864–1953*, by A. W. Ledbrooke, a satisfying and illuminating review. *A History of Leicestershire County Cricket* by the county treasurer, E. E. Snow, is another well-made book, something of a model of its kind. He has continued it in the club's centenary year, with *Leicestershire Cricket 1949 to 1977*.

The 3 volumes – *Middlesex CCC, 1864–1899*, by W. J. Ford, *1900–1920*, by F. S. Ashley-Cooper, and *1921–1947*, by Nigel Haig, are careful collections of scores; more pleasantly readable is *Middlesex County Cricket Club* (1951) by the Hon T. C. F. Prittie. *Northamptonshire Cricket: a History*, is a careful record by J. D. Coldham. Thanks to the efforts of the tireless and enthusiastic publisher, C. H. Richards, of Nottingham, his county has been well chronicled. Richards's own *Nottinghamshire Scores and Biographies* covered the period 1838 to 1925 in adequate detail. Then, in 1923, F. S. Ashley-Cooper published his *Nottinghamshire Cricket and Cricketers*, a characteristically meticulous work, full of well-marshalled facts from the earliest days of play in the county until 1922. That book now deserves continuation. *Sixty Years of Somerset Cricket*, by R. A. Roberts, was issued in 1952, and is a pleasant and readable history. *Surrey Cricket*, by Lord Alverstone and C. W. Alcock, in 1902, was the first of the really ambitious county histories and remains the bulkiest. It has been continued in *The Story of the Oval, 1902 to 1948*, by Louis Palgrave, and Gordon Ross's *The Surrey Story*, which latter follows the team through to its great peak under Stuart Surridge.

There have been many books about cricket in Sussex: F. S. Ashley-Cooper, A. J. Gaston and A. D. Taylor, the well-known cricket collectors and students, all issued small studies of the subject but, until the Second War, A. E. R. Gilligan's *Sussex Cricket* was the most substantial. Then, in 1950, Sir Home Gordon wrote *Sussex County Cricket* in the Convoy Press's series, and in 1959 came John Marshall's more comprehensive review *Sussex Cricket: a History*. The Warwickshire club predictably commissioned a major work of history called *The Story of Warwickshire Cricket* (1974) by Leslie Duckworth: it is a handsome 691-page volume. W. R. Chignell was responsible for *History of Worcestershire CCC*, carefully written out of quite considerable research and in 1969 he produced a sequel, *Worcestershire Cricket 1950 to 1968*.

Yorkshire has been the best served of the counties in terms of histories. There have been numerous pamphlets and smaller books about play there, but the authoritative account, with the official support of the county club, has been maintained in the only practicable way, by a series of volumes. *History of*

There was never a more devoted nor meticulous student of cricket than F. S. Ashley-Cooper, who in 1925 in a biographical last volume (xv) wrote 'finis' to *Scores and Biographies*. He compiled, and collaborated in, innumerable books and brochures. A selection of his essays *Cricket Highways and Byways* reflects the range of his knowledge and a singular feeling for the game.

Yorkshire County Cricket, 1833 to 1903, was written by the Rev R. S. Holmes; the second volume, 1903 to 1923, by A. W. Pullin; and the latest, 1924 to 1949, by J. M. Kilburn. All three are satisfying and well presented. J. M. Kilburn's *Yorkshire County Cricket* (1950) is a good shorter survey and *Talks with Old Yorkshire Cricketers*, published by A. W. Pullin under the pseudonym of 'Old Ebor', contains much useful, illuminating and, in some cases, tragic information elicited from many of the county's early players in interviews conducted in their old age. The latest updatings are *A History of Yorkshire Cricket* (1970), a rounded and complete story to that date by J. M. Kilburn; and *Yorkshire Cricketers 1839–1939*, a voluminous series of biographical studies by Peter Thomas.

Only two of the English minor counties have histories of any size – *Herefordshire Cricket*, by Edwyn Anthony (1903), still makes pleasant reading, blending its facts with chatty digressions; and *Staffordshire Cricket* (1924), by W. G. Watson, marshals its many facts in good order. There are smaller, but quite workmanlike, histories of Durham (W. R. Bell, 1932) and, published in year-book form, Suffolk (A. Wade and D. F. Durham, to 1938) and Lincolnshire, 1843 to 1959, with supplement to 1960, by R. J. Charlton.

A History of Queensland Cricket (E. H. Hutcheon) is the only Australian publication on the scale of the better English county accounts. It sprang out of an original plan to compile a complete history of Australian cricket in a series of state-sections, then the Board of Control decided that such a work would be unwieldy and suggested that the states should publish their own individual books; only Queensland has, so far, done so. There are, however, two earlier and smaller volumes on the game in South Australia, by Clarence Moody (1898) and C. B. O'Reilly (1930), and in 1957 Roger Page published *A History of Tasmanian Cricket*, a better record than that of any of the Sheffield Shield states, apart from Queensland.

West Indies have *Jamaica Cricket, 1863 to 1926*, by J. C. Beecher, and *Cricket in Barbados* by Bruce Hamilton (1947), while there was a souvenir brochure on the Diamond Jubilee – 1956 – of the Border Cricket Union in South Africa. Otherwise few of the major overseas units have produced anything to compare with *Cricket Centenary*, a 300-page book with which F. F. Cane marked, in 1955, a hundred years of cricket in Hawke's Bay, New Zealand.

The positions of the two major universities in terms of histories differ widely. For years *A History of the Cambridge University Cricket Club, 1820–1901*, a very full account by that gifted cricketer and writer W. J. Ford, was something of a reproach to Oxford. But in 1962, *History of the OUCC*, Geoffrey Bolton's devoted and friendly book, emphasized that Cambridge are now, by almost half their existence, unrecorded.

Public school cricket history, as a whole, is unwieldy, because it includes so many, and constantly varying, standards of performance and importance. The best – virtually the only – general book on the subject is *Public Schools Cricket 1901–1950*, in which W. N. Roe brought together essays, by undoubted authorities, on the cricket of seventeen major schools. The 3rd volume of *Fifty Years of Sport at Oxford and Cambridge and the Great Public Schools*, an elaborately produced work, edited by A. C. M. Croome in 1913, recorded, with generous illustration, cricket between Eton, Harrow and Winchester. There have been numerous books of scores of matches of many schools and W. S. Patterson's *Sixty Years of Uppingham Cricket* (1909) places the cricket of those years in a warm and well-observed background. For the moment, however, Repton and Winchester – through supplements to the earlier works – and Denstone are the only schools with generally available and up-to-date histories. The student of the subject can find full information in the magazines of the schools concerned – but even to bring them all together would be a dismaying task and he will probably find the widest manageable coverage in Lillywhite's *Companions* and *Annuals*, *Wisden* and the often overlooked, but valuable, *Ayres' Cricket Companion*, which, from its 4th – 1905 – issue until it ceased publication in 1932, devoted often valuable attention to the game in the schools.

There is no department of cricket literature more varied or more rewarding than the histories of the clubs. From the several imposing volumes devoted to MCC to the souvenir leaflets with which village clubs have marked their centenaries or jubilees, the field is wide, full of pleasures and surprises, cheaply priced rarities, human and social documents and, for the collector, opportunities to beat the bibliographers by finding an unrecorded item from some local printing press. The subject is too vast to be treated generally but, in the booklet *Famous Cricket Clubs*, H. E. Powell-Jones collected a series of essays on MCC and a dozen other of the well-known clubs, usually, if loosely, described as 'peripatetic', such as I Zingari, Incogniti and Free Foresters. *The Weekend Cricketer*, by A. C. L. Bennett, one of the most distinguished captains of the Club Cricket Conference, ranged more widely, and studied more deeply, most of the major, and many of the minor, clubs of Middlesex, Essex, Kent and Surrey, with emphasis on Conference members and standards.

League Cricket in England by Roy Genders, is a spirited and somewhat controversial argument for the major Leagues which, perhaps, puts their case too strongly. There are several accounts of specific club competitions. The Huddersfield and District League celebrated its Diamond Jubilee with a booklet which could treat of such great clubs as Kirkheaton, home of George Hirst and Wilfred Rhodes, and Lascelles Hall which, at least twice, had 6 of its members in the Yorkshire XI. *The First History of the Doncaster & District Cricket League* (1951) covered 72 clubs, and also includes some famous names. *Yorkshire Cricket Council, 1899–1951* deals in orderly fashion with the growth of that famous competition. A southern title to claim entry is *A Cup for Cricket*, which marked 50 years of the I'Anson Trophy, a competition for village clubs in the area of the Hampshire-Surrey border.

MCC, by its age and seniority, has given rise to a considerable amount of writing. Sir Pelham Warner's *Lord's*, the most important, has been followed by *Lord's 1946–70* by Diana Rait-Kerr and I. A. R. Peebles. Of the rest *Annals of Lord's and History of the MCC* is the most appreciable work of Alfred D. Taylor. *Lord's and the MCC* (1914), produced in the 'de luxe' manner fashionable at the time, is the joint work of Lord Harris and F. S. Ashley-Cooper; exceptionally well documented, it provides the basis for any subsequent writing on the subject. *MCC 1787–1937* appeared first as a special supplement to *The Times* and then was made into a well-illustrated and produced book by several hands, reflecting the wide influence of MCC over the world of cricket.

The first cricket classic is the reminiscent view of the players of the Hambledon Club in the 54 small pages 'added to' *The Young Cricketer's Tutor*, credited to John Nyren – 'The Whole Collected and Edited by Charles Cowden Clarke'. No one will ever know how much was done by author or amanuensis, but neither ever proved remotely so impressive alone as in this collaboration. Constantly reprinted, discussed and quoted, these studies have proved wonderfully enduring, as stimulating now as when they were first written. Nyren, and most of the relevant associated material, was collected by E. V. Lucas with his own characteristically felicitous observations, under the title *The Hambledon Men*. An admirable companion to Nyren is *The Hambledon Cricket Chronicle, 1772–1796*, printing some happily preserved Minute and Account Books of the club and admirably edited by F. S. Ashley-Cooper. Many club records consist solely of score-sheets and averages, like *Scores of the Incogniti Cricket Club* but, from the start – first printed 1871 but dating back to 1861 – they take up an impressive amount of shelf-space and a complete set is not easy to find. Some of these early lists of scores are extremely scarce – like the little oblong *Lansdown Cricket Club: Matches 1829 to 1851* and the slightly more explanatory record of the *7th (QO) Hussars Cricket Club Matches 1873 to 1888*, written by H. M. Ridley in Secunderabad and printed in Wincanton.

More important in this class is *Shadows Over the Wicket*, an account by E. Hoskin, the team's scorer, of the 6 seasons, from 1940 to 1945, of the British Empire XI, which played much of the best cricket seen in England during the last war. Some 30 Test players and many county 'caps' played for this 'scratch' side, which raised thousands of pounds for charity and gave much pleasure to a cricket-starved country.

The more expansive club histories are mainly early; few of them could be commercially practicable nowadays. The most ambitious is *The Eton Ramblers Cricket Club*, the first volume, 1862 to 1880, by Philip Norman, the second, 1881 to 1914, by G. A. Foljambe, altogether over 600 pages of scores, comment and biography. *Annals of the Free Foresters from 1856 to 1894* is another massive work, by W. K. R. Bedford and W. E. W. Collins, written largely from first-hand knowledge – personal, sometimes slightly pompous in a 'period' fashion, but entertaining and occasionally genuinely, if not sophisticatedly, funny. *Records of the Harlequin Cricket Club 1852–1926* was the last book of Alfred Cochrane, who had genuine gifts as both a cricketer and a writer. Because so many Harlequins played in first-class cricket, this book with its weight of personal observation, has much valuable criticism of well-known cricketers.

Yet the most pleasing of these large histories of major clubs is *Annals of the West Kent Cricket Club 1812–1896*, by Philip Norman; its wealth of detail bespeaks much patient inquiry, but it is lightly borne in a book at once sound, easily readable, anecdotal, reminiscent, humorous and, at times, deeply nostalgic. Open it where you will and put it in the hands of any reader, whether cricketer or not, and, once started, he will read on, for it is personally written, and essentially about people, rather than scores.

Cricket literature yields many such labours of love, undertaken with no hope of profit and little but very local glory, some of them rare, yet not regarded as sufficiently important to be costly. Such are *The History of Cricket in Kendal* (1906), *The Lancaster Cricket Club 1841–1909*, *The Leicester Ivanhoe Cricket Club 1873–1923*, *Nottingham Forest Amateur CC 1877–1901*, *The Walsall CC 1833–1909*, *Rochdale CC 1824–1902*, and, a rare bird to arrive so late, *The History of the Hampstead Cricket Club* (1949). Four pleasantly produced club histories since the war have been in limited editions, confined to members: they are of the Band of Brothers, Butterflies, and Lloyd's Register Clubs, and on Lords and Commons cricket.

No review of club histories would be just which ignored the excellence of the Scottish productions, which, in proportion to the amount of cricket played there, are more impressive than those of any other club cricket. There are competent studies of the Brechin, Grange, Perth, Kirkcaldy, Uddingston, Penicuik, Kilmarnock, Manderston, Selkirk, Gala, Clydesdale and Ayr clubs, and a quite huge tome on Drumpellier. No club anywhere else in the world, apart from MCC, can equal the 5 solid volumes of history and scores – the last four by T. C. Riddell – devoted to the Greenock Club; while Dr N. L. Stevenson, captain of the Carlton Club, in addition to his history of Scottish cricket, has devoted at least a dozen slim booklets of pleasant and friendly prose to the doings – and especially the tours – of that club.

From club cricket have come the most convivial books on the game: social, sometimes uproarious, their appeal has little to do with excellence of performance. First among them must come *Black Hats v White Hats*, by Fred Cobley (1895), with the sub-title 'or Ilkley Tradesmen at the Wickets and Around the Festive Board'. It is difficult to imagine a clearer picture of life in a small Yorkshire town during later Victorian days than this happy account of cricket – sometimes more than twenty-a-side – and huge suppers, followed by local songs and monologues composed for the occasion. *Some Cricket Outings of the Goldsmiths' Institute Cricket Club* (1892–1898) changed its title in the 2nd volume to *Cricket Tours of the Goldsmiths' Institute Cricket Club* (1899–1904) – 'Printed for Private Circulation only'. Both were by 'their Hon. Sec.' and both reflect the spirit of holiday cricket with many good meals, much good fellowship and an admirable – or reprehensible? – lack of anxiety about match-results. *A Short Account of the Origin of the Kilkenny Cricket Club and of its Proceedings in the Years 1830–1* seems also to have been a private matter, briefly recording some uproariously bibulous occasions for which cricket was the excuse.

No one perhaps made such a complete impact on the game as H. S. Altham – player of distinction, coach, historian, speaker, administrator and elder statesman, his breadth of knowledge was only equalled by his facility in expressing it.

There is a humorous note of limitation to J. C. Squire's small book *The Invalids: a Chronicle*, recounting the activities of a team of men of letters, including A. G. Macdonell, who is said to have based his account of a cricket match in *England, Their England* on one of these games. G. K. Chesterton was once their host and contributed a piece of light verse to the book to mark the occasion. The whole is a pleasantly irreverent corrective to over-seriousness about cricket. So, too, are the 6 volumes of *The Old Broughtonians Cricket Weeks*, published between 1921 and 1938, recording matches played by many of the same players as composed the Invalids. The text is largely confined to scores with occasional laconic comment. The books were elegantly printed by the Favil Press and, since there were only about 50 copies of any volume, they tend to be rare and expensive. The latest of this kind to come to my hand is called *Welsh Wanderings or Thro' Wales with Bat and Bottle*, a gay account of a Scottish tour against some extremely strong – cricketing – opposition, by an arch cricket-enthusiast, the late J. M. Fleming.

Among the many pleasant, but relatively small, histories put out since the war we may notice – with regret for many omissions – those of the clubs of Bath, Beverley, Clontarf, Corsham, Reading, The Frogs, Harborne, Sevenoaks and Leamington. Notable overseas club histories have come from Australia – East Melbourne, Western Suburbs, Mosman, Richmond; West Indies – Kingston; South Africa – Port Elizabeth and the Wanderers; Ceylon – Sinhalese, Bloomfield and Colombo Colts; New Zealand – Parnell, Southland; Amsterdam (in Dutch), Hong Kong, Toronto and Germantown (USA). Most happily free from controversy and 'newsworthiness', this is the section of cricket literature most concerned with the game for its primary object which, surely, is human pleasure.

Accounts of major – Test-playing – tours form, nowadays, with the exception of the autobiographies of 'star' players, the largest body of cricket publishing. Until the Australian season of 1932–33 – the occasion of the so-called 'Body-line' series – tours had been reported – with a few admirable exceptions important in the history of cricket writing – largely by participants. Sir Jack Hobbs once remarked, 'The first time I went on an overseas tour there were only two people reporting the cricket back to England: one only cabled the scores, and the other was our manager.'

It is important for any follower of cricket under 30 or so to realize that, until 1914, the basis of reporting the game was that the reporter found enjoyment which he attempted to communicate to his readers. That attitude persisted in a substantial degree even after the upsets of the 'Body-line' tour, and still endures strongly in some quarters. But after the Second War publishers, the ultimate arbiters of what shall, and what shall not, be published, apparently decided that public demand is for tour-reports from the press and commentary boxes. Publishers, the management of popular newspapers, radio and television are professionally required to assess public taste. Thus, in reporting the change, the only qualification must be the old one – 'I neither praise nor blame, I merely relate'. So, since 1946, a spate of books on major tours has been turned out, at a pace which only professional writers could maintain, to catch the presses so quickly that the books are available bare days after the last ball of a Test series has been bowled.

Such developments, however, were not dreamt of in 1860, the year of the first tour account, called *The English Cricketers' Trip to Canada and the United States*, written by 'Fred Lillywhite, who, with his tent, press, etc., accompanied the expedition in his professional capacity of reporter of the matches to be played across the water'. It is an ingenuous piece of writing but, with its simple illustrations and description of the travel, social functions and the human side of the tour, it gives a genuinely illuminating – and, to the modern reader, often surprising – account of the tour. R. A. Fitzgerald – secretary of MCC – described another American visit in *Wickets in the West*, a story altogether different in character, relaxed, social, light-hearted, with some sharp observation and friendly humour.

A third type of account appeared when the match reports written by Charles F. Pardon for *Bell's Life* on the Australian tours in England of 1882 and 1884 were reprinted in book form. The accounts are full, carefully observed and soundly written: a landmark in cricket literature. 'The Cricket Press' covered the same tours at almost equal length but with greater attention to biographies of the players and less to the actual matches. *Shaw and Shrewsbury's Team in Australia* (1884–85) was published by Shaw and Shrewsbury, who contributed interesting 'background' letters on the voyage and the personalities of the players, while the matches were satisfyingly reported by the Special Correspondent of *The Sporting Life*; it, and Pardon's two books, remain among the best of all about tours.

There are some rarities on the subjects of non-Test-playing travels – such as *The Tour of the West Indian Cricketers* (Canada and the USA, 1886), *Irish Cricketers in the United States* (1879), *Cricket Across the Sea* (Gentlemen of Canada in Great Britain, 1887), *English Cricketers at Barbados* (two books, 1895 and 1897) and *English Cricketers in the West Indies* (1895). Many a cricketer, too, must have let his eye slip uninterestedly past the unlikely title, *Ten Thousand Miles through India and Burma*, which is Cecil Headlam's pleasant and full account of the Oxford Authentics' Eastern tour in 1902–03. But these are largely collectors' items, often pleasant and sometimes revealing, but not important in the main stream of cricket history. *The Cricketing Record of Major Wharton's Team, 1888–89*, describing the first tour of South Africa, is also scarce, but larger and more important.

Strangely, in view of the excellence and success of the books of Charles Pardon and *The Sporting Life* reporter, the professional cricket correspondents did not return significantly to the field of tour accounts for another 50 years. Instead, for the obvious reasons that their travelling and living expenses were already paid, participants – players and managers – took up the thread and it was Sir Pelham Warner who, after some experiment, evolved the accepted modern form. His *Cricket in Many Climes* (1900), covering 5 tours – in West Indies, United States, Canada, Portugal and South Africa – and *Cricket Across the Sea* (1903), which dealt with the non-Test-playing visit of Lord Hawke's team to Australia and New Zealand, were trial runs. *How We Recovered the Ashes* (1904) and the *The MCC in South Africa* (1906) established the method which he employed in one of the best of all cricket accounts – *England v Australia*, which recounts the epic tour of 1911–12.

After the First World War, the number of tours – and tour-books – steadily increased. P. G. H. Fender wrote shrewdly analytical examinations of the England-Australia Tests of 1920–21, 1928–29, 1930 and 1934 and M. A. Noble came into the field with some similarly technically astute accounts. 1926 saw the beginning of the series of England-Australia tour accounts under the title *The Fight for The Ashes*, of which there have now been 11 volumes, distinguished by the date of the series, from the hands of M. A. Noble, P. F. Warner, J. B. Hobbs, A. G. Moyes, Peter West, I. A. R. Peebles and R. A. Roberts. They have been uniformly sound reports, covering every match played throughout the tour and with good background material.

The Tests between England and Australia in 1932–33, the so-called 'Body-line' series, gave rise to at least 13 titles, from pamphlets to full-scale books, varying in attitude and degree of partisanship. The best probably was Arthur Mailey's sage and witty *And Then Came Larwood*, while D. R. Jardine's *In Quest of the Ashes* and J. H. Fingleton's much later *Cricket Crisis* argue the two opposing cases.

That series of 1932–33 proved a dividing line, not immediately nor sharply apparent, but, viewed now in retrospect, definitive. From that time the official attitude towards players writing about cricket in which they had taken part developed from coolness, through disapproval, to contractual preclusion. Therefore there is a sense of loss in recognizing two of the merriest of all cricket books – *The Book of the Two Maurices* and *The Two Maurices Again* – in which M. J. Turnbull and M. J. C. Allom recorded the MCC tours, of Australia and New Zealand, 1929–30, and South Africa, 1930–31, with perky humour and intelligent appreciation of the play.

It was after the Second War, with the vast increase of Test cricket involving, with the entry of Pakistan in 1954, 7 countries, and a far wider press coverage, that tour accounts increased to such an extent as to produce, within 15 years, far more books than in the 60 preceding years of Test cricket. Merely to name them all would occupy considerable space and fog all critical comment. It must, therefore, be sufficient to say that considerable writing skill has been brought to bear on more than a hundred books. J. H. Fingleton has written at

Jack Fingleton, who has written books on 5 Test rubbers, at Cranbrook School, Sydney, with the famous playwright Ben Travers, an avid follower of the game who was still to be seen at Lord's past the age of 90.

unhurried length, but with considerable power, on 5 Test rubbers, and another former Australian Test player, W. J. O'Reilly, has observed two others with an expert eye.

Among English writers, Neville Cardus has written some of his most evocative prose about Tests between England and Australia, E. W. Swanton has reprinted his *Daily Telegraph* reports of some tours and written at greater length on others; Alan Ross, with an eye to, and feeling for, wider issues, has reported 4 tours in 3 books. A. G. Moyes combined a sense of historic perspective and undoubted enthusiasm in accounts of several visits to Australia and R. T. Brittenden was at his best in *Silver Fern on the Veldt*, report of New Zealand in South Africa, 1953–54. Richie Benaud, Charles Fortune, Alex Bannister, Bruce Harris, Alec Bedser, Louis Duffus, John Kay, Bill Bowes, Pat Landsberg, R. S. Whitington, A. W. Mitchell, Margaret Hughes, L. D. Roberts, E. M. Wellings, Rex Alston and Christopher Martin-Jenkins have dealt at length with major Test tours.

Since the Second World War, through the sheer volume of Test cricket – 549 matches in 32 years after it compared with 274 in 62 before, has made it impossible to chart every tour book (there were, for instance, 9 on the 1978–79 England tour in Australia). Neither is a critical standard of any value for the demand must always be for an account of one particular tour. There are now so many titles that *The Bibliography of Cricket* is the only valid guide.

Readers and students will do well, too, to ensure through the major cricket booksellers – usually to be found advertising in the cricket magazines – what titles are available, new or second-hand. There are, too, regular publications by the (new) Association of Cricket Statisticians; and notable contributions to cricket research by such students as J. F. Mandle, Irving Rosenwater and J. Goulstone, not always published separately but often appearing in journals.

Fred Gale, a leading light among the original reporters, covered the game from the days of the All-England XI of William Clarke almost to the Golden Age: a trenchant but respected critic who wrote under the pseudonym 'The Old Buffer'.

Literature

DAVID RAYVERN ALLEN

'Writings of country or period whose value lies in beauty of form or emotional effect': a dictionary definition of literature that perhaps is only partly true in respect of the works on cricket. Whereas there may be some reservations about the former qualification, excepting the best of its kind, surely there are none regarding its emotive power. The long-standing, continuing affair between bat, ball and pen shows no signs of abating – in fact, quite the reverse.

Much early writing on the game was confined to verse, and sometimes the baldly stated match results found a new, more memorable level in poetic licence. So we have *Surry Triumphant or the Kentish-Men's Defeat* (1773), a ballad by the Rev John Duncombe, being a parody of a game played at Bishopsbourne Paddock; and also its sequel *The Kentish Cricketers*, a poem by John Burnby in the same year.

The antics of cricketers had been noted in books of the 17th century and before – albeit very briefly: *The Life of Thomas Wilson, Minister of Maidstone*; Timbs's *School Days of Eminent Men*; *The Works of Rabelais* by Sir Thomas Urquhart; Henry Teonge's *Diary*; and *Mysteries of Love and Eloquence or the Arts of Wooing and Complementary* by Edward Phillips, a nephew of John Milton, are a few. There is even a solitary reference to be found in *The Voyages and Travels of the Ambassadors from the Duke of Holstein to the Grand Duke of Muscovy, and the King of Persia* by Adam Olearius. Davies's translation shows how Persian grandees kept fit in 1637, 'They play there also at a certain Game, which the Persians call Kuitsckauken, which is a kind of Mall, or Cricket.'

A convenient starting point for 18th-century cricket verse was *In Certamen Pilae* (1706) from *Musae Juveniles* by an old King's man, William Goldwin. It was to be around 150 years before Latin again found so permanent a place in the library of cricket, with the imaginary burlesque by Frederick Gale bemoaning the discontinued matches between Eton and Winchester at Lords, *In Memoriam gloriosam ludorum Etoniensium Harroviensium, Wykehamicorumque*, when in desperation 'the two elevens drove to Blackwell and sailed for America in hopes of happier times.' There were a number of mainly insubstantial references to cricket during the 1700s, in plays, mock operas, magazines, pamphlets and books of verse, and it is worth indicating some of these if only to show that cricket can lie in surroundings 'passing strange': *A Rod for Tunbridge Beaus, bundl'd up at the Request of the Tunbridge Ladies*, and Baker's *Humour of the Age* (both 1701), *Lewis Baboon turned honest* (1712); *Pills to Purge Melancholy* (1719); *The Rape of Helen* (1737); *The Dunciad* (1742) by Alexander Pope; *Maxims, Characters, and Reflections, Critical, Satyrical, and Moral* (1757); *Wit at a Venture* (1764); and *The Torpedo*, a poem to the Electrical Eel, dedicated to Lord Cholmondeley in 1777. In the same year were printed *Heath Hill*, a poem in 4 cantos by W. Hurn; and *Box Hill* by Edward Beavan which gives an account of a match at Colman's Green. *The Galaxy* issued by W. Belcher and others in 1790, tells us that 'Cricket:– being a game peculiar to Kent, and a few other counties, I subjoin a short description of it, by way of episcode, or rather detachment.'

It was a game between Kent and England at the Artillery Ground 46 years earlier that had inspired *Cricket: an Heroic Poem* by James Love (Dance). Dance, who had studied at St John's College, Oxford, became bankrupt, joined 'rogues and vagabonds' on the stage, and apparently played Falstaff with some success. The poem is probably the most famous of all early cricket writing and has appeared in 6 known editions. We also have the advantage of a totally different look at this mostly pre-Hambledon period of cricket in England in the letters of the Swiss traveller Monsieur Cesar de Saussure to his family, *A Foreign View of England in the Reigns of George I and George II*, translated and edited by Madame Van Muyden, and published in 1902.

Cricket literature paused for reflection at the turn of the 18th and 19th centuries. Apart from various editions of the laws of the game, and pocket handbooks of scores and instruction by such as Britcher, Epps, Boxall and later Lambert, Bentley, Cole, Wallis, Dean, Limberd, Lea and Tyas, there was little of note to record until Mary Russell Mitford's *Our Village* appeared in book form in 1824. These sketches of rural England had been serialized 5 years previously in *The Lady's Magazine*, and have earned a description as the first major prose on the game. A pattern of village cricket was formed that has since been re-enacted many times and interpreted many ways, in books of fiction, fact and faction; always, however, the traditional tapestry remains. A. G. Gardiner, A. G. Macdonell, A. A. Milne and Alec Waugh have used the theme – it has remained close to the literary heart.

It was at this period that the other cricketing Mitford, the Rev John, who was educated at Oriel College, Oxford, was contributing articles to *The Gentleman's Magazine*. In July and September of 1833, he reviewed *The Young Cricketer's Tutor*, by John Nyren, *to which is added 'The Cricketers of My Time' by the same author, the whole collected and edited by Charles Cowden Clarke.*

Cowden Clarke was a contributor to a weekly periodical called *The Examiner*, which was edited in the 1830s by one Albany Fonblanque, and according to F. S. Ashley-Cooper, *The Cricketers of My Time* appeared also in its pages. This is surprising in view of the fact that the content had formed an irregular series of articles in *The Town* newspaper, toward the end of 1832, and was issued as a supplement. That most knowledgeable of cricketing 'dons', Leslie Gutteridge, who provided this information, notes a number of differences from the edition of 1833, some of which help to clarify the text. As for *The Tutor*, there has been speculation concerning how much, if any, was penned by Nyren, and how much by Clarke. We do know that Nyren had been the recipient of an old cricketer's manuscript given to him by William Ward, MP, and the information therein must have helped considerably in the writing of the book.

Nyren, born at Hambledon in 1764, was the son of Richard Nyren, the club's 'general' in the great years. *The Tutor*, reproduced in many editions, has been called the *'locus classicus'* of cricket, and the most quoted passage refers to 'high-feasting held on Broad-Halfpenny, during the solemnity of our grand matches'. There are other descriptions to relish; of Tom Walker:

> Tom's hard ungain, scrag-of-mutton frame; wilted, apple-john face . . . his long spider legs, as thick at the ankles as at the hips, and perfectly straight all the way down. Tom was the driest and most rigid-limbed chap I ever knew; his skin was like the rind of an old oak, and as sapless. I have seen his knuckles handsomely knocked about from Harris's bowling; but never saw any blood upon his hands – you might just as well attempt to phlebotomise a mummy.

Nyren, 'good Catholic, musician, and philanthropist', moved in a celebrated circle. Cowden Clarke, Charles Lamb, Malibran, William Hazlitt and Leigh Hunt all gathered for 'Sunday Soirées' at his friend Vincent Novello's house, and cricket was one of the common interests for several in that group. Besides reviewing Nyren's *Tutor* for the *London Journal* in 1834, Leigh Hunt had written an article on *Cricket and exercise in general* which later appeared in his book *The seer, or Common places refreshed*, and Hazlitt's *Sketches and Essays* included 'Merry England' incorporating an appreciation of Long Bob Robinson.

The Rev John Mitford, who, as we have seen, twice reviewed Nyren's book, renewed his connexion with cricket classics in a rather exceptional manner. When he was the Vicar of Benhall in Suffolk, he had provided a roof for the famous old player William Fennex, and wisely committed their conversations to paper. He gave this manuscript to a James Pycroft, who had obtained a cricket blue at Oxford, and seemed destined to have a career in Law, but had instead chosen a different order and cloth. Pycroft was so enthused by the Fennex memoirs that he started garnering even more information concerning 'the good old days', and this eventually reached fruition with *The Cricket Field* in 1851. This book was another landmark in cricket literature, and followed the course set by *The Young Cricketer's Tutor* in regard to reprint.

Pycroft, who in 1835 had produced *The Principles of Scientific Batting* (with further editions in 1844 and 1845), wrote and made contributions to a number of books on the game, notably *The Cricket Tutor* (2 editions, 1862); 2 issues of *Cricketana* (1865), originally published as a series of papers to *London Society* in 1863/4; *Beeton's Cricket book* (Frederick Wood, 1866 and 1869); and *Reminiscences of the old players* (1868). Pycroft's *Table Talk* (nd), and *Oxford Memories* (2 vols, 1886), also had material of cricket content.

Books on cricket proliferated from around the time William Denison provided *Sketches of the Players* (1846). Academic, artist and musician, Nicholas Wanostrocht, brought out *Felix On the Bat* the year before. Arthur Haygarth was busy compiling his invaluable *Scores and Biographies* – 15 volumes in all, the first being published in 1862; the biographical side being relevant to this piece, although more details will be found elsewhere.

Echoes from old Cricket Fields were sounded out in 1871 by Frederick Gale, whose humorous if heavy literary style occasionally found outlet in pamphlets such as *The Alabama claims* (1872), and *Mr Pepys on cricket* (1873), which Gale informs us was an addition to Pepys's *Diary* discovered in the Mitcham Parish fire-engine where it had been hidden for 2 centuries. In more serious vein he produced *The Game of Cricket (1887)* 10 years after *The English game of cricket*, a worthy tome by Charles Box, had been issued by *The Field* office.

Cricket by its very nature has always attracted the nostalgic memoir, and such is in evidence in *Old Cricket and cricketers* (1890) by H. H. Montgomery, a reprint of the chapters on cricket in the author's *History of Kennington*, issued the previous year; *Kings of Cricket* (1893) by Richard Daft; *71 Not Out* (1899) by William Caffyn; and *Chats on the Cricket Field* (1910), by W. A. Bettesworth, the author also of the important *The Walkers of Southgate*. Montgomery was at one time Bishop of Tasmania, and also father of 'Monty' of Alamein; Daft and Caffyn were notable cricketers, and reported the activities of the 'All England' and 'United' XIs.

The prolific F. S. Ashley-Cooper was Editor of *Cricket* for 5 years from 1907, the year the 'American Cricketer Office' in Philadelphia produced his *Cricket and Cricketers* which, as in all his writing, contains fascinating and well researched data on various aspects of the game. He was one of the greatest authorities on his subject for a period of over 30 years, and *The Observer* review of his book *Cricket Highways and Byways* (1927) refers to him as 'the Polymath of Cricket'. He was fond of producing booklets in limited edition, mostly published by Merritt and Hatcher, Ltd, of London, and one privately circulated limited edition of 30 copies was *Cricket and the Church* (1904), a dissertation that had originally graced the pages of *Cricket*. It is a reminder of the continuous connexion between the clergy and cricket on the field of play as well as in literature from the days of *The Sabbath-breakers* (1712), which records the dreadful fate of 4 young men who dared to play the game on a Sunday, through to Norman Grubb's offerings from the Religious Tract Society on C. T. Studd, cricketer and missionary, and *Parson's Pitch* by the Rev David Sheppard. Studd himself had delivered *Quaint Rhymes by a Quondam Cricketer* in 1914, and was one of three brothers, two of whom were in the Church, and one, in 1928–9, Lord Mayor of London. The verse of that provider of *Cricket Songs* (1894), Norman Gale, somehow seems appropriate, even with a little imaginative licence ('The Church Cricketant'):

> I bowled three sanctified souls
> With three consecutive balls!

The aptly named E. B. V. Christian includes a chapter on cricket books in his essays *At the Sign of the Wicket* (1894),

Ian Peebles here aged 43, soon after the war – one of the select company whose distinction as writers has matched their prowess on the field. His autobiography, *Spinner's Yarn*, won the Cricket Society's Literary Award.

It has been truly said of Sir Neville Cardus that his *Manchester Guardian* reports from 1920 onwards transformed the art of cricket writing.

and, appropriately for a poet, also some thoughts on the poets of cricket. He says of Andrew Lang, whose output was too diverse for him to be characterized as a cricket poet, 'that he once gave to cricket an admirable ballade, but of late he has declined miserably upon golf.'

The game worldwide, or at least as far as the pink had run on the map – virtually the same thing – was represented in Pelham Warner's *magnum opus*, dedicated by gracious permission to the King-Emperor, *Imperial Cricket* (1912). This had an impressive list of contributors, and not surprisingly, in view of Warner's own aspirations, opened with a chapter from F. S. Ashley-Cooper on 'Cricket and the Royal Family.' Warner produced many books on the game – *My Cricketing Life* (1921), *Lord's 1787–1945* (1946), and *Long Innings* (1951), spring readily to mind. Diana Rait Kerr and Ian Peebles provided a welcome continuation to Warner's book on Lord's with *Lord's, 1946–1970*.

Before surrendering entirely to contemporary writers, mention must be made of some eminent literary figures who have enhanced cricket with their thoughts in print. The writings of E. V. Lucas on many subjects are scattered with cricketing gems, and have been partly collected in *Cricket all his Life* (1950), by Rupert Hart-Davis; yet with such a plentiful array, 3 wholly cricket titles must suffice. First *Willow and Leather* (1898), described as a book of praise with essays and verse; *The Hambledon Men* (1907), which even now seems a delightfully unpredictable foray into much-trodden ground; and *A Hundred years of Trent Bridge*, which was privately printed for Sir Julien Cahn in 1938, just before Lucas died. Sir Julien, of course, ran his own team for many years, an enterprise which had attracted another knight with a love of the game, Sir James Barrie. The seemingly indescribable goings-on of 'The Allahakbarries' were twice condensed into small booklets by Barrie, and are now scarce, sought-after trove for avid and affluent collectors. Clifford Bax was another who organized his own side, and survived to relate the experience towards the end of his life in 'An Author's eleven' from *Some I knew well*. He also edited *The Old Broughtonians* cricket weeks into 6 volumes, and found himself appearing in the pages of Sir John Squire's privately printed chronicle of *The Invalids* (1923).

The activities of *The Invalids* gained immortality through delineation in *England, Their England* by A. G. Macdonell. Squire led a team of 'London Bohemians' that 'boasted' A. P. Herbert, Walter Monckton, Howard Marshall, Alec Waugh, E. N. da C. Andrade and Edmund Blunden, and it was the poet and scholar Blunden, who was later to reflect his own feelings for the game in *Cricket Country* (1944). In the early 1950s he was appointed Head of the English Department at the University of Hong Kong, and it was from there in 1961, that the English Society produced a *festscrift* entitled *Edmund Blunden, Sixty Five* honouring his 65th birthday, composed of tributes from a distinguished cast including the Crown Prince of Japan and the British Prime Minister.

The village match found a lasting interpreter in Hugh de Selincourt. *The Cricket Match* (1924), has been called cricket's greatest novel – not without justification. Fictionalized cricket inevitably encouraged a high proportion of 'Boy's Own' titles. *Allison of Avonshire* or *Wanderlust's Third Innings* leave little doubt as to what to expect, and a few writers even enveloped real characters into their stories as in Lennie Lower's *Bradman and the Burglar*, in order, perhaps, to add authenticity, and at the same time make the product more marketable. Cricket in fiction is worth a book in itself, and indeed, it has a bibliography by Gerald Brodribb, listing examples of the genre. The immortal humorist P. G. Wodehouse has provided some of the best in cricket fiction – *The Gold Bat* (1904), for instance, and 3 books involving Psmith.

The modern era of writing on the noble game has been dominated by Neville Cardus and John Arlott and, in 1969, they collaborated to produce a book of fine prints, *The Noblest Game*, which contains a reflective view of cricket's historical span from Cardus, with authoritative introductions to 60 beautifully reproduced old prints and paintings from Arlott. For the connoisseur of cricketing art it forms a natural relationship with *The Noble game of cricket* (1941), which was composed of superbly illustrated drawings and prints from the Sir Jeremiah Colman collection. Any 'Cardus on cricket' bears witness to the high plateau of prose that is within. To search through *Days in the Sun* (1924), *The Summer Game* (1929), *Cricket* (1930), *Autobiography* (1947), *Second Innings* (1950), *Close of Play* (1956), *Full Score* (1970), is to discover the essential Neville Cardus.

John Arlott has a unique place in cricket literature. He has an enviable ability to 'bring alive' any incident or situation, and yet place it in perspective with brevity. The Arlottian phrase is unmistakable, and has the advantage of replaying 'The Voice' already heard over the airwaves. A prodigious output on many subjects including infantile paralysis, topography, wine, cheese and snuff, produced over some 35 years, makes restricted coverage of even his cricket writing somewhat unrepresentative. It ranges from book journals to reader's guides, from biography to history, from poetry and anthology to monographs of the players, mostly but not exclusively Hampshire, produced (often as an off-print from a *County Yearbook*) in limited edition. Space permits but one title; the almost psychological study of *Fred* (1971) reveals not only the subject (F. S. Trueman), but also the author at his most compelling.

One of the most important books on the game, not only of recent but written times, arrived from the West Indies in 1963. *Beyond a Boundary* by the scholarly C. L. R. James is exceptional because it does not confine its philosophy to just

A. A. Thomson's easy nostalgic style had a large following. A writer on many subjects, he concentrated latterly on cricket, and actually published 10 cricket books in his sixties.

cricket. It explores in depth the interrelation of the game and racial politics in the Caribbean, and, with the benefit of hindsight, one can see pointers of today and the future for other parts of the cricket world.

Other notable additions that deserve to be charted have come from the novelist A. A. Thomson. A rich vein of humour is apparent in *Cricket My Pleasure* (1953), *Cricket My Happiness* (1954), and *Cricket the Great Captains* (1965). In 1933 R. C. Robertson-Glasgow compiled a selection of prose and verse sketches, gleaned mostly from *The Cricketer*, in *The Brighter Side of Cricket*; over the next 30 years he produced several collections of his own humourous and highly individual newspaper writings and a charming autobiography, *46 not out*. Denzil Batchelor edited and introduced in 1967 some *Best Cricket Stories*. *The Story of Continental Cricket* by P. C. G. Labouchere, T. A. J. Provis and P. S. Hargreaves made a novel appearance in the bookshops in 1969, the three authors possessing between them greater or lesser mastery of 14 European languages, plus a superficial knowledge of Slavic and Celtic tongues. A cataloguist might be tempted to bracket this offering with *Strangers' Gallery* (1974), by Allen Synge, which looks at some foreign views of English cricket, although there is little similarity. J. M. Kilburn said *Thanks to Cricket* in 1972, a book 'compounded of autobiography, biography, appreciation, history, evaluation, philosophy, sometimes wise, sometimes nostalgic, always traditional and idealistic'. *Fingleton on Cricket* was available in the same year, and so was *Sort of a Cricket Person* which was more than an autobiography of E. W. Swanton. The book, titled from a remark made by a child, encompassed a range of experience and activity that knew no boundaries. Written in that incomparable conversational style that is distinctly his own, Jim Swanton covers all sides of the media, sports other than cricket, social life, as well as a moving insight of his time as a POW of the Japanese. *Follow On* (1977) is a companion volume containing informed, charming and civilized reminiscences on a variety of topics – Lord's, aspects of Oxford, Body-line, and a few 'old buffers'.

Recently there has been *Cricket Addict's Archive* by Benny Green and *In Celebration of Cricket* by Kenneth Gregory, 2 fascinating anthologies which prove that there is still a rich well of untapped material in store. In *Cricket in Isolation (the Politics of Race and Cricket in South Africa)*, edited and published in Cape Town by André Odendaal, the author sets out 'to record for posterity the wide spectrum of views held by a number of leading personalities, representatives of their respective groups, at this historic juncture in time'. *The Packer Affair* by Henry Blofeld covers comprehensively the whole sorry saga. *Sir Donald Bradman* is a remarkable biography by Irving Rosenwater. *The Golden Age of Cricket 1890–1914* by David Frith, with a foreword from J. B. Priestley, has rare photographs, most of them unpublished before, pleasing colour reproductions from *Vanity Fair* and Chevalier Taylor, informative cameos, and general presentation give convincing support to the author's contention that 'of all the phases in Cricket's history none has the seductive charm of the late-Victorian and Edwardian period'.

And so the writings of cricket multiply year by year. The total output on the game has made deep inroads into 5 figures, and therefore the literature in this piece can barely touch the fringe. It is mortifying to have found no room for Francis Thompson, Alfred Cochrane, Conan Doyle, Dudley Carew, Bernard Darwin – there are many more.

The only consolation is to climb a metaphysical plane as did 'Dwarpa' in 'Cricket as allied to the Heavens', or to come down to earth with *Certain Personal Matters* by H. G. Wells. 'The Veteran Cricketer' was 'seized', he says, 'some scores of years ago now, by sciatica, clutched indeed about the loins thereby, and forcibly withdrawn from the practice of the art; since when a certain predisposition to a corpulent habit has lacked its natural check of exercise, and a broadness almost Dutch has won upon him'. When, as sometimes happens, that day finally arrives, at least still try and emulate Blunden's friendly poet:

> Have you not ever felt the urge to write
> Of all the cricket that has blessed your sight?

Reference

JOHN ARLOTT

No game has ever thrown up so many books of reference as cricket. A reasonable library of the hard facts of the first-class game would run to between three and four hundred volumes; and it could be widened substantially if it were to cover public school and club cricket. The hundred plus volumes of *Wisden* are, of course, the accepted foundations for such a collection: they are dealt with here under a separate heading.

Doctor Johnson once remarked, 'Knowledge is of two kinds. We know a subject ourselves, or we know where we can find information upon it.' Irving Rosenwater, followed by the late Roy Webber, were the only men I have ever known who remembered enough cricket figures with sufficient accuracy to approach the Doctor's first category. For the rest of us, it is enough to know 'where we can find information upon it'. It is, however, also important to know where *not* to look. There has been so much research and collection of figures on the subject of cricket, often done for amusement, by cricket enthusiasts; and as amusement it did no harm. Yet a surprising amount of it has been published undeservedly or without adequate checking. Few books of figures are completely accurate, and it would be unwise to describe even the best of cricket reference books as perfect.

The student of cricket about to build a library may be sure that more than half the reference books he finds offered in catalogues and on book-shop shelves can be left where they are. The vast majority of them he can reject for the simple reason that they have been superseded; books of Test Match scores are out of date as soon as they are printed – if not before.

Once more, the student will need to limit his field. The studies and prolific writings of S. P. Foenander provide statistics about cricket in Ceylon down to levels on which few, if any, students in other countries will want to work. Some books of 'records' have been issued which merely plagiarise, with less accuracy, the standard works; while others go rambling off into the compilation of figures which reveal nothing. So the cricket reference library should be built carefully, avoiding duplication, seeking the authoritative work in each field.

The first edition of this work, *The World of Cricket* (1966), was by far the widest ranging and most authoritative cricket reference book ever published and this edition should maintain that standard.

Probably the most frequent demand of the man reaching for a cricket reference book is match-scores. Once more, as in all cricket chronicles, we begin with Haygarth's *Scores and Biographies*. Absorbing the early records of Epps, Britcher and Bentley, *S. & B.* gives match-scores from the start of recorded cricket to 1878, and continues with biographies of players who appeared up to 1898. Most of its gaps in respect of scores have been made good by Waghorn (in *The Dawn of Cricket* and *Cricket Scores 1730–1773*) and Buckley (*Fresh Light on 18th Century Cricket* and *Fresh Light on Pre-Victorian Cricket*). *Wisden*, beginning in 1864, maintains a fairly complete coverage of play all over the world until to-day. Yet it must be emphasized that the spread of the game in recent years has strained even *Wisden's* capacity and a number of scores in major overseas competitions are not now available in it; those for Australia, India, South Africa, West Indies and New Zealand are now to be found in their own year-books; Pakistan, however, is not so well covered. To clear the backlog will entail an immense amount of research and to publish it would involve a completely uneconomic operation. Nevertheless, it is said that it is to be attempted.

Wisden gives averages of the minor counties and the second XIs of the first-class counties, but their full scores can only be found in the year-books of those counties. Public schools averages and summaries of their seasons appear in *Wisden*. *The Cricketer* treats of public school, league and club cricket in a review fashion. Anyone who wants hard figures on matches at this level, though, must usually go to school magazines and local newspapers. Complete scores outside county and representative play can only be maintained on a scrapbook or filing-system method.

As soon as the reader is content with reviews – a season summed up in a few lines – he can turn, prior to *Wisden*, to *Denison's Cricketer's Companion* (1844 to 1847), and, more lengthily and thoroughly, to Frederick Lillywhite's *Cricketer's Guide* (1848 to 1866). The other 2 'Lillywhites' – the *Companion* and the *Annual* running, between them, to 1900, add little to *Wisden*.

Detailed reference to week-by-week events are covered most impressively by 2 periodicals. *Cricket* began in 1882 – the year of the invention of 'The Ashes' – and, changing its name in the last year to *The World of Cricket*, carried on until 1914. After the First World War – to be precise, in 1921 – *The Cricketer* started publication and, with some changes, has continued ever since. Until recent years, these two periodicals – *Cricket* as a weekly, *The Cricketer* (now *Cricketer International*), first as a weekly and then a fortnightly during the summer, experimenting with a winter monthly, winter and spring annuals, and now monthly issues – gave most first-class scores. *Cricket* was usually bound up with an index for the year while H. A. Cohen compiled an index to *The Cricketer* from 1921 to 1960 which The Cricket Society published, in instalments, in its *Journal*. But no normal-sized index can include all the smaller items of gossip and information contained in these 2 publications. Still, it is reasonably certain that any item of even passing importance will be found reported, and often commented upon, in the issue following its occurrence.

From 1960 to 1973 *The Playfair Cricket Monthly*, its scores and statistics based on the method of the late Roy Webber, followed by Michael Fordham, also provided periodical reference. *The Wisden Cricket Monthly*, edited by David Frith, began with the issue of June 1979. In this category should be noted the publications of what is now The Cricket Society. The first, under its early name, was *The Society of Cricket Statisticians News Letter No. 1*, a single printed sheet which appeared in 1948. It soon changed its name and, as *The Cricket Society News Letter* ran until its 60th issue, of 16 pages, by the end of 1960. It then changed its format to become *The Journal of The Cricket Society* averaging 76 pages, appearing half-yearly. From its first appearance in 1977 *Cricket News* weekly during the season, sporadically out of it, concentrated largely on scores.

The Cricket Quarterly (1963 to 1970), founded and edited by the eccentric Rowland Bowen had primarily a scholarly outlook; but it printed much which more 'popular' publications would not have included. Much of its content is of real value to the deeper student of cricket.

Since 1968 *Australian Cricket* (founded by Eric Beecher and subsequently edited by Phil Tresidder), and *Cricketer* (from 1973) edited by Eric Beecher, have provided coverage during the season of the game in Australia. From 1974 *The Cricket Player* (in succession to *New Zealand Cricketer*) has rendered a similar service in New Zealand.

One of the commonest queries that sends cricketers to their reference books is 'Did so-and-so ever play first-class cricket?' No single book will answer that question. *Bat v Ball – 'The Book of Individual Cricket Records 1864–1900'* – by J. H. Lester was an early ambitious attempt to set out players' figures. It included those of every player who had played an innings of 50 or more, or taken 50 wickets in first-class games, and ran to 366 pages of text; it is a convenient, season-by-season record for its period. In one volume – *Cricket Form at a Glance for Sixty Years 1878–1937* – Sir Home Gordon set out the nearest approach there has yet been to a complete statistical record of first-class cricket. Unfortunately his starting date – 1878, based on the first Australian visit – is 5 years later than the latest date ever accepted for the start of the County Championship; and, though he began to make the notes to keep it up to date, it is now far, far behind the times. His main aim was to give the date of birth – and of death where applicable – the schools and first-class clubs, years of first and last first-class matches, appearances in Tests and in Gentlemen v Players at Lord's, aggregates and averages of runs and wickets and the catches and stumpings – *in English cricket* – of all who played in any *two* seasons between 1878 and 1937, who came to England with a first-class touring side, or who were awarded blues. Astonishingly enough, Sir Home's figures balance. But they are by no means always correct.

To trace a player not in that record – who may have played only 1 or 2 matches or in a single season in the period – is a more complicated task. A number of county histories – to their date – include complete lists of every player who ever appeared for them.

A development relatively recent (except in the case of Yorkshire), of considerable use to the searcher for statistical information, is the inclusion of full figures in county year-books of the figures for every player who has ever appeared for that county. The trap here for the unwary, however, is that the figures usually refer only to the player's performances for that county and do not include his record in Tests, Gentlemen v Players, on tour or in festival or other matches and sometimes not in *non*-Championship matches for his county.

One work of statistics, now scarce, but diverting and revealing, was called *Our Leading Cricketers* for 3 years, 1924 to 1926, and was then continued in *The Cricket Spectator* from 1927 to 1931. It was compiled by 'H.P.-T.' (P. F. Thomas) and was based on 5-year comparison tables.

To refer to a player's career is less easy. The monumental *S. & B.* must again be our first choice. Although Haygarth's list of matches ended at 1878, he continued his notes on all the players of any importance up to 1900. F. S. Ashley-Cooper, editing Haygarth's notes for the publication of Volume XV – biographies only – in 1925, still included only men who made their first appearances by 1898, but he continued, and often amplified, Haygarth's notes on them to maintain the records of their careers to virtually the date of publication. So *S. & B.* provides biographies of the leading players who began their careers between 1744 and 1898. It is generally regarded as a safe rule, when working from *Scores and Biographies*, to

LEFT In *Cricket Form at a Glance for Sixty Years 1878–1937* Sir Home Gordon aimed at a complete statistical record of first-class cricket. As a copious writer his work was described in our 1st edition as 'gossipy, readable and inaccurate', with the saving grace that 'he was a great lover of the game.'

RIGHT Roy Webber established a remarkable mastery of cricket statistics as the official BBC scorer and the author of many books of reference before his early death in 1962.

assume that, unless a player is specified as batting or bowling left-handed, he was right-handed or so dimmed by the distance of time that no one could recall which hand he used. But this may not be always safe, and it is perhaps the one flaw in both Haygarth's and Ashley-Cooper's otherwise meticulous work that they do not always state whether their players are right- or left-handed.

That same flaw occurs in almost every 'Who's Who' of cricketers ever published. It is annoying to find a batsman described as 'successful' or 'accomplished', a bowler as 'persevering' or 'sometimes deadly', without any reference to left or right, or type of bowling. For instance, H. V. Dorey published *Cricket Who's Who*, subtitled 'The Cricket Blue Book', for 5 years from 1909 to 1913, partly repetitious but useful except that he does not define right-hand or left. The same fault is apparent in S. Canynge Caple's later *The Cricketer's Who's Who* (1934), which otherwise deals generously with its subjects, as does his later (1947) volume of the same title which, however, ends at 'E'. J. D. Betham's *Oxford and Cambridge Scores and Biographies* ran only to 1904; his subsequent records were never published, but for its period it is good on university cricket, though, again, no definition is given of the player's method.

The late Roy Webber, his successor, Michale Fordham, and Bill Frindall are the only compilers of such books who virtually never fail to define. Webber published his *Who's Who in World Cricket* in 1952 and followed it with a substantially revised edition in 1954 dealing with leading players. In addition, from 1950 until 1962 (the year of his death), he prepared a 'Who's Who' section of English players, including lesser names, in *The Playfair Cricket Annual*. Michael Fordham has continued it. All the entries in these compilations deliberately avoid flights of fancy but provide, tersely, all the basic information any reasonable inquirer could demand. They refer only to players active from 1950. Dorey's and Caple's books almost close the gap between *S. & B.* and Webber.

Cricket Records with a commentary by A. C. Coxhead (1899) was an early and intelligent attempt to set out records, but it is, of course, far out of date. In this field there have been a number of diffuse and inaccurate books.

Roy Webber, who was trained as an accountant, devoted his life, after the Second World War, to cricket statistics, which must have seemed to everyone else an extremely hazardous venture. He succeeded for 4 reasons: the first was his own determination to do so; the second was the high standard of his accuracy; the third the extent of his search and research – which was backed by a sound filing system; and, finally, his ability to present statistics in fresh and genuinely revealing fashions. His 'Career Records' were not entirely original – in fact they were inherited from Sir Home Gordon – but he kept them valuably up to date in *The Playfair Cricket Annual*. So far as major collections of statistics were concerned, he made an impressive trial run with *The Playfair Book of Cricket Records* (1951, with appendix to 1953) and then, in 1961, he produced *The Book of Cricket Records*, so extensively revised as to be virtually a different work. It has been succeeded and superseded by *The Kaye Book of Cricket Records* (1968, with supplement to 1970) by Bill Frindall, based largely on the Webber method but now much overdue for revision.

Another useful book of statistics by Roy Webber, simple enough in conception but not duplicated elsewhere, is *County Cricket Championship 1873–1956*, which, among its other facts, gives every County Championship table between those years – a constantly useful source of reference.

The field of cricket annuals is heavily cluttered with the fallen: for over 100 years publishers have put out yearly gatherings of facts sadly lacking in originality which, in many cases, lived a bare 1 or 2 years. Few of them did more than précis *Wisden*; so we may confine our attention to the pre-*Wisden* era, overseas countries and the few publications which had something fresh to add to the basic information of the 'Cricketer's Bible'.

Of the early books, *The Cricketers' Register for 1833* is somewhat unusual: it was published in a series of monthly instalments with consecutive pagination – to 32 – and dealt, in terse, but often useful, fashion with matches of varying importance. *The Cricketers' Companion*, compiled by William Denison, ran for 4 years, containing the scores of matches played from 1843 to 1846: it is largely a collection of scores of which the more important were reprinted by Haygarth, and its chief point of interest lies in the reviews of the seasons which Denison wrote for the last 3 issues.

Lillywhite's *Guide to Cricketers*, which began in 1849, endured only 3 years in competition with *Wisden* but for the preceding 16 seasons it improved steadily and has much useful information on play and the general pattern of the game over that period. A set – 22 editions in 18 years – is rare and extremely valuable. John Lillywhite's *Cricketers' Companion* (1863 to 1885) and James Lillywhite's *Cricketer's Annual* (1872 to 1900) provide some important first-hand comment to play and background.

Once *Wisden* was established, few of the other annuals mattered much, though *The Athletic News Annual* had good statistics. But the adequate reference library ought to include *Ayres' Cricket Companion*; it started as a pamphlet in 1902 but in the next year was far more substantial and continued to grow until it ended in 1932. It is particularly valuable for its slightly out-of-the-way, magazine-type articles.

In recent years, *The Playfair Cricket Annual*, first issued in 1948 – until 1963 when, though it kept its name, it was virtually swallowed up by the former *News Chronicle Cricket Annual* – proved fresh and different.

When one comes to overseas annuals, the casualty list again was murderously heavy. Only one country – Australia – maintained an annual for as much as 20 years to the 1960s; and, prior to the last war, there was nothing of any consistent weight from any of them. So no complete reference can be built up even remotely comparable with a run of *Wisden* for any of the other cricketing countries.

Australia

Until the *New South Wales Cricket Year Book* took on the role of a national record – at least so far as Sheffield Shield and Test play are concerned – in 1927–28, only one Australian annual had survived as long as 5 years; and since 1900 there had been virtually no publication of that type apart from the State yearbooks.

Biers and Fairfax put out *The Cricketer's Guide for Australia* as early as 1857, with some very good match accounts and biographical notes, but it only lived for 3 issues and is now a rarity. There were *The Cricketers' Register for Australasia* (2 issues), *Ironside's Handbook* (14 years), Davis's *Australian Cricket Annual* (1896–1898) and others, edited by T. W. Wills, J. Fitzpatrick, and Conway, plus Whitbridge's *South Australian Cricketer's Guide*. But they were all dead by 1900. The best of them were Davis's *Annual* and the workmanlike Boyle and Scott's *Australian Cricketer's Guide*, which ran for 5 years from 1879 to 1884. In 1896, a weekly called *Australian Cricket* was launched. It lasted 18 weeks only. *The Australian Cricketer* – 6 monthly issues covering the Australian season – was started in 1930 and carried some unique supplements, but it came to an end in 1934.

The first Australian reference annual of modern times is *The N.S.W. Cricket Year Book*, which, with the issue dated 1927–28, began its coverage of the main play there and gradually extended its national character. It has had some breaks, due to war, but the next copy made good the backlog each time. It should be noted by researchers that after the 1948–49 edition the titling method was changed. The next issue was called the 15th edition. In 1970 *Australian Cricket Yearbook*, began publication edited first by Eric Beecher and then by Phil Tresidder and has continued to give admirable coverage. It has been followed by *Cricket Close Up* (Eric Beecher).

South Africa

Here, again, the early story is one of struggle, but little continuity. Fortunately there is good coverage, particularly of the earlier years, in the 3 volumes of the Luckin-Duffus *History of South African Cricket* and in recent years there has been promise – not always fulfilled – of some degree of regularity. *The Natal Cricketers' Annual* ran for 4 seasons, from 1884–85 to 1887–88 and continued as *The South African Cricketers' Annual* for another 4, to 1891–92. A brave isolated effort was made with *The South African Cricket Almanac*, 1949–50, but it lived only that one season. For 1951–52, Geoffrey Chettle produced *The South African Cricket Annual*, which missed publication for 1958 but included most of the material that would have gone into that issue in 1959, appeared again in 1960, then appeared under the date 1961–62 with, apparently, official support and has since been kept up to date most healthily: it is now (1979) subsidized and known as *The Protea Cricket Annual of South Africa* and edited by Denys Heesom.

West Indies

This was, perhaps, the saddest story of all: West Indian cricket, which captured the imagination of followers of the game all over the world, was dismally badly documented. *The Barbados Cricketers' Annual* survived 20 issues, from 1894–95 to 1913–14 but it was, reasonably enough, almost entirely concerned with cricket in that island and dealt briefly even with inter-colonial matches not played in Barbados. Then came *The Sporting Chronicle Souvenir Annual*, published in Trinidad, which first appeared in 1921, and certainly came out regularly until 1929, possibly thereafter. While it dealt with all sports, it devoted most attention and space to cricket and afforded valuable coverage of inter-colonial tournaments. Unfortunately it had little currency outside Trinidad and copies are hard to find. Happily in 1970 Tony Cozier founded and edited *The West Indies Cricket Annual*, a flourishing and authoritative publication.

New Zealand

New Zealand had a good *New Zealand Cricketers' Annual* for 4 years from 1895, then nothing of note until A. H. Carman and N. S. MacDonald launched *The Cricket Almanack of New Zealand* in 1948. Since that date it has appeared steadily, increasing in scope and improving in layout, year by year, and providing first-class reference to cricket in that country on all levels. It is now subsidized and published as *The Shell Cricket Almanack of New Zealand*.

India

India has always evinced an eagerness to produce cricket books. P. N. Polishwalla put out the first edition of his *India Cricket Annual* in 1917 and it continued, somewhat erratically, with some changes of format and, latterly, under the title of *All India Cricket* until the 1930s, providing variable, but often valuable, data on cricket in India. *The Crickinia*, with many useful scores, and information not available elsewhere, ran for 6 years from 1939–40.

Indian Cricket, edited by S. K. Gurunathan (now T. N. Sundaresam), first appeared, under the title *Indian Cricket 1946–47*, in 1948 – that is to say, contrary to the usual method of dating, it gave the reports and results of cricket played during the season of 1946–47. The same method of dating was followed to 1960–61, then the issue covering the season of 1961–62 was titled 1962. *Indian Cricket* has clearly been modelled on *Wisden* and is highly factual, well indexed and, except for its title, up to date. It continues regularly and solidly.

Pakistan

Because no commercial publication could maintain regular publication of a chronicle of play in Pakistan, the Board of Control undertook the responsibility. The assistant secretary of the Board, Ghulan Mustafa Khan, produced 7 volumes covering the seasons 1965 to 1975 up to 1978. It provides scores only.

Sri Lanka

Cricket in Ceylon, now Sri Lanka, has been better served in terms of annual records of matches and players than at least 2 of the Test-playing countries. *Handbook to Ceylon Cricket* first appeared in 1901 and, changing its title to *Ceylon Sports Annual* in 1907, continued until 1914; *Ceylon Cricketers' Almanack*, 1911, 1912 and 1913 (E. W. Foenander) and *Ceylon Cricketers' Companion*, 1925, 1926, 1927 (S. P. Foenander) provided match accounts and scores until 1927.

North America

The American Cricketer – a full set of which is now a scarce item – ran from 1877 to 1929, the longest sequence ever maintained by a cricket periodical, *The Cricketer* excepted. It covers American cricket for its time and provides much other material for students. *The American Cricket Annual* was first issued in 1890 and there are other publications on the game there but *The American Cricketer* is adequate. Since 1959 the Canadian Cricket Association has issued a cyclostyled annual report covering their – steadily extending – cricket.

Other Countries

John Lawrence's *Handbook of Cricket in Ireland* dealt with cricket there from 1865 to 1881 and there have been a number of books dealing with the game in Scotland, the latest – and statistically the best – was *The Scottish Cricket Annual*, edited by James Cowe and A. M. C. Thorburn (1962–1968).

There have been cricket publications in Dutch and Danish as well as from some of the African countries but to follow play there is, as yet, somewhat unusual.

It may be well to note, however, *Imperial Cricket* by P. F. Warner (1912), in style a 'presentation volume' but providing good early reference on cricket not only in the main and Test-playing countries but also in Scotland, Ireland, Tasmania, Egypt and the Sudan, West Africa, East Africa, Hong Kong and the Far East, Malaya, Samoa and the Islands of the South

Seas, Fiji, the Solomon Islands, Canada, Bermuda. A long essay entitled 'A Girdle Round the Earth' in *Cricket Highways and Byways* by F. S. Ashley-Cooper also contains some valuable researches on the beginnings of play in lesser centres of the game.

Collections of Test cricket scores and averages were frequent in the years when they were also simple. From Brumfitt and Kirby's *England v Australia at the Wicket* (1887) there was a constant stream of books containing the scores of the Tests between the 2 senior countries in that field. *History of the Tests 1877–1947*, by Sydney Smith, Jnr, was superseded by *Test Cricket: England versus Australia* (to 1968) by Ralph Barker and Irving Rosenwater, with full statistics but also sound reviews of each series, and the pictorially impressive *England v Australia* (1977) by David Frith with outstanding pictorial content.

Except in such cases of additional quality, it obviously had become altogether too parochial to limit Test Match coverage. Hence, most valuable in filling the wide gap since the records of Webber and Arthur Wrigley was *The Wisden Book of Test Cricket* by Bill Frindall covering the 824 matches between all countries until May 1978; with its junior *Test Cricket Records from 1877* by James Gibb continuing, though with 'potted' scores, to September 1978.

Gentlemen v Players

The previous records were superseded by Sir Pelham Warner's *Gentlemen v Players 1806–1949* which contained full scores and statistics of the match to that date; it is impracticable, or at least, it would prove uneconomic from a publishing point of view, to bring it up to date to the end of the fixture in 1962.

The University Match

J. D. Betham's *Oxford and Cambridge Scores and Biographies* gives scores and concise biographical notes about all players in that match to 1904. There have been several lists of scores but the most up to date is now in *History of the O.U.C.C.*, by Geoffrey Bolton, complete to 1960.

Public School Matches

Full scores of public schools matches played at Lord's are given in *Wisden* for the following year. Others can be found regularly in school magazines. But there are a number of books which bring together scores of specific schools over long periods. The most notable are *John Wisden's Public School Matches* (all between Eton, Harrow and Winchester, 1805 to 1897); *Eton v Harrow at the Wicket*, by F. S. Ashley-Cooper (complete to 1921, ample biographical notes); *Repton Cricket 1865–1905*, by A. H. J. Cochrane (all matches with Uppingham and Malvern); *The Elevens of Three Great Schools 1805 to 1929*, by W. R. Lyon (Eton, Winchester and Harrow, scores and biographies); *Scores of the Principal Cricket Matches Played by Cheltenham College*, by An Old Collegian (Past v Present and Cheltenham v Marlborough, to 1867); *Clifton College Cricket Records 1863 to 1891*, by E. L. Fox (all matches with Sherborne and Cheltenham); *Charterhouse Records 1850 to 1890*, by B. Ellis (all matches with other public schools); *Bradfield v Radley Cricket*, 1853–1920, by T. Steele (includes Bradfield's matches with other schools also); *Rugby Cricket Scores 1831 to 1893*, compiled for the Old Rugbeian Society; *History of Winchester Cricket*, by E. H. Fellowes (with supplements to 1951); *Scores of the Cricket Matches between Rugby and Marlborough*, by E. S. Andrew (to 1903).

J. M. Kilburn, for 40 years cricket correspondent of the *Yorkshire Post*, has written a dozen books on the game including *Homes of Sport – Cricket* (with N. W. D. Yardley), *History of the Yorkshire County Cricket Club*, and two volumes of memoirs, *Thanks to Cricket* and *Overthrows*.

Touring Teams

Australian Cricketers on Tour 1868–1974 by Les R. Hill (1974) superseded the earlier records by Rex Pogson and Roy Webber.

The Language of Cricket, by W. J. Lewis, is one of the few cricket books to bear the imprint of the Oxford University Press, and it maintains the academic standards of its publisher. It is a most faithful alphabetical reference to the terms used in cricket, giving their meaning, derivation where possible, and the earliest traceable use of them in print. No other book like it has been attempted in cricket and it forms a unique and often quite invaluable work of reference.

Cricket Grounds

Wisden includes a plan of one of each county's grounds each year in its county review section. *Homes of Sport: Cricket*, by N. W. D. Yardley and J. M. Kilburn, discusses most of the first-class grounds in England with comment on their pitches, characteristics, amenities, plans of many of them and routes to them.

The Laws

There are several books of reference on the Laws of cricket: they are of different types, of service to different types of inquirers and researchers. The first must be Colonel R. S. Rait Kerr's *The Laws of Cricket* which traces, dates and describes every change and every significant publication of the Laws from 1744 to 1947. *The Umpire's Decision*, by Frank Lee, sets out the duties of an umpire with notes and comments on a practical level. *Cricket and Scoring* is the official Handbook of the Association of Cricket Umpires, compiled by Colonel R. S. Rait Kerr in consultation with the Association and numerous other experts. It deals in full detail with the Laws and with the umpire's interpretation of them. *Watson's Index to the Laws of Cricket* – 3 times revised to 1950 – is an Australian publication, conveniently arranged in alphabetical order of subject with cross-reference to the relevant Law and notes.

Curiosities

Cricket Extraordinary, by A. D. Taylor, *Curiosities of Cricket*, by 'An Old Cricketer' (A. L. Ford), and *Curiosities of First-Class Cricket*, by F. S. Ashley-Cooper, are 3 relatively small books which marshal oddities of the game such as are discovered by long and deep researchers in the dimmer files. Each will provide amazing occurrences not to be found in the normal record books.

Bibliography

In 1977 the issue of *A Bibliography of Cricket*, compiled by E. W. Padwick and published by the Library Association for The Cricket Society, gave cricket students a superlative instrument of research. It has 8,294 entries, is skilfully cross-referenced, expertly made and even wider in its coverage than the most experienced students had anticipated. Mr Padwick is a professional bibliographer and he has put all cricket students in his debt.

His work renders its predecessors, by A. D. Taylor, J. Goldman, A. J. Gaston, Gerald Brodribb, Neville Weston or

Since the war no one has communicated cricket more prolifically or more acceptably, over the air and in books and newspapers, than John Arlott. He is shown here in the earlier years of his career when his name was becoming a household word.

C. J. Britton, collectors' items; but should not cause such early Cricket Society researchers as J. D. Coldham, Geoffrey Whitelock, J. P. Everitt, and Michael Pearce to be forgotten.

Other lists of value to the collector are – *Catalogue of the Collection at 'The Yorker', Tate Gallery Exhibition of Cricket Pictures from the Collection of Sir Jeremiah Colman* (1934), *Catalogue of Historic Bats* (the Green-Cahn Collection); *Catalogue of the Rural Game of Cricket*, a loan exhibition by the Museum of Rural Life, Reading University (1957); *Catalogue of the Imperial Cricket Memorial Gallery at Lord's; Catalogue of Two Centuries of Cricket Art* – Sheffield Art Gallery, 1955; *Catalogue of Cricket Exhibition, National Gallery of Sports and Pastimes* (1950); *Catalogue of the Pictures, Drawings etc., belonging to the MCC* (1912).

Still the list expands, until it is obvious that, bibliography apart, a complete reference library on cricket has yet to be compiled.

Text-Books

G. H. G. DOGGART

Every schoolboy knows – or is at least the poorer for not knowing – that long, long ago a Greek lay bruised and buffeted among the bushes by a river, and that with the dawn came lovely maidens to the meadow, washed their clothes, then played their game of ball – for fun and not for points. It was an age of innocence before words like 'textbook' or 'manual of instruction', with their pedagogic overtones, had been minted; and we are told, possibly because she had not received the benefits of Group Coaching, that one of Nausicaa's girls threw badly and the ball fell into the stream. Nor – to move forward in time – were the Sons of Kent dependent on manuals of instruction when, in 1744, they defeated All-England by 1 wicket only. Victory was due, the story goes, to a dropped catch during the last-wicket partnership when 'the erring ball, amazing to be told! slipped through his outstretch'd hand and mock'd his hold'. Poor Waymark! How many times must the 'immortal butterfingers', as Andrew Lang called him, have relived that moment in an agony of reminiscence and reflected sadly on cricket's cruel way of correcting pride.

All of us have our private Utopias, either because we yearn for a past that the present can never live up to or because they offer in themselves 'a cordial for drooping spirits'. Sydney Smith's idea of heaven, we are told, was to eat *paté de foie gras* to the sound of trumpets; a distinguished literary critic has expressed a preference for a deck-chair in a summer garden with a beer and a book about the inimitable Jeeves by the inimitable Wodehouse. And in more practical vein there must be many who would choose to sit, like the Persian poet, beneath their favourite bough, possibly forgoing their jug of wine, their loaf of bread and their musical companion, but accompanied by a carefully chosen pile of books on our 'beautiful, difficult summer game'. And when we make our choice, surely, you will say, no books of instruction would qualify, with their clinical approach and analytical prose? – but you would be wrong – for from first to last, from the book by T. Boxall published in *c.* 1801, with its high-sounding title *Rules and Instructions for Playing at the Game of Cricket, as practised by the most Eminent Players*, down to the most recent edition of *The MCC Cricket Coaching Book*, the authors have infused into their works a warmth and a wisdom that make them admirable companions.

Two 19th-century gems must take pride of place in my collection. In the year after the Great Reform Bill there appeared, with considerable editorial help from Charles Cowden Clarke, John Nyren's *The Young Cricketer's Tutor: full directions for playing the elegant and manly game of Cricket*. And in addition to instruction what splendid tales it tells of the men of the Hambledon era, they who in H. S. Altham's phrase, 'raised the game into an art'.Even more evocative, surely, is this title: *Felix on the Bat – being a scientific enquiry into the use of the Cricket Bat together with the History and Use of the Catapulta.* Published in 1845, and full of humour, shrewd advice and period charm, it was the work of Felix, or, as he was called outside the cricket world, Nicholas Wanostrocht, a schoolmaster and a notable Kent player in the halcyon days of Alfred Mynn and Fuller Pilch.

'N. Felix' of Kent, whose real name was Nicholas Wanostrocht, was a cricketer of rare versatility, artist, musician, schoolmaster, and author of the treatise *Felix on the Bat.*

The author begins with a characteristically modest prologue, and there follow 7 chapters entitled 'Dress, etc.', 'Play', 'The Home Block, Hanging Guard or Back Play, as it has been variously called', 'Forward!', 'The Draw', 'Off-Cut Half-Volley and Leg-Hit Half-Volley' and 'The Cut', the sound practical advice being couched in a fluent and allusive prose style with occasional built-in moral overtones. Each chapter is headed by an apt quotation from 'The Bard' himself and illustrated by pictures, some in pale water-colours, from originals by G. F. Watts, and others in simple black and white, all of them as charming as they are instructive.

In one illustration, for instance, a young man lifts his bat in practice towards gully and makes contact with a Pickwickian figure whose face is barely visible behind the blade – the caption reads disarmingly: 'Some people stand very near to the striker when at practice: the consequence is occasionally serious as above.' In another, watched by 3 admiring spectators, his arms akimbo, his body at an angle of 45° to the horizontal ('literally inclined', as a pupil wrote recently about Hilaire Belloc), a deep fielder is shown in the act of receiving a ball full in the teeth – the caption reads: 'We are told, "Stop the ball anyhow, so you stop it". In any case excepting in the above, perhaps, it may be advisable. This is, however, entirely left to your discretion. In a third – a wonderful study in power and grace – the position for the hitting of the half-volley on the

This standard work on the technique of cricket is in its 4th edition, with sales so far around 70,000.

leg stump would satisfy the most demanding of coaches today, in particular the way (as *The MCC Cricket Coaching Book* put it over 100 years later) 'the left shoulder has dipped and the left foot has opened to lead the line of balance on to the line: the bat has been pushed back by the left arm towards first slip'. There is much cricket wisdom within its covers: 'A grand secret of comfort is to have spikes put into shoes which you have worn for some time.' 'The leg stump is usually and justly considered to be the most vulnerable.' 'The half-volley off-cut and the half-volley leg-hit are both the result of well-timing the ball; and upon a just appreciation of this fact is founded the apparent contradiction that some of the weaker men hit harder than their more muscular competitors.' 'So in the contingencies of this peaceful warfare, beware of too sudden rush into the violence of your desperate deed: but, being resolved, STRIKE! that the opposers may beware of thee.' We have moved many moons from the age of innocence; an age of sophistication, with its attendant strengths and weaknesses, has undoubtedly arrived.

Sixty years later, there appeared *Great Batsmen – Their Methods at a Glance, Illustrated by 600 photographs*. It was followed closely by *Great Bowlers and Fieldsmen*, both by Charles B. Fry and George W. Beldam. We are here in a different world to that of Felix, for not only has the art of photography transformed the technique of pictorial exposition, but also the game of cricket, owing to the great improvement in wickets and consequently also in batting, has become more complex and more subtle. C. B. Fry's acute and highly analytical mind (did he not achieve eternal fame by defeating F. E. Smith in the scholarship list for Wadham?), his wide learning, his lucidity of expression and his Olympian self-confidence give to his writings an exceptional quality. For sustained allusive brilliance, for instance, read his prologue and epilogue to E. W. Swanton's account of the recovery of the Ashes in 1953. *Great Batsmen* and its successor (as well as his later and often recondite book called *Batsmanship*) remained until recently in a class of their own for their shrewd observation and subtle analysis of the techniques of batting, bowling and fielding. A comment on page 139 of *Great Batsmen*, opposite a photograph of the secondary position at the wicket, indicates his careful and observant approach: 'The crease in the sweater proves the slight inclination at the waist – The manner of lifting the bat suggests a predilection for driving and for strokes played with a full arm swing.' The photographs themselves are inspiring to this day: they include pictures of all the great batsmen in batting's golden age, 3 of them, those of 'W.G. and the backlift', 'V. T. Trumper and the start of a straight drive' and 'K. S. Ranjitsinhji and the finish of a leg-glide', being included in the *MCC Cricket Coaching Book*. The presentation of both books is redolent of a more leisurely and gracious age.

But Felix and Fry have no monopoly of books which offer the reader a satisfying blend of instruction and entertainment. In 1897 Prince Ranjitsinhji's *The Jubilee of Cricket* was first published, and many will agree that it remains one of the best books yet written on the game. Much of it is given up to shrewd technical instruction – for instance: 'straight' play must be acquired as a habit. The lesson must be so well learnt that the necessary movements of the arms and the body become perfectly natural instead of laborious and difficult. Nature must give way to art till, to quote the Hon Edward Lyttelton's words, 'art becomes nature'. But it includes also much of historical and general interest, as when we read 'W. L. Murdoch has many amusing stories of how "Spoff" used to lie awake at night wrestling with bowling problems, and trying to think how best to get rid of certain batsmen'. Perhaps this gives us a clue to the attraction of so many cricket text books which on first appearance have but a limited appeal? For in the communication of technique authors are forced to refer constantly to the noted players of past and present, and to intersperse their teaching with anecdote and allusion.

The 6th edition of *Cricket* (edited by A. G. Steel and the Hon R. H. Lyttelton) in the Badminton Library of Sports and Pastimes dates from 1901. Here again one is struck by the masterly way in which literary ability is made the handmaid of technical instruction. There are 14 chapters in all, including one on 'Single Wicket matches' and another on 'Border Cricket' by Andrew Lang, one of a fine company of literary men devoted to the game. In his article on Batting Mr Lyttelton starts by describing 3 especially delightful moments in life connected with games, the third of which is the crack to square-leg off a half-volley just outside the legs. 'When once', he writes, 'the sensation has been realized by any happy mortal, he is almost entitled to chant in a minor key a Nunc Dimittis, to feel that the supreme moment has come, and that he has not lived in vain'. He then proceeds to examine the grip and the stance subscribing, incidentally, to 'The Champion's' theory that the right foot should never be moved when playing fast bowling except to cut or to pull a very short ball. He goes on to discuss forward and back play with much shrewdness, though without, perhaps, quite the fascinating insight shown by Fry into the perennial dilemma which faces batsmen during an innings and which it is the bowler's primary object to provoke – whether to play forward or back to the particular ball that has been bowled. This is a book to treasure, not least for the splendid picture on page 139 of a thickly-moustachioed wicket-keeper, his eyes glued to a ball that is out of the picture but dropping, one guesses, at a speed of 32 feet per second, eyeing a similarly equipped batsman who, despite his ample form, we learn from the caption, is 'A pokey batsman dealing with a high-dropping full-pitch'.

In *The Art of Cricket* Sir Donald Bradman made a characteristically thorough contribution to a full understanding of the game: it should be a 'must' in any cricket library.

Other works jockey for position – a beautifully bound Crown Quarto Edition, de Luxe, dated 1891, No. 622 out of 652 copies of his book called *Cricket*, signed by W. G. Grace himself, which contains much wise advice (including, in the chapter on Fielding, the 9th of 11 points for beginners: 'Do not go into the field with a cigarette or a pipe in your mouth'); a slim volume written, with characteristic modesty, by J. B. Hobbs, as he then was, entitled *Cricket for Beginners*, first published in 1922, reprinted in 1932, and one of the first books on the game one young aspirant was happy to acquire; *The Book of Cricket* by Sir Pelham Warner, whose unquenchable love for the game shines forth from every page; *The Game of Cricket* in the Lonsdale Library, in which the game is discussed, as its cover impressively tells us, by 'many authorities'; 2 books by T. E. Bailey, one entitled *Cricket* which is admirably lucid and informed, the other *Cricketers in the Making* written in collaboration with D. R. Wilcox, whose son posed for its striking photographs; a most wise book for coaches called *Cricket – Can it be taught?* by G. A. Faulkner, one of the finest all-rounders of all time, who later started his own cricket school in Fulham; *Cricket Practice and Tactics* by B. W. Hone, scorer of a century in the University Match of 1932; an admirably balanced *Cricket Dialogue* between 2 Eton masters, both Oxford blues in their day, one a batsman, the other a bowler, C. H. Taylor and D. H. Macindoe; Sir Donald Bradman's *The Art of Cricket*, a remarkable book by a remarkable man whose mastery of the game is reflected in its pages; *Teach Yourself Cricket* by F. N. S. Creek; a book called *Attacking Cricket* by the current Warden of Radley (who has yet to explain to me why someone so enthusiastic about the game should write a book attacking Cricket!); *Your Book of Cricket* by 2 Malvern coaches, A. R. Duff and G. H. Chesterton; coaching books by former England captains, books on every aspect of the game – all these, and others denied a mention for obvious reasons of space, cry out for a place in the sun.

There are many cricket books which I shall have with me, not only beneath my bough but also when, like Clarence, I have 'passed the melancholy flood, with that grim Ferryman that poets write of'. I shall be ready when I reach the Custom House which Maurice Baring once dreamed of, and reply to the official who asks me 'Have you anything to declare?' Among my cricket baggage will be found, not only the writings of those authors who have set out solely to amuse and entertain, but also, surprising perhaps to relate, a textbook or two, and one in particular, whose primary object it was 'to review the whole field of the game's technique'. In so doing MCC produced something far greater than a mere book of instruction, for *The MCC Cricket Coaching Book*, now revised and reprinted with the advice and active involvement of the National Cricket Association's 3 national coaches, surpasses any other similar work for the combined quality of its technical advice and literary skill, its photography and drawings, its production and presentation – for all of which H. S. Altham, G. O. Allen, H. P. Crabtree and the artist Bruce Drysdale, as well, of course, as the publishers and the printers, deserve the gratitude of all who love the game.

Broadcasting

Sound

H. F. ELLIS

A hot day and a slow crawl in congested traffic along the Mile End Road and Bow Road and all the rest of that grisly route that leads one eventually from the centre of London to Gidea Park and Chelmsford and places east – the very essence of tedium, one would say. But the car wireless (for such, in the days I am thinking of, we sensibly called it) was crackling away and Denis Compton was approaching a double-hundred and indeed, perhaps along Eastern Avenue or thereabouts, actually attaining it. When was this, and whose the running commentary that made the long grind not merely bearable but enjoyable? Memory is at fault on both points. The records show that Compton made 207 against South Africa at Lord's in 1947 and 278 at Pakistan's expense in 1954 at Nottingham, and of the two I incline to opt for the latter, having no recollection that the stream of reported boundaries came to a halt soon after the magic total. The commentator could, I suppose, have been Rex Alston or E. W. Swanton or John Arlott, or all 3 in turn, and now, a little belatedly, I extend my grateful thanks to whichever it was for shedding a kind of glory even over Leytonstone.

To another cricket commentary, altogether less satisfactory in the upshot, I have no difficulty in attaching a date. On the last day of the Fourth Test against Australia in 1961 I was picnicking with my family somewhere in Wales, or possibly the Wye Valley – a fairish way at any rate from Old Trafford where sterner matters were afoot. We had a portable radio (so called by this time) balanced on the car roof and tuned in to hear whether England, faced with an improbable 256 to make in less than 4 hours, were managing to save the game. Astonishingly, instead of saving the game, we were winning it. Dexter, with Subba Row comfortably installed at the other end, was lambasting the bowling in all directions. The score was approaching 150 for 1, well over halfway with not much under 2 hours still to go and May to come in next in case some trifling mishap occurred. The sun shone, the sandwiches tasted good, the tea less conscious than usual of having existed in a vacuum. So for about 5 happy minutes. Then Richie Benaud put himself on, to bowl leg-breaks round the wicket into the rough, a most unseemly manoeuvre. Almost instantly the sun went in, the tea grew cold, the sandwiches curled sardonically at the edges, the score degenerated to 160-odd for 5. I am glad to have no idea which commentator cast such a blight over a one-time contented country idyll.

Casting much further back, to the very early days of cricket broadcasting, memory for some reason calls up consistently sunnier pictures. In the beginning there was the Voice, and it always seemed to be giving me good news. Of course, the voice itself was measured, calm, reassuring: never intended by nature to be a vehicle for panic or dismay. But there must have been times in those middle 1930s when Howard Marshall had evil tidings to impart. I do not remember them. The note that echoes down over more than 40 years – apart from the majestically inevitable 'Over goes his arm . . . and he *Bowls*' – is 'Well, Leyland and Ames are still there', richly enunciated, utterly consoling. And tensely awaited. Because non-stop commentaries had not then come into being, so that the listener had to endure long intervals between transmissions with no clue to what was going on, what disasters had befallen. When the time came for switching on again it was a moment of truth indeed, often a moment of dread. What better instrument than the voice of Howard Marshall to tell you that all was well, that Leyland and Ames were still there, batting with great solidity and composure?

Howard Marshall (right), the original 'voice of cricket', who more than anyone established the style and technique of sound broadcasting on cricket, with another famous BBC sporting figure, John Snagge.

Running commentary on cricket, as opposed to broadcast 'eye-witness' reporting, began only in 1935, though rugby football and association football had their first 'ball-by-ball' baptism a good 8 years earlier. The delay was due, of course, to a feeling that too little happened at cricket, too slowly, to make instant commentary a feasible entertainment. Once it was tried, however, the expertise of men like H. B. T. Wakelam and Michael Standing, in addition to Marshall, proved that the thing could be done – and done so successfully that in 1939, when the West Indians were here, the BBC were emboldened to launch out on the uncharted seas of daylong ball-by-ball commentaries on a Test series. By the following season there were even sterner preoccupations than cricket, and the only scores widely listened to were those of enemy planes destroyed as against our own losses of Hurricanes and Spitfires.

After the war continuous commentaries on Tests became such an established feature of the summer scene that the BBC could hardly have stopped them without risk of a protest march on Broadcasting House by millions of deprived listeners. New voices took up the task of conveying to an unseen and unseeing host the flavour of a cover drive by Len Hutton or Trevor Bailey's forward defensive prod. To the nucleus of John Arlott, Rex Alston and Jim Swanton (the last-named's imperial tones and admirably succinct summaries already familiar from prewar days) were added as time went by Peter West, Brian Johnston (the perennial rambler), Robert Hudson, Alan Gibson, with welcome interpolations from such overseas visitors as Alan McGilvray and Jack Fingleton. 'Scorers' also proliferated. The need for an assistant in the box, to keep track of significant details and remind the commentator that 11 no-balls had been bowled since lunch, had been realized as early as the mid-1930s and the names of Arthur Wrigley, Roy Webber, Jack Price and (more recently) Bill Frindall became familiar to the public. At first, as I remember, the scorer was unheard as well as unseen: a mere passer of notes, less vocal and more shadowy even than the old 'Square Three' man in broadcasts from Twickenham, at most a faint background whisper of 'His third four' or 'An hour and twenty minutes'. Nowadays he emerges quite boldly into the open, and is expected moreover not just to keep notes of everything that happens *as* it happens but to be omniscient about everything that *has* happened over the last 50 years or so. Thus it is nothing to hear Bill Frindall volunteer a statement about the last occasion on which an Indian bowler under 21 took 5 wickets in the first innings of a Test match. I do not believe Howard Marshall would have cared for that.

There have been other changes since his time. Sometime after the war 'experts' in the shape of old, or not-so-old, cricketers of renown were introduced to make their more or less revealing comments, at intervals between overs, on the general situation or the merits of this or that player. A. E. R. Gilligan, N. W. D. Yardley and F. R. Brown, former England captains, were among the pioneers in this field, to be followed (whether on sound or television) by Denis Compton, Richie Benaud and Ted Dexter among others. In their varying styles the resident professors on radio, such as Trevor Bailey and Fred Trueman, superimpose a majestic authority on the ceaseless chatter of each new generation of commentators, including, more recently, Henry Blofeld, Christopher Martin-Jenkins, Don Mosey and Tony Lewis.

Amid this mighty cloud of witnesses the listener sometimes has difficulty in determining just how many and who are in the box together. Writing some years ago Rex Alston observed that

> Test Match commentary has tended in recent years to concentrate on keeping listeners aware of the score rather than on entertaining them with descriptive material. It is perhaps a more professional method, but the human touch is lacking. Commentators tend to become a type rather than individuals with distinctive styles.

The BBC Radio 'Test Match Special' commentary team.

I doubt whether he would feel that to be still true today. The present band of happy warriors, swapping jokes and leg-pulls, reading postcards from correspondents, enlivening the longueurs of a fast bowler's walk back with instalments of anecdotes ('I'll come back to that in a moment'), can hardly be accused of lacking the human touch. They seem to enjoy being on the job together, and like to share their enjoyment with anybody listening. Nor do they neglect their duty to inform us about what is actually happening on the cricket field and its environs. Sometimes one may feel that the family atmosphere is a shade over-insistent; sometimes it might be better to let the witticisms arise naturally from the context or not at all. But on the whole this modern development of the difficult art of continuous commentary works pretty well. Many viewers of the almost equally continuous presentation of Tests on television like to turn from time to time from the technicalities of Messrs Benaud and Laker to hear what the Sound Gang are on about or to revel in the splendidly dictatorial pronouncements of Trevor Bailey. Some even switch the picture off as well for a few minutes rest. One thing about cricket on sound only is that you don't have to read 'Make Someone Happy' or 'Gas Gets On With It' every time the bowler walks back to his mark.

We have been fortunate, over the years, in the quality of our commentators. There have been, and are, tiresome mannerisms of the kind to which we are all subject (but do not get paid for them), endless repetitions of pet phrases or near-meaningless introductory or interjected conjunctions and adverbs that are no more than stutters, so that one wonders why some Head of Outside Broadcasting does not intervene with an occasional kindly word of advice or veto. But, on the whole, the admixture of information, technical or statistical, of straight reporting, of scene-setting, character sketches, background and so on is remarkably satisfying. The voices are pleasant. There is no screeching, no attempt to arouse vicarious excitement of the kind deemed essential in the broadcasting of many, if not most, other sports. Of course the very nature of cricket helps to preserve its interpreters from the worst excesses, but we should be thankful that those who select them have, almost without exception, chosen men who understand the game and love it. From the all-round entrepreneurs, the inevitable omniscients prepared to become enthusiastic, to say the least, about tennis, golf, football, athletics, gymnastics, swimming, show jumping, boxing, ice-hockey – from the Colemans, Carpenters and Vines of this world – cricket has been spared.

Television

PETER WALKER

The impact of television on all sports has been enormous. As a result of this kind of exposure, table tennis, show-jumping and snooker have been elevated from the ranks of minority interests to favourite viewing times, with United Kingdom audiences frequently topping the 8 million mark. Cricket too has been a beneficiary the world over. At one stage of the 1978–79 season in Australia it was possible to switch from channel to channel and watch a Test between Australia and England on one, a Sheffield Shield match between 2 States on another and a Packer game on a third.

In the United Kingdom cricket coverage, to date, has been a virtual monopoly of the BBC. Except in isolated regional instances ITV has shown scant interest in bidding for the TCCB's contract which comes up for renewal every 3 years. Consequently the BBC have built up an unrivalled reputation for their coverage but even this has been the subject of reappraisal after the innovations brought to the presentation of World Series Cricket in Australia.

The first-ever match televised was the Second Test at Lord's between England and Australia in 1938. It was transmitted in the London area only and although the viewing figures were measured in thousands only, television, of course, was still in its infancy. However, the response was sufficiently encouraging for the BBC to screen the Fifth Test at the Oval as well. The commentator on both occasions was H. B. T. Wakelam (maker of the first of all sporting commentaries at Twickenham on sound radio 11 years earlier) who witnessed Hutton's innings of 364 as England totalled 903 for 7 declared.

In 1939 the Second and Fifth Tests of the England v West Indies series were covered, again for London viewers only. After the war, technical developments in the highly costly world of television hardware were slow and it was not until 1950 and the opening of the BBC's Sutton Coldfield transmitter on the outskirts of Birmingham that a match outside the metropolitan area was televised – the Third Test between England and the West Indies at Trent Bridge. Two years later, further expansion enabled Tests at Headingley and Old Trafford to be brought into the fold. By modern standards coverage was miserly – 1.00 pm–1.30 pm and 4.30 pm–6.30 pm on Mondays. Wednesdays and Thursdays. There were even stricter limitations on Saturdays; 4.30 pm–6.30 pm. It was only on Tuesdays and Fridays that the number of hours televised began to approach today's figures . . . any time between 11.30–6.30 pm but no more than 4½ hours in all.

In 1959 an increased fee between the BBC and the Board of Control for Test Matches greatly extended the permitted hours of Test coverage. Since then the BBC has steadily expanded its output and range of competitions covered so that now, in addition to all the Test matches in a series, BBC channels 1 and 2 provide either live coverage or recorded highlights for transmitting late at night of selected Schweppes County Championship games, the Gillette Cup, the Benson and Hedges Cup and the John Player League. This last competition is played on Sunday afternoons, and BBC 2 covers every ball from one selected match each weekend. At the end of a close-run season such as those of 1976 and 1978 when any one of 3 teams could have won the title, all the likely contenders' matches were covered, with pictures and commentary switching from one ground to the other across the length and breadth of Britain.

This of course was a vastly expensive operation yet on the BBC 1 and 2 networks sport contributes 13% of the overall output, and total licence revenue is approximately £250 million per year. At £10,000 per hour running costs, sport is indeed the cheapest form of television available. By way of comparison, a drama production averages out at £81,000 per hour, light entertainment at £45,000 per hour.

Let us now consider the problems of presentation. The preparation for any match to be televised, be it a 5-day Test or a Sunday afternoon JPL game, is fundamentally the same and involves roughly the same number of people. Some weeks before the event the producer and the Engineering Manager who is responsible for the technical equipment will gather on site for a planning meeting. At this are decided all the important issues such as where the 4 or 5 cameras will be sited, the laying of the several miles of cabling and the placement of the control vehicles, as well as the more mundane items such as where the crew will eat.

A key factor is the getting of the signal out of the ground to the nearest BBC transmitter: no major problem at the Test grounds but a ticklish business at an outlying venue like say Darley Dale in Derbyshire where a series of small link vans have to be scattered up the hillside, relaying the signal to the top of the slope from where a 'booster dish' throws the picture and sound to a transmitter mast on the horizon.

The day before a match the riggers arrive bringing with them the necessary equipment which, besides the zoom lens electronic colour cameras (£40,000 apiece), includes an emergency generator in case the mains supply fails. The total capital equipment costs involved in covering a cricket match is in the region of £850,000.

Although the viewer at home will usually see only one person – the presenter plus any of his interviewees, around 50 people are actually involved on the day(s) of transmission. The normal complement of commentators is 2 who work in 20-minute shifts supported by an ex-Test player who adds further analysis and comment. From the postwar resumption until the mid-1960s, Brian Johnston and E. W. Swanton were the principal television commentators, the latter also contributing the in-vision summaries. For Tests against Australia they were joined by the famous Australian, Jack Fingleton. For the past 10 years their role has been filled by Jim Laker, the great England off-spinner, and Richie Benaud, the Australian all-rounder and captain. Analytical help has come at various times from Denis Compton, Ted Dexter, Brian Close and Ray Illingworth as well as overseas Test cricketers commenting on their countrymen's performances. Since 1952 the presenter or 'linkman', who also occasionally helps out with commentary, has been Peter West.

The scorer sits alongside the commentators endlessly providing them with the minute-by-minute statistics so necessary for the factual representation of the progress of the game. The scorer is also a source of historical reference as to previous matches and the career records of the players

Brian Johnston was permanent commentator in the formative years of television cricket, now perennially active on sound.

involved. To be able to do this on demand – and some of the questions asked are obscure in the extreme – requires a man with a tremendous love and knowledge of the game. Irving Rosenwater has scored for BBC television since 1970 and meets all these requirements with speed, good humour and an unerringly accurate service.

The televising of a match revolves around the control centres called a 'scanner'. Roughly the size of a large furniture removal van, upwards of £600,000 worth of equipment and 10 people work in an air-conditioned but very restricted space. In addition to the main van, a vital unit is the caption scanner. This is either a separate small hut or a specially cordoned off section in the pavilion. Up to 6 people beaver away in this environment making up the batting scorecards, bowling analyses, name captions and other visual printed information which is fed in from a special camera in the room. This can be superimposed over the pictures of the game in progress at the director's discretion.

In the main control scanner itself sits the producer/director – often one and the same person in television outside broadcasts – his secretary, who is responsible for making sure the programme runs to time and who liaises with the main continuity studio based in London, the engineering manager whose responsibility covers the entire range of the technical output from the ground, and the sound supervisor who controls the commentator's microphones, the effects mikes around the ground and the internal communications between the main scanner and the rest of the crew outside. Several other engineers keep a watching eye on the quality and colour composition of each camera.

The cameramen work on a shift basis, usually an hour on followed by half-an-hour off. This break is necessary because the intense concentration required to peer through a small viewfinder is extremely tiring. In the scanner the director can see the output of all his cameras on eye level monitors. By depressing one of a row of buttons in front of him on the control panel he selects which camera's output the viewer sees at home. There are all sorts of additional visual gimmicks available to the director, but the basic coverage is usually kept along fairly simple lines to avoid confusion.

This selection needs split-second decision-making and great skill and judgement which come only after long experience. The top-class director is always at least one picture further ahead in his mind than the one he's offering to the person at home. Throughout the transmission he gives a running stream of verbal instructions to his cameramen, who wear headphones, telling them the kind of picture composition he wants. He can also talk to his commentators, and they to him, on a special microphone called a 'lazy' – conversations which naturally do not go out on air. Throughout the day there is a constant interchange between all the people covering the game, making suggestions for future shots, close-ups of individual players or specific items of interest around the ground. For the past 10 years the leading cricket producer/director at the BBC has been David Kenning who has travelled the world looking and learning from the way other countries cover cricket.

Kenning freely admits that the experiments carried out by the Kerry Packer organization in Australia have added to the previously rather fixed ideas on match coverage.

Now for the camera positions: the main one is sited immediately behind the wicket at the lowest possible height to give an uninterrupted view over the umpire's head. This camera (1) covers the whole pitch including the batsman and bowler at the moment he releases the ball. It also has the option of zooming in to isolate the batsman. Alongside camera (1) is another camera (2), usually called the fielding camera. It operates on a wider angle than (1) and once the ball has been hit the director invariably cuts to this camera to give the viewer a perspective of where it's gone. This also allows (1) to refocus on the whole length of the pitch to illustrate the batsmen running between the wickets.

These two main cameras are augmented by 2 more at ground level. Camera (3) is usually placed alongside the sightscreen at the same end as the 2 cameras aloft. It is there principally to follow the fielder in pursuit of the ball, close up of individual players, crowd shots and between-over pictures of the scoreboard. Camera (4) is usually at right angles to the pitch and has a similar rôle to that of (3). These 2 cameras are there to help create and build up the atmosphere surrounding a game leaving the coverage of the match itself to the 2 main cameras, (1) and (2).

In the hands of skilled cameramen and an alert director, minor miracles are worked every hour of the transmitting day. The time-lapse between the ball being released, skied by the batsmen and caught by a fielder 30 yards from the bat can be less than 4 seconds. It is not unknown for a director to get 5 different shots into that period: 1) The bowler delivering the ball at the batsman; 2) the batsman in close-up striking it; 3) the ball in the air with the fielder waiting for it; 4) the anguish of the batsman waiting to see the outcome; 5) the fielder making the catch.

Creating television programmes is all about story telling and the visual idea and compositions of the director and his crew can enhance or mar a gripping yarn. Action replays have become an integral part of sporting coverage. There are 2 ways of doing this. By replaying a video-tape recording of the incident at normal speed or by looking at it in slow motion. The equipment which provides this particular facility is known as a slow motion disc. Moving pictures are basically a collection of still frames run together at high speed to give the impression of movement. A variable speed disc has the electronic ability to separate each frame and reproduce it at any speed selected, right down to a 'freeze frame' dead stop. This expensive bit of gadgetry,

Jim Laker's laconic style of television commentary has been identified especially, since its beginning, with the John Player League. He is seen here with Mike Procter, who is receiving the Walter Lawrence Trophy for the fastest hundred of 1979 from Colin Ingleby-Mackenzie.

without which no director would dream of covering a major sports event, costs in the region of £100,000, while a standard VTR (video-tape recorder) machine is about half that amount. With television engineering in a constant state of improvement, the future hardware of the business is virtually impossible to forecast.

Every ball bowled is recorded on at least one VTR machine but, because of the wastage, if nothing happens in an over the tape is then rewound and recorded over – just like an ordinary sound tape recorder. If something of interest does happen the incident is recorded again onto a separate compilation tape from which are assembled the late-night edited highlights programme of the day's play.

For all its 2 dimensional limitations there can be no doubt that in the hands of a well-trained crew, an intelligent director, and a skilled commentator televised cricket has become the next best thing to being actually there and often provides an extra dimension missing from the game itself.

Cricketers in Other Fields

KENNETH GREGORY

Wilde's Lady Bracknell opined that 3 addresses always inspire confidence even in tradesmen. But pity the Cambridge shopkeepers of the late 1940s who had to remember whether to send G. H. G. Doggart's bills to Fenner's, or to the University headquarters of Association football, Rugby fives, rackets or squash. '*Five* blues? Now that I come to look at him, he seems an ostentatiously eligible young man.' Of such stuff are potential headmasters made. Another 5-blues man, and a double-international, was the Hon Alfred Lyttelton, who in due course became a King's Counsel, a Privy Counsellor and a member of the 20th-century's most famous Cabinet.

Yet neither Lyttelton nor Doggart impressed by the sheer magnificence of their appearance as did a certain bowler. Less than a decade after taking 5 South African wickets for 19 runs at Port Elizabeth in 1889, C. A. Smith was a member of George Alexander's company at the St James's Theatre where Bernard Shaw attended a performance of *As You Like It* and decided that no man could ever act as superbly as C. Aubrey Smith's Duke looked. Clearly Smith had to be an actor, the only alternative roles open being Viceroy of India or Commissioner of the Metropolitan Police. More than 40 years after his success in South Africa, he was in Hollywood – with another keen cricketer Boris Karloff, formerly W. H. Pratt of Uppingham – preparing to play against Bradman. Still a Broadway star in his late 70s, and filming with Laurence Olivier, Sir Aubrey made a point of not working during the summer if the Australians were due at Lord's.

The grand and universal manner was once more common than it is today. C. B. Fry not only finished his on-drive as though awaiting the attentions of a sculptor, played for England at the Association game and appeared in a Cup Final, set a world record for the long jump, and took a 'first' in Honour Mods, he was recognized as a moral force. He also wrote like an angel – albeit one whose style relied less on the New Testament than on Thucydides, his message reflecting the latter's 'For we are lovers of the beautiful, yet simple in our tastes, and we cultivate the mind without loss of manliness.' Almost exactly contemporary with Fry at Oxford in the 1890s were G. O. Smith, a greater footballer, and R. E. Foster, as great a batsman and expert at rackets and golf. All scored hundreds against Cambridge, in fact the only thing they could not do was sing. This was left to B. S. Foster, 4th brother in the magnificent 7. Some felt he let his family down by neglecting county cricket, though ladies disagreed with this after a visit to Daly's where the hero of many a musical, Basil Foster, made swooning quite the done thing.

No one swooned, and many slept, when H. Makepeace batted. But his record was impressive: FA Cup winners' medal, League champion's medal, 4 international 'caps', membership of Lancashire's triumphant sides of 1926–1928, a century against Australia. H. T. W. Hardinge, A. Ducat, D. C. S. Compton and, more recently, C. A. Milton attained the highest honours at these 2 games, the Compton brothers achieving their Wembley summit with Arsenal in 1950. (As Leslie was centre-half and not goalkeeper, Denis had no opportunity to put one past his brother, football's equivalent of the fraternally bestowed run out in Leslie's benefit match).

The Hon Alfred Lyttelton, celebrated in many fields, is seated to the left of his brother Edward, himself also a noted all-rounder and captain of the famous Cambridge XI of 1878 which defeated the first Australians.

In the amateur sphere, and had not chronology ordained otherwise, the vintage Pegasus sides must have gazed with rapture on the Ashton brothers – unless Hubert was playing hockey – and A. T. Barber. But with the elegant stroke-player, D. B. Carr and H. A. Pawson, as fleet on the wing as he was between wickets, and F. C. M. Alexander, Pegasus were quite good enough. In the latter they boasted a full-back who was later to captain West Indies and keep wicket, and score a hundred in the immortal 1960–61 series in Australia. Not surprisingly, the Nawab of Pataudi, senior, brought his eastern magic to the hockey field, and gained a half-blue for billiards where breaks of 238 doubtless satisfied him. J. W. H. T. Douglas was not renowned for delicacy of touch; on taking over the MCC side from an indisposed Warner in Australia, his mind was fully occupied. Or did he sometimes reflect on the Olympic Games middle-weight final of 1908, when a straight left and a right cross subdued one 'Snowy' Baker, and conclude that Baker was easier to handle than was S. F. Barnes?

Cricketers who excel in other fields are generally batsmen, bowlers tending to hibernate out of season, feet up. True R. O. Schwarz, purveyor of googlies (Bedi's pace through the air, Chandrasekhar's off the pitch), played rugby for England, as did S. M. J. Woods who, anyway, must be classed as an eccentric like his fellow Australian, R. H. Bettington. How

Arthur Milton, of Gloucestershire and the Arsenal, is the last man to have played cricket *and* association football for England.

Oxford club selectors managed to avoid squinting with self-pity in the early 1920s has never been explained, Bettington's habit being to play golf for the University one Saturday, and rugby the next. Clearly an addiction to back of the hand profundities does something to a man's mental balance, such as encouraging the study of Sanskrit in the bar parlour of the 'Goose and Grasshopper'.

Not that Bettington was as fine a golfer as L. G. Crawley – 'he could become one of *the* players in the world' wrote Bernard Darwin – who, after a double-hundred for Essex, wandered off to become English Amateur Champion and a Walker Cup stalwart. E. R. Dexter, of course, remains the great enigma, a man who appeared to have the natural talents of a Wethered or Tolley but who did not, save too briefly on the cricket field, concentrate his genius. Once, prior to an MCC tour, he girded his Conservative principles and descended on Cardiff, South-East where he outdrove his opponent, L. J. Callaghan, but found himself too often stymied on the greens: Dexter whose golf began by playing the dinner match for Cambridge.

As bowlers rarely succeed in other games, so one remarks on the relative paucity of rugby forwards among batsmen. But consider the glut of full-backs, among them M. B. Hofmeyr (once noted by the General Editor of this book, who paled beneath his tan, as a prospective opening partner for Bruce Mitchell), V. G. J. Jenkins, A. M. Jorden, H. G. Owen-Smith, G. W. Parker and T. U. Wells. Indeed it is impossible to resist choosing the non-scrummagers of an International XV from cricketers, that mighty full-back Jenkins being omitted as he would add lustre and weight to the pack: Owen-Smith; R. H. Spooner, W. Wooller, C. B. van Ryneveld, A. E. Stoddart; M. J. K. Smith, M. J. Turnbull. If Smith should withdraw on the grounds that a man who partnered O. L. Brace must find any other scrum-half monotonous, his place will go to M. P. Donnelly.

Had not C. B. Fry missed a rugby blue through injury – and the short step from Oxford to England would have been no problem for him – he might have graced the right wing. Imagine a golden autumn afternoon, players not yet in the pink and so grateful for any respite, with Fry pausing before each throw-in to debate with the linesman who, since we are considering cricketers in other fields, will be Neville Cardus. Fry on the impossibility of being bowled by an off-break, Cardus on the quiddity of Mahler – and 16 forwards happily recumbent.

The hero is he who knows immortal days. Perhaps in the present context he was an Oxford University and St Mary's Hospital welterweight boxer better known outside the ring. Aged 20 in 1929, he made 52 not out for South Africa at Lord's (off Larwood, Tate, Hammond, J. C. White and R. W. V. Robins, some of whom could bowl), causing *The Times* to hail 'a Trumper in the making'. In the next Test at Leeds he flayed the bowling for 129 in one of cricket's finest rearguard actions, the same newspaper adding 'I told you so'. Less than 7 years later, by now a doctor, he was England's full-back in 'Obolensky's match' against New Zealand at Twickenham, where he enjoyed himself by delaying his kicks to touch until he had dodged several opponents. When he returned home, a replacement was sought, someone perhaps 'an Owen-Smith in the making'. Which is a happy note on which to end, or would be but for shrill mutterings on Mount Olympus.

'Can't have it! Shan't have it! Won't have it!'

Before me stands a massive figure, hand plucking at beard.

'Look here, young feller.'

I rise, bow, and trust he is permitted to bat and bowl at both ends.

'I'm captain! The other day I took my cleaver and hit a golf ball off the summit, went two miles. There're bottles down wells all over Olympus. Just played against XXII of Hades. Ever heard of Attila? plays with a cross-bat like brother Edward. Got him caught at deep square-leg, my "bread and butter ball".'

I murmur congratulations.

'BOWLS! Who was responsible for the first bowls match between England and Scotland?'

'You, Doctor.'

'Who captained England?'

'You, Doctor.'

'Whose rink was never beaten in six matches?'

'Yours, Doctor.'

'Don't want 'em to forget me down there.'

LEFT Leonard Crawley might well have played for England in the 1930s but for the competing claims of golf.

RIGHT Ted Dexter is every bit as powerful and correct a striker of a golf as of a cricket ball, and might have attained a similar eminence in golf had he not concentrated on cricket. He was also a promising rugby footballer and rackets player.

Ducks

GERALD BRODRIBB

It is characteristic of the nature of cricket that the unpleasant business of being dismissed without scoring should be referred to as 'making a duck's egg' (a term coined in the 1860s), or more commonly 'a duck', and some clubs have extended the idea by putting on the score-board an actual likeness of a duck instead of the dismal figure 0. Even in first-class cricket ducks are by no means uncommon. In all Test Matches between England and Australia the batsman has been dismissed without scoring in about 12% of all fallen wickets. The greatest succession of consecutive ducks in first-class cricket is 6 – a doubtful distinction by A. Wright, of South Australia, in the season of 1905–06. Several batsmen (including such a good one as G. W. Parker of Gloucestershire) have failed to score in 5 consecutive innings, but perhaps the most notable example of unsuccessful batting was the performance in 1907 of G. Deyes, of Yorkshire, who in 14 consecutive innings had scores of 0, 0 and 0 not out, 1, 1 not out and 0, 0, 0 and 0, 1 not out, 0, 0, 0 and 0.

The serving of ducks is not confined to poor batsmen; even such great players as Trumper, Hammond, R. H. Spooner, Hutton (twice), W. Gunn, D. Kenyon and Ames have at one time suffered 3 consecutive ducks, Ames indeed being thrice dismissed first ball. One of Hutton's bad spells came right in the middle of his record-breaking batting of June 1949, in which month he scored 1,294 runs. J. H. Brain in 1885 was considered a batsman good enough to open the innings for the Gentlemen at Lord's, but in the same year he had an astonishing run of misfortune which brought him consecutive scores of 1 and 0, 0 and 2, 0 and 0 – a mere 3 runs in 7 innings. In 1946 the great Compton had a disastrous spell in which he suffered consecutive innings of 0, 0, 8 and 0, 1, 0.

If not-out innings are included, the greatest number of unproductive innings in succession is 10, by B. J. Griffiths (Northants) in 1974–77 (during a spell of 17 out of 19). Nine in succession have been made by J. P. Candler (Cambridge) in 1894–1895 (his whole career consisted of these 9 innings followed by a score of 8); by T. W. Goddard (Gloucester) in 1923; by A. H. S. Clark (Somerset) in 1929 (his whole career was made up of these 9 innings); by B. S. Boshier (Leicester) in 1955; by O. S. Wheatley (Glamorgan) in 1966 (during a spell of 12 in 13); and by M. W. W. Selvey (Middlesex) in 1972.

A batsman's first innings in big cricket is always a great ordeal and, of course, many batsmen have made ducks on their debut. Among those who have thus failed are such distinguished names as W. G. Grace, J. Gunn, R. Relf, Clem Hill, W. R. Hammond, C. B. Fry, F. E. Woolley, L. Hutton, D. R. Jardine, W. A. Brown, T. W. Graveney, E. R. Dexter, W. J. Stewart, M. J. K. Smith, L. N. Constantine, J. D. Robertson, N. W. D. Yardley, D. S. Sheppard, E. Weekes, N. C. O'Neill, B. C. Booth, P. F. Warner, R. W. V. Robins and E. R. T. Holmes. R. A. Sinfield, who later became a very useful batsman, actually made 7 ducks in the course of his first 11 innings in first-class cricket. One duck is depressing enough, but to score 2 in the same match is a grim fate which has befallen even the great. With the exception of Grace, Hobbs, K. S. Ranjitsinhji, Sutcliffe, Bradman and Compton, almost every other player has at one time or another 'bagged a brace', or, to use another euphemism, got a 'pair of spectacles'. One was a most notable entry: 'Shrewsbury – b Turner – 0', which twice appeared in a score-sheet of the 1887–88 season, and has been matched more recently in the entry 'Simpson – b Brown – 0' at Lord's in 1964.

Of all batsmen Hobbs was the most reliable starter, for in only 3% of his 1,315 innings in first-class cricket was he dismissed without scoring. For a great batsman to 'bag a brace' in a Test Match is very rare, but in the Test at Leeds in 1899 M. A. Noble and S. E. Gregory both did so, while Clem Hill in one of his 2 innings also made a duck. Thus 3 great batsmen in 5 innings out of 6 between them failed to produce a single run. Sometimes a team appears to be afflicted by what may be called a plague of ducks. On 5 occasions 8 batsmen have been dismissed in an innings without scoring a run between them; on one of these in 1872, when Surrey bowled out MCC for 16 runs, all the first 7 batsmen made ducks. Six years later when the Australians defeated MCC in a famous match no fewer than 16 of the 31 wickets which fell resulted in ducks. The greatest number of ducks ever produced in a match is 18, when Middlesex lost a county game to Yorkshire in 1891.

Not all scores of 0 have been entirely useless. Barlow, of Lancs, once wore down the bowling for 65 minutes before being out without scoring, and both Humphreys and Ernest Smith have played match-saving innings of 0 not out which lasted an equally long time. In 1946 J. A. Young's innings of 0 not out enabled R. W. V. Robins to put on 75 runs for the last wicket for MCC v Yorkshire; Robins made all 75 runs while Young kept his end up. R. S. Machin, of Cambridge University, once went in last and helped in a last-wicket stand of 69 without himself scoring a run. T. G. Evans in the 1946–7 Adelaide Test batted defensively for 95 minutes before opening his score.

There are various candidates for the doubtful honour of

O. S. Wheatley, an admirable bowler for Cambridge and Glamorgan, in 1966 made 9 ducks in a row, and 12 out of 13.

'worst-ever' batsman, among them J. C. Shaw, who in all the 109 innings which he played for Notts reached double figures only once. In the course of consecutive innings played for Northants between 1925 and 1927 the fast bowler, E. W. Clark, once batted 65 times without reaching double figures. His batting figures for 1926 read: 45 – 12 – 74 – 8 – 2·05. A similar absence of batting form was once showed by E. Hollies, whose top score in the 42 innings he played in 1946 was only 5 not out. Hollies belongs to that distinguished band of cricketers who in the course of their first-class career have captured a greater number of wickets than they have made runs. Among these are W. E. Bowes, C. S. Marriott, H. D. Read, L. Fleetwood-Smith and F. Morley.

It is with no sense of ridicule that these unsuccessful batsmen are mentioned; they have all won considerable distinction in other spheres of the game. Their batting misfortunes are probably easier to bear than the failures of the great, from whom so much is always expected. Let them remember how Hendren and Mead, the heaviest scorers of 1923, made scores of 0 & 0 and 0 & 1 in the Test Trial of that year, and how Gibbons of Worcestershire in 1939 made 2 not-out centuries in one match, and then 2 ducks in the next one.

Gentlemen v Players

GEOFFREY MOORHOUSE

By the time the last contest between first-class amateur and professional cricketers took place in 1962, many people had long concluded that the Gentlemen v Players match was an anachronism, if not a titular affront to those who earned their living by playing the game. That the fixture spanned 157 years was mainly due to cricket's notable (and blessed) regard for its own traditions, its reluctance to change merely for the sake of contemporary appearances. It can be argued that few genuine first-class amateurs – men who received neither direct nor indirect financial reward for playing cricket – survived the Second World War outside schoolmasters and the university teams though a handful certainly remained through the 1950s including such as Robins, Insole, George Mann, Palmer, Warr and Clark (all of whom, as it happens, have since been prominent in the councils of cricket). To that extent the disappearance of Gents v Players from the fixture list was inescapable.

Yet a number of the postwar matches between the 2 sides were among the most vivid games of cricket played in those years, and they added much to the enjoyment of the English season. They were worthy reminders of the period, which stretched for more than half-a-century before Test matches occurred, when Gentlemen v Players enabled Englishmen to see the best available cricketers pitting themselves against each other in one match. Apart from anything else, the fixture exhibited the specifically amateur ingredient of cricket, a lightness that professionalism can rarely afford to the same degree. A certain amount of humbug went with it at times, latterly identified as 'shamateurism', and Gents v Players by definition always embodied a number of caste marks that had become progressively unacceptable to the nation at large. None the less the genuine amateur gifts to the game have been sorely missed since the genuine amateur disappeared.

Gentlemen v Players was essentially an English cricketing occasion, although a similar match was played in Philadelphia for many years after 1885, and Melbourne had seen a short series with the same title in the 1860s before Australians decided that it was not to the colonial taste. The first of all such games, however, was played for 3 days in July 1806 on Thomas Lord's first ground in Dorset Square, at a time when betting was as much a part of cricket organization as sponsorship has become today. In order to produce reasonable odds for this match, the Gentlemen were fortified by the loan of 2 professionals, the Surrey all-rounder William Lambert and Hambledon's illustrious 'Silver Billy' Beldham, and it was largely their performance that caused the Players' defeat by an innings. Lambert's skill was also instrumental in winning the return match by 82 runs a fortnight later, though scores of 58 and 38 came from the bat of the Rev Lord Frederick Beauclerk, descendent of Charles II's and Nell Gwynn, who estimated that he made 600 guineas a year from his cricket yet described the game as one 'unalloyed by love of lucre and mean jealousies.'

Thirteen years passed before the contest was renewed, this time on Lord's present ground, where the Players won easily, though again lending men to the opposition. Out of the first half-dozen encounters, the Gentlemen won 4 times, but for 19 years after 1823 they were outclassed by the Players in spite of various devices to supplement their amateur capacities. A rare victory to the Gentlemen of 1829 was mostly the work of William Lillywhite's professional round-arm bowling, which more frequently demolished them when the Sussex man appeared for the Players. Sometimes the Gentlemen were allowed as many as 17 cricketers, while their opponents were confined to 11. Once, in 1837, they were permitted to defend conventional wickets while the Players had to bat in front of 4 stumps measuring 36 inches by 12 inches overall. They still lost that notorious 'Barndoor Match' (otherwise known as Ward's Folly) by an innings. The fixture, in short, had become such a nonsense by 1841 that the MCC disowned it and it was saved only by means of a public subscription.

W. G. Grace's years of greatness were the only ones in the long history of Gentlemen v Players when the advantage lay with the former. This perfect defensive back-stroke shows one facet of his armoury.

In 1934 this Gentlemen's side, all but 2 of them Test cricketers, beat the Players at Lord's by 7 wickets, their first victory since 1914. Back row: W. H. V. Levett, E. R. T. Holmes, A. Melville, F. R. Brown, J. H. Human and A. D. Baxter; front row: B. H. Valentine, C. F. Walters, R. E. S. Wyatt (captain), G. O. Allen and M. J. Turnbull.

E. Hendren led the Players in this match. Next to him (from the right) are: M. Leyland, W. R. Hammond, J. O'Connor, A. Mitchell, H. Verity, M. S. Nichols and J. Smith. Unseen are H. Sutcliffe, T. B. Mitchell and L. E. G. Ames.

Alfred Mynn, the Lion of Kent, was responsible for restoring amateur fortunes on the field. The Gentlemen won in 1842 and 1843, with Mynn's 46 runs and 9 wickets in one match, followed by 47 runs and 8 wickets in the other. More victories came in that decade and the fine left-hand batting of Nicholas Wanostrocht, Blackheath schoolmaster and author of the classic manual *Felix on the Bat*, had much to do with some of them, aided by the stonewalling of Arthur Haygarth, another of cricket's great bookmen. For the Players, William Clarke of Nottingham, creator of the Trent Bridge ground and leader of the touring 'All England XI', bowled strongly, and the professionals at this time also included the likes of John Wisden, Fuller Pilch and George Parr. From 1854 to 1864 the Gentlemen failed to win a single match, even though the Lord's game was often augmented from 1857 by a second contest at the Oval, which lasted until 1934 (Scarborough was to be another venue from 1885 to 1962, and there were occasional sallies in Brighton, Hastings, Bournemouth, Folkestone, Canterbury and Prince's ground in Chelsea). Then 1865 came, and with it the start of a long amateur supremacy inseparable from the name of W. G. Grace.

He was only 16 years old when he joined his elder brother E.M., 'the Coroner', in the 1865 fixtures, taking 7 wickets in the Oval match and making 34 as an opener in the 2nd innings at Lord's. These were but a modest foretaste of what was to come. As H. S. Altham wrote, 'Nothing in all his monumental history is more remarkable than the stark figures which illustrate W.G.'s decisive impact on the Gentlemen v Players match.' From the moment he began to appear in the lists, the Players won at Lord's only twice before 1885, and only 3 times in 16 games played during that period at the Oval or at Prince's. Grace scored a total of 6,008 runs for the Gentlemen, more than twice as many as any other batsman on either side; and he took 276 wickets, when only 3 other bowlers in the history of the contest even reached 100. He made 15 centuries against the Players, including 134 not out on a dreadful Lord's pitch in 1868, when the next highest score in the match was 29 and Grace himself took 10 wickets for 81. He was the only man who twice made a double-hundred in these matches. On his 85th and last appearance for the Gentlemen in 1906, which was also his 58th birthday, he was top scorer for his side with 74 runs at the Oval. On his last appearance in the Lord's match, in 1899, he had scored 78. C. B. Fry made a hundred in that game and the Gentlemen won it by an innings and 59 runs after some remarkable – and anachronistic – under-arm lob bowling by D. L. A. Jephson (Cambridge and Surrey), who took 6 for 21 in the Players' first innings.

The dominance of Grace from the mid-1860s until almost the end of the century, which made the match the classic of the English season, should not obscure the fact that there were fine performances by other men on both sides. If George Lohmann and Johnny Briggs won the match for the Players by their bowling in 1889, S. M. J. Woods and F. S. Jackson did the same to secure an innings victory for the Gentlemen in 1894, by bowling unchanged throughout the match. The fixture now illustrated all the appeal of cricket's Golden Age, and the fine talents available to both sides caused results to fluctuate more than at any other period. In the drawn game at Lord's in 1903, Fry hit 232 not out and joined Archie MacLaren in an unbroken partnership of 309 in just under 3 hours. Next year the Gents won by 2 wickets, in spite of Leicestershire's J. H. King scoring 2 hundreds for the Players to 1 from Ranjitsinhji for the amateurs. In 1906 the Gentlemen triumphed again, though Arthur Fielder of Kent took all 10 of their first innings wickets. The 1909 match went to the Players, with Sydney Barnes taking 8 for 55. Two years later, at Lord's, the Gentlemen won a game notable for being the last cricket match Tom Hayward played in and the first G v P in which Jack Hobbs scored a hundred – Hobbs going on, in the 1925 match at Scarborough, to hit 266 not out, the highest score ever made in Gents v Players. The Gentlemen were to have a thin time in results when the Golden Age passed, though often holding their own in a growing abundance of draws. Duleepsinhji scored a hundred in each innings in 1930 off the googlies of 'Tich' Freeman, who was then the terror of the counties. By 1937 the talk was all of Leslie Ames dismissing 8 amateur batsmen from behind the stumps, which equalled the record of Warwickshire's Lilley in the 1904 match. Hammond captained the victorious Players in Ames's year; 12 months later, having turned amateur, he led the Gentlemen to an equally decisive win thanks to Kenneth Farnes's fast bowling and an astonishing 175 by H. T. Bartlett.

It says much for the quality of cricket seen in modern times between the Gentlemen and Players, as well as for the hold the fixture maintained on the public imagination, that great crowds rolled up to Lord's for the event for several years after the Second World War. Some 28,000 watched the 1948 contest (when a Hutton century led to a win for the Players), which may be compared with the 33,000 who saw the 1904 match. Although the weight of professional experience told more and more as the 20th century advanced – indeed, the Gentlemen recorded only 4 victories in all the matches played at Lord's after the First War – the games after 1945 were often stirringly fought. In 1950 Hollies and Wright, last men in for the Players, were still defying the bowlers when time ran out, after C. J. Knott had done the hat-trick for the Gentlemen. In 1957 Trueman and Hollies (again) held on for the professionals when the scent of an amateur victory was in the air. In 1960, with 8 wickets down, Moss was going for the winning run off the last ball of the match when Dexter threw him out from long-on. Of the Players' 8 postwar victories, none was more thrilling than that of 1952, when Laker bowled Marlar with the first ball of the last over, only 2 runs short of an amateur success. Within a few years the long agonizing over amateur and professional status would begin, eventually resolved by the Advisory County Cricket Committee on 26 November 1962.

Gentlemen v Players was over, and the final tally of the principal match results was this: of 137 games at Lord's, Gentlemen won 41, Players 68, and 28 were drawn; of 72 games at the Oval, Gentlemen won 16, Players 34, 21 were drawn, and the match of 1883 was tied; of 39 matches at Scarborough, Gentlemen won 4, Players won 15, and 20 were drawn.

In the very last encounter at Lord's in 1962, the 2 sides were captained by (in the usage of the event) Mr E. R. Dexter and F. S. Trueman, and the match ended in a rain-swept draw. But the last words on it must be those of H. S. Altham.

On the first day the Rev D. S. Sheppard, returning to cricket after a break of some years, played an innings of 112 sound and resolute enough to ensure his place for Australia, and with Dexter and M. J. K. Smith helping him in partnerships of over 90 each, the Gentlemen's total was 323. Bailey made full use of a heavy atmosphere on the second day to take 6 for 58 and only some good hitting by Trueman and Titmus got the Players out of serious trouble and within 63 of their enemy. The third morning was dominated by an impressive century by Prideaux, which enabled Dexter to declare, setting the Players 236 to get in 3 hours. Enterprising and attractive play by J. H. Edrich, Parfitt and Graveney carried them well ahead of the clock, but then the clouds opened, and Gentlemen and Players left the field at Lord's together for the last time.

The Christopher Morris Library Haverford USA

E. ROTAN SARGENT

The C. Christopher Morris Cricket Library and Collection is housed in its own wing and exhibition room adjoining Haverford College's Library in Haverford, Pennsylvania. It was officially opened in March 1969, after one of America's most distinguished cricketers, Dr John A. Lester, had proposed in 1964 that a 'cricket alcove' be planned in the then expanding College library. Mr Morris, one of Philadelphia's and America's greatest all-round cricketers, and others acted upon the suggestion and the present facility is the result.

During its formative stages the enterprise was administered by a committee composed chiefly of Haverford College cricketers and chaired by Professor Howard Comfort, a former Haverford cricket captain. Subsequently the management passed to a more inclusive C. C. Morris Cricket Library Association formed in 1970 and separate from the College. The present Association is a non-profit organization with virtually world-wide membership.

A nucleus of cricket literature already existed in the College library but this has now been greatly expanded from many other sources, especially by the donation of Christy Morris's own extensive cricket library. There are approximately 1,500 volumes on the shelves and several hundred pamphlets, treatises, letters, score cards, etc., contained in catalogued box files. Outstanding items include a complete set of *Wisden's Cricketers' Almanack* (1864 to date) and 2 complete sets of *The American Cricketer* (1877 to 1929). With cataloguing of its original acquisitions completed, the Association has continued to add a substantial number of volumes, together with many items of cricket memorabilia, to its shelves and display cases. It is the Association's intent to make the collection as complete a record as possible of the story of cricket in the United States and Canada. As Philadelphia has often been referred to as 'America's nursery of cricket', it is not surprising that the local area is the best documented, but the larger intention is the ultimate goal. In addition, the collection includes considerable material from all parts of the cricketing world.

The Library and Collection also includes memorabilia of numerous cricketers, such as scrapbooks kept by Philadelphians on their various tours of England in the late 19th and early 20th centuries; trophies presented to Dr Lester and the great bowler, J. Barton King, by Prince Ranjitsinhji; a bat presented by W. G. Grace to G. L. Jessop and by him to the Merion Cricket Club in 1897, after he had made 1,541 runs with it in only 9 innings; the bat with which Christy Morris himself at the age of 20 contributed 164 runs to a handsome victory over Notts at Trent Bridge; and a number of blazers and club ties. There are also 2 holograph letters from Dr Grace; a number of prints and paintings; petit point belts such as young ladies of the last century made for their favourite cricketers; autographed cricket balls, cups, medals, and many other trophies.

A feature of the Library's memorabilia is the very large collection of photographs of American cricket teams and of teams which have toured the USA from abroad. These pictures date from Civil War days to the present. Within its scope, the Morris Library and Collection is unique in North America and, with the exception of the museum at Lord's, perhaps in the world.

In keeping with the terms of its charter, the association has been active in the promotion of the game particularly in the Philadelphia area, providing publicity and other services in connection with visiting teams on tour and furthering interest in the sport among younger people in clubs and schools in the vicinity. The Library and Collection is open to the public by application to the circulation desk of the Haverford College Library at any time when the latter is open. At present the administrative secretary is in the room on Monday, Wednesday and Friday afternoons, 1.00 pm to 4.00 pm. Access at other times for research purposes is also available by contacting the College Library which will make an appointment with the Curator (Mr E. R. Sargent).

The cricket library at Haverford College, USA, was set up as a memorial to one of the best Philadelpian cricketers, Christy Morris.

Periodicals

IRVING ROSENWATER

The Cricketer

Founded in April 1921, by Sir (then Mr) Pelham Warner on his retirement from the first-class game, *The Cricketer* has enjoyed an unbroken existence approaching 60 years. During this period it has established itself as the premier cricket journal. Dignified and authoritative in style, it has sought to be primarily a journal of record, and contains a virtual history of the game over the period it covers. Especially valuable has been its attention to minor – particularly school and club – cricket, and the widespread coverage it has afforded the game abroad. In the late 1920s A. W. T. Langford joined 'Plum' Warner as his assistant editor and from the early war period he became effectual editor, continuing his close association with the paper until he retired in the autumn of 1966. Up to the Second World War, the normal publishing programme consisted of weekly issues in the summer with a Winter and Spring Annual; today the journal is published monthly throughout the year, the April and November issues taking the form of the Spring and Winter Annuals respectively. Its contributors have included many of the most eminent names in the world of cricket.

From the May 1973 issue, *The Cricketer* – by then with B. G. Brocklehurst, the former Somerset captain, as managing director, and E. W. Swanton as editorial director (posts still held by both) – incorporated *Playfair Cricket Monthly* without sacrificing its traditional character; and thenceforth advanced, by the end of the 1970s, to the highest circulation in its history.

B. G. Brocklehurst, managing director of *The Cricketer*, assists Comtesse Lecointre, of Moët & Chandon to draw lucky tickets at a *Cricketer* Cup Final. Behind her is C. G. A. Paris, then President of MCC.

In the summer of 1973 a publishing offshoot was launched – *The Cricketer Quarterly*, edited, as it still is, by Gordon Ross, and presenting the facts and figures of contemporary cricket in all parts of the world. As a factual adjunct to *The Cricketer* itself, it has proved extremely popular (even though, within less than 3 years, it was obliged to double its cover price).

The Cricketer launched The *Cricketer* Cup for invited Old Boy teams in 1967; the number doubled 2 years later to 32. It has also organized, from its first year in 1972, the Haig – since 1979, the Samuel Whitbread – Village Cricket Championship, now comprising some 750 village teams, and which sees its final at the end of the season at Lord's.

Playfair

Playfair is the distinctive name applied to a series of sporting publications which have arisen in England since the Second World War. In cricket, the *Playfair* legend is associated with a cricket annual, first published in 1948. In its old, octavo style, the first 6 issues (1948–1953) were edited by Peter West, and the last 9 (1954–1962) by Gordon Ross.

It assumed a fresh format in 1963 on coming under the aegis of the Dickens Press, with Gordon Ross continuing as editor from that time to the present day. Since 1975 the annual has been sponsored by Gillette Industries Limited. In May 1960, the *Playfair Cricket Monthly* was founded and served as a record of the game under the editorship of Gordon Ross and, until his death in 1962, Roy Webber. It ceased publication after the April 1973 issue and was incorporated in *The Cricketer*.

Wisden Cricket Monthly

Wisden Cricket Monthly began publication in 1979 under the imprint of Wisden Cricket Magazines Ltd. Like the former *Playfair Cricket Monthly* it concentrated on Test and first-class cricket. It has no connexion, other than the trade-name leased from the copyright owners, with the famous *Almanack*.

Reporting

GERALD PAWLE

More than 40 years ago R. C. Robertson-Glasgow, sent to cover Surrey's match against the New Zealanders for the *Morning Post*, began by observing that since there were 2 widely divergent types of reader he would do his best to satisfy both. He therefore split his contribution into 2 sections. Report Number One was severely factual, recording that persistent rain overnight and during the morning had prevented play on the final day, the game being abandoned as a draw. Report Number Two amply compensated his readers:

> Having twice been carried past his station on the Underground Railway – on the first occasion because the train did not stop, and on the second owing to the density of passengers – your Correspondent, whose umbrella had been broken in the general push, arrived wet at the Oval to find one spectator in the pavilion consulting the tape machine.

He met A. Gover, the Surrey fast bowler, who expressed the view that even if Surrey, who led by a bare 43 runs with four men out, should continue to fare indifferently he (A. Gover) felt able and inclined to bowl out New Zealand at moderate cost.

Your Correspondent then conversed with the umpires, Buswell and Lee, who stated that this was no day for the crowds sight-seeing in London. Also with A. Peach, coach to the Surrey club, who recalled notable matches between Surrey and Somerset. Mr Page, captain of the New Zealand team, made some interesting remarks on bowling round the wicket with off-breaks. By this time the rain had, if anything, increased and luncheon was served. Soon after, the company dispersed.

Nowadays, when only Senior Citizens recall the *Morning Post* and the high quality of its cricket coverage under its scholarly Sports Editor, T. K. Hodder, I fear that this charming vignette would be considered woefully irrelevant, but 'Crusoe's' engaging flight of fancy is certainly relevant to the task of surveying Cricket Reporting in general. In this wider field I am uneasily aware that there are probably several kinds of reader to be considered, if not necessarily placated.

Some will wait hopefully for a discursive historical study of the game and its chroniclers since the birth of the 18th century. They may well advance the view that anyone, poet or scribbler in prose, who mentioned cricket in a published work should be taken into account in tracking down the first reporter of all. So without conviction I record the suggestion of G. D. Martineau that one William Goldwin, born in 1682, has some claim as the progenitor of all of us in the Press Box today. He is hardly a convincing candidate, however, for his sole contribution which I can trace was not only composed entirely in Latin verse but failed to identify either the match or any of the players. Indeed, in the Dark Ages of cricket it was largely left to minor poets to sing its praises, and not until midway through the nineteenth century do we find the prototype of the genuine newspaper reporter.

Perhaps this is hardly surprising, for even at Lord's there was no accommodation for the Press until a Grand Stand was built in 1868. Prior to this Mr W. H. Knight, who, according to Sir Pelham Warner was 'the only recognized newspaper representative' had to stand all day in the shrubbery at the end of the Pavilion. He had no scoreboard or cards to assist him; every run had to be recorded in his own scorebook.

The painstaking Mr Knight, employed by *Bell's Life*, forerunner of the *Sporting Chronicle*, is surely, a more convincing father figure of the modern cricket correspondent than any of the troubadours who described the game in verse 150 years earlier. His special accreditation at Lords suggests that he was recognized as a genuine professional journalist providing contemporary reports of the day's play, and since I am dealing with the development of newspaper coverage, as distinct from the more leisurely forms of writing on the game in books and periodicals, I shall leave these broader acres in the vast field of cricket literature to better qualified assessors.

Throughout the Victorian and Edwardian era newspaper reports of cricket matches, mainly anonymous, lacked style, shape, and character. They also lacked the insight and analytical quality which marked the new generation of correspondents who came to the fore after the first World War. Before that many reports were padded out with weird metaphor and a florid jargon which reads strangely today. Fielders 'chased the crimson rambler to the confines' and 'the willow' was wielded with tiresome repetition. Small wonder that 'journalese' was scornfully coined to chide such solecisms.

The First World War accelerated the social revolution which has been gathering momentum ever since. From the 1920s fewer Gentlemen appeared on the cricket fields of England, but more gentlemen appeared in the Press Box, and because men like Warner, Robertson-Glasgow and C. B. Fry had themselves been fine players their informed criticism raised the general standard of reporting.

Undoubtedly, however, the most significant newcomer of all was Neville Cardus, who between 1920 and 1939 wrote nearly two million words for the *Manchester Guardian* under the *nom de plume* of 'Cricketer'. G. D. Martineau has rightly said that the reports of Cardus influenced cricket writing all over the world as no journalism had done before. By temperament and self-education a music critic, who regarded cricket purely as a means to a musical end, this man of extraordinary talents had at least a cricket genesis, taking a lowly job at Shrewsbury School before the 1914–18 war as assistant coach and groundsman to pay for his musical education. But he arrived in the cricket press box almost by accident, when the *Guardian* sent him to spend a summer at Old Trafford following a breakdown in health.

In less than a year his name was made, for he wrote like a dream, getting right away from slavish recording of facts and figures. Combining wit and imagery with keen observation of character and human foibles he raised daily reporting to a literary art form of a quality not hitherto attempted in sporting journalism. His favourite performers sprang to vivid life. Of Emmott Robinson, the perky, bow-legged Yorkshireman, he wrote:

Emmott cherished the new ball clearly; he would carry it between overs in person to the next bowler needing it after himself; and he would contain it in the palms of his hands shaped like a sacred chalice.

The method of another Yorkshireman, the great Wilfred Rhodes, he described with acute perception:

Flight was his secret, flight and the curving line, now higher, now lower, tempting, inimical; every ball like every other ball, yet somehow unlike; each over in collusion with the others, part of a plot. Every ball a decoy, a spy sent out to get the lie of the land; some balls simple, some complex . . . and one of them – ah! which? – the master ball.

Grant Richards, his first publisher, described Cardus as 'an austere and sensitive figure' and this he remained. Music was always his first love but, he once conceded, 'I have met far more interesting characters than among musicians of England', and he did more than anyone else to make them interesting to the lay reader.

Robertson-Glasgow, too, had style and wit, and an engaging sense of the ridiculous which made him such a hilarious conversationalist; his reports of the dullest proceedings were a recurring delight.

In an entirely different way to Cardus and 'Crusoe' C. B. Fry created a minor revolution of his own, bringing to his commentaries for the *Evening Standard* a glorious inconsequentiality which won him an entirely individual following. Scholar and athlete extraordinary, proconsul, sailor, and prodigious talker, Fry came to journalism late in life, and blandly ignoring accepted technique he used his daily platform to blend shrewd comment on the play with startling digressions and often obscure classical allusions. His presence in any press box guaranteed a day of unique theatrical entertainment.

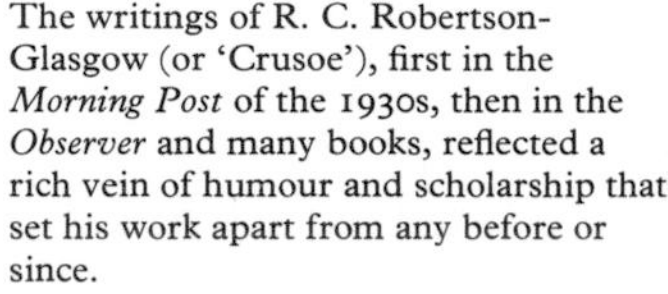

The writings of R. C. Robertson-Glasgow (or 'Crusoe'), first in the *Morning Post* of the 1930s, then in the *Observer* and many books, reflected a rich vein of humour and scholarship that set his work apart from any before or since.

The actual mechanics of transmitting a cricket reporter's 'copy' to his newspaper have become much more complicated during my lifetime. When I joined one of the great provincial dailies in 1931 I was shown the pigeon loft on the roof where the reports of the paper's august cricket correspondent, Mr A. W. Pullin ('Old Ebor') used to arrive after the bird had been launched from one of Yorkshire's grounds. For the vast Yorkshire cricketing public Old Ebor wrote at inordinate length, unhampered by any consideration of literary style – he was one of the severely factual school – and it amazed me how any pigeon ever struggled into the air when shackled to one of his weighty effusions.

By the time I arrived in Leeds the pigeons had been banished by the postal telegraph and telephone, but in most other respects our days were probably just as arduous as Old Ebor's. Writers from the national papers might arrive late at the ground, weave their elegant essays, and depart early, but most of the large Yorkshire press party who travelled with the team from May to September had to face a very different task.

First they had to turn out a lengthy report for their evening paper, dictated every hour or so up to tea. After completing at least a column of this running commentary it was time to turn to a more demanding exercise. With play still in progress one was expected to write a further column and a half of detached and critical comment for the morning paper and a different, far more critical, readership.

In one respect we were luckier in those days. We were not personally responsible for the transmission of our 'copy', for perched at the back of the Press Box, like sparrows on a branch with beaks wide open, were the messengers, waiting to pounce and bear off the news of another century by Holmes, another bowling feat by Verity, to the nearest telephone.

When play ended for the day at, say, Bramall Lane, they would snatch my morning paper story, enclose it in a large blue envelope labelled 'NEWS INTELLIGENCE. NOT TO BE DELAYED' and cycle to the railway station where they handed it to the guard of the Leeds train. If Yorkshire were playing on some remote foreign ground like Hove or Bristol one's report was typed on a Press Telegram form, franked by a yellow pass guaranteeing deferred payment, and entrusted to the General Post Office. The GPO rarely let us down. Occasionally folio 10 might reach the office before folio 2, but a provincial morning paper went to press so late in those days that there was always time in hand. Nowadays no Union would allow a staff writer to produce 2 different reports for his employer for the same salary. It was, however, a form of slavery which I, for one, thoroughly enjoyed.

When, a war and 30 years later, I returned unexpectedly to cricket writing I encountered different problems altogether. To my dismay the sturdy race of telephonist-messengers, with their flat caps and bicycle clips, had vanished without trace. In the brave new world nobody was anxious to do a day's work of this kind for one pound. At 3.30 on my first afternoon I dialled Fleet Street. 'Pawle at Taunton – Yorkshire v Somerset', I said defensively. There was an ominous pause. 'Can you ring back in half an hour?', replied a brisk, businesslike voice; 'we haven't quite worked it out. Space is a bit tight'. This seemed odd. No one on the *Yorkshire Post* had ever told my messenger that space was tight. They merely cleared the decks by spiking anything which might have come in about Association Football, Bowls, or Speedway Racing; they were not considered gentlemanly pursuits, anyway.

When I rang back the anonymous Voice issued a stream of meaningless instructions. 'You'd better Top and Tail it today. Can you give us 3-7-2? And don't forget to let Manchester have it. Oh, and by the way, we'd better have a check call, just in case.'

It transpired that my new masters wished me to supply them with the middle of my report first, dictating precisely 245 words at the tea interval. At the close of play they wanted a general introduction of 105 words, followed by a further 70 which had to cover the last 2½ hours of play. I then had to telephone the Top and Tail to Manchester where a different staff fashioned their own headlines and allocations of space for the Northern editions.

Reporting in Australia: two great Australian spinners – Clarrie Grimmett and Bill O'Reilly.

Eventually I finished with London and turned to Manchester where I found to my alarm that I was dictating to a woman, but not only did she seem to know the names and initials of every player, and every position on the field; she even knew about Check Calls. 'You just ring up to see if they've lost your report', she explained consolingly. When, an hour later, I rang London I was asked if I had enjoyed my day. 'It's a bit different since I last did this sort of thing', I ventured. 'I never had to write a report backwards for the *Yorkshire Post*. They didn't go in for this Topping and Tailing . . .'

'Yes, I expect things have changed a bit since Lord Hawke's day' said the Sports Editor unfeelingly. 'You'll get used to it, though . . .'

Writers reminiscing about their youth habitually claim that there are few 'characters' left, few glorious eccentrics, and I must admit that the modern cricket press box has no one quite like Fry, Robertson-Glasgow or 'Beau' Vincent of *The Times* who once announced during a Test Match at Manchester that as the cricket was unbearably dull he proposed to return temporarily to London to present his expense sheet to the cashier. There was much gaiety and laughter in those days. Now frivolity is curbed by the new, statistical school of cricket writers, grimly intent on recording every mathematical triviality and alarming people like me by suggestions that we might have missed some peculiar landmark like Boycott's 7,000th boundary, or Underwood's 3,500th maiden over. The random reflections of a now part-time observer of the cricket scene professionally should not, however, obscure the positive and beneficial developments which have taken place in cricket reporting since the last war.

The public following of cricket today is far larger than it has ever been, and the game's popularity has been immensely increased by both press and radio. In spite of unrelenting pressure on space, which particularly affects the popular press, quality papers like *The Times*, *Daily Telegraph* and *Guardian* have continued to cover cricket responsibly and well, and new reputations have been made. In the immediate postwar decade writers like Ian Peebles and Alan Ross brought to readers of *The Sunday Times* and *Observer* respectively the style, wit and charm of 'Crusoe's' younger days. In the *Daily Telegraph*, and in his masterly summings up on the television screen, E. W. Swanton earned a unique repute for balanced judgment,

In 1958–59 the English press entourage was considerably larger than the MCC team. This group of 18 lacks, among others, several famous players and their 'ghosts'. Back row: J. H. Wardle, John Woodcock, Charles Fortune, Brian Chapman, Ian Peebles, Charles Bray, Alex Bannister, John Clarke and Frank Rostron; middle row: Bill Bowes, Crawford White, John Kay, L. N. Bailey, E. W. Swanton and Alec Bedser; in front: R. A. Roberts, Denys Rowbotham and Harry Gee.

shrewd insight into technique and tactics, and an encyclopaedic knowledge of every aspect of the game. This he put to good use in his weekly commentary for the newspaper which has covered cricket more widely than any in Britain.

Though it may be invidious to single out correspondents still writing regularly, the name of John Woodcock deserves recording for the consistently sound judgment which he employs in the service of *The Times*. In the same way exception should also be made for John Arlott, doyen of radio commentators, prolific cricket historian, and the *Guardian*'s chief cricket writer to boot.

It is an interesting commentary on the increased public interest to reflect that only 2 journalists accompanied D. R. Jardine's team to Australia in the 1930s. One, Bruce Harris of the *Evening Standard*, was primarily a lawn-tennis writer; his only Fleet Street companion was sent out to ghost the daily reports of Jack Hobbs. Two decades later the English press party was larger than the MCC team itself, and although modern social trends have encouraged a shift of emphasis from straightforward sports reporting towards concentration on 'the news angle' in the popular dailies, many of the latter are well served by journalists with a genuine dedication to cricket, a notable example being the late Clive Taylor, of the *Sun*.

The fundamental nature of the game, its subtleties, and its demands on skill, perseverance, and an equable temperament set it apart from contests which place a premium on strength and stamina, crowd-provoking theatricalism, and all too often the exaltation of the individual to an absurd degree. The game of cricket has its own distinctive pattern and a constantly changing rhythm which holds its own fascination. Economic pressures have forced changes, some of which make a mockery of basic principles in batting, bowling, and intelligent field-placing to accommodate the one day 40-over extravaganzas which have so greatly eased the County Treasurers' burden. In consequence it is difficult to write a worthwhile account of the Sunday afternoon league match where the result is greater than the game or any of its players, and artistry and intelligence are squandered in the quest for action at all costs.

Being an adaptable fellow the cricket writer today takes the rough with the smooth. Happily there will always be other games to cover when artistry can take precedence over mere frenetic endeavour. Admittedly modern production problems often complicate his task, but he accepts the curbs on space and the constant indignities of inaccurate typesetting with commendable philosophy. And so he should, for he still has one of the most pleasant duties in the world.

Scarborough Festival

T. N. PEARCE

When a cricket enthusiast says 'See you at Scarborough' he means one thing and one thing only – that he is going to the Scarborough Festival and he expects to see you there. The idea of promoting a week of first-class cricket in Scarborough was first considered in 1872 when several cricketers on holiday in the town suggested to Robert Baker, the secretary of the Scarborough Cricket Club, that they should raise a side to play the local club. Baker was quickly impressed with the possibilities of the idea, so together with the help of Lord Londesborough, and after 3 years of negotiations, he brought his cherished scheme to fruition and the first Festival games were played in 1876.

Since those early days the character of the Festival has shown many changes so far as players and ground facilities are concerned. In the first Festival the takings amounted to about £30 but in recent years these have reached over £10,000. All the profits have been ploughed back into the amenities of the ground, which is now one of the best equipped in the country and has a perfect playing surface. But for all the changes and improvements that have taken place on the ground, with its President's tent, Yorkshire County Cricket Club tent and the Mayor's tent, together with the band, there still exists the same charm that brings spectators from all over the country to Scarborough year after year.

C. I. ('Buns') Thornton was the father of the Festival, having played for the Scarborough Cricket Club before the Festival was born. Thornton played for Eton, Cambridge University, Kent and Middlesex and was well known as a terrific hitter. As an undergraduate he hit a ball over the pavilion at Lord's – not the present one – and for many years held the distinction of being the only man to have cleared the roofs of the houses to the south of the Scarborough ground and landed the ball in Trafalgar Square. This feat was equalled in 1945 by C. Pepper of the Australian Forces XI at the expense of Eric Hollies. It is something which to anybody standing at the wicket appears absolutely impossible. On his retirement from active association with the Festival, Thornton recommended as his successor H. D. G. ('Shrimp') Leveson Gower, under whose guidance the Festival went from strength to strength.

In 1950 Leveson Gower was invited to be President of the Festival and he then handed over to the writer the duties of Festival Teams organizer. In recognition of their services to the town and to cricket all three have been honoured with the Freedom of the Borough of Scarborough. The President of the club and of the Festival is elected annually, and the club can boast as distinguished a list of Presidents as any in the country. They include HRH The Duke of Edinburgh, the Duke of Norfolk, Lord Derwent, Lord Grimthorpe, the Earl of Halifax, the Earl of Londesborough, Lord Hawke and Viscount Downe besides many others whose names are famous in cricket and Yorkshire circles. There have, of course, been some wonderful and outstanding performances in the Festivals. Undoubtedly its popularity stems from the fact that during the years all the greatest players of their day have played there, and have been pleased to return and play again whenever possible. These players, unhampered by the restrictions of playing for points or Ashes, have been and are willing to display their great ability to the obvious enjoyment of themselves and the spectators.

Practically all the principal touring teams to visit this country have played in the Festival, as well as most of the best England cricketers during the years.

Unfortunately, owing to the reorganization of the first-class county programme and the extension of the Sunday League matches into September it became very difficult to arrange suitable matches. However this has been largely overcome by some generous sponsorship in the form of the Fenner Trophy originated in 1971 by S. B. Hainsworth, President of J. H. Fenner Ltd of Hull and a great supporter of cricket. This competition consists of 3 knock-out one-day matches spread over 3 days involving 4 of the leading counties for a trophy and substantial prize money.

The ground authorities make every effort to see that as much cricket as possible is presented to the public, and no bowler can nowadays hope to find a sticky wicket during the Festival. All the wickets for the Festival are covered whenever possible from the middle of August, every night during the Festival, and at any time during the match when it rains. The covers, which are quite infallible, take the ground staff nearly 3 hours to erect for the complete overnight covering and when in position resemble a marquee. Spectators are allowed on the ground during the lunch and tea intervals, and so many old acquaintances meet at these times that it is most unusual to be able to clear the ground in time for cricket to restart punctually. As seats are bookable there are numerous parties who book identical seats year after year, and always ensure from the secretary that other parties of friends have as usual booked the seats adjoining and around them. Anyone who has not been to the Scarborough Festival has missed one of the most enjoyable institutions in the cricket year.

C. I. Thornton (known as 'Buns') was the father of the Scarborough Festival, and in his own right a great hitter. Surrounding him are the team he chose to play the South Africans there in 1924: back row: C. W. L. Parker, P. Holmes, A. Kennedy, A. P. F. Chapman, A. Dolphin, E. Tyldesley and G. O. Allen; seated: Hon C. N. Bruce, E. Hendren, C. I. T., J. W. H. T. Douglas, and W. Rhodes.

Scoring

MICHAEL FORDHAM

The earliest known cricket match to have taken place was in 1646 at Coxheath, near Maidstone, between 2 players against 4 of Maidstone, but it was not until 1744 when England played Kent at the Artillery Ground in Finsbury, London, that the full score of a match was preserved. There are earlier references to cricket than 1646, and it will never be known when it developed from a mere encounter between ball and bat or stick to a game when runs were scored and matches between sides were arranged, which led to the need to keep a permanent or quasi-permanent record of the game. The first known method of scoring was to cut notches on a stick with a larger notch for, say, every 5th or 10th run. It will also never be known when a change from this method to scoring on paper took place; no doubt the change was gradual rather than immediate.

Scoring-law Changes

The following shows how the scoring laws of the game were gradually introduced:

1744 The first known copy of the Laws refers to notches instead of runs, but does not state how they were made. The umpires adjudicated on good or bad runs, which presumably included the instance of a short run. If the bowling side obstructed a run, the umpires could order a notch to be scored as a penalty.

1774 Short runs referred to for the first time.

1788 No runs to be scored if the striker is caught, and the run in which a batsman is run out is not to be counted.

1798 5 run penalty if a fielder stopped the ball with his hat.

c 1809 Lost ball Law allowed the striker to score all the runs he made with a minimum allowance of 4 runs.

c 1811 Striker may play at a no-ball and score any resulting runs. One run penalty for a wide introduced, but to be scored as byes. The term 'run' instead of 'notch' was used for the first time; it became general by 1823.

'The Scorer,' William Davies of Lewes Priory (Thomas Henwood 1842).

c 1823 Lost ball allowance increased from 4 to 6 runs.

1828 The allowance for a wide to be scored as a wide and no longer as byes.

1829 One-run penalty for a no-ball introduced.

1835 The ball to be called dead after a wide, so that only one run could be scored.

1836 Bowlers given credit for all wickets caught or stumped off their bowling.

1840 Bowling analyses kept for the first time, though for some years this was not general.

1844 Batting side to score all runs resulting from a wide.

1884 Boundaries officially mentioned for the first time, but they had been general in first-class or important cricket for many years. Byes and leg-byes separated for the first time in the Laws, although they had been scored separately since 1848.

1910 Allowance of 6 for a hit out of the playing area introduced for the first time; until this date only hits right out of the ground had counted 6.

At this point it is relevant to quote Law 4 of the 1980 Code of Laws:

1 *Recording runs*

All runs scored shall be recorded by Scorers appointed for the purpose. Where there are two Scorers they shall frequently check to ensure that the score sheets agree.

2 *Acknowledging Signals*

The Scorers shall accept and immediately acknowledge all instructions and signals given to them by the Umpires.

The only other point in the new Laws which is of vital interest is that the responsibility for determining the correctness of the scores has now passed from the captains to the umpires (see the new Law 21). How satisfactory this change may prove in minor cricket only experience will show.

Scoring Methods

The simplest form of scoring is in books which have been used in school and club matches for very many years. These provide for runs to be entered against the batsman's name as they are scored, and each ball, whether scored off or not, is entered in the bowling analysis at the bottom of the page. The various extras are entered in the appropriate section, and all runs, irrespective of how they are made, are crossed off on a chart, numbered from 1 to say, 499, so that the innings total can be determined immediately. Byes and leg-byes are not entered as such in the bowling analysis, but no-balls are, either as a figure, if runs have been scored, or as a dot if no run is scored, ringed by a circle in either case. All runs scored as wides are counted as extras and only a cross is entered in the bowling analysis.

The score at the fall of each wicket is recorded, and at the end of the innings the number of runs scored is totalled up and checked against the chart, and the bowling analysis is completed and, with the addition of the extras, checked against the innings total. This should be a simple task if the 2 scorers have checked with each other at the end of each over as to the number of runs scored off the over, the innings total and the batsmen's totals. Scorebooks that are used in County and Test cricket are somewhat larger and more detailed, with spaces provided for time, such as when a batsman began and finished his innings, for each 50 of the innings and for the score of the

Herbert Strudwick, the great Surrey wicket-keeper, was after his retirement for many years a scorer in the old style.

not-out batsman as each wicket falls. The score chart is dispensed with and the bowling analysis is enlarged because of the longer innings that are played in 3 and 5-day cricket. Most, if not all, county scorers keep the batsmen's and the innings totals progressively on a plain sheet of paper or pad to enable them to ensure that the scoreboard is correct.

An alternative method of scoring is by entering each over in descending order across a series of columns, hereafter referred to as line-by-line scoring. The origin of this method is not certain, but it is known that it was used at an early stage of his career by W. Ferguson ('Fergie'), an Australian who came to this country with the 1905 touring side as scorer and baggage-master and performed the same function for touring teams to this country, Australia, New Zealand and South Africa for over 50 years. Roy Webber, in a previous article on this subject, admitted to having it explained to him at school, and it is known to have been used by P. G. H. Fender when he watched England v Australia Test Matches in the 1920s and 1930s as an author and journalist. After the last war, K. McCanlis, an umpire, had scorebooks printed in this style, but their use never became widespread.

In one of its simplest forms, some 7 columns are needed on lined paper. The first column will show the number of the over being delivered, the name of the bowler and the number of his over, with the name being entered on the left or right hand to indicate the end at which he is bowling. The next 2 columns are the bowling analysis appropriate for each batsman. The striker will have the runs entered and a nought for each ball he does not score off. The other batsman will have a dot entered for each ball he does not receive. At the end of each over, the total number of balls received by each batsman in his innings is entered. Extras are entered as appropriate. The 4th column shows the score at the end of the over and the time. The 5th and 6th columns relate again to the batsmen and show their scores at the end of the over with the number of minutes they have been batting. The number of fours and sixes hit is entered when appropriate with a ring or square round the totals respectively. The 7th column can show the time of the innings and contain notes on such items as chances missed, stoppages of play and runs needed to win. A similar sheet can be used to record over by over figures for each bowler. As play progresses it is possible to look back and see the state of the game at any given moment of the day and also when one batsman has received considerably more bowling than his partner, as well as the number of balls he has received or the runs he has scored off a particular bowler.

Radio and Television Scoring

In the early broadcasting of cricket, the commentator worked by himself and gave reports rather than commentary. However, in the Lord's Test match of 1934, the late Howard Marshall found himself in some difficulty when Hedley Verity took 14 wickets on the 3rd day. It was agreed that for the next Test at Old Trafford, he should have an assistant to keep the score for him and Arthur Wrigley, a young player on the Lancashire staff, was given the job. Wrigley scored in each subsequent Test until the war, and afterwards, when a further scorer was needed for television, Roy Webber established himself and was followed by Jack Price, who became a third scorer at this level. All three realized the inadequacy of the ordinary scorebooks and gave much thought to modifying the line-by-line system to meet their individual needs, the primary purpose always being to give information readily to the commentator. They were household names in cricket broadcasting until all three died between 1962 and 1965. They were succeeded by Bill Frindall on sound radio and on television by Irving Rosenwater, who have both become equally well known. The former has refined the line-by-line scoring method and has marketed loose-leaf sheets printed in this style. With these and the articles that the various scorers have written over the years describing the system, it has had much publicity and many young enthusiasts now use it.

Scoring Charts

Another aspect of scoring is the compiling of scoring charts for a batsman's strokes. The most illustrated method is to draw a line away from the wicket to the approximate position where the ball is fielded, adding the value of the stroke at the end of the line and the initial of the bowler off whom the stroke is made. For a hundred it can be of great interest, though for some of the very large innings played in the past the result becomes somewhat overwhelming. The other method is to note each stroke as the runs are scored, with the direction and value of the runs, and transfer to a chart afterwards. The Test match scorers for radio and television incorporate this into their line-by-line scoring.

Score-Boards

The most common and long-established score-board at school or club level is one that gives the total (often put up in tens), the number of wickets down and the score of the last man to be dismissed, the actual score being displayed when a wicket falls. The wealthier clubs, and all grounds on which county cricket is played, have a more detailed type of board which gives the innings total and the score of each batsman, put up run by run, details of the dismissal of the last batsman and the scorecard number of the bowler operating at each end, with various individual refinements. In recent years, these boards have been modified or extended to provide for the number of overs bowled by each bowler in limited-over matches. The only English ground ever to be equipped with a complete score-board of the type used on the major Australian grounds, and in more modest versions in the other Test playing countries, was Trent Bridge. This was brought into use in 1951, but became too expensive to operate and was replaced in 1973 by a streamlined board which is mainly operated electrically.

The Australia **Cricket Club** *v.* **the** England **Cricket Club.**

Match Played at Sydney on 14 · 15 · 17 · 18 December 1894

1st Innings of Australia Result

Time		BATSMAN.	RUNS SCORED.	HOW OUT.	BOWLER.	TOTAL.
12·12 12·20	1 · 1	Lyons J	1	Bowled	Richardson	1
12·12 2·34	2 · 2	Trott H	2114121	Bowled	Richardson	12
12·22 5·47	5 · 3	Giffen G	1442224411114114214421111124 12444411114211114111422244131214231441111211124	caught Ford	Brockwell	161
2·36 12·37	3 · 4	Darling J		Bowled	Richardson	0
2·39 ·57	4 · 5	Iredale F	42241141114444111111411233241134441	Caught Stoddart	Ford	81
·18 ·16	9 · 6	Gregory S	21414434211414241144142411114224343 3314342342242441441111222242244214214231324111111	caught Peel	Stoddart	201
5·49 2·30	6 · 7	Reedman J	4121153	caught Ford	Peel	17
12·32 2·55	7 · 8	McLeod C	2112321111	Bowled	Richardson	15
1·10	8 · 9	Turner CTB	1	Caught Gay	Peel	1
1·12 ·26	10 · 10	Blackham J	1114132211221244231412412134224111141	Bowled	Richardson	74
3·18	11	Jones E	443	Not out		11

UMPIRE

Byes	44	8
Leg Byes	111	3
Wide Balls	1	1
No Balls		

Runs at the fall of each Wicket	1	2	3	4	5	6	7	8	9	10	Total of Innings.
Time	12·28	12·34	12·37	3·57	5·43	12·30	12·55	1·10	3·16	3·26	
Runs	10	21	21	192	331	379	400	409	563	586	586

Total time at wkt – 7 hours 11 mins

BOWLING ANALYSIS.

BOWLER.	RUNS FROM EACH OVER.	Overs	Maidens.	Wides	No Balls.	Runs.	Wickets.
Richardson	[illegible]	55·3	13	·	·	181	5
Peel	[illegible]	53	14			140	2
Briggs	[illegible]	25	4			96	–
Brockwell	[illegible]	22	7			78	1
Ford	[illegible]	11	2	1		47	1
Stoddart	[illegible]	3	·			31	1
Lockwood		3	2			1	–

Published by ALFRED SHAW & ARTHUR SHREWSBURY, Football and General Athletic Sports Warehouse, Carrington St. Bridge, Nottingham.

ABOVE An orthodox score-sheet of the kind now out of fashion in first-class circles though otherwise still in universal use: England v Australia at Sydney in 1894–95. BELOW The more informative version, compiled by Michael Fordham, from an analysis sheet which no photograph can make intelligible to the ordinary reader: Sussex v Northants in a Gillette Cup semi-final, 1979.

GILLETTE CUP SEMI-FINAL
22 August 1979

SUSSEX V NORTHAMPTONSHIRE AT HOVE
NORTHAMPTONSHIRE - WON TOSS

IN at	OUT at	MINS. BATTED	No.	BATSMAN	HOW OUT	BOWLER	RUNS	W KT	TOTAL	6s	4s	NOTES
10·30	10·44	14	1	COOK	C LONG	ARNOLD	5	1	13	–	1	4TH OVER
10·30	10·52	22	2	LARKINS	RUN OUT		11	2	16	–	2	5TH OVER
10·45	12·00	75	3	WILLIAMS	BOWLED	SPENCER	16	3	77	–	2	24TH OVER
10·53	2·37	184	4	LAMB, A.J.	C PIGOTT	ARNOLD	101	4	234	–	11	56TH OVER 50 IN 97 MINUTES OFF 89 BALLS, 8 4's 100 IN 180 MINUTES OFF 146 BALLS, 11 4's
12·01	2·40	119	5	WILLEY	BOWLED	ARNOLD	89	5	234	–	10	56TH OVER 50 IN 72 MINUTES OFF 86 BALLS, 6 4's
2·38	2·58	20	6	YARDLEY	C SPENCER	PHILLIPSON	7	7	255	–	–	60TH OVER
2·41	2·49	8	7	SHARP	RUN OUT		4	6	241	–	–	58TH OVER
2·50	–	8	8	WATTS	NOT OUT		8			–	–	
			9	HODGSON	DID NOT BAT							
			10	LAMB, T.M.								
			11	GRIFFITHS								

EXTRAS (b. , l.b. 9 , n.b. 5 , w.) 14

TOTAL 255 FOR 7 WICKETS OFF 60 OVERS IN 228 MINUTES

OVERS PER HOUR = 15·78
RUNS PER OVER = 4·25
RUNS PER HOUR = 67·10

FALL OF WICKETS: 1-13, 2-16, 3-77, 4-234, 5-234, 6-241, 7-255

BOWLER	O.	M.	R.	W.
IMRAN KHAN	12	1	55	0
ARNOLD	12	2	45	3
PIGOTT	6	0	39	0
SPENCER	12	2	34	1
PHILLIPSON	6	1	27	1
BARCLAY	12	0	41	0

Hrs.	Overs	Runs
1	15	42
2	18	58
3	17	90
4		
5		
6		
7		
8		
9		
10		

Runs	Mins.	Overs	Last 50
50	68	16·3	
100	120	33	52
150	151	44	31
200	183	50·4	32
250	225	59·1	42
300			
350			
400			
450			
500			

LUNCH SCORE:
125-3 OFF 38 OVERS, LAMB 64, WILLEY 25

Wkt.	Partnership Between		Runs	Mins.
1st	COOK	LARKINS	13	14
2nd	LARKINS	WILLIAMS	3	7
3rd	WILLIAMS	LAMB	61	67
4th	LAMB	WILLEY	157	116
5th	WILLEY	YARDLEY	0	2
6th	YARDLEY	SHARP	7	8
7th	YARDLEY	WATTS	14	8
8th				
9th				
10th				

Some Cricket Curiosities

GERALD BRODRIBB

The game has produced an unending number of strange and unusual happenings, and every season provides some new curiosity. Here is a random selection of oddities from first-class cricket.

Nicholas Felix, the great Kent and All-England batsman of the 1840s, used to keep a note of his score by writing it on his stiff shirt-front.

S. T. Callaway on his debut for New South Wales v Queensland in 1914–15 made 207 in what turned out to be his only innings in first-class cricket.

During the Notts v India match at Trent-Bridge in 1974 play was stopped by parachutists who landed near the pitch when aiming for the nearby River Trent.

When E. W. Dillon bowled his first over for Kent v Surrey at the Oval in 1902 every ball was hit for a single down to C. J. Burnup fielding at deep third-man.

W. H. Ponsford when playing for Victoria v Tasmania at Melbourne in 1922–3 scored 429 – a new record score – in what was only his 4th innings in first-class cricket.

The pioneers of protective headgear seem to be R. Daft, who swathed his head with towels when batting for Notts v MCC at Lord's in 1870, and E. Hendren, who wore a cap with attached side-flaps in several matches in 1933.

George Brown when playing for Hampshire v Warwickshire at Southampton in 1926 was sent in later than usual. He showed his annoyance at batting at No. 10 by hitting a ball from Howell over the wicket-keeper's head and sightscreen for 6; he then split his bat, tore the blade in two, handed one half to the umpire, and continued to bat on successfully with the other half.

G. E. Vivian's debut in first-class cricket was for New Zealand in the 2nd Test against India at Calcutta in March 1965. He was aged 18: his father was chosen to tour England after playing in only 3 first-class matches, and also played for New Zealand at the age of 18.

In the First Test between England and India at Old Trafford in 1974, S. Madan Lal, 'b. Hendrick 2', had his off- and leg-stumps knocked out with the middle stump left standing.

When bowling for Notts v Northants at Kettering in 1932 H. Larwood knocked his right hand on the stumps and cut his finger so badly that he was unable to take further part in the match.

In 1926-7 at Melbourne, Victoria made a record score of 1107 against New South Wales: a month later, in the return match at Sydney, they were all out for 35.

C. P. Foley when batting for Middlesex v Sussex at Lord's in 1893 picked up a fallen bail, and after an appeal he was given out by umpire Henty; he was then recalled by the Sussex captain.

R. H. Moss on leaving Radley went to Oxford where he won a blue in 1889. On becoming ordained he later played for Bedfordshire, but retired from minor county cricket in 1910, and moved to Worcestershire. In 1925, 36 years after his last first-class appearance, he was called upon by Worcestershire to play against Gloucestershire at Worcester. He was then aged 57 – the oldest man ever to play in a County Championship match.

In the Test series against Australia in 1956 P. E. Richardson, the England opening batsman, was out caught at the wicket in every one of his 8 dismissals.

When playing for England against Australia at the Oval in 1880 G. F. Grace caught G. J. Bonnor for 2 when fielding at long-on at a distance reckoned to be 115 yards from the wicket. The batsmen had turned for their third run when the catch was made.

When fielding at short-leg for Surrey at Kingston in 1946 A. R. Gover took a catch from R. N. Exton (Combined Services) by closing his legs on the ball. He could see nothing, as he was in the act of putting his sweater over his head. It was J. C. Laker's first wicket in first-class cricket.

Alfred Gover, Surrey and England bowler, distinguished coach, one-time president of the Lord's Taverners, has a more esoteric claim to distinction. At the Kingston-on-Thames Festival he made an unusual catch between his thighs while in the act of pulling on his sweater. Thus R. N. Exton was dismissed and J. C. Laker claimed his 1st first-class wicket.

J. N. Shepherd, for D. H. Robins's XI v Orange Free State at Bloemfontein in October 1973 scored 54 – all in boundaries, 3 sixes and 9 fours.

When playing for British Guiana v Barbados in September 1946 D. F. Hill bowled an over of 14 balls. There were no wides or no balls, and the 6 extra balls (the 8-ball over was in use) were the result of the umpire miscounting. The 14th ball of this over had E. Weekes lbw.

Clem Hill made scores of 99, 98 and 97 in three consecutive innings for Australia v England in the Test series of 1901–2.

During Kent's 2nd innings v Leicester at Tunbridge Wells in 1975 the umpires cancelled the 3 runs scored by M. H. Denness when his partner Asif Iqbal ran one short. The umpires considered the short run was deliberately made.

Three of the first 4 Middlesex batsman were out 'Hit wicket' to A. P. Freeman of Kent at Lord's in 1921.

J. K. Moss fielding for Victoria v Queensland at Brisbane 1976–77 jammed his right boot into a boundary gutter when trying to stop a hit from G. S. Chappell: with the ball just out of Moss's reach the batsmen ran four.

V. M. Merchant after scoring 128 for India v England at the Oval in 1946 was, as non-striker, run out by D. Compton kicking the ball into the wicket at the bowler's end.

In the final of the Quaid-I-Azam Trophy at Karachi in 1958–9 the score-book entries for Abdul Aziz read:

1st innings . . . retired hurt 0
2nd innings . . . did not bat, dead 0

In the Second Test between England and New Zealand at Christchurch 1977–78 R. G. D. Willis was no-balled in the first innings because the short-leg, P. H. Edmonds, was too close and moved during Willis's run-up.

In 1868 during the Surrey v Lancashire match at the Oval play was suspended for 1 hour because of the excessive heat.

C. W. L. Parker when taking 9–36 for Gloucester v Yorkshire in his benefit match at Bristol in 1922 once hit the stumps 5 times in 5 consecutive balls, but the 2nd ball was a no-ball.

When playing for Somerset v Gloucester at Taunton in 1919, A. E. S. Rippon scored 92 and 58 not out, under the assumed name of 'S. Trimnel'.

After two overs of play in the Yorkshire v Derbyshire match at Chesterfield in 1946 it was discovered that the pitch had been marked out 2 yards too long.

The most runs made off a single hit is the 10 credited to S. Hill-Wood (Derbyshire) off the bowling of C. J. Burnup (MCC) at Lord's in 1900 in one of the games in which the experimental 'net-system' (all hits run out) was being used.

In the Yorkshire v Leicestershire match at Huddersfield in 1919 the Yorkshire 12th man, A. C. Williams, acted as a substitute for Leicestershire and caught out 4 of his own side.

In their 2nd innings v the West Indies in the Fourth Test match at Kingston in 1975–6 India were all out 97, 5 batsmen being recorded as 'absent hurt'. In their 1st innings of 306–6 declared the declaration was made to prevent further injury after two batsmen had retired hurt.

W. D. Hamilton when playing for Oxford v Cambridge at Lord's in 1882 was so nervous that at one time he ran in the opposite direction. His scores were 9 and 0.

According to R. C. Robertson-Glasgow, in the match against Somerset at Weston in 1920 P. S. E. Toone, of Essex, a mighty thrower, once threw the ball in so high and wide that it cleared the wicket-keeper's head and landed on the sight-screen.

Playing for Mahasashtra at Poona in 1948–49, B. B. Nimbalkar's score at lunch time was 443 not out: he seemed set to break Bradman's world record score of 452 not out, but the fielding side, Kathiawar, had had enough, refused to come out again, and conceded the match.

At Lord's in 1948 M. P. Donnelly (Warwickshire) was out 'bowled J. A. Young . . . 55'. The ball hit him on the foot, bounced right over the top of the stumps, and then spun back into them from behind.

C. C. Case when playing for Somerset v Notts at Taunton in 1930 was out 'hit wicket' to a ball from Voce. When he fell on his stumps he was so disturbed that he left carrying a stump under his arm instead of his bat.

F. Buckle had an unfortunate match when playing for Middlesex v Surrey in 1869. His score-book entries read:

1st innings . . . not sent for in time 0
2nd innings . . . absent unwell 0

When scoring 211 against Leicester at Leicester in 1967 all the Northants batsmen fell to catches by 10 different fielders.

W. A. Johnston (Australia) on his tour of England in 1953 had batting figures for the season of:

17 – 16 – 102 – 28 not out – 102

W. A. ('Bill') Johnston, the Australian Test bowler, saw the funny side of most things, not least the fact that as the regular No. 11 batsman he headed the batting averages of the 1953 side to England with 102·00. In his 17 innings he was not out 16 times.

In the match Somerset v Notts at Taunton in 1930 G. Hunt (Somerset) found the vicious in-swingers of W. Voce (Notts) so troublesome that he changed over to left-hand batting when facing Voce, but continued to bat in his normal right-handed way to the other bowlers.

D. W. Carr, aged 37, made his debut in first-class cricket for Kent v Oxford University on 27 May 1909, and on 9 August played for England v Australia in the Fifth Test at the Oval, thus rising to Test cricket within 10 weeks of his debut.

T. J. E. Andrews in making 164 for Australians v Middlesex at Lord's in 1926 was three times caught off a no-ball.

K. C. Ibrahim began the season of 1947–8 in India with scores of 218 not out and 36 not out, 234 not out and 77 not out, 144; his average for the season then stood at 709.

In 1866 G. Wells, for Sussex v Kent at Gravesend, hit his wicket while the bowler was running up to bowl and was given out: he was therefore out from a ball that was never actually delivered.

A. E. Watt's 2 innings of 24 and 54 for Kent v Gloucester at Gravesend in 1936 included 10 hits for six.

V. T. Trumper's first 8 hundreds in first-class cricket were scores of 292 not out, 253 not out, 135 not out, 104, 300 not out, 208, 165, 230.

W. M. Woodfull in scoring 118 for the Australians v Surrey at the Oval in 1926 hit only one 4 – his last scoring stroke.

In 1923 A. H. H. Gilligan of Sussex had 70 innings – the most ever in a first-class season.

In 1899 an amendment to Law ordained that a ball lodged in clothing was deemed dead: in earlier days W. Ward was concerned in an incident when he played the ball 'into the inclosure of his pantaloons'.

Some Cricket Eccentrics

BENNY GREEN

Although there is no question that the patron saint of eccentricity resides somewhere in the Grace family, it is not easy to decide on whose shoulders the mantle falls, on Edward Mills the Coroner, or William Gilbert the Doctor. Which of these two astonishing originals embodies the more succulent absurdities, E.M., whose irascible romanticism was reflected not only in his persistent pulling of balls outside the off-stump to the leg boundary but also in his pursuit of barrackers in the crowd, or W.G., who contradicted the classical orthodoxy of his own batting technique with his slyly comic bending of the rules?

The secret of both brothers was a simplicity of approach amounting to pure genius, a slapstick pragmatism harking back to the Georgians. In this regard it is much to the point that their maternal grandfather George Pocock, whose favourite mode of transport was kite carriage, was the sometime organist at Portland Wesleyan Church at Kingsdown near Bristol, and that, after a skirmish between organists and deacons, he left for ever, taking the organ with him; years later E.M., as a schoolboy at Long Ashton, was given out lbw by a dubious decision and applied the family precedent by walking off the field with the stumps under his arm.

The same cavalier attitude to both the spirit and the letter of the law persisted throughout E.M.'s long career, and with typical Gracean gusto he not only refused to conceal his chicanery but actually revelled in it, whether as player or as administrator. F. A. Leeston-Smith, playing for Weston-super-Mare against Thornbury, once hit E.M. for 4 successive sixes, an event which the Coroner later recalled as follows:

F. L. Cole made one off my first ball, Leeston-Smith six off my second, six off third, six off fourth, six off fifth, when the umpire said, 'I'm afraid it is over, Doctor'. I said, 'Shut up. I am going to have another, and off this one he was stumped'.

It was hardly likely that such a man, when appointed to the secretaryship of a county club, would bother with the conventional proprieties; the minutes of a Gloucestershire session of 1873 read as follows:

Committee meeting held at the White Lion Hotel, Bristol, on Thursday, November 25 at 3 o'clock. Present: E. M. Grace and that's all.

Naturally the alliance of the Coroner and the Doctor was many-faceted; in 1882 the Australian G. J. Bonnor, asked how he had been dismissed in a match at Clifton, replied, 'I was talked out by the fielders'. Bonnor, however, was no pillar of orthodoxy himself, being rumoured to have come out to bat for Non-Smokers against Smokers with a large cigar clamped between his teeth. As for W.G., his place as the champion of sporting perversity is too secure to require further documentation, but it is worth saying that he remains the only published author of the 19th century who believed that no good could come of reading books, that he once raided the Lord's pavilion and kidnapped William Midwinter for a match at the Oval, that among his sporting accomplishments was the ability to empty a magnum of champagne and then balance the bottle on his head, and that A. J. Webbe remembered at his mother's home in Eaton Square, 'W.G. marching round the drawing room after dinner bearing the coal scuttle on his head for a helmet, with the poker carried as a sword'.

Eccentrics generally may be sub-divided into the Expert-technical, the Inept-Aspiring, and the Dotty-Idolatrous. In the first category falls Charles Burgess Fry, who, on being no-balled for throwing, tied his bowling arm in a splint, buttoned down his shirt-sleeve and was only frustrated in his plan to reduce the umpires to absurdity through the refusal of his captain, W. L. Murdoch, to put the plan into operation. Later Fry, the only opening batsman ever to be offered the throne of Albania, summed up his own technique by saying that he had only one shot but could make it go to 9 different parts of the field. Eccentricity of subtly differing kind must be attributed to the aforesaid Midwinter, who not only indulged in wilful dissimulation himself, but induced the administrators of two hemispheres to indulge in it also, which explains how he found himself playing for Australia against England in 1876, for England against Australia in 1881, and for Australia against England in 1882. Midwinter, the first inter-continental cricketer, is famous for a miraculous metamorphosis achieved in his travels, having embarked for Australia in 1880 as 'W. Midwinter' and returned the following April as 'W. Midwinter; Gent'. This elevation, however, pales before the bewildering social fluctuations of Grace's cousin, W. R. Gilbert, who was listed by *Wisden* as an amateur until 1886, as a professional 1887–1923; as an amateur again in 1924; as a professional again posthumously from 1925–34; as an amateur again 1934–40; and subsequently as nothing at all.

Intermittent idiosyncracy must be ascribed to Robert Peel, the Yorkshire bowler who could on occasion drink himself into a condition more or less indistinguishable from eccentricity, who was described in one *Wisden* match report as 'having to go away' and who was eventually ushered out of the first-class game by Lord Hawke, for a nameless misdemeanour often said to have been his running in the wrong way and bowling at the pavilion in the mistaken belief that it was a batsman. On a less secular level there was the curious case of the Leicestershire batsman Albert Knight, who was in the habit of placing a request for extra-terrestrial assistance from the Almighty before facing his first delivery, a tactic of such manifest unfairness that the Lancashire bowler Walter Brearley was moved to complain to the MCC.

There was George Gunn, one of the most brilliant of batsmen, whose great century for England against Australia at Sydney in 1908 was marred, he always said, by the congenital inability of the cornetist in the orchestra on the ground to play in tune. His successor at Trent Bridge, Charlie Harris, often expressed the sterner tendencies of a more utilitarian age by remarking to the fielders as he walked in to bat, 'Good morning fellow-workers'.

One must also nod at the great hitter C. I. Thornton, who was once seen at Sittingbourne dressed in a borrowed nightshirt stalking wild duck; of more relevance was his wonderful plan to play an innings 'ball by ball in the manner of certain well-known batsmen'. Sadly he was out first ball 'when leaving the ball alone in the customary manner of a certain defensive player'. Hesketh Pritchard forsook a successful career by going to Patagonia in the mistaken conviction that when he arrived there he would find a Giant Sloth; Billy Buttress of Cambridgeshire, a gifted ventriloquist, enjoyed sitting in railway carriages causing other passengers to search their luggage for non-existent mad cats and dogs; Charles Newhall of the Philadelphians always went in to bat carrying a lemon, which he placed by stumps so that he might suck it for inspiration before each stroke; T. C. O'Brien spent part of the 1891 season appearing, for no discernible reason, as one J. E. Johnston; the Hon Lionel Tennyson, said to have beguiled the longeurs of a Gentlemen v Players match by laying odds of 10–1 that his grandfather had written 'Hiawatha', was never clear in his mind, as Hampshire captain, if he had hired his valet as wicket-keeper or his wicket-keeper as valet.

Although E. H. D. Sewell was a good player, it is as an honorary member of the Inept–Aspiring group that he has endeared himself to posterity. Sewell, who was once no-balled for delivering with both feet off the ground, said it was the first time in his life that he had been mistaken for an acrobat. He published several books; these tended to be discursive. One volume included a team of bearded players, the menu for a banquet, a plea for the smashing of more pavilion windows, a rewriting of Kipling's verse, a discussion of dress waistcoats, and a photograph of himself wearing a gas mask. One wonders what he would have made of Lord Frederick Beauclerk, who batted in a beaver hat.

When on overseas tours the slow bowler Julius Caesar

George Gunn's individuality extended to getting out (or staying in) more as the spirit moved him than by any merit in the bowling. In days when bands commonly played at cricket matches it might be that the cornet-player was out of tune: or it might simply have been 'too 'ot.' His eccentricity has in this photograph extended somewhat to the photographer – good likenesses proved hard to come by.

Gerry (G. J. V.) Weigall, who rates high among the cricket eccentrics (in bowler hat), is in august company here at a Trent Bridge Test. The others from left to right are Arthur Mailey, R. H. Spooner, A. C. MacLaren, Plum Warner, H. D. G. Leveson Gower and Wilfred Rhodes. Usually Weigall illustrated his technical comments with an umbrella, here forsaken for a walking stick.

always cried when required to sleep alone. This problem never worried the Yorkshireman Ted Wainwright, who always took his bat to bed with him; an interesting variation on this theme was provided by the New York millionaire Hesketh K. Nayler, who treated his own impotency with homeopathic doses of fat ladies with no clothes on playing cricket with balloons; sadly his case never came to the attention of Dr Freud. Further sexual innuendo is provided by the Duke of Dorset, who in 1754 sacked his mistress, the ravishing Bacelli, for running him out. Even worse running between wickets was committed by John Boot of Newark, who in 1737 died in a collision with his batting partner.

Harry Bagshaw (Derbyshire) was buried in 1927, in accordance with his instructions, dressed in his umpire's coat holding a cricket ball. Walter Cave (Surrey) invented the idea of candleholders on pianos. T. A. Fison (Highgate School) once scored as follows: '264 Retired to catch train for Continent', while G. E. Hemingway, having hit the ball into a bed of nettles, ran 250 while the fieldsmen debated who should retrieve it. Charles Absolom, a famous London club cricketer, took 100 wickets in a season when he was 80 years old. G. J. V. Weigall (Cambridge and Kent) described the omission of Frank Woolley from the England side as 'the worst crime since the Crucifixion', refused to eat veal-and-ham pie during a match, and once, on arriving at a village ground to be told there was no clock, complained, 'No clock, sir? The clock is more important than a lavatory.'

Finally there are the Dotty-Idolatrous, whose passion for the game is equalled only by their inability to excel at it. These include the dramatist Sir James Barrie, who claimed to be a slow bowler so slow that if he produced a delivery of which he disapproved, he could run down the pitch and fetch it back; he once described a perfect wicket as being 'a little on the creamy side'. The poet J. C. Squire would put himself on to bowl at one end, saying 'At the other end the glint of the sun on the stumps would put me off'. Sir Julien Cahn batted in inflatable pads, and is said to have bowled 'not so much up and down as to and fro'. No summary of cricketing eccentricity would be complete without reference to Lord Justice Norman Birkett, who as a small boy said his prayers every night by asking the Deity to look after the entire Surrey XI, which he named, man by man, ending with 'and God bless leg-byes'; also to an Epsom stockbroker called Arthur Courcy, who was so stirred by the climactic moments of the England v Australia 1882 Test match at the Oval that he bit through the handle of his brother-in-law's umbrella; last of all to the poet Robert Graves, who has recorded as follows a lull in the fighting on the Western Front:

> 24 June, 1915. Vermelles. This afternoon we had a cricket match, officers v sergeants, in an enclosure between some houses out of observation from the enemy. Our front line is three-quarters of a mile away. I made top score, 24; the bat was a bit of a rafter, the ball a piece of rag tied with string; and the wicket a parrot cage with the clean, dry corpse of a parrot inside. Machine-gun fire broke up the match.

Throwing

E. W. SWANTON

There have been occasional outbreaks of feeling against suspect bowling actions ever since the no-balling of John Willes at Lord's in 1822. There was some controversy in the 1880s. The 1882 Australians commented bluntly on certain actions while James Lillywhite's criticisms in his *Companion* of 1883 were subsequently supported by the Hon R. H. Lyttelton, V. E. Walker and H. H. Stephenson. At Lord Harris's instigation the 'absolutely fair' clause was added at this time to the bowling Law. Yet although Lancashire had one notorious thrower in Crossland and a widely suspect man in Nash neither seems to have been no-balled. Several counties contented themselves with cancelling their matches with Lancashire who eventually took the hint and dispensed with these men's services. The matter came to a head again in

1897–1898 when several famous cricketers were no-balled including C. B. Fry and the Australian fast bowler, Ernest Jones.

J. Phillips, an Australian who alternated between England and his home country, umpiring in the first-class seasons of each, showed himself fearless in applying the Law. Other umpires, fortified by the support of Lord Harris, and perhaps encouraged also by the outspoken comment of S. H. Pardon, editor of *Wisden*, followed suit. By 1903 the trouble had been eliminated, and for the following half-century there was only one isolated case in English first-class cricket of a bowler being no-balled for throwing. There were a few instances elsewhere in the world, and in 1941–42 in Barbados a certain Mabarak Ali, of Trinidad, set up a melancholy sort of record by being no-balled 30 times in one innings.

In 1952 G. A. R. Lock, of Surrey, was no-balled in a county match (immediately after the first of his 47 appearances for England). He was also no-balled in a Test Match by a West Indian umpire in Jamaica in 1954. Yet Lock bowled on, murmured against but unchecked. Nor was he the only suspect in the 1950's. In 1958 at their customary meeting at Lord's the umpires were warned to be on their guard. It was, however, the press criticism of I. Meckiff and certain others during the MCC tour of Australia in 1958–59 that put an effective spotlight on throwing and, incidentally, underlined the damage to international sporting relations which alleged infringement of this Law can cause.

There were 4 throwing prosecutions in England in 1959, and in 1960 came the regular no-balling of the South African, G. Griffin. Jones and Lock were hitherto the only bowlers in Test history to have been no-balled while playing for their countries. Griffin was selected for the Second Test at Lord's, he within the previous few weeks having been no-balled for throwing 17 times in 3 matches of the South African tour by 6 English umpires. In this Test he was no-balled 11 times.

The ICC (*qv*), meeting shortly after this affair, having been made specially conscious of the need to strengthen the umpires in an unpalatable duty, framed an explanatory note to the Law which was accepted by all members for experimental use (*i.e.* it was not to be added to the statute book), as follows:

A ball shall be deemed to have been thrown if, in the opinion of either umpire, the bowling arm having been bent at the elbow, whether the wrist is backward of the elbow or not, is suddenly straightened immediately prior to the instant of delivery. The bowler shall nevertheless be at liberty to use the wrist freely in the delivery action.

The Conference statement went on to say:

It is considered that the pregoing definition will result in a more uniform interpretation of what constitutes a throw and should assist greatly in achieving the object all have in mind. The question of throwing is, however, a complicated and difficult problem, especially for the umpires who are solely responsible for interpreting the Laws. The whole problem has been complicated by modern methods of publicity resulting in a danger of prejudgment. The Conference, therefore, having reached a unanimous conclusion in a most amicable spirit, hope that all those who may be concerned with the future welfare of cricket will do all in their power to assist those whose admittedly difficult task is to adjudicate on this problem.

With the prospect of Australia on their forthcoming visit to England in 1961 bringing Meckiff and possibly other bowlers concerning whom doubts had been raised among cricketers and critics of both sides, MCC and Australia in a decision without precedent agreed on a moratorium until the First Test Match. Umpires would report to the English and Australian authorities, but would not no-ball for throwing. In the event the Australian team chosen contained none to whose action exception could be taken and the tour passed off happily. The climax to the case of Meckiff (who had been no-balled twice, by different umpires, in Sheffield Shield matches in 1962–63) came at Brisbane in the first Australia-South Africa Test of 1963–64 when he was no-balled 4 times in his opening over. He was not subsequently put on in the match, after which he announced his retirement from cricket.

The problem of throwing is still not far below the surface. Sir Donald Bradman's comment on his return home from the 1960 Conference will have been widely echoed:

It is the most complex question I have known in cricket, because it is not a matter of fact, but of opinion and interpretation. It is so involved that two men of equal good will and sincerity could take opposite views.

In recent years, however, the policy followed by the TCCB of having suspect actions filmed and examined in slow motion has kept trouble at bay in England. Nor can one recall any flagrant cases abroad. If any should arise it must be hoped that umpires will act with the moral courage of such men as the late Sid Buller, of F. S. Lee, C. Egar of Australia and C. Jordan of Barbados during the outbreak which came to a head at the historic ICC meeting of 1960.

Geoff Griffin's action, in 1960 the cause of a furore; and bowling under-arm after he had been no-balled during the England v South Africa Test at Lord's.

Umpires

ALEX BANNISTER

In the innocent beginnings of cricket there seem to have been no umpires as we know them today. A rough form of justice was dispensed in matters of dispute by an old player or an experienced onlooker.

As William Goldwin wrote in his famous verse 'The Cricket Match' in 1706:

> Now some grey veteran intercedes,
> And wins their love, the while he pleads:
> A Daniel come to judgment, he to all around speaks equity.
> Though now his arms he laid aside,
> And marred by years his early pride,
> Yet rich is he in cricket lore,
> And proves that they need strive no more.

The words 'rich in cricket lore' have survived the centuries as the perfect description of dedicated men, eternally criticised, seldom praised and much misunderstood.

In 1727, some time before the original Code of Laws of 1744, umpires were employed for two matches between teams raised by the Duke of Richmond and Mr Brodrick. As was customary at the time heavy bets were placed on the result, and carefully drawn-up Articles of Agreement provided for the umpires' protection – 'If any of the Gamesters shall speak or give their opinion on any point of the game they shall be turned out and voided in the match.' With the highly-regrettable development of 'sledging' – slang to cover verbal abuse on the field, not always directed at the opposition – the atmosphere might be sweetened if a modern culprit were to be 'voided in the match.'

In the Code of 1744 umpires were made the judges of all 'frivolous delays of all hurts whether real or pretended' – a forerunner of the current Law covering Fair and Unfair Play and an indication that human nature changes little. A stick or bat was carried by the first umpires, which had to be touched by a batsman to signal the completion of a run. Fortunately for such a cumbersome method there were, as yet, no Bradmans or Comptons on the scene. No doubt the umpire's stick was a symbol of his authority and, in moments of stress, a useful weapon to have in hand. The imperative role of the umpire was soon recognized. Much of the game's enviable reputation for fair play has been founded on his honesty and integrity, and the acceptance by players that the infallible umpire has yet to be born. The best are those who make the fewest mistakes. Probably the most cogent words in the Laws are concentrated in the part-sentence 'in the opinion of the umpire.' No other opinions matter, a simple fact of cricket summed up in the old chestnut:

> Batsman departing to pavilion: 'That wasn't out, umpire.'
> Umpire: 'No? Well look in tomorrow's paper.'

Provided he keeps his sense of humour the umpire can always get his own back. 'I could see he was from here' shouted an angry fielder from mid-off in a Test Match. Nothing was said until the player came in to bat. Then a straight-faced umpire asked: 'Would you like guard from over the stumps or from mid-off?' The umpire's duties have multiplied alarmingly over the years. The comments on this of the top-hatted 'Honest Will' Caldecourt, who umpired with his right arm encased in his waistcoat in a Napoleonic pose more than a century ago, would be interesting to hear. So would those of the great Frank Chester it he had been handed a modern protective helmet during overs.

Sid Buller leaving the field for the last time. Within minutes of this photograph being taken, coming off for rain in the County Championship match between Warwickshire and Nottinghamshire at Edgbaston in August 1970, he had collapsed and died.

Even the comparatively recent stalwarts would find almost intolerable pressures if they returned to the game now. In the final of the Prudential World Cup at Lord's in 1975 H. D. Bird and T. W. Spencer stood from 11 am to 8.43 pm – apart from arriving early for their pre-match supervision – while 118·4 6-ball overs were bowled and 18 wickets fell, including five close run-outs in the Australian innings. The demands on their concentration and judgment on a highly exciting occasion was severe – greater than on any of the 22 players. One lapse could have led to uproar, and while it is beyond dispute that television, radio, long-range high-speed cameras, crammed press boxes and modern publicity, have greatly increased the burdens of umpiring, it is also a fact that the instant play-back has more often than not confirmed a decision to be right.

The playback is a monstrous weapon for the critic. For one thing it is two-dimensional, making no allowance for the position of the bowler and conveying deceptive angles. Basically it is an unjust intrusion on the umpire as the sole and instant judge. It is a development which must earn sympathy for umpires, who have become the target for increasing pressure from players not over-caring about how a wicket is obtained. Experience counts for so much, which is where English umpires have the advantage. The majority are drawn from the playing ranks and apart from their invaluable contact with first-class cricket and cricketers they have a feel and sixth sense for right and wrong. They are not pressurized by constant appealing – a practice regrettably on the increase –

and umpiring is their full-time occupation. In other countries this is seldom so.

A candidate for the first-class list in England is nominated by a county. In rare cases an outstanding umpire might be promoted from the minor counties. Once accepted by a special committee of the Test and County Cricket Board he is obliged to maintain a high standard of competence. A report on his performance is submitted at the end of each match. There is an annual eye and hearing test, and the retiring age is 65, to be extended only in exceptional circumstances.

By common consent the modern umpire, though given more and more responsibility, has a better deal than his predecessors, and his pay, notably at Test level, has been greatly improved. He deserves every penny he gets.

At international level the home authority draws up a panel of umpires available for a Test series, and the visiting side is given the chance of vetting each member before a Test. The tourists also have the right to object to a nominated umpire. In recent years several objections have been lodged, some with good reason. In England at least two umpires have been withdrawn from a Test and financially recompensed by a sympathetic committee who did not agree with the complaints.

Such is the strain of a 5-day Test that it is customary for the duties to be shared during a series. In Australia in 1974–75, however, R. C. Bailhache and T. F. Brooks stood in all six matches. In the next home series with England, in 1978–79, Brooks was so severely criticized that he retired after one Test, and, what was more, made public his decision while the game was still in progress. His premature retirement was an unhappy example of the pressures an umpire is obliged to bear.

As the aspiring official is soon to discover, a mastery of the Laws is but a starting point, a basic requirement. The difficulty is putting theory into practice, to interpret all 42 Laws 'within the meaning of the act' faithfully and accurately. Special regulations and notes to the Laws also have to be digested, and there are separate conditions of play for every competition. An encyclopaedic memory and a legal training might be recommended. An umpire's duties in the course of an English season could embrace a 5-day Test Match, the Prudential Trophy, one-day internationals, 3-day fixtures with the touring team, the 3-day Schweppes County Championship, the Gillette Cup, the Benson and Hedges Cup, the John Player League and the so-called 'friendlies' involving MCC and the Universities. Little wonder that the first question of the day an umpire might ask himself is: what's the competition today? Followed by a prudent revision of the match conditions.

Ground, weather and light conditions on less than summery days are an important umpiring responsibility. Whatever the decision it seldom satisfies both teams and spectators. After one contentious argument during a Test between England and New Zealand at Trent Bridge in 1978 it was decided to arm umpires with light meters for the final Test of the series at Lord's. Some years earlier meters had been used by a few selected umpires as an experiment. It was not a conspicious success, and although it was stressed that the meters were to be used only as a guide at Lord's it appeared more of a public relations exercise than a serious bid to solve a nagging problem. The final decision, meter or not, still rests with the umpires.

Law 3 deals with duties of the Umpires. For 'starters' it stipulates that before the toss for innings they shall acquaint themselves with any special regulations and agree with both captains on any other conditions affecting the conduct of the match; they must satisfy themselves that the wickets are properly pitched and agree between themselves on the watch or clock to be followed during play.

On to Law 42:

'The Umpires are the sole judges of fair and unfair play . . . The Umpires shall intervene without appeal by calling and signalling "dead ball" in the case of unfair play but should not otherwise interfere with the progress of the game . . .' except where required to do so by the Laws.

In short they control the conduct of the game, even before the first ball and right to the last. If there is a more onerous occupation in a major sport it has been well hidden.

Occasionally even the most experienced are caught out, and it is not to be wondered at. Homer, posing as Frank Chester, nodded at Lord's in a Test between England and New Zealand when an illegal declaration was permitted on the first day. Nor was the error spotted immediately in the pavilion. However, Chester and Dai Davies were equal to a highly uncommon situation when Sir Leonard Hutton, playing against South Africa at the Oval in 1951, attempted to hit the ball a second time. Hutton was rightly given out for 'obstructing the field'. The players are not always as conversant with the Laws as they should be. An instance of this happened in a prewar match at the Oval when Chester no-balled the late Hedley Verity, who, as a protest against the perfection of the pitch, had bowled an under-arm delivery without notifying the batsman of a change of action. At the first interval the Yorkshire players, led by Herbert Sutcliffe, descended on the secretary's office for a copy of the Laws, to prove Chester wrong. Instead they found Chester to be right.

At Sydney in 1979 there was the curious incident of Graham Yallop, Australia's captain, being allowed the use of an old and worn ball when England in the 4th innings of the Sixth Test Match needed 32 runs to win. There was a 6 minute delay while England unsuccessfully argued that Law 5 did not permit such a tactical ploy, attempted because the pitch was taking spin. The Law states that subject to agreement to the contrary either captain may demand a new ball at the start of each innings. As no agreement had been made England's protest should have been upheld. As it was the runs were scored for the loss of one wicket, but had there been a larger target and Australia had won, the authorities would have had a problem on their hands.

In the 1964–65 series between the West Indies and Australia a local umpiring dispute left the Test Match at Georgetown short of an umpire. Eventually one of the West Indies selectors G. E. Gomez, the former Test all-rounder, filled the vacancy and was to be seen racing off the field at the end of play to do a

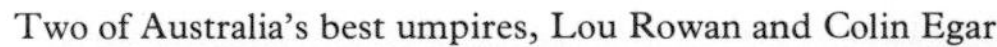

Two of Australia's best umpires, Lou Rowan and Colin Egar.

radio summary. While Gomez did an exceptionally good job, and earned the admiration of the players of both sides, it did not pass unnoticed by the Australians that they – and Gomez – were placed in an invidious position. Playing for the West Indies was Charlie Griffith, the fast bowler whose action was a permanent source of controversy. The Australians argued with cold logic that as Gomez had been a party to Griffith's selection he was unlikely to find fault with his action as an umpire. A more honest character than Gomez never trod the earth, but the imagination boggles at the furore he would have provoked had he no-balled Griffith for throwing!

The West Indies is not the easiest place to umpire. Once after play had been suspended for a riot following a run out decision England's captain, Hutton, trying to inspire confidence in the unfortunate official, said: 'We have every faith in you. Carry on as if nothing had happened.'

'That's all very well, Mr. Hutton' was the reply. 'I've got to stay on here after you have left!'

Experience, a philosophic attitude and a firm will – as distinct from the 'personality' who puts himself above the game – are priceless virtues. Team work is an integral part of successful umpiring for it is plain common sense to seek help in settling a doubtful point, particularly catches which might not have carried to the wicket-keeper standing back. It stands to reason that the square-leg umpire is sometimes in a better position to judge.

But even two heads can be confused at odd times. Two tail-enders in a county match became involved in a hilarious tangle while running for a long hit. In utter confusion and rather like Siamese inseparables they ran up and down the pitch several times while both wickets were broken. While fielders and spectators were enjoying the confusion the two umpires earnestly conferred and eventually confessed to the panting batsmen: 'We don't know which of you is out. What about a volunteer?'

Hardly a month of the season passes without a worried umpire contacting the secretary of the Test and County Cricket Board on some moot point of Law or a condition of play.

Umpires have to be concerned at the practice, whether by design or not, of bowlers following through in their delivery and creating a rough patch within a prescribed area. Leniency can create problems as was demonstrated in a Test at Wellington between England and New Zealand, in 1978, when bowlers of both sides were at fault.

As sole judges of fair and unfair play umpires have a thankless task and regrettably the day seems long gone when players were above making claims for a doubtful catch. In some instances only the catcher knows whether it is a fair dismissal; yet there is a growing tendency to make all kinds of spurious and excitable appeals, particularly for the bat-pad snick. The practice of appealing for leg-before decisions from all parts of the field has also grown. At one time only the bowler and wicket-keeper were considered to be in a position to 'ask'.

The more frequent use of the emotive bumper has brought endless problems in modern cricket from arguments on the actual length of a delivery to angry charges of uncontrolled intimidation. There are many who believe the onus of control should not rest entirely with umpires, but that it is the equal responsibility of team managers and controlling authorities. It was too much to expect that the violence of the age should pass cricket by. Nonetheless, firm control is imperative and not everything should be left to the umpires.

Nothing causes umpires more anxiety than having to decide whether it is 'unreasonable or dangerous' (in the words of the Law) to continue playing. In deteriorating light the batsman does not want to risk his innings. The bowler, on the other hand, is invariably happy to play on, though when play does continue in poorish light the fielding captain dislikes it if he is denied the use of his fast bowlers.

The umpire has to consider, among other things, how long a batsman has been at the wicket; the longer he has the less he might be inconvenienced by bad light. Also taken into consideration are the size and effectiveness of the sightscreens and the general state of the background. Being human, umpires are sometimes conscience-stricken when a batsman is dismissed after a light appeal has been turned down. Over the years the regulations governing appeals against the light have changed several times. Once, immediately after the Second War, when unlimited appeals were allowed, the late Sidney Barnes, Australia's opening batsman, appealed after every other delivery.

There was also a time when no appeals at all could be made. Then, too, the game's comedians were in their element. One batsman flashed a torch; another lit matches on the way to the wicket, while the umpires, enjoying the joke, watched impassively but unimpressed. A retort by Jack Newman, a renowned Hampshire player, became a classic. Hampshire were not keen on continuing in a doubtful light, but all their hints had fallen on deaf ears. When Newman arrived at the wicket his captain, Lord Tennyson, bellowed:

'Can you hear me, Newman?'

'Yes, I can hear you, my lord' came the reply 'but where are you speaking from?'

Every umpire has to have a sense of humour, and to learn to laugh at himself. Alex Skelding, a great character with his white boots, snowy hair and fog horn voice, was handed a stray dog by an Australian fielder Sidney Barnes. 'The white stick comes later,' promised Barnes. Skelding was something of a poet and his 'An Umpire's Lament', if not Shakespearian in style, won considerable notoriety. At the close of play he made a ritual of taking off the bails and saying: 'And that concludes the entertainment for the day, gentlemen.' A Leicestershire bowler in his day Skelding wrote a report on his benefit match which began: 'Play began in a biting wind before a sparse crowd.'

What makes the retired player enter such a thankless job? Certainly it is not the thought of money – though payments have improved – or the glory and satisfaction of being in the public eye. For many there is no other reason than to continue to be a part of a game which, for all the knocks and disappointments, is a good life and infinitely better than the office or the workshop floor. The freemasonry of the game still appeals and draws. There is, though, no cosy security, and a place on the list may be abruptly withdrawn.

The hours are long, the winds can be cold, and the travelling arduous – the late Paul Gibb's caravan was a common sight on the county circuit. Eddie Paynter, the little England and Lancashire left-hander, gave up umpiring because he said he couldn't afford to continue. He met so many old pals that it cost him too much money. Most, on graduating to first-class umpiring, no matter how long and distinguished their playing experience, soon realise they have to cope with something new and challenging. One former wicket-keeper was embarrassed to find himself joining in an appeal on his first outing; another was taken aback when the bowler handed him his false teeth for safe keeping during the opening overs. The newcomer discovers that it is an invitation to disaster to be hurried into making decisions; he learns to ignore the vehemence of an appeal. Attention must be paid to what might appear to a layman as trivialities. Who would imagine, for instance, that breath control can play a part in umpiring? Yet to shout 'No-ball' instantly and with a strong voice an intake of breath is needed as the bowler takes his final strides to the wicket.

Concentration is imperative – of a discreetly relaxed kind. To doze if even for a split-second invites a mistake. To be caught napping is a sin, every decision being important not only to the individual but to his team. The instinct to follow the flight of the ball all the time once it is hit has to be overcome. Apart from the possibility of the bail being dislodged, and a good or bad appeal being made, it is necessary to see every run is properly completed.

Keeping an eye on the score-board and being satisfied that all signals are properly accepted by the scorers is routine, and becomes particularly important in a close finish. The last thing anyone wants is a disputed finish with arguments raging about a lost extra, but it can easily be done if signalling is slipshod, or the scorers, with heads down, miss an umpire's call. On major Australian grounds signals are acknowledged by a red light, the next ball being delayed until a response is made. At Sydney and Melbourne the distance from umpire to scorers is considerable, and it is a sound system. That lovable character Bill Reeves was said once to have signalled to a beer tent at Canterbury in the mistaken belief he was in touch with the scorers.

A ball can be put through a gauge to ensure it is the proper shape and size. In recent years the ball has tended to fall out of shape, and umpires need to be alive to the tactical ploy of a try-on in the hope that a replacement might swing more, or have a more pronounced seam, or be less worn, or even be easier to grip.

Above all an umpire cannot panic. If he does he is lost. Always the benefit of the doubt should go to the batsman. The umpire, for example, should both hear the snick and see the deflection to be satisfied a batsman has been caught.

Frank Lee once came in for criticism at Trent Bridge when he turned down an appeal from the entire Glamorgan team. Although there was a sound of ball on wood Lee was sure the batsman had not hit it, and at the end of the over his suspicions were confirmed by a mark on the outside of the off stump. The ball had missed the bat and brushed the stump, producing a click as if it had touched the edge of the bat.

Further evidence of good umpiring – and the luck of the game – came from J. T. Murray, the Middlesex wicket-keeper, after his century for England against the West Indies at The Oval in 1966. Murray scored 112; yet he might have gone to the first ball he received from Griffith. Playing back he edged it on to his pads. There was a confident appeal, which was turned down to the disappointment of the fielders. Yet Buller was right. 'Considering the noise that was going on from the crowd at the time it was a wonderful piece of umpiring', said Murray. 'I wouldn't have complained if I'd gone first ball'. Unhappily, in an imperfect world the public hear only of the allegedly bad decisions. Good decisions seldom make news.

Practical demonstrations of how the lbw law is interpreted have surprised players and umpires alike. One of the difficulties facing international cricket is the acceptance of a common interpretation of the Laws. On one England tour of Australia off-break bowlers were, as a matter of course, denied leg-before decisions to the sweep shot – to the particular consternation of Fred Titmus. Batsmen were allowed to plant a leg down the pitch and sweep with impunity, aware that if they missed they were safe. It amounted to a free hit and was a negation of the off-spinner's art.

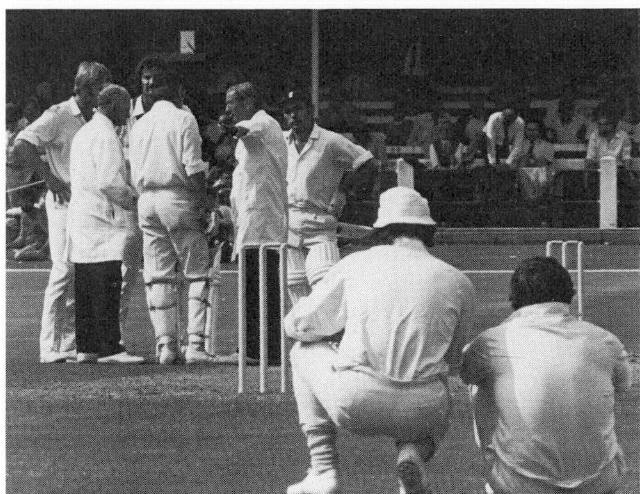

Complaints by bowlers to umpires that balls have lost their shape are a modern frustration. Though sometimes justified they can be an excuse for a 'breather', or just to break a batsman's concentration. A. E. G. Rhodes and T. W. Spencer are involved here, the scene England v Australia at Trent Bridge 1972.

An umpire never involved in a controversy has yet to be born. It is part of his trade to have a broad back and suffer the taunts of those who think they know better. His one dread is to be let down by authority.

As far back as 1862 John Lillywhite, umpiring a match between Surrey and England, no-balled Willsher 6 times in succession. The England players left the field in protest and the game restarted the next day with a replacement for Lillywhite. Happily the status of and supporting sympathy for the umpire have grown, and there is a universal acknowledgment of the debt the game owes him. The physical and mental stamina necessary for any major game is considerable; only the dedicated could face the task season after season. Players and critics are inclined to forget that the umpire does not make the Law. He only strives to interpret it to the best of his ability and judgment, fearlessly and without prejudice.

In March 1953, the Association of Cricket Umpires was formed with the objective of raising the standard of club umpiring, and it has been of immense value. Regular meetings and discussions are held, examinations conducted, and help and advice are freely given to club umpires by their professional colleagues. From the parent organisation have sprung up regional Associations not only at home but abroad. The devotion and interest of the amateur umpire is as necessary to club cricket as the efficient professional is to the upper echelons.

War Casualties

E. W. SWANTON

The toll that the two World Wars exacted among cricketers is faithfully related in the *Wisdens* of 1915–1920 and of 1941–46. At a range of 60 years and more it is a melancholy exercise to peruse the endless pages under the inscription 'Roll of Honour' telling of the slaughter of a generation on the fields of Flanders, at Gallipoli and elsewhere. The lists extend from the greatest to those of modest attainment and a few of whom it was said that but for the war they might have played for England. Nor is the record in any way insular, the names of many cricketers from overseas – not least Canadians – bearing tribute to the meticulous eye for fact and detail that Sydney Pardon and his fellow-compilers of the *Almanack* brought to their work.

Two great Kentish cricketers, Colin Blythe and K. L. Hutchings, head the list of the First War fallen, among whom is another Test player, the Yorkshireman M. W. Booth. Australia subscribed Albert Cotter, their famous fast bowler, and South Africa two of the googly quartet who made history in Edwardian days, R. O. Schwarz and G. C. White. In rough chronological order came E. Crawley (Cambridge), A. Jaques (Hampshire), Alan Marshal, the Australian who played for Surrey, R. O. Lagden (Oxford), G. G. Napier (Oxford), W. S. Bird (Oxford and Middlesex), W. J. H. Curwen (Oxford and Surrey), G. B. Davies (Cambridge and Essex), W. B. Burns (Worcestershire), Sir Francis Cunliffe (Oxford and Middlesex), Percy Jeeves (Warwickshire), L. J. Moon (Middlesex), E. A. Shaw (Oxford), H. G. Garnett (Lancashire), J. E. Raphael (Oxford and Surrey), J. H. Hunt (Middlesex), Rev H. Staunton (Notts), L. G. Colbeck (Cambridge and Middlesex), A. Hartley (Lancashire), D. W. Jennings (Kent), C. E. Hatfeild (Oxford and Kent) and E. L. Wright (Oxford and Lancashire).

A. E. J. Collins, the Clifton boy whose 628 not out is still the highest score ever made, was a First War casualty. One learns that F. O. Grenfell, who topped the Eton averages as a boy, was the first Army officer to win the VC, and that the New Zealander, R. G. Hickmott, was 'probably the most promising young cricketer in the Dominion.'

The long list of casualties in 1915 includes a line which, read at this distance, touches the sublime in bathos. Sub-Lieut Rupert C. Brooke, of the Royal Naval Division, died at Lemnos of sunstroke. Though unsuccessful in the Marlborough match at Lord's he headed the Rugby School bowling averages in 1906, and 'had gained considerable reputation as a poet.'

Of John Howell, younger brother of Miles and generally reckoned the most promising of all the young cricketers killed without having the chance to make their name it is recorded that in the August of his penultimate year at Repton 'he journeyed up to Walsall with Surrey's Second XI for the express purpose of playing Barnes's bowling and had the satisfaction of scoring 45.' What touching precocity! Within a few months the world's greatest bowler was due in South Africa to take 49 wickets in 4 Tests, a record that must be secure for ever.

It was a sombre coincidence that possibly the 2 most distinguished England cricketers to fall in action in the two World Wars were the great slow left-arm bowlers, Colin Blythe (1917) (above) and Hedley Verity (1943) (below).

Although British and Commonwealth casualties were lighter over all in the Second World War they were still especially heavy among the best fighting troops among whom many of the younger cricketers were to be found. *Wisden's* final Roll of Honour lists some 200 players of note, not by any means all first-class, though many would undoubtedly have become so. They included 11 Test cricketers: G. B. Legge, K. Farnes, G. G. Macaulay, M. J. Turnbull and H. Verity of England; Ross Gregory of Australia; A. B. C. Langton, A. W. Briscoe and C. M. Francois of South Africa; and D. A. R. Moloney and W. N. Carson of New Zealand. A distressing feature was the loss of so many former captains of counties and universities, in two cases of both: notably C. T. Ashton (Cambridge), F. G. H. Chalk (Oxford and Kent), E. J. H. Dixon (Oxford), P. T. Eckersley (Lancashire), G. D. Kemp-Welch (Cambridge), G. B. Legge (Kent), R. P. Nelson (Northants), M. J. Turnbull (Cambridge and Glamorgan) and D. F. Walker (Oxford).

Other well-known English names of the 1930s to be found on the list included T. G. L. Ballance (Oxford), P. H. Blagg (Oxford), J. P. Blake (Cambridge and Hampshire), R. E. C. Butterworth (Oxford and Middlesex), R. A. Gerrard (Somerset), the rugby international, J. W. T. Grimshaw (Cambridge and Kent), J. G. Halliday (Oxford), C. P. Hamilton (Army and Kent), B. Howlett (Kent), R. H. C. Human (Cambridge and Worcestershire), J. W. Lee (Somerset), brother of Harry and Frank, F. M. McRae (Somerset), M. H. Matthews (Oxford), C. W. C. Packe (Leicestershire), W. J. Pershke (Oxford), P. W. Rucker (Oxford), K. B. Scott (Oxford), R. G. Tindall (Oxford), D. F. Walker (Hampshire), P. M. W. Whitehouse (Oxford) and R. de W. K. Winlaw (Cambridge and Surrey). The number of inter-war blues was 20, 14 of them Oxonians.

Among other well-known players from other countries were L. C. Bell (Canada), P. H. B. Cloete (Western Province), R. Crook (Wellington, NZ), G. L. Cruikshanks (Eastern Province), C. Doyle (Orange Free State), R. J. Evans (Border), J. D. E. Gartley (Transvaal), F. S. Haden (Auckland), E. P. Hamilton (Transvaal), G. C. Hart-Davis (Natal), N. H. McMillan (Auckland), A. P. Monteath (Otago), C. F. B. Papenfus (OFS), D. Price (Western Province), K. L. Ridings (South Australia), W. A. Roach (Western Australia), P. F. Seagram (Canada), F. Thorn (Victoria), and C. W. Walker (South Australia), of the 1930 and 1938 Australian teams to England.

Of those, killed in their teens or early twenties, who might have been destined for great things in the game one can only speculate. Certainly amateur cricket was more or less deprived of half a generation. As an example affecting one school, nearly 20 members of the Eton XIs of the 1930s were killed. The Harrow casualties were also heavy, and other schools may well have been hit equally hard or even harder.

Wisden Cricketers' Almanack

R. L. ARROWSMITH

Wisden Cricketers' Almanack, first published in 1864 and produced annually ever since, takes its name from one of the best players of the years immediately preceding its birth. Born at Brighton in 1826, John Wisden played his first match for Sussex in 1845 and his last in 1863, and between those dates was one of the most formidable players in England. Although he was a small man, he was, in his younger days at any rate, a fast bowler, but straighter and steadier than anyone else of his pace. Even considering the low-scoring standards of the times, his record is remarkable and one of his feats is unique. Playing, by virtue of owning a ground at Leamington, for North v South at Lord's in 1850, he clean bowled all 10 of his opponents in the second innings, and it is stated in *Scores and Biographies* that 'without exaggeration his balls turned a yard from the off'. He was, moreover, a good bat, with a couple of hundreds to his credit at a period when hundreds were rare, and we can well believe the popular opinion that around 1850 no one would have had a chance against him at single wicket.

But quite part from his cricket he was clearly a man of considerable character. He and James Dean, also of Sussex, were the prime movers of the revolt against Old Clarke in the All-England XI and it was they who in 1852 founded the United England XI, which proved every bit as successful as its rival. Wisden was also, with George Parr, largely responsible for the first important tour abroad, when in 1859 they took twelve professionals to play in Canada and the United States. How profitable this was financially can be seen when one learns that each of the players made about £90 out of the two months' trip.

Before this in 1855 Wisden had set up with Frederick Lillywhite a cricket and cigar business in New Coventry Street, London. Lillywhite was a difficult and quarrelsome person and the partnership was dissolved three years later, Wisden continuing the business on his own. Like his other ventures, it prospered and, when he died in 1884, he was a comparatively well-to-do man.

John Wisden, founder of the *Almanack*.

It was in 1864 that he published the first of his *Cricketers' Almanacks*. It seems unlikely that he himself ever wrote for them, as the elder James Lillywhite did for his annuals. Indeed for the first 6 years there was no writing to do. In 1866 it is expressly stated,

> John Wisden and Co., have carefully avoided making any remarks upon the play or players, as the purport of this little work is to record the scores of the matches published as a book of reference.

The first issue, published at one shilling, a price that was to remain unchanged until 1915, is a curious compilation. It contains the almanack proper, with an entry for each day in the year, the births and deaths of cricketers being intermingled with festivals of the church and the anniversaries of historical events. This feature was retained until 1878, though it was considerably reduced in size in 1870. At times the compiler was obviously hard put to it to find suitable events: thus in 1875 under 20 August we have 'Burning hot day, 1874' and under 21 August 'Ten clergymen played in match, 1851'.

After the almanack in the original issue came the Laws of Cricket, a list of first appearances at Lord's, centuries scored since 1850, extraordinary matches and scores of Gentlemen v Players and of the matches between the two great travelling XIs. There followed a bewildering hotch-potch of miscellaneous information including the winners of classic races and of 'Varsity Boat races, the rules of bowls, quoits and knur-and-spell and an account of European relations with China and of the trial of Charles I. The whole comprised 112 pages.

Next year the non-cricket information was dropped except from the almanack, scores of 'Varsity Matches from the beginning were added and the scores of MCC matches and of matches played between the first-class counties. In 1867 the births and deaths of cricketers first appeared and the results of matches played by Anomalies, Butterflies, Cambridge University, Civil Service, Free Foresters, Gravesend and Milton, Incogniti, I Zingari, Kensington Park, Longsigns, Oxford University, Quidnuncs, Royal Artillery, Southgate and Upper Tooting. In the following year the information about club cricket was drastically reduced and soon disappeared entirely with the exception of the results of I Zingari matches, which have been retained to the present day.

In 1870 came the first great change: accounts of matches were introduced, to be followed in 1872 by an introductory account of the season of each county. These were written until his death in 1879 by W. H. Knight, and if one were seeking for a well of pure Victorian journalese undefiled, one could not do better than turn to him.

> James Phillips averaged in '76 about the same as he did in '75: but his fine cover-point fielding was right up to top-class county form, and

saved many runs. His brother – the famous 'Little Harry' – has been moved up to 'first man in' position, and his average has 'moved up' proportionally from 5·9 in 1875, to 11·3 in 1876. His accident at Tunbridge Wells was indeed 'a sad blow to himself' and 'a sore discouragement' to his county. As to the rest of the team, space bids Mr Compiler to refer readers to the County scores and summaries, and to heartily wish a pleasant and successful season to Sussex cricketers in 1877.

But the chiefest gem has been preserved by F. S. Ashley-Cooper from an account of a match in 1877 in which Dr E. M. Grace, going in first, had made 200 not out and Dr A. Grace was left with 28 not out – 'A doctor at the beginning, and a doctor at the end. Such is life.'

Poor Mr. Knight! It is easy to make fun of him. But he was a genuine lover of cricket; with the limited county programmes of those days he had ample space at his disposal (an account of an ordinary county match sometimes covers two pages of small print) and he really does tell one what happened. Thus in an account of North v South at the Oval in 1878 –

Shrewsbury was fielding deep long-on in front of the people by the tavern; Mr Thornton let out powerfully at one from Morley, Shrewsbury ran to the front of the pavilion, and there, with back hard up against the paling, he caught the ball and tumbled over – *head first, heels in the air form* – into the lap of some old member, cosily enjoying the cricket on a front seat; but Shrewsbury held the ball all the while, and came up smiling and tossing the ball up in the usual neat form that Shrewsbury displays in all his cricket.

How vividly we can see the whole incident! Indeed for one who wishes to be transported for a while to those carefree days when averages counted for little and Championship points for nothing, when each match was an entity in itself like many a modern club match and there were plenty of amateurs with unlimited time to play, when the news that Grace was batting produced a stream of hansoms from the City to Lord's and when London had a third great ground in Prince's, I know nothing better than an evening spent quietly savouring the accounts of matches in a *Wisden* of the 1870s.

After Knight's death *Wisden* fell for a time upon evil days. The form remained much the same, but the accounts are colourless and the general conduct of the almanack was unbusinesslike. The climax seems to have come when the 1886 volume was a year late in appearing and, in a happy moment, the proprietors appointed C. F. Pardon as editor, with his brothers, E.S. and S.H., and C. Stewart Caine to help him. C. F. Pardon remained editor for four years only (he died in 1890) and his fame has long since been eclipsed by that of his brother, but there can be no doubt how much *Wisden* owes to him.

It increased rapidly in both size and circulation, new features were introduced (the Cricketers of the Year dates from his time) and the accounts of the county season began to contain really informed and informative criticism. For instance, in the account of Sussex in 1890 there is as fair a statement of the case for residential qualification under proper safeguards as will be found anywhere and the county is urged to take full and legitimate advantage of the residential law, though the writer makes it clear that he would not have been in favour of anything approaching the modern system of registration. Within a few years Sussex, reinforced by Ranji, Fry and W. L. Murdoch, to say nothing of pros such as Marlow and Bland, were a side to be reckoned with.

Whether C. F. Pardon would, if he had lived, have acquired as great a reputation and prestige in time as his brother, Sydney, was destined to do, it is impossible to say. As it is, Sydney Pardon is unquestionably the greatest name in the history of *Wisden*. He was a man of real ability and wide interests, who contributed articles to *The Times* not only on cricket, but also on music, racing and the drama, on all of which subjects he was an authority. He had too a considerable knowledge of athletics, rowing, boxing and billiards, and his encyclopaedic memory made him a mine of information about persons and events.

Sydney H. Pardon, editor of *Wisden* from 1891 to 1925.

For years his Notes in *Wisden* carried a weight and attracted an attention which is quite extraordinary when one considers that he had never himself been a serious player. The proof of the pudding is in the eating and on almost every major subject over the years on which he expressed a decided opinion time has proved him right. He consistently opposed tampering with the laws; since his death a whole host of experiments have been tried and almost every one has turned out to be a failure. In 1907 he wrote of a suggestion for shorter boundaries,

Nothing could be worse for the game than to make boundary hits easier than they are at present. . . . To my mind it is essential that boundaries should be as deep as possible so that hits may be worth the runs given for them. One has only to watch a day's cricket at the Oval, with deep boundaries all round, and then see a game on a small ground to appreciate enormous difference. Short boundaries, by decreasing the opportunities for good fielding, rob cricket of half its charm.

In the last Notes he wrote, in 1925, Pardon expressed himself strongly against the covering of the whole wicket. He was always lukewarm beforehand about the Triangular Test conception, though its complete failure in the event was largely due to two causes which he could not have foreseen – the weather and the refusal of 6 of the leading Australian players to make the trip. In 1919 he opposed uncompromisingly the scheme for 2-day matches: before the end of the season the Advisory Committee had decided unanimously to revert to three-day matches in 1920.

Again in 1921 he objected strongly to the importation of Australians:

Clubs with money to spend should encourage native talent and not buy cricketers of established reputation. Partly for the reason that it would open the door to financial dealings I was glad that the registration scheme, drawn up at the request of the counties by Lord Harris and brought forward in December, was rejected by the Advisory Committee. . . Even at the risk of being described, as I have been before now, as a hide-bound Tory, I must affirm my belief that the two-years residential qualification is a great safeguard in preserving the true spirit of county cricket.

Pardon never did greater service to cricket than by his uncompromising condemnation of unfair bowling. For almost 20 years he campaigned against it in *Wisden* and elsewhere, and when in 1901 the captains of the first-class counties and MCC between them stamped it out so effectively that for 50 years it ceased to be a problem, he legitimately prided himself on having contributed to the result. Indeed perhaps only Jim Phillips, the famous umpire, could have been said to have done more to bring it about.

Pardon had spoken out fearlessly and constantly:

We have not the least hesitation in saying that a fast bowler with the action of Jones, or a slow bowler with a delivery so open to question as McKibbin, would have found no place in the earlier elevens that came to England. Jones's bowling is, to our mind, radically unfair, as we cannot conceive a ball being fairly bowled at the pace of an express train with a bent arm.

To the argument that it is impossible to distinguish between throwing and legitimate bowling, I attach no importance whatever. I wonder what my old friend Bob Thoms would say if anyone told him he could not tell a throw from a fairly bowled ball. A throw may be difficult to define in words, but to the eye of a practical and unbiased cricketer it is, I think, very obvious.

I regard Mold as the luckiest of men to have gone through nearly a dozen seasons before being no-balled.

It was typical that on matters of public policy Pardon never minced his words. Of the 1909 Selection Committee he wrote,

To this day the extraordinary blundering in connection with the team for the Test Match at Lord's . . . remains unexplained. Lord Hawke was away from England at the time, the responsibility for the selection of the eleven resting entirely on C. B. Fry, H. D. G. Leveson Gower and A. C. MacLaren. How these three gentlemen came to make such a muddle of the business no one has ever been able to understand.

At the Oval a fatal blunder was committed in leaving out Buckenham – a blunder for which it was generally understood that MacLaren was responsible. Experts occasionally do strange things and this was one of the strangest. The idea of letting England go into the field in fine weather on a typical Oval wicket with no fast bowler except Sharp touched the confines of lunacy. The despised man in the street could not have been guilty of such folly.

Individuals Pardon criticized kindly unless some principle was at stake. Over teams he was more outspoken. For instance of the England side at Lord's in 1921 he wrote,

To be quite candid, an England side so slow and generally inefficient had never previously been seen against Australia.

Many years before he had written of Leicestershire,

It was a matter of common knowledge that there was a lack of discipline among the professionals, and it is fair to assume that much of the ill-success attending the later efforts of the eleven can be attributed to this cause. The committee even went to the length of leaving one or two men out of matches. It is to be hoped the punishment, light as it was, will have taught the delinquents the error of their ways before another season opens: otherwise even more drastic measures may have to be taken to prevent a recurrence of what was really a scandal.

Pardon's kindliness and fairness as a critic can nowhere be seen better than in the obituary notices, which first appeared in 1891, and the more important of which at least he wrote himself. These were rightly described in *The Cricketer* after his death as 'gems of biography'. He had been watching first-class cricket since 1863 and reporting it since 1872 and had thus himself seen most of the players on whom he was writing.

Pardon was succeeded on his death in 1925 by C. Stewart Caine, who had been associated with *Wisden* ever since the Pardons took it over, and it was natural that under him the almanack should remain largely unchanged, though it increased in size. Stewart Caine was a man greatly respected and trusted by those in authority in the cricket world, who knew that he would never betray their confidence. Only a shrewd critic could tell his work now from Sydney Pardon's. Again it is fascinating to see how time has confirmed his judgments.

Is there not a danger of this Test match cricket becoming rather a fetish? It produces some wonderful struggles, it is true, and is immensely popular not only here but even more so, if possible, in Australia, but it tends to make cricket more of a spectacle than a game and one may question whether the feverish atmosphere it creates is altogether healthy.

This was written in 1926. Five years later he wrote,

It is to be hoped that when representatives of the commonwealth come here again, the over-preparation of pitches which obtained last summer, will have been abolished and a return made to conditions that admit of an even fight between bowler and batsman. . . . Finally I trust that we have seen the last of playing a match to a finish, however many days may be required for that purpose. Given normal circumstances, four days are quite sufficient for the decision of a game contested in reasonably enterprising spirit – the real cricket spirit.

Stewart Caine died in 1933 and was succeeded by S. J. Southerton. A son of the famous Surrey bowler, Southerton had been bred on Mitcham Green, then a great nursery of Surrey cricket, had acted as scorer to the Australian side of 1893 and had himself been a useful club cricketer who once performed a hat-trick for the Press Club against the Authors at Lord's. Moreover, he had accompanied the MCC side to Australia in 1928–29 and so had had experience of conditions there. Like his predecessors he had a long association with *Wisden* dating from 1894, but his own tenure of office was destined to be short and he died in March 1935. He, too, was greatly respected and trusted and he maintained the tradition of being completely outspoken where the interests of the game demanded it. No fairer view of the Body-line controversy can be found than his in *Wisden* for 1934, and a year later he criticized fiercely journalists who concerned themselves more with tittle-tattle than with what happened on the field of play.

And here it may be said that anything in the nature of tittle-tattle and especially any prying into the private lives of players has always been studiously avoided in *Wisden*. Historical accuracy may have made some reference unavoidable, but the policy has always been a decent reticence. Thus of a player who was found stealing in the dressing-room, *Wisden* wrote at the time, 'About his subsequent disappearance from cricket there is no need to speak', and years later in his obituary all we find is, 'His career in first-class cricket ended abruptly.' Take again what is said of the last years of Pooley:

Of the faults of private character that marred Pooley's career and were the cause of the poverty in which he spent the later years of his life there is no need now to speak. He was in many ways his own enemy, but even to the last he had a geniality and a sense of humour that to a certain extent condoned his weaknesses.

At times indeed this reticence is tantalizing:

An unpleasant incident marred the concluding portion of the match. There was a delay of a quarter of an hour, the Lancashire captain offering to give up the match, but being eventually prevailed upon to proceed with it.

But we are not told what the incident was.

Wisden has also been characterized since the time of the Pardons by a decency and dignity of style and has never descended to the current jargon of the popular journalist. Indeed one great teacher of history was for years accustomed to read to his pupils accounts of matches from old *Wisdens* as models of what concise historical narrative should be.

Already in 1929 it had been necessary to curtail the births and deaths and in 1938, under Southerton's successor, W. H. Brookes, the first large-scale reorganization of *Wisden* took place. The old division into two parts was abolished, the contents were rearranged, the counties were put in alphabetical order and not in the order of the Championship, and more photographs were introduced. At the same time the cover of the paper-backed edition was changed and happily made more durable and the almanack was published for John

Wisden and Co by J. Whitaker and Sons. From 1944 to 1978 the publishers (still on behalf of John Wisden) were Sporting Handbooks Ltd. In 1979 the publication was taken over by Macdonald & Janes.

No doubt much was to be said logically in favour of the changes and the present form of the almanack may be more convenient for those who simply read the current number. But to those many who are constantly delving into old *Wisdens* the necessary adjustment from one form to the other is undeniably tiresome. Meanwhile the omission of more and more of the earlier births and deaths though inevitable (clearly this section could not have been allowed to swell indefinitely) is a grave inconvenience. However at last these have been selected on a more logical basis than before and in the 1979 edition the section was far more satisfctory than for many years.

Brookes resigned in 1939 and from 1940 to 1943 the duties of editor were undertaken by Haddon Whitaker, who modestly referred to himself as merely 'co-ordinating the contributions from various sources and presenting them as a whole'. During these years 'Notes by the Editor' disappeared, their place being taken by notes on the previous season by R. C. Robertson-Glasgow. In 1944 Hubert Preston, who had been closely associated with the preparation of *Wisden* since 1895, took over the full duties of editor and resumed the Notes. He was succeeded in 1952 by his son, Norman Preston, and who in 1977, to the delight of his many friends, was deservedly awarded the MBE.

Norman Preston was editor of *Wisden* following the retirement of his father Hubert in 1952 until his death in 1980. He is succeeded by John Woodcock.

It is perhaps presumptuous to criticize the reigning dynasty. Much that has been done is clearly in accordance with modern demands and was no doubt inevitable in any publication which seeks to pay its way, and for some features, the detailed index and the often extremely interesting articles by famous players, one has nothing but praise. But the summaries of county seasons in these days lack authority and distinction and give a general impression of being written by people whose judgment of a player depends wholly on his figures. None the less *Wisden* remains the recognized authority on each year's cricket and, as a record of first-class cricket in every part of the world, is more nearly complete now than at any period of its history.

The earliest issues of *Wisden* down to 1878 are very rare, so rare indeed that a facsimile edition has been published to enable collectors to complete their sets. However, it may safely be said that, whatever the money value of the first 6 issues, their practical value, at least to anyone who possesses the relevant volumes of *Scores and Biographies*, is small. The real interest begins with the accounts of matches in 1870. From then on *Wisden* is indispensable to anyone who wishes to study cricket history. There is no adequate substitute.

Nowhere else can one be sure of finding the full score, with an account, of every first-class match played in England and, at least for many years past, in Australia or by English touring sides abroad; nowhere else can one trace so fully the career of any first-class player of the period and nowhere else is one so likely to find, if one is prepared to search a bit, a reliable and informative account of his methods.

It is a bad book to turn to in a hurry, not because it is hard to find what one wants, but because in looking for that one's eye is sure to fall on something which suggests another fascinating line of inquiry and soon one is off, like a dog with his nose to the ground investigating one smell after another, forgetful of all else, forgetting even for what purpose one originally took a volume from the shelf.

Part X
Laws

The 1980 Code Introduced

S. C. GRIFFITH

AT THE International Cricket Conference of 1973 member-countries invited MCC to recodify the Laws of Cricket, in order to bring the 1947 Code of the Laws up to date. Since 1947 many Notes had been added to the Laws and the Conference felt that it was time to consolidate the various amendments and Notes in order to achieve greater clarity and simplicity in a new Code. It was agreed that I should be invited to prepare the first draft, but I could not undertake to begin the task until the autumn of 1974. At the same time, all member-countries of the International Cricket Conference, that is to say both full and associate members, were invited to examine the existing Laws of Cricket (including the Notes) and to recommend any deletions, additions and amendments thereto. It was also thought desirable for me, as Secretary of the Conference, to collate these recommendations from member-countries before the task was begun.

In the event, it took me a year, in collaboration with T. E. Smith (the former General Secretary of the Association of Cricket Umpires), to produce the first draft, which was submitted to MCC in December of 1975. My first job was obviously to collate the recommendations and also to consider the many suggestions – *e.g.* some 300 from the ACU – received, both from other organizations and individuals throughout the cricketing world. Before getting down to the first draft I came to the following general conclusions, with which Tom Smith agreed:

1 That the vast majority of the Notes to the Laws were, in themselves, Laws and should be included as such in any re-draft.
2 That the Laws themselves should be paragraphed under suitable headings for ease of reference.
3 Certain Laws should be merged, not only for ease of reference, but for the sake of clarity. For instance, some of the Laws in the 1947 Code had no heading and were difficult to locate.
4 That in any redraft the irritating habit of not describing the cross-reference, using the Law number only, be eliminated.
5 That such Laws as were redrafted should be applicable as far as possible to all levels of cricket in whatever cricketing country.
6 That an attempt should be made to clarify those situations in the playing of the game which had given rise to the largest number of queries on the Laws received by MCC and ACU during my time at Lord's.

Quite clearly it would have been helpful had one been able to retain the existing numbering of the Laws, but, as time went by, this became more and more difficult to achieve, and eventually the idea was discarded. In fact, we were able to reduce the 47 Laws contained in the 1947 Code to 42, including an entirely new Law, to which I will refer later.

The Laws of cricket have stood the test of time remarkably well, and I feel very strongly that the reason for this is that the Law-makers have never attempted to legislate for every possible happening in this wonderful but complicated game of cricket. Were one to try to do so, the Laws would be unmanageable in size and would perhaps never succeed in achieving their object. Another reason for the strength of the Laws has been the determination of almost every cricketer in the world to do his best to play, not only within the Laws, but, just as importantly, within the spirit of the game. For this reason, sanctions have rarely been imposed, although as the game has evolved some form of sanction in certain circumstances has become necessary.

There is one other point. The production of the 1980 Code has been the result of consultation throughout the cricketing world. A tremendous amount of time and trouble has been taken to ensure that the views of cricketers at every level have been sought. There comes a time, however, in an exercise of this sort when the MCC Committee felt that a date for publication had to be fixed. This Code was, therefore, introduced to the Members of MCC after consideration of several drafts by all cricketing countries. Many members put in suggestions, almost all of which were drafting points, and most were included when the final draft was approved at a Special General Meeting of MCC on the 21 November 1979.

Besides the paragraphs already referred to and the incorporation of many of the Notes into the Laws themselves, the vast majority of the changes relate to arrangement in a more logical order; merging certain Laws – *e.g.* Laws 14 and 16 of the 1947 Code into one Law, namely Law 13 – in the new Code; rewording for the sake of clarity; some small additions – *e.g.* 'Signals' under Law 3.13; and the exclusion of Laws which apply only to one country or first-class cricket.

There is, however, one new Law – 'Timed Out', Law 31 in the new Code, which to some extent replaces Law 17 in the 1947 Code. This new Law makes it possible for a batsman to be given out on appeal if he wilfully takes longer than two minutes to reach the wicket. Hitherto, the batting side as a whole have lost the match – the batting side being deemed to have refused to play. It has been felt that such a penalty has been unjustified, even taking into account the damage which can be done by deliberate time-wasting. The new Law has the further advantage of encouraging batsmen to acquire a sense of urgency.

Certain other Laws were the subject of final discussion at the 1979 International Cricket Conference.

(a) Fitness of Ground, Weather and Light. The discussion here mainly centred on the question of appeals, particularly against the light. The view is taken that allowing the batting side one appeal per session of play would result in more play taking place. The practice whereby the umpires take the initiative and only continue play if the batting side so request can prompt batsmen to go off on occasions on which they might not have exercised a right of appeal.

An attempt has been made to take account of exceptional circumstances arising, and enabling the umpires in such cases to suspend play – a sad reflection on modern trends in crowd behaviour.

(b) Consistency has been achieved in regard to the mowing of the pitch in a match of 3 or more days' duration. Hitherto, there has been a difference in practice in this respect.

(c) Law 32 ('Caught') has been the subject of long and complicated debate, principally because of the difference of opinion as to whether or not a fieldsman should remain wholly within the boundary after 'completing a catch'.

(d) Polishing the ball (Law 42.5). Certain countries were anxious to impose a ban on polishing the ball, taking the view that such polishing retarded the growth of spin-bowling. As most spin-bowlers tend nowadays to polish, it was finally agreed that, provided no time was wasted, polishing should be allowed. The difficulties for the umpires in detecting polishing were appreciated and to allow a bowler only to polish would, in practice, tend to waste time rather than to save it.

(e) The bowling of fast, short-pitched balls presented the Law-makers with the greatest problem of all, and, following experiments in various parts of the world, it was finally agreed that the basic problem was to attempt to eliminate any form of intimidation. It was felt that the words 'systematic or persistent' to some extent missed the point. A definition of a fast, short-pitched ball has been included and to transgress in this respect could be as a result of one ball so bowled.

Furthermore, the procedure to be adopted by the umpires in the event of transgression has been laid down and applies equally to other Laws where applicable.

(f) The bowling of fast, high full pitches has been severely dealt with for the first time – see Law 42.9 in the new Code.

In the new Code, mention had been made in regard to the wearing of helmets. In debating the issue of wearing helmets in the field consideration was given to the possible discouragement of the practice, and it was partly for this reason that the new Law was introduced. MCC did not feel able to ban the use of helmets by fieldsmen because of the legal implications and the awful repercussions if a fieldsman was badly injured as a result of that ban. At the same time, it is reasonable to suppose that nobody wants positively to encourage their use in the field and for that reason Law 32.2(a) is included.

It is clear from the foregoing that the new Code must be read in conjunction with the old and cannot be dealt with by simply relating the 1947 Code in detail with the 1980 Code. There are many points which became apparent in a detailed examination – toleration in the specification of the ball for manufacturing reasons; bats to be made of wood; players showing dissent; and many other small but important changes.

Cricket, like every other art-form, is constantly evolving, and in due course this code, like its predecessors, will stand in need of modification. Yet it is only the 4th full revision to be undertaken of the original Laws of 1744. It is my earnest hope that the code of 1980 will stand the test of time as well as those that have gone before.

The Laws of Cricket (1980 Code)

Preface

During the last 200 years the conduct of the game of Cricket has been governed by a series of Codes of Laws. These Codes were established as indicated below, and were at all times subject to additions and alterations ordained by the governing authorities of the time. Since its formation in 1787 the Marylebone Cricket Club has been recognized as the sole authority for drawing up the Code and for all subsequent alterations. It is of interest that the development and revision of the Laws was essential as a method of settling debts resulting from gambling associated with the more important cricket matches. The Club also holds the World Copyright.

There is little doubt that cricket was subject to recognized rules as early as 1700, though the earliest known Code is that drawn up in 1744 by certain noblemen and gentlemen who used the Artillery Ground in London. These Laws were revised in 1755 by 'Several Cricket Clubs, particularly that of the Star and Garter in Pall Mall.'

The next arrangement was produced by 'a Committee of Noblemen and Gentlemen of Kent, Hampshire, Surrey, Sussex, Middlesex and London', at the Star and Garter on 25 February 1774, and this in turn was revised by a similar body in February 1786.

On 30 May 1788, the first MCC Code was adopted, and remained in force until 15 May 1835, when a new Code of Laws was approved by the Committee. The Laws appear to have been first numbered in 1823.

The 1835 Code, amended in detail from time to time, stood until 21 April 1884, when, after consultation with cricket clubs both at home and overseas, important alterations were incorporated in a new version adopted at a Special General Meeting of the MCC.

By 1939, these Laws, supplemented as they had been by the inclusion of many definitions and interpretations in the form of Notes, were in need of revision, and immediately on the conclusion of the World War the opinions of controlling bodies and clubs throughout the world were sought, with the result that the present Code was adopted at a Special General Meeting of MCC on 7 May 1947.

The revision in the main aimed at the clarification and better arrangement of the previous laws and their interpretations, but did not exclude certain definite alterations designed firstly to provide greater latitude in the conduct of the game as required by the widely differing conditions in which it is played, and secondly to eliminate certain umpiring difficulties.

During the last 30 years, however, changes and Notes have been included requiring the publication of 5 editions of the 1947 Code. At the International Cricket Conference of 1972, MCC suggested that the stage had been reached where, for the purposes of removing anomalies, consolidating various Amendments and Notes, and of achieving greater clarity and simplicity, the 1947 Code of the Laws of Cricket should be revised and rewritten. As a result of this suggestion, MCC were asked to undertake the task beginning in the autumn of 1974 following a period of consultation throughout the cricket-playing world.

After initial consideration, MCC decided that the original point of the Notes to the Laws – that of providing interpretations of difficulties arising from the Laws – had to some extent been lost. Many notes were, in themselves, Laws, and, as such should be included in the Laws. In addition to the object of recodification, MCC have attempted to make this important change.

The Laws of Cricket apply equally to women's cricket as to men's. As in the past, however, this New Code refers to the male person only, for convenience and brevity.

Many queries on the Laws are sent to MCC for decision every year, and it is from these sources that the chief difficulties arising from the Laws have become manifest. MCC, as the accepted makers of the Laws, which can only be changed by the vote of two-thirds of the members present and voting at a Special General Meeting of the Club, have always been prepared to answer these queries and to give interpretations on certain conditions which will be readily understood, *i.e.*:

(a) In the case of League or Competition cricket, the enquiry must come from the Committee responsible for organizing the league or competition. In other cases, enquiries should be initiated by a representative officer of a Club, or of an Umpires' Association on behalf of his or her Committee, or by a master or mistress in charge of school cricket.

(b) The incident on which a ruling is required must not be merely invented for disputation, but must have actually occurred in play.

(c) The enquiry must not be connected in any way with a bet or wager.

The basic Laws of Cricket have stood remarkably well the test of well over two hundred years of playing the game; and it is thought that the real reason for this is that cricketers have traditionally been prepared to play in the spirit of the game, as well as in accordance with the Laws. The unique character and enjoyment of cricket depends upon all cricketers, at whatever level, continuing to preserve this spirit.

J. A. BAILEY
Secretary MCC

Contents

LAW 1: THE PLAYERS

1 *Number of Players and Captain*

A match is played between 2 sides each of 11 Players, one of whom shall be Captain. In the event of the Captain not being available at any time a Deputy shall act for him.

2 *Nomination of Players*

Before the toss for innings, the Captain shall nominate his Players who may not thereafter be changed without the consent of the opposing Captain.

NOTES

(a) *More or less than 11 players a side*

A match may be played by agreement between sides of more or less than 11 players but not more than 11 players may field.

LAW 2: SUBSTITUTES AND RUNNERS: BATSMAN OR FIELDSMAN LEAVING THE FIELD: BATSMAN RETIRING: BATSMAN COMMENCING INNINGS

1 *Substitutes*

Substitutes shall be allowed by right to field for any player who during the match is incapacitated by illness or injury. The consent of the opposing Captain must be obtained for the use of a Substitute if any player is prevented from fielding for any other reason.

2 *Objection to Substitutes*

The opposing Captain shall have no right of objection to any player acting as Substitute in the field, nor as to where he shall field, although he may object to the Substitute acting as Wicket-Keeper.

3 *Substitute not to bat or bowl*

A Substitute shall not be allowed to bat or bowl.

4 *A Player for whom a Substitute has acted*

A player may bat, bowl or field even though a Substitute has acted for him.

5 *Runner*

A Runner shall be allowed for a Batsman who during the match is incapacitated by illness or injury. The person acting as Runner shall be a member of the batting side and shall, if possible, have already batted in that innings.

6 *Runner's Equipment*

The person acting as Runner for an injured Batsman shall wear batting gloves and pads if the injured Batsman is so equipped.

7 *Transgression of the Laws by an injured Batsman or Runner*

An injured Batsman may be out should his Runner break any one of Laws 33 (Handled the Ball), 37 (Obstructing the Field) or 38 (Run Out). As Striker he remains himself subject to the Laws. Furthermore, should he be out of his ground for any purpose and the wicket at the Wicket-Keeper's end be put down he shall be out under Law 38 (Run Out) or Law 39 (Stumped) irrespective of the position of the other Batsman or the Runner and no runs shall be scored.

When not the Striker, the injured Batsman is out of the game and shall stand where he does not interfere with the play. Should he bring himself into the game in any way then he shall suffer the penalties that any transgression of the Laws demands.

8 *Fieldsman leaving the field*

No Fieldsman shall leave the field or return during a session of play without the consent of the Umpire at the Bowler's end. The Umpire's consent is also necessary if a Substitute is required for a Fieldsman, when his side returns to the field after an interval. If a member of the fielding side leaves the field or fails to return after an interval and is absent from the field for longer than 15 minutes, he shall not be permitted to bowl after his return until he has been on the field for at least that length of playing time for which he was absent. This restriction shall not apply at the start of a new day's play.

9 *Batsman leaving the field or retiring*

A Batsman may leave the field or retire at any time owing to illness, injury or other unavoidable cause, having previously notified the Umpire at the Bowler's end. He may resume his innings at the fall of a wicket, which for the purposes of this Law shall include the retirement of another Batsman.

If he leaves the field or retires for any other reason he may only resume his innings with the consent of the opposing Captain.

When a Batsman has left the field or retired and is unable to return owing to illness, injury or other unavoidable cause his innings is to be recorded as 'retired, not out'. Otherwise it is to be recorded as 'retired, out'.

10 *Commencement of a Batsman's innings*

A Batsman shall be considered to have commenced his innings once he has stepped on to the field of play.

NOTES

(a) *Substitutes and Runners*

For the purpose of these Laws allowable illnesses or injuries are those which occur at any time after the nomination by the Captains of their teams.

LAW 3: THE UMPIRES

1 *Appointment*

Before the toss for innings two Umpires shall be appointed, one for each end, to control the game with absolute impartiality as required by the Laws.

2 *Change of Umpire*

No Umpire shall be changed during a match without the consent of both Captains.

3 *Special Conditions*

Before the toss for innings, the Umpires shall agree with both Captains on any special conditions affecting the conduct of the match.

4 *The Wickets*

The Umpires shall satisfy themselves before the start of the match that the wickets are properly pitched.

5 *Clock or Watch*

The Umpires shall agree between themselves and inform both Captains before the start of the match on the watch or clock to be followed during the match.

6 *Conduct and Implements*

Before and during a match the Umpires shall ensure that the conduct of the game and the implements used are strictly in accordance with the Laws.

7 *Fair and unfair play*

The Umpires shall be the sole judges of fair and unfair play.

8 *Fitness of Ground, Weather and Light*

(a) The Umpires shall be the sole judges of the fitness of the ground, weather and light for play.

(i) However, before deciding to suspend play or not to start play or not to resume play after an interval or stoppage, the Umpires shall establish whether both Captains (the Batsmen at the wicket may deputize for their Captain) wish to commence or to continue in the prevailing conditions; if so, their wishes shall be met.

(ii) In addition, if during play, the Umpires decide that the light is unfit, only the batting side shall have the option of continuing play. After agreeing to continue to play in unfit light conditions, the Captain of the batting side (or a Batsman at the wicket) may appeal against the light to the Umpires, who shall uphold the appeal only if, in their opinion, the light has deteriorated since the agreement to continue was made.

(b) After any suspension of play, the Umpires, unaccompanied by any of the Players or Officials shall, on their own initiative, carry out an inspection immediately the conditions improve and shall continue to inspect at intervals. Immediately the Umpires decide that play is possible they shall call upon the Players to resume the game.

9 *Exceptional circumstances*

In exceptional circumstances, other than those of weather, ground or light, the Umpires may decide to suspend or abandon play. Before making such a decision the Umpires shall establish, if the circumstances allow, whether both Captains (the Batsmen at the wicket may deputize for their Captain) wish to continue in the prevailing conditions: if so their wishes shall be met.

10 *Position of Umpires*

The Umpires shall stand where they can best see any act upon which their decision may be required.

Subject to this over-riding consideration the Umpire at the Bowler's end shall stand where he does not interfere with either the Bowler's run up or the Striker's view.

The Umpire at the Striker's end may elect to stand on the off instead of the leg side of the pitch, provided he informs the Captain of the fielding side and the Striker of his intention to do so.

11 *Umpires changing ends*

The Umpires shall change ends after each side has had one innings.

12 *Disputes*

All disputes shall be determined by the Umpires and if they disagree the actual state of things shall continue.

13 *Signals*

The following code of signals shall be used by Umpires who will wait until a signal has been answered by a Scorer before allowing the game to proceed.

Boundary – by waving the arm from side to side.
Boundary 6 – by raising both arms above the head.
Bye – by raising an open hand above the head.
Dead Ball – by crossing and re-crossing the wrists below the waist.
Leg Bye – by touching a raised knee with the hand.
No Ball – by extending one arm horizontally.
Out – by raising the index finger above the head. If not out the Umpire shall call 'not out'.
Short run – by bending the arm upwards and by touching the nearer shoulder with the tips of the fingers.
Wide – by extending both arms horizontally.

14 *Correctness of Scores*

The Umpires shall be responsible for satisfying themselves on the correctness of the scores throughout and at the conclusion of the match. See Law 21.6 (Correctness of Result).

NOTES

(a) *Attendance of Umpires*

The Umpires should be present on the ground and report to the Ground Executive or the equivalent at least 30 minutes before the start of a day's play.

(b) *Consultation between Umpires and Scorers*

Consultation between Umpires and Scorers over doubtful points is essential.

(c) *Fitness of Ground*

The Umpires shall consider the ground as unfit for play when it is so wet or slippery as to deprive the Bowlers of a reasonable foothold, the Fieldsmen, other than the deep-fielders, of the power of free movement, or the Batsmen the ability to play their strokes or to run between the wickets. Play should not be suspended merely because the grass and the ball are wet and slippery.

(d) *Fitness of Weather and Light*

The Umpires should only suspend play when they consider that the conditions are so bad that it is unreasonable or dangerous to continue.

LAW 4: THE SCORERS

1 *Recording Runs*

All runs scored shall be recorded by Scorers appointed for the purpose. Where there are two Scorers they shall frequently check to ensure that the score sheets agree.

2 *Acknowledging Signals*

The Scorers shall accept and immediately acknowledge all instructions and signals given to them by the Umpires.

LAW 5: THE BALL

1 *Weight and Size*

The ball, when new, shall weigh not less than $5\frac{1}{2}$ oz/155·9 g, nor more than $5\frac{3}{4}$ oz/163 g: and shall measure not less than $8\frac{13}{16}$ inches/22·4 cm, nor more than 9 inches/22·9 cm in circumference.

2 *Approval of Balls*

All balls used in matches shall be approved by the Umpires and Captains before the start of the match.

3 *New Ball*

Subject to agreement to the contrary, having been made before the toss, either Captain may demand a new ball at the start of each innings.

4 *New Ball in Match of 3 or More Days Duration*

In a match of 3 or more days duration, the Captain of the fielding side may demand a new ball after the prescribed number of overs has been bowled with the old one. The Governing Body for cricket in the country concerned shall decide the number of overs applicable in that country which shall be not less than 75 six-ball overs (55 eight-ball overs).

5 *Ball Lost or becoming Unfit for Play*

In the event of a ball during play being lost or, in the opinion of the Umpires, becoming unfit for play, the Umpires shall allow it to be replaced by one that in their opinion has had a similar amount of wear. If a ball is to be replaced, the Umpires shall inform the Batsman.

NOTES

(a) *Specifications*

The specifications, as described in 1 above shall apply to top-grade balls only. The following degrees of tolerance will be acceptable for other grades of ball.

(i) *Men's Grades 2–4*
Weight: $5\frac{5}{16}$ oz/150 g to $5\frac{13}{16}$ oz/165 g. Size: $8\frac{11}{16}$ inches/22·0 cm to $9\frac{1}{16}$ inches/23·0 cm.
(ii) *Women's*
Weight: $4\frac{15}{16}$ oz/140 g to $5\frac{5}{16}$ oz/150 g. Size: $8\frac{1}{4}$ inches/21·0 cm to $8\frac{7}{8}$ inches/22/5 cm.
(iii) *Junior*
Weight: $4\frac{5}{16}$ oz/133 g to $5\frac{1}{16}$ oz/143 g. Size: $8\frac{1}{16}$ inches/20·5 cm to $8\frac{11}{16}$ inches/22·0 cm.

LAW 6: THE BAT

1 *Width and Length*

The bat overall shall not be more than 38 inches/96·5 cm in length; the blade of the bat shall be made of wood and shall not exceed $4\frac{1}{4}$ inches/10·8 cm at the widest part.

NOTES

(a) *The blade of the bat may be covered with material for protection, strengthening or repair. Such material shall not exceed $\frac{1}{16}$ inches/1·56 mm in thickness.*

LAW 7: THE PITCH

1 *Area of Pitch*

The pitch is the area between the bowling creases – *see* Law 9 (The Bowling and Popping Creases). It shall measure 5 ft/1·52 m in width on either side of a line joining the centre of the middle stumps of the wickets – *see* Law 8 (The Wickets).

2 *Selection and Preparation*

Before the toss for innings, the Executive of the Ground shall be responsible for the selection and preparation of the pitch; thereafter the Umpires shall control its use and maintenance.

3 *Changing Pitch*

The pitch shall not be changed during a match unless it becomes unfit for play, and then only with the consent of both Captains.

4 *Non-Turf Pitches*

In the event of a non-turf pitch being used, the following shall apply:
(a) Length: That of the playing surface to a minimum of 58 ft (17·68 m)
(b) Width: That of the playing surface to a minimum of 6 ft (1·83 m)
See Law 10 (Rolling, Sweeping, Mowing, Watering the Pitch and Remarking of Creases) Note (a).

LAW 8: THE WICKETS

1 *Width and Pitching*

Two sets of wickets, each 9 inches/22·86 cm wide, and consisting of 3 wooden stumps with two wooden bails upon the top, shall be pitched opposite and parallel to each other at a distance of 22 yards/20·12 m between the centres of the 2 middle stumps.

2 *Size of Stumps*

The stumps shall be of equal and sufficient size to prevent the ball from passing between them. Their tops shall be 28 inches/71·1 cm above the ground, and shall be dome-shaped except for the bail grooves.

3 *Size of Bails*

The bails shall be each $4\frac{3}{8}$ inches/11·1 cm in length and when in position on the top of the stumps shall not project more than $\frac{1}{2}$ inch/1·3 cm above them.

NOTES

(a) *Dispensing with Bails*

In a high wind the Umpires may decide to dispense with the use of bails.

(b) *Junior Cricket*

For Junior Cricket, as defined by the local Governing Body, the following measurements for the Wickets shall apply:

Width – 8 inches/20·32 cm
Pitched – 21 yards/19·2 m
Height – 27 inches/68·58 cm
Bails – each $3\frac{7}{8}$ inches/9·84 cm in length and should not project more than $\frac{1}{2}$ inch/1·3 cm above them.

LAW 9: THE BOWLING, POPPING AND RETURN CREASES

1 *The Bowling Crease*

The bowling crease shall be marked in line with the stumps at each end and shall be 8 ft 8 inches/2·64 m in length, with the stumps in the centre.

2 *The Popping Crease*

The popping crease, which is the back edge of the crease marking, shall be in front of and parallel with the bowling crease. It shall have the back edge of the crease marking 4 ft/1·22 m from the centre of the stumps and shall extend to a minimum of 6 ft/1·83 m on either side of the line of the wicket.

The popping crease shall be considered to be unlimited in length.

3 *The Return Crease*

The return crease marking, of which the inside edge is the crease, shall be at each end of the bowling crease and at right angles to it. The return crease shall be marked to a minimum of 4 ft/1·22 m behind the wicket and shall be considered to be unlimited in length. A forward extension shall be marked to the popping crease.

LAW 10: ROLLING, SWEEPING, MOWING, WATERING THE PITCH AND RE-MARKING OF CREASES

1 *Rolling*

During the match the pitch may be rolled at the request of the Captain of the batting side, for a period of not more than 7 minutes before the start of each innings, other than the 1st innings of the match, and before the start of each day's play. In addition, if, after the toss and before the first innings of the match, the start is delayed, the Captain of the batting side shall have the right to have the pitch rolled for not more than 7 minutes.

The pitch shall not otherwise be rolled during the match.

The 7 minutes rolling permitted before the start of a day's play shall take place not earlier than half an hour before the start of play and the Captain of the batting side may delay such rolling until 10 minutes before the start of play should he so desire.

If a Captain declares an innings closed less than 15 minutes before the resumption of play, and the other Captain is thereby prevented from exercising his option of 7 minutes rolling or if he is so prevented for any other reason the time for rolling shall be taken out of the normal playing time.

2 *Sweeping*

Such sweeping of the pitch as is necessary during the match shall be done so that the 7 minutes allowed for rolling the pitch provided for in 1 above is not affected.

3 *Mowing*

(a) *Responsibilities of Ground Authority and of Umpires*

All mowings which are carried out before the toss for innings shall be the responsibility of the Ground Authority thereafter they shall be carried out under the supervision of the Umpires, *see* Law 7.2 (Selection and Preparation).

(b) *Initial Mowing*

The pitch shall be mown before play begins on the day the match is scheduled to start or in the case of a delayed start on the day the match is expected to start. *See* 3(a) above (Responsibilities of Ground Authority and of Umpires).

(c) *Subsequent Mowings in a Match of 2 or More Days' Duration*

In a match of 2 or more days' duration, the pitch shall be mown daily before play begins. Should this mowing not take place because of weather conditions, rest days or other reasons the pitch shall be mown on the first day on which the match is resumed.

(d) *Mowing of the Outfield in a Match of 2 or More Days' Duration*

In order to ensure that conditions are as similar as possible for both sides, the outfield shall normally be mown before the commencement of play on each day of the match, if ground and weather conditions allow. *See* Note (b) to this Law.

4 *Watering*

The pitch shall not be watered during a match.

5 *Re-marking Creases*

Whenever possible the creases shall be re-marked.

6 *Maintenance of Foot Holes*

In wet weather, the Umpires shall ensure that the holes made by the Bowlers and Batsmen are cleaned out and dried whenever necessary to facilitate play. In matches of 2 or more days' duration, the Umpires shall allow, if necessary, the re-turfing of foot holes made by the Bowler in his delivery stride, or the use of quick-setting fillings for the same purpose, before the start of each day's play.

7 *Securing of Footholds and Maintenance of Pitch*

During play, the Umpires shall allow either Batsman to beat the pitch with his bat and players to secure their footholds by the use of sawdust, provided that no damage to the pitch is so caused, and Law 42 (Unfair Play) is not contravened.

NOTES

(a) *Non-Turf Pitches*

The above Law 10 applies to turf pitches.

The game is played on non-turf pitches in many countries at various levels. Whilst the conduct of the game on these surfaces should always be in accordance with the Laws of Cricket, it is recognized that it may sometimes be necessary for Governing Bodies to lay down special playing conditions to suit the type of non-turf pitch used in their country.

In matches played against Touring Teams, any special playing conditions should be agreed in advance by both parties.

(b) *Mowing of the Outfield in a match of 2 or more days' duration*

If, for reasons other than ground and weather conditions, daily and complete mowing is not possible, the Ground Authority shall notify the Captains and Umpires, before the toss for innings, of the procedure to be adopted for such mowing during the match.

(c) *Choice of Roller*

If there is more than one roller available the Captain of the batting side shall have a choice.

LAW 11: COVERING THE PITCH

1 *Before the Start of a Match*

Before the start of a match complete covering of the pitch shall be allowed.

2 *During a Match*

The pitch shall not be completely covered during a match unless prior arrangement or regulations so provide.

3 *Covering Bowlers' Run-Up*

Whenever possible, the Bowlers' run-up shall be covered, but the covers so used shall not extend further than 4 ft/1·22 m in front of the popping crease.

NOTES

(a) *Removal of Covers*

The covers should be removed as promptly as possible whenever the weather permits.

LAW 12: INNINGS

1 *Number of Innings*

A match shall be of one or two innings of each side according to agreement reached before the start of play.

2 *Alternate Innings*

In a 2 innings match each side shall take their innings alternately except in the case provided for in Law 13 (The Follow-On).

3 *The Toss*

The Captains shall toss for the choice of innings on the field of play not later than 15 minutes before the time scheduled for the match to start, or before the time agreed upon for play to start.

4 *Choice of Innings*

The winner of the toss shall notify his decision to bat or to field to the opposing Captain not later than 10 minutes before the time scheduled for the match to start, or before the time agreed upon for play to start. The decision shall not thereafter be altered.

5 *Continuation after one innings of each side*

Despite the terms of 1, above, in a 4 innings match, when a result has been reached on the 1st innings the Captains may agree to the continuation of play if, in their opinion, there is a prospect of carrying the game to a further issue in the time left. *See* Law 21 (Result).

NOTES

(a) *Limited Innings – One Innings Match*

In a 1 innings match, each innings may, by agreement, be limited by a number of overs or by a period of time.

(b) *Limited Innings – Two Innings Match*

In a 2 innings match, the 1st innings of each side may, by agreement, be limited to a number of overs or by a period of time.

LAW 13: THE FOLLOW-ON

1 *Lead on First Innings*

In a 2 innings match the side which bats first and leads by 200 runs in a match of 5 days or more, by 150 runs in a 3-day or 4-day match, by 100 runs in a 2-day match, or by 75 runs in a 1-day match, shall have the option of requiring the other side to follow their innings.

2 *Day's Play Lost*

If no play takes place on the 1st day of a match of 2 or more days' duration, 1 above shall apply in accordance with the number of days' play remaining from the actual start of the match.

LAW 14: DECLARATIONS

1 *Time of Declaration*

The Captain of the batting side may declare an innings closed at any time during a match irrespective of its duration.

2 *Forfeiture of Second Innings*

A Captain may forfeit his 2nd innings, provided his decision to do so is notified to the opposing Captain and Umpires in sufficient time to allow 7 minutes rolling of the pitch. *See* Law 10 (Rolling, Sweeping, Mowing, Watering the Pitch and Re-Marking of Creases). The normal 10-minute interval between innings shall be applied.

LAW 15: START OF PLAY

1 *Call of Play*

At the start of each innings and of each day's play and on the resumption of play after any interval or interruption the Umpire at the Bowler's end shall call 'play'.

2 *Practice on the Field*

At no time on any day of the match shall there be any bowling or batting practice on the pitch.

No practice may take place on the field if, in the opinion of the Umpires, it could result in a waste of time.

3 *Trial Run-Up*

No bowler shall have a trial run-up after 'play' has been called in any session of play, except at the fall of a wicket when an Umpire may allow such a trial run-up if he is satisfied that it will not cause any waste of time.

LAW 16: INTERVALS

1 *Length*

The Umpire shall allow such intervals as have been agreed upon for meals, and 10 minutes between each innings.

2 *Luncheon Interval – Innings ending or Stoppage within 10 minutes of Interval*

If an innings ends or there is a stoppage caused by weather or bad light within 10 minutes of the agreed time for the luncheon interval, the interval shall be taken immediately.

The time remaining in the session of play shall be added to the agreed length of the interval but no extra allowance shall be made for the 10-minute interval between innings.

3 *Tea Interval – Innings ending or Stoppage within 30 minutes of interval*

If an innings ends or there is a stoppage caused by weather or bad light within 30 minutes of the agreed time for the tea interval, the interval shall be taken immediately.

The interval shall be of the agreed length and, if applicable, shall include the 10 minute interval between innings.

4 *Tea Interval – Continuation of Play*

If at the agreed time for the tea interval 9 wickets are down, play shall continue for a period not exceeding 30 minutes or until the innings is concluded.

5 *Tea Interval – Agreement to Forego*

At any time during the match, the Captains may agree to forego a tea interval.

6 *Intervals for Drinks*

If both Captains agree before the start of a match that intervals for drinks may be taken, the option to take such intervals shall be available to either side. These intervals shall be restricted to one per session, shall be kept as short as possible, shall not be taken in the last hour of the match and in any case shall not exceed 5 minutes.

The agreed times for these intervals shall be strictly adhered to except that if a wicket falls within 5 minutes of the agreed time then drinks shall be taken out immediately.

If an innings ends or there is a stoppage caused by weather or bad light within 30 minutes of the agreed time for a drinks interval, there will be no interval for drinks in that session.

At any time during the match the Captains may agree to forego any such drinks interval.

NOTES

(a) *Tea Interval – One-Day Match*

In a one-day match, a specific time for the tea interval need not necessarily be arranged, and it may be agreed to take this interval between the innings of a one-innings match.

(b) *Changing the agreed time of intervals*

In the event of the ground, weather or light conditions causing a suspension of play, the Umpires, after consultation with the Captains, may decide, in the interests of time-saving, to bring forward the time of the luncheon or tea interval.

LAW 17: CESSATION OF PLAY

1 *Call of Time*

The Umpire at the Bowler's end shall call 'time' on the cessation of play before any interval or interruption of play, at the end of each day's play, and at the conclusion of the match. *See* Law 27 (Appeals).

2 *Removal of Bails*

After the call of 'time', the Umpires shall remove the bails from both wickets.

3 *Starting a Last Over*

The last over before an interval or the close of play shall be started provided the Umpire, after walking at his normal pace, has arrived at his position behind the stumps at the Bowler's end before time has been reached.

4 *Completion of the Last Over of a Session*

The last over before an interval or the close of play shall be completed unless a Batsman is out or retires during that over within 2 minutes of the interval or the close of play or unless the Players have occasion to leave the field.

5 *Completion of the Last Over of a Match*

An over in progress at the close of play on the final day of a match shall be completed at the request of either Captain even if a wicket fall after time has been reached.

If during the last over the Players have occasion to leave the field the Umpires shall call 'time' and there shall be no resumption of play and the match shall be at an end.

6 *Last Hour of Match – Number of Overs*

The Umpires shall indicate when one hour of playing time of the match remains according to the agreed hours of play. The next over after that moment shall be the first of a minimum of 20 6-ball overs (15 8-ball overs), provided a result is not reached earlier or there is no interval or interruption of play.

7 *Last Hour of Match – Intervals between Innings and Interruptions of Play*

If, at the commencement of the last hour of the match, an interval or interruption of play is in progress or if, during the last hour there is an interval between innings or an interruption of play, the minimum number of overs to be bowled on the resumption of play shall be reduced in proportion to the duration, within the last hour of the match, of any such interval or interruption.

The minimum number of overs to be bowled after a resumption of play shall be calculated as follows:

(a) In the case of an interval or interruption of play being in progress at the commencement of the last hour of the match, or in the case of a first interval or interruption, a deduction shall be made from the minimum of 20 6-ball overs (or 15 8-ball overs).

(b) If there is a later interval or interruption a further deduction shall be made from the minimum number of overs which should have been bowled following the last resumption of play.

(c) These deductions shall be based on the following factors:

(i) the number of overs already bowled in the last hour of the match or, in the case of a later interval or interruption, in the last session of play.

(ii) the number of overs lost as a result of the interval or interruption allowing one 6-ball over for every full three minutes (or one 8-ball over for every full four minutes) of interval or interruption.

(iii) any over left uncompleted at the end of an innings to be excluded from these calculations.

(iv) any over left uncompleted at the start of an interruption of play to be completed when play is resumed and to count as one over bowled.

(v) an interval to start with the end of an innings and to end 10 minutes later; an interruption to start on the call of 'time' and to end on the call of 'play'.

(d) In the event of an innings being completed and a new innings commencing during the last hour of the match, the number of overs to be bowled in the new innings shall be calculated on the basis of one 6-ball over for every 3 minutes or part thereof remaining for play (or one 8-ball over for every 4 minutes or part thereof remaining for play); or alternatively on the basis that sufficient overs be bowled to enable the full minimum quota of overs to be completed under circumstances governed by (a), (b) and (c) above. In all such cases the alternative which allows the greater number of overs shall be employed.

8 *Bowler unable to complete an Over during last hour of the Match*

If, for any reason, a Bowler is unable to complete an over during the period of play referred to in 6 above, Law 22.7 (Bowler Incapacitated or Suspended during an Over) shall apply.

LAW 18: SCORING

1 *A Run*

The score shall be reckoned by runs. A run is scored:

(a) So often as the Batsmen, after a hit or at any time while the ball is in play, shall have crossed and made good their ground from end to end.

(b) When a boundary is scored. *See* Law 19 (Boundaries).

(c) When penalty rules are awarded. *See* 6 below.

2 *Short Runs*

(a) If either Batsman runs a short run, the Umpire shall call and signal 'one short' as soon as the ball becomes dead and that run shall not be scored. A run is short if a Batsman fails to make good his ground on turning for a further run.

(b) Although a short run shortens the succeeding one, the latter, if completed, shall count.

(c) If either or both Batsmen deliberately run short the Umpire shall, as soon as he sees that the fielding side have no chance of dismissing either Batsman, call and signal 'dead ball' and disallow any runs attempted or previously scored. The Batsmen shall return to their original ends.

(d) If both Batsmen run short in one and the same run, only one run shall be deducted.

(e) Only if 3 or more runs are attempted can more than one be short and then, subject to (c) and (d) above, all runs so called shall be disallowed. If there has been more than one short run the Umpires shall instruct the Scorers as to the number of runs disallowed.

3 *Striker Caught*

If the Striker is Caught, no run shall be scored.

4 *Batsman Run Out*

If a Batsman is Run Out, only that run which was being attempted shall not be scored. If, however, an injured Striker himself is run out, no more runs shall be scored. *See* Law 2.7 (Transgression of the Laws by an Injured Batsman or Runner).

5 *Batsman Obstructing the Field*

If a Batsman is out Obstructing the Field, any runs completed before the obstruction occurs shall be scored unless such obstruction prevents a catch being made in which case no runs shall be scored.

6 *Runs Scored for Penalties*

Runs shall be scored for penalties under Laws 20 (Lost Ball), 24 (No Ball), 25 (Wide Ball), 41.1 (Fielding the Ball) and for boundary allowances under Law 19 (Boundaries).

7 *Batsman Returning to Wicket he has left*

If, while the ball is in play, the Batsmen have crossed in running, neither shall return to the wicket he has left even though a short run has been called or no run has been scored as in the case of a catch. Batsmen, however, shall return to the wickets they originally left, in the cases of a boundary and of any disallowance of runs and of an injured Batsman being, himself, run out. *See* Law 2.7 (Transgression by an Injured Batsman or Runner).

NOTES

(a) *Short Run*

A Striker taking stance in front of his popping crease may run from that point without penalty.

LAW 19: BOUNDARIES

1 *The Boundary of the Playing Area*

Before the toss for innings, the Umpires shall agree with both Captains on the boundary of the playing area. The boundary shall, if possible, be marked by a white line, a rope laid on the ground, or a fence. If flags or posts only are used to mark a boundary, the imaginary line joining such points shall be regarded as the boundary. An obstacle, or person, within the playing area shall not be regarded as a boundary unless so decided by the Umpires before the toss for innings. Sight-screens within, or partially within, the playing area shall be regarded as the boundary and when the ball strikes or passes within or under or directly over any part of the screen, a boundary shall be scored.

2 *Runs scored for Boundaries*

Before the toss for innings, the Umpires shall agree with both Captains the runs to be allowed for boundaries, and in deciding the allowance for them, the Umpires and Captains shall be guided by the prevailing custom of the ground. The allowance for a boundary shall normally be 4 runs, and 6 runs for all hits pitching over and clear of the boundary line or fence, even though the ball has been previously touched by a Fieldsman. 6 runs shall also be scored if a Fieldsman, after catching a ball, carries it over the boundary. *See* Law 32 (Caught) Note (a). 6 runs shall not be scored when a ball struck by the Striker hits a sight-screen full pitch if the screen is within, or partially within, the playing area, but if the ball is struck directly over a sight-screen so situated, 6 runs shall be scored.

3 *A Boundary*

A boundary shall be scored and signalled by the Umpire at the Bowler's end whenever, in his opinion:

(a) A ball in play touches or crosses the boundary, however marked.

(b) A Fieldsman with ball in hand touches or grounds any part of his person on or over a boundary line.

(c) A Fieldsman with ball in hand grounds any part of his person over a boundary fence or board. This allows the Fieldsman to touch or lean on or over a boundary fence or board in preventing a boundary.

4 *Runs Exceeding Boundary Allowance*

The runs completed at the instant the ball reaches the boundary shall count if they exceed the boundary allowance.

5 *Overthrows or Wilful Act of a Fieldsman*

If the boundary results from an overthrow or from the wilful act of a Fieldsman, any runs already completed and the allowance shall be added to the score. The run in progress shall count provided that the Batsmen have crossed at the instant of the throw or act.

NOTES

(a) *Position of Sight-Screens*

Sight-screens should, if possible, be positioned wholly outside the playing area, as near as possible to the boundary line.

LAW 20: LOST BALL

1 *Runs Scored*

If a ball in play cannot be found or recovered any fieldsman may call 'lost ball' when 6 runs shall be added to the score; but if more than 6 have been run before 'lost ball' is called, as many runs as have been completed shall be scored. The run in progress shall count provided that the Batsmen have crossed at the instant of the call of 'lost ball'.

2 *How Scored*

The runs shall be added to the score of the Striker if the ball has been struck, but otherwise to the score of byes, leg-byes, no-balls or wides as the case may be.

LAW 21: THE RESULT

1 *A Win – Two Innings Matches*

The side which has scored a total of runs in excess of that scored by the opposing side in its two completed innings shall be the winners.

2 *A Win – One Innings Matches*

(a) One innings matches, unless played out as in 1 above, shall be decided on the first innings, but see Law 12.5 (Continuation After One Innings Of Each Side).

(b) If the Captains agree to continue play after the completion of one innings of each side in accordance with Law 12.5 (Continuation After One Innings of Each Side) and a result is not achieved on the second innings, the first innings result shall stand.

3 *Umpires Awarding a Match*

(a) A match shall be lost by a side which, during the match,

(i) refuses to play, or

(ii) concedes defeat,

and the Umpires shall award the match to the other side.

(b) Should both Batsmen at the wickets or the fielding side leave the field at any time without the agreement of the Umpires, this shall constitute a refusal to play and, on appeal, the Umpires shall award the match to the other side in accordance with (a) above.

4 *A Tie*

The result of a match shall be a tie when the scores are equal at the conclusion of play, but only if the side batting last has completed its innings.

If the scores of the completed first innings of a one-day match are equal, it shall be a tie but only if the match has not been played out to a further conclusion.

5 *A Draw*

A match not determined in any of the ways as in 1, 2, 3 and 4 shall count as a draw.

6 *Correctness of Result*

Any decision as to the correctness of the scores shall be the responsibility of the Umpires. *See* Law 3.14 (Correctness of Scores).

If, after the Umpires and Players have left the field, in the belief that the match has been concluded, the Umpires decide that a mistake in scoring has occurred, which affects the result, and provided time has not been reached, they shall order play to resume and to continue until the agreed finishing time unless a result is reached earlier.

If the Umpires decide that a mistake has occurred and time has been reached, the Umpires shall immediately inform both Captains of the necessary corrections to the scores and, if applicable, to the result.

7 *Acceptance of Result*

In accepting the scores as notified by the scorers and agreed by the Umpires, the Captains of both sides thereby accept the result.

NOTES

(a) *Statement of Results*

The result of a finished match is stated as a win by runs, except in the case of a win by the side batting last when it is by the number of wickets still then to fall.

(b) *Winning Hit or Extras*

As soon as the side has won, see 1 and 2 above, the Umpire shall call 'time', the match is finished, and nothing that happens thereafter other than as a result of a mistake in scoring, see 6 above, shall be regarded as part of the match.

However, if a boundary constitutes the winning hit – or extras – and the boundary allowance exceeds the number of runs required to win the match, such runs scored shall be credited to the side's total and, in the case of a hit, to the Striker's score.

LAW 22: THE OVER

1 *Number of Balls*

The ball shall be bowled from each wicket alternately in overs of either 6 or 8 balls according to agreement before the match.

2 *Call of 'Over'*

When the agreed number of balls has been bowled, and as the ball becomes dead or when it becomes clear to the Umpire at the Bowler's end that both the fielding side and the Batsmen at the wicket have ceased to regard the ball as in play, the Umpire shall call 'over' before leaving the wicket.

3 *No Ball or Wide Ball*

Neither a no ball nor a wide ball shall be reckoned as one of the over.

4 *Umpire Miscounting*

If an Umpire miscounts the number of balls, the over as counted by the Umpire shall stand.

5 *Bowler Changing Ends*

A Bowler shall be allowed to change ends as often as desired, provided only that he does not bowl 2 overs consecutively in an innings.

6 *The Bowler Finishing an Over*

A Bowler shall finish an over in progress unless he be incapacitated or be suspended under Law 42.8 (The Bowling of Fast Short Pitched Balls), 9 (The Bowling of Fast High Full Pitches), 10 (Time Wasting) and 11 (Players Damaging the Pitch). If an over is left incomplete for any reason at the start of an interval or interruption of play, it shall be finished on the resumption of play.

7 *Bowler Incapacitated or Suspended during an Over*

If, for any reason, a Bowler is incapacitated while running up to bowl the first ball of an over, or is incapacitated or suspended during an over, the Umpire shall call and signal 'dead ball' and another Bowler shall be allowed to bowl or complete the over from the same end, provided only that he shall not bowl 2 overs, or part thereof, consecutively in one innings.

8 *Position of Non-Striker*

The Batsman at the Bowler's end shall normally stand on the opposite side of the wicket to that from which the ball is being delivered, unless a request to do otherwise is granted by the Umpire.

LAW 23: DEAD BALL

1 *The Ball becomes Dead, when:*

(a) It is finally settled in the hands of the Wicket-Keeper or the Bowler.
(b) It reaches or pitches over the boundary.
(c) A Batsman is out.
(d) Whether played or not, it lodges in the clothing or equipment of a Batsman or the clothing of an Umpire.
(e) A ball lodges in a protective helmet worn by a member of the fielding side.
(f) A penalty is awarded under Law 20 (Lost Ball) or Law 41.1 (Fielding the Ball).
(g) The Umpire calls 'over' or 'time'.

2 *Either Umpire shall call and signal 'Dead Ball', when:*

(a) He intervenes in a case of unfair play.
(b) A serious injury to a Player or Umpire occurs.
(c) He is satisfied that, for an adequate reason, the Striker is not ready to receive the ball and makes no attempt to play it.
(d) The Bowler drops the ball accidentally before delivery, or the ball does not leave his hand for any reason.
(e) One or both bails fall from the Striker's wicket before he receives delivery.
(f) He leaves his normal position for consultation.
(g) He is required to do so under Laws 26.3 (Disallowance of Leg Byes), etc.

3 *The Ball ceases to be Dead, when:*

(a) The Bowler starts his run up or bowling action.

4 *The Ball is not Dead, when:*

(a) It strikes an Umpire (unless it lodges in his dress).
(b) The Wicket is broken or struck down (unless a Batsman is out thereby).
(c) An unsuccessful appeal is made.
(d) The wicket is broken accidentally either by the Bowler during his delivery or by a Batsman in running.
(e) The Umpire has called 'no ball' or 'wide'.

NOTES

(a) *Ball finally Settled*

Whether the ball is finally settled or not – see 1(a) above – must be a question for the Umpires alone to decide.

(b) *Action on call of 'Dead Ball'*

(i) *If 'dead ball. is called prior to the Striker receiving a delivery the Bowler shall be allowed an additional ball.*
(ii) *If 'dead ball' is called after the Striker receives a delivery the Bowler shall not be allowed an additional ball, unless a 'no ball' or 'wide' has been called.*

LAW 24: NO BALL

1 *Mode of Delivery*

The Umpire shall indicate to the Striker whether the Bowler intends to bowl over or round the wicket, overarm or underarm, right or left-handed. Failure on the part of the Bowler to indicate in advance a change in his mode of delivery is unfair and the Umpire shall call and signal 'no ball'.

2 *Fair Delivery – The Arm*

For a delivery to be fair the ball must be bowled not thrown – see Note (a) below. If either Umpire is not entirely satisfied with the absolute fairness of a delivery in this respect he shall call and signal 'no ball' instantly upon delivery.

3 *Fair Delivery – The Feet*

The Umpire at the bowler's wicket shall call and signal 'no ball' if he is not satisfied that in the delivery stride:

(a) the Bowler's back foot has landed within and not touching the return crease or its forward extension

or

(b) some part of the front foot whether grounded or raised was behind the popping crease.

4 *Bowler Throwing at Striker's Wicket before Delivery*

If the Bowler, before delivering the ball, throws it at the Striker's wicket in an attempt to run him out, the Umpire shall call and signal 'no ball'. *See* Law 42.12 (Batsman Unfairly Stealing a Run) and Law 38 (Run Out).

5 *Bowler Attempting to Run Out Non-Striker Before Delivery*

If the Bowler, before delivering the ball, attempts to run out the non-Striker, any runs which result shall be allowed and shall be scored as no balls. Such an attempt shall not count as a ball in the over. The Umpire shall not call 'no ball'. *See* Law 42.12 (Batsman Unfairly Stealing a Run).

6 *Infringement of Laws by a Wicket-Keeper or a Fieldsman*

The Umpire shall call and signal 'no ball' in the event of the Wicket-Keeper infringing Law 40.1 (Position of Wicket-Keeper) or a Fieldsman infringing Law 41.2 (Limitation of On-side Fieldsmen) or Law 41.3 (Position of Fieldsmen).

7 *Revoking a call*

An Umpire shall revoke the call 'no ball' if the ball does not leave the Bowler's hand for any reason. *See* Law 23.2 (Either Umpire Shall Call and Signal 'Dead Ball').

8 *Penalty*

A penalty of 1 run for a no ball shall be scored if no runs are made otherwise.

9 *Runs From a No Ball*

The Striker may hit a no ball and whatever runs result shall be added to his score. Runs made otherwise from a no ball shall be scored no balls.

10 *Out from a No Ball*

The Striker shall be out from a no ball if he breaks Law 34 (Hit the Ball Twice) and either Batsman may be Run Out or shall be given out if either breaks Law 33 (Handled the Ball) or Law 37 (Obstructing the Field).

11 *Batsman given Out off a No Ball*

Should a Batsman be given out off a no ball the penalty for bowling it shall stand unless runs are otherwise scored.

NOTES

(a) *Definition of a Throw*

A ball shall be deemed to have been thrown if, in the opinion of either Umpire, the process of straightening the bowling arm, whether it be partial or complete, takes place during that part of the delivery swing which directly precedes the ball leaving the hand. This definition shall not debar a Bowler from the use of the wrist in the delivery swing.

(b) *No Ball not counting in over*

A no ball shall not be reckoned as one of the over. See *Law 22.3 (No Ball or Wide Ball).*

LAW 25: WIDE BALL

1 *Judging a Wide*

If the Bowler bowls the ball so high over or so wide of the wicket that, in the opinion of the Umpire it passes out of reach of the Striker, standing in a normal guard position, the Umpire shall call and signal 'wide ball' as soon as it has passed the line of the Striker's wicket.

The Umpire shall not adjudge a ball as being a wide if:

(a) The Striker, by moving from his guard position, causes the ball to pass out of his reach.

(b) The Striker moves and thus brings the ball within his reach.

2 *Penalty*

A penalty of one run for a wide shall be scored if no runs are made otherwise.

3 *Ball coming to rest in front of the Striker*

If a ball which the Umpire considers to have been delivered comes to rest in front of the line of the Striker's wicket, 'wide' shall not be called. The Striker has a right, without interference from the fielding side, to make one attempt to hit the ball. If the fielding side interfere, the Umpire shall replace the ball where it came to rest and shall order the Fieldsmen to resume the places they occupied in the field before the ball was delivered.

The Umpire shall call and signal 'dead ball' as soon as it is clear that the Striker does not intend to hit the ball, or after the Striker has made one unsuccessful attempt to hit the ball.

4 *Revoking a Call*

The Umpire shall revoke the call if the Striker hits a ball which has been called 'wide'.

5 *Ball not Dead*

The ball does not become dead on the call of 'wide ball' – *see* Law 23.4 (The Ball is Not Dead).

6 *Runs resulting from a Wide*

All runs which are run or result from a wide ball which is not a no ball shall be scored wide balls, or if no runs are made one shall be scored.

7 *Out from a Wide*

The Striker shall be out from a wide ball if he breaks Law 35 (Hit Wicket), or Law 39 (Stumped). Either Batsman may be Run Out and shall be out if he breaks Law 33 (Handled the Ball), or Law 37 (Obstructing the Field).

8 *Batsman given Out off a Wide*

Should a Batsman be given out off a wide, the penalty for bowling it shall stand unless runs are otherwise made.

NOTES

(a) *Wide Ball not counting in Over*

A wide ball shall not be reckoned as one of the over – see Law 22.3 (No Ball or Wide Ball).

LAW 26: BYE AND LEG-BYE

1 *Byes*

If the ball, not having been called 'wide' or 'no ball' passes the Striker without touching his bat or person, and any runs are obtained, the Umpire shall signal 'bye' and the run or runs shall be credited as such to the batting side.

2 *Leg-Byes*

If the ball, not having been called 'wide' or 'no ball' is unintentionally deflected by the Striker's dress or person, except a hand holding the bat, and any runs are obtained the Umpire shall signal 'leg-bye' and the run or runs so scored shall be credited as such to the batting side.

Such leg-byes shall only be scored if, in the opinion of the Umpire, the Striker has:

(a) attempted to play the ball with his bat, or

(b) tried to avoid being hit by the ball.

3 *Disallowance of Leg-Byes*

In the case of a deflection by the Striker's person, other than in 2(a) and (b) above, the Umpire shall call and signal 'dead ball' as soon as one run has been completed or when it is clear that a run is not being attempted or the ball has reached the boundary.

On the call and signal of 'dead ball' the Batsmen shall return to their original ends and no runs shall be allowed.

LAW 27: APPEALS

1 *Time of Appeals*

The Umpires shall not give a Batsman out unless appealed to by the other side which shall be done prior to the Bowler beginning his run-up or bowling action to deliver the next ball. Under Law 23.1(f) (The Ball Becomes Dead) the ball is dead on 'over' being called; this does not, however, invalidate an appeal made prior to the first ball of the following over provided 'time' has not been called. *See* Law 17.1 (Call of Time).

2 *An Appeal 'How's That?'*

An appeal 'How's That?' shall cover all ways of being out.

3 *Answering Appeals*

The Umpire at the Bowler's wicket shall answer appeals before the other Umpire in all cases except those arising out of Law 35 (Hit Wicket) or Law 39 (Stumped) or Law 38 (Run Out) when this occurs at the Striker's wicket.

When either Umpire has given a Batsman not out, the other Umpire shall, within his jurisdiction, answer the appeal or a further appeal, provided it is made in time in accordance with 1 above (Time of Appeals).

4 *Consultation by Umpires*

An Umpire may consult with the other Umpire on a point of fact which the latter may have been in a better position to see and shall then give his decision. If, after consultation, there is still doubt remaining the decision shall be in favour of the Batsman.

5 *Batsman leaving his Wicket under a misapprehension*

The Umpires shall intervene if satisfied that a Batsman, not having been given out, has left his wicket under a misapprehension that he has been dismissed.

6 *Umpire's Decision*

The Umpire's decision is final. He may alter his decision, provided that such alteration is made promptly.

7 *Withdrawal of an Appeal*

In exceptional circumstances the Captain of the fielding side may seek permission of the Umpire to withdraw an appeal providing the outgoing Batsman has not left the playing area. If this is allowed, the Umpire shall cancel his decision.

LAW 28: THE WICKET IS DOWN

1 *Wicket Down*

The wicket is down if:

(a) Either the ball or the Striker's bat or person completely removes either bail from the top of the stumps. A disturbance of a bail, whether temporary or not, shall not constitute a complete removal, but the wicket is down if a bail in falling lodges between two of the stumps.

(b) Any player completely removes with his hand or arm a bail from the top of the stumps, providing that the bail is held in that hand or in the hand of the arm so used.

(c) When both bails are off, a stump is struck out of the ground by the ball, or a player strikes or pulls a stump out of the ground, providing that the ball is held in the hand(s) or in the hand of the arm so used.

2 *One Bail Off*

If one bail is off, it shall be sufficient for the purpose of putting the wicket down to remove the remaining bail, or to strike or pull any of the three stumps out of the ground in any of the ways stated in 1 above.

3 *All the Stumps Out of the Ground*

If all the stumps are out of the ground, the fielding side shall be allowed to put back one or more stumps in order to have an opportunity of putting the wicket down.

4 *Dispensing with Bails*

If owing to the strength of the wind, it has been agreed to dispense with the bails in accordance with Law 8, Note (a) (Dispensing With Bails) the decision as to when the wicket is down is one for the Umpires to decide on the facts before them. In such circumstances and if the Umpires so decide the wicket shall be held to be down even though a stump has not been struck out of the ground.

NOTES

(A) *Remaking the wicket*

If the wicket is broken while the ball is in play, it is not the Umpire's duty to remake the wicket until the ball has become dead – see LAW 23 (DEAD BALL). *A member of the fielding side, however, may remake the wicket in such circumstances.*

LAW 29: BATSMAN OUT OF HIS GROUND

1 *When Out of his ground*

A Batsman shall be considered to be out of his ground unless some part of his bat in his hand or of his person is grounded behind the line of the popping crease.

LAW 30: BOWLED

1 *Out Bowled*

The Striker shall be out bowled if:

(a) His wicket is bowled down, even if the ball first touches his bat or person.

(b) He breaks his wicket by hitting or kicking the ball on to it before the completion of a stroke, or as a result of attempting to guard his wicket. *See* Law 34.1 (Out – Hit the Ball Twice).

NOTES

(a) *Out Bowled – Not LBW*

The Striker is out Bowled if the ball is deflected on to his wicket even though a decision against him would be justified under Law 36 (LBW).

LAW 31: TIMED OUT

1 *Out Timed Out*

An incoming Batsman shall be out Timed Out if he wilfully takes more than 2 minutes to come in – the 2 minutes being timed from the moment a wicket falls until the new batsman steps on to the field of play.

If this is not complied with and if the Umpire is satisfied that the delay was wilful and if an appeal is made, the new Batsman shall be given out by the Umpire at the Bowler's end.

2 *Time to be Added*

The time taken by the Umpires to investigate the cause of the delay shall be added at the normal close of play.

NOTES

(a) *Entry In Score Book*

The correct entry in the score book when a Batsman is given out under this Law is 'timed out', and the Bowler does not get credit for the wicket.

(b) *Batsmen crossing on the Field of Play*

It is an essential duty of the Captains to ensure that the in-going Batsman passes the out-going one before the latter leaves the field of play.

LAW 32: CAUGHT

1 *Out Caught*

The Striker shall be Out Caught if the ball touches his bat or if it touches below the wrist his hand or glove, holding the bat, and is subsequently held by a Fieldsman before it touches the ground.

2 *A Fair Catch*

A catch shall be considered to have been fairly made if:

(a) The Fieldsman is within the field of play throughout the act of making the catch.

(i) The act of making the catch shall start from the time when the Fieldsman first handles the ball and shall end when he both retains complete control over the further disposal of the ball and remains within the field of play.

(ii) In order to be within the field of play, the Fieldsman may not touch or ground any part of his person on or over a boundary line. When the boundary is marked by a fence or board the Fieldsman may not ground any part of his person over the boundary fence or board, but may touch or lean over the boundary fence or board in completing the catch.

(b) The ball is hugged to the body of the catcher or accidentally lodges in his dress or, in the case of the Wicket-Keeper, in his pads. However, a Striker may not be caught if a ball lodges in a protective helmet worn by a fieldsman, in which case the Umpire shall call and signal 'dead ball'. *See* Law 23 (Dead Ball).

(c) The ball does not touch the ground even though a hand holding it does so in effecting the catch.

(d) A Fieldsman catches the ball, after it has been lawfully played a second time by the Striker, but only if the ball has not touched the ground since being first struck.

(e) A Fieldsman catches the ball after it has touched an Umpire, another Fieldsman or the other Batsman. However a Striker may not be caught if a ball has touched a protective helmet worn by a Fieldsman.

(f) The ball is caught off an obstruction within the boundary provided it has not previously been agreed to regard the obstruction as a boundary.

3 *Scoring of Runs*

If a Striker is caught, no run shall be scored.

NOTES

(a) *Scoring from an Attempted Catch*

When a Fieldsman carrying the ball touches or grounds any part of his person on or over a boundary marked by a line, 6 runs shall be scored.

(b) *Ball still in Play*

If a Fieldsman releases the ball before he crosses the boundary, the ball will be considered to be still in play and it may be caught by another Fieldsman. However, if the original Fieldsman returns to the field of play and handles the ball, a catch may not be made.

LAW 33: HANDLED THE BALL

1 *Out Handled the Ball*

Either Batsman on appeal shall be out Handled the Ball if he wilfully touches the ball while in play with the hand not holding the bat unless he does so with the consent of the opposite side.

NOTES

(a) *Entry in Score Book*

The correct entry in the score book when a Batsman is given out under this Law is 'handled the ball', and the Bowler does not get credit for the wicket.

LAW 34: HIT THE BALL TWICE

1 *Out Hit the Ball Twice*

The Striker, on appeal, shall be out Hit the Ball Twice if, after the ball is struck or is stopped by any part of his person, he wilfully strikes it again with his bat or person except for the sole purpose of guarding his wicket: this he may do with his bat or any part of his person other than his hands, but see Law 37.2 (Obstructing a Ball From Being Caught).

For the purpose of this Law, a hand holding the bat shall be regarded as part of the bat.

2 *Returning the Ball to a Fieldsman*

The Striker, on appeal, shall be out under this Law, if, without the consent of the opposite side, he uses his bat or person to return the ball to any of the fielding side.

3 *Runs from Ball lawfully struck Twice*

No runs except those which result from an overthrow or penalty, *see* Law 41 (The Fieldsman), shall be scored from a ball lawfully struck twice.

NOTES

(a) *Entry in Score Book*

The correct entry in the score book when the Striker is given out under this Law is 'hit the ball twice', and the Bowler does not get credit for the wicket.

(b) *Runs credited to the Batsman*

Any runs awarded under 3 above as a result of an overthrow or penalty shall be credited to the Striker, provided the ball in the first instance has touched the bat, or, if otherwise, as extras.

LAW 35: HIT WICKET

The Striker shall be out Hit Wicket if, while the ball is in play:

(a) His wicket is broken with any part of his person, dress, or equipment as a result of any action taken by him in preparing to receive or in receiving a delivery, or in setting off for his first run, immediately after playing, or playing at, the ball.

(b) He hits down his wicket whilst lawfully making a second stroke for the purpose of guarding his wicket within the provisions of Law 34.1 (Out Hit the Ball Twice).

NOTES

(a) *Not Out Hit Wicket*

A Batsman is not out under this Law should his wicket be broken in any of the ways referred to in (1a) above if:

(i) *It occurs while he is in the act of running, other than in setting off for his first run immediately after playing at the ball, or while he is avoiding being run out or stumped.*

(ii) *The Bowler after starting his run-up or bowling action does not deliver the ball; in which case the Umpire shall immediately call and signal 'dead ball'.*

(iii) *It occurs whilst he is avoiding a throw-in at any time.*

LAW 36: LEG BEFORE WICKET

1 *Out LBW*

The Striker shall be out LBW in the circumstances set out below:

(a) *Striker Attempting to Play the Ball*
The Striker shall be out LBW if he first intercepts with any part of his person, dress or equipment a fair ball which would have hit the wicket and which has not previously touched his bat or a hand holding the bat, provided that:

(i) The ball pitched in a straight line between wicket and wicket or on the off side of the Striker's wicket, or in the case of a ball intercepted full pitch would have pitched in a straight line between wicket and wicket.
and
(ii) The point of impact is in a straight line between wicket and wicket, even if above the level of the bails.

(b) *Striker Making No Attempt to Play the Ball*
The Striker shall be out LBW even if the ball is intercepted outside the line of the off-stump, if, in the opinion of the Umpire, he has made no genuine attempt to play the ball with his bat, but has intercepted the ball with some part of his person and if the circumstances set out in (a) above apply.

LAW 37: OBSTRUCTING THE FIELD

1 *Wilful Obstruction*

Either Batsman, on appeal, shall be out Obstructing the Field if he wilfully obstructs the opposite side by word or action.

2 *Obstructing a Ball from being Caught*

The Striker, on appeal, shall be out should wilful obstruction by either Batsman prevent a catch being made.

This shall apply even though the Striker causes the obstruction in lawfully guarding his wicket under the provisions of Law 34. *See* Law 34.1 (Out Hit the Ball Twice).

NOTES

(a) *Accidental Obstruction*

The Umpires must decide whether the obstruction was wilful or not. The accidental interception of a throw-in by a Batsman while running does not break this Law.

(b) *Entry in Score Book*

The correct entry in the score book when a Batsman is given out under this Law is obstructing the field, and the bowler does not get credit for the wicket.

LAW 38: RUN OUT

1 *Out Run Out*

Either Batsman shall be out Run Out if in running or at any time while the ball is in play – except in the circumstances described in Law 39 (Stumped) – he is out of his ground and his wicket is put down by the opposite side. If, however, a Batsman in running makes good his ground he shall not be out Run Out, if he subsequently leaves his ground, in order to avoid injury, and the wicket is put down.

2 *'No Ball' Called*

If a no ball has been called, the Striker shall not be given Run Out unless he attempts to run.

3 *Which Batsman is Out*

If the Batsmen have crossed in running, he who runs for the wicket which is put down shall be out; if they have not crossed, he who has left the wicket which is put down shall be out. If a Batsman remains in his ground or returns to his ground and the other Batsman joins him there, the latter shall be out if his wicket is put down.

4 *Scoring of Runs*

If a Batsman is run out, only that run which is being attempted shall not be scored. If however an injured Striker himself is run out, no runs shall be scored. *See* Law 2.7 (Transgression of the Laws by Injured Batsman or Runner).

NOTES

(a) *Ball played on to opposite Wicket*

If the ball is played on to the opposite wicket neither Batsman is liable to be Run Out unless the ball has been touched by a Fieldsman before the wicket is broken.

(b) *Entry in Score Book*

The correct entry in the score book when the Striker is given out under this Law is 'run out', and the Bowler does not get credit for the wicket.

LAW 39: STUMPED

1 *Out Stumped*

The Striker shall be out Stumped if, in receiving a ball, not being a no-ball, he is out of his ground otherwise than in attempting a run and the wicket is put down by the Wicket-Keeper without the intervention of another Fieldsman.

2 *Action by the Wicket-Keeper*

The Wicket-Keeper may take the ball in front of the wicket in an attempt to Stump the Striker only if the ball has touched the bat or person of the Striker.

NOTES

(a) *Ball rebounding from Wicket-Keeper's person*

The Striker may be out Stumped if in the circumstances stated in 1, above, the wicket is broken by a ball rebounding from the Wicket-Keeper's person or equipment or is kicked or thrown by the Wicket-Keeper on to the wicket.

LAW 40: THE WICKET-KEEPER

1 *Position of Wicket-Keeper*

The Wicket-Keeper shall remain wholly behind the wicket until a ball delivered by the Bowler touches the bat or person of the Striker, or passes the wicket, or until the Striker attempts a run.

In the event of the Wicket-Keeper contravening this Law, the Umpire at the Striker's end shall call and signal 'no ball' at the instant of delivery or as soon as possible thereafter.

2 *Restriction on actions of the Wicket-Keeper*

If the Wicket-Keeper interferes with the Striker's right to play the ball and to guard his wicket, the Striker shall not be out, except under Laws 33 (Handled the Ball), 34 (Hit the Ball Twice), 37 (Obstructing the Field), 38 (Run Out).

3 *Interference with the Wicket-Keeper by the Striker*

If in the legitimate defence of his wicket, the Striker interferes with the Wicket-Keeper, he shall not be out, except as provided for in Law 37.2 (Obstructing a Ball from being Caught).

LAW 41: THE FIELDSMAN

1 *Fielding the Ball*

The Fieldsman may stop the ball with any part of his person, but if he wilfully stops it otherwise, 5 runs shall be added to the run or runs already scored; if no run has been scored 5 penalty runs shall be awarded. The run in progress shall count provided that the Batsmen have crossed at the instant of the act. If the ball has been struck, the penalty shall be added to the score of the Striker, but otherwise to the score of byes, leg-byes, no balls or wides as the case may be.

2 *Limitation of On-Side Fieldsmen*

The number of on-side Fieldsmen behind the popping crease at the instant of the Bowler's delivery shall not exceed two. In the event of infringement by the fielding side the Umpire at the Striker's end shall call and signal 'no ball' at the instant of delivery or as soon as possible thereafter.

3 *Position of Fieldsmen*

Whilst the ball is in play and until the ball has made contact with the bat or the Striker's person or has passed his bat, no Fieldsman, other than the Bowler, may stand on or have any part of his person extended over the pitch (measuring 22 yards/20·12 m × 10 ft/3·05 m). In the event of a Fieldsman contravening this Law, the Umpire at the bowler's end shall call and signal 'no ball' at the instant of delivery or as soon as possible thereafter. *See* Law 40.1 (Position of Wicket-Keeper).

NOTES

(a) *Batsmen changing Ends*

The 5 runs referred to in 1 above are a penalty and the Batsmen do not change ends solely by reason of this penalty.

LAW 42: UNFAIR PLAY

1 *Responsibility of Captains*

The Captains are responsible at all times for

ensuring that play is conducted within the spirit of the game as well as within the Laws.

2 *Responsibility of Umpires*

The Umpires are the sole judges of fair and unfair play.

3 *Intervention by the Umpire*

The Umpires shall intervene without appeal by calling and signalling 'dead ball' in the case of unfair play, but should not otherwise interfere with the progress of the game except as required to do so by the Laws.

4 *Lifting the Seam*

A Player shall not lift the seam of the ball for any reason. Should this be done, the Umpires shall change the ball for one of similar condition to that in use prior to the contravention. *See* Note (a).

5 *Changing the condition of the Ball*

Any member of the fielding side may polish the ball provided that such polishing wastes no time and that no artificial substance is used. No one shall rub the ball on the ground or use any artificial substance or take any other action to alter the condition of the ball.

In the event of a contravention of this Law, the Umpires, after consultation, shall change the ball for one of similar condition to that in use prior to the contravention.

This Law does not prevent a member of the fielding side from drying a wet ball, or removing mud from the ball. *See* Note (b).

6 *Incommoding the Striker*

An Umpire is justified in intervening under this Law and shall call and signal 'dead ball' if, in his opinion, any Player of the fielding side incommodes the Striker by any noise or action while he is receiving a ball.

7 *Obstruction of a Batsman in running*

It shall be considered unfair if any Fieldsman wilfully obstructs a Batsman in running. In these circumstances the Umpire shall call and signal 'dead ball' and allow any completed runs and the run in progress or alternatively any boundary scored.

8 *The Bowling of fast Short Pitched balls*

The bowling of fast short pitched balls is unfair if, in the opinion of the Umpire at the Bowler's end, it constitutes an attempt to intimidate the Striker. *See* Note (d).

Umpires shall consider intimidation to be the deliberate bowling of fast short pitched balls which by their length, height and direction are intended or likely to inflict physical injury on the Striker. The relative skill of the Striker shall also be taken into consideration.

In the event of such unfair bowling, the Umpire at the Bowler's end shall adopt the following procedure:

(a) In the first instance the Umpire shall call and signal 'no ball', caution the Bowler and inform the other Umpire, the Captain of the fielding side and the Batsmen of what has occurred.

(b) If this caution is ineffective, he shall repeat the above procedure and indicate to the Bowler that this is a final warning.

(c) Both the above caution and final warning shall continue to apply even though the Bowler may later change ends.

(d) Should the above warnings prove ineffective the Umpire at the Bowler's end shall:

(i) At the first repetition call and signal 'no ball' and when the ball is dead direct the Captain to take the Bowler off forthwith and to complete the over with another Bowler, provided that the Bowler does not bowl two overs or part thereof consecutively. *See* Law 22.7 (Bowler Incapacitated or Suspended during an Over).

(ii) Not allow the Bowler, thus taken off, to bowl again in the same innings.

(iii) Report the occurrence to the Captain of the batting side as soon as the Players leave the field for an interval.

(iv) Report the occurrence to the Executive of the fielding side and to any governing body responsible for the match who shall take any further action which is considered to be appropriate against the Bowler concerned.

9 *The Bowling of fast high Full Pitches*

The bowling of fast high full pitches is unfair. *See* Note (e).

In the event of such unfair bowling the Umpire at the bowler's end shall adopt the procedures of caution, final warning, action against the Bowler and reporting as set out in 8 above.

10 *Time Wasting*

Any form of time wasting is unfair.

(a) In the event of the Captain of the fielding side wasting time or allowing any member of his side to waste time, the Umpire at the Bowler's end shall adopt the following procedure:

(i) In the first instance he shall caution the Captain of the fielding side and inform the other Umpire of what has occurred.

(ii) If this caution is ineffective he shall repeat the above procedure and indicate to the Captain that this is a final warning.

(iii) The Umpire shall report the occurrence to the Captain of the batting side as soon as the Players leave the field for an interval.

(iv) Should the above procedure prove ineffective the Umpire shall report the occurrence to the Executive of the fielding side and to any governing body responsible for that match who shall take appropriate action against the Captain and the Players concerned.

(b) In the event of a Bowler taking unnecessarily long to bowl an over the Umpire at the Bowler's end shall adopt the procedures, other than the calling of 'no ball', of caution, final warning, action against the Bowler and reporting.

(c) In the event of a Batsman wasting time (*See* Note (f)) other than in the manner described in Law 31 (Timed Out), the Umpire at the Bowler's end shall adopt the following procedure:

(i) In the first instance he shall caution the Batsman and inform the other Umpire at once, and the Captain of the batting side, as soon as the Players leave the field for an interval, of what has occurred.

(ii) If this proves ineffective, he shall repeat the caution, indicate to the Batsman that this is a final warning and inform the other Umpire.

(iii) The Umpire shall report the occurrence to both Captains as soon as the Players leave the field for an interval.

(iv) Should the above procedure prove ineffective, the Umpire shall report the occurrence to the Executive of the batting side and to any governing body responsible for that match who shall take appropriate action against the Player concerned.

11 *Players damaging the Pitch*

The Umpires shall intervene and prevent Players from causing damage to the pitch which may assist the Bowlers of either side. *See* Note (c).

(a) In the event of any member of the fielding side damaging the pitch the Umpire shall follow the procedure of caution, final warning and reporting as set out in 10(a) above.

(b) In the event of a Bowler contravening this Law by running down the pitch after delivering the ball, the Umpire at the Bowler's end shall first caution the Bowler. If this caution is ineffective the Umpire shall adopt the procedures, other than the calling of 'no ball', of final warning, action against the Bowler and reporting.

(c) In the event of a Batsman damaging the pitch the Umpire at the Bowler's end shall follow the procedures of caution, final warning and reporting as set out in 10(c) above.

12 *Batsman unfairly stealing a Run*

Any attempt by the Batsman to steal a run during the Bowler's run-up is unfair. Unless the Bowler attempts to run out either Batsman – *see* Law 24.4 (Bowler Throwing At Striker's Wicket Before Delivery) and Law 24.5 (Bowler Attempting to Run Out Non-Striker Before Delivery) – the Umpire shall call and signal 'dead ball' as soon as the Batsmen cross in any such attempt to run. The Batsmen shall then return to their original wickets.

13 *Players' Conduct*

In the event of a player failing to comply with the instructions of an Umpire, criticizing his decisions by word or action, or showing dissent, or generally behaving in a manner which might bring the game into disrepute, the Umpire concerned shall, in the first place report the matter to the other Umpire and to the Player's Captain requesting the latter to take action. If this proves ineffective, the Umpire shall report the incident as soon as possible to the Executive of the Player's team and to any Governing Body responsible for the match, who shall take any further action which is considered appropriate against the Player or Players concerned.

NOTES

(a) *The Condition of the Ball*

Umpires shall make frequent and irregular inspections of the condition of the ball.

(b) *Drying of a Wet Ball*

A wet ball may be dried on a towel or with sawdust.

(c) *Danger Area*

The danger area on the pitch, which must be protected from damage by a Bowler, shall be regarded by the Umpires as the area contained by an imaginary line 4 ft/1·22 m from the popping crease, and parallel to it, and within two imaginary and parallel lines drawn down the pitch from points on that line 1 ft/30·48 cm on either side of the middle stump.

(d) *Fast Short Pitched Balls*

As a guide, a fast short pitched ball is one which pitches short and passes, or would have passed, above the shoulder height of the Striker, standing in a normal batting stance at the crease.

(e) *The Bowling of fast Full-Pitches*

The bowling of one fast, high full pitch shall be considered to be unfair if, in the opinion of the Umpire, it is deliberate, bowled at the Striker, and if it passes or would have passed above the shoulder height of the Striker when standing in a normal batting stance at the crease.

(f) *Time Wasting by Batsmen*

Other than in exceptional circumstances, the Batsman should always be ready to take strike when the Bowler is ready to start his run-up.

Part XI
Glossary

All-Rounder A phrase long in common usage. It generally denotes utility in the departments of batting and bowling.

Amateur Literally 'one who is fond of' (*C.O.D.*). Used in English cricket until 1962 to differentiate the cricketer who took nothing out of the game except his out-of-pocket expenses from the professional who took wages and/or match fees. The distinction was abolished 'by a clear majority' at the Advisory County Cricket Committee on 26th November 1962, the decision being subsequently ratified by MCC. Outside first-class cricket – as, for instance, in the Leagues – the words 'amateur' and 'professional' are still, however, in common use.

Analysis A summary of the detail of a bowler's performance over an innings or period, thus:

MELFORD 11 overs, 4 maidens, 18 runs, 4 wickets: or, more commonly,

MELFORD 11–4–18–4

Also the detail itself as written in the scorebook over by over.

Artificial Pitches A surface made of some substance other than turf. It can be of concrete or asphalt, with or without a coconut or jute fibre matting overlay; or of a chemical compound; or it can be a fine gravel preparation, watered and rolled, and covered with a mat. The Dutch play on matting, mostly over a preparation of this kind. Much cricket overseas, and some in England, is played on an artificial surface. In South Africa all cricket took place on matting until the late 1920s. In Trinidad the change to turf dates from the early 1950s. Generally speaking, cricket is a better game on a true artificial pitch than on an indifferent grass one.

The proliferation of Indoor Schools has encouraged manufacturers towards research into such surfaces. The MCC Indoor School has a floor of *Uniturf* and pitches of two paces, one more susceptible than the other to spin. Pitches are also made by *Recticel, Truturf, Polygrass, Polyturf* among others. Details of cost and general advice can be obtained by affiliated clubs from all County Associations affiliated to the NCA.

Ashes, origin of After Australia had beaten England for the first time in 1882 *The Sporting Times* printed a mock obituary notice lamenting the death of English cricket and adding that 'the body will be cremated and the ashes taken to Australia'. When, in the following winter, the Hon Ivo Bligh (later Lord Darnley) took a team to Australia and reversed the result, certain ladies burned a bail, sealed the ashes in an urn and presented it to him. In his will Lord Darnley bequeathed the urn to MCC. It is to be seen now in the Memorial Gallery at Lord's. Thus 'the Ashes' are not mythical. They do not, however, change hands, but are kept permanently at the Headquarters of Cricket. *N.B.* From *Recovering the Ashes* (Warner): 'The rubber was won: the "Ashes" were in my cricket-bag: the hour of my Nunc Dimittis had arrived.'

Attack, the The bowling and fielding effort.

Appeal A call made by a player to an umpire for a decision on any matter affecting play, usually as to whether a batsman is out in the ways calling for arbitration: caught at the wicket, stumped, lbw, run out, handled ball, obstructing the field.

Average The mean number of runs per innings over a period, found by dividing the aggregate by the number of completed innings; of a bowler, the mean cost of runs per wicket, made by dividing the number of runs scored off his bowling by the number of wickets taken.

The averages. Comparative tables of batting and bowling averages.

Away-Swinger The ball that moves in the air from leg to off. It is effected by the bowler gripping the ball with the first 2 fingers on top, and to either side of the seam, which is slightly canted so that at the moment of delivery it lies in the direction of 1st slip. The right side of the thumb will be on the bottom side of the seam directly beneath the first 2 fingers.

Back Play The second part of the basic batting method. '*Unless a batsman can, by playing forward, command the pitch of the ball, he must play back and so have time to watch whatever it may do after pitching. The slower and more difficult the wicket, the more he must rely on back play. The right foot moves well back and just inside the line of the ball with the toe pointing parallel to the crease. The weight is transferred on to this foot but the balance of the head remains slightly forward. The left foot, eased up on to the toe, acts as a balancer. The ball should be met just below the eyes which should be as level as possible as they watch the ball down the pitch. The stroke is controlled by the left wrist and arm with the elbow high. The right hand relaxes into a thumb and finger grip. The body must be kept sideways as much as possible.*

'*Where the ball is short enough for the batsman to feel in real command, he can lengthen and quicken the swing of his back stroke to force it for runs. The body must be kept sideways and the left arm must still control the stroke, but the right hand should reinforce it with a "punch" just before impact. There will be a strong follow-through in the direction in which the ball has gone.*' – MCC's *Cricket – How to Play*.

Back Spin An under-spin occasionally given to the ball by certain slow bowlers, causing it to come more slowly from the pitch.

Back up, to To assist a colleague or colleagues in the field or at the wicket. In the field it involves any action by a fielder designed to prevent overthrows or extras. This normally consists in standing behind another fielder or the wicket-keeper to stop the ball in case he misses it, and in supporting another fielder in the case of a long throw-in.

In batting, to make ground down the pitch, when at the non-striker's end, as soon as the ball leaves the bowler's hand, in order to shorten the distance in the event of a run.

Backward Point The phrase is rather out of fashion, having given place to 'gully' (*qv*).

Bails The apex of the wickets is formed by the 2 bails, each of $4\frac{3}{8}$ inches in length. They shall not project more than $\frac{1}{2}$ inch above the stumps. Record distance for sending a bail in first-class cricket is 67 yards, 6 inches by R. D. Burrows (Worcestershire) at Manchester in 1911.

Ball The instrument propelled. Made of hand-stitched leather dyed red, the interior being of cork wound with twine. Weight not less than $5\frac{1}{2}$ not more than $5\frac{3}{4}$ ounces. Circumference not less than $8\frac{13}{16}$ inches nor more than 9 inches.

CHRONOLOGY

1744 The weight was the only consideration. It had to be between 5 and 6 ounces.

1774 The limits of weight were established as above.

1838 The circumference to be between 9 and $9\frac{1}{4}$ inches.

1927 The limits of the circumference were altered to the present figures, *i.e.* not less than $8\frac{13}{16}$ inches nor more than 9 inches.

1980 A note to Law 5 prescribes $5\frac{1}{16}$ ounces as the maximum weight in Junior Cricket.

Barrack, to To make comment on the play of a disparaging kind, audible to fellow-spectators and to the players. Of 19th-century Australian origin it varies in quality in that country from the rare gem of wit to the inevitable adjuration, 'Get a bag, you mug', when a catch is dropped. The practice has become more prevalent and the noise much greater in most Test-playing countries, to the distress and annoyance of many.

Bat The weapon of propulsion. The blade or striking part is of willow, the handle of cane layered with thin strips of rubber, bound with twine, over which is a sheath, also of rubber. The cane extends from the shoulders into the heart of the willow to the extent of a sharp point, this projection being known as the splice. The rounded back nowadays assumes several shapes. Maximum dimensions 4¼ inches in width, 38 inches in length. The weight of the average full size bat varies from just over 2 lbs to a little under 3 lbs. No limit has ever been set regarding weight. A hundred years ago a 4-lb bat was no rarity. The new Law 6 prescribes that the bat be made of wood.

Batter In north-country usage nowadays, the batsman. A common term from the 18th century.

Batting The art of using the bat.

Batting-Gloves Generally of leather or fabric with tubular or spiked leather sewn to the back, worn to protect the hands.

Beamer A fast full pitch which, whether by accident or design, imperils the batsman's head. There has long been an unwritten convention among cricketers against bowling of this kind that is widely respected, on the grounds that it is dangerous. It is now categorically forbidden in Law 42.

Bite, to When the turf is responsive the ball on pitching is said to 'bite', *i.e.* to grip the surface, and either turn or lift unduly, or do both.

Blazer The conventional off-field uniform of the cricketer.

Blind Spot That small area of the pitch, whereon when the ball lands the batsman is in momentary doubt whether to play forward or back, being often thereby undone.

Block The mark made by the batsman on taking guard. Also to play with great care, merely to stop the ball with the bat.

Blue One who plays for either Oxford or Cambridge in the University Match.

'Bosie' An Australian word for the googly, the ball with the leg-break action that turns from the off. Named after its originator, B. J. T. Bosanquet, who used his invention to good effect on the first MCC tour to Australia in 1903–04.

Bouncer A short fast ball bowled with the intention of discomposing the batsman and/or causing him to mistime a hook-stroke.

Boundary The limit of the playing area on all sides. May be marked by a fence, rope or line. The stroke that hits the ball past or over the boundary. Normally 4 runs are allowed for a hit that passes over after pitching, 6 for one that clears the boundary full pitch.

Bowl, to To propel the ball fairly at the wicket.

Bowled A means of dismissal. (*See* LAWS)

Bowler He who propels.

CHRONOLOGY

1744 All bowling was under-arm. The bowler was allowed to change ends only once during the innings.
1811 The Law was slightly altered to underline the necessity for a bowler to bowl with the hand below the level of the elbow.
1817 A new bowler was allowed two trial balls.
1835 The Law was altered to allow round-arm bowling. The hand was not to be above the level of the shoulder.
1838 Trial balls no longer allowed.
1864 Over-arm bowling allowed.
1870 Bowler could change ends twice provided he did not bowl more than 2 overs in succession.
1889 He could change ends as often as he pleased provided he did not bowl 2 overs in succession.
1933 MCC resolved that any form of direct attack by the bowler upon the batsman was against the spirit of the game.
1936 Umpires were instructed on action to take in the case of 'persistent and systematic bowling of fast short-pitched balls at the batsman standing clear of the wicket'. The bowler was to be cautioned, and if this was ineffective, the captain was to be informed. If this also had no effect, the umpire's duty was to forbid the bowler to bowl for the remainder of the innings.
1939 The above made law.
1980 The wording of the law regarding fast short-pitched bowling has been simplified and the umpire's powers strengthened thereby. He is required to consider both the skill of the batsman and the cumulative effect throughout the innings. The new Law 42 also prohibits fast high full-pitches.

Bowling-Crease (*See also* LAWS)

CHRONOLOGY

1744 It extended 3 feet on either side of the wicket.
1902 The extent of the crease was increased to 4 feet on either side of the wicket. (When the width of the wickets was increased in 1931 no alteration to the full length of the crease was made. Therefore it now measures 3 feet 11½ inches on either side).

Box, the An old-fashioned term for the position that used also to be called backward point, and has now become gully (*q.v.*). Also the name used for the shield to protect the genitals.

Break The deviation of the ball from the straight after pitching, caused by the bowler's spin or cut.

Break-back The off-break. Rather old-fashioned phrase today but useful to identify the ball which is brought back by cutting the fingers across the seam as distinct from the finger-spinning action.

Bump-ball What is to some apparently a catch, the ball having, however, been played directly from the bat to the ground whence it has rebounded.

Bumper A short ball bowled by a fast bowler that bounces around or over the batsman's head or shoulders.

Butter-fingers An old-fashioned epithet applied to a fielder who has missed an easy chance. Used in *Pickwick Papers* (1837) by Mr Jingle.

Bye A run obtained from a ball (other than a Wide or No-Ball) which passes the striker without touching either his bat or his person. (*See* LAW 26.)

Call A batsman's command to his partner to run. The captain's nomination of a fielder to attempt a catch. An umpire's cry of no-ball.

Cap The headgear of the cricketer. It denotes also a distinction in that it comprises the colours and/or badge of a particular club or institution, and is awarded for service.

Carrying One's Bat is to return not out at the end of a completed innings, after having gone in first.

Castle (*Colloq.*) The Wicket.

Century Colloquial term for a hundred runs.

Champion, the W. G. Grace's title.

Change Bowler He who is brought on after the opening bowlers.

Chop Stroke through the slips made as the word implies; a variant of the late cut.

Chucker One who infringes the Bowling Law.

Closure Declaration.

Cob Obsolete phrase for a very slow ball. Tom Brown bowled cobs to old Mr Aislabie in the MCC match at Rugby.

Cow Shot An unorthodox stroke to leg, rustic in character. Hence the alternative phrase, Hay-maker.

Crack Of a player: high-class. A favourite phrase of the old writers, *e.g.* of Hobbs: 'Before the luncheon adjournment the Surrey crack dispatched the crimson rambler to the confines on no fewer than 9 occasions. Afterwards the Oval idol, etc. etc.'

Cradle A contraption of slatted wood on an iron frame, concave in shape, on to which cricketers throw the ball with a low trajectory to give one another catching practice.

Creeper A ball that shoots along the ground.

Creases Lines painted with whitewash on the pitch according to the Laws (q.v.) to define the bowler's permitted area of delivery and the ground within which the batsman is safe from stumping or from being run out.

Cricketana The collective noun embracing all manner of relics, from the game's equipment and dress to pictures, china, and esoteric bric-a-brac, for which cricket addicts keep up a brisk demand.

Cross-bat, to play with a *i.e.* not perpendicular. To aim thus across the flight of the ball.

Crumbler A pitch that is disintegrating

Cut The stroke played with a horizontal bat to a short or shortish ball outside the off stump. '*Cutting is a very effective way of getting runs off short balls outside the off stump, especially from quick bowling. According to whether it is played early or late, the ball can be hit as square as cover or as fine as second slip. But for the cut to be made safely, the ball must be short enough for the batsman to watch it rise off the pitch, and wide enough to give him plenty of room for the stroke. For all cuts, the bat must be picked well up and rather towards fine-leg, with the right elbow well clear of the body and the back of the left shoulder slightly turned on the bowler*' – MCC's *Cricket – How to Play*..

Cut through, to Describes the ball which on hitting a wet wicket comes through straight and relatively quickly rather than turning and/or lifting.

Cutter A fairly new term to denote a bowler who turns the ball, or the ball that turns. An off-cutter is simply an off-break bowler, or the off-break itself. The phrase springs from an effort to describe the method by which the faster bowlers most usually try to make the ball deviate after pitching, by drawing the hand one way or the other across the seam of the ball rather than oscillating the fingers and/or the wrist. To the more old-fashioned it is just another item in a terminology that tends increasingly to daunt devotees with its complexity.

Also one who cuts.

Cut up, to Said of a pitch that becomes defaced when played on after rain.

Dead The ball becomes dead (*i.e.* out of play) at certain points defined in the Laws, (*qv*)

Declare, to The act of the captain in bringing his side's innings to an end when wickets are still standing. Following is the evolution of the declaration law.

CHRONOLOGY

1744 No provision
1889 Declaration authorized on last day only.
1900 Declaration could take place after lunch on 2nd day
1910 Declaration at any time on second day
1951 Experiment to allow declaration at any time on first day
1957 Experiment incorporated into Laws

Deep The field near the boundary. Also called the 'country'.

Defence Used of batsman. His stopping power.

Deliver, to To bowl

Delivery The action of bowling.

Devil Used of a bowler. 'He has a lot of devil', *i.e.* pace off the pitch, general hostility.

Donkey-drop A high innocent-looking ball.

Drag, to Of a bowler, to impart back spin. E. R. Wilson and C. V. Grimmett were exponents of drag.
To put the drag on=to pull.
To drag into the wicket=to play on.
To drag the rear leg when bowling.

Draw The old-fashioned stroke, hard now to imagine (especially since it was most common before the advent of pads), whereby the batsman deflected the ball by a late turn of the wrists between his legs and the wicket. Also used of old to describe a stroke whereby the batsman cocked his left leg and deflected the ball underneath.

Dress The evolution of cricketing dress has to some extent been dictated by the modes of contemporary costume throughout the ages. Styles have naturally varied at different periods, but a feature of successive changes has always been an increase in convenience to the cricketer, so that his movements on the field have progressively become less encumbered. At the time of the growth of organised cricket around the middle of the eighteenth century, knee-breeches, silk stockings and silver-laced hats – despite the discomfort such apparel must have afforded – were in general use; prints show shirts to have been normally frilled and buckles on players' shoes. The first major advance came with the introduction of trousers soon after the turn of the 19th century. They were always white (for important games, at least), and by the 1820s high-collared shirts with a prominent bow-tie were the general fashion. Even the leading players wore braces at that time, a feature that time was to prove inexpedient with the advancement of bowling techniques in the 19th century.

Technique, indeed, as well as experience, brought further changes in cricketers' apparel, but for many years up to the end of the 1840s, the tall top-hat – normally a black or white 'beaver' – was worn by batsmen, bowlers and fielders alike. Apart from the danger of such a hat falling on the wicket, it could not have made running easy and must have caused fatigue in hot conditions. After a short 'pill-box' vogue, the soft flannel cap was a natural and sensible replacement, and though the straw hat had a brief vogue, the club cap – in much the form that we know it today, except that the peaks were smaller – had become a regular feature by the 1870s. Meanwhile coloured shirts, often spotted, together with belts, were worn for about twenty years from 1850. Cricket blazers made their appearance in the 1860s. Boots began to replace shoes, and by the 1880s the modern 'sweater' had appeared. White shirts were by now the rule, and by the close of the 19th century, with buckskin boots and self-supporting trousers in general use – though sashes were also commonly worn – the uniform of the cricketer had reached very much the pattern that is now common. Styles of umpires' dress have varied from the tall hat and black coat of the middle of the last century to the normal white coats that were first worn (but by no means generally) in the 1860s. In Australia, South Africa and in some parts of the West Indies, the umpires wear half-coats, a style also introduced in first-class cricket in England in the late 1960s.

In Australia from 1977–78 and in England from 1978, protective headgear became common for many batsmen in important matches, taking the form of steel helmets, often with a visor and additional face protection. Such helmets have also been worn by some fielders close to the bat.

Draw, a Unfinished match.

Drive, to To hit at the pitch of the ball with a free swing of the bat. '*The drive is the most exhilarating stroke in cricket and an invaluable weapon in any batsman's armoury of attack. The technique of the drivers, whether straight, on or off, is really the same as that for the forward strokes, except that the bat lift is higher and the ball is hit just beside the left toe rather than met in front of it. The power of the drive comes from a lengthened and accelerated swing in which arms, wrists and hands all take part. The arc of this swing must be as long, smooth and flat as possible; the left arm and hand must control it; the right hand will reinforce it just before the bat meets the ball, but it must not come in too early or it will tend to pull the swing across the line of the ball. As in the forward stroke, lead with your head, left shoulder and hip on to the line of the ball.*' – MCC's *Cricket – How to Play*.

Driver One who specializes in hard, straight hitting, *e.g.* C. B. Fry, K. R. Miller, P. B. H. May, C. H. Lloyd.

Duck A score of 0.

Eleven, or XI A team.

Extra Any run not scored from the bat. Extras comprise no-balls, byes, leg-byes and wides. In Australia called 'sundries'.

Fast-footed Of a batsman. One who declines to leave his crease.

Fast-medium A recognized bowling pace.

Fetch, to Describes the stroke whereby the batsman stretches on the off for the purpose of pulling the ball to leg.

Field The arena. Also a fielder: *e.g.* He is a good field.

Fielding One of the 3 basic arts of cricket.

Fiery Used of a pitch of uncertain disposition.

Fine At a narrow angle. Of a fieldsman; the reverse of square.

Finger-spin One of the bowler's ways of making the ball turn, as distinct from wrist-spin (though here, too, the fingers come into play) and 'cut'.

First-class As distinct from lower forms of cricket. Matches of three days and more as listed by the ICC are considered first-class and the players' achievements therefore qualify for inclusion in the first-class averages. When the quality of the players concerned is questionable the appropriate national authority becomes the arbiter.

Flight The quality possessed by some bowlers that induces the batsman to attempt the wrong stroke because he has been deceived in the air. It is achieved by subtle changes in speed and trajectory, based on an apparently identical action.

Floor Colloquial term for the pitch or the field. *e.g.* he put it on the floor = he dropped or 'grassed' a catch.

Fly Slip An occasional position some 20 or 30 yards in rear of the slips used in the case of a batsman who is inclined to slice or snick the ball over their heads.

Follow On, to Of a side; to bat a 2nd time out of turn when ordered to do so by the opposition according to the Laws (*qv*).

The evolution of the Follow-on Law is as follows:

CHRONOLOGY

1744 No provision.
1835 Compulsory if 100 runs or more in arrears.
1854 Deficit reduced to 80, Follow-on still compulsory.
1894 Deficit increased to 120.
1900 The Follow-on was made optional and the margins became 150 in a 3-day match, 100 in a 2-day match and 75 in a 1-day match.
1946 Experimental law allowed declaration on first day after batting side had scored 300.
1951 A side could declare at any time.
1957 Above made law. Declarations not to be made as a result of agreement with the opposing captain.

1961 In County Championship matches only, the Follow-on Law was suspended.
1962 Follow-on in a match of more than 3 days' duration to be 200 runs.
1963 Follow-on in County Championship matches reintroduced.
1980 In the new code the Follow-on was defined thus:– 5-day match 200 runs, 4-day and 3-day match 150 runs, 2-day match 100 runs, one-day match 75 runs.

Follow-Through The aftermath of delivery. '*As the right arm comes through after delivering the ball the body continues to pivot until the right shoulder is pointing to the batsman. By this time the right arm has carried across in front of the left thigh and the left arm has swung back close to the body until it is well up and clear from it. The follow-through will be continued for several strides and should be as straight as is consistent with not cutting up the playing area of the pitch with spikes.*' – MCC's *Cricket – How to Play*.

Force, to To force the game is to press for runs quickly, usually at the expense of risk.

Forcing Batsman A quick scorer. The reverse of a defensive one: *e.g.* G. L. Jessop, F. E. Woolley (generally), S. J. McCabe, E. R. Dexter, Sir Garfield Sobers and C. H. Lloyd. The difference between a forcing batsman and one of less aggressive inclination is a matter of degree and, to some extent, of method also.

Forward Play The first part of the basic batting method. '*The forward stroke is not only invaluable in defence, but the basis of all the drives. The object is to play the ball as near as possible to the point where it pitches. The weight should be right forward over a bent left knee. For this the right foot will naturally ease up, and when the ball is met, only the toe will be on the ground. The left hand and wrist must control the stroke, the right hand relaxing into a thumb-and-finger grip. The longer the left hand keeps the full-face of the blade moving down the line of the ball, the safer the stroke. The head should be behind the top of the bat handle and over the point of contact, with the eyes watching the ball as long as possible.*' – MCC's *Cricket – How to Play*.

Free Unrestricted, uninhibited. Of a batsman.

Full pitch The ball that can be hit before it bounces.

Game Style of play, *e.g.* forcing game, defensive game.

Gardening The act of repairing a wet pitch by flattening it with the bat.

Gate The sum collected at the turnstiles or at the gate.

Gauge Instrument for measuring the width of the bat to guard against its transgressing the maximum.

Gauntlets Manufacturer's term for wicket-keeping gloves.

Gentleman The ancient characterisation of the amateur, unpaid cricketer as distinct from the professional. Deriving from an age of clear-cut class distinctions, the phrase survived in the traditional title 'Gentlemen v Players' (*qv*) until the abolition of the amateur in English first-class cricket after the 1962 season. Thus passed the oldest first-class fixture, dating back to 1806.

Ghost In the terminology of cricket one who writes a book or article that appears under the name of a well-known player. Cricket ghosts represent no modern development. John Nyren's *The Cricketers of My Time*, perhaps the finest piece of descriptive writing on the game ever written, was compiled in association with a professional man-of-letter, Charles Cowden Clarke. The talk that inspired the writer no doubt was the talk of Nyren, but the finished piece was set down and edited by Cowden Clarke. Many of the books and articles attributed to cricketers since Nyren (1764–1837) have been the work of other hands, either wholly or in part.

Ghost-writing first aroused controversy and strong criticism when Harold Larwood, one of the central figures in the Body-line row, gave his name to some inflammatory material after the 1932–33 tour of Australia. More recently some newspapers and publishers have sought sensational writing in the form of disputes and alleged off-the-field scandals. MCC and the counties, considering that this practice had reached a stage when it was bringing the game into serious disrepute, in 1959 framed a regulation that required cricketers registered with county clubs to submit to them for approval all writing intended for publication. The penalty for failure to comply is loss of registration, that is to say banishment from English first-class cricket. The provision has been incorporated, since 1961, in the Rules of County Cricket.

Give the Ball Air, to Of a bowler, to give the ball a parabolic trajectory as distinct from a 'flat' one.

Glance A deflecting stroke to leg. Its possibilites were made apparent by K. S. Ranjitsinhji.

Go Away, to Of the ball that goes from leg to off after pitching.

Going-In, order of Batting order.

Googly The off-break bowled with the leg-break action. The deception is caused by a slight dropping and further turning of the wrist which causes the ball to emerge from the back as opposed to the front of the hand. Its inventor was B. J. T. Bosanquet (*qv*) in honour of whom Australians call this ball the 'Bosie' (*qv*).

Googly Bowler One who purveys the googly, usually in conjunction with the leg-break.

Go With the Arm, to Of a ball that on pitching continues to follow the course of the bowler's arm. Generally used to describe the trajectory of a bowler bowling round the wicket, and thus making a wider angle than he who bowls close to the stumps.

Greasy Said of a pitch affected by rain.

Ground-Fielding A sub-division of fielding; not catching.

Groundsman He who tends the fields and looks after the premises.

Ground-staff The cricketers employed by a county. Applied nowadays to the juniors outside the county team who bowl in the nets, perform duties under the direction of the groundsman and are the special care of the coach.

Grub An underhand ball that runs along the ground. Rarely seen.

Guard The position of the bat as held upright by the batsman on coming in, so that he may make his block. He asks the umpire to align the bat with one of the stumps, normally leg or middle or 'middle-and-leg'. The batsman adjusts its position according to the umpire's signal.

Gully The short catching position wide of the slips but fine of point. Gully forms an angle with the direction of the ball of between, say, 100 and 140 degrees. Like all fielding positions it is slightly elastic, according to the other dispositions at a given moment. It is synonymous with the older-fashioned backward point and box. (*qqv*).

Half-cock An improvised stroke neither forward nor back, made when the batsman finds, too late to change the movement of the feet, that the ball is not sufficiently far up for a full forward stroke.

Half-volley The ball that allows the batsman to reach it easily on the forward stroke at or the instant after the moment of pitching. In theory an easy ball to drive hard as distinct from the one of good length which the batsman must either stretch out at or meet after it has risen by playing back.

Hambledon The home of the famous club of that name on the Hampshire Downs which was the chief focal point of cricket from about 1768 to 1788, immediately prior to the founding of the Marylebone Cricket Club (1787). The doings of the Hambledon Club were immortalized by John Nyren, whose father, Richard, kept the *Bat and Ball* Inn overlooking the ground, in *The Cricketers of my Time*. John Nyren's book was collected, along with other writing by the Rev John Mitford and the Rev James Pycroft, under E. V. Lucas's editorship into one volume: *The Hambledon Men*. These countrymen, from this and adjacent villages, raised the game into an art, achieving such a standard over this period that they were more than a match for All-England. As told by Nyren their story makes one of the most romantic chapters in the history of sport.

Harrow-Bat A size of bat, suitable for a teenage boy.

Hit the Ball Twice A highly uncommon mode of dismissal. A batsman may hit the ball twice only in defence of his wicket. See Law 34.

Hook The MCC definition in *Cricket – How to Play* is: '*The hook is the name commonly given to the stroke by which a short ball on the wicket, or even to the off-side of it, is hit round to the on-side with a cross bat.*' This covers every stroke to the on-side played off the back foot except the leg-glance. Certain writers (especially Australians) refer to many such strokes as pulls, but it seems that the only way to avoid confusion in the minds of reader or listener is to describe such on-side strokes off the back foot as hooks, and to confine the term 'pull' to the forceful on-side strokes played in front of the wicket off the front foot. C. B. Fry's description made 50 years ago still stands: 'The hook-stroke is a forcing variation of the back-stroke.'

How's that? This, with many minor variations and a multiple of inflections, is the standard form of appeal.

Ice Cricket on ice was a regular winter diversion in the 19th century. The 1880 *Wisden* gives details of a dozen matches played in the severe winter of 1878–79, making it clear that this was only a selection from the many that had taken place. Two were played by the light of a full moon, and none had to be left drawn (as was one in earlier times recorded by F. S. Ashley-Cooper) because of a thaw. Ashley-Cooper in an essay entitled 'Winter Cricket' in his *Cricket Highways and Byways* gives a diverting account of the difficulty of playing on skates, and instances among other unusual events a match played between units of the Royal Navy at Spitzbergen by the light of the midnight sun. The game on ice was once even popular at Davos.

In-field The field close to the wicket bounded by a rough imaginary circle that passes through the normal positions of square-leg, mid-on, mid-off and cover-point.

In-swinger The ball that swings in the air from off to leg. The method of bowling it is as follows: '*The seam of the ball will be "canted" slightly towards fine leg. The second finger will lie along the inner side of the seam with the first finger, and more or less parallel with it; the ball of the thumb will be on the bottom side of the seam more or less directly beneath them. In the delivery stride the front foot will land slightly to the off-side of the right foot, and the arch of the back should be slightly exaggerated. The arm must come over as high, i.e. as close to the head, as possible, and instead of swinging across the body must come down in front of it and finish by the right thigh.*' – MCC's *Cricket – How to play*.

The first man to develop the in-swinger was the American, J. B. King (*qv*) of Philadelphia around 1895. It was bowled, left-handed, to much effect a little later by G. H. Hirst. Another early right-handed exponent was A. Jaques of Hampshire. These men and others used strong leg-side fields of 5 or 6, and this bowling development was partly responsible for a more open batting stance sometimes called 'two-eyed'.

The change in the lbw law (1937) encouraged in-swing bowling, as did the more frequent taking of the new ball in English first-class cricket from 1947 onwards. In efforts to counter the subsequent dominance of this type of bowling in England the number of leg-side fielders behind the wicket has been limited to two and the new ball has been made less frequent.

Innings The outcome of a tenure of the batting crease, whether by a batsman, or by a team.

Knighthoods Nine cricketers have been knighted for their services to the game, either as players or administrators, or as something of both. Details of their careers may be found under BIOGRAPHIES They are:

Sir Francis Lacey (1926)
Sir Frederick Toone (1929)
Sir Pelham Warner (1937)
Sir Donald Bradman (1949)
Sir Henry Leveson Gower (1953)
Sir Jack Hobbs (1953)
Sir Leonard Hutton (1956)
Sir Frank Worrell (1964)
Sir Garfield Sobers (1975)

Knock (*Colloq.*) Innings.

Lap, the A colloquial term for an unorthdox stroke aiming across the flight of the ball in the rough direction of square-leg. It is in type somewhere between the pull and the sweep (*qv*). Hence 'To put the lap on him'.

Last Over Following are the regulations that have applied regarding the bowling and completion of the last over. Before 1947 an over had to be started if time had not expired. It had to be finished unless a wicket fell within 2 minutes of time. If the over was the last one on the last day of a match the batting side could claim the finishing of the over even if a wicket had fallen and time had now expired. In 1947 it was decreed that either captain could claim that the final over of a match be completed. In 1959, and since, instead of the players being ready to start the final over the square-leg umpire's position was made that criterion. If he, walking at his normal pace, was in position at the bowler's end before time was reached the over should be bowled. (*See* Law 17).

Late Cut (*See also* CUT) In this finer version of the stroke the ball is met with a horizontal bat and a flourish of the wrist when it is almost level with the stumps.

lbw There have been only 3 alterations to the Law since lbw was first made an offence in 1774, the last in Law 36 of the new code.

CHRONOLOGY

1744 No mention as such but umpires were allowed to adjudicate on 'standing unfair to strike'.
1774 The striker was out if he 'puts his leg before the wicket with a design to stop the ball and actually prevents the ball from hitting the wicket'.
1788 Ball to be pitched in a straight line to the wicket. The 'design clause' omitted.
1929 Experimental Law whereby the batsman was out lbw even if the ball first hit his bat or hand.
1933 Above experiment discontinued.
1937 Extended to include ball pitched on the off side of the wicket provided the intervening pad was between wicket and wicket. This had been tried experimentally in the previous 2 years.
1980 In addition to the 1937 provision the batsman may also be adjudged out *if he has made no attempt to play the ball* even if it is intercepted outside the line of the off-stump.

Leg-break The ball that turns from leg to off. It is normally bowled thus: '*The top joint of the thumb and first two fingers are spaced naturally apart gripping across the seam. The third and little fingers are bent, with the third finger cupping the ball and lying* along *the seam. For this break it is the third finger that imparts the main spin though the first two fingers help. The wrist is bent inwards and only flips straight as the ball is delivered. The third and fourth finger flick upwards and forwards, whilst the thumb side of the hand cuts downward. After delivery the hand will finish palm downwards.*' – MCC's *Cricket – How to Play*. This manner of delivery involving a partial turn of the wrist restricts the speed of the ball to slow-medium. Certain accomplished bowlers, for instance S. F. Barnes and A. V. Bedser, have turned the ball from leg at a faster pace than this, by the action of strong fingers on the seam without the turning of the wrist.

Leg-bye A run obtained from a ball (other than a no-ball) that touches a part of the striker's dress or person, other than his hand, but has made no contact with the bat. (*See* LAW 26).

Leg hit An inexact term which, however, is generally used to describe a full-blooded pull in the area of mid-wicket or square-leg.

Leg-side The side of the pitch and field (if a line be drawn from middle stump to middle stump) that contains the batsman's legs.

Leg-theory A concentration of the attack towards the leg-stump and the pads with a strong supporting field encircling the batsman on the leg-side. It may be used in conjunction with off-breaks, especially on a turning wicket, or with in-swingers, or with left-arm bowling of all types and paces, generally, but not always, delivered over the wicket. These variations are not to be confused with Fast Leg Theory, which was one of the names given to the English method of attack used in Australia in 1932–33, discussed and described under Body-line.

Leg-trap The close crescent of fielders that are the normal adjunct of in-swing and of off-break bowling.

Length The basis of bowling and the root of all good cricket. '*The real test of a good ball is that it should present the batsman with a problem; the problem of deciding whether he should play forward or back to it. This means that it must not be so far up that he can really command it by a properly played forward stroke, or so short that he can watch it comfortably off the pitch when he plays back. But the area within which the ball can drop and present this problem cannot be laid down mathematically: it will vary according to a bowler's pace and the pace of the pitch, and even according to the batsman's build and reach. The faster the bowler and the faster the pitch, the bigger is the margin within which a ball can be reckoned a good length. The slower the bowler and the slower the pitch, the smaller must that margin be. The margin for a really fast bowler on a fast pitch can be as much as 9 ft., whilst for a slow bowler on a dead wicket it can be little more than 3 ft. But length is also to some extent relative to the batsman; the taller the batsman and the more he really uses his reach in playing forward, the more he can reduce the 'upper' limit of the bowler's margin of length; to a short batsman, or the one who relies chiefly on back play, the bowler will be able to pitch the ball further up.*' – MCC's *Cricket – How to Play*.

Light The constantly varying factors affecting play are wicket, weather and light. The evolution of the Law in relation to the light is as follows:

1884 Umpires to be the sole judges of the fitness of weather conditions, including the light.
1892 Umpires could be appealed to as to whether the light was fit for play.
1946 Special regulation disallowed appeals against the light. The umpire became the sole judge.
1948 In matches against the Australians either side could make one appeal per day.
1953 Same conditions as in 1948 for matches concerning the Australians.
1956 In matches concerning the Australians one appeal per batting side per session was allowed. After the one appeal had been

made further decisions were the responsibility of the umpires.
1957 For Test Matches against the West Indies one appeal per session was allowed.
1958 One appeal per session in Test Matches. No appeal in other matches.
1963 One appeal per session allowed in all matches.
1980 Law 3 of the new code makes the umpires the sole judges of the fitness of the light without appeal from the batting side. If however both captains wish the game to continue it shall do so.

Long Field The area around the sightscreen at the bowler's end; also an alternative name for the fielders who patrol there, long-off and long-on.

Long Handle Taking the long handle is to adopt a free and aggressive attitude, so called because the driver in full cry naturally slips his hands to the top of the handle to increase the arc of his swing and therefore the power of his stroke.

Long Hop A ball short enough to be safely punished off the back foot on one side of the wicket or the other.

Long Leg The position on or near the boundary behind the wicket on the leg-side.

Long-off The position on or near the boundary on the off-side of the sight-screen at the bowler's end.

Long-on The position on or near the boundary on the on-side of the sight-screen at the bowler's end.

Long Stop The position behind the wicket-keeper once universally necessary and a place of much distinction. Long obsolete except in very junior cricket.

Lost Ball See Law 20. This archaic provision is a relic of the days before boundaries when all hits had to be run out. Its retention in the Laws is a reminder that they must make provision for the playing of the game in unusual circumstances.

Maiden An over in which no runs are scored from the bat.

'Man in' The cry that recalls the fielders to their places after the fall of a wicket.

Match A contest of two innings per side, except in the case of a one-day game where the result *may* depend on one innings each. (*See* LAW 21).

Match-card A card giving the names of the players of both sides in the order of their going-in, with sufficient space opposite the names to enable full scoring details to be written down. A peculiarity of the match-card is that although it is universally provided in first-class matches in England – and also in many second-class, club and school matches – it is hardly ever seen abroad.

Matting An alternative surface for the pitch. Has been used until comparatively recently for Test Matches in certain countries abroad (South Africa, the West Indies, Pakistan). The tendency now is to prepare grass pitches for all high-class cricket everywhere. Some overseas cricket of good quality is still played perforce on matting, and it is also used in England where there are serious difficulties in the production of a good grass pitch. The mat is made of either *coir* (coconut fibre) or jute, the *coir* giving a lively, responsive surface, the jute a more placid one. An evenly laid, well-stretched mat makes for a more skilful game than an inferior grass pitch.

Meat Of the bat. The middle of the blade at its thickest point.

Minor Counties The English counties not recognised by the TCCB as first-class. There is a Minor Counties' Championship (*qv*) in which at present 19 counties participate.

Mishit A faulty stroke.

Mow A bucolic sort of leg hit.

Nets The parallel lengths of string netting, upheld by supports, between which practice wickets are pitched.

New Ball Regulations concerning the changing of the ball have varied constantly over the years.

CHRONOLOGY

1744 Ball to be marked by the umpires so that it could not be changed during a match.
1798 A new ball could be demanded by either side at the start of each innings.
1907 The fielding side could demand a new ball after 200 runs.
1946 A new ball could be taken after 55 overs.
1949 Taking of the new ball was delayed until 65 overs.
1955 The basis of overs bowled was abolished, and a return made to the 200 runs rule.
1956 A further change allowed for a new ball after 200 runs or 75 overs, whichever came first.
1961 The Law was amended once more, the basis for taking the new ball being 85 overs. The alternative of 200 runs was abolished.
1980 In the new code Law 5 leaves governing bodies to determine the availability of the new ball in matches of 3 days or upwards, but lays down a minimum of 75 overs.

Note: If a ball becomes damaged it can be replaced by one having had an equal amount of wear and tear.

Night-watchman A lower-order batsman sent in late in the evening to tide over the remaining time, and so prevent the possible loss of a better player.

No-ball The umpire's cry to denote an illegal delivery; the ball itself.

Following is the evolution of the No-ball Law, other than that applying to Throwing (*qv*).

1744 If the bowler bowled with his 'hinder foot' over the bowling crease the umpire was to call no-ball. There was no penalty. Presumably the ball was bowled again.
1811 The batsman was allowed to hit a no-ball and count any runs resulting.
1829 No-ball penalized one run.
1899 Either umpire could call no-ball if not entirely satisfied with fairness of delivery.
1912 Batsman could be run-out but not stumped off a no-ball.
1947 The bowler's foot, whilst still to be behind the bowling crease, need not be grounded at time of delivery.
1963 As an experiment in first-class cricket the bowler was judged on the position of his front foot. The front foot was required to be grounded within the popping crease and within a line drawn from the end of the bowling crease at right angles to the popping crease.
1980 In the new code Law 24 prescribes that some part of the front foot whether grounded or raised must be within the popping crease, and that the back foot must land within, and not touching, the return crease or its forward extension.

Notch The mark made by a knife on the stick in primitive scoring.

Not out To remain undismissed. The negative reply to an appeal by the umpire.

Obstructing the Field A highly unusual mode of dismissal. (*See* LAW 37.) L. Hutton was thus given out by F. Chester batting for England v South Africa at the Oval in 1951.

Off-break The ball that turns from off to leg. '*The main spinning "lever" is the top joint of the first finger lying across the seam and pressing hard on to it. The thumb and second finger are placed naturally on each side of it. The third and little finger are bent up to "cup" the ball from below. At the start of the action the wrist is bent back, i.e. towards the back of the forearm. As the ball is bowled it flicks forward and at the same time the first finger drags sharply downwards and thumb flips upwards. The action of the hand and wrist is the same as that of turning a door knob to open a door. After delivery the hand cuts across the body and finishes with palm pointing upward.*' – MCC's *Cricket – How to Play*.

Off-drive The forceful off-side stroke off the front foot. '*The most important thing in off-driving is to get your head, left shoulder and hip over on to the line of the ball; if they are right, the left foot will look after itself. The wider the ball, the more should the back of the left shoulder be turned on the bowler and the wider on the off-side should the stroke be aimed. The bat will in fact start its downward swing from the line of fine leg. Keep the full face of the bat moving through the line of the stroke as long as possible.*' – MCC's *Cricket – How to Play*.

Off-side That side of the pitch or field whereon the batsman does not take his stance. The ground to the right of a line drawn to the bowler's wicket as the batsman makes his survey.

Oldest Cricketer E. A. English, who played for Hampshire between 1898 and 1901, is the only English first-class cricketer known to have reached three figures. He died aged 102 and 8 months, having remained an active sportsman almost to the end. When 82 he did a hole in one, played his last golf aged 91 and 2 years later reached the final of the Alton Conservative Club snooker championship. J. Wheatley, who played for Canterbury (NZ) from 1882 to 1906, died in 1962, also aged 102.

Oldest Umpire Joseph Filliston, a former professional slow-bowler, umpired for the BBC Cricket Club after passing his 100th birthday. He is the only centenarian to have umpired at Lord's, 'standing' in the Lord's Taverners v Old England match there in

1962. He died following an accident in October, 1964, aged 102.

On-drive The forceful leg-side stroke off the front foot. '*The first movement is a slight dipping of the left shoulder; this will allow the left foot and the line of balance, with the head leading, to come out on to the line of the ball; the left foot will land just outside that line. The straighter the ball, the straighter must the stroke be aimed and the longer will the full face of the bat be moving down the line. The batsman must strongly resist the tendency to "pull" his on-drives by allowing the right hand and right shoulder to play too big a part; he must not allow his left hip to fall away.*' – MCC's *Cricket – How to Play*.

Out-cricket The broad effort of a team when in the field.

Out-field That part farthest from the pitch.

Out-fielder Strictly any fielder on or near the boundary, but more usually denotes one such fielding in front of the wicket.

Over The period of play, or the aggregate of the balls themselves, from one changing of ends to the next. The over now consists uniformly of 6 balls in first-class cricket throughout the world although Law 22 in the new Code specifies 6 or 8.

CHRONOLOGY

In England

1744 The over consisted of 4 balls.
1889 5 balls.
1900 6 balls.
1939 The 8 ball over was adopted for 1 year in *English first-class cricket as an experiment. It was not re-introduced after the war.*

Abroad

1887 Australia increased number from 4 to 6.
1918 Australia adopted 8 ball over. Until the season of 1979–80 they have used it since except for matches against MCC in 1920–21 and in the Test Matches of 1928–29 and 1932–33.
1924 New Zealand experimented with the 8 ball over, but reverted to 6 in 1927.
1937 South Africa experimented with the 8 ball over in 1937–38 and in 1938–39 for the MCC tour. They then reverted.
1980 Australia announced that they would revert to the 6 ball over for the 1979–80 season.

Other countries have followed the Laws applying in matches in England.

Over-pitch, to Of a bowler to exceed the good length.

Over the wicket The method of bowling wherein the operative arm is near to or over the stumps.

Overthrow The throw which, not having been gathered at the stumps after a piece of fielding, enables the batsmen to complete a run, or further runs. Also the run or runs so made.

Pad-play The act of stopping difficult balls deliberately with the pads.

Pads The batsman's leg-protectors, made of buckskin, canvas or synthetic substance extending from ankle to thigh. Their interior consists of a 'cushion' of hair and/or rubber, stiffened with cane.

Pair Two scores of 0 in the same match. Hence a pair of spectacles.

Pavilion The permanent structure on a cricket ground wherein members of the club change, wash, eat, drink, watch, converse, dispute, and otherwise disport themselves.

Pitch, care of the In recent years regulations concerning covering of the pitch have varied too frequently to be all listed here. The more crucial changes only are given. Law 11 in the new code (*qv*) allows complete covering before the start of a match but leaves other detailed provisions in the hands of responsible authorities.

CHRONOLOGY

1744 No mention is made. The pitch was left untouched during the whole of the match.
1788 Rolling, covering and cutting were allowed when necessary.
1849 At the demand of either side the pitch could be swept and rolled before each innings.
1860 The option for sweeping and rolling was restricted to the side who were to bat next.
1883 Rolling for ten minutes before the commencement of each day's play allowed.
1913 Covering of end of pitch allowed.
1924 The whole of the pitch could now be covered from 11 a.m. on the day preceding a match until the match actually started. After the beginning of play the ends of the pitch could again be covered when necessary and each night. Such covering might not protect a larger area than 18 feet by 12 feet at each end and might not extend more than 3 feet 6 inches beyond the popping crease.
1927 Where a pitch was wholly covered before the beginning of a match it could be similarly covered during the whole of Sunday in the case of a weekend match.
1931 Period of rolling reduced to 7 minutes.
1932 Artificial drying of the pitch allowed.
1934 The covering of the pitch for 24 hours prior to the beginning of a Test allowed.
1955 If both captains and umpires were in agreement that the pitch was so saturated that any further rain would delay the restart, the whole of the pitch could be covered, and for as long as the umpires decided.
1956 The pitch could be covered for any period prior to the bowling of the 1st ball.
1959 The pitch must be covered from the moment play was abandoned for the day.
1960 Pitches for Tests in England to be covered, if necessary, not only prior to the first ball but following any abandonment of play for the day and at weekends. This was a compromise arrangement (due to last 20 years) whereby the variety which derives from differing conditions was to some extent at least retained.
1963 Optional covering by countries was supplanted by a uniform restriction of complete covering only prior to the match and over the weekend.
1980 Pitches for Tests in England to be completely covered throughout, as had long been the practice in other countries. The provision for county matches remained as in 1963.

Pitch The specially prepared area between the wickets. It is, and has always been, 22 yards long, this being the length of the agricultural chain.

Pitch, to Of a bowler: *e.g.* he pitched a good length.

Pitch Up, to To keep the ball at least on a good length or beyond.

Play The umpire's call to begin. The action of the game.

Played On The batsman is said colloquially to have played on when the ball hits the stumps after contact with his bat.

Plumb Of a wicket, true. Of a decision, palpably out (in the estimation of the speaker).

Point The position square of the wicket, and close, on the off side 'at the point of the bat'. Once very popular it has now been largely superseded by gully. Is used however in Australia to denote a man square at the range of cover-point: *i.e.* theoretically just saving 1 run.

Popping-crease The line marking the extent of the batsman's safe ground. (*See* LAWS)

CHRONOLOGY

1744 This crease, of unlimited length, to be parallel to the return crease and 46 inches away from it.
1819 Distance increased to 48 inches.
1963 The experiment of judging a no-ball by the position of the bowler's front foot made it necessary to draw a line from the end of the return crease to the popping-crease, and at right angles to both.

Professional The time-honoured appellation of the paid player as distinct from the amateur before the distinction was abolished in English first-class cricket in 1962. The arts and skills of the game were fostered and refined, with like effect if somewhat different emphasis, both by those who approached the game as a pastime and those who followed it as a livelihood. The phrase is now confined to those employed to coach and/or to play by clubs and schools.

Pull A forceful stroke to leg played off the front foot aimed to some extent across the flight of the ball. Thus it differs from the on-drive. It can be played from the line of the off-stump or even outside it.

Put In, to To require the opposition to bat first on winning the toss.

Put On, to Of a bowler.

Reach A property of batsmanship. The distance which, according to his build, a batsman can stretch forward and still either hit the ball on the half-volley, or smother it.

Retire Hurt The phrase used in the score-card when a batsman is unable to continue his innings. Note that he may do so at any subsequent time, but only after the fall of a wicket and with the consent of the opposing captain.

Return The throw back to the stumps at either end after the ball has been fielded.

Return Crease The lines extending backwards at right-angles from the bowling crease and 4 feet 4 inches from the middle stump at each extremity of it. They describe the lateral limit beyond which a bowler's rear foot may not land in the delivery stride. (*See* LAW 9).

Round the Wicket The method of bowling wherein the operative arm is the farther from the stumps.

Rubber A series of Test Matches.

Run The scoring unit.

Runner The man allocated to run for a batsman who has been incapacitated.

Run Out Form of dismissal. (*See* LAW 38)

Run the Ball Away, to To cause it to move off the pitch towards the slips.

Score-book The repository of the score.

Score-card The printed card of the score, sold on the ground.

Scorer The recorder of the details of the game.

Scratch side A personally collected side with no bond of common membership.

Seam The stitching around the ball's circumference that holds together its leather segments. It is used by bowlers of whatever kind to obtain a better purchase of the ball.

Seam bowler Modern phrase used to describe any bowler, of medium pace or above, who aims to make the ball deviate otherwise than by finger-spin. Hence 'seamer'.

Second slip The fielder just wide of first slip.

Selector He who, usually with two or more colleagues, chooses a team for a particular game or series or tour. Hence Selection Committee.

Send back, to To decline one's partner's call when batting.

Shooter A ball that fails to rise after pitching.

Short-leg The close catching positions on the leg-side all the way round from short mid-on to the wicket-keeper come under the generic title of short-leg. Where there are several such fielders, they must be further characterized as being backward (*i.e.* of square) or forward. For the finer angles, the phrase leg-slip is often preferred.

Short run There are two uses. When either batsman turns for a second, or subsequent, run without having grounded his bat or either foot behind the popping-crease, the umpire shall call 'one short', and the run shall not be counted. (*See* LAW 18)

A quickly taken single for a tap or short hit is also described as a short run.

Side An XI or team. Prior to 1884 the Laws failed to specify the size of a team. The number was then laid down as 11 (unless otherwise agreed).

Sight-screen The expanse of white (or sometimes nowadays duck-egg blue) screen on the boundary sited immediately behind the bowler in order to give the batsman the clearest possible view of the ball. There are many forms of screens, most of them being on wheels and accordingly mobile.

Silly Applied to several fielding positions to denote 'close'.

Single One run.

Single Wicket A form of cricket once common, and revived in amended form in the 1960s, wherein only one batsman operates at a time. In the early 19th century the title of the Champion of England was decided by single wicket. Alfred Mynn (1807–1861) was the most redoubtable performer.

The Laws varied with the times, and the number of contestants might be anything from one only on each side to five. There were sometimes no fielders, and seldom more than five. In Mynn's day the batsman could not leave his ground before making his stroke. Runs accrued only for hits in front of the wicket (i.e. of an extension of the popping-crease). All the separate codes of laws from the first in 1744 down to that of 1884 specified the special provisions applying to single wicket. But when the 1947 code was formulated (the first complete revision in over 60 years) single wicket was ignored since it had long ceased to be played.

In 1963 a tournament took place at the Scarborough Festival between 16 selected cricketers, under rules laid down by the sponsors, the brewers of Carling Black Label Lager Beer. Following this initial effort Bass Charrington became sponsors, and the event moved to Lord's where it attracted fair crowds and was rated very good fun. The basic rules were that a batsman could bat for a maximum of 8 overs unless previously dismissed. There was a full complement of fielders (provided from the MCC ground-staff) and a first-class wicket-keeper. It was discontinued after 1969.

The winners were: 1963, K. E. Palmer; 1964, B. R. Knight; 1965, Mushtaq Mohammad; 1966, F. J. Titmus; 1967, G. S. Sobers; 1968, rained off; 1969, K. D. Boyce.

Skittle, to To dismiss summarily.

Sky, to To make a high hit. Hence skier.

Slasher A type of batsman inclined to hit hard and hazardously with a horizontal bat.

Slice A stroke on the off-side made with the face of the bat unduly open.

Slinger A bowler with a low delivery.

Slip The position next to the wicket-keeper, and fine, on the off-side.

Sticky wicket A pitch made soft and treacherous in behaviour by rain.

Stone-waller A notoriously slow scorer. There have always been men with a particular reputation in this respect, beginning perhaps with Tom Walker of Hambledon. W. H. Scotton (Notts), R. G. Barlow (Lancashire), A. C. Bannerman (New South Wales), and B. Mitchell (Transvaal) are other names. In recent times T. E. Bailey is perhaps the most conspicuous example. Their kind is somewhat at a discount in these limited-over days.

Stumps Three, surmounted by two bails, form the wicket. Their dimensions are 28 inches in height, 9 inches in breadth. Stumps are normally made of polished ash.

Swerve A somewhat dated term: synonymous with swing (*qv*).

Swing The lateral movement of the ball in the air, caused by a particular grasp of the seam in the hand of the bowler.

Test Match An international contest played between two full member countries of the International Cricket Conference.

Toss The method of determining choice of innings.

CHRONOLOGY

1744 The winner of the toss to have choice of innings and pitch.

1774 Visiting team to have choice of innings and pitch.

1809 Independent selection of pitch. The toss once more to decide choice of innings.

Tour An expedition wherein a team fulfils a fixed playing itinerary.

Umpires' Signals The following umpiring signals are laid down in Law 3 of the new code:

Boundary by waving the hand from side to side.

Bye by raising an open hand above the head.

Dead ball by crossing and re-crossing the wrists below the waist.

Leg-bye by touching a raised knee with the hand.

No-ball by extending one arm horizontally.

Out by raising the index finger above the head.

Short run by bending the arm upwards and by touching the nearest shoulder with the tips of the fingers of one hand.

Six by raising both arms above the head.

Wide by extending both arms horizontally.

Wicket or Pitch What is called in the Laws the pitch is also commonly referred to as the wicket. This is a source of understandable confusion to the uninitiated.

Wicket-keeper He who, fortified by pads and gauntlets, fields behind the stumps at the batsman's end. There have been specialist wicket-keepers since the end of the eighteenth century, their equipment having, of course, improved with the years.

Wide A ball that passes so wide of the wicket, or so high over it, that in the umpire's opinion it is out of reach of the batsman, he having taken guard in the normal position. (*See* LAW 25).

Yorker A ball designed to pitch at the instant when the bat on the downswing becomes vertical, and so to pass underneath it. If the batsman has remained in his ground it will therefore land on or adjacent to the popping crease. Thus it is fuller than a half-volley and less far up than a full-pitch. Hence, of a batsman, to be yorked.

Statistical Appendix

All statistics in this appendix are taken to the end of the 1979 English season

Career Records

Ten Thousand Runs in a Career

	YEARS	INNS	RUNS	AVERAGE
Abberley, R. N.	1964–1979	439	10082	24·47
Abel, R.	1881–1904	1007	33124	35·35
Ackerman, H. M.	1963–64 to 1978–79	377	11410	32·69
Alderman, A. E.	1928–1948	529	12376	25·94
Allen, B. O.	1932–1951	512	14195	28·85
Alley, W. E.	1945–46 to 1968	682	19612	31·88
Amarnath, L.	1933–34 to 1960–61	277	10269	42·08
Ames, L. E. G.	1936–1951	951	37248	43·51
Amiss, D. L.	1960–1979	783	30038	43·53
Armstrong, N. F.	1919–1939	637	19002	32·98
Armstrong, W. W.	1898–99 to 1921–22	406	16158	46·83
Arnold, E. G.	1899–1913	592	15853	29·91
Arnold, J.	1929–1950	710	21831	32·82
Ashdown, W. H.	1914–1947	812	22589	30·73
Asif Iqbal	1959–60 to 1979	621	20745	37·37
Astill, W. E.	1906–1939	1153	22731	22·55
Atkinson, G.	1954–1969	608	17654	31·13
Avery, A. V.	1935–1954	455	14137	33·65
Baig, A. A.	1954–55 to 1975–76	391	12367	34·16
Bailey, T. E.	1945–1967	1072	28642	33·42
Bakewell, A. H.	1928–1936	453	14570	33·98
Balderstone, J. C.	1961–1979	354	10193	32·25
Barber, R. W.	1954–1969	653	17631	29·43
Barber, W.	1926–1947	526	16402	34·38
Bardsley, W.	1903–04 to 1927–28	376	17031	49·94
Barker, G.	1954–1971	809	22288	29·21
Barling. T. H.	1927–1948	609	19209	34·61
Barlow, E. J.	1959–60 to 1978	440	16330	39·34
Barlow, R. G.	1871–1891	598	10762	20·11
Barnes, W.	1875–1894	725	15425	23·20
Barnett, C. J.	1927–1953–54	821	25389	32·71
Barrick, D. W.	1949–1960	490	13970	32·64
Barrington, K. F.	1953–1968	831	31714	45·63
Bartlett, H. T.	1933–1951	350	10098	31·95
Bates, L. T. A.	1913–1935	749	19371	27·85
Bates, W.	1877–1887–88	494	10214	21·54
Bates, W. E.	1907–1931	685	15884	24·25
Bear, M. J.	1954–1968	562	12564	24·25
Bedser, E. A.	1939–1962	692	14716	24·00
Benaud, R.	1948–49 to 1963–64	365	11719	36·50
Bennett, D.	1956–1968	612	10656	21·88
Berry, G. L.	1924–1951	1056	30225	30·26
Birkenshaw, J.	1958–1979	637	12203	23·51
Board, J. H.	1891–1914–15	906	15675	19·37
Bolus, J. B.	1956–1975	833	25598	34·03
Bond, J. D.	1955–1974	548	12125	25·90
Booth, B. C.	1954–55 to 1969–70	283	11265	45·42
Booth, B. J.	1956–1973	600	15298	27·91
Booth, R.	1951–1970	671	10139	18·91
Borde, C. G.	1952–53 to 1973–74	370	12821	40·96
Bosanquet, B. J.T.	1898–1919	382	11696	33·42
Bowell, H. A. C.	1902–1927	810	18510	24·13
Bowley, E. H	1912–1934	853	28163	34·89
Bowley, F. L.	1899–1923	738	21121	29·62
Boycott, G.	1962–1979	739	35761	56·94
Bradman, D. G.	1927–28 to 1948–49	338	28067	95·14
Brann, G.	1885–1905	475	11201	25·92
Braund, L. C.	1896–1920	752	17801	25·61
Brearley, J. M.	1961–1979	654	20878	36·75
Briggs, J.	1879–1900	821	14002	18·25
Broadbent, R. G.	1950–1963	520	12800	27·58
Brockwell, W.	1886–1903	539	13285	27·00
Brookes, D.	1934–1959	925	30874	36·10
Brown, A. S.	1953–1976	808	12851	18·12
Brown, F. R.	1930–1959	534	13303	27·43
Brown, G.	1908–1933	1012	25649	26·71
Brown, J. T.	1889–1904	633	17850	30·46
Brown, S. M.	1937–1955	580	15756	29·17
Brown, W. A.	1932–33 to 1949–50	284	13840	51·44
Burge, P. J. P.	1952–53 to 1967–68	354	14640	47·68
Burnup, C. J.	1895–1907	395	13614	36·79
Buse, H. T. F.	1929–1953	523	10623	22·65
Buss, M. A.	1961–1978	547	11996	23·99
Butcher, B. F.	1954–55 to 1971–72	262	11628	49·90
Buxton, I. R.	1959–1973	579	11803	23·94
Cadman, S. W. A.	1900–1926	690	14068	21·44
Calthorpe, Hon F. S. G.	1911–1935	576	12596	24·03
Carpenter, H.	1893–1920	551	14939	28·45
Carr, A. W.	1910–1935	709	21051	31·61
Carr, D. B.	1945–1968	745	19257	28·61
Cartwright. T. W.	1952–1977	737	13710	21·32
Chapman, A. P. F.	1920–1939	554	16309	31·97
Chappell, G. S.	1966–67 to 1979	425	18685	50·91
Chappell, I. M.	1961–62 to 1979	425	18790	48·80
Charlesworth, C.	1898–1921	632	14289	23·61
Chatterton, W.	1882–1902	507	10863	23·21
Clark, T. H.	1947–1959–60	426	11490	29·38
Close, D. B.	1949–1978	1217	34833	33·23
Coe, S.	1896–1923	775	17438	24·73
Compton, D. C. S.	1936–1964	839	38942	51·85
Congdon, B. E.	1960–61 to 1977–78	395	12545	34·84
Constable, B.	1939–1964	701	18849	30·45
Cook, T. E. J.	1922–1937	730	20198	30·37
Cooper, E.	1936–1951	444	13304	31·98
Cowdrey, M. C.	1950–1976	1130	42719	42·89
Cowper, R. M.	1959–60 to 1969–70	228	10595	53·78
Cox, G.	1931–1960	752	22912	32·96
Cox, G. R.	1895–1928	978	14643	18·74
Crapp, J. F.	1936–1956	754	23615	35·03

Crawford, V. F. S.	1896–1910	479	11909	26·64
Croom, A. J. W.	1922–1939	628	17692	31·43
Cutmore, J. A.	1924–1936	595	15975	28·58
Dacre, C. C. R.	1914–15 to 1936	439	12230	29·18
Daniell, J.	1898–1927	531	10468	21·94
Darling, J.	1893–94 to 1907–08	334	10637	34·42
Davies, D.	1923–1939	698	15458	24·30
Davies, E.	1924–1954	1033	26566	27·84
Davison, B. F.	1967–68 to 1979	498	17304	38·03
Dawkes, G. O.	1937–1961	736	11411	18·08
Dawson, E. W.	1922–1934	482	12597	27·09
Dempster, C. S.	1921–22 to 1947–48	306	12145	44·98
Denness, M. H.	1959–1979	808	25081	33·57
Denton, D.	1894–1920	1163	36479	33·37
Dews, G.	1946–1961	642	16803	28·52
Dexter, E. R.	1956–1968	565	21093	40·79
Dillon, E. W.	1900–1923	414	11006	28·29
Dipper, A. E.	1908–1932	865	28075	35·27
Dodds, T. C.	1943–44 to 1960	691	19384	28·80
Doggart, G. H. G.	1948–1961	347	10054	31·51
d'Oliveira, B. L.	1961–62 to 1979	564	18882	39·66
Dollery, H. E.	1933–1955	717	24413	37·50
Douglas, J. W. H. T.	1901–1930	1035	24530	27·89
Ducat, A.	1906–1931	669	23373	38·31
Dudleston, B.	1966–1979	467	13920	32·90
Duleepsinhji, K. S.	1924–1932	333	15485	49·95
Dyson, A. H.	1926–1948	697	17922	27·15
Eagar, E. D. R.	1935–1958	599	12178	21·86
Ealham, A. G. E.	1966–1979	430	10007	27·41
Eastman, L. C.	1920–1939	696	13438	20.80
Edmeades, B. E. A.	1961–1976	555	12593	25·91
Edrich, G. A.	1946–1958	508	15600	34·82
Edrich, J. H.	1956–1978	979	39790	45·47
Edrich, W. J.	1934–1958	964	36965	42·39
Edwards, M. J.	1960–1974	452	11378	26·70
Elliott, C. S.	1932–1953	468	11965	27·25
Emmett, G. M.	1936–1959	865	25602	31·41
Engineer, F. M.	1958–59 to 1976	510	13436	29·52
Evans, T. G.	1939–1969	753	14882	21·22
Fagg, A. E.	1932–1957	803	27291	36·05
Fane, F. L.	1895–1929	723	18567	27·34
Favell, L. E.	1951–52 to 1970–71	347	12379	36·62
Featherstone, N. G.	1967–68 to 1979	442	11578	29·01
Fender, P. G. H.	1910–1936	783	19034	26·65
Fishlock, L. B.	1931–1952	699	25376	39·34
Fletcher, D. G. W.	1946–1961	519	14461	30.25
Fletcher, K. W. R.	1962–1979	868	28521	38·38
Flowers, W.	1877–1896	696	12891	19·77
Foster, H. K.	1894–1935	523	17154	34·17
Fredericks, R. C.	1963–64 to 1979	344	14565	46·53
Freeman, J. R.	1905–1928	579	14604	27·88
Fry, C. B.	1892–1921–22	658	30886	50·22
Gale, R. A.	1959–1968	439	12505	29·35
Gardner, F. C.	1947–1961	597	17905	33·71
Gavaskar, S. M.	1966–67 to 1979	333	15508	52·05
Geary, G.	1912–1938	820	13504	19·80
Gibb, P. A.	1934–1956	479	12520	28·07
Gibbons, H. H. I.	1927–1946	671	21087	34·34
Giffen, G.	1877–78 to 1903–04	421	11757	29·61
Gilliat, R. M. C.	1964–1978	441	11589	29·33
Gillingham, F. H.	1903–1928	352	10050	30·64
Gimblett, H.	1935–1954	673	23007	36·17
Goddard, T. L.	1952–53 to 1969–70	293	11203	40·88
Grace, E. M.	1862–1896	555	10025	18·67
Grace, W. G.	1865–1908	1493	54896	39·55
Graveney, T. W.	1948–1971	1223	47793	44·91
Graves, P. J.	1965–1979	495	11870	26·73
Gray, J. R.	1948–1966	818	22650	30·73
Green, D. M.	1959–1972–73	479	13383	28·83
Greenidge, C. G.	1970–1979	410	16594	43·10
Gregory, R. J.	1925–1947	646	19495	34·32
Gregory, S. E.	1889–90 to 1912–13	592	15303	28·49
Greig, A. W.	1965–66 to 1978	579	16660	31·19
Grieves, K. J.	1945–46 to 1964	746	22454	33·66
Gunn, G.	1902–1932	1061	35208	35·96
Gunn, G. V.	1928–1950	395	10337	29·37
Gunn, J. R.	1896–1932	845	24557	33·19
Gunn, W.	1880–1904	850	25791	33·15
Haig, N. E.	1912–1936	779	15224	20·91

Haigh, S.	1895–1913	747	11715	18·65
Hall, I. W.	1959–1972	483	11666	25·86
Hall, L.	1873–1894	538	10853	22·84
Hallam, M. R.	1950–1970	905	24488	28·84
Hallows, C.	1914–1932	586	20926	40·24
Hamer, A.	1938–1960	515	15465	31·17
Hammond, W. R.	1920–1951	1005	50551	56·10
Hampshire, J. H.	1961–1979	765	22743	33·54
Hanif Mohammad	1951–52 to 1975–76	371	17059	52·32
Hanumant Singh	1956–57 to 1977–78	329	12404	44·53
Hardinge, H. T. W.	1902–1933	1021	33519	36·51
Hardstaff, J., sr	1902–1926	620	17146	31·34
Hardstaff, J., jr	1930–1955	812	31847	44·35
Harris, C. B.	1928–1951	601	18823	35·05
Harris, M. J.	1964–1979	548	18630	37·40
Harvey, R. N.	1946–47 to 1962–63	461	21699	50·93
Hassan, S. B.	1963–64 to 1979	402	10565	28·86
Hassett, A. L.	1932–33 to 1953–54	322	16890	58·24
Hawke, Lord	1881–1911	920	16506	20·25
Hayes, E. G.	1896–1926	896	27318	32·21
Hayes, F. C.	1970–1979	329	10313	36·57
Hayward, T. W.	1893–1914	1138	43551	41·79
Hazare, V. S.	1934–35 to 1966–67	366	18569	58·02
Headley, R. G. A.	1958–1974	758	21695	31·12
Hearne, A.	1884–1910	825	16287	21·74
Hearne, J. W.	1909–1936	1025	37252	40·98
Hedges, B.	1950–1967	744	17733	25·22
Hendren, E. H.	1907–1938	1300	57611	50·81
Hill, A. J. L.	1890–1921	389	10141	27·93
Hill, C.	1892–93 to 1925–26	417	17216	43·47
Hill, M.	1953–1971	484	10722	24·09
Hill, N. W.	1953–1968	518	14303	29·43
Hirst, G. H.	1891–1929	1215	36323	34·13
Hitchcock, R. E.	1947–48 to 1964	517	12442	27·89
Hobbs, J. B.	1905–1934	1315	61237	50·65
Holland, F. C.	1894–1908	429	10384	25·96
Holmes, E. R. T.	1924–1955	465	13598	32·84
Holmes, P.	1913–1935	810	30574	42·11
Hopwood, J. L.	1923–1939	575	15548	29·90
Hornby, A. N.	1867–1899	710	16108	24·08
Horner, N. F.	1950–1965	656	18533	29·79
Horton, H.	1946–1967	744	21669	32·83
Horton, M. J.	1952–1971	724	19944	29·55
Howarth, G. P.	1968–69 to 1979	335	10187	32·65
Howorth, R.	1933–1951	611	11479	20·68
Hubble, J. C.	1902–1929	528	10935	23·61
Humphreys, E.	1899–1920	639	16603	27·95
Hutchings, K. L.	1902–1912	311	10054	33·62
Hutton, L.	1934–1960	814	40140	55·51
Ibadulla, K.	1952–53 to 1972	702	17039	27·30
Iddon, J.	1924–1945	712	22681	36·76
Ikin, J. T.	1938–1964	554	17968	36·81
Illingworth, R.	1951–1978	1051	23977	28·40
Imtiaz Ahmed	1944–45 to 1964–65	311	10383	37·57
I-Mackenzie, A. C. D.	1951–1966	574	12421	24·35
Inman, C. C.	1956–57 to 1971	422	13112	34·50
Insole, D. J.	1947–1963	743	25237	37·61
Intikhab Alam	1957–58 to 1979	682	13646	22·37
Iremonger, J.	1899–1914	534	16622	35·06
Jackson, F. S.	1890–1907	500	15824	34·03
Jackson, G. R.	1919–1936	468	10288	23·06
Jackson, V. E.	1936–37 to 1958	605	15698	28·43
Jaisimha, M. L.	1954–55 to 1975–76	387	13515	37·54
Jameson, J. A.	1960–1976	611	18941	33·34
Jardine, D. R.	1920–1948	378	14848	46·84
Jenkins, R. O.	1938–1958	573	10073	22·23
Jessop, G. L.	1894–1914	855	26698	32·63
Johnson, H. L.	1949–1966	606	14286	26·40
Johnson, P. R.	1900–1927	488	11931	25·71
Jones, A.	1957–1979	1006	30914	32·64
Jones, A. O.	1892–1914	774	22955	31·57
Jones, W. E.	1937–1958	563	13535	27·12
Jupp, H.	1862–1881	677	14817	23·44
Jupp, V. W. C.	1909–1938	876	23278	29·39
Kallicharran, A. I.	1966–67 to 1979	438	17150	43·30
Kanhai, R. B.	1954–55 to 1977	663	28639	49·29
Keeton, W. W.	1926–1952	657	24276	39·53
Kennedy, A. S.	1907–1936	1025	16586	18·53
Kenyon, D.	1946–1967	1159	37002	33·63

Key, K. J.	1882–1909	560	12925	26·32
Khan, Majid	1961–62 to 1979	602	23955	43·08
Killick, E. H.	1893–1913	770	18768	26·17
Kilner, N.	1919–1937	619	17522	30·36
Kilner, R.	1911–1927	540	14422	29·73
King, J. H.	1895–1926	988	25122	27·33
Kinneir, S.	1898–1914	525	15641	32·72
Kippax, A. F.	1918–19 to 1935–36	254	12747	57·69
Kitchen, M. J.	1960–1979	612	15230	26·25
Knight, A. E.	1895–1912	702	19357	29·24
Knight, B. R.	1955–1969	602	13336	25·69
Knight, R. D. V.	1967–1979	474	13512	30·99
Knott, A. P. E.	1964–1979	571	14243	30·49
Langdon, T.	1900–1914	519	10723	21·23
Langridge, James	1924–1953	1058	31716	35·20
Langridge, J. G.	1928–1955	984	34380	37·45
Lawry, W. M.	1955–56 to 1971–72	417	18734	50·90
Leary, S. E.	1951–1971	627	16517	31·10
Lee, C.	1952–1964	472	12129	26·59
Lee, F. S.	1925–1947	586	15310	27·93
Lee, G. M.	1910–1933	622	14858	25·84
Lee, H. W.	1911–1934	720	20007	29·82
Lenham, L. J.	1956–1970	539	12796	26·16
Lester, E. I.	1945–1956	347	10912	34·20
Lester, G.	1937–1958	649	12857	21·60
Lewis, A. R.	1955–1974	708	20495	32·42
Leyland, M.	1920–1948	932	33660	40·50
Lightfoot, A.	1953–1970	495	12000	27·64
Lilley, A. A.	1891–1911	639	15597	26·30
Lilley, B.	1921–1937	512	10496	24·24
Livingston, L.	1941–42–1964	384	15260	45·01
Livingstone, D. A.	1959–1972	519	12722	27·89
Llewellyn, C. B.	1894–95 to 1912	461	11425	26·75
Lloyd, C. H.	1963–64 to 1979	524	22401	49·89
Lloyd, D.	1965–1979	536	15442	32·44
Lock, G. A. R.	1946–1970–71	812	10342	15·88
Lockwood. E.	1868–1884	566	11344	21·52
Lockwood, W. H.	1886–1904	531	10673	21·96
Lowson, F. A.	1949–1958	449	15321	37·18
Lucas, A. P.	1874–1907	435	10263	26·38
Luckhurst, B. W.	1958–1976	660	22293	38·17
Lyon, B. H.	1921–1948	448	10694	24·98
Macartney, C. G.	1905–06 to 1926–27	360	15020	45·79
MacBryan, J. C. W.	1911–1936	362	10322	29·52
McCabe, S. J.	1928–29 to 1941–42	262	11951	49·39
McCool, C. L.	1939–40 to 1960	413	12420	32·94
McCorkell, N. T.	1932–1951	696	16108	25·60
McDonald, C. C.	1947–48 to 1962–63	307	11375	40·48
McEwan, K. S.	1972–73 to 1979	320	11305	38·32
McGahey, C. P.	1894–1921	751	20723	30·20
McGlew, D. J.	1947–48 to 1966–67	299	12170	45·92
McIntyre, A. J. W.	1938–1963	567	11145	22·83
Mackay, K. D.	1946–47 to 1963–64	294	10823	43·64
MacLaren, A. C.	1890–1922–23	699	22022	34·03
McLean, R. A.	1949–50 to 1965–66	318	10969	36·80
Makepeace, H.	1906–1930	778	25799	36·23
Manjrekar, V. L.	1949–50 to 1967–68	295	12832	49·92
Mankad, A. V.	1963–64 to 1979	291	11356	49·37
Mankad, M. H.	1935–36 to 1963–64	359	11554	34·69
Mann, F. T.	1908–1933	612	13237	23·43
Marner, P. T.	1952–1970	680	17513	28·33
Marshall, R. E.	1945–46 to 1972	1053	35725	35·94
Martin, S. H.	1925–26 to 1949–50	457	11491	26·97
Mason, J. R.	1893–1919	557	17337	33·27
May, P. B. H.	1948–1963	618	27592	51·00
Mead, C. P.	1905–1936	1340	55061	47·67
Melville, A.	1928–29 to 1948–49	295	10598	37·85
Merchant, V. M.	1929–30 to 1951–52	221	12876	72·74
Milburn, C.	1960–1974	435	13262	33·07
Miller, K. R.	1937–38 to 1959	326	14183	48·90
Milton, C. A.	1948–1974	1078	32150	33·73
Mitchell, A.	1922–1947	593	19523	37·47
Mitchell, B.	1925–26 to 1949–50	281	11395	45·39
Morgan, D. C.	1950–1969	882	18356	24·94
Morris, A. R.	1940–41 to 1954–55	250	12614	53·67
Mortimore, J. B.	1950–1975	989	15891	18·32
Morton, A.	1901–1926	625	10933	19·21
Murdoch, W. L.	1876–77 to 1904	684	17070	26·83
Murray, D. L.	1960–61 to 1979	514	12380	28·45
Murray, J. T.	1952–1975	936	18872	23·59
Mushtaq Mohammad	1956–57 to 1979	819	30315	42·10
Nayudu, C. K.	1916–17 to 1963–64	305	10159	35·03
Neale, W. L.	1923–1948	700	14752	23·75
Newham, W.	1881–1905	633	14318	24·26
Newman, J. A.	1906–1930	837	15333	21·65
Nicholls, R. B.	1951–1975	954	23607	26·17
Nichols, M. S.	1924–1939	758	17843	26·51
Noble, M. A.	1893–94 to 1919–20	378	14034	40·79
Norman, M. E. J. C.	1952–1975	640	17441	29·26
Nourse, A. D.	1931–32 to 1952–53	269	12472	51·53
Nourse, A. W.	1896–97 to 1935–36	371	14216	42·81
Oakes, C.	1935–1954	474	10893	25·09
Oakman, A. S. M.	1947–1968	912	21800	26·17
O'Brien, T. C.	1881–1914	452	11397	27·01
O'Connor, J.	1921–1939	903	28764	34·90
Oldfield, N.	1935–1954	521	17811	37·89
Oldroyd, E.	1910–1931	511	15929	35·16
O'Neill, N. C.	1955–56 to 1966–67	306	13859	50·95
Ord, J. S.	1933–1953	459	11788	27·80
Ormrod, J. A.	1962–1979	679	18230	30·48
Outschoorn, L.	1946–1959	595	15496	28.59
Padgett, D. E. V.	1951–1971	806	21124	28·58
Page, M. H.	1964–1975	451	11538	28·55
Palairet, L. C. H.	1890–1909	488	15777	33·63
Palmer, C. H.	1938–1959	588	17458	31–74
Parfitt, P. H.	1956–1974	845	26924	36·33
Parker, J. F.	1932–1952	523	14272	31·57
Parkhouse, W. G. A.	1948–1964	791	23508	31·68
Parks, H. W.	1926–1949–50	725	21725	33·57
Parks, J. H.	1924–1952	758	21369	30·74
Parks, J. M.	1949–1976	1227	36673	34·76
Parsons, J. H.	1910–1936	557	17983	35·69
Nawab of Pataudi, jr	1957–1975–76	500	15425	33·60
Paynter, E.	1926–1950–51	533	20075	42·26
Payton, W. R. D.	1905–1931	770	22132	34·36
Pearce, T. N.	1929–1952	406	12060	34·26
Pearson, F. A.	1900–1926	811	18735	24·23
Peel, R.	1882–1899	689	12135	19·46
Perrin, P. A.	1896–1928	918	29709	35·92
Phebey, A. H.	1946–1964	599	14643	25·91
Pilling, H.	1962–1979	536	15199	32·40
Place, W.	1937–1955	487	15609	35·63
Pollock, R. G.	1960–61 to 1978–79	322	15721	55·16
Ponsford, W. H.	1920–21 to 1934–35	235	13819	65·18
Poole, C. J.	1948–1962	637	19364	32·54
Prentice, F. T.	1934–1951	421	10997	27·70
Pressdee, J. S.	1949–1969–70	581	14213	28·83
Prideaux, R. M.	1958–1974–75	808	25136	34·29
Procter, M. J.	1965–1979	568	19324	37·44
Pullar, G.	1954–1970	672	21528	35·34
Quaife, W. G.	1894–1928	1203	36016	35·38
Radley, C. T.	1964–1979	612	18304	34·53
Randall, D. W.	1972–1979	342	10714	34·33
Ranjitsinhji, K. S.	1893–1920	500	24692	56·37
Read, J. M.	1880–1895	599	13570	24·31
Read, W. W.	1873–1897	738	21568	31·62
Redpath, I. R.	1961–62 to 1975–76	391	14993	41·99
Reid, J. R.	1947–48 to 1965	418	16128	41·35
Relf, A. E.	1900–1921	900	22176	26·68
Relf, R. R.	1905–1933	527	14441	28·37
Revill, A. C.	1946–1960	654	15917	26·48
Reynolds, B. L.	1950–1970	737	18824	28·01
Rhodes, W.	1898–1930	1528	39802	30·83
Rice, C. E. B.	1969–70 to 1979	310	10075	38·01
Richards, B. A.	1964–65 to 1979	543	27293	55·70
Richards, I. V. A.	1971–72 to 1979	319	14108	47·34
Richardson, D. W.	1952–1967	660	16303	27·40
Richardson, P. E.	1949–1965	794	26055	34·60
Richardson, V. Y.	1918–19 to 1937–38	297	10727	37·63
Robertson, J. D. B.	1937–1959	897	31914	37·50
Robins, R. W. V.	1925–1958	565	13884	26·40
Robson, E.	1895–1923	761	12620	17·62
Rogers, N. H.	1946–1955	529	16056	32·04
Roope, G. R. J.	1964–1979	552	16652	37·50
Rowan, E. A. B.	1929–30 to 1953–54	258	11710	48·58
Roy, P.	1946–47 to 1967–68	298	11868	42·38
Russell, A. C.	1908–1930	719	27564	41·73
Russell, W. E.	1956–1972	796	25525	34·87

Ryder, J.	1912–13 to 1935–36	274	10494	44·28
Sadiq Mohammad	1959–60 to 1979	495	17940	38·49
Saeed Ahmed	1954–55 to 1977–78	348	12866	39·83
Sainsbury, P. J.	1954–1976	948	20176	26·86
Sandham, A.	1911–1937–38	1000	41283	44·82
Santall, F. R.	1919–1939	797	17730	24·93
Sardesai, D. N.	1960–61 to 1972–73	271	10231	41·75
Seymour, J.	1900–1926	911	27238	32·08
Sharp, J.	1899–1925	805	22715	31·11
Sharpe, P. J.	1956–1976	811	22530	30·73
Shepherd, D. R.	1965–1979	476	10672	24·47
Shepherd, J. N.	1964–65 to 1979	461	10116	25·80
Shepherd, T. F.	1919–1932	531	18715	39·81
Sheppard, D. S.	1947–1962–63	395	15838	43·51
Shipman, A. W.	1920–1936	661	13682	23·22
Shrewsbury, A.	1875–1902	811	26439	36·67
Simpson, R. B.	1952–53 to 1977–78	436	21029	56·22
Simpson, R. T.	1944–45 to 1963	852	30546	38·32
Sinfield, R. A.	1921–1935	696	15674	25·69
Smedley, M. J.	1964–1979	604	16482	31·21
Smith. A. C.	1958–1974	611	11012	20·93
Smith, D.	1927–1952	753	21843	31·65
Smith, D. V.	1946–1962	625	16960	30·34
Smith, E. J.	1904–1930	814	16997	22·42
Smith, H.	1912–1935	656	13413	22·35
Smith, M. J.	1959–1979	698	19731	31·82
Smith, M. J. K.	1951–1975	1091	39832	41·84
Smith, R.	1934–1956	682	12042	20·27
Smith, S. G.	1899–1900 to 1925–26	379	10918	31·28
Smith, T. P. B.	1929–1952	692	10170	17·98
Sobers, G. S.	1952–53 to 1974	609	28315	54·87
Spooner, R. H.	1899–1923	393	13681	36·28
Spooner, R. T.	1948–1959	580	13851	27·27
Sprot, E. M.	1898–1914	458	12328	28·66
Squires, H. S.	1928–1949	658	19186	31·24
Stackpole, K. R.	1959–60 to 1973–74	279	10100	39·29
Staples, A.	1924–1938	512	12762	28·23
Steele, D. S.	1963–1979	637	18565	33·45
Steele, J. F.	1970–1979	409	11047	30·26
Stephenson, H. W.	1948–1964	749	13203	20·06
Stevens, G. T. S.	1919–1933	387	10376	29·56
Stewart, M. J.	1954–1972	898	26492	32·90
Stewart, W. J.	1955–1971	491	14826	34·08
Stocks, F. W.	1946–1957	430	11397	29·60
Stoddart, A. E.	1885–1900	537	16738	32·12
Stone, J.	1900–1923	526	10362	22·38
Storer, H.	1920–1936	517	13515	27·69
Storer, W.	1887–1905	490	12966	28·87
Storey, S. J.	1960–1978	492	10776	25·06
Subba Row, R.	1951–1964	407	14182	41·46
Sugg, F. H.	1883–1899	510	11653	24·22
Sutcliffe, B.	1941–42 to 1965–66	405	17283	47·22
Sutcliffe, H.	1919–1945	1088	50138	51·95
Suttle, K. G.	1949–1971	1064	30225	31·09
Tarrant, F. A.	1898–99 to 1936–37	540	17900	36·38
Tate, M. W.	1912–1937	970	21717	25·02
Taylor, B.	1949–1973	949	19094	21·79
Taylor, H. W.	1909–10 to 1935–36	340	13105	41·87
Taylor, K.	1953–1968	524	13053	26·74
Tennyson, Lord	1913–1937–38	759	16828	23·33
Thompson, G. J.	1897–1922	606	12018	21·97
Timms, J. E.	1925–1949	847	20457	25·03
Titmus, F. J.	1949–1979	1135	21564	23·16
Todd, L. J.	1927–1950	727	20087	31·73
Tolchard, R. W.	1965–1979	541	12022	31·30
Tompkin, M.	1938–1956	655	19927	31·83
Townsend, A.	1948–1960	553	12054	24·95
Townsend, L. F.	1922–1939	786	19555	27·54
Tremlett, M. F.	1947–1960	681	16038	25·37
Tribe, G. E.	1945–46 to 1959	454	10177	27·35
Trimble, S. C.	1959–60 to 1975–76	262	10282	41·79
Trott, A. E.	1892–93 to 1911	602	10696	19·48
Trumper, V. T.	1894–95 to 1913–14	401	16939	44·57
Tunnicliffe, J.	1891–1907	806	20268	27·13
Turnbull, M. J. L.	1924–1939	626	17543	29·78
Turner, D. R.	1966–1979	441	11384	28·10
Turner, G. M.	1964–65 to 1979	681	28797	48·72
Tyldesley, E.	1909–1936	961	38874	45·46
Tyldesley, J. T.	1895–1923	994	37897	40·66
Ulyett, G.	1873–1893	912	20484	23·46
Umrigar, P. M.	1944–45 to 1967–68	350	16155	52·28
Valentine, B. H.	1927–1950	645	18306	30·15
Vine, J.	1896–1922	920	25171	29·94
Virgin, R. T.	1957–1977	773	21930	29·87
Viswanath, G. R.	1967–68 to 1979	343	13284	42·44
Wadekar, A. L.	1958–59 to 1974	358	15377	47·31
Wainwright, E.	1888–1902	603	12485	21·82
Walcott, C. L.	1941–42 to 1963–64	238	11820	56·55
Walker, I. D.	1862–1884	508	11399	24·51
Walker, P. M.	1956–1972	788	17650	26·03
Walker, W.	1913–1937	624	18259	32·37
Walters, C. F.	1923–1935	427	12145	30·74
Walters, K. D.	1962–63 to 1976–77	390	14802	43·40
Ward, A.	1886–1904	642	17783	30·08
Warner, P. F.	1894–1929	875	29028	36·33
Washbrook, C.	1933–1964	906	34101	42·67
Watkins, A. J.	1939–1963	753	20362	30·57
Watson, F.	1920–1937	688	23596	36·98
Watson, W.	1939–1964	753	25670	39·86
Watts, P. J.	1959–1979	592	14229	28·17
Webbe, A. J.	1875–1900	641	14466	24·81
Weekes, E. D.	1944–45 to 1964	241	12010	55·34
Wellard, A. W.	1927–1950	679	12515	19·73
Wensley, A. F.	1922–1939–40	590	10735	20·40
Wharton, A.	1946–1963	745	21796	32·24
White, J. C.	1909–1937	765	12202	18·40
White, R. A.	1958–1978	639	12442	23·29
Whitehead, H.	1898–1922	680	15112	23·07
Whysall, W. W.	1910–1930	601	21592	38·74
Wight, P. B.	1950–51 to 1965	590	17773	33·09
Wilson, A. E.	1932–1955	502	10744	25·28
Wilson, J. V.	1946–1963	770	21650	31·33
Wilson, R. C.	1952–1967	647	19515	32·09
Wolton, A. V. G.	1947–1960	478	12930	31·00
Wood, B.	1964–1979	484	14261	33·79
Wood, C. J. B.	1896–1923	823	23879	31·05
Woodfull, W. M.	1921–22 to 1934–35	245	13392	65·00
Woods, S. M. J.	1882–1910	690	15352	23·43
Wooller, W.	1935–1960	677	13586	22·64
Woolley, C. N.	1909–1931	658	15395	24·67
Woolley, F. E.	1906–1938	1532	58969	40·75
Woolmer, R. A.	1968–1979	404	11410	33·55
Worrell, F. M. M.	1941–42 to 1964	326	15025	54·24
Worthington, T. S.	1924–1947	720	19221	29·07
Wrathall, H.	1894–1907	509	11023	22·54
Wright, L. G.	1883–1909	593	15166	26·10
Wyatt, R. E. S.	1923–1957	1142	39470	40·07
Yardley, N. W. D.	1935–1955	658	18173	31·17
Young, A.	1911–1933	537	13159	25·55
Young, D. M.	1946–1964	842	24555	30·69
Younis Ahmed	1961–62 to 1979	555	17806	37·32
Zaheer Abbas	1965–66 to 1979	494	22339	50·31

One Thousand Wickets in a Career

	YEARS	WKTS	AVGE
Allen, D. A.	1953–1972	1209	23·64
Arnold, E. G.	1899–1913	1069	23·14
Arnold, G. G.	1963–1979	1037	21·53
Astill, W. E.	1906–1939	2432	23·76
Attewell, W.	1881–1900	1949	15·34
Bailey, T. E.	1945–1967	2082	23·13
Bannister, J. D.	1950–1968	1198	21·92
Barratt, F.	1914–1931	1224	22·71
Bedi, B. S.	1961–62 to 1979	1507	21·71
Bedser, A. V.	1939–1960	1924	20·41
Bestwick, W.	1898–1925	1458	21·33
Birkenshaw, J.	1958–1979	1050	26·91
Blythe, C.	1899–1914	2506	16·81
Bowes, W. E.	1928–1949	1639	16·76
Boyes, G. S.	1921–1939	1472	23·51
Braund, L. C.	1896–1920	1113	27·30
Briggs, J.	1879–1900	2212	15·95
Brown, A. S.	1953–1976	1230	25·64

Brown, D. J.	1961–1979	1161	24·76	Mead, W.	1892–1913	1916	18·99
Brown, F. R.	1930–1959	1219	26·19	Mercer, J.	1919–1947	1593	23·41
Buckenham, C. P.	1899–1914	1152	25·31	Mitchell, T. B.	1928–1939	1483	20·58
Cartwright, T. W.	1952–1977	1536	19·11	Mold, A. W.	1889–1901	1673	15·54
Chandrasekhar, B. S.	1963–64 to 1979	1032	24·00	Morgan, D. C.	1950–1969	1248	25·08
Clark, E. W.	1922–1947	1203	21·54	Morley, F.	1872–1883	1270	13·45
Clay, J. C.	1921–1949	1315	19·77	Mortimore, J. B.	1950–1975	1807	23·18
Close, D. B.	1949–1978	1167	26·42	Moss, A. E.	1950–1968	1301	20·78
Coldwell, L. J.	1955–1969	1076	21·18	Newman, J. A.	1906–1930	2032	25·20
Cook, C.	1946–1964	1782	20·52	Nichols, M. S.	1924–1939	1834	21·66
Copson, W. H.	1932–1950	1094	18·96	Paine, G. A. E.	1926–1947	1021	22·85
Cornford, J. H.	1931–1952	1019	26·49	Parker, C. W. L.	1903–1935	3278	19·47
Cottam, R. M. H.	1963–1976	1010	20·91	Parkin, C. H.	1906–1926	1048	17·58
Cox, G. R.	1895–1928	1843	22·86	Peate, E.	1879–1890	1076	13·48
Dean, H.	1906–1921	1301	18·14	Peel, R.	1882–1899	1754	16·21
Dennett, E. G.	1903–1926	2147	19·82	Perks, R. T. D.	1930–1955	2233	24·07
Dooland, B.	1945–1957	1016	21·98	Pocock, P. I.	1964–1979	1257	25·47
Douglas, J. W. H. T.	1901–1930	1894	23·32	Pollard, R.	1933–1952	1122	22·56
Durston, F. J.	1919–1933	1329	22·03	Preston, K. C.	1948–1964	1160	26·33
Eastman, L. C.	1920–1939	1006	26·81	Procter, M. J.	1965–1979	1231	19·09
Emmett, T.	1866–1888	1582	13·36	Relf, A. E.	1900–1921	1897	20·94
Fender, P. G. H.	1910–1936	1894	25·05	Rhodes, H. J.	1953–1975	1073	19·70
Field, E. F.	1897–1920	1026	23·48	Rhodes, W.	1898–1930	4187	16·71
Fielder, A.	1900–1914	1277	21·02	Richardson, T.	1892–1905	2105	18·42
Flavell, J. A.	1949–1967	1529	21·48	Richmond, T. L.	1912–1932	1176	21·22
Flowers, W.	1877–1896	1187	15·91	Ridgway, F.	1946–1960	1067	23·72
Freeman, A. P.	1914–1936	3776	18·42	Robinson, E. P.	1934–1952	1009	22·58
Geary, G.	1912–1938	2063	20·03	Robson, E.	1895–1923	1147	26·44
Gibbs, L. R.	1953–54 to 1975–76	1024	27·22	Root, C. F.	1910–1933	1512	21·11
Giffen, G.	1877–78 to 1903–4	1022	21·31	Ryan, F. B.	1919–1931	1008	21·14
Gifford, N.	1960–1979	1565	21·68	Sainsbury, P. J.	1954–1976	1316	24·14
Gladwin, C.	1939–1958	1653	18·30	Santall, S.	1894–1914	1220	23·98
Goddard, T. W. J.	1922–1952	2979	19·84	Shackleton, D.	1948–1969	2857	18·65
Gover, A. R.	1928–1948	1555	23·63	Shaw, A.	1864–1897	2027	12·12
Grace, W. G.	1865–1908	2876	17·99	Shepherd, D. J.	1950–1972	2218	21·32
Grimmett, C. V.	1911–12 to 1940–41	1424	22·28	Sims, J. M.	1929–1953	1581	24·92
Grundy, J.	1850–1869	1125	13·05	Sinfield, R. A.	1921–1939	1173	24·49
Gunn, J. R.	1896–1932	1242	24·53	Smith, D. R.	1956–1970	1250	23·72
Haig, N. E.	1912–1936	1117	27·48	Smith, E.	1951–1971	1217	25·84
Haigh, S.	1895–1913	2012	15·94	Smith, H. A.	1925–1939	1076	25·99
Hallam, A. W.	1895–1910	1012	19·02	Smith, R.	1934–1956	1350	30·56
Hearne, A.	1884–1910	1144	20·03	Smith, T. P. B.	1929–1952	1697	26·63
Hearne, J. T.	1888–1923	3061	17·75	Smith, W. C.	1900–1914	1077	17·55
Hearne, J. W.	1909–1936	1839	24·43	Snow, J. A.	1961–1977	1174	22·72
Herman, O. W.	1929–1948	1045	27·00	Sobers, G. S.	1952—53 to 1974	1043	27·74
Higgs, K.	1958–1979	1524	23·56	Southerton, S. J.	1854–1879	1626	14·30
Hilton, M. J.	1946–1961	1006	19·41	Spencer, C. T.	1952–1974	1367	26·69
Hirst, G. H.	1891–1929	2739	18·72	Staples, S. J.	1920–1934	1331	22·85
Hitch, J. W.	1907–1925	1398	21·48	Statham, J. B.	1950–1968	2260	16·36
Hobbs, R. N. S.	1961–1979	1056	26·71	Tarrant, F. A.	1898–99 to 1936–37	1489	17·65
Hollies, W. E.	1932–1957	2323	20·94	Tate, F. W.	1887–1905	1331	21·55
Howorth, R.	1933–1951	1345	21·87	Tate, M. W.	1912–1937	2784	18·16
Illingworth, R.	1951–1978	2031	19·93	Tattersall, R.	1948–1964	1369	18·04
Intikhab Alam	1957–58 to 1979	1469	27·96	Thompson, G. J.	1897–1922	1591	18·89
Jackman, R. D.	1964–1979	1122	23·15	Titmus, F. J.	1949–1979	2815	22·34
Jackson, H. L.	1947–1963	1733	17·36	Townsend, L. F.	1922–1939	1088	21·12
Jackson, P. F.	1929–1950	1159	26·33	Tribe, G. E.	1945–46 to 1959	1378	20·55
Jenkins, R. O.	1938–1958	1309	23·62	Trott, A. E.	1892–93 to 1911	1674	21·09
Jepson, A.	1938–1959	1051	29·08	Trueman, F. S.	1949–1969	2304	18·29
Jupp, V. W. C.	1909–1938	1658	23·01	Tyldesley, R.	1919–1935	1509	17·21
Kennedy, A. S.	1907–1936	2874	21·24	Underwood, D. L.	1963–1979	1840	19·28
King, J. H.	1895–1925	1204	25·15	Venkataraghavan, S.	1963–64 to 1979	1196	24·13
Knight, B. R.	1955–1969	1089	24·06	Verity, H.	1930–1939	1956	14·90
Laker, J. C.	1946–1964–65	1944	18·40	Voce, W.	1927–1952	1558	23·08
Langford, B. A.	1953–1974	1410	24·79	Wainwright, E.	1888–1902	1062	18·20
Langridge, James	1924–1953	1530	22·56	Walsh, J. E.	1936–37 to 1956	1190	24·55
Larwood, H.	1924–1938	1427	17·51	Wardle, J. H.	1946–1958	1842	18·95
Lees, W. S.	1896–1911	1402	21·39	Wass, T. G.	1896–1920	1666	20·46
Lillywhite, James	1862–1881	1140	15·38	Watson, A.	1872–1893	1351	13·41
Llewellyn, C. B.	1894–95 to 1912	1013	23·41	Wellard, A. W.	1929–1950	1614	24·35
Loader, P. J.	1951–1963–64	1326	19·04	Wensley, A. F.	1922–1939–40	1135	26·42
Lock, G. A. R.	1946–1971–72	2844	19·23	Wheatley, O. S.	1956–1969	1098	20·81
Lockwood, W. H.	1886–1904	1376	18·34	White, J. C.	1909–1937	2356	18·57
Lohmann, G. A.	1884–1897–98	1805	13·91	Willsher, E.	1850–1874	1188	13·07
Macaulay, G. G.	1920–1935	1837	17·65	Wilson, D.	1957–1974	1189	21·00
McDonald, E. A.	1909–10 to 1935	1395	20·76	Woods, S. M. J.	1886–1910	1040	20·82
McKenzie, G. D.	1959–60 to 1975	1218	26·98	Woolley, F. E.	1906–1938	2068	19·85
Martin, F.	1885–1900	1317	17·38	Wright, D. V. P.	1932–1957	2056	23·98
Mayer, J. H.	1926–1939	1144	22·20	Young, J. A.	1933–1956	1361	19·68

Fifty or More Hundreds in a Career

	INNS	100S		INNS	100S		INNS	100S		INNS	100S
Hobbs, J. B.	1327	197	May, P. B. H.	618	85	Marshall, R. E.	1053	68	Hanif Mohammad	371	55
Hendren, E. H.	1300	170	Wyatt, R. E. S.	1141	85	Zaheer Abbas	494	68	Watson, W.	753	55
Hammond, W. R.	1004	167	Hardstaff, J., Jr	812	83	Harvey, R. N.	461	67	Chappell, G. S.	425	54
Mead, C. P.	1340	153	Kanhai, R. B.	663	83	Holmes, P.	810	67	Insole, D. J.	743	54
Sutcliffe, H.	1087	149	Turner, G. M.	681	81	Robertson, J. D. B.	897	67	Keeton, W. W.	657	54
Woolley, F. E.	1537	145	Leyland, M.	932	80	Perrin, P. A.	918	66	Bardsley, W.	376	53
Hutton, L.	814	129	Richards, B. A.	543	79	Simpson, R. T.	852	64	Dipper, A. E.	865	53
Grace, W. G.	1493	126	Barrington, K. F.	772	76	Gunn, G.	1062	62	Jessop, G. L.	855	53
Compton, D. C. S.	839	123	Langridge, J. G.	984	76	Majid Khan	602	62	Seymour, J.	911	53
Graveney, T. W.	1223	122	Washbrook, C.	902	76	Hirst, G. H.	1215	60	Bowley, E. H.	853	52
Bradman, D. G.	338	117	Hardinge, H. T. W.	1021	75	Lloyd, C. H.	524	60	Close, D. B.	1217	52
Boycott, G.	739	115	Abel, R.	994	74	Simpson, R. B.	436	60	Ducat, A.	669	52
Cowdrey, M. C.	1130	107	Amiss, D. L.	783	74	Warner, P. F.	875	60	Dexter, E. R.	565	51
Sandham, A.	1000	107	Kenyon, D.	1159	74	Hassett, A. L.	322	59	Gavaskar, S. M.	333	51
Hayward, T. W.	1138	104	O'Connor, J.	906	72	Shrewsbury, A.	801	59	Parks, J. M.	1227	51
Edrich, J. H.	979	103	Quaife, W. G.	1203	72	Fagg, A. E.	803	58	Whysall, W. W.	601	51
Ames, L. E. G.	950	102	Ranjitsinhji, K. S.	500	72	Parfitt, P. H.	843	58	Cox, G., Jr.	752	50
Tyldesley, E.	961	102	Brookes, D.	925	71	Rhodes, W.	1528	58	Dollery, H. E.	717	50
Hearne, J. W.	1025	96	Russell, A. C.	719	71	Hazare, V. S.	355	57	Duleepsinhji, K. S.	333	50
Fry, C. B.	658	94	Mushtaq Mohammad	803	70	Chappell, I. M.	425	56	Gimblett, H.	673	50
Edrich, W. J.	964	86	Denton, D.	1163	69	Fishlock, L. B.	699	56	Lawry, W. M.	417	50
Sobers, G. S.	609	86	Smith, M. J. K.	1091	69	Milton, C. A.	1078	56	Watson, F. J.	688	50
Tyldesley, J. T.	994	86				Hallows, C.	586	55			

All-Rounders

10000 RUNS AND 1000 WICKETS

	RUNS	WKTS		RUNS	WKTS		RUNS	WKTS
Arnold, E. G.	15853	1069	Hearne, A.	16287	1144	Relf, A. E.	22176	1897
Astill, W. E.	22731	2432	Hearne, J. W.	37252	1839	Rhodes, W.	39802	4187
Bailey, T. E.	28642	2082	Hirst, G. H.	36323	2739	Robson, E.	12620	1147
Birkenshaw, J.	12203	1050	Howorth, R.	11479	1345	Sainsbury, P. J.	20176	1316
Braund, L. C.	17801	1113	Illingworth, R.	23977	2031	Sinfield, R. A.	15674	1173
Briggs, J.	14002	2212	Intikhab Alam	13646	1469	Smith, R.	12042	1350
Brown, A. S.	12851	1230	Jenkins, R. O.	10073	1309	Smith, T. P. B.	10170	1697
Brown, F. R.	13303	1219	Jupp, V. W. C.	23278	1658	Sobers, G. S.	28315	1043
Cartwright, T. W.	13710	1536	Kennedy, A. S.	16586	2874	Tarrant, F. A.	17900	1489
Close, D. B.	34833	1167	King, J. H.	25122	1204	Tate, M. W.	21717	2784
Cox, G. R.	14643	1843	Knight, B. R.	13336	1089	Thompson, G. J.	12018	1591
Douglas, J. W. H. T.	24530	1894	Langridge, James	31716	1530	Titmus, F. J.	21564	2815
Eastman, L. C.	13438	1006	Llewellyn, C. B.	11425	1013	Townsend, L. F.	19555	1088
Fender, P. G. H.	19034	1894	Lock, G. A. R.	10342	2844	Tribe, G. E.	10177	1378
Flowers, W.	12891	1187	Lockwood, W. H.	10673	1376	Trott, A. E.	10696	1674
Geary, G.	13504	2063	Morgan, D. C.	18356	1248	Wainwright, E.	12485	1062
Giffen, G.	11757	1022	Mortimore, J. B.	15891	1807	Wellard, A. W.	12515	1614
Grace, W. G.	54896	2876	Newman, J. A.	15333	2032	Wensley, A. F.	10735	1135
Gunn, J. R.	24557	1242	Nichols, M. S.	17843	1834	White, J. C.	12202	2356
Haig, N. E.	15224	1117	Peel, R.	12135	1754	Woods, S. M. J.	15352	1040
Haigh, S.	11715	2012	Procter, M. J.	19324	1231	Woolley, F. E.	58969	2068

Wicket-Keeping

MORE THAN 750 VICTIMS IN A CAREER

	YEARS	TOTAL	CT	ST		YEARS	TOTAL	CT	ST
Murray, J. T.	1952–1975	1527	1270	257	Elliott, H.	1920–1947	1195	895	300
Strudwick, H.	1902–1927	1493	1235	258	Parks, J. M.	1949–1976	1182	1089	93
Huish, F. H.	1895–1914	1328	925	376	Booth, R.	1951–1970	1122	946	176
Hunter, D.	1889–1909	1327	955	372	Ames, L. E. G.	1926–1951	1113	698	415
Taylor, R. W.	1960–1979	1315	1172	143	Duckworth, G.	1923–1947	1090	751	339
Taylor, B.	1949–1972	1270	1064	206	Stephenson, H. W.	1948–1964	1084	752	332
Butt, H. R.	1890–1912	1262	971	291	Binks, J. G.	1955–1975	1071	895	176
Board, J. H.	1890–1914–15	1206	852	354	Evans, T. G.	1939–1969	1060	811	249

Knott, A. P. E.	1964–1979	1048	943	105
Dawkes, G. O.	1937–1961	1042	896	146
Long, A.	1960–1979	1014	892	122
Cornford, W. L.	1921–1947	1000	656	344
Oates, T. W.	1897–1925	984	751	233
Price, W. F. F.	1926–1947	977	665	312
Andrew, K. V.	1952–1966	903	721	182
Lilley, A. A.	1891–1911	899	709	190
Smith, E. J.	1904–1930	875	719	156
Tolchard, R. W.	1965–1979	857	757	100
Murray D. L.	1960–1979	854	755	99
Pooley, E.	1861–1883	850	492	358
Wood, A.	1928–1947	848	603	245
Sherwin, M.	1876–1896	834	607	227
Murrell, H. R.	1906–1926	831	563	268
Luckes, W. T.	1924–1949	827	586	241
Meyer, B. J.	1957–1971	825	708	117
Engineer, F. M.	1958–59 to 1976	824	703	121
Brooks, E. W. J.	1925–1939	819	724	95
McIntyre, A. J. W.	1938–1960	791	634	157
Davies, H. G.	1935–1958	788	584	204
Lilley, B.	1921–1937	786	655	131
Smith, A. C.	1958–1974	776	715	61
Jones, E. W.	1961–1979	765	689	76
Spooner, R. T.	1948–1959	765	585	180

Catches

MORE THAN 500 IN A CAREER

	YEARS	CT
Woolley, F. E.	1906–1938	1015
Grace, W. G.	1865–1908	877
Lock, G. A. R.	1946–1970–71	830
Hammond, W. R.	1920–1951	819
Close, D. B.	1949–1978	810
Langridge, J. G.	1928–1955	786
Hendren, E. H.	1907–1938	755
Milton, C. A.	1948–1974	755
Rhodes, W.	1898–1930	708
Walker, P. M.	1956–1972	697
Tunnicliffe, J.	1891–1907	691
Mead, C. P.	1905–1936	668
Cowdrey, M. C.	1950–1976	638
Stewart, M. J.	1954–1972	634
Seymour, J.	1900–1926	622
Sharpe, P. J.	1956–1976	617
Sainsbury, P. J.	1954–1976	616
Grieves, K. J.	1945–46 to 1964	599
Hayes E. G.	1896–1926	598
Oakman, A. S. M.	1947–1968	594
Smith, M. J. K.	1951–1975	593
Morgan, D. C.	1950–1969	573
Parfitt, P. H.	1956–1974	564
Fender, P. G. H.	1910–1936	558
Graveney, T. W.	1948–1971	550
Hirst, G. H.	1891–1929	550
Jones, A. O.	1892–1914	548
Braund, L. C.	1896–1920	547
Wilson, J. V.	1946–1963	545
Edrich, W. J.	1934–1958	526
Kennedy, A. S.	1907–1936	523
Barrington, K. F.	1953–1967	511
Cox, G. R.	1895–1928	510
Carr, D. B.	1945–1968	501

Test Career Records

These figures embrace official Test Matches. Amended records where applicable inclusive of the unofficial Test series of 1970 between England and the Rest of The World are appended separately in order to prevent confusion.

2500 Runs in Tests

ENGLAND

	TESTS	INNS	NO	RUNS	HS	AVGE	100S
Cowdrey, M. C.	114	188	15	7624	182	44·06	22
Hammond, W. R.	85	140	16	7249	336*	58·45	22
Hutton, L.	79	138	15	6971	364	56·67	19
Barrington, K. F.	82	131	15	6806	256	58·67	20
Boycott, G.	84	145	17	6316	246*	49·34	18
Compton, D. C.S.	78	131	15	5807	278	50·06	17
Hobbs, J. B.	61	102	7	5410	211	56·94	15
Edrich, J. H.	77	127	9	5138	310*	43·54	12
Graveney, T. W.	79	123	13	4882	258	44·38	11
Sutcliffe, H.	54	84	9	4555	194	60·73	16
May, P. B. H.	66	106	9	4537	285*	46·77	13
Dexter, E. R.	62	102	8	4502	205	47·89	9
Knott, A. P. E.	89	138	14	4175	135	33·66	5
Amiss, D. L.	50	88	10	3612	262*	46·30	11
Greig, A. W.	58	93	4	3599	148	40·43	8
Hendren, E. H.	51	83	9	3525	205*	47·63	7
Woolley, F. E.	64	98	7	3283	154	36·07	5
Fletcher, K. W. R.	52	85	11	2975	216	40·20	7
Leyland, M.	41	65	5	2764	187	46·06	9
Washbrook, C.	37	66	6	2569	195	42·81	6

FOR ENGLAND INCLUDING V REST OF THE WORLD 1970

	TESTS	INNS	NO	RUNS	HS	AVGE	100S
Cowdrey, M. C.	118	196	15	7865	182	43·45	22
Boycott, G.	86	149	17	6576	246*	49·81	18
Edrich, J. H.	79	131	9	5234	310*	42·90	12
Knott, A. P. E.	94	147	16	4385	135	33·47	5
Amiss, D. L.	51	90	10	3736	262*	46·70	11
Greig, A. W.	61	98	4	3695	148	39·30	8
Fletcher, K. W. R.	56	93	12	3315	216	40·92	7

AUSTRALIA

	TESTS	INNS	NO	RUNS	HS	AVGE	100S
Bradman, D. G.	52	80	10	6996	334	99·94	29
Harvey, R. N.	79	137	10	6149	205	48·41	21
Lawry, W. M.	67	123	12	5234	210	47·15	13
Chappell, I. M.	72	130	9	5187	196	42·86	14
Walters, K. D.	68	116	12	4960	250	47·69	14
Simpson, R. B.	62	111	7	4869	311	46·81	10
Redpath, I. R.	66	120	11	4737	171	43·45	8
Chappell, G. S.	51	90	13	4097	247*	53·20	14
Morris, A. R.	46	79	3	3533	206	46·48	12
Hill, C.	49	89	2	3412	191	39·21	7
Trumper, V. T.	48	89	8	3163	214*	39·04	8
McDonald, C. C.	47	83	4	3107	170	39·32	5
Hassett, A. L.	43	69	3	3073	198*	46·56	10
Miller, K. R.	55	87	7	2958	147	36·97	7
Armstrong, W. W.	50	84	10	2863	159*	38·68	6
Stackpole, K. R.	43	80	5	2807	207	37·42	7
O'Neill, N. C.	42	69	8	2779	181	45·55	6
McCabe, S. J.	39	62	5	2748	232	48·21	6

SOUTH AFRICA

	TESTS	INNS	NO	RUNS	HS	AVGE	100S
Mitchell, B.	42	80	9	3471	189*	48·88	8
Nourse, A. D.	34	62	7	2960	231	53·81	9
Taylor, H. W.	42	76	4	2936	176	40·77	7
Barlow, E. J.	30	57	2	2516	201	45·74	6
Goddard, T. L.	41	78	5	2516	112	34·46	1

WEST INDIES

	TESTS	INNS	NO	RUNS	HS	AVGE	100S
Sobers, G. S.	93	160	21	8032	365*	57·78	26
Kanhai, R. B.	79	137	6	6227	256	47·53	15
Lloyd, C. H.	65	113	8	4594	242*	43·75	11
Weekes, E. D.	48	81	5	4455	207	58·61	15
Fredericks, R. C.	59	109	7	4334	169	42·49	8
Kallicharran, A. I.	51	86	8	3869	187	49·60	11
Worrell, F. M.	51	87	9	3860	261	49·48	9
Walcott C. L.	44	74	7	3798	220	56·68	15
Hunte, C. .C	44	78	6	3245	260	45·06	8
Butcher, B. F.	44	78	6	3104	209*	43·11	7
Nurse, S. M.	29	54	1	2523	258	47·60	6
Richards, I. V. A.	28	47	2	2500	291	55·55	8

NEW ZEALAND

	TESTS	INNS	NO	RUNS	HS	AVGE	100S
Congdon, B. E.	61	114	7	3448	176	32·22	7
Reid, J. R.	58	108	5	3428	142	33·28	6
Turner, G. M.	39	70	6	2920	259	45·62	7
Sutcliffe, B.	42	76	8	2727	230*	40·10	5
Burgess, M. G.	47	86	5	2562	119*	31·62	5

INDIA

	TESTS	INNS	NO	RUNS	HS	AVGE	100S
Gavaskar, S. M.	50	93	7	4947	221	57·52	20
Viswanath, G. R.	56	101	7	4241	179	45·11	9
Umrigar, P. R.	59	94	8	3631	223	42·22	12
Manjrekar, V. L.	55	92	10	3208	189*	39·13	7
Borde, C. G.	55	97	11	3061	177*	35·59	5
Nawab of Pataudi Jnr	46	83	3	2792	203*	34·90	6
Engineer, F. M.	46	87	3	2611	121	31·08	2

PAKISTAN

	TESTS	INNS	NO	RUNS	HS	AVGE	100S
Hanif Mohammad	55	97	8	3915	337	43·98	12
Mushtaq Mohammad	57	100	7	3643	201	39·17	10
Asif Iqbal	52	89	6	3308	175	39·85	11
Majid Khan	44	77	3	3140	167	42·43	7
Saeed Ahmed	41	78	4	2991	172	40·41	5

FOR OWN COUNTRY AND REST OF THE WORLD

	TESTS	INNS	NO	RUNS	HS	AVGE	100S
Sobers, G. S.	98	169	22	8620	365*	58·63	28
Kanhai, R. B.	84	146	6	6511	256	46·50	16
Lloyd C. H.	70	122	9	4994	242*	44·19	13
Mushtaq Mohammad	59	104	7	3672	201	37·85	10
Barlow, E. J.	35	66	2	2869	201	44·82	8
Engineer, F. M.	48	90	3	2614	121	30·04	2
Pollock, R. G.	28	49	4	2506	274	55·68	8

100 Wickets in Tests

ENGLAND

	TESTS	WKTS	AVGE
Trueman, F. S.	67	307	21·57
Underwood, D. L.	74	265	24·90
Statham, J. B.	70	252	24·84
Bedser, A. V.	51	236	24·89
Snow, J. A.	49	202	26·66
Laker, J. C.	46	193	21·23
Barnes, S. F.	27	189	16·43
Willis, R. G. D.	50	181	24·38
Lock, G. A. R.	49	174	25·58
Tate, M. W.	39	155	26·16
Titmus, F. J.	53	153	32·22
Verity, H.	40	144	24·37
Greig, A. W.	58	141	32·20
Bailey, T. E.	61	132	29·21
Old, C. M.	41	129	27·86
Rhodes, W.	58	127	26·96
Allen, D. A.	39	122	30·96
Illingworth, R.	61	122	31·20
Briggs, J.	33	118	17·74
Arnold, G. G.	34	115	28·29
Lohmann, G. A.	18	112	10·75
Wright, D. V. P.	34	108	39·11
Botham, I. T.	21	107	19·61
Peel, R.	20	102	16·81
Wardle, J. H.	28	102	20·39
Blythe, C.	19	100	18·63

FOR ENGLAND INCLUDING REST OF THE WORLD 1970

	TESTS	WKTS	AVGE
Underwood, D. L.	77	272	25·30
Snow, J. A.	54	221	27·45
Greig, A. W.	61	152	31·76
Illingworth, R.	66	133	32·09
Old, C. M.	42	131	28·83

AUSTRALIA

	TESTS	WKTS	AVGE
Benaud, R.	63	248	27·03
McKenzie, G. D.	60	246	29·78
Lindwall, R. R.	61	228	23·05
Grimmett, C. V.	37	216	24·21
Davidson, A. K.	44	186	20·53
Lillee, D. K.	32	171	23·49
Miller, K. R.	55	170	22·97
Johnston, W. A.	40	160	23·90
Thomson, J. R.	32	145	25·51
O'Reilly, W. J.	27	144	22·59
Trumble, H.	32	141	21·78
Walker, M. H. N.	34	138	27·47
Mallett, A. A.	35	125	27·95
Noble, M. A.	42	121	25·01
Johnson, I. W.	45	109	29·19
Giffen, G.	31	103	27·09
Connolly, A. N.	29	102	29·22
Turner, C. T. B.	17	101	16·53

SOUTH AFRICA

	TESTS	WKTS	AVGE
Tayfield, H. J.	37	170	25·91
Goddard, T. L.	41	123	26·22
Pollock, P. M.	28	116	24·18
Adcock, N. A. T.	26	104	21·10

WEST INDIES

	TESTS	WKTS	AVGE
Gibbs, L. R.	79	309	29·09
Sobers, G. S.	93	235	34·03
Hall, W. W.	48	192	26·38
Ramadhin, S.	43	158	28·98
Valentine, A. L.	36	139	30·32
Roberts, A. M. E.	27	134	24·61
Holder, V. A.	40	109	33·27

NEW ZEALAND

	TESTS	WKTS	AVGE
Collinge, R. O.	35	116	29·25
Taylor, B. R.	30	111	26·60
Hadlee, R. J.	26	107	30·14
Motz, R. C.	32	100	31·48

INDIA

	TESTS	WKTS	AVGE
Bedi, B. S.	67	266	28·71
Chandrasekhar, B. S.	58	242	29·74
Prasanna, E. A. S.	49	189	30·38
Mankad, V.	44	162	32·31
Gupte, S. P.	36	149	29·54
Venkataraghavan S.	47	139	33·35

PAKISTAN

	TESTS	WKTS	AVGE
Fazal Mahmood	34	139	24·70
Intikhab Alam	47	125	35·93
Sarfraz Nawaz	34	120	30·56

FOR OWN COUNTRY AND REST OF THE WORLD

	TESTS	WKTS	AVGE
Gibbs, L. R.	83	312	29·79
Sobers, G. S.	98	256	33·01
McKenzie, G. D.	63	255	29·84
Intikhab Alam	52	139	36·89
Pollock, P. M.	29	118	24·71

Notes on Chief Contributors

General Editor

SWANTON, E. W. (Jim) OBE (b. 1907). Author and retired cricket writer and broadcaster. *Evening Standard* 1927–39; *Daily Telegraph* Cricket 1946–75 and rugby correspondent 1948–64. Books: *A History of Cricket* (jt author with H. S. Altham); *Sort of a Cricket Person*; *Follow On*, etc. President of The Cricket Society.

Associate Editor

WOODCOCK, JOHN (b. 1926). Cricket Correspondent of the *Manchester Guardian* 1952–53 and of *The Times* since 1954. Has covered all major Test tours of the last 25 years and reported more than 250 Test Matches. Ed *Wisden* from 1980.

Assistant Editors

PLUMPTRE, GEORGE (b. 1956). Read Modern History at Cambridge. Contributor to *The Field.* Currently writing book on *Royal Gardens of British Isles.*

WINLAW, A. S. R. (Tony) (b. 1938). Cofounder The *Cricketer* Cup 1967; Cricket, rackets and rugby football for *Daily Telegraph* since 1959. Assistant Ed 1st edn *The World of Cricket* (1966). Son of R. de W. K. Winlaw (Cambridge and Surrey). Handicapper for The Jockey Club since 1966.

Statistician

COPINGER, G. A. (b. 1910). Associated with *Wisden* since 1934, in charge of 'Records' section 1947–1963; responsible for 'Cricket Averages' for Press Association 1947 to date. Chairman of The Cricket Society 1947–53. President Club Cricket Conference 1976. Has an extensive cricket library and a wide collection of cricketana.

Chief Contributors

ALSTON, REX (b. 1901). Cambridge Athletics blue. Captained Bedfordshire at cricket. Bedford Sch staff 1924–41. BBC staff 1942–61, specializing in broadcasts on cricket, rugby, athletics and lawn tennis. Cricket and rugby for *Daily Telegraph* and *Sunday Telegraph.* Books: *Taking the Air*; *Over to Rex Alston*, etc.

ALTHAM, H. S. (*see* PART III).

ARLOTT, JOHN (*see* PART III).

ARROWSMITH, R. L. (Bob) (b. 1906). Schoolmaster: Lancing Coll (1929–38), Charterhouse Sch (1938–66, housemaster, 1950–65). Hon Sec Charterhouse Friars 1929–49. Squash for Sussex 1934–35. Contributor to *Wisden* and *The Cricketer.* Books: *History of Kent County Cricket*; *The Charterhouse Register, 1769–1872.*

BAILEY, TREVOR (*see* PART III).

BANNISTER, ALEX (b. 1914). Cricket correspondent *Daily Mail* 1947–79. Many overseas tours in every major cricketing country. Managed Commonwealth side to Pakistan 1968. Contributor to *Wisden, The Cricketer*, etc.

BENAUD, RICHIE (*see* PART III).

BISSEKER, TREVOR (b. 1936). Journalist since age of 18: *Daily News*, Durban 1955–60; *Johannesburg Star* 1960–70; succeeded Louis Duffus as cricket correspondent of the *Argus* Group 1968–70; *Rand Daily Mail* 1970–79, Sports Ed 1970–75; Dep Ed *Port Elizabeth Evening Post* from 1979. Contributor to many cricket books and journals.

BLOFELD, HENRY (b. 1939). Cricket blue at Cambridge 1959, and first kept wicket for Norfolk aged 16. Journalist and broadcaster: cricket for *Sunday Express, The Times, Observer* and *Guardian*; broadcast many Test series for BBC both at home and abroad. Books: *Cricket in Three Moods*; *The Packer Affair*, etc.

BOLTON, GEOFFREY (1893–1964). Schoolmaster: Summerfields Sch, Oxford 1919–60, partner 1930–56, Headmaster 1956–60. President Sussex Martlets 1950–64. Books: *Sussex Martlets 1905–1955; History of the OUCC* (1962).

BOSE, MIHIR (b. 1947). Chartered Accountant. Cricket correspondent of London Broadcasting 1973–75; since then general foreign correspondent for *Sunday Times*, and general freelance journalist for LBC. Has written for *Daily Express, Guardian, Sunday Times* and *New Society.* Books: *Keith Miller* (a cricketing biography, 1979); working on a book on the history of Cricket for Quartet.

BOWLES, WILLIAM, BEM (b. 1900). Groundsman Eton Coll from 1936. Founded Nat Assoc of Groundsmen (now Institute of Groundsmen) 1934. Book (co-author): *Practical Groundsmanship* (1952).

BREARLEY, MICHAEL (*see* PART III).

BRIDGER, KENNETH (b. 1920). Dir of Research in Ceramics at Ferro Enamel, Argentina. Long-standing contributor on cricket and rugby football to *Buenos Aires Herald.* Book: *North and South* (a history of Argentina's annual cricket 'classic').

BRITTENDEN, R. T. (Dick) (b. 1919) Sports Ed *The Press*, Christchurch, from 1956. Twice winner of national journalism awards. Regular overseas tours with NZ teams. Books: *New Zealand Cricketer*; *Great Days in New Zealand Cricket*, etc.

BROCKLEHURST, B. G. (Ben) (b. 1922). Played for Somerset 1952–54 (capt 1953–54). Man Dir and proprietor of *The Cricketer.* Hon Sec Anglo-Corfiot Cricket Assoc.

BRODRIBB, GERALD (b. 1915). Schoolmaster: St Peter's, Seaford; Canford Sch; and Hydneye House (Headmaster 1954–70). Books: *The English Game* (anthology); *Cricket in Fiction*; *Next Man In*; *Hit for Six*; *The Croucher* (biography of G. L. Jessop); *Maurice Tate*, etc.

BULLOCK, KENNETH (b. 1927). Manager, Fiber Optics, Phillips Cables, Brockville, Ontario. Ed *Canadian Cricket Annual* 1958–65; and *Canadian Cricketer* from 1972. Director of Canadian Cricket Assoc from 1972; Vice-Pres 1977 and 1978. Chm Selectors and Manager of the Canadian team 1977 and 1978. Canada's delegate to ICC 1979.

BURNET, J. F. (b. 1910) Cambridge Rugby Fives blue. Founder The Jesters CC and The Jesters Club (1928). Fell Magdalene Coll Cambridge from 1949 (Bursar 1949–77). Books: *The Public and Preparatory Schools Yearbook* (Ed since 1948); *An Account of The Jesters Club, 1928–79.*

CARDUS, NEVILLE (*see* PART III).

CAREY, MICHAEL (b. 1936). Cricket commentator and writer: Yorkshire and Granada TV; BBC; *Observer, Guardian*; *Daily Telegraph* (as Henry Bevington); *Wisden*, etc. Books: *In Search of Runs* (with Dennis Amiss).

CARR, MAJOR D. J. (b. 1920). Cricket for the Army and Berkshire. Assist Sec Derbyshire CCC 1960–62, Sec 1962–75.

COLE, ADRIAN (b. 1936). Certified Public Accountant. Vice-Pres Hollywood Cricket Club. Has toured regularly with the USA cricket team as a player or official scorer.

COWDREY, COLIN (*see* PART III).

COZIER, TONY (b. 1943). Originator and Ed *The West Indies Cricket Annual* from 1970. Has covered all recent West Indian tours and broadcast for the BBC and around the world. Books: *The West Indies: Fifty Years of Test Cricket*, etc.

DAVIES, J. G. W. (Jack) (b. 1911). Cambridge cricket blue 1933–34; played for Kent, intermittently, 1934–51. Treasurer Cambridge Univ CC 1958–76; Treasurer MCC from 1976. Sec Cambridge Univ Appointments Board 1952–68. Dir Bank of England 1969–76.

DE MESQUITA, NORMAN (b. 1932). BBC Radio London since 1970, currently Sports Ed. Cricket and football for *The Times*. Ice Hockey referee for 15 years.

DEXTER, TED (*see* PART III).

DOGGART, G. H. G. (Hubert) (b. 1925). Housemaster at Winchester; now Headmaster of King's Sch, Bruton. Won 5 blues and captained Cambridge in 4 games (including cricket). Played for England in 1950; led Sussex in 1954, and MCC in South America 1959. President of ESCA from 1965; Cricket Council 1968–71; MCC committee from 1975. Edited *The Heart of Cricket* (a memoir of H. S. Altham).

DOLMAN, F. L. J. (Frank), MBE (b. 1904). A lifetime in London club cricket: Sec, Pres, Chm and now Life Vice-Pres Club Cricket Conference. Chm Assoc of Cricket Umpires from 1970.

DUFFUS, LOUIS (b. 1904). Cricket, rugby (and war) correspondent for South African *Argus* group of newspapers for many years. Reported over 100 Tests played by South Africa, 1929–70. Books: *Cricketers of the Veld* (1947); *South African Cricket 1929–1947* (1948); *Springbok Glory* (1955).

DUNSTAN, KEITH (b. 1925). Correspondent for *Melbourne Herald* group in New York, London and currently Los Angeles. Columnist for *Courier-Mail*, Brisbane 1954–58 and *Sun-News Pictorial*, Melbourne 1958–77. Books include: *The Paddock that Grew (A History of the Melbourne Cricket Club)* (1962); *Supporting a Column* (1966); *Wowsers* (1968); *Knockers* (1972); *Sports* (1973, 1st Braille Book of the Year Award).

EAGAR, DESMOND (1917–1977). Oxford blues for cricket (1939) and hockey; cricket for Gloucestershire (1935–39) and Hampshire (1946–57). Sec Hampshire CCC 1946–77; Assist Manager MCC to Australia and New Zealand 1958–59. Hockey Correspondent *Sunday Telegraph* 1961–1977. Books: jt author of *Hampshire County Cricket* (the official history: 1957).

ELLIS, H. F. (Humphry) MBE (b. 1907). Joined *Punch* 1933 (Dep Ed 1949–53); Ed *The Manual of Rugby Union Football* 1952; contributor to *New Yorker, Countryman, Cricketer*, etc. Books: *Twenty-five Years Hard* (1960); *Mediatrics* (1961); *The World of A. J. Wentworth* (1964).

FINGLETON, JACK (*see* PART III).

FLEMING, A. W. P. (Tony) (b. 1931). Cricket for RAF (capt 1974 and 1975), and Combined Services. Manager of Lord's Indoor Sch since it opened in 1977.

FORD, W. R. (Ronnie), CBE (b. 1913). Group-Captain (ret). Played cricket for RAF and Combined Services. Assist Sec MCC 1970–79.

FORDHAM, MICHAEL (b. 1926). Local Govt Offr, Kent CC. A BBC scorer for Sound and TV from 1958. Contributor to former *Playfair Cricket Monthly*; compiler for *Playfair Cricket Annual* from 1963 and of 'Cricket Records' for *Wisden* from 1979.

FORRESTER, R. A. C. (Reggie) (b. 1907). Solicitor. Hon Sec Wiltshire CCC 1929–64, capt 1947–49, Pres 1964–65. Chm Minor Counties CA from 1963. Member TCCB and Cricket Council.

FRITH, DAVID (b. 1937). Ed *The Cricketer* 1972–78; founder and Ed *Wisden Cricket Monthly* from 1979. Played Sydney Grade cricket. Books: biographies of A. E. Stoddart and A. A. Jackson; *The Fast Men*; *The Ashes '77* (with Greg Chappell); *The Golden Age of Cricket; The Ashes '79*, etc.

GAUNT, DAVID (b. 1934). Teacher and lecturer in Teachers' Training Colls. PE Education Adviser with Humberside Education Authority from 1976. Chairman of BCSA Cricket Association from 1972. Manager of BCSA sides to West Indies 1978, 1979 and 1980.

GIBSON, ALAN (b. 1923). Author and broadcaster. Joined BBC, West Region, as producer and compère of radio programmes before becoming an all-round freelance. Test, county cricket and rugby football commentator. Contributor to several newspapers and magazines including *The Times, Sunday Telegraph, Guardian, Spectator* and *The Cricketer*. Books: *Jackson's Year* (1965); an autobiography, *A Mingled Yarn* (1976); and *The Cricket Captains of England* (1979).

GREEN, BENNY (b. 1927). Professional jazz musician 1946–61. Broadcaster; TV Critic *Punch*; columnist *Daily Mirror* and *What's On in London*; contributor to *Spectator*, etc. Ed *Cricket Addicts' Archive* (1977); *Shaw's Champions* (1978); *Wisden Anthology* (1979), etc.

GREGORY, KENNETH (b. 1921). Writer, including cricket, at different times, for *The Times, Guardian, Spectator, Illustrated London News*, etc. Books: *The First Cuckoo* (1976); *In Celebration of Cricket* (1978).

GRIFFITH, S. C. (Billy), CBE, DFC, TD (b. 1914). Cricket for Sussex; toured with MCC: to Australia 1935–36; West Indies 1947–48; South Africa 1948–49. Sec Sussex CCC 1946–50, President 1975–77. Cricket Correspondent *Sunday Times* 1950–52. Assist Sec MCC 1952–62, Sec 1962–74. Member ICC 1962–74; Cricket Council 1969–74. President MCC 1979–80.

HAINSWORTH, SIDNEY B., CBE (b. 1899). From 1945 Man Dir, Chm and now Pres of J. H. Fenner. For 6 years on the committee of Yorkshire CCC. In 1970 worked on the declining Scarborough Festival, persuading 4 of the leading counties to play in the Fenner Knock-out Competition. Pres at Scarborough 1972 and 1973.

HARDY, DAVID (b. 1949). Town planning in London 1972–74; in Holland from 1974. Ed cricket and squash club magazines in Holland. Contributor to *The Cricketer*.

HARGREAVES, PETER (b. 1928). Coach and cricket administrator in Denmark. Books: 20 works, mostly on the English language; *The Story of Continental Cricket*.

HAYWARD, SIR RICHARD, CBE (b. 1910) Pres Civil Service CA from 1966. President Assocn of Kent Cricket Clubs from 1970. Chm Civil Service Sports Council 1968–73.

HAZELDINE, REX (b. 1939). Head of PE Dept, King's Sch, Worcester 1962–68; Snr Lecturer in PE, Loughborough Coll 1968–78; Lecturer in PE and Sports Science, Loughborough Univ of Technology from 1978. NCA Advanced coach. Manager and selector UAU. Cricket XI.

HILL, ERIC, DFC, DFM (b. 1923). Played cricket for Somerset 1947–51; capt Somerset 2nd XI 1954–55. *Somerset County Gazette* 1952–63; freelance cricket and rugby writer from 1963 for *Sunday Telegraph*, Press Association, etc. Toured South Africa (1956–57) and Australia (1962–63) as writer.

INSOLE, D. J. (*see* PART III).

JAMES, C. L. R. (b. 1901) Political and cricket journalist; occasional cricket reports for the *Manchester Guardian* 1933–54; Ed *The Nation* (Trinidad) 1958–60. Books: *Beyond a Boundary* (1963), and works on politics and history.

KAY, JOHN (b. 1910). Played for Middleton in Central Lancashire League 1925–45. Hon Sec Central Lancashire League 1943–59. Lancashire CCC Committee. For 35 years cricket correspondent *Manchester Evening News*. Books: *Cricket in the League*; *A History of Lancashire CC*.

KEATING, FRANK (b. 1937). Sports journalist and broadcaster: contributor to *Guardian, The Cricketer*. 'Sportswriter of the Year' 1977 (Astroturf Prize).

KENNEDY, MICHAEL (b. 1929). Northern Ed *Daily Telegraph* from 1960; Music Critic from 1950. Author of Books on Elgar, Vaughan Williams, Barbirolli and Manchester.

KILBURN, J. M. (Jim) (b. 1909). Played cricket for Barnsley in the Yorkshire League and Bradford in the Bradford League. Cricket correspondent *Yorkshire Post* 1934–76. Sec Cricket Writers Club 1954–69. Books: *In Search of Cricket* (1937); *Homes of Sport: Cricket* (with N. W. D. Yardley) (1952); *History of Yorkshire Cricket* (1969); *Thanks to Cricket* (1972), etc.

MACDONALD, TREVOR (b. 1939). Born and educated West Indies. Sports broadcaster and producer of current affairs for BBC Overseas Service. Has lived in England since late 1960s. Currently newscaster and reporter for ITN; as ITN sports correspondent covered the Packer series.

McLEAN, TERENCE (b. 1913). Leading New Zealand sporting journalist, has toured worldwide (36 International Rugby tours), and written more than 20 books since 1954. Contributor on games to *The Times* and *Sunday Times*.

MAIR, NORMAN, G. R. (b. 1928). Won 4 caps for Scotland at rugby football in 1951; cricket for Scotland. *Sunday Telegraph*, 1961–64. A leading sporting journalist with *The Scotsman* since 1964. Scots 'Sports Journalist of the Year' 1980.

MARDER, JOHN I. (1908–76). Born at Nottingham, emigrated aged 18 to USA, and helped revival of cricket in Missouri and California. Pres of USA Cricket Assoc from its formation in 1961 until his death. Represented USA on ICC from their election as associate members in 1965 until his death.

MARLAR, ROBIN (b. 1931). Played for Cambridge 1951–53 (capt 1952) and Sussex 1951–62 (capt 1955–59). Between 1951 and 1962 took nearly a thousand wickets. Parliamentary Candidate, Bolsover 1959. Wrote cricket and rugby football for *Daily Telegraph* before joining the *Sunday Times* as cricket correspondent. Hon Sec Cricket Writers' Club. Book: *The Story of Cricket* (1979).

MARTINEAU, G. D. (1897–1976). Regular soldier and schoolmaster; began to concentrate in 1949 on a wide range of freelance writing in both prose and verse. A contributor and book reviewer to *The Cricketer* for many years. Books: *Bat, Ball, Wicket and All* (1950); *They made cricket* (1956); *The Valiant Stumper* (1957), etc.

MARTIN-JENKINS, CHRISTOPHER (b. 1945). Played cricket for Surrey 2nd XI. Assist Ed *The Cricketer* 1968–70. Joined BBC 1970; BBC Cricket Correspondent from 1973. Books: *Testing Time* (1974); *Assault on the Ashes* (1975); *The Jubilee Tests* (1977); *In Defence of the Ashes* (1979), etc.

MASON, RONALD (b. 1912). Civil Service 1931. Called to the Bar 1935. Staff Tutor in Literature London Univ 1969–79. Books: *Batsman's Paradise* (1955); *Jack Hobbs* (1960); *Walter Hammond* (1962); *Sing All a Green Willow* (1967); *Warwick Armstrong's Australians* (1971), etc.

MELFORD, MICHAEL (b. 1916). Oxford Athletics blue 1936–38. Cricket and rugby football for *The Observer* 1946–50; joined *Daily Telegraph* 1950; cricket and rugby correspondent *Sunday Telegraph* 1961–75; cricket correspondent *Daily Telegraph* from 1975. Has reported frequent MCC tours, as well as Olympic Games in Melbourne (1956) and Rome (1960). Ed *Pick of The Cricketer*. Assoc Ed 1st edn *The World of Cricket* (1966).

MOORHOUSE, GEOFFREY (b. 1931). Formerly chief feature writer of the *Manchester Guardian*. Author of books on monasticism, Calcutta and British diplomacy; made 2,000 mile journey through the Sahara. A compulsive cricket watcher, wrote *The Best Loved Game* (1979) (Cricket Society Literary Award).

ODENDAAL, ANDRÉ (b. 1954). Author of 2 books – *God-Forgotten Cricketers* (1976) and *Cricket in Isolation* (1977) – while a student at Stellenbosch University. Assist Ed *South African Cricketer* 1976–77. At present taking a PhD in History at Cambridge.

OWEN-SMITH, MICHAEL (b. 1949). Son of 'Tuppy' Owen-Smith. Sports journalist on *Cape Argus* from 1970; Dep Sports Ed from 1979. Currently editing *Protea Cricket Annual*.

PAWLE, GERALD (b. 1913). *Yorkshire Post* sports staff 1931–39; later *Sunday Times* and Kemsley Newspapers; Ed Dir Beaverbrook Western from 1968; cricket for *Daily Telegraph*. Squash for England 1949; open champion of Ireland (1939) and France (1939). Books: *The Secret War* (1956); *The War and Colonel Warden* (1963).

PEARCE, T. N. (Tom), OBE (b. 1905). Played cricket for Essex 1929–50 (captain 1933–50); Pres Essex CCC from 1970. Test Selector 1949–50; Manager MCC team to India, Pakistan and Ceylon 1961–62. Hon Organizer Scarborough Festival from 1951. Rugby for Middlesex and London Counties; international rugby referee. Hon Sec British Sportsmen's Club.

PEEBLES, IAN (*see* PART III).

PERERA, S. S. (Chandra) (b. 1922). Member Exec Committee Board of Control for Cricket in Sri Lanka from 1975. Assist Manager Sri Lanka Under-19 team to Pakistan 1973. Regular contributor on cricket to various magazines and newspapers in Sri Lanka.

PRABHU, NIRANJAN ('Prab') (b. 1923). Sports Ed *Times of India* from 1959. Regular reporter of Indian tours to Australia, England, New Zealand, Pakistan and West Indies.

PRESTON, NORMAN, MBE (1903–1980). Cricket Reporting Agency 1933–65; Cricket and Football Ed Press Association for 25 years. Joined *Wisden* 1933; Ed 1952–80. Reuters correspondent to Australia 1946–47, 1954–55; West Indies 1947–48.

RAYVERN ALLEN, DAVID (b. 1938). BBC staff producer on Sound and TV. Musician and playwright. Contributor to *The Cricketer* and *Wisden Cricket Monthly*. Currently writing biography of C. Aubrey Smith and book on cricket songs.

REA, HON FINDLAY (b. 1907). Civil servant with Central Office of Information until retirement in 1972. Chelsea Borough Council 1945–51; twice Labour Parliamentary candidate. Organizer, for *The Cricketer*, of National Village Competition and Lord's Taverners Colts Trophy from 1973.

RHEINBERG, NETTA (b. 1911). Pres Gunnersbury Women's Cricket Club; Chm Middlesex WCA 1948–77; Sec WCA 1947–1939; Manager international cricket teams. Played for England. Editor *Women's Cricket* 1950–67. Vice-Chm The Cricket Society since 1967. Books: *Fair Play*; *The Story of Women's Cricket* (with Rachael Heyhoe Flint).

RICE, TIM (b. 1944). Runs Heartaches CC. Libretti of: *Joseph and the Amazing Technicolour Dreamcoat; Jesus Christ Superstar; Evita*, etc. Co-author *Guinness Book of British Hit Singles* (2 edns). Ed *Lord's Taverners' Sticky Wicket Book*.

ROBERTS, R. A. (Ron) (1927–65). Freelance journalist and broadcaster. Overseas tour manager to South Africa, Rhodesia, Kenya, Tanzania, Greece, India, Pakistan, Malaysia, New Zealand and Hong Kong. After early experience with *Somerset County Herald* and *Bristol Evening News*, wrote for many English and overseas newspapers. Books include: *Sixty Years of Somerset Cricket* (1952), and *The Fight for the Ashes* (1961).

ROBERTSON-GLASGOW, R. C. ('Crusoe') (1901–65). Classical scholar at Charterhouse and Oxford. Cricket for Charterhouse, Oxford, Somerset and the Gentlemen. One of the game's great essayists, Cricket correspondent *Morning Post* (1933–37), *Daily Telegraph* (1937–38), *Observer* (1938–50), Books include: *The Brighter Side of Cricket* (1933 and 1951), *Cricket Prints* (1943), *46 Not Out* (1948), *Rain Stopped Play* (1948).

ROBINSON, RAY (b. 1905). Prolific cricket writings since 1930; Cricket Society Jubilee Literary Award 1977; Australian Correspondent for *Daily Telegraph* and *The Cricketer* for many years. Books: *Between Wickets* (1946); *From the Boundary* (1951); *The Glad Season* (1955); *The Wildest Tests* (1972–1979); *On Top Down Under*, etc.

ROBSON, J. D. (Don) (b. 1934). Chm Durham County Council 1973–74. Chm NCA from 1977. Company Sec construction firm and sports retail firms. Contributor to various sporting publications.

ROSENWATER, IRVING (b. 1932). One of the Assist Eds 1st edn of *The World of Cricket* (1966). Formerly Assist Ed of *The Cricketer*; contributor from 1955. Founder and 1st Ed *The Journal of The Cricket Society*. BBC TV scorer from 1971. Books: *A Portfolio of Cricket Prints* (1962); *England v Australia* (jt author with Ralph Barker, 1969); *Sir Donald Bradman: A Biography* (1978) (Cricket Society Literary Award).

ROSS, ALAN (b. 1922). Cricket and squash rackets for Oxford and Royal Navy, both during the Second War. Cricket correspondent *The Observer* 1954–72. Ed *London Magazine* and Man Dir London Magazine Editions from 1965. Books: *Australia '55*; *Cape Summer*; *Through the Caribbean; Australia '63*; *West Indies at Lord's*; *The Cricketers' Companion* (Ed), etc.

ROSS, GORDON (b. 1919). Cricket Consultant to Gillette since beginning of the Gillette Cup in 1963. Ed former *Playfair Cricket Monthly*. Assoc Ed *The Cricketer*; Exec Ed *Wisden*; Ed *Playfair Cricket Annual* and *Cricketer Quarterly Facts and Figures*. Books: *The Surrey Story* (1957); *A History of Cricket* (1972); *A History of West Indies Cricket* (1976), etc.; and many brochures and handbooks.

RUTNAGUR, D. J. (Dicky) (b. 1931). Cricket correspondent *Hindustan Times* 1958–66; Ed *Indian Cricket-Field Annual* 1956–64; freelance cricket reporting since 1966, widely travelled; cricket, squash and badminton for *Daily Telegraph*.

SARGENT, EDWARD ROTAN (Tanny) (b. 1914). Played squash and tennis for Harvard, US Inter-collegiate singles squash champion, Canadian squash doubles champion. Chm Merion Cricket Club, Philadelphia since 1972. Curator, C. C. Morris Memorial Library at Haverford College.

SCOTT, DEREK (b. 1929). Hon Sec Irish Cricket Union from 1974. Cricket correspondent *Evening Press*, Dublin 1960–72. 'Irish Notes' in *Wisden* for 20 years.

SHORT, P. D. B. (Peter) (b. 1926). British Army 1945–57; twice mentioned in despatches (Cyprus). Played for The Army. Sec West Indian Board of Control 1966–72; Pres Barbados Cricket Assoc from 1973. Hon Life Member MCC.

SINGLETON, A. P. (Sandy) (b. 1914). Cricket for Oxford 1934–37 (capt 1937). Played for Worcestershire 1934–46 (capt 1946); emigrated and played for Rhodesia 1947–48. Hockey for Derbyshire. Schoolmaster.

SMITH, A. C. (Alan) (b. 1936). Played cricket for Oxford 1958–60 (capt 1959–60). Played for Warwickshire 1958–74 (capt 1968–74); 6 Tests – 4 v Australia (1962–63), 2 v NZ (1963); MCC to Canada and USA 1959; Capt MCC to South America 1964–65. Assist

Manager MCC to Australia and New Zealand 1974–75; Test Selector 1969–73. Gen Sec Warwickshire CCC from 1976.

SMITH, LESLIE (b. 1914). Press Association, cricket and football 1932–79; represented Reuters on 5 overseas tours with MCC. Contributed to *Wisden* for 40 years.

SMITH, M. J. (Mike) (b. 1942). Played for Public Schools at Lord's, 1959. Middlesex XI 1959–1979 (vice-capt 1974–1977); played for England in 5 1-day Internationals. Nearly 20,000 runs; 40 hundreds. Committee of the Cricketers' Association.

SNOW, E. E. (b. 1910). Cricket for Leicester CC, Leicester Nomads. Hon Sec Leicestershire CCC 1957–59; Chm Ground Committee Leicestershire from 1968. Brother of C. P. and P. A. Books: *A History of Leicestershire Cricket* (1949); *Sir Julien Cahn's XI* (1964), etc.

SNOW, PHILIP, MBE (b. 1915). Captained Leicestershire CCC 2nd XI 1936–37. Administrator Fiji and Western Pacific 1938–52. Founded Fiji Cricket Association 1946; captained Fiji 1942 and to New Zealand 1948; Permanent Fiji rep on ICC since 1965. Bursar Rugby Sch 1952–76. Brother of C. P. and E. E. Books: *Cricket in the Fiji Islands* (1949); *The People from the Horizon: An Illustrated History of Europeans among South Sea Islanders* (1979), etc.

STEVENSON, M. H. (Mike) (b. 1927). Played cricket for Cambridge 1949, 1950, 1952; and Derbyshire. Schoolmaster for 17 years: Bromsgrove, Pocklington and Queen Elizabeth's GS, Blackburn. Cricket and rugby for *Daily* and *Sunday Telegraph*; regular contributor *The Cricketer*, *Rugby World*. Books: *History of Yorkshire Cricket* (1975); *Life of Ray Illingworth* (1978), etc.

STOLLMEYER, J. B. (*see* PART III).

STREETON, RICHARD (b. 1930). Reuters 1958–1969, covering MCC in Australia and New Zealand (1965–66), West Indies (1967–68) and Olympic Games in Tokyo and Mexico City. Staff of *The Times* from 1969; general sports writer from 1977.

THICKNESSE, JOHN (b. 1931). On *Daily Express* 1957–58; *Daily Telegraph* 1958–61; *Sunday Telegraph* 1961–66; cricket correspondent of *Evening Standard* from 1967.

THOMSON, A. A. (1894–1968). Author and Journalist. President of the Cricket Society 1963–68. Wrote on cricket for *The Times* and *Punch*. Books: *Cricket My Pleasure* (1953); *The Great Cricketer* (1957); *Hirst and Rhodes* (1959); *The Golden Ages* (1961); *The Great Captains* (1965); *The Wars of the Roses* (1967), etc.

TYSON, FRANK (*see* PART III).

VOCKINS, MICHAEL (b. 1944). Sec Worcestershire CCC since 1971. Helped devise and establish indoor cricket 1970; member Cricket Council's Enquiry into Youth and Junior cricket. Book: *Indoor Cricket* (1973).

WALKER, PETER (b. 1936). Played for Glamorgan 1956–72; 3 Tests for England v S. Africa 1960. In 1961 achieved notable treble of 1,600 runs, 101 wickets, 73 catches. Regular BBC TV and radio commentator; Welsh Rugby Correspondent *Sunday Telegraph* 1964–76. Books: *Winning Cricket* (1964); *Cricket Conversations* (1978); *The All-Rounder* (1979), etc.

WARR, JOHN (*see* PART III).

WHITE, CRAWFORD (b. 1910). Retired cricket writer. Played for Lancashire 2nd XI which won Minor Counties' Championship 1934. Cricket Correspondent of the *News Chronicle*, *Daily Mail* (briefly) and for 17 years of *Daily Express*. Made 25 overseas tours and covered nearly 300 Test Matches.

WHITING, STEVE (b. 1938). Cricket for KCS Wimbledon, Merton College Oxford, Byfleet, Guildford, etc. On *Sun* since 1965; Assist Sports Ed until 1977; cricket correspondent since then.

WOOLLER, WILFRED (b. 1912). Played for Cambridge at cricket; and at rugby 1933–35, also for Wales 1933–39 (capt 1938–39). Welsh squash international 1946–47. Captained Glamorgan at cricket 1947–60. Test Selector 1955–62. Sports writer for *Sunday Telegraph* from 1961. Books: *History of Glamorgan CCC; Fifty Years of the All Blacks*, etc.

WYNNE-THOMAS, PETER (b. 1934). Hon Sec Assoc of Cricket Statisticians; Librarian Trent Bridge Cricket Ground; Ed *Notts Yearbook* from 1975. Books: *Notts Cricketers 1821–1914* (Cricket Society Award, 1971); *History of Forest Wanderers CC*.

YEOMANS, C. R. (Ron) (1908–1980). Hon Sec Northern Cricket Society 1948–79; Chm Council of Cricket Societies 1969–79. Yorkshire CCC committee 1956–80. Derbyshire squash champion 1935, 1936 and 1938. Contributed on cricket to *Yorkshire Post* 1947–73; *Daily* and *Sunday Telegraph* 1973–79.

Photograph Acknowledgments

Where there is more than one source on a page, the credits start with the picture furthest to the left and nearest the top of the page and work down each column – a, b, c, d, etc.

Willie Alleyne Associates: 38, 129
Associated Press: 613*a*
Associated Newspapers, Sydney: 151*a*
Australian Information Service: 193, 244, 486*b*, 355*b*
BBC: 586*b*, 592*a*, 594*a*
BBC Hulton Picture Library: 412
The Beldam Collection: 24, 25, 136*b*, 141*a*, 174, 211, 219*b*, 262*b*, 288*a*
Bert Butterworth: 59
Cape Herald: 110
Cape Argus: 107, 235
Central Press: 27, 30*b*, 33, 51*b*, 56*b*, 58, 60*a*, 64, 84*b*, 93, 97*a*, 112, 123, 138*b*, 141*b*, 152*b*, 158*a*, 166*a*, 170, 172, 173, 182, 183*b*, 185*c*, 187*a*, 199, 202, 204*a*, 209*b*, 215, 219*a*, 221, 223, 224*b*, 225, 226, 227*a*, 228, 231, 258, 264, 268*b*, 271, 273, 276, 279, 295*a*, 299, 310, 312, 321, 322, 326, 333, 368*b*, 372*a*, 374, 377, 380, 388, 396, 409*a*, 410, 413*b*, 419, 420, 422*c*, 429, 434, 439, 448, 487*a*, 500, 514, 515, 516*ab*, 525*b*, 532*a*, 533*b*, 557, 568*a*, 596*a*, 597, 607, 610
N. Chadwick: 364*b*
R. A. Christopher: 520*a*
Crown Copyright: 516*c*
Daily Herald: 455*a*
Daily Mail, Manchester: 36
Die Burger: 109*b*
Luis Druetta: 53
Patrick Eagar: 6, 39*b*, 40, 43, 46, 49, 60*b*, 99, 126, 135, 136*a*, 137*a*, 143, 145*a*, 148, 149, 157, 164*a*, 166*b*, 168, 176*b*, 179, 184, 185*b*, 200, 201, 204*b*, 205, 206*b*, 209*a*, 210, 217, 218, 229, 238, 246, 247, 249, 252, 280*bc*, 281, 282*a*, 283, 303, 307, 313, 314, 315, 319, 323*b*, 331, 338, 354, 355*a*, 356, 357, 373, 376*b*, 382, 385*b*, 386, 390*b*, 403*a*, 411, 414, 426*b*, 435, 438*b*, 440, 443*b*, 453*b*, 459, 460, 461, 465*b*, 468, 472, 475, 481, 482, 484, 488, 489*b*, 490, 491, 493*a*, 494, 496, 499, 502, 505*b*, 530, 574, 579, 590*b*, 616
The Echo, Sunderland: 450
Fox Photos: 114, 145*b*, 163, 171, 198, 394*a*, 479, 486*a*, 495, 558, 562, 565
Fox Waterman Photos: 594*b*
The Friend (South Africa): 113
David Frith: 56*a*, 261*a*
Stanley Glazer: 583*a*
Henry Grant: 501
Guardian, Manchester: 525*a*
G. Hallawell: 394 *bc*
Huddersfield Examiner: 528*b*, 532*b*
Pauline Johnston: 74
Ken Kelly: 45*b*, 68, 69, 72, 75, 89, 94, 100*a*, 102, 115, 120, 127, 140*a*, 369, 370, 425, 426*c*, 430*b*, 431, 464*b*, 465*a*, 466, 473, 474, 480, 483, 504*b*, 614
Kentish Gazette: 390*a*, 391
Lord's Taverners: 359, 363
Peter Mackinnon: 580
MCC: 1, 2, 3, 4, 8, 9, 10, 11, 12, 14, 15*a*, 16, 17, 18, 21, 23, 26, 28, 32*a*, 42*b*, 44, 45*a*, 48, 52, 80, 140*b*, 177, 186, 187*b*, 195, 221, 233, 240, 242, 259, 261*b*, 280*a*, 282*b*, 291, 295*a*, 383, 387, 392, 401, 402*b*, 409*b*, 535, 569, 571, 572*a*, 575, 577, 589*b*, 606, 608*a*, 611, 619
Adrian Murrell: 224*a*, 477
National Film Board of Canada: 71
Northern Counties Photographers: 526
M. L. Pecker: 188, 334, 405
Press Association: 29, 97*b*, 105, 121, 216, 222, 302, 323*a*
Sydney Riley: 62*a*
The Scotsman: 512
Sky Fotos: 487*b*
Bill Smith: 381*b*, 398*b*, 415, 423
Philip Snow: 77
Southern Newspapers: 384*b*, 385*a*
Sport and General: 32*b*, 51*a*, 81, 82, 84*a*, 98, 106*b*, 131, 133, 137*b*, 139*b*, 144, 146, 150*a*, 151*b*, 155, 169, 176*a*, 192*a*, 214, 263*a*, 274, 327, 372*b*, 398*a*, 403*b*, 404, 406*b*, 407, 426*a*, 445, 470, 471, 528*a*, 544, 613*b*
The Star, Johannesburg: 237*b*
Sun-Herald: 160, 192*b*, 197, 272, 485
Syndication International: 150*b*
The Times: 78*a*, 106*a*, 153, 183*a*, 185*a*, 196*a*, 269, 317, 376*a*, 384*a*, 430*a*, 493*a*, 521*b*, 523, 540*a*, 543, 549, 550, 555, 556*a*, 559, 563, 567, 568*b*, 602, 615
Universal Pictorial Press: 194, 196*b*, 329
Walker Studios: 413*a*, 443*a*
Western Australian Newspapers: 66, 604
John Woodcock: 62*b*, 130, 156, 158*b*, 190, 489*a*, 505*a*, 603
Yorkshire Post: 588

Index

This index, compiled by J. D. COLDHAM, *Editor of the* Cricket Society Journal, *is of course selective. A completely exhaustive index, such as that of* Wisden *which signposts everything with a clarity making all things evident to the veriest moron, would scarcely have either been practicable or necessary. The more significant references to persons and places, clubs and other kindred institutions, happenings on the field and in the councils of the game, and other events in due order, are noted. References to contributors are given in bold numerals and to illustrations in italic numerals.*